BLOOMSBURY CLASSICS

NEW CLASSICA… BOOKS FO…

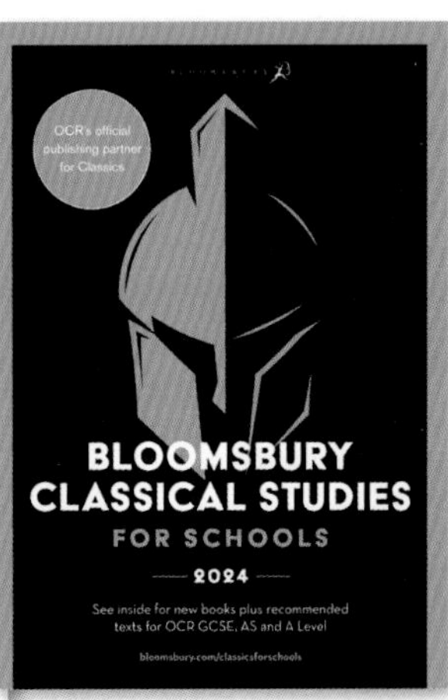

Browse the latest and bestselling textbooks in our online catalogue

Download yours at: **bloomsbury.com/ClassicsForSchools**

ISYB Special Offer: **20% off** online when using code **ISYB24** until 31.12.24

2024 HIGHLIGHTS

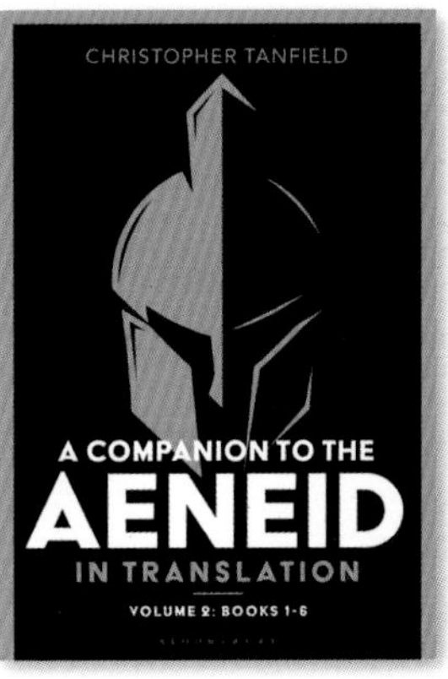

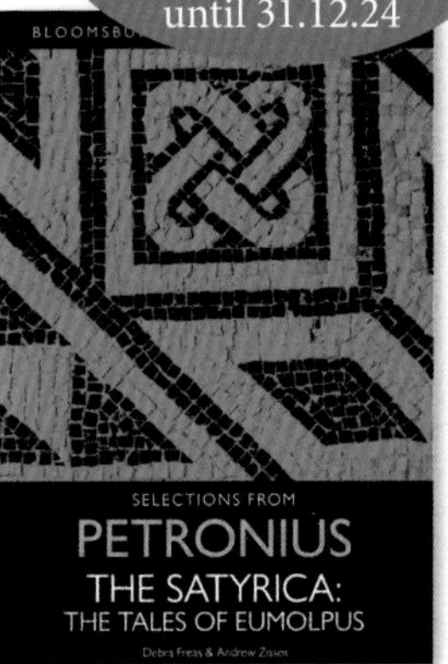

Find out more: **bloomsbury.com/ClassicsForSchools**

Sign up for the latest news and additional teacher resources at **bloomsbury.com/ClassicsSignUp**

BLOOMSBURY

INDEPENDENT SCHOOLS YEARBOOK

2023–2024

Boys Schools, Girls Schools,
Co-educational Schools and
Preparatory Schools

Details of Schools whose Heads are in membership of
one or more of the following
Constituent Associations of the
Independent Schools Council (ISC):

The Heads' Conference (HMC)
Girls' Schools Association (GSA)
The Society of Heads
Independent Association of Prep Schools (IAPS)
Independent Schools Association (ISA)

Edited by

JULIE BENNETT

Tel: 020 3745 9354; email: isyb@acblack.com
website: www.independentschoolsyearbook.co.uk

BLOOMSBURY YEARBOOKS
LONDON • OXFORD • NEW YORK • NEW DELHI • SYDNEY

BLOOMSBURY YEARBOOKS
Bloomsbury Publishing Plc
50 Bedford Square, London, WC1B 3DP, UK
29 Earlsfort Terrace, Dublin 2, Ireland

First published in Great Britain 1889
This edition published 2024

A catalogue record for this book is available from the British Library.

ISBN: PB 978-1-3994-0946-9

2 4 6 8 10 9 7 5 3 1

Printed and bound in Great Britain by CPI Group (UK) Ltd,
Croydon CR0 4YY

To find out more about our authors and books visit www.bloomsbury.com and sign up for our newsletters.

INDEPENDENT SCHOOLS YEARBOOK 2023–2024

CONTENTS

. . . /continued

PART III: THE SOCIETY OF HEADS

73 schools for pupils from age 11 to 18 whose Heads are members of The Society of Heads. The majority are co-educational schools, but Membership is open to boys and girls schools. Many of the schools also have a Preparatory/Junior school or department.

PART IV: INDEPENDENT ASSOCIATION OF PREP SCHOOLS

459 schools whose Heads are members of IAPS; 16 of these are overseas members. Most of the schools are co-educational; some cater for boys only or girls only. The preparatory school age range is 7 to 11/13, but many of the schools have a pre-preparatory department for children up to age 7.

PART V: INDEPENDENT SCHOOLS ASSOCIATION

192 schools in membership of ISA. Schools in this Association are not confined to one age range and can cater for any age range of pupils up to 18/19 years.

ISC

INDEPENDENT SCHOOLS COUNCIL

www.isc.co.uk

The ISC is established:

- to support the aims and objectives of its member associations
- to provide authoritative research and intelligence about the sector
- to promote public affairs and parliamentary engagement on behalf of the sector
- to provide online access and support informing parental decisions
- to promote the sector through agreed national messaging and communications

The Constituent Associations of the ISC are:

Association of Governing Bodies of Independent Schools (AGBIS)
Girls' Schools Association (GSA)
The Heads' Conference (HMC)
Independent Association of Prep Schools (IAPS)
Independent Schools Association (ISA)
Independent Schools' Bursars Association (ISBA)
The Society of Heads

The ISC's Affiliated Associations are:

Boarding Schools' Association (BSA)
Council of British International Schools (COBIS)
Scottish Council of Independent Schools (SCIS)
Welsh Independent Schools Council (WISC)

Secretariat

Chairman
Barnaby Lenon

Chief Executive
Julie Robinson

Independent Schools Council
First Floor, 27 Queen Anne's Gate, London SW1H 9BU

Tel: 020 7766 7070
Website: www.isc.co.uk

HMC

THE HEADS' CONFERENCE

www.hmc.org.uk

HMC is the world's first Heads' association dating back to 1869 when Edward Thring of Uppingham School convened the first Conference. Since that time, Conference has convened annually and it is a condition of membership that Heads attend, so that the association retains its sense of collegiality and common purpose.

There are currently over 300 members leading in the UK and Ireland and serving 270,000 young people, making it by far the largest Heads' association in the independent sector. HMC welcomes many different types of school, including day and boarding schools, senior and through schools as well as boys', girls', co-educational and diamond schools. In addition, 50 international members represent schools throughout the world.

UK and Ireland schools must operate on a not-for-profit basis, and they must also meet stringent requirements to ensure educational quality and breadth. HMC schools are prominent supporters of state sector partnerships and several sponsor state-maintained academies. All HMC schools are committed to the safeguarding of children and young people.

The aims of the association have changed relatively little since its foundation and it continues to support its members, to represent their views and to exemplify excellence in education. It has an extensive professional development programme for Heads, aspiring heads, senior leaders, governors and others. The Education team, with senior and junior school specialists, provides advice and support on a variety of school-related issues. Most recently HMC has published helpful guides on university access, bursaries, digital skills in schools, the future of assessment and much more.

The Communications team supports members with issues from crisis communications and political engagement to website design and social media strategies. HMC has a Partner Directory, offering members direct access to high quality and recommended suppliers and advisers, ready to support schools with excellent services.

HMC is closely associated with the other independent sector associations within the Independent Schools Council (ISC), and with the Association of School and College Leaders (ASCL), which represents the Heads and senior staff of secondary schools and colleges in both the maintained and independent sectors. HMC schools make up more than 50% of the student body within ISC, and 54% of all pupils on fee assistance in ISC schools are at an HMC school.

The HMC Board and Council 2023–2024

Elected Board Members

Chair	Sue Woodroofe	The Grammar School at Leeds
Vice-Chair	Melvyn Roffe	George Watson's College
Chair-Elect	Jaideep Barot	Bristol Grammar School
Treasurer	Brendan Wignall	Ellesmere College
Members	George Hartley	The King's School, Chester
	Sally-Anne Huang	St Paul's School
	Lisa Kerr	Gordonstoun
	Geoff Thompson, MBE	
	Arun Kanwar	

Council Members

Chair – East	Simon Lockyer	Royal Hospital School
Secretary – East	Andrew Holman	Wellingborough School
Chair – Irish	Robert Robinson	Campbell College
Secretary – Irish		
Chair – London	Fionnuala Kennedy	Wimbledon High School
Secretary – London	Alastair Land	Harrow School
Chair – North East	Anthony Jackson	Barnard Castle School
Secretary – North East	Alexandra Wilson	Tranby
Chair – North West	George Hartley	King's School Chester
Secretary – North West	Paul Vicars	Birkenhead School
Chair – Scottish	Mark Lauder	Strathallan School
Secretary – Scottish	Matthew Pearce	The Glasgow Academy
Chair – South Central	Alastair Chirnside	St Edward's School
Secretary – South Central	Elaine Purves	Queen Anne's School
Chair – South East	Shaun Fenton	Reigate Grammar School
Secretary – South East	Tom Lawson	Eastbourne College
Chair – South West	Rupert Heathcote	Queen Elizabeth's Hospital
Secretary – South West	Louise Simpson	Exeter School
Chair – West	Charles Fillingham	Solihull School
Secretary – West	Jon Pitt	RGS Worcester
Chair – International	Vanita Uppal, OBE	The British School, New Delhi
Secretary – International	Nicholas Hammond	The British School of Paris

Co-opted Members

Chair of Education	Christopher Stevens	Bradfield College
Chair of Professional Development	Ben Vessey	Canford School
Chair of Universities	Nick Weaver	Ipswich School
Chair of Inspection	Jason Slack	The King's School in Macclesfield
Chair of Communications	Philip Britton, MBE	Bolton School
Chair of Membership & Professional Standards	George Hartley	The King's School, Chester
Chair of Sports	Kevin Knibbs	Hampton School
Chair of Pastoral & Safeguarding	Sarah Kerr-Dineen	Oundle School

General Secretary & CEO: Simon Hyde

Director of Finance & Operations: Chris Silver

HMC - The Heads' Conference

12 The Point, Rockingham Road, Market Harborough, Leicestershire LE16 7QU

Tel: 01858 465260 · email: office@hmc.org.uk

website: www.hmc.org.uk

GSA

GIRLS' SCHOOLS ASSOCIATION

gsa.uk.com

The Girls' Schools Association is a membership organisation that champions girls and their teachers so that they have the best chances to excel in the lives they choose to lead. An expert in girls' education, GSA defends girls' best interests and regularly commissions rigorous research to demonstrate the modern relevance and enduring power of a girls-only education.

Its 152 schools-strong membership is made up of Heads from a diverse range of independent and state girls' schools, including many of the top performing in the UK. Together they educate over 90,000 students.

Rigorous research compellingly proves the power of a girls' education built for girls. The facts are that girls' schools are crucial to achieving gender equality; they level the playing field for girls and consistently campaign for the benefit of girls and women, and always have. The data consistently shows that girls thrive in all-girls educational environments: girls in girls' schools are more confident and emotionally in control; girls in GSA schools are significantly more likely to study STEM (science, technology, engineering and maths) subjects, and take up and continue to play sport. Combining exceptional academic provision (most progress to top universities) with a deep understanding of what girls need to thrive, GSA schools put girls first to foster their courage, curiosity, and self-belief in their abilities, and ambitions.

Modern girls' schools offer an array of options to suit every family and pupil including day, boarding, junior, senior, large, small, urban or rural, with each offering every girl numerous opportunities to fully realise their potential as active, equal, confident and competent women. GSA alumnae are testament to the power of an all-girls education, and many are world-renowned women forging brighter futures for the next generation of change makers. Excelling in all careers, including the traditionally male-dominated professions, they include scientists, international campaigners and activists, artists and actresses, foreign correspondents, Olympic medallists, and businesswomen.

GSA schools are similarly respected internationally and have an impressive global reputation. Fostering the highest standards of education, pastoral care and co-curricular activity, alongside a wealth of extra-curricular opportunity in art, music, drama, sport and more. They share experience, specialisms, events, and facilities in a variety of cross-sector school partnerships, and many GSA schools offer bursaries to extend the opportunity further to more families and pupils.

A powerful, well-respected association within the educational establishment, GSA is committed to enhancing the understanding of the benefits of girls' schools, always working to inform and influence the national and international education debate, and commissioning, conducting, and collating pertinent research. In addition to acting as advocate, GSA provides its members and their schools with professional development courses, conferences, advice, and opportunities to debate and share best practice.

The GSA works closely with the Association of School and College Leaders, is a member of the Independent Schools Council, and joins hands with organisations in the UK and internationally – such as the Association of State Girls' School (UK), the National Coalition of Girls' Schools (US) and the Alliance of Girls' Schools Australasia – in the interests of girls' education worldwide.

GSA's goal is to create the world as it should be, a place where every girl can achieve and lead; and it is GSA's belief that a girl's education gives girls the skills and appetite to recognise their full talents, and rightfully realise brilliant lives.

Officers 2023–2024

President	Marina Gardiner Legge	Oxford High School GDST
Vice-President	Heather Hanbury	Lady Eleanor Holles School
Treasurer	Sarah Matthews	Truro High School for Girls
Committee Chairs		
Boarding	Liz Hewer	St George's School, Ascot
Education	Helen Jeys	Manchester High School for Girls
Inclusion	Heidi-Jayne Boyes	Wakefield Girls' High School
Junior and Prep	Nina Kingsmill Moore	Glendower Preparatory School
Membership & Accreditation	Jane Prescott	Portsmouth High School GDST
Research	Fionnuala Kennedy	Wimbledon High School GDST
Safeguarding & Pastoral	Will le Flemming	The Abbey
Sport and Wellness	Sarah Rollings	Heathfield School
Universities	Matthew Shoults	Notting Hill & Ealing High School GDST
Regional Representatives		
East	Jo Cameron	Queenswood
London	Richard Tillett	Queen's College London
Midlands	Fiona Miles	Loughborough High School
North East	Carole Cameron	Queen Mary's School, Thirsk
North West	Nicola Smillie	Alderley Edge School for Girls
Scotland	Anna Tomlinson	St Margaret's School for Girls, Aberdeen
South Central	Jo Duncan	Wycombe Abbey School
South East	Anna King	Notre Dame School
South West & Wales	Jessica Miles	Monmouth School for Girls

Secretariat

Chief Executive: Donna Stevens
Operations Director: Imogen Vanderpump
Membership Director: Sue Hincks
Executive Assistant to the Chief Executive: Jeven Sharma
Membership Manager: Jannette Davison
Conference & Events Manager: Jennifer Purser
Head of Media & Communications: Rachel Donati
Events & Communications Officer: Alicia Buckleberry
Membership & Research Officer: Mandy Lam
Accounts: Rehana Alimahomed

Girls' Schools Association
Suite 105, 108 New Walk, Leicester, LE1 7EA
Tel: 0116 254 1619 · email: office@gsa.uk.com
website: gsa.uk.com

THE SOCIETY OF HEADS

www.thesocietyofheads.org.uk

The Society is an Association of Heads of just over 140 well-established independent schools. It was founded in 1961 when a group of Heads decided they needed a forum in which to share ideas and experience. Since then the Society has grown substantially in size, reputation and effectiveness and represents a vibrant community of independent schools throughout England and Wales with some additional overseas members.

The Society's policy is to maintain high standards in member schools, to promote independent education, to provide an opportunity for the sharing of ideas and common concerns, to foster links with the wider sphere of higher education and to strengthen relations with the maintained sector by promoting partnerships.

Within the membership there is a wide variety of educational experience. Some schools are young, some have evolved from older foundations, some have behind them a long tradition of pioneer and specialist education; a number are at the leading edge of education in music, dance and the arts; and several are well known for their effective support for those with specific learning difficulties. The great majority are co-educational but we also have some all-boys and all-girls schools. Many have a strong boarding element; others are day only. All offer a stimulating sixth-form experience and give a sound and balanced education to pupils of widely varying abilities and interests.

The Society is one of the constituent Associations of the Independent Schools Council. Every Full Member school has been accredited through inspection by the Independent Schools Inspectorate (or Estyn in Wales and HMIE in Scotland) and is subject to regular visits to monitor standards and ensure that good practice and sound academic results are maintained. The Society is also represented on many other educational bodies.

All members are in membership of the Association of School and College Leaders (ASCL) or other union for school leaders and Full Member schools belong to AGBIS or an equivalent professional body supporting governance.

The Society hosts the autumn meeting, summer meeting and the annual conference for members. The Society also provides an extensive professional development programme.

Officers 2023–2024

Chair: David Gajadharsingh, The Royal Ballet School
Vice-Chair: Sue Hannam, Lichfield Cathedral School
Chair Designate: Gareth Doodes, The King's School, Worcester
Hon. Treasurer: Christine Cunniffe, LVS Ascot

Committee 2023–2024

Sue Hannam, Lichfield Cathedral School
Sarah Raffray, King's International School, Bangkok
Dr Andy Kemp, The National Mathematics and Science College
Adrian Meadows, The Peterborough School
Christine Cunniffe, LVS Ascot
Damian Ettinger, Cokethorpe School
David Gajadharsingh, The Royal Ballet School
David Tickner, Newcastle School for Boys
Gareth Doodes, The King's School
James Davies, Halliford School
Jessica Ward, Elmhurst Ballet School
Judith Fremont-Barnes, St Paul's Cathedral School
Julian Noad, Queen's College, Taunton
Richard Notman, Stover School
Rob Jones, Rendcomb College
Silas Edmonds, Ewell Castle School

CEO: Clive Rickart

The Society of Heads
Office 101B, Harborough Enterprise Centre,
Compass Point Business Park, Market Harborough, Leicestershire LE16 9HW
Tel: 01858 433760 · email: info@thesocietyofheads.org.uk

IAPS

INDEPENDENT ASSOCIATION OF PREP SCHOOLS

iaps.uk

IAPS is the leading association for Heads of independent prep and junior schools in the UK and internationally, providing its members with a range of support services, advice, professional development and a voice with government.

Headteachers can only join IAPS if they have been accredited through a range of measures of quality of the schools that they run. They must demonstrate the highest standards of education and care, and that their school offers an all-round, values-led, broad education which produces confident, adaptable, motivated children with a lifelong passion for learning.

While the values may be the same, each of our schools is independent and distinct: we have single-sex and co-educational, boarding, day and mixed, urban and rural. Sizes vary from more than 800 pupils to around 100.

We have one of the independent sector's top training programmes which includes a broad range of professional development courses. New members are offered a highly qualified IAPS coach as support and members are divided into district groups by geographical location, giving them the chance to meet with fellow heads on a regular basis. We organise sporting tournaments for pupils to a national standard in a wide range of sports. Our annual conference brings together members and leaders in educational thinking, politics and business.

With over 600 member schools in the UK and around 50 beyond it, IAPS offers excellent opportunities to members for fellowship and networking.

The Board and Officers for 2023–2024

Chair: Andrew Nott

Members of the Board:

Elected Board Directors

Emma Goldsmith

Charlotte Johnson

Elaine Rawlings

Maxine Shaw

Tim Smith

Bill Toleman

Jim Walton

Independent Board Directors

Mojca Lozar

Lucy Murphy

Camilla Gray Muir

Caroline Townsend

Dean White

Officers:

Chief Executive: Dominic Norrish

Director of Education: Mark Brotherton

Director of Membership Services: Emilie Darwin

Head of Finance: Jackie Moore

Membership Secretary: Petra Hancock

Facilities Manager: Christine McCrudden

Independent Association of Prep Schools

Bishop's House, Artemis Drive, Tachbrook Park, Warwick, CV34 6UD

Tel: 01926 887833 · email: iaps@iaps.uk

Facebook: @UKIAPS · LinkedIn: /company/iaps

X/Twitter: @iapsuk · X/Twitter (Sport): @iapsuksport

ISA
INDEPENDENT SCHOOLS ASSOCIATION
www.isaschools.org.uk

The Independent Schools Association (ISA) brings the Headteachers of over 650 independent schools together, representing the diverse range of independent education practised across the UK and overseas. Established in 1878, ISA is one of the oldest of the associations that make up the Independent Schools Council (ISC).

ISA exists to provide professional support, fellowship and opportunity to their 651 members who nurture and develop over 130,000 pupils within their schools. Promoting best practice and fellowship remains at the core of ISA, as it did when it began over 145 years ago.

ISA supports Headteachers using their independence to meet the specific needs of their pupils. At ISA there are schools with different approaches to the curriculum, schools with different religious characters, and none, and schools with different ways of operating. This all contributes to a wide-ranging membership, not confined to any one type of school, but including all: nursery, pre-preparatory, junior and senior, all-through schools, coeducational, single-sex, boarding, day, bilingual, performing arts and specialist provision.

As well as tailored professional development opportunities for ISA Members through their programme of courses and conferences, pupils in ISA schools benefit through their Head's membership with access to the extensive ISA Sport and Arts programmes. ISA Sport champions inclusion in physical activity for young people across 54 national (and over 150 regional) events. ISA Arts helps schools inspire creativity, expression and individuality across the arts with both virtual and in-person events. Also, the annual ISA awards ceremony celebrates excellence and innovation across Members' schools.

The ISA central office also provides advice to Members in areas such as HR, curriculum, finance, leadership and governance, and represents the views of its membership at national and governmental levels. A strong regional network of fellow Heads supports each Member, and all Members receive a complimentary compliance check in the run-up to their next scheduled inspection, as well as an annual pastoral visit from a dedicated regional ambassador.

Membership is open to independent school Heads and Proprietors provided they meet the necessary criteria, which include accreditation by any government-approved inspectorate.

Council and Officers for 2023–2024

President: Lord Lexden OBE

Independent Trustees:
Andrew Hampton
Claire Osborn
Richard Walden

Honorary Officers:
Chair: Jeff Shaw
Vice-Chair: Phil Soutar
Vice-Chair: Natasha Dangerfield

Elective Councillors:

Matthew Burke
Allan Cairns
Helen Chalmers
Lawrence Collins
Andrew Hammond
Christopher Hammond
Sue Knox
Irfan Latif
Stephen McKernan
Geraldine Maidment
Kevin Samson
Oliver Scott
James Wilding

Area Coordinators:

East Anglia: Pauline Wilson
London North: Amanda Campbell
London South: Dominic Price
London West: Jonathan Hetherington
Midlands: David Preston
North: Jeremy Duke
South West: Dionne Seagrove

Officials

Chief Executive Officer: Rudolf Eliott Lockhart
Deputy Chief Executive Officer: Peter Woodroffe
Director of Education and Inclusion: Helen Stanton-Tonner
Professional Development Officer: Alice Thompson
Office Manager and PA to the CEO: Karen Goddard

Independent Schools Association
ISA House, 5–7 Great Chesterford Court, Great Chesterford, Essex CB10 1PF
Tel: 01799 523619 · email: isa@isaschools.org.uk
X/Twitter: @isaschools · LinkedIn: /company/independent-schools-association

AGBIS

ASSOCIATION OF GOVERNING BODIES OF INDEPENDENT SCHOOLS

REGISTERED CHARITY NO. 1108756

www.agbis.org.uk

The Association of Governing Bodies of Independent Schools (AGBIS) supports and advises governing bodies of schools in the independent sector on all aspects of governance.

The charitable objects of AGBIS are the advancement of education and the promotion of good governance in independent schools.

AGBIS offers a number of services* to their members including:

- Training seminars and webinars for new and experienced governors, on a variety of topics, and free eLearning courses on safeguarding and for new governors.
- An advisory service on all aspects of governing schools via telephone, email and the website.
- 'Guidelines for Governors' a manual of good practice.
- Annual survey of salaries and benefits of heads and bursars.
- eNewsletters to keep governors informed on current topics of interest and/or concern.
- Bespoke on-site and virtual training for governing bodies, leading governors' strategy days and reviews of governance for schools.
- Annual conference and AGM for representatives of member schools.
- Support for governor recruitment including: a list of potential new governors; an online Vacancies Board where members can advertise their governor vacancies; and a member discount on support from board-level search specialists.

* Some of the AGBIS services are offered for a fee.

Board

AGBIS is a registered charity (No 1108756) and company (No 0521716) limited by guarantee governed by a Board which meets at least once every school term. Board members are nominated by school governing bodies and serve initially for a three year period. The Board is advised by three committees: Training and Membership, Nominations and Governance and Finance.

The AGBIS Board includes three honorary officers:

Chair: Mark Taylor (Tring Park School for the Performing Arts)
Deputy Chair: Mike Gregson (The Edinburgh Academy Foundation)
Treasurer: Sarah Phillips (King Alfred School)

Chief Executive: Richard Harman
Director of Training and Membership (Deputy CEO): Cheryl Connelly

Association of Governing Bodies of Independent Schools
The Grange, 3 Codicote Road, Welwyn, Hertfordshire AL6 9LY
Tel: 01438 840730 · email: enquiries@agbis.org.uk
X/Twitter: @AGBIS2 · LinkedIn: /company/agbis

ISBA

INDEPENDENT SCHOOLS' BURSARS ASSOCIATION

www.theisba.org.uk

The Independent Schools' Bursars Association (ISBA) is the only national association to represent school bursars and business managers of independent schools, providing them with the professional support they need to manage their schools successfully and provide a world class education to their pupils.

The association can trace its history back to the founding of the Public Schools Bursars' Association which held its first general meeting on 26 April 1932 at the offices of Epsom College. Its name then changed to the Independent Schools' Bursars Association in 1983.

The ISBA now has more than 1,100 independent school members, including international associate members, from smaller preparatory schools to larger and well-renowned senior schools, including both boarding and day schools. Although it is the school and not the bursar who becomes a member of the association, it is usually the bursar or equivalent who is the school's nominated representative.

The association is one of the constituent members of the Independent Schools Council (ISC) and also works closely with the other seven constituent associations of the ISC. It is represented on the ISC Governing Council and a number of ISC committees and is also often called on to represent the ISC at meetings with the Department for Education, Health & Safety Executive and Teachers' Pensions providing advice on bursarial matters.

Full membership of the ISBA is open to schools who are members of one of the constituent associations in membership of the ISC. Associate membership is open to certain other schools/organisations which are recognised as educational charities.

Day-to-day the ISBA advises many different staff within a school's senior management team including the bursar, finance director, chief operations officer, business manager, deputy or assistant with areas of responsibility encompassing accounting, financial management and reporting, risk management, regulatory compliance, facilities management, HR, technology, environmental sustainability, auxiliary services and more. As part of its range of support services the association offers schools:

- guidance and legislative briefings, and model policies to download from its online reference library;
- a comprehensive professional development programme covering finance, legal, HR, inspections and other key operational issues and tailored to suit staff at all levels;
- information, advice and networking opportunities at the ISBA Annual Conference (the 2024 conference will take place from 20 to 22 May 2024);
- a 'Bursar's Guide' – providing the latest information on legislation affecting schools;
- termly copies of the ISBA's magazine – The Bursar's Review – and weekly and monthly e-bulletins covering the latest legal, financial and HR news and more;
- an online job vacancies page where schools can advertise any of their vacant bursary management roles for free.

The ISBA Board consists of the Chair of the Association, Neil Cufley, Director of Operations at Royal Russell School, and the bursars of between eight and 12 other leading independent schools.

The Independent Schools' Bursars Association is a Registered Charity, number 1121757,
and a Company Limited by Guarantee, registered in England and Wales, number 6410037.

Chief Executive: Mr David Woodgate

Independent Schools' Bursars Association
167-169 Great Portland Street, 5th Floor, London, W1W 5PF
Tel: 01256 330369 · email: office@theisba.org.uk
X/Twitter: @the_isba · LinkedIn: /company/703763

COBIS
COUNCIL OF BRITISH INTERNATIONAL SCHOOLS

www.cobis.org.uk

X/Twitter: @COBISorg · @COBIS_CEO

Representing over 400 members and supporting associates, COBIS is the global association for international British schools overseas. The organisation has developed markedly since its foundation, changing to meet the needs and aspirations of its growing global school membership base.

COBIS exists to serve, support and represent its member schools – their leaders, governors, staff and students by:

- Providing Quality Assurance in member schools via the Accreditation and Compliance scheme
- Representing member schools with the British Government, educational bodies and the corporate sector
- Providing effective professional development for senior leaders, governors, teachers and support staff
- Facilitating, coordinating and supporting professional networking opportunities for British International schools
- Promoting child protection and safer recruitment and employment practices
- Engaging, challenging and inspiring students of all ages and abilities by delivering excellent interschool student competitions and events
- Providing access to information about trends and developments in UK education
- Facilitating high impact 'Member to Member' professional networking
- Promoting career opportunities within the global COBIS network
- Connecting suppliers and companies operating in the education sector with international British schools overseas in its role as Trade Challenge Partner of the Department for International Trade (DIT)

Council of British International Schools
55-56 Russell Square, Bloomsbury, London WC1B 4HP
Tel: +44 (0)20 3826 7190 · email: pa@cobis.org.uk

BSA

BOARDING SCHOOLS' ASSOCIATION

www.boarding.org.uk

The Boarding Schools' Association (BSA) is part of the BSA Group. BSA Group supports excellence in boarding, safeguarding, inclusion and health education, serving more that 1,500 organisations and people in 40 countries worldwide. Since it's foundation in 1965-6, BSA has promoted boarding education and the development of quality boarding through high standards of pastoral care and boarding accommodation.

A UK boarding school can only be a full member of the BSA if it is also a member of one of the Independent Schools Council (ISC) constituent associations, or in membership of the BSA State Boarding Forum (SBF). These two bodies require member schools to be regularly inspected by the Independent Schools' Inspectorate (ISI), Care Inspectorate (Scotland), Care Inspectorate (Wales) or Ofsted. Other boarding schools who are not members of these organisations can apply to be affiliate members. Similar arrangements are in place for international members. Boarding inspection of ISC accredited independent schools has been conducted by ISI since September 2012. Ofsted retains responsibility for the inspection of boarding in state schools and non-association independent schools.

Boarding inspections must be conducted every three years. Boarding in England is judged against the National Minimum Standards for Boarding Schools which were last updated in September 2022.

Relationship with government

BSA is in regular communication with the Department for Education (DfE) on all boarding matters in England and with devolved governments for other parts of the UK. The Children Act (1989) and the Care Standards Act (2001) require boarding schools in England to conform to national legislation. The promotion of this legislation and the training required to carry it out are matters on which the DfE and BSA work together. BSA worked especially closely with the DfE and other government departments during the coronavirus pandemic, supporting the safety and continuity of education for its member schools' pupils and staff. Other governmental departments BSA work with are the Home Office, Ministry of Defence and the Foreign, Commonwealth & Development Office.

Boarding training

BSA delivers the world's largest professional development programme for boarding staff. It offers:

- Two-year courses for graduate and non-graduate boarding staff – these involve eight study days and two assignments, each about 4,000 words long. This is the flagship training opportunity for staff seriously interested in boarding excellence
- A Diploma course for senior experienced boarding staff, involving three study days and three assignments. We run two modules each year starting in November and March
- MA in residential education
- A broad range of day seminars and webinars on topics of particular interest to boarding/pastoral staff – e.g. Essentials of Boarding, Leading a Boarding Team
- Meeting the Needs of International Boarders
- Specialist one or two-day conferences for Boarding Staff, Heads, Health & Wellbeing staff**, Marketing and Admissions staff* and State Boarding Schools staff and Safeguarding Leads***
- A course for new and aspiring boarding Heads
- Certificates in Mental Health, Safeguarding, Inclusion, School Nurses, Coaching and Mentoring
- Basic training online, for those very new to boarding.

* With SACPA (Safeguarding and Child Protection Association), part of the BSA Group

** With HIEDA (Health in Education Association), part of the BSA Group

*** With BAISIS (British Association of Independent Schools with International Students), part of the BSA Group

In 2022, BSA Group also launched, The Institute of Boarding (TIOB), a dedicated association for supporting and recognising professional boarding school staff.

State Boarding Forum (SBF)

BSA support state boarding school members through the State Boarding Forum. There are a total of 44 state boarding schools across England, Scotland and Northern Ireland. At these schools, parents pay for boarding but not for education, so fees are substantially lower than in an independent boarding school. The latest BSA State Boarding Forum Census was published in January 2023.

Legal Services

BSA Group Legal is the trading name of BSA Group Legal Services Ltd, a law firm authorised and regulated by the Solicitors Regulation Authority of England and Wales. The BSA Group Legal team works closely with the Home Office to support members with UK immigration matters relating to independent schools. In 2023 the BSA also partnered with Verisio to provide a Due Diligence service to support schools carrying out background checks on future students and their families.

BSA Group Leadership Team

Chief Executive: Robin Fletcher

Deputy Chief Executive and Chief Operating Officer: Aileen Kane (Maternity Leave)

Director, Heida and Group Services Director: Lee Glaser

Senior Director: Dale Wilkins

Legal and Public Affairs Director: Kate Hollyer

Director, BSA: David Walker

Director of Operations: Chris King (Maternity Cover)

International and Membership Director: Caroline Nixon

Director of Safeguarding and Director, Sacpa: Claire Dan

Director of Engagement and Director, TIOB: Gaelle Sullivan

Programmes Director, BSA Group and Director, BAISIS: Beth Waddington

The Boarding Schools' Association
167-169 Great Portland Street, 5th Floor, London, W1W 5PF
Tel: +44 (0)20 7798 1580 · email: bsa@boarding.org.uk
website: www.boarding.org.uk

ISEB

INDEPENDENT SCHOOLS EXAMINATIONS BOARD

Common Entrance (CE)
Common Academic Scholarship (CASE)
IESB Common Pre-Tests
ISEB Project Qualification (iPQ)

www.iseb.co.uk

Chief Executive:
Julia Martin, MA, BA, PGCE, FRSA
Chair:
Wendy Griffiths, BSc, PGCE

COMMON ENTRANCE (CE)

The Independent Schools Examinations Board (ISEB) was founded in 1903 to design and deliver a 'common' entrance examination for independent senior school admissions. ISEB's Common Entrance (CE) examinations were first introduced in 1904, and are still taken around the world 120 years later.

CE has evolved and expanded over the last 120 years and now produces examinations for ten subjects at 13+, from English, mathematics and science, through to geography, history, modern foreign languages, classical civilisation, and theology, philosophy and religion. The paper-based examinations remain an important and highly-regarded milestone in the independent academic calendar, and offer fantastic preparation for pupils ahead of GCSEs.

Candidates are entered for CE 13+ examinations if they attend a prep school that uses CE as part of its curriculum, or if they have been offered a place at a senior school subject to their passing the examinations.

Candidates will usually be entered by and take the examinations at their current prep school, however, if they attend a state or international school that does not use CE as part of their curriculum, they may need to be entered by a parent or guardian. In these cases, the senior school to which the candidate is applying will be able to advise which CE 13+ examinations the candidate should be entered for. Parent/guardian registration for CE 13+ is completed via the Family Hub on the ISEB website.

Full information, including subject specification and examination timetables, is available from the ISEB website. Past CE 13+ examination papers can be purchased from the ISEB online shop. Visit www.iseb.co.uk/common-entrance.

COMMON ACADEMIC SCHOLARSHIP (CASE)

Common Academic Scholarship (CASE) examinations are used by independent senior schools to access scholarship candidates at 13+. CASE papers are set in English, mathematics, science, history, geography, theology, philosophy and religion, French and Latin.

Candidates taking CASE examinations will be entered by the senior school to which they have applied, and will usually sit the examinations at the senior school.

Full information, including subject specifications and examination timetables, is available from the ISEB website. Past CASE examination papers can be purchased from the ISEB online shop. Visit www.iseb.co.uk/common-academic-scholarship.

ISEB COMMON PRE-TESTS

The ISEB Common Pre-Tests are shared 11+ assessments used as part of senior school admissions processes. The Pre-Tests are used by UK's leading independent senior schools, including Eton College, Harrow, Charterhouse, Marlborough College, Brighton College, Lady Eleanor Holles, and James Allen's Girls' School. The Pre-Tests are flexible, shared assessments, designed to reduce the test burden on families and support pupil wellbeing.

Comprising four tests in English, mathematics, verbal reasoning and non-verbal reasoning, the ISEB Pre-Tests are taken by pupils once during the academic year, usually in years 6 or 7. Their results are shared with any senior schools they have applied to that use the Pre-Tests as part of their admissions processes.

The results are age-standardised across each cohort of pupils, ensuring there are no benefits or disadvantages for candidates who are older or younger at the point at which they take the tests. The ISEB Pre-Tests are adaptive, which means that pupils are presented with questions based on their previous answers. This ensures that the difficulty remains at the right level to demonstrate the best of each pupil's ability and potential, and that they feel confident and have an enjoyable test experience.

The ISEB Pre-Tests online test player offers a range of flexible features, so pupils can tailor the test experience to their individual needs. All candidates can hide the onscreen timer and adjust font size and colour overlays, and candidates with SEND requirements can request further access arrangements.

Candidates usually take the ISEB Pre-Tests at their current prep school or at the senior school to which they are applying. Pupils outside of the UK, or that do not attend a school that hosts the tests can contact VICTVS to arrange an invigilation centre. VICTVS has a global network of exam venues and invigilators, all of whom are highly trained to coordinate ISEB assessments. Visit www.victvs.co.uk/iseb-exam-invigilation.

Candidate registration for the ISEB Pre-Tests is completed by parents or guardians through the Guardian Admin Portal. Registration is quick, simple and free. Please visit the ISEB Pre-Tests Admissions Toolkit for additional guidance on the registration process. Visit www.iseb.co.uk/pre-tests-admissions-toolkit.

Additional test practise and preparation is not a requirement of the ISEB Pre-Tests. However, ISEB understands that many families choose to engage in additional practice at home. ISEB advocates a holistic approach to preparation and practice, taking into consideration overall mental, emotional and physical wellbeing. Families can find a range of free online support resources through the Pre-Tests Admissions Toolkit, alongside information about the only test practice platform endorsed by the examination board, Bond Online Premium Plus. Visit www.iseb.co.uk/pre-tests-admissions-toolkit.

ISEB PROJECT QUALIFICATION (iPQ)

The ISEB Project Qualification (iPQ) provides a framework for teaching and assessing the development of independent, pupil-led project-learning skills, taking the form of a 15-20 hour-long project. The iPQ can be used as a stand-alone addition to a school's existing curriculum or as an alternative to one or more subjects and is usually completed in Years 5 to 8. Children are registered for the iPQ by their school, and receive a certificate from ISEB recognising their achievements. Further information can be found at www.iseb.co.uk/iPQ.

Past papers, family resources, and endorsed support materials:

The ISEB online shop provides a wide range of support and preparation material for ISEB examinations and qualifications, including printed packs of past papers for CE and CASE. Families will also find endorsed and quality-assured test practice materials for the ISEB Pre-Tests, and the ISEB Parent Power Toolkit, a set of premium pupil wellbeing resources designed to support their children throughout their assessment and admissions journeys. Visit www.iseb.co.uk/shop.

Bond Online Premium Plus is a test practice platform for the ISEB Pre-Tests. It is the only platform endorsed by ISEB, as it most closely aligns to the questions and format of the Pre-Tests. Featuring questions written by ISEB, as well as mock tests, Bond Online Premium Plus is produced by Bond, Oxford University Press, and utilises cutting-edge technology from CENTURY. Parents and guardians can try it free for seven days. Visit www.iseb.co.uk/shop.

The ISEB Parent Power Toolkit has been produced in partnership with Dr Kathy Weston from Tooled Up Education. It provides a range of online, research-backed videos and activities designed to give agency to parents and guardians through strategies and practical ideas to support children prepare for important tests while prioritising their mental wellbeing. The resources are flexible and easy to integrate into busy family life. There are four parts to the toolkit, so families are supported throughout their assessment journeys. Visit www.iseb.co.uk/shop.

Contact

ISEB can be contacted through our dedicated customer support portals. Visit www.iseb.co.uk/contact for links to our support portals and knowledge bases.

Independent Schools Examinations Board

Suite 3, Endeavour House, Crow Arch Lane, Ringwood, Hampshire BH24 1HP

Tel: 01425 470555 · email: enquiries@iseb.co.uk

website: www.iseb.co.uk

INDEPENDENT SCHOOLS INSPECTORATE

www.isi.net

ISI provides assurance on the standards and quality of school life for children and young people in association independent schools in England. The inspectorate reports to the Department for Education on the extent to which these schools meet the statutory Independent School Standards.

For schools providing pupil accommodation, ISI also inspects against additional requirements set out in the National Minimum Standards (NMS) for Boarding Schools. All inspection reports are published on the ISI website.

In September 2023, ISI introduced a new inspection framework. Preparations for this started almost two years ago and included a seven-month consultation and a four-phase pilot programme. ISI will continue to inspect schools routinely twice within a six-year inspection cycle or as directed by the Department for Education. Under this framework, ISI has moved to a single type of routine inspection to promote clarity and consistency in their reporting over time and simplify the inspection process for school.

There are also three types of non-routine inspection, including 'additional inspections' where the Department for Education have reason for a school to be inspected urgently. This could be due to concerns raised by parents, staff or pupils.

Safeguarding is a focus of all inspections. Inspectors review evidence relating to a school's safeguarding arrangements and report to the Department for Education on the extent to which schools meet their responsibilities. Listening to pupils is central to this process, and every inspection uses anonymous pupil, parent and staff questionnaires as a crucial part of the inspection evidence. Inspectors also speak to pupils in groups on inspection.

Quality assurance is embedded at every stage of ISI's inspection process. This includes a high-quality training and development programme for their 700-strong inspector workforce. Every year ISI delivers, on average, over 300 hours of qualification, induction and annual training.

ISI's independence is essential to delivering reliable and valid judgements on the schools they inspect. Their governance structure and policies ensure they operate as a fully independent inspectorate. They have an independent Board of Directors, which holds the senior management team to account for the delivery and quality of inspections.

Independent Schools Inspectorate
CAP House, 9-12 Long Lane, London EC1A 9HA
Tel: 020 7600 0100 · email: info@isi.net

METHODIST INDEPENDENT SCHOOLS TRUST

www.methodistschools.org.uk

Trust Schools

Culford School, Bury St Edmunds, Suffolk
Farringtons School, Chislehurst, Kent
Kent College, Canterbury, Kent
Kent College Pembury, Tunbridge Wells, Kent
Lorenden Preparatory School, Faversham, Kent
Moorlands School, Leeds, West Yorks
Queen's College, Taunton, Somerset
Shebbear College, Beaworthy, Devon
Truro School, Truro, Cornwall
Woodhouse Grove School, Apperley Bridge, West Yorks

Associated Schools

Ashville College, Harrogate, North Yorks
Kingswood School, Bath, Somerset
Rydal Penrhos School, Colwyn Bay, North Wales

Affiliated Schools

The Leys School, Cambridge
Queenswood School, Hatfield, Herts
St Faith's School, Cambridge
Kent College Dubai
Kent College West Cairo

In cases of need applications may be made to a Methodist Bursary Fund for financial help to enable Methodist children to attend these schools. This fund is available to day pupils as well as boarding pupils. Details are available from the Schools.

Information regarding other sources of assistance with fees may be obtained from The Independent Schools Council, First Floor, 27 Queen Anne's Gate, London SW1H 9BU. Tel: 020 7766 7070; email: office@isc.co.uk.

Methodist Independent Schools Trust
27 Tavistock Square, London WC1H 9HH
Tel: 020 7935 3723 · email: admin@methodistschools.org.uk

GDST

THE GIRLS' DAY SCHOOL TRUST

www.gdst.net

The Girls' Day School Trust (GDST) is the UK's leading family of independent girls' schools. We also have two academies. We have over 150 years of experience educating girls. In all of our schools, academic excellence is a given, but GDST girls also learn to be confident, happy and fearless, prepared for the opportunities of the future.

We tailor our approach to how girls learn best, providing them with the attributes they need to excel. We focus not only on what is learned but *how* it is learned.

We concentrate on creating an environment where all can thrive and learn from one another. Physical and emotional wellbeing is paramount, which is why every GDST school provides an incredible array of extra-curricular activities and wellbeing programmes.

Nothing holds our girls back – they're encouraged to embrace every role and subject. As a result, they trust their own abilities and are alive to every opportunity. At GDST schools, girls learn without limits.

GDST schools

Blackheath High School
Brighton Girls
Bromley High School
Croydon High School
Howell's School Llandaff, Cardiff
Kensington Prep School
Newcastle High School for Girls
Northampton High School
Northwood College for Girls
Norwich High School for Girls
Notting Hill & Ealing High School
Nottingham Girls' High School
Oxford High School
Portsmouth High School
Putney High School
Royal High School, Bath
Sheffield High School for Girls
Shrewsbury High School
South Hampstead High School
Streatham & Clapham High School
Sutton High School
Sydenham High School
Wimbledon High School

GDST academies

The Belvedere Academy, Liverpool
Birkenhead High School Academy

Information on the schools and academies can be found in the Yearbook or on the GDST website: www.gdst.net.
The Girls' Day School Trust is a Registered Charity, number 306983.

The Girls' Day School Trust
10 Bressenden Place, London SW1E 5DH
Tel: 020 7393 6666 · email: info@gdst.net
X/Twitter: @GDST · Instagram: @gdstgirls

CISC

CATHOLIC INDEPENDENT SCHOOLS' CONFERENCE

www.catholicindependentschools.com

The Catholic Independent Schools' Conference is a dynamic and forward-thinking family of schools with members in England, Scotland, Ireland, France, Spain, Gibraltar and Italy. There are 112 schools in CISC, educating more than 36,000 pupils from nursery age through to eighteen.

There is a wide variety of types of school in CISC, with co-educational, single-sex, day, boarding, junior, prep, senior and all-through. We also have in our family of schools ten special schools (two independent and eight non-maintained special schools) serving a wide range of complex needs from profound physical disability to visual impairment and autism.

Most of our schools have their foundation in a Religious Order or Congregation. These orders, many from the Continent, set up Catholic schools in Britain when there was little educational provision for the Catholic population. Despite the great variety of these religious foundations there is a strong common goal to serve the mission of the Church by educating young men and women to take their place in society as young disciples, or for those who are not of the Catholic faith, principled citizens with values based on the Gospel who will work for the common good.

CISC is very much part of this living tradition and is committed to playing its part in the mission of the Church in education. A priority for us is to support the formation of our members, the heads of our Catholic independent schools. We are also committed to developing the next generation of leaders and and collaborate with EducareM (educarem.org.uk) on a personalised journey of formation at each stage of career progression, including recently qualified teachers, those leading and those aspiring to leadership of a Catholic school.

CISC sees itself as a distinctive, traditional, yet forward thinking part of the Catholic educational landscape, which enriches and is enriched by collaborations across all elements of Catholic education, namely the maintained sector, dioceses and the Catholic Education Service (CES). As such, CISC works closely with the CES across a range of policy areas and supports and contributes to their Formatio programme, developed specifically for those in executive leadership.

CISC is a charitable organisation and the main beneficiaries are our members and their colleagues. CISC is governed by a committee of serving heads who are trustees of the charity. It employs a Secretariat who is responsible for delivering on the strategic aims of the organisation.

For more information, please visit our website or contact Dr Maureen Glackin: info@catholicindependentschools.com.

Officers for 2023–2024

Chair: Mr Antony Hudson, MA, PGCE, NPQH – St George's Junior School

Committee

Treasurer: Mr Matthew Burke, BA, PGCE, Adv.Dip, NPQH – St Edward's School
Fr Chris Cann, MA, MTh – Stonyhurst, St Mary's Hall
Mrs Sarah Conrad, BA, PGCE, NPQH – St Teresa's Prep School
Mrs Margaret Giblin, BATh, HDipEd, MA – Marymount International School, London
Mr Jon Reddin, BSc, MSc, NPQH – Ratcliffe College
Mrs Annie Sutton, BA, NPQH – St Joseph's Specialist Trust

General Secretary: Dr Maureen Glackin, BA, PGCE, MA, PhD, SFHEA, FCCT

Catholic Independent Schools' Conference
40 Bramwell Close, Sunbury-on-Thames, Middlesex TW16 5PU
Tel: 07595 089928 · email: info@catholicindependentschools.com

CHOIR SCHOOLS' ASSOCIATION

www.choirschools.org.uk

Patron: The Duchess of Kent
Committee:
Chairman: Yvette Day, King's College School, Cambridge
Vice-Chair: David Morton, The King's School, Gloucester

Neil Chippington, St John's College School, Cambridge
William Goldsmith, St George's School Windsor
Simon Larter-Evans, Tring
Richard Murray, Christ Church Cathedral School, Oxford
John Attwater, King's School, Ely
Gareth Doodes, The King's School, Worcester

CSA Full and Associate Members

Ampleforth College
Bristol Cathedral Choir School
Chapel Royal, Hampton Court
Chetham's School of Music, Manchester
Christ Church Cathedral School, Oxford
City of London School
Croydon Minster
Dean Close Preparatory School, Cheltenham
Durham Cathedral Schools Foundation
Exeter Cathedral School
Framlingham College
Frideswide Voices, Oxford
Hereford Cathedral School
King's College School, Cambridge
King's Ely
King's Rochester Preparatory School, Kent
The King's School, Worcester
Leicester Cathedral
Lichfield Cathedral School
Lincoln Cathedral
Lincoln Minster School
Magdalen College School, Oxford
Merton College, Oxford
New College School, Oxford
Norwich School
Old Palace School, Croydon
Reigate St Mary's Preparatory and Choir School
RGS Prep, Guildford
Ripon Cathedral
Runnymede St Edward's School, Liverpool
Salisbury Cathedral School
Saint Thomas Choir School, New York, USA
St Edmund's Junior School, Canterbury
St Edward's College, Liverpool
St George's School, Windsor
St John's College, Cardiff
St John's College School, Cambridge
St Mary's Music School, Edinburgh
St Nicholas Cathedral, Newcastle upon Tyne
St Paul's Cathedral School, London
St Peter's School, York
St Peter's Collegiate Church, Wolverhampton
St Cedd's School, Essex
The Cathedral School, Cardiff
The King's (The Cathedral) School, Peterborough
The King's School, Gloucester
The London Oratory School
The Minister School Southwell
The Pilgrims' School, Winchester
The Portsmouth Grammar School
The Prebendal School, Chichester
Truro School
Wells Cathedral School
Westminster Abbey Choir School, London
Westminster Cathedral Choir School, London
Whitgift School, Croydon

The Choir Schools' Association celebrated its Centenary in 2018.

55 schools in the UK educate some or all of the choristers at cathedrals, churches or college chapels all over the country. Between them they educate more than 25,000 pupils, including some 1,200 choristers. Westminster Abbey Choir School is the only school in the UK to educate choristers and probationers only; Saint Thomas Choir School in the USA similarly only educates those who sing in the choir. The Association's associate membership includes cathedrals and churches without choir schools.

Choir schools offer a very special opportunity for children who enjoy singing. They receive a first-class academic and all-round education combined with excellent music training. The experience and self-discipline choristers acquire remain with them for life. There is a wide range of schools: some cater for children aged 7–13, others are junior schools with senior schools to 18; most are Church of England but the Roman Catholic, Scottish and Welsh churches are also represented.

Most CSA members are fee-paying schools. Deans and Chapters may provide fee assistance while Government support comes in the shape of the Choir Schools' Scholarship Scheme. Under the umbrella of the Music and Dance Scheme, funds are available to help those who cannot afford even the reduced school fees. Government funding through the Music and Dance Scheme (MDS), along with other monies in its Bursary Trust Fund, is administered by the CSA. Applications are means-tested; awards are only made once a child has secured a place at a choir school.

Every year, members of the CSA are looking for children to join their various foundations as probationer (trainee) choristers. Many of these positions come with boarding options, which reduces the commuting commitment if you don't live nearby.

Each CSA member school has its own particular admissions procedure for choristers, including musical and academic assessments. A number of foundations offer informal voice tests which enable the organist or director of music to judge whether a child has the potential to become a chorister even before the more formal process might begin. Sometime, a child may be offered a place immediately; more usually they will be invited to enter the more formal voice trial organised by the school, but sometimes too, a family may be advised not to proceed with an application.

A good chorister applicant will show potential, a keen musical ear and an eagerness to sing. A clutch of music examination certificates is not vital – good reading skills, alertness and enthusiasm are! At the same time, school staff must be satisfied that a potential chorister would be able to cope with their school work and with the many other activities on offer as well as the demanding choir workload.

To find out more generally about choir schools please visit the CSA website: **www.choirschools.org.uk**
Or make an enquiry via: **info@choirschools.org.uk**

CIFE

COUNCIL FOR INDEPENDENT EDUCATION

www.cife.org.uk

President:
Lord Lexden, OBE

Vice President:
Hugh Monro, MA

Chairman:
Tom Caston, BA, GTP, MSc

Vice-Chairman:
Dr Seán Buckley

Independent sixth-form colleges are extremely well placed to offer what is needed for students preparing for university and beyond. The best such colleges are generally members of CIFE, the Council for Independent Education, an organisation which was founded more than 50 years ago. There are 22 CIFE colleges, geographically spread across the country, each one offering individual features but all subject to high standards of accreditation. For example, there are some colleges that specialise in students wishing to retake in order to improve exam grades, some offering GCSE and pre-GCSE programmes as well as full A Level courses, which may be residential, homestay, day, or a mix of all three. Several colleges offer foundation programmes and are twinned with universities. In short, CIFE colleges offer a wide range of educational environments in which students can succeed.

Teaching in CIFE colleges really helps and supports students since teaching groups are small and teachers highly experienced and specialists in their subject. The 'tutorial' system derives directly from Oxbridge where it continues to be world famous. A student in a small group receives a greater degree of individual attention. Regular testing ensures that she/he maintains good progress, and the emphasis on study skills provides essential support for the AS/A Level subjects.

It is not surprising that a student gains confidence and self-belief within such an environment. Colleges engender a strong work ethic in their student communities. Many of the minor rules and regulations essential for schools are not necessary at CIFE colleges. Good manners and an enthusiastic attitude are every bit as important, but uniform, strict times for eating or homework, assemblies or games participation are not part of the picture. It can be seen from the large numbers of students going on to higher education from CIFE colleges that universities regard our students highly.

Increasing numbers of young people are deciding to move school at the age of 16, not because they are unhappy with their school, but because they see the need for a change at this stage. It may be that they wish to study a subject which their school does not offer, such as Accounting, Law, Psychology or Photography. Perhaps they are looking for a more adult environment or one where they can focus on their academic subjects to the exclusion of other things. However, it would be misleading to suggest that CIFE colleges are lacking in extracurricular activities, as every CIFE college recognises the need for enrichment of all sorts, sporting, social and creative. The difference is that activities are at the choice of the student.

As with schools, choosing a college calls for careful research. CIFE colleges undergo regular inspection either by the Independent Schools Inspectorate, Ofsted and/or the British Accreditation Council, recognised bodies which regulate the provision and standards of teaching, safety and pastoral care. While each college has its own individual character, all share the desire to provide each individual student with a superb preparation for higher education.

Members of CIFE

Ashbourne Independent Sixth-form College, London
Bales College, London
Bath Academy, Bath
Bosworth Independent College, Northampton
Brooke House College, Market Harborough
Cambridge Tutors College, London
Carfax College, Oxford
CATS College, Cambridge
Cherwell College, Oxford
Collingham, London
David Game College, London
Guildhouse School, London
LSI Independent Sixth Form College, London
Mander Portman Woodward, Birmingham
Mander Portman Woodward, Cambridge
Mander Portman Woodward, London
Oxford Sixth Form College, Oxford
Padworth College, Reading
Regent College, London
Rochester Independent College
Westminster Tutors, London
The Worthgate School, Canterbury

Further information can be obtained from:

CIFE

Tel: 020 8767 8666 · email: enquiries@cife.org.uk

UNITED LEARNING

www.unitedlearning.org.uk

Patrons

The Most Revd & Rt Hon Justin Welby, Archbishop of Canterbury
The Most Revd & Rt Hon Stephen Cottrell, Archbishop of York

United Learning – Group Board

Chair of the Group Board:
Richard Greenhalgh

Chair of United Church Schools Trust:
Dr Rosalind Given-Wilson

Zoe Asensio Sanchez
David Brown
Sir Jon Coles
Karima Fahmy
Melissa Geiger
Ben Gordon
Dame Sue John
Dame Reena Keeble
Neil MacDonald MBE
Dr Rania Marandos
Christie Spurling MBE

Executive Team

Chief Executive: Sir Jon Coles
Chief Transformation Officer: Lauren Thorpe
Director of Secondary Academies: Ben Antell
Chief Financial Officer: Louise Johnston
Director of Primary Education: Darran Ellison-Lee
Interim Director of Independent Schools: Fiona Boulton
Director of Strategy and Performance: Anna Paige
Director of HR: Kate Bradley
Director of Professional Development: Suzanne Howard

United Learning Independent Schools

AKS Lytham (HMC, day)
Ashford School (HMC, IAPS, boarding and day)
Banstead Preparatory School (IAPS, day)
Coworth Flexlands Preparatory School & Nursery (IAPS, AGBIS, ISBA, day)
Dunottar School (The Society of Heads, day)
Embley (The Society of Heads, IAPS, boarding and day)
Guildford High School (HMC, IAPS, day)
Lincoln Minster School (HMC, The Society of Heads, IAPS, boarding and day)
Rowan Preparatory School (IAPS, day)
The Royal School (ISC, IAPS, GSA day/boarding)
St Ives School for Girls (IAPS, day)
Surbiton High School (HMC, IAPS, day)
Tranby (HMC, The Society of Heads, IAPS, ISA, day)

Our Ethos

United Learning is a group of schools committed to providing excellent education through which all pupils are able to progress, achieve and go on to succeed in life. Our approach is underpinned by a sense of moral purpose and commitment to doing what is right for children and young people, supporting colleagues to achieve excellence and acting with integrity in all our dealings within and beyond the organisation, in the interests of young people everywhere. We summarise this ethos as 'The Best in Everyone'.

This ethos underpins our core values:

- Ambition – to achieve the best for ourselves and others;
- Confidence – to have the courage of our convictions and to take risks in the right cause;
- Creativity – to imagine possibilities and make them real;
- Respect – of ourselves and others in all that we do;
- Enthusiasm – to seek opportunity, find what is good and pursue talents and interests;
- Determination – to overcome obstacles and reach success.

As a single organisation, we seek to bring together the best of independent and state sectors, respecting both traditions and learning from each. We believe that each of our schools is and should be distinctive – each is committed to developing its own strengths and identity while sharing our core values as institutions which promote service, compassion and generosity.

Academic scholarships, exhibitions and bursaries are awarded at all schools. The tuition fees vary according to age and school; for example, tuition fees per annum in the senior schools range from £13,008 to £19,290 (day), and £29,190 to £38,778 (full boarding).

United Learning comprises: UCST (Registered in England No: 2780748. Charity No. 1016538) and ULT (Registered in England No. 4439859. An Exempt Charity). Companies limited by guarantee. VAT number 834 8515 12.

United Learning
Worldwide House, Thorpe Wood, Peterborough, PE3 6SB
Tel: 01832 864444 · email: enquiries@unitedlearning.org.uk

High quality education in an actively Christian environment for all

www.woodardschools.co.uk
X/Twitter: @WoodardSchools

Members of the Board
Chairman: Mr R S Morse

The Rt Revd Dr J Inge, BSc, MA, PhD, DLitt, Bishop of Worcester (*President*)
Mr H J Dellar, BA Hons, MA
Mrs A C Hogg
Mrs M Holman, MA
Mr M H Mortimer, FCA
Mr B M Newman, MA, MBA, CEng, FIMechE, FIET, FIoD, FRSA
Mrs F Orchard
Mr W G Pecover
Mrs S C Pelham

Key Officers:
The Revd Justin White, MEng, MA (*Senior Provost*)
Mr C Wright, MA, FRSA (*Director of Education*)
Mr M Corcoran, BSc, ACA (*Director of Finance/Company Secretary*)

Incorporated Schools (*independent*)

Ardingly College
Ardingly College Preparatory School
Bloxham School
The Cathedral School, Llandaff
Denstone College & the Prep at Denstone College
Ellesmere College
Hurstpierpoint College
Hurstpierpoint College Preparatory School
King's College, Taunton
King's College Preparatory School, Taunton
Lancing College
Lancing College Preparatory School at Hove
Lancing College Preparatory School at Worthing
The Peterborough School
Prestfelde School, Shrewsbury
Queen Mary's School, Thirsk
Ranby House, Retford
Worksop College

Information on all of the schools can be found at www.woodardschools.co.uk.

Woodard schools form the largest group of Anglican schools in England and Wales. In addition to the above list of incorporated schools, a number of schools in the independent and maintained sectors choose to be associated or affiliated, respectively. Woodard also sponsors academies. The schools are not exclusive and take pupils of all faiths and of none. In total over 30,000 pupils are taught in schools throughout the group.

This unique partnership of schools, independent and state, boarding and day, junior and senior, co-educational and single-sex, is united by a determination to provide a first-class holistic education within a distinctive Christian ethos. The schools were founded by Nathaniel Woodard in the nineteenth century and aim to prepare children from a wide variety of backgrounds for responsibility, leadership and service in today's world.

The schools seek to provide flexible, stimulating, demanding and appropriate schemes of academic study together with a rich variety of sporting, artistic and recreational opportunities. We encourage personal success, self-confidence and self-respect whilst also stressing the importance of responsible citizenship, high moral values and a commitment to use one's gifts in the service of others.

With the geographical spread and diversity of schools included in the group it is able to offer parents a wide range of educational options for their children. Woodard incorporated schools operate bursary and scholarship schemes including all classes of concession. Fees vary from school to school and are set locally.

The Woodard Corporation is a Registered Charity (No. 1096270) and Company (No. 4659710). The objects of the charity are to promote and extend education (including spiritual, moral, social, cultural and physical education) in accordance with the doctrines and principles of the Church of England/Church in Wales by directly or indirectly carrying on schools.

Woodard Schools
High Street, Abbots Bromley, Rugeley, Staffordshire WS15 3BW
Tel: 01283 840120 · email: john.sherratt@woodardschools.co.uk

AMCIS

ASSOCIATION FOR ADMISSIONS, MARKETING AND COMMUNICATIONS IN INDEPENDENT SCHOOLS

FOUNDED 1993

www.amcis.co.uk

Objectives:

- To promote and develop good marketing practice in admissions, marketing and communications in independent education
- To help increase the effectiveness of the admissions, marketing and communications representatives of member schools
- To encourage personal development within the schools' admissions, marketing and communications professionals

Achieved through:

- Seminars, webinars and workshops on a variety of admissions, marketing and communications-led subjects held throughout the year
- Annual residential conference
- Online networking meetings
- Training – Diploma in Schools' Marketing & Diploma in Admissions Management
- Helpline
- Website with member-only resource section
- LinkedIn Group Forum
- Twitter feed
- Facebook Group
- On-line News bulletins throughout the year
- Speakers provided for conferences, inset days and similar

Membership:

- School Membership, renewable annually by subscription
- Corporate Membership, renewable annually by subscription

The Association is directed by a Chair, Vice Chair and Treasurer together with a Board of Directors.

CEO: Tory Gillingham

AMCIS

57A Market Place, Malton, North Yorkshire YO17 7LX

Tel: 01653 699800 · email: enquiries@amcis.co.uk

X/Twitter: @AMCISNews · LinkedIn: /company/amcis

AROPS – THE SCHOOLS' ALUMNI ASSOCIATION

FOUNDED 1971

arops.org.uk

President:

Peter Jakobek (Old Bristolians)

Vice-Presidents:

Margaret Carter-Pegg (Old Crohamian)
Guy Cliff (Old Silcoatian)
Bill Gillen (Old Arnoldians and Belfast Old Instonians')
John Kidd
Tim Neale (Radleian Society)
Anthony Phillips (The Lancing Club)
Q D Seymour-Smith (Old Decanian and Old Millfileldian)
Trish Woodhouse

Committee

Chair: Alan Cooper (Old Waynfletes)
Secretary/Administrator: Rosie Findlay
Treasurer: Vijay Khullar (Old Roffensian)
Registrar: Keith Balkham (KGS Friends)
and up to 10 committee members

AROPS was founded in 1971 by Mike Comer of the Old Johnians, St John's School, Leatherhead.

Aim: To provide a friendly forum in which to exchange views, share experiences and ideas, between representatives of school alumni societies and school development offices to enhance the offering to both alumni and current pupils.

Membership: Open to representatives of any school alumni society and school development officers. One membership covers both the school and the alumni society. New members are always welcome. Details are available on the website – arops.org.uk – where you can also find information on events and member societies' news, regularly updated. Please contact us by email: arops@arops.org.uk.

Meetings: AROPS organises a series of in-person Regional Network Meetings hosted by member schools. These explore current issues and also allow members to discuss items concerning alumni engagement on an informal basis. Additionally there are ad hoc on-line events too. Please check website for latest details of events: arops.org.uk.

Additionally there is an AGM in November followed by a dinner which any member may attend.

Subscription: £50 per year. Please email the Administrator, at arops@arops.org.uk, including a name and telephone contact number along with your enquiry.

MOSA
MEDICAL OFFICERS OF SCHOOLS ASSOCIATION

FOUNDED 1884

www.mosa.org.uk

Today MOSA is a professional organisation concerned with providing medical care for mainly but not exclusively, independent schools, boarding and day. In 2015, membership was opened to any healthcare professional currently or previously registered with an appropriate, professionally recognised organisation.

This meant that, for example, school nurses were eligible to join as full members. The number of nurse members has steadily increased and four nurses are now members of MOSA council. As a result, the Association has gone from strength to strength with the nurses bringing a new breadth of knowledge and skill to the Association's activities. The membership is now a mix of general practitioners who are medical officers to schools in their practice areas and school nurses, as well as some non-clinicians working in a school setting such as members of the teaching profession who are eligible to join as associate members.

The business of the Association is conducted by Council of MOSA, which meets three times a year and is made up of current and retired school medical officers and nurses. The day-to-day running of MOSA is the responsibility of the executive secretary together with one of the officers, the executive officer, who is a practicing healthcare professional. The current membership stands at 261.

Who Runs MOSA?

President

Dr Stephen Haynes, SMO, Bloxham School and GP, Oxford

President-elect

Dr Jim Ropner, GP and SMO, Cheltenham College

MOSA Executive Officer

Mrs Liz Carey, Former Chief Nurse, Charterhouse

MOSA Trustees

Dr Neil Arnott, Former SMO, Sevenoaks School

Dr Rebecca Pryse, Former SMO, Stowe School, Buckinghamshire

MOSA Educational Lead

Dr Rene Skule, SMO, Bryanston, Canford and Clayesmore Schools, Dorset

Council Members

Mrs Bev Gilbert, Former Lead Nurse, Wellington College

Mrs Alice Lyons, Lead Nurse, Chafyn Grove

Mrs Fiona Parry, Lead Nurse, Cheltenham College

Mr Nate Kelly, Lead Nurse, St Mary's, Calne

Dr Steve Brown, SMO, Rugby School

Dr Sue Xavier, Public Health Consultant and Governor, Ashdown House Prep School

Current benefits of joining:

- Full access to all members' educational meetings with reduced registration fee. MOSA events and webinars that the nurse team have attended can be recorded as evidence to ISI inspections.
- Access to a wide range of clinical and administrative guidelines on subjects relevant to school health for all members of the team.
- A private forum for health professionals to seek advice and share good practice around specific school health issues. Peer support for school health teams.
- A specialist consultancy service for an school that requires a review of their medical and nursing provision. With a pool of highly experienced school doctors and nurses, MOSA are able to offer support with nursing development reviews, nursing revalidation and assist schools with the employment for school nursing positions.

How to join/costs of joining:

Clinical membership is £185 per annum (reviewed annually). However, if joining as part of a school group or GP surgery, the first member is £185 and all additional members are half price £92.50. www.mosa.org.uk/become-a-member.

THE ENGLISH-SPEAKING UNION

ENGLAND & WALES REGISTERED CHARITY NO. 273136

www.esu.org

Oracy Education with the English Speaking Union

ESU education programmes support the development of vital oracy skills for all children and young people. Our resources, programmes and competitions all teach two things. First, they teach students *how* to talk - how to structure a speech, summarise information, listen critically and to consider and address different audiences. Second, they help students to learn *through* talk. By discussing current affairs and topical issues, in any class or subject, students not only acquire deeper subject knowledge, but a greater awareness of the world around them. Their horizons broaden and they improve their ability to consider and evaluate diverse opinions and points of view.

Debate Academy

Debate Academy is a friendly, immersive summer school for 14 to 8 year olds. It offers top-quality coaching in debate skills to all ability levels, delivered by some of the best coaches and debaters in the world. Whether students have little to no experience or are getting ready from trials for their national debating team, this summer school has something to offer.

As well as offering important debate tips and debate skills training, Debate Academy is a wonderful opportunity to make friends with like-minded people, to learn more about the wider world through our elective sessions and spend a week away from home developing confidence and independence. It's a summer camp like no other, and we hope to see you there!

Find out more: www.esu.org/programmes/debate-academy.

Discover Your Voice

The ESU's Discover Your Voice oracy workshops are available for learners in Key Stages 2-5, providing oracy skills development opportunities tailored to age, ability and school or setting requirements.

Suitable for: Beginner (Years 5-6); Intermediate (7-8) and Advanced (Years 9-10) in schools or youth groups/ informal education settings or for groups of home schooled children and young-people.

Workshop length: Workshops last 2.5 hours (but multiple options can be combined to create a full-day programme).

Delivery: ESU oracy experts.

Using the ESU's century of oracy education, we support schools to develop their oracy provision through the lens of debate or public speaking - but ever workshop provides all learners with a thorough understanding of core oracy skills and workshop 1 in each stream provides a general oracy skills introduction for students of all ages.

Choose a one-off workshop or work with us over a longer period with sequenced series of sessions, building to a capstone oracy even day, facilitated by ESU oracy experts.

Each of the workshops are structured around the ESU key skill sets of:

- reasoning and evidence;
- listening and response;
- expression and delivery;
- and organisation and prioritisation.

Customisable to specific curriculum areas or projects, all Discover Your Voice workshops build learners' ability to communicate and reason effectively, to listen, and to understand and respond to others' points of view. All workshops last 2.5 hours, but multiple options can be combined to create a full-day programme (or longer).

Find out more: www.esu.org/programmes/discover-your-voice-oracy-workshops.

PART I

Schools whose Heads are members of the The Heads' Conference

ALPHABETICAL LIST OF SCHOOLS

The following schools, whose Heads are members of both HMC and GSA, can be found in the GSA section:

Badminton School
Edgbaston High School
Howell's School Llandaff
Lady Eleanor Holles
Notting Hill and Ealing High School
Redmaids High School
The Royal High School Bath
St Paul's Girls' School
St Swithun's School
South Hampstead High School
Wimbledon High School

HMC
GEOGRAPHICAL LIST OF SCHOOLS

PAGE

ENGLAND

Symbols used in Staff Listings

* Head of Department § Part Time or Visiting
† Housemaster/Housemistress ¶ Old Pupil
‡ See below list of staff for meaning

Individual School Entries

The Abbey

Kendrick Road, Reading RG1 5DZ
Tel: 0118 987 2256
email: schooloffice@theabbey.co.uk
website: www.theabbey.co.uk
X/Twitter: @theabbeyschool
Facebook: @theabbeyschoolberkshire
Instagram: @theabbeyschoolreading
LinkedIn: /company/the-abbey-school-reading

The Abbey is a remarkable all-girls community of learning and scholarship. It is a place of curiosity, adventurous spirits, and the excitement of discovery. We foster an atmosphere of warmth and support, full of fun and laughter. As a result we develop the assurance for students to take risks, explore interests and passions, and engage generously with the world in our girls-only environment.

Our outlook is internationally-minded and collaborative. Our goal is to prepare students to live with confidence, purpose, and joy. To support this philosophy we offer International Baccalaureate programmes at our Junior School and Sixth Form.

This means providing exceptional single-sex opportunities across the widest spectrum of curricular and co-curricular activities. Our job is to find, encourage and broaden each individual's talents and interests. Therefore it is a privilege to witness our students' liveliness of mind and help that to develop as they become resilient young people with the enthusiasm and tenacity to make a difference.

At the heart of The Abbey community lies a shared enthusiasm for lifelong learning, underpinned by a relentless intellectual curiosity and spirit of discovery encouraged at every stage of the educational journey. Supported by a proactive and compassionate pastoral system, every girl from Nursery through to Sixth Form is encouraged to explore her passions, embrace new challenges and question her assumptions.

Located within walking distance of Reading Station, the School provides an extensive coach network across Berkshire and Oxfordshire for both Junior School and Senior School girls. A range of scholarships are available, as well as financial assistance offered via means-tested bursaries.

We have played a leading role in all-girls education for over 130 years. During that time, we have adapted and innovated, preparing students for the always-changing world that lies ahead of them. That is true now more than ever. We seek to equip girls to face the future on their own terms, driven by courage, honesty and kindness above all else.

Number of Pupils. 1,005.

Fees per term (2023–2024). Reception £4,500, Lower Preparatory (Year 1) £5,150, Upper Preparatory (Year 2) £5,500, Lower I – Lower III (Years 3–6) £5,900, Upper III – Upper VI (Years 7–13) £7,250.

Scholarships & Bursaries. We offer Academic and Specialist scholarships at entrance to encourage excellence and aspiration and to celebrate students whose commitment to learning is exceptional.

An Abbey scholarship is confirmed for 3 years (Years 7–9) and then reviewed (www.theabbey.co.uk/the-abbey-all-girls/admissions/scholarships).

Bursaries are provided to assist Senior School students who would benefit significantly from an education at The Abbey and whose parents could not otherwise afford to send them. Every case will be taken on its individual merits but, among those who qualify financially, the academic potential will be the overriding factor (www.theabbey.co.uk/the-abbey-all-girls/admissions/bursaries).

Charitable status. The Abbey is a Registered Charity, number 309115.

Board of Governors:
Mrs Elizabeth Harrison (*Chair*)

Mr Simon Dimmick	Mr Colin Singer
Mrs Julie Butler	Ms Robyn Field
Mr Michael Emmanuel	Mrs Jo Jolly
Mrs Susan Colebrook	Mr Andrew Peach
Mrs Elisabeth West	Dr Harriett Kemp
Miss Sanya Burgess	

***Executive Head*: Will le Fleming**, BA Hons, MA Cambridge

Head of the Junior School: Nisha Kaura, BSc Hons, DMS, PMQ, PGCE, MEd

Head of Finance & Resources: Nadine Doble, BSc Cardiff, ACMA

ACS International School Cobham

Heywood House, Portsmouth Road, Cobham, Surrey KT11 1BL
Tel: 01932 867251
email: cobadmissions@acs-schools.com
website: www.acs-schools.com/cobham
X/Twitter: @ACSintschools
Facebook: @ACSCobham
Instagram: @acscobhamschool
LinkedIn: /school/acs-international-schools

ACS Cobham is a co-educational school for 1,300 students aged 2–18 and 300 expert faculty and staff, representing over 70 nationalities.

Far more than just a school, ACS Cobham is a friendly, vibrant international community with a global outlook that guides our world-renowned curriculum. Based on US educational best practice, we offer a new kind of learning for a new kind of world citizen. Our goal is as simple as it is inspiring: to make our students ready for the challenges of tomorrow, so they thrive at every stage of their lives.

Our teaching and academic credentials are second to none. Our students are encouraged to tailor their studies to suit their talents and ambitions, while a wealth of outstanding support amenities help deliver a well-rounded educational experience. Equally important is our beautiful, leafy campus, just 30 minutes from central London. Our location offers students the best of both worlds – the stimulation of one of the world's great cities, combined with the charms of the English countryside.

Unique amongst our four schools, ACS Cobham offer boarding as an option for students aged 13 to 18, who enjoy state-of-the-art facilities in our recently opened boarding house.

Academic programme. At ACS Cobham, your child has access to an independent and flexible curriculum, underpinned by the International Baccalaureate (IB) Diploma, Advanced Placement (AP) courses and the ACS High School Diploma (US). These opportunities develop your child's learning and life skills. ACS graduates have established a tradition of attaining excellent exam results, enabling them to continue their studies at top universities around the world, including the US and UK.

Facilities. Situated on 128 acres approximately 30 minutes by train from Central London, ACS Cobham enrols over 1,300 students. Exceptional facilities include an Early Childhood village; purpose-built Lower, Middle, and High School buildings; gymnasium and cafeteria complex and two world-class boarding houses. All Lower, Middle and High School buildings have separate classrooms, science labs, libraries, computer labs, art and music studios and access to the school's state-of-the-art Interactive Learning Centre.

Enrichment activities. ACS Cobham offers extensive and varied extracurricular clubs and community service activities both locally and internationally, which encourage students to participate in the richness of school life. Students also participate in international theatre arts programmes, maths, literature and music competitions in the UK and across Europe.

Sports. Our 128-acre campus is home to the best range of quality sports facilities of any international school in Europe, with soccer and rugby fields, softball and baseball diamonds, an all-weather Olympic-sized track, tennis courts, and a six-hole golf course. Our Sports Centre comprises a 25-metre competition indoor swimming pool, basketball/volleyball show courts, dance and fitness studios, and a café.

Boarding at ACS Cobham. As part of an increasingly mobile world, the ACS Cobham Boarding House has established itself as a genuine champion of internationalism, with students representing more than 30 countries. We are proud of our multicultural identity, and celebrate the things that make us different as an integral part of boarding life.

Expert residential house parents and nurse ensure our students have the constant support, guidance, and care to be happy, inspired, and ready to make their mark on the world.

A multi-million pound refurbishment of the existing boarding house Fields is now complete and features a new walk-in medical centre with a fully-trained medical team. All study-bedrooms are either single or twin, and all have a private bathroom. Furnishings are to a very high standard and include wall-to-wall carpeting, built-in wardrobes (closets), desks, lamps, bookcases, beds and bedside units. There is WiFi throughout. There are spacious lounges with large screen television and DVD players, laundry facilities, and kitchenettes. Main meals are taken in the school's stunning dining hall located next to the Boarding House.

Boarders are allocated bedrooms on their own or with other boarders of the same age. Boys and girls are accommodated in separate areas, with some shared common rooms.

Accreditation. ACS Cobham is accredited by the New England Association of Schools and Colleges (NEASC) and is authorised by the International Baccalaureate (IB) to offer the International Baccalaureate Diploma Programme (IBDP). The school holds memberships in the US College Board Advanced Placement (AP) Program, the European Council of International Schools (ECIS), the Council of International Schools (CIS) and the Independent Schools Association (ISA).

Four schools, one world-class education. ACS Cobham is part of ACS International Schools. Founded in 1967 to serve the needs of international and local families, ACS International Schools now educates 3,500 students up to age 18, from more than 70 countries, at three London area campuses in England and one in Doha, Qatar.

Contact the admissions team. The admissions team is available throughout the year to answer questions, book campus visits, and assist families through the enrolment process. Students are accepted in all grades throughout the year, on non-selective criteria.

Age range. 2–18.

Number in school. Day: 647 Boys, 601 Girls; 190 Boarders.

Fees per annum (2023–2024). Tuition: £9,120–£32,030. Boarding (including tuition fees): £51,920–£55,330 (full), £45,620–£49,030 (5-day).

***Head of School*: Barnaby Sandow**

Head of Senior School: Robert Crowther
Assistant Head, Wellbeing: Sara Thomas
Assistant Head, Teaching and Learning: Kristie Sheard
Assistant Head, Operations: Ian Ahmet

High School Principal: Michelle Quirin
Upper School Principal: Luke Welch
Middle School Principal: Darren Sheldrake
Lower School Principal: Judith Kingsbury

Albyn School

17–23 Queen's Road, Aberdeen, Aberdeen City AB15 4PB

Tel: 01224 322408
email: admissions@albynschool.co.uk
website: www.albynschool.co.uk
X/Twitter: @AlbynSchool
Facebook: @AlbynSchool
Instagram: @albynschool
LinkedIn: /school/albyn-school

Motto: *Vigor et Juventas (Vigour and Youth)*

Albyn School is an independent day school for boys and girls aged 2–18 located in the heart of Aberdeen's West End.

Vision. Albyn School is educating for life. Its progressive philosophy is centred on being stronger together with a focus on building academic excellence, growing community spirit and engendering social conscience.

Headmaster Stefan Horsman said: "We want our pupils to be self-aware, ambitious and outward-looking, so they can contribute to the world as global citizens. In order to achieve this, we seek to help them develop six key qualities: curiosity, resilience, confidence, endeavour, empathy and teamwork."

Everything the School does is underpinned by its ethos of community spirit, love of learning and mutual respect.

Nursery. Albyn School Nursery comprises two phases: Toddlers (age 2–3 years) and Preschool (age 3–5 years). The Nursery plays an important role in the School as it is the beginning of the Albyn journey which will take the majority of the children through to their final year of school, S6.

With an emphasis on the importance of play, children learn language and literacy skills, develop their first steps towards numeracy and build a strong foundation for future learning. The School also instils habits of good health and wellbeing while providing a calm, stimulating and secure environment in which children can grow in confidence, make friends and most importantly, have fun.

Lower School. The Lower School curriculum has at its core the School's goal for every pupil to develop a love of learning and grow the skills, knowledge and understanding they need to be confident learners, ready to progress to the next level of education. Albyn School's small class sizes mean that teachers can gain an in-depth understanding of all pupils in their class.

There are three different components to the Lower School curriculum which allow pupils to develop a strong foundation in the key areas of literacy and numeracy, while providing the opportunity to grow their understanding of the world around them.

Curriculum for Excellence. Albyn School's core curriculum is informed by aspects of Scotland's Curriculum for Excellence, especially in literacy and numeracy, but goes above and beyond it in many important areas.

International Primary Curriculum. Albyn's curriculum is also influenced by the International Primary Curriculum which is a comprehensive, thematic, creative curriculum with a clear process of learning and specific learning goals for every subject. Every year group works on diverse, carefully selected units throughout the school year. Each unit begins with an exciting Entry Point and ends with an Exit Point to showcase a child's learning journey.

Albyn Curriculum Enrichment Programme. Albyn School wants their pupils to have a healthy balance between a love for learning and curiosity beyond the classroom. With that in mind, they introduced the Albyn Curriculum Enrichment Programme (ACE for short) which is built into the day for P1–7 pupils. All children take part in a range of activities including sport, music, cooking and crafts during the school day.

Additional visits by specialist teachers in Art, Drama, French, Music and PE enhance the learning provided by Lower School classroom teachers.

Upper School. In the Upper School children continue to explore their own potential, discover the world around them and embrace the opportunities available to them. The Upper School curriculum allows pupils to discover their passion as they learn across a broad range of subjects initially which are refined as pupils progress.

Albyn School follows the Scottish system of education, with Upper School pupils being entered for National 5 examinations (equivalent to GCSEs), Highers and Advanced Highers (equivalent to A Levels).

Co-curricular activities. Albyn School pupils have the opportunity to choose from 100+ co-curricular activities. They are encouraged to get involved in different activities to develop their interests beyond academic study. These activities may remain as a hobby or could inspire pupils to consider careers which they may not otherwise have thought of.

Some of the most popular co-curricular activities are The Duke of Edinburgh's Award, Combined Cadet Force, and Formula 24. The co-curricular landscape at Albyn School extends beyond STEM activities, encompassing diverse interests such as music (choir, jazz, orchestra, sound engineering), sport (football, golf, hockey, netball, cricket, athletics, cross country), languages (French, Spanish, German and Latin), and a myriad of other clubs including Model United Nations, debating, Young Enterprise, and gardening, offering pupils a rich tapestry of opportunities for personal and collective enrichment.

Trips. In Upper School, Albyn's annual Activities Week offers pupils a diverse range of experiential learning opportunities as well as providing the chance for pupils to forge friendships across year groups and create lifelong memories.

Beyond Albyn School. Every year, Albyn School pupils choose a variety of different subjects and destinations as they continue their educational journey. Nearly all pupils exit to universities – mostly in Scotland but also around the UK and abroad.

Pastoral care. Albyn School provides an environment where pupils feel safe, secure and comfortable in an atmosphere of mutual respect and trust. Each pupil is assigned to one of four Clans (Douglas, Forbes, Gordon or Stuart) when they join Albyn School. The School believes that its strong Clan system helps foster relationships between pupils and staff and creates community spirit within the School. Regular Clan events such as sport, singing, and debating allow for interaction between pupils of all ages.

Student numbers. 772 (Nursery, Lower School and Upper School), 663 (Lower School and Upper School).

Nursery Fees per annum (2023–2024). Albyn Toddlers: Year round Full day: £74; Year round Half day (session 1 or session 2): £42 Term time Full day: £80; Term time Half day (session 1 or session 2): £45 Lunches and snacks are included in the above fees. Albyn Preschool: Year round Full day: £74; Year round Half day (session 1 or session 2): £42 Term time Full day: £80; Term time Half day (session 1 or session 2): £45 Lunches and snacks are included in the above fees.

Lower School fees per annum (2023–2024). P1–P2: £9,995; P3–P5: £12,995; P6–P7: £13,995. School meals are an additional charge of £4.65 per day.

Upper School fees per annum (2023–2024). S1–S6 £15,995.

Admission. Albyn School's main P5–7 and S1 assessments take place in January. Entry to all years is also possible throughout the year and the offer of a place is subject to satisfactory performance in an entrance test and interview (Upper School pupils). Albyn School hosts a number of Open Days throughout the year, and its Admissions Team also offers private tours. Please email admissions@albynschool.co.uk for more information and to arrange a visit.

Curriculum. Albyn School follows the Scottish system of education, with Upper School pupils being entered for National 5 examinations (equivalent to GCSEs), Highers and Advanced Highers (equivalent to A Levels).

Scholarships and Bursaries. Albyn School aims to provide opportunities for all children who would benefit and thrive from the educational experience they offer. In order to do that, the School supports a range of Bursary Awards for children who might not otherwise be able to attend the School. Albyn School Bursary Awards are available for pupils entering P6 and above. Bursaries are awarded according to both academic ability and financial need. A financial assessment determines whether a full or partial award is made. As a general guide, these awards are made to families whose total gross annual household income does not exceed £80k.

For further details please visit: www.albynschool.co.uk/admissions/bursary-awards-financial-assistance-albyn-school/

Charitable status: Albyn School is a Registered Charity, number SCO 08392

Chair of Governors: Mr Colin Boag, FCCA

***Head*: Mr Stefan Horsman**, MA Oxon, FRGS, PGCE

Senior leadership team:

Head of Lower School and Nursery (*Deputy Child Protection Coordinator & Named Person*): Mr Nathan Davies, MA Hons

Senior Deputy Head: Mr David Starbuck, MA Hons, PGCE

Deputy Head: Mr John Blunsdon, BSc Hons, PGCE

Deputy Head (*Child Protection Coordinator & Named Person*): Mrs Nichola Crawford, BA/BSc Hons, QTS

Lower School Deputy Head (*Nursery–P2, Deputy Child Protection Coordinator & Named Person*): Miss Zibby Brown, BEd Hons

Lower School Deputy Head (*P3–7*): Mrs Ailey Smith, BEd Hons

Senior Teacher and Exams Officer: Miss Carly Blair, BSc PGDE

Bursar: Mr Chris Simpson, MA Hons ACMA, CGMA

Director of Digital Strategy: Mr Dave MacDonald, BSc Hons, PGDE

Development Director: Ms Frances Loughrey, MA Hons

Director of Marketing and Admissions: Mrs Fleur Murdoch, MA Hons, PG Dip

Human Resources Manager: Mrs Susan Allan

Alleyn's School

Townley Road, Dulwich, London SE22 8SU

Tel: 020 8557 1500
email: enquiries@alleyns.org.uk
website: www.alleyns.org.uk
X/Twitter: @AlleynsSchool
Facebook: @Alleynsschool
Instagram: @alleynsschool

Motto: *All We Can Be*

Set in the heart of South London and dating back to 1619, Alleyn's School takes pride in its commitment to providing an excellent education that prepares students for the challenges of a rapidly changing world, while at the same time preserving a love of learning for learning's sake. With a keen eye on the future, Alleyn's ambition is to instil a sense of entrepreneurship, philanthropy and community within each child, mirroring the values embodied by its founder, Edward Alleyn.

As one of the country's leading co-educational independent schools with a history of outstanding academic achievement and co-curricular success on the stage, pitch, page and screen, the School recognises that wonderful results are a by-product of an outstanding values-driven education. At the core of an Alleyn's education are shared values of Respect, Opportunity, Courage, Curiosity and Kindness. These principles, which are embedded across the school and serve as a place of from which staff and pupils can draw power and purpose, shape the character of every Alleyn's pupil, empowering them with the confidence and skills to be 'All They Can Be.'

Alleyn's pupils are encouraged to 'find their thing' whether through sport, the arts, student leadership or debate. The School offers a wide range of co-curricular activities to complement the academic curriculum and provide pupils with experiences and opportunities beyond the formal classroom, which include extensive Duke of Edinburgh, CCF and outreach programmes.

Admissions. We welcome applications from boys and girls from all backgrounds, with bursaries as well as academic and specialist subject scholarships available. We look for candidates who will respond to the School's care, opportunities and values, and who will, in return, contribute to the School with their talents and enthusiasm. Regular admission to Alleyn's Junior School occurs at 4+, 7+ and 9+. The main entry points to the Senior School are 11+ and 16+.

Curriculum. We aim to nurture holistic excellence for all, developing curiosity, reflection, determination, independence and a lifelong love of learning. All pupils follow a broad and balanced curriculum; pupils are invited to discover and develop their interests, knowledge and skills within a safe and supportive environment. As students advance through their educational journey, they are progressively given more opportunities to make choices from a diverse array of subjects.

Most of our pupils go on to top UK universities, including Oxford and Cambridge. However, each year several students also successfully gain places on prestigious music and drama courses, Foundation Art programmes, or choose to study overseas at institutions such as Harvard, Yale, and McGill. Every pupil is encouraged to apply for the path that best suits them.

Careers. A dynamic and evolving careers programme focuses on pupils' career curiosity and career exploration throughout their time at school. Co-created with pupils, parents and staff and led by a qualified careers guidance professional, this includes work experience, guidance interviews and aptitude tests, interaction with employers, employability programmes, exploration of how careers link to the academic curriculum and a programme of careers lessons and talks, culminating in an annual Festival of Inspiration and Enterprise, which features an interesting mix of hands-on interactive workshop style sessions and industry/career stalls.

Facilities. The School enjoys first-class facilities within its 28-acre campus, including a professional theatre, the MCT, and sporting facilities, such as a swimming pool with Olympic timing system, Astroturf and MUGA, all of which are made available to local schools and community groups throughout the year.

A School Council and Learning Council, with members from each section of the School, represent pupils' views to the Head. Other pupils' committees discuss life at School, including the Gender Equality Champions, the Minorities Student Union and the Eco Committee.

Alumni community. All former pupils, parents and staff are warmly encouraged to remain part of the Alleyn's community. The School has a strong and thriving alumni community that remains engaged and connected with both each other and the School. Alumni receive regular communications and publications and attend a wide range of events and reunions throughout the year.

Charitable status. Alleyn's School is a Registered Charity, number 1161864, and a Charitable Company Limited by Guarantee, registered in England and Wales, number 09401357. Registered office: Townley Road, SE22 8SU.

Fees per term (2023–2024). £8,340 (£25,020 per annum).

Bursaries. The Senior School offers means-tested bursaries to children who might flourish here, but whose financial circumstances may not allow them to meet the full school fees.

Scholarships: Scholarships (which can be worth up to a maximum of £5,000 per year and are not means tested) may also be awarded in conjunction with bursaries.

Chair of Governors: Mrs Laura Malkin, BA

***Head*: Mrs Jane Lunnon**, BA Bristol

Senior Deputy Head: Mr Andy Skinnard, MA Oxon (*Designated Lead for Safeguarding*)
Deputy Head (*Personnel & Administration*): Ms Sue P Chandler, BSc, PG Dip
Deputy Head (*Academic*): Dr Tom Durno, PhD Cantab
Deputy Head (*Pastoral*): Mr Gavin English, BAA
Head of Alleyn's Junior School: Mr Simon Severino, MA Oxon

Assistant Heads:
Head of Upper School: Ms Alex C Smith, MA, MA
Head of Middle School: Mrs Mel A Joel, BA
Head of Lower School: Mrs Helen E Lawrence, BA

Co-curricular & Partnerships: Mr Neil J G Green, BEd
Teaching & Learning: Mrs Claire L Heindl, BA
Director of Studies: Mr Aidan J Sproat-Clements, MA Cantab.
Chief Operating Officer: Mr Guy Collins-Down, BSc
Chief Finance Officer: Mrs Claire M Morgan, BSc, FCA
Director of Development & Alumni Relations: Mr Frank E Keenan, BA, MBA
Director of External Relations: Ms Isabella Sharp, MA Cantab, MSc
Director of People: Mr Andrew Lawson, BA, FCIPD
SMT Secondee, Director of Academic Performance, Analysis and Administration: Mr Paul Ryder, BEng
Registrar: Ms Louise Mawer, LLB

Ashford School

United Learning

East Hill, Ashford, Kent TN24 8PB
Tel: 01233 625171
email: admissions@ashfordschool.co.uk
website: www.ashfordschool.co.uk
X/Twitter: @AshfordSchool
Facebook: @AshfordSchool
Instagram: @AshfordSchool
LinkedIn: /ashford-school

Founded in 1898, Ashford School is a dynamic environment in which our students are inspired by our adventurous approach to learning.

Ashford School is a leading independent co-educational day and boarding school for children from 3 months to 18 years old, situated in the heart of Kent and just 37 minutes from London. We offer an exceptional and inspiring education that promotes the happiness and success of all pupils.

Based on two sites, the School includes: Bridge Nursery (3 months to 3 years) and Ashford Senior School (Years 7–13) on East Hill in Ashford, and 2½ miles away we have The Stables Nursery (3 months to 3 years) and Ashford Prep School (3 to 11 years) in the neighbouring leafy village of Great Chart.

Parents choose Ashford School for many reasons: we achieve high academic success; we work very closely with our students giving attention to the needs of the individual; our class sizes; our challenging and supportive environment; our wide range of co-curricular activities; and our energetic, specialist teachers. We pride ourselves in selecting highly capable adults who are experts from a variety of backgrounds.

At Ashford School we celebrate individuality and provide adventurous learning opportunities. We currently have over 80 co-curricular activities on offer from Combined Cadet Force, badminton and chamber choir, to debating, jazz band, ceramics, graphic design, food studies, table tennis, modern pentathlon, and Young Enterprise.

We are also extremely proud of the facilities at Ashford School which include a brand new state-of-the-art sports pavilion; sports centre; two indoor swimming pools; two flood-lit astro turfs for hockey, netball and tennis; all-weather netball, basketball and tennis courts; gyms; specialist art, design technology, ICT and science labs; a well-stocked learning centre; a café and atrium; a dining hall; pupil common rooms; playing fields for cricket, football and rugby; an auditorium and theatre; and a music School with several performance areas. We are also one of only 18 All-Steinway Schools in the UK.

Our learning is underpinned by four key factors, namely *Celebrating Individuality, Optimising Potential, Academic Rigour* and *Adventurous Learning*. We believe that learning should be challenging, motivating and lead to a sense of fulfilment, which is why we strive to provide an inspiring environment that encourages growth and adventure so that our students can develop into all they are capable of being.

Our School is made up of a diverse community of staff and children from all over the world. We embrace individual talent and consider our School to be a place where students and staff are inspired and in turn inspire others.

There are over 500 students in the Senior School (11–18) and a similar number in the Prep School and Nurseries (0–11). We have capacity for up to 170 boarders in the Senior School, cared for by several resident teachers and support staff; a mix of nationalities represented.

Academic Success. In 2023, 90% of GCSE grades were awarded between grade 9 and grade 5, and over half of the results graded 7 or higher. At A Level in 2023, 63% of pupils achieved grades A*–B, 85% of pupils gained A*–C, 80% achieved A*–A in English Literature and 100% of students gained A*–B in Art, English Literature and Drama. We are incredibly proud that 71% have confirmed places at their first-choice university, and 84% have places at their first- or second-choice university. The vast majority are continuing their studies at Russell Group universities, many reading STEM subjects such as Biochemistry, Medicine, Optometry, Physiotherapy and Veterinary Science.

Entry Requirements. Please visit the Admissions section of our website for all details about entrance requirements and the process you will need to follow to apply for a place at Ashford School.

Scholarships. Academic, Art, Sport, Music, and Drama scholarships are available for Years 7, 9 and 12. Please visit our website for further information.

Fees per term (2023–2024). Day: Prep £4,050–£5,787; Years 7 to 13: £6,342; Senior: £6,786. Full boarding (from 11 years): £13,830; Weekly boarding (from 11 years): £9,932.

Where relevant, fees include lunches for day pupils/children and all meals for boarders, as well as most books, equipment, and compulsory visits. Public examinations, such as GCSEs, A Levels and music exams, are charged as extras in arrears. All fees are payable in advance of the start of each term in September, January, and April.

Charitable Status. Ashford School is part of United Learning which comprises: UCST (a Company Limited by Guarantee, Registered in England, number 2780748, and a Registered Charity, number 1016538) and ULT (a Company Limited by Guarantee, Registered in England, number 4439859, and an Exempt Charity).

Governing Body:
Chair: Mrs D Geering
Professor P Freemont
Mr A Richards
Mr J B Rimmer
Mrs E Rose
Mr M Sutton
The Ven S Taylor
Ms S Morris
Ms N Ratchford

***Headmaster*: Mr Michael Hall**, BA Liverpool, MA

Head of the Senior School: Mr Michael Hall, BA Liverpool, MA
Senior Deputy Head: Ms N Timms, BEng Loughborough
Deputy Head (*Academic*) *& Director of Staff Development & Training*: Mrs J Russell, BA Leeds
Deputy Head (*Operations Co-curricular & Community Partnerships*): Mr T Grieves, BA Durham
Head of Ashford Prep School: Mr N Tiley-Nunn
Deputy Head (*Teaching & Learning*): Mrs R Clifford, BSc
Deputy Head (*Pastoral*): Mr C Neesham, BA

Bablake and King Henry VIII School

Part of the Coventry School Foundation

BKHS Bablake Senior
Coundon Road, Coventry CV1 4AU

Tel: 024 7627 1200
email: info.bablake@bkhs.org.uk
X/Twitter: @BKHSBablake
Facebook: @BKHSBablake

BKHS King Henry VIII Senior
Warwick Road, Coventry CV3 6AQ

Tel: 024 7627 1111
email: info.khviii@bkhs.org.uk
X/Twitter: @BKHSKHVIII
Facebook: @BKHSKingHenryVIII

website: www.bkhs.org.uk

BKHS brings together the rich heritages of Bablake and King Henry VIII schools. The School continues the tradition of an exceptional education within the city, built upon outstanding opportunities, superb teaching and learning, and strong pastoral care.

The School is represented on the Headmasters' Conference and on the Association of Governing Bodies of Independent Schools. The governing body is the Coventry School Foundation, on which are represented Sir Thomas White's Charity, the Coventry Church Charities, Coventry General Charities and Birmingham, Coventry, Oxford and Warwick Universities. There are also several co-opted Governors.

BKHS Bablake was originally part of the College of the same name founded by Queen Isabella in 1344. After the dissolution of the monasteries, it was refounded in 1560 by the city; it is chiefly associated with the name of Thomas Wheatley, whose indentures of 1563 put its finances on a firm foundation.

Number in School. There are approximately 746 Day Pupils (including 198 in the Sixth Form) and 360 in the Preparatory School and Pre Prep.

BKHS Bablake Facilities. On the 11-acre site stands the main buildings, which have been considerably extended to include a Sports Centre, heated indoor swimming pool and a purpose-built Modern Languages Block and a purpose-built English, Music and Drama Block. For further details of the Prep and Pre Prep, also on this site, *see* BKHS Prep and Pre Prep entry in IAPS section. There are 27 acres of playing fields, a large pavilion, and two all-weather hockey pitches located a mile from the School.

BKHS King Henry VIII was founded in 1545 by John Hales, Clerk of the Hanaper to the King, under Letters Patent of King Henry VIII.

Number in School. There are approximately 611 Day Pupils (including 202 in the Sixth Form) and 380 in the Preparatory School.

BKHS King Henry VIII Facilities. The School moved to its present site in Coventry in 1885. The Governors have continually improved, extended and restored the buildings which are well equipped to cope with the demands of an up-to-date, relevant and challenging curriculum. The School has extensive playing fields, some of which are located on the main site, other fields are ten minutes away by minibus.

The School has an Art facility, a Sixth Form Centre, a Sports Hall, a six-lane, 25m swimming pool, and fitness suite. There is also a dedicated Archive room containing a timeline from 1545 to 2014 and original Tudor artefacts.

BKHS Curriculum. The curriculum is broad and balanced, integrating National Curriculum principles and practices where appropriate. The Senior School curriculum provides courses leading to the GCSE examinations and A levels. Subjects available currently are Art, Biology, Business Studies, Chemistry, Classical Civilisation, Computer Science, Drama and Theatre Studies, Economics, English, French, Food and Nutrition, Geography, German, History, Latin, Law, Mathematics (and Further Mathematics), Music, Philosophy, Religion and Ethics, Photography, Psychology, Physics, and Spanish. All pupils follow a structured PSHE course. Separate sciences are taught up to IGCSE. Most pupils study 10 subjects at GCSE, the majority progressing into the Sixth Form where the A level curriculum is followed, with three subjects being examined at the end of the two years. All students study an academic enrichment programme, leading to an additional qualification, for example an Extended Project Qualification (EPQ). Physical Education and Sport are also considered to be a vital part of the curriculum and are available as an A level option.

Courses in Key Skills/Complementary Studies and Critical Thinking are offered in the Sixth Form. There is a wide range of Enrichment Studies options including Art, Astronomy, Chinese, Computing, Cookery, Design, Drama, Music, Photography and many others.

Examination results at all levels are excellent.

BKHS Games. Rugby, Hockey, Netball, Basketball, Cross-Country, Athletics, Rounders, Tennis, Cricket, Swimming, and Orienteering. The School has an extensive artificial turf games area, used mainly for hockey, but providing an additional 24 tennis courts (in the summer).

BKHS Co-Curricular Activities. The School is noted for the excellence of its sport, music, drama, debating, public speaking and outdoor pursuits. All pupils are encouraged to contribute to the extracurricular life of the School. The School has close connections with many universities including Oxford and Cambridge. All pupils are involved in the charity work of the School and there is a large Community Service programme for the Senior pupils in Year 11 and the Sixth Form.

BKHS Admission. Entry is via the School's own Entrance Examination held annually in October for entrance the following September. The normal age of entry is 11 but there are smaller intakes at 12, 13 and 14.

Entry to the Sixth Form is based on gaining at least five GCSE passes at grade 6 or above (with a grade 7 preferred in the subjects chosen to study at A level, and required in some cases) and an interview with the Headmaster and Head of Sixth Form.

Enquiries about admissions should be addressed to the Admissions Office: admissions@bkhs.org.uk.

BKHS Scholarships. Academic, Art and Music scholarships are available for entry into Year 7.

Academic, Sport and Music scholarships are available for Sixth Form entry.

The Governors also annually award a number of bursaries for those entering at Year 7 and Sixth Form; these are dependent on academic ability and parental means.

BKHS Fees per term (2023–2024). Senior School £4,595; Prep School £3,640; Pre Prep £3,185.

Charitable status. Coventry School Foundation is a Registered Charity, number 528961. It exists to provide quality education for boys and girls.

Chair of Governors: Mr I Dunn

***BKHS Principal*: Mr C Staley**, BA, MBA

***BKHS Bablake Headmaster*: Mr A M Wright**, BSc

Pastoral Deputy Head: Mrs G Press, BEd

***BKHS King Henry VIII Headmaster*: Mr P Dearden**, MEd, BA

Deputy Head: Dr M Cuthbert, BSc, MEd, HDipEd, WITS

Deputy Head: Mr R Sewell, BA

Deputy Head: Mrs C Dowding, BSc

Badminton School

Westbury-on-Trym, Bristol BS9 3BA

Tel: 0117 905 5200
email: admissions@badmintonschool.co.uk
website: www.badmintonschool.co.uk
X/Twitter: @BadmintonSchool
Facebook: @BadmintonSch
Instagram: @BadmintonSchool
LinkedIn: /school/badminton-school-limited

See full entry in the **GSA** section, on **p. 419**.

Bancroft's School

High Road, Woodford Green, Essex IG8 0RF

Tel: 020 8505 4821
email: office@bancrofts.org
website: www.bancrofts.org
Facebook: @bancroftsschool
Instagram: @bancroftsschool

Motto: *Unto God only be honour and glory*

Bancroft's school is an HMC co-educational school for approximately 1,100 pupils aged 7–18. Founded by the Drapers' Company in 1737, as a result of a bequest from Francis Bancroft, the school still maintains its historic links with the City, combining the best of traditional values with innovative practices. The school moved to its present site at Woodford Wells in 1889. The fine Victorian quad was designed by Sir Arthur Blomfield, and provides a dining hall, chapel, library and classrooms. There have been many additions to the original buildings over the years, which have ensured that Bancroft's has first-rate facilities, including a swimming pool and sports hall on site. Bancroft's became fully co-educational in 1979. In 1990, a Preparatory school was opened, providing education for children aged 7–11. The school is committed to providing excellent value for money, as well as offering Assisted Places to those who could not otherwise attend the school.

The School offers a wide range of subjects at GCSE and A Level and has a strong record of academic success. Virtually all Bancroftians progress to university, with about 15 each year to Oxford or Cambridge. On average, 75% of pupils will go on to study at Russell Group institutions. Bancroft's has a very strong record of pupils studying medicine and dentistry.

The major sports for girls are hockey, netball, tennis and athletics; the main curricular games for boys are football, rugby, hockey, cricket and athletics. Swimming, badminton and basketball are also provided. The Physical Education programme includes gymnastics, trampolining, basketball and badminton.

The School has a Contingent of the CCF (both Army and RAF sections), a Sea Scout Unit, and a branch of the Duke of Edinburgh's Award Scheme. The wide programme of concerts and plays throughout the school year offers opportunities for pupils of all age groups.

Preparatory School. The Prep School opened in September 1990, occupying purpose-built accommodation on a separate site within the school grounds. There are 12 classrooms, a hall, a library, a performing arts studio and specialist rooms for art and science. Although self-contained, the Prep School makes extensive use of the Senior School's sports, music and drama facilities.

(*For further details, see Preparatory School entry in IAPS section.*)

Admission. 66 places are available each year for boys and girls wishing to enter the Preparatory Department at 7+; entry tests take place in the January. Transfer to the Senior School is guaranteed. At 11+, there are another 60 places available for children entering Bancroft's who sit an examination in Mathematics, English and a computer-based reasoning test in January. For candidates of other ages, individual arrangements are made. Applications for 7+ and 11+ entry must be made before 1 December in the year prior to entry. There is a direct entry for boys and girls into the Sixth Form dependent upon GCSE results and performance in the School's 16+ entrance examination which is sat in the November of Year 11.

Scholarships. Academic awards are awarded on an honorary two-year basis at 11+ and 16+. Music awards are awarded at both 11+ and 16+, again for a two-year period; Music awards include tuition fees on one or two instruments. Drama, Art, Sports and Community awards are awarded to pupils already at Bancroft's from Year 8 onwards. Pupils may be given awards at other points in their school careers. None of these awards carry fee remission.

Assisted Places, are available at age 11, which can cover the full fees. These are awarded based on disclosure of family finances and performance in the Entrance Examination. Two means-tested Assisted Places are available for entrants to the Prep School at age 7; these only cover Prep School fees. Assisted

Places may also be available for entrants into the Sixth Form.

Fees per term (2023–2024). Senior School: £7,590, Prep School: £6,365. Fees include lunch and books.

Charitable status. Bancroft's School is a Registered Charity, number 1068532. It exists to provide an academic education to able children.

Chairman of the Governors: Sir Andrew Ford

***Head*: Mr S R J Marshall**, MA, MA, MPhil

Senior Deputy Head: Mrs K Shapiro, MA
Deputy Head Academic: Dr M Lim, PhD
Deputy Head Pastoral & Safe Guarding Lead: Mrs E F de Renzy Channer, MA
Senior Tutor: Mr R B de Renzy Channer, MA
Assistant Heads:
Mr J T M Barr, MEng (*Pastoral*)
Ms E C Burnside, MA (*Activities & The Co-Curriculum*)
Mr A Gocoldas, BSc (*Academic*)
Mr J P Dickinson, MEng

Barnard Castle School

Newgate, Barnard Castle, County Durham DL12 8UN
Tel: 01833 690222
email: genoffice@barneyschool.org.uk
website: www.barnardcastleschool.org.uk
X/Twitter: @barney_school
Facebook: @BarnardCastleSchool
Instagram: @barnardcastleschool
LinkedIn: /company/barnard-castle-school

Motto: *Parvis imbutus tentabis grandia tutus*

The St John's Hospital in Barnard Castle was founded in the 13th century by John Baliol, whose widow founded the Oxford College. By a Scheme of the Charity Commissioners, bequests under the will of Benjamin Flounders of Yarm were combined with the funds of the St John's Hospital and public subscriptions to build and endow the present foundation in 1883. Originally known as the North Eastern County School, the name was changed to Barnard Castle School in 1924.

'Barney', as it is affectionately known, is a day and boarding school for boys and girls between the ages of 4 and 18.

Organisation and numbers. There are 512 pupils aged 11–18 in the Senior School, of whom 110 are boarders. The Preparatory School comprises a Pre-Prep Department of 48 pupils between the ages of 4 and 7, and 132 pupils between the ages of 7 and 11, of whom 13 are boarders. (*See also Preparatory School entry in IAPS section.*) The Senior and Preparatory Schools are located on adjacent sites and operate separately on a day-to-day basis while enjoying the mutual benefits of being able to share a number of resources and facilities. Girls were first admitted in 1981 and the School has been fully co-educational since 1993.

Location. The School is situated on its own extensive grounds on the outskirts of an historic market town in an area of outstanding natural beauty. The area is well served by Teesside International and Newcastle airports as well as Darlington railway station. The School also operates its own bus service for pupils from a wide area.

Curriculum. This is designed to provide a broad, balanced and flexible programme, avoiding undue specialisation at too early a stage. In the Prep School, emphasis is given to literacy and numeracy skills, as well as Science, History, Geography, French (from age 8), Religious Education, Technology, Art, Music, Information Technology, Physical Education (including swimming) and Games. These subjects are developed further in the Senior School, with the addition of Latin or Classical Civilisation, Personal, Social and Health Education, and three separate sciences. German or Spanish is added at age 12, while Business Studies and Engineering increase the list of GCSE options at age 14. There are some twenty A, AS or Pre-U Level subjects, which give a wide choice in the Sixth Form. Almost all Sixth Form leavers go on to University or College courses. A Learning Support Department provides specialist help for those who need it in both the Preparatory and Senior Schools, and tuition is offered in English as a Second Language.

Religious Education. The School is a Christian foundation and the Chapel stands at the heart of the School in more than just a geographical sense. The School Chaplain, who plays an important role in the pastoral structure of the School, as well as being responsible for Religious Studies and Chapel worship, is an ordained member of the Church of England, but the School is a multi-denominational one which welcomes and supports pupils of all faiths and none. Pupils attend weekday morning assemblies in Chapel, and there is a Sunday service for boarders.

Boarding and Day Houses. There are eight single-sex Houses within the Senior School – three boarding and five day – each small enough for pupils to know each other well, but large enough to allow a mixture of interests, backgrounds and abilities, as well as opportunities for leadership. Housemasters and Housemistresses, each supported by a team of Tutors and Assistants, are responsible for the welfare and progress of each pupil in their charge.

Junior Boarders (boys and girls aged 7–11) and Senior Girl Boarders live in their own modern Houses in the School grounds, alongside their Houseparents, Boarding Tutors and Matrons. The two Senior Boys' Boarding Houses have recently undergone a major programme of restructuring and refurbishment, and offer comfortable accommodation within the main building of the School. The resident Housemasters are supported by resident boarding tutors and matrons, and by the School Sister in the School's Medical Centre. The School Doctor visits daily.

Cultural and other activities. The School has a flourishing music department in which the Chapel Choir, Orchestras, Wind and Jazz Bands and smaller ensembles perform regularly.

Drama is also prominent, with a regular programme of productions taking place throughout the year. There is a strong tradition of after-school activities; both day and boarding pupils take part in a wide range of clubs and societies, selecting from over 100 weekly activities.

Games. Rugby, Hockey, Netball, Cricket, Athletics, Squash, Cross-Country Running, Tennis and Swimming are the main sports, and other options such as soccer, badminton, basketball and golf are available. The School has extensive playing fields, a modern Sports Hall, and Fitness Centre, squash and tennis courts, and a heated indoor swimming pool. A full-size, floodlit AstroTurf-style pitch is available for all to use. Regular inter-school matches are arranged at all levels.

Outdoor activities. There is a strong emphasis on providing instruction, opportunity and challenge in a wide range of outdoor activities. Much of this takes place under the auspices of a flourishing Cadet Force (Army and RAF sections) or The Duke of Edinburgh's Gold and Silver Award schemes.

Careers. There is a well-equipped Careers Room, and a team of careers staff work together with the Higher Education Coordinator to provide pupils at all stages of the School with expert advice and help in decision-making and application procedures.

Admission. Pupils are admitted at all stages via the School's own Entrance Assessments. There is also direct entry into the Sixth Form subject to satisfactory performance at GCSE level. Details of the application procedure are obtainable from the Registrar (admissions@barneyschool.org.uk).

Scholarships and Assisted Places. Academic Scholarships and Exhibitions are awarded to entrants to the Senior School at Year 7, Year 9 and the Sixth Form, on the basis of the School's own entrance examinations held in February.

Music scholarships and exhibitions: There are two music exhibitions available in Year 7, a further two scholarships in Year 9 and in the Sixth Form.

Sport exhibitions based on potential are available at Year 7 and scholarships are available at Year 9 and in the Sixth Form. Four exhibitions may be awarded in Year 7, followed by up to four scholarships in Year 9 and a further two scholarships in the Sixth Form.

Art scholarships and exhibitions are available from Year 9 and in the Sixth Form.

Drama scholarships and exhibitions are available to candidates entering the Sixth Form.

Awards may be supplemented by means-tested Bursaries.

The School is also able to offer a small number of means-tested assisted places. Details are available from the Admissions Secretary.

Fees per term (2023–2024). Senior School (Years 7–13): Day £5,665; Junior Boarders (Years 7–8): £10,100; Junior International Boarders (Years 7–8): £11,780; Senior Boarders (Years 9–13): £10,810; International Boarders: £12,500. Fees are inclusive and subject to annual review.

Charitable status. Barnard Castle School is a Registered Charity, number 1125375, whose aim is the education of boys and girls.

The Governing Body:
Chair: Mrs C J Sunley
Vice-Chairs: Mr N Bliss; Dr J Elphick
Chair of Finance & Estates Sub-Committee: Mr I Moffat
Chair of Education, Welfare and Staff Development Sub-Committee: Mr P Kelsall
Chair of Strategy, Marketing & Development Sub-Committee: Mr E Rendall
Chair of Governance Sub-Committee: Dr J Elphick

Mr M Allison
Mr P Hodges
Mrs K Marshall
Mr P Mothersill
Ms C Newnam
Mr D C Osborne
Councillor G Richardson
Mr D F Starr
Mrs D Vinsome

Clerk to the Governors: Mrs S Metcalf, BA, FCCA

***Headmaster*: Tony C Jackson**, BA

Second Master: Martin Pepper, BA
Deputy Head (*i/c of Sixth Form*): Fiona Beadnell, MA
Deputy Head (*Pastoral*): Carrie J Riley
Deputy Head (*Academic*): Matthew Corke, BA Hons

Registrar: Bronwyn Huddleston
International Registrar: Nicola Slater

Housemasters/mistresses:
Bowes: Janey Dolby, BA
Dale: Joseph Pickering, BSc
Durham: David Riley, BA Hons
Marwood: Elizabeth Heward, BA
Longfield: Peter Lavery, BA Hons
Northumberland: Luke D Monument, BSc
Tees: Henry W Fairwood, BSc
York: Martin Pepper, BA

Assistant Director of Studies: Mark D Robson, BSc, MEd

Heads of Departments:
Art: Kate Baptist, BA
Biology: Rebecca K B Gibson, MSc, BSc
Business Studies: Paul Easton, BA Hons
Chemistry: Janine Wilson, MA
Classics: John D N Gedye, BA
Design & Technology: Alan M Beaty, BSc
Drama: Scott Edwards, BA
English: Helena Langford, PhD
Geography: David W Dalton, MA
History: Huw Bradbury, MA
ICT: Judith Brown, MSc
Maths: Mike Nicholson, BSc, MEd
MFL: Helen D Kent, MPhil, BA
Music: Richard J Dawson, BA Hons
Physics: Christopher Butler, MSc, MA
Politics: Andrea J Campbell, BA
Psychology: Jamie Sinar, BSc Hons
Religious, Ethics & Philosophy: Rachel Romano, BA Hons
SEN: Deborah Wafer, BSc Hons
Sport: Rachael S Masterman, MA, BSc

Teaching Staff:
Charles H Alderson, BSc
Charlotte Bates, MA
Erin E Beaty, BA
Lesley Burgess, BEd
Sarah Burnham, BA Hons
Dr Ian Butterfield, PhD, BSc
Lee Clough, BEd
Caroline Connor, BSc
Nick J Connor, BA
Kevin B Cosstick, JP, PhD, BSc
Isobel Dawson, BA Hons
Anna Dias, BA Hons
Lee Dickson
Mick Donnelly, FLCM, Cert Ed
Andy M Dunn, MSc, MPhil
George Ford, BMus Hons
Sam S Forsyth, BSc
Elizabeth Gorman-Tysoe, MA
Elizabeth Heward, BA

Martin Ince, BA
Carla Lavery, BSc
Adriana Longo, MA
Alan J Maude, BSc
Chris Misiak, BA Hons
Sebastian T Nichols, PhD
Fiona Norrie, BEd
Sarah Rothwell, MA
Emma Taylor, LLB
Ben C Usher, BSc

Combined Cadet Force:
Commanding Officer: Lt Col Caroline E Connor, BSc
SSI: Tony Wardman

Medical Centre:
School Nurse: Mrs Bethan Cummins, BSc Hons
School Nurse: Mrs Suzanne Newbrook, BSc
School Counsellor: Mrs Gaynor Murray, BA Hons

Bedales School

Church Road, Steep, Petersfield, Hampshire GU32 2DG

Tel: 01730 300100
01730 711733 (Admissions)
email: admissions@bedales.org.uk
website: www.bedales.org.uk
X/Twitter: @BedalesSchool
Facebook: @BedalesSchool
Instagram: @BedalesSchool
LinkedIn: /school/bedales-school

Number in school. 472 pupils: 231 boys, 241 girls; 317 boarders.

Fees per term (2023–2024). Bedales Senior: Boarders £14,185, Day £11,145. Bedales Prep: Boarders £9,750, Half-boarding (3 nights) £8,680, Day £6,745–£7,335. Bedales Pre-prep: £3,945–£5,150.

Established in 1893 as a humane alternative to the authoritarian regimes of late-Victorian public schools, Bedales maintains its founding values of innovation and liberalism in its approach to education. Students thrive in an environment that fosters individual expression and critical thinking and develops a lifelong love of learning.

The Bedales estate is situated in 120 acres of farmland, orchards, woodland and playing fields in the South Downs National Park. The school is only an hour's train journey from London, yet charmingly captures rural living in the British countryside. Students take pride in their contributions to Outdoor Work at Bedales, from tending to the variety of livestock on the estate and beekeeping, to demonstrating practical skills in blacksmithing and using homegrown produce in the Bakehouse.

The school is continuously shaped by what is considered best for the educational welfare and happiness of the students as individuals. Listening to the views of pupils is a fundamental aspect of the school's progressive ethos and led to Bedales' creation of one of the first school councils in 1916. The students' voices are valued and assist in forging the framework in which the school community lives, learns and grows.

Senior School (13–18).

Curriculum. Bedales is committed to offering students a balanced and stimulating curriculum that broadens their learning beyond the classroom and prepares them for their individual journeys in the world.

The Block 3 (Year 9) curriculum is a rich, experiential project-based year. At the beginning of the academic year, there is a challenging week of outdoor pursuits and team-building in the Lake District. Here, students work with tutors alongside the dedicated and professional staff at the centre. On their return, they are introduced to the curriculum so they can make informed subject choices and have greater autonomy over what they would like to learn. During this first year at Bedales, students study the Humanities through an interdisciplinary 'real-world' approach, which culminates in the Bedales Humanities Research Project and combines History, Geography, Global Perspectives and Philosophy, Religion and Ethics (PRE).

The school has created a unique selection of its own courses to complement a core of five i/GCSEs: Bedales Assessed Courses (BACs). Students pursue their educational interests with a choice of five of the 14 BACs which include English Literature, Sports Science and Digital Game Design. Well regarded by Universities, BACs comprise continuous assessment and provide meaningful and detailed content to promote collaboration, intellectual ambition and creative thinking. The provision of a more rigorous and project-based alternative to exam-only assessments seeks to educate the whole individual and broaden their educational horizons. The school will be expanding the number of BACs that it already offers to include the Sciences and Languages in a move toward a two-GCSE model from 2026.

Bedales also supports students through its wellbeing programme, in which individuals in Blocks 3–5 (Years 9–11) have weekly wellbeing lessons, to increase awareness of emotional health and to build resilience and self-esteem.

The subjects offered at Bedales Sixth Form allow a high degree of flexibility to provide for individual students' needs and consider the requirements of universities and colleges in the UK and overseas. Inspired by the success of BACs, Bedales has developed an additional strand of the Sixth Form curriculum to replace a fourth A Level. The Bedales Enrichment Programme is Bedalian in its idealism, breadth and content, and each student's programme combines academic study, sport and global awareness among others. Structured around the conviction that education should be about 'head, hand and heart', it prepares students for life after Bedales, by developing the skills of independent learning that are vital in higher education and beyond.

Facilities. Within the school's 120-acre setting is a broad range of facilities to support the co-curricular activities that take place at Bedales. The school has a wide selection of sporting facilities that are used to host fixtures and lessons throughout the year, with multiple football pitches and tennis courts, a cricket pitch and pavilion and 25 m swimming pool. The school is also home to a modern Art & Design Building and the Memorial Library, a Grade I listed Arts & Crafts building, constructed using traditional materials and methods. The series of bays, large windows and beautiful wooden interior create a quiet haven for studying or reading. Bedales takes pride in its award-winning theatre that offers an atmospheric venue for school performances and conferences. The Olivier

Theatre seats 300 and boasts a professional-standard lighting rig and sound system.

Community. Pertaining to the school's motto 'Work of Each for Weal of All', students at Bedales are encouraged to explore their individuality, while also valuing their involvement within the community. Notably, the school holds an annual community day where students and staff work in collective endeavour to celebrate key founding figures and the current community by contributing to a 'whole-school effort'. These may entail a united effort to fundraise for a chosen charity or working on a communal project on the school's estate. With mutual respect being a cornerstone of the school's culture, students and staff are addressed using first-name terms and students choose what to wear to school. This enriches Bedales' inclusive and welcoming atmosphere that is underpinned by a clear structure of values, rules, guidance and support. Sixth Form students are also expected to take on positions of responsibility in the school, such as contributing to one of the many student committees, and acting as role model and mentor to younger students.

Environment. Bedales is dedicated to protecting the environment and continuously reviews and adapts sustainability initiatives implemented. Members of the school value the environment in which they live, learn and grow and take active responsibility to protect it. The school is developing a sustainability co-curriculum, focused on growing more of its own food and involving students in the reduction of food waste and composting. This will complement the planned expansion of the school's solar power programme and the move to an electric fleet of school vehicles.

Admission. Entry to the school is from 3+, 7+ (Bedales Pre-prep), 8+, 11+ (Bedales Prep), 13+ and 16+ (Bedales Senior). Once in the school, students are assessed before proceeding to the next stage.

Entry Tests. Entry for newcomers at 10+ and 11+ takes the form of residential tests in the January before entry; 13+ assessments take place approximately 20 months before entry. Entry at 16+ is by a series of interviews on a single day. Ad hoc testing is also offered if places are available. Contact the Admissions team in the first instance.

Bedales Prep School (8–13). (See Bedales Prep, Dunhurst entry in IAPS section.)

Bedales Pre-prep School (3–8).

Number in school. 91: 45 girls; 46 boys.

Entrance at 3+ is by date of registration; after this, acceptances are made following informal assessments, should vacancies arise.

Bedales Pre-prep is the foundation of the children's education, and the beginning of their journey through Bedales. It forms an introduction to the underpinning principle rooted in the school: learning as part of a wider community characterised by trust, mutual respect and shared creative endeavour.

The school aims to nurture children to be rounded, confident, inquisitive and kind to others, and to challenge themselves in a safe environment without a fear of failure.

Bedales Pre-prep places an emphasis on outdoor learning, utilising the open orchard and wooden playground within the estate for learning, playing and growing, across all four seasons. The children engage in Outdoor Work and are enthusiastic about planting, growing and eating fruits and vegetables from the nursery garden, greenhouse and vegetable plots.

The curriculum at the Pre-prep is wide and encourages the development of lifelong skills to cultivate a lasting love of learning. Children are supported in an explorative approach to their early education, with the aim for pupils to be fluent readers, spontaneous and literate writers and sound mathematicians as they progress to Bedales Prep. Equal value is placed on intellectual, creative, emotional, social and physical development, promoting the application of rigorous imagination to practical and theoretical challenges. The children benefit from the vast curriculum that introduces them to the Humanities, Arts, Sciences and Languages. Integration is a strength at Bedales, allowing all pupils to benefit from the range of resources and facilities on the estate. Pre-prep children have regular visits across the school, investigating in the Prep school's science labs and using the shared sports facilities, as well as exploring the world beyond Bedales on residential and day trips. These close links between the Pre-prep, Prep and Senior school allow children in Year 3 to automatically transfer from the Pre-prep to the Prep unless there are exceptional circumstances. Year 3 children have opportunities for more challenges and often join together with Prep pupils in lessons, matches and games. A comprehensive sports programme including swimming, tennis, gymnastics, netball and football promotes the enjoyment of movement from an early age.

Scholarships. Personal development is central to the Bedales concept of scholarship, with the objective of aligning scholarship beneficiaries with the school's desire to develop inquisitive thinkers with a love of learning.

The school has introduced a scheme for students with particular talents in Art, Design, Music, Dance, Drama, Sport and other academic subjects to foster their appetite for research, enquiry and development. Depending on their specialist subject, most scholarship holders have access to a research fund to support their individual scholarly projects. There is no reduction in school fees; research grants are non-means-tested and hence have a relatively small financial value (up to £500 per year for 2023/24). The award of a scholarship is reviewed annually based on student performance.

Bursaries. Ranging from part-fee contributions up to full 100% bursaries (with further support for additional costs), these awards enable pupils (generally from 11+ upwards) with an appetite for learning to attend Bedales Prep and Bedales Senior, who otherwise would have been unable to pay the fees. Awards are based on an assessment of the family's financial means. The school's John Badley Foundation charity supports 100% bursaries.

Pupils can benefit from the award of either a scholarship or a bursary, or both. Although bursary financial assistance is not dependent on a scholarship award, the school aims to enable pupils with particularly strong talents to attend the school, therefore a number of bursary beneficiaries also benefit from scholarship awards. Please contact the Head of Admissions (email: admissions@bedales.org.uk; tel: 01730 711733) if you would like to discuss suitability for a scholarship or bursary to Bedales Prep or Bedales Senior.

Charitable status. Bedales School is a Registered Charity, number 307332. Its aims and objectives are to educate children as broadly as possible in a creative and caring environment.

Governors:
Claudia Arney, MBA
Clare Bradbury, BSc, PGCE
Edward Impey, DPhil
Edward Rees, BA Ed Hons
Felix Grey, MChem, MPhil
Isabella [Issie] Myers, MsC, MRSB
Jessica Boyd, PhD
Mark Hanson
Owen Jonathan, LLB Hons
Stephen Lehec, BA, PGCE
Stephen Nokes (*Chairman*)

***Head*: Will Goldsmith**, MA Edinburgh, Graduate Teacher Programme with QTS Brunel, PGCAEP Oxford Brookes

***Head, Bedales Prep, Dunhurst*: Colin Baty**, NPQH, BEd, Dip Teach Waikato University NZ, BPP Roehampton

***Head, Bedales Pre-prep*: Fiona Read**, BEd Hons Kingston, PGDip Open University

Bursar and Clerk to the Governors: Richard Lushington, BA, MCIPD Thames Polytechnic London

Director of External Relations: Rob Reynolds, BSc Royal Holloway London, MBA Strathclyde, MCIM

Bede's Senior School

Upper Dicker, East Sussex BN27 3QH

Tel: 01323 843252
email: school.office@bedes.org
website: www.bedes.org
X/Twitter: @bedesnews
Facebook: @bedesseniorschool
Instagram: @bedesseniorschool

Bede's Senior School is an independent, co-educational school for pupils from the age of 13 to 18, offering both day and boarding places. Bede's is located in the heart of the beautiful Sussex countryside, in the rural village of Upper Dicker in East Sussex, just over an hour from London.

At Bede's, we believe that every child is unique, each possessing individual and sometimes hidden talents. Bede's fosters a community of curiosity which encourages every individual to find and develop their passions, seek new horizons, develop lasting friendships and achieve their potential.

The school champions choice at every turn. Each Bedian is nurtured to find joy in their pursuit of brilliance, to develop a genuine love of learning. This culture of compassion and conscientiousness enables Bede's to nurture inquisitive minds and, in combination with the opportunities its campus provides, create unforgettable memories.

The Senior School owes its existence in part to the success and vitality of Bede's Preparatory School in Eastbourne, one of the first boys' Preparatory Schools to become fully co-educational and now one of the largest co-educational Preparatory Schools in the country. The Senior School has 815 students. Of these, 330 are boarders (full and weekly), 485 are day students, 309 are Sixth Formers, and there are pupils of 46 different nationalities.

The School takes great pride in the variety of its students and the outstanding range of opportunities available to them. Bede's is a place where every pupil is truly treated as an individual and where they are enriched in a holistic way – enabling them to flourish in all aspects of life.

Facilities. Bede's Senior School has five stunning boarding houses, the latest of which was built in 2022 and includes modern facilities, accommodates 70 beds as well as a stunning atrium, and additional breakout and learning spaces. Two of the boarding houses were recognised by the Institute of Chartered Surveyors in 2013 for their outstanding design and innovation. The multi-purpose Hall is used for School Assemblies, examinations and many sports, including basketball, badminton, cricket, football, netball and tennis. The Performing Arts Centre, in a beautiful setting next to the lake, provides studio space for both drama and dance. A new multi-purpose games area, water-based astro and cricket pavilion were all opened in 2015. Bede's has its very own zoo – which originally opened in 2011 – and currently hosts over 70 species of mammals, birds, amphibians, reptiles, fish and invertebrates. In 2018, it was extended with six brand-new enclosures, housing African birds, Madagascan lemurs, and South American squirrel monkeys.

Academic. As no two pupils are the same, Bede's is geared towards enabling everyone to identify their personal passions and then acquire expertise in their specific areas of interest. Bede's offers a considered and diverse array of high-quality courses, both within the academic timetable and as part of a unique co-curricular programme.

In Year 10, all pupils study English and Maths GCSE along with a Science GCSE/BTEC, and most pupils study at least one language. Bede's offers a carefully curated range of GCSE and BTEC options in a wide variety of subjects, including Business, Ceramics, Computer Science, Performing Arts and many more. The Fifth Form years are full of personal growth and development as pupils seek real areas of specialisation. They will emerge, at the end of two years' study, ready to face the challenges of the Sixth Form and life beyond.

Bede's offers an exciting curriculum of 35 subjects at A Level/BTEC, designed to educate, engage and enthuse. There is a supportive Sixth Form, Universities and Careers team to help pupils in their transition to higher education and the world beyond studying. The Sixth Form provides an exciting time for pupils, who can flourish in subjects that they have chosen. Sixth Form subjects include BTEC Dance, Economics, BTEC Animal Management and BTEC Production Arts.

Vocational provision: BTEC National Certificate in Sport, Music Performance, Animal Management and Business Management.

Bede's also runs the Legat Dance Academy which is fully integrated with the academic programme.

Current class sizes average 16 up to GCSE level and 12 at A Level.

Co-Curricular. Bede's provides a holistic approach to education. It is our strong belief that learning takes place beyond the confines of the classroom. With this in mind, Bede's places creativity, service and action at the heart of the pupil experience.

Bede's pupils pick from a wide array of over 100 clubs and activities that include climbing, e-sports, downland walking, mixed martial arts, debating and music. Activities slots occur three times a week and allow pupils to explore a range of interests. Every pupil is able to pursue their talents via our specialist staff, unbeatable facilities and an innovative timetable.

The Emerging Talent Programme brings together pupils across different sports who have potential to become professional sports people and provides training in areas such as nutrition, sports psychology and media handling.

Pastoral Care. Our exceptional pastoral care is evidenced as happy pupils who are engaged in their learning and actively involved in the wider life of the school, embracing every opportunity provided to them. Pupils who are kind to themselves and each other and are gracious about success and failure.

At the Senior School, the House system, which sees pupils from all year groups integrated into a family unit, ensures that each pupil feels familiar and grounded from day one. The Housemaster or Housemistress is supported by their team of House Tutors as well as House Prefects.

Tutors typically oversee 10–12 tutees and meet with them daily, either in their tutor groups or one to one. This regular contact time ensures that tutors get to know their tutees quickly, supporting them in all aspects of their life at Bede's Senior School.

Religion. The School maintains the Village Church for the local community. Confirmation classes are available, if requested. All students attend weekly meetings in the church which are appropriate to boys and girls of all religions and are of outstanding variety. Bede's does not impose any singular religious observance on its students but would rather either that their existing faith is further strengthened by their being full members of the congregation of local churches or that they grow to appreciate and value the importance of a strong spiritual life through the thoughtful and varied programme of 'School Meetings'.

Admission. The usual points of entry are at Year 9 and Year 12, although a small number of places are usually available for entry into Year 10. Pupils entering Year 9 will be invited to attend a Bede's Experience Day in Year 7 when pupils will take part in group activities, take a cognitive test, be interviewed and participate in an activity of choice. School reports and references are also taken into account. Entry into the Sixth Form will be conditional on GCSE results, reports and references.

Scholarships and Bursaries. Bede's invests in excess of ten per cent of its annual income in means-tested fee remission and academic, art, dance, drama, music and sports scholarships. Prospective students who wish to join outside of the scholarship process are able to apply for means-tested fee remission.

Further details regarding scholarships and bursaries are available from the Admissions Office, email: admissions@bedes.org.

Fees per term (2023–2024). Termly Tuition Fees (Day Fees): £8,990. In addition to the Tuition Fees (Day Fees), the following Termly supplements also apply: Day Boarding Supplement £250, Sixth Form Supplement £4,260, Legat £310, Weekly Boarding Supplement £4,260, Full Boarding Supplement £5,090.

Charitable status. St Bede's School Trust Sussex is a Registered Charity, number 278950. It exists to provide quality education.

Governors:
Mrs Geraldine Watkins (*Chair*)
Mr John Burbidge, BA Hons, ACA
Mr Stephen Esson
Mrs Sarah Jelly
Mr Guatam Kakar
Mr Dermot Keegan
Dr Charlotte Lemaigre, MA Hons, DClinPsychol
Mr Nicholas Mercer, BA Hons
Mrs Katherine Nash, BEd
Mrs Victoria Parker, BSc, MRICS
Mr Marios Pattihis
Mr Kyle Siwek
Mr Simon Smith, FRSA
Revd Jeremy Sykes, MA Hons

***Headmaster*: Mr P Goodyer**, BSc, MBA, FRSA

Senior Management:
Deputy Head: Mr J Tuson, MA, GTP (*English*)
Deputy Head, Operations: Mr P Wise, BSc Hons, MA, PGCE
Assistant Head (*Teaching & Learning*), Mr N Abrams, BSc Hons, PGCE
Assistant Head (*Innovation & Development*), Mr S Choithramani
Director of Summer School: Mr R Edwards, BSc, Msc
Assistant Head (*Day*): Mr N Driver, BCom, PGCE
Assistant Head (*Boarding*): Mr P Juniper, BSc Hons, PGCE, CBiol, MRSB
Director of Communications, Admissions and Development: Mrs R Nairne, BA Hons
Director of Safeguarding: Mrs A Hodge, RMA, CYP
Director of People: Emma Maynard, MCIPD
Bursar: Dr J Northway, MB, FRCS

Housemasters and Housemistresses:
Bloomsbury: Mrs M-J Newbery, BA Hons
Camberlot: Mr S Brown, BSc Hons, PGCE
Crossways: Mrs L MacKenzie, BA, PGCE
Charleston: Mr T Mpandawana, BSc, DipEd
Deis: Mr L Pianet, BA Hons
Dicker: Mr C Abraham, BSc Hons, Dip Law, PGCE
Dorms: Mr R Hickman BA Hons, GTP
Dorter: Mrs R Weston-Betts, MA, PGCE
Knights: Mr A Waterhouse, HDE Secondary
Stud: Mr P Jones, BSc Hons, MSc, PGCE

Heads of Departments/Subjects:
Mr J Turner, BA Hons, PGCE (*Creative Arts Faculty*)
Mrs E Excell, BA Hons, GTP (*Photography*)
Mr N Potter, BSc Hons, PGCE (*Design & Technology*)
Mr R Williams, BA Hons, GTP, Dip Media Ed (*Film & Media Studies*)

Mr J Whittaker, BA Hons, PGCE (*Humanities Faculty, History & Politics*)
Mr B Jackson, BSc, PGCE (*Business & Economics*)
Miss H Worrall, BSc Hons, MA (*Geography*)
Mr S Costi, BA Hons, PGCE (*Religion & Philosophy*)
Ms G Wainwright, MAES, BA Hons, PGCE (*Inquiry Learning*)
Mr P Juniper, BSc Hons, PGCE, CBiol, MSB (*Assistant Head (Boarding), Animal Management*)
Miss A Rowsell, BA Hons, MA Ed (*Physical Education*)
Mrs P Nikiteas, BA Hons, TEFL, Cert in SEN, CICTL (*PSHE*)
Mr M Oliver, BA Hons, PGCE (*Languages Faculty*)
Miss P Saoulidou, BA, MSc (*Classics*)
Mr J Cook, RSA, TEFLA (*EAL*)
Ms V Ganivet (*MFL*)
Mrs K Lewis, BA, PGCE (*Director of Performing Arts*)
Mr W Rennison, BA Hons, PGCE (*Academic Drama*)
Miss S Pennington, AISTD (*Legat School of Dance*)
Mr R Scamardella, MMus, MMP, FRSM, FRCO (*Director of Music*)
Ms J French, BSc, PGCE (*STEM Faculty*)
Mr C Betts, BSc Hons (*Computing and Information Technology*)
Mr S Manos, BSc Hons, PGCE (*Maths*)
Mrs Y Stainsby, MSc, PGCE (*Psychology*)
Ms L Finat-Duclos (*Chemistry*)
Mr O Froom, MPhys Hons, PGCE (*Physics*)
Mrs N Morton-Freeman, BSc Hons, PGCE (*Biology*)
Mrs C MacGregor, BSc, QTS, PGCE (*Director of Learning Enhancement*)
Mr D Byrne, BA Hons (*Director of Sport*)
Mr C Borsoi, BA Sports Coaching & Development (*Director of Hockey*)
Ms F Byrne, LTA Level 4 performance coach, MSc (*Senior School Tennis*)
Mr D Caryer, BA Hons, UEFA B Licence (*Director of Football*)
Ms J Kavanagh, Level 2 Netball Coach (*Head of Netball*)
Mr P Osborn, ASA Level 3 Swim Coaching (*Performance Swimming*)
Mr A Wells, ECB Level 4 & PGDip (*Director of Cricket*)

Year Heads:
Mr L Backler, BA Hons, PGCE, MA Ed (*First Year*)
Mr D Cheshire, BA Hons, MA, GTP (*Deputy Head of Sixth Form*)
Mr J Henham, BSc Hons, PGCE (*Sixth Form (Academic Progress)*)
Dr E Onofeghara, LLB, LLM, PGCE (*Assistant Director of Studies (GCSE)*)
Mr J Sealey, MA, BA Hons, PGCE (*Sixth Form (Engagement)*)
Mrs M Waterhouse, H Dip, FDE (*Director of Studies (GCSE)*)

Bedford Modern School

Manton Lane, Bedford, Bedfordshire MK41 7NT
Tel: 01234 332500
email: reception@bedmod.co.uk
website: www.bedmod.co.uk
X/Twitter: @BedfordModern
Facebook: @BedfordModernSchool
Instagram: @bedfordmodern
LinkedIn: /bedford-modern-school

Bedford Modern School (BMS) is one of the Harpur Trust Schools in Bedford, sharing equally in the educational endowment bequeathed for the establishment of a school in Bedford by Sir William Harpur in 1566. Bedford Modern School was a Direct Grant Grammar School which became independent in 1976. It became co-educational in September 2003.

Number of Students. There are 268 students in the Junior School (aged 7–11) and 1,014 students in the Senior School and Sixth Form (aged 11–18).

(*See also Bedford Modern Junior School entry in IAPS section.*)

Facilities. The school occupies an attractive forty-acre wooded site to the north of Bedford. The main buildings date from 1974 and there have been substantial additions since that time, most notably an assembly hall and classrooms to the Junior School (2002); a Sixth Form Study Centre and Refectory (The Rutherford Building – 2006) and Library Resource Centre (2007). There are extensive facilities for Science, Design Technology, Information Technology, Music and Performance Arts. Each year group has its own common room.

A state-of-the-art Science Centre opened in September 2017. The exciting design provides current and future generations of BMS students with an inspirational learning environment.

The playing fields are all on the school site with extensive facilities for rugby, hockey, football, cricket and athletics, among other sports. There is also a large swimming pool, fitness suite, gym and sports hall. Recent additions include two large all-weather training areas and netball courts. The school shares a large and well-stocked boathouse with the other Harpur Trust Schools on the River Great Ouse.

Admissions. Students are admitted between the ages of 7 and 16. The School conducts its own entrance assessments which are held in January of the year prior to September entry.

Registration fee is £125.

Fees per annum (2023–2024). Tuition: Junior School £12,324, Senior School and Sixth Form £16,908.

Assistance with Fees. The school offers both academic and subject-specific bursaries in Sport, Art, Performance Arts, Music, IT and Design Technology. All bursaries are means-tested and are also dependent on a student's academic success in the entrance assessments. Further details can be obtained from the BMS website at www.bedmod.co.uk/admissions/bursaries.

Curriculum. The Junior School (ages 7–11) curriculum covers Mathematics, English, Humanities

(History, Geography and RE), Science, ICT, Design Technology, Modern Foreign Languages, PE and Games, Art, Drama, PSHE and Swimming.

In the Senior School, the curriculum includes all of the core subjects, as well as Design Technology, ICT, RE, PE, Music, Art and Drama. All students study French, German, and Spanish in Year 7 and Latin in Year 8 before making their GCSE subject choices. Students opt for ten GCSE subjects.

In the Sixth Form, students select four from a wide range of 27 subjects. The choice of subjects includes Computer Science, Politics, Economics, Business, Religious Studies, Philosophy, Design Technology, Classical Civilisation, Drama and Theatre Studies, PE, Psychology, and Film Studies. The majority will continue three subjects to A Level.

ICT Facilities. The school boasts a range of ICT facilities offering both staff and students an individual network account and email address so that they are able to access over 400 networked PCs across the school in addition to high-speed broadband internet access, wireless classroom laptop sets, networked printing, and an extensive subject software library including a range of training courseware material.

All standard classrooms are equipped with a computer linked to ceiling-mounted data projector and speakers. There are a number of interactive whiteboards and additional presentation equipment is also available for use.

Religious and Moral Education. The school is multi-faith and multicultural and personal, social and health education is a fundamental and well-established part of the timetable. There is also a dedicated Head of Equality, Diversity and Inclusion in post who leads this important agenda.

Individual Care. Every student has a personal tutor, who supervises and takes an interest in their academic progress, co-curricular activities and sporting interests. Tutors meet with their tutees on a daily basis and there is at least one longer pastoral session each week. Each year group has its own common room for use at break and lunchtimes and other non-taught times with a study area and recreational facilities.

We believe that common sense and courtesy lie at the heart of pastoral care. We stress self-discipline and high standards of personal conduct. The tutorial system and the academic organisation are discrete, working in parallel to complement each other. We aim to provide a relaxed but purposeful environment; a culture in which all feel at ease and are ambitious to achieve their best.

Drama. Throughout the year there are several large-scale productions, a Drama Festival hosted for local schools and several smaller events. There are separate drama and dance studios and a 300-seat theatre. Speech and Drama is offered throughout the school, leading to LAMDA examinations. Ballet, tap and modern dance lessons follow the ISTD syllabus.

Music. Students can learn all of the orchestral and band instruments as well as piano, keyboard, guitar, electric guitar and singing. The school has a large variety of choirs, orchestra, bands and ensembles. Students can follow courses for GCSE and A Level Music. Music accommodation includes a music technology suite with ten MacBook Pro computers and state-of-the-art recording facilities.

Activities. There are many school societies and clubs catering for a variety of tastes and interests. The voluntary Combined Cadet Force is strong with Army, Navy and RAF sections. There is a structured programme of outdoor education which includes residential trips in Years 6, 7 and 8 with international expeditions available for older students. Outreach including community service and the Duke of Edinburgh's Award scheme are very popular.

Sport. The major sports are rugby, football, cricket and rowing for boys and hockey, cricket, netball and rowing for girls. Additional activities include: table tennis, water polo, badminton, squash, cross-country, weights and fitness, fives, sevens, swimming, dance, athletics, rounders, tennis, climbing and gymnastics. There is regular representation at national, divisional and regional levels.

Higher Education. In 2023, 82% of Sixth Form students achieved grades awarded at A*-B and 80% of students went on to a degree course at their chosen university. This includes five students who achieved places at either Cambridge or Oxford, and ten students who secured courses to study Medicine or Veterinary Sciences.

Old Bedford Modernians' Club. For further details on the school's alumni association, please visit www.obmclub.bedmod.co.uk.

Charitable status. Bedford Modern School is part of the Harpur Trust which is a Registered Charity, number 1066861. It includes in its aims the provision of high quality education for boys and girls.

Governors and Staff:
Chair of School Governors: Shirley Jackson

Leadership Team:

***Headmaster*: Mr D Payne**, MA Hons, PGCE, MEd

Senior Deputy Head: Mr A Whomsley, BA, QTS
Deputy Head (*Academic and Innovation*): Mr M Price, MA Cantab, PGCE
Deputy Head (*Pastoral and Student Progress*): Mrs J Goodacre, BA Hons, PGCE, MBA
Head of Junior School: Mrs P Pacyna, BA Hons, QTS
Director of Sixth Form: Mr J White, BEd Hons
Director of External Relations: Ms J Ridge, BA Hons
Director of Operations: Mr M Horn BEng Hons, PGDip, MA, CEng, FIMechE

Bedford School

De Parys Avenue, Bedford MK40 2TU

Tel: 01234 362216
email: admissions@bedfordschool.org.uk
website: www.bedfordschool.org.uk
X/Twitter: @bedfordschool
Facebook: @Bedford-School-100057414311854
Instagram: @bedfordschool_uk
LinkedIn: /school/bedfordschool

Bedford School is a leading boarding and day school for boys aged 13–18. The school, which was established in 1552, is situated in an extensive 50-acre estate in the heart of Bedford and is just 40 minutes from London by train.

'That they be good men'. Bedford School recognises that every single boy is different, and, indeed is proud to observe that there is no one 'Bedford boy'. Instead, with both inspiration and support, they seek to nurture each boy's individual interests and encourage him to develop them as far as he can take them. They aim for balanced, outward-looking, forward-thinking, kind and sociable young men who are comfortable in their own skins. When it is time to take the next step, each boy leaves as a good man, secure in his values, happy and ready to take his place in the world.

Number in School. 727 boys aged between 13–18 years: 220 flexi, weekly and full boarders, 507 day boys.

Boarders and Day Boys. There is a balanced mix of day boys, flexi, weekly and full boarders, who combine in lessons, games and all other school activities. There are six Senior Boarding Houses, each containing up to 51 boys.

Academic. Academic excellence is central to life at Bedford School. Consistent high exam results at GCSE, A Level and the IB set the standard for academic achievement throughout the school. The curriculum extends learning well beyond the national requirements and is structured to provide a balanced and varied choice of subjects, which will challenge each boy's strengths.

Boys are encouraged to achieve through a balance of different teaching techniques, small class sizes and (where appropriate) setting, well-resourced and subject-specific classrooms, specialist teachers, prep setting, regular lecture series and visiting speakers, lunchtime and after school academic clinics. Technology is used extensively to support and enhance learning.

University and careers. A strong careers and UCAS provision enables all boys, throughout their school years, to access tailored, professional experience and advice. In addition to an annual careers fair, regular information evenings, lectures and seminars are also held. The school is a member of the Independent Schools Careers Organisation and holds E2E Gold status and a gold Career Mark.

Almost all leavers go on to higher education. In 2023, 75% of boys took went on to Russell Group and/or Times Top 30 universities.

Co-curricular. The school offers a diverse programme of co-curricular activities every evening between 4.15 pm and 6.00 pm for boarders and day boys alike, many of which involve girls from Harpur Trust sister school, Bedford Girls' School. Activities include the Combined Cadet Force (CCF), Duke of Edinburgh's Award scheme, community partnership work, fundraising groups, and more than 60 other clubs and societies from Astronomy to Young Enterprise. Concerts, plays, lectures and film performances are given in the Great Hall, the Recital Hall, the Erskine May Hall and the Quarry Theatre.

Service. The school's Community Partnership Programme, launched in 2019, creates true partnerships that are valued and respected equally by the boys, the school and those that are supported. Every boy leaving the school in the Upper Sixth has the opportunity to contribute to his local community through a long-term and meaningful partnership. The boys' community partnership work sits alongside a wide range of charity work that pupils throughout the school already undertake, including ongoing support for the men's health charity: Movember, House charity fundraising events, Duke of Edinburgh and IB CAS.

Sport. The school aims to inspire a lifelong interest in sport for all, promoting teamwork, wellbeing, fitness and fun. A team of dedicated, passionate specialist teachers and coaches are on hand to provide high-quality guidance and help each boy to develop his skills. Many boys go on to excel at sport, and the majority of major sport first teams are of county standard or beyond.

The school's major sports are rugby, hockey, rowing and cricket but the range of sports on offer extends to athletics, badminton, basketball, cross country, fencing, fives, golf, sailing, soccer, squash, swimming, tennis, water polo and weight training/conditioning.

First-class facilities include a twin AstroTurf complex with floodlights, an indoor 25 m swimming pool, 28 tennis courts, four squash courts, a golf development centre with golf simulator, a climbing wall and acres of immaculate grass pitches.

Music. All boys have the opportunity to explore and perform, with a wide range of musical instruments and groups from which to choose. As well as the two Senior Symphony Orchestras, a Chamber Orchestra, a Concert Band and a large Choral Society, there is a Chapel Choir trained in the English Cathedral tradition, two Junior Orchestras, a Dance Band, Jazz Band, Rock Band, a large number of chamber music groups, and a Music Society. There is a full music programme throughout the year, with at least one concert a week.

The Music department is situated in a £3 million, state-of-the-art, purpose-built development, which includes a superb recital hall, music technology suite, multi-track recording studio and the school's radio station.

Drama. All boys can get involved in Bedford School's vibrant drama scene, whether on stage or behind the scenes. Each year a range of formal and informal dramatic productions are performed by all age groups.

The drama department is housed in the school's Quarry Theatre. The 286-seat theatre and 60-seat studio-theatre provide a superb venue for school productions and the extensive programme performed by visiting touring companies.

Art and Design. The art department works to develop each boy's individual artistic talents and encourages pupils to engage with and appreciate the world around them. Boys are encouraged to develop a lifelong appreciation of the creative arts with visits to museums and galleries, annual study tours abroad, weekly life drawing classes and a series of art lectures.

The Art School, located in a characterful mid-1750s Georgian building, has three specialist studios for painting, printmaking and sculpture. All three Art staff are practising artists.

Admissions. The majority of boys enter Bedford Prep School from the age of seven and the Upper School at 13 or 16 years of age. The Prep School has its own Headmaster and specialist staff. (*See Bedford Preparatory School entry in IAPS section.*)

Parents wishing to send their sons to Bedford School should apply to the Director of Admissions. All applicants are expected to provide evidence of good character and suitability from their previous school. Year 9 applicants from Preparatory Schools wishing to enter the Upper School are assessed in Year 6 or Year 7 by an initial Pre-test and interview. In Year 8 all applicants undertake a computer-based test (designed to measure raw academic potential) at the school, along with written English and Mathematics papers.

Boys looking to join the Sixth Form are invited for an assessment day in the January before entry. Applicants sit a Verbal Reasoning paper and have an interview with a senior member of staff. The school also takes up a reference with the boy's current school and considers his application along with his predicted grades at GCSE.

Additional information is available on the website: www.bedfordschool.org.uk/admissions.

Scholarships and bursaries. The school offers a range of generous scholarships and bursaries to boys who excel academically or show outstanding talent in art, drama, music or sport (including golf).

Awards are available for boys joining the school at 13+ and 16+ entry points. For more information, please visit www.bedfordschool.org.uk/scholarships.

Fees per term (2023–2024). Day Boys: £8,157; Full Boarders: £13,794; Weekly Boarders: £13,338; Flexi Boarders: £10,540 (two nights per week) to £11,540 (three nights per week).

Old Bedfordians Club. For further details, visit www.bedfordschool.org.uk/association/ob-club.

Charitable status. Bedford School is part of the Harpur Trust which is a Registered Charity, number 1066861.

Chairman of Governors: Sir Clive Loader, KCB, OBE, ADC, FRAeS

***Head Master*: Mr J S Hodgson**, BA

Vice Master: Mr S Baldock, MA, FRSB

Deputy Head (*Academic*): Mr L Rogers, BA, MBA

Assistant Head (*Teaching & Learning*): Mr W Montgomery, BSc

Assistant Head (*Pastoral*): Mr M Gracie, BSc, MEd

Director of Finance and Operations and Clerk to the Governors: Mr A Macfarlane, BSc, MSc

Director of Marketing and Communications: Mrs J Dickson, BSc

Director of Bedford School Association: Mr H Maltby, BA

Director of Admissions: Mr R Midgley, BA Ed

Berkhamsted Schools Group

Overton House, 131 High Street, Berkhamsted, Hertfordshire HP4 2DJ

Tel: 01442 358000 (General enquiries)
01442 358001 (Admissions)

email: enquiries@berkhamsted.com
admissions@berkhamsted.com
boys@berkhamsted.com
girls@berkhamsted.com
sixth@berkhamsted.com

website: www.berkhamsted.com
X/Twitter: @berkhamstedsch
Facebook: @berkhamstedschool
Instagram: @berkhamstedschools
LinkedIn: /Berkhamsted-School

Our family of six schools offers a 'Diamond model' with co-educational and single-sex tuition for boys and girls, providing the best of both worlds in one family of Schools. At the Pre-Prep and Prep, boys and girls are taught together until the age of 11, separately from 11–16 (Berkhamsted Boys and Berkhamsted Girls), enabling them to flourish academically, with numerous co-educational activities, trips and events, before coming back together again in a joint Sixth. Heatherton provides a co-educational nursery class (3–4) and single-sex education for girls from age 4 to 11. *Please also refer to separate entries for Berkhamsted Prep, Berkhamsted Pre-Prep and Heatherton.*

We are a family of Schools with a long history and proud traditions, yet we have a firm eye on current best educational practice and use of leading-edge teaching technologies. We are proud of our excellent academic standards without being academic hothouses. The Berkhamsted family of Schools have all the advantages of access to large-school resources with a small school sense of community and individual care. Our House system places academic progress and pastoral care at the centre of your child's education. There is a range of options to make life easier for time-pressured families: a day nursery that operates 50 weeks a year from 07.30 to 18.00, wrap-around care and extended hours, the choice of flexible, weekly or full boarding, coach routes and a multi-activity holiday camp and other courses on offer during the main school holidays through Camp Beaumont: Berkhamsted.

There are 443 pupils in the flourishing co-educational Sixth. Between the ages of 11 and 16, 544 boys at the Boys School (Castle) and 430 girls at the Girls School (Kings), are taught in single-sex groups.

The Principal is a member of both HMC and GSA.

Aims. At Berkhamsted we believe that excellent academic results do not have to be won at the expense of the wider attributes of a good education. All pupils are supported and encouraged to reach their full potential, with appropriate teaching environments for each age group and a structure that offers the best of both co-educational and single-sex tuition. In addition to the development of the intellect, social, sporting and cultural activities play an important part within the framework of a disciplined and creative community based on Christian values. It is important that pupils come to value both the individual and the Community through school life. The School seeks to encourage spiritual and moral values and a sense of responsibility as an essential part of the pursuit of excellence.

Location. The School stands in the heart of Berkhamsted, a historic and thriving town only 30 miles from London. It enjoys excellent communications to London, the airports, to the Midlands and the communities of Buckinghamshire, Bedfordshire and Hertfordshire.

Facilities. The original site has at its heart a magnificent Tudor Hall used as a schoolroom for over 300 years. Other buildings are from late Victorian to modern periods and of architectural interest (especially the Chapel modelled on the Church of St Maria dei Miracoli in Venice). With separate Pre-Prep and Prep sites, and two Senior School campuses, the School is well equipped with a range of facilities. There are new Science laboratories, Library and Learning Resources Centres, Information Technology suites, Sixth Form centres located on the two Senior School campuses, Careers libraries, Dining halls, Medical centre, House rooms, Deans' Hall (an Assembly Hall) and Centenary Theatre (a modern 500-seat theatre also used for concerts and theatre productions). Recreational and sports facilities include extensive playing fields, Eton Fives courts, Squash courts, Tennis courts, Gymnasium, Drama studio, Music school and Art studios. Additional facilities include a Sports Hall and 25m indoor swimming pool and a state-of-the-art Design Centre as well as the Nash-Harris Building at Kings comprising a new dining facility, classrooms and Chapel. More recent additions include a new sports pavilion and changing rooms at the School's Chesham Road Playing Fields and upgrades to the Football and Rugby pitches, as well as a high ropes course at the Haresfoot site and a brand new, floodlit 4G AstroTurf sports pitch at Kings.

Curriculum. The Senior School curriculum includes: English, English Literature, Mathematics, Biology, Chemistry, Physics, History, Geography, Religious Studies, French/Spanish, Latin/Classics, Mandarin, Music, Art, Physical Education and Design and Technology. Up to eleven subjects may be taken for GCSE. In the Sixth Form, courses are offered in 28 subjects and all students benefit from an Enrichment Programme with the option to complete an Extended Project Qualification. Pupils are prepared for university entrance, including Oxbridge. Careers guidance and personal tutoring are offered throughout.

Day and Boarding. Pupils may be full boarders, weekly boarders, flexible boarders or day pupils. The two Boarding houses, accommodating boys and girls separately, are well-equipped and within a few minutes' walk of the main campus. There are up to 60 boarding places. Day pupils come from both Berkhamsted and the surrounding areas of Hertfordshire, Buckinghamshire and Bedfordshire.

Pastoral Care and Discipline. The School Houses are the main social and pastoral unit; the Head of House and House Tutors. They provide continuity of support and advice and monitor each individual pupil's progress. The aim is to encourage self-discipline so that pupils work with a sense of responsibility and trust. Pupils are expected to be considerate, courteous, honest, and industrious.

Pupil wellbeing is of vital importance at Berkhamsted. The Deputy Heads, alongside the Pupil Wellbeing and Personal Development team, support teaching staff across the whole school in implementing a proactive strategy that focuses primarily on keeping pupils well and looking for early signs of potential issues. There is a Medical Centre with qualified staff. The School Medical Officer has special responsibility for boarders. Qualified Counsellors are available to all pupils for confidential counselling. The School also has a full-time Chaplain.

Sport and Leisure Activities. Major sports for Girls are Lacrosse, Netball and Tennis and for Boys, Rugby, Football and Cricket. A number of other sports are also pursued including Athletics, Badminton, Cross-Country, Equestrian, Eton Fives, Golf, Hockey, Judo, Rowing, Shooting, Squash and Swimming. Team games are encouraged and pupils are selected for regional and national squads.

There is a flourishing Duke of Edinburgh's Award at all levels. The CCF, community service, work experience and Young Enterprise are offered. The format of the school day allows pupils in the Senior School to choose from a wide range of clubs, societies or courses, which are attended during school hours. Regular school theatre productions, orchestral and choral concerts achieve high standards of performance.

Enrichment. At Berkhamsted, we recognise that intelligence takes many forms and we encourage all our pupils to pursue their talents and interests through the many enrichment opportunities on offer for each age group. These opportunities are available for academic subjects and co-curricular topics. For the more academically adventurous, there are a number of avenues through which to fulfil their potential at each school.

Careers. A team of advisors, internal and external, is directed by the Head of Careers who also arranges Careers Lunches, Applying to Higher Education training sessions, Medicine and Law Careers Taster Days and an annual Higher Education, Careers, Apprenticeships and GAP Year Fair. Heads of House oversee pupils' applications for higher education, together with parents and Careers advisors. The great majority of leavers proceeds to university and higher education.

Entry. Entry to the Pre-Prep School is from the age of 3, entry to the Prep School from 7, and entry to the Senior Boys & Girls from 11. Children are assessed for entry to the Nursery year group during a meeting with the Headteacher and attend an informal assessment day for Year 2 entry. The School's Entrance Assessments and an interview are required for entry to the Prep and Senior Boys and Girls.

Berkhamsted Prep pupils entering Berkhamsted Senior Schools will not be required to take any entrance exams from the 2025 Year 7 entry onwards: this affects pupils in Year 3 in September 2021, and following years. Additionally, Heatherton pupils entering Berkhamsted Girls will not be required to take entrance exams for the Senior School, this affects pupils in Year 3 and Year 4 in September 2022, and following years, making the journey through to Berkhamsted Girls as smooth and seamless as possible.

In order to gain admission to Berkhamsted Sixth, students require 43 points across their best 8 GCSE subjects with a minimum requirement of a Grade 6 in the subjects they wish to study. There are also specific admission requirements relating to certain courses, although competition amongst external candidates means that it is the norm that top grades are required.

Scholarships and Bursaries. It is the Governors' policy to award Scholarships and Exhibitions on merit to pupils whom the Governors wish to attract to Berkhamsted because of the contribution that they are able to make to School life, be that academic, musical, sporting, creative or as potential leaders.

Academic Scholarships are awarded on the basis of academic merit alone on entrance to the School.

Who can apply? Applications are welcome from pupils who qualify from their performance in the Entrance Examination and sit Scholarship Examinations in English, Mathematics and other appropriate subjects. These are usually only at 11+, 13+ and 16+.

Incent Awards are made to talented pupils from financially or socially disadvantaged backgrounds.

They are awarded to enable pupils who would not otherwise be able to attend Berkhamsted, to afford to do so.

Candidates must demonstrate academic potential or have a particular talent(s) or skill(s) so that they will make a significant contribution to some other area of School life.

The Award shall be up to 100% of the school fees, and, where appropriate, will also include financial assistance for School uniform and sports kit, travel to and from school, school trips and expeditions, extra lessons e.g. Music, Drama etc if applicable.

Whilst most applications for Incent Awards will be received from candidates who are presently in maintained sector schools, Berkhamsted does work with a number of feeder schools in the independent sector who offer awards on a similar basis and thus will entertain applications from pupils who are presently in receipt of means-tested awards of this nature.

Music, Drama, Art and Sports Scholarships are also offered.

Where there is a demonstrated need, additional means-tested funding may be available to those awarded Scholarships.

More information about Scholarships and Bursaries may be obtained from the Admissions Manager or on the School website.

Fees per term (2023–2024). Day Pupils (Reception–Sixth Form) £3,675–£8,425; Boarding Pupils £13,770 (full), £11,550 (weekly).

Further information about the School's aims, its academic curriculum, facilities, activities, admissions, scholarships and awards is published in the School's prospectus and is available on the School website. Admissions enquiries should be made in the first instance to the Admissions Manager, who will be pleased to arrange for parents to visit the School.

Old Berkhamstedians. There is a vibrant and growing community of Old Berkhamstedians: www.theoldberkhamstedians.org. President: Mrs Emma Jeffrey.

Charitable status. Berkhamsted Schools Group is a Registered Charity, number 310630.

Chair of the Governors: Mrs C Copland

***Principal*: Mr R P Backhouse**, MA Cantab

Vice Principal: Mr A Ford, BA
Chief Operating Officer: Mr J Anthony, BSc, FCA
Chief People Officer: Mrs T L Evans, CIPD, FInstLM
Headteacher, *Berkhamsted Sixth*: Mr M Walker, BA
Headteacher, *Berkhamsted Boys* (*Boys 11–16*): Mr T Hadcroft, MSc, MRes, MA
Headteacher, *Berkhamsted Girls* (*Girls 11–16*): Ms E Watson, BEng, MBA

Birkdale School

Oakholme Road, Sheffield S10 3DH

Tel: 0114 266 8408
0114 266 8409 (Admissions)
email: headmaster@birkdaleschool.org.uk
admissions@birkdaleschool.org.uk
enquiries@birkdaleschool.org.uk
website: www.birkdaleschool.org.uk
X/Twitter: @BirkdaleSchool
Facebook: @BirkdaleSchool

Motto: *Res non verba*

Birkdale School is an HMC day school for 750 pupils, co-educational at the Prep School and with a Sixth Form of around 200 pupils. The age 4–11 Prep School is on a separate campus nearby. (*For further details see IAPS section.*) Birkdale is in the process of becoming fully co-educational by admitting girls into Year 7 in 2024. The Governing Body is in membership of the Association of Governing Bodies of Independent Schools.

Set in a pleasant residential area near the University 1.5 miles from the city centre, and 5 miles from the Peak District National Park, the school has expanded in recent years to provide for Sheffield and South Yorkshire the only independent secondary school for boys, with a co-educational Sixth Form. Birkdale Prep School for 250 pupils is on a separate campus half a mile from the Senior School. School coaches bring pupils from Worksop, Chesterfield, North Derbyshire, Rotherham and Barnsley.

Birkdale is a Christian school, reflecting its foundation in the evangelical tradition. There is nothing exclusive about this: entrance is open to all, and there is no denominational emphasis. We seek to develop the full potential of each individual: body, mind and spirit. Within a framework of high academic standards, pastoral care is given a high priority, balanced by an emphasis on sport and outdoor pursuits, music and drama with a wide range of extracurricular activities available.

At 18, over 95% of pupils go on to university, with a good proportion each year gaining places at prestigious universities including Oxford and Cambridge.

Admission. The main ages of admission are at 4, 7, 11 and 16, although it is possible to admit pupils at other ages if a place is available. Entrance examinations for candidates at 11 are held annually towards the end of January. Entrance to the co-educational Sixth Form is subject to interview and a satisfactory performance in GCSE examinations. In the first instance, enquiries should be addressed to the Registrar.

Academic curriculum. Over 25 subjects are offered at A Level. A full range of academic subjects are offered to GCSE. All pupils study English Language and Literature, Mathematics, Double Award Science, at least one Modern Foreign Language (French, German, Spanish) and at least one of the Humanities subjects (Classical Studies, Geography, History, RE). Optional subjects include Art, Design & Technology, Latin, Drama and Music. The wider curriculum includes ICT, Religious Education, Health Education, Careers and Economic Awareness. Latin, German and Spanish are compulsory subjects in the Lower School (11–13) in addition to the usual range of National Curriculum subjects.

Games and outdoor pursuits. The major games are Rugby, Soccer, Cricket and Athletics, with Cross Country, Hockey, Netball, Tennis, Squash, Basketball, Volleyball, Swimming and Golf also available. The playing fields are a short bus ride away from the school. A 10-lane cricket net facility, constructed to full English Cricket Board standards was opened in 2012. The netting system is retractable and so the area can also be fully utilised for football and hockey outside of the cricket season. All members of the school play games weekly. Additional team practices take place on Saturdays or at other times, and there is a full fixture list in the major sports. The school uses two local international venues, Ponds Forge and the English Institute of Sport for netball, dance and athletics. Birkdale's Sports Hall is at the centre of the Senior School campus.

Outdoor Pursuits play an important part in the overall leadership training programme. All members of the school participate in regular training sessions leading in each age group to a major expedition. This programme culminates in the 4th Form camp held annually. Virtually all members of the Third Form undertake the Bronze Award of the Duke of Edinburgh's Award scheme, and an increasing number progress to Silver and Gold awards.

Music and the Arts. Music, Art and Drama flourish both within and outside the formal curriculum. A full annual programme of dramatic and musical productions is arranged. Over 120 pupils receive weekly instrumental music lessons at school, and a wide range of orchestras and choirs provide opportunities for pupils to experience group musical activities at an appropriate level.

Extracurricular activities. In addition to the activities above there is a broad range of clubs and societies which meet at lunchtime and outside the formal school day, providing opportunities for members of the school to explore and excel in activities such as Chess, Debating and Design as well as in the usual activities such as Sport, Drama, Outdoor Pursuits, Art and Music. Awards are often won in local and national competitions.

Careers. The school is a member of the Inspiring Futures careers guidance service and there is a well equipped Careers Centre on site. A biennial Careers Convention is held in the school and regular visits are made by services liaison officers and others to give advice and help to pupils under the guidance of the school's careers staff.

Fees per term (2023–2024). Sixth Form: £5,414; Senior School: £5,351 (Years 9–11), £5,265 (Years 7 and 8); Prep School: £4,397; Pre-Prep Department: £3,586. Including lunches, textbooks and stationery (with the exception of Sixth Form textbooks).

Scholarships and bursaries. Academic, Music and Sports Scholarships are normally available at 11 and 16. Bursaries are available to increase awards up to 100% of fees in cases of proven financial need. In addition we offer the Arkwright Scholarship at 16+.

Charitable status. Birkdale School is a Registered Charity, number 1018973, and a Company Limited by Guarantee, registered in England, number 2792166. It exists to develop the full potential of its members within a Christian community.

Chairman of Governors: P Houghton, FCA

Bursar and Clerk to the Governors: R Wade

***Head Master*: P Harris**, MSc

Deputy Head (*Pastoral*): P R King, BA

Deputy Head (*Academic*): R D Becks, BSc

Heads of Departments:
Art: A Armitage, BA, Dip Ed Management
Biology: Mrs B Holder, MA, BSc
Careers: C J Cook, BSc
Classics: Ms M Fforde, MA, BA
Design & Technology: P S Offer, BA
Drama: A G Low, BA
Economics & Business Studies: S B Stoddard, BA
English: Mrs S J Burt, BA
Geography: H Parker, BSc
History: M S Clarke, MA
ICT: G Morton, BSc
Mathematics: M E Roach, BSc
Modern Languages: Mrs K M Higham, BA, MEd
Music: A M Jordan, BMus
Outdoor Pursuits: S Watchman, BA
Physical Education: S C Depledge, BSc
Psychology: M D Downs
Science & Physics: Dr P C Jukes, PhD, MA
Religious Education: T J Pearson, BA
Chemistry: Dr P D Myatt, BSc, DPhil
SENCO: L E Marsh, BA
Counsellor: M Armour-Brown

Prep School:
Head of Prep School: C J Burch, BA, PGCE
Deputy Head (*Pastoral*): J M G McDermott, BEd
Deputy Head (*Academic*): S Lambert, BA Hons, PGCE
Senior Mistress: Mrs E J Arcari, BA

Birkenhead School

58 Beresford Road, Oxton, Birkenhead, Merseyside CH43 2JD

Tel: 0151 652 4014
email: enquire@birkenheadschool.co.uk
website: www.birkenheadschool.co.uk
X/Twitter: @BirkenheadSchl
Facebook: @birkenheadschool
Instagram: @birkenheadschool
LinkedIn: /school/birkenhead-school

Motto: *Beati mundo corde*

Birkenhead School is a leading co-educational independent school situated in Oxton, Wirral. The School offers outstanding educational opportunities for girls and boys from three months to eighteen years and attracts students from Wirral, Cheshire, Liverpool and North Wales.

The School was established in 1860 and at the heart of the School is a strong and welcoming student and parent community.

The *Good Schools Guide* comments 'Birkenhead is riding high. A bustling, traditional and community-driven school with happy, diligent pupils and a growing focus on extracurricular. Super campus and excellent rapport with teachers too. First rate and first choice not only for local families but increasingly those from further afield.'

School buildings are grouped around a spacious campus with a beautiful 'village green' at the centre. The different parts of the School have their own distinct areas and the School offers an educational journey from Nursery to Sixth Form and children move seamlessly from one year to the next.

Exam results position the School as one of the leading independent schools within the North-West. The aim is academic excellence for all through inspirational teaching that looks to embed a lifelong love of learning. By knowing each individual, the School aims to recognise and celebrate each student's unique skills and passions, adding value at every stage of the educational journey. Details of the curriculum at each key stage are available on the school website.

The education goes beyond the confines of the National Curriculum and students enjoy an extensive co-curricular programme of clubs and activities alongside programmes such as 'Enrich and Explore', 'Future Skills' and 'Beyond the Curriculum'.

Music plays an important role at the School, with students encouraged to learn a musical instrument from a young age. There is a wide range of musical bands to join including both Prep and Seniors Orchestras, Concert Band, Big Band and various ensembles. The School hosts an annual Festival of Arts that includes a wide range of concerts, exhibitions, lunchtime recitals and musical workshops which are open to both the School and wider community.

The School has a reputation for Choral music and offers a Chapel Choir that sings at weekday services and the weekly Sunday Evensong service in its on-site Chapel.

Sports offered at the School include rugby, hockey, netball and lacrosse during the winter terms and cricket, athletics, tennis and rounders during the summer. There are representative teams at all levels and the playing fields cover approximately 40 acres on three different sites. Facilities include a floodlit AstroTurf surface, strength and conditioning gym, cardio gym, squash court, fitness suites and a climbing wall. The School has its own Duke of Edinburgh's Award scheme.

There is a strong tradition of drama, now offered as a GCSE subject, with regular Prep and Senior productions, alongside annual House Drama and House Music competitions.

The School's 'Inspiring Talks Series' encompasses the Nicholls Lecture Series for Sixth Form students, the Boumphrey Lecture Programme for younger pupils in Prep and a 'No Limits' Series in Seniors. The School also regularly welcomes high-profile public figures and authors to the School for events that are open to members of the public.

The School works closely within its community and has links with a number of business organisations, the Chamber of Commerce and many local charities. The School offers a range of events for children across Wirral including author talks, science events for local Brownies and Cub groups and has launched its 'Be Inspired' programme for pupils in Years 5 and 6 with a focus on social mobility through education.

The legacy of an education at the School is about confidence, social awareness, and a breadth of skills and knowledge that will stay with students for a lifetime and set them apart from their peers. The majority of students continue their learning at Russell Group universities including Oxbridge and the School has a long tradition of producing Medical students. Upon leaving the School, The Old Birkonian Society offers young people membership of an established and extensive community and a range of alumni events provide valuable networking opportunities.

Fees per term (2023–2024). Seniors £4,520–£4,955; Prep £3,235–£3,695.

Admissions. Both the Headmaster and Head of Prep meet personally with prospective parents to discuss individual children's passions and abilities and admissions are managed by their respective PAs. Prospective families are welcomed and encouraged to visit the School for a personalised visit at any time during the year and early application is encouraged. The School hosts Open Events during the Michaelmas, Lent and Summer terms. Entrance into the Prep is through individual assessments and interviews. Entry into Seniors at age 11 is by progression from the Prep and, for external applicants, through Assessment and Taster Days hosted by the School in Years 5 and 6. Entry into the Sixth Form is based on GCSE grades and an interview.

Charitable status. Birkenhead School is a Registered Charity, number 1093419. The charitable status means the School not only accepts fee-paying pupils, but can offer places to able children from less advantaged backgrounds.

President: Sir Andreas Whittam Smith, CBE

Chair of Governors: Mr A J Cross, LLB Hons

Company Secretary and Clerk to the Governors: Mr M J Turner, MA Oxon, MInstLM (*Bursar*)

***Headmaster*: Mr P R Vicars**, MA

Deputy Head (*Pastoral*): Mrs K Pankhurst, BA
Deputy Head (*Academic*): Mr T Whitworth, BA
Head of Prep: Mr H R FitzHerbert, BA
Deputy Head of Prep: Mr R A Halpin, BSc

Bishop's Stortford College

School House, Maze Green Road, Bishop's Stortford, Hertfordshire CM23 2PQ

Tel: 01279 838575
email: admissions@bishopsstortfordcollege.org
website: www.bishopsstortfordcollege.org
X/Twitter: @BSCollege
Facebook: @bishopsstortfordcollege
Instagram: @thebishopsstortfordcollege
LinkedIn: /school/bishops-stortford-college

Motto: *Soli Deo Gloria*

Academic qualifications are a prime focus for us, yet we know that qualifications alone will not suffice for a life fully lived. Together, qualifications and qualities are what an education for today and tomorrow must deliver.

There are opportunities. So many opportunities. In the classroom, on the sports fields, in the clubs and societies. We offer every pupil the chance to unearth new talents and to develop valuable life skills.

Underpinning everything is a strong, community spirit that empowers each pupil to thrive and succeed. We have created a community of togetherness where none of us is as important as all of us.

Our strategic objectives and projects ensure we are creating the Bishop's Stortford College of tomorrow. These days standing still is moving backwards. Bishop's Stortford College is not standing still. It is as simple as that.

We are the modern face of independent education.

Prep School. The organisation of the Prep School (for pupils up to age 13+) is largely separate from that of the Senior School, but the curricula of the two schools are carefully integrated. Pupils share resources in sport, design and technology, and music.

(*For further details see entry in IAPS section.*)

Admission. The main ages of admission are 4, 7, 11, 13 and 16, but entry at intermediate stages is possible. Entry to our Senior School at 13+ is based on school reference, interview and entry test results. Sixth Form Entry interviews and examinations are held in the November before year of entry.

Scholarships. The following annual awards are available:

10+ (Year 6): Academic, Music
11+ (Year 7): Academic, Music, Art, Sport
13+ (Year 9): Academic, Music, Art, Sport
Sixth Form: Academic, Music, Art, Sport, Drama

Financial Assistance. Means tested financial assistance is available.

Fees per term (2023–2024). Senior School: Full Boarders £13,698; Overseas Boarders £14,238; Weekly Boarders £12,540; Day £8,162.

Prep School: Full Boarders £10,215; Overseas Boarders £10,430; Weekly Boarders £9,738; Day £6,141–£6,473; Pre-Prep £3,983. There are no compulsory extras.

Pre-Prep: £3,983.

Fees are inclusive except for individual music tuition.

Charitable status. The Incorporated Bishop's Stortford College Association is a Registered Charity, number 311057. Its aims and objectives are to provide high quality independent day and boarding education for boys and girls from age 4 to 18.

Governing Council:

G E Baker, BSc, MRICS (*Chairman*)
I M Pearman, MA, MRICS (*Vice Chairman*)
D Alexander
J Gammage
P J Hargrave, BSc, PhD, FREng
S R Lehec, BA
P Mullender, MA
I Silk
D F Thomson, BAcc, CA

Representative Governors Appointed by the Council:
A J W Conti, BEng, FCA (*Parent Representative*)
R C V Harrison, BCom, ACA (*United Reformed Church Representative*)
C P Solway, BSc, MRICS (*Baptist Union Representative*)
S Nurbhai, MB ChB, MRCP UK
P Dodd, BSc
G Barker, CBW, FBA, FSA, FRGS

***Head*: Kathy Crewe-Read**

Senior Deputy Head (Boarding): Graham Brooks
Deputy Head (Pastoral) & Senior Designated Safeguarding Lead: Jane Pawulska
Deputy Head (Academic): Peter O'Connor
Head of Sixth Form: Katie Banks
Assistant Head (Operations): Matt Drury
Assistant Head (Academic): Mark McGrath
Assistant Head (Co-curricular): Paul West
Assistant Head (Partnerships): Emma Bowater

Prep School:
Head of Prep School: William J Toleman
Senior Deputy Head: Graham Millard
Deputy Head (Operations): Adrian Hathaway
Deputy Head (Academic): Wendy Sharman
Deputy Head (Pastoral) and Designated Safeguarding Lead: Imogen Cowan
Head of Shell and Deputy Designated Safeguarding Lead: Kirsty Brooks
Assistant Head (Academic): Emmanuelle Carme
Assistant Head (Boarding): Ed Jones
Assistant Head (Communications and Operations): Julie Pickard

Pre-Prep:
Head of Pre-Prep: Jo Wallace
Charlotte Cuthbert
Francesca Mann
Kate Howes
Emily Hathaway
Rebecca Smith
Nicola Rossington
Katherine Prowse

College Chaplain: Ian Morris
Bursar: Paul Stanley
Head of Admissions: Vickie Warburton
Director of International Relations: Tony Evans
International Admissions Officer: Jaimie Kwan
Prep School Admissions Officer: Fiona Brett
Pre-Prep Admissions Officer: Sally McGuiness
Director of Marketing and Communications: Polly Bridgman

Bloxham School

A Woodard School

Bloxham, Banbury, Oxon OX15 4PE

Tel: 01295 724301
email: admissions@bloxhamschool.com
website: www.bloxhamschool.com
X/Twitter: @BloxhamSchool
Facebook: /bloxhamschool
Instagram: @bloxhamschool

Motto: *Justorum Semita Lux Splendens*

Bloxham School is an independent, co-educational boarding and day school for students aged 11 to 18. Situated in north Oxfordshire, Bloxham offers a rural setting whilst being easily accessible from London and the Home Counties.

A Bloxham education provides students with enriching educational experiences that help them to mature intellectually, physically, emotionally and spiritually. A balanced curriculum encourages the students to become leaders and creative thinkers, foster their passions, and be compassionate to others. Bloxham's outstanding teaching standards enable students to fulfil their academic potential, opening the doors of opportunity beyond the school gates and into their future careers.

An education from Bloxham School encapsulates the following five hallmarks:

- **A Passion for Learning:** fostering creativity and the capacity for dynamic, independent and critical thought. At the heart of Bloxham's teaching is the belief that all students should be inspired and encouraged to explore their learning further. Students learn to develop independent critical thought, reflect on their learning and use their intellect to problem solve.
- **A Balanced Curriculum:** academic rigour sits high on the agenda, but it is complemented by the broader curriculum to develop qualities like resilience, communication, teamwork and tenacity. Bloxham's broader curriculum ranges from mainstream sports to minor ones, and from music, drama and art, to astronomy and kayaking.
- **A Gold Standard of Pastoral Care:** a commitment to every child's wellbeing creates the strong foundations on which Bloxham's reputation for a gold standard of pastoral care has been built. We are proud to offer full, flexi and day boarding options.
- **The Development of Character:** through promotion of responsibility, generosity, resilience, and imagination. The broad and balanced curriculum, along with the experience of being part of a boarding community, creates opportunities for students to be of service to others, to lead by example, and to be part of a team. By working with others they learn to communicate, to listen, to be generous in their support and to develop empathy.
- **Christian Values:** nurturing a compassionate spirit so that students become a force for good in an ever-changing world. Bloxham aims to develop "spiritual intelligence" alongside intellectual and emotional intelligence, where students can think for themselves, question what they believe and formulate their core values, perhaps for the rest of their lives. Although the school has been built on a Christian ethos, those of faith, no faith and other faiths are welcomed and Bloxham openly encourages understanding, diversity and tolerance for all.

Admissions. Students join Bloxham at 11+, 13+ and 16+. 11+ entry is based on performance in the school's entrance exam, whilst 13+ entry is based on common entrance results (if appropriate). Students looking to join at 16+ should be predicted at least six 9–5 grades, including Maths and English. Students should have at least 6s in their option subjects, with 7s desirable for Maths and Sciences.

Bloxham welcomes international students and supplementary English lessons are available for an additional fee if required.

Full details can be obtained from the Admissions Department.

Fees per term (2023–2024). Senior School: Overseas Boarders £13,990; Full Boarders £13,390; Day Boarders £10,270; Day £6,990 (includes all meals except breakfast and supper for Day students).

Lower School: Weekly Boarders £8,990; Day Boarders £8,190; Day £6,990 (includes all meals except breakfast and supper for day pupils).

Scholarships and Bursaries. Students are invited to apply for Academic, Art, Drama, DT, Music and Sport Scholarships, which bring a fee remission of up to 10%.

Bursaries based on financial need are considered on an individual basis. They can be received in conjunction with a Scholarship or without.

The Development Office. The Development Office and the Old Bloxhamist Society work together to coordinate a rich programme of social and careers-orientated events for Bloxham alumni.

Charitable status. Bloxham School Limited is a Registered Charity, number 1076484. Its aim is to provide high quality academic education in a Christian environment.

Council of Governors:
Chairman: Lis Lewis-Jones

Lance Anelay	Andrew Nott
Paul Clayson	Steve Richards
Lizzie Coles-Kemp	Carol Shaw
Hermione Harper	Martin Ward
Colin MacIntosh	Simon Wood
Jonathan Meyrick	

***Headmaster*: Mr Paul Sanderson,** MSc, MEd

Deputy Head Curriculum: Mr Matthew Buckland, MEd, BSc
Deputy Head Pastoral: Mrs Louise Ladds, BA, MA
Deputy Head (*External Communications*): Mr Matt Bull, BSc
Assistant Head (*Student Welfare & Pastoral Care*): Mrs Jacqui Skevington, BEd
Assistant Head (*Staffing & Wellbeing*): Mrs Jane Cochran, BA
Bursar: Mr David Ramm

Heads of Departments:
Art: Mr Robert Matthew, BA, MDes, FRGS
Biology: Dr Karla Perera, BSc, PhD

Business Studies & Economics: Mrs Sara Clitheroe, BA
Chemistry: Dr Simon Floate, BSc, PhD
Computing: Mr Luke Harris, BSc
Design & Technology: Mr Mark Skevington, BEd
Drama: Mr Joe Hornsby, BA
English: Mrs Clare Summers, MA
Food Technology: Mr Peter Harvey, Cert PCE
Geography: Dr Clare Evans, MSc, PhD
History and Politics: Mr Robert Hudson, BA, MA
Latin: Mrs Victoria Moir, BA
Learning Support: Mrs Natalie Long, BSc
Mathematics: Sam Moulder, BSc
Modern Languages: Mrs Jenny Rose, BA
Music: Mr Alex Redpath, BMus RCM (*Director of Music*)
PE: Mr Ben Ford, BSc
Physics: Mr James Richardson, BSc
Psychology: Mrs Nichole Guzenda, BA
Sport: Mr James Walker, BA (*Director of Sport*)
Theology: Dr Debbie Herring, BTh, PhD

Head of Careers: Mrs Nichole Guzenda, BA
Head of Sixth Form: Mrs Emma Exelby, BA, MA

Houses and Housemasters/mistresses:

Boys' Houses:
Crake: Mr Robert Hudson
Egerton: Mr David Best
Seymour: Mr Matt Bull
Wilson: Mr David Bowden

Girls' Houses:
Raymond: Mrs Jude Single
Stonehill: Mrs Harriet Woodward
Wilberforce: Mrs Pippa Duncan-Jones

Day House:
Merton: Mrs Cheryl Linton

Lower School: Mrs Clare Bridge
Park Close: Mrs Sophie Heathcote

Headmaster's PA: Mrs Julie Morris
Admissions Registrar: Mrs Fay Hand
Medical Officer: Dr Stephen Haynes, MBBS, MRCGP, DFFP
Chaplain: Rev. Alex Ladds, MA

Blundell's School

Tiverton, Devon EX16 4DN
Tel: 01884 252543
email: info@blundells.org
website: www.blundells.org
X/Twitter: @BlundellsSchool
Facebook: @blundellsschool
Instagram: @blundellsschooldevon

Blundell's is a thriving co-educational day and boarding School combining strong academic achievement and excellent co-curricular activities in a secure and happy environment. The deep friendships that are formed at Blundell's fostered by the great community, together with the intellectual, physical and cultural interests, provide pupils with skills for life. The School was built and endowed in 1604 at the sole charge of the estate of Mr Peter Blundell, Clothier, of Tiverton, by his executor the Lord Chief Justice, Sir John Popham. In 1882 the School was moved to its present site on the outskirts of Tiverton.

Admission. Entry is at 11, 13 and 16 for most pupils. This is via the Blundell's Entrance Test or the Common Entrance Examination. Most join the School in September, though a January entry is welcome.

Numbers. There are 634 pupils of whom 279 are girls; 353 board (full, weekly, flexi). There are three boys' Houses and two girls' Houses for Years 9–12 and a separate Upper Sixth House. Years 7 and 8 have a separate House with separate pastoral and academic leadership.

Fees per term (2023–2024). Full Boarding £10,175–£14,530; Weekly Boarding £8,770–£12,410; Day £5,780–£8,865. Flexi boarding is also available.

Scholarships and Bursaries. Open Scholarships and Exhibitions: Up to half of the chosen designation fee (i.e. boarding, weekly, flexi, day) are offered on the basis of our own examinations held in January (13+) and November (Sixth Form). Awards for Art, Music, Drama, Sport and All-round ability are also made. At 11+ Junior Exhibitions only are awarded for academic and musical ability (January examination) and are deducted from the basic tuition fees.

Services Package available to the children of serving members of the Armed Forces and Diplomatic Corps.

Awards may occasionally be supplemented by means-tested bursaries at the discretion of the Head.

Full details of all scholarships and bursaries are available from the Registrars' Office.

School Work. There are four forms at age 11 and five at age 13. During the first three years most pupils will study Art, Biology, Chemistry, Design and Technology, Divinity, Drama, English, French, Geography, History, Information Technology, Mathematics, Music (Class), Personal and Social Development, Physical Education and Physics. Latin, Greek, German and Spanish are also available.

During the GCSE years the range of subjects remains broad. Extensive advice is provided by the School to assist both GCSE and A Level choices.

Sixth Form options enable a wide combination of subjects to be taken. Four of the following are taken to AS Level and three to A Level: Art, Biology, Business Studies, Chemistry, Classical Civilisations, Design Technology, Drama, Economics, English, Film Studies, French, Geography, German, History (Modern & Early Modern options), ICT, Latin, Mathematics and Further Mathematics, Music, Photography, Physical Education, Physics, Psychology, Religious Studies (Ethics) and Spanish.

Mark Orders, Tutorial System and Reports. Good communication is a central concept. Frequent Mark Orders and Staff Meetings are held to monitor each pupil's work. All pupils have academic tutors. Parents receive termly formal written feedback in addition to receiving Mark Order summaries every few weeks. There are regular parents' meetings and information forums.

Music and Drama. Blundell's music is excellent. Based in our own music school there are several choirs, an orchestra and varying musical ensembles. These range from a jazz band through a chamber choir to brass, woodwind and string groups. The Department has state-of-the-art recording equipment. In addition to School concerts there are visits from professional musicians. The Choir recently performed in Carnegie Hall in New York.

Similarly, Drama plays a key role in the School. There are three major School Plays each year, as well as House plays. The magnificent, purpose-built Ondaatje Hall offers the combined facilities of a theatre, a concert hall and an art studio. Frequent visits are made by theatre companies and Blundell's is a cultural venue for Mid-Devon.

Games and Physical Training. Boys play rugby in the Autumn Term whilst girls play hockey. Spring Term sports include cross-country, squash, rugby, fives, hockey, soccer, fencing, basketball, netball and rugby sevens. In the Summer Term cricket, tennis, swimming, athletics and golf take place. The Sports Hall gives further scope to the range of sport, as does the all-weather floodlit pitch; there is also a Fitness Suite. Elite sportsmen and women are supported with specialised fitness programmes. A variety of other sports, such as clay pigeon shooting, fly fishing, canoeing and miniature range shooting, are available through the extensive activity programme.

Computing and Technology. All pupils have access to the school IT network and will develop a range of skills during their time at school to support their studies.

Recent New Facilities. There have been extensive developments at Blundell's over the past two decades which include upgrading the Science Departments, provision of advanced technological and careers arrangements as part of the resources included in the redesigned Library, a new Modern Languages block, ongoing refurbishment of all boarding houses, a Fitness Suite, a Music School, IT suites and extension to Westlake (Y13 Boarding House) to incorporate new study areas and a library. With Blundell's Preparatory School on site, the whole campus provides education from the age of 3 to 18 years.

Community Service. The School is involved in a wide variety of activities, both local and national, and pupils regularly raise around £20,000 per annum for a variety of charities, as well as taking part in practical tasks locally.

Adventure Training. Blundell's is well placed to make full use of Dartmoor and Exmoor, the coast and rivers of the area, for academic fieldwork or adventure training. For many years the School has entered teams for the Ten Tors Expedition on Dartmoor, canoes the Devizes–Westminster race and takes part in The Duke of Edinburgh's Award scheme up to Gold level.

CCF. Everyone in Year 10 serves for a year in the CCF. Thereafter it is voluntary and comprises senior pupils who provide the NCO Instructors. There are links with the 18 Cadet Training Team, Derriford, and the Rifle Volunteers.

Boarding. Blundell's is built around the ethos of boarding and all pupils (full boarding, weekly, flexi boarding and day) are accommodated in one of seven houses on the campus. A full range of weekend activities is offered including a Leadership Programme, Ten Tors, sport and a range of local trips and activities.

Religion. The School maintains a Christian tradition, while welcoming members of other faiths. All pupils are expected to attend weekday morning Chapel and boarders go to the School Service on Sundays. The Chaplain prepares pupils who wish to be confirmed; the Confirmation Service takes place annually in the Spring Term.

Accessibility. Blundell's is close to the M5, and is served by Tiverton Parkway Station, under two hours from Paddington, London. Airports at Bristol and Exeter are close at hand.

Prospectus. Fuller details of School life are given in the prospectus, available from the Registrars. Prospective parents are invited to visit the School, when they will meet the Head and a Housemaster or Housemistress and have a full tour of the School with a current pupil. The Blundell's website (www.blundells.org) is regularly updated throughout the academic year.

Preparatory School. Blundell's Preparatory School for children aged 3 to 11 years is part of the site at Blundell's. For further information apply to the Headmaster, Mr A D Southgate. *(See also entry in IAPS section).*

Charitable status. Blundell's School is a Registered Charity, number 1081249. It exists to provide education for children.

Board of Governors:

Mr N P Hall	Rt Revd N McKinnel
Dr S B Ansell	Mrs D L Rees
Ms A Crosse	Dr A Smith
Mr N J Cryer	Mr R W Thane
Mr G L Howe	Mr I R G Thomas
Mr M Huntingford	Mrs J S Thomson
Mr M J Lovett	Dr M E Wood
Mrs J M A Mannix	

Mr R W Thane (*Representative Governor*)
Sir Christopher Ondaatje, OC, CBE (*Honorary Governor Emeritus*)

Bursar and Clerk to the Governors: Mrs Annika Hedrich-Wiggans

***Head*: Mr Bart Wielenga**

Second Master: Mr Matt Radley
Deputy Head (*Academic*): Mr Charles List
Deputy Head (*Co-curricular*): Mr Ed Saunders
Designated Safeguarding Lead: Mrs Nicky Klinkenberg

Heads of Department:
Art: Gil Armstrong Williams
Biology: Jonathan Ratcliffe
Careers Education & Advice: Pippa Bucknell
Chemistry: Andy Mead
Classics: Becky Milne
Design & Technology: Tom Frappart
Drama: Tammy Winsley
Economics & Business Studies: Tom Candler
English: Leah Thomas
Examinations: Katie List
French: Kate Wheatley
Geography: Guy Bucknall
German: Isobel Scott
History & Politics: Richard Moore
IT: Martin Dyer
Learning Support: Sara-Jane Soutar
Mathematics: Adam Simson

Modern Languages: Nick Lecharpentier
Music: Oliver Leaman
PHSE: Belinda Jones
Physical Education: Rebecca Manley
Physics: Douglas Morrison
Psychology: Emma Weaver
Religious Studies: Andrew Berrow
Science: Georgina Batting
Sport: Ed Saunders

Director of Development: Mr Ben Boswell
Director of Marketing: Mr Dylan Smart
Head's PA: Mrs Heather Vincent

Registrars:
Mr Peter Klinkenberg
Mrs Charlotte Botting

Preparatory School
***Headmaster*: Mr Andy Southgate**

Julie Aldridge (*Art & DT*)
Joshua Allen
Susie Allen (*Mathematics & Music*)
Lisa Baily (*Girls' Games*)
Bronte Barber
Jo Carter
Bronte Chalk
Sue Clark
Laura Clifford (*Head of Pre-Prep*)
Bethan Cracknell (*Music*)
Julian Fawkes
Edward Frances
Claire FitzHerbert (*French*)
Tim Genders (*English*)
Bethany Harris
Simon Howkins (*Deputy Head*, *PSHEE*)
Jessica Lampard (*Food Technology*)
Jane Lawrence (*Geography*)
Hannah Mahon (*Science*)
Laura McGowan
Lee Moore (*Academic Leader*, *RE*)
Charlotte Morris (*Drama*, *Outdoor Learning*)
Daniel Morris (*Assistant Head Curriculum*, *Mathematics*, *ICT*)
Joanne Read
Joanna Richardson
Jane Roberts
Jessica Roberts
Sarah Southgate
Alison Spencer
Alexandra Steel (*RE*)
Izzy Stribling
Simon Swain (*Boys' Games*)
Emma Thornton (*Geography & History*)
Clare Whitten

Miss Gloria Butt (*Administration*)
Miss Beverley Stone (*Headmaster's PA*)

Bolton School Boys' Division

Chorley New Road, Bolton BL1 4PA

Tel: 01204 840201
email: seniorboys@boltonschool.org
website: www.boltonschool.org/seniorboys
X/Twitter: @BoltonSch
Facebook: @BoltonSch
Instagram: @bolton_sch
LinkedIn: /school/boltonsch

Motto: *Mutare vel timere sperno*

Bolton School Boys' Division, founded ante 1516 as Bolton Grammar School for Boys, was rebuilt and endowed by Robert Lever in 1644. In 1913, the first Viscount Leverhulme gave a generous endowment to the Bolton Grammar School for Boys and the High School for Girls on condition that the two schools should be equal partners known as Bolton School (Boys' and Girls' Divisions).

Bolton School today – the TES' Independent School of the Year in 2019 – is a family of schools, where children enjoy an all-through education, joining our co-educational Nursery or Pre-School Class for 3 and 4 year olds or Infant School (ages 4–7) before moving up to our single-sex Junior and Senior Schools with Sixth Forms. We are strong believers that girls and boys from 7+ perform best in a single-sex environment, but one where there are co-educational activities – the best of both worlds.

Situated in imposing sandstone buildings on a thirty-two acre site, Bolton School Boys' Division, which comprises a Senior School and Sixth Form, educates over 950 day pupils. The Senior School is fed by our Junior Boys' School (200 boys aged 7–11 years), which is part of Bolton School's Primary Division.

Bolton School seeks to realise the potential of each pupil. We provide challenge, encourage initiative, promote teamwork and develop leadership capabilities. It is our aim that students leave the School as self-confident young people equipped with the knowledge, skills and attributes that will allow them to lead happy and fulfilled lives and to make a difference for good in the wider community.

We do this through offering a rich and stimulating educational experience which encompasses academic, extra-curricular and social activities. We provide a supportive and industrious learning environment for pupils selected on academic potential, irrespective of means and background.

Curriculum. The GCSE programme comprises a core curriculum of English Language, English Literature, Mathematics, Biology, Chemistry, Physics and Sport. In addition, pupils select a further 4 options chosen from Art and Design, Classical Civilisation, Electronics, French, Geography, German, Greek, History, Latin, Music, Physical Education, Product Design, RS, Russian, Science Enrichment and Spanish. Pupils must choose at least one foreign language and one Humanities subject. At A Level, approximately 30 different subjects are on offer. Boys generally begin by studying 4 subjects, with the majority reducing to 3 A Levels in Year 13. A small number of subjects offer the

AS level qualification. While many boys elect to take standard combinations of either Arts or Science subjects in the Sixth Form, a high degree of flexibility ensures that any desired combination of subjects can be offered. Our enrichment programme allows students to pursue other qualifications. Examples include the Extended Project Qualification, Artsmark, Science Crest Award and a Youth Leadership Award among others. All students participate in sports lessons and in community service work. In 2017 the School won the Queen's Award for Voluntary Service, the MBE for organisations.

Facilities and organisation. The Boys' and Girls' Divisions of Bolton School are housed in separate buildings on the same site and, although the organisation of the two Divisions provides single-sex schools, there are many opportunities for boys and girls to meet and to collaborate. This is particularly so in the Riley Sixth Form Centre, where boys and girls share a Common Room, café and learning areas equipped with the very latest technology. Single-sex teaching remains the norm in the Sixth Form, although in a very few subjects co-educational arrangements are in operation. The buildings of the Boys' Division include the Great Hall, two libraries, gymnasium, sports hall, swimming pool, laboratories, art rooms, sixth form common room, ICT learning centre, design technology centre, performing arts centre, MFL laboratory, classrooms and dining hall. The Junior School building has recently been extended and refurbished and contains eight form rooms and specialist rooms for ICT, art & design and science & technology together with a gymnasium, library and its own dining accommodation. Use of the new £1m all-weather sports surface, the sports hall, the adjacent 25-metre swimming pool and the arts centre is shared by all sections of the school.

Games and PE. The extensive playing fields which adjoin the School contain thirteen pitches. Principal games are football, rugby and cricket. Tennis, hockey, swimming, water polo, badminton, athletics, golf and orienteering are also all played at representative school level. All boys also undertake a gymnastics programme and play volleyball and basketball. The School is divided into four Houses for the purpose of internal competitions.

Art, Drama, Design, Music. In addition to timetabled sessions in each discipline, there are many opportunities for extracurricular activities in these pursuits. Facilities in the art department include a pottery room with kiln; within the very active musical life of the School there are choral groups, orchestras and ensembles catering for all ages and abilities. In addition arrangements can be made for individual lessons on all orchestral instruments, piano, organ and in singing. Drama is an important part of the work of the English department and boys are encouraged to develop their talents in the drama studio and arts centre. The annual major school play, musical or opera is produced in cooperation with the Girls' Division. Design and technology features strongly in the curriculum in both Junior and Senior Schools with considerable success each year in the A Level technology courses, many boys gaining industrial sponsorships as a result. In addition, a wide variety of extracurricular opportunities exists in both the design technology base and the computer rooms. All boys are encouraged to take part in the extensive lunchtime programme when over 120 clubs, societies and practices are offered to different groups. The School has Platinum Artsmark status.

Outdoor pursuits. Outdoor adventure learning plays an important role in developing our pupils' resilience, independence and leadership skills. All junior school and senior school pupils up to Year 12 in the senior school undertake an annual period of outdoor education within curriculum time. In addition, camps, trips, exchanges and expeditions ordinarily go to over 60 destinations over two years, many of them abroad. The School has its own 60-bed Adventure Learning Centre, Patterdale Hall in Cumbria, used by parties of boys for curriculum, weekend, holiday and fieldwork expeditions. Lunchtime and after-school clubs offer opportunities to take part in further outdoor learning, from archery and orienteering to climbing, canoeing and kayaking. In Year 8, boys have the opportunity to camp at Saundersfoot, and to undertake sail-training lessons on Tenacity of Bolton, the boat built by boys at the School. In Year 9, all pupils work towards the DofE Bronze Award and many go on to achieve Silver and Gold. There is a large and active Scout Group with its own modern headquarters on school premises.

Religion. The School is non-denominational; all boys have periods devoted to religious education. In assemblies the basic approach is Christian although a great variety of readings and methods of presentation are adopted.

Careers and Higher Education. In Lower School, the Careers Education Programme is primarily delivered through SPACE and pastoral periods. Boys are introduced to the Unifrog system in Year 7 (they use this through to Sixth Form) and start to explore skillsets and personality traits that may link into future careers. In Upper School, boys complete a Morrisby profile which serves to form part of their Careers interview when they are selecting A levels. Each boy is provided with personal data that can help provide a base to explore potential careers. In the Sixth Form, through Unifrog, boys learn about careers that link to their educational choices; they also complete an interview and CV-training day which includes a bespoke interview from a professional in their chosen field. Former pupils are invited to sign up for the *Find Your Path* mentoring scheme, where recent leavers benefit from support and guidance by Old Boy mentors. There are also biennial Careers Fairs and regular careers talks, often from inspirational former pupils.

Transport. The School provides an extensive coach service covering 20 routes which offers secure and easy access for pupils from a wide surrounding catchment area.

Admission. An entrance examination is held in January annually for boys over 7 and under 8 on 31 August of the year of admission. Fifty places are available at 7+ and a few additional places thereafter. Admission to the first year of the Senior School (140 places) is by entrance examination held annually in mid-January. Boys who are over 10 and under 12 on 31 August of the year of entry are eligible. Entry to the Sixth Form is available to boys who have taken GCSE examinations elsewhere on the basis of interview and agreed levels of performance in these public examinations. Boys are also admitted at other ages when vacancies occur; in these cases, admission is gained through satisfactory interview and test performances. There is a co-educational pre-preparatory section – Beech House Infants' School – which has recently moved to new purpose-built, state-of-the-art premises. Admission is from the age of 4 and enquiries should be made to infants@boltonschool.org. There is also a nursery providing facilities for children from 3 months to 4 years old.

Fees per term (2023–2024). Senior School and Sixth Form: £4,544; Infant and Junior Schools: £3,632. Fees include lunches.

Fee Assistance. Means-tested Foundation Grants are available and one in five Senior School pupils receives assistance with fees. Scholarships are also available and are offered regardless of parental income, to those pupils whose achievement in the Entrance Examination and the interviews places them at the top of the cohort.

Prospectus and Open Day. The School holds an annual Open Morning in mid-October for the benefit of prospective candidates and their parents. Individual tours can be arranged on working days throughout the year. Further information concerning all aspects of the School is contained in the digital prospectus, copies of which may be obtained from the Admissions Registrar. Enquiries concerning admission are welcome at any time of the School year.

Charitable status. Bolton School is a Registered Charity, number 1110703.

Chairman of Governors: Mr I Riley, MEng, MBA

***Head of Foundation*: P J Britton**, MBE, MEd

***Head of Boys' Division*: N L Ford**, BSc

Deputy Head (*Pastoral*): Mrs H M Brandon, MA
Deputy Head (*Admissions & Achievement*): Dr F H Mullins, BSc, PhD
Foundation Head of Educational Research and Innovation: Ms H Bradford-Keegan, BA Hons, MA
Assistant Head (*Student Well-being & Behaviour*): P Davidson, MA
Assistant Head (*Operations*): D L Stevens, BSc
Assistant Head (*Co-Curricular*): Miss H Tunstall, BSc, MSc
Assistant Head (*Achievement & Assessment*): Mrs C L Waller, BA
Assistant Head (*Acting*): P Newbold, BA
Head of Sixth Form: M H J Prentki, BA
Foundation Head of Compliance: J D Williams, BSc

Heads of Department:
Art and Design: Mrs M A Ryder, BA & Mrs L Turner, BA
Biology: Dr N Morgan, BSc, PhD
Business Studies and Economics: D W Kettle, BA
Chemistry: Dr R Kell, MChem, DPhil (*Acting*)
Classics: D V B Lamb, MA
English: Ms J Z Sigrist, BA
French: A C Robson, BA
Geography: P Newbold, BA
German: Miss K Roddy, MA
History: Miss S V Burgess, MA
ICT: P J Humphrey, BSc
Mathematics: D N Palmer, BSc
Music (*Curriculum*): Miss H Sherry, BMus
Physical Education:
P Fernside, BA (*Head of Games*)
M Johnson, BSc (*Head of PE*)
Physics: M R Ormerod, BSc
Religious Studies: Miss A Ali, BA & Miss J Choudhury, BA
Russian: N R W Wyatt, MA
Spanish: Mrs J L Cotton, BA, MA
Technology: C J Walker, BA

Instrumental Music Staff:
Brass, Cello, Clarinet, Guitar, Oboe, Organ, Percussion, Piano, Saxophone, Singing, Viola, Violin

Junior School (*Age 7–11*):
Head: Mrs S Faulkner, BA, MAEd (*Acting*)
Deputy Head: Mrs Winstanley, BCom

Head of Boys' Division's Personal Assistant: Mrs J Higham
Admissions Registrar: Miss A Fenton

Bootham School

Bootham, York YO30 7BU
Tel: 01904 623261 (School)
01904 623261 (Headmaster)
email: office@boothamschool.com
website: www.boothamschool.com
X/Twitter: @BoothamSchool
Facebook: @BoothamSchool
Instagram: @boothamschool
LinkedIn: /school/bootham-school

Bootham offers Full, Weekly and Flexi Boarding and Day Education to students from ages 11–18, together with day education from the age of 3 at Bootham Junior School. There are now over 500 pupils in the Senior School and 150 day pupils in the Junior School (*see entry in IAPS section*).

The School was founded in 1823 by Quakers, but pupils of all denominations or none are welcomed. All pupils attend Meetings for Worship and arrangements are made for pupils to be prepared for confirmation or membership of their own churches.

Curriculum. In Schoolrooms (Years 7–9) all pupils pursue a course of study which includes English, Mathematics, Physics, Chemistry, Biology, Geography, History, Latin or Classics, French, German or Spanish, Philosophy and Religious Education, Design Technology, Computer Science, Physical Education, Music, Art, Drama and Personal, Social and Health Education (PSHE).

In Seniors (Years 10 and 11) pupils follow a curriculum leading to 10 subjects at GCSE.

College (Years 12 and 13) is preparatory to university entrance. The majority of pupils remain at school until the age of 18 and each year there is a strong Oxbridge entry. A wide choice of subjects is offered. It is usual to study 3 or 4 examination subjects and to study subjects of wider interest.

Students are able to choose from a wide variety of subjects. These are: Mathematics, Further Mathematics, Computer Science, Physics, Chemistry, Psychology, Biology, English, French, German, Spanish, History, Classics, Latin, Geography, Economics, Business Studies, Music, Art, Design Technology, Religious

Studies, Drama and Theatre Studies, Politics, and Physical Education.

Site and Buildings. The School is situated close to York Minster. From the road it appears as an impressive line of Georgian houses but behind this is the spacious main school campus. There is a steady programme of development, and the buildings now include fully refurbished College facilities (2021/22), 8 well-equipped Laboratories, an impressive Arts Centre (open 2014) with Auditorium and Darkroom (photography), 2 ICT Suites, 2 DT workshops, an Astronomical Observatory, an up-to-date Physical Education Department with Sports Hall, Indoor Swimming Pool, Fitness Suite and Squash Court, and a modern Assembly Hall, which received a national RIBA award. The buildings are complemented by formal gardens and playing fields, overlooked by York Minster. Further playing fields are situated nearby, in Clifton, which also houses Bootham Junior School in a new purpose-built complex.

Pastoral Care. As a Quaker School, Bootham places great emphasis on caring relationships within a friendly community. There are three boarding houses, under the special care of House staff. Each House has its own recreational facilities. Throughout the School, both boarding and day pupils are supervised and guided by form tutors. In College, pupils have Personal Tutors who are responsible for both academic and pastoral matters, and guidance towards Higher Education or other alternatives.

Admission. Pupils usually enter Bootham in Lower Schoolroom (Year 7/Age 11). Entry is also usually possible in Middle & Upper Schoolrooms (Years 8 & 9) and Lower Seniors (Year 10/Age. The main entrance assessment is held annually in January and this forms the basis of Scholarship and Bursary selection. Sixth form entry is welcomed and selection is on the bases of school report and GCSE performance. In special circumstances late entrants can be considered.

Leisure Time Activities. The School has long been recognised as a pioneer in the provision of enrichment activities. The Natural History Society, founded in 1832, is the oldest society of its kind in this country. Other clubs and societies include Social Action, Debate, Drama, Drone Flying, Chess, Cookery and Orchestra. There are over 100 activities offered each week. Pupils follow the Duke of Edinburgh's Award scheme and are involved in Community Services.

Music. The Director of Music is supported by peripatetic teachers. Tuition is arranged in a wide variety of instruments and a strong tradition of music in the School is maintained. Recent leavers have secured places at the Royal College of Music and there is a strong tradition of students gaining places and scholarships at music colleges.

Games. Football, Hockey, Tennis, Fencing, Cricket, Swimming, Athletics, Netball, Basketball, Badminton, Squash, Rounders. There is no cadet force.

Fees per term (2023–2024). Full Boarding: £7,300–£11,540. Day: £6,225–£6,810.

Fees for instrumental music lessons are extra. Enquiries for up-to-date information are welcome.

Scholarships and Bursaries. *Academic* Scholarships (honorary and without fee reduction) are awarded on an annual basis at the end of each academic year and are based on performance throughout the year. Academic Scholarships are subject to annual reviews.

Means-tested Bursaries (supported by the Bootham Trust) are available:

- to assist Friend (Quaker) children, or the children of Friend (Quaker) parents, to attend the School;
- to assist children, whose families would not be able to afford an independent school education, to attend the School.

For full details please see separate Scholarships and Bursaries section.

Bootham Old Scholars' Association. There is an annual Reunion in York during the second weekend in May, as well as a Sports Reunion in March. The Bootham Old Scholars' Association has branches in all parts of the country and Eire.

Charitable status. Bootham School is a Registered Charity, number 513645.

***Head*: Deneal Smith**

Deputy Head: Martyn Beer, BA, PGCE, NPQH

Head of Junior School: Helen Todd, BA, MA Ed, QTS

Assistant Heads:
Madeline Bowley
William Lewis, MA
James Ratcliffe, BSc

Bursar: Gavin Blackstone, CPFA, BA

Admissions Registrar: Fiona Ward, MA, PGCE

Bradford Grammar School

Keighley Road, Bradford, West Yorkshire BD9 4JP

Tel: 01274 542492
email: admissions@bradfordgrammar.com
website: www.bradfordgrammar.com
X/Twitter: @BradfordGrammar
Facebook: @bradfordgrammarschool
Instagram: @bradfordgrammarschool
LinkedIn: /bradfordgrammar

Motto: *Hoc Age*

With a heritage dating back to 1548, Bradford Grammar School (BGS) is one of the oldest and most respected institutions in Yorkshire. Our illustrious past spans hundreds of years. In 1662, Charles II granted BGS's Charter, a document that the school proudly displays. Having occupied three locations since our establishment, the iconic building that BGS inhabits today was opened in 1949. A long history of excellence inspires BGS pupils to fulfil their potential and make their own mark upon the future of BGS.

With a 'first-class, academic and outward-looking approach' (*Good Schools Guide*), BGS is one of the UK's leading independent schools, providing an outstanding education for 1,054 girls and boys aged six to 18 (from age 4 in September 2024). The school is fully co-educational: girls have been admitted to the Sixth Form since 1984 and in all intakes from 1999.

BGS provides every opportunity for its Junior, Senior and Sixth Form pupils to embrace academic, sporting and creative excellence within an aspirational, caring environment in which happiness is the key to an individual's success. With its impressive 'value added' provision, academic excellence is available to all.

Pupil numbers. 1,054 day pupils (571 boys, 483 girls). Junior School (6–11): 151 pupils (79 boys, 72 girls). Senior School (11–18): 903 pupils (492 boys, 411 girls).

Location and facilities. The school, comprising six main buildings and a separate junior school building, stands in extensive grounds situated just a mile from Bradford city centre. The School thrives upon the opportunities created by this dynamic hub of enterprise and innovation.

The majority of our pupils travel by bus or train from areas such as Ilkley, Skipton, Leeds, Halifax and Huddersfield. We provide dedicated buses from a number of locations, including Oakwood, Headingley, Adel, Oxenhope, Huddersfield, Batley, Luddendenfoot, Halifax, Brighouse and Ilkley. Frizinghall train station is within a five-minute walk of the school and we provide a daily patrol team who ensure that pupils walk between the station and the school safely and sensibly. There are direct rail connections from Frizinghall train station to Leeds, Airedale and Wharfedale, Skipton, Ilkley and Apperley Bridge.

Nestling on the edge of the Yorkshire Dales, and within striking distance of the Lake District, opportunities abound for outdoor visits and residential trips.

Facilities include a dedicated Sixth Form centre with full Wi-Fi, the Hockney Theatre, Design Technology workshops, Computer Aided Design (CAD) suites, fitness suite with rowing machines, cycling machines, treadmills and weights, a music auditorium, recording studio, debating chamber, dedicated Science building, a state-of-the-art library, a 25 m competition swimming pool, sports pavilion, and squash courts, and our new outstanding £4m sport facilities – comprising cricket lanes, netball and tennis courts and astro-turfed hockey pitches, as well as our all-weather sports barn. The Price Hall is the centrepiece of the main school building and provides a magnificent setting for assemblies, concerts and other major events.

Bradford Grammar Junior School occupies Clock House, a seventeenth century Manor House within the wooded and tranquil school grounds, where it enjoys its own assembly hall, Computing and Design Technology facilities and teaching accommodation. *For further details, please see separate entry in IAPS section.*

Senior School curriculum.

In *Years Seven and Eight* all pupils study English, Mathematics, French, German, Latin, Biology, Physics, Chemistry, Geography, History, Art, Music, Design and Technology (DT), Religious Studies (RS), Personal Development, Drama, Computing and PE/Games.

In *Year Nine* pupils follow a common core of English, Mathematics, Geography, History, Physics, Chemistry, Biology, RS, Personal Development and PE/Games, choose one core Modern Foreign Language from a choice of French, German or Spanish and choose three optional subjects from a choice of German, Spanish, Latin, Greek, Art, Music, DT and Computer Science.

In *Years Ten and Eleven* pupils follow ten GCSE courses. All pupils follow a common core of English Language, English Literature, Mathematics, Biology, Chemistry, Physics, and PE/Games, choose a core Modern Foreign Language from French, German or Spanish, and choose three optional subjects from Geography, History, French, German, Spanish, Computer Science, Drama, Physical Education, Latin, Greek, Art, Music, DT and RS.

Year 12 (Lower Sixth Form). Pupils choose *either* three subjects and complete the EPQ *or* choose four subjects from Art, Biology, Business Studies, Chemistry, Classical Civilisation, Computer Science, Drama & Theatre, DT, Economics, English Literature, English Language, Extended Project Qualification (EPQ), French, Further Mathematics, Geography, German, Greek, History, Latin, Mathematics, Music, Music Technology, Physical Education, Physics, Politics, Psychology, RS and Spanish. The AS Level exam is available in some subjects. In addition, they also take one or two Enrichment courses from a wide range of certificated or non-examined options.

Year 13 (Upper Sixth Form). Pupils usually take three of their Year 12 courses through to A Level. Some pupils take a fourth A Level or complete the EPQ.

For further details please see the booklets *A Guide to GCSE Courses* and *A Guide to Sixth Form Courses*, both of which can be downloaded from our website at www.bradfordgrammar.com.

Results.

A Level: Terrifically successful at A and AS Levels, BGS has been recognised as having one of the highest average university admission points per student of any school in West Yorkshire. In 2023, 152 A Level students celebrated outstanding success with 55% of all exams awarded A*/A grades, overall, 94% of students at BGS secured A–C grades.

GCSEs: At GCSE, our results far exceed the national average. In 2023, 52% were awarded 9/8 and 97% grades 9–4.

Co-curricular activities. We actively encourage pupils to engage in co-curricular activities. Pupils in the Senior School normally have a choice of over 50 clubs and societies covering a wide range of sports, drama, music, academic subjects and other areas of interest – from rowing, orienteering, war games, debating, Biomedical and Classics Societies to Micro:bit, Games, volunteering, fundraising and Handmade Clubs, there is something for everyone. Pupils can take part in The Duke of Edinburgh's Award scheme, the Combined Cadet Force (both RAF and Army) and World Challenge expeditions. There are many exciting and enriching school trips and tours, domestic and overseas.

Pastoral care. Outstanding pastoral support contributes to the happiness of Bradford Grammar School pupils, creating a positive, friendly atmosphere for all. The School works closely with parents to ensure each child receives the best possible pastoral care during their time at BGS. The team of form tutors, Heads of Year, school nurses, school counsellor, Learning Support Department and pastoral prefects work together to promote pupils' happiness and progress and ensure that every child receives the attention they deserve. Pupils who need extra support are quickly identified by our pastoral team and given the help they need as they make their way up the school. The BGS Personal Development (PSHE) programme includes modules on wellbeing and mental health as well as RSHE for every year group.

The School encourages pupils to participate in physical exercise and a wide range of co-curricular opportunities, so that they are further developed beyond the classroom too.

Admission. Boys and girls can join the school at the ages of 6, 7, 8, 9, 10 in the Junior School (this will include ages 4 and 5 from September 2024) or 11, 12, 13 or 16 in the Senior School. Pupils are admitted into the Sixth Form on the basis of their GCSE results (at least 20 points, grade B, preferably A, in sixth form subjects), an interview and a satisfactory reference from the candidate's current school. Candidates for entry into Year 2 (6+), Year 3 (7+) and Year 4 (8+) will be invited to spend an informal day in the Junior School. Admission for all other ages is by examination in Mathematics and English in January each year.

Assisted places. Places are awarded on a means-tested basis, each case being reviewed annually. The award depends on parental circumstances, the amount of capital available at the time of the examination and the academic ability of the candidate.

Scholarships. Needs-blind academic scholarships up to 25% of the fee are available for Year 7 entry.

Fees per term (2023–2024). Junior School: £3,665 (Year 2) and £3,863 (Years 3–6), Senior School: £4,937, Sixth Form: £4,937.

Former pupils include trail-blazing artist David Hockney, Chancellor of the Exchequer Denis Healey, Olympic champions Alistair and Jonny Brownlee and Team GB Performance Analyst Dr Deborah Sides.

Old Bradfordians Association. President: Mr I Holland, c/o Bradford Grammar School.

The Parents' Association (previously BGS Society). Chairperson: Mrs J Pine, c/o Bradford Grammar School.

Charitable status. Bradford Grammar School (The Free Grammar School of King Charles II at Bradford) is a Registered Charity, number 529113. It exists to provide education for children.

Governors:

Chairman of Governors: Lady Morrison, LLB
Vice-Chairman: Professor C Mellors, OBE, BA, MA, PhD, FAcSS, FHEA, FRSA
Life President: A H Jerome, MBE, MA [OB]

Ex-officio:
The Very Reverend Andy Bowerman

Co-optative:
C Beck, FCCA
P Cogan, BA, FCA
D J Davies, MBE, BEng, MA
S R Davies, BA, FRSA
J E Disley, BA
C Hamilton Stewart, MBE
His Honour J A Lewis
Professor Sir A F Markham, BSc, PhD, MB, BS, DSc, FRCP, FRCPath
I McAleese, FCIPD
District Judge A Pema [OB]
T Pugh, BA
Dr A Qasim, BA, MB, BChir, MA, PhD, FRCP [OB]
C M Wontner-Smith, BA, FCA [OB]
Sir D Wootton, MA [OB]

Representing the University of Bradford:
vacant

Representing the University of Leeds:
Dr A Mighell, BSc, BChD, MBChB, PhD, FDSRCS, FHEA

Representing Chamber of Commerce:
S Needham, OBE, DL

Governors Emeriti:
J E Barker, MA [OB]
P J M Bell, JP, FCIS, CText, FTI, FRSA [OB]
R G Bowers, DL, BSc, CEng, FRSA [OB]
I Crawford, FCA
J D Fenton, MCSP, SRP
Professor A Francis, BSc, ACGI, CCMI, AcSS
J G Ridings, FCA

[OB]: Old Bradfordian

Bursar and Clerk to the Governors: H Najib

***Headmaster*: Dr S Hinchliffe**, BA, MEd, PhD, FRSA

Deputy Headmaster: J Boardman

Assistant Head, Pastoral: M J Chapman, MA
Assistant Head, Curriculum: G P Woods, MA
Assistant Head, Development: P Merckx, BSc

Headmaster, Junior School: R Ribeiro

Brentwood School

Middleton Hall Lane, Brentwood, Essex CM15 8EE

Tel: 01277 243243
email: headmaster@brentwood.essex.sch.uk
website: www.brentwoodschool.co.uk
X/Twitter: @Brentwood_Sch
Facebook: @BrentwoodSchoolUK
Instagram: @brentwood_sch
LinkedIn: /school/brentwood-school-uk

Motto: *Virtue, Learning and Manners*

Brentwood School was founded in 1557 and received its charter as the Grammar School of Antony Browne, Serjeant at Law, on 5th July, 1558. The Founder became Chief Justice of Common Pleas shortly before the death of Queen Mary, and was knighted a few months before his death in 1567. The Foundation Stone over the door of Old Big School was laid on 10th April, 1568, by Edmund Huddleston and his wife Dorothy, who was the step-daughter of the Founder. The Elizabethan silver seal of the School Corporation is still in the possession of the Governors. In 1622 Statutes were drawn up for the School by Sir Antony Browne, kinsman of the Founder, George Monteigne, Bishop of London, and John Donne, Dean of St Paul's.

Brentwood School is a co-educational school with a total of 1,925 pupils including 572 in the Preparatory School. The Preparatory School is fully co-educational as is the Sixth Form (of 399 pupils), but boys and girls are taught separately between the ages of 11 and 16. Boarding is available for boys and girls from age 13.

Buildings and Grounds. The School occupies a 75-acre site on high ground at the northern end of the town some 20 miles north-east of London. Old Big School, the original School room, is still in regular use, thus maintaining a direct link with the School's founder. Over recent years, a major building programme has seen extensions to the Philosophy and Mathematics buildings, Dining Halls, Library and Reception. In November 2011, HRH Prince Edward The Earl of Wessex formally opened the School's new Sixth Form Centre and Wessex Auditorium. The Sixth Form Centre, which has become the intellectual powerhouse of the School, provides an exemplary educational environment for the International Baccalaureate Diploma programme. Facilities include common rooms and private study areas, 16 additional classrooms, a dedicated computer suite and multi-purpose 400-seat auditorium. The award-winning Bean Academic Centre was opened to pupils at the end of March 2016. With large classroom spaces, a lecture theatre and café, it provides a state-of-the-art environment within which pupils can develop independent learning. A multi-million pound development, revealing an Aladdin's cave of the latest educational facilities and resources, was completed at the Preparatory School and formally opened in November 2021. Facilities include a new reception area; a new Foundation Year facility with outside play space; a Futures Room and eight specialist classrooms; a new Hall and performance space, which can seat an audience of over 500 and provides space for assembly, PE and clubs; and a new dining facility and kitchen.

Organisation. The School is one community within which, for good educational reasons, girls and boys are taught separately from age 11 to 16. They are encouraged to participate together in all co-curricular activities. The Senior School is divided into Year Groups. Each Year Group has a Head of Year and Deputy who oversees it. The vast majority of pupils join the School at 11 after successfully completing the Entrance Examination. A broad curriculum is followed through the first three years and this continues through careful choice of GCSE and IGCSE subjects to the end of the Fifth Year. Entry to the Sixth Form is conditional upon success in the GCSE examinations. There is a wide choice of subjects, whether students want to follow the International Baccalaureate Diploma Programme (IBDP), BTEC Extended Diploma (Sport and Business) or A Levels. Most go on to University and many pupils gain places at Oxford and Cambridge each year.

Religion. Although Brentwood is a Christian School, pupils and staff from all faiths, or none, are welcome. There is a resident Chaplain and pupils attend the Chapel weekly. Regular Communion Services are held.

Boarding. There are two Boarding Houses. The boys reside in Hough House which currently accommodates 39 students; the girls reside in Mill Hill House where 26 are accommodated. The public rooms are spacious and both Houses are generously staffed. Full and weekly boarding are available. A qualified Matron runs an efficient Sanatorium.

Pastoral Care. Brentwood School has an outstanding level of pastoral care which is provided by Heads of Year, Tutors and our Pastoral Team, ably supported by the Senior Deputy Head (Pastoral), Mrs Jenkin, and by all colleagues. Together they support the wellbeing of all pupils, enabling each pupil to thrive in a kind, caring and inclusive community. Their encouragement to their pupils to participate in a wide range of activities successfully engenders greater self-confidence and self-awareness. In addition to Mrs Jenkin, Heads of Year and Tutors, there are three pastoral managers in the Senior School and a Director of Pastoral Care and Safeguarding, Miss Bishop.

Performing Arts. We are proud to be a Steinway School, enabling our pupils to learn on the very best-made pianos in the world, as well as some rare instruments otherwise unavailable to them. Brentwood is also a partnership school with the Guildhall School of Music and Drama, one of the finest musical institutions in the world. Music plays an important part in the life of the School, as do Drama and Dance. There are four orchestras and several ensembles and jazz groups. The Big Band is internationally acclaimed. There are at least three dramatic productions each year, together with regular Dance shows.

Careers. There is an excellent University Entrance and Careers Department where students receive advice and can obtain information about courses and/or careers. Aptitude Tests; Work Experience; visits to colleges, universities and places of work; and visiting speakers are all part of the provision. A careers convention is held each year.

CCF, VSA & DofE. All pupils either join the Combined Cadet Force or, through the Voluntary Service Activity, engage in a wide-ranging series of activities, which bring them into contact with the Community. The Duke of Edinburgh's Award scheme runs alongside these activities.

School Societies. There are many flourishing societies covering a wide range of interests, catering for all ages. The ACES programme in the Prep School encompasses the areas of Arts, Community, Enrichment and Sports, and the Sir Antony Browne Society (SABS) is a society for Sixth Form students, which provides them with an opportunity for intellectual discussion and cultural interest.

Sports Facilities. Brentwood School was one of the official training venues for the London 2012 Games. The playing fields are part of the School complex and provide ample space for football, cricket, hockey, rugby and tennis. There is a world-class all-weather athletics track. The Brentwood School Sports Centre includes an indoor football/hockey pitch, six badminton courts, indoor cricket nets, basketball courts and a fencing salle, as well as squash courts and a fitness suite. There is an Olympic-sized heated indoor swimming pool and an all-weather pitch. Provision is made for golf, horse riding, skiing and table tennis. The two AstroTurfs and netball courts are floodlit for use in winter.

Preparatory School. *See* entry in IAPS section for details.

Entry. Entrance Examinations for both boys and girls aged 11 are held at the School in December each year. Entries are also accepted at 13 plus, following the ISEB Common Pre-Tests, vacancies permitting. Transfers at other ages are also possible. Sixth Form entry is through GCSE success, a consultation interview and a Headteacher's confidential reference.

Scholarships and Bursaries. In addition to Academic scholarships, the School offers Chess, Dance,

Drama, Music and Sport scholarships at 11+. These may be supplemented by means-tested Bursaries. Art, Dance, Drama, Music and Sport scholarships are offered for Sixth Form. There are also academic scholarships available for entry into the Sixth Form.

The School offers a considerable number of Bursaries in addition to the awards described above.

Fees per term (2023–2024). Day: £7,824; Boarding: £15,332.

Old Brentwoods Society. There is a flourishing Society for pupils to stay in touch once they have left School; email: oldbrentwoods@brentwood.essex.sch.uk.

Charitable status. Brentwood School (part of Sir Antony Browne's School Trust, Brentwood) is a Registered Charity, number 1153605. It is a Charitable Trust for the purpose of educating children.

Governors:
Sir Michael Snyder, DSc Hon, FGS, FCA, FRSA [OB] (*Chairman*)
Lord Black of Brentwood, MA, Hon FCIPR, FRSA [OB] (*Vice Chairman*)
Mr P C Beresford, FNAEA, MARLA
Mrs J Bryan, LLB, CTA
Mrs S Dalgarno, MA, PGCE, JP
Mr D J Elms, MA, FCA, FCSI
Professor B J W Evans, BSc Hons, PhD [OB]
Dr M Fenton, MA, MSc, MA, PhD, DipEdLaw, FRSA [OB]
Mr J Fergus, FCIMSPA
Mr J Griffith-Jones, MA, ACA, TD
Mr M Hampson, BEng Hons, FBCS
Mrs A Hardy QC, LLB Hons, LLM, AKC
Mrs J M Jones, BA Hons, ARCM, NPQH
The Venerable D Lowman, BD Hons, AKC
Mr P Machray, BA Hons, ACA, BFP
Mr R I McLintock, MSc, DMS, Dip Ed
Mr S Norris, BSc Hons [OB]
Professor C A Tout, MA, PhD [OB]
Cllr J R Tumbridge, CC, MCIArb, LLB Hons
[OB] *Old Brentwood*

Senior Leadership Team (*Central*):

***Headmaster*: Mr M Bond**, BA

Senior Deputy Head (*Pastoral*): Mrs N Jenkin, BA, MA
Deputy Head (*Academic*): Mr J Barfield Moore, MA
Deputy Head (*Staffing, Co-Curricular & Operations*): Mrs A Goodfellow, BA, MA, MA
Bursar and Clerk to the Governors: Mr J Blunden, CBE, LVO, BSc Hons
Finance Director & Deputy Bursar: Mrs Sarah Carswell, BA Hons, ACA
Prep Headmaster: Mr Jason Whiskerd, BA Hons
Director of Development: Mr S Mason, BA Hons

Heads of Department:
Art: Mr C Lonsdale, MA, BA
Biology: Mrs P Ebden, BSc, MSc
Business Studies: Mrs K Giles, BA (*Head of Equestrian*)
Chemistry: Dr N Law, MA, PhD
Classics: Mr S Hitchings, BA, MA
Computing & ICT: Mr G Kiff, BSc
Co-Curricular Activities: Mrs J McLeod, BSc
Dance: Mrs M Carabache, BA, MA, AMTLA
Design & Technology: Miss L Hall, BA, MA
Drama: Mrs S Hermosa, BA
EAL: Mr B Clements, BA, MPhil, DipRSA
Economics: Mrs C Micallef, B Com, BAcc, MSc
English: Miss A Cooper, BA, MA
Food & Nutrition: Miss M O'Rourke, BA
Geography: Miss J Collins, BA
History & Politics: Mr D Rogers, BA
Learning Support: Mrs R Harvey, BA
Mathematics: Miss E Warnes, BSc, MEd
Modern Languages: Mrs M Morris, BA, MA Maîtrise (*Head of Languages and German*)
Music: Mr F Cooper, BA [OB] (*Director of Performing Arts and Director of Music*)
Outdoor Education: Dr A Moxon, BSc, MA
Physics: Mr C Beadling, BSc
Psychology: Miss J Atkinson, BSc, MSc
Theology & Philosophy: Miss S Boyle, BA
Sports & Games: Mr N Gamester, BSc (*Director of Sport*)

Head of Admissions: Mrs D Cook
Headmaster's PA: Mrs J Beazley

Brighton College

Eastern Road, Brighton BN2 0AL

Tel:	01273 704200
	01273 704339 Head Master
	01273 704260 Bursar
	01273 704210 Prep School
	01273 704259 Pre-Prep School
email:	admissions@brightoncollege.net
website:	www.brightoncollege.org.uk
X/Twitter:	@BrightonCollege
Facebook:	@BrightonCollegeUK

Motto: ΤΟ Δ'ΕΥ ΝΙΚΑΤΩ – *Let right prevail*

Thoroughly progressive, academic, inclusive and, above all, focused on the importance of kindness, Brighton College has become a powerhouse in independent education. Founded in 1845 in the heart of Brighton's Kemptown area, its historic quad and listed buildings speak of a rich educational heritage. Its dynamic head teacher Richard Cairns, however, is far more interested in the future and has become known nationally for his ground-breaking approach, both educationally and pastorally.

Mr Cairns has overseen an ambitious capital project during his tenure which includes the new 20-classroom Yeoh Building, including a Creative Learning Centre, and the School of Science and Sport, including 18 university-standard laboratories, 25-metre swimming pool and double height sports hall.

The College regularly achieves the best GCSE and A Level results in Sussex and some of the highest in the country. In the most recent exam results, the school's Sixth Formers achieved 97% A*–B in their A Level, while the most common grade at GCSE was the top grade of 9, with 94% of exam grades being 9–7/A*–A. The top destination for Brighton College pupils is Oxford and Cambridge, with 290 attending Oxbridge from 2013–2023.

The school has been the recipient of many awards: named 'United Kingdom Independent School of the

Decade' in 2020 and 'United Kingdom Independent School of the Year' in 2019 and 2013 by *The Sunday Times*, Mr Cairns was named 'UK Head of the Year 2023' by *Tatler* magazine. *The Week* called Brighton College 'Top School in Britain for STEM' in 2023 and the 'Most Forward-thinking School in Britain' for two years running in 2018 and 2019.

There is a wealth of extracurricular activities on offer, in particular sport, music and the performing arts. There are now 1,250 pupils, of whom a third are boarders. In its most recent inspection in 2021, the Independent Schools Inspectorate gave Brighton College and its Prep School a perfect score in every category, including 'Excellent' (the highest possible rating) in the quality of pupils' achievements, and the quality of pupils' personal development.

Buildings. An extensive programme of development has taken place which has seen many of the new builds win architectural awards. In 2020, The School of Science and Sport opened, containing 18 university-standard labs, plus a 25-metre pool and rooftop running track; in 2015, the Music School opened, home to state-of-the-art recording facilities and a 150-seat recital hall. In September 2017, the tenth new building in ten years opened, the Hopkins-designed Yeoh Building, with its innovative top-floor double-height Creative Learning Centre.

Admission. Pupils are admitted to the Lower Third at the age of 11 via assessments held at the College in January; to the Fourth Form between the ages of 13 and 14 via the Common Entrance examination, the Academic Scholarship examination or by special assessment and interview; and into the Sixth Form for A Levels between the ages of 16 and 17. In all cases pupils must also produce evidence of good character and conduct from their previous school. The College prospectus and registration form can be obtained from the Director of Admissions.

Houses. An extensive refurbishment programme is nearing completion across the day and boarding houses. A third of the pupils are boarders in the school and weekly boarding is increasingly popular, giving pupils the opportunity to go home on Friday afternoon and return either on Sunday evening or Monday morning.

Health. There is a Central Health Centre with a team of qualified nurses, and the Medical Officer visits regularly.

Catering. There is self-service dining room, managed by a qualified Catering Manager.

Holidays. School holidays are around three weeks each at Christmas and Easter, and eight weeks in the Summer. There is a half-term holiday of one week in all three terms.

Religion. A short morning service is held in Chapel on two days a week, with one service aimed to embrace all faiths.

Curriculum. The School is divided into seven forms: Lower Third, Upper Third, Fourth, Lower Fifth, Upper Fifth, Lower Sixth and Upper Sixth. In the Sixth Form, 28 subjects are available at A Level. For GCSE, pupils select their subjects – usually 10 – at the end of the Fourth Form. 99% of pupils proceed to university. Preparation for the UCAS process begins in the second term of the Lower Sixth, and pupils are guided towards appropriate choices by the Head of Sixth Form in conjunction with the individual pupil's tutor.

Sport. The College enjoys a strong record of excellence at sports. The main playing field (the Home Ground) is part of the College campus and the large Jubilee Ground is a mile away at East Brighton Park. All pupils take part in the College's extensive games programme. The main sports for boys are rugby, football and cricket and for girls, netball, hockey and cricket. In addition, a host of other options are available including basketball, squash, tennis, golf, beach volleyball, athletics and cross country.

Service. All pupils from the Lower Fifth onwards are expected to participate in a service activity on one afternoon a week. Pupils may participate in charity work or, in the Sixth Form, Community Service; alternatively they may join The Duke of Edinburgh's Award scheme or enter one of the three sections of the CCF.

Music. There is a strong musical tradition and pupils reach a very high level of performance. The award-winning Chamber Choir, Chamber Orchestra, Symphony Orchestra, Concert Band and Swing Band perform regularly both inside and outside the College. There are several Chamber groups, and the Choral Society and Orchestra usually perform major works at the annual Brighton Festival.

Drama. The College has a strong tradition of excellence in drama, and there are opportunities for anyone to be involved. In addition to the regular calendar of a musical, Sixth Form studio production, Sixth Form play, Fourth Form play, Lower School play and House Drama festival, there are also many productions mounted entirely by pupils.

Activities. Creative activities are encouraged both in and out of school time, and the College has its own Art School and Gallery. Dance is a very popular activity, with many boys and girls performing in regional and national productions.

Careers. The Head of Careers with a team of tutors advise pupils on careers. The College is a member of the Independent Schools Careers Organisation.

Scholarships. The following Scholarships are available:

11+ Entry: Academic, All-Rounder (Art, Dance, Drama, Music and Sport), Chess and Choral.

13+ Entry: Academic, All-Rounder, Art & Photography, Chess, Choral, Dance, Drama, DT, Music and Sport.

Sixth Form Entry: Academic, Sport and Expressive Arts (Art, Dance, Drama, Music) and Opening Doors.

For further details about scholarships, please contact the Admissions Office.

Fees per term (2023–2024). Boarding (Fourth Form to Upper 6th): Weekly £14,000–£14,420; UK Full Boarding £16,590–£17,520; International Full Boarding £20,540–£21,640. Day (Lower Third to Upper 6th): £7,310–£10,080.

Old Brightonians, the College's alumni network, has annual dinners and a number of flourishing sports clubs.

Preparatory School. The College has its own co-educational Nursery, Pre-Prep & Prep School. (*For details see entry in IAPS section.*)

Charitable status. Brighton College is a Registered Charity, number 307061.

Chair of Governors: The Lord Mogg, KCMG

Senior Management Team:

***Head Master*: Mr R J Cairns**, MA, FRSA

Group Chief Operating Officer: Mr P Westbrook, BA, FCA
Second Master: Mr S Marshall-Taylor, BA
Executive Head of Prep Schools: Mr J Weeks, BA

Deputy Heads:
Mr C Fowler, BA
Mr N J Fraser, MA
Miss L Hamblett, MA
Mr A T Patton, MA
Mrs J A Riley, MA

Bursar: Ms E Dobson, MA, CIMA
Assistant Head (*Sixth Form*): Ms O Upchurch, MEd
Assistant Head (*Middle School*): Ms P Alisse, MA
Assistant Head (*Co-Curriculum*): Mr J Cornish, MSci
Assistant Head (*Outreach and Partnerships*): Miss D Parkes, MEd
Assistant Head (*Director of Boarding*): Mrs J Hamblett-Jahn, LLB
Assistant Head (*Director of Studies*): Mr G Brocklesby, BA
Assistant Head (*London Academy of Excellence*): Mr J Carr-Hill, MSc

Director of Admissions/Registrar: Mr A Merrett, BSc
Chaplain: Canon D Stone, MA, BM, BCh

Bristol Grammar School

University Road, Bristol BS8 1SR

Tel: 0117 973 6006
email: headmaster@bgs.bristol.sch.uk
website: www.bristolgrammarschool.co.uk
X/Twitter: @bgsbristol
Facebook: @bgsbristol

Motto: Ex Spinis Uvas

'The Grammar School in Bristowe' existed under a lay master in 1532 in which year, under a charter of Henry VIII, it was endowed with the estates of St Bartholomew's Hospital by the merchant and geographer Robert Thorne and others. The trust was placed in the care of the Corporation of Bristol and then the Trustees of the Bristol Municipal Charities. In September 2004 the School incorporated as a company limited by guarantee with registered charitable status and is now governed under Memorandum and Articles of Association approved by the Charity Commission in 2004.

Co-educational since 1980, Bristol Grammar School is a day school providing a wide-ranging and challenging education for c. 1,000 boys and girls aged between 11–18, while BGS Infants and Juniors, based on the same site, caters for those in the 4–11 age range.

Pupils learn in an atmosphere that motivates them to enjoy their education and as a result BGS has a deserved reputation as one of the leading academic schools in the South West. The School has a friendly and lively environment and pupils are encouraged to make the most of the wide-ranging opportunities available to them. When pupils join the School at 11+, they are based in the same building in their House form groups, which helps ease their transition to Senior School, as well as providing an important opportunity for the year-group to bond socially. In Years 8–11, each House group has its own base, although teaching is spread throughout the School's specialist facilities.

Close to the city centre and adjacent to Bristol University, Bristol Grammar School is well placed to take advantage of the city's many amenities. It is also committed to a continuing programme of investment to ensure its own facilities continue to offer the best possible opportunities to its pupils.

The Houses. The School is divided into six Houses, each organised by a Head of House with the assistance of a Deputy Head of House and House Form Tutors. Form Tutors will typically remain with pupils throughout their time in the Senior School from Years 7–11. Older pupils become leaders within their House, while social, theatrical, musical, sporting and other opportunities allow those from all year-groups to work together in a friendly and cooperative atmosphere. As well as providing continuity of pastoral care and enhancing school/home links, the Houses operate as families within the School community, encouraging a real sense of belonging among pupils.

Curriculum. The School takes note of the National Curriculum but – in keeping with its academic ethos and focus on every learner being enabled to make the most of their individual ability – a far wider range of subjects and opportunities is offered. Setting is used in Maths, the Sciences and some Modern and Classical languages to ensure optimal individual progress, but there is no streaming. In Year 7 all pupils follow a curriculum which includes English, Mathematics, Science, French, Spanish, History, Geography, Design & Technology, Food & Nutrition, ICT, Latin, PRE (Philosophy, Religion and Ethics), Art, Music, Drama, Dance, and Physical Education. In Year 8 the core curriculum is continued but pupils are offered a further choice of languages to include German and Russian. In Year 9 pupils personalise their curriculum, making choices from all subjects studied thus far and other areas such as Classical Civilisation, Greek, Business Studies and Computer Science, and pupils then choose their GCSE options from this broad base. Most pupils take ten GCSEs at the end of Year 11 in the core subjects of English, Mathematics, Biology, Chemistry, Physics, a humanities subject and a modern language, together with a selection of other subjects, chosen from a carefully balanced range of options.

BGS currently offers IGCSEs in Mathematics; the Sciences; Geography; History; French; German; Spanish; Business Studies; Food & Nutrition; and Philosophy, Religion & Ethics (PRE). The Sixth Form provides the opportunity to study either A levels or the International Baccalaureate (IB) Diploma Programme. There are a wide range of subjects on offer in the Sixth Form: English Language (A level only), English Literature, Mathematics and Further Mathematics, Biology, Chemistry, Physics, Design & Technology (A level only), French, German, Russian, Spanish, Latin, Greek, Classical Civilisation (A level only), History, Politics (A level only), Geography, Economics, Business Studies (A level only), Computer Science,

Psychology, Philosophy, Drama & Theatre Studies, Dance, Physical Education, Art, Music, and Music Technology (A level only). In addition, many pupils take an elective course; their options include the Extended Project Qualification, a Sports Leadership award, Creative Writing, Further Mathematics, and Mathematical Studies. Many also choose to complete their Gold Duke of Edinburgh's Award. All Sixth-form pupils follow enrichment courses and attend a richly diverse programme of weekly lectures by visiting speakers. Many also attend enrichment lessons to support university preparation for Russell Group and Oxbridge Universities, including for Medicine, Veterinary Science and Law. Our experienced Higher Education and Careers Advisors guide pupils to proceed on a pathway that is best suited to their ambitions, whether that be an apprenticeship, the world of work or attending one of the wide range of universities in the UK and abroad, with the majority securing places at their first-choice universities.

There are frequent opportunities for parents to consult Form Tutors and Heads of Houses and regular meetings are held for parents to meet the teaching staff. The School also has three teachers to support pupils with SEN (including dyslexia and EAL).

Games. The Games options – which vary for different age-groups – include rugby, hockey, netball, football, cross-country, cricket, athletics, tennis, and weight training. Facilities for orienteering, aerobics, climbing, dance, judo, fencing, badminton and squash are also available. There is a Pavilion and extensive playing fields at Failand, which includes an all-weather 3G pitch, two AstroTurf hockey pitches and netball and tennis areas. Below the Sixth Form, all pupils participate in School games sessions; the full range of sports is available to Sixth-form pupils. Major sports tours are run on a three-year cycle: recent destinations have included New Zealand, South America, South Africa, and Sri Lanka and Malaysia.

Activities and Societies. Pupils take part in a wide-ranging programme of activities (this forms part of the compulsory curriculum for some year-groups), and there are many clubs and societies at lunchtimes and after school, including Astronomy Club, Model United Nations (MUN), Beekeeping, and Architecture Club. There are flourishing choirs and orchestras; individual tuition can also be arranged on a large number of instruments. Drama and Dance productions are regularly staged by different age levels and by the Houses. Pupils may join the Duke of Edinburgh's Award scheme in Year 10 and there is an active Community Service unit.

Admission. Entry to the School is normally in September at age 11+ following a satisfactory performance in the entrance examination held in the previous spring and a creditable school report or reference. All Year 7 applicants are also invited to meet with a member of staff to discuss their school work, interests and hobbies. A small number of places become available each year at age 13+, with a further thirty–forty places at 16+. Pupils may also be accepted into the School during the year at other points, subject to the availability of places.

Applications should be made to the Admissions Office at the School. Prospective entrants and their families are always welcome to visit; please see the website for information about open days, tours and taster days.

Bursary Awards. The School's Bursary Award scheme is able to offer substantial financial assistance towards the fees of able pupils whose parents have limited means. The scheme is kept under regular review by the Governors who constantly seek to extend it.

Scholarships. Scholarships are available for entry at 11+ and 16+ and are awarded for academic ability; all applicants who take the entrance assessments in January are automatically considered for these, there is no separate assessment. Scholarships are also available at 11+ for Sport and Creative & Performing Arts.

From September 2023 onwards pupils awarded a BGS scholarship will receive an annual grant to support development in the field of their award, and join our Scholars Programme. The scholarships will no longer carry an automatic fee reduction, but all pupils (including those awarded scholarships) are eligible for fee assistance through the Bursary Award scheme.

Our Scholars Programme is designed to meet the educational needs of its most gifted pupils. This programme offers extended individual learning opportunities, group activities and mentoring in and out of School by the Heads of Scholars. At 16+ pupils may apply to become specific Subject Scholars and work more closely with Heads of Subject.

Fees per term (2023–2024). Senior School £5,975. Juniors: Years 3–6 £3,951. Infants: Years 1 & 2 £3,671, Reception £3,362. Fees include the cost of most textbooks and stationery and lunch for Reception to Year 11 pupils.

BGS Infants and Juniors. The Junior School extended its provision to include Infants, with its first Reception class in September 2010. The School admits children from 4–11 and is housed in its own buildings on the same site as the Senior School. (*For further details see entry in IAPS section.*)

Old Bristolians Society. Close contact is maintained with former pupils through the Old Bristolians Society whose Honorary Secretary can be contacted at the School.

Charitable status. Bristol Grammar School is a Registered Charity, number 1104425. It has existed since 1532 to provide an education for Bristol children.

Governors:
M Alkerstone
Dr M Boulton
I Chesham
Ms M Crayton
Miss H Drake
Dr M Gainsborough
S Harvey
P Huckle
Mrs S Hutchison
Mrs E Leggate
J May
A Moore
Mrs L Parr
N Pickersgill,
Ms K Redshaw
D Shelton
Mrs M Simmons-Bird
J Sisman

Ms S Speake
Dr D Thompson
R Vaitilingam
M Wilson

Senior Leadership Team:

***Headmaster*: J M Barot**, MA, MSc

Head of BGS Infants and Juniors: Miss H Hughes, BSc, MEd
Deputy Head: P R Roberts, BSc, MSc
Deputy Head: Ms R L Davies, BA, MSc
Deputy Head: M L Pattie, MA MLitt
Deputy Head: Miss F A Ripley, BSc
Deputy Head: D J Stone, BSc
Bursar: G Mitchell, BA

Assistant Head: G S Clark, BSc
Assistant Head: J S Harford, BSc
Assistant Head: O L Chambers, BSc
Assistant Head: A N Gunawardana, BA
Assistant Head: B Schober, BSc, MA
Assistant Head: T Yates, BA

Bromley High School
GDST

Blackbrook Lane, Bickley, Bromley, Kent BR1 2TW
Tel: 020 8781 7000
email: bhs@bro.gdst.net
website: www.bromleyhigh.gdst.net
X/Twitter: @bromleyhs
Facebook: @bromleyhighschoolGDST
Instagram: @bromleyhighschoolgdst
LinkedIn: /school/bromley-high-school-gdst

Bromley High School is a selective school offering an exceptional education to girls aged 4–18 years. Set in leafy parkland and benefitting from first rate facilities, both Junior and Senior Schools provide a beautiful and buzzy environment where bright girls flourish.

The school is part of the GDST (Girls' Day School Trust), the leading network of independent girls' schools in the UK. Founded in 1883, Bromley High School was originally situated in the centre of Bromley. In 1981 it moved to Bickley to occupy modern purpose-built buildings set in 24 acres of leafy parkland.

In the classroom, each girl's intellectual potential is challenged and developed by inspirational teachers whose concern for your daughter ranges infinitely beyond her performance in examinations; teachers who have a capacity to develop a love of learning, a spirit of enquiry and an independence of mind. Girls learn to collaborate and to compete; to be creative and intellectually curious and their learning is underpinned by the school's ethos of achievement for all and by the subject passion, enthusiasm and expertise of their teachers.

Results are consistently superb. In 2022, 80% of new GCSE Grades were 8–9. Achievement at A Level was 43% A*, 80% A*/A and 92% A*–B. The school is most proud of its consistently impressive Value Added results at GCSE and A Level which demonstrate the care taken to bring out the best in every girl. In the 2016 ISI Inspection Report, Learning and Achievement were graded as Exceptional.

However, outstanding success at Bromley High School is not purely academic. Bromley High girls are resilient and well-rounded young women participating with enthusiasm and commitment in Music, Drama, Sport, Duke of Edinburgh's Award and an overabundant range of activities – and where they have interest or talent or enthusiasm, it is nurtured so that they learn to excel. Sport is exceptional with recent leavers gaining sports scholarships to Princeton and Yale.

Pastoral care is thoughtful and developmental, actively encouraging girls to develop key attributes: Confidence, Courage, Composure, and Commitment. Every house takes on the responsibility of supporting its own charity and the school has a highly valued tradition of volunteering and charitable activity.

Bromley High School pupils are confident, cheerful, considerate and enthusiastic about the myriad of opportunities their school has to offer.

Pupil Numbers. Senior School (ages 11–18): 571 (including the Sixth Form). Junior School (ages 4–11): 303.

The Junior School. Our two-form entry Junior School provides a stimulating and happy environment in which our pupils are encouraged to strive for excellence in all they do and to derive satisfaction from their achievements both great and small. From the earliest years we offer a broad curriculum which encourages, challenges and excites the young mind. Our aim is to foster a love of learning, develop independent thinking and promote a spirit of enquiry that leads to a depth of understanding. In our approach to teaching and learning we blend the traditional with progressive insights into learning styles and the particular needs of young girls as learners in a modern world. We teach the full range of the National Curriculum, including French, Spanish, German and also Latin and accord sports and the creative arts a significant place in the timetable, whilst ensuring that the foundations of the core subjects are well established. Class lessons are differentiated and we offer extension and support where appropriate and specialist teaching, sometimes from Senior School staff, in a number of subjects.

Bromley High believes in preparing girls for the challenges beyond school and values the importance of a holistic approach. The school provides many varied opportunities within a vibrant co-curricular programme including sporting, musical, dramatic and other creative activities. We make the most of our beautiful school grounds to provide opportunities for outdoor learning, in which our Forest School is a vital part.

Forest School is a planned programme that takes place in a woodland environment with the aim of developing opportunities for the learner to encounter the beauty, joy, awe and wonder of the natural environment. The approach is 'hands on' and seeks to promote the holistic development of the unique child, including physical, spatial, linguistic, emotional and spiritual aspects. Self-confidence and independence are increased through freedom, time and space to learn. A safe and secure environment allows the girls to extend their learning beyond their comfort zone; to challenge their existing boundaries and ideas and to tackle investigations and tasks which in the classroom may not be possible. Collaboration and cooperation between the learners, their peers and the forest school leader is at the core of the Forest School programme. Social skills develop through risk-taking and an understanding of the consequences of your own actions, whilst self-awareness, self-regulation and empathy for others are also developed. Forest School enables children to be active participants in their own education and development.

In the delivery of our curriculum we are well served by outstanding facilities which, in addition to comprehensively equipped classrooms, include a music wing, a library, ICT suite, a science room, an art and technology room, a sensory garden and outdoor 'classrooms'. Our new multi-million pound extension and refurbishment of the Junior School offers specialist teaching spaces which reflect the importance we place on providing the best possible learning environment, alongside our exceptional teaching. The girls are all enjoying our new Science Lab, Digital Hub and light-filled Art Studio and Design and Food Technology room, which look onto fields and woodland. We share many other facilities with the Senior School including a swimming pool, gymnasium, sports hall, tennis courts and an all-weather pitch.

The Senior School. Bromley High combines a tradition of scholarship with an innovative curriculum and expansive co-curricular provision. In the classroom, an emphasis on independent learning and growth mindset is designed to inculcate a spirit of enquiry, an independence of mind and a love of learning. Girls participate with enthusiasm and commitment in Music, Drama, Sport and an overabundant range of activities – and where they have interest or talent or enthusiasm, it is nurtured so that they learn to excel.

Consistent investment has developed new science facilities, library, sixth form centre, drama studio, and specialist teaching rooms for the creative arts enabling departments to have their own dedicated spaces for teaching and extracurricular activities. Visual and creative arts are highly valued with Photography, Drama and Dance offered to A level and students regularly progressing to study at Central St Martin's and other prestigious Arts Foundation courses and to Ballet Schools.

Academic. Languages, both ancient and modern, are a particular strength, with French, German and Spanish offered from Year 7. Latin and Classics are both popular A Level choices, with Ancient Greek offered as an optional extra GCSE. As a girls' school, Bromley High lays great emphasis on STEM subjects – Science, Technology, Engineering and Mathematics. Teaching rooms are equipped with Smart Boards and all have Wi-Fi and digital projector facilities which allow pupils to use iPads, Chrome Books, or their own mobile computer devices. Teachers are encouraged to enrich the curriculum and teach lively, challenging lessons. Myriad trips and activities, including music tours abroad from Year 7, and Lower School trips to Florence, Venice and Iceland. The modern foreign languages department has links with France, Germany and Spain and arranges exchanges, visits and work experience placements.

Girls study 10 GCSE subjects including Mathematics, Biology, Chemistry, Physics, English and English Literature and a Modern Language. Three further options are chosen from French, Spanish and German, Latin and Classical Civilisation; Computer Science, Music, Art, Photography, Drama, Dance, Design Technology, Economics, Geography, History, Physical Education.

Sport. Sports facilities on the school's 25-acre site are superb, including a large, well-equipped Sports Hall, a new fitness suite, a gymnasium, a 400-metre athletics track, two grass hockey pitches, a fine indoor heated swimming pool, and floodlit AstroTurf pitches and courts. Sport is both integral to the curriculum and an important part of the extracurricular life of the school. The school is proud of its tradition of producing national level athletes and swimmers and the number of girls who play county level hockey, netball, swimming, tennis and athletics.

Sixth Form. The Sixth Form Centre provides a bright, modern setting for traditional scholarship. Students select from a broad range of A Levels supplemented by Extended Project, AS Thinking Skills and electives such as Young Enterprise, Magazine Editing, Fashion, etc. Careers education is supported by the extensive GDST network of more than 70,000 alumnae. Sixth Formers benefit from GDST-wide initiatives, such as leadership and Oxbridge conferences and residential course on topics such as Engineering and Environmental Sustainability.

Extracurricular Activities. A great emphasis is put on an enthusiastic involvement in music, art, sport and drama. The annual Dance production is a significant event in the school calendar, and in recent years the school has staged concerts in major London venues such as the Royal Albert Hall, Southwark Cathedral and The Swiss Church.

Girls contribute to local, national and international charities and to community service. Almost all girls participate in the Duke of Edinburgh's Award scheme in Year 10, with some continuing to completion of Gold Award in Sixth Form. The Eco Society promotes a keen interest in environmental issues. There are regular exchanges to France, Germany and Spain as well as Geography and Biology field trips as far as Iceland. Annual World Challenge expeditions have recently visited Madagascar, Mongolia and Costa Rica. The Year 6 and 7 Music Tours have recently visited Paris, Brussels, Normandy and Bruges with the Senior Music Tour performing in Berlin, Prague, New York and Los Angeles. It is first only all-girls senior school in the world to have all Steinway status and musicians benefit from a Musician-in-Residence.

Fees per term (2023–2024). Senior School £6,375, Junior School £5,141.

Fees cover tuition, stationery, textbooks and scientific and games materials as well as entry fees for GCSE and GCE Advanced Level examinations. Extra tuition in Music and Speech and Drama is available at recognised rates.

Bursaries. Bursaries are means-tested and provide, for successful applicants, assistance with fees to enable bright girls to benefit from a GDST education. For those receiving full remission of fees, the award may include uniform and trips allowances.

Scholarships. There are Academic, Art, Music and Sport scholarships for the most successful candidates in the assessments at 11+ and for entry into the Sixth Form.

Admission and Entrance Examination. Admission into the school is at 4+ (Reception) and 7+ (Year 3) by assessment and testing. Pupils from the Junior School progress automatically to the Senior School but external applicants, or those wishing to be considered for scholarship or bursary are assessed at 11+. The examination tests verbal and non-verbal skills, as well as creative writing. Entry to the Sixth Form is dependent on interview and school reference, including predicted grades and is contingent on results at GCSE.

Charitable status. Bromley High School is part of The Girls' Day School Trust, which is a Registered Charity, number 306983.

Chair of the Local Governors: Mr Dominic Broom, LLB

***Headmistress*: Mrs E Codling**, BSc Southampton, MA Goldsmiths London, PGCE, NPQH

Deputy Head (*Pastoral*): Mrs T Hathway, BA Greenwich
Deputy Head (*Academic*): Dr S Lindfield, BSc Oxon, PhD Liverpool
Assistant Head (*Head of Sixth Form*): Mrs C Bird, BA Manchester
Assistant Head (*Organisation*): Mr P Isted, BA Bristol

Director of Finance & Operations: Mr R Taylor, MA

Head of Junior School: Mrs C Dickerson, BA Anglia
Deputy Head of Junior School: Mrs K Powell, BEd Primary Ed Greenwich

Director of Marketing and Communications: Ms N Messih, BA Leeds

Admissions Registrar: Mrs L Clarke

Bromsgrove School

Worcester Road, Bromsgrove, Worcestershire B61 7DU

Tel: 01527 579679
email: admissions@bromsgrove-school.co.uk
website: www.bromsgrove-school.co.uk
X/Twitter: @bromsschool
Facebook: @bromsgroveschool
Instagram: @bromsgroveschool
LinkedIn: /school/bromsgrove-school

Motto: *Deo Regi Vicino*

The date of the School's Foundation is unknown but it was reorganised by Edward VI in 1553 and was granted a Royal Charter 6 years later. It was refounded in 1693 by Sir Thomas Cookes, at the same time as Worcester College, Oxford (formerly Gloucester Hall). The link between School and College has been maintained ever since.

Location. This co-educational boarding and day school is situated some 13 miles north of the Cathedral City of Worcester and an equal distance south of Birmingham. Birmingham International Airport and Station are a 20-minute drive by motorway. The M5, M6, M42 and M40 motorways provide easy access to the School.

The School stands in 100 acres of grounds on the south side and within walking distance of the market town of Bromsgrove.

Facilities. The School has outstanding academic facilities including an award-winning Art, Design and Technology building, a twenty-classroom Humanities building and eighteen recently built or refurbished Science laboratories. Latest developments include a new Performing Arts complex, which was formally opened in November 2017. The complex includes two 300-seat venues: historic Routh Hall on the Senior campus and Cobham Theatre based within the Preparatory campus.

Sports facilities are extensive with a major sports complex which houses an arena large enough for eight badminton courts, and bleacher seating for 500. Dance studios, gym, teaching rooms and hospitality suite/sports viewing room enhances the existing all-weather, floodlit sports facilities which sit comfortably alongside the extensive grass pitches.

Boarding. The boarding environment at Bromsgrove is happy, stable, disciplined and nurturing. Bromsgrove Senior School's boarding community is made up of boarders from over 55 nationalities accommodated between five Houses, one of which is Housman Hall a Sixth Form co-ed house, formerly home of OB and poet A E Housman, which has been sympathetically refurbished and is situated just off the School campus. All accommodation is finished to a very high standard. The stability and continuity that enable boarders to thrive are provided by resident houseparents (all academic members of staff) and their families, assistant houseparents, housemothers, and a team of house-based tutors. All meals are taken centrally in the School, with the exception of the evening meal at Housman Hall.

Day pupils also benefit from the House system and all belong to one of seven day-houses: there are four boys houses and three houses for girls including the newly opened Ottilie Hild House. Houseparents and tutors work in each House and give pupils the pastoral and academic support they need. Pupils are very loyal to their House and competitions between day and boarding Houses, including sport, music, drama and debating, are keenly contested.

Numbers. There are 1,060 pupils in the Senior School, of whom over 490 are boarders. The Preparatory, Pre-Preparatory and Pre-School have a further 720 pupils aged 7 to 13, including 100 boarders aged 7+. (See also Preparatory & Pre-Preparatory School entry in IAPS section.)

Curriculum. In the Preparatory School, a broadly based curriculum is followed. In addition to the usual academic subjects, time is given to Art, Music, ICT, Drama, Design Technology and to a full programme of Physical Education. Languages on offer include French, German, Spanish and Latin.

As pupils move up the School, GCSE choices are made for the start of Year 9. Eleven subjects is the norm at GCSE, with a broad core including the three separate sciences, a modern language and three further optional subjects. The minimum qualification for automatic entry into the Sixth Form is a six-point average at GCSE with areas of strength also evident. Pupils may study the IB Diploma or take the A Level route whilst BTECs are also available in Sports Science and Business Studies. Flexibility in timetabling aims to ensure that all pupils' subject choices are catered for whatever the combination. Many A Level subjects are available including, Art, Biology, Business, Chemistry, Classics, Computer Science, Design and Technology, Drama and Theatre Studies, Design, Economics, Engineering, English, French, Geography, German, Latin, Mathematics and Further Mathematics, Music, Physical Education, Physics, Politics, Religious Studies, Spanish and Textiles. Under the IB umbrella, Italian, Environmental Systems, Mandarin, Global Politics and Psychology are also on offer. With two-thirds of students achieving A*/A at both GCSE and A Level and an IB average of 38.0 points in 2023, virtually all pupils proceed to degree courses, many at Russell Group universities. The most popular university destinations in recent years have been University and King's Colleges in London followed by Exeter, Bath and Bristol with an increasing number continuing to a QS World Top 100 university.

Performing Arts. The performing arts are well supported at Bromsgrove School and rightly thrive. The School boasts a fantastic Performing Arts Centre which includes a state-of-the-art concert hall, full-sized theatre, a large drama studio and a suite of music classrooms and practice areas. Historic Routh Hall has been transformed into a concert hall, tuned exclusively for musical performances and making use of its exceptional acoustic qualities. Adjacent, a new Music School houses a suite of specialist classrooms, recording studios and 12 instrumental practice rooms, as well as a reception foyer and box office. The Performing Arts Avenue leads to an equivalent home for Drama. Cobham Theatre has flexible seating (with a capacity of 300), the hydraulic thrust stage allows for a wide range of dramatic and dance performances. The facility also boasts a 90-seat performance studio, with large scenic workshops, props stores and modern dressing rooms available for both lessons and productions.

Music and Drama flourish both within and outside the formal curriculum. House Music Competitions, Jazz Gigs and a variety of informal concerts happen throughout the year. There is plenty of scope for involvement in the School Orchestra and String, Wind and Brass Ensembles, Chamber Groups, Jazz Bands, a 50-strong Chapel Choir and large Choral Society. The timetable is sufficiently flexible to allow special arrangements to be made for outstanding musicians. Each year, the Chamber Choir takes the opportunity to sing in some spectacular cathedrals and chapels, including singing Evensong at Worcester College Oxford, Hereford Cathedral and St Paul's Cathedral. Major musical productions such as *Grease* and *Hairspray* are also highlights of the school year with extensive casts and backstage crew made up of pupils. School musicians take part in festivals, which have included the Upton Jazz Festival and Cheltenham Festival of Arts and there is a strong Choral Society which performs in venues including Birmingham Town Hall.

Discrete Drama forms part of the curriculum for every student from Year 5 to Year 8. The option is available for students to take the subject to GCSE level and at A Level the school offers Theatre Studies. Senior, Fourth Form and Prep School productions, alongside a number of House Drama Competitions at all levels, form the main spine of co-curricular Drama at Bromsgrove which has a reputation for very high production standards. A high level of training for aspiring theatre technicians and designers ensures a vibrant dramatic life within the School for both performers and those wishing to work backstage.

Drama Scholarships are awarded to students joining at 13+ and 16+ whilst Music Scholarships are available at 11+, 13+ and 16+.

Careers. The School employs a full-time Careers Advisor and a comprehensive careers counselling programme, called Bromsgrove Futures is available to pupils of all ages. Many former pupils return to talk to and advise current pupils about university courses and careers possibilities.

Co-curricular activities. A wide range of sports and activities is offered, giving opportunities to participate at a competitive level in Athletics, Badminton, Basketball, Clay Pigeon Shooting, Climbing, Cricket, Cross Country, Debating, Fencing, Golf, Hockey, Horse Riding, Netball, Rugby, Rounders, Soccer, Squash, Swimming, Table Tennis, Tennis, Volleyball and Young Enterprise.

The Saturday timetable, in conjunction with the weekday programme, allows the activities programme more flexibility to offer both recreational and academic choices. Pupils may select from a diverse range of recreational activities including Academic extension and support, Revision for GCSE, A Levels, IB, SATs and Oxbridge, Biology, Chemistry and Physics Olympiad, Aerobics, Art, Architectural Modelling, Astronomy, Badminton, Beekeeping, Board Game Design, Body Balance, Chess, Coding, Cookery, Corps of Drums, CREST Science, Design Technology, Drama, EPP (Economics, Politics and Philosophy), Engineering, Forest Schools, Flourishing Fiver, Golf driving range, Handicrafts, History Society, Horse Riding, ICT, Investment Club, Karate, Literary Society, MedVet Society, Military skills, Music, Outdoor pursuits (including climbing, high ropes, kayaking, orienteering, raft building, sailing), Mahjong, Park Run, Photography, Plaster Modelling, School Magazine, School Gardens, Trampolining, Ultimate Frisbee, Upcycling, Website design and Weight training. There are opportunities to gain qualifications in Life saving, First Aid, LAMDA, Sports/Dance Leader Awards and Martial Arts. In addition to the activities programme, Year 9 pupils participate in Bromsgrove Badge, comprising a selection of activities that help to prepare them for the Bronze Duke of Edinburgh's Award and culminating in a four-day camp at the end of the year. There is a thriving Combined Cadet Force (Army and RAF), and many pupils are involved in The Duke of Edinburgh's Award scheme. The School's Bromsgrove Service programme caters for large numbers of pupils and provides a wide range of activities; examples include working in local schools and charity shops, visiting residential homes, acting as Learning Mentors and Student Listeners, helping in animal sanctuaries, supporting conservation projects and fundraising for charities.

Admission. Entrance at 13 is by Bromsgrove School Entrance Examinations. Boys and Girls may be admitted to the Preparatory School at any age from 7 to 12 inclusive. 11+ and 13+ Entrance Tests take place in November and mid-January for entry into other years.

Places are available in the Sixth Form for boys and girls who have had their GCSE education elsewhere.

Scholarships and Bursaries. Awards are made on the results of scholarship examinations held at the School in November. A significant number of scholarships, means-tested bursaries and Foundation bursaries for pupils of academic ability are awarded at 11+, 13+ and 16+. A number of Music scholarships and exhibitions are awarded each year at ages 11, 13 and 16, offering free tuition on up to two instruments. Scholarships for pupils talented in Arts/Textiles, Sport or Drama are awarded at 13+ and 16+. Means-tested bursaries may be used to supplement any scholarship. Full details are available from the Admissions Department.

Fees per term (2023–2024). Senior School (age 13+): £15,040 full boarding, £9,965 weekly boarding, £6,720 day inc. lunch. Preparatory School (age 7–13): £9,770–£12,055 full boarding, £7,125–£8,630 weekly boarding, £4,690–£6,080 day inc. lunch. Pre-Preparatory (age 4–7): £3,250–£3,580 day. Nursery (age 2–4): £68.20 per full day session.

Charitable status. Bromsgrove School is a Registered Charity, number 1098740. It exists to provide education for boys and girls.

Patron: A Denham-Cookes
President: S Towe

A Vice-President: V S Anthony
A Vice-President: N J Birch
A Vice-President: R D Brookes
A Vice-President: J A Hall
A Vice-President: T M Horton
A Vice-President: R Lane

Governing Body:
M Luckman (*Chair*)
Lt Col M Ballard
C Cameron
J P Campion
A Cleary
Dr D Cunningham
Dr C Lidbury
J Loynton
D Morton
J W Roden
I Stringer
C Thompson
D Walters
D Waltier
A Willcox

Company Secretary: J Sommerville

***Headmaster*: M Punt**, BA, MA Oxon, MSc, PGCE

Bursar: Mrs L Brookes, ACMA
Assistant Head: Miss R M Scannell, BA, PGCE
Deputy Head (*Academic*): P S Ruben, BSc, MPhil, MBA
Deputy Head (*Co-Curricular*): P S T Mullan, BA, PGCE
Deputy Head (*Pastoral*): A McClure, BA, PGCE
Deputy Head (*Teaching*): Mrs J Holden, MA Oxon, PGCE
Director of Wellbeing: Miss Z Leech, BA
Senior Master: S Matthews, BA, PGCE

School Medical Officer: Dr D Law, MA, MBChB Oxon, MRCGP, DRCOG, DFFP

Staff:
* Head of Department
† Houseparent

S J Kingston, BEd
Mrs S Shinn, BSc, PGCE (*Timetabler*)
Ms S J Cronin, BA, DMS, PGCE
Mrs F K Bateman, BSc, PGCE
Mrs S E Ascough, BSc, PGCE (*Director of Operations*)
D G Wilkins, BA, SCITT
M A C Beet, MA Cantab, PGCE (**German*)
Miss F E Diver, BA, PGCE
N C J Riley, BSc, PGCE (**Mathematics*)
Mrs E L E Buckingham, BA (**Girls PE & Games*)
Miss S A Franks, BSc, PGCE
Miss M M Smith, BA, PGCE (**Spanish*)
Mrs T L Helmore, BA, PGCE
O A Matthews, BEng, PGCE (**Design and Technology*)
Dr M Thompson, BSc, PhD, MInstP, PGCE (*IB Coordinator*)
Revd P Hedworth, BEd, BA (*Chaplain*)
Dr M K Ruben, BA, PhD, PGCE (**Gifted and Talented*)
G N Delahunty, BA, PGCE (**Politics*)
Ms E L Densem, BA, PGCE (**Sixth Form Enrichment*)
H Bell, MA, PGCE
Miss J Zafar, BA, PGCE (**History*)
S Broadbent, BA, QTS
D Tamplin, BSc, PGCE
Mrs K Hands, BA, PGCE (**Religious Studies*)
Ms G Tyrrell, BA, PGCE (**French*)
D Williams, BA, PGCE
A Carrington-Windo (*Director of Rugby*)
Miss L Davenport, BSc, PGCE
S Noble, BSc, PGCE
Miss A Baker, BSc, MMath, MEd
J Baldrey, BA, PGCE
Mrs L Newton, BEng, PGCE
Mrs E Gill, BA, PGCE
A Helmore, BA, MA, PGCE
J Holdsworth, BSC, PGCE
Mrs D Sutherland, BA, HDipMaths, QTS
Mrs J Holdsworth, BA, PGCE
J McKelvey, BA, PGCE (*Director of Music*)
Mrs K Hannah, BA, PGCE
T Clinton, BSc, PGCE
Mrs J Boonnak, BA, MA, PGCE (**International Education*)
L Mullan, BSc, PGCE (**Boys PE & Games*)
Miss L Hunter, BA, PGCE
M Giles, BSc, PGCE
Miss S Hankinson, BSc, PGCE
Miss R Green, BSc, PGCE (*Director of GCSE*)
S Higgins, BEd (**PE*)
Miss N Langford, BA, GTTP
Miss F McCanlis, BMus, PGCE
H Pothecary, BSc, PGCE (**TOK*)
Mrs G Wright, BSc, PGCE
Mrs V Adams, BA, MA, PGCE
D Atkinson, BSc, MSc, PGCE
Mrs A Eaton, MA, GTP
G Evans, BSc, PGCE
T Hinde, BA, MA

A Kelly, BSc, MDip Ed (*Examinations Officer*)
Ms A Linehan, BSC, MEd, PG Dip Ed
Mrs N Reid, BA, PGCE
Dr D Rimmer, PhD, MA (*Master of Scholars*)
Dr R Short, MChem, PhD, PGCE (*i/c DofE Silver*)
Mrs C Wadley, BA
Miss P Woolley, MChem, PGCE (*i/c Bromsgrove Service*)
Mrs J Bradford, BA (*Drama*)
O Spencer-Burton, BA, PGCE
P Dinnen, MA (*English*)
S Kettle, BSc, PGCE (*Science, *Physics*)
Mrs J Talbot, MA, PGCE
T Norton, BA (*Director of Performing Arts*)
A Gooderham (*Director of Hockey*)
S Coleman, BSc, PGCE
Dr A Davies, PhD, PGCE
Miss E Hill, BSc, PGCE
A Summerfield, MSc, QTS, PGCE
G Tasker, BSc, PGCE
R Unterhalter, BA, PGCE (*President of the Common Room*)
B Vice, MChem (*Chemistry*)
Mrs A Webb, BA, PGCE
Miss G Aust, BA, PGCE
Dr M Jewkes, BA, MA, PhD
I Jones, BSc, MSc, PGCE
Dr D West, BSc, PhD, MA, PGCE (*CAS*)
Miss G Farrell, BA, MA, PGCE (*Life Skills*)
Dr K Morris, BSc, PGCE, PhD (*Extended Essay*)
G Patel MSc, BSc, PGCE
D Pover, BA, PGCE
G Young, BSc, PGCE
Mrs F Linfield, BA (*Economics*)
Mrs J McCarthy (*Curriculum Support*)
P Prouse, MSc, PGCE, DipNLP, FRAS, MIstP
J Snelling, BSc, PGCE, CGeog, FFCCT
Mrs J Tidmarsh, BA, PGCE
Dr E Jones, BA, PhD, PGCE
Mrs J Williams, BA, PGCE
Miss L Blakeley, BA, MA, PGCE (*Art*)
W Colson, BSc, PGCE
Ms S Palitti, BA, PGCE
Ms R Williams, BA, PGCE
Miss F Bates, BSc
Miss R Elwood-Adams, BSc
T Milnes, MSc Director of Cricket
Mrs R Parveen, BA (*EAL*)
A Phillips, BSc (*Biology*)
Miss H Popescu, BSc
Mrs F Round, BSc, PGCE
Miss H Swift, BSc
Dr D Tchakhotine, BSc (*Director of A Level*)
A Arnold, BA, PGCE
L Bradbury, BA, PGCE
L Brown, BSc, PGCE
S El Hanibali, BA, PGCE
G Hatfield, BA
S Hopkins, BSc, PGCE
A Hutsby, BSc, PGCE
K Kinsella, BA, PGCE
A Osorio-Martinez, BA, PGCE
J Palmer, BSc, PGCE
W Pardoe, BSc, PGCE
H Pemberton, BA, PGCE
E Perez-Higueras Gomez-Escalonilla, BA
J Traynor, BA
A Wolverson, BA, PGCE
H Xu, BSc, PGCE

Houses and Houseparents:
Boarding:
Elmshurst (*Boys*): M Giles
Housman Hall (*Sixth Form*): G Tasker
Mary Windsor (*Girls*): Mrs C Matthews
Oakley (*Girls*): Mrs V Adams
Webber (*Sixth Form*): Mrs J Courtney
Wendron-Gordon (*Boys*): D Farnfield

Day:
Hazeldene (*Girls*): A Linehan
Lupton (*Boys*): G Evans
Lyttelton (*Boys*): J Holdsworth
Ottile HIld (*Girls*): Miss Ruth Powell
School (*Boys*): G Young
Thomas Cookes (*Girls*): Mrs K Hannah
Walters (*Boys*): H Bell

Music Staff:
J McKelvey, BA, PGCE (*Director of Music*)
Mrs M Corrie (*Music, Preparatory School*)
Ms F McCanlis, BMus, PGCE
T Martin, BA, Dip ABRSM (*Head of Jazz*)
Mrs J Russell, BA, PGCE
Miss H Bool, GBSM, ABSM, BTech Nat (*Head of Percussion*)
J Dunlop, BA, GBSM, ABSM (*Head off Wind and Brass*)
Ms F Swadling, BA, ABSM, GBSM (*Head of Strings*)
Mrs J Parsons, BMus Hons, PGDip, ALCM (*Head of Keyboard*)
S Cowperthwaite (*Organist*)
Mrs M Cullen, BA (*Music Administrator*)
Mrs C Hinde, MA (*Performing Arts Administrator*)
Visiting Music Staff:
Mrs J Allin (*Clarinet*)
N Barry, GGSM, LTCL (*Piano*)
M Broadhead LTCL, DipTCL (*Cello*)
Mrs R Brown, BMus (*Singing*)
P Campbell-Kelly, GMus, RNCM, PG Dip RNCM, PPRNCM (*Violin*)
Ms J Chaddock (*Double Bass*)
Mrs S Chatt, GBSM (*Percussion*)
Miss P Cheng (*Double Bass*)
Miss S Clarke, GBSM (*Violin*)
Mrs K Fawcett, BA, MA, PG Dip (*Viola, Violin*)
A Gittens, BTec, HND (*Electric Guitar*)
Mrs J A Hattersley, CT ABRSM, LRSM (*Brass*)
Mrs J Hiles, GBSM, ABSM (*Flute, Piano*)
Mrs J Porter, BMus (*Piano*)
R Tattam (*Bassoon*)
W Theunissen (*Singing*)
J Topp, Bmus, LGSMD (*French Horn*)

Preparatory & Pre-Preparatory School
Headmaster: M Marie, BA, PGCE
Deputy Head (*Academic*): Mrs T Hill, BA, PGCE
Deputy Head (*Operations*): Mrs K Ison, BEd
Head of Junior Department: Mrs R Ivison, BA, PGCE (*Year 3*)

Dr V Barron, BA, MA, PGCE, PhD (*Wellbeing*)
Mrs A Davis, BA, PGCE, CCET (*Curriculum Support*)
Mrs C S Abraham, BA, MA, QTS

J Amphlett, BA, PGCE (**Drama*)
Miss J Balkham, BA, PGCE (**Year 7*)
R Barnett, BSc, GTP
M Barratt, BA, MA, QTS
Mrs G Billig, BSc, PGCE
Mrs R Boardman, BA, PGCE (**Spanish/German*)
Mrs L Campbell, BEd
G Clark, BEd
Mrs M Corrie, GTCL, LTCL (**Music*)
Mrs S Dakin, BA (**Forest School*)
Mrs J Danks, BMus, PGCE (**Girls PE*)
Mrs J Drury, BSc, PCGE
Mrs T Faulkner-Petrova, BA, BSc, MSc, PGCE (**EAL*)
Mrs K Finnegan, BA, PCGE (**French*)
Mrs C Goodall, BA, PGCE
Mrs Y Griffiths, BSc, PGCE
Mrs S Grove, BEd
J P Grumball, BSc, PGCE (**IT*)
Miss K Guest, BSc
Mrs C Hathaway, BA, PGCE
Mrs D Hepburn, BSc, MA, PGCE
Miss E Hubbard, BA, PGCE
Mrs S James, BSc, MA, QTS (**Geography*)
Mrs S Jeffrey, BSc, PGCE (**Science*)
G Jones, BA, PGCE
Mrs G Judson, BSc, PGCE (*President of the Common Room*)
C D Kippax, BA, PGCE (**MFL*)
Mrs R Laurenson, BA, PGCE (**Year 4*)
Mrs Z Lawton, BA, QTS
Mrs C Leather, BSc, PGCE (**PSHEE*)
J Liqurish, BA, PGCE
Revd Dr S J P Loone, Mphi, MEd, BA, BTheol, PhD. PGCE, CTC, NPQH
Miss M Mimberg, BA, PGCE
Miss A Read, BTec, BA, PGCE (**Art*)
Miss C Roskell, BEng, PGCE
Mrs J Russell, BA, PGCE
R Shone, BA, PGCE
Mrs L Singh, BDes, PGCE (**RE*)
Mrs V Sitlu, BA, PGCE (**Year 5*)
G Snelling, MA, PGCE
P Sutherland, HD Ed (**Design & Technology*)
J Thornely, BSc, PGCE
Mr M Turner, BSc, PGCE (**Mathematics*)
Miss S Watson, BA, PGCE (**English*)
Mrs S Webley, BSc, PGCE, MEd (**Year 8*)
M Wilkinson, BSc, PGCE
Mrs H Worton, BA, PGCE (**Year 6*)

Boarding House and Houseparents:
Page: Mr & Mrs R Lawton
Conway Page: Mr S Jenkins & Ms T Salt

Pre-Preparatory Staff:
Deputy Head (*Pastoral*): B Etty-Leal, BSc, PGCE
Deputy Head (*Academic*): Mrs K Western, BEd

Mrs J Townsend, BA, PGCE (**Early Years*)
Mrs C Cattell, BA, PGCE (**Key Stage 1*)
Mrs J Kingston, BMus, PGCE
Miss E Lewis, BA Ed
Mrs J Lockhart, BEd
Mrs N Marie, BA, PGCE
Miss E Marrs, BA, PGCE
Mrs M Martin, BA, GTP
Mrs N St John, BA, PGCE

Bryanston School

Blandford, Dorset DT11 0PX
Tel: 01258 484632
email: head@bryanston.co.uk
website: www.bryanston.co.uk
X/Twitter: @BryanstonSchool
Facebook: @bryanstonschool

Motto: *Et nova et vetera*

Bryanston is a leading co-educational boarding and day school for pupils aged 3–18, based in Dorset.

Inspired by over 90 years of innovative practice, our approach to education and our distinctive culture nurtures purposeful, curious, and well-rounded individuals.

We work tirelessly to ensure that each pupil not only achieves the results they deserve, but also learns to think independently, be self-reliant and explore new interests. At the heart of our approach is the 'Bryanston Method', a one-to-one, five-year duration relationship for every pupil with a hand-picked tutor who acts as champion, mentor, and enabler.

This has been the keystone of the School's philosophy since our foundation, tailored to the needs and interests of each pupil. There is no Bryanston 'type' – we want our pupils to think for themselves. Alongside high academic standards and expectations, we provide an emotionally and intellectually supportive environment, allowing pupils to develop independent, creative, and unbounded thinking.

Bryanston is a place where children learn to love their minds, free their spirits, and find their mission.

Situation. The School is located in beautiful Dorset countryside near the market town of Blandford. There are 400 acres of grounds, which include a stretch of river used for rowing and canoeing, playing fields, woodland, and parkland.

Numbers. There are approximately 405 boys (30 in Prep) and 392 girls (83 in Prep).

The size of Bryanston Prep ensures that each pupil is known by everyone; each child has an identity and is respected for their individuality.

Admission. At 13, assessments and interviews. At 16, entrance tests and interviews.

For Bryanston Prep, assessment is conducted via taster days and informal interviews.

Scholarships. Academic, Art, Computer Science, Design & Technology, Music, Performing Arts, Sport, and the Richard Hunter All-Rounder Scholarships are available annually for entry at 13+.

Academic, Art, Drama and Music Scholarships, plus Udall Awards for Sport are available annually for entry to the Sixth Form.

Scholarships range in value and may be supplemented by means-tested bursaries. Music Scholarships carry free musical tuition, optional Alexander Technique lessons and a weekly accompaniment lesson.

Further details may be obtained from the Director of Admissions. Email admissions-prep@bryanston.co.uk for Bryanston Prep and admissons@bryanston.co.uk for the senior school.

Organisation. Bryanston Prep keeps pace with the expectations of 21st-century learning, while nurturing traditional values and a strong ethos. We pride ourselves on our pastoral care and the opportunities we offer children through a crucial developmental stage of their life. We encourage independent thinking and creative learning, and outdoor play is a key part of the school day. In a delightful country setting, the school provides a safe but challenging environment in which children can discover their strengths, take risks, and make friends.

The senior school is organised on a house basis with five senior boys' houses, five girls' houses, and two junior boys' houses, although the house system is less rigid and formal at Bryanston than in many senior schools.

All pupils have a personal tutor throughout their time in the school, with whom they meet on a one-to-one basis at least once a week. One-to-one tutoring starts in Year 6 at Bryanston Prep as the School begins to equip pupils with the skills they need to become independent learners.

All sixth-form pupils in their final year have individual study-bedrooms, while lower-sixth formers usually share study-bedrooms. All meals are served centrally in the Dining Hall, providing additional opportunities for friendships to be formed across house and year groups.

Religion. Christian inspiration and Christian ideals are fundamental to the Bryanston philosophy, but the school recognises that pupils may come from homes which follow other faiths or have no strong religious affiliation. There is, therefore, no attempt to impose worship on pupils, rather the intention is to provide an atmosphere in which spiritual values can be discovered and developed.

School Work. The school encourages innovation in all areas of the curriculum, passionately believing that it is not what you learn, it is how you learn.

The School aims to lead pupils to a position where they are capable of working on their own, for a university degree or professional qualification, or in business. In addition to traditional class teaching, there is, therefore, increasing time given to private work as a pupil moves up the school in the form of assignments to be completed within a week or a fortnight. Teachers are available to give individual help when required, and tutors supervise pupils' work and activities in general on a one-to-one basis.

Pupils experience more freedom than at many schools, yet the safety net of the one-to-one tutor system and one-to-one subject tutorials is also sturdier than most.

Every pupil is encouraged to explore a range of opportunities. At Bryanston Prep, the small class sizes and high staff-to-pupil ratio ensures individual attention.

All pupils follow the same broad and challenging curriculum in D (Year 9), if at all possible. This curriculum includes Latin, Modern Languages, three separate Sciences, Creative Arts, Technology and Music as well as English and Mathematics. GCSEs are taken after three years when a pupil is in B (Year 11). There is a highly flexible choice of subjects at this level and subjects are set independently.

In the sixth form pupils can choose between A Levels and either the International Baccalaureate Diploma or the International Baccalaureate Career-Related Programme. All lower-sixth formers follow a compulsory Personal and Social Education course, and the academic enrichment programme provides supplementary sessions to develop key skills and approaches to learning.

Music. Bryanston has an exceptional musical tradition, and music is at the heart of school life.

The scholarships and awards won by Bryanston Prep pupils reflect academic, musical, artistic and all-rounder prowess; there is a strong artistic and musical tradition.

Inclusion and participation, as well as excellence, are core values and to achieve these every pupil in D (year 9) learns an instrument for the entire year. An extraordinary range of concerts, recitals and musical groups take place, with over 600 individual music lessons taught each week.

Drama. A well-equipped, modern theatre provides the venue for the many school productions which take place during the year as well as for touring professional companies. In addition to acting, pupils are involved in stage management, stage lighting and sound, and front-of-house work. There is also a large Greek Theatre in the grounds.

Sport and Leisure. A wide variety of sports is on offer at the school, including athletics, archery, badminton, canoeing, climbing, cricket, cross country, fencing, fives, hockey, indoor hockey, kayaking, lacrosse, netball, riding, rowing, rugby, rugby 7s, sailing, squash, swimming, and tennis.

Extensive playing fields between the school and the River Stour provide 42 tennis courts, two AstroTurf pitches, nine netball courts, a grass athletics track and grass pitches for all major sports, an all-weather riding manège and cross-country course.

A sports complex provides an indoor heated 25m, six-lane swimming pool, Performance Sports gym with dual axis force platforms and 360-degree motion cameras, 40m indoor sprint track, two large indoor sports halls, four squash courts, three indoor fives courts, spinning studio, 200m^2 fitness suite, bouldering wall, multi-purpose studios, analysis room, physio room, and an outdoor and adventure hall and storage.

At Bryanston Prep, team sports and swimming have an all-year-round place in the timetable. There are many extracurricular activities including riding, triathlon, dance, drama, and outdoor environmental pursuits.

Additional Activities. Pupils are encouraged to contribute to their community, using their time proactively and developing a growing self-reliance. All pupils take part in all or some of the following:

- Community and Social Service
- Extracurricular activities chosen from a wide range of options
- The Duke of Edinburgh's Award
- Adventure Training

This careful balance of academic subjects and extracurricular activities encourages all aspects of personal growth.

Dress. At Bryanston Prep, the uniform is practical, comfortable, and smart, suitable for both boys and girls.

At the senior school, there is no uniform but there is a dress code and firm expectations for academic achievement.

Careers. The Sixth Form and Careers Department work closely with tutors, houses, and departmental heads to provide guidance for pupils at every academic age and stage of development, at a pace that is right for each individual.

Our goal is to empower pupils to develop confidence and self-awareness, to reflect on their abilities and aspirations, and to gain insights into their future career options and higher education pathways.

Work-related learning is actively included as part of curriculum development, with psychometric profiling offered in Year 11. Higher Education and 'next steps' events are organised annually, providing the chance to meet with employers, academic subject specialists and overseas universities. Ongoing support is provided one-to-one, in small groups, via PSRE and guidance events. Bespoke support is available for those who are applying to university overseas.

Further Education. The vast majority of pupils in the sixth form gain admission to universities or other academies of further education.

Fees per term (2023–2024). Senior: £15,534 for boarders, £12,738 for day with bed and £10,350 day only pupils.

Prep: Boarders: £6,656–£8,710; Day: Prep £4,548–£5,671, Pre-Prep £3,095. There are no compulsory extras.

Charitable status. Bryanston School Incorporated is a Registered Charity, number 306210. It is a charitable trust for the purpose of educating children.

Governors:
J R Greenhill, MA, KC (*Chair*)
N Bickford, BA
B P Broad, BA
A Browning
S O Conran
J A F Fortescue, BA
C G Martin, ACA, MA
M E McKeown, BA, MSc
L M V Soden, BA, MA
R Swallow

***Head*: R G Jones**, BA, MEd

Deputy Head, Academic: M S Deketelaere, BA, MSc & DIC, PGCE

Head of Bryanston Prep: W Lockett, BA, PGCE

Staff:
* *Head of Department*
† *Housemaster/Housemistress*

Art:
*D G Knight, BA, PGCE
G J Cedeira, BA
A Connolly, BA, PGCE
†H E Dean, BA, PGCE
†J A K Dickson, BA, PCGE
J E Jehu, BA, PGCE

Classics:
*B Pullan, BA, MA, PhD, PGCE
†Dr H L Fearnley, BA, PhD
D Fowler-Watt, MA (*Director of Performing Arts*)
L M Jones, BA, MA
A J Sanghrajka, BA (*IB ToK Coordinator*)

Drama, Theatre Studies and Film:
J F Quan, BA, MA (*Director of Drama*)
H Simmonds (**Academic Drama*)
S N Wheeler, BA, PGCE (**Film*)
G A Martin, BA Videographer

Economics and Business Studies:
*R H Ings, BSc, PGCE
Dr P S Bachra, MA, EdD (**Pastoral*)
A N R Bray, BA (**Work-Related Learning*)
†J J A Beales, BA, PGCE
†M S Christie, MA, PGCE
G E S Drake, BSc, PGCE
N L Payne, BA, PGCE

English:
*H E J Weatherby, MA
M Belassie
L R Boothman, BA, PGCE
†S H Davies, MA
N M Kelly, BA, PGCE
A Matthews
O Nicholson, BA, MA, PGCE
L Perry

Geography:
*K E Andrews, BA, PGCE
M S Deketelaere, BA, MSc & DIC, PGCE (**Curriculum Planning*)
J E G Ralphs, BA, PGCE (**Sixth Form*)
R J Boulton, BA, PGCE
L C Kearney, BEd (*International Coordinator*)

History and Politics:
*W J Bridges, BSc, PGCE
*J G Strange, MA, PGCE
A B L de Steiger Khandwala, MA, MA, MPhil, PGCE
P Quarrell, BA, PGCE (*Senior Tutor*)
T Strongman, BA, PGCE
S M Vincent, BA, PGCE (*Admissions Tutor*)
J Waters, BA

History of Art:
*S A Wilson, BA, MA
S A E Stacpoole, BA

Mathematics:
*D Banham, BSc, PGCE
†C B Craig, BSc (*B/C Coordinator*)
S B Green, BA, MA
P A Griffin, BSc, PGCE
C L Kean, BSc, PGCE (*C Coordinator*)
C E Murray, BSc, PGCE
V R M Peck, BSc
E Pyke, MEng, PhD
T Reynolds, MA, MSc
A K Tarafder, BSc, PGCE

Modern Foreign Languages:
*L C Johnson, MA (**Modern Languages*, *Senior Tutor*)
C Dechirot, BA, MA (**French*)
E Flitters, BA, MA (**German*)
M Sanger, BA (**Spanish*)
L C Blanco, BA
L Diaz Perez
A J Gilbert, BA, PGCE
L R Haynes, BA, PGCE
F Mateo Sanz
R A Pakenham-Walsh, BA, PGCE
L Tate, BA, PGCE

†J M I Velasco, BA, PGCE

Music:
X Illes, BA, PGCE (*Director of Music*)
G M Scott, BA, PGCE, Premier Prix, ARCO, LTCL (*Assistant Director of Music*)
D Andrews (**Jazz*)
A Dickinson (**Singing*)
C S Scott, BMus, PGCE, FTCL, ARCM, LTCL (**Strings*)
R B K Rowntree, BMus (*Singing Coordinator*)

PE and Sport Studies:
R McCann, BSc, MA (*Director of Sport*)
B C Rodford, BSc, PGCE (*Assistant Director of Sport*)
*S E Morris, BSc, PGCE
M Foster (**Football*)
C L Miller, BA Ed (**Boarding*)
C L Bray, BSc, PGCE
J E Morris

Philosophy and Religious Studies:
*L J D Pollard, BA
Revd J Davis (*Chaplain*)

Psychology:
*Dr H A Hogarth, BSc, MSc, PhD (*IB Extended Essay Coordinator*)

Science:
*A J Elliot, BSc, PGCE (**Chemistry*)
C A Çava, MPhys (**Physics*)
S H Jones, BSc, PGCE (**Biology*)
C G Bloomfield, BSc, PGCE
R J Collcott, MEng, MSc, PGCE
G S Elliot, BA, PGCE
A M Harwood, BSc, PGCE
P L Haywood, BSc, PGCE
†R J Johnson, BSc, PGCE
Dr M T Kearney, MA, PhD, CEng, MRAeS, CPhys, MInst
†E Morris, BSc, PGCE, DipEd
J D Pritchard, MSc, PGCE
†N G Welford, BSc, PGCE

Technology:
A J Barnes, BA, CertEd (*Director of Technology*)
M J Davis, BSc, PGCE (**Computer Science*)
C J Mills, BA, PGCE (**Design and Technology*)
N J Davies, BEd
R H Ings, BSc, PGCE
J Ladd-Gibbon, BA, MA

Careers:
A N R Bray, BA (**Work-Related Learning*)
L C Kearney, BEd (*International Coordinator*)

Academic Support:
*A Hicks
J S Bell, MA
K E Heminsley
C Steven-Fountain, BA, PGCE, Cert SpLD

Library:
E C Minter, BA, PG Dip ISM, MCLIP

Outdoor Education:
D P T Curry, BSc

Head of Admissions: M Burke

Bury Grammar School

Tenterden Street, Bury, Greater Manchester BL9 0HN

Tel: 0161 696 8600
email: schooloffice@burygrammar.com
website: www.burygrammar.com
X/Twitter: @BuryGrammar
Facebook: @BuryGrammarSchool
Instagram: @burygrammarschool
LinkedIn: /burygrammarschool

Motto: *Sanctas clavis fores aperit*

Bury Grammar School was founded in 1570 during the reign of Queen Elizabeth I by Reverend Henry Bury, a wealthy philanthropic clergyman who was committed to educating the people of Bury, Reverend Peter Shaw, the Rector of Bury, and Edward Stanley, the third Earl of Derby, who gave the land on which the School was built.

The School was first located on land beside the Rectory in Bury near what is now Bury Parish Church. One of the earliest known pupils was a local boy called Thomas Wilde, whose father was given financial help for his son's education at the School. It is likely that at the start Bury Grammar School only employed one school master and concentrated on teaching basic skills of reading and writing. Bury Grammar School was a school for boys only until 1884.

Today, Bury Grammar School is an ambitious school with an uplifting, positive and life-affirming ethos. We believe utterly in the transformative power of education and we always have high aspirations for our young people. We are an all-through school for pupils aged 3 to 18.

Pupils begin their BGS journey of educational excellence in our co-educational Kindergarten from three years of age. They then progress to single sex education in our Senior Schools from age 11 through to 16, and coeducational teaching in our Sixth Form. The single sex set-up in the Senior Schools gives boys and girls the freedom to be themselves, to focus on their learning and growth without distractions, and to develop into confident and well-balanced young people. Outside the classroom, there are plenty of co-educational activities on offer, for example in Drama, Art, Music and the Combined Cadet Force giving pupils the best of both worlds. Transition from one key stage to the next is also made easy as individual pupils' potential and talents are very well known to us.

In the Sixth Form, boys and girls are ready to learn alongside one another as they prepare for university and life beyond BGS.

Every one of our Schools has a caring family environment where each pupil is known and nurtured as an individual. They make friends easily and many friendships formed at BGS often last a lifetime.

Curriculum. We are immensely proud of our 450+ year history and the traditions that make us unique. As a confident and forward-looking school, our strong foundations provide the perfect springboard from which to innovate as we prepare our pupils for successful, productive, and happy lives in a global 21st century.

'Quality is never an accident: it is always the result of intelligent efforts.' Quality is the common thread running through our history and into our future: this is the hallmark of a Bury Grammar School education.

Our 'all-through' curriculum best prepares our children for the challenges which lie ahead and at the same time remains true to our tradition of providing an independent, unique and inspirational grammar school education.

Our curriculum model allows our pupils to meet the changing demands of Higher Education and of life beyond BGS; it delivers an impressive enrichment offering, true to our strong tradition of nurturing fully-rounded individuals who have the edge when it comes to embracing life's opportunities.

BGS is the leading school in the area where pupils continually reach outstanding academic standards, achieving exceptional examination results at GCSE and A Level and gaining places on competitive courses at elite universities.

Facilities and Development. Bury Grammar School has a distinguished history of excellence dating back to the 1570s. Proud of its historic links with the town of Bury and the surrounding area, Bury Grammar School possesses a full range of modern facilities. These facilities enable the School to offer a broad and rich academic curriculum and extra-curricular programme. We have a co-educational Primary Division, single sex Senior Schools and a co-educational Sixth Form. This is a structure which allows pupils to develop into confident, happy learners in environments which are perfect for their age and conducive to a high-quality education. Our senior school pupils thrive in the single sex teaching groups, making spectacular progress at every level. Outside the classroom, all our extra-curricular activities are mixed. The best of both worlds, in our view. There is in effect five small schools within one big School at BGS, which means we know every child well. At the same time, each child benefits from the fact that we have so many expert teachers on site, with many of them teaching in more than one area of the School. Every pupil feels at home in their own area of school, but also has access to all our facilities on our 45-acre site.

Art. Well-equipped facilities allow all pupils to develop skills in print making, ceramics, sculpture, painting, drawing, textiles, new media, and animation. There are frequent visits to galleries, both locally and further afield. Pupils' artwork is proudly displayed throughout the school and BGS hosts regular exhibitions which are opened to the School community.

Music and Drama. Music infuses every aspect of our School and is an integral part of every day. Whether it be performances in assembly, performing at a community event or taking part in one of the plentiful concerts that fill our school calendar. Our Music Department values all, whatever their experience and whatever style of music they are interested in and encourages them on their musical journey. We aim to develop the potential of every pupil, no matter what their ability. Pupils with musical talent are encouraged by the whole school community to flourish and to achieve great things. The emphasis is firmly placed on diversity and versatility, which is evident in the varied and challenging music enrichment programme both within and outside of school.

Physical Education and Sport. Sport at Bury Grammar School embodies the core aims of participation, performance, enjoyment, health and partnerships. The School has a long-standing reputation for sporting endeavour and prowess and strives to provide excellent sporting opportunities for all pupils. We offer a diverse and inclusive programme of activities in which every pupil participates, through our curriculum and extensive enrichment programme. All our pupils are encouraged to try their hand at a range of sports and physical activities, whatever their level of ability. We believe that physical health and wellbeing play a crucial role in the educational journey of young people, developing leadership, teamwork, communication skills and self-discipline.

BGS pupils have been successful at local, regional and national level in netball, basketball, rugby, football, swimming and athletics and many of our pupils attain representative honours, including international selection. Other sports on offer include table tennis, badminton, rounders, tennis, handball, and yoga.

Essentially, we strive for all our pupils to be physically active, whilst at the same time aspiring to the highest level of elite performance.

Our sports facilities:

- 3G All Weather Pitch
- Spring & Jump Track
- Multi Use Games Area (MUGA)
- Sports Hall (Tenterden Street)
- Cricket & Athletics Field
- Cricket Nets
- Swimming Pool
- Hockey & Athletics Field
- Buckley Wells Playing Fields
- Tennis & Netball Courts
- Sports Hall (Bridge Road)
- Gymnasium
- Climbing Wall
- Fitness & Dance Studio
- Infant School Sports Hall

Outdoor Education. In the senior school a residential course is offered to Year 7 pupils at an outdoor centre to participate in water and land-based activities. We are delighted to offer participation in the Duke of Edinburgh's Award Scheme at Bronze, Silver and Gold level and also long and short haul expeditions with World Challenge.

CCF. The Bury Grammar School CCF was established in 1892 and is one of the oldest CCFs in the country. BGS is immensely proud of its CCF, the largest voluntary CCF in the country. It brings together an Army section (Royal Regiment of Fusiliers) and an RAF section. The current strength of the Contingent is 300+ cadets. The CCF helps pupils develop qualities such as self-discipline, resourcefulness and perseverance, a sense of responsibility and skills of management and leadership.

Pastoral Care. Bury Grammar School prides itself on excellent pastoral care and its ability to work as a family to nurture and care for every individual. It cares for and respects its pupils and, in turn, expects them to care for and respect others. The BGS philosophy for pastoral care is simple: BGS pupils should be happy, secure and ready for all that life has to offer. BGS offers individualised pastoral support for every pupil and is always keenly aware that it is a privilege to work alongside young people. BGS is fortunate to have on site a highly dedicated and skilled School Health Team who work closely with pupils, parents and staff to ensure that medical, health and wellbeing needs are met. BGS also offers the services of a qualified counsellor who is on site on a weekly basis to provide confidential support and advice to those pupils who need it. Each pupil has a Form Tutor who has primary responsibility for their pastoral care and for oversight of their academic progress and their extra-curricular programme. Form Tutors are led by Heads of Year who also oversee a pupil's academic progress. There is also a strong House system for a wide range of sporting, musical and cultural inter-house competitions.

Careers. The Careers Department aims to provide all pupils with access to the information and advice they need to make informed and sensible decisions about their futures. Guidance is provided by individual interviews and regular careers conventions and mock interview mornings. All pupils are also required to complete a period of work experience during Year 10 and Year 12.

Bury Grammar School Alumni Associations. The BGS journey carries through to our Alumni Associations; friendships formed at Bury Grammar School really do last a lifetime.

BGS Old Boys' Association Secretary: Matt Cooke, email: mjcooke01@aol.com

BGS Old Girls' Association Secretary: Suzanne Gauge, email: suzanne.gauge@btinternet.com

Admission, Scholarships and Bursaries. Admission is by examination/assessment and interview. A number of means-tested bursaries, based on academic performance and financial need, are awarded each year, in Year 7 and Year 12.

Fees per term (2023–2024). Senior School and Sixth Form £4,363; Primary Division £3,316.

Charitable status. Bury Grammar Schools Charity is a Registered Charity, number 526622. The aim of the charity is to promote educational opportunities for boys and girls living in or near Bury.

Governing Body:

Chair of Governors: Mr R Smyth
Vice Chair of Governors: Mr M Edge

Mrs S Gauge	Ms S McNeill
Dr S Hyde	Ms N Smith
Mr P Lee	Mr S Wild
Mr D Long	Mr G Yeung
Mr T McDougall	

Finance Director: Mr R Berry, BA

Clerk to the Governors: Mrs A Cloke

***Principal of Bury Grammar School*: Mrs J Anderson**, BA, PGCE, MEd

Deputy Principal, Director of Academic Provision, IT & Operations: Mrs V Leaver, BSc (*Geography*)

Head of Sixth Form: Mrs H Simmons, BA (*Drama*)

Senior Deputy Head, Enrichment and Partnerships: Mr R Lees, BA (*MFL*)
Senior Deputy Head, Pastoral: Mrs R Newbold, BSc (*Physical Education & Geography*)
Deputy Head, Educational Visits and Health & Safety: Mr A Dennis, BSc (*Mathematics, Head of Outdoor Activities*)
Director of Studies: Mrs K Lewis, MSc (*Physics*)
Director of Communications & School Information: Mrs C Lynskey, BA

***Principal of Bury Grammar Primary Division*: Mrs C Howard**, CIPS

Principal's PA: Mrs A Cloke
Deputy Principal's PA: Miss E McDonnell

Campbell College

Belmont Road, Belfast, Co Antrim
BT4 2ND, Northern Ireland

Tel: +44 (0)28 9076 3076
email: hmoffice@campbellcollege.co.uk
website: www.campbellcollege.co.uk
X/Twitter: @CampbellCollege
Facebook: @CampbellCollege1894
Instagram: @campbellcollege
LinkedIn: /school/campbell-college-belfast

Motto: *Ne Obliviscaris*

Campbell College, which was opened in 1894, was founded and endowed in accordance with the will of Henry James Campbell, Esq (Linen Merchant) of Craigavad, Co Down. It has a reputation as one of the leading educational environments in the country. Our commitment is to welcome, challenge and inspire each and every pupil to be the very best they can be, to push themselves and to stand tall as contributors to a global society.

Ethos. Our commitment is to welcome, challenge and inspire each and every pupil to be the very best they can be, to push themselves and to stand tall as contributors to a global society.

Confidence, commitment and achievement are at the heart of everything we do. From the classroom to the extracurricular activities, we are dedicated to ensuring that boys make the most of their talents within Campbell and beyond.

We nurture the individual and prepare them for the world. Academic achievements are important and we expect our pupils to strive for high grades; it is also our duty to harness the potential in every pupil whether it is academic, creative, physical or otherwise.

We want boys to leave the school with an assured set of values; we want them to believe they can truly make a difference in society. We want our boys to leave the school with things that are going to matter to them for the rest of their lives.

Pastoral Care. We believe that pupils learn best when they are happy, safe and secure and the purpose of our pastoral care is to provide such an environment. The strong, caring ethos of the College is demonstrated by its commitment to the welfare of the pupils and staff.

In Senior School all boys are allocated a Personal Tutor as the first point of contact for parents and our comprehensive Child Protection Policy is issued to all parents before their child commences school. Above and beyond this level of care we have a dedicated medical centre on campus led by the College Matron and a School Doctor who visits our boarders three times a week.

Boarding. We have a successful boarding department which brings an international dimension and unique character to the College; this will enable our pupils to thrive in the increasingly global world in which we all must live and work. We have approximately 150 boarders.

The Curriculum. This is focused upon giving our boys the maximum opportunity to produce the best possible examination results from a varied choice of subjects which meet the needs of the 21st century.

Class sizes are capped at 26 throughout Key Stage 3 to allow boys to grow in confidence and security in their learning as they make the transition from Primary School to Senior School. The teacher to pupil ratio is a generous 1:14, and the curriculum followed at Year 8 comprises English, Maths, Science, Geography, History, Religious Education, French, Art, Drama, Music, Technology, ICT, PE and Learning for Life and Work.

The Campus. Campbell College stands in a secure and impressive 100-acre wooded estate where the academic, boarding, artistic and sporting pursuits are all catered for on site. The College has its own indoor swimming pool, AstroTurf pitches, squash courts, shooting range, running track and numerous rugby and cricket pitches. It has a variety of sports and assembly halls, drama studio, computer suites and technology areas.

Other Activities. Campbell College is able to provide boys with a host of activities which naturally complement the culture of learning promoted within the school. Whilst the College is widely acknowledged for its sporting excellence, especially in rugby, hockey and cricket, there are many other opportunities available. Alongside a diverse range of sports there are opportunities to participate in The Combined Cadet Force, Duke of Edinburgh's Award scheme, Drama and Music productions and the Charity Action Group.

A competitive House system allows all boys to compete, with camaraderie and collegiality, in numerous inter-House competitions so all have an opportunity to represent their House as well as their school.

Holidays. There are three annual holidays: two weeks at Christmas and Easter, and eight in the summer. In the Christmas and Easter terms there is a half-term break of one week, during which parents of boarders are required to make provision for their sons to be away from school.

Admissions. Campbell College welcomes students at a variety of entry levels. Day boys can begin in Kindergarten and stay through to Sixth Form; boarders may start at Year 8. The school structure is designed to offer our students easy transitions as they grow and mature; they begin in Junior School, then move aged 11 to Middle School, before progressing to Senior School to prepare for their public examinations (GCSE, AS and A2 Level).

There are approximately 1,000 students in the Senior School of whom 150 are boarders, and 267 students in the Junior School.

Fees per annum (2023–2024) Boarding (Years 8–14): £19,970 (UK & Irish Citizens), £22,370 (EU citizens), £27,700 (Rest of the World). Day: £3,470.

As a Voluntary B Grammar School, Campbell College charges an annual fee to all pupils for development and maintenance. The Board of Governors seeks to support applications to the College by offering scholarships and bursaries, the details of which may be found in the Prospectus.

Prospectus. Further information is included in our prospectus which can be obtained from the College Office or you may download a copy from the College website.

Old Campbellian Society. There is a link from the College website.

Charitable status. Campbell College is registered with the Inland Revenue as a charity, number XN45154/1. It exists to provide education for boys.

Governors:
A W J Wilson, BA Hons, MSc, ACMA (*Chair*)
J Andrews, BSc Hons, FCA (*Vice-Chair*)
G C Browne, BEng Hons, CEng, FIStructE, MICE, MaPS, MConsE
A Colmer, LLB, Barrister at Law
His Honour Judge A F W Devlin
G Elliott, BSc Hons, MRICS
M E J Graham, BSc Hons, MSc, FCIOB, FICE
J R Hassard, MA, BEd, DASE, AdvCertEd, PQH
I D Jordan, MA Cantab, FCA
Mrs J Kelly, BA Hons, FCA
H J McKinney, BSc, Cert Ed (*Teacher Governor*)
J Parks, BSc, MAC, MANLP (*Parent Governor*)
H R H Wilson, BA Hons, FCA, FCG, CDir, FIoD, CMgr, FCMI, FInstLM, FRSA

***Headmaster*: Mr R M Robinson**, MBE, BSc, PGCE, MEd, PQH NI

Vice-Principals:
Mr W E Keown, MA, PGCE
Mr C G Oswald, BSc, PGCE, AdvCertEd, MEd

Senior Teachers:
Mr H J McKinney, BSc, CertEd
Mr H H Robinson, BSc, PGCE
Mrs K E Sheppard, MSc, BSc, PGCE (*Learning Support*)
Mrs S L Coetzee, BMus, PCGE, PGCE Careers
Mr C McIvor, MA, PGCE

Assistant Teachers:
Mr A Doherty, BMus Hons, PGCE
Mr C G A Farr, BA, DASE, AdvCertEd, MEd, CertPD
Mr D M McKee, BA, PGCE, DipModLit
Ms B M Coughlin, BEd, PGCertComp
Mrs G E Wilson, BMus, MTD
Mr D Styles, BA, PGCE, Dip IndStudies
Mr B F Robinson, BA, PGCE, MSc
Mr A W Templeton, BSc, PGCE
Mr N R Ashfield, BSc, PGCE
Mr S P Collier, BA, PGCE
Mrs R McNaught, MA, PGCE
Mr G Fry, BA, PGCE
Mr D Walker, BEd

Mr J McCurdy, BD, MA, PGCE
Mr M Cousins, BSc, PGCE
Mrs L Haughian, BA, PGCE
Mr M G Chalkley, BA, PGCE, MEd, PQH
Mr N McGarry, BA, PGCE
Mrs M Debbadi, BA, PGCE, MSc
Dr J A Breen, BSc, PGCE, PhD
Mr R D Hall, BSc, PGCE
Mrs E McIlvenny, BA, PGCE
Mrs K Magreehan, BA, PGCE
Ms L Anderson, BA, QTS
Mrs J Bailie, BA, PGCE
Mrs C A M Irwin, BSc, PGCE
Mr P D A Campbell, BEd
Mr T R Thompson, BSc, PGCE
Mr A McCrea, BEng, PGCE
Mrs W Pearson, BEd
Mr J H Rea, BSc, PGCE
Mrs K Murphy, BSc, PGCE
Mrs V Spottiswoode, BA, PGCE
Mr F N Mukula, BSc, AssDipTh, PGCE
Miss G Lamont, BEd, MSSc
Mr G P Young, BEd
Mr J P Cupitt, BSc, PGCE
Mrs W Shannon, BA, PGCE
Ms K M Marshall, MA, QTS
Mrs K McGarvey, MSci, PGCE
Mr J McNerlin, BSc, PGCE
Mr J Smyth, BSc, PGCE
Mrs J L Hempstead, MA, PGCE
Ms S Kirsch, BA, PGCE
Dr A Dunne, MA, PhD, PGCE
Mrs E McInerney, BSC, MEd
Mr M Brown, MA, PGCE
Ms L Donly, MA, PGCE
Ms D Chada, MA, PGCE
Ms P McCaul, MA, PGCE
Mrs E Reynolds, BSc, PGCE
Mr R McMaster, BSc, PGCE
Miss A Beckett, BSc, PGCE
Mr D Ledwich, BSc, PGCE
Ms E Anderson, BA, PGCE
Mr M Snodden, BA, PGCE
Miss V Wightman, BSc, PGCE

Visiting Music Teachers:
Mrs M Fenn (*Woodwind*)
Mrs J Leslie (*Brass and Piano*)
Mrs K Lowry (*Lower Strings*)
Mrs H Neale (*Upper Strings and Piano*)
Mr M Wilson (*Brass*)
Mrs L Lynch (*Percussion*)
Mr R Nellis (*Guitar*)

Bursar: K J Wilson, FCA
Headmaster's Secretary: Mrs L Crawford
Medical Officer: Dr G Millar, BMSc, MBChB, MRCGP
Matron: Mrs E M Hoey, SRN

Junior School:
Head: Miss A Brown, BA, PGCE, MEd, PQH
Mrs E M Gwynne, BEd
Mrs H M Jennings, BEd Hons, Dip PD
Mrs S Lismore, MEd, BEd Hons
Mr A Russell, BA Hons, PGCE
Mr M Boyd, BEd Hons
Mr A P Jemphrey, BEd, DASE
Mr S Bolingbroke, BA Hons, PGCE
Mr C Irvine, LLB, QTS
Mrs S Nickels, BSc, PGCE
Miss K Courtney, MA, PGCE
Mrs P McGarry, BEd
Mrs L M Leyland, MEd, BEd
Miss K Courtney, MA, PGCE
Miss L Reid, LLB, PGCE
Ms C Martin, BA, PGCE
Mrs S Smith, BSc, PGCE
Mr P Martin, MEd, BA Hons, PGCE

Canford School

Wimborne, Dorset BH21 3AD
Tel: 01202 841254
email: admissions@canford.com
website: www.canford.com
X/Twitter: @CanfordSchool
Facebook: @CanfordSchool
Instagram: @CanfordSchool
LinkedIn: /school/canford-school

Motto: *Nisi Dominus Frustra*

Set in over 250 acres of landscaped grounds in Dorset, Canford, founded in 1923, is among the top UK co-educational boarding schools for children aged 13–18. Its vision is for every pupil to be '*inspired to explore, empowered to express and challenged to excel*'. This is underpinned by our values of courageous attitude, humble ambition, gracious leadership and purposeful engagement which we seek to instil in every Canfordian. The school celebrated its centenary with the highest roll in its history at 663 pupils.

Academic. Examination results and higher education offers are consistently excellent. The school is a leader regionally in A Level and GCSE success. Over 95% of pupils move on to top universities each year and as a SAT testing centre, a number choose further study internationally, most recently gaining scholarships to top US colleges. Pupils also move on to degree apprenticeships, creative arts foundation courses and into the world of work. These outcomes are due to the dynamic, vibrant nature of the education we offer, where learning is cross-curricular. We are ambitious for our pupils, and Canfordians are encouraged to develop their interests both within and beyond the classroom within a supportive, inclusive environment.

Co-curricular. Pupils benefit from excellent sporting and arts facilities and a broad choice of activities. Learn Real Tennis on one of the few original school courts in the country, ascend Mont Blanc with the CCF Army corps, leap from great heights on the school climbing tower, take to the stage in dramatic or musical roles, or even indulge a passion for beekeeping.

The lively cultural enrichment programme includes visiting lecturers and inspirational trips designed to encourage pupils to debate and challenge perceived wisdom and broaden their intellectual and cultural horizons.

A Canford education is a great privilege and central to our ethos is making a difference, not only to our own lives but also to the lives of others. The school is one of only a handful of UK independents which fully sponsors an Academy school – The Bourne Academy in East Howe, one of the most deprived areas of the country. Over 8,800 hours annually are given by pupils and staff in Community Action projects, including working in primary schools, visiting the elderly, taking groups of inner-city pupils on trips to the beach and outdoor activity centres and helping maintain hedgerows and green spaces in the local area.

Each year, a group of Sixth Formers raise money themselves and visit orphanages, most recently in India, Ghana and Cambodia, to assist with building projects, and to teach and play with the children. This experience has such a profound effect that some pupils choose to return to further their work in the orphanages after they leave Canford.

As a parent commented: '*It is such a privilege for a child to be educated at Canford. The school has managed to instil a sense of appreciating that privilege without the arrogance that can accompany a private education at some other top boarding schools.*'

Facilities are first class, with a mix of Grade 1 listed buildings and modern teaching and boarding spaces. A sports centre, gym and swimming pool complex, an original Real Tennis court, a 9-hole golf course, school Boathouse, floodlit astros, netball and tennis courts and rugby and cricket pitches are among our sports facilities. Creative Arts are well served through a 300-seat theatre, dedicated Music School and Art Gallery.

A new library building opened in September 2021, offering over 300 metres of shelving and a multimedia area with access to multiple online resources. Breakout seminar spaces with video conferencing facilities allow for meetings both onsite and with schools and organisations across the globe through our Global Connections programme. A redesigned Assembly Hall to meet the school's growing numbers opened in 2021. Two new boys' boarding houses opened in 2023. The next project is the Sixth Form, with a careers and future life centre opening in the 2024/5 academic year and Upper Sixth house accommodation in 2026.

Awards

- Sunday Times Parent Power – Top Co-ed Independent School in South West for A Level Results (2023/2024)
- HIEDA Health and Wellbeing Champion for All Round Excellence winner (2023)
- BSA Boarding Excellence in Mental Health and Wellbeing winner (2023)
- School House Community Partnerships winner (2023)
- TES Boarding School of the Year finalist (2023)
- Talk Education Innovation in Creative Arts finalist (2023)
- ISP Drama/Creative Arts School of the Year finalist (2023)
- The Week Best of the Best for School Campus Setting finalist (2023)
- Tatler Public School of the Year (2019)
- ISP Boarding School of the Year (2018)

Number of Pupils. 663.

Admissions. At 13+ prospective pupils sit the ISEB pre-test at their schools, and, if successful, are invited to a pre-assessment day called 'The Headmaster's List'; a mix of individual and group interviews and written and online assessments.

At 16+, pupils sit Canford's own entrance tests and attend interviews at the school. They also have to meet the GCSE criteria for entry – currently 42 points, plus an 8 minimum at GCSE in the four subjects chosen to study at A Level.

Fees per term (2023–2024). Boarders £15,173, Day £11,497.

Scholarships & Bursaries. At 13+ there are Academic, Art, Design Technology, Drama, Music and Sport awards. At 16+ there are Academic, Music and co-curricular (Assyrian) Scholarships. Awards are between 5% and 20% of fees, and can be supplemented with a means-tested bursary if applicable.

Canford is committed to broadening access to the education it offers, with means-tested bursaries worth up to 110% of fees. The Martin Marriott Foundation, named after a former Headmaster, was established in 2017 with the specific purpose of raising funds to support bursary pupils. In the past year it has raised sufficient funds to sponsor two SpringBoard pupils at 13+ entry. Around 6% of our pupils receive means-tested support and 35 pupils are currently benefiting from 80% or more bursary funding.

Charitable status. Canford School is a Registered Charity, number 306315.

Chair of Governors: Lieutenant General Sir Gary Coward, KBE, CB

***Headmaster*: B A M Vessey**, BA, MA, MBA

Managing Director & Bursar: D Brook, OBE, FI MarEST, CEng, MA, BSc

---

The Cathedral School Llandaff
A Woodard School

Llandaff, Cardiff CF5 2YH

Tel: 029 2056 3179
email: registrar@cathedral-school.co.uk
website: www.cathedral-school.co.uk
X/Twitter: @cslcardiff
Facebook: @cslcardiff
Instagram: @cslcardiff

Set in 15 acres of parkland and playing fields within minutes of Cardiff city centre, The Cathedral School was founded in 1880. Acknowledged by Estyn as "excellent" in all five inspection areas (2018), there are currently nearly 800 pupils at the co-educational school between the ages of 3 and 18 years. The Cathedral School is a member of the Woodard Corporation and is underpinned by a strong Christian ethos. Pupils of all faiths and none are welcomed.

Track record for excellence. Excellent academic results and an exceptional co-curricular programme foster the growth of intellectual curiosity at The Cathedral School, which offers enormous breadth of opportunity. Named third best private school in the UK by A Level results this year by *The Telegraph*, The Cathedral School was also named best independent school in Wales in 2023 by the *Sunday Times*. High quality pastoral care and the School's caring Christian ethos give pupils the opportunity to reach their full potential in a vibrant, fun and supportive environment. Our beautiful campus and our links with Llandaff Cathedral inspire a sense of heritage, whilst our first-class curriculum enables our young people to look confidently to the future.

Nursery, Infants & Juniors. Strong academic skills and an appetite for learning are developed from a very young age. Nursery starts this journey of exploration and pupils are prepared for a seamless transition into Senior School, building confidence and a zest for life. The partnership between home and school starts on day one and the well-being and happiness of its pupils are the highest priority. Working closely with parents, the Nursery provides for the needs and interests of each child as an individual.

Beyond the classroom, there are extensive opportunities to enjoy competitive sport, especially team games which have busy and challenging fixture lists; opportunities to perform music at an excellent standard including opportunities for boys and girls to join choirs, orchestras, ensembles and to sing as choristers in Llandaff Cathedral; drama and dance thrive; there are opportunities to enjoy the outdoors, wildlife, outward bound activities; opportunities to get involved in action for good causes, including environmental awareness and charity work. There are also plenty of inter-house activities to get involved with which create a vibrant atmosphere. Nearly all pupils transfer into the Senior Section to continue their educational journey through to 18.

The Seniors. We pride ourselves upon being a strong learning community. It is important that everyone feels valued and that they have a meaningful part to play. From the initial Year 7 bonding weekend creating new friendships, to the caring house system, a mutually supportive environment means that every pupil's skill, interest, talent and potential are nurtured. Regularly recognised, whether by the education inspectorate Estyn, or in newspaper league tables, as one of the highest achieving schools in Wales academically, a great emphasis is also placed upon the co-curricular. For Years 10–13 the Duke of Edinburgh's Award (DofE) is hugely popular and delivered by our own dedicated staff. For Years 7–9, the Head's Award, underpins what we do, recognising character and breadth of achievement and celebrating our pupils' sense of motivation, organisation and willingness to be involved.

The quality of music at the Cathedral School is outstanding. It is our boys and girls who sing Llandaff Cathedral's choral services day by day, and the same excellence of musicianship rubs off in school within a wide range of genres, from the classical to rock and pop, chamber music to jazz. The School is equally proud of its sporting tradition. With a very high coach to player ratio and a busy, competitive fixture list, rugby, football, sevens, cricket, hockey, netball, cross-country and tennis all thrive here. Equally, participation in public speaking and debating competitions, challenging drama productions and various genres of fine art all add to the opportunities for all pupils to achieve standards which help them grow in confidence.

Sixth Form. We were incredibly proud of the outstanding results achieved by our A Level cohort this year. 98% of university applicants gained a place at their first-choice university, with five students taking up places at Oxford or Cambridge and seven going on to study medicine or veterinary medicine. Our students progress to the most selective and sought after universities, including Oxford, Cambridge, Imperial College London, Bristol, Cardiff, Bath, Leeds and Nottingham. With small classes, a full range of academic subjects and highly experienced staff with close university links, the Sixth Form culture is ambitious and supportive in equal measure. A Level Subjects: Art, Biology, Business, Chemistry, Computer Science, Design & Technology, Drama & Theatre, Economics, English Literature, French, Geography, German, Politics, History, Latin, Mathematics, Further Mathematics, Music, Physical Education, Physics, Psychology, Religious Studies, Spanish, and the Extended Project Qualification (EPQ).

Scholarships & Bursaries. Financial support via means-tested bursaries is available at Year 7 and 12 entry, with academic, sport and music scholarships available.

School Transport. School transport is available with bus routes from Brocastle, Caerphilly, Castleton, Miskin and Penarth. Working parents are helped by wraparound care from 8.00 am to 6.00 pm and a holiday club for our pupils and their siblings.

Fees per term (2023–2024). Years 12 & 13 £5,308, Years 7–11 £5,232, Years 5 & 6 £4,795, Years 3 & 4 £4,256, Reception, Years 1 & 2 £3,732 Nursery £3,205.

Charitable status. The Cathedral School Llandaff Limited is a Registered Charity, number 1103522. It exists to provide a high standard of education for girls and boys underpinned by a caring Christian ethos.

Chairman of the Council: M R Havard

Senior Management Team:

***Head*: Mrs Clare Sherwood**, MA

Acting Deputy Head Pastoral: Dr Stuart Bailey, MEng, PhD
Acting Deputy Head Academic: Mr Lawrence Moon, BA, MA

Head of Sixth Form: Mrs Catrin Ellis-Owen, BA
Head of Primary: Mrs Sally Walsh, BEd, NPQH
Assistant Head (*KS2*): Mr Chris Morgan, BA
Assistant Head (*EYFS & KS1*): Mrs Karen Price, BA, MA
Acting Assistant Head (*Safeguarding*): Mrs Sarah Howell-Jones, BA
Bursar: Mr Robert Leek

Charterhouse

Godalming, Surrey GU7 2DX
Tel: 01483 291501 (Admissions)
01483 291500 (General Enquiries)
email: admissions@charterhouse.org.uk
reception@charterhouse.org.uk
website: www.charterhouse.org.uk
X/Twitter: @CharterhouseSch
Facebook: @charterhousesch
Instagram: @charterhousesch
LinkedIn: /charterhouseschool

Motto: *Deo Dante Dedi*

Founded in 1611, Charterhouse is one of the UK's leading coeducational independent schools, with a prestigious global reputation.

Surrounded by a world of opportunity and connected by a feeling of belonging, each pupil is educated to embrace life's full potential, and empowered to carry this into their future.

A Charterhouse education prepares for both academic success as well as laying the foundations for future professional, social and personal fulfilment. Shared values are central to school life, enabling each pupil to be themselves. Everything at Charterhouse begins with kindness.

Campus. Charterhouse is set in a beautiful 250-acre campus located on the edge of the attractive market town of Godalming, in the south of England. Conveniently close to London and within 50 minutes of both Heathrow and Gatwick airports, the campus provides an environment that is safe, rich in heritage and an inspiring setting for the whole community to live and work together.

With 17 grass sports pitches, 3 full-sized Astroturf pitches, an athletics stadium, a sports centre, 24 tennis courts and a 9-hole golf course, not to mention beautiful lawns and gardens, the campus is one of the best, if not the best, in the UK. Combined with a 235-seat theatre and separate music performance and art display spaces, the School's setting encourages pupils to contribute, and provides a feeling of space in which pupils can discover new opportunities and explore their potential.

Pupil numbers. Charterhouse has 950 pupils – 557 in the Under School (Years 9–11) and 393 in the Sixth Form.

Academic. The School is academically ambitious for all pupils, with each strand of a Charterhouse education combining to ensure that they are 'future-ready' – fully prepared for the real world of tomorrow and equipped to seize future opportunities as they present themselves. The curriculum is all about choice for the individual and is firmly rooted in academic rigour, intellectual curiosity and independent learning, though it is the breadth of options available to each pupil at every stage of their education that make it stand out from the rest.

The curriculum includes an innovative course in Informatics (computational sciences) for all its youngest pupils, and having completed their GCSEs, pupils benefit from the dual offer available in the Sixth Form: A Levels with an Extended Project Qualification or the breadth of the IB Diploma Programme. A wonderful range of additional academic electives are also on offer, including the Charterhouse Entrepreneurship Diploma (accredited by the Institute of Enterprise and Entrepreneurs) and the Ivy House Leadership Award.

Co-curricular. From an outstanding and varied academic education to the raft of co-curricular options – opportunities abound at Charterhouse. Our co-curricular activities are an essential strand of a Charterhouse education, combining opportunities for leadership development, creativity, exercise and team work. They are also great fun.

The timetable enables all pupils to regularly enjoy a wide range of activities, making use of the School's impressive facilities. More than 80 different sports and activities are on offer, including outdoor pursuits, music, drama and other creative opportunities. All pupils are encouraged to develop existing interests to exciting levels and to take up new ones.

A great many clubs and societies are pupil-led and, alongside our sport and outdoor education programmes, offer real leadership opportunities and there are few limits to what can be pursued.

No two Charterhouse educations are the same: every pupil will have the chance to find their passions, often in the most unexpected of places, which many will carry with them into later life.

Future-ready. Charterhouse pupils are amongst the most future-ready young people in the UK. The School's FutureU activities are a central element of the Carthusian experience, aimed at ensuring pupils can proactively develop the transferable skills, professional knowledge, experiences and mindset required to thrive throughout their later lives. Every pupil accesses FutureU content throughout their time at School via a dedicated programme led by the School's Futures Team as well as elements being delivered within the academic curriculum, co-curricular and PSHE programmes. The new Business, Leadership and Entrepreneurship Hub is the centre of the Futures programme, providing spaces to facilitate collaboration and help pupils to develop the presentation and communications skills required in the world of work.

Houses. The intangible sense of community and togetherness are often the starting point when describing the Charterhouse experience. All pupils experience a true sense of collective belonging, independence and identity.

The House is the centre of every pupil's time at Charterhouse. Their House is a welcoming home from home, with the resident Head of House becoming their day-to-day mentor, with responsibility for looking after them throughout their time at the School.

The Heads of Houses are supported by a team of pastoral staff and tutors. Every pupil is matched with a tutor who takes a particular interest in their academic progress, co-curricular commitments and also guides them through the PSHE programme. Tutors meet with their tutees formally three times a week as well as meeting informally on the tutor's weekly duty evening in House.

The House Teams are supported by a 24-hour Health Centre and pupils also have access to support through the Wellbeing team, counsellors and chaplaincy.

Admissions. Inclusivity sits at the heart of life at Charterhouse and the School welcomes children from all educational and cultural backgrounds. Families are warmly invited to visit Charterhouse to meet the Head, Dr Alex Peterken, and his staff, and to experience a glimpse into School life.

The School welcomes boarders and day pupils at 13+ entry and 16+ entry. The Admissions process is academically selective by competitive assessment, interview and subject to a reference from a child's current school.

13+ entry. Children need to be registered by 1 October, when they are in their Year 6, prior to taking the ISEB pre-test. The School reserves 35% of places for assessment in Year 7. This is for children who have just missed out on places in Year 6 and also for those who registered too late to be assessed in Year 6.

Sixth Form. Charterhouse welcomes around 50 new pupils into the Sixth Form each year. Registrations open in the spring term of the year prior to entry.

Full details on the Admissions processes are available on the School website: www.charterhouse.org.uk/admissions.

Fees per term (2023–2024). Boarders: £15,845, Day Boarders: £12,789.

Scholarships and bursaries. Charterhouse offers a range of scholarship awards to pupils joining the School across academic study, music, sport, art, dance and drama. These awards are earned through open competition and are based on merit. They can be supported by bursaries, where there is a need.

Over the course of four centuries, the School's scholarship programme has flourished. Today, scholars continue to make significant contributions to the vibrant school community. Scholarships retain their immense worth, not only in enriching School life but also in showcasing an individual's talents when applying for universities and when stepping into the professional world.

All bursaries are means tested and are subject to funds being available. The award is reviewed annually for changes in parents' financial circumstances and may be adjusted as a result. Awards may cover up to 100% of the school fees.

Charitable status. Charterhouse School is a Registered Charity, number 312054.

Governing Body:
Mr John Olsen, BA (*Interim Chair*)
Mr Mark Bishop, BA, MA, PGCE, MBA (*Chair from 1 March 2024*)
Mr Kwaku Awuku-Asabre, BSc, DipLaw
Mr Durell Barnes, BA
Mr Mark Bishop, BA, MA, PGCE, MBA
Mrs Caroline Brown, MA, PgoL, LPC
Mr Stephen Browne, MA, MBA, PGCE, MCSI
Professor Vince Emery, PhD, FSB
Mrs Helen Goatley, BA LLB
Mr James Goldsmith, BSc, MRICS
The Very Revd Dianna Gwilliams, BA, MA
Dr Nihara Krause, BSc, MSc, PsychD, CPsychol, CSci
Mr David Macey, FCA
Mr Pete Malcolm
Mr Jeremy McIlroy, FCA, ATII
Mr Andrew Reid, MA, MBA, FCA
Mr David Royds, BSc
Mr Michael Walton, MA, MBA, FRICS

Clerk to the Governing Body: Mrs Alex Warburton, BA

Senior Leadership Team:
***Head*: Dr Alex Peterken**, BA, MA, EdD
Director of Finance and Operations: Mr Phil Grainge, MA, ACMA, CGMA
Senior Deputy Head: Mr Andrew Turner, BA, LLM
Deputy Head (*Academic*): Mr Duncan Byrne, MA, MEd, MBA
Deputy Head (*Pastoral*): Mr Edward Poynter, BA, MEd
Assistant Head (*Sixth Form & Futures*): Mr Simon Allen, MA, MEd
Assistant Head (*Pastoral*): Miss Leanne Rowlands, BSc, PCET
Assistant Head (*Under School*): Mr Sam Cooke, MA
Assistant Head (*Co-Curricular*): Mrs Jani Lambeth, BSc
Assistant Head (*Teaching & Learning*): Mrs Rebecca Markham-Jones, MA
Assistant Head (*Senior Tutor*): Mrs Louisa Wilkins, MA
Director of Safeguarding: Mrs Alex Colclough, BA
Senior Head of House (*Girls*): Mrs Rebecca Pugh, BA
Senior Head of House (*Boys*): Mr Sam James, MA
Director of Admissions: Mrs Iona Hutchinson, BA
Director of Foundation and External Relations: Mr Chris Hibbs, BA, MCIOF, FRSA
Director of Wellbeing & Inclusion: Mrs M Jolly, BA, MA
Director of International & Online Education: Ms Karen Davies, MA, MBA

Heads of Houses:
Bodeites: Mr David McCombes, MA
Chetwynd: Mrs Michelle Creer, BA
Daviesites: Mr Sam James, MA
Fletcherites: Mrs Catherine McDonald, MA
Girdlestoneites: Mr Charlie Sparrow, MA
Gownboys: Mr Andrew Marshall-Taylor, MA
Hodgsonites: Mr Ian Richards, MA
Lockites: Mr Andrew Hunt, MA
Northbrook: Mrs Rebecca Pugh, BA
Pageites: Mr Paul Martin, BSc, MA
Robinites: Mr Jason Ellis-Woodley, MSc
Saunderites: Mrs Suzanne Allen, MA
Sutton: Mrs Alice Evans, BA, MA
Verites: Mr Edward Reid, MMath
Weekites: Miss Georgia Gordon-Martin, BA

Cheadle Hulme School

Claremont Road, Cheadle Hulme, Cheadle, Cheshire SK8 6EF

Tel: 0161 488 3330
0161 488 3345 Senior Admissions Manager
email: admissions@chschool.co.uk
website: www.cheadlehulmeschool.co.uk
X/Twitter: @CheadleHulmeSch
Facebook: @CheadleHulmeSchooll
Instagram: @CheadleHulmeSchool
LinkedIn: /Cheadle-Hulme-School

Motto: '*In loco parentis*'

A challenging, dynamic and relevant education for every student lies at the heart of Cheadle Hulme School. Set in 83 acres of Cheshire countryside, near Manchester, the School offers an inspiring education that not only instils in its pupils a deep love of learning, but also the ability to adapt to change and think creatively and critically about the world around them. From Pre-School to Sixth Form, pupils learn together and independently and their broad timetables encompass all aspects of the wider CHS experience. Through an Academic, Active and Altruistic curriculum, underpinned by a strong set of values, each learner is provided with opportunities to help them make the very best of their journey.

Means-tested bursaries at Year 7 and Sixth Form entry are available and High Potential Programmes in Sport, Music and Art and Drama.

Number in School. 1,542 (818 boys 724 girls) of whom 309 are in the Junior School and 318 in the Sixth Form.

Location. The School which is about 10 miles south of Manchester, 3 miles from the Airport and 10 miles from the Derbyshire Hills consists of the original Victorian and many new buildings in its own 83 acres of open land.

Admission. There are four main points of entry to Cheadle Hulme School.

The Junior School takes pupils from 3 years of age into Pre-School and age 4 into Reception and there are a few places available to join at age 7 into Year 3.

In the Senior School the largest intake is at 11+ into Year 7. We also welcome academically-able students to join us in the Sixth Form at 16+. There may be opportunities to join CHS in other Year groups, subject to places being available.

The assessment process is competitive because many more children apply than places exist, is designed to determine that the child can profit from the type of education provided.

Organisation and Curriculum. For pastoral care and administrative purposes the School is divided into Sixth Form; Upper School (Years 9–11); Lower School (Years 7 and 8); Junior and Infant. The curriculum is kept as broad as possible to KS3 and students choose 9 subjects at GCSE. In Sixth Form, extension classes form part of the Year 13 curriculum in all subjects.

On leaving the majority of pupils progress to University.

Clubs and Societies. There are many co-curricular activities that students are encouraged to participate in and there are many annual dramatic and musical productions. Large numbers of pupils undertake the Duke of Edinburgh's Award Scheme which introduces them to a variety of new skills and expeditions to develop organisational and leadership abilities. Student leadership opportunities in numerous co-curricular clubs give older pupils the opportunity to gain experience and skills working with and coaching younger pupils.

Games and Physical Activities. There is a full range of the field and team games. Swimming is for all in the School's heated indoor pool. Students are encouraged to participate in all sports and to perform to the highest standard.

Fees per term (2023–2024). Subject to termly review: Pre-School £3,667; Junior School £3,515–£3,776; Senior School £4,864.

New parents, who are not already in membership of the Foundation Scheme, will automatically be enrolled in it. The aim of the scheme is to assist pupils to remain in the School in the face of financial difficulty following the incapacitation or the death of a parent. Benefits cannot be guaranteed, but in recent years no deserving case has been refused.

Bursaries. Bursaries are offered at 11+ based on academic merit and financial eligibility. A number of other Bursaries are available for entry to the Sixth Form on the same basis.

Charitable status. Cheadle Hulme School is a Registered Charity, number 1077017.

Governing Body:

Mrs Catherine Boyd (*Chair*)	Mr Stuart Abraham
	Ms Jodie Birkett
Mr Chris Roberts	Mrs Claire Thompson
Dr David Riley	Mr Martin Tyley
Mrs Joanne Squire	Mr Richard Oman
Mr Michael Bolingbroke	Mrs Belinda Matthews

Chief Operating Officer: Mr Warren James

***Head*: Mr Neil Smith**

Senior Deputy Head: Mr Lee Richardson
Deputy Head (*Pupil Progress and Welfare*): Mrs Susan James
Deputy Head (*Teaching and Curriculum*): Mr Nick Axon
Deputy Head (*Co-curricular and Partnerships*): Mrs Caroline Dunn
Head of Junior School: Mr Vincent Weightman
Head of Infants: Mrs Anneliese Pye

Heads of Departments:
Art & Design: Mr Adam Hayley
Biology: Mrs Melissa Bates
Careers: Mrs Clare Haffner
Chemistry: Mrs Rachel Gray
Classics: Ms Elizabeth Meehan
Director of Sport: Mr Giles Hegarty and Mrs Emma Bebbington
Drama: Mrs Louise Bailey
Economics Business Management: Mr Will Haines
English: Mrs Alex Vyce
Food & Nutrition: Mrs Kathryn Vlastos
Geography: Mrs Corrie Shallcross
History: Mr Matt Bell
Learning Support: Mrs Clare Hughes
Mathematics Mr Steven Norton
Modern Languages, French: Mr Oliver Abbott
Modern Languages, German: Mrs Emma Hayward
Modern Languages, Spanish: Mrs Jemma Becker
Music: Mr Andrew Pettit
Politics: Mr Peter Thorn
Physics: Mrs Jade Johnstone
Psychology: Mrs Kris Gilbertson
Religious Studies: Mrs Rebecca Lothian
Sports Science: Mr Andy Wrathall
Technology: Mr Luke Dunn

Senior Admissions Manager: Mrs Berni Pickford

Cheltenham Ladies' College

Bayshill Road, Cheltenham, Gloucestershire GL50 3EP

Tel: 01242 520691
email: enquiries@cheltladiescollege.org
website: www.cheltladiescollege.org
X/Twitter: @cheltladiescoll
Facebook: @CheltLadiesColl
Instagram: @cheltladiescoll
LinkedIn: /school/the-cheltenham-ladies-college

A College education gives pupils the best possible opportunities to achieve their potential in both the academic and personal spheres.

Academic excellence forms the basis of College life, but just as important is the formation of character. We recognise that a 21st-century education needs to inspire, prepare and equip young people to sustain a lifetime of independently sought learning, and to give them the flexibility and resourcefulness to flourish in our rapidly changing world.

We believe that the wellbeing of our students is as important as their academic outcomes; it has a direct bearing on the quality of the engagement and interactions, including their receptiveness as learners. Pupils are encouraged to be self-determining and caring towards others, building the foundations of character and self-sufficiency for success and fulfilment in the years beyond school.

Students are encouraged to embrace a broad range of co-curricular activities to suit their interests, from the sporting to the intellectual and cultural. A global outlook encourages them to play a part in the wider world, creating young women who value and contribute to their communities. Life at College promotes mutual respect, integrity and courage, while nurturing intellectual curiosity, creativity, confidence and an enduring love of learning.

Our pupils are at the heart of all College does; we are ambitious for their futures, collectively and individually.

Numbers. Approximately 192 day and 670 boarding.

Fees per term (2023–2024). Day: £9,900, Boarding: £15,050. New Entrants to Sixth Form: Day £11,300, Boarding £16,900. Some extras are charged, e.g. music, riding.

Admission. Entry at 11+, 13+ and 16+ via College's own examinations. An interview is also required for some entry points.

Academic. Our curriculum aims to instil in each student a curiosity about the world in which she lives and equip her with tools to question, reason and communicate articulately. Our Lower College curriculum provides exceptional breadth, building foundations for the GCSE years. Pupils study separate sciences, computing, humanities and a language acquisition course, as well as music, drama, art and design, and engineering, enterprise and technology. As a large school, College is able to offer extraordinary advantages in resources and choices. Pupils have a free choice of options for GCSE but are encouraged to maintain a broad curriculum, tailored to their individual strengths and interests. In Sixth Form, they have the option of taking A Levels or the International Baccalaureate (IB) Diploma Programme. Our exam results for GCSE, A Level and IB are consistently excellent, leading to College winning a number of awards for academic excellence over the last five years, including being named *South West Independent Secondary School of the Decade* by Parent Power, The Sunday Times Schools Guide 2021.

Pastoral care and wellbeing. As a large school, College is able to offer extraordinary advantages in resources and choices, but we are also divided into small groups too, through the three academic Divisions (LC, UC & SFC), Tutor groups and Houses. These create interlocking layers of pastoral care, which work alongside our whole-school Wellbeing Programme, to enable every pupil, the reserved as well as the extrovert, to find opportunities to lead a confident, fulfilled and enjoyable life at College. This network is backed up by an experienced and well-resourced Medical Centre based in College, an informed and skilled Catering Department and the support of the College Chaplain. Pastoral care isn't something that happens when things go wrong; it's a constant support network for every student throughout her time in College.

Buildings and grounds. College is set in a 36-acre dispersed estate in the centre of Cheltenham. The single teaching site is built in a Gothic revival style, complete with the stunning Princess Hall. It is complemented by the more recent Art and Technology block, housing College's Engineering, Enterprise and Technology Department, the Parabola Arts Centre, with a 325-seat theatre, and College's Health and Fitness Centre, which opened in 2018. This sports complex and the Day and Boarding Houses are located in nearby residential areas within a short walking distance of the main site.

Houses. There are six Junior Boarding Houses and three Junior Day Houses. All students then move into one of six Houses in Sixth Form, which is an excellent stepping stone to university life. Each House is run by a Housemistress, Deputy Housemistress and a team of staff, as well as a dedicated Chef. All Houses have dining rooms, common rooms, prep rooms, computer rooms, space for music practice and laundry facilities. Day girls are fully integrated into all College activities, regularly joining boarders on weekend trips and expeditions.

Music, drama and dance. More than 1,000 individual music lessons take place each week, which are scheduled around the curriculum to ensure girls do not miss academic lessons. There are also many choirs, orchestras and concerts throughout the year and at least five drama productions, with Sixth Form girls performing an open-air Shakespeare play in the Summer Term. Dance and gymnastics are also available and very popular.

Sport and co-curricular. At College, we are deeply committed to promoting the health, fitness and wellbeing of all pupils and to developing talent and a lifelong enthusiasm for sport and exercise, regardless of ability or expertise. The main sports are hockey, lacrosse, netball, swimming, athletics and tennis, but College aims to provide activities pupils enjoy and more than 30 different sports are offered. Alongside the existing 25 m swimming pool, tennis and netball facilities, and AstroTurf pitches, the new Health and Fitness Centre includes a second sports hall, multi-purpose studios, a dance studio, and a gym and fitness suite. More than 140 co-curricular opportunities are on offer, including astronomy, life drawing, hip hop dance, beginner's Russian, fencing, debating, journalism, yoga, ethical hacking, martial arts, Model UN, philosophy, engineering, Young Enterprise, medical and ethical club and international society.

Scholarships and bursaries. A number of Academic, Art, Music and Sport Scholarships and other awards are made annually for pupils of all ages.

Applications for bursaries are welcome from girls whose parents require financial assistance in order to help their daughter join College.

Beyond College. Our dedicated Professional Guidance Centre provides specialist careers and higher education advice to pupils throughout their time at College. Sixth Form tutors also provide significant support in this area. The majority of our girls gain places at Russell Group universities, including Oxbridge, or at top US universities to study a diverse range of subjects.

Former pupils (Guild). There are over 8,000 Guild members in more than 70 different countries across the world, and many are actively involved in helping current girls prepare for the future, including supporting networking dinners, interview preparation, hosting careers and networking events, and arranging speakers from universities and the professions.

Charitable status. Cheltenham Ladies' College is a Registered Charity, number 311722. It exists to provide a high standard of education for girls.

Chair of Council: Mr Nick Baird, MA, CMG, CVO

***Principal*: Ms Eve Jardine-Young**, MA

Vice-Principal: Mr Richard Dodds, BSc
Vice-Principal (*Academic*): Dr David Gamblin, MChem, MRSC

Chief Operating Officer: Mr Nigel Richards, BSc
Director of Admissions: Mr Richard Houchin, BA, MSc, PGCE, PGCER, ACEM
Director of External Relations: Mrs Dragana Hartley, BSc, FCIM, FRSA
Co-Curricular Director: Mr James Pothecary, MSci
Head of Pastoral Care: Miss Caroline Ralph, BEd
Head of Sixth Form College: Mr Josh Sumner, BA, MA
Head of Upper College: Dr Bethan Coupland, BA, MA
Head of Lower College: Ms Charlotte Woodhead, BEd Hons

Chetham's School of Music

Long Millgate, Manchester M3 1SB

Tel: 0161 834 9644
email: chets@chethams.com
website: www.chethams.com
X/Twitter: @Chethams
Facebook: @ChethamsSchoolofMusic
Instagram: @Chethams_school
LinkedIn: /chethams-school-of-music

Chetham's School of Music is a co-educational school for boarding and day students aged eight to eighteen. The School teaches a broad curriculum set within a framework of music. At the centre of every child's course is a 'musical core' of experiences rooted in a determination to educate the whole person. There are two Principals, one focusing on Academic and Pastoral Care, the other on Music. Originally founded in 1653, through the Will of Humphrey Chetham, as a Bluecoat orphanage, the School was reconstituted in 1969 as a specialist music school.

The School numbers 335 students and there are 200 boarders. Admission is by musical audition, and any orchestral instrument, keyboard, guitar, voice, Jazz or composition, may be studied. Each student studies academic courses which lead to GCSE and A Levels, and to university entrance and conservatoire. The School stands on the site of Manchester's original 12th century Manor House adjacent to the Cathedral and is housed partly in the fine 15th century College Buildings, and partly in the New School Building which houses all the instrumental, musical and academic teaching. The building also includes an Outreach Centre and two Concert Halls: the Carole Nash Hall and The Stoller Hall.

Music. Instrumental tuition is guided and monitored by Heads of Department in each specialism, they survey students' work, conduct internal examinations and arrange for external professionals to give masterclasses. Internationally renowned musicians hold residences at the School and there are three Music Courses throughout the year. The Joint Principal (Director of Music) has responsibility for the full-time Music Staff and for about 130 visiting tutors. All students receive three sessions of individual instrumental tuition each week. Practice is rigorously set and supervised. Academic Music is studied at GCSE and A Level.

Boarding. There are two boarding houses for girls and boys aged 13 to 18 and one for Juniors aged 8 to 13. Each House is run by Heads of House in residence, with resident assistants. All full-time teachers act as Tutors and are involved with pastoral care. In addition, there is a well-staffed Medical Centre with Nurses, School Doctor, Counselling, Psychotherapy, Hearing Nurse and Physiotherapy.

Recreation. Chetham's School of Music offers students a 'Health and Fitness' programme, which includes sports and fitness, conditioning and health, but also in respect of injury prevention as young musicians.

Chetham's as a specialist music school has student well-being at its heart. Our holistic approach to student well-being is delivered by personal trainers and specialist activity leaders throughout the day and evenings following individual, initial information-gathering and needs analysis. The School's medical staff, physiotherapist and caterers also contribute to the programme.

Applications, Visits. Entry is by audition only. Preliminary assessment auditions are held throughout the year, with final auditions in the Christmas and Spring terms.

The Prospectus and application forms are available on the School's website. Parents and prospective students are welcome to visit the School by arrangement with the Auditions Administrator.

Fees, Grants. All entrants from the United Kingdom are eligible for grants under the Department for Education's Music and Dance Scheme. Parental contributions are calculated according to means and parents on low incomes qualify automatically for full fee remission. The Bursar will be glad to advise about the scales.

Choristers. The School is a member of the Choir Schools' Association and Choristerships at Manchester Cathedral for day boys and girls are available under a separate scheme. Choristers' Fee: £10,764 pa (subject to Cathedral Bursaries).

Charitable status. Chetham's School of Music is a Registered Charity, number 526702. It exists to educate exceptionally gifted young musicians.

***Joint Principal*: Miss N Smith**, BA, NPQH
***Joint Principal*: T Redmond**, BA
Assistant Principal and Head of Sixth Form: Mrs J Harrison, MA
Assistant Principal and Head of Brass and Percussion: D Chatterton, BAMus Hons, GRNCM, Hon ARAM
Director of Finance: A Ross, MBA, ACMA, CGMA, CPFA, FCMI
Head of Middle School: A Henderson, BA
Head of Lower School: Mrs A Price, MA

Christ College
Brecon

Brecon, Powys LD3 8AF

Tel: 01874 615440
email: enquiries@christcollegebrecon.com
admissions@christcollegebrecon.com
website: www.christcollegebrecon.com
X/Twitter: @ChristColBrecon
Facebook: @christcolbrecon
Instagram: @christcolbrecon
LinkedIn: /company/Christ-College-Brecon

Motto: *Possunt quia posse videntur*

Founded by Henry VIII, 1541. Reconstituted by Act of Parliament, 1853.

Christ College, Brecon lies in a setting of outstanding natural beauty at the foot of the Brecon Beacons on the edge of the small market town of Brecon, two minutes' walk away on the opposite side of the river.

The school was founded by King Henry VIII in 1541 when he dissolved the Dominican Friary of St Nicholas. The 13th Century Chapel and Dining Hall are at the centre of school life and the school's mix of important, historic buildings and modern architecture represents the continuity of education at the school.

In 2017, when the school was last inspected by Estyn it was rated 'Excellent'.

Organisation. Christ College has on average 400 pupils from 4–18 divided into three

sections – Prep (4–13), Senior (13–16) and Sixth Form (16–18).

Pupils aged 4–11 are based in St Nicholas House and are mainly day pupils. 11–13 year old pupils are based in Alway House which is for both day and boarding pupils.

There are two senior girls boarding houses (de Winton & Donaldson's) and two senior boys boarding houses (Orchard & School House) along with a Middle School Hub for 13–16 year old day pupils and the Senior Hub for Sixth Form day pupils.

Pupils can choose to be day pupils, flexi boarders, weekly boarders or full boarders. We run a comprehensive daily minibus service for pupils who wish to travel in each day.

Chapel. Chapel services are conducted in accordance with the liturgy of the Anglican church, but entrance to Christ College is open to boys and girls of all faiths. The ownership of Chapel by the boys and girls, demonstrated through their participation in services and their singing both as a congregation and by being members of the Chapel Choir is a feature of the school. Pupils are given the option to prepare for Confirmation by the School's Chaplain annually.

Curriculum. Pupils follow a balanced, varied curriculum during the Key Stage 3 years (Years 7–9). GCSE options are chosen at the end of Year 9 with most pupils opting to take 10 subjects including both core and specialist options. Our Sixth Form curriculum is a hybrid of traditional linear A-Level specifications, BTEC courses (Sport, Performing Arts & IT) and subjects which adopt a modular structure (notably Maths and each of the separate Science subjects). The EPQ is available to all pupils in the Sixth Form and is an optional qualification that can be pursued alongside A-Level courses.

Games. The main school games are Rugby, Cricket, Hockey and Netball. In addition, there are many other games on offer including tennis, basketball, swimming and golf at nearby Cradoc Golf Club.

Music. The Chapel Choir enjoys an excellent reputation. As befits a school in Wales, singing at all school occasions is committed and energetic. The school has a Chamber Choir, plus multiple wind, brass and string ensembles and its pupils play a prominent role in the South Powys Youth Orchestra. There are many other opportunities to play in ensemble groups throughout the school. Individual instrumental and singing lessons are delivered by visiting musicians.

Activities. In addition to sporting pastimes, a wide range of activities are available to pupils as part of the 2nd curriculum as well as opportunities to participate in the Duke of Edinburgh's Award scheme and CCF.

Overseas Travel. There are many opportunities to travel overseas with exchanges to Japan, sports tours, ski trips and trips associated with academic study.

Entrance. Pupils are admitted to the prep school between the ages of 4–10 years.

Pupils enter the school aged 11, 13 or 16. Pupils are admitted to other year groups after discussion with the Head and Deputy Head Academic.

Pupils entering at 11 and 13 are expected to take entrance tests in Mathematics and English. A school report is requested.

Pupils entering at 16 are expected to gain 6 GCSEs at Level 5 (grade C) or better. Pupils should ideally have at least a Level 6 (grade B) in GCSE in the subjects they wish to take at A Level. A report from the previous school is also requested.

Term of Entry. Pupils are accepted in the Michaelmas, Lent and Summer terms.

Scholarships. Scholarships are available for entry at age 11, 13 and 16 and hold a maximum value of up to 20%.

Scholarships available: All-rounder, Academic, Sport, Art, Music, Drama, Outdoor Adventure, Science.

Process: Interview and Assessment.

Bursaries are available from Year 7 onwards and are subject to a means test.

10% bursaries are available each year for the children of serving members of the Armed Forces in receipt of CEA (available from Year 9 onwards).

Fees per term (2023–2024). Years 1–6: Day from £3,304, Boarding (for Years 5 & 6) from £6,329; Years 7–11: Day from £6,139, Boarding from £9,973; Years 12–13: Day £7,335, Boarding £13,382.

Charitable status. Christ College, Brecon is a Registered Charity, number 525744. Its aims and objectives are to provide a fully rounded education for boys and girls between the ages of 4 and 18.

Chair of Governors: Professor M C R Davies, BSc Eng
***Head*: Mr Gareth Pearson**, BEng

Deputy Head (*Academic*): Mr H G Mackridge, MA
Deputy Head (*Pastoral*): Mr S D Hill, BA Hons
Bursar: Mr M Allen, MA
Head of Admissions: Mrs M L Stephens
Development Director: Mr G M Thomas, MBE, BSc

Churcher's College

Ramshill, Petersfield, Hampshire GU31 4AS
Tel: 01730 263033
email: admissions@churcherscollege.com
website: www.churcherscollege.com
X/Twitter: @churchers1722
Facebook: @churchers1722
Instagram: @Churchers1722
LinkedIn: /churcher's-college

Motto: *Limitless Potential*

Churcher's College is an independent day school for girls and boys offering Nursery, Junior, Senior and Sixth Form education. With 1,050 pupils at the Senior School and 250 pupils at the Junior School (excluding the Nursery) of approximately equal numbers of boys and girls aged 3 to 18 years old, Churcher's College enjoys recognition as one of the most accomplished independent, co-educational day schools in the country.

The school is hosted on two campus sites in Hampshire enabling the Junior School and Nursery pupils to flourish in their own beautiful grounds in Liphook, whilst maintaining close links with the Senior School and Sixth Form located in nearby Petersfield. Both sites offer on-site playing fields and unrivalled facilities, providing the comfort and opportunities of an open, healthy environment.

Senior School Admissions. We welcome girls and boys at 11+ (Year 7) and 16+ (Sixth Form) at the Senior School. Entry at other points may be possible, depending on availability of places.

Our Admissions Team are always happy to help, so for any enquiries please contact admissions@churcherscollege.com.

Years 1–5: From the 11+ entry, pupils follow an academic programme comprising of Mathematics, English, Physics, Chemistry, Biology, Latin, Classical Civilisation, Geography, Religion & Philosophy, Music, Art & Design, Design & Technology, Computer Science, Drama and Sport Science. In the First Year pupils study Spanish alongside their personal choice between French and German. In the Second Year an additional Modern European language (German or Spanish) is added to the programme. All pupils follow a broad curriculum and are not asked to specialise until they reach GCSE.

All pupils follow GCSE courses in Mathematics, English Language and Literature, a Modern Language, a Humanity and at least two additional optional subjects. All pupils begin the AQA GCSE 'Trilogy' course in the third year, which leads to two GCSE grades, but at the end of the Third Year, some pupils are offered the opportunity to transfer onto the Separate Sciences course, based on aptitude and ability.

Pupils are tested and examined regularly with formal assessment procedures each half term and each end of term.

The Sixth Form. The Sixth Form offers a wide variety of strong, widely-recognised A Level courses. The Churcher's Sixth Form curriculum allows you to build a portfolio of excellence, demonstrating to university admissions tutors and employers a depth and breadth of understanding in a wide range of fields.

Although precise programmes of study vary, based on the individual, most students will study three A Level qualifications, with Further Maths being taken as an additional fourth. In addition to this, a number of the most academically-inquisitive pupils will complete the Extended Project Qualification.

A Level course subjects include: Ancient History, Art, Biology, Business, Chemistry, Computing, Design & Technology, Drama, Economics, English Literature, French, Geography, German, History, Latin, Mathematics, Further Mathematics, Music, including the Advanced Musicians Course, Physics, Politics, Psychology, Religion & Philosophy, Spanish, Sports Science.

There is a fully equipped Sixth Form Centre, for both study and recreation, a floor of the Library dedicated to Sixth Form private study, an excellent Careers Library and full-time Careers Officer and specialist Sixth Form teaching rooms and ICT facilities.

Facilities. Churcher's academic facilities include a Music School and auditorium, state-of-the-art D&T workshops, Computing suites, Drama studios, Art & Design studios and an impressive Science block. Sports facilities include a 25-metre swimming pool, tennis courts, netball courts, rugby pitches, all-weather hockey pitches, cricket squares, fitness suite, sports hall and gymnasium (including a climbing wall).

Games and Other Activities. The major sports played are Rugby, Hockey, Netball and Cricket. Pupils also have the opportunity to enjoy Water Polo, Dance, Swimming, Badminton, Volleyball, Tennis, Strength & Conditioning, Athletics, Aerobics and Cross-country, and many more. The School has a strong CCF unit with Army, Air Force and Naval Sections, and a Duke of Edinburgh's Award programme (Bronze, Silver and Gold). Other activities include Mountain Biking,

Canoeing, Gliding, Climbing, Adventurous Training, Tycoon Enterprise Competitions, Karate, Fencing, Football, Sailing, Table Tennis, Basketball, Chess, MUN, Drama, Textiles, Pottery and Photography.

Music and drama are very strong in the school with highly acclaimed school productions and music performances plus opportunity to work on lighting and sound backstage. The school also has a significant range of orchestras, rock, jazz and wind bands, choirs and ensembles.

Careers. An extensive Careers & Higher Education Programme, delivered by a dedicated team, ensures all pupils get excellent advice and guidance. Highlights include an annual Careers Convention, specialised careers testing and talks from guest speakers from different industries, in addition to an Oxbridge, Medics, and full UCAS programme available to all. Advice on apprenticeships, plus talks, tutorials and various external conventions and exhibitions ensure a comprehensive programme. CV writing, interview practice and more are also delivered.

Parents' Association. A thriving Parents' Association is at the heart of the school community, contributing to an effective partnership between home and school, raising funds for various initiatives, events or needed school items.

Fees per term (2023–2024). Senior School & Sixth Form: £6,245.

Charitable status. Churcher's College is a Registered Charity, number 1173833, and is a Charitable Company Limited by Guarantee, registered in England and Wales, company number 10813349.

Governing Body:
Chair: Charles Strick, BSc MechEng, MBA, CEng
Vice-Chair: Jo Bloomer, LLB Hons
Co-Opted Governors:
Stephen Barrett
Sinclair Beecham
Cathryn J D Bush, MBSS, BSc, DFFP, MRCGP
John Franklin, MA, MEd Admin
Tarquin Henderson
Cindy Herraman-Stowers
Robert Ingram, MA
Chloe Jay, BA GDL
Walter A Jones, MA
Peter Lawrence, BA Hons
Mark Leigh, BA Hons Econ, FCA
Robert May, MIOD
Diane Moses, FCA
Parents' Association Nom, Junior School: Richard Oates, BA Hons, CFA
Parents' Association Nom, Senior School: Matthew Steven, MEng

Clerk to the Governors: N Medley, MPhys

***Headmaster*: Simon H L Williams**, BSc, MA

Deputy Heads:
Sarah M J Dixon, BSc (*Staff and Co-curricular*)
Chris D P Jones, MA (*Pastoral*)
Ian G Knowles, BSc (*Academic*)

Head of Sixth Form: William Baker, BA Lancaster, MSc Portsmouth, FRSA

Senior Teachers:
Gary M Glasspool, BSc St Andrew's, MEd Bristol, EdD Bristol (*Teaching & Learning*)
Suzanne Herrington, BA Staffordshire (*Pastoral*)
Richard M Hoe, BSc Liverpool (*Well-being, Inclusion and Safeguarding*)
Louisa J A Taylor, BSc Bath (*Co-ordinator of Community Partnerships and Outreach*)

Director of Studies: Sarah L Cockerill, BSc Exeter
Academic Registrar: I M Crossman, BA Lancaster
To see the full list of staff, please visit our website: www.churcherscollege.com.

City of London Freemen's School

Ashtead Park, Ashtead, Surrey KT21 1ET
Tel: 01372 822400
email: admissions@freemens.org
website: www.freemens.org
X/Twitter: @HelloFreemens
Facebook: @HelloFreemens
Instagram: @hellofreemens

Motto: *Domine dirige nos*

An independent co-educational day and boarding school for children aged 7 to 18.

Freemen's is a school where open-hearted children are happy to be; where academic excellence is an expectation but is rooted in a supportive environment where every child matters. We place particular emphasis on the individual and their needs, and in providing the opportunities to identify and develop their skills to flourish throughout their time at Freemen's, and beyond.

Our mission is to learn, lead and make a difference. This ethos is felt throughout the School, from Juniors to Seniors and beyond into Sixth Form. We are fortunate to have a wonderful sense of community in our beautiful patch of Surrey parkland, with a diverse and welcoming cohort of students; expert, trailblazing teaching staff; an active and engaged parent body and a wealth of friends and supporters in the local area, the City of London and as part of our burgeoning alumni community.

Our founding ethos was all about community and that remains at the forefront of our thinking almost 170 years later. City of London Freemen's School was set up to look after the orphaned children of Freemen of the City. The school was founded in Brixton in 1854 to educate boys and girls; we have always been co-educational – it is an essential part of our character, even before that was commonplace. As well as committing right from our foundation to a charitable, co-ed, broad education, we have also continuously admitted boarders alongside our day pupils, and they remain an integral part of what makes Freemen's the community it is.

In 1926, the City of London Corporation moved the school to Ashtead Park. We really do enjoy the best of locations – a leafy Surrey Hills site, but wholeheartedly connected to the Square Mile and only a short train journey into Waterloo or Victoria. We are located between Epsom and Leatherhead with easy access to Heathrow and Gatwick – both of which are only 22 miles away – via the M25. Since then, our site has expanded to accommodate numbers and to support our children's development in excellent facilities. You can be sure that the interests of the children will always come first here.

School buildings include a central Georgian Mansion, a floodlit all-weather pitch, Sports Hall, an Art and Design Centre, a Science and Technology Centre and a Studio Theatre. A state-of-the-art music school – including a Steinway-D concert grand piano – and a co-educational boarding house for 60 pupils were completed and opened in 2014. An award-winning swimming pool was opened in 2017 and an ambitious refurbishment project on the Main House building, which houses a state-of-the-art Sixth Form Centre, was completed in 2021.

Junior School. The Junior School provides 20 classrooms for up to 400 pupils. and is fully integrated within the framework and policies of the whole school. Its facilities include specialist rooms for Art and Design, Science and STEM learning, as well as an Assembly Hall and Library. See Junior School entry in IAPS section.

Organisation and entry. Freemen's is divided into two sections but is administered as a single unit. The Junior School has its own specially trained staff and its own self-contained building, but otherwise all staff teach throughout the school. Pupils seeking entry to the Junior School sit the school's own entrance assessments at 7+ (held in December). Pupils seeking entry to the Senior School take the school's own entrance assessments at 11+ and 13+ (held in November). Freemen's Junior School pupils may expect to transfer directly to the Senior School at 11+ without sitting further examinations.

Sixth Form applicants do not need to sit entrance assessments if they are sitting 7 or more GCSEs (including GCSE English). Entry requirements for Sixth Form include:

- a minimum Grade 7 in seven subjects and specific requirements in the subjects you wish to study at A Level
- completion of a Sixth Form Questionnaire after applying
- a one-to-one interview with a member of the Sixth Form team
- a confidential report from pupil's current school.

Curriculum. The first four years (Years 3 to 6) are largely taught by class teachers following the broad outlines of the National Curriculum. Up to the age of about 14, all pupils have substantially the same curriculum which comprises English, French/German/Spanish, Mathematics, Physics, Chemistry, Biology, History, Geography, Religious Education, Latin, Design Technology, Computing, Food Technology, Art, Music, PE and Games

Thereafter, apart from a common core of English, French or German or Spanish, Mathematics and the three separate Sciences, GCSEs can be selected from subjects including Art and Design, Business Studies, Computer Science, Design Technology, Drama, Food Preparation and Nutrition, French, Geography, German, History, Latin, Music, Philosophy, Ethics and Religion and Spanish, so that most pupils will take 10 subjects. Physical Education and Personal, Social and Health Education are included in the curriculum at all levels and all age groups have an Enrichment afternoon.

Sixth Form courses include the following: Art, Biology, Business, Chemistry, Classical Civilisation, Computer Science, Design and Technology, Drama, Economics, English Literature, French, Further Mathematics, Geography, German, Politics, History, Latin, Mathematics, Music, Philosophy Ethics and Religion, Physics, Psychology, Spanish and Sport Studies.

The Sixth Form curriculum is designed to ensure that Freemen's students are well prepared for university entry and future employment. The range of subjects available aims to allow all potential Sixth Formers to follow a programme that meets their interests, abilities and career aspirations. For each Sixth Form student, three pathways are offered through the curriculum:

- Pathway 1: Four A levels to include Mathematics and Further Mathematics
- Pathway 2: Three A Levels + EPQ + Free Minds
- Pathway 3: Three A levels + Free Minds.

This is complemented by enrichment mornings, a varied programme of games afternoons, careers guidance and personal, social and health education.

The School has an excellent academic record. Recent GCSE results have been excellent, with 39% of students achieving the highest grade (9) and 84% of examinations awarded grades A*/A or equivalent (7–9).

A Level results have been equally impressive with 23% of grades at the highest level (A*) and 87% of examinations awarded A*–B grades. Nearly all leavers go on to degree courses at universities or other higher education institutes. 2023 saw 64% of students receive an offer at a Russell Group university and 93% of students were placed at their university of choice.

Games. Each pupil is treated as an individual and we give them the opportunity to forge their own path of physical activity to suit them. To do this we ensure our programme is broad, to enable pupils to try numerous sports, and give our pupils a choice of activity in Games for their latter years at the school, making our programme more relevant to each of our pupils.

Freemen's sports programme for Junior and Senior pupils includes football, rugby, netball, hockey, cricket, athletics, tennis, boys hockey and girls' touch rugby.

Pupils in Year 11 to Year 13 are given the option of selecting from 14 different activities in Games each term. There are competitive fixtures in fencing, football, netball, rugby, swimming, squash, tennis, athletics, cricket, cross country, fencing, indoor hockey and rugby sevens.

Co-curricular. The co-curricular programme offers a huge choice of activities and covers everything from performing arts and sport to the enrichment, elective activities and House programmes.

The Duke of Edinburgh's Award is a very popular option in the Senior School. Students may also participate in the Army or RAF Sections of the Combined Cadet Force (CCF).

All pupils belong to one of three Houses in which they will take part in a range of competitions including music, drama, sport as well as cookery, photography, debating and more. Pupils are based in form groups aligned with their house as they move up through the key stages. The house system also gives pupils leadership opportunities throughout each key stage.

Fees per term (2023–2024). Junior School: £5,856–£6,505 (day); Senior School: £7,861 (day), £12,568 (weekly boarding), £13,958 (full boarding); Sixth Form: £8,214 (day), £12,921 (weekly boarding), £14,311 (full boarding). Instrumental Music lessons: £288 per term. School lunches: £258 (day pupils) per term.

Scholarships and bursaries. Scholarships are awarded in recognition of excellence, achievement and potential in academic study or music. They carry considerable prestige for the award holder but are of limited financial value (up to 5% discount of the fees). Academic Scholarships and Music Scholarships are available for entry into Year 7, Year 9 and Year 12 to internal and external pupils. Bursaries are offered based on the amount of need required and the child's performance in our entrance assessments. The level of bursary will depend on each family's circumstances, but transformational bursaries are available and could be up to 110% of the school fees. All applications are strictly confidential and will be reviewed on a case-by-case basis.

Board of Governors:
Deputy Philip Woodhouse (*Chairman*)
Jamel Banda (*Deputy Chairman*)
Deputy Graham Packham
Alderman Robert Howard
Alderman Tim Levene (*ex-officio*)
Alderman Christopher Makin
Councillor Chris Townsend
Roy Anklesaria
John Foley
Nicholas Goddard
Michael Hudson
Andrew McMillan
Clare Verga
Lady Gillian Yarrow
Support Officer: Melanie Peel

Executive Leadership Team:
***Headmaster*: Mr Roland Martin**
Deputy Head: Mr Stuart Bachelor
Academic Deputy Head: Mr Paul Bridges
Bursar: Mrs Oonagh O'Mahoney

Senior Leadership Team:
Assistant Head (*Head of Sixth Form*): Mrs Sarah Stewart
Assistant Head (*Head of Upper School*): Ms Sophie Blair
Assistant Head (*Head of Junior School*): Mr Matthew Robinson
Assistant Head (*Head of Boarding*): Mr Alan Auld
Assistant Head (*Learning, Teaching and Innovation*): Mr James Felgate
Assistant Head (*Co-curricular*): Mr Jamie Shore-Nye
Assistant Head (*Staff and Staff Development*): Mrs Emma Smith
Director of External Relations: Mr Jason Harrison-Miles
Director of HR: Mrs Anna Atkins
Director of Learning Support: Mrs Sarah Bailey
Director of Operations: Mr Ed Kennedy

Boarding:
Deputy Houseparent: Miss Georgina Farrington
Deputy Houseparent: Mrs Katie Moilliet

Heads of Year:
Assistant Head of Upper School: Mrs Joanne McCullagh [maternity cover]
Head of Year 9: Mr Tim Deakin
Head of Year 10: Dr Beatrice Blucke
Head of Year 11: Mr Peter McKee
Head of Year 12: Mr Daniel Moran
Head of Year 13: Mrs Nicola Bax

Heads of Department:
Art: Mrs Rebecca Houseman [maternity cover]
Biology: Mr John Graham
Business and Economics: Mrs Justine Marvin
Chemistry: Dr Julia Lister
Classics: Mrs Romer Attenborough
Computer Science: Mrs Ghadah Ibrahim
Drama: Mr Jeremy Colton (*Director of Drama*)
English: Mr James Smith
Examinations: Mrs Sufiah Wallace
Food Preparation and Nutrition: Mrs Tina Judge
Future Pathways: Mrs Lucy Ryckeart
Geography: Mrs Ofelia Bueno-Lopez
History and Politics: Mr Andrew Weston
Languages: Alicia Palomo Lopez
Mathematics: Mrs Marie Cast
Music: Mr Anthony Merryweather (*Director of Music*)
Philosophy and Religion: Mr Tim Wright
Physics: Mr James Hallam
PSHE: Mrs Philippa Whiteley
Psychology: Miss Joanna Vinall
Spanish: Mrs Christina Salisbury
Sport: Mr Edward Smith (*Director of Sport*)
Design and Technology: Mr Steve Sarsfield

Junior School:
Assistant Head of Junior School: Mrs Louise Jowitt
Head of Year 3 (*Form 1*): Mrs Emma Smith
Head of Year 4 (*L2*): Mrs Vanessa Symonds
Head of Year 5 (*U2*): Mrs Janet Wilby-King
Head of Year 6 (*L3*): Mrs Sarah Gillespie
Head of Year 7 (*U3*): Mr Haydon Jones
Head of Year 8 (*L4*): Mrs Fiona Moncur

Duke of Edinburgh's Award:
DofE Senior Coordinator: Revd Jon Prior

Combined Cadet Force:
CCF Contingent Commander: Mr Alexander Truelove

Medical Centre:
School Nurse Managers: Ms Kate Lynch; Mrs Elizabeth Holmden
School Nurses: Mrs Diana Carter; Mrs Priscilla Mills

Professional Services Staff:
Executive Assistant to the Headmaster: Mrs Tracie Bruce
Executive Assistant to the COO: Mrs Katie Reeves
Safeguarding Coordinator: Mr Nigel Legg
HR Officer: Miss Helen Lambert
HR Administrator: Mrs Gillian Anklesaria
Finance Manager: Mrs Angela Bulkeley
Finance Officers: Mrs Debra Widmer; Mrs Jane Arnett; Mrs Natalia Schutte; Mrs Suzanne Wilding
Head of Admissions: Ms Debbie Bellenger
Head of Marketing and Communications: Mrs Nicola Warren

Marketing and Communications Officer: Ms Gemma Roberts
Digital Marketing Officer: Ms Katherine Alano
Admissions Officer: Mrs Cheryl Turnbull
Development Officer: Mrs Sabina Lillyman
Office Manager: Ms Sonia Oke
SLT Secretary: Mrs Julia Donovan
Senior School Receptionist and Administrator: Mrs Karen Shelton
PA to Head of Junior School: Mrs Kathy Hurst
Junior School Administrator: Mrs Michelle Grasty
Sports Administrator: Mrs Tracey Clarke
Music Administrator: Mrs Patricia Barrie
Librarians: Mrs Ashley Bate; Ms Charlotte Bellsham-Revell
Director of Digital Services: Mr Paul Hykin
Data Manager: Mr Anthony Richmond
Technology, Enhanced Learning and Training Manager: Mr Matt Skilton
Head of Operations: Mr Edward Kennedy
Head of Grounds and Gardens: Mr Gary Marshall
Facilities Manager: Mr Gyorgy Simon
Chaplain: Rev Jonathan Prior

Technicians:
Mrs Joanna Wojcik (*Senior Technician, Physics*)
Mrs Mary Marrett (*Senior Technician, Biology and Chemistry*)
Mrs Christine Foster (*Science, Junior School*)
Mr Lewis Grover (*Biology and Physics*)
Mrs Emma Eshelby (*Chemistry*)
Ms Emma Hughes-Phillips (*Art and Design*)
Mr Daniel Barter (*Art and Design*)
Mr Chris Ruby (*Facilities*)
Mr David Holloway (*Technologies*)
Mrs Eileen Enright (*Food Technology*)

City of London School

Queen Victoria Street, London EC4V 3AL
Tel: 020 3680 6300
email: admissions@cityoflondonschool.org.uk
reception@cityoflondonschool.org.uk
website: www.cityoflondonschool.org.uk
X/Twitter: @CityofLdnSchool
Facebook: @CityofLondonSchool

City of London School understands that for pupils to thrive, they must be happy. It is why we cherish individuality, shun stereotypes, and encourage every pupil to be the very best version of themselves. With a vibrant, diverse, multicultural city on our doorstep, we draw strength from difference, recognising that diverse perspectives can help answer big questions.

We aspire to be a school that fully prepares respectful, optimistic and inquisitive boys for the rapidly changing demands of the twenty-first century. We aim always to provide an education in the broadest sense, combining academic excellence with exceptional pastoral care, framed by an outward-looking and forward-thinking approach. We also strive to make that education available to as many talented boys as possible, including through transformational bursaries for those who may not otherwise be able to afford the fees.

We occupy a unique river side location in the heart of the capital. We trace our origins to a bequest left by John Carpenter (Town Clerk of the City of London) in 1442 for the education of 'four poor boys'. The City of London Corporation was authorised by an Act of Parliament in 1834 to use this and other endowments to establish and maintain a School for boys. The current School lies in the heart of the City next to the Millennium Bridge, with St Paul's Cathedral to the north and the Globe Theatre and Tate Modern across the Thames to the south. A new Library was added in 2016 and a new on-site fitness centre was inaugurated in 2022. Our sibling schools, City of London School for Girls (CLSG) and City Junior School are located a short walk away.

Admissions. Pupils are admitted aged 10, 11 and 13 (as on 1 September of year of entry), on the results of the School's own entrance examinations held each year. Note that pupils applying for entry at age 13 are examined when they are in Year 6. Those admitted at 16 into the Sixth Form are selected by test and interview in the previous November. Applicants must register for examinations using the School's online system.

Fees per term (2023–2024). £7,545.

Scholarships. Academic, Music and Sports Scholarships are awarded annually.

Bursaries. We offer transformational bursaries, up to the value of full fees, to assist families of academically very bright pupils, who otherwise could not ccess private education. Candidates for entry to the School may also apply to be a chorister in the Choir of Her Majesty's Chapel Royal, St James's Palace for which they will receive a Choral Bursary. Potential choristers may also take voice auditions and academic tests in Year 4; the School also has a number of choristers who sing in the Temple Church Choir.

Curriculum. All pupils follow the same broad and engaging curriculum up to and including the Third Form (Year 9). In the Third Form pupils spend eight afternoons throughout the year exploring the world around them on educational visits to institutions and places of interest in and around the City. Latin, French and Mandarin are started by all in the First Form. Choices are made from Latin, Latin/Greek, Classical Civilisation, Spanish, German or Mandarin, along with at least one from Music, Drama, Art or an exciting bespoke course on Design, Computing & Robotics. Fourth and Fifth Form pupils take a core of English, Mathematics, three Sciences, at least one Modern Foreign Language (which can include Russian), at least one humanity (History, Geography, R&P, Classical Civilisation) and choose two other subjects from a wide range of subjects available for study to GCSE/IGCSE. In the Sixth Form, pupils study either four A level subjects, or three and an EPQ (Extended Project Qualification). Virtually all pupils leaving the Sixth Form proceed to their first or second choice of Russell Group University, with a large number applying successfully overseas.

Games. Our 20 acres of playing fields, at Grove Park in south-east London, offer excellent facilities for football, cricket, athletics, and tennis. Sporting facilities on the School site include a newly opened fitness and conditioning suite, an astroturf pitch, sports hall, a gymnasium and a 25-metre swimming pool.

School societies. There is a large number of School clubs and societies, catering for a very wide range of interests, and a Freshers' Fair is held early each year to allow societies to promote themselves. Every opportunity is taken to benefit from the School's central position by participation in the cultural and educational life of London, and of the City in particular. We have a strong musical tradition; tuition is available in a large range of instruments (all First Form (Year 7) pupils are given the opportunity to be taught a musical instrument as part of the normal curriculum), and membership of the School choirs and orchestras is encouraged. The School also has a fully-equipped Theatre and a Drama Studio. There is a large CCF Contingent run jointly with CLSG which pupils may join from the age of 13, with Army, Navy and RAF Sections. There is also a successful Community Service programme. Many pupils also take part in the Duke of Edinburgh's Award scheme.

Alumni, known as Old Citizens, enjoy a programme of year reunions careers and networking events throughout the year and receive regular e-news and an annual alumni magazine. Members of this vibrant alumni community also deliver varied talks to pupils throughout the year and mentoring support to Sixth Formers contemplating university and career choices.

Chairman of Governors: Mr T Levene

***Head*: A R Bird**, MA, MSc

Senior Deputy Head: M Wardrop, M Chem
Deputy Head (*Pastoral*): Mrs A K Martineau, MA
Deputy Head (*Co-Curricular & Operations*): A J V McBroom, BA
Deputy Head (*Academic*): G Y Bezalel, MA
Director of Studies & Senior Mistress: Miss N H Murphy, BA
Director of Admissions & Communications: P S Marshall, MA
Director of Development: Ms K Ostermann, BA
Head of Sixth Form: C R Webb, BSc
Head of Middle School: B S Savage, BA
Head of Lower School: P P Sanders, MA, MEd

Head of Senior Sixth Form: Ms T R Tooze
Head of Junior Sixth Form: M N Everard-Pennell
Assistant Head of Sixth Form: T L Robinson
Head of Fifth Form: T H White
Head of Fourth Form: Ms K A Saunt
Head of Third Form: J E McArdle
Assistant Head of Third Form: F J Isaac
Head of Second Form: B A Medlock
Head of First Form: Miss F G Eason
Head of Old Grammar: J Findlay

* *Head of Department*

Classics:
*Mr S A Swann
Miss Z L Connolly
Ms V Herrenschmidt
Mr J E McArdle
Mr J E Pile
Miss C L Rose

Drama:
*Miss S H Dobson
Miss J R Martin
Mr B S Savage

Economics:
*Mr D P Rey
Mr J Chamberlain
Mr M Wacey
Mr C R Webb

English:
*Mr R J Bryant
Mrs L V Bartlett
Ms A C Cann
Miss E J Green
Ms L E Hynes
Mr F J Isaac
Mr J Norman
Mrs H Sebban
Ms I L Taylor
Ms T Tooze

Future Guidance:
*Mrs B A Chambers (*Director of Future Guidance*)
Mr J P Santry

Geography:
*Mr G Wagg
Ms A D Edkins
Mr O J Ignotus
Mr P S Marshall

History and Politics:
*Mr A J Bracken
Ms S H Badr
Mr R G Brice
Mr S J Brown
Mr A J V McBroom
Miss N H Murphy
Mr A A Powrie
Ms K A Saunt
Mr P J Wright

Innovative Design and Visual Arts:
*Mr M Jones (*Director of IDVA*)
*Mr S Beresford-Zahra (*Head of Art*)
*Mrs S L Ralph (*Head of IT&C*)
Miss B Easton
Miss A E Gill
Mr S R Lewington
Mr P P Sanders
Miss S J Tomlinson
Ms G Trueman
Mr M Wells-Gray

Mathematics:
*Mr B P Broadhurst
Mr T G Betchley
Mrs E M Betchley
Dr S J Dugdale
Miss Y Feng
Mr S S Fernandes
Miss S Golleck
Miss C A Hudson
Mr D S Littlestone
Miss E L McCallan
Miss J C L Mesure
Mr S Mozakka

There are Visiting Music Teachers for Bassoon, Cello, Double Bass, French Horn, Flute, Guitar, Jazz, Oboe, Organ, Percussion, Piano, Saxophone, Singing, Trombone, Trumpet, Tuba, Viola, Violin.

Learning Support:
*Ms A C DiStefano
M C Biltcliffe
Ms M Bousiopoulou
Mrs C S Musgrove

Modern Languages:
*Mr R Edmundson
Mr P R Eteson (**French*)
Mr B Pollard (**German*)
Mrs E Bunnage (**Mandarin*)
Miss F G Easton
Miss B L Manion
Mr T A Pandolfino
Mr B S Savage
Ms N Tebib-Deverson
Mr A M Thomson
Miss V Vincent
Ms A Waugh
Mr T H White

Music:
*Mr R Quesnel
Mr A J Crockatt
Miss J E Jones

Physical Education:
*Mr N F Cornwell
Mr S Dorrington
Mr B A Medlock
Mr S E Robinson
Mr J P Santry
Mr B J Silcock
Mr H G Sutcliffe

Religion & Philosophy
*Mr J M Fenton
Mr J Findlay
Mrs A Giannorou
Ms A K Martineau

Science:
*Dr C S Bradford (*Mr*)
Dr K L Pattison (**Biology*)
Miss E M Reilly (**Chemistry*)
Mr A A Wood (**Physics*)
Ms O R Babb (*Junior Science*)
Mr T F Beck
Mr N A Boney
Mr G H Browne
Mr S L Clifford
Mr G W Dawson
Mr R J Dharamsh
Dr M N Everard-Pennell
Mr S A Hall
Mr N J Lowe
Mr R Mackrell
Mr T L Robinson
Mr M Wardrop
Mr A Zivanic

Mrs A J Fountaine
Mrs K J Ireland

Library:
*D A Rose
Mr M Evans
Ms J Grantham
Mrs R Howley
Mr T J Osborne (*Bookshop Manager*)

Admissions Registrar: Mrs V J Haley

Director of Partnerships: Ms L E Hynes

Head of Finance: Mr N Basye

Head of People: Ms K Kerr

City of London School for Girls

St Giles' Terrace, Barbican, London EC2Y 8BB

Tel: 020 7847 5500
email: reception@clsg.org.uk
website: www.clsg.org.uk
X/Twitter: @clsggirls
Instagram: @cityoflondonschoolforgirls

City of London School for Girls is an independent day school for pupils aged 11–18 situated in the heart of the Barbican. Opened in 1894, the school provides an outstanding education for able students from all backgrounds, cultures and faiths. We capitalise on our location to attract students from all over Greater London and beyond, and give them access to every learning opportunity our capital has to offer.

Academic yet unstuffy, modern yet acutely aware of its history, diverse yet with a strong sense of identity, our school defies easy categorisation. This is best demonstrated by our unique geography, nestled between the brutalist Barbican and looming Roman walls. Ours is an intellectually edgy, unassuming and unpretentious environment, unshackled by tradition, and imbued with a relaxed excellence. This is a refreshing and modern place in which to learn.

Our school is a kind and compassionate place, and our values of respect, responsibility and resourcefulness course through the concrete of our famous Barbican site. We are proud of our outstanding and individualised pastoral care, which encourages pupils to understand themselves and take considered and reflective ownership of their lives. We nurture an inclusive and kind community, which embraces the cultural and social mix in the school and world around us.

At City we aim to provide an intellectually exciting and rigorous learning environment, where students are constantly encouraged to interrogate their knowledge and understanding, to take risks and to experiment. We seek to provide them with a deep knowledge-based curriculum, but also the skills to scrutinise, synthesise and apply that knowledge in a wide variety of contexts. Discussion is at the heart of every lesson, and we are keen to inculcate in our students a familiarity and ease with ambiguity. They are unfazed by the more complex and nuanced areas, and are encouraged to grapple with these issues head on.

Admission. Main entry points to the school are at 11 and 16 years of age. For other entry points, vacancies are only occasional. The initial entrance assessments for 11+ and 16+ entry are held in the autumn term.

Applications for all applicable entry points open in spring the year before entry. Specific deadlines can be found on the website.

Scholarships and bursaries. The school offers music scholarships for entry at 11+ and 16+. There are also art, sport and drama scholarships available at 16+. City is committed to enabling access to the school for those for whom its education will be most transformational and offers means-tested bursaries for entry at 11+ and 16+.

Fees per term (2023–2024). £7,926. Optional extras: individual music lessons: £349 (ten lessons) per term.

School Governors:
Chair: Alderman Robert Howard

***Headmistress*: Jenny Brown**, MA Oxon

Senior Deputy Head (*Staff and Special Projects*): Justine Venditti, BEng Swansea

Deputy Head (*Academic*): Neil Codd, BA Oxon
Deputy Head (*Pastoral*): Susannah Gilham, BA Oxon
Deputy Head (*Partnerships and Co-Curricular*): Rosie Lockyear, BA Cantab

Chief Operating Officer: John Hall, MA Cantab, MInstRE, MBPsS

Assistant Head Teaching, Learning and Research & Development: Kay Hotchkiss, MChem Oxon
Assistant Head of Diversity & Inclusion: Soumia Arif, BA London

Head of Sixth Form: Georgie Hankinson, BSc Staffordshire
Acting Head of Senior School: Victoria Bradford, MPhys Oxon
Head of Lower School: Elly Nicoll, MA Oxon, MA London

A full staff list can be found on our website: www.clsg.org.uk/about-us/our-staff

Clifton College

Guthrie Road, Clifton, Bristol BS8 3EZ

Tel: 0117 315 7110
email: admissions@cliftoncollege.com
prepadmissions@cliftoncollege.com
website: www.cliftoncollege.com
X/Twitter: @Clifton_College
Facebook: @CliftonCollegeUK
Instagram: @CliftonCollegeUK
LinkedIn: /Clifton-College

Motto: *Spiritus Intus Alit*

Clifton College is a top co-educational boarding and day school for pupils aged 3–18, founded in 1862 and incorporated by Royal Charter in 1877. The school is nestled in the heart of Clifton, and takes advantage of the many cultural and educational activities on offer in the modern and vibrant city of Bristol, with plenty of countryside nearby.

Admission. Pupils are normally admitted in September for the Upper School, between the ages of 13 and 14. Most are required to pass the Common Entrance examination, which can be taken at their Preparatory Schools. Each pupil is assessed by considering their academic potential, along with their educational background and profile, including conduct and attitude. Their current school's recommendation is an important part of this process. For an applicant resident overseas, the entry requirements will be appropriate to previous educational experience. Such pupils for entry into Years 9, 10 and 11 will normally be asked to sit UKISET entry tests, focusing on aptitude.

Interested families should get in touch with the College's admissions team on 0117 3157 110 or admissions@cliftoncollege.com who will then provide an application form to complete. Once the non-refundable registration fee has been paid, the arrangement of interviews and appropriate entry tests will begin.

Age range. 13–18.

Number of pupils. 778.

Fees per term (2023–2024). Years 9–11: Boarders £14,875; Flexi Boarders (4 nights) £13,410; Day Pupils £9,890. Sixth Form: Boarders £15,480; Flexi Boarders (4 nights) £13,915; Day Pupils £10,045.

Houses. Pupils are assigned a House when they join the College, where they will meet their Tutors, spend time with their peers and benefit from a supervised environment in which they can meet, work or relax, providing a true home away from home. Each House is led by a Housemaster/Housemistress and their spouse, along with Tutors, Matrons and the occasional House dog.

There are four boarding Houses for boys; Moberly's, Wiseman's, School House and Watson's House and three Houses for girls; Hallward's, Oakeley's and Worcester. There are a further three day Houses for boys, and two for day girls, these have the same status as Boarding Houses and day pupils are encouraged to take part in the abundant activities available as an active member of their House.

Catering. In-house catering is managed by Sodexo, with pupils and staff enjoying a wide variety of food. All meals are eaten in the main dining hall, this includes supper for Boarders, and day pupils if pre-arranged.

Academic structure. While the College strongly believes a first-rate education is not something which can be measured in league tables alone, a strong emphasis is placed on academic standards. It is these rigorous standards that enable Clifton pupils to go on to pursue the future they choose, whether that is attending Oxbridge or a Russell Group university, or diving straight into the world of industry or commerce.

Pupils enter the Upper school in Year 9 and follow a general course for their first year, with GCSEs chosen at the end of Year 9.

Pupils then move up to the Sixth Form and typically choose four A Level subjects in the Lower Sixth, before narrowing this to three in the Upper Sixth. A great many combinations of subjects are available, including a number of BTEC Level 3 qualifications.

Service. The Outdoor Education Department at Clifton College facilitates and develops teamwork, leadership, confidence and self-esteem. Various outdoor activities are available that include; geocaching, archery, low ropes, initiative tasks, bouldering, indoor climbing, first aid and mountain biking. As well as the weekly programme, pupils also participate in 2 field days where they get to work as a team in height based and water based activities. Kayaking and Canoeing, the Duke of Edinburgh Award, Overseas Expeditions, Winter Mountaineering and Wilderness and Survival Skills are also encouraged.

Combined Cadet Force (CCF) is offered at the College, and provides a disciplined youth organisation, enabling pupils to develop powers of leadership. All pupils may join any of the three sections: Army, Royal Navy and Royal Air Force. The Army concentrates on the self-discipline of field tactics; the Navy provides the opportunity to engage in a wide range of maritime activities, using the College's own boats located in the nearby docks; whilst the RAF takes full advantage of the availability of local air experience flights.

There is a certain amount of military training, which is designed to give young people a chance to exercise responsibility and leadership, to provide them with some knowledge of our defence forces, and to encourage those who might be interested in becoming members of the Armed Services.

Societies. The College provides a varied programme of events for day and boarding pupils, ensuring each child is given the opportunity to develop and nurture lifelong interests. More than just add-on 'extras', the societies and clubs form a central part of the well-rounded education that is the Clifton College Experience. Mid-week activities take place in the Art, Technology and Music departments. These are complemented by physical activities such as dance, basketball, real tennis, fencing, volleyball, swimming, horse riding and fitness. At the weekend, pupils can take part in organised voluntary activities such as theatre or cinema trips, horse riding or dry-slope skiing.

Music and Art. The musical activities of the school are wide and varied, and are designed for musicians of all standards. They include the Chapel Choir, Choral Society and Chamber Choir, a full orchestra, two string orchestras, two wind bands, a jazz band, as well as numerous chamber music activities. Visiting concert artists regularly run masterclasses, and there are numerous opportunities to perform. Music lessons are available for virtually all instruments, across many styles. Annual instrumental and vocal competitions are held both at House level and individually. The well-equipped and recently refurbished Joseph Cooper Music School includes practice facilities, computers, a dedicated recording studio.

Drawing, Painting, Sculpture, Pottery, Textiles and various Crafts are taught under the supervision of the Director of Art in the Art School. There is an annual House Art Competition and various exhibitions throughout the year, with many pupils also choosing Photography.

Theatre and Drama play an important part in the life of the school with an increasing number of pupils achieving success in LAMDA and PCERT LAM examinations. The Redgrave Theatre is used for the

House Drama Festival, the annual school musical and for plays prepared and performed by individual Houses, the staff or the Modern Languages Society. It is also used for teaching purposes, and in addition for concerts, lectures and meetings.

Physical Education. Clifton College offers a proven pathway to excellence in Sport and has produced many international and current professional players. High Performance Sports Programmes and player-specific conditioning is offered by professional coaches such as a GB Hockey Olympian, former Superleague Netball player, former Welsh Cricketer and former players for England, Bristol and Ireland Rugby.

In the Michaelmas Term, boys play Rugby and girls play Hockey, with an extensive multi-sport option for seniors who are not in team squads. In the Lent Term, Hockey and Football are the main options for boys whilst girls mostly play Netball. Rowing, Running, Squash, Swimming, Shooting, Climbing and Rackets are among the alternative options.

In the Summer Term, Cricket is the main sport for boys and Tennis for girls, with Athletics, Rowing, Swimming and Shooting as alternatives for seniors. The College's 90 acre sports complex at our Beggar's Bush site includes three floodlit all-weather Hockey and Football pitches, six floodlit Tennis courts, a 3G artificial pitch for Football and Rugby, a water-based Hockey pitch with training D, and a Real Tennis court.

The development of a new state-of-the-art sports complex at Beggar's Bush, 'The Chellaram Sports Complex', will house an eight court hall for netball, tennis, basketball and badminton amongst other sports, as well as extensive hospitality and catering facilities, and is set to be completed for the 2024 school year.

Careers. Careers advice is led by a dedicated staff member in charge of Careers, with Housemasters/mistresses overseeing individual applications. Tutors, Heads of Departments and the Head of Sixth Form also offer a wealth of support. The College hosts an excellent Careers Fair in the Summer Term, alongside careers seminars and events throughout the year. The Old Cliftonian community offers a host of advice and work experience opportunities which pupils are encouraged to explore. The school is a subscribing member of the Independent Schools Careers Organisation and of the Careers Research and Advisory Centre at Cambridge.

Clifton College Preparatory School. *Headmaster:* J Walton, BA

There is no 'one size fits all' approach at Clifton College Preparatory School, a friendly and inspiring co-educational boarding and day school for pupils aged 8–13. Each child is considered and treated as an individual with a unique profile of skills, passions, talents and undiscovered potential. Clifton College offers a stimulating and challenging curriculum, which combines traditional methods with programmes of study relevant to the needs of the next century.

For further details see entry for Clifton College Preparatory School in IAPS section.

Charitable status. Clifton College is a Registered Charity, number 311735. It is a charitable trust providing boarding and day education for pupils aged 3–18.

Chairman of College Council: Mr Nick Tolchard

Council:
President: Mr Stephen Zimmerman
Chair: Mr N Tolchard, BSc
Vice-Chair: Mr M Eldridge
Treasurer: Mr M Howard-Cairns

***Head Master*: Dr T M Greene**, MA, DPhil
Senior Deputy: Mr G Simmons, BSc
Deputy Head (*Academic*): Mr G Turner, MSc
Deputy Head (*Co-curricular & Planning*): Mr J Mather, MSc
Deputy Head (*Pastoral*): Mrs R Coomber, BSc

Head of Sixth Form: Mr N Mills, MA
Director of Admissions: Mr J Hills, MA
Chaplain: Revd Mel Parkin

Clongowes Wood College

Clane, Co Kildare W91 DN40, Ireland

Tel:	00 353 45 868202
email:	reception@clongowes.net
website:	www.clongowes.net

Motto: *Aeterna non Caduca*

Clongowes Wood College was founded in 1814 in a rebuilt Pale castle – Castle Brown in North Kildare, about 25 miles from Dublin. A boarding school for boys from 12–18, the school has developed steadily ever since and now has circa 500 pupils on the rolls, all of whom are seven-day boarders.

The College is situated on 150 acres of land, mostly comprising sports fields and a 9-hole golf course. It is surrounded by about 300 acres of farmland. Clongowes is listed as an historic building.

Admission. Application for admission should be made to the Headmaster. There is a registration fee of €50. An assessment day is held in May prior to the year of entry and entry is determined by a variety of factors including: suitability of the student to boarding life, family association, geographical spread including Northern Ireland and abroad, date of registration, and an understanding of the values that animate the College. Normal entry is at the age of 12; entry in later years is possible if a place becomes available.

Curriculum. A wide choice of subjects is available throughout the school and pupils are prepared for the Irish Junior Certificate and the Irish Leaving Certificate. This latter is the qualifying examination for entry to Irish Universities and other third-level institutions. It is acceptable for entry to almost all Universities in the United Kingdom, provided the requisite grades are obtained. All pupils take a Transition Year programme following the Junior Certificate. This programme is recommended by the Department of Education in Ireland. Work experience modules, social outreach programmes, exchanges with other countries and opportunities to explore different areas of study are all included in this programme.

Religious teaching. Clongowes is a Jesuit school in the Roman Catholic tradition and there are regular formal and informal liturgies. Boys are given a good grounding in Catholic theology and are encouraged to participate in retreats, prayer groups and pilgrimages

(Taize, Lourdes). Social Outreach is part of the curriculum in Transition Year and is encouraged throughout the school. A small number of boys of other faiths are pupils in the school.

Sport. All boys play rugby in their first year in school. They then have the choice to continue in that game or to play other games. There are several rugby pitches, a golf course, tennis courts, soccer pitches, squash courts, a cross-country track, an athletics and cricket oval, a gymnasium and a new swimming pool; these facilities provide plenty of opportunity for a variety of activities. Athletics, Gaelic football and cricket are popular activities in the third term. Clongowes has a strong rugby tradition and has won the Leinster Championship twice in the last decade.

Other activities. Following the Jesuit tradition, the school has a fine reputation for debating and has won competitions in three different languages (English, Irish, French) in the last decade. A large school orchestra and school choir gives a formal concert at Christmas and another before the summer holidays. Drama productions take place at every level within the school. A large-scale summer project for charity has been undertaken each year. A residential holiday project for children with disabilities takes place in the school each summer and is animated by teachers and pupils. The College has recently created link programmes with schools in Hungary and Romania.

Pastoral care. The school is organised horizontally into Lines. Two 'prefects', or housemasters look after each year within a Line, composed of two years, with a Line Prefect in charge of the Line itself. In addition, an Academic Year Head oversees the academic work of each of the 70 pupils within each year. A Spiritual Father or Chaplain is attached to each line. There is a strong and positive relationship with parents and a good community spirit throughout the school. The school seeks to foster competence, conscience and compassionate commitment in each of the boys in its care.

Fees per annum (2023–2024). €23,150. Students with English as a second language pay an additional 10% fee premium per annum. Students entering at Senior Cycle only (Senior Cycle begins at 4th Year) pay an additional 15% fee premium per annum.

Clongowes Union. This association of past pupils of the school can be contacted through: The Secretary, The Clongowes Union, Clongowes Wood College, Clane, Co Kildare; email: development@clongowes.net.

Trustee of the School: Fr Leonard Moloney, SJ, Provincial of the Society of Jesus in Ireland

Chairman of the Board of Management: Mr Daire Keogh

***Headmaster*: Mr Chris Lumb**, BSc, HDip, MEd

Assistant Headmaster: Mr Paul McCormack, BA, HDip Ed

Head of Boarding: Mr Steven Gray, BA, HDip Ed, ATPLs

Director of Studies: Ms Helen Hickson, BA, HDip Ed, MA, MSc

Cokethorpe School

Witney, Oxfordshire OX29 7PU

Tel: 01993 703921
email: hma@cokethorpe.org
admissions@cokethorpe.org
website: www.cokethorpe.org
X/Twitter: @CokethorpeSch
Facebook: @CokethorpeSch
Instagram: @CokethorpeSch
LinkedIn: /company/cokethorpe-school

Motto: *Inopiam Ingenio Pensant*

Founded in 1957, Cokethorpe School provides a liberal education to roughly 630 boys and girls aged four to eighteen in a dynamic and vigorous day school environment. Set in 150 acres of parkland, the School sits two miles from Witney and just ten from Oxford.

Aims. The School creates a community of rounded, considerate and confident young people with high personal expectations. The pupils are provided with an exceptional breadth of opportunities to further their learning and expand horizons, whilst the individual focus afforded to pupils ensures that they are supported in making the right choices for their development.

These qualities are formulated in the School's leadership traits: integrity, courage, empathy, judgement, ambition, and responsibility. These are characteristics the School instils in every pupil. In the Prep School, these take the form of the Cokethorpe Characters, with attributions reflecting attitudes to learning.

Curriculum. Whilst the National Curriculum is broadly followed throughout the Prep School and on to GCSE, there is plenty of space afforded to push beyond, providing plentiful scope for intellectual challenge and curiosity to flourish. An exceptional breadth of subjects is offered at age groups across the Prep and Senior Schools.

At GCSE, all pupils study core subjects of English, Maths and Science and have a wide choice of subject options in addition. Sixth Formers typically choose to either study three subjects at A Level and complete the EPQ or select four A Level subjects. A further group opt to follow the Extended Diploma in Business programme. The small size of teaching groups is particularly conducive to rigorous individual attention and encouragement. Students can select from 24 subjects for Sixth Form, including, to name but a few: Philosophy, Politics, Economics, Latin, Further Mathematics, Psychology and Sociology.

Admissions. The main entry points are: Reception (4+), Year 3 (7+), First Form (11+), Third Form (13+) and Sixth Form (16+). Places in other year groups are considered if a place becomes available during the academic year. For the specific requirements of each entry point, please refer to the School's website.

Bursaries and scholarships. Financial assistance is available to parents of pupils who meet the required standards but require a bursary award to take up a place. All awards are means tested and the number and value of awards will vary according to the family circumstances and availability of funds. Bursary funding is prioritised for pupils in the senior school and applications are required in the Michaelmas term prior to entry. Scholarships are assessed separately and awarded annually and worth between £200 and £300 each. A pupil may hold multiple scholarships. Holders of all awards are expected to contribute fully to the life of the school and work to their academic capacity as they progress through the school.

Setting. The elegant Queen Anne Mansion House is both home to the Prep School and entrance to myriad facilities beyond. A range of modern buildings host the Senior School's academic endeavours around a series of quads, and beyond, a 200-seat black-box theatre is the perfect setting for the Performing Arts and visiting speakers. The core sports are complimented by the Outdoor Education programme, which includes clay pigeon shooting, climbing, sailing, and a popular and hugely successful kayaking programme. The extensive extra-curricular programme (known as 'AOBs') plays a prominent part in a pupil's timetable and includes over 160 weekly activities to select and savour.

Fees per term (2023–2024). Prep School: Reception–Year 2 £5,075, Years 3–4 £5,445, Years 5–6 £5,675.

Senior School: £7,735.

Fees include lunch. Extras are kept to a minimum.

The Cokethorpe Society. Director of Development: Nicola Wynne, Cokethorpe School, email: development @cokethorpe.org.

Charitable Status. Cokethorpe Educational Trust Limited is a Registered Charity, number 309650.

Governing Body:
Chairman: Mr J Bennett, BSc

Dr C Easmon, MBBS, MRCP, MSc Public Health, DTM&H, DOccMed
The Right Revd C Fletcher
Mrs W E Hart, CFQ, MA, ICAEW
Dr W W Lau, PhD, MSc, BSc
Mrs J Norris, BA Hons, Dip TP, MSc, MRTPI
Mr P Tolley, BSc, FRICS
Mr K Walton, Cert Ed
Mr M Wannell, FCCA
Governor Emeritus: Mr M St John Parker, MA

***Headmaster*: Mr D J Ettinger**, BA, MA, PGCE, FRSA

Deputy Headmaster: Mr J C Stevens, BEng, FRSA
Bursar: Mrs H J Stapleton, FCCA
Head of Prep School: Mrs N A Black, BA
Director of Studies: Mr A E Uglow, BA, PGCE
Director of Co-Curricular: Mr G J Sheer, BA, PGCE
Head of Sixth Form: Mr E J Tolputt, BA, MA, MEng
Director of Development: Ms N A Wynne, BA, MA
Head of Staff Development: Mrs S A Orton, BA, PGCE, SpLD Cert
Deputy Head of Sixth Form: Mrs M H D Cooper, BA, PGCE
Deputy Head of Sixth Form: Mr A P Gale, BSc, PGCE

Housemasters and Housemistresses:
Feilden: Mr J E Hughes, BA, BMus
Gascoigne: Mrs E Semenzato, DLit, PGCE
Harcourt: Miss A M Woodcock, BSc
Queen Anne: Mrs L Bowden, BSc, QTS GTP
Swift: M Joiner, BSc, MA, PGCE
Vanbrugh: Ms L A Mountain, MA, PGCE
Lower House: M J P O'Connor, BEd

Heads of Departments:
Art: Ms E F Williams, BA, PGCE
Business Studies and Economics: Mrs N Silversides, BEd, CELTA
Classics: Mr S Oliver, BA, MLitt, PGCE
Design Technology: Mrs H V Brown, BA, PGCE
Drama: Mrs C L Hooper, Dip Act, DCL
English: Mr S P Howells, BA, NPQLT
Geography: Mr J E Bown, BSc, PGCE
History: Mr C M Tyer, BA, MSt, PGCE
Learning Development: Mrs S J Arbuckle, BA, PGCE, NASENCO
Mathematics: Mr A G M Ladell-Stuart, MMath, PGCE
Modern Foreign Languages: Miss M Boubkari, BA, PGCE
Music: Dr E J Winkley, BA, PHD, QTS
Philosophy, Religion and Civics: Mr A D Waldron, BA
Physical Education: Mr J P Gallagher, BSc, MA, PGDipEd
Psychology and Sociology: Mrs K J Rogers, BSc, PGCE
Science: Mr O L Richards, BA, MA

Colfe's School

Horn Park Lane, London SE12 8AW

Tel: 020 8852 2283
email: head@colfes.com
website: www.colfes.com
X/Twitter: @ColfesSchool
Facebook: @ColfesSchool

Colfe's is an independent day school for girls and boys from age 3–18. It is one of London's oldest schools and was nearly 100 years old when Abraham Colfe, Vicar of Lewisham, re-established it in 1652. In his will, he entrusted the care of Colfe's to the Leathersellers' City Livery Company, which governs the school to this day.

Entrance is selective and academic standards are high. Over the last four years, 88% of A Level results have been A*–B, with over 60% of grades either A* or A. In 2023, over 95% of students went to their first-choice university. At GCSE in 2023, 59% of grades were 9–8 and nearly 80% were 9–7*. We have an exceptional and popular programme of activities outside the classroom.

Colfe's has a strong reputation for all-round quality and innovation – in December 2016 the school was rated as 'Excellent' by the Independent Schools Council following an ISI inspection. We have also been awarded two TES Awards for Education Initiative of the Year (2014 and 2016) for our outstanding pastoral programmes.

We offer a number of fully funded means-tested scholarships in the Sixth Form. In so doing we draw on strong working relationships with a number of local comprehensive schools in two of London's most deprived boroughs.

We are proud of our 360-year history but we are not burdened or defined by it. Colfe's doesn't promote a single mould. It is very much a school of the present day.

Admissions. There are approximately 800 pupils in the Senior School, including 220 in the Sixth Form. The Junior School caters for a further 460 pupils. All sectors of the school are fully co-educational. The main points of entry to the Junior School are 3+ and 4+ (EYFS). The majority of the Junior School pupils transfer to the Senior School at 11. Approximately 60 to 70 pupils from a range of local state primary and prep schools enter the Senior School directly at 11 and there are a limited number of places available to pupils wishing to join in the Sixth Form at Year 12.

Buildings. All the teaching accommodation is modern and purpose built. Specialist on-site facilities include the Sports and Leisure Centre, comprising sports hall, swimming pool, and fitness suite. The Leathersellers' Sports Ground, located less than a mile from the main school campus, provides extensive playing fields and related facilities. There is also a dedicated forest school nearby for younger pupils. The school also holds the freehold of the Old Colfeians ground at Horn Park. The opening of the Stewart Building in 2015, comprising a purpose-built Sixth Form suite and eight hi-tech classrooms, marked the end of a £10 million phase of site improvement.

Curriculum. The curriculum follows the spirit of the National Curriculum in both Junior and Senior Schools. Pupils are entered for the separate Sciences at GCSE and follow the IGCSE Mathematics course. A wide range of subjects is available at A Level, 27 in total, including Drama, Politics, Media Studies, Psychology and Philosophy.

Physical Education and Games. Physical Education and Games are compulsory for all pupils up to and including Year 11. Full use is made of the wide range of facilities available on site, including a fully-equipped Sports Centre, swimming pool and all-weather surface.

Both boys and girls play rugby, cricket, football and athletics. Other sports available include swimming, gymnastics, basketball, health-related fitness and tennis.

Music and Drama. Music and Drama thrive alongside each other in the purpose-built Performing Arts Centre. The music department is home to a wide range of performance groups ranging from beginners to advanced ensembles in both classical and contemporary genres. There are regular performance opportunities given throughout the year, some held in the purpose-built recital hall and others in external venues. A team of visiting instrumental teachers provide further opportunities for pupils to enjoy making music. Drama is a popular subject at both GCSE and A Level, with large numbers of pupils also involved outside the classroom.

Careers. The Careers and Higher Education Department is staffed on a full-time basis. Regular events include University Information Evenings and Careers Fairs.

Fees per term (2023–2024). Senior School: £6,820 (excluding lunch); Junior School (KS2): £5,640 (excluding lunch); KS1: £5,335 (including lunch); EYFS: £5,110 (including lunch).

Devices. On entry to the school, parents will be asked to purchase a device for their children to use in lessons and for homework.

Scholarships. Scholarships are awarded mainly on the basis of outstanding performance in the Entrance Examination. The exam is designed to identify and reward academic potential, as well as achievement.

Means-tested scholarships are also available at 11+ and 16+. These may, in exceptional circumstances, cover the total cost of tuition fees. Applications can be made online via the Colfe's School website.

A limited number of Art, Drama, Music and Sports awards are also available at 11+ and 16+. In the case of Music scholars, free instrumental tuition may accompany the award. Details of Music and Sports awards can be obtained from the website.

The Colfeian Society. Enquiries to the Alumni Relations Officer, Colfe's School, London SE12 8AW; email: development@colfes.com.

Charitable status. Colfe's School is a Registered Charity, number 1109650. It exists to provide education for boys and girls.

Visitor: HRH Prince Michael of Kent

The current Governors provide between them a broad range of relevant experience and qualifications. A majority are Members or appointees of the Leathersellers' Company to which Abraham Colfe entrusted the School in his will when he died in 1657.

The activities of the Leathersellers are many and varied but the School and its fortunes continue to feature prominently on the Company's agenda. The Master of the Company is, *ex officio*, a member of the Board of Governors.

Board of Governors:
Mr Mark Williams (*Master of the Leathersellers' Company*)
Mr Matthew Pellereau, BSc, FRICS (*Chairman*)
Mrs J Bradley, LLB
Mrs Belinda Canham, BA Hons
Ms S Cooke
Mr Daniel Coulson, BSc Hons, MA, MRICS
Mr E Dove
Dr Nicola Jones, BA Hons, MPhil, PhD Cantab
Mr Timothy Lister, FCA
Mr Joseph Mafe, BSc
Mr Christopher Ramsey, MA Cantab
Mr James Russell, BA
Mr Mark Russell
Prof. Laura Tunbridge, FBA

***Headmaster*: Mr R Russell**, MA Cantab

Deputy Head: Mrs D Graham, GRSM, LRAM
Bursar and Clerk to the Governors: Mr M Adamson, MA Cantab, FCA
Director of Studies: Ms M Schramm, BA, MA
Director of Pastoral Care: Mrs J German, BA Hons
Director of Sixth Form: Mr S Drury, BA Hons, MA
Director of Teaching and Learning: Mrs J Sansome, BSc Hons, MSc
Head, Junior School: Mrs M-C Gilfedder-Bonnar, LLB, BSc, PGCE
Director of Admissions and Communications: Mrs K Bridgman, BA Hons

Heads of Departments:
Art & Photography: Mrs N Gudge, BA Hons
Head of Faculty Business, Economics and Politics: Mr Nathan Carter, BA
Business: Mr M Cox, BSc Hons
Classics: Mr H Biggs, MA Oxon
Design & Technology: Mrs C Cox, BA Hons
Drama: Mrs N Maher, BA Hons, Acting Dip
Economics: Mr C Emmerich, BA, MA, MSc
English: Mrs K Guy, BA Hons
Geography: Mrs H Nissinen, BSc Hons, MA
History: Ms O Crummay, MSc
Learning Support: Miss A Coode, BA Hons, DTLLS Literacy
Maths: Mr A Guy, MEng Hons
Media Studies: Mr C Foxall, BA Hons
Modern Languages: Mr M Koutsakis, MA
French: Mrs C Davies, BA Hons
German: Mr M Koutsakis, MA
Spanish: Miss L Chapman, BA Hons
Music: Mr T Newberry, BA Hons, Dip ABRSM
Outdoor Education: Major C Cherry, BSc Hons
Physical Education: Mrs N Rayes, BEd Hons, EMBA
Politics: Mr M Poolton, BA Hons, MSc
Religion & Philosophy: Miss Z Kendrick, BA Hons, MEd
Biology: Dr G Zimmermann, BSc, PhD
Chemistry: Mr T Armstrong, BSc
Physics: Mr J Fishwick, BSc Hons
Psychology: Dr J Lea, PhD, BSc Hons

Collegiate School Bristol

Bell Hill, Stapleton, Bristol BS16 1BJ

Tel:	0117 965 5207
email:	admissions@collegiate.org.uk
website:	www.collegiate.org.uk
X/Twitter:	@CollegiateSB
Facebook:	@CollegiateSchoolBristol
Instagram:	@collegiateschoolbristol

Motto: *Go and Do Thou Likewise*

Collegiate School is a thriving co-educational day school for pupils aged 3 to 18 located on a spacious 30-acre site in Stapleton village, north Bristol. It is less than one mile from Junction 2 of the M32 and therefore easily accessible from north Bristol and South Gloucestershire.

There are approximately 800 pupils at Collegiate School – the Prep School (230 pupils), which caters for the 3–11 age range and includes a pre-school, is adjacent to the main site which accommodates the Senior School (570 pupils), where pupils attend from 11–18 (Year 7 to Sixth Form). *For details of the Prep School, see entry in IAPS section.*

A Collegiate education extends far beyond the classroom with opportunities for sport, music, service and co-curricular activities all playing their part in creating the unique experience on offer at the school.

In 2019, the ISI rated Collegiate School as 'Excellent' in all areas. In their report they captured the true essence of the school, highlighting its unique culture as well as the less easy-to-measure elements, which combine to make a Collegiate education so special. The statistics have long shown that Collegiate pupils achieve outstanding exam results and make excellent progress. However, it is the strong values pupils develop; their self-confidence, well-developed communications skills and the resilience they show when things get tough, that produce what is known as the Collegiate character.

Curriculum. Collegiate School offers a wide-ranging and engaging curriculum in line with the provisions of the National Curriculum. To support the core subjects, a wide range of optional subjects can also be taken, including art, business studies, computing, drama, design technology, music, physical education and religious studies. There is a wide choice of A Level subjects available in the Sixth Form including BTECs and CTECs in business, music and sports and exercise science.

Extracurricular. Collegiate School is fortunate to have all facilities on a 30-acre site, meaning students can seamlessly combine academic studies and sporting pursuits. With over 50 clubs to get involved in each week, the Collegiate experience is designed to allow students to find and develop their passion beyond the classroom, whether through the pride and spirit displayed on the sports field; the exciting array of activities in Combined Cadet Force; or in the first-rate creative spaces including art studios, the music technology classroom, or design technology workshop.

Pastoral. The Collegiate philosophy is quite simple: happy children do well. This makes the provision of pastoral care of great importance in the school. At the very heart of this provision is the house system. Four co-educational houses covering all year groups provide a structure through which the development, wellbeing and happiness of all young people is monitored and supported.

Sport and games. Collegiate School has a shining sporting legacy, perhaps unsurprisingly given the impressive on-site facilities that are unique in Bristol. Sport plays a huge part in the life of pupils and while excellence is pursued for those with talent, everyone is encouraged, regardless of ability, to get involved. Opportunities to represent the school are abundant and an impressive number of teams are fielded each week. The main sports for boys are rugby, hockey, cricket and tennis and for girls it is hockey, netball, cricket and tennis.

Future leaders. The Collegiate Future Leaders programme was developed with local universities and companies to help ensure sixth form pupils are equipped with the right skills and knowledge for a rewarding life beyond school. The programme comprises six areas with pupils benefitting from taught sessions each week run by a specialist team of tutors, senior staff members and instructors from the world of work and academia. The areas include academic excellence, extended project qualification, careers guidance, professional projects, employability skills and UCAS support.

Service and community. Pupils are given many opportunities to contribute to the wider community. Collegiate School's Combined Cadet Force, one of the most successful in the South-West, allows cadets to regularly take part in expeditions and activities. Pupils also have the opportunity to undertake The Duke of Edinburgh's Award which seeks to develop lifelong skills. Pupils relish the opportunity to get involved in a diverse range of volunteering projects across the city.

Admission. Pupils are admitted at 11+ through the school's own examinations. Pupils also join the school for the Sixth Form. Academic scholarships are available as well as scholarships for pupils excelling in art, drama, music and sport. Bursaries are also available which are means tested.

Religious denomination. The school's religious affiliation is to the Church of England, and use is made of neighbouring Stapleton Parish Church for morning assemblies and other services. Pupils of other denominations are also warmly welcomed.

Fees per term (2023–2024). £5,750.

Charitable status. Collegiate School is a Registered Charity, number 1079552. Its aims and objectives are the provision of education.

Governors:
Chair of Governors: Mr N Baker
Mrs B Allpress
Mrs K Bishop, CBE
Mr M Burchfield
Mrs A Burrell (*Deputy Chair*)
Mrs G Cross
Mrs C Duckworth
Mr R Foley
Mr C Green, CBE
Mr M Hughes
Dr S Patel
Dr M Sooriyabandara
Mrs C Tilley
Mr J Wright

***Head*: Mr J McCullough**, MA Oxon

Deputy Headmaster: Dr P Hill, BSc, PhD

Assistant Head, Academic: Dr J Tovey, BA, PhD
Assistant Head, Co-Curricular: Mr E Beavington, MA
Assistant Head, Curriculum: Dr Z Bell, PhD
Assistant Head, Equality, Diversity & Inclusion: Miss C Flay, BA
Assistant Head, Pastoral: Mr D Boyce

Head of Sixth Form: Ms K Porter, MA

Director of Finance: Mrs K Fisher, ACA, BA
Director of Facilities: Mr S Crossman

Cranleigh School

Horseshoe Lane, Cranleigh, Surrey GU6 8QQ
Tel: 01483 276377
email: admissions@cranleigh.org
website: www.cranleigh.org
X/Twitter: @cranleighschool
Facebook: @cranleigh-school
Instagram: @cranleighschool
LinkedIn: /cranleigh-school

Motto: *Ex cultu robur*

Cranleigh is a leading co-educational weekly boarding and day school set in a stunning rural location in more than 280 acres on the edge of the Surrey Hills. Cranleigh's beautiful campus is exceptionally well equipped, with outstanding classrooms, studio, performance and sports facilities, including three theatres, twelve rehearsal and performance spaces, competition pitches, stables, sports centres, golf course, outdoor education centre and swimming pool.

There are strong links between the School and nearby Cranleigh Preparatory School and pupils also join from a wide variety of other prep schools across London and the home counties, creating a lively, House-based community of young people who are drawn together by their inherent love of life and getting involved in everything Cranleigh has to offer.

Cranleigh School's principal aim is to provide an environment in which pupils can flourish, enabling them to capitalise on the diverse range of opportunities offered by the School and to achieve to the best of their ability within a framework of shared values and standards. The School's 280-acre site, situated eight miles from Guildford on the Surrey/West Sussex border, lies on the outskirts of Cranleigh Village and within 45 minutes of London. The School is fully co-educational, with some 288 girls and 408 boys between the ages of 13 and 18, including a Sixth Form of about 280. It is a predominantly boarding community, attracting boarders from both the local area and further afield; it also, however, welcomes day pupils, who are fully integrated into the Cranleigh community, playing their part in the activities of their respective houses and benefiting from the advantages thereby offered.

Each house (separate for boys and girls) has a resident Housemaster or Housemistress, a resident Deputy, Matrons and a team of Tutors for both the Lower School and Sixth Form. There is also a strong and active partnership between parents and the School.

Cranleighans are encouraged to relish a challenge, to feel they are known as individuals, and to become talented and wise adults with the ability to adapt to a fast-changing world. Both the Prep and the Senior Schools are proud of their excellent academic track records, culminating in outstanding performances at Common Entrance, GCSE and A Level. 99% of pupils go onto Higher Education and Cranleigh also has a consistently strong Oxbridge contingent.

Academic patterns. Cranleigh enjoys an academic life that is both exciting and demanding. We have high expectations of our pupils, our academic results are strong and teachers are committed to ensure Cranleighans appreciate that acquiring a love of learning is crucial in leading a personally fulfilled and professionally successful life. Indeed, education finds its purpose in the value of the well-lived lives it makes possible, a value which goes far beyond economic prosperity. Our aim is to act within the spirit of the National Curriculum, but to offer more, taking full advantage of our independence and the extra time available to a boarding school. We, therefore, retain a very broad curriculum in the Fourth Form and have an options system in the Lower and Upper Fifth Forms which enables a pupil to take between nine and eleven GCSE subjects before moving on to A Levels in the Sixth Form. In the Sixth Form, pupils can select from a wide choice of subjects.

Lessons are focused, pacey and engaging, with the focus being on how the pupils learn, as opposed to how the teachers teach. Traditional teaching methods absolutely have their place, but we strongly advocate lessons in which pupils are actively involved in a dynamic process of thinking. Learning, it is said, is 'supervised trying' and we insist that working hard and working intelligently must always be the root of our success. We also know that learning is most rewarding in a community that is lively, co-operative, critical and, fundamentally, engaged with the joy of discovery.

Independent learning is a hugely important aim for us. With this in mind, all year 10 pupils have taken the Higher Project Qualification since September 2017 and from September 2016 onwards, the majority of our Sixth Formers have taken the Extended Project Qualification. These qualifications encourage pupils to think for themselves and come to answers through discussion and reflection.

We believe that education is richer and deeper when students approach their learning philosophically, asking themselves questions that lead to deeper thinking, and engaging with problems to which there may be no agreed answers. Education in this rich sense is more than a preparation for future work: it is a preparation for life in the complex and uncertain world that our students will enter.

Of course, examination success is important too and whilst pupils are encouraged to learn independently, they are also taught the knowledge and skills required for excellent performance in examinations. Independent learning is excellent preparation for examination success, but there will always be a place for precise instruction in the requirements of different assessment types, the essentials of examination technique, and the analysis of past examination performance.

Creative and Performing Arts. Cranleigh has maintained an enviable reputation for music over many years, and the Merriman Music School offers pupils some of the finest facilities available. We send choral scholars to Oxford, Cambridge and major music departments and colleges elsewhere; boys and girls of all ages successfully take part in national competitions and well over a third of the School learns a musical instrument. Keyboard players have access to our Mander two-manual tracker organ, purposefully designed for versatility and teaching, and to two Steinway concert grand pianos. Our exciting Cranleigh Music initiative is now well established, bringing together the Music departments of Cranleigh School and Cranleigh Preparatory School under a single performing, management and administrative structure. While facilities remain on separate sites (both sides of Horseshoe Lane), the ethos is that of a single music faculty encompassing the full 7–18 age range, whose cohesive structure will help to nurture and progress talent from a very young age, so ensuring that all pupils are able to perform in an environment commensurate with their individual ability.

Cranleigh also boasts a strong Drama department. Regular large-scale productions take place in the Speech Hall, to which is linked a studio theatre, the Vivian Cox Theatre, while a flourishing technical theatre department encourages the development of 'backstage' skills. The School's proximity to London allows for regular attendance at professional theatre, music and opera productions.

Art and Design Engineering. Both subject areas house a talented mix of practising artists, teachers and designers. The Woodyer Art Studios provide some of the best school art facilities in the country and is spread over several buildings, with a mix of dedicated airy studios. Six large art studios provide specialist provision for painting, printmaking, photography, sculpture and ceramics. A Sixth Form studio enables each student to have their own working space; two suites of computers provide digital facilities while photography is also equipped with a traditional darkroom. The printmaking studio is equipped for relief printing, acid-based etching, and screen-printing. A large project studio provides for a weekly Sixth Form life class and for exhibitions of student work.

The Design Engineering department boasts three fully equipped design studios and workshops. Each design studio features a suite of both PCs and Macs running the latest 2D and 3D CAD software, alongside ample space for the delivery of theoretical content and sketching. Each studio is equipped with a 3D Printer allowing for the rapid prototyping of 3D models created on Autodesk Fusion 360. The department also features a CAM mezzanine which is an excellent space for building 3D printers, housing the large format printer and vinyl plotter. The main Design Engineering workshop is housed within the school's original sports hall which allows for a considerably sized, open-plan workshop kitted out with the required tools and machinery. Branching from the main workshop space is an electronics lab for soldering and electronic circuit development, a CAM area consisting of a large format CNC router and a laser cutter, and a heat treatment bay for welding and brazing.

The studios are open every day and appropriate use is made of the faculty library, ICT and digital video and photo facilities. External visits are encouraged (both nationally and internationally) and all students exhibit throughout the year.

Sport. Cranleigh has an extensive range of extremely high-standard sporting facilities. During their time at Cranleigh, pupils have the chance to try a variety of sports. Due to our Sport for All philosophy, all pupils have the opportunity to train and compete regularly as part of a team throughout the year.

The School possesses an impressive array of sports facilities, including three full-size Astroturf pitches (one of which is floodlit), a 9-hole golf course, Cricket Pavilion and five outdoor cricket squares, with one all-weather match pitch, an Equestrian Centre with two sand schools, one 30 m x 60 m, one 20 m x 40 m, both with floodlights, cross-country jumping field and on-site hacking, six fives courts, twelve hard tennis courts, nine Astro tennis courts, eight netball courts, an indoor swimming pool and eco-friendly, purpose-built fitness gym with a range of cardiovascular and weighted equipment as well as a physiotherapy room. For Rugby, Football and Cricket, Cranleigh also has ten grass pitches on site, including an International standard 1st XV pitch. The large Sports Hall complex, the Trevor Abbott Sports Centre, provides a popular venue for netball, tennis, badminton and basketball, and also includes a separate dance studio. There is also a separate Indoor cricket bubble for year-round development.

High standards are set for the numerous competitive teams, with an extensive programme of fixtures at all levels and for all ages. 'Sport for All' is a key philosophy at the School, supported by an experienced and talented team of coaches, many of whom have competed themselves at county, national and Olympic level. The School has witnessed some outstanding team and individual successes in recent years, including National representation in hockey, rugby, riding and cricket; taking National titles in horse riding (show jumping and dressage), kayaking, cricket, rugby 7s, swimming and hockey and also seeing several recent Old Cranleighans continue to compete in the international arena and as Olympic hopefuls.

In the Michaelmas term the majority sports are hockey for girls and rugby for boys; in the Lent term, the majority sports are netball for girls and hockey for boys. During the winter terms, pupils can also compete in lacrosse, cross country, golf, water polo, football, fives, and riding, plus badminton and canoeing for the Sixth Form. All pupils in the Fourth and Lower Fifth Forms take part in the majority sport, while an element of choice is gradually introduced for the older pupils. All pupils in the School take part in sport, even in the Sixth Form. In the Summer term, the main team sport for boys is cricket, whilst some boys compete in tennis, swimming, athletics and golf. For girls, the main sport is tennis, with competitive swimming, athletics, rounders and cricket popular additional offerings.

Service activities. There are opportunities for pupils to take part in a range of 'service' activities. Boys and girls may join the CCF or get involved with Voluntary Action or the Cranleigh School Environmental Action Group. Cranleighans help local people in community settings and also have links with local schools for children with learning difficulties and with a home for adults with similar difficulties. All houses and the Fundraising Group raise money for various charities.

Wider initiatives also include the School's 'Beyond Cranleigh' partnership – a key partnership between Cranleigh School and Beyond Ourselves, a London-based charity that works to improve the lives of disadvantaged young people in both London and in Zambia. This partnership has led to Cranleigh's sponsorship of a primary school in Kawama, to which Sixth Form pupils regularly make visits to help with building and teaching initiatives. Cranleigh has also pledged to support social enterprise projects in Kawama to provide jobs and skills training for locals post-education. Such initiatives are designed to focus pupils' thoughts on life beyond the School.

Outdoor education. Cranleigh operates a large Duke of Edinburgh's Award scheme, with many pupils completing the Gold Award before leaving school. By way of introduction, all Fifth Form pupils undergo an Outdoor Education programme in order to improve their self-awareness and confidence. There are many other opportunities for Outdoor Education through the CCF, and there is a well-attended climbing club (which has its own bouldering wall).

Religion. The striking, neo-Gothic Chapel was built as a central point of the School, and Cranleigh maintains its concern to present the Christian way of life. It welcomes pupils of all faiths and none.

Developments. The Cranleigh School Development Plan of 2015 initiated the production of a master plan. The results of this master plan were to take a phased approach to campus development with the first phase commencing in 2016 and taking broadly four years. The overall theme of the Development Plan was to enhance pastoral support, and teaching and learning. It was considered that the girls' boarding houses, at around 110 pupils, were too large and that two new boarding houses for girls should be developed, leading to four girls' houses, each for around 75 pupils, in addition to the four boys' houses, each of around 100 pupils.

The teaching facilities in the Connaught Block (to the right of Speech Hall) were considered to be past their best and so a decision was made to build a new teaching facility for English, the Humanities, Economics and Business Studies as well as Learning Support and Careers; the latter being broadened to Cranleigh Futures. A need was also identified at the Senior School for new squash courts and a modern café for pupils. At the Prep School, a number of the older buildings in the middle of the campus were outdated and it was decided to build new teaching facilities for Science, Design Technology and Art.

Girls' boarding houses. The first major project was the creation of a third girls' boarding house, Rhodes. This project was completed in October 2017 and after one year it has bedded into the Cranleigh landscape seamlessly. The opening of the van Hasselt Centre allowed existing classrooms in the Connaught Block to be converted back to their original use as boarding accommodation. We were delighted to open a fourth girls' house in September 2019, named Martlet (after the birds on the School's shield).

New teaching buildings. The building of the two new teaching buildings, one at each school, started in early 2017. The Prep School building progressed on schedule and their exciting new facility, including a flexible area for staff known as the Hub, was opened in early July by the former Chair of the Governing Body, Anthony Townsend, whose name the building takes. The new van Hasselt Centre at the Senior School, which includes both new classrooms and social spaces in the old squash courts, was completed in November 2018 and is now in full use. The centre is named after Marc van Hasselt, Cranleigh's Headmaster from 1970–84. These two new facilities are both spectacular and evidence of the School's strong commitment to core academic subjects.

Squash courts. The final element of the master plan was the building of new squash courts to replace the old courts which were subsumed into the van Hasselt Centre. Completed in 2023, these were built onto the side of the Trevor Abbott Sports Centre and include a new gym.

These new facilities add to the already impressive campus and take Cranleigh School forward as a leading co-educational dedicated boarding community. It is an exciting time to be at Cranleigh.

Planning for our pupils' future. Cranleigh takes the future of its pupils very seriously. It maintains good contacts with various professions, industry and commerce, through links developed as part of the careers advice structure. All pupils are regularly assessed during their time at the School, and this process includes a period of Work Experience at the end of the Upper Fifth year. Closely linked with the Old Cranleighan Society and the School, the Cranleigh

Network oversees skills training, CV advice, postgraduate work experience and mentoring.

Admission and registration. If you do not already know Cranleigh, we strongly recommend an initial visit during one of our small group visits or open mornings, dependent on age of entry. These will enable you and your child to have a tour of the school, ground and facilities and meet a few key members of staff to answer any initial questions. Our visits and open mornings are very popular and so advance booking via the Admissions office is essential to avoid disappointment. Please call the Admissions Office for more information on 01483 276377.

Awards. The Master of Scholars has a specific responsibility for all Scholars. They are members of their houses and attend normal lessons, but also have an additional programme throughout their time at the School that covers a wide variety of academic, cultural, social and commercial areas beyond the syllabus and which encourages independent thinking and research.

At age 13, Cranleigh School offers a variety of awards and scholarships. In certain circumstances, additional consideration may be given to sons or daughters of public servants, members of the armed forces and the clergy of the Church of England.

Fees per annum (2023–2024). Boarding: £46,035. Day: £37,905. It is the policy of the School to keep extras down to an absolute minimum, and limited to such charges as individual music tuition. Textbooks are supplied until the Sixth Form, at which point pupils are encouraged to buy their own so that they may take them on to university. A scheme is available for the payment of fees in advance.

Preparatory School. Cranleigh is closely linked with Cranleigh Preparatory School, where boys and girls are normally admitted at seven or eight, but also at other ages. For further information, apply to the Headmaster of the Preparatory School (*see entry in IAPS section*).

Charitable status. Cranleigh School is a Registered Charity, number 1070856. It exists to provide education for children aged 13–18 and the Preparatory School for those aged 7–13.

***Headmaster*: Mr Martin Reader**, MA Oxon, MPhil, MBA, QTS

Deputy Head: Mr S D Bird, BA, MEd, QTS
Deputy Head (*Pastoral*): Dr A P Saxel, BSc, PhD
Deputy Head (*Academic*): Mr D R Boggitt, BEng, PGCE, MEd

Assistant Head (*Co-Curricular*): Mr C H D Boddington, BA, PGCE, MEd
Assistant Head (*Director of IT*): Mr D J Futcher, BSc, MBCS, QTS
Assistant Head (*Learning, Teaching and Innovation*): Dr J L Taylor, BA, BPhil, PhD, PGCE
Assistant Head (*Liaison*): Mr S J Batchelor
Assistant Head (*Pastoral*): Mr D J Mulae, BSc

Director of Operations: Mr P A Dunn, BA
Director of Finance: Miss J A Underdown, BA, CIMA
Director of External Relations: Mrs J R Cooksley, MA, BA Hons, NCJT Prof Cert
Director of Admissions: Mr A P Forsdike, MA, PGCE
Strategic Development Director: Mr J Dale-Adcock, BA, PGCE
Chair of Common Room: Miss S L Greenwood, BA

Culford School

Bury St Edmunds, Suffolk IP28 6TX

Tel: 01284 728615
email: admissions@culford.co.uk
website: www.culford.co.uk
X/Twitter: @CulfordSchool
Facebook: @officialculfordscool
Instagram: @culfordschool

Motto: *Viriliter Agite Estote Fortes*

Culford School was founded in 1881 in Bury St Edmunds and moved to its present site on the Culford estate in 1935. The School is one of eight owned by the Methodist Independent Schools Trust and is administered by a Board of Governors, to whom local control is devolved.

About Culford School. Culford is a co-educational boarding and day school for 850 pupils aged between 1 and 18 across three schools: the Pre-Prep & Nursery, Prep and Senior Schools, all of which are situated within 480 acres of beautiful Suffolk parkland.

Where is Culford School? Culford is conveniently located four miles north of Bury St Edmunds and is within easy reach of Cambridge and Norwich (to which the school runs a daily bus shuttle service), Ipswich and Stansted Airport, and Heathrow and Gatwick airports are within two hours of Culford.

Teaching & Learning. We believe education should be challenging, enriching and fun and are committed to helping our pupils achieve excellence in all areas of school life. Hard work in the classroom is complemented by full sporting and extracurricular programmes.

Curriculum. We aim to give a broad and balanced education that enables every pupil to fulfil their academic potential. Core subjects at GCSE are English language and literature, mathematics, the three sciences and a foreign language. Pupils can choose additional subjects from a wide range of options and receive guidance from the Deputy Head, their teachers and personal tutor, who, along with their Housemaster or Housemistress, has responsibility for their academic and social progress.

Culford Sixth Formers usually study three or four subjects. The majority of students go on to university, including Oxbridge and the prestigious Russell Group universities. Sixth Formers may also study for a Culford Independent Research Project which enables students to study beyond the confines of A Level specifications; it can be an essay, a film, a composition or even something created in Design and Technology.

Facilities. Culford is centred on the magnificent Culford Hall, an 18th century mansion formerly the seat of Marquis Cornwallis and Earl Cadogan. The Hall houses Culford's music department and purpose-built Studio Theatre. Further facilities include a new £2.2m landmark library at the academic heart of the school and a brand new art centre, a modern, dynamic space that can be used for lessons, exhibitions and events. More recent developments include: a state-of-the-art, 24-track recording studio; the installation of two dance studios which both include a high sprung Harlequin floor, the same used by professional dancers. More recently a state-of-the-art Creative Technology Centre was opened which includes DT, digital media and innovation facilities.

Teaching Facilities. Teachers are specialists in their fields and are united by a passion to help the children in their care achieve their goals, whatever they may be. Classrooms are modern and well equipped, and in the case of specialist subjects, such as languages and sciences, have the latest technologies installed.

Sports Facilities. Culford's fantastic Sports and Tennis Centre is a state-of-the-art facility which comprises a four-court, championship-standard Indoor Tennis Centre, a 25m heated indoor pool, gym, strength and conditioning suite, golf swing studio, golf short game area, driving range and a large sports hall with a climbing wall and indoor cricket nets. Outside there are further tennis courts, two of which are seasonally covered, two artificial turf pitches (one in partnership with Bury Hockey Club) and numerous rugby and hockey pitches. In September 2021, we opened a renovated Strength & Conditioning suite alongside a new fitness gym.

Pupils can also pursue athletics, horse riding, archery, CCF and the Duke of Edinburgh's Award. Culford launched a new Football Academy programme to sit alongside its already well-established tennis, golf and swimming programmes.

Boarding. Culford accepts boarders aged 7 to 18 and for a whole host of reasons, including an 'Excellent' ISI rating, boarding is extremely popular with over half of Senior pupils boarding. Boarders enjoy an amazing range of weekend activities and have full access to Culford's impressive Sports and Tennis Centre.

Culford's boarding Houses offer children a comfortable, secure and fun place to live during term time. Culford offers flexible arrangements for other boarders where possible: part and occasional boarding is available providing space is free. We do not have an enforced exeat at the weekends; children may stay at school throughout the term, going home at the weekend or to stay with friends when they or their parents wish them to.

All pupils have access to our fully-equipped Medical Centre, supervised by a resident nurse, and this includes provision for residential care when necessary.

Culford Pre-Prep & Nursery School. Our purpose-designed Nursery accepts children from age 1 to 3 and perfectly prepares them for School life. Culford's Nursery is available for 50 weeks per year.

Culford Pre-Prep provides teaching for 80 children from Nursery at age three through to age seven in a delightful setting within the grounds.

Both Pre-Prep and Nursery schools take part in Forest School activities, a way of learning outdoors that helps children to develop personal, social and technical skills in a woodland setting.

Music & Drama. Music plays an important part in the life of the School. There are numerous choirs, orchestras and bands and regular concerts are held to give pupils the chance to perform in public. Individual music tuition is offered in voice, piano, organ and all orchestral instruments. Drama is also very popular and there are regular House plays and concerts as well as major productions: these include musicals and plays for different sections of the School.

Activities. There is a huge array of clubs and societies on offer – from academic and creative to sporting and community. Pupils are encouraged to take part in Community Service Activities and many participate in the Duke of Edinburgh's Award Scheme or choose to join the Combined Cadet Force (CCF).

Culford's popular Dance Programme features a professional high-sprung floor and classes in all types of dance, including ballet, contemporary, jazz and choreography.

Staff regularly take pupils out on visits and expeditions too, and every summer a group of Sixth Formers and teachers spend 3 weeks in Malawi helping with various development projects; a trip that is universally viewed as a life-changing experience. Other recent trips have included tours to New York, skiing in France and scuba diving in Tobago as well as sports tours worldwide.

Entry. The majority of pupils join in September at ages 1–7 (Pre-Prep), 7+, 8+ and 11+ (Preparatory School); and at 13+ and 16+ (Senior School). Entry to the Sixth Form is on the basis of GCSE performance or its equivalent for overseas candidates.

Entry to Culford Pre-Prep School is by informal assessment just prior to enrolment.

Applications are welcome from individuals throughout the year, subject to places being available.

Visiting Culford School. If you would like to visit Culford please contact the Admissions Office to arrange an appointment and a tour on 01284 385308 or to request a copy of the School prospectus. We also hold regular Open Mornings each term, please visit www.culford.co.uk to find out more.

Scholarships and Exhibitions. Culford holds its Scholarship examinations between November and January for entry for the following September. Scholarships are awarded according to merit in the following categories:

11+: Academic, Music, Swimming, Tennis, Cricket and Golf

13+: Academic, Art, Design & Technology, Drama, Music, Hockey, Rugby, Swimming, Tennis and Sport

16+: Academic, Art, Drama, Music, Design & Technology, Hockey, Rugby, Swimming, Tennis, Golf and Sport

Swimming and Tennis Scholarships may be available at any age from 10+.

Bursaries are available to those in genuine financial need.

A generous Forces Allowance is available to parents who are serving members of the Armed Forces and are in receipt of the MOD CEA.

For further details please apply to The Registrar, Tel: 01284 385308 or email: admissions@culford.co.uk.

Senior School Fees per term (2023–2024). Day: £7,885, Full Boarding: £12,385.

Charitable status. Culford School is part of the Methodist Independent Schools Trust, which is a Registered Charity, number 1142794.

Chair of Governors: Mr Mark Donougher, BSc, ACA

***Head*: C Bentley**, MEd
Deputy Head: Dr J Guntrip, BSc, PhD
Assistant Head: D V Watkin, BEd

Dauntsey's

West Lavington, Devizes, Wiltshire SN10 4HE

Tel: 01380 814500
email: info@dauntseys.org
website: www.dauntseys.org
X/Twitter: @DauntseysSchool
Facebook: @DauntseysSchool
Instagram: @dauntseysschool
LinkedIn: /dauntsey's-school

Founded in 1542, Dauntsey's is a leading co-educational boarding and day school for 11–18 year olds, set in a 150-acre estate on the edge of Salisbury Plain in Wiltshire. We offer our 860 pupils challenge and inspiration, both inside and outside the classroom.

Academic endeavour is at the heart of all that we do, and we expect pupils to leave with strong exam results and a love of learning. But our ethos is about much more than exam grades. Drama, music, art and sport all flourish here and the rural surroundings provide an ideal setting for many outdoor activities. Our extensive adventure education programme encourages our pupils to develop important life skills, such as resilience, communication, creativity and teamwork.

The school's uniquely lively and friendly atmosphere encourages pupils 'to have a go', try new things and so develop their self-confidence and self-belief. Our school community thrives on a culture of kindness and mutual respect which leads to a real sense of belonging.

For more information please visit our website www.dauntseys.org which provides a real flavour of life at Dauntsey's.

'Our ultimate priority is the happiness and fulfilment of every person in our community. In our experience, if our pupils are happy, then success will follow.' Mark Lascelles, Head Master, Dauntsey's

The community. Our house system is the cornerstone of our community, giving pupils a secure source of support and guidance on every aspect of life, as well as the chance to get together and have fun. Every pupil joins either a boarding or day house, which are co-educational in the Lower School (ages 11 to 13) and single sex in the Upper School (ages 14 to 18). Each house is run by a housemaster or housemistress and a team of tutors who take a close and active interest in pupils' academic and social development, as well as encouraging them to make the most of the activities on offer. Above all, they really do make sure that the house is a home from home.

Curriculum. Throughout the school, the curriculum is broad and balanced, offering the opportunity to study an extensive range of subjects. The academic curriculum is well balanced, wide-ranging and offers a good amount of choice. The timetable offers a great deal of flexibility, with well-structured weekly lessons and extensive options that cater for the different interests and aptitudes of all our pupils. Dauntsey's promotes independent learning, enabling pupils to fulfil their potential and develop the key skills they will need in later life. Gifted and talented pupils have access to work and experiences at the higher cognitive levels, to stimulate interest and develop advanced thinking skills, while pupils with mild learning difficulties get expert help and support from a dedicated team of specialist teachers.

Games. The major sports are Rugby, Football, Hockey, Cricket and Netball. Other games options include Tennis, Squash, Athletics, Swimming, Soccer, Water Polo, Fencing, Badminton and Basketball. In the Sixth Form further options include Triathlon training, Canoeing, Basketball, Rifle-shooting, Yoga, Cross-Country, Ballet and Dance. Sixth Formers can also choose to do volunteer work within the community.

Extracurricular activities. Our adventure education and extracurricular programmes set us apart, encouraging pupils to try new experiences. From drama, dance, music, sport and a huge range of clubs and societies, to our lecture series, adventure programmes and volunteering initiatives – there are opportunities to suit everyone. We aim to push our pupils out of their comfort zone, inside and outside the classroom, and we bring that spirit of adventure to everything we do.

Fees per term (2023–2024). Boarders: £12,580; Day Pupils: £7,600. There are no compulsory extras.

Admission. Boys and girls are admitted at 11 and 13 (boarding only) by examination, school report and interview; to the Sixth Form by I/GCSE grade predictions or equivalent and interview.

Scholarships and bursaries. Scholarships and awards are available for boarding and day places at 11+, 13+ and 16+ and carry a maximum fee remission of 10%. Scholarship supplements are available to those who have been awarded a scholarship and provide financial help with the school fees. For further details please contact the Registrar.

Charitable status. Dauntsey's School is a Registered Charity, number 1115638. It is dedicated to the education of boys and girls.

Chair of Governors:
Veryan Nield, BSc, MBA

***Head Master*: Mark Lascelles**, BA

Deputy Head (*Pastoral*): Mrs A L Jackson, BA

Second Master: Mr A Collins, BA, MSc Oxon

Deputy Head (*Academic*): Mr D Noble, MA Oxon, MA, MBA

Head of Lower School: Miss E S Conidaris, BSc

Bursar: Mr James Davey, MEng
Head of Admissions: Mrs H Sullivan
Head Master's Secretary: Mrs C Holgate

Dean Close School

Shelburne Road, Cheltenham, Gloucestershire GL51 6HE

Tel: 01242 258000
email: registrar@deanclose.org.uk
website: www.deanclose.org.uk
X/Twitter: @DeanCloseSchool
Facebook: @DeanCloseSchool

Motto: *Verbum Dei Lucerna*

Sitting on a beautifully landscaped 50-acre site in the Regency town of Cheltenham, Dean Close School is an attractive mixture of old, traditional buildings and modern, hi-tech facilities. The School was opened in 1886 in memory of Francis Close, Rector of Cheltenham 1826–55 and later Dean of Carlisle, and has been co-educational since 1967. Dean Close is a Christian school which believes that education is as much about building character and relationships as it is about gaining knowledge. Dean Close Preparatory School was established in 1949.

Admission and Withdrawal. Admission to the Senior School at 13 is through Common Entrance or direct entrance tests in English, Maths and Verbal Reasoning. Sixth Form: examination and interview, 6 grade 6s minimum at GCSE. We advise pupils to have at least an A in the subjects they wish to study at A Level. Prospectus and application forms are available from the Registrar who is also happy to arrange a visit at a time to suit. There is a non-returnable registration fee of £100 and a deposit is payable one year before entry. One term's notice is required before a pupil is withdrawn from the School.

Fees per term (2023–2024). Boarding £14,250, International Boarding £15,500, Flexi Boarding £11,175–£13,395, Day £9,595.

Term of Entry. We prefer to accept pupils in September but will make exceptions at any time of year, even in the middle of a term, if a good reason exists.

Scholarships and Bursaries. The School offers scholarships, exhibitions and bursaries at age 13 and for entry into the Sixth Form. The six areas of talent which are recognised are academic, music, sport, drama, art and design technology. The size of award is set according to performance. Dean Close Preparatory School also offers scholarships at ages 7 and 11.

Academic: The 13+ ISEB Common Scholarship Examination, for which specimen papers are available from the ISEB, is held annually at the school in February. Candidates for academic scholarships from state schools should contact the Admissions team. The Sixth Form Scholarship examination takes place in November.

Music (including Choral and Organ) and Drama Scholarships are based on audition, interviews and exam (Drama). Individual specialist tuition is free to all scholars and exhibitioners.

Art and Design Technology Scholarships may be awarded, based on portfolio, drawing / technical test and interview.

Sports Scholarships are awarded to reflect all-round sporting ability and commitment. Assessment by conditioning tests, skills tests in two or more sports and interviews.

Means-tested bursaries for sons and daughters of clergy and missionaries. Automatic discounts, known as Thierry Awards, are offered to parents serving in HM Armed Forces on a scale according to rank. Foundation Bursaries for families in the locality unable otherwise to benefit from a Dean Close education.

Number and Organisation. There are 490 in the Senior School (13–18). The Sixth Form comprises approximately 40% of the School. There are ten Houses: three for boy boarders (one Sixth Form only), three for girl boarders (one Sixth Form only) two day houses for boys and two day houses for girls. Houseparents take immediate responsibility for pupils' work, careers, applications for universities and further education. A tutorial system ensures that all pupils have a member of the teaching staff who takes a particular interest in them, both academically and pastorally. There is a Futures department giving advice on careers, university programmes and choices on leaving school. The Preparatory School (2–13) has approximately 453 pupils of whom 222 are girls.

Work. In the lower part of the School, pupils are set rather than streamed; included in the timetable is a Creative Studies course introducing pupils to a wide range of artistic and creative subjects, embracing Art, Drama, Music, PDT and Physical Education. The language centre, music school, art school, sports hall, modern laboratories, IT Suite, electronics and creative workshops combine excellent teaching and leisure facilities which are available both in timetabled and extra-curricular time. Much of the accommodation has been built in the last twenty years and is modern and purpose-built. A professional 550-seat theatre houses an ambitious programme of productions. There is also an open-air theatre. As well as several orchestras, wind band, many ensembles and the Chapel Choir, the School has a Choral Society which performs a major work at least once a year. The Strings Department is headed up by the internationally renowned Carducci Quartet. Tuition in any number of musical instruments is available as an extra. Free tuition is provided for music award holders and high-grade musicians. The theatre also affords first-class concert facilities.

Religious Education. The teaching and Chapel services are in accordance with the Church of England and the School's strong Evangelical tradition is maintained. The Chaplain prepares members of the

School for confirmation each year. Most services are in the School Chapel.

Games. The School has a 25m indoor swimming pool and a £3m sports hall, both used year round. There are two international standard AstroTurf pitches, a large number of tennis courts and grass pitches for rugby, cricket and athletics. Hockey, rugby, cricket, netball, athletics, tennis, and cross-country are the main sports.

Health. The School has three qualified Sisters with Assistants and visiting Doctors. There is a surgery and a medical centre.

Outside Activities. There is a huge range of clubs, activities and societies, from climbing to creative writing, salsa dancing to Warhammer, theatre tech to horse riding. A very active Combined Cadet Force with RN and Army sections trains every Wednesday afternoon and some pursue Bronze and Gold Duke of Edinburgh's Award. There is an active outward bound club and a large Community Action group gets involved with projects on a local, national and international level, particularly with a link school in Uganda.

Charitable status. Dean Close School is a Registered Charity, number 1086829. It exists to provide education for children.

President of Council of Members: The Lord Ribeiro, CBE

Board of Trustees:
Revd M Allen
Mr S Bullingham, MSc, BSc
Mrs K Carden, MPhil, BA (*Chairman*)
Mrs H S L Daltry, BA
Mr C S S Drew, MA
Mr L Glaser, MA, BSc
Mr S Holliday, MA
Mr M Hughes
Mrs F L Knight, BA
AVM R Lock, CBE, BSc
Mr G McDonald
Mr M P Smith, MA
Mr M Smith
Lt Col ET Taylor, BA, RA

The Trustees are elected by the Members of Council and oversee the overall governance of the School. They carry a substantial burden of financial and legal responsibility on an entirely voluntary basis and the School is greatly indebted to them.

***Warden*: Mrs Emma Taylor**, MA Oxon, PGCE

Headmaster: B J Salisbury, MEd, PGCE

Deputy Headmaster: A S Hall, BA HMS, MA
Deputy Head Pastoral: Mrs J A Davis, MA, PGCE
Deputy Head Academic: J A Hole, MA
Director of International Pupils: Mrs R J Vest, BA, PGCE, MAELT

Bursar: A P Bowcher, MBA, FCIB, DipFS
Chaplain: Revd J C Ash, BA

Preparatory School:
(see entry in IAPS section)
Headmaster: P Moss, BA
Deputy Head Operations: J Harris, BA, PGCE
Academic Director: J Gould

Pre-Preparatory School:
(see entry in IAPS section)
Head: J E Cowling, BA, PGCE
Early Years Foundation Stage Coordinator: Miss A Moorhouse, BEd

Director of Admissions: Mrs R Chaplain, BSc
Registrar, Pre-Preparatory: Lesley Miller
Head of Admissions, Preparatory: Mrs K Fergusson
Head of Admissions, Senior: Mrs K Serjeant, BA

Downe House

Hermitage Road, Cold Ash, Thatcham, Berkshire RG18 9JJ

Tel: 01635 200286
email: registrar@downehouse.net
website: www.downehouse.net
X/Twitter: @DowneHouse
Facebook: @downehouse
Instagram: @downe_house
LinkedIn: /downe-house-school

At a glance. Established in 1907, Downe House is one of the top all girls' boarding schools in the UK, offering a world-class traditional independent education with a modern twist. With a focus on excellence and the individual, girls are encouraged to make the most of the exceptional academic, co-curricular and enrichment opportunities on offer and to create their own paths, authentic to themselves. Situated in a beautiful Berkshire 110-acre woodland estate, Downe House offers family-friendly boarding balanced with an exceptional wealth of opportunities.

Supported by personal tutors, girls excel not only in their studies but in Sport, Creative and Performing Arts and Music, going on to study at the top universities in the world. A Microsoft Showcase school, girls are equipped with outstanding digital skills, preparing them for a fast-developing modern workplace.

We have a **strong global outlook** that prepares our young women to be world-ready, offering them opportunities to study and work abroad. In Year 8, all girls spend a term at our school in France, and in Years 10 and 12, girls can take part in our Global Exchange Programme, with 16 schools across five continents. The Sixth Form takes this further, offering global internships, which in 2023/24 featured more than 25 internships spanning five continents, alongside a Mini MBA, the Ivy House Leadership Award and our Sixth Form Interview Training Programme, which uses VR and AI technology. Girls leave Downe House with confidence – empowered to succeed.

Academically, we encourage ambition and ignite a love of learning through a supportive community. Although personal triumphs and individual achievements are the most celebrated within the School, the foundation of academic success is evident from our GCSE and A Level results.

In 2023, at I/GCSE 81% of all grades were at 9–7 grades (A*+, A* and A). In addition to success in the core subjects, we are delighted to have seen impressive results across the curriculum with many faculties achieving a high % of 9–7 grades (A*+, A* and A), including Science (87%), Languages (86%), Creative Arts (83%) and Performing Arts (94%).

At A Level, 27% of all grades were A*, 64% A*–A and 84% A*–B. 46% of our students achieved 3 or more A*–A grades and these outstanding results have enabled our girls to secure places at some of the world's top universities.

Over 20% of our girls are heading to Oxford, Cambridge and the top London universities to study a remarkable breadth of courses, including: Fine Art, Engineering, Music and English Language and Literature at Oxford; Natural Sciences at Cambridge; PPE and Biomedical Sciences at King's College London; Chemistry with Molecular Physics and Maths at Imperial College London; Medicine at Queen Mary University London, and Robotics & AI, English, Global Humanitarian Studies and French and German at UCL.

As well as leading universities across the length and breadth of the UK, some students are heading to prestigious destinations across the world, including The New School (Parsons) USA, UCLA, Semmelweiss, and the University of Hong Kong.

What makes Downe House special? The answer is in the Downe House DNA:

- Collaboration
- Resilience
- Creativity
- Aspiration
- Compassion
- Communication
- Outward-looking

In the classroom, on the pitch, on stage and everywhere in between, these values are the hope and aspiration for every pupil. Upon stepping through the School gates, everyone is treated and celebrated as an individual. Whether she is an artist with an aptitude for mathematics, a scientist with a love of music, or an athlete with an interest in politics, she will be nurtured and encouraged to discover her passions and talents.

The dynasty of Downe House women who preceded, and the sheer variety of career paths and achievements of our alumnae, is testimony to our ethos. They all carry with them the imprint of the Downe House DNA.

Pastoral Care

'*Downe House was everything we hoped for in the next step for our daughter's education. You have evidently done a wonderful job of creating the right environment to foster achievement and happiness.*' (DH parent, 2021)

Downe House was founded as 'a school where every individual within the community matters', and this has not changed. We work in partnership with parents to ensure that every Downe House pupil leaves school with a lifelong intellectual curiosity, the confidence that she can face life's challenges, and a steadfast place in a lively school community.

Boarding. Downe House offers idyllic accommodation onsite, with a wealth of activities as part of our boarding model. So well-suited to the needs of a busy modern family, that over 90% of pupils are boarding students. Offering both boarding and day places, Downe House provides every pupil with the gift of time and space for extra-curricular activities balanced with important family time.

Fees per term (2023–2024). £15,920 for boarders, £11,840 for day.

Admissions. Pupils may enter the school at 11+, 12+ or 13+ upon successful assessment, interview and ISEB Common Pre-Test. Pupils can also join the Sixth Form after completing our interview and entrance test.

Application for entry should be made well in advance. Prospective parents are asked to make an appointment to visit the School and meet the Headmistress prior to their daughter's start date.

Scholarships. The School offers a number of Academic Scholarships at 11+, 12+, 13+ and for entry into the Sixth Form. Scholarships are also awarded in Music, Creative Arts and Sport (11+ and 13+) and Drama (13+ and 16+) and there are Headmistress's Awards for outstanding all-round performers. As a Scholar or Exhibitioner, pupils have access to our specialist Scholarship programme which offers a range of specialist enrichment activities to inspire her and extend her knowledge. A mentor is provided to guide and encourage her on her journey as well as important leadership opportunities, designed to stretch and challenge her. For more information on Scholarships please visit the website: Scholarship Programme | Downe House School

Bursaries. Downe House is committed to extending access to the education and welcoming pupils who would otherwise be denied the opportunity of a boarding experience of the highest calibre and quality. For more information on Bursaries please visit our website: www.downehouse.net/downe-house-admissions/bursaries

Location. An easy drive from London takes you to our beautiful, secure school campus in the heart of rural West Berkshire. Our stunning 110-acre woodland estate overlooks the historic Berkshire Downs.

Pupils enjoy the close proximity to other schools for match fixtures and academic enrichment events, as well as hosting and attending socials with local prep schools and independent schools such as Eton College, Radley College, Bradfield College and Harrow School.

Find your Downe House. As one Sixth Former summed up the experience, '*I left Downe House with the feeling there was nothing I couldn't achieve.*'

Charitable status. Downe House School is a Registered Charity, number 1015059. Our aim is the provision of a sound and broadly based education for pupils, which will equip them for university entrance and beyond.

Governors:

Ms Fru Hazlitt, BA (*Chair of Governors*)
Mr Timothy Boucher, BA, FCA (*Chairman of Finance & General Purposes Committee*)
Ms Elizabeth Clarke, BA, CPE
Ms Paola Diana, BA, MA
Ms Veryan Exelby, MA
Mrs Fiona Holmes, BComm
Ms Sally McNair Scott, LLB (*Chair of Business Development Committee*)
Dr Christopher O'Kane, MA, MB BChir, MSc, DPhil
Dr Clare Ratnage, BSc, MBChB, MRCP, MRCGP (*Chair of Safeguarding Committee*)
Mr Mark Ridley, BA, MA, MRICS (*Chairman of Estates Sub-Committee*)

Ms Caroline Ross, LLB, CIPD
Mr Joe Smith, BA, MEd, PGCE (*Chairman of Education Committee*)
Mr Nick Woods, BSc, FCA

Clerk to the Governors: Mr Edward Valletta

Leadership Team:

***Headmistress*: Mrs Emma McKendrick**, BA, PGCE, FRSA

Deputy Head: Mr Matthew Godfrey, BA, MA Ed, PGCE
Deputy Head (*Academic*): Mr Hugh Grant, MA, PGCE
Deputy Head (*Pastoral*): Mrs Genevieve Ford, BA, PGCE
Assistant Head (*Sixth Form*): Miss Georgiana Taylor, BA Hons, PGCE
Assistant Head (*Upper School*): Mrs Anna Dourountakis, BA, HDE Post Graduate
Assistant Head (*Lower School*): Miss Kate Eaves, MA, PGCE
Assistant Head (*Operations*): Mrs Philippa Toogood, BA, MSt, PGCE
Director of Finance and Business Enterprise: Mr Kevin Elliott, BA, MA, MEd, MBA
Director of Digital Delivery and Innovation: Mr David McClymont, PG Dip, MCITP EA
Director of HR: Ms Kate Tuttle, MCIPD
Director of Estates and Services: Mr Alasdair Heath
PA to the Headmistress: Ms Judy Davies

Admissions:
Registrar: Miss Angela Nutt
Registrar@downehouse.net

Dulwich College

Dulwich Common, London SE21 7LD

Tel: 020 8693 3601
email: info@dulwich.org.uk
website: www.dulwich.org.uk
X/Twitter: @DulwichCollege
Facebook: @DulwichCollege
Instagram: @dulwichcollege
LinkedIn: /school/dulwich-college

Motto: *Detur gloria soli Deo ~ Let Glory be given to God alone*

Dulwich College was founded in 1619 by Edward Alleyn, the Elizabethan actor, and marked its 400th anniversary in 2019.

The College is an academically selective, independent day and boarding school for boys aged 7–18; full, weekly and flexi boarding is available for boys aged 11–18. Situated in over 70 acres of grounds and playing fields, the campus is just 10 minutes by train from London Victoria. A Dulwich education ensures each pupil fulfils their academic potential whilst taking advantage of the wide range of sporting, cultural and adventurous activities on offer.

Boys move on to universities, medical and dental schools, music and art colleges. Almost all enter higher education, but an increasing number of boys are following vocational paths including Degree Apprenticeships. Pupils are prepared for entry to the most competitive universities such as Oxford, Cambridge and Imperial, where a very good record of places is maintained each year.

The College's principal aims for all its boys are:

- to offer an appropriate academic challenge which enables each pupil to realise his potential;
- to create an environment which promotes an independent work ethic and encourages all boys to acquire a love of learning;
- to provide a wide range of sporting, cultural and adventurous activities for pupils to enjoy and through which they can learn to work cooperatively and to take a lead;
- to nurture a supportive community that encourages a sense of social responsibility and spiritual and personal development;
- to ensure that pupils from a broad variety of backgrounds can feel equally secure and valued;
- to offer boys and staff opportunities to benefit from and contribute to the College's international and UK educational partnerships.

Organisation. The College, comprising some 1,600 boys, has four specific schools: Junior School, Lower School, Middle School and Upper School. Each of these has its own Head who is responsible to The Master for that part of the College. Within each School there are Heads of Year and Form Tutors who have daily contact with boys in their care. These teams are responsible for overseeing the pastoral and academic welfare of the boys and they ensure that close links are fostered between parents and the College.

DUCKS. Nestled within the leafy grounds of Dulwich College, DUCKS, the Infants' school and Kindergarten, fondly referred to as the 'jewel on the hill', stands as a beacon of co-educational excellence. Here children aged 6 months to 7 years embark on a journey of early education within an environment of expansive outdoor spaces and attractive learning environments. Moreover, DUCKS children enjoy the rich array of facilities and resources available within the 70 acre Dulwich College campus.

Day House system. A thriving Day House system offers boys the opportunity to take part in a wide range of competitive activities including art, chess, poetry, general knowledge, debating, drama and music. They can also compete in a number of sports throughout the academic year, including rugby, soccer, hockey, cricket and athletics.

Curriculum. In Years 7 and 8 all boys follow a broad and balanced curriculum, including all standard core subjects and French or Spanish, Chinese, Latin, Wellbeing, PE, Computing, Drama, DT, Art and Music. In Year 8, boys make a choice between Latin, Chinese or German; this reduces the number of languages studied to two, allowing boys the time to engage rigorously in their chosen languages and make significant progress. In Year 9 boys continue with the core subjects, Wellbeing and PE together with French or Spanish, and they choose a second language from German, Chinese, French, Spanish, Latin or Italian. This second language may be a continuation of languages they have previously studied, or they may start them from scratch. In Years 10 and 11 boys take between nine and 10 GCSE subjects, comprising English, English Literature, Mathematics, Biology, Chemistry, Physics and French or Spanish plus three optional subjects; they all continue with Wellbeing and PE. In the Upper School (Years 12 and 13), there is a free choice of three A Level subjects (four if they are studying Further Mathematics) and since 2017 every pupil has opted for an A Level 'Plus' option which is an in-house qualification that aims to provide enrichment, cross-curricular links and programmes that reflect the likely courses boys choose at university. Boys will also choose a 'Link' course in conjunction with James Allen's Girls' School that will provide breadth to their educational profile, including a regular lecture series and community service options. The concept of Free Learning (supra-curricular and other learning beyond the curriculum) is now fully embedded in the life of the College across all year groups.

Facilities. Over the years the College has developed its complex of buildings to meet the needs of boys' education in the twenty-first century, and this development continues. In the summer of 2022, work began on the complete refurbishment of the Lower School for Years 7 and 8.

One of these developments is The Laboratory, a new state-of-the-art building that brings together the twin cultures of Science and Art. There are 21 laboratories, three preparation rooms and the James Caird Hall, which houses the rescue boat of one of the College's most famous Old Alleynians, Sir Ernest Shackleton. There are five adaptable 'Informatics' suites with free-thinking spaces for creative learning and cross-curricular collaboration and a seminar room with full videoconferencing facilities. In addition, there is a versatile 240-seat auditorium which is available to the whole Dulwich community for events and exhibitions and an outdoor piazza for recreation and performance.

Extensive IT facilities are available to all pupils. The IT network gives pupils and staff access to a wide range of centrally stored learning resources through the College's own virtual learning environment, 'MyDulwich'. Three separate libraries, all staffed by professional librarians, cater to the specific needs of different age groups. Exhibitions, drawn from the College archive, are regularly mounted in the Wodehouse Library.

The College has two separate dining areas which provide a wide choice of food, including a vegetarian option, on a cafeteria basis for both pupils and staff. The College also has its own shop, the Commissariat, where uniform, equipment and stationery can be purchased. The Medical Centre provides professional nursing care on a round-the-clock basis for boarders and day boys. The College Counsellor, based in the Medical Centre, provides confidential consultation for pupils and parents.

Sport is integral to life at Dulwich College both within the curriculum and as part of the wider co-curricular programme. There are over 70 acres of playing fields. The Sports Centre includes a substantial sports hall and a modern indoor 25-metre swimming pool. The College owns a boathouse on the Thames, accommodating the thriving Boat Club, and an Outdoor Centre in the Brecon Beacons which is used for a variety of activities and residential courses.

- **1,215 pupils (75%) represent Dulwich at sport**
  We have a breadth and depth of opportunities for all pupils to participate in sport with a commitment to educating pupils about why physical activity is important and the positive effects of sport through our physical wellbeing programme.
- **A multi-sport approach**
  This includes Rugby, Football, Hockey, Cricket, Athletics, Rowing, Tennis, Badminton, Fencing, Swimming, Water Polo, Squash, Basketball, Cycling and Cross Country.
- We run a **High-Performance Programme** tailored to meet the needs of the individual; pupils don't, however, have to be sports scholars to access this programme.
- Pupils have gained **scholarships to top universities** both in the UK and abroad, and a number have gone on to full-time careers playing sport.

Music and Drama. A professionally equipped, purpose-built Music School provides all pupils with the opportunity to study a musical instrument. More than 600 pupils receive individual tuition every week from 35 experienced specialist musicians, led by the Heads of Strings, Wind, Brass, Keyboard and Singing. The College Chapel Choir, an ancient foundation, leads regular services in the Foundation Chapel (Christ's Chapel) and also at other venues throughout the country. The Edward Alleyn Theatre is a fully rigged auditorium with a capacity of 250; over 50 events are staged annually and the facility includes rehearsal and teaching spaces, as well as dressing rooms. In 2019 Dulwich College was awarded 'Independent School of the Year for the Performing Arts', acknowledging the work and talent of the Drama and Music departments. The award was conferred by *Independent School Parent* magazine.

- The College offers Music Awards at 11+, 13+ and 16+. Music Scholarships are awarded up to 33% remission of fees and include free tuition on 2 instruments. Music Exhibitions offer free tuition on two instruments.

Art and DT. At Dulwich College, we are not necessarily in the business of turning every student into a professional artist. Instead, we endeavour to instil a life-long love, respect and understanding of the arts as a whole. We strive to ensure our challenging curriculum and diverse co-curricular and enrichment opportunities appeal to the wide range of students who come into our care. We believe art allows students to go on a journey into unknown territories, to discover a passion and niche within the world of cultural possibility, in turn helping them to gain confidence in their ability to create, take risks and problem solve.

- **The Store Gallery**
  Our 'rough magic' space The Store hosts exhibitions and events by emerging artists and collectives. These have included *Evolving Spaces* with Almanac architects, *Make a Mark* with a collective of artists both London based and international and *Interview – prototype* with Harrison Pearce. The space is also used for artists in residence and to showcase work by pupils providing them with the skills and experience of being the maker, curator, and technician.
- **Partnerships**
  As part of a collective of art and art history departments we work with our local partnership

schools on **art, photography and design projects and competitions**. We come together to both host and attend talks and lectures, most recently **Michael Landy** gave a talk and interview at the College hosted by a pupil panel made up of our pupils and those from partnership schools.

- **Community Art**
  Two students were commissioned by the Camberwell Society to paint an optical illusion of the Jamaican poet, writer, and activist Una Marson at Denmark Hill Station. Their art installation, an anamorphic illusion of the BBC trailblazer, was seen by 10,000 daily commuters.
- **Prize winners**
  Two A level Art pupils won the judges prize for the London Schools Sovereign Art Prize and many of our students are awarded top place at the Young Art competition.

Clubs and Societies. A wide variety of clubs and societies, many run by the pupils themselves, take place during the lunch break and after school. These range from Lego for the younger boys to the Political Society which is responsible for inviting prominent public figures to speak. The College is particularly renowned for its Debating success that in 2016 culminated in a Year 12 pupil captaining Team England to victory in the World Schools Debating Championships. The College encourages boys to take part in expeditions as well as many community-based activities which can include membership of the Combined Cadet Force, Scouts, the Duke of Edinburgh's Award scheme and Community Action. Academic, cultural and sporting excursions take place at various points throughout the school year.

Careers. Specialist careers staff, professional external advisors, dedicated IT facilities and an accredited library provide an up-to-date service assisting boys in planning higher education and careers. Boys and their parents attend the annual Courses and Careers Convention to consult with representatives from key employers, professional institutes and around 25 universities. Upper School boys receive guidance on how degree course choices might influence their future careers. Regular networking events and groups have the aim of allowing Old Alleynians (OAs) and Alleynians to share experiences and expertise and to develop their network of professional contacts. Alumni of all ages can benefit from membership and are encouraged to join.

Mentoring is widely recognised as an effective tool for enhancing career prospects and ensuring informed choice. The Mentoring Programme is offered to Dulwich College pupils and OAs and brings together mentors and mentees in purposeful, mutually rewarding relationships. It is designed to provide additional support for OAs as they progress through their careers.

Boarding. There are three boarding houses in Dulwich College, all situated within or close to the campus. Each house has a Housemaster who is resident with his family. Boys in Years 7–13 live in Old Blew and The Orchard and boys in the Upper School live in Blew House and Ivyholme, where each boy has his own room with en-suite facilities. At present, there are around 140 boarders. Boarding at Dulwich is truly international with boys coming from all over the world and this adds to an atmosphere of cultural tolerance and intellectual curiosity.

ISI Inspection November 2014. ISI Inspectors awarded Dulwich College, Dulwich College Junior School and DUCKS 'Excellent' in every category, 'Exceptional' for 'the quality of pupils' achievements and learning' for the senior school – the only category for which this grading can be given – and 'Outstanding' for the EYFS (Kindergarten, Nursery and Reception).

Entry. Pupils are admitted to the College as day pupils, boarders, weekly boarders or occasional boarders. Places are available at age 7, 11, 13 and 16. Casual vacancies occur from time to time at ages 8, 9, 10 and 12. At age 7 places are awarded on the basis of interview, report and practical assessment during the Lent Term. At age 11 places are awarded on the results of the Combined Entrance and Scholarship Examination held in the Lent Term. Candidates take papers in English and Mathematics and also a Verbal/Non-Verbal Reasoning test. At age 13 boys may take the College's own Entrance Examinations held in the Lent Term. Entrance is by examination and interview. At 16+ places are offered on the results from subject specific tests, interview and GCSE grades. Application should generally be in the year before desired date of entry. For further information please see the Admissions section on the College website. A non-refundable registration fee of £160 is charged for all applications and £320 for overseas applications.

Fees per term (2023–2024). Day: £8,231 (includes lunch for Junior and Lower School pupils up to Year 8); Full Boarding: £17,182; Weekly Boarding: £16,108.

Scholarships and Bursaries. We warmly welcome applications from parents with academically strong boys who need full or partial financial support to send their son to Dulwich College. Bursaries provide financial assistance with school fees. Whilst the majority of bursaries are offered on entry to Year 7 (11+), we also award bursaries to boys joining in Years 3 (7+), 4 (8+), 5 (9+), 9 (13+) and 12 (16+).

We also offer a range of scholarships. Please refer to our scholarships pages for more information about how we acknowledge academic, sporting and cultural excellence. Thanks to the generosity of our benefactors, we are able to give over £4 million every year to support 200 bursary awards.

All applicants are considered on the basis of their performance in the entrance examination and interview. A Bursary and a Scholarship might be awarded together up to a maximum value of 100% of the school fees. In addition to school fees, means-tested support may be available for trips and other enrichment activities.

Old Alleynians. Founded in 1873, The Alleyn Club is a flourishing former pupils' association with over 10,000 Old Alleynian (OA) members living in more than 90 countries. The club's name acknowledges the founder, Edward Alleyn, actor, theatre manager and contemporary of William Shakespeare.

Charitable status. Dulwich College is a Registered Charity, number 1150064.

The Governing Body:
Chair: Adrian JS Carr, PhD [OA]
Vice Chair: Dr Irene Bishop, CBE, BEd, MA, LLD
Fred Binka [OA]
Ben Dean, BA, MProf [OA]
Keri Elborn, BA, FCA
Karen Fowler, MA

Randa Hanna, BA, AA Dipl RIBA
Howard Kerr, MA, MBA
David Parfitt
Catherine Polli, LLB
Tim Pethybridge
Malik Ramadhan, OBE [OA]
Kirsty Rutter, BSc, ACMA
Nic Weatherhead, BSc, MCIPD

Honorary International Advisor to the Governors: His Excellency Khun Anand Panyarachun, Hon KBE, MA [OA]
Special Advisor to the Governors: Sir John H Riblat, FRICS, Hon FRIBA [OA]

[OA] *Old Alleynian*

Clerk to the Governors: Ms K Jones, LLB

***Master of the College*: Dr Joe Spence**, BA Hons, PhD

Deputy Masters:
Mrs F M Angel, BA (*Senior Deputy*)
Mr A Threadgould, BSc (*Academic*)
Dr C S B Pyke, MA, MMus, PhD (*External*)
Mr E Read, MA (*Pastoral and Co-curricular*)

Chief Operating Officer: Mr G Keogh-Peters, BA, ACA
Chief Financial Officer: Mr B Hoo, ACA
Director of Communications: Ms J M Scott, MA, MBA
Director of Development: Mr M Jarrett, BA
Director of Admissions, Libraries & Archives: Dr N D Black, BA, PhD

Head of Upper School: Mr C O Siochru, MA, MPhil
Head of Middle School: Mr S Tanna, BA
Head of Lower School: Ms F Cooke, BA
Head of Junior School: Dr T G A Griffiths, PGCE, MA, MSc, DPhil
Head of DUCKS (*Kindergarten and Infants' School*): Mrs J Parker, BEd

Registrars: Mrs A Williams and Mrs P Twisk
Archivist: Mrs C M Lucy, BA, MCLIP

PA to the Master: Mrs M Wood
PA Governance & Finance: Ms S White

The High School of Dundee

Euclid Crescent, Dundee, Tayside DD1 1HU

Tel: 01382 202921
email: enquiries@highschoolofdundee.org.uk
website: www.highschoolofdundee.org.uk
X/Twitter: @HSofDundee
Facebook: @highschoolofdundee
LinkedIn: /high-school-of-dundee

Motto: *Prestante Domino*

The present School traces its origins directly back to a 13th-century foundation by the Abbot and Monks of Lindores. It received a Royal Charter in 1859. Various Acts of Parliament in the 19th century were finally consolidated in an Order in Council constituting the High School of Dundee Scheme 1965, which was revised in 1987.

Admission. The School comprises three sections:

The Nursery – 62 pupils (age 3–5; pre-school and ante pre-school).

The Junior Years – 269 pupils (Primary 1 to Primary 7).

The Senior Years – 598 pupils (S1 to S6).

The normal stages of entry are Nursery, Primary 1 and S1. Entry to Primary 1 (age 4½ to 5½ years) is by interview held in January and to S1 (age 11 to 12 years) by an Entrance Assessment held in January. Where vacancies exist entrance is usually available at all other stages subject to satisfactory performance in an entrance assessment.

Bursaries. A number of means-tested bursaries are provided for entry to P6/7 and from S1 in the Senior Years, to help those who otherwise could not afford the fees.

Fees per term (2023–2024). Primary: £3,770 (P1 to P3), £3,950 (P4 to P5), £4,488 (P6 to P7); Secondary: £5,350. Nursery varies according to the number of sessions selected.

Buildings. The six main school buildings are in the centre of the city and form an architectural feature of the area. Two excellent, extensive playing fields – Dalnacraig and Mayfield – are situated some 1½ miles to the east of the school. As well as grass pitches, the facilities include an international standard synthetic water-based hockey surface and a sand-dressed synthetic hockey pitch which is up to national standard. The school's Mayfield Sports Centre, comprising a state-of-the-art games hall, dance studio, gymnasium and fitness suite, is adjacent to the playing fields. The Nursery is also located at Mayfield.

Curriculum. The Junior Years follow a wide-ranging primary curriculum. Subject specialists are employed in PE, ICT, Music, Science, Modern Languages, Art, Drama and Health and Food Technology.

In the Senior Years, after two years of a general curriculum, some specialisation takes place with pupils currently being prepared for the Scottish Qualifications Authority examinations at National 5, Higher and Advanced Higher which lead directly to university entrance. Results in public examinations are amongst the best in Scotland, with pupils regularly achieving the top marks nationally in individual subjects, and 90–95% of leavers enrolling at universities in the UK or abroad.

Co-Curricular Activities. Almost 100 co-curricular activities are offered. Sports teams compete at the highest levels and each year a number of pupils represent their country in a wide range of sports. Music plays an important part in the life of the school, with a large number of orchestras, bands, choirs and musical ensembles to choose from. Special tuition is provided in a wide variety of instruments.

There is a flourishing contingent of the Combined Cadet Force including a pipe band. Drama, Public Speaking and Debating, Chess and The Duke of Edinburgh's Award scheme are examples of the wide variety of activities available.

Charitable status. The Corporation of the High School of Dundee is a Registered Charity, number SC011522. The school is a charity to provide quality education for boys and girls.

The Board of Directors comprises:
Chairman, 2 ex officiis Directors, viz, The Lord Dean of Guild and The Parish Minister of Dundee. The Guildry of Dundee, the Nine Trades of Dundee, the Old Boys' Club and the Old Girls' Club and the Parents' Association each elect one Director. Six Directors are elected by Friends of the High School and up to 6 co-opted by the Board.

School Staff:

***Rector*: Mrs L A M Hudson**, MA
Deputy Rector (*Senior Years*): Mrs S J Watson, MA
Deputy Rector (*Junior Years*): Mrs J Rose, BEd
Chief Operations Officer: Mrs S Locherty, BA, CA
Deputy Heads – Senior School:
Mr N R Clarke, BSc, MSc
Mr D G Smith, BSc
Deputy Head – Junior Years: Mrs C E Proudfoot, MA, DELL
Director of ICT: Mrs W Wilson, BSc

Junior Years:
Mrs O Cannon, MA
Miss M Cardno, MA, CEEd
Miss L Carrie, MA, MPhil
Mrs L Coupar, MA
Miss C Devlin, MA
Mrs S Fish, BEd
Mrs K Goldie, BEd
Mrs A J Gruar, BA
Miss E Innes, BSc
Mrs G Johnson, BEd
Mr N W Joss, MA
Mrs M R Leburn, MA
Mrs E Morenikeji, BEd
Mrs J Palmer, BEd
Mrs C E Proudfoot, MA, DELL
Mrs C E Rankin, BA
Miss K A Reith, MEd, DELL
Mrs F A Trotter, BSc

Nursery:
Acting Manager: Mrs S Yule, BA
Acting Deputy: Miss A Mackie
Miss A Bajwa
Miss A Balfour
Miss E Cahill
Mrs S Crotti
Miss K Hodgkinson
Miss C Hutton
Mss R Lakshimi
Miss R McGarrity
Miss Z Millar
Miss J Paton
Miss N Stewart
Miss J Wakeford

Senior School:
* *Head of Department*

English:
*Mrs A Tevendale, BA Hons, MEd
Mr C Anderson, MA
Mr D P Campbell, MA
Mr D M Finlay, MA
Ms J Fulton, MA
Dr J M Morris, MA, MLitt, PhD
Mr M A Stewart, MA, MPhil

Drama and Media Studies:
*Mrs L M Drummond, Dip Drama
Mrs L E Sangster, BA

History and Modern Studies:
*Mr G Fyall, BA, Dip Ed
Miss K H E Douglas, MA
Mrs L A Hudson, MA
Mrs L Jack, MA
Mr A Kent, MA

Geography:
*Miss J L Stewart, BSc
Mrs R Lloyd, MA, MSc
Mrs S J Watson, MA

Business Education:
*Mr N S Higgins, BSc
Miss A Campbell, MA Hons
Mr N Duncan, BA Hons

Classics:
*Mr E Faulkes, BA
Dr A Lazani, BA, MA

Modern Languages:
*Mr N A MacKinnon, MA
Mrs J Brown, BA
Mrs Y Murdoch, MSc
Mrs L C Smith, MA
Mrs D M Wedderburn, MA

Mathematics:
*Mrs L A Craig, BSc
Mr N R Clarke, BSc, MSc
Dr S Ferguson, MA, MSc, PhD
Miss D Macdonald, BSc
Dr N McReynolds, MPhys, PhD
Mr R C Middleton, BSc
Dr P A Smith, BA, MEng, MA, PhD
Dr F Spiezia, MSc, PhD

Chemistry:
*Dr N Kiernan, MChem, PhD
Mrs R J Broom, BSc
Mr A S Downie, BSc
Dr E R T Robinson, MChem, PhD

Biology:
*Mr R H Bunting, BSc
Dr M W Fotheringham, MA, PhD
Mr G M S Rodger, BSc

Physics:
*Mr J Darby, BSc
Dr D G Brown, BSc, PhD
Mr D J A Finch, MSc, PGDE
Mr A Vicat-Brown, MEng

Technologies:
*Mr S McBride, BSc
Mr S Holden, BSc
Mr D G Smith, BSc

Art and Design:
*Mr A Kerr, BA
Mrs M Angus, BA
Mrs J Cura, MDes

Music:
*Dr L S Steuart Fothringham, MA, PhD, FRCO
Mr S Armstrong, Dip RSAMD
Mr J Christie, BMus, MMus
Miss P de Villiers, BMus, MMus
Miss A Evans, BA, LTCL
Miss R R McDonald, BMus, PGCert
Ms S Morgan, BMus
Ms G Simpson, Dip Mus, ALCM
Mrs S Sneddon, LTCL, ALCM
Mrs E M J Stevenson, MA
Mr D W S Wilton, BA

Learning Skills:
*Mrs J M Downie, MA, Dip ASL
Mrs L Duff, MA
Mrs S M Guy, MA
Mrs C McDonald, BEd
Mrs K L Whiting, BSc

Physical Education:
*Mr E D Jack, BEd
Mr R A Aitken, BSc
Mr C K Allan, BSc
Mrs L Anderson, BEd (**Hockey*)
Mrs L S L Baxter, BEd
Miss R Flack, MA
Miss P Geatons, BEd
Mr P J Godman (**Rugby*)
Mr G R E Merry, BSc
Miss A A Robinson, MA
Mrs L A Southern, Dip Ed

Home Economics:
Mrs L J Ross, MA

Library:
*Miss I McFarlane, MA, MSc
Mrs J S Hutton, MA

Pastoral Care and Support
*Mr N R Clarke, BSc, MSc (*Deputy Head with responsibility for Pastoral Care & Support*)
Mr C K Allan, BSc
Mrs L S L Baxter, BEd
Mr A S Downie, BSc
Ms J Fulton, MA
Mrs S M Guy, MA
Mrs L Jack, MA

Head of Careers:
Mr C K Allan, BSc

Outdoor Activities Coordinator:
Mr G M Ross, BA

Eastbourne College

Old Wish Road, Eastbourne, East Sussex BN21 4JX

Tel: 01323 452323 (Admissions)
01323 452300 (Headmaster)
01323 452300 (Bursar)
email: reception@eastbourne-college.co.uk
website: www.eastbourne-college.co.uk
X/Twitter: @EBCollegeLife
Facebook: @EastbourneCollege
Instagram: @eastbournecollege
LinkedIn: /eastbourne-college

Founded 1867; incorporated 1911.

Endless horizons endless opportunities

Few top senior independent schools in Britain offer a six-minute stroll to the doorstep of a national park, an international tennis venue, a county cricket ground, two challenging golf courses, award-winning beaches, theatres, a modern art gallery, a brand new shopping centre with state-of-the-art cinema, and a mainline station to London (85 minutes), London Gatwick Airport (55 minutes) and Ashford International (direct trains to Europe).

Independently minded since 1867

Founded over 150 years ago, today Eastbourne College reaches out like never before, connecting its boarding and day pupils with a raft of opportunities that abound within a few hundred metres of the school. The College's learning environment is second to none thanks to a recently completed £33 million development, an outstanding, supportive house system, and a timetable which optimises educational contact time, provides guided optional Saturday morning enrichment sessions, and promotes a busy calendar of competitive sport and time to socialise.

A traditional heart. A modern mind.

We've always done things differently at Eastbourne College. We're proud of our heritage, but always looking forward. Progressive and innovative. Empowering our pupils to question the answers and find their own path in life. Set in idyllic coastal surroundings, this is a place that truly makes a lasting impression. We encourage children to be confident and also teach them to be kind, courteous and considerate of others, put simply, good people that others want to be around.

Why Eastbourne College?

- Holistic approach to learning, nurturing success in and out of the classroom.
- Over 57% of grades achieved 7, 8 or 9 (equivalent to A or A*) at GCSE and over 75% of grades were awarded at A* to B at A Level in 2023.
- We sit in the top 4% of schools nationally for academic 'value added' which means on average our pupils achieve one grade above their predicted grade.
- Diverse and exciting co-curriculum, offering everything from Art to Zumba.
- Strong support network where pupils feel at home from day one.
- Flexible, family-friendly for both boarders and day pupils, and those that need a combination of the two.

World-class campus

In 2019, Dame Katherine Grainger DBE officially opened Eastbourne College's Project 150. The £33 million P150 development places the College at the forefront of learning environments in the UK.

Facilities include:

- 32 state-of-the-art classrooms
- two technology suites
- cricket pavilion with live-stream match video analysis
- dance studio with sprung floor and ceiling recess for ballet lifts and throws
- large Sport England-compliant sports hall (5 badminton courts long); year-round multi-sport training
- Sport England-compliant six-lane 25 m indoor swimming pool
- fitness suite for elite and inclusive participation
- two glass-backed squash courts
- alfresco-feel dining hall
- Tim's café
- stunning entertainment and exhibition spaces.

Admissions

Year 9 entry. Early registration for a place is recommended in Year 5/6. The College runs an Early Offer system which uses underlying ability score data and a detailed headmaster/mistress reference about a Year 6 or 7 pupil who is registered with us and whom we have been able to meet during a personal visit in order to make a firm offer of a place. Please contact the Admissions Department for more information.

Sixth form entry. Applicants for the sixth form should be predicted a GCSE grade average of 6.5 or above and receive a very positive reference from their current school. We normally expect sixth form applicants to complete a minimum of 8 GCSEs. If you would like to be considered for entry to the sixth form at the College in August 2024, please contact us to arrange a visit. This should be done as early as possible and certainly no later than by the end of the first term of Year 11.

Scholarships and bursaries. Academic, creative arts and sports awards are offered. In line with most top independent schools, the great majority of awards given at the College are valued at between 5% and 20% of the day or boarding fees, but more may be offered in exceptional circumstances and awards may be supplemented by a means-tested bursary.

Bursaries are means tested according to the Charity Commission criteria.

Entry forms for scholarships can be obtained from the Admissions Department.

Fees per term (2023–2024). Boarding: £14,580 (Years 9–11), £14,805 (Sixth Form); Day: £9,570 (Years 9–11), £9,755 (Sixth Form). An additional supplement for overseas pupils applies. Fees include meals and most extras.

Preparatory School. The charitable bodies governing Eastbourne College and the independent prep school, St Andrew's Prep, amalgamated in February 2010 to become one charity. Collaboration between the two schools had always been extremely close but, until then, there had been no formal financial or governance links between them. This was a change of governance and not of the school. The schools continue to operate independently and St Andrew's prepares boys and girls for a variety of schools including the College.

The **Eastbournian Society** brings together all those with a College connection: parents of current and former pupils, current and former staff, Old Eastbournians, friends, neighbours and local businesses. In particular, strong links are maintained with former pupils who offer careers assistance to current pupils (there is a convention every year to support the careers and higher education programme). The Society provides a series of social events and career and business networking opportunities. It comprises also the College's fundraising activity, providing funds for bursaries and new developments.

The **Devonshire Society** (legacy club) meets annually.

Charitable status. Eastbourne College Incorporated is a Registered Charity, number 307071. It exists for the purpose of educating children.

Board of Governors:

President: His Grace The Duke of Devonshire, KCVO, CBE, DL

Vice-Presidents:
The Earl of Burlington
His Excellency Nasser Judeh, BSc
General The Lord Richards of Herstmonceux, GCB, CBE, DSO, DL

Chairman: Mr P A J Broadley, MA Oxon, MSc, FCA
Vice-Chairman: Mr J P Watmough, LLB

College Chaplaincy:
Chaplain: Revd D J Merceron, BA Institute of Archaeology

Chief Operating Officer and Clerk to the Board of Governors: Abbey Gough, BA, FCA

Senior Management Team:

***Headmaster*: The Hon T N M Lawson**, MA Christ Church Oxford

Second Master: Mr C W Symes, BSc, MEd, MCGI Edinburgh
Deputy Head (*Academic*): Mr J M Gilbert, BSc Cardiff, MBA, MRSC
Deputy Head (*Co-curricular*): Mr A T Lamb, MBE, BA University of New England NSW Australia, Dip Ed, DL
Deputy Head (*Pastoral*): Mrs G E Taylor-Hall, BA Liverpool
Development Director, *Eastbournian Society*: Mrs E C B Garrett, BA Warwick
Director of Marketing and Admissions to the Eastbourne College Charity: Mrs G L Crowhurst, BA Oxford Brookes

Edgbaston High School

Westbourne Road, Edgbaston, Birmingham, West Midlands B15 3TS

Tel: 0121 454 5831
email: admissions@edgbastonhigh.co.uk
website: www.edgbastonhigh.co.uk
X/Twitter: @Edgbaston_High
Facebook: @Edgbaston-High-School-Official-430788326941674
Instagram: @edgbastonhighschool

See full entry in the **GSA** section, on **p. 431**.

The Edinburgh Academy

42 Henderson Row, Edinburgh EH3 5BL

Tel: 0131 556 4603
0131 624 4987 (Admissions)
email: seniorschooloffice@edinburghacademy.org.uk
admissions@edinburghacademy.org.uk
website: www.edinburghacademy.org.uk
X/Twitter: @edinburghacad
Facebook: @TheEdinburghAcademy
Instagram: @edinburghacad
TikTok: @TheEdinburghAcademy

The Edinburgh Academy is a co-educational day school for pupils aged 2 to 18 with a proud history and outward vision. Founded in 1824 with the aspiration to create a school where excellence could always be achieved, the School motto translates as 'Always Excel'. The Edinburgh Academy is built on strong traditions but is always seeking to innovate.

The Edinburgh Academy consists of a Nursery of 110 children, a Junior School of 400 children and a Senior School of 660. The School's size allows it to cater for the individual needs and ambitions of each child while high staff ratios mean that at each stage it can tailor the teaching and pastoral care to the needs of each pupil, giving them the best possible chance to develop their unique talents. Through a rounded education, Academy pupils enhance their social, emotional and spiritual capacities; equipping them for citizenship in a challenging and changing world. The attributes of an Academy Learner are that they are curious, creative, independent, collaborative and resilient.

Campus. A strength of the Academy is the split campus. This allows for purpose-built facilities and high-quality teaching at each age and stage through which all children can flourish.

Situated in Edinburgh's New Town since 1824, the Senior School is a stunning architectural blend of traditional and modern buildings. The most recent additions have been the Hockey Pavilion, indoor climbing wall, Henry Marsh Golf Centre and the Learning Commons, which provides multipurpose lecture and STEM learning spaces.

The Junior School, Nursery and Playing Fields occupy 26 acres on Arboretum Road: next to the world-renowned Royal Botanic Gardens. Outdoor learning and learning through play are central factors for educating children on our spacious campus while the purpose-built Nursery provides a bright, functional and fun environment ensuring the best of opportunities for learning both inside and out.

Academic. The Academy supports each child on their preferred education path and gets to know each individual extremely well in helping them to reach their personal goals and achieve to the best of their ability. The pre-14 curriculum offers flexibility; giving a very good grounding in basic skills while allowing pupils to progress through developing the critical higher order skills inherent in the best parts of 'A Curriculum for Excellence'. Older Senior School pupils present for exams in a wide range of subjects at National 5, Higher and Advanced Higher.

In keeping with the stated vision of producing children who are 'Grounded in Scotland, Ready for the World', the school takes pride in the fact that there are Academicals (alumni) around the globe who look back on their Academy education as their first crucial step on the ladder to success.

Class sizes. Class sizes are kept relatively small to allow teachers to identify and nurture each child's strengths. In the Junior School, the aim is to keep class sizes of around 22 children. In the Senior School, no teaching group is larger than 20 pupils, and most are substantially smaller.

Courses of study. A very wide general curriculum is taught at the Edinburgh Academy between the ages of 2 and 14. Away from the valuable lessons taught by their class teacher, Nursery pupils receive specialist teaching in Science, PE, Modern European Languages and Music. In Junior School, this is further complimented by Art and Mandarin (from Primary 5) while in Senior School, specialist Latin, Drama and Design Technology are introduced. Maths is set from Primary 3 and all subjects are taught by Secondary School specialist teachers from Primary 7 (Geits).

Eight subjects are taken for National 5 (GCSE equivalent): English, Maths, a foreign language and a science must be taken and it is recommended that pupils complete the balance by adding either History or Geography, and one of Art, Music, Drama, PE or a technical subject.

In the final years of the Senior School, the emphasis increasingly moves towards preparing young people for higher education and beyond. The penultimate year sees the breadth inherent in Scottish Highers followed by the greater depth of Advanced Highers. In Art and Music, a two-year A Level course is offered in the belief that this is better suited to the needs of pupils looking to progress in those specialisms.

Physical Education. All Academy pupils are encouraged to stay active and healthy. Over 25 acres of sports pitches, including four all-weather surfaces, squash, tennis and fives courts and a sports centre, are coupled with top-class coaching to help them enjoy their chosen sports. Pupils can choose from a full range of winter and summer sports and teams represent the School in rugby, hockey, football, cricket, tennis, squash, badminton, fives, athletics, skiing, golf, swimming, cross country running, netball and dance.

The Academy also has a state-of-the-art Climbing and Bouldering Facility that is without doubt the best school arena of this type in the country.

Outdoor education. The Edinburgh Academy has invested significantly in its 'Spirit of Adventure Fund'. As well as the Climbing Wall, this has allowed for the recruitment of both a Director of Adventure and Character Education and an Early Years Outdoor Learning specialist. This example of 'EA Innovation' means that all Academy children from the youngest in the Nursery to those completing their Gold Duke of Edinburgh's Award benefit from the resilience and character most easily developed in the outdoors.

Music, Drama, Art. The Creative Arts are an important part of Edinburgh Academy life and pupils are encouraged to take part from Junior School and beyond. Most pupils learn a musical instrument and are members of the various choirs, orchestras, bands and ensembles. All Junior School pupils take part in an annual drama production while the Senior School produces extremely high-quality performances at regular intervals throughout the year.

In Art, a large number of pupils take the A Level and the success rate for being accepted into Art College is very high. A number of students join the Academy each year with their primary objective being to study Fine Art. This is complemented in Design and Technology where there is a fully furnished Jewellery Studio. At the end of each year there is a major exhibition in these subjects where pupils' work is displayed and sold.

Extracurricular. The Academy recognises that significant learning takes place outside the formal classroom and believes in a balance between academic and co-curricular activities; offering a wide range of opportunities to participate and represent the Academy in sport, music and a variety of expressive and creative arts.

There is an extremely broad range of co-curricular activities available including Debating, Photography, Computing, Model United Nations, Modern Languages, Jazz, Politics, Scripture Union, Film Club, Chess, Pipes and Drums, Public Speaking, Eco Group, Diversity Group, Gender Equality Group, Media Group, Sailing, Cross Country, Climbing, Football and many, many more.

Combined Cadet Force and The Duke of Edinburgh's Award. All pupils over the age of 14 must participate in either the CCF (Army, RAF or Pipe Band sections) or The Duke of Edinburgh's Award scheme for a period of three terms after which further participation is voluntary. The CCF sections offer training in field craft, flying, weapons handling, orienteering, drill and first aid and affords young people the opportunity to develop their leadership potential.

Fees per annum (2024–2025). Nursery: £3,385–£14,680. Junior School (P1–P6): £10,870–£13,284, Senior School (P7–7ths/S6): £14,321–£17,541. For further details about the financial package available please contact Accounts on 0131 624 4916.

Scholarships and bursaries. Means-tested bursaries of up to 100% of fees are offered to pupils who are most able to benefit from an Edinburgh Academy education; irrespective of financial means. These are generally available to Senior School pupils.

A number of scholarships (age 11+) are offered to candidates of very high ability either academically or in Art, Music or Sport. Examinations and assessments are held in January.

Admissions. The majority of new pupils join at the beginning of the autumn term in late August though some also join during the session. Other than for Nursery, all candidates for admission to the Edinburgh Academy must be assessed by the School and assessment days are held in November (Junior School P2–6) and January (P1 and Senior School). The Academy is always delighted to welcome families outwith this time. Initial enquiries should be made to the Admissions Registrar: Tel: 0131 624 4987; email: admissions@edinburghacademy.org.uk.

Edinburgh Academical Club. There is a strong alumni community and the Club works hard to remain in contact with former pupils all over the world. They host events each year, both from a social and career perspective, and have established a career mentoring and internship service to help former pupils. Contact: Tel: 0131 624 4958, email: accies@edinburghacademy.org.uk.

Charitable status. The Edinburgh Academy is a Registered Charity, number SC016999. It exists for the advancement of education and the contribution to the educational life of Scotland in its widest sense.

Court of Directors:

Nicholas Bobb	Ruari Mackenzie
Richard Bogie	Emma Marshall
Gary Connel	Steven Maxwell
Tony Cook	Sheriff Principal C A L Scott, KC
Anjali Dholakia	Sally Sutherland
Richard Fletcher	Dr Fiona Wilson
Mark Galloway	
Fiona Lane	

Chair: Mark Galloway

Bursar and Clerk to the Court: Guy Cartwright, MA, CA

***Rector*: Barry Welsh**

Junior School Staff:

Head of the Junior School: Mr G A Calder, MA Hons, PGCE, Dip Ed Leadership; Mrs L Htet Khin, LLB Hons [from April 2024]

Deputy Head of the Junior School: tbc

Senior School Staff:

Deputy Rector (*Director of Studies*): Mr T J Halsall, BA, MEd, PGCE

Deputy Rector (*Pastoral and Personnel*): Mr M Bryce, BSc

Deputy Rector (*Learning and Teaching*): Mrs C E Hancox, MA, PGCE

Elizabeth College

The Grange, St Peter Port, Guernsey, Channel Islands GY1 2PY

Tel: 01481 726544
email: office@elizabethcollege.gg
website: https://elizabethcollege.gg
X/Twitter: @Eliz_Coll
Facebook: @ElizabethCollegeGuernsey

Motto: *Semper Eadem*

Elizabeth College, founded in 1563 by Queen Elizabeth I, is a selective day school. We are a vibrant community with a challenging and stimulating academic and co-curricular programme for children between the ages of 2 and 18. EC Junior School is co-educational and provides a pre-school, infant and junior school education for children aged 2½ through to 11. The Upper School is phasing in co-education from Years 7 and 12 and works in partnership with The Ladies' College at Sixth Form.

Buildings and grounds. The Upper School (for students over 11 years) with its imposing main building (1829) overlooks the town and harbour of St Peter Port. The classrooms and laboratories (all of which are equipped with appropriate modern teaching facilities), the Hall and Sports Hall are accommodated on this site. Improvements in recent years have included a new Refectory, six fully refurbished Science Laboratories, the creation of the Science Quad and outdoor learning spaces at both the Upper and Junior School sites. There are two large games fields, one of which includes an artificial pitch for hockey. Elizabeth College Junior School (ECJS) comprises ECJS Queen's Road, the Junior School (Years 3–6) and ECJS Kings Road, our infant school and pre-school. The Junior School has its own site ten minutes' walk from Elizabeth College. It takes boys and girls from 4 to 11 years old and also has a pre-school facility for younger children.

Perrot Court. There have been a number of landmark moments in the lifetime of the College; self-evidently the most important is its foundation in 1563 with the grant of the original site. The purchase of the adjacent building, Perrot Court, allows us to enhance the facilities at the College to ensure that we are able to fully support the educational demands of current and future students. The new building will give a 40% increase in floor space and, most importantly, the opportunity to create new, flexible spaces for learning and being, something which has become more challenging in the constrained environs of an historic College main building and site originally intended for 150 students.

Academic curriculum. In Years 7 and 8, students follow a broad curriculum which is common to all, covering English, Mathematics, Sciences, Creative and Performing Arts, Humanities and Social Sciences, IT and Modern Foreign Languages. In Year 9, the Key Stage 3 curriculum remains broad, but choices are made from the Humanities, Social Sciences, Creative and Performing Arts. The core remains common to all: English, Mathematics, the Sciences and RS. In Years 10 to 11, the aim is to produce a high level of achievement and choice at GCSE by offering flexibility wherever possible. Three sciences are studied to Separate or

Trilogy GCSE. At least one Modern Language is taken, although more are available as options. English Language, Mathematics and RS are also core subjects. English Literature is studied within the English teaching groups, but is not compulsory for all and Additional Mathematics FSMQ is studied by some within their Maths teaching group. Other GCSE options combine the traditional with the contemporary: Art and Design, Business Studies, Classical Civilisation, Computing, Dance, Drama, Geography, History, Music and PE are currently offered. The Sixth Form is run in partnership with The Ladies' College with interchange of students between schools and shared teaching of many groups. The Sixth Form offers a very broad array of subjects across the two schools enabling a wide variety of choices, with all GCSE subjects carrying on into Key Stage 5 and new ones introduced: Economics, Film Studies, Further Mathematics, Photography and Psychology. Tutorial periods provide pastoral guidance while PSHE and Life Skills, which included Futures Education (Careers and University courses), PE and Games are timetabled throughout Key Stages 3, 4 and 5.

Music. There is a lively extracurricular music programme which includes the College Orchestra, Wind Ensemble and Pop and Jazz Bands, with numerous small ensembles running alongside these larger groups. There is a variety of choral groups ranging from the fun and inclusive College Choir to the more selective College Chapel Choir and the senior Close Harmony Group. The latter two groups appear regularly in events around the island and usually take part in visits to France to sing in Cathedrals and at concerts. Individual instruction is available in instrumental and vocal studies, catering for a wide range of interests including piano, organ and traditional orchestral studies as well as contemporary and jazz styles. The Junior School has its own choirs, orchestra, recorder group and steel pan band.

Games. The sports fields cover some 20 acres. The Junior School has its own small playing field, and also has access to the facilities of the Upper School. The major College games are Association Football, Hockey and Cricket. Athletics, Badminton, Basketball, Cross-country Running, Fencing, Golf, Rugby Football, Motor Sports, Netball, Sailing, Shooting, Squash and Swimming also flourish. Physical Education forms a regular part of the curriculum for all students up to the end of Year 11. Some seniors specialise in Outdoor Pursuits as their Games option under the guidance of a fully qualified expert. Despite the size of the Island, plentiful opposition for sports fixtures is available. The College competes against other Island schools, has a traditional rivalry with Victoria College in Jersey, makes regular tours to the UK mainland and hosts return visits from UK schools.

Combined Cadet Force. This is voluntary and optional from Year 10 and is Tri-Service. Cadets commit for two years with the option to extend their service for a further two years in Sixth Form. Cadets travel regularly to the UK and beyond for proficiency training, camps, courses, qualifications and competitions, as well as adventurous training. Competition shooting forms a major part of the CCF and there is a long and distinguished record at Bisley. The CCF has an important role in providing Guards of Honour for Island ceremonial occasions.

Duke of Edinburgh's Award. Students are encouraged to participate in this scheme. Both Bronze and Gold Awards are offered as extra-curricular activities. Bronze expedition work takes place locally in the Channel Islands whilst the expedition work necessary for the Gold Award takes place on the UK mainland during the Easter and Summer holidays.

Community service. We encourage students in all year groups to support our regular charity days that are led and run by a Sixth Form team. All students in Year 9 will take a five-week activity on conservation and eco awareness; including a visit to the school allotment. From Year 10 onwards, students can opt to serve in the CCF, where they will be involved in numerous island parades and ceremonies; Sports Leadership, whereby students are encouraged to coach and take charge of sports fixtures and games for younger teams on the island; and conservation, in which students are involved in growing crops that can be used by themselves, the College kitchen and others; or working with a local charity such as Health Connections. The College also runs an annual trip to Kenya where Sixth Form students spend some time teaching in local Primary schools, working with a local charity for children; there is also an educational bursary linked to this charity, that has been set up and organised by students from the College.

Scouts. There is an active Elizabeth College Scout and Explorer Group, which meets on Friday evenings at the College Field. There is a Cub Scout Group for ECJS students, also based at College Field.

Clubs and societies. The College stresses the importance of co-curricular activity. All Year 9 students have an opportunity to take part in DofE as part of Friday afternoon activities and many opt to take on the challenge of Gold in Sixth Form. The Elizabethan Award encourages KS3 students to work towards certificates and badges at Bronze, Silver and Gold level in six key strands (physical, skills, service, creative, cultural and reading). This initiative was launched in 2019 in conjunction with our whole-school Friday afternoon activities programme – which means the whole College (staff and students) are all involved in learning through activities and non-examined subjects at the end of the week. Years 10 to 13 can work towards committing to fewer activities but becoming more committed to them and aiming for excellence in their chosen areas. Students can be awarded half or full College colours for extended commitment and excellence. Clubs and societies help students to achieve these awards and there is an extensive selection run at lunchtime, after school and at the weekends. Everything from bell-ringing, sea swimming, hockey, football, cricket, netball debating, music ensembles, outdoor pursuits, ceramics, science club, shooting, sailing, model train club, chess and numerous others.

Pastoral care. At Elizabeth College each year has a Head of Year assisted by four Tutors. Students attending Elizabeth College Junior School also have Form Tutors. All these staff provide pastoral care and academic guidance for their own sections of the College. They are supported by a School Listener who offers emotional support for the school and a Chaplain who conducts services in all three schools as well as preparing students for Confirmation.

Parental involvement. Parents are strongly encouraged to take an active part in their child's education. There are regular assessments and reports, parents' evenings, pastoral information evenings and parent workshops. Heads of Year keep in regular contact with parents through newsletters and email. The Heads of Year and students' tutors are always available to meet with parents to discuss any concerns.

Admission. The principal ages for admission into the school are 4, 11 and 16, but there are sometimes vacancies for entry at other ages. Entry is by means of assessment and/or interview which are adapted to the age of the applicant. There is a £110 non-refundable registration fee. Applications for entry should be addressed to the Registrar.

Scholarships to the College. The Gibson Fleming Trust provides Awards on a means-tested basis for current students to support them in their involvement with extra-curricular activities.

Foundation bursary scheme provides means tested bursaries to students who would not be able to access a College education without additional financial support. We currently offer the equivalent of five full bursaries for entry into Year 7 and two full bursaries for entry into Year 12. We welcome applications from children with enquiring minds who would benefit from our broad curriculum, outstanding extracurricular and enrichment activities, diverse community and inspirational environment.

Choral and instrumental scholarships. The Gibson Fleming Trust provides Choral and Instrumental Scholarships to current students with some financial assistance available alongside the awards. Details of the scholarships may be obtained from the Director of Music.

Scholarships to the universities. The College Exhibitions, Scholarships and Prizes include the Queen's Exhibition, the Lord de Sausmarez Exhibition, the Mainguy Scholarship, the Mansell Exhibition, the University of Winchester prize.

Travel. There are several flights each day from Southampton, Gatwick and Stansted. There are also regular flights to the West Country and to Midlands and northern airports. There are frequent sailings to and from Portsmouth and Poole, which offer vehicle transportation.

Alumni. The Honorary Secretary of the Old Elizabethan Association is Kin Tang who may be contacted via www.oea.org.gg.

Fees per term (2023–2024). Acorn House (Pre-Prep): £4,340; Beechwood (Prep): £4,678; Upper School (11–18): £4,907.

Directors:
The Very Revd T Barker, Dean of Guernsey (*Chairman*)

Mrs R Bowyer
Mrs K Bray
D Crook
M Ferbrache
Mrs M Galpin
K Lord
J Roche
S Sharman
A Tautscher
L Trott

***Principal*: Mrs J M Palmer**, BA

Head of the Junior School: R I Fyfe, BA
Vice-Principal (*Academic*): T I Addenbrooke, BEng, MSc, PhD
Vice-Principal (*Pastoral*): C D Eyton-Jones, BA Ed
Assistant Principal (*Sixth Form*): Mrs J A Dittmar, BSc
Assistant Principal (*Training, Development and Engagement*): Mrs J F Roberts, MA, MA, PGDip
Foundation & Marketing Director: Mrs D A Carruthers, BSc
Bursar & Clerk to the Directors: J G Couchman, BA

Members of Teaching Staff:
E C Adams, BA
Ms M L Adkins, BA
B E H Aplin, BSc
Mrs A M Baker, BSc
Mrs E F Blazina, BA
Mrs C S Buchanan, BA
M A M Buchanan, BA
R G Campbell, BSc, MSc
J J Conner, BSc
M R Copeland, BA, MA
Mrs P S Copeland, BA
D J Costen, BA
Mrs G Dallin, BSc
P G Davis, BSc
R M Davis, BA
Ms F De Garis
Miss A C M Demongeot, BA, MA
J A Depnering, MA, DPhil
T R de Putron, BSc
T P Edge, BA, MA
A Ellis
L R G Garland, BSc, MA
M Garnett, BA
A J Good, BSc
S J Huxtable, MA
D R L Inderwick, BA, MA
M Johnson, BA
C Johnston
Mrs G Laird, BMus, MA
Mrs R Lee
Mrs S Lee, Mgr
R G Le Sauvage, BSc
Ms E A Loveridge, BA
D R Loweth, MA, MEd
Mrs H M Mauger, BA
Mrs E C S Meijer, BA
Miss R E Merrien, BSc
R A Morris, BA
A R Mulholland, BSc, MA
Miss C B Newall, BA
Mrs K A Norman, BA
Mrs S Ozanne, BA
Ms J M Pendleton, BA
Mrs P J Read, MSci, MA
J R D Rowson, BA
Miss M Schofield, BA
D Scott, BA
Miss R L Seymour, BSc
T C Slann, Dip NEBSS
Ms T L Smith, BA, MA
M A G Stephens, BA
A G Stewart, BSc
Ms S L A Tribe, BA
M I Walters, BA, MEd

Chaplain: The Revd P A Graysmith, BSc
Director of Music: Miss E D Willcocks, BMus, MA
Games and Physical Education: T P Eisenhuth, BPhysEd

Prep:
Deputy Head Pastoral: Mrs E Bott, BEd
Deputy Head Academic: Mrs E J Spiller, BSc
Mrs E Chapman, BSc
Mrs D Dowding, BA
Mrs S Ellis
Mrs C Hervé, BA
Ms J Lavery, BSc
Mrs C Martel, BA Ed
Mrs E Parkes, BEd
Mrs A M Pollard, BEd
Miss E Randall, Bsc
Mrs K Reed, BA
Mrs J Ricketts, BA
Mrs B Santi, BSc, MA
P Sargent, BA
Mrs N Stevens, BEd
M Stokes, BA
R Sutton, BA
Mrs C Wray, BSc

Pre-Prep:
Deputy Head: Mrs J Atkinson, BEd
Mrs C Bowden, BEd
Miss R Curtis, BA Ed
Miss S Dorey, BEd
Mrs L Du Port, BA
Mrs J Hamilton, BA
Mrs E Jones, BA Ed

Ellesmere College
A Woodard School

Ellesmere, Shropshire SY12 9AB
Tel: 01691 622321
email: hmsecretary@ellesmere.com
website: www.ellesmere.com
X/Twitter: @ellesmerecoll
Facebook: @Ellesmere-College
Instagram: @ellesmere_college
LinkedIn: /school/ellesmere-college

Motto: *Pro Patria Dimicans*

Ellesmere College is a fully co-educational school set in the beautiful Shropshire countryside in North-West England. As one of the leading independent schools in the region, it offers students between the ages of 7 to 18 the chance to achieve both personal and academic success in their studies and a wide range of activities, including music, art, sport and drama, in a happy, friendly atmosphere. **In 2021, Ellesmere College was accredited as a High Performance Learning World Class School – one of only 39 schools worldwide to hold the distinction.** We prepare students for their i/GCSEs, A Levels, BTEC and the International Baccalaureate (IB), as well as giving them the opportunity to enjoy a full and varied sports and co-curricular programme. Founded in 1884 and standing in its own stunning grounds covering more than 50 hectares, the school is conveniently located near the small, historic town of Ellesmere, with easy access to Manchester, Birmingham, Liverpool and London.

The house systems. The Lower School (ages 7–13) has a competitive system based on 3 houses – Brownlow, Phillips and Heywood.

The Senior School (Yr 9–13) has a competitive 'house point' system – academic and sporting – based on 4 houses, all of which are co-educational and combine boarding and day pupils:

- Meynell House
- Talbot House
- Wakeman-Lambart House
- Woodard House.

Separate from the *competitive* houses is the *residential* house system for day and boarding arrangements:

There are 3 girls' boarding houses:

- St. Aidan's – Middle School (13–16 years)
- St. Oswald's & St. Hilda's – Sixth Form.

There are 4 boys' boarding houses:

- St. Patrick's & St. Cuthbert's – Middle School (13–16 years)
- St. Bede's & St. Luke's – Sixth Form.

Curriculum. In the first year in the Senior School, a full range of subjects is studied, designed to give all pupils a comprehensive introduction before focusing on their core elective subjects for i/GCSE. At i/GCSE all pupils take English, Mathematics, and either Dual Award Science or the three Sciences studied separately. Other subjects depend on individual aptitude and choice.

In the Sixth Form, over 24 academic subjects are available for study to A Level, BTEC Diploma or International Baccalaureate (IB) Diploma to prepare for university entrance, the Services and the Professions, or to the USA degree system via our SATs pathway.

Ellesmere College will be launching its International Foundation Programme (IFP) for entry into university as a one-year foundation programme course soon.

Music. The College has very strong musical traditions and has been awarded Artsmark Platinum in recognition of the award-winning arts provision at the College. It possesses two of the finest organs in the country, including the internationally renowned St Mary Tyne Dock Schulze Organ. The Chapel Choir has a wide repertoire of Church Music and a number of other ensembles, all of which give regular concerts. There are House Music Competitions every year, Celebrity concerts, and the community Sinfonia Orchestra.

The Music School is part of the College Arts Centre which provides first-class facilities, including a 220-seat theatre, 8 Practice Rooms, a Recording Studio and Teaching Rooms.

Arts Centre. This purpose-built complex hosts Drama, Dance, Film, Music and Art Exhibitions. A programme is organised in which international artists in all these fields visit the Centre, which shares its facilities with the local community.

Careers. At all levels pupils are encouraged to seek advice from the College careers Masters and Mistresses as well as representatives from the Independent Schools Careers Organisation. A Careers Convention is held each year for pupils in Year 11. Students also take ESB (English Speaking Board), ILM (Institute of Leadership & Management Level 3), SATs and mentoring programmes.

Games and Physical Education. Ellesmere has a long tradition of sporting excellence and has a total of 7 Sporting Academies: rugby, football, tennis, swimming, golf, cricket and shooting. The sporting excellence is supported by the Rugby Academy programme, the Tennis Academy and the Ellesmere College Titans Swimming Team. The Cricket Academy was launched in 2009, the Shooting Academy in 2010, Golf Academy in 2015 and the Football Academy in 2016. The LTA approved indoor Tennis Centre was completed in 2017 and there is also a High Performance Hockey Programme with a pathway to international progression.

All members of the School are required to participate in a regular programme of games, though particular inclinations and aptitudes are taken fully into consideration. Facilities include two sports halls, floodlit multi-sports AstroTurf pitches, a fitness centre, squash courts, a heated indoor swimming pool, indoor and outdoor shooting ranges, two high-tech gymnasia, a purpose-built LTA-accredited indoor 4-court tennis centre, 6 floodlit all-weather tennis courts, a golf course, indoor golf Sky-Trak, rugby pitches, all-weather hockey pitches, cricket squares and an athletics track. The school also has access to nearby lakes, rivers and hills providing opportunities to develop other skills including sailing, canoeing and horse riding.

All pupils are expected to join one of the following: D of E (Duke of Edinburgh's Award – Bronze, Silver & Gold), Outdoor Training Unit, Combined Cadet Force (CCF – Army, Navy, RAF), Social Service. These activities occur on one full afternoon a week, but, in order to extend their activities, twice a year 3 days are set aside when all members of the College participate in 48-hour expeditions. In the Lent Term a single day is devoted to expeditions.

Admission. Students are admitted at all points of entry into the school. Entrance examinations are held in February for Lower School entry. Scholarships for Prep School candidates are held in May, while others take the Common Entrance Examination in June.

Scholarships and bursaries. A wide range of awards recognising a range of talents are available:

- *Academic:* a maximum of 50% fee remission.
- *All-Rounder:* a maximum of 25% fee remission.
- *Art:* a maximum of 25% fee remission. Applications welcome for the The Adlard Scholarship.
- *Drama:* a maximum of 25% fee remission.
- *Music:* a maximum of 50% fee reduction and free tuition in two instruments. Exhibitions are worth up to a maximum of 25% fee reduction and free tuition in one instrument.
- The *Schulze Organ Award* is for Sixth Form candidates only – valued at 50% of fees.
- *Sports:* a maximum of 50% fee remission.

In cases of need, all awards may be supplemented by means-tested bursaries.

There are reduced fees for children of the Clergy and Service personnel.

Foundation and Regional awards are also available for local children.

Fees per term (2023–2024). Upper School: Boarders £13,545, Weekly Boarders £9,670, Day £7,450.

Lower School: Boarders £10,855, Weekly Boarders £9,170, Day £4,565–£5,250.

Fees are inclusive of general College charges.

For more information visit: www.ellesmere.com/the-schools/all/admissions/fees

'Old Ellesmerians' Former pupils of the school become members of The Ellesmerian Club, which in turn enables them to take part in a number of societies and activities. For further information, contact: external.relations@ellesmere.com

Charitable status. Registered Charity, number 1103049. It exists to provide education for children.

Founder: The Revd Nathaniel Woodard, DCL, then Dean of Manchester

Visitor: The Rt Revd The Lord Bishop of Lichfield

College Council:

D C Brewitt
Mrs F M Christie
The Reverend Canon B C Clover
Mrs S Connor
J S Hopkins
R A K Hoppins
C E Lillis
A L Morris
Mrs R E Paterson
The Reverend M J Rylands
M D T Sampson

***Headmaster*: B J Wignall**, BA, MA, MCMI, FRSA

Deputy Head (*Pastoral*): Dr R Chatterjee, BSc, MSc, PhD, Cert SpLD

Deputy Head (*Academic*): Mrs S V Pritt-Roberts, BEd, MEd, NPQH

Deputy Head (*External Relations*): Mr S B Mullock, BA

Head of Sixth Form: Dr T Gareh, BSc, MSc, PhD, CSci, CChem, MRSC

Head of Middle School: Mrs S Phillips, MA

Head of Lower School: Mrs S Morgan, BEd

Director of Activities: Mr C Davies, BA

Chaplain: The Revd Phillip Gration

Director of Operations: M McCarthy, BSc, DMS

Registrar: Ms K Randall, BSc

Eltham College

Grove Park Road, Mottingham, London, LONDON SE9 4QF

Tel: 020 8857 1455
email: mail@eltham-college.org.uk
website: www.eltham-college.org.uk
X/Twitter: @ElthamCollegeUK
Facebook: @ElthamCollegeOfficial
Instagram: @ElthamCollegeLondon
LinkedIn: /Old-Elthamians

Eltham College is a thriving co-educational independent day school for students aged 7 to 18.

Set on a spacious and green campus of nearly 70 acres in south-east London, Eltham College is a highly successful school which aims to provide a broad and balanced education for girls and boys to prepare them to prosper as adults in a modern and fast-changing world. The College is academically selective and is one of the leading academic schools in the country, as but also with a rich and varied co-curricular programme including Sport, Music, Drama and Art. The school is a Top 20 London day school in the Sunday Times Parent Power Good Schools Guide and has been named as their "Independent Secondary School of the Year 2024 (London)." We are also a Microsoft-accredited Showcase School, one of only 50 across the UK.

Eltham College has a distinct character, born out of its Christian heritage, and it continues to focus on the care of the individual. Strong pastoral care and a relaxed and unpretentious atmosphere make the school a happy and vibrant place.

There is an ambitious programme of development and expansion as well as a strong emphasis on staff development to ensure students benefit from a dedicated team of staff – experts in their field, and passionate about their subject.

History. The College was founded in 1842 as the 'School for the Sons of Missionaries'. It began life as a small boarding school catering for the children of missionaries whose parents were serving overseas including, famously, GB gold medal winning Olympic athlete Eric Liddell. The College moved to its present site in Mottingham, south-east London, in 1912. The school's extensive playing fields surround an elegant 18th century mansion, itself a former naval college, as well as many much more modern buildings.

The College has developed into a day school for nearly 1,100 boys and girls – with nearly 800 pupils in the Senior School and approximately 260 in the Junior School. Most recently, the school has merged with Blackheath Prep School to form the Eltham College Family of Schools.

Location. The College is located on a spacious 70-acre site with extensive playing fields in the London

Borough of Bromley, adjacent to the boroughs of Royal Greenwich and Lewisham. It lies within easy reach of both central London and the Kent countryside. There are regular and fast train services to London Bridge, Charing Cross and Cannon Street stations (@20–25 minutes) while the nearby A20 main road links to the M25 in less than 15 minutes. Students come from a wide local area that includes Blackheath, Bexley, Bromley, Chislehurst, Dartford, Dulwich, Greenwich, Sydenham and London Docklands.

Facilities. The College has superb facilities which have been improved considerably in recent years. These include the Gerald Moore Art Gallery, newly refurbished Science laboratories, two floodlit all-weather AstroTurf pitches and an extended Dining Hall. The award-winning Turberville Centre, opened in 2019, houses Languages and Maths classrooms, a seminar room, and a new Sixth Form Centre including a café, dedicated study areas and a seminar room. Nearby, a £3 million Medical and Wellbeing Centre provides an integrated hub for the school nursing team, counsellors and Chaplain. The Eric Liddell Sports Centre comprises a sports hall, dance studio and fitness suite and a 25 metre swimming pool.

Curriculum. The curriculum is broad and balanced, incorporating both traditional and modern elements. For example, all students in Year 7 study French, Latin, German and Spanish, and all students go on to study at least one Modern Language to GCSE, and separate Sciences are available to all. Most students take ten GCSEs and three A Levels, chosen from a wide range of subjects, plus the EPQ. Recent examination. Results place Eltham amongst the best schools in the country: in summer 2023, nearly a third of all GCSE grades were grade 9 and more than 80% of all grades were 9/8/7 across a broad range of subjects.

A Level results are consistently high: in 2023, more than one third (34%) of all grades were A* and nearly 75% were A*/A. 96% of our students secured a place at their chosen university that included Oxbridge, other leading Russell Group universities, and a number of specialist colleges and conservatoires in the UK and overseas universities. Popular degree courses include Engineering, English, Drama, Music, Medicine, and Sports Science with others also choosing Psychology, Economics, Computing, and various Modern Languages.

Co-Curricular. The co-curricular activities provide an impressively wide range of opportunities while ensuring that academic potential is fulfilled. The College has an enviable reputation in Sport, Music, Art and Drama. There are a number of international and Olympic standard sports coaches; the quality and range of Music participation and performance is strong and rising; and audiences are frequently treated to spectacular Drama productions in the school's purpose-built theatre.

The majority of students participate in a wide range of clubs and societies including (to name but a few): Duke of Edinburgh's Award, Bloodbowl, Chess, Debating Society, Eco-Eltham, Entreprenerds, FemSoc, Japanese Club, Rocket Club and Water Polo. There is also a School Congress that meets regularly every term to discuss, debate improvements to the school and to put forward ideas and proposals. Students are encouraged to help those less fortunate than themselves by taking part in charity fundraising events. The Lower Sixth take part in a Community Service scheme helping local charities.

Trips and expeditions are a major feature of life at Eltham College. These range from the traditional UK visits to more ambitious overseas trips which in recent years have included: Uganda, China, Germany, Iceland, Switzerland and the United States. Language trips and exchanges are encouraged and these have included visits to Bordeaux, Spain, Beijing and Cologne. Sport, Drama and Music tours are frequent occurrences, both in the UK and overseas, and these have included Spain, South Africa, and The Netherlands.

Admissions. Students are admitted at 7+ (Year 3), 11+ (Year 7) and 16+ (Sixth Form) via an entrance examination and interview. Occasional vacancies do sometimes occur outside of the traditional entrance points. The College is academically highly selective, and there are many more applicants than places. Approximately half of students come from local primary schools and half from the independent sector. The College has a wide social mix, thanks, in part, to our Bursary scheme which provides financial assistance for those unable to afford the full fees.

Scholarships. The College offers a number of scholarships and bursaries to attract the brightest and most talented students to the College. Scholarships and Bursaries (financial assistance) are available to all students applying to the Senior School and Sixth Form. Scholarships offering fee remission are awarded on Academic performance at 11+ and 16+. There are also scholarships in Music, Drama, Art and Sport.

Bursaries. As befits a school founded for the sons of missionaries and a former Direct Grant School, a significant number of students receive financial support to attend the College. Bursaries are available up to 100% of fees subject to ISBA confidential means-tested criteria.

Term of Entry. The College normally accepts students only for the beginning of the academic year in September but, if gaps in particular year groups occur, it is willing to interview and test at any point in the year with a view to immediate or subsequent entry. However, the school is usually over-subscribed.

Junior School. The Junior School is based on the main school campus in a separate building sometimes known as The Grange. This is a large specially converted and fully-equipped school house on the College site which accommodates about 260 day pupils in classes of around 22 children. In addition to classrooms are an Assembly and Games Hall, Science Room, Music Room, and an Art, Design and Technology Room. With an emphasis on English and Mathematics, the curriculum (which includes Mandarin, French and German), provides an excellent foundation for the academic journey on through the Senior School. Excellence and variety is also pursued outside the classroom whether on the sports field, stage or concert hall. The Junior School is managed by its own Head, who is responsible to the Headmaster.

Admission is at 7+ (into Year 3) by entrance assessment, though there are occasional places at 8+. There is no entrance test for students from Eltham College Junior School wishing to move up to the Senior School from Year 7. Recommendation for continuing to the Senior School is made on the basis of a student's performance during their time in the Junior School and on their potential to flourish in the Senior School. Almost all students progress seamlessly through to the Senior School.

Applications for places in the Junior School should be made to the Head of Admissions (details on the school website).

Fees per term (2023–2024). Senior School/Sixth Form £7,929; Junior School £6,518. Lunch £363.

Charitable status. Eltham College is a Registered Charity, number 1058438. It exists to provide education for boys and girls.

Governors:
The Governing Body comprises the Chairman and Vice Chair, ten Trust Governors and eight Nominated Governors representing the Baptist Missionary Society, the Council for World Mission, the United Reformed Church, the London Boroughs of Bexley and Bromley, the Parents (two representatives elected by the parental body) and the Staff Common Room (one representative elected by the Teaching Staff).

Chairman of the Board: Mr P Doyle

***Headmaster*: Mr G Sanderson**, MA Oxon, FRSA
Bursar: Mr R Wilkinson
Senior Deputy Head (*Senior School*): Mr J Martin
Deputy Head (*Curriculum*): Ms K Nutbeem
Deputy Head (*Pastoral*): Mrs A Massey
Deputy Head (*Co-Curricular*): Mr J Willatt
Head of Junior School: Ms V Meier

Senior School Teaching Staff:
* *Head of Department*

Art:
*Miss S Heraghty, BA (*Director of Art*)
Miss K Duke
Miss Y Shin
Mr D Hughes (*Theatre Technician*)
Mr L Burton (*Artist in Residence*)

Biology:
*Mr S Marlow, BSc
Mrs N Colwell, BSc
Mr A Merrett
Miss J C Perry, BSc

Chemistry:
*Mr H Hawkridge, BSc
Ms S Baig
Mrs N Colwell
Mr H Nicholls
Dr J N Hill, BSc (*Technician*)
Mrs J C Perry, BSc
Mrs K Pender

Classics:
*Dr E Michalopoulou, BA, MA, PhD
Ms M Cogni
Mr C Nicholls

Computing and Computer Science:
*Mr T Collins, MSc, BEng
Mr T Manuell
Miss J Muirhead

Design and Technology:
*Mr C Quinton
Mr N Dale
Miss M Johnson
Mr P Wren

Drama:
Mrs K Robinson, BA, MA (*Director of Drama*)
Miss E Coleman (*Head of Academic Drama*)
Miss I Tyner
Mr R Warren (*Technical Manager*)
Mr M Curley (*Theatre Technician*)

Economics:
*Mr M Sanusi
Mr T Midgley
MIss A Hampton-Armstrong

English:
*Mr C Cook
Mr T C Mitchell, BA (*Head of Creative Writing*)
Mr J Stephenson
Miss V Barsby, BA
Miss E Bush
Ms E Tournes
Mrs N Whittaker
Miss T Patel

Geography and Geology:
*Mr P Angel, MA, BSc, NPQSL
Ms M Calwell
Mr A D Beattie, MA
Mr J P Chesterton, BSc
Mrs L Clough
Miss K Richard, BSc
Mr J Willatt, BSc (*Deputy Head – Co-curricular*)

History:
*Dr A Davies, BA, MA, PhD
Mr M E R Chesterton, BA
Mr E Cavendish
Mr A Higginson
Mr J Martin (*Deputy Head*)
Mr R Green

Mathematics:
*Mr T Brook
Mrs R E Bevington, BSc
Mr A Astbury-Palmer
Mr J Capocci
Mrs N Bilsby, BSc, MA (*Head of Wellbeing*)
Mr B Eastley
Mr J P Crowley, BEng
Ms R Gordon, BSc (*Assistant Head – Teaching and Learning*)
Mr A Hon
Ms A Tysba
Mrs S Wood, BSc [part-time]

Modern Languages:
*Miss L Scarantino, BA
Mrs F Archdale
Miss C Franz, MA (*Head of German*)
Mrs B Hazeldine
Ms E Paull (*Head of Spanish*)
Ms M Su, BA, MA (*Head of Mandarin Chinese*)
Mrs E Brooke
Mr J Houghton, MA (*Chaplain*)
Mr A Johnston
Ms H Pan
Mr F Nieto Almada, MA
Mrs S Chevrier-Clarke

Music:
Mr S Johns (*Director of Music*)
Ms E Potter-Hicks (*Head of Academic Music*)
Ms J Lewis (*Administrator*)
Ms A Bryans
Mr C Nall
Mrs D Nall
Mr S Thompson
Mr T Bullard
Miss J O'Leary
Mrs D Bailey
Mrs J Brits

Physics:
*Mr A Hindocha, BSc
Ms S Baig
Mr A Chan, MEng
Dr M Cianciaruso, PhD
Mr J Crowley, BEng
Mr S Whittaker, MSc

Politics:
*Mr M Chesterton
Mrs A Massey
Mr T Midgley

Psychology:
*Ms M M Pokorny, BSc (*Head of Middle School*)

Philosophy and Theology:
*Mr H Burling
Mr E Cavendish (*Head of Scholarship*)
Ms E Haste (*Head of Year 7*)

Sport:
*Mr M Edwards (*Director of Sport*)
Mr Y Arafat (*Cricket Pro*)
Miss E Evans (*Head of Ski Racing*)
Miss K Harding (*Head of House – Chalmers*)
Mr J Halls (*Hockey*)
Ms B Holmes (*PE*)
Mr S Florescu-Serban (*Fencing*)
Mr J Hill (*Water Polo Coach*)
Mr R Hills (*Cricket Coach*)
Miss B Holmes (*Head of Skiing*)
Mr J Kelly (*Head of Cricket*)
Mr B King (*Head of Year 8, Head of Rugby*)
Mrs K Parkin (*PE and Sports Psychologist*)
Mr S Perfect (*Head of Aquatics*)
Mr L Petrozzi (*Rugby*)
Mr E Thorogood (*Head of HPAP*)
Miss L True (*Head of Netball*)
Mr A Witchell (*Rugby Coach*)

Learning Support:
*Mrs M Franklin
Ms N Reynolds
Ms N Macaulay
Ms S Kilford
Ms T Patel

Library:
Mrs C M Roche, MiL

EPQ:
Mrs J Angel

Sixth Form:
Ms C Scott-Blount (*Head of Sixth Form*)
Mr J Stephenson (*Head of Year 12*)
Mrs K Powis-Holt (*Head of Year 13*)

Development Director: Ms S O'Donovan
Head of Admissions: Mrs C St Clair-Charles
Head of Communications: Mr E Funnell

Junior School:
Head of the Junior School: Mrs V Meier, MA
Deputy Head of the Junior School (*Academic*): Ms J Dudley
Deputy Head of the Junior School (*Pastoral*): Mr A Taylor

Junior School Teaching Staff:
Mrs N J Chamberlain, BEd (*Head of Years 3 and 4*)
Mr I Wearmouth (*Head of Years 5 and 6*)
Mr M Alexander, BA (*Head of Junior School Music*)
Mrs A Wearmouth, BA (*Head of English*)
Mr N Dale, BA (*Head of History*)
Miss M S Johnson, BA (*Head of Design and Technology*)
Mrs B Martin (*Head of Modern Foreign Languages*)
Mr M O'Dwyer, BEd (*Head of Co-curricular*)
Mr S Oliver, BSc (*Head of Mathematics*)
Mrs H Pan (*Head of Junior School Mandarin*)
Mrs H L Sargeant, BSc (*Head of Computing*)
Mr W Schaper, BEd (*Head of Geography*)
Miss N L Tutchings, BEd (*Subject Leader PSHE, Form Tutor Year 4*)

Emanuel School

Battersea Rise, London SW11 1HS

Tel: 020 8870 4171
email: enquiries@emanuel.org.uk
website: www.emanuel.org.uk
X/Twitter: @Emanuel_School
Instagram: @Emanuel.school

Motto: *Pour bien désirer – the noble aim*

Emanuel School was founded in Westminster by Lady Anne Dacre in 1594 and moved to its present site on the north side of Wandsworth Common in 1883 as one of the five schools of The United Westminster and Grey Coat Foundation.

Emanuel is a fully co-educational day school for ages 10–18. We have approximately 1,080 pupils across the school.

Admission. Each September, 48 pupils are admitted into Year 6 (10+), 96 pupils into Year 7 (11+) and 30 into the Sixth Form.

Applicants will be required to submit their last full year school report. We will also request a reference from their current headteacher (or equivalent) and they will sit entrance exams. A number of pupils are then invited back to interview with a member of staff.

Registration for all entry points closes in mid-October the year before entry.

Prospective parents are warmly encouraged to visit the school and there are many opportunities to do so. Please see our website for details.

Fees per term (2023–2024). £7,687 covering tuition, books and lunch. Extras charged are for individual instrumental tuition and some external visits and trips.

Site and buildings. Emanuel School is located on a beautiful, leafy, 12-acre site in Battersea, on the north edge of Wandsworth Common, only 10 minutes' walk from Clapham Junction rail station. The original Victorian building is the core of the school, with teaching and learning space, a large and well-stocked library, theatre and a beautiful chapel. The Dacre building opened in 2017, with outstanding art and design facilities and a film studio, and the newly extended and improved sixth-form centre reopened in the autumn term 2022. The school has begun work on a masterplan to improve and further develop teaching and learning facilities over the coming years.

The school's playing fields adjoin the school buildings together with a sports hall, full-sized indoor swimming pool and fives courts. The school has a boathouse on the Thames by Barnes Bridge and a further 16-acre off-site sports ground near Raynes Park, where a new all-weather pitch for hockey, netball, tennis, cricket and football, as well as 3 new cricket practice nets were added for use this autumn term.

Scholarships and assistance with fees (bursaries). Academic and co-curricular scholarships are available and pupils may hold more than one type of scholarship. The fee remission for scholarships is typically 10% but in exceptional circumstances, can be up to 25% or 50%.

All applicants are considered for academic scholarships, which are awarded on the basis of outstanding performance in the school entrance examinations.

Applicants applying for Music, Art, Drama and Sports scholarships must pass the entrance exams before a scholarship can be awarded. Thereafter, each department has specific criteria for their scholarship requirements.

As well as awarding academic and co-curricular scholarships, Emanuel School is committed to widening access by offering fee assistance. Fee-assisted places (bursaries) are available dependent on financial need and can hold the value of up to 100% of the school fees, including covering the costs of uniform and school trips.

Please see our website for more details about scholarships and fee assistance.

Organisation. There are two forms for pupils who join at Year 6 (10+). Pupils joining at Year 7 (11+) are placed into six forms. Primary responsibility for their care rests with the form tutor and the head of year, under the overall supervision of the Head of Lower School, who deals with Years 6, 7 and 8. As all pupils move from Year 9 into Year 10 there is a regrouping along the lines of the subjects chosen for GCSE examinations. The tutor system continues throughout the school.

Pupils are placed in houses when they join the school and they stay in these houses throughout their school career. Although originally intended as a means of fostering competition in games, these houses have developed a strong community spirit over many years. Pupils join a house-led peer mentoring group which meets fortnightly and is led by at least two students from the Upper Sixth. Specially trained, the Sixth Form mentors, with the support of the heads of house, organise discussions and short activities designed to help pupils with day-to-day school life, make friends across the years, and informally share advice on future academic plans.

Times. The normal school day runs from 8.25 am to 3.50 pm, but many activities take place after school. Some school activities, especially sports fixtures, but also music and drama rehearsals, take place at the weekend.

Curriculum. Pupils in the Lower and Middle School study a wide range of subjects, including English, Mathematics, Biology, Chemistry and Physics (as separate sciences), Geography, History, Religious Studies, Computing, Design and Robotics (CDR), Music, Art and Design, Drama, Latin and Modern Languages (French, Spanish and German). There is a double period PE lesson, a Games afternoon and a Life Education lesson each week. Pupils also have a weekly lesson called 'Ethos'; this is an introduction to critical thinking, informed discussion and debating, aiming to develop independence and resilience in our younger pupils.

In the Sixth Form, pupils choose three A Level subjects from 26 on offer (including additional options such as Psychology, Politics, Economics and Photography) and also complete the Extended Project Qualification (EPQ). Sixth Form leavers go on to a variety of institutions, including Oxbridge and Russell Group universities, art college, music and drama conservatoires or universities overseas.

Art, Music & Drama. Emanuel has a long-standing tradition of excellence in Art, Music and Drama and all pupils are encouraged to participate in the breadth of opportunities available.

The music department caters to a wide range of musical interests, from choral and orchestral to contemporary music. Pupils take part in concerts, workshops and ensembles including rock and pop concerts, house music competitions and DJing workshops. The music department collaborates with the drama department to produce an annual whole-school musical.

Drama is taught throughout the school with many pupils continuing through GCSE and A Level. There are many opportunities for co-curricular participation through year-group productions and trips. Every other year, the Emanuel Theatre Company takes over 20 students to the Edinburgh Fringe Festival to perform two shows.

Art facilities include specialist paint and print studios, a dark room for photography, a ceramics room with dedicated kiln and glazing rooms and a sculpture studio. Pupils follow a broad syllabus where they can develop a range of creative skills. There are plenty of extracurricular opportunities for budding artists to enjoy, including trips, drawing masterclasses and exhibitions. Emanuel students gain places to study at some of the best art colleges in the country.

Sport & Activities. Rugby, cricket, rowing and football are the main school games for boys. For girls, the main activities are netball, cricket, hockey and rowing. Many other activities become available as a pupil moves up the school. Each pupil will have one games afternoon each week and other opportunities for physical education and swimming. The school has its own playing fields, sports hall, mini astro, swimming pool, fives, netball and tennis courts and boathouse on the Thames.

There are over 50 weekly clubs and activities taking place over lunchtime and after school as well as over 40 subject clinics. The most popular clubs include Film and Media Club, Bouldering Club (on our climbing wall), Costume Making Club, Junior Equality Club and Dr Who Club, as well as a number of sports and performing arts clubs.

The Duke of Edinburgh's Award scheme is offered to pupils from Year 9 upwards. Community outreach is arranged for senior pupils and can involve hospital visiting or voluntary work in local primary schools, charity shops or our local hospice.

Partnerships and Outreach. A central point of our ethos is the cultivation of an altruistic, caring and outward-looking community. All Lower Sixth students are involved in our award-winning outreach initiative, Primary Ambitions. Each Friday, our students spend one hour teaching a variety of subjects to Year 6 children from our local partner schools. Students gain confidence as well as developing their leadership and organisational skills. In turn, we hope that the programme will inspire and challenge young people within our community to develop some new skills, relish newfound opportunities and explore new friendships – and most importantly, have fun!

Careers. Careers and higher education advice is readily available from an experienced team. There is an annual careers convention for senior pupils where many representatives from a wide variety of industries and professional areas visit the school to talk about career options.

More formal work experience is offered as part of an extensive careers and further education advice programme from Year 9 upwards. There is a very strong Young Enterprise programme in the Lower Sixth; Emanuel has a good record and has been within one round of the national finals for the last two years.

Old Emanuel Association. *Membership Secretary*: oe@emanuel.org.uk

Charitable status. Emanuel School (administered by The United Westminster and Grey Coat Foundation) is a Registered Charity, number 1181012.

Chairman of the Governors: Mr M Jaigirder, MA

***Headmaster*: Mr Robert Milne**, MA King's College London

Senior Management Team:

Bursar: Mr M Russell, ACMA
Senior Deputy Head: Mrs J L Peters, MA Oxon
Deputy Head (*Pastoral*): Mr R Kothakota, MEd Buckingham
Deputy Head (*Co-curricular*, *Partnerships & Admissions*): Mr S W Turner, MEd Birmingham
Deputy Head (*Academic*): Dr R M Evans, DPhil Oxon
Director of Studies: Mrs R Brown, DPhil Oxon
Head of Sixth Form: Ms J A Johnson, MA Oxon
Head of Middle School: Mrs J McIsaac, MA Lond
Head of Lower School: Ms H Windsor, BA Cardiff
Senior Tutor: Mr S P Andrews, BA Swansea

Epsom College

College Road, Epsom, Surrey KT17 4JQ

Tel: 01372 821004 (Head)
01372 821234 (Director of Admissions)
01372 821133 (Bursar)
email: admissions@epsomcollege.org.uk
website: www.epsomcollege.org.uk
X/Twitter: @EpsomCollegeUK
Facebook: /Epsom-College

Motto: *Deo non Fortuna*

Founded in 1855, Epsom College is a boarding and day school for girls and boys aged 11–18, situated in 72 acres of parkland estate close to Epsom Downs and is only 15 miles from central London. The College was voted Independent School of the Year in 2022 (both as the overall winner, and as school of the year for student wellbeing).

In 2022, A Levels were 62% A*-A, and 85% A*-B. Over half of all students achieved a clean sweep of A*-As. At GCSE, 54% of all grades were 9–8 (A*) and 74% were 9–7 (A*-A).

Almost all leavers go on to degree courses, especially at research-led universities. The Russell Group universities are particularly popular, with Bristol, Durham, and Oxford and Cambridge strongly represented each year. Increasingly our pupils study overseas, with places at US universities on the rise.

Boarding is central to the College with many of our boarders – both weekly and full boarders – living within 25 miles. The House system ensures a strong sense of community and support. All pupils, whether day, weekly or full boarders, are placed within one of our 13 Houses. Year groups mix, and a strong sense of pride in the House, and care for fellow pupils of all ages is encouraged.

All pupils, no matter whether they board, benefit from our traditional boarding school model which features longer days and Saturday school. This creates space in our timetable for pupils to benefit from more than academic studies alone.

In any given week, pupils will have their Duke of Edinburgh, CCF or volunteering in the local community programme as part of their timetabled routine. They will also enjoy an abundance of sport and co-curricular activities (ranging from activities that earn valuable UCAS point, to activities that stimulate mind, body and soul – such as yoga, dance, art, photography, debating, first aid, and much more besides).

Numbers and Houses. There are 1,100 pupils in the School, around 60% are day pupils. There are 382 in the Sixth Form and 180 in the Lower School (Years 7 and 8).

Around 16% of pupils are from overseas and there is a spread of 38 nationalities.

The school is fully co-ed, with a 50/50 split in Years 7 and 8, and a 60/40 male to female split in the senior years. There are 6 separate houses for girls: two boarding houses, Crawfurd and Wilson; three day houses, Murrell, Raven and Rosebery; and White House, for both boarding and day girls.

The boys' boarding houses are: Fayrer, Forest, Granville and Holman. All boarding Sixth and Fifth Formers and Upper Fourth Formers have study-bedrooms in the modernised Houses.

In the Michaelmas Term there are two weekend exeats roughly halfway through each half term, in addition to a two-week half-term holiday. In each of the other two terms there is one exeat in the first half followed by a one-week half-term holiday. Weekly boarders can go home every weekend.

The day boy Houses are: Carr, Propert and Robinson. Day boys and girls are full members of the School community and have lunch and tea in College. All members of the School, boarders and day, eat centrally in the Dining Room which makes for efficiency and strengthens the sense of community.

Pupils who are ill are looked after in the School Medical Centre which has a qualified sister always on duty.

Academic Work. In the Lower School the design of the curriculum follows a number of key principles: Skills for the future, learning to learn, well-being and 21st century education. Outside of the normal curriculum, all pupils have timetabled wellbeing and mindfulness, service in the community, and are able to select from a carousel of 150 co-curricular activities, encompassing everything from gardening to STEM.

Middle Fourth (Year 9) pupils take English, Mathematics, Physics, Chemistry, Biology, Religious Studies, Drama, Geography, History, Art, Music, a Modern Language (French, German, Spanish or Mandarin), Computer Science and Design Technology. Pupils can then choose to study a second modern language, Latin or Classical Civilisation, or an additional Creative Arts subject (Design & Technology, Art or Music). With the exception of Maths and Languages, setting continues to be mixed ability.

Pupils will choose their GCSEs at the end of Year 9 to commence study in Year 10. They take 10 subjects, seven are compulsory, three can be chosen. The compulsory subjects are English Language, English Literature, Mathematics, Biology, Chemistry, Physics and a Modern or Classical Language (from French, German, Spanish, Mandarin, Latin or Classical Civilisation). The optional three subjects are taken from Art, Computer Science, Design & Technology, Drama, French, Geography, History, Latin, Music, Photography, PE, Religious Studies or Spanish.

Almost everyone then enters the Sixth Form. Students will choose 3 principal subjects to study at A Level. These will then be enhanced by choices from the core curriculum where they can choose from: Core Maths, US College Board Advanced Placement in English Language and Composition, Extended Project Qualification, International Certificate in Digital Literacy or Young Enterprise. They will also benefit from a varied lecture programme and Epsom's award-winning service programme. A wide range of A Level subjects are offered. Options in Business, Politics and Government, Photography, Psychology and Economics are introduced to complement the broad range of subjects already available at GCSE. The courses are linear meaning all examinations are taken at the end of Upper Sixth.

There are excellent facilities for work in one's own study, in the main Library or one of the specialist Departmental Libraries.

Higher Education. Almost all students go on to university, with the occasional student choosing to follow another path, such as Art Foundation. In recent years, Medicine, Law, Engineering, Economics and Business degrees have proved particularly popular degree options, but Epsom students have been successful in gaining places on a broad variety of competitive courses. 82% of all pupils go to Russell Group universities each year. Overseas universities – particularly in the US – are increasingly popular, with 11% of 2022's leavers choosing this route. Epsom has a dedicated programme to support overseas applications.

Careers. Careers education is offered from the first term at Epsom and is particularly well developed in the Sixth Form. Epsom has an experienced team of careers tutors with specialists in Medicine, Oxbridge Entrance, Engineering and American University Entrance. Much care is taken to assess a pupil's potential and aptitude and to provide proper guidance on careers. All pupils belong to Inspiring Futures and all Fifth Form pupils take careers aptitude tests through their Futurewise programme. There is a well-established work experience programme and a Careers Convention is organised each year for the Fifth Form and Lower Sixth. The College also hosts a GAP Year Fair.

The **Religious Teaching** and the Chapel Services follow the doctrines of the Church of England, but there are always pupils of other denominations and faiths. Multi-faith services take place regularly. There is a Senior Chaplain who works together with a visiting Rabbi and a Hindu priest to ensure a multi-faith approach. Muslim pupils attend prayers at the College.

Games and other Activities. Games contribute much to the general physical development of girls and boys at Epsom and the College has a strong tradition of high standards in many sports. The very large number of teams means that almost all pupils are able to represent the School each year. A wide range of sports is available: Rugby, Hockey, Netball, Cricket, Tennis, Athletics and Swimming, Squash (6 courts), Target Rifle Shooting (with an indoor range), Football, Cross-Country, Golf, Badminton, Rounders, and Basketball. The Indoor Sports Centre, housing two sports halls, squash courts, a fitness centre and gym, and climbing wall, was opened in 1989 by the Patron of Epsom College, Her Majesty The Queen.

The Target Rifle Team has a long history of excellence at Target Rifle Shooting, both small-bore and full-bore, and over the last 20 years has consistently been the premier rifle shooting school in the UK. The College Rifle team has won the National Championships – the Ashburton Shield – 14 times in the past 26 years and 15 times overall. The College holds the record for the highest number of Ashburton wins by a single school.

The CCF has Naval, Army and RAF Sections and pupils over the age of 14 are expected to join for 2 years when much time is spent on camping and expeditions. Older boys and girls may join instead The Duke of Edinburgh's Award scheme, while others are involved with the service programme in Epsom where they contribute to the community and take a leadership role in service projects.

The College ensures that all pupils take advantage of an extensive range of activities from Dance to Design Textiles. Over 150 clubs and societies are accessible each week, and the co-curricular programme at the College has been ranked as the 'best of the best in UK independent education' by *The Week* magazine.

Music, Art and Drama. There are three full-time Music teachers and a large staff of visiting music teachers. Over one-third of the pupils learn musical instruments and virtually any instrument can be taught, and many take singing lessons. There are four Choirs, a School Orchestra and seven major instrumental ensembles, including Big Band, Clarinet, Saxophone and Classical Guitar. Visits are arranged each term to concerts in London and elsewhere. The Music School has a Concert Hall and 18 practice rooms. Recent productions have included *Footloose, Spamalot, The Sound of Music, Les Misérables, Jesus Christ Superstar* and *Cabaret*.

Art, which includes pottery, printing and sculpture as well as painting and drawing, is housed in a spacious building with 8 studios, a Library, an Exhibition Room and an Exhibition Hall. There are two full-time Art teachers and one part-time, and Art is studied up to GCSE and A Level.

There are several major Drama productions each year, from classical theatre to the modern musical, produced by a range of staff and pupils. These give boys and girls an opportunity to develop their talents and interests in Drama.

Admission. Almost all pupils enter Epsom College in September. There are 3 entry levels: 11+, 13+ and 16+.

For those entering at 11+ candidates will be assessed for entry in January of Year 6. They will sit papers in English, Mathematics non-verbal and verbal reasoning, and these tests will be supported by a short interview and a report from their current school.

Pupils wishing to enter at 13+ sit our entrance exam in their Year 6 and are offered a deferred place, conditional upon maintaining the same standards at the present school. Some enter the school later than this and there is always a direct entry into the Sixth Form, both for girls and boys.

A boy or girl may be registered at any age by sending in the registration form and fee. All enquiries should be sent to the Director of Admissions from whom a prospectus may be obtained.

Fees per term (2023–2024). Boarders £15,511; Weekly Boarders £13,801; Day Pupils £10,303. Lower School: Day pupils £7,726.

The fees are inclusive and cover the normal cost of a pupil's education. The main extras are for examination fees, private tuition and a pupil's personal expenses. Fees for day pupils include lunch and tea.

There is a College Store for the provision of uniform, clothing and other requirements.

Entrance Scholarships. Scholarships are available at 11+, 13+ and 16+ entry for excellence in academic study, performing arts (drama or music) and sport.

Girls and boys holding awards invariably go on to contribute much to school life throughout their time at Epsom. The College community holds them in high regard.

Candidates may apply for more than one award. Scholarships and Exhibitions will only be awarded if candidates of sufficient merit present themselves.

If a Scholarship or Exhibition is not awarded on entry to the College in Year 7 or 9, there is a further opportunity to be promoted to the status of an award holder in Year 12 (Lower Sixth).

Bursaries. Over the past six years, Epsom has reduced the value of non means-tested Scholarships and Awards, which can be worth up to 10% a year. This has enabled us to double the bursary fund which is allocated to families with demonstrable financial need.

In turn this has helped us, with Educational Trust support, to widen our access to disadvantaged families. This is one of the College's declared aims in line with both Government and HMC guidance. Potential scholarship applicants are encouraged to seek extra financial support, if appropriate, by way of a means-tested Bursary. Application forms are available on request from the Bursar or Admissions Registrar.

Old Epsomians. The Old Epsomian Club promotes sporting activities, social gatherings and networking events among its former pupils, with eight international chapters and an online database. On leaving the College, all pupils automatically become lifelong members of the OE Club and they are invited back regularly for reunions, the OE Dinner and Founder's Day. They also receive several publications each year, including the OE magazine. Bursaries are available for the sons and daughters of OEs who wish to attend the College.

Charitable status. Epsom College is a Registered Charity, number 312046. It exists for the advancement of education.

Patron: Her Most Gracious Majesty The Queen

Chair: Mr Alex Russell, OBE
Vice-Chair: Mrs Karen Thomas
Treasurer: Mr Andrew Pianca
Mrs Sarah Blaney
Dr Jeremy Bolton
Mr John Bowerman
Mrs Tania Botting
Mrs Fiona Boulton, OBE
Mrs Vivianne Gordon-Pullar
The Very Revd Dianna Gwilliams
Mr John Hay
Mr Ashley Head
Mr Dej Mahoney
Mr Julian Mount
Mr Anish Patel
Mr George Pincus, MBE
Mr Alex Vartevanian
Mr Clive Watson
Dr Alastair Wells

***Head*: Sir Anthony Seldon**, BA Oxon, PhD LSE

Second Master: Mr Paul Williams, BSc Dunelm
Bursar: Mr Paul Ratcliffe, BSc Winchester, CMgr, FCMI
Deputy Head Digital Education: Mr Richard Alton, MA Cantab, MPhys
Deputy Head Pastoral: Ms Marisa Bosa, BA Trent University, Canada, BEd Queen's University, Canada
Deputy Head Academic: Mrs Becky Brown, MChem Oxon

Assistant Head Total Curriculum: Mr Andy Bustard, BA Swansea
Assistant Head Digital Learning: Mr Ollie Fernie, BA Dunelm
Assistant Head Futures & Progression: Mr Ed Lance, BSc Dunelm
Assistant Head Pupil Wellbeing & DSL: Mr Chris Filbey, BA Dunelm
Assistant Head Systems: Mr Stuart Head, BSc (*University of the West of England*)
Assistant Head Teaching Staff and Examinations: Mr Will Keat, BSc UCL, MA King's College London
Assistant Head Sixth Form: Mr Nick Russell, MA (*Liverpool*)
Assistant Head Lower School: Mrs Leah Skipper, BA Queen Mary, University of London
Director of Marketing and Communications: Mr Mark Tobin, BA East Anglia

Heads of Year:
Head of Third Form: Mr Mark Farmer, BA Exeter
Head of Lower Fourth: Mrs Katie Eysenck, BA Oxon, MA Birkbeck
Head of Middle Fourth: Mr David Nuthall, BA Nottingham
Head of Upper Fourth: Dr Rachael Storey, BSc Dunelm, PhD King's College London
Head of Fifth Form: Mr Jim Stephens, BSc Liverpool
Head of Lower Sixth: Miss Ceara Kelly, BSc National University of Ireland, Galway, BSc Hons Institute of Technology, Sligo
Head of Upper Sixth: Mr Nick Russell, MA Liverpool

Chaplaincy:
Senior Chaplain: Revd Canon A M J Haviland, BEd Leeds, PGDipCMM Surrey, FCCT, FRSA, CF(v)
Assistant Chaplain: Mrs R Catterall
Hindu Chaplain: Ms M Joshi
Muslim Chaplain: Dr H Hammuda

Headmaster's Office:
Headmaster's PA: Mrs S Lawrence
Deputy Heads' Secretary: Mrs V Bogie

Admissions Office:
Director of Admissions: Mrs C Kent
Admissions Registrar: Mrs L Watkins

Bursars Office:
Bursar's PA: Miss F Storr

Epsom College Education Trust and OE Club:
Development Director: Ms H Tranter

Epsom Library:
Librarian: Mrs S Perry

College Archive:
College Archivist: Mrs R Worthy

Eton College

Windsor, Berkshire SL4 6DW

Tel: 01753 370611 (Admissions)
01753 370100 (Head Master)
01753 370540 (Bursar)
email: admissions@etoncollege.org.uk
website: www.etoncollege.com
X/Twitter: @Eton_College
Facebook: @Eton-College-117613119649208
Instagram: @eton.college

Eton College is a full boarding school for boys with 1,345 boys, situated next to the historic town of Windsor, Berkshire. It was founded in 1440 by King Henry VI. The school's ethos is to take talented boys with character and give them the skills to progress through life as happy, successful and socially responsible adults. Academic results are important but so too are the skills gained from co-curricular activities including music, drama, art, sports, Combined Cadet Force, outdoor education, the many different societies and our community engagement programme. At Eton, the emphasis is on finding, nurturing and giving value to each pupil's unique talents.

Approximately one fifth of the boys at the school currently receive financial aid. See our website www.etoncollege.com for further details.

The Tony Little Centre for Innovation and Research in Learning. The world of teaching and the way young people learn is being transformed through the advent of new technologies and a better understanding the neuroscience and psychology of learning. Our Centre for Innovation and Research in Learning puts Eton at the forefront of global teaching and learning developments.

The Centre works alongside partner schools and schools and universities around the world to exchange ideas and share best practice, carry out research and analyse new developments – with the aim of continually improving our outstanding teaching and learning experience for our boys as well as society more widely.

Academic achievement. Academic excellence is central to Eton life, with the vast majority of our boys going on to attend leading universities, as well as top universities in the United States. Our boys go on to study a range of subjects as undergraduates, for instance, the sciences (including medicine), humanities/English, modern languages and economics/business. Eton also has its own dedicated Learning Support Centre for boys with special educational needs.

Sport. Sport plays a central role in school life. There are nearly 30 different activities on offer, ranging from the more familiar football, rugby, cricket and rowing to Eton's own unique sports – the Wall and Field Games.

We have many highly skilled Masters and professional coaches involved in our extensive sports programme. At Eton, our main goals in sport relate to participation, performance and enjoyment. Success in this respect is evident through the amount of pupils that take part in School and House teams throughout the year and the improvement seen in their time here. Achievement is evident at all ability levels including at national level, where our top teams and high-ability sportsmen regularly compete favourably and with no small degree of success.

The arts. Over 1,300 music lessons are taught each week at The Music Schools. The majority of our 78 teachers balance their work at Eton with successful performing careers in the music industry, with many holding positions at leading music colleges. Our facilities include three concert halls, a recording studio, three music technology suites, drum suites, a music library, and a large number of teaching and practice rooms. Around 50 ensembles and choirs rehearse each week. Senior boys regularly put on their own concerts – a tradition initiated by Hubert Parry during his time as a boy at Eton. Around 25 music scholarships and exhibitions are awarded each year.

Eton's Director of Drama is Rebecca Farley MA (Acting Director of Drama until November 2024 is Hailz Osborne MA). More than 20 theatrical productions are staged at the school each year, affording boys the opportunity to take part both onstage and behind the scenes; these opportunities have seen a number of alumni forging very successful careers in the industry. Facilities include the 400-seat Farrer Theatre, a flexible auditorium with state-of-the-art lighting and sound, a scenic workshop, wardrobe, make-up studio and dressing rooms. The smaller Caccia Studio and Empty Space Theatre seat 100 and 60 people respectively. There is also a film unit and radio drama opportunities.

The Drawing Schools have opportunities for printmaking, computer graphics and digital photography, painting and drawing. There are 3D studios with facilities for sculpture (in wood, metal, plaster) and ceramics. Regular professional art exhibitions are staged and there is also an ambitious Artist-in-Residence programme. Art and design feature in the curriculum and consistently achieve high examination standards. Boys are also encouraged to use the Drawing Schools as a leisure and hobby area in their free time.

Additional activities. Eton hosts over 200 society meetings every year covering a broad range of topics from eminent speakers. A diverse programme of meetings is drawn up by boy secretaries of some 70 societies including Environment Society, Journalism Society, the African & Caribbean Society and the Psychological Society.

Eton also offers boys a choice between joining a very successful Combined Cadet Force or being part of a thriving department for community engagement, allowing boys to balance their co-curricular programme, with volunteering valued as much as individual endeavour. Boys are encouraged to develop a sense of social responsibility and give back in a number of ways, including volunteering with school children or the elderly and taking part in charity fundraising events, such as the annual Eton Action Fair.

Pastoral care. The welfare of boys at Eton College is taken extremely seriously and a robust system is in place, specifically designed to enable staff to spot problems as early as possible. The House structure, Tutor groups, our own health centre (at which boys are treated by nurses and GPs), our consultant adolescent psychiatrist, the Stephenson Centre for Wellbeing (which houses two psychologists and two counsellors) and the chaplaincy teams (with representatives of multiple faiths) all play a role within this system. Our pastoral care procedures are reviewed regularly by the Head Master, Lower Master, Deputy Head (Pastoral) and Director of Safeguarding.

Admissions. The majority of boys are admitted to the school aged 13. For entry up to and including 2026, registration is required by 30 June in UK School Year 5 (the academic year in which a boy reaches the age of 10) and related bursary applications must reach us by 15 September of UK School Year 6; please note these are strict deadlines. There are scholarships for entry aged 13 – the academic King's Scholarship and various Music Awards. These do not come with any automatic fee remission; however, it is possible to apply for a means-tested bursary in connection with an application for a Kings or Music Scholarship. There are also a small number of places available in the Sixth Form, namely Orwell Awards (funded places for boys for whom studying at Eton would be a transformative experience) and additionally up to four fee-paying places.

The Admissions process for entry up to and including 2026 consists of two stages. The first consists of the ISEB Common Pre-Tests and a report from the boy's current school, and the second stage, held at Eton, consists of a specially designed computer test and an interview.

A visit to the school either before registration or before assessment is recommended. Please contact the Admissions Team via www.etoncollege.com for further details.

Fees per term (2023–2024). £16,666.

Charitable status. Eton College is a Registered Charity, number 1139086.

Provost: The Lord Waldegrave of North Hill, PC, MA
Vice-Provost: Peter McKee, MA

Leadership Team:

***Head Master*: Simon Henderson**, MA

Lower Master: Paul Williams, BA

Bursar: Janet Walker, MA, FCA

Deputy Head (*Academic*): Tom Hawkins, MA
Deputy Head (*Boarding*): James Fulton, MA
Deputy Head (*Co-Curricular*): Jonathan Newton, MA
Deputy Head (*Curriculum Staff*): Jeanette Thorne, BSc
Deputy Head (*Partnerships*): Tom Arbuthnott, MA, MPhil
Deputy Head (*Pastoral*): Mike Grenier, MA

Director of Communications, Engagement & Development: Justin Nolan, MA
Director of Safeguarding: Alice Vicary-Stott, BA

Clerk & Legal Advisor to Provost & Fellows: Karen Neale, BA
Buildings & Facilities Director: Christopher Reeve, BSc, MRICS
Director of Admissions: Paul Smith, MA, MSt
Finance Director: Catherine Taylor, BA, ACA
HR Director: Anna Tomlinson, BA, MSc, MCIPD

Exeter School

Victoria Park Road, Exeter, Devon EX2 4NS
Tel: 01392 273679 (Head/Director of Admissions & Marketing)
01392 258712 (Bursar/Office)
01392 307080 (Admissions office)
email: admissions@exeterschool.org.uk
website: www.exeterschool.org.uk
X/Twitter: @ExeterSchoolUK
Facebook: @ExeterSchoolUK
Instagram: @exeterschooluk
LinkedIn: /exeter-school

Motto: *ΧΡΥΣΟΣ ΑΡΕΤΗΣ ΟΥΚ ΑΝΤΑΞΙΟΣ*

Founded in 1633, Exeter School occupies a 25-acre site, located within a mile of the city centre, having moved from its original location in the High Street in 1880. Some of its well-designed buildings date from that time but many new buildings have been added over the past twenty years and the school now enjoys first-rate facilities on a very attractive open site.

The school is fully co-educational and offers education to boys and girls from 7 to 18. It has its own junior school of around 200 pupils, nearly all of whom transfer to the senior school at the age of 11. The senior school has around 720 pupils, including a sixth form of 220. (*For further information about Exeter Junior School, see entry in IAPS section.*)

The New School joined the Exeter School family in March 2021 and was then rebranded as Exeter Pre-Prep School in September 2023. This offers a co-educational nursery and pre-prep for girls and boys aged 3–7 meaning that Exeter School can offer more as a through school.

Exeter School is a well-run setting with high all-round standards and very good academic results – 4 out of the UK's 126 pupils that achieved eleven grade 9s at GCSE in 2023 were Exeter School pupils. It prides itself on strong cultural, sporting and extracurricular achievement. Its music is outstanding and there is a strong tradition of performance drawn from all age groups, with over 500 instrumental lessons a week being covered by 26 visiting music teachers. It offers a very wide range of sports and maintains consistently high standards especially in hockey, rugby and cricket. It is well placed for outdoor pursuits (e.g. Duke of Edinburgh's Award scheme and Ten Tors on Dartmoor) and has its own very large voluntary CCF unit. The school is closely involved with the life of the City of Exeter and its university and it has a substantial commitment to support the local community.

Buildings, grounds and general facilities. The senior school block includes a large multi-purpose assembly hall, a library, a private study area, dining hall and Sixth Form Centre as well as many well-appointed classrooms. A major refurbishment of the former boarding accommodation to include a new library and study centre was completed for September 2006 and the outdoor swimming pool has been transformed into a welcoming admissions reception in 2022. There are separate buildings on the site housing the Chapel, the Music School, the Science Centre, Art Studio, Drama Studio, Design and Technology Centre and Exonian Centre. The Science Centre provides 14 laboratories and there are four fully equipped computer rooms with innovative renovations being rolled out constantly. All departments have access to their own computers and the School has a wide, controlled access to the internet. In 2005, the school opened a new dance studio and a fitness suite to add to the existing sports facilities of a large modern well-equipped Sports Hall with its own squash courts and access to on-site floodlit all-weather sports arena, top-grade all-weather tennis/netball courts and a 25m indoor swimming pool, built in 2017. The playing fields, which are immediately adjacent to the school buildings, are well kept and provide, in season, rugby, cricket, hockey, football, rounders and athletics areas. The junior school, which was extended in 2017 to provide additional changing room facilities and a STEAM room for DT, science and cookery, has access to all the senior school facilities but is self-contained on the estate. The playground benefitted from a substantial refurbishment over the summer of 2021, including bespoke wooden playground equipment and an outdoor classroom.

Admission. The majority of pupils enter the Pre-Prep first and transfer up to Exeter School at age 7. If transferring into Exeter School from another institute, they mostly enrol into the junior school at 7 or 9 and the senior school at 11 or 13. Admission is also possible at other ages where space allows and a significant number of pupils join at the age of 16 for sixth-form studies.

Entrance to the junior school is by assessment in January. This includes a report from the child's previous school, classroom sessions in the company of other prospective pupils, and literacy and numeracy tasks.

Entrance examinations for the senior school are held in January.

Assessment for entry to the sixth form at 16 is by interview and a report from the applicant's previous school. Dedicated interview days are held monthly from December to March each year and the entry requirement is a minimum of 3 passes at grade 7 and 3 passes at grade 6 at GCSE, including English and mathematics, with normally a grade 7–9 in the subjects chosen for study.

Registration Fee: £150 (£100 for Pre-Prep).

Fees per term (2023–2024). Junior School: Years 3 & 4 £4,400, Years 5 & 6 £4,600 (Overseas £18,630 per annum). Senior School: £5,570 (Overseas £22,950 per annum).

Sibling discount of 5% for the second child and 10% for the third or subsequent child attending concurrently. Fees are collected termly.

Scholarships and financial awards.

Academic scholarships for 7+ pupils new to Exeter Junior School are awarded based on the results of the entrance assessments sat in January of the year of entry. Exeter School offers a range of scholarship opportunities to pupils who are talented in their chosen discipline. Scholarships are available at 11+, 13+ and 16+ for pupils who show excellence in art, drama, music, and sport. Academic scholarships for pupils new to Exeter School are awarded based on the results of the entrance assessments sat in January of the year of entry. All registered candidates for the 11+, 13+ and 16+ examinations are automatically considered for an academic scholarship or exhibition based on their performance in the examinations and interviews.

Bursaries are means-tested awards based on parental circumstances and are awarded on an annual basis. They are available to external candidates who meet the school's academic entry requirement and whose parents could not afford to send their child to Exeter School without financial assistance.

Free places – As part of its bursary programme, Exeter School is able to offer up to nine free places in the senior school and sixth form as a result of donations and legacies from former pupils and grants from a local charity.

Curriculum. In the first three years in the senior school all pupils take English, history, geography, two modern foreign languages (French, German or Spanish), classical studies, mathematics, IT, physics, chemistry, biology, art, design technology, drama, music and religious and physical education. After this there is a wide choice of subjects at GCSE level, including English, one compulsory modern foreign language, mathematics, dual or triple award science and three of the following: Latin, French, German, Spanish, classical civilisation, religious studies, history, geography, music, drama, art, design and technology, and computer science.

Pupils enter the sixth form choosing over 20 different subjects for A Level study and are prepared for university scholarships, university entrance and admission to other forms of further education or vocational training. Over 95% go on annually to degree courses.

Houses. There are ten pupil houses. Each is under the personal care of a Head of House and his/her deputy, with whom parents are invited to keep in touch on any matter affecting their child's general development and progress throughout the school.

Religion. All pupils attend religious education classes, which include sixth form discussion groups.

Games. Rugby, hockey, cricket, swimming, athletics, dance, cross country, tennis, badminton, squash, shooting, basketball, netball and golf. Further activities are available for the sixth form, including football and multi-gym sessions. Recent sports tours have included a trip to Canada.

Community and other service. All pupils learn to serve the community. Many choose to take part in social service, helping old people and the handicapped young. There is a voluntary CCF Contingent with thriving RN, Army and RAF Sections. The CCF offers a large variety of outdoor activities, including adventure training camps, Ten Tors Expedition training as well as specialist courses. Pupils are encouraged to participate in the Duke of Edinburgh's Award scheme.

Music. Pupils are taught singing and musical appreciation and are encouraged to learn musical instruments. More than one third of all pupils have individual lessons on at least one instrument. There are four orchestras, a Choral Society which annually performs a major work in Exeter Cathedral and four choirs, three jazz bands, and numerous smaller groups from string quartets to rock bands. There are over 30 visiting instrumental teachers. Over 20 public concerts are given each year. Recent summer music trips have included Barcelona, Salzburg and New York.

Drama. Drama is developed both within and outside the curriculum. The School Hall with its large and well-equipped stage provides for the dual purpose of studio workshop and the regular production of plays and musicals. The recently refurbished Drama Studio is used for smaller productions.

There are three productions every year: the senior school play operates on a three-year rotation (Shakespeare, straight play, musical), embracing a variety of styles, genres and challenges; the lower school play (Years 7–11) is performed in the summer term in the main school hall and offers a very exciting opportunity for pupils to get on stage and show their talents and the Middle Fifth play, which is performed in February in the drama studio, is open to Year 10 only, meaning actors don't miss out in the transition between the seniors and the juniors. The drama department hosts National Youth Theatre auditions every year and has introduced LAMDA as an extracurricular option.

Art and Design. Art lessons are given to junior and senior forms. Apart from the formal disciplines of GCSE and A Level, which can be taken by those who choose, all pupils have opportunity for artistic expression in painting, print-making, photography and construction in many materials. All younger pupils learn to develop craft skills in wood, metal and plastic and to use them creatively in design work. Some then follow GCSE or A Level courses in design and technology. There is an annual art exhibition in July.

Expeditions. Throughout the school a large number of residential field trips and expeditions take place each year including a Third Form residential camping on the school field, various departmental excursions, several foreign exchanges and Duke of Edinburgh's Award expeditions. In recent summers, the school has run its own adventure trips to Namibia, Peru, Vietnam, the Himalayas, Cuba and Borneo. There is a programme of major and minor sports tours.

Societies and clubs. Pupils are encouraged to pursue their interests by joining one of the school societies. Groups of enthusiasts can form new societies or clubs, but the following are at present available: art, badminton, basketball, chess, Choral Society, computing, dance, drama, electronics, model railway, MUN, music, politics, shooting and squash.

Social. Close contact is maintained with the city and the university. Association between members of the school and the wider society outside is fostered wherever opportunity offers.

The staff believe strongly in the value of association with parents, who are invited to meetings annually throughout their sons' or daughters' time at the school. A termly lecture by a visiting speaker is provided for parents.

Careers. Careers education begins at the age of 7 and continues on a progressive programme until pupils leave the school. Careers evenings are held annually when pupils and their parents have the opportunity to consult representatives of the professions, industry and commerce. A work experience programme is organised for Year 11 pupils each summer, and a scheme of mock interviews with career professionals for pupils in the sixth form. A major Careers Convention is held at the school each Autumn for pupils from Years 9 to 13.

Honours. Pupils regularly gain admission to Oxford and Cambridge. The school encourages application to the leading universities, including the Russell and 1994 Groups.

Leading musicians have gained places at the Royal College of Music and the Royal Academy of Music.

Charitable status. Exeter School is a Registered Charity, number 1093080, and a Company Limited by Guarantee, registered in England, number 04470478. Registered Office: Victoria Park Road, Exeter, Devon EX2 4NS.

Patrons:
The Lord Lieutenant of the County of Devon
The Right Reverend the Lord Bishop of Exeter
The Right Worshipful the Lord Mayor of Exeter

Governors:
James Gaisford, BSc, ACA (*Chair*)
Gillian Hodgetts MSc, MCIPR, BA Hons, DMS, DN, RGN (*Vice-Chair*)
Ruth Vigers (*Vice-Chair, Nominated Safeguarding Governor*)
Rowan Edbrooke, BEd Hons (*Vice-Chair*)
Claire Baillie
Adrian Burbanks, BA
Helen Clark
Catherine Gibaud, KC, BBus Sc Hons, MA
Stephen Hodder, BSc
Michael Johnson, BA, PGCE
Dominic Kalantary, BSc
Richard May, BA, MRICS
David McGahey, MA, PGCE
Andrew Richards, FCA, CTA, TEP

***Head*: Ms L A Simpson**, BSc

Deputy Head: Miss A Dunning, BA
Deputy Head: G S Bone, BSc
Deputy Head: Dr J L Wilson, MPhys, DPhil
Assistant Head, Character: Miss B Rose, MA
Assistant Head, Head of Sixth Form: Mr L Chu, BA

Assistant Staff:
* *Head of Department*
[OE] *Old Exonian*

Art & Design:
*Mrs J Brewer, BA
Ms C Brownsey, BA
Mr J Mason
Mrs J H Rafferty-White, BA

Biology:
*Mrs J H Metcalf, MA (*Director of Science*)
Mr P J C Boddington, BSc
Mrs K Britton
Mrs K A Coe, BSc
Mrs A C Johnson, BSc
Ms M E Montagu
Mrs J M Seaton-Burn, MSc (*Chair of Teaching and Learning Committee*)

Chemistry:
*Mr R F J Tear, BSc
Mr P I O'Connor, BSc
Dr S P Smale, PhD (*CCF Contingent Commander and Head of RAF section, CCF*)
Mrs F J Tamblyn, BSc
Ms D H Wilson, MBA

Classical Subjects:
*Mrs E K J Dunlop
Dr E L Keane, DPhil
Mrs S T Trica, MA

Computer Science:
*Ms A O Pinches, BEng
Mr G J McGrath, BSc

Design Technology
*Mr R A Collard, BSc
Mr L Mc Menamin

Drama:
*Mr J S Brough, BSc, LAMDA
Mr C C Harknett, BA
Mr A G Sorlie-Pring

Electronics:
*Mr M E Schramm (*see Physics*)

English:
*Mr A S Dobson, MA
Mr S R Butler, BSc
Mrs J H Daybell, BA, MA
Mrs E K J Dunlop, BA, MA, MPhil
Mr R O Evans, BA
Mr C C Harknett (*see Drama*)
Mr C O'Rooke
Mrs K L Ridler-Murray, BA, MA
Mr E J Seaton-Burn, BA

Geography:
*Mr P M Hyde, BSc
Mr S Munday, BA
Mrs A Roff, BSc, MSc
Mrs H M Sail, MA

Careers and Higher Education
Mrs M Szender

History:
*Mr G N Trelawny, BEd, MA
Mr R J Baker (*see Social Studies*)
Mrs S Bartholomew
Mrs A-J Culley, BA, BSc
Miss M Nye, BA
Mrs M F Sheehan (*see Social Studies*)

Languages:
*Ms L Trotman, BA
Mr R A Charters, BA
Mrs N H R Cushion, BA
Miss A Dunning (*see Deputy Heads*)
Mrs A M Francis, MA
Mr M F Latimer, MA, MSt
Mrs D D S Masters, BA
Mrs S C Wilson, BA

Learning Support:
Mrs H E Coogan, BEd
Mrs A L Reeves, BSc (*Head of RN Section, CCF*)

Mathematics:
*Mrs E V Cartwright, BSc
Miss A C Blackmore, MSc
Mr T Bowler, MSc
Dr G J D Chapman, BSc, PhD, MSc
Mr M F C Glanville, BSc
Mr B M Hall, BA
Mr M J Hughes (*see Senior Deputy Head*)
Ms M McCluskey, BA, MSc
Mr A J Reynolds, BSc (*Examinations Officer*)

Music:
*Mr P Tamblyn, MA, MMus (*Director of Music*)
Mr G M Davies, MA (*Assistant Director of Music*)
Mr P J Adcock, MA
Mrs R Allnatt, Dip RCM, Cert Adv Study
Mr D Bowen, BEd
Mr M R Cann, BA
Mr S J Crossen
Mr A Daldorph, BA
Mr A Gillett, ARCM
Mr M F Greenwood, LRAM
Miss C A Hayek, LRAM
Mrs S L Jenkins, MA
Mrs R E A Molins, BA
Mr B R Moore, BA, MA
Mr P K Painter, Dip Mus Ed
Mrs R L Willson, BA

Physical Education:
*Mr D J Gibson, BSc (*Director of Sport*)
Miss L Barnes, BSc
Miss R A Carter, BSc
Mrs H L Hayden, BSc
Miss E Horn, BSc
Miss B G Johnson
Mr E P M Jones, BSc (*Head of Raleigh House*)
Mr A C F Mason, BA
Mr T N Ross, BSc
Mr G Skinner, BEd [OE]

Physics:
*Mr D L N Tuohey, BSc, MA
Mr G S Bone (*see Deputy Heads*)
Dr M J Commin, MA, PhD
Dr G B N Robb, MA, PhD (*Master i/c Aquatics*)
Mr M E Schramm, BSc
Mr D I Trim, BSc (*Head of Army Section, CCF*)
Dr J L Wilson (*see Deputy Heads*)

Psychology:
*Mrs C Gooddy, MSc
Mrs A M Godfroy, BA

Religious Studies:
*Mr J F M Gooddy, MA
Mrs J M K Murrin, BA

Social Studies:
Mr S K Mackintosh, BA (**Economics*)
Mr R J Baker, BA (**Politics*)
Mrs M F Sheehan, BA (**Politics*)
Mr P Bell, MA, BA
Mr M J G Connolly, BA

Junior School

Headmistress: Mrs Saskia van Schalkwyk, BA Hons, QTS

Deputy Head: Mr J S Wood, BA

Assistant Staff:
Ms A Ager
Ms J A Barnes, BA
Mrs H E Coogan, BEd
Miss E C Cox, BA
Mr A P Cunningham, BA
Mr C Dutch
Mr R W I Evans, MA
Mrs C H Handley, BEd
Mrs L L Hardy, MA
Mrs K L Jones, BSc
Mrs S S Morgan, BA
Mrs R E Pettet, BA
Mr R J Pidwell, BA
Mrs H D Russell, BA
Ms S Withers, Dip

Bursar and Clerk to the Governors: M C M MacEacharn, FCA, BSc
Deputy Bursar and Company Secretary: Mrs G M Robins, BA, FCCA
Operations Manager: C A Stewart
Director of Development and Alumni: Miss A S A Holohan, BA
Director of Admissions and Marketing: Mrs E S Williams
Admissions Manager: Mrs A O C Irons
Communications Manager: Mrs L K Bates, BA
Headmaster's PA: Mrs K Leach
Bursar's PA: Mrs L M Stewart
Information Manager: Mr A D R Carter, BEng
Network Manager: Mr P D Sprake, MCSA
Librarian: Mr T Halpin, MA
School Nurse: Mrs L J Barlass, BSc

Farringtons School

Perry Street, Chislehurst, Kent BR7 6LR

Tel: 020 8467 0256
email: fvail@farringtons.kent.sch.uk
website: www.farringtons.org.uk
X/Twitter: @OneFarringtons
Facebook: @OneFarringtons

Farringtons School is situated in 25 acres of green belt land in Chislehurst, which provide attractive surroundings while still being within easy reach of London (25 minutes to Charing Cross), the south coast and Gatwick airport (45 minutes), and Heathrow airport via the M25 (1 1/4 hours).

The School is committed to providing a first-class education for pupils of all ages in a caring community which supports all its members and helps each pupil to achieve his or her full potential both academically and personally. After-school care is available until 6.30 pm.

The School offers an enhanced National Curriculum, with a wide range of GCSE and A Level subjects available. Nearly 100% of Sixth Form leavers customarily go on to degree courses at Universities or Higher Education Colleges. Academic standards are high from a comprehensive intake of pupils and in 2023 a 98% pass rate was achieved at A Level.

The excellent facilities include a Technology building, a large Sports Hall with Dance Studio and Fitness Suite, splendidly equipped Science and Modern Language departments, a well-stocked library, Careers Room, indoor heated swimming pool and extensive playing fields, as well as a School Chapel, where the School regularly comes together.

The main sports are netball, tennis, football, swimming and athletics, but badminton, volleyball and table tennis are also undertaken and other extracurricular activities available include The Duke of Edinburgh's Award scheme, various choirs and instrumental ensembles, gymnastics, dance, ballet, drama club, fencing, etc.

The School also offers an exciting Floreat Programme, where pupils have the opportunity to experience new activities such as archery, scuba diving and bee-keeping during the school day.

To obtain a prospectus and further information or to arrange a visit, contact the Registrar: admissions@farringtons.kent.sch.uk.

Fees per term (2023–2024). Day: £4,020 (Pre-Reception, full time), £4,960 (Prep), £6,240 (Senior); Weekly Boarding: £10,590; Full Boarding: £13,290.

Charitable status. Farringtons School is part of the Methodist Independent Schools Trust, a Registered Charity, number 1142794. It exists solely to provide a high-quality, caring education.

Governing Body:
Chairman: Mr A Harris
Vice-Chairman: Mr Ric Hinton

Members:
Mrs S Donaldson
Mr S Herd
Mr P Johnstone
Mrs J King
Dr A Squires
Mr M Vinales
Revd Dr J Zihle

Bursar and Clerk to the Governors: Mrs Sally-Anne Eldridge

***Headmaster*: Mr David Jackson**, BA, MEd

Deputy Head: Mr N Young
Assistant Head (*Curriculum*): Mr L Garwood
Assistant Head (*Pastoral & Head of Boarding*): Mr S Palacios
Head of Sixth Form: Ms V Jackson
Head of Prep School: Mr R Boyjoonauth
Deputy Head of Prep School: Mrs J Cryan

Director of Marketing & Admission: Mrs F Vail
Registrar: Mrs B Thompson
Prep School Registrar: Ms V Standing

* *Head of Department*

English:
*Miss S Bliss
Mr B Coulthard
Mrs V Denman
Ms K Evans
*Mrs K O'Neil
Ms N Ramsden
Mrs E Russell
Mr P Scowen
Ms Mingyue Yang
Ms C Lewington
Mrs M McEvilly
Mrs V Owen
Mrs L Sriram
Mr L Templeman

Mathematics:
*Mr F Gray
Mrs I Haider
Mrs Z Hanson
Ms M Jeffrey
Mrs M Mahil
Mr R Nagrra
Mr H Silo

Science:
*Mr D Foster
Mrs J Daws
Miss F Evans
Mrs M Haughney
Mrs R Ashworth
Ms Sheronett Brown
Mr J Gardner
Mrs R Miah
Mr S Owen
Mr N Varley
Mrs L Williamson
Mrs S Watson
Mrs P White

Modern Languages:
*Mlle I Mosqueron
Mr J Hernando
Mrs F Jackson
Ms V Jackson
Mr P Scowen

Humanities:
*Mr G Curran
Mr C Catling
Miss E Choi
Mr A Essex
Mr K Jones
Mrs R Saunders
Miss A Sawyer
Mr K Wilson

Business, Finance & Technology:
*Miss K Ootim

Performing & Creative Arts:
*Miss J Warburton
Mrs G Allen
Miss R Azulay
Mrs S Freeston
Mrs D Humphrey
Mr R Matthews
Mrs S Molyneaux
Mr N Raynor
Miss I Smith

Learning Development:
*Ms N Palmer
Mr S Flashman
Miss M Gill
Ms K Miles
Mrs J Pyle

Sport:
*Mr C Doyle
Mrs S Arnold
Mrs E Broughan
Mr A Doherty
Miss B Farrant
Mrs J Sherwood
Miss K Southward

Prep School:
*Mr R Boyjoonauth
Mr A Alansari
Ms F Alexander
Mrs G Bastos
Mrs L Benjamin
Mrs K Breen
Mrs P Brookman
Mrs S Coop
Miss S Cox
Mrs C Crouser
Mrs J Cryan
Mrs T Devaux
Mr A Doherty
Mrs C Fitzpatrick
Mrs C Frisby
Mr H Hadfield
Mrs h Harry
Mrs J Hurst
Ms S Johnson
Ms H Kearns
Ms H Khurana
Mrs M Levey
Mrs L Long
Mrs E Loosen
Mrs A Lopez
Mrs J Oliver
Miss K Randall
Mrs H Reynolds
Mrs H Roberts
Mr J Shimmin
Ms K Streeter
Ms C Steel
Mrs S Vickers
Mrs A Vinales
Ms S Watts
Miss E Webber
Mrs L Webster

Felsted School

Felsted, Dunmow, Essex CM6 3LL

Tel:	01371 822606 (Head) 01371 822608 (Admissions Registrar)
email:	reception@felsted.org
website:	www.felsted.org
X/Twitter:	@felstedschool
Facebook:	@felstedschool
Instagram:	@felsted-school
LinkedIn:	/felsted-school

Founded in 1564 by Lord Richard Riche, Felsted educates boys and girls aged 4 to 18. Felsted is ideally situated in a safe, picturesque North Essex village, close to both London and Cambridge, and within easy reach of Stansted and other international airports. Felsted is a Church of England foundation but welcomes pupils from all religious traditions and none. The Senior School, for 13 to 18 year olds, has around 570 pupils; the majority are boarders and weekend arrangements are flexible. The Prep School is also home to approximately

500 pupils, with a buoyant boarding house, home to full, weekly and flexible boarders.

Felsted seeks to develop the character of every student, to help prepare them for life beyond school. This is done through a broad and holistic education with strength in Music, Drama, Sport, The Arts, Leadership and Service. Felsted seeks to develop and stretch students academically, to be lifelong learners, well-rounded, aspirational and globally minded, with the skills to flourish beyond school, applying the principles of a growth mindset, to be the best they can be.

Felsted celebrated its 450th anniversary in 2014, and was honoured by a visit from HM Queen Elizabeth II and HRH Prince Phillip.

The School is a Global Member of the Round Square Organisation offering international exchanges and collaboration, and offers both A Levels and the International Baccalaureate Diploma in the Sixth Form, plus the Extended Project Qualification (EPQ). The website hosts much information about the school plus many videos, including one called 'Boarding at Felsted'. A Boarding Schools' Association (BSA) member school, Felsted had an Ofsted boarding and welfare inspection in 2011 and was rated 'outstanding' in every aspect, and also received an 'excellent' rating in all aspects in the Independent Schools Inspectorate inspection in 2019. The school also passed with flying colours in a full compliance inspection across both the Preparatory and Senior Schools in 2019. Details are available on our website, and directly on the ISI website. Felsted was awarded the TES Boarding School of the Year award in 2023 and is featured in the Tatler Schools Guide 2024 as one of the top schools in the United Kingdom.

The Houses. There are ten Houses at Felsted, a day house for boys, a day house for girls, three boarding houses for boys, three boarding houses for girls, an Upper Sixth House for boys and an Upper Sixth House for girls. Each House is under the direction of a resident Housemaster or Housemistress.

Each Boarding House is supported by a pastoral team comprising a resident Assistant House Parent, a matron responsible for overseeing the domestic arrangements, and several House tutors, a number of whom are resident.

The Curriculum. All pupils study English Language, English Literature, Mathematics and Sciences (Double or Triple Award) to GCSE and choose a further four subjects from the following: History, Geography, TEP (Theology, Ethics and Philosophy), French, German, Spanish, Latin, Classical Civilisation, Art and Design, Music, Drama, Triple Science, Design & Technology (Resistant Materials), Physical Education and Computer Science.

One of the options is expected to be a Modern Foreign Language and one is expected to be a Humanities subject.

In the Sixth Form pupils have a choice between A Levels and the International Baccalaureate Diploma.

Those studying A Levels normally choose three subjects to study along with an Extended Project Qualification (EPQ). The following subjects are offered: Art and Design, Business, Classical Civilisation, Computer Science, Design Technology, Drama and Theatre, Economics, English Literature, Geography, History, Latin, Mathematics, Further Mathematics, Media Studies, Modern Foreign Languages (French, German, Spanish), Music, Physical Education, Politics, Psychology, Sciences (Biology, Chemistry, Physics) and TEP (Theology, Ethics and Philosophy).

IB pupils study six subjects, one from each of the following categories: Language and Literature (English, German, Italian, Self-Study Language, Spanish and French), Language A (English, German, Italian, Self-Taught), Language (Other) (French, German, English, Spanish, Latin and Italian 'ab initio'), Humanities (Economics, Geography, History, Philosophy, Psychology), Sciences (Biology, Chemistry, Design Technology, Physics, Sports Exercise and Health Science), Mathematics (Maths Analysis and Approaches or Maths Applications and Interpretation), The Arts/Elective (Music, Visual Arts, Biology, Economics, French B, Spanish ab initio). They also follow a course on the Theory of Knowledge, write an extended essay and are fully involved in the Creativity, Action and Service Programme.

Scholarships, Awards and Bursaries. Academic, Music, Drama, Art, Design/Technology/Engineering and Sports Scholarships are awarded annually for entry into Year 7, 9, 10 and 12, up to the value of 20% of the fees.

The assessments for Year 7 entry take place in November and the following January. For Year 9, 10 and 12 in November and February (Academic only) in the year preceding entry.

Awards recognising all-round ability or a specific ability in one area, are also available.

Means-tested Bursaries may be available to increase an award.

At least two Open Bursaries (100%) each year may be available to those who might otherwise not be able to consider Felsted, due to financial circumstances, as well as a Royal Docks Scholarship (100%) and the school has recently developed a link with the Royal Springboard Foundation to support a further two pupils a year.

Talented students in Design are also entered at 16+ for Arkwright Foundation Scholarships.

Fee reductions are available for children of those serving in the Armed Services, or the Foreign Office.

Full details are available at www.felsted.org and from the Admissions Office.

Registration and entry. Registration fee is £125. Registration can be completed whenever a family is ready, but this is usually completed around 1 year in advance, subject to year group of entry. Application deadlines and further details of registration for each entry phase can be found on www.felsted.org/admissions

Before admission to Felsted Senior School, prospective pupils must pass the Felsted Entrance assessment, provide a Head Teacher's report and have an interview with the Felsted School Head. For Sixth Form entry, a minimum of 32 points must be gained across their best six subjects at GCSE, with at least a 6 in the subjects to be studied at A Level or at Higher Level in the IB Diploma.

Fees per term (2023–2024). Senior School: Full Boarding (7 nights): £14,700, Weekly Boarding (5 nights): £13,620, Contemporary Boarding (3 nights): £11,770, Day: £9,605. Prep School: Day: £3,705–

£7,275, Weekly Boarding: £9,415, Full Boarding: £9,995.

Felsted Prep School, whose Head is a member of IAPS (The Independent Association of Prep Schools), shares the same governing body with Felsted School. It has its own campus, with approximately 500 pupils aged 4 to 13. There is a dedicated teaching centre for 11–13 year-olds and a state-of-the-art Pre-Preparatory Department, which opened in 2011. (For further information, see entry in IAPS section.)

The Old Felstedian Society organises both social and sporting activities, plus networking opportunities across a variety of industries. The Development & Alumni Relations team would be pleased to answer queries about the Alumni (ofs@felsted.org) and further information can be found via the school's website.

Charitable status. Felsted School is a Registered Charity, number 310870. The charity is based upon the Foundation established by Richard Lord Riche in 1564 with the objective of teaching and instructing children across a broad curriculum as ordained from time to time by its Trustees.

Governing Body:
Chair of Governors: Robert Brown
Julia Abel Smith
Mike Beale
Geoffrey Boult
Ann Carrington
Jane Crouch
John Davies, OBE
Bobbi Davy
Dr James Nicholson
Lucilla Poston
Alison Sefton
Oliver Stocken, CBE
Revd Nic Stuchfield
Patricia Wardell
Jason Windsor
Stephen Wolfe

Bursar and Clerk to the Governors: Andrew Clayton, MA

***Head*: Christopher Townsend**, BA

Bursar: Andrew Clayton, MA
Senior Deputy Head: George Masters, BA
Deputy Head (*Academic*): Lorne Stefanini, MA
Director of Safeguarding (*DSL*): Nicola O'Brien
Director of Global Education: Robin Hancock, MA, EdD
Prep School Head: Miranda Norris, BEd, ILMP, MEd

Art:
J N Buniak, MA
E A M Jackson, BA
A V Warner, BA

Business:
E Grant, BSc
A T Mohindru, LLB
J K Peddy, BA

Classics:
E J Clark, BA
E M McLaren, MA (*Head of Roberts Society*)
A J Quinlan, BA (*Head of Andrew Society*)

Computer Science:
J I Poston, BSc
A V Price, MA (*Physics*)
A A Ross, BSc
M White, MA

Design and Technology:
M D Cudjoe, BA
D M Maclean, MA
H K Pheloung, BA

Drama:
C Bartlett, BA
M C Donaldson, BA (*Assistant Head – Academic*)
L Macey, BA
L J Mann, BA

Economics:
F M Barrett, BBS (*Assistant Head – Boarding*)
R Castle, BSc
M L McIlvenna, BA, MEd
S D Wilson, BA

English and Media:
M R Crossley, BA
C A Croxson, BA
C A Drake, BA
C M James, BA (*Head of Project Qualifications*)
A J MacLeod, BA (*Head of Girls' Cricket*)
A MacMillan, BA, MA
E L Predebon, MA (*Director of Teacher Development*)
R J Purdy, BA, MEd (*PSHE, Assistant Head – Staff & Co-curricular*)
N M Sunshine-Harris, BA (*Assistant Director of Professional Guidance & Support*)
A J Townsend, BA, MA

Geography:
A McCaughern, BSc
G R Stringer, BSc
O G Thomas, BSc
N Thompson, BSc, GRA

History & Politics:
B R Maude-Barker, MA (*Head of Politics*)
R Pathak, BA
L M Scofield, BA (*Director of Professional Guidance*)
T Strange, PhD (*Academic Enrichment Co-ordinator*)
J C E Strong, PhD, MA

Mathematics:
J W Adams, PhD
J C Andrews, MEng
M J Campbell, MSc
C Donaldson, BSc
J M Finch, BSc
J M Jevons, BA (*Timetabler*)
A Munns, MA
N Pritchard, BSc
H J Rendall, BSc

Modern Languages:
G M Bermejo Gonzalez, BA (*Spanish*)
A N Fazekas, MA (*German*)
V Grandi, BA, MA (*French*)
G E Kehoe, BA (*French & Spanish*)
N F S O'Brien, MA (*Spanish, EAL, DSL*)
A J Pallot, BA (*German*)
R Perez Cabrera, MA (*Spanish, Round Square Co-ordinator*)

K L G Reddey, BA (*Spanish & French*)
F Sanchez del Rio, Licenciatura (*Spanish, Editor of 'The Felstedian'*)
P M Torres Vaquero, BA, MA (*French*)
Music:
W J Warns, MA, DipABRSM, FNCM (*Director of Music*)
R J Thear, BA (*Assistant Director of Music*)
S Tan, BA, BMus, MMus GRA
Physical Education and Sport:
S Barrett, BSc (*Senior HM*)
B J Bury, BA
W H Croft, BA GRA
G C Ellis, BA GRA
J E R Gallian (*Director of Cricket*)
Z V Griffith
C S Knightley, BA (*Director of Sport*)
A Le Chevalier, PGCE (*Director of Rugby*)
R Marriott-Cox (*Director of Tennis*)
D L C Nelson, BSc
N J Phillips, BA (*Head of Boys' Hockey*)
J R Westwood (*Director of Hockey*)
L Willis, BSc, MS (*Director of Girls' Sport & Head of Girls' Hockey*)
Project Qualifications:
C M James, BA
PSHE and RSE:
L M Keable, BA (*2 i/c*)
R J Purdy, BA, MEd (*Assistant Head – EDI, Staff & Co-Curricular*)
Psychology:
M Cacace, BA Exeter (*Head of IB Core*)
V L Smith, BSc, MEd
Science:
L E Barden, BSc (*Chemistry*)
L T Barrett, BSc (*Chemistry*)
J Entwistle, BSc (*Biology*)
K J Farr, MSc (*Biology*)
H J Mollison, BSc, MEd (*Head of Science, Chemistry*)
C H Palmer, MA (*Physics*)
A J A Pask, BSc (*Chemistry*)
A V Price, MA (*Physics, Business Intelligence Reporting Manager*)
A L F Simpson, BSc (*Biology, Director of Exams*)
D T Smith, BSc (*Physics*)
R L Williams, BSc (*Biology, Assistant Head Academic*)
K L Woodhouse, BSc (*Physics, Director of IBDP*)
Theology, Ethics and Philosophy:
L M Keable, BA
S R Lambert, PhD
N J Little, BA (*Chaplain, i/c Charities*)
G W S Masters, BA (*Senior Deputy Head*)
L K Stefanini, BSc, MA (*Deputy Head – Academic*)
J C Turner Jones, BA
Wellbeing Centre:
C J Croll, MBACP Accred
R K S Love, BSc, MBACP
J M Miller, PDC, PDD, PGCert, MBACP reg
K J Newnham, MBACP, reg
Support for Learning:
S J Beale, BA Bristol
C M Dungey, RSciTech
J W Hipkin, BA Manchester QTS, MEd
N J Johnson, CDip
E L Masters, MA Aberdeen
C M Phillips, MCILIP W London
A L Salmon, BA Leicester, MEd Middlesex
J C Turner Jones, BA Birmingham
EAL:
D K Guerrero, BA Middlesex, Dip TEFLA
CCF:
L W Jay
C H Palmer, MA Cambridge (*CCF Contingent Commander*)
Duke of Edinburgh's Award & Educational Visits:
D L Whittock
Library:
N S Howorth, BA Edge Hill, Dip Lib, MCLIP

Houses and Housemasters/mistresses:
Boys' Houses:
Deacon's: Barny Bury
Elwyn's: Elliott Grant
Gepp's: Luke McIlvenna
Montgomery's: Andrew Le Chevalier
Windsor's: Clifford Palmer
Girls' Houses:
Follyfield: Sonia Wilson
Garnetts: Sarah Barrett
Manor: Carolyn Phillips
Stocks's: Loren Willis
Thorne: Connie Donaldson
Director of Marketing: Mr Jack Dougherty
Head of Admissions: Miss Gemma Kilby
School Chaplain: Reverend Nigel Little
Medical Officer: Mrs Sally Staines

Fettes College

Carrington Road, Edinburgh EH4 1QX

Tel: +44 (0)131 311 6744
email: admissions@fettes.com
website: www.fettes.com
X/Twitter: @Fettes_College
Facebook: @FettesCollegeFettesPrep
Instagram: @fettes.college
LinkedIn: /school/fettes-college

Motto: *Industria*

Fettes College – A place to live. A place to learn. A place to grow.

Situated in a stunning 100-acre campus, close to the heart of Edinburgh, Fettes College enjoys a reputation as one of the pre-eminent co-educational boarding schools in the UK. Fettes is a collaborative community in which every member is working towards fully realising their potential while supporting those around them.

- Excellent GCSE, A Level and IB results
- Co-educational 7–18
- Full boarding ethos
- Sector leading pastoral care
- Extensive co-curricular programme

- Proudly Scottish with a global outlook
- Easy access to Edinburgh Airport

Curious, creative and kind, Fettesians are inspired to aim high while understanding what it means to be a good person and give back.

Following the English examinations of GCSE, and dual pathway of A Level and IB in the Sixth Form, we offer each of our students the opportunity to make the most of their talents and gain a wealth of new experiences in a happy, encouraging environment where innovation and creativity are key.

'*Our students will leave the school knowing themselves, looking out for others, capable of thinking critically and ready to make a positive mark on their rapidly changing world. They will be bold and visionary yet compassionate; they will possess a global perspective and be ready to embrace the opportunities of the future.*' Helen Harrison, Head.

Offering each student the opportunity to make the most of their talents and to gain a wealth of new experiences in a happy, encouraging environment, Fettes College maximises students' potential by affording them all the opportunities that a full boarding ethos offers, delivering excellent outcomes for the individual, while ensuring the highest levels of care. Each boarding house is like a family and the boarding houses are at the heart of Fettes life. All senior school students – day and boarding – are part of a boarding house and each firmly believes their house is the best house! House spirit is strong. Lifelong friendships are made, trust is fostered and loyalty forged. With over 60 co-curricular activities on offer, weekends at Fettes are vibrant and fun-filled.

As part of our – *Fettes Moving Forward* – vision for the future we have already introduced Engineering, Enterprise and Technology (EET) into our curriculum, featuring lessons in Robotics, Structural Engineering, programming and 3D printing. All Third Form students receive this education. From September 2024, students will have the option to take EET as an alternative to one of their GCSE options and will qualify for a Higher Project Qualification (HPQ).

Fees per term (2023–2024). Fettes Prep: Boarders £10,230; Day Pupils £6,970. Fettes College: Boarders £14,700; Day Pupils £12,350.

There are three terms per academic year. Fees include the cost of all meals.

Chair of Governors: The Rt Hon Lady Morag Wise

***Head*: Mrs Helen Harrison**

Forest School

Snaresbrook, London E17 3PY
Tel: 020 8520 1744
email: admissions@forest.org.uk
website: www.forest.org.uk
X/Twitter: @ForestSchoolE17
Facebook: @ForestSchoolE17
LinkedIn: /company/forest-school

Motto: *In Pectore Robur*

Established in 1834, Forest is an outstanding all-round school, offering a breadth and depth of opportunity in which pupils' personal development is exceptional and academic attainment very high. It is, above all, a happy school which understands the rich inter-relationship between curricular, the co-curricular and the pastoral. The school is located on a 45-acre site at the edge of the capital's largest open space, Epping Forest.

There are currently 1,502 pupils in the School – 783 boys and 719 girls. All pupils share the main school campus and facilities such as the Chapel, Dining Hall, Sports Hall, playing fields, Deaton Theatre, and the Martin Centre for Innovation. Sixth Form pupils enjoy use of a dedicated Sixth Form Centre, including collaborative IT workspaces, group study areas and a careers room.

Curriculum. Academic enrichment, learning and personal development are the natural outcomes of Forest's holistic approach to education, which enables our pupils to grow in a diverse and progressive community before they progress beyond our 'White Gates' to a career or university of their choice. A rich core academic curriculum in the first years of the pupils' time at Forest is progressively augmented by opportunities to make personal choices, reflect thoughtfully on personal development and form a more individualised academic curriculum as they progress and grow.

In Y7–Y9 a broad range of core subjects is taught, including Modern and Classical Languages, incorporating Mandarin Chinese, and the three Sciences. Options in Y9 include Computer Science, Ancient Greek and Food & Nutrition, as well as more traditional subjects. At GCSE, all pupils follow a core curriculum of English Language & Literature, a Modern Foreign Language, Maths and Science (separate or Double Award, according to preference) as well as a choice from around 15 optional subjects. A distinctive feature of the curriculum is that all pupils also submit work for the Higher Project Qualification (HPQ) – a research-based dissertation on a subject of the pupil's own choosing, following a taught course of critical thinking and project skills, and then assessed at GCSE level.

In the Sixth Form, pupils take the Sixth Form Curriculum which has a particular emphasis on Personal Development. A Levels provide the core academic element and Sixth Formers can choose from 28 different A Level subjects, with most choosing three main subjects, examined at the end of the two-year course, and taught in small teaching groups of typically around ten to fifteen pupils. All Sixth Form Curriculum pupils begin a course in Project Skills in Year 12 and will produce an Extended Project Qualification (EPQ), which may take the form of a dissertation-style essay, or 'creative artefact', such as a film, composition or even a computer program. Sixth Formers Personal Development curriculum is centred on the seven core values of Forest School: Community, Diversity, Growth, Hard Work, Learning, Responsibility and Wellbeing.

The School places considerable emphasis on teaching the effective use of Information and Communications Technology. Every pupil in the Senior School is required to have with them a keyboard-enabled device in school, and all pupils are trained in the use of mobile devices as an appropriate tool to best leverage learning. All teachers incorporate digital materials and applications within their teaching, when the learning task would stand to benefit from it. Computer Science, with an emphasis on programming, is available from Y9 as an academic subject.

Additionally, all pupils – from Year 7 to Year 13 – are engaged in a robust and sequenced programme of reflection, study and assessment in Relationships, Sex and Health Education. This is a critical subject at Forest and ensures that all of our learners are able to fully understand and be equipped for the increasingly complex world which they inhabit.

The curriculum is augmented by a wide range of timetabled academic super-curricular activities which supplement the core curriculum and which cultivate cultural and aesthetic appreciation, critical thinking and develop problem solving skills. Lessons in additional languages such as Italian and Russian are offered, as well as opportunities to develop skills through Science and Maths competitions, partnership work with universities, participation in MOOCs and multiple opportunities to attend 'Lookout Lectures' featuring diverse national and international leaders from the realms of business, civil society, science and culture.

Co-Curriculum. The School has a large music department with more than 50 visiting staff teaching a wide range of instruments and voice. Regular concerts take place in School venues and outside including House Music and national competitions. Drama offers three major productions per year alongside House Drama competitions, and regular showings for curricular Drama. Art presents exhibitions and cross-curricular projects with English and other departments. The PE department boasts a heritage of sporting excellence for both girls and boys in a wide range of both mainstream and less conventional sports with pupils regularly selected at district, county, and national level. Other activities include Forest's Combined Cadet Force, which is linked to the Royal Green Jackets, and The Duke of Edinburgh's Award scheme which offers Bronze, Silver and Gold levels with high completion rates at all stages. Pupils can choose anything from chess to technology, debating to drama, a wide range of musical activities to some of the best sporting offerings. Pupils participate in a diverse programme of activities that encourage the learning of physical, cultural and leadership skills throughout their time at Forest. The co-curricular programme at Forest builds and develops five core principles – Creativity, Challenge, Culture, Community and Careers.

Games. The main games for boys are association football, hockey, cricket, and athletics. The main games for girls are hockey, netball, cricket, football, and athletics. The sporting facilities are extensive and include an all-weather AstroTurf facility, tennis and netball courts, indoor and outdoor cricket nets, gym, sports hall, two swimming pools, strength and conditioning suite, 5-a-side 3G and acres of sporting fields. Additional sports such as swimming, tennis, basketball, fencing, rowing, golf, squash, mountain biking, table tennis, badminton and water polo are also available to boys and girls.

Fees per term (2023–2024). Reception to Year 2: £5,749, Year 3: £6,132, Year 4 to 6: £6,625, Year 7 to 13: £8,185. Fee reductions are available for children of the Clergy.

Careers. Many of the pupils go on to take up places at Oxford, Cambridge, Russell Group universities, Conservatoires, and prestigious Arts colleges. However, Forest is successful at placing pupils in professional apprenticeships with companies including PricewaterhouseCoopers and Morgan Stanley.

Admission – Preparatory School. The only entry point to the Prep School is 4+. In principle, pupils are assessed on the basis of:

4+ entry

A series of low-key activities which include: picture recognition, some letter recognition, following a pattern, knowing colours, counting, drawing, naming simple shapes, sequencing, listening to a story, playing and responding sensibly to the adults who are present.

Admissions – Senior School. In principle, pupils are assessed based on:

11+ entry:

- Performance in an entrance assessment
- Performance in a collaborative task
- An interview with a senior member of staff
- A written confidential report from the present school

16+ entry

- Performance in an entrance examination
- An interview with a senior member of staff
- A written confidential report from the present school
- Predicted Grades
- Recent School report

Entry into the Forest Sixth Form requires at least three grade 7s or above; and at least three grade 6s or above; and at least grade 5 in English and Maths; and the required grade at I/GCSE in the qualifying subject/s required for their chosen courses.

Full GCSE grade requirements can be found on the School website: www.forest.org.uk.

Scholarships and Bursaries are available at 11+ and 16+ entry. Scholarships are awarded for outstanding academic ability and exceptional attainment in Art, Drama, Music and Sport. The maximum non-means-tested fee remission awarded in respect of any one pupil is 20% of full fees, whether in one area of excellence or in a combination of one or more areas of excellence.

Bursaries are means-tested and are awarded in addition to Scholarships, up to and including the total remission of fees; in other words, a free place. Bursaries are only given in conjunction with a Scholarship.

In addition, seven 11+ Assisted Places may be awarded annually to pupils who pass the entrance exam and have the greatest financial need.

For full details visit www.forest.org.uk.

Charitable status. Forest School, London is a Registered Charity, number 312677. The objective of the School is Education.

Governing Council:
Chairman of Governors: David Wilson, LLB Hons, FRSA, FRGS
Geraldine Atlee
Dr Steven Berryman
The Venerable Elwin Cockett
Jane Davies
William Fuller
Yemisi Gibbons
Dr Saniya Hadi, BSc Hons, MBBS, MRCOG

Simon Perry
Paul Sampat

Leadership Team:

***Warden*: Mr M Cliff Hodges**, BA University College Cardiff, MA University College London

Bursar: Mrs D E Coombs, BSc Cape Town, Hons B&A, MBA Stellenbosch

Head of Preparatory School: Mr J E R Sanderson, BMus Perf Hons Elder Conservatorium, BMus Adelaide, FRSA, FCCT

Deputy Head Staffing and Operations: Mrs J A Stewart, BA, University of the West of Scotland, MEd, The University of Buckingham, FCCT, CMgr

Deputy Head Academic: Mr M E Key, BA Birmingham, MA Warwick, MSt Harris Manchester College, Oxon

Deputy Head Pastoral: Mrs N Milton, BA Roehampton, NPQH

Deputy Head Safeguarding. Designated Safeguarding Lead: Mr J H Kayne, BSc Nottingham Trent, NPQH

Deputy Head Co-Curricular: Miss G Van Praagh, BA American Academy of Dramatic Arts

Head of Sixth Form: Ms K Spencer Ellis, MA Christ Church Oxon

Head of Middle School: Ms L E Lechmere-Smith, BA Sheffield

Head of Lower School: Mr J T Sloan, BA Royal Holloway, University of London

Heads of Subject Departments:

Art: Mr J W Stevenson
Biology: Ms A Plumb
Chemistry: Mr A Barlow
Classics: Ms R K Jeffries
Computer Science: Mr M S Jalowiecki
Design and Technology: Mr H Ibrahim
Drama: Mrs S Moon
Economics and Business: Ms C Morgan
English: Mrs C L Nightingale
Food & Nutrition: Mr B T Ojewunmi
French: Dr A Gray
Geography: Mr E W Morris
German: Mrs H P R Miller
Politics: Mr L Flynn
History: Mr H W Clough
Learning Support: Mrs M Wright
Mandarin: Mrs L Chen
Mathematics: Mr A Ashiq
Music: Mr L A Pares
Physical Education: Mr M L Broughton
Physics: Mr P T S Aspery
Projects: Ms E E Newman
Religious Studies & Philosophy: Miss R Mackie
Science: Miss J White
Spanish: Ms P Cordon
Wellbeing: Mrs L Parrales

Houses:

Boys' Houses:
Bishop's: Mr O E Ling
Copeland's: Mrs H P R Miller
Doctor's: Mr D A Cawley
Guy's: Mr L Bouzguenda
Johnians: Mr J Miller
Miller's: Ms S A Taylor-Denton
Poole's: Mr H Hughes

Girls' Houses:
Astell: Miss C A Heath
Baylis: Mrs J Wyn-Thomas
Eliot: Ms H R Bettridge
Franklin: Mrs H Cole
Hepworth: Ms F C Rae
Kingsley: Ms G H Green
School: Ms K E Brosnan

Support Staff:

Admissions:
Registrar: Ms D Cleveland-Hurley
Assistant Registrar: Miss R Begum
Admissions Administrator: Mr C Cheung

Director of Communications: Mrs S Gautama (*Alumni, Marketing and Outreach*)

Bursar's Office:
Chief Accountant: Mr N Asghar, BA East London
Assistant Accountant: Ms T Jones
Accounts Clerk: Mrs E Kearney
Assistant Accounts Clerk: Ms S Morl

Clerk to the Governors: Ms A Crawley

Francis Holland School, Regent's Park

Ivor Place, London NW1 6XR

Tel: +44 (0)20 7723 0176
email: admin@fhs-nw1.org.uk
website: www.fhs-nw1.org.uk
X/Twitter: @FHSRegentsPark
Facebook: @FHSRegentsPark
Instagram: @fhsregentspark
LinkedIn: /company/francis-holland-school-regent's-park

Founded 1878.

There are 554 day girls and entry by examination and interview is normally at 11+, with a number joining at 16+ for the Sixth Form. The School was founded in 1878 and is affiliated to the Church of England, but girls of all Christian denominations and other faiths are welcomed. The School is part of the London 11+ Consortium, an association of 14 independent London day schools for girls, operating one entrance exam across the group.

Curriculum and Aims. Girls are prepared for GCSE, A Levels, and for admission to Universities, and Colleges of Art and Music. Full use is made of the museums, theatres and galleries in central London. Extra lessons are available including fencing, music, Speech and Drama, kickboxing, Mandarin Chinese, cookery, street dance, yoga and cheerleading. For the first five years, to GCSE, girls follow a broad curriculum and normally take between 9 and 11 GCSE subjects. Careers advice is given from the third year, and all pupils receive individual guidance through to the Sixth Form. Sixth Formers can study three subjects or four subjects plus an elective. Some of these additional courses lead to a qualification and all of them are designed both to extend and to enrich learning. All Sixth Formers have the opportunity to take an Extended Project Qualification.

Physical Education. Sport takes place in Regent's Park. Netball, Hockey, Tennis and Cricket are our main sports. Girls also have the opportunity to partake in Gymnastics, Athletics, Football and Swimming, which takes place in the onsite swimming pool. Senior girls have a choice of additional activities including spinning, Judo, pilates, strength and conditioning and use of the fitness suite.

Scholarships and Bursaries. Francis Holland is committed to widening access to the local and wider community. Bursary awards up to 100% fees are typically offered at Year 7 and on entry to the Sixth Form and are reviewed annually. The number of bursaries awarded each year is at the discretion of the Governors and may vary.

There are the following competitive awards each year:

- 11+ Academic, Music, and Art scholarships are available to the value of 5% of fees
- Sixth Form: Academic scholarships (internal and external) up to the value of 25% of fees, Music, Art and Sport scholarships up to the value of 25% of fees
- Remission of a third of the fees is available to places offered to daughters of the clergy.

Fees per term (2023–2024). £7,630.

Situation. The School is situated across 4 buildings on Ivor Place and Linhope Street, just outside Regent's Park and three minutes from Baker Street and Marylebone stations. Victoria and Hampstead buses pass the school.

Charitable status. The Francis Holland (Church of England) Schools Trust Limited is a Registered Charity, number 312745. It exists to provide high quality education for girls.

Patron: The Right Revd and Right Hon The Lord Bishop of London

Council of Governors:
Chairman: Patrick Sherrington, LLB, LLM, FCI, Arb
Ms F Angel, BA Hons, PGCE
Dr F Baawuah, MB, ChB, MRCGP, MRCP
Mr R Backhouse, MA
Dr C Barker, MA, BM, BCh, MRCPCH, PhD
Mr M Cuthbert, FRICS, BSc, MBA, DipProjMan
Mr A Fincham, MA
Prof C Gwenlan, MSci, PhD
Dr S Hay, PhD, MA, BSc
Mrs S Nedas
Mrs N du Preez, MA, BSc
Ms E Regina, MSc Arch, ARB, RIBA
Mr I Ramsay, BSc, FCA
Ms N de Renzo, MSc, Bocconi
Dr Mary Short, BA, PGCE, PhD
Dr H Spoudeas, MBBS, DRCOG, FRCPCH, FRCP, MD
Revd A Walker
Ms J Woodham-Smith, MA

Bursar: Mr G Wilmot, BA, ACA

Clerk to the Governors: Ms E Wilkinson, CILEX

Senior Leadership Team:

***Head*: Mrs K Woodcock**, BA Bristol, PGCE

Senior Deputy Head: Ms A Slocombe, MA Magdalene College Cambridge
Academic Deputy Head: Miss J Zugg, BSc Cape Town, South Africa
Pastoral Deputy Head: Miss C Mahieu, BEd Sydney, Australia
Assistant Head (Operations): Ms S Hack, BA Portsmouth, FRGS
Assistant Head (Teaching & Learning): Miss Cherish Bere, PGDip KCL
Assistant Head (Sixth Form): Mr N Gridelli, BA Bologna, Italy
Director of External Relations: Mrs V McKinley, BA Business School Greenwich

Francis Holland School, Sloane Square

39 Graham Terrace, London SW1W 8JF

Tel:	020 7730 2971
email:	office@fhs-sw1.org.uk
website:	www.fhs-sw1.org.uk
X/Twitter:	@FHSSloaneSquare
Facebook:	@FHSSloaneSquare
Instagram:	@fhssloanesquare
LinkedIn:	/company/francis-holland-school-sloane-square

Founded 1881.

There are 739 Day Girls in the School. Entry is at 4+ for the Junior School, which currently has 165 pupils, 11+ for the Senior School, and 16+ for Sixth Form. The Senior School has 574 pupils. The School was founded in 1881 and is affiliated to the Church of England, but girls of all Christian denominations and other faiths are welcomed. The School is part of the London 11+ Consortium, an association of 14 independent London day schools for girls, operating one entrance exam across the group.

Curriculum and Aims. Excellent academic standards are achieved through the provision of a challenging academic curriculum and talented staff who encourage an enthusiasm for learning, intellectual curiosity and creativity as well as encouraging entrepreneurship through our double award-winning Creative Enterprise programme. This allows our girls to thrive in a relaxed and happy environment where they are respected as individuals and able to fulfil their unique potential. Sixth Formers can study three, or occasionally four, subjects over the two years, and all have the opportunity to take an Extended Project Qualification. The Sixth Form has dedicated careers and universities support, with girls prepared for university entry both in the UK and overseas, including US colleges.

Junior School. Francis Holland Junior School (age 4–11) shares the same site as the Senior School at Sloane Square.

Physical Education. Netball, Hockey, Football and Cricket are our main sports. Girls also have the opportunity to partake in Gymnastics, Athletics, Tennis and Swimming. Senior girls have a choice of additional activities including spinning, Judo, pilates, strength and conditioning and use of the fitness suite. There is a Sixth Form gym in the Sixth Form Centre, the Old School House.

Scholarships and Bursaries. Francis Holland is committed to widening access to the local and wider community. Our Foundation Scholarship Bursary Programme supports girls who display outstanding promise to succeed at Francis Holland, but whose parents might not have sufficient financial means. Bursary awards up to 100% fees are typically offered at Year 7 and on entry to the Sixth Form and are reviewed annually. The number of bursaries awarded each year is at the discretion of the Governors and may vary.

There are the following competitive awards each year:

11+ Academic, Music, Drama, Art, and Sport scholarships are available to the value of 5% of fees. One Classical Ballet scholarship is available up to the value of £2,000.

Sixth Form: Academic scholarships (internal and external) up to the value of 25% of fees, Music and Drama scholarships up to the value of 25% of fees.

Remission of a third of the fees is available for places offered to daughters of the clergy.

Fees per term (2023–2024). £7,050–£7,750.

Situation. The School is situated in Belgravia on Graham Terrace, a two-minute walk from Sloane Square station and 10 minutes from Victoria, which has major rail links around London and the South West. Buses to Clapham, Battersea, Wandsworth, Hammersmith, Fulham and Putney pass the school.

Charitable status. The Francis Holland (Church of England) Schools Trust Limited is a Registered Charity, number 312745. It exists to provide high quality education for girls.

Patron: The Right Revd and Right Hon The Lord Bishop of London

Council of Governors:
Chairman: Patrick Sherrington, LLB, LLM, FCI, Arb
Ms F Angel, BA Hons, PGCE
Dr F Baawuah, MB, ChB, MRCGP, MRCP
Mr R Backhouse, MA
Dr C Barker, MA, BM, BCh, MRCPCH, PhD
Mr M Cuthbert, FRICS, BSc, MBA, DipProjMan
Mr A Fincham, MA
Prof C Gwenlan, MSci, PhD
Dr S Hay, PhD, MA, BSc
Mrs S Nedas
Mrs N du Preez, MA, BSc
Ms E Regina, MSc Arch, ARB, RIBA
Mr I Ramsay, BSc, FCA
Ms N de Renzo, MSc, Bocconi
Dr Mary Short, BA, PGCE, PhD
Dr H Spoudeas, MBBS, DRCOG, FRCPCH, FRCP, MD
Revd A Walker
Ms J Woodham-Smith, MA

Bursar: Mr G Wilmot, BA, ACA

Clerk to the Governors: Ms E Wilkinson, CILEX

Senior Leadership Team:

***Head*: Mrs A Haydon**, MSc Oxford, BSc Durham

Senior Deputy Head Academic: Mr R Cawley, MA, BA Lancaster, FRSA

Senior Deputy Head Pastoral: Mrs S Pittaway, BA Reading

Deputy Head of Operations and Co-Curricular: Mrs R Floyd, BA Durham

Head of Junior School: Mrs S Dixon, MA King's, BA Leeds

Head of Sixth Form: Ms C Stansfield, MA Courtauld, BA Oxford

Head of Futures (*Careers and Guidance*): Mrs C Wilkes, MSc LSE, BA Cantab

Director of External Relations: Mrs V McKinley, BA London

Development Director: Mr T Robertson, MA Edinburgh

Director of Information Systems and Digital Strategy: Mr M Britland BSc

Frensham Heights

Rowledge, Farnham, Surrey GU10 4EA

Tel: 01252 792561
email: admissions@frensham.org
website: www.frensham.org
X/Twitter: @FrenshamHeights
Facebook: @frensham
Instagram: @frensham_heights
LinkedIn: /frensham-heights-school

Frensham Heights is a highly distinctive day and boarding school in the beautiful Surrey Hills.

Founded in 1925, we welcome students from the age of 3 to 18. Located close to the beautiful Georgian market town of Farnham and 15 miles from the historic city of Guildford, we are about an hour from London, Heathrow and Gatwick airports.

Our Approach. A progressive approach to education transcends the school years and aims to prepare each child for their future, both along whatever path they may choose and also as part of society as a whole. Students are asked to be active participants in their learning, challenging themselves and taking risks. They're asked to question and explore – to develop as individuals, as part of our school community and as engaged citizens of the wider world.

Our Teaching & Learning. We pride ourselves on looking at the whole child. Body, mind and spirit. Every child has potential. Not just a narrow potential to do well in academic tests or behave in a classroom, but each has their own potential far wider than this. An amazing imagination. A keen eye for colour or ear for rhythm. A passion for the environment, for numbers, for human rights, for literature. A natural grace on stage or one that's still developing. We can miss the mark hugely if we judge children with easy to tick boxes when they undoubtedly have so much more to offer. And so we offer them a very broad curriculum to let each child follow their own path towards fulfilling their unique potential. Until the end of Year 9, all students will explore a diverse timetable made up of mathematical and scientific, creative and performing, linguistic and literary, physical and technological, moral and spiritual, social and human subjects. All held in equal importance. Our GCSEs and A Levels are equally broad and are supported by a growing number of BTEC and alternative qualifications – allowing students to create a tailor-made curriculum supporting their passions, strengths and goals.

Our Learning Relationships. With a more informal setting and smaller classes, the teachers and students really get to know each other. Literally on a first-name basis. This is important because we ask our students to step up and be more responsible and self-motivated than they may need to be elsewhere. We don't micro-manage, we do support, but ultimately it's down to each child to take control of their learning. Teachers learn each child's strengths and weaknesses. They reinforce where needed and push where they can, but most importantly, they are a friendly face. They genuinely want to help, not to intimidate or belittle.

We welcome boarders from Year 7 upwards. As with most things at Frensham, we understand that one size never fits all so we have a few different boarding options for Years 7 and up – Full Boarding, Weekly Boarding, 3 Day Boarding and Occasional Boarding. Alongside our many and varied extracurricular activities, boarders are offered additional activities and trips. Our co-educational boarding houses are relaxed, warm, lively and supportive with boys and girls accommodated in separate areas, but sharing comfortable common rooms where they can study and socialise.

Student numbers. 500 boys and girls aged 3 to 18 years. Average class size: 18.

Admissions. Children entering Nursery and Reception will be invited in for a short informal visit to meet our Teacher in Charge of Early Years. Children entering Years 1 to 6 will be invited to spend a day with us in their current year group to join in with the usual class activities. They will also spend a short time with a teacher working through some core numeracy and literacy activities. Students looking to join in Years 7–9 will join us for our assessment day in January which involves short tests in Maths, Spelling, English Reading Comprehension and Creative Writing (and Science for Year 9) plus an afternoon of team building activities. Candidates will also be invited for informal small-group interviews. Those looking to join us for Sixth Form must have achieved, or be likely to achieve, at least six GCSE passes at grades 9–4, of which a minimum of a 4 is required in both English Language and Mathematics. Candidates will be invited to our assessment/interview day in November.

Curriculum. Our curriculum is intentionally broad to offer each student both a thorough grounding in a diverse timetable of creative, scientific, physical and theoretical subjects, but also to give them each the chance to find their own passions and interests. Subjects are interwoven, giving a depth of understanding and experience that is often lacking in a more traditional curriculum. Most students take 10 GCSEs (or alternatives) – English Language, English Literature, Mathematics and Science (Trilogy or Separate Science) are compulsory; PE, Games, Outdoor Education, PRE and PSHE continue to be an integral part of the curriculum through GCSE and A Level years.

Extracurricular Activities. An extensive and varied selection of activities includes sports of all sorts, outdoor education, art, music, dance, drama, hobbies and clubs. Clubs run at lunch and after school.

Religion. Frensham Heights is non-denominational and there are no religious services.

Dress. No uniform. Dress code is based on respect for others and suitability for purpose.

Welfare and Discipline. Discipline is founded on exceptional staff–student relationships reflecting school values: originality of thought, spirit of togetherness, respect of individuality, courage to try. Every student has a personal tutor. There is a school nurse and a counsellor.

Learning Support. We can support a limited number of children with mild learning difficulties.

Overseas Students. We admit boarders from overseas and provide tuition in English as a Second Language as part of their curriculum. All boarders must have a UK based guardian.

Fees per term (2023–2024). Nursery fees: EYFE session (free from 8.30 am–11.30 am) plus £23.50 (morning session, including lunch), £41.50 (afternoon session, including lunch), £44.50 (EYFE full day), £78 (full day); Reception £2,855; Years 1–2: £3,340; Years 3–4: £4,085; Years 5–6: £5,080; Years 7–8: £7,255 (day), £10,550 (full boarding); Years 9–11: £7,615 (day), £11,940 (full boarding); New Sixth Form Entrants: £8,085 (day), £15,615 (full boarding).

Scholarships and Bursaries. Honorary scholarships are awarded for academic distinction or exceptional promise in Music, Art, Dance, Drama and Sport and scholars access dedicated enrichment activities. A small number of means-tested bursaries are available.

Charitable status. Frensham Heights Educational Trust is a Registered Charity, number 312052. It exists to provide a high quality, progressive education for boys and girls.

Governors:
Chair: Simon Wilcox, FInstLM, MSc, CMgr
Vice Chair: Phil Ward, BEd
Treasurer: TBC
Clerk to the Governors: Susie Birdsall, BA Hons
Richard Fry, MA, MEng Cambs
Kate Love, MA Oxon
Sally Marriott
Will Marriott
Danuta Staunton, MA, PGCE
Jackie Nickson, MRICS
Gregory West, BA
Joris Wonders, BA, MSc, ACC

***Head*: Andrew Fisher**, BA Hons, PGCE

Assistant Head (*Operations & Cocurricular*): Andy Spink, BSc, QTS
Assistant Head (*Pastoral, Progress & Behaviour*): Jo Dalziel, BEd Hons, PGCE
Head of Junior School: Nick Oram-Tooley, BA, QTS

George Heriot's School

Lauriston Place, Edinburgh EH3 9EQ
Tel: 0131 229 7263
email: enquiries@george-heriots.com
website: www.george-heriots.com

Motto: *I distribute chearfullie*

George Heriot's School was founded in 1628 to care for the fatherless children of Edinburgh. Today it is a modern, fully co-educational day school for children aged 4–18 which continues to fund the education of children who have lost a parent under its Foundation.

The School is situated on a world heritage site in the centre of Edinburgh, within easy walking distance of bus and rail terminals – a number of bus routes service the School. Edinburgh Castle forms a magnificent backdrop, and Edinburgh's flourishing financial centre, the University of Edinburgh, the College of Art, the National Library and the National Museum of Scotland are located close by.

The original building, described as a 'bijou of Scottish Renaissance Architecture', forms the centre of this bustling school, with the Chapel, Council Room and Quadrangle of particular historical note. Over the years, a succession of new buildings has provided the full complement of educational facilities. A state-of-the-art sports centre was opened in 2012 and new Refectory and Wraparound Care facility in 2018. The School has excellent sports fields and facilities at Goldenacre.

Our aim is to introduce all pupils to a broad spectrum of academic, cultural and sporting interests and experiences, enabling them to develop into articulate, self-reliant, hard-working and kind adults who play their full part in an ever-changing society.

Heriot's has long enjoyed a reputation for academic excellence, with outstanding examination results; we value scholarship and effort. In the same spirit, every pupil is encouraged to participate in an extensive array of co-curricular activities. We encourage participation and success in an unusually wide range of sports including cricket, basketball, football, cross-country running, hockey, rowing, rugby, athletics and tennis, we also strongly encourage more minority sports.

We have an outstanding record in music, both choral and instrumental, and in drama. Junior and Senior schools boast a huge range of clubs, with particular strength in our Debating Society, Pipe Band, Drama productions, the Duke of Edinburgh's Award and Combined Cadet Force. The School proudly holds Gold level in UNICEF's Rights-Respecting Schools Award. There is a heavy emphasis throughout the School on charitable fundraising and community service including our award-winning S6 Voluntary Service programme, in line with our motto: *I Distribute Chearfullie*.

The Nursery (32 children). The Nursery accommodates children in their pre-school year. It is part of the Early Years Department. Admission to the Nursery is open to all.

The Junior School (585 pupils). The Junior School follows a bespoke curriculum with a focus on academic rigour and solid subject content, particularly with regard to literacy, numeracy and science. Art, drama, modern languages, music, computing and all areas of physical education are taught by specialists. Philosophy is a key strength in the Junior School through the delivery of its unique Learning Enhancement programme.

The Senior School (1,048 pupils). For the first two years, a broad curriculum is followed. An unrivalled choice of subjects is available from S3 to S6 in preparation for Scottish Qualifications Authority examinations. Most pupils remain for our carefully designed Sixth Year and proceed to university or other forms of tertiary education.

Heriot's enjoys a reputation as a caring community. Great importance is given to pastoral care and a sophisticated careers advisory programme is in place. The Support for Learning Department provides invaluable help to many Junior School and Senior School pupils.

Admission: Admission (other than for Nursery) is by assessment. Application for occasional places is welcome at any time, but for the main entry stages the application deadline is 1 December the year preceding entry.

Fees per annum (2023–2024). Junior School: £10,962 (Nursery, P1 & P2), £13,309 (P3 to P7); Senior School: £16,440.

A limited number of bursaries is available from Primary Six and there are Scholarships for entry at Senior One. Children who have lost a parent may qualify for free education and other benefits through the Foundation. Full information is available from the Finance Office on request.

Charitable status. George Heriot's Trust is a Registered Charity, number SC011463. It exists to provide education for children.

***Principal*: Mr G Warren**

Giggleswick School

Giggleswick, Settle, North Yorkshire BD24 0DE
Tel: 01729 893000 Headmaster's Office
01729 893012 Bursar's Office
email: admissions@giggleswick.org.uk
website: www.giggleswick.org.uk
X/Twitter: @giggschool
Facebook: @GiggleswickSchool
Instagram: @giggschool
LinkedIn: /company/giggleswick-school

Giggleswick School is based on the edge of the Yorkshire Dales National Park, offering affordable independent education and academic excellence for girls and boys aged 2 to 18. The school was awarded 'excellent' in an impressive six aspects of provision by the Independent Schools Inspectorate (ISI).

Located on the edge of the beautiful Yorkshire Dales National Park, the school sits within a 200-acre campus of stunning countryside, where you'll find 500 years of heritage, exceptional modern facilities and a happy, welcoming community.

334 boys and girls attend Giggleswick, either as full-time or flexi boarders or day pupils. It is a traditional British boarding school with 65% of pupils boarding (increasing to 80% in Sixth Form), 17% of whom are from military families and 17% from the international community. The approach to education combines excellent academic achievement, ambition and strong self-belief, with a strong focus on personal development. The school's core values are participation, ambition and respect.

In 2021, 83% achieved A*–B grades at A level. BTEC options continue to deliver excellent results for our students and this year 93% of our pupils achieved the D*D or D*D* (A*/A or A*/A* equivalent) grade. At GCSE, 51% achieved 7–9 grades. Our dramatists were among the top performers with 80% achieving the higher grades 7–9. Classified as the hardest subjects by the CEM Centre, Physics and German have been an area of strength with 50% achieving grades 7–9 in Physics and 71% in German.

However, life is about more than great grades at Giggleswick. The extended day and boarding ethos gives all pupils the chance to participate in any of over 70 co-curricular activities that encourage pupils to explore new horizons, challenge themselves and often achieve beyond their expectations. 50% of pupils take part in music lessons at Grade 6 or above with 120 pupils in drama productions. Average class sizes are 13.5 in Key Stage 3 and 4 and 6.5 in Sixth Form.

All boarders live in one of seven boarding houses with a dedicated co-ed house for young boarders in Years 6 to 8. The first phase of a multimillion pound investment in boarding facilities was completed in September 2018, which is shaping a new family-friendly model of boarding to create a modern home away from home with a real focus on community and wellbeing.

There are excellent sports coaches at all levels, superb facilities and regular programmed training sessions. Each year a number of pupils gain representative honours in a range of sports and a place on the Elite Sports Programme. This includes specialist coaching, mentoring, professional sports visits and strength and conditioning training.

Facilities include a floodlit AstroTurf, a state-of-the-art fitness centre, two indoor sports halls and an indoor swimming pool. The Outdoor Pursuits Department is staffed by a Mountaineering and Climbing instructor and eleven Mountain, Hill and Moorland Leaders and climbing Instructors. Staff also hold Paddlesports, Mountain Biking and Caving qualifications. The school has its own indoor climbing wall, crag, 10km mountain bike trail and a shooting range on campus. There are a number of local, nationally recognised, crags and caves and the hills of the Yorkshire Dales.

Giggleswick's Art Department provides a lively and stimulating environment where pupils can explore and develop their creative skills. The department includes a resident ceramic artist, who works and teaches in the Department. There is a well-equipped ceramics studio, a vacuum silkscreen printing bed, plus facilities to make photo silkscreens, and a large etching press.

Drama takes place in the state-of-the-art Richard Whiteley Theatre, a 250-seat professional venue. There are opportunities to develop skills in stage management, sound and lighting as well as acting in productions such as *Much Ado About Nothing*.

In the music department there is a Head of Instrumental Music as well as a Head of Department and four full-time musicians. They are assisted by a team of 13 visiting teachers, and ensembles include the School Orchestra, Concert Band, Chapel Choir, Concert Choir, a Brass Ensemble and a String Quartet as well as a number of rock bands. Numerous performance opportunities are offered including trips abroad.

Giggleswick is not a selective school. The school has an equal opportunities policy and is happy to consider applications from any child so long as other entrance criteria are met. Various scholarships and bursaries are also available.

The school is an hour's drive from Leeds, Manchester and The Lakes. It can be reached from the M6 or M1 motorways or by rail via Settle or Giggleswick stations. Overseas students fly to Leeds/Bradford or Manchester Airports.

Fees per term (2023–2024). Reception–Year 2: Day £2,260; Years 3 & 4 Day £5,200; Years 4–6 Boarders £8,600, Day £5,200; Years 7 & 8: Boarders £9,835, Day £6,395; Years 9–11: Boarders £12,855, Day £7,940; L6–U6: Boarders £13,305, Day £8,600. 5-night and 3-night flexi boarding also available.

Charitable status. Giggleswick School is a Registered Charity, number 1109826.

The Governing Body:
Chair: A V Thursby, BBA
Vice-Chair: R R Waldie, BA

Bursar & Clerk to the Governors: Khashi Sharifi

***Headmaster*: S Hart**, BEng

Deputy Head: C A San José, MA

Senior Master: N A Gemmell, BA

Deputy Head (*Academic*): Miss A L Wood, MA

PA to the Headmaster: Mrs C A Jowett

The Glasgow Academy

Colebrooke Street, Glasgow G12 8HE
Tel: 0141 342 5494
email: admissions@tga.org.uk
website: www.theglasgowacademy.org.uk
X/Twitter: @glasgowacademy
Facebook: @glasgowacademy
Instagram: @glasgowacademy
LinkedIn: /school/the-glasgow-academy

Motto: *Serva Fidem*

Founded in May 1845, The Glasgow Academy is the oldest continuously independent school in the west of Scotland. It has been co-educational since 1991, when it merged with Westbourne School for Girls. Mergers with Atholl Preparatory School in Milngavie (1999) and Dairsie House School in Newlands (2005) have given parents a choice of three locations for their children in the Nursery to Prep 4 age group, contributing to the school's enduring success as a school covering the whole of west central Scotland. Children from The Glasgow Academy Milngavie and Newlands transition to our west end campus at Kelvinbridge in Prep 5. The school's affairs are managed by The Glasgow Academicals' War Memorial Trust, formed to commemorate the 327 former pupils killed in the war of 1914–18.

Organisation. The Preparatory School roll is 812 pupils (392 boys, 420 girls) between the ages of 3 and 11 and educates pupils from the earliest stages for the work of the Senior School. The Senior School roll is 840 pupils (435 boys, 405 girls). They are prepared for the National Qualifications at National 5 level at the end of S4, Higher at the end of S5 and Advanced Higher or Higher at the end of S6. The Sixth Form provides courses in most subjects leading to presentation at Advanced Higher. Pupils are prepared for entrance to Oxford and Cambridge. The Academy has a history of successes at Oxford, Cambridge and the Scottish Universities. It aims to offer a unique combination of academic, musical, dramatic, sporting, co-curricular, social and outdoor education opportunities, backed up by high levels of pastoral care. There are numerous opportunities for children to develop leadership skills and take on responsibilities.

Buildings. The magnificent main building (1878) contains the Senior School library as its centrepiece and classrooms. Recent purpose-built facilities include a Music School (1994), Art and Design School (1998), Preparatory School (2008) and multiple award-winning science centre, auditorium and hospitality/social area (2015). Two drama studios, a dance studio, rowing studio, medical centre and fitness area were also created in 2015. There are extensive sports facilities, including new astros, rugby/cricket pitches and a water-based hockey pitch.

Health and wellbeing. The school places great importance on supporting pupils' health and wellbeing. Pupils are at the heart of this with an influential School Council meeting each week, with a HWB sub-committee working in partnership with staff to lead improvement in safeguarding, a regularly reviewed and evolving PSE curriculum, and provision of assemblies and guest speakers on a range of topics relevant to young people's lives. S6 pupils lead a school buddy system, including the delivery of digital awareness and online safety workshops to younger pupils and parents. The school website features information for parents on how to support their child's wellbeing.

Music and Drama. Music tuition is offered in a wide range of instruments by 21 tutors. There are Senior, Junior and Theatre Choirs, a Concert Band, Pipe Band, Brass Group, Percussion Ensemble, Orchestra and various Prep School groups. Concerts and large-scale drama productions take place regularly and are supplemented by plays mounted by smaller groups. There are music tours to places such as New York, Rome and Barcelona.

Societies and activities. These range from Basketball, Chess, Debating and Public Speaking to Engineering, Fairtrade and Research clubs. Very large numbers of pupils undertake each section of the Duke of Edinburgh's Award and there is a thriving Young Enterprise group. Residential education is an integral part of the curriculum at various stages of both the Prep and Senior schools. These experiences augment the PSE programme by promoting team-building and personal and social development through outdoor challenges.

Games. Teams represent the school in Hockey, Rugby, Cricket, Swimming, Golf, Tennis, Athletics, Netball, Basketball, Rowing, Football, Shooting and Squash. Options include Badminton, Cross-Country running, Dance and Outdoor education.

Combined Cadet Force. The Academy has a strong voluntary contingent with Royal Navy, Army and RAF sections.

Childcare outside school hours. The Academy provides care before and after school for its younger pupils. There is also provision for children between the ages of 3 and 12 through the holidays.

Entrance. Pupils may be registered at any age. The main entry points are (a) in the Preparatory School: age 3, 4 and 10; (b) in the Senior School: age 11 or 12 or for Sixth Form. Bursaries are available for P7–S6.

Fees per term (2023–2024). Preparatory School: P1 £3,335–£3,630, P2 £3,435–£3,738, P3–P4 £3,798–£4,0799, P5 £4,079 P6–P7 £4,778. Senior School: S1–S2 £4,561, S3–S5 £4,950, S6 £4,950 (Autumn & Spring Terms), £4,037 (Summer Term).

Charitable status. The Glasgow Academy is a Registered Charity, number SC015638. It exists to provide education for girls and boys.

Secretary: Thomas W Gemmill, LLB, NP

***Rector*: M K Pearce**, BA Dunelm

Deputy Rector and Head of Senior School: M Gibson, BSc Edinburgh, PhD Edinburgh

Deputy Heads:
Academic: A N MacRae, BSc Strathclyde
Pastoral: Mrs K R Graham, BSc Newcastle-upon-Tyne, MEd Aberdeen
Senior Phase: G Spreng, MA Glasgow
Operations: I Mackie, BSc Glasgow

Heads of Department:
Art & Design: Ms N Umer, MA Kingston
Biology: J Laycock, BSc Edinburgh
Chemistry: C A Main, MSci, PhD Glasgow
Classics: S A A McKellar, MA Glasgow
Computing Science: Mrs J E McDonald, MA Glasgow
Drama: G E Waltham, MA Glasgow
Economics & Business Studies: A Taylor, BA Glasgow
English: Mrs A F Watters, MA St Andrews
Food Technology: Ms C Dolan, BSc Manchester Metropolitan
Geography: Mrs V Magowan, MA Glasgow
History & Modern Studies: S M Wood, MA St Andrews
Mathematics: K.M Russell, BSc Heriot-Watt, PG Advanced Dip Mathematics Hull
Modern Languages: Mrs E B Holland, MA Glasgow
Music: T E Mills, BMus Bangor
Physics: Mrs H McMillan, BSc Strathclyde

Physical Education/Sport:
Director of Sport: Mrs R Toft, BEd Heriot-Watt
Head of PE: M A Manson, BA Strathclyde
Head of Rugby: J Gordon, BSc Edinburgh Napier

Outdoor Education: Ms R Goolden, Mountain Instructor Certificate, Outdoor Education Dip. & National Governing Body Awards, Newbury College

Learning Support: Mrs A A Harvie, BA Strathclyde, PGDip Ind Admin Glasgow Caledonian

Careers: A J McCaskey, MA Glasgow

Counsellor: Mrs A F Young, MA Glasgow, MRes Strathclyde, PGDip Psychodynamic Counselling West of Scotland, BACP

Preparatory School:
Head: A Mathewson, BEd Strathclyde
Head of Lower Prep: Miss L Smith, MA Glasgow
Head of Upper Prep: S Fairlie-Clarke, BSc Glasgow, PGDip Napier

The Glasgow Academy Milngavie:
Head: Miss J McMorran, DCE, PGDip, DipTEFL

The Glasgow Academy Newlands:
Head: Mrs A MacLeod, BA Strathclyde, PGDE

After-school Care:
After-school Care Manager: Mrs C Bremridge, BA Childhood Practice Glasgow

Administration/Finance:
Chief Operating Officer: G Halliday, FCBI

Admissions/Development:
Director of External Relations: S A Dignall, BA Strathclyde

Rector's PA: Mrs L Fletcher
Administration Manager and PA to COO: Mrs C McLaren
Combined Cadet Force:
Contingent Commander: Major A Mathewson
SSI: Major C J Duff

Chaplains:
Revd D J M Carmichael, MA, BD
Revd A Frater, BA, BD
Rev. N Galbraith
Revd G Kirkwood, BSc, BD, PGCE
Revd S Matthews, BD, MA

The High School of Glasgow

637 Crow Road, Glasgow G13 1PL

Tel: 0141 954 9628
email: admin@hsog.co.uk
website: www.highschoolofglasgow.co.uk
X/Twitter: @HSofG
Facebook: @TheHighSchoolofGlasgow
Instagram: @thehighschoolofglasgow
LinkedIn: /school/the-high-school-of-glasgow

Motto: *Sursum semper*

The High School of Glasgow is a vibrant, caring and high-achieving co-educational day school, which has been part of Glasgow's story since the 12th century and is the oldest continuous school in Scotland. Its present incarnation came into being in 1976 following a merger involving the Former Pupil Club of the High School, then a selective state grammar school, and Drewsteignton School in Bearsden.

Buildings. The Senior School occupies modern purpose-built buildings at Anniesland on the western outskirts of the city immediately adjacent to twenty-three acres of playing fields. The Junior School is in the extended and modernised former Drewsteignton School buildings in Bearsden about three miles away. New facilities opened during the last few years include a purpose-built Science extension, a water-based artificial pitch and 3G multi-sports area, a Junior School extension, a Drama Studio, a Refectory, a Fitness Centre, a Grandstand and an Information and Communications Technology building, and in 2017 a Health and Wellbeing Centre.

Organisation. The School is a day school with 968 boys and girls. The Junior School, which includes a pre-school Kindergarten, has 280 pupils (aged 3–10). Primary 7 pupils are included in the Senior School which has 685 pupils (aged 11–18). A general curriculum is followed until the Third Year of the Senior School when, with the Scottish Qualifications Authority examinations in view, a measure of choice is introduced. In Fifth Year Higher examinations are taken and in Sixth Year courses for Advanced Highers are offered. While the majority of pupils are aiming for the Scottish universities, places are regularly gained at Oxford, Cambridge and other English universities.

Throughout the School, time is allocated to Art, Music, Personal, Social and Health Education, Physical Education and Religion and Philosophy. All pupils will also take courses in Computing Studies, Drama and Health and Food Technology at various stages in their school careers.

Games. The main sports are hockey, rugby, athletics, cricket, tennis and swimming. Pupils participate in a wide variety of other sports, including badminton, basketball, netball, football, volleyball, golf, cross-country running and skiing.

Activities. Pupils are encouraged to participate in extracurricular activities. Clubs and societies include debating, Scripture Union groups, computer, table tennis, chess, art, bridge, chemistry, electronics, drama and film clubs. Pupils take part in the Duke of Edinburgh's Award Scheme and the Young Enterprise Scheme, and parties regularly go on tour. There are choirs, orchestras, jazz and concert bands and a pipe band and tuition in Instrumental Music is arranged as requested. Each year there are several concerts and dramatic productions. The Chamber Choir was BBC Songs of Praise Senior School Choir of the Year 2013.

Admission. Entrance tests and interviews are held in January. The principal points of entry are at Kindergarten (age 3–4), Junior 1 (age 5), Transitus (age 11) and First Year (age 12) but pupils are taken in at other stages as vacancies occur.

Fees per term (2023–2024). Junior School: £4,159–£4,856; Senior School: £5,157–£5,653.

Bursaries. The School operates a Bursary Fund to give assistance with fees in the Senior School in cases of need.

Former Pupils' Club. The Glasgow High School Club Limited is the former pupils' association of the old and new High Schools. Former pupils all over the world maintain an interest in the life and work of the School. *Secretary*: Murdoch C Beaton, LLB.

Charitable status. The High School of Glasgow Limited is a Registered Charity, number SC014768. It is a recognised educational charity.

Governing Body:
Honorary President: Mr Raymond Williamson
Chair: Mrs M A Stewart, LLB Hons, Dip LP, DEM
Vice Chair: J G Williamson
DR N Crick, BA Hons, MA, DPhil
P B Gray
Dr M N Gupta, BSc Hons, MBChB, MD, FRCP
Mr Michael Hutcheson, MA Hons, CA
Mr S C Miller, WS, LLB Hons, Dip L
Mrs J K Panesar, BSc
Mr S Pengelley, BA, PGCE
Mrs Julie Rose, BEd
Dr C M Stephen, MBChB, DGM
Mrs Karen Trickett, MA Hons
Mr N Watson
Mr S Wilson, BComm Hons
Mr Guy Worthington, MSc, BA Hons, PGCE

Adviser to the Board: Professor Sir V A Muscatelli, MA Hons, PhD, FRSE, FRSA

***Rector*: J O'Neill**, MA Hons, PGCE Dist

Head of Senior School: K J A Robertson, BSc Hons

Deputy Heads:
Mrs S Sangster, BEd Hons
P Graham, BSc Hons
I S Leighton, BSc Hons

Staff:
* *Head of Department*
† *House Staff*

Art:
*Mrs C J Bell, BA Hons
Miss N J Henderson, BDes
Mrs J Stewart, BA Hons

Classics:
*Mr J Bullen, BA Hons
Mrs C Bell, MA Hons
Mrs J Deeks-Nisbet, BA Hons

Computer Studies:
*Mrs S E Sterkenburg, BSc Hons, PgC MLE
Mr K Kyle, Masters in Data Analytics, BA, PGDE
I R Purdie, BSc Hons

Economics and Business Studies:
*Mr T J Jensen, MEd, BComm
Mr P Graham, BSc Hons
C Hutchison, BA Hons

English:
*P A Toner, MA Hons
Mrs R A Baynham, MA Hons
†P D C Ford, MA Hons
Mrs S de Groot, MA Hons
Ms K Head, PGDE
Mrs N Lawther, MA Hons, MPhil
T Lyons, MA Hons
Ms A Marshall-Black, BA Hons (*Drama*), BTEC
Miss K Melville, BA Hons
Mrs M Noonan, BA Hons (*Drama*)
Mrs A Viswanathan, MA Hons (*Drama*)

Geography and Modern Studies:
*Miss N L Cowan, MA Hons
Mr I S Leighton, BSc Hons
Mrs K Rinaldi, MA Hons
Dr H Ross, MA Hons
Mr C Totten, BSc Hons

Health and Food Technology:
*Miss K D Moore, BA Hons
†Mrs C Elsby, BA Hons
Mrs C N Mitchell,

History:
*Mr C MacKay, BA Hons
Ms G A C Clare, MA Hons
Miss E McGrath, PGDE, MLitt, MA Hons
Dr H Ross, MA Hons
†Miss N Sutherland, MA Hons

Learning Support:
*Mrs J Dougall, MA Hons
Mrs S de Groot, MA Hons
Mrs D McCluskey, BSc Hons
Mrs S Mitchell, BEd Hons
†Mrs R Owen, BEd Hons

Mathematics:
*Mrs C V M Anderson, BSc Hons
Mrs J B Armstrong, BSc Hons
Mrs E Clark, BSc Hons
D K Hamilton, BSc Hons, PhD
†T A Lockyer, LLB
J G MacCorquodale, BSc Hons
D R MacGregor, BSc Hons
Mrs H S Mills, MEng
Mrs G Wimpenny

Modern Languages:
*Mr N F Campbell, MA Hons, LLB
Mrs K J Bhatia, BA Hons
†Miss M B Cranie, BA Hons
Mrs A M T Drapeau-Magee, L-ès-L, M-ès-L
Mrs K Evans, MA Hons (**Careers*)
Ms M-A Kennedy, PC Sec Ed
Mrs K McCartney, MA Hons
Mrs V MacCorquodale, MA Hons
Ms Y Song, PGDE

Music:
*Mrs S C Stuart, MA Hons/Mus Oxon, MSt Oxon, PG Adv Dip RCM
Mr L D Birch, BA Hons, LRAM, DRSAMD
Mr B Docherty, DRSAM MMus, BMus

Mr B Parker, BMus
Mrs J Tierney, BMus
Mr F Walker, BA Hons, ARCO

Religion & Philosophy:
*Ms G A C Clare, MA Hons
Mrs Stacey Greenlay, MEd

Science:
N M E Dougall, BSc Hons, MSc, (**Biology*)
Dr N J Penman, BSc Hons, PhD (**Chemistry*)
Dr D R Went, MSc, PhD (**Physics*)
Mr J Campion, BSc Hons
Dr J Clark, PGDE, Doctor of Philosophy for Research, Master of Chemistry
Miss J Horn, PGCE
Dr M McKie, BSc Hons, PhD
Mrs A E McNeil, BSc Hons, MSc
Dr L Parsons, PhD
†Mrs M R Peek, MSc

*Dr N J Penman, BSc Hons, PhD
Mr K J A Robertson, BSc Hons
Mr I J Smith, BSc Hons

Sport and Physical Education:
*Mr P J Smith, BEd Hons
Mrs R Bruce, BSc Hons
Mrs A Cox, BEd Hons (**Girls' PE*)
Mrs S Dougan, BEd Hons
K F FitzGerald, BSc Hons
F J Gillies, BSc Hons
Ms J Hood, BEd Hons
G Hunter, BSc Hons
Mr M Lang
†S Leggat, BEd Hons
J McCarthy, BEd Hons
Mrs D McCluskey, BSc Hons
Miss S McGilverary
Mrs S Mitchell, BEd Hons
Mrs R Owen, BEd Hons
Mrs S Sangster, BEd Hons

Junior School Staff:
Head Teacher: Miss H Fuller, BEd Hons
Mrs G Morrans, BEd Hons (*Deputy Head*)
Mrs M Pollock, BA Hons, PG Dip Mus, MMus (*Deputy Head*)
Miss C Bertram, BA Hons
Miss C E Carnall, BMus, MA Hons (*Music*)
Mrs L Cowan, BEd Hons
Mr B Docherty, DRSAM
Mrs A M T Drapeau-Magee, L-ès-L, M-ès-L (*French*)
Miss A Downie
Mrs M Duncan, SVQ3 Social Services
Mrs H M Eustace, BEd Hons
Mrs S A Foster, MA Hons
Miss K Hallam, BEd Hons
Mrs L A Lambie, BEd Hons
Mrs N Livingston, BEd Hons
Mrs K McCartney, MA Hons
Mrs E J McConechy, BEd Hons
Mrs J MacLaren, BEd Hons, MA Hons Cert (*Principal Teacher*)
Miss R McLean, MA
Mrs C Mitchell, BLE Hons
Mrs M I Moreland, DCE, AEE
Ms C Nicol, MEd, PGDE
Ms K Nolan, PGDE, BA
Miss I Rashid, BA Hons
Mrs G Reid, MA Hons (*Principal Teacher*)
Mrs E Robertson-Sword, PGDE, BA Hons
Mrs P Rooney, MA Hons, Dip SfL (*Principal Teacher*)
Miss R Saunders, BEd Hons
Mrs S Spinks, MA Hons
Mrs J Steel, BSc Hons
Mrs S Spinks, MA Hons
Miss S Tonge, MSc, PGCE, BA Hons

Bursar: Mrs J M Simpson, BAcc, CA
Rector's PA: Miss P McConnell

Glenalmond College

Glenalmond, Perth, Perthshire PH1 3RY

Tel: 01738 842000 (Reception)
01738 842144 (Admissions Office)
email: registrar@glenalmondcollege.co.uk
website: www.glenalmondcollege.co.uk
X/Twitter: @GlenalmondColl
Facebook: @GlenalmondColl
Instagram: @GlenalmondColl
LinkedIn: /school/glenalmondcollege

Motto: *Distinctly Glenalmond*

Religion. The College has an Episcopalian foundation and has a splendid Chapel. However, pupils from a wide range of ethnic, religious and cultural backgrounds are welcomed.

Admission. Glenalmond offers both day and boarding. There is Second Form entry for pupils in Primary 7 and Glenalmond College is becoming increasingly popular as a Sixth Form option and admission is welcome at any year.

Curriculum. In the Second and Third Forms (Years 8 and 9, S1 and S2) all pupils take a wide range of subjects including English, Mathematics, History, Geography, French, Spanish or German, Latin or Ancient Civilisation, Biology, Chemistry, Physics, Technology, Music, PSHCE, Drama, Art and ICT. In the Fourth and Fifth Forms pupils may choose three options from a wide range of subjects (including Latin and Greek), along with the core subjects of Mathematics, English Language and Literature, French, and the three Sciences. Each pupil is guided by an academic tutor who meets regularly with their tutor group.

The Sixth Form curriculum is designed to allow pupils as wide a choice as possible with 21 A Level subjects being offered and 4 Higher subjects. There are weekly lectures from outside speakers on social, economic, and cultural subjects that foster academic excellence across the age ranges and the William Bright Society promotes cross-year group discussions on relevant academic and moral issues.

Careers. Over 98% of pupils continue to university and around half of pupils go to Russell Group universities, with a good number gaining places at Oxbridge each year.

Art, Drama and Music. Music plays a central part in the life of the school: there is an Orchestra as well as smaller String, Woodwind, and Brass Groups, the pipe band and choirs. The Drama and Art departments flourish, in conjunction with the well-established Design and Technology Centre.

Sport and Recreation. There is a wide variety of sporting activities to choose from including Rugby, Hockey, Lacrosse, Cross-Country, Cricket, Athletics, Basketball, Shooting, Sailing, Tennis and Golf. There is a large indoor heated Swimming Pool and Squash Courts, Tennis Courts, a nine-hole (James Braid designed) Golf Course, and a world-class, water-based astroturf pitch for Hockey. The school has recently built a new indoor golf hub, complete with simulation screens. The ski slopes of Glenshee are just over an hour away.

Combined Cadet Force. There is a contingent of the Combined Cadet Force with strong links with the Armed Forces.

Fees per term (2023–2024). Boarding fees range from £9,650 to £14,935 with full details available at: www.glenalmondcollege.co.uk/admissions/fees-scholarships-bursaries. Our school fees are as inclusive as possible and cover all of the teaching, accommodation and living costs.

Scholarships. Pupils with exceptional potential, who intend to join Glenalmond in our Second or Third Form, can apply for Scholarships in their area of excellence. As well as the kudos of being a Glenalmond Scholar, successful applicants also benefit from a fee remission of up to 10%. The Scholarships come in two forms: named Academic Scholarships; and College Scholarships in Art, Drama, Music, Piping or Sport. Sixth Form Scholarships are also available.

Remissions. A sibling discount policy recognises the burden of fees for more than one child at a time and is applied with a 5% remission for a second child, 20% remission for a third child, and 50% remission for a fourth (or more) child. Financial assistance is provided for serving members of the Armed Forces and members of the Clergy, both attracting an automatic 10% remission on fees.

Council:
President of Council: The Primus of the Episcopal Church in Scotland, The Most Reverend Mark Strange, Bishop of Moray, Ross and Caithness
Chairman of Council: I Grey, OBE

***Warden*: M Mortimer**, MBA, BA

Deputy Warden: Mrs J Davey, MA Edinburgh, PGCE
Sub-Warden, Academic: Mr Craig Henderson, BSc, PhD St. Andrews, PGCE
Sub-Warden, Pastoral: Mrs S Sinclair, BSc Edinburgh, PGCE

Bursar & Clerk to the Council: R Garnish
Director of Admissions: Mrs R Maga
Chaplain: Reverend S A Graham, SSC, BA MA Belfast, PGDip, PGCE

Godolphin and Latymer School

Iffley Road, Hammersmith, London W6 0PG

Tel: 020 8741 1936; 020 8735 9595 (Bursar)
email: office@godolphinandlatymer.com
website: www.godolphinandlatymer.com
X/Twitter: @GandLSchool
Facebook: @GandLSchool
Instagram: @GandLSchool

Motto: *Francha Leale Toge*

Foundation. Godolphin and Latymer became a girls' day school in 1905. It was aided by the London County Council from 1920 onwards and by the Inner London Education Authority when it received Voluntary Aided status after the 1944 Education Act. Rather than become part of a split-site Comprehensive school it reverted to Independent status in 1977.

Godolphin and Latymer is an independent day school for approx. 800 girls, aged 11 to 18. The school stands in a six-acre site in Hammersmith, near Hammersmith Broadway and excellent public transport. Historic buildings – including a converted church – sit side-by-side with modern facilities interconnected by tranquil gardens and courtyards. Facilities include a pottery room, computing classes, science and technology laboratories, art studios, a dark room, an ecology garden, all-weather surface for hockey and tennis and netball courts The Rudland Music School opened in the Autumn Term 2008 and the renovated church, The Bishop Centre for the performing arts, was completed in early Spring 2009. These state-of-the-art developments provide a range of teaching and performance spaces, recording studios and a music technology suite. The Bishop Centre provides an auditorium to seat over 800. In September 2015 the Sports Complex, the Hampton Centre, was opened and a new Sixth Form Centre, Library and extended dining facilities will open in Autumn 2023.

At Godolphin and Latymer the academic and pastoral aspects of school life operate in tandem and we strive for a love of learning and academic excellence whilst emphasising the development of the individual, within a happy, supportive community.

There is an emphasis on choice and opportunities with the option of both the A Level and IB pathways in the Sixth Form and an extensive extra-curricular and G&L Futures programme. The school aims to develop the girls' self-respect, self-confidence and resilience, together with consideration and care for others so that they feel a sense of responsibility and are able to take on leadership roles within the school and the wider community.

Pastoral care. The school has a close relationship with parents, and every member of the staff takes an interest in the girls' academic and social welfare. Each girl has a co-form teacher and a deputy form teacher and there is a Head of Lower School, Head of Middle School and a Head of Sixth Form, each with at least two deputies.

Curriculum. We offer a broad, balanced curriculum including appropriate education concerning personal, health, ethical economics and social issues. During the first three years, girls study: English; Mathematics; French, Spanish or German; Mandarin; Latin; History; Geography; Religious Studies; Physics; Chemistry; Biology; Computing; Food Preparation and Nutrition; Design Technology; Art; Music; Drama; and Physical Education. In Year 8, students can choose to continue with Mandarin and their European language or study two European languages. In Year 9, students may study Latin or Classical Civilisation; they also undertake three 8-week programmes exploring Computing, PSHE and our bespoke Futures Programme. In Year 10, Italian and Classical Greek become available and Computer Science is available for GCSE and A Level. Girls take ten subjects to GCSE.

In the Sixth Form, there is a choice of curriculum between the A Level and the International Baccalaureate Diploma. All subjects (except PE, Food Preparation and

Nutrition and Design Technology) offered to GCSE can be continued into the Sixth Form with the addition of Ancient History, Economics, Politics and History of Art. Sixth Formers also undertake the Extended Project Qualification (AL) or Extended Essay and Theory of Knowledge (IB) and attend lectures given by outside speakers.

The Sixth Form. The new Sixth Form Centre opened in Autumn 2023. The 210 girls in the Sixth Form play a leading role in the school, taking responsibility for many extracurricular activities, producing form plays and organising clubs. They undertake voluntary work and lead our Social Impact Committee.

Higher Education and careers advice. A strong careers team offers advice to girls and parents with specialists for Oxbridge, Vet/Med and Overseas destinations. Almost all girls proceed to their first-choice Higher Education degree course (including around 25% to Global Top 10 universities).

The Creative Arts. Music and Drama flourish throughout the school. The Rudland Music School has outstanding facilities for music: 20 soundproofed rooms for individual or group work, a recording studio, ICT suite and two classrooms which open out into a very large rehearsal space for choirs and orchestras. There are numerous choirs, two orchestras and several small ensembles. Individual music lessons are offered in many different instruments. Each year there is a Year 7 play, Year 10 and Sixth Form plays as well as the school productions. The Bishop Centre offers a superb performing arts space for music, drama and dance.

Physical Education Teams regularly achieve success at regional and national level in netball, hockey, rowing, athletics, cross-country and cricket and students also enjoy badminton, basketball, dance, fencing, football, gymnastics, Karate, kickboxing, pilates, rock-climbing, rounders, skiing, swimming, tennis, trampolining, volleyball, yoga, as well as Boom cycle and squash in the Sixth Form. A state-of-the-art Sport and Fitness Centre provides a Sports Hall, climbing wall, dance studio and fitness suite. Tennis/netball courts and an astroturf hockey pitch are also on site.

Extracurricular activities. The many opportunities for extracurricular activities include Dissection Club, Wild Aspirations, Computing, Chess, Model United Nations, Debating, Creative Writing, Classics Club and the Duke of Edinburgh's Award scheme, as well as a wide range of sporting activities such as karate, fencing, rowing and trampolining.

Activities outside the School. Students enjoy language exchanges to Germany and a musical exchange to Hamburg. There are study visits to Spain, Italy, Germany, France, Greece, Norway and a ski trip to the US. We take advantage of our London location by arranging visits to conferences, theatres, exhibitions and galleries. Field courses are an integral part of study in Biology and Geography.

Admission. Girls are normally admitted into Year 7 (First Year Entrance) or into our Sixth Form. We are a member of the London 11+ Consortium and 11+ examinations take place in December and interviews in January. 16+ tests and interview take place end October/November. There are occasional vacancies in other years. Entry is on a competitive basis.

Fees per term (from January 2024). £9,218. Fees are liable to change each January. Private tuition in music and speech and drama is extra. Most girls have school lunch.

Scholarships. Music scholarships are available on entry to Year 7 and in the Sixth Form and include free tuition in one instrument.

An Art scholarship is available in the Sixth Form.

All scholarships are worth up to 30% of fees and may be topped up by means-tested bursaries in cases of need. For all awards, candidates must satisfy the academic requirements of the school.

Bursaries. A number of school bursaries are available annually.

Uniform. Uniform is worn by girls up to and including Year 11.

Charitable status. The Godolphin and Latymer School is a Registered Charity, number 312699. It exists to provide education to girls aged 11 to 18.

Governors:
Chair: Mr S Davies, BA Oxon
Ms S Davies, BA Wimbledon College of Art, MA London
Mr M Esiri, LLB London, MBA Greenwich
Mrs Mary Hill, BSc Bristol PsychD, AFBPsS, MBACP, HCPC
Mrs S Kinross, BA Exeter
Mr K Knibbs, MA Oxon
Dr L Magrill, BSc Edinburgh, MCom Birmingham, PhD Bradford
Mr N McLaughlan, BA Durham
Mrs J McNeill, QC, MA Oxon, GDL City
Ms T Meller, BA Glasgow School of Art, Dip Arch Oxford Brookes, RIBA
Mrs E Watson, BA Exeter

Clerk to the Governors: Mrs D Lynch, BSc Kingston, FCCA

Staff:

***Head Mistress*: Dr F Ramsey**, MA, DPhil Oxon
Senior Deputy Head (Academic): Dr S Harnett, MA, DPhil Oxon
Deputy Head (Pastoral), Deputy Designated Safeguarding Lead: Dr J Carter, BA Oxon, MA Chicago, MSt, DPhil Oxon

Assistant Heads:
Learning and Teaching and New Technologies: Dr C Badger, MSci, PhD Cantab, FCCT, MA UCL
Co-Curricular and Educational Development: Mr J Carroll, BSc Durham
Staff and student wellbeing and development, including Designated Safeguarding Lead: Mrs J Smart, BSc Birmingham

Heads of Departments:
Art and Design: Miss L Cooper, BA Staffordshire, MA Wimbledon School of Art
Classics: Mrs L Duffett, BA Oxon, MA London
Computing: Mrs G Oliver, MA Cantab
Design and Technology: Ms M Martins, BA Leeds
Drama: Ms S Adams, BEd Melbourne
Economics: Mrs M Koutsiouki, BA Athens, MSc Warwick
English: Mr C Griffin, BA Exeter

Geography: Mr M Golland, BA London, MEd Cantab, FCCT
History and Politics: Mrs A Armstrong, BA York
History of Art: Dr G Williams, BA Leeds, MA UCL, PhD York
Individual Learning Needs: Ms A Clark, BA Oxon, BSc Open University
International Baccalaureate Coordinator: Ms A Dubois, BA, MA Le Littoral
Mathematics: Mr J Ramsden, BSc Durham
Modern Foreign Languages: Mrs C Corcoran, MA Orléans, MA Southampton
French: Mrs C Corcoran, MA Orléans, MA Southampton
German: Miss A Page, BA Oxon
Italian: Miss L Padalino, BA Bologna
Mandarin: Mrs S Whittaker, BA Durham
Spanish: Mr D Rees-Williams, BSc Bath
Music: Mr C Langworthy, BMus Manchester
Philosophy and Religion: Mrs M Davis, BA, MA Surrey
Physical Education: Miss E Elfick, BEd Exeter
Science: Ms G Andrade, BSc London, MA East London
Biology: Mr T Juvanendran, BSc UCL
Chemistry: Mrs A Swann, MChem Oxon
Physics: Mr J McGrath, BSc Wales, MSc Cranfield

Bursar: Mrs D Lynch, BSc Kingston, FCCA
Registrar: Mrs F Lundberg, CIPD
Higher Education and Careers: Mrs A Armstrong, BA York
PA to the Head Mistress: Miss V Stearns

Senior School Nurse:
Mrs T Vardigans, RN, SpCPHN-SN Brunel

Gordonstoun

Elgin, Moray IV30 5RF

Tel: +44 (0)1343 837837
email: admissions@gordonstoun.org.uk
principalpa@gordonstoun.org.uk
website: www.gordonstoun.org.uk
X/Twitter: @gordonstoun
Facebook: @GordonstounSchool
Instagram: @gordonstounschool
LinkedIn: /company/gordonstoun-school

Gordonstoun is a Scottish original. It's the global pioneer of character education – the first school to build an international reputation for academic rigour with unrivalled outdoor experiences. Founded in 1934 by German educator Dr Kurt Hahn, Gordonstoun's enduring character has evolved to meet the needs of the modern world. Hahn asked his students to never settle for less. Gordonstoun continues his challenge today, with its uniquely broad curriculum. The close-knit boarding community is immersed in a huge range of testing activities from classroom study to ocean sailing, on the 220-acre woodland campus, the local community and across the wider world.

"Gordonstoun doesn't have to try to be different – it just is. It's the original holistic education, using outdoor challenges and service to others to build confidence and improve academic performance… if you want an escape from the academic sausage factory and the chance to think out of the box, sign up now." *Good Schools Guide 2020*

The school is unapologetic in developing original characters and original thinkers. The school's motto – *Plus Est En Vous* – asks students to discover more inside themselves. A rich programme of academic and practical discovery helps students find their own passions and reveal their potential. They leave school ready to face life with purpose and determination. They take with them a lifelong resilience, equipping them for the world beyond its walls.

'It wasn't until we saw the curriculum and the schedule of what they would be doing each day that we truly understood the difference between Gordonstoun and other schools.' *Current parent.*

Active engagement in service to the local community comprises a core part of Gordonstoun's 'working week', further expanding the students' sense of personal and social responsibility and building self-esteem. Students volunteer for one of nine services and it is the only school in the UK to have its own Fire Engine, staffed by senior students who respond to genuine emergencies.

"The extensive range of opportunities for personal achievements in the senior school, as part of the Gordonstoun broader curriculum, is outstanding." *HM Inspectors, 2019.*

The School. Gordonstoun is a co-educational boarding and day school for children aged 4–18. There are approximately 130 pupils in the Junior school and a further 440 in the Senior School. Gordonstoun prides itself on the balanced make-up of the student body with approximately one third from overseas, one third from Scotland and one third from the rest of the UK. Gordonstoun is the birthplace of the Duke of Edinburgh Award. In 2023, 62 students journeyed across the highlands by foot or canoe for their assessed expeditions. Gordonstoun is also a founding member of The Round Square Organisation and in the Spring Term Year 12 students have the opportunity to spend a part of the term on exchange with Round Square schools around the world; they can also take part in International Service Projects, providing support to communities as far afield and Thailand, India and closer to home in the Northern Isles.

Boarding. Gordonstoun is one of the few remaining full-boarding schools in the UK and nearly 90% of students in the Senior School are full boarders. A full programme of activities is offered throughout weekends and day pupils join in with weekend activities.

Pastoral Care.

"The positive, caring, family ethos of Gordonstoun School promotes a sense of trust, respect and kindness for all." *HM Inspectors, 2019*

Our systems are built around our pastoral aims, which closely reflect the Gordonstoun ethos and our aim of developing the whole person. As well as house parents, tutors and every member of staff are trained to look after the children. There is a secure online system to keep track of every child and share necessary information.

"The pastoral set up is the best I've seen. Well planned, supportive and built around the child." *Good Schools Guide, 2020*

Curriculum. Gordonstoun follows the English National Curriculum of GCSE and A Level examinations. There are a wide range of subjects available at both levels.

In Year 12 students choose three or four A Level subjects and are encouraged to undertake an optional EPQ. BTEC's are also offered. Most non-English speaking students also take their native language at A Level.

Gordonstoun has a wide support network for those students requiring Learning Support and there is the opportunity to receive one-to-one or small-group teaching.

"My son came from a school down south. He's a different boy without the pressure. In fact, his work is improving simply because he's happy." *Current parent.*

Academic Results. 2023 saw the return of grade boundaries to pre-pandemic levels and Gordonstoun saw a 30% increase in A levels at grades A*-A. There was a 36% increase in the top grade at GCSE and 45% of their students achieved the equivalent of A*-A in BTECS. Gordonstoun is a non-selective school with clear academic ambition; ensuring that their students meet, or exceed, their own, individual baseline testing which is recorded and carefully monitored throughout their careers at school. 89% of this year's final-year students achieved a place at a university of their choice.

Destination of Leavers. Students go on to universities, colleges, and art schools all over the world, including Oxford, Cambridge and the UK's Russell Group universities.

The wide range of activities students undertake during their school years, including training with the Coastguard Service, Fire Service and as Lifeguards, help them to stand out at interview and ensure they have the right skills for rewarding careers.

Sport and Activities.

"Outdoor pursuits are huge and every single student gets involved. Sailing, skiing, hillwalking, climbing. The school owns a 80ft sail-training-vessel, Ocean Spirit, which makes annual trips to destinations such as the Arctic. Sailing is taught in the same kind of cutters as those used by Prince Philip when he was at Gordonstoun. Why? Because they have a crew of eight and teamwork is integral. All pupils are trained in expedition skills and try everything from backpacking and canoeing to exploration. And of course, the school offers a full DofE programme – they did invent it after all, naming it after their most famous alumnus." *Good Schools Guide 2020*

In addition to sailing and expeditions, which form an integral part of the curriculum, the school has competitive teams in rugby, football, hockey, basketball, cricket, tennis, athletics and squash for the boys; hockey, netball, tennis, athletics and squash for the girls; and mixed teams in golf and tennis. These teams participate in national competitions and players are regularly chosen to represent district and regional teams. There are also opportunities to compete in swimming galas, cross-country running, skiing, sailing and adventure races. There is a wide range of recreational sports available including: target shooting, badminton, golf, aerobics, yoga, mountain biking, cycling, climbing, kayaking, orienteering, table tennis and horse riding. Indeed, Gordonstoun is, for the second year running, the Scottish School's Champions in Prelim Dressage and 85 cm Show Jumping.

Gordonstoun prides itself on the strength of its performing arts. dance, drama and Music are available to all students and there are regular collaborations between the three departments to produce major theatrical productions. A weekly dance activity is available to all students and there is also an annual Dance Show, a Senior School musical and regular productions of Shakespeare. The School routinely takes shows to the Edinburgh Fringe Festival. Most recently, they staged a unique adaptation of Macbeth with music by Scottish rock band Biffy Clyro, which played to packed houses. Music students are encouraged to become accustomed to performing in front of audiences large and small via a weekly series of relaxed lunchtime concerts as well as full-scale, formal musical events. Nearly half of the student body receives individual musical tuition in a wide range of instruments. The art department has a teacher from virtually every discipline: fine art to photography.

Wednesday afternoons are also dedicated to working in one of the school's nine rescue or community services. Service to others develops a sense of responsibility and requires each student giving up his or her time and effort to benefit others without expecting return or reward. It fosters links with the local community and includes training which leads to nationally recognised qualifications which prove useful beyond School life.

Admissions. Gordonstoun will be different from any other school you have looked at or visited. We run regular Virtual Taster Days as well as hosting personal visits to our campus.

We do not hold Open Days as we like to tailor-make your visit and we are happy to advise on your travel plans. Please contact admissions@gordonstoun.org.uk

Fees per term (2023–2024). Senior School: Day £10,850, Boarding £15,300; Year 12 & 13 Direct entry: Day £11,867, Boarding £16,330. Junior School: Day £6,450 (Y3–Y8), £4,750 (Y1–Y2), Weekly Boarding (from age 8) £10,350.

Scholarships and Bursaries Awards are generally for 10% of the annual fee. Additional awards may be available based on means-testing.

Charitable status. Gordonstoun Schools Limited is a Registered Charity, number SC037867.

Chair of Governors: David White

***Principal*: Lisa Kerr [until August 2024]; Peter Green [from September 2024]**

Head of Senior School: Simon Cane-Hardy
Head of Junior School: Cath Lyall

Deputy Head (*Pastoral Care*): Philip Schonken
Deputy Head (*Curriculum*): Danielle Cowan

Key Stage 5 Leader: Mel James
Key Stage 4 Leader: Kim Barton
Key Stage 3 Leader: Emma Murray

Director of Admissions: Sabine Richards

Financial Director: Pamela Muir

Director of Gordonstoun International Summer School: Jo Shirriffs

The Grange School

Bradburns Lane, Hartford, Northwich, Cheshire CW8 1LU

Tel: 01606 539039
email: office@grange.org.uk
website: www.grange.org.uk
X/Twitter: @Grange_Cheshire
Facebook: @GrangeCheshire
Instagram: @Grange_Cheshire
LinkedIn: /the-grange-school

Motto: E Glande Robur – 'From an acorn, an oak'

The Grange School is a co-educational independent school for 4–18 year olds. We are located in the heart of Cheshire, in the semi-rural village of Hartford, just south of Northwich.

At The Grange we ensure that our young people live their education by creating a learning environment where they are fully immersed in their school experience. Our hard-working, learner-focused teachers, outstanding facilities and broad enrichment opportunities ensure that every child receives an education that prepares them for life after school. They leave equipped with the tools to become ambitious, respectful and confident adults.

Junior School. The Grange Junior School provides an outstanding start to any child's educational journey. We understand the importance of these formative years in the development of each young person and want every child to develop a love for school and for learning.

Our first priority is to provide a caring atmosphere in which the children can thrive and learn. This requires staff that welcome and understand each and every child, giving them – and their parents – the attention that they deserve. This allows us to help them successfully navigate their way through the inevitable difficulties of growing up and life in general. Happy children will learn.

We offer a learning programme from Reception to Year 6 that is designed to be both broad and flexible, creating a full, balanced education. Children develop particular academic interests and passions; ensuring they attain at the highest level of which they are capable. With a focus on staff development, an average class size of 21, a teaching staff: child ratio of 1:12 and modern, well-equipped facilities, it is no surprise our children consistently attain beyond expectation.

We enable our children to flourish as individuals; encouraging children to pursue their own interests and strengths. As well as sports and creative arts we offer leadership opportunities, the chance to engage in charitable events and hear from guest speakers. We also arrange numerous day trips and offer residential stays both in the UK and overseas.

Senior School. A Grange Senior School Education is all about unleashing our students' creative minds and developing their passions and skills to aid them in their futures through a curriculum that inspires.

Before students select their GCSE options, we make sure they have the opportunity to try every subject, from Maths to Food & Nutrition. We understand the value of educating students through a wide and varied curriculum. It is this that lets young people discover an unknown talent they can pursue and thrive in.

Students participate in the many Enrichment opportunities we provide and they understand the importance of this as a part of their education. We also have a dedicated Student Welfare and Support Team who are here for students to help them through any challenges they face.

We believe in educating the whole child. When students leave us, they are fully prepared for the adult world as open-minded, confident individuals because they were given the chance to live their education at The Grange.

Sixth Form. The Grange Sixth Form is transformational. Through developing their leadership and academic skills, our students leave as young, motivated individuals ready for adult life. We have an enviable academic record in helping our students achieve outstanding results and the majority go on to secure university places at the country's top institutions. With a dedicated Careers Department, advice is always available. Whilst students are offered unrivalled support for their academic studies, they also enjoy greater freedom and independence, to prepare them for life after The Grange. The modern Sixth Form Centre provides a stimulating atmosphere where students can study, meet and socialise; further developing a deeper experience and community spirit based on the principles of self-management as well as collective responsibility.

Beyond the academic arena, there is a broad range of enrichment and leadership experiences for students. These include the Duke of Edinburgh scheme, a Peer Support scheme, our Extended Project Qualification as well as drama, music and sporting opportunities. Tolerance and mutual respect of others, in line with our values, are promoted and students are encouraged to support the wider community through volunteering and charitable activities. Above all, the Sixth Form is a happy place where students can explore academic curiosity in a motivating environment.

Results

A Level results 2023:

- 21% of grades were A*
- 60% of all grades A*–A more than twice the national picture
- 81% of all grades A*–B versus 53% nationally
- 80% of students heading to their first choice university

GCSE results 2023:

- 61% of this year's results were at grades 9–7, almost 3 times the national figure
- 43% of all GCSE entries were at the top grades of 8 or 9
- 83% of all GCSE grades in Art, Graphic Design, 3D Design and Textiles were at 7–9
- 55% of all grades in Biology, Chemistry and Physics were at grade 9

Fees per term (2023–2024). Junior School: £3,520 (Reception & Year 1), £3,820 (Years 2–6); Senior School & Sixth Form £4,715.

Scholarships. Several scholarships are offered for entry to the Senior School for exceptional academic ability and music. A number of Sixth Form Scholarships are awarded for outstanding academic potential after an examination held at the end of spring term preceding Sixth Form entry.

Bursaries worth up to the full fee, and assessed according to means, are available to new entrants to the Senior School.

Charitable status. The Grange School is a Registered Charity, number 525918. It exists to provide high-quality education for boys and girls.

Chair: Mr T Brocklebank

***Head*: Dr L Earps**

Senior School:
Senior Deputy Head: Mr R Oakes
Deputy Head Pastoral: Mrs H Eaton
Deputy Head Academic: Mr J Walker
Director of Teaching and Learning: Mr J Gribben
Director of Enrichment and Co-Curriculum: Mrs H Hackett
Director of Post-16 Education: Mrs H Horsley
Director of Finance and Operations: Mr S Gauller

PA to the Head: Mrs J Ward
Head of Finance: Mrs V Williams
Estates Manager: Mr J Birdsey
Marketing Manager: Dr S Thistleton
Admissions Registrar: Miss L Hough

Junior School:
Head of Junior School: Mr B Tagg
Deputy Head Pastoral Care: Miss A Evans
Deputy Head Academic Development: Mr M Pearson

PA to the Junior School Headmaster/Admissions Coordinator: Mrs N Pratt

Guildford High School – Senior School

United Learning

London Road, Guildford, Surrey GU1 1SJ
Tel: 01483 561440
email: guildford-admissions@guildfordhigh.co.uk
website: www.guildfordhigh.co.uk
X/Twitter: @guildfordhigh
Facebook: @GuildfordHigh
Instagram: @GuildfordHigh

Age Range. Girls 11–18.

Number of pupils. 700.

Fees per term (2023–2024). £6,949. Fees exclude lunches. Textbooks and stationery are provided.

Guildford High School consistently boasts some of the best academic results in the country and has recently been awarded *Independent School of the Year 2024* and *South East Independent School of the Decade* by the *Sunday Times*. We are proud to be a local school serving the local community since 1888. Located next to London Road train station, our pupils travel in from the surrounding towns and villages each morning and a successful train buddy scheme ensures our younger pupils do not travel alone.

Pastoral care is woven into the fabric of Guildford High School. We believe that young people learn best when they are happy and, with that in mind, we have carefully created an environment in which pupils feel safe to push their boundaries and challenge themselves. Our annual 'Well-being Week' is an established highlight of the school calendar and in previous years has featured yoga, circus skills, a silent disco and mindfulness. Our pastoral staff, led by our Deputy Head Pastoral, are second to none.

Creating an environment in which pupils feel safe and valued allows them to throw themselves into their learning. Joining the Senior School in Year 7, pupils will find themselves studying Current Affairs, Philosophy and Latin in addition to the more traditional subjects you would expect to find on the timetable. As they go through the school, subject options increase again and new subjects such as Greek are offered at GCSE and Psychology, Politics and Economics at A Level.

Homework is kept to a minimum at Guildford High School. In Years 7–9, our pupils spend no more than one hour per evening on homework and no homework needs to be handed in the next day. This allows time for extracurricular activities to be enjoyed and new skills developed. Similarly, no homework is set for holidays – this is time for family visits, relaxing and enjoying hobbies.

Pupils joining us in Year 7 or for Sixth Form come from a huge number of schools throughout the local area and there is no one type of 'GHS pupil'. We are a community of actors, musicians, artists, scientists, bookworms and sports women. In an environment that buzzes with creativity and rings with laughter, pupils are unlimited in their belief in each other and themselves. Our former pupils go on to achieve great things in all walks of life.

Facilities. Facilities include a brand new state-of-the-art Performing Arts Centre and Recital Hall, libraries, 11 well-equipped laboratories, whiteboards in every classroom, an Information Technology Centre, a Design Technology Centre, Art and Design Studios, a Food Technology Room, Music Technology Studio, a Careers Room and Dining Hall. A large Sports Hall with indoor courts, gymnasium and 25m indoor swimming pool is surrounded by the school's own outdoor pitches.

Charitable status. Guildford High School Senior School is part of United Learning which comprises: UCST (a Company Limited by Guarantee, Registered in England, number 2780748, and a Registered Charity, number 1016538) and ULT (a Company Limited by Guarantee, Registered in England, number 4439859, and an Exempt Charity).

Governing Body: The Council of United Learning

Patron: The Most Revd and Rt Hon Justin Welby, Archbishop of Canterbury

Local Governing Body:
Ms Kate Richards (*Chair*)
Ms Karen Braganza
Mrs Anna Lise Gordon (*Child Protection Representative*)
Ms Zip Jila (*EYFS Representative*)
Dr Sian Jones (*Health and Safety Representative*)
Mr Robert Turnbull
Mr Richard Webb (*E-safety Representative*)
Mr Nigel Wickham (*Health and Safety Representative*)

Head: **Mrs Karen Laurie**, BA Hons Leeds

Deputy Heads:
Pastoral: Mrs Catherine Gilmore, BSc Hons Bath
Academic: Mr Duncan Peel, BA Hons Bristol, MA London
Co-curricular: Mr William Saunders, BA Hons Bristol, MA St Mary's Twickenham

Haberdashers' Boys' School

Butterfly Lane, Elstree, Hertfordshire WD6 3AF

Tel: 020 8266 1700
email: office@habsboys.org.uk
website: www.habsboys.org.uk
X/Twitter: @habsboys
Facebook: @habsboys
Instagram: @habsboysschool
LinkedIn: /school/habsboys

The School was founded in 1690, in 1898 it was transferred from Hoxton to Hampstead and in 1961 to Aldenham Park, Elstree, Hertfordshire.

The aim of the School is the fullest possible development of the varied talents of every boy within it, and to this end a broad curriculum is provided, together with extensive facilities for the development of each boy's cultural, physical, personal and intellectual gifts. The School sets out to achieve high academic standards and sets equally high standards in cultural and other fields. In matters of behaviour a large degree of self-discipline is expected, and of mutual tolerance between members of the School community.

Organisation. The School, which is a day school, has 120 boys in the Pre-Prep (ages 5–7) and over 200 boys in the Preparatory School (ages 7–11), and over 1000 in the Senior School (ages 11–18). There are 6 Houses. The School regards pastoral care as important; all the Heads of House, Deputy Heads of House and Heads of Section have a large responsibility in this field but so also do House Tutors and the Chaplain, as well as other members of the staff.

Forms. In the Pre-Prep School there are two forms in Reception, Year 1 and Year 2 with approximately 20 boys in each form. In the Preparatory School there are three forms in Years 3, 4, 5 and 6 each with about 18 boys. In the Senior School there are six forms in Years 7 and 8 with approximately 25 boys in each form. There are twelve forms in Year 9 each with about 15 boys. Years 10 and 11 are divided amongst eighteen forms each with 14–16 boys. The usual size of teaching groups in the Sixth Form is about 10–15.

Facilities. The School and its sister School, Haberdashers' Girls' School, enjoy the use of a campus of over 140 acres with extensive woodlands. The playing fields surround the buildings, which in the Boys' School include the following: Assembly Hall, Dining Hall, Sixth Form Common Room, Music Auditorium, special accommodation for Classics, English (including a Drama Room), History, Geography, Mathematics, Information Technology, Modern Languages including 2 Languages Laboratories, Music School, Science and Geography Centre with 19 laboratories and 8 classrooms, a Design Centre for Art, Craft and Technology, state-of-the-art Sports Centre, Gymnasium, Indoor Swimming Pool, Climbing Wall, Squash Courts, two Artificial Grass Pitches and much more.

The Prep School is situated on the same campus in a building of its own. (*For further details, see Prep School entry in IAPS section.*) As of January 2023, the Pre-Prep is also situated on the same campus in a newly purpose-built building.

The Curriculum up to the age of 13 is common for all, with no streaming or setting except in Mathematics in Year 8. From the age of 11 in addition to the usual subjects it includes three separate Sciences and two foreign languages which are taught as a carousel to ensure all boys have sampled all languages before making informed choices. From the age of 13, subjects are taught in sets of mixed abilities. GCSE courses start in Year 10, when boys take ten subjects. In the Sixth Form students study four subjects to AS in the Lower Sixth, narrowing to three A2 subjects in the Upper Sixth. The School takes seriously its commitment to Enrichment and Enhancement; this non-examined part of the curriculum occupies 10% of the week in both Upper and Lower Sixth. Boys are entered for the GCE examination at A Level at the age of 18 and are prepared for entry to degree courses at Universities. The wide scope of the School's curriculum gives ample opportunity for all its boys whether preparing for University (overwhelmingly their primary interest), for a profession, for the services, or for commerce or industry. The University Applications and Careers Departments have their own modern facilities, and careers advice is readily available to parents and to boys.

Religious Education. The School is by tradition a Church of England school, but there are no religious barriers to entry and no quotas. It is part of the ethos of the School that all its members respect the deeply-held beliefs and faith of other members. The School Chaplain is available to, and holds responsibility for, all boys in the School of whatever faith. He prepares for Confirmation those who wish it, and there are weekly celebrations of Holy Communion and an annual Carol Service in St Albans Abbey. The morning assembly and class teaching, however, are non-denominational in character. Faith assemblies are held on Thursday mornings, and comprise separate meetings for Christians, Jews, Muslims, Hindus, Jains, Sikhs, Buddhists and Humanists.

Physical Education. A wide variety of sports is available, including Athletics, Badminton, Basketball, Cricket, Cross-Country Running, Fencing, Golf, Gymnastics, Hockey, Rugby, Football, Sailing, Squash, Shooting, Swimming, Tennis, Table Tennis and Water Polo. All boys are expected to take part in physical education unless exempt on medical grounds.

Out of School Activities. The extensive range includes a period of two hours on Friday afternoon when boys can choose one of a large variety of activities of a service nature. This includes Community Service, both on the School campus and among those who need help in the surrounding district. It also includes the Combined Cadet Force, which has Royal Navy, Army and Royal Air Force sections, and Adventure Training.

Music and Drama. Both have a prominent place in the School. The Music School has a Recital Hall and some twelve other rooms; 20 visiting instrumental teachers between them teach 500 instrumental pupils each week covering all the normal orchestral instruments together with Piano and Organ. There is a Choir of 250, and several orchestras. For Drama the facilities include a generously equipped stage and a separate Drama Room with its own lighting and stage equipment.

School Societies. School Societies and expeditionary activities in term time and holidays include Amnesty, Archery, Art, Badminton, Bridge, Canoeing, Chess, Choral, Classical, Crosstalk, Debating, Duke of Edinburgh's Award, Dramatics, English, Football, History, Jazz, Jewish Society, Life-saving, Life Drawing, Modern Languages, Mountaineering, Philosophical, Photography, Politics, Puzzles and Games, Rifle, Sailing, Science, Squash, Stamp Club, Windsurfing and many more.

Transport. There is a joint schools coach service providing an extensive network of routes and some 110 pick-up points, to enable boys and girls to attend the School from a wide area, and to remain for after-school activities.

Admission. Boys are admitted only at the beginning of the school year in September. They may be admitted at the age of 4 and may remain in the School until the end of the academic year in which the age of 19 is attained, subject to satisfactory progress at each stage of the course and to compliance with the School Rules currently in force. Each year approximately 36 boys are admitted at age 4, a further 18 boys at age 7, approximately 100 at age 11 and approximately 25 at age 13. There are competitive examinations including written and oral tests of intelligence, literacy and numeracy at the ages of 7 and 11, held in December for admission in the following September. Applicants aged 13 also take examinations at the beginning of January and are interviewed later in the month for entry in September. Registration Fee: £150.

An Open Day for prospective parents is held each year early in October.

Scholarships and Bursaries. A number of Academic Scholarships are awarded annually to pupils entering the Senior School. A smaller number of Creative Writing, Music, Art, Drama and Sports Scholarships are awarded each year to students who show additional special promise in these specific areas.

A significant number of means-tested Governors' Bursaries are awarded at age 11+, valued from a few hundred pounds to full fees, depending upon financial need. Open equally to boys progressing from the Prep School and to those applying from other Schools.

Full details of all these awards are included in the prospectus available from the School Registrar who is happy to answer enquiries.

Fees per term (2023–2024). Main School £8,183 exc. lunch; Prep School (Years 3–6) £7,747 exc. lunch; Pre-Prep (Reception–Year 2) £6,384 inc. lunch.

Instrumental lessons (individual tuition) £245 per instrument; Group classes £150; Aural & Theory classes £75; Instrument hire £35.

Charitable status. The Haberdashers' Aske's Charity is a Registered Charity, number 313996. It exists to promote education.

Chair of the Board of Governors: S Cartmell, OBE

Executive Principal: Mr A R Lock, MA

***Headmaster*: R Sykes**, BA

Head of the Prep School: K Umpleby, BSc Hons
Senior Deputy Head: N Hamshaw, MA
Deputy Head Pastoral: C E Shooter, BA
Acting Deputy Head Academic: M Brennan, BA
Chief Operating Officer: R Dunn, MA
Director of Co-curricular: A J Simm, BA
Director of Teaching: J S Bown, BA

Head of the Sixth Form: G Noble, MEd
Head of the Middle School: A M Lawrence, MA
Head of the Lower School: T B Hardman, BEd
Director of Admissions: R Shaw, BA Hons
Joint Schools Director of Development: W Friar, MS
Director of Foundation: R de H Llewellyn, MA
Joint Schools Director of Marketing and Communications: A Tooley, BA
Director of People: Dr R McKenzie-Young, PhD
Director of Outreach & Partnership: J Plotkin, MA
Director of Finance and Resources. L Karfoot, BA

Heads of Department:

Academic Support: F McEwan-Cox, MEd
Art: K Barron, BA Hons
Classics: C Joyce, PhD
Computing & ICT: C Ovia, MA
Design & Technology: S Vincent, MA
Economics: J Wolfson, BSc Econ Hons
English & Drama: I D Wheeler, BA Hons
Examinations: A Thakar, BSc Hons
Geography: S C Edwards, BSc Hons
History: S P Clark, BA Hons
Libraries & Archives: T Chan, BSc Hons, MA MHLA
Mathematics: K Harrison, BSc Hons
Modern Languages: R J Thompson, BA Hons
Music: D O'Hare, BA Hons
Performance Music: T Taylor, MMus
Director of Sport: R J McIntosh, MEd
Politics: S P Clark, BA Hons
Science: G R Hobbs, PhD
Theology & Philosophy: R Davis, MA

Heads of House:
Calverts: K Barron, BA Hons
Hendersons: T Jones, BSc
Joblings: G Chapmen, PhD
Meadows: D C Taberner, MSc
Russells: M Broadwith, MSc
Strouts: A F Metcalfe, BSc

Prep School:
Head: K Umpleby, BSc Hons
Deputy Head (Academic): M Best, BA Hons
Deputy Head (Pastoral): P Swindell, BA

Pre-Prep School:
Head: V Huggett, BSc

Haberdashers' Monmouth School

Almshouse Street, Monmouth, Monmouthshire NP25 3XP

Tel: 01600 713143
email: admissions@habsmonmouth.org
website: www.habsmonmouth.org
X/Twitter: @Habsmonmouth
Facebook: @Habsmonmouth
Instagram: @habsmonmouth
LinkedIn: /Haberdashers'-Monmouth-Schools

Motto: *Serve and Obey*

Age range. 3–18.

Haberdashers' Monmouth School is a co-educational day and boarding school situated in the beautiful Wye Valley. Pupils gain a real sense of identity, a grounding and sense of belonging that only comes from a school with a rich history that extends over 400 years. During that time, countless young men and women have passed through its doors and gone onto do amazing things, in the knowledge that they are part of the unique Haberdashers' family, providing a support system which will be with them for life, transcending boundaries, cultures and ages. This is known as the Haberdashers' Advantage.

Sixth Form. We are investing enormously into our Sixth Form to not only provide superb facilities but also ensure that every student can participate in a simply outstanding enrichment programme, all whilst achieving academic excellence.

Boarding. Our vision is simple: every pupil who calls Haberdashers' Monmouth School their home will leave with an unwavering sense of fulfilment. Here it's more than just a home away from home; it's a safe and supportive environment, where our dedicated staff make you feel like family. We take immense pride in providing the optimum setting to cultivate the perfect balance between academic endeavours and a diverse array of engaging extra-curricular activities. It's a place where lifelong friendships are forged within our inclusive community.

Buses. We run an extensive bus service that covers a large area.

Admissions. We have multiple entry points for children applying to join us and we welcome applications throughout the year (subject to availability). Early application is encouraged wherever possible at our key entry points. We hold open events in September, January and May, but families are welcome to visit at any time.

Curriculum. Our pupils are introduced to a wide range of subjects in their early years and they usually go on to take 9 or 10 subjects at GCSE. We offer almost 30 A level courses in our Sixth Form. Music, Performing Arts and Sport play a huge part in school life and the school prides itself in the quality in all these areas.

Extra-curricular activities. We offer a wealth of lunchtime and after-school opportunities catering for all interests. We run many trips and expeditions, events and community projects, giving students life-affirming opportunities and experiences.

Pastoral care. Our staff are caring and supportive both in and out of the classroom, helping each pupil to feel valued as an individual. Our pastoral philosophy is to develop resilience, personal management, confidence and a sense of community that will take our girls and boys through later life.

Fees per term (2023–2024). Day £6,659, Boarding £12,847–£13,948; Monmouth Prep School: Day £3,187–£4,670, Boarding (Years 3–6) £8,572.

Scholarships and Bursaries. Various Scholarships and Awards are available for pupils joining in Year 7 (11+), Year 9 (13+) and Year 12 (16+) and applications are open for all candidates, whether boarders or day pupils. Academic Scholarships are awarded on consideration of entrance examination results, interview and school report. Scholarship allocation is based on entrance results, an interview, an audition or trial, and a clear display of outstanding potential. Scholarships usually hold a value of a maximum of 10% of the school fees. Means-tested Bursaries and Assisted Places of up to 100% of fees are also available at all entry points.

Charitable Status. Haberdashers' Monmouth School is part of a group of schools under the umbrella of the Worshipful Company of Haberdashers. Started in 1614 by Haberdashers William Jones, the school is extremely fortunate to have a substantial endowment income that ensures regular investment into our school facilities as well as enabling us to keep our fees very competitive and offer generous bursaries and scholarships in academia, sport, drama, music, dance and the creative arts. William Jones's Schools Foundation is a Registered Charity, number 525616.

Board of Governors:
Chairman of Governors: Lord Colin Moynihan

Mrs J Booth	Mr N Manns
Professor R Carwardine	Mr R Miners
Professor A Davies	Mr A Mohindru
Mr S Garratt	Mr N Waters
Mr T Haden-Scott	Dr R Weeks
Dr S Honeywill	Mr I de Weymarn
Mr A Lock	Mrs R Williams
Mr J McLaren	

Clerk to the Governors: Mrs C Stansfield, BA

Staff:
Executive Team:
***Headmaster*: Mr S Dorman**, MA Oxon, MPhil
Headmaster Prep Department: Mr N Shaw, MA
Foundation Bursar: Mrs T Norgrove, MBA
Director of External Relations: Mrs N Muir, BSc

Senior Leadership Team:
Deputy Head (*Pastoral*): Mrs R Rees, BA, MEd, PGCE
Deputy Head (*Pastoral*): Mr D Edwards, BA
Deputy Head (*Academic*): Mrs E Arrand, BA
Director of Sixth Form: Mr A Peace, BSc
Director of Boarding: Mrs G Peace, BA, MA
Assistant Deputy Head (*Academic*): Dr E Evans, BSc, PhD
Head of Progress & Assessment: Mr D Evans, BA, MA
Head of Wellbeing: Miss S Fowler, BSc
Head of Extra-Curricular: Mr G Stentiford, BSc, MSc

Haileybury

Haileybury, Hertford SG13 7NU
Tel: 01992 706200 (Reception)
01992 706353 (Admissions)
email: admissions@haileybury.com
website: www.haileybury.com
X/Twitter: @HaileyburyUK
Facebook: @HaileyburyUK
Instagram: @haileyburyuk
LinkedIn: /school/haileybury-uk

Haileybury is a leading independent co-educational boarding and day school, situated on 500 acres of beautiful Hertfordshire countryside, just 20 miles north of London.

Haileybury's spectacular grounds are home to excellent teaching, outstanding facilities, and superb pastoral care for its community of 11–18 year old pupils.

Academic Opportunity. The school offers a dedicated Lower School for Years 7 and 8 and a wide range of GCSEs and IGCSEs.

In the Sixth Form, pupils can select to study for A levels or the International Baccalaureate (IB) Diploma.

Haileybury's unrivalled curriculum allows pupils to select personal pathways, such as coding and global civilisations, based on their individual passions. In the Sixth Form, electives include criminology, geopolitics and music technology.

Boarding and Day. More than two-thirds of pupils are boarders and school life is centred around 12 boarding houses, Lower School benefitting from having their own house. Pupils join at 11+, 13+ or 16+ entry points.

For Lower School pupils, flexi-boarding is available which means families do not have to commit to full boarding at this stage, and pupils return home for the weekend.

From Year 9 onwards, there is the additional flexibility of pupils being able to return home after sporting commitments on Saturday afternoons.

Exceptional Opportunities. Beyond the academic curriculum, pupils benefit from a vast array of activities, including professional sports coaching and regular visits from speakers and performers from the arts, sporting and academic worlds. The co-curricular programme is packed with opportunities, from Climbing and Scuba Diving to Film-Making and the Model United Nations – and countless more activities in between.

Haileybury also encourages pupils to immerse themselves in the Creative Arts both academically and as part of their co-curricular options. Drama, Music, Dance, LAMDA and Art are at the heart of school life. The School takes pride in hosting spectacular arts productions with multiple showcases per term and pupils are able to take part in music concerts, drama productions and public performances throughout the year.

The first school to do so in the UK, Haileybury is also taking part in the global Stan-X programme, a pioneering study of genetics. Working from a purpose-built lab, Haileybury pupils are contributing to efforts to find cures for diseases such as pancreatic cancer and diabetes.

Excellent Facilities. Adding to the already existing outstanding teaching facilities, Haileybury's new state-of-the-art Science and Technology Centre opened in November 2023, doubling the size of the School's previous provision and offering pupils the very best environment and resources available.

Supportive Environment. At Haileybury, a caring environment is crucial to a pupil's happiness and fulfilment. There is an emphasis on pastoral care with around-the-clock support from housemasters and housemistresses, the chaplain and tutors, as well as an on-site health centre providing a circle of care. The School is a home-from-home, with a warm and friendly feel.

Fees per term (2023–2024). Senior boarding £14,900, Senior day £10,785, Lower School boarding £9,455, Lower School day £7,170.

Scholarships. We welcome applications from those who demonstrate excellence, talent, outstanding achievement and promise. Scholarships available:

- 11+ entry: Academic, Music, Sport
- 13+ and 16+ entry: Academic, Drama, Music, Sport, Art, Design Technology

Bursaries. Bursaries are offered to make it possible for talented pupils or those in significant pastoral need, whose parents could not otherwise afford the fees, to benefit from an education at Haileybury.

For further information please visit: www.haileybury.com/admissions/scholarships-and-bursaries/.

Charitable status. Haileybury is a Registered Charity, number 310013.

Governing Body:
Chair of Council: Martin Rayfield, BSc Econ, ACA
Deputy Chair of Council: Charles Sherwood, MA Cantab, MSc, MBA
Treasurer: Richard Munn, MA Cantab, FRGS

Leadership:

***The Master*: Martin Collier**

Deputy Master: Simon Heard

Deputy Heads:
Academic: Miles Tomkins
Co-curricular: Angus Head
Pastoral: Laura Pugsley
Director of Marketing and Admissions: Georgina Collicutt
Chief Financial Officer: Michael Schofield
Chief Operating Officer: Catrin Mills
Estates Director: Simon Brophy
Director of International Partnership: Mark Smith
Director of Development: Amy Ledingham

Assistant Heads:
Digital Learning: Tom Wade
Pastoral: Peter Blair
Pupil Progress and Behaviour: Olivia Firek
Head of Sixth Form: Sarah Webb

Halliford School

Russell Road, Shepperton, Middlesex TW17 9HX
Tel: 01932 223593
email: registrar@hallifordschool.co.uk
website: www.hallifordschool.co.uk
X/Twitter: @hallifordhead
Facebook: @hallifordschool
Instagram: @hallifordschoolshepperton
LinkedIn: /halliford-school-limited

Halliford is a warm-hearted School founded on strong family values where we are proud to know and be respectful of every student as an individual. Our theme 'Come as you are. Go as all you can be' perfectly encapsulates our mission to encourage and support Hallifordians to flourish and become the best version of themselves that they can possibly be. Our boys join us for their seven-year journey from 11 to 18 and we warmly welcome girls to join our co-educational Sixth Form, which provides our senior students with the opportunities to excel in a more independent environment. Halliford is an incredible community to belong to and spend part of their only childhood. Halliford School was founded in 1921 and moved to its present site in 1929. The Headmaster is a member of both HMC and the Society of Heads.

Facilities. Halliford School is situated on the Halliford bend of the River Thames. The old house, a graceful eighteenth-century building, which stands in six acres of grounds, is the administrative centre of the School. There are six additional acres of sports fields 500 yards from the school gates. Over the years, there has been a steady development programme, including the 320-seat theatre, a refurbished kitchen and dining room, new classrooms, and a new Science laboratory. There is an impressive Sports Hall with a climbing wall and changing facilities. The Philip Cottam building was further developed and incorporates the Sixth Form Centre and Café, the Art Studios, and the Music Centre, including the Recital Hall. There is also a wonderful design studio and workshop for the Design & Technology students. As part of our Centenary celebrations, a brand new £3 million building opened in November 2021 featuring a state-of-the-art Learning Resource Centre and six new classrooms. We proudly consider ourselves a small school, without any apologies. The advantage of our size is our deep familiarity with one another. We see and know each student beyond the crowd; no one ever gets lost here. Despite our size, we are well equipped, both on site and through extensive partnerships worldwide.

Admission. There are approximately 460 students on roll with a three-form entry at Year 7 (approximately 60 students). There is a further entry at Year 9, and admission is possible into other year groups dependent on the availability of places. Entrance is by interview followed by examination (English, Mathematics and Reasoning). Siblings are given priority as long as they can benefit from a sound academic education. This policy creates a strong feeling of a family community and helps reinforce the close partnership that exists with parents. Girls and Boys are admitted into the Sixth Form based on their GCSE predictions, a report from their current school and an interview. Our pursuit of excellence is characterised by academic ambition balanced with academic sensitivity.

Curriculum. In Years 7 to 9, students study the following subjects: English, Mathematics, two languages (French, German or Spanish), Latin/Classical Civilisation, Biology, Chemistry, Physics, History, Geography, Art, Drama, Music, Design and Technology, Computing, Religious Studies, and Physical Education. In Years 10 and 11 (GCSE), there is a compulsory core of English Language and Literature, Mathematics (some also take Further Mathematics), a Modern Foreign Language (French, German or Spanish), and the three separate Sciences. Students choose a further three subjects: a second Modern Foreign Language, Latin, Classical Civilisation, History, Geography, Religious Studies, Art, Drama, Music, PE, Business Studies, Design Technology (either Resistant Materials or Graphic Products) or Computing Science.

Some 22 subjects are available at A Level in the Sixth Form, and all teaching is co-educational. Students also complete an extended project.

Games. Rugby, Football, and Cricket are the main games played at Halliford. Athletics, Basketball, Tennis, Badminton, Table Tennis, Volleyball and Golf are available, plus a large number of other activities.

Pastoral organisation. The health and wellbeing of our students are paramount to everything we do at Halliford. Our students are designated a House that will act as both pastoral support and a community throughout their time at the School. Houses have a tutor in each year group and a Head of House. In addition, we have a Head of Year for Year 7 to ensure our students have a positive transition into the School. Likewise, we have a Head of Sixth Form to support the students who choose Halliford for the final two years of their school career. Tutors are always willing to see parents, and the Headmaster can usually be seen at very short notice. We have two part-time Matrons covering the full week who look after our students, alongside staff who are all first aid trained. We have a school counsellor available to our students, plus our Sixth Formers act as mentors to the younger students.

Out-of-school activities. These include very successful Drama, Music, Sport and Art Departments.

There is a long list of clubs including Chess, Design, Computing, Film, Creative Writing, Modern Languages, Science and Art. In addition, there are Senior and Junior Debating, Academic Societies, Inter-House Public Speaking and Singing Competitions. The Duke of Edinburgh's Award is available as an additional activity.

School Council. Each Tutor group elects a representative to the School Council. This is not a cosmetic exercise, and in recent times, the School Council has effected real changes. Halliford believes that students have good ideas which can be implemented for the wellbeing of the School as a whole.

Prospective parents. The main School Open Mornings are held on the last Saturday in February and the first Saturday in October. Further Visitor Mornings are held in November, March and May during the school week. Also, the School holds Sixth Form Open Evenings in May and October. Prospective parents are welcome at other times by appointment for personal tours.

Fees per term (2023–2024). £6,950.

Scholarships and bursaries. The School offers scholarships up to the value of 10% per annum of the annual tuition fees for entry at Year 7, Year 9 and in the Sixth Form. The scholarships awarded are Academic, Art, Drama, Music, and Sport, plus STEM for Sixth Form.

The School is also keen to help those who could not otherwise afford the fees, and means-tested bursaries are available on application.

Old Hallifordians. Chairman: Sam Lawrence.

Charitable status. Halliford School is a Registered Charity, number 312090. It exists to provide high-quality education.

Governors:
Chairman: Mr K Woodward
Deputy Chairman: Mr C Squire
Mr M Crosby
Mr R Davison
Mr B Harris
Mr A Hirst
Mrs P Horner
Mr A Lenoel
Dr M Sachania
Mr J Sharp
Miss A Wallace

***Headmaster*: Mr James Davies**

Bursar: Mrs Elspeth Sanders
Deputy Head Academic: Mr Richard Fulford
Deputy Head Pastoral: Mr James Norman
Assistant Head Co-Curricular: Mr Sean Slocock
Head of Sixth Form: Mr Andy Carroll
Director of Student Welfare: Mr Matt Shales
Director of Teaching and Learning: Mr Guy Boyes

Hampton School

Hanworth Road, Hampton, Middlesex TW12 3HD
Tel: 020 8979 5526
email: headmaster@hamptonschool.org.uk
admissions@hamptonschool.org.uk
website: hamptonschool.org.uk

Motto: *Praestat opes sapientia*

Founded in the academic year of 1556/57 by Robert Hammond, a Hampton merchant, and re-established in 1612. From 1910 the School was administered by the local authority, latterly as a voluntary aided school.

Hampton is a lively, friendly and caring day school where innovative teaching is underpinned by strong shared values and complemented by outstanding pastoral care. Currently around 1,300 boys aged 11 to 18, including a Sixth Form of about 400. The School achieves all-round excellence, encouraging academic ambition, personal responsibility and independent thinking in an energetic, happy and well-disciplined community. It aims to provide a challenging and stimulating education for boys of high academic promise from the widest possible variety of social backgrounds.

Consistently in the top academic echelon nationally, Hampton is distinctive in being concurrently one of the country's most successful sporting schools and among the leading educational settings for music, drama and community partnerships. The School places paramount importance upon striking the right balance between academic and cultural, sporting and artistic endeavours, allowing boys to be happy and to fulfil their potential wherever their interests may lie. No pupil is funnelled down a particular route; boys are allowed to follow their own path in a nurturing, inspiring and aspirational environment. Standards are extremely high and result naturally and organically from the fun boys have at Hampton and their enthusiastic, well-balanced involvement in the huge range of opportunities on offer. The School places fundamental emphasis upon the importance of boys being personally ambitious while supporting those around them (in the School community and beyond) with kindness and compassion.

In the most recent ISI integrated inspection (May 2023) Hampton was awarded the highest judgement possible in each individual category. Pupils' achievements are exceptional across the broad academic curriculum, in co-curricular activity and in the extensive enrichment programmes. Inspectors concluded that outstanding analytical and thinking skills lead to academic achievements far and above national and worldwide averages. Alongside excellence across the curriculum, the School was praised for pupils' excellent personal development along with their pronounced sense of acceptance of the rich diversity in society. It was also noted that the curriculum is enriched by an extensive, varied range of co-curricular activities and strong links with the community. The inspection report confirmed the School's success in meeting its aim of producing mature, confident yet grounded young people who aim for personal success while supporting those around them with kindness.

Hampton is academically selective and virtually all boys go on to leading Russell Group or equivalent universities, with increasing numbers to American Ivy League Universities. Examination results in 2023 at A Level (70% A*–A grades, 32% at A*) and GCSE (75% 9–8, 45% at grade 9) were extremely strong. Over 95% of boys gained places at Russell Group Universities or equivalent. The Sixth Form has a strong emphasis on deep academic enquiry, breadth of study, critical thinking and independent learning.

An annual exchange programme offers boys the chance to visit Spain, Germany, France, Italy and Russia as well as Asia, Africa and the Far East. Boys visit many countries through academic and sporting initiatives and there is an extraordinary range of trips available.

The extensive co-curricular programme forms an essential part of the balanced education which Hampton provides and includes a diverse range of clubs from beekeeping and archaeology to radio, Lego robotics and drone club. Music and drama are central to the character of the School and concerts, musicals and plays involve all age groups throughout the year. Over half the boys learn musical instruments and there are frequent music and choir tours abroad. A notable number of Organ and Choral Scholarships to Oxbridge colleges have been won over recent years.

Drama is included in the curriculum, in addition to regular School and year group productions. There are major joint music and drama productions regularly with neighbouring LEH. Recent highlights include *Little Shop of Horrors, Guys and Dolls, Return to the Forbidden Planet, Crazy for You, Anything Goes, West Side Story, Mack & Mabel, Jekyll & Hyde,* Shakespeare's *The Tempest, Joseph Kesselring's Arsenic and Old Lace,* Jez Butterworth's *Jerusalem* and *Oliver Twist* and *The Wizard of Oz*, both the latter being joint productions with one of the School's partnership schools, Waldegrave School for Girls.

Hampton has an outstanding reputation for sport and standards are very high indeed; many boys play at county and national level in a wide range of sports. Particular strengths are cricket, football, rowing, rugby, tennis and chess. The First XI's were crowned national U18 English Schools FA (ESFA) Cup Final in 2023 and 2019, the Second XI, Under 16As and Under 16Bs secured the English Schools FA (ESFA) title in 2020 and the Under 13As champions in 2022. Chess players also brought home the English Chess Federation (ECF) schools' trophy in June 2023. A multi-year group team comprising First Year to Sixth Form topped a table of leading schools to claim the ECF title and record what is possibly a unique Chess-Football double! In rugby, the First XV reached the semi-final in the prestigious RFU Champions Trophy and the U15As have reached the final eight in the Rugby Football Union National Cup competition. Boys benefit from superb facilities and specialist coaching. Hampton has produced many schoolboy internationals in a wide range of sports and also Olympic rowers; the School shares a nearby boathouse on the River Thames with LEH.

Integrity and social conscience are encouraged implicitly through the daily interaction of boys and teachers, as well as explicitly through School assemblies, PSHE lessons, extensive Charity, Environment and Community Service programmes, and long-standing links with the Hampton Safe Haven, now a government approved primary school in Malawi. The School was one of the two founding schools of the 'Mindfulness in Schools Project' promoting pupil well-being and emotional resilience.

Hampton School and LEH are served by 23 coach routes across south-west London, Surrey and Berkshire.

Buildings and Grounds. The School has been situated on its present site since 1939.

Set within grounds of some 27 acres, all facilities (with the exception of the Boat House) are on site including four rugby pitches, seven football pitches, six cricket squares, six hard tennis courts and a rock climbing wall. Buildings include an Assembly Hall, Dining Hall, large multi-purpose Sports Hall, fully-equipped Library and specialist facilities for Art, Science, Technology, Computing and Coding and Languages. A rigorous development programme ensures that all boys continue to benefit from first-class facilities. More recent additions include; a three-storey Atrium extension providing further classrooms and a large display area; a multi-use ball area, state-of-the-art all-weather 3G sports ground for football, rugby and recreational use and a bespoke Sixth Form Study & Careers Centre.

The magnificent Hammond Theatre provides exceptional facilities for the performing arts, doubling as a theatre and concert hall.

The Millennium Boat House, located on the nearby River Thames and shared with LEH, was opened in 2000 by Sir Steve and Lady Redgrave and provides the focal point for the popular and highly successful Boat Club.

Community. Community is integral to life at Hampton and the School's aim is for boys to leave as happy, educated and well-rounded young men with a sense of social responsibility and the desire to make the world a better place.

The School is deeply committed to playing a full role within the wider community and enjoys a wide range of thriving partnerships with local schools, charities and other organisations. In 2023, over 1,800 pupils from 80 different schools took part in 67 different partnership activities, including GCSE and A level revision classes for local secondary school pupils; Music and Drama workshops university preparation assistance; Hampton senior pupils also visit Hampton High and Twickenham Academy to provide peer mentoring for Maths.

Strong links are also maintained with the numerous local state primary schools which provide around 50% of the First Year intake. Year 5 and Year 6 pupils from a number of local state primary schools attend teaching sessions in a range of subjects on Saturday mornings as part of the School's Lion Learning Programme and regular Maths, English and Science competitions and workshops are held. Hampton teachers also undertake outreach work in local schools offering support in the Sciences, English and Maths.

Hampton Sixth formers undertake placements in local primary schools as part of their Curriculum Enrichment Programme, working with young children on literacy, numeracy, computing and sport. Many boys in the Fourth Year and above volunteer their assistance in primary schools, residential homes for the elderly and local charities. Various joint activities are run with LEH, including an annual autumn tea party and a Christmas Party for local senior citizens, together with trips for children with special needs to LEGOLAND and the Discovery Centre.

The School enjoys particularly strong links with their immediate neighbouring schools, Hampton High and LEH. These two schools participate in a wide range of activities with Hampton pupils including Drama, Music and CCF and the very popular visiting speakers 'Talk!' programme.

Hampton is one of the foundation partners, in collaboration with LEH and Reach Academy, a new sixth form college which opened in September 2022. Feltham College is an exciting new model of post-16 education, which brings together a powerful partnership of education, business and health service providers to broaden choice for local young people and offer them transformative opportunities. The College is a centre of academic and vocational excellence at the heart of the town, playing a key role in rejuvenating a historically deprived area that has experienced significant pandemic-related job losses.

Curriculum. Boys in the Lower School follow a wide curriculum, including Design Engineering, Computing and Coding, Physics, Chemistry, Biology, a Modern Language (French, German or Spanish), Latin, Art, Drama and Religious Studies. Mandarin, Greek and Russian are optional subjects available from the Third

Year. In the Fourth and Fifth Years all boys continue to study, in addition to PE, Sport and Mindfulness, the following: English Language, English Literature, a Modern Language, Mathematics and the three sciences for (I)GCSE. They choose three subjects from the following: Art, Ancient History, Computer Science, Design Engineering, Drama, French, Geography, German, Greek, History, Latin, Mandarin, Music, Religious Studies, Russian and Spanish. Most of these (I)GCSEs are taken at the end of the Fifth Year. The most able mathematicians also take Additional Mathematics GCSE.

The Sixth Form offers a free choice of A level subjects, in addition to a wide range of courses delivered through the Curriculum Enrichment Programme taught jointly with neighbouring LEH, including Critical Thinking and Oracy. Pupils in the Lower Sixth study at least three A levels, which continue to be studied in the Upper Sixth and a further course, which may lead to an internal or external qualification. Additional teaching and preparation is provided for boys seeking entrance to highly-selective universities, nearly all Hamptonians secure places at Russell Group or equivalent settings, with many moving on to read their chosen subject at one of the global top-10 universities, including Oxford and Cambridge. About fifty boys a year also opt for the Hampton Extended Project, a substantial piece of independent research of around 5,000 words.

Sport. Sport and Physical Education are part of every boy's School week and the sporting programme combines strength, depth and breadth. All Hamptonians have a free choice of sport and pupils can choose between football and rugby in the autumn and spring terms; cricket, athletics and tennis are offered in the summer term. From the Third Year upwards, a large number of pupils chose to join the Boat Club. A broad programme of specialist sports provides opportunities for boys to involve themselves in basketball, cross-country, swimming, badminton, volleyball, golf, table tennis, squash, sailing and skiing. A large number of boys take part in voluntary sport on Saturdays; fixtures, at a range of ability levels, are arranged for each age group.

Careers. Each boy receives advice from the Careers and UCAS department at those points when subject choices should be made. The School is a member of Inspiring Futures, who provide Morrisby testing and interviews as part of the Fifth Year curriculum. A Higher Education Fair is held annually and there are advice evenings for parents and pupils on Sixth Form choices and on university decision-making.

Pastoral Care. Pastoral provision is embedded within the day-to-day life of the School, through Form Tutors, Heads of Year, School Nurses and outstanding counsellors. A well-established mentoring system provided by our Sixth Formers, provides much-valued pupil to pupil support to our Lower School boys. Pupils' wellbeing is of paramount importance and focus on adolescent mental health has strengthened in recent years supported by our expert on-site School Counsellors, annual wellbeing surveys and bespoke PSHE sessions.

The newly-developed PSHE provision also plays a pivotal role focusing on six specific strands: Health & Wellbeing, Relationships and Sex Education, Digital Wellbeing, Living in the Wider World, Universities & Careers, and the Hampton Curriculum. We host a range of speakers covering a broad range of topics, including sex and relationships, gender equality, mental health, gaming, and safe driving. We are also adding a series of pupil-led sessions, including a session in collaboration with neighbouring girls' school Lady Eleanor Holles.

At Hampton, Mindfulness and Wellbeing education is a compulsory, timetabled part of the curriculum for our boys.

The School also runs a LGBTQ+ group and a Diversity & Inclusion group.

Societies. The very active Adventure Society provides opportunities for kayaking, climbing, orienteering, camping and expeditions both in the UK and abroad. An exceptionally large number of boys undertake The Duke of Edinburgh's Award – Gold and Silver.

The musical programme is extremely rich and varied and includes a New Boys' Concert, two Christmas Concerts in addition to a Carol Service, Jazz in the Park, a Summer Concert and two Rock Concerts. The School's 45-strong male-voice choir Voices of Lions perform annually at the Edinburgh Fringe, regularly attracting audiences of over 100 per day. 30% of pupils take lessons in School on at least one instrument, with a significant number of these learning more than one; in addition there are over 35 ensembles and choirs that perform regularly. The Joint Choral Society, with the neighbouring LEH, gives a performance of a major choral work annually. There are numerous drama productions, with at least one dramatic production each term, and also an annual musical. In all these activities, as in the Community Service work, the School enjoys close cooperation with LEH. Hampton is also an All-Steinway school.

A programme of visiting outside speakers, 'Talk!', is open to pupils and members of the local community. Recent contributors include Olivier Evans (leading civil servant), Biologist and wildlife photographer David Fettes, Diplomat and Former Ambassador to Germany and France, Sir Christopher Mallaby, British climber Neil Gresham and BBC Foreign Correspondent Nick Bryant. During the national lockdowns we hosted virtual events with celebrity and author Gyles Brandreth and ITV News at Ten anchor Julie Etchingham.

There is an extensive range of 100+ co-curricular clubs and societies, among which Chess, Beekeeping, Debating, Lego Robotics, Drone Club and The Writers' Room are particularly strong.

The pupil-led campaign group, Genocide80Twenty, aims to raise awareness of recent genocides among younger people and attracts national and international plaudits from politicians, journalists and public figures.

Admission. Boys are usually admitted to the School into the First Year (Year 7), Third Year (Year 9) and the Sixth Form. Approximately 160 boys join the First Year at 11+ each September and a further 40–45 join the Third Year at 13+. A small number join the Sixth Form each year.

Candidates for entry at 11+ and 13+ sit the School's own entrance examination when they are in Year 6. Approximately half of those who sit the assessments are invited for interview and a confidential reference is sought from the current Head. A 10+ Advance Place exam is open to boys in Year 5 for deferred entry to the

First Year (Year 7) and a further Pre-test is held in Year 7 for those who sat the Year 6 Pre-test for 13+ entry without gaining an offer, as well as to those who have not sat before. Full details regarding admissions procedures are provided on the School's website.

Boys may also be admitted to fill occasional vacancies at other ages at the discretion of The Headmaster. Further details may be obtained from the Head of Admissions (Tel: 020 8979 9273).

Fees per term (2023–2024). £8,240 inclusive of books and stationery.

Scholarships and Bursaries. Hampton welcomes applications from boys whose parents cannot afford fees (in full or in part) and the School awards a significant number of bursaries each year. The Hampton School Trust is fully committed to continuing to increase the number of transformative bursaries (i.e. free places) at the School for boys whose parents cannot pay any fees. The value of the award, which may be up to 110% of the tuition fees, is related to a family's financial circumstances. In addition, a growing number of transformative Fitzwygram Foundation free place Scholarships are awarded each year. The Fitzwygram Foundation, established as a separate linked charity in 2016, works alongside the School to increase the number of free places offered to boys of families in genuine need. All Fitzwygram Foundation Scholars receive full fee remission and additional financial assistance with other costs (e.g. coach travel, lunches, uniform, School trips).

Scholarships (remitting between 5% and 15%, and in exceptional circumstances, 25% of tuition fees) are awarded for academic merit and to boys demonstrating exceptional ability in art, chess, drama, music and sport at 11+ and 13+. Choral Scholarships, awarded in conjunction with the Chapel Royal, Hampton Court Palace, are also available at 11+ entry.

Further details on all Awards may be obtained from the Admissions Office.

Hampton School Alumni. Hamptonians join a successful global alumni network of 11,500+. The lifelong relationship with the School provides opportunities for mentoring and a programme of alumni events. The Alumni Office is located in the heart of the School and regularly welcomes Hamptonians back to their School.

Charitable status. Hampton School is a Registered Charity, number 1120005.

Governors:
Chairman: A H Munday, LLB, KC
R G Alexander, MA Oxon, OH (1989)
O J C Boardman, OH (1996)
S A Bull, BSc, ACA
Mrs E M L Cremin, BA Hons
J A Gore-Randall, MA Cantab
M J Grieveson, BA Hons, FRICS
R J Harris, MA Cantab, KC FRSA
Revd B R Lovell, BEng Hons, BA Hons, MA
R Mercer, BA Hons, PGCE
D N Rey, BA Hons, OH (1988)
F A Steadman, MEd
C P Walsh, BSc, FCA, CFA, OH (1996)
L H Welch, BArch Hons, RIBA, RIAS
M A Woolhouse, FCMA, CGMA, OH (1989)
A Yandle, MA Oxon

Clerk to the Governors: M A King, BSc (*Bursar*)

OH – *Old Hamptonian*

Senior Leadership Team:

***Headmaster*: Kevin Knibbs**, MA Oxon

Deputy Heads:
Dr Sarah A Hendry, PhD
Pippa Z S Message, BSc
J Owen Morris, MA Cantab
Mark A J Nicholson, BA

Assistant Heads:
Dr J C Flanagan, PhD
Miss P A Holmes, BSc
Mr R T Scarratt, MA Cantab
Mr S A Wilkinson, MA Oxon

Bursar: Mike A King, BSc

Departmental Staff:
* *Head of Department*

Art:
*Karen A Williams, BA
Adrian J Bannister, MA
L A Carolan, BA
Stephanie Kirby, BA
Joanna G Moore, MA Cantab
Jerry Blighton (*Technician*)

Biology:
*Phil H Langton, BSc, Dip EnvSci (*Head of Tennis*)
Guy K Baker, MBiochem Oxon (*Head of Lower Sixth, Online Safeguarding Officer*)
Joseph B Cumberbatch, BSc
Richard J Davieson, BSc (*Online Safeguarding Officer*)
E Eamens, MA
Victoria Halford, MSc (*Head of PSHE and eSafety*)
Sarah Hendry, PhD (*Deputy Head*)
Polly A Holmes, BSc (*Assistant Head, Deputy Designated Safeguarding Lead*)
Katya L Martin, MA Oxon
Pippa Z S Message, BSc (*Deputy Head, Designated Safeguarding Officer*)
Harry Moore, BSc (*Asst Head of Third Year*)
E Towler, BSc
Janice Green (*Senior Technician*)
Milagrosa Estavillo (*Technician*)

Chemistry:
*Mr D A Mitchell, BSc
David Schofield, MA Oxon (*Asst Head of Careers & UCAS*)
Neil J I Double, BSc (*Asst Head of Upper Sixth*)
Aidan Doyle, BSc (*Asst Head of Careers & UCAS*)
Anthony F Ellison, BSc
J C Flanagan, PhD (*Assistant Head*)
Polly A Holmes, BSc (*Assistant Head, Deputy Designated Safeguarding Lead*)
S Y James, BA Cantab
Vonn Jimenez, MSci
J Francesca Knibbs, BSc
Jonathan Neville, MChem (*Head of Fifth Year*)
Lelja Puljic, DPhil
Delith Wainer (*Technician*)
S Masterson, MA (*Technician*)
A Meyers (*Assistant Technician*)

Classics:
*J Wesley Barber, MA Oxon
A R Hall, MA (*Asst Head of Fifth Year*)
V O Berezhnoi, MA
A H Jacobs, MA
Amy Winstock, BA Oxon
Alex Ziegler, MPhil Cantab (*Asst Head of First Year*)

Computer Science:
*Gordon Clark, BSc
C H Hui, BEng
Tanya Scorer, BSc
Vincent Ting, MSc
Y H Wong, BSc

Design & Engineering:
*Jason Holdaway, BEng
J A Lee, BSc
S McKitrick, MEng
Diane C Woodward, BSc
S Zannettou, BSc
A [Tony] Barun (*Technician*)
Oliver Keattch (*Technician*)

Drama:
*A E Jones, BA
N C Richardson, BA
Elizabeth Tiller, BA (*Asst Head of Second Year*)
C S Watkins, BA

Economics:
*Ski Paraskos, MA Oxon
E C Astrup, BA
Alexandra M Hopton, MA
Cem Kandemir, BSc
Eileen Mullan, BSc
Tom F Rigby, BA (*Joint Head of Third Year*)

English:
*Catherine E Rigby, BA
I H Alexander, BA
Michael M Baker, MA
Tessa Bartholomew, BA (*Asst Head of Lower Sixth*)
Martha B Bedford, BA (*Joint Head of Third Year*)
Caroline Ruth Bellingan, BA
M J Bradley, MA
Toby Green, BA (*Asst Head of Third Year*)
Will S Leafe, BA (*Asst Head of Fourth Year*)
Alexandra C McLusky, BA
Carli Minchin, BA
Rachel L Morse
R E Pickford Scienti, BA
Victoria Whitwam, BA Cantab (*Arts' Award Coordinator*)
J J Willoughby, BA

Geography:
*T M Townshend, BA
Charlotte Brown, BA (*Asst Head of Fifth Year*)
C A Harrison, MA
Frances Highton, MA
R Hill, MSc (*Asst Head of Second Year*)
Thomas E Hill, BA (*Joint Head of First Year*)
Ladea Michelsen, BSc (*Joint Form Charity Co-ordinator*)
E M Murfin, MA

History:
*O G Roberts, BA
Caroline R Bellingan
Martin P Cross, BA
J R Fryer, MA
Shelley Ann Havord, MA
Kevin Knibbs, MA Oxon (*Headmaster*)
Andy J Lawrence, BA Oxon
J Owen Morris, MA Cantab (*Deputy Head, Designated Safeguarding Lead*)
Jim Parrish, BA (*Head of Lower Sixth*)
H E Partridge, BA (*Asst Head of Lower Sixth*)
Jennifer L Peattie, BA (*Joint Head of First Year*)
Victoria M Smith, BA (*Joint Head of Third Year, Deputy Designated Safeguarding Lead*)
Sarah Willcox, MA

Learning Support:
*Caroline Conway
Nicola Day, BEd
Sylvia Garrido-Soriano, BA (*Academic Extension & Think! Coordinator KS3*)
Caroline King (*Cover Supervisor*)
Sian Reeve, BA (*Cover Supervisor*)
J Moffitt, ACIS (*Learning Support & SEN Administrator*)
A Veliu, BA

Library:
*Karl Hemsley, MA
Emma Rommer (*Joint Form Charities Coordinator*)

Mathematics:
*J R Archer, MMath Oxon
C A Alishaw, BA
Christopher G Aubrey, MA Oxon
Gareth Bailey, BSc
Ami Banerjee, MBA (*Head of Cricket*)
Jon Barnes, BSc (*KS5 Mathematics Co-ordinator*)
S P Bracken, Higher Diploma
Adrienne S Burke
Hannah Clarke, BSc
Anna Czumaj, BSc (*KS3 Mathematics Co-ordinator*)
A J Dalton, BA
E Delamare, BSc
Bernadette K Frith, BSc
Daniel Griller, BA Cantab (*Oxbridge and Olympiad Coordinator*)
George R Haynes, BSc
A W Kershaw, BSc
C J Lee, BSc
Hannah M Mason, MA
Caroline H Reyner, MSc Oxon
M O Rudajev, MEd
Christopher M Schurch, BSc
Verity Short, MA Cantab
Nick Stebbings, BEng (*Asst Head of Lower Sixth*)
Rohit R Trivedi, MA Cantab (*KS4 Mathematics Coordinator*)
Nivetha Vasanthakumar, BSc
M J Waldon, MSc
Marta Watson-Evans, MA (*KS5 Coordinator*)

Modern Languages:
*T R Aucutt, BA
Isabell Jacobson, BA (*Head of Spanish*)
Katya White, BA (*Head of Russian*)
Katherine Willett-Pecnik, BA Oxon (*Head of German*)
Yi Hong Zhang, MA (*Head of Mandarin*)
Christopher J Blachford, BA
Margaret Chandler, MA

M J Ciechanowicz, MA Cantab (*Asst Head of Careers & UCAS*)
Maria Doncel-Cervantes, BA
A E Embiricos, BA
L Fan
Silvia Garrido-Soriano, BA (*Academic Extension & Think! Coordinator KS3*)
Charles Malston, BA (*Head of Fourth Year*)
Sophie E May, BA Oxon (*Asst Head of Careers & UCAS*)
Jill C Owen, BA (*Head of Second Year*)
H L Peel, MA
Philipp Studt, MA (*Asst Head of Fifth Year*)
G J Todd, BA
Sophie C Yoxon, MA
Joan Herrero Burguillos (*Spanish Assistant*)
M F Conques (*French Assistant*)
C Cox (*French Assistant*)
Yulia Isaeva (*Russian Conversation*)
S Lenck (*German Assistant*)
D J Porras (*Spanish Assistant*)

Music:
*Daniel E Roland, MusB
James C Ferrier, BA
Sarah Mattinson, BA
Ewan J Zuckert, BMus (*Asst Head of Lower Sixth*)

Personal, Health & Social Education:
*Victoria Halford, MSc
D Fuldner, MSc (*Asst Head of First Year*)
G R Haynes, BSc
Rebecca J Nicholson, MPhys Oxon (*Asst Head of PHSE and eSafety*)
R J Singleton, BEng (*Asst Head of Fifth Year*)

Physics:
*Mark G Yates, PhD
Gordon H Clark, BSc (*Head of Computer Science*)
Dan J Fendley, BEng (*Senior Tutor, Induction Tutor*)
Daan Fuldner, MSc (*Asst Head of First Year*)
Stephen Gray, BSc
Rebecca J Nicholson, MPhys Oxon (*Asst Head of PHSE and eSafety*)
Christine Reilly, MSc
Rebecca Singleton, BEng (*Acting Joint Head of PSHE, Asst Head of Fifth Year*)
T L Walsh, MPhys
Amy White, MA Cantab
Tim E Wilson, MPhys
Ollie M Worrall, MSc (*Cantab*)
David A Hughes, HNC (*Senior Technician*)
Rebecca Galan (*Technician*)

Politics:
*W S Leafe, BA
Jenny A Field, MA Cantab
Will S Leafe, BA (*Asst Head of Fourth Year*)
Tom F Rigby, BA (*Joint Head of Third Year*)

Psychology:
*Rachael O'Connor, MA (*Acting Head of Psychology*)
M Fakatou, BSC
Holly Peck, MSc

Religious Studies & Philosophy:
*Ben Clark, MSt
E C Holt, BA
Mark A J Nicholson, BA (*Assistant Head, Deputy Designated Safeguarding Lead*)
M L Parkes, MA
R T Scarratt, MA Cantab (*Assistant Head*)
Rupert Vann-Alexander, BA
S Andrew Wilkinson, MA Oxon (*Assistant Head, Head of Careers & UCAS*)

Sport and PE:
*Carlos Mills, BSc (*Director of Sport*)
Andrew Beattie, BSc (*Director of Rugby*)
David Burke, BEd (*Director of Football*)
Colin Greenaway (*Director of Rowing*)
H P Hooper, BA (*Acting Head of Specialist Sports*)
M K Sims, BSc (*Head of PE, Sports Rehabilitation*)
G J Todd, BA (*Head of Tennis*)
C Hurst (*Asst Director of Football*)
S John (*Head of Outdoor Pursuits & Duke of Edinburgh Award*)
J Butler (*Senior Rowing Coach*)
T Crook (*Outdoor Activities Specialist*)
Geoffrey Jones (*Boatman*)
P Hope (*Rowing Coach*)
Harry Perry (*Rowing Coach*)
A Ward (*Rowing Coach*)
J Hood, MSc (*Sports Assistant, Cover Supervisor*)
D E Boyes, BSc (*Graduate Sports Assistant, Cover Supervisor*)
D C Towl, BSc (*Graduate Sports Assistant, Cover Supervisor*)

Administrative Staff:
Examinations Officer: Michelle Barnes
Headmaster's PA: Clare Espley, BA
Head of Admissions & Marketing: Dorothy Jones, BA, Dip Mar
Admissions Assistants: Karen Saul; A White
School Nurses: S Rivers; Elizabeth Searle; A Johnson-Adegoke

Harrow School

Harrow on the Hill, Middlesex HA1 3HP

Tel:	+44 (0)20 8872 8000 (Enquiries)
	+44 (0)20 8872 8003 (Head Master)
	+44 (0)20 8872 8007 (Admissions)
	+44 (0)20 8872 8320 (Bursar)
email:	harrow@harrowschool.org.uk
website:	www.harrowschool.org.uk

Mottos: *Stet Fortuna Domus* (May the fortune of the house stand); *Donorum dei dispensatio fidelis* (The faithful stewardship of the gifts of God).

Harrow School is a full-boarding school for boys aged 13 to 18. It was founded in 1572, under a royal charter from Queen Elizabeth I, by a local landowning farmer, John Lyon, whose original intention was to provide 30 boys of the parish with a classical education. Today, the School's purpose is to prepare boys with diverse backgrounds and abilities for a life of learning, leadership, service and personal fulfilment; distinguished Old Harrovians include seven British prime ministers and the first prime minister of India, Pandit Nehru, as well as poets and writers as diverse as Byron, Sheridan and Richard Curtis. This statement of purpose is borne out through our various areas of activity: teaching that helps boys achieve their best academically, pastoral care that matures them both emotionally and spiritually, and an extra-curricular programme that develops their characters and interests. The School's 324 acres have a collegiate feel, its historical architecture complemented by modern buildings that meet its pupils' developing needs. Approximately 840 boys attend Harrow, from across the UK and further afield.

Academic. Harrovians routinely progress into higher education that ranks among the best the world has to offer. The vast majority of boys who go to university attend either Oxbridge, Russell Group or well-known international institutions, particularly in the USA. These include Stanford, Harvard, Yale, Princeton and Cornell. Following 2022 A Level results, Harrovians will be attending six of the world's top ten universities, including Oxford, Cambridge and Ivy League institutions, and nearly 130 Harrovians are taking up places at Russell Group universities. However, no two Harrovians are the same: some live in London, others much further afield in the UK or overseas; a number come from established Harrow families, others have no experience of public schooling; many excel in sport or the arts, others are very strong academically. What Harrovians experience through their extra-curricular activities, and by leading and serving others, are just as important as their lessons.

The Super-Curriculum. Beyond the examination syllabus, our Super-Curriculum focuses on the aspects of scholarship that are not formally assessed: habitual reading, independent research, reflection and debate. Central to this is the electives system, in which boys select a challenging off-syllabus course that is taught in small groups. These courses promote lateral thinking, problem-solving and the articulation of profound thought, while also allowing boys to lead their own learning. On virtually every night of the week, there are seminars and society meetings, and we are able to attract eminent speakers from all walks of life to enrich and broaden the boys' experience of academic and cultural life.

Boarding. Our leafy 300-acre estate contains 12 Boarding Houses. The buildings are quite individual, with their own gardens and facilities, helping to set each one apart. The Houses inspire fierce loyalty from the boys and old boys, who take pride in their own part of Harrow. House Masters and their families live in the Houses, and are assisted by an Assistant House Master, Matron, Year Group Tutors and Health Education Tutors. In addition, the chaplaincy, full-time psychologist and pastoral support committee provide further layers of nurturing and support. Approximately 70 boys live in in each House. There are no dormitories: a boy shares his room with a boy of the same age for the first year or so, and thereafter has a room to himself. Every boy has a computer in his room and each House has common rooms and shared kitchens. All teachers live in the School. Typically, for the first two weekends of a term, all pupils are in the School. If they are able to, parents come and visit. On the third weekend – an exeat – all pupils go home or to friends; the weekend starts around noon on Friday and ends at 9.00pm on Sunday. The next two weekends are followed by a nine-day half term.

Sport. With afternoon games available in around 30 sports, five times a week, sporting fixtures against other schools and the chance to compete regularly in House matches, boys are kept healthy and active. Under the expert guidance of some of the country's leading coaches, boys develop their skills, character and confidence. Through games such as rugby, soccer, cricket and Harrow football, they learn how to be team players. Equal emphasis is placed on the many individual sports offered here that cultivate resilience, self-discipline and enjoyment. Surrounded by acres of sports fields, AstroTurf pitches, a golf course, swimming pool, sports centre, tennis, rackets and fives courts, Harrow has a breadth of sporting opportunities. Our elite sportsmen have an impressive record of achieving excellent standards and some go on to enjoy successful, professional sporting careers. Unique occasions like the annual cricket match versus Eton provide memorable highlights in the School year.

The Arts. The arts are an extremely important part of Harrow's packed calendar of activities. Whether it's learning a musical instrument, playing in orchestras and ensembles, singing in choirs or in houses, performing in plays or discovering beauty in fine art, sculpture and ceramics, the opportunity for creative expression at Harrow not only sets our boys on a lifetime of personal enrichment and enjoyment, but also teaches them to be more self-disciplined, attentive and better at planning and organising their busy lives. Boys who participate in the vast spectrum of Harrow's creative and performing arts also find that this involvement has a broader, more beneficial effect on their overall academic performance. By encouraging boys to perform in the highest-quality School and house concerts, plays and competitions, we see them finding their own voice and the confidence to express their individual creativity, regardless of innate talent.

After Harrow. Virtually all of our boys take up places at selective universities. Boys who are heading towards Oxbridge, Ivy League and other competitive institutions are given specific guidance and preparation from their House Masters and our dedicated Universities Team.

The Harrow Association, Harrow's Old Boys' Society, has a thriving membership of over 10,000. Tel: 020 8872 8200, email: ha@harrowschool.org.uk.

Admission. Boys are typically admitted for entry at 13 and a smaller number at 16. Visit www.harrowschool.org.uk/admissions/admissions-home for more information.

Fees per term (2023–2024). £16,850, including board, tuition, textbooks, a stationery allowance and laundry. For any subject requiring additional tuition, there is an extra charge.

Scholarships and Bursaries. A large number of scholarships are awarded every year. Scholarships have a value of 5% of the fee and are held throughout a boy's time at Harrow, subject to satisfactory performance. Boys may apply for more than one of the different types of scholarship, which include Academic, Music, Art, Sport and Outstanding Talent. Boys do not necessarily need to be awarded a scholarship to be considered for a bursary. In this case, bursary support is considered for strong candidates upon application to the School. Sometimes, candidates will be asked to achieve a scholarship to be eligible for a bursary. More than 10% of boys in the School receive support with their fees.

Charitable status. The School is constituted as a Royal Charter Corporation known as The Keepers and Governors of the Possessions Revenues and Goods of the Free Grammar School of John Lyon, which is a Registered Charity, number 310033.

Senior Management Team:

***Head Master*: W M A Land**, MA

Deputy Head Master: S Harrison, PhD

Director of Studies: C E G Bailey, BA, FCCT

Director of Pastoral Care: S Taylor

Director of Safeguarding: Dr D R Wendelken, BA, MPhil, PhD

Academic and Universities Director: Ms H R Fox, MA

Director of Shaftesbury Enterprise: T M Dalton, BSc

Registrar: Dr E R Sie, BSc, PhD, CChem

Bursar: J Wood

Chief Executive of the Harrow Development Trust: D L Collins

Director of Operations: R G Arundell

Highgate School

North Road, London N6 4AY

Tel: 020 8347 3564 (Admissions)
email: admissions@highgateschool.org.uk
website: www.highgateschool.org.uk
X/Twitter: @highgate1565
Facebook: @HighgateSchoolLondon
LinkedIn: /school/highgate-school

Motto: *Altiora in votis*

Founded over 450 years ago, Highgate is one of the UK's leading co-educational independent schools, located close to Highgate village and Hampstead Heath. Our Senior School was awarded the *Sunday Times* London Independent Secondary School of the Decade in 2021 and was placed in the Top 10 independent London schools and Top 20 national schools in the 2024 *Sunday Times* Schools Guide.

Our pupils come from a diverse range of backgrounds across North London and beyond and attend our Pre-Preparatory School (ages 4–7), Junior School (ages 7–11) and Senior School, including the Sixth Form (ages 11–18). Our Senior School was awarded The Sunday Times London Independent Secondary School of the Decade in 2021.

Our teachers are enthusiastic, experienced and well-qualified subject specialists. Pastoral care is at the heart of all we do, and we provide extensive co-curricular activities, including sport, music and drama.

Our School has three principal aims:

- To be a place for learning and scholarship

Learning at Highgate is not about meeting other people's expectations but discovering and pursuing intellectual passions. Helping pupils pursue subjects they love gives them the experiences of using discretionary effort to succeed and makes them brilliantly employable: they choose to go beyond to fulfil their own dreams.

- To be a reflective community

We encourage our pupils to take responsibility for themselves and for their role in society. Through community action groups, volunteering, fundraising, bursaries, local school partnerships and sustainability actions, we strive together as a School to make a positive impact on the world around us.

- To be an exemplar for the healthy life

We want our pupils to enjoy their childhood to the full, to develop and pursue their academic and co-curricular passions, and to lead fulfilling exciting lives as thoughtful and open-minded young adults. Pupils leaving school will be intellectually, emotionally and practically equipped for the world of work and the challenges of day-to-day life.

Admissions. Prospective pupils are assessed at the different entry points. Pre-Prep children are invited to a group assessment; Junior School entry is normally at the age of 7, with candidates taking an entrance examination, with a proportion interviewed in groups. For pupils joining our Senior School at 11, there are tests and a significant proportion are then interviewed. Pupils from other schools are admitted to our Sixth Form following an interview. We offer means-tested bursaries at 7+, 11+ and 16+ and music scholarships (11+ and 16+).

Wellbeing is at the heart of our school. We understand that developing the whole person, a child who feels happy, healthy and confident in themselves, with skills to manage ups and downs, is of utmost importance, not only during their time here but when they leave and move into the adult world. We nurture confidence and strength of character, supporting pupils to grow and thrive in their emotional, mental and physical health.

Sport and Exercise is taught by specialist coaches and teachers to ensure a high-quality experience with 25 different sporting pathways available. We have a High Performance Programme for top pupil-athletes and currently have 43 pupils playing sport at County level and 9 at National level. Our extensive playing fields are complemented by indoor facilities in the Mallinson Sports Centre which includes a 25-metre swimming pool and sports courts, all-weather pitches for football, netball and hockey and cricket nets. We are fortunate to be within a short distance of Hampstead Heath for walks and cross country running.

Co-curricular activities provide countless opportunities for pupils to have fun, make new friends and learn something new. With over 150 clubs, societies and activities to choose from and that continue to evolve and develop in response to the changing interests of our pupils and the world around us.

Community partnerships are integral to our school's ethos. We encourage pupils to play an active role in their community, both in school and wider society. Within the Senior School, there are several pupil working groups to help steer and drive initiatives, along with a wide-reaching programme of community engagement, from volunteering with local charities to fundraising events.

Buildings and Facilities. The main Senior School site is on North Road and combines historic buildings (Chapel, central classrooms and Sir Martin Gilbert Library) with modern facilities such as a 200-seat auditorium, music recital spaces, drama studio, science laboratories, modern language classrooms, and ICT suites. Our Mills Centre for Art and Design on Bishopswood Road provides studio and gallery space, with facilities for printmaking, sculpture and filmmaking, plus an IT suite for graphics and computer aided design. The well-equipped design and engineering workshops features 3D printers, laser cutters, an electro-pneumatic lap and an automotive workshop.

Junior School is on Bishopswood Road in a spacious, modern building which opened in 2016. Offering specialist facilities for computing, science, art, DTE, drama and music, as well as a large retractable-seat hall, outside play spaces and a small amphitheatre.

Pre-Prep School is on Bishopswood Road in an airy and colourful building which underwent an extension and refurbishment in 2022. Overlooking our sports grounds, pupils benefit from their own playground, dining hall, a library with enclosed terrace, and secure area to observe a green planted roof. Within the safety of our grounds, we have a woodland area where pupils explore the natural world through Forest School lessons.

Transport links include several bus routes and the Northern line on London Underground, with central London 15–20 minutes away. We also offer a school bus service for Junior and Senior School pupils.

Pupil Numbers. 1,930 (985 boys, 945 girls).

Fees per term (2023–2024). Senior School: £8,505; Junior School: £7,800; Pre-Preparatory School: £7,365 (Reception–Year 2).

Bursaries. Our website has further information about applying for bursary places and our Admissions team can answer any specific questions.

Charitable status. Highgate School is a Registered Charity, number 312765

Chair of Governors: Bob Rothenberg, MBE, BA, FCA, CTA

***Head*: A S Pettitt**, MA

Hill House School

Sixth Avenue, Auckley, Doncaster, South Yorkshire DN9 3GG

Tel: 01302 776300
email: info@hillhouse.doncaster.sch.uk
website: www.hillhouse.doncaster.sch.uk
X/Twitter: @HillHouseSchool
Facebook: @hillhouseschool
Instagram: @hillhouseschool
LinkedIn: /school/hill-house-school-doncaster

Hill House was founded in 1912 and occupies the site of the former RAF Officers' Quarters of RAF Finningley. The school provides a seamless, fully co-educational day education from age 3 to 18, and aims to provide a top-class holistic education where extracurricular success and personal development stand alongside academic excellence.

Number of pupils. There are 800 pupils, with an equal number of boys and girls.

Education. Children enter the School at 3 years of age via Nursery where structured play and learning are the order of the day. As children progress through the School there is a gradual change to subject-based teaching in specialist rooms, in preparation for GCSEs at 16 and A Levels at 18. Upon leaving the Junior School, children enter a full house system for pastoral care. All main school subjects are offered, including individual Sciences, French, Spanish and Latin.

Facilities. The school is based in an historic building with new, purposely renovated classrooms. The site includes a large hall, dining room and theatre. In 2011, Hill House Sixth Form was launched, housed in its own new Sixth Form Centre, including classrooms, coffee shop and large common room. A new Music School contains practice rooms, a recording studio and a performing studio. 2013 saw the opening of the school's sports grounds at Blaxton, where a new Sports' Pavilion opened in Lent 2023. In 2015, the blue AstroTurf Paver Hockey Pitch was opened, and in 2017 a new Dining Hall was created. In 2023, a new Pavilion was opened at Blaxton Sports Grounds.

Extracurricular activities. Music, Drama, Art and Sport play an important part in the life of the School. Throughout the year, over 100 academic, recreational, musical and sporting activities per week are also offered in extracurricular time. The major sports undertaken include rugby, netball, hockey, cricket, and tennis. There is a competitive fixture list including a number of overseas tours. There are four orchestras and five choirs within the school, who enjoy the newly built Music School. Drama productions and concerts are undertaken on a regular basis. Residential trips and sports tours are undertaken at most age levels.

The School day. School opens at 8.00 am, with lessons from 8.40 am to 4.00 pm. Activities run from 4.00 pm, and a before- and after-school club operates from 7.30 am and until 6.00 pm. The school operates a five-day week, with a full games afternoon for all ages above 7. There are some activities and fixtures at weekends. Sixth Formers also have an Enrichment Afternoon, where they spend time exploring university admissions and undertaking internships at local businesses, hospitals, etc.

Fees per term (2023–2024). £3,467–£5,333 according to age. Fees include lunch and most extras.

Scholarships. Scholarships are available at 11+ for Academic, Sport, Art, Music and Performing Arts, and at 16+ for Academic and Leadership.

Charitable status. Hill House School Limited is a Registered Charity, number 529420.

Governors:
Mrs J Fearns (*Chair*)
Mrs R Blakemore
Dr A Cooper
N Ebden
A Joshi
R Leggott
A Ogley
Dr J Pickering
Dr K Rao
J Sprenger

***Headmaster*: David Holland**, MA Cantab

Head of Senior School: Mrs Caroline Rogerson, BSc Hons
Head of Junior School: Mr Jonathan Hall, BEd Hons
Deputy Head of Senior School: Mrs Helen Jones, MA Cantab
Second Master: Mr Simon Hopkinson, BA Hons
Senior Mistress: Mrs Christine Havard, BA Hons
Deputy Head of Junior School: Mrs Charlotte Leach, BA Ed Hons

Bursar and Clerk to the Governors: Mrs Karen Wigglesworth, ACMA Hons

Heads of Departments:
Mr Mark Birch, MA (*English*)
Mr Mark Brannan, BSc Hons (*Science*)
Mr Victoria Bodman, BA Hons (*Practical Music*)
Miss Jo Chappell, BA Hons (*Religious Studies, Head of Sixth Form*)
Mr Richard Dorman, BA Hons (*History*)
Mr Graham Green, MA (*Geography*)
Mrs Anna Helliwell, BA Hons (*Modern Foreign Languages*)
Ms Heather Lindsay, BA Hons (*Classics*)
Mr Richard Otley, BA Hons (*Business and Economics*)
Mr Samuel Owen BA Hons (*Director of Cricket*)
Mrs Wendy Parkhurst, BA, MA (*Art*)
Mr Christopher Rose, BSc Hons (*Director of Rugby*)
Mrs Mahjabeen Thomas, BSc Hons (*Mathematics*)
Mrs Katie Vickers, BA Hons (*Sport*)

Housemistress (*Field House*): Mrs Susannah Otley, BA Hons
Housemaster (*Master House*): Mr Peter Shipston, BA, MA
Housemistress (*New House*): Mrs Sarah Green, BA Hons
Housemistress (*School House*): Mrs Catherine Mann, BA Hons

Howell's School Llandaff GDST

Cardiff Road, Llandaff, Cardiff CF5 2YD
Tel: 029 2056 2019
email: admissions@how.gdst.net
website: www.howells-cardiff.gdst.net
www.howellscoedcollege.gdst.net
X/Twitter: @HowellsSchool
Facebook: @Officialhowells
Instagram: @howellsschoolgdst
LinkedIn: /howell-s-school-llandaff

See full entry in the **GSA** section, on **p. 441**.

Hulme Grammar School

Chamber Road, Oldham, Lancs OL8 4BX
Tel: 0161 624 4497
email: admin@ohgs.co.uk
website: www.hulmegrammar.org
X/Twitter: @OldhamHulme
Facebook: @hulmegrammarschool
LinkedIn: /hulme-grammar-school

The school, founded in 1611, was reconstituted in the 19th century under the Endowed Schools Act. The main buildings of Hulme Grammar School were opened in 1895 on a commanding south-west facing site overlooking the city of Manchester.

The Oldham Hulme family of schools is renowned for delivering outstanding levels of education at each stage of a child's development. With unbeatable standards and outstanding achievements, the schools cater for boys and girls aged 2 to 18 and offer a caring, orderly and academically stimulating environment.

Life as part of the Hulme family begins at our Pre-Prep School, which sits in a purpose built, modern building. Confidence and a broad, balanced education is then instilled in pupils throughout our flourishing Prep School, our thriving Senior School and finishing at our outstanding Sixth Form, creating well rounded young adults ready to achieve their full potential as they transition into adult life.

At Hulme Grammar, we believe in the power of curiosity, critical thinking, and creativity. Our dedicated teachers are passionate about igniting the spark of curiosity within each student, encouraging them to question, explore, and develop a love for learning that extends far beyond the classroom and which they will carry with them forever.

In the past school year, students at Hulme Grammar School have continued to aim high and achieve higher, with GCSE and A Level grades outperforming many other schools, as well as sporting prowess, with 2 students winning medals at the English Summer National Swimming meet, one student going reporting on the Women's World Cup Final and our Young Entrepreneurs team, Foxglove Papers, reaching the final of the Side Hustle Initiative, winning countless awards in the process.

Beyond individual achievements, the school also raised over £5,500 for charity in the last school year, with events held for a local hospice, a care facility for children with complex disabilities, LGBT+ charities, as well as students volunteering their time to support disabled pilgrims at Lourdes in France.

At Hulme we expect much of our pupils in the classroom. However, we also expect much of them outside of it as well! We take a holistic approach to education and a dynamic and vibrant extra-curricular programme is a key part of what we can offer your child. Our extra-curricular programme is rich and varied and runs across the age range.

We believe that what sets Hulme apart in this regard is the level of participation in our extra-curricular programme – it's not just the preserve of the few. Our PE departments run teams in sports that are too numerous to list here; 115 of our students take instrumental music lessons, our Combined Cadet Force is flourishing and challenges its cadets in a range of exciting ways. We are always looking to add new and interesting clubs to our programme; recent additions include a team for the Moon Camp Challenge, E-Sports, Anime & Japanese club, Robotics club and Eco club. We also encourage healthy competition, with Mock Trials, School Masterchef and Hulme's Got Talent being firm favourites of students.

The pastoral structure is crucial to the support given to our pupils. The form tutor is the first point of call for parents and pupils and each year group has a dedicated head of year supported by the Assistant Principal Pastoral.

We have small forms allowing us to know our pupils well and to give individual care. We are able to respond quickly to issues and are very supportive in our approach. There is close communication with parents and our pupils are nurtured in a caring environment.

We have three school counsellors and a school nurse who augment the pastoral care and the support on offer. We have a peer mentor scheme, reinforced through our PSHE course. We also have Tootoot where students can discuss their problems anonymously and receive immediate support.

We tailor the curriculum to individual needs and circumstances. For example, some year 8 & 9 students have Learning Support in place of a second foreign language. We ensure that the most able students are fully challenged by their academic work. And in the planning of lessons, the aptitudes, needs and prior attainments of pupils are taken into account.

Fees per academic year (2023–2024). Pre-Prep (see website), Prep School £9,840, Senior School and Sixth Form £13,470; International Students £18,000 per annum payable in advance.

A number of bursaries are awarded annually to pupils entering at the ages of 11 and 16. These awards are based on parental income and academic ability and will remain in place for the time in school subject to satisfactory progress by the pupil.

Charitable status. Hulme Grammar School is a Registered Charity, number 526636. It exists to provide a balanced academic education for pupils aged 2 to 18.

Chair: Mrs V Stocker LLB (*Chair of the Steering Committee and contactable via the School's Clerk to the Governors*)
Vice Chair: A Richards BSc Hons (*Child Protection Governor*)

Elected Governors:
Mr J Greenwood, BA Hons, MRICS, MCIOB (*Chair of the Property Committee*)
Mr R S Illingworth, BSc Hons (*Acting Treasurer*)
Mr W Ley ICAA, BCOM (*Chair of the Finance & Commercial Committee*)
Mr R Lobley, MRICS (*Chair of the Health, Safety & Environment Committee*)
Mr D Spencer, FPFS, IMC
Mr J Sutcliffe, BA Hons, MEd
Mr G Wheeldon, CDir, FIoD
Representative Governors Metropolitan Borough of Oldham: Dr Z Chauhan, MD, MRCGP

School Leadership Team 2023–2024:
***Principal*: Mr T Oulton**, MA Oxford
Mrs N Duncalf AAT, FCCA (*Director of Finance and Operations*)
Miss N Begley MA Middlesex, BSc Limerick (*Director of Marketing, Admissions and Communications*)
Mr R B Hobson-Williams, BSc Leeds (*Assistant Principal Additional Needs, DDSL*)
Mrs A Berry BSc Nottingham (*Assistant Principal Sixth Form, DDSL*)
Mr A H Marshall, BSc Hull (*Deputy Principal – Pastoral, DDSL*)
Mr M C Jones, MPhys Manchester (*Deputy Principal – Academic*)
Dr C R Millington, BSc, DPhil, MEd Durham, Oxford, Cambridge (*Assistant Principal Outreach, Head of Year 13*)
Miss R L Turner, BSc Loughborough (*Assistant Principal – Academic*)

Senior School Leadership Team 2023–2024:
Mr J C Budding, BEd Sheffield Hallam (*Head of Senior School – DSL*)
Mr N P Buckley, BA Sheffield (*Senior Pastoral Lead Years 10 & 11, Business Studies and Economics*)
Miss L Lavin, BSc Manchester Metropolitan (*Senior Pastoral Lead Years 7–9, Biology*)
Mr S Norbury, BSc Liverpool John Moores (*Senior Teacher Digital Strategy*)
Mrs R Ford, BA Leeds (*Senior Teacher Co-Curriculum, Physical Education*)

Prep School Leadership Team 2023–2024:
Mrs Z Ward, LLB Liverpool (*Head of Prep School*)
Mrs A Thorpe, BA Lancaster (*Deputy Head of Prep School*)
Miss K V Evans, BA Sheffield Hallam (*Assistant Head of Prep EYFS*)

Hurstpierpoint College Senior School and Sixth Form

A Woodard School

College Lane, Hurstpierpoint, West Sussex BN6 9JS
Tel: 01273 833636
email: admissions@hppc.co.uk
website: www.hppc.co.uk
X/Twitter: @Hurst_College
Facebook: @HurstCollege
Instagram: @hurst_college
LinkedIn: /school/hurstpierpoint-college

Motto: *Beati mundo corde*

Founded 1849 by Nathaniel Woodard, Canon of Manchester.

Hurstpierpoint College is a co-educational day and boarding school for pupils aged between 4 and 18 years. There are currently 507 boys and 433 girls in the Senior School and Sixth Form, 50% of whom are boarders.

The school is truly co-educational throughout. Boarding is a particularly popular option. In their Upper Sixth year at Hurst, students join St John's House—a co-educational day and boarding house where, appropriately supervised, they enjoy greater freedom and are encouraged to further develop their independent learning skills in preparation for university.

Buildings and Facilities. At the heart of the school's large country campus lie the core school buildings and Chapel arranged around three attractive quadrangles built of traditional Sussex knapped flint. Key facilities nearby include three floodlit AstroTurfs, an art school, sports hall, music school, dance and drama studios, 320-seat theatre, indoor swimming pool, and Medical Centre. The extensive grounds are laid mainly to playing fields and include one of the largest and most attractive school cricket pitches in the country.

Chapel. As a Woodard School, Hurstpierpoint has a Christian foundation and underpinned by Christian values, although pupils of other faiths or of no faith are warmly welcomed. Pupils attend up to three assemblies during the week. The main Eucharist takes place early on Friday evenings. Pupils who wish to do so are prepared in small classes for the annual confirmation taken by one of the bishops of the diocese.

Curriculum. The five-day academic week is structured to allow pupils to study a variety of subject options that can be adapted to suit their natural ability. The Senior School entry year (Shell) provides students with the chance to experience most of our GCSE subjects before they choose their options. In the second year (Remove) and third year (Fifth), the curriculum is split into two parts: core subjects (English, Maths, three sciences) and optional subjects such as Art & Design, Classical Greek, Computer Science, Dance, Drama, Humanities, Modern Foreign Languages, Design Technology, and Latin.

Students entering the Sixth Form study A Levels, with the majority selecting three subjects, and many Sixth Form students take the EPQ as an extension of one of their A Level subjects. The subject choice is wide and in addition to traditional subjects you can choose Economics, Politics, Psychology, and Sociology.

All pupils' work is overseen by academic tutors, and we take particular care to ensure that university applications are properly targeted to suit the students' aspirations and talents.

Games. The College operates a "no-one on the bench" policy that seeks to place pupils in sporting activities most suited to their tastes and abilities. During the first two years they are expected to take part in at least some of the major sports, including rugby, netball, athletics, and hockey, but thereafter a greater element of choice occurs. A varied array of sporting activities makes up the wider programme, ranging from equestrian to swimming, mountain biking, and sailing. Recent tours for major sports include to Italy (rugby), Barbados (netball), Dubai (cricket), and South Africa (hockey).

Service Afternoons. From Remove (Year 10) onwards, pupils take part in service activities every week, including Combined Cadet Force (Army, RAF, and RN sections), Community Service, and Environmental Conservation.

Music. There has always been a strong musical tradition at Hurstpierpoint with an orchestra and other more specialised ensembles. A large proportion of the pupils take individual instrumental lessons and give frequent recitals. The Chapel Choir plays a major part in regular worship and there are several other choral groups.

Drama. The Shakespeare Society is the oldest such school society in the country and organises an annual production and an annual musical. Drama covers a wide range and varies from major musicals to more modest House plays and pupil-directed productions. The new 320-seat Bury Theatre also gives the more technically minded ample opportunity to develop stage management, lighting, and sound skills.

Other Activities. The afternoon activity programme includes Art, Climbing, Dance, Self-Defence, Car Maintenance, Girls' Football, Hurst Farm, Robotics, Japanese, LAMDA, Ninjitsu, Shooting, Horse Riding, Polo, Karate, Golf Range, Squash, Clay Pigeon Shooting, Dinghy Sailing, and Surfing, alongside a variety of music clubs and literary clubs.

Fees per term (2023–2024). Senior School: Weekly Boarding £12,340 (Years 9–11), £12,205 (Sixth Form); Flexi Boarding £11,585 (Years 9–11), £11,450 (Sixth Form); Day £9,640 (Years 9–11), £9,505 (Sixth Form).

Scholarships and Bursaries. Awards available at 13+: Academic, Art, Dance, Drama, Music and Sports. Awards available at 16+: Academic, Art, Drama, Music, Sports, and Dance.

Means-tested bursaries may be available to pupils who hold an academic award.

Admission. For 13+ entry, pupils must be registered on the College's list and will sit the Common ISEB Pre-Test in Year 6. Candidates are then invited to attend an assessment day and offers are made following this in March of Year 6.

To matriculate into the Sixth Form at Hurst, pupils require at least 4 Level 7 GCSEs. They should achieve a Level 7 or above in the subjects that they intend to study and, where a pupil wishes to start a new subject which they have not studied before, they need to have achieved a Level 7 or above in a GCSE subject closely related to it (i.e., for Economics, ideally a pupil should have a Level 7 in Maths GCSE). Students should also have a minimum of a Level 5 at GCSE in Mathematics and English.

Please contact the Senior School Admissions Office for further information.

Preparatory School. *See entry in IAPS section.*

Charitable status. Hurstpierpoint College is a Registered Charity, number 1076498. It aims to provide a Christian education to boys and girls between the ages of four and eighteen in the three schools on the campus.

Governors:
Chair: Mr A Jarvis, BEd, MA, FRSA

***Head of College*: Mr Dominic W Mott**, MA Queens' College, Cantab, Spanish
Deputy Head of College: Mr Lloyd P Dannatt, MEng Imperial College, London, Physics
Head of Sixth Form: Mr Brian T Schofield, BA Pembroke College, Oxon, Politics
Head of Middle School: Mr Owain J Jones, MA St Edmund Hall, Oxon, Biology

Hymers College

Hymers Avenue, Hull, East Yorkshire HU3 1LW
Tel: 01482 343555
email: enquiries@hymers.org
website: www.hymerscollege.co.uk
X/Twitter: @Hymers_College
Facebook: @HymersCollege
Instagram: @hymers_college

Hymers College is a co-educational day school offering the very best for young people from the age of 3 to 18 years. Since September 2022 Hymers has owned Hymers Hessle Mount Preparatory School, and together we offer an education from Pre-School through to and including Juniors, Seniors, and Sixth Form, providing supportive pastoral care, outstanding academic teaching, wide-ranging co-curricular activities and first-rate facilities.

Hymers College was originally opened as a school for boys in 1893 when the Reverend John Hymers, Fellow of St John's College Cambridge and Rector of Brandesburton, left money in his will for a school to be built 'for the training of intelligence in whatever social rank of life it may be found among the vast and varied population of the town and port of Hull'. Although the school has remained true to its Founder's intentions through a generous fee remission scheme, the catchment area now stretches across the city of Hull, East Yorkshire and North Lincolnshire, and the School became fully co-educational in 1989.

Number of Pupils. 1026.

Hymers Hessle Mount (Pre-School, Reception, Years 1 and 2) total 83.

The Junior School (Years 3–6 inclusive) has 212 pupils aged 7–11 and offers a full range of academic, sporting, music and co-curricular activities.

The Senior School has 575 pupils aged 12–16 and the Sixth Form has 156 pupils aged 16–18.

Admission is usually by assessment at ages 7, and 11 and 13, together with an interview with the Headteacher. Places may also be available in other year groups. Pupils at Hymers Hessle Mount do not sit an assessment for entry to the Junior School. In addition, pupils in Hymers College Junior School do not sit an assessment for entry to the Senior School.

Almost all pupils qualify for the Sixth Form through GCSE results. Pupils from other schools are admitted to the Sixth Form on the basis of good GCSE results, an interview with the Headmaster and a computer-based assessment.

Pupils are prepared for the GCSE in a broad curriculum including music, business-related subjects, computer science, technology and the arts.

There is a full range of courses leading to A Level examinations, and special preparation is given for Oxford and Cambridge entrance, as well as for medicine, dentistry and veterinary science.

Facilities. Set in 45 acres of grounds the buildings consist of 35 classrooms, 11 specialist laboratories, extensive ICT facilities, audio-visual room, 200-seater theatre, Art/Design Technology Centre, a gymnasium and a large sports hall. There is a specialist music block providing a full range of music facilities including a recital hall, rehearsal and music technology rooms and a recording studio. The award-winning Learning Resources Centre, the most recent building addition to the School, houses a café, library and study area and break out rooms. In recent years the school has refurbished many science laboratories as well as the Sixth Form Common Room and Reception areas. The Junior School building contains 9 classrooms and specialist rooms for music, DT, art and science, along with a library, sports hall and changing rooms. All Senior School pupils are issued with a chromebook and there are class sets of digital devices to enhance the learning of Junior School pupils. The grounds include a recently upgraded all-weather astro pitch, upgraded tennis and netball courts, rugby and cricket pitches and a swimming pool and sports centre including a fitness suite.

Co-curricular Activities. All pupils are strongly encouraged to participate in the very wide range of co-curricular activities and a longer lunch break allows adequate time for pupils to do this. The main school games are rugby, cricket, hockey, netball, tennis and athletics. The school regularly competes at national level and provides members of county and national teams. Many pupils take part in The Duke of Edinburgh's Award scheme and Hymers is the only independent school to host the National Citizen Service (NCS) which encourages a huge amount of community engagement which has led to a national award. Over 80 clubs and activities are offered throughout the School including British Sign Language, water polo, chess, Law Society, debating and Time Capsule Club. Drama is particularly strong, with several productions a year. Music is a major school activity: from full orchestras to choir and chamber groups in each part of the school. Individual tuition is available in most instruments.

Fees per term (2023–2024). Senior School including Sixth Form £4,735; Junior School (Years 3–6) £3,956–£4,182; Hymers Hessle Mount Years 1 and 2 £3,066, Reception £2,738, Pre-School £information available upon request. Hymers Bursaries are typically awarded at ages 11 and 16.

The Old Hymerians' Association, c/o Development Manager, Hymers College, Hull HU3 1LW.

Charitable status. Hymers College is a Registered Charity, number 529820-R. Its aims and objectives are education.

Governors:
Mr J M V Redman, BSc, FIDM, MIOD (*Chair of Governors*)
Mr M P Astell, BEng, MBA, FIMechE, CEng (*Vice Chair*)
Mrs S Anwar West, LLB, LLM
Mr P A B Beecroft, BSc, MA, MBA, FInstP
Professor P G Burgess, BA, MA, PhD Cantab, FRHistS
Mr A H Chicken, BA Hons, MEd
Mr J F Connolly, BSc
Mr D A Gibbons, BSc, MRICS
Mrs G A Greendale
Mr M C S Hall, BSc
Mr J G Leafe
Mrs E A Maliakal, LLB
Mr C M Read, MA Oxon, MRICS
Mr D U Rosinke, BSc, ACA

Mrs N Shipley, FCA
Mrs G V Vickerman, BSc, MSc, MRICS
Mr J R Wheldon, LLB Hons, MRICS, ACI Arb
Mrs E A Wilson, BEd, AGSM

***Headmaster*: Mr J P Stanley**, MA, MBA
Deputy Head (*Management*): Mr R Wright
Deputy Head (*Pastoral*): Mrs H Jackson
Directors of Teaching & Learning: Dr M Pickles and Mr R Simpson
Director of Co-Curricular: Mr D Thompson
Director of Finance: Mrs K F Walker
Head of Junior School: Mr P C Doyle, BSc
Interim Head of Hymers Hessle Mount: Mr A Copeland

Immanuel College

Elstree Road, Bushey, Hertfordshire WD23 4EB
Tel: 020 8950 0604
email: enquiries@immanuelcollege.co.uk
website: www.immanuelcollege.co.uk
X/Twitter: @ICBushey
Facebook: @ImmanuelCollegeUK

Motto: *Torah im Derech Eretz ~ Jewish learning leading to secular success*

Immanuel College is a selective, co-educational day school founded in 1990 by the late Chief Rabbi, Lord Jakobovits to fulfil his vision of a school affirming modern orthodox Jewish values and practice in the context of rigorous secular studies. The College aims at giving its pupils a first-class education that encourages them to connect Jewish and secular wisdom, to think independently and to exercise responsibility. Its ethos is characterised by attentiveness to individual pupils' progress, high academic achievement and the integration of Jewish and secular learning. There are both Jewish and non-Jewish teachers at the school, the common element being enthusiasm for their work and concern for their pupils. Its results at GCSE and A Level have been increasingly impressive in recent years. In 2023 two thirds of GCSE results were graded 7 or higher and 57% of A Levels were graded A* or A. The majority of Immanuel College students have proceeded to their first choice of university to include two top-ten American universities, numerous Russell Group settings, a coveted degree apprenticeship in industry, and one of the world's most elite degree programmes for Art and Design.

Age Range. 4–11 and 11–18. The Preparatory School opened in September 2011 and now includes Reception to Year 6 classes.

School Roll. There are 583 pupils on roll. There are 123 pupils in the Sixth Form.

Buildings and Grounds. The College is situated in a tranquil 11-acre site dominated by Caldecote Towers, a Grade II-listed 19th-century mansion. Facilities include the Joyce King Theatre, two suites of science laboratories, a fitness suite, a large all-weather surface for tennis and netball, cricket and football pitches, and grounds for field events and athletics. Professor Lord Winston opened a new multi-functional 8-classroom building in September 2010, and a further building incorporating an enhanced Jewish Learning facility (Atar-Zwillenberg Beit K'nesset), additional classrooms and state-of-the-art laboratories was opened in November 2014 by Chief Rabbi Ephram Mervis. Dining room facilities were upgraded in 2017, along with a new Sixth Form Art Studio and an expanded library. In 2019 a completely refurbished computing suite was installed, along with a new music technology facility, and there have been further improvements to playgrounds and security features.

Admissions (Senior School). Most boys and girls enter in September, though pupils are accepted in all three terms. Admission into the Senior School is on the basis of performance in the College's entrance examination and interview. The principal entry is at 11+, but the School considers pupils for admission at any point. A growing number of boys and girls join the College in the Sixth Form; offers of places are gained by entrance examinations and interview and are conditional upon GCSE results and suitability for A Level courses.

Admissions (Preparatory School). Admission into Reception and Year 1 is on the basis of informal assessment consisting of a play session and a focus activity. For Year 2 there is a short Mathematics activity and a reading/writing task.

Fees per annum (2023–2024). Senior School: £22,509; Lunch £360 per term. Preparatory School: £12,506; Lunch £244 per term.

Scholarships and Bursaries. Academic and Jewish Life & Learning Scholarships are awarded on a competitive basis to outstanding 11+ entrants. Exhibitions to the value of £2,000 per annum are awarded to pupils who show exceptional promise in Art and Music. Means-tested bursaries are awarded to a number of boys and girls from less affluent families who are academically and personally suited to the education the College provides.

Curriculum. The articles of the College's faith are that Jewish and secular learning shed light on one another, that the appreciation of each is deepened by study of the other, and that the life of the mind and spirit should not be compartmentalised but holistic. As such, the school offers a wide range of secular subjects, including English, Mathematics, Further Mathematics, Computing, Sciences, as well as Art and Design, Photography, Drama, Geography, History, French, Spanish, Modern Hebrew, Music, Personal Development Education, Physical Education and Relationship and Sex Education. At A Level, additional subjects include Economics, Government & Politics, Media Studies, Sociology, Business and Psychology. Throughout a pupil's time at Immanuel, Jewish Studies forms part of the core curriculum. Jewish ethics, philosophy, history and religion and Israel Education are studied by way of close textual learning and through guest speakers and seminars, developing *Chochma* (wisdom) and well-founded Jewish identities. All members of the College have informal and formal opportunities to deepen their understanding of Jewish faith and practice with team members from the School's Jewish Life & Learning Centre, the Beit.

Pastoral Care. The College prides itself on attentiveness to the needs of individual pupils. The Pastoral Team includes Form Tutors and Heads of Section, who in Years 7 to 11 work under the direction of the Deputy Head for Pastoral Care. The Director of Sixth Form is in charge of a team of Sixth Form Tutors. Parental consultation evenings take place regularly, through a hybrid model of online and in-person appointments. The Pastoral Hub, staffed by people outside the teaching faculty, provides important individual support. The Student Council, which meets frequently, gives pupils the opportunity to express their views and make suggestions about further improving school life.

Religious Life. The College commemorates and celebrates landmarks in the Jewish and Israel calendar such as Purim, Chanukah, Succot and Yom Ha'atzmaut. Each January, on Holocaust Memorial Day, Lower Sixth Form students share the knowledge and insights that they have gained on their trip to Poland with pupils in the first five years of the Senior School. The College also commemorates Yom Hazikaron. Pupils attend morning and afternoon prayers on a daily basis.

The Inclusion and Learning Support Department supports teachers to help pupils become independent and successful learners. In addition to the programme followed by all pupils, the Department provides a range of tailored programmes to pupils whose learning needs are more specific. Pupils with a variety of learning profiles are thereby helped to develop confidence and to exceed their predictions and reach their potential.

Art, Music and Drama. The College enjoys a tradition of excellence in the visual arts (the annual Gottlieb Art Show being the highlight of the artistic year) and drama (recent school productions have included *Beauty and the Beast, Anastasia, Macbeth, An Inspector Calls, The Happiest Days of Your Life, Pygmalion, The Trojan Women, Twelfth Night, Three Sisters, The Crucible, Rumours, Mary Poppins, My Fair Lady, Annie Jr, Fiddler On The Roof* and *The Sound of Music*). There is a yearly Music Festival and the calendar includes a number of concerts and recitals involving soloists, ensembles and orchestra.

Games. The PE and Games staff involve pupils in activities that range from aerobics, golf, and trampolining to athletics, cricket, football, hockey, lacrosse, table tennis, netball, badminton and tennis. Over twenty sports clubs meet weekly. Physical Education may be studied for GCSE and A Level. Sports facilities include an all-weather surface and a fitness suite. The College has won trophies in many sporting competitions in recent years and were recently crowned District Cricket Champions at Years 7, 8 & 10.

Enrichment Activities. The many co-curricular activities on offer include opportunities for pupils to participate in leadership programmes, volunteering schemes, charity fundraising (Shevet Achim), The Duke of Edinburgh's Award, public speaking, debating competitions and The Alan Sennit Programme. There are also clubs in areas such as philosophy, medicine, law, chess, art, STEM, military history, Jewish life and learning, world affairs, modern European languages and Model United Nations.

Educational Trips. In Year 7 pupils visit Amsterdam; in Year 8 they visit an outward-bound centre in France; in Year 9 they spend three weeks in Israel; in Year 10 they visit Strasbourg and Madrid; in Year 11 they have the opportunity to take part in a cultural trip to Berlin and in the Lower Sixth they spend eight days in Poland, although the Covid Pandemic has interrupted these visits in the recent years. These experiences encourage pupils to understand themselves, bond with one another and comprehend the forces that have shaped contemporary Jewry. Photography students benefit from trips to foreign locations of great natural beauty.

Careers. The guidance provided by the College supports pupils in their research about choices beyond Immanuel. Through assemblies, the lower years are encouraged to start thinking about their own strengths and weaknesses and likes and dislikes which lead to discussions about future pathways. Even at this stage, any experience in the labour market is encouraged and supported. By the time GCSE subject choices need to be made, pupils are aware of the wider world around them and are closely monitored throughout the process. During Year 10 and Year 11, pupils make use of the weekly Careers Clinic, where they may collect information about relevant courses, one-day events and other opportunities to engage directly with people from specific areas of work. Year 11 pupils may also undertake testing by My Future Choice (formerly known as Cambridge Occupational Analysts) and this, along with a personal interview after mock examinations, helps pupils and their parents to feel confident about making the right A Level choices. Pupils continue to enrol in career-specific courses and events throughout the Sixth Form, and all are welcomed to our Careers Fair.

Charitable status. Immanuel College is a Registered Charity, number 803179. It exists to combine academic excellence and Jewish tradition in a contemporary society.

The Board of Governors:
Mr Daniel Levy (*Chairman*)
Mrs Hannah Boyden
Mr Henry Bennett
Mrs Mandy Berkman
Rabbi Jacob Ebrahimoff
Mr Neal Menashe
Dr Nina Robinson
Rabbi Shaul Rosenblatt
Mrs Jodi Schajer
Mr David M Smith
Mr Daniel Tannenbaum
Mrs Lisa Zimmerman

Clerk to the Governors: Mrs Isabel Arbisman

***Head Master*: Dr Millan Sachania**, MA Cantab, MPhil, PhD, FRSA

Senior Leadership Team:

Second Master: Mr Daniel Endlar MChem Oxon

Acting Deputy Head Mistress (*Pastoral*) *& Designated Safeguarding Lead*: Mrs Sharron Shackell, BA, MEd, CMgr, FCMI

Deputy Head Master (*Jewish Life & Learning*): Rabbi Yoni Golker, BSc, MA

Head of Preparatory School: Mrs Alexis Gaffin, BEd Cantab

Assistant Head: *Director of Studies*: Mrs Jo Fleet, BA

Assistant Head: *Director of Sixth Form*: Mrs Nicola Fahidi, BA

Assistant Head: *Head of Inclusion and Learning Support*: Mr Aryeh Richman, BA

Director of Finance & Operations: Mr Nicholas Brann, MA Oxon

Director of Human Resources: Ms Rachelle Hackenbroch, BA

Director of Strategic Communication & Development: Ms Mary Beer FRSA, BA *cum laude*

James Allen's Girls' School (JAGS)

144 East Dulwich Grove, London SE22 8TE

Tel: 020 8693 1181
email: enquiries@jags.org.uk
website: www.jags.org.uk
X/Twitter: @JAGSschool
Facebook: @JAGSschool
Instagram: @JAGSschool

At JAGS, pupils flourish in an environment which nurtures self-confidence and independence, while feeling supported through outstanding pastoral care from dedicated members of staff and their peers.

The school is exceptionally proud of the strong, contemporary pastoral systems in place, and the care that each member of staff takes to ensure that they know each student as an individual.

JAGS recognises that these ingredients are key to the happy and inclusive community it is renowned for. It is a nurturing environment in which all pupils can thrive.

At GCSE and A level the school consistently achieves among the highest results in the country, particularly in STEM subjects, and pupils regularly go on to study at some of the world's most prestigious universities.

The school recently celebrated its best ever A Level results, with one in five Year 13 leavers going onto Oxbridge.

JAGS Senior School has approximately 900 pupils with 200 in the Sixth Form. About a third of girls come up from our Junior School, James Allen's Junior School, with about two-thirds entering from other preparatory and state primary schools.

Based in Dulwich, the 22-acre campus includes pristine playing fields and historic botany gardens. The state-of-the-art sports centre features a 25-metre swimming pool, climbing wall, floodlit artificial turf pitch, dance studio, squash court, fitness studios and gym. Elsewhere, the school's Prissian Theatre (which can be set up traditionally or in the round) offers the perfect arena for both lessons and stage shows.

Over the summer break, the school's iconic Holst Hall was transformed into a multifunctional space ideal for House Assemblies, lessons, workshops, or students socialising at lunch.

JAGS is fully committed to offering the full breadth of holistic learning. At every turn, there are a myriad of co-curricular clubs and activities on offer which allow pupils to indulge any interests and passions they may have.

As opposed to a timetable of extracurricular activities, which may be viewed as an additional part of school life, JAGS promotes co-curricular activities to highlight how these operate in tandem with the rest of school life, helping pupils build new friendships and develop skills for the future.

If a club does not already exist, pupils are encouraged and empowered to simply start their own.

The list is almost too long to count, as girls constantly set up new clubs and societies either to give themselves a chance to build on their academic learning (Biology Club, Robotics Club, History Clinic, Law Society), take up charitable endeavours (Charity Club, Link Age, Saturday Literacy Scheme), or pursue recreational passions (Italian Film Club, Bel Canto Club, Fashion Society, Code Breaking Club).

Pupils have also started several societies which celebrate the school's unique and diverse community. These include the African Caribbean Society (ACS), Islamic Society (ISOC) and the LGBTQ+ Society.

In recent times, a raft of new societies championing sustainability has emerged in line with the school's renewed commitment to sustainability.

These include the Eco Champions; who work with the dedicated Sustainability Lead to develop school-wide initiatives, Incredible Edibles; who work with the Botany Manager to grow a wide range of foods and vegetables on-site, and The Repair Club; who breathe new life into staff's and students' damaged or worn items, improving waste reduction and sustainability.

This is, of course, alongside dozens of co-curricular sports clubs on offer, such as football, netball, table tennis, Zumba, swimming, water polo, rowing, hockey and rock climbing.

Fees per term (2023–2024): £7,575.

Admission: Students are mainly admitted at 11+ and 16 +. Casual vacancies at other ages.

Entrance Examination: For details and method of admission, please visit **www.jags.org.uk**

Scholarships and bursaries:

Since 1741, James Allen's Girls' School has been guided by a singular forward-thinking and philanthropic approach to education.

At the heart of this vision is an extensive and generous bursary scheme which allows the school to continue attracting intellectually curious girls, regardless of their economic background.

More than one in six students studying at the Senior School receive this transformational, life-changing bursary provision. The majority of these financially assisted students are supported with more than 90% of fees, as well as the costs of uniform, travel, school trips, activities and lunches.

A means-tested bursary scheme is available to all year groups from 11+ entry onwards. Scholarships are also available to students who show exceptional potential academically, and in Art, Music and Sport, at 11+, deferred 13+ and 16+ entry. Sports scholarships are also offered at 11+ and deferred 13+ entry.

Charitable status:

James Allen's Girls' School is a Registered Charity, number 1124853.

Governors:

Dr Jane Marshall, FRCPsych (*Chair*)

Mr Alan Bird, MA Cantab, MSc
Mr Richard Collins, MA Oxon, FCA, CF
Mr Robert Cunningham, ACA
Mr Milind Dhuru, BA Hons, FCA, MBA
Ms Sarah Drennan-Jones, LLB Hons
Mr Adrian Floyd, BSc Hons, PGCE
Ms Tory Hyndman, BA Hons, MBA
Ms Alexandra Loydon, BA Hons
Mrs Geraldine McAndrew, OBE, HonMLitt, BA Hons, CQSW
Dame Erica Pienaar, BA Hons, MBS, FRSA
The Hon Dr Rema Kaur Wasan, MA Cantab, MBBS Lon, MRCP, FRCR UK
Mr Jason Peck, Chartered Accountant, Member of the ICAEW, BSc Hons, Clerk to the Governors

Staff:
***Head*: Mrs Alex Hutchinson**, MA Oxon, PGCE
Head of Junior School: Ms Victoria Goodson, BA, MA
Senior Deputy Head, Designated Safeguarding Lead: Rhona Muir, MA Oxon, MSc
Director of Finance & Clerk to the Governors: Mr Jason Peck, Chartered Accountant, Member of the ICAEW, BSc Hons
Deputy Head Academic: Ben Chappell, MA London
Deputy Head, People: Paul O'Dwyer, MA Oxon, MA London
Director of Operations: Justine Addison, MA

John Lyon School

Harrow-on-the-Hill, Middle Road, London HA2 0HN

Tel: 020 8515 9400
email: admissions@johnlyon.org
website: www.johnlyon.org
X/Twitter: @JohnLyonHarrow
Facebook: @johnlyonharrow
Instagram: @johnlyonharrow
LinkedIn: /school/johnlyonharrow

Motto: Stet Fortuna Domus

John Lyon is an academically selective, co-educational independent day school in Harrow-on-the-Hill in northwest London.

We became co-ed from 2021, with girls joining the School in Year 7 for the first time in our 145-year history. We also now offer an all-through education from Nursery, aged 3, to A Level, aged 18, thanks to our coming together with Quainton Hall School in central Harrow. Quainton Hall became John Lyon's Prep School.

Academic excellence is at the very heart of what pupils who study here seek to achieve. With the opportunity to explore a broad curriculum and gain a solid grounding in all the major academic subjects, pupils work alongside dedicated teachers to develop learning skills, creativity and the ability to fully apply themselves in all areas of life.

Building on this platform, pupils perform well from the point they join the School – whether at age 11, 13 or 16 – and achieve excellent results in public examinations at GCSE and A Level. Most students are rewarded for their hard work by gaining places at leading UK universities, before moving on into the workplace in a huge and varied range of valued professions.

John Lyon pupils also gain from their time outside the classroom. The School has a strong reputation for opportunities and success in Music, Art, Drama and Sport. Add to this an exciting Co-Curricular Programme focusing on each pupil's sense of community, achievement and wellbeing, a range of more than 100 extra-curricular activities, and pastoral care that is second to none, a John Lyon education is designed to nurture high-achieving and happy children.

Admission. John Lyon offers a broad education to pupils who aspire to achieve excellence in all they do. As such, the admissions procedure is designed both to reveal applicants' ability as well as to judge their potential. The School offers places to able young pupils who have a great attitude to learning combined with a desire to be the best that they can be.

Pupils typically join John Lyon in Years 7, 9 and the Lower Sixth, largely from a northwest London catchment area, including the Boroughs of Harrow, Hillingdon, Ealing, Brent, Barnet, Camden, Westminster, Kensington & Chelsea and Hammersmith & Fulham, as well parts of Middlesex, Berkshire, Buckinghamshire and Hertfordshire.

The School prides itself in its welcoming and helpful approach to admissions, for children at 11+, 13+ and at 16+ into the Sixth Form.

11+ selection is based on English and Mathematics examinations, participation in a group activity and an interview. 13+ selection includes examinations in English, Mathematics, French and Science, as well as an interview with the Head. 16+ entry is by interview and results at GCSE.

Curriculum. The academic curriculum is at the heart of every working day at John Lyon – it forms the core of all the School seeks to achieve as a leading place of learning. English, Mathematics, the sciences, humanities, creative arts, languages and digital learning form a curriculum designed to educate and inspire, giving knowledge and a desire to want to know more.

The School places a large emphasis on Learning Skills, which apply to all areas of a pupil's experience and success at John Lyon, both inside and outside the classroom. With a focus on reading, the chance to work on extra projects and through the wide range of activities on offer, Learning Skills enhance each pupil's communication, self-reflection and evaluation, logical and critical thinking, independent learning, academic writing and transferable skills.

John Lyon is also a proudly digital school, recognised as one of the leading 50 digital innovation schools in the UK and praised for its use of technology in the classroom to enhance learning outcomes. A School Managed Device policy means all students have a laptop or tablet with them during the School day, allowing them to access content and complete assessed work online while taking more ownership and responsibility for their learning. Pupils in Years 7, 8 and 9 follow a Digital Learning curriculum beginning with essential skills such as online safety training to understand how to use the internet and digital technology responsibly.

Scholarships. All pupils who take the 11+ or 13+ entrance examination will be considered for an

Academic Scholarship. Their performance in the examination, their school reference and their interview will all be taken into consideration. Sixth Form Scholarships are awarded dependent on GCSE results. The School also awards a small number of Scholarships to candidates of outstanding ability and potential in Drama, Music, Sport, Art and STEAM.

Bursaries. In line with the purpose of the School at its founding almost 150 years ago, John Lyon remains committed to widening access for local families. Each year, the School makes available a number of means-tested bursaries to pupils who demonstrate exceptional talent and potential.

School Buildings. The main School buildings house the Science and STEAM laboratories, Drama studios, Art studios, gallery and the Boyd Campbell Hall. The Music School has a 120-seat recital hall, a recording studio and eight individual practice studios. The sports complex comprises a 25-metre indoor swimming pool, fitness studio and sports hall.

Games. A floodlit multi-use games area allows for all-weather Hockey and Tennis at the 25-acre Sudbury Playing Fields, a short distance from the main School site. There are four main Cricket squares, seven Football pitches, a challenge course, pavilion and Archery range. Pupils also use sporting facilities at Harrow School including Cricket nets, Athletics track, nine-hole Golf course, Tennis, Squash and Badminton courts.

The main Sports are Association Football and Hockey in the Autumn and Spring Terms, and Cricket, Athletics, Tennis and Swimming in the Summer Term, supported by Badminton, Basketball, Archery, Water Polo, Golf and other games.

Co-Curricular Programme. On Friday afternoons at John Lyon all pupils put their Academic timetables to one side and participate in the School's broad, engaging and fascinating Co-Curricular Programme.

The Co-Curricular Programme offers something different to pupils beyond the classroom and is aimed at developing a sense of achievement, wellbeing and enjoyment, while gaining practical skills and engaging with the eight School Values. The John Lyon Co-Curricular Programme is an important and integral part of the School timetable and wider School life, designed to add to pupil learning and introduce pupils to exciting new ideas and opportunities, which will help them in School, outside School and beyond into higher education and the workplace.

Extra-Curricular. John Lyon's extra-curricular sports practices, clubs and activities are a much-loved element of School life, aimed at encouraging curiosity, furthering knowledge and nurturing passions outside the timetable. The School's extra-curricular activities are second to none and allow every pupil to flourish as an individual. John Lyon believes that options beyond the classroom are essential to balance the learning in class. They help pupils build resilience, teamwork and leadership, and are seen by many as a distinguishing feature on a university application form and then on a CV. But above all, a well-rounded pupil is a happy pupil. John Lyon typically offers more than 100 clubs and societies every week that provide a wealth of experiences and opportunities to every pupil.

Charity and Community. The charitable ethos that has run through John Lyon since its founding in 1876 shows no sign of slowing, and this generation of pupils, like their predecessors, engage in numerous charitable and community projects, giving time and raising money for projects in Harrow and beyond.

John Lyon's public benefit objectives are to support the wider community through the sharing of expertise and facilities in Sport, the arts and academia. The School has strong links with schools in the maintained sector, who regularly join events; facilities are used by local schools and community groups; pupils raise significant sums for local, national and international charities; access to a John Lyon education is widened through scholarship and bursary awards; and pupils are seen out in the community all year round, giving their time to local initiatives.

The School is part of John Lyon's Foundation, an educational foundation also consisting Harrow School and John Lyon's Charity. The Foundation aims to maximise the opportunities for children and young people by enabling them to realise their potential, broaden their horizons and ultimately enable them to experience and enjoy a better quality of life.

Careers. Specialist advice concerning entrance to Higher Education is given and there is a team of specialists in the Sixth Form Centre to offer guidance and support with UCAS, university choices, Oxbridge preparation and careers.

Entry to University. University destinations included a broad range of Russell Group universities such as Oxford, Durham, Warwick and Imperial, and especially institutions within the University of London, notably UCL and KCL.

The Lyonian Association. All pupils leaving the School become life members of the Association. The Association has shared use of the School's sports ground and its own pavilion at Sudbury Fields.

Fees per term (2023–2024). Year 7 to Upper Sixth £7,632 (including lunch) (www.johnlyon.org/admissions/bursaries-scholarships-and-fees).

Charitable status. The Keepers and Governors of the Free Grammar School of John Lyon is a Registered Charity, number 310033.

Governors:
Mr Giles Goodfellow, KC, MA, LLM (*Chairman*)
Mr Neil Enright, MA Oxon, MBA, NPQH, FRSA [OL] (*Deputy Chairman*)
Mr Ian Kendrick, BEd Hons, MA
Mr David Tidmarsh, BSc Hons, PGCE
Mr Liam Halligan, MPhil Econ, BSc Hons [OL]
Mr Richard Winter, CBE, FCA
Mrs Catherine Southgate, BBus Acc, FCA
Professor John Greenwood, PhD, FRCPath
Mr Anup Vyas, LLB Hons [OL]
Mrs Kay Burnaby, MRICS
Mr Matthew L S Judd, BA Hons, FRGS
Mr Chinmay M Gupta, PHD, FRCS Tr & Orth, MA, BMBCH Oxon
Mrs Joanne Owens, LLB Hons
Mr Simon Flamank, LLB Hons

Clerk to the Board of Governors: The Hon Andrew Millett, MA [OL]

[OL] *Old Lyonian*

***Head*: Mrs Rose Hardy**, MA Oxon, MEd

Chief Operating Officer: Mr G Mawdsley, MA Cantab
Deputy Head: Mr A Sims, MA, MEng Cantab

Assistant Heads:
Mr T Lewis, MA, MEng Cantab (*Academic*)
Mr J Rowe, MA UEA (*Pastoral*)
Mr H Jones, MA Cantab, FRCO, FCA (*Quainton Hall Links*)
Director of Studies: Mr R Lokier, BA Cantab
Director of Admissions: Dr F Weinberg, BSc, MSc, PhD Imperial
Director of Finance: Mrs T Dovey, FCCA
Director of Marketing & Communications: Mr J Suchak, BA Hertfordshire, MCIM
Director of Operations: Ms Destiny Belle, CWIFM

Head of HR: Mrs C Bertie, CIPD
Head of Sixth Form: Revd S Mepham, BDiv King's College, London, AKC, MA London

Kelvinside Academy

33 Kirklee Road, Glasgow G12 0SW

Tel: 0141 357 3376
email: rector@kelvinside.org
website: www.kelvinside.org
X/Twitter: @kelvinside1878
Facebook: @Kelvinside1878

Motto: ΑΙΕΝ ΑΡΙΣΤΕΥΕΙΝ

Kelvinside Academy was founded in 1878. Since May 1921, it has been run by the Kelvinside Academy War Memorial Trust, which was formed in memory of the Academicals who gave their lives in the War of 1914–18. The affairs of the Trust are managed by a Board of Governors.

Kelvinside Academy is a co-educational day school for some 650 pupils, aged 3 to 18.

The main building is in neo-classical style and Grade A listed but has been extensively modernised within. Further buildings and extensions provide excellent facilities for all subjects and interests, and are symptomatic of the school's progressive approach. Recent additions include Scotland's Innovation School, state-of-the-art IT and multimedia suites, custom-built nursery, library upgrade and sports pavilion.

Curriculum. Junior School pupils (from J1) benefit from specialist input in Innovation, Art, Music, PE and Modern Languages. The Senior Prep (P7) year is a transitional year with a core curriculum taught by the class teacher but science, languages, art, music and PE are delivered by secondary specialists. Computing is a core compulsory subject up to S4.

Senior 3 and 4 pupils follow eight National 4 or 5 courses, followed by Higher and Advanced Higher courses in Senior 5 and 6.

Combined Cadet Force. The hugely popular CCF is compulsory for one year in Senior 3. Pupils also embark upon The Duke of Edinburgh's Award scheme at this stage.

Games. Rugby and hockey are the principal team games in the winter terms with athletics, tennis and cricket in the summer. A range of additional sports and games, from handball and football to basketball and dance, is offered.

Activities. A rich programme of extracurricular and House activities contributes significantly to the broad educational experience enjoyed by all pupils.

The Expressive Arts. Music, drama, dance and the visual arts have a central role in both the curriculum and the co-curriculum.

Fees per term (2023–2024). Nursery: dependent on number of sessions attended; Junior School: £3,497–£4,700; Senior School: £5,050–£5,317.

Admission. For Nursery and P1, children undergo an informal assessment. For P2 to Senior 3, children sit an entrance test and informal interview. For Senior 4 to Senior 6, entry is by interview, school report and exam results.

Bursaries. Financial support with fees (ranging from 10%–100%) is available to P7 and Senior School pupils.

Charitable status. The Kelvinside Academy War Memorial Trust is a Registered Charity, number SC003962. The purpose of the Trust is to run a combined primary and secondary day school in memory of those former pupils of the school who gave their lives in the war of 1914–18.

Board of Governors:
Mr A McKendrick, LLB, Dip LP, NP (*Chair*)
Mr A Tear (*ex officio*)
Mr C J Mackenzie, LLB, Dip LP, NP
Mr G Bisset, BAcc, CA
Mrs N Hinde
Mr M Scott
Mrs Y Craig
Mrs L Faulkner
Ms L Baxendale, LLB Hons, Dip LP, NP
Ms M Carey, MA Hons

***Rector*: Mr D J Wyatt**

Chief Operating Officer: Mr D Pocock
Deputy Rector: Ms D Gallacher
Academic Deputy: Mr C Derrick
Assistant Deputy: Mr J I Cuthbertson
Head of Junior School: Mrs C Sweeney
Director of Admissions & Communications: Mrs K Bottomley

Kent College

Canterbury, Kent CT2 9DT

Tel: 01227 813906
email: admissions@kentcollege.co.uk
website: www.kentcollege.com
X/Twitter: @kentcollegehm
Facebook: @kentcollege
Instagram: @kentcollegecanterbury
LinkedIn: /Kent-College-Canterbury

Motto: *Lux tua via mea*

This outstanding boarding and day school is situated on the edge of the beautiful City of Canterbury. Students can join the Nursery from three months old and continue through the Junior School and the Senior School until the age of eighteen. Parents choose the school not only for its excellent academic results and wide range of co-curricular activities but also for its warm, friendly and welcoming atmosphere. Students are encouraged to achieve all that they can, in a happy and supportive environment.

Boarding at KC. We are proud of the international nature of the school with over 40 countries represented. While most day students live within an hour of the school, our thriving boarding community makes up a third of the College. Boarders live in six boarding houses which are all on site and are managed by experienced House Parents and their teams. Boarders are fully integrated into the day-to-day life of the school but also have their own specially arranged activities in the evenings, from basketball to archery, trips to the Natural History Museum in London, or Go Karting at the weekends.

Campus. The Junior and Senior schools occupy two independent sites just five minutes apart by car. Both schools are surrounded by extensive playing fields which are used throughout the school day. Modern classrooms and a forward-thinking approach to technology throughout the school distinguishes Kent College as a market leader in education. Excellent sport, music and drama facilities are augmented by the highest level of teaching and coaching. The recently opened Great Hall is an impressive 600-seat auditorium that provides cutting-edge facilities for worship, concerts, and the performing arts. The music and drama departments host some 13 concerts and drama performances in the theatre during the school year.

Farm and horse riding. Our working farm provides an opportunity for students to take Green Studies as part of the curriculum but also to enjoy learning about animal welfare and care as part of our Young Farmers Club. Our students can take horse riding lessons throughout the year in our riding arena with our experienced riding instructors and can also take stable management courses.

Curriculum. The school offers GCSEs, iGCSEs (as part of a pre-Sixth Form year), 23 A Levels, the International Baccalaureate and a number of Cambridge Technical courses. For the IB the school has consistently ranked in the top 10 UK small cohort schools with an average score of 37. Most school leavers go on to Russell Group and other top universities both in the UK and abroad. Each year a number of pupils secure offers of places at Oxford and Cambridge. The curriculum is aligned to the National Curriculum but a greater range of subjects is provided. It is not the aim to specialise in any one group of subjects but to provide a balanced curriculum, which will give full opportunity for students to get a good grounding of general knowledge and then later to develop particular talents to a high standard. We pride ourselves on being able to provide a personalised learning experience, where we can organise the curriculum to suit the student.

Learning Support Centre. The Learning Support Centre is a haven of help for those among the school intake that need extra support. Students are taught all the mechanisms that they need to access the whole curriculum. Support remains a constant throughout the child's time here.

International Study Centre. Small group lessons and specific language assistance provide a useful platform for those students who need to improve their English. These students are integrated into the mainstream classes at a pace that suits them.

Pastoral care. The school operates closely with each student and the student's parents to ensure that there is an open line of communication. Each student is individually supported by a strong team: house parents; deputy head of wellbeing and pastoral; heads of house and lower school heads of house; tutors; teachers and peer mentors; all of whom take a significant interest in looking after the needs of each individual.

Religion. As a Methodist school, a strong Christian ethos purveys all that the school does. Students of all faiths and no faith are welcomed in the school.

Co-curricular activities. The school possesses 28 acres of playing fields and a floodlit all-weather hockey pitch, netball courts and tennis courts. The major games for boys are Rugby, Hockey, Tennis, Cricket and Athletics and for girls are Netball, Hockey, Tennis, Cricket and Athletics. Hockey is a particular strength, with teams regularly attaining National championship status. Representative honours are common occurrence in all sports. The boarding community enjoys full use of the facilities in the evening with regular activities in Basketball, Football and Fitness Training. Senior pupils take part in various forms of community service in the City and the school also has its own Duke of Edinburgh's Award group. There are over 100 co-curricular activities available, including Art, Debating, Chess, Conservation, CDT and Photography, and every student is expected to participate in 2 co-curricular activities per week.

Music and drama. Music and drama play an important part in the life of the school. There are four choirs, two orchestras, a jazz band, rock groups and a variety of other specialist ensembles and singing groups. Many concerts are given each year, including the annual Carol Service in Canterbury Cathedral. Whole-school productions occur every term as well as Arts week in the Spring term.

Scholarships. Realising the potential within young people is something that is incredibly important at KC. Our scholarship programme allows us to nurture those that already have talents in particular areas. The school awards academic, music, sport, drama, art and design scholarships to pupils for entry into Years 7, 9 and 12. Full details may be obtained from our Admissions team.

Bursaries. It is central to our ethos that the school provides opportunities to make a Kent College education accessible to many who would not normally be able to afford full tuition fees. Parents will be invited to complete a financial assessment form and the scale of bursary awarded will be based on the information provided and the financial criteria which the school applies to all bursary awards. In addition, the school operates an awards system for the children of HM Forces, NATO, the Foreign and Commonwealth Office personnel, as well as providing a Methodist Ministers' Allowance.

Fees per term (2023–2024). Day Pupils: £6,511–£7,487; Boarders: £10,072–£13,860 (full). International Study Centre: £1,350 extra.

Admissions. The usual ages of admission to the Senior School are 11, 13 and 16. Entrance Assessments usually take place in the Spring Term for admission the following September. Contact admissions@kentcollege

.co.uk to arrange a personal visit or for more information.

Charitable status. Kent College, Canterbury is part of the Methodist Independent Schools Trust, which is a Registered Charity, number 1142794. The School was founded to provide education within a supportive Christian environment.

Governors:
Chair: Mrs L Cocking
Secretary to the Governors and Bursar: Mrs B McCafferty

***Head*: Mr M Turnbull**

Deputy Head, Learning: Mr G Letley
Deputy Head, Wellbeing and Pastoral: Mr D Bennett

Chaplain: Revd Alison Walker

Director of External Relations: Mrs Andrea Warden
Head's PA: hm@kentcollege.co.uk

Head of Junior School: Mr S James
Head of Junior School's PA: Miss H Bayly
(See entry in IAPS section)

Kent College Pembury

Old Church Road, Pembury, Tunbridge Wells, Kent TN2 4AX

Tel: 01892 820218
email: admissions@kentcollege.kent.sch.uk
website: www.kent-college.co.uk
X/Twitter: @KentCollegePemb
Facebook: @KentCollegePemb
LinkedIn: /kent-college-pembury

Kent College Pembury is a leading day and boarding school for pupils aged 3 to 18. The Prep School accepts boys up to Year 2 (2023) and each subsequent year until the Prep School is fully coeducational by 2027. The Senior School is girls only 11 to 18.

Kent College is forward-thinking school with high academic standards and a flexible and personalised approach for each pupil. At GCSE, pupils achieve, on average, one grade higher than predicted which puts the school in the top 7% in the UK for 'Value Added'.

The recent ISI inspection awarded Kent College the highest possible grading of 'Excellent' in Academic Achievement and Personal Development, as well as being fully compliant. The report showed that "pupils achieve high levels of knowledge, skills and understanding across all areas of the curriculum" and that "pupils are highly confident and are well prepared for the next stage of their lives".

Set in 75 acres of beautiful countryside, Kent College has excellent facilities which ensure it provides outstanding opportunities for pupils so they can approach life and learning with creativity and adventure.

The boarding community is an integral part of the school and boarders take part in a wide range of activities, sports, and trips to ensure their time at Kent College is maximised and they are equipped with the necessary skills to excel in their lives beyond school.

The school is accredited by HMC, GSA, BSA and IAPS.

Ethos and Aims. The Prep School (ages 3–11) and the Senior School (ages 11–18) are part of the Methodist Independent Schools Trust, whose schools have an ethos of being caring, Christian environments, and welcome pupils from all faiths or none. The Methodist value of 'doing all the good you can,' sits at the very heart of Kent College and ensures every pupil can be the absolute best they can be, not only for themselves but for the community and the world around them.

Location and Facilities. The Prep School and the Senior School share the site which is set in 75 acres of beautiful green countryside in Pembury, three miles from Royal Tunbridge Wells. It is just 35 minutes to London by train and within easy reach of Heathrow and Gatwick airports, channel ports and the Channel Tunnel. The school campus comprises the original Victorian manor house and purpose-built facilities that include a Music Centre, Sixth Form Centre, Science block, a 200-seat theatre, Dance studio and on-site outdoor confidence course. The Susanna Wesley Arts and Library Centre provides an open-plan library space, computer rooms and bright and spacious Art studios. For sport, the school has two large sports halls, an all-weather Astro pitch, fitness suite, netball and tennis courts and a brand new, indoor 25m swimming pool.

The junior boarding house, Hawkwell and Hargreaves, is home to all boarders from Year 4 to Year 9 while the senior boarding house, James and Osborn, is for boarders in Year 10 to Upper Sixth. Boarders come from across the world with many from countries including Hong Kong, China, Spain, Singapore, Thailand, South Africa as well as the UK. Flexi-boarding is a popular option for local day pupils.

The Prep School is based in its own modern, purpose-built building with art rooms, language laboratories, computer rooms and library inside and spacious playgrounds, forest school and netball and tennis courts outside. Prep School pupils additionally have all the sports, music and drama facilities of the Senior School at their disposal. The Prep School has its own wide range of after school clubs and offers flexible wraparound care from 7.30am-7.30pm. (See also Prep School entry in IAPS section.)

Curriculum. In the first years of the Senior School all pupils follow a wide curriculum which includes academic as well as creative and practical subjects. At GCSE, all pupils take English Language, English Literature, Mathematics, separate Sciences, and select from a wide range of other GCSE option subjects including Textiles, Food Technology, Spanish, Computer Science, Physical Education and Art. In the Sixth Form, pupils take 3 or 4 A Levels and/or BTECs. Sixth Form pupils take part in the KC Honours programme, participating in extracurricular activities such as The Ivy House Award, a transformational personal and professional development programme which aims to develop extraordinary leaders, the Extended Project Qualification designed to develop analytical, critical thinking and research skills, the CREST Gold Award in Science and The Duke of Edinburgh Award Scheme. These are all focused on improving pupils' skills such as confidence, leadership, innovation, creativity, problem solving and intrapersonal skills, which are in demand by employers.

Academic Results. Kent College is a leading school in the UK for 'Value Added', currently ranked in the top 7% of schools at GCSE, with pupils achieving at least one grade higher than predicted. The school is at the very top in several subjects, such as Food Technology and English.

Sixth Form leavers head to leading universities across the UK to study a wide range of subjects. In 2023, 83% were accepted into their first-choice university.

A recent *Good Schools Guide* review commented; "if you're looking for an injection of optimism, it's right here: bold, courageous and resilient learning where the message emblazoned on the school minibuses – 'We Are The Future' – really does apply to these pupils, who we felt are more than ready to 'smash the world'."

Sport. Sporting activities include hockey, netball, cricket, football, athletics, cross country, tag rugby, horse riding, swimming, tennis, trampolining, dance and gymnastics. The school has a strong history of producing national and international players and athletes.

Extracurricular Activities, Music and Drama. The school prides itself on offering an extensive programme of extracurricular activities at lunchtimes, after school and at weekends which are open to day pupils and boarders. There are frequent visits to London theatres, art galleries, lectures and places of cultural interest, overseas trips including Pompeii, Ypres, South Africa and Dublin, and residential trips with a broader educational remit. Music and Drama are performed to West End standard in the two school productions each year (from Sweeney Todd to Six), and a myriad of concerts, musicals night, open mic and opera nights allow pupil to showcase their exceptional ability and talent.

Entrance. Main intakes to the Prep School are to Nursery (age rising 3) and Reception (age 4) classes. The school will take pupils into other year groups subject to places being available. Entrance into Years 3–6 is based on the school's own entrance tests.

The main entries to the Senior School are at Year 7, Year 9 and the Lower Sixth. The school is gently selective and entrance is by a computer-based test, interview and a reference from the previous school. Boarders are welcomed from age 8.

Scholarships and Bursaries. Academic, Art, Dance Drama, Music and Sport Scholarships are awarded to outstanding entrants at 11+, 13+ and 16+.

Bursaries: Kent College is committed to broadening access to the school by offering to eligible parent or guardians means tested financial support towards the payment of school fees in the form of bursary awards. Fee assistance may be offered to those applying to the Senior School.

Fees per term (2023–2024). Senior: Day £8,460, Full Boarders £13,500, Weekly Boarders £11,500. Prep: Day: £3,890–£5,850. Full Boarders £11,500, Weekly Boarders £9,900. Sixth Form Entrant: £9,040. Discounts for siblings.

Charitable status. Kent College Pembury is part of the Methodist Independent Schools Trust, which is a Registered Charity: number 1142794.

***Head*: Miss Katrina Handford**, BA Hons, MEd, PGCE

Deputy Head – Academic: Mr James Mossman, BA Hons, MA, PGCE

Deputy Head – Pastoral: Mrs Louise Payne, BA Hons, MBA, PGCE

Head of Prep School: Mrs Salli Hall, BSc Hons, PGCE

Head of Sixth Form: Mrs Wendy Young Min, BA Hons, PGCE

Bursar: Mrs Angela Jenkins, BA Hons, ACA

Chair of Governors: Mrs Jane Day

Chaplain: Rev'd Kate Osweiler

Director of External Relations: Mrs Sara Ward, BSc Hons

Kimbolton School

Kimbolton, Huntingdon, Cambs PE28 0EA

Tel: 01480 860505
email: headmaster@kimbolton.cambs.sch.uk
website: www.kimbolton.cambs.sch.uk
X/Twitter: @KimboltonSchool
Facebook: @KimboltonSchool
Instagram: @Kimbolton_School

Motto: *Spes Durat Avorum*

The School was founded in 1600 and was awarded Direct Grant status as a boys' day and boarding school in 1945. Girls were first admitted in 1976. The Preparatory School (ages 4–11) and the Senior School are fully co-educational with day boys and girls (4–18) and boarding boys and girls (11–18). As a result of the withdrawal of the Direct Grant the School assumed fully independent status in 1978. There are around 300 pupils in the Prep School and 760 pupils in the Senior School. There is almost a 1:1 ratio of girls to boys.

Mission Statement. Kimbolton School creates a caring, challenging environment in which all pupils are encouraged to fulfil their potential and are given opportunities to flourish in a wide variety of curricular and extra-curricular interests.

It provides a close family environment where young people are educated to be tolerant, socially responsible and independent of mind, equipping them for our changing world. It is a community that challenges pupils to discover their talents, develop socially and excel.

Facilities. The Senior School facilities are situated in and around the main school building, Kimbolton Castle, once the home of Queen Katharine of Aragon and for three centuries the home of the Dukes of Manchester. Now, with its Vanbrugh front and Pellegrini murals, it is a building of considerable beauty and architectural importance. The former State Rooms are study areas for senior pupils and the Castle Chapel is used each day for prayers.

The Queen Katharine Building is a state-of-the-art teaching and learning centre, complete with a 120-seat multimedia lecture theatre. Its two-storey Science and Maths wing provides outstanding facilities including 12 laboratories and a digital learning suite. The Lewis Hall caters for the performing arts and daily assemblies and provides modern theatre and concert facilities. The Design Technology Engineering Centre is up-to-date and well-equipped, as is the Music School.

A large sports complex, incorporating squash courts, gymnasium, sports hall, multi-gym and changing rooms stands in the Castle's parkland. Closer to the Castle itself, lie a modern Art Centre, Library and a 25m indoor swimming pool. The School has two fine all-weather hockey pitches, one of which is floodlit.

Our separate girls' and boys' boarding houses stand adjacent to the grounds in the picturesque Kimbolton High Street. The boarding community is an important part of the School.

The Prep School is located to the west of Kimbolton village, at the opposite end of our 120 acres of parkland and playing fields. It has, on site, a dining hall, library, digital suite, assembly hall, music teaching and practice rooms, science laboratory, art and design technology room, and sports hall, as well as large, light and airy classrooms.

We are very much one school: the curricula of the Prep and Senior Schools are aligned, our warm caring ethos starts at Reception Year and continues through to the Upper Sixth; and some of our staff teach at both the Prep and Senior Schools.

Admission and Organisation. The Prep School admits children at 4+, and 7+ (as day pupils) with the expectation that they will complete their education in the Senior School. Entry at other ages is sometimes possible. Tests for entry at the Prep School are held in February. Entry into the Senior School at the age of 11 is open to boarders and day pupils; the Senior School Entrance examinations are also held in February. There are also entries at 13+, usually by the Common Entrance Examination in June. Those not preparing for Common Entrance may sit the School's own 13+ examination in February. Entry into the Sixth Form is based on interview and GCSE/IGCSE results.

Arrangements can be made for overseas candidates to take the entrance examination at their own schools.

Pupils are accepted in September at the start of the academic year, but a few places may be available for entry in other terms.

The relationship between the Prep and Senior Schools is a close one and contributes to the strong 'family' atmosphere of the whole School. In the Senior School, there are four senior houses and one junior house. It is an important element of our pastoral care that boarding pupils and day pupils are together – there are no day houses. Housemasters/Housemistresses, assisted by Tutors, look after the general well-being and progress of their charges.

Work and Curriculum. For the first two years in the Senior School there are usually five parallel forms; in each of the third, fourth and fifth years there are usually six forms with sets for most subjects. Boys and girls entering at 13 join one of the Third Forms. An option scheme is introduced in the Fourth Form. In the Sixth Form specialisation occurs, and pupils will usually study three subjects from the following list: English Language; English Literature; History; Geography; French; Spanish; Maths; Further Maths; Physics; Chemistry; Biology; Music; Art (Fine Art); Art (Photography); Art (Critical and Contextual); Design Technology and Engineering; Drama and Theatre; Physical Education; Economics; Business; Politics; and Philosophy, Religion and Ethics.

Each A Level has a period of subject enrichment, allowing students to explore topics beyond the curriculum. To widen their interests and experience, all students also choose to take an Extension Course in subjects typically including Astronomy, Classics, Robotics, Cooking For Life, Creative Writing, Debating, Digital Media, Ethical Philosophy, Film-Making, Music Technology, Political Ideas and Psychology. All Sixth Formers follow a 'Preparing for Citizenship' series of lectures, seminars and debates. Almost all leavers gain places at the universities of their choice, with many heading to Oxbridge colleges and Russell Group universities

Religious Teaching. Our school is non-denominational with a Christian ethos and attracts children of all religions and none. Pupils attend Chapel once a week and have PRE lessons each week in the First to Third Form. Other services are held in the School Chapel during each term for pupils and parents to attend. Sunday Services are held in the Chapel and occasionally the School worships in the Parish Church.

Sport and Activities. The School owns over 120 acres of land, more than 20 of which are laid out as playing fields. The major sports for boys are association football, hockey and cricket. For girls the main sports are hockey, netball and tennis. Other sports include girls' cricket, girls' football, athletics, gymnastics, dance, climbing, archery, swimming, golf, fitness training, clay pigeon shooting, squash, badminton, basketball and rounders. Swimming is popular with before and after school sessions and numerous galas. Extensive use is also made by the sailing club of nearby Grafham Water, both for recreational sailing and inter-school matches. Canoeing is popular and each year a team competes in the highly demanding 125-mile Devizes–Westminster challenge. The equestrian club competes in around twenty fixtures during the course of the year. The aim is to find a sport that each pupil loves and will continue to enjoy long after leaving Kimbolton.

Music and drama play an important part in the life of the School and almost half of the pupils take lessons in a great variety of instruments. There is a Choral Society, two orchestras, several bands and many ensemble groups. The School stages plays, musicals or concerts each term.

The School contingent of the CCF is a voluntary, keen and efficient body, divided into Navy, Army and RAF Sections with a national reputation for excellence; Community Service is an alternative. There is a successful Duke of Edinburgh's Award scheme with a large number of participants.

There are many other activities and societies that meet on a regular basis, such as debating, public speaking, forensic science, photography, chess, robotics, motor vehicle engineering, bookworms, dance, beekeeping, gardening, medical society, modelling, pottery and philosophy.

All pupils are able to participate in the large number of trips in the UK and abroad.

Careers. Advice can be sought at any time by pupils or their parents from the Careers staff and we have excellent resources in the Careers Room. All pupils undertake an online profiling test at the end of the Fourth Form, which results in a personal careers guidance report. This is the basis for an individual, half-hour interview with a visiting Careers Guidance Institute-qualified interviewer early in the Fifth Form. Morrisby membership gives our pupils access to a lifelong range of resources and guidance. An annual HE, Gap and Careers Fair is held for Fourth to Sixth Formers.

Dress. The School colours are purple, black and white. Boys wear blazers and grey flannels (shorts until the final year in the Prep School). The girls' uniform includes a standard skirt, blouse and blazer. Sixth Formers wear a black suit.

Scholarships and Bursaries. A number of scholarships are awarded at 11+ and 13+ to candidates who perform with distinction in the Entrance Examination or in Common Entrance.

In addition, William Ingram Scholarships are awarded for 13+ entrants who excel at Music, Art or Games and Leadership.

Sixth Form Scholarships and Exhibitions are awarded to those who achieve outstanding results in GCSE.

There is a bursary scheme for deserving candidates aged 11 or over; bursaries may be awarded on their own or in addition to scholarships.

Fees per term (2023–2024). £4,150 (Lower Prep), £5,385 (Upper Prep), £6,590 (Senior Day), £11,175 (Senior Full Boarding), £10,485 (Senior Weekly Boarding). These figures include a 2% discount which is applied if fees are paid by termly direct debit.

The fees are inclusive of lunches and there is no charge for laundry, books and stationery.

There is a reduction of 2½% in tuition fees when siblings attend at the same time.

Music tuition Fee: £275–£350 per term for individual lessons. (Half a term's notice must be given in writing before a pupil discontinues music lessons.)

Old Kimboltonians Association. All correspondence to: Ms V Wakefield, Alumni Officer, OKA, Kimbolton School, Kimbolton, Huntingdon, Cambridgeshire PE28 0EA; email: alumni@kimbolton.cambs.sch.uk.

Charitable status. Kimbolton School Foundation is a Registered Charity, number 1098586.

Governing Body:
Cllr J A Gray (*Chairman*)
Mr J W Bridge, OBE, DL (*Vice Chairman*)
Mrs S M Brereton
Mrs J L Doyle
Mr P J Farrar
Cllr I D Gardener
Cllr Mrs D Hellett
Mrs K E S Lancaster, MC Cantab, LPC/CPE
Dr P Loughna
Mr S J F Page, BA Hons, Cert Ed
Mr G K Peace
Mrs T Reid
Dr R Smith
Mr D J Suckling
Mr G R Yeandle

***Headmaster*: Mr W Chuter**, BA

PA to the Headmaster: Mrs J Nelson-Lucas

Senior School:

Senior Deputy Headmaster: Mr L G d'Arcy, MChem
Deputy Head (*Academic*): Mrs R H Taylor, MA
Assistant Head (*Extension & Enrichment*): Mr C W Smith, MPhys
Assistant Head (*DSL*): Mrs L A Hadden, BA
Assistant Head (*Staff*): Mrs C E Thomas, MA
Director of Activities: Mr D Koch, D Phil
Head of Sixth Form: Mr M S Gilbert, BEd

School Chaplain: Ms C Brazier, BA, MSSCh, MBChA
Head of Careers: Ms G A Jackson, BSc

Heads of Departments:
Art: Mrs L D Bamford, BA, MA
Biology: Mr P J Whatling, BSc
Chemistry: Mr E C Drysdale, BSc
Design, Technology & Engineering: Ms M Flack, BA
Digital Learning: Mr M Reed, MEng
Drama: Ms N L Akielan
Economics & Business Studies: Mrs J A Powell, BA
English: Mrs A E O'Donnell, MA
Food & Nutrition and Textiles: Mrs L King, BSc
Geography: Mr S Wilson, BA
History: Mr O J Chipperton, MA
Maths: Mr A S Jessup, BSc, MA
Modern Foreign Languages: Mrs M Viruete Navarro, MA
French: Mr R E Knell, BA
Spanish: Mrs M Viruete Navarro, MA
Music: Mr D Gibbs, MA, FRCO
Philosophy, Religion and Ethics: Mrs C E Thomas, MA
Physical Education: Miss T M Lloyd, BSc
Physics: Mr C M Holmes, BSc, BA
Politics: Mr F W B Leadbetter, MA, BD, AKC, FRSA, FRHistS
Academic Support: Ms R Stewart, BEd
Director of Sport: Mr C K Lawrence, BSc
Boys' Games: Mr A S Lawless
Girls' Games: Mrs E L R Lawless
Outdoor Pursuits: Mr J Sweet, BA

Preparatory School:

Headmaster of Preparatory School: Mr J P Foley, BA
Senior Deputy Head (*DSL*): Mr O C Stokes, BEd, MEd
Deputy Head (*Academic*): Mrs R L Lambert, BEd
Head of Lower Prep: Mrs L K Collins, BA

Bursar & Clerk to the Governors: Mrs J F Agnew, LLB Hons, LLM
Registrar: Mrs R White

King Edward VI School

Southampton

Wilton Road, Southampton, Hampshire SO15 5UQ

Tel: 023 8070 4561
email: registrar@kes.hants.sch.uk
website: kes.school
X/Twitter: @KESSouthampton
Facebook: @KESSouthampton
Instagram: @kessouthampton

'After seven years of being a KES student, I can say for certain that I made the right choice of school. I was never the most academically able or sporty student but the culture here is one of developing existing skills, encouraging new talent and never leaving any individual to settle for anything less than that of which they are capable.' – *Upper Sixth Student*

King Edward VI School was founded in 1553, making it the oldest in Southampton, with a long and distinguished history stretching back over 460 years. We are extremely proud of these traditional roots, but we are prouder yet to be recognised as a vibrant, modern institution, dedicated to equipping our pupils with the skills to thrive in the 21st century.

Admission. An entrance examination is held in January for boys and girls seeking to enter Year 7 at age 11 or Year 9 at age 13 that September. Applications from able under-age candidates will also be considered. Smaller numbers of entrants are accepted into the other school years if there is space, provided the applicants are of suitable academic ability. Students may also apply to join the Sixth Form. In order to qualify for entrance to the Sixth Form a student will normally be required to have grade B (or a 6) or above in six subjects at GCSE, including English Language and Mathematics, and A grades in the subjects to be studied at A Level.

Registration for entry may be made at any time on a form obtainable via the school website or from the Registrar, who can supply current information about fees, bursaries and scholarships.

Class sizes average 22; the average size of Sixth Form sets is 8.

Curriculum. All pupils follow a common course in the first two years: this includes French or German or Spanish with Latin or Classical Civilisation, Mathematics, Science and an Extended Studies programme. In years 3, 4 and 5 all pupils study eight 'core' subjects to IGCSE: Biology, Chemistry, English Language, English Literature, a Modern Foreign Language, Mathematics, Religious Studies and Physics. In addition there is a range of 'option' subjects: Art, Computer Science, Design and Technology, Economics, Dance, French, Geography, German, History, Italian, Music, PE, Philosophy, Spanish, Sports Science and Theatre Studies. The syllabus leading to the IGCSE Examinations, in which most pupils take eleven subjects, is designed to avoid any premature specialisation. In the Sixth Form, students study four A Level subjects in the Lower Sixth and then at the end of this year choose to continue with all four or just to continue with three of the subjects. In addition, all have an afternoon of Games in both years and follow a Foundations Studies programme in both the Lower and Upper Sixth Year.

On entering Year 7, pupils join a form of about 22, with a Form Tutor responsible for their general welfare and progress. The other years are organised on a system of pastoral groups of about 16. Each group has its own Year Head. In addition there is a Head of Lower School who has general responsibility for the first three years; a Head of Upper School and a Director of the Sixth Form have similar responsibilities in their respective areas.

Our aim is to provide a congenial atmosphere and a disciplined environment in which able pupils can develop as individuals.

Academic. As a leading co-educational independent day school, King Edward's undoubtedly has high academic standards and expectations. Under the guidance of expert teaching staff, our pupils consistently excel in public examinations, and both GCSE and A Level results are exceptional. As a result, Sixth Form students regularly gain admittance to leading universities in this country and abroad; in 2022, 63% of students went on to study at a Russell Group University.

School Activities. 10% of a student's timetable is devoted to physical education as sport and games are regarded as forming an integral part of life at King Edward's. The major sports played in the three terms are rugby, hockey, cricket and tennis for boys; and netball, hockey, tennis and rounders for girls; other sporting activities include athletics, basketball, badminton, fencing, squash, swimming and a number of other games. The School has a large sports hall, a dance studio, and a fully equipped fitness studio and an all-weather pitch for hockey and similar games which provides twelve tennis courts in summer. There are a further 33 acres of off-site sports fields which include a second astro pitch and floodlit netball and tennis courts.

A considerable range of clubs and societies meets during lunchtime, after school, at weekends and in school holidays, catering for pupils of all ages and many differing tastes. All are encouraged to join some of these societies, in order to gain the greatest advantage from their time at the School.

In addition to a large number of sporting teams representing the School, there are such activities as charitable and community work, dance, drama, debating, chess, Duke of Edinburgh's Award scheme, international expeditions, sailing and numerous superb musical opportunities. The School has flourishing choirs, as well as orchestras and a large number of smaller instrumental groups. We have a brand new bright and large Art department and vibrant and well-equipped Design and Technology premises. The studios and workshops are usually open during lunchtimes and after school. Over the past few years, the whole school has been expanded and refurbished with modern classrooms and specialist rooms. The Dobson Theatre was remodelled and refurbished in 2017, the dining room extended in 2018, and our central library was remodelled and extended in September 2019. In 2022, the Sixth Form Concourse was redeveloped. In 2023, there was a renovation of the Fitness Suite.

Fees per term (2023–2024). £6,665. Fees can be reduced in appropriate cases by the award of Bursaries and Scholarships. Scholarships are available on entry at age 11, 13, and 16. Further Scholarships may be awarded during a pupil's career in the School. Some Scholarships are awarded for proficiency in the Creative Arts. Foundation Bursaries are available at age 11, 13 and into the Sixth Form.

Charitable status. King Edward VI School Southampton is a Registered Charity, number 1088030. The object of the Charity is to advance education and training in or near Southampton or elsewhere, including the carrying on of school or schools or other educational establishments and ancillary or incidental educational or other associated activities for the benefit of the community.

Patron: The Lord Lieutenant for the County of Hampshire, Mr Nigel Atkinson

Governors:
Chair: A J Morgan, MA Oxon, FCA, ATII
Vice-Chair: I H Rudland

Cllr M Chaloner, MA Cantab, Barrister-at-Law
Mr A Connell, BSc
Mr G C B Davies, BSc, FCA
Mr R Dhanda
Reverend J M Finch
Mr D P Geddes
Mr J J Gray, BSc, FCA
Mr A Jones
Miss P S Kirk, BEd, CertEd
Mr A Knibb, BA Hons, B Arch, ARB, RIBA
Dr J E Mitchell, MA Cantab, MBBS, DRCOG, DCH
Mrs C G Musker, Chartered MCIPD
Mrs H V Nicholson, MA Oxon, MSc
Cllr N S Penman
Mr T A M Steele, FCA
Miss V C Stuart-Taylor
Mrs W P Swinn, BDS, LDS, RCS
Dr A L Thomas, MA PhD Cantab, CBiol, MRSB

Bursar and Clerk to the Governors: Mr R Maher, BA Econ, ACA

***Head*: Mr N Parker**, MA Ed, MBA

Senior Deputy Head: Mr A Dellar, BSc
Deputy Head (*Academic*): Dr B Waymark, BA, MA Ed, PhD
Deputy Head (*Pastoral*): Mr W Collinson, BA

Assistant Head (*Registrar*): Mrs E Sheppard, BSc
Assistant Head (*Co-curricular*): Miss C Forsey, BMus, PGDip
Assistant Head (*Teacher Development and Pedagogy*): Mrs P Burrows, BSc
Assistant Head (*Digital Strategy*): Mr O Rokison, MEng
Assistant Head (*Director of Sixth Form*): Dr E Thomas, MChem, PhD
Head of Upper School: Mrs H Searles, BA, MA
Head of Lower School: Mrs L Henderson, BEd

Teaching Staff:
* *Head of Department*

Art:
*Mr G Piggott, BA (*Head of Creative Arts*)
Miss C Jones, BA
Mr E Lewis, BA
Miss A McGinn, BA
Mrs N Moxon, BA
Mrs S Peterson, BA

Biology:
*Dr N Wortham, PhD, MBioChem
*Mr S Aellen, BSc (*Head of Science*)
Mrs J Barnes-Wardlaw, BSc
Mrs L Burnett, BSc
Miss C Cooper, BSc
Miss H Crompton, BSc
Mr M Miller, BSc, MPhil
Mrs S J Peterson, BA
Mrs F Taylor, BSc

Chemistry:
*Mrs L Millington, BSc
Mrs J Collinson, MChem
Mr R Cross, BSc
Mr A Dellar, BSc
Mrs G Dellar, BSc
Dr S Gamblin, BSc, PhD
Mrs E Sheppard, BSc
Mr A Smith, BSc
Dr E Thomas, MChem

Classics:
*Miss I Painter, BA
Mr C Giles, BA
Mr J Halls, MA

Computer Science:
*Mr D Cutler, MPhys
Mr L Hall, BEng
Mrs F Price, BA
Mr M Willis, BEd

Design & Technology:
*Mrs A Blow, BSc
Mrs S Channers, BEng
Mrs A Herbert, BA
Mrs S Peterson, BSc

Drama:
*Mrs L Gilmour, BA (*Director of Drama*)
Mrs H Arnold, BA
Mrs H Hawker, BA

Economics & Business:
*Mr P Sheppard, BSc
Mr N Culver, BA
Mr M Laverty, BA
Mr R Nicholas, BA
Mrs S Quinn, BA
Mr S Ritchie, BA

English:
*Dr A Schofield, BA, MA, PhD
Mrs H Arnold, BA (*Second i/c*)
Mr W Collinson, BA
Ms L S Dara, MA
Mrs S Evans, BA
Miss H Goodsell, MA
Mrs J Gunton, BA
Ms C Pyne, BA, MA
Miss E Rawson, BA, MA
Mr B Reekes, BA, MA
Dr A Wilson, PhD

Geography:
*Ms T King, BA
Dr T Fewtrell, BSc, PhD
Miss L-J Gibbs, BA
Mr G Havers, BSc
Mrs A Penfold, BA
Mrs E Walls, MSc

History:
*Mr N Diver, BA (*Head of Humanities*)
Miss J Barron, BA
Mrs S Burt, BA
Mr C Dormehl, BA
Mrs A Leathem, MA
Mrs R Potter, BA
Mr G Potter, BA

Mathematics:
*Mr G Eyssens, BEd
Mrs C Asiki, BA, MA (*Second i/c*)
Mr S Barley, BSc, MSc
Ms C Dolan, BSc
Mr C Jackson, BSc
Mrs L Matthews, BSc

Mr R Nichols, BA
Miss E Ridley, BSc
Mr P Robinson, BEng, MSc, MA
Mr I Rosenburg, BEd
Mrs J Thimbleby, BSc (*Second i/c*)
Mr M Willis, BSc

Modern Languages:
*Mr A Sinclair, BA
Ms K Clement, MA (**French*)
Ms M Gorbat, BA (**German*)
Mrs E Ladislao, BA (**Spanish*)
Miss V Berrueco Pastor, MA
Miss L Breheny, BA
Mrs H Deng, MA
Miss A Galan, PGCE
Mr A Kendall, BA
Mr G Lawson, BA, MA
Mrs S Rugge-Price, MA
Mr R Soames, BA

Music & Dance:
*Mr A Eadon, BA (*Director of Music*)
Miss S Barnett, BA
Ms T Hayden, MA, BMusEd
Mr M Kelly, BA
Miss B Wu, BA

Physical Education:
*Mr D Kent, BA (*Director of Sport*)
Mr M Mixer, BSc (**PE & Games*)
Miss L Cole, BSc (**Netball*)
Mr C Crichton, BA (**Hockey*)
Mr A Penn, BA (**Cricket*)
Mrs L Henderson, BEd
Mr A Leathem, BA
Miss L Lister, BSc
Mrs H Penn, BA
Mr A Powell, BSc, MSc

Philosphy & Religious Studies:
*Mr A Cross, BA
Mrs R Kairis, BA
Mr G Potter, BA
Mrs H Searles, BA, MA

Physics:
*Mr R Simm, BSc
Mrs P Burrows, BSc, MSc
Mr D Lawson, MEng
Mrs M Mahdavi, BSc
Dr M Mayor, MSc, PhD
Mrs C Ribas de Oliveria, BSc, MSc

Psychology:
*Mrs E Brindley-Ewan, MA
Mr C Jackson, BSc
Mr M Miller, MSc, MPhil

Curriculum Support:
*Mrs Z Ramshaw, BA
Ms C Boyle, BEd
Miss N Collings, BEd
Mrs R Whitfield, BA, MA Hons, MPhil

King Edward's School
Bath

North Road, Bath BA2 6HU

Tel: 01225 464313 (Senior School)
01225 463218 (Junior School)
01225 421681 (Pre-Prep School)
email: reception@kesbath.com
website: www.kesbath.com
X/Twitter: @KESBath
Facebook: @kesbath
Instagram: @kesbath

As the city's former grammar school, founded in 1552, KES has a very healthy tradition of nurturing academic excellence and ambition, reflected these days in the School's outstanding results which consistently place us in the top five independent schools in the South West. The ethos of the School is one that encourages all pupils to play as hard as they work and to make the most of all the wonderful opportunities here, both in and out of the classroom, that enable them to grow and thrive within a supportive and caring framework. We set the bar high, but we also give our pupils all the tools that they need to reach those ambitious standards. We aim to foster talent in all its forms and to open doors to enquiry and discovery. Independent-mindedness and creative spirit are strong suits, but so too is the sense of community that seeks to respect and value all its members.

As a family of three schools, the Pre-Prep, Junior and Senior sections of King Edward's offer an inspiring and supportive environment for children age 3 to 18. Some join us just for the Sixth Form, many stay for their entire school career. All pupils are encouraged to be the best they can be and all are nurtured along the pathway to leading happy, fulfilled and successful lives at school and beyond.

ISI Inspection report. In 2023, the School was inspected by the ISI and was judged as 'excellent' in all areas. In relation to the 'Excellent' quality of KES pupils' academic and other achievements, the ISI noted that 'pupils' overall achievement across all age groups is outstanding and represents [the] successful fulfilment of the School's aim for pupils to strive for excellence', adding that 'this level of attainment is a consequence of the pupils' highly positive attitudes to learning, supported by teaching which shows strong subject knowledge combined with comprehensive learning resources'.

Organisation. King Edward's is a co-educational day school. The School consists of a Senior School of 884 pupils, a Junior School of 195 pupils and Pre-Prep & Nursery of 85 pupils.

Facilities. The Senior School is situated on a 19-acre campus with stunning views across Bath. A further 17-acre site at nearby Bathampton is home to the School's playing fields and sports pavilion. Senior School buildings include the Wroughton Theatre, extensive refurbished laboratories for Biology, Chemistry, Physics and ICT & Creative Media Suite and a designated Modern Foreign Languages building. The newly refurbished Holbeche building includes an extensive

Sixth Form Centre with adjoining café, an extended Careers and Higher Education Centre, a refurbished Design Suite and Design Technology studios. There is also a modern Sports Hall, together with an all-weather sports pitch. One of the most iconic buildings on the site is the stunning Wessex Building: a three-storey, glass-fronted structure with a dining room and servery on the first floor, a multi-purpose second floor for assemblies, presentations, concerts and social gatherings, and a state-of-the-art Library on the ground floor. The Senior School also has a state-of-the-art purpose-built Drama Centre.

Admission. King Edward's Pre-Prep and Nursery: Most pupils start at the Pre-Prep in Nursery in the September after they turn three years old. Thereafter, children progress to Reception and then on to Years 1 and 2. Space allowing, children are also welcomed throughout the academic year.

Junior School: Children joining from our own Pre-Prep do so via internal assessment. They do not sit an entrance examination. Pupils from other primary schools and preparatory schools are offered places based on assessment and interview. Main entry is in Year 3 and Year 5 but other vacancies may occur.

Senior School: All potential Year 7 pupils are interviewed and assessed via an entrance examination testing Verbal Reasoning, Mathematics and English. Older pupils may enter the Senior School, if and where places are available, by sitting an entrance examination appropriate to their age.

Pupils may also seek direct entry into the Sixth Form. Such pupils are expected to acquire a sound set of GCSE passes before transfer for advanced study. Applicants are interviewed and a reference is sought from their present schools.

Application forms and further information concerning entry are obtainable from the Registrar or available online. Open Days are held in the Autumn and Spring terms.

Fees per term (2023–2024). Pre-Prep: starts from £3,330, Junior School: £4,470, Senior School: £5,650.

Scholarships. Scholarships are awarded in Year 7, either for academic excellence or for an outstanding special talent in art, drama, music and sport.

Bursaries. Means-tested Bursaries may be awarded to children entering Years 7 and 12, whose parents are unable to pay the full fee. A general Bursary fund is also available to assist parents during times of unforeseen family circumstances, when they may find themselves unable to fund full school fees. Further details are obtainable from the Bursar's office.

Senior School curriculum. We start in Years 7 and 8 with a broad range of subjects, to which we add choice and greater range in Year 9. By the time pupils are choosing their GCSE options, they will have a clearer idea of their strengths and enthusiasms and be able to select the best range of subjects to go alongside the core subjects of English, Maths, all three sciences and a modern foreign language.

For A Level, further specialisation and greater focus on personal interest and academic strengths come into play as pupils look to their education and potential careers after life in the Sixth Form. We offer careers guidance and testing to support these fundamental choices and then UCAS and Higher Education guidance as they look to make the move to their chosen degree subject from the A Levels they will complete in Year 13.

No two pupils are the same and so we work to provide as much choice and flexibility as we can in our options schemes for Years 9, 10 and 12. All combinations are possible in principle and a broad mix of subjects is as supported as more traditional routes of sciences, languages or humanities.

Throughout, there is an underlying appreciation that pupils succeed best when taught interesting and engaging lessons by enthusiastic, specialist staff. We want our pupils to leave here with valuable study skills, having found their intellectual and academic passion and having fulfilled their potential in that area.

Music and Drama. There is a healthy musical tradition in the School, with over 20 instrumental and choral groups affording opportunities to explore differing musical styles. Partnerships with Bath Abbey and Bath Philharmonia Orchestra help to further extend the experience of our musicians and choirs. Pupils are also regular recipients of the Bath Young Musician of the Year.

King Edward's is known for producing exceptional theatrical work and is regarded as a centre of excellence for its creative and challenging performance work, the professional standards of its productions, and its consistently outstanding academic results. In addition to two big productions each year, the Senior School also offers inter-form competitions, Duologue performances, drama clubs and drama tech club. The School has also introduced LAMDA exams and taken several shows to the Edinburgh Fringe.

Sport. Sport plays a significant role in the life of King Edward's School. The School enjoys a strong sporting tradition, where all pupils are encouraged to take an active role in the curricular and co-curricular opportunities available to them. Each pupil is encouraged to develop their potential, creating the opportunity to allow later involvement at recreational level or within a competitive environment. We aim to nurture teamwork, leadership, commitment and a passion for sport through the opportunities available to all pupils at KES. The major games are rugby, hockey, cricket and netball. Minor sports include athletics, cross-country, tennis, soccer, badminton, golf, dance, gymnastics and table tennis.

School societies and activities. The School aims to challenge and stimulate all pupils by offering a wide range of activities and experiences beyond the classroom. The 2023 ISI Report praised the range of opportunities and quality of achievement available to all pupils beyond the classroom, with inspectors observing that, 'pupils' engagement with the broad and varied extracurricular programme is outstanding'.

Outward-bound opportunities include joining the School's CCF, founded in 1896, or taking part in the Duke of Edinburgh's Award scheme. The School also enters the Ten Tors Competition each year. Lunchtime clubs include Esports Club, KES Pride, Creative Writing Club and a Literary Discussion Group.

Pastoral care The Deputy Head (Pastoral) coordinates the pastoral team. Every child has a Form Teacher who is at their foremost contact during daily life at school. Tutors work in teams managed by Heads of Year or Senior Tutors who are in turn assisted by Heads of Sector (Lower, Middle School and Sixth Form). The pastoral staff are ably supported by a Health and Wellbeing Centre. The School prides itself on its family atmosphere and the excellent relationships between pupils of all ages and staff.

Honours. In 2023, pupils performed exceptionally in their A Levels: 87% A*–B grades. At GCSE: 84.1% of grades awarded 9–7.

King Edward's Junior School and Pre-Prep and Nursery. For further details please see separate entries for the Junior School and Pre-Prep and Nursery under IAPS.

The Association of Old Edwardians of Bath. c/o The Development Office.

Charitable status. King Edward's School Bath is a Registered Charity, number 1115875. It is a charitable trust for the purpose of educating children.

Chair of Governors: Mrs W Thomson, MEd, BEd Hons, LLCM TD

***Headmaster*: Mr M Boden**, MA

King Edward's School
Birmingham

Edgbaston Park Road, Birmingham B15 2UA

Tel: 0121 472 1672
email: admissions@kes.org.uk
website: www.kes.org.uk
X/Twitter: @KESBham
Facebook: @KESBham
LinkedIn: /company/king-edwards-school-birmingham

Motto: *Domine, Salvum fac Regem*

King Edward's School, Birmingham, was founded in 1552 and occupied a position in the centre of the city until 1936 when it moved to its present 50-acre site in Edgbaston, surrounded by a golf course, lake and nature reserve and adjacent to the University. It is an independent day school with 908 boys aged 11 to 18. Approximately 35 in each year receive financial assistance with fees, from scholarships and the Assisted Places Scheme. The School belongs to the Foundation of the Schools of King Edward VI in Birmingham (two independent, six grammar schools and five academies), and its sister school, King Edward VI High School for Girls, is on the same campus. Academically one of the leading schools in the country, King Edward's is also renowned for the scale of its provision and its excellence in sport, music, drama, outdoor pursuits and trips and expeditions.

Admission. Most boys enter the school at 11+. In addition, applications at 16+ to enter the Sixth Form are encouraged. 11+ candidates take papers in Mathematics, English and Verbal Reasoning at a level appropriate to the National Curriculum. A large number of pupils are also interviewed as part of the admissions process. The admissions process for 16+ applicants consists of interviews, examinations in Higher Level IB Diploma subject options, predicted GCSE results and a headteacher's report.

Please note the school will sometimes consider applicants for entry at 13+, if spaces is available.

Scholarships and Assisted Places. Approximately 25 academic scholarships varying in value from 5% to 50% of the fees are awarded each year. Most of these scholarships are awarded at 11+, but awards are also made to outstanding candidates at 16+ and, very occasionally, at 13+. Music scholarships are also available.

The Assisted Places Scheme offers means-tested support to up to 20 boys a year. The majority of Assisted Place pupils join at 11+, but Assisted Places are also available to those joining the Sixth Form.

Fees per term (2023–2024). £5,682.

Academic success. The school's 2023 International Baccalaureate Diploma results were strong with an average point score of 35.9, surpassing the global average of 30.24 points. One in five of the cohort achieved 40 points or above, which is higher than the UK national average of 16%, and several students achieved exceptional scores, including eight boys who attained either 44 or 43 points.

At GCSE, 44% grades were 9s, 69% were 9–8s and 88% were 9.7. Furthermore, 13 pupils achieved 10 straight grade 9s and 33 pupils achieved all 9/8s across their 10 GCSEs.

Curriculum. *Lower School*: The following subjects are studied by all boys to the end of the third year: English, Mathematics, French, Geography, History, Physics, Chemistry, Biology, (General Science in first year), Latin, Art, Design, Drama, Music, PE and Religious Studies. All boys study one of German, Spanish or Classical Greek in the third year and may take their choice to GCSE or IGCSE and beyond. In addition, boys are required to undertake familiarisation courses in Information Technology. In the Fourth and Fifth year, boys take 10 subjects. All boys must study Mathematics, English Language, English Literature, a Modern Foreign Language and at least two sciences, plus three or four other optional subjects at GCSE or IGCSE.

Sixth Form: All pupils study for the International Baccalaureate Diploma in the Sixth Form, being able to select three High Level subjects and three Standard Level subjects from across the IB Diploma's six subject groups, and also taking the IB Core (Theory of Knowledge; Extended Essay; and CAS – Creativity, Activity and Service).

The School's curriculum goes beyond preparation for examinations. For example, PE and games are compulsory for all and Friday afternoon is set aside for the entire school to pursue non-academic activities: Combined Cadet Force, Leadership, service in the community, outdoor pursuits, Art, Information Technology etc.

Music and drama. The School has a very rich musical and dramatic life. Many of the musical groups and theatrical productions take place jointly with King Edward VI High School for Girls. There are over ten different musical groups and choirs. The School's Performing Arts Centre has main hall seating for up to 500 and excellent facilities for music and drama.

Games. Rugby, cricket, hockey, and water polo are the major team games in the School. However, many other games prosper including archery, athletics, badminton, basketball, chess, cross-country, cycling, fencing, fives, golf, kayaking, squash, swimming, table tennis and tennis. The School has extensive playing fields for all these activities plus its own swimming pool, international-standard athletics track, sports hall, gymnasia and squash courts. In 2015 the School opened a new hockey pavilion and astro pitch, and in 2019 it opened a new sports centre, which includes a sports hall, cardiovascular fitness room, multipurpose space, classroom and changing rooms.

Societies and clubs. The School has a very wide range of clubs and societies including Christian Union, Islamic Society, Literary Society, History Society, Bookworms, Economics and Business Society, Senior and Junior Dramatic Societies, Art Society, Geographical Society, Debating Society, Mentoring Society, Mathematical Society, Modern Languages Society, Sustainability Society, Writers' Society, Lifeguarding, Chess Club, Model United Nations, Spectrum, School Chronicle and Hillwalking.

CCF, Outdoor pursuits and expeditions. The Royal Naval, RAF and Army Sections of the Combined Cadet Force are very popular amongst pupils. In addition, the KES Award and the Duke of Edinburgh's Award scheme have grown substantially in recent years, so that the majority of pupils in the third year gain the KES Award and over 40 each year undertake the Gold Duke of Edinburgh's Award. All of this forms part of a strong tradition of trips and expeditions, ranging from cycling and caving and walking and skiing trips, to language trips to Europe, to major expeditions to Ecuador and the Galapagos Islands, Guyana and Madagascar. There have also been very successful rugby tours to Australia, India, Canada, South Africa and China.

Forms and houses. In the first five years, each form has an average of 25 pupils. In the Sixth Form, forms are on average 12 in number, and often comprise pupils together from the Lower and Upper Sixth. There is also a house system, comprising eight houses, which continues to provide an important element of pastoral support and competition in sport, music, drama, debating and general knowledge.

Charitable status. The Schools of King Edward VI in Birmingham is a Registered Charity, number 529051. The purpose of the Foundation is to educate children and young persons living in or around the City of Birmingham.

Governing Body of The Schools of King Edward the Sixth in Birmingham:
Chair of Governors: Mrs Lucy Williams

***Chief Master*: Dr Katy L Ricks**, MA, DPhil

Deputy Chief Master: Ms D E McMillan, BSc

Deputy Head (*Academic*): Dr J R Evans, BSc, PhD
Deputy Head (*Pastoral*): Mr T Quayle, BA, MSt, MBA
Deputy Head (*Co-curricular*): Mr M J Bartlett, BA
Deputy Head (*Digital, Data and Systems*): Mr H M Coverdale, BSc Econ
Director of External Relations: Mrs Jo Bullock, BSocSc, CIPR Diploma
Director of Admissions: Mrs Neelam Hall, BA
Director of Development: Mrs Adelaide Bailey, BA, CSBM
Bursar (*Operations*): Mrs Jenny Butterworth, BSc, FCA
Bursar (*Estates and Finance*): Mrs Zoe Robinson, BSc, ACA

King Edward's Witley

Petworth Road, Godalming, Surrey GU8 5SG

Tel: 01428 686700
email: admissions@kesw.org
website: www.kesw.org
X/Twitter: @KESWitley
Facebook: @KESWitley
LinkedIn: /king-edward's-school-witley

King Edward's Witley, a Bridewell School, was founded in 1553 by King Edward VI as Bridewell Royal Hospital. Originally housed at the Bridewell Palace, which was given under Royal Charter to the City of London, the School moved to Witley in 1867, simultaneously changing its name; it became co-educational again in 1952. The School is an independent boarding and day school for girls and boys aged 11–18. The School has 484 pupils; approximately 70% are day pupils. There are a substantial number of bursaries, currently around 50, available to help girls and boys whose home circumstances make a boarding style of education a particular need.

The School is situated in a 100-acre campus in an Area of Outstanding Natural Beauty in the Surrey countryside, approximately ten miles south of Guildford, with Heathrow and Gatwick international airports both within a 45-minute drive.

King Edward's Witley is steeped in history, but combines its traditional strengths with a modern outlook. The School prides itself on its ability to provide a school community that reflects the real world, admitting pupils from a broad range of academic, social, economic and cultural backgrounds – 80% are English native speakers and 40 countries are represented. All children are nurtured to encourage independent thinking and a spirit of respect and understanding for others, resulting in a mature and well-rounded outlook on life and a commitment to upholding the strongest moral values.

King Edward's takes pride in its academic, socio-economic and cultural diversity. The School ensures that all pupils are congratulated for their effort and dedication to achieving personal success. King Edward's Sixth Form offers A Levels and BTECs. In 2023, IB pupils achieved an average score 32.3 out of a possible 45; the world average is 32. A Level results – 29.1% A*–A, 59.5% A*–B, 77.2% A*–C.

In 2023, at GCSE, 95.1% of pupils achieved 5 or more grades at 9–4 (A*–C) including English Language and Mathematics. 40.2% of grades were 9–7 (A*–A), 60.5% of grades were 9–6 (A*–B).

The School also runs a one-year Pre Sixth Form course for overseas pupils, representing an opportunity to improve English language skills and trial the A Level subjects on offer, allowing for more Sixth Form choices.

Renowned for its ability to nurture pupils so they excel in their academic studies, King Edward's Witley also provides a highly motivating and inspiring environment for children to equally thrive in other sporting/creative activities. The School has an excellent reputation for its welcoming community and the provision of high-quality pastoral care.

Years 7 and 8 constitute the Lower School and are accommodated in Queen Mary House with shared communal facilities for boys and girls. From Year 9 upwards, boys and girls live in six modern, purpose-built paired houses where the accommodation and study areas are completely separate but everyone can come together in the shared communal facilities on the ground floor.

Facilities at the School are second to none and include a state-of-the-art Business and Finance Centre, indoor swimming pool, gym, all-weather hockey and tennis playing fields and a central dining hall, which delivers an outstanding standard of catering. The School pioneered paired boarding houses with communal areas, where everyone can come together in their spare time to enjoy games, TV, music and conversation in the common rooms, kitchen, music and television rooms. For the Sixth Form, a lively common room, Sixth Form prefects' room, study area and careers library provide an environment for independent learning and recreation.

Admission. Children are normally admitted at 11+, 13+ and 16+, but if there is room they may be admitted at other times, and occasionally a child who should clearly be working alongside older children is admitted at 10+. Admission is by pre-testing or by the School's own entrance examination and interview taken normally in the January prior to entry.

Fees per term (2023–2024). Boarders: Lower School £12,735, Year 9–11 £12,735, Pre-Sixth Form and Sixth Form £12,985, including all boarding and tuition fees.

Day Pupils: Lower School £6,675, Year 9–11 £7,835, Pre-Sixth Form and Sixth Form £7,995 including meals. Individual music tuition in piano, organ, singing and all orchestral instruments is available.

Bursaries. Bursaries are available for both boarding and day pupils. The School has an endowment providing support for children whose circumstances make boarding a particular need. Awards are reviewed annually with regard to parental circumstances and to school fees. They may be given in conjunction with Local Education Authority grants or help from a charitable trust. The School has a dedicated Bursaries Officer who works with applicants to source the financial support needed to enable worthy candidates to join the School.

Scholarships. Academic, Art, Drama, DT, Music and Sports Scholarships are offered at 11+, 13+ or 16+ for entry to the Sixth Form. These awards will be up to a maximum of 10% of full fees but may be augmented in case of financial need. Children of serving members of the armed forces will be considered for a discount.

Charitable status. King Edward's Witley is a Registered Charity, number 311997. The Foundation exists to provide boarding education for families whose circumstances make boarding a particular need, though the excellent facilities and the high standards of academic achievement and pastoral care make it attractive also to any family looking for a modern and distinctive education.

Treasurer and Chairman of Governors: Mrs J Voisin, BA

***Head*: Mrs Joanna Wright**, BA, PGCE

Deputy Head: D Corran
Deputy Head Co-Curriculum: M Harrison
Assistant Deputy Head (Academic): R Davies

Academic Staff:
* *Head of Department*
† *Housemaster/mistress*

J A J Allen, BA (*English*)
Mrs S Antill, NatDip (*ICT*)
R Arch, MA, MSc (**Economics & Business Studies*)
Ms R Archer (*Design & Technology, Food & Textiles*)
B Arthey, BA (*Guitar*)
Dr P Attwell, BSc, PhD (*Science*)
A Bardell (*Technician – Art & Photography*)
A Baynes, MA (**Modern Languages*)
Dr C Brockhaus, MA, PhD (*Language Assistant*)
Ms H Browning (*Learning Support & EAL*)
Mrs A Butler (*School Office Administrator*)
T Campbell, BA (**Geography*)
E Cathro (**Chemistry*)
Miss E Cattle, MA (**Classics*)
Dr P Cave, LRAM, GRSM, ARAM, PhD (*Piano*)
Mrs L Cleaves, BA, MA (**Drama*)
Miss S Condy, BTh, MA (†*Elizabeth, Religious Studies & Philosophy*)
Miss T Cowell, BMus, MMus (*Brass*)
J G Culbert, BSc, Dip Comp Sc (**Science, *Physics*)
Mrs M Davies (**Careers and Higher Education*)
R Davies, BSc, MLitt, MA (**Mathematics*)
Miss F de Bray (*Music*)
Miss J Dibb-Fuller, BSc (*Learning Support and EAL*)
Mrs S Ellison, BA, LRAM (*Bassoon*)
N Emsley, BSc, Dip Com (†*Grafton, Mathematics, Science, Theory of Knowledge and Critical Thinking*)
Mrs F Fitch, BA (*Head of Hockey*)
M Fox, BSC (*Science*)
Mrs E Francis, BA (*History*)
T Frazer, BA (*Assistant Director of Music*)
Mr A Guthrie (*Science Technician*)
Ms C Harding, BA, ACRM (*Double Bass*)
Mrs E Harman, BSc (†*Ridley, Economics & Business Studies*)
Mrs J Harris, BA (**Library & Resources, Extended Essay Coordinator*)
Ms R Harris, PGDip, BMus (*Voice*)
M Harrison, BA (*Director of Co-Curriculum and Leadership, Modern Languages*)
Mrs L Harris-Jones, BA, MA, MBA, (**Religious Studies & Philosophy, *Theory of Knowledge & Critical Thinking*)
G Haylock, BA (*Head of Football*)
P W Head, BEng, MPhil (**Mathematics*)
J Hennessey-Brown, ARCM, BMus (*Cello*)
Mrs A Hill, BSc (*Science Technician*)
Mrs R Hillage, PGCE, BA (*Learning Support and EAL*)
Mrs S J Hinde-Brown, BA (*Modern Languages*)
Mrs J A Hinton, BSc (*Modern Languages*)
Mrs A Hobbs (*Sports Coach*)
Miss R Hodges, MA (*Science*)
Mrs G Holtham, BA (*Modern Languages*)
Mrs J Hooker (*Design & Technology Food and Textiles*)

Miss S Hughes, MChem (*Science*)
Ms U John, GMD, RNCM (*Violin and Viola*)
A N K Johnson, BSc, MSc (**Design & Technology Resistant Materials*)
D Laurence, BA (*Economics & Business Studies*)
Mr S Laurent (*Teacher of Sports, Cricket specialism*)
Dr A Lennard, PhD, BSc (**ICT*)
Mrs J M Lyttle, BA (*†Tudor, English & Drama*)
A Macmillan, BA (*†Wakefield, Design & Technology Resistant Materials*)
Mrs Z Marsden, BA (**Learning Support and EAL*)
Ms R McNaught, BA, MA, Dip RAM
Mrs A Meyer, BSc, BEd (*Mathematics, Assistant Head of Sixth Form, Pre Sixth Coordinator*)
P Miller, MSc, BSc, (**Director of Sport*)
Dr H Mir, PhD (*Mathematics*)
Mrs L Moore, BA (*Art & Photography*)
Miss N Nishizono-Miller (*Organist in Residence*)
Ms A Ochoa-Fagan, BA (*Language Assistant*)
Mrs M Pevreall, BSc, MSc (**Biology*)
Mrs M Phillips, BA (**History*)
Mrs D Pickering, MA (*Teacher of French and Subject Co-ordinator*)
Mrs M A Plana Duran, BA (*Language Assistant*)
Ms O Pocock, MA (*Classics*)
Reverend J Radcliffe, MA (*Religious Studies & Philosophy*)
C Robinson (*Technician, Design & Technology Resistant Materials*)
Mr A Ryman (*Teacher of Sports*)
Mrs C Shouksmith, BA (**Art & Photography*)
A Sibacher, BSc (*Mathematics*)
B Simmonds, BMus, Dip ABRSM, LLB, MPerf (*Piano*)
D Slater, BA (*English*)
S Sliwka, BMus, FRCO, LRSM (**Director of Music*)
D Standing, MA RAM (*Voice*)
Mrs S Styles, BEng (*Science*)
Mrs H Thorpe, BA (*Geography*)
D Tobias, BA (*†Edward, English, Theory of Knowledge and Critical Thinking*)
Mrs J Todd (*Examinations Officer*)
Mr F Tontoh (*Percussion and Drums*)
Ms E Trussler (*Artist in Residence*)
Mrs E Turnbull, BSc (*Mathematics*)
Mrs A Valentino, BA, MEd (*English*)
Mrs C van der Vijer, BA (*Language Assistant*)
Mrs A Webster, BA (*Learning Support and EAL*)
Ms J Webster, BMus (*Flute*)
Mrs C Wickramasinghe De Silva, BA QTS (*Learning Support and EAL*)
H Wiggin, BMus, Grad Dip, MPerf (*Clarinet, Flute & Saxophone*)
Mrs S Witherby, BA, MSc (*Learning Support and EAL*)
Mrs J Worrall (*Science Technician*)

King Henry VIII School

Part of the Coventry School Foundation

Warwick Road, Coventry CV3 6AQ
Tel: 024 7627 1111
email: info.khviii@bkhs.org.uk
website: www.kinghenrys.co.uk
X/Twitter: @KHVIIISchool
Facebook: @KingHenryVIIISchool
Instagram: @kinghenryviiischool

Founded in 1545 by John Hales, Clerk of the Hanaper to the King, under Letters Patent of King Henry VIII, King Henry VIII School has a deserved reputation as one of the finest independent, co-educational day schools in the UK.

Learning, wellbeing, and respect – these are our prime aims.

The school is represented on the Headmasters' Conference and on the Association of Governing Bodies of Independent Schools. The governing body is the Coventry School Foundation, on which are represented Sir Thomas White's Charity, the Coventry Church Charities, Coventry General Charities and Birmingham, Coventry, Oxford and Warwick Universities. There are also several co-opted Governors.

There are 317 boys and 255 girls in the Senior School, and 135 boys and 102 girls in the Junior School.

Facilities. The school moved to its present extensive site in a pleasant part of Coventry in 1885. The Governors have continually improved, extended and restored the buildings which are well equipped to cope with the demands of an up-to-date, relevant and challenging curriculum. The school has extensive playing fields, a six-lane, 25m swimming pool and fitness suite. The school has a brand new, state of the art Robotics Hub providing a resource for students and local primary schools in the community. The school has its own museum featuring a timeline from 1545 and contains original Tudor artefacts.

Curriculum. The curriculum is broad and balanced, integrating National Curriculum principles and practices where appropriate. The Senior School curriculum provides courses leading to the GCSE examinations and A Levels. Subjects available currently are Art, Biology, Business Studies, Chemistry, Classical Civilisation, Computer Science, Design and Food Technology, Drama and Theatre Studies, Economics, English, French, Geography, German, History, Latin, Law, Mathematics, Music, Photography, Philosophy, Religion and Ethics, Physics, Politics, Psychology and Spanish. Physical Education and Sport are also considered to be a vital part of the curriculum and are available as an A Level option. All students follow a structured PSHE course.

Courses in Key Skills/Complementary Studies and Critical Thinking are offered in the Sixth Form. Year 12 pupils achieve great success in The Extended Project Qualification.

Examination results at all levels are excellent.

Games. Rugby, Hockey, Netball, Basketball, Cross-Country Running, Athletics, Rounders, Tennis, Cricket, Swimming, Golf and Orienteering. Junior School games include Tag Rugby, Swimming, Soccer, Rounders, Athletics, Cricket and Cross-Country Running. The school has one of the largest artificial turf games area in the country, used mainly for hockey, but providing an additional 24 tennis courts in the summer.

Extracurricular Activities. The School is noted for the excellence of its sport, music, drama, debating, public speaking and outdoor pursuits including DofE. All pupils are encouraged to make a contribution to the extracurricular life of the school. The School has close connections with many universities including Oxford and Cambridge.

Admission. Admission is via the School's own Entrance Examination, held annually in October for entrance the following September. The normal age of entry is 11, but there are additional intakes at other ages and also at Sixth Form level. All enquiries about admission to the school should be addressed to henrysadmissions@bkhs.org.uk.

Scholarships. The Governors award annually a number (not fixed) of entrance bursaries and scholarships. Full details regarding financial assistance are available on the website www.kinghenrys.co.uk.

Old Coventrians Association. Email: alumni@bkhs.org.uk; website: www.kinghenrys.co.uk.

Junior School. The Junior School is based on the same site and enjoys excellent facilities which include a Library, ICT rooms with networked PCs, an Art and Design rooms, a Science room, Astroturf and Sports Hall and a Music room. Children are accepted by assessment from 7+ to 10+. The emphasis is on a broad education based upon the National Curriculum and children are prepared for entry to the Senior School.

Fees per term (2023–2024). Senior School £5,050; Junior School £4,000; Pre Prep & Nursery (5 full days) £3,500.

Charitable status. Coventry School Foundation is a Registered Charity, number 528961. Its aim is to advance the education of boys and girls by the provision of a school or schools in or near the City of Coventry.

Chair of Governors: Mr Ian Dunn

Principal, Coventry School Foundation: Mr C Staley, BA, MBA

***Senior School Headmaster*: Mr Philip Dearden**, MA Ed, BA

Deputy Heads:
Dr Michele Cuthbert, BSc, MEd, HDipEd, WITS
Mr Richard Sewell, PGCE, BA Hons
Mrs Carrie Dowding, PGCE, BSc Hons

***Junior School Headmaster*: Mr Josh Holtby**, BA, MA

King William's College

Castletown, Isle of Man IM9 1TP
Tel: 01624 820110
email: admissions@kwc.im
website: www.kwc.im
X/Twitter: @kwciom
Facebook: @kwciom/
Instagram: @kwcandthebuchanschool
LinkedIn: /school/king-william's-college

Motto: *Assiduitate, non desidia*

King William's College owes its foundation to Dr Isaac Barrow, Bishop of Sodor and Man from 1663 to 1671, who established an Educational Trust in 1668. The funds of the Trust were augmented by public subscription and the College was opened in 1833 and named after King William IV, 'The Sailor King'.

In 1991, the College merged with the Isle of Man's other independent school, The Buchan School, Castletown, which had been founded by Lady Laura Buchan in 1875 to provide education for young ladies. The Buchan School has been reformed as the junior section of the College for boys and girls up to age 11. (*For further details of The Buchan School, see entry in IAPS section*).

The College is set in superb countryside on the edge of Castletown Bay and adjacent to Ronaldsway Airport. The Isle of Man is approximately 33 miles long and 13 miles wide and is an area of diverse and beautiful scenery.

There are approximately 340 pupils at College and a further 160 pupils at the Preparatory School. There is also a Nursery School for 2 to 4 year olds on the Buchan site. Both King William's College and The Buchan School are fully co-educational.

Entry. New pupils are accepted at any time, but most begin at the start of the September Term. Boys and girls are admitted to the Preparatory School up to the age of 11, at which point transfer to King William's College is automatic. Entry to College, including Sixth Form level, is by Head's report and interview.

Further details and a prospectus may be obtained from the Admissions Office to which applications for entry should be made.

Organisation. The school is divided into three sections: Fourth Form (Years 7 & 8), Fifth Form (Years 9, 10 & 11) and Sixth Form (Years 12 & 13). Each section is led by a Head of Year, assisted by a team of tutors who monitor the academic progress and deal with all day-to-day matters relating to the pupils in their charge. In addition, all pupils are placed in one of three co-educational Houses for internal competitive purposes, which provides an important element of continuity throughout a pupil's career at the School.

Boarders. There are two houses: one for boys and the other for girls. The living and sleeping accommodation is arranged principally in study-bedrooms for senior pupils, with junior pupils sharing with one other student. Each House has its own Houseparent who is responsible for the pastoral welfare of the pupils. He or she is assisted by two or three tutors, of whom at least two are resident.

Chapel. The College is a Church of England foundation but pupils of all denominations attend Chapel; the spirit of the services is distinctly ecumenical.

Curriculum. Pupils at both Schools follow the National Curriculum in its essentials.

The curriculum is designed to provide a broad, balanced and challenging form of study for all pupils. At 11–13 pupils take English, Mathematics, French and Spanish or Latin, Science, History, Geography, Design Technology, ICT, Art, Music, Drama, Religious Studies, Physical Education, PSHE. Pupils then go on to study typically 9 or 10 subjects at (I)GCSE level from a wide number of options.

In the Sixth Form King William's College offers the **International Baccalaureate**. Students choose 6 subjects, normally 3 at higher level and 3 at standard level, which must include their first language, a second language, a science, a social science and Mathematics. In addition, students write an extended essay (a research piece of 4,000 words), follow a course in the Theory of Knowledge (practical philosophy) and spend the equivalent of one half day a week on some form of creative aesthetic activity or active community service (e.g. Duke of Edinburgh's Award fulfils this requirement).

Music and Drama. There are excellent facilities for Drama with House plays and at least one major school production each year, together with regular coaching in Speech and Drama. There are Junior and Senior Bands and Choirs, and a very flourishing Chapel Choir. The House Music competition is one of the many focal points of House activity.

Games. The College has a strong tradition and a fine reputation in the major games of rugby, hockey, netball and cricket. There are regular fixtures with Isle of Man schools and schools in other parts of the British Isles. Athletics, football, cross-country and swimming all flourish and there are both House and College competitions. Senior pupils may opt to play golf on the magnificent adjoining Castletown Golf Links or to sail as their major summer sport. There are approximately thirty acres of first class playing fields, an indoor heated swimming pool which is in use throughout the year, a miniature rifle range, a gymnasium for basketball and badminton, hard tennis courts, two squash courts and an all-weather pitch and outdoor cricket nets.

Other Activities. There is a wide range of societies and activities to complement academic life. The Duke of Edinburgh's Award Scheme flourishes and expeditions are undertaken regularly both on the Island and further afield. There is a thriving Combined Cadet Force and Social Services group. There are strong links with the Armed Services who help regularly with Cadet training. There are regular skiing trips, choir tours and educational trips to the UK and abroad.

Travel. King William's College is easily accessible from the UK and abroad. Some boarders come by sea from Heysham or Liverpool using the regular service to Douglas but the majority of boarding pupils and parents come by air from the British Isles and much further afield. There are direct flights to London, Belfast, Birmingham, Dublin, Liverpool, Manchester and other UK cities. Boarding House staff are fully experienced in arranging international flights and younger pupils are met at the airport.

Health. The health of all pupils is in the care of the School Doctor. There is a sanatorium supervised by a qualified nursing staff and high standards of medical care are available at Noble's Hospital in Douglas.

Fees per annum (2023–2024). Day: £20,345 (Years 7 & 8), £24,545 (Years 9–11), £26,995 (Years 12 & 13). Boarding Fee: £14,595 in addition to Day Fee.

A reduction of one-third of the fee for boarders and one half of the fee for day pupils is allowed for children of clergy holding a benefice or Bishop's licence and residing in the Isle of Man. There is a similar arrangement for children of Methodist Ministers.

A reduction of 10% is allowed for serving members of the Armed Forces of the Crown. Once a pupil is accepted, the reduction continues even though the parent may leave the Services.

A reduction is allowed for the second, third and fourth child.

Scholarships and Bursaries. Year 7 Academic Scholarships are available. Our Scholarships & Awards are honorary. There is also a Bursary fund to support students if the financial circumstances of parents make this necessary. Further details of all scholarships may be obtained from the Principal's Office and on the website: kwc.im/scholarships/.

Charitable status. King William's College is a Manx Registered Charity, number 615 and is operated as a Company limited by guarantee.

Visitor: The Lord Archbishop of York

Council Members of Bishop Barrow's Foundation:
His Excellency Sir John Lorimer, Lieutenant Governor of the Isle of Man (*Chairman of Council Members*)
The Lord Bishop, Rt Revd P Eagles
Mr G C Kinrade, Chief Executive Officer, Department of Education and Children, BEd
Mr S G Billinghurst, BA Hons, ACA
Mr P B Clucas, BA, BSc Hons, MICA
Mr A C Collister
Mrs A V Craine
Mr T W B Cullen, MBE, MA
Mrs E J Higgins, BSc, ACA
Dr M J Hoy, MBE, MA, PhD
Mr N H Wood, ACA, TEP

Governors:
Mr P B Clucas, BA, BSc Hons, MICA
Mr S Billinghurst, BA Hons, ACA
Mr Y C D Chan, BA Hons, MEd, ACA, DChA, MBE
Mr A C Collister
Mrs S M Dean, BA Hons, FCCA
Mrs C Edmundson, BMus, MBA, PGCE, LRAM, ARCM
Mr R W Flower, BSc Hons, MEd
Mr P L Harwood, BSc Hons, FIA
Mrs E J Higgins, BSc, ACA
Dr L V Hulme, MB, BS, LRCP, MRCS
Miss S J Leahy, LLB, Dip LP
Dr M Drijfhout, MRCGP, DRCOG, DFFP, DPalMed, DOcMed

Bursar and Clerk to the Governors: Ms M Mackie, FCCA

***Principal*: Damian Henderson**, MA Cantab

Deputy Head Academic: Mr M Roberts
Deputy Head Pastoral: Mr S L Corrie, BMus Hons

* *Head of Department*
† *Housemaster/mistress*
§ Head of Year

Full Time:
Helen Allan, BSc Hons, CPT3A
Kathy Bailey
Amanda Barber, BSc Hons, PhD†
Amy L G Beesley, BA Hons, PGDip
Amy Benziane, BA Hons
Catrin Beswick, MSci
Clare Broadbent, MA
Katharine M Brown, MPhys*
Harry Brindle, BA Hons
Madeleine J Burger, BEd
Amy-Jayne Clark, BA Hons, MA
Stephen N Cope, BA Hons*
Matthew Crabtree, BSc Hons
Emma Craine, BA Hons*
Helen Crosbie
Colin Davidson, MA Hons
Steven Daykin, BMus, PgDip, MISM*
Claire Duffy
Sonja M Ellson, MA*
Carolina Ganzo-Perez, MA*
Donné Gerry, BEd Hons
Lauren Groom, BA*
France Heckel, MA*
Vikki Hope, BSc Hons
Niall A Howell Evans, BA
Paula Howell Evans
Edmund J Jeffers, BA Hons*
Sara A Jeffers, BA Hons
Stephen B Jelly, BA Hons*§
Stephen P Kelly, BA Hons*
Amanda Kerr, BA Hons, MA, MAEd*
Bethan Kneen, BSc§
Ella Magee
Anya L Morgans, BA Ed Hons, BSc Hons*§
Paul H Morgans, CChem, CSci, PhD, MRSC*
Mark Moss, MArt Hons
Susie Parry, BA Hons*†
Riaan Riekert, BComm*
María Sánchez de la Blanca García, BA
Alison M Schreiber, MA
Erica J Scott, BA Hons (*Chaplain*)
Kirry K Shimmin, BSc*
Zoë E Shimmin-Mann, BSc Hons, MSc*
Clare V Singleton, BA*
Alasdair D Ulyett, BSc*
Philip Verschueren, BSc, MSc
Anouk de Vos, BSc Hons, MA*
Zoe E A Watterson
Schalk de Wet, BA Hons

Principal's PA: Mrs Jo Bateson & Mrs Denise Jones
Admissions Registrar: Mrs Marion Clifford-Taggart
School Medical Officer: Dr Marijtje Drijfhout, MRCGP, DRCOG, DFFP, DPalMed, DOcMed

King's College School

Wimbledon Common, London SW19 4TT

Tel: 020 8255 5300 (Senior School)
020 8255 5335 (Junior School)
email: admissions@kcs.org.uk (Senior)
jsadmissions@kcs.org.uk (Junior)
website: www.kcs.org.uk
X/Twitter: @KCSWimbledon
Facebook: @kingscollegeschool

Motto: *Sancte et Sapienter*

King's College School Wimbledon is a friendly, kind, inclusive and purposeful community where pupils' enthusiasm and creativity shine in every corner of the school. Founded by royal charter in 1829, as part of the university of King's College London, intellectual endeavour and a progressive spirit have always been at the heart of the life of King's. While pupils' exceptional success in public examinations makes King's one of the world's leading schools, a true King's education is so much more. The school motto, 'sancte et sapienter' (with holiness and with wisdom), encapsulates the importance we place on both the mind and the spirit of the whole person. King's prepares pupils to forge their own path with the confidence and heart of our lion, guided by their learning and strong values. We want them to lead meaningful, fulfilling lives in the world beyond school.

Organisation. King's College School is a day school. Boys only are admitted below the sixth form while the sixth form is co-educational. The school consists of a senior school of 1,221 pupils aged 11 to 18 and a junior school of 287 pupils aged 7 to 11 who are prepared for entry to the senior school.

Pastoral care is delivered in forms until Year 8. From Year 9 (fourth form), pupils are allocated a tutor in a house who is responsible for their progress and welfare throughout the rest of their school career.

Admission. Entrance at 11+ into Year 7 is via an entrance exam which boys sit in year 6.

Entrance at 13+ into Year 9 is via a pre-test which boys sit in Year 6 followed by the CE or scholarship in Year 8. Should a boy's prep school no longer be preparing pupils for CE, the conditional Year 9 place is subject to satisfactory reports from his prep school head.

Places for girls and boys are available each year for entry to the sixth form via 16+ entrance tests. Preliminary enquiries about entry should be made to the admissions registrar.

Junior School. Entrance examinations, graded according to the ages of the pupils, are held in the January of the year of entry. Enquiries should be made to the junior school secretary. *(For further details of the junior school refer to entry in IAPS section.)*

Scholarships. A number of academic, music, sport, drama and art scholarships are available at 11+, 13+ and 16+ entry points. For further details, visit the school website or contact the admissions registrar.

Bursaries. King's is keen to provide financial support to families whose only barrier to joining the school is the cost of fees. We offer free (100% bursaries) and subsidised places (partial bursaries) at the main entry points to the senior school, Year 7 (11+), Year 9 (3+) and lower sixth (16+). We can also offer extra support with additional costs like uniform, sports kit, trips, lunches and textbooks. For further information, please visit the school website.

Fees per term (2023–2024). The senior school (Year 9 onwards): £8,630; the lower school (Years 7–8): £7,805; the junior school (Years 5–6): £7,805; the junior school (Years 3–4): £7,250.

The Curriculum – Junior School. The curriculum of the junior school is designed to lead naturally into that of the senior school in content and style. All boys within a year group follow the same timetable.

Transition and first form (Years 3 and 4):

English; Mathematics; Science; History; Geography; Religious Studies; Music; Drama; Art; Technology (Year 3 only); ICT; Personal, Social, Health and Economic Education (PSHEE); Think Tank (in Years 3 and 4); three double sessions of Physical Education and Games.

Second and third forms (Years 5 and 6):

English; Mathematics; Science; French; Latin; History; HOTEL (History of the English Language); Geography; Religious Studies; Music; Drama; Art; Design and Engineering; ICT; Personal, Social, Health and Economic Education (PSHEE); Physical Education and two afternoons of Games. Boys are set French and Mathematics from Year 6.

The Curriculum – Senior School. The lower and middle school curriculums offer a wide range of options which enable the maximum choice of subjects in the sixth form. A very wide range of subjects is available at GCSE and IGCSE (International GCSE). In the sixth form, pupils choose to study either A Levels or the International Baccalaureate Diploma Programme (IBDP).

Religious Education. King's is an Anglican foundation but welcomes pupils from all churches and faiths, and the practice of other faiths is encouraged. The school has a Chaplaincy through which pupils are prepared for confirmation and there is a Chapel for voluntary worship and communion

Music. A state-of-the-art music school, with a 200-seat concert hall, was opened in September 2018 by HRH The Duchess of Gloucester. Four orchestras, six choirs, big band, chamber ensemble, as well as various smaller groups and jazz groups, perform a number of major choral and orchestral works each year. There are regular performances at major London venues including Westminster Abbey, Cadogan Hall, St Paul's Cathedral and St John's Smith Square. The choir and orchestra also undertake international tours. Approximately 30% of the pupils have individual music lessons at the school.

Games. A multi-function sports and swimming complex was opened in September 2019. It provides a six-court sports hall, a 25 m swimming pool, aerobic areas, a strength and conditioning room and a large studio amongst other facilities. There are two all-weather surfaces for hockey and tennis at the Kingsway ground. The school's boathouse is on the Tideway at Putney Bridge. After an introduction to a range of games in the fourth form, pupils have a free choice of termly sports. The major sports are rugby, hockey, netball, football, tennis and cricket and the games programme also includes athletics, badminton, basketball, cross-country running, fencing, golf, rowing, squash, swimming, table tennis and water polo.

School Societies and Activities. King's is renowned for its co-curricular programme; the importance we attach to this dimension of a pupil's education is recognised by the dedication of an entire afternoon's timetable on Friday to activities. Alongside this programme, a huge variety of sporting, drama, musical and other activities is offered throughout the school week. King's extensive partnerships and outreach programme reflects a strong belief in the benefit of educational partnerships and a permanent commitment to sharing our resources with the local community. The community projects are the most popular co-curricular activity at King's, with over 400 of our pupils and teachers volunteering to work in their community every Friday afternoon.

Honours. Places offered at Oxford and Cambridge for 2016: 57, 2017: 51, 2018: 44, 2019: 46; 2020: 39, 2021: 25; 2022: 39; 2023: 40.

Charitable status. King's College School is a Registered Charity, number 310024. It exists to provide education for children.

Governing Body:
The Archbishop of Canterbury (*Visitor*)
The Rt Revd Christopher Chessun, Bishop of Southwark (*Ex Officio*)
Lord Deighton, KBE (*Chairman*)
G C Slimmon, MA, MBA (*Vice Chairman*)
S A Bennett, BA
C G Hale, MA, LLM
S A B Hobbs, BA, PGCE
D G Ingram, MA
Sir Robert Jay, KC
J Larizadeh
I A Macmillan, BSc, ACA, MBA
A Ng, BSc, FCA
T Oki
R J Parker, MA
J-A Prager
J L Robinson, BA, PGCE, MEd
J G Sarpong, BSc, MBA
T Stockil
P J L Strafford, BA, MBA

Acting Bursar & Clerk to the Governors: Mr A R M Stewart

***Head*: Dr A K Cotton**

* *Head of Department*

Junior School Headmaster: E H Lougher
Senior Deputy Head: Ms M J Clarke, MA

Deputy Heads:
Mr R H Amlot, MA
Dr R C J Atkinson
Mr K Gross, BEd

Director of Studies: Mr M Stables, MA

Assistant Heads:
Mr B M Baulf, MA (*Head of Teaching and Learning*)
Mr J S Gibson, BA (*Head of Lower School*)
Mrs J M Lawton-Cook, BSc (*Head of Sixth Form*) [maternity leave]
Mr D Miller, BSc (*Innovation*)

Miss A L McGarvey, BSc (*Enrichment & Pupil Progress*)
Mr C P Sandels, MSc (*Head of Middle School and Acting Assistant Head of Sixth Form*)

Directors:
Mr D I Cass, BA (*IB*)
Mr T J Davies, BA (*Digital Learning and Innovation*)
Miss R M Davis, BA (*Staff Welfare*)
Mr P A Hatch, MusB (*Partnerships and Outreach*)
Mr H M Lam, MA (*Higher Education*)
Mrs H M Lindsey-Noble, BA (*Equality, Diversity and Inclusion*)
Miss C A Ramgoolam, MA (*Public Occasions*)
Mr J M A Ross, BA (*Acting Director of Mental Health and Wellbeing*; *Acting Deputy Head of Modern Languages and Head of Italian*)
Miss E R Tozzi, BA (*Mental Health and Wellbeing*) [maternity leave]
Mrs S Willis (*Safeguarding*)

TEACHING STAFF

Art:
*Mrs G A Yuille, BA
Mrs E J Halliday, BA
Miss E R McIllroy, BA
Mr N Pollen, MA (*Head of Lower School and Junior School Art*)
Miss H J Williamson, BA
Miss B B Yardley, BA

Biology:
*Dr J E Blythe
Miss J Brown, MA
Ms S L Burnham, BSc
Mr J E Grabowski, BSc (*Head of Layton*)
Miss A M Lethbridge, BSc
Mrs R G O'Brien, MA
Mr J Painter, MA
Mrs R F A Rose, BSc (*Head of Year 7*)
Mr A I C Stockley, BSc
Mrs E M Taylor, BSc
Miss E J C Witney-Smith, BSc

Chemistry:
*Dr A M Hayes
Miss R L Alexander, BSc
Ms K P C Anderson, MSc
Dr R C J Atkinson
Mr T D E Bithell, MA
Dr I I F Boogaerts (*Deputy Head of IB*)
Ms C M Burke, MSc
Mr C P R Crow, MSc
Miss A M Dawe, BSc [maternity leave]
Mr E Josypenko, MSc (*Head of Maclear*)
Ms M E Sanford, BSc (*Head of Glenesk*)
Dr R A L Winchester
Miss R Y Yang BSc

Classics:
*Mr S L C Young, BA
Miss F T I Barwick Ward, BA
Mr B M Baulf, BA (*Assistant Head, Head of Teaching and Learning*)
Mr G E Bennett, BA (*Deputy Head of IB*)
Miss E A Garnett, MA (*Head of A Level*)
Mr A L V Karski, BA
Mr J A Pinder, BA

Computer Science:
*Mr D Haxton, BSc
Mrs E P Hedley, MSc
Miss C A Ramgoolam, MA (*Director of Public Occasions*)

Design & Engineering:
*Miss L E L Spicer, MS
Mr J D Broderick, MA (*Head of US and overseas universities*)
Mr H Chandler, MA
Mrs H M Gallagher, BSc
Mr T E Phillips, BEng

Drama:
Ms D J Barron, MA (*Director of Drama*)
Miss H Feeny, MA (*Head of Lower School Drama*)
Mr J L B Trapmore, MA (*Head of Curricular Drama*)
Mr P H Dyer, MA (*Director in Residence*)

Economics & Social Sciences:
*Ms A M Troy, BA
Miss N A l Khalifa, BSc
Mrs S M Danaher, BA
Mr F R C Jones, BA
Mr H M Lam, MA (*Director of Higher Education*)
Mrs H E Marion, MA
Mr L F Rees, MSc (*Deputy Director of Overseas Schools*)
Mr G J A Simpson, BSc
Mrs S Williams, BCom

English:
*Dr J P D Cannon
Mr R H Amlot, MA (*Deputy Head, Pastoral*)
Miss S L Bailey, BA
Mr B L Bransfield, MA
Mr D I Cass, BA (*Director of IB*)
Miss C F Crothers, BA
Miss H E L Jay, MA
Mr P W Ost, BA (*Deputy Head of English*)
Mr J D Statham, MSc
Mr H R Trimble, BA
Mr R C Yule, BA

Geography:
*Mr M V Christou, MA
Ms M J Clarke, MA (*Senior Deputy Head*)
Miss T J Evans, BSc
Mrs J M Lawton-Cook, BSc (*Assistant Head, Head of Sixth Form*) [maternity leave]
Miss L M Nahorniak, BA [maternity leave]
Mr J F Odling, BSc
Mrs K E Potts, MA
Miss F L M Smart, BA
Mr K H Tipping, BA

History & Politics:
*Mrs F A Ring, MA
Dr O J Blaiklock
Miss R M Davis, BA (*Director of Staff Welfare*)
Mrs S A Maurice, BA
Mr B E F Reekes, BA
Mr T D Rendell, BA
Dr A C Ruddick (*Deputy Head of History and Politics*)
Mr M A Stephenson, MA

Learning Enrichment:
*Miss E Sadler, BA
Ms H Hughes-Waage, SpLD

Ms M S Murphy, MA
Mrs L J Pearson
Mrs A L J Sandwell, BA (*Deputy Head of Learning Enrichment*)

Mathematics:
*Mr S J Nye, BSc
Dr C G Bell
Miss R Bhattacharya, BA
Mr A J Bray, BSc
Dr A Charafi
Miss L K Cooke, BSc (*Head of Year 7*)
Dr S Coury
Mrs S Y Han, BSc
Mr A Haria, MA
Mr D J G Iles, BSc
Miss J E James, BSc
Dr H K B Metrebian
Mr M J Poole, BSc
Dr A Schmidtmann
Dr T R Squires, BA (*Head of Alverstone*)
Mr M Stables, MA (*Director of Studies*)
Mr M J Stenning, BSc (*Deputy Director of Studies*)
Mr A M R Trosser, MSci, ARCS
Mr O Vella, MSc, CTeach
Mr S A Williams, BSc (*Deputy Head of Mathematics*)

Modern Languages:
*Mrs H M Mulcahy, BA
Mrs A J Ansbro, MA
Miss B P Cerda Drago, BA (*Deputy Head of Modern Languages, Head of Spanish*) [maternity leave]
Dr F A Cheung (*Head of French*)
Mr S A Etienne, MA (*Deputy Head of Education – King's International*)
Mr K Gross, BEd (*Managing Director of King's International*)
Mrs S Jin, MA
Mr S C Kent, MA (*Head of Chinese*)
Miss M M E Kidwell, MA
Mrs P Liberti
Mrs H M Lindsey-Noble, BA (*Director of Equality, Diversity and Inclusion*; *Head of German*)
Miss J A Maxwell, BA
Mr P Moren, BA
Miss R C Peel, BA (*Head of Major*)
Ms C O H Robinson, BA (*Head of Russian*)
Mr J M A Ross, BA (*Acting Director of Mental Health and Wellbeing, Acting Deputy Head of Modern Languages and Head of Italian*)
Mr J R C Saxton, BA
Miss A Strachan, BA
Mr D Starrett, BA
Ms S A J G Toussaint, BA

Music:
*Mr D G Phillips, MA (*Director of Music*)
Mr N E Bricht (*Head of Wind & Brass*)
Mr J A Cotton, BA
Mr G R F de Voil, BA (*Head of Lower School Music*)
Mr P A Hatch, MusB (*Director of Partnerships and Outreach, Assistant Director of Music*)
Mr M L Nixon, BMus (*Head of Keyboard*)
Miss L A Scotchmer (*Head of Strings*)

Physical Education:
*Mr R P McCluskey, BA (*Director of Sport*)
Mr J J Barrington, BSc (*Head of Football*)
Mr C J S Beck, BPEd
Mr E W Bowden, MSc (*Director of Rugby*)
Mr J S Gibson, BA (*Assistant Head, Head of Lower School*)
Mr T Gwynne, BSc (*Head of Year 8, Head of Cricket, Head of Lower School PE & Games*)
Miss J L Leach, BSc (*Deputy Director of Sport and Head of Girls' Games*)
Mr L O'Sullivan (*Head of Aquatics*)
Mr T P Rogers, BSc (*Head of Kingsley and Academic PE*)
Mr K G Tuck, BSc

Physics:
*Miss J L Duncombe, MPhys
Mr M S Benyohai, MA
Mr S M Burditt, BSc
Mr T H Davies, MA
Miss E L Geraghty, MA (*Head of Education – King's International*)
Mr D Miller, BSc (*Assistant Head – Innovation*)
Mr S W Newton, MSc
Mrs R F A Rose, BSc (*Assistant Head of Lower School*)
Mr A L Rothman, MEng
Mr C P Sandels, MSc (*Assistant Head – Head of Middle School and Acting Assistant Head of Sixth Form*)
Mr J M B Short, BEng
Ms M A G Spottiswoode, BSc

PSHE:
*Mrs S E Wiseman
Miss A M Dawe, BSc [maternity leave]
Mr C Li, MEng
Miss A M Lethbridge, BSc
Mr L L Massey, MSc
Mr J F Odling, BSc

Psychology:
*Miss F M Donohue, BSc
Mrs R C A Lawrence, MSc
Miss A L McGarvey, BSc (*Assistant Head – Enrichment & Pupil Progress*)

Theology & Philosophy:
*Mr A J Wood, MA
Mr F J Barber, BA
Dr H M Cocksworth, MA [maternity leave]
Mr T J Davies, BA (*Director of Digital Learning and Innovation*)
Ms M C E Miller, BA (*Chaplain*)
Mr J H Renwick, MA (*Director of co-curricular Education*)
Miss E R Tozzi, BA (*Director of Mental Health & Wellbeing*) [maternity leave]
Miss K Y Williams, MA

Support Staff:
PA to the Headmaster: Mrs S Carrett
Admissions Registrar: Ms S J W Dowling, BA
PA to Junior School Headmaster: Mrs S Richards

King's College, Taunton
A Woodard School

South Road, Taunton, Somerset TA1 3LA
Tel: 01823 328210 (Headmaster)
01823 328200 (Reception)
email: admissions@kings-taunton.co.uk
website: www.kings-taunton.co.uk
X/Twitter: @KingsTaunton
Facebook: @kingscollegetaunton
LinkedIn: /school/kings-college-taunton

Motto: *Fortis et Fidelis*

King's College is a co-educational boarding school that comprises King's Prep for children from nursery to Year 8 and King's College senior school from Year 9 to Sixth Form. The schools are situated on separate sites in the heart of the Somerset countryside, only three hours from London by train.

King's College seeks to develop well-rounded, balanced individuals with a love of learning and academic curiosity. Boarding and pastoral care are core to life at King's, and with so many pupils and staff living on-site in centrally located boarding houses, there is a strong sense of community.

The school holds the position of being one of the top academic secondary institutions in the county, regularly leading the tables in both GCSE and A-level results. As well as academic excellence, the breadth of sport and other co-curricular activities are unparalleled for a school of King's size.

As well as being an exceptionally happy school, we are busy and purposeful. Pupils leave well qualified, but more importantly, they leave as well-rounded, intellectually curious and balanced individuals who have been nurtured and encouraged to grow, develop and explore.

Boarding. Much of what sets us apart from other schools stems, we believe, is our strong boarding ethos. Our houses are centrally placed (two are in the main school building) and boarding is central to what we are. Our boarders come from far and wide. Many are local – a few live closer to school than some of their day pupil friends. Others come from the south west of England, while others are from further afield in the UK and some from overseas. This makes for a varied and vibrant community within the houses. Wherever pupils come from, they soon develop a strong sense of loyalty to their house, which makes for exciting and hotly contested inter-house competition in sport and many other activities.

We believe that boarding is a rich and life-affirming experience for our pupils. We know that they leave us well prepared for the demands and challenges of university life. Their friendships are extraordinarily long-lived. They are independent, resilient, resourceful, cheerful, tolerant, pro-active, kind, capable young men and women who go on to make their mark on the world.

The Curriculum. Pupils are challenged by enthusiastic and dedicated specialist teachers both inside and outside the classroom. Careful planning has devised a programme of visits, lectures, tutoring and prep to support learning. House-based tutors each support seven or eight boys or girls throughout their time at the school. Pupils are also prepared with care for examinations (GCSE and A-levels) and university, and are encouraged to develop independent thought and inquiring minds. This ethos resulted in pupils gaining the top A-level results in the area.

Sports and Activities. Sport is pivotal at King's, and the school aims to engage and develop all pupils so they have fun. First class facilities include two floodlit Astroturfs, a tennis/netball dome, 25m swimming pool, strength and conditioning suite, a climbing wall and an equestrian centre. For those with elite aspirations, excellent technical coaching is backed up by mentoring and support maintaining a healthy life balance. The school has a Cricket Performance Centre and is an accredited England hockey performance centre.

King's also has a vast array of co-curricular activities unparalleled for a school of its size, from drama, music, outdoor pursuits and CCF, to dance, cookery and debating. Outdoor activities are well catered for under the umbrella of the CCF (Royal Navy, Royal Marines and Army sections), and alongside that are the Duke of Edinburgh Bronze and Gold award schemes. Kayaking and water polo are popular, as is climbing – we have our own indoor wall and climbing club.

Fees per term (2023–2024). UK boarders £13,785. Day pupils £9,160.

Charitable Status. Woodard Schools Taunton Ltd is a Registered Charity, number 1103346. King's College exists to provide high quality education for boys and girls aged 13–18.

***Headmaster*: Mr Michael Sloan**

Deputy Head (*Pastoral*): Mrs Karen McSwiggan
Deputy Head (*Academic*): Mr Jonty Lawford
Head of Sixth Form: Mr Oliver Elsworth
Head of Boarding: Mr Dafydd Jones
Director Finance & Operations: Mr Simon Worthy
Director of Admissions & Marketing: Mrs Kate Rippin
Director of Development: Mr Phillip Rothwell
Chaplain: The Revd Mark Smith
PA to the Headmaster: Melissa Catton

King's Ely

The Old Palace, Palace Green, Ely, Cambridgeshire CB7 4EW
Tel: 01353 660701 (Principal's PA)
01353 660707 (Admissions)
email: admissions@kingsely.org
website: www.kingsely.org
X/Twitter: @Kings_Ely
Facebook: @KingsElyOfficial
Instagram: @kingselyofficial
LinkedIn: /kingselyofficial

Energy, Courage, Integrity

King's Ely is a leading independent, co-educational day and boarding school in Cambridgeshire which serves the academic and pastoral needs of children aged 2 to 18, with boarders from 8 years old.

Nestled in the beautiful and tranquil cathedral city of Ely, King's Ely is a vibrant, nurturing, inclusive and forward-looking community which has prepared children's futures for a millennium, making it one of the oldest schools in the world.

Ely is just 15 minutes from Cambridge and 1 hour from London, with direct rail links to both. The school is a 5 minute walk from Ely train station and King's Ely's privately-run school buses stop at key locations around Cambridgeshire, Suffolk and Norfolk.

King's Ely is delighted to be a finalist in the recent Independent Schools of the Year Awards, and its latest Independent Schools Inspectorate (ISI) inspection (November 2021) resulted in the school achieving the highest grading possible in every single category.

Inspectors said that "pupils throughout King's Ely make excellent progress across all areas of learning and at all ages and ability ranges", and that "pupils show a keen appreciation, respect and support for the diverse nature of their community".

King's Ely is a school where learning really is an adventure. Students are encouraged to take risks in their learning, pushing themselves beyond the boundaries of their expectations, discovering more about the world around them, and, in doing so, more about themselves. What makes King's Ely special is its determination to instil in the young people in its care a real enthusiasm for learning and a belief that all students can achieve if the teaching is approached in a way that suits the learning style of each pupil. This is not easy necessarily; it is challenging, often uncomfortable, but King's Ely students know that they are well supported, that their teachers believe in them, and so they are willing to step out of their 'comfort zone' and take the very risks that will bring about high-level learning.

Whether a student shines in a classroom, in a laboratory, on a stage, on a pitch or on a mountainside, King's Ely promises an abundance of opportunity for personal development, both academically and socially.

Organisation. King's Ely is fully co-educational from the ages of 2 to 18. The total roll is 1,050 and around a quarter of pupils over the age of 8 are boarders.

The school is divided into four parts: King's Ely Acremont, the Nursery and Pre-Prep for children aged 2 to 7, which stands in its own grounds at Acremont House; King's Ely Junior for children aged 7–13 (Years 3–8); King's Ely Senior for students aged 13–16 (Years 9–11) and King's Ely Sixth Form for students aged 16–18 (Years 12–13).

Buildings. The Old Palace on Palace Green, home for centuries to the Bishops of Ely, serves as the entrance to the school, housing the Sixth Form Centre, the Head's Offices and Admissions, as well as the Development Office. The school still uses many of Ely's medieval monastic buildings – as boarding houses, as classrooms and as the dining hall. The 14th century Porta, the great gateway to the monastery, has been converted into a magnificent Senior School Library. Other recent buildings show the continuing and substantial investment in modern facilities: the renovated Georgian villa that now houses the Nursery and Pre-Prep section of King's Acremont; a new Art School and Performance Studies block, housing the new Dance Studio and 'Black Box' Drama Studio; a Technology Centre; a Senior Music School and Recital Hall and a self-contained, two-storey accommodation including seven classrooms and a science laboratory for Years 7 and 8.

King's Ely Acremont. At King's Ely Acremont, children thrive in a happy, safe environment where they feel secure and valued and quickly develop a sense of belonging. Children from the ages of 2 to 7 are encouraged to question, explore and have the confidence and security to take risks in their learning. A rich, creative curriculum sets the children on the road to becoming lifelong thinkers and learners. Courage and courtesy are valued, encouraged and celebrated publicly.

Children may start in King's Ely Nursery in the term in which they turn 2. The Nursery is sessional and it is recommended children attend three sessions a week from the outset. However, flexibility to suit the needs of each individual child is important. As children progress through the Nursery, the number of sessions should increase to a minimum of five sessions per week. The children are very well prepared for a smooth transition into Reception through regular visits ensuring that they are very familiar with both staff and setting in the next stage of their journey through King's Ely. Please contact Admissions to discuss suitable sessions for your child.

Children start Reception in the September following their 4th birthday. Reception, Year 1 and Year 2 are all taught in Acremont House. Small class sizes, with a Teacher and Teaching Assistant in each, allow children to flourish, preparing them well for the transition to King's Ely Junior.

King's Ely Acremont offers working parents the option of an 8am Breakfast Club, After School Care until 6pm and Holiday Club. Forest School, Science Club and Musical Sparklers are just some of the clubs on offer.

King's Ely Junior. King's Ely Junior celebrates the many ways that students learn and is keen to embrace different learning styles. Students are encouraged to develop their autonomy as they mature and there is an expectation of an ever-increasing use of information literacy, technology and study skills during the students' time at King's Ely Junior. Individual responses, such as films being made for homework, or a computer generated response to a task are equally as welcome as a formal written piece of work. Students can be characterised by their flexibility of approach and it is seen as an important life skill for the next generation.

Ensuring that every student is challenged to fulfil their potential and encouraged along the way, requires that the progress of each student is measured and supported well at all times. Form Tutors shoulder this role on a day to day basis. However, each student has a Head of Year who monitors their work and considers how well they are progressing against the school's predictions. Weekly meetings ensure that speedy intervention is offered to support or extend students appropriately.

From Year 5 onwards, students are set for Maths and English. At this point the students are split between four sets of about 14. These groups are reviewed frequently by the subject teachers and the Head of Year and any adjustments to the sets are made by the Director of Studies, following discussion with parents. As students progress through the school more subjects are set, such as Languages and Science. In Years 7 and 8, subjects are linked according to the English, Maths and Science or Language sets. Students are taught in four or five groups, depending on subject.

Every term is punctuated by a host of academic challenges that serve to inspire the pupils and encourage them to push the parameters of their learning. Examination results are high and the school prides itself on being at the forefront of developments in the educational world.

During the school day all children are divided among four co-educational Houses for pastoral and competitive purposes; each of these Houses is staffed by male and female members of the teaching staff. King's Ely Junior has one co-educational boarding house and one for the boy choristers of Ely Cathedral who are all pupils of King's Ely Junior. There is a wide range of extra-curricular opportunities both at lunch times and after school – Archery, Pottery, Golf, Engineering Club – the choices are endless!

King's Ely Senior. The amount of academic choice that pupils can exercise grows as they move through the Senior School. Options in the Sixth Form are very flexible and the sets are often small. Up to GCSE (Year 11) there is a compulsory core of English, Mathematics, Religious Studies and Sciences. In addition, every pupil chooses up to four option subjects from: Art, Business Studies, Classical Civilisation, Design and Technology, Food and Nutrition, Drama, English as a Foreign Language, French, Geography, German, History, Latin, Music, Physical Education, Spanish. Inter-House competitions in disciplines such as singing, Ely Scheme and debating are keenly participated in.

King's Ely International. At King's Ely International, students are welcomed from all over the world to engage with the unique community that is King's Ely. The aim is to ensure a smooth and successful transition into the vibrant environment of a UK boarding school, steeped in history but offering an innovative educational experience.

Although fully integrated with the main school, King's Ely International offers effective support academically for international students between the ages of 14 and 16 who may be studying for the first time in the UK. The one-year intensive GCSE course suits students who wish to complete their GCSEs in a year. The Pre-GCSE programme is for students between the ages of 14 and 15 who need support in their English. It is also a "stand-alone" course and may be seen as a sabbatical year, especially for European students who wish to return to their home countries after a year abroad improving their English.

Extra-Curricular Activities. King's Ely has a holistic approach to education and this is reflected in the school's thriving co-curricular scene, for which it is renowned. Music, Art, Drama, Ely Scheme (outdoor education), Sports, practical hobbies and interests – all are catered for in a large range of lunchtime and after-hours activities.

Ely Scheme. All pupils in Year 9 are introduced to the school's distinctive outdoor pursuits programme, Ely Scheme, which provides a training in practical and personal skills and in teamwork, initiative and leadership. For some pupils it leads on to the Duke of Edinburgh's Award Scheme or to specialised activities such as climbing, kayaking or pioneering.

Art, Drama and Music. Music is strong, as one would expect in a school that is so closely linked to the cathedral. There is a full programme of performances for school and public audiences, and regular tours overseas. Nearly half of all pupils have personal tuition in a musical instrument; many learn two or even three. An outstanding Art School, opened in March 2010, inspires Fine Art, Sculpture, Photography and Textiles. All parts of the school present plays every year in addition to productions by year or ad hoc groups.

Games. The school's main sports are Rowing, Rugby, Football, Netball, Hockey and Cricket. Athletics, Badminton, Basketball, Tennis, Sailing, Squash, Swimming, Golf, Clay Pigeon Shooting and Horse Riding are also available. All pupils are encouraged to take part in team games, and there is a full programme of fixtures against other schools.

Religious Worship. The Junior and Senior Schools worship regularly in Ely Cathedral. Other services weekly are also in accordance with the principles of the Church of England. The Bishop conducts a confirmation service for pupils in the Lent Term. However, all denominations (or none) are warmly welcome.

Exeats. Boarders are granted weekend exeats on the written request of a parent or guardian. Weekly and flexi boarding are increasingly popular.

Admission. Registration forms can be obtained from the Admissions Department and a £100 (£150 for non-EU) fee is payable at first registration.

Admission to King's Ely Acremont is by interview.

Admission to King's Ely Junior is by interview and INCAs in English and Maths. There is also Lucid screening for dyslexia. King's Ely Junior entrance assessments are held in January prior to the following Michaelmas Term. Small groups of children are invited to attend assessments throughout January. Offers are made for the beginning of February.

Admission to King's Ely Senior at 13+ entrance is by the school's entrance examination consisting of English, Maths, Science and Lucid in late January.

Admission to Year 12 at 16+ is by interview with the Principal and predicted GCSE grades. The entry qualification for the Sixth Form is not less than six C grades with B grades in subjects selected for A Level. Twenty-seven AS/A2 Level subjects are offered in Years 12 and 13. Taster Days are held throughout November and December.

Pupils may enter the school at any time, depending on availability of space and assessment.

Scholarships and Exhibitions. Entrance Scholarships and Exhibitions up to a cumulative total of 10% of tuition fees are awarded for achievement and potential in academic work, music and sport, and 5% in art, design technology, drama.

A competitive examination is held in January each year and successful candidates enter Year 9 the following Michaelmas Term. These Scholarships will be continued until the end of Year 11, subject to satisfactory progress, after which an application for a Sixth Form Scholarship may be made.

King's Ely Senior:

Academic Scholarships are for the three years from Year 9 leading to the GCSE examinations and are made on the basis of a competitive examination set by the school in January. Successful candidates are also interviewed.

Music Scholarships are available for choral and/or instrumental excellence, including organ-playing, and may include free weekly tuition on two musical instruments. Candidates for entry into Year 9 are invited to the school for auditions in January.

All boy Choristers of Ely Cathedral are full boarders of King's Ely Junior and receive a choristership worth 50% of fees while they remain in the choir and a bursary worth 33% of fees on transfer to King's Ely Senior. Members of the Cathedral Girls' Choir are all boarders in King's Ely Senior and receive a bursary worth 33% of boarding fees. Additional means-tested funding may be available. Chorister auditions are held in February for boys who will be aged 8 and for girls who will be 13 by the following September.

Sports Awards, for entry into Year 9, are open to boys and girls with potential for major county, regional or national representation or with all-round sporting excellence. Reports will be sought from the candidates' coach(es) and practical tests, if required, will be held at the school in January.

Art, Drama and Design Technology Exhibitions are available for entry into Year 9 and assessments are held in January.

Sixth Form:

Academic Scholarships are for the two years of the A Level course and are made following an examination in November and an interview with the Vice Principal (Academic) and Head of Sixth Form (Academic). Candidates should be on course for at least six A* or A passes at GCSE.

Music Scholarships are available for choral and/or instrumental excellence, including organ-playing, and may include free weekly tuition on two musical instruments. Candidates for entry into Year 12 are invited to the school for auditions in November.

Sports Awards, for entry into Year 12, are open to boys and girls with potential for major county, regional or national representation or with all-round sporting excellence. Reports will be sought from the candidates' coach(es) and practical tests, if required, will be held at the school in November.

Art, Drama and Design Technology Exhibitions are available for entry into Year 12 and assessments are held in November.

Full particulars of all awards are available on the King's Ely website.

Bursaries. Awards may be supplemented by a means-tested Bursary if there is genuine financial need. Bursary support may be available to new pupils over the age of 7 whose parents are unable to pay the full tuition fee.

Fees per term (2023–2024). King's Ely Acremont Nursery and Pre-Prep: Nursery places are booked by the session; Daily rates range from £35 (mornings), £79 (extended day). The fee for Pre-Prep Reception to Year 2 is £4,159 per term (no boarding). Pre- and after-school care and holiday club are available at extra charge.

King's Ely Junior per term: Years 3 and 4: £5,832 (day); £9,281 (boarding); Years 5 to 8: £6,332–£6,411 (day); £9,795–£9,939 (boarding).

King's Ely Senior per term: Years 9 to 13: £8,738 (day); £12,885 (boarding).

Flexi boarding: It may be possible to offer overnight accommodation for day pupils on an occasional basis at a cost of £50–£60 per night. The cost of extended flexi boarding will be quoted in advance upon application to Admissions.

Concessions: A generous discount in fees is available from age 4 for children of clergy serving the Christian faith and boarders who are children of Services personnel in receipt of CEA and also for children of FCO employees. Sibling discount on the third child is available. Bursaries are available to those entering Year 7 or beyond.

Old Eleans. Former pupils receive news of the school and of their contemporaries and are invited annually to events.

Charitable status. The King's School, Ely is a Registered Charity, number 802427. Its aims and objectives are to offer excellence in education to day and boarding pupils.

Chairman of Governors: Mr David Day

***Principal of King's Ely*: Mr John Attwater**

Head of King's Ely Acremont Pre-Prep and Nursery: Mrs Faye Fenton-Stone

Head of King's Ely Junior: Mr Richard Whymark

Head of King's Ely Senior: Mr Jonathan Shaw

Vice Principal Academic (*Whole School*): Mrs Jane Thomas

Director of Boarding: Mr Andy Thomas

Director for International Students: Mr Matthew Norbury

Director of Admissions and Marketing: Mr Nick Tappin

King's School
Bruton

The Plox, Bruton, Somerset BA10 0ED

Tel: 01749 814200
email: office@kingsbruton.com
website: www.kingsbruton.com
X/Twitter: @kingsbruton
Facebook: /kings.bruton

Motto: *Deo Juvante*

An HMC boarding and day school educating 370 boys and girls aged 13 to 18.

Headmaster's Welcome: Community. Quality. Success.

King's Bruton is a remarkable school with over 500 years of history. We are blessed with a wonderful location in South Somerset. There are 370 pupils at King's and the key to our success, and increasing popularity, is to combine our relatively small size with a high quality education. In recent years we have had outstanding GCSE, A Level and BTEC results with the vast majority of our pupils going on to their first choice of university. Our hockey teams have reached 12 National Finals with our U16 girls winning the English Schools' National Indoor Hockey Championships in 2017. There are over 70 pupils in our full Choir, our Chapel Choir sing Evensong in regional cathedrals every term, whilst our 200-seat theatre is the venue for outstanding drama. Our thriving CCF is one of the oldest in the country, whilst over half of our senior pupils undertake Silver and Gold Duke of Edinburgh Awards.

I asked a pupil to describe King's Bruton to me in three words and she said, without hesitation, "Caring. Community. Happy". I would like to add, "Quality. Excellence. Achievement". Your son and daughter will not be allowed to drift, to hide or to get lost at King's. As Headmaster I set myself two challenges: I want all pupils to leave King's saying firstly, "I enjoyed School" and secondly, "I couldn't have done any more".

King's pupils are encouraged to respect themselves and others, to adopt a positive attitude, and to strive to be the best they can be. Pupils leave here confident but not arrogant and fully prepared to contribute to life beyond the School gates. King's is a busy, happy and thriving community and we would be delighted to welcome you for a visit, I am confident that you will be impressed.

Ian Wilmshurst – Headmaster

Link to Headmaster's Welcome Video: www.kingsbruton.com/about-us/headmaster-s-welcome.

Further details can be obtained by emailing the Registrar on registrar@kingsbruton.com.

Aims of the School. King's Bruton is a boarding and day school, which places a very high value on a genuinely holistic education in which every individual pupil is given an opportunity to flourish and develop. The School constantly strives to set standards that are well beyond what might normally be expected. The five main aims of the strategic development plan are:

- To develop further the School's warm and supportive boarding community, and to provide a comprehensive all round education in which pupils of all ages are valued as individuals.
- To continue to raise the academic expectations of all pupils at GCSE, BTEC and A Level, and in terms of their higher education and career aspirations within a broad and balanced curriculum.
- To ensure that, within the School's resources, access to a King's education and facilities are as open as possible to the wider community.
- To aim for excellence in the fields of sport and the performing arts.
- To enhance the School's strong Christian ethos, and to continue to encourage and support pupils in their spiritual growth and faith.

School Values. These school values are outlined every year by the School Prefects. They are the values that the Prefects want upheld by the rest of the King's community. As a school community we aspire to uphold:

- A sense of community. In a small school like King's, the community spirit is what makes us stand out from the rest. We are a close-knit school so no one is left out. The friendly atmosphere allows individual personalities to develop.
- Punch above our weight. Our size does not hold us back. We have the willingness and determination to go the extra mile and to achieve the best of our abilities both inside and outside the classroom.
- Modesty in victory and graciousness in defeat. At King's, we believe encouraging involvement in all areas of school life leads to a more rounded individual. We acknowledge the humility and enthusiasm necessary to do better in the future.
- Acceptance and equality. King's prides itself on the equality and fairness of its pupils. Diversity is accepted and valued equally so no one feels excluded or less important than anyone else.
- Loyalty. Loyalty drives life at King's: this is not only loyalty to friends and staff but also loyalty to Houses, teams and ultimately oneself. Whether it's on the sports field, or halfway through the toils of the School year, our loyalties will be what inspire us.
- Respect. We believe King's shows respect in all aspects of school life; this includes respect towards the School grounds, each other and any member of staff while also being able to enjoy fun and friendly relationships across the age groups.
- Pride. We feel all members of King's, staff and pupils alike, are proud to be part of our school community. This leads to a desire to excel in the School and help us to make the School the best it can be.

Scholarships & Bursaries

Scholarships and Exhibitions are awarded to recognise talent and potential and we encourage boys and girls entering the 3rd Form and 6th Form to apply for our various scholarships. The maximum value of any non means-tested Scholarship or Award, or combination thereof, is 20% of fees.

Scholarships and Awards are available at 3rd Form entry in the following subjects: Academic, Art, DT, Drama, Music, Sport, All Rounder.

Scholarships and Awards are available at L6th Form entry in the following subjects: Academic, Art, Drama, Music, Sport

Overseas Applicants

King's Bruton continues to welcome pupils from all countries of the world and encourages applications from interested families and agents. Our European and international pupils bring great benefits to the School in all aspects of school life. We have never differentiated school fees between UK, Europe or international pupils and continue to ensure the fees remain consistent across all nationalities. Boarding is an essential part of life at King's Bruton, and currently boarders and day pupils are fully integrated into all of the Boarding Houses.

Armed Forces Families

King's Bruton has a long tradition of welcoming children from serving Forces families and with ex-Service men in teaching and support roles, as well as at Senior Management level and on the Board of Governors, we have a deep understanding of the unique circumstances associated with military life.

The School works hard to ensure our provision remains affordable for Service families whilst ensuring the best levels of education and care. A Forces discount of 20% is currently available for all Forces families, irrespective of whether they are in receipt of CEA. With a Bursar who has spent 25 years in the Army, many of them as a CEA claimant, there is an intimate knowledge of the CEA system and understanding of the process. The emphasis is on flexibility and recognising the unique circumstances of every family.

Additionally, we have a specially designated member of staff who acts as the focus for Forces families ensuring that the School understands the specific requirements of our various Forces families and their children, and the pressure that comes with Service life both in the UK and abroad.

The King's Bruton Foundation

The King's School, Bruton Foundation comprises three schools – King's Bruton, Hazlegrove Prep and Sunny Hill Nursery – and offers the opportunity for a continuity of outstanding education for girls and boys age 2 to 18. The schools are united by a common set of values and principles and bound by a shared history that stretches back to the foundation of King's in 1519. A junior school was started at King's in 1902 and was established as an IAPS Preparatory School in 1947 when it moved to Hazlegrove House, which the Foundation purchased in 1953. Sunny Hill Nursery joined the Foundation in 2022.

Charitable status. King's School, Bruton is a Registered Charity, number 1071997. It exists to provide education for boys and girls from 13–18.

Mr Stephen Edlmann, MA (*Senior Warden*)
***Headmaster*: Mr I S Wilmshurst**, MA Cantab

The King's School

Canterbury

25 The Precincts, Canterbury, Kent CT1 2ES

Tel: 01227 595501 (Reception)
01227 595544 (Bursar)
01227 595579 (Admissions)
email: info@kings-school.co.uk
website: www.kings-school.co.uk
X/Twitter: @KingsCanterbury
Facebook: @KingsCanterbury
LinkedIn: /the-king's-school-canterbury

St Augustine's foundation of a monastic school in Canterbury in 597 AD marks the origin of The King's School: hence, its claim to be the oldest school in the country. It was re-founded by King Henry VIII in 1541. More recently, a Junior School has been established on the former estate of Lord Milner outside the city. The close relationship with the Cathedral Foundation has been there throughout.

King's Scholars. Many schools cherish the notion that they are the oldest school in the country, but there is little doubt that there has been a school on the present World Heritage site of King's School, Canterbury since the Augustinian mission to England in 597 AD. The name of the school and its intimate relationship with the Cathedral community of the mother church of the Anglican Communion date from the Henrician settlement, as do the King's Scholars who, along with the Headmaster and the Senior Deputy Head, form part of the original Foundation of Christchurch, Canterbury. So much for the history, the King's Scholars continue to occupy buildings and be taught in classrooms that predate the Reformation. Besides their function in the Cathedral, the King's Scholars are at the heart of the vibrant and open-ended academic life of the school. Each year, some of the King's Scholars are on full means-tested bursaries, keeping alive the original vision of the school. The modern King's Scholar discovers a school which is fully co-educational, diverse in its catchment and intentions, as well as in tune with the wider life of the city of Canterbury and national/international context beyond its immediate compass.

Scholarships and Bursaries. Up to twenty King's Scholars and Exhibitioners are elected each year following competitive examinations and interviews in February. A further group of King's Scholars are added at the Sixth Form entrance stage (competitive examination and interviews in the November preceding entry). These academic awards have a meritocratic value of 10% of the fees, but the crucial thing is that they can be augmented by means-tested bursaries up to 100%. The extremely strong tradition of music at King's, both instrumental and choral, means that Music Scholarships (about 20 are awarded annually) are generously provided for. The school is particularly welcoming for those who have come on to King's from the choir schools of Cathedrals and Colleges. There are further Music Scholarships made for Sixth Form entry.

There are further Scholarships and Exhibitions at 13+ for exceptional ability in Art and Sport – the Gower Sports Scholarships named after the former England cricket captain – and the school also grants awards for DT, Drama and Dance.

Academic Life. The King's curriculum is distinct for its combination of striving for the very highest standards in the most appropriate Public Examinations (IGCSEs at the end of Year 10 for a few subjects, but mainly at the end of Year 11; A Levels and Pre-U courses in the Sixth Form) on the one hand, and the pursuit of learning and the development of the intellect for its own sake (self-standing courses, tutorials and lectures in the evenings and extended project qualifications, as well as independent research). The school puts particular emphasis on studying Mandarin, German and Russian, as well as 'new' subjects like Photography and Computer Science. A wide degree of choice of subject in the Sixth Form (Earth & Planetary Sciences and Philosophy, for example) is often an engine for academic success.

Some 20–25 offers of admission to Oxford and Cambridge are received each year.

All-round Vision. Christopher Marlowe, William Harvey and Thomas Linacre number amongst King's pupils and the pursuit of the Renaissance ideal still resonates in the contemporary school. The strongest encouragement is given to Music, Drama, Sport, CCF and the Visual Arts. This stems from belief in the value of these activities in themselves, but also since recreation and success in these fields leads to growth in self-confidence and better academic performance. Alongside these activities are opportunities to get involved in Partnership projects and pursue the Duke of Edinburgh's Award.

Numbers and Organisation. There are currently 947 pupils on the school roll, 485 boys and 462 girls. There are 6 boys' boarding houses, 7 girls' boarding houses and 3 (mixed) day houses. To the east of the main school buildings in the Cathedral Precincts is St Augustine's, home to 5 boarding houses, the original Medieval Hall and magnificent school library. There are 2 major sites for sport, Birley's and Blore's, each with extensive sports facilities. Junior King's School, the prep school of King's, occupies a site on the River Stour, in Sturry, three miles from Canterbury. There are currently 376 pupils at Junior King's, 207 boys and 169 girls of whom 73 are boarders.

Admission. Application should be made to the Assistant Registrar. It is advisable to register pupils at an early age. Admission is normally through the Common Entrance Examination, the King's School entrance examination (for non-CE candidates) or, if academically appropriate, through the King's Scholarship Examination. The age of entry is about 13.

Fees per term (2023–2024). Senior School: £14,830 for boarders and £9,275–£10,300 for day pupils. Junior School: £10,165 for boarders and £5,890–£7,225 for day pupils.

OKS (Old King's Scholars). *Coordinator*: Molly Burgess, OKS Association Office, Tel: 01227 595669; email: oks@kings-school.co.uk.

The King's Society exists for all parents, past and present. A termly programme of social and cultural events is open to all members and is published on the school website.

Charitable status. The King's School of the Cathedral Church of Canterbury is a Registered Charity, number 307942. It exists to provide education for boys and girls.

Visitor: The Lord Archbishop of Canterbury

Governors:
Interim Chairman: Count Benoit de Vitry D'Avaucourt
Dame F J Judd, KC [OKS] (*Vice Chair*)
The Venerable Dr Will Adam
M W S Bax, FRICS [OKS]
Mrs Clare Cowburn Baker
Mrs Angela Culley
Revd Canon Andrew Dodd
Dr Henrietta Hughes, OBE, FRCGP
Ms Fionnuala Kennedy
Mr Wol Kolade
The Very Reverend David Monteith
Mr Robert Moulsdale
Revd Canon Dr T Naish, MA, PhD
Revd Canon Dr Emma Pennington
Mr Andrew Stewart
Dr Michael Sutherland
Clerk to the Governors: M R Taylor, FRSA

Governors Emeriti:
The Very Revd J A Simpson, OBE, MA, DD
The Lady Kingsdown, OBE, DCL

[OKS] *Old King's Scholars*

***Head*: Ms Jude Lowson**

Head's PA: Mrs L Hutchinson
PA to Senior Deputy Head & Lattergate Office Administrator: Mrs A Goodier
Lattergate Receptionist: Miss A Comber

Senior Deputy Head: Mrs E A Worthington, MA

Deputy Head Academic: L G Bartlett, BA, MRSC
Deputy Head Pastoral: Miss T Lee, BA
Deputy Head Co-Curricular: G Hunter, BEng, Grad Dip Ed
PA to Deputy Head Pastoral/Deputy Head Co-Curricular: Mrs F Bird
PA to Deputy Head Academic & Academic Assistant: Mrs P Phillips
Academic Assistant: Mrs G V Hone, BSc Econ
Examinations Officer: Mrs S Reid

Head of Sixth Form: A J Holland, BSc
Heads of Middle School: D Galmes-Gazapo, BA; J M Maréchal, BA, MSc; M Mawby
Head of Lower School: M H Henderson
Head of Oxbridge: H L Warwicker MA
Head of Extended Projects: Dr L Hynes

Bursar: M R Taylor, FRSA

Director of Development and Alumni: Mrs J Grant
Deputy Development Director: Mrs S Tingle

Head of Marketing: K L Orwin, BA

Registrar: J W Outram, BA
Assistant Registrar: Mrs B Skilton

Senior Chaplain: The Revd L R F Collins, BD, AKC, MTh
Chaplain: The Revd T Pote
Graduate Assistant Chaplain: S Thorne

Librarian: Miss P K Rose, FDA, MA, PGCHE, ACLIP

Medical Officer: Dr D Gregory, MB BS, MRCGP, DRCOG

* *Head of Department*
† *Housemaster/mistress*

Art:
Mrs G C Burrows, BA
*Mrs I A Dutton, BA
M McArdle, BA
Mrs G Farrell, BA
D K Willis, BA
Mr J Dutton

Classics:
*M W Browning, BA
W Corbyn, BA
Miss H L Warwicker, BA

Design & Technology:
*M J Rolison, BEd
V Caspary, MFA

Drama:
*Mrs R J Beattie, BA, FRSA
Ms R Frances, BA

Economics:
*J Pope
Mrs L A Horn, BSc
J Hounsell, BA
A Rodriguez, MSc
M D Bell, BCOM, CIMA

English:
Dr H Barton, MA, PhD
Mrs L Carlyle, BA, DPhil
†Mrs J M Cook, BA
*Dr L Grindlay, MA, PhD
A J W Lyons, BA, MA, FRSA
Dr J P Wilper, BA, MLitt, PhD
†Mrs A L Young, MA
L J Benson, BA, MA

Geography:
A J Holland, BSc
†M E Lister, BSc, MSc
J A Lloyd, BSc
†R P Sanderson, BA
Mrs S J Sensecall, BSc
*Ms Freyja Dolan, BA

History:
*Miss C E Anderson, BA, MA
†G W H Harrison, MA
Dr D J C Perkins, BA, MA, Dip Law, PhD
Mrs E A Worthington, MA
I Bannerman, BA

History of Art:
*Dr H Barton, MA, PhD

ICT and Computing:
A J Holland, BSc
*C P Wooldridge, BSc

Mathematics:
†Mrs E R Bell, MSci
M O Cox, MA, MEng, Dip ITEC
Dr R A B Johnson, MSc, PhD
Mrs J Gorman, BSc
A McFall, BSc
*S P Ocock, BA
Dr K J Palmer, BSc, PhD
M Henderson, BA

Ms E Berry, BA
Ms F Walton, BA
E Triffault, BA

Learning Support:
Mrs D J Ardley, BA
Mrs S Burke, MA
Ms G R Moorcroft, BEd, MA
Mrs M L Orders, BA
*Mrs C R Titterton, BA
Mrs B Raffety, BA
Mrs K Rothwell, BA

Modern Languages:
Mrs Z T Allen, MA
Miss L N Bernardo Otamendi, Lda, MPhil, MA
*Miss H C Davies, MA
Mrs M B Garcés-Ramón, Lda
Mrs N Geoffroy, L-ès-ScEd
R T M Harrison, BA
†Mrs R E Heskins, BA
Dr J R Karolyi, BA, PhD
*Mrs L Liu, BA, MPhil
Miss J M Maréchal, BA, MSc
Miss F Zanardi, MA
D Galmes-Gazapo
E McCaffery, BA
A A T Blum
N Madeley
J Bao, BA, MA

Music:
K Abbott, Dip RCM
*W Bersey, BMus
Mrs A Caldon, BA, PDM
G R Swinford, BA
N G Todd, MA

Politics:
E N Nilsson, BA, MA

Physical Education:
*C Lewis-Gardiner
†M E Lister, BSc, MSc
†R A L Singfield, BEd (**Sport*)

Religious Studies and Philosophy:
*Dr D Cardinal, MA, PhD

The Revd L R F Collins, BD, AKC, MTh
Mrs C A Cox, BA, MPhil
Miss A K Fraser, MA, MPhil
Mrs C A Hayes, BA
*Miss T Lee, BA
J W Outram, BA

Science:

Biology:
Ms K Budden, BSc
J M Hutchings, BA
*Mrs E H Lockwood, MA, BSc
Dr M A McVeigh, MSc, PhD
†M J W Smiley, MA
M J Thornby, BSc
B A Landymore
E Rooms, BA

Chemistry:
L G Bartlett, BA, MRSC
R P Cook, BSc
*Dr S T Hayes, MSci, PhD, MRSC
Dr L W Hynes, BSc, PhD
Dr L E J Jones, MChem, PhD
D A Scott, BSc, MSc, MA Ed, MRSC (**Science*)
†A S D Stennett, BSc
Mrs H Hunter

Physics:
*Miss L M Comber BSc (**Science*)
F Elias, Ldo, PhD
Miss L M Kendrick, BSc
†Mrs E S Ladd, BEng
†M C Orders, BSc

Earth & Planetary Sciences:
*M R Mawby, BSc

Psychology:
*J M Hutchings, BA
I Williamson, BSc, MA, MSc

Houses and Housemasters/mistresses:
School House: A Vintner
The Grange: M Orders
Walpole: Mrs N Ridley
Meister Omers: R A L Singfield
Marlowe (*day*): G W H Harrison
Luxmoore: J P Wilper
Galpin's: R P Sanderson
Linacre: M Lister
Tradescant: R T M Harrison
Broughton: Dr D McVeigh
Mitchinson's (*day*): Mrs E S Ladd
Jervis: Mrs R E Heskins
Harvey: Mrs J M Cook
Bailey (*Sixth Form*): Mrs E Bell
Carlyon (*day*): M J W Smiley
Kingsdown: Mrs C A Hayes

The Junior King's School
Milner Court, Sturry, Nr Canterbury, CT2 0AY
Tel 01227 714000

Headmistress: Mrs E J Károlyi, MA

(For further details see Junior King's School entry in IAPS section.)

The King's School
Chester

Wrexham Road, Chester CH4 7QL
Tel: 01244 689500
email: info@kingschester.co.uk
website: www.kingschester.co.uk

Motto: *Rex Dedit, Benedicat Deus*

The School was founded AD 1541 by King Henry VIII, in conjunction with the Cathedral Church of Chester. It was reorganised under the Endowed Schools Act in 1873, and by subsequent schemes of the Ministry of Education. The School is now Independent. The aim of the School is to prepare pupils for admission to Universities and the professions, and at the same time provide a liberal education.

Organisation. The School, which at present numbers 1154, consists of (i) an Infant School for pupils aged 4 to 7 years, (ii) a Junior School for pupils aged 7 to 11 years, and (iii) the Senior School. The Infant and Junior Schools are housed in separate buildings, but are run in collaboration with the Senior School. On entry to Shells (2nd year of the Senior School) pupils are placed in one of eight houses; every student has a tutor who oversees their progress and welfare throughout their school career.

Admission. Please refer to our admissions policy which outlines the criteria and selection process for entry: www.kingschester.co.uk/policies. Selection is by academic merit alone.

Academic. Departments are grouped into four Faculties whose Heads report to the Academic Deputy Head. The subjects offered for study in the Sixth Form are – on the Arts side: Art, Business, Classical Studies, Drama, Economics, English, English Language, French, Geography, German, History, Latin, Music, Philosophy, Politics, Religious Studies, Spanish; and on the Science side: Biology, Chemistry, Computing, Further Mathematics, Mathematics, Physics, Psychology, Sports Science and Design Technology. It is possible to take most combinations of subjects in the Sixth Form.

Spiritual life. The School is part of the Cathedral Foundation and regularly holds its own services in the Cathedral. Spiritual assemblies are held regularly in school.

Music. Music is part of the general curriculum for all pupils up to the age of 14. After this music may be taken at GCSE and A Level. Private tuition in orchestral instruments, piano and organ is available. There are many musical ensembles and choral groups including the Schola Cantorum which leads the worship in Cathedral services.

Cadet Corps. There is a CCF contingent which gives pupils opportunities to develop leadership skills and to undertake adventurous training.

Outdoor education. Opportunities are provided both within and outside the curriculum for outdoor education, and all pupils in each of the first three years of the senior school spend some days away at centres specialising in outdoor activities. In addition many pupils participate in the Duke of Edinburgh's Award Scheme at all levels.

Games. Football, Hockey, Netball, Rugby, Cricket, Rowing, Swimming, Badminton, Basketball, Athletics, Netball, Tennis, Squash, Golf, Rounders.

Buildings. Formerly situated adjacent to the Cathedral, the school moved into new buildings in 1960 situated in rural surroundings nearly 2 miles from the centre of Chester. Since then there has been an impressive programme of additional building development. These include the Wickson Library, a new Music School, the Vanbrugh Theatre and extensions to the Sixth Form Centre. In September 2014 the Junior School was extended to provide a new Junior School Library and Learning Centre, and in September 2015 a purpose-built Infant School was opened by the Duke of Westminster. A state-of-the-art Sports Centre opened in April 2019, The Rohan Ingley Pastoral Centre in 2021 and the redevelopment of the sixth form centre is underway with completion due in 2023.

Alumni associations. Please see the website (www.kingschester.co.uk/alumni) for details of OAKS (the Organisation for the Alumni of the King's School) and CAOKS (Chester Association of Old King's Scholars).

Fees per term (2023–2024). Tuition: Senior School £5,260; Junior School £4,032; Infants £3,557.

The School offers a small number of bursaries annually.

Scholarships. Academic scholarships of up to £500 are awarded to pupils during their early years in the Senior School. Scholars carry the title 'King's Scholar' throughout their time at the school.

Tenable in the Sixth Form: A number of scholarships are awarded to students on entry to the Sixth Form and during their Sixth form years. These include: (1) Keith Oates Scholarship: £1,000; (2) Investec Scholarship: £1,000; (3) King's School Parents' Association Scholarship: £500.

Tenable at Universities: (1) Old King's Scholars Exhibition: £750; (2) Robert Platt Exhibition: £500; (3) John Churton Exhibition: £500; (4) Haswell Exhibition: £500; (5) Finchett Maddock Exhibition: £500.

Charitable status. The King's School, Chester is a Registered Charity, number 525934. The aim of the charity is to provide a sound education to all boys and girls who can benefit from it regardless of their economic and social background.

Governors:
Mrs S J Verity, BSc (*Chair*)
A J Bartley, KC
A Bentley
Mrs J M Carr, BA, FCA
J B Ebo
Mrs N Dowling
Mrs C A Edwards, MA
Miss C Gillies
Mrs D Leonard
D K Rowlands
M Sayer
The Venerable T R Stratford, BSc, PhD, Dean of Chester
Ms M Troy
J Walsh

Clerk to the Governors: Mrs H A Jordan, FInstML, MCGI

***Headmaster*: G J Hartley**, MA Cantab, MSc

Deputy Head (*Operations*) T M Gill, MA
Deputy Head (*Academic*): J E Millard, BA
Deputy Head (*Pastoral*): Mrs C Sumner, BA
Head of Sixth Form: J P Carter, MA
Director of Studies: A J Dewbery, MA
Assistant Head (*Pastoral*): S F Prest, MA
Director of Learning Support: Mrs S Glass, BA

Assistant staff:
* *Head of Department*

Art and Design:
*S Downey, BA (*Head of Faculty – Creative Arts & PE*)
Ms L Black, BA
Mrs A L Hollingworth, BA (*Assistant Head of Sixth Form*)
R Conroy, BA
M Harris, BA
Miss R Hillier, BA, MSc
Mrs C A Rule, BA

Biology:
*R H Jones, BSc, PhD
J A Dunn, MSc
Dr H C Faulkner, BSc, DPhil (*Head of Faculty – Science*)
L A Parkes, BSc, MSc (*Assistant Head of Sixth Form*)
Mrs O Wilkinson, BSc

Chemistry:
*A Cook, BSc, PhD
Dr C A Gleave, BSc, PhD
Dr J R Macnab, BSc, PhD
Mrs K L Russon, BSc
Dr S Wharton

Classics:
*Mrs K Birch, BA
Mrs C Collier, BA

Design Technology:
*R J Curtis, BSc
Ms L Black, BA
Miss S J Champion, BA
Ms N Corrigan

Drama:
*Mrs C L Howdon, BA
Mrs R Hamer
Mrs J Williams, BA, MA

Economics & Business:
*S D Walton, BA, MSc

English:
*R J Aldridge, BA, MBA
M A Boyd, BA (*Head of Werburgh House*)
Mrs C Ditchburn
Mrs E Howard
Ms P McKeown
Miss E Sherriff (*Head of Removes*)
C Tomkins

Geography:
*M J Prestshaw, BSc MEd, MRes
Mrs R H Aldridge, BA (*Head of Walsh House*)
J A D Blackham, BA (*Head of Grosvenor House*)
Mrs A M McNabb, BA (*Head of Bradbury House*)

History & Politics:
*P G Neal, BA
J P Carter, MA (*Head of Sixth Form*)
Mrs G K Chadwick, BA
R J M Hensman, BA, MA, PhD
S Neal, BA (*Head of Faculty – Languages & Humanities*)

Information Technology:
*O Hall, BA
A J Dewbery, MA
A Phoenix Holland

Mrs E E Simpson, BA, MBA

Mathematics:
*Mrs C E Lanceley, BSc
S D Bibby, BSc
Mrs S Cooper, BSc
A J Dewbery, MA
D Gibbon, BSc
Mrs A Ignata, BSc
Mrs C Plass, BSc
Mrs C N Ranson, BSc
Miss D Roberts, BSc
Mrs H E Sugarman, MMath

Modern Languages:
*Miss L E McCutcheon
M D Bircham, BA
Mrs M R Hartley, BA
Miss E Higgins
Mrs C Irvine, BA
Mrs M Rowley Williams, BA, MEd [maternity leave]
Mrs R E Webb, BA (*Head of Gladstone House*)

Music:
*Ms D L Neal, BMus, MA (*Director of Music*)
Mrs K Bannerjee, BMus
M Lansom, BSc (*Head of Strings*)
Mrs V L S Latifa, BMus (*Head of Dutton House*)

J E Millard, BA

Personal & Social Education:
*M S Lee, MA

Philosophy & Theology:
*J R Rees, BA
M S Lee, MA
Ms J E Rutberg, MA (*Head of Faculty – Social Sciences & Maths*)

Physical Education:
*R Lunn, BEd (*Director of Sport*)
Mrs K Jones, BA (*Assistant Director of Sport*; *Head of Fox House*)
S Egerton, BA
Miss E L Halstead, BA
B Horne, BSc
R I Hornby, BA

Physics:
*S Bosworth, MA, DPhil, FRAS
Ms H M Davies, BSc, MSc
N Heritage, MSc, PhD, MInstP, CPhys
B Horne, BSc
Mrs K Scutter, BSc

Psychology:
*R Hornby, BA
Miss G Bramham, BSc

Head of Junior School & Infant School: Mrs M A Ainsworth, LLB, MEd
Deputy Head (*Junior School*): A Griffiths, BA
Director of Studies (*Junior School*): T W Griffin, BA
Deputy Head (*Infant School*): Mrs J C Callaghan, BEd

Assistant Staff (*Junior School & Infant School*):
Miss J M Anderson, BA, CertEd
Mrs J Benson, BA
T Blakemore, BA Ed
Miss J Davies, BA
H J Duncalf, BEd
Mrs D Grove, BA
Miss J M L Hartley, BA
K A Hollingworth, BEd
Miss S Ley, BA
J B Melville, BEd
Mrs N C M Moffatt, BA
Mrs L Morrice Evans, BA
Mrs M D O'Leary, BA
D M O'Neil, BSc
Mrs S Parker, BEd
Miss K A Savage, BA
J N Spellman, BEd
Mrs N J Stevens, BMus
Mrs A Stevenson, BEd
Mrs N M Tomlinson, BA
Mrs S Tomlinson, BEd
Mrs C Williams, BA
Mrs K Williams, BEd

Visiting Music Teachers:
W Armstrong, BA, PGRNCM (*Oboe*)
Ms M Blythin, BA (*Harp & Piano*)
Miss B Griffiths, BMus (*Piano*)
S J Hall, BSc (*Bass Guitar*)
Ms S Marrs, FTCL (*Voice*)
N Middleton, BA (*Drums*)
D Ortiz, BMus (*Head of Brass*)
A Parker, MA (*Saxophone*)
M Reynolds, BA (*Piano*)
Mrs J Richardson, CT ABRSM, ATCL (*Flute*)

Extra-Curricular Staff:
Director of Rowing: J A D Blackham, BA
Contingent Commander, CCF: Maj M S Lee, MA
Duke of Edinburgh's Award Coordinator: D A Brown
Educational Visits Coordinator: R I D Hornby, BA

Director of Finance & Operations: Mrs H Jordan
Director of Human Resources: Mrs A H Millard, BSc, MCIPD
Director of Marketing, Communications & Partnerships: Mrs S O'Donnell
Director of ICT: J K Warne, BSc, MCSA
Admissions Manager: Mrs E R Sears, BA
Head Librarian & Archivist: vacant
Examinations Officer: vacant
School Nurse: Mrs L Jones, RN
Care Scheme Manager: vacant

Headmaster's PA: Mrs E Paul, BSc

The King's School
Macclesfield

Alderley Road, Prestbury, Macclesfield, Cheshire SK10 4SP

Tel: 01625 260000
email: mail@kingsmac.co.uk
website: www.kingsmac.co.uk
X/Twitter: @kingsmac
Facebook: @kingsinmacc
Instagram: @explore/tags/kingsmac

The King's School is the top performing independent school in Cheshire East for GCSE and A Level results and is listed in The Sunday Times ParentPower 2024 League table as being in the Top 5 Independent Schools in the North-West for academic results.

Founded in 1502, King's relocated in 2020 to a new, purpose-built and eco-friendly school campus. The school sits on a stunning 80-acre rural campus just outside Macclesfield/Alderley Edge.

King's offers an exciting co-educational learning environment for boys and girls aged 3–18. It strives for excellence across all areas of teaching and learning, as well as in sporting, musical and creative endeavours. Exceptional pastoral care is a defining feature of the school. The last ISI Inspection in 2022 awarded King's the highest grading of 'Excellent' in all aspects.

Number in school. Infants age 3–7: 168 boys and girls. Juniors age 7–11: 256 boys and girls. Senior pupils age 11–16: 722 boys and girls. Sixth Form: 190 boys and girls. Total: 1,336.

Organisation and curriculum. The King's School is a co-educational day school and is organised into three Divisions: the Infant & Junior Division; the Senior Division; and the Sixth Form. Each Division is run by a Principal, who is responsible for day-to-day organisation and wellbeing of pupils, and the Principals are supported by Vice-Principals, Heads of Year and a pastoral team.

Girls and boys from 3–18 enjoy a broad curriculum and the same extensive range of opportunities.

The King's School has one Board of Governors and one Head of Foundation, plus a Senior Management Team, who manage the school.

King's aims include 'to challenge our pupils to aspire, work hard and achieve' and 'to develop lively and enquiring minds'. The curriculum is broad and rich throughout all year groups offering pupils of all ages choice and a range of experiences.

The School's most recent ISI Inspection Report (2022) graded King's as 'Excellent' – the highest ranking – in all aspects. As well as teaching and pupils' achievements being excellent, so too is pastoral care, which is a high priority within the school. The divisional structure is key to enabling each unit to be small and operate as a community. Coupled with the aim of 'fostering a friendly, polite and caring community', King's is definitely a happy place to be a pupil.

Infant & Junior pupils enjoy the highly engaging 'Learning Challenge Curriculum', which is an enquiry-based approach to learning and delivers cross-curricular learning in humanities, languages, science and creative subjects.

Senior pupils enjoy a broad and balanced curriculum, which covers English, Maths, three humanities, four languages, four creative subjects, Computer Science, Critical Thinking, PHSE, PE, Games, three Sciences and outdoor learning. Senior pupils are able to study 10 or 11 GCSEs.

Sixth Form students are assigned to a personal tutor responsible for a group of 10–15 pupils throughout their Sixth Form course. Any justifiable combination of available A Level subjects may be pursued, complemented by an IGCSE Global Perspectives (in Year 12), and a wide range of options from the Extended Studies Programme in Year 13, including the EPQ, Japanese, the Arts Award, Sports Leadership and others. Students choose from these options, which are designed to extend their breadth of cultural interest and intellectual inquiry, while Recreational Activities are designed to encourage the positive use of leisure time and offer experience in a range of sports and activities. Pupils are supported by an excellent Careers service and are well prepared for University Entrance Examinations, competitive entry to university and higher-level apprenticeships.

In 2023, the school won the Wellbeing Award in the Education Awards 2023, for its work around pupil wellbeing and outdoor learning.

New campus. The King's school moved to its new £60m campus in the summer of 2020. The new 80-acre campus offers state-of-the-art facilities to enhance the educational experience of all pupils. The new campus contains a dedicated Sports Centre, with a 25 m swimming pool, indoor cricket facilities, large indoor hall with six courts, a martial arts studio, gym and café.

Arts and craft. Well-equipped, spacious Art rooms and Design & Technology (DT) workshops include an Innovation Suite, and are used for teaching as well as being available for use by the members of the Art Club, STEM Club, Textile Club and Craft societies outside the timetable.

Music. Over 400 pupils receive tuition in the full range of orchestral instruments, the Piano, Organ, Classical Guitar and Singing. A scheme in Year 4 allows all pupils to receive tuition (free) in an instrument of choice. There are three orchestras, a Concert-band, two Jazz bands, three Choirs and many ensembles, all of which provide regular performing experience. The Foundation Choir was the first BBC Songs of Praise Choir of the Year in 2003. Choir tours to Europe take place alternate years. Pupils regularly enter the music profession in addition to those pursuing academic training. Music Scholarships are available.

Drama. Theatre Studies is an important creative option at GCSE and covers all aspects of the theatre. Great importance is attached to the regular production of school plays and musicals, which involve large numbers of pupils and enjoy a distinguished reputation. Facilities include a large Performance Hall, as well as a main hall (950 seats). Pupils regularly take examinations and study for LAMDA qualifications in performance and public speaking.

Sport. The school has extensive sporting facilities and a large Games Department with around 20 staff. The school offers Sports Scholarships and has an Elite Athlete Programme (KEAP). All pupils take part in Games and PE activities appropriate to the season. Junior School sports include Football, Cricket, Netball, Hockey, Tennis, Rounders, Rugby, Swimming, Athletics and a wide range of individual games. In the Senior School, boys' sports include Rugby, Hockey, Cross-Country, Squash, Badminton, Cricket, Tennis, Athletics and Basketball; the girls' sports include Hockey, Cricket, Netball, Tennis, Football, Cross-Country, Volleyball, Rounders, Dance, Gym and Athletics. In addition there is a varied programme of sports in the Sixth Form, including activities such as Caving, Fell Running, Sailing, Yoga and Rock Climbing which are actively pursued by boys and girls.

Outdoor pursuits. This is a thriving part of the school. There is a regular programme of activity weekends including canoeing, gorge scrambling, surfing, coasteering, etc. In addition, numerous expeditions are arranged in the many favourable areas near the school and also abroad. Sailing and Orienteering are popular and The Duke of Edinburgh's Award scheme attracts around 300 pupils each year. King's is one of the largest DofE authorising centres in the north of England.

Clubs and societies. There is a wide range of clubs catering for most interests and hobbies, ranging from Astronomy, Debating, Dance, Chess and Squash to Sailing, STEM Club, Equestrian Society, Electronics Club, Coding Club and Taekwondo.

Fees per term (2023–2024). Senior School and Sixth Form: £5,105, Infants & Junior School: £4,140. Sibling discount scheme available.

Scholarships and bursaries. Bursaries are available for entry at 11 and 16 years of age. In addition, a number of Academic Scholarships are awarded based on performance in the Entrance Examination. Senior School Music Scholarships are available for pupils joining Year 7 (in instrument or singing). Music and Organ scholarships are also available in the Sixth Form. Places on the King's Elite Athlete Pathway (KEAP) are available to pupils joining Year 7.

Admissions. King's is a selective school. Admission to the Infants, Juniors and Seniors is normally for

September each year through competitive examination of age-appropriate entrance assessments. Pupils are admitted to the Sixth Form subject to academic attainment at GCSE, interview and meeting course entry requirements. Entry requirements are an average of grade 6 or higher across eight GCSE subjects, with a minimum of a grade 5 in both Mathematics and English Language (university matriculation requirements). Most A Level subjects require a grade 7–9 in a subject to be studied at A Level, and this is compulsory for Mathematics and Science subjects. Further details of Admission arrangements are available on the website and upon request. Immediate admission, e.g. for new arrivals in the area, is possible if places are available.

Former Pupils' Association. Chairman: Amber Owens, email: formerpupils@kingsmac.co.uk. An annual magazine and twice yearly newsletter are provided to former pupils alongside a full programme of events.

Visit the website. The award-winning website is found at www.kingsmac.co.uk.

Charitable status. The King's School, Macclesfield is a Registered Charity, number 1137204. It exists for the education of pupils between the ages of 3 and 18.

Chairman of the Governors: Mr A Higginson, BSc Hons, FCMA
Vice-Chair of Governors: Ms J White, BSc Hons, CBE

Senior Management Team:

***Head of Foundation*: Mr Jason Slack**, BSc Hons, MA Ed

Deputy Head (*Academic*): Mr R Griffiths, MA Cantab
Deputy Head (*Operations*): Mr P J Cooper, BSc
Director of External Relations: Mrs C Johnson, BSc, DipM
Director of Finance: Mr J M Spencer Pickup, BSc Hons, ACA
Senior Teacher: Mr R Davies, MA
Principal of Seniors: Mrs H L Broadley
Principal of Infants & Juniors: Mrs R Cookson, BA
Principal of Sixth Form: Miss D Jestin

Vice-Principal of Seniors (*Lower School*): Mrs E Smith
Vice-Principal of Seniors (*Middle School*): Mr S Mattingly
Vice-Principal of Infants & Juniors: Mrs E L Warburton, BEd
Vice-Principal of Infants & Juniors: Mr P Boardman

Heads of Departments:
Art & Design: Mrs D Inman, BA
Classics: Mr A Mallin, BA
Computing: Mr P Mackenzie, BSc
Design & Technology: J Nichols, BEd
Drama: Mrs C Deva, BA
Economics & Business Studies: Mr J S MacGregor, MA
English: Mr R Kellett, BA, PGCE
Geography: Mr A S Puddephatt, BA
Geology: Dr J A Fitzgerald, BSc, MSc, PhD
History: Miss L Hughes, BA
Learning Support: Mrs J Fletcher

Modern Languages: Mr I E Dalgleish, BA
German: Mrs Slack
French: Mdm Schue
Spanish: Ms S Bailey

Director of Music: Mr I Crawford, BMus
Physical Education (*Director of Sport*): Mr C S Thompson, BA, PGCE
Physics: Dr S J Hartnett, BSc, DPhil, PGCE
Politics: Mrs L Christie, BA
Psychology: Mrs C Bell, BSc, PGCE, MA Ed
Religion & Philosophy: Mr R N Jackson, BA

Science: Mr J Street, BSc, PGCE
Biology: Mrs K Byrne
Chemistry: Miss L C Watkins, BSc

The King's School Worcester Foundation

Senior School
5 College Green, Worcester WR1 2LL

Tel: 01905 721700
email: info@ksw.org.uk
website: www.ksw.org.uk
X/Twitter: @KingsWorcester
Facebook: @KingsWorcester

King's St Alban's Prep
Mill Street, Worcester WR1 2NJ

Tel: 01905 354906
email: ksa@ksw.org.uk

King's Hawford Prep
Hawford Lock Lane, Claines, Worcester WR3 7SD

Tel: 01905 451292
email: hawford@ksw.org.uk

A Cathedral School appears to have existed at Worcester virtually continuously since the 7th century. In its present form, however, The King's School dates from its re-foundation by King Henry VIII in 1541.

This Foundation of Schools has a history dating back to the 7th Century and close links to the Cathedral. The King's School has a strong sense of tradition combined with a modern and successful approach to learning, inspiring pupils to aim higher, shaping the character to go further, and instilling the values to lead lives of purpose. The King's School is well known locally for its friendly atmosphere and excellent relationships between staff and pupils.

Today, The King's School, Worcester is a Foundation comprising two preparatory schools and a senior school – all three are co-educational day schools.

The Senior School, for pupils from 11–18, still occupies its original site adjacent to Worcester Cathedral and sits on the banks of the River Severn. The buildings are grouped around College Green and the School Gardens. They range in date from the 14th century College Hall and Edgar Tower through the 17th and 18th century buildings surrounding College Green, to a range of modern, purpose-built buildings including an award-winning boat house, a modern ECO Sports Hall and Performing Arts Centre, an enviable well-resourced School Library and a recently refurbished Modern Languages Department.

King's St Alban's stands in its own grounds adjacent to the main school site, offering education from age 2–11, with a purpose-built pre-prep department for girls and boys aged 4–7 and a teacher-led nursery for children from 2 years. The school has a large hall, a dedicated Science Laboratory, an IT suite, an Art and Technology Room, Libraries, Music Rooms, Sports Hall and 25 metre Swimming Pool. In the grounds stand the Chapel, the main buildings of the Prep School with the Nursery and Pre-Preparatory Department on an adjacent, self-contained site. Frequent use is made of the Senior School facilities, such as the 300-seat Theatre and Dance and Drama Studios.

King's Hawford is set in a spacious rural setting just to the north of the city and offers education from age 2–11. The school has a strong focus on outdoor learning and holds the LoTC (Learning Outside the Classroom) Award, for its outstanding outdoor learning provision. The school is accommodated within an elegant and recently refurbished Georgian house surrounded by playing fields, a heated enclosed swimming pool, a multi-purpose sports hall and performance space and secure play area for younger children. The school has a double-decker bus that has been converted into an amazing library. The children's weekly radio show is posted on the website.

The nurseries at the Prep Schools are well regarded and rated highly amongst parents. In 2021 they received the UK Top 20 Group Award.

Numbers and Admission. The King's School is fully co-educational. King's St Alban's has 182 pupils. King's Hawford has 283 pupils. The Senior School has 881 pupils, including 269 in the Sixth Form.

Entrance to the King's School is by the Prep Entrance Test at 7, 8 or 9, or by the School's Examination at 11, 12 and 13. Boys and girls also join the School at Sixth Form level; this entry is by test, interview and GCSE results.

Religion. The King's School has an historic connection with Worcester Cathedral. Religious education, given in accordance with the Christian faith, is non-denominational. Pupils of all denominations and faiths are welcomed.

Curriculum The Senior School offers GCSE and A Level examinations in preparation for Higher Education. The curriculum is designed to give all pupils a general education and to postpone specialisation for as long as possible. Further details will be found in the Prospectus and on the School's website.

Games. The major sports are Rugby, Netball, Hockey, Football, Rowing and Cricket. Other sports include Tennis, Athletics, Cross Country, Badminton, Rounders, Fencing, Golf, Swimming, Sailing and Canoeing. PE and games are compulsory for all: a wide choice is offered to Sixth Formers.

Other Activities. The Senior School organises a contingent of the Combined Cadet Force (CCF) and provides an outstanding programme to enable pupils to engage in the Duke of Edinburgh's Award scheme.

Pupils undertake Community Service within and beyond Worcester and our Charity Committee organises a series of events across the year to fundraise and raise awareness of wide-ranging issues.

Regular drama performances are of an exceptional standard and our accommodation for them is superb with a fully equipped theatre seating 320, a black box studio which seats 80, and also a dance studio complete with mirrors and a sprung floor. Music is similarly impressive with a broad range of ensembles, choirs, orchestras, bands, quartets and groups.

Sport is very strong among both boys and girls and benefits from some outstanding facilities, including a swimming pool, three-storey climbing wall and an industry-standard Boathouse.

As well as a thriving Lego Robotics Club, School Radio and participation in the Engineering Education Scheme and Young Enterprise, pupils are offered the chance to undertake Model Union Nations (MUN) and debating.

Scholarships and Bursaries. Both Music and Academic Scholarships are available at 11+, 13+ and 16+ in the Senior School, value up to one third of tuition fees. Academic scholarships at 11+ and 13+ are awarded on the basis of the Entrance Test and an interview: at 16+ on the basis of an aptitude test and interview.

Fees per term (2023–2024). Senior School £5,765, Prep Schools £2,925–£5,340.

Charitable status. The King's School Worcester Foundation is a Registered Charity, number 1098236. It exists to provide high-quality education for boys and girls.

Chair of Governors: Mrs P Preston, MA Oxon, DipM

***Chief Executive and Headmaster of The King's School Worcester Foundation*: Mr G E Doodes**, MA, FRSA

Senior Deputy Head: Dr A Oliver, BA, MSc, EdD
Deputy Head Pastoral: Miss H Dyke
Deputy Head Academic: Mrs K Beever, MA, CEng

The King's Prep Schools:

King's St Alban's:
Head: Mr N Hawker, BMus, MPhil
Assistant Head, Pre-Prep: Miss B Cartwright, BEd
Deputy Head: Mr A Kent
Director of Sport: Mrs J Clark
Academic Deputy: Mrs K Beauchamp

King's Hawford:
Head: Mr T Butt, BSc
Deputy Head: Mrs C Knight, BEd
Assistant Head: Mr L Stigant
Head of Lower School: Mr O Roberts, BEd
Head of Early Years: Miss A L Kingston, BA

Kingston Grammar School

London Road, Kingston-upon-Thames, Surrey KT2 6PY

Tel: 020 8546 5875
email: enquiries@kgs.org.uk
website: www.kgs.org.uk
X/Twitter: @KGS1561
Facebook: @KingstonGrammar
Instagram: @KGS1561
LinkedIn: /school/kingston-grammar-school/

Motto: *Bene agere ac laetari*

The school has existed since the fourteenth century when it was located in the Lovekyn Chantry Chapel. In 1561, Queen Elizabeth I, in response to a humble petition from the Burghers of Kingston, signed Letters Patent establishing the 'Free Grammar School of Queen Elizabeth to endure for ever'. In 1944, the School accepted Direct Grant Status, becoming fully independent in 1976. Two years later it became co-educational, initially with girls in the Sixth Form followed by girls joining the First Year the following year. There are still close links with the Royal Borough of Kingston upon Thames, but no residential qualification for entry to the School. There are around 881 pupils and the current proportion of boys to girls is 50%–50%.

Buildings. Starting with the medieval Lovekyn Chapel, the site of Kingston Grammar School has been developed over 450 years. The refurbishment of the Fairfield Building has provided modern, energy-efficient classrooms and science laboratories. The Queen Elizabeth II building, opened by Her Majesty in 2005, has a Performing Arts Centre, a Music Technology Suite, Sixth Form Centre and classrooms. Pupils have access to an extensive networked computer system which they can access from home. The school is easily accessible by road and there are good rail links to Kingston. The 22-acre sports ground includes an indoor sports pavilion, 4 cricket squares, 6 netball courts, 8 tennis courts, 6 cricket nets, 2 hockey pitches plus practice area, 4 football pitches, an Olympic gym and the KGS boathouse.

Entry to the School. Admission to the School at 11+ and 13+ is by examination and interview, and at 16+ by written application, interview and GCSE results. Candidates sit the School's own examination papers in November prior to year of entry. We also hold a 10+ deferred entry exam for candidates in Year 5 at primary school to join the School in the First Year (Year 7).

Term of Entry. Pupils enter in September. Occasional vacancies are considered.

Fees per term (2023–2024). £7,820; this covers all charges excluding public examination fees, trips and lunch.

Scholarships and Bursaries. The Governors award Co-curricular scholarships (on merit) and means-tested fee assistance to pupils entering the School at 11+, 13+ and 16+.

The School encourages academic aspiration in all its students, and has recently moved to offering Academic Scholarships to the highest achieving students following their first two years of study.

Additional Academic Scholarships are also awarded at 16+ including for new entrants to the school on the basis of outstanding GCSE results in August.

Art Scholarships may be awarded at 11+, 13+ and 16+ following a practical test, interview and submission of a folder of work.

Design & Technology Scholarships may be awarded at 16+ following an interview and submission of a folder of work.

Drama Scholarships are also available at 16+, based on auditions and an interview.

Music Scholarships, plus free tuition on one instrument, are available. Auditions are held in November for candidates who are applying for entry at 11+, 13+ or 16+.

Sport Scholarships are also awarded for candidates demonstrating outstanding sporting potential. These are available at 11+, 13+ and 16+, based on practical assessment.

Curriculum. The academic curriculum through to GCSE emphasises a proper balance between varied disciplines and a range of intellectual experience, with all students taking Maths, English, the three sciences and at least one modern foreign language as part of 10 IGCSE/GCSE subjects. Maths IGCSE may be taken early by the most able candidates who then proceed to the Additional Maths qualification. There is a Learning Support Department and mentoring for pupils with specific needs. A full Careers Programme is offered with ongoing support for university entry from a dedicated Director of Higher Education & Careers. Growing numbers of students choose to study outside the UK and are fully supported in their applications. Pupils are encouraged to view academic pursuit as a desirable end in itself. In the Sixth Form, students choose either three or four A Level subjects in the Lower Sixth and continue with three into the Upper Sixth (with the exception of those studying Further Maths as a fourth A level throughout). In addition, students in the Lower Sixth undertake an academic enrichment programme, designed to develop the skills necessary to learn independently and to broaden their horizons. They are able to choose from courses such as the Extended Project Qualification (EPQ), Leadership & Management and Critical Thinking. They also engage in community service. All Sixth Form students attend fortnightly lectures on wider social issues and international themes. Almost 100% of the Sixth Form elect to proceed to higher education, including Oxford and Cambridge, with a high proportion gaining entry to Russell Group as well as overseas institutions.

Care. A pupil's Form Tutor is responsible for welfare and progress. Experienced Heads of Year, supported by Assistants, coordinate the work of Form Tutors. There are two full-time qualified nurses working in a dedicated medical area. Two school counsellors visit during the week to support any pupils who have concerns in and out of school. Parent consultation evenings are held regularly and pupils receive a number of written reports per year, in addition to twice-termly grade cards. Pastoral evenings are also held covering a wide range of topics using a variety of external and internal speakers. Sessions are also held where parents can discuss with each other and staff the difficulties and anxieties faced by young adults. Pastoral education takes place in all year groups through dedicated lessons and lectures, supplemented by high-quality outside speakers on a wide range of subjects. There is also a wellbeing strategy, and regular surveys and focus groups assist the school to formulate procedures to work on this key area of school life.

Sport. The School's sports grounds are beautifully situated at Thames Ditton, next to the River Thames, opposite Hampton Court Palace. Kingston Grammar School not only prides itself on the high percentage of students engaged in competitive sport, but the large number who go on to obtain county, regional and international honours. Hockey (winter/spring terms), rowing (all three terms) and cricket (summer term) are the focus sports, with teams/crews competing at all levels in friendly fixtures as well as county, regional and national championships. The School also has representative sides in football, athletics, cross country running, golf, netball and tennis, with an emphasis on creating sporting opportunities for all, as well as focussed training and support for its performance athletes.

Societies. The School is proud of its extensive co-curricular provision and its programme of House-based activities. A large number of school societies provides for the interests of students of all ages. They range from Chess and Debating to STEAM and Young Enterprise. The Duke of Edinburgh's Award scheme is popular and overseas travel is a regular feature of many activities. The Music Department has a vigorous programme of concerts and tours, and a flourishing Drama Department provides a wealth of opportunity for students in all aspects of dramatic production.

Community Service. A large number of pupils volunteer through our partnerships with local schools and charities as part of the Community Service Programme at KGS. These programmes include pupils preparing food for a community soup kitchen, working with Elmbridge Community Link to support young people with special educational needs, hosting 'tea parties' with our students for residents of local residential care homes, online maths mentoring with a local secondary school, and a range of opportunities to support a local primary school through a reading project, a drama club and support for their sport activities. Whilst these opportunities are primarily aimed at older students, younger students participate in activities hosted in school. Volunteering is challenging and rewarding, and helps to foster compassion, empathy and a sense of social justice, while enabling students to develop skills such as teamwork, responsibility and resilience. Although KGS already offers a wide range of activities to choose from, staff are also willing to help pupils find other projects.

Careers. The Careers & Universities Department assist students with their options at all levels, are available at parents' evenings and give advice on possible future careers. They are in close contact with employers in professions, commerce and industry through a strong alumni department. All pupils undertake the Morrisby Profile at the end of the Fourth Year to assist with career and study choices, whilst in Fifth Year pupils have an opportunity to undertake work experience after their GCSE examinations. An annual Careers Fair and other specialist careers seminars are offered during the academic year. Particular attention is given to the advice on entry to universities to which the majority of Sixth Formers go and students are also encouraged to explore apprenticeship routes.

Parents' and Staff Association. The Association exists to further the interests of the School in the broadest possible way and does much to strengthen the links between staff, parents and students. The Sherriff Club (rowing), The Hockey Society, Music Society and Drama Society also support school activities.

KGS Friends (our alumni society) is the umbrella organisation of former students, parents and staff. It works to keep alumni connected with the school and with each other, raising awareness of all that the school does and helping alumni support each other throughout their lives. Alumni can join at any time by contacting the alumni office and students and parents leaving the school are encouraged to join.

Honours. Around 10% of the cohort achieve places at Oxford and Cambridge.

Charitable Status. Kingston Grammar School is a Registered Charity, number 1078461, and a Company Limited by Guarantee, registered in England, number 3883748. It exists to enable children to adapt their talents to meet the needs of an ever-changing world, whilst holding fast to the principles of self-reliance, a sense of responsibility and a determination to seize opportunity.

Governing Body:
Mr R O'Dowd, BSc, RSA *(Chair)*
Mr J Harchowal, MRPharmS, MSc, BPharm Hons *(Vice Chair)*
Mr V Agarwal, ACA, MBA
Dr N Ahmed, BSc, PhD
Mr E Bowyer, BA
Mrs C Chevallier, MA, CIPD
Mr N Cole, MA, MPhil, DPhil Oxon
Mrs L Dux, LLB
Mr A D Evans, BSc, ACA
Mr P Kelk, BA
Mr N Khandan-Nia, BSc
Ms B Lelyveld, MA
Mrs J Mikardo, BA, CQSW, Member of ACP
Mrs D Rose, MA Cantab

Clerk to the Governors: Ms D Coomes

***Head Master*: Mr S R Lehec**, BA

Deputy Head, Director of Development: Mrs V S Humphrey, BA (*Geography*)
Deputy Head Academic: Mr W Cooper, MPhil (*Religion & Philosophy*)
Assistant Head: Mrs D M Sherwood, BSc (*Geography*)
Assistant Head: Mr A J Beard, MA (*History*)
Assistant Head: Mrs A D Lett, BSc (*Chemistry*)
Assistant Head: Ms A L Williams, BSc (*Biology*)
Assistant Head: Mr N C Hudson, BA (*English*)
Assistant Head: Mr A S House, MSc (*Geography*)

Teaching Staff:
* *Head of Department*

Miss H Airbright, BSc (*Biology*)
Ms I Albayrak, MSc (*Economics*)
Ms L R Andrew, MSc (**Classics*)
Mrs A Angell, BA (*History*)
Miss A Arcos Villanueva, BA (*Spanish*)
Mrs S E Bailey, BA (*Art*)
Mrs J Barkey, BA (*Art*)
Mr T Beaumont, BSc (**Boys' Hockey*)
Miss B Beeharry, BSc, MBA (*Economics and Business*)
Mr A Beggs (*Contingent Commander CCF*)
Mr M Behnoudnia, BSc (*Second in Physics, Assistant Head of Academic Scholars*)
Mr T G Benson, MSci (*Physics, *STEAM*)
Mr W Bohanna, BA (**Economics*)
Mr D Brook, MA (*English*)
Mrs J Butcher, BA (*History & Politics, Head of Third Year*)
Miss S J Butler, BA (*PE, Head of First Year*)
Mr N Casasanto, BA (*Chemistry*)
Mr I Chiew, MSc (*Mathematics*)
Miss M Christmas, MA (*Drama*)
Miss A Clarkson, BA (*Chemistry*)

Ms S Clifford, BSc (*Mathematics*)
Mrs M Collins, MA (*History*)
Mr K Connor, MEng (**Mathematics*)
Ms M Cope, BA (*History*)
Dr A Crampin, BSc, PhD (*Physics, Head of Lower Sixth*)
Mr S R Crohill, BA (*Drama*)
Mr M Daly, BSc (*Hockey, PE*)
Mr I Deepchand, BSc (**Physics, Assistant Head of Year*)
Miss A Dion-Jones, BA (*Design Technology*)
Mr J A Dyson, BA (**Art*)
Mr B Edwards (*Director of Sport*)
Mrs A L Edwards, MA (**Psychology*)
Miss L Emm, BA (*Design Technology*)
Mr M B Emmerton, MEng (*Second in Mathematics*)
Mrs A Evans, MA (*German*)
Mrs R A Faiz, MA (*Mathematics*)
Mr D Farr, BA (**Design Technology*)
Mr A R Fitzgerald, MA (*Director of Careers & Universities*)
Mr N S Forsyth, BSc (*Biology, Head of Wellbeing*)
Mr O P Garner, BA (*French & Italian, Head of Fifth Year*)
Mrs P S Garside, MA (**English*)
Mr A Gautam, MA (*Computing*)
Mr R M Gee, BA (*Director of Drama*)
Mr F A Geron, MSc (*Computing*)
Mr M S Grant, MA (*History, Head of Second Year*)
Mr E Green (*Director of Rowing*)
Mr M Hall, MSc (*PE, Football*)
Mr J Halls, BA (*Design Technology*)
Mrs S Hassan, MSc (*Mathematics, *Community, Action and Service*)
Miss A Henderson, BA (*History*)
Mr A B G Henderson, MSc (*Psychology, EPQ Lead*)
Miss A L Hicks, BSc (*Biology, Head of Fourth Year*)
Ms R K Hill, MSc (*Biology*)
Mrs L Hobbs, MA (*English*)
Miss C Hurley (*Geography*)
Miss O Jackson, MA (*English*)
Ms M Jimenez, BA (*Spanish*)
Mrs C A Jones, BSc (*Mathematics*)
Dr K Kennedy, DPhil (**History, Young Enterprise*)
Mrs J King, MA, MEd (**Learning Support*)
Mr M Laflin, BA (**Director of Music*)
Mr S Lavery, MSc (*Assistant Director of Sport*)
Mr H R Lawrence, BSc (*Religion & Philosophy*)
Ms A Lenzi, BA, MA (*Learning Support*)
Mrs L M Macfarlane, MSc (**Geography*)
Mrs O Maclay, BA (*Spanish, Assistant Head of Year*)
Miss A E Maclean, BA (*French & German*)
Mrs P Mayor, BSc (*Physics*)
Ms F McBride, BA, MA (*Librarian*)
Mrs R H McCulloch, MA (*Geography*)
Mr S R Morris, BSc (*Mathematics, Deputy Director of Careers & Universities*)
Miss H M Naismith, MSc (**Girls' Hockey, PE*)
Mr C O'Collins, BSc (*Chemistry*)
Mr J Orr, MA (*Mathematics*)
Miss M Parry, BSc (*Mathematics*)
Miss V Paterson, MA (*Classics, *Community Service*)
Mrs A S Phoenix, BSc (*PE*)
Mrs K D Pinnock, BA (*French & Italian*)
Mrs E Pytel, BA (*Classics, Head of Academic Scholars*)
Mrs N A Reilly, MSc (*Mathematics*)
Mrs M Robinson, BSc (**PSHE*)
Mr M J C Rodgers, MSc (**Biology, Golf Programme*)
Mrs T M Russell, Mag Phil (**Modern Foreign Languages*)
Miss R J Sharp, BA (*French & Spanish, Second in Modern Foreign Languages*)
Dr P Sheehy, MA, PhD (*Religion & Philosophy*)
Mr P J Simmons, BSc (*PE, Assistant Head of Year*)
Mr J W Skeates, MA (*Mathematics*)
Mrs L Slezak, BSc (*Mathematics*)
Mr D A R Sorley, BA (**Politics, History, Professional Tutor*)
Mrs P W E Stones, MA (*Second in English*)
Miss K Tamblyn, BA (*English*)
Ms F S Thomas, MRes (*Biology*)
Mr J J Tierney, BMus (*Music*)
Mrs R Wakely, BA (*Art*)
Mr C G Wenham, BA (*Second in Chemistry, Head of Upper Sixth, Head of CU*)
Mrs C Williams, BA (**Religion & Philosophy*)
Dr L H Winning, MChem, DPhil (**Chemistry*)

Director of Finance & Operations: Mr D Leen
Director of Human Resources: Mrs N Sloan
Director of IT: Mr N Baxter
Facilities Manager: Mr D Harris
Head Master's PA: Dr S Warne
Head of Marketing: Mrs T Phillips
Senior Registrar: Mrs J Shalgosky

Kingswood School

Lansdown, Bath BA1 5RG

Tel: 01225 734200
email: admissions@kingswood.bath.sch.uk
website: www.kingswood.bath.sch.uk
Facebook: @KingswoodSchool
Instagram: @kingswoodschool
LinkedIn: /kingswoodschool

Motto: *In via Recta Celeriter*

Kingswood Senior School is a thriving independent co-educational day and boarding school like no other, welcoming children from 11–18 years old. As a busy boarding and day school, we offer a staggering range of co-curricular opportunities, celebrating both cultural and sporting achievement.

Whilst some pupils continue their journey from Kingswood Prep School, we welcome many new students at our various entry points (Years 7, 9 and 12) and they settle into life at Kingswood seamlessly which is testament to the strength of our inclusive community.

Pastoral care. Pastoral care is central to everything we do at Kingswood and we all want our pupils to feel good about themselves, recognise their strengths, constantly develop any areas that they find challenging and have a positive impact on the community and world around them.

Site and facilities. With an abundance of space on our 200-acre site in Lansdown, Bath, we are within easy reach of the M4 and M5 motorways, as well as having great transport links to Bristol and London. The School sits alongside original Victorian buildings and a host of modern developments, including boarding houses, a theatre, a sports hall, a sixth form centre, dining area and a cafe with stunning views of Bath below. The six boarding and day houses are located within the school campus. Sporting facilities also include a swimming pool, two floodlit AstroTurfs, extensive playing fields and a modern pavilion.

Curriculum. Our curriculum is engaging and interactive, enabling us to build on our pupils' past educational experiences and allows them to achieve a deeper understanding of, and greater competence in, each aspect of the curriculum as they move through the School. At Sixth Form, the core curriculum consists of the study of three A Levels, selected from over twenty subjects and complemented by Advanced Elective courses. Students also benefit from a General Studies and Life Skills programme and many pursue an Extended Project Qualification.

Co-curricular. Pupils benefit from a vibrant and extensive co-curricular programme which enhances their learning experience at Kingswood. There are over 100 activities each term and the provision for sport, music and drama is outstanding. Many pupils participate in The Duke of Edinburgh's Award and the school hosts the annual Bath Schools Model United Nations conference.

Sports and games. Kingswood is widely recognised as one of the top schools for sport in the South-West, with students competing at both national and international levels. We are fortunate to have strong links with various professional clubs such as Bath Rugby; we work with Team Bath at Bath University so that we can support gifted and talented sportsmen and women in fulfilling their athletic potential. However, our games philosophy at Kingswood is very much "sport for all", and we believe in encouraging all students, whether they be on the A, B, C or D teams, to be the best they can.

Sustainability. At Kingswood, we are passionate about the future and contributing to a fair and sustainable future for all. We recognise that we have a unique opportunity to educate and empower our pupils and wider community to share this vision and deliver this future. To this effect, the School offers a wide variety of activities, projects and programmes that engage with the many facets of sustainability.

Leavers. The vast majority of Kingswood sixth formers go on to university, either immediately after school or after a gap year. Much support is given to all Sixth Form students, including guidance on writing personal statements and interview practice. As a result of this support, the overwhelming majority of Kingswood students achieve a place at their first-choice university.

Fees per term (2023–2024). £6,146 (day); £9,707–£12,025 (weekly boarding); £11,112–£13,310 (full boarding); £9,933–£13,619 (international boarding).

EAL teaching is provided for students who do not speak English as their first language – this is invoiced separately as required. HM Forces families receive a reduction in boarding fees of up to 20% for each child.

Entry requirements. Entry at 11+ and 13+ is based on Kingswood's own entrance examination, a report from the candidate's current school and, where possible, a personal or group interview. Sixth Form entry is dependent on performance at interview, current school report and GCSE achievement.

Scholarships and bursaries. Academic and Special Talent scholarships (up to a maximum of 25% of the basic fees) are available annually to our day and boarding pupils entering Years 7, 9 and Lower Sixth. Special Talent scholarships are awarded for excellence in a particular field: Art, Drama, Music, Sport, Design Technology. John Wesley Awards are also available for boarders. Means-tested bursaries, worth up to 100% of fees, are available in Years 7, 9 and 12.

Charitable status. Kingswood School is a Registered Charity, number 309148.

Chairman of the Governing Body: Mr T Lindsay

***Headmaster and Principal of the Kingswood Foundation*: Mr A Gordon-Brown**

Senior Deputy Head & Vice Principal: Mr J M Davies

Deputy Head Academic: Dr R McIlwaine
Deputy Head Co-Curricular: Mr J W Davies
Deputy Head Pastoral: Mr J Matthews

Head of Lower School: Mr S Pentreath
Co-heads of Middle School: Mrs S Hurlinger & Mrs L Smyth
Head of Sixth Form: Mr C Woodgate
Head of Boarding: Mr D Harding

Director of Marketing, Admissions and Communications: Mrs H Drew
Head of Marketing & Communications: Mrs C Flynn

Lady Eleanor Holles

Hanworth Road, Hampton, Middlesex TW12 3HF

Tel: 020 8979 1601
email: office@lehs.org.uk
website: www.lehs.org.uk
X/Twitter: @LEHSchool
Facebook: @LEHSchoolOfficial
Instagram: @lehschoolofficial
LinkedIn: /school/the-lady-eleanor-holles-school

See full entry in the **GSA** section, on **p. 446**.

Lancing College

Lancing College – Senior School and Sixth Form, Lancing, West Sussex BN15 0RW

Tel: 01273 452213
email: admissions@lancing.org.uk
website: www.lancingcollege.co.uk
X/Twitter: @lancingcollege
Facebook: @lancingcollege
Instagram: @lancing_college
LinkedIn: /company/lancing-college

Motto: *Beati mundo corde*

Founded in 1848 by the Revd Nathaniel Woodard, Lancing College is one of the first schools of the Woodard Foundation.

There are 600 pupils in the school, accommodated in ten houses.

Location. The school stands on a spur of the Downs, overlooking the sea to the south and the Weald to the north, in grounds of several hundred acres, which include the College Farm.

By train, Lancing is 10 minutes from Brighton, 30 minutes from Gatwick Airport and 75 minutes from central London.

Buildings and Facilities. The main school buildings, faced with Sussex flint, are grouped around two quadrangles on the lines of an Oxford or Cambridge College.

The College has extensive laboratories, a purpose-built Music School, a Theatre with a full-time technical manager and a modern Design and Technology Centre with computerised design and engineering facilities. Alongside this, a strikingly modern Art School provides vast studio space and a photography suite. A café is located in the centre of the school for use by pupils and staff. There are over 350 private studies for boys and girls, many of which are study-bedrooms. There is a sports hall, indoor swimming pool and a miniature shooting range. Sporting facilities also include Squash, Tennis and Fives courts and an all-weather surface and full-sized AstroTurf hockey pitch. The Equestrian Centre provides livery as well as additional horses for co-curricular activities.

The Chapel, open to visitors every day, has the largest rose window built since the Middle Ages. In 2022 the west end of the Chapel was completed with an elegant three-arched porch to provide an entry worthy of this Grade 2 listed national monument.

Admission. Boys and girls are normally admitted at the beginning of the Autumn Term in their fourteenth year. The Advance (Pre-Test) Programme provides an early entry route for pupils, who can apply in the Advent Term of Year 6 and Year 7.

A registration fee of £200 is paid when a child's name is entered in the admission register. Entries should be made via the Director of Admissions, who will assign a House, following as far as possible the wishes of the parents. After a pupil has joined the school, parents usually correspond with the Housemaster or Housemistress directly.

Sixth Form Entry. Applications for entry should be made to the Director of Admissions one year prior to the year of entry. Testing takes place in November or by private arrangement.

Curriculum. Designed as far as possible to suit every pupil's potential with a wide range of subjects on offer including over 20 at A Level. Pupils work closely with academic staff and personal tutors to help them consider future options, entry to universities and to a wide range of professions. The College prides itself on the individual support available for pupils.

In a pupil's first three years, the curriculum provides a broad, balanced education without premature specialisation. The total of subjects taken at GCSE is limited to about nine or ten, the object being to promote excellence in whatever is studied and to lay firm foundations for the Sixth Form years.

The following subjects are studied in the Senior School: English Language and Literature, Religious Studies, Mathematics, Physics, Chemistry, Biology, French, Spanish or German, Geography, History, Physical Education, Music, Art, Design and Technology, Photography, Latin, Greek or Classical Civilisation, and Drama.

In the Sixth Form there is a choice of over 20 subjects which can be studied to A Level. A BTEC qualification is also available in Business and Sport. Pupils are also encouraged to carry out an EPQ (Extended Project Qualification) to enhance their studies.

A close connection has been established with schools in Germany and Spain, with which individual and group exchanges are arranged.

Tutorial System. In addition to the Housemaster or Housemistress, there are pastoral Tutors attached to each House who act as Academic Tutors to individual pupils. The Tutors' main functions are to supervise academic progress and to encourage general reading and worthwhile spare time activities. A pupil usually keeps the same Tutor until he or she moves into the Sixth Form, where this function is taken over by an Academic Tutor chosen from one of the specialist teachers.

Music and Art form an important part of the education of all pupils. There are orchestras, bands, ensembles and choirs. Organ and Choral awards to Oxford and Cambridge and Colleges of Music are frequently won. There is a full programme of extra-curricular **Drama**. The **Art School** and **Design & Technology Centre** provide for a wide range of technical and creative work.

Other Activities. Boys and girls in their first year are given the opportunity to sample the many activities on offer at the College. A well-organised co-curricular programme is followed by pupils of all age groups and participation is strongly encouraged under the supervision of the Assistant Head, Co-curricular.

Several plays are produced each year and pupils are able to write and perform their own plays and to learn stagecraft.

In the Advent Term the main sports are Association Football for boys and Hockey for girls; in the Lent Term Hockey for boys and Netball for girls. Squash, Fives, Badminton, Basketball, Volleyball, Cross Country and Shooting (the College has an indoor range) take place during both terms for boys and girls. Rugby Sevens is played in the Lent Term. Cricket, Tennis, Sailing, Athletics and Rounders take place in the Summer Term. There is Swimming all year round in the College's indoor heated pool; Lancing College Swimming Club, affiliated with Swim England, supports the development of county, regional and national swimmers.

The College has a CCF contingent (with Army and RAF sections) and takes part in the Duke of Edinburgh's Award scheme. There's an option to join Explorer Scouts, which supports focus on life skills, leadership, teamwork and volunteering. There is also a flourishing Outreach group, which works in the local community. Pupils help to run a small farm (including sheep, goats, pigs and chickens) and participate in conservation projects under the supervision of the Farm Manager. Links have been established with local industries and pupils are involved in business experience through the Young Enterprise scheme.

Careers and Higher Education. A number of the teaching staff share responsibility for careers advice and there is a well-equipped careers section in the Gwynne Library. Popular universities include Imperial College, Manchester, Bristol, Durham, UCL, LSE and Sheffield; three to Oxbridge in 2023; several to other international universities. All members of the Fifth Form attend the annual Careers Fair and enrol in the 'Morrisby' online profiling programme. Pupils in the Sixth Form take part in the 'Leaving Lancing' programme with activities to help pupils develop practical, team working and leadership skills.

Scholarships and Exhibitions. Candidates for the following awards must be under 14 years of age on 1st September in the year of the examination. The age of the candidate is taken into account in making awards. A candidate may enter for more than one type of award, and account may be taken of musical or artistic proficiency in a candidate for a non-musical award; but no one may hold more than one type of award, except in an honorary capacity.

A number of scholarships in Academic subjects, Art, Drama and Sport are offered every year, ranging in value up to a maximum 10 per cent of the annual school fee. In very exceptional cases, awards of up to 25 per cent are made.

A number of Music and Choral Scholarships ranging in value up to a maximum 10 per cent of the annual school fee (25 per cent in very exceptional cases). Scholarships may be offered to pupils from schools where the time for Music is less than in some others, and where a candidate may have less musical experience but greater potential.

One Professor W K Stanton Music Scholarship for a Chorister from Salisbury Cathedral School, or failing that any Cathedral School. A Stanton Exhibition may also be awarded. There is one Peter Lewis Scholarship for a promising horn player.

The Peter Robinson Cricket Scholarship is awarded to an outstanding young cricketer at 13+ and 16+ entry.

A number of Ken Shearwood Awards, ranging in value up to a maximum 10 per cent of the annual school fee (25 per cent in very exceptional cases), are made to pupils of all-round ability and potential who have made outstanding contributions to their present schools.

Entry Forms for Academic, Art, Music, Drama, Sport and All-Rounder (Ken Shearwood) awards are obtainable from the Admissions Office.

Sixth Form Awards: Scholarships are available for new entrants to the Sixth Form with special proficiency in Academic subjects, Art, Music, Drama and Sport. There is also one Organ Scholarship. The candidate's general ability to contribute to the life of a boarding school community will also be taken into account. A small number of Scholarships is also available internally on the strength of GCSE results.

The value of all Entrance Scholarships may be augmented by bursaries, according to parental circumstances.

Fees per term (2023–2024). Boarding: £14,850; Flexi-Boarding: £12,480 (subject to availability); Day: £10,150.

Further details about fees, including the scheme for payment in advance of a single composition fee to cover a pupil's education during his/her time in the school, are available from the Bursar.

Charitable status. Lancing College is a Registered Charity, number 1076483. It exists to provide education for boys and girls.

Governing Body:
The Provost and the Directors of Lancing College Ltd

Visitor: The Archbishop of Canterbury

Governors:
Mr Martin Slumbers, BSc, ACA [OL] (*Chairman*)
Mr Henry Lawson, MA Cantab, MBA Harvard [OL] (*Deputy Chairman*)
Mr David Austin, BSc
Mrs Jenny Brown, MA Oxon
Mr Robert Crawford Clarke, BSc Agric, MRICS
Mrs Pippa Cleeve, BA Hons, Cert Mgmt Open
Mr Andrew-Dane Fairclough, BA
Professor Michael Farthing, MD, DScMed, FRCP, FMedSci
Mr Tim Hancock, MA [OL]
Mr Justin Higgo, MA Oxon, Dip. Law [OL]
The Venerable Luke Irvine-Capel, MA Oxon, MA Leeds
The Rt Revd Jonathan Meyrick, MA Oxon, OL (*Provost*)
Dr John Scott, BA Oxon, PhD, MBA [OL]

Clerk to the Governing Body: Mrs Benita Hibbert, MSc

[OL] *Former Pupil*

***Head Master*: Mr D T Oliver**, BA, MPhil

Bursar: Mr M B Milling, CA
Senior Deputy Head: Mrs H R Dugdale, MA
Deputy Head: Mr J R J Herbert, BA, PhD
Executive Director External Relations and Communications: Mrs Diana Cree, BA, MBA, MRS, CIM
Assistant Head (*Academic*): Mrs P S Faulkner, BSc
Director of Admissions: Ms Maggie Roberts, BA, MEd
Director of IT: Mr A C Brown, MBCS
Chaplain: Fr J C Pottinger, MA, MTh Oxon
Foundation Director: Ms Catherine Reeve, BA [OL]

Houses & Housemasters/mistresses:

Boys:
Head's: Mr G D Bird
Second's: Mr D J Harvey
School: Mr N L Payne
Gibbs': Mr M J H Smith
Teme: Mr T P Atkinson

Girls:
Field's: Mrs E Campbell
Handford: Ms A McKane
Manor: Ms K V Edwards
Sankey's: Mrs F Britnell

Co-ed:
Saints': Mrs M S Porter

Head Master's PA: Ms Annabel Wade
Admissions Manager: Ms Sarah Gittus
Deputy Admissions Manager: Mrs S Pinto

Latymer Upper & Prep School

Upper School
King Street, Hammersmith, London W6 9LR

Tel: 020 8629 2024
email: head@latymer-upper.org
website: www.latymer-upper.org
X/Twitter: @LatymerUpper
Facebook: @latymerupper
Instagram: @latymerupperschool
LinkedIn: /latymer-upper-school

Prep School
36 Upper Mall, Hammersmith, London W6 9TA

Tel: 020 7993 0061
email: principal@latymerprep.org
website: www.latymerprep.org
X/Twitter: @latymerprep

Latymer Upper and Prep School, governed by the Latymer Foundation, dates back 400 years when founder, Edward Latymer, donated funds to 'to clothe and educate eight poore boies' from Hammersmith. Situated on the banks of the River Thames in West London, it is one of the country's leading co-educational, independent day schools. Visitors frequently refer to the 'palpable buzz' and energy they experience when they come on site and this vitality is one of the many characteristics of Latymer that makes studying and working here so stimulating. Latymer values and respects diversity; it is modern and forward-thinking; it promotes a global outlook; and has a dynamic community of talented people who combine the highest academic achievement with excellence in the arts and sport.

In 2023, Latymer Upper & Prep School won the Independent School Parent Award for Social Mobility, with the Prep School a finalist for Prep School of the Year. Our long-running bursary scheme ensures a first class education to academically able students from all walks of life. Currently 1 in 5 pupils are in receipt of a bursary – on average 83% of fees – which are funded wholly through the donations of the Latymer community.

The vibrant student body consists of more than 1,400 girls and boys from all walks of life, of which 400 students are in the Sixth Form and 176 are in the Prep. The two schools share the same grounds and excellent sports, music and theatre facilities.

Admission is by competitive examination and interview.

Candidates for the Prep School are required to sit a 7+ entrance exam and, once in the Prep School, are not required to sit the 11+ entrance exam, being automatically accepted to the Upper School.

For candidates hoping to join the Upper School, the 11+ examination is usually taken in the December of Year 6. Successful candidates are then invited for interview, which takes place in January.

Entry to the Sixth Form is based on an exam, followed by an interview in November of the year before entry, and conditional offers at GCSE.

Details of Open Days and Entry are on the School's website.

Tuition fees per term (from September 2023). Upper School: £8,074; Prep School: £7,353.

Bursaries. A number of means-tested bursaries are awarded every year assessed on academic merit and family circumstances. These range from 25% to 100% of fees and are available at 7+, 11+ and 16+. The culmination of the Inspiring Minds campaign is close to achieving its aim to raise enough funds to offer 1 in 4 pupils a means-tested bursary in 2024, making Latymer one of the most inclusive independent schools in the country.

Scholarships. 11+ Entry: Music Scholarships of varying amounts are offered, together with music awards of free tuition on two instruments. Scholarships will only be offered to candidates who are successful in the school's competitive entrance examination.

16+ Entry: Scholarships for Music, Drama, Art and Sport. Candidates who have satisfied the academic requirements will be invited to an interview and assessment in December of the year preceding entry.

Further details are available from the Director of Admissions and Bursaries (020 8148 4519; admissions@latymer-upper.org).

Curriculum. A full range of academic subjects is offered at GCSE and A Level. Languages include Spanish, Mandarin, Latin, French, German and Greek (European Work Experience and exchanges are run every year). Science is taught as separate subjects by specialists from Year 7. Form sizes in the Prep and Lower School of around 22 and smaller teaching group sizes ensure the personal attention of staff. The World Perspectives Course, now UCAS accredited, comprising elements of Geography, History, RS, Politics, Philosophy, and Economics is enjoyed by Years 10 and 11. Year 9 students take our 'Global Goals' sustainable development course.

From 2027 Middle School pupils (Y9–11) will take two GCSEs – Maths and English – then they will choose subjects from a reformed curriculum that you may expect to see at GCSE (long courses) as well as short courses (in cross-curricular themes e.g. climate change). Subjects traditionally studied at A Level, e.g. Politics, Economics and History of Art, will also be brought into the Middle School. Assessments will be varied; some traditional written exam-style assessments, as well as presentation work, vivas, group work, digital production. In 2027 a new Middle School curriculum will be introduced and students will study Maths and English GCSE plus a school-designed long and short courses following traditional courses plus a range of subjects that include AI, coding, climate change, or literature in translation.

Pastoral Care. The School takes pastoral care very seriously. Each pupil has a tutor, and tutor groups are small, meaning that each pupil can receive individual care and attention. Tutors see their pupils very frequently, monitor their academic progress and help them with day-to-day issues. Form Tutors deliver a coherent PSHE programme which promotes involvement in the community, charity work, and the personal, social and academic development of the Form. Tutors are supported by experienced Heads and Assistant Heads of Year, who have significant pastoral expertise and, along with tutors, are the first port of call for parents' and pupils' concerns. Three Heads of Division (Lower School, Middle School and Sixth Form), the Deputy Head (Pastoral), Pupil Welfare Officer and a Safeguarding Officer, both of whom are non-teaching staff with expertise in supporting individuals and families, complete the pastoral team. Additionally, many specialists also support the teaching staff in caring for our pupils including a team of three counsellors, two registered nurses in the Medical Centre, a Chaplain and the Head of Wellbeing and PSHE.

Much of this is echoed in the Prep, which also has access to the on-site counsellors and nurses. The Prep provides a caring, happy and safe environment, promoting high quality personal development alongside independent learning. While Form tutors have primary pastoral responsibility – in terms of pupils' academic and social life at the school – wellbeing is a whole school responsibility. As we are a small school, the staff all know the children and their families well and there is a continuous sharing of information among staff.

The Academic Mentoring Department (AMD) is integral to the academic and pastoral structures at both Latymer Upper and Prep School. With a deep understanding of current thinking on neurodiversity and growth mindset, the AMD team embraces a creative approach to teaching and learning. Using assistive technology – iPads, laptops and a range of software – AMD support enhances the academic work of pupils across the age ranges, providing an education that will enable all our pupils to achieve the highest academic standards, while simultaneously maintaining excellent mental health. There is also a highly effective Prefect and peer mentor system where the more senior students provide advice and a listening ear for our younger pupils, as well as demonstrating leadership across the school community.

Music and Drama. The Performing Arts play a large part in the life of the School. The Latymer Arts Centre houses music practice rooms and a 300-seat theatre in addition to increased facilities for Art. The Latymer Performing Arts Centre houses a 100-seat recital hall, music classrooms, and more practice rooms and a dance/drama studio. The installation of a 5-metre-wide drop screen, laser projector and surround-sound system in the Recital Hall means that at the 'click of a button' the Recital Hall transforms into a Cinema. This supports the School's new courses and competitions in film-making and history of film.

Across Prep and Upper schools there are several orchestras and bands and a number of major concerts each term, both in-school and in Central London venues. There are a number of major drama productions each year, and opportunities for all pupils to perform in events. The School also has its own recording studios and record label.

Science and Library. A state-of-the-art building, housing three floors of science laboratories. The spacious library on the ground floor is popular with all year groups and is overseen by a dynamic and multi-award-winning Librarian.

Sport. In the Upper and Prep Schools, the emphasis is on engagement, inclusion, participation, and opportunity at every level with county, regional, national and international success.

Upper School teams enjoy great success in the major sports of rugby, football, hockey, netball, rowing, fencing, cricket and tennis; with other sports such as athletics, basketball, badminton, dance, climbing, swimming and water polo, volleyball, triathlon, pilates and yoga providing for individual interests. The School maintains an excellent fixture card for all major sports.

The major sports played at the Prep School are football, rugby, cricket, athletics, hockey and netball, in addition to various PE activities such as basketball, badminton and gymnastics. Each year the whole school participates in the 'Bandstand Cup' cross country race. There is also a thriving swimming club.

The Sports Centre – opened by Sir Steve Redgrave in 2017 – features outstanding facilities including a 6-lane, 25m pool with an adjustable floor, a large sports hall, fitness suite, climbing wall and three studios all providing a full programme of indoor sporting activities and fitness training throughout the year for pupils in both schools.

In addition, the School has netball courts and an on-site Boat House with direct river access and a large pontoon installed in 2021. At Quintin Hogg Sports Ground in Chiswick, plans are approved for redevelopment of cricket nets, tennis courts, football and hockey pitches as well as the pavilion and changing rooms. The Wood Lane complex (a short coach drive away) features all-weather, floodlit playing surfaces, including 4 rugby/football pitches, 3 cricket squares, a floodlit AstroTurf for hockey, netball, football and tennis and a modern pavilion with changing rooms. Out of school hours the facilities are used for training by the England Rugby Team and visiting international teams.

Sixth Form. In the large co-educational Sixth Form, all students will follow the core curriculum, studying three full A Levels from a choice of 24 – the academic requirement that universities expect – with the option to do a fourth A Level as an elective course. In addition, we help to prepare students for university study by including a 10-week course on Research Skills and different types and theories of knowledge. All students take Games once a week, undertake at least a term of Service in the Community and complete a series of Life Skills units. Students also have the opportunity to take a number of exciting elective courses, giving breadth to their studies beyond their core subjects. We are especially keen for students to pursue the Extended Project Qualification or the slightly shorter Latymer Research Report, and to take a selection of the non-examined Latymer Designed Courses that are a distinctive, enriching component of our Sixth Form provision.

In 2023 89% of students who applied to university (UK and International) secured their first choice; 21 students secured places at Oxbridge; 80 offers from International Universities – including Brown, Bocconi, Carnegie Mellon, Dartmouth, Duke, McGill, Notre Dame, NYU, UChicago, UPenn and Yale. The newly refurbished Sixth Form Centre opened in September 2021; the new Centre includes quiet study spaces, a café and an attractive area for socialising and relaxing. Students also have access to expert advice in the University and Careers Centre. Our Sixth Form is an excellent preparation for university life: an academically rigorous, emotionally nurturing space in which our community of bright young people form firm friendships for life.

Extra-Curricular Activities. There is a fantastic choice of around 150 clubs and societies for pupils to enjoy at lunchtime and after school. From chess to dance, aerospace to Japanese puzzles, life-drawing to water polo, each student is encouraged to try new activities, be it for one term or longer – with some going on to become lifelong passions. All pupils are encouraged to join at least two different clubs and societies.

In addition, every pupil in Upper School has the opportunity to have residential experiences and to take part in outdoor pursuits as part of the annual Activities Week. The Prep runs residential courses and an annual overseas trip.

The Duke of Edinburgh's Award scheme flourishes with a number of students achieving the Gold Award each year.

Fundraising by a very active Parents' Gild ensures that nobody is excluded from an activity for financial reasons. The Parents' Gild is an integral part of the school community, organising a variety of fundraising and social events ensuring opportunities occur frequently to meet with staff socially.

Community Partnerships. Community service is an important part of a Latymer education and the School works in partnership with 250 local schools, charities and community organisations to deliver a wide variety of projects both in the UK and abroad. The partnerships with local schools benefit more than 3000 children each year.

Alumni. Upon graduation, Latymerians join a successful global network of nearly 6,000 alumni. This lifelong relationship with the School provides career opportunities, mentoring, an exclusive alumni networking platform, regular news updates and a popular programme of events. The Alumni team is part of the Foundation Office based within the School.

Charitable status. The Latymer Foundation is a Registered Charity, number 312714. It exists to provide a first class education to academically able students from all walks of life.

Chairman of Governors: Kieran Murphy

Co-opted Governors:
Mark Brewer
Chantal Free
Robert Lewis
Annamarie Phelps
Alex Plavsic
G David Price
Charles Wijeratna
Pauline Campbell
Jamie Grant
David Benson
Mark Edwards

Clerk to the Governors: Lucinda Evans

***Head*: Susan Wijeratna**, BA

Deputy Heads:
Matthew Chataway, BA, MA (*Pastoral*)
Ian Emerson, MA, BSc (*Academic*)
Lucy Cole, BSc, MA Ed (*Co-curricular and Operations*)

Assistant Heads:
Charles Ben-Nathan, BA, MBA (*Director of Studies*)
Rachel Marley, BSc (*Middle School*)
Yuvraj Nirwal, BSc, MA (*Director of Teaching and Learning*)
Sam Adams, BA, MA (*Sixth Form*)
Amy Sellars, BSc (*Lower School*)
Debbie Kendall, BA (*Middle School*)

Prep School Principal: Andrea Rutterford, BEd Hons, Dip SpLD

Prep School Deputy Principal: Victoria Penney, BEd

Director of Studies: Charlotte Hurst, BA, MA

Heads of Year:
Andrew Copeman, BA, MSc (*Upper Sixth*)
Jon Haines, BSc (*Acting Head of Lower Sixth*)
Katie Temple, BA (*Year 7*)
Gareth Cooper, BSc (*Year 8*)
Lucy Snooks, BA (*Year 9*)
Kathleen Webb, BA (*Year 10*)
Kat Burns, BA (*Year 11*)

Heads of Departments:
Academic Mentoring: Nina Devereux, LLB Dip, Level 7 SpLD PATOSS
Art and Design: Leslie Farago, BA
Biology: Elizabeth Hansford, BSc, MSc
Chemistry: Ed Forbes, MChem
Classics: Marcel Lewis, BA
Computing: Jackie Price, BA
Design: Elizabeth Green, BA
Drama: Justin Joseph, BA
Economics: William Wearden, BA
English: Jon Mitropoulos-Monk, MA
Extended Project: Helen Doyme, MSci
Geography: Amy Case, BA
History: Jonathan White, MA
History of Art: Ruth Taylor-Bell, BA, PGDip
Mathematics: Patrick MacMahon, MA, MSc
Modern Languages: Cameron Palmer, BA, MA
Music: Tony Henwood, MA, ARCO, FRSA
Physical Education and Games: Natalie Maclean, BSc
Physics: James Hunt, BSc
Politics: Paul Goldsmith, BA, MBA, FRSA
PSHCE and Wellbeing: Charlotte Jennings, BA
Religion & Philosophy: Elizabeth Dunleavy, BA
World Perspectives: Laura Leicester, BA

The Grammar School at Leeds

Alwoodley Gates, Harrogate Road, Leeds LS17 8GS

Tel:	0113 229 1552
email:	enquiries@gsal.org.uk
website:	www.gsal.org.uk
X/Twitter:	@theGSAL
Facebook:	@TheGSAL
Instagram:	@thegsal
LinkedIn:	/the-grammar-school-at-leeds

The Grammar School at Leeds (GSAL) is one of the UK's leading independent day school, helping girls and boys aged 3–18 develop into happy, confident, curious and kind young people. By nurturing their interests and talents in a stimulating setting, our caring, dedicated staff encourage pupils to answer inspiration's call.

We are committed to caring for our pupils as well as educating them. Our aim is to help them develop their individual abilities and talents within an ethic of teamwork, friendship and mutual respect. We have a generous teacher–pupil ratio and small class sizes, which means that every student receives personal and individual attention. There are common rooms and dedicated outdoor areas for specific year groups.

At GSAL, your child will discover a world of opportunity. The school's extensive 128-acre campus at Alwoodley Gates offers world-class facilities, including an indoor swimming pool, 3G pitch, astros and expansive playing fields. Pupils also have access to an art and design centre, 16 fully-equipped science laboratories and a recently redeveloped library with collaborative and individual learning spaces. In 2024–25 will see the unveiling of our new Performing Arts Centre – a purpose-built, world-class music, drama and performance hub with 350-seat theatre, studio and rehearsal space. The breadth of academic and co-curricular activities is breathtaking with pupils typically partaking in 4–5 hours of enhanced provision every week.

Exam results and awards. Exam results are consistently outstanding. In 2023 52% of A-level grades at A*/A and 70% of GCSE grades at 7–9 (A/A*). GSAL was named the North Independent Secondary School of the Year in 2024 and of the decade in 2021 by the *Sunday Times*.

GSAL Primary. For younger learners, the school offers the very best start in an environment rich in language, music, creativity and outdoor play. Inspiring teachers will encourage your child to be curious, brave, to express themselves, care for others and to treat learning like one big adventure. We support them to grow a little every day to prepare them for their years at senior school and beyond. Primary School has its own dining room for younger pupils, specialist classrooms for science, food technology and music, a drama studio, sports hall and two libraries.

The diamond model. At GSAL, pupils are educated in co-educational classes in up to age 11 whilst they are in Primary School and again from 16–18 in Sixth Form. From 11 to 16 (years 7 to 11) pupils are taught in single-sex classes for their academic lessons, which follows the diamond model of learning but still have co-educational pastoral provision, social time and co-curricular activities.

Heritage. GSAL's founding schools, Leeds Grammar School and Leeds Girls' High School, were established on principles of philanthropy and scholarly endeavour. We remain dedicated to these principles to this day, all the while ensuring that GSAL's educational offering remains fit for a changing world.

Equity, Diversity and Inclusion. We are resolutely a multi-faith school with a large multi-cultural community which helps promote our culture of tolerance and understanding. GSAL is accredited by the National Centre for Diversity (NCFD), the first independent school to do so.

If you're inspired by this snapshot of GSAL, come and see what we have to offer for yourself and visit us at one of our open events or taster sessions for nursery and reception.

"I look forward to meeting you and your family and welcoming you to this very special place, where we celebrate your child's individuality as part of a thriving and dynamic school community." *Sue Woodroofe, Principal, The Grammar School at Leeds*

Admission. Applying for a place at GSAL is a simple process and for most, starts a year in advance of entry. We hold a number of open events throughout the autumn term which families are encouraged to attend. Parents must then complete our online application form and pay a non-refundable £75 application fee before their desired year group's application deadline. Parents will be sent details of their child's entrance assessments which, for most, take place in the January prior to entry. Following the entrance assessments, parents will be sent the outcomes of their child's application within two weeks.

Details of the entrance procedure, together with copies of sample papers, are available on the school website: www.gsal.org.uk.

Admissions Manager: Alice Atkinson, admissions@gsal.org.uk.

Fees per term (2023–2024). Senior School (Years 7–13): £5,463. Primary School: Years 3–6 £4,080, Reception–Year 2 £3,738. Nursery: 5 days £3,330, 4 days/week £2,664, 3 days/week £1,998.

Bursaries. A number of means-tested bursaries (some full-fee) are currently awarded each year to pupils entering the school in Year 7 and Year 12. Visit https://gsal.org.uk/admissions/bursaries/ for more information.

Alumni. Alumni include former pupils of Leeds Grammar School, Leeds Girls' High School and The Grammar School at Leeds. Further information can be found in the alumni section of the school website, email: alumni@gsal.org.uk.

Charitable status. The Grammar School at Leeds is a Registered Charity, number 1048304. It exists for the advancement of education and training for boys and girls.

***Principal*: Sue Woodroofe**

Vice Principal and Head of Primary School: Gabrielle Solti
Vice Principal & Head of Senior School: Graham Purves
Senior Deputy Head (*Pastoral Care*): Helen Stansfield
Senior Deputy Head (*Academic*): Debbie Danks
Director of External Relations: Helen Clapham
Director of Finance and Operations: Steve Kingston
Whole School Director of Sport: Lorcan O'Brien
Head of Human Resources: Rachel Cooper
Director of Sixth Form: Rachel Purcell
Principal's Executive Assistant: Nina Coltman Leigh

Leicester Grammar School

London Road, Great Glen, Leicester LE8 9FL
Tel: 0116 259 1900
email: admissions@leicestergrammar.org.uk
website: www.lgs-senior.org.uk
X/Twitter: @LGS_Senior
Facebook: @Leicester-Grammar-School
LinkedIn: /leicester-grammar-school

Leicester Grammar School was founded in 1981 as an independent, selective, co-educational day school to offer able children in the city and county a first-class academic education. Its founders sought to create a school which would maintain the standards and traditions of the city's former grammar schools lost through reorganisation, and to develop them to meet the demands of a rapidly changing environment. The School moved to a new state-of-the-art building on the south-east side of Leicester in September 2008.

There are 882 day pupils in the Senior School, of whom 223 are in the Sixth Form. A further 409 pupils, aged 3–11, attend the Junior School.

Admission. An entrance examination is held in the Lent Term for boys and girls seeking to enter the Preparatory (10+) and Year 7 (11+) forms in the following September. Papers are taken in Reasoning, English and Mathematics. In addition, admission into Years 9 and 10 takes place at ages 13 and 14 and there is provision for direct entry into the Sixth Form, offers of a place being conditional upon the GCSE grades gained. The normal entry requirement to the Sixth Form is a minimum of three GCSEs at Grade 7 or better accompanied by a minimum of three further GCSEs at Grade 6 or better. Visitors are always welcome to make an appointment to see the school and meet the Headmaster. All applications are handled by the Head of Marketing & Admissions, from whom all application forms are obtainable. Candidates at all levels may be called for an interview.

Scholarships and bursaries. The School offers a range of scholarships for pupils of outstanding academic, musical, sporting or artistic talent. These are awarded on the basis of examination and assessment. Awards cover entry at all ages from Year 7 including sixth form entrants.

The fee remission associated with scholarships is not means dependent and is usually worth no more than 5–10% of the termly fee.

Bursary support is available either for new applicants to the School or for existing pupils whose circumstances have changed. Bursaries are available only to pupils in Year 7 and above at Leicester Grammar School. Bursaries of up to 100% of the termly fee are available, subject to rigorous testing of financial need and limited by the overall bursaries budget.

Curriculum. Class sizes are about 20 to 24 in the first three years; the average size of a GCSE group is 19; of a Sixth Form group 12.

All pupils in the first three years (and those entering the preparatory form) follow a balanced curriculum covering the National Curriculum core and foundation subjects, Religious Studies and Latin (Classical Studies in the preparatory form). Classes are split into smaller groups for the creative and technological subjects, so that all pupils can gain practical experience, whether in the School's ICT suite or on its extensive range of musical instruments. From Year 8, the three science subjects, Biology, Chemistry and Physics, are taught separately. There is no streaming, and setting occurs only for Mathematics and French from Year 8. In Year 9, an element of choice is introduced and pupils must opt from a choice of third languages and from a list of five creative subjects.

In Years 10 and 11, pupils prepare for GCSE or GCSE equivalent examinations in ten subjects, as well as doing PE/Games. All study a 'core' of three subjects: Mathematics and English Language and Literature. The range of 'options' includes Art, Biology, Chemistry, Classical Civilisation, Computing, Design and Technology, Drama, French, Geography, German, Greek, Religious Studies, History, Latin, Music, Physics, Spanish and PE. Students will normally follow at least two Science subjects and at least one Modern Foreign Language.

Students in the Sixth Form normally study 3 A Levels from a choice of 21 subjects, including Further Mathematics, Psychology, Economics, Physical Education, Politics, Computing and Theatre Studies. There is no rigid division between arts and science sides. To ensure that breadth of education does not suffer, a proportion of the Sixth Form complete an Extended Project. The school has an excellent record of success at public examinations and university admissions, including Oxbridge. The Careers Department is very active in giving help and advice to students.

School activities. A broad range and variety of activities complements the academic curriculum. Participation rates are high.

Music, drama and sport form an integral part of life at LGS. Every pupil in the First Year learns a musical instrument and a high proportion continue afterwards with private weekly lessons. The School Orchestra gives two major concerts a year, while a training orchestra, a jazz band, a dance band, recorder groups and various chamber ensembles explore other avenues. The School Choir is the resident choir for the Crown Court Services and tours regularly. Links are strong with the Leicestershire School of Music orchestras and several pupils play in national orchestras. Senior and junior drama clubs function throughout the year; a major play or musical and a junior play are staged regularly and house drama extends the opportunity to act to most pupils.

Games are seen as an important means not only of promoting health and fitness but also of inspiring self-confidence. Major winter games are hockey, netball and rugby and in summer athletics, cricket and tennis. Opportunities occur for individuals to follow their interest in badminton, basketball, squash, golf, table tennis, gymnastics, dance, sailing and cross-country running while swimming is an integral part of the PE programme. The school's own facilities are extensive and meet all modern standards for sport. Teams represent the School in the main games at all age groups and several students achieve recognition at county or even national level. The school is proud of the fact that it is one of only eight other schools to have been awarded the Sportsmark Gold with Distinction, for the quality of the delivery of sport within the school.

Societies and clubs complement these activities, ranging from chess to The Duke of Edinburgh's Award scheme, history and Lit Soc to model aeroplanes, debating to art, design and technology, for which the workshop and art rooms are usually open during lunchtimes and after school.

Religion. The school espouses the principles of the Church of England, teaching the Christian faith, its values and standards of personal conduct, but also prides itself on welcoming children of all faiths, who play a full part in the life of the community. Very strong links exist with Leicester Cathedral and there is a flourishing Guild of Servers and University of Leicester clergy participate in school life and prepare confirmation candidates.

Pastoral care. Responsibility for a wide-ranging system of pastoral care and for the creation of the caring, friendly and disciplined environment, resides in eight Heads of Year, assisted by form teachers, personal tutors and a very active house system.

Junior School. Entry to the Junior School is by interview and, where appropriate, assessment at 3+, 4+, 7+ and into other school years, when places are available. Pupils are prepared for entry to the Senior School. A balanced curriculum is followed covering National Curriculum Key Stages 1 and 2 and beyond; French (from 5 years), classical studies and ICT are also taught. A wide range of activities complements the academic curriculum, with a strong stress on music and a rapidly growing games programme. The School is a Christian foundation and lays great emphasis upon the pastoral care of young children. (*See also Junior School entry in IAPS section.*)

Fees per term (2023–2024). Senior School: £5,306; Junior School (Years 3–6): £4,586; Kinders to Year 2: £4,316.

Old Leicestrians Association. All correspondence to the OL Secretary, c/o the School.

Charitable status. Leicester Grammar School Trust is a Registered Charity, number 510809. Its aims and objectives are to promote and provide for the advancement of education and in connection therewith to conduct, carry on, acquire and develop in the United Kingdom or elsewhere a School or Schools to be run according to the principles of the Church of England for the education of students and children of either sex or both sexes.

Trustees:
Steven Gasztowicz, KC (*Chair*)
Mrs Julia Burns, BA (*Vice Chair Academic*)
Michael Holley, MA Cantab, ACA (*Vice Chair Financial*)
Mrs Elisabeth Bailey, MA Cantab
Mr Mukesh Bulsara, FICA
Prof Deborah Cartmell
Duncan Green, Esq
Dr Susan Hadley
Nathan J Imlach, MA, CA, FCSI, CF
Dr Deenesh I Khoosal, MB, BCh, LLM RCS, FRCPsych
Mrs Kerry Law
Mr Alex Osiatynski, BA, MA, MA, PGCE
Dr Rohan Saigal
Prof Jim Saker, BSc, MSc
The Venerable Richard Worsfold

Senior Leadership:

***Headmaster of Leicester Grammar School and Principal of the Leicester Grammar School Trust*: Mr John Watson**, MA Hertford Oxon

Director of Finance and Operations: Mr Stephen Jeffries, LLB Leeds, FCA (*Law*)
Senior Deputy Head: Mr Magnus Anderson, MA Pembroke Cantab (*Physics*)
Deputy Head Curriculum: Mr Carl James, MA Girton Cantab (*Mathematics*)
Deputy Head Pastoral: Miss Jennifer Young, MA Exeter (*History*)
Director of Wellbeing and Co-curriculum: Mrs Angela Ewington, MA Nottingham (*Biology*)
Head of Sixth Form: Mr James Hunt, BA Reading (*English*)

Heads of Year:
Miss Jo Mould, BEd Bedford College of HE (*Head of Prep, Year 6*)
Miss Caitlin Jeffries, BSc West of England (*Head of Year 7*)
Mr Nathan Grimadell, BSc Derby (*Head of Year 8*)
Mrs Nikki Laybourne, BSc Hons, MSc Loughborough & Mrs Helen Martin, BSc Nottingham, MA Open (*Joint Heads of Year 9*)
Mrs Jane Tompkins, BA Leicester, MA Heythrop London (*Head of Year 10*)
Mrs Marie McNally, BA Westminster (*Head of Year 11*)
Mr James Hunt, BA Reading (*Head of Sixth Form*)
Mrs Zoe Village, BSc Leicester (*Assistant Head of Sixth Form*)

Academic Staff:
* Head of Department

Art and Design:
*Miss Katie-May Driver, BA University of the Arts
Mrs Amanda Davies, MA De Montfort
Miss Jennie Knight, BA De Montfort
Mr Richard Sekhon, BA Loughborough

Biology:
*Dr Kathryn Fulton, BSc Dunelm, PhD Nottingham
Mrs Philippa Clare, BSc, ARCS Imperial College, MSc Leicester
Mr Peter Cox, BSc University College of Wales, Bangor (*Learning Technologies Co-ordinator*)
Dr Sharon Dunham, BSc Glasgow, PhD Glasgow
Mrs Angela Ewington, MA Nottingham (*Director of Wellbeing and Co-curriculum*)
Ms Gillian Hancock, BSc Nottingham
Mr Paul Lawrence, BSc Leicester

Business & Economics:
*Mr Peer Moore-Friis, BA De Montfort, PGDIP Oxford, CIM DIP (*Young Enterprise Co-ordinator*)
Mr Khuzema Esmail, BA Portsmouth, (*Head of Life Education*)

Careers:
Mrs Clare Scott, BA Hons (*Careers Leader*)

Chemistry:
*Dr Simon Ainge, BSc, PhD Newcastle, CChem, FRSC, ARSM Organ (*School Organist*)
Dr Adrianne Kendall, MA, DPhil Oxon

Mr Andrew King, MChem Loughborough (*Assistant Timetabler*)
Mrs Helen Martin, BSc Nottingham, MA Open (*Duke of Edinburgh Award, Joint Head of Year 9*)
Dr Shalini Singh, MSc Punjabi, PhD Leicester

Classics:
*Mr Philip Pratt, MA Harvard
Ms Marysia Bancroft, BA Bristol, MA Bristol
Dr Peter Donnelly, MA Dunelm
Mr Christopher Gilham, BA London
Dr Anastasia Vassilliou, BA Athens, MPhil, PhD Birmingham

Computing:
*Mrs Maskean Sian, BA Middlesex
Mr Lee Kelham, BEng Cranfield

Design and Technology:
Miss Katie Campbell, BA Nottingham Trent (*Head of Design and Technology*)
Mr Nathan Grimadell, BSc Derby (*Head of Year 8*)
Mrs Selina Moore, BSc DeMontfort
Mr Robert Parkin, BEng Nottingham Trent

Drama:
Ms Annette Hulme, BA Essex, MA Loughborough (*Head of Academic Drama*)
Miss Rachel Adams, BA Italia Conti Academy (*Head of Performance Drama*)
Dr Julian Griffin, MA Cantab, PhD OU (*Head of English*; *Theatre Studies*)
Miss Emma Rowbotham, BA Birmingham

English:
*Dr Julian Griffin, MA Cantab, PhD OU, (*Theatre Studies*)
Mrs Rachael Kendall, BA Dunelm, MA Goldsmiths (*Deputy Head of English*)
Mrs Catherine Barnes, BA De Montfort, MA Birmingham
Miss Rebecca Hadfield, BA Exeter (*Charity & Community Service Co-ordinator*)
Mrs Marlene Higginson, BEd, MA Toronto (*Editor of Leicestrian*)
Miss Nicola Hughes, BA London (*Head of Initial Teacher Training*)
Mr James Hunt, BA Reading (*Head of Sixth Form*)

Food and Nutrition:
Mrs Elaine Nisbet, BEd Trent Polytechnic
Mrs Selina Moore, BSc DeMontfort
Mrs Rebecca Pole, BSc Sheffield Hallam

Geography:
*Mr Richard Campbell, MA Edgehill
Mrs Heather Feasey, BA Cape Town
Miss Emma Hill, BSc Reading (*Head of House – Vice Chancellors*)
Mrs Marie McNally, BA Westminster (*Head of Year 11*)
Mrs Sophie Sharp, BA Leeds, MSc East Anglia, MA Anglia Ruskin

History:
*Mr Andrew Picknell, MA University of London
Miss Aviyah Butt, BA Leicester
Mrs Vicky Hird, BA Leicester
Mrs Amanda McHugh, MA Anglia Ruskin

Miss Jennifer Young, MA Exeter (*Deputy Head Pastoral*)

Learning Development:
*Miss Joy Clapham, BA Hons, MBAEd, PGC SpLD Leicester, PGC SENCO Northampton, SpLD, TPC Patoss

Life Education:
*Mr Khuzema Esmail, BA Portsmouth

Mathematics:
*Dr David Crawford, MA, DPhil Oxon, MEd Bristol, MA Ed OU, MSc OU
Mr Graham Inchley, BSc Hull, MSc Bristol (*Deputy Head of Mathematics*)
Mr Carl James, MA Cantab (*Deputy Head Curriculum*)
Miss Ramandeep Kaur, BSc Leicester
Mrs Roxanne King, BSc Birmingham (*Head of House – Dukes*)
Mrs Cristina Margiax Lopez, MSc Universidad Politecnica de Valencia
Mr Michael Moore, BSc Loughborough
Mr Neil Murray, BSc Imperial, MA London, MSc Sheffield Hallam
Mrs Kerry Pollard, BSc Loughborough
Mr Joey Radford, BSc Sheffield (*Head of House – Judges*)
Mrs Brin Rai, BSc Birmingham
Mrs Zoe Village, BSc Leicester (*Assistant Head of Sixth Form, Duke of Edinburgh Award*)

Modern Foreign Languages:
*Mrs Sylvie Lopez-Correia, MA Université de Picardie Jules Verne
Mrs Emma Nelson, BA Northumbria (*Deputy Head of Modern Foreign Languages*)
Miss Alex Chell, MPhil Trinity College, Dublin (*French & German, Duke of Edinburgh Award*)
Mrs Amy Dewe, BA Warwick (*French*)
Mrs Catriona Purdon, BA Sheffield (*Spanish*)
Mrs Katharine Douglas, BA Liverpool (*French & Italian, EAL*)
Miss Charlotte Julian, BA Birmingham (*French & Spanish*)
Mrs Francoise Paton, DEUG and Licence Bordeaux (*French*)
Mrs. M. Siegfried-Brookes, MSc Zurich (*German Assistant*)

Music:
*Mr John Barker, BMus, MMus Royal College of Music, PGCE, MTeach UCL IOE
Mrs Amy McPherson, BA Oxon, St Anne's (*Deputy Director of Music, Able, Gifted and Talented Co-ordinator*)
Ms Elizabeth Carpenter, BA Birmingham

Physical Education:
*Mr James McCann, MA Bath
Mr Graeme Blackhall, BSc Edinburgh (*Assistant Director of Sport, Head of Rugby*)
Mrs Fiona-Lisa Beaumont, MSc Central Lancashire (*Head of Netball*)
Mr Harry Ellis, BSc Loughborough
Mr Conor Geier, BSc Nottingham Trent
Miss Caitlin Jeffries, BSc West of England (*Head of Hockey, Head of Year 7*)

Mrs Nikki Laybourne, BSc Hons, MSc Loughborough (*Head of Girls Cricket, Joint Head of Year 9*)
Miss Maisie Regan, BSc
Miss Amy Rothwell, MSc Loughborough (*Head of House – Dukes*)
Mr Matthew Stubbs, BEd Sheffield Hallam (*Head of Academic PE*)
Mr Troy Thacker, BEd, CNAA: Crewe & Alsager College (*Middle School Mentor*)

Physics:
*Mr Philip Reeves, BSc Manchester
Miss Ellen Allcoat, BSc Bristol (*Senior House Co-ordinator, Head of House – Masters*)
Mr Magnus Anderson, MA Cantab (*Senior Deputy Head*)
Mrs Fiona Johnston, BSc Thames Polytechnic
Miss Kate MacLeod, BSc University College London (*EPQ Co-ordinator*)

Politics:
*Dr Sarah Yeomans, MA, PhD Loughborough

Psychology:
*Ms Kat Lovelock, BA Warwick
Dr Kathryn Fulton, BSc Dunelm, PhD Nottingham (*Head of Biology*)

Religious Studies:
*Ms Jane Ford, BA Newcastle
Mrs Eva Brookes, BA Sheffield, MA London
Mrs Jane Tompkins, BA Leicester, MA Heythrop London (*Head of Year 10*)
Mr Duncan Whitton, BA Leicester Polytechnic

Textiles:
Mrs Amanda Davies, MA De Montfort
Miss Jennie Knight, BA De Montfort

Leighton Park School

Shinfield Road, Reading, Berkshire RG2 7ED
Tel: 0118 987 9600
email: admissions@leightonpark.com
website: www.leightonpark.com
X/Twitter: @LPSchool
Facebook: @leightonparkschool
Instagram: @leightonparkschool
LinkedIn: /leighton-park-school

Leighton Park is a leading co-educational day and boarding school for students aged 11–18 based in Reading, Berkshire and the winner of the Independent Schools Association Best Senior School of the Year 2023–24.

Leighton Park exists to form young people of real character and confidence, with a determined desire to change the world, reflecting the school's Quaker values and forward-looking approach. We are a school that inspires achievement with values, character and community and academic excellence is the consequence of our approach.

Our vibrant learning community empowers each student to achieve excellent outcomes, through supporting their choices, nurturing individuality and encouraging talent in whatever direction it may lie. Ours is an education for succeeding in life, as well as in academic assessments. Set in 65 acres of beautiful parkland, our students have an enriching environment in which to learn, reflect and grow.

With Quaker values held strongly at the centre of all that we do, our emphasis is on our students loving their learning, encouraging them to try a huge range of new experiences and developing their greatest talents. You will be struck on visiting us by the warmth of relationships that characterise the school, the wealth of opportunities for development of body and mind, and the sense of calm and space in which that development takes place.

Academic. The success of our approach is demonstrated by the latest UK Government 16–18 league tables, which place the school in the top 100 in England, or top 1%, for the academic progress made by our students. Despite being among the top performing schools in the country, we are no results factory. We believe a school must be judged by the full range and depth of achievements of its students, and at Leighton Park we develop young people who understand, cherish, and make a difference to the world which they inherit. Leighton Park is particularly known for STEAM (Science, Technology, Engineering, Arts and Maths), with a particular emphasis on creative problem-solving and interdisciplinary approaches.

Sixth Form. In Sixth Form, students can choose between the International Baccalaureate Diploma Programme (IB) and A Levels with or without an Extended Project Qualification (EPQ) which carries UCAS points worth half an A Level.

Co-Curricular programme. Our wraparound provision, which welcomes day students from 7.20 am to 9.00 pm, offers all our pupils the time to discover and develop their greatest talents. The school's curriculum positions students for success in a fast-changing world, where many of today's jobs will not exist in 30 years' time. Students have the time and space to understand and enjoy their learning and extend their passions through over 90 different co-curricular hobbies. Central to the school's approach, we teach leadership, creative thinking and risk-taking, empowering students to be a force for good in the world and reflecting the school's Quaker ethos. The range of choice and the school's focus on the individual create a fun, supportive and nurturing experience.

Sports. Sport plays an important role in life at Leighton Park with many individual performers and teams reaching county and regional level in sports. The School's Advanced Performer Programme (APP) supports elite athletes. While the School does very well in traditional sports such as rugby, netball, cricket and hockey, it also offers alternatives such as yoga, judo and basketball. The School is very supportive of individual talents and interests from equestrian sports to gymnastics. First-rate coaching and facilities ensure that talented and enthusiastic students can develop their sporting abilities to the full.

Music. Music is another particular strength of the School with a stunning Music and Media Centre providing students with exceptional facilities, including a Yamaha Live Lounge recording studio and a media production suite. Our Music Department is accredited as a Flagship Music Education Partner, the only school in

Europe to hold this status, with 60% of students studying an instrument and 27 music teachers on staff. We also partner with Sontronics and are a certified Steinberg Training Centre, providing exposure to industry-standard music technology for our students.

Location and school life. The school is set in 65 acres of beautiful parkland in Reading, 25 minutes from London and 30 minutes from London Heathrow Airport. A significant proportion of the park is dedicated to sport and outdoor learning opportunities, but it also provides that all-important space in which students can take some time for peaceful reflection.

Facilities. Leighton Park has the facilities you would expect of a leading independent school, including a brand-new Sixth Form Centre (opening September 2024). This project will develop an historic building designed by one of the UK's most celebrated Victorian architects, Alfred Waterhouse, and imbue it with beautiful study spaces and cutting-edge learning technology. A new whole-school library will also be housed here. Our Music and Media Centre opened in 2019, provides fabulous music and creative media facilities for students, In recent times, investments have been made to support the school's Science, Technology, Engineering, Arts and Maths focus, placing the creative arts at the heart of the traditional STEM approach. This includes modern science labs, a wonderful Design Technology centre and impressive mathematics facility. The school's innovative use of the latest teaching and learning technologies is supported by continuous investment in technology, including Google Classroom, Clever Touch screens in classrooms and the use of personal laptops.

Boarding. Our Weekly or Full Boarding students enjoy the very best of Leighton Park, benefitting from a wonderful sense of calm, balanced with an incredible amount of activity and dynamism. There is a co-educational Lower School Boarding House for Years 7 and 8, Fryer House, with two Senior Houses for boarders in Year 9 and above; School House for boys and Reckitt House for girls. Students come from 41 different countries, with strong UK representation.

Housemasters and Housemistresses create homely environments supported by tutors and House Managers, ensuring each student feels relaxed and comfortable. With a dedicated staff and plenty of opportunity to socialise with other students, each Boarding House is very much its own community.

Entry. Entry to the school includes consideration of school reports, tests in English, Maths, essay-writing and an interview, with an additional English test where appropriate. Pupils are normally admitted at one of three points: Year 7 (age 11); Year 9 (age 13), and the Sixth Form. Entry to the Sixth Form requires 5 GCSE passes or equivalent at Level 6 / Grade B or above, with a Level 7 required in certain subjects. Students can opt for A Levels or the IBDP in Sixth Form. We also offer a Pre-Sixth course of 5 GCSEs in one year.

Fees per term (2023–2024). Full Boarding: £12,095–£15,390; Weekly Boarding: £10,500–£13,070; Day: £7,720–£9,810.

Scholarships and bursaries. We award academic, art and design, dance, drama, music and sport scholarships to students entering Years 7, 9 and Sixth Form based on a competitive exam. These represent up to 30% of a day student's fees. We also offer scholarships in STEAM, Ethical Enterprise and IB Scholarships which are intended for Sixth Form applicants. Just as important as the financial incentive is the support they receive to develop their talents and excel in their field. Candidates may apply for any combination of scholarships but can only receive the financial benefits of one. Bursaries may be available, in cases of financial hardship, to existing and prospective pupils. Bursaries are always means tested and subject to annual review. Additional awards may be made by the David Lean Foundation or by the Ian Austin Bursary Fund.

Charitable status. The Leighton Park Trust is a Registered Charity, number 309144. It exists to provide education for young people.

Chair of Governors: Eme Dean-Lewis

***Head*: Matthew L S Judd**

The Leys

Trumpington Road, Cambridge CB2 7AD

Tel: 01223 508904
email: admissions@theleys.net
website: www.theleys.net
X/Twitter: @LeysCambridge
Facebook: @TheLeysSchoolCambridge
Instagram: @instagram.com/leyscambridge

Motto: *In Fide Fiducia*

The Leys is situated half a mile from the centre of the university city of Cambridge, close to the River Cam and Grantchester Meadows. The School was founded in 1875 on the initiative of a group of leading Methodists to provide a liberal Christian education, establishing a tradition which has continued unbroken to this day. The School was incorporated as a Charitable Trust in 1878. All the buildings are grouped around the Main Field and lie within the estate originally acquired for the purpose; there is a second extensive playing field nearby.

The Leys is a friendly, caring and happy community, large enough to offer many opportunities, but not so large as to lose sight of the individual. The School is fully co-educational; of a total of over 560 pupils, 200 are in the Sixth Form. Girls and boys are accommodated in separate houses. 70% of the pupils are accommodated in the boarding houses, but all, including the 160 day pupils, are able to enjoy all the opportunities offered by boarding school life.

Buildings and facilities. There is a continuing development programme involving all areas of the School. A state-of-the-art Music School was opened in 2005. There is an excellent Humanities Building with first-class facilities for Geography, History, Classics and Divinity together with a Museum and Archives Centre, and an award-winning Design Centre, which contains workshops (metal, plastic and wood), a 3D printing and laser cutting area, Art School, Ceramics Studio, Computer Centre, together with facilities for Design, Photography, Cookery and an Exhibition Centre. A Sports Hall and all-weather pitch were built in 1995. In 2008 the Sports Hall was extended to include a superb fitness suite and cricket pavilion, and a second Astroturf pitch was added. A new climbing wall was constructed in summer 2007. A major capital development has been added, which provides a new theatre, Assembly Hall, Drama and Dance Studios, Drama Department, School Café and three new Science Laboratories. This project, known as Great Hall, was completed in summer 2013. There are 40 acres of playing fields, an indoor heated swimming pool open all the year, a recently refurbished boat house on the Cam shared with King's, Selwyn and Churchill Colleges, and synthetic as well as grass tennis courts. A radical redesigning and refurbishment of all boarding houses began in summer 2006, with the aim of providing the most comfortable and homely of boarding facilities. To date six of the seven Senior Boarding Houses have been refurbished. The School Library underwent a major refurbishment in 2008.

Admission. Admission for girls and boys is mainly at 11+, 13+ and 16+. Entrance tests for 11+ and 13+ entry are held in the January prior to entry. Places in the Sixth Form are available for both girls and boys who have successfully completed their GCSE or equivalent courses elsewhere. Application for admission should be made to the Admissions Office in the first instance.

Scholarships. Scholarships are available for entry at 11+, 13+ and to the Sixth Form, valued at a maximum of 5% fee remission, which can be supplemented by means-tested bursaries up to a total concession of 100%.

Academic Scholarships are available for entry at 11+, 13+ and for entry to the Sixth Form at 16+. Scholarships are also available for entry at 13+ in Music, Art, STEM, Sport, Drama and all-rounders, and for entry to the Sixth Form at 16+ in Music, Art, Sport and Drama.

The School also participates in the Arkwright Scholarship Scheme, which is an external examination offering Scholarships for those wishing to take Design and Technology in the Sixth Form and who are aiming to read Engineering, Technology or other Design-related subjects in Higher Education.

The Scholarship Examinations at 11+ and 13+ take place in the Spring Term and the Sixth Form Scholarship Examination takes place in the November of the year prior to entry.

Bursary awards are made on a means-tested basis, and applications for bursaries must be made before entrance tests are taken.

Special awards for children of Methodist Ministers and members of HM Forces are available. Special consideration is given to the sons and daughters of Old Leysians.

Further particulars may be obtained from the Registrar.

Curriculum. The academic curriculum broadly conforms to the National Curriculum but is not restricted by it. Each pupil has an Academic tutor who, in conjunction with the Director of Studies and the Housemaster or Housemistress, works to tailor the pupil's programme to suit the needs of the individual wherever possible. Pupils follow a broad programme in the first three years (Years 7, 8 and 9). At the end of Year 9 they choose three from a wide range of options to add to the basic core of IGCSE English Language and Literature, separate Sciences and a Modern Foreign Language, and GCSE Mathematics and Religious Studies. The GCSE examinations are normally taken at the end of Year 11, but Religious Studies is taken by all pupils in Year 10.

In the Sixth Form, a similar option scheme operates with pupils choosing from a total of 25 subjects to take normally 3 A Levels in the Sixth Form. Double Maths (Maths and Further Maths) is regarded as one subject leading to two A Levels.

There is considerable flexibility of combinations possible at both levels, and choices are made after consultation between parents, tutors, careers staff and subject teachers. The most able pupils are given an enrichment programme under the guidance of the Director of Academic Development, including extension projects, visits to Gifted and Talented seminars, and seminars with Cambridge undergraduate or postgraduate students. In addition, departments organise extension groups and societies and the school has a thriving Debating Society and a Model United Nations group. The school runs its own Independent Research Project to help senior pupils develop independent study skills.

About 95% of the A Level candidates proceed to degree courses. A Reading Party for potential Oxford and Cambridge candidates is held during the Summer Term.

Personal and Social Education forms an integral part of the curriculum at all levels. In the Sixth Form this is supplemented by a year-long programme that draws on the cultural resources of Cambridge University and the city as a whole.

The Chapel. The School Chapel is at the heart of the community in every sense. From the time of its Methodist foundation The Leys has been firmly based on non-sectarian Christian principles. It welcomes boys and girls of all denominations and religions, encouraging them to see the relevance of a personal faith of their own. Religious Education forms part of the curriculum. Preparation is also given for Church membership, and a combined confirmation service is held.

Physical Education. The physical education/games programme aims at introducing a wide variety of physical activities. Sports available are Rugby, Hockey, Cricket, Tennis, Athletics, Netball, Badminton, Basketball, Gymnastics, Golf, Rowing, Sailing, Dance, Shooting, Climbing, Squash, Swimming, Volleyball, Water Polo. Outdoor activities such as Camping, Orienteering, Canoeing, and Climbing are also encouraged through CCF and The Duke of Edinburgh's Award. PE is offered at GCSE and A Level. The School has close links with many Cambridge University Sports Clubs, with the Sixth Form competing in University Leagues.

Careers. In the Lower School, careers guidance forms part of the PSHE programme and is carried out by tutors and members of the Careers Department. Year 9 are supported in their option choices by tutors and Careers staff and are introduced to the Careers Library. Year 11 take the Preview Careers Selection Programme. It matches pupils' interests and abilities to appropriate career fields and is followed up by two individual interviews with career specialists. Year 11 pupils are also encouraged to participate in the Work Experience scheme. Support continues into the Sixth Form with all Lower Sixth being interviewed by Careers staff. An annual Careers Forum is organised in the Lent term, enabling pupils to investigate various career paths before embarking on their UCAS applications. Work experience is organised throughout the Sixth Form.

Societies. All are encouraged to participate in out-of-school activities of their choice. These range from Literary, Philosophical, Scientific, Mathematical, Languages, Debating, Music and Drama societies to any of the activities available in the Design Centre, which are available after School and at weekends. The life of the School is enriched by its proximity to Cambridge; distinguished visiting speakers are available, and pupils are encouraged to go to plays, concerts and lectures in the town. The programme of visiting speakers is largely run by the pupils themselves, overseen by a member of staff. A programme entitled the Cambridge Experience ensures that all Sixth Form pupils avail themselves of the cultural opportunities afforded by the school's location.

Combined Cadet Force. Except in special circumstances, pupils in Year 10 join the CCF (Army or Navy section) and also follow The Duke of Edinburgh's Award scheme. CCF camps take place annually. There is a miniature range, and a Rifle Club exists for small-bore shooting. The School is an authorised centre for the organisation of activities within The Duke of Edinburgh's Award scheme and pupils work towards the Bronze, Silver or Gold awards in the four sections: community service, expeditions, physical recreation and skills or hobbies.

Fees per term (2023–2024). Years 7 and 8: £10,185 (Boarders), £6,655 (Day); Years 9–13: £13,960 (Boarders), £10,365 (Home Boarders), £9,220 (Day).

St Faith's Preparatory School is part of the same Foundation. It was founded in 1884 and acquired by the Governors of The Leys in 1938. There are 570 boys and girls, aged 4–13 years. The buildings, which include the Keynes Building opened in 2006 and a new Sports Hall opened in May 2011, stand in 10 acres of grounds. *For further details, see entry in IAPS section.*

The Old Leysian Society. *Secretary*: Karen Sears, The Leys School, Cambridge CB2 7AD.

Charitable status. The Leys and St Faith's Schools Foundation is a Registered Charity, number 1144035. It aims to enable boys and girls to develop fully their individual potential within a School community firmly based on Christian principles.

Chair of The Leys Committee: Mr J Gladwin, BSc, MEd

***Headmaster*: M J Priestley**, MA Oxon

Lincoln Minster School

Part of United Learning

The Prior Building, Upper Lindum Street, Lincoln, Lincolnshire LN2 5RW

Tel: 01522 551300
email: admissions@lincolnminsterschool.co.uk
website: www.lincolnminsterschool.co.uk
X/Twitter: @MinsterSchool
Facebook: @LincolnMinsterSchool
Instagram: @LincolnMinsterSchool
LinkedIn: /Lincoln-Minster-School

Lincoln Minster School is an independent co-educational HMC day and boarding school for pupils aged 4–18 years. We aim to provide an inspirational all-round education that combines academic achievement with a wealth of co-curricular opportunities.

We offer an all-through education, where the nurturing, stimulation and development of our pupils in all areas of school life, overseen by inspiring and caring staff, is at the heart of what we do.

Our intention is to provide an inspiring 'Education for Life', from Reception all the way through to our A Level pupils. Individual needs are catered for across all age groups where boys and girls, of differing abilities and interests, excel in our vibrant community and where pupils have the opportunity to develop their leadership, mentoring and communication skills.

Structure and Organisation. Set in Lincoln's Historic Quarter, our Preparatory and Senior School sites are fully equipped to prepare our pupils for the careers of tomorrow, providing pupils with an inspiring environment in which to fulfil their potential.

The Preparatory School is a short walk from Lincoln's Bailgate, has been extensively redeveloped and was opened in September 2014.

Our Senior School site is made up of a number of buildings, both new and old. The main Prior Building was purpose built and opened in 2002 by the former Archbishop of Canterbury, Lord Carey. The sweeping, curved building overlooks the city and boasts fully equipped science labs, art studios, IT suites and our dedicated Sixth Form Centre. Our latest addition, the Harper Building, is dedicated to music and performance and includes an impressive Recital Hall, music practice rooms and a fully-equipped Drama Studio, as well as a Sports Hall.

The sight of our pupils in their distinctive blazers and staff in their academic gowns processing to the Galilee Porch at Lincoln Cathedral for our End of Term Services and Prize Giving Ceremonies is a special one; a reminder of how important a sense of tradition is in a modern world and a modern school.

Lincoln Minster School is a member of United Learning, which owns and manages independent schools and academies across England. There is no doubt that membership of a group of this size gives Lincoln Minster School strength and breadth of contact.

Curriculum. A full range of subjects is offered and the school is proud of its excellent track record of examination success.

We specialise in finding the best in every pupil and place equal value on cultural, technological, scientific, linguistic and creative subjects.

The curriculum is supported by a wealth of trips, visits and activities. We offer over 150 different clubs and activities to pupils including a comprehensive sports programme to cater for all tastes.

We are proud to offer a number of exciting specialist programmes in Golf, Tennis and Squash. In partnership with industry specialists, our exclusive Sport Performance Programmes offer young potentially elite players the opportunity to train on world-class facilities.

Pupils on these tailored programmes benefit from high-quality coaching and opportunities to compete alongside their studies.

We encourage all of our pupils to stretch and challenge themselves, to test new skills outside their comfort zone, and not to worry when they make a mistake, but to learn from it. This way, our pupils develop a resilience, grow in self-esteem and become more equipped to face the challenges that lie ahead.

Music. Music is a key component of the school's curriculum throughout all year groups. Whether it is the Year 5/6 orchestra, strings ensemble, jazz band or Prep choir, our pupils are encouraged to involve themselves fully.

Our Harper Building benefits from individual practice rooms, classrooms and a purpose-built Recital Hall – the ideal venue for concerts, performance rehearsals and workshops.

We also hold memorable concerts throughout the year in the nave of Lincoln Cathedral.

Boarding. Our boarding house is just a short walk to school sites and is overseen by highly experienced and approachable boarding staff. We pride ourselves on making every pupil's boarding experience a happy and productive one and have a range of boarding options to suit every family.

We have an inclusive boarding culture where each boarder, whether termly, weekly or flexi, are all treated as equal members of our boarding family.

We have a blend of day pupils and boarders, both from overseas and from the UK. This broad social and cultural mix ensures the school has a truly national and global outlook.

Admissions. Once you have decided to join the Lincoln Minster family, our staff will support you throughout the entire application process.

We are a proudly non-selective school with no entrance exams. We welcome pupils who will support the aims, ethos and expectations to which we aspire. We are confident that we can fully provide any child with a true education for life in line with their potential.

Scholarships. Each year, we are proud to award Scholarships to pupils who are capable of extremely high levels of achievement and who we believe will make a significant contribution to the life of the school.

Scholarships are offered at entry into Years 7 through to 12. Awards vary and are dependent on a variety of factors, including references and assessment performance. Once awarded, they will be reviewed on a termly basis. If the criteria are met at every review, scholarships will continue for the duration of another term during the pupil's time at Lincoln Minster School.

Fees per term (2023–2024). Day (including lunch): Reception to Year 2 £3,759, Year 3–6 £4,835, Year 7–13 £5,524. Weekly Boarding: Year 3–6 £8,471, Year 7–13 £9,802. Occasional Boarding: £57 per night.

Charitable Status. Lincoln Minster School is part of United Learning which comprises: UCST (a Company Limited by Guarantee, Registered in England, number 2780748, and a Registered Charity, number 1016538) and ULT (a Company Limited by Guarantee, Registered in England, number 4439859, and an Exempt Charity).

Chair of Local Governing Body: Kate Richards

Members:
Susie Mooney
Elaine Rose
Mark Tottman

Senior Leadership Team:
***Head*: Jon Tyler**
Executive Principal: Mike Buchanan
Deputy Head Teaching and Learning: Alex Sandbrook
Deputy Head: *Pastoral & Head of Boarding*: Charlotte Brigden
Head of Preparatory School: Mark Burton
Bursar: Jane Stone

Heads of Department:
Mr M Barrett (*IT*)
Mr N Boot, BA Hons, DipLaw, QTS (*History*)
Mrs C Cobo (*Modern Foreign Languages*)
Mr J Cochrane, BSc, PGCE (*Mathematics*)
Mrs K Cook-James, BEd (*Learning Support*)
Mr T Eves, BSc Hons, PGCE (*Acting Head, PE & Games*)
Mrs R Gladwin, BA Hons, PGCE (*Social Sciences*)
Mrs J Glenn-Batchelor, BA Hons, GTP (*Geography*)
Mrs R Hewitt, MEd, BA Hons, PGCE (*English*)
Mrs N Hutchinson, MEd, BMus Hons, PGCE (*Music*)
Mrs H Mason, BSc Hons, PGCE (*Science*)
Mr D Osborne, BSc, QTS (*Head, Geography*)
Mrs C Servonat-Blanc, BA Hons, PGCE (*Art, Graphics & Photography*)
Miss A Tweedale, BA Hons, PGCE (*Head of Business, Sixth Form*)
Ms R Viscomi (*Food Science*)
Mrs J Wafer, BA Hons, PGCE (*Drama*)

Examinations Officer: Mr J Hart, MSc, BSc Hons, PGCE

Lingfield College

St Piers Lane, Lingfield, Surrey RH7 6PH

Tel: 01342 832407
email: office@lingfieldcollege.co.uk
website: www.lingfieldcollege.co.uk
X/Twitter: @LingfieldColl
Facebook: @LingfieldCollege
Instagram: @lingfieldcollege
LinkedIn: /company/lingfield-college

Age range. 0–18.
Number in school. 948.

Fees per term (2023–2024). £3,500–£6,810. Nursery according to sessions attended.

Situation. The School is located just outside the village of Lingfield on the Surrey, Sussex, Kent border. Lingfield station has a line to London Victoria via Hurst Green, Oxted and Woldingham and is 5 minutes' drive or ten minutes' walk. The School also operates an extensive bus service.

Entry. Senior School: at 11+ and 13+ by Entrance Examination and report from previous school. At 16+ by 6+ GCSEs results and school report.

Scholarships. Prep School: available from Year 5. Senior School: at 11+, 13+ and 16+ (Academic, Art, Drama, Music and Sport). Means-tested Bursaries may also be available to Scholars.

Academic. In Years 7–9, pupils study the core subjects and a range of other options within the Lower School Curriculum. Pupils typically take 10 GCSEs which consist of English Language and Literature, Triple Science (although some may take Dual Science), at least one Language and 3 other subjects of their choice which include Computing, Media and Economics. IGCSEs are taken in the majority of subjects. The top Maths set take Additional Maths as well as IGCSE Mathematics. 23 subjects are offered at A Level and many students also sit the Extended Project Qualification.

The School offers an extensive Scholars' Programme for its Academic Scholars and Award Holders. Seminars are held and special excursions planned as part of the Scholars' enrichment programme. Headmaster's Lectures are held every term. The School is dedicated to a progressive and innovative approach to learning and has invested heavily in digital learning (including refurbished Media Suites and iPads plus an interactive lecture theatre), whilst valuing traditional methodology.

Pastoral. Pastorally, the School was considered 'outstanding' in its last inspection. Since then, improvements such as smaller tutor groups, more parent focus groups, regular school council and House meetings have further enhanced the feel of a forward-thinking, family-focused school. Communications between the Lingfield village community, staff, students and parents are both open and honest. The School has a 'Whole School' approach to support wellbeing and mental health, working in a proactive and preventative way to support every student to stay emotionally healthy, as well as supporting specific needs. The School employs a comprehensive team of welfare support including 2 school councillors.

Sport. The School has a sporting ethos of 'Opportunity, Participation and Excellence' and students have access to a wide range of sporting activities which take place at lunchtime and after school. Students represent the School across a full range of sports at all levels and age groups, as well as participating in regional and national competitions. Hockey, netball and football form the core of major team sport representation in the autumn and spring terms whilst cricket, athletics, tennis and rounders provide the main options for the summer term.

The Rugby Club runs for both the autumn and spring terms and provides an option for those who want to play rugby to represent the School. Golf, equestrian, swimming, cross country, badminton, basketball and table tennis are some of the other competitive team sports available.

Pupils who hold Sport Scholarships benefit from the Elite Sports Mentoring Programme which helps aspiring young athletes fulfil their potential.

Co-curricular. The School has an extensive co-curricular programme with over 140 clubs on offer, taking place both at lunchtime and after school. The clubs vary from arts and crafts to sporting and practical activities and have been designed to help pupils develop their hobbies, strengths and skills. Recent additions to the Senior School program include fencing and paddleboarding clubs. There are also numerous trips for the students to go on; these include departmental trips, language exchanges and sports tours.

The Duke of Edinburgh's Award programme is particularly popular. More than 90% of pupils take the Bronze Award in Year 9 & 10 and about 40% of them proceed to the Silver and Gold Awards.

In the Sixth Form, students can participate in a wide programme of activities such as Zumba, Ballroom Dancing, Self-Defence, Car Maintenance, Orienteering, Cooking, Youth Parliament, Debating, Public Speaking, Critical Thinking and Safe Driving Talks. In addition to this, an extensive range of outside speakers visit the School to hold seminars and lectures, offering pupils the chance to broaden their horizons.

Music. A substantial number of students subscribe to instrumental lessons and participate in musical ensembles. The School maintains two orchestras, two choirs, a Jazz Band, Ukulele Group, Acoustic and Electric Guitar Groups, Street Band, Rock/Pop Bands, Saxophone Quartet, Woodwind Orchestra and String Ensemble, all run by a team of specialist instrumental teachers. As well as the main school concerts and productions, regular informal recitals are given.

Drama. The Drama Department offers a full range of theatrical experience to its actors and audiences, exploring challenging texts from classics to modern writers, pushing both the academic and performance boundaries of the students. All pupils are taught Drama in the Lower School and it is a popular and successful option at both GCSE and A Level. They are all accommodated in the School's fully equipped studio spaces, technical, costume and make-up workrooms, as well as a specialist Speech and Drama room.

Religion. Lingfield transferred to a lay management in 1987. It maintains its Christian ethos and welcomes students and staff of all faiths, and of none. Its philosophy is based on a strong belief in the development of the whole person. The School has a tradition of providing a caring, friendly and disciplined environment.

Buildings. In 2023, the School opened the Cocoon, a brand new baby suite catering for babies from 6 months to 2 years. In 2022, Nursery and Reception classrooms underwent an extensive refurbishment to provide light, colourful learning spaces with interactive teaching walls. In the same year, Nursery, KS1 and KS2 playgrounds were resurfaced and equipped with high-quality play equipment. In the summer of 2022, the Senior School completed a pitch redevelopment project to resurface the hockey pitch, netball courts and expansion of the cricket nets. The School comprises a purpose-built Performing Arts Centre, Sports Hall,

Science Rooms and Art and Photography facilities. The state-of-the-art Sixth Form Centre offers a university-style lecture theatre, modern, interactive classrooms, Atrium coffee shop and student-designed common room. There are 40 acres of grounds which include 4 football pitches, a floodlit astro and cricket nets.

Charitable status. Lingfield Notre Dame is a Registered Charity, number 295598. It exists to provide education.

Chair of Governors: Mrs F Halpin

***Headmaster*: Mr R W Bool**, BA Hons, MBA

Headmaster's PA and Clerk to Governors: Mrs T Unwin

Deputy Heads:
Mr C Fast, BEd, BSc
Mrs A Folkard, BSc
Mrs E Parsons, BA, MA

Assistant Head: Mr S Hofmann, BSc

Director of Sport and Co-Curricular: Mr S Casey, BA

Prep School:
Head of Prep School: Mrs J Shackel, BA Hons (*SENDCO*)
Prep School Head's PA: Mrs K Rider
Director of Studies, Prep School: Mrs C Hubbard, BA Hons

Head of Finance & Resources: Mrs A Brassett
Head of Organisational Development: Mrs C Wren, Chartered MCIPD
Registrar: Mrs J Armstrong
HR Manager: Mrs C Marsden, HND, MCIPD
Marketing Manager: Miss C Whitlock, BA Hons, CIM cert
Head of Estates and Facilities: Mr A Taylor, BEng, MSc

A full list of teaching staff is available on the website.

Lomond School

10 Stafford Street, Helensburgh, Argyll and Bute G84 9JX

Tel: 01436 672476
email: admin@lomondschool.com
website: www.lomondschool.com
X/Twitter: @LomondSchool
Facebook: @LomondSchool
Instagram: @lomond.school
LinkedIn: /school/lomond-school

A superb quality of life. Lomond School is a co-educational independent school, for children aged 3 to 18, positioned in the elegant suburbs of Helensburgh, a coastal town located only 10 minutes from Loch Lomond and the Trossachs National Park. We make the most of our unique location by providing and encouraging participation in a wide range of opportunities for outdoor learning, sports and activities. Our young people enjoy a superb quality of life in a beautiful and safe environment.

Personalised Education. At Lomond School we believe passionately that education should be about supporting our young people to develop and grow, both academically and personally, as rounded individuals with strong values who are ultimately prepared to embark confidently and successfully on their life beyond Lomond School.

We uphold this commitment with six **Guiding Principles** which are delivered throughout our curriculum and co-curriculum. These include: Internationalism; Environmentalism; Adventure; Leadership; Lifelong Learning and Service. To find out more visit our website at www.lomondschool.com.

As an International Baccalaureate World School we are proud to offer our Senior Pupils the choice of studying the IB Diploma Programme, IB Career-related Programme or SQA Qualifications.

Inclusive Ethos. Our focus is on preparing our students for their future by ensuring that they learn the skills necessary to be successful in the 21st century whilst developing the traditional values and qualities that they require to be responsible and active global citizens.

We provide small class sizes, an extensive programme of extra-curricular activities, attention to the individual and a strong record of academic achievement which opens the door to allow new experiences, skills and talents to be explored. All aspects of development are accorded importance, be they academic, musical, dramatic, sporting or in wider outdoor activities.

The Lomond Family. Our experienced pastoral care team ensures the welfare and onward progression of all of our students. Our young people are well known by staff and teachers and we see ourselves as a large family where any issues or problems are identified and dealt with promptly and effectively.

Extra-curricular and Outdoor Learning. Our location means that there is a particular emphasis on outdoor pursuits. The Duke of Edinburgh's Award is, without doubt, a significant feature and we have enjoyed great success carrying out expeditions both locally and abroad. Many of our trips and excursions revolve around our passion for the outdoors and have included trekking in Morocco, canoeing in Norway, skiing in Austria and travelling to Africa to help a number of educational charities there.

We also build many cultural and educational trips into the school year with visits to Paris, Berlin, Brussels and Iceland, as well as Hockey and Rugby tours to South Africa or more locally. We support and encourage our young people to make the most of the opportunities available, recognising both the immediate and long-term benefit of the personal development these experiences and activities can offer.

Living at Lomond. Our boarding facility adds a distinctive dimension to the school; the mix of cultures and backgrounds enriches our curriculum and co-curriculum, supporting all of our pupils to develop their global awareness and understanding.

Our infrastructure boasts a mix of modern, purpose-built structure and characterful listed buildings, which make for an inspirational setting for our young people. We continually invest in our facilities and take a cutting-edge approach to every new project we initiate.

Entry and Scholarships. Means-tested bursaries are available for entry between T2 and S6 with fee assistance ranging from 10% to 100% depending on circumstances. In addition, we offer discounts for the Armed Forces and are a CEA approved school. Scholarships are also available in the fields of academic excellence, creative arts, music and sport.

Lomond is a non-selective school. Part of our admission process, however, is an assessment in Mathematics and English for 11 to 18 year-olds. For younger pupils, placement in classes is the main requirement, whilst for senior pupils reports and examination results are given due weighting.

Fees per annum (2023–2024) – monthly amount by direct debit over 10 months. Tuition: Nursery – Local Authority Funded with priority given to those entering our Junior School. £1,066 (Junior 1–2), £1,271 (Junior 3–5), £1,385 (Transitus 1), £1,468.50 (Transitus 2), £1,513.50 (Senior School).

Boarding (inc. Tuition Fees): Full Boarding £3,641; Weekly Boarding £2,596; Occasional Boarding £65 per night.

All fees are inclusive of the annual Capital Levy (£210).

Charitable status. Lomond School Ltd is a Registered Charity, number SC007957. It exists to provide education for boys and girls.

Board of Governors: Mr A Hart (*Chair*)

***Principal*: Mrs C Chisholm**

Lord Wandsworth College

Long Sutton, Hook, Hampshire RG29 1TB

Tel: 01256 862201 (Main Office)
01256 860385 (Admissions)
email: info@lordwandsworth.org
website: www.lordwandsworth.org
Facebook: @LordWandsworth
Instagram: @lordwandsworth
LinkedIn: @lordwandsworth

Motto: *Vincit Perseverantia*

Lord Wandsworth College is a co-educational secondary school for 680 pupils between the ages of 11 and 18. Approximately 60% of the pupils are boarders, either full, weekly or flexi.

LWC is thriving under the leadership of Adam Williams who became Headmaster in 2015. Its increasing popularity has been reflected in rising pupil numbers, and a transformational vision for education has led to major investment in the campus and facilities. The latest, and most significant, of these capital projects is an £8 million state-of-the-art Science Centre that opened in January 2022. This is a dynamic and highly successful school on a clear upward trajectory.

Location and accessibility. Situated in a magnificent 1,200 acre campus of rolling countryside, woodland and a working arable farm, Lord Wandsworth College provides an inspiring education to 650 boarding and day pupils, aged 11–18. LWC is just five miles from Junction 5 of the M3 and only one hour from London by road or rail.

History. Lord Wandsworth College is named after Baron Sydney Stern, a Liberal MP and the son of a City banker. Granted a peerage after winning the seat of Stowmarket in 1891, Stern took the title of Lord Wandsworth in reflection of his many links with the area. When Lord Wandsworth died in 1912, he left a generous bequest to educate the children of agricultural workers – children who had lost one or both parents and needed the support of a boarding environment. Lord Wandsworth's Trustees purchased the site on which the College now stands and the first Foundationers arrived in 1922, followed by fee-paying pupils in 1945.

Committed to upholding the wishes of Lord Wandsworth, every year the Lord Wandsworth Foundation offers approximately 50 assisted Foundation places. 2,500 Foundationers have passed through the College since its inception. The Foundation exists to help children who have lost the support of one or both parents through death, divorce or separation and require a caring and supportive boarding environment in which to thrive.

Mission statement. For 100 years, Lord Wandsworth College has helped young people become confident, curious and compassionate men and women, ready to seize the opportunities of an ever-changing world.

On our stunning 1,200 acre campus in North Hampshire, we've created an extraordinary educational community of staff and 680 boys and girls, offering both boarding and day options.

Our pupils consistently excel in traditional testing, with more than half scoring A* to A at GCSE and A Level. More importantly, they are given an education of opportunities, through inspirational teaching, helping pupils discover their passions and overcome their doubts. We teach through care, giving the support pupils need to achieve their goals; an ambition stemming from our Foundation heritage. Our exceptional character-driven philosophy has been nationally recognised by the Association for Character Education, which shapes confident and resilient young people who are ambitious to go and make a positive difference in the world.

The outstanding features of the school are:

- that almost all academic staff live on campus allowing them to provide a high level of pastoral care;
- that Character Education is imbedded into the curriculum and co-curriculum. By promoting Character Education, we believe we will give all pupils the best chance of realising their full potentials.
- that all pupils, whether full, weekly, flexi boarding or day, belong to one of the eight houses and are fully integrated into the social life of the school;
- that the school is purpose-built with an outstanding range of facilities for both academic and extracurricular activities;
- that the school is an unusually unpretentious, happy and caring community.

Curriculum. The aim of the curriculum is to provide a full and flexible range of subjects to fit the needs of each individual. The school's policy is to follow closely the National Curriculum.

Subjects taught to GCSE are: English (Language and Literature), French, Geography, Mathematics, History, Latin, Classical Civilisation, Drama, Physics,

Chemistry, Biology, Spanish, Art, Music, Design & Technology, Computer Science and Religious Studies.

Most pupils continue into the Sixth Form where the subjects taught at A Level are: English, History, Geography, Economics, Business Studies, Classical Civilisation, Music, French, Spanish, Politics, Physics, Chemistry, Biology, Mathematics, Further Mathematics, Art, Design, Theatre Studies, PE, Psychology and Photography. We also offer the EPQ and BTECs in Sport, Enterprise and Entrepreneurship and Creative Digital Media.

Games. The school provides incredible sports facilities and has a local and national reputation for many of its pursuits. The main boys' games are rugby, hockey and cricket and for girls hockey, cricket and netball with many pupils reaching County and National level. In addition swimming, athletics, tennis, football, golf, cross-country running, horse riding and canoeing are all on offer.

Drama. Drama has a high profile and several shows are staged each year. A new performing arts space, The Nadine Uppal Theatre, opened in 2021. There is a musical production every other year as well as showcases, reviews and workshops. Pupils are encouraged to participate in all fields of drama either acting, writing, set design, tech support, lighting, stage management, prop-making or sound.

Music. There is a large variety of instrumental ensembles, including a swing band, concert band and rock groups. Pupils have the opportunity to sing in various choirs. Tuition is available in singing, all orchestral instruments, piano, percussion and guitar. Musicians regularly perform formally and informally both within school and at local venues.

Other activities. There is an extensive co-curricular programme. Some of the activities on offer are: Mandarin, Cookery, Chess, Community Service, Pottery, Drama clubs, Mountain Biking, Dance, Photography, Art Clubs, Riding, Life-saving, Debating and Climbing.

The Duke of Edinburgh's Award scheme is thriving and the College has its own licence to run the scheme. There is an active CCF programme for Year 10 pupils and above which has an Army and Air Force Section.

Organisation. There are three main entry points to the College: 11+, 13+ and 16+. Students are accepted at other entry points provided there is a vacancy. The completion of a Registration Form is the first step for all years. A £350 non-refundable registration fee is charged to cover the cost of administration and entrance testing.

Scholarships and Awards on offer are:

First Form (Year 7): Academic, Performing Arts (Music, Drama and Dance) and Sport.

Third Form (Year 9): Academic, Performing Arts (Music, Drama and Dance), Art, Sport and All-Rounder

Sixth Form (Year 12): Academic, Performing Arts (Music, Drama and Dance), Art, Sport and All-Rounder

Foundation Awards are available for children who have lost the support of one or both parents through death, divorce or separation.

Further details for all scholarships and awards may be obtained from the Admissions Office.

Fees per term (2023–2024). Senior Full Boarding £14,000, Senior Weekly Boarding £13,390, Senior Flexi Boarding £12,080, Senior Day £9,880, Junior Full Boarding £12,350, Junior Weekly Boarding £11,930, Junior Flexi Boarding £10,750, Junior Day £8,400.

Charitable status. Lord Wandsworth College is a Registered Charity, number 1143359. It exists to provide education for boys and girls.

Chairman of Governors: R J Hannington

The Governing Body consists of 16 Governors.

***Headmaster*: Adam Williams**, MA

Senior Deputy Head: Alex Battison, MA
Deputy Head, Teaching and Learning: Stephen Badger, MA Cantab
Deputy Head, Pastoral: Alexandra Cocksworth, MA
Chief Operating Officer: Baz Bennett, MA
Marketing and Admissions Director: Pete German, BA
Development Director: Samantha Corfield, BEng
Head of Sixth Form: Tom Rimmer, BSc
Director of Compliance and Projects: Collette McDonald, MA
Director of People: Dawn Wilde, CIPD

Teaching Staff and Assistants:
* *Houseparent*

Marie-France Allen (*EAL Assistant*)
Chris Andrews, BA (*Director of IT Services*)
Sarah Badger, MA (*Head of Modern Languages*)
Adam Ball, BSc (*Chemistry & Academic Enrichment*)
Natalie Bastiman, PGCE (*Mathematics*)
Thomas Batchelor (*Business Studies, Economics, Entrepreneurship & Enterprise*)
Pippa Battison, BA (*Classics & History*)
Anna Berney (*Interim Head of Business, Economics, and Enterprise & Entrepreneurship*)
*David Beven, MA (*Sport*)
Georgia Bowers (*Sport*)
Gemma Burns, MSc (*Design & Textiles*)
Aubrey Collins, BSc (*Head of Physics*)
Mark Collins, BSc (*Geography*)
*Kate Cuff, BA (*Drama*)
Sally Dawson-Couper, MEd (*Head of Mathematics, Assistant Deputy Head, Director of Studies*)
Rachel De La Cruz, MA (*Head of Spanish, Head of 5th Form*)
Paul Donald, MA (*English*)
Jennifer Edgar, MSc (*Chemistry*)
Michael Firth (*Religion, Philosophy & Ethics*)
Ed Firth, BA (*Geography*)
*Russell Fisher, MA (*Design & Technology*)
*Max Gaulton (*Mathematics*)
Alex Hamilton, MA (*Head of Latin & Classics*)
Lee-Anne Hampson, BA (*Art*)
Esther Haydock, PhD (*Science, Head of Academic Enrichment*)
Ben Hazell (*Sports*)
Hannah Hendrick, BA (*Sports Science & Academic PE*)
Katherine Henley, MA (*Spanish & French*)
James Hine, BA (*History*)
*Holly Hunter-Wright, BA (*Art*)
Kirsty Jackman (*Head of Wellbeing & PSHEE*)
Nick Jenkins, BSc (*Science*)
Nicole Jinadasa, BSc (*Chemistry, Head of 1st & 2nd Form*)
Gitte Kenning, MSc (*Business Studies & Economics*)
Richard Kimber, BEng (*Mathematics, Senior Master*)
Poppy Lake, BSc (*Head of Girls Sport*)

Tanja Lambe, MA (*Mathematics, Head of Outreach*)
Katia Lannon (*Science*)
Claire Liggins, BA (*Head of Design & Technology*)
Jonathan Lilley, BA (*Head of History*)
Rebecca Lodge-Maynard (*Design & Technology*)
Jeni Loud, BSc (*Physics, Assistant Deputy Head, Staff*)
Richard Lovell (*Head of Outdoor Learning*)
Audley Lumsden, BSc (*Physics*)
Joanne Mackenzie, MSc (*Biology*)
Laurie Macvean (*English*)
*Pete Maidment, BA (*Head of Junior House*)
Jack Malden, BA (*Business Studies & Economics*)
Peter McNeely, MA (*Classics and Latin, Assistant Deputy, Teaching & Learning*)
Graham Mobbs, BA (*Head of Art*)
Andrew Molin (*Biology*)
Veronique Morris-Aloni, BA (*Head of Curriculum Support*)
Vincent Murtagh, BSc, PhD (*Head of Chemistry*)
Clare Mutch, BA (*French & Spanish*)
Thelma Naidoo, MA (*English*)
Jan Norgaard, BSc (*Head of Geography*)
Craig O'Nions, BSc (*Mathematics*)
Laura Osborne, BA (*English, Assistant Head of Sixth Form*)
Liza O'Shea, BA (*Art*)
Angharad Packer (*Psychology*)
Aaron Parker, MMus (*Acting Director of Music*)
Harriet Paskell, BSc (*Geography*)
Susan Penny, BSc (*Science*)
Sanna Pollard (*Biology*)
Chris Radmann, BA (*Head of English*)
*Lesley Radmann, BA (*English*)
James Rayner, BA (*Head of Academic PE*)
Gemma Reeks, BA (*Head of Performing Arts*)
Tim Richardson, BA (*Assistant Director of Co-Curricular*)
Tom Rimmer, BSc (*Geography, Head of Sixth Form*)
Patricia Risley, BSc (*Computer Science*)
Daniel Rodriguez (*French & Spanish*)
Thomas Rowland (*Science*)
Helen Shedden, BA (*English, EPQ Coordinator*)
*Tom Shedden, BA (*History, Head of Boarding*)
Lauren Showell (*French*)
Eloise Shrimpton, BA (*Sports Science & Academic PE*)
Soma Singh, BA (*Director of Sport*)
Mark Smith, MA (*Geography*)
Sophie Springer, BA (*History, Head of 4th Form*)
Lewis Starbuck, BSc (*Sport, Head of Rugby*)
Thomas Starnes, MA (*Head of Religion, Philosophy & Ethics*)
Melisia Swaby (*Computer Science*)
Alexandra Tarsey (*Head of Futures*)
Sophie Townsend, BA (*Spanish & French*)
Ian Watson, MEng (*Mathematics, Head of 3rd Form*)
Holly Welham, BSc (*Head of Science*)
Zoe Wheddon (*Spanish*)
Christian White, MA (*Head of Politics*)
David Widdowson, BSc (*Mathematics*)
Timothy Willis (*Music*)
Chloe Wilson, BA (*Classics & Latin*)
Jack Wrenn (*Sport*)
Louis Yates (*Head of Psychology*)

Loretto School

1–7 Linkfield Road, Musselburgh, East Lothian EH21 7RE

Tel: 0131 653 4444 (Senior School Reception), 0131 653 4570 (Junior School Reception), 0131 653 4455 (Admissions)
email: admissions@loretto.com
website: www.loretto.com
X/Twitter: @LorettoHead
Facebook: @LorettoSchool
Instagram: @LorettoSchool
LinkedIn: /company/loretto-school

A small School, big on heart, big on ambition.

Our changing world is full of challenges and opportunities for young people. Finding a school that can provide an all-round education to fully prepare them for what lies ahead is vital. Loretto is that school.

Founded in 1827, Loretto is Scotland's first boarding school. Today an independent, private, boarding and day school, it welcomes girls and boys, from 3 to 18 years.

Set in a safe, leafy 85-acre campus just six miles from Edinburgh, Loretto enjoys all the advantages of this rural setting while being globally connected – the School is just nine kilometres/six miles from Scotland's capital city, its international airport, rail, and road networks.

Welcoming just over 500 pupils across the Junior School and Senior School, the first thing you notice when you enter Loretto's campus is the warmth and energy of both pupils and staff. Relationships are marked by kindness, care and respect; a truly special environment for providing the confidence and know-how to thrive in life beyond Loretto. More than nine pupils out of ten achieve places at their chosen onwards destination, many attending top universities such as, Oxford, Cambridge, St Andrews, Newcastle, and Durham, as well as American universities.

Loretto's foundational belief is that each child has unique potential. The small nature of Loretto allows staff to individually know each child, whether they be our youngest pupils in Loretto's Pre-School, or our oldest pupils in Upper Sixth. Our staff will help find where a pupil's interests may lie and there is a distinct emphasis on the individual development of each child in mind, body, and spirit.

Loretto has a whole-school approach and Junior School pupils, or 'The Nippers' as they are affectionately known, enjoy the same, safe, supporting and stimulating environment as Senior School pupils. They also benefit from exceptional shared facilities such as the playing fields, Theatre, Sports Hall, and Music School.

Loretto, with its superb location on Scotland's Golf Coast, also has a strong tradition of top-level golf. The school's surrounding area of East Lothian offers a choice of magnificent links courses, and in 2002 this tradition blossomed into The Golf Academy. The Academy is now regarded as one of Europe's leading golf academies where pupils can develop their sporting talent in tandem with an exceptional education.

Directed by a team of top-class PGA Professional coaches, Loretto offers golfers access to state-of-the-art practice centres, and an abundance of local, accessible golf courses. With innovative practice facilities, including a nine-hole artificial putting green, several driving bays, bunker and chipping areas, and a putting studio with video analysis and Trackman.

From day one, Loretto's founder was dedicated to blending academic excellence with a wealth of experiences beyond the classroom. The enormous range of co-curricular activities offered ensures that each pupil can grow and develop wherever their interests and talents may lie. The School's achievements in music, art, drama and its strong reputation in sporting endeavours – both in major team sports and other sports, are testament to that.

Ultimately, to really understand the warm and welcoming atmosphere that makes Loretto different, you have to experience the School in person. So please come along for a visit – you will soon see why our pupils are so proud to be called Lorettonians.

Fees per term (2023–2024). Day: £3,212–£9,182 per term; Full Boarding: £8,782–£13,485 per term; Flexi Boarding: £7,479–£11,191 per term.

Admission. Applications are accepted for entry into most years in the School from aged three upwards, except Upper Sixth (Year 13). Loretto's Admissions team work alongside families through the whole admissions process to ensure pupils are happy, successful and secure within Loretto's academic, cultural and pastoral environment, whether they are boarders, flexi or day pupils.

Scholarships and Bursaries. Academic, Music, Piping and Sports Scholarships are available from 12+ entry, with Art and Drama Scholarships also available from 13+ entry. Means-tested bursaries are available for up to 105%.

Chairman of Governors: Mr Peter McCutcheon

***Headmaster*: Dr Graham R W Hawley**

Head of Junior School: Mrs Catherine Beddison

All Senior School staff: please visit www.loretto.com/senior-school-staff-directory
All Junior School staff: please visit www.loretto.com/junior-school-staff-directory

Loughborough Grammar School

Burton Walks, Loughborough, Leicestershire LE11 2DU

Tel: 01509 233233
email: grammar.admissions@lsf.org
website: www.lsf.org/grammar
X/Twitter: @LboroGrammar
Facebook: @LboroGrammar
Instagram: @LboroGrammar
LinkedIn: /loughborough-schools-foundation

Motto: *Vires acquirit eundo*

Loughborough Grammar School was founded in 1495 by Thomas Burton, Merchant of the Staple of Calais. The School is part of the Loughborough Schools Foundation, a foundation of four schools comprising: Fairfield Prep School (boys and girls 3–11), Loughborough Grammar School (boys 10–18), Loughborough Amherst School (boys and girls 4–18) and Loughborough High School (girls 11–18). The schools operate under one governing body and are situated on two neighbouring campuses in the town. The Foundation also includes The Loughborough Nursery for children from 6 weeks to 4 years.

There are just under 1,000 boys in the School, including over 60 boarders.

The School moved to its present site of some 27 acres in 1852 and is situated away from the centre of the town in attractive grounds containing the beautiful avenues of trees known as Burton Walks. At its centre is a handsome Victorian College quadrangle. There has been an impressive development programme in recent years – a new Music department was opened in September 2006; a new state-of-the-art Chemistry building in September 2009; a refurbished and extended Biology building in September 2011; a new Physics building in September 2012 and a new Mathematics building and boarding provision in 2013, completing the Science Park.

Admission. Entry to the School is by the school's own examination at all levels and also by Common Entrance at 13+. Sixth Form entry is dependent on GCSE results and interview with the Headmaster and other senior staff.

Boarding arrangements. Boys are admitted to Denton House at the age of 10 or over; Sixth Form boys are in School House. Termly and Weekly boarding is available.

Fees per term (2023–2024). Day without EAL: £5,300–£5,390, Weekly Boarding: £11,310–£11,400, Full Boarding without EAL: £13,000–£13,090, Full Boarding with EAL: £13,500–£13,590. Music (individual instrumental lessons): £275 (for 10 lessons).

The School offers a 25% boarding fee remission to sons of HM Forces and sons of Clergy.

Scholarships and bursaries. A number of Scholarships are offered, based on performance in the Entrance Examination. Sixth Form scholarships are based on GCSE results. Music Scholarships are also awarded at 11+, 13+ (Common Entrance), and 16+ (Sixth Form). There are also a number of bursaries, dependent on parental income.

Foundation bursaries. School Assisted Places (up to 100% fee remission) are based on financial need and Entrance Examination performance. Such places are means-tested and an application for one requires the completion of a form declaring income and a home visit.

Religious teaching. The School is non-denominational though there is a strong Christian tradition. The Chaplain teaches Religion and Philosophy but is available for boys at any convenient time. On Wednesdays, Boarders attend the School Chapel and, on request, are prepared for Confirmation by the Chaplain.

Curriculum. The aim of the School is to give a broad and balanced general education to GCSE with greater specialisation afterwards. In Year 6, boys follow a curriculum similar to that of their last year of junior school; subjects included are English, Mathematics, French, Art, Sciences, Drama, Design and Technology,

Geography, IT, History, Music, PE, RE. In Year 7, all boys study English, Mathematics, Science, French, History, Geography, Latin, and Music. Additionally, all boys have lessons in RE, PE, PSHE and Games. In Year 8, Design and Technology is introduced and, in addition to French, boys choose a second language from either German or Spanish. In Year 9 pupils continue with both MFLs, and make some choices from their existing subjects as well as Ancient Greek and Drama.

In Years 10 and 11, for GCSE, boys study English Language and Literature, Mathematics, a modern Foreign Language, and at least two sciences. They also choose three subjects from an extensive options list. Some more able boys study a tenth subject.

The Sixth Form contains 300 boys. A wide range of A Level subjects and combinations is available, along with General Studies, EPQ, Games and other activities. There are some joint teaching lessons with the Girls' High School.

Learning support is available to pupils with diagnosed Special Educational Needs or Disabilities (SEND). We offer targeted support from our experienced and well qualified Learning Support teachers and assistants.

Games. The School has an excellent First XI field and a junior field of over 13 acres within its precinct and within two miles are well-equipped playing fields extending to nearly 70 acres.

The School runs teams in Rugby, Soccer, Hockey, Cricket, Athletics, Tennis, Cross Country, Swimming, Badminton, Fencing and Squash. In addition, there is a Sailing and Canoe Club. The School prides itself in an array of Mind Sports, with teams in Bridge, Chess, Go and Chinese Chess.

Combined Cadet Force. There is an efficient and keen CCF of about 250 boys from Year 10 onwards, run on an optional basis, with 17 Officers, an SSI and a RQMS. Boys have the choice of joining the RAF, Army or Royal Navy Sections. The CCF complex is purpose-built with excellent facilities and many varied and Adventurous Training courses are available to members.

Scouts. There is a flourishing Scout Troop of 35 boys and 1 Scouter.

The Duke of Edinburgh's Award. Over 250 boys are actively involved in the scheme and each year a large number earn Gold, Silver and Bronze awards.

Music (of which much is joint with the Girls' High School) takes place in our award-winning Music department, which has 'All-Steinway School' status, and instrumental ensembles involve all the schools in the Foundation. For boys at LGS, there are 4 Choirs and 26 instrumental ensembles, including 3 Orchestras, 2 Wind Bands, 2 Jazz Bands and nearly twenty smaller instrumental ensembles, which each rehearse weekly. Our top ensembles perform on the national stage regularly, including in the MfY Schools' Prom at the Royal Albert Hall (2017), and there are annual music tours for instrumental and vocal groups alike: recent tours have taken in Barcelona (2014), Truro (2015), Prague (2016) and Belgium (2017). Our sacred choirs sing services regularly at cathedrals around the UK, having performed in Southwell Minster, as well as Coventry, Birmingham, Leicester, Gloucester and Worcester Cathedrals in the past couple of years. We put on a large-scale concert each spring at De Montfort Hall, involving all Year 7 pupils and other choirs performing a choral masterpiece (Carmina Burana, Mozart's Requiem, Verdi's Requiem) with our symphony orchestra.

Drama. The School has a fine Studio/Theatre and all boys in Years 6, 7 and 8 participate in a dramatic production. After that, there are productions for other age groups in conjunction with the Girls' High School each term.

Careers. Careers advisors are available to inform boys on options for their futures, with special regard to University or Professional careers. The School is a member of the Independent Schools Careers Organisation.

Academic successes. An average of 10 boys per year gain admission to Oxford and Cambridge, and over 98% each year begin degree courses at Universities.

The Loughburians Alumni Association. All former pupils of the Loughborough Schools Foundation have automatic free membership to the alumni association. All enquiries to loughburians@lsf.org.

Charitable status. Loughborough Schools Foundation is a Registered Charity, number 1081765, and a Company Limited by Guarantee, registered in England, number 4038033. Registered Office: 3 Burton Walks, Loughborough, Leicestershire LE11 2DU.

Chair: Mr Roger Harrison, MA Cantab, DipArch RIBA

***Headmaster*: Mrs H M Foster**, BA Greenwich, MEd Buckingham

Senior Leadership Team:
Deputy Head Academic: Mrs M C Herring, BSc St Andrews
Deputy Head Pastoral: Mr T Emmet
Assistant Head Operations: Dr T G Willmott, BSc, PhD London, MBA Leicester
Assistant Head Pupil Experience: Dr A D Waters, BSc Cantab, PhD Bristol

Magdalen College School
Oxford

Cowley Place, Oxford OX4 1DZ

Tel: 01865 242191
email: enquiries@mcsoxford.org
website: www.mcsoxford.org
X/Twitter: @MCSOxford
Facebook: @MCSOxfordUK
Instagram: @mcsoxford
LinkedIn: /school/magdalen-college-school-oxford-limited

Motto: *Sicut Lilium*

Magdalen College School consists of 640 boys aged 7–16 with a co-educational Sixth Form of 324. Academic standards are amongst the highest in the country and there is a strong emphasis on study beyond the syllabus, especially in the Waynflete Studies programme. This allows Sixth Formers to develop a personal project, which is finally supervised by university academics. Almost all pupils go on to higher education with about a third each year progressing to Oxford or Cambridge. The school seeks to develop the individuality and interests of each pupil. There is a strong emphasis on extracurricular activity, with particularly proud traditions in sport, music and drama.

History. Founded by William of Waynflete, Magdalen College School opened in 1480, and rapidly acquired an international reputation. Early Masters included Thomas Wolsey, early pupils Richard Hooker, John Foxe, Thomas More and William Tyndale. The school, which from an early stage provided choristers for the College choir, was accommodated entirely in College until the late 19th Century, when expanding numbers led to the acquisition and erection of buildings on the other side of the Cherwell, opposite the University Botanical Gardens and adjacent to St Hilda's College. Today's school still occupies this picturesque site.

Buildings. The school buildings include a Chapel which also serves as a theatre, a library, classrooms, science laboratories, Music School, Sports Complex, Design and Technology Rooms and an art department. In June 2001, a £2m sports complex was opened and in 2005, the school opened its new Sir Basil Blackwell Library. In Autumn 2008, The Michael Peagram Building was opened which houses a modern dining hall, the Art and Design department, Senior Common Room and reception area. In 2012, the Sports Hall was extended to incorporate a studio and additional classrooms, and a climbing wall was added. The state-of-the-art Richard Record Sixth Form Centre was completed in October 2017, including a cafeteria, study space and offices as well as the central social space.

Pastoral. From 7–11, boys are in form groups. Their Tutor is responsible for day-to-day care, pastoral welfare and academic progress. Boys from age 11 and Sixth Form girls are allocated to one of the six Houses. A Housemaster or Tutor in charge of each section is responsible for the pastoral and academic welfare of pupils in his or her Houseroom. The Heads of Departments, SENCO, Chaplain and Matron also play key roles in the pastoral organisation.

Organisation and Curriculum. All boys study a core of subjects to GCSE level, consisting of English, Maths, Science and at least one modern foreign language. In addition, there is a wide variety of options taken by pupils in their GCSE years including Latin and Greek, Geography, German, Spanish, History, Computing and Art. There is no streaming and very little setting.

Pupils study four subjects in the Lower Sixth and sit rigorous internal exams in the Trinity Term. Pupils have the opportunity to focus on three subjects in the Upper Sixth, but a significant proportion sit four or even five A Levels. MCS has a busy curriculum in the Sixth Form; as well as their A Levels, all pupils complete an independent research project (Waynflete Studies), have Games sessions and take part in our Community Service Programme. The provision is further enriched by a Thinking Skills programme and by regular seminars and lectures delivered by members of the MCS community and visiting speakers.

Careers. Careers Aptitude Tests are offered to all boys in the Upper Fourth Form, and there is a regular programme of careers workshops with support programmes for specific careers, e.g. Medicine. Most pupils undertake a work experience placement at the end of the Fifth Form; an extensive programme offering entrepreneurship opportunities from Year 9 upwards is in development.

Sports and Societies. In addition to Physical Education, which is taught in the curriculum, games play a major part in the School. Major sports are rugby in the Michaelmas Term, hockey and rowing in Hilary, and cricket, rowing and tennis in the Trinity Term. Other sports include basketball, netball, football, fencing, cross-country, sailing and athletics. There are Army and Air Force sections of the CCF and a Community Service Organisation. Many pupils participate in the Duke of Edinburgh's Award scheme.

The main playing field, surrounded by the River Cherwell, adjoins the grounds of School House and covers 11 acres. The school also enjoys the daily use of the adjacent Christ Church playing fields and regularly uses a number of other university sporting and cultural facilities. In addition, the school has use of the Magdalen College sports fields one mile from the School. Rowing takes place on the Cherwell from the school grounds.

Music is extremely important in the school and there is a large Choral Society, a Madrigal Group, Senior and Junior Orchestras, a Jazz Band and other ensembles. Many pupils are involved in drama and there are several productions in the year, including performances at theatres around Oxford. There are many other societies and clubs covering cultural and recreational activities. The main school concert is held annually in the Sheldonian Theatre. The school is the founder and main sponsor of the Oxford Festival of the Arts, an annual multi-disciplinary celebration, which features events, performances and community projects throughout the City.

Admissions. The main entry points are at 7, 11, 13 and 16. Around 25 boys are taken at 7, a further 15 or so at 8 and 9, and about 70 at the age of 11. Up to 25 boys are taken at 13. Around 60 boys and girls join the school directly into the Sixth Form.

Admission at ages 7, 8, 9 and 11 is by a School Entrance Examination held in January or February each year.

Admission at age 13 is by pre-test at 11 followed by the Common Entrance Examination for most candidates at preparatory schools and by a School Entrance Examination held in March each year for candidates at maintained schools.

Offers of Sixth Form places are made after interview, and are conditional on GCSE grades.

Candidates can be registered at any age. Full particulars can be obtained from the Registrar, email registrar@mcsoxford.org.

Term of Entry. Pupils enter the school in September. Exceptionally, for example if parents move into the Oxford area, other arrangements can be made.

Fees per term (2023–2024). £6,992 (Year 3 to 4); £7,259 (Year 5 to Sixth Form). They are payable in advance and are inclusive of textbooks and stationery. The Registration Fee (non-returnable) is currently £100 or £200 for overseas candidates. For the latest fees look at www.mcsoxford.org/fees.

Scholarships, Exhibitions and Bursaries. Scholarships, Exhibitions and Governors' Presentation Awards are awarded at all points of entry.

Bursaries are available subject to testing of parental means and many bursaries are supported through alumni gifts.

At age 13, up to 16 Scholarships of up to £300 are awarded each year based on the results of a two-day scholarship examination in February. Candidates should be under 14 on the subsequent 1 September. Closing date for entries: 11 January.

Music, Art, Drama and Sports Scholarships are awarded each year on the results of assessments held in January (Music), February (Art and Drama) and November (Sports). Music award holders also receive free tuition in one instrument.

Further information can be obtained from the Registrar.

Choristerships. There are 16 Choristerships. Entry is by Voice Trial and candidates should normally be between the ages of 7 and 9. For a Chorister two-thirds of the tuition fee is remitted. All enquiries about Choristerships should be addressed to the *Informator Choristarum, Magdalen College, Oxford OX1 4AU.* Choristers normally continue at the school after their voices have broken. In deserving cases, further financial help may be available.

Honours. Almost all pupils go on to higher education when they leave – to Oxford, Cambridge and other universities.

Old Waynfletes. The school has an active alumni network which supports social and professional activities and fundraising projects. Representative Old Waynfletes of the 20th century include Olympic athlete and soldier, Noel Chavasse, VC and bar; bookseller Sir Basil Blackwell; Nobel Prize winner Sir Tim Hunt; composer Ivor Novello; educationalist Tom Wheare; theatre director John Caird, film and theatre director Sir Sam Mendes, visual artist Julian Opie and sports commentators Nigel Starmer Smith and Jim Rosenthal.

Contact: Waynflete Office, Magdalen College School, email: waynfleteoffice@mcsoxford.org.

Charitable status. Magdalen College School Oxford Limited is a Registered Charity, number 295785. Its aims and objectives are to promote and provide for the education of children.

Governors:
Mr R J Price (*Chairman*)
Mr A D James (*Vice Chair*)
Mrs J A Phillips (*Vice Chair*)
Professor M R Bridson
Professor C C Coussios
Mr J M Hawker [OW]
Mr S R Hope
Mrs S Khan
Mr R J Langley
Mrs A F La Trobe Weston
Dr R R Phillips
Dr R A Saldanha
Mr B A M Vessey [OW]
Mr M Whitmore
Dr P N Withers

***Master*: Miss Helen L Pike**, MA Oxon, MA Michigan, MA London (*History*)

Usher: Mr T G Beaumont, MA Cantab (*History, Safeguarding Officer*)

Deputy Head (*Academic*): Mr B D White, BA Oxon (*Mathematics*)

Deputy Head (*Education Development*): Dr S R Crawford, BA Oxon, PhD (*Biology*)

Clerk to the Governors and Bursar: Mrs A H West, MA

PA to the Master: Mrs A Sweeney, BA

Registrar: Mrs A Green, BA

Director of the Waynflete Office: Mrs S J Baker, MA

The Manchester Grammar School

Old Hall Lane, Manchester M13 0XT

Tel: 0161 224 7201
email: general@mgs.org
website: www.mgs.org
X/Twitter: @mgs_1515
Facebook: @p/The-Manchester-Grammar-School-100088001140121
Instagram: @mgs_1515
LinkedIn: /the-manchester-grammar-school

Motto: *Sapere Aude – Dare to be Wise*

The Manchester Grammar School was founded in 1515 to promote 'godliness and good learning', and it has endeavoured throughout its history to remain true to these principles, whilst adapting to changing times. It is now an independent boys' day school with around 1,600 pupils. Almost all leavers go on to university, and there is a strong tradition of boys progressing to Oxford and Cambridge and other leading Russell Group universities. A number of pupils each year obtain offers from prestigious US universities. Over 150 qualified teaching staff provide all pupils with a broad, traditional and flexible curriculum; for example, boys may study up to five languages at GCSE, from a choice of Latin, Greek, French, German, Italian, Mandarin, Russian and Spanish. Courses studying Archaeology and Anthropology and Cyber Security and Cryptography are also available as part of the enrichment programme in the Sixth Form. The School offers a vast and diverse range of co-curricular opportunities.

The tradition of offering places to clever pupils regardless of their background is maintained by MGS bursaries. Approximately 200 pupils in the school receive means-tested bursaries. Our pupils come both from primary and preparatory schools and represent a wide variety of cultural, ethnic and religious backgrounds.

Registration and Entry. Entry to the Junior School is considered at age 7, 8, 9 and 10, subject to availability at any stage during the academic year. Junior School pupils progress automatically to the Senior School. Entry for most other boys joining the School is at age 11, although entry at other ages is considered, subject to availability and applicants for Sixth Form entry are particularly welcomed. At all levels the normal assessment for entry involves prospective pupils spending a day in School, being taught and assessed in small groups. Alongside these assessment days, there is an entrance exam for entry at age 11. Sixth Form entrants have to meet GCSE grade requirements. Further details are available from the Admissions Office.

Fees per term (2023–2024). £15,180 per year, or £5,060 per term.

Bursaries. 200 pupils currently receive full or partial bursaries. Bursary places are available for boys joining Years 3 and 4, Year 7 and the Sixth Form, with the majority of funding being offered for entry in Year 7, and are only offered to families who are permanently resident in the UK, and living the North West of England, at the point of application. The School's ability to offer bursaries depends upon the level of funding available. The School does not offer academic scholarships.

Junior School. The Junior School opened in September 2008 in award-winning accommodation. It admits boys from age 7 and currently has approximately 240 pupils. There is a strong focus in its curriculum on creativity, academic enrichment and skills-based learning. Specialist teachers from the Senior School contribute to the academic enrichment in Years 5 and 6.

Senior School Organisation and Curriculum. During the first two years, the boys will study English, Mathematics, a modern foreign language (French, German, Russian, Spanish and Mandarin Chinese are offered), Classics (including Latin) History, Geography, General Science, Religious Studies, PSHE, Computing, Music, Art & Design, Drama, PE, Swimming and Games. Greek, Italian and Electronics are introduced as options in Year 9; there is also the opportunity for pupils who have not already done so to take up languages offered in Year 7. In Year 10, pupils may opt to study for an AS Extended Project Qualification; Classical Civilisation is also offered. Pupils make GCSE choices towards the end of Year 9 and typically take ten subjects, including Mathematics, English, English Literature, a language and at least one science subject.

In the Sixth Form, A Level and Pre-U courses are offered, with each department selecting the course which offers the best preparation for university; in addition, all pupils participate in the School's own non-examined enrichment programme, which includes a philosophical and critical thinking course (Perspectives).

Pastoral Care. Each form in the school is looked after by a Tutor, who is responsible, with the appropriate senior members of staff, for the academic and general progress of each pupil. In the Senior School Tutors work with no more than 13 boys. Regular written reports are supplemented by Parents' Evenings. The School Medical Room is staffed by a part-time doctor and two full-time Nursing staff. The older pupils selected as prefects are encouraged to help younger pupils in running societies and other co-curricular activities.

Creative Arts. All pupils experience Music, Art & Design and Drama within the curriculum; in addition, each of these areas offers activities to large numbers of pupils during the lunch-hour and after school. There are choirs, orchestras and instrumental tuition; plays, drama workshops and musicals; clubs for art, pottery, and computer design. There are regular exhibitions and public performances both in school and in public venues. The School has a well-equipped theatre and drama studios, providing many opportunities for pupils both to perform and provide technical support for productions.

Sport. All boys take part in timetabled games and the school produces successful teams in most sports. A new sports hall opened in 2015 and a water-based hockey pitch was added in 2018; there are extensive playing fields, a gymnasium, indoor swimming pool, squash courts, tennis courts and fitness suite. The choice of sport increases with age, to include rowing and climbing in addition to mainstream sports. The importance of positive competition and the value of teamwork are understood very strongly here. Our philosophy in sport is that every boy is important to us and can develop as sportsmen irrespective of his starting point. We also have sporting programmes in place which enable the better sportsmen to achieve their true potential. Specialist coaches help develop the skills of players, and many members of the teaching staff manage teams and deliver coaching sessions themselves, helping to form close bonds between boys and teachers. Boys in the Junior School also participate in a range of sports (with a 100% participation rate in our major games of rugby, football, hockey, and cricket), with current pupils performing at an Elite level within Gymnastics, representing GB U12 Tennis and affiliated to elite football clubs. Swimming and Water-Polo are a cornerstone of PE & Sport at MGS including our individualised swim development programme which caters for those less able in the water. Water-Polo teams enjoy national success across all age groups while our swimmers attend all ESSA and HMC national competitions. We do not offer sports scholarships; however, our Elite Performer Programme supports our high-achieving sportsmen and balances the demands on leading performers in multiple sports. In recent years, we have supported our national individual sportsmen in sailing, windsurfing, cycling and fencing, to complement the achievements of boys within teams.

Outdoor Pursuits. The school has a long tradition of camping and trekking and there are numerous weekend and holiday excursions. The School is the largest centre for D of E in the North West. Mountain activity days are offered most weekends, free of charge. Four annual camps cater for the full age range and offer a wide choice of activities. In recent years expeditions have visited the Alps, the Pyrenees, Morocco and Scandinavia. The School has two centres in Cumbria and one in Derbyshire.

Foreign Visits. Many trips abroad are organised each year, providing enjoyable holidays of broad educational value. Destinations include France, Germany, Spain, Russia, Italy, Greece, Mexico, Argentina, Peru, Mexico, Egypt, Tunisia, South Africa, India and China.

Societies and Activities. There are over 100 clubs and activities available to boys at The Manchester Grammar School, and pupils can also start their own clubs. Across the school, there are over 70 regular clubs and society activities, over and above those connected with Music, Sport, Outdoor Pursuits and Volunteering. These mainly take place at lunchtime and after school. Post-covid there has been a huge resurgence, especially in Chess, Pottery and Bridge among others. It is a joy to watch boys duelling at chess while eating their sandwich lunches or the ever present Latin Scrabble Club! Boys often organise new activities, for example, the new Year 7 Engineers are currently dreaming of launching a rocket. At the senior end, MUN is very popular and busy, while clubs such as Berkeley Society, Wildlife Soc, Pi Shop (Mathematics), Doc. Soc. and Eng. Soc., which are all led by pupils, flourish.

Prizes and Scholarships. In addition to bursaries, funds are provided for grants to help deserving pupils with the expense of a range of co-curricular activities. Prizes are awarded in all subjects in the curriculum.

Old Mancunians' Association and MGS Parents' Society. The Old Boys' Association has a well developed network all over the world. There is an annual Old Boys' Dinner in Manchester with further events in the UK and overseas. The Development Office Administrator is Julie Wright, who can be reached at the School.

The MGS Parents' Society has a membership of parents and friends and exists to support school activities and promote a programme of social events.

Charitable status. The Manchester Grammar School is a Registered Charity which provides Public Benefit. The aim of the School is to prepare able boys from the Manchester area, regardless of their financial background, to proceed to university and make a positive contribution to society in their adult life.

Governors:
Dr David Barker
Mr Allan Beardsworth
Mrs Clare Bolton (*Chair*)
Professor David A Cardwell
Ms Joy Kingsley
Mr Brandon Leigh (*Treasurer*)
Mrs Jane Luca
Dr Helen Moore
Dr Jonathan R W Prag
Mr Robert Race
Mr Michael Robinson
Mr John Young

Ex officio Governors:
The Dean of Manchester
The Lord Mayor of Manchester

Bursar and Clerk to the Governors: Mrs G M Batchelor, BSc

***High Master*: Dr M A Boulton**, BEng, PhD

Deputy High Master: Mrs M A S Lowe, BA, MPhil, MEd

Academic Deputy Head: B Bowles, MEng, MMath
Academic Deputy Head Teaching and Learning: D O Lacey, BA, MEd
Deputy Head Safeguarding & Designated Safeguarding Lead: D Farr, MA
Deputy Head Pastoral & Deputy Designated Safeguarding Lead: S Crawshaw, BSc, MA, PhD
Surmaster & Head of Co-Curriculum: J W Mangnall, MA
Head of Junior School: E R Losse, MA
Director of Development: S P Jones, BA, MBA
Head of Lower School: P W Freeman, BSc, MSc
Head of Middle School: P J Higgins, BSc
Head of Sixth Form: M D Corbett, BSc
Assistant Head: S Foster, BA, MA
Proctors: S E Jones, BA; D M Taylor, BA
Director of Admissions: D L Virr, BSc
Director of Studies: D Jeys, BSc, MA

Academic Staff:
* *Head of Department/Subject*

Art and Design:
R E Berry, BA
K Davidson, BA, MA
J Dobbs, BA, MAEd
L J Murphy, BA, MA*
S Taylor, BA

Biology:
J Blair, BSc*
S G Crawshaw, BSc, MA, PhD
P W Freeman, BSc
E Loh, BSc, MSc, PhD
N A Loughlin, BSc
C Morgan, BSc
N Rowlands, BSc, MSc
E Tal, BA
A Wicking, BA

Chemistry:
I Airth, BSc
C Buckley, BSc
M Facchini, BSc, MSc
S Graham, MSci, PhD
H M Hughes, BSc
T C James, BSc
H Martin, MChem
F C Roberts, MChem*
G M Tinker, MEng

Classics:
L D Hopkins, BA, MPhil, DPhil
F E Hunt, BA
E Nabney, BA, MA, PhD
C A Owens, BA, MA*
S R Sharma, BA, MPhil
C Sykes, BA, MA
N G Williams, BA

Computing:
R Brown, BSc
B J Charlton, MSci
D E Millington, MSc, BSc*
D Soon, BSc, MBA, MBCS

Duke of Edinburgh:
M D Rollinson, BSc, MEd
S Wild*

Drama:
H Baldwin, BA
J Best, BA
M J Nichols, BA*
J Sherratt, BA
K Tetley, BA

Economics:
I Iliffe, BA, MBA
G R McSherry, BSc*
A E Rigler, BA
D Wilson, BA, MA

Electronics:
D P Smith, MEng, PhD*

English:
R E Adams, MA, MA
E C Appleton, BA, MA
A Dixon, BA
J L Geldard, BA, MA, MA
J Grant, BA, MEd
R Keep, MA Cantab, PGDipEd
A Lloyd-Hughes, BA
C E McCarthy, BA, MA
I McConnell, BA, MA
H Sargeant, BA, MA
B Townsend, BA
S Van der Ouderaa, MA
J Welsh, BA, MA
L F Williamson, BA, MA*

General Science:
H Beaumont, MEng
D W Inglis, BSc, PhD*
D L Virr, BSc

Geography:
F C G Baker, BA
M D Corbett, BSc
A Curry, BSc
P J Higgins, BSc
J W Mangnall, MA
M A Nowell, BSc
L E Price, BA, MA, PhD
M D Rollinson, BSc, MEd
S P G Spratling, BA
P J Wheeler, BSc*

History:
G R Barker, MA
N Carter, MA
K Edwards, BA
A R T Hern, BA MPhil, MPhil*
J Hopkins, BA, MA, PhD
D O Lacey, BA, MEd
M A S Lowe, BA, MPhil, MEd
S Orth, BA, MA, PhD
W B Pye, BA
A M Smith, MA
M G P Strother, MA, MPhil, MSt
D M Taylor, BA

Junior School:
C T Ashurst, BA, MEd
J M Aspinall, BA
K V Atty, BA
D R Barnett, BEd
J M Barnett, BA
A J Bentley, LLB
A G Bird, BSc
C E Boddington, BSc
S C Callaghan, BA
C Daly, BA
L I Doyle, BEd

D D Freeborn, BA
T O Glennie, BA
N J Grundy, BA
F E Jones, BSc
E R Losse, MA* (*Head of the Junior School*)
S Mercer-Murray, BMus
J Robinson, BA
E Thompson
L Wass, BEd

Teaching Assistants:
L L Birch[2]
C M Burke[2]
S Butt[2]
J S Caverly[2]
K Faulkner[2]
E Malik[2]
C Mercer[2]
S Reed[2]
N Reynolds[2]
J Robinson[2]
C Shovlar[2]
V Tierney[2]

Mathematics:
J K Allinson, BA, MA
J P Barker, BSc
B Bowles, MEng, MMath
A E Carolan, BSc
A R Davies, BSc, MSc
T J Dessain, MMATH, PhD
L Devlin, MSci
A Graham, BA, MA, PhD*
D Jeys, BSc, MA
I Z Khan, BSc
M Lawley, MSci, PhD
L Lawrence, MMath
S J Leigh, BEng
O W J Llewellyn-Smith, BSc
J L McMillan, BSc, MA
G J Morris, BSc
D V Naughton, MM, PhD
J Parkinson-Jones, MMATH
T J Pattison, BSc, MIMA, CMath
R Varro-Zelena
R T Watt, BSc

Modern Foreign Languages:
D Bannatyne, MA
P J Chadwick, BA, MA, DPhil
K David, MA
A P Dobson, BA, MA
A V Hemsworth, BA*
J A Houghton, BA*
A Jacinto, BA*
S E Jones, BA, MEd
R Lan, BA, MA*
S Lu, BA
D Minguito-Pantoja, BA
M Morato
R J Neal, BA, MA, MEd
S J Paulson, BA
E Rayers, BA
G Rrugeja
N J Sharples, BA, MA*
C J Shaw, BA
L Speed, Mosc Dipl*
E Stafford, BA

Language Assistants:
G Bozzi[1]
C Granger[1]
G Hernandez
A Schutz[1]
N Vazquez Miro[1]
E Velardi[1]
M Zhao[1]

Music:
G Blackwell
F A Bradley, BMus
H Butchart, BA, LTCL, ARCM
R M Carey, MA*
E L Jackson, BMus

PSHE:
C E McCarthy, BA, MA*

Physical Education:
T A Grainger, BSc, MA
R F Jennings, BA
A Khares
J L Leggett, BA
D R Paddon
M J Roe, BSc
S Swindells, RFU II, RFU III
W Van Zyl, BSc
M Watkinson, Levels 1–4 Coaching Cricket*
G Wilson, Euro I
T C Young, BA

Physics:
M A Boulton, BEng, PhD
N W Davenport, BEng
J Holt, BSc, DPhil*
A J Marsden, MSc, PhD
S H McGarry, BEng, MSc
R W Morley, BSc, MA
S U Riley, BEng, PhD
M Saghir, MSc, BSc, PhD
D P Smith, MEng, PhD
L Thewles, BSc

Politics:
S Foster, BA, MA, LLB
E C Kilheeney, PhD, BA, MA*

Religion and Philosophy:
M W Bolton, MA
A Brower Latz, BA, MA, PhD*
M P A Coffey, MA, MA
D Farr, MA
A Greggs, BA
J Kenny, BA, MA
N D Raven, BD, MTH
A N Smith, BA
R Malhotra[2]
I Merlo[2]
L Merlo, BA, MA
H E Sargeant, BA, MA

SEND:
A V Batchelor, BSc, MA
H Butchart, BA, LTCL, ARCM*
R Daws, BSc, MEd

* head of department
[1] language assistant
[2] teaching assistant
[2] SEND assistant

PA to the High Master: P Harrison
Admissions Office Manager: K Heathcote

Marlborough College

Bath Road, Marlborough, Wiltshire SN8 1PA

Tel: 01672 892200 (Main Switchboard)
01672 892400 (The Master's Office)
01672 892300 (Admissions)
email: master@marlboroughcollege.org
admissions@marlboroughcollege.org
website: www.marlboroughcollege.org
X/Twitter: @marlboroughcol
Instagram: @marlboroughcollege

Founded 1843. Incorporated by Royal Charter.

The College is fully co-educational and full boarding. There are 1,015 boys and girls in the 16 Houses and the usual age of entry is either 13 or 16.

Registration. For entry to the College at 13+ registrations are accepted from four years before entry. The College assesses the majority of applicants in the January of Year 6 and offers are made for approximately 75% of places. There is a second entry point in the January of Year 7 when approximately 20% of places will be offered. The final 5% of places will be offered in Year 8. All applicants to the College must meet our entry criteria and take either the Academic Scholarship or the Common Entrance examination. Children whose schools do not prepare them for Common Entrance will have alternative arrangements and parents should contact the Admissions Department directly. The 13+ Scholarship examinations take place in March prior to entry in September. Sixth Form entry and Scholarship examination is in the November before entry. Registrations for entry at 16+ must be made before the 1st of October in the year before entry.

Bursaries. Bursaries of up to 100% of the fees are available for candidates for both 13+ and 16+ entry and the College offers a limited number of bursaries for the children of Clergy. Uniform and other costs can also be included dependent on need. All bursaries, including those for Clergy places, are awarded on a means-tested basis and applications must be submitted by the 1st July of the academic year in which the child takes their entry assessment. Places for candidates requiring a bursary grant are awarded via our standard assessment procedures according to our Bursary Policy, which is available on the website.

Scholarships. There are up to 8 Academic Scholarships at 13+ and a further 22 Awards in Music, Art, Design Technology, Drama and Sport. Up to 20 awards are made at Sixth Form entry.

A Scholarship Prospectus and copies of past papers may be obtained from the Admissions Office. Applications and enquiries about entries and scholarships should be addressed to The Director of Admissions, tel: 01672 892300; email: admissions@marlboroughcollege.org.

Academic. The College's curriculum follows and extends the National Curriculum to allow for a proper combination of breadth and specialisation. It is designed to stimulate, challenge and support all pupils and to ensure that they maximise their potential. There is a clear focus placed upon success in public examinations, where standards are very high, but the College prioritises pupil success at higher education and in their subsequent careers.

Almost all pupils go on to study at university either in the United Kingdom (approximately 80% annually to Russell Group universities) or, increasingly, overseas with destinations ranging from Europe to North America and beyond.

In the Lower School a wide-ranging curriculum is followed. Central to this is "Form", an innovative and unique humanities course which embraces English, History and Religious Studies. It gives pupils a sense of the history, the evolution of human culture and our place within it. It aims to develop the skills and habits of mind that will lead to success at the College and beyond – wide reading, critical analysis, synthesis and evaluation of ideas, the confidence to have a go and voice their opinions. Choices are made at the end of the Shell (Year 9) leading to 10 or 11 GCSEs and IGCSEs. In the Sixth Form, pupils choose from over 30 A Levels, as well as having the option to take an Extended Project (in which the College is a large and successful centre) and further language options, including Arabic and Hebrew.

The curriculum is supported by an enormous range of academic extension and enrichment activities through societies, lectures, theatre trips, museum and gallery visits, debates, poetry readings, conferences, and concerts, creating a full co-curriculum which recognises that qualifications alone do not produce an educated person.

Careers. Nearly all pupils who come to Marlborough go on into the Sixth Form and virtually all proceed to degree courses. The well-resourced Futures Department is located at the heart of the College and assists Housemasters and Housemistresses in advising boys and girls and their parents about Sixth Form subject selection, higher education options, gap year projects, work experience and careers. Each year, a good number of pupils take up Oxbridge and medical places, and around 10% move on to universities overseas. The College is an ACT testing centre (for those considering North American universities).

Sports and Activities. Sports facilities are outstanding. There are two first class floodlit AstroTurf pitches, acres of sports pitches, allowing for at least 20 simultaneous games in the field sports, a newly re-laid athletics track, a sports hall, an 8-lane 25m swimming pool with hydraulic floor, 24 tennis courts, six fives courts, four squash courts, two rackets courts and nine netball courts. The main sports for boys are rugby, hockey, cricket, athletics, tennis and football, and for girls, hockey, netball, cricket, tennis, lacrosse and athletics. Alternative sports include aerobics, badminton, basketball, clay pigeon shooting, dance, fencing, fishing, fives, golf, jiu jitsu, rackets, riding, rugby sevens, shooting, squash, swimming, water polo, watt biking and yoga. There are regular fixtures in many of these sports and several run sports tours and pre-season trips. Tours have included boys' and girls' cricket to South Africa, netball to Barbados, lacrosse to the USA, rugby to France and hockey to the Netherlands and Spain (both boys' and girls'). The shooting team enters both the Schools' Cup and the Imperial Cup at Bisley each year.

An Outdoor Activities Department offers the Gold and Silver Duke of Edinburgh's Award, canoeing, climbing, kayaking and mountain biking. The annual Devizes to Westminster kayak race has become a feature of the Lent Term for up to 10 Upper School crews. The school has its own indoor climbing wall and there is a weekly Climbing Club. There are numerous OA activities each Sunday in term-time in House groups and more adventurous trips further afield in the school holidays. Recent trips have been to the Brecon Beacons, Snowdonia, Nepal, Peru and Iceland. The Gold Duke of Edinburgh's Award Training, Practice and Assessed Expeditions take place in school holidays and half-terms.

The College's Combined Cadet Force is thriving. It is compulsory for part of Year 10 and optional thereafter. It provides excellent leadership training and there is a strong record of College pupils winning Sixth Form Army Scholarships. All year groups take part in Field Days or CCF Camps both in the UK and abroad; the Upper School cadets have visited the US Navy Seals in California on four recent occasions.

Outreach and Partnerships. The College also offers a comprehensive Outreach Programme in the local community. The mantra "with privilege comes responsibility" is the underlying philosophy. Many of the pupils are involved with local primary schools, Riding for the Disabled and local environmental projects, amongst others. The College has a partnership with Swindon Academy which involves College staff and pupils providing academic support. Swindon Academy Year 7 and Year 8 pupils visit the College weekly and also attend some themed residential weekends at the College. In the Summer Term, the Lower Sixth pupils help to run a Primary Club for local 4–7 year olds.

Recently the College has started to provide Maths mentoring to pupils in Slough and Swindon, using the Colet Mentoring platform. In addition, pupils use TWIN science kits to capture the interest of talented local primary school children in STEM subjects. EdClub, an online mentoring scheme with children in Kenya, was founded at the College and pupils in the Hundred and Lower Sixth are in contact with their mentees on a weekly basis.

Trips and Societies. The College has a large array of thriving academic and intellectual societies which complement and support the academic programme, attracting impressive speakers each term from across a broad section of disciplines. There is a programme of Day Trips in term time and, usually, Study Trips in the holidays, which support and enrich the academic curriculum. Recent examples include Geography to China, Iceland and Tenerife, History of Art to Italy, Politics to Bosnia, Classics to Greece, English to Ireland, and Physics to CERN and Florida. The Modern Languages Department runs a series of exchanges and trips to language schools in the target country.

Music. Marlborough nurtures every level of musical talent through inspired coaching within a dynamic and energetic environment. Access to a diverse range of solo, chamber, ensemble, band, choral and orchestral mediums provide invaluable experience to perform. We regularly gain excellent academic results both for GCSE Music, A level Music and Music Technology. A high percentage of pupils go on to study Music at conservatoire or university and we celebrate Oxbridge entrance success and choral scholarship awards most years. Approximately 55% of our pupils have music lessons, and highlights of the music calendar include a Music Scholars' Gala Concert at the Royal Academy, our annual collaboration with the Southbank Sinfonia and our whole-school events such as the House Harmony and the House Shout. We have a world-class concert facility in the Memorial Hall, our magnificent Chapel for choral concerts and two additional theatre spaces, plus informal recital areas.

Drama. Drama at Marlborough is all about collaboration, creative debate, experimentation and excellence. With many productions every year, diversity of style is at the heart of what we offer; from contemporary productions of classical tragedy to musicals and farcical comedy. Independent productions give the opportunity for pupils to write, direct and produce, working alongside visiting practitioners and influenced by the wide range of touring productions that visit our three well-equipped theatres. Trips to the theatre are enjoyed frequently being within visiting distance of London, Bristol, Oxford and Stratford. Drama is offered as an option in the Shell (Year 9) and then is a popular choice at both GCSE and A Level.

Fine Art and Photography. Art at Marlborough has been respected nationally and internationally across the last half century for the delivery of visual excellence. Our success lies in the fact that Art staff believe in every pupil's individuality and potential to fully realise their artistic ambitions. Pupils are able to steer their creative journey through an exploration or 2 & 3D processes including sculpture, ceramics, textiles, drawing, printmaking, painting and film, along with digital and traditional darkroom photography.

The Art School is a happening place with a plethora of activities: visiting artists, exhibitions and trips. We have forged strong and lasting links with the British Museum, the Royal Society of Painter-Printmakers in London, Verso Art Charity, Preshute Primary School, Aberystwyth University St Barbe Museum and Art Gallery, and Eames Fine Art.

Our Art department has an exceptional track record in preparing pupils for first choice destinations in higher education. Over the past two years we have placed 28 pupils on a range of leading foundation and degree courses all over the world.

Opened in 2005, our purpose-built Art School houses five open-plan studios for painting, drawing, relief and intaglio printmaking, screen printing, a photography darkroom and studio; lecture room and a computer suite and a well-resourced Art library. Two buildings adjacent to the Art School accommodate the ceramics and sculpture studios as well as a 'large scale drawing' studio. A particular bonus for our Upper Sixth Art pupils is that they are each given their own individual studio work-station. We also have a dedicated gallery and archive space in 'The Mount Gallery'.

Design and Technology. The Design Department recently located to the Beko Innovation Centre and consists of a large multi-disciplinary design studio with integrated digital design tools. The main studio offers a flexible space for large-scale prototyping and focused design education, as well as a base for engineering, computer science, entrepreneurship and other disciplines, to engage with the space. We also have a separate workshop area with our new CNC machine and an array of more manufacturing-focused equipment. The department has invested in 3D-printing equipment which is used across all year groups and by wider members of the Marlborough community and this is housed in our Design Study; a space intended for sixth form to engage in independent design practice which also houses our design library. We also have outbuildings which accommodate our wood preparation equipment, spray booth, metalworking and heat treatment areas.

Fees per term (2023–2024). £15,665.

The Marlburian Club. www.marlburianclub.org.

Charitable Status. Marlborough College is a Registered Charity, number 309486 incorporated by Royal Charter to provide education.

Visitor: The Most Revd The Lord Archbishop of Canterbury

Council:
President: The Rt Revd The Lord Bishop of Salisbury
Mrs P Cameron Watt, MA Hons (*Acting Chair*)
M Birkin, BA
J P W Coleman, LLB
P Denton, MSc, ACA
Mrs T Freeman, BA
The Revd S Gray, BA, MA, PGCE
K Kabwe
T D Martin-Jenkins, MA, MBA
Ms R King, MA
R Perrins, BSc, FCA
Mrs S Reeves, MA, MPhil

International Council:
Y A M Tunku Ali Redhauddin ibni Tuanku Muhriz, BA, MC/MPA

***Master*: L J Moelwyn-Hughes**, MA, MEd

Second Master: S M Wessels, BSc
Bursar: A Hart, BA
Deputy Head (*Academic*): D T Clark, MTheol
Deputy Head (*Pastoral*): E C Nightingale, MA
Deputy Head (*Co-Curriculum*): J R B Scragg, MA
Director of Admissions: J J Lyon Taylor, BSc
Director of Safeguarding: Mrs C Kane, BA, MSc
Assistant Head (*Teaching & Learning*): Mrs B E A Nightingale, BA
Assistant Head (*Inspection*): T C M Lauze, BA, MBA
Head of Boarding: Mrs J A Hodgson, BSc, MA

Assistant Staff:
* *Head of Department*
† *Housemasters/Housemistresses*

Miss A L Adderley, BA (†*New Court*)
B R Allen, MA
M W Alleyne (**Cricket*)
N M Allott, BSc
D I Andrew, MA, MSci (**Economics & Business*)
A J Arkwright, BA (**Instrumental Studies*)
D R Armitage, MA (†*B House*)
Miss S H Bingham, BA
J M Birchall, BSc
T A Birkill, BSc (**Biology*)
M B Blossom, MA
Ms V R Brown, MA
Mrs R L T Bruce, BA
A A Burke, MA
M P L Bush, BA
M Butterfield, MA (*Organist*)
J P Carroll, BEd (**Upper Sixth*)
S C Clayton, BA
M Conlen, BSc
Mrs H A M Cox, BSc (†*Elmhurst*)
J R Cox, BA
Ms M A D'Angelo, BA (**Spanish*)
Miss J Darby, BA, GMus
R G De Rosa, BSc (**Geography*)
A H de Trafford, MA (†*Turner House*)
Miss V G M Delalleau, BA
S J Dennis, MBE, MSc
T J Dolan, MSc (**Computer Science*)
Dr G A Doyle, MSc, PhD, DIC, CChem, MRSC (**Science*)
P T Dukes, FGSM, ARAM (**Artistic Director*)
J J Duplock, MA
S Earwicker, MPhil
O P Elton, BA (**Mathematics*)
M A Eysele, BSc
Dr S D Flatres, MSci, PhD
C A Fraser, MA
Mrs J L Fruci, BA (†*Morris*)
Miss O Gallagher, BSc
W H Gibbs, BSc
B W Giles, MA
T P Gilmour (**Rugby*)
N O P Gordon, MA (**English*, *Form*)
Miss L S Gray, BSc
Mrs H Green, MSc (**SENDCO*)
P E D Green, MA
Miss O F Grimley, BSc
C L Harrison, BSc (†*Summerfield*)
S R Hawthorn, BSc (†*Preshute*)
Mrs E R Hayes, MA (**French*)
Mrs K Heaton, MA (**Politics*)
J Hodgson, BSc (**PSHEE*)
Mrs K Holder, MA (**Chemistry*)
Mrs R F Horton, MA (**Director of Sport*)
Miss K J Hvass, BA
Miss J C Isitt, BA
G James, BSc (**Astronomy*, *Director of the Blackett Observatory*)
Dr R J Justice, MA, DPhil
D Kenworthy, BA, MFA (**Drama*)
Mrs K J Kiggell, MA (†*Dancy House*)
T A Kiggell, MA
G D M Lane, BSc (†*C3*)
J T W Lane, BA
Miss A C Langdale, MSc (**Futures*)
Ms Q Li, MA (**Mandarin Chinese*)
Mrs D L Lilley, MA
J F Lloyd, MPhil (**Classics*)
Mrs J L Luker, BSc (**Psychology*)
G I Macmillan, BA (†*Cotton House*)
D J Madden, BEng (**Design and Technology*)
Mrs H J C Marvin, BSc (**Lacrosse* †*Ivy House*)
T G R Marvin, MA
Mrs J McClean, BA
Dr F S McKeown, BA, PhD (**History of Art*)
M McNally, BSc
G J McSkimming, BSc (†*Barton Hill*)
A O J Meehan-Staines, BA (*Choirmaster*)
Mrs H L Meehan-Staines, BSc (**Director of Digital Learning*)
B H Miller, BSc
W J Molyneux, BA
J J L Moore, MA
N J L Moore, MA
P N Morley-Fletcher, MA (**Italian*)
C A F Moule, MA (**History*, *Academic Scholarship & Leadership Programme*)
Mrs E J P Moule, MA
J N Newman, BSc
P J Newman, BA
P J O'Sullivan, BA
A G Oxburgh, BA (**Oxbridge*)
J H Parnham, MA
Mrs E J Penrose, MA
G R Playfair, MA (†*C2*)
J M Quinn, BA
Miss T C Rainer, MA (**German*)
M S Ramage (**Hockey*)
Dr L J Richards, BSc, PhD
Dr D G Roberts, MSc, PhD
Dr E Ryder, BSc, PhD
Mrs M C Sandall, BA
R A Sandall, BCom, BA
Mrs R Scott, MA
M J Sharrad, BSc (**PE*)
C S Smith, BEng, MSc
Mrs E C Smith, BA
K G A Smith, BA
Dr J P Swift, BSc, PhD (†*C1*)
I R Thorp, MMath, PhD
H L R Tilney, BA (†*Littlefield*)
R Tong (**Outdoor Activities*)
Miss C Toomer, GGSM (**Academic Music*)
E F J Twohig, MA, MFA (**Art*)
Mrs S K Walker MSc (†*Mill Mead*)
C J Wheatland, MPhys (**Physics*)
R D Willmett, BA (**Lower Sixth*)
Mrs A T Woodford, BA (**Modern Languages*)
Miss B L Woods, MSc (**Religious Studies*)
J Wright, BSc

Senior Chaplain: The Revd T W G Novis, BA, Mdiv
Medical Officer: Dr A Collings, MB, BS, DCH
Librarian: J E Burton, BA
Master's Assistant: Mrs G Milne

Merchant Taylors' School

Sandy Lodge, Northwood, Middlesex HA6 2HT

Tel: 01923 821850 (Head Master's PA)
01923 820644 (Reception)
01923 845514 (Admissions Officer)
01923 825669 (Bursar)
email: info@mtsn.org.uk
website: www.mtsn.org.uk
X/Twitter: @MerchantTaylors
Facebook: @MerchantTaylors
Instagram: @merchanttaylorsschool
LinkedIn: /merchanttaylorsschoolnorthwood

Motto: *Concordia parvae res crescunt*

The school has enjoyed a distinguished history since its foundation by the Merchant Taylors' Company in 1561. It was one of the nine original "Clarendon" public schools and its pupils have achieved distinction throughout its history. The school enjoys close links with the Company, which, to this day, constitutes its Governing Body. In 1933 the school moved from central London to its present superb, rural setting of 280 acres at Sandy Lodge, Northwood. We are within easy reach of parents in Buckinghamshire, Hertfordshire, Middlesex and North-West London by car, train or school coach service, as well as a mere half hour by tube from Baker Street.

Four distinct boys' day schools share the campus. The nursery school, pre-prep and prep cater for 330 boys from 3 to 13 years of age (the prep school shares some of its facilities with the senior school, but is a separate school in its own right), while the senior school has approximately 890 pupils from 11–18, with over 300 in the sixth form.

All pupils have an individual tutor who looks after them during their school career in small House tutor groups. They are encouraged to cultivate interests at which they can excel, to have confidence in their abilities and to gain self-knowledge as well as knowledge. The academic achievements of the school are first-rate and are achieved in a humane, civilised and unpressured atmosphere. We place a great emphasis on encouraging boys to organise many activities themselves and to take responsibility for others.

Admission. Entry to the senior school at 11+ and 13+ is by the School's own Entrance Examinations, together with an interview; for entry to the Prep school, see Merchant Taylors' Prep entry in the IAPS section. 16+ applications are invited after the publication of GCSE results. Applicants should have at least seven top grades at GCSE.

Term of entry. September unless there are very special circumstances.

Scholarships and Bursaries. There are no separate Scholarship papers in the Entrance Examinations. We make awards to boys who perform exceptionally well in these examinations and at a separate interview; we take into account information received from the boy's current school.

11+ entry: At least 5 major Academic Scholarships are awarded, each up to a maximum value of 50% of the School fee. Up to 5 minor Academic Scholarships each to the value of £200 per annum. Up to 2 All-Rounder scholarships, each up to a maximum value of 50% of the School fee. Scholarships for Sport, Art, Design Technology & Drama (a maximum of 2 per subject) each to the value of a £200 department programme and associated materials.

13+ entry: At least 5 major Academic Scholarships are awarded, each up to a maximum value of 50% of the School fee. Up to 12 minor Academic Scholarships each with a minimum value of £200 per annum. Up to 2 All-Rounder scholarships each up to a maximum value of 50% of the School fee. Up to 8 scholarships for Sport, Art, Design Technology & Drama (a maximum of 2 per subject) each to the value of a £200 department programme and associated materials.

16+ entry: Entrance Scholarships are available across the disciplines of Engineering; Bio-Medicine; Finance and Economics; Languages; Humanities; Creative Arts and Technology. Each up to a maximum value of 50% of the School fee. One bursary up to the value of the full School fee is available.

Music Scholarships: Four Music Scholarships (one of up to 25% of the School fee; one of up to 15% and two of up to 10%) awarded across 11+, 13+ and 16+. A Scholarship includes free instrumental and/or singing tuition on two instruments (or instrument and voice). Additional awards of free tuition may be made if there are boys of sufficient merit.

All Scholarships can be supplemented by means-tested bursaries should there be a proven need.

Bursaries: The School welcomes applications from parents whose sons would benefit from attending Merchant Taylors' School, and who will contribute strongly to the life of the community, but who require financial assistance. Means-tested bursarial support is available up to the value of 100% of the School fee; further details can be obtained from the Admissions Office.

Scholarships at Oxford and Cambridge Universities. At the end of their first undergraduate year, Old Boys are eligible for election to a maximum of three Sir Thomas White Scholarships at St John's College Oxford, a Matthew Hale Scholarship at The Queen's College Oxford and a Parkin & Stuart Scholarship for Science or Mathematics at Pembroke College Cambridge.

Curriculum and Organisation. The curriculum in years 7, 8 and 9 (Thirds, Upper Thirds and Fourths) is a broad one: Art and Design, Biology, Chemistry, Computing, Design Technology, Drama, English, French, Geography, History, Latin, Mathematics, Music, Physical Education, Physics, PSHCE, and Religious Studies. Greek, German, or Spanish are started when 13+ boys enter the school. All boys take nine or ten GCSEs, chosen from the subjects above. Boys are entered for IGCSEs and GCSEs. A student entering the Lower Sixth embarks upon a two-year course in which all boys initially study four subjects to A Level, with most certifying three and some four. An extensive choice of super-curricular options is available, including the EPQ, Thinking and Study skills and Careers Preparation.

Music. All orchestral and band instruments, piano, organ, percussion and guitar are taught to boys throughout the school. Choirs, orchestras, bands and chamber groups give frequent concerts throughout the year.

Games and Physical Education. Magnificent playing fields include over 55 acres dedicated to rugby, cricket, soccer and hockey. There are fives, squash and tennis courts; an athletics track and two floodlit, all-weather pitches. The Sports Hall accommodates four badminton courts, a multi-gym, a climbing wall, a fencing salle and indoor cricket nets. The school's lakes provide a marvellous facility for our sailing club, canoeing and windsurfing. Physical Education is compulsory for all pupils, and all pupils learn to swim. There is an indoor swimming pool and water polo is offered. Coaching in fencing, basketball, judo and karate is excellent. MTS is one of only two schools in the country to host first-class cricket fixtures and is the home of Middlesex Youth Cricket.

Service Sections. The school has a Contingent of the Combined Cadet Force with RN, Army, and RAF Sections. The CCF includes girls from St Helen's School, Northwood. There is a rifle range for the use of the Contingent (and we send a team to Bisley every year). The Duke of Edinburgh's Award scheme allows boys to achieve Bronze, Silver and Gold Awards, and the Community Service programme provides an opportunity for a wide range of activities in the local area. All boys in Years 10 and 11 take part in the CCF, The Duke of Edinburgh's Award scheme or Community Service teams.

The school places great emphasis on charitable endeavour and the boys run a great many societies to support good causes. A special feature of the school's charity work is Phab, a week-long residential holiday for handicapped children held every Easter and organised by Sixth Form boys together with the girls of St Helen's School. The school also has a charitable partnership with two schools in India.

School Societies. A large number of societies cover a wide field of interests and activities.

Careers. There is an outstanding Careers Advisory Service, which organises annual Careers and Higher Education Conventions at the school and a range of work experience.

House and Tutorial Systems. The school is divided into eight Houses. Each House is under the care of a Head of House and a team of tutors, who are responsible for the pastoral care of boys in that House.

Fees per term (2023–2024). £10,148 (Autumn Term), £7,611 (both Spring Term & Summer Term); these cover not only tuition, games, and lunch but also a lifetime alumnus subscription (OMT). There is a non-refundable registration fee of £100; separate admission fee deposits are charged later.

Merchant Taylors' Prep, the Preparatory school to Merchant Taylors', adjoins the senior school.

(*For further details see Merchant Taylors' Prep entry in IAPS section.*)

Charitable status. Merchant Taylors' School Charitable Trust is a Registered Charity, number 1063740. It exists to provide a first-class all-round education for boys, irrespective of their background.

The Governors of the School:
Chairman: D G M Eggar

P Barefoot
R J Brooman
G B du Parc Braham
Dr J Cox
Commodore A Cree, CBE
A Eastwood
D Haria
Mrs S A Morgan
The Hon R H E Newall
J C Oram
Ms L E Orr
V Paul
Mrs J Redman
J Twining

Clerk to the Governors: E Valletta

***Head Master*: S J Everson**, MA

Bursar: I D Williams, MBA, CMgr, GCMI, MAPM, MCIL
Second Master: M C Husbands, MA
Deputy Head (*Academic*): R C Garvey, MA
Deputy Head (*Pastoral*): Dr C L Harrison, BSc, PhD
Deputy Head (*Co-Curricular*): T C H Greenway, BSc
Senior Master: Dr A R H Clarke, MA, DPhil
Director of Studies: D J Spikings, BA, MEng
Assistant Head, Teaching and Learning and innovation: LV Smith, MA, ACC
Development Director: N J Latham, LLB Law
Director of Marketing and Admissions: A J Brackin, BA
School Chaplain: The Reverend J T Fields, MA, STM
Acting Head of Upper School: M T Herring, BA
Head of Middle School: J D Manley, MA
Head of Lower School: Dr R B C B Hesketh, MA, PhD

Assistant Staff:
* *Head of Department*

Art & Design:
Mr S N Leech, BA (*Acting Head of Art*)
Ms I Lumsden, BA
Mr A C Cataldo, BA
Mrs A Speker, BA

Careers:
*Ms S Grice, BSc
Mrs M Thobani (*Work Experience Co-Ordinator*)
Mrs R Marsh, BA (*Careers Co-Ordinator*)

Classics:
Mr E H Gazeley, MA (*Acting Head of Classics*)
Miss Z Binji, BA, MA
Ms N Cebon, BA
Miss A Gurmail-Kaufmann, BA
Mr M C Husbands, MA (*Second Master*)
Mr J Hedges-Robinson, MSt (*Graduate Teacher*)

Computing:
*Mr G N Macleod, BA
Mr J E Firestone, MA (**CCf and Outdoor Education*)
Mr E E W Williams, MEng, MBCS, CITP, FCCT (*Director of Digital Strategy*)

Design, Engineering and Technology:
*Mr W Yu Hin Tang Meng
Mr C Docherty, BA
Miss H M Park, BSc (*Head of Walter House*)
Mr S J Reid, BSc
Mr G A Wilson, BA (*Head of Community Service*)

Drama & Theatre Studies:
Miss C L Clarke, BA (*Director of Drama*)

Economics & Politics:
Dr M I Beacham, BA, MSc, PhD (**Economics*)
Mr R C Garvey, MA (*Deputy Head Academic and Teacher of Religion and Philosophy*)
Mr J P Martin, BA (**Politics*)
Ms S Rochow, MA

Mrs H Hall, BA, (*Head of Charity Drive*)
Mr C J Oey, MA

English:
*Mr M G Hilton-Dennis, BA (*SCR Representative On Governing Body*)
Miss L Green, MA (*Joint Deputy Director of Communications*)
Miss M J Fitzpatrick, BA [family leave]
Mr J D Manley, MA (*Head of Middle School*)
Mrs S Moss, Bed [maternity cover]
Mr A J Richardson, BA (*international Universities Coordinator*)
Mr D G Robinson, BA (*Joint Head of Communications*)
Ms D Scott, MA (*Assistant Head of Lower School*)
Mrs K Shockley, BA (*Second in English*)
Ms LV Smith, MA (*Assistant Head, Teaching and Learning and innovation*)
Mrs L Solomon, MA
Miss E K Trafford, MA (*Deputy Director of Co-Curriculum*)
Mrs K Younge, BA

Geography:
*Mr A Murray, MA
Mrs S R Burnham, BA
Mrs E J Lemoine, BA (*Head of Raphael House*)
Miss H J Maxfield, BA (*Assistant Head of Middle School*)
Mrs S A Riddleston, BA (*Senior Teacher*)
Mr R Simmonds, BSc (**PSHCE and Head of Andrewes House*)

History:
*Mr M W S Hale, MPhil
Mrs F E Blatchford Pace, BA
Mr R Evans, BSc
Mr M T Herring, BA (*Assistant Head of Upper School*)
Dr R B C B Hesketh, MA, PhD (*Head of Lower School*)
Mr P A Hoyle, BA, MSt (*Head of Scholarship*)
Mr J G Taylor, MA (*Registrar*)

Information Services:
Dr A R H Clarke, MA, DPhil (*Senior Master, Deputy Head of information Services*)
Mr J P Beck (*IT Manager*)
Mx B Butler (*IT Technician*)
Mr R Dixon (*Network Engineer*)
Mr N Evans (*IT Engineer*)
Mx A Laver Junior (*IT Technician*)
Mr E J Roberts (*IT Technician*)
Mr I Rudling (*Webmaster*)

Learning Support:
*Ms E J Sadler, BA, MEd
Ms K L Bowman, BA (*Specialist Teacher*)
Mrs D D Kotecha, MSc MTS (*Executive Functions Specialist-Learning Support*)
Mrs N Lakhani, BSc (*Learning Support Specialist Mentor*)
Mrs T Hasnain, MBA (*Learning Support Specialist Mentor*)
Miss L Gadd, BSc (*Learning Support Assistant*)

Library:
Mrs A J South, BSc, Diplib (*Senior Librarian*)
Mrs P J Jones, BA Pgdip (*Library Assistant*)
Mrs R J L Millard, BA, MA (*Assistant Librarian*)
Miss R Agajanian, PhD (*Assistant Librarian*)

Mathematics:
*Mr A S Miller, BSc
Mr A P Carroll, BA
Mr S J Coles, BSc
Mr M A Fothergill, BSc (*Head of Manor House*)
Mrs H E Ezomo, BA (*Assistant Staff Tutor*)
Mrs D C Gedalla, BA
Mrs S M Hale, BSc, MSc (*Head of Hilles House*)
Mr S F Hardman, BSc (*Second in Mathematics*)
Mrs G M Hazan, BA (*Joint Head of Phab*)
Mrs N Manek, BA (*Examinations officer*)
Ms N Monteiro, MSc (*Assistant Head of Upper School, Head of Oxbridge*)
Mrs T A Omert, BEng (*Joint Head of Phab*)
Mr K Prashar, BA (*EPQ Co-Ordinator*)
Mr S L Rowlands, BSc, MSc
Mr K Thomas, BSc

Modern Foreign Languages:
*Mr R P Bailey, BA
Mrs M C R Castro, BA (*Spanish*)
Ms E Danis, LLCE (**French*)
Miss R G Haye, Licence LCE
Miss A Gurmail-Kaufmann (*German*)
Ms V A Kotsuba, BA, MA (*French*)
Mr M W Pacey, BEd (**German*)
Ms N Rittey, BA (**Spanish*)
Mrs C E Udell, MA (*German*)
Mr T M Wells, BA (*French*)
Mrs E J White, BA (*French, Assistant Head of Lower School*)

Music:
Mr S J Couldridge, Dip TCL (*Director of Music*)
Mrs J H Stubbs, MusB ARCO, ALCM (*Assistant Director of Music*)
Ms F Martin, Med [maternity cover]
Mr D Tonks, MSt
Miss S Walsh, MA [family leave]

Physical Education:
Mr G Roots, BSc (*Director of Sport*)
Mr A C Bruce, MSci, MSc, ASCC (*Physical Education and Psychology*)
Mr E Conway, BSc, MSc (*Director of Rugby*)
Mr P J Davies, BSc, MSc (**Sport Science*)
Mr S De Weymarn, BSc (*PE*)
Mr I Mcgowan, BSc, MSc (*Director of Cricket and Assistant Head of Middle School*)
Mr J O Middleton, BSc (*Director of Hockey*)
Mr A Hayes, MSc (*Performance Coach – Hockey*)
Mr J Richardson, BSc (*Graduate Assistant – Sport*)
Mr C Tod, BSc (*Graduate Assistant – Sport*)

Psychology:
*Miss K Chakraborty, BSc

Religion & Philosophy:
*Ms G C Solomons, BA
Mr R C Garvey, MA (*Deputy Head Academic*)
Mr T J Lightfoot, MPhil
Miss S Wallace, BA, MA (*Acting Head of Upper School*)

Science:
*Mrs F A Rashid, BSc

Biology:
*Mrs S N Stuteley, BSc
Mr T C H Greenaway, BSc (*Deputy Head Co-Curricular*)
Dr C L Harrison, BSc, PhD (*Deputy Head Pastoral*)
Dr A Komissarova, MA, PhD
Ms O Lo, BSc
Mrs S C Pratt, MA
Mr B J Simpson, BSc (**PSHE*)

Chemistry:
*Mr M P Powell, MA
Mr M S Hughes, BSc (*Assistant Head of Lower School, Head of White House*)
Dr M M Lohr, PhD (*Staff Tutor*)
Dr M Lomas, BSc, PhD (*Head of Spenser House*)
Miss M Knight, BSc
Mrs F A Rashid, BSc (**Science*)
Mr J R Talboys, BSc (*Assistant Head of Middle School*)

Physics:
*Mrs A Mayadeen, MPhys
Mr R Aniolkowski, BSc
Dr A R H Clarke, MA, DPhil (*Senior Master, Deputy Head of information Services*)
Mr A Cummings, BSc
Miss K N Hustwitt, BSc
Mr A Sa'id, BSc
Mr D J Spikings, BA, MEng (*Director of Studies*)
Mr B Waterhouse, BSc (*Head of Mulcaster*)

School Counsellors:
Ms P Llewellyn, BSc Hons, PG Dip (*Lead School Counsellor*)
A Mullen (*BACP Accredited Counsellor/Psychotherapist*)

Visiting Teachers:
W Alexander, DipTCL (*Guitar*)
J Atkins, DipRAM (*Trumpet*)
Miss C Barry, BA (*Cello*)
S Byron, BMus Hons RCM (*Trombone*)
Miss P Beddoe, MA (*Clarinet*)
Miss S Clark, MA, LRSM, ARCM, DipRCM, CTABRSM (*Piano*)
Miss K Cormican, GTCL, PDOT (*Violin*)
Mrs R Couldridge, GTCL (*Violin, Viola and Piano*)
A Gathercole, GGSM (*Trumpet*)
Ms N Hawkins (*Guitar*)
D Hester, LTCL, DipTCL (*Bassoon and Music Technology*)
R Hobson (*Organ*)
J Lawrence, BA (*Percussion*)
Mrs N Manington, BMus, LGSM (*Piano and Jazz Piano*)
B Marshall, MMus (*Oboe*)
N Martin (*Percussion*)
Ms Z Matthews, MMus (*Viola*)
Mr D Robb (*Clarinet*)
Mrs C Ridout (*Cello*)
D Saunderson, GGSM (*Singing*)
Mrs M Stone, MMus (*Piano*)
Mrs N Tait, LRAM Hons (*Cello*)
Mr R Wainwright (*Organ*)

Sports:
P Adams (*Badminton*)
M Barrell (*Cricket*)
H Battram (*Sports & Conditioning*)
L Bilyard (*Hockey*)
P Butcher (*Tennis*)
S Butcher (*Tennis*)
G Calway (*Cricket*)
A Chowdhury (*Tennis*)
R Croxon (*Hockey*)
G Davis (*Rugby*)
A Edge (*Squash*)
S Galloway (*Cricket*)
H Haynes (*Hockey*)
G Mandair (*Hockey*)
J Moore (*Cricket*)
A Morrison (*Squash*)
C O'Connor (*Rugby*)
M Patel (*Cricket*)
R Patel (*Cricket*)
M Ramshaw (*Hockey*)
D Samuel (*Rugby*)
R Sanghera (*Cricket*)
G Summerfield (*Cricket*)
S Thanki (*Cricket*)
M Wheeler (*Strength & Conditioning*)
A Wijesuriya (*Cricket*)
L Wooldridge (*Cricket*)

Head Master's PA: Mrs J Jolliff
Admissions Officer: G McCann
Bursar's Secretary: Mrs A Johnson

Merchant Taylors' Prep:
Head of School: Dr Karen McNerney, BSc Hons, PGCE, MSc, EdD
Senior Deputy Head: Antony McConnell, MA Hons, PGCE, FHA
Deputy Head: Andrew Crook, BA Hons, PGCE

Merchiston Castle School

294 Colinton Rd, Colinton, Edinburgh EH13 0PU

Tel: 0131 312 2200
0131 312 2201 (Admissions)
email: admissions@merchiston.co.uk
website: www.merchiston.co.uk
X/Twitter: @MerchiNews
Facebook: @MerchistonEdinburgh
Instagram: @merchinews
LinkedIn: /merchistoncastleschooledinburgh

Motto: *Ready Ay Ready*

The School was established in 1833 and moved in 1930 from the centre of the city out to its present spacious and attractive site, bordered by the Water of Leith and close to the Pentland Hills.

There are 400 boys in the School, of whom 260 are boarders.

Admission. The normal ages of entry are 7–14 and 16, though from time to time there may be vacancies at other ages. Entry at 7–12 is by entrance assessment, interview and current school report; entry at 13 by the Common Entrance or Merchiston entrance examinations and current school report. Entry at 14 is by Merchiston entrance examinations. Entry to the Sixth Form at 16 depends on a successful showing in GCSE or National 4 and National 5 examinations as well as on interview, internal examination and a school report. Our approach to examination is very personable and we strive to make this as accessible as possible by facilitating online testing wherever possible. Entry is possible in all three terms, where vacancies permit.

A prospectus and further details may be obtained from the Admissions Office. Prospective parents are encouraged to visit the School. Information may be also found on our website (www.merchiston.co.uk) and via these links:

Admissions: www.merchiston.co.uk/admissions

Order a Prospectus: www.merchiston.co.uk/admissions/order-a-prospectus

News Centre: www.merchiston.co.uk/about/news-centre

Courses of study. In the Juniors the curriculum comprises English, English Literature, Mathematics, Biology, Chemistry, Physics, History, French, Latin, German, Spanish, Mandarin, Geography, Religious Studies, Art and Design, Music, PE, Electronics, Design and Technology, and Information Technology.

In the Middle School a 2-year course leading to GCSEs is followed, consisting of a core curriculum: English, English Literature, Mathematics, a foreign language (French, Spanish, Mandarin), IGCSE Biology, Chemistry and Physics, and a wide range of optional subjects, including History, a second foreign language, Electronics, Information Technology, Geography, Latin, Religious Studies (Philosophy and Ethics), Art and Design, Design and Technology, and Music.

A Level options include English Literature, Mathematics, Further Mathematics, Biology, Chemistry, Physics, French, Mandarin, Spanish, History, Geography, Economics, Government and Politics, Classical Civilisation, Religious Studies, PE, Information Technology, Latin, Design and Technology, Electronics (AS only) and Art. Other languages at A Level (including German and Russian) are available on request. In addition to his main subjects, each boy follows a General Studies course offering Moral and Social Studies and Careers Guidance. Classes are small throughout the School, and all subjects are set by ability. The School prepares boys for entry to Oxford and Cambridge, as well as American colleges and universities (our students can now choose SAT prep as one of their Saturday Electives modules).

The School makes provision for specialist ESOL teaching for International students, including an opportunity to study GCSE English in the Upper Sixth year.

In 2023, university destinations included Glasgow, Edinburgh, St. Andrews, Nottingham, Exeter, Newcastle, Aberdeen and Manchester. Overseas university destinations include Germany, the Netherlands and the USA.

Houses. Fully refurnished Middle Year Boarding Houses and dedicated Sixth Form Boarding House with single, ensuite rooms. The Houseparents and House Tutors pay special attention to the care of the individual and to the development of both his studies and interests.

Day boys. The life of day boys is fully integrated with that of the boarders: all boys spend time together in class, on the sporting field and during extra-curricular activities.

Games. The principal games are rugby, played in the Autumn and Lent Terms, and in the Summer Term cricket and athletics. Basketball and other indoor sports are houses in the sports hall, and there are great on-site facilities for other sports including hockey, football, squash, fives, and badminton. Our renowned Tennis and Golf Academies, led by expert coaching, can take full advantage of our on-site indoor Tennis Dome and of a strong partnership with a local Golf Club. Merchiston prides itself on fostering the pursuit of excellence in a sport-for-all environment. The School is currently represented nationally and internationally in many sports, such as athletics, cricket, golf, rugby and target shooting.

Music. Music plays an important part in the life of the School. Tuition is available in all keyboard and orchestral instruments; currently about fifty per cent of the School learn a musical instrument, and two choirs flourish. There is also a School orchestra, a close harmony group, a jazz band and two pipe bands. The choir and instrumentalists frequently go on tour, e.g. to the USA, the Far East, and Europe.

Drama. There is at least one major drama production a year, jointly staged with our sister school, as well as frequent House plays or drama workshop productions in a well-equipped, purpose-built theatre.

Art, Craft, Design and Technology, and Ceramics. The Art and Design Centre offers scope both within the curriculum and in the pupils' free time for painting, pottery, metalwork, woodwork and design work. Courses in Computing and Electronics are also available both within the curriculum or in free time. Our state-of-the-art Design & Technology department benefit from both a traditional and modern set-up with pupils able to access laser cutters as well as 3D rapid prototype printers.

Societies. There is a wide variety of clubs, including chess, debating and electronics. Visits to theatres, concerts and exhibitions are a frequent part of a boy's life at Merchiston. The Enlightened Curriculum uses Edinburgh as a prime resource for cultural experiences for all age groups.

CCF participation is voluntary (except for Shell form). CCF includes outward bound activities such as climbing, hillwalking, canoeing and camping. All senior boys at Merchiston also undertake a Bronze Duke of Edinburgh's Award expedition, with participation at Silver and Gold level on a voluntary basis.

The School is also very active in community service work and they boys themselves are often involved in fundraisers for community projects and charitable causes.

Girls. The School does not accept girls but has a special relationship as brother/sister school with St George's School for Girls, Edinburgh and Kilgraston School in Perthshire. This includes joint expeditions, concerts, tours, seminars, debating, drama, social events and study courses. Merchiston operates a joint fee scheme with both schools.

Careers advice. An expert careers adviser supplements the advice of the Academic Leadership Team, Houseparents and Academic Tutors. In the LVI year, pupils attend timetabled lessons in Careers as part of the General Studies Programme of the Sixth Form, where they are also encouraged to take a Work Experience placement and to visit local universities in the month of June. When pupils start in the Shell, they undertake Cambridge Occupational Analysts (COA) Preview and Profile assessments. These assess each individual's interests and abilities in several key cognitive areas. In the Fifth Form each individual has a discussion with the Head of Careers, during which interests are explored and feedback from the COA assessments is given. The discussion is focused on career areas of interest – as identified by the individual and the COA feedback – and identifying areas to be investigated, as well as touching on potential A Level programmes. There is an annual HE & Careers Fair to which other local schools are invited. Merchiston also offers a Careers Café, a series of appointments throughout the year hosted by Alumni working in different fields to give our students advice for their future professional life.

Health. There is a medical centre in the charge of Registered Nurses and a Health Assistance; the School Doctor visits regularly.

Fees per term (2023–2024). Junior School: Day boys £5,730; Forms II and III: Boarders £9,610; Day boys £6,480. Senior School (Forms IV and above): Boarders £13,440; Day boys £9,750.

Sibling, Forces and Teaching Profession (means-tested) fee reductions are available.

Scholarships and Bursaries. A range of scholarships are offered each year across different subject areas and carry a 5% reduction in school fees (this reduction is being introduced from September 2024 with no retrospective financial reduction). Our Scholarships are awarded at two main entry points: Sixth Form Scholarship (16+) and Senior School Scholarship (13+). All applicants must also satisfy the academic entrance requirements for their age.

For further information see: www.merchiston.co.uk/admissions/scholarships.

Means-tested financial assistance: where parental income is not sufficient to allow the pupil to attend Merchiston, parents may apply for means-tested financial assistance. Contact the Admissions Team for more information.

Forces: 10% fee remission is available to the sons of serving members of HM Forces.

Old boys. Known as Merchistonians and part of the Merchistonian Club. Former pupils include: The Rt Hon Lord John MacGregor, MP; Sir Peter Burt, former Chief Executive, Bank of Scotland; The Rt Hon Lord Kenneth Osborne PC, longest-serving judge of the current Scottish bench; Air Marshal Sir John Baird, Surgeon General of the British Armed Forces between 1997 and 2000; International Rugby Union players: N G R Mair, W S Glen, I H P Laughland, A C W Boyle, A H W Boyle, Q Dunlop, G R T Baird, J Jeffrey, P Walton, C Joiner, B R S Eriksson, D W Hodge, N J Mayer, I A Fullarton, P J Godman, F J M Brown, Sam Hidalgo-Clyne, Zach Mercer; Shane Corstorphine, former Senior Vice-President Skyscanner.

Charitable status. Merchiston Castle School is a Registered Charity, number SC016580. It aims to give each boy in his way the capacity and confidence to live in an uncertain world and to make that life as rich as possible; more specifically, to encourage him to work hard and to take pride in achievement, to think independently, to face up to challenges, to accept responsibility, to show concern for others and the environment, and to develop wider skills and interests.

School Leadership Team:

***Headmaster*: J Anderson**

Deputy Head Teaching & Learning: Dr D D J Cartwright
Deputy Head Wellbeing: D Rowlands
Bursar: Mrs P Axon

Pupil Support Leadership Team:
Senior Deputy Head: D Rowlands
Assistant Head Pupil Support: W Ogilvie-Jones

Mill Hill School

The Ridgeway, Mill Hill Village, London NW7 1QS

Tel: 020 8959 1176
email: office@millhill.org.uk
registrations@millhill.org.uk
website: millhill.org.uk
X/Twitter: @MillHillSenior
Facebook: @MillHillSenior
Instagram: @MillHillSenior

Motto: *Instilling values, inspiring minds*

Fees per term (2023–2024). Day (including lunch) £8,600, Full Boarding £14,530, Weekly Boarding £12,265. Fees include additional charges for curriculum expenses and additional contributions towards basic sports trips and visits.

Overview. With its aims of instilling values and inspiring minds, Mill Hill School offers education to boys and girls aged 13–18 and offers day places, weekly and full boarding. Mill Hill School seeks to equip pupils for life, both now and in the future. Its stimulating academic environment and numerous activities outside the classroom encourage learning and personal growth. They are committed to the development of every pupil and believe that their friendly and supportive community helps this to happen. Situated in Mill Hill, the school occupies a magnificent 115 acres of beautiful grounds, just 10 miles from Central London with easy access to underground and main line stations.

The grounds provide a spacious setting for the academic buildings and boarding and day houses and offer extensive facilities for sports and activities. A part of the Mill Hill Education Group, a charitable collection of independent schools.

Houses. There are 888 pupils in the school, of whom 115 are boarders. Weekly and Full boarding is available for entry at Year 9, Year 10 and Sixth Form. There are four Boarding Houses and eight Day Houses, all of which have been recently refurbished.

Boarding. Full boarders have a large range of activities and workshops on Saturday mornings. These sessions are also optional for day and weekly boarding pupils.

The boarding community is co-educational and multi-cultural. This allows pupils to gain a greater understanding and respect for people of any gender, all races, faiths and nationalities, enabling pupils to welcome diversity of opinions. Pupils are encouraged to develop moral integrity and the confidence to stand up for what they believe in, which enables them to make a positive influence in their lives at school and beyond.

Admission. The main entry point is at 13+, with the majority of pupils joining from Belmont Mill Hill Prep. External candidates are selected on the basis of assessments, a Head's reference and interviews.

Pre-testing for external candidates is offered in Year 6 for unconditional places at Year 9 (13+) entry. For Year 6 Track candidates there are two assessment rounds. The first round involves computer-based assessments of aptitude in verbal, non-verbal reasoning and numerical skills. Results are age-standardised, enabling us to accurately compare candidates born at different times of the year. Round two sees the candidates complete group interviews, a team working task and a creative writing activity. Only chance vacancies apply to Year 8 Track prospective 13+ pupils, with candidates registering their interest in the Autumn Term and a waiting list being drawn up based on computer-based assessments, school reports, references and interviews.

Sixth Form (16+) Entry: Admission to the Sixth Form is based on an entry requirement of five GCSE passes, at least two at Grade 7 plus three at Grade 6, together with at least Grade 5 in Mathematics and English, or equivalent qualifications or written examinations for overseas pupils, as appropriate. More detailed entry requirements for specific A Level courses are given in the School's Sixth Form Curriculum Guide. Candidates unable to offer the range or number of subjects required (e.g. some overseas candidates) will be considered on their individual academic merit. In 2023, the School introduce the Level 3 BTEC in sport. This pathway is designed to support pupils within elite sporting programmes and has an entry criteria of 5 level 5s.

Selection is made on the basis of predicted grades, a general interview with a senior member of the School, and a reference from the candidate's present school. Offers made are conditional on meeting the entry requirements detailed above. International candidates are interviewed either in person or online. All pupils with English as a second language will be asked to sit an EAL paper and a spoken English interview. Scholarships are awarded on the basis of examinations and subsequent interviews in the Autumn Term.

Curriculum. The School's academic curriculum is broad, flexible and forward-looking. It is designed to encourage pupils' intellectual curiosity, sound learning and a spirit of inquiry in the pursuit of academic excellence. The curriculum seeks to enable pupils to acquire core knowledge and skills in English, Mathematics, Science and a Modern Language, and to develop their own particular academic interests. It also incorporates a full programme of Personal, Social and Health Education, appropriate guidance and information for pupils on subject choices, higher education and careers.

Music, Drama and Art. The Creative Arts have a long and successful tradition at Mill Hill School and are a key part of the academic curriculum. In addition to achieving excellent results in public examinations, relevant academic departments have a high success rate in preparing pupils for further study in the Arts.

Alongside academic successes, there is a substantial and varied programme of co-curricular activities in these subjects. The Art Department offers multiple facilities and a teaching staff with knowledge and expertise in many disciplines. Pupils are encouraged to develop their interest and skills in painting and drawing, moving image, photography, printmaking, sculpture and textiles.

In addition to the extensive range and number of Drama performances relating to examination courses, there are multiple school productions each year, ranging from Shakespeare to musicals. A highlight is the biennial Inter-House Drama Festival, which attracts hundreds of pupil participants, including actors, directors, and playwrights.

The School's Music Department arranges an extensive programme of concerts, competitions, and recitals throughout the year, some of which include recitals by professional performers. Individual tuition in most instruments and singing is available from high-quality specialist teachers. There are also a large number of musical ensembles, these include several orchestras and bands, two jazz ensembles, four choirs and numerous ad hoc pupil bands and chamber ensembles.

Sport. Mill Hill School is renowned for its sporting excellence, aiming to equip Millhillians for a healthy life now and in the future. Achieved through the dual stream approach; 'Fit for Performance' and 'Fit for Life'. Every pupil, regardless of physical ability or experience, is encouraged to participate in both competitive and non-competitive sports and activities. The core sports for boys are rugby, hockey, football and cricket, and for girls are hockey, netball, and cricket. Elective sport opportunities include athletics, badminton, basketball, climbing, cross country, dance, Eton Fives, golf, rugby 7s, swimming, table tennis, tennis, triathlon volleyball and yoga. For most able pupils, there is an innovative Sports Scholarship programme where pupils have access to the Performance Department, which includes a full-time Physiotherapist, Nutritionist, Mental Skills Coach and two Strength & Conditioning Coaches. Junior Sports Scholars work alongside the Performance Department during their time-tabled sessions in the week, whilst the Senior Sports Scholars have their own individual mentors who work with them on a one-to-one basis, designing individual programmes and workshops.

There are a range of awards and Bursaries available for talented sporting pupils, designed to supplement the home-grown talent. Through the continued commitment to delivering an outstanding coaching provision and drive for pupil progression, there has been a unique portfolio developed of partnerships with professional clubs and coaches across many sports. The impressive list of full-time coaches includes an England & Mavericks netball player, Saracens Premiership rugby player, Middlesex County Cricket Coach, Tottenham Hotspur Premiership Academy Coaches, Great Britain Hockey Coach, Great Britain athlete, and PGA Advanced Golf Pro, alongside club partnerships, which include Saracens Rugby, Middlesex Cricket, Hampstead & Westminster Hockey Club and Tottenham Hotspur FC. The links pupils have with professional players and coaches ensures that they receive the highest level of support, driving innovation and collaboration.

The School's facilities are both extensive and impressive; they include: a modern sports complex incorporating a recently refurbished indoor sports hall; indoor cricket nets; a fully-equipped fitness suite and conditioning centre. There is also a newly laid floodlit AstroTurf; 25 metre swimming pool; three fives courts; six outdoor tennis courts; four netball courts; an indoor golf teaching suite incorporating a golf simulator and an outdoor golf centre; and numerous cricket, football and rugby pitches across the 115-acre site.

Scholarships and Bursaries. Scholarships and Bursaries. Scholarships are available to pupils entering the Fourth and Sixth Forms (Years 9 and 12) at both 13+ and 16+. Awards are allocated to pupils showing exceptional talent in a variety of areas, both in the classroom and on the sports field. Academic, Music, Drama, Art, Design Technology and Sports Awards are available.

Academic Scholarship candidates are identified through sitting exams in English, Mathematics, Science, French and Latin (optional). Candidates are called back for interviews on the strength of their scores. A Full Academic Award may be given, or single-subject awards may be made. It is important to highlight that there is no fee remission associated with Scholarships, the primary benefit being the increased level of support, challenge and provision that is offered to successful applicants.

Means-tested bursaries are available to new entrants to the School. These are intended to extend the benefits of a Mill Hill education to pupils whose families would not otherwise be able to afford the School's fees. Bursary awards are made by the Court of Governors upon the recommendation of the Foundation Bursary Committee.

Further information can be found on the School website.

Charitable status. Mill Hill Education Group is the brand name for The Mill Hill School Foundation, a Registered Charity, number 1064758.

***Head*: Mr David Benson,** BSc Hons

Millfield

Street, Somerset BA16 0YD

Tel: 01458 442291
email: admissions@millfieldschool.com
website: www.millfieldschool.com
X/Twitter: @millfieldsenior
Facebook: @MillfieldSchool
Instagram: @millfieldschool

The school was founded in 1935 by R J O (Jack) Meyer with the philanthropic aim of using its resources to generate places for boys who were gifted but not wealthy. The school became co-educational in 1939. Millfield's vision is to be the world leader for the development of children, offering an environment where students are immersed in limitless academic, artistic and sporting opportunities and individually supported to discover their brilliance. Set in over 100 acres of grounds, the facilities are unmatched in the UK: an Olympic-sized swimming pool, indoor Equestrian Centre, a 500-seat theatre, golf courses, art gallery, state-of-the-art cricket and golf centres and a music school housing a 350-seat Johnson concert hall, recording studios and numerous practice rooms.

The school is fully co-educational with approximately 1,330 students, 54% boys and 46% girls; 75% of whom are boarders.

Day and Boarding Houses. There are 19 boarding houses, situated on or within easy reach of campus, with separate houses for boys and girls. Most Sixth Formers have their own rooms whilst younger students share either in pairs or fours. As part of the Nine at Millfield programme, Year 9 have dedicated boarding and day houses. All Year 9 houses lie in the heart of the campus and have a higher staff to student ratio to oversee every aspect of each student's wellbeing and academic progress. There are four day houses for Year 10 to Upper Sixth; they have their own base on site and may stay in the evenings to do supervised prep.

The Curriculum. We have a broad, unrivalled choice for GCSE, BTEC and A level options.

All students entering Year 9 (at age 13), regardless of ability, study English, mathematics, three sciences, at least one language, art, design and technology, IT, food and nutrition, geography, history, religious studies, physical education and music. The student to teacher ratio is 6.5:1. Students have a structured co-curricular programme.

In Years 10 and 11, students follow courses leading to GCSEs in the core subjects of English, mathematics, science and a language. In addition, there is a wide choice of options: art & design, business studies, Chinese, computer science, drama, economics, BTEC enterprise, food and nutrition, French, geography, German, history, Italian, Latin, music, physical education, product design, religious studies and Spanish.

The school offers a wide range of A level subjects to Sixth Formers. These include art, biology, business, chemistry, Chinese, drama, economics, English literature, French, further mathematics, geography, German, history, IT, classical civilisation, Latin, mathematics, media studies, music, philosophy, physical education, physics, politics, product design, psychology, religious studies and Spanish. Also on offer are the vocational courses of BTEC business and BTEC enterprise and entrepreneurship (both equivalent to two A levels), BTEC National Diploma in Art & Design (equivalent to three A levels), BTEC Diploma in Sport (equivalent to two A levels), BTEC Music (equivalent to one A level) and Leiths Introductory Certificate. Most students will study three A level courses (or equivalent) in the Lower Sixth and continue with all of these courses into the Upper Sixth. Wider enrichment opportunities are available to all Sixth Formers. The curriculum offers breadth, depth and flexibility in course choice. Students are also prepared for STEP papers and Scholastic Aptitude Tests (SAT exams) for American Universities. English as an additional language (EAL) and Learning Support is available at all levels.

Sport and Activities. Millfield runs an unparalleled range of sports and activities to engage all students. Those in Years 9, 10 and 11 generally choose from one of the core games of the term, including rugby and basketball (boys) and hockey and dance (girls) in the autumn term. Football and hockey (boys) and netball, dance and football (girls) in the spring term, and athletics, cricket and tennis (both boys and girls) in the summer term. In Sixth Form, the range extends to include all of the above plus badminton, canoeing, chess, clay shooting, climbing, karate, sailing, skiing, squash, trampolining, triathlon, and various fitness activities such as aerobics, pilates, spinning and yoga. Throughout the school, students may also specialise in one of our high-performing programmes including athletics, cricket, fencing, golf, modern pentathlon, squash, swimming and tennis.

Students in Years 9, 10 and Lower Sixth take part in the Millfield Activity Programme (MAP) where they can further broaden their experiences through a choice of more than 100 activities, ranging from athletics and

British Military Fitness to film clubs, dissection, lacrosse, beekeeping and falconry.

Fees per term (2023–2024). Boarding £15,925; Day £10,365.

Scholarships and Bursaries. Scholarships carry a fee reduction of up to 10%, awarded to students who display exceptional talent in academic, all-rounder, art, drama, dance, design & innovation, music and sport. A limited number of Headmaster's Scholarships of up to 50% are also available. Where parental resources are limited, these may be augmented by means-tested bursaries of up to 100%.

Charitable status. Millfield is a Registered Charity, number 310283. Its aim is to provide independent boarding and day education for boys and girls, and to maintain an extensive system of bursary aid to gifted students or those in financial need.

Governors:
Chair of Governors: R Rudd

R Abernethy	C Hirst
B Alizadeh	C Macdonald
W Bushell	N Maddock
R Clark	J Maudslay
Mrs N Della Valle	Mrs J Mitchell
F Dickens OBE	D Pinto
S East	M Simon
R Exley	R Soluade
T Griffiths	P Warner
Mrs K Griggs	O Welsby
C Harvey MBE	

Clerk to the Governors: Mrs R Summerhayes

***Headmaster*: Gavin Horgan**, MA Oxon

Finance Director: Mrs M Johnson, BSc Hons, ACA
Deputy Head (*Academic*): Mr David Brooke, MMath Oxon, PhD
Deputy Head (*Pastoral*): Mrs S Quenault [from September 2024]
Deputy Head (*Enrolment and Outreach*): J Postle, BA Hons, PGCE, FRSA
Assistant Head (*Academic*): Dr A Gutteridge, MPhil, PhD
Assistant Head (*Middle School*): R Furlong, BSc Hons, MEd, PGCE
Assistant Head (*Sixth Form*): E James, BA Hons, MSc
Director of Sport: Dr S Drawer, MSc, PGCE, PhD
Head of Marketing: Mrs L Webb, BA Hons
Head of Millfield Prep: D Thornburn, MEd
Head of Human Resource: Mrs C Hawksworth, BSoc Sci
Director of IT: G Henderson, BA Hons, MA
Financial Controller: K Hawkins
Assistant Head (*Pastoral and Staff*): C Middleton, BSc Hons, PGCE
Assistant Head (*Student Welfare and DSL*): A Whatling, MSc
Director of Enterprises: Miss H Angelinetta, BA Hons

Heads of Department:
Art, Design & Technology: Mrs I Meakin
Biology: Mrs L McEwen, BSc
Chemistry: Mr J Casalis De Pury
Computing and ICT: Ms K Rogers
English as an Additional Language (*EAL*): Ms J White
Economics: A Shaw, MA Oxon, PGCE
English and Media: J C Baddock, BA Hons
Geography: D Barry
History and Politics: Mr M Howard
Food and Nutrition: P Reeves, BA Hons, DTLLS, MA
Languages: M Nash, BA Hons, MA, ATCL, PGCE
Learning Support Centre: Ms J White, BSc Hons, MEd, QTS, PG Dip, MDG
Library: S Bull, BA, PGDE
Mathematics: Dr C Fiddes, BA Oxon, PhD
Music: K Barry
Physical Education: S Maddock, BA Hons, MEd
Physics: Mr C Davies
Religious Studies and Philosophy: T Churchill, BA Hons, MA, PGCE

Houses and Housemasters/Housemistresses:

Boarding Houses:
Abbey: Ms C Rose
Acacia: Miss J Moore
Butleigh: Mrs E Watambwa
Etonhurst: Ms K Lloyd
Holmcroft: R Owlett
Joan's Kitchen: M Speyers
Keen's Elm: S Lane
Kernick: Ms C Coutand-Moore
Kingweston: D Askham
Martins: Ms C Garcia
Millfield: T Bowley
Orchards: S Robertson
Portway: Miss L Chamberlin
Shapwick: T Kingsford
St Annes: T Stokes
Southfield: Ms T Allen
The Grange: T Neal-Smith
Walton: J Lewis
Warner: Mrs J Weare

Day Houses, Boys:
Great: Mr J Bishop
Mill: Mr M Frost

Day Houses, Girls:
Overleigh: Mrs A Brade
The Lakes: Mrs J Gray

Day House (*Year 9 Girls & Boys*):
Ivythorn: Mrs K Butt

Heads of Sport:
Director of Athletics: N Wheeler
Tutor i/c Badminton: K Lloyd, BSc
Head of Basketball: C Seeley
Director of Cricket: M Garaway, ECB Level 4 Coach
Master i/c Cross Country: J Allen
Director of Dance and Drama: R Fox
Director of Fencing: M Cleary
Head of Football: S Perkins
Director of Golf: K Nicholls, PGA/LET member
Director of Hockey: R Keates, HA Coach Level 2
Head of Karate: T Cheung, purple belt in Washinkai Karate and Kickboxing, blue belt in Shotokan karate
Head of Modern Pentathlon: A Cord
Director of Netball: J Adamson
Head of Outdoor Adventure: N Woodall
Head of Equestrian Sports (*Riding & Polo*): M Wilder
Director of Rugby: J Mallett, RFU Level 4
Sailing: P Williams
Skiing: M Patel
Director of Squash: I Thomas, High Performance Coach

Director of Swimming: E Dale, BSc
Director of Tennis: D Manlow
Head of Trampolining: J Boyd
Head of Triathlon: C Brown

Moreton Hall

Weston Rhyn, Oswestry, Shropshire SY11 3EW
Tel: 01691 773671
email: admin@moretonhall.com
website: www.moretonhall.org
X/Twitter: @moretonhall
Facebook: @moretonhall

One of the UK's highest achieving schools, Moreton Hall was founded in 1913 by Ellen Lloyd-Williams (Aunt Lil) in Oswestry and moved to its present location in 1920. In 1964, the school became an educational trust. Although the school is predominantly boarding, a number of day pupils are admitted each year.

Member of HMC, GSA, The Society of Heads, IAPS, and AGBIS.

Admission. Moreton Hall Prep is the preparatory school of Moreton Hall, sharing not only its extensive facilities but also a commitment to nurture and celebrate the talents of each child. Moreton Hall Prep takes girls and boys from Pre-Prep (age 3) to Year 6 and offers a unique start to their education, ensuring academic rigour goes hand in hand with encouragement to achieve success in all creative and sporting fields.

Girls and boys are admitted to Moreton Hall, normally in September at age 11 by the School's entrance examination which is held at the end of January each year. This examination requires no knowledge of foreign languages and is designed to test potential ability rather than factual recall. This examination can be taken by pupils at 10+, with supplementary papers at 12 and 13. Sixth Form entrance is by entrance examination, current school report and interview, and numbers are limited. All applications should be addressed to the Principal.

Though predominantly boarding, day pupils are welcomed. Boys may board from the age of 8–13.

Scholarships and bursaries. A number of academic scholarships worth up to 20% of fees will be awarded to pupils at ages 11+, 12+, 13+ and 16+. Scholarships for Music, Drama, Art and for outstanding Sporting talent are also available. Pupils may apply for more than one scholarship. Means-tested bursaries may be awarded up to the value of 100% of fees.

Fees per term (2023–2024). Boarders: £8,600 (Moreton Hall Prep), £11,995 (Years 7 and 8), £12,995 (Years 9–13). Day pupils: £3,845–£5,460 (Moreton Hall Prep), £7,540 (Years 7 and 8), £8,695 (Years 9–13).

Curriculum. Going well beyond the National Curriculum, some 20 subjects are available at GCSE, varying from traditional academic subjects such as Latin and the Sciences, to practical subjects such as Drama, Dance and Physical Education. Modern Languages available include French, Spanish, Mandarin Chinese and Russian. A Levels in History of Art, Social Biology, Business Studies and Theatre Studies extend the range of the curriculum. Information Technology is a compulsory subject up to Sixth Form, optional thereafter.

Examinations offered. GCSE, A Level, ABRSM, ESB (English Speaking Board). Over 95% of Upper Sixth go on to University.

Religious activities. Non-denominational. Weekday service, longer service on Sunday, visiting preacher.

Academic, sporting and extracurricular facilities. Moreton Hall is engaged in an ambitious development programme and has facilities of the highest quality designed to provide the right environment for the education of pupils in the twenty-first century.

Younger pupils are housed in the Stables building under the supervision of resident houseparents and assistants. The building is designed to create a family atmosphere with dormitories split into smaller units, close to common rooms, washrooms and staff accommodation.

As pupils progress up the school, the dormitories are gradually replaced by double and finally single study-bedrooms. The Sixth Form Houses provide single and double en-suite facilities. Here, within the structure of a boarding school, senior girls are given the necessary freedom to prepare for the next stage in their careers.

The Centenary Science Centre is a unique Medical Science Faculty. The Science Centre, Information Technology rooms and Art and Design Centre are housed within a short distance of the central classroom, careers and library complexes.

All classrooms, libraries and boarding houses are networked and all Sixth Formers have internet access from their study-bedrooms.

An exceptionally well-equipped Sports Centre comprising a sports hall and floodlit tennis courts along with a heated indoor swimming pool, nine-hole golf course, an all-weather surface, and playing fields are set in one hundred acres of beautiful parkland at the foot of the Berwyn hills. The school offers a wide range of sporting options including Lacrosse, Netball, Hockey, Cricket, Tennis and Athletics. Sailing and Riding are also popular.

The Holroyd Community Theatre, Musgrave Theatre, Outdoor Theatre and Music School stimulate theatrical and musical activities ranging from house plays, lunchtime shows and jazz evenings through to ambitious school plays and orchestral concerts. Great emphasis is placed on girls taking part in as wide a range of extra-curricular interests as possible.

The nationally acclaimed Moreton Enterprises offers students real business experience. Supervised by professional advisers, but all run by the students themselves.

Old Moretonian Association. c/o Moreton Hall.

Moreton Hall Education Ltd. Company registration number 14232201

Board Members:
Chair: Mr D Murphy
Mr R Carryer
Mrs R Clacher, CBE

***Principal*: Mr Michael Brewer**, BA, MA

Deputy Head of Academic: Mrs S Champion, BSc, MSc
Head of Moreton Hall Prep: Mrs D Speakman, MA

International Director: Miss E Conlon, BA
Operations Director: Mr A McTaggart, FCMA, CGMA

Morrison's Academy

Ferntower Road, Crieff, Perthshire PH7 3AN

Tel: 01764 653885
email: enquiries@morrisonsacademy.org
website: www.morrisonsacademy.org
X/Twitter: @macmorrisons
Facebook: @morrisonsacademy
Instagram: @morrisonsacademy
LinkedIn: /morrison's-academy

Motto: *Ad summa tendendum ~ Striving for the highest*

The School. Morrison's Academy is a vibrant co-educational day school located in Crieff, Scotland. Founded in 1860 and an integral part of the community in Crieff, the school comprises a 10-acre main campus supplemented by 45 acres of sports fields and main hall. Morrison's Academy provides a quality education for over 530 boys and girls from 2 to 18 years, delivering a contemporary Scottish curriculum.

The school's strong academic foundations are supplemented by numerous skills based educational programmes including our Outdoor Adventures and Activities programme, our Learning for Life programme and the Peter Jones Enterprise Academy, the first in Scotland. Each programme has been carefully developed to provide pupils with life skills: resilience, perseverance, problem solving and social skills – preparing Morrisonians for big futures.

Morrison's Academy's Nursery is housed in a purpose-built facility with an extensive garden on the main campus. The Nursery benefits from access to the school's wider campus, facilities and specialist teaching staff. There is a well established transition programme for pupils leaving Nursery and entering into Primary School, preparing them for Primary One.

The Primary School, housed in a separate building on the main campus, educates pupils in small classes. Pupils also benefit from access to the wider school facilities and specialist subject teaching. Transfer between primary and secondary is helped by the Transitional Year (P7), which provides literacy and numeracy teaching in the Primary School by a class teacher with all other lessons being provided in the Secondary School taught by subject specialists.

The Secondary School supports pupils to fulfil their academic potential, gain Scottish qualifications and entry to universities in both the UK and abroad. Academic expectations and achievements are high and small groups encourage individual learning and development. On average 95% of S6 go on to University.

Situation. Situated in Crieff, surrounded by stunning Perthshire countryside, Morrison's Academy has one of the most beautiful locations of any school in Britain. The stunning mountain scenery provides the backdrop for the school and offers outstanding locations for outdoor learning. Pupils attend from the local area and travel from Perth, Pitlochry, Dunkeld, Aberfeldy, Auchterarder, Stirling, Dunblane and Falkirk.

Curriculum. Morrison's Academy follows a modern, Scottish curriculum; its dynamic and varied teaching methods support pupils to fulfil their academic potential and encourage every individual to strive for their highest. Pupils in Primary and lower Secondary follow the Scottish 5–14 programme of study, leading in upper Secondary to National 5 and then to Higher and Advanced Higher National Qualifications.

Emphasis is placed upon academic achievement, but is coupled with numerous enriching educational skills-based programmes including the Outdoor Adventures and Activities programme, the School's unique Learning for Life programme and, more recently, the Peter Jones Enterprise Academy, the first in Scotland which develops entrepreneurial skills. The School has a range of subjects that they call their Golden Thread subjects, which feature heavily from Nursery through to Secondary school, supplementing the core academic subjects – Music, Art, Sport, STEM, Enterprise, Learning for Life and Outdoor Adventures and Activities which ensure a well rounded education and allow and encourage every child to flourish and grow in their areas of interest and develop their talents.

Pupils are encouraged to develop broad skills and interests outside the classroom. Co-curricular activities (available to primary and secondary pupils) are extensive and Morrison's Academy makes good use of its glorious location. The Morrison's Academy education is further enhanced through local, national and international educational visits.

Houses. All pupils are placed in one of the four houses named after local families: Campbells, Drummonds, Grahams and Murrays. There is healthy, competitive rivalry between the houses and senior pupils are encouraged to take charge of teams for sporting, music, debating and other events. The house system also forms the basis for the pastoral care system in the Secondary school; giving pupils and families one point of contact for all pastoral matters throughout their secondary educational journey.

Games and Activities. Morrison's Academy encourages pupils to participate in a wide range of co-curricular opportunities, offering over 90 different sports, activities and clubs to its Primary and Secondary pupils.

All pupils use the playing fields and facilities on the main campus or walk to the 45 acres of playing fields, including an artificial pitch and cricket wicket for all-weather playing, and pavilions at Dallerie. There is also a Strength and Conditioning Suite, a Climbing Wall, a Bouldering Room and a good number of Tennis Courts. Main sports are rugby, hockey, cricket, tennis and athletics. From upper primary fixtures against other schools take place, generally on Saturday mornings.

Other sporting activities include mountain biking, golf, football, basketball, netball, swimming, golf, weight training, skiing, climbing, orienteering, hill walking, kayaking, karate and more. To complement the sporting activities, pupils are active in The Duke of Edinburgh's Award Scheme, the Combined Cadet Force, drama, music – with a variety of choral, ensemble, band and orchestral opportunities available, debating, chess, Pipe Band, Eco club, Enterprise club, charity fundraising, art, photography and more. Pupils are challenged to make the most of their time and all within the wonderful environment of Perthshire.

Fees per term (2023–2024). Day: Primary £3,900–£5,533, Secondary £5,858.

The fees include tuition, textbooks, stationery, external examination fees, sports and curriculum-related travel.

Where 3 or more children are enrolled coterminously, families will be awarded the following sibling discounts: 3rd child at school – 25% discount & 4th and subsequent children – 50% discount.

Admission Procedure. Admission to the school is by entrance assessment and school report and/or exam results and entrance interview. Entrance assessments can take place throughout the year as required.

For a prospectus pack and any queries, please contact the Admissions Registrar on admissions@morrisonsacademy.org.

Scholarships and Financial Assistance. At Morrison's Academy we would like as many children as possible to benefit from the opportunities that a Morrison's Academy education provides. Consequently, a number of means-tested bursaries are awarded each year.

Bursaries are awarded using a combination of academic merit (as tested in the Entrance Assessment) and financial need. Awards take the form of a discount on tuition fees and will be subject to annual testing of parental means, with changes to financial circumstances required to be notified in between. In exceptional cases, full fee awards may be available, but the majority of awards fall in the range of 20% to 60% of the tuition fee.

There are also a number of Sixth Form Scholarships which are awarded after examination and interview in May. The awards, which carry a nominal financial value, recognise both achievement and potential.

Charitable status. Morrison's Academy is a Registered Charity, number SC000458. The school is a recognised charity providing education.

Board of Governors:
Chairman: Mr D Glen

Mrs I Beveridge	Bailie C McLaren
Ms S Brooks	Mr E McLellan
Mrs L Butler	Prof T Moran
Mr D Cloy	Mr J O'Neill
Mrs K Cook	Mr J Stewart
Mr C Dolby	Mr J Taylor
Mr G Martin	Mr R White

Clerk to Governors: Mr G Sutherland

***Rector*: Mr A McGarva**

Senior Leadership Team:
Depute Rector: Mr D Johnston
Assistant Rector: Ms E McCormick
Assistant Rector: Mr C Nicoll
Head of Nursery & Primary: Ms M Bulloch
Head of External Relations: Mrs M Gardi McGregor
Head of Finance: Mrs J Lochhead
Head of Operations: Ms M Smith
Admissions Registrar: Mrs C Elliott

Mount Kelly

Parkwood Road, Tavistock, Devon PL19 0HZ

Tel: 01822 813193
email: admissions@mountkelly.com
website: www.mountkelly.com
X/Twitter: @Mount_Kelly
Facebook: @MountKellyFoundation
Instagram: @mount.kelly
LinkedIn: /mount-kelly

Motto: *#itstheclimb*

If you like the outdoors, have a sense of adventure and are keen to take advantage of every opportunity that comes your way, then Mount Kelly is the school for you.

Our spectacular location means that we are well known for our strong commitment to co-curricular activities and we encourage all pupils to take part, whether it be camping out on the moor, paddling a canoe or riding the waves on a surf board. We call it the 'Mount Kelly Spirit', an attitude to life that develops here, one that allows pupils to really experience the life-defining educational experience that we promise.

With a high standard of academic schooling and a proven track record in public examination results, over 82% of our pupils gained places at their top choices of universities in the UK and overseas, with more achieving places at Russell Group, Bath and Loughborough universities compared to last year.

The School has an internationally recognised coaching facility for swimming with a four-lane 25 m pool and an eight-lane 50 m pool and has had alumni at the last six Olympic and Paralympic games. In 2023, it topped the medal table at the British Summer Nationals for the second year running, confirming its place as having the top swimming programme in the UK.

In association with Chelsea FC Foundation, the School runs a girls' performance football programme for 16–18 year olds. Two fully FA licensed coaches offer at least 16 hours coaching a week. The squad reached the 2022/23 Season Semi-Finals in the ISFA U18 Girls National Cup and six of the players represented England ISFA in the U16 and U18 girls squad.

Our swimmers and footballers board and are taught alongside their contemporaries.

The College Chamber Choir is the flagship ensemble of the School. The group perform challenging music from all periods and in a huge variety of styles, but mostly *a cappella*. They won the Barnardo's School Choir of the Year Competition in London in 2020.

The success of our swimmers, footballers and singers create a culture in which the level of commitment and dedication required to excel are not considered out of the ordinary but are qualities to which everyone can aspire.

The School was selected as one of the World's Leading Boarding Schools by Fortune in 2023; highly commended for Happiest Boarding School and Originality in Teaching Music and Arts in 2022 by Muddy Stilettos; and selected as a finalist for the Independent School Parent magazine's Independent School of the Year Award in 2019 and in Performing Arts in 2020.

Site and buildings. Mount Kelly is set in over 100 acres of green fields and woodland on the edge of Dartmoor National Park and on the outskirts of the historic town of Tavistock, Devon. The buildings comprise the School Chapel, Assembly Hall, Performing Arts Centre, Dining Rooms, Libraries, Art Studios, Technology workshops, Science Laboratories, Swimming Pools (50 m, 25 m indoor and 25 m outdoor), Sports Hall, Gym, Climbing Wall, Fives and Squash Courts, floodlit All-Weather Pitches.

Term of entry. Pupils may be accepted at any stage in the school year from reception though to Year 12.

Scholarships. Each year, Mount Kelly makes available a number of scholarships and awards to pupils hoping to join us in Year 9 or the Sixth Form. Scholarships and awards are competitive on entry, and provide exceptional opportunities for able pupils. Awards may be given in the following disciplines: Academic, Art, DT, Music (inc. Choral), Sport, Football and Swimming. Means-tested fee assistance is available to all applicants who qualify.

Curriculum. The GCSE curriculum is flexible and aims to stretch each pupil appropriately. The core subjects are Mathematics, English (Language and Literature) and Science. The range of option subjects include Art & Design, Business Studies, Computer Science, Drama, DT, EAL, French, Geography, History, Music, Physical Education, Philosophy, Religion and Ethics (PRE) and Spanish.

Pupils entering the Sixth Form need to possess six GCSE passes with at least a grade 6 for any subject they wish to study at A Level and a 7 for Mathematics and the Sciences. Mount Kelly pupils study for three A Levels. A Level option subjects include Mathematics, Further Mathematics, English Literature, Biology, Physics, Chemistry, Fine Art, Photography, Business Studies, Economics, Geography, History, Music, Physical Education, Politics, Product Design, Psychology, Religious Studies, Modern Foreign Languages and EPQ. Mount Kelly also offers a range of BTEC courses including Sports Coaching, Applied Science and Performing Arts. All pupils in Year 12 year receive tuition in Public Speaking.

Co-curricular activities. Mount Kelly has a strong commitment to co-curricular activities and the majority of College pupils are involved with the Duke of Edinburgh's Award programme, the Devizes to Westminster International Canoe Race, or the Ten Tors Challenge. There is also a strong Naval section of the Combined Cadet Force.

Academic staff run the innovative Learning Outside the Classroom Programme from Year 3 to Year 9. Children in the Pre-Prep attend forest school on a daily basis as weather permits.

All pupils are encouraged to explore new interests and to make the most of their spare time. Societies and activities include LAMDA, Debating, Current Affairs, Drama, Choir, Orchestra, Ensembles, Chess, Computer Programming, Photography, Fine Arts, Surfing and Textiles.

Sport. Mount Kelly has a strong sporting tradition. Sports undertaken are Rugby, Hockey, Netball, Cricket, Football, Tennis, Athletics, Swimming, Cross Country, Squash, Basketball, all of which are played competitively with over 700 fixtures a year.

Fees per term (2023–2024). Day Pupils: £2,850 to £6,990, Full Boarding: £7,580 to £12,320.

Charitable status. The Mount Kelly Foundation is a Registered Charity, number 306716.

Chair of the Governors: Mr Ian MacQueen

***Head Master and Principal of the Foundation*: Mr Guy Ayling**, MA

Senior Deputy Head: Mrs Laura Tabb, BSc, MBa

Deputy Head (Academic),:Mr James Dixon, MA, PGCE

Assistant Head (Safeguarding): Maddy Carr, BA, MA

Head of Prep: Mr Dominic Floyd, BA, PGCE, QTS

Mount St Mary's College

College Road, Spinkhill, Sheffield, Derbyshire S21 3YL

Tel: 01246 433388
email: head@msmcollege.com
website: www.msmcollege.com
X/Twitter: @MountSpinkhill
Facebook: @MSMBHS
Instagram: @mountsaintmaryscollege
LinkedIn: /mount-st-mary-s-college-barlborough-hall-school

Motto: *Sine Macula*

Welcome to Mount St Mary's College

Mount St Mary's College is an idyllic place for children to grow into the fullness of our Jesuit vision, becoming good 'Men and Women for Others' from the moment they join us through to the end of Sixth Form aged 18.

We hope that as you read more about 'The Mount' as it is affectionately known, you will gain insight into just what it is that makes this such a special place to learn, live and work – a sense of our well-known 'Mount Spirit', which makes the Mount feel like home.

We are a Jesuit school, and our vision upholds these values. In that spirit, we welcome students of all faiths and none to become:

- **Grateful** for their own gifts, for the gift of other people, and for the blessings of each day; and generous with their gifts, becoming men and women for others;
- **Attentive** to their experience and to their vocation; and discerning about the choices they make and the effects of those choices;
- **Compassionate** towards others, near and far, especially the less fortunate; and loving by their just actions and forgiving words;
- **Faith-filled** in their beliefs and **hopeful** for the future;
- **Eloquent** and truthful in what they say of themselves, the relations between people, and the world;
- **Learned**, finding God in all things; and **wise** in the ways they use their learning for the common good;
- **Curious** about everything; and **active** in their engagement with the world, changing what they can for the better;

- **Intentional** in the way they live and use the resources of the earth, guided by conscience; and **prophetic** in the example they set to others.

We very much look forward to welcoming you at Mount St Mary's, a place truly inspiring young hearts and minds to go forth and set the world on fire.

Our cosmopolitan boarding community of British and overseas students is at the heart of College life. It is a place where memories and friendships are made that last a lifetime, where opportunity is around every corner and possibilities are endless.

Students gain so much from this diversity, not least an understanding of and a respect for cultural differences, which has never been more important in today's global society. The linguistic benefits are huge, as immersion in an English speaking environment makes perfecting the language a very real possibility.

Boarding at the Mount means a home away from home. Our younger students typically share 2–3 per room, and this is where the foundations of lifelong friendships and connections begin. The rooms are warm and cosy, providing every home comfort and aspect of modern-day living. Our older students have their own room for quiet work and privacy.

The houses all have communal spaces for study, relaxation and socialising, with laundry handled by our boarding parents, and all meals prepared freshly and on-site in our expansive kitchens and served in the refectory.

Our boarding students say that the Mount is their family, and this is certainly how our boarding parents feel. They provide a welcoming and nurturing environment for each student who walks through our door. We all care for one another, in the true spirit of a Jesuit institution.

The boarding houses are found at the heart of campus, which is set in acres of beautiful and safe countryside, housing our numerous sports fields and Olympic-standard athletics track. All this provides a stunning view from your new bedroom window.

The school day. One of the many benefits of boarding is that whilst your classmates are rising early to travel to school, you are already there! You are relaxed and ready for the day ahead, which typically looks like this:

- 7.30 am Breakfast together in our refectory

- 8.30 am School Lessons begin (morning break and lunch taken)

- 4.30 pm School Lessons finish

- 4.45 pm–5.40 pm After School Activities (Boarders choose at least 3 per week)

- 5.45 pm Supper

- Study and free time follow before lights out (time varies per year group).

Beyond the classroom. Life outside the classroom is busy but balanced for our boarders. They experience everything the Mount has to offer, with weekend excursions, activities, sporting fixtures, mass, and a bond with new friends that last a lifetime.

After lessons during the week, boarders can take full use of our on-site, fully equipped gym and swimming pool, and enjoy group sessions ranging from strategy games to gardening! You can choose a minimum of three activities at least three times a week. Options typically on offer include: Games, Study, Swimming, Gardening, Chaplaincy, Music, Drama.

Weekend trips include outings to local national parks, cinema trips and days out at theme parks. These usually take place on Sundays after mass, as Saturdays are generally spent either participating in sports fixtures, or cheering on your peers with the true embodiment of Mount Spirit.

Applying for a place. To study at the Mount is to become a Mountaineer, or an OM as they are more widely known. It is a special thing to become a Mountaineer, and once you attend the Mount, you are an OM for life.

We are currently accepting places for September 2023. We'd love to have you join us and become part of a community that spans every continent across many generations.

Starting a new school can be a little daunting, especially when looking at studying abroad. Our friendly admissions team are on hand to discuss any further questions you may have about life at the Mount.

Please contact admissions@msmcollege.com to apply for your place at Mount St Mary's. You can also start the application process online at www.msmcollege.com/admissions/internationaladmissions

Fees per annum (2023–2024). Day: Years 7–8 £14,610; Years 9–13 £16,770; Boarding: Years 7–8 £28,110; Years 9–13 £36,810.

Talk to us.

Dr Caroline Routledge, Head of Admissions (admissions@msmcollege.com)

Dan Wright, Headmaster (head@msmcollege.com)

Leadership Team:

***Headmaster*: Dan Wright**

Headteacher, Barlborough Hall School: Karen Keeton

Deputy Head (*Pastoral*)/*Head of Boarding*: Jack Murphy

Head of Admissions: Caroline Routledge

New Hall School

The Avenue, Boreham, Chelmsford, Essex CM3 3HS

Tel: 01245 467588
email: admissions@newhallschool.co.uk
website: www.newhallschool.co.uk
X/Twitter: @NewHallSchool
Facebook: @newhallschool
Instagram: @newhallschool_1642
LinkedIn: /school/new-hall-school

Pupil numbers. Senior Divisions (11–16): 637. Sixth Form (16–18): 240. Preparatory Divisions (4–11): 377. Nursery (1–4): 98

Day 1,025, Boarding 327.

Location. New Hall School benefits from a magnificent campus and stunning heritage setting, with a grade I listed main building part of a former Tudor palace occupied by King Henry VIII.

We aim to educate the whole person: academically, creatively and socially, in a community which also nurtures the spiritual dimensions of human life. All benefit from the outstanding facilities on offer within our stunning 70-acre campus.

New Hall is set in an idyllic and convenient location, just 25 minutes by train from London Stratford and within easy reach of all major airports. We offer a distinctive education of real quality that is designed to give students the best start in life.

Diamond Model. At New Hall, students are educated in co-educational classes up to age 11 and again at Sixth Form, however, from 11 to 16 they are taught in single-sex lessons.

The main benefits of the 'diamond model' and five years of single-sex teaching derive from the ability to tailor pastoral and academic provision more sensitively and expertly to the needs of young people going through the physical, emotional and social upheaval of adolescence. Young teenagers are liberated from the negative peer pressure of having to perform in mixed classes.

Gender stereotyping of subjects is also removed. Girls and boys follow an identical curriculum and do not learn to perceive subjects as being more suited to either girls or boys.

Curriculum. New Hall Preparatory Divisions curriculum is enriched by specialist subject teachers for French, Computer Science, Latin, Drama, Music, Physical Education, Art and Dance. Their expert knowledge and passion for their subjects greatly enhance the children's learning experience.

The extensive co-curricular activities on offer set New Hall Preparatory Divisions apart; from Philosophy and Latin, to Mandarin and Poetry, there is always something to do.

Creative subjects including Music, Drama, Dance, Art and Design Technology all form part of the mainstream academic curriculum, and also feature in activities offered outside normal lessons. We have three choirs, infant, junior and chamber, as well as a Preparatory Orchestra. Our pupils regularly perform at prestigious venues, which include the O2 Arena and the Royal Albert Hall.

The Senior Divisions curriculum is distinctive in its breadth and academic rigour. An imaginatively taught and well-balanced curriculum is appropriately tailored to the needs of the individual. The experienced and dedicated staff endeavour to bring out the best in everyone.

New Hall has its own Most Able and Talented programme, which is proven to add exceptional value at GCSE and A Level. We believe that giftedness can be created and that students' academic skills can be developed at ever higher levels if they are given intellectual challenges.

New Hall encourages able students to apply for Oxford or Cambridge universities. The school has a good track record of students winning Oxbridge places in a wide range of subjects, including sciences, arts, humanities and languages.

We are proud that our examination results are consistently among the best of any independent school in the area.

Co-Curriculum. Our co-curricular programme is designed to add breadth to the New Hall education, which enables us to develop the well-rounded young men and women of whom we can be proud.

Our educational philosophy is reflected in the extensive array of challenging co-curricular activities. Educational visits in the Senior Divisions to countries such as India and China, alongside our societies and clubs, create a stimulating environment for your son or daughter to develop his or her passions, learning and talents.

Through activities such as debating, Model United Nations and political philosophy, students can become independent thinkers with a broad and rich experience of social and academic life.

Our Ethos. Our Catholic foundation and ethos is central to all that we do, supported by the work of our lively Chaplaincy Team. At New Hall, a special value is placed on love and forgiveness, which encourage relationships based on trust, kindness, self-respect and care for those in need.

All students participate in our award-winning New Hall Voluntary Service (NHVS), where they gain confidence, leadership and team-working skills and a desire to serve others. They will develop a sense of charity and community that will remain with them beyond their years at New Hall.

Boarding. We have a thriving full boarding community and options for full or flexible boarding. The four boarding houses offer their members a strong sense of identity and opportunities to forge new friendships. There are dedicated boarding provisions for students aged 7–16 and for Sixth Form students.

Although each of our boarding houses has its own individuality, a common theme throughout is the exceptional pastoral care and dedication of the residential team. This is a significant strength of our school.

Music and Performing Arts. Our dedicated Performing Arts Centre and theatres allow students opportunities for group or individual performances, which develop talent and encourage confidence.

Music has a long and fine tradition at New Hall. There is a host of performing groups, including choir, chapel choir, senior orchestra, strings academy and jazz band. Students can participate in the Trinity Drama programme, which develops presentation and public speaking skills. Drama performances range from Shakespeare to modern plays and musicals. Dance is a particular strength, with the annual dance show attracting a cast of more than 200 girls and boys.

Students take part in regional and national festivals and competitions and groups regularly perform in major venues across Europe.

Sport. New Hall students are able to develop their team spirit and physical development through our rich programme of sporting opportunities.

Under the guidance of expert coaches, including former international sportsmen and women, New Hall balances first-class training for those with particular sporting talents, with an inclusive 'sport for all' approach.

Our elite sportsmen and women compete at county, regional and national levels, at which they have enjoyed individual team success.

Our facilities set us apart and the rich variety of sports on offer include rugby, hockey, netball, cricket, swimming, athletics, golf, skiing and tennis.

Fees per term (2023–2024). Senior Divisions: Day £6,960–£7,539; Full Boarding £9,900–£11,991.

Preparatory Divisions: Day: £3,537–£4,878; Full Boarding (from age 7): £7,818.

Nursery Division: £1,710–£4,068.

Entry requirements. ISEB Common Pre-Test assessment, school report, supplementary piece of creative writing, and interview.

Scholarships and Bursaries. Scholarship candidates follow the normal entrance procedure and, dependent on the type of scholarship, a further assessment. All candidates for Year 7 entry are entered for the Academic Scholarship, which is awarded to the highest achieving student from the ISEB Common Pre-Test results. Other scholarships at Year 7 entry 2022 are available in Music, Modern Languages, All-Rounder and Sport. There are also scholarships available for Catholic students. Similar scholarships are available for Year 9 entry. For Sixth Form entry, there are scholarship awards available based on GCSE examination results as well as an All-Rounder scholarship, Modern Languages, Classical Languages, Music, Sport and STEM.

Further information on Admissions, Scholarships and Bursaries is available from the Admissions Team and on the school website.

Charitable status. New Hall School Trust is a Registered Charity, number 1110286. Its aim is the education of children within a Christian environment.

Chair of Governors: Mr Philip Wilson

Senior Leadership & Management Team:

***Principal*: Mrs K Jeffrey**, MA Oxon, PGCE Surrey, BA Div PUM, MA Ed Mgt OU, NPQH

Deputy Principal: Mr Andrew Fardell
Head of Sixth Form DSL, Sixth Form: Mrs Natalia Andrews
Nursery Manager, DSL Nursery: Mrs Lynne Baines
Head of Digital Technology: Mr Matt Charlesworth
Head of Finance: Mr Andy Findlow
Deputy Head of Sixth Form: Dr Stephanie Foster
Director of Learning & Teaching, DDSL Prep: Mrs Alison Hilder
Vice Principal: Mr Vincent Holden
Head of HR: Ms Francesca Martin
Head of Girls' and Boys' Divisions, Lead DSL: Mrs Suzanna Minnis
Executive Assistant and Clerk to the Governors: Mrs Elizabeth Murphy
Vice Principal: Mrs Katherine Reading
Head of Pre-Prep Division, DSL Pre-Prep: Mrs Rachel Tagoe
Vice Principal Curriculum, Growth & Innovation: Dr Paul Tiffen
Head of Preparatory Division, DSL Prep: Mrs Samantha Twomey
Head of Theology: Miss Maria Webb

Newcastle-under-Lyme School

Mount Pleasant, Newcastle-under-Lyme, Staffordshire ST5 1DB

Tel: 01782 631197
email: info@nuls.org.uk
website: www.nuls.org.uk
X/Twitter: @NuLSchoolUK
Facebook: @NewcastleunderLymeSchool
Instagram: @nulschooluk

Newcastle-under-Lyme School, which attracts pupils from a large area of Staffordshire, Cheshire and Shropshire, is a co-educational day school for 800 pupils aged 2–18. The present School was formed in 1981 through the amalgamation of Newcastle High School and the Orme Girls' School, two schools which were endowed under an educational charity scheme for children in Newcastle-under-Lyme which has its roots in the 1600s. The two schools enjoyed a reputation for scholarship and for service to the community throughout North Staffordshire, a reputation which has continued with the formation of Newcastle-under-Lyme School. The School is also well known for its high standards in sport, music and drama, which play a major part in the co-curricular life of the School. The Prep School is adjacent to the Senior School and has some 300 pupils aged 2–11. The School is rated as 'Excellent' by ISI in both inspection categories.

Buildings and grounds. Set in 30 acres, the School is pleasantly situated in a quiet conservation area close to the centre of Newcastle-under-Lyme. The original buildings still form part of the School and extensions have been added from time to time. A fine dining hall was opened in one of the wings of the original building, part of the continuing programme of development and refurbishment which was begun when the School reverted to full independence in 1981. The Millennium Sixth Form Centre opened in 2000 affording spacious new accommodation for senior students. The new Stinton building was opened in September 2014. Newcastle-under-Lyme School is home to excellent sports facilities, including pool, Astroturf and a new £3.5-million sports centre. The School has a Language laboratory, workshops, a Music School, an Art and Design Centre and a gymnasium. There are also tennis and netball courts and extensive playing fields adjacent to the School.

Organisation. The School is organised in two sections: the Preparatory School – Nursery (2004), Pre-Prep (2004) and Prep (1982) – which has up to 300 pupils in the age range 2 to 11, and the Senior School of some 500 pupils, including the Sixth Form numbering more than 150 students.

Form Tutors and Heads of Year have particular responsibility for pastoral welfare.

Curriculum. A broad curriculum in the first five years has English (Language and Literature), Mathematics, Biology, Chemistry, and Physics as core subjects. All pupils also take a Modern Foreign Language, Latin, Greek, History, Geography, Religious Education, Music, Art, Food and Nutrition, Design and Technology, Computer Science, PE, Swimming and

Games. Pupils have the option of taking Biology, Chemistry and Physics as a dual-award GCSE or as three separate GCSEs in Year 10 and Year 11.

Pupils take nine GCSEs and the great majority will proceed to take three A Level subjects in the Lower Sixth Form. There is the possibility of taking the Extended Project Qualification.

Choices in the Sixth Form include A Level Business Studies, Psychology, Philosophy, Economics, British Government and Politics and Physical Education in addition to the subjects available at GCSE. Pupils access our Aspire programme for Oxford and Cambridge Entrance and a specialist programme for Medicine, Dentistry, Veterinary Science applications.

Co-curricular activities. The main school games are Rugby, Cricket, Hockey, Athletics, Tennis and Cross-Country for the boys and Hockey, Athletics, Netball, Tennis and Rounders for the girls. Swimming and Life Saving also feature strongly and there are opportunities for Aerobics, Basketball, Badminton, Golf and other physical activities in the Sixth Form.

There are also strong traditions in both Music and Drama and standards are very high. More than 200 pupils receive instrumental tuition and there are a number of concerts in each year with major performances being given locally. There are three major drama productions each year including one each at Upper School and Lower School levels plus a whole-school production.

The flourishing Combined Cadet Force has naval, army and air-force sections and there is also a Scout troop. Pupils also participate in the Duke of Edinburgh's Award scheme with great success.

Clubs and Societies meet during the lunch hour and after school.

Careers. The School places much emphasis on the importance of careers guidance, both in the GCSE years and in the preparation for higher education.

Admissions. Entry to the Nursery is on a first-come first-served basis. Entry to the Prep School and Years 7, 8, 9 and 10 of the Senior School is by examination/assessment only. Pupils moving into the area may be considered for entry at any time.

Entry at Sixth Form level is by interview and GCSE qualifications.

Registration forms are available on request.

Scholarships and bursaries. The offer of a number of prestigious Scholarships has recently been enhanced with a range available at Year 7 and Sixth Form entry. They include academic, sports, music, art and drama Scholarships and Exhibitions.

Bursaries: A number of Bursaries are available for pupils applying for entry to the Senior School and Sixth Form. Bursaries offer assistance with School Fees, depending upon parental income.

Further details may be obtained from the Registrar.

Fees per term (2023–2024). Senior School: £5,033; Prep School: Prep £4,115, Pre-Prep £3,664, Nursery £50 per day.

Charitable status. Newcastle-under-Lyme School is a Registered Charity, number 1124463. The object of the Charity shall be the provision and conduct in or near Newcastle-under-Lyme of a day or a day and boarding school or schools for boys and girls.

Chair of Governors: Mr D P Wallbank, BA

***Headmaster*: Mr M Getty**, BA Hons, NPQH

Deputy Heads:
Mrs J A Simms, BA, MSc (*Pastoral*)
Mr I S Dicksee, BA, MA (*Academic*)

Head of Sixth Form: Mr A Poole, BSc, MA

Finance Bursar: Mr A Cryer

Newcastle-under-Lyme Preparatory School:

Head of Preparatory School: Mrs K Thomson, BA, MEd

Nursery Manager: Mrs E Taylor, EYPS

Norwich School

70 The Close, Norwich, Norfolk NR1 4DD
Tel: 01603 728430
email: admissions@norwich-school.org.uk
website: www.norwich-school.org.uk
X/Twitter: @NorwichSchool
Facebook: @NorwichSchool
Instagram: @norwich_school

Norwich School is a co-educational, independent day school for pupils aged four to eighteen. Currently there are 1,200 pupils attending the school. Set in the Cathedral Close, Norwich School is a traditional, yet lively place where boys and girls enjoy a rounded and stimulating education. The school is characterised by strong, warm relationships and a profound appreciation of scholarship.

The school achieves exceptional results but we believe that an education for life is about more than statistics. Here we enjoy local character, beautiful surroundings and a remarkable history. Staff and pupils together create a supportive atmosphere and boys and girls benefit from specialised facilities and a broad curriculum.

Ethos. Learning is at the heart of the broad education we offer at Norwich School. This invaluable asset is underpinned by strong Christian values, especially those of love, care and compassion; which we emphasise in all activities and relationships within our community.

Aims. Norwich School is committed to: Nurturing and developing knowledgeable, reflective young people who are capable of understanding difficult concepts and expressing complex and profound ideas; Providing a rich, broad and varied education that develops the diverse talents of all; Equipping our young people for a lifetime of leadership and service.

Pastoral. The Senior School is organised by Houses. Pupils are allocated to a House upon joining the school, and stay with that House as they move up through the year groups. Many of a pupil's first and firmest friendships will be forged within the House.

Each of the eight Houses is managed by a Head of House – a senior member of staff who comes to know the pupils and their parents very well during their years of association with the House, and who brings compassion and continuity to a pupil's life. If a problem arises, the tutor will involve the Head of House in its resolution; they are familiar figures in the school who offer a blend of experience and encouragement.

Sixth Form. Life in the Sixth Form is a busy and rewarding experience, combining rigorous academic scholarship and commitment to a range of extra-curricular activities, as well as leadership and service roles. Our aim is to ensure that all pupils reach their potential and are able to apply for the university courses and career paths of their choice.

Extra-curricular activity. There are many areas of life beyond the classroom that serve to fulfil the aim of a broad and varied education. Encompassed within the programme are challenges, opportunities for service, group cooperation, team participation and leadership. All are seen as central to the educational experience of each school member.

It is hoped that every pupil will find something from the programme which will influence and stay with them far beyond their school days.

Bursaries. Norwich School sets aside generous funds to enable pupils to attend the school who would otherwise not be able to do so without financial help. Bursaries are available in the Senior School only.

All bursaries are means-tested and can result in a reduction in fees of up to 100%; there is a sliding scale based on family income and finances and resources of the school.

Scholarships. The school offers a range of awards for excellence in five areas: academic excellence (11+, 13+ & 16+), music (11+, 13+ & 16+), sport (11+, 13+ & 16+), performing arts (16+ only) and art & design (16+ only). A place on one of our scholarship programmes is made available to Senior School pupils with outstanding ability, potential and flair, which the school assesses by examination, interview, portfolio and audition, as appropriate.

Means tested financial support is also available to candidates applying for these awards.

Admission. The main points of entry are at ages 4, 7, 11, 13 and 16. Applications to other year groups are also considered.

Fees per term (2023–2024). Senior School: £6,659; Lower School (Years 3–6): £6,069; Lower School (Reception–Year 2): £4,516.

Partnerships. Norwich School is committed to providing partnership opportunities and carrying out outreach work with both local, national and international organisations. Our ethos talks of a loving and compassionate community and one of our key aims is to prepare our young people for a lifetime of leadership and service.

Our pupils and staff are actively encouraged to undertake voluntary activities in the wider community, from fundraising to offering practical help, and sharing curriculum and staff development opportunities.

The school's commitment to making a positive impact in the community drives our decision-making and our activities reflect the breadth and depth of our relationships with the schools, charities and organisations we work with.

Old Norvicensians. All former pupils automatically become Old Norvicensians (ONs for short) for their life beyond school. Our Development Office runs a busy schedule of alumni engagement: reunions, networking events and publications, as well as a well-supported public lecture series with external partner organisations.

Charitable status. Norwich School is a Registered Charity, number 311280. It exists solely to provide education.

Chair of Governors: Mr P J E Smith

***Head*: Mr Steffan D A Griffiths**, MA Oxon

Notting Hill and Ealing High School
GDST

2 Cleveland Road, Ealing, London W13 8AX
Tel: 020 8799 8400
email: enquiries@nhehs.gdst.net
website: www.nhehs.gdst.net
X/Twitter: @nhehs
Facebook: @nhehsGDST
Instagram: @nhehsgdst

See full entry in the **GSA** section, on **p. 458**.

Nottingham High School

Waverley Mount, Nottingham NG7 4ED
Tel: 0115 978 6056
email: info@nottinghamhigh.co.uk
enquiries@nottinghamhigh.co.uk
website: www.nottinghamhigh.co.uk
X/Twitter: @NottsHigh
Facebook: @nottshigh
Instagram: @nottshigh
LinkedIn: /nottshigh

Motto: *Lauda Finem*

This School was founded in 1513 by Dame Agnes Mellers, widow of Richard Mellers, sometime Mayor of Nottingham. The first Charter was given by Henry VIII, and supplementary Charters were given by Philip and Mary, and by Queen Elizabeth. The School, which remains independent, is now administered under the terms of a scheme issued by the Charity Commissioners.

Organisation. There are 1,180 day pupils, of whom 329 are in the Infant and Junior School and 262 in the Sixth Form. Nearly all Junior School pupils go on to complete their education in the Senior School. (*For further details about the Infant and Junior School, see entry in IAPS section.*) From 2015 the school became co-educational in the Sixth Form and Infant school, followed by the other year groups from 2016.

Curriculum. The Senior School curriculum leads to examinations at GCSE in the normal range of subjects. The Sixth Form are prepared for A Levels. The range of subjects is wide: Latin, Drama and Theatre Studies, Modern Languages, English Literature, English Language, History, Economics, Politics, Design Engineering, Geography, Mathematics and Further Mathematics, Physics, Chemistry, Biology, Music, Art,

Philosophy, Religion & Ethics, Psychology, RS, Music, Physical Education and Computer Science.

Admission. Entrance Examinations and assessments are held in January each year. Applicants for the Infant School should be between the ages of 4 and 7 years, for the Junior School between the ages of 7 and 11 years, and for the Senior School/Sixth Form between 11 and 16 years on 1 September of the year of entry subject to places being available and a successful interview (entry to Sixth Form is also dependent upon a minimum of 5 7s at GCSE).

Fees per term (2023–2024). Tuition: Senior School £5,979; Junior School £4,763; Lovell House Infant School £4,094.

Entrance Scholarships and Bursaries.

Nottingham High School has its own means-tested Bursaries to be awarded to pupils entering the Senior School at age eleven. All Bursaries will be awarded at the Headmaster's discretion and will normally continue until a pupil leaves the School.

Academic Part Scholarships are a fixed sum automatically awarded to the top performing students at the end of Year 7. These cannot be applied for – every student who joins Year 7 will be entered for this.

Games. The Playing Fields, covering 20 acres, are situated about a mile and a half from the School with excellent pavilion facilities. There are also indoor cricket nets at the school. The School games, in which all pupils are expected to take part unless medically exempted, are Rugby, Hockey, (together with Association Football in the Junior School) in the winter, and Cricket or Tennis and Athletics in the summer for boys. Girls play Hockey (The School has 2 brand new purpose built Hockey pitches), Netball and Rounders in the winter and summer terms respectively. Other alternatives provided for seniors include Cross Country, Squash, Association Football (Sixth Form), Badminton, Golf, Shooting, and Basketball. Swimming (the School has its own 25m pool) forms part of the Physical Education programme.

Combined Cadet Force. The School maintains a contingent of the CCF based on voluntary recruitment and consisting of Navy, Army and Air Force sections. There is a small bore range, and the School enters teams for various national competitions.

Societies. Individual interests and hobbies are catered for by a wide range of Societies which meet in the lunch break or at the end of afternoon school. These include and are not limited to Drama, Modern Languages, Mathematics, Chemistry, Biology, English, Politics, Arts, Music and Debating Societies, the Chess Club, the Bridge Club, Christian Union, and the Scout Troop. Over 160 pupils a year participate in the Duke of Edinburgh's Award scheme. The Community Action Group and the Explorer Scouts are alternatives to this.

Music. Apart from elementary instruction in Music in the lower forms, and more advanced studies for GCSE and A Level, tuition is offered by 3 full-time and 18 part-time teachers in the full range of orchestral instruments. There are 2 School orchestras of 50 and 30 players, 2 Choirs, a concert band (wind) of 50, a Training Band and Big Band and choral and orchestral concerts are given each year. There are a number of instrumental bursaries, covering fee tuition on one instrument, available to pupils entering Year 7.

Wellbeing Centre. Nottingham High School opened it's Wellbeing Centre in 2023, promoting a balanced, healthy experience for students' academic and personal lives. Features include Oasis Room and Garden, a Spirituality Space, the School Counselling service, physiotherapy, and a Flexible space for activities such as yoga and pilates classes.

Honours. 8 Places at Oxford and Cambridge in 2023.

Charitable status. Nottingham High School is a Registered Charity, number 1104251. It exists to provide education for pupils between the ages of 4 and 18 years.

Governing Body:
The Lord Lieutenant of Nottinghamshire
The Lord Mayor of Nottingham
Two Representatives of the City Council
One Representative of the Nottinghamshire County Council
Four Representatives of the Universities
Eleven Co-optative Members

Chairman of the Governors: Mr Steven Banks

***Headmaster*: Mr Kevin Fear**

Deputy Head (*Academic*): Mr Paul Spedding
Deputy Head (*Pastoral*): Miss Lisa Gritti
Assistant Head (*Co-Curricular*): Mr Richard Alexander
Assistant Head (*Director of Studies*): Dr Katharine Linton
Deputy Head (*International and Strategic Projects*): Mrs Angharad Simpson
Assistant Head (*Pastoral*): Ms Michaela Smith
Head of Sixth Form: Mr David Gillett
Head of Infant & Junior School: Mrs Clare Bruce
Director of Finance and Operations: Mrs Harriet Avison

Headmaster's EA: Miss Rebecca Winch
Head of Marketing: Mrs Claire Sneddon
Head of Admissions and Partnership: Mrs Ruth Boxer

Head, Infant and Junior School: Mrs Clare Bruce
Deputy Head (*Academic*): Miss Lucy Thorpe
Deputy Head (*Pastoral*): Mr Christian Cordy

Oakham School

Chapel Close, Oakham, Rutland LE15 6DT

Tel: 01572 758500
01572 758758 (Admissions)
email: admissions@oakham.rutland.sch.uk
website: www.oakham.rutland.sch.uk
X/Twitter: @OakhamSch
Facebook: @OakhamSchool
Instagram: @oakhamschool
LinkedIn: /oakhamschool

Motto: *Quasi Cursores Vitai Lampada Tradunt*

The possibilities for learning really are limitless at Oakham School. As a large co-educational boarding and day school with over 1,000 pupils aged 10–18 and a 50:50 split of boys and girls and boarders and day pupils, we are proud to be able to offer a truly staggering range of experiences, activities and opportunities.

Whilst academic excellence lies at the heart of everything we do, our focus goes far beyond helping our students to achieve outstanding examination results. The Arts flourish and we have an enviable reputation for excellent coaching in a variety of sports. Activities are also an integral part of life beyond the classroom.

Oakham School is an exceptionally caring community. Our unique House structure ensures we nurture all aspects of our pupils' well-being throughout their Oakham journey; students are surrounded by staff who are expertly trained to both support their needs and to challenge them to become independent, thoughtful, and responsible young adults.

Oakham is well known and loved for being a friendly and unpretentious school. Whilst we are proud of our 400-year heritage, our priority is always to be at the forefront of educational developments. We were one of the first independent schools to move to co-education in 1971 and we were also one of the first schools to introduce the IB Diploma, alongside A Levels. We continue to look to the future and our focus now, in today's digital world, is on effectively teaching students Information Literacy.

Facilities. Oakham's facilities include one of the best school libraries in the country, state-of-the-art Science and Design Technology facilities, an art gallery, a new Faculty of Social Sciences, a theatre, and a music school. The sports facilities are extensive with 40 acres of superbly maintained fields, all-weather pitches for hockey and tennis, a recently refurbished sports complex with an indoor swimming pool, squash courts, fives courts and fitness centre, and access to nearby Rutland Water for sailing and Luffenham Heath for golf. A new Medical and Pastoral Centre opened in 2017.

Organisation and Curriculum. Oakham has 16 houses: four in the Lower School (ages 10–13), 10 in the Middle/Upper School (ages 13–17), and two houses for final year girls and boys, where they can concentrate more closely on their studies and enjoy increased freedom in preparation for university. The Housemaster or Housemistress is responsible for pastoral support. Each pupil has a tutor, who is responsible for pupils' personal and academic development, and for keeping a balance between academic, creative and social activities.

The curriculum is tailored so that an education at Oakham develops the potential of all our pupils, opening up academic and commercial opportunities around the world. The Lower School offers a unique and exciting programme combining the full range of traditional subjects with the development of essential learning habits. In the Middle School, pupils can choose their GCSEs and IGCSEs from a comprehensive range of subjects. In the Upper School Oakham is unusual in offering a choice between A Levels and BTECs or the highly-regarded IB Diploma Programme.

GCSE/IGCSE: All pupils take English Language, English Literature, Dual-Award Science (which comprises Biology, Chemistry and Physics), with the possibility of studying separate Sciences, and Mathematics. They also choose from History, Geography, Religion and Philosophy, French, Spanish, German, Drama or Music and a variety of Creative Arts subjects (Fine Art – Painting and Mixed Media, Textile Design or Sculpture, Design Technology or Electronics). Other options include: Citizenship Studies, Classical Civilisation, Computer Science, Creative iMedia, Greek, Latin and Physical Education. We expose pupils to a rich cultural environment, providing an exciting programme of projects and visits to enhance learning beyond the classroom and the exam syllabus.

16+: Upper School pupils may opt either for A Levels and equivalent stand-alone qualifications or the International Baccalaureate Diploma. A Level subjects on offer include: Art: Critical and Contextual Studies, Art and Design, Biology, Business (A Level and BTEC), Chemistry, Classical Civilisation, Computer Science, Design Technology, Drama and Theatre Studies, Economics, English Literature, French, Geography, German, Classical Greek, History, Latin, Mathematics, Further Mathematics, Music, Philosophy, Physics, Politics, Psychology, Spanish, Sport Science (A Level and BTEC). The International Baccalaureate Diploma Programme offers a similar range, but students study six subjects: three subjects are studied at Higher Level and three at Standard Level. Additionally, all students take the three Core Elements of the Diploma: Theory of Knowledge, the Extended Essay and a programme of Creativity, Activity and Service.

Music. Around half of all pupils play in musical ensembles, choirs, bands, orchestras, and musical theatre productions. Over 80 concerts each year present a wide variety of performing opportunities both in and out of School, as well as international tours. Pupils are regularly selected for national youth ensembles and the School Chamber Choir has a national reputation for excellence.

Drama plays an important part in the life of the School with five major productions each year. A majority of pupils at all levels takes part in at least one dramatic production a year.

Art, Design and Technology. The Richard Bull Centre and the state-of-the-art Jerwood School of Design together offer an extensive array of creative and Design Technology opportunities, including painting, pottery, sculpture, textiles, print-making, photography, computer-aided design and electronics, working in wood, metal and plastics. Pupils regularly compete for and win nationally recognised awards and scholarships, such as the Arkwright Scholarship.

Sport and Activities. Our major sports are rugby, hockey, cricket, athletics, netball and tennis. Some 30 other sports options are also offered. A typical year will see over 100 pupils progress to the national finals in 10 different sports. Oakham is proud to be a well-recognised training ground for national squads.

We offer a comprehensive activities programme (over 125 on offer) and each week pupils follow an activity (or hobby) and, from the Middle School upwards, a Service Option. They can try something new or pursue an existing passion. Our Service Options develop skills and values for life. Pupils choose from an extensive volunteering programme, the Combined Cadet Force or the Duke of Edinburgh's Award.

Entry. Normal entry points are 10+, 11+, 13+ and 16+. Pupils are accepted mainly in September at the start of the academic year. Full admissions information is available from the Director of Admissions.

Scholarships and Bursaries. The following scholarships/awards are available: Academic and Music (11+, 13+ and 16+), Performing Arts and Sporting

Talent Awards (11+), All-Rounder (13+), Art, Design and Technology, Drama and Sport (13+ and 16+). The basic value of a scholarship/award is up to 10% and top-up means-tested support may be available. For further information, including bursaries, please request an information booklet from the Director of Admissions, Tel: 01572 758758.

Fees per term (2023–2024). Lower School (age 10–13): £10,500–£11,485 (full boarding), £8,225–£11,000 (weekly boarding: 2 to 6 nights), £6,845–£7,510 (day).

Middle and Upper Schools (age 13+): £14,635 (full boarding), £13,685 (weekly boarding: up to 6 nights), £8,700 (day).

Honours 2023. Overall 42% of all exams taken at A Level, Pre-U, BTEC or in the IB Diploma were awarded A* or A or equivalent. At A Level 68% gained A*–B grades or equivalent. Five pupils scored 100% in Art and two got 100% in Critical & Contextual Studies. In the IB Diploma, our average point score was 34.5, compared with the worldwide average of 30. 15% of pupils achieved 40 or more points (equivalent to 4 A*s at A Level) and one pupil achieved a perfect score of 45 points. At GCSE, 49% of pupils gained A*/A/9–7 grades. Eleven pupils left to study at 'Loxbridge' universities and 21 pupils are now at overseas universities. Six leavers are now on clinical courses and 12 are following specialist art and design courses.

Charitable status. Oakham School is a Registered Charity, number 1131425, and a Company Limited by Guarantee, registered in England and Wales, number 06924216. Registered Office: Chapel Close, Market Place, Oakham, Rutland LE15 6DT. It exists for the purpose of education.

Trustees:
Chairman: Professor Neil T Gorman, DL, BVSc, PhD, DVSc, DVM, DACVIM, Dip-ECVIM, FRCVS, FRSA

Ex officio:
The Lord Lieutenant for Rutland, Dr Sarah Furness, PhD
The Very Revd Christopher Dalliston, Dean of Peterborough

Co-optative:
David Allsop, BA Dipl Arch. RIBA
Professor Philip Baker, BMedSci, BM, BS, DM, FRCOG, FRCSC, FRANZCOG, FMedSci
Peter Boddy, MBA, BA Hons
David F Crean, BSc
Mark Dorsett, FCIPD
Professor Neil T Gorman, DL, BVSc, PhD, DVSc, DVMS, DVM, DACVIM, Dip-ECVIM, FRCVS, FRSA
Julia H Grundy
Dr Simon Hyde, MA, DPhil
Mrs Obi Jegede, LLB, LLM, GDip
Stephen Jones, MSc, MLitt
Natasha F Marshall, BA
Margaret Miles, BSc
Josephine Osborne, BA Hons, LLM
Rashmi Patel, BA Hons, Grad IPD
Roger Summerton, FCA
Stephen Woolfe, LLB

***Headmaster*: Henry Price**, MA Oxon

Chief Operating Officer: William Hawkes, BA
Senior Deputy Head: Arthur Mayhew, MSc
Deputy Head (Pastoral): Mrs S J Gomm, BSc
Deputy Head (Academic): Dr Leo Dudin, PhD
Deputy Head (Co-curriculum): James Robinson, BA

Senior Members of Staff:
Head of Upper School: Mrs M Fairley, BA
Head of Middle School: N Favill, BA
Head of Lower School: J Cure, BA
Senior Housemaster: T Dixon-Dale, BA
Director of Admissions: Mrs A Steiger
Director of External Relations: Mrs S Rowntree

Heads of Department:
Activities: M J Powell, HND BSA
Biology: Dr P J Ingles PhD
Business: Mrs S D Donlevy, BA
Careers: Dr R Pearson, RCDP
Chemistry: Mrs J E Griffiths, MChem
Citizenship: Miss V Lamb, BEd
Classics: Dr W G Leveritt, BA, MPhil
Computer Science: Mrs N Deacon, BSc
Creative Arts: Ms E Brass, MA
Drama: Mrs G Norell, BA
Economics: Mr S J Janes, BA
English: Dr E Reddy, MA, PhD
Geography: H A Collison, BSc, MPhil
History: J N J Roberts, MA
Languages: E J Milner, MA
Learning Support: Dr E Stanley Isaac, BSc, PhD, NASENCo, PGCertv SpLD, AMBDA
Mathematics: M J H Coman, BSc (*Acting*)
Music: P Davis, MA, ARCO
Politics & International Relations: L Ward, BA
Physics: TBC
Psychology: Miss C Findlay, BA, MEd
Religion and Philosophy: Mrs K Brett, BA
Sport: Dr I Simpson, BSc, Med, DProf

Chaplain: The Revd T F Tregunno, MTh

Housemasters/Housemistresses:
Lower School:
Ancaster: Mrs K Gibbons, BSc
Lincoln: Mrs W Singhal, BSc
Peterborough: M M Fairweather, MA
Sargants: D Williams, BA

Middle School:
Barrow: A S Denman, BA
Buchanans: Miss L Aherne, MA
Chapmans: O Hughes, BA, MA
Clipsham: S Dachtler, BA
Gunthorpe: Mrs Lydia Dunbavand, BSc
Hambleton: Miss S Angove, MA
Haywoods: G Gelderbloom, HDE Dip RSA
Rushebrookes: Mrs K M Robinson, MA
Stevens: Mrs E Roe, BEng
Wharflands: T Dixon-Dale, BA

Upper School:
Round House: Mrs H J Cannie, BA
School House: A Ross, BSc, MA

The Oratory School

Woodcote, Reading, South Oxfordshire RG8 0PJ
Tel: 01491 683500
email: enquiries@oratory.co.uk
website: www.oratory.co.uk
X/Twitter: @oratoryschool
Facebook: @TheOratorySchool
Instagram: @theoratoryschool
LinkedIn: /company/the-oratory-school

Motto: *Cor ad cor loquitur*

The Oratory School was founded in 1859, by Saint John Henry Newman. It is an HMC Co-educational Catholic boarding and day school for pupils aged 11–18.

Location. The school is situated in an 'Area of Outstanding Natural Beauty' (AONB) in grounds of approximately 100 acres in South Oxfordshire, yet is within easy travelling distance of London, major motorways and airports.

Ethos. The Oratory has high academic standards, but an Oratory education is about developing young people in a much deeper sense than exam results alone can demonstrate. An Oratory education gives our young people every opportunity to draw out and find their individual innate talents and qualities and instils in them a sense of joy and a genuine love of learning. At The Oratory everyone will find their place to shine, encouraged through our vast array of co-curricular activities. The Oratory is not a large school and this enables each and every pupil to be known, valued and stretched as an individual within our nurturing community. Strong pastoral care is at the heart of what we do. As a Catholic school that welcomes pupils of all faiths or none, visitors often comment on the inclusive family atmosphere of our school; it is this supportive environment that nurtures the confidence, self-expression and resilience that are vital for success and happiness in the world of today.

Organisation. Four Senior Houses and one Junior House, St Philip House, both day and boarding. There are currently 377 pupils: 137 boarding, 41 weekly boarding, 17 flexi boarding and 240 day pupils.

Health. The school's Medical Centre is permanently staffed during term time by a team of Registered Nurses and a duty nurse is present night and day.

Admission. Pupils enter at 13+ through the Scholarship or Common Entrance Examinations, or at 11+ or 16+ by entrance exam. Pupils also enter in the 6th Form and in other year groups subject to availability. All pupils are expected to take an assessment prior to entry.

Academic. All pupils follow the internationally recognised and intellectually rigorous GCSE (or IGCSE in a number of subjects) and A Level curricula, with the Extended Project Qualification (EPQ) also offered at 6th Form. We have a rich and varied curriculum that is enhanced by masterclasses, workshops, lectures and field trips to inspire and enthuse our pupils.

All academic subjects are taught in small classes by specialist teachers who have a real drive to instil a genuine love of learning in all our pupils. As The Oratory is a smaller school, the pupils have the benefit of developing excellent relationships with their teachers and tutors, who know their strengths and their weaknesses, and who can support them throughout their entire school journey, ensuring that all our pupils are set challenging targets.

We are a selective school. Academic endeavour is very much encouraged; we want our pupils to work hard, take responsibility for their own learning, and strive to achieve everything of which they are capable. Having reached their academic potential, the majority of our pupils gain entry to their first choice of university, including many Russell Group universities. They then go on to pursue a wide range of exciting careers.

Religious Education. The school is an HMC Catholic school which welcomes pupils of all faiths or none. There is a resident Chaplain who looks after the spiritual needs of both pupils and staff.

Art, Drama and Music. *The Good Schools Guide* describes our Art Department as a 'hive of energy, where everybody finds their niche' and The Oratory has won top accolades both for A Level and GCSE Art and Design, confirming our place nationally as one of the top schools for Art in the country. In 2023, A Level exam results were 100% A*–A in 3D Design A Level and 78% A*–B in Art A Level. The department believes that anyone can be an artist and film-making, textiles, coding and animation are all possible alongside traditional Art media. In an age where creative thinking is becoming increasingly important in the workplace, The Oratory Art Department is well placed to equip our pupils for the future.

The Drama Department is an active, flourishing department at The Oratory, and Drama provision is outstanding, helping pupils to develop their imagination and self-expression, confidence and public-speaking skills. All pupils have the opportunity to perform in our Theatre and Performing Arts Centre. If they are not involved in LAMDA, GCSE, or A Level Drama performances, pupils can still participate in the main school production or in our popular inter-house Drama Competition. There is also a Drama club that focuses on improvisation techniques, and we run regular theatre trips.

Music touches the lives of everyone at The Oratory and is an integral part of life at the school. Our aim is to build a musical journey for every pupil in the school, whatever their level of musical ability or particular musical interest. There are rehearsals for ensembles every day of the week, and individual lessons on instruments ranging from the piano to the bagpipes. We have a strong tradition in both choral and jazz music; however, the repertoire encountered by our pupils encompasses everything from plainsong to punk. There is a strong emphasis on performance and providing abundant opportunities to shine at all levels of ability. There are frequent enrichment visits to venues such as the Wigmore Hall and English National Opera.

Sports. The Oratory has a 9-hole golf course and a Sports Centre that includes a 25 m swimming pool, indoor sports hall, gym, ergo room, indoor cycling studio, 2 squash courts, 6 lawn tennis courts and we are one of only five schools in the country to have a Real Tennis court. We also have a boathouse on the River Thames for our rowers.

In addition to the main games of Rugby, Football, Cricket, Hockey (Berkshire League winners for 2023 and 2022), Netball and Rowing, pupils take part in Athletics, Cross-Country Running, Swimming, Tennis, Badminton, Basketball, Squash, Golf and Real Tennis. There is a co-educational programme for Cricket, Football, Real Tennis, Rowing and Swimming, and Horse Riding is available.

Co-curricular. Enrichment activities take place three or four times every week, with a vast array of activities to choose from, encouraging our pupils to try new things.

Leadership skills are encouraged by our flourishing contingent of Oratory CCF, which includes Army, RN, RAF and Adventure Training. The Duke of Edinburgh's Award scheme is popular with the Gold expedition going to various locations in the UK and overseas.

Careers guidance. Almost all students at The Oratory go on to higher education. Advice and guidance is readily available for our students, who are helped through the process by their tutor, as well as the rest of the 6th Form team. We provide guidance to achieve smooth and successful applications to the institutions and courses to which our students aspire: Careers advice; UCAS preparation and advice; Specialised Oxbridge preparation; Medic preparation.

There is also guidance on careers (including visiting guest speakers and a Careers Fair), apprenticeships and more vocational courses.

Fees per term (2023–2024). Boarders: £14,437 (Junior House: £9,878); Day Pupils: £9,920 (Junior House: £7,155).

The fees include board, tuition, consolidated extras and games. Means-tested bursaries are offered on a discretionary basis.

Scholarships. A number of Academic Scholarships and Awards in Art, Music, Drama, DT and Sport are offered. Awards are of varying values. All-rounder Awards are made on the recommendation and reports from a pupil's current Headteacher. 6th Form Scholarships are also available.

Alumni. Oratory School alumni are called Old Oratorians. There is a Development Office that keeps in touch with the alumni through a programme of events and communications.

Charitable status. The Oratory Schools Association is a Registered Charity, number 309112. It is a charitable trust dedicated to continuing the aims of its Founder, Saint John Henry Newman.

Governing Body:

President: The Rt Hon Lord Judge, MA Cantab, PC

Vice-Presidents:
M H R Hasslacher
N Purnell, KC, MA Cantab

Chairman: P Lo, BA, PGCE
Vice-Chairman: P M Sieyes, Esq.

Clerk to the Governors & Bursar: F Yates, MA Oxon, ACA

***Head Master*: Dr Julian Murphy**, DPhil Oxon

Deputy Head Academic: M Syddall, MA Oxon, MSt
Deputy Head Pastoral: M B Fogg, BA

Chaplain: Fr D Rocks, OP

Oundle School

Oundle, Peterborough, Northamptonshire PE8 4GH
Tel: 01832 277125
email: info@oundleschool.org.uk
website: www.oundleschool.org.uk
X/Twitter: @oundleschool
Instagram: @oundleschool

Motto: *God Grant Grace*

Founded in 1556, Oundle School is one of Britain's leading co-educational independent schools for boarding and day pupils aged 11–18. Situated in the small, charming market town of Oundle, Northamptonshire, travel from London is less than an hour by train yet the School enjoys a beautiful setting in the heart of the UK countryside. The School and town are closely entwined, with Oundelians taking their place within this wider community, not isolated from it.

The Best of Modern Boarding. Oundle has long been associated with the very best of modern independent boarding education, with an approach that means, while there are regular exeats, pupils are either all in or all out. The result is a full and varied seven-day-a-week programme with endless opportunities and a real buzz to the weekends. The House system is at the heart of both School life and pastoral care, with each boarding House being home to those who live and work there. All meals are taken together in House dining rooms and every pupil is part of a small, carefully structured House tutorial group which spans all years, reflecting a family feel and allowing older pupils to act as mentors to the younger ones.

Number of Pupils (2023–2024). 810 boarders and 310 day pupils.

Academic Success. Oundle has long shown itself to be open to innovation and change, combining a strong and traditional educational model with new disciplines, techniques and facilities. The curriculum offers a huge breadth of subjects and opportunities; eight timetabled languages, twenty-nine A Level options, twenty-six GCSE/IGCSE options and over forty academic societies. Oundelians are encouraged to look beyond their current strengths and interests, harness their natural intellectual curiosity and explore new avenues for learning.

Oundle's academic results are steadfastly excellent. In 2023, 26% of A Level grades awarded were A* or equivalent, with 63% A*/A and 83% A*–B. At I/GCSE, 27% achieved 9 (A**), 54% were awarded 9 or 8 (A**/A*), while 74% were graded at 9–7 (A**–A). On average, 10% of Oundelians gain Oxbridge offers and 75% take up Russell Group university places, with increasing numbers looking across the Atlantic for higher education with a more global approach.

Co-curricular Activities. A vast range of enriching co-curricular opportunities encompass three development strands: Leadership and Adventure; Service; and Creativity and Culture. The School is proud of being the largest DofE centre in Central England and having the largest School CCF in the country. The Arts also play a huge role in the life of Oundelians, with around 20 School, House and professional touring productions performed annually in the Stahl Theatre; over 50% of pupils learning at least one musical instrument; and the Yarrow Gallery playing host to spectacular pupil exhibitions. Sport is flourishing; the Sports Masterplan has recently been completed and the pursuit of sporting excellence and elite performance sits comfortably alongside a vision for all pupils to benefit from a wide selection of team and individual sporting options.

Partnerships and Outreach. As a founding member of the Oundle, Peterborough and East Northants (OPEN) Learning Partnership, Oundle is committed to increasing opportunity, raising aspirations and allowing the sharing of best practice between both state and independent schools. A unique partnership with Imperial College London sees the School employ an Imperial College London Outreach Fellow who teaches Science both at Oundle and at its partner schools. There is also a valuable link with Swansea University's Engineering department and a further formal partnership with the Royal College of Music.

Admissions. Main entry is at 11+, 13+ and 16+ (boarding and day), with a small number of places available at other stages, including boarding places at 12+. At 11+ pupils join either the junior boarding House or junior day House, before moving to a senior House at 13+, alongside pupils joining from a range of prep schools at this key entry point.

Depending on the stage of entry and current school, applicants sit Common Entrance or Oundle's own entrance test, alongside an interview.

Scholarships. An extensive series of entrance scholarships is offered each year.

Scholarships at 11+:

- Junior Academic
- Junior Music

Scholarships at 13+:

- Academic
- Oundle (for those with talents in two or more disciplines)
- Music
- Drama
- Art
- Design, Engineering and Technology
- Sport

Scholarships at 16+:

- Academic
- Music
- Art
- Design, Engineering and Technology
- Sport

Bursaries. Bursaries vary in size according to circumstance; ranging from 10% to 100% or more, to ensure a pupil does not miss out on the broad range of co-curricular opportunities Oundle offers. Pupils must comfortably satisfy the academic entry requirements but equally be able to demonstrate they will contribute fully to the life of the School.

Parents who feel that they may need the support of a bursary are encouraged to discuss the matter with the School, through the Admissions Office in the first instance, well in advance of the due date of entry. Decisions regarding bursary assistance are made approximately two years ahead of entry.

Fees per term (2023–2024).

UK Boarders: First Form – 3 Day (Year 7): £9,210, First Form – Full or Weekly (Year 7): £11,505, Second Form (Year 8): £13,355, Third Form to Sixth Form (Years 9–13): £15,145.

Day Pupils: First Form (Year 7): £7,450, Second Form (Year 8): £8,635, Third Form to Sixth Form (Years 9–13): £9,790.

Overseas Boarders: First Form – Full or Weekly (Year 7): £11,771, Second Form (Year 8): £13,621, Third Form to Sixth Form (Years 9–13): £15,411.

Laxton Junior School caters for 4 to 11-year-old boys and girls and has 250 pupils on roll. *(For further details, see entry in IAPS section.)*

Charitable status. Oundle School is a Registered Charity, number 309921.

The Governing Body:
Mr Robert Ringrose (*Chairman*)
Mr Ian Hodgson (*Vice Chairman*)
Sir Charles Bowman
Mr Oliver Brettle
Mr Edward Campbell-Johnston
Mr Neil Chippington
Mr Guy Chisenhale-Marsh
Mr Howard Clayden
Mr Timothy Coleridge
Mrs Suzanna D'Oyly
Mr Jason Hill
Mr Alasdair Kennedy
Mr Charles McAndrew
Mrs Debbie McGregor
Mr Ben Shepherd-Smith
Mr Dominic Toriati
Mr Chris Tyler
Mr James Whitmore

Ex-Officio:
Sir Charles Bowman (*Master*)
Mr Guy Chisenhale-Marsh (*Second Warden*)
Mr Edward Campbell-Johnston (*Third Warden*)

Leadership:

***Head*: Mrs S Kerr-Dineen,** MA Cambridge

Deputy Head: Mrs D L Watt, MA Oxford
Deputy Head Academic: Dr A Baragwanath, Msci, PhD Durham
Deputy Head Pastoral: Mrs A E Meisner, BA Nottingham
Deputy Head Co-Curricular: Mr A J Sherwin, MA Edinburgh
Deputy Head Admissions: Mr A B Burrows, MAEd Open, BSc York
Deputy Head Partnerships and Outreach: Mr G Montgomery, MSci Queen's, MA Bath

Senior Chaplain: Revd Maria Coulter, MTh London

Bursary:
Bursar: Mr D J Toriati, MA King's College
Director Finance: Eleanor Charlton

Admissions:
Registrar: Mr J Hammond Chambers, MA Nottingham
Assistant Registrar: Miss S Johnson, BA Durham
Assistant Registrar: Miss T Dorman, MChem Leeds

The Perse Upper School

Hills Road, Cambridge CB2 8QF
Tel: 01223 403800
email: schooloffice@perse.co.uk
website: www.perse.co.uk
X/Twitter: @ThePerseSchool
Facebook: @theperseschool
Instagram: @theperseschoolcambridge
LinkedIn: /school/the-perse-school-cambridge

The Perse School is Cambridge's oldest secondary school, founded in 1615 by Dr Stephen Perse, a Fellow of Gonville and Caius College. The School still maintains close links with both Gonville and Caius and with Cambridge University.

The Perse Upper School is a co-educational independent day school for pupils aged 11–18.

Ethos. The Perse is a very special school which is both traditional and innovative, academic and caring, understanding and structured, industrious and fun. While our excellent academic results are well-known, prospective pupils and their parents can be surprised to discover the exciting extra-curricular opportunities also on offer. Beyond the classroom there is a wealth of opportunity in music, drama, sport and outdoor pursuits, along with a vibrant programme of over 100 clubs and societies. The Perse is a supportive community characterised by mutual respect, encouragement and care. Our diverse pupil body sets us apart from the stereotypical image of independent schools. Students come from a wide range of backgrounds thanks to our significant bursary programme and a commitment to delivering an outstanding education whilst keeping a downward pressure on fee increases. The School's vision is: '*To love learning and strive for the greater good*'.

History. The School remains true to its historic roots, with close links to the University of Cambridge and a £1 million a year means-tested bursary programme that supports more than 90 pupils.

Admission. There are approximately 1,250 students in the Upper, including 370 in the Sixth Form. The main entry points are Year 7, Year 9 and the Lower Sixth. Our entrance assessments involve a combination of tests, group activity and a short informal interview. All candidates sit papers in English, maths and verbal reasoning. Year 9 candidates sit an additional humanities paper. Sixth Form applicants sit entrance tests and offers are conditional on GCSE results.

Facilities. The Perse has invested more than £40 million in new facilities over the last decade. In 2021, a new Sixth Form Centre opened, together with a refurbished lecture theatre and dining facilities. The Upper occupies an attractive 27-acre greenfield site with extensive on-site playing fields and recreational areas. In addition, the School has recently acquired and developed a 45-acre site at Abington, 6 miles from the School, for additional sports and outdoor pursuits activities. Pupils enjoy high specification science labs and classrooms; a purpose built sports centre, fitness suite and studio, extensive netball and tennis courts and 3 all-weather Astroturf surfaces; a recently extended music centre including a rehearsal hall; art studios and a gallery; a lecture theatre; and an outdoor pursuits centre, climbing wall and shooting range. In the heart of the School, the Rouse Library and the award-winning Peter Hall Performing Arts Centre overlooks Ellison Court. During 2023–24, further major projects include a new swimming pool, sports centre and climbing wall. We will also be increasing the number of science labs we have at the Upper School and will be adding an additional floor onto our Design and Technology building.

Academic excellence. Perse pupils learn in a purposeful and supportive environment where they are taught to think independently and to make sense of a diverse and complex world. The School achieves some of the best A Level and Pre-U results of any co-educational school in the country, regularly appearing in the top 10 schools nationally. Pupils regularly excel in science and maths Olympiads, economics and business challenges, drama and poetry contests and essay and fiction writing competitions.

Rounded education. There is a buzz about daily life at The Perse. There are more than 100 clubs and societies on offer. Nearly 450 pupils, several of whom are involved in national ensembles, take part in 70 school ensembles, with 60 concerts, masterclasses and competitions organised throughout the year, including recent high-profile performances at Saffron Hall, Ely Cathedral and Westminster Abbey. There are at least 10 drama productions each year led by a Theatre Practitioner in Residence and based in a state-of-the-art Performing Arts Centre. A wide range of other performance, literary and debating opportunities are also available. The main sports are cricket, hockey, netball, rugby and tennis. There is an extensive fixtures list; the School fields more than 160 teams in 30 different sports and regularly enjoys regional and national success. More than 600 pupils are involved in the Outdoor Pursuits programme, developing personal confidence, team working and leadership skills. There are a wide range of trips on offer from weekend outings in the UK's national parks to adventurous international expeditions. Popular groups include the Perse Exploration Society, Paddle-sport Club and Climbing Club.

Pastoral care. We know that happiness is a prerequisite to academic and extracurricular success, and to personal development. Each student has a tutor who provides pastoral and academic care. The tutor is at the heart of our approach to pastoral care. Through daily contact, tutors and their tutees develop a strong bond, setting targets and celebrating success or helping pupils overcome challenges. Tutors are someone the students can trust and talk to. There are also peer listeners, form prefects and a system of heads of year, heads of section, senior tutors and school counsellors.

Supportive community. The Upper is a happy school where pupils feel safe, secure and supported. The School works hard to strike the right balance of work and play, comfort and challenge, instruction and discovery, rules and common sense, and guidance and independence. The Perse has a very active programme of charitable fundraising and outreach, and pupils have the chance to become involved in the wider community. Perse pupils work with children from over 20 local primary schools and support charitable fundraising projects, such as Christel House and East Anglia's Children's Hospices.

Global perspective. The Perse has strong international links including foreign language and cultural exchanges, a partnership with Christel House (a charity that educates some of the world's poorest children) and membership of the SAGE global alliance of leading schools. Pupils regularly travel overseas and increasingly collaborate remotely through the latest technology.

Fees per term (2023–2024) School fees per term: £7,061.

Bursaries and scholarships. Means-tested bursaries are available, ranging from 5% to 100% of annual tuition fees. For Year 7 and 9 entry there are no scholarship awards on entry as emphasis is placed on ensuring as many means-tested (bursary) awards are made. Pupils have the opportunity to apply for a music scholarship at the end of Year 7 or 9. Scholarships are available on entry to 6th form for Music, Drama, Art and Sport, as well as Academic Scholarships and Dr Perse Awards. All scholarships are currently one-off payments of £500.

The Perse Prep is a co-educational preparatory school for pupils aged between 7 and 11. Tel: 01223 403920; email: prep@perse.co.uk. (*See The Perse Prep School entry in IAPS section.*)

The Perse Pelican School is for children aged 3 to 7. Tel: 01223 403940; email: pelicanschoolsec@perse.co.uk. (*See The Perse Pelican School entry in IAPS section.*)

Alumni & development. The Perse develops relationships with Old Perseans and Friends around the world. Tel: 01223 403808; email: perseado@perse.co.uk.

Charitable status. The Perse School is a charitable company limited by guarantee (company number 5977683, registered charity number 1120654) registered in England and Wales whose registered office is situated at The Perse School, Hills Road, Cambridge CB2 8QF.

Governing Body:
A Au, MA, FCA
H Bettinson, MA, PhD
S Boyle, MA
K Davies, MA, FCA
W Dawkins, BA
D Ferguson, MA
N Finlayson-Brown, BA
S Freestone, OBE, DL, MEd, GRSM, LRAM, ARCM
C Hancock, KC, MA, LLM [OP]
J Hawkes, PHD, FSA, FRAS
S Lebus, MA
A Oliver MA, MPHIL, PHD, LITTD
G Proudfoot, MA
S Roberts, MA
J W Scott, MA (*Chair*)
M Singh, MBA, Master Mariner
S Steele, CTA
D Williams, MB, BCh, FRCP, FRCPH

Clerk to the Governors: Maggie Hastings

***Head*: Ed Elliott**

Bursar: Alison Shakespeare
Senior Deputy Head: Dan Cross
Deputy Head (*Pupil Development and Welfare*): Ed Wiseman
Deputy Head (*Operations and Outreach*): Gavin Richards
Deputy Head (*International and Educational Opportunities*): Simon Armitage
Deputy Head (*Teaching and Learning*): Tanya Khimyak
Director of Communications: Claire Ziwa
Deputy Bursar and Chief Financial Officer: Ginni Carroll
Director of HR: Cheryl Few
Business Development Director: Kathy Sawtell
Director of ICT: Fraser Robertson

Plymouth College

Ford Park, Plymouth, Devon PL4 6RN
Tel: +44 (0)1752 505100
email: admissions@plymouthcollege.com
mail@plymouthcollege.com
website: www.plymouthcollege.com
X/Twitter: @PlymouthCollege
Facebook: @PlymouthCollege
Instagram: @plymcollege

Plymouth College, based in the maritime city of Plymouth with the moorland, countryside and coastal landscapes of Devon and Cornwall close to hand, has been at the forefront of education in South West England since its foundation in 1877. It amalgamated in 1896 with Mannamead School for boys in Plymouth, founded in 1854. The School became fully co-educational in 1995 and in 2004 merged with St Dunstan's Abbey for Girls.

Numbers. Currently there are 510 pupils in the school (300 boys and 210 girls) from ages 3 to 18.

Buildings. The Senior School stands on high ground in Plymouth. The buildings include Science Laboratories, Art and Craft rooms including extensive facilities for photography and print-making, the Dining Hall, an Assembly Hall in which concerts and plays are performed as well as a well-equipped Design and Technology Block. The grounds in Ford Park include a rifle range and an indoor, 25m heated swimming pool. Playing fields at Ford Park are supplemented by two other fields close by. There is an on-site astro surface and the school has use of a full-size AstroTurf pitch for hockey nearby. In 2004 a hospitality suite and Music School opened and in 2011 two new boarding houses were established. The Boarding Houses have undergone a two-year refurbishment programme since 2016. The Sixth Form has its own dedicated Centre with its own Bistro and 2016 saw the opening of the Michael Ball Drama Studio, opened by its namesake who is an old boy of the school. Another old boy, Tom Daley, opened the new Strength & Conditioning Gym in 2018. There is also an outdoor education centre located on Dartmoor.

The Preparatory School, for pupils aged 3–11, is on the same site as the Senior School and benefits from the extensive facilities.

Organisation. Below the Sixth Form, pupils are set in some areas so that pupils may proceed at a pace best suited to their abilities. Pupils are organised in 4 Houses and participation in house events is actively encouraged. Each pupil is under the supervision of a Tutor and Head of Year who report to the Assistant Head. In Years 7–10 Form Prefects are appointed. Every pupil is expected to play a full part in games and other school activities outside the classroom. Pupils in Years 10 and above also take part in our enrichment programme which includes The Duke of Edinburgh's Award, CCF (all 3 sections), Sports Leaders Award and a wide range of other activities. All pupils take part in a PSHEE programme, with careers advice starting in Year 7. English (Language and Literature), a Modern Language, Mathematics, Physics, Chemistry and Biology are taken by all to GCSE. Normally three more are chosen by the pupils

Sixth Form. The Sixth Form is based on tutor groups with approx. twelve pupils in each group. Pupils usually study three subjects at A Level, with four being studied in exceptional circumstances. In addition, our Sports Baccalaureate is an alternative to A Levels and includes a BTEC in Sport & Outdoor Education as well as qualifications in other sporting and outdoor activity areas. Tutors keep a pastoral and academic watch on the pupils' performance, feeding information to the Head and Assistant Heads of Sixth Form.

Sixth Formers are well prepared for universities and careers both in the UK and overseas, including scholarship advice for the US, with detailed university advice starting in Year 9.

Games. Rugby, Football, Cricket, Hockey, Netball and Swimming are the major sports. There is also Athletics, Badminton, Basketball, Cross-Country Running, Fencing, Sailing, Shooting and Tennis. Games are compulsory but more senior pupils have a wide range of options available to them.

School Activities. Pupils take part in a wide range of activities. There is a contingent of the CCF with Navy, Army and Air Force Sections. There is also The Duke of Edinburgh's Award scheme and adventure training as well as participation in Ten Tors each year. Pupils in Year 10 participate in a Sports Leaders scheme with local primary schools. A number of overseas expeditions are also organised each year. School Societies cover a range of activities from Mountain Biking to Young Enterprise. There is also a very good and active Outdoor Education department which offers pupils opportunities in such activities as Bushcraft, Caving and Kayaking.

Music & Performing Arts. There is an excellent school choir that sings at all major school events, concerts, and church services throughout the school year. The school orchestra, like the choir, provides music at school events and concerts. In addition to these groups the school has various small ensembles that are run by the visiting specialist instrumental teachers. The school has a thriving house drama and music competition that attracts whole school support. As well as the formal/organised music making there are innumerable student-led bands that help to ensure that the music department is a vibrant environment. Tuition is provided on all orchestral instruments, including percussion. Voice, piano, organ and all types of guitar lessons are also available. Speech and drama lessons (LAMDA) are offered to all students. The music and drama departments work together on large-scale productions. The drama department offers drama clubs to all year groups. Both departments work with a number of visiting performers/practitioners throughout the year; these are usually focused on specific year groups or examination groups. There are annual music and drama scholarships and instrumental exhibitions.

Boarders. With pupils from all over the world, the boarding houses are run by an enthusiastic, experienced and friendly team who are responsible for all aspects of boarders' welfare. There is also a good mix of activities at the weekends including ten-pin bowling, ice skating, beach visits, cinema trips, surfing, moorland walking and horse riding.

The Boarding Houses are situated on the senior school campus: one for boys, one for girls (approximately 40–50 in each) and two smaller satellite houses.

Admission. Admission to the Senior School is normally based on the College Entrance Examination for boys and girls over 10½ and under 12 on 31st August of the year of entry, but it is also possible to enter at other points during the academic programmes. Admission to the Preparatory School is from the age of rising 3. For admission to the Senior and Prep School, please contact admissions@plymouthcollege.com.

Scholarships and Bursaries. There are a variety of Scholarships and Awards for Academia, Art, Music, Drama and Sports and High Performance Sports. These are typically awarded for Year 7, 9 and Sixth Form Entry. In addition to scholarships, means tested bursaries of up to half fees are available. Further information, email admissions@plymouthcollege.com.

Bursaries are means tested.

Fees per Term (2023–2024). Prep School from Reception £3,257 to years 5 & 6 £4,494. Senior School: Day: Years 7–8 £5,608, Years 9–11 £6,390, Sixth Form £6,643. Boarding: Years 7–8 £11,437, Years 9–11 £12,501, Sixth Form £13,110. Weekly Boarding: Years 7–8 £9,177, Years 9–11 £9,976, Sixth Form £10,229. Occasional boarding is available at £60 per night and for up to a maximum of 14 nights a term.

Fees include stationery and games. There are no supplementary lunch charges for full boarding pupils. Music lessons are extra.

Armed Forces and sibling discounts are available.

Charitable Status. Plymouth College is a Registered Charity, number 1105544. Its aim is to provide private education for boys and girls.

***Head*: Mr A Carr**, MA St Andrews

Head of Prep School: Mr H Thomas, BSc Exeter
Deputy Head (*Pastoral*): Mr C Irish, BSc Birmingham
Assistant Head (*Academic*): Mr P Grey, BSc Open, AMInstP
Assistant Head (*Co-curricular*): Mr P Mutlow, BA Durham (*Director of Sport*)
Bursar: Mr T Williams (*Prep and Senior School*)
Head of Marketing and Admissions: M P Gilchrist, BSc Loughborough

Teaching Staff:

Mr E S Agobiani, LLB Leicester (*Classics*, *History and Head of Year 11*)
Miss P J Anderson, MA Emmanuel College Cambridge (*Head of Classics*)

Mr R Atkinson, BA Exeter (*History and Assistant Head of Year 10*)
Mrs E Bales, BA Warwick (*Year 3*)
Mrs A C Blunden-Currie, BA Exeter (*Biology*)
Mr K C Boots, BA Wales, MEd Exeter, AMBDA (*Head of Psychology*)
Mr B Bryan, BSc Northampton (*Head of Psychology*)
Mrs S Chapman, BA Exeter (*Head of Learning Support/SENCo*)
Mrs A-L Chubb, BA Wolverhampton (*Head of History and Head of Year 10*)
Mrs R L Connor, BA Nottingham (*Head of EAL and Deputy Head of Sixth Form*)
Miss A R Croot, BA Plymouth (*Head of English*)
Mrs P de Jager, BPrimary Ed, Rhodes University (*Assistant SENCo, Form Teacher Year 5*)
Mrs S Dutta, BA Brighton (*Pre-School*)
Mr R L Edwards, BA Wales (*English, Director of Rugby and Deputy Head of Sixth Form*)
Mrs J Eglinton, BMus Royal Northern College of Music, MMus (*Director of Performing Arts and Director of Music*)
Miss C Ellis, BA Leeds (*Year 3*)
Mrs A J Escott, BA Plymouth (*Head of Art and Photography*)
Mrs E Fabian, BEd St Mark & St John (*PE*)
Mr S Fenwick, BA Exeter College of St Mark & St John (*PE and Games, Head of Hockey and Assistant Head of Year 9*)
Mrs B Field, BSc York (*Chemistry, Head of Girls' Boarding*)
Mr M Gibbs, BSc Exeter, BSc Oxford (*Head of Biology*)
Mrs A E Green, BSc Nottingham (*Maths*)
Mr J Gregory, BA Birmingham (*Business and Economics*)
Mrs C Haffenden, BA Cardiff (*Art*)
Mrs F Hanvey, BEng Strathclyde (*Prep STEM*)
Miss K Haynes, BSc Plymouth (*Geography*)
Miss N S L Husband, BA Queen Margaret (*English and Drama*)
Mr L Ilott, BEd De Montford (*Head of Boarding, PE and English*)
Mr D A Jones, BSc Birmingham (*Head of Mathematics*)
Dr S Jordan, PhD Dundee (*Biology*)
Mrs N Lisney, BA Plymouth (*Head of Design Technology*)
Mrs F Lister, BEd St Mark & St John (*Pre-School*)
Mr G J Llewellyn-Rees, BEng Brunel, MEng Heriot Watt, MBA Imperial College (*Head of Physics*)
Mrs J Manuel, BEd Exeter (*Year 4*)
Mr D J Martin, BA Warwick (*Head of Religious Studies*)
Mr P J McCormack, BSc Exeter (*Head of Chemistry*)
Mrs F McWilliam, BA University of West of England (*Reception and Head of EYFS*)
Mr J Moate (*IT*)
Mrs R Moore, BA Open (*Head of English and Head of Lower School*)
Mrs C Murray, BSc Warwick, BSc Queen's College Cambridge (*Biology*)
Miss J Newnham, BEd Cheltenham & Gloucester College of Higher Education (*Maths, Form Teacher Year 6 and Deputy Head of Preparatory School*)
Dr A Norris, BSc Liverpool, PhD (*Maths*)
Miss L M Odendaal, BA Stellenbosch (*Maths and PE*)
Mrs N Paice, BA College of St Mark & St John (*Head of Geography*)
Mr C Paull, BA Plymouth (*Year 4*)
Mr P J Randall, BA Oxford Brookes (*French, Spanish, German and Head of MFL*)
Mr O Rees (*OED Manager*)
Mrs C Riley-Harling, BSc St Mark & St John (*PE and Head of Netball*)
Miss L M Russo, MSci Imperial College (*Physics*)
Miss C P Sherratt, BSc Plymouth (*Maths*)
Mrs J Smith, BA University of London (*Year 2*)
Mrs C Spence, BA Manchester (*Year 4*)
Mr R Stubbs, GMus Hartlepool, FTCL, ARCM (*Music and Form Teacher Year 6*)
Mrs S Sullivan, BA Glasgow School of Art (*Art*)
Mr A G Summons, BSc, MSc Exeter (*Head of Business & Economics and Head of Sixth Form*)
Mrs R J Thomas, BA Exeter (*KS2/3 English and Humanities*)
Miss E D Tremaine, BEd De Montfort (*Head of PE and Sport, Sports Baccalaureate*)
M P Underwood, BEd St Mark & St John (*PE, English and Form Teacher Year 6*)
Miss F Venon, Licence D'Anglais Universitie de St Etienne, Maitrise (*French and Exams Officer*)
Mrs C Wesley, Licence Université de Caen Basse-Normandie (*KS2/3 French and Boarding Parent*)
Mr M P Wesley, BSc Nottingham Trent (*DT and Head of Year 10*)
Mrs V J Willden, BA Plymouth (*LDD and Religious Studies*)

Pocklington School

West Green, Pocklington, York, East Yorkshire YO42 2NJ

Tel: 01759 321200
email: admissions@pocklingtonschool.com
website: www.pocklingtonschool.com
X/Twitter: @pockschool
Facebook: @PocklingtonSchool
Instagram: @pockschool
LinkedIn: /school/pocklington-school

Pocklington is an inclusive, family focused and academic school that offers incredible experiences inside and outside the classroom for children aged 2–18 years. We believe in encouraging pupils to seize opportunities from the broad range of activities we offer. Along with our approach to teaching and learning, these help to form the bedrock of our young Pocklingtonians' character and grow the qualities that support our values. Our sense of community, care for each other and pride in the school is tangible. This is no more evident than in our outstanding boarding provision. At the heart of this ethos lie our Values and Virtues. They drive all that we do at Pocklington and mean our pupils leave with a deep sense of social responsibility and the ability to shape their own future, ready for happy, fulfilling and successful lives.

Pocklington School lies 12 miles east of York on the edge of a vibrant, friendly market town, on a 50-acre campus with good public transport links and its own bus service. The school, founded in 1514, blends strong traditions with innovation and flexibility, encouraging pupils to have the courage to take chances with their learning and achieve the best that they can.

Numerous co-curricular activities for day and boarding pupils take place every day until 5pm, and each pupil is encouraged to pursue their own interests to help develop the depth of character and self-awareness to tackle life's challenges on their own terms. Facilities include a 300-seat theatre, an indoor sports hall, strength and conditioning room and swimming pool, plus 21-acres of grass sports pitches and two full-sized synthetic pitches.

Our boarding provision is designed to be as flexible as possible, to best suit the individual needs of pupils and their families. Full, weekly and part-time boarding options are available in our four, beautiful boarding houses located either on or adjacent to the school campus, which create a home from home for all our boarders.

Right through from Prep School, where the Curiosity Project curriculum enables children to expand their critical thinking skills through structured and creative enquiry, to the Sixth Form where independent thought is prized, our pupils are encouraged to be resilient, resourceful learners. To support the school's strategic goal of further improving academic performance, increasing pupils' independence and meeting the needs of modern family life, pupils engage in a 5-day academic week, Monday to Friday. Saturdays are reserved for sports fixtures, and boarders enjoy a full weekend programme of activities and trips.

We employ the best educational tools and new technology to ensure youngsters are enthused and inspired by the world of knowledge available to them. Our Art and Design Technology Centre has every facility to encourage the pursuit of traditional arts and crafts, as well as providing cutting-edge equipment for digital and computer design, and manufacturing technology. An individual approach, supported by flexible learning platforms allows each pupil to progress at their own pace, boosting their confidence and self-esteem so they often exceed their expectations.

We take great pride in our Health and Wellbeing Centre, which opened in 2023, and is staffed by a dedicated team of professionals. As well as pastoral house teams, teachers and support staff, pupils can seek help from our chaplain, medical team and independent clinical psychologists. Our house system fosters a sense of community and belonging. Inter-house challenges encourage pupils to work together across year groups and our Sixth Form students are encouraged to take on responsibilities and leadership roles.

Our Sixth Form offers an exciting and wide-ranging educational experience which aims to challenge and support students in equal measure. With spacious communal areas, a study centre and a comprehensive library, students are encouraged to be aspirational in setting their personal goals; independent, enquiring and self-motivated in their studies; and in possession of the integrity, resilience and compassion needed to become responsible young adults. With 25 A levels, four BTEC Level 3 courses and an enrichment programme to select from, students can personalise their academic study programme to suit their interests, skills and career aspirations.

Recent former pupils who retain links with the school include Davis Cup winner Kyle Edmund, England rugby star Rob Webber and world-renowned concert pianist Alexandra Dariescu.

We aim to instil the Pocklington Values and Virtues into all our pupils, to engage with our families and support them in raising the Pocklingtonians of tomorrow and to be open to innovation, conscious of tradition and so secure our Foundation's future.

Fees per term (2023–2024). Day: £3,432–£6,266, Boarding: £8,899–£11,552, Weekly Boarding Plus (Mon–Fri Nights): £8,261–£10,625. Other boarding options are available – *see* website for details.

Chair of Governors: Mr J V T Tilsed, MB, BS, MS, FRCS Eng, FRCS Gen Surg, FEBS EmSurg

***Headmaster*: Mr T Seth**, MA Cantab

Head of Pocklington Prep School: Ms S Ward, LLB PgDip

The Portsmouth Grammar School

High Street, Portsmouth, Hants PO1 2LN

Tel: 023 9236 0036
email: admissions@pgs.org.uk
website: www.pgs.org.uk
X/Twitter: @PGS1732
Facebook: @ThePortsmouthGrammarSchool
Instagram: @theportsmouthgrammarschool
LinkedIn: /school/pgs1732

Motto: *Praemia Virtutis Honores*

The Portsmouth Grammar School is a happy and vibrant independent school located in the historic heart of Portsmouth and only a few minutes' walk from the Solent.

The Portsmouth Grammar School was founded in 1732 by William Smith: Mayor of Portsmouth and Physician to its Garrison. Of humble origins, Smith flourished through spirit, vision, and learning. He was determined that, like him, the young people of Portsmouth should have access to a transformative education. And so, in his will, he asked his Oxford college, Christ Church, to establish a school in the town where he had prospered.

We remain true to William Smith's vision today. A forward-looking school located in the historic heart of Portsmouth, we encourage our pupils to envision their life at 25, and we prepare them to make a positive contribution in whatever pathway they choose. Portsmouth is, after all, a city concerned with destinations.

We do this by nurturing the individual potential of each of our pupils. Our success in public examinations and in securing places at first-choice universities is combined with attention to personal flourishing and to the joy of lifelong learning. In our caring, family community, pupils develop through academic challenge, an astonishing breadth of co-curricular activity, and opportunities both to lead and to serve. Our guiding commitment is to support every pupil to be happy and successful; in that order.

The Portsmouth Grammar School is a fully co-educational independent day school. There are 1,351 pupils in the School.

The Pre-School offers outstanding care for girls and boys from age 2½ to 4, supporting them to become confident and happy children who are active, independent learners.

The Junior School at The Portsmouth Grammar School is a happy and dynamic place for children aged 4–11 (Reception–Year 6) to learn. We like to think of it as a 'Eureka' school, where every day our children are challenged to 'find things out'. Children in the Junior School excel academically and grow into happy, confident, individuals. The main ages of entry are 4 and 7, however there are places available for intermediate entry.

Pupils in the Junior School no longer sit the 11+ entrance assessments for entry in to the Senior School. The Head of the Junior School will recommend entry to the Senior School following its programme of continuous assessment.

The Portsmouth Grammar Senior School offers girls and boys aged 11–16 outstanding academic, pastoral and co-curricular opportunities. Pupils flourish in a supportive and caring environment, achieving excellent results at GCSE. Pupils are enthusiastic and committed learners. They enjoy supporting others in their learning, using information and communication technology to enhance their understanding. Admission is by the School's Entrance Assessment at 11+ and at 13+. Entrants at 13 are usually pre-tested at 11 to accommodate high demand for places. Pupils are admitted at other ages, should vacancies occur, subject to assessments and satisfactory reports from previous schools.

PGS offers a broad Sixth Form curriculum, which places a strong emphasis on academic challenge and enrichment. Admission to the Sixth Form is subject to satisfactory standard at GCSE and interview.

Curriculum. The Portsmouth Grammar School aims to create an environment in which pupils are keen to develop a range of analytical skills and creative talents. We encourage pupils to be enquiring and independent in their learning. We want our learners to evaluate their progress critically and learn to optimise their potential by setting themselves challenging goals and adopting effective study techniques. They should be willing to work collaboratively, with proper respect for each other's different talents and mindful at all times of academic honesty. The Sixth Form A Level curriculum offers all pupils the opportunity to undertake an Extended Project Qualification (EPQ), which may be essay-based, creative or practical. They will have access to a wide range of taught academic enrichment courses, to extend their learning beyond their core subjects, through our Ignite! programme. Students may choose from a broad range of community partnership projects and work experience, receiving skills coaching and opportunities for leadership development.

A Level subjects include: Art, Biology, Business Studies, Chemistry, Classical Civilisation, Design and Technology, Drama, Economics, Electronics, English Literature, French, Geography, German, Government and Politics, Greek, History, Latin, Mathematics, Further Mathematics, Music, Physical Education, Psychology, Religious Studies and Spanish. The Personal Enrichment Curriculum offers pupils the resources, opportunities and coaching to develop and build personal qualities, personal perspective and ideas, extended thinking, confidence, the ability to take control of life and an understanding of what they enjoy. It is focused on personal development through exciting, rewarding and hugely enjoyable opportunities, providing an inspiring platform for the future.

The Sixth Form prepares candidates for entry to Higher Education, and the Universities and Careers Department provides excellent support with UCAS applications and close relations with various forms of employment.

Religion. The Portsmouth Grammar School is non-denominational.

Pastoral Care. We firmly believe that a child's happiness is an essential foundation for their wellbeing and to their progress in learning. It is also vital to their preparation for a flourishing and fulfilled life beyond school, as individuals, as lifelong learners, as citizens and within the world of work. Individualised care is at the heart of PGS life; our staff are enormously dedicated and go above and beyond to support the pupils in their care.

Sport. Rugby football, netball and hockey are the main games in Winter and Spring; cricket (boys and girls), tennis and athletics in the Summer. Cross-country running, squash, judo, badminton, gymnastics, basketball, aerobics, swimming and sailing are also available. The School has enjoyed national success in recent years in sports such as football, hockey, netball, athletics, and cricket.

The Co-Curriculum. There are significant opportunities for co-curricular involvement at the school. Music, Sport, Drama, CCF and Outdoor Pursuits including Ten Tors and participation in the Duke of Edinburgh's Award scheme, play a huge role in the development of pupils and provide them with a diverse and popular range of activities. Service to the local community and charity work is also an important feature of the school's ethos. Many clubs and societies cater for a considerable range of co-curricular interests from the Model United Nations to Wildlife Club. Numerous expeditions, holiday activities and trips are actively encouraged and include many foreign tours for sports teams and music ensembles. The School has a flourishing exchange scheme with French, German and Spanish schools. Sports teams have recently gone on tour to Singapore, Malaysia and South Africa. Recent expeditions have seen pupils travel to Madagascar, Uganda, Cambodia, Argentina and Cuba.

Fees per term (2023–2024). Senior School £6,315; Junior School £4,052–£4,494. (Fees quoted include direct debit discount.)

Scholarships and Financial Assistance. An extensive programme of scholarships and means-tested financial assistance is offered in the Senior School from 11–18 years and we are extremely grateful to all those whose generosity makes it possible for a growing number of pupils to join PGS each year, regardless of their financial situation.

Scholarships are non means-tested and awarded to recognise exceptional academic or co-curricular ability. Where appropriate, these awards may be augmented by a bursary.

Financial assistance (bursaries) is entirely means-tested and reflect the outstanding academic potential of an individual pupil regardless of ability to afford the school's fees.

All candidates are automatically considered for academic scholarships at 11+, 13+ and 16+.

Additionally, scholarships can also be awarded for excellence in Art, Drama, Music and Sport at 11+, 13+ and 16+. Existing PGS pupils may also apply for consideration for these awards once they become eligible during their time at the school.

Full details of all scholarships and bursaries are available on the School's website.

Buildings. The School is located within the historic quarter of Portsmouth. The Grade II listed buildings of the Junior and Senior School sit comfortably next to modern developments, including a Sixth Form Centre and Science Centre, a Music School, a modern dining and theatre complex and a fully refurbished library. The School sports facilities are located at the Hilsea Playing Fields and include an all-weather pitch and Sports Pavilion.

Honours. Just under 90% of pupils win a place at their first or insurance choice university and we have frequent success in helping our pupils secure offers for prestigious degree apprenticeship schemes with organisations such as Dyson, Rolls Royce and Unilever.

Sportsmen include England Cricket Captain Wally Hammond and England Women's Team Cricket Player Charlie Dean, Athletics International Roger Black, and Paralympian Ross Morrison. Military distinction in abundance, including 3 VCs (one the first VC submariner), several Admirals, Generals and Air Marshals. Medicine is also a continuing theme – from pioneer ophthalmologist James Ware to Viagra researcher Ian Osterloh. Arts are well and diversely represented: dramatist Simon Gray, poet Christopher Logue, novelist James Clavell, film director James Bobin, Sky News entertainment reporter Joe Michalczuk, cathedral organist Christopher Walsh, and pop singer Paul Jones. Civil Servants, Judges and barristers galore, plus entrepreneur industrialist Alan Bristow.

Charitable status. The Portsmouth Grammar School is a Registered Charity, number 1063732. It exists to provide education for boys and girls.

Governing Body:
Chairman: Mr W J B Cha, BA
Mrs S Baker, MA
Mrs K Bishop, BA
Mr T W Burden, MA
The Very Revd Dr Anthony Cane, BA, MPhil, PhD
Mr M R Coffin, BA Econ, FCA
Mrs V Durham, MA Oxon
Mrs S Gingell, MSc, DIPSW
Dr M Grossel, BSc, MA, PhD
Ms C Harries
Mr N D Latham, CBE, MSc, CEng, FIMarEST, FIMechE
His Honour Judge Lodder, KC, LLB
Mr P G Parkinson, BA, Dip Arch
Mr J D Poulton, BA Cantab
Dr S Ross, MB ChB, MRCGP

Senior Team:

***Head*: Mr D Wickes,** MA

Senior Deputy Head: Mr R Bristow, MA (*Oxon*), PGCE, FRSA, MCCT
Deputy Head (*Academic and Staff Welfare*): Mrs S Haslam, BA Hons, MA, QTS
Deputy Head (*Teaching and Learning*): Mr J Andrews, BA, MSc
Deputy Head (*Pastoral*): Ms L Ryan, BA, MA
Assistant Head (*Sixth Form*): Mrs R Clay, BA
Assistant Head (*Pastoral*): Miss F E A Bush, BA
Assistant Head (*Admissions and Partnerships*): Mrs J Jackson, BSc
Assistant Head (*Co-Curriculum*): Mr M Murray, MA
Assistant Head (*Pupil Progress*): Mr Martin Hill, BA Hons, MEd

Bursar: Mr J Read

Junior School and Nursery

Head of the Junior School: Mrs A Wilson-Smith, BA, PGCE
Deputy Head: Mr J Ashcroft, BSc, PGCE
Head of Pre-School & Infants, Mrs J Millward, BEd

Assistant Heads:
Mrs R Evans, BA, QTS (*Pastoral*)
Mrs G Radford, BA (*Academic*)
Pre-School Lead: Mrs C Eastburn, BA, PGCE

Princethorpe College

Princethorpe, Rugby, Warwickshire CV23 9PX

Tel:	01926 634200
email:	post@princethorpe.co.uk
website:	www.princethorpe.co.uk
X/Twitter:	@PrincethorpeCol
Facebook:	@princethorpecollege
Instagram:	@ThePrincethorpeFoundation

Princethorpe College is a Catholic, co-educational, HMC independent day school and welcomes members of all faiths and backgrounds. The school was founded as a boys' school in 1957 in Leamington Spa by the congregation of the Missionaries of the Sacred Heart (MSC), moving to its present site, a former Benedictine monastery, in 1966. The College became co-educational in 1996, and in September 2001 formed a partnership with Crackley Hall School in Kenilworth in order to provide continuous education from 2 to 18 years. A further merger took place in September 2016 with the Crescent School, Rugby. All schools are members of an independent trust – The Princethorpe Foundation.

Number in school. The school has around 900 day pupils from 11 to 18 years with some 200 in the Sixth Form. An extensive network of private coaches transports pupils from a wide area.

Aims. The College provides a caring, Christian environment for children where their needs can be met and their talents, confidence and self-esteem developed.

There is a healthy balance between freedom and structure and an emphasis on self-discipline through responsibility and trust, which develops confidence and independence.

The College draws on a rich tradition of Catholic teaching and the spirituality of the Missionaries of the Sacred Heart, whose ethos is central to its character. In welcoming families of a variety of faiths and none, the school community is a living example of ecumenism. The College motto, *Christus Regnet* – let Christ reign – is a reminder of Christ's love, service, forgiveness and generosity of spirit.

Academic. A broad-based, stimulating curriculum satisfies a wide range of ability and fosters a love of learning. A favourable pupil to teacher ratio, permitting personal attention, contributes to impressive value-added achievements. High fliers are stretched and provided with intellectually challenging assignments through our da Vinci Programme, ensuring that they achieve at the highest possible levels. The curriculum is well supported by a magnificent library and ICT. Qualified specialists give tuition to pupils with special educational needs.

Pupils in Years 7 to 9 have a broad-based curriculum which avoids early specialisation and usually go on to take nine or ten GCSEs.

Supervised homework and free extended day are offered until 6.00 pm.

The Sixth Form. Students in the Sixth Form are prepared for A Level examinations after which the vast majority proceed to university. The Head of Sixth Form and the team of tutors monitor the academic progress of Sixth Formers through regular discussions with the students and their teachers. Visits to university Open Days, together with professional careers advice enables students to make the best choices about their next stage of education.

Our Sixth Form enrichment programme puts a strong emphasis on the acquisition of key skills and the education of the whole person. Sixth Formers are offered residential outward bound courses, training programmes and retreats which provide an opportunity for reflection and exploration, to develop a mature and balanced perspective. Guest lecturers, debates and trips all enhance Sixth Form life.

All Sixth Formers enjoy privileges and have the responsibilities of leadership and example; certain members are elected to perform prefectorial duties. Prefects attend a leadership course and learn valuable management skills. They organise activities for younger pupils and chair the School Council, which offers a forum for lively discussion and gives the students an influential voice in the running of the College. The House Captains have a pivotal role in the organisation of inter-house events.

Careers. The Careers Advice Programme commences in Year 9 and regular tutorials are held concentrating on option subject choices and developing careers awareness. Interview technique is developed and students are assisted with work experience placements which are undertaken at the end of Year 10 and Lower Sixth. The College also holds a biennial Careers Fair for pupils in Year 10 to Sixth Form and their parents.

Art & Design. A feature which immediately strikes all visitors to the College is the outstanding display of canvases. Superb examination results and successes in national competitions are commonplace. The study of drawing, painting, graphics and ceramics are central and they are enhanced by using the work of great artists as stimulus material.

Technology includes Food, Graphics, Resistant Materials, Textiles and Electronics. Pupils can work with a variety of materials, realising their technical designs in the well-resourced workshops, which includes CAD/CAM facilities.

Music and Drama. Music is studied by all pupils in their first three years and as an option at GCSE and A Level. The College choir gives regular performances and tours. Many pupils learn instruments and are encouraged to join the orchestra. Peripatetic staff offer tuition in most instruments. There is a state-of-the-art studio with digital recording facilities for Music Technology and there is an acclaimed Binns organ in the magnificent Chapel built by Peter Paul Pugin.

The College has a theatre and regular productions are staged including musicals and revues. Productions involve a large number of pupils and staff and provide an excellent way for pupils of different years to get to know each other. There are thriving Dance and Drama Clubs. Theatre Studies is offered in the Sixth Form.

Physical Education. All pupils participate in games and Physical Education classes. Physical Education can also be studied as an examination subject at GCSE and A Level as can a BTEC in Physical Education. The major sports are rugby, netball, hockey, cricket, rounders, tennis and athletics; they are run in tandem with badminton, soccer, squash, basketball and trampolining.

The Sports Centre has a sports hall, fitness gym and a climbing wall. Extensive outdoor facilities include an internationally recognised cross-country course, floodlit all-weather pitch, tennis courts and over sixty acres of games pitches.

Sports Clubs include Rugby, Football, Hockey, Netball, Climbing Wall, Badminton, Archery, Golf, Fitness, Running, Trampolining, Cycling, Athletics, Rounders and Tennis.

Co-curricular activities. There is always a wide range of clubs, societies and activities such as Airgineers, Art, Beekeeping, Book Club, Chess, Cookery, Craft, Creative Writing, Dance, Darts, Debating, Drama, Electric Car Club, Equestrian Club, Film Review, Green Team and Wildlife Club, History Club, ICT, Language Conversation – Spanish and French, MEDSOC. Mindfulness, Model UN, Photography, Poetry, Project Club, Psychology, Science, Technical Theatre, Textiles, Young Designers, Youth Chaplaincy and Youth St Vincent de Paul. The Duke of Edinburgh's Award, World Challenge, Camps International and Outward Bound courses are also offered. The Arts Society provides a cultural programme of lectures, poetry evenings, music recitals and play readings.

Admissions. Admission is by examination, in November, for entry the following September, generally at 11 and 13 and at other ages as space allows. Students from other schools join the Sixth Form after their GCSE courses.

Scholarships. There is a variety of Scholarships available for particularly able or talented candidates, ranging from Academic, Art and Sports to a range of Performing Arts including Choral, Drama, Music and Musical Theatre (including dance). Additionally, for the Sixth Form there are Academic, Art, Music, Organ and Sports Scholarships available. Scholarships to a maximum reduction of 50% of tuition fees are on offer.

Academic Scholarships: Candidates applying for entry in Years 7, 8, 9 and 10 will be considered automatically for an academic scholarship when taking the Entrance Examination.

Art Scholarships: Candidates must submit a portfolio and attend an Art Scholarship day. Further details and an Art Scholarship application form are available from the Registrar.

Performing Arts Scholarship – Choral: Candidates must attend an audition. Further details and a Choral Scholarship application form are available from the Registrar.

Performing Arts Scholarship – Drama: Candidates must attend an audition. Further details and a Drama Scholarship application form are available from the Registrar.

Performing Arts Scholarship – Music: Candidates must attend an audition. Further details and a Music Scholarship application form are available from the Registrar.

Performing Arts Scholarships – Musical Theatre (including Dance): Candidates must attend an audition. Further details and a Musical Theatre application form are available from the Registrar.

Sports Scholarship: Candidates must attend a live assessment session. Further details and a Sports Scholarship application form are available from the Registrar.

All Rounder Scholarships: In addition to the scholarships that can be applied for, exceptional candidates who are both academically able and gifted and talented across a number of areas may be considered for an All-Rounder Scholarship, which is awarded at the discretion of the Headmaster.

Sixth Form Academic Scholarships: Sixth Form Academic Scholarships are open to all external candidates who are expected to achieve 9–7 grades at GCSE. Applicants will be invited to the Academic Scholarships Day where they will sit a Verbal Reasoning examination and have an interview with the Headmaster. More details are available from the Registrar.

Sixth Form Sports Scholarships: Senior Sport Scholarships may be awarded to internal or external candidates entering the Sixth Form. Full details are available from the Registrar.

Sixth Form Music – Instrumental, Choral and Organ Scholarships: Candidates must attend an audition. Full details are available from the Registrar. In the Sixth Form there is also an Organ Scholarship of up to 50% of tuition fees available to candidates who have a high level of ability and are committed and enthusiastic performers. Again details are available from the Registrar.

Sixth Form Drama Scholarships: Students will be required to attend an audition. Further details available from the Registrar.

Sixth Form Art Scholarships: Students will be required to attend an Art Scholarship Day. Further details available from the Registrar.

Fees per term (2023–2024). £5,280 excluding transport and meals. Instrumental tuition, external examinations and some targeted support for those with learning needs are charged as extras.

Charitable status. The Princethorpe Foundation is a Registered Charity, number 1087124. It exists solely for the education of children.

Governing Body:
Trustees:
Chair of Trustees: Mrs Elizabeth Griffin, BSc, PGCE, CTC
Jatinder Birdi
John Fisher
Mrs Barbara Forster, Cert Ed
Richard Harcourt, MBA
Charlie Jenkinson, BA, CIPS, MILT
Rowland Johnson, BCom, MSocSc
Mrs Helen Knight, BA, PGCE, MA, NPQH
Robert Lee, LLB
Kieron Shaw, MBE, MSc, FCIS
Commodore Bernard Warner

Staff:

***Headmaster*: Grove du Toit**, BA Ed, BA, BEd, MA, MBA

Deputy Heads:
Pastoral: Mrs Beth Sharpe, BSc, PGCE, PGCert Ed (*Special Needs and Inclusion*; *Design and Technology*; *Designated Safeguarding Lead*)
Academic: Michael Spencer, BScm, PGCE (*Physics*)

Assistant Heads:
Co-curricular: Neil McCollin, BA, QTS
Director of Digital Strategy: Andy Compton, BA, PGCE, MA (*Modern Languages*)
Teaching and Learning: Dr Liz Pyne, BA, MA, PGCE, PhD (*History*)
Marketing, Admissions and Communications and Old Princethorpians Secretary: Mrs Melanie Butler, BA

Head of Sixth Form: Ben Collie, BSc (*Biology*)
Foundation Principal: Ed Hester, MA Oxon, PGCE (*Mathematics*)
Foundation Assistant Head: Alex Darkes, BEd
Foundation Bursar, *Company Secretary and Clerk to the Trustees*: Eddie Tolcher, BA, ACIB, MCMI, TechIOSH
Foundation Development Director: Steve Kowal, BSc
Foundation Director of Estates: Robert Heath, BSc, PGCE

* *Head of Department*
Art:
*Paul Hubball, BA, PGCE (*Head of Photography*)
Mrs Rebecca Blunsom-Washbrook, BA, GTP (*Photography*)
Mrs Susan Harris, BA, PGCE (*Head of Transition and Induction*)
Miss Helen Plenderleith, BA

Careers:
*Mrs Jacqui Quinney, BA, PGCE
Mrs Kerry Low, BA, Dip CG (*Careers Adviser*)

Classics:
*Mrs Laura Rindler, MA Oxon, PGCE, MBA
Mrs Rachel Taylor, BA, QTS

Computer Science:
*Edward Musson, BA, PGCE
Steve Carter, BSc, PGCE

CoRE Programme:
Mrs Anne Allen, BSc, PGCE (*Assistant Head of Sixth Form*; *Geography*)
Kieran McCullough, BA, PGCE (*House Activities Co-ordinator for Fisher*; *Religious Studies and Games*)
Adam Rickart, BSc, PGCE (*Head of Austin House*)
Mrs Joanne Smith, MChem, PGCE (*Chemistry*; *Assistant Head of Sixth Form Academic*)

Design and Technology:
*Paul Scopes, BEd, AST
Mrs Catherine Morrish, BSc, PGCE
Mrs Kati Nelson, BA, PGCE (*Teacher in Charge of Textiles*)
William O'Hara, BSc, PGCE
Ms Jacqui Scott, BSc, PGCE (*Teacher in Charge of Food Technology*; *Games*)
Mrs Beth Sharpe, BSc, MA, PGCE, PGCert – Education (*Special Needs and Inclusion*; *Deputy Head – Pastoral and Designated Safeguarding Lead*)
Tom Walton, BSc, PGCE (*Games*)

Drama and Theatre Studies:
*Ms Aileen Cefaliello, BA, PGCE (*English*)
*Miss Vicky Roberts, BA, PGCE
Mrs Celia Scott, BA, ALA Associate

Economics and Business:
*Mrs Elizabeth Gane, BA, PGCE
Mrs Helen Baker, BA, PGCE (*Geography*)
Ms Helen Essery, LLB, PGCE (*Head of Law*)
Mrs Louisa Fielding, BA, PGCE (*Senior Head of House*; *Head of Fisher House*)
Daniel Lumb, BA
Mrs Laura Wilford, BSc, QTS

English:
*Mrs Helen Pascoe-Williams, BA, PGCE
Mrs Joanna Evans, BA, PGCE (*Whole School Language for Learning Lead inc VESPA*)
Miss Rachael Mack, BA, QTS (*Games*)
Mrs Fiona Moon, BA, Post Grad Cert in Dyslexia and Literacy (*Second in Department*; *Special Educational Needs*)
Mrs Jessica Newborough, BA, PGCE (*Head of More House*)
Jack Parker, BA, PGCE
Miss Lydia Petrucci, BA, PGCE
Mrs Jessica Proudlock, BA, PGCE

Geography:
*Mrs Helen Baker, BA, PGCE (*Economics and Business*)
Mrs Anne Allen, BSc, PGCE (*Assistant Head of Sixth Form*; *CoRE Programme*)
Stewart Dear, BSc, QTS (*Games*)
Mrs Sarah Evans, BSc, PGCE

History:
*Mrs Adelaide Fretwell, BA, MA, PGC (*Head of Politics*)
Mrs Katharine Darwood-Bredin, BSc, GTP
Mrs Tracey Hester, BA Oxon, PGCE (*Oxbridge Co-ordinator*)
Mrs Julia Lindsay, BA, MA, PGCE (*Challenge Curriculum Co-ordinator*; *Politics*)
Greg Lyttle, BA, MA, PGCE (*Teacher in Charge of Politics*)
Dr Liz Pyne, BA, MA, PGCE, PhD (*Assistant Head – Teaching and Learning*)

Law:
*Mrs Helen Essery, LLB, PGCE (*Business*)

Mathematics:
*Mrs Sharon McBride, BSc, PGCE, ALCM
Mrs Tanya Cowan, BSc, PGCE
Ed Hester, MA Oxon, PGCE (*Headmaster*)
Ms Helen Lewis, BA (*Second in Mathematics*)
Ms Davinya Munford, BSc, PGCE
Alex Phillips, BSc, PGCE (*Games*)
Mrs Leanne Rickart, BEd
Alef Rosenbaum, MA Oxon, PGCE
Theodoros Scoutas, PGCE (*KS5 Mathematics Coordinator*)
Gabor Toth, MSc
Mrs Isobel Turner-Pryce, MA, PGCE

Modern Languages:
*Mrs Stella Keenan, MA, PGCE (*Spanish Subject Leader and French*)
Andy Compton, BA, MA, PGCE (*Assistant Head – Director of Digital Strategy*)
Mrs Sarah Duran, Licence LLCE Anglais, PGCE (*Second in Department*)
Mrs Heather Foulerton, BA, PGCE
Mrs Bérénice Galano, Licence LLCE Anglais (*House Leader – Austin*; *French and Spanish*)
Mrs Michele Gawthorpe, MA Oxon, QTS
Mrs Kate Ingram, BA, PGCE
Mrs Natalie Shedden, BA, PGCE

Music:
*Gil Cowlishaw, BMus (*Director of Music*)
Mrs Alison Wakeley, BMus, MMus, PGCE (*REAL Time Coordinator*)

Photography:
*Paul Hubball, BA, PGCE (*Head of Art*)
Mrs Rebecca Blunsom-Washbrook, BA, GTP (*Art*)

Physical Education and Games:
*Lee Cassell, BA, PGCE (*Foundation Director of Sport*)
Will Bower, BSc, Post Grad Dip with QTS (*Head of Outdoor Education*)
Miss Ellie Callan, BSc, NQT (*House Leader – Fisher*; *Acting Primary School Sport Liaison*)
Ms Hannah Carminati, BSc, QTS (*House Leader – Benet*; *Primary School Sport Liaison*) [maternity leave]
Ben Collie, BSc (*Biology*, *Head of Sixth Form*)
Stewart Dear, BSc, QTS (*Geography*)
Mrs Sarah Evans, BSc, PGCE (*Geography*)
Stuart Friswell (*Rugby Coach*)
Mrs Elizabeth Gane, BA, PGCE (*Head of Economics and Business*)
Thomas Gleghorn, BSc, PGCE (*Head of Academic PE*)
Miss Natalie Hardy, BTEC (*Sports GTA*)
Miss Victoria Howell, BSc (*Acting House Leader – Benet*)
Joe Jackson, BSc, PGCE (*Head of Boys' Games*)

Miss Rachael Mack, BA, QTS (*Hockey Coach*; *English*)
Neil McCollin, BA, QTS (*Assistant Head – Co-curricular*)
Miss Megan McDonagh, BSc, PGCE (*PE and Games Coach*)
Dr Dominic Phelps, BA, MA (*Religious Studies*)
Alex Phillips, BSc, PGCE (*Mathematics*)
Gavin Rooney (*Sports Coach*)
Ms Jacqui Scott, BSc, PGCE (*Design and Technology*)
Cyprian Vella, BA, MA, PGCE (*Assistant Head of Sixth Form*; *Head of Religious Studies*)
Tom Walton, BSc, PGCE (*Design and Technology*)
Mrs Clare White, BSc, PGCE (*Science*; *Psychology and Sociology*)
Harry Walters, BSc, PGCE
Miss Carly Walton, BA, PGCE (*Head of Girls' Games*)
Paul Whitehead (*Hockey Coach*)

Politics:
*Greg Lyttle, BA, MA, PGCE (*Teacher in Charge of Politics*; *History*)
*Mrs Katharine Darwood-Bredin, BSc, GTP (*History*)
Mrs Julia Lindsay, BA, MA, PGCE (*History and Games*)

Psychology and Sociology:
*Mrs Fionnuala Schofield, BSc
Miss Lizzie Caisey, BA, MA, PGCE
Adam Rickart, BSc, PGCE (*Head of Austin House*; *CoRE Programme*)
Mrs Clare White, BSc, PGCE (*Science and Games*)

Religious Studies:
*Cyprian Vella, BA, MA, PGCE (*Assistant Head of Sixth Form*; *Games*)
Miss Elizabeth Hester, BA, PGCE
Kieran McCullough, BA, PGCE (*House activities Coordinator Fisher*; *CoRE Programme*)
Miss Megan O'Gorman, BA, QTS
Dr Dominic Phelps, BA, MA (*Games*)
Mrs Marianne Tallis, BA, PGCE

Special Educational Needs Department:
*Mrs Natasha Warwood, BA, QTS, NASENCO (*Head of Learning Support and SENCo*)
Ms Lorna Prestage, BSc, PGCE, PG Dip, ADG (*Special Educational Needs Coordinator*)
Mrs Kayley Arkesdon, MBA (*Learning Support Assistant*)
Miss Emilie Bergerat, HND (*Learning Support Assistant*)
Mrs Naomi Chard, BA, PGCE (*Learning Support Assistant*)
Mrs Rebecca Gonan, BA, PGCE (*Learning Support Assistant*)
Mrs Anne Marie Isaacs (*Learning Support Assistant*)
Mrs Amanda Kelly (*Learning Support Assistant*)
Mrs Fiona Moon, BA, PG Cert SpLD (*English*)
Mrs Lee O'Gorman (*Learning Support Assistant*)
Mrs Angela Ritson, BA, QTS (*Learning Support Teacher*)

The Sciences:
*Miss Emma Cooper, BSc, PGCE (*Head of Chemistry*)
Ben Collie, BSc (*Biology*; *Head of Sixth Form*; *Games*)
Mrs Sam Curtis, BSc, PGCE (*Chemistry*)
Dan Lee, MEng, PGCE (*Second in Science*; *Head of Physics*)
Dr Emilie Onyekwe, BSc, QTS (*Chemistry*)
Miss Faye Roberts, BSc, MSc, PGCE (*Biology*, *Head of Benet*)
Simon Robertson, BSc, PGCE (*Head of More House*; *Biology*)
Mrs Sophie Rose, BSc, PGCE (*Physics*)
Mrs Joanne Smith, MChem, PGCE (*Chemistry*)
Rob Southern, BSc, PGCE (*Physics*)
Michael Spencer, BSc, PGCE (*Physics*; *Assistant Head – Director of Studies*)
Mrs Catherine Warne, BSc, PGCE (*Biology*)
Mrs Clare White, BSc, PGCE (*Science*; *Psychology and Sociology*)
Dan White, BSc, PGCE (*Biology and Chemistry*)

Prior Park College

Ralph Allen Drive, Bath BA2 5AH
Tel: +44 (0)1225 835353
email: office.ppc@priorparkschools.com
website: www.priorparkcollege.com
X/Twitter: @priorpark
Facebook: @prior.park.37
Instagram: @priorpark_college
LinkedIn: /school/prior-park-college-schools

Motto: *Deo Duce, Deo Luce*

Prior Park College is a co-educational Catholic boarding and day school. Founded in 1830 by Bishop Baines, it was under the control of the Bishops of Clifton until 1924, when it passed to the Congregation of Christian Brothers. Since 1981, Prior Park has been under lay management.

The College is housed in magnificent Palladian architecture, built by John Wood for Ralph Allen, with glorious views of the UNESCO World Heritage City of Bath. The 57-acre site combines an elegant setting for boarding and day education with access to Bath and its numerous cultural attractions. Proximity to the M4 and M5 motorways places the College within easy reach of London, the Midlands, the South-West and Wales. Good rail links and proximity to Bristol, Heathrow and Gatwick international airports allow easy transfer for our international students.

Structure of the School. Prior Park is a friendly, thriving community of approximately 600 pupils. The two boarding houses are home to approximately 145 full and weekly boarders. Flexi boarding is also available if space is available.

Objects of the College. The school's primary aim is to provide a genuine all-round education and whilst academic endeavour remains at the school's core, Prior Park encourages its students to embrace all the opportunities on offer. It is a school that cares. The school's renowned pastoral system provides space and support for each of its students and enables our leavers to be capable, confident and compassionate adults.

Buildings and Grounds. Ranked by the Oxford Royale Academy as the UK's most beautiful boarding school. The Houses, Administration and College Chapel are to be found in the fine 18th-century architecture grouped around Ralph Allen's celebrated Palladian Mansion. A major refurbishment programme of boys' and girls' boarding accommodation has provided comfortable study-bedrooms, quiet areas and recreational rooms. On-site facilities are excellent and include a state-of-the-art sports centre with fitness suite, indoor swimming pool, all weather pitches, 160-seat theatre, recording studio, Chapel, an industry standard A Level D&T workshop and a brand-new Sixth Form Centre.

Curriculum. The academic curriculum conforms to and goes beyond the requirements of the National Curriculum. The curriculum in Year 7–9 is broad. Great care is taken to ensure that careful guidance is given to pupils in Year 9 and Year 11 when GCSE and A Level choices are being made. The majority of pupils will study ten GCSE subjects. In Sixth Form students mostly take three A Level subjects plus another qualification, e.g. an Extended Project Qualification (EPQ).

Music. The College has a highly-deserved reputation for musical excellence. Orchestras, band, choirs, shows, chamber music, jazz, African drums; the Music department covers every musical genre. Two chapel choirs provide high quality music for the weekly sung Mass in the glorious surroundings of the Chapel of Our Lady of the Snows.

The Music Department houses a recording studio and teaching and practice rooms. Around half the pupils learn a musical instrument. Several Prior Park musicians have gone on to Oxbridge. Other graduates go to major conservatoires and play in NYO, NCO, etc.

Drama. The Drama department is proud of its reputation for putting on diverse and impressive productions each year, including works by Beckett, Ibsen, Miller, Shakespeare and Stoppard. The school has its own professionally equipped 160-seat Julian Slade Theatre and Mackintosh Dance Studio.

Visual Arts and D&T. The Visual Arts department comprises Fine Art, Photography and Textiles. Student work is showcased in the gallery spaces throughout the College. The D&T department is highly respected, with facilities on a par with neighbouring universities and many industrial workplaces. For many years, Prior Park Students have been awarded a prestigious Arkwright Engineering Scholarship.

Physical Education and Games. Physical Education is included in the curriculum. Games are an important part of school life. Focus sports are Rugby, Hockey, Cricket, Netball and Tennis. From Year 9, students are also offer elective sports: Swimming, Badminton, Cross-Country, Football, Basketball, Table Tennis, Athletics, use of Fitness Studio, Sailing, Stand Up Paddleboarding.

Clubs and Societies. There are daily clubs ranging from Astronomy to Amnesty International.

The voluntary Combined Cadet Force includes Navy and Army Sections. Adventure training takes place both in the UK and overseas. Cadets are encouraged to participate in the Service and Contingent Camps and Courses.

The Duke of Edinburgh's Award scheme operates at Bronze and Gold Award level. Participants work on the four sections: volunteering, skills, physical, and expeditions; plus a residential project section at Gold Award level.

Saturday Active is a programme of courses that take place every Saturday morning. There are over 20 courses to choose from, including Sailing, Golf, Archery and Yoga.

Boarders and day pupils alike participate in a wide range of activities after school. Public speaking and debating thrive. All younger full-time boarders take part in Saturday Active.

Admission. Main points of admission are at 11+, 13+ and 16+ but pupils may transfer into the College at other times if places are available. Early registrations are encouraged. Prospective families are encouraged to visit the College on Open Days or by arranging an individual visit.

Entrance and scholarship examinations for 11+ and 13+ take place in December and January prior to entry in September. 16+ scholarship examinations and interviews take place in November. Please contact the Registrar, admissions@priorparkschools.com, for the relevant entrance/scholarship admission booklet.

Scholarships and Bursaries. Academic Scholarships are available at 11+, 13+ and 16+. Art, D&T, Drama, Music and Sporting awards are available at 11+, 13+ and 16+. Awards can carry with them a fee remission.

Bursaries are available, including HM Forces Bursaries. The Bursar is pleased to discuss individual cases. Sibling discounts apply.

Fees per term (2023–2024). Full Boarding: £12,878; Weekly Boarding: £9,990; Day: £5,874–£6,483.

The Paragon School, Bath – Junior School of Prior Park College. The Paragon School is part of Prior Park Educational Trust. Housed in an impressive Georgian mansion, the co-educational school for 3–11 years is set in beautiful wooded grounds, only a few minutes drive from Prior Park College. A broad and balanced curriculum is delivered within a happy, caring environment.

Head: Mrs Rosie Allen

For further details, see entry in IAPS section.

Prior Park School, Gibraltar. Opened in September 2016, Prior Park School is the first Independent co-educational senior school in Gibraltar for children 12–18 years.

Headmaster: Mr Peter Watts

For further details please visit: www.priorparkschools.com

Charitable status. Prior Park Educational Trust is a Registered Charity, number 281242.

Mrs M Moore
Revd Prebendary N Rawlinson
Mrs J Singleton

***Headmaster*: Mr Ben Horan**

Deputy Head Academic: Mr C Gamble
Deputy Head Pastoral: Mrs I Burton
Assistant Head (Activities): Mr M Bond
Assistant Head (Progress and Tracking): Mr M Blaikley
Assistant Head (Director of Studies): Mr K Chard
Assistant Head (Tracking): Mrs R Lennon
Assistant Head (Teaching and Learning): Miss N Cordon
Assistant Head (Well Being): Mr D Sackett
Assistant Head (Sixth Form): Mrs A Colquhoun
Director of Operations and Finance: Ms E Sandberg
Head of Compliance: Miss E Wickham
Digital Learning Lead: Mr J Gibbons

Heads of Departments:
Biology: Mr G Price
Chemistry: Dr R Archer
Classics: Mrs S Hearn
Design & Technology: Mr R Faulkner
Computer Science: Mr J Gibbons
Drama & Theatre Studies: Mr D Langley
Economics and Business: Mr M Kerr
English: Dr K McGowran
English as an Additional Language (EAL): Mr P Stroud
Eurasian Studies: Ms B Main
Geography: Mr S Burt
History: Mr M Bishop
Learning Development Programme (LDP): Mrs J Bendry
Mathematics: Mrs J Jones
Modern Languages: Mr T Barrat
Music: Mr M Nicholls
Physics: Ms C Ellis-James
Psychology: Mrs F Evans
Theology and Philosophy: Mr T Maxwell
Visual Arts: Ms S Seville

Visiting Music Staff for Acoustic/Electric Guitar, Bass Guitar, Bassoon, Cello, Clarinet, Drums, Flute, Oboe, Piano, Saxophone, Trumpet, Violin, Viola, Voice.

Executive PA to Headmaster and Director of Operations and Finance: Ms D Miller
Registrar: Mrs V Quinn
Lay Chaplain: Mrs T Tunbridge
Director of Development: Mr D Rainey

Queen Anne's School

6 Henley Road, Caversham, Berkshire RG4 6DX

Tel: 0118 918 7300
email: office@qas.org.uk
website: www.qas.org.uk
X/Twitter: @QASCaversham
Facebook: @QASCaversham
Instagram: @qas_caversham
LinkedIn: /school/queen-anne's

An innovative education for an ever-changing world.

Set in 35 acres and just a short walk from the River Thames, Queen Anne's School, Caversham, is an independent boarding and day school for girls between the ages of 11–18. The school prepares 450 students for an ever-changing world through an exciting and continually evolving education, steeped in excellence and innovation.

"There's something magical about the place, it's as much about life preparation as academics. With such an array of first class facilities, tip top pastoral care, plus a culture of female empowerment, we think it's definitely one for the list of any parent for whom happiness & roundedness are top priorities." – Good Schools Guide

In 2023, Queen Anne's School was awarded the prestigious Microsoft Showcase School Award for the fifth year running. This award acknowledges the extensive digital teaching and learning that has become integral to the school's approach. The leading girls' day and boarding school became one of just a small group of schools in the UK to be recognised by the international tech giants as leaders in digital learning. The school is also at the forefront of innovation with Artificial Intelligence (AI) and leads the Thames Valley AI in Education Network.

With over 100 co-curricular activities available, the school offers a holistic approach to the girls' learning, both in and outside the classroom. From animation to swimming and The Duke of Edinburgh's Award to Beekeeping Club, there is a wealth of opportunities for students to discover their passions and their strengths.

The outstanding facilities include the Scott Music Centre, boasting a state-of-the-art recording studio, a suite of 24 iMacs and an impressive recital hall. The award-winning Sixth Form Centre, with themed breakout spaces, tech-filled study pods and a café, provides Sixth Formers with a dedicated space to learn, revise and relax.

The 2023 GCSE results saw 45% of students achieve 9/8 (A**/A*) and 96% achieve 9–4 (A**–C) across 25 subjects. At A Level, 49% of all grades awarded were A*/A and 88% received A*–C. The 2023 cohort went on to attend top universities, including Oxford, Birmingham, Cardiff, Exeter and Berklee College of Music in Boston.

Queen Anne's School strives to support busy families and offers and an extensive transport network with buses covering areas in Berkshire, Oxfordshire, Buckinghamshire and London including along the new Elizabeth line. The flexibility of day, flexi and full boarding options allow families to choose the right balance for their needs.

Visit www.qas.org.uk or contact the admissions team on 0118 918 7333.

Student Wellbeing. Queen Anne's has an excellent reputation for pastoral care. The staff believe that students perform best when they are happy and secure, and Queen Anne's has effective pastoral systems in place to ensure this. The support network includes House Parents and the House Pastoral Team, Academic Staff and Tutors as well as Heads of Year.

Curriculum. All girls follow a broad and varied curriculum up to GCSE. Separate subject sciences are taught, along with English Literature, English Language and Mathematics; French, Spanish, German or Mandarin may be taken from Year 7. Music and

Technology, Art and Drama form part of the girls' timetable until the end of Year 9. Computer Science is taught throughout the school. A programme of personal, social and health education is followed by all girls. A wide range of A Level subjects is offered; Music Technology, Film Studies, Media Studies, Criminology, Sociology and Environmental Science were introduced in September 2022.

Careers. Girls go on to Higher Education courses at Russell Group and Ivy League universities, and also take up places on Degree Apprenticeship schemes, for example, at Dyson and Coca-Cola.

Co-curricular activities. Queen Anne's offers a full extracurricular programme and excellent opportunities for sport, including tennis, lacrosse, swimming and netball. Students interested in music, drama and art can pursue their passions with a number of clubs available to join and performance opportunities each term. The Duke of Edinburgh's Award, Young Enterprise, public speaking and debating, Model United Nations events, dance, riding, socials and many more activities are available.

Admission. Girls are admitted at 11+, 13+ and at Sixth Form by Queen Anne's Entrance Examination or by Common Entrance. Sixth Form places are offered on the basis of GCSE predictions and results. For further information please contact the Head of Admissions.

Scholarships are offered for entry at 11+, 13+ and 16+ and are awarded for excellence in one or more fields of school life. Awards may be made for Academic Excellence, Sport, Art, Drama, Music or All-Round Contribution

Fees per term (2023–2024). Full Boarding: £14,983; Flexi Boarding: £13,759–14,510; Day pupils: £8,962.

Charitable status. Queen Anne's School is part of The United Westminster and Grey Coat Foundation, which is a Registered Charity, number 1181012.

Board of Governors:
Chair: Miss M Corbally, FCCA, CTA

Board members:
Mrs S Roberts, BA, DMS
Mr D Charles, BSc, ACA
Mr W Goldsmith, BA, MSc, QTS, FCCT, FRSA
Mr M De Mello, BSc
Mrs C Gray, BA
Mrs I Millard, BA, PGDip, PGCE
Mr R F Penfold, MBE
Mrs C Pampe, MBA, BA Hons
Mrs S Gold, BA
Mrs A Chandaria, MPHARM, MBA, CPC
Mr D Ferguson, BA

Leadership Team:

***Head*: Ms Elaine Purves**, BA Hull, PGCE Durham

Senior Deputy Head (*Academic*): Mr Mark Richards, BMus Wales, MMus King's London, Research Fellowship Cardiff, FRSA, MCCT
Deputy Head (*Pastoral*): Mr Andy Towse, BSc, MA
Director of Finance and Strategy: Mrs Rebecca Patton, BA Oxford, Diploma in Corporate Finance ICAEW, MSc [pending]
Human Resources Manager: Mrs Judith Tremayne, Dip Performance Management, Dip Advanced Performance Management, Dip Change Management

Senior Managers:
Head of Digital/Strategy and Computing: Mr Andrew Dax, BSc Oxford Brookes, MEd University of Buckingham
Director of Lower School: Ms Daniela Vought, BSc Open University, GTP
Director of Middle School: Mrs Linda McGrenary, BEd Strathclyde
Director of Sixth Form: Mr Ben Stephenson, BSc Warwick, MSc Loughborough, GTP
Head of Teaching and Learning and Assistant Head: Mrs Anna Spellman, BA, PGCE Reading
Head of Monitoring and Tracking: Mr Derek Bottomley, BSc Leeds, PGCE Oxford

Queen Elizabeth Grammar School
Wakefield

Senior Section (Boys 11–18)
154 Northgate, WF1 3QX

Tel:	01924 373943
email:	qsoffice@wgsf.net

Junior Section (Boys 7–11)
158 Northgate, WF1 3QY

Tel:	01924 373821
email:	qjoffice@wgsf.net
website:	www.wgsf.org.uk
X/Twitter:	@QEGSYorkshire
Facebook:	@QEGSYorkshire
Instagram:	@QEGSYorksire
LinkedIn:	/school/queen-elizabeth-grammar-school-wakefield

Motto: '*Turpe nescire*'

Steeped in over 430 years of history, yet recognised as a school at the forefront of educational thinking, QEGS is continually refreshing its facilities and resources, to enable students to excel in every area of academic and co-curricular achievement, in line with its School Values: Care, Contribute, Aspire.

Facilities. The Junior Section is housed in its own building and enjoys specialist facilities, including a purpose-built STEM block, a swimming pool and the school's very own Forest School, "Owl's Den".

Across the drive in its inspiring Senior Section building, boys enjoy access to specialist areas for 25 academic departments. Students also have access to an indoor gym, fitness suite, sports pavilion and sports fields.

Curriculum. At QEGS boys follow a wide-ranging curriculum, tailor-made to each student's specific needs.

In the Junior Section boys enjoy active, well-paced practical learning with frequent brain breaks and opportunities for movement. Every lesson in and out of the classroom is buzzing with curiosity and enthusiasm.

In the Senior Section, there's a palpable sense of discovery and exploration as boys from 11–18 enjoy a broad range of unique learning experiences. The school's unique enrichment and development programme provides no fewer than 80 enrichment activities, enabling boys to customise a corner of their timetable and add that vital edge to an already high-octane academic diet.

Pastoral Care/Wellbeing. QEGS creates a secure environment where students gain a true sense of their own worth and feel a real sense of belonging, fostered through small form groups, affiliation to a house, twice-weekly assemblies and dependable peer and staff support.

In addition to its in-school counsellor and matron, boys enjoy a number of wellbeing initiatives, including a weekly enrichment afternoon and a dedicated wellbeing day complete with lessons, online resources and mindfulness practices.

Physical Education and Games. Countless opportunities exist at every level of sport at QEGS. All boys can get involved either individually or as part of a team in Athletics, Badminton, Basketball, Climbing, Cricket, Cross-Country, Cross-Fit, Fitness Training, Football, Hockey, Judo, Mountain Biking, Rugby, Swimming, Table Tennis, Tennis and Volleyball.

The school's excellent sports facilities include a sports hall with fitness suite, games fields, swimming pool, athletics track, sports pavilion and all-weather Astroturf, providing the perfect environment for sporting achievement.

Athletics, Cricket, Hockey and Rugby teams regularly reach regional finals and latter stages of national competitions, and boys compete at international level.

Music and Drama. The school has a full programme of musical and dramatic activities. Throughout the year, all age groups in the Junior Section take part in a stage production, and the Senior Section stages major productions with its sister school, Wakefield Girls' High School.

Students can also access individual instrument or singing lessons, with a team of over 30 visiting instrumental musicians working with the school's music department.

There are numerous choirs in the Junior Section and a highly talented barbershop group in the Senior Section. The school's ensembles take part in local festivals and National Competitions.

The school's orchestras and swing band involve boys from Year 3 upwards and give performances of the highest standard at musical events throughout the year within school and in the local community.

Clubs and Societies. Over 100 clubs and societies are held during the school week, encouraging involvement, firing passions and igniting new interests. The various music groups include brass, woodwind, string ensembles and choirs. The school also participates in the Duke of Edinburgh's Award Scheme and is now officially recognised as an official DofE Centre. There is also a significant programme of charity collections and related activities.

Admissions. Entry into the Junior Section is usually at 7, although places are retained for entry at 8, 9 and 10 years.

Entry into the Senior Section is normally:

- at 11 based on each boy's performance in his entrance exam and how he presents himself in his personal interview. Or as a result of good academic performance in the Junior Section
- at 16 after a satisfactory performance in the GCSE examinations and personal interview.

Enquiries about entrance to the school should be made to the Admissions Manager (qegsadmissions@wgsf.net).

Fees per annum (2023–2024). Junior Section: Years 3 & 4 £12,168, Years 5 & 6 £12,846. Senior Section (Years 7+): £16,248.

Scholarships and Bursaries. The school is committed to helping students from all backgrounds to explore their full capabilities and enjoy the best educational start in life. Each year, the Governors award a limited number of academic scholarships to boys entering the Senior Section at 11.

Means tested awards are also available to students joining at Year 7 or Year 12, covering up to 75% of their school fees under the Wakefield Grammar School Foundation Awards Scheme. Enquiries about awards should be made to the Admissions Manager (qegsadmissions@wgsf.net).

The Old Savilians' Club. President: Mr R Ackroyd

Charitable status. Wakefield Grammar School Foundation is a Registered Charity, number 1088415.

Chair of Governors: Mr Martin Shevill, BEd, MSc, FCCT

Bursar and Clerk to the Governors: Mrs J Cocker

***Head*: Dr R Brookes**, MChem

Deputy Head (*Pastoral*): Mr J Palin, BEng

Assistant Head (*Co-curricular*): Mrs C Palin, BA

Director of Studies (*Operations*): Mr M Fitzsimons, MA

Director of Studies (*Staff*): Mrs A Eggleston, BA, MEd

Director of Junior Section: Mr R Thompson

Queen Elizabeth's Hospital (QEH)

Berkeley Place, Clifton, Bristol BS8 1JX

Tel: 0117 930 3040
email: head@qehbristol.co.uk
office@qehbristol.co.uk
website: www.qehbristol.co.uk
X/Twitter: @QEHSchool
Facebook: @QEHSchool
Instagram: @QEHSchool

Motto: *dum tempus habemus, operemur bonum*

By his will dated 10 April 1586, John Carr, a Bristol merchant, founded Queen Elizabeth's Hospital, a bluecoat school in Bristol on the lines of Christ's Hospital which was already flourishing in London. The Charter was granted to the School by Queen Elizabeth I in 1590. Originally composed entirely of boarders, the School continued so until 1920 when foundation day boys were admitted. Direct Grant status was accorded in 1945. The School is now independent and day only and, as of September 2017, has a co-educational Sixth Form.

Admission. There are 669 pupils in the Senior School, ranging in age from 11 to 18. Entrance examinations for both Year 7 and Year 9 applicants are held in January each year; Sixth Form and other Years by arrangement. Girls are able to join the co-ed QEH Sixth Form.

Term of entry. Usually September.

Entrance scholarships. Scholarships run alongside the means-tested bursary programme. Pupils awarded a music, sport or academic scholarship receive an annual grant for their development.

Assisted places. There are many School assisted places available. The School has a substantial foundation income and is able to give generous support to parents whose means are limited. All pupils (including those awarded a scholarship) are eligible to apply for financial support based on an assessment of the family's means which takes parents' income and the value of capital assets into consideration.

Buildings. The School was originally close by the City Centre but moved to new premises on Brandon Hill in 1847. A major building and improvement programme has included the building of the QEH Theatre (1990), refurbishment of the Art School (2000), new Mathematics rooms and heavy investment in ICT (2004). An 80-strong Junior School opened in 2007 (increasing to over 100 in 2012) along with a new Sixth Form Centre. In 2008 a multimillion pound development programme, in conjunction with Bristol City Football Club, saw new football pitches on 23 acres at the Sports Ground at Failand. A further £2.7 million has been invested at the Failand for a 3G artificial surface for rugby and football, sand-dressed artificial surfaces for hockey and tennis as well as tarmac surfaces for netball and tennis. A new £3 million Science and Art Building was opened in October 2016 and future development plans include improvements to Music and Art facilities and other areas of the school. An expanded Sixth Form Centre opened in September 2017.

Curriculum. Students are prepared for the GCSE and GCE A Level, and for university entrance. The usual school subjects are offered at GCSE level, and the A Level subjects are: English Literature, English Language, Drama, Economics, Classics, Classical Civilisation, History, Geography, French, German, Spanish, Art, Photography, Film Studies, Design and Technology, Music, Mathematics, Further Mathematics, Music Technology, Physics, Chemistry, Biology, PE and Sport, Business Studies, Computer Science, Ethics and Philosophy, Government & Politics and Psychology.

Music & Drama. There is a School Orchestra, Choir, Jazz Band, Brass Group, and Wind Band among the twenty or so ensembles. Music is included in the timetable for all the junior forms. GCSE and A Level music are part of the School curriculum, and tuition is arranged for a wide range of instruments. The Choir and Instrumentalists perform regularly and also undertake joint ventures with other schools in Bristol. Drama flourishes and the school has its own high-tech purpose-built theatre which seats 220.

Art. The Department is well equipped and offers ceramics, screen printing, photography and computer imaging.

Religious Studies. The School is a Christian one which welcomes students of all faiths, or none. Religious Studies is part of the curriculum and students attend two services a year in Bristol Cathedral.

Games. Rugby, Football, Athletics, Cricket, Swimming, Tennis, Hockey, Netball, Badminton, Squash, Judo, Climbing and Mountain Biking. A large number of students also participate in The Duke of Edinburgh's Award and Ten Tors.

Dress. Boys wear either grey trousers and a blazer or a plain dark suit. Sixth Form student wear smart business dress. Traditional bluecoat uniform is worn by some for special occasions.

General. All parents are encouraged to join the Friends of Queen Elizabeth's Hospital, a society whose aim is to promote a close relationship between parents and staff and to further the welfare of the School. There is a flourishing Elizabethan Society for alumni, which holds regular meetings and circulates a newsletter. A panel of former pupils, formed from all professions, and working with the Head of Futures, is available to give advice on careers to students.

The School has long been known in Bristol as 'The City School' and its links with the Lord Mayor and Corporation are strong. Students read the lessons and sing in the Lord Mayor's Chapel, and groups are in attendance for such occasions as Mayor-making and Council Prayers.

The central position of the School, close to the University, the Art Gallery and Museum, the Central Library, the Bristol Old Vic and the Bristol Beacon, affords ready access to a wide range of cultural facilities which students are encouraged to use.

Junior School. 110 Boys aged 7–11. (*For further details see QEH Junior School entry in IAPS section.*)

Fees per term (2023–2024). Senior School: £5,695, Junior School: £3,895. Fees include text and exercise books, and essential educational trips but do not include public examination fees or lunches (which are £280 per term).

Charitable status. Queen Elizabeth's Hospital is a Registered Charity, number 1104871, and a Company Limited by Guarantee, number 5164477. Queen Elizabeth's Hospital has existed since 1590 to provide a first class education.

Governing Body:
Mr P A Keen, FCIB (*Chairman*)

Mrs C Bateson, MA, BA Hons
Ms S Blanks, MSc
Mr J Buchanan, LLB Hons, CTA
Mr A Cherry
Mr E Corrigan, BA, FCS, MAE
Mr T Davis, BSc, MRICS
Mr J Hirst
Mr J Hollingdale, MA Oxon, FCA, MCIArb
Mr M Jones, BSc
Mr J Milne, MA, MBA
Mr K Riley, BA Hons, MA
Mrs J Sadler
Mrs A Woodward
Ms P Yianni

Bursar: Mr M K Suddaby, MA, ACA

***Head*: Mr R D Heathcote**, BSc

Deputy Head (*Academic*): Mr J Martin, MA
Deputy Head (*Pastoral*): Mr N Pursall, BA
Assistant Head (*Staff Development*): Mr C Brotherton, MA
Assistant Head (*Sixth Form*): Mr R Porter, MA

Assistant Head (*Logistics and Co-curricular*): Mr T J Dunn, BSc
Assistant Head (*Equality and Pupil Wellbeing*): Miss L Mantle, BA, MA

Mr S Albon, BSc
Mr P M Amor, BA
Mrs A L Baker, BA
Ms C R Bernstein, MA
Ms H Bosson, BSc
Miss J Bowkett, BSc
Mr F Burns, MSc
Miss T Cardale, BSc
Mr R D Carr, BA
Ms L Carter, BA
Mr D J Chalmers, BSc
Mr A C Clements, BSc
Ms C Coleman, BA
Mr C B Conquest, BEd
Mr R Cope (Bristol Old Vic)
Miss A Cottingham, BA
Mr J Cox, BSc
Ms O Darkes-Sutcliffe, BA
Mr A Donald, BA
Mrs K Ellis, BA
Mrs K Emery
Ms A Feledziak, BA
Miss L Fenner, BA
Mrs C Gardner, BA
Mr E M Gent, BA
Mrs D Guthrie, BSc
Mr R J Harris, BA
Mr S A Harris, BSc
Mr T Harrison, BA
Mr D T Hawkes, BSc
Miss C Hiles, PGDip
Mrs P Hockenhull, BA
Mrs N Holcombe, BA
Mr K M Holmes, BA
Miss E Hunter, BSc
Mrs K Izzard-Clark, BSc
Mr A Jarvis, BA
Dr J Jönsson, MSc, PhD
Mr P E Joslin, BEd
Mr J Kelly, BSc
Mrs J Kerslake, BSc
Ms T R Kibblewhite, BSc
Dr H L Kyle, BSc, PhD
Ms S K Liddle, BSc
Mrs H Mann, MA
Mr R Martineau, MEng
Mrs M McGowan, BA
Ms H McKellar, MA
Miss C McQuaid, BA
Mr S Mitchell, BSc
Mr P C Moore, BEd
Mrs S Moritz, BSc
Mr S J Munnion, BA
Dr V Neild, BA
Mr A Paltzer, BA
Mr J Parsonage, MA
Mrs A Pegg, BA
Mr W G Plowden, BA
Mrs I Porter, BA
Ms C A Rostron, MA
Mr C Ryan, BSc
Ms K E Ryan, BA
Mrs H Shields, BA
Mr M Sloan, BSc
Mr A W H Swithinbank, BA
Mrs N Taylor, BA
Miss G Tyler, MSc
Mr Z Verry, BA
Mrs F Waite-Taylor, BA
Mr R J Waldron, BA
Mr G S Westwater, BSc

Junior School:
Headteacher: Mr D M Kendall, MA, MEd

Visiting Music Teachers:
Mr J Bacon, MMus
Mr P Barrett, BA, PG Dip
Mr R Grist, BA Hons, BMus Hons
Miss C Lindley, BA
Mr N Malcolm
Mr B Mullan, BMus
Mrs O Parfitt
Mr A Purnell, BMus Hons RWCMD
Mr G Sterland
Mr N Shipman, BMus LGSMD
Mr A Stewart, BMus
Mr R Webb
Mr J Whitfield, BMus

Chaplain: The Revd C M Pilgrim
Headmaster's Secretary: Mrs E Davies
Admissions Registrar: Mrs C Matthews
Librarian: Miss H Richardson

Queenswood School

Shepherd's Way, Brookmans Park, Hatfield, Hertfordshire AL9 6NS

Tel: 01707 602500
email: admissions@queenswood.org
website: www.queenswood.org
X/Twitter: @QueenswoodSch
Facebook: @QueenswoodSch
Instagram: @queenswoodschool
LinkedIn: /company/queenswood-school

Motto: *In Hortis Reginæ – In the Queen's Gardens*

Queenswood is a progressive boarding and day school for around 490 girls, aged between 11 and 18, where boarders make up around half of the School. The School was founded in 1894 in Clapham Park and moved to its current site in Hertfordshire in 1925. An all-round education focuses on equipping the girls with all the life skills required of women in the 21st century. Within a caring and supportive framework, the girls enjoy a dynamic academic curriculum, supported by a diverse and exciting co-curricular programme.

Queenswood has exceptional value-added results, with our pupils always performing beyond their predicted grades, particularly at GCSE. We believe that every girl should follow her own individual learning journey, so we set development targets that suit her learning style and potential. The Personalised Learning Team works with our teaching staff to integrate this bespoke approach into lessons, whilst simultaneously providing 1:1 support for girls with a high standard of academic achievement and for those who need a little more assistance in certain subjects.

It is a warm and friendly community where everybody knows each other. Girls thrive within a nurturing House structure tailored to meet their needs as they progress from the Lower School, through the Middle School, and on into the Sixth Form. Day girls are fully integrated within the Houses, are able to enjoy all the facilities and opportunities available to the boarders, but choose to go home at night after a packed school day. There is a flexible approach to boarding to meet the varying needs of individual families; girls may choose to flexi board for 1, 2 or 3 nights, weekly board or be full boarders.

Here at Queenswood, we know that happy girls are successful girls and so we place paramount importance on pastoral care. The Good Schools Guide states that 'Queenswood is all about kindness and support and it shows in every nuance of school life'. Queenswood parents enthuse about the proactive approach to mental health, highlighting our mentoring programme. On entrance to the school, Year 7 girls are mentored by a fellow pupil in Year 8 and Year 13, with these girls going above and beyond to help one another. This peer-support complements our fantastic pastoral staff, such as our boarding assistants and resident full-time counsellor, who ensure that someone is always looking out for your daughter.

Queenswood is proud to be an international community with an outward-looking approach; overseas girls make up around 15% of the pupils. We welcome girls of all faiths and none, recognise and support an individual's adherence to her own faith, but expect all girls to embrace the School's broad spiritual ethos.

The girls are ambitious high achievers, winning places at the top universities both at home and abroad prior to embarking upon a range of exciting careers. Individual talent also flourishes in sport and the creative and performing arts. The extensive co-curricular programme helps develop the girls' soft skills in a wide variety of ways and significantly contributes to their excellent academic results. As important as individual achievement is the development of a sense of responsibility for each other and the world in which they live. Queenswood girls are thoughtful young people with a secure set of values and self-confidence.

The beautiful Queenswood estate provides the perfect educational environment. Being just 20 minutes from central London, it also has the advantage of easy access to the cultural richness of the capital. At the same time, its proximity to major international airports provides ease of travel for both our overseas girls and for those participating in the School's foreign exchange and visit programmes.

Curriculum. With over twenty-five subjects in the curriculum and more than one hundred co-curricular activities available, girls have every opportunity to discover their strengths and to become exceptional learners and leaders. We offer a holistic educational experience which supports and encourages intellectual, physical, moral and spiritual development.

Life. Queenswood encourages intellectual curiosity, of which the spiritual dimension is an important part. Girls are therefore welcome to discuss their thoughts, feelings and faith in an open and supportive context. Since true education is holistic it includes spiritual and moral development. All pupils of the School, whatever their religion, are encouraged to explore and develop their own faith in an atmosphere of tolerance. We accept girls of all faiths and none.

Boarding. We strongly believe that fun and friendship should be the foundation of our boarding community. So, we invite you to enter a world where your daughter will be able to embrace diversity, firmly establish her independence while still fostering a sense of care and concern for the community, sample more to achieve more and certainly make friends for life.

Lower School. Our ultimate aim in the Lower School is to help girls to become independent students with enthusiasm for learning and the ambition to develop their skills and qualities to their fullest extent. Beyond the classroom, there is a wealth of opportunities for younger girls to enrich their education. These include a wide range of co-curricular clubs and activities and a diverse programme of House outings and excursions.

Entry. Entrance to Queenswood is by examination (Common Entrance Exam or Queenswood's papers), interview and a report from the pupil's current Headteacher.

Scholarships. Queenswood Scholarships are awarded in recognition of outstanding achievement or promise in a particular sphere. The majority of our Scholarships are honorary and do not attract financial support; however, a small number of awards with fee remissions may be available for candidates applying for a music Scholarship who demonstrate exceptional potential.

Fees per term (2023–2024). Day: Years 7–8 £8,120, Years 9–13 £9,460. Boarders: Years 7–8 Flexi boarding (1–3 nights) £8,375–£8,800, Weekly boarding £9,155, Full boarding £10,235; Years 9–13 Flexi boarding (1–3 nights) £10,170–£11,330, Weekly boarding £12,115, Full boarding £13,950.

Old Queenswoodians' Association. The OQA has 4,000+ members and an active young membership that supports current Queenswoodians after their time at School has come to an end.

Charitable status. Queenswood School Limited is a Registered Charity, number 311060, which exists to provide high-quality education for girls.

Governors:
Mr H J de Sausmarez, BA, FCIS (*Chair*)
Mr T C Garnham, BSc (*Vice Chair*)
Mr R Baines, BSc, CIMA, CEng, MICE
Mrs K Belshaw, LLB Hons, PGLDip, LLM, AKC
The Reverend Dr D M Chapman, BSc, MA, MPhil, PhD
Ms J Fenn, MA, PGCE, FCCT
Mr R Garwood, BA Hons, Dip MRS
Dr O McGuinness, BSc, MB BS, FRCP, DCH, DRCOG
Mr S Morris, MA, PGCE, NPQH
Mrs C Norman, BSc, CIMA
Mrs N Penny
Mr J Phelan, MA Ed, BA Hons, PGCE
Mr A D Poppleton, BEng, CEng, AKC, FIET, FBSC
The Honourable N Stamp
Mrs P M Wrinch

***Principal*: Mrs J Cameron**, BSc Hons Surrey, PGCE

Bursar and Clerk to the Governors: Mr I Williams, BEng Hons, RMCS Shrivenham, CEng
Director of External Relations: Mrs D Cresswell, BA Hons York, DipM
Deputy Head Academic: Mr I Sheldon, MChem Oxon, PGCE, MRSC
Deputy Head Pastoral: Mrs C Stokes, BEd Hons
Assistant Head, Pupil Data, Teaching and Learning: Mr S Daughton, BA Hons, PGCE, MRHS, MA London
Assistant Head, Boarding: Mrs V Ludwick, BA Hons, PGCE
Head of Sixth Form: Mr C Fox, BA Hons Sheffield, MA Warwick, MSc Oxon
Assistant Head Digital Strategy: Mr S Lovell, BSc Hons Southampton, PGCE
Chaplain: The Reverend K Douglas, MBA
Head of PR, Digital and Print: Mr N Kelley, BA Hons Oxon

Admissions Team:
Head of UK Admissions: Miss C Noone
Head of International Admissions: Ms A George
Admissions and Marketing Assistant: Mrs V Leigh

Further details can be found at www.queenswood.org/explore/staff-and-governors

Radley College

Abingdon, Oxfordshire OX14 2HR

Tel: 01235 543127 (Warden)
01235 543122 (Bursar)
01235 543174 (Admissions)
01235 543000 (General Enquiries)

email: warden@radley.org.uk
website: www.radley.org.uk
X/Twitter: @RadleyCollege
Facebook: @RadleyCollege
Instagram: @radleycollegeoxon

Motto: *Sicut Serpentes, sicut Columbae*

Radley College was founded by the Reverend William Sewell, Fellow of Exeter College, Oxford, to provide an independent school education on the principles of the Church of England. It was opened on 9 June 1847 and incorporated by Royal Charter in 1890. It stands in a park of some 800 acres.

General arrangements. There are 770 boys in the school, all of whom board. On admission, boys enter one of the 11 houses known as Socials. All are close together within the grounds. All meals are served in Hall on a cafeteria system. There is a daily Chapel Service for all boys.

Admission. The 13+ admissions process is held when boys are in Year 6. Boys are assessed using the ISEB Common Pre-Test, a current school report and an interview with the Warden or Senior Master at Radley. Those who have registered early on the Radley List (generally before a boy is 3 years old) will go through this process in the Michaelmas Term of Year 6 with offers being made in March of Year 6. Those who have not registered early go through the same pre-test assessment and are interviewed in the Lent Term of Year 6 with offers being made in March of Year 6. This process is called Open Entry. Offers will be unconditional, but boys are required to sit either 13+ Scholarship or Common Entrance (or Maths and English exams for those abroad) and Radley reserves the right to refuse entry in exceptional circumstances.

Places are also available for Sixth Form entry and, occasionally, in Year 10 (Removes): details are available on our website.

Scholarships and bursaries. Academic, Music, Sport, Drama and Art Awards (Scholarships and Exhibitions) are all available every year. Radley launched a new award, the Innovation Scholarship, for September 2024. All awards may be supplemented by a means-tested bursary. Details are available on our website or from Admissions: admissions@radley.org.uk. Further means-tested bursaries (11+ Funded Places) of up to 115% of the fees are available for boys who would otherwise be unable to afford to come to Radley and applicants are assessed in Year 6.

Academic: Around 10 Academic Awards are offered annually.

Music: On average five Instrumental Scholarships and several Exhibitions are offered annually with free tuition.

Sport: At least five sport awards are offered annually.

Drama: Around two awards will be offered annually.

Art: Around two awards will be offered annually.

Innovation: Up to five awards annually.

Work. In the Shells, Removes and Fifth Form a broad curriculum is followed. There is some choice at GCSE with boys generally taking nine or ten subjects.

In the Sixth Form a boy can specialise in a combination of Classics, French, Spanish, German, Theatre Studies, English, History, Religious Studies, Geography, Geology, Biology, Chemistry, Physics, Mathematics, Economics, Politics, Economics and Business, Music, Art or Design, leading to A level qualifications. An AS in Art is also available, being part of a Sixth Form Curriculum Extension Programme, which also includes the Extended Project Qualification (EPQ), a mini-MBA and an International Relations Course.

Futures. Radley Futures is our comprehensive careers programme which runs through all years and is designed to prepare students for higher education and work. This includes writing CVs, psychometric testing and profiling, UCAS and international university application support and interview practice. All students can access professional advice and gain exposure to a wide variety of careers through talks, visits and work experience. In the Sixth Form, boys are given the opportunity to join our business networking platforms where they can interact with Old Radleians and Radley parents, developing their early networking skills and starting to build a lifelong network before they leave.

Games. In the Michaelmas Term rugby is the major school sport. In the Lent Term the 'wet-bobs' row and the 'dry-bobs' play hockey (the major sport) and football. In the Summer Term cricket and rowing are the major sports alongside athletics and tennis. There are also numerous minor sports which involve boys in competition with other schools. The playing fields are close to the main buildings.

The College has its own boathouse, and the use of a stretch of the River Thames between Sandford and Abingdon. The VIIIs compete in regattas and Head of the River races.

There are three all-weather hockey pitches, an athletics track, five squash courts, a Real Tennis court, a rackets court, two covered Fives courts, 20 hard tennis courts and a 9-hole golf course. There is a large, well-equipped gymnasium and an indoor, heated swimming pool attached to a multi-purpose sports hall and a Strength and Conditioning Centre situated near a state-of-the-art rowing tank.

CCF and Duke of Edinburgh's Award. All boys, in their fourth term, join the Radley College Contingent, Combined Cadet Force (Army, Navy and Air sections). They work for the Proficiency examination, which takes three terms. When they have passed Proficiency and done a week's Corps Camp in the holidays they either stay on in a special section for further training or join one of the many Partnership Projects on offer. There is a thriving Duke of Edinburgh's Award scheme.

Fees per term (2023–2024). £16,025. There is available a system of insurance against loss of fees caused by illness, accident, or infection. Particulars can be obtained from the Bursar.

Charitable status. St Peter's College, Radley is a Registered Charity, number 309243. It exists for the purpose of the education of youth in general knowledge and literature and particularly and especially in the doctrines and principles of the Church of England.

Visitor: The Rt Revd The Lord Bishop of Oxford

Council:
Chairman: D C S Smellie, MA
Vice-Chairman: G A Kaye, BSc

M Breen
J C Bridcut, MA
T M Durie, BA, ACA, FSI
Revd Dr S Hampton
N J Henderson, MA, FRCS
Sir J Holmes
R N L Huntingford
E J Martineau, FRGS
H J R Morris
C H Palmer
D J Pluck, FCA
M J W Rushton, MA
S J B Shaw
C M A Sweetnam
R H Warner, MA, ACA
H J R Willis, MA

***Warden*: J S Moule**, MA

Sub Warden: B J Holden, MA, BTech
Sub Warden (*Designate*): N Murphy, MA

Deputy Heads:
H Crump, LLB, BA
J Porter, MA
R D Shaw, MA

Directors:
E Anderson, BA
S Langdale, BA

Under Master:
T R G Ryder, BA, MFA

Teaching Staff:
P Asbury, BA
O Astley, BA Hons
S Barlass, BA
R Beattie, BA
C M Bedford, BA, PhD
A C Bibby, BA
M C F Brown, BA
V K Buse, BA
I K Campbell, BA
M M Carter
R Catmull
O W Choroba, MPhil, PhD
L J Clogher
G C Dalrymple, MA, MSc
S H Dalrymple, BA
T J Deasy, BA, MA
J de Ritter, BA
E Ellis
P M Fernandez, MA
J A Gaunt
J E Gearing, BA
†S R Giddens, BSc, MSc, PhD (*C Social*)
M G D Glendon-Doyle, BA (*K Social*)
R J Grice, BA
†A M H Hakimi, BSc, MPhil (*L Social*)
M C Hart, BA
A J Hibbs, MPhys
M P Hills, MMath
E O Holt, BA
T Horacek
†R E P Hughes, BSc (*A Social*)
M Hurley, BA
K C Ison, BA
M R Jewell, BA
R Johnson, BSc
†W A Jolly, BSci (*E Social*)
†G R King, BA (*G Social*)
B T Knowles, BA
Dr P J Langman, BSc
T C Lawson, BA
Dr M Lebedeva, MSc
C D Lloyd, BSc
C R Mason, MMath Hons
S Matthews
†C P McKegney (*D Social*)
R K McMahon, MA, MPhil, DPhil
P J Miron, BSc, DPhil
K A Mosedale, MA, MSc
A F C Nash, BA
M G Noone, MA
A C N Norman, MSc
†T C H Norton, MA (*F Social*)
A P Pancrazi, Lycee
S J Perkins, BSc
Dr C Ploix, DPhil
D J Pullen, BSc
O J Purslow
C Robinson, BA
Dr D I Robinson, MEng
L P Robinson, BA
D W S Roques, MA
M I Rumbold, BA
L Ryan, BSc
D Scott, BA
†C E Scott-Malden, BA, MA (*B Social*)
J A S Sheldrake
E Simpkins
J M Sparks, BSc
W Swain, BA
F E Taylor, BA
S W Townsend
R Tufnell, BA
A A Vaan, BSc
M E Walker, BA, MA, PhD
A Wiles, BA
†K W S Willis-Stovold, BSc (*J Social*)
O D Wills, MEng
B L Wilson, BA Hons
J A D Wilson, MChem
†N Wood (*H Social*)
G Wiseman, BA
R D Woodling, MChem
Dr D Zimmer, MChem

Chaplain: The Revd Dr R A H Evans
Librarian: Ms A Stead
Music:
Precentor: S J Gladstone, MA
T M Morris, MA, DPhil, FRCO
S-L Naylor, MA

There are 36 peripatetic music staff.

Bursar and Secretary: A Ashton, MA, ACIB
Development Director: E Anderson, BA
Director of Admissions: S Langdale, BA

Ratcliffe College

Fosse Way, Ratcliffe on the Wreake, Leicester, Leicestershire LE7 4SG

Tel: 01509 817000 School Office
01509 817072/817031 Admissions Office
email: admissions@ratcliffecollege.com
website: www.ratcliffecollege.com
X/Twitter: @RatcliffeColl
@RatcliffePrep
@RatcliffeSport
Facebook: @RatcliffeCollege
Instagram: @RatcliffeCollege
LinkedIn: /school/ratcliffe-college

Motto: '*Legis Plenitudo Charitas*'

Founded in 1847 by the Rosminian Fathers, Ratcliffe is steeped in history and tradition. Set in 200 acres of beautiful grounds, students benefit daily by working and playing within a truly inspirational physical environment.

The College's inclusive Catholic ethos is complemented by the outstanding quality of the College's community through which the College's Mission, "Learning and Growing in the Light of the Gospel", serves to nurture resilience and develop maturity. Young people leave Ratcliffe with a strong sense of who they are and their purpose in the world, equipped to make a difference to the communities in which they live and work.

Ratcliffe College has been judged 'Excellent' in all areas, following the recent Focused Compliance and Education Quality ISI Inspection, held in May 2022.

Academic Excellence

We are committed to getting the very best out of our students and provide every opportunity for them to exceed expectations, realise their full potential and achieve the highest grades possible.

With a winning combination of excellent teaching, small class sizes and state-of-the-art facilities, our pupils benefit from a rich learning environment and consequently attain significantly higher grades than predicted. In the summer of 2023, 81% of all A-Level grades were A*-C and 32% achieving A*/A, with a pass rate of 99.5% overall.

Co-Curricular Programme

To succeed academically, we believe that young people need to grow and learn outside the classroom too. Our programme provides the perfect balance of academic and co-curricular activities. Pupils have choice from an enormous range of clubs, societies and new experiences weekly. Our co-curricular programme revolves around the "Big Six" – Chaplaincy, Sport, Music, Drama, Combined Cadet Force, and the Duke of Edinburgh's Award.

Outstanding Facilities and Campus

Ratcliffe College benefits from outstanding facilities and cutting-edge academic spaces, inspiring a love of learning for all. The College campus and facilities encourage students to excel and provides a safe community and environment in which to live and grow.

State-of-the-art facilities, include:

- Sixth Form Centre, with a modern business café and independent study facilities
- Refurbished Boarding accommodation and communal spaces
- Indoor swimming pool
- Carbon-zero English Language Centre
- A £1.3 million Fitness Suite
- The tranquil Lockhart Garden
- Athletics Track
- Two sports halls
- Floodlit and all-weather pitches (Tennis, Rugby, Hockey and Netball)

The campus also benefits from a high-performance theatre, creative art spaces, galleries, and excellent music facilities.

Boarding at Ratcliffe

Our vibrant, warm and welcoming boarding community enjoys a strong international flavour, something that has long been part of the College's history. Students aged 11 and above can choose from full, weekly, regular, and occasional boarding, becoming part of a diverse boarding community. Our boarders are supported by a dedicated pastoral team and enjoy a comprehensive programme of activities and excursions, arranged for evenings and weekends.

"Pupils have excellent attitudes to learning and considerable willingness to participate across all areas of their education." – ISI Inspection Report 2022

For further enquiries, please contact our Admissions Team on 01509 817072 or admissions@ratcliffecollege.com.

Nearest International Airport: East Midlands (40km).

Number of Pupils. 915 (81 boarders).

Fees per term (2023–2024). Day: £3,780–£6,563 (Per Term) Boarding: £8,566–£12,870.

Charitable status. Ratcliffe College is a Registered Charity, number 1115975, for the education of children.

Governing Body:
Mrs S Spillane (*Chair*)
Mr S Burns (*Vice-Chair*)
Mr M Cummins (*Chair of Education and Co-Curricular Committee*)
Mrs T Gamble (*Chair of Pastoral, Chaplaincy, Safeguarding and Boarding Committee*)
Mrs M Kewell (*Chair of Preparatory School Committee*)
Dr M Riley (*Vice Chair of Pastoral, Chaplaincy, Safeguarding and Boarding Committee*)
Mr P Rudd (*Foundation Governor*)
Fr P Sainter (*Foundation Governor*)
Mr S Astill (*Chair of F & GP*)
Mr M Wells (*Governor*)
Mr A C Smith (*Eco Governor*)
Mr D Amies (*Governor*)

***Headmaster*: Mr J Reddin**, BSc, MSc, NPQH

Senior Deputy Head: Mr K Ryce, BA, MSc
Deputy Head Pastoral: Mr J Rainer
Director of Finance & Operations: Mr C Bellamy, HND
Head of Preparatory School: Mrs S Minford
Assistant Head Academic: Ms J Davis, BA, MSc
Assistant Head, Head of Sixth Form: Mr B Harrison, BA
Deputy Head of Preparatory School: Mrs M Markham, BMus
Father President: Fr P Sainter, IC, BSc, BPhil, MA, STL

Teaching Staff:
* *Head of Department*

Miss E Bakewell-Voss, BA (*Physical Education*)
Dr D Barrett, PhD, BSc (*Mathematics*)
Ms E Battrum, MA, MEd (*Geography*, *Head of Year 8*)
Mr R Beach, BA (*Preparatory School*)
Miss S Bolivar-Medina (*MFL*)
Mrs K Bradbury, BSc (*Mathematics*)
Mrs V Breward, BSc (*Science & Food Science*)
Dr K Brouilette, PhD, MA, BSc (*Science & Food Science*)
Mrs K Burton, BA (*Food Science & Nutrition*)
Mr J Cantrill, BA (*History**)
Mrs J Cartwright (*Head of Curriculum, Preparatory School*)
Miss L Chapman, MChem (*Chemistry**, *Boarding Assistant*)
Mr A Chorley, MSc (*Science**)
Mrs S Clarke, BA (*Mathematics*)
Mrs C Cole, MA (*Mathematics*)
Mr M Cole, BSc (*Director of Co-Curriculum & Wellbeing*)
Mrs R Cook, BA (*Preparatory School, Music*)
Miss A Corbinzolu, BA (*Head of Year 9, Religious Studies*)
Mrs C Craven, BA (*Drama**, *Head of Year 7*)
Mrs A Crebbin, DEUG (*French, Spanish*)
Mr M Darlington, BSc (*Physics**, *Curriculum Director*)
Mrs L Davids, BSc (*Learning Support, English*)

Mrs N Dexter, BSc (*EYFS*)
Mrs C Dimilta-Jones (*Economics & Business Studies*)
Mr C Doherty, BEng (*Mathematics*)
Mrs K Don (*Preparatory School*)
Mrs K Donegan, BA (*Director of Music**)
Mrs A Dungey, BSc (*Science*, *Food Technology*)
Mr P Enoux, BA (*Preparatory School*)
Mr C Farbrother, BSc (*Chemistry*)
Mr W Faulconbridge, BSc (*Preparatory School Sport**)
Mr A Ferrari, BSc (*Preparatory School*)
Dr S Ferguson, PhD, BSc (*Biology*)
Mr J Finn, BA (*Preparatory School*)
Miss D Gatt, BSc (*Biology*)
Miss L Gentle, BSc (*Physical Education*, *Head of Girls' Netball*)
Mrs N Gilchrist, BEd (*Preparatory School*)
Mr J, Estevez (*Senior Boys' Housemaster*)
Mrs D Grant, BEd (*Preparatory School*)
Ms S Griffin, BSc (*Head of Girls' Games*, *Preparatory School*)
Mr T Hallam-Jones, BA (*Religious Studies*)
Mrs A-L Harrison, BA (*Art & Design*, *Assistant Head Year 7*)
Miss V Hobbs, BA (*English*)
Ms E Johanson, BA (*SENCo/Learning Support**)
Mr M Jones, BSc (*Computer Science & Information and Communication Technology**, *ECDL Centre Manager*)
Dr S Jones, PhD (*Mathematics**)
Mr M Kaye, BA (*Physical Education*, *History*)
Mrs A Keeling, BEd (*Reception*, *Preparatory School*)
Mr D Kent, BA (*Preparatory School*)
Mr M Lambert, BSc (*Geography**)
Miss N Langton, BA (*EYFS*)
Dr C Latham, BSc, MSc, PhD (*Preparatory School Learning Support*)
Mr J Litchfield, BSc (*EYFS*)
Miss C Llewelyn, BA (*Preparatory School*)
Mr M Lucas, BSc (*Academic PE**)
Mrs H Macfarlane, BA (*MFL*)
Mr P McCrindell, BA (*Languages*)
Mrs L McCue, BEd (*Preparatory School*)
Mrs J Munton, BA (*Drama*)
Mr M Newman, BA (*Head of Year 13*, *2nd i/c History & Politics*)
Mrs Y O'Connor, BA, MEd (*Religious Studies*)
Mr S Pattni, BSc (*Physics*)
Miss E Radford, BA (*MFL*)
Miss R Ravat, BSc (*EYFS**)
Mrs J Reddin, BA (*French*)
Mrs M Reeves, BA, MSc (*EAL*, *English*)
Mrs E Richardson-Cauldwell, BA (*Art & Design**)
Miss B Robinson, BA (*English*)
Dr A Robinson, BSc, PhD (*Science*)
Mr P Rogers, BA (*Design & Technology*, *Head of Year 11*)
Mr A Seth, BSc (*Design & Technology**)
Mrs K Shepherd, BSc (*Preparatory School*)
Miss C Simms, BA (*Media Studies**)
Ms C Slusarenko, BSc (*Psychology*)
Mrs E Smith, BSc (*Physics*)
Mrs P Smith, BA (*Religious Studies*)
Mr T Snowden, BA, MA (*History*, *Geography*, *Religious Studies*)
Mr P Spencer, ACIB (*Head of Year 12*, *Business/Economics**)
Miss T Spencer, BA (*PSHCE**, *Business Studies*)
Dr S Standen, BSc, PhD (*Science*)
Dr L Stannard, BA, MA, PhD (*English**)
Dr J Summers, BA, PhD (*MFL**)
Mr S Thorpe, BSc (*Biology**, *LCFC Academy Liaison*, *Assistant Boys' Housemaster*)
Miss S Tidy, BA (*English*)
Miss J Truman, BSc (*Academic PE*)
Mr D Turner, BEd (*Preparatory School*, *Assistant Boys' Housemaster*)
Mrs A Turns, BSc (*Director of Sport**)
Miss K Vickers, BMus (*Music*)
Ms W Walker, BA, MA (*Librarian*)
Mr N Walsh, LLB (*Religious Studies**)
Mr T Wardle, BA (*Computer Science*, *Information Communication Technology*, *Head of Year 10*, *Digital Learning Co-ordinator*)
Mrs V Warman (*EYFS*) [maternity cover]
Mrs E Waters, BEd (*Learning Support*, *Deputy SENCo*)
Mrs L Wetton, BA (*Preparatory School*)
Mrs L Whieldon, BA (*English*)
Mr D Willcock (*Hockey**, *Learning Support*)
Mrs K Williams (*EYFS*)
Mr W Wong, BSc (*Mathematics*)
Mr E Woodcock, BA, MSc (*Cricket**, *Physical Education*)
Dr L Wilson, BA, MA, PhD (*Latin*)
Miss A Wright, BA (*Art & Design*)

Sports Coaches:
Mr M Birr, Miss G Brock-Taylor, Mr J Chapple, Miss B Cobden, Ms S Freeman, Miss C McGlynn, Mr J Nightingale, Mr N Taylor

Peripatetic Music Staff:
Mr P Bennett, Dr M Bonshor, Mr J Boyd, Mrs S Cheeseman, Mr C Earp, Mr R Finn, Mrs S Forrester, Miss S Hall, Mr G Henderson, Mrs C Lee, Ms C Pascall, Mrs R Provost, Miss R Reedman, Mr M Shaw, Mrs K Thompson

Graduate Assistants:
Miss K Taylor (*Sports*)
Mr J Atkins (*Sports*)
Mr S Palucki (*Sports*)
Mr R Jawurek (*German*)
Miss L Refflard (*French*)
Mrs M Salazar (*Spanish*)

Teaching Assistants (*Preparatory School and Nursery*):
Mrs S Allen, Level 3
Miss C Croxall, Level 3
Mrs R Deacon, BA
Miss L Driver
Mrs A Hailes, Level 3, BA
Mrs P Heir, BA
Miss E Lacey, Level 3
Mrs A Leake, Level 2
Mrs M Karanja Phombeah, Level 3
Mrs E Kavanagh, BSc, MSc
Mrs M Rushin
Miss C Stone
Mrs J Yapa, BA

Head of Marketing & Admissions: Mrs C Bradley
Development Manager: Mrs L Liston

Reading Blue Coat School

Holme Park
Sonning Lane, Sonning-on-Thames, Berkshire
RG4 6SU

Tel: 0118 944 1005
email: reception@rbcs.org.uk
website: www.rbcs.org.uk
X/Twitter: @ReadingBlues
Facebook: @ReadingBlueCoat
Instagram: @readingbluecoatschool

Reading Blue Coat is an independent day school with almost 800 students aged 11–18, set in an attractive 46-acre site reaching down to the banks of the River Thames in the village of Sonning-on-Thames in Berkshire. The School was founded in 1646 by Richard Aldworth, a merchant of London and Reading, and a Governor of Christ's Hospital. In September 2023, the School extended the long-established co-education of the Sixth Form and welcomed girls into Year 7 and will be fully co-educational in all years by 2027.

Aims. The School aims to provide a stimulating and friendly atmosphere in which each student can achieve their full intellectual, physical and creative potential. Students are encouraged to be self-reliant and adaptable and we hope that they will learn the basis of good citizenship founded on honesty, fairness and understanding of the needs of others. At Reading Blue Coat, students have access to extensive co-curricular opportunities including music, drama, public speaking and sport, as well as in the community – all of which celebrate our values of aspiration, compassion, courage, integrity and service. To be kind and engaged is what we expect of every member of our community. Kind to one another and to ourselves, and engaged with learning and the wealth of opportunities that can be enjoyed in and away from the classroom.

Pastoral Care. At Blue Coat, our philosophy is that every student should be known and cared for as an individual. Good relationships are everything. Our focus in getting to know young people, enjoying their company, and finding out what makes them tick. With our low staff-to-student ratio, expert teachers, and individualised tutoring, we care for our students deeply and thoughtfully. That could be experienced in a House Family meeting, a one-to-one with a tutor, or just a good chat with a friend. What makes Blue Coat special is the personal touch.

Academic. The academic life of the School is defined by its commitment to excellence and sharing of high expectations. The learning habits of our students, and the development of their curiosity, knowledge and creativity are all considered to be essential elements of our academic curriculum. Expert staff help to unlock the potential in every student, seeking to instil a love for learning and develop flexible, independent thinkers.

Curriculum. In Years 7 to 9, students study core subjects of English, mathematics and sciences along with a broad range of subjects, including Classics, modern foreign languages and philosophy, religion and ethics. In Years 10 and 11, students follow courses in mathematics and sciences and also opt to complete four further courses in a wide range of additional subjects, such as history, geography, geology and physical education. A wide range of subjects is offered at A Level, including Psychology, Economics, Business, Politics and Drama, with nearly every student going on to university, including Oxford and Cambridge. Adventure Education has also been introduced as a compulsory part of the curriculum and is providing students with opportunities to flourish away from the classroom.

Sixth Form. The co-educational Sixth Form Centre accommodates more than 250 students. Students choose from a range of 26 subjects, including subjects most will not have studied before, such as business, economics, government and politics, drama and psychology. The Extended Project Qualification option is much valued in Higher Education. In addition to A Level courses, all Sixth Formers follow compulsory careers and enrichment programmes.

Sports and Activities. Competitive sport plays a key part in developing a Blue Coat student's potential, no matter at what level, nor in which sport. Respect, belief, commitment, and sportsmanship are the characteristics we aim to nurture in each student. Main sports are athletics, cross country, cricket, football, girls' hockey, netball, rowing, and rugby. All our main sports have a highly competitive and extensive fixture list and compete both at local and national level. Other popular competitive sports include badminton, basketball, golf, rugby sevens, swimming, table tennis, tennis, and touch rugby. Our highly qualified, experienced and enthusiastic coaching team, encourages every student to maximise their potential, as well as enjoy their experience regardless of ability.

The Combined Cadet Force includes Army, Royal Air Force and Royal Navy sections and The Duke of Edinburgh's Award, provide many opportunities for expeditions, trips, community service and leadership.

In our time-tabled Adventure Education and Activities programmes, students enjoy time away from the classroom to learn valuable lessons in leadership, communication, and resilience, as well as exploring the wider world in a variety of ways.

The arts. Music, Drama and Dance enjoy a high profile in the life of the School. Well over a third of the students receive individual instrumental lessons and are encouraged to join in activities such as the choir, Chamber Choir, Piano Trio, String Ensemble, Concert Band, Saxophone Group, Brass Group, Swing Band, Wind Band, Junior Strings, Treble Choir, rock bands, Senior Brass Group and Blue Coat Big Band. Concerts, drama productions and musicals are presented regularly throughout the academic year. The popular drama productions are all supported by a strong student technical theatre team.

Location and Facilities. The School is situated in the Thames-side village of Sonning-on-Thames, 10 minutes from Reading and close to the Regatta town of Henley-on-Thames. School House, originally built in the eighteenth century, stands at the heart of the School. The School's facilities have undergone a continuous programme of improvement over the last decade, including a new IT Centre, a new Design Technology Centre, a new Geology and Psychology block and a Grounds, Maintenance and Activities Centre, which provides a shooting range and CCF and Adventure Education facilities. The three-classroom Coach House was also opened in 2021, and provides space for pupils to work collaboratively. The School has recently expanded its facilities for the Sixth Form and has plans for further development of a Performing Arts Centre. Our extensive sports facilities include an on-site boathouse, eight outstandingly maintained rugby and football pitches, six cricket squares, four netball courts, three tennis courts, a swimming pool, a multi-use Sports Hall, a multi-use games area (MUGA), an athletics track with a dedicated jumping area and a fitness suite. We also share facilities with Reading RFC, Reading Hockey club, Sonning Cricket club and Berkshire County Sports Club.

Admissions. The three main points of entry in September are at 11+, 13+ and 16+. 11+ entry is by assessments taken in the previous autumn term, and 13+ assessments take place during the autumn term of Year 7. Entry at other levels is by assessment and interview and is subject to vacancies. Entry to the sixth form for girls and boys is by formal letter of application, interview and conditional on GCSE results. From September 2023, the School extended its co-educational provision to welcome girls into Year 7.

Scholarships and Bursaries. The award of scholarships and bursaries, including academic scholar, art, dance, drama, music and sports awards, are based on merit and need. Foundation Scholarships up to 100% of fees are available according to financial need.

Fees per term (2023–2024). £6,655.

Charitable status. Reading Blue Coat School is a Registered Charity, number 1087839.

Chairman of Governors: Howard Williams

***Headmaster*: Pete Thomas**

Redmaids' High School

Westbury Road, Westbury-on-Trym, Bristol BS9 3AW

Tel: 0117 962 2641
email: admissions@redmaidshigh.co.uk
website: www.redmaidshigh.co.uk
X/Twitter: @RedmaidsHigh
Facebook: @redmaidshighschool
Instagram: @redmaidshigh
LinkedIn: /redmaids'-high-school

See full entry in the **GSA** section, on **p. 469**.

Reigate Grammar School

Reigate Road, Reigate, Surrey RH2 0QS

Tel: 01737 222231
email: info@reigategrammar.org
admissions@reigategrammar.org
website: www.reigategrammar.org
X/Twitter: @ReigateGrammar
Facebook: @ReigateGrammarSchool

Reigate Grammar School (RGS) is a co-educational day school for pupils aged 11 to 18. It is a multi-award winning school proud of its track record in being recognised by many national awarding bodies for: Wellbeing and Pastoral Care (TES); Community Outreach (ISP); UK Social Mobility Awards (SOMO); Community Engagement and Outreach (Education Today); Highly Commended Sixth Form (Muddy Stilettos); Leading Parent Partnership for engagement with parents; and Creativity, to name a few.

RGS is regularly listed in the Times league tables as amongst the highest attaining schools in the country. In 2023, 95% of A Level grades were A*–B and 85% of GCSE grades were 7–9. 95% of students received university offers from Oxford, Cambridge, Russell Group, medical schools and prestigious universities in America or Europe.

The school is situated in the historic market town of Reigate, just outside the M25, yet with easy transport links into London, Surrey and Sussex. There is also a popular coach service spanning a 20-mile radius across 12 routes, including late buses, enabling even more students to benefit from the school's strong tradition of excellence in a wide variety of extracurricular activities, including an enviable reputation in sport, music and drama. Large numbers of pupils participate in the Combined Cadet Force and in The Duke of Edinburgh's Award. The school raises a significant amount of money each year for local and national charities and students give thousands of hours to volunteering locally.

Admissions. Pupils are normally admitted to the School at 11+, 13+ or 16+, although vacancies occasionally occur at other ages.

Fees per term (2023–2024). Years 7–8: £7,510; Years 9–13: £7,665. Sibling discounts are available.

Scholarships and bursaries. The school offers a wide range of scholarships and bursaries.

Junior School. Reigate St Mary's Preparatory and Choir School and Chinthurst School, Tadworth (see entries in IAPS section) are the junior schools of Reigate Grammar School.

Charitable status. Reigate Grammar School is a Registered Charity, number 1081898. Its aim is to provide high quality education for boys and girls.

Governing Body:
Chair: Mr M Elsey

Mr M Adshead	Mr L Herbert
Dr S Banerjee	Mrs M Hulme
Mr M Benton	Miss L Page
Mr C Cobain	Mrs M Stilwell
Mr B Day	Mr N Weber
Mr C Dixon	Mr E Wheeler
Mrs M Edmunds	

Headmaster: **Mr S Fenton**, OBE, BA, MA, MEd Oxon

Deputy Head: Mrs M-A Collins, BEng Bristol
Deputy Head: Miss S Arthur, BA Durham
Deputy Head: Dr B Stones, BSc, PhD Edinburgh
Assistant Head: Mrs C Hosegood, BSc Durham
Assistant Head: Mrs C Lawson, BA Liverpool
Assistant Head: Miss M Pope, MA, MSci, MA Cantab, Sussex
Assistant Head: Miss L Robertson, BA East Anglia, MA Lancaster

Director of Sixth Form: Mrs E Taylor, BA Nottingham, MA UCL
Head of Sixth Form: Mrs M Mitchell, BEd Exeter
Head of Sixth Form: Mr R Verdon, BA Nottingham, MBA Macquarie

Head of Upper School: Mr M Hetherington, BA Nottingham
Head of Fifth Form: Mr N Newman, BA Newcastle
Head of Fourth Form: Mrs C Cline, BSc St Mary's
Head of Third Form: Ms C Case, BA Canterbury

Head of Lower School: Mrs S Leck, MA Cambridge
Head of Second Form: Miss S Carraro, BA Ca Foscari
Head of First Form: Miss H Rose, BSc Chester

Chaplain: Rev P Jackson, BA Cheltenham, BA Bristol
Bursar & Clerk to the Governors: Mr S Douty, FCMA
Head of Foundation and Business Development: Mr S Davey, MA

Heads of House:
Bird: Miss E Paine, BA Chester
Cranston: Mr J Leck, BA East Anglia
Hodgson: Miss G McGregor, BA Newcastle
Williamson: Mr M O'Donnell, BSc Kent

Teaching Staff:
A list of teaching staff is available on the website.
PA to the Headmaster: Mrs B Eustace

Rendcomb College

Rendcomb, Cirencester, Gloucestershire GL7 7HA

Tel: 01285 831213
email: admissions@rendcombcollege.org.uk
website: www.rendcombcollege.org.uk
X/Twitter: @RendcombCollege
Facebook: @Rendcombcollege
Instagram: @rendcombcollege
LinkedIn: /rendcomb-college

Rendcomb College is a co-educational, independent day and boarding school for children aged 3 to 18 in the heart of the Cotswolds, UK. The College was founded in 1920 by Noel Wills and is set within a stunning 230-acre parkland estate which is equidistant from Cheltenham and Cirencester.

Our Mission. Our mission is to develop thoughtful, adventurous and ambitious young people who are lifelong learners. We aim to prepare them with the character and skills to succeed in the ever-changing world after school. Our pupils have the freedom to experience, explore and enquire about the world around them. We aim to encourage independence and tolerance in a safe, caring community and magnificent natural environment.

To achieve this we will:

- Promote a growth mindset, where abilities can be developed through dedication and hard work;
- Provide a co-curriculum that will challenge and support character development, leadership and teamwork;
- Encourage individualism, creativity and contribution to a nurturing and collaborative community;
- Engender physical, spiritual and mental wellbeing through a strong pastoral system;
- Prepare pupils for life beyond school;
- Develop an appreciation for and responsible attitude towards their environment and surroundings.

Admission. Pupils join the Junior School from Nursery or Reception or join the Senior School at age 11, 13 or 16. The entrance examination at 11 is taken at Rendcomb and comprises three papers: English, Mathematics and Verbal Reasoning. At 13, pupils are admitted by Common Entrance or Rendcomb Examination and at 16 by interview, school reports and GCSE results.

Curriculum. Rendcomb College's curriculum extends well beyond the confines of the classroom and the core teaching day. Our small size in both the Junior and Senior schools enables all students to participate in a number of sports, in addition to a wide range of activities which begin after the end of formal lessons each day. Our philosophy is to consider these to be co-curricular, aimed at combining with the academic elements to genuinely develop the whole person and ensure that we provide a fully-rounded education.

University Entrance. In the last three years, leavers have gone on to a number of prestigious universities including Oxford, Cambridge, Swansea, Keele, Cardiff, Royal Holloway and Durham. Popular course choices by Rendcomb College students at these universities include Law, Medicine, Chemistry, Modern Language, and Computer Science.

Houses. Both Day pupils and Boarders share the same Houses, enabling strong friendships and comradery to flourish among all pupils throughout the College.

Pupils can board when they join the Senior School in Year 7 through to Sixth Form. From Year 10 upwards, all Boarders have their own study bedrooms which can be personalised, whilst the younger pupils share dormitories with two or three other students.

Our boarding is very flexible, especially at weekends; from Saturday teatime onwards, Boarders choose to stay at school to work, relax or join in family life at home. There are beds for Day pupils too if they wish to try boarding, or if they need to stay over.

In September 2019, the Year 7–9 house, Godman, opened following an extension and refurbishment. In Years 10 and 11, pupils are split by gender until they reach Sixth Form when they join the co-educational Park House.

Boarders' weekends are full, busy and purposeful through the provision of an extensive programme of activities run by our Boarding Activities Coordinator.

The four Houses at Rendcomb College are located on the school's campus and within easy reach of classrooms and sports facilities. The Houses offer an ideal setting for all pupils to thrive and develop under the guidance of the Houseparents and their pastoral and domestic teams.

Bursaries. A number of bursaries are awarded in keeping with the original charitable aims of the College's Founder. The amount of the bursary award is not influenced by the level of the child's academic ability but by the extent of need and each case is assessed on its own merits with awards being made accordingly.

Scholarships. A number of Scholarships (Academic, Art, Music, Drama and Sport) are awarded each year at Year 7, 9 and 12 with additional Scholarships awarded in Year 3. Scholarships are based on the assessment of a pupil's potential and the value that we believe they will add to the life of our school. We also award the Noel Wills Scholarship and the Rendcomb Scholarship at Year 7.

Rendcomb celebrated its 100th birthday in 2020 and the Governors secured the launch of a number of 100% fully-funded scholarships for entry into Year 4 and Year 12.

Fees per term (2023–2024). Senior School: Boarding £10,140–£14,785, Day £6,850–£9,275. Junior School: Day £2,650–£4,999. We accept the Government's 30 hours scheme in Nursery and Reception for qualifying families.

Charitable status. Rendcomb College is a Registered Charity, number 1115884.

Chairman of Governors: Mr Nicholas Ford

***Head of College*: Mr Rob Jones**, BA, MEd

Head of Juniors: Mr Gavin Roberts, BA, PGCE

Bursar: Mrs R Elliott-Jones, BA

Repton School

Repton, Derbyshire DE65 6FH

Tel: 01283 559222 (Admissions)
01283 559200 (Reception)
email: admissions@repton.org.uk
website: www.repton.org.uk
X/Twitter: @ReptonSchool
Facebook: @ReptonSchool
Instagram: @ReptonSchool
LinkedIn: /school/repton-school

Founded in 1557, Repton School was established on the site of a 12th century Augustinian Priory in the Derbyshire village of the same name. Today Repton is a modern community with a clear sense of purpose and momentum. As a pre-eminent co-educational boarding and day school in the heart of England, Repton provides a balanced, broad-based education, blending heritage with the pursuit of excellence in a 21st century context, offering world-class facilities alongside high quality teaching and pastoral care.

Repton is home to around 620 pupils, making it large enough to achieve excellence in and out of the classroom, yet small enough for individuals to grow and flourish. Each pupil, whether day or boarding, is a member of a House, of which there are ten (six for boys and four for girls). Repton Prep is situated two miles from the Senior campus and is home to enviable, age-appropriate facilities set in the beautiful 55-acre grounds of a Palladian manor house.

Academic standards are high and because most of the teachers, tutors and coaches live in the village, Reptonians never have to prioritise academic achievement over their love of the theatre or rank their aptitude for sport above their passion for music.

Both campuses are situated in picturesque locations whilst offering extensive travel links. Repton and Repton Prep can be easily reached by road from the M1, M6 and M5 via the A50, by rail from East Midlands Parkway and Lichfield, or from nearby Birmingham and East Midlands airports.

Admissions. Pupils from a wide range of prep schools are admitted to Repton at 13+ (Year 9). Pupils can also join the School at 14+ (Year 10) and 16+ (Year 12). Repton invites prospective pupils to take part in GL Assessment's CAT4 Tests that focus on a pupil's potential, skills and abilities. Along with the completion of these assessments, Repton will also request school reports and a reference from your child's current school.

Fees per term (2023–2024). Boarders: £14,560; Day pupils: £10,800. Some additional expenses (for trips, sports kit, pocket money, etc.) will be incurred.

Houses and Pastoral Care. There are ten Houses – six for boys and four for girls, each home to approximately 60 pupils. Day pupils are fully integrated with the boarders, who make up around 70% of the Repton community.

In-House dining is one of the most highly treasured aspects of Repton life, with day and boarding pupils dining with teachers and staff in their own House three times each day. Each of the Houses has its own in-House catering team, including a Head Chef, providing delicious home-cooked food sourced from local producers.

The House is in a true sense every Reptonian's home in the School – the place where pupils eat, sleep, work and live. The Housemaster or Housemistress has overall responsibility for an individual pupil's work and development, lives in the House with their own family and is supported by a resident Matron, resident Tutor and a team of Duty Tutors. The size of the House is carefully calibrated to allow for individualised care. Repton's pastoral care combines the best of traditional care with a systematically proactive approach aiming to pre-empt problems and support each pupil. By interweaving scientific and data-driven measures, the Pastoral team has developed highly tuned pastoral care provision.

Curriculum. The Curriculum at Repton includes both the Academic Curriculum and Co-Curriculum. It gives pupils experience in linguistic, mathematical, scientific, technological, human and social, physical and creative education. It also provides for the spiritual, social and cultural development of pupils.

The Co-Curriculum provides a rich programme of activities appropriate to pupils' educational needs in relation to personal, social, emotional and physical development. It is Repton's aim to run a varied programme of sport and other extracurricular activities and all pupils are expected to participate.

Pupils joining Repton in B Block (Year 9) study Biology, Chemistry, English, Geography, History, Mathematics, Physical Education, Physics, PSHE, Religious Studies, Art, Design Technology, Drama and Music. They also opt to study a combination of modern foreign languages and classical subjects.

In A and O Block (Years 10 and 11) all pupils will study Mathematics, English Language, English Literature and the sciences. Pupils also choose from French, Spanish, German, Art, Business, Design, Drama, Geography, History, Music, Latin, Physical Education and Religious Studies. Pupils can opt to take Music, Art, Textiles and Photography 'off timetable'.

Most Sixth Formers study three subjects at the start of Lower Sixth, though some take four. Pupils can opt from the following subjects: Art, Biology, Business, Chemistry, Design Technology, Drama, Economics, English Literature, French, Geography, German, History, Latin, Mathematics and Further Mathematics, Music, Physical Education, Photography; Physics, Politics, Psychology, Religious Studies, Spanish, Sport (BTEC), Business (CTEC) and Textiles.

Pupils have the opportunity to take the Extended Project Qualification and in the Lower Sixth, pupils follow a programme devised by the School, 'Future Leaders', which covers public-speaking, careers and higher education, personal finances, geopolitics, and prepares Sixth Formers for life beyond Repton.

Across all year groups specialist learning support lessons are also offered, including English as an additional language (EAL).

Beyond Repton. In 2023, 16% of pupils achieved an A* and 68% of pupils A*–B, with 83% of pupils achieving their first-choice university destination and 57% placed at one of the Russell Group establishments. Reptonians go on to study at a wide range of universities, with US universities proving increasingly popular. Of those, three candidates chose to study abroad at US Ivy League University, which included Cornell, Dartmouth and Princeton. They form a growing cohort of Old Reptonians in the US at prestigious universities including Harvard and Stanford.

Facilities at Repton are of a world-class standard and significant investments in recent years give pupils, partner schools and the wider community access to state-of-the-art facilities. This includes the newly refurbished Sports Centre and the Science Priory which offers pupils access to an observatory, outdoor classrooms and a university-style lecture theatre.

Repton is fortunate to possess outstanding all-weather water-based hockey pitches, indoor hockey, an indoor swimming pool, strength and conditioning suites, and a cricket ground that is the envy of many schools and clubs; a Music School with a plethora of practice rooms, concert hall, performance areas and recording studio; the 400 Hall Theatre with a versatile, purpose-built Studio space; and a stunning Art School with two art galleries, dedicated workshops for 3D work, ceramics, and photography.

Creative Arts. Music is at the heart of Repton and all pupils are encouraged to participate in a wide variety of classroom and extra-curricular music activities. The Music Department is housed in an impressive building which features a purpose-built concert hall, a fully equipped recording studio, a computer suite specifically for composition and a variety of academic and instrumental teaching spaces. The department's six full-time members of staff are joined by Heads of Strings, Wind & Brass and Singing and there are 30 specialist Visiting Music Teachers.

The Drama department offers many opportunities for all pupils to perform and work backstage in the vast array of productions that take place during the School year. It is housed in the award-winning 400 Hall Theatre with an auditorium, studio theatre, and a number of dressing room spaces. The theatre facilities were designed specifically as learning spaces for independent practice, thus allowing pupils to be heavily involved in production as well as in performance. Extra-curricular activities include all aspects of theatre production including acting, assistant directing, stage management, sound, lighting design and operation, hair and make-up and costume design.

The LAMDA qualification is offered to pupils to improve their confidence and self-efficacy and lessons are available flexibly to fit around pupils' individual programmes.

In addition to its timetabled curriculum, the philosophy of the Art School encourages 'Art for all' outside formal lessons. The department organises a bi-annual Fashion Show of collections made by the pupils, in addition to numerous exhibitions including works from both national and local art companies. The Artists-in-Residence scheme enables pupils, both on and off the academic timetable, to benefit from the expertise and inspiration of recent graduates and practising artists.

The Design and Technology Centre is home to two workshops, a CNC and 3D printing area, alongside a lecture room and classroom teaching spaces. The department encourages O Block (Year 11) pupils to apply for the Arkwright Scholarship every year; a prestigious national scheme which rewards excellence in design and engineering disciplines and leads to exciting opportunities with local and national industry leaders.

Sport. At Repton, you will find a balanced approach to sporting success. Achieving in sport at the highest levels of performance and participation for all are in no way mutually exclusive. Over 80% of Reptonians represent the School in at least one sport and every Reptonian participates in sport at least three times per week. The School's illustrious sporting heritage is matched by the achievements of their pupils today. It is Repton's aim to discover and develop the sporting and athletic potential within every pupil, as part of a balanced and challenging curriculum encouraging a lifelong love of sport and the benefits it brings.

Repton has amassed an enviable collection of silverware across their focus sports (cricket, football, hockey, netball, swimming and tennis), but above all, it is about what sport brings out in pupils: teamwork, dedication, resilience, leadership and a sense of achievement – both collectively and individually.

The redeveloped Sports Centre includes two floodlit water-based Astroturf hockey pitches, a state-of-the-art, full size indoor hockey facility, a 25m indoor swimming pool with spectator area, two indoor and 12 outdoor floodlit tennis courts, netball and squash courts as well as a specialist strength and conditioning suite.

Combined Cadet Force. All pupils join the CCF in A Block, joining either the Army or RAF section for a year's basic training. Repton also has excellent in-house facilities for the CCF including an indoor 0.22 rifle range, a climbing wall and the Old Trent for rafting. After A Block, continued membership of the CCF is voluntary, either as part of The Duke of Edinburgh's Award or as Community Service.

Scholarships. A range of scholarships and exhibitions are offered annually at 13+ and 16+. A number of awards are available for pupils joining Repton from both the maintained and independent sectors. These include:

C B Fry All Rounder Award is an award worth up to 25% of the Repton boarding fee offered at 13+ to candidates exhibiting outstanding all-round leadership potential. Pupils are required to be nominated by their current Headteacher and will undertake assessments in academia, sport and one of the creative arts.

Music Scholarships and Exhibitions are awarded at 13+ and 16+, with examinations taking place in November (16+) and January (13+).

Drama Scholarships and Exhibitions are also offered at 13+ and 16+, with auditions and interviews taking place in November (16+) and January (13+).

Art Scholarships and Exhibitions are offered at 13+ and 16+. Examinations take place in November (16+) and January (13+). Candidates will be assessed by examination, interview and an assessment of their portfolio.

Design and Technology (DT) Scholarships and Exhibitions are offered at 13+ and 16+. Examinations take place in November (16+) and January (13+). Candidates will be asked to complete a practical session, interview, and to provide a folder of work for assessment.

Sports Scholarships and Exhibitions are offered at 13+ and 16+, to pupils of exceptional talent. Assessments are held in October (13+) and November (16+).

For further information email: admissions@repton.org.uk

Bursaries may be available to those who would not otherwise be able to attend an independent school. These may, in appropriate circumstances, be used to supplement Academic or non-academic awards. Means-tested bursaries are also available to Forces families.

Charitable status: Repton (1093166) is a Registered Charity. The School exists to provide high quality education for boys and girls.

Chairman of Governors: E M Shires, BA, FCA

***Headmaster*: M Semmence**, BA Durham, MA, MBA Warwick
Principal Deputy Head: J G Golding, BA King's College London
Deputy Head (*Academic*): A Currie, MPhys, MEd, DipLCM Durham
Deputy Head (*Pastoral*): T H Naylor, BSc Reading
Deputy Head (*Safeguarding*): S J Lees, BA Leeds
Deputy Head (*Admissions and Marketing*) *& Director of Digital Development*: J D Wilton, MA Lady Margaret Hall Oxford
Deputy Head (*Inclusion and Wellbeing*): A F Parish, BA Durham
Assistant Head (*Academic*): Dr N F Pitts, PhD Leeds
Assistant Head (*Operations*): A J Smith, BSc Loughborough

Heads of Department:
Art: I J Whitfield, MA Royal College of Art
Business: M K Court, BA Durham
Biology: N J Gardner, BSc Birmingham
Chemistry: R G Dexter, BSc Royal Holloway
Classics: C S Dammers, BA Late Exhibitioner of Worcester College Oxford
Design and Technology: L E Politowski, BDes, Dundee
Drama: J P Cooper-Richards, BA Wales
Economics: J N Kyte, BA Keele
English: B Miller, BA St Anne's College Oxford
Ethical & Religious Studies: B Eades, BA Kent
Geography: T Howell, MA, MSc, FRGS, Cambridge
History & Politics: Dr N F Pitts, BA, PhD Leeds
Mathematics: E L Bywater, BSc Reading
Modern Languages: B Page, BA Warwick
Music: O M Walker, BA Late Scholar of Keble College Oxford
Physical Education: R G Clarke, BSc, MA Loughborough and Warwick
Physics: T M Lewis, MEng Cardiff
Psychology: E K Browne, BSc, Birmingham
Science: Dr S M Ingleston-Orme, BSc, PhD Nottingham

Boys' Boarding Houses:
The Cross: M R Wilson
Latham House: M W T Hunt
New House: R G Embery
The Orchard: I M Pollock
The Priory: D A Exley
School House: S D Goudge

Girls' Boarding Houses:
The Abbey: H C Pettit
The Garden: G L Hill
Field House: C R Watson
The Mitre: C J Jenkinson

Admissions Manager: J Bird
Executive Assistant to the Headmaster: D Cameron

RGS Worcester

Upper Tything, Worcester WR1 1HP

Tel: 01905 613391
email: office@rgsw.org.uk
website: www.rgsw.org.uk
X/Twitter: @RGSWorcester
Facebook: @rgsw.org.uk
Instagram: @rgs_worcester

Age Range. 11–18.

Number of Pupils. 939.

Fees per term (2023–2024). £5,598.

School Aims. RGS Worcester Family of Schools provides an excellent all-round education for children aged 2–18 years, developing character, intellect, physical and emotional well-being and cultural understanding within a supportive community.

The Schools aim to cultivate an ethos in which each pupil is cared for individually, valued equally and achieves their potential by:

- Encouraging the growth of intellectual curiosity, creativity and a positive attitude to learning, through a broad, coherent and balanced curriculum, the use of digital technology to enhance teaching and learning, and educational and enrichment opportunities
- Developing in every child quiet self-confidence, aspiration, responsibility, resilience, spiritual values and a personal moral code, consideration for others, tolerance and understanding of other cultures
- Offering a wide range of co-curricular activities which children can develop their social, sporting and cultural interests, explore and enhance their leadership skills and learn the importance of working together
- Promoting opportunities for higher education and career options, and creating an awareness of the world beyond the School and a sense of service to the local and wider community

History. The Royal Grammar School Worcester was founded around 1291, received its Elizabethan Charter in 1561 and was granted its 'Royal' title by Queen Victoria in 1869. The Alice Ottley School was founded in 1883 as Worcester High School for Girls. The two schools merged to form RGS Worcester & The Alice Ottley School in September 2007 and was renamed RGS Worcester in September 2009.

Location and Buildings. The Senior School is situated a few minutes' walk from the centre of the City and is convenient for rail and bus stations.

Educational facilities are outstanding: Sports Halls, specialist Art, IT, Technology and Textiles rooms, a Performing Arts Theatre, Library, Science Block, Music Technology room, and a Lecture Theatre, as well as several assembly halls. The playing fields and boathouse are close by.

There are three co-educational Preparatory Schools: RGS The Grange, set in 50 acres of grounds to the north of the city; RGS Springfield, housed in a beautiful Georgian building in the centre of the nearby Britannia Square, secluded and secure, it benefits from its close proximity to the Senior School; and RGS Dodderhill in Droitwich Spa, Worcestershire. All three have a co-ed nursery from the age of 2. RGS Dodderhill also has a Senior School for girls only from 11–16.

Curriculum. Pupils follow a common curriculum for the first three years in the Senior School which includes the usual academic subjects, plus IT, Design Technology, Music, Drama and PE. The GCSE option arrangements (Years 10 and 11) allow a wide choice, giving a balanced curriculum which does not prejudice subsequent career decisions. Most members of the Sixth Form study at least three subjects to A Level, a BTEC and CTEC are also on offer. The School's Digital Learning Programme is an integral part of the teaching and learning experience.

Careers. A member of Inspiring Futures, the award-winning careers service is readily available and the Head of Careers is responsible for ensuring that all pupils receive basic careers education, and subsequently, access to all the necessary information and experience on which a sound decision may be made regarding future career and Further or Higher Education.

Physical Activities. A wide range of sporting interests and abilities is catered for. Sports include: Rugby Football, Association Football, Cricket, Athletics, Netball, Hockey, Cross-Country Running and Rowing.

Outdoor Pursuits. Combined Cadet Force comprises Royal Navy, Army and Air Force sections. Good opportunities exist for attachments to regular units in the UK and abroad for flying, leadership and adventure training. Those who choose The Duke of Edinburgh's Award scheme may work for their Bronze, Silver and Gold Awards, and undertake adventure training and community service.

Other Activities. There is a wide range of clubs and societies, with school productions taking place each term. School music is also strong: there is a Big Band, several brass ensembles, choirs and smaller vocal ensembles, and a very popular Jazz Band. The School fosters a range of international links including regular exchanges with schools in France, Germany, Spain, China and the USA.

September Admission. This is by examination held in January/February, mainly at 11+ but also at 12+ and 13+. Admission into the Sixth Form is on the basis of a test, interview and GCSE results. Exceptionally, pupils may also be examined and admitted at other points in the year. Admission to the Preparatory Schools is by an assessment from age 6+ and by classroom visit before this age.

Scholarships and Bursaries. Scholarships are offered for academic achievement as well as for music, art, design, textiles, drama and sport of up to 50% remission of fees. Bursaries of up to 100% are also available according to parental means and academic potential.

Charitable status. RGS Worcester is a Registered Charity, number 1120644. The aim of the charity is the education of boys and girls.

Chair of Governors: Mr Quentin Poole
Consultant Director of Finance & Operations and Clerk to the Governors: Mr Ben Edwards

***Headmaster*: Mr John Pitt**

Deputy Heads:
Senior: Mr Lloyd Beecham
Academic: Ms Rebecca Roberts Gawen

Preparatory Schools:
RGS The Grange:
Headmaster: Mr Gareth Hughes

RGS Springfield:
Headmistress: Mrs Laura Brown

RGS Dodderhill:
Headmaster: Mr Thomas Banyard

Robert Gordon's College

Schoolhill, Aberdeen AB10 1FE
Tel: 01224 646346
email: enquiries@rgc.aberdeen.sch.uk
website: www.rgc.aberdeen.sch.uk
X/Twitter: @robertgordons
Facebook: @robertgordonscollege
Instagram: @robertgordonscollege
LinkedIn: /robertgordonscollege

Motto: '*Omni nunc arte magistra*' – Be all you can be

Robert Gordon's College is a remarkable school which places a strong emphasis on community. Renowned for being a large school with a vibrant environment and high academic achievement, it is also recognised for its ethos of being a caring, inclusive and respectful community.

At Robert Gordon's College you can do it all! Explore languages, sport, technology, science, social, practical and creative subjects that will open up new ways of thinking and learning.

It is an exciting time for you as a family, as you begin your journey at Robert Gordon's College – a time where your curiosity allows you to make the most of a wide and varied curriculum. When you love learning you can take on any challenge the world sets you.

Talking about the strong awareness and appreciation of what is best for each individual, Robin Macpherson, Head of College highlights: "At Robert Gordon's College we instill confidence and respect in all our pupils as they discover their potential in the world. We believe that you will achieve academically and enjoy your time here if you are in a caring, supportive environment and that's what we aim to provide.

"We encourage pupils to develop their own sense of identity, discover who they are and what their place in the world is. We want them to be brave and adventurous, with a focus on learning how to learn, so they can adapt and thrive in an ever-changing world."

The Robert Gordon's community is passionate about sparking curiosity and inspiring appetites for growth through engaging learning environments where pupils can explore and be all they can be.

Mrs Sarah Webb, Head of Junior School shares: "Getting the best start for every child is really important to us. Our aim is for children to be happy, safe and in a nurturing environment."

"We provide a stimulating and inspiring learning experience within our purpose built classrooms and flexible learning spaces where children are motivated, value hard work and strive to achieve their best."

Highlighting the strong support for pupils' emotional, education and career development, Mrs Clare Smith, Head of Senior School says: "Our pupils build their knowledge and confidence as they begin to discover more about themselves as learners and explore options for new pathways for the future. Leadership is a key element of these final years at school, where pupils are supported by the wider community of alumni and partners across the world who are extraordinary in their support to assist the next generation of Robert Gordon's College pupils."

"We believe that exposing pupils to others who have experienced life beyond school, perhaps moving to a new city or region of the world, experiencing new industries and perhaps even connecting with alumni for work experience, is a critical part of preparing them for the future."

Learning at Robert Gordon's is a partnership between home and school that helps pupils discover their strengths and what they enjoy.

Bryan Fagan, Junior School parent adds: "Our children enjoy all aspects of school life at Robert Gordon's and are heavily involved in lunchtime and after school clubs such as choir, storytelling, movie club and the active sports at Countesswells, and as a parent, it really is hard not to become part of the Gordon's community."

Talk to our Admissions team and take the next step in making that journey for your child and we'll be with you every step along the way. Contact us at +44 (0)1224 646346, email admissions@rgc.aberdeen.sch.uk or visit www.rgc.aberdeen.sch.uk/beginyourjourney.

Number of Pupils. 1,540.

Admission. The main entry points are Primary 1, Primary 6 and Secondary 1. Entry to Primary 1 (age 4½–5½ years) is by interview held in January/February, and to Primary 6 (age 9½–10½ years) by Entrance Test held in January. Entry to Secondary 1 is by an Entrance Examination held in January. Entry at other stages depends upon vacancies arising, and the offer of a place is subject to satisfactory performance in an Entrance Test and interview.

Fees. Please visit our website for information: www.rgc.aberdeen.sch.uk/beginyourjourney/fees.

Bursaries. Our new Junior Foundationer Awards offer fee assistance to applicants entering Robert Gordon's College Junior School. The Foundationer Awards offer pupils the opportunity to be part of a supportive community, whatever their background or interest, they can find their niche and excel.

Robert Gordon's College offers free places and reduced fee places to pupils every year for entry into Secondary 1. These Bursaries are awarded after jointly assessing financial need and academic merit. Burnett Scholarships offer up to half-fee discounts to pupils of outstanding talent in academic subjects, in music, or in sport and are available to pupils currently in Fourth or Fifth Year at other schools.

Charitable status. Robert Gordon's College is a Scottish Charity, SC000123, regulated by the Scottish Charity Regulator (OSCR).

Chairman of Governors: Kevin Reynard, BCom, CA

***Head of College*: Robin Macpherson**, BA, MSc, FRSA

Head of Junior School: Jane Tulloch, MA Hons
Deputy Head of Junior School: Sally-Ann Johnson, BEd, MEd
Deputy Head of Junior School: Varie MacLeod, BEd
Head of S1: Mrs Stacey Hardie
Deputy Head and Head of S2 & S3: Mr Neil Buchanan
Deputy Head and Head of S4 & S5: Mrs Claire Cowie
Deputy Head, Pastoral: Mr Robin Fish

Head of S6: Mr Stewart Hardie
Director of Finance: Andrew W Lowden, MA, CA
Director of Development, Marketing and Admissions: Laura Presslie, BA
Director of IT Services: David Stone, BSc, MSc

Roedean School

Roedean Way, Brighton, East Sussex BN2 5RQ

Tel: 01273 667500
email: admissions@roedean.co.uk
website: www.roedean.co.uk
X/Twitter: @RoedeanSchool
Facebook: @RoedeanSchool

Roedean is a globally recognized girls' senior school situated on the enchanting south coast of Brighton, UK. Going beyond traditional academics, Roedean is committed to nurturing talents and igniting curiosity. Our uniquely academic environment cultivates a caring and friendly community where girls not only excel academically but also explore their passions and embrace challenges.

Nestled in a breathtaking location with sea views and a charming farm, Roedean offers day and boarding options for girls aged 11 to 18. Conveniently located just 30 minutes from Gatwick and an hour from London, our school provides easy accessibility. At Roedean, girls are encouraged to pursue intellectual challenges, resulting in outstanding examination results—a testament to the resilience, curiosity, and confidence instilled by our approach.

We take pride in our exceptional pastoral care system, ensuring the well-being of every student. Combined with a diverse sports offering and vibrant visual and performing arts programs, Roedean creates an environment where girls thrive academically, emotionally, and socially. Roedean provides a truly holistic education in an inspirational setting.

Founded in Brighton in 1885 by the three Lawrence sisters and incorporated by Royal Charter in 1938, Roedean's original aims still resonate today. The school has grown from 360 to 700 girls in the last decade, fostering a community of over 45 different nationalities, committed to independent learning and the development of self-confidence.

Philosophy. As an academic institution, we aim to inspire curiosity and a love of learning in all our girls. At Roedean, discussion and debate are at the heart of learning, creating thought-provoking and meaningful lessons. Whether in the Sciences or Humanities, collaboration, cooperation, challenge, and discussion with peers are integral to our approach. Our girls eagerly think, learn, explore, and develop intellectually, socially, and emotionally, resulting in exceptional achievements and placements in top institutions in the UK and beyond.

Our holistic vision extends beyond the classroom, emphasizing the value of experiences in Sport, Art, Drama, Music, and Dance. The diverse on-site facilities, including a Chapel, all-weather pitch, indoor swimming pool, professional theatre, and more, contribute to an environment where girls can excel in various fields.

Roedean's curriculum provides a structured grounding in basic skills while offering a broad program covering 30 subjects. The emphasis on traditional subjects is balanced by offerings like Psychology, Russian, and Philosophy. Small class sizes ensure individual attention, and the academic enrichment program, HHH (Heads, Hands, and Hearts), further enriches the learning experience.

Results from our GCSE program reflect outstanding achievement, with 32.1% of grades at the highest Grade 9 and 57.7% at Grades 9–8. The Sixth Form offers over 28 A Level subjects, and our Year 13 cohort achieved remarkable results, with 28.2% of all grades at A* and 55.5% at A*-A.

Co-curricular Activities and Physical Education. Roedean offers a wide range of music, art, design, speech, debating, drama, and dance opportunities, supported by optional private tuition and club activities. The school excels in the performing arts, boasting a top-class Theatre where girls gain experience both on stage and behind the scenes.

Our commitment to co-curricular activities extends to sports, with facilities for netball, hockey, swimming, cricket, and more. Inter-school fixtures and participation in local, county, and national tournaments enhance the overall experience.

Boarding. Roedean's boarding options cater to different preferences, ensuring a homely environment for every girl. The four Houses in the main school and two Houses in the Sixth Form provide varying levels of independence. Boarders can engage in activities on weekends, enjoy communal spaces like the Old Dining Room, and participate in a diverse Weekend Programme.

Health. The School Health Centre, run by a Registered General Nurse, ensures the well-being of students. Regular clinics by a visiting doctor and counselling sessions further support the holistic development of each student.

Religion. Roedean welcomes students of all faiths or none, offering arrangements for religious practices based on individual preferences.

Facilities. Set in 118 acres of grounds, Roedean boasts spectacular facilities, including sports fields, a theatre, dance studios, art studios, science labs, and more. After a £1.5 million refurbishment, the Sixth Form Centre provides an independent and focused space for learning and socializing.

School Year and Leave Out. Roedean operates on a three-term system, with summer holidays lasting eight weeks and Christmas/Easter breaks up to four weeks each. Boarders enjoy flexibility with two weekend exeats each term and the option to go home on weekends.

Admission. Entry at 11+, 12+, 13+, and 16+ is through Roedean Entrance Examination papers in English, Mathematics, and Non-Verbal Reasoning. The school also admits suitably qualified girls each year to the Sixth Form. Scholarships and bursaries are available, covering various fields such as academics, arts, dance, drama, music, performing arts, and sports.

Scholarships and Bursaries. Academic, Art, Dance, Drama, Music, Performing Arts and Sport scholarships are available for girls entering Year 7, Year 9 and the Sixth Form.

Sixth Form Scholarship examinations are held in November; Junior Scholarship examinations are held in January.

Means-tested bursaries are available. Details of scholarships and bursaries may be obtained from the Director of Admissions.

Fees per term (2023–2024). Full Boarders: £13,275–£15,925; Weekly Boarders (5 days): £12,120–£13,515; Flexi-Boarders (3 days): £9,855–£11,915; Day Girls: £6,730–£8,795. For girls entering the Sixth Form from other schools, there is an additional supplement of £1,730 per term (boarding). Parents who wish to pay a single composition fee should apply to the Director, Finance and Administration.

Extra fees are charged for individual tuition in musical instruments, speech training, ballet, and some athletic activities.

For further details, please contact the Director of Admissions.

Charitable status. Roedean School is a Registered Charity, number 307063. It exists to provide quality education for girls.

President:
Ms Mary Henderson [OR]

Vice-President:
Mrs Virginia Stephen [OR]

Chair of Council (*interim*):
Mr Guy Perricone

Vice-Chair of Council (*interim*):
Ms D Patman, FRICS, ACIArb

Council:
Mr John Cain, FCA
Miss Frances Graham, BSc, PG, MCIPD [OR]
Miss Claire Jenkins, MTheol [OR]
Miss Victoria Jenkins, MA, PGCE, MEd [OR]
Ms Samantha J Louis, SA [OR]
Mr Cornelius Medvei
Mr Anthony Millard, BSc, PGCE
Ms Karoline Molberg, BA Hons [OR]
Mrs Teresa Outhwaite, BA PGDip [OR]
Mrs Vivien Smiley, BA, MA DipIPR [OR]
MRs Gaelle Sullivan, PGCE, PGDip (*SEND*), Med

Staff:

***Head*: Mrs Niamh Green**

Senior Deputy: Mrs Jane Sharp
Deputy Head, Pastoral: Miss Rachel Hart
Deputy Head, Academic: Dr John Hobbs
Deputy Head, Co-Curriculum and Partnerships: Dr Ross Barrand
Director of Finance and Administration: Mr Richard Poffley
Assistant Head, Futures: Ms Helen Boobis
Assistant Head, Pastoral: Ms Kate Orrells
Assistant Head, Pastoral: Mr Nathan Wriglesworth
Assistant Head, Teaching and Learning: Mrs Sarah Black
Director of Sixth Form: Miss Carmel Carragher
Director of Studies: Mr Dom Orys
Director of Admissions and Marketing: Mrs Alison Wienekus

Heads of Department:
Art: Ms Sarah Strachan
Business Studies: Mr Stjohn Rowlands
Classics: Miss Charlotte Allen
Dance: Miss Sophie Abaza
Design Technology: Mrs Helen Quirk
Drama: Mrs Susan Woodbridge
Economics: Mr Paul Clingan
English: Mr Darren Woodhouse
Geography: Mr Guy Carter
History: Mrs Sarah Black
Mathematics: Mr Andy Lutwyche
Modern Languages: Mr Julien Sampieri
Music: Mr Benjamin Rous
Philosophy & Religious Studies: Mr Steve Megahey
Physical Education: Miss Kate Wakeling
Psychology: Mr Phil Harrison, BA Middlesex
Natural Sciences: Mrs Lauren Bond

Rougemont School

Llantarnam Hall, Malpas Road, Newport, South Wales NP20 6QB

Tel:	01633 820800
email:	registrar@rougemontschool.co.uk
website:	www.rougemontschool.co.uk
X/Twitter:	@RougemontSchool
Facebook:	@RougemontSchool
Instagram:	@rougemontschool

Rougemont School was founded in a house named 'Rougemont' in Clevedon Road, Newport in 1925. Mr and Mrs Evans bought it in 1931 and, expanding to the house next door, the school gained a reputation for sound teaching in the 3Rs and was directed towards grammar school entrance.

In 1948, Nant Coch House, Risca Road, was purchased for the school. The number of pupils increased to around two hundred and, as the grammar schools started to close, the emphasis moved towards obtaining places in independent senior schools.

When Mr and Mrs Evans retired in 1974, a group of parents raised a loan to buy the school and a board of nine governors was elected. The Stow Hill buildings, formerly housing the Convent of St Joseph, were purchased and provision was extended first to Common Entrance level, then to O levels. Finally, the first A levels were taken in 1983 under the leadership of Mr Frank Edwards.

The strength and reputation of the school was continuing to grow with the Headmasters Mr Richard Ham (1988–1991) and Mr Graham Sims (1991–1995), when Llantarnam Hall, a large Victorian mansion set in 50 acres of parkland on the outskirts of Newport, became available. Mr Ian Burge, who was Chair of Governors at the time, saw an opportunity to establish the long-term future of the school, and together with the other governors, purchased the Hall and moved in the junior section in September 1992.

Mr Ian Brown – formerly Bursar and Development Manager – took the helm in 1995 and by the end of the same year all the pupils had been moved to the present site. Since then, we have seen non-stop development of permanent purpose-built accommodation, and the school now houses around 550 pupils, with competition for places growing all the time.

Following the retirement of Mr Brown, Dr Jonathan Tribbick was appointed Headmaster from September 2002. After 12 years' service and outstanding achievements, Dr Tribbick retired in 2014, succeeded by Mr Robert Carnevale who retired in 2023.

Mrs Lisa Pritchard was appointed as the new overarching Head of Rougemont School in 2023.

Admission to the Preparatory and Senior Schools is by interview and assessments. Entry to the Sixth Form is dependent on GCSE results.

The following paragraphs refer mainly to the Senior School although peripatetic specialists work in both and there is some interchange of teachers.

Curriculum. Pupils follow a wide syllabus to age 14. For the two years to GCSE pupils normally study ten subjects of which English Language and Literature, Mathematics and Numeracy, a language, science and a humanities subject are normally compulsory. 18 subjects are available.

Sixth Form. 22 AS/A2 Levels are available. Sixth Form pupils have their own common room and study area. Sixth Form pupils can also take part in a range of extracurricular activities and games.

Religion. Rougemont School is non-denominational.

Careers. The School belongs to the Independent Schools Careers Organisation. The Senior teachers advise on all aspects of further education and careers.

Music. In addition to specialist teachers of music, a large number of peripatetic teachers cover the range of orchestral instruments. There are choirs and instrumental ensembles for all ages.

Drama. In addition to the Infant Department's Spring Festival and the Senior School Eisteddfod, two large-scale productions and two musical events take place each year.

Elocution and dance. Visiting staff hold weekly classes for LADA courses, ballet and modern dance.

Sport. The School has developed a high standard of performance in most major sports. There is a wide fixtures programme for both boys and girls, as well as the opportunity to participate in numerous coaching courses.

Clubs. A wide variety of extracurricular activities and clubs are available at lunch time and after school, as is supervised prep.

The Duke of Edinburgh's Award. This is a very successful activity within the school and over 60 pupils have gained the Gold Award in the last twenty years.

Fees per term (2023–2024). From Nursery to Sixth Form, fees range from £2,990–£5,322.

Scholarships. Academic, Sport and Performing Arts Scholarships are available for entry into Year 7, between 5%–20%. A limited number of means-tested bursaries are offered from Year 7 upwards. The School offers Academic, Sporting and Creative Arts Scholarships to the value of 5–20% for Sixth Form entry.

Further information. A prospectus and other details are available from the Registrar (Tel: 01633 820800, email: registrar@rougemontschool.co.uk).

Charitable status. Rougemont School is a Registered Charity, number 532341. It exists to provide education for boys and girls.

Governors:
Chair: Mr P Harris
Vice-Chair: Mr M Cordner
Mrs F Bennett
Mr H Clark
Mr R Green
Mr I Hoppe
Dr A Kotecha
Mr D Lunt
Mr D McClelland
Mrs C McNamara
Mrs W Williams

***Head of Rougemont*: Mrs L Pritchard**, BA, PGCE

Director of Infants: Miss L Hallas, BA, PGCE
Director of Juniors: Mr A Bevan, BA, PGCE
Director of Seniors: Mrs S Archer, BSc, PGCE (*Biology*)
Director of Sixth Form: Mr H Singer, MA Ed, BA, PGCE
Director of Inclusion and Assessment: Mr A Griffiths, BEng, PGCE (*ALNco*)
Director of Operations: Mr P Rich
Director of Business and Finance: Mr A Knight

Senior School:
Mrs L Bateman, BA, PGCE (*Head of Art*)
Mr K Bell, BA, PGCE (*Head of Boys' Sport*)
Mrs S Boon, BA, PGCE (*Art, DT*)
Mr M Bowman, BSc, PGCE (*Mathematics*)
Mrs K Bridges, BSc, PGCE (*Science, Maths, IT*)
Ms C Bromley, BSc, PGCE (*Mathematics*)
Dr S Brown, BA, BSc, PhD, PGCE (*Senior Laboratory Technician*)
Mrs J Caddick, BA, PGCE (*English, UCAS & HE Coordinator*)
Mrs E Carnevale, BSc, PGCE (*Geography*)
Mr B Cheung, BA, PGCE, QTS (*Physics*)
Ms A Clason-Thomas, BA, MA, PGCE (*Assistant Head of KS3, Pupil Coordinator KS3, French, English*)
Mr R Cording, BSc, QTS (*Design and Technology*)
Mr P Daley, BA, PGCE (*Latin*)
Ms M Davies, BA, PGCE, QTS (*Music*)
Mrs L DeCruz, BA, PGCE (*Head of Religious Studies, Curriculum Coordinator*)
Mr C Dobbins, BMus, DepMus, LRSM, PGCE (*Director of Music*)
Miss C Dugdale, BA, PGCE (*PE, Religious Studies*)
Mrs K Elms, BA, PGCE (*English, Film Studies, House Tutor Coordinator*)
Mrs R Garrod, BA, PGCE (*History, KS3 History Coordinator*)
Mr M Grimes, MSc, BSc, PGCE (*Head of Physics*)
Mr J Hardwick, BSc, PGCE (*Biology, Science, Careers*)
Mr J Hawkins, BSc (*Physical Education*)
Miss R Hayes, BA, PGCE (*Head of Design & Technology, DofE*)
Mrs E Hughes, BA, PGCE (*English*)
Mrs K Hughes, BSc, PGCE (*Head of Geography, Clubs Coordinator*)
Ms L Jones, BA, PGCE (*Physical Education*)

Mrs A Jenkins, BSc (*Assistant Head of KS5, Chemistry, Physics*)
Mr M Jenkins, MA Cantab, PGCE (*Head of History, Geography, House Tutor*)
Mrs C Langford, BSc, PGCE (*Head of Chemistry, Curriculum Administrator*)
Mr S Mansfield, BSc, PGCE, (*Head of Biology*)
Ms K Marshall, BSc, PGCE, (*Director of Sport*)
Mr P McMahon, MSc, BSc, QTS (*Head of Computing and IT, Google Administrator, ECDL Coordinator*)
Miss A Mintowt-Czyz, BA, PGCE (*Head of English*)
Mrs D Morgan, BA, PGCE (*French*)
Mrs S Munro, DEUG, Licence, PGCE (*Head of French, Year 7 Pupil Progress Coordinator*)
Mrs L Nepean, BA, PGCE (*Head of Drama, House Tutor, Performance Coordinator*)
Miss C Owen, BA, PGCE (*Assistant Head of KS4, Head of Business Studies*)
Mr W Price, BA, PGCE (*Head of KS4, Head of Spanish*)
Mr A Richards, BSc, PGCE (*Head of Mathematics*)
Mr M Savery, BA, PGCE (*Head of Economics, Spanish, EPQ Co-ordinator*)
Mr J Steadman, BSc, PGCE (*Physical Education*)
Mrs T van der Linde, MA Ed, BSc, PGCE (*Mental Health and Wellbeing Lead, Chemistry*)
Ms M Williams, BA, PGCE, QTS (*Computing and IT*)

Juniors:
Mr A Bevan, BA, PGCE (*Director of Juniors*)
Mrs A Burridge, BSc, PGCE (*Junior Class Teacher, DofE*)
Mr C Dobbins, BMus, DipMus, LRSM, PGCE (*Director of Music, Games*)
Mrs S Evans (*Junior Class Teacher, Music*)
Mrs A Exley (*Art*)
Mrs K Galloway, KS2 (*Teaching and Learning Assistant*)
Mrs R Hale, BA, PGCE (*Junior Class Teacher, Able and Talented Coordinator*)
Mrs K Jones (*HLTA*)
Mrs L Kelley, BA, QTS (*Junior Class Teacher, Coordinator of Science*)
Mrs R Manley, BA, QTS (*Junior Class Teacher*)
Mrs R Morgan, BA, PGCE (*Learning Development Centre*)
Mrs R Payne, NNEB (*Teaching and Learning Assistant*)
Mr A Pritchard, BSc, PGCE (*Mathematics, PE*)
Mr S Rowlands, BA, QTS (*Junior Class Teacher, House Tutor*)
Mrs L Singer, MA Ed, BSc, PGCE (*Junior Class Teacher, PE Prep School Coordinator*)
Mrs K Williams, BEd (*Junior Class Teacher*)

Infants:
Mrs H Ashill, NNEB (*Teaching and Learning Assistant*)
Ms C Burdett, BA, PGCE, QTS (*Infant Class Teacher, Leader of Digital Learning and Innovation*)
Mrs B Cobner-Matthews, LLB (*HTLA*)
Mrs C Devine, BA, QTS (*Infant Class Teacher*)
Mr C Dobbins, BMus, DipMus, LRSM, PGCE (*Director of Music*)
Mrs A Exley (*Art*)
Mrs L Kelley, BA, QTS (*Infant Class Teacher, Coordinator of Science*)
Mr G Morgan BSc, PGCE (*Infant Class Teacher*)
Mrs T Mountford, BEd (*Primary Sport*)
Mrs N Noor, BA, PGCE (*Infant Class Teacher*)

Nursery:
Mrs E Beale (*Teaching and Learning Assistant*)
Mrs J Forouzan, NNEB (*Nursery Teacher*)
Mrs E Mian, NNEB (*Teaching and Learning Assistant*)
Miss L Wiseman (*Teaching and Learning Assistant*)

Registrar: Mrs N Bates

Royal Grammar School
Guildford

High Street, Guildford, Surrey GU1 3BB
Tel: 01483 880608 (Headmaster)
01483 880600 (School Office)
email: rgs-office@rgsg.co.uk
website: www.rgsg.co.uk
X/Twitter: @RGSGuildford
Facebook: @RGSGuildford
Instagram: @rgs_guildford

Located in the centre of the historic town of Guildford, the RGS is an independent day school for around 970 boys aged 11 to 18, some 280 of whom are in the Sixth Form. As a flagship for boys' education, the School has a national reputation for academic excellence but also prides itself on its traditional values of decency and respect, supported by outstanding pastoral care. RGS boys have the opportunity to experience the widest range of enriching activities providing them with a broad and balanced education. Academic excellence is at the very heart of the School's philosophy. The RGS aims to encourage the growth of intellectual curiosity and creativity and to inculcate a life-long love of learning in the boys. The RGS is consistently one of the top five boys' schools in the country at both A Level and GCSE and is extremely proud of its Oxbridge record; in the last decade 293 places have been secured.

Buildings and Facilities. The Tudor buildings in Guildford's High Street have been at the very heart of the RGS for over five centuries. The School was founded by Robert Beckingham in 1509 and established by King Edward VI's Charter of 1552, which decreed that there should be "…one Grammar School in Guildford …for the Education, Institution and Instruction of Boys and Youths in Grammar at all future times for ever to endure". Among the first in the country to be purpose-built, the original buildings contain a remarkable Chained Library, which is now the Headmaster's Study. The School enjoys facilities appropriate to education in the 21st century, including a state-of-the-art Music School, Art School, purpose-built Sixth Form Centre, Sports Hall and the John Brown Building which houses the innovative Design and Technology centre. The Sports Ground at Bradstone Brook provides twenty acres of pitches, tennis courts and a pavilion overlooking the pitches. The School also benefits from the use of nationally renowned sports facilities in the immediate proximity, including Surrey Sports Park.

Curriculum. The school day is from 8.45am to 4.00pm; there are no lessons on Saturdays. Many co-curricular activities and clubs take place after school, however. In the first two years (Years 7 and 8 nationally), all boys follow a common curriculum embodying the programmes of study for Key Stage 3 of the National Curriculum. The subjects studied are English, French or Spanish, Geography, History, Latin, Maths, Information Technology, RE, PE, Art, Music, Drama, Design and Technology, and Science. In the Second Form, the boys study the separate sciences.

In the Third Form (Year 9) the boys continue to follow a core curriculum of study for Key Stage 3, but also begin to specialise by choosing to study from a pool of options, providing the opportunity to explore subjects in more depth. These optional subjects include additional languages – German and Ancient Greek. In addition, all boys study Computational Thinking.

GCSEs and IGCSEs are offered with boys taking ten subjects out of the 23 available. At GCSE additional subjects include PE and Computer Science, as well as a range of ancient and modern languages. The opportunity exists to study Arabic, Mandarin, Japanese and Russian off timetable.

All Sixth Form boys take four subjects in the Lower Sixth Form and then three or four at A Level. A broad range of subjects are offered, all of which are well-regarded by the leading universities. The Sixth Form curriculum also includes a rigorous, in-house research project and a General Studies programme organised in conjunction with Guildford High School.

Religion. The ethos of the RGS is firmly based on traditional Christian principles and the School has strong links with Holy Trinity Church in the centre of the town and Guildford Cathedral; however, as a non-denominational school, boys from all faiths are welcomed. A diverse, stimulating assembly programme provides the opportunity for collective worship and broadens the boys' horizons while establishing a tolerant set of values. Religious Education lessons, which are an integral part of the School's curriculum, further contribute to developing each individual's moral compass.

Pastoral Care. Respect, tolerance and understanding of others characterise daily life at the RGS and the very strong rapport between boys and teachers makes for a vibrant environment. The boys establish lasting relationships within the year group; in addition, the house system, mentoring, and role of all senior boys as prefects ensure friendships are forged throughout the School. The outstanding pastoral care on offer from dedicated form tutors, heads of year and personal tutors, all overseen by the Senior Deputy Head, enables the boys to thrive in a mutually supportive environment where every boy can flourish as an individual.

Co-curricular Activities. The exceptional range of co-curricular activities offered is one of the greatest strengths of the School; there are currently over seventy societies at the RGS. These range from air rifle, chess, Christian Union, drama, Model United Nations, music, philosophy, squash to Young Enterprise. Boys have the opportunity to take Bronze, Silver and Gold Duke of Edinburgh's Award through the Combined Cadet Force or Outdoor Pursuits. Over 30% of students learn a musical instrument and they can join a variety of instrumental groups including Big Band, School Orchestra, Choir and a strong Choral Society. There are many opportunities for boys throughout the School to get involved in drama productions, both for the School and their house.

Games. The School's principal games are rugby, hockey and cricket, although as boys move up the School their sporting options widen considerably. Sports available include athletics, badminton, basketball, cross-country running, fencing, football, golf, sailing, shooting, swimming and tennis. Professional coaching and outstanding facilities develop the skill levels of boys of all abilities; the School takes pride in providing competitive sport and opportunities for all while also nurturing the very best of sporting talent. The School currently has a significant number of boys who are competing for county, national and international honours.

Admission. Boys may be considered for entry to the RGS at any age between 11 and 18. The usual ages of entry, however, are at 11+, 13+ and 16 into the Sixth Form. All applicants wanting a place at 11+ or 13+ take the entrance examinations in the November of Year 6; those for holding a deferred place for 13+ entry will also take the Common Entrance examination or Scholarship papers in Year 8. New boys are admitted in September of each year. The Headmaster is pleased to meet parents in small groups, arrange for them to see the School, and discuss the possibility of their son's entry to the School. Small group appointments are made through the Head of Admissions (Registrar and Marketing), who can supply a hard copy of the School's prospectus; it is also available on the RGS website.

Fees per term (2023–2024). £7,524 (plus £329 for lunches, which are compulsory for First and Second Forms), inclusive of all tuition, stationery and loan of necessary books.

Scholarships. Scholarships of up to 10% fee remission are awarded in recognition of outstanding academic merit. For boys entering the First Form at 11 there is a competitive examination in English and Mathematics, held in January. For boys entering the Third Form at 13, the Common Academic Scholarship Examinations (CASE) are taken in May. The top scholar of a year group is designated the King's Scholar.

Music scholarships of up to 10% fee remission are available at 11 and 13. It is hoped that a King's Scholarship can be awarded each year to a boy of outstanding musical potential.

One Art Scholarship and one Sports Scholarship of 5% fee remission at 13+ is available annually.

Full details of Scholarships and Fee Assistance (Bursaries) are available from the Head of Admissions (Registrar and Marketing).

Charitable status. Royal Grammar School Guildford is a Company Limited by Guarantee. Registered in England, Company Number: 10874615. Registered Office: High Street, Guildford, Surrey, GU1 3BB. Registered Charity Number 1177353

Governing Body:
Chairman: Mrs S K Creedy, MA Cantab
Vice-Chairman: Mrs H Styche-Patel, BSc, MBA
Mrs K T Atkinson, BDS
Mrs F E Carter, BA

The Earl of Onslow, High Steward of Guildford
Mr J D Fairley, BA
Mr S G S Gimson, MSc Def Tech
Professor M Humphreys, MBE, PhD, LLB, PFHEA
Mr T E Lingard, BSc, MInstP [OG]
Dr L S K Linton, MA, MB ChB, MRCP
Mrs M-L Logue, MA Cantab
Mr S J Meredith, BA, FCA, ChA
Mr M More-Molyneux, HM Lord-Lieutenant of Surrey
Mrs N Nelson-Smith, BA
Professor S Price, MSc, PhD, FBTS, ERT, FHEA
Ms K Spasić, ACMA, CGMA
Professor H E Treharne, BSc, MSc, PhD, SFHEA, FBCS
Mr N E J Vineall, KC, MA Cantab and Pittsburgh [OG]
Mr M J Windsor, BA, MA

[OG] *Old Guildfordian*

Chief Operating Officer: Mr R A Ukiah, MA
Bursar and Clerk to the Governors: Mrs C M Perceval, BA

***Headmaster*: Dr J M Cox**, BSc, PhD (*Biology*)
Senior Deputy Head: Mr A U Woodman, BSc, MA (*Biology*)
Deputy Head: Mrs J S R Thorpe, BSc (*Biology*)
Senior Master: Mr J W Pressley, MA (*Classics*)

Assistant Head (*Pastoral DSL*): Mr N W Gough, BSc, MSc (*Economics*)
Assistant Head (*Teaching and Learning*): Miss N S Goul-Wheeker, MA (*Classics*)
Assistant Head (*Partnerships*): Mr T W Shimell, MChem (*Chemistry*)
Assistant Head (*Operations*) : Mr N E Wild, BA (*Religion and Philosophy*)
Assistant Head (*Curriculum*): Mr D S J Wright, BA (*Economics*)
Assistant Head (*Co-curricular*): Mr S J H Yetman, BSc

* *Head of Department*

Art:
*Mrs R F Shepherd, BA
Mrs F Khan-Evans, BA, MA
Mr K A Trim, BA
Mrs A A Wood, BSc, MPhil

Biology:
*Mr S Burns, MBiochem
Mrs A Battersby, MA
Mr M Chamberlain, BSc, MSc
Miss E L Cuthbertson, BA
Mr I P Rossiter, BSc

Chemistry:
*Mr W-S Lau, MChem, MRSC
Dr J S Braithwaite, BSc, PhD
Miss N G Dann, MChem
Dr S Khan, BSc, MSc, PhD, MRSC
Dr C C McGeady, BSc, MRes, PhD
Dr L A Whall, BA, PhD
Mr M C Williams, BSc [OG]

Classics:
*Mr E K D Bush, MA
Mr B J Callaghan, BA
Dr G I Fanti-Byrne, MA, MA, PhD
Mr P G Nathan, BA, LIB
Mr P L Palmer, BA

Design & Technology:
*Mr J B Kelly, BA, MA, MA RCA
Mr M Bailey, BSc [OG]
Mr A J Colebrook, BSc
Mr K A Trim, BA

Drama:
*Ms N C McClean, BA, MA
Miss S J Cox, BA
Ms A L Tamblyn, BA

Economics:
*Mr J D Stratford, BSc
Mrs G S Bownes, BA
Mr D T Chapman, BSc
Mr R E Presley, MA

English:
*Ms T T Wijesinghe, MA
Mr D Amis, BA
Mrs H M Curtis, BA
Dr E A McEwan, BA, MA, PhD
Mrs C E Moon, BA, MA
Mr J G Muchmore, BA
Mr N M Patel, BA, MSt

Geography:
*Mrs R G Waters, MA
Mr W D Cowx, BSc, MSc
Mr T E Fishpool, BA
Mrs G M Richards, BA
Mrs H E Tarasewicz, MA
Mrs A L Woodman, BSc, MSc
Mr J C Witts, BSc

History:
*Mr J M Davies, MA
Mr A C Dodd, BA, MA [OG]
Mr F C B Evans, BA
Mr D N Holliday, BA
Mr T J J Owens, BA (*Politics*)
Mr W H N Spouge, BA, MA

Mathematics:
*Mr S G Black, MMath
Mrs I E Busby, BA
Mr J A Casale, BSc, MBA
Mr R D Crew, BTech
Mr P J Dunscombe, BSc
Mr C George, BSc
Mr A R Gyford, MSc
Mr A W J Hadley, MMath
Mr M Hanak-Hammerl, MSc
Dr D J Jackson, MSc, PhD
Mr M R Jenkins, BSc
Mr P M Johnson, BEd
Mr A B Kirkland, BSc
Dr L A Kurian, BSc, MSc, PhD
Mr S H Ling-Winston, BSc, MSc, MPhil COS
Mr N C Pinhey, BSc
Dr J P Varney, MSc, PhD
Mr C H Wakeling, BSc
Mrs D B Webster, BA

Modern Languages:
*Mr W Dugdale, BA, MA
Mr S J Baker, BA
Dr M M Creagh, BA, MSc, PhD
Mrs E J Kenyon, MA
Mr R J A Lemaire, BA
Mr A R Lowe, BA
Mr J Marchiafava, Lic
Mrs R J Rathmell, BA
Miss G E Spencer, BA
Mrs N Wilson, BA

Music:
*Mr S J Orchard, BMus, MMus (*Director of Music*)
Miss L A Eaton, BMus, MMus
Mr D H Chambers, BMus, PCASS
Ms I Garvie, BMus, MMus, PGDip
Miss J E Newman, AGSM, CRD
Miss L J A Wild, Lic, MMus
Mr P H White, MA

Physical Education:
* Mr G D G Cover, BSc (*Director of Sport*)
Mr M F Baggs, BA
Mr D J Bartram, BSc (*Hockey*)
Mr R C Black, BSc (*Cricket*)
Mr B Dudley, BSc (*Rugby*)
Mr S D Gaynor, BSc
Mr J D N Lythgoe, BSc
Mr B J D Rogers, BSc
Mr I Wilkes, BEd

Physics:
*Mr J P Hood, MA, MSci
Mr M A Burbidge, BSc, BA
Mr J J H Holland, BEng
Mr L M Holland, BSc
Mrs N L Odhams, MA, MEng
Mr M R F Royds, BSc
Dr R Sisca, NSc, MSc, PhD

Religion and Philosophy:
*Mr R B Meadowcroft, BA, MA
Mr T F Foster, BA [OG]
Mr K J Galpin, BA [OG]
Mr K Tayar, BA [OG]

Head of Admissions (*Registrar and Marketing*): Mrs K L Sweet, BA, MCIPD

Royal Grammar School
Newcastle upon Tyne

Eskdale Terrace, Newcastle upon Tyne NE2 4DX

Tel: 0191 281 5711
email: communications@rgs.newcastle.sch.uk
website: www.rgs.newcastle.sch.uk
X/Twitter: @RGSNewcastle
Facebook: @newcastleroyalgrammarschool
Instagram: @rgs_newcastle
LinkedIn: /school/royal-grammar-school-newcastle

Thomas Horsley, the original settlor of the Royal Grammar School Newcastle (RGS), pledged his legacy to the School in 1525. Almost 500 years later, RGS continues to flourish as the premier independent school in the North-East of England and as one of the country's leading schools. As The Sunday Times' North East Independent School of the Decade, we regularly lead all northern schools in national league tables and pride ourselves on academic excellence, a high level of pastoral support, involvement in a wide range of sports and other co-curricular activities, and our commitment to bursaries and partnerships.

The RGS has grown substantially and has now been fully co-educational for over 20 years. There are now some 1,320 students, nearly 270 of whom are in the Junior School. The Sixth Form of over 320 students is one of the largest in the independent sector.

The school is based in the heart of the City, immediately opposite Jesmond Metro station. The school occupies over 30 acres of land and has state-of-the-art facilities, including five brand-new art studios, a new library, a new Sixth Form Centre, a 25 m swimming pool, two Sports Halls, a Performing Arts Centre, outdoor football/rugby pitches at Mooracres, an artificial turf pitch for hockey and the former County Cricket Ground.

Curriculum. The aim of the curriculum up to Year 11 is to offer a general education, culminating in GCSE in a wide range of subjects. All students study English (Language and Literature), a Modern Language (French, German or Spanish), Mathematics, Biology, Physics and Chemistry to this level and three further examination subjects are taken at GCSE level from Ancient History, Art, Computing, Economics, Geography, German, Greek, History, Latin, Music, Spanish, Engineering Design & Technology and Drama. Additionally, there is a programme of Art, Drama, Music and Technology for all in Years 7 to 9.

Sixth Formers will normally choose three A Level subjects. In addition, students will be required to select either a fourth A Level or a combination of two complementary courses from EPQ or non-examined subject. The range of A Level subjects currently: Ancient History, Art, Biology, Chemistry, Computing, Engineering Design Technology, Economics, English, Film Studies, French, Geography, German, Greek, History, Latin, Mathematics, Further Mathematics, Music, Philosophy, Physics, Physical Education, Politics, Psychology, Spanish and Theatre Studies. There is also a compulsory series of lectures and talks/workshops designed to provide cultural and personal broadening and development.

Almost all Sixth Formers go on to University, and success in gaining entry at Oxford and Cambridge, and medical schools, has been an outstanding feature of the school's record.

Physical Education. All students are required to take part in a Physical Education programme which, up to Year 10, includes Rugby, Football, Cross Country, Cricket, Athletics, Gymnastics, Hockey, Netball, Tennis, Swimming. At the upper end of the School a wider range of activities is offered: in addition to the above students may opt for Badminton, Basketball, Climbing, Fencing, Fitness training, Karate, Orienteering, Squash, Tennis, Table Tennis, Volleyball and Dance. A wide range of activities is available to all through voluntary membership of various Sports Clubs.

Activities. Art, Drama and Music are strong features in the life of the School, all of them overflowing from scheduled lessons into spare-time activity. There is a large number of wide-ranging music groups and ensembles from choirs and orchestras to bands, jazz ensembles and rock groups. There are several productions in the theatre each term. Numerous societies meet in the lunch-break, before or after school, some linked with school work but many developing from private enthusiasms. There is a thriving Duke of Edinburgh's Award scheme. There is an entirely voluntary Combined Cadet Force Contingent. Annual overseas visits include ski-parties, sporting tours, Classics trips, visits to art galleries and to the battlefields of World War I.

Supervision and pastoral care. Each student is within the care of (a) Form Supervisor and (b) Tutor. The latter will normally be associated with the student throughout their school career, and the aim is to forge a personal link with students and their families.

The Careers programme begins in Year 9; in Year 11 and the Sixth Form every possible care is taken to advise each student individually about Careers and Higher Education.

The School's Medical Officers are available regularly for consultation; there are also male and female School Counsellors.

Buildings. Some of the School's buildings date from 1907 and are described by Pevsner as 'friendly neo-Early-Georgian'. Recent years have seen many developments and improvements, including the opening in February 1996 of a new Sports Centre, a new Science and Technology Centre which opened in 1997, and new Maths and ICT departments in 1998. A new Junior School extension opened in 2005 and a Performing Arts Centre opened in 2006. A new 6-lane, 25 m swimming pool was completed in August 2015 as part of an additional sports complex, which includes a second sports hall, a dance and fitness suite and new indoor and outdoor changing facilities.

A new building on the main site was completed in September 2019 and houses a new library, a suite of rooms for Art, Maths, Science, Engineering Design Technology, and a home for the new Digital Technology and Computing Department. Similarly, a new Pastoral Centre will link this new building with the rest of the School.

In January 2020, we opened our new Sixth Form Centre, which saw the combination of the old Sixth Form Common Room and old Library into a much larger, and modern area. The open-plan style centre comprises individual study pods, a Sixth Form only bank of computers, a space for collaborative working, printing facilities and a new coffee bar.

Junior School. Years 3 and 4 of the Junior School are separately housed in Lambton Road opposite the Senior School playing fields. Years 5 and 6 are housed in a purpose-built extension on the main school site. Junior School students use the Sports Centre, Swimming Pool, games fields and dining hall. English and Mathematics are taught by Form Teachers, while History, Geography, French, Science, Religious Education, Music, Art and Physical Activities are taken by specialists.

Entrance. Entry is by examination. Application is via an online form: www.rgs.newcastle.sch.uk/prospective-families/admissions.

Junior School at 7+ and 9+. Prospective students attend Assessment Days held in November (9+) and January (7+) when they take part in a number of activities and sit a number of short tests. A reference is sought from previous/current school.

Senior School at 11+. The Senior School examination is held each January for prospective students who will be 11 on 1 September of the year in which entry is desired. Applications by December (later application at School's discretion). A reference is sought from previous/current school.

Sixth Form at 16+. Applicants are considered for direct entry to the Sixth Form if their GCSE results are likely to form an adequate basis. A reference is sought from the previous/current school, prior to interview.

Each year a small number of places may be available at entry points other than the main ones listed. Please contact the Head of Admissions for details.

Term of entry. Autumn, although a small number of places may become available throughout the year.

Fees per term (2023–2024). Senior School: £5,507, Junior School: £4,639.

Bursaries. Some bursaries, awarded on the basis of parental income, are offered. Details are available from the Head of Admissions.

Charitable status. The Newcastle upon Tyne Royal Grammar School is a Registered Charity, number 1114424.

Governing Body:
Mr A Fletcher (*Chair*)
Mrs S Green (*Vice-Chair*)
Mrs J Berry
Mr R H Fell
Mr J Fitzpatrick
Professor M Haniffa
Mr N McMinn
Ms S Milligan
Mr M Robinson
Mr R Sanghera
Councillor T Thorne
Mrs S Woodroofe

***Headmaster*: Mr G Stanford**, MA Oxon, MBA, FRGS

Deputy Head: Mr T E Keenan, BSc Bradford, MSc Northumbria, PGCE
Deputy Head (*Academic*): Mr C Quayle, BA Durham, PGCE, MEd
Deputy Head (*Pastoral*): Miss S J Longville, BA Newcastle, PGCE
Deputy Head (*Co-Curriculum*): Mr A McBride, BA Hons Durham, MEd Northumbria, PGCE Northumbria
Head of Junior School: Mr J N Miller, BA Northumbria
Head of Sixth Form: Mrs N McGough, MSc Imperial College, PGCE, MRes

Director of Finance & Operations: Mrs R Amey, MEng Nottingham, ACMA
Director of Development and Communications: Mrs S Beck, MSc London Southbank, MCIOFCert
Director of Partnerships: Mr J A Smith, BSc Edinburgh, MEd Newcastle, PGCE

Royal High School Bath GDST

Lansdown Road, Bath BA1 5SZ

Tel: 01225 313877
email: royalhigh@rhsb.gdst.net
website: www.royalhighbath.gdst.net
X/Twitter: @RoyalHighBath
Facebook: @TheRoyalHighSchoolBath
Instagram: @royalhighschoolbath
LinkedIn: /company/royal-high-school-bath

See full entry in the **GSA** section, on **p. 471**.

Royal Hospital School

Holbrook, Ipswich, Suffolk IP9 2RX

Tel: 01473 326200
email: admissions@royalhospitalschool.org
reception@royalhospitalschool.org
website: www.royalhospitalschool.org
X/Twitter: @RHSSuffolk
Facebook: @RoyalHospitalSchool
Instagram: @royalhospitalschool
LinkedIn: /Royal-Hospital-School

The Royal Hospital School was founded in 1712 in Greenwich, London, to 'improve navigation' through education and, as it prepared boys for a life at sea, many went on to become explorers and pioneers of their time. The school is immensely proud of these historic links and discovery, exploration and challenge continue to shape its ethos. The traditional values of loyalty, commitment, courage, respect, service and integrity have underpinned the school's core aims and philosophy from the very beginning. Three hundred years later, they are still as relevant to the education it provides as they were then. Today the school is set in 200 acres of Suffolk countryside overlooking the Stour Estuary and it is a co-educational HMC boarding and day school for approximately 700 pupils providing a full and broad education, fit for the modern world. It aims to inspire its pupils to have the courage and commitment to be ambitious for their futures, whichever path they choose, challenging pupils of all academic abilities, steering them to look beyond the moment, and beyond the confines of the classroom, and to approach life with an open and receptive mind.

House System. 57% of pupils board and there is a strong diamond-shaped House System. An ongoing programme of refurbishment and development provides superb facilities and accommodation for both boarders and day pupils.

Pupils joining the school at 11+ are accommodated in the Junior House purpose-built with 4/6-bedded rooms and facilities, routines and pastoral care that assist the transition between junior and senior school. Weekly boarding and the opportunity to stay overnight on an ad hoc basis are available.

Pupils then join one of eight Senior Houses. Three are co-educational day houses and five are boarding houses (3 for boys and 2 for girls), home to approximately 60 boarders. Boarders in the lower years share rooms with up to four other pupils whilst older pupils have double or single studies with en-suite facilities.

In the Upper Sixth both boarding and day boys and girls join Nelson House, where they learn to live more independently in preparation for university.

Curriculum and Academic Development. The school's curriculum shadows the National Curriculum Key Stages 3 and 4. On joining the school, pupils are placed in forms based on assessed ability from entrance testing or at 13+ the results of Common Entrance examinations. The school subscribes to the Durham University Value Added Measuring Scheme at all levels, allowing tutors to map pupil progress. In core subjects setting takes place from the outset and at GCSE level setting occurs in all core curriculum subjects. There are 66 x 55 min periods over a two weekly timetable.

Lower School (Years 7–8): The subjects studied are English, mathematics, science (biology, physics and chemistry), modern foreign languages (French and Spanish), Latin, geography, history, design technology, art, drama, music, religious studies, RHS Compass (digital literacy, Personal, Social and Health Education, Computing and study skills) and PE. There are four forms in Years 7 and 8 and the average class size is 18 pupils. Homework is set daily and completed within supervised sessions during the working day by both boarders and day pupils. All junior pupils must take part in at least three co-curricular activities after lessons.

Middle School (Years 9–11): The subjects studied in Year 9 are the same as in the Lower School and a further intake of pupils from prep schools means that there is an additional class. GCSE courses start in Year 10 and most pupils will study 9 subjects including English language and literature, mathematics, physics, chemistry, biology (either as three separate sciences or as the dual award) as the core subjects and four options from science (if taking separate sciences), history, geography, PE (Physical Education and Sports Science), French, Spanish, media studies, religious studies, art, music, theatre studies, design technology and business studies.

Sixth Form (Years 12 and 13): Pupils choose three from approximately 27 A Level and BTEC subjects. Subject choice depends upon average point scores at GCSE and grades gained in specific subjects. As well as three A Level or BTEC subjects, pupils must choose one from a range of academic Elective subjects which can range from an Extended Project Qualification to a BTEC Level 2 First Award in Information and Creative Technology. RHS+ provides sessions on careers, managing finances, cooking on a budget, digital effectiveness and safety and coping with stress and mindfulness. RHSXtra runs a series of talks and seminars on topics aimed at broadening horizons and inspiring curiosity. Around 90% of pupils go to the University or Higher Education institution of their choice and approximately 50% to Russell Group and other top-class universities. An increasing number of pupils are gaining places on Higher Degree Apprenticeship schemes with leading corporations, whilst a few join the Armed Forces or gain direct workplace appointments.

Pupil progress is formally monitored by means of at least two assessments or reports per term which grade the academic performance of the pupil against their target or challenge grades, as well as looking at their attitude to learning. Every pupil has a personal tutor and daily tutorial meetings are an opportunity to deal with any problems and check on progress.

All pupils have access to an electronic device (Microsoft Surface) and Wi-Fi throughout the site. Additional networked computers are available in Boarding or Day Houses as well as in computer suites around the school. Mobile learning is embraced by the teaching staff with the aim of enhancing teaching and learning. Recent remote and hybrid learning allowed a full, unadapted timetable of lessons to be delivered during the pandemic via MS Teams and OneNote.

Through high quality, enthusiastic teaching, excellent resources and dedicated tutorial support, every pupil is encouraged to aim high and achieve his or her personal best. The most able pupils' potential is realised through the mentoring of scholars, the Riddle and Studd Societies for gifted and talented pupils and Oxbridge preparation for those pupils requiring it, led by a dedicated Head of Academic Challenge.

Sport and Leisure. Facilities include ninety-six acres of playing fields, a golf course, shooting range, sports hall, fitness suite, gym, climbing wall, large heated indoor swimming pool, squash courts, tennis and netball courts and an all-weather sports surface.

The school has a strong sailing tradition and all pupils joining in Year 7 receive sailing instruction to RYA Level 2. Through the school's RYA-accredited Sailing Academy, pupils have access to a fleet of 40 racing dinghies on adjacent Alton Water reservoir, as well as traditional Cornish Shrimpers on the River Stour and Orwell. The school is widely known as one of the top in the country for both fleet and team sailing and offers an elite training programme for those wishing to follow an Olympic pathway.

Other main sports include cricket, rugby, hockey and netball where the school has an excellent group of coaching staff as well as strong links to academy and high-performance centres in the region. Kayaking, athletics, cross country, climbing, basketball, football, golf, kickboxing, tennis, riding and swimming are also sports on offer and are popular with a number of pupils at the school. The swimming pool also offers opportunities for kayak-polo, life-saving training and sub-aqua.

Music and Drama. The school has a particularly strong musical tradition and the state-of-the-art Music School provides a recital hall, specialist rooms, recording studio and technical suite. Almost half the pupils in the school are involved in music on a regular basis and regularly perform both at and outside of school. Recent highlights include playing at Westminster Cathedral, on HMS Diamond for HM The King's Coronation celebrations and a music tour to Washington. The school Chapel is of cathedral proportions and has one of the finest organs in Europe, much used by pupils as well as professional performers. Peripatetic teachers offer tuition in a wide range of instruments and the choir and chamber choir perform both nationally and internationally. As well as drama in the curriculum and LAMDA classes, productions are often combined with the music department for whole-school performances and there is a full programme of plays, competitions and festivals each year.

CCF and Community Service. All pupils participate in the Combined Cadet Force in Years 9 and 10 and are able to choose between Army, Navy, RAF and Royal Marine sections. The emphasis is on adventure training and personal development. More than 300 pupils take part in The Duke of Edinburgh's Award scheme and 100 of these to Gold Award. The Community Action Team promotes the school's social responsibility and is actively involved in a wide range of charitable activities in the local community.

Religion. The core values of the school are based on the Christian faith but pupils from a variety of religions and cultural backgrounds attend the school and all beliefs are respected. The magnificent Chapel, that holds over 1,000 people, is the spiritual hub of school life and the whole community gathers twice weekly for morning worship.

Admission. Entry to the school is normally at 11, 13 and 16 years. Pupils are asked to sit an entrance examination, comprising papers in English, mathematics and verbal reasoning, in the November prior to the September of the year of entry unless following Common Entrance for entry in Year 9. Entry into the Sixth Form is subject to a minimum average GCSE point score and specific grades in chosen A Level subjects. Entry is also subject to an interview and satisfactory reference from the pupil's current school.

Fees per term (2023–2024). Full Boarding: £10,692 (Years 7 and 8), £13,767 (Years 9–13). Weekly Boarding: £10,184 (Years 7 and 8), £12,642 (Years 9–13). Day: £6,373 (Years 7 and 8), £7,413 (Years 9–13). 3-Night Boarding: £9,150 (Years 7 and 8), £10,974 (Years 9–13).

A Boarding Bundle is available to parents of day pupils or 3-Night Boarders who want to take advantage of the flexibility of buying units of 15 nights purchased in advance.

Discounts are available for services families eligible for the MOD Continuity of Education Allowance (CEA), naval seafarers and siblings where two or more children are in the school at any time.

Scholarships, Exhibitions and Awards are awarded annually for academic excellence, musical talent, drama, art, sport and sailing. All scholarship candidates are required to sit the school entrance examination (unless taking Common Entrance or GCSE examinations), have an interview and undergo an assessment in their relevant field. Full details from the Admissions Office, Tel: 01473 326136 or email: admissions@royalhospitalschool.org.

Bursaries. Pupils in receipt of a scholarship or award are eligible to apply for additional assistance by way of a means-tested bursary, should the financial circumstances of the family necessitate it. The school's parent charity, Greenwich Hospital, can award generous means-tested bursaries to the children of seafarers, particularly serving or retired Naval or Royal Marines personnel, of up to 95% of fees.

Charitable status. The Royal Hospital School is owned by Greenwich Hospital which is a Crown Charity.

Director, Greenwich Hospital: Mrs Deirdre Mills

Governors:
Chair of Governors: Mr M Pendlington

Prof T Arulampalam	Mr A Kerr
Mrs T Bartlett	Mr O Peck
Commodore R Bellfield	Mrs N Probert
Ms J Dow	Mr T Stenning
Prof R Harvey	Mr P Torrington

Senior Management Team:

***Headmaster*: Mr Simon Lockyer**, BSc, MEd

Chief Operating Officer: Mr G Tunnicliffe, CB, CVO, MA, BA, DiploD, MAPM
Second Master: Mr S J Dixon, MA
Deputy Head (*Academic*): Mrs C A Stevens, BSc
Deputy Head (*Pastoral*): Mrs Z S King, BSc
Director of Admissions & Marketing: Mrs S Walker, BA Hons, DipM, FCIM
Director of Learning: Mr M R Routledge, BA, MSc
Director of Academic Systems: Mr J R W Battman, MEng
Director of Finance: Mrs C Wood, ACA
Assistant Head (*Co-curricular*): Mr B Martineau, BA Hons, PGCE, MBA
Deputy Bursar (*Operations*): Mr J Reid, OBE, MA
IS Manager: Mr A Davison

Chaplain: Rev L E Mumford, BA
Directors and Programme Heads:
Head of Sixth Form: Mrs H Izod-Miller, MEng
Head of Futures: Miss L Bayliss-Fuller, CEIAG, BA Hons
Head of Digital Learning: Mr M Vickers, MA
Examinations Officer: Mrs J Rooney
Academic Challenge Co-ordinator: Mr G N G Johnson, BA
Director of Music: Mr E C Allen, BA
Director of Sport: Mr N L Cooper, BA
Director of Sailing and Water Sports: Mr E M G Sibson, MSc
CCF Contingent Commander: Capt M Ward, RE, BSc Hons
Assistant Head of Sixth Form: Mrs M Price, BA

Heads of Department:
Art: Mrs H L Barber, BA
Biology: Mr B A Raybould, BSc
Business and Economics: Ms C Fairley
Chemistry: Mr M Coventry, BSc

Classics: Dr P Taraskin
Climbing: SSgt P Ryan
Head of Cricket: Mr C Nortje
Design Technology: Mr O Millington, BA
Drama: Mr D Kerr, BA
Duke of Edinburgh's Award & CCF: Sgt P Ryan
English: Ms J L Stone, BA
English as an Additional Language: Mr D P Coleman, BA
French: Mrs A Barth, BA
Geography: Mrs A C Lockyer, BSc
History and Politics: Mr O Roe, BA
Learning Support: Mrs E Burge, MA
Mathematics: Ms S C Botley, BSc
Media Studies: Mr K Gurur
Netball: Miss J Holden
PE (Academic): Mrs S Daley
Physics: Dr M R Gibbs, BSc
PSHE: Ms M R Hemmens, MA
Psychology and Sociology: Mrs M R Price, BA
Religious Studies: Mrs K O'Callaghan, MA
Science: Mrs K Finlay
Spanish: Mr A E Gutierrez-Aldana, BA

CCF School Staff Instructor: WO1 (RSM) K Weaver

Support Staff:
Deputy Bursar (Finance): Mr S Hall
Headmasters PA: Ms C Farmer
Marketing Manager: Mrs L Bolton
Commercial Manager: Mrs C Fitzpatrick
HR Manager: Mrs J Roberts
Head of Admissions: Mrs E Allinson
UK Admissions Manager: Ms A McDonnell
International Admissions Manager: Ms L Warner
Community and Alumni Relations Manager: Mrs L Baylis-Fuller
Health Centre: Sister D Sweeney, RGN

The Royal Masonic School for Girls

Rickmansworth Park, Rickmansworth, Herts WD3 4HF

Tel: 01923 773168
email: admissions@rmsforgirls.com
website: www.rmsforgirls.com
X/Twitter: @RMSforGirls
Facebook: @RMSforGirls
Instagram: @RMSforGirls
LinkedIn: /school/rmsforgirls

There are 990 pupils in school between the ages of 2 and 18. Approximately 10% of the current school population are boarders.

Premises and Facilities. Founded in 1788, the School came to Rickmansworth in 1934. Purpose-built, the school stands in over 300 acres of parkland on an elevated site overlooking the valley of the River Chess. The buildings are spacious and well-appointed. They include excellent ICT facilities, a dedicated Science building, a Planetarium, an Observatory, Chapel and Library.

The Sports Hall is equipped to the highest international standards and includes a gym and fitness suite. There is a heated indoor swimming pool, 12 tennis courts, four squash courts, superb playing fields and an All-Weather pitch. The School has been awarded Sportsmark status. The state-of-the-art Performing Arts Centre includes a recording studio and green room facilitating learning about production, as well as performance.

Location. Central London is 15 miles to the south and Amersham is just north of the town. The M25 is one mile from the school and links it to London (Heathrow) – 30 minutes, London (Gatwick) – 50 minutes, and Luton Airport – 30 minutes. London Underground services (Metropolitan Line) and British Rail from Marylebone enable Central London to be reached by train in 30 minutes.

General Curriculum and Aims. The first three years of Senior School provide a broad general education that fulfils the requirements of the National Curriculum and reaches far beyond it. Students cover a wide range of subjects including English, Mathematics, Science, History, Geography, Philosophy, Ethics and Religion, Design Technology, Computer Science, Food and Nutrition, Art, Drama, Physical Education and Life Skills. Language Studies begin with French, Spanish, German, and Mandarin, Latin and Ancient Greek are also offered. The academic curriculum is supported by a vast range of co-curricular opportunities and Sixth Form Studies are enhanced with the RMS Edge programme designed to provide a bespoke timetable for each student.

GCSE options are chosen from among all the subjects taught in Years 7 to 9 and new possibilities, such as Business, Economics, Creative Media and Astronomy. Most pupils take nine or ten GCSE subjects and girls are guided in their choices by subject teachers, in full consultation with parents. Triple Science is available.

The Sixth Form. The School offers 29 subjects in flexible combinations. Politics, Classical Civilisation, Photography, Sociology, and Psychology are all new additions to the curriculum at this stage. Virtually all Sixth Formers go on to higher education.

Religion. Girls of all faiths and none are welcome.

Health. The School Doctor attends the Health Centre regularly. There are three nurses on duty every day.

Admission. Please contact the Admissions Department admissions@rmsforgirls.com or visit the school website for further information. The main entry points are 3+, 4+, 11+, 13+, and 16+, although students may join in other year groups subject to assessment and space being available. Families can book private tours at any time.

Scholarships and Bursaries. Scholarships are offered by the School to encourage and reward excellence. Scholarships are awarded in recognition of outstanding achievement, or promise in a particular area. Scholarship awards do not exceed 25% of the annual fee but may be supported with a means-tested bursary.

At 11+: Awards are given in recognition of excellence with regard to academic achievement in the entrance examination, Sport, All-Rounder potential, Art, Drama, and Music.

At 16+: Awards are given for academic excellence, Music, Visual Arts, Sport, and Performing Arts.

A number of means-tested, fully funded bursaries are available each year to candidates who are successful in the entrance assessment and where the family is eligible for financial assistance. Priority is given to applicants for whom the bursary will be most transformational.

Fees per term (2023–2024). Senior School: Full Boarders £13,140; Weekly Boarders £12,115; Day Pupils £7,315–£7,490.

Cadogan House Prep School: Full Boarders: £9,095 (Years 3–6); Weekly Boarders: £8,625 (Years 3–6); Day Pupils: £4,530–£5,670. Ruspini House Nursery School (boys and girls aged 2–4): ££1,660–£ 5,840. Please see the website for the full range of nursery fees.

Charitable status. The Royal Masonic School Limited is a Registered Charity, number 276784. Its aims are the advancement of education.

Board of Governors:
Mr Simon Staite (*Chair*)
Mr K S Carmichael, CBE (*Honorary Life President*)

Mr S Brew	Mrs S Shackell
Mrs C Shorten Conn	Mr A Wauchope
Mr R Garvey	Mr I Williams
Mr B Saini	Mrs H Wilson

Clerk to the Governors: Mrs D Robinson, BSc Bristol, ACA

***Head Teacher*: Mr K Carson**, BA Liverpool, MPhil Cantab, PGCE

Head of Senior School: Ms R Bailey, BSc York, PGCE
Head of Sixth Form: Mrs C Freeman, BSc Durham, PGCE
Head of Prep School: Mrs M Horn, BEd
Head of Nursery School: Mrs V Greig, BA

Director of Finance and Operations: Mrs E Gosht
Director of Marketing and Admissions: Mrs A Nicoll

Deputy Head, Academic: Mrs S Hardy, BA
Deputy Head, Pastoral: Mrs A Davies, BA

Assistant Head, Academic: Mrs H Roberts, BA Durham, PGCE
Assistant Head, Co-Curricular: Mr D Cox, BEng Brunel, MEd Cantab, PGCE

Head of Admissions: Mr M Carter

Head's PA: Mrs S Clifford

Royal Russell School

Coombe Lane, Croydon, Surrey CR9 5BX

Tel: 020 8657 4433
email: headmaster@royalrussell.co.uk
website: www.royalrussell.co.uk
X/Twitter: @Royal_Russell
Facebook: @RoyalRussellSchool
LinkedIn: /royal-russell-school

Motto: *Non Sibi Sed Omnibus*

Royal Russell is different by design. We are a co-educational family school, for children aged 3 to 18 years with boarding and day facilities, set in 110 acres of beautiful woodland, enjoying excellent access to London and Gatwick and Heathrow airports.

Royal Russell's motto is '*non sibi sed omnibus*' which translates as 'not for oneself, but for all' and our commitment to each other is to help our happy and vibrant community to strive for their vision of success. Our extensive campus facilities and state-of-the-art technology blend effortlessly to inspire learning and personal growth.

We encourage pupils to extend their learning beyond the curriculum through enrichment activities and cultural experiences, learning together in an open community that reflects the real world and celebrates both individual and collective achievements. As a school with a truly international outlook, we are proud of our links with campuses in China, Lithuania and South Korea.

Number in School. There are 1,225 pupils in the school: 899 pupils in the Senior School; 711 day pupils and 188 boarders. There are 279 in the Sixth Form, and 326 in the Junior School.

Admission. Pupils enter in the Autumn term at the age of 3+, 11, 13 or 16. Space permitting, pupils may be considered and admitted at other ages, and there is a direct entry into the Sixth Form for eligible pupils.

Curriculum. Our broad and stimulating curriculum combines to spark imaginations, inspire creative thinking and broaden horizons. We know that at Royal Russell, the best progress takes place with girls and boys learning together, problem solving and benefiting from different interpretations, perspectives and approaches.

Facilities. Our campus provides excellent academic and sporting facilities which include a well-resourced School Library, a new Science block, a Performing Arts Centre, spacious areas for Art, Design Technology, Food Science and Photography, a Media Studies Suite, a multi-million pound sports complex including a full-size floodlit Astroturf pitch, three all-weather training pitches and a swimming pool. Sixth Form pupils enjoy use of a Sixth Form Study Centre and Drapers' Cafe.

Organisation. Pupils perform best when they feel secure, accepted and supported. Our pastoral approach is highly valued by our pupils and their parents and is strengthened by our House System. The houses are at the centre of school life, with each pupil allocated to one of nine houses, led by a dedicated team including a personal tutor who gets to know each child well and understand their interests, aspirations and concerns.

Games. We offer an extensive range of sports for quality participation, fitness and fun including football, hockey, cricket, netball, tennis, swimming and athletics. Badminton, basketball, table tennis, trampolining and volleyball are also played.

Music, Drama and Art. Music and Drama play a prominent role at Royal Russell. Our Performing Arts Centre is at the heart of our campus and the Drama Department is lively and dynamic, offering all pupils the opportunity to take part, both within the curriculum and as a co-curricular activity. Our thriving Music Department has a reputation for excellence with many pupils achieving significant musical success. Pupils have opportunities to perform in many concerts, with Jazz, Swing and Samba Bands, Orchestra and the Chamber Choir and Barbershop. Our Art, Photography, Media, Food and Design Technology departments nurture the creative streak in every pupil.

Careers. The Head of Careers coordinates careers advice, giving individual counselling and helping with university applications and the School is a member of the Career Development Institute whose services are available to all pupils.

Clubs and Activities. With a programme of over 100 clubs and activities, all pupils are encouraged to participate. The School's involvement in the Model United Nations programme is renowned, with our annual International MUN conference, attracting over 500 student delegates from all over the world. There is a flourishing voluntary Combined Cadet Force and Duke of Edinburgh's Award scheme; the Theatre Society takes advantage of the School's proximity to London's theatres, and the annual ski trip is always oversubscribed.

Junior School. The aim in the Junior School is to instil a lifelong love of learning with a strong academic focus and extensive range of clubs and activities. Breakfast Club and after-school care is available. The Junior and Early Years Section provides a happy, secure and purposeful environment and the majority of children transfer to the Senior School after Year 6. (*For full details please see our* entry in the IAPS section.)

Scholarships. A number of scholarships are available each year to pupils aged 11+ to 13+, in music, drama, art or sport. Sixth Form scholarships are also awarded annually.

Fees per term (2023–2024). Senior School: Boarders £14,864 (Years 7–13); Day £7,520 (Years 7–13 inclusive of lunch). Junior School: Years 5–6 £5,665 and Years 3–4 £5,444 (inclusive of lunch, after-school clubs and supper), Reception to Year 2 £4,444 (inclusive of lunch), Nursery £2,668 to £4,444.

Religion. The school's religious affiliation is to the Church of England but pupils of all faiths and none are welcome. Our approach to daily life is founded on Christian principles and we maintain an atmosphere of mutual respect and understanding.

Charitable status. Russell School Trust is a Registered Charity, number 271907. It exists solely for the education of boys and girls.

Patron: Her Late Majesty, Queen Elizabeth II

Board of Governors:
Chair: Mr A Merriman

Prof Ali Ansari	James Lacey
Olivia Bedell-Pearch	Andrew Lorie
Nicholas Cobill	Sir Philip Moor
Peter Dawson	James Penny
Dr Angelo Fernandes MBE	Nicola Rabson
Michelle Grant	Andrew Roach-Bowler
Cecile Halliday	Jennifer Smith
Lisa Jessup	Shirley Thompson

Senior School:

***Headmaster*: Mr Chris Hutchinson**, BMet, FRSA

Senior Deputy Head: Mr Sam Powell
Deputy Head Learning: Mrs Clare Tovey

Director of International Relations: Mr Graham Moseley, BEd Hons, MA
Director of International Relations: Mr David Selby, BA Hons
Director of Operations & Clerk to the Governors: Mr Neil Cufley
Senior School Registrar (*Boarding*): Mrs Karen Sanchez
Senior School Registrar (*Day*): Mrs Jo Doble

The Royal School Dungannon

2 Ranfurly Road, Dungannon BT71 6EG, Northern Ireland

Tel: 028 8772 2710
email: info@rsd.dungannon.ni.sch.uk
website: www.royaldungannon.com
X/Twitter: @RoyalDungannon

Motto: *Perseverando* (*Excellence through Perseverance*)

In 1608 James I made an order in Privy Council establishing six Royal Schools in Ulster of which Dungannon became, in 1614, the first to admit pupils. In 1983 plans were first drawn up to incorporate the neighbouring girls' grammar school and to use both campuses' excellent facilities for co-educational purposes. This development came to fruition in 1986. A £9 million building and refurbishment programme began in 2000 and was completed in 2003, providing very high-tech specialist accommodation in science, technology and IT. In 2007 an international standard Astroturf hockey pitch was completed with flood lighting and four new all-weather tennis courts were opened. Annual investment by Governors in the school's infrastructure has continued allowing RSD staff and pupils to enjoy excellent facilities.

For nearly four centuries the Royal School has aimed at providing an education which enables its pupils to achieve the highest possible standards of academic excellence and at developing each pupil into a mature, well-balanced and responsible adult, well-equipped for the demands of a highly complex and technological world.

There are four Houses which foster the competitive instincts and idiosyncrasies of young people. Pastorally, each year is supervised by a Head of Year who guides his/her pupils throughout the child's career in a caring school environment.

The Boarding Department provides accommodation for 54 Boarders with the Girls and Boys housed in separate wings of the modernised Old School building dating from 1789. The recently refurbished facilities include a new kitchen/dining area, recreation area with flat screen TV and games console, new furniture in all dormitories and fully regulated wireless internet throughout. There are a number of staff who assist in the Boarding Department, including a Head of Boarding, a team of seven resident teaching staff, a team of 5 day and evening matrons, and a large number of support staff. These staff all work together to ensure that high standards of care and support are maintained. The School is also serviced by a team of local doctors and dentists who support the Boarders. A major hospital is less than 30 minutes from the campus.

The extensive buildings are a mixture of ancient and modern, with recently opened technology and science accommodation. Eight well-equipped Science Laboratories, Audio/Visual Room, two Libraries, Sixth Form Centre and Study Rooms, Technology, two Music and Art Studios and two Information Technology Suites are supplemented by a Boarding Department housed in well-appointed accommodation which has been completely renovated in the recent times. Boarders are able to make use of a wide range of facilities such as Sports Hall, Computer Laboratory, Multi-gym, Badminton Courts, Television Lounges, satellite TV, high-speed broadband (including Skype) and nearby facilities such as the local swimming pool and extensive parkland walks. Situated in its own spacious grounds in a quiet residential area of this rural town, the School is linked directly by motorway to Belfast (40 minutes), two airports, cross-Channel ferries and railway stations.

The establishment of good study skills and practices is considered to be of crucial importance. The size of the School ensures that no child is overlooked in any way.

At A Level new subjects are offered such as Economics and, in collaboration with partner schools, Media Studies, Politics, Psychology and Business Studies.

Pupils are prepared for GCSE and A Levels under all the major UK Examination Boards and there is a tradition of Oxbridge successes as well as a high rate of entry to the University of Ulster, Queen's University Belfast and other leading British Universities. In most years around 95% of the Upper Sixth Form proceed to Higher Education. The School's overseas students typically choose to enrol both at UK universities and universities in their home country.

Many co-curricular pursuits are encouraged during lunchtime or after school, such as Choir, Orchestra, Duke of Edinburgh's Award scheme, Chess, Charities, Debating, Public Speaking and many more.

Alongside the School's academic achievements in both Arts and Sciences may be placed its record in the sporting world: in Rugby, Hockey, Cricket, Badminton, Shooting, Table Tennis and Tennis.

Fees per annum (2023–2024). Day: £150. 7-Day Boarding: £13,650 (UK Passport holder). 7 days a week (EU passport holder) £19,275 – the tuition fee to EU citizens of £5,625 per annum is not currently chargeable until such times as the local government in Northern Ireland enacts Brexit legislation. In the current situation EU tuition remains free, however this may change at a later stage. 7-Day Boarding including Tuition £24,000 (non-UK/non-EU citizens). 5-Day Boarding: £9,150 (UK Passport holder).

Charitable status. The Royal School Dungannon is a Registered Charity, number XN46588 A. It was established by Royal Charter in 1608 for the purpose of education.

Board of Governors:
Chairman: Dr P G Steen, PhD, BSc, CPhys, MInstP
Vice Chairman: Dr G Walsh, BEd, PhD, ALCH, FHEA
Members:
Mrs J Anderson, BA Hons, MCIPD
D N Browne, MIB, MIMgt
R J Clingan, BSc, MEd, PGCE, PQH NI
J C M Eddie
Mrs R Emerson, BSc, CSP
G Ferry, BSc
Dr J M Hagan, MB, BCh, BAO, BSc Hons, PgDip, PgCert
Mrs R Hampton, BSc, CSP
Mrs C L Kerr, BA, MEd, PGCE
Mrs G Leonard
Lord Maginnis of Drumglass, PC
Dr L Maguire, BDS, LLM
Dr D Maguire, BDS
Revd B Martin, BTh, Dip Miss
Mrs L McDonald
N H McLean, LLB, MBA
R B K McLean, MRICS
Mrs E Patterson, BA, MSSC, Dip IT
R F Patton, LLB
Mrs K Rainey, BA Hons, MSc, ACMA, CGMA
D Thompson, BEd, DipASEd, PQH (NI)
Mrs J Williamson, BA, MSc, PGCE, CPsychol AEP, HPCP
J G Willis LLB
J W Willis, BEd

Secretary to the Governors: The Headmaster

***Headmaster*: Dr D A Burnett**, BA, PhD, NPQH

Teaching Staff:
* *Head of Department*
[1] *Head of Year*
[2] *Head of House*

Deputy Head: R J Clingan, BSc, MEd, PGCE, PQH NI

Senior Teacher: *G R Black, BSc, PGCE
Senior Teacher: *Miss A E Chestnutt, BSc, MEd, PGCE
Senior Teacher: Mrs C L Kerr, BA, MEd, PGCE

Head of Boarding: Miss S Winslow, BDes
Assistant Head of Boarding: M J Black, MSci, PGCE

Miss A Anderson, BA, PGCE. ARSM, DipLCM
Mrs A Best, BA, PGCE
*N J Canning, BEng, PGCE
*R E Chambers, BSc, PGCE
*Mrs W Y Chambers, BSc, MEd, PGCE, Dip IT
Miss K L Clarke, BMus, PGCE
Miss S A Colgan, BSc, PGCE
*S J Cuddy, BMus, PGCE
[1]Mrs A Gilkinson, MSc, PGCE
J R Graham, BA, MSc, PGCE
*Mrs R L Hampton, BSc, PGCE
*Mrs S J Jackson, BA, MEd, PGCE
*P S Kerr, BA, MSc, PGCE
[1]G S R Lucas, BSc, PGCE
[2]Mrs P L Matthews, BEd, PGCE
*[2]G W McClintock, BSc, PGCE
Miss D McCombe, BSc, PGCE
Mrs C E McMcCormick, BA, PGCE
[1]Mrs S J McCullough, BA, PGCE
M McDowell, BA, MA, PGCE
Mrs S J McGrath, BSc, PGCE
Mrs L McGurk, BSc, PGCE
*G M McLoughlin, BSC, PGCE
Mrs C S Montgomery, BSc, PGCE, DASE
*Miss H Montgomery, BSc, PGCE
*P G Moore, MA, PGCE, GC, TEFL
Mrs N G Peden, BEd
*Ms A M Prescott, BEd, MEd
[2]A S Ritchie, BSc, PGCE
Mrs L Shaw, BA Hons, PGCE

Mrs A V Simpson, BSc, PGCE
*Mrs J Stewart, BSc Hons, PGCE, DIS
[1]Mrs E V Stitt, BA, PGCE
*Mrs A R Straghan, BSc Econ, PGCE
Mrs V I Troughton, BA, PGCE
A T Turner, BSc, PGCE
[1]G T Watterson, MSc, PGCE
[1]J W Willis, BEd Hons
I A Wilson, BSc, PGCE

Chaplain: Vacant

Administrative Staff:
Bursar: Mr D Wheeler, BSc Econ, FCA
Headmaster's Secretary: Mrs L Martin

Matrons:
Mrs J Byrne, BSC, PGDip, SRN (*Day*)
Mrs C Saygi (*Evening*)
Mrs J Caddoo (*Evening*)
Ms M Campbell (*Evening*)

Rugby School

Rugby, Warwickshire CV22 5EH
Tel: 01788 556216 (Head Master)
01788 556260 (COO)
01788 556273 (Director of Admissions)
email: head@rugbyschool.net (Head Master)
coo@rugbyschool.net (COO)
admissions@rugbyschool.net (Director of Admissions)
website: www.rugbyschool.co.uk
X/Twitter: @RugbySchool1567
Facebook: @RugbySchool1567
Instagram: @rugbyschool1567
LinkedIn: /school/rugby-school

'*If variety is the spice of life, then Rugby is on to a winner*' (*Tatler Schools Guide* 2024)

Ethos. Rugby, probably more than any other school in the land, focuses on helping our students become 'whole' people – people who are multifaceted in their interests, talents and ambitions. Here, we do not just say 'the whole person is the whole point', we live it, every hour of every day.

Here, students flourish in a supportive and spiritually aware community, which challenges learners, develops resilience and encourages intellectual risk-taking. We foster academic excellence and nurture individual talents enabling our students to develop a lifelong love of learning, while achieving outstanding results.

Head Master, Gareth Parker-Jones, said he believes Rugby to have succeeded when a spark is created in the mind of the student, be it in the classroom, on the sports field, in the music rooms, on stage, in the art studios, or around any sort of activity.

'What I see here, time and time again, is that once a student becomes good at one thing and enjoys doing it, they soon become good at something else. And then something else again. In this way, Rugby helps our students form the habit of doing things well – of being good at life,' he added.

This, of course, owes a huge amount to Rugby being a true seven-day-a-week boarding school, along with two day houses open from 7.00 am to 22.00 pm, there is the space and time to accommodate hundreds of activities – some academic, many not. Rugbeians are very busy, and that teaches vital life skills of prioritisation and organisation.

Academically, Rugby's consistently excellent results place it as among the best performing co-educational boarding schools in the UK, but while excellence is celebrated, nobody is ever on the bench. If 32 netball teams are needed to ensure every student gets to play a fixture, that is what happens.

And this is why we are the leading co-educational boarding school in the country.

Number of Students. 868 (45% girls, 55% boys).

Location. Enjoying a central location just 48 minutes by train from London and close to the M6, M1 and Birmingham Airport, Rugby School offers the best of all worlds – a leafy green 150-acre campus on the edge of the countryside but still part of the town.

Facilities. A rich, cultural heritage runs through the core of the School with many buildings of architectural distinction, from the impressive Chapel to the splendid Temple Speech Room. Step away from the town and enter another world of ancient cloisters and elegant quads punctuated by swathes of green.

The facilities are, however, state of the art, including a purpose-built Modern Languages building, an impressive Science Centre, a Design Centre featuring The Lewis Gallery with its dedicated art and exhibition space, and a huge new sixth form centre for studying the IB Diploma Programme and A Level subjects.

The Music Schools feature 40 teaching/practice rooms, technology classrooms, recording studio and a small concert hall. More than 120 music performances happen every year and students regularly get to perform with the School's professional orchestra.

Sports facilities are equally impressive, including a modern Sports Centre, with its 25 m pool, fitness suite and courts, three new AstroTurf hockey pitches, soccer and rugby fields, and hard courts for tennis and netball. A state-of-the-art gym will open shortly. Our polo fields mark the boundary of this wide-reaching campus. Sport at Rugby includes athletics, badminton, basketball, cricket, cross-country, fencing, fives, football, golf, gymnastics, hockey, netball, polo, rackets, rugby, sailing, squash, swimming and tennis. Every student has access to professional sports coaching and conditioning, and there is a dedicated athletes programme.

Boarding Houses. The House structure at Rugby is central to our strong sense of community. Ideas flourish best where they were originated and it was our pioneering Head Master, Dr Thomas Arnold, who initiated the boarding house system to ensure exceptional pastoral care and provide the ideal social environment in which young people could thrive.

Much copied but never bettered, more than 200 years of 'House' experience has resulted in a genuine and uncompromised care plan which supports every single student.

The 13 Boarding Houses at Rugby, each with their own unique character, in different locations and of varying sizes, all offer a true home away from home, a real family to which every student belongs and is rightly proud of. An ambitious programme of improvements is currently under way.

The ethos at Rugby that the whole person is the whole point is undeniably apparent within this perfected and seamless House structure. The role of Housemaster or mistress as head of the 'family' is to create and maintain a happy and balanced home with the able support of their deputy and the Matron who, importantly, are all resident. Totally committed to the wellbeing of their young people, this nucleus of staff provides 24-hour care that is second to none.

Day Houses. Rugby's two Day Houses, one for girls and one for boys, were recently expanded to provide even better facilities and space to meet increased demand for places. They now accommodate 200 day students who all benefit from the depth and breadth of a boarding experience.

Academic. *GCSE*: All the usual subjects are offered, as well as Computing, German, Spanish, Latin, Greek, Design, Art, Music, PE, Theatre Studies and Religious Studies.

IB and A level: Rugby offers the IB Diploma. Alongside the core, CAS, Theory of Knowledge, Extended Essay and the traditional subjects, the list extends to far more, including Theatre, Literature and Performance, Mandarin and Italian *ab initio*, Psychology, Global Politics and Environmental Systems and Societies. A level is offered in all the GCSE subjects, as well as in Business Studies, Economics, Graphics, Textiles and Politics. Students also have the opportunity to pursue an Extended Project.

All go on to Higher Education with an impressive number of students achieving Oxbridge and Russell Group places, while an increasing number achieve offers in Canada, the US and Europe.

A diverse programme of academic enrichment is an integral part of a Rugby education, with all students attending a wide range of clubs and activities. Academic societies, many of which are student-driven, invite a wide range of eminent figures to the School – speakers have included Rowan Williams, Anthony Horowitz and Poet Laureate Carol Ann Duffy.

In addition, all Year 9 students embark on the Rugby Learner Profile. Unique to Rugby School, this cross-curricular method of teaching and learning transcends the traditional classroom formula, helping to develop key dispositions that encourage maturity and promote engagement.

Spiritual Life. A well-balanced individual needs a sense of spiritual awareness, along with academic achievement and physical ability. The experience of holiness, an understanding of right and wrong, and respect for the worth of each human being; these things are the invisible glue holding our community together. These values are learned in every part of our lives, but the School Chapel and the activities connected with it are a particular focus for our spiritual development.

The Chaplains get to know the students by sharing meals, visiting the Houses and involving themselves with all the School's activities. They also share the teaching of the younger students, giving them regular contact with the entire Lower School.

Co-curricular. With more than 200 activities on offer, the co-curricular programme plays a huge part in the meaning of 'Whole' in our Whole Person Whole Point ethos. Our community is thriving, exciting, inclusive and full of opportunities for students to find inspiration, fun, challenge, curiosity, confidence and fulfilment. We believe growing as a person, developing into the type of adult students want to be, involves making choices, especially in how you spend your time.

Our sporting philosophy of 'nobody on the bench' sees our students represent the School in a significant range of sports as we stick to our core principle which nicely moulds excellence with opportunity. Our CCF is thriving with over 200 cadets and our Performing Arts Faculty sends productions to the Edinburgh Fringe and Bloomsbury Festival. The Music Schools are a hive of activity and the recently launched chorister programme seeks to secure choral singing within schools. You'll hear our choirs perform evensong on BBC Radio 3, as well as in the local churches. Our Rugby 360 service programme sees 550 students out engaging with meaningful service in the local community each week. Our DofE completion rates are amongst the highest in Central England. We have over 70 clubs and societies on offer. The Lewis Gallery is open throughout the year showcasing student work and we have strong community links in all of our co-curricular areas. There truly is something on offer for everyone within our co-curriculum at Rugby School.

Admission. At 13+, offers of day places are made in Year 6 and boarding places in Year 7, on the basis of previous school's report and interviews, subject to gaining at least an average of 55% in CE, or the School's own Maths and English tests, or via scholarship application entry.

At 16+, places for boarders and day students are offered on the basis of previous school's report, interview and written entrance tests during Year 11 (including English and Mathematics) in the subjects chosen for IB and A level. Offers are subject to at least three grade 6 and three grade 7 GCSEs, or equivalent.

Scholarships. Our scholarship provision is designed to attract boys and girls of outstanding talent and skill in a variety of fields. We value scholarship of all sorts. Through the excellence of our academic provision and our facilities we aim to foster high achievement at all levels and to challenge expectations. The interplay of teaching and learning, and the experiences to be gained from being part of a rich and diverse community, encourage all students to develop their talents and to emerge as confident, well-rounded individuals.

13+ (Year 9) Academic Scholarships: Examinations are held in February of Year 8.

16+ (Year 12) Academic Scholarships: Scholarship interviews are held in mid-November of Year 11. Candidates must first take the Sixth Form Entrance Examination and those showing scholarship potential will be called for Scholarship interviews.

Music Scholarships: Awarded each year at 13+ and 16+. At 13+ with assessment auditions held at Rugby School in late January of the year of entry. At 16+ the audition is held in November as part of the 16+ entrance procedure.

Art Scholarships: Awarded each year at 13+ and at 16+. At 13+ the assessment takes place in March of Year 8. At 16+, it is in November as part of the 16+ entrance procedure.

Design and Technology Scholarships: Awarded each year at 13+ and at 16+. At 13+ the assessment takes place in March of Year 8. At 16+ it is in November as part of the 16+ entrance procedure.

Sports Scholarships: At 13+ and 16+ for candidates with outstanding ability or potential in the major team games for boys (rugby, hockey, cricket and tennis) or girls (hockey, netball and tennis). At 13+ the assessment takes place in November of Year 8. At 16+ it is in October of Year 11.

Performing Arts Scholarships: A number of Performing Arts Scholarships are awarded each year at 13+ and 16+ to candidates with outstanding acting ability or potential. At 16+ there are also scholarships for technical ability in performing arts. At 13+ the assessment takes place in February of Year 8. At 16+ it is in February of Year 11.

Computing Scholarships: Awarded each year at 13+ and 16+. At 13+ the assessment takes place in May of Year 8. At 16+ it is in November as part of the 16+ entrance procedure.

Foundation Awards: Several Foundation Awards are made annually to day boy and day girl candidates at 13+ and 16+. These candidates must live within a radius of 20 miles from the Rugby Clock Tower – excluding the city of Coventry.

Awards and Augmentation: The value of a Scholarship Award or a Foundation Award (including more than one award) is a maximum fee concession of 5%. Support can be augmented up to 100% of the day fees subject to means assessment.

The Arnold Foundation aims to raise funds through charitable donations to support the education of talented students whose families would not be able to fund boarding school fees. Funds are available for several awards for entry to the sixth form and at 13+. Students offered a place through this scheme may be awarded up to 100% of the full boarding fee plus extras. The final selection is through interviews. Candidates are expected to pass the school's normal entrance requirements. Initial enquiries should be made via the Admissions Office.

For further information and details of all Scholarships, Foundation Awards and The Arnold Foundation please contact the Director of Admissions, Tel: 01788 556273, email: admissions@rugbyschool.net.

Fees per term (2023–2024) The consolidated termly fee for boys and girls: £15,330 (boarding), £9,630 (day).

Further Information. Visit: www.rugbyschool.co.uk. Enquiries and applications should be made in the first instance to the Director of Admissions.

Charitable status. The Governing Body of Rugby School is a Registered Charity, number 528752. It exists to provide education for young people.

Governing Body:

Mr B J O'Brien (*Chair*)
Ms C J Marten, MA (*Deputy Chair*)
Mr R Aggarwal, MA, MBA
Mr N Bacon, FCA, CTA
Mr J C F Barwell, BA, FCSI, OBE
Ms C A Coates, LLB
Mr R J A Elmhirst, LLB (*Deputy Chairman, Finance & Audit*)
Dr C Greenhalgh, BA, PGCE
Mr A Habib, Bsc, MSc
Mr J R Moreland, MA, PGCE, NPQH
Mr S R T Penniston (*Associate Governor for RS Thailand*)
The Reverend Canon Dr R M Pryce
General (*retd*) Sir Tim Radford, KDB, DSO, OBE
Mr D Skailes, BSc, FCA
Mr P Smulders, BA, MBA
Mrs C Wills

Chief Operating Officer and Clerk to the Governing Body: Mr P A Nicholls, MA, FCA

Medical Officer: Dr H Collier, MB, ChB, DRCOG, MRCGP

Rugby School Group

Executive Principal (*International*): Dr N G Hampton, MA, PhD, PGCE
International Development Director: Mr I M McIntyre, MA
Governor (*International*): Mr P R A Green, MA, PGCE

Rugby School

***Head Master*: Mr G Parker-Jones**, MA, MA, PGCE

Deputy Heads:
Mr E S Davies, BA, MSc, PGCE (*Academic*)
Mrs L M Hampton, BEd, MSc
Mr L D Shepherd, BSc, PGCE (*Co-Curricular*)

Assistant Heads:
Mr P K Bell, MA, MSc, PGCE (*Houses*)
Miss R J Force, BSc (*Middle School*)
Dr G C E Joyce, BSc, PhD, PGCE (*Upper School*)
Dr J D Muston, MA, MPhil, DPhil (*Formation*)

Head of Safeguarding:
Mrs E L Sale, BSc, PGCE

Director of Admissions: Mrs L J Bursey Faulkner, BA, BMus QTS, LRSM

Teaching Staff:
* *Head of Department*

Chaplaincy:
The Revd R M Horner, BSc (*Chaplain*)*
Miss L Greatwood, BSc, DipMin, PGCE

Classics:
Mr W D Nicholl, BA, MA, MEd*
Dr F B Chesterton, BA, MA, PhD, PGCE
Mr A W Chow, BA
Mr S A Lambert, BA
Mr T J Morrison, MA, PGCE

Computer Science:
Mrs L A Bell, BEng*
Mr I Kurgansky, MSc, PGCE
Mr T E Rennoldson, BSc, PGCE

Design:
Mrs A K Merlarkey, BA, PGCE (*Design*)*
Mr J D Brown, BA, MA, PGCE
Mr M Cuff, BA, PGCE
Miss J E Harrington, BA, MA PGCE
Mrs H Lambie-Jones, BA, MA, PGCE
Mr J Ryan, BA, B-Tech, PGCE, MFA
Mr O Selfridge, BA, MA, PGCE
Mr B J Welch, BEng, PGCE
Mr D H Wright, BA, MA, PGCE

Economics and Business:
Mr A M Burge, BSc, PGCE (*Business*)*
Miss H Burrows, BA, PGCE (*Economics*)*
Mr A J I Baird, MA
Mr H J Higginson, BA
Ms H L McPherson, BSc, MSc, PGCE

English:
Mr T Eyre-Maunsell, MA, MA, PGCE*
Mrs M Baker, BA, PGCE
Mr H Dhesi, MA, BA, PGCE (*Head of TOK*)
Mrs N B Lockhart-Mann, BA, HDipEd, MSc
Mrs E M Moyle, BA, MA, PGCE
Dr J H Moyle, BA, MA, PhD
Ms A Scott-Martin, MA, MA, PGCE
Dr A T Shaw, BA, MA, PhD, PGCE
Mr A N Smith, MA, MTeach, PGCE
Dr J A Sutcliffe, BA, PhD, PGCE

Futures Advisory Service:
Mrs D Horner, BA*
Ms L Waweru, BPhilEd, PQCG
Mrs C Wheeler, BSc, PGDip, QCG

Geography:
Mrs J Brett, BA, PGCE*
Mrs C M Dow, BA, PGCE
Mr J C Evans, BA, PGCE
Miss L A Grieve, BA, MA, MSc, BSc, PGCE
Dr L E Milner, MA, MSc, PhD
Mr L D Shepherd, BSc, PGCE
Mr D W Wood, BA, PGCE

History:
Dr T D Guard, MA, MSt, DPhil, PGCE*
Miss C V Barnett, BA, PGCE, NPQH
Mr E S Davies, BA, MSc, PGCE
Dr M E Fowle, BA, MA, PhD, PGCE
Miss K Hollings, BA
Mrs M H Mahalski, MA, GDL, LPC, PGCE
Dr J D Muston, MA, MPhil, DPhil
Mr G Parker-Jones, MA, MA, PGCE
Dr T W Smith, BA, MA, PhD, PGCE, FRHistS, FRAS
Mr J M Stedman, BA

IB Co-ordinator:
Mrs N B Lockhart-Mann, BA, HDipEd, MSc

Keeper of Scholars and Oxbridge:
Dr A G Davies, BSc, PhD, PGCE (*Science & Mathematics*)
Dr T W Smith, BA, MA, PhD, PGCE, FRHistS, FRAS (*Arts & Humanities*)

Learning Development:
Mr I W L Murdoch, BA, PGCE, NASENCO, CPT3A*
Miss R S Cave, BSc, PGCE
Mrs A Dhesi BA, PGCE
Mrs N A Snowden, BEd, Hon Inclusive Education
Miss L Woodford, BA, PGCE

Mathematics:
Mr N Jones, MA, MEng, PGCE*
Mr W Uglow, BSc, PGCE (*Second i/c*)
Mr M R Baker, BA, PGCE
Mr P K Bell, MA, MSc, PGCE
Ms H C S Casson, BA, MA, FRSS, PGCE
Miss R J Force, BSc
Mrs N Good, MA, MMath, PGCE
Mr I Kurgansky, MSc, PGCE
Mr B L Lane, MA, MSc, PGCE
Mr A Langstone, MA, BSc, PGCE
Mrs S C McGuirk, BEng, PGCE, NPQML
Dr W P Murphy, BSc, MSc, PhD
Mr B J Rigg, MA, ACA
Mrs L J Sheehan, MA, BA, PGCE
Mr A J Siggers, BSc, PGCE

Modern Languages:
Mr L Callan, BA, MA, PGCE*
Mrs K Adams, BA, PGCE (*Spanish*)*
Mr C M Brown, BA, PGCE (*German*)*
Dr B Parolin, BA, MA, PhD, PGCE (*Italian*)*
Ms C Piquard, BA, MA (*French*)*
Mr G Arnoux, BA, MAm PGCE
Mr S Foulds, BA, PGCE
Mrs C A O'Mahoney, BA, PGCE
Ms C A Piton, MA, PGCE
Mr E Rico
Ms B S Sanchez Alonso, BA, BA, PGCE

Music:
Mr R J Tanner, MA, FRCO, ARAM, Hon FGCM (*Director of Music*)*
Miss R Taylor, MA, MA, DipABRSM, LRAM, ATCL (*Deputy Director of Music*)
Mr J J Conway, BA, ARCO, PGCE (*Academic Music*)
Mr A R Davey, LTCL (*Head of Co-Curricular Music*)
Mr I Foster, BMus, PGDip (*GSMD*), QTS (*Head of Music Partnerships*)
Mrs S Sanders, BMus
Mr M Sandy, MMus, MA Cantab, DipABRSM (*Head of Vocal Studies*)
Mr I M Wicks, BEng, PGCE (*Head of Keyboard*)
Mr J A Williams, BA, MA, Dip ABRSM, PGCE, ACIEA (*Head of Academic Music*)

Philosophy and Theology:
Mrs A L Parker-Jones, MA, PGCE*
Mr A B Birch, BA, MLitt
Miss L J Greatwood, BSc, Dip Min, PGCE
Revd R M Horner, BSc
Ms M J Rule, BSocSci, MA, PGCE

Politics and International Relations:
Mr P Teeton, BA, MA*
Miss C V Barnett, BA, PGCE, NPQH
Miss A F Griffiths, BA, MSc

PSHE:
Miss L J Greatwood, BSc, DipMin, PGCE

Science:
Mr S P Robinson, BSc, PGCE, MRes*
Mr P M Gillam, MA, PGCE (*Biology*)*
Dr S R Belding, MChem, DPhil (*Chemistry*)*
Mr R Parker, BSc, PGCE (*Physics*)*
Mr T J Batchelor, MA, MChem
Mr H E Burke, BSc
Mrs K Carter, BEng, CEng, MRAeS, PGCE
Dr S A Crabb, BSc, PhD
Dr A G Davies, BSc, PhD, PGCE
Mr R Dhanda, BSc, QTS
Mr A D Ellis, BSc, MEd, PGCE
Mr N A Fisher, BSc, MSc, MA, FInstP, PGCE
Miss L J Greatwood, BSc, Dip Min, PGCE
Mrs L M Hampton, BEd, MSc
Dr G C E Joyce, BSc, PhD, PGCE
Mrs R J Lam, BSc, PGCE

Mr R B McGuirk, BSc, MSc, PGCE
Mr M A Monteith, BSc, PGCE
Dr N J Morse, BSc, PhD, CChem, FRSC
Dr G Nelson, BSc, MSc, DPhil
Mrs E A Robinson, BSc, PGCE, MEd
Dr A M Thompson, BSc, PhD, PGCE (*Biology*)
Dr M A Thompson, BSc, PhD, PGCE (*Chemistry*)
Dr A A Wheatley, MA, MSci, PhD, PGCE

Sport:
Mrs D L Skene, BSc, PGCE (*Director of Sport*)*
Mr M Bayly, BSc (*Director of Rugby*)
Mr C Folker, BCom Acc (*Director of Rackets Sports*)
Mr M J Powell (*Director of Cricket*)
Mr J M Stedman, BA (*Director of Hockey*)
Mr N T Atley, MSc (*Strength & Conditioning Coach*)

Sports Science:
Mr H C Chamberlain, BSc, PGDip, PGCE*
Mr B D Adams, BSc, PGCE
Mr H E Burke, BSc
Miss E M Watton, BA, PGCE (*PE*)
Mrs L M Hampton, BEd, MSc
Mrs D L Skene, BSc, PGCE

Theatre Studies & Performing Arts:
Dr T D Coker, BA, MMus, MPhil, PhD (*Artistic Director*)*
Mr C J Browning (*Head of Co-Curricular Performing Arts*)
Mr A K Chessell, BA, MSc, PGCE
Mrs S J Farmer, BA, PGCE (*Head of Academic Drama*)
Ms E Finlay, BA, MA (*Head of Dance*)
Mrs F Passmore, BA, PGCE, MTL

Houses and Housemasters/mistresses:

Boarding Houses (*boys*):
Cotton: Mr Michael Powell
Kilbracken: Mr Saul Foulds
Michell: Mr Ben Welch
School Field: Dr Mark Fowle
School House: Mr Andrew Smith
Sheriff: Mr Maurice Monteith
Whitelaw: Mr Ashley Ellis

Day Boy House:
Town: Mr Andrew Chessell

Boarding Houses (*girls*):
Bradley: Mrs Caroline Dow
Dean: Mrs Felicity Passmore
Griffin: Miss Lisa Greatwood
Rupert Brooke: Miss Katie Hollings
Stanley (*Sixth Form only*): Ms A Scott-Martin
Tudor: Mrs Debbie Horner

Day Girl House:
Southfield: Mrs Michelle Baker

Ryde School with Upper Chine

Queen's Road, Ryde, Isle of Wight PO33 3BE

Tel: 01983 562229
email: school.office@rydeschool.net
website: www.rydeschool.org.uk
X/Twitter: @RydeSchool
Facebook: @RydeSchool
Instagram: @rydeschoolwithupperchine
LinkedIn: /school/rydeschool

Motto: '*Ut Prosim*'

Ryde School with Upper Chine is a coeducational day and boarding school providing education for pupils aged 2 to 18. Situated on the South Coast of England, Ryde is a ten-minute boat ride from Portsmouth. Ryde School was founded in 1921 as a grammar school for boys. Upper Chine was founded as a girls' school in Shanklin on the Isle of Wight in 1914. The two schools merged in 1994 to form Ryde School with Upper Chine and in 1996 the School acquired the buildings of Bembridge School. As a result of these acquisitions and mergers, the School became fully coeducational. Boarding provision is now on the main school site in Ryde in two new boarding houses; the beautifully renovated Victorian 'Millfield' for pupils to Year 10 and the new purpose-built 'Centenary' for Years 11 to Upper Sixth.

Situation and Buildings. The School stands in its own grounds of around 17 acres in Ryde with stunning views over the Solent and is easily accessible from all parts of the Island. It is within walking distance of the terminals which link Ryde to Southsea by hovercraft (10 minutes) or Portsmouth by catamaran (25 minutes) and a number of pupils travel daily from the mainland. In recent years there have been many additions to the School facilities with a new Performing Arts Centre in 2022, modern Art and DT departments, eight science labs recently fully refurbished, a new Health and Wellbeing Centre, new tennis and netball courts, a new coffee shop for parents, staff and pupils, a new gym and a dedicated Sixth Form Centre. Two newly opened boarding houses, a new Cookery School and a new Nursery have recently been added.

Organisation and Curriculum. As an IB World and Round Square School, the School aims to provide a world-class education on the Isle of Wight enabling boarders and day pupils to flourish in mind, body and soul, nurturing the character, skills and values to help them make a positive difference and embrace the opportunities of the wider world.

In the Pre-Prep and Prep, strong emphasis is placed on core skills, proficiency in reading, writing and number work with a strong focus on STEM, sports and outdoor learning. All pupils in the Prep School get the opportunity to sail. Pupils are prepared for entry into the Senior School, and following a recommendation from the Prep School, they are offered places in the Senior School at the age of 11. We also prepare pupils to move to specialist mainland schools and pupils have recently won scholarships to Winchester and Millfield.

In Years 7 and 8 we run a two-year diploma programme authorised by the PSB (Pre-Senior Baccalaureate), "Ryde Global". The programme of work in the Senior School is designed to provide a broad but challenging education up to the end of Year 11. The subjects taught to IGCSE/GCSE level are English Language and Literature, Mathematics, Physics, Chemistry, Biology, French, German, Latin, Mandarin, Spanish, ESL, Geography, History, Business Studies, Art, Music, Academic PE, Drama, Computer Science and Design Technology. All pupils select an elective subject from: Global Perspectives, Arts Award, Science CREST Award, Informatics or additional English and Maths to add breadth. All pupils also follow a programme of Personal Development (PD) and Games.

In the Sixth Form, pupils choose from three routes: the IB Diploma Programme, 'A Level Plus' (3 A Levels plus various enrichment and extension options) and the IB Careers-related Programme (An IB certificate that combines academic courses alongside vocational qualifications in one of Business, Art or Sport). In addition, A Level students are encouraged to take the Extended Project Qualification, designed to add breadth to their academic studies. Careers advice and guidance is given to all pupils. Students go on to a variety of universities and careers, including Oxbridge, medical schools, arts colleges and other Russell Group Universities, apprenticeships and straight into employment.

Tutorial System. Each pupil has a tutor who is responsible for his or her academic and personal progress and general pastoral welfare. The tutorial system encourages close contact with parents, which is further reinforced by parents' meetings, which are held at regular intervals, and a parent portal.

The School aims to maintain sound discipline and good manners within a traditionally friendly atmosphere and encourages pupils to live up to the School motto "Ut Prosim".

Our values underpin our community, shaping everything we do and how we go about our daily lives.

AMBITION – We are ambitious both individually and for our School. We have high expectations and aspirations.

RESPONSIBILITY – We take responsibility for our own actions and decisions. We value integrity and self-discipline.

COURAGE – We have the courage to be adventurous and to be risk-takers. We have the tenacity to keep trying and to overcome challenges.

RESPECT – We respect ourselves, each other and our community as a whole. We expect kindness, inclusivity, empathy and open-mindedness.

Games. The main games in the Senior School are hockey, rugby and cricket for the boys, and hockey, netball and cricket for the girls with sailing and athletics also a big focus. Girls' football and rugby are also offered. In the Prep School, football is also played. Other games include basketball, rounders, croquet, squash, golf, swimming, rowing and tennis. Regular matches are arranged at all levels against teams both on the Island and the mainland. There are many opportunities for sailing, both keel boats and in the School's own fleet of dinghies. Many pupils compete for the School and for local clubs and at county and national level.

Music and Drama. The Music Department incorporates practice and teaching facilities and a well-equipped recording studio. The School has a flourishing choral tradition, with opportunities for participation in a variety of choirs and instrumental groups. Concerts and musical plays are performed in both Senior and Prep Schools, and concert tours abroad have taken place in recent years. Full-length plays are produced each year by both Senior and Prep Schools, and special attention is given in the English lessons of the younger forms to speaking, lecturing and acting. Musical Theatre is a particular strength. The School has its own Performing Arts Centre and a School Poet. In 2021 one of our music scholars won the Keyboard section of the BBC Young Musician.

Activities. Pupils are expected to take part in extracurricular activities and there is a wide range to choose from, including the Combined Cadet Force, Duke of Edinburgh's Award scheme, a flourishing debating and public speaking programme, riding, art and design clubs, sports clubs, numerous trips and the opportunity for exchange visits. The school is particularly proud of the number of pupils undertaking Gold DofE.

Boarding. Boarding for both boys and girls is available from Year 6. Full, weekly and flexi boarding options are available in two boarding houses in the school grounds.

Fees per term (from September 2023). Tuition: Foundation Stage – please see School website; Pre-Prep £3,128–£4,415; Prep School £5,358; Senior School £5,542.

Boarding (inc. tuition): Prep/Senior School: £12,099–£12,283 (full), £10,766–£10,950 (weekly).

Rates are for payment by Direct Debit.

Scholarships and Bursaries. Scholarships may be awarded on merit to external or internal candidates for entry at 11+, 13+ and 16+. All scholarships open up bursaries, which are means-tested.

Charitable status. Ryde School is a Registered Charity, number 307409. The aims and objectives of the Charity are the education of boys and girls.

Governors:
Chairman: Mr C Lees
Vice-Chairman: Dr M Legg
Hereditary Governor: Mr A McIsaac
Chair of Finance & General Purposes: Mrs D Haig-Thomas
Chair of Education Committee: Mr P Hamilton
Mr A Crawford
Ms C Doerries, KC
Mrs M Esfandiary
Mrs Caroline Jacobs (*Safeguarding and Staff Liaison*)
Mrs J Wallace-Dutton
Mr P Weeks (*Health and Safety Committee*)
Mr G Whitefield

Clerk to the Governors: Mrs S Webb

***Head Master*: Mr W Turner**, BA Hons, PGCE

Deputy Head (*Boarding, Staffing & Enrichment*): Mr A Daville, MA Oxon, QTS
Deputy Head (*Safeguarding*): Mrs J Harding, BSc Hons, PGCE
Deputy Head (*Academic*): Dr G Speller, BSc, MPhil, PhD Cantab
Head of the Senior School: Mr P R Moore, MA, BSc

Head of Prep: Mr E Marsden, BSc Hons
Head of Pre-Prep: Mrs E Willetts, BA, PGCE
Finance Director: Mrs R Kennedy, BSc
Director of Learning: Mr D Shapland, MEd
Head of Sixth Form: Mr M J Windsor, BSc
Head of Pastoral Care: Miss C B Vince, BA Hons, PGCE
Assistant Head (Academic): Miss G S Stenning, BA Hons, PGCE
Head of Section 7–9: Mr M Whillier, BSc, QTS
Head of Year 7: Mrs Rebecca Daville MA Oxon, PGCE
Head of Years 8 & 9: Mrs P Ball, BA
Head of Section 10 & 11: Miss J Dyer, BA

Senior Teachers:

Mr A Jackson, BA, PGCE, NPQH (*Head of Modern Languages*)
Mr P Pavlou, BA Hons, PGCE (*Head of Group 5, Mathematics*)

§ *Part-time*

Senior School Teaching Staff:

Mr M Alderton, MPhys (*Centenary Housemaster, Physics*)
Mr L Attrill, MBE, MEng, Pg Dl, PGCE (*Head of Chine, Physics*)
Mr F Bagnall, BSc, PGCE (*Director of Sport & Fitness, PE, Head of Rugby*)
Mrs P Ball, BA Hons (*Head of Years 8 & 9, English*)
Ms K E Bishop, BSc, BA Hons (*Head of Psychology, Science*)
Mrs N Broughton, BA Hons, MA, PGCE (*Head of Art*)
§Miss S Broyé, BA, MA, PGCE (*Languages, CCF Contingent*)
Mr T Bull, BA (*Head of Academic Drama, Dance Live, Theatre Manager*)
Mrs P Bussell (*Teacher of PE & Girls Games, Assistant to Head of Pastoral Care/PE*)
Miss V Cave, MA, PGCE (*History*)
Mr M G Chalmers, BSc Hons (*Head of Chemistry, Rowing*)
Mrs S Chapman BSc Hons, PGCE (*Mathematics*)
Mr J C Comben, BA Hons (*Head of History, Bronze Duke of Edinburgh's Award*)
Mr A Daville, MA Oxon, QTS (*Deputy Head (Boarding, Staffing & Enrichment), Physics*)
§Mrs R Daville MA Oxon, PGCE (*Head of Year 7, English*)
Mr T Dumbach, AB Harvard Hons, MSt Oxon (*i/c Latin, US University Entrance, Scholarship*)
Miss G Dye, BTEC, PE (*Sports Coach, Head of Football, Girls Cricket*)
Miss J A Dyer, BA (*Head of Section 10 & 11, Languages, i/c Spanish*)
Mr H Edwards, BSc Hons, PGCE (*Millfield Housemaster, i/c Academic PE*)
Dr Flaherty, MA Hons, MPhil, PGCE, PhD (*i/c Politics/MUN*)
Dr B Foreman, BSc Hons, PhD, PGCE (*Head of Science*)
Mr A M Graham, BA, HNTD (*Mathematics*)
§Mrs N Green-Appleton, BSc, MSc (*Science*)
Ms M Grice (*Languages*)
§Ms H Ham, MSc, PGCE (*Mathematics, Psychology*)
Mrs Jemma Harding, BSc Hons, PGCE (*DSL, Deputy Head (Pastoral), Psychology*)
§Mrs K Hayter, BA Hons, PGCE (*Geography, Politics, Classics*)
§Mr J Henson, BA Hons, DipHE (*Music*)
Mr M Hooper, BA, MA, PGCE (*Head of Economics & Business, BTEC Quality Nominee*)
Mr Richard Hughes, BSc, PGCE (*Geography*)
Mr A Jackson, BA, PGCE, NPQH (*Head of Modern Languages Faculty, Gold DofE, Senior Teacher – ECTs & PGCE*)
Mr A Johnston, BA Hons (*Head of Computer Science*)
Ms E C Jones, BA Hons, PGCE (*English*)
Ms J Jones, BSc, MA (*Head of Learning Support, Geography*)
§Miss A Lengersdorf, BA (*Languages, i/c Cookery*)
Miss M Lopez-Vilar, BA Hons, PGCE, QTS (*Languages*)
Mrs C Manser, BSc Hons, PTLLS (*Director of Sailing, Economics & Business Studies*)
Mr J McCormack (*Sports Coach*)
Mr P R Moore, MA, BSc (*Head of Senior School, Deputy DSL, Mathematics*)
Ms A J Newman, BA Hons, PGCE (*i/c Mandarin*)
Mr Alastair Nye, BA Hons, QTS (*Mathematics*)
Mr M Osbourne, BA Hons, MA (*Design & Technology Technician*)
Mrs L E O'Sullivan, BSc Ed Hons (*Head of Trinity, Mathematics*)
Mr J Parry (*Graduate Teacher, Music & Sport*)
Mr P Pavlou, BA Hons, PGCE (*Senior Teacher – Timetable, Mathematics*)
Ms E Penner, BA Hons, PGCE (*Head of English*)
§Ms R Perkins, MA (*ESL/SEN*)
Dr Marie Pointer, BSc Hons, PGCE (*Science*)
Miss Poppy Price, BA Hons, PGCE (*English/Learning Support*)
§Miss J Rann, BA, PGCE (*Art*)
Mrs J Ratcliff, BA Hons, PGCE (*Art*)
Ms C Rose, BA Hons (*Head of Design Technology*)
Mr D Shapland, MEd (*Director of Learning, IB Coordinator, RE, TOK, Director of Studies – Sixth Form*)
Dr G R Speller, BSc, MPhil, PhD Cantab (*Deputy Head Academic*)
Mrs P Spibey-Dodd (*Games Coach*)
Miss A Starling, BA Hons, PGCE (*Head of Geography*)
Miss G S Stenning, BA Hons, PGCE (*Assistant Head Academic*)
Mr P G Swann, BSc Hons, PGCE (*Head of Physics*)
Mrs Begona Tarrago (*Spanish Language Assistant*)
Miss Beatriz Teotónio-Pedrosa, MSc, PGCE (*Science*)
Mr C G S Trevallion, BSc (*Head of Biology, Duke of Edinburgh's Award Coordinator*)
Mr W Turner, BA Hons, PGCE Head Master
Mrs R F Tweddle, IPGCSE, GTCL, LTCL (*Head of Music, Choral Director*)
Miss C Verleure, BA, PGCE (*Head of Chine, Languages, i/c French*)
Miss C Vince, BA Hons, PGCE (*EPQ Coordinator, Head of Pastoral Care, English*)
Mrs L L Waldron, BA Hons, MEd, PGCE (*2nd in Dept, Mathematics, Internal Exams*)
Mr G Watson, BA Hons, QTS (*History*)
§Mrs J J Whillier, BSc, QTS (*Mathematics*)
Mr M Whillier, BSc, QTS (*Head of Section 7–9, Chemistry*)

Mrs Y Wiggins, PGCE, (*Languages, Extended Essay Coordinator, Scholarship, i/c German*)
§Mr J Willetts, BSc (*Head of Religious Studies, Economics, Careers & HE Advisor*)
Mr M J Windsor, BSc (*Head of Sixth Form, Geography*)
Mr A Woodward (*Cricket Professional*)
Mr C Youlten, BA, PGCE (*Head of Arts Faculty, Performance, Drama*)
Mrs W Youlten, BA Hons, PGCE (*2nd in Dept, English, Assistant Head of Sixth Form*)
Ms H Young, BSc Hons, MA, PGCE (*Head of Hanover, Chemistry*)

Prep School:

Head of Prep: Mr E Marsden, BSc Hons

Ms C Armstrong
Mrs E Dickson, BA Hons, PGCE
§Mrs S Flux, BA
Mr A Gallerwood, BA, Hons, QTS
Mrs G Gallerwood, BA, Hons, QTS
Mrs J Jeffery
§Ms L Kirkby, OND
Mrs M Langshaw, BA Hons, PGCE
Mrs G Marsden, BA Hons
Mr J Mathrick, BSc Hons, PGCE, QTS
Mr N McCall
§Miss O Newnham, BEd Hons
Mrs E Shaw, BA Hons
Miss R Shaw, BEd Hons
§Mrs T Simons, BEd
Mrs M Walker, BMus Hons, MMus, PGCE

Nursery and Pre-Prep:

Head: Mrs E Willetts, BA Hons, PGCE (*DSL*)

Mrs C Callaghan, Diploma in Montessori Early Years
Miss K Clarke, BA Hons, PGCE, NNEB
Ms P Evans, BEd Hons
Ms E Cooke
Mrs S Hickmott, AMI TQUK Level 2
Mrs L Hughes, BA Hons, QTS
Mrs S Lea, NTD, CPHCC
Miss V Lovell, BEd Hons
Mrs C O'Donnell, BSc Hons, MSc Res, PhD
Mrs P Ong, DPP
Ms T Squire, NNEB
Miss A Townson, NVQ3
Ms V Winter

St Albans School

Abbey Gateway, St Albans, Herts AL3 4HB
Tel: 01727 855521
email: hm@st-albans.herts.sch.uk
website: www.st-albans.herts.sch.uk
X/Twitter: @SASHerts
Facebook: @stalbansschoolherts
Instagram: @sasherts
LinkedIn: /school/st-albans-school

The origins of the School date back to the monastic foundation of 948, and today, St Albans School is a day school of just over 900 pupils. Girls have been admitted into the Sixth Form since 1991. Whilst maintaining a high standard of academic achievement, the School aims to foster the development of talent and responsibility, along with the fulfilment of individual potential.

Buildings. For more than three centuries, the School was located in the Lady Chapel of the Abbey. It moved in 1871 into the Monastery Gatehouse, a building of considerable historic and architectural interest, where teaching still continues. There were extensive additions made to the campus during the twentieth century, which in recent years has been extended significantly by the purchase of a very large building on an adjacent site and its conversion to a superb Art school, Sixth Form Centre and a suite of classrooms and the building of a Sports Centre.

The School's new Mathematics and CCF building, the Corfield Building, opened in January 2020, which, as well as significantly improving the home of the School's ever-popular CCF unit, provides the Maths Department with a building worthy of its outstanding results. The Corfield building houses a brand new CCF shooting range and office space on the lower ground floor, and a bespoke two-storey Maths Faculty on the upper ground and first floors.

Additionally, the School's new Computer laboratories opened in September 2020 and new, open plan Science laboratories opened in September 2021 in the area vacated by the Maths Department.

The Music Department moved into a brand new Music School in 2018, which includes a new classroom, a Chamber Music performing space complete with a Steinway Grand piano, a state-of-the-art recording studio, nine practice rooms and a large ensemble rehearsal room.

The School has close historical and musical ties with the Cathedral and Abbey Church of St Alban. By permission of the Dean, assembly takes place twice weekly in the nave, where the School Choir sings regularly and an annual concert is performed in collaboration with St Albans High School for Girls.

Admission. The majority of boys enter at the age of 11 or 13. There is a further admission at 16+ into the Sixth Form when girls are also admitted; candidates are accepted occasionally at other ages. For the main entry at age 11, an Assessment Day is held at the School each year in January, and parents of interested candidates can find more information on the School's website, along with online registration. Candidates at age 13 enter through the 12+ and 13+ Assessments. Unconditional offers of places are made at 12+ in the June of Year 7, with the remainder of places for Year 9 being offered in the January of Year 8 through the 13+ Assessment. Ideally, parents should apply to the School at least 2 years in advance for entry at 13.

Pupils are admitted only at the start of the Autumn Term unless there are exceptional circumstances.

Fees per term (2023–2024). £7,732.

Bursaries and scholarships. Assistance with tuition fees may be available in cases of proven need from the School's own endowments. Such Bursaries are conditional upon an annual means test and will be awarded according to a balance of merit and need.

Numerous Academic scholarships are awarded on academic merit at each age of entry. At 11+ entry, Choral, Music and Art scholarships are available. At 13+ entry, Art, Music, Sport and Academic scholarships are available. At 16+ entry to the Sixth Form, Academic and Music scholarships are available to external candidates only.

Curriculum. The curriculum for the first three years is largely a common one and covers a wide range. All pupils study Maths, English, Biology, Chemistry, Physics, History, Geography, Religious Studies, French and Latin. Students choose an additional two languages from German, Mandarin Chinese and Spanish. The timetable also includes Art, Drama, Music, Computer Science and Design and Technology. At GCSE Maths, English Language and Literature, Biology, Chemistry and Physics are compulsory subjects and pupils have four further options. In the Sixth Form, pupils study four subjects at A Level from the start of the Lower Sixth Form. Most students will continue with three of these chosen subjects in the Upper Sixth Form, along with an Extended Project. The vast majority of Sixth Form leavers go on to Russell Group or similar universities.

Co-curricular activities cover a wide range and there are 200 clubs and societies to cater for most interests. Musical activities are many and varied and include regular concerts and recitals by the School Choir, Choral Society and ensembles and by professional artists. Plays are produced three or four times a year, and there is ample opportunity for creative work in the Art school and the Design Technology Centre. There is a strong contingent of the CCF with sections representing the Army and RAF. Many pupils join the Duke of Edinburgh's Award scheme and do various forms of social service and conservation work in and around St Albans. The School owns a Field Centre in the Brecon Beacons in Wales, which is used for curricular and co-curricular trips during term time and school holidays.

Games. The School competes at a high level in Rugby, Hockey, Cricket, Cross-country, Swimming, Tennis, Athletics, Netball and Lacrosse, in addition to a range of other sports including Football, Rugby Sevens, Shooting, Basketball, Badminton, Golf, Skiing and Table Tennis. The School's Sports Centre offers a swimming pool, sports hall, fitness centre and studio and climbing wall. The School also owns the Woollam Playing Fields, comprising an Astroturf all-weather pitch and a superb state-of-the-art pavilion, 6 laser levelled rugby pitches, 7 football pitches and 8 cricket squares (5 grass and 3 all-weather). A video of Woollams' facilities can be viewed on the School's website. There are good links with Saracens RUFC, whose training is based at the Woollam playing fields.

Pupils are transported to Woollam's for Games and Co-Curricular sport daily and the School also utilises local facilities in the adjacent Verulamium Park for athletics, cross country and golf. Within the games programme the school looks to provide competitive sport options alongside more activities focused on engagement and encouraging lifelong leisure participation.

Charitable status. St Albans School is Registered Charity, number 1092932, and a Company Limited by Guarantee, number 4400125.

Board of Governors:
Chairman: Mr N Osborn, MA Oxon
Vice Chairs: Miss A Philpott and Mrs C Pomfret, MA Oxon, ACA
Lt Col M W S Cawthorne, RM (*retd.*)
Mrs F Lightowler
Prof J P Luzio, MA, PhD, FMedSci
Mr S Majumdar, BA
Ms C Millington, BSc
Mr N C Moore, LLB, MA, CNAA
Mr C Oglethorpe, BCom
Mr M E Punt, MA Oxon, MSc, PGCE
Mr B C Walker, BA, PGCE, CELTA
Mr A Woodgate, BA, MRICS
Advisory Panel:
Mr P G Brown
Mr O King, MRICS
Ms B Mehta-Parmar
Mrs C Preston, BSocSc
Mr P M Rattle, BA
Mr L Sinclair, BSc, MRICS
Mr M Sutton, BA, FCA, FRSA
Bursar and Clerk to the Governors: Mr R J Hepper, MA Cantab, FCA

Staff:

***Headmaster*: Mr J W J Gillespie**, MA Cantab, FRSA
Second Master: Ms M Jones, BSc
Deputy Head – Academic: Mrs V J Saunders, BA, MEd Cantab
Deputy Head – Staff: Mr G D Nichols, BA, MEd
Head of Sixth Form: Mr G J Walker, MA Cantab, FRSA
Head of Middle School: Mr C C Johnston, MA, FRGS
Assistant Head – Co-Curricular and Head of Third Form: Mr G S Burger, HDip Ed SA, MEd
Head of Lower School: Mrs R C Harris, MA Oxon
Assistant Head – Higher Education and Careers: Dr R G Hacksley, BA, FRSA
Assistant Head – Data and Curriculum: Dr J H Saunders, MA Cantab, PGDip GSMD
Assistant Head – Safeguarding and Wellbeing: Mrs H J Robertson, BEng
Director of Marketing, Admissions and Communications: Mrs J L Morrison, BA
A full staff list is available on our website: www.st-albans.herts.sch.uk/about-us

St Aloysius' College

45 Hill Street, Glasgow G3 6RJ
Tel: 0141 332 3190
email: mail@staloysius.org
website: www.staloysius.org
X/Twitter: @StAlsGlasgow
Facebook: @StAlsGlasgow
LinkedIn: /st-aloysius'-college

Motto: *ad majora natus sum* (I was born for greater things).

Founded in 1859, St Aloysius' College is a Catholic school for boys and girls aged 3 to 18. The school is fully co-educational at all stages (Kindergarten to S6) with a roll drawn from a wide catchment area in and around Glasgow.

As Scotland's only Jesuit school, St Aloysius' College shares a tradition of educational excellence that is almost 500 years old. It is part of a worldwide network of schools and universities whose mission is the "*Improvement in living and learning for the greater glory of God and the common good*" (*St Ignatius Loyola*).

The College creates an environment that is underpinned by mutual respect, friendship, and care for others. It prides itself on upholding a clear set of religious, moral, and spiritual values.

Five Jesuit values underpin life at the College: Delight in Learning, Personal Excellence, Make a Difference, Care and Respect, and Faith and Values.

Great importance is placed upon educating the whole person, with pupils encouraged to develop confidence, leadership, and teamwork through sport, outdoor activity, music, drama, and many other activities.

Buildings. St Aloysius' College is located in the historic Garnethill area of central Glasgow with additional facilities in Millerston. The College's main Garnethill campus is made up of a number of school buildings and is well served by public transport.

The College campus is varied, providing examples of both award-winning modern architecture and construction, as well as historic listed buildings. The original Jesuit residence, now part of the school, is a listed building, as is The Mount where Art and Music are taught, and the magnificent St Aloysius' Church which the College uses regularly.

Two further additions to the St Aloysius' College campus, The Junior School and The Clavius Building used for Maths, Science and Computing, have attracted widespread critical acclaim. The buildings have been the subject of great praise and won many architectural awards, including the Best New Building in Scotland 2004.

The Kindergarten building is located beside the Junior School and is the ideal place for younger pupils to learn and play.

Completed in 2017, the state-of-the-art sports complex is situated adjacent to the original College building. It comprises a large games hall, dance studio, cardio and weights room, viewing gallery, and a café.

Curriculum. The Junior School and lower years of the Senior School follow internally devised courses that are suitable for academically able children. All Junior School pupils study specialist subjects such as science, art, music, IT, and languages from Kindergarten and P1. National 5 is taken at the end of S4 and pupils take five Highers in S5. A wide range of Advanced Highers and other courses are available in S6.

Music and the Arts. At St Aloysius' College, pupils are taught the art of self-expression through the development of the imaginative, the affective, and the creative. These three elements of Jesuit education are essential to the formation of the whole person. Art is taught from Junior School by specialist teachers and there is an established music department with instrumental lessons from P3, orchestras, and the unique Schola Choral Programme.

Sport and Outdoor Education. St Aloysius' College offers an outstanding programme of sport and physical education. Rugby and Hockey remain the College's principal sports from P6 to U18 level. Cross-country and athletics are also offered at all levels, while Senior School pupils have the opportunity to represent the college in basketball, football, and swimming.

The College also offers opportunities to learn wider Outdoor Education and pupils have enjoyed great success in the Duke of Edinburgh's Award programme.

Co-Curricular. As well as Music and the Arts, and Sport, St Aloysius' College has an extensive co-curricular programme designed to encourage personal excellence and a delight in learning. This begins at Junior School, where children can participate in the likes of STEM club, and continues in Senior School where pupils are involved in Public Speaking and Justice and Peace to name but a few.

Admission. Entrance assessments are held in January and informal meetings with parents form part of the application process at all stages. Pupils from Primary 4 upwards will also be asked to send in a 'Your Green Blazer Story' as part of their application.

Fees per annum (2023–2024). £11,421–£14,976.

Bursaries are available on consideration of parents' income.

Charitable status. St Aloysius' College is a Registered Charity, number SC042545.

Board of Governors:
Fr Peter Gallagher SJ (*College President*)
Dr Isabelle Cullen (*Chair of Governors*)
Fr Simon Bishop SJ
Mrs Tina Campbell
Mrs Natalie Finnegan
Ms Nicola Gallen
Mr Greg Hannah
Ms Sophie Harkins
Mr Ben McLeish
Mrs Jennifer Quinn
Mr Damian Ralph
Mrs Catherine Teenan
Mrs Angela Vickers

Bursar and Clerk to the Board: Mrs Kathleen Sweeney, FCCA

***Head Teacher*: Mr Patrick Doyle**

PA to the Head Teacher: Mrs Monica Harper

St Bede's College

Alexandra Park, Manchester M16 8HX

Tel: 0161 226 3323 (Senior School)
0161 226 7156 (Preparatory School)
email: headteacher@sbcm.co.uk
prepschool@sbcm.co.uk
admissions@sbcm.co.uk
website: www.sbcm.co.uk
X/Twitter: @StBedesCollege
Facebook: @St-Bedes-College-Manchester
LinkedIn: /Bedian-Alumni

Motto: '*Nunquam otio torpebat*'

St Bede's is a Catholic HMC Independent Co-educational Grammar School welcoming Catholic and non-Catholic children from Nursery to Sixth Form. We are celebrating over 140 years of history set in a magnificent Grade II listed building in the heart of Manchester.

The College is widely recognised for the calibre of its students who leave as well-rounded, polite and articulate young adults who are academically successful and ready to meet the demands of life at university and beyond.

Each year there are one hundred coveted places available ensuring each student is guaranteed individual attention and personalised support.

We believe passionately in the importance of traditional family values and in encouraging every pupil to develop genuine friendships. Each child in the College is known and valued in a community where there are no barriers to learning. Whilst academic success is a high priority, focus on developing lifelong learning is of greater significance. Ultimately we want to develop young men and women who are constructive and compassionate members of our society.

Admission. Children may join the College at different stages in their academic journey, where children can enjoy an all-through education, joining our co-educational Nursery for 3 year olds before moving up to our co-educational Prep School. and then on to the main College. It is assumed that all Prep pupils will transfer automatically into the Senior part of the College.

The College Entrance Examination for external candidates wishing to join the College at 11+ takes place in January each year. Details of the examination may be obtained from our Admissions team, email: admissions@sbcm.co.uk. There is also direct entry to the Sixth Form. Interviews are held from the beginning of the Easter Term.

Curriculum. Curriculum provision is constantly monitored to ensure the best possible educational provision for all students.

The Lower School curriculum offers the core subjects of English, Mathematics, Sciences and RE together with Latin, Computer Science, Technology, History, Geography and PE/Games and tutor time. In the Middle School four subjects are chosen from French, German, Spanish, Latin, Classical Civilisation, Economics, Business, Computer Science, Design & Technology, Art and Music for a one-year course to further enhance GCSE options.

At GCSE/IGCSE, ten subjects are taken in varied combinations supported by a programme of academic enrichment.

Students must achieve 7 GCSE passes (grades 9–4) to be admitted to the Sixth Form. At A Level approximately 23 different subjects are currently on offer. Many students also opt to study the increasingly popular Extended Project Qualification. Flexibility ensures that any desired combination of subjects can be offered.

A strong learning support department ensures that all pupils fulfil their educational potential.

Co-Curriculum. There is an extensive weekly programme of extra-curricular provision that complements learning from outside the classroom and all pupils are encouraged to try new activities or extend their leadership by organising new ones for their peers.

Our goal is to develop wider skills for lifelong learning as well as helping to prepare students for the major ideas, innovations and challenges that they face in a rapidly-changing society. Bedians are confident in their ability to make a difference once they have left the College fully prepared for top universities and the world of work.

Fees per term (2023–2024). Senior School £4,436.34, Prep School £3,175.

Charitable status. St Bede's College Limited is a Registered Charity, number 700808. Its aims and objectives are the advancement and provision of education on behalf of St Bede's College.

Governance: The School is governed by a Board of Trustees. The Chairman of the Board is Mr Xavier Bosch.

***Headteacher*: Mrs M Kemp**, BA Hons, UNED

Academic Deputy Head: Mr T Sanders, BA Hons

Assistant Heads:
Strategy & Innovation: Mr F Calmaestra, BA Hons, MA, MBA, MSc
Safeguarding & Ethos: Mrs C Boylan, BA Hons
Academic: Mr C S Wright, BSc Hons

Head of Sixth Form: Dr Anne McMonagle, BA Hons, MA, PhD

Preparatory School:
Head of Prep: Mrs C Hunt, BEd Hons

St Benedict's School

54 Eaton Rise, Ealing, London W5 2ES

Tel: 020 8862 2000 (School Office)
020 8862 2010 (Headmaster's Office)
020 8862 2254 (Admissions)
020 8862 2183 (Finance Director)
email: seniorschool@stbenedicts.org.uk
admissions@stbenedicts.org.uk
website: www.stbenedicts.org.uk
X/Twitter: @stbenedicts
Facebook: @StBenedictsSchool
Instagram: @StBenedictsSchool
LinkedIn: /st-benedicts-school

Motto: *a minimis incipe*

St Benedict's is London's leading independent Catholic co-educational school, situated in leafy Ealing. The School is a successful blend of the traditional and the progressive; proud of its heritage but also forward thinking and innovative. A seamless education which can begin at the age of 3 and continue through to the Sixth Form, in a caring, happy community, enables our pupils to thrive.

Academic standards are high: inspirational teaching, tutorial guidance and exceptional pastoral care are at the heart of the education we offer, allowing children to develop their full potential.

The Junior School and Nursery provide a supportive and vibrant environment in which to learn. Sharing excellent facilities with the Senior School and a programme of cross-curricular activities help ease the transition at 11+ to the Senior School, which is on the same site.

At St Benedict's, there is a vital focus on personal development, and our outstanding co-curricular programme helps pupils to thrive by enabling them to find and develop their unique gifts and talents. St Benedict's has a distinguished sporting tradition, and Music and Drama are both excellent, with a strong choral tradition and termly drama productions.

We encourage principled leadership, resilience and character in our pupils, and promote the Christian values of integrity, fairness and generosity to others. This is a hallmark of the School and there could be no better way of equipping young people for the future.

Recent developments include a new Nursery and Pre-Prep Department, providing our youngest pupils with a first-rate learning environment. This is in addition to a new Sixth Form Centre and Art Department.

St Benedict's School is unique. Come and visit, and see what we have to offer.

Fees per term (2023–2024). Senior School: £6,969, Junior School: £5,914, Pre-Prep: £5,321, Nursery: £3,850–£5,789.

Charitable status. St Benedict's School Ealing is a Registered Charity, number 1148512, and a Charitable Company Limited by Guarantee, registration number 8093330.

Governing Body: The Governing Board of St Benedict's School

***Headmaster*: Mr Joe Smith**

Deputy Heads:
Ms F Allen
Mr L Ramsden

Bursar: Mrs C Bedwin

Headmaster's PA: Mrs R Wynne

Registrar: Mrs L Pepper

St Columba's College

King Harry Lane, St Albans, Hertfordshire AL3 4AW

Tel: 01727 855185
email: admissions@stcolumbascollege.org
website: www.stcolumbascollege.org
X/Twitter: @StColumbasHerts
Facebook: @StColumbasCollege
Instagram: @stcolumbascollege
LinkedIn: /school/stcolumbascollege

Motto: '*Cor ad Cor Loquitur*'

St Columba's College is located twenty-five miles from central London in the Cathedral City of St Albans, Hertfordshire. SCC is a thriving 4–18 Catholic, independent, coeducational day school comprising 800 pupils.

Originally founded in 1939, the school was re-established by the Brothers of the Sacred Heart (United States) in 1955. Its educational philosophy emanates from the traditions and religious values of the order. The College welcomes children and families of all faiths as well as those of no particular persuasion. The school prides itself on its family, community ethos, engaging with parents and pupils on a personal level, so they are known, treasured, and loved. It is a welcoming, dynamic, forward thinking school. Formation of the whole person is at the root of its educational ethos and mission.

Columba's is an academic and aspirational school with a mixed ability intake devoted to scholarship and the holistic development of each individual child. Its pastoral provision is exemplary. Academically, the College has exceptional value-added results, with pupils largely performing beyond their predicted grades particularly at GCSE. The College challenges students to be the best they can be in intellectual achievement and their person and character. It has just undergone an ISI Inspection, in May 2022, and judged in every respect as excellent. *"Quality of pupils' academic and other achievements is excellent"* ISI Report

Whilst confident that this will continue to be the case, the College is now embarking on a significant teaching and learning development in the phased introduction over two years of 1:1 devices using surface pro laptops to be completed for September 2023. The College is transitioning from an all-boys establishment to one that is coeducational, and currently has girls in the Prep school, a small number in Form 1 (yr7) in the senior and with a significant cohort in Lower and Upper 6th. Our hope is that those who enter the College will remain with us until 18.

We aim to provide an educational environment which will motivate and captivate students so that they develop a love of learning and enquiry, becoming truly independent learners who take control of their educational pathways. *"Pupils have strong study skills and demonstrate excellent attitudes to learning."* ISI Report

Individuals are encouraged to regard challenge as healthy and something to manage and control rather than something to prevent growth. The development of a strong moral compass is also a significant priority as part of the holistic education. Individuals develop a *"strong understanding of right and wrong... develop a deep moral compass"* ISI Report

The College's atmosphere, in which healthy relationships are based on respect and the three Cs of Courage, Courtesy and Compassion, is underpinned by the belief that if children are happy then they will be successful. They are encouraged to take full advantage of the opportunities afforded them, directed to engage in activities and interests to extend their experiences and skills within and beyond the curriculum.

This diet is wide and engaging whether immersed in academic research, participating in charitable activities, supporting local community and international initiatives, acting, playing music in various ensembles and choral activities, involvement in the multitude of clubs and societies, or by engaging in the wide range of sporting activities, our children are challenged to extend themselves and learn by experiencing the breadth of in school life. Every individual is required to contribute to this vibrant community in action and spirit.

Columba's believes in traditional values, underpinned by its religious roots of Catholicism. It is determined to be forward looking and engaging to the 21st Century parent and pupil. We have a diverse intake of pupils of mixed ability, valuing pupils and staff, of differing race, sexualities, religious persuasion, gender, learning needs and academic strengths. One of the core strands of the success of the College is that of community, and unity, irrespective of individual uniqueness whilst respecting those characteristics and talents that make us different.

Students develop a *"deep spiritual understanding and a profound appreciation of non-materialistic aspects of life."* ISI Report

Columba's values inclusion because of the benefits of roundedness that this can bring to an individual's life. In this way we develop individuals who are confident but never arrogant about themselves and their life chances. *"Students develop notably strong levels of self-belief and esteem."* ISI Report

The College stands in its own grounds overlooking the picturesque St Albans Abbey. In recent years, extensive improvements have been made to include a state of the art Science Centre, English suite, Music and Drama facilities, a spacious and bright Art Department and a complete modernisation of the Sixth Form Centre. The Prep has upgraded the Science and Laboratory provision, the soft-play and playground and reconfigured and upgraded teaching classrooms to enhance the learning environment. Improvement to the sports facilities continues with A Multi Use Grass area (MUGA), an Artificial Grass Pitch (AGP) and seeded grass pitch coming into play for April 2023.

Entry. St Columba's College admits pupils from 4–18, and there are currently 800 students in the Prep and Senior School. Whilst the main entry point for the Prep tends to be Reception, we welcome applications throughout the year, places gained being dependent on assessment and suitability. The main entry point for the Senior school is September at 11+, by entrance test and interview, with a smaller group being offered entry at 13+. Internal and external entrants to 6th Form must have a minimum of six grades at 6 or above. Applications for places occasionally available in other year groups and times of year are welcome.

Scholarships. Academic and Music scholarships are awarded at 11+, 13+ and Lower 6th. Drama and Sports Scholarships are also available at 13+ and Lower 6th. Means-tested Bursaries are offered at all levels of entry.

The Curriculum. The Prep school follows a framework designed to implement future world skills via the Prep School Baccalaureate (learning skills trust). The Prep offers a broad curriculum providing Subject Specialism in Sport, Music, Science, Languages, ADT, Computing, and Life Skills alongside excellence in core subjects. In the senior school the curriculum is kept as broad as possible up to GCSE, pupils usually taking 9 to subjects from the traditional range of Humanities, Social Sciences, Arts, Modern Foreign Languages and Science options. There are twenty-two A Level subjects currently on offer, and the Sixth Form is complemented by an enrichment course which prepares students for extra qualifications including the Extended Project Qualification (EPQ) and Personal Finance. Oxbridge potentials are provided with support of their application by an individually tailored programme. Almost all of the Sixth Form students go on to universities including the Russell group, as well as Oxford and Cambridge, and diverse other institutions as individual choices are followed. High quality apprenticeships to prestigious companies are part of the career progression for a number.

Careers. The College has a qualified Head of Careers and Higher Education who works from a fully equipped Careers Centre using the latest technological software, search engines, and reference and application packages, to support students in discerning their career pathways. High-quality individual guidance is provided to ensure students make fully informed decisions about subject choices and university courses mindful of potential subsequent career options.

Pastoral Care. The Pastoral life and care of the students is a significant priority in ensuring that schooling is enjoyable. *"Excellent personal development."* ISI Report. Prep school care is based around their class groups whilst a House system does operate for purposes of competition. In the Senior school, the six Houses operate vertically and continue to operate in the 6th Form where the team is augmented by the Head of 6th and two Deputies. The Houses and their teams are supported by a Ministry Team. Relations between the staff and parents are open – a strength of the College – they are in regular contact with each other in monitoring the progress of the students in seeking to nurture the academic and personal talents of each individual. The College operates an age specific tailored Pastoral Programme addressing social and moral issues as well as education on health and well-being, internet safety and respond dynamically to address contemporary issues.

Sporting Provision. All students participate, and the College has a strong sporting reputation. It seeks to offer the opportunity to participate in a wide range of disciplines, promotes competition, and actively encourages high performance both in individual and team sports. A rich variety is available at all levels, including Rugby, Hockey, Basketball, Football, Tennis, Cricket, Netball, Athletics, Swimming, Cross Country, Dance and Golf. Facilities include a large gymnasium, a fully equipped fitness suite and all weather and grass pitches on site. The Sports Department makes extensive use of significant local facilities of soccer and rugby pitches, an athletics track, swimming pool and a golf course which are all immediately adjacent to the College site.

Extended and Extra-Curricular Activities. The College offers a wide variety of activities both at lunchtime and after school. These fall under the SHAPE (Service, House, Pastoral and Extra-curricular) portfolio of activities designed to engage and challenge all pupils into participation. These include clubs such as STEM, Maths Challenge, rugby, football, basketball, cricket and athletics, drama, art, chess, computing, Young Enterprise, Combined Cadet Force, Duke of Edinburgh's Award and many others, as well as a variety of academic and social clubs and charity work opportunities.

There are a number of music ensembles, including a choir, barbershop group, orchestra, flute quartet, jazz band and bell choir. Cultural, adventurous and sporting trips are part of this programme and there are strong associations and joint ventures with the Brothers schools in the United States to add to the international dimension of the opportunities. *"Students participate with obvious enthusiasm in the broad extra-curricular programme"* ISI Report

Charities & Service. Part of our ethos is a commitment to charitable giving and action. Central to this is educating the whole community to an appreciation of the differing social and economic circumstances in the world, and an engagement in the ways and means of supporting those in some way disadvantaged. Service opportunities are available at all ages and compassionate service is lived out according to the College motto of 'Cor ad Cor Loquitur' – heart speaking to heart. *"Service is a key part of the school's ethos"* ISI Report

Preparatory School. The Preparatory School is on the same site as the Senior School and shares many of its facilities. The Prep has a strong family atmosphere, providing a secure and purposeful environment in which expectations are high. It admits students by assessment into the Lower Prep and Upper Prep. In their final year, most Preparatory School pupils are offered unconditional places at St Columba's College Senior School, following recommendations by Prep School staff.

(*See also St Columba's College Preparatory School entry in IAPS section.*)

Alumni. St. Columba's College Alumni is an engaging, thriving and committed arm of the school which continues that familial engagement and strength of the College. It naturally welcomes former students, staff and governors to interact with its many social, community and networking events throughout the year. It also provides access to the College business directory to build a lifelong network of friendships and call upon Alumni members for career development. Alumni are active in charitable events, specialists talks to school members, Inspirational Days, work experience, apprenticeship placement and offer careers advice and mentoring amongst many other offerings.

Fees per term (2023–2024). Senior School £6,446, Prep 4–6 £5,502, Prep 3 £4,998, Reception–Prep 2 £4,238.

Charitable status. St Columba's College is a Registered Charity, number 1088480. It exists to provide a well-rounded Catholic education for pupils from 4–18 years of age.

Governors:
Mrs Barbara Elliot, MA Cantab (*Acting Chair*)
Mr Oli Adams, BA Hons
Br Ronald Hingle, SC, BS, MEd
Br Joseph Holthaus, MA
Br Ivy LeBlanc, SC, BS, MEd, MPS
Mrs Nicola Lloyd, BA Hons, LLB
Mrs Ruth Loveman, BSc, PGCE
Mr Stephen Watson, BA, FCA

Bursar and Clerk to the Governors: Mrs Rachel McHattie, BA Hons, ACMA

***Headmaster*: Mr Karl Guest**, MA

Deputy Head, DSL: Mrs K Marson, MA
Assistant Head (*Director of Studies*): Ms Lucy Cronin, MA
Assistant Head (*Learning, Teaching & Professional Development*): Mr Nick Hele, BA
Assistant Head (*Student Formation*): Mr J Tatham, BA
Head of Sixth Form: Mr D Waters, BA
Head of Prep: Mr Richard McCann, BA
Deputy Head of Prep: Mr K Boland, BA
Deputy Head of Prep and SENCo: Miss C Maton, BA

Administration:
Headmaster's PA: Mrs B Coakley
Head of Prep's PA: Mrs E McConachie
Bursar's PA: Mrs M Clinch
Admissions Registrar: Mrs K Dell

St Columba's School

Duchal Road, Kilmacolm, Inverclyde PA13 4AU
Tel: 01505 872238
email: admissions@st-columbas.org
website: www.st-columbas.org
X/Twitter: @StColSchool
Facebook: @stcolumbasschool
Instagram: @stcolumbasschool
LinkedIn: /st-columba-s-school-kilmacolm

Motto: *Orare Laborare Literisque Studere*

Founded in 1897, St Columba's School is a non-denominational day school for boys and girls aged 3–18 years and is renowned for its first-class education and academic excellence. Situated at the heart of Kilmacolm, yet within easy reach of the city of Glasgow and the surrounding areas, it is a forward-looking, vibrant and dynamic school.

The first thing you notice at St Columba's is the warm welcome and the strong sense of community. This is in part the result of its size where teachers know each pupil by name. Indeed, considerable effort is made to create an environment which allows the School to identify and nurture the unique talents and skills of each pupil, and encourage each one of them to realise their full potential, grow and flourish.

St Columba's success is evident not only in its excellent academic results, regularly placing St Columba's as one of the highest-achieving schools nationally, but in the impressive young people you will meet in a classroom, at an international debate, or on a rugby field: they are polite, articulate and quietly self-assured. The School combines the pursuit of academic excellence with a range of opportunity and challenge to develop self-confident and independent young people who have a strong sense of community and who will become responsible and reflective future leaders. High-quality teaching, a strong sense of belonging and the space for pupils to grow and achieve their full potential is what St Columba's offers. The School's Pipe Band is known for its success, most notably becoming World Champions in 2023 in the Novice A category.

St Columba's offers wraparound care from 7.30am to 6.00pm, financial assistance and a dedicated coach service.

Facilities. Our school campus sits within the heart of the village of Kilmacolm and easy travelling distance of Glasgow. Junior School is nestled in a woodland setting filled with light and colour and caters for our children in Early Years to Junior 6. Senior School is located a third of a mile from Junior School and caters for pupils in Transitus (J7) to Senior SVI.

Over the last 8 years we have invested £7 million to provide the Senior School Girdwood Building that houses Transitus (Primary 7), English, Languages, the Pastoral Care Suite, a Library and 13 classrooms; revamped our 6 science laboratories; and landscaped our Junior School grounds. Our most recent investment is our modern Wellbeing Centre. This new resource at the heart of the school reflects the values of St Columba's where we recognise that, for children to flourish and for staff to support them, health and wellbeing is paramount.

Sports facilities include: gym area for gymnastics and dance, large purpose-built sports hall including fitness suite, all-weather floodlit hockey/tennis ground, access to three rugby pitches and a large playing field used for athletics and cross-country running.

Curriculum. St Columba's School follows the Scottish Curriculum at all stages. Junior School pupils are taught French, music, drama and PE by specialist staff. Transitus (P7) is a transitional year with the core curriculum taught by the class teacher and science, languages, art, music and PE delivered by specialist secondary teachers. Pupils in Senior IV are presented for National 5 examinations followed by Higher Grade and Advanced Higher Grade examinations in Senior V and Senior VI.

Games. Rugby, hockey, tennis, athletics, badminton, gymnastics, swimming, volleyball, basketball, soccer, dance (girls), orienteering. Optional: netball, squash, cricket, golf, skiing/snowboarding, curling, street dance, weight-training.

Extra-Curricular. Throughout the whole school there are approximately 60 clubs and societies. They range from athletics and orchestra, gardening and science, STEM and enterprise, debating and Lego club, through to coding and philosophy covering most letters of the alphabet. There is truly something for every child. Individual tuition in a wide range of instruments is available. Public performances and school shows are arranged on a regular basis.

Our progressive outdoor education programme allows pupils to develop resilience and the ability to problem solve; and learn to work as part of a team in some of Scotland's most beautiful locations. We are proud to be sector leaders running one of the most successful DofE Award programmes in Scotland, with Mini Duke and Junior Duke Awards offered to children in Junior 2–6 whilst Transitus and Senior I pupils take part in the John Muir Award. Over 90% of Senior III pupils enrol in the Bronze Award each year.

There is a very strong tradition of fundraising for charity and community service within the School.

St Columba's has strong links with schools in France.

Organisation. The school is organised into four Houses for both pastoral and competitive purposes. Each house has a Head of House as well as a pupil Captain and Vice-Captain. Career guidance is supported by an external adviser.

Admission. Entry to St Columba's is by a combination of entry test, interview and, where applicable, a report from the applicant's previous school. Open events are held in November and entrance tests are held in January. The main entry points are Early Years, Junior 1 and Transitus, however, pupils are taken in at other stages as places become available.

Fees per annum (2023–2024). Early Years 1,140 hours of free EYC in partnership with Inverclyde Council, J1 & J2 £11,335, J3 £12,410, J4 £13,190, J5 & J6 £13,865, Transitus–Senior VI £15,610.

A number of bursary places, ranging from 10–100% of fees are available.

Charitable status. St Columba's School is a Registered Charity, number SC012598. It exists to provide education for pupils.

Chairman of the Board of Governors: Mr D Girdwood, DL, BSc, MEd, SQH

***Rector*: Mrs V Reilly**, MA Edinburgh
Depute Rector: Mr M J McLaughlin, MA Greenwich, BA Thames
Depute Rector: Ms A Berry, BA MRes Kent, MEd Buckingham
Depute Rector: Ms J Fulton, MA Stirling, MA Durham
Depute Rector – Junior School: Mr Allan McKay, BEd Strathclyde
Bursar: Mrs U Telfer
Admissions Registrar: Mrs L Mathie
Rector's PA: Mrs A Maxwell

St Dunstan's College

Stanstead Road, London SE6 4TY

Tel: 020 8516 7200
email: collegeoffice@stdunstans.org.uk
admissions@stdunstans.org.uk
website: www.stdunstans.org.uk
X/Twitter: @StDunstansColl
Facebook: @StDunstansColl
Instagram: @stdunstanscollege
LinkedIn: /st-dunstans-college/

Motto: '*Albam Exorna*'

The College was founded in the 15th Century in the Parish of St Dunstan-in-the-East, part of the Tower Ward of the City of London. In 1888 the school was re-founded in Catford, South East London. It became co-educational in 1994.

Buildings. The College is located on a 15-acre site three minutes' walk from Catford and Catford Bridge railway stations. Facilities include an imposing Great Hall, a well-equipped Learning Resource Centre, Performing Arts Centre, three state-of-the-art ICT suites and a brand new Junior School, STEM block and Sixth Form Centre which opened in 2021. The College celebrated the opening of the Performing Arts Centre in April 2022. The Performing Arts Centre is home to all Music, Drama and the Performing Arts departments and features large studios, practice rooms, LAMDA spaces and a MAC classroom for musical tech. The Performing Arts Centre also is home to the school's 170-seat theatre which stages large-scale productions, conferences and community events. There is also a Wellness Centre for physical and mental first aid, counselling, chaplaincy and peer mentoring. To complement extensive playing fields on site, St Dunstan's has a sports hall, fully-equipped fitness rooms, floodlit netball/tennis courts and an indoor swimming pool, along with a 20-acre sports facility on nearby Canadian Avenue called the Jubilee Ground. This site provides playing fields, multi-use games areas, a gym, dance studio and function rooms, further enhancing the sporting and other facilities available to its pupils and the wider community. The College also has two climbing and bouldering walls.

One is a lead climbing wall made from real rock, including crack and abseil ledges. The second, donated by the Friends of St Dunstan's, is a moonboard made for bouldering. It is fitted with an LED system and is fully Bluetooth compatible, allowing students to create their own routes and challenges.

Organisation and Curriculum. The College educates boys and girls from the ages of 3 to 18. The Junior School comprises a nursery class for 20 children (3+), a Pre-Prep Department for 120 children aged 4–7 and a Prep Department of 160 children aged 7–11.

In the Junior School great emphasis is placed on letting children learn in a friendly, caring and stimulating environment. Pupils study a broad curriculum and participate in a wide variety of extra-curricular activities. The Head of the Junior School is a member of IAPS (*see entry in IAPS section*).

The Senior School, with a total of 826 pupils, comprises Key Stage 3 (Years 7–9), Key Stage 4 (Years 10 and 11) and Key Stage 5 (Years 12 and 13). A considerable choice of subjects is on offer – Art & Design, Biology, Business Studies, Chemistry, Classical Civilisation, Computing Science, Design & Technology, Economics, English, Drama, Geography, History, Latin, Mathematics, Modern Foreign Languages, Music, Philosophy, Religion and Ethics, Physics, Psychology, Sport and Exercise Science. Alongside the academic curriculum sits an additional curriculum named the Stuart Curriculum which covers three key strands of Relationships (including Sex Education), Skills for the Future (including Careers guidance) and Critical Thinking and Rhetoric (including Public Speaking and Debating).

The College is a vibrant, academic community with a friendly atmosphere. It values cultural diversity and has a reputation for high academic standards and excellent pastoral care. This continues into the Sixth Form where students are supported to achieve outstanding academic results (88% A*–B in 2022), whilst developing each individual's distinctive talents and skills. This philosophy has been the basis for the College's flagship St Dunstan's Diploma programme – a flexible, innovative and exciting programme designed to inspire, challenge and assist all Sixth Formers achieve their unique ambitions and potential.

Pupils have the opportunity to join a very broad range of co-curricular activities through its Forder Programme. It forms a central part of each school day with activities taking place during a dedicated timetabled period. This allows all pupils to immerse themselves in creative, active and service activities along with opportunities to develop leadership skills and a greater understanding of the wider world for the older year groups.

Combined Cadet Force. The CCF is extremely popular and comprises the Royal Navy Section, the Army Section and the Corps of Drums. Typically, cadets join the CCF in Year 9 and by Year 11 become responsible for training younger cadets. The activities undertaken are designed to develop qualities of leadership, resourcefulness, self-reliance, responsibility, confidence and a sense of community service.

Community Service. The College has a strong tradition of service and involvement with the local community. Pupils from Year 9 upwards form a Community Service group that provides various types of help and support to the local community.

Drama. There are opportunities for pupils to be involved in drama productions to suit all ages and abilities. These range from small scale informal performance to larger whole College musicals. Pupils can study towards and be entered for LAMDA examinations. The College hosts an annual 10-day Festival in the summer.

Duke of Edinburgh's Award scheme. The College has very strong numbers of pupils involved at all Award levels.

Music. Pupils from all parts of the school participate in a variety of choirs, orchestras and instrumental ensembles. Pupils have the opportunity to perform at a wide variety of events, both at the College and at a number of prestigious London venues including St John's Smith Square and Cadogan Hall.

Sport. The chief sports are cricket, hockey, netball, rounders, soccer and swimming. Pupils also have opportunities to take part in rugby, cross-country running, tennis, basketball, badminton, sailing, golf, fitness training and yoga.

Entrance. The main entrance points are at the age of 3, 4, 7, 11, 13 or 16. Admission to the College is competitive in all years with the exception of the Nursery, and depends on academic ability and the demonstration of potential. At 11+ an Entrance Examination is held annually in January.

Entrance Scholarships. Scholarships are offered for academic merit and also for excellence in Music, Sport, Art & Design and Drama. Means-tested bursaries are available. There is also a Design Engineering Scholarship available at 16+.

Fees per annum (2023–2024). Nursery, Reception & Years 1–3: £16,011–£16,461; Years 4–5 £18,312; Year 6: £20,172; Senior School £21,321.

The Dunstonian Association. The DA has 5,000 members. All pupils subscribe to the DA while at school and automatically become life members when they leave.

The Friends of St Dunstan's. This parent–school association works to support the educational, social and extra-curricular activities of the school for the benefit of all pupils. All parents are automatically members of the Friends of St Dunstan's.

Charitable status. St Dunstan's Educational Foundation is a Registered Charity, number 312747.

Governors:
Chairman: Mr P Durgan, BA, FCA
Safeguarding Link: Mr J Ronan
Dr Aman Bhandari
Dr Y Burne, JP, OBE
Dr A Cairns, MRSC, MIMMM
Mr N Crawford
Revd K Hedderly
Mr N Lyons, MA
Mrs R Meredith
Mr D Probert, BA Hons, MBA
Mr S Rahman, BA, LLB, LLM
Mr T Shave
Mr N Sheera, MA, MBA
Prof M Van Hemelrijck

Clerk to the Governors: Mr D Richards

Chief Operating Officer: Mrs S Hutt

Senior School Academic Staff:

***Head*: Mr N Hewlett**, BSc, PGCE

Deputy Head (Academic): Mr J Holmes, MA
Deputy Head (Pastoral): Mrs J McLellan, MSc, MA (*Designated Safeguarding Lead DSL*)
Head of Junior School: Miss L Whitwood
Head of Sixth Form: Mr A Brewer, BA
Co-curricular and Staff Development: Mr D Gower, BSc
Director of Studies: Mrs E Latham, BSc
Director of Teaching and Learning: Miss H Riddle, MA

* *Head of Department*

Dr S Adeoya-Osiguwa, BSc
*Mrs J Anderson, BSc
Miss S Arajian, BSc
*Ms S Atkinson, BA
Mrs H S Baptiste, BSc
Mr J Bell, BA
Miss A Biggs, BSc
Mr L Blair, BSc
Ms E Bocarro-Ashford, BSc
*Mr N Bocarro-Ashford, BSc
Mr A Brewer, BA
Mrs K Browne, BSc
*Mr D Butcher, MSc
*Ms R E Butryn, MA
Dr J Bunzl, PhD
*Miss L Clewley, BSc
Miss A Collard, BA
Mr L Corbin O'Grady
*Mr C Cox, BSc
Mr A Currie, BSc
Mrs G L Davies, BSc
Mr R W Davies, BA
Mr P Dawson, BA
Ms S Eiles, BSc
Mr J P H Elmes, MA
Miss G Entwisle, BMus
Mr G Gibb, BSc
*Mrs E Goakes, BEng, MA
Mr L Golding, BSc
Mr D Gower, BSc
*Mr R Gregg
Miss C Harrison, BA
Miss E Harrison, BA
*Mr S Healy, BA
Ms D Hernandez-Alarcon, BA
Mr J Holmes, BA
Miss H Hughes, BA
Miss S Jones, BSc
*Miss A Karmock-Golds, BA
Miss L Kilbey, BA
Mrs E Latham, BSc
*Mr J Lavery, BA
Miss M Lopez, BA
Miss C Lucas, MSc
Ms S Lukins Segerstrom, BSc
Miss O McConnell-Wood, BA
Mrs J McLellan, BA
Ms K Melhorn, BA
Miss T Miah, BA
Mrs S Mitchell, BSc
Miss R Money, BMus
Ms K Nelson, BSc
Mr Z Ng, MSc
*Mr D Oldfield, BA
*Miss E Partridge, BSc
Ms V Permanand, SENDCo
Mrs N Peposhi-Robertson, BA
Miss M Pridmore, BA
Dr R Qadiri, PhD
*Mr J Randall
Ms R Redding, BA
Ms S Reece, BA
*Miss J Restivo, BA
Ms N Rich, BA
Miss H Riddle, MA
Mr R Risebro, BSc
Miss A Sengupta, BSc
Mr G Szell, BSc
*Mr M Thain, BA
Miss E Tournes, BA
Miss W Tseng, BA
Miss R Turner, BSc, MSc
Miss C Wang, BSc, MSc
Miss C Westrip, BA
Mrs L Williams, BSc
Mrs B Wilson, BSc
Ms C Winder, BSc
Miss E Wood, MA, MA
Dr J Yu, DPhil

PA to the Head: Mrs V Hearn
Director of Development and Dunstonian Relations: Mrs I Blake-James
Director of Communications: Mr J-L Squibb
Director of Administrative Services and Events: Miss T Beard
Director of Digital Services: Mr J Hanson
Director of Estates: Mr M Bacon
Director of Admissions: Miss G Morrison
PA to the Head of the Junior School: Miss D Jackson

St Edmund's College

Old Hall Green, Ware, Hertfordshire SG11 1DS

Tel:	01920 824247
email:	admissions@stedmundscollege.org
website:	www.stedmundscollege.org
X/Twitter:	@StEdmundsWare
Facebook:	@stedmundscollegeandprep
Instagram:	@stedmundscollegeandprep
LinkedIn:	/company/st-edmund's-college

Motto: *Avita Pro Fide*

St Edmund's College, England's oldest Catholic school, is a leading Independent day and boarding, co-educational Catholic School for boys and girls aged 3–18. From the Nursery to the Sixth Form, St Edmund's College offers an education that challenges and stimulates, developing the whole person in the intellectual, physical, emotional and spiritual areas of life; the richness of our extracurricular provision and our high academic standards are testament to the College's success and popularity.

Located on a beautiful site in rural East Hertfordshire, only 40 minutes to London by train, St Edmund's has outstanding transport links to the surrounding area and makes full use of the excellent facilities on its 450-acre site including floodlit astroturf pitches and indoor swimming pool.

Scholarships are available at 7+, 11+ and 16+ and we welcome applications for entry to all years if places are available. St Edmund's welcomes students from all faiths who support our ethos.

Admission. Students are mainly admitted at the ages of 11, 13 and 16, although entry is always considered at other ages if there are spaces available.

Scholarships. The College offers the following scholarships:

St Edmund's College 11+ Scholarships:

Douay Academic Scholarships are decided by the mark in the 11+ Entrance Exam, the school report, the confidential school report and the interview with the Headmaster.

Old Hall Academic Scholarships are restricted to Catholic students who are in a Catholic school (and have been for the last two years). As above, this award is decided by the mark in the 11+ entrance exam, the school report, the confidential school report and the interview with the Headmaster or a College Senior Leader.

All Rounder Scholarships are decided by interview, school report, confidential report and mark in the Entrance Exam. For this award, the child will be competent academically and also be able to make a substantial contribution to other areas of life at St Edmund's. This will be as agreed with the Headmaster but contributions might be to one or more aspects, such as drama, music, technology, the Catholic life of the College, specialised sports or outdoor pursuits.

Art Scholarships are decided by examination of a portfolio and a test. Scholars are required to make a significant contribution to the artistic life of the College.

Music Scholarships are decided by audition and include the provision of free tuition in two instruments. Scholars will normally be required to play two instruments with at least one being Grade 4 certification level (voice can be counted as one instrument).

Music Exhibitions may also be awarded which give free tuition in either one or two instruments. Those in receipt of Music Scholarships and Exhibitions are required to make a significant and sustained contribution to the musical life of the College.

Sport Scholarships are decided by open competition and references from sports clubs or teachers where the child is already involved in sport at a very high level, for example, County level. Scholars will be expected to play a full and sustained role in the sporting life of the College.

The closing date for Year 7 scholarship applications is in early December for entry the following September.

Sixth Form Scholarships:

At 16+, the Cardinal Allen Academic Scholarships are decided by open competition using the results of specially set scholarship examinations, interview and previous school reports. Candidates for these scholarships would be expected to achieve all A/A* grades in their GCSEs. Music, Sport and Art scholarships may also be offered through competitive test.

The closing date for Year 12 scholarship applications is in early December for entry the following September.

Bursaries. We also offer a limited number of means-tested Bursaries at 11+, of up to 100% of fees. The closing date is in early December.

Further details are available from the Admissions Office on 01920 824247.

Fees per term (2023–2024). College: Day Pupils: £6,164–£7,245; Weekly Boarders: £8,549–£10,495; Full Boarders: £10,255–£12,821.

There are reductions for siblings and for sons and daughters of serving members of the Armed Forces.

Curriculum. All pupils follow the National Curriculum. At the end of Year 11, pupils take GCSE examinations in all courses that they have followed, usually more than is required by the National Curriculum.

In Rhetoric (Sixth Form), students study A Levels and the majority leave St Edmund's to progress to Russell Group universities including some to Oxford and Cambridge.

Religious Instruction. St Edmund's is a College for all those who appreciate the values of a Catholic Education. All students receive instruction in Christian doctrine and practice from lay teachers. Importance is attached to the liturgical life of the College and the practical expression of faith. All faiths and denominations are welcomed.

Sport. Great importance is attached to sport and physical education throughout the College. All pupils are required to participate in a variety of sports. The major sports for boys are rugby, football, cricket and athletics, while for girls they are hockey, netball, rounders and athletics. The other sports available are cross-country, tennis, swimming, basketball and badminton. A floodlit astroturf pitch, large sports hall, indoor swimming pool, tennis courts, strength and conditioning suite and cardiovascular fitness suite, together with 450 acres of grounds, provide excellent facilities.

Extracurricular Activities. At St Edmund's we believe our responsibility reaches far beyond the academic success of our students. We have a commitment to the whole person, which is reflected in the broad range of activities on offer to everyone and we wish to encourage the notion that success can be achieved in many ways, not just in the classroom.

Each day between 3.30pm and 4.30pm, time is set aside for students to pursue an interest or activity. Wednesday afternoons are also dedicated to our activities programme.

The CCF (RAF and Army sections), Community Service and The Duke of Edinburgh's Award play a prominent part in developing a self-reliant and confident individual.

Careers. There is a Head of Careers and Careers Library. Careers advice is available to pupils from the age of 13. There are regular careers lectures and visits to industry and universities. The Director of Sixth Form is also an integral part of the careers team offering advice and structured support for University choices and applications.

Prep School. St Edmund's also includes a Prep situated on the same estate. It consists of a Nursery, Infants and Junior School for pupils from age 3 to 11, which feeds into the Senior School at 11. The pupils are able to make use of many of the amenities of the Senior School such as the Refectory, Chapel, Swimming Pool and Sports Hall. There is no boarding at the Prep School.

(*For further details, see entry in IAPS section.*)

Charitable status. St Edmund's College is a Registered Charity, number 311073. It aims to provide a Catholic Education for students of all faiths between the ages of 3 and 18.

President & Patron: His Eminence Cardinal Vincent Nichols, Archbishop of Westminster

Governors:
Mr Paul Raynes, MA Cantab (*Chair*)
Mrs Jane Ranzetta (*Deputy Chair and Chair of Academic Sub-Committee*)
Mr John Bryant (*Chair of Prep School Sub-Committee*)
Mr Stephen Grounds, BSc, DPhil
Fr Alban McCoy, OFM Conv, BA, MLitt
Ms Nichola Walsh, BA Hons, MA
Dr Veronica Fulton, FCA, MA, DSG

Clerk to the Governors: Mrs K Pugsley

Senior Leadership Team:

***Headmaster/DSM Child Protection*: Mr M Mostyn,** BA Hons Exeter, MA Ed

Headmaster of Prep School: Mr S Cartwright, BSc Surrey

Bursar: Mr P Watkinson, MBA London, BSc Reading

Deputy Head Academic: Mrs S Sanders, BA Hons London, PGCE Cantab
Deputy Head Pastoral: Mr C Upton, BA Hons Durham, PGCE Sunderland, PGDM Open
Deputy Head Religious Life: Mrs P Peirce, BD AKC London
Deputy Head St Edmund's Prep/DSL Child Protection: Dr F J F McLauchlan, MA, PhD Cantab
Assistant Head Academic Timetable, Curriculum & Data: Mrs R A K West, BEd Hons Exeter
Assistant Head Academic Teaching and Learning: Mrs C Noble, BA Hons Exeter, PGCE Canterbury
Assistant Head Community Life/Deputy DSL Child Protection: Mrs L Dunhill, BSc Hons, PGCE Nottingham
Assistant Head Pastoral/DSL Child Protection: Mr G West, BSc East Anglia
Assistant Head Co-Curricular: Mr N Lee, BSc Hons Birmingham
Assistant Head of St Edmund's Prep: Mr G Duddy, BEd Wales

Director of External Relations: Mrs J Ariano, MBA Heriot-Watt Edinburgh, MA London, BA Hons Anglia Ruskin
Head of Boarding: Mr A Smerdon, BSc Hons St Mary's Twickenham, PGCE South Bank
Head of Finance/Deputy Bursar: Mrs N Castle, FCCA
Human Resources Director: Mrs H Duffy, LLB Hull, PGDL
Priest in Residence: Revd Father P H Lyness, MA Rhodes
Technical Projects Director: Mr S Winfield

Heads of Department:
Art, Design and Technology: Miss A M Healy, BA Luton
Business Studies and Economics: Miss E Chilton, MEd Cantab, BA Lancaster
Drama: Mrs N Schiff, MA Herts, BA Plymouth, PGCE Reading
English and Media Studies: Mr A Hay, MEd Cantab, PGDip London, BA Hons Oxford Brookes
Geography: Mr P Bittles, BSc Hons Belfast, PGCE Liverpool Hope
History and Politics: Mr C Berkley, BA Liverpool, PGCE ARU CELTYL Seoul, TESOL Trinity College London, CELTA Cantab
Information Technology and Computing: Mr K R Fry, BSc Brunel, MSc Herts, PGCE Exeter
International Department: Miss Z Hibbert, BA Hons Portsmouth, PGCE Cantab, Delta M1 & M2 Seville Cert, TESOL UCL
Languages:
French: Mrs F Harvey-Keenan, BA Hons Durham, PGCE Nottingham
German: Mrs J Gardner, BA Bradford, PGCE Herts
Italian and Latin: Miss S Rinaldi, BA Hons Open
Spanish: Ms E Gambino, BA Hons Manchester, PGCE Middlesex
Mathematics: Mrs H Fraser, BSc, PGCE East Anglia
Music: Mr A O'Brien, MA London, MMus City, MPerf City, BA Hons East Anglia
Physical Education: Mr K Dixon, MSc Brunel, MSc Oxon, BSc Manchester (*from April 2023*)
Psychology: Mr N Eliasson, MA Birmingham, PGCE Canterbury, BSc Hertfordshire
Religious Studies: Miss A Moloney, BA Hons Surrey, PGCE Roehampton
Science: Miss M Towns, BSc UWE Bristol, PGCE London
Cardinal Hume Centre, Learning Support: Mrs N Wells, BSc Hons Hertfordshire, PGCE Greenwich
Careers: Mrs E Thomas, BA Hons Lincolnshire & Humberside

A full staff list is available at: www.stedmundscollege.org/information/staff-and-vacancies/who-we-are/staffing.

St Edmund's School Canterbury

St Thomas Hill, Canterbury, Kent CT2 8HU

Tel:	01227 475601 (Admissions)
	01227 475600 (General Enquiries)
email:	admissions@stedmunds.org.uk
website:	www.stedmunds.org.uk
X/Twitter:	@StEdsCanterbury
Facebook:	@StEdsCanterbury
Instagram:	@stedscanterbury

Motto: *Fungar Vice Cotis*

St Edmund's is an independent, co-educational day and boarding school for pupils aged between 2 and 18 years, comprising the Pre-Prep, Junior and Senior Schools. Its aim is to provide varied opportunities for academic, sporting, artistic, musical and dramatic achievement. The school has excellent teaching facilities and numerous options for extracurricular activities.

First established in 1749 as the Clergy Orphan School in Yorkshire, the School later moved to London and settled in its present location in 1855. The School's commitment to its origins endures, as does its Christian ethos. However, the School welcomes pupils from all backgrounds and places a particularly strong emphasis on pastoral care.

St Edmund's is situated on a beautiful site at the top of St Thomas Hill, adjacent to the University of Kent and overlooking the historic city of Canterbury. It is within easy reach of the towns of East Kent, and is just over an hour from London. The proximity to London's airports, the Channel ports and Eurostar stations at Ashford and Ebbsfleet gives international pupils convenient access to the School.

St Edmund's is a distinctive and historic boarding and day co-educational school where a family atmosphere is fostered, individuals are valued, the spiritual element is explored, and pupils enjoy a rich academic and cultural experience. We are committed to producing happy and successful pupils who can access a high quality education, while enjoying a wealth of stimulating and exciting extracurricular activity. Set within a beautiful and extensive green field site affording spectacular views of the city and Cathedral of Canterbury, St Edmund's not only enjoys a stunning location, but also offers a happy, vibrant and creative environment within a supportive community.

The school offers a nurturing, yet challenging, environment where an emphasis is placed upon academic rigour and co-curricular involvement. Its co-curricular provision is broad, but also encourages excellence in each individual area. Its tradition of housing and educating the Choristers of Canterbury Cathedral brings much to the richness and diversity of our community.

Academic standards are set high. Its dedicated and talented teaching and support staff work alongside pupils to encourage them to develop into caring, resourceful and confident young men and women who are well equipped to tackle the demands of the modern world.

Organisation. The Nursery, Pre-Prep, Junior and Senior Schools are on the same site and are closely integrated, using the same Chapel, music and art facilities, theatre, dining hall, science laboratories, sports facilities, and so on. However, for practical day-to-day purposes the Junior School is led by the Head of the Junior School and the Nursery and Pre-Prep under the Head of Pre-Prep. St Edmund's derives much of its strength and its capacity to work efficiently and economically from its close-knit structure.

The Senior School is divided into four Houses: Baker, Wagner, Warneford and Watson, the respective Housemasters each being assisted by a team of Deputies and Tutors.

The chapel. All pupils attend at least two of the morning services a week. Confirmation is conducted annually by the Archbishop of Canterbury (as Patron of the School) or by the Bishop of Dover acting on his behalf; the candidates are prepared by the School Chaplain. The School Carol Service is held in Canterbury Cathedral, by kind permission of the Dean and Chapter.

Buildings and facilities. Over the past twenty years there have been extensive additions to and modernisation of the school's buildings and facilities: a new Junior School building; a purpose-built music school; a new Sixth Form Centre; the main hall with tiered auditorium and exhibition area; the sports hall; the technology department; additional classrooms and major extensions to science, art, IT and the Pre-Prep School; as well as the conversion of all Senior School boarding accommodation to study-bedrooms and refurbishment of Junior boarding premises. Recent additions include: phase one of the Academic Hub with 8 classrooms; new recreational facilities for Senior School boarders; a refurbished theatre and library; an AstroTurf pitch; a new medical centre; upgrading of classrooms, boarding and House facilities.

Academic organisation. At St Edmund's, the academic expectations are high. The breadth and balance of the academic programme exceeds the requirements of the National Curriculum and pupils begin to be grouped by ability while they are in Junior School. This approach encourages children to apply their talents and aptitudes with diligence and perseverance. Comprehensive reports are sent regularly throughout the school year. A system of interim reports, as well as regular parents' meetings, ensures close communication with parents.

Nursery and Pre-Prep Schools: The Nursery and Pre-Prep Schools have their own classroom buildings and playground, creating a warm, secure and friendly learning environment in which pupils can develop to the full. The happy and purposeful atmosphere helps pupils develop their confidence.

The School has a wide range of excellent activities and teaches a broad-based curriculum that emphasises academic development as well as art, music, drama, outdoor education and sport. The teachers have many years' experience of working with Early Years' children and the small classes allow staff to focus on the needs of every pupil.

Junior School: The aim of the Junior School is to produce independent learners who are confident and motivated. In Forms 3 to 5, the National Curriculum is broadly followed and, while placing particular emphasis on English, Maths and Science, there is also focus on subjects such as Art, Drama, French, Geography, History, Information Technology, Latin and Music. Subject specialists teach Forms 6 to 8, helping to prepare pupils for Senior School. Music (from Form 3), Drama, Technology and Art (from Form 6) and Science (from Form 7) is taught in specialist facilities.

The House system gives older pupils the opportunity to experience the skills of organisation, cooperation and leadership, by helping and encouraging younger members of their Houses and assisting with the organisation of House teams and events. Taking on more responsibility and developing greater initiative is valuable in smoothing their passage to Senior School.

Choristers: The choristers of Canterbury Cathedral are all members of the Junior School. They board in the Choir House (in the Cathedral Precincts) in the care of Houseparents appointed by the school. All their choral training is undertaken in the Cathedral by the Master of Choristers and Cathedral Organist; the remainder of their education takes place at St Edmund's.

Senior School: In the first year of the Senior School (Year 9) pupils follow a core curriculum in English, Mathematics, French, Physics, Chemistry, Biology, History, Geography, Art, Music, Information Technology, Religious Education, PSHEE, Physical Education, and Technology. Drama, Spanish and Latin are options.

GCSE core subjects are: English, English Literature, Mathematics and the three (separate) Sciences. Options include French, German, Latin, Spanish, History, Geography, Art (Ceramics), Art, Food Technology, Product Design, Computer Science, Music, Drama, Dance, Physical Education and Religious Studies.

The following subjects are offered for A Level examinations: Art, Biology, Business Studies, Ceramics, Chemistry, Classical Civilisation, Design and Technology, Economics, English Literature, Film Studies, French, Geography, German, Government and Politics, History, Mathematics and Further Mathematics, Music, Music Technology, Photography, Physics, Psychology and Theatre Studies. In addition to their A Level choices, Lower Sixth pupils have the option to undertake an EPQ (Extended Project Qualification) and the Leiths Academy Diploma.

Careers and Higher Education. The School is affiliated to the Independent Schools Careers Organisation and the Careers Research and Advisory Centre. Pupils have the opportunity to undergo careers aptitude testing in the GCSE year, and all pupils are assisted in finding a placement for a week or more of work experience in the GCSE year. The careers and higher education staff give all possible help in the finding of suitable careers and in selecting appropriate universities and colleges of further education. Most A Level candidates go on to degree courses after leaving school; others join Art or Music conservatoires, or Drama schools.

Music. Music is woven into the fabric of school life at St Edmund's, reinforced by the presence of the Canterbury Cathedral Choristers. In the purpose-built Music School, specialist teachers give lessons to pupils from Pre-Prep through to the Sixth Form. Pupils of all ages participate in numerous musical ensembles which cater for a range of vocal and instrumental abilities. As a result, there is an exceptional practical examination record, with more than 80% of entrants achieving Distinction or Merit. Over twenty-five concerts and performances take place each year, from small lunchtime recitals in the Recital Hall to large gala concerts in Canterbury Cathedral. The school acts as a focus for musical excellence for children throughout East Kent and enjoys a creative partnership with the Tippett Quartet.

Performing Arts. Dramatic performance is included in the curriculum from the earliest years. Every term, the Pre-Prep School holds thematic drama workshops. Pupils in Junior and Senior Schools participate in school plays and other performances with vitality and enthusiasm, as an outlet for expressing their talents in acting, dancing, singing, music, choreography and technical production. The consistently outstanding GCSE and A Level results are testament to the emphasis placed on drama within the curriculum and school life in general.

St Edmund's has recently been awarded the Independent Schools of the Year Best Performing Arts school in the UK for 2023.

Art. The emphasis St Edmund's places on creative subjects means that art is embedded in the curriculum across the three Schools. Pupils studying Art and Design enjoy excellent facilities and teaching. Drawing, painting, print-making, photography (traditional and digital), sculpture and ceramics are offered to pupils in the Junior and Senior Schools.

Sport. Association football, hockey, cricket, athletics, tennis, squash and (for girls) netball and rounders are the principal sports but there are opportunities for many other forms of exercise, including cross-country running, indoor rowing, golf, badminton, basketball, volleyball, swimming and gym-based fitness training. There is an AstroTurf pitch and large playing fields that adjoin the school buildings. There is an open-air heated swimming pool. The sports hall is well-equipped. There are eight tennis courts (both hard and grass), a compact golf course and a rifle range.

Activities. For those in the first four years of Senior School one afternoon a week is given over specifically to a broad range of activities. A number involve helping the local community, while other pupils learn new skills, e.g. archaeology, broadcasting, Eco-Schools, Japanese language and culture, kite making, literary and debating societies, photography, Rotary Interact and yoga.

In the second year all Senior School pupils join the Combined Cadet Force, a highly successful unit commanded by a member of the teaching staff and administered by an ex-soldier. There is an annual camp in the summer and an adventurous training camp at Easter, attendance at which is voluntary. Cadets may remain in the CCF for the duration of their school career if they wish, and are encouraged to do so if contemplating a career in the armed forces.

Pupils may also participate in The Duke of Edinburgh's Award scheme and the British Association of Young Scientists. There are regular field trips, choir and music tours, sports tours and many other one-off trips.

In Junior School, too, there is a diverse range of extracurricular activities, many of which draw on the school's excellent facilities for sport, music and drama. There is a Year 8 outdoor activities week in Spain, an annual sports tour and skiing trip.

Health. The School Medical Centre is staffed by state registered nurses and provides medical care at all times. The health of the pupils is supervised by a senior local general practitioner under the NHS. A counselling service is available.

St Edmund's Festival of the Arts. Established in 2017, the Festival was planned and delivered with a clear and single aim: to celebrate the fantastic talents of young people by bringing to Canterbury an event as new and fresh as it was creative and innovative with a line-up of world-class artists. To date guest artists have included Freddy Kempf, Tasmin Little, Jess Gillam, Curtis Stigers and Sheku & Isata Kanneh-Mason and it has become a fixture in the Canterbury arts calendar.

Admission. *Nursery and Pre-Prep School:* Entry at any age from 2–7. Once registered, children are invited to visit the School for informal assessment.

Junior School: Entry at any age from 7–12. Candidates will sit entrance tests and all prospective pupils will be interviewed or attend an assessment day.

Choristers: St Edmund's is the school of the Canterbury Cathedral choristers. For details of the voice trials please contact the Junior School Secretary.

Senior School: Entry at 13 from preparatory schools is through the Common Entrance Examination. Candidates from other schools will be tested appropriately or sit the School's own entrance tests. There is also a large entry of pupils into the Sixth Form, usually on the basis of interview and GCSE grade estimates from their present school.

Fees per term (2023–2024). Senior School: Boarders £14,498; Weekly Boarders £13,514; Day pupils £8,120. Junior School: Boarders £11,040; Weekly Boarders £10,061; Choristers £9,714; Day pupils £6,186–£5,989. Pre-Prep: £3,725–£4,306. Nursery £30.59 per day in receipt of Free Early Education. Extras have been kept to the minimum.

Entrance scholarships. Competitive scholarships of up to 25% of tuition fees are offered in academic achievement, music, drama and sport at 11+, 13+ and 16+. In addition, art scholarships and choral exhibitions are available at 13+ and 16+. At the discretion of the Head an All-Rounder scholarship may be made to a candidate whose combination of talents merits an award. Such a candidate will have sat the academic scholarship paper and been assessed for a scholarship in at least one other discipline.

Bursaries and fee concessions. Originally founded to provide a free education for the fatherless sons of the clergy of the Church of England and the Church of

Wales, St Edmund's now accepts applications from boys and girls for Foundationer status. Bursaries to provide a temporary (no more than 12 months) cushion are granted on a means-tested basis to existing pupils. Fee concessions, also means-tested, can be provided to the children of the clergy, members of the armed forces and to the third and subsequent children of the same family in the school at the same time.

Charitable status. The school is owned by St Edmund's School Canterbury, which is a charitable company limited by guarantee, registered in England and Wales, and a Registered Charity, number 1056382. It exists to educate the children in its care.

Patron: The Lord Archbishop of Canterbury

Governors:
Chairman: Air Marshal C M Nickols, CB, CBE, MA, FRAeS
Deputy Chair: Mr Q L Roper, BA Hons, MA, NPQH
Dr M Carnegie, MB BS
Mr R Dodgson
Dr P Eichorn, MD
Mr C Harbridge, FRICS
Mrs N Leatherbarrow, BSc, MBA
The Revd Canon Dr T J N Naish, BA, MA, PhD
Mr S M Sutton, BA, FCA
Councillor P A Todd

***Head*: Mr E G O'Connor**, MA Cantab, MPhil Oxon, MEd Cantab

Head of The Junior School: Mr Ross Comfort, MA

Head of The Pre-Prep School: Mrs Sarah Bartholomew

Chaplain: The Revd Joy Atkins

Bursar: Mr N C Scott-Kilvert, FCCA

Deputy Head: Mrs C J Shearer, BA Bangor, PCGE Leeds

Assistant Head Co-Curricular: Mr N Hodge

Please refer to the school website for the full staff list.

St Edward's, Oxford

Woodstock Road, Oxford OX2 7NN
Tel: 01865 319323 (Warden)
01865 319321 (Bursar)
01865 319200 (Registrar)
email: registrar@stedwardsoxford.org
website: www.stedwardsoxford.org
Instagram: @stedwardsoxford

Motto: *Pietas Parentum*

St Edward's was founded in 1863 by the Revd Thomas Chamberlain to educate the sons of middle class clergy in the Anglican tradition. The somewhat cramped original premises in the centre of Oxford soon proved inadequate for the growing School, so the decision was taken in 1873 to move to what were then the farmlands of Summertown. Today, the School sits on a vast 100-acre estate, complete with the Christie Academic Centre, the impressive Olivier Hall, the innovative North Wall Arts Centre, the high-specification Music School, a fully-equipped sports centre, a riverside boat house, pitches, courts, elegant Quad, golf course and canalside towpath. It is unusual to find such extensive grounds in a city boarding school; St Edward's is less than a mile from the university city of Oxford and only a 2-minute walk from the busy urban village of Summertown. The School has around 810 pupils, 86% of whom board, and 45% of whom are girls. Pupils live in one of 13 houses (five for girls, four for boys and four boys' houses with a co-educational Sixth Form), and enjoy outstanding academic and co-curricular opportunities.

Ethos. We seek to educate pupils at St Edward's in a liberal and open community, in which scholarship is promoted, in which there is excellence in every area of school life, and in which there is a culture of service within and outside the School. We celebrate scholarship not only for the acquisition of knowledge through study but also for the development of a life-long interest in the life of the mind. We seek excellence for pupils in learning and in teaching, in pastoral care, in co-curricular opportunity, in diversity, in sustainability and in all school facilities. We believe that real public benefit comes not only from the sharing of resources and from working in partnership with others outside the School, but also – and more importantly – from the commitment to serving others which pupils will develop during their time at Teddies. We also believe in allowing pupils to be themselves and to chart their own course through the many opportunities available to them at Teddies, as the School is also affectionately known, so developing the confidence and the independence to thrive at university and in their professional and personal lives. At the same time, we ensure that pupils take full advantage of the facilities and opportunities available to them at the School, because we know that academic success and personal fulfilment follow from breadth of interest and engagement.

Pastoral care. The comprehensive pastoral care system at St Edward's has long been regarded as one of the School's great strengths – a point highlighted by successive ISI reports. The system is underpinned by a highly-effective network of relationships offering distinct but interwoven levels of care. Each pupil sits at the centre of his or her network, surrounded by a range of people who can offer guidance and support. The Housemaster or Housemistress is a vital member of that architecture for pastoral care, and in this role they are supported by an Assistant HM and a Matron. Also key are Tutors who monitor the academic and pastoral life of six to 10 pupils, meeting with them regularly to offer advice and guidance across the full range of a pupil's experience of living and learning at Teddies. Within the school community, Sixth Formers are trained to offer a peer listening service and a great many other leadership and support roles; the two Heads of School meet regularly with senior staff to discuss all aspects of school life. The Deputy Heads Pastoral and Safeguarding, the School Doctor, the Director of Wellbeing, the School Psychologist, the School Counsellor, School Nurses, the Health Centre and the Chaplaincy Team are also part of the comprehensive pastoral care network.

Academic work. Academically, it would be hard to overstate the importance to St Edward's of being in Oxford, within easy reach of the stimulating academic life of the university. Academic endeavour lies at the heart of the School; pupils are expected to work consistently hard, to take responsibility for their own learning and to engage actively in the many opportunities open to them for broadening their intellectual horizons. The school offers GCSE/IGCSE, A Level with the Extended Project and the IB Diploma. The GCSE programme is enhanced by St Edward's own optional Pathways and Perspectives courses – designed to stretch and inspire – two of which may be taken alongside GCSEs. The Sixth Form community is split 50/50 between A Levels and the IB. The Learning Support Department ensures the provision of support for pupils with special educational needs and disabilities, both through direct support of pupils and their parents and through the teaching staff.

In 2023, just under half of all Sixth Form grades were A*–A or Levels 7–6 (A Level or the IB Diploma) and 83% were A*–B or Levels 7–5. Around two thirds of all grades at GCSE and in our own Pathways and Perspectives courses were Levels 9–7. Most Sixth Form leavers take up places at Russell Group or equally prestigious universities, including Oxford and Cambridge and, increasingly, pupils look to study overseas. In recent years, pupils have gone on to study at US and Canadian universities, including Harvard, Brown, Columbia, Dartmouth and UCAL Berkeley. Pupils have also been successful in their applications to universities in Hong Kong and Japan, and to universities in a number of European cities including Dublin, Amsterdam, Leiden and Madrid. Their success comes partly from the specialist support which we provide for them in their applications to universities outside the UK.

To extend academic opportunities for all pupils, outstanding university-level facilities have just opened at the heart of the School in the Quad. The Christie Centre features The Oxley Library, The Roe Reading Room, flexible new classrooms and a social learning space. Alongside the academic facilities is the stunning new Olivier Hall which hosts countless concerts, performances and gatherings for our growing community.

Higher Education and careers. Provision in this area is managed by a team with a wide range of experience and expertise. A Head of Higher Education and Careers, a Head of Employability and Careers Education, and a Head of Overseas Applications are supported by external guidance from a US universities expert. Higher Education and Careers advice is highly personalised and quite exceptional. The Shell Curriculum and our Pathways and Perspectives courses are designed to feed directly into pupils' career planning by teaching explicitly the skills required for today's workplace: research, self-regulation, innovative thinking, presentation, collaboration and teamwork. Pupils are given every assistance in choosing the right course of further study and in preparing a strong application, including visits by representatives of UK and US universities, mock interviews and personal statement workshops. Tailored advice is given to Oxbridge and Ivy League candidates and to those aiming for highly-competitive courses, such as Medicine or Veterinary Science.

Music, Drama and the Arts. The cutting-edge programming of the award-winning North Wall Arts Centre enriches the cultural life of both the School and the wider community, placing St Edward's at the forefront of developments in arts education. As a result, the arts are highly valued and enormously successful at St Edward's. The Drama Department is flourishing: main school productions, including musicals, are complemented by devised pieces, House plays, Shell plays and a Speech and Drama programme. The Art Department is strong and vibrant, benefiting from recently enhanced facilities and a stream of visiting exhibitions to The North Wall. The Dance programme is extensive, with over 120 classes every week for more than 200 pupils – covering styles from ballet to hip hop – generating a range of material for regular dance shows. The Music Department, housed in the elegant Music School, delivers about 500 lessons every week, taught by a team of 40 visiting specialists. The main school groups include the Orchestra, Chamber Orchestra, Chapel Choir, Chamber Choir, St Edward's Singers (a choir for the School and the local community), Concert Band, Big Band, Jazz Band and various Chamber Music groups. There are around 60 concerts a year, in School and further afield, with occasional foreign tours.

Sport, games and activities. A wide variety of sports, games and activities is on offer. We compete at the highest level in several sports and can boast of county and national representatives. We encourage all our pupils to participate and to enjoy playing at all levels. We have fielded as many as 27 teams on one day – over 400 children representing the school. These sports, games and activities include rugby, football, hockey, cricket, rowing, athletics, netball, squash, tennis, swimming, cross-country running, sailing, golf, football, canoeing, ceramics, theatre crew, filmmaking, debating, investment, textiles, cycle maintenance, volunteering, charitable challenges, community service – and much more. We operate a Combined Cadet Force with Navy, Army and RAF sections, and offer The Duke of Edinburgh's Award.

Admission to the School. St Edward's admits pupils at three entry points each year: approximately 150 into the Shell (Year 9), around 20 into the Fourth Form (Year 10) and some 65 into the Lower Sixth (Year 12). Formal registration, for which a fee is charged, takes place online via the school website. Full details of the application process for all entry points are available on the website under the Admissions tab.

Scholarships. Academic and Music Scholarships, and Art and Sports Awards are available at both Shell (Year 9) and Lower Sixth (Year 12) entry. At Shell entry, Arts Awards cover Art, Dance, Drama and Design Technology; and at Lower Sixth entry, Arts Awards cover Art, Dance and Drama.

Scholarships come with fee remission of 5% per annum. Exhibitions (the second level of Scholarship), and Sports and Arts Awards attract fee remission of 2.5% per annum. Full details of the application process, selection criteria, assessments and closing dates are available on the website under the Admissions tab.

Bursaries. Any pupil applying to St Edward's in Years 9, 10 or 12 may apply for means-tested fee support up to 100% of fees through our Bursary programme. Applications should be made by 1 October in the year of application. Bursaries are unrelated to Scholarships and Awards.

Fees per term (2023–2024). Boarding: £15,660; Day: £12,528.

Charitable status. St Edward's, Oxford, is a Registered Charity, number 309681. The vision for the School is to be fully co-educational, taking every advantage of its location in Oxford, to which access is broad and balanced, in which staff and pupils together make up a diverse and mutually supportive community of learners, in which pupils develop self-agency through opportunity, in which there is a culture of service, from which pupils graduate with values for life and skills for the 21st century, and in which the estate and all operational structures facilitate sustainable excellence.

Visitor:
The Right Revd The Lord Bishop of Oxford

Governing Body:
Chris Jones, MA FRSA [OSE] (*Chairman*)
Wilf Stephenson, MA (*Vice Chair*)
John Adedoyin, MA, MBA [OSE]
Sarah Ainsworth, MA, MSc, CQSW (*Churchill Fellow*)
Caroline Baggs, BSc
Joe Burrows, MA
The Venerable Jonathan Chaffey, CB, Archdeacon of Oxford
Helen Cook, BEd, FCIPD [OSE]
Georgina Dennis, MA [OSE]
Professor Louise Fawcett-Posada, MA, DPhil
Kenneth MacRitchie, MA, BD, LLB
Clare Robertson, MBChB, MRCP Paeds, FRCPCH
Michael Roulston, MBE, BPhil, MEd
Philip Winston, MA, PhD

[OSE] *Former Pupil*

***Warden*: A J Chirnside**, MA Oxon

Bursar & COO: E G B Hayter, MVO, BSc Southampton

Sub-Warden: C Hamilton, MSc Southampton
Sub-Warden Academic: D J Flower, MA Oxon

Deputy Heads:
Pastoral: R Bellamy, BA Loughborough, MA Open
Safeguarding: J E B Cope, MA, Late Exhibitioner of Keble College, Oxon, MA Open
Co-Curriculum: N H C Coram-Wright, MA St Andrews
Assistant Heads
Curricular: J Young, BSc Warwick
Academic: L L H Tao, BA Durham
Co-Curriculum: A C W Tester, MA Late Organ Scholar of Fitzwillam College, Cantab
Registrar: N C A Jones, BEd Hons London

Development Director: R J Henshilwood, BA Hons Nottingham Trent
Head of Communications: T van der Heiden, BA Oxon

Chaplain: Revd. E M V Boughton, BA Oxon

Directors:
Teaching and Learning: R H Stephens, BSc Southampton, MA Durham
IB: A Fielding, BA York, MSc Oxon
Behaviour & Standards: E Singfield
Music: Peter Clements, BA Oxon
Organisation: P C Gowen, BSc Leeds
Sport: N J Bond, BSc Cardiff Metropolitan

Head of Higher Education: M Gillingwater, BSc, MSc Edinburgh, MEd Cantab

School Analyst: M J Golesworthy, MChem Oxon, DPhil Oxon, FRSM, FTCL
Head of Pupil Transition: R M Storey, BSc Edinburgh
Head of Super Curriculum: S C S Waldock, BSc Durham
Head of Pupil Progress: K L Newson, BA Sheffield
Head of Pupil Voice: F L Wickens, MA Oxon

Teaching Staff:
J Adlam, PhD Hamburg
S K Arbuthnot, BA Queen's Belfast
M E L Austen, BA Cantab
L Barr, BA London
O J Barstow, MEng Nottingham Trent
O S Bartholomew, MA Oxon
M. Blackham, BSc Southampton Solent
H Bond, BSc Bath
N J Bond, BSc Cardiff Metropolitan
L Bray, MA York
M E Bunch, BA, MA Durham
J J Burbidge, MA, PhD Ohio
S Cabello Malfetano, BA Malaga
D Caro Solano, BA Western Australia
J A Cazabon, MSc Wales
H Chitsenga, BSc Instituto Superior Pedagogico EJ Varona, Cuba
J E Clapham, MAM Edinburgh, MSc Kingston
R F Cottrell, BA Southampton
N C Creed, MA Late Choral Exhibitioner of Trinity College, Cantab
G Damiani, BMus Guildhall School of Music & Drama, ARCO
A-L Davies, MA, University of Pau
C A Davies, BA York, MA Open
J M Davies, MA, BA Swansea
M-L Delvallée, Licence d'Anglais, MA Université du Littoral, MA Canterbury
P Diaz Rogado, MA Salamance
R E Drury, BSc Leeds
L C Duffy, BA Hull
T W Duncan, BA Kingston
K J Eden, BA Winchester, MA City, London
L Elkins, Italia Conti Academy
A N Elliott, BA Oxon
D Finamore, BSc Bath
M D Fletcher, MA Cantab, PhD Bath, CSciTeach, CSci, CChem, MRSC
L K French, BSc Bangor
A D M Friend, MA Edinburgh
E W B Friend, MEarthSci, Oxon
M D G Glover, BSc Oxford Brookes
A M Goldsmith, BA Newcastle
A R Griffiths, BSc Loughborough
K L Grinyer-Bouwer, BA Bristol
A J Grounds, BA Brunel, MSc Oxon
A R Hahn, BA Glasgow School of Art
A J T Halliwell, BA Loughborough
L Hamblin-Rooke, BSc St Mary's Twickenham
C Hanly, BA Rhodes University
M J Hanslip, BEd Greenwich
J L Harris, BSc Leiden, MSc Sheffield
P Herring, BA Hons Cantab
F Higgins, MA Birmingham, MPhil Dublin, BA Oxon
C Holder, BA Brighton, MFA Slade School of Fine Art
T E Holdsworth, BEng Cranfield
S C Holland, BSc Nottingham Trent
C M Holliday, BA Bournemouth

J N Hooper, MA Reading
N F Hunter, BA Courtauld Institute, London
J E Ingram, MMath Warwick, MEd University College London
H Irving, BA, Nottingham
M Islam, BSc Imperial College
R Jackson, BA Oxon
C M James, BSc Kent
S James, BEng Kent
R Jerstice, BA Cantab
A Kenny, BA Exeter
J Law, BSc Brunel
A Mango, BA La Sorbonne, Paris
B C Marett, MA The Royal College of Art
A E Moffatt, BA Oxford Brookes
S J M Munday-Webb, BA Central School of Speech and Drama
H S Murphy, BSc Nottingham
G E Nagle, MA, DPhil Oxon
M F Narajos, BA, BM, BCh, PGDip Oxon
L O'Rourke, BSci St. Andrews
C Ord, MA Heidelberg, DPhil Oxon
V Patel, MA Warwick, DPhil Oxon
L L A Paul, BA Manchester
R Perry, BA Oxon
J R Powell, GRSM, LRAM, ARCM
M Powell, BA Oxon
A L Qui, BSc Warwick
Y S Ramadharsingh, BSc West Indies
K J Reid, MSc St Andrews
R Ritchie, BSc, Warwick
S J Roche, BA, MEd Leeds
E P Scates, BA Bournemouth, MA Canterbury Christ Church
C S Schofield, MA Cantab
A E D Scott
J Sephton, BA Oxon
J E Sinclair, BA Oxon
N M Simborowski-Gill, MA Oxon
R M Simmonds, BA Exeter
J A Simpson, MA Oxon
A E Smith, MEng Bristol
H Stanley, MPhys, Warwick
S D Symington, BA Exeter, MSc Bath
M J Taylor, MA Durham, ALCM
H D Thomas, LLB Birmingham, MEd Cantab
R K Thomas, BSc Liverpool
A Todd, BA Sterling
P Torri, MA Milan, PhD Leuven
W H Truter, BSc Stellenbosch
L R Turley, BA, PGDip Glasgow School of Art, PGDip Oxford Brookes
C A Wallendahl, MA Oxon
A P Waring, BSc Birmingham
B R Watts, BSc Bristol, PhD Oxon
S J Wheeler, BSc Leeds, PhD Sheffield
A J Wiggins, MA Oxon
T Wyatt, BA Oxon

Post-graduate Teachers:
V Abreu, MSc Birmingham
M Birtles, MA Oxford Brookes
I Cervera, BA Bordeaux
S Cole, BA Exeter
L Cowlishaw, BA Oxford Brookes
B Evans, BSc Hons Loughborough
J M Gomez, BA Pablo De Olavide
H Holbech, BA Falmouth
M V Koch, MA Humbolds-Universitat, Berlin
E Miles-Kingston, BMus University of London
J Miller, BA Loghborough
F Pietersen, BA Exeter
P Salmond Smith, BA University of London
K Shepherd, BSc Oxford Brookes
N Sinclair, BA Leicester, MA Oxon
C Wukics, BSc, Oxford Brookes

Examinations Officer: M Islam, BSc
Director of Finance & Corporate Services: K Pearce MA Cantab, FCA
Head of HR: C Waterfield, BSc, Assoc CIPD
Estates Bursar: R A Hayes
CCF, Contingent Commander: Sqn Ldr N H Coram-Wright, RAFAC, MA
CCF, School Staff Instructor: Captain O Perera
Librarian: S A Eldred, BA, MSc

School Doctor: Dr Olivia Beardmore

St George's College, Weybridge

Weybridge Road, Weybridge, Surrey KT15 2QS

Tel: 01932 839300
email: contact@stgeorgesweybridge.com
website: www.stgeorgesweybridge.com
X/Twitter: @sgweybridge
Facebook: @stgeorgescollegeuk
Instagram: @stgeorgesweybridge
LinkedIn: /company/st-george-s-weybridge

Motto: *Amore et Labore*

The College was founded by the Josephite Community in Croydon in 1869, and moved to its present 100 acres of beautiful grounds on Woburn Hill, Weybridge in 1884. Within its unique family orientated ethos, the College seeks to encourage a wide, balanced Christian education in the Catholic tradition, encouraging excellence and achievement across a broad spectrum of academic, sporting and extra-curricular activities. Almost all pupils move on to higher education, the vast majority gaining places at Russell Group universities, including Oxford and Cambridge. The College is co-educational throughout, and there are over 1,000 students.

Admissions. Entry is mainly at age 11 (First Year), with smaller cohorts at 13 (Third Year) and 16 (Sixth Form). Students are enrolled in September each year after successfully completing entrance examinations and interviews the previous winter. Entry is occasionally possible during an academic year.

Full details on the admissions process can be found on St George's website or by contacting their Admissions team.

Entrance Scholarships. Scholarships for Art, Music, Drama, Sport and Academic can be awarded on entry to the school at 11, 13 and 16 and carry a 10% remission of the basic school fees.

Scholarships in these areas can also be awarded at any point throughout a student's time at the College. These are classed as 'Honorary' scholarships and do not carry any fee remission, but are identical in every other respect to scholarships awarded on entry.

Scholarships gift students a programme that develops and nurtures their talent, in addition to the College's normal curriculum. The College's scholarships programme very much underscores their mission for students to be the very best version of themselves.

There is no set number of scholarships awarded for each year group. Across the whole College, there will be well over 350 scholars at any one time.

Details on the process for application and guidance on expected standards are to be found on our website under the Admissions section. A certain number of scholarships are allocated to our Junior School candidates each year.

Bursaries. We offer fee remission of up to 110% for children at the College at 11+ and 16+. Remission may include additional assistance with uniforms, school bus, compulsory school lunches, essential academic trips and exam fees. Children undergo our normal entrance assessment and Bursary applicants are also subject to a full financial assessment to measure eligibility. Please contact Admissions admissions@stgeorgesweybridge.com for non-standard entry applications.

Short-term Financial Assistance. The College provides short-term financial assistance for existing families who find themselves in difficult financial circumstances. Further information is available from the Bursar.

Facilities. St George's College is embracing sustainability across its campus, and in spring 2022 was able to complete its Ground Source Heat Pump project to heat and cool much of the College.

The College's world-class Activity Centre was built to mark their 150th anniversary in 2019, and offers an exceptional array of facilities for dynamic use. This ambitious building was designed to provide several flexible and varied environments to cater for many different types of activity, now and in the future. Spaces include a glassfloor in the main hall for multi-sport use, dance studio, climbing wall, mental performance studio, and a gym; all helping to inspire students to excel throughout their school life and beyond. In addition to the Activity Centre facilities, the College has 19 tennis courts, including three international standard grass courts, clay courts and an impressive four-court Indoor Tennis Centre. There are floodlit netball courts, an all-weather athletics track and two astroturf hockey pitches. The College Boat Club is situated nearby on the Thames.

Our modern Sixth Form building provides group and silent study rooms, social space, five History and five Geography classrooms, staff offices and meeting areas.

Refurbishment over the past three years has provided modern facilities for Science, Music, Languages, English, Mathematics, Theatre and Technology.

There is an extensive Arts Centre, and an impressive Library.

A new building project to further enhance teaching and learning spaces for History, Classics, Art, Drama, Food Technology, Computing and SEND is due to be ready for September 2025, and will be carbon net zero once operational.

The Curriculum. This is kept as broad as possible up to GCSE, with a balance between Arts and Science subjects. Students usually take a maximum of 10 GCSEs, while A Level candidates may choose from over 20 subjects. The vast majority of our Sixth Form students go on to Russell Group universities, including Oxford and Cambridge.

Careers. Guidance is given throughout a student's career at St George's, but particularly while students are making GCSE, A Level and university choices. The Careers Coordinator has a contemporary, well stocked Careers Room and makes effective use of testing, portfolios, work experience, trial interviews, Challenge of Industry days and computer software to support students.

Art. The Art Department attracts large numbers of students at GCSE and A Level who achieve consistently high results in their examinations. A large proportion of A Level candidates successfully apply to Art Colleges, often each receiving several offers in this highly competitive field.

Music. Music plays a vital part in school life. There is a wide range of music-making encompassing early music, madrigal groups, jazz, rock, African Drumming as well as more traditional ensembles, orchestras and wind bands. The choir and orchestra give regular performances (including radio broadcasts), and usually tour Europe annually. Tuition is available on all orchestral instruments from a team of 36 visiting specialists who teach over 400 students each week. Students play in youth orchestras and have gained scholarships to the major conservatoires.

Responsibility and Service. Many students engage in care for elderly people at home or in care homes, as well as those with disabilities. Groups of Sixth Form students accompany people with disabilities to Lourdes in the Easter and Summer terms, and for two weeks each Summer term, students from the Junior School and College take part in GO! (Georgian Outreach); an abundance of community projects that range from gardening and conservation to helping the elderly and local state schools. Students find these activities a rewarding exercise in Christian service. More recently, Sixth Form students have supported refugee children with online weekly tutoring to support their transition to British schools, and their BBC Award Winning Sixth Form Kennedy Club embraces providing hospitality and entertainment for displaced and refugee young people each Thursday evening.

There is a flourishing College Council, and the Prefect and Mentor system offer positions of responsibility to the oldest students.

The Duke of Edinburgh's Award scheme is offered at Bronze, Silver and Gold levels and all students are encouraged to take part.

Pastoral Care. The spiritual, moral and academic wellbeing of the students is the concern of every member of staff at the College. Nearly all academic staff act as Group Tutors with particular responsibility for the daily care of their students and for forging links with parents.

St George's are the only independent school of their size that allocated two tutors to each tutor group in the First and Third Years. This allows far richer personal attention in these key starting points for students.

Each Year Group is led by a Head of Year, and the three Chaplains have a general pastoral role. All groups have a day of retreat away each year. The College also has six Houses to which the students are affiliated, and all students have one period per week as part of their PSE programme. St George's also has pastoral specialists, an in-house counsellor and a peer-support network.

Extracurricular Activities. A very wide range of clubs and societies take place both at lunchtime and after school. In addition to music and sport, a broad range of interests is catered for. Some examples include Lego Robotics, Young Enterprise, Philosophy and Mindfulness, and new clubs are added each year.

Sport. All students participate in the wide variety of sports offered at St George's: rugby, hockey, netball, cricket, tennis, rowing, and rounders, plus a wide range of other activities such as golf, athletics, badminton, basketball and cross country. Each student has the opportunity to develop their own talents in small coaching groups. The College has its own Activity Centre, Boat House on the Thames, 19 tennis courts (including four indoor), two floodlit artificial pitches with viewing stand, floodlit netball courts, six artificial cricket nets, one main pavilion and two smaller cricket pavilions, and eight rugby pitches. The College has access to the Junior School's heated outdoor swimming pool. Attendance at national hockey finals is an annual event and the College hosts a very popular Under 18 Hockey Sixes every year. International honours have recently been gained in hockey, cricket, rowing and tennis.

Junior School. St George's Junior School is located nearby in Thames Street, Weybridge, and is co-educational for children aged 3 to 11.

(*For further details, please see Junior School entry in IAPS section.*)

Fees per term (2023–2024). First Year to Upper Sixth: £8,055. Lunches are optional at £425.

Charitable status. St George's College Weybridge is a Registered Charity, number 1017853, and a Company Limited by Guarantee. The aims and objectives of the Charity are the Christian education of young people.

Governing Body:
Chair: Mr D Nowlan
Mrs S Allom
Mr D Bicarregui
Mrs T Bowden
Mrs C Burnham
Mrs M Fawcett
Dr L Gordon
Mr J Hood
Mr T Kirkham
Mr N Lemmon
Mrs S Munk
Mr C Prescott
Mrs M Satchel
Mrs C Shevlin
Mr K Gosal
Clerk to the Governors: Mrs C Punt

***Headmistress*: Mrs R F Owens**, MA Oxon, PGCE, NPQH

Deputy Head, Academic: Mr H Warner, BA Hons, PGCE
Deputy Head, Pastoral: Miss S L Hall, BSc, PGCE
Deputy Head, Staff: Mr A Cornick, BA Hons, PGCE
Assistant Head, Extra Curricular & College Entry: Ms H Taylor, BA Hons, PGCE
Assistant Head, Pastoral: Mrs T A Hall, BSc, MSc, PGCE
Assistant Head, Academic: Mr J E Davies, BA, PGCE
Assistant Head, Sixth Form: Mr J D Carr, BA Hons, PGCE
Assistant Head, Curriculum: Mr R H Cheney, BSc, QTS

College Chaplain: Fr Martin Ashcroft, CJ, MA, MA, STB, BPhil, BA CertEd
Assistant Chaplain: Mrs J Mall
Assistant Chaplain: Mr K Mendes
Heads of Department:
Academic Support: Miss R M Kippin, BA, PGCE
Art: Mr T A Mcllwaine, BA Hons, PGCE
Biology: Mr M T Stather, BSc Hons, PGCE
Business & Economics: Mr D P Danaher, MTL, BA, PGCE
Chemistry: Ms S E Goodfellow, MA Oxon, BA Hons, PGCE
Computing: Mrs L Bahrami, BSc, PGCE
Design & Technology: Mrs E M Larkin, BA Hons, PGCE
Director of Drama: Mr J R Garbett, BA Hons, PGCE
English: Mr N Waight, BA Hons, PGCE
Food & Nutrition: Mrs J B Weaver, BA Hons, PGCE
Geography: Miss L Hamer (*Christmas Term*); Mr J F Odling, BSc, PGCE (*from 1/1/2024*)
History: Mr M J Barham, BA Hons, PGCE
Languages: Mr T Deive, BA, PGCE (*i/c Spanish*)
Latin: Mrs S Carpenter, BA Hons, PGCE
Mathematics: Miss S H Arif, MEd, BSc Hons, PGCE
Director of Music: Miss K B Wardil, BA Hons, PGCE
Physics: Mr B J Peake, BSc, PGCE
Politics: Mr P Gillingham, BA Hons, PGCE,
Psychology: Mr W B Harrison, BA Hons, PGCE
Religious Studies: Mr S W McAndrew, BA Hons, PGCE, QTS
Director of Sport: Mrs L E Gibson, BSc, PGCE

St Helen and St Katharine

Faringdon Road, Abingdon, Oxfordshire OX14 1BE

Tel:	+44 (0) 1235 520173
email:	admissions@shsk.org.uk
website:	www.shsk.org.uk
X/Twitter:	@SHSKSchool
Facebook:	@StHelenStKatharine
Instagram:	@shskschool
LinkedIn:	/shskschool

Founded in 1903, St Helen and St Katharine is an independent day school for girls and young women aged 9–18 in Abingdon, just south of Oxford. Our 720+ students study in a campus-style environment with beautiful Edwardian and modern buildings – including a brand-new Sixth Form Centre, the Benedict Building – set in 22 acres of grounds. We offer students the best possible experience at each stage of their educational journey, from our Junior Department through to Sixth Form.

St Helen's is a school where bright girls with enquiring minds thrive, as they grow into intellectually curious and erudite young women. Academic life is full, vibrant and spirited, both within and beyond the classroom, combining to stimulate intellectual endeavour and inquisitive independence which embody the ethos of our school. Our goal is to ensure that every student achieves success as she defines it so that she can believe in herself, her talents and abilities, and feel prepared and equipped for life beyond school.

Academic. Ranked top independent girls school in Oxfordshire (*The Times Parent Power 2023*), our academic results are excellent and consistently place us among the best schools in the country. In 2023, 92% of A level grades were A*–B, and 73% were A*–A. 82% of (I)GCSE grades were 9–7, while 61% were 9–8.

Our curriculum offers a full, broad and stimulating range of subjects at all ages as well an extensive range of opportunities for academic enrichment beyond lessons, such as attending specialist lectures and conferences, discussion dinners and Oxbridge preparation.

Our vision for St Helen's Sixth Form is to create an environment for our students that will spark their intellectual spirit and imagination. We offer students the chance to create a programme of four individual elements of study where they choose three or four A levels as the core of their academic work, some taught jointly with Abingdon School. They can then add a St Katharine's Study option – for example, an EPQ, Ethics for Scientists or Mandarin – to complement or contrast their A level subjects.

Pastoral. Behind everything we do at St Helen's is a deeply held belief in the value of kindness. Working with families, it is our intention that every student leaves the School valuing the power of being kind to themselves and to others. We want them to be confident in creating and maintaining secure, appropriate and positive relationships with other people as they travel through life. We support them in developing an increased self-understanding and to be able to savour the best of times and weather the more challenging moments.

We do a lot of talking and listening. Students have a range of people with whom they can share their world in addition to their friends. At the heart of the pastoral system, Form Tutors are the first port of call alongside an extensive network of support including the Head of Section, Pastoral Deputy Head, Health Centre, Counselling team and Chaplain.

We are truly ambitious for every student, pastorally surrounding them with kind, consistent and dedicated people who want to help them have a happy school experience and the foundations in place to thrive in the world beyond school.

Extracurricular activities, trips and visits. Our broad and exciting extracurricular programme, Beyond, plays a central role within school life. Students are offered myriad opportunities to explore and extend their interests as we actively encourage them to give new things a go. We host 70+ sports clubs for elite competition as well as for leisure, 300+ music lessons per week and at least six drama productions every year. There are clubs and societies from cricket and debating to philosophy and Minecraft, as well as activities such as DofE and the Tycoon Enterprise competition.

First-hand experiences and opportunities to travel give students a chance to broaden their understanding of themselves and the world, and play their part in developing self-reliance. Whether joining a netball, cricket and tennis tour to Sri Lanka, a volunteering expedition to Eswatini or studying volcanic and glacial landscapes in Iceland, going on trips provides lifelong memories through the fun and activities they involve.

Facilities. Over the last decade, an extensive building programme has been undertaken with many new additions to the School, including our Sports Centre, Performing Arts Centre, state-of-the-art Library, Science Centre and a 3D Design Centre. Our new Sixth Form Centre, the Benedict Building, opened in January 2023 and features nine spacious classrooms, a range of individual and group study spaces, a flexible hall and a café.

Admissions. Students are admitted to the Junior Department at either Years 5 or 6, and to the senior school at Years 7, 9 or Lower Sixth. It may be possible to admit students into other years should a place be available.

Scholarships. Our scholarship programme seeks to recognise excellence and potential across academic ability, music, art, drama and sport. Our scholarship programme is not subject to means testing and varies in duration and value.

Bursaries. Opening access for families who would not otherwise be able to afford school fees has always been central to our ethos. If a student has the ability, imagination and drive to grasp the opportunities on offer at St Helen's, we would like to give her that opportunity We offer means-tested bursaries from 20–100% of fees from Year 7, as well as transformational bursaries at A level.

Fees per term (2023–2024). £6,895.

Charitable status. The School of St Helen and St Katharine Trust is a registered charity, number 286892.

Chair of Governors: Mr Kevan Leggett

***Headmistress*: Mrs Rebecca Dougall**, MA London, BA Bristol

Director of Finance and Operations: Mrs Nicola McAvoy, BSc London
Senior Deputy Head: Mr John Hunt, MA St Andrews
Pastoral Deputy Head: Mrs Elizabeth Bedford, MA Oxford Brookes, BA Durham

Assistant Head, Academic Enrichment and Extracurricular Activities: Dr Abbie Pringle, DPhil, MSc Oxon, BSc Oxford Brookes
Assistant Head, Futures and Partnerships: Mrs Heather Darcy, MA Warwick, BSc London
Director of Communications and Marketing: Ms Lea Askgaard, MA Southern Denmark

St Lawrence College

Ramsgate, Kent CT11 7AE

Tel: 01843 572900 (Head of College)
01843 572912 (Junior School)
01843 808080 (Bursar/General Office)
01843 572931 (Admissions)

email: bursar@slcuk.com
admissions@slcuk.com

website: www.slcuk.com

X/Twitter: @slcMain

Facebook: @slcukofficial

Co-educational, Day: age 3–18 years, Boarding: age 7–18 years.

Number of Pupils.

Senior School 388 pupils in total: 95 boy boarders, 72 girl boarders, 221 day pupils.

Junior School 148 pupils: 4 boarders (3 boys, 1 girl), 144 day pupils.

Educating children from the age of 3 to 18 years, this safe and caring school is set in over 80 acres of spacious, stunning grounds which house beautiful old architecture combined with new modern builds and facilities. Founded in 1879, it is home to 536 day and boarding pupils from local, UK and international families and welcomes boarders from 7 years of age.

High Performance Learning is embedded in our supportive, caring environment, which is founded on traditional Christian values. We have small class sizes where each child is an individual, nurtured to succeed in all aspects of life, ranging from progress in their studies to empathy, resilience and leadership.

Academic. St Lawrence has a long record of providing an excellent academic education within a supportive community, but is also modern in its outlook and very well suited to preparing pupils for a rapidly changing world. Class sizes are small and pastoral support is strong. Academic standards are high and impressive results are achieved across all years in the school. An extensive choice of GCSEs and A Levels are offered, with an excellent success rate of pupils going on to their first-choice university, including Oxbridge.

In the Junior School pupils are given the opportunity to explore new experiences such as Forest School, Thinking and Learning Skills and STEAM enrichment subjects. Pupils are expected to become independent learners and participate in STRETCH homework projects; we do not have Gifted and Talented for the few but rather we have STRETCH for all.

Boarding. Boarding pupils enjoy a 'home from home' experience, both in terms of comfort and atmosphere. In recent years, a massive programme of investment has created some truly remarkable facilities for boarders. All senior boarders are housed in single or double rooms with en-suite facilities and younger boarders are placed in rooms of between two and five pupils with modern streamlined en-suite bathrooms and Junior boarders (from age 7–11) enjoy living in Kirby House, a modern, purpose-built development which offers en-suite accommodation of exceptional quality.

Facilities & Extracurricular. Continued investment saw a new Science, Art and Design Centre opened in May 2018. Sporting facilities are exceptional and expert coaching is provided at all levels in a variety of disciplines including hockey, rugby, netball and cricket. There is an Olympic-standard waterbased hockey pitch and the Sports Centre houses a fitness suite, squash courts, climbing wall, dance studio and a large sports hall for badminton, basketball, etc. Music and drama flourish, enhanced by a 500-seat Theatre. Alongside the traditional chapel and library sits the school's modern coffee shop and boarders are able to use all of the facilities in the evenings and at weekends. All pupils benefit from an extensive activities programme which includes the CCF (Combined Cadet Force) and the Duke of Edinburgh's Award scheme, as well as chess, climbing, archery, golf, fencing, horse riding, table tennis, musical theatre, and many more activities.

Membership of the wider College community gives Junior School pupils the best of both worlds, and they are able to share many of the Senior School's excellent specialist facilities, including the Sports Centre and Theatre. The wide range of sports on offer includes rugby, hockey, cricket, netball, football, athletics, cross-country and swimming. There are plenty of fixtures against other schools, but, most importantly, children learn the value of fitness, cooperative teamwork and good sportsmanship. There is a proud musical tradition, and plenty of scope for drama and the creative arts, including LAMDA lessons. Some extra-curricular activities take place at the end of the school day, but most are concentrated into the popular, informal varied Saturday morning programme.

Location. The school is set in a safe, self-contained campus situated within easy walking distance of the historic seaside town of Ramsgate, home to the stunning Royal Harbour – currently the only Royal Harbour in England. It has excellent transport links to the continent, being near both Dover and the Channel Tunnel. London is only 75 minutes away by high-speed rail link to St Pancras International. Both Gatwick and Heathrow are under 2 hours away.

Exam Results. Outstanding results are achieved by the most academic students who progress to top universities. In 2019/20 the school entered the High Performance Learning (HPL) Fellowship of World Class Schools, confirming that our approach enables students to develop the cognitive skills, values, attitudes and attributes needed for high academic performance and lifetime success.

2023 Exam results – GCSE (9–7) 33%, GCSE (9–6) 49%, GCSE (9–4) 85%, A Levels (A*-A) 17%, A Levels (A*-B) 40%, A Levels (A*-C) 64%.

Admissions.

Junior School

An initial parental tour with the Head or Admissions Officer will be followed by a Pupil Taster Day, which allows the prospective pupil to be assessed in numeracy and literacy as well as getting to know the school from the inside.

Subject to a satisfactory meeting and supporting documentation, the Head of the Junior School may offer a place.

All parents will be asked to complete and return a Registration Form and a £100 Registration Fee (non-refundable).

Upon receipt of the Registration Form, the Terms and Conditions of the School will be sent with an Acceptance Form. The Acceptance Form must be completed and returned together with a deposit. This will secure a place at the School.

The deposit will be held for the duration of the child's time here and will be returned when all outstanding accounts have been settled in full. It does not form part of the payment for school fees or boarding fees that are charged termly in advance.

Senior School

Admission to St Lawrence College requires completion of the Registration Form and a £100 Registration Fee (non-refundable). The admissions process includes return of the form, along with the most recent School report for the student. Completion of assessments, where required CAT tests and an Interview with the Head of College form part of the admissions process for all students.

At 16+ the offer of a place will be dependent on the above processes and a meeting with the Deputy Head responsible for Academics and/or Head of Sixth Form.

EU and Overseas Students will be admitted on the same basis as above, however an EAL paper is included. Our special EFL centre will assess and integrate overseas pupils into the curriculum by offering a range of English teaching options, including an intensive English course.

Fees per term (2023–2024). Senior School: Boarders £11,242–£13,633, Day £6,421–£6,959.

Junior School: Boarders £9,818, Day £2,938–£4,597.

Fees are due and payable before the commencement of the relevant school term. St Lawrence College offers generous sibling allowances.

Individual Private Tuition: £60 per hour. Individual Instrumental Music: £41 per hour.

Bursaries. Parents in HM Forces pay the MOD CEA (Continuity of Education Allowance) plus 10% of our main boarding and tuition fees. Bursaries are awarded annually to pupils in need of financial assistance and who are likely to make a positive contribution to the life of the school. Bursaries may be awarded to new or existing pupils of the College and pupils who have been awarded a scholarship that requires supplementing. Parents may apply to the Governors' Bursary Committee for assistance and will be required to complete a confidential grant application form. Bursaries are means tested.

Scholarships. Scholarships can be offered in Years 7–11 for outstanding academic ability, art, drama, music or sports disciplines, worth up to 25% of fees. Sixth Form scholarships are also available.

Charitable status. The Corporation of St Lawrence College is a Registered Charity, number 307921. It exists to provide education for children.

Clerk to the Governors and Bursar: J A Connelly, MA, MBA, BEng, CEng, MIET

***Head of College*: Barney Durrant**, MA

Deputy Head (*Academic*): B Pennells, BA Hons
Assistant Head (*Academic*): K B Parker, BA Hons, PGCE (*Head of Design & Technology*)
Deputy Head (*Pastoral*): T Moulton, BA
Chaplain: Revd J P Goodwin-Hudson (*Religious Studies*)
Assistant Head, 6th Form: E Matthews, BA (*Drama*)
Director of Marketing, Admissions and Development: E Taker, BSc Hons

Junior School
Head: Mrs E Rowe, BA Hons, PGCE

St Leonards School

St Andrews, Fife KY16 9QJ

Tel: 01334 472126
email: contact@stleonards-fife.org
website: www.stleonards-fife.org
X/Twitter: @StLeonards_Head
Facebook: @stleonardsschool
Instagram: @stleonardsschool
LinkedIn: /school/st-leonards-school

Motto: *Ad Vitam*

Situated in the heart of St Andrews, St Leonards offers an outstanding co-educational boarding and day education for pupils aged five to 18, combining high academic achievement and opportunity with an inspirational atmosphere.

There are approximately 600 pupils in the School, of 35 different nationalities, with an equal number of boys and girls and around 145 boarders.

St Leonards was named Scotland's *Independent School of the Year 2019* by the Sunday Times Schools Guide.

Ethos. Founded in 1877, St Leonards aims to prepare young people for the challenges of life ahead, in line with the School's motto 'Ad Vitam', and to provide them with the skills to step into the world with confidence and integrity. We offer a broad, rigorous education and exceptional opportunities, while instilling confidence, responsibility and independence.

Location and Campus. St Leonards combines a beautiful, historic campus with the cultural and academic buzz that comes from being in the heart of the seaside university town of St Andrews.

The School is situated in a secure campus within the medieval walls of the former St Andrews Priory. The site has served as a place of learning since the 16th century and contains several buildings of historical significance, including our library, a building once used by Mary Queen of Scots as lodgings.

Students at St Leonards have sandy beaches, historic landmarks and world-famous golf courses on their doorstep, as well as the friendly town of St Andrews itself, in which our pupils are made to feel very much part of the community.

St Andrews is less than an hour from Edinburgh and just 20 minutes from Dundee (a one-hour flight from London).

Curriculum. St Leonards was the first school in Scotland to be accredited as an all-through International Baccalaureate School, delivering the inspiring Primary Years Programme, Middle Years Programme and IB Diploma and Career-related Programme in the Sixth Form.

In Years 7–11, pupils follow the MYP, followed by IGCSEs – typically around ten. A one-year Pre-IB course is also offered (equivalent to Year 11).

Years 1–6 follow the PYP, with all our IB Programmes ensuring a seamless learner journey, from Year 1 up to Year 13.

University Connection. The School has close links with the University of St Andrews, which was named top UK university by The Times Good University Guide for 2022. Each year, St Leonards appoints an Associate Researcher, a postgraduate student who provides a link for the pupils to the research community at the University. St Leonards students also have access to the University Library and Sports Centre and attend a range of lectures.

Sport, Drama, Art and Music. Students regularly enjoy success on the playing field in sports including rugby, lacrosse, hockey, tennis and football. They are encouraged to make the most of living just a few hundred yards from the most famous golf links in the world. The School runs a leading five-tier Golf Programme, delivered in partnership with St Andrews Links Golf Academy, and catering to all levels, from the complete beginner to the scratch golfer.

Pupils have the opportunity to learn a wide variety of musical instruments, leading to ABRSM recognition, while Drama students can take part in a number of professional-standard productions, staged both in School and at the neighbouring Byre Theatre. Art students show off their inspiring work every year in an exhibition that is open to the public, as well as gaining national recognition in photography awards.

Co-Curricular. There is an extensive range of over 50 different activities, including the Duke of Edinburgh's Award, sailing, beekeeping and debating. Trips abroad are organised throughout the school year, with recent destinations including Venice and Verona, skiing in the Alps, golf in La Manga, Spain, and a German exchange in Dresden. Community is central at St Leonards, with recent projects ranging from collecting supplies for Ukraine, to cooking and distributing fresh meals to families in need.

Boarding. St Leonards excels in its boarding provision. Thanks to an ambitious £5m refurbishment programme, students live in modern, stylish comfort in a country house setting. According to a recent Care Commission inspection report, St Leonards offers its boarding pupils, 'an outstanding, Scottish, boarding experience', with the quality of care and support and the quality of the environment rated as 'excellent'. Full, flexi and weekly boarding is available from the age of 10.

Fees per term (2023–2024). Years 1–3: £3,862, Years 4–6: £4,787 (day) or £9,464 (boarding), Years 7–9: £5,886 (day) or £11,504 (boarding), Years 10–13: £6,255 (day) or £14,744 (boarding). Weekly and flexi boarding fees are also available.

Admission. Applications can be considered for any year group, at any time during the school year, although some year groups do have waiting lists and early application is recommended. Financial assistance may be given, based on need. Full details are available from the Registrar.

Charitable status. St Leonards School is a Registered Charity, number SC010904.

Members of Council:
Chair: Col Martin Passmore, MA, GCGI, FRSA
Mr Philip Petersen, BSc, MBA
Ms Charlie Wilson, BSc, FCCA
Mrs Carole Arnot
Ms Christine Bowie, MSc, PQD, MDACP Accred
Mr Danny Campbell
Mrs Victoria Collison-Owen, MA
Mr Ken Dalton, BSc Hons, CEng
Mr Paul Dollman, BSc Hons, CA
Mr Neil Donaldson, MSc
Mrs Laura Jacks, JD
Mr Alistair J Lang, BLE Hons, LLB, Dip LP
Mrs Heidi Purvis, BA, PGCE
Mr Andrew Peddie
Mrs Fenella Taylor, BA Hons

Academic Staff:

***Head*: Simon Brian**, MA Hons Edinburgh

Senior Deputy Head: Dawn Pemberton-Hislop, BA Hons Sheffield, MBA Keele
Deputy Head (*Academic*): Will Gaisford, BA Oxford
Deputy Head (*Wellbeing*): Andrew Durward, BEd Hons Edinburgh
Deputy Head (*Boarding*): Gerry Young, BSc Strathclyde
Head of Sixth Form: Aileen Rees, MA Hons Cambridge
Assistant Head of Sixth Form: Jill White, BSc Hons Aberdeen
Head of Years 10 & 11: David Blair, BSc Hons Stirling
Head of Years 8 & 9: Fiona McGregor, BSc Hons St Andrews
Assistant Head of Years 8 & 9: Paul Shiells, BEd Hons Aberdeen
Acting Head of Years 4–6: Nicola Arkwright, BEd Hons Coventry
Head of Years 1–3: Claire Boissiere, MA Hons Dundee
Diploma & Career-related Programme Coordinator: Ben Seymour, BSc Hons UEA Norwich
GCSE Coordinator: Michael Dick, BSc Hons St Andrews

Middle Years Programme Coordinator: Kathryn McGregor, BA Hons Southampton
Primary Years Programme Coordinator: Catherine Brannen, MEd Aberdeen, MA Madrid

Art & Design:
Donna Rae, MA Glasgow, BFA Chicago
Margaret Behrens, BA Hons, Dip PG Edinburgh
Camilla Fyfe, BA Hons Oxford
Winsome Hardie, BA Hons DJCA Dundee
Linda Jackson, BA Hons DJCA Dundee
William Clark, MA Winchester, BA Hons Dundee

Classics:
Vitalii Berezhnoi, BA Hons Kaluga State
Dora Burbank, MA Hons St Andrews

Computer Science:
Gus Ferguson, MBChB Cape Town, MSc Heriot Watt

Economics:
Pablo Funcasta, BA Cambridge, MSc LSE
Paula Prudencio-Aponte, BSc Bolivia, PG Dip St Andrews, MSc Manchester

EAL and English B:
Dawn Cremonese, MA Hons St Andrews, MA TESOL Leicester
Nicola Greener, BA Hons Newcastle

English:
Alfonso Iannone, MA Hons, PG Dip Edinburgh
Katharine Gilbertson, MA Hons St Andrews
Denise Johnston, BA Hons Cardiff
Imogen Mowbray, BA Hons Birmingham
Vanessa Samuel, BA Hons Cambridge
Andrew Proudfoot, BA Hons Liverpool

Geography:
Amy Henderson, MA Hons Dundee
Jill White, BSc Hons Aberdeen
Victoria Sherwood, BEd Hons Manchester Metropolitan

History:
Damian Kell, BA Hons, MA Hons Oxford
Susannah Adrain, MA Hons Dundee
David McLeish, MA History Dundee
Lorna Greenwood, MA Hons Edinburgh, Cert Ed Studies London
Jennifer Murray-Turner, BEd British Columbia, BA Hons Toronto

Learning Support:
Gillian Greenwood, MA Hons Cambridge
Aisling Bonner, BA Dublin City
Catherine Gratwick, MA Hons St Andrews
Anna Radons-Harris, BSc Hons Lancaster
James Turner, BEd Toronto, BSc Hons Nottingham Trent, MSc Brunel
Ann Stephens, BEd Dundee

Library:
Angela Tawse, MA, PG Dip St Andrews, MA UCL, MCLIP

Mathematics:
Russell Hall, BSc Hons St Andrews
Jonathan Edwards, BEd Hons Wales
Hilary Ballantine, BSc Hons Edinburgh
Michael Dick, BSc Hons St Andrews
Stuart Reilly, BSc Hons, BA Hons OU
Kristina Struck, State Exam MA Berlin
Sean Pennycook, BEng Hons Napier

Modern Languages:
Nora Gannon, MA Aix-Marseilles
Kathryn McGregor, BA Hons Southampton, MEd Buckingham
Mary Bradley, BA Hons Durham
Rie Adya, BA, MA Rissho, MPhil, PhD Delhi
Susana Aranzana-Gonzalez, BA, MA, CAP Valladolid
Anne Bavaj, First State Examination, MA Bonn, Second State Examination Aachen
Anna Beck, BA Columbia, MBA Cornell
Marion Dalvai, MA Trento, MPhil Dublin, PhD Dublin
Jennifer Michels, MA Dundee
Ayah Durkawi, PhD Newcastle
Andrea Morris, MA Hons Glasgow
Marije Sneddon, BEd Ede
Louise Lacaille, MA Hons St Andrews, MSt Oxford
Elena de Celis Lucas, BA Hons A Coruna
Eulalia Grifell, MA Hons Heriot-Watt
Rebecca Masson, MA Hons, MLitt St Andrews
Max Sutherland, BSc OU, MA Hons St Andrews
Andrea Viggiano, BA Florence, PhD Bologna, PhD Cornell
Haiyan Wang, BA, MA Sichuan, Chengdu, MSc Dundee

Music:
Fiona Love, BMus Hons Glasgow
Annie Harratt, MA St Andrews
Liam Brolly, BMus Hons RCM
Kat Chisholm, GRNCM, PG Dip RSAMD
Douglas Clark, Dip Mus Ed RSAMD
Martin Dibbs, MA, MLitt, PhD St Andrews, DMS ARMC
Darryl Ritchie, BMus Hons Birmingham
Winston Emmerson, BSc Hons Rhodes, MSc, PhD UPE
Stuart Foggo
James Lind, BMus Hons, MMus RCS
Ruairidh Geddes, Dip ABRSM
Kenneth Letham, BMus Hons, PG Dip RCS
Kirstie Logan, BSc Hons OU, Graduate RNCM
Jessica Long, MA Hons St Andrews, Dip ABRSM, PG Dip RCS
Dorothy McCabe, GRSM, ARCM, ATCL, Cert Ed London
Mairi McCabe, BMus Hons Napier, ATCL, Dip ABRSM
Melanie O'Brien, Dip TCL TCM London, ALCM, LLCM Napier
Megan Read, MA Glasgow, PG Dip Mus RSAMD
Suzannah Rice, BA Hons Southampton
Lynne Ruark, DRSAM, LRAM, Glasgow, CertEd Edinburgh
Toni Russell, BA Hons Applied Music Strathclyde
Paul Shiells, BEd Hons Aberdeen
Sally Shiells, BEd Hons, MMus Aberdeen
Dorine Sorber, MA RC Brussels
Anthony White, BMus Hons Aberdeen

Physical Education:
Mark Baxter, BEd Hons Edinburgh
David Blair, BSc Hons Stirling
Fintan Bonner, BA Ireland
Andrew Broadhurst, BA Manchester Metropolitan
Louise Carroll, BEd Hons Edinburgh

Rosie Dawson, BA Hons Bangor
Neil Hislop, BEd Hons Jordanhill
Callum Parsons, BSc Abertay, HNC Fife College, UKCC Level 2 Coaching (*Scottish Rugby*)
Dylan Suttie, HNC Fife College, BSc Hons Abertay
Andrew Turnbull, BSc Napier

Psychology:
Rachael Cave, BSc Aberdeen

Science:
Sharon Moan, BSc Hons Manchester Metropolitan
Patrick Smith, BSc Glasgow
Rachel Deegan, BA Oxford
Emma Coyle, BSc Hons Edinburgh
Mary Kennovin, BSc Hons Portsmouth Polytechnic, PhD St Andrews
Charlotte Kirby, BSc Hons St Andrews
Fiona McGregor, BSc Hons St Andrews
Robert MacGregor, BSc Hons Edinburgh
Christopher Meighen, BSc Hons Edinburgh
Rebecca Patterson, BSc QMUC
Aileen Rees, MA Hons Cambridge
Sara Tedesco, MSc Taranton, PhD Cork
Mark Arnold, HNC Dundee
Alison Hill, MSc Glasgow, BSc Hons Aberdeen PhD Belfast
Paul Jardine, BSc Hons St Andrews

Theatre:
Nichola McQuade-Powell, BEd Hons London
Christian Olliver, BA London RCSSD, BA Hons Birmingham Trent, MA London City
Laura Stewart, MA Hons Kent
Eva Walker, BA Hons West of Scotland

St Leonards Years 1–6

Hannah Anderson, MA Hons Aberdeen
Nicola Arkwright, BEd Hons Coventry
Marina Barclay, PDA (*Classroom Assistant*)
Ailsa Beebee, BEd Dundee
Lauren Clements, BEd Strathclyde
Dianne Cormack, BSc Hons St Andrews
Anna Fisher, MA Hons Dundee
Annabel Lindsay, BA Hons Oxford Brookes
Georgina Majcher, BSc Hons Northumbria
Caz McIntee, MFA New York, BA Hons DJCAD (*Classroom Assistant*)
Adele Neave, BSc Hons Glasgow School of Art
Caroline Souter (*Classroom Assistant*)
Marije Sneddon, BEd Ede
Nicola Steven, BSc Hons Glasgow, PGDip QMU (*Classroom Assistant*)

Chief Operating Officer: Andrew Maitland
Head of External Relations: Sarah Proudfoot, MA Hons Edinburgh

St Mary's School Ascot

St Mary's Road, Ascot, Berkshire SL5 9JF
Tel: 01344 296600 (Main Switchboard)
01344 296614 (Admissions)
email: admissions@st-marys-ascot.co.uk
website: www.st-marys-ascot.co.uk

St Mary's School Ascot is a Roman Catholic boarding school founded by the Religious of the Institute of the Blessed Virgin Mary. St Mary's today is a self-governing, self-financing school.

Founded in 1885, the school is set in 55 acres within easy reach of London and Heathrow and close to the M4, M3 and M25 motorways.

Numbers on Roll. Boarders 365, Day pupils 23.

Age Range. 11–18.

Method of Entry. 11+ and 13+ School's own examination and interview. There is a small entry at Sixth Form.

Scholarships and Bursaries. At 11+ and 13+, there are three Academic Scholarships available worth up to 5% of the fees.

At 16+, there is one Academic Scholarship available worth up to 5% of the fees.

One Music Scholarship, worth 5% of the fees and free of charge musical instrument or vocal tuition for up to three 30-minute lessons per week, is awarded annually to a pupil entering the School at 11+ or 13+. Candidates must have qualified to at least Grade V on the first study instrument at the time of application.

One Art Scholarship worth up to 5% of the fees is awarded annually to a pupil entering the School at 11+, 13+ or 16+.

One All-Rounder Scholarship is is awarded annually to a pupil entering the School at 11+ and another at 13+.

One Sports Scholarship worth up to 5% of the fees is awarded annually to a pupil entering the School at 13+.

Means-tested bursaries are available.

Fees per term (2023–2024). Boarders £16,710, Day pupils £11,900.

Curriculum. All pupils follow a broad curriculum to GCSE including Religious Education, English, History, Geography, Maths, Biology, Physics, Chemistry, French, German, Italian, Spanish, Latin, Music, Drama, Art and Design, Computer Science and Physical Education. Tuition is also available in Piano, most String and Wind Instruments, Ballet, Tap Dancing, Speech and Drama, Ceramics and Craft activities, Tennis, Photography.

All pupils are prepared for GCSE at 16+ and typically take 10 subjects.

Sixth Form pupils have a choice of 25 A Level subjects and normally study 4 subjects. Interview, CV and course choice preparation is offered to all Upper Sixth pupils, including Oxbridge candidates. They are encouraged to undertake some of the many extra activities on offer and develop skills outside their A Level curriculum. Sixth Form pupils also have their own tutor who liaises closely with the Careers Specialist. Careers advice forms an integral part of the curriculum. This is supported by work experience, work shadowing placements and talks from external speakers, including

Ascot Alumnae. The majority of sixth form pupils go on to university, and preparation is offered to Oxbridge candidates.

The School is a member of Inspiring Futures, which provides careers information, advice and guidance.

Religious Education is an integral part of the curriculum and the chapel holds a central position in the life of the school.

Sport. A varied programme is offered depending on age group. It includes Netball, Hockey, Gym, Swimming, Cricket, Tennis, Squash, Badminton and Athletics.

Purpose-built sports complex with sports hall, dance studio, squash courts and fitness suite. A floodlit 400m athletics track and hockey pitch provides a year-round, all-weather sports facility.

Drama. Performing Arts Centre which includes a flexible auditorium with lighting catwalks and control room with teaching facilities, fully-equipped drama studio and make-up and dressing rooms.

Art, Drama, Music, Science, Modern Languages and English. Specialist buildings are provided for all of these subjects and all pupils are encouraged to develop their musical, artistic, scientific and linguistic skills.

Libraries. The senior and junior libraries form the academic heart of the school. The senior library was built to meet the specific needs of Year 11 and Sixth Form girls and includes seminar rooms, which are used for teaching and careers advice.

Other Activities. Senior pupils are encouraged to participate in Community Service Projects, and those interested may enter The Duke of Edinburgh's Award scheme. There is a wide range of club activities for all ages, and, as a termly boarding school, generous provision is made for evening and weekend activities.

Charitable status. St Mary's School Ascot is a Registered Charity, number 290286. Its aim is to provide an excellent education in a Christian atmosphere.

Board of Governors:
Ms C Vaughan (*Chair*)
Mr C Beirne
Mrs A Clementi
Mr M Hattrell
Ms A Lee
Mr P McKenna
Ms S Meadway
Mr A Neil
Ms A Polizzi di Sorrentino
Sr M Robinson
Ms G van Maaren
Mr J Weaver

Council:
The Lord Hemphill (*Chair*)
Mr M Armour
Mrs C Colacicchi
Mr N Davidson
Mr P Davis
Baroness S Hogg
The Hon Mrs O Polizzi

Senior Management Team:
***Headmistress*: Mrs D Staunton**, BA York, MA York, PGCE
Senior Deputy Head: Ms R Toner, BA Cantab, MA London, PGCE
Pastoral Deputy Head: Dr R Peat, BMus, MA, PhD City
Academic Deputy Head: Mrs B Breedon, BEd Queen's Belfast, MSc Ulster
Bursar: Mr G Brand, BA Leeds
Director of Sixth Form: Mr L Higgins, BA Nottingham, MEd Cantab, PGCE
Director of External Communications: Mr C Ellott, LLB UCL, BA OU, PGCE
Director of Co-Curricular: Mr A Smith, BA Warwick, MA Royal Holloway, PGCE

Catering Manager: Mr R Hope
Estate Manager: Mr T Clark
Finance Manager: Mr J Jordan
Registrar: Mrs S Young

A full staff list can be obtained on request on: 01344 296600

St Mary's Calne

Curzon Street, Calne, Wiltshire SN11 0DF

Tel: 01249 857200
email: admissions@stmaryscalne.org
website: www.stmaryscalne.org
X/Twitter: @StMarysCalne
Facebook: @stmaryscalne
Instagram: @stmaryscalne
LinkedIn: /school/st-mary's-calne

St Mary's Calne (founded in 1873) is an independent boarding and day school for girls aged 11–18, a happy, purposeful and flourishing community of around 360 pupils with an 80% to 20% boarding-to-day ratio. St Mary's welcomes cultural diversity and around 15% of the students come from overseas.

The school is located in the market town of Calne amidst the Wiltshire Downs, an area of stunning natural beauty and historical significance. The school is within easy reach of the university towns of Bath, Bristol and Oxford and just over an hour by train from London. This ideal location means that the girls benefit from a huge range of co-curricular opportunities.

Focus on the individual. Small by design, St Mary's provides exceptional all-round education in a warm, nurturing environment. It is the individualised approach to every aspect of school life that makes St Mary's Calne special. The pastoral care is outstanding. Every girl has a Tutor to support her through aspects of school life, from organisational skills and subject choices through to university application.

Academic Excellence. St Mary's Calne has a well-deserved reputation for academic excellence and is committed to providing an education that will challenge and inspire its pupils. In the *Sunday Times Parent Power Schools' Guide 2024*, St Mary's was ranked 1st independent school in Wiltshire and 2nd in the South West. St Mary's is also the first independent school in the UK to be awarded the Platinum Science Mark Award.

In 2023, students went on to study at a range of leading universities including Oxford, St Andrews, Durham, Edinburgh, Exeter, King's College London (KCL), London School of Economics (LSE) and, in recent years, have gained places at prestigious universities in the USA. They will be reading a broad range of subjects including Architecture, Biology, Business & Management, Classics, Computer Science, Engineering, English, Film & TV Production, Fine Art, History of Art, Law, Materials Science, Modern Languages, Music, Philosophy & Theology, Psychology, Sport & Exercise Science.

Co-Curricular Opportunities. Opportunities in sport, music, art and drama abound and the facilities are superb, including a £2.55 million sports complex and full-size astro, a purpose-built theatre, a Sixth Form Centre and a state-of-the-art new library, overlooking the orchard.

80% of girls play musical instruments and take part in a wide variety of ensembles. The girls perform at many events, both in the local community and further afield.

Drama productions in the purpose-built theatre are of the highest standard. In Year 9, students perform at a professional theatre and senior students perform annually at the Edinburgh Fringe. In Art, in addition to holding a triennial exhibition in London, the girls have received numerous awards, including having artwork selected for the Young Artists' Summer Show at the Royal Academy of Arts.

The girls excel at sport, and the school is represented at county level in several major sports, nationally in athletics and lacrosse and internationally in horse riding, with all girls taking advantage of the superb sports facilities.

The girls also enjoy many other sports, including tennis (the St Mary's Calne Tennis Academy was a National Finalist for 'School of the Year' 2021 at the LTA Tennis Awards), hockey, horse riding, swimming, badminton, kayaking and ski racing.

Outreach. The girls are very active in the local community and have helped in local hospitals and schools, performed concerts for the elderly in residential care homes and read to younger children in the community library. In addition, the girls help to raise awareness of, and funds for, local charities, such as Doorway, a charity which helps the homeless in North Wiltshire.

Fees per term (2023–2024). Boarding: £15,575, Day: £11,620.

Scholarships and Bursaries. Scholarships and Exhibitions are available to new entrants at 11+, 13+ and at Sixth Form. Any girl who is awarded a Scholarship or an Exhibition may apply for a means-tested Bursary.

We also offer Foundation Scholarships at entry to the school at 11+ for girls applying from the State sector.

Please contact Admissions for further details and key dates regarding our Scholarships and Bursaries on: admissions@stmaryscalne.org.

Charitable status. St Mary's School (Calne) is a Registered Charity, number 309482 and exists for the education of children.

Chair of Governors: Mr S Adde

***Acting Head*: Mrs D Harrison**, MA Cantab, PGCE Bristol, CPP Roehampton

Deputy Head Academic: Mr M Smyth, BSc Newcastle, PGCE Cantab, MSc Oxon

Deputy Head Pastoral: Mrs S Toland, MA Cantab, PGCE Brunel, CPP Roehampton

Director of External Relations: Mrs C Depla, MA St Andrews

Director of Sixth Form, High Education & Professional Guidance: Ms L Holloway, MA Oxon, MA Oxford Brookes

Head of Community Outreach: Mrs Claire Bolton, BA Leeds, PGCE Sheffield

School Chaplain: Revd J Beach, BSc Essex, BA Bristol, MTh Cardiff

St. Mary's College

Everest Road, Crosby, Merseyside L23 5TW

Tel: 0151 924 3926
email: office@stmarys.lpool.sch.uk
website: www.stmarys.ac
X/Twitter: @stmarys_college
Facebook: @stmaryscollegecrosby
Instagram: @stmaryscollegecrosby

Motto: *Fidem Vita Fateri*

St. Mary's College is an Independent Catholic School for boys and girls of all faiths aged 0–18, rated 'Excellent' in all areas by the Independent Schools Inspectorate (ISI). We are a thriving community which places a high value on outstanding academic achievement and all-round personal development. Our school is built on strong values which emphasise the importance of caring for others and striving for excellence in all we do. Boys and girls can start at our Bright Sparks & Early Years department (0–4 years) soon after birth and progress to our Preparatory School (4–11 years) before moving on to the College (11–18 years), where they achieve excellent public examination results. Our rich programme of extracurricular activities equips our pupils with the skills and values which will guide and support them throughout their lives. Scholarships and bursaries are available.

Numbers. There are 492 pupils in the Senior School; 169 pupils in the Preparatory School and 192 children in the Early Years department. There are no boarders.

Preparatory School. St. Mary's Prep offers an outstanding and inspiring primary education to 4–11 year olds. We provide individual attention, challenge and support which enables each child to achieve their own personal excellence, whatever that might be.

The academic thrust of the school is central with a strong focus on the key enabling skills of reading, writing and mathematics. Our curriculum is designed to give our pupils the best opportunity to succeed academically and develop a lifelong love of learning. Pupils are given a solid foundation in literacy and numeracy whilst developing skills in Science, History, Geography, Art, Design and ICT. These skills are developed through 'themes' chosen to capture the pupils' imagination and offer them the opportunity to explore different ways of learning. Specialist tuition in

French, Spanish, Music, PE and Games is also an integral part of our curriculum.

We also provide an extensive programme of extra-curricular activities, and pupils are encouraged to take advantage of these opportunities to develop their confidence and extend their experience.

The Head of the Preparatory School, Mr Jonathan Webster, will be pleased to meet you and show you round.

Senior School. At St. Mary's College, pupils benefit from small class sizes and excellent facilities, including specialist IT, design and technology and learning resource centres, a well-equipped sports centre and our specialist music school.

We pride ourselves on our inspirational approach to education, and the focus for our highly qualified and experienced teaching staff is a combination of academic excellence with modern and imaginative teaching methods. We teach pupils how to think, not what to think. A rigorous yet broad and balanced curriculum is provided across the range of the humanities and sciences. During their first three years our pupils study 14 distinct subjects including separate sciences, Classics, Latin and two foreign languages. In their fourth year – after thorough consultation with pupils and parents – they begin two-year GCSE courses in a minimum of ten subjects, which must include English, English Literature, Mathematics, Religious Studies, and Science (either 3 or 2 GCSEs). A foreign language is strongly recommended to be one of the choices.

As well as academic excellence, we place a lot of emphasis on the cultural life of our pupils, with every child entering the college being given the opportunity to play a musical instrument. Drama and dance are also important features of life at St. Mary's, and our pupils are not afraid to tackle the classics, from Ajax and Electra to Grease and Oliver!

Specialist coaching is provided in numerous sports, including Rugby, Cricket, Football, Hockey, Netball, Swimming, Athletics and Cross-Country, and we have excellent facilities at our 20-acre playing fields, sports centre and brand new state-of-the-art gym.

A wide range of other student interests are catered for by a large number of clubs and societies meeting at lunchtimes or after school. Our Combined Cadet Force (Army and Royal Air Force) offers opportunities including adventure training and air experience flying, while there is also strong participation in the Duke of Edinburgh's Award Scheme.

Another important objective of the college is to broaden the horizons of our pupils and we do this via regular foreign trips, language exchanges and sport and music tours which have, in recent years, ventured as far afield as the United States and Australia.

St. Mary's is easily accessible to pupils throughout Merseyside and West Lancashire thanks to our extensive transport network of school coaches.

The Principal, Mr Michael Kennedy, will be pleased to welcome you to St. Mary's College for an informal meeting and a tour of the school.

Fees per term (2023–2024). Senior School: £4,421; Preparatory School: £3,044.

Scholarships & Awards. We offer a number of Academic Scholarships, which can be worth up to half fees and will be tenable throughout a pupil's career in the senior school (including Sixth Form), provided the pupil's efforts and behaviour remain consistent with the standard expected of scholars. The awards are based on academic merit alone and will be irrespective of income. There is no need to make a separate application: offers will automatically be made to parents whose children come top of the field in the entrance examination. Our Edmund Rice Scholarships (Assisted Places) are won by academic ability but also take a family's earnings into consideration.

We also award scholarships for those gifted in art, music and sport although the financial value of these Excellence Awards, as they are collectively known, is more modest; our Art, Music and Sport Scholarships are typically worth a £1,000 discount off annual fees.

Sixth Form Scholarships. Edmund Rice Scholarships are available on merit, and are awarded on the basis of a Scholarship Examination.

Charitable status. St. Mary's College Crosby Trust Limited is a Registered Charity, number 1110311. The aims and objectives of the Charity are to advance religious and other charitable works.

Governors:
Mrs S Ward, FCMA, BSc (*Chair of Governors*)
Mr M McKenna, LLB (*Deputy Chair*)
Mrs L Martindale, MA, BEd
Mr D McCaughrean, MSc
Mrs P Old, LLB
Mr C Platt, FIIRSM, CMIOSH
Mr A Symons, BSc
Mrs H Thompson, ACA, BSc
Mrs S Tsao, BSc
Mr C Wright, BSc, MRSC, MIoD

***Principal*: Mr M Kennedy**, BSc, MA, NPQH, CChem, MRSC

Vice Principal: Mrs J Thomas, BSc

Senior Leadership Team:
Mrs S Bartolo, BEd (*Head of Lower School*)
Mr A Byers, BA (*Head of Middle School, Head of Music*)
Mr P Duffy, MPhil (*Head of Sixth Form*)
Mr S Gray (*Business Director*)
Mr J Quint, BA, PGCert (*Director of Marketing, Admissions & Development*)
Mr N Rothnie, MA Oxon (*Extended Learning Coordinator, Head of History*)

Preparatory School Headmaster: Mr J Webster, BA

Head of Early Years: Mrs A Haigh, BEd

St Paul's Girls' School

Brook Green, Hammersmith, London W6 7BS
Tel: 020 7603 2288 (Front Office)
020 7605 4882 (Admissions)
email: admissions@spgs.org
frontoffice@spgs.org
website: www.spgs.org
X/Twitter: @SPGSMain
Facebook: @StPaulsGirlsSchool
Instagram: @stpaulsgirlsschool
LinkedIn: /stpaulsgirlsschool

See full entry in the **GSA** section, on **p. 486**.

St Paul's School

Lonsdale Road, Barnes, London SW13 9JT
Tel: 020 8748 9162
email: reception@stpaulsschool.org.uk
website: www.stpaulsschool.org.uk
X/Twitter: @StPaulsSchool
Facebook: @StPaulsSchool1509
Instagram: @stpaulsschoollondon
LinkedIn: /St-Paul's-School

Motto: *Fide et literis*

St Paul's School is one of the UK's leading independent schools, offering an outstanding all-round education for some of the brightest boys in the country.

Founded in 1509 by John Colet, Dean of St Paul's Cathedral, to educate boys 'from all nations and countries indifferently', regardless of race, creed or social background, St Paul's School remains committed to his vision today.

Erasmus, the greatest scholar of the northern Renaissance, advised Colet in the original planning of St Paul's School and wrote textbooks for the School's use. Today, a sense of scholarship, a commitment to all-round excellence and a culture of venturing beyond the syllabus continues to pervade life at St Paul's, which is known for its inspirational and responsive teaching, outstanding academic results and a commitment to contribute to the local community, as well as national and international charities.

University destinations. The most recent year for which the school has a full list of the destinations of St Paul's leavers is 2022. Typically around 50% of Paulines attend the top 10 universities within the 'QS World Rankings'. Of those that choose to study in the UK, the largest proportion go to Oxford or Cambridge, with more than one quarter of all pupils gaining places each year. In 2022, 35 pupils headed to top North American universities including MIT, Stanford, Harvard and the University of Chicago, which are also within the top 10 in the 2022 QS World University rankings, and seven to other international institutions.

A small number of pupils choose to take GAP years, paid employment, apprenticeships or internships.

Admission. Application for Admission to St Paul's is made via the online application form on the school's website. 13+ candidates can register when they are in Year 5. In the Autumn Term of Year 6, three years before entry, they must take the ISEB Online Pre-Test. The results of this, together with a detailed report from their current school, will be used to select candidates for interview and written assessments. Following the interview and written assessments, boys may be offered a Main List place which is conditional upon continued good conduct and academic progress at their existing school, including an unreserved reference of support from their Head Teacher in Year 8.

There is a registration fee of £175 at 13+.

For 16+ applications should be made one year in advance. Further details can be found on the School's website. No registration fee is required at the time of applying. Successful applications will pay the fee when accepting their place.

A deposit of £3,200 is required when a parent accepts the offer of a place for their son after interview. The Deposit will be returnable only if the boy fails to reach the necessary standard prior to entry or when the final account has been cleared after the boy leaves St Paul's.

Fees per term (2023–2024). The Basic Fee for St Paul's is £9,895 and £7,910 for St Paul's Juniors. This covers tuition, games, loan books, stationery, libraries, medical inspection, a careers aptitude test in the GCSE year, certain school publications and lunch, which all boys are required to attend. Charges are made for the purchase of some books (which become the personal property of boys) and public examination fees.

There are facilities for up to 35 boarders (ages 13 to 18) and boarding is flexible, allowing boys to go home at weekends as they wish. The Boarding Fee is £14,891 per term. Boys joining at age 13 can only be weekly boarders and must return to a family member or approved guardian at weekends. Boys joining at age 16 can be full boarders. Boarding is not available for pupils below Year 9. There is a second boarding house for 11 pupils to accommodate flexi-boarders.

Assistance with fees – bursaries. St Paul's takes pride in giving the best possible education to talented boys, irrespective of their family's financial circumstances. Each year there are funds available for free and subsidised places for those with a household income below £120,000. Bursaries are means-tested each year and may change as a family's financial situation improves or deteriorates. More information can be obtained from the school's website.

Scholarships. St Paul's School offers a number of honorary Academic Scholarships annually at 13+ and 17+. These are worth £60 per year. For external candidates entering at 13+, the scholarship examination is held annually in May. There are also a number of music scholarships awarded annually at 11+ and 13+. Each Scholarship is worth £60 per annum, plus free tuition on two instruments. Exhibitions consist of free tuition on one instrument only.

Curriculum. All boys follow a broadly based course up to IGCSE/GCSE. Thereafter in Year 12 and Year 13, A Level subjects are arranged so that boys can combine a wide range of Arts and Science subjects if they so wish. In Year 12, nearly all boys take four subjects and may also undertake an Extended Project Qualification, followed by three or four subjects in Year 13. Subjects are all taken in a linear way and there are no public exams in Year 12.

Games. Physical Activities offered include: Athletics, Badminton, Basketball, Cricket, Cross-Country, Fencing, Fives, Futsal, Golf, Judo, Rackets, Rowing, Rugby, Rugby Sevens, Sculling, Soccer, Swimming, Tennis, Table Tennis, Ultimate Frisbee and Water Polo. In addition, Climbing, Cycling and Sailing take place off site. The school has its own Swimming Pool, Fencing Salle, Tennis, Fives and Rackets Courts, Dojo, Fitness Centre and its own Boat House. The Sports Centre also comprises a Main Hall and Gymnasium. The Sports Hall is equipped for Tennis, Badminton, Basketball and has five indoor Cricket nets.

Music. All boys are taught music in the classroom in the first year. In subsequent years, GCSE is taught as a two-year course, and A Level taught in the final two years. Additional tuition is available in piano, organ, all the standard orchestral instruments, jazz, music theory and aural. There is a wide range of ensemble activities – chamber music, jazz and big band, two full orchestras, two training orchestras and several choral/vocal groups. The music school contains a professional standard concert venue, the Wathen Hall, several rehearsal rooms, two large teaching rooms and a music technology suite. There are regular concerts and recitals, as well as music competitions, musicals and external engagements, workshops and festivals.

School Societies. There is a wide choice of more than 30 Societies, including Musical, Artistic and Dramatic activities, Debating, Historical and Scientific Societies, Politics and Economics, Bridge, Chess, Natural History, Photography, European Society, a Christian Union and Social Service.

St Paul's Juniors adjoins the school. (*For details see entry in IAPS section.*)

Charitable status. St Paul's School is a Registered Charity, number 1119619. The object of the charity is to promote the education of boys in Greater London.

Governors:
Chairman: Richard Cassell, BA, LLB
Deputy Chairman: Tim Haynes, BA

Tom Adeyoola, MA
Sarah Barker, LLB
Veryan Exelby, MA
Andrew Fenwick, BA
Lord Grabiner, KC
Harry Hampson, MA, MEng
Joanne Harris, BSc, MBBS
Sam Newhouse, MA
Alison Palmer, BSc
Aisha Sanusi, BA
Rupert Tate, MA
Sarah Thomas, MA
Mark Tuffney, BSc
Rt Hon Lord Vaizey of Didcot, BA

Clerk to the Governors: Elizabeth Wilkinson

St Paul's Teaching Staff:

***High Master*: Sally-Anne Huang**, MA Oxon, MSc Leicester, MA Roehampton

Surmaster: Fran Clough, BSc Dunelm, PhD Cantab

Deputy Head – Academic: James Gazet, MA Cantab
Deputy Head – Co-Curricular: Thomas Killick, MA, PhD Cantab
Deputy Head – Pastoral and Boarding: Nick Watkins, MA Oxon, PGCE IoE
Deputy Head – Mental Health, Wellbeing & Life Skills: Samuel Madden, BA Exeter, MA LSE

Director of Admissions: Andy Mayfield, BSc Manchester, MSc, DPhil Oxon
Director of Teaching and Learning: Tahmer Mahmoud, BA Oxon, PGCE Leeds, MA London
Director of Assessment And Data: Simon Holmes, MPhys, DPhil Oxon
Director of Careers & Universities: Rebecca McGreevy, MA Edinburgh, PGCE IoE
Director of Partnerships and Public Service: Stuart Block, MA Cantab, PGCSE Buckingham

Head of Eighth Form: Naomi McLaughlin, BA Cardiff, PGCE Goldsmiths
Head of Middle School: Douglas Perrin, MA, PGCE Cantab

Undermasters:
James Blurton, BSc St Mary's, PGCE Brunel
Kerilynne Cloete, BSocSci Cape Town, MA UCL, PGCE IoE
Sarah Field, BSc Edinburgh, DPhil Oxon
James Gilks, MSc, PhD Nottingham, PGCE KCL
Caroline Gill, MA Cantab, PGCE Chelteham
Glenn Harrison, BSc Brunel, PGCE Cantab
Hugo Nilsson, BA Warw, PGCE Bristol
Hannah Warner, MA Cantab, MA Dunelm

Heads of Faculty:
Creative and Performing Arts: Daniel Pirrie, MA Edinburgh
English: Matthew Gardner, MA Oxon, MA Manchester, MA London
Humanities: Alexander Isaac BSc, MSc Bristol, MA London, PGCE London, FRGS
Languages: Alexander Tofts, BA Dunelm, PGCE Canterbury Christchurch
Mathematics: Andrew Ashworth-Jones, BSc North London, PGCE Exeter
Science, Technology, Engineering, ICT & Computing: Camille Shammas, BSc Sheffield, PhD Bristol

Chaplain: The Rev'd Matthew Knox, BSc Manchester, BA, MA Dunelm, PGCE Newcastle

St Peter's School, York

Clifton, York YO30 6AB

Tel: 01904 527300
email: enquiries@stpetersyork.org.uk
website: www.stpetersyork.org.uk
X/Twitter: @stpetersyork
Facebook: @stpetersschoolyork
Instagram: @stpeters.york
LinkedIn: /school/stpetersyork

Motto: *Super antiquas vias*

Founded in 627AD, St Peter's is one of the world's oldest schools. It provides outstanding boarding and day education for boys and girls from 13 to 18. Pupils at St Peter's School achieve some of the best grades in the North of England at GCSE and A Level. It has a co-educational prep school, St Peter's 8–13, which admits boarding and day pupils, and a day pre-prep and nursery, St Peter's 2–8. (*See separate entries in IAPS section*).

St Peter's is a co-educational boarding and day school with 604 boys and girls aged 13–18. There are just over 126 boarders housed in four boarding houses, and all day pupils are assigned to a day house, all of which are on the campus. St Peter's offers full boarding and part-time boarding options.

Buildings & Facilities. The School occupies an impressive 47-acre site just a few minutes' walk from the historic centre of York. Playing fields stretch down to the River Ouse and the School boat house, and the sports facilities are further supplemented by three sports halls, a fitness suite, an astro pitch and a 25 m 6-lane swimming pool.

There are three performance spaces of varying capacities, a music school, an outstanding art school with its own exhibition gallery and an extensive library. The school's sports pitches have been recognised for their excellence by the Institute of Groundsmanship, and a Maths and Modern Foreign Languages block opened in September 2018.

Entrance. Pupils are admitted through the School's entrance examinations held at the end of January for 13+ and in mid-November for 16+. The School is oversubscribed and application before the entrance exam is strongly recommended.

Curriculum. St Peter's offers a very broad middle-school curriculum, including Music, PE, Art, Design & Technology, Community Action, and courses in personal and social education, among many others.

Nearly all pupils proceed into the Sixth Form, and A Level courses are available in all subjects studied for IGCSE/GCSE, and in Economics, Politics, Business Studies, Further Mathematics and PE.

Academic and pastoral care. A comprehensive house and tutorial system with interim assessments and reports during the term ensure the close scrutiny by all the teaching staff of pupils' academic and general development.

Religious education and worship. Religious Studies are part of the curriculum, and Chapel is seen as an opportunity for pupils to be made aware of the School's Christian heritage.

Careers and university entrance. The School is an 'all-in' member of the Independent Schools Careers Organisation. Careers staff are available for consultation, maintaining an extensive library relating to careers and higher education, and organising a full programme of events for the Sixth Form. In 2015, the School's Careers Department was accredited by Career Mark, 'The mark of Quality for Careers Education and Guidance'. Approximately 90% of Sixth Form pupils go straight on to further or higher education study, with over 60% of pupils progressing to elite and Russell Group universities in the UK (including Oxford and Cambridge).

Games and Physical Education. Physical education is a significant part of the curriculum. There is an extensive games programme, 250 sports teams and excellent sports facilities. Rugby, netball, hockey, cricket and rowing are major sports, and many other options including swimming, athletics, cross country, basketball, squash, yoga, badminton, tennis, fencing, golf, mountain biking, trampoline, fitness and weight training are available.

Combined Cadet Force. A flourishing and voluntary CCF contingent, with army and air sections, allows the pursuit of many activities including a full programme of camps, expeditions and courses.

The Duke of Edinburgh's Award is also on offer with expedition training for all levels as part of the activities programme and 150 pupils are currently participating.

Music. Musical ability is encouraged throughout the School. There is an orchestra, bands, choirs, choral society, Barbershop and Barbieshop groups and numerous smaller activities. Concerts and tours abroad are a regular feature of the school year. Tuition in all instruments is provided, and music is offered at GCSE and A Level.

Art. Drawing, painting, print-making, ceramics and sculpture may all be taken up both in and out of school hours in an outstanding department.

Drama. The School has three performance spaces: the Memorial Hall, the Shepherd Hall and the smaller, more flexible Drama Centre. There are various productions through the year giving opportunities for acting and backstage skills.

Clubs and societies. Over 80 flourishing clubs and societies are available, including chess, debating and Radio 627. The Community Action programme has over 100 regular participants.

Travel and expeditions. Opportunities for trips and tours have included skiing trips, Classics trips to Greece, trekking in Morocco, a Rugby tour to Canada and the USA, among many others.

The Friends of St Peter's. Parents are encouraged to join the Friends, a society whose aim is to promote a close relationship between parents and staff.

Fees per term (2023–2024). Full Boarding: £12,440–£12,555, Non-EEA Full Boarding: £13,410–£13,530, Day: £7,260–£7,330. Tuition fees include the costs of stationery and textbooks. There are no compulsory extras except for examination fees. Lunches are included in day fees.

Scholarships and Bursaries. Honorary scholarships are awarded to those performing extremely well in the entrance examination.

Various music awards covering a proportion of the fees and free tuition on up to three musical instruments are available for entrants at 13+ or Sixth Form. Interviews and auditions for these awards are held in January or February.

Help with Fees is available at 13+ and 16+. Full particulars on Help with Fees and scholarships are available from the Admissions Officer, Mrs Gillian Bland, Tel: 01904 527305 or email: g.bland@stpetersyork.org.uk.

Further information. Prospectuses are available on request: tel: 01904 527305, email: enquiries@stpetersyork.org.uk, or via the website: www.stpetersyork.org.uk.

Charitable status. St Peter's School, York, is a Registered Charity, number 1141329.

Board of Governors:
Chairman: Mr W Woolley
Vice Chair: Dr N Durham

Members of the Board:

Ms C Baker	Ms C Smart
Mr M Calvert	Mr A Taylor
Mrs J Copley-Farnell	Sir J Townsley
Mr J Gill	Ms G Vidic Cattorini
Dr S Hinchliffe	Mr P Widdicombe
Revd Canon Dr V Johnson	

Clerk to the Board: Ms K Hodges

***Head Master*: Mr J M P Walker**, MA Oxford, MA London

Chief Operating Officer: Mrs R Desport, BSc
Director of Admissions, Marketing and Communications: Ms S T Opie, BSc
Pastoral Deputy: Miss T M Mounter, BA
Academic Deputy: Mr D H Gillies, BA, MSc Oxon
Director of Finance: Mrs R Johnson, BA, FCA
Head Master's PA: Mrs C E McTurk
Admissions Officer: Mrs G Bland

The Prep School – St Peter's 8–13
Head: Mr P C Hardy, BA, PGCE

Deputy Head: Mr M C Ferguson, HDE

The Pre-Prep and Nursery – St Peter's 2–8
Head: Mrs A M Clarke, BA

A full staff list is available on the school website.

St Swithun's School

Alresford Road, Winchester, Hampshire SO21 1HA

Tel:	01962 835700
email:	office@stswithuns.com
website:	www.stswithuns.com
X/Twitter:	@StSwithunsGirls
Facebook:	@StSwithunsSchool
Instagram:	@StSwithunsGirls
LinkedIn:	/school/st-swithun's-school

See full entry in the **GSA** section, on **p. 488**.

Seaford College

Lavington Park, Petworth, West Sussex GU28 0NB

Tel:	01798 867392
email:	info@seaford.org
website:	www.seaford.org
X/Twitter:	@seafordcollege
Facebook:	@seafordcollege
Instagram:	@seafordcollege
LinkedIn:	/company/seaford-college

Motto: *Love to learn*

The College was founded in 1884 at Seaford in East Sussex and moved to Lavington Park at the foot of the South Downs in West Sussex in 1946. The picturesque grounds cover over 400 acres with Prep School (*see IAPS entry*), outstanding Performing Arts Centre, extensive sports facilities, a superb Art and Design hub, a modern Sixth Form Centre, purpose-built boarding houses, a state-of-the-art Mathematics, Science and Music School.

Seaford is controlled by an independent non-profit-making Charitable Trust approved by the Department for Education and the Charity Commissioners, and is administered by the College Board of Governors.

Students. Day and boarding facilities, with options of full, weekly and flexi boarding. Over 950 students of which 265 in the Sixth Form. Two boys' houses, a girls' house, a junior house and two Sixth Form boarding houses.

Aims. Seaford College's aim is to bring out the best in each individual, by helping every pupil to reach their full potential and to achieve personal bests both inside and outside the classroom. The aim is to enable students to leave the College feeling confident in their own abilities and able to contribute in the external world.

Academic. The Prep School (Years 1–8) offers a wide-ranging curriculum, which includes the core subjects of English, Mathematics, Science, Spanish, French and Information Technology, as well as Geography, History, Art, Music, DT, Sport, Forest School and PSHCE.

Years 9, 10 and 11 lead up to the GCSE examinations. Students study the core subjects of English Literature, English Language, Mathematics and Science and then choose four other syllabuses to follow from a comprehensive list of subjects, which include: Art, Business Studies, Computer Science, Dance, Design and Technology, Drama, Fine Art, Food Prep/Nutrition, French, Geography, History, Music, Physical Education, Religious Studies, Spanish and Textile Design.

The A Level subject list is comprehensive and students choose three subjects to study. In their first year of Sixth Form, students may undertake The Duke of Edinburgh's Silver/Gold Award or start an Extended Project Qualification (EPQ).

Music. An important part of life at Seaford, with the Music School offering the latest in recording and performing facilities. The College boasts an internationally renowned College Chapel Choir, who have sung on tour with Gary Barlow and have performed many concerts for charity. The College also has an orchestra and offers lessons for all instruments. Music can be studied at GCSE and A Level.

Sports. With superb facilities available in the grounds; staff have coached and played at international level, the college has a reputation for sporting excellence. Facilities include: eight rugby pitches, eight tennis courts, five cricket pitches, a water-based all-weather hockey pitch, enclosed swimming pool, a large indoor sports hall that allows tennis, netball and hockey to be played all year round, and a 9-hole golf course and driving range.

Art. The Art department's excellent reputation allows students to exercise their talents to the fullest in every aspect of art and design, whether it is ceramics, textiles, fine art, animation, or any other medium they wish to use. Many students go on to study at design school, work for design and fashion houses or advertising companies. Students' work is displayed throughout the year in the department's large gallery.

Combined Cadet Force. Strong ties with the military shown in a very well-supported Combined Cadet Force (CCF) with each wing of the armed forces represented. Weekend exercises and training include canoeing, climbing, sailing, adventure training and camping.

Admission. Entry at age 6 consists of a visit to the school, reports and references from current school. Entry at age 10 and 11 consists of reports, references and cognitive ability testing. 13+ students sit the ISEB pre-test in Year 6, a school visit, reports and references. Offers are made in the January of Year 6 and are unconditional and deferred until Year 9. Sixth Form entry is dependent upon GCSE results, informal school visit, reports and references, and a conditional offer is made in the year of entry based on a minimum point system at GCSEs and including English and Mathematics. Overseas students are required to take a written examination to determine the level of comprehension in English.

Scholarships and bursaries. Academic, Music, Drama, Dance, Art, Design Technology and Sports scholarships may be awarded to girls and boys entering the Prep and Senior School at 11+, 13+ and 16+, with the exception of DT which is only available at 13+ and 16+. These scholarships offer up to 10% discount on fees per annum at the discretion of the Scholarship committee.

Bursaries are available on a means-tested basis. A potential scholarship recipient in need of further financial assistance may apply for a means-tested bursary.

Sibling and Forces discounts are also available. Please contact our Admissions team for details.

Fees per term (2023–2024). Years 9–13: £12,690 (Full Boarding), £11,115 (Weekly Boarding), £8,210 (Day). Years 7 & 8: £8,735 (4-Day Monday–Thursday Boarding), £6,570 (Day). Year 6: £8,245 (4-Day Monday–Thursday Boarding). Years 3–6: £3,960–£6,045 (Day).

Extras. Drama, Clay Pigeon Shooting, Duke of Edinburgh's Award, Golf, Sailing, Kayaking, Museum & Theatre trips, Creative Writing, Debating Club, Rock Climbing, Martial Arts, Chess, etc.

Charitable status. Registered Charity, number 277439. To provide education for children.

Governing Body:
R Venables Kyrke (*Chairman*)

J Cooper	R Norton
Mrs G Gordon-Thomson	Mrs V Padgham
Mrs J Hall	H A Phillips
A Hayes	J Scrase
N Karonias	Dr J Slater

***Headmaster*: J P Green**, BA Hons, PGCE

Senior Deputy Head: W Yates, BSc Ed
Deputy Head: A Arya, BEng Hons
Deputy Head: S D'Agar, BSc Hons
Assistant Head: Mrs S Butler, BA, MA
Assistant Head: Mrs J Forman, BA
Prep School Head: A Brown, BEd
Deputy Head Prep School: J Harte, BSc

Sevenoaks School

High Street, Sevenoaks, Kent TN13 1HU
Tel: 01732 455133
email: regist@sevenoaksschool.org
admin@sevenoaksschool.org
website: www.sevenoaksschool.org
X/Twitter: @SevenoaksSchool
Facebook: @SevenoaksSchoolUK
Instagram: @sevenoaksschooluk
LinkedIn: /sevenoaks-school

Motto: *Servire Deo Regnari Est*

Sevenoaks (founded in 1432) is a co-educational day and boarding school for students aged 11 to 18. Just half an hour from Central London and Gatwick International Airport, its superb 100-acre campus is set in the Kent countryside.

Sevenoaks is one of the world's leading IB schools, having taught the International Baccalaureate for over 40 years.

Sevenoaks is among the top schools in the UK. It is the *Sunday Times* Co-educational Independent School of the Year 2023 and *Spear's* School of the Year 2022. The UK Independent Schools Inspectorate (ISI) awarded Sevenoaks the rare accolade of 'Exceptional' for its pupils' achievement.

In 2022, its average IB Diploma score was 40.3 points, about eight points above the world average, and consistent with previous years. The Higher Education department supported successful applications to universities in the UK, USA, Canada, Europe and Hong Kong. An outstanding 92 per cent progressed to their firm choice university.

Sevenoaks proudly publishes the university destinations of leavers every year. Given its global perspective, it supports about 20% of students to universities in another country, with increasing numbers going to North America, specifically Ivy league and top universities in the United States.

The majority go to Oxbridge, London universities or other top universities in the UK, such as Bristol or Durham.

Sevenoaks students have access to world-class facilities for co-curricular pursuits, including sport, music, drama and art, at least 70 clubs and societies, a wide range of study trips and exchanges, and a well-established community service programme.

There is a strong emphasis on the co-curriculum, from sport to music, drama and art. Pupils are regularly selected for regional and national orchestras and choirs, the NYT, and compete at county, national and international level in a number of sports.

Sevenoaks was one of the first UK schools to incorporate voluntary service as a compulsory element of the co-curriculum, pioneering a local Voluntary Service Unit in the 1960s and continuing with a strong service programme today. There is also a CCF and The Duke of Edinburgh's Award scheme; with Gold expeditions abroad as well as in the UK.

In 2017 the school launched its Middle School Diploma for Year 9, which records pupils' academic and co-curricular achievements in creativity, action and service as well as in the enriching Sevenoaks core courses, Ten Ideas That Changed the World and Critical Perspectives.

There are lessons and sport for all pupils on Saturdays and a full programme of activities for boarders on Sundays.

The facilities are first-class. In 2018, a state-of-the-art science and technology centre opened, uniting the four core fields of science, with an innovative new Sixth Form Global Study Centre alongside, providing the school's first dedicated space for the IB and higher education. Other recent developments include a sports centre providing outstanding facilities and an award-winning, world-class performing arts centre.

With seven distinctive and comfortable boarding houses, and a new girls' boarding house opening in 2023, its boarding community is fun, friendly and busy.

The school's international outlook promotes the principles of tolerance and open-mindedness. Ambitious but principled, confident and compassionate, Sevenoaks pupils are prepared for leadership in an ever more complex world.

Admission. The main points of entry to the school are at 11, 13 and 16 years. A small number are admitted at other levels. At 11+, pupils are admitted on the basis of a competitive examination held in January, an interview and school report. At 13+, candidates take part in an assessment process in May of their Year 7. A reference from their current school is also required. Academic and Co-Curricular scholarship examinations are held in the May of Year 8. At 16+ students are admitted into the Sixth Form based on their performance in interview and academic entrance tests, and on the strength of their current school reports. All applications for entry should be addressed to the Director of Admissions (regist@sevenoaksschool.org).

Fees per term (2023–2024). Boarders £15,595; Day Pupils £9,709 (including lunch). Fees for pupils entering directly into the Sixth Form are £16,919 (boarding) and £11,206 (day).

Scholarships and Bursaries. Sevenoaks offers scholarships to students joining at 11+, 13+ and 16+. These scholarships honour and celebrate exceptional talent in academia, music, sports, drama and art.

In recent years we have reduced the financial element of our scholarships, as we have embraced a principle of awarding financial assistance according to need. We are now taking the final step and removing the financial element entirely for all candidates applying from 2022 onwards, although Music Scholars will still receive free tuition on one instrument.

This move will enable us to direct all our financial resources to supporting families who otherwise could not afford for their child to benefit from a Sevenoaks education. We firmly believe this is the right and equitable thing to do. Over the years, many families of scholars have taken the same view and waived their fee reduction to donate it to our financial assistance fund; we are most grateful to them.

Financial Assistance. Currently more than 60 pupils are in receipt of financial assistance with fees, with some receiving additional support to cover the cost of uniform, trips and other extras. It is a key priority to significantly increase the number of students receiving financial assistance over the coming years.

All awards of financial assistance are means-tested, which requires parents to answer detailed questions and provide evidence of their financial circumstances.

Families interested in applying for financial assistance are invited to read about the eligibility criteria and process in our Financial Assistance with Fees Policy.

Further details can be obtained from Lorna Dolan, Director of Admissions, Sevenoaks School, High Street, Sevenoaks, Kent, TN13 1HU. Tel: 01732 467703; Email:regist@sevenoaksschool.org

Charitable status. Sevenoaks School is a Registered Charity, number 1101358. Its aims and objectives are the education of school children.

Governing Body:
Chair: A Beckett
Vice-Chair: C Gill

Governors:
K Allen
R Best
J Davies
A Eastman
E Ecclestone
C Houghteling
G Innes
J London
P Luxmore
M McInerney
M Merson
A Timms
A Yuravlivker

Interim Bursar and Clerk to the Governors: D Davies

Academic Staff:

Senior Leadership Team:

***Headmaster*: J R Elzinga**

Senior Deputy Head: C Ives
Deputy Head (*Pastoral*): J Lidiard
Deputy Head (*Academic*): C Taylor
Deputy Head (*Co-curriculum*): S Walmsley
Deputy Head (*Staff*): H Tebay
Deputy Head (*Boarding*):N Haworth

Director of Admissions: L Dolan
Executive Director of Advancement: M Joyce
Director of Institute for Teaching & Learning: M Beverley
Director of Institute for Higher Education and Professional Insight: W Heydorn
Director of International Baccalaureate: T Haworth
Head of Sixth Form Admissions: S Coquelin
Head of Sixth Form: M Edwards
Head of Middle School: R McQuillin
Head of Lower School: M Capelo

Sherborne Girls

Bradford Road, Sherborne, Dorset DT9 3QN

Tel: 01935 818224 (Admissions)
01935 812245 (School)
01935 818206 (Bursar)
email: admissions@sherborne.com
website: www.sherborne.com
X/Twitter: @sherbornegirls
Facebook: @sherbornegirls
Instagram: @sherbornegirls
LinkedIn: /Sherborne-Girls

Sherborne Girls, founded in 1899, provides an outstanding education for 11 to 18 year olds in the beautiful county of Dorset and is proud of its co-curricular programme and exceptional pastoral care. Girls are welcomed at 11+, 12+, 13+ and into the Sixth Form. There are 474 girls: 426 boarders, 48 day girls. A close relationship with Sherborne School allows co-ed opportunities including music, drama, activities, clubs and societies and social occasions. The schools have the same term dates.

Terms. Three terms of approximately 12 weeks each. Christmas holidays 3 weeks; Easter holidays 3 weeks; Summer holidays 9 weeks. Term dates are in common with those of Sherborne School.

Admission. Online assessments in Year 6 plus interviews at the School, or remotely where necessary. Girls should be registered in advance and reports will be requested from their current school. For entry into the Sixth Form, girls are required to gain six good passes (grade six or above) in relevant subjects. See the "entry at 16+" page on the website for more details regarding the GCSE points.

Registration fee: £250. A deposit of £2,000 is required before entry (a term's fees for overseas pupils).

Scholarships and Bursaries. Academic Scholarships are offered at 11+, 13+ and 16+ annually as a result of examination and interview. There are also scholarships offered for outstanding promise in Music, Art and Design, Drama and Sport. All examinations are held in January and February apart from Sixth Form in November. Scholarship awards are made on merit. Scholarships may be combined with means-tested bursaries which can raise considerably the effective amount of an award. Bursarial support (up to 100%) may be available in cases of demonstrable need.

Music Awards (Junior and 16+): Music scholars receive free music tuition for up to three lessons per week. Music Exhibitions offer free music tuition for up to three lessons per week. Junior scholarships receive up to £3,000 fee remissions (all disciplines).

Art and Design Scholarships (13+ and 16+): Candidates will be required to bring a portfolio with them and would be asked to do some work in the Art Department while they are here. Junior scholarships receive up to £3,000 fee remissions (all disciplines).

Sport Scholarships (Junior and 16+): Candidates should offer one or more sports, preferably reaching county standard or higher. Junior scholarships receive up to £3,000 fee remissions (all disciplines).

Drama Awards (13+): Drama scholars receive free drama tuition for one lesson per week. Drama Exhibitions also offer free drama tuition for one lesson per week. Junior scholarships receive up to £3,000 fee remissions (all disciplines).

Fees per term (2023–2024). 13+: boarders £14,950, day boarders* £12,250, day girls £9,600. 11+: boarders £12,250, day girls £9,600.

*Day boarders are girls who wish to stay overnight (£55 per night) on the odd occasion and for whom a bed space will be made available on request.

Houses. There are five houses for 13–17 year olds and one Upper Sixth house. Girls who are aged 11 and 12 years old spend their first two years together in Aldhelmsted West House, our Junior Boarding House.

Religion. The School has a Church of England foundation, but it values the presence and contribution of members of all the Christian traditions and of other faiths. Regular services are held in the Abbey, some jointly with Sherborne School.

Examinations. Girls are prepared for I/GCSE and A Levels. There is a wide choice of subjects to be studied.

Games. Hockey and Lacrosse/Netball are played in the Michaelmas and Lent terms and Tennis, Rounders, Cricket and Athletics during the Trinity term. Oxley Sports Centre in partnership with Sherborne Girls contains a 25 m pool and state-of-the-art fitness suite. There are Squash Courts, floodlit Astroturf, Sports Hall, Dance Studio and Climbing Wall. Riding, Badminton, Cross-Country Running, Golf, Aerobics, Sailing, Trampolining are some of the alternative games.

Sherborne Old Girls. All enquiries should be made to Mrs Fiona James at the School, Tel: 01935 818329.

Prospective parents and their daughters are invited to the School's Tour Mornings or private visits by appointment. Please visit the school's website or telephone Admissions on 01935 818224 for further details.

Charitable status. Sherborne School for Girls is a Registered Charity, number 307427. It exists to provide education for girls in a boarding environment.

Council:
Chair: Mrs L Hall
Members:

Ms J Blanch
Dr S Connors
Mrs S Craig-McFeely
Canon N Edwards
The Rt Revd K Gorham
Mrs A Harris
Mrs A Hughes
Mr R A L Leach
Mrs J Massey
Mrs K Saker
Mr M Scott
Mr M Taylor
Dr P Williams
Mrs M Wingfield Digby
Mr N Wordie
Life President: Mr S Wingfield Digby

Clerk to the Council: Mrs F Clapp

Senior Staff:

***Head*: Dr Ruth Sullivan**, BSc, PGCE Edinburgh, MSc, PhD London School of Hygiene and Tropical Medicine

Bursar: Mrs Fiona Clapp, MBA, BSc Hons London, PGCE

Senior Deputy Head, Teaching and Learning: Mrs Louise Orton, BSc Swansea, PGCE

Deputy Head, Pastoral: Mrs Jessica Briggs, BA Hons Reading
Deputy Head, Operations and Co-Curricular: Mrs Jayne Dart, BSc Hons Oxford Brookes
Director of Sixth Form: Mr David Banks, Cardiff
Director of Studies: Mr Richard Barnes, LLB Hons Liverpool, MEd, PGCE
Director of Admissions: Mrs Karen Williams, MBA Brunel
Director of Development and Marketing: Mrs Katherine Massey, BA Hons Oxford Brookes

For full list of staff please go to the school's website www.sherborne.com

Sherborne School

Abbey Road, Sherborne, Dorset DT9 3AP

Tel: 01935 812249
01935 810403 (Admissions)
email: admissions@sherborne.org
website: www.sherborne.org
X/Twitter: @SherborneSchool
Facebook: @SherborneBoysSchool
Instagram: @sherborneschool
LinkedIn: @sherborneschool

Royal Arms of Edward VI: *Dieu et mon droit*.

The origins of Sherborne School date back to the eighth century, when a tradition of education at Sherborne was begun by St Aldhelm. Edward VI refounded the School in 1550. The present School stands on land which once belonged to the Monastery. The Library, Chapel, and Headmaster's offices which adjoin the Abbey Church, are modifications of the original buildings of the Abbey. Sherborne School merged with Sherborne Prep School in 2021.

Situation. The School lies in the attractive Abbey town of Sherborne with a direct train to London taking two hours.

Organisation. There are just under 600 boys at Sherborne with 90% of them being full boarders. Boys are accommodated in eight houses, all of which are within easy walking distance of the main school.

Admission. Entry is either at 13+ (Year 9) or 16+ (Sixth Form) with a small number of places available at 14+ (Year 10). Assessment days take place for 13+ entry when pupils are in year 6 or 7. Pupils may then sit scholarship examinations or Common Entrance in year 8. Late applicants may be assessed after this time subject to places being available.

Scholarships and Exhibitions. Sherborne offers a wide range of scholarships and exhibitions at 13+ entry: Academic, Music, Art, Design & Technology, Drama and Sport. Sixth Form Academic, Sports and Music awards are also offered annually.

Closed Awards: A Raban Exhibition of up to 10% of fees for the sons of serving or ex-services officers; a Nutting Exhibition of up to 10% of fees for sons of RN Officers. A military discount is available for sons of serving officers.

Sixth Form Entry. Places are available for boys who wish to join the Sixth Form to study A Levels for two years. Scholarship and entrance examinations take place by arrangement with the Director of Admissions.

Curriculum. All pupils follow a broadly based curriculum for their first three years to GCSE. In the Sixth Form boys study at least three A Levels drawn from a wide choice of available courses, BTECs are also offered to further diversify the curriculum. There is also a stretching enrichment programme as a part of the compulsory curriculum and a scholars programme.

Careers and Universities. The Careers Department has an enviable reputation. Boys experience work shadowing programmes in the fifth and lower sixth forms – these are followed by careers conventions, university visits, parents' forums and lessons in interview techniques. Virtually all leavers go on to university.

Pastoral Care. The boys in each house are in the care of a Housemaster and their family, an Assistant Housemaster, a resident tutor and a resident matron. In addition, a team of tutors assists the Housemaster in the running of the House and boys have many avenues of support and advice available to them. The School Chaplain also plays a major role and will talk with a boy whenever required. A School Counsellor is available, and boys may book appointments directly and confidentially.

Tutor. Each boy has a personal Tutor who monitors his academic progress and provides a useful contact point for parents.

Religion. The weekly pattern of Christian services in the school Chapel or Sherborne Abbey underpin the spiritual rhythm of the school. There is a wide variety of voluntary Christian groups and services including a Friday night candlelit Eucharist which is well attended. Boys can be prepared for Confirmation into the Church of England and the Roman Catholic Church.

Community Service. Boys take part in a busy programme aimed at encouraging a sense of responsibility towards the local community.

Art. The Art School is a dynamic and highly successful department achieving outstanding academic results at all levels. The core disciplines are based around the study of Fine Art, with an eclectic mix of approaches such as painting, photography, 3D, digital media, printing, pottery and performance.

Design and Technology. The subject is taught from year nine right through to A Level and pupils can go on to higher education courses in Product and Aeronautical Design, Architecture and Engineering. The department has developed links with local industries where pupils can see CAD/CAM production, commercial furniture design and precision casting in process.

Music. There is a strong music tradition in the School – over 400 music lessons take place every week. There are two full orchestras, various chamber music groups, many different types of jazz band, a brass group, a swing band, Chapel choir and a choral society, not to mention rock bands. Much of this is run in conjunction with Sherborne Girls. Numerous concerts, recitals and musical productions are held throughout the year. Lunch time concerts take place every Friday.

Drama. Drama productions of all kinds are a major feature of school life, from large scale musicals to classical drama, substantial modern works and fringe performances, many staged with Sherborne Girls. The sophisticated technical resources of the Powell Theatre attract programmes from professional touring companies.

Information Technology. The school has a fast, wireless network that is available throughout the school, including in boarding houses. Safe filtering systems and time restrictions are in place to protect pupils and all pupils have their own devices.

Sports. There are over fifty acres of sports fields, where, at any one time, seventeen various games or matches can take place. Other facilities include two AstroTurf pitches, twenty tennis courts, Rugby fives courts and a shooting range. There is a brand new state-of-the-art Sports Centre with a twenty-five metre swimming pool, a fitness suite, squash courts, golf simulator, and much more. A wide variety of sports and activities are offered including athletics, badminton, basketball, canoeing, cricket, cross-country, fencing, fives, golf, hockey, polo, riding, rugby, sailing, shooting, soccer, sub-aqua, swimming and tennis.

Societies and Activities. In addition to a full sporting, music and drama programme, numerous academic societies meet regularly throughout the term. Over 100 clubs are offered for boys including bridge, chess, computing, debating, photography, dining, life drawing, cooking for university, film making, community service, speech and drama and United Nations.

The school has a strong tradition of outdoor education and, in addition to The Duke of Edinburgh's Award scheme, there are walking, climbing, kayaking and sailing trips. These are local or further afield in Scotland, the Lake District, Wales, Exmoor, Dartmoor and occasionally abroad. Boys also take part in the annual Ten Tors Challenge.

Membership of the Combined Cadet Force is voluntary and the Army, Royal Navy and Royal Marine sections attract about 150 boys and girls from Sherborne Girls each year. A large number of trips and camps are arranged during the term time and the holidays.

Old Shirburnian Society. Mr John Harden, Secretary, tel: 01935 810557, email: OSS@sherborne.org.

Girls' School. Sherborne School's unique partnership with Sherborne Girls offers collaborative opportunities and social events for its pupils throughout the year.

Fees per term (2023–2024). Boarders: £15,200; Day Boys: £12,050.

Charitable status. Sherborne School is a Registered Charity, number 1081228, and a Company Limited by Guarantee, registered in England and Wales, number 4002575. Its aim and objectives are to supply a liberal education in accordance with the principles of the Church of England.

Governors of the School:

Chair: Lt Gen David Leakey, CMG, CVO, CBE, MA

***Headmaster and CEO*: Dr Dominic Luckett**, BA, DPhil, FRSA, FHA, FCCT

Deputy Head (*Academic*): Dr Tim Filtness, BA, MA, PhD

Deputy Head (*Co-curricular*): Tim Bennett, BA Ed, NPQH

Deputy Head (*Pastoral*): Allister Sheffield, BSc

Deputy Head (*Sixth Form*): Alex Boyd-Williams, BA, MEd, PGCE, DipEFC

Director of Operations: Matthew Jamieson, BA

Assistant Head (*Academic*): Lindsey Millar, BA

Director of Boarding: Ben Sunderland, BEng

Bursar: David Cole, BSc, MSc, PhD

Director of Admissions: Anne Megdiche

For a full Staff List please visit: www.sherborne.org/about-sherborne/staff

Shiplake College

Henley-on-Thames, Oxon RG9 4BW
Tel: 0118 940 2455
email: registrar@shiplake.org.uk
website: www.shiplake.org.uk
X/Twitter: @ShiplakeCollege
Facebook: @ShiplakeCollege
Instagram: @ShiplakeCollege
LinkedIn: /shiplakecollege

Motto: *Exemplum docet – The example teaches*

Shiplake College is an independent co-educational boarding and day school for nearly 520 pupils aged 11–18, based in the Oxfordshire countryside on the banks of the River Thames. There has been a co-educational Sixth Form since 1998 and in September 2023, girls joined in Year 7 (making up 42% of the cohort) as the College goes fully co-educational.

Ethos. The central pillars of Shiplake are its core values, the 3I's, 'Inclusive, individual, inspirational'. We ensure that every pupil is challenged and supported according to their need and ability. We firmly believe that in addition to a solid academic grounding, sporting, social and cultural achievements are vital to a pupil's long-term development. Shiplake offers a wide range of challenging enrichment activities to ensure an all-round education.

Academic. We aim to admit a well-balanced intake of pupils with a variety of skills and talents. Pupils are selected on his or her potential to make the most of the opportunities that Shiplake can offer.

Pastoral Care. Shiplake is renowned for delivering outstanding pastoral care. Houses are a huge part of the Shiplake community. Each house is run by a Housemaster/mistress who is supported by a strong team of staff including the Matron, Tutors, Medical Staff and the Chaplain. The houses provide excellent support for the pupils in addition to ensuring a comfortable, homely environment for pupils to study or relax. There is a strong house spirit in evidence with competitions organised for arts, games and academic progress.

A Church of England school, there is a programme of worship. The Chaplain, whose role is purely pastoral, is always available to any member of the College community. Shiplake also welcomes pupils of other faiths or no particular faith.

Boarding. Boarding is an integral part of life at Shiplake. Full, weekly, flexi boarding and overnight stays allow pupils to benefit from all the academic and co-curricular opportunities offered. 130 weekly and full boarders enjoy a busy weekend and evening programme, which covers a mixture of cultural, social and sporting trips and activities. International pupils, including a balance of British and non-British students resident abroad, represent approximately 5% of the current school population.

Location. Two miles upstream of the famous Regatta town of Henley-on-Thames, Shiplake is conveniently close to the M4 and M40 and Reading railway station. This idyllic countryside location is just an hour from London and within easy reach of Heathrow and Gatwick airports.

Facilities. Shiplake House, built in 1889 as a family home, is at the heart of the school. The College uses the twelfth-century Parish Church for assemblies and worship. In addition to the main school buildings, Shiplake boasts a range of facilities including a Sixth Form centre and a multi-activity centre with boathouse (Davies Centre) which both opened in 2020.

Academic Structure. Pupils entering the College in Year 7 follow the specially designed curriculum for Years 7 and 8. Pupils enjoy the broad and balanced Year 9 curriculum which provides a strong foundation for GCSE. Sixth Form pupils select three subjects from a choice of 28 and also complete a qualification such as an EPQ.

Learning Development. Shiplake has a dedicated Learning Development Department to provide help for those who are academically gifted and those who find certain subject areas difficult to access. About 12% of pupils receive additional support, to improve pupils' confidence and self-esteem and equip them with the necessary skills. All pupils are able to approach their subject teachers for additional support whenever necessary.

Sport. Sport is an integral part of life at Shiplake. The College has an excellent sporting reputation and most pupils take part in a sporting activity every day. The College enjoys direct access to the river, sports pitches, tennis courts and an outdoor swimming pool. The sports hall offers a variety of indoor sports, a weight-training gym and a fitness room. The Davies Centre includes over 30 ergometers, weights room, two-storey climbing wall and an archery/rifle range.

Music, Art and Drama. The College has a thriving Arts programme. The annual House Music Competition ensures that every pupil in the school is involved in preparing for a performance and every term there is at least one concert. The Drama Department provides a range of opportunities for the theatrically inclined, to explore and experiment with the subject beyond the constraints of the curriculum. Art exhibitions take place throughout the year.

Activities. Two afternoons are dedicated to a Co-Curricular programme where pupils choose from a wide range of activities including art, cookery, debating and canoeing. The College has a thriving CCF, with Air Force, Army and Navy sections, and a Duke of Edinburgh's Award scheme with a number of pupils each year collecting Gold Awards. The school has links to a Kenyan School for which fundraising activities are regularly undertaken.

Careers. An experienced Head of Careers with a careers programme from Year 10.

Admission. The Registrar is the first point of contact for all admissions enquiries. Pupils are admitted at 11+ into Year 7, at 13+ into Year 9 and at 16+ into the Sixth Form. Places are offered following an assessment day. Occasional places arise in other years. See the website for details.

Scholarships. Means-tested scholarships and bursaries are offered for academic excellence and to outstanding sportsmen, artists, actors or musicians.

Fees per term (2023–2024). Years 7–8: Day £7,400; Years 9–13: Full Boarders £14,665, Weekly Boarders £13,200, Flexi (2 nights) £11,520, Day £9,410.

Alumni. The Old Viking Society has a programme of sporting and social events and sends frequent e-newsletters.

Charitable status. Shiplake College is a Registered Charity, number 309651. It exists to provide education for children.

Chairman of Governors: Sir David Tanner, CBE
***Headmaster*: Tyrone Howe**

Shrewsbury School

The Schools, Shrewsbury, Shropshire SY3 7BA

Tel: 01743 280500 (Switchboard)
01743 280525 (Headmaster)
01743 280820 (Bursar)
01743 280552 (Director of Admissions)
email: admissions@shrewsbury.org.uk
website: www.shrewsbury.org.uk
X/Twitter: @ShrewsburySch
Facebook: @ShrewsburySchool
Instagram: @ShrewsburySchool
LinkedIn: /school/shrewsbury-school

Motto: *Intus si recte, ne labora*

Founded by Edward VI by Royal Charter in 1552, Shrewsbury School combines tradition with a vibrant, modern co-educational vision and a strong sense of community.

The School sits on a 110-acre campus perched above the banks of the River Severn, overlooking the historic market town of Shrewsbury, approximately 50 miles west of Birmingham. It is surrounded by glorious unspoilt countryside, close to the Shropshire Hills and the nearby Welsh Marches, and just a short drive away from Snowdonia National Park. All offer countless opportunities for walking, rock-climbing, field trips and expeditions, while the School's grounds host pitches described as 'the most beautiful playing fields in the world' (Sir Neville Cardus).

Shrewsbury is fully co-educational, with a seven-day boarding heartbeat and an integral day community. There are 12 integrated houses: seven boys' houses; and five girls' houses, including Queen Elizabeth Hall which was opened in September 2023.

It is associated with Packwood Haugh, a co-educational prep school for pupils aged 3 to 13 (*see IAPS entry*).

Number in School. There are 841 pupils in the School (618 boarding and 223 day).

Admission. Most admissions are in September. Girls and boys are admitted at 13 or 14 or into the Sixth Form at 16. Registration forms and other information can be obtained from the Admissions Office. The registration fee, which is non-returnable, is £100.

Entry at 13: Pupils usually take the Common Entrance Examination or the Scholarship Examination in the term preceding that in which they wish to come. The School has its own entrance test for pupils who have not followed the Common Entrance syllabus.

Sixth Form Entry: Direct entry into the Sixth Form depends on examination at Shrewsbury, an interview, and a favourable report from the applicant's present school.

Scholarships. Shrewsbury School has had a tradition, since its founding Charter in 1552, of making generous scholarship awards. Scholarships fall into various categories – Academic, Music, Art, Drama, Design & Technology, Sport and All-Rounder. Awards are made either to pupils under the age of 14 joining the School in the Third Form, or to those entering the School at Sixth Form level.

Statement of aims. Shrewsbury School has a strong vision, derived from its position as a major co-educational boarding school of international reputation. It aims to instil a rigorous approach to academic work, based on the encouragement of independent thinking and intellectual curiosity. The School believes that learning should be a habit that is inculcated for life, not only a means to short-term examination success.

Through its diverse opportunities, Shrewsbury School aims to encourage and enable pupils to become caring, thoughtful, confident members of society. Ambitious yet not arrogant, generous in spirit, interesting, interested and able to respect and communicate effectively with people of all backgrounds.

To this end, Shrewsbury will always strive to achieve the highest possible standards in the breadth and quality of its curriculum, the provision of its facilities and resources, and the achievements – whether academic, sporting, musical, theatrical or artistic – of its pupils and staff. Shrewsbury delights in the uniqueness of its education; a blend of values, traditions, inspiring people, a beautiful location, participation in the world beyond school, and a strong belief that life is what you make of it.

Academic curriculum. Shrewsbury's academic provision endeavours to be exciting, challenging, responsive and versatile. We want pupils to be engaged in a learning process that combines inspirational experience with the sort of rigour and precision that will prepare them not only to produce excellent results in public examinations, but also to be empathetic, innovative and leading contributors to the world beyond the school gates.

We actively encourage cross-curricular thinking – synthesising ideas between Faculties and encouraging the transference of skills. Our classrooms are warm, welcoming environments in which pupils can expect to have their thoughts and opinions heard and in which they will certainly be pushed to meet and exceed their potential. Above all else, we aim to engender excitement and enjoyment and to cultivate a love of learning for its own sake both in the classroom and well beyond it.

An academic programme entitled 'Origin' has been introduced for pupils in their first year at Shrewsbury (Third Form). The key motivator for this is a desire to ignite a passion for learning that will transcend the mechanics of examinations and remain with the pupils long after they have left the school. Alongside the core disciplines from which pupils make their GCSE selections, there are also 'Reading the World' sessions during the year which offer them the opportunity to consider problem-solving, current affairs, social change and the world of economics. In order to promote independence in learning, pupils undertake a key project, the Third Form Portfolio, which requires them to make a presentation and produce a written report on two self-selected areas about which they feel passionate. Pupils also follow a fortnightly programme of Personal and Social Development which promotes self-esteem, respect and tolerance.

All pupils take English, Mathematics, French, Physics, Chemistry, and Biology to GCSE. They are required to take at least one Modern Foreign Language, chosen from French, German and Spanish. Study of a second (or third) modern language can be undertaken in the option blocks, where the other choices are Latin or Ancient History, Greek, German, Spanish, History, Geography, Art, Design, Philosophy & Theology (RS), Music, Computer Science, Astronomy and PE. All pupils also study a non-examined course in Personal and Social Development.

All pupils in the Lower Sixth embark on four qualifications leading to at least three A Level qualifications at the end of their two years in the Sixth Form. The fourth option choice may be an Extended Project Qualification, a further A Level course, or the Global Perspectives Qualification. Subjects offered at A Level are: Art, Biology, Business, Chemistry, Classics (Latin, Greek, Classical Civilisation), Design and Technology, Drama, Economics, English, French, Geography, German, History, History of Art, Mathematics, Further Mathematics, Music, Philosophy and Theology, Physical Education, Physics, Politics and Spanish.

For those pupils who need it, there is a well-equipped team of Learning Support specialists who work with teachers and pupils. English Language support is available for those for whom English is an additional language.

The Moser Library was extensively refurbished in 2017. It houses the School Library, the Moser collection of watercolours and the Ancient Taylor Library, which contains a large and important collection of medieval manuscripts and early printed books.

Sport. With nine full-size grass pitches, two AstroTurf pitches, 3G football pitch, an indoor Cricket Centre, two boathouses with an indoor tank and ergos, 14 fives courts and an indoor 25-metre deck-level pool, the sports facilities at Shrewsbury are of an exceptional standard.

Shrewsbury's renowned sporting reputation embodies Serious Fun; empowering our sportsmen and women to flourish while instilling an enjoyment of sport for life.

Sport plays an important part of a healthy lifestyle and a well-balanced education allowing individuals to thrive in our whole-person education. Whether participating at a high performance or recreational level – we will help you find your sport.

Salopians compete internationally, particularly in rowing and cricket, and we are one of the strongest football schools in the country. Shrewsbury is also one of the top schools in the country for boys' and girls' running and for Eton fives. Pupils also achieve great levels of success in hockey, netball, rugby, racket sports, fencing, athletics, basketball and swimming.

Music. Inclusivity is central to the ethos of Shrewsbury School's Music Department. The Music Faculty aims to give as many pupils as possible the opportunity to take part in the rich musical life on offer, and music of all styles and genres is encouraged. Approximately 45% of pupils receive individual music lessons, often in more than one instrument. Teaching is available in any orchestral instrument, as well as in singing, percussion, piano (classical and jazz), organ, guitar, harp and music theory. There are a large number of instrumental and choral groups and pupils are given regular opportunities to perform in public, ranging from Friday lunchtime concerts, chamber music evenings and pupil-led open mic nights in the Music School's own 200-seat auditorium, through to full orchestral concerts in Birmingham Town Hall or Cadogan Hall in London

A purpose-built music school provides a small concert hall, 20 practice and teaching rooms, two classrooms, and an IT suite equipped with the latest hardware and software. Larger concerts are held in the School's main assembly hall, the Alington Hall, which seats 500.

Drama. Drama is an important part of school life, with four major school productions, dance showcases, student-directed work, new writing and a range of house plays every year. Alongside the many opportunities for pupils to perform on stage as actors or dancers, they can also learn the technical theatre skills of designing and operating lighting and sound, and supporting with costume, hair, make-up and stage-management. Additionally the School hosts at least one professional visiting company or artist in the theatre each year.

Shrewsbury has built up a strong reputation for producing original musicals, with lyrics and music written by members of staff. On alternate years since 1994, these have toured to the Edinburgh Fringe Festival, where they have attracted great critical acclaim.

All pupils in the Third Form experience a module of Drama as part of the English syllabus, and pupils may study Drama as an academic subject at GCSE and A Level.

Our brand new Barnes Theatre features a 250-seat auditorium with state of the art equipment, a dance studio, a new entrance foyer and further studio spaces for drama.

Other co-curricular activities. Co-curricular activities are a fundamental part of life at Shrewsbury and an extensive range of possibilities are offered to pupils, with one afternoon each week and a full day each term dedicated to these. Many of the activities make use of the unspoilt countryside on the doorstep and the easy access to the Welsh hills: the Combined Cadet Force, leadership courses, the Duke of Edinburgh's Award scheme, mountain biking, gliding, scuba diving, the Rovers (adventure club), the Natural History Society.

Arts-based activities include dance, creative arts, creative writing, film and video, music technology, and there are also opportunities to learn skills such as lifeguarding, judo, cooking, horse riding. Many pupils volunteer in the local community and many devise projects of their own through the pupil-led Global Social Leaders programme.

Societies. There is a wide variety of thriving clubs and societies at Shrewsbury. These range from Literary, Historical, Political, Debating, Model United Nations, STEM, Drama and Language societies to those catering for practical skills, including Beekeeping and Technical Theatre. Most academic faculties run their own societies, and their meetings often welcome distinguished academics to give lectures at school. These are also open to members of the public.

Field study centre. Shrewsbury owns a farmhouse in Snowdonia, which is used at weekends throughout the year as a base for expeditions and house trips.

Careers. The Futures Department plays an important part in preparing pupils for the world beyond Shrewsbury School. Led by the Head of Futures and the Head of Higher Education, the Department works as part of the whole school team, supported by the Salopian Club, to provide advice to pupils on course choices, universities, work experience and co-curricular activities. Old Salopians also benefit from access to support from the Department.

Careers education at Shrewsbury is embedded within the Third Form through the Personal and Social Development (PSD) and Tutorial programmes. The focus at this stage is on self-discovery and exploration, and enabling pupils to link the key skills they are developing through school life to the world of work. In the Summer Term they undertake pupil-led social action projects which benefit the local community.

Careers education through the PSD and Tutorial programmes continues in the Fourth Form. Pupils are introduced to external speakers from several contrasting professional areas and take part in the National Enterprise Challenge as part of National Careers Week and. During the Easter holidays, they are expected to take part in work experience.

At the beginning of the Fifth Form, pupils take a careers profiling test. The detailed personalised reports provide the stimulus for one-to-one interviews with qualified advisers, and the Tutorial and PSD programmes enable further exploration and support.

The focus in the Sixth Form is on supporting pupils to research information on all the options open to them. The Higher Education Adviser and the Head of Futures, with support from external speakers, deliver a full range of advice through lectures, workshops and one-to-one guidance to enable pupils to identify their strengths, vocations and ambitions. These include presentations and workshops on UCAS, Degree Apprenticeships / School Leaver programmes, LNAT, UCAT, BMAT, studying abroad and gap years. Upper Sixth pupils are guided through the application processes for universities, including Oxbridge, and are given assistance to plan effective and fulfilling gap years if they choose that option.

The Department has seen a continued upward trend of Salopians choosing to study abroad at top universities across North America, Europe, Asia and Australia. The support offered to students has provided them with the opportunities of pursuing their passion across the globe.

Community Service. Through an extensive range of volunteering opportunities and projects, including the pupil-led Global Social Leaders initiative, pupils play an active part in the local community. These include volunteering at Shrewsbury Food Bank, in the local hospital, in primary schools, care homes, charity shops and at Shrewsbury Ark for the homeless.

Shrewsbury House. Founded in Everton, Liverpool as a Club for boys in 1903 by masters from Shrewsbury School, Shrewsbury House was rebuilt as a Youth and Community Centre in association with the Local Authority and the Diocese in 1974. It runs Junior and Senior Clubs for local young people throughout the week. Links between Shrewsbury School and Shrewsbury House are strong, and the Headmaster and three members of staff sit on its Committee. Fundraising takes place at the School throughout the year and there are regular exchange visits, including opportunities for Lower Sixth Formers to take part in residential Social Studies courses at Shrewsbury House.

Shrewsbury International Schools. The school has close links with Shrewsbury International Schools in Bangkok and Hong Kong. Shrewsbury International School Bangkok opened in 2003 and an additional primary school was opened in the city centre in Bangkok in September 2018. Shrewsbury International School Hong Kong opened its doors to primary school children in September 2018. Shrewsbury International School Phnom Penh opened its early years' provision in the heart of the city in 2022 with the main campus due to open in August 2024. In 2023, Shrewsbury was delighted to announce a new partnership that will see Shrewsbury International School India open in Madhya Pradesh in 2025. Teaching and pupil exchanges take place between the schools, and Governors of Shrewsbury School serve on the boards of management of the International Schools.

Fees per term (2023–2024). Boarders: £14,660–£16,004 including tuition, board and ordinary School expenses. There are no other obligatory extras, apart from stationery. Day Pupils: £10,054–£10,599.

Application for reduced fees may be made to the Governors through the Headmaster.

Old Pupils' Society. Most pupils leaving the school join the Salopian Club, The Schools, Shrewsbury SY3 7BA; email: oldsalopian@shrewsbury.org.uk.

Charitable status. Shrewsbury School is a Registered Charity, number 528413. It exists to provide secondary education.

Governing Body:
J Pitt, BSc Hons, MBA (*Chairman*)
D Chance, MBA, Deputy Chair
R Boys-Stones, BSc, FCA
J R Clark, MA, PGCE
Diana Flint, DL (*Appointed by the Lord Lieutenant of Shropshire*)
Mrs S Hankin, BA
Carla Howarth, LLB, MA
Dr S Jones-Perrott, MBBS, FRCP, BA Hons Oxon
Will Kenyon, MA Oxon, FCA
Canon Jonathan Leigh, MA, FRSA
Professor A J McCarthy, BSc, PhD
J M H Moir, BA Hons Architecture, MBA
Councillor D Morris, BA
Councillor C M Motley, BA Hons (*Appointed by Shropshire Council*)
Mrs F Schofield, BA Hons, PGCE
D Stacey, DL
Mrs G Walters, BBLS

***Headmaster*: N L Winkley**, MA, MEd

Bursar and Clerk to the Governors: M J Ware, MA, ACA

Senior Deputy Head: K Brennan, MSc, PGCE
Senior Master and Director of Admissions: M J Cropper, MA
Deputy Head (*Academic*): R A Kowenicki, MSci, PhD
Deputy Head (*Pastoral*): Ms A R Peak, BA
Deputy Head (*Co-Curricular*): H R Brown, MA, PhD, FTCL
Head of Partnership and Community Engagement: S H Cowper, MA
Director of Shrewsbury School Foundation: O A Jackson-Hutt, MA, MSt
International Development Director: Dr M Tamilarasan, BEng, PhD, FRAeS
Director of Marketing and Communications: G Ferriday, BA, FCIM

Assistant Masters/Mistresses:
* *Head of Faculty/Department*
† *Housemaster/Housemistress*

R Adams, BEc, BEd (*Business*)
G Ansell, MA, CertTESOL (**English as an Additional Language, Chinese*)
J Armstrong, MA (*Mathematics*)
R Arrol, BA (*English as an Additional Language*)
G G Bandy, MA (*English*)
M Barrett, BSc, MA (*Business, Economics, †Rigg's*)
Dr R Barrett, MSc, PhD (*Physics, Safeguarding Team*)
A Baxendale, MA (*English*)
L Baxendale, BA (*History*)
G J F Bell, BA (*Senior Admissions Tutor*)
H O M Bennett, MA (*Philosophy & Theology, i/c Tennis*)
M C Bird, BA (*Philosophy & Theology, †School House*)
Dr A D Briggs, BSc, PhD, MRSC, ACIEA (**Science, *Chemistry*)
A Brogan, BSc (**Mathematics*)
L A Caddel, BA (**Art*)
Dr R A J Case, BSc, PhD (*Biology*)
C L Cissone Hunter, BA, PgDip (*Drama*)
M D H Clark, MA (*Classics, Sixth Form Admissions Tutor*)
C E Cook, MA (*History, i/c Rugby*)
S K P Cooley, MEng (*Mathematics, Physics*)
L A E Corcoran, BA (*Politics, History*)
Dr A R Currie-Jordan, MSc, PhD (*Biology*)
L Dale, BSc (*Chemistry*)
N P David, BSc, MRICS (*Business, Economics, *Director of Activities*)
G M Davies, BSc (*Head of Girls' Cricket*)
J Davies, BSc (*Mathematics*)
B Degalet, BA (*French*)
A R Duncan, BA (*Economics, †Severn Hill*)
Dr M S Elliot, MA, PhD, CPhys, MInstP (**Astronomy & EPQ, Physics*)
C English, BA (*Learning Support*)

R F Evans, BSc (*Geography*)
H S M Exham, BSc (*Biology*, **Digital Learning*, †*Oldham's*)
H Farmer, BA (*Modern Languages*, **Pupil Wellbeing*, *Safeguarding Team*)
T Fitton, BA (*Philosphy & Theology*)
R T Fitton, MEng (*Mathematics*)
P G Fitzgerald, MA (**Classics*)
T Folker (**Adventure*)
J R Fraser-Andrews, MA, MMus (*English*, *Latin*)
J A Gabbitas, BA, MA (*Art*)
H L Gale, BSc (*Chemistry*)
V R Garcia, BA (*Modern Languages*)
E A Gibbons, BA (*Art/Photography*)
S C Griffiths, MSc (*History*, *Politics*, †*Ingram's*)
M H Hansen, BSc, MSc (*Mathematics*)
M J Harding, BA, ACA (*Business*; *Economics*)
I P Haworth, MA (*History*, *Politics*)
E Hellyer, MA, MA (*Philosphy & Theology*; **Academic Innovation*)
L Hennessy, BA (*Assistant Director of Sport*)
C E Hopkins, BA (*Futures Fellow*)
W A Hughes, BA (*Physical Education*, *i/c Cricket*)
A T Hundermark, BSc (*Geography*, *i/c Rowing*)
Í J López Iglesias, BA, MA (*Spanish Fellow*)
M D B Johnson, BA (*Mathematics*, **Pupil Behaviour*, *Safeguarding Team*)
S Jones, BSc (*Physical Education*)
D M Joyce, DipRCM, ARCM (*Music*)
P A Kaye, BEng (**ICT & Computing*)
C W Kealy, BComm (**Business*)
Revd A Keulemans, BSc, BTh (*Chaplain*, *Philosophy & Theology*)
V L Kirk, BSc (*Chemistry*)
M von Kuk, MA (*Modern Languages*)
S G Latcham, BA (*Classics*)
K Leslie, BA (**English*)
A H Livingstone, MA, RSA CELTA, PGCert DLD PAPAA (*Deputy Head of Learning Support*)
K M Lloyd, BA, MA (*Design & Technology*)
R E Lloyd, BA (*Art Fellow*)
J V Lucas, LLB, BSc (*Mathematics*, *Head of Third Form*)
Dr E Lyell, BA, MRes, PhD (*Philosophy & Theology*)
J A Matthews, BSc (*Biology*)
Dr F Matthews-Bird, BSc, PhD (**Geography*)
G L J McGee, BA (*Classics*)
M L McKenzie, BMus, MMus, LTCL (**Director of Music*)
P A Merricks-Murgatroyd, BA (**Economics*)
E D Micklewright, BA, MA (*Biology*)
K V Mitchell, MA, DipEd, AMBDA, APC (**Learning Support*)
R Moreno, BA (**French*)
Dr T S Morgan, BSc, PhD (**Biology*)
H J Morrey, MLitt (*English*)
A P Morris, BA (*Spanish*, *i/c Fives*)
D Morse, BA (*English*)
A X Murray, BSc (*Chemistry*)
G E Murray, BSc, PGCert SpLD, AMDBA, APC (*Learning Support*)
G L Muston, MA (*Humanities Fellow*)
Dr C W Oakley, MMath, DPhil (*Mathematics*, **Academic Administration*)
Dr J L Pattenden, MA, DPhil (*Physics*)
Dr P Pattenden, MA, DPhil, C Phys, MInstP (*Physics*, *Head of Elite University Applications*)
I W Payne, BSc, MA (*Mathematics*)
S E Pearson, BA, MA (*English*, *Safeguarding Team*)
A P Pedraza, MA (**Spanish*)
A S Pembleton, BSc (**Director of Sport/*Physical Education*)
T P Percival, MA (*Classics*, *Head of Higher Education*)
N J Perkins, BSc (**Design & Technology*)
E Phillips, MA (*English*, †*Ridgemount*)
H E Pook, BA, OCR Dip SpLD (*Learning Support*)
D Portier, MA, DEA (*French*, *Head of Sixth Form*)
N M Pritchard, BA, PGDip (*Business*, *Admissions Tutor*, *i/c Volunteering*)
M J Raven, BA (*Geography*)
I Reade, BA (*Drama*)
W R Reynolds, BSc (*Design & Technology*, †*Emma Darwin*)
R R C Robbins, BMus, MA, LRAM (**Choral Music*)
D M Roberts, BSc, MEd (*Mathematics*, *Computing*)
P J B Rudge, BA, MA (**History & Politics*)
M Schofield, BSc (*Chemistry*)
A J Shantry, PGDip (*Cricket Professional*)
S L M Shantry, BSc (*Mathematics*)
C Shelley, BA, HNC, MinstAM (*Music*, *Music Technology*, *Guitar*)
W M Simper, BSc (*Biology*)
M S Skipper, BMus (**Academic Music*)
A Smiter, MSc (*Physics*, **Science Outreach*)
A E Smiter, MSc (**Physics*)
G Smith, BA (*Geography*)
M D Spencer, BSc (*Mathemaics*, *Physics*)
S Stanhope (**Dance*)
R Stockburn, BA (*French Assistant*)
L R Temple, BA (*English*, †*Moser's*)
F W Tickner, BA (*English*, *i/c The Hunt*)
M J Tonks, BA (**Philosophy & Theology*, **Guardianship & International Family Liaison*)
J Turney, MA (*Biology*)
T D J Warburg, MA (*Modern Languages*)
N J Welch, BSc (*Mathematics*)
T C Whitehead, BA (**Modern Languages*, *French*)
S P Wilderspin, BA (*Physical Education*, *i/c Football*)
S E Williams, MChem (*Chemistry*, *Head of Middle School*)
C H Wilson, BA (*Philosophy & Theology*, †*The Grove*)
R M Wilson, MEng, MA (*Mathematics*)
I A Winkley, BA, MA (*History of Art*, *Philosophy & Theology*)
R Witcombe, BSc (*Design & Technology*)
G Y Y Woo, MSc (*Chemistry*)
C I U Wordie, TEFL, ACES (*German Assistant*)
D M Wray, MChem, MRSC (*Chemistry*)
J J C Wright, BSc (*Geography*; †*Churchill's*)
A J Wyatt, BA (*Art*, †*Mary Sidney*)
R Yardley, BA, MEd (*Acting Head of French*, *Modern Languages*)
N N Zafar, BA, MA (*Economics*, *Politics*)

School Doctors:
The General Practitioner Team, Radbrook Green Surgery, Bank Farm Road, Radbrook, Shrewsbury

Headmaster's Personal Assistant: F Nicholas

Solihull School

Warwick Road, Solihull, West Midlands B91 3DJ

Tel: 0121 705 0958
email: admin@solsch.org.uk
website: www.solsch.org.uk
X/Twitter: @solsch1560
Facebook: @SolihullSchool
Instagram: @solsch1560
LinkedIn: /SolihullSchool

Motto: '*Perseverantia*'

Solihull School was founded in 1560 with the income from the chantry chapels of the parish of Solihull. The school is particularly proud of the richness and diversity of the education that it provides. The school has always been closely involved with the community, making its sporting and theatrical facilities available for local schools. In September 2020, the school merged with Saint Martin's to create a leading 3–18 independent co-educational day school across two campuses. Solihull Senior School on the Warwick Road campus and Solihull Preparatory School on the Saint Martin's campus.

Organisation. Solihull provides education for over 1,500 children aged between 3 and 18. The Headmaster of Solihull School is Mr Charles B Fillingham. Mr M P Penney is Head of the Preparatory School, which occupies a 20-acre campus on Brueton Avenue and has more than 430 pupils aged from 3 to 11. Mr S A Morgan is Head of the Senior School attended by 1,100 pupils aged 11–18. In 1973, girls were accepted into the Sixth Form. In September 2005, the school became fully co-educational.

Site and Facilities. Solihull moved to its present site in 1882 and the original school building, School House, survives. The Senior School campus now comprises over 40 acres of buildings and playing fields. Over the last 20 years there has been a very substantial building programme. This originally involved the extension of the Science Department and Design and Technology Centre, the laying of an artificial turf pitch and three squash courts, and the redevelopment of School House. In 2002 a new theatre, the Bushell Hall, was built, which can accommodate an audience of 600 and an assembly for 1,000. At the same time, the old hall was transformed into a library and IT rooms. In 2003, the Alan Lee Pavilion, was completed. In September 2005 a new teaching area, the George Hill Building, was unveiled to provide 16 classrooms and an extensive social space. The David Turnbull Music School was unveiled in September 2009. In September 2015, a four-floor, state-of-the-art Sixth Form centre, The Cooper Building, opened. It was designed to transform Sixth Form teaching and learning and to incorporate the latest multimedia technology. A second artificial turf pitch was completed in 2017. In November 2019, the school opened its refurbished Refectory. In September 2020, Solihull merged with Saint Martin's school and opened Solihull Preparatory School on the Saint Martin's campus. During the summer of 2020, the Junior School building on the Warwick Road campus was repurposed for Senior School use and renamed The Mark Hopton Building. In September 2022, a new dance studio opened in The Mark Hopton Building. The Preparatory School on the Saint Martin's campus has been redeveloped as a 3–11 school with substantial building work and modifications such as bespoke specialist teaching rooms for Art, Design and Technology, ICT, Music and Science and Clevertouch boards. Prep School facilities include a full sized floodlit artificial pitch, a 25m swimming pool, a large recently built library of over 8,000 books and a SMArt Performing Arts Centre that incorporates an auditorium and a dance studio. In October 2021, development work commenced on a car park expansion, extensive grounds facilities and new playing fields. This latest construction project on the Saint Martin's site was completed in September 2022. In September 2023, Solihull was confirmed as a Microsoft Showcase School 2023–2024.

Curriculum. In the Prep School particular emphasis is placed on establishing high standards in core subjects and key skills that permeate the children's learning across the curriculum. The Prep School has specialist teaching rooms for Art, Design and Technology, ICT, Music and Science. EYFS and Infant pupils enjoy the 'Alice House Guide to Living Well' programme – covering Happy, Engaged and Meaningful Living – and Junior School pupils learn resilience skills as part of the Prep School's Wellbeing and Personal Development programme.

At the beginning of the Senior School, all pupils take at least one year of Latin and Spanish. In the second year French and German are optional subjects. English Language and Literature, Mathematics, a Modern Foreign Language, Physics, Chemistry and Biology remain compulsory subjects to GCSE. Three other subjects are chosen from a wide range of options.

The size of the Sixth Form enables the school to offer a very wide range of subjects and combinations. These subjects are Art, Biology, Business, Chemistry, Classics, Dance, Design and Technology, Economics, English Literature, French, Greek, Geography, German, History, Latin, Mathematics, Further Mathematics, Music, PE, Physics, Psychology, Religious Studies (Philosophy and Ethics), Spanish and Theatre Studies. There is also a substantial programme of Enrichment for all pupils in the Sixth Form, ranging from Debating and Creative Writing to Cookery and Theatre Design.

Academic Success. In 2023, Solihull recorded another set of outstanding A Level results with a 100% pass rate; 77% A* to B grades and 52% of all grades falling into the A* or A category. At GCSE, 67% of the 2023 grades were at 9–7.

Games. Games are an integral part of the school curriculum and all pupils in the school are involved. PE is compulsory until Year 11 and all pupils in the school have a games afternoon. The school has a very strong tradition in the major team games, but also offers a very wide range of other options. The principal team games are rugby, cricket, hockey and netball. The Prep School pupils play football in addition to these sports. The school also has teams in tennis, athletics, swimming, clay-pigeon shooting, cross-country, badminton, basketball and fencing to name but a few. In recent years the school has organised very extensive tours for pupils of differing ages: in 2023 our senior rugby and netball teams toured South Africa. Individual and team success in national competitions is a regular feature of Solihull sporting life.

Music, Drama and Dance. The school has a very strong tradition in Music and Drama, which has been enhanced since the building of the Bushell Hall, The David Turnbull Music School on the Warwick Road campus and the SMArt performing arts centre on our Saint Martin's campus. Over a third of all pupils learn a musical instrument and there are over 25 different musical groups in the Senior School. This ranges from orchestras, bands and choirs to piano, string and wind ensembles. Several of these groups are very successful in competition at local festivals. There are many opportunities for pupils to perform at concerts, both formal and informal, throughout the year. A busy programme of masterclasses is given by visiting professional musicians. There is also an excellent Chapel Choir that performs during the school week and at the chapel services each Sunday. Each term the choir sings Evensong in a cathedral (including an annual visit to St Paul's in London) and performs on BBC Radio 4's Daily Service. In 2015, the school joined the Steinway Initiative, purchasing three new Steinway grand pianos.

The Drama and Music departments come together each year for the staging of an ambitious musical, which always involves a large number of pupils. There are two major dramatic performances each year: a school musical (*Twelfth Night, Nell Gwynn, Little Shop of Horrors, Fame* and *The Addams Family*) and a school play (*Fuente Ovejuna, The Royal Hunt of the Sun* and *Goodnight Mr Tom*). In 2023 Solihull was privileged to welcome Holocaust survivor Eva Schloss MBE for the British Premier of 'My Brothers' Gift' and Susan Pollack OBE for a performance of Kindness: A Legacy of the Holocaust. In addition, there are several other productions throughout the course of the year, including a recent highlight the 9 Teens World Premier. Solihull expanded its Performing Arts offering with the addition of Dance in 2020.

Outdoor Education. Outdoor Education plays a major part in the school's life. In the Third Form pupils take part in an outdoor activities programme called Terriers. In the Shell Form every pupil spends a week at the school's David Fricke mountain cottage in Snowdonia. From the Shell Form pupils are able to participate in the CCF, which has an Army and an RAF section, and from the end of the Fourth Form, they can pursue the Duke of Edinburgh's Award scheme. There are approximately 80 pupils in the CCF and 160 are involved at different stages of the Duke of Edinburgh's Award scheme.

Admissions. Pupils are accepted into Solihull School through assessments at 3+, 4+, 5+ and 6+ and examination at 7+ to 14+. A major point of entry to Senior School is at 11+ (Year 7). Places are awarded on the basis of written exams in English and Mathematics, verbal and, in some cases, non-verbal reasoning plus an interview. Some pupils are also accepted to enter the school at 12+, 13+ and 14+. A substantial number of pupils enter the school at Sixth Form level. Offers for admission to the Sixth Form are made on the basis of an interview, predicted GCSE grades and a personal profile. Such offers are conditional on receiving a pupil's school report which should indicate high levels of effort and attainment, excellent conduct and a positive attitude to school life plus achieving a minimum of two grade 7s and four grade 6s at GCSE, normally including grade 6 in Mathematics and English.

The dates for entrance examinations and the Sixth Form scholarship examinations are available on the school website.

Fees per term (2023–2024). Nursery fees are available on our website. Reception/ Infant 1/ Infant 2 £4,143; Junior School £4,733–£4,917; Senior School £5,625.

Scholarships and Bursaries. The number of awards and their value is at the discretion of the Headmaster. As well as Academic, there are Art & Design, Music and Sport Scholarships which are awarded at 11+. At Sixth Form Solihull awards Academic, Art & Design, Music, Performing Arts and Sport Scholarships.

In addition to scholarships, means-tested bursaries are available to offer opportunities to pupils with financial needs. Applicants for such assistance are considered at Senior School and Sixth Form entry.

The Development and Alumni Relations Office at Solihull School. Solihull School Community Network alumni.solsch.org.uk is a network bringing together alumni, parents past and present, former and current staff and friends of both Solihull and Saint Martin's schools. It is a place to share memories, forge careers and social connections and offer support to current students and recent leavers. Email moseleyl@solsch.org.uk or call 0121 703 2963.

Old Silhillians Association. The Old Silhillians Association support and maintain links with the school. They also have their own clubhouse and extensive sports facilities. Website: www.silhillians.net; email: osa@silhillians.net.

Charitable status. Solihull School is a Registered Charity, number 1120597. It exists to provide high-quality education for pupils between 3 and 18 years old.

Chairman of the Governors: Mr Damian Kelly, BA

Bursar and Clerk to the Governors: Mr Richard Bate, MA Cantab, ACMA

***Executive Headmaster*: Mr Charles B Fillingham**, MA King's College London, MSc Oxon

Head of the Senior School: Mr Sean Morgan, BA
Head of the Preparatory School: Mr Mark Penney, BA
Senior School Deputy Head (*Teaching & Learning*): Mrs Katherine Robinson, BSc
Senior School Deputy Head (*Pastoral*): Mrs Rachael Speirs, BA
Preparatory School Senior Deputy Head (*Pastoral & Staff Welfare*): Mr Michael Jones, BA, MA
Preparatory School Deputy Head (*Academic*): Mrs Janet Humphreys, BEd

Director of Development and Alumni Relations: Ms Lucy Lunt, BA, PGDip
Assistant Head (*Co-Curricular*): Mrs Hannah Fair, BA, MA
Assistant Head (*Staff Welfare*): Mrs Emma Jones, BA
Assistant Head (*ICT Strategy*): Mr Matthew van Alderwegen, BA, MA
Preparatory School Assistant Head: Mrs Emma Inglis, BEd
Junior School Assistant Head: Mrs Suzannah Farnan, BSc

Alice House Assistant Head: Mrs Helen Coleman, BSc

Head of Sixth Form: Mrs Natasha Evans, BA, MA
Head of the Middle School: Dr Peter Spratley, BA, MA
Head of the Lower School: Mr Michael Gledhill, BA, LLB
Head of EYFS: Mrs Julie Litwinko, BPhil
Head of Infants: Mrs Hannah Grace, BA, QTS

* *Head of Department*

Mr Gareth Affleck, BA (**History & Politics*)
Mr Nick Adams, BA
Miss Mia Agudo-Dunn, BA
Miss Rachel Airdrie, BA
Mr Oliver Anderton, BSc
Mrs Joanne Ashton, BA
Mrs Nicola Atkins, BEd
Mr Matthew Babb, BSc
Mrs Katie Baden, BSc
Miss Emma Baker, BA
Mr Owen Bate, BSc
Mrs Rebecca Beavon, BA
Miss Claire Bednall, BSc, MSc
Mrs Jennifer Bernamont, BSc
Mr Mark Bishop, BSc, MSc (**Mathematics*)
Mrs Claire Black, BA
Mrs Laura Blackburn, BSc
Mr Mark Briggs, BSc
Mr Darryl Brotherhood, BSc (**Health & Fitness*)
Mr David Brough, BSc
Mr James Brown, BA
Mrs Alison Burt, BSc
Ms Libby Campbell, BA
Mr Edward Carne, BA
Dr William Carroll, PHD
Mrs Rhian Chillcott, MA
Mr Samuel Chillcott, MSci, MEng (**Physics*)
Mrs Jackie Clark, BA, MA
Miss Beth Cobden, BA
Mrs Kirsty Cooke, BA
Mr Neal Corbett, BA (**Design Technology*)
Miss Alexia Coste, BA, MA
Mr Martin Covill, BSc
Mr Geddes Cureton, BSc
Mrs Hannah Davidson, BSc
Mr Mark Davies, BEng
Mr Paul Delaney, BA (**French*)
Mrs Pelvinder Deu, BSc
Mrs Nicola Dickerson, BA
Ms Claire Dignon, BA, MA
Dr Amy Eagleton, PhD
Mr Alex Eden, BSc
Mrs Janine Elkington, BSc
Mrs Tracey Farnell, BSc (**Prep School Sport, Health & Fitness*)
Mr Francisco Fernandez-Valverde
Dr Sian Foster, MA, MPhil, DPhil, MBA
Mrs Joanne Francis, BA, MPhil
Mrs Bettina Freeman, MA
Mrs Tracy Gallagher, BEd
Mrs Corinne Goodman, BSc (**Chemistry*)
Mrs Caroline Graham, BA
Mr Simon Grove, LLB
Mr Christopher Guy, BSc
Mrs Saranne Haley, BSc, MA
Mrs Helen Hallworth, BSc
Mr James Hands, BA
Mrs Lucy Harper, BA
Mrs Jennifer Hart, BA, QTLS
Dr Stuart Hart, BA, MPhil, PhD (**English*)
Mrs Mieke Hartland, BA
Mrs Louise Haynes, BSc
Mr John Henderson, BA (**Art & Photography*)
Mrs Kim Higginson, BA
Reverend Rachel Hill-Brown, MTH, BEd
Mrs Kate Hull, BSc
Mr Matthew Imison, BA, MBA
Mrs Iryna Igoe, BEd
Mrs Elzabe Jansen van Rensburg, BSc
Mr Gareth James, BA
Dr Amelia Jennings, BA, DPhil
Dr Richard Jennings, BSc, PhD
Miss Azahara Jimenez Fuentes, DipHE
Mrs Joanna Johnson, BA, MPhil (**Classics*)
Mr Conor Joyce, BSc
Mr Tim Kermode, MA (**Director of Music*)
Ms Natalie Leeson, BSc
Mr Nick Leonard, BEd
Mr Nicholas Linehan, BA
Mrs Alexandra Longden, BA
Mrs Gabrielle Lowe, BSc, PGDip
Miss Lydia Lynch, BSc
Mr Andrew MacArthur, MMath
Mr Andrew MacKenzie, BA
Mr Darren Maddy
Mrs Jane Mander, BA
Mrs Hanlie Martens, MMus
Mrs Julie Massarella, BEd (**Food & Nutrition*)
Mr Cameron May, BSc
Mr Philip May, BSc
Mr Tim Mayled
Mr Christopher Mayer
Mrs Kirsty McAlister, MA
Mrs Colette McArthur, BA
Mrs Wendy Meigh, BEd (**Economics & Business*)
Mrs Hayley Middleton, BEng, BCom
Mr Stephen Mitchell, BSc
Mr Junaid Mohammed, BA
Mrs Clare Mollison, BA
Mr Paul Morgan, BA (**Spanish*)
Mrs Rachel Morgan, BEd
Miss Rebecca Noon, BA
Mrs Dawn Parker, BSc (**Biology*)
Dr Mary Partridge, BA, MA, PhD
Mr Owen Parsons, MSci
Mrs Vanessa Patel, BA (**Computer Science*)
Mrs Donna Penney, BSc, NASENCo
Mr Simon Phillips, BA, MMus (**Academic Music*)
Mrs Emma Pimlott, BSc
Miss Tegan Pike
Mr Alex Poole, BSc
Mr Ali Raza
Mr Richard Reed, BSc
Mr David Rice, BA, MA
Mr Brett Richmond, BSc
Mrs Catherine Ridout, BEng
Mr William Rigg
Mrs Helen Roberts, BMus, MMus
Mrs Alex Roll, BA
Mrs Louise Rooney, Level 5 Dip Ed, MBACP (**Wellbeing & Personal Development, Anti-discrimination Lead*)

Ms Laura Rutherford, MA Cantab, MEd (**Religious Studies*)
Dr Fran Ryland, BSc, MPhil, PhD (**Combined Science*)
Miss Jenna Sainsbury, BA
Miss Eloise Saunders, BSc
Mr Daniel Shodipo, MSc, MA
Mrs Elizabeth Shearing, BA, SENCo, APC, AMBDA (**Learning Support*)
Mrs Jane Sixsmith, MA & Honorary Doctorate
Mr Keith Slade, BMus, RNCM
Miss Jessica-May Smith, BA
Miss Rebecca Smith, BSc
Mrs Joanne Spencer, BA
Mrs Julie Spraggett, BMus
Mrs Laura Spratley, BA
Mrs Kirsteen Stafford, BA, MA (**Drama*)
Mr Leo Tat, MSc
Miss Rebecca Taylor, BA
Miss Amy Thacker, BA, MA
Mr Steve Thompson, BSc (**Sport*)
Mr Matthew Tibbitts, BSc
Mrs Raminder Trainor, BSc
Mr Jack Vaabel, BA
Ms Sarah Vaughan, BA, MEd
Mrs Danielle Wana, BA (**Academic PE*)
Miss Stephanie Waldron, BSc
Mr Joseph Walker, BA
Mrs Sarah Watton, BA
Mrs Laura Webb, BA
Mrs Ruth Whaley, MA
Mr David Whiting, BSc
Miss Anna Wilkie, BSc (**Psychology*)
Miss Rebecca Windmill, MSci, MA (**Geography*)
Miss Helen Winn, LLB
Miss Mia-Rose Yates, BA
Ms Zhe Zhou, BSc, MSc

Assistant Staff:

Human Resources Manager: Mrs Hayley Miles, MCIPD MA, BA
Assistant Human Resources Manager: Mrs Joanna Barrett, CIPD

Admissions Registrar: Mrs Nicolette Mullan
Admissions Officer: Mrs Allison Morris
Admissions Administrator: Mrs Linda Bevan

Assistant Bursar (*Operations & Staff*): Ms Julie Henrick, ILM
Assistant Bursar (*Facilities, Compliance & Transport*): Miss Gemma Deery, BSc, IOSH
Headmaster's PA: Mrs Lisa McGann
PA to the Bursar: Ms Suzanne Baldwin
PA to the Head of the Senior School: Mrs Tracey Duggan
PA to Head of the Preparatory School: Mrs Jessica Harris

Director of Academic Guidance & Administration: Mrs Rhian Chillcott, MA

Alumni Events & Communications Manager: Mrs Lynn Moseley

Head of Technical Support: Mr Martin Moseley

Head of Marketing: Mrs Lucie Ray-Barrett
Marketing Assistant: Mrs Julia Ackroyd, BSc

SSI & DofE Manager: Mr Philip Dean, MBE

Medical Officer: Dr Sunil Kotecha, MBChB, FRCGP, MSc
School Nurse Team Leader: Mrs Helen King, RGN
School Nurse: Mrs Liz Munro, BSc, RGN, DN, QN
School Nurse: Mrs Claire Evans, RGN

Librarian: Mrs Alison Vaughan, BA

South Hampstead High School GDST

3 Maresfield Gardens, London NW3 5SS

Tel:	020 7435 2899
email:	senioradmissions@shhs.gdst.net
website:	www.shhs.gdst.net
X/Twitter:	@SHHSforgirls

See full entry in the **GSA** section, on **p. 492**.

Stamford School

Southfields House, St Paul's Street, Stamford, Lincolnshire PE9 2BQ

Tel:	01780 750300
email:	ses@ses.lincs.sch.uk
website:	www.stamfordschools.org.uk
X/Twitter:	@SpedeNews
Facebook:	@stamfordendowedschools
Instagram:	@StamfordSchools

Motto: *Christ me spede*

Founded by William Radcliffe, of Stamford, 1532.

Introduction.

Stamford Endowed Schools have been educating students since 1532. Our Schools have a long and prestigious heritage, but everything we do at Stamford is focused on preparing young people to lead happy and fulfilling lives in the 21st century. At the start of the academic year 2023–2024 Stamford Schools opened its doors for the first time to teach students co-educationally at all stages as Stamford High School and Stamford School merged.

We strive to offer an outstanding, contemporary education in which students develop the ability to think for themselves and to interpret the world around them. Every child at Stamford is encouraged to be an independent thinker and take the lead in their own education. The Stamford Endowed Schools comprise of Stamford Junior School from ages 2–11, Stamford School from ages 11–16 and Stamford Sixth Form from ages 16–18. All three Schools are located throughout the historic Lincolnshire town of Stamford on our 55 acre site. Stamford is a dynamic, vibrant, modern, and exciting school, built on the strengths of five centuries of learning, with a resolute focus on preparing our students for 2030 and beyond. Our students leave Stamford as rounded and grounded young people, ready for life beyond education. At the heart of all our Schools is the focus on academic ambition, pastoral excellence, and the opportunity for students to become the very best version of themselves.

Buildings and Grounds.

Our School sites are embedded in the heart of Stamford, covering just over 55 acres of the town. We are an intrinsic part of the local community, with the Nursery and Junior School located to the west of the town, and Stamford Sixth Form (St Martin's) and Stamford School (St Paul's) situated in the centre of Stamford.

St Paul's proudly forms the foundation of the Stamford School site, now home to Year 7–11 students, upholding the legacy of the former boys' school before its co-educational merger with Stamford High School. The Chapel, formerly St Paul's Church, from which the site takes its name, is the oldest part of our School. In 1532 teaching began in the Corpus Christi chapel of St Mary's, but in 1553, the School moved to the remaining portion of St Paul's. The Chapel dates as far back as the Domesday Book of 1086. Elsewhere at St Paul's you will find the Oswald Elliott Hall, Performing Arts Centre, Sports Centre, Swimming Pool, and Playing Fields. The footbridge across East Street links the St Paul's site, where you will find three of our Boarding Houses, with the Sports facilities and School buildings.

St Martin's was home to the Stamford High School until September 2023 when Stamford School and High School merged. It is now home to the Stamford Sixth Form where Year 12 and 13 are based. The School buildings were originally part of Browne's Hospital, which first opened its doors in 1877. Former High School students include Frances Chapman (OS 1884) who later became piano teacher to the famous composers, Sir Malcolm Sargent (OS 1910) and Sir Michael Tippet (OS 1922). Three of our Boarding Houses are based at St Martin's, along with the Ancaster Studio, Birkbeck Drama Studio and Spires Café. The Wothorpe Sports Centre and Astro Pitches are based between the St Martin's site and Stamford Junior School, just five minutes' walk from the main reception along Kettering Road.

School Structure and Curriculum.

The Schools educate over 1,200 students co-educationally from Years 7 to 13. Years 7–11 learn predominantly at the St Paul's site of Stamford School, moving to the Stamford Sixth Form at St Martin's in Years 12 and 13. At Stamford we want our students to take the lead in their own education. At the heart of what we offer at Stamford is the opportunity for children to thrive, and to help them become the best version of themselves. Every student at Stamford, from Nursery through to Sixth Form, is encouraged to be an independent thinker. At Stamford we offer young people opportunity and breadth of experience, which combined gives them an education that develops their ability to think for themselves.

ACADEMIC CURRICULUM

We offer a wide and detailed curriculum to suit all students. Enabling a stronger academic focus, tailored to every pupil, gives our students balance. Our curriculum incorporates linguistic, mathematical, scientific, technological (including computing), human and social, physical, aesthetic and creative, spiritual, moral, ethical and personal education. Teachers and parents work together, identifying each student's personal strengths and ensuring they achieve what they are capable of – their progress is proactively tracked through both formal and informal reporting.

APPROACH TO LEARNING

Our approach to learning is formed around a framework of four guiding principles that include creativity, collaboration, critical thinking and complex problem-solving. Lessons are designed to be engaging, and to challenge and stretch your child. Our 'ideal classrooms' provide an innovative environment that promotes collaboration between students, their peers and their teachers.

STAMFORD SIXTH FORM

The Stamford Sixth Form programme offers 28 different subjects at A Level and 3 BTEC courses plus 1 Cambridge Technicals course. This means students can choose the subjects they love, as well as ensuring they are equipped with the knowledge and qualifications needed to enter further education or the workplace in the future. Around 90% of our Sixth Form who apply to UCAS go on to university, including Oxford, Cambridge, and Russell Group universities. Whether students are interested in a career, degree apprenticeships, further education, travel, gap years or volunteering, our priority is to work with you to help you understand the right options available. We support all our students in exploring all routes. At Stamford Sixth Form our aim is to ensure that students don't lose their breadth of learning, and have a range of opportunities once they begin their further education. Funnelling down from a broad range of subjects at GCSE, we understand that moving to a narrower range of subject choices can often limit breadth. We want our scientists to still have a passion for literature; we know our language students still need numeracy skills for adult life when managing money for the first time; and we also still need to have fun, relax and unwind.

We have designed our timetable to increase contact time for key subjects. Our unique life skills programme offers students a range of taught, short courses in areas such as finance for the real world, how to cook for yourself at university, how to prepare a business pitch, how to dance and how to rewire a plug, or change a tyre once you've learnt to drive! Students will be encouraged to manage their own time, to make appointments with their individual form tutors and work in a more flexible way to study, whilst remaining in the structured setting of a school environment. We hope that offering a flexible and varied programme to our students will ensure their time at Stamford is valuable, life-affirming and enjoyable.

Stamford has a robust pastoral structure, ensuring students have a learning environment where they are happy, secure, feel listened to and cared for. As a school we know that happy, cared-for students are most likely to thrive. Our pastoral system means that day to day our students have access to a year group Student Support Manager, a Head of Year as well as their Form Tutor. The students are also supported by our school counsellors, safeguarding, health and wellbeing and behaviour teams who all work together under one Pastoral umbrella. This ensures care is consistent and timely, providing an environment for our students to build resilience and strengthen their own wellbeing. At Stamford, we believe collaboration with parents, tutors, staff and our wider community, is important. This gives our students the tools they need to cope with the challenges life can throw at them and ensure they feel fully supported throughout. We also provide a modern PSHE programme that is challenging, informative and inspirational. The programme is embedded into our curriculum and an important part of our day.

Activities.

At Stamford we believe co-curricular activities build inclusivity, community and teamwork. Being involved in our co-curricular programme helps our young people support and respect each other, their peers and wider community around them. It gives them the ability to try new things, and unlock their team spirit. At Stamford, we believe that our co-curricular offering is an essential part of a child's schooling with us and that our co-curricular activities help students to develop important life skills such as leadership, confidence, and teamwork.

We strive to create as many opportunities as possible for students to extend their learning and passions beyond the classroom. Our extensive range of co-curricular activities, from CCF and debating, to photography and cooking, all promote a love of learning beyond the academic programme. There are also opportunities for students to reinforce their curriculum learning and extend their experience with clubs such as Drama and Dance as well as Music lessons. These clubs give the students an ability to try new things and with over 400 clubs and activities a week at Stamford, there is something for everyone.

Careers.

Our Head of Futures, Higher Education advisors and Stamford Alumni are on hand to help ensure students' next steps are tailored to individual pathways and that each student gets the best bespoke advice and support. At Stamford we offer a unique, tailored approach to Futures, with our Head of Futures, a Level 6 qualified careers advisor and member of the Careers Development Institute, along with a knowledgeable and experienced Higher Education advisory team on hand to guide students through their post-16 options. We offer Morrisby profiling and 1:1 careers advice which, combined with students' academic data, helps us guide and support students with their important decision making. Stamford's Futures ethos is simple: We believe that the purpose of school is to connect the past, present and future for our young people. In our Futures programme we guide and empower our students to become the best possible version of themselves as they leave Stamford and take first steps into their future beyond school. We ask our students, 'who could you be, and would you like to be'? We work alongside them to help them find the best next steps to take towards their future fulfilment.

House Structure.

The Stamford boarding community is small with seven boarding properties, which ensures students and our boarding Houseparents feel part of a close-knit community. Our boarding houses are age-appropriate and single-sex to ensure the need for privacy is respected and the right community atmosphere is created for our students. We offer full, weekly, flexible and occasional boarding, so there is something for everyone, depending on circumstances. Our Houses are full at the weekends, with students enjoying a social life rich in after-school clubs, sports, fun-packed trips and activities tailored to their age group. Boarders can also make use of our leisure centre and pool, or take advantage of support and advice from tutors and Houseparents during homework time.

Sixth Form Boarding – St Martin's and Welland House Y11–12

Both Welland House and St Martin's are home to our senior girls in Year 11–12. Both Houses are best described as a home from home. Both offer a nurturing, kind and caring community, with positivity and fun at their core, and a true sense of belonging and camaraderie at their heart. Park House is the home for our eldest female students in Year 13, located close

to the Burghley Estate. Park House is a safe and quiet space away from the town centre for students to study, relax and unwind.

Senior Boarding

St Paul's is our house for younger female students and Byard House is the home of lower school boys. Both houses are located in the heart of the Senior School campus and for students in Year 7–10. The neighbouring houses team up for social activities and weekend trips to encourage a really dynamic and energetic community atmosphere. The pastoral care given to students is second to none, with Houseparents, tutors, matrons and support staff on hand for anything the students need.

Browne House is home to our senior boys in Year 11–13. Located on the St Paul's site, the house is perfectly positioned close to the large playing fields and sports centre, whilst being close to the town centre and social elements of Stamford to allow for some independence. Stamford is a safe and inclusive town, with the School's embedded within, so students are always safe and looked out for.

Admission.

At Stamford School there are three main points of entry in Year 7, Year 9 and Year 12. We can admit students into Year 8 and Year 10 when space allows. In these cases, the entrance exam and interview will be arranged on an ad-hoc basis.

Our admissions procedures are designed to be as straightforward as possible for all applicants, whilst also enabling us to gain a full understanding of each applicant's academic potential and suitability to Stamford Schools.

Of the 160 year group total, approximately half will join Year 7 from Stamford Junior School and the other half will come from a wide range of primary and preparatory schools across the region. The entrance examinations take place in January of the year of entry, when an applicant is in Year 6. All applicants will be invited to Stamford School to undertake; an interview with a member of our teaching staff; an inhouse English and Maths computerised assessments, (based on the current Year 6 curriculum) and a short piece of creative writing. The computerised assessments measure verbal and non-verbal reasoning, quantitative and spatial skills.

Applicants cannot prepare for these tests which are designed to assess their inherent (rather than taught) aptitude. They will use a school device to complete the assessments. For the written assessments (creative writing) students will be under examination conditions; they will be given a subject and will be asked to plan and write a short story based on this topic, within 30 minutes.

We admit around 30 students each year into Year 9. They will join the students who have come through from Year 7 to form a year group of around 180 students. The Main Entrance Examinations for Year 9 entry are held early in the Summer Term of Year 7 (age 11+). Following the Main Examinations, Stamford School will continue to accept registrations and make offers for as long as places remain available. Depending on the number of applicants and spaces available, the school may arrange a late exam day in the Autumn Term of Year 8 (age 12+).

Year 12 Entry

All applicants will be invited to Stamford Sixth Form to undertake; An interview with a member of our teaching staff; An inhouse computerised assessments (based on the current Year 11 English and Maths curriculum) This test assesses verbal and non-verbal reasoning, quantitative and spatial skills. Applicants cannot prepare for these tests which are designed to assess their inherent (rather than taught) aptitude.

Interview candidates will be interviewed by a member of the Sixth Form team. The focus of this interview is to get a better understanding of the candidate as a learner, but questions are likely to also explore other interests, achievements and skills to give us a more rounded impression of the individual.

International candidates must have a minimum English language level of B2 CEFR Level (IELTS equivalent 5.5–6.5). Following receipt of their application, the Admissions team will be in touch to guide them through the Year 12 entrance assessments and interviews, which will be held in the November of their Year 11.

Following the November assessment day, Stamford Schools will continue to accept registrations and make offers for as long as places remain available.

Fees.

Day student, Years 7 & 8, including lunch – termly £6,650, annual Fee £19,950.

Day student, Years 9 to 11, including lunch – termly £6,833, annual fee £20,500

Day student Years 12 and 13, including lunch – termly £6,833, annual fee £20,500

Boarding ranges from £9,233 for a three day boarding option termly (£27,700 annually) to £12,825 for a full boarding package of a non-UK resident (£38,475 annually).

Applicants are required to pay a non-refundable registration fee of £100.

Scholarships and Bursaries.

The Stamford Schools Scholarship provision is designed to recognise boys and girls with outstanding talents and skills in a variety of fields, and to help develop those talents and skills during their time at the school. Scholarships are awarded on entry to Stamford School, although there are later opportunities to gain a Scholarship once a pupil is at the school. Scholarship Awards will be made to students entering in Years 7, Year 9 and Year 12.

Stamford Scholars benefit enormously from the additional opportunities and enrichment programmes offered to them. Scholarships are awarded on merit and do not carry a fee remission or financial award. All scholarships are kept under review and are reassessed after a period of two years. At Stamford we offer Scholarships in Art, Drama, Music, TADA (Talented Athlete Development Award) in Year 7 and 8, and a Sports Scholarship from Year 9.

Currently, we provide more than £2m of bursary support to students. At Stamford we are proud of maintaining the wide socio-economic background of our students. Life-changing bursaries are available for talented students who otherwise would not be able to afford the fees to attend our School, giving them the opportunity to benefit from a Stamford education.

Each year we offer support to families of the brightest students whose financial resources are limited. Financial assistance is based on means-testing the household income and assets using a standard formula widely used within the independent schools sector.

Assistance with fees is available for students joining our Senior School in Years 7 to 13 and is means-tested, therefore the process will involve a home visit. The vast majority of our bursaries are awarded to children joining us at the key entry points of Year 7 and Year 12. Other years of entry are considered by exception only. Bursary applications should be submitted at the same time as you apply for a place. All bursaries are reviewed annually, and the student's suitability will be considered through an academic assessment as well as reviewing previous school results and the child's school report.

Charitable status. As part of the Stamford Endowed Schools, Stamford School is a Registered Charity, number 527618.

Chair of the Governing Body: Mr Tom Cartledge

Bursar and Clerk to the Governing Body: Dean White

***Principal*: William Phelan,** MBA

***Deputy Head*: Nicholas Davies**

Stephen Perse Foundation

Union Road, Cambridge, Cambridgeshire CB2 1HF

Tel: 01223 454762
email: admissions@stephenperse.com
website: www.stephenperse.com
X/Twitter: @SPFSchools
Facebook: @stephenpersefoundation
Instagram: @stephenpersefoundation
LinkedIn: /stephen-perse-foundation/

Stephen Perse is a family of independent schools, educating boys and girls from nursery and early years to sixth form, in Cambridge and Saffron Walden. We seek to educate and inspire the change-makers of tomorrow: intelligent young people with the creativity, compassion, confidence and conviction to improve society and the world.

Our vision is to create and sustain an outstanding educational environment that fosters modern scholarship through exceptional teaching and a dynamic, flexible and rigorous academic curriculum. Added to this, the breadth and quality of our pastoral care and extensive co-curriculum serve to nurture and celebrate our students' individuality and personal development.

Our community of staff, students and parents places great emphasis on our values, which include: scholarship, excellence and creativity in teaching and learning, kindness, self-reliance and social and environmental responsibility.

Our inspirational environment includes immersive digital engagement and the provision of dynamic spaces to encourage learning and curiosity. Extensive sport, music, drama, art and wider creative opportunities across all age groups support and enhance our students' experiences and achievements.

Our results are exceptional, placing us among the best independent schools in the country by any measure: at GCSE and A level; our leavers' university destinations; and in what our students go on to achieve beyond their formal education.

Students leave us ready to take their place in a complex, changing global society, with all of the attributes and attitudes they need to make a positive difference in the world.

Our history. Founded in 1881 as the Perse School for Girls, our history is part of Cambridge's rich academic past. Since evolving into the Stephen Perse Foundation in 2001, we have grown significantly, opening our doors to boys as well as girls and providing a complete educational pathway to inspire and guide young learners from early years to sixth form.

In 2008, we successfully set up a co-educational Sixth Form; in 2010, we acquired our Madingley site; in 2013, we merged with Dame Bradbury's School in Saffron Walden.

Our outstanding leadership and strategic vision has been acknowledged through awards and accolades including, in 2014, being named both Independent School of the Year at the TES Independent School Awards and the Sunday Times Schools Guide 2021 East Anglia Independent Secondary School of the Decade.

Admissions. Our pupils and students are as mixed as any group of young people – but they all have bright, enquiring minds, whether they're artistic or academic, sporty or in need of educational support.

There are many entry points across our schools, ranging from early years to sixth form. Please see our website for details, dates and FAQs. We hold our own entrance tests and interviews, held annually, usually in January for a September start. Entry is available outside of these testing dates if places allow; please contact the Admissions office if you would like more information.

Boarding is available for our Sixth Form students.

Pastoral care. We place a great emphasis on pastoral care and the wellbeing of all our students. Established pastoral structures support the students and foster personal development, responsibility and informed choices. Subject teachers and year staff care for the academic progress and individual welfare of each student.

All schools tell you they're wonderful but the only way to know if they're right for you is to see for yourself. At Stephen Perse you'll find pupils and students who bubble with enthusiasm, teachers who love what they do and a place where young people blossom and have amazingly good fun. They'll be delighted to show you what being here is really like.

Results. Our students achieve top results and go on to study at world-leading universities. Just as importantly, they are encouraged to pursue their dreams and follow the path that's right for them. Last academic year's results were outstanding with 71% of GCSE entries graded at 7, 8 to 9; 58% of grades A*–A at A Level or IB equivalent.

Our leaver destinations represent the best, most exciting opportunities the world has to offer. In 2023, our students have secured places at prestigious universities, including world-leading Russell Group institutions University of Cambridge, University of Oxford, Durham University, University of Edinburgh and Imperial College London.

Fees per term (2023–2024). Early Years £92 per day (Age 1–2) and £89 per day (Age 2–3); Stephen Perse Cambridge, Junior School: £4,875–£6,163; Stephen Perse Dame Bradbury's Saffron Walden, Junior School: £4,875–£5,839; Stephen Perse Cambridge, Senior School: £7,128 and Stephen Perse Cambridge, Sixth Form (Day): £6,841 and (Boarding): £14,705.

Charitable status. The Stephen Perse Foundation is a Registered Charity, number 1120608, and a Company Limited by Guarantee, number 6113565.

Governors:
Dr Vicky Mills (*Chairman*)
Ms Lavinia Abell
Mr Ray Anderson
Mr Paul Beastall
Mrs Leah Bramwell
Dr Victor Christou
Mr Munish Datta
Ms Jessica Farrimond
Prof Rob Foale
Mr David Gill
Ms Janet Magee
Prof. Alexander Routh
Ms Sara Russo
Dr Hugh Shercliff
Mr Simon Thorley KC
Mr Sven Töpel

***Principal*: Mr Richard Girvan**

Chief Financial and Operating Officer: Sarah Bonnett

Executive Director: Heidi Hall

Head of Early Years: Mrs Sarah Holyoake

Head of Junior School Dame Bradbury's Saffron Walden: Mr James McCaughran

Head of Junior School Cambridge: Mr David Hewlett

Head of 11–18: Mr Stephen Ward

Stowe School

Stowe, Buckingham, Bucks MK18 5EH

Tel: 01280 818000
email: enquiries@stowe.co.uk
website: www.stowe.co.uk
Facebook: @stoweschool
Instagram: @stoweschool

Motto: '*Persto et Praesto*'

Our purpose is to create a community of Change Makers ready to transform the world.

We are opportunity-led and believe that schools must equip pupils to thrive in a fast-moving, ever changing world. We prepare Change Makers for jobs that don't yet exist, using technology which hasn't yet been invented, to solve problems which we haven't yet thought about. We can't compete on labour costs or raw materials, but we can set the pace in intellectual capital, creativity and entrepreneurial flair. Yes, we teach pupils numeracy and literacy and how to excel in exams, but we also teach them how to collaborate, to solve problems, to think critically and to reflect. We equip them with the skills, resilience and ideas they need to adapt and flourish.

It is what pupils do with the knowledge they acquire which will turn them into Change Makers. Emotional intelligence, teamwork and thought-leadership enable pupils to take advantage of new technologies, limitless access to information and advances in engineering, robotics and artificial intelligence. With empathy, versatility, originality and creativity, Stowe's inclusive community is transforming how young people are prepared to enter the world beyond the school gates. We have created a fully integrated programme of interventions: putting Change Makers at the centre of everything we do and providing transformational opportunities in and outside the classroom.

We offer co-curricular breadth and depth with a sports programme which encourages full participation while developing the talents of our elite athletes (which include Olympic medallists such as James Rudkin for rowing and Marilyn Okoro for track and field). Music, art, drama and creative writing encourage Change Makers to express themselves in diverse ways, transcending political, social and cultural boundaries while bringing a greater understanding of human experience.

We catalyse change by providing generous Change 100 bursaries, inspirational teaching and coaching, infrastructural investment, treating our work force as valued colleagues and prioritising social and environmental impact. By promoting equality and inclusion we move forward to realise our dream, every pupil at Stowe should go into the world to make positive change, create new opportunities and build a better future for all.

Stowe is a boarding and day School with boys and girls from 13 to 18. The School roll is 905, comprising 620 boarders and 285 day pupils. Pupils are also accepted each year for two-year A Level courses.

Houses. There are ten boys' and six girls' Houses.

The Curriculum. The academic experience at Stowe is designed to encourage intellectual curiosity, a thirst for knowledge and understanding and independence of thought and expression. Stoics are asked to be committed and enthusiastic learners, to embrace challenge and to see failure as a necessary step in achieving progress. They are urged to be ambitious, make the most of their academic opportunities and to continually strive to improve their skills.

Art, Design and Information Technology. All pupils are introduced to these subjects in their first year at Stowe. Art and Design are popular both for those pursuing hobbies and for those studying for formal examinations. Traditional skills are covered alongside more modern techniques such as computer-aided design and desktop publishing.

Music and Drama. These subjects flourish as important and integral parts of the School's activities both within and outside the formal curriculum. There is plenty of scope to get involved in the School Orchestras, Jazz Band, Clarinet Quartet, Choirs, School plays, House plays and House entertainments. The timetable is sufficiently flexible to allow special arrangements to be made for outstanding musicians to study outside School. Drama Clubs and Theatre Studies groups have a fully-equipped theatre at their disposal. The refurbishment of the Theatre and classrooms, alongside a purpose-built Music School, allows these creative arts to flourish.

Careers Guidance. Careers education forms a continuous thread throughout a Stoic's time at Stowe. It aims to provide a framework within which each can develop the self-awareness and experience necessary to make balanced decisions at each stage during their time at the School and, hopefully, after they leave. Stowe's Careers Education & Guidance Programme begins when pupils join the Third Form at 13. It aims to provide increasing contact with the world outside, throughout a Stoic's time at School and to help reach those decisions which affect their future in as well-informed and balanced a way as possible. Every encouragement is given to discuss the various options with Houseparent, Tutor and Careers Staff.

Religion. The School's foundation is to provide education in accordance with the principles of the Church of England and this is reflected in its Chapel services on Sundays. Pupils of other faiths and other Christian Churches are welcomed and, in some cases, separate arrangements are made for them on Sundays. Every pupil attends the chapel services on weekdays.

Games. The main sports for boys are rugby, hockey and cricket; for girls, hockey, netball, lacrosse and tennis. Stowe also offers an exceptionally wide range of other sports, giving everybody the opportunity to take part in an activity they enjoy.

Significant investment has been made in our sports facilities in recent years and Stowe has some wonderful facilities which include:

- 8 Rugby Pitches
- 7 Cricket Squares
- Double floodlit AstroTurf
- 4 Football Pitches
- Eight-lane Athletics Track with comprehensive field event facilities
- Four-court Badminton Sports Hall
- BHS highly commended Equestrian Centre, including a cross country course and a floodlit arena
- 3 Lacrosse Pitches
- 11 lanes of turf cricket nets & 10 lanes of AstroTurf nets
- 3 Squash Courts
- State-of-the-art Gym
- 3 Fives Courts
- 25m six-lane Competition Pool
- Clay Pigeon Shooting Range
- 4 Netball Courts
- 27 Tennis Courts
- 12 Spinning Bikes
- 9 Hole Golf course and Teaching Studio

Other Activities. Pupils complement their games programme with a broad variety of extra-curricular activities, including clubs and societies.

On Mondays a special activities programme is based on Service at Stowe and at the heart of this is the Combined Cadet Force with all three service arms, the Duke of Edinburgh's Award scheme, Community Service (in the neighbourhood) and Leadership skills.

The Award at Stowe. This is designed to encourage Stoics to see the benefits of engaging fully in all areas of School life and to ensure that Stoics finish their time at Stowe with valuable experience and qualifications which will help them stand out in a fast-changing world, whilst also offering the opportunity to learn through positive experience. Stoics engage with The Award at three different levels during their time at Stowe. At all levels they will be expected to engage in eight key areas of School life; Academic Achievement, Achieving, Beyond Term-Time and Citizenship, Sport and Physical Activity, The Arts, In the Community and Thinking Differently.

Fees per term (2023–2024). Boarders £14,686, Day in Boarding pupils £10,558, Day House pupils £8,503 payable before the commencement of the School term to which they relate. A deposit is payable when Parents accept the offer of a place. This deposit is repaid by means of a credit to the final payment of fees or other sums due to the School on leaving.

Scholarships and Bursaries. A range of Scholarships and Exhibitions are offered at Stowe. Scholarships may be supplemented by means-tested bursaries, with a limited number of fully-funded places, where there is proven financial need.

Academic Scholarships

Academic Scholarships are awarded to those applicants who can demonstrate very high levels of academic attainment (Academic Scholars tend to achieve eight or more GCSEs at grade 8 or 9 by Year 11), as well having as a real enthusiasm for learning and showing a genuine commitment to academic pursuits and extension.

Art Scholarships

Art Scholarships are offered to pupils who show an exceptional ability to think and create with skill, imagination and passion. The committed Art Scholar will be a leader in their Year Group and beyond, organising and participating in exhibitions, entering competitions and pushing the boundaries of their working practice at all times. Art Scholars are exemplary in their commitment to the Art School, taking full advantage of daily activity sessions and weekend workshops.

Chess Scholarships

Stowe runs an active and successful Chess Club which meets weekly throughout the year. There is an Inter-House Chess Tournament and the Club regularly plays team fixtures against other schools. Stowe also plays host to two open Chess tournaments per year for primary and secondary pupils, which usually attract between 80–120 players. Each year we award a single Chess Scholarship to a pupil joining our Third Form. The successful Chess Scholar will be expected to play an active role with the Chess Club, to represent the School in Chess fixtures against other schools and to play in the two open tournaments hosted by Stowe.

Drama Scholarships

Drama Scholars are expected to take the subject at GCSE and to audition for all co-curricular School productions including Congreve and Junior Congreve. Academically, Drama Scholars are expected to show devotion and enthusiasm, maintaining high standards of academic achievement throughout the GCSE course, with the expected outcome of a Grade 9/8 A*/A. In School productions, Scholars are expected to show commitment to the development of skill and dedication to the process of making theatre, setting an example both on stage and in the rehearsal room and acting as ambassadors in the wider School body and as representatives of the School at public performances.

Design Scholarships

Alongside our Scholars deepening their knowledge of the subject through the study of the GCSE in Design Technology (Edexcel), they also develop an appreciation of various architectural styles; experiencing first hand an understanding of what constitutes beautiful design. Scholars engage in our termly manufacturing and disassembly projects with the intent of improving the aesthetic and mechanical properties of existing products, as well as learning about the precision involved in world-class engineering.

Equestrian Scholarships

Equestrian Scholars, along with their own pony/horse, are expected to play an active role in participating and promoting Equestrian sport both within Stowe as well as externally. Equestrian Scholars will regularly represent the School at competitions, including National School Equestrian Association (NSEA), be role models to others in the team by displaying strong teamwork skills and will use their own growth and development to inspire others. We are looking for candidates who have a strong bond with their pony/horse and who are able to demonstrate their passion and commitment to the sport.

Golf Scholarships

Candidates must possess a demonstrable track record of golfing achievement at a high level. This would normally include evidence of success at County/Regional level, along with being in possession of an established official WHS golf handicap. Golf Scholarships will only be awarded to candidates who are outstanding golfers or good golfers that show serious potential.

Music Scholarships

A number of awards are made each year, ranging from Exhibitions (free instrumental tuition on one or two instruments) to Scholarships (a Scholarship plus free instrumental tuition on two instruments). A candidate's musicianship and practice ethic will have a direct bearing on any award granted, and successful candidates will be expected to play a full and active role in the Department, including membership of our choirs.

Sports Scholarships and Exhibitions

These may be awarded to exceptional candidates at 13+ and 16+ showing outstanding potential in at least one of Stowe's key sports: boys: rugby, hockey and cricket; girls: hockey, netball, lacrosse and tennis. Exceptional ability in individual sports may also be considered. Each application is reviewed on its merits and due consideration is given to the contribution they would make to sport at Stowe.

Roxburgh Scholarships

In addition to strong academic potential which will be demonstrated by exams in English, Maths and Science (in which we would expect candidates to achieve 70%+), it is expected that candidates will display excellence in at least one of the following: Art, Design, Drama, Music or Sport. Due to the high academic standard required, candidates cannot be awarded both an Academic Scholarship and a Roxburgh Scholarship.

The Sixth Form Berry Scholarship for Original Thinking reflects the importance of original and creative thinking, not just in itself but, crucially, to the future needs of business and wider society. Macro-level changes to the world's economic make-up, coupled with technological advancement, changing workforce demographics, global integration and increased competition have meant that approaches and attitudes towards work have transformed – indeed, the world of work is almost unrecognisable compared with that of just a few years ago. We want pupils to leave Stowe, not only with an ability to adapt and thrive in that volatile world, but with the confidence to make positive change. Their ability to use the skills of original thinking will be key to that – and so we seek candidates who will be 'constructive non-conformists' within our community, and set an example for others to follow.

Change 100. Our ambition and mission is to raise an endowment fund of £100 million over the next ten years. This will transform our long-term ability to provide the life-changing chance of a Stowe education to talented and deserving children from socially diverse and financially disadvantaged backgrounds. This endowment will provide 100 free places in the School at all times, and forever, enabling 20 children in each year group to attend the School on a fully-funded place. To ensure that Change 100 has an immediate impact, we have also pledged to spend the first £1 million raised each year on places the following September. We are delighted that in September 2021, the first ten children joined us on our Change 100 programme and look forward to growing that number significantly in the years to come.

Full details may be obtained from The Registrar.

Admissions. Boys and girls can be registered at any age. Full details can be obtained from the Admissions Department (admissions@stowe.co.uk), who will supply registration forms. The School is always prepared to consider applications from pupils to enter the School at 14 if places are available. The date of birth should be stated and it should be noted that boys and girls are normally admitted between their 13th and 14th birthdays.

The Old Stoic Society. Director: Anna Semler. Old Stoic Society Office: Tel 01280 818252, email oldstoic @stowe.co.uk.

Charitable status. Stowe School Limited is a Registered Charity, number 310639. The primary objects of the charity, as set out in its Memorandum and Articles of Association, are to acquire Stowe House, which was achieved in 1923, and to provide education in accordance with the principles of the Church of England.

Governing Body:
Mr Simon C Creedy Smith, BA, FCA (*Chairman*) [OS]
Mr Christopher J Tate, BA, MIMC (*Vice Chair*) [OS]
The Rev Peter Ackroyd, MA, MBA, PhD
Mr Patrick Bradshaw, BA
Ms Rebecca Brown, BA
Ms Julie C Brunskill, BSc, MRICS
Mr Simon Cuerden
Ms Elizabeth J de Burgh Sidley, BA, FRICS
Mr Rupert Fordham, BA Cantab
Mr John Frost, BSc, MRICS, MNAEA, MARLAz [OS]
Mr Richard Greaves, BA
Mr Will Jakeman, BSc, PGCSE
Mr Sunjeewa Jayawardena BSc, MBA
Mrs Andrea Johnson, BSc, PGCE
Mrs Mairi Johnstone, LLB, DipLP, BSc, MBA, GradCG
Mrs Catriona Lloyd, MA Cantab
Mr Doug Muirhead
Jena Ntumba
Ms Emma Taylor MA, PGCE
Mr Chris Wheeler BA, MBA, PGCE, FRSA
Mr Michael B M Porter, BA, MSc (*Secretary to the Governors*)

[OS] Old Stoic

***Head*: A K Wallersteiner**, MA, PhD

Senior Deputy Head: L Copley
Deputy Head (*Academic*): Dr J A Potter
Deputy Head (*Pastoral*) *& Designated Safeguarding Lead*: M Rickner
Director of Sport: C Sutton
Co-curricular Coordinator: G D Jones

* Head of Department

Art:
*Scott, Daniel
Arlington, Joanna
Corthine, Fiona
Grimble, Chris J

Biology:
*Carter, Louise
Abbott, Leah
Black, Georgina
Blake, Natasha
Blatchford, Abbey
Lyons, Dr Sinéad
Newlin, Elspeth

Business Studies & Economics:
*West, Dr Gordon D J
Ashfield, Anthony
Bristow, Angela
Corthine, Richard
Freeman, William
Hare, Timothy
Tompkins, Jenny
Wicks, Kate

Chemistry:
*Waine, Dr Alexandra
Douglas, Sara
Gracie, Judy
Radley, Luke A
Teasdale, Matthew
Wakeford, Dr Joanna L

Classics:
*Sheppe, James
Bradshaw-Gibson, James

Computer Science:
*Gupta, Aditya
Acquaah, Ebo
Gabriel, Adam
Martin, Glen

Design & Technology:
*Quinn, Martin K
Davies, Christopher
Peratopoullos, Costas
Treen, Victoria
Webster, Thomas
Whitby, Stephen J
Williams, Samuel E

Drama & Theatre Studies:
* Parker, Laura
Ackroyd, Emma
Miller, Lucy I
Miller, Simon
Wrigley, Janice

EAL:
*Carter, Sharon
Hipson-Holder, Jen

English:
*Borman, Nicola
*Ackroyd, Emma J (*Head of Media & Film Studies*)
Bodor, Gabrielle
Cook, Jonathan M
Hipson-Holder, Jen
Keenan, Niamh
Kerrigan, Chris

McNeill, Owain
Pearson, Georgina
Peppiatt, James W H
Pickering Polláková, Vlasta
Rickner, Sophie C
Smith, Fitzpatrick
Webber, Andrew

Games:
Calland, Charlotte (*Netball*)
Coote, Becky (*Equestrian*)
Coote, George D (*Athletics*)
Corthine, Fiona E G (*Polo*)
Davis, Cheryl S (*Swimming & Water Polo*)
Gavrilovic, Dusan (*Golf*)
Ingham Clark, Rob (*Lacrosse*)
Kennedy, Philip (*Beagles*)
Knott, James (*Cricket*)
Michael, Isaac (*Badminton & Basketball*)
Rudkin, Andrew (*Rowing*)
Scott, Ben M O (*Hockey*)
Seely, Grant (*Rugby*)
Syme, Duncan (*Sailing*)

Geography:
*Elliott, Francesca
Campbell, Lorraine C
Elwell, Thomas
Rowley, Shelley
Stanworth, Becky

History:
*Griffin, Paul J
Bonomi, James
Green, Dominic
McNeill, Owain
Potter, Julie
Righetti, James
Shah, Francesca L
Stafford-Smith, Rhea

History of Art:
Christie, Elliott
Hope, Rhiannon

Library:
Keiller, Samantha
Stockley-Battams, Lucinda

Mathematics:
*Møller, Mikkel B
Adkins, Charles
Arnold, Andrew
Ayres, Amanda
Brown, Rebecca
Bulwa, Felix
Calland, Paul
Geyton, Henry
Heaven, Susan
James, Fiona
Lee-Stevens, Victoria
Nichols, Jessica R
Penrhyn-Lowe, Sophie L
Perea, Vanesa
Stanworth, Alec M

Modern Languages:
*Tearle, Alice R G (*German*)
Arroyo, Aimi
Bernal-Guerrero, Andrea
Ferrero, Isabel
Herrbach, Mathilde
Holland, Rachel
Hutchin, Brigitte
Jones, Tracy L
*Leluan, Fanny (*French*)
*Morales-Shearer, Julio (*Spanish*)
Pena, Maria
Podesta, Desirée
Thevenet, Pauline
Windett, Emma

Music:
*Bryden, Emma
Andrew, Ben
Hawkes, Thomas
Horwood, Jane
Kingston, Jonathan
Rana, Leena
Weston, Ben

Philosophy and Religion:
*Holloway, Francesca L
Adkins, Dr Imogen H
Bray, Colin S
Rickner, Michael P

Physics:
*Thompson, Paul A
Davis, Jonathan B
Fathulla, Kamaran
Gardner, Dean
Hart, Brian J
Lee-Stevens, Victoria
Reinhold, Jessica

Politics:
*Cole, Simon R
Shah, Francesca L

PSHE:
Huxley Capurro, Liz

Psychology:
*Harvey-Craig, Aiden
Barbeli, Talia

Skills Development:
*Carter, Sharon
Ivory, Rhian
Tracey, Rhian
Wright, Adam

Sports Science:
*Dias, Victoria L
Arnold, Philip R
Dias, Patrick J
Sutton, Craig
Sutton, Sarah E
Taylor, Ruth

Houses and Houseparents:
Boys' Houses:
Bruce: P Arnold
Temple: B J Hart
Grenville: Whitby, S
Chandos: A Ashfield
Cobham: R Corthine
Chatham: P Dias
Grafton: S Fitzpatrick
Walpole: G D Jones

Girls' Houses:
Nugent: Mrs T Jones & Z Jones
Lyttelton: Dr S Lyons, Ross Deyzel
Queen's: Mrs S Rickner & M P Rickner
Stanhope: Mrs L M Carter
Sixth Form House:
West: S Sutton
Day Houses:
Cheshire: C Davis
Winton: J Peppiatt

Medical Officer: Dr Victoria Morrell, MA DFSRH, MRCGP
Director of Development: C Dudgeon
Group Director of Marketing and Admissions: T Roddy
Group Director of Finance: M Greaves

Strathallan School

Forgandenny, Perth, Perthshire PH2 9EG
Tel: 01738 812546
email: admissions@strathallan.co.uk
website: www.strathallan.co.uk
X/Twitter: @StrathallanSchl
Facebook: @strathallanschool
Instagram: @Strathallanschoolofficial
LinkedIn: /company/strathallanschool

Motto: *Labor Omnia Vincit*

Strathallan School is an independent boarding and day school whose mission to provide an outstanding education for all stands true to its original foundation over 100 years ago. Harry Riley founded Strathallan in 1913 with the ambition to create a school where there would be opportunities for every pupil to excel, and the vision is one held true today.

The School is fully co-educational and numbers 580 pupils, of whom 270 are day pupils and 310 are boarders.

Situation. Strathallan School is located 6 miles south of Perth in the village of Forgandenny. It occupies an idyllic rural location, situated in 150 acres of richly wooded estate on the northern slopes of the Ochils and overlooking the Earn valley. At the same time, Strathallan is within easy reach of the international airports – Edinburgh (35 minutes) and Glasgow (1 hour).

At the centre of the School is the main building which dates from the 18th century and was formerly a country house and home of the Ruthven family. The School continues to invest in outstanding facilities, which have seen a £23m investment since 2005. These include modern laboratories, a Theatre, Computer Centre, Library, Design Technology Centre, Sports Hall, Fitness and Weight Training Room, 2 Floodlit Synthetic Hockey Pitches, Indoor Multi-Sports Facility, Dance and Drama Studio, Medical Centre, Art School and newly refurbished Boarding Houses. All boarding houses have been built within the last thirty years with modern facilities and a single study-bedroom for every boarder in their last four years.

Aims. The school's mission is to provide an outstanding education that gives opportunities for all pupils to perform to the very best of their abilities. Each individual, no matter their passion or interest, is supported and inspired to shine during their time at school. Our aim is to send pupils out into the world with close friends and the ability to make new ones, and with the knowledge and skills to succeed at university and beyond.

Organisation. The School is primarily a boarding school yet also takes day pupils who are integrated into the boarding houses. There are four Senior boys' houses (Ruthven, Nicol, Freeland and Simpson). There are three girls' houses (Woodlands, Thornbank and Glenbrae). All boarding houses have their own resident Housemaster or Housemistress, assisted by House Tutors and a Matron. Boys have single study-bedrooms from the Fourth Form and girls have single study-bedrooms from the Third Form.

Strathallan Prep School, launched in September 2020, has its own Head Teacher and has Riley as its boarding house. It is designed to cater for boys and girls wishing to enter the School at age eight. Riley is run by a resident Housemaster, assisted by House Tutors and two Matrons. After Riley, pupils move directly to one of the Senior houses. Strathallan Prep School is the perfect balance of small classes with big resources. Its pupils enjoy the expertise of dedicated primary school teachers and the specialist input of subject teachers from the senior school. Strathallan Prep School and Riley House are situated within their own area of the campus, yet also enjoy the facilities of the main School.

The whole School dines centrally and there is a wide choice of hot and cold meals as well as vegetarian and vegan options. All boarding houses have small kitchens for the preparation of light snacks.

Religion. Strathallan has a Chapel and a resident Chaplain who is responsible for religious studies throughout the School.

Curriculum. Two of the keys to academic success are an ethos of continuous improvement and support from high quality, passionate teachers, and we pride ourselves on providing just such a learning environment. In addition, all pupils receive support from a tutor linked to their house and there is a full-time Careers Advisor to help with opportunities available beyond school. In 2020, the School became the first in Scotland to offer a triple pathway, including A Levels, one- and two-year Highers, and Advanced Highers, providing choice and flexibility in the face of a diverse range of tertiary education and employment options after school. In 2023, 85% of pupils achieved their first choice university.

Junior. Boys and girls entering Strathallan Prep School follow a course designed for the transition between their previous school and joining the senior part of Strathallan School at the age of 13. The following wide range of subjects is taught: Art, Computing, Design Technology, Drama, English, French, Geography, History, Latin, Maths, Music, PE, Personal and Social Development, Religious Education and Science. Courses are generally based on English Key Stages Two and Three.

The aim is to ensure pupils have an appropriate basis in the core subjects to move on to further study whilst also providing experience in specialist areas taught by subject experts. Teachers are careful to take account of ability and previous learning, guaranteeing each pupil works at an appropriate level for them and progresses at the right pace.

Third Form. Pupils in the Third Form participate in the following wide range of subjects: Art, Biology, Chemistry, Computing, Design & Technology, Drama, English, French, Geography, German and Spanish, History, Latin, Mathematics, PE, Physics and Religious Education. They are given a grounding in the skills necessary to pursue the subjects in the future should they wish, and an experience which is worthwhile in itself. All subjects are taught by specialists.

Fourth Form and the start of GCSE study. The two year GCSE course begins in the Fourth Form. All pupils study English, Mathematics, at least one Modern Language and two of the three Sciences. In addition, each pupil studies History or Geography (and can study both), plus two other subjects from an extensive choice. The aim is to ensure that pupils keep their options open, pursue a well-rounded curriculum, and establish a good basis for Sixth Form study.

Pupils are supported in their study not only by the individual teachers and the Heads of Department but also by a tutor who is linked to their house. A system of Merits and Distinctions rewards both individual pieces of outstanding work and continuous hard work and achievement. It is a central aim of the academic programme that pupils' efforts and achievements are recognised.

Sixth Form. Nearly all pupils stay on into the Sixth Form where the normal entry requirement is five passes at grade C or above at GCSE level. It is a special feature of Strathallan's Sixth Form that there is the flexibility to choose either A Levels or Scottish Highers. The choice is determined by the needs of the individual pupil. There is a wide range of subjects (currently the widest curriculum in Scotland), including: Art & Design, Biology/Human Biology, Business Management/Business Studies, Chemistry, Classical Civilisation/Classical Studies, Computing Science, Design & Technology/Design & Manufacture, Drama, Economics, English, French, Geography, German, Graphic Communications, History, Latin, Mathematics, Modern Studies, Music, Music Technology, Physical Education, Physics, Psychology, Religious Studies/RMPS, Spanish and Theatre Studies, with the option to include an EPQ.

The formal academic curriculum is supplemented by an extension programme of talks, visits and exchanges. We have well-established links with continental schools, and visits to theatres, galleries, courses and conferences in the UK and abroad often take place. Extracurricular activities and societies complement academic study and enhance pupils' interest in learning and discussion through activity beyond the classroom.

Each pupil is allocated a tutor who is a member of the academic staff and one of the duty staff of the boarding house. The tutor monitors pupils' academic and social progress and is responsible for discussing their regular reports with them.

Games. The main School games are rugby, cricket, hockey, netball, athletics and tennis, and standards are high. Other sports include skiing, squash, rounders, football, fencing, judo, badminton, table tennis, basketball, swimming, golf, horse riding and cross-country running in all of which national and regional success have been achieved in recent years.

Strathallan has two squash courts, 15 hard tennis courts, three netball courts, two floodlit synthetic pitches, a heated indoor swimming pool, two sports halls, gymnasium, a fitness and weight training room and a dance and drama studio. One sports hall comprises a basketball court, three badminton courts, a rock-climbing wall as well as facilities for six-a-side hockey and indoor cricket coaching, while the other has three full-size indoor tennis courts, with a multi-play surface, allowing a multitude of sports to be accommodated. Sailing, canoeing and skiing are recognised pastimes, and pupils participate in School ski days in the Spring term. Strathallan also has its own nine-hole golf course as well as Tennis and Shooting Academies.

Activities. All pupils are encouraged to take part in a range of activities for which time is set aside each day. There are over 50 weekly activities to choose from including dance, drama, pottery, chess, photography, first aid, lifeguarding, judo, horse riding, shooting (both clay pigeon and small bore) and fishing. There are also many societies and a programme of external speakers who visit the School. Pupils can also work towards awards under The Duke of Edinburgh's Award and John Muir Award schemes and are encouraged to take part in community service.

Music. The Music department has its own concert room, editing suite, keyboard room and classrooms, together with a number of individual practice rooms. Music may be taken at GCSE, Higher and AS/A2 Level. Over 40 different ensembles rehearse every week, including choirs, traditional music ensembles, jazz band, wind band, an orchestra, folk bands and rock bands. A house music competition takes place annually and there are regular concerts throughout the term. Individual tuition is available for virtually all instruments.

Piping. The Piping and Drumming Department have two full-time piping instructors and a full-time drumming instructor, as well as visiting staff. Individual lessons take place in our designated department and are available throughout the year. Pupils can work towards SQA qualifications in Piping and Pipe Band Drumming. We have three prize winning Pipe Bands which take part in events across the world including the Barbados Celtic Festival and the New York Tartan Day Parade as well as appearances at Hampden Park and Murrayfield Stadium.

Art. Art is recognised as an important part of the School's activities and there are opportunities to study the subject at GCSE and AS/A2 Level. Pupils benefit from regular art trips abroad and have the opportunity to exhibit their work both locally and further afield. A purpose-built Art School features facilities for ceramics, sculpture and print-making. National awards reflect pupils' achievements in this area.

Drama. Drama thrives throughout the School and the department makes full use of the Theatre as well as the purpose-built Dance and Drama Studio. There are junior and senior performances each year and pupils are encouraged to become involved in all aspects of production. The School also provides tuition in public and verse speaking and pupils regularly win trophies at the local festivals. There is also an annual Musical and pupils enter musical theatre exams.

Combined Cadet Force. There is a large voluntary contingent of the Combined Cadet Force with Navy, Army and Marines Sections.

Careers. Careers guidance begins in the Third Form. The Careers Adviser maintains close links with universities and colleges and regularly visits industrial firms. We have exchange programmes with schools in Australia, New Zealand and South Africa. There is a dedicated Careers Library, well-stocked with prospectuses, reference books and in-house magazines. Strathallan is a member of the Independent Schools Careers Organisation, a representative of which visits regularly and of the Scottish Council for Development and Industry.

All pupils have the opportunity to gain work experience in the Fifth Form, after their GCSEs. There is also a GAP year programme which provides placements for pupils to work overseas prior to going to university. Strathallan has particularly strong links with charities in Kenya.

Pastoral care. At Strathallan, there is a strong emphasis on pastoral care. The School has drawn up its own welfare guidelines in consultation with parents, governors and Perth and Kinross Social Work Department, and was rated 'Excellent' by the Care Inspectorate in 2019.

Health Centre. Strathallan has its own purpose-built Health Centre with consulting and treatment rooms. There are nursing staff at the Centre and the School's Medical Officers visit four times a week. Physiotherapy, chiropody, and relaxation also take place in the Centre during term time.

Entrance. Strathallan Prep School Entrance – Boys and girls are admitted to Strathallan Prep School at either age 5, 6, 7, 8, 9, 10, 11 or 12. An Entrance Day is held in early Spring each year for those who are available. Entry is based on a satisfactory school report and assessments in Maths and English.

Entry to the Senior School – Candidates for entry into the Senior School at age 13 may enter via the Open Scholarship examination in February, Common Entrance or a satisfactory school report.

Sixth Form – Boys and girls may also enter at Sixth Form level, either via the Sixth Form scholarship examination in November or on the basis of a satisfactory school report and GCSE/Standard Grade results.

Scholarships. Awards are made on the basis of competitive examination/assessment. Bursary help is available to supplement awards for outstanding candidates on a financial need basis.

Awards are available in the following categories to candidates entering the school at three levels:

Junior School: Academic, Music and Sport. Candidates should be under 13 years old on 1 September in the year of entry. Scholarship Examination: January.

Third Form: Academic, Music/Piping, Art, Performing Arts, Drama, All Rounder and Sports. Candidates should be under 14 years old on 1 September in the year of entry. Scholarship Examination: February.

Sixth Form: Academic, Music/Piping, Art, Performing Arts, Drama and Sports. Candidates should be under 17 years old on 1 September in the year of entry. Scholarship Examination: November.

Further information is available on the School's website, www.strathallan.co.uk, or from The Admissions Office, Tel: 01738 815091, email: admissions@strathallan.co.uk.

Bursaries. Bursaries are awarded dependent on financial circumstances and are available to pupils who have qualified for entry through assessment, scholarship or school report or a combination. It is not necessary for successful candidates for bursaries to have achieved scholarship standard but it may be possible to add a bursary award to a scholarship to enable a pupil to come to Strathallan. Armed Forces fee remission available.

Fees per term (2023–2024). Strathallan Prep School (Riley House): £9,727 (boarding), £5,766 (day), Junior School: £9,950 (boarding), £5,982 (day). Senior School: £13,943 (boarding), £9,120 (day).

Prospectus. Up-to-date information is included in the prospectus which can be obtained by contacting the Admissions Office or via the School's website.

Charitable status. Strathallan School is a Registered Charity, number SC008903, dedicated to Education.

Board of Governors:
Chairman: Mr M Griffiths, LLB Hons, CA
Prof E Alton, MA, MD, FRCP, FHEA, FERS, FMedSci
Mr E Anderson, MA
Mr N M Campbell, Bacc CA
Ms Alison Clark, BA Hons, MSc
Mrs C Clark
Professor J Crang, BA, PGCE, PhD, FRHist, FRSA
Dr E Doherty, BSc, MBCHB, DFSRH, MRCGP
Mr S Fairbairn, MA, LLB, Dip LP NP
Mr R Gibson
Mr D Gillanders
Mr S J Hay, BA, MSc
Mr I Hutchison, Ceng FIMechE
Mr P Johnston, FCCA
Mrs E Lister, BSc, DipEd
Mr A Naasan
Professor G Paton, BSc, PhD
Mr A Sinclair, BSc
Mr A Wood, MRAC, FRICS

***Headmaster*: Mr M Lauder**, MA

Assistant Staff:
Mrs T Ailinger, Staatsexamen, Cert TESOL
Mr J Ambrose, BA Hons
Mrs C Angus, MA, PGCE Primary
Mrs F Barker, MA, BD, MTh
Mr D J Barnes, BSc, PGCE, PGCG, FRGS (*Deputy Head Pastoral*)
Mr I Barrett, BA Hons, PGCE
Mr G J Batterham, BSc, PGCE (*Simpson Housemaster*)
Mrs K Bergin, BEd Hons
Mr M Bergin, BSc, PGCE (*Nicol Housemaster*)
Ms S Birrell, BA Hons
Dr K E M Blackie, PhD, PGDE, BSc
Dr B Cooper, BSc, PhD, PGCE
Mrs M-L Crane, BA, PGCE
Mr S Dick, BEd (*Riley Housemaster*)
Mr A L M Dunn, MA, PGCE
Mrs Z Ettle, LLM, PGCE, PGDip (*Woodlands Housemistress*)
Mr J Fraser, BMus
Mr G N Gardiner, BSc, PGCE
Mr D R Giles, BA QTS, Cert PP
Mr F Glancy, BA Hons, PGDE
Dr K Goundry, MA, PhD, PGDE
Miss E Grubb, BA Hons, MSc, PGDE
Ms K Haddick, MA Hons, PGDE
Mrs S E Halley, BSc, PGDE
Mr S Hamill, BA (*Deputy Head Academic*)
Mr N A Hamilton, BMus
Mr A D Henderson, UKCC
Mr W Herbert, BA Hons
Mr D M Higginbottom, MA, PGCE
Mrs J Higginbottom, MA, PGCE
Mrs R Hodson, MA, PGCE, MSc
Mrs C G Howett, BA, Dip Ed
Mr J Johnston, BA, PGDE
Mr E Kalman, BSc, MPhil
Mr P J S Keir, BEd, Cert SpLD
Mr L Kent, BSc, PGCE (*Thornbank Housemaster*)
Mrs C Laird-Portch, BA Hons, PGCE
Mrs E C Lalani, BEd, Dip Man (*Head of Strathallan Prep School*)
Mrs C Leadbetter, BSc Hons, PGDE, MEd
Mr E Lee, MA, PGCE
Miss R Leese, BSc Hons, PGCE
Mrs C Marjoribanks, BSc Hons, PGCE
Mrs F MacBain, MA (*Assistant Head, Sixth Form*)
Dr J Mace, BA Hons, MA, DPhil (*Deputy Head Pastoral*)
Mr R Macleod, BSc Hons, PGDE
Mr J McAuley, BA Hons, PGDE
Mr R McDermott, BEd, MEd
Mr I McGowan, BCom Dip Teaching (*Ruthven Housemaster*)
Ms S Mackay, BA, MSc, PGCE
Miss B McKay, MA Hons, PGDE
Mr K McKinney, BSc, BEd
Mr B Miles, BA Hons
Ms G Miles, MSc PGCE
Dr I Mitchell, BSc, PhD
Mr S Mitchell, BSc, PGCE
Mr C Muirhead, BA
Mr T Ogilvie, LTA CC
Ms A Pfupajena, BSc Hons, PGDE
Mrs T Rankin, BSc Hons
Mr D Richardon, BA
Mr G S R Robertson, BA, DMS
Miss C Roome, MA, MLitt, PGDE
Mr S Rose, BEng Hons, PGCE (*Freeland Housemaster*)
Mr G Samson, BSc Hons, PGCE
Dr F Sapsford, MA Hons, MPhil Cantab
Dr T Sharples, MChem Hons, DPhil, PGDE
Mrs H Shere, BA Ed Hons
Miss A Sime, BEd (*Assistant Head, Co-curricular*)

Mrs S Simon, BMus Hons, PGCE
Mr C Swaile, MA Hons, PGDE
Mr J Thompson, BSc
Mrs A J Tod, MA, PGCE
Mr M R A J B Tod, BSc, PGDip
Mrs K Troup, BS, MA, PgCert
Mr P M Vallot, BSc
Ms A Wardlaw, BSc
Miss C Warren, BSc Hons
Mr A Watt, BComm, HDE (*Assistant Head Organisation, Director of Studies*)
Mrs L Waugh, BA, PGDE
Ms K Wilson, BSc, PGCE (*Glenbrae Housemistress*)
Revd J Wylie, BSc, BD, MTh
Dr T Zhou, MSc, PhD

Bursar and Clerk to the Governors: Mr A C Glasgow, MBE, BEng, MSc, CEng

Director of External Relations: Mrs C Bath, BA Hons
Admissions Manager: Mrs A Johnstone, BA Hons
Alumni & External Relations Manager: Mrs A Wilson , BA Hons, MBA
Digital Media Manager: Mr D Glasgow, MA Hons
Marketing Manager: Mrs H Lewis-McPhee, MA Hons, MLitt

Medical Officers:
Dr L D Burnett, MBChB, BSc, DRCOG, MRCGP
Dr A M Lewis, MBChB, MRCGP

Streatham & Clapham High School GDST

42 Abbotswood Road, London SW16 1AW

Tel: 020 8677 8400 (Senior School)
020 8674 6912 (Prep School & Nursery)
email: senior@schs.gdst.net
prep@schs.gdst.net
admissions@schs.gdst.net
website: www.schs.gdst.net
X/Twitter: @SCHSgdst
Facebook: @SCHSgdst
Instagram: @schsgdst

Motto: *ad sapientiam sine metu*

Streatham & Clapham High School is a distinguished historical foundation. It was founded as Brixton High School in 1887 by the Girls' Public Day School Trust as one of its earliest member schools. In 1895, HRH Princess Louise, Duchess of Argyll, opened its buildings in Wavertree Road, London SW2, now the site of the Prep School. In 1994 the Senior School moved to Abbotswood Road, London SW16, into the imposing buildings of the former Battersea Grammar School.

The School offers an inspiring, enlightened and intellectually challenging education for its pupils in a lively, vibrant and warmly supportive environment. The family ethos of Streatham & Clapham High School enables its masters and mistresses to know, value and nurture each pupil as an individual. The School celebrates diversity and draws strength from its rich social and cultural mix.

The School's core belief is that all members of its community should be inspired to outperform expectations on a daily basis. The pursuit of excellence is thus the School's defining feature. It nurtures pupils to attain success across the widest spectrum of activity, extending far beyond the conventional 'academic' horizon. In so doing, they learn the beauty of reason, the allure of the aesthetic, and the vitality of the physical. The School's pupils thus learn to navigate the landscape of the human spirit and achieve beyond the realms of expectation.

The School's vision: to be unrivalled in empowering its young women to discover, nurture and project their unique identities and character.

The School's purpose: to enable every girl to achieve beyond the bound of expectation on a daily basis, across the spectrum of endeavour.

The School's salient and distinctive features:

- It nurtures, not coerces, excellence
- It is a family, not a factory, school
- It celebrates difference through its buzzy, diverse community, drawing strength from all that is great about London
- It has an unstinting commitment to innovation; the School does not stand still but is a trailblazer
- It draws strength from being part of the GDST family of schools, being pioneers in, and the shapers of, girls' education.

General information. Streatham & Clapham High School is an independent, academically selective school for girls aged 3–18, with just under 900 pupils on the roll. Girls aged 3–11 attend the Nursery and Prep School, located in spacious buildings with outstanding facilities on Wavertree Road in Streatham Hill. The Senior School inhabits a four-acre site focused on a symmetrical 1930s building designed by J E K Harrison, FRIBA, in a delightfully tranquil and leafy oasis of south London, next to Tooting Bec Common, where the soundscape is dominated by birdsong. Many girls live locally and an increasing number walk or cycle to School, encouraged by the School's commitment to sustainable travel. The Senior School is ten minutes' walk from Streatham Hill National Rail station and seventeen minutes from Balham National Rail and Underground. Other pupils come from further afield, including Battersea, Clapham, Wandsworth, Dulwich, Tooting and Brixton. The School is also within easy reach of the theatres, museums and galleries of central London.

Facilities. The School has first-class facilities for learning, providing an environment that enables girls to develop their interests and strengths both inside and outside the classroom. The School keeps up-to-date with new teaching methods and innovative techniques, such as interactive online learning, and uses them to engage and extend its pupils. Its facilities include a computer room, a music suite including a dedicated music technology room, a Recital Hall and black-box theatre, two design & technology workshops, a full-size indoor Sports Hall, Dance and Art studios, and sports pitches and netball/tennis courts. In 2017, the school occupied a stunning state-of-the-art sixth form centre on a new floor of the main building (which constituted the first phase of the £13 million building project), and the final phase of the building work, an architecturally innovative and spacious new dining hall and a striking new reception at the front of the school, together with a fountain atrium, was completed in March 2018. The new facilities have won a number of architecture awards, including the Building Design Awards, a RIBA Award, and the Architects' Journal Retrofit Awards (School Project of the Year).

Academic matters. The ability profile of the school is significantly above the national average, with a proportion of pupils being far above the national average. The school is in the top tier of independent schools in terms of its public examination results. Pupils do well: in 2023 at GCSE, over 22% of results were Grade 9 and 68% were Grades 9 to 7.

At A Level there has been a commendable upward trend in performance, with the percentage of A*–B grades rising from 68% in 2019 to an impressive 73% in 2023.

A significant milestone was reached with 88% of grades attaining A*–C. 11% of grades attained the highest accolade of A*, reflecting a subset of exceptional individual achievements. Continued success in STEAM subjects with over a third of pupils going on to study STEAM related subjects, including Biochemical Engineering at University College London, Maths and Statistics at the University of Newcastle and Biomedical Science at the University of Surrey. Physical Education (PE) stands out with an exceptional achievement, where a remarkable 100% of students secured A*–A and 75% A* grades, reflecting their dedication to excellence in this field.

Curriculum. The School offers a wide range of subjects. Pupils in the Upper Third, Lower Fourth and Upper Fourth (Years 7 to 9) study the core disciplines of English, Mathematics, and Science. Other subjects offered include Art, Mandarin and Sinology, Computing, Design & Technology, Drama, French, Geography, History, Italian, Latin, Music, Philosophy, Religion and Ethics, Physical Education, and Spanish. All of these subjects, as well as Ancient Greek, are available at GCSE or IGCSE in the Fifth Form (Years 10 and 11). The School offers a range of subjects for study at A Level, including Art & Design, Biology, Chemistry, Classical Civilisation, Latin, Critical Thinking, Design & Technology, Drama & Theatre Studies, Economics, Engineering, English Literature, Geography, Government & Politics, History, French, Italian, Spanish, Mathematics, Further Mathematics, Music, Physical Education, Physics, Psychology and Religious Studies. The majority of sixth-form students also pursue the Extended Project Qualification to extend their interests and knowledge. Virtually all sixth-form students proceed to the most competitive Russell Group universities (including Oxbridge).

Enrichment programme ('Kinza'). Kinza, an Arabic term meaning 'hidden treasure', is the School's unique enrichment programme of which there are timetabled weekly sessions throughout the year. Every Kinza course is designed to encourage a love and respect for learning for its own sake, utilising the interests and expertise of staff. The activities cover an extremely broad range of activities. In recent years, these have included Anthropology, Art History, Engineering, Crime Fiction, Fashion, Film and Society, Islamic Art, Young Money and much more. Opportunities to deepen aspects of the broad knowledge acquired through Kinza are afforded through individual research and collaborative working processes. Each girl participates in several different activities during the course of the year. At the same time of the week, the sixth-form students engage in the School's community service programme, 'Lux'.

Activities. The School has a thriving co-curricular life, with over 100 societies and clubs, ranging from academic fields to more specialised activities. There are a very large number of activities in the performing arts; pupils having the opportunity to perform in a number of dramatic productions during the school year or to belong to around 15 music ensembles, including choirs and orchestras, which annually lead the School's Carol Service at Southwark Cathedral. Pupils may belong to a legion of sporting clubs (including hockey, netball, gymnastics, rowing, cricket, football, badminton, athletics and many more), and have the opportunity to participate in a number of outdoor educational activities, such as the Duke of Edinburgh's Award. A busy programme of trips and expeditions is scheduled, for instance a cultural trip to China, a flagship sixth-form expedition to Cambodia, geography trips to Iceland, sports tours and language trips abroad. The School's proximity to central London makes possible many excursions to concerts, museums, art galleries and theatres.

Pastoral care. The School does not view outstanding pastoral care as an 'add-on' to its academic programme. Neither does it believe that a 'hothouse' atmosphere is desirable or healthy. The School's core belief is that girls achieve best if they are happy and settled in their social relationships. Hence the 'family' ethos of the School, which holds that the way in which individuals are nurtured and valued is intrinsic to the pupils' progress and success. All pupils are under the care of one of five Heads of House, and all members of staff, up to the Head, are easily accessible to pupils. To ensure that the School's social and emotional care is comprehensive and alert, the School has a Deputy Head (Pastoral) with oversight of pastoral matters. In conjunction with the work of the Heads of House and the sixth-form mentoring scheme, this enables the School to identify challenges or problems early and then work with pupils and where necessary their parents to overcome them. It also helps the School to encourage and celebrate real progress and achievement every day. The strong prefectorial system and school council under the leadership of the Head Girl ensure that the pupil voice has suitable influence in shaping the life and work of the School.

Admission. There are six principal admission stages: by assessment for the Nursery (3+ years), 4+ and 7+, and by competitive entrance examination at 11+ and 13+ and at Sixth Form level. Occasional places sometimes arise at any age; interested parents are advised to contact the Registrar. 11+ candidates will undertake an interview and creative writing session. Applicants for 13+ entry will have individual interviews after the 13+ entrance examination. Applicants for 11+ entry sit the ISEB Common Pre-Test, comprising English, Mathematics, verbal and non-verbal reasoning exercises. Applicants for 13+ entry sit papers in English, Mathematics and Science. The transfer of a pupil from the Prep to the Senior School is contingent on the School's assessment of the pupil's suitability for admission into the Upper Third Form (Year 7).

Fees per term (2023–2024). Senior School: £7,001, Prep School: £5,441, Nursery: £4,114. The fees are inclusive of non-residential trips and extras, but exclude the cost of lunch.

Scholarships. A number of scholarships, worth up to a maximum of 25% of fees, are available for 11+ and 16+ entrance. They are not means-tested. Academic scholarships are awarded on the basis of individual candidates' performance in the entrance examination and interview. A number of sixth-form academic scholarships are also available, on the basis of a written assessment and interview. Specialist scholarships, in Art, Drama, Music and Sport, are also available for 11+ entrance.

Bursaries. A small number of means-tested bursaries are available at 11+ and at 16+ for students applying for the Sixth Form. All requests are considered in confidence and application forms are available from the Registrar.

The Board of Local Governors:
Mr Angus Wrixton, BSc Hons (*Chair*)
Miss S Campbell, BA, MA
Mrs R Chowdhury, BA, MSc, CMRS
Mr Dan Clay
Mrs E Gibson, BA, LLB
Mr Simon Packard

***Head*: Ms Cathy Ellott**, BA Oxon, MA London, PGCE Cantab

Deputy Head (*Academic*): Mr M Weatherhead, BEng De Montfort, MA St Mary's, NPQH

Deputy Head (*Pastoral*): Ms A Smith, BSc Glamorgan, PGCE Science

Director of Finance & Operations: Miss A Bullock

Director of Marketing & Communications: Mrs D Young, BA Northampton, MSc Surrey

Assistant Head (*Co-Curricular and Community*): Mrs T Philipsen-Allen, BA AUB, PGCE French, NPQSL

Assistant Head (*Sixth Form*): Miss Camilla Simpson, BA Oxon, PGCE

Acting Assistant Head (*Teaching & Learning and Staff Development*): Mrs S Elliot, BA Cantab, PGCE Classics

Head of Prep School: Mrs H Loach, BEd Cantab

Deputy Head of Prep (*Academic*): Ms Z Simpson, BA Roehampton, PGCE, NPQSL

Deputy Head of Prep (*Pastoral*): Mrs J Hayes, BA Oxon, PGCE

Teaching Staff (*Senior School*):
* *Head of Department*
Ms Sharon Akintunde, BSc UCL, MSc, GTP (**Chemistry*)
Miss Leah Anderson, BA Brighton, PGCE (*Assistant Director of Sport*)
Miss Fouziah Arshad, BSc Kingston (*Mathematics*)
Mr Paul Baker, BA Colchester, PGCE (*English*)
Miss Rebecca Baker, BA Falmouth, PGCE (**Art*)
Miss Emma Barnard, BA Keele, MA Sussex, PGCE (*English*)
Miss Grete Barzdenyte, BSc Canterbury, PGCE (*Physical Education*)
Mrs Anusha Burton, BA Birmingham, PGCE (*Philosophy*, *Religion & Ethics*)
Mme Catherine Casset, BA Paris, MA, PGCE (*French*)
Ms Mengmeng Cheng, BSc Bath, MSc Loughborough
Dr Sadaf Choudhry, MEng QMW, PhD, PGCE (*Chemistry*, *Physics*)
Mrs Laura Cooper, BA Nottingham, QTS (**Futures & Aspirations*, *French*)
Mrs Jennifer Crane, MA Cantab, MSc London, PGCE (*Biology*)
Mr Andrew Doddridge, BSc UCL, PGCE (**Geography*)
Mrs Sarah Donnan, BA Durham, PGCE (*Deputy Head of Sixth Form*, *English*)
Mrs Susannah Douglas, MA London, PGCE (*Art*)
Mrs Elizabeth Esser, BA Cantab (*Director of Music*)
Ms Hannah Evans, BA Kings College, PGCE (*English*)
Mrs Mary Evans, BA Exeter, PGCE (*House Mistress*, *Drama*)
Mrs Ciara Eves, BA St Mary's London, QTS (*Director of Sport*)
Mrs Katherine Ferguson-Burke, MA Glasgow, PGCE (**Biology*)
Mrs Rachel Ferguson, BA Manchester, PGCE (*English*)
Miss Sarah Fitzgibbon, BSc Leeds, PGCE (**Science*, **Physics*)
Mrs Jane Flanagan, BA Nottingham, MSc, QTS (*House Mistress*, *Geography*) [maternity cover]
Mr Paul Frost, BA Lancaster, ACMA, PGCE (**Digital Learning and Computing*)
Miss Carmen Garcia-Gomez, BA Southampton, PGCE (*Second in Modern Foreign Languages*, *Spanish*) [maternity cover]
Mr Matthew Gibson, BA Oxon, PGCE (**Academic Music*)
Mrs Rachel Grant, BSc Loughborough, PGCE (*House Mistress*, *Physical Education*, *Science*)
Miss Jennifer Green, BA Swansea, PGCE (*Classics*)
Mr Christopher Haynes, PGCE (**DT & Engineering*)
Ms Fiona Helszajn, BA Edinburgh, PGCE (**Modern Foreign Languages*, *Spanish*) [maternity cover]
Dr Nazish Khan, BSc Manchester, MSc Coventry, PGCE (*Chemistry*)
Mr Benjamin Kirby, BSc, Msc Cardiff, PGCE (*Economics*)
Mrs Juliana Kirby, BA Leicester, PGCE (**Mathematics*)
Mr David Lee, BA Manchester, PGCE (**History and Politics*)
Miss Dior-Jade Lewis, BA Leicester, PGCE (**PSHCE*)
Mr Patrick Lynch, BA London Metropolitan, PGCE (*Design & Technology*)
Mr Tito Newell, BA Surrey, PGCE (*Philosophy*, *Religion & Ethics*)
Ms Thu Ha Nguyen, BSc Queen Mary's, PGCE (*Mathematics*, *KS4 Mathematics Co-ordinator*) [maternity cover]
Mrs Caroline Pearman-Gibbs, BA Oxford (**Modern Foreign Languages*) [maternity cover]
Mr Phillip Powell, MSc Bristol, PGCE (*Biology*)
Mr Thomas Punt, BA Lancaster, PGCE (**Philosophy*, *Religion & Ethics*)
Mr Adam Razaq, BA Kingston, PGCE (*KS3 Co-ordinator*, *Mathematics*)
Mr Duncan Reader, BA Cantab, MA, MSc, PGCE (*Mathematics*)

Ms Rose Ren, BA Shanghai, PGCE (*Lead in Mandarin & Sinology, EPQ Co-ordinator*)
Mr James Robinson, MA Oxon, PGCE (*Mathematics*)
Miss Ananya Sengupta, BSc Nottingham, PGDip (*Physics*)
Miss Jasmeet Soor, BA Nottingham, PGCE (*History & Politics*)
Mr Michael Spooner, BSc Bristol, MA, PGCE (*House Master, Physics*)
Ms Violet Tabrizi, BA Vancouver, PGCE (*History*)
Ms Penelope Thane-Woodhams, BA Loughborough, PGCE (*Director of Drama*)
Mrs Laura Tuggey, MA Edinburgh, QTS (*Geography and History*)
Ms Lily Vigor, BA Central Saint Martins, PGCE (*Art*)
Miss Hayley Walker, BA King's College London, PGCE (**Classics*) [maternity cover]
Mr Frederic Ward, BSc Leeds, PGCE (*Mathematics, Science*)
Mrs Carol Weatherhead, BA London, MA Warwick, PGCE (**Learning Support, History*)
Mrs Florence West, MSc Cardiff, BSc Durham, PGCE (*Science*)

Teaching Staff (*Prep School*):
Miss Lucy Baker, BA Warwick, PGCE (**Upper School, Year 5*)
Ms Emma Baldwin, BA Southampton, PGCE (**RE, Year 4*)
Ms Rachel Barnes, BA Exeter, PGCE (**Transition, *Humanities; Year 5*)
Mrs Kate Belshaw, BA Leicester, PGCE (**English, Year 6*)
Mr Padraig Carr, BA Carlow College, Eire, PGCE (**Mathematics, Year 6*)
Miss Taibah Cashmiri, BA St Mary's, PGCE (*Reading Lead, Year 2*)
Miss Millisa Dolke, PGCE (*Teacher of Prep PE*)
Miss Sophie Dowler, BA Sheffield, PGCE (**EYFS/ Lower School, Nursery*)
Mrs Victoria Henderson-Cleland, BA Bristol (**Latin*)
Mme Emmanuelle Koeb, BA London Met, PGCE (**French*)
Miss Sarah McKee, BA Oxford Brookes, PGCE (*Reception*)
Ms Alice Markes, BSc Leeds, PGCE (*Year 3*)
Ms Sally Maskell, BEd Exeter (**Science & Digital Learning*)
Miss Alexandra Nicholson, BA Liverpool Hope, PGCE, QTS (**Art, Year 4*)
Miss Claire Pandey, BA London, BA Metropolitan, PGCE (*Eco Lead, Year 1*)
Ms Agnieszka Dziamalek, BSc Opole, Poland, MA, QTS (**Prep PE*)
Mrs Robyn Pressley, LTCL Cape Town, SA, MA, PGCE (**Drama, Year 4*)
Miss Robyn Sullivan, BA Worcester, PGCE (**Gifted and Talented, *House & Charities, Year 3*)
Ms Anna Tabor, GGSM, LGSM, MMus Surrey, PGCE (**Music*)
Mrs Rachael Watson, BA Brunel, CCET, PGCE (**Supported Learning Needs & Academic Welfare*)

Head's Executive Assistant: Ms Shirley Halm
Head of Admission: Mr Anatoly Reeves BA Manchester

Sutton Valence School

North Street,
Sutton Valence, Maidstone, Kent ME17 3HL

Tel: 01622 845200
email: enquiries@svs.org.uk
website: www.svs.org.uk
X/Twitter: @SVS_News
Facebook: @SuttonValenceSchoolNews
Instagram: @explore/locations/675880073/sutton-valence-school

Motto: *Where each cares for all and individuality is cherished*

Founded in 1576 by William Lambe, Sutton Valence School has over 425 years of proud history. Today the School is co-educational and includes a preparatory school on a neighbouring site. Both schools are situated on the slopes of a high ridge with unequalled views over the Weald of Kent in the historic, beautiful and safe village of Sutton Valence.

Our greatest strength is our community. The relationships we enjoy between staff, pupils and parents allow us to craft an educational journey that is individually suited to every pupil. During a family's association with the School we hope they will feel involved, listened to and informed.

Through the high expectations and standards we set, all our young people are encouraged and helped to go further than they had thought possible in their academic, co-curricular, community and leadership journeys. We want them to become confident, civilised, tolerant and open-minded individuals who possess a love of learning and a strong sense of self-discipline along with a set of values reflecting our principles as a Christian Foundation.

Ethos. A community where each cares for all and individuality is cherished.

Results. Sutton Valence School has an inclusive intake, however, our academic strength lies in enabling our students to achieve beyond their benchmarked potential, whatever their ability. On average, our students will gain results at A Level that outperform their predicted grade on entry to the School by 0.5 of a grade per subject. As measured by Durham University's Centre for Evaluation and Monitoring, Sutton Valence School has an outstanding record for adding academic value.

Curriculum. The academic curriculum is innovative and aims to achieve a balance between the needs of the individual and demands of society, industry, universities and the professions. Classes are small and the graduate teaching staff to pupil ratio is 1:9.

Our First and Second Forms (Years 7 and 8) follow our innovative, challenging and stimulating Junior Curriculum, which has academic excellence at its heart and continues to promote our pupils' love of learning. We also ensure that the fundamental study skills required for success are mastered so that our pupils can move on fully prepared to excel at GCSE and beyond. These pupils also pursue our excellent Junior Leadership programme.

Many pupils join us in the Third Form (Year 9) from other schools. In this form, we concentrate on developing a high level of competence in the essential numeracy, literacy and ICT skills across all subjects, in targeted-ability groups, in preparation for GCSEs which are then studied in the Fourth and Fifth Forms.

In Fourth and Fifth Form (Years 10 and 11) pupils usually study nine or ten subjects at GCSE level. These are divided between the core subjects – English and English Literature, Mathematics, Science, PSHE and ICT – along with option groups. Each group contains a number of subjects, offering a choice which allows every pupil to achieve a balanced education whilst, at the same time, providing the opportunity to concentrate on his or her strengths.

Sixth Form Pupils (Years 12 and 13), either progressing from our Fifth Form or joining us from elsewhere, pursue an A Level course in three or four carefully-chosen subjects, along with an extended project qualification (EPQ). They receive individual support and expert, bespoke, advice on appropriate Higher Education applications, interview practice, CV writing and careers in general. Whilst the vast majority continue their academic journey at university level, employment-based training routes are becoming an increasingly popular option for some.

Potential Oxbridge candidates are identified in the Lower Sixth year and suitable tuition is arranged.

Setting, Promotion, Reporting. In First to Fifth Form Mathematics and French are setted. Academic progress is monitored by tutors and, at regular intervals throughout the term, every pupil is graded for achievement and effort in every subject for their classwork and effort in their prep.

Higher Education and Careers. Sutton Valence School has a modern and well-equipped Sixth Form Centre which incorporates a careers library and the latest technology to help in degree and career selection.

Music. Music plays a very important part in the life of the school, and we have a deservedly fine reputation for the quality and range of our music-making. Approximately 40% of the pupils learn a musical instrument or have singing lessons; there are four choirs, an orchestra, wind band, string group, jazz band, and a full programme of concerts. Music tours to Europe are arranged, and the Music Society organises a programme of distinguished visiting performers every year.

Drama. As with Music, Drama is central to the life of the School and the creative expression of our students. Every year there will be a number of productions, in addition to theatre workshops and reviews. Pupils may choose to receive one-to-one drama coaching lessons in preparation for LAMDA exams. The Baughan Theatre provides an adaptable venue, seating up to 200 for Drama, Music and lectures, along with rehearsal rooms, technical gantry and scene dock.

Sport and Physical Education. Sutton Valence School has a deserved reputation as a strong sporting School, competing in 17 sports. On average, 40 pupils will have representative honours at County, Regional and National levels in the main sports as well as in other disciplines. On a typical Saturday afternoon, half the school will be engaged in matches.

Our 100-acre site has one of the best Cricket squares in Kent, two floodlit Astroturf pitches for Hockey, a six-lane indoor swimming pool, Tennis, Netball and Squash courts, a sports hall encompassing a full-size indoor Hockey pitch, sprung-floor Cricket nets and fitness suite, six Golf practice holes and a floodlit all-weather running track. Additional sports, such as Football, Judo, Dance, Horse riding, Badminton, Basketball, Fives and Fencing are offered through our activities programme.

Pastoral System. The School is arranged vertically in houses, with the Juniors (Years 7 and 8) in a separate house. Each House has a Housemaster or Housemistress and is divided into Tutor Groups containing pupils from each year and from day and boarding.

The School is a Christian foundation, however, our values are very much based on openness, tolerance and inclusivity. As such, we welcome students from all faith backgrounds, as well as those families who have no faith commitment.

Community Service, CCF and Duke of Edinburgh's Award. The CCF provides an organisation within Sutton Valence School which enables boys and girls to develop self-discipline, responsibility, self-reliance, resourcefulness, endurance, perseverance, a sense of service to the community and leadership. It complements the academic and other co-curricular aims of the School in preparing our pupils for adult life. All three services are offered – Army, Navy and RAF. Pupils are encouraged to join the Duke of Edinburgh's Award scheme where there is the opportunity for planning and undertaking expeditions. On average, 15 Gold Awards are achieved each year.

Clubs and Activities. Time is specifically set aside each week for clubs and activities. Every pupil spends time pursuing his or her own special interests, and with up to 40 clubs or activities from which to choose, the range and scope is very wide. In addition, various school societies and some other activities take place out of school hours, for example, the Kingdon Society for Academic Scholars.

Scholarships and Bursaries. Academic, Art, Design Technology, Music, Sport and Drama Scholarships are awarded at 11+, 13+ and Sixth Form entry. Candidates may apply for a maximum of two non-academic scholarships.

The Westminster Scholarship supports well-motivated and able pupils who enter Sutton Valence School at Sixth Form level and who are expected to achieve at least six GCSE passes at Grade 8 or 9.

Bursaries are awarded according to financial need at the discretion of the Scholarship and Bursaries Committee, and are reviewed annually. Forces bursaries are available.

Further details may be obtained from the Admissions Office.

Fees per term (2023–2024). Tuition: £7,362 to £8,748. Senior Boarding (in addition to Tuition): £4,784 (Full), £2,554 (three, four or five nights p/w), £64 (occasional boarding – per night)

Instrumental Music: £313 per term (ten lessons).

Charitable status. The United Westminster Grey Coat Foundation is a Registered Charity, number 1181012.

Governing Body:
Mrs G Swaine, BSc Hons, MEd (*Chair*)
Mr C C Baxter

Mr R W Blackwell, MA
Mrs J D Davies, BSc
Mrs A F Dawson, MA
Dr R E Densham, BA, MSc, MSc DCounsPsych
Dr M J Heber, MB, BS, FRCGP
Mr A J Hutchinson, MA Cantab
Mr P P Sherrington, LLB, LLM, FCIArb
Mrs A J Storey-Mason, MA

***Headmaster*: J A Thomas**, MA Cantab, MA London, NPQH

Senior Staff:
Senior Deputy Headmaster: J J Farrell, MA Cantab, MEd Buckingham (*History*)
Deputy Head (*Academic*): Mrs R K Ball, BA Wales Lampeter (*English, Media Studies, Film Studies*)
Deputy Head (*Staff and Student Development*): Mr D R Sansom, BSc Wales Swansea (*Geography*)
Assistant Head (*Safeguarding*): Ms L Austen, BA Portsmouth, MA Portsmouth (*Designated Safeguarding Lead, English, Media*)
Assistant Head (*Wellbeing*): Mrs M Trachonitis, BSc Cardiff Metropolitan (*Games, PSHE*)
Bursar: Mr S R Fowle

Administrative and Admissions Office Staff
Headmaster's PA: Mrs S Bishop
Director of Admissions and Development: Mr W Radford
Admissions Officer: Mrs H Skinner
Admissions Assistant: Mrs D Child

Tonbridge School

Tonbridge, Kent TN9 1JP

Tel:	01732 365555
email:	schooladmin@tonbridge-school.org
website:	www.tonbridge-school.co.uk
X/Twitter:	@TonbridgeUK
Facebook:	@tonbridgeschool
Instagram:	@tonbridge.school

Motto: '*Deus dat incrementum*'

Tonbridge has a distinctive mixture of boarders and day boys and enjoys superb indoor and outdoor facilities on a 150-acre site, which lies only 40 minutes by train from central London. It currently has just over 800 boys, who come from a variety of backgrounds.

The School is highly respected, both in the UK and internationally, for providing a world-class education. Boys are encouraged to be creative and intellectually curious; to approach new opportunities with confidence; and to learn to think for themselves and develop leadership skills, while being mindful of the needs and views of others. A Tonbridge education includes a vibrant programme of co-curricular breadth and depth.

Tonbridge is renowned for its high-quality, innovative teaching and learning, and for academic achievement. Exam results at A Level and GCSE are outstanding each year. In 2023, 43 per cent of all A-level grades awarded were at the very highest grade of A*. In total, 80 per cent of all grades were A* or A, while nearly all grades (97 per cent) achieved by Tonbridge A-level students were either A*, A or B.

In GCSEs for 2023, 48 per cent of grades were at 9, the highest possible grade, and more than three quarters (77 per cent) were at 9 and 8 (with both grades the equivalent of A*). Overall, 94 per cent of grades were at 9, 8 or 7.

In the *Sunday Times* 'Parent Power' Schools Guide 2024, Tonbridge is ranked as the sixth best independent school nationally, and is placed second overall in the south-east.

Each year the School's Upper Sixth leavers gain places at the UK's leading universities, including Oxford, Cambridge and Russell Group institutions, with the large majority securing their chosen destination. Those opting to study abroad also attend prestigious institutions, most commonly in the USA. Tonbridge boys have recently gained places (and scholarships) at Princeton, Chicago, Duke, Colombia, USC and New York University Abu Dhabi, as well as at universities in Austria, the Netherlands, Australia, Canada and Hong Kong.

Pastoral care is based around an outstanding House system. Strong and positive relationships between boys, staff and parents are central to its success, and the School ensures that each pupil, whether a boarder or a day boy, feels fully at home and well supported.

The School has a genuine commitment to widening access: a key part of its ethos is to ensure that any bright, talented boy has the opportunity to benefit from a Tonbridge education, regardless of background or financial situation. The School aims to increase the number of boys on significant financial support (including the full-fee 'Foundation Awards') to at least 100 by the time of its 475th anniversary in 2028. Tonbridge also supports families that need more limited help. Fee remissions each year, for bursaries, scholarships and other awards exceed £2.8 million.

Location. Tonbridge School is just off the M25, on the edge of the Kent / Surrey / Sussex borders, and attracts families from all over southern England and beyond. It lies in 150 acres of land on the edge of the town of Tonbridge, providing a good balance between town and country living.

Admissions. www.tonbridge-school.co.uk/admissions.

About 155 boys are admitted at the age of 13 (Year 9) each year. An additional 20 or so places are available for entry to the Sixth Form at the age of 16 (Year 12). We also have up to 6 places for boys aged 14 (Year 10).

Registration for a boy at 13+ entry should be made, preferably, not later than three years before the date of intended entry. Boys will then be asked to complete the ISEB pre-test and to visit Tonbridge for an assessment afternoon, usually during the Autumn Term of Year 6. The information collected from these assessments, in conjunction with the current school Head's report, will determine whether the offer of an unconditional or provisional place may be made. Those receiving an unconditional offer will be required to complete no further assessment. Those receiving a provisional offer will be invited to take a further assessment (in Maths and English) during the Summer Term of Year 7, after which a provisional offer may be converted to an unconditional offer.

Later registration for Year 9 entry is possible during Year 7, with such candidates following a modified entrance procedure. Details of this procedure can be found on our website or obtained from the Admissions Office: Tel: 01732 304297; E-mail: admissions@onbridge-school.org.

Applications for 14+ (Year 10) and Sixth Form (Year 12) entry are best made by 1 September a year before entry, but may be considered later. Admission at 14+ is gained via our own Maths and English exams. Boys sitting for entry at 16+ will take papers in the 4 subjects they wish to study in the Sixth Form, in addition to an English Language paper.

Please see the school website to view an online a copy of the prospectus. The Admissions pages of the site give full details of the registration procedure.

Scholarships and Bursaries. Some 45 scholarships overall are offered each year to boys in either Year 6 (the Junior Foundation Scholarship) or in Year 8.

Up to 6 Junior Foundation Scholarships are available to candidates in Year 6 who are attending a state primary school or to those attending a prep school, but who would require financial support in order to attend Tonbridge. Candidates should register by early October during Year 6 and will be invited to attend an assessment afternoon in November, with the stronger candidates returning to take tests in Maths and English in February. Such scholarships, which are confirmed in Year 6, may provide financial support of up to 100% to allow boys not currently in the independent sector attendance at prep school for Years 7 and 8, as well as at Tonbridge from Year 9.

In Year 8, a further 21 Academic Scholarships are awarded (following examination in early May) as well as 10 or more Music Scholarships (for which auditions are held in early February), up to 10 Art, Drama or Technology Scholarships (assessed in early February) and up to 4 Cowdrey Scholarships, for sporting ability and sportsmanship (also assessed in early February). The award of any scholarship opens up eligibility for a means-tested bursary of between 10% and 100% of school fees, as agreed by the Bursar following a confidential review of financial circumstances.

Entry forms and full particulars of all Scholarships and Foundation Awards are available on the school website.

Fees per term (2023–2024). £16,648 for a boarding place and £12,490 for a day place.

Charitable status. Tonbridge School is a Registered Charity, number 1097977.

Governors:
G M Rochussen (*Chairman*)

C Ashton
T M Attenborough
Mrs S Bishop
D P Devitt
M Dobbs
M E Fry
Professor H Gaunt
S Hall
H Hamilton-Turner
J G Leahy
Dr N Perry
Dr V Rangarajan
J Rogers
Dr M S Spurr, DPhil
J Thorne
Mrs K Wheadon
G White

Clerk to the Governors: Major General A Kennett, CBE

***Headmaster*: J E Priory**, MA Oxon

Second Master: J R Bleakley, BA
Deputy Head Academic: M J Weatheritt, MA
Director of Admissions: Mrs H F McLintock, BA
Deputy Head Co-Curricular: J A Fisher, BSc
Deputy Head Pastoral: C J C Swainson, MA
Lower Master: Mrs J H McNeil, BA
Director of Learning & Academic Enrichment: Mr J Blake, BA, MSc
Tonbridge Society Director: A Ballard, BA

Assistant Staff:
* *Head of Department/Subject*

Art:
*F J Andrews, MA, BA
W D F Biddle, BSc
Miss E H Lycett, BA
Mrs B L Waugh, BFA
Art Librarian: Mrs M P Dennington
Art Technician: Mrs J M Brent

Classics:
*Dr J A Burbidge, BA, MSt, DPhil
Mrs C C Campbell, BA
S G Ginns, MPhil, BA
A P Schweitzer, MA
Ms L H Shackleton, MA
R J M Stephen, MA
L F Walsh, BMus

Computer Science:
*Dr J E Robertson, BSc, MSc, PhD
W S Chiu, BA

Design Technology and Engineering:
*R L Day, BSc
W D F Biddle, BSc
Dr A O Cooke, MEng, DPhil
J M Woodrow, BA
Technology Technicians: R Davies; O Longson
Teaching Assistant: C Martin

Digital Creativity:
*P J Huxley, BSc
C D Walker
W S Chiu, BA

Divinity:
*J C F Dobson, MA
B C F Bennet, BA
R Burnett, MA
The Revd A P Law, BA
L U Masters, BA
The Revd D A Peters, MA
R H Sheemar, BA
Dr H J M Swales, MA, MPhil

Drama:
*G D Bruce, MA
*S U Hussain, MA, BA (*Head of Academic Drama*)

Director in Residence: Mrs F R Bailey, MSc, BA

English:
*Dr J G Reinhardt, BA, MSEd, MA, PhD
J R Bleakley, BA
Miss L C Clubb, BA
Mrs K A Crowley, BA
R H Evans, MA
S J Farmer, MA
P F Houston, MA, BA
Dr J D Shafer, PhD, MA, BSc
N J Waywell, BA

Extended Project Qualification:
Mrs R Davis, BSc

Geography:
*C M Battarbee, BA
C M Henshall, BA
Mrs J H McNeil, BA
Mrs J M Watson-Reynolds, MA, BA

History:
*N Hillyard, BA, MSt
Dr J M T Dixon, BA, MPhil, PhD
Mrs F C Dix Perkin, MA
C W Eades, BA
Mr R A Haines, MA, BA
Dr C D Thompson, BA, MPhil, PhD

Mathematics:
*J M Ashton, BSc
T G Fewster, BSc
K A Froggatt, MA
Miss J A D Gent, BA
Dr I R H Jackson, MA, PhD
B D M Katz, MSc, BA
Dr J D King, MA, PhD
Mrs P M King, MA, BA
M J Lawson, BA
N J Lord, MA
V Myslov, BA
Dr A A Reid, MChem, PhD, AFHEA
S J Seldon, MA, MEng
Dr J D Shafer, PhD, MA, BSc
Dr Z Wang, MMath, PhD

Modern Languages:
*W H C Law, BA (**French*)
S Kerr, BA (**German*)
Miss M del Mar Ponce Galan, BA, GCTSA (**Spanish*)
X J Wu, MA (**Mandarin Chinese*)
Mrs M F D Brenchley, BA
R Burnett, MA
R D Hoare, MA
J C Ortega, BA
J A Storey-Mason, BA
J-P Vieu, BA, MA
C E Wright, BA
Ms X Yu, BA

Music:
*M A Forkgen, MA, ARCO (*Director of Music*)
J R P Thomas, MA, FRCO (*Head of Academic Music & Choirmaster*)
D L Williams, GRSM, ARCM, LRAM (*Piano*)
S J Hargreaves, MA, MEd
L F Walsh, BMus

Pastoral Education (PSHEE):
*Mrs C C Campbell, MA
R Burnett, MA
A G McGilchrist, MEng
Mrs J M Watson-Reynolds, MA, BA
P J North, MA, BA
J C Ortega, BA
F J Andrews, MA, BA
W D F Biddle, BSc

Science:
*N C Waite, BSc

Physics:
*C T E Powell, BSc, MA, MRes
G M Barnes, BSc
Dr S Chalk, PhD, BSc
Dr A O Cooke, MEng, DPhil
C G Curtis, BA
R L Fleming, MA, MInstP
A G McGilchrist, MEng
N C Waite, BSc
M J Weatheritt, BSc, MA

Chemistry:
*Dr D P Robinson, MEarthSci, DPhil
A T J Byfield, MA, BTh, PGDip
G C Fisher, BSc, MA
J A Fisher, BSc
Miss G G Gao, MChem
Miss H A Hayward, MChem
Dr C R Lawrence, MA, PhD
Dr S X Sneddon, PhD, BSc
K J Walsh, MSci

Biology:
*Dr W J Burnett, PhD, BSc
Ms A R Cooper, MBiochem
Mrs C A Felstein, BSc
Miss H A Hayward, MChem
P M Ridd, MA
A T Sampson, BSc
C J C Swainson, MA
K J Walsh, MSci

Social Science:
*S M Cleary, BSc (*Social Science & Economics*)
Miss K E Moxon, MA (**Politics*)
C M Ashurst, BA (**Business*)
J Blake, BA, MSc
L U Masters, BA
P J North, MA, BA
N R V Rendall, BA
Dr J D W Richards, MA, PhD
K M Seecharan, BSc
A J Sixsmith, BA

Sport, Health and Fitness:
Director of Sport: C D Morgan, BSc
Assistant Director of Sport & Hockey Coach: Mrs L Maasdorp
Rugby Academy Director: R H Crane, BSc

Director of IT & Digital: A W Milgate

Head of Communications: Mr N J Ellwood, MA
Head of Marketing: Mrs K Dimnik

Head of Universities & Careers: Mrs R Davis

Learning Strategies and EAL:
*Mr J D C Lewis, BSc
Mrs C Clugston, MA
Mrs L A Fry, MA
Mrs N M Gerard, BA, DipSPLD
Mrs H F McLintock, BA
R J M Stephen, MA
Mrs R Thomson, BA, DipHE, TESOL

Houses & Housemasters:
Boarding:
School House: K M Seecharan
Judde House: J A Storey-Mason
Park House: A T Sampson
Hill Side: P J North
Parkside: Dr C D Thompson
Ferox Hall: C W Eades
Manor House: S J Hargreaves

Day:
Welldon House: R H Evans
Smythe House: G C Fisher
Whitworth House: C M Ashurst
Cowdrey House: N R V Rendell
Oakeshott House: G M Barnes

Librarian: Mrs H Precious, BA, MSc, MCLIP

Admissions Secretaries:
Miss R G Hearnden (*Senior Admissions Officer*)
Mrs V C Larmour (*Admissions Officer Lower Sixth Entry*)
Mrs R Griffiths (*Foundations Awards Manager*)
Mrs L Coakley (*Admissions Officer (Year 6)*)

Examinations Officer: Miss B J Shepherd

Administration:
Headmaster's PA: Mrs J T Bishop
PA to the Second Master & School Administrator: Miss E J Day
PA to the Bursar: Mrs D J Shepherd
Music Dept Administrator: Mrs J Marsh

Trinity School
Croydon

Shirley Park, Croydon CR9 7AT

Tel:	020 8656 9541
email:	lowerschooladmissions@trinity.croydon.sch.uk
website:	www.trinity-school.org
X/Twitter:	@TrinityCroydon
Facebook:	@Trinity-School
LinkedIn:	/Trinity-School

Motto: *Vincit qui Patitur*

The School was founded by Archbishop John Whitgift in 1596. The full title of the school is Trinity School of John Whitgift.

One of the three governed by the Whitgift Foundation, the School is an Independent Day School for boys aged 10–18 with a co-educational Sixth Form. The School aims to give a wide education to students of academic promise, irrespective of their parents' income.

Buildings and grounds. Trinity School has been in its present position since 1965, when it moved out from the middle of Croydon (its old site is now the Whitgift Centre) to a completely new complex of buildings and playing fields on the site of the Shirley Park Hotel. The grounds are some 27 acres in extent, and a feeling of openness is increased by the surrounding Shirley Park Golf Club and the extensive views to the south up to the Addington Hills. There are additional playing fields in Sandilands, ten minutes' walk from the School.

The resources of the Whitgift Foundation enable the School to provide outstanding facilities. All departments have excellent and fully equipped teaching areas.

Admission. The main ages of admission are at 10, 11 and 13. Entry is by competitive examination and interview. A reference from the feeder school will also be required. The School attracts applications from over 150 schools, with approximately 60% entering from state primaries. Entries of boys and girls into the Sixth Form are also welcomed.

Fees per term (2023–2024). £7,561 covering tuition, books, stationery and games.

Bursaries. Whitgift Foundation Bursaries (means-tested) are available providing exceptionally generous help with fees.

Scholarships. Academic, Art, Design Technology, Drama, Music and Sport Scholarships are available annually to boys applying for entry at 10+, 11+ or 13+. Boys must be the relevant age on 1 September of the year of entry. Awards are based on the results of the Entrance Examination, interview and current school reference. They are awarded without regard to parental income and are worth a percentage (maximum 50%) of the school fees throughout a pupil's career.

Academic, Art, Music and Sport Scholarships are also available for entry to the Sixth Form, based on GCSE results.

Scholarships may be supplemented up to the value of full fees if there is financial need.

Music Scholarships of up to 50% fee remission include free tuition in two instruments. Applicants are required to play two pieces on principal instrument and show academic potential in the Entrance Examination. Awards are available for all instruments and singing ability can be taken into consideration. Further details from the Director of Music.

Organisation and counselling. The School is divided into the Lower School (National Curriculum Years 6–9) and the Upper School (Years 10–13). The Pastoral Leader in charge of each section works with the team of Form Tutors to encourage the academic and personal development of each boy. There is frequent formal and informal contact with parents.

A counselling service is provided to pupils as part of the pastoral provision and a fully qualified School Counsellor is on hand to help students with their individual needs. Pupils can refer themselves to the Counsellor or they may be referred by staff.

There is a structured and thorough Careers service, which advises boys at all levels of the School and arranges work experience and work shadowing.

While the academic curriculum is taught from Monday to Friday, there is a very active programme of sports fixtures and other activities at the weekend, and all boys are expected to put their commitment to the School before other activities.

Curriculum and staffing. The School is generously staffed with well qualified specialists. The organisation of the teaching programme is traditionally departmental based. The syllabus is designed to reflect the general spirit of the National Curriculum while allowing a suitable degree of specialisation in the Upper School.

The normal pattern is for pupils to take 9 or 10 GCSE subjects, and to proceed to the Sixth Form to study an appropriate mixture of AS and A2 level subjects, complemented by a wide-ranging General Studies programme, before proceeding to university.

Games and activities. The main school games are Rugby, Football, Hockey, Cricket and Athletics, with the addition of Netball for girls in the Sixth Form. Many other sports become options as a boy progresses up the School. Games are timetabled, each pupil having one games afternoon a week.

At the appropriate stage, most boys take part in one or more of the following activities: Community Service, CCF, Duke of Edinburgh's Award scheme, Outdoor Activities. There are many organised expeditions during the holidays.

Music. Music at Trinity has an international reputation, and every year Trinity Boys Choir is involved in a varied programme of demanding professional work. The Choir has performed at the BBC Proms for the past seven years and sings at the Royal Opera House, the English National Opera, Glyndebourne or Garsington 3–4 times each year. Recently the choristers have travelled to Vienna, Brussels, Venice, Dusseldorf and Wachock Abbey, Poland. They also appear regularly on radio and television. Trinity Choristers, who specialise in religious music, hold an annual residential Easter Course at a British cathedral. Choral Scholarships are awarded annually and enable boys to receive additional professional voice training without charge.

Many boys learn at least one musical instrument, and a large visiting music staff teach all orchestral instruments, piano, organ and classical guitar. There are numerous orchestras, bands and other instrumental groups for which boys are selected according to their ability. Musicians recently travelled to Canada and instrumentalists are regular finalists in the Pro Corda National Chamber Music competition.

Drama. There are two excellently equipped stages in the school and a lively and developing programme of formal and informal productions directed by pupils, staff and members of the Old Boys Theatre Company. Drama forms part of the formal curriculum in Years 6–9 and can be studied for GCSE and A Level.

Art and Design Technology. As well as the formal curriculum, which has led to 70% of the School taking a GCSE in art or design technology, pupils are encouraged to make use of the excellent facilities to develop their own interests.

Charitable status. The Whitgift Foundation is a Registered Charity, number 312612. The Foundation now comprises the Whitgift Almshouse Charity for the care of the elderly and the Education Charity which administers three schools.

Visitor: His Grace the Archbishop of Canterbury

Chairman of the Court of Governors: Mr C J Houlding

Court Governors:
Revd Canon Dr Andrew Bishop
Mr P Cornforth
Mr N Edwards, BA Dunelm, ACA
Ms S Fisher
Mr C J Houlding
Mr W Jones
Mr M Long
Ms J MacKenzie
Revd Dr Rosemary Mallett

Dr A Mehta, FRCP
Mr D A Metha
Mr A Patel, ACA, MSc
Ms D Payne, MA
Mr D Seymour, CB
Ms A Wright

Chief Executive of the Whitgift Foundation: Mr M C Corney

School Committee:
Chairman of the Trinity School Committee: Mr D Seymour, CB
Revd Canon Dr Andrew Bishop
Chris Butler
Marcie Buxton
Mr J Crozier
Mr S Jetha
Mr W Jones
Dr B MacEvoy
Mr A Patel
Mr T Perrin

***Headmaster*: Mr A J S Kennedy**, MA Cantab

Senior Deputy Head: Mr T T Rounds, BA Birmingham
Deputy Head, Pastoral, Designated Safeguarding Lead: Miss S Ward, BSc Birmingham
Deputy Head, Academic: Mr A J Corstorphine, MA, MBA, MPhil Cantab
Deputy Head, Head of Lower and Middle Schools: Mr J Munnery
Director of Co-Curricular Activities: Mr M D Richbell, BSc Liverpool
Bursar: Mr D Navarro, BCom Hons/LLB Auckland
Director of Teaching and Learning: Mr R Hardman, BA, MA Leeds
Head of Sixth Form: Mr J Pietersen, BA Cantab

Teaching Staff:
* *Head of Department*

Mr M I Aldridge, BEd London (*Design Technology, Head of UCAS*)
Mr S R Allison, BA Durham (*Spanish**)
Dr M S Asquith, BA, MA, PhD London (*English*)
Miss C Atkinson, BA, UCL (*French**)
Miss R C Bainbridge, MA Durham (*Mathematics*)
Ms D S Bala, BDS Chennai (*Biology*)
Mr R Barlow, BSc Bristol (*Mathematics*)
Mr E Beesley (*Saturday School Teacher*)
Mrs S Baulf, BA Reading (*Economics & Business*)
Ms N M Beaumont, MA, MSc Oxon (*Mathematics**)
Mr D Beavan, MA UCL, MSc Cantab, PhD Woolongong (*Mathematics*)
Mr O J Benjamin, BA Durham (*German**, *Spanish, Junior Languages Co-ordinator*)
Mrs I M Bennett, BEd Leeds Beckett (*Biology, Head of Netball*)
Ms H A Benzinski, BSc London (*Mathematics, DofE Co-ordinator*)
Mr G C Beresford-Miller, BA Rhodes (*Physical Education, Head of High Performance and Head of Games*)
Mrs K A Beresford-Miller, BA King's London (*Religious Studies**)
Mr R M Biggs, BSc Cardiff (*Design Technology*)
Mrs N Blamire-Marin, BA Granada (*Spanish*)
Mr P J Blanchard, BSc Exeter, MBA Warwick (*Chemistry*)
Miss E Bodinier, BA Hons, Worcester, MA Angers, France (*German, French*)
Miss V J Boorman, BA King's London (*Classics, Head of Upper Sixth*)
Mr N D Borley, BSc Manchester (*Chemistry*)
Mrs N Boyce, BA Rhodes (*Religious Studies, Head of Lower School*)
Mr M Brennan, BA Hons Warwick, MA Oxon (*History**)
Mr M M Bright, MSc Bristol (*Physics*)
Mrs M Bromberg, MSc Imperial (*Biology MFB*)
Ms Q Cao (*Mandarin*)
Mrs H C Carey, BSc Durham (*Religious Studies, Deputy Head of Lower School*)
Mr C S Chambers, BA Cantab (*Drama Productions**)
Mr S W Christian, BA Liverpool (*French, Spanish*)
Mr W A Coma, BA Leeds (*Art, Assistant Head of Mentoring, Head of Junior Year*)
Ms A Costello, BA Roehampton (*Learning Support*)
Mr D W G Currigan, BA Chelsea, MA Kingston (*Design Technology**)
Miss A E Davis, BA Manchester (*Maths*)
Mr T J Desbos, LCE Lille (*French, i/c DLL*)
Ms A Donkin, MChem Durham (*Chemistry**)
Mr A B Doyle, MA Glasgow, MA Open (*English**)
Mrs R Doyle, BEd Glasgow (*SEN*)
Mrs Z Dungerwalla, MSc, BSc Nottingham (*Chemistry*)
Mr M El Moudden, BSc London (*Computer Science*)
Miss J S Eminsang, BA Manchester (*Mathematics, Head of Junior Maths*)
Mr R E Evans, Dip Perf RCM (*Head of Piano*)
Mr L M Flanagan, BA Cantab (*Physics**, *Head of Science*)
Mrs K Fuge, BSc City (*Music, Head of Singing*)
Mrs A A Fulker, BA Oxford Brookes (*Art, Head of Personal Development*)
Mr N A Giles, BA Liverpool John Moores (*Head of Hockey**)
Ms A E Gilmour, BSc, Loughborough (*Physics, Head of Diploma*)
Miss R M Goddard, Portsmouth (*Biology, Head of Diving, Head of Third Year*)
Mr B Goode, BA London (*English*)
Mrs E Gornall, BA, MA Durham (*Spanish*)
Mr T Guise-Brown (*Physical Education*)
Mr M Hammond, BSc Hons Sussex (*Maths*)
Mr R D G Haythorne, BA, MA Oxon (*Maths, Physics & Computer Science*)
Mr T Heath, BSc Sheffield, MSc Bristol (*Biology, Junior Science**, *MDV Assistant*)
Mr T Heaton, BA Essex (*Psychology*)
Miss C Herdman, BSc Manchester (*Business*)
Mr S M Hodge, BA Exeter (*Religious Studies, Head of Fifth Year*)
Mr R M Holdsworth, BA, MA Oxon (*Music**)
Mr O J Hutchings, BA, MA York, MA London (*History, Politics & i/c Politics, Head of EPQ & SFP*)
Mr I Kench, BSc Loughborough, MSc Oxon (*Physical Education, Director of Sport*)
Mr G Kimmins, Exeter (*Physical Education, Head of Rackets, Head of Second Year*)

Mr S D King, BA Manchester Metropolitan (*Physical Education, Head of Performance Sport & Head of Aquatics*)
Mrs R E Lattery-Lee, BA SOAS (*History, Head of Fourth Year*)
Ms A Long (*Physical Education, Head of Girls Games*)
Mr D J P Lydon, BA, MA Dublin (*English, Head of Mentoring*)
Mr R Malde, BSc Bristol (*Economics*)
Mr A E Magee, MA St Andrews (*English*)
Dr J Manchester, PhD Birmingham (*Chemistry*)
Miss K J Manisier, MSc Imperial (*Physics, ITT Lead, STEM Engagement Coordinator*)
Dr M Mariani, BSc Kent, PhD UCL (*Physics*)
Mr O Marriott, BSc Exeter, MSc Buckingham (*Physical Education**)
Mr P Mazur, BA Wales, MA London (*Drama, Contingent Commander CCF*)
Mrs S J McDonald, MA St Andrews (**Learning Support*)
Mr S A McIntosh, MA Oxon (*German, Timetabler*)
Mrs K Molteni, BA Hull, MA UCL (*History*)
Mr R D Moralee, BSc Johannesburg (*Biology**)
Miss E Moreno (*Spanish*)
Mr N Mulroy (*Music*)
Mr J C Munnery, BSc Nottingham (*Geography, Deputy Head Middle School*)
Mr S Orungbamade, BEd Nigeria (*Economics and Business**)
Mr S D Page, BSc Sussex (*Computer Science**)
Mr T D Parkins, BA (*English*)
Miss C A Parkinson, BSc Sussex, MSc UCL (*Psychology*, Science*)
Mr B J Patel, MA Cantab (*Mathematics, Physics*)
Mr B Patel, MSc UCL (*Mathematics*)
Mr J A Paterson, BA Cantab (*Classics, Assistant to Head of Sixth Form*)
Mr F Peronius (*Mathematics*)
Mr C P Persinaru, DipRAM, LRAM RAM (*Music, Head of Strings*)
Mr J Pettitt, BMus Trinity (*Music, Head of Jazz, Rock and Pop*)
Mr H P Petty, BA Bristol (*English, MAT and Enrichment Coordinator*)
Mrs R J Petty, MA Oxon (*English, Drama, Deputy Designated Safeguarding Lead*)
Mrs X L Phasey, MA Schiller International (*Chinese*)
Ms E Poole, BA Exeter (*History*)
Mrs A Prestney, BA Durham (*Geography*)
Mr D K Price, BA Wimbledon School of Art (*Design Technology, Director of Admissions*)
Mrs S J Rapoport, BEd Twickenham (*Academic Mentor*)
Mr S Reck, BMus Perf Hons, MMus, DipLCM, ALCM (*Music, Head of Guitar*)
Mrs L Regan, BMus, LRAM (*Music, Assistant Director of Music*)
Mr S H Richards (*Head of Cricket*)
Mr T M G Richmond, BSc Manchester (*Biology, Head of S&C*)
Mr P J Roberts, BSc Bath (*Physical Education, Economics & Business, Head of Rugby*)
Mr J Robertson, BA Hons UCL, PGDip Royal Academy (*Director of Art**)
Miss L P Robinson, BA Birmingham (*Drama**)
Miss S Rossitter, BA Manchester (*Economics*)
Mr C P Ruck, BSc Southampton (*Geography**)
Mr N Russell, MA St. Andrews (*History*)
Mr R M Salmanpour, BSc London (*Chemistry*)
Mr J B Savile, BSc Durham (*Geography, Head of Sailing, Head of First Year*)
Ms I S Sher, MA Edinburgh (*English*)
Mr A E Smith, BA, MA York, MSc London (*Religious Studies*)
Mr M Stacpoole, BA Twickenham (*PE*)
Dr E W Steer, PhD, MA Oxon (*Chemistry*)
Mrs B J Steven, BA Cape Town (*English*)
Ms T Stevens-Lewis, BA, MA Goldsmiths (*Art, i/c Photography*)
Mr J E Stone, BA Cantab (*Classics*)
Ms C S Story, BA Durham (*English*)
Ms E M Suarez, BA Juan Carlos 1 (*German, Spanish*)
Mr D J Swinson, MA, FRCO, ARCM, LRAM (*Director of Music**)
Mr P G Tattersall, BMus Hons RNCM (*Music*)
Mrs S Z Taylor, BSc Exeter (*Mathematics, Professional Co-ordinating Mentor*)
Mr J G Timm, BA Cantab (*History, Politics*)
Mr C H Todd, BMus, MMus, LRAM, ALCM (*Music, Head of Brass**)
Mr J Townsend, (*Design Technology*)
Mr W S Tucker, BSc Exeter (*Physics*)
Mrs T A Upton, BSc Warwick (*Mathematics*)
Miss S T Van Dal, BA Cantab, MA UCL (*Classics**)
Mr R van Graan, BA Canterbury Christchurch (*Director of Digital Strategy**)
Mr M D Waller, MA St Andrews (*Religious Studies*)
Mrs Q Wang, BA Henan Institute of Finance (*Chinese*)
Mrs C E Webb, BSc Bath (*Mathematics*)
Miss G E Webber, BA, MA Nottingham (*Economics & Business, Head of Lower Sixth*)
Mrs C-J Wilkinson, BSc Glasgow (*Biology*)
Miss N Wiltshire (*Chemistry, Mental Health Lead*)
Miss J Wiskow, MA Wuppertal, Berlin (*German*)

Admissions Registrar: Ms M-A Costart
Sixth Form Admissions: Ms S Redican
Headmaster's PA: Mrs K Walsh

Truro School

Trennick Lane, Truro, Cornwall TR1 1TH

Tel: 01872 272763
email: enquiries@truroschool.com
website: www.truroschool.com

Motto: *Esse quam videri*

Truro School was founded in 1880 by Cornish Methodists. In 1904, it came under the control of the Methodist Independent Schools Trust (MIST) and is now administered by a Board of Governors appointed by the Methodist Conference. Although pupils come from all parts of the country and abroad, the roots of the school are firmly in Cornwall and it is the only HMC school in the county.

The religious instruction and worship are undenominational though the school is conscious of its Methodist origins.

There are 855 pupils (511 boys, 344 girls; 790 day, 65 boarders) in the Senior School (age 11+ and above).

There are another 290 pupils in the Preparatory School, where boys and girls may start in the Nursery at the age of 3.

The school is fully co-educational throughout and there is a strong Sixth Form of some 180 pupils.

Boarding. The Senior School has two girls boarding houses: Malvern House (Sixth Form) and Pentreve House; boy boarders live in Trennick House. All the Houses have Boarding Staff who live onsite with their families, helping to ensure a home from home feel. Pupils eat in the central dining room with a cafeteria system. There is a School Medical Centre on site and the boarders have full use of all the School facilities.

Campus and Buildings. The Prep School campus is built around a country house acquired by the school in the 1930s. It has an indoor heated swimming pool and extensive areas for science, modern languages, computing, art and crafts, as well as a modern sports hall, new Dining Hall and a new Assembly Hall. The Pre-Prep is housed in a purpose-built unit within the grounds of the Prep School.

The Senior School occupies an outstanding site overlooking the Cathedral city of Truro and the Fal Estuary. It is only five minutes from the centre of the city, but the playing fields reach into the open countryside. The school is excellently equipped. There is a first-class Library, extensive science laboratories, excellent Technology and Art facilities, a computer centre, Music School, Sixth Form Centre and a Sixth Form Café and a range of classroom blocks. The fine block containing the Burrell Theatre, six classrooms and a drama centre has been extended to provide a Modern Languages Centre in The Wilkes Building. An attractive and newly refurbished chapel provides a focus for the life of the school. The Sir Ben Ainslie Sports Centre, completed for September 2013, provides an eight-court multi-use sports hall, two county-standard glass-backed squash courts with viewing gallery, large fitness suite with a range of aerobic, strength and conditioning equipment, a multi-purpose dance and exercise studio with a sprung wooden floor, adding to the existing excellent facilities of 25m swimming pool, cricket nets, tennis courts, 40 acres of pitches and cricket pavilion. Following a link with Truro Fencing Club in September 2014, the school has its own designated Fencing Salle. In September 2018, the School opened its new Cookery School, in association with Leiths School of Food & Wine – a state-of-the-art 10-bay facility for co-curricular cookery and delivery of the Leiths Introductory Certificate to Food and Wine during the Sixth Form.

Organisation and Curriculum. Our academic programme up to GCSE provides a balance between the three Sciences, Humanities, Creative Arts and Modern Languages. In the 1st to 3rd Year, pupils study English, Mathematics, Biology, Chemistry and Physics, French, Spanish and German, Geography, History, Religious Studies, Art, Design & Technology, Drama, ICT and Music. All pupils have PE as well as Games each week.

At GCSE the norm is to study ten subjects at full GCSE. Compulsory subjects are English Language, English Literature, Mathematics, Religious Studies, Double Award or Triple Award Science; the options include French, German, Spanish, Geography, History, Art and Design, Design and Technology, Music, Drama, Computer Science, PE and Geology.

A Levels include the same subjects as at GCSE, but with the introduction of Further Mathematics, Religious Studies (with Philosophy and Ethics), Economics, Business Studies, Psychology and the Extended Project Qualification. Our Extension Studies programme includes modules on Photography, Philosophy and Film Studies. As part of this we provide advice on careers and university applications, with a specialised programme for potential Medics, Dentists and Vets and Oxbridge. Three subjects will be most commonly continued into the Upper Sixth at A Level and the vast majority of Sixth Formers go on to further education when they leave. In addition to A Levels, we offer the five-term Leiths Introductory Certificate which carries UCAS points as well as the CTECH in Sport and Physical Activity.

Out-of-School Activities. Co-curricular life is rich and varied. There is a choir, school orchestra, a jazz group, a brass band and many other ensembles. Facilities such as the ceramics room, the art room and the technical block are available to pupils in their spare time. A huge variety of activities includes fencing, squash, sailing, golf, basketball, debating, surfing, and many others. Many pupils take part in the Ten Tors Expedition, an exceptional number are engaged in the Duke of Edinburgh's Award scheme, as well as local Community Service.

Games. All the major team games are played. Badminton, cross-country, hockey, netball, squash and tennis are available throughout most of the year. Rugby and Girls Hockey are played in the Winter Term and Soccer and Netball in the Spring Term. In the summer, cricket, athletics and tennis are the major sports. The covered pool is heated. The School also has its own Fencing Salle, with our fencers competing nationally and internationally.

Admissions. Pupils are able to join the Prep at any age from 4 to 11 years and at any point in the academic year, subject to availability. Admission to the Senior School's 1st to 4th Years is by entrance exam, school report and interview. Admission to the Sixth Form is by school report and interview with the Head, and is based on predicted GCSE grades or equivalent.

Scholarships and Bursaries. Truro School has linked with Truro Cathedral to offer chorister scholarships for girls (ages 13–18) and boys (ages 7–13). Fencing Scholarships are also available. Academic, Sporting and Music scholarships are awarded in the form of enhanced educational opportunities, and not as a reduction in fees. The School also offers a small number of means-tested bursaries up to the value of full fees.

Fees per term (2023–2024). Senior School: International Boarders £12,275; Full Boarders £11,099; Weekly Boarders £9,535; Day Pupils (including lunch) £5,585. Prep (including lunch): £4,940 (Years 3–4); £5,130 (Years 5–6). Pre-Prep (including lunch): £3,655 (Nursery and Reception); £3,480 (Years 1 and 2).

Academic results. A number of pupils proceed to Oxbridge every year, along with overseas universities. Around 95% of the Sixth Form proceed to degree courses. In 2022 81% of A Levels were at A* to B grades with 63% at A*/A. At GCSE in 2022, over 60% were at grades A*/A, 9–7 and 37% at grade 9 or 8.

Former Pupils' Association. There is a strong Former Pupils' Association and it has its own webalumnus. The "Friends of Truro School" involves parents, staff, old pupils and friends of the school in social events and fundraising.

Charitable status. Truro School is part of the Methodist Independent Schools Trust, which is a registered Charity, number 1142794.

Visitor: The President of the Methodist Conference

Administrative Governors:
Chairman: R Thomas, BSc, MRICS
N Ashcroft, MBE
M Aliffe, BA Hons, BSC, FRICS
R Cartwright, CTA
B Dolan, LLB Hons
Revd Mark Dunn-Wilson
Mrs E Garner, BA Hons, MEd
R Griffin, MA
Mrs L Howard, BSc, MEd
A Luck
M MacDonald, BEng, FCA
A Murray, MA
R Raistrick, BA, PGCE
Mrs B Scarsbrook, BA Hons, BCL, BPTC
Mrs H Sullivan, MA
Mrs C White, MSc, BA Hons, FCIPD, FLPI

***Headmaster*: A Johnson**, BA

Deputy Heads:
R Murphy (*Pastoral*)
Dr S K Pope, BSc, PhD (*Academic*)
Mrs Z Jobling (*Co-Curriculum & Partnerships*)

Assistant Heads:
Mrs E Ellison, BSc (*Director of Studies*)
Miss E Mitchell (*Teaching & Learning*)

Chaplain: Revd Helen Byrne

Business Director: K Topping

Boarding House Staff:
D McKeown, MSc, MEd
Mrs S Mulready, BA Malvern

Heads of Year:
R Williamson, MA (*Head of Sixth Form*)
R T Picton, MPhys (*Head of Middle School*)
T H Copeland, MA (*5th Year*)
Miss J R Egar, BA (*4th Year*)
G D Hooper, PGCE (*3rd Year*)
Miss D Overend (*2nd Year*)
Mrs F L Thurlow (*1st Year*)

Heads of Department:
D Meads, BA (*Art*)
Ms S Havis (*Biology*)
Dr J Older, BSc, PhD, PGCE (*Chemistry*)
B Oldfield, BA (*Drama*)
C Baker, BSc (*Design and Technology*)
J Whatley, BSc (*Economics, Business Studies and Politics*)
Mrs A L Selvey, BA, MA (*English*)
Mrs J Wormald, BSc (*Geography*)
Ms J Hope, BSc (*Geology*)
Dr M H Spring, MA, PhD (*History*)
J Butterworth, BA, MEd, PGCE (*Mathematics*)
Ms C Le Bihan, PGCE (*Modern Languages*)
Richard Osmond (*Music*)
D J Sanderson (*Director of Sport*)
A L Laity, BSc (*Physics*)
Mrs B L Richards, BA Hons, PGCE (*Religious Education*)

Truro School Preparatory School
(see entry in IAPS section)

Prep School Head:
Mr R Morse

University College School

Frognal, Hampstead, London NW3 6XH

Tel: 020 7435 2215
email: seniorschool@ucs.org.uk
website: www.ucs.org.uk
X/Twitter: @UCSHampstead
Instagram: @ucshampstead

University College School is a leading London day school providing places for approximately 600 boys aged 11–16, with a co-educational Sixth Form of approximately 350 places. UCS admitted its first cohort of girls into the Sixth Form in September 2008 and around 60 girls join UCS each year.

University College School was founded in Gower Street in 1830 as part of University College, London and moved to its current location in Hampstead in 1907. The UCS Foundation comprises three separate schools offering education to children at each stage of their development from the ages of 3–18, founded to promote the Benthamite principles of liberal scholarship and education. Intellectual curiosity, breadth of study and independence of mind combine to achieve academic excellence; they are not subordinate to it.

Selecting children with no regard to race or creed, UCS fosters in them a sense of community alongside a tolerance of and a respect for the individual. By offering the fullest range of opportunities for personal and for group endeavour, it teaches the value of commitment and the joy of achievement. It is a place of study, but also of self-discovery and self-expression; a school that places equal value on learning with others as on learning from others.

Admission. UCS Pre-Prep accepts boys at the age of 4 to join Reception. Boys join the Junior Branch at the age of 7 and the Senior School at the age of 11. We invite both boys and girls to apply at 16 for places in our Sixth Form. We always advise parents to check the admissions pages on the UCS website for the most up-to-date information.

Curriculum. The UCS curriculum is designed to match the educational needs of pupils at all stages of their development. At the Pre-Prep, the mix of formal and informal learning develops independent and enquiring thinkers. At the Junior Branch, whilst the emphasis is on breadth, boys are also prepared for Key Stage 2 Tests in English, Maths and Science.

The Lower School: In the first years at the Senior School boys aged 11–13 follow a broad, common curriculum founded on the best features of the National Curriculum but enriched to develop a love of learning and positive study skills. These traits enable our pupils to develop their own academic specialisms as they go up through the school, whilst also ensuring that they receive a rounded academic education.

Mathematics is taught in banded groups related to boys' ability and progress. There is otherwise no streaming and subjects are studied within form groups. Homework is set each day, and usually takes between 45 minutes and one hour.

The Middle School. The curriculum is deliberately broad, in order to provide a suitable basis for further study leading to GCSE and Sixth Form courses. Pupils are divided into sets in Mathematics according to ability. More time is devoted to Science and boys may take up a further Classical or Modern Language (Greek, German, Spanish or Mandarin). In addition boys choose one option from Music, Drama and Computing. PSHE continues in Year 9 in the classroom and in the following two years, through a programme of presentations, discussions and visits from outside speakers. Homework tasks include a wider range of topics and activities than before.

For the two years leading to GCSE, boys continue with English and Mathematics. They may then choose freely a further seven subjects with the only proviso that, to maintain a sufficient breadth to their studies, they must include at least one Modern Language from those they have previously studied and at least one science subject. Boys in the top two Mathematics sets also take the Additional Mathematics qualification alongside their GCSE.

The GCSE subjects offered are: Biology, Physics, Chemistry, French, German, Spanish, Italian, Mandarin, Latin, Greek, History, Geography, Art, Design and Technology, Drama, Dance, Music and Computer Science.

The Sixth Form. Pupils may study any combination of four subjects in the Transitus (Year 12) and may freely mix Arts and Science subjects if they wish. Careful guidance is provided to ensure that the course upon which they embark will provide an appropriate basis for an application to the Higher Education course and institution of the individual pupil's choice. After one year of study, pupils may continue with three or four subjects in the Sixth Form (Year 13). Sixth Form sets normally include 8–10 pupils who, in preparation for Higher Education, are encouraged to take greater personal responsibility for study.

The A Level subjects available are: English, Mathematics, Further Mathematics, Biology, Physics, Chemistry, French, German, Spanish, Mandarin, Latin, Greek, History, Geography, Economics, Politics, Philosophy, Psychology, Drama and Theatre Studies, Computer Science, Design and Technology, Art, Music and History of Art.

Pastoral Care. We regard the personal, emotional and moral development of our pupils as a major priority at every single stage of the education that we offer. The aim of our pastoral system is to encourage pupils to develop their own identities and to express them with a proper regard for the feelings and sensitivities of others. Pupils are encouraged from an early age to develop a sense of responsibility for their own behaviour. Much stress is laid upon tolerance of and respect for one another. Considerable effort is made to build a sense of community within the school. To this end, two days a week the school starts with a whole school, deme or year assembly of a non-denominational character. Pupils and their parents know the identity and the responsibilities of the members of staff concerned for their care. Parents are involved as fully as possible in pastoral matters and will always be informed and consulted.

Careers. Pupils are guided by means of interviews and tests towards careers appropriate to their gifts and personalities. Pupils are given opportunities to attend holiday courses directed towards specific careers. Also, visiting speakers are invited to the School and there are frequent Careers events. There is a full Careers Library and a comprehensive programme of Work Experience. The Parents' Guild and Old Gowers' Club (alumni organisation) also provide advice and support.

Physical Education and Games. The state-of-the-art Sir Roger Bannister sports complex opened in December 2006. The pupils have periods of Physical Education within their normal timetable in the sports complex. The School playing fields cover 27 acres and are situated a mile away in West Hampstead. In addition to grass surfaces, there is a large all-weather pitch and two pavilions. An impressive new double pavilion was opened in 2019 and the fields have recently undergone major levelling and drainage works. The major sports for Lower and Middle school boys are Rugby, Football, Hockey and Cricket with increased choices from Year 9. The School has its own Tennis and Fives courts at Frognal, together with an indoor heated Swimming Pool. Other sports include Athletics, Squash, Badminton, Basketball, Climbing, Fives and outdoor pursuits. For sixth form boys and girls there is a wide choice of indoor and outdoor sports.

Music and Drama. There is a strong musical tradition at UCS and many pupils play in the Orchestras, Wind Band and a great variety of groups and ensembles. Choral music is equally strong and Jazz is a particular feature. Instrumental tuition is given in the Music School, opened in 1995, and this and Ensemble Groups are arranged by the Director of Music. The School's Lund Theatre, opened in 1974, is the venue for a range of Drama from major productions to experimental plays, mime and revue. An open-air theatre was completed in 1994. A regular programme of evening events is arranged for the Autumn and Spring terms.

Other School Societies. These cover a wide range of academic interests and leisure pursuits, including the Duke of Edinburgh's Award scheme. There is a very active Community Action Programme, which works in the local community and there are regular fundraising initiatives for both local and national charities.

Philanthropy at UCS. Philanthropy has played a significant role in modernising the UCS estate and providing exceptional spaces for its pupils. Three major new facilities have opened in recent years which provide modern and up-to-date environments for pupils and staff alike. The Kantor Centre delivers sporting facilities fit for the capacity of the school, visitors and the local community it serves. The AKO Centre for Innovation in Learning and Teaching saw the entire refurbishment of the school library along with establishment of a research fellow into cutting edge teaching methods. Philanthropy has always played its part in the site of the Sixth Form Centre, and some 50 years after the original appeal was made to build this, the AKO Foundation provided a much needed full refurbishment. The generosity of donors, alongside revenues from our commercial activities, has enabled UCS to commit significant sums to funding bursaries, the majority of which provide wholly free places to talented young people. It continues to be the mission of UCS to substantially increase these sums year on year, working to widening access to a UCS education wherever possible.

Fees per term (2023–2024). Senior School: £8,471, Junior Branch: £7,757, Pre-Prep: £7,077.

Scholarships and Bursaries. UCS is firmly committed to promoting and increasing access to our unique education through fee assistance. From its beginning in 1830 UCS has had at its core a commitment to access, with a pledge that religion should be no bar to entry. In the 21st century, we add a further commitment – that the education we provide will not be restricted solely to those who can afford it and each year we commit £1.2 million to bursary support. We offer bursaries of up to 100% and UCS consistently ranks at the top of independent schools in London for the number of 100% bursaries awarded each year. The School also offers music scholarships which award the holder a reduction in the annual school fees of between 10% and, in exceptional cases, 50%. The precise value will depend upon the standard of applicants and the competition in any one year. Music scholarships entitle the holder to free instrumental tuition at school on an instrument (including voice) of the candidate's choice, which will remain in place throughout a pupil's time at UCS.

Alumni Association, the Old Gowers' Club. There are almost 9,000 current Old Gowers living in countries all across the world. Many are actively involved in helping current pupils prepare for the future, including supporting networking, interview preparation, attending careers events, and volunteering as speakers from universities and wide ranging professions. Amongst the Old Gowers are Nobel Prize winners, Olympic medalists, leaders in the arts, science and law as well as entrepreneurs in a diverse range of areas, to name but a few.

Charitable status. University College School, Hampstead is a Registered Charity, number 312748. Its aims and objectives are the provision of the widest opportunities for learning and development of students without the imposition of tests and doctrinal conformity but within a balanced and coherent view of educational needs and obligations.

Governors:
Mr Stephen Warshaw, BA (*Chair*)
Mr Stephen Adams, RIBA, FRSA [OG]
Mr Andrew Brem, MA, MSc, MBA
Mr Joe Cohen
Mr Richard Donner, BA
Ms Reena Gogna, LLB Hons
Mr Robert Gullifer, MA, FRSA
Mr Avi Rao, MBA, BEng
Mr Christopher Rodrigues, CBE
Mrs Angela Ryker Gallagherm, JD, MBA
Ms Shirley Soskin
Professor Li Wei, PhD, FBA, MAE, FAcSS, FRSA
Dr Paul Wood, PhD, MA, BA
Dr Edward Ziff, OBE, DL, Hon DBA

[OG] *Old Gower*

Senior School:

***Headmaster*: M J Beard**, MA, MEd

Vice Master & Academic Director: M T English, BA, MA

Deputy Head (*Pastoral*): A R Wilkes, BA

Assistant Heads:
R H Baxter, BA, MA
S E Bennett, BA
S A P FitzGerald, BA
J E L Lewis, BA
P S Miller, BSc
E D Roberts, MSci
T P Underwood, BA

Deme Wardens:
Baxters: S C Walton, MusB
Black Hawkins: A M Mee, MA
Evans: S D Maze, BA
Flooks: J P Cooke, BA
Olders: M Foster, BSc
Underwoods: Dr K Bugler, BSc, MSc, PhD

Sixth Form:
Head of Sixth Form: R H Baxter, BA, MA

Lower School Wardens:
Head of Lower School: E D Roberts, MSci
Entry: E A Barnish, BA, MA
Shell: Mr L N Hughes, BA

Senior School Heads of Departments/Subjects:

Art: Mr L A Farago, BA
Art History: Mr A M Mee, MA
Biology: Miss R A Potter, BSc
Chemistry: Dr S K Hoyle, MSci, PhD
Classics: Mr A R McAra, MA
Computer Science: Mr C Spence-Hill, BSc, MA
Design & Technology: Mr H J Franks, BA, MA
Drama: Mr C M Abbott, BA (*Director of Drama*)
Economics: Ms K Shah, BSc, MPhil
English: Mr H Hardingham, BA, MA
Geography: Mr M B Murphy, BA
History: Mr A G Vaughan, BA
Politics: Mr L A Smith, BA
Learning Support: Mr P G P Milton, BSc, MSc
Mathematics: Mr D J Armitage, MEng
Modern Languages: Mrs S Hess, BA (*Head of Modern Languages and Head of German*)
Miss C Bandera, BA, MA (*Head of Italian*)
Miss K Cieslak, MA (*Head of French*)
Miss M R Maggioni, BA (*Head of Mandarin*)
Ms L V Tyson, BA (*Head of Spanish*)
Music:
Mr C R Dawe, BA, MA, MMus (*Director of Music*)
Mr I C Gibson, MA (*Head of Academic Music*)
Philosophy: Dr K S Viswanathan, BSc, MA, PhD
Physical Education: Mr E P Sawtell, BA (*Director of Sport*)
Physics: Dr P D Edmunds, MSci, PhD
PSHE: Mr D J Bluck, MA
Psychology: Mrs C E Hawes, BSc, MSc

Junior Branch:
Headmaster: Mr L Hayward, MA
Deputy Head (*Academic*): Mr M Miles, MSc
Deputy Head (*Pastoral*): Mr D J Edwards, BA
Assistant Head (*Admin*): Ms P Gaglani, BSc

Pre-Prep:
Headmistress: Dr Z Dunn, BEd, PhD, NPQH
Deputy Head (*Head of EYFS*): Ms N Watt, BEd
Director of Learning Support and SENCO (*Pre-Prep and Junior Branch*): Ms S Ryan, MA

Uppingham School

Uppingham, Rutland LE15 9QE
Tel: 01572 822216
email: admissions@uppingham.co.uk
website: www.uppingham.co.uk
X/Twitter: @UppinghamSchool
Facebook: @UppinghamSchool
Instagram: @uppinghamschool
LinkedIn: /uppingham-school

Uppingham is a boarding and day school for boys and girls aged 13–18. There are around 850 pupils in the School, of which some 375 are in the Sixth Form.

From September 2024, Uppingham will be opening a 13+ co-educational Day House. For children who live locally to the School, being a day pupil at Uppingham offers the perfect blend of a truly expansive and holistic education with the flexibility of going home each evening.

Uppingham School's foundation dates from 1584, the year in which Archdeacon Robert Johnson, a local puritan rector, obtained a grant by Letters Patent from Queen Elizabeth I to found a free grammar school for the male children of poor parents. In 1853, this small local school was transformed into one of the foremost public schools of its time by the remarkable educational thinker and headmaster, Edward Thring. His pioneering pastoral ideas and belief in the values of an all-round education shaped the School then and continue to define it now. Small, family-like boarding houses that offer children individual space, an all-round education that caters for a broad range of pupils, and inspiring surroundings in which children are happy and learn better – all of these lie at the heart of Uppingham's identity.

Uppingham is a school of Christian foundation, and the whole School meets in the Chapel five days a week. Pupils forge a deep affection for Chapel – with hymn-singing a particularly distinctive feature – always enthusiastic and joyful. Uppingham welcomes all faiths, and while many Uppinghamians would not claim any kind of Christian faith, we believe that the traditions and stability represented by Chapel offer value and relevance to all.

Situation. Uppingham is a small market town set in the beautiful Rutland countryside. It is about 100 miles north of London, roughly equidistant from the M1 and A1/M11, and midway between Leicester and Peterborough on the A47. The A14 link road makes connections with the Midlands and East Anglia easier and faster. It is served by Kettering, Oakham, Corby, Peterborough and Leicester train stations, and by London (Stansted, Luton, Heathrow), Birmingham and East Midlands airports.

The buildings. At the heart of the School are the impressive buildings of the main quadrangle: the Victorian School Room and Chapel designed by the architect of the Law Courts in the Strand, George Edmund Street, the Library housed in a beautiful building dating from 1592, the Memorial Hall and the fine classroom blocks where the Humanities are based. The three Music Schools on this campus reflect the vitality of a musical tradition dating back to 1855. Edward Thring appointed the first Director of Music in any English public school. Nearby are the central Buttery, the Language Centre and the Sixth Form Centre.

At the western end of the town lies the Western Quad, the School's inspiring architectural vision of a space that unites Arts, Sciences, Theatre and Sport. The Science Centre contains 17 laboratories (including an environmental studies lab, outdoor classroom and project room), a lecture theatre, library, offices and meeting rooms. The Leonardo Centre, for Art, Design and Technology, and Textiles, looks across an open space studded with contemporary sculpture, and to the east sits the 300-seat Theatre with adjoining Drama Studio, workshops and Theatre Studies classrooms. To the north, overlooking an expanse of playing fields, lies the Sports Centre with a contemporary design that complements the central quad, which houses state-of-the-art sporting facilities, a swimming pool and a fitness suite.

Academic matters. While the School is noted for its strong commitment to all-round education, the depth of its pastoral care and wealth of facilities, academic study is the priority. Pupils move around the School campus during the working day, and the 55-minute lessons encourage detailed and developed learning.

Until GCSE, specialisation is minimal and pupils are taught in sets for most subjects. Most take a minimum of nine GCSE/IGCSE subjects. Members of the Sixth Form study three subjects alongside a parallel curriculum enriched by lectures and a variety of extracurricular activities. Extended Project Qualifications (EPQ) are also offered.

Each pupil's progress is monitored by a Tutor and the Housemaster or Housemistress – there are regular reviews of academic progress, in addition to pastoral reports.

At all stages of a pupil's career the Housemaster/Housemistress and Tutor are in regular contact with parents. Parent–teacher meetings take place annually for all year groups, and additional discussions are held regarding GCSE and A Level options and higher education.

The School's expansive Higher Education and Careers programme, overseen by professional advisers and staff, ensures that pupils know the full range of opportunities available to them after they complete their secondary education. Parents and pupils may call on the School's Higher Education and Careers advisers alongside additional professional services. Visiting speakers from universities and careers are featured throughout the year, and the School offers advice on GAP year planning.

Beyond the curriculum. As part of the School's enrichment programme, Uppinghamians get involved in an extensive range of additional pastimes and hobbies, based on the values of Be Inspired, Thrive, Make An Impact. The UPP&Out programme runs on Friday afternoons, and is central to developing courageous, curious, compassionate, adaptable and passionate young people. UPP&Out activities include Combined Cadet Forces (CCF), the Duke of Edinburgh's Award, Community Service, specialised Scholars Programmes and UppSkill – where pupils have the opportunity to learn new skills and challenge themselves.

Music. Uppingham has always had a very distinguished reputation for music, being the first school to include music on its curriculum for all pupils. More than 50% of pupils learn an instrument, and a busy programme of weekly public recitals, house and year group concerts, and performances in the UK and abroad offer pupils of all abilities regular chances to perform. Pupils receive conservatoire-style tuition at the school for a faculty comprised of nine full-time staff and more than 45 visiting music teachers, including current professors at the Royal College of Music, The Guildhall School of Music and Drama, and the Royal Birmingham Conservatoire of Music.

Uppingham is home to three music schools, with The Paul David Music School offering an inspirational centre for learning and rehearsal, with cutting-edge music technology suites. The School has an outstanding Chapel Choir, accomplished orchestras and national prize-winning chamber groups, a slick and polished Jazz Orchestra, and a thriving Alternative Music Society promoting rock concerts.

Sports and games. Uppingham has a strong tradition of sporting excellence, and pupils have gained county and national honours in a variety of sports. Sports on offer include rugby, hockey, cricket, tennis and athletics plus squash, badminton, swimming, football, sailing and dance.

Sport is for everyone at Uppingham, with all pupils encouraged to try their best and achieve to their fullest potential. We are driven by values, and not results, creating an environment where all pupils can achieve success and enjoyment at whatever level they wish to participate.

Talented athletes and sports scholars are offered a high level of coaching from experienced coaches and professionals in all major sports, often going on to represent club, academy, county, regional or national teams.

The Sports Centre includes a sports hall, six-lane 25 m swimming pool, fitness studio, gym, squash courts and dance studios. There are more than 65 acres of playing fields, three Astroturf surfaces (one floodlit), tennis, netball and fives courts, a shooting range and climbing wall.

The Leonardo Centre. The striking design of the Art, Design and Technology Centre allows the broad range of creative activities taking place to interact and stimulate each other. The Centre houses a fine art and printing space (with 3D printing), studios for design (including CAD design), textiles, ceramics, sculpture, photography and workshops primarily for wood, metal and plastic, and teaching rooms. The Warwick Metcalfe Gallery displays the work of pupils, staff and visiting artists.

Drama. Uppingham Theatre is a flourishing professionally equipped 300-seat theatre, with a stylish adjoining Drama complex with an 80-seat 'black box' studio, workshops, classrooms and offices. Major school productions open to all pupils are staged annually, including the recent original production of Manderley, based on Daphne du Maurier's Rebecca. Audiences are often struck by what many describe as 'West End-standard performance' in Uppingham Theatre. The programme also features Junior and Senior plays and joint boarding-house productions, and pupils are an integral part of the running of the theatre. Drama and Theatre is taught at GCSE and A Level.

Boarding and pastoral. There are fifteen boarding houses dotted around the town and School estate: nine for boys, one for Sixth Form girls and five for 13–18-year-old girls. Houses are small, most being home to around 50 children, 45 in the case of the Sixth Form girls' house. All pupils eat their meals in their own house dining room and are joined at lunch by teaching and non-teaching staff.

Much of the non-teaching life of the School is organised around the houses and they inspire strong loyalties. In addition to excursions and social events, there is a long-standing tradition of inter-house competitions (House Challenge, singing, debating and sports), house concerts, and some ambitious drama productions.

Pupils are supported by a wide-ranging pastoral network. The Housemasters and Housemistresses are resident, and lead a team of at least five tutors, including a Deputy Housemaster/Housemistress. Assigned to particular pupils, tutors help to monitor academic progress and social development. Each house is supported by experienced matrons providing medical support and supporting the pastoral care of the pupils. Any pupil may use the services of a professional psychologist or the School's qualified counsellor. The School's Medical Centre is open 24 hours a day in term time, with qualified medical staff in attendance.

When our new Day House opens in September 2024, day pupils within the Day House will experience the same exceptional pastoral support that is offered within our boarding houses.

Technological environment. Uppingham provides outstanding technology facilities for pupils in both academic and boarding areas. Resources include the online Encyclopedia Britannica and JSTOR, an online collection of over 1,000 academic journals and one of the most trusted sources of academic content.

In the classroom, academic departments have the tools to ensure that IT complements teaching and learning.

Admission. Most pupils are admitted to Uppingham in the September following their thirteenth birthday. Prospective pupils and their parents usually visit the School three years prior to entry. If not already registered, prospective pupils should be registered then. Two years before entry, all registered pupils complete pre-tests, with interviews at Uppingham. All applications should be supported by a satisfactory reference from the current school. The Headmaster offers conditional places to successful candidates after this process has concluded. Parents then complete and return an acceptance form together with an entrance deposit. Receipt of the entrance deposit guarantees a place in the School subject to the pupil qualifying for admission with tests in Year 8, often Common Entrance. In completing the acceptance form parents also confirm that Uppingham is their first choice of school. Full details are available on the School's website.

To continue into the Sixth Form the minimum grade requirement is three 7s and three 6s at GCSE. It is recommended that pupils have at least 7 at GCSE in the subject they wish to continue at A Level. In some subjects (Mathematics, the Sciences and MFL) an 8 or 9 grade is required (full details are available on the School's website).

There are a limited number of places available for entry into the Sixth Form. Pupils may register an interest in Sixth Form entry to Uppingham at any time and formal registration should be completed by the end of September, eleven months prior to entry. The test, interview and offer procedures take place in October and November ten months before entry. Admission at this level is dependent on tests and interviews at Uppingham, and then achieving at least three 7s and three 6s at GCSE (or equivalent), excluding short course GCSEs.

Details about admissions can be found on the school website or may be obtained from the Admissions Department.

Scholarships and bursaries. At 13+, Academic, Art, DT and Textiles, Drama, Music, Sport and Thring (Leadership) scholarships are available. Scholarship exams are held in the February/March preceding entry; the deadline for applications is typically in mid-January.

At 16+, Academic, Art, DT and Textiles, Drama, Sport and Music scholarships are awarded in the November preceding entry. The deadline for applications is typically the end of September.

At Uppingham, a candidate may only hold one scholarship award at any one time so that they can specialise in their area of talent. Candidates are not permitted to sit scholarships in more than two disciplines.

Where a family's financial means leaves them unable to afford a place at Uppingham, they may be eligible to receive support via a means-tested bursary. All candidates seeking a bursary should be registered with the School and need to fulfil the same entrance criteria as described above.

Details of all scholarships and bursaries may be found on the school website or obtained from the Admissions Department.

Fees per term (2023–2024). Boarding: £15.174; Day (in a boarding house): £9,858. There is a scheme for paying fees in advance.

For the 2024–2025 academic year, the fees per term for day pupils joining the Day House (opening in September 2024) will be £9,790. The 2024–2025 fees for boarding and day (in a boarding house) will be confirmed in April 2024.

Former pupils. The Uppingham Association was founded in 1911 to maintain the link between OUs and the School. All pupils may become life members when they leave and a database of their names, addresses, school and career details is maintained at the School by the OU Administrator. In addition to a range of OU events that are organised each year for members, a magazine is published annually, which contains news about OUs and activities at the School, and all members are encouraged to make full use of the OU Website.

Charitable status. Uppingham School is a charitable company limited by guarantee registered in England and Wales. Company Number 8013826. Registered Charity Number 1147280. Registered Office: High Street West, Uppingham, Rutland LE15 9QD.

Bursar/Finance Director, Clerk to the Trustees: S C Taylor, MA, ACA

***Headmaster*: Dr R J Maloney**, MTheol St Andrews, MA, PhD King's College London

Senior Deputy Head: K M Wilding, BA
Deputy Head Academic: B Cooper, MA
Registrar: C S Bostock, MA, MSc
Chaplain: The Revd Dr J B J Saunders, BA, PhD
Assistant Head: *Co-Curricular*: Dr Kyi Muller, BSc, PhD
Assistant Head: *Teaching and Learning*: M J Melville-Coman, BSc, MCCT
Assistant Head: *Pastoral Care*: R H Kay, BA, MA
Assistant Head: *Safeguarding*: C L Senogles, BSc, MSc
Assistant Head: *Sixth Form*: R J O'Donoghue, MA
Assistant Head: *Data/Academic Management*: P J Nicholls, BSc

Assistant Staff:
* Head of Faculty/Department
† Housemaster/mistress

Art, *Design & Technology*:
*C P Simmons, BSc
*M E Boyce, BA, MA (*Textiles*)
*H J Harrison, BA (*DT*)
*A R Reid, BA (*Art*)
S N Jarvis, BA, MA
J Luckhurst, BA
†K Wells, BA
A G Zanetti, BA

Biology:
*H E Holroyd, BSc
Y L Guy, BSc
Dr K Muller, BSc, PhD
Dr C L Pemberton, BSc, PhD
A Rajput-Buckland, MA
H J Robinson, BSc

Chemistry:
*R A King, BSc (*Science*)
Dr A J Dawes, MChem, MA, PhD
Y L Guy, BSc
A Kowhan, BSc
Dr N L Singleton, BSc, PhD

Classics:
*D W J Addis, BA, MA
S W Clark, BA, MA
S G Dewhurst, BA
D J H Draper, MA Oxon
Dr D C Oliver, PhD, MSc
†G S Tetlow, MA

Computer Science:
*S E L Webster, BSc

Drama and Theatre:
*S A Barker-Doherty, BA (*Director of Theatre*)
†J Holroyd, BA

Economics & Business:
*G D Hook, BSc
N J King, BA
T G MacCarthy, BA
S Raguseelan, BSc
G L Watt, BSc

English:
*Miss N Abdul-Karim, MA, MPhil
N G Fletcher, BA, MA
C S Greenlaw, BA
V L Kinmond, BA, MA
M B Sherwin, BA
K L Tetlow, BA
T R Tolond, BA, MA

Geography:
*T P Davies, BSc
†C C Breakwell, BSc, MSc
†T Hollyer, BA
†A N Huxter, BSc, MSc
S J Kowhan, BA
R J O'Donoghue, MA
K M Wilding, BA

History:
*B M Kirkby, MA
†J S Birch, MA
R B Fitzsimmons, BA
I C Neilson, MA
J A Reddy, BA

History of Art:
*D S R Kirk, BA
Dr E E Wilce, BA, MA, PhD

Learning Support & EAL:
*Z Jenkins, BSc (*Learning Support and SENCO*)
*A Rawlins, BEd (*EAL*)
J A Wilding, BSc

Mathematics:
* J W Partridge, MA (*Acting Head*)
L J Allen, BSc, MBCS
S J Bradley, BEng
P Gomm, BSc
†K F Hanrahan, MSc
C L Halliday, BSc
M J Melville-Coman, BSc
A S M Moosajee, BSc
E O'Brien, BSc
P J Nicholls, BSc
†A D Parker, BSc
J W Partridge, MA
L K Whiteside, BSc
H M Whittle, BSc

Modern Languages:
*A J Dowsett (*Languages, German*)
*A Gadd BA, MA, MSc (*Spanish*)
* Z J R Hunter, BA (*Acting Head of French*)
*Z B Zeng, BA, MA (*Mandarin*)
M A B Davies, BA
A M O Fritschy-Haramburu
†H M Johnstone, BA
I Miller
K M Turney
R M B Wilkinson, MA

Music:
*A J Kennedy, MA, PGDip (*Director of Music, Voice*)
*T Moore, BA (*Academic Music*)
*A P Webster, GGSM, ARCM, PDOT (*Instrumental Music, Clarinet*)
*M P Ćwiżewicz, MEng, ACGI, PGDip (*Strings*)
*D A Revels, BA Oxon, MA Oxon (*Singing*)
*W F J Smith, BMus, PGCE (*Jazz, Pop and Tech*)
S A Smith, BA, PPRNCM
J Stevens, GGSM, MA

Philosophy and Religious Studies:
*S L Colbourne, BA
B Cooper, MA
†R C Hegarty, MA
Dr R J Maloney, MTheol, MA, PhD
The Revd Canon Dr J B J Saunders, BA, PhD
†P M Shacklady, BA

Physical Education & Sport:
*N Gandy (*Director of Sport*)
*J M Baker, BSc (*Deputy Director of Sport, Coach Development, Hockey*)
*C A R Esson, BSc (*Deputy Director of Sport, Participation*)
*R G M Surtees (*Deputy Director of Sport, Performance, Racquets*)
*K J Borthwick, BSc, MSc (*Athletic Development*)
*H N Costello, BA, MA (*Physical Education*)
*H E V Joseph (*Netball*)
*I R Smith (*Rugby*)
*R M L Taylor, BA (*Cricket*)
†D J Bartley, BSc
†C C Breakwell, BSc, MSc
T Jarvis, BSc
A C Welch, BEd
†J R Welch, Bed
N L Williams, BSc

Physics:
*E L Ellis, BA
Dr D D Boyce, PhD, MPhys, CTeach, CPhys, CMath, CSci, CSciTeach, FInstP, FCCT, FIMA, ML, RCI, CWI, CWIA, CL, PSI
M E Dalzell, BSc
G S Wright, BSc

Politics:
*H J Barnes, MA
†T Makhzangi, BA
T P Prior, BA, MA

Wellbeing:
*R K G Hannigan, BA
†T C Hollyer, BA
R H Kay, BA, MA

Houses and Housemasters/mistresses:
Brooklands: James Holroyd
Constables: Katherine Hanrahan
Fairfield: Jo Welch
Farleigh: James Birch
Fircroft: Tom Hollyer
Highfield: Richard Hegarty
Johnson's: Alex Parker
The Lodge: Helen Johnstone
Lorne House: Andrew Huxter
Meadhurst: Patrick Shacklady
New House: Christina Breakwell
Samworths': Kitty Wells
School House: Simon Tetlow
West Bank: David Bartley
West Deyne: Toby Makhzangi

Victoria College
Jersey

Mont Millais, Jersey, Channel Islands JE1 4HT

Tel:	01534 638200
email:	admin@vcj.sch.je
website:	www.victoriacollege.je
X/Twitter:	@VictoriaCollege
Facebook:	@VictoriaCollegeJersey

Motto: *Amat Victoria Curam*

The College was founded in commemoration of a visit of Her Majesty Queen Victoria to the Island and opened in 1852. It bears the Arms of Jersey and the visitor is Her Majesty The Queen.

There are currently 680 boys in College and 275 in the Preparatory School.

The College is situated in extensive grounds above St Helier and commands spectacular views south and west over the Bay of St Aubin.

The fine building of 1852, with its Great Hall, de Quetteville Library and administrative areas, is set at the centre of new teaching accommodation, including classrooms, a music centre, an extensive Science suite opened by Her Royal Highness The Princess Royal, a Sixth Form Centre, Art and Design Technology suite, computer suites and the Howard Davis Theatre, refurbished in 1996 and updated in 2019. A suite of 4 new English classrooms were finished in 2014 along with a new Sixth Form Centre. House rooms (now Year Group rooms) were added in 2015.

College Field is adjacent to the main buildings and includes an all-weather hockey pitch.

Located in the grounds is a 25-yard shooting range, squash courts and CCF Headquarters. A multimillion pound sports complex with swimming pool was opened in 2003.

Education. There is a strong focus on adding value in all aspects of educational provision. The Combined Cadet Force, The Duke of Edinburgh's Award and a wide-ranging co-curricular programme helps provide opportunities for all students, catering to all interests and skill levels. Academic excellence, focusing on supporting students to achieve their personal academic bests, is a core goal. The curriculum conforms to the requirements of the Jersey Curriculum. From September 2022 at GCSE, students study English Language and Literature, Mathematics and at least two Science subjects from Biology, Chemistry and Physics. They also select from Spanish, French, History, Drama, Geography, an additional Science, Music, Art, Computer Science, DT, Food & Nutrition, Sports Science and Classical Civilisation. Boys select their optional subjects from those which best suit their aspirations, passions and abilities, the choice being guided by teaching staff in consultation with students and parents.

Boys study three A Level subjects (from a choice of 23) suited to their interests and future career options. Students from 3 other collaboration schools on Island share provision at Key Stage 5, to widen the choice of subjects available, and students visit other schools for those lessons. A wide ranging Sixth Form enrichment programme is offered, including lecture series and careers programme, Extended Project Qualification, and a significant number of options, many of which carry formal qualifications outside of the traditional academic sphere (e.g. sports coaching).

Prizes. Her Majesty The Queen gives three Gold Medals annually for Science, Modern Languages and Mathematics as well as two Prizes for English History. The States of Jersey offers a Gold Medal and a Silver Medal annually for French.

Physical Education and Games. Sport is enjoyed and promoted across all Key Stages at the College, and consistent success in both on and off Island competitions is the norm. Many students represent the Island in chosen sports.

Winter games include Association Football, Rugby, Hockey and Squash. Summer games include Cricket, Swimming, Shooting, Tennis and Athletics. Matches are played against Elizabeth College, Guernsey and numerous English Independent Senior Schools.

Combined Cadet Force. The College has an excellent CCF Contingent with an establishment of approximately 135 across three sections: Army, Navy and RAF. It is commanded by Sqn Ldr S Blackmore.

Admission. The age of admission is 11 years though boys are considered for entry at all ages. Entrants that do not come directly from the associated Victoria College Preparatory School must pass the College Entrance Examination.

Fees per term (2023–2024). £2,504. A grant is payable by the States of Jersey to supplement fees.

Preparatory School. The College has its own Preparatory School which stands in the College grounds. Boys progress to the College at the age of 11. *(For further details see entry in IAPS section)*.

Leaving Scholarships. There are a number of Scholarships for further education (of varying amounts). The Queen's Exhibition is tenable for three years at certain Universities; the Wimble Scholarship, the Sayers Scholarships and the De Lancey and De La Hanty Scholarship, tenable at British Universities, and the Rayner Exhibitions are recent additions to the rich endowment of Scholarships enjoyed by the College for its students.

Visitor: His Majesty The King

Governing Body:
Richard Stevens (*Chair*)
Paul Willing
Simon Marks (*Joint Vice Chair of Governors*)
Nick Cawley (*Joint Vice Chair of Governors*)
Colin Smith
Alexandra Ruddy (*Joint Vice Chair of Governors*)
Lee Bosio
Susana Rowles
Tina Caldeira
Becky Kane
Sofia Nicolle
Jon Cartmell
Melanie Grandfield

***Headteacher*: Dr Gareth Hughes**, PhD, MPhil Cantab, MSc, MA Oxon, PGCE, NPQH (*Geography*)
Deputy Head Teacher: Mr Patrick Crossley, MA Cantab, MEd, BTh, FRSA, GTP
Assistant Head – Curriculum, Teaching & Learning: Mrs Karen Palfreyman, BA Hons, MA Cantab
Assistant Head – Sixth Form: Mr Alan Falle, BA Hons, PGCE
Assistant Head – Staffing: Mrs Parmjeet Plummer, BA Hons, PGCE, FRSA, FCCT, NPQH
Assistant Head – Student Progress: Mr Anthony Griffin, BA Hons, PGCE
Assistant Head – Supercurriculum: Ms Rebecca Kane, BSc Hons
Assistant Head (secondment): Mr Jonathan Kellett
Bursar: Carolyn Ferguson, CAT, MIAB

Teaching Staff:
Emma Aikenhead, BEng, QTS (*Head of Design & Technology*)
Kieran Akers, BA Hons (*Design and Technology*)
Miranda Blackmore, BSc Hons, PGCE (*Geography*)
Gareth C Bloor, MA, BD Hons (*Head of RE*)
Tom Broad, BSc Hons (*Physics*)
Jacqueline Bryan, BA Hons (*English*)
Leah Channing, PGCE (*Drama*)
Steven Cooke, PhD, BEng Hons (*Head of Physics*)
David Cox, BA, BEd Hons (*Biology*)
Joseph Crill, BSc Hons (*Head of Hockey, Sports*)
Iain Durkin (*Head of Mathematics*)
Emma Davies, BA Hons, PGCE (*Music*)
Nicole Edgecombe, MA, BA Hons (*Modern Foreign Languages*)
Elise Falla, BA Hons, PGCE (*Head of Student Voice & Head of PSHE, English*)
Alan Falle, BA Hons, PGCE (*Assistant Head of Sixth Form*)
Miss Amy Flack, BSc Hons, PGCE (*Head of Psychology*)
Jodi Fowler, BEd Hons (*Design & Technology*)
Jose Galan, BSc, PhD (*Computer Science*)
William Gorman, BA Hons (*Design & Technology*)
Samuel Habin, BA Hons (*Director of Sports*)
Daniel Hodder, BSc, PGCE (*Head of Geography*)
Mr Tim Hutton, BA, PGCE (*Head of Business Studies & Trident Co-ordinator*)
Maria Innes BA, PGCE (*Modern Foreign Languages*)
Rebecca Kane, BSc Hons (*Assistant Head Supercurriculum, Biology*)
Stephanie Kellett, BA Hons, PGCE (*RE*)
Rachel Kemp, MA, PGCE (*English*)
Adam Lester, BSc Hons (*Sport*)
Vanessa McGrath, BSc Hons (*Mathematics*)
Nataly Miorin, BA Hons, PGCE, MA, NPQSL (*Head of History*)
Dawn Murphy, BA Hons, PGCE (*Head of Economics & Deputy Head of Sixth Form*)
Francis Murton, BMus, LRAM, LTCL, ARCO, ACIEA, PGCE (*Director of Music*)
Lucy Ogg, BA Hons, PGCE (*Drama*)
Eimear Pallot, MChem, QTS (*Chemistry*)
Ozzy Parkes, BA Hons, PGCE (*Head of Computer Science*)
Monica Perestrelo, BA Hons, PGCE (*Head of Modern Foreign Languages*)
Richard Picot, BSc (*Head of Celebrations & Rewards, Sports*)
David Pinto, MA, PGCE
Parmjeet Plummer, BA Hons, PGCE (*Assistant Head – Staffing, History*)
Mrs Maggie Quinn, BA Hons, PGCE (*Head of English*)
Majella Raindle, MSc, BSc Ed Hons (*Mathematics*)
Jefferson Randall, BA Hons (*Head of Art*)
Jane Richardson, PhD, BSc Hons, PGCE (*Head of Biology*)
Anna Robinson, BA Hons (*English*)
Andrew Royle, BSc Hons (*Sports*)
Helen Ryan, BA Hons (*Head of Photography*)
Clare Scott, BA Hons, PGCE, PGC Dyslexia & Literacy
Mahmoud Shahin (*Mathematics*)
Holly Shrimpton, BA Hons (*English*)
Rachel Smith, BA Hons (*History*)
Thomas Smith, BEng Hons (*Physics*)
James Townsend, BA Hons (*PSHE, Sport*)
Olivia Varney, BA Hons (*English*)
Valérie Videt, Licence-ès-Lettres (*Modern Foreign Languages*)
Adam Warburton, BA Hons (*Head of Theatre Studies*)
Andrew Ward (*Chemistry*)
Matthew Widdop, MChem, MRSC (*Head of Chemistry*)
Carys Williams, BEng Hons, PGCE (*Mathematics*)
Catherine Woodward, BSc, PGCE (*Science*)

Preparatory School
Headteacher: Dan Pateman, BA Hons

Wellingborough School

London Road, Wellingborough, Northamptonshire NN8 2BX

Tel: 01933 222427
email: admissions@wellingboroughschool.org
website: www.wellingboroughschool.org
X/Twitter: @wboroschool
Facebook: @WboroSchool
Instagram: @wboroschool
LinkedIn: /wellingborough-school

Founded in 1595, Wellingborough School prides itself on its rich history and enduring traditions which are visible today in its architecture, House system and, most importantly, values. The School's mindset, however, is thoroughly progressive and, as an organisation, is keen to embrace innovations which strengthen the ethos and integrity of the School. Families are reassured by the School's longevity and the body of knowledge it has developed over time about how best to educate boys and girls.

Wellingborough School is a co-educational school for boys and girls from the age of 3 to 18, and is divided into a Preparatory School (age 3–11: 225 pupils), and Senior School (age 11–18: 625 pupils, including 168 pupils in the Sixth Form).

Curriculum. The Prep School follows the International Primary Curriculum which gives a thorough grounding in the core subjects, while offering the pupils a broad spectrum of experience in Languages, Art and Design, Music, Drama and Sports as well as an international perspective on global issues.

The School's academic standards and expectations are high, based to a large extent on the National Curriculum. In the Senior School, quality learning and teaching enables pupils to take ownership of their future as they make decisions about their curriculum. Pupils in Years 7 and 8 have the opportunity to study a full range of subjects before spending more of their time on the subjects they enjoy in Year 9 (through our mini-options system) before choosing from over 20 GCSEs for Year 10.

Students in Sixth Form can choose from 25 A Level options including an Extended Project Qualification.

Sport. The playing fields, over 40 acres in extent, are used for the main boys' sports of rugby, football and cricket, and hockey and netball for girls; cross country, athletics, and tennis are also highly popular. The School site also boasts two AstroTurf pitches, five all-weather tennis courts, a shooting range and Sports Hall. The latter has four badminton courts, indoor cricket nets and facilities for fencing, table tennis, basketball and a dedicated fitness suite.

Co-Curricular Activities. The School's Co-Curricular programme blends inside the classroom with outside the classroom and is an extremely important part of the life and ethos of Wellingborough School. Pupils can choose from a wide variety of co-curricular activities, which aim to accommodate all abilities and most interests, at lunchtimes, after school and at weekends for all year groups.

During their time in the Prep School, the children can experience specialist dance lessons, individual music lessons, ensemble practices and frequent plays. Other activities include Art, Chess, Lego, Gardening, Cookery, Choir, Jigsaw, Touch-typing, Mindfulness, Reading and many more.

Pupils in the Senior School participate in lunchtime enrichment activities such as forensic science, chess, dance, first aid and public speaking, community cohesion projects are also popular.

The School's Drama Department produces an annual production each year, recent performances have included *Les Misérables*, *Oliver* and *Sweeney Todd*. The Music Department benefits from a variety of visiting music teachers offering individual lessons and ensemble practices in 25 different instruments.

Pupils from Year 9 onwards join one of four CCF Sections: Royal Navy, Royal Marines, Army or Royal Air Force, with the aim of developing cadets' personal qualities and leadership skills. The School also offers pupils the opportunity to achieve the Duke of Edinburgh Award at Bronze, Silver or Gold levels.

Admission. All applications for entry should be made to Admissions.

Pastoral Care. In the Prep School pupils are assigned to one of six Clubs. The vertical structure of the Club system means that pupils of all ages integrate with one another and older pupils can share their experiences and help and support our younger pupils.

In the Senior School, all pupils are allocated a House on entry. The single-sex House system includes 4 boys' Houses and 3 girls' Houses. Each House has its own character, colour, charity and history and is led by a Housemaster or Housemistress. The School also has an award-winning Wellbeing Team offering guidance and support to pupils of all ages and their families.

Scholarships are offered to external candidates for entry at 11+ and 16+. These Scholarships are awarded in the following subjects; Academia, Music, Drama, Art & Photography and Sports. Applications are required by the beginning of January and assessments take place in the following weeks.

Bursaries. Wellingborough is a diverse and welcoming community, a School which believes that its fees should not present a barrier to children who are in a position to benefit from the opportunities that it offers. The School offers eligible parents or guardians financial assistance with tuition fees, usually aimed towards the Senior School. Bursaries are awarded as a discount of between 10% and 100% of tuition fees, depending upon the financial, compassionate or other pertinent circumstances of the applicants. The parents of over 60 Wellingborough School pupils, aged 11 to 18, are currently in receipt of a means-tested Bursary.

Fees per term (2023–2024). Preparatory School: £3,743 (Nursery & Reception), £3,910 (Years 1–2), £4,553 (Year 3) £5,202 (Year 4), £5,794 (Years 5–6); Senior School: £6,057 (Years 7–8), £6,537 (Years 9–13).

Term of Entry. New pupils are accepted throughout the year. The largest entry is in September at the beginning of each academic year.

Old Wellingburian Club. All former pupils who have spent at least one year in the School are eligible for membership. Correspondence should be addressed to the OW Club Secretary at the School.

Charitable status. Wellingborough School is a Registered Charity, number 1101485.

Governors:
Mr P Tyldesley, Esq, BA, MRICS (*Chairman*)
Mrs D Line, BA, CA, CA SA
Mrs C Bruce, MA
Mr I M Cantelo, BEng Hons, CEng, MIET
Dr C Duncan, MBBS, DRCOG, MRCGP
Mr N M Lashbrook, BA Hons
Mr S Marriott, Esq
Mr J Smith, BSc Hons, MRICS
Ms Susan Tafeni, MBA, MA, BSc, RN
Mr R Thakrar, Esq, BSc Hons, MBCS
Miss R Turner, BA Hons
Mr D Waller, Esq, MA Oxon, MA London

Staff:
***Headmaster*: A N Holman**, MA Cantab, MEd

Bursar: N A Johnson, MA Cranfield
Head of the Prep School: K Owen, BSc Exeter
Deputy Head (*Academic*): C A Gamble, MA Cantab
Deputy Head (*Operations*): R Spiby, MA Cranfield
Deputy Head (*Pastoral*): Q Wiseman, BA Newcastle
Head of Lower Prep: R M Girling, BEd Cambridge
Deputy Head (*Prep School*): C Petrie, BSc Loughborough
Director of Learning & Teaching: S R Medley, BSc Durham

Wellington College

Duke's Ride, Crowthorne, Berkshire RG45 7PU

Tel: 01344 444101 (The Master)
01344 444013 (Director of Admissions)
01344 444020 (Chief Operating Officer)
01344 444000 (Reception)
email: info@wellingtoncollege.org.uk
website: www.wellingtoncollege.org.uk
X/Twitter: @WellingtonUK
Facebook: @WellingtonCollege
Instagram: @wellingtoncollege
LinkedIn: /school/wellingtoncollege

Set within 400 acres of parkland in Berkshire and less than an hour's drive from London and Heathrow, Wellington College is one of the UK's and the world's great co-educational boarding and day schools. It seeks to provide young people with the knowledge, skills and character to serve and help shape a better world. Its innovative and interesting use of technology in the classroom, combined with its emphasis on pedagogical research, outstanding teaching, and pupil-centred learning, ensures that Wellington is at the forefront of educational advance.

An exciting fusion of heritage and modernity characterises our educational philosophy. Our curriculum, facilities and teaching methods are constantly adapting to the challenges of preparing young people for an ever-changing world. Wellington College is a school which is dynamic in every sense of the word, and yet all that we do is rooted firmly in our five College values – kindness, courage, respect, integrity and responsibility – values which underpin every aspect of life at Wellington.

Organisation. There are approximately 1,100 pupils, with 580 boys and 520 girls, spread across all age groups. All pupils belong to one of seventeen houses: seven within the main College buildings, ten in the grounds. An eighteenth House, a new co-educational sixth form house, will open in 2024. Fifteen of the houses accommodate the 80%+ who board at Wellington. There are two specific day houses, one each for girls and for boys. Year 9 boarders share rooms in their first year and may do so in a second or third year, but then move on to their own room. There is a central dining hall and meals are taken here on a cafeteria basis, although three houses have their own dining facilities. The V&A café is open during school hours for drinks and snacks. The school has its own medical officer and a 9-bed health centre constantly staffed by fully qualified nurses.

Pastoral. Wellington prides itself on its outstanding levels of pastoral support. Pupil and staff-led Mental Health initiatives, alongside our nationally recognised Wellbeing curriculum not only help our pupils successfully navigate their teenage years, but also prepare them for healthy, happy and successful lives. House life lies at the heart of each pupil's experience, and it comes as no surprise that every Wellingtonian is convinced that their house is the best. Housemasters and housemistresses, dedicated tutor teams, matrons and housekeepers all ensure that the House truly is a home away from home.

Academic. Wellingtonians study GCSEs, followed by the IB Diploma or A Levels and, whichever route they take, results are superb. In 2023, 37% of grades at GCSE were 9s (the most common grade for Wellingtonians) and 86% 9–7, with 10 students achieving a clean sweep of 9s. The combined total of IB and A Level grades was impressive: 31% of grades achieved were A*/7 and 74% A*A/76. 100 Wellingtonians have been offered Oxbridge places over the past five years, while 25–30 move on each year to American universities, including several to Ivy League universities.

Sport. In 2022/23 there continued to be over 20 different sports on offer at Wellington, involving 200 teams in around 1,500 fixtures, and it was yet another bumper year for Wellington Sport. Over 30 Wellingtonians were involved in national level sport, with 12 teams or individuals taking part in national finals.

Performing Arts. Music, Dance and Drama are stunning, with 60% of pupils taking instrumental or speech and drama lessons with some 1,000 lessons taking place each week and over 50 visiting teachers. 2022/23 was an outstanding year for the Arts at Wellington. Not only have we continued to provide a whole range of activities for our students, but we have been externally recognised by being awarded Artsmark Platinum and being nominated for a TES Excellence in Creative Arts Award for our Festival of Musical Theatre, the finale of our wonderful Arts Festival in October.

Co-curricular. Leadership, service to others and developing an international outlook are also central to the College's core values which is why co-curricular activities include CCF, Duke of Edinburgh's Award, and a pioneering Global Social Leaders scheme, in which pupils learn to create and run innovative social action projects, tackling local and global issues.

Clubs and societies range from Green Power Racing to the Field Gun team, from WTV (Wellington's own television company) and its pupil-run radio station DukeBox, to a full range of more traditional pastimes such as Photography, Creative Writing, Debating and the Model United Nations society.

Admission to the School. Most pupils enter the school in September (at the start of Year 9) when they are between 13 and 14 years of age. There are occasionally places available for pupils at 14+ (Year 10). Around 50 pupils join the College for the Sixth Form (applications open at the end of Year 10). Registration (with £300 fee) is online. Those registered for 13+ entry (by the end of Year 5) sit the ISEB Common Pre-Test in the Michaelmas term of Year 6. Selection for a subsequent assessment day (usually in the Lent term of Year 6) is based in small part on the results of the Pre-Test and in much larger part on a school reference. Those who are successful are then offered a place conditional on a satisfactory reference from their current school at the end of Year 8. A waiting list also operates. Pupils who have missed the registration date for 13+ entry have the opportunity to go via a Late Admissions Route. All details and registration forms are to be found on the website.

Scholarships. Detailed information about the scholarships available on entry at age 13+ or 16+ can be found on our website. Scholarships at 13+ are only awarded in Academics and Music. The most prestigious, named Academic scholarships and scholarships in other disciplines (Art, Drama, Dance and Sport) are awarded at the end of Year 9 to reward not only ability but also scholarly attitude. Prospective scholars are invited to participate in Inspire Days in their areas of particular interest during Year 8.

For entry at 16+, scholarships are awarded in the above areas as part of the full application process.

As well as it being a great honour and accolade, pupils awarded scholarships upon entry to the College, and those awarded at the end of Year 9, are expected to be leaders and role models within their field of interest. They will also take part in a programme of extension activities and opportunities appropriate to their particular area of talent. Music scholars, for example, attend regular masterclasses with visiting professionals and Academic award holders partake in an extension programme of study designed by our Director of Academic Extension.

Scholarships do not carry any financial benefit. The only exception to this is Music Scholarships which allow for free tuition in two instruments and free composition and Alexander Technique lessons.

Fee-assisted places. Widening access to Wellington is at the heart of the Governors' and Master's vision for the future of the College. All financial aid in terms of fee reduction is therefore awarded via a means-testing procedure (details on our website and from the Chief Operating Officer's office). Our aim is to enable an increasing number of families, who otherwise would not be able to afford the fees at Wellington, to send their son or daughter to the College. Means-tested bursaries may be up to 100% of College fees, depending on individual family circumstances.

Foundation places. Very generous remission, including free places based on means-testing, are available for the sons and daughters of deceased military servicemen and servicewomen and of others who have died in acts of selfless bravery, subject to entry requirement and according to the rules of the Foundation. Further details are available from the Chief Operating Officer's office.

The Prince Albert Foundation. The Prince Albert Foundation is a scholarship programme aimed at widening participation to families who would not normally consider or be able to access independent education, and for whom we can offer a genuine shift in opportunity. Currently there are 10–15 fully funded Prince Albert Scholarships awarded each year, predominantly at 16+. Children who are eligible for Prince Albert Scholarships are those whose families are at a socio-economic disadvantage; all families are means assessed by the Chief Operating Officer. There is often a further relevant need/desire for boarding. Candidates must meet our minimum academic criteria for entrance; we assess potential as well as current achievement, and actively encourage applicants who will maximise opportunities at the College – including academic, sporting, music and student leadership. The Prince Albert Foundation is not a programme designed to recruit pupils with a significant sporting talent.

Fees per term (2023–2024). Boarders: £16,310, Day: £11,920. Separate charges totalling £366 per instrument are made for musical tuition (10 lessons). The school runs an attractive fees in advance scheme for parents with capital sums available.

The Wellington Community. Our role is to build a supportive, global professional and social network of students, Old Wellingtonians, parents (current and past), grandparents, staff and partner schools. We deliver a diverse programme of engagement events and offer careers support, guidance and mentoring opportunities by drawing on our incredible resources within the Community; we truly champion the diverse skill sets our unique Community has to offer. We also run Wellington College's own networking website, Wellington Connect, where all members of our Wellington Community can share expertise, find (or offer) mentoring opportunities, and make connections with friends past and present. To find out more please email the Wellington Community office on community@wellingtoncollege.org.uk or go to the Wellington Community website www.wellycom.net or sign up to Wellington Connect at www.wellingtonconnect.co.uk

The Wellington Group. Wellington builds strong external partnerships to broaden its impact in education and continues to have mutually beneficial partnerships with a wide variety of schools, including Special Schools, Secondary and Primary schools. The Wellington family of schools includes Eagle House prep school and eight schools in China, India and Thailand, with new schools in development. This network supports opportunities for cultural dialogue and understanding and broadens access to world-class education including through bursaries and regional education initiatives.

Further information including details of Visitors Days can be found on the website, and the Admissions Office can be contacted on 01344 444013.

Charitable status. Wellington College is a Registered Charity, number 309093. It exists to provide education for boys and girls aged 13–18.

President: HRH The Duke of Kent, KG, GCMG, GCVO, ADC, DL

Vice-President & Chairman of Governors: Mr William Jackson, MA

Ex officio Governors:
The Archbishop of Canterbury, MA, BA, DipMin
Arthur Charles Valerian Wellesley, 9th Duke of Wellington, MA, Hon DLitt, OBE, DL

Governors:
Lord Karan Bilimoria, CBE, DL
Ron Dennis, CBE
James Garvey, BA, BAI, MA
Dr Emma Judge, CPsychol
Mrs Felicity Kirk, LLB
Dr Christie Marr, BA Hons, MSc, DPhil, MBA
Mrs Jill May, BA
Mrs Emma McKendrick, BA, FRSA
Mark Milliken-Smith, KC
Ms Virginia Rhodes, BA Hons
Ms Helen Stevenson, MA
The Rt Hon The Lord Strathclyde, CH
Lt Gen Sir Christopher Tickell, KBE, MA

***Master*: James Dahl**, MA
Second Master: Mrs Cressida Henderson, BA
Director of Safeguarding: Mrs Delyth Lynch, BSc
Director of EDI & Social Responsibility: Mrs Naima Charlier
Director of Admissions: Phil Mann, BSc
Deputy Head (Academic): Benjamin Evans, BSc
Deputy Head (Co-curricular): Nick Creed, BA, MEd
Deputy Head (Pastoral & Wellbeing): Tom Wayman, BA, MPhil
Director of The Bridge: Iain Henderson, BA
Head of the Wellington Community & Director of Strategic Advancement: Murray Lindo, BA, MA, MSc, CIPD
Deputy Head (Teacher Development & Character Education): Mrs Katy Granville-Chapman, BA, MSc

Director of Academic Extension: Mrs Amanda Campion, MA
Director of Arts & Music: Simon Williamson, MA, FRCO
Director of Digital Learning: Dr Julian O'Loughlin, MSc, PhD
Director of HE, Careers & International Universities: Dr Emma Ramsey, BA, MA, PhD
Director of IB: Richard Atherton, BSc, MPhil
Director of Organisation: Dr Will Heathcote, MPhys, DPhil
Director of Performance: John Rawlinson, BSc
Director of Science, Technology & Engineering: Mrs Miranda Patterson, BSc
Director of Sport: Dan Pratt, MSc
Director of Teaching & Learning: Dr Rachelle Kirkham, MA, PhD
Director of Wellington Leadership & Coaching Institute: Mrs Emmie Bidston, BA

Heads of Department:
Art: Mrs Alice Carpenter, BA Hons
Biology: Mrs Astrid Edmunds, BSc
Business: Simon Roundell, MA
Chemistry: Dr Caroline Evans, MChem, PhD
Classics: Dr Matthew Johncock, MA, PhD
Computer Science: Stephen Barraclough, BSc
Dance: Mrs Caroline Kenworthy, BA; Mrs Clare Cooke, BA
Design, Engineering & Technology: Robert Winter, BSc
Drama: Nick Huntington, BA Hons
Economics: Dushy Clarke, BA, MSc
English: Ms Estella Gutulan, BA
EPQ & HPQ: Ms Cherry Briggs, MBiochem, MSc, MA
French: Mrs Sandra Aktas, BA, BSc
Geography: Timothy Rothwell, MA
German: Simon Kirkham, BA Hons
History: Ben Lewsley, BA
Mathematics: Paul Cootes, MA, MSc
Modern Foreign Languages: Dr Rachelle Kirkham, MA, PhD
Music (Academic): Sean Farrell, BA
Philosophy & Religion: Tom Kirby, BA, MSt
Physical Education: Mrs Kate Pratt, BSc
Physics: Adam Hicks, MEng
Politics: Paul Dunne, BA, MSc
Psychology: David Rea, BSc
Spanish: Mrs Catherine Willis-Phillips, MA
Theory of Knowledge: Dr James Tapley, BSc, MA, PhD
Wellbeing: Ian Morris, BA
Academic Support & SEND: Mrs Kam Opie, BSc, MSc, SpLD Diploma; Mrs Ellie Farrell, SpLD Diploma, PG Dip, GTCL

CC CCF: Sam Wilson, BSc
Chaplain: Fr Adrian Stark-Ordish, BA
Chief Operating Officer: Stephen Crouch, BA, ACA
Operations Bursar: Brian Cannon, MSyl, MCGI
Group Estates Bursar: Edwin Wai, BA Hons, MSc
Director of Finance: Mrs Laura Tamplin
Head of Prince Albert Foundation: Ms Sarah Miller
Legal & Compliance Director: Mrs Katherine Baker, MA
International Managing Director: Scott Bryan
Director of IT Services & Development: Tony Whelton
Medical Officer: Dr Helen Rutherford
Health Centre Nurse Manager: Mrs Tracey Coles
Head of Student Emotional Health & Wellbeing: Dr Jenny Griggs
Head of Marketing: Mrs Vicky Williams, BA
Registrar: Mrs Louise Peate, BSc
EA to the Master: Mrs Angela Reed
EA to the Chief Operating Officer: Mrs Lisa Thompson

Wellington School

South St, Wellington, Somerset TA21 8NT
Tel: 01823 668800
01823 668803
email: admissions@wellington-school.org.uk
website: www.wellington-school.org.uk
X/Twitter: @wellingtonsch1
Facebook: @WellingtonSchool
Instagram: @wellingtonschool1

Motto: *Nisi dominus frustra*

Founded in 1837, Wellington School is a co-educational, academically selective school providing a friendly, disciplined environment and a wide range of co-curricular opportunities. The School was this year shortlisted for several awards and was the winner of the Boarding Schools Association for Best Community Work.

Situation. Located on the southern edge of Wellington, at the foot of the Blackdown Hills, this fully co-educational School is equidistant from Tiverton Parkway and Taunton Railway Stations. The M5 approach road (Junction 26) is within a mile. Currently there are 600 pupils in the Lower and Upper Schools (11–18 years), of whom 20% board.

Buildings. The School has witnessed an extensive building programme over recent years with a state-of-the-art study centre in the Duke's Building, brand new floodlit all-weather hockey pitch, refurbished Sixth Form Centre and cafe.

The John Kendall-Carpenter Science Centre has state-of-the-art laboratories and lecture theatre, a multimillion pound sports complex, a purpose-built Prep School and a new classroom block and examination hall. Major improvements to Performing Arts facilities, includes a new theatre space. In 2017 a new junior girls' boarding house with en-suite rooms was opened.

Grounds. There are 35 acres of playing fields as well as a new floodlit all-weather hockey pitch, squash court, an indoor swimming pool and an indoor and outdoor climbing wall.

Houses. There are mixed School Houses including Day and Boarding pupils, with many inter-house competitions. In addition, there are 5 boarding houses in total.

There is a central Dining Hall and all meals are served on a cafeteria basis. The School also has its own well equipped laundry.

There is a fully equipped Health Centre, with a trained staff under the direction of the School Medical Officer.

Academic Organisation. The School is divided into the Lower School (Year 7–9), Upper School (Year 9–Year 11) and the Sixth Form. The Prep School (Nursery–Year 6) is on a separate, adjoining campus.

Most pupils enter the Senior School at Year 7, 9 or 12. The curriculum in Years 7, 8 and 9 is designed to allow pupils to develop the skills needed to succeed at GCSE and features a good range of practical and more academic subjects including Latin. At GCSE all pupils study English, English Literature and Mathematics and a further six subjects. Pupils have a free choice of studying three sciences separately or as Dual Award Science. The Mathematics and Science courses lead to IGCSE qualifications. The most able mathematicians take IGCSE at the end of Year 10 before taking Additional Mathematics in Year 11. Students have a free choice from a wide range of subjects in the Sixth Form as well as the Extended Project Qualification. A system of grades every term and tutor groups ensure that academic monitoring of pupils is supportive and effective.

Religious Education is part of the curriculum in the Lower School and is an option for study at GCSE and A Level. The School is Christian in tradition and there is a short Act of Worship in the School Chapel on each weekday with a longer Sunday service. The content and form of these services are based on contemporary Anglican procedures. Attendance is expected although sensitivity is shown towards pupils of other faiths for whom alternative provision can be made.

Music. Tuition is available on all orchestral instruments, as well as piano, organ, drum kit and percussion, classical and electric guitars and voice. The department consists of 2 full-time, 1 part-time and 25 specialist instrumental staff. The School is equipped with Bosendorfer and Yamaha pianos. There is a large Rodgers Digital Organ in the Chapel. Some 30 ensembles rehearse each week, giving plentiful opportunities to performers of all ages and all instruments. The department currently runs a wide range of choirs of various genres including the renowned Chapel Choir. Concerts of all kinds take place throughout each term and world class musicians to the School to give recitals and masterclasses. Pupils are entered for ABRSM, Trinity Guildhall and Rockschool exams each term.

Physical Education and Games. Pioneering Sport and Wellbeing Department with all pupils playing games regularly, unless exempt for medical reasons. Wellbeing, which is also part of the curriculum for Years 7 to 11, takes place in the Sports Complex and includes nutrition, psychology and mental health with the aim of embedding physical activity as part of a healthy lifestyle. All pupils learn to swim and are given the opportunity to take part in as many sports as possible. In the winter term, rugby and hockey are the main sports; in the spring term hockey, netball and cross-country running; in the summer term athletics, girls and boys cricket, tennis and swimming. Team practices take place throughout the week with matches on Saturday afternoons.

Out of School and CCF Activities. All pupils from Year 10 upwards either join the large CCF contingent, with army, naval and RAF sections, or are engaged in Citizens Wellington with volunteering activities on a weekly basis, ranging from community services and conservation, to music, art and creative activities such as producing school radio podcasts. Outdoor Education, both within the CCF and as part of the School's extensive programme to introduce all students from Year 7 upwards, includes camping trips, Duke of Edinburgh's Award and climbing and caving clubs are very popular, with many trips organised for all year groups. The CCF also has a highly respected Corps of Drums, which frequently features in local ceremonial events. Societies, in addition to the above, include art, chess and drama at various levels, STEM, computing and others.

Careers. A careers and higher education coordinator offers a guidance service including visits to and from employers and universities, a careers speed-dating event, careers talks, a careers networking dinner and careers fair with local schools.

Entry. Entrance exam for Year 7, 9 and Sixth Form. There is a registration fee of £100 for all pupils and a refundable deposit of £400.

Scholarships and Bursaries. A number of academic and sport, drama, performing arts and art and design scholarships are offered each year for entry at 11+ and 13+. Music scholarships are awarded for entry at 11+, 13+ and above. Awards may be increased by an income-related bursary. A small number of awards are offered for the Sixth Form.

Fees per term (2023–2024). Boarders: £10,120–£13,330, Weekly Boarders: £8,425–£10.420, International Boarders: £10,930–£13.895. Fees include tuition, board, laundry, medical attention and Health Centre and books. Day pupils: £5,995–£6,895 (excluding lunch).

Extras. Apart from purely personal expenses, the termly extras are private music lessons from £31.00 per 40 minutes; EAL lessons at various rates depending on need.

Charitable status. Wellington School is a Registered Charity, number 1161447. It aims to provide a happy, caring co-educational day and boarding community, where pupils are provided with the opportunity of making best use of their academic experience and the School enrichment activities, in order to enhance their overall preparation for life after the age of eighteen.

Governing Body:

Chairman: Mrs A Govey, MSc
Vice Chairman: Mr R Palfrey, MA, PGC
Mrs S Page, MA, PGCE
Rear Admiral R Harding, CBE, FRAeS
Mr D James, MEng, CEng, MiMechE, MBA Ess
Mr M Rowe
Mr P Tait, MA
Mr J Vick, MA, PGCE
Mrs S Merry, BSc, RGN
Mr K Wheatley, LLB, PGCE, NCTJ

***Headmaster*: Mr Eugene du Toit**, MA, MBA

Academic Deputy Head: Dr H Barker, BA Hons, PhD
Deputy Head (*Pastoral*): Mr A Kemp, BSc, PGCE
Deputy Head (*Co-curricular*): Mr N Renyard, BA Hons, MSc, PGCE
Head of Sixth Form: Mrs L MacAlister, BA Hons
Head of Lower School and Co-curricular: Mr J Swarbrick, BEd, BSc
Head of Upper School: Mrs S A Dean, BA, PGCE
Head of Boarding: Mr S Costello, BA Hons, PGCE

Academic Staff:
Mr C A Askew, BA, PGCE
Miss I Askew, BA
Dr H Barker, BA Hons, PhD
Mrs J Berron
Mr J Bird, MSc, MA, PGCE, BSc
Mrs K Bishop, BA Hons, MA, PGCE
Mr D Brammall
Mr P J Buckingham, MA, PGCE
Mrs G Burtchaell, BA, PGCE
Mr S Campbell, CELTA, MBA, BA, PGCE
Mr J Caulfield, BA, QTS, NPQSL
Mrs D Clarke, BA Hons, PGCE
Mrs N Clewes, BEng Hons, PGCE
Mr D Cole, BA
Miss M Collins, BA, MA, PGCE
Mr S Costello, BA Hons, PGCE
Mrs V Daley, BSc, PGCE
Mrs C Davies, BA, PGCE
Mrs S A Dean, BSc, PGCE
Mr M E Downes, BSc, PGCE
Mr G Durston, BSc Hons
Mrs H Durston, BA, PGCE
Mr B Elkins, BD Hons, PGCE
Mr T Fasham, BSc, PGCE
Mr L Foot, BSc
Dr P T Galley, BSc, DIC, PhD, PGCE
Mr W Garrett, BA, PGCE
Mr A Gerolemou, BA, MA
Mr E Gillett, BA, MSCi, PGCE
Mr D Goodchild, BSc Hons, MSc
Mr L Greany, BSc Hons, PGCE
Miss E Greenway, BSc Hons, PGCE
Mrs E Gumbrell, FdA, BA, PGCE
Mrs L Gurney, BSc
Mr C Hamilton, MChem, ACA, PGCE
Mrs I Hare, BA Hons, PGCE
Mrs S Harrod-Booth, BEng, PGCE, MA
Mrs L Hayward, BSc
Mr D Healey
Dr K A Hodson, BA, MA
Mr B Hopgood, BSc
Mr B House, BSc
Mrs L Howe, BSc Hons, MRAC
Mr J Ilett, BA, PGCE
Miss R Isdell-Carpenter, BA, PGCE
Mrs C James, BA Hons, PGCE
Mr T Johns, MBA, PGCE, BSc
Dr A R Jolliffe, BA, MA, DPhil
Mrs T Kaya, BA, TESOL
Mr A Kemp, BSc, PGCE
Mr P Lawrence
Mr J-M Legg, BA, PGCE
Mrs L E Leonard, BA
Mrs L MacAlister, BA Hons
MIss L Marref
Miss R L Marsden, BA, PGCE
Mr R Marsh, BA, PGCE
Ms K McClelland, BA
Mrs C Merrett, PGCE, BA
Mrs G Michael, LAMDA, BA Hons, PGCE
Miss S Middleton, BA, PGCE
Mr M Milne, BA, PGCE
Mr A Moy, BSc Hons, PGCE
Mr S Nash
Miss E Paget, PGCE, MSc, BSc
Ms H Payne
Mr A Phillips, BSc, PGCE
Mr H Phillips, BEd
Ms G Redman, BA Hons
Mr N Renyard, MSc, BA, PGCE
Mrs T Robertson, BA Hons, MPhil, PGCE
Mr C J Sampson, BMus
Mr T Sampson
Mrs A Sands, MA Hons, PGCE
Miss K Sass, BA Hons, PGCE

Mr I Schmidt, BA, PGCE
Miss E Scott, BSc, PGCE
Mr A C Shaw, BA, MSci, PGCE, LCGI
Mrs R Shaw, LTCL, GTCL
Mrs K Stent, BA, PGCE
Mr R E Stevens, BSocSc, PGCE
Mrs R Stratton, BA
Mr J Swarbrick, BSc, QTS
Miss S F L Toase, BSc, PGCE
Mrs E Trace
Mr A J Trewhella, BA, ARCO, PGCE
Miss C Walker, BA
Miss R Watson, MSc Hons, PGCE
Mr B Wilkinson, BMus, PGCE
Mr A Wilson, BA
Mr J Wright

Head of Admissions: Mrs R Debenham, BA, FCIPD
Medical Officer: Dr R Yates

Wells Cathedral School

The Liberty, Wells, Somerset BA5 2ST
Tel: 01749 834200
email: admissions@wells.cathedral.school
website: wells.cathedral.school
X/Twitter: @wellscathschool
Facebook: @wellscathedralschool
Instagram: @wellscathedralschool
LinkedIn: /school/wells-cathedral-school

In 909AD Wells Cathedral School was formed to provide education for the choir boys at Wells Cathedral. Today, Wells Cathedral School is a family-orientated co-educational boarding and day school for 2–18 year olds which provides an all-round education alongside world-class Specialist Music and Chorister training. Their vision is to inspire every individual pupil to nurture their talents in a vibrant, creative, spiritual and stimulating environment to become a responsible global citizen. Their core values are Creativity, Aspiration, Responsibility and Endeavour (CARE).

There is a Senior and Prep School with over 700 boys and girls aged from 2 to 18. Boarders number around 240, while the remainder are day pupils (about 40% of pupils in the Senior School board), and a Prep School aged boarding option for pupils from Year 4. Once accepted, a child normally remains in the School without further Entrance Examination until the age of 18+.

Fees per term (2023–2024). Sixth Form: Boarders £13,343, Day £8,186. Years 9–11: Boarders £12,529, Day £7,480. Years 7–8: Boarders £12,065, Day £7,231. Years 4–6: Boarders £9,553–£10,604; Day £5,211–£6,261; Reception–Year 3: £3,112–£4,686. Nursery: various sessions available.

Scholarships and bursaries. Scholarships are awarded to recognise current talent and potential in the fields of Academics, Art, Drama, Mathematics, General Music (for those not looking to join our Specialist Music Scheme) and Sport, for pupils joining the School in Years 7, 9, 10 and Lower Sixth. In addition to a financial award of up to 50% for truly exceptional candidates (the majority of Scholars are awarded 10%), Scholars receive enhanced educational opportunities and privileges to help them develop their talents. In addition, means-tested bursaries may also be available. The deadline to apply is early December. Scholarship Days are held in January, and decisions are announced in February.

For pre-professional musicians wishing to join our Specialist Music Programme, we offer a number of music awards based upon the standard and quality of applicants (assessed at Music Auditions held three times throughout the year) and individual financial circumstances. We also offer places to 'general' musicians who might wish to take advantage of the wealth of musical opportunity here, but who might not wish to enrol on the Specialist pathway.

The School is one of only four in England designated by the Department for Education to provide specialist musical education. The DfE therefore provides generous assistance (up to 100% of fees) with tuition, boarding and music fees for up to 80 gifted musicians per year. These grants are means-tested according to parental income, and are provided by the DfE Music & Dance Scheme.

In addition, all choristers automatically benefit from a 25% discount on tuition fees and a 50% discount on boarding fees, and may also be considered for further bursaries and financial assistance (on average, Choristers receive around 50% off their School fees). Once they have left the Choir at the end of Year 9 (or sometimes earlier if voice changes necessitate), they receive a discount worth 5% of their School fees for each year they were in the Choir, worth up to 20%, for the rest of their time at the School. We welcome enquiries and chorister applications at any point. Special arrangements can be made for children from overseas.

For further details of awards, contact the Admissions team, Tel: 01749 834441, email: admissions@wells.cathedral.school.

Situations and buildings. The medieval city of Wells, with its famous Cathedral and a population of only 10,500, is the smallest city in England. It is just over 20 miles from Bath and Bristol where there is a good rail service, and easily accessed from the M4 and M5 motorways. Bristol International Airport is a 40-minute drive away.

The School occupies all but one of the canonical houses in The Liberty, keeping its medieval and 18th-century atmosphere, whilst providing for the needs of modern boarding education. There are modern classrooms and science laboratories built amongst walled gardens. There is a 25-metre covered swimming pool, tennis and netball courts, brand new astroturf pitch, three sports fields and an all-weather hard play area. A sports hall provides indoor facilities for tennis, badminton, cricket, basketball, volleyball, hockey, five-a-side football, climbing and a multi-gym. There are theatrical and concert facilities, including an award-winning concert hall, a music technology centre, a computer studies centre, art, design and technology department, drama studio, dance studio, library and sixth form centre.

There are eight boarding houses; one for prep boarders, one for Upper Sixth boarders and a further six in the Senior School, three for boys and three for girls, the most senior pupils having study-bedrooms. The aim is to give security to the younger pupils and to develop a sense of responsibility in the older pupils.

Organisation and curriculum. Despite its national and international reputation, the School has retained close links with the local community, and its fundamental aim is to provide all pupils with an education consistent with the broad principles of Christianity. More specifically, the School aims to be a well-regulated community in which pupils may learn to live in harmony and mutual respect with each other and with the adults who care for them. The curriculum has been designed to enable all children who gain entry to the School to develop fully all their abilities, and to take their place in due course in tertiary education and the adult community of work and leisure.

The emphasis is on setting by ability in particular subjects rather than streaming. There is every attempt to avoid early specialisation. There is a Sixth Form of some 200 taking A Level courses in all major academic subjects.

The majority of pupils take up places at Russell Group Universities, with between 5 and 10% of the Upper Sixth being offered places each year at Oxford and Cambridge. The majority of Music Specialists will be offered places at the leading conservatories in the UK and globally, often with scholarship awards.

Societies. There is a wide range of indoor and outdoor activities in which pupils must participate, although the choice is theirs. Outdoor education is an important part of the curriculum. Besides a Combined Cadet Force with Army and Navy sections, and a Duke of Edinburgh's Award scheme, activities as diverse as photography, sailing and golf are also on offer. Ballet and riding lessons can also be arranged.

Music. The School is one of four in England designated and grant-aided by the Department for Education (DfE) to provide special education for gifted young musicians, who are eligible for substantial financial assistance. Wells is unique in that both specialist and non-specialist musicians are able to develop their aptitudes within a normal school environment. These talents are widely acknowledged by audiences at concerts given by pupils from Wells throughout the world.

There are over 130 talented pupils following specially devised timetables which combine advanced instrumental tuition and ensemble work with academic opportunity. More than half of the School learns at least one musical instrument. Children in Year 1 are given the opportunity to learn a string instrument, usually cello or violin, as part of their music curriculum, which they can choose to continue in Year 2 as a paid lesson should they wish. Pupils receive the highest quality teaching, often leading to music conservatoires and a career in music. Central to specialist music training are the opportunities to perform in public and there is a full concert diary. There are also regular concerts by the many ensembles in the School.

The Wellensian Association. Old Wellensians, Wells Cathedral School, Wells, Somerset BA5 2ST.

Charitable status. Wells Cathedral School Limited is a Registered Charity, number 310212. It is a charitable trust for the purpose of promoting the cause of education in accordance with the doctrine of the Church of England.

Patron: HM King Charles III

Governors:
Chair of Governors: Mr David Brown, OBE
Prebendary Harry Musselwhite
Prebendary Emeritus Barbara Bates
Mr Andrew Campbell-Orde
Mr Martin Cooke
Canon Dr Megan Daffern
Mr Andrew Gummer
Mr Tim Lewis
Mrs Dorothy Nancekievill
Mr Robert Powell
Mr Kris Robbetts
Professor Jeffrey Sharkey
Mrs Elizabeth Shelton

***Head Master*: Alastair Tighe**

Deputy Head (*Pastoral*): Martin Ashton
Deputy Head (*Academic*): Natalie Perry
Director of Music: Alex Laing

Senior School Teaching Staff
Claudia Alabiso (*Modern Foreign Languages*)
Helen Arendse (*Mathematics*)
Martin Ashton (*Deputy Head (Pastoral), Designated Safeguarding Lead, English, Media Studies, Christian Union*)
Lucy Balderson (*Music*, *Head of Year 10/11*, *Retention Officer*)
Jonathan Barnard (*Science*)
Julia Bird (*Head of EAL*, *Head of Upper Sixth Form, including WISC*)
Jeremy Boot (*Head of Humanities*, *Geography*)
Neil Bowen (*Head of English*)
Harvey Brink (*Head of Academic Music*)
Samuel Broderick (*History with Politics*)
Kate Brown (*Learning Support*, *Modern Foreign Languages*)
Ross Brown (*Coordinator of Brass Studies*)
John Byrne (*Coordinator of Keyboard Studies*)
Raul Cabarcas-Barros (*Spanish*, *French*)
Louise Cannon (*Dance*)
Nicola Connock (*Head of Mathematics*)
Jack Coward (*Music Technology*)
Sarah Cowell (*EAL*)
Andrew Davies (*Head of Year 9*, *Religion*, *Philosophy & Ethics*)
Fiona Davies (*Chemistry*)
Shelley Deans (*Drama*, *Theatre Studies*)
Isabel Dempster (*PSHE*)
Jules Desmarchelier (*Director of Languages*)
Mark Dignum (*Head of Learning Support*)
Christopher Dine (*Head of Academic & Co-Curricular Operations*, *Physics*)
Luke Dosanjh (*EAL*)
Christopher Eldridge (*Head of History*)
Mandy Fielding (*Food Technology*)
Christopher Finch (*Head of Pupil Programmes*, *Leader of Vocal Studies*)
Janice Gearon (*English*, *History of Art*)
Dominic Grass (*Mathematics*)
Helen Gray (*Head of Chemistry*, *Assistant Head of Lower Sixth*)
Mark Grinsell (*Chemistry*)
Penny Hall (*Learning Support*)
Stephen Harvey (*Private Learning Coordinator*)

David Heath (*Head of Art*)
Gemma Heath (*Art*)
Gill Hoadley (*Mathematics*)
Naomi Holland (Teacher of Speech and Drama: Peripatetic)
Aryana Hsieh (*Chinese*)
Lauren James (*Learning Support*)
Violaine James-Cudworth (*Cover Supervisor*)
Teresa Jarman (*Business Studies & Computing*)
Jessica Jarvis (*Biology*)
Echo Kenny (*Cantonese*)
Oliver Kershaw (*Head of Outdoor Education*)
Alex Laing (*Director of Music*)
Edward Leaker (*Head of Instrumental & Vocal Coaching (VMS), Coordinator of Woodwind Studies*)
Lucy Lee (*English*)
Jane Lipton (*Badminton*)
Simon Lloyd (*Academic Music*)
Wendy Mahon (*Business & Economics*)
Heidi Martini-Smith (*Learning Support*)
James Mayes (*History, Classics, Latin and Head of Hockey*)
Neil McPherson (*English*)
Daniel Meehan (*PE*)
Kathryn Mitchell (*Subject Leader KS3 Science, Head of Academic Enrichment*)
Bryan Moore (*Head of Computing, Mathematics*)
James Moretti (*Mathematics*)
Rebecca Murdoch (*Religion, Philosophy & Ethics, Geography, Head of Lower Sixth Form*)
Robin Murdoch (*Mathematics Department Coordinator*)
Alison Nash (*Music*)
Eliana Nelson (*Head of Photography*)
Jayne Obradovic (*Head of Pupil Experience & Wellbeing Coordinator, Percussion Coordinator, Summer Schools*)
Kenneth Padgett (*Head of Science, Head of Biology*)
Clare Pattemore (*Boarders Activities*)
Natalie Perry (*Deputy Head, Academic*)
Lawrence Plum (*Head of Classics, CCF*)
Brian Poxon (*Head of Religion, Philosophy and Ethics*)
Gemma Pritchard (*Head of Academic PE, Head of Girls' Tennis*)
Elsbeth Ralls (*Assistant Head of Years 10/11*)
Kimberley Richards (*EAL*)
David Rowley (*Geography, Geology, Head of Years 7/8*)
Sally Rowley (*English, Head of Sixth Form*)
Constantine Sillem (*Spanish, French*)
Geoffrey Smith (*Mathematics*)
Simon Smith (*Coordinator of Strings Studies*)
Saffron Stockall (*Psychology*)
Letty Stott (*Head of Music Performance*)
Emi Thornburn (*Mathematics*)
Charlotte Tibbs (*Sport*)
Damian Todres (*Head of Creative Arts, Director of Drama & Theatre Studies*)
Rosie Watch (*Learning Support*)
Tom Webley (*Director of Sport*)
Adam West (*Science*)
Georgina Wheeler (*Head of Physics*)
Mark White (*Head of Music Technology*)
Laurence Whitehead (*Academic Music*)
Lara Williams (*English*)
Tammie Williams (*Head of Netball*)
Veronica Zausmer (*EAL*)

Prep School
Head of Prep School: Jody Wells
Deputy Head: Karl Gibson
Head of Pre-Prep: Rebecca Perdrix

Laura Bain (*Head of Girls' Games*)
Sarah Jane Beats (*Mathematics, Head of Computing*)
Steve Bratt (*Head of Sport & PE*)
Rebecca Bridgford-Whittick (*Head of SEND*)
Rachel Coling (*Art*)
Kelly Fairey (*KS1*)
Karl Gibson (*Deputy Head of Prep School, Science Coordinator*)
Marie Gibson (*Head of English*)
Kateley Kinnersley (*French*)
Carina Morgan (*Dance*)
Clare Rowntree (*Head of Music & Performance*)
Emily Scott (*KS1*)
Fiona Shaw (*KS1*)
Sarah Swarfield (*PE and Sport*)
Lesley Wanklyn (*Head of Geography*)
Jonathan Ward (*Mathematics Coordinator*)
Rosie Warner (*History Coordinator*)
Charlotte White (*KS1*)

Bursar and Clerk to the Governors: B McCartney
Admissions Registrar: J Prestidge
Head's PA: Mrs C Edwards
Director of Admissions and Marketing: J Fosbrook
School Doctor: Dr J Machling

West Buckland School

Barnstaple, Devon EX32 0SX

Tel: 01598 760000
email: admissions@westbuckland.com
website: www.westbuckland.com
X/Twitter: @westbuckland
Facebook: @wbsdevon
LinkedIn: /westbuckland

Motto: *Read and Reap*

West Buckland School is an independent day and boarding school set in 90 acres of beautiful North Devon countryside in the South West of England. Founded in 1858, the school has always stressed the importance of all-round character development alongside good academic achievement. Our size allows pupils to receive plenty of individual care and attention to their needs and talents.

West Buckland Preparatory School educates children between the ages of three and eleven. There is strong cooperation and support between the schools which share the same grounds, so making the transition as easy as possible.

West Buckland is fully co-educational.

Situation. The school stands in 90 acres of beautiful North Devon countryside on the edge of Exmoor. Barnstaple is 10 miles away and the M5 motorway can be reached in 35 minutes. Boarders arriving by train at Exeter station are met by coaches.

Buildings and grounds. The central range of buildings, dating from 1861, still form the focus of the school, and now includes an arts centre. Other developments include a Library and Study Centre, Sixth Form boarding house, learning support centre and student cafe. The campus offers outstanding sports facilities, including an indoor heated 25-metre swimming pool, squash courts, 19 tennis courts and an Astroturf hockey pitch. The Jonathan Edwards Sports Centre opened in 2008 and the award-winning 150 Building for Art, Design Technology and the 150 Theatre opened in 2010. A new study centre for all senior school pupils and a co-educational Sixth Form boarding house with single en-suite bedrooms opened in 2015.

Admission. Boys and girls are admitted as boarders from Year 7 or day pupils from age 4 onwards. The present number of pupils is: 142 boarding, 514 day.

Entrance to the Preparatory School is by interview and assessment of school reports. Entry to the Senior School is by assessment or to the Sixth Form upon interview, GCSE results and school report.

Fees per term (2023–2024). Senior: Full Boarding £11,088–£11,825, Weekly Boarding £1,613 (5-night stay), Day £5,786. Preparatory: Day £2,860–£4,580.

Scholarships and bursaries. A number of scholarships are awarded for entry at 11+, 13+ or 16+ (value at the discretion of the Headmaster). Candidates must be under 12, 14 or 17 years of age on 1st September for entry the following year. Applications are welcomed throughout the year – see our website for details.

Academic, Music, Drama and Sports scholarships are available for entry at 11+, 13+ and 16+. At 16+ there is also an Art scholarship. Details and deadlines are available on our website.

With the support of the West Buckland School Foundation, means-tested bursaries are available for boarders and day students at all ages.

Curriculum. In the Preparatory School, the main emphasis is upon well-founded confidence in English and Mathematics, within a broad balance of subjects, including modern languages, music, IT, sciences and arts. Particular attention is given to the development of sporting, artistic and musical talents.

In the Senior School, breadth is complemented by specialisation. All students study the three separate sciences from Year 7, while both French and Spanish are the principal languages offered from Year 7. Our flexible options arrangements at GCSE respond to students' individual strengths and preferences. A wide range of A Level subjects is offered to sixth formers whose results uphold the high academic standards of the school; the school is launching the IB Career Programme from September 2023. More information on curriculum is available on the school website.

Careers. The Careers Staff advise all pupils upon the openings and requirements for different careers. They make full use of the facilities offered by Connexions and host regular careers events, further education advice and visits and career presentations.

Games, the Performing Arts and other activities. One of the most impressive features of life at West Buckland is the quality and range of extracurricular activities, with a high level of involvement from pupils and staff.

The school has a strong sporting tradition. Rugby, hockey, cricket, netball, tennis, athletics, swimming, cross-country, squash, golf, shooting, badminton, basketball and many other sports offer opportunities for inter-school and inter-house competition and for recreation.

About a third of all pupils receive instrumental and singing tuition from specialist teachers. The wide range of choirs and instrumental groups give concerts at least once a week throughout the year. Drama is a strength of the school with productions of many kinds throughout the year. The Performing Arts are complemented by the exceptional facilities provided by the school's award-winning 150 Building which houses an impressive studio theatre.

Music. Tuition is available on all instruments. Pupils are encouraged to perform in concerts, in choirs and instrumental groups. Music Technology is also a strong feature of the department's work.

Outdoor education. Much use is made of the proximity to Exmoor and the coast for climbing, kayaking, mountain biking, surfing, coasteering, scuba diving and other adventurous activities. All pupils receive instruction in camp craft, first aid and map reading. The Combined Cadet Force has Army and Royal Air Force sections, and offers a range of challenging pursuits. Our students succeed at all levels in The Duke of Edinburgh's Award scheme each year, and there is a regular programme of expeditions in this country and overseas.

Religion. The tradition is Anglican but the school welcomes children from all denominations and faiths – or none. Services of worship are held on a regular basis at East Buckland Church.

Attitudes and values. The school sets out to be a friendly and purposeful community in which happiness and a sense of security are the foundation on which young lives are built. At all levels, members of the school are asked to lead a disciplined way of life, to show consideration for others, to be willing to be challenged and to recognise that the success of the individual and the success of the group are inextricably linked.

Charitable status. West Buckland School is a Registered Charity, number 1167545. Its purpose is the education of boys and girls from 3 to 18.

The Governing Body:

Patron: P D Orchard-Lisle, CBE, TD, DL, LLD [hc], DSc [hc], MA, FRICS

President: The Countess of Arran, MBE, DL

Vice Presidents: Mr B Green, Mr J M H Light

Chair of Governors: Mr Ian Blewit

Governors:
Dr T Brummitt, MBCHB, BSc Hons, MRCGP
Georgie Cotton
Dr R J Fisher-Smith, BA, MA, PGCE, PhD
Mr J Hall
P Hevingham, LLB Hons, MRICS, FCIARB
Mr G C James
N Kingdon, BDS, MOrthRCS
J Palk

Mrs S C E Salvidant, BEd Hons
P Stucley, BA Hons
Mrs N J Wild, BA Hons, MRICS
Mr J Wilson, MA
Interim Bursar and Clerk to the Governors: C Candlish, BSc, PGCE, ACMA

***Headmaster*: Mr Phillip Stapleton**, BSc, MA Durham, MBA, PGCE, MRSC

Deputy Head Academic: Mr R Paler, BA Hons Kent, MA SOAS London, PGCE Institute of Education London

Deputy Head Pastoral: Mrs K Corbin, MEd Exeter

Head, Prep: Mrs S Atkinson, BA Hons,
Day Houses & Housemasters/mistresses:
Brereton House: Dr E N D Grew, PhD Exeter
Courtenay House: D Brown, BSc Hons Bournemouth
Fortescue House: Mrs J Keech
Grenville House: Dr J McKerrow, PhD McMaster Ontario

Head of Boarding: Mr Richard Boyle
Admissions Manager: Mrs J Omar

Westminster School

Little Dean's Yard, Westminster, London SW1P 3PF
Tel: +44 (0)20 7963 1000
email: registrar@westminster.org.uk
website: www.westminster.org.uk
X/Twitter: @wschool
Facebook: @WestminsterSchoolUK
Instagram: @westminstergram__
LinkedIn: /westminster-school-london

Motto: *Dat Deus Incrementum*

Westminster School is an independent day and boarding school for boys aged 13–18 and girls aged 16–18, with a long history, a distinctive ethos, and a unique sense of place in the very heart of London.

About the School. Westminster is a leading academic school in the centre of London. Pupils achieve exceptional examination results and entrance to some of the top universities in the world. It is a busy, passionate and purposeful place where independent and deep thinking is enjoyed, encouraged and respected by all, and where holistic excellence is nurtured and valued. At the heart of London, adjacent to Westminster Abbey and the Houses of Parliament, the School's origins can be traced to a charity school established by the Benedictine monks of the Abbey of St Peter. After the dissolution of the monasteries in 1540, King Henry VIII personally ensured the School's survival. His daughter, Queen Elizabeth I confirmed royal patronage in 1560 and is celebrated as the School's Foundress. For several hundred years the School continued to be joined with Westminster Abbey, forming one collegiate foundation, until the 1868 Public Schools Act established the School as an independent body.

Academic. Westminster is one of the foremost centres of academic excellence in the country. However, our commitment to academic life does not manifest itself in an educative style that revolves around the passing of examinations. Our pupils' success in public examinations and in gaining entry to leading universities is a result of their enjoyment of academic enquiry and debate, as well as their curiosity and passion for subjects well beyond the content of the published syllabuses. The aim of the School is to instil in our pupils a deep love of learning and respect for the tradition of scholarship, as well as an openness to fresh ideas and innovative ways of thinking. Pupils are taught to appreciate and learn from the knowledge of those who came before them, yet we also ensure that they have ample opportunity to engage with current political, cultural and academic developments.

When pupils first arrive at the school, aged 13, they follow a common yet comprehensive programme of study. This includes English, Mathematics, the Sciences, Geography, History, Theology and Philosophy, French, Classics, Art, Drama, Music, Computer Science and RSHE. In the co-ed Sixth Form, pupils usually study four A Levels, which are supplemented by Cultural Perspectives and Options courses of their choosing. In addition, pupils are encouraged to take part in Mathematics, Science and Linguistics Olympiads and many other academic competitions too.

Admissions. The two main points of admission at Westminster School are 13+ for boys and 16+ for boys and girls.

About 125 to 130 boys join each year at 13+, both boarding and day pupils. About half come from Westminster Under School with others from a wide range of schools, mainly in London. Entry for 13+ begins with visiting the School for the first time in Year 5. In Year 6, boys take ISEB Common Pre-tests in Mathematics, English, verbal reasoning and non-verbal reasoning. Interviews follow, as well as further tests in Mathematics and English, and a report from the boy's current school. Unconditional offers are then made for entry into Year 9 aged 13. The system described above is for boys who can remain at their prep schools until they are 13. Boys who attend primary schools, finishing in Year 6, should be registered for 11+ entry to Westminster Under School. Candidates who are not offered an unconditional place may be placed on a waiting list.

Registration for 16+ entry opens in the summer a year before entry. Entry is by competitive examination and interview. Candidates choose four entry examination subjects, usually the four subjects they plan to take for A Level. The offer of a place is conditional on a candidate achieving a minimum of eight (I)GCSE passes at A/7 grade, of which at least four are at A*/8–9, preferably in the subjects to be studied at A Level.

Boarding. Boarding has been central to life at Westminster since the School was founded. Between a quarter and a third of pupils choose to board and many members of staff live within the precincts to enable a flourishing boarding life. This means that activities continue into the evening, with a full programme of society meetings, lectures, school plays and concerts, and cultural trips to London events. There are six residential boarding houses, including one which is a co-educational house for day pupils, but only has girl boarders.

Bursaries and Scholarships. Since its foundation, Westminster School has made it possible for academically able and musically-gifted pupils to attend the School, who would not otherwise have been able to do so without financial support. Bursaries of up to 100% are available and are awarded to pupils according to individual need, at both 13+ and 16+.

King's Scholarships are the School's much-coveted academic scholarships. There are 48 King's Scholars, with 12 chosen every year: eight boys at 13 and four girls at 16. King's Scholars board at the School and all belong to College, one of the six boarding houses. An examination entitled 'The Challenge' is held annually to determine which pupils are elected as King's Scholars for entry at 13+. The Challenge consists of papers in Mathematics, English, French, Science, Latin, History, Geography and an optional Greek paper. For King's Scholarships awarded to girls entering at 16+, selection is based on the overall performance in the Sixth Form Entrance Exam papers and interviews. The School also awards up to eight Music Awards annually for 13+ entry and up to four Music Scholarships for 16+ entry. The Henry Purcell Organ Scholarship is awarded biennially to a pupil in the Sixth Form.

Co-Curricular and Sport. To balance the academic pursuits of our pupils, Westminster offers a wide variety of activities to complement our curriculum. These provide pupils with new and different opportunities to engage with less familiar concepts, with one another and with the world around them.

The School is renowned for its culture of music and theatre, and pupils are encouraged to take music lessons, to join orchestras and choirs and to take part in musicals, plays, concerts and other projects.

Each week, pupils in Years 9 and 10 take part in Lower School Activities, after School on Mondays, Wednesdays, and Fridays, with options such as bookbinding, debating, The Duke of Edinburgh's Award, and robotics. Pupils in the sixth form often lead lunchtime and after-school societies, focused on subjects that are important to them, which are overseen by a member of teaching staff and to which all members of the school community are invited. The School also runs many expeditions in the UK and overseas.

In the sixth form, our Options programme enables boys and girls to study an additional language such as Arabic or Japanese, learn a new skill such as electronics or computer programming, or complement their studies in a particular area of interest such as an Introduction to Political Philosophy or studying British Sign Language. A more intensive volunteering option also exists, where pupils can not only give their time to local projects but also take specific courses to equip them for their chosen community outreach.

Two entire afternoons each week are dedicated to sport, known as 'Station' at Westminster, and pupils compete in fixtures against opposing teams in and around London, with cricket, football, netball and rowing being the School's major competitive sports. We have the unusual feature that all pupils have a free choice as to which Station option they participate in. We are extremely fortunate, in the centre of London, to have a great deal of outdoor space for Station: pupils have a shooting gallery and several Fives courts, in addition to our playing fields at Vincent Square; which together with the School's Victorian sports pavilion has just been renovated and reopened. We also have a Sports Centre that offers over 6,000m^2 of indoor space, housing a multi-use movement studio, a rowing training suite, fencing pistes, indoor cricket nets, a fully-equipped gym, two climbing walls, a dojo and a table tennis area and courts for basketball, netball, five-a-side football, volleyball, hockey and badminton.

Pastoral care. All pupils at Westminster have a weekly timetabled RSHE and Wellbeing lesson, delivered by trained and resourced staff, to help guide them and to help them make constructive choices in their lives. Topics are designed to be engaging and age-appropriate, with depth, substance and relevance to the daily lives of today's young people. Pupils themselves have had input into the curriculum design and will continue to do so.

The well-established community of houses enables a strong, well-integrated system of pastoral care, to ensure the needs of each individual pupil are addressed, and that all pupils – whatever their age, background or gender – enjoy their time at School. When issues occur, they are communicated swiftly to the Housemaster, who talks with the pupil's parents, teachers and Tutor, to devise the best way forward.

All houses have a Matron and all pupils have access to our state-of-the-art Health Centre, run by an experienced Nursing Sister and visited regularly by the school GPs. We have the full-time support of School Counsellors, and the Chaplaincy also plays an important role in ensuring the welfare of the community. Senior pupils from each house are trained as Peer Supporters to provide additional support and advice.

Community, Partnerships and Charity. At Westminster we are fortunate to enjoy some of the highest quality teaching and facilities in the country, so we are committed to making sure that others have the chance to access and benefit from our resources. There are a number of established schemes in place to help children outside Westminster School. Platform is an academic programme created and provided by Westminster School and Westminster Under School that inspires Year 5 pupils from state schools who show exceptional academic potential and energy for learning. School headteachers nominate participants every year, and the pupils then participate in a free one-year programme of Saturday morning sessions and a two-day course, to fuel their ambition and to allow their academic potential to flourish. Alongside the Platform programme, we introduced Platform Plus, a tailored programme, specifically designed for intellectually inquisitive Year 10 students who have an all-round curiosity and passion for either STEM or Liberal Arts subjects. Our most recent addition is Platform Pups, which is the programme for Year 2 pupils whose teachers think would greatly benefit from the extra opportunity to develop and stretch their fundamental English and mathematical skills.

Westminster pupils enjoy a wide variety of volunteering opportunities and there is an emphasis on pupil-led fundraising to help to ensure that contributing to society in holistic and generous ways forms a key part of our pupils' educational experience.

We also maintain a close relationship with nearby Harris Westminster Sixth Form (HWSF), which was created in partnership with not-for-profit organisation The Harris Federation in 2014 to offer an outstanding education to students from all backgrounds and neighbourhoods in London. HWSF combines the Federation's experience of establishing outstanding academies in and around London with Westminster School's ability to teach and develop exceptional pupils.

Fees per term (2023–2024). Day fees: £11,433–£12,495; Boarding fees: £16,506. For more information see www.westminster.org.uk/admissions/fees.

Preparatory Department. Westminster Under School is Westminster School's preparatory equivalent. The Under School admits day boys only and currently has 286 pupils in attendance. Entry to the Under School is at 7+, 8+ and 11+. For further information, please see Westminster Under School's entry.

Charitable status. St Peter's College (otherwise known as Westminster School) is a Registered Charity, number 312728.

Visitor:
His Majesty The King

Governing Body:
Mr Mark Batten [OW] (*Chair*)
Ex Officio and Nominated:
The Dean of Westminster, The Very Reverend Dr David Hoyle, MBE (*Ex Officio Member*)
Ms Emily Reid [OW] (*Nominated Common Room Governor*)
The Reverend Canon David Stanton (*Nominated Abbey Governor*)
Appointed Members:
Mr Basi Akpabio [OW]
Dr Sarah Anderson
Mr Nabeel Bhanji [OW]
Mr Edward Cartwright [OW]
Ms Jessica Cecil
Mr John Colenutt (*Deputy Chair*)
Professor Maggie Dallman OBE
Dr Tristram Hunt
Dr Dominic Luckett
Mr Richard Neville-Rolfe [OW]
Mrs Claire Oulton
Ms Joanna Reesby
Ms Grace Yu

Clerk to the Governing Body: Mrs Diana Robinson

[OW] Old Westminster

Senior Management Committee:
***Head Master*: Dr Gary Savage**, PhD
Under Master: Mr James Kazi, MA
Bursar: Mrs Amanda Oakley Smith, FCA

Deputy Head (*Academic*): Ms Clare Leech, MA
Deputy Head (*Co-curricular*, *Events and Planning*): Dr Vivienne Horsfield, EdD
Deputy Head (*Boarding*, *Diversity and Inclusion*, *Partnerships*): Mr Jeremy Kemball, BSc
Director of Upper School: Dr Tasos Aidonis, PhD
Director of Teaching and Learning: Ms Abigail Farr, MA

Wimbledon High School GDST

Mansel Road, London SW19 4AB
Tel: 020 8971 0900 (Senior School)
020 8971 0902 (Junior School)
email: info@wim.gdst.net
website: www.wimbledonhigh.gdst.net
X/Twitter: @WimbledonHigh
Instagram: @wimbledonhighschoolgdst
LinkedIn: /school/wimbledon-high

See full entry in the **GSA** section, on **p. 500**.

Winchester College

College Street, Winchester, Hampshire SO23 9NA
Tel: 01962 621247 (Admissions)
01962 621100 (Office)
email: admissions@wincoll.ac.uk
website: www.winchestercollege.org
X/Twitter: @WinColl
Facebook: @WinchesterCollegeOfficial
Instagram: @WinchesterCollege
LinkedIn: /school/winchester-college/people

Motto: *Manners Makyth Man*

Winchester College is a leading independent senior school in Hampshire, UK, set in beautiful, historic surroundings, and renowned for academic excellence. The school offers full boarding for boys in Years 9 to 13, with day girls and boys in the Sixth Form. This exciting new development is part of the school's Vision for the 21st Century, which embodies a significant programme of change, and also includes increased bursary provision, broadening of the curriculum, and further investment in technologies and the school's facilities.

At Winchester there is a thriving culture of curiosity and exploration. Pupils are chosen for their ability to think; dons are selected for their enthusiasm, dedication and expertise. Put simply, inspiring teachers inspire learning.

Outside study time, pupils have a huge choice of extracurricular activities, clubs and societies within which to find like minds and fresh challenges. Whether broadening or intensifying their interests, Winchester pupils take part in a stimulating range of activities that enriches their studies and their school life, including politics, rock climbing, natural history, scuba diving, literature, CCF, charities and expeditions.

Div. Div is at the heart of a Winchester education, defining the liberal character of academic life at the school. Pupils engage in discussion and debate, and embrace the idea of learning for its own sake, unrestrained by any examination syllabus.

Div is multi-disciplinary in scope. In Years 9 to 11, it provides pupils with an introduction to the broad sweep of History, from classical times to the Early Modern period. It also encompasses English literature and language, the History of Science and Art, Religious Studies and PSHEE.

In the Sixth Form, each Div don determines the programme. The material selected for inclusion is equally likely to be artistic, literary, philosophical, political, sociological, art-historical, ethical, religious or musical.

Through this combination of disciplines, the school helps develop discriminating learners. Div helps pupils to think critically, to question and assimilate complex ideas, and to articulate their thoughts with clarity and confidence, both on paper and orally in front of their peers.

Academic. At Winchester College, academic expectations are high, and success is achieved through a genuine curiosity and love for learning. A Winchester education therefore combines cultural studies in Div with a conventional curriculum of examined subjects. Examined courses are taught by highly qualified subject specialists.

In addition to Div, pupils begin at Winchester in Year 9 studying Mathematics, Biology, Chemistry, Physics, French or German, Geography and Latin. They also study one of the following: Ancient Greek, Spanish, Russian or Chinese, and choose two subjects from Art, Design and Music.

GCSEs: Towards the end of Year 9, pupils express their preferences for GCSE study. The majority of pupils complete a minimum of nine GCSEs and IGCSEs (all graded 9–1). The compulsory subjects (in addition to Div) are English, Mathematics, Latin, French or German, and two or three Sciences. Pupils also choose from among the following to bring the total to nine: History, Geography, Ancient Greek, Art, Design, Music, Spanish, Russian and Chinese.

A Levels: Pupils ordinarily study three A Level subjects and, to foster independence and responsibility, an Extended Project Qualification (EPQ), alongside Div. Linear A Levels are complemented by the flexibility of the EPQ, where pupils are able to explore more deeply their cross-curricular research interests. The EPQ encourages pupils to develop first-class research skills, to synthesise information from a variety of differing sources, and to become accustomed to the demands of independent study.

Sixth Form. We believe that Sixth Form should be the most interesting, enriching and academically demanding years of school life. There is no better place to spend these years than within the motivated and supportive community of Winchester College.

Learning alongside like-minded individuals, Sixth Form pupils enjoy inspirational teaching in small classes with outstanding resources. Each year, pupils join us with the intellectual spark and curiosity to take advantage of everything Winchester has to offer, and leave with the drive and determination to give something back. Winchester provides an intellectually stimulating environment in which conversation and debate are encouraged, and individual scholarship is nurtured. Subject specialists stretch individuals well beyond A Level syllabuses, providing the perfect preparation for university.

Fees per term (2023–2024). £16,384 per term for boarding, £12,123 for day.

For more information see www.winchestercollege.org/admissions/fees.

Boarding. Boarding at Winchester offers an unmatched experience of focused learning and friendship. Discussions in class can continue in the house, instilling a lifelong love of debate. In consultation with parents and pupils, the school accommodates boarders with care, getting to know them first through a personal admissions process. There are approximately 60 boarders in each house.

Admissions. We spend time getting to know each prospective family during the admissions process. It is a unique system, focused on potential, not merely prior attainment. It is based substantially on interview and ensures that by the time a pupil joins Winchester, they will often have had a number of years to get to know us.

13+ (boys only). When your son reaches Year 4, attend one of our two Open Days or a weekly Registrar's Tour. Registrar's Tours will start in the summer term of Year 4. In Year 5, select from one of our two Open Days or a weekly Registrar's Tour, then explore your choice of boarding house with a 'Housemaster at Home' visit, which introduces you to up to three Housemasters.

16+ (boarding boys only, day girls and boys). The dedicated Sixth Form Open Day is held in September or October each year. Examinations and interviews take place in November.

For more information see the Admissions page on our website www.winchestercollege.org/admissions.

Scholarships and Exhibitions are awarded to pupils who successfully pass the Winchester College 'Election' for entry at 13+, a unique selection process involving written examinations and interviews.

Headmaster's Nominations may be awarded to pupils not previously offered a conditional place or Scholarship, but whose exam results are deemed strong enough.

Scholarships, Exhibitions or Headmaster's Nominations do not carry a remission of school fees.

Music Scholarships and Exhibitions are available to any candidate who shows exceptional musical talent. Scholarships offer free tuition in two instruments (including singing) and Exhibitions offer free tuition in one instrument.

In addition, up to three Choral Scholarships and one Organ Scholarship are available for 16+ entrants. These carry free tuition in two instruments, one of which must be singing or the organ.

Sports Scholarships offer successful candidates at 13+ and 16+ specialist coaching sessions, regularly assessed strength and conditioning programmes, and a dedicated Sports Department tutor.

New Sixth Form scholarships for 2023 admission are available for Modern Languages, Classics and Entrepreneurship.

More information on Scholarships: www.winchestercollege.org/admissions.

Bursaries. Winchester College is committed to maintaining the founder's intention of offering an education to any pupil who would benefit from it, regardless of their financial circumstances. Awards range from 5–100% of the school fee and are means-tested.

The Wykeham Award is a dedicated bursary available for those pupils who join us in the Sixth Form and are currently studying at a UK state secondary school.

More information on Bursaries: www.winchestercollege.org/admissions/bursaries.

Charitable status. Winchester College is a Registered Charity, number 1139000. The objects of the charity are the advancement of education and activities connected therewith.

Visitor: The Lord Bishop of Winchester
Warden: Sir Richard Stagg, KCMG
Sub-Warden: Mr Andrew Sykes, MA

Fellows:
Mr Robert Lee Allen, BSc, CA
The Hon Sir Stephen Cobb, Hon LLD
Ms Clarissa Farr, MA
Mr Nicholas Ferguson, CBE, FSA Scot, BSc, MBA
Mr David Goodhew, MA, FRSA
Prof Helen Higson, OBE, DL
Mr William Holland, BA, FCA
Mr Brian Li Man-Bun, JP, MA Cantab, MBA, FCA
Mrs Alison Mayne, MA, PGCE
Dr William Poole, MA, DPhil, FSA
Dr Magnus Ryan, MA, PhD
Mrs Laura Sanderson, MA, MPhil
Mr Roland Turnill, MA
Mr Miles Young, MA Oxon

Bursar and Secretary: P D Thakrar
***Headmaster*: Ms E A Stone**

Alumni, Winchester College Society Director: A J C Normand, Donovan's, 73 Kingsgate Street, Winchester SO23 9PE

Wisbech Grammar School

Chapel Road, Wisbech, Cambridgeshire PE13 1RH

Tel: 01945 583631
01945 586750 Admissions
email: office@wisbechgrammar.com
website: www.wisbechgrammar.com
X/Twitter: @wisbechgrammar
Facebook: @wisbechgrammar
Instagram: @wisbech_grammar

Founded in 1379, Wisbech Grammar School is a co-educational day and boarding school. It draws around 600 pupils aged 3 to 18.

The School is set in 34 acres of magnificent grounds in a conservation area. Open, friendly and welcoming, the School is small enough for staff to know all the pupils individually, but large enough to provide an impressive range of opportunities. All members of the Senior School and Preparatory School are encouraged to develop their confidence and unlock their true potential, both inside and outside the classroom, as well as engaging with the wider community.

'*On visiting for the first time, our immediate impression was of a school where pupils showed a real sense of purpose and where they were clearly enjoying their lessons and activities.*' This comment, by parents looking for a school, is typical of the feedback we are delighted to receive.

Recently, the School has been through a number of transformation projects which include:

- An upgrade of the whole school IT infrastructure in summer 2021 to support a more technological approach to teaching and learning. All new 1st Form pupils receive iPads as part of the everyday school toolkit and AI has been introduced into online and classroom teaching via platforms such as Century.
- The redesign of school classrooms based around Harkness tables – a method of teaching and learning that involves 12–14 pupils seated around a large oval table which encourages pupils to discuss ideas, work collaboratively and shifts the focus away from the more traditional, teacher-at-the-front-of-the-class approach.
- A new 6th Form Centre which allows pupils to have a dedicated space for specialist 6th Form subjects, collaborative and silent working spaces, a lecture facility, plus a café and common room space; all with the aim of supporting academic success at A Level.
- The transformation of the old 6th Form house into a new International Boarding House for overseas pupils.
- The establishment of Science, Maths and Humanities Creative Hubs, so pupils benefit from having focused academic environments that utilise the expertise of specialist teaching staff and resources.

Senior School admission. The main entry is at age 11 by a competitive entrance examination. The test, which consists of verbal and non-verbal reasoning, spatial, quantitative tests and English, is designed to discover potential. Pupils can also enter at 2nd, 3rd and 4th Form levels. Offers of 6th Form places are made on the basis of interview and a report from a pupil's current school and final GCSE results.

Fees per term (2023–2024). Senior School (including 6th Form): £5,333; Prep School: £3,699–£3,799.

Bursaries and scholarships. Wisbech Grammar School offers a bursary programme which provides financial assistance to pupils who would not otherwise be able to take up the offer of a place, allowing them to achieve their full potential. Bursaries are means tested and will require the parents to make a detailed statement of their income and assets. Awards range from 5% to 85%. In exceptional cases, an award of 100% may be granted.

The School also offers scholarships for children entering Year 7, Year 9 and Year 12. Scholarships are awarded to children who excel in a number of areas (Academic, Music, Art, Drama and Sport); this includes financial support and may be awarded alongside a bursary.

Application forms for Bursary Assisted Places are available from the Admissions Team: admissions@wisbechgrammar.com.

Travel to school. The School's catchment area embraces King's Lynn, Hunstanton, Downham Market, March, Whittlesey, Peterborough, and Spalding and Long Sutton. School buses run from a number of these places, visiting villages en route. The School is also well served by local buses.

The 6th Form experience. The School has a first-class track record in enabling pupils to realise their university and career aspirations. Entrusted with a greater degree of independence, 6th Formers are encouraged to make their mark and develop leadership qualities, both within the house system and at a wider level. The 6th Form centre has been transformed into a modern contemporary space for pupils.

Sport. WGS offers an all-inclusive sports curriculum that gives every pupil the opportunity to engage in sports at all levels. The School offers team sports including Rugby, Hockey, Netball, Cricket, and Athletics, as well as a range of individual sport and fitness sessions.

With the Elite Sports Programme, pupils can pursue sports at a higher level with expert coaching and player pathways with Northampton Saints and Northamptonshire County Cricket Club.

Performing Arts is an extremely popular element of our extended curriculum and many of our pupils take advantage of the variety of school productions and stage performances; *Joseph and the Amazing Technicolor Dreamcoat* and *Shout*, were a huge success and played to a nightly full house at The Angles Theatre in Wisbech.

The Music Department also plays a prominent role, with orchestras, choirs, steel bands, bespoke instrument tuition and performances throughout the year, showcasing the multitude of musical talents within the School. Our Dance Studio offers pupils access to top level coaching from visiting dance companies.

Co-curricular. We offer many options for pupils to enjoy an extensive array of clubs as part of their timetabled curriculum within the school day – from Archaeology to Astronomy, Philosophy to Politics, Shakespeare to Steel Band and Young Enterprise to Young Engineers.

The Art and Design department is a highly visible presence in the School, mounting exhibitions on-site and at the Reed Barn at the neighbouring National Trust property, Peckover House. Our talented artists and designers regularly win places at the top art colleges.

Around 130 pupils participate in the Duke of Edinburgh's Award, with those at the highest level mounting expeditions to the Lake District, Snowdonia and Mont Blanc. The Senior School adventure begins with an outdoor activity weekend for the 1st Form.

Wisbech Grammar School Prep caters for pupils from Kindergarten (age 2) to Prep 6. As well as access to many of the Senior School facilities, they also have their own dedicated computer room and a light and spacious hall.

Wisbech Grammar School is a trading name of Wisbech Grammar School Limited. The Company is registered in England and Wales with company number 11454188.

Registered Office: Chapel Road, Wisbech, Cambridgeshire PE13 1RH

Senior Team:

***Headmaster*: Mr B J Rimmer**, BSc, NPQH

Bursar: Mrs N J Miller

Senior Deputy Head, Prep School: Mrs K Neaves, BEd

Senior Deputy Head, Senior School: Mr P W Timmis, BSc

Deputy Head Academic: Mrs V A Garment, BA, MA, NPQSL

Assistant Head Data and Digital Innovation: Mr R D Killick, BSc

Assistant Head Staff Development, Teaching and Learning: Ms E Semper, MA

Assistant Head Sports & Partnerships: Mr P J Webb, BA

Assistant Head Pupil Development and Leadership: Dr S J Miller, BSc, PhD, DIC

Head of Marketing and Admissions: Mr P A Lewis, MCIM

Withington Girls' School

Wellington Road, Fallowfield, Manchester M14 6BL

Tel: 0161 224 1077
email: office@wgs.org
website: www.wgs.org
X/Twitter: @WGSManchester
Facebook: @withingtongirlsschool
Instagram: @withingtongirlsschool
LinkedIn: /withington-girls-school

Motto: *Ad Lucem – Towards the light*

Since its foundation in 1890, Withington has remained relatively small and now has around 740 pupils, with over 150 in the Junior Department and a Sixth Form of over 160. This size allows a friendly, intimate environment together with a broad and balanced curriculum. Withington provides a wide range of opportunities for girls, helping them to achieve their potential, academically, socially and personally. Withington attracts pupils from a wide geographical area and from many different social and cultural backgrounds, producing a diversity in which the school rejoices.

The School's A Level and GCSE results have been consistently outstanding. Girls who gain a place as a result of the entrance examination normally take GCSE/IGCSE examinations in 9/10 subjects, followed by 3 or 4 A Levels. An exciting and varied Enrichment programme offers Sixth Formers courses such as mindfulness, financial literacy and leadership skills. In addition to the Enrichment Programme, which all Sixth Formers follow, many also complete an Extended Project Qualification (EPQ). Studies are directed towards encouraging a love of learning for its own sake, frequently going beyond the confines of the examined curriculum, as well as towards the ultimate goal of university entrance, including Oxford and Cambridge (11.7% of the cohort in 2023).

The School enjoys excellent facilities and has an ongoing programme of major developments. Recent projects have included a purpose-built Junior School building, a central, enclosed 'Hub' area at the heart of the school and an expanded and refurbished suite of university-standard Chemistry laboratories, all of which were completed in 2015. During 2018, a significant new sports facilities development was completed, reflecting the school's ongoing commitment to the promotion of physical activity for girls, one of the school's founding principles. In 2019, the outdoor netball courts and all-weather pitch were resurfaced to a high specification, bringing Withington's sports facilities to an excellent standard across all areas. A project to extend and refurbish the ground floor dining area, and to create additional space in a first floor extension that incorporates a new conference room, pastoral offices and a learning support centre, was completed early in 2022.

Withington fosters all-round development and the girls' academic studies are complemented by an extensive range of over 100 extracurricular activities. Music is strong and very popular; there is a comprehensive range of choirs and orchestras, involving all age groups. Drama also thrives with regular productions including original works. Girls play a variety of sports, including hockey, lacrosse, netball, rounders, tennis, athletics and football. Pupils are selected to represent county and national squads and there are regular sports tours within Europe and further afield such as the USA and South Africa. In addition to fixtures with other schools, pupils compete in a variety of sports within the School's House system. The four Houses, named after Withington's founders, also provide a focus for dramatic, musical and other activities.

The Duke of Edinburgh's Award and the Young Enterprise scheme, Model United Nations conferences, voluntary work in the local community, science, mathematics, linguistics Olympiads and a wide range of academic extension activities, residential activity weekends, foreign trips and local fieldwork all feature prominently in the School's provision. Numerous extracurricular clubs and societies include: musical theatre, African & Caribbean Society, engineers club, computer coding, drama tech club, sign language, Arts Award and chess. Awareness of the wider world is encouraged and girls have a strong sense of social responsibility, participating in many fundraising activities. Sixth Formers use their holiday time to participate in community projects in The Gambia; others participate in expeditions (to Malaysia and Borneo in 2016, Sri Lanka in 2017 and Kenya in 2019 and an 18-day expedition to Morocco in 2023). Preparation for life after school starts early and involves a programme of careers advice, work experience and UCAS application guidance. Older girls work with younger girls in numerous ways, through the House system, extracurricular activities, peer support and mentoring.

Visitors are warmly welcomed and Open Days are held in the Autumn term. A number of means-tested bursaries are awarded annually together with awards from various external Trusts. Entrance at age 7–11 is by Entrance Assessment/Examination, held in January, together with interview (11+ entry only) and a reference from current school. Admission to the Sixth Form is by interview and is conditional upon GCSE results. For entry at other points, please don't hesitate to contact the Admissions Team for further information.

The School has a thriving alumnae network with regular events, with many alumnae offering help and inspiration to current pupils. The School engages in a number of partnership projects with local State schools and has strong links with the local community. Withington has earned a number of accolades from The Sunday Times Schools Guide; ranked first for academic results in the North-West in the 2024 and 2022 editions, named as North-West Independent School of the Decade in the 2021 edition, North-West Independent School of the Year for 2012, 2020 and 2023, and Top Independent Secondary School of the Year nationally 2009/10. Withington was the Financial Times Best Value Independent Day School in 2012 and was ranked as the best value independent school in the country by The Daily Telegraph in June 2023, based on an analysis of results in public examinations and fees. Consistently featured in the annual Tatler Schools Guide of the top independent schools in the UK, Withington was named as a Runner-Up for Public School of the Year 2015 by Tatler.

Fees per annum (2023–2024). Senior School: £15,573, Junior School: £11,910, including lunches and insurance. LAMDA, individual instrumental music lessons and Arts Award are charged separately. Before- and after-school care are not charged.

Charitable status. Withington Girls' School is a Registered Charity, number 1158226. It aims to provide an exceptional quality of opportunity, to encourage independence of mind and high aspirations for girls from seven to eighteen.

¶ *Alumnae*

Board of Governors:
Chair: Mr M Pike, LLB
Mr C Poston, BSc, FCA (*Hon Treasurer*)
Dr J Allred, MB ChB, MRCGP, DRCOG, DFFP
Mr A Chicken, BA, MEd, FRSA
Dr R Dev-Jairath, MBChB, MRCGP, DCH, DRCOG, DPD, FHEA
Mr M Griffin
¶ Mrs D Hawkins, DL, JP, LLB
Prof D Leigh, BSc, PhD, CChem, FRS, FRSE, FRSC, MAE
Dr L Maynard-Atem, MSc, PhD
Mr A Pathak, BSc
Mr H Sinclair
¶ Mrs S Stuffins, BA, MSc, MRICS
Mr M Torevell, BA, ACA

***Headmistress*: Mrs S J Haslam**, BA Lancaster (*English*)

Deputy Head Pastoral: ¶Ms J M Baylis, MA Manchester (*English and Drama*)

Deputy Head Academic: Mr T Bennett, MA Cambridge (*Geography*)

Assistant Head: Dr S E Madden, PhD Newcastle (*Biology*)

Bursar: Mrs A Cohen, LLB Liverpool

Full-time Teaching Staff:
* *Head of Department/Subject Lead*
Mr N Aguilera, BA Almeria (*Spanish*)
Miss K L Browning, BA London (*Geography*)
¶ Miss D Bruce, BA Birmingham (**Religious Studies*)
Miss S Choudhury, BA Manchester (*English*)
Mrs A Clark, MA Manchester (*English*)
Mrs E Corrigan, MSc Durham (**Biology*)
Mr C Eccles, MSc Manchester (*ICT & Computer Science*)
Mr K Eckersall, BSc Leicester, MA Durham (*Chemistry*)
Mrs S E Fletcher, BEd Brighton (*Mathematics*)
Mr C Forrest, MPhys Manchester (*Physics*)

Mrs S E Hamilton, MA Aberdeen (**Geography*)
Dr Z Hawke, PhD Edinburgh (*Biology*)
Miss L Hegarty, BA Sheffield (**French*)
Mrs J C Howling, MA Cantab (**Classics*)
Mr S Humphrys, BA Leeds (*Religious Studies, *PSHCE*)
Ms L Johnson, BA Manchester (**Physical Education*)
Mrs J Johnston, BA MMU (**Art, Assistant Head Pastoral*)
Mrs N Kimpton-Smith, BA Durham (*History, Religious Studies, Politics*)
Ms A Kusznir, Dip Mech Moscow (*Mathematics*)
Miss E Lowe, MA Edge Hill (*Physics*)
Mrs K Michael, MA Open University (**Physics*)
Miss K Mottershead, BA Brighton (*Physical Education*)
Mrs S I Mounteney, BSc London (**Mathematics*)
Miss A Noya, BA Santiago de Compostela (**Spanish*)
Mrs M Parker, BA Leeds (*History*)
Dr L Pitts, PhD Leicester (*Chemistry*)
Mrs S J Rigby, BA Nottingham (**Learning Support*)
Ms E K Robinson, MA Cantab (*Classics, Director of Sixth Form, Enrichment*)
Mrs G E Sargent, BMus London (**Music*)
Dr J Smiles, PhD Manchester (**Science, Chemistry*)
Mr A Snowden, BSc Warwick (**ICT*)
Mrs E Suttle, MSc Manchester Metropolitan University (**English, Assistant Head Academic*)
Miss R Thorpe, BSc Manchester (*Biology*)
Mrs N Toubanks, BSc Manchester (**Economics*)
Dr C P G Vilela, PhD Lisbon (**Chemistry*)
Mrs J C Wallis, BA Leeds (**Politics, Deputy Head of Sixth Form*)
Mrs N Watson, BA Leeds (**Food & Nutrition*)
Miss F Whiteley, BSc Lancaster (**Psychology*)
Miss B Wilson, BA Sheffield (*History*)

Junior School:
Head of Junior School: Ms Bridget Howard, BEd Exeter
Ms J Arschavir, MA Liverpool (*Year 4*)
Mrs S Birch, BEd Edge Hill (*Year 3*)
Mrs L Cordrey, BA York (*Deputy Head of Juniors*)
Mr M Dunn, BSc Sheffield (*Year 5, Junior School Coordinator of Assessment and Pupil Tracking*)
Mr N Goodwin, BA Manchester (*Year 4*)
Miss L Gorman, BA Edge Hill (*Year 4*)
Mrs A Harris, MSc MMU (*Year 6*)
Mr J Lazenby, BA Liverpool (*Year 6*)
Mrs B Lowe, BSc Northumbria (*Year 3*)
Mrs K McCulloch, MA Manchester (*Year 5*)

Part-time Teaching Staff:
Mrs C Air, BA Oxon (**History*)
Mrs L Berry, BA Manchester (**Drama*)
Ms S Bickley, BSc Durham (*Mathematics*)
Mr M Boyle, BSc Wales (*Biology, *EPQ*)
Miss H Brown, MA MMU (*Art*)
Mrs K Carter, MA Oxford (*Languages*)
Mrs J Carter, BSc Leeds (*Physical Education*)
Mrs R Corner, MA Exeter (*Drama*)
Mrs F Cotton, BA Heriot-Watt (**Design Technology*)
Mr A Cumberford, BA Oxon (**German*)
Mrs D Da Silva, BA Portsmouth (*Design Technology*)
Mrs C E Edge, MA Leeds (*English, Partnerships Coordinator*)
Mr R Edge, BSc Hull (*Mathematics*)
Mrs R Fildes, MA MMU (*Art*)
Ms A Godwin, BA Oxon (*Learning Support*)
Miss I Gonzalez, PGCE (*Spanish*)
Mrs S Hetherington, BA Leeds Beckett (*Physical Education*)
Miss R Hylton-Smith, MA Goldsmiths (*Music*)
Mr M Houghton, BA Oxford (*Classics*)
Mrs A Humblet, BA University of Dijon (*Spanish*)
Mrs V Kochhar, BSc Exeter (*Mathematics*)
Mr C Lambert, BA Sheffield (*English*)
Mrs K Levene, BA Liverpool John Moore's (*Design Technology*)
Mrs N Morgan, BMus Lancaster (*Music*)
Mrs D Odeyinde, BSc Queen's Belfast (*Learning Support*)
Ms S Pym, BSc Bath (*Mathematics*)
¶ Mrs S Roberts, MA Manchester (*Physical Education*)
Ms A Siddons, BA Bath (*German*)
Mrs R Statter, BSc Warwick (*Mathematics*)
Mrs J Stockton, BA Leeds (*English*)
Mrs Z Taylor, BA MMU (*Art*)
Dr E L Terrill, DPhil Oxon (*Mathematics*)
Mrs A Walker-Holland, BMus Birmingham (*Music*)
Mr M Williams, BSc Manchester Metropolitan University (*Chemistry*)

Executive Assistant to Headmistress: Mrs L Thomas, BSc Sheffield Hallam
Head of Futures: Ms N Kober, BSc Bristol
Librarian: Mr D Whelan, BA MMU
Archivist: Miss H Brown, MA MMU
School Health Lead: Sister J Lees, RGN
Development Director: Mrs L Dowdall, BSc Leeds
Director of Admissions and Marketing: Mrs C Dow, BA Witwatersrand
Office Manager: Ms S Kennedy, BA Manchester
Director of Digital Services: Mr A Lockett, BSc Bradford
Site Manager: Mr M Morris, NEBOSH

Woldingham School

Marden Park, Woldingham, Surrey CR3 7YA

Tel: 01883 654206
email: registrar@woldinghamschool.co.uk
website: www.woldinghamschool.co.uk
X/Twitter: @WoldinghamSch
Facebook: @woldinghamschool.co.uk
Instagram: @woldinghamsch
LinkedIn: /company/woldingham-school

A leading day and boarding school for girls aged 11–18 set in 700 acres of the most beautiful Surrey countryside, Woldingham is an inspiring place for students to become confident, compassionate and courageous young women. It's a place where students learn to 'write your own story' through excellent teaching, boundless opportunities and first-rate pastoral care.

Despite Woldingham's rural and peaceful location, the school is remarkably easy to get to. With Woldingham station adjoining the school grounds, London is just 30 minutes away by train and the school is only 30 minutes from Gatwick and 45 minutes from Heathrow airports.

Main House, the stunning 19th century mansion at the centre of the school, sits alongside purpose-built science labs, humanities and language hubs, and studios for art, drama and music. With a professional standard auditorium seating 630, it's no surprise that award-winning actors Emma Corrin and Carey Mulligan both attended Woldingham.

Students achieve outstanding GCSE and A Level results to secure places at leading UK and international universities, opening doors to exciting careers. Students choose from a wide range of academic enrichment opportunities, including a vibrant talks programme from leading academics, annual philosothon, and dynamic scholarship programme to stretch and challenge scholars.

Woldingham has an exceptional programme of sport, clubs, performing arts and outreach into the local community, enabling students to develop an excellent range of skills, expertise and interests. In 2022, Woldingham opened an Outdoor Education & Adventure Centre – a perfect addition to the school's wonderful 700 acres.

Woldingham has excellent indoor and outdoor sports facilities onsite. Hockey and netball teams compete locally and regionally with first-class training from specialist coaches. The tennis dome means tennis can be played year round, as well as on outside courts in the summer. There is an indoor swimming pool, squash courts, fitness suites, dance studio and newly refurbished sports hall with cricket nets.

The beauty and peace of Woldingham in the Surrey Hills makes it the perfect place to board. Boarders live with their own year group in comfortable and well-equipped boarding houses, and there is a great sense of community. Enthusiastic and experienced housemistresses understand how to help new girls settle in quickly and make the most of school life. Flexi boarding is a great option and weekly boarding, where students spend their weekends at home, is increasingly popular.

One of the UK's oldest girls' schools, Woldingham is proud to be a pioneer of women's education and its staff are experts in teaching in an all-girls environment. Woldingham's supportive and stimulating single-sex environment enables students to become authors of their own life story, growing into independent women who make a positive contribution to the world.

Woldingham is a Sacred Heart Catholic school, warmly welcoming students of all faiths and none.

Admissions. Main entry is via the Woldingham School Assessment in the autumn prior to entry for 11+, 13+ (standard and deferred entry) and 16+ candidates.

Scholarships. We offer the following academic and co-curricular scholarships, designed to recognise exceptional achievement, intellectual curiosity and persistence:

Academic, Art, Music, Drama and Sport Scholarships are offered at 11+, 13+ and 16+. In addition, a Local Girl Scholarship (means tested) is offered at 11+, Performing Arts Scholarships at 11+ and 13+ and Science Scholarships at 16+.

Bursaries. We are committed to providing bursaries, depending upon the financial and other pertinent circumstances of applicants. They are intended for girls who demonstrate strong academic potential and where the financial circumstances of the family will make attending Woldingham impossible.

Fees per term (2023–2024). Full boarding: £14,195–£15,450; Weekly boarding: £12,470–£13,610; Day (tuition): £8,030–£9,130; Flexi-boarding: £72.50 per night (max. 2 nights per week).

Charitable status. Woldingham School is a Registered Charity, number 1125376.

Chair of Governors: Ms C Berwick, BSc SocSci Southampton

***Interim Head*: Mrs J Harrington**, BA Exeter, NPQH

Deputy Head Academic: Ms N Weatherston, BSc Newcastle
Deputy Head Operations & Co-curricular: Mrs S Woolaway, BSc Open University
Deputy Head Wellbeing (*acting*) *and Head of Marden*: Ms K Renshaw, BSc Leeds
Deputy Head Safeguarding & Boarding (*acting*): Miss T Bennett, BSc Durham, MSc Oxon
Head of Sixth Form: Mr P Abbott, BSc Cardiff
Bursar: Mrs A Higgs, BSc, LSE, FCA
Director of Communication: Ms J Rawlinson, BA Hull, MA Florida
Foundation Director: Mrs C Mair, BA London
Director of Admissions: Mrs L Underwood

Heads of Department:
Art: Miss S Campbell, BA London Metropolitan
Biology: Mrs E Petty, BSc Birmingham
Business: Mrs C Abbott, BA Westminster
Chemistry: Mr P Currie, Graduate RSC Kingston
Classics & Latin: Dr J Dixon, PhD Manchester, BA, MA Liverpool
Computer Science: Mr T Rattle, BA Exeter, MA Brighton
Design & Technology: Mr D Wahab, BA Brighton
Drama: Miss S Williams, BA Italia Conti Academy
EAL: Mrs T Carrilero, BA Spain
Economics: Mr I Smith, BA Liverpool, MEd Greenwich
English: Ms B MacLean, BA, MA Canada
French: Mrs C Maillot, BA equiv. France
Geography: Mr D Lock, BA London
German: Mr V Ceska, BA Czech, MA France
Higher Education & Careers: Mrs M Young, BA Durham, MA Durham
History: Mrs A Housden, BA Kent
History of Art: Mr A Cullen, BA SOAS
Learning Enhancement: Ms R Moorvan, BA South Africa, MEd OU
Mathematics: Mrs R McKenna, BSc Cardiff
Media Studies: Mr S Maunder, BA Sheffield
Music: Ms R Ives, BMus, ARCM, DipRCM perf Royal College of Music
Physical Education: Mrs C Treacy, BSc Gloucestershire
Physics: Mrs M Clayton, BSc Birmingham
Politics: Mrs K Payne, BA Durham
Psychology: Mrs R Deaney, BSc Open University, BMus, PG Dip RCM
Science: Mr P Rickard, BSc Bristol, BSc Liverpool
Spanish: Mr A Lopez, BA Oviedo
Theology: Mr A Ross, BA Lancaster, MA St Mary's, AIDTA [B]

Wolverhampton Grammar School

Compton Road, Wolverhampton, West Midlands WV3 9RB

Tel: 01902 421326
email: admissions@wgs.org.uk
website: www.wgs.org.uk
X/Twitter: @WGS1512
Facebook: @WolverhamptonGrammarSchool
Instagram: @wolverhamptongrammarschool
LinkedIn: /company/wolverhampton-grammar-school

Wolverhampton Grammar School was founded in 1512 by Sir Stephen Jenyns – a Wolverhampton man who achieved success as a wool merchant, became a member of The Merchant Taylors' Company, then Lord Mayor of London. He decided to benefit his hometown by founding a school 'for the instruction of youth in good manners and learning'. The school retains close links with the Company.

Wolverhampton Grammar School is an all-through independent, selective day school for boys and girls aged 4–18 from a wide catchment area throughout the West Midlands, Staffordshire and Shropshire. It is ranked in the top 10 independent schools for academic performance in the West Midlands by the Sunday Times Parent Power Guide 2024.

The School's vision is to deliver 'an education that transforms lives as well as minds'. A personalised curriculum provides an education and learning experience that is unique. Students achieve excellent GCSE and A Level exam results alongside an experience that includes the largest range of extracurricular activities of any school in the area.

In its last ISI inspection, WGS was judged to be 'Excellent' in all areas. The report can be read on the ISI website: www.isi.net.

Buildings. The stunning 25-acre site includes a purpose-built Sixth Form Centre and Learning Hub, a Design Studio with CAD/CAM modelling suite and workshop and the £3.8 million Arts and Drama Centre. A Sports Centre and floodlit all-weather AstroTurf pitches offer some of the best sporting facilities in the area, with a Sports Pavilion providing panoramic views of the playing fields. Chemistry, Physics and Biology laboratories have been refurbished to the highest modern standards. Technology is integrated seamlessly into lessons using iPads as an effective educational tool. All pupils from Year 3 upwards have their own iPad which allows them to access specialist apps and bespoke textbooks. The learning experience is enhanced further through virtual and augmented reality.

Admission. The School accepts applications to the Junior, Senior and Sixth Form (Reception to Year 13) throughout the year, although new students usually join in September. The School's own Year 7 entrance tests are held in the preceding January. Offers for the Sixth Form are made subject to GCSE results and interview. Applicants are advised to apply early and before the end of the Autumn term.

Fees per term (2023–2024). Reception: £3,300; Years 1 & 2: £3,300; Years 3 to 6: £4,000; Senior School and Sixth Form: £5,200.

Entrance scholarships. The Jenyns Scholarship is a means-tested award for Year 7 applicants living in a Wolverhampton (WV) postcode. It may be offered as one full fee-paying place or shared between multiple students as a proportion of fees. As a guideline, family household income should not exceed £60,000. A Year 7 Music Scholarship worth up to 25% fee remission is awarded annually to a candidate working towards Grade 5 in their chosen instrument. The successful candidate must also pass the School's Entrance Test.

For students entering at 16+, a Music Scholarship worth up to 25% fee remission is awarded annually to a candidate working at Grade 6 standard in their chosen instrument. The successful candidate must meet the Sixth Form entry requirements and be aiming to reach Grade 8 by the end of Upper Sixth. A means-tested, OW Sports Scholarship is offered to one student playing at county, regional or national level in their chosen sport. It is equivalent to one full fee-paying place and is for applicants living in the Wolverhampton area (WV postcode). Applicants must fulfil the entry criteria for the Sixth Form and take a practical assessment with the Director of Sport.

Assistance with fees. The School offers several means-tested bursaries to children from less affluent families who can demonstrate that they will benefit from the opportunity of an education with Wolverhampton Grammar School. Contact the Admissions team to find out more.

Curriculum. The curriculum is delivered using a two-week timetable and covers a broad range of academic subjects including language choices and Computer Science. Sixth Formers have a choice of 20+ A Level subjects and Cambridge Technical qualifications as well as the Extended Project Qualification (EPQ). Students go on to excellent universities including Oxford, Cambridge and other Russell Group institutions.

Games and outdoor activities. Students benefit from over 140 extracurricular activities, clubs, societies, trips, international expeditions and sport tours. Sport has a long tradition at the school and students compete at city, regional and national level. The 25-acre site includes rugby, cricket, hockey and football pitches, netball courts, an all-weather Astroturf and athletics track as well as a fully equipped sports centre with dance studio, multi-gym and indoor courts for badminton, squash and nets. A 'sport for all' attitude exists in games and PE, where the staff endeavour to match the student to a sport or activity in which they can succeed. There is a commitment to the highest standards of skill and sportsmanship but the emphasis is also placed on enjoyment. The School participates in The Duke of Edinburgh's Award scheme and there are opportunities to undertake field trips and foreign exchanges. The School also has Fives Courts as well as a purpose-built climbing wall.

Dyslexia. The School's OpAL (Opportunities through Assisted Learning) department is designed to allow bright children with Specific Learning Difficulties (Dyslexia) to enjoy the challenge of a first-rate academic education. OpAL students achieve notable success at GCSE and A Level; grades are consistently above the national average. Students also have access to additional 1-2-1 and small group teaching around core curriculum subjects.

Arts and other activities. Purpose-built facilities for art, music and drama provide the best venues possible for exhibitions and school productions. The professional art gallery known as the Viner Gallery is used by students and commercial artists alike, whilst the contemporary Hutton Theatre is home to exceptional performances by students from across the School. A thriving music department is at the heart of the campus and students take part in the many music groups and ensembles before and after school. An active student Charity Fundraising Committee ensure that all students are involved in working for the good of others.

Pastoral Care. The School's first priority is the happiness of its students. Overseen by an Assistant Head with responsibility for Pastoral Care, WGS has a dedicated, expert pastoral team, a school counsellor, Wellbeing department and Sixth Form mentors. An important forum is the Student Parliament which consists of elected representatives from all year groups who are encouraged to suggest improvements to school life.

Charitable status. Wolverhampton Grammar School Limited is a Registered Charity, number 1125268.

Chair of the Board of Directors: Mr James Sage

***Head of Wolverhampton Grammar School*: Mr Nic Anderson**

Head of Wolverhampton Grammar Junior School: Mr Dan Peters

Finance Director: Mrs Shona Hemmings

Deputy Head: Mr Toby Hughes

Assistant Head (*Teaching & Learning*): Mr Alex Yarnley

Assistant Head (*Academic Administration*): Mr Jon Wood

Assistant Head (*Pastoral*): Miss Claudine Jones

Director of Marketing and Communications: Mrs Jenny Dredger

Woodhouse Grove School

Apperley Lane, Apperley Bridge, Bradford, West Yorkshire BD10 0NR

Tel: 0113 250 2477
email: enquiries@woodhousegrove.co.uk
website: www.woodhousegrove.co.uk
X/Twitter: @woodhouse_grove
Facebook: @woodhousegroveschool
Instagram: @woodhouse_grove

Motto: *Bone et fidelis*

Woodhouse Grove was founded in 1812 and is situated in the heart of Yorkshire. A co-educational day and boarding school for pupils aged from 2 to 18 years. Boarding pupils are taken from the age of 11 years.

Our hard work has been recognised by the latest Independent Schools Inspectorate inspection which rated Woodhouse Grove as Excellent. The inspectors came away with very clear evidence of the Grovian Values that we seek to promote. They recognised our outstanding academic and co-curricular programme and our aim to ensure that all our pupils reach their full potential.

At Woodhouse Grove, we appreciate that every child is a unique individual and this is at the heart of everything we do. We aim to motivate pupils academically and beyond the classroom and to provide an educational environment designed to allow students to fully participate in school life.

We offer a rich, challenging and dynamic curriculum and want our students to ask questions of the world around them with an open mind; to have the character to listen to others, but also to stand up for their beliefs. We encourage our pupils to 'give back' to their community and we believe that this well-rounded, diverse approach is the key to building academic and personal confidence. Ultimately, our objective is to provide our students with the drive and aspiration to become the very best version of themselves that they can be.

Set in idyllic grounds near Leeds, the school is opposite Apperley Bridge train station and within four miles of Leeds Bradford Airport. We have high standards and an all-encompassing approach to education and our outstanding facilities reflect this. A recording studio, 220-seat theatre, sports halls, swimming pool and climbing wall are all within our 70-acre campus.

Numbers. There are 782 pupils in the Senior School including 64 boarders and a Sixth Form of 223 students. Brontë House (age 2–11 years) has 308 pupils.

Buildings. Our facilities include a purpose-built sports centre with a multi-functional sports hall, a fully-refurbished fitness suite, a dance studio, a 25m competition swimming pool, squash courts, floodlit and covered outdoor courts, floodlit all-weather pitch, performing arts centre and climbing wall. We have fully equipped science laboratories, a state-of-the-art DT and Art centre, a spacious music and drama block, language suite and fully-equipped IT rooms. We have a modern spacious Sixth Form block with a brand new corporate style study centre and refurbished boarding houses which provide a separate sixth form annexe for boys.

Sport. We have approximately 40 acres of playing fields including grounds for Cricket, Rugby, Football and Athletics as well as indoor Squash, Basketball and Swimming facilities. There are several all-weather Tennis Courts, newly installed outdoor cricket nets, a floodlit, covered outdoor court for Netball and Tennis and a floodlit all-weather pitch.

Music. A high percentage of pupils have instrumental or vocal tuition and pupils can perform in a wide variety of music, drama and dance groups. Accredited exams offered include ABRSM & Trinity Guildhall Speech and Drama. There are a number of high-profile annual performances taking advantage of the dedicated theatre and recording studio. Music tours take place every two years. Sixth form courses are available in Music and Music Technology.

Curriculum. Boys and girls can enter the Senior School at any age but mainly at the age of 11, 13 and 16 and the curriculum is arranged to provide a seamless transition through from Brontë House and upwards through the Sixth Form to University entrance. A wide range of GCSE (and IGCSE) courses are offered and currently we are offering 24 subjects at A Level plus additional BTEC options and the opportunity to gain work experience within local business partners as part of the sixth form experience. Specialist support is offered to meet EAL, dyslexia and other learning needs. All students get the chance to study French, Spanish and German. The campus is served by full-site Wi-Fi.

Sixth Form Entry. Places are available for students who want to come into the School at the Sixth Form stage subject to entry requirements.

Scholarships and Bursaries. Scholarships can be applied for directly from the headmaster for academic, all-rounder, art, sport and music. In addition, bursaries can be awarded following the offer of a place, in cases of financial need (plus allowances for children of ministers and of service personnel). Extras include excursions and extra tuition, such as music.

Admission. Places are offered subject to availability and based on our own entrance exam, in-school interview and previous school report. Pupils are usually accepted in September, although arrangements can be made for entry throughout the school year.

Brontë House is our Preparatory School and takes boys and girls from the age of two years old. Fees include wrap-around care from 7.30am until 6.00pm. Ashdown Lodge Nursery takes pupils, on a day or part-day basis, with a choice of term time only or, a 51-week contract.

Fees per term (2023–2024). Main School: £11,765–£11,830 (full boarders), £5,430–£5,500 (day). Brontë House: £3,900–£4,650 (day). Ashdown Lodge Nursery and Reception: £3,640–£3,900 (day). Fees include all meals, books, stationery, examination fees and careers tests.

Extra Subjects. There are a wide range of extra subjects available including individual music lessons, singing, speech and drama, extra sports coaching, debating, Duke of Edinburgh's Award, photography and fencing.

Old Grovians Association. email: oga@woodhousegrove.co.uk.

Charitable status. Woodhouse Grove School is part of the Methodist Independent Schools Trust, which is a Registered Charity, number 1142794.

Governors:
Mr C Allen, LLB
Mr M Best, ACA
Mr S Burnhill, BSc
Mr R S Drake, LLB Hons, ACIArb
Rt Revd C P Edmondson
Mrs P M Essler, BSc
Mrs S Huby, BA
Dr K Johal, PhD, BSc
Prof M Manogue, BDS, MDSc, PhD
Mr S Morris, MA, PGCE, NPHQ
Mr M Pearman, MA
Ms M Phillips, MBA, Registered Nurse
Mrs B Proctor, BA, CIPD
Revd K Tankard, BA, MA
Mr A Wintersgill, FCA (*Chair*)
Mr A Wood, BA, ACA

Staff:

***Headmaster*: Mr J A Lockwood**, MA

Deputy Head: Mrs E Nulty, BA
Deputy Head (*Academic*): Mr E J Wright, BSc
Deputy Head (*Pastoral*): Mr A M Cadman, BSc

Assistant Head (*Boarding and Compliance*): Mr D King, MA
Assistant Head (*Curriculum*): Mrs C Nott, MA
Assistant Head (*Organisation*): Mr K D Eaglestone, BSc
Assistant Head (*Staff Development*): Mrs V Limbert, BA
Assistant Head (*Sixth Form and Futures*): Mr C Softley, BA

Chaplain: Revd R Drost
Operations Director: Mrs V Bates, ACA
Director of Marketing and Commerce: Mrs S Cadman, BA

* *Head of Department*
† *Head of House*

Mr J Allison, BA (**Design Technology*)
Ms M Barnes (*Modern Languages*)
Mr N Barr, BA (*Assistant Director of Sport, PE and Games, Mathematics*)
Miss A Barron, BA (*French, German*)
Mr E Bean, BSc (**Co-Head of Science, Physics*)
Mr J Bedford (*Head of Rugby*)
Mr J Birkett (*Design and Technology*)
Ms G Bond (*Modern Languages*)
Mr D Bradburne (*Director of Sport, Health and Fitness*)
Mrs N Bradburne (*Head of Girls' Boarding, Sports coach*)
Mr A Cadman, BSc (*PE*)
Ms B Carey (*German*)
Mrs P N Charlton, MA (*Art & Design*)
Mrs K Curtis, BSc (**Academic PE, Games*)
Mr T Davis, BA (*Director of Academic Systems, Chemistry*)
Mr M Dawson, BA (*History*)
Mrs S Dawson, BA (*Mathematics*)
Mr M Dobson, BSc (*Head of Boys' Boarding, PE and Games*)
Revd R Drost (*School Chaplain, PSHE*)
Ms L Dudley (*PE and Games, Psychology*)
Mr K Eaglestone, BSc (*Mathematics*)
Mrs J L Edger, BSc (*Physics*)
Miss E Emmott, BA (*Art*)
Miss K England, BSc (*Chemistry*)
Miss L Evers, MA (*English, Media Studies, Drama*)
Mr T Exeter (*Science, †Head of Vinter House*)
Mr I Fernandez (*Drama, Spanish*)
Mr R Firbank (**History*)
Mrs H Fisher, BSc (**Psychology*)
Mr C Garbutt, BSc (*Biology, Chemistry*)
Mr M Gill, BSc (*Computing*)
Mrs K L Goodwin-Bates, MA (*English*)
Ms S Habergham (*English, Drama*)
Miss S Harder, BSc (*Science, †Head of Findlay House*)
Mr T Hicks (*Sports Coach*)
Mr D Higgins (*Maths, Computing*)
Mrs E Hodson, BA (*Modern Foreign Languages*)
Miss L Holloway, BA (**RS, †Head of Atkinson House*)
Miss L Hughes, BA (*English*)
Dr A Ingham, BSc (*Biology*)
Mr C Jackson, (*Games, PSHE, †Head of Stephenson House*)

Miss C D Jemmett, BA (*English*)
Mr A Jennings, BA (*Religious Studies*)
Mrs K Jennings, BEd (*PE*)
Mr M Keegan, BA (*English*)
Mrs A Kerr, BSc (**Mathematics*)
Mrs V Limbert, BA (*English*)
Mr O Mantle, BA (*Business Studies*)
Mr L McNeil (*Economics*)
Mrs H Mitchell, BA (**Modern Foreign Languages*)
Mr P J Moffat, BA (*Geography*)
Miss B Monk, BA (**EAL, English, *Learning Support*)
Mr M F Munday, BA (*Geography*)
Mr C Norris (*Maths, Science*)
Mrs C Nott, MA (*Mathematics*)
Mrs E Nulty, BA (*Business Studies*)
Miss L Oakley, BA (**English*)
Miss C Pearce, BA (*PE and Games, Geography*)
Mr G Randhawa (*Head of Cricket*)
Mrs L Richardson, BSc (**Co Head of Science, Biology*)
Mr J B Robb, BA (*RS, Philosophy*)
Mr J Shah (*Chemistry*)
Mrs R Sharpe, BA (*English*)
Mrs D L Shoesmith-Evans, MA (*History, Politics*)
Mrs K Simpson (**Art*)
Mrs D Smith, BA (*Design and Technology*)
Mrs L Smith, BA (*Modern Languages*)
Mr C Softley, BA (*PE & Games*)
Mrs C Spencer, LLM (*Business Studies, Economics, †Head of Towlson House*)
Miss H Spiller, BA (*Art*)
Ms V Strachen (*English, EAL*)
Mr D Sugden, BSc (*Mathematics*)
Mr J P A Tedd, MA (**Performing Arts, Music*)
Miss G Thompson, BA (*PE and Games, Head of Netball*)
Mrs R Vernon, BSc (*PE and Games, PSHE*)
Mr T Walker (*Maths*)
Mrs R Warner, BA (*Politics, History*)
Mrs L Watmough, BA (**Business Studies, †Head of Southerns House*)
Mrs P L Watson, MA (*Business Studies, Economics*)
Mrs R Wickens, BA (**Geography*)
Mr B Wilson (*Music*)
Mr E Wright, BSc (*Mathematics*)
Mr M Yam (*Science*)
Headmaster's Secretary: Ms K Fleming
Admissions Manager: Mrs J Amos

Brontë House
Head of School: Mrs S Chatterton, BEd
Deputy Head (Pastoral): Mrs F Pearson, BA
Deputy Head (Academic): Mrs H J Simpson, BA
Assistant Head (Operations): Mr J Gallucci
Head of Early Years: Mrs H Foster

Worth School

Paddockhurst Road, Turners Hill, West Sussex RH10 4SD

Tel: 01342 710200
email: admissions@worth.org.uk
website: www.worthschool.org.uk
X/Twitter: @worthschool
Facebook: @worthschool
Instagram: @worth.school
LinkedIn: /worth-school

Worth is a Catholic Benedictine boarding and day school for boys and girls aged 11–18 where those of any faith, or none, are welcome. It is a truly distinctive school, known for its strong community values, friendly atmosphere and the excellence of its all-round education. The school has been under the leadership of Mr Stuart McPherson (formerly at Eton College) since September 2015 and in the Head Master's words is: "a place where we seek to uncover and ignite children's passions and talents. The path a life takes often begins at school, and this is why we do not just provide education, we offer learning with heart and soul, and this gives Worth a difference of kind that sets us apart."

This magnificent school is in the heart of the Sussex countryside, about halfway between London and Brighton, and less than 15 minutes from Gatwick airport. We are ideally placed to allow students to sample some of the cultural highlights that Britain has to offer, while providing a beautiful environment in which to learn.

In an Independent Schools Inspectorate (ISI) Report in November 2017, Worth was judged to be excellent – the highest possible grade – for the quality of the pupils' academic and other achievements and personal development. A review by the *Good Schools Guide* in 2017 concluded that "This school has everything going for it...". The latest review in the *Tatler Schools Guide* refers to Worth as a "school on the up".

The school offers a broad curriculum, where students can opt for the International Baccalaureate Diploma or A Levels. The School has offered the IB since 2002 and a pre-IB course was introduced for non-UK students in Year 11 in 2015. Examination results are excellent and pupils enter the best universities in the UK and abroad, including Oxford, Cambridge, Russell Group universities and Ivy League institutions.

The wider curriculum is rich and varied with a huge range of activities, societies, lectures and trips from which to choose. There is also a lively sporting programme which has produced students of national and county standard, and the school's reputation for performing arts is outstanding.

History. Worth welcomed girls into Years 7 and 9 in September 2010. They joined other girls in an already thriving co-educational Sixth Form, and the school has been fully co-educational since 2012 with girls integrated into all aspects of school life.

Courses of study. At GCSE level, students usually take ten subjects. The compulsory core is: English, Mathematics, Sciences, French or Spanish or German (plus PE and SMSC).

There is a wide choice of subjects at A Level and there is also the opportunity to take the Extended Project Qualification (EPQ). A BTEC in Business is available subject to demand. Full details of subject choices can be found on the School website.

Alternatively, Sixth Form students may study the International Baccalaureate. This involves the study of six subjects, three at Higher Level and three at Standard Level. Details can be found in the Sixth Form Subject Options booklet on the Worth School website.

Thanks to the generosity of a former student, a multi-million pound new Sixth Form Centre and School Library opened in April 2022. Sixth Form students may also choose to study for Oxbridge entrance and a number gain places at either Oxford or Cambridge.

Pastoral Care. Care of each student is of central importance throughout the school, as evidenced by our 'Outstanding' Ofsted grading for Boarder provision. Each pupil is a member of a House and has a personal tutor who monitors work progress and assists the Housemaster/Housemistress with overall care. The House support structure also includes a Chaplain and a matron, supported by an assistant matron in each of the Boarding Houses. There is a counsellor available to pupils.

Sport. Worth loves its sports. The main sports are: rugby, football, hockey, netball, cricket, tennis and athletics. Other sports played at competitive level include fencing, squash, golf, basketball, lacrosse and swimming, and sports are also available through school clubs and activities (see below). There is a floodlit Astropitch, a nine-hole golf course, squash courts, tennis courts, fencing salle, golf simulator, dance studio and fitness suite. The school also makes use of the excellent athletics facility and 50m swimming pool at a multi-sports centre nearby.

Performing Arts. Music is important at Worth. There is a flourishing choir, the *Schola Cantorum*, that is involved in tours and makes regular appearances in the Abbey Church. The school orchestra performs regularly, as does the Jazz Band. The annual House Music and Young Musician of the Year competitions provide all pupils with an opportunity to perform and encourage an interest in music.

Drama also flourishes with regular dramatic and musical productions at all levels and the standard of performance is exceptional. There are three major productions a year, taking place in the purpose-built Performing Arts Centre which comprises a 250-seater theatre, box office, drama office and workshop, dressing rooms, recording studio, a sound-proofed 'rock room', rehearsal rooms, a recital room and music classrooms.

Extracurricular activity. Pupils of all ages take part in activities one afternoon, and clubs and societies at least twice a week, as part of the academic timetable. There are more than 150 activities, clubs and societies to choose from each week, ranging from helping with the local primary school and photography to sailing, clay pigeon shooting and chess. There is a horse riding school for students nearby and there are stables on the campus. Worth is also a centre of excellence for The Duke of Edinburgh's Award scheme. There are lectures by external speakers and a wide array of trips, visits and exchanges both at home and abroad.

Weekends. In September 2022 Saturday morning academic lessons, previously compulsory for all pupils in the senior school, moved into the Monday to Friday timetable. This change presents a range of new opportunities for boarders and an exciting new structure for the weekend boarding experience at Worth with a dynamic programme of activities, clubs, revision classes and more, as well as compulsory sports fixtures.

Admissions Policy.

Entry at 11+: Entrance tests in English, Maths and Non-Verbal Reasoning are held in January each year. Offers are based on test results, a report from the student's current school and an interview with the Head Master. Annual promotion is subject to the pupil having shown satisfactory academic performance as determined by the Head Master, and a good disciplinary record.

Entry at 13+ (Year 9) for 2024–2025: Admission at 13+, after visits and registrations, is via Worth's own assessment tests and interviews held at the school in the Lent Term of Year 6 or, occasionally, Year 7. Admission for overseas candidates is via separate assessment tests and interviews held in their own countries.

Entry at 16+: Admission is by means of reports and references from the candidate's current school, assessments and interviews held at Worth during the year prior to entry. Entry is competitive, and successful applicants will usually be predicted to gain top grades in most of their GCSEs or equivalent examinations, but we recognise the central value of Art, Drama, Music, Sport and other co-curricular activities, and enthusiasm in these fields is expected and encouraged.

Scholarships. Scholarships at Worth are highly prestigious awards available to students demonstrating outstanding talent and ability in the spheres of Academic Study, Art, Design and Technology, Drama, Music or Sport. Candidates must be registered with the school prior to entering the scholarship process and applications for bursaries should be made at the same time as applications for scholarships.

For all types of scholarships, awards can range in value and a candidate may also hold one or more awards, so that Academic, Art, Design and Technology, Drama. Music or Sport awards may be held concurrently. Additionally, at the Head Master's discretion, exceptional awards with a fee concession may be made where, during the assessment process, we identify exceptional potential or need. Tenure of any award depends upon continued satisfactory progress. The school reserves the right to vary the number of awards according to the strength of applications. The level of fee concession provided can be augmented by bursary support which is subject to means assessment.

For further information on scholarships and bursaries, please see the school website.

Fees per term (2023–2024). Years 9–13: Boarding £14,390, Day £9,800; Years 7 & 8: Day £6,605.

Friends of Worth. The parents of children at Worth run their own programme of social events to which all parents are invited.

Worth Society. All Old Worthians are entitled to join the alumni society which organises events as well as assisting with individual work experience and ongoing careers guidance. Contact Mary Lou Burge at worthsociety@worth.org.uk.

Charitable status. Worth School is a Registered Charity, number 1093914. Its aims and objectives are to promote religion and education.

Board of Governors:
Rt Rev Abbot Mark Barrett, OSB, MA Cantab, MA, PhD (*President*)
Mr Jeremy Fletcher, BA (*Chair*)
Mrs Brenda Alleyne, LLB
Ms Mary Coller, BSc
Dr Bridget Dolan, QC
Mr George Fitzsimons, MA, FCA
Mr Peter Green, Cert RE, MA
Mr Gavin Hamilton-Deeley, FCA
Dom Martin McGee, BA, MA, MSt
Ms Alison Palmer, BSc
Mrs Helen Parry, BSc
Mr Tim Pethybridge, MA
Dr Cameron Pyke, MA, MMus
Mr Geri Silverstone, MSc
Dom Peter Williams, OSB

***Head Master*: Mr Stuart McPherson**, MA
Second Master: Mr André Gushurst-Moore, MA
Interim Deputy Head (*Academic*): Dr Daniel Coughlan, BA, MA, PhD
Deputy Head (*External*): Mr Gordon Pearce, MA
Deputy Head (*Co-Curricular and Partnerships*): Mr Julian Williams, BSc, MA, Dip TESL
Assistant Head (*Pastoral*): Mr Mark Macdonald, BSc
Assistant Head (*Pupil Progress*): Mrs Sarah Flint, BA
Assistant Head (*Sixth Form*): Mr Matthew Doggett, MA, MSc
Director of Mission: Mr Dan Harris
Chief Operating Officer: Mr Jim Francis, MA Cantab, ACMA

Teaching Staff:
* *Head of Department/Subject*

Miss Sarai Adams, LLB, MA (*English*)
Mr Paul Ambridge, BA (*Physics*)
Mr Roger Appleton, BA (*French*)
Mrs Esme Mustian Atkinson, BA (*Librarian*)
Mr Garry Backshell, BSc Hons, MSc (*Physics*)
Mrs Frances Baily, BSc, MSc (**Physics*)
Mrs Andrea Beadle, BA, MA (**German*)
Mrs Sophie Belloul, BA (**French*)
Mr Jonathan Bindloss, BA, MA (**Religious Studies, Theory of Knowledge*)
Mr Stuart Blackhurst, HND (*Head of Digital Strategy*)
Mr Lewis Brito-Babapulle, MA (*Director of Music*)
Mrs Bethany Browning, MA (*Mathematics*)
Mr William Burch, MSc (*Maths*)
Mrs Caroline Burton, MSc (*Biology, St Anne's Housemistress*)
Mr David Burton, BEd (*Director of Sport*)
Mrs Lucinda Button, BA (*Art & Design*)
Mrs Katie Camp, BA (*Art*)
Mrs Olivia Carter, BSc (*Mathematics, Assistant to Head of Sixth Form A Level*)
Mr Raj Chaudhuri, BCom, ECB Level 4 (*Master in charge of Cricket*)
Mr Paul Cheeseman, BA (*Design and Technology*)
Miss Sarah Clarke, BA (**History*)
Mrs Dawn Clubb, BA, MA (**English*)
Mr James Coleman, BA (*Religious Studies, Assistant to Head of Sixth Form IB*)
Miss Karen Collingwood, BA (*Art*)
Mr Daniel Collins, LLB (*Head of Football*)
Mrs Camilla Cook, BA, MA (*English, Extended Essay Coordinator*)
Miss Hannah Coulson (*Graduate Sports Assistant*)
Mr William Crénel, LLCE (*French, St Bede's Housemaster*)
Mrs Claire Cross, BA (*Religious Studies*)
Miss Stephanie Dawes, BSc (*Psychology*)
Miss Maria Isabel Del Valle, BA Hons (*Spanish, French*)
Mr John Dent, MEng (*Mathematics*)
Mr Kieran Elson, BA, MA (*History*)
Mr John Everest, BA (**Photography, Assistant to Head of Middle School*)
Mrs Julie Fleming, LLB (*Business Studies*)
Dr Barbara Gehrhus, Diplomchemiker, PhD (*Chemistry*)
Mr Calum Giles (*Head of Hockey and Master in Charge of Golf*)
Mrs Sarah Glanville, BA (*English*)
Mrs Danielle Gwynne, BSc (**Mathematics*)
Mr Paul Harrison, BSc (*Geography*)
Mrs Jo Harvey-Barnes, Cert Ed (*Games & Physical Education, Biology, St Catherine's Housemistress*)
Ms Sabina Hickmet, BA (*French Teaching Assistant*)
Miss Hannah Higgins, BSC Hons, MSc (*Physics*)
Mrs Luthfa Hood, BA (*Computer Science*)
Mr Andrew Hunter, BA, MA, MSc (*English*)
Mr Joseph Huntley, BA (*Religious Studies, Head of PSHE*)
Mr Lewis Kelly, BA (*Graduate Sports Assistant*)
Mrs Jo-Anne Kennedy, BA (*Art*)
Mrs Andrea Kirpalani, BSc (**Science, *Chemistry*)
Miss Naomy Larkin, BA (*English*)
Mrs Catherine Latham, BSc, MSc (*Head of Learning Support and SENCO*)
Miss Amelia Lawson, BA (**Visual Arts*)
Mrs Rachel Le Mare, BA, MA (*Business Studies*)
Mrs Daniele Lloyd (*French*)
Miss Lucy Lockwood, BA (*Music Technology*)
Miss Elizabeth Longstaff, BA (*Learning Support Maths*)
Mrs Natalie Lynch, BA (*Director of Drama*)
Mrs Anna MacMahon, BA, MEd (*Austin Housemistress*)
Mr Alick Macleod, MSc (*Geography, Gervase Housemaster, Head of Boarding*)
Mrs Helen Macleod, BA (*History*)
Mr David Marks, BA, MA (**English as an Additional Language*)
Mrs Claudine Maude, BSc (*Biology, Interim Assistant to Head of Sixth Form A Level*)
Mrs Gemma McCabe, BSc (*Mathematics*)
Mr David McColl, BSc (*Sports Coach, Higher Level Teaching Assistant*)
Mrs Sigrid Moiseiwitsch (*German*)
Mrs Maria Molinero, BA (**Modern Foreign Languages, *Spanish*)
Mr Bruce Morrison, BEd (*Games & Physical Education, Mathematics, Butler Housemaster*)
Mr Robin Moss, BSc (*Chemistry & Science*)
Miss Tola Olawuyi, BEng (*Mathematics*)

Mr Andrew Olle-Nasim, BSc (*Games & Physical Education, Chapman Housemaster*)
Miss Amahlia Parkinson, BSc (*Religious Studies*)
Ms Elizabeth Peters, BA (*History & Politics*)
Mr Richard Phillips, BSc (**Economics and Business Studies*)
Ms Alessandra Pittoni, Laurea in Lingue (*Italian*)
Mr Thomas Richardson (*Head of Rugby Development*)
Mr Liam Richman, BSc (*Mathematics, Rutherford Housemaster*)
Mrs Beverley Rodwell, BA (*Learning Support, Deputy SENCO*)
Mr Stephen Rodwell, Cert Ed (*Assistant Director of Music*)
Miss Kathryne Rosati, BSc (*Science*)
Miss Eleanor Ross, BSc (*Chemistry, St Mary's (Middle) Housemistress*)
Miss Charlotte Rule, BSc (*Geography, St Mary's (Sixth Form) Housemistress*)
Ms Victoria Sadler, MA (*Geography*)
Dr Peter Scott, BSc, PhD (**Biology*)
Mrs Kirstie Smith (*Sports Coach*)
Mr Bevan Soga, BA (*Mathematics, Farwell Housemaster*)
Mrs Geeyoung Steele, BA (*Religious Studies*)
Mr Ben Taylor (*Games & Physical Education*)
Dr Bianca Thomas, BSc Hons, MSc, PhD (*Biology*)
Mrs Charlie Todman, BSc (*Mathematics*)
Mr Philip Towler, BA (**Classics*)
Mr Michael Turner (*Graduate Performing Arts Assistant*)
Mrs Averil Waghorne, BA (*Higher Level Teaching Assistant*)
Mr Matthew Walsh, BSc (*Assistant Director of Sport, Head of Academic and Core PE*)
Mr William Warwick, MA (*History*)
Mr Edward Watson, BSc (*Economics*)
Mr Dan Weaver, BA (**Design and Technology, *ICT*)
Mr Matthew Wellman, BA, MA (*Drama*)
Mr Tom Wilkinson, BSc (*Sports Coach – Performance*)

Registrar: Mrs Jo Everett
Head Master's Secretary: Mrs Samantha Braund
Head of Pupil Healthcare: Miss Tania Murphy

Wrekin College

Wellington, Shropshire TF1 3BH

Tel: 01952 265600
01952 265602 (Headmaster's Office)
01952 265603 (Admissions)
email: admissions@wrekincollege.com
website: www.wrekinoldhall.com
X/Twitter: @WrekinCol
Facebook: @WrekinCollege
Instagram: @wrekincollege
LinkedIn: /school/wrekincollege

Motto: *Aut vincere aut mori*

Wrekin College was founded in 1880 by Sir John Bayley and in 1923 became one of the Allied Schools, a group of independent schools.

Wrekin is a highly successful independent co-educational day and boarding school for children aged 11–18. Boasting an extensive campus in a beautiful part of Shropshire, Wrekin opened a new Dance Studio in September 2021, and its state-of-the-art Music School in January 2020. Wrekin now turns its attentions to its new Design and Technology Centre, its next major project. These additions come after the launch of Wrekin's enviable Business School, in January 2017, which has the future of Wrekin's pupils at its heart. The recent and future developments reflect the school's guiding principle to help every child achieve the most they are capable of, prepare them for the competitive world they will enter, and give them a lasting sense of the joy and value of learning that will enrich their future lives. Other facilities include a purpose-built Theatre, a double Sports Hall, Astroturf (a second all-weather playing surface opened in January 2022), 25m indoor swimming pool, together with all the expected classrooms, ICT facilities and a dedicated Sixth Form Centre. Co-educational since 1975, there are seven Houses, which cater for both day and boarding pupils, and these include dedicated junior Houses for the 11 to 13 intake. Everyone eats together in a central dining room and a Health and Wellbeing Centre is available to all pupils. The Chapel is central to the school both geographically and in the impact it makes on the ethos of the school.

Admission. Wrekin is non-selective; boarders and day pupils are admitted at 11+ and 13+ after sitting the Entry Examination or Common Entrance. There is also a Sixth Form entry based on GCSE achievement. Entry into other years is possible, dependent on places being available.

Term of Entry. The normal term of entry is the Autumn Term but pupils may be accepted at other times of the academic year.

Academic Matters. The core purpose of the school is teaching and learning to support each child in reaching his or her academic potential. Wrekin is proud of its academic record, based on stimulating intellectual curiosity, providing excellent and inspiring teaching, and making learning exciting.

Teachers are experienced, expert and approachable, and give a great deal of time to pupils both inside and outside the classroom. Our tutoring system means each pupil has personalised academic and pastoral support throughout the year. Our Support for Learning staff can help those with additional needs, and our enrichment programme stimulates and stretches our more able students.

Our curriculum is constantly reviewed in the light of changes in educational policy and philosophy, but we are committed to offering our pupils a solid and broad academic foundation. We offer a wide range of subjects for GCSE, A Level and BTEC exams, and guide pupils in choosing subjects that suit their interests, abilities and future plans. Our Head of Sixth Form offers expert advice on life after Wrekin, including university applications.

Sport. For a 'small' school, our sporting prowess is remarkable. We aim for very high standards in our core sports and a very wide range of options. We believe in excellence but also in participation – sport for all, and for life.

Educating the Whole Person. The outdoors is one of Wrekin's most valuable classrooms. The skills learned and adventures experienced during pupils' participation in the Combined Cadet Force and the Duke of Edinburgh's Award scheme stay with them for life. Both are enthusiastically supported by highly dedicated staff, and the take up among our pupils is impressive. We are very proud that Wrekin's 'completion rate' at all levels of the scheme is substantially above the national average.

What happens outside the classroom is just as important a part of a Wrekin education. The range and quality of activities available to every pupil is outstanding. Our pupils' development and achievements in these areas are supported by wonderful facilities and highly dedicated staff.

Scholarships and Bursaries.

Academic Scholarships are awarded at our normal entry points of 11, 13 and 16.

Music and Art/Design Scholarships: As for all other scholarships, Music and Art Awards will not exceed twenty five per cent of the fees. However, Music Scholarships carry with them a specified amount of free instrumental and/or vocal tuition. Candidates must also satisfy the school's normal academic entry requirements.

Sports Awards: Sports Scholarships may be awarded to candidates with outstanding ability in Sport. Applicants must attend a sports assessment day and satisfy the school's normal academic entry requirements. Candidates should be capable of a very significant contribution to the sporting success of Wrekin College. Typically candidates will have representative success at regional or National level.

Pendle Awards may be offered to all-rounders who have high academic standards and excellence in other areas such as sport, music or art. Those seeking a Pendle Award must sit the academic Scholarship Examination, either at 11+, 13+ or 16+ level and meet scholarship standard in at least one other area.

Bursaries may be awarded on entry and can be awarded in addition to a scholarship. All bursaries are means-tested.

For further information please visit our website www.wrekinoldhall.com

Fees per term (2023–2024). Years 7 and 8: £5,850 (day), £8,450 (weekly boarding), £10,350 (full boarding UK), £11,200 (full boarding international). Years 9–13: £7,050 (day), £9,900 (weekly boarding), £12,110 (full boarding UK), £13,100 (full boarding international).

Music lessons: £29.25 per 30-minute session; Extra tuition: £29.25 per 30-minute session.

Sibling discounts are available when three or more siblings are enrolled in the Trust; details on request.

Old Wrekinian Association. A flourishing Wrekinian Association of over 3,500 members exists to make possible continuous contact between the School and its old pupils, for the benefit of both and to support the ideals and aims of the school. It is expected that pupils will become members of the Old Wrekinian Association when they leave Wrekin.

Charitable status. Wrekin Old Hall Trust Limited is a Registered Charity, number 528417. It exists to provide independent boarding and day co-education in accordance with the Articles of Association of Wrekin College.

Visitor: The Rt Revd The Lord Bishop of Lichfield

Governors:
R J Pearson, BSc (*Chair*)
Revd M Beer
E Crawford, MB, ChB, BSc, MRCP [OW]
A J Dixon, LLB
T Edwards
J A Grant, BSc [OW]
N Griffiths [OW]
R M L Jones, FCA, BA Hons
P Mack, BSc, ACA, CTA
M Samra, FRGGP
D Styles
L Welsby
R Yates-Ward

[OW] Old Wrekinian

***Headmaster*: T Spence**, BA, MEd

Senior Deputy Head: Mrs A Wright, BSc

Deputy Head (*Teaching and Learning*): B Smith, BA, MPhil

†*Assistant Head* (*Head of Boarding*): Dr G Roberts, BSc, PhD
Assistant Head (*Co-Curricular*): D Winterton, BA
Assistant Head (*Director of Planning*): P M Stanway, BSc
Assistant Head (*Director of Music and Head of Middle School*): S Platford, MBE, BA, LTCL, ABSM

Head of Sixth Form: T Southall, BSc

Bursar: D Brown, BA, ACMA, CGMA

Assistant Staff:
† *Housemaster/mistress*

E Anastasi
T Asch, BA
J Ashington-Carter
D Blanch, MA, MBA, MA (*Cantab*)
†E Boffey, BSc
J Boulter, BA
R Brock, BSc
†H S R Brown, BA
S Carter, BEng, MBA
S E Clarke, BA, FRGS
M Crone, BA
K Davies, BSc
C Del Manso
R Edge, BSc
R Evans, BA
S Hammerton, BSc
R Harrison, BA
S-B Holder, BA
L Howsam
A Jagger, BA
W Jennings
R Johnson
A King
A Knight, BSc
†J D Kotas, BA
B Lambert
T Lintern, BSc
K B Livingstone, BA
†J Longfellow, BA, MEd Cantab
C Manganaro
†J Mather, BSc
D Mathias, BSc
S Mathias, BA
†H Milton, BA
F Milton, BA
R Norval, BSc
J G Phillips, BA
A Pitchford, BSc
K Richards, BSc
C A Ritchie-Morgan
R Salano Marin, BA
J Shaw, BA
J Shindler, BSc
A Thomas
C Thust, BSc
A Tickner, MSc
S Trask, BEng
G Walker
A Walsh, BA
†M N J Warner, BSc
A E Wedge, BSc
S Williams
Dr A Woodshore-Gray, BA, MA, PhD

Support for Learning:
M Beattie, BA, TEFL
H Ingoldby, BA, TEFL
J Roberts, BA, BSc, TEFL
D Tunnah, BSC, QTS, NASENCO, CPT3A
French Assistant: F Kennedy

Visiting Music Staff:
L Adamson (*Voice – Classical, Music Theatre, Rock and Pop*)
J Burgess (*Flute*)
R Ellis (*Voice – Music Theatre, Rock and Pop*)
M Giles (*Piano*)
C Hickman (*Low Brass*)
Dr M Hall (*Piano*)
T Hall (*Percussion*)
O James (*Percussion*)
A Jones (*Guitar*)
C J Jones (*Piano, Clarinet and Saxophone*)
L Jones (*Violin*)
Y Kagajo (*Piano*)
J Magee (*Cello*)
P Parker (*Guitar*)
A Pinel (*Organ and Piano*)
F Stubbs (*Bassoon*)
M Svensson (*Strings*)
G Wilkes (*Upper Brass*)

Games:
C A Ritchie-Morgan (*Head of Girls' Games*)
J Shaw (*Director of Sport*)

Sports Coaches:
T Asch (*Rugby*)
J Ashington-Carter (*Rugby*)
K Bennett (*Girls' Games*)
G Bush (*Athletics*)
D Clarke (*Swimming*)
L Coop (*Hockey*)
P Dean (*Netball*)
F Edwards (*Tennis*)
T Ettridge (*Cricket*)
J Gwynne (*Sports Graduate*)
B Lambert (*Rugby*)
P Lauder (*Badminton*)
J Longfellow (*Rugby*)
D Mathias (*Rugby*)
S Mathias (*Hockey*)
J Mostyn (*Senior Options*)
K Richards (*Football*)
T Simms (*Basketball*)
O Stevenson (*Sports Graduate*)
L Toor (*Sports Graduate*)
I Williamson (*Cross Country*)
S Williams (*Hockey*)
V Woodman (*Netball*)

CCF:
SSI & Outward Bound Activities Instructor: A Chwalinski
Secretary OWA: M de Weymarn

Deputy Bursars:
Operations and Head of Estates: H Hyde
Facilities: B C Crone
Chaplain: Revd L Plummer, BA, LTh

Director of Marketing: C Hendy, BA
Head of Admissions (*UK*): R Curel
Head of Admissions (*Int*): E Cornaby
Headmaster's Personal Assistant: K Daniels, BSc

HMC International

ALPHABETICAL LIST OF SCHOOLS

HMC Schools in Europe

The British School of Brussels

Pater Dupierreuxlaan 1, 3080 Tervuren, Belgium
Tel: 00 32 2 766 04 30
email: admissions@britishschool.be
website: www.britishschool.be
X/Twitter: @BSB_Brussels
Facebook: @britishschoolbrussels
Instagram: @bsb_brussels
LinkedIn: /the-british-school-of-brussels

Creation. The British School of Brussels (BSB) was founded in 1969 as a non-profit making organisation in Belgium and was opened in 1970 by HRH The Duke of Edinburgh. It is run by a Board of Governors, comprising distinguished British and Belgian citizens from both the professional and business worlds, together with parent and staff representatives.

Site. The school occupies a beautiful site of ten hectares, surrounded by woodlands and lakes near the Royal Museum of Central Africa in Tervuren, which is 20–25 minutes by car from the centre of Brussels. The site belongs to the Donation Royale, the Foundation which manages the estates left to the Belgian people at the beginning of the 20th century by King Leopold II.

Facilities. The school has excellent modern specialist facilities, situated on a green and spacious campus. These facilities include dance and drama studios, a university standard music suite as well as eleven science laboratories, four art studios and seven technology workshops. The campus is also home to an Early Childhood Centre for children of 1–3 years. The sporting facilities of the school have been extensively developed to include world class amenities such as a multi-purpose sports hall, gymnasium, and fitness suite. In addition, the BSB is the only international school in Belgium to have its own competition standard swimming pool. The school's outdoor sports facilities were redesigned in 2019 and now include multiple sports pitches, tennis courts and the largest free-standing bouldering wall in any school in Europe. As well as the exterior sports grounds, students also enjoy outdoor learning in the campus grounds and the adjoining forest. To aid learning at most stages of their development, students in most year groups are issued with either their own iPad or laptop computer.

Organisation. The British School of Brussels is an independent, fee-paying, non-profit-making international school. The School is a co-educational, non-selective day school for students from 1 to 18 years of age, with a roll of approximately 1,350. Around 30% of the students are British and there are approximately 70 other nationalities represented. The curriculum, both in the Primary School and Secondary School, is a British-based curriculum up to age 16, adapted to suit the needs of our European context and international students. In the Secondary School, students sit GCSE/IGCSE examinations at the end of Year 11 (aged 16). Senior students then have the choice of three pre-university qualifications: The International Baccalaureate (IB) Diploma (with English/French or English/Dutch bilingual options), GCE A Levels or BTEC courses in business, sports, applied science, and hospitality prior to moving on to Higher Education in the UK, USA, Belgium and beyond. Provision is also made for Oxbridge tuition and US university applications.

Our examination results, year on year, are very impressive and place us in the top performing schools globally. At A Level in 2023, over half of the total grades attained ranged between A* and B, with an outstanding 32% attaining the coveted A or A* grade – these exceptional results, contributing to BSB's 99% pass rate. The 2023 IB results contributed to an impressive three-year average of 37 points. Many students surpassed the 40-point threshold, securing admissions to renowned global universities. With a pass rate of 97%, BSB students again surpassed the global average of 79%. At BTEC level in 2023, 56.5% of all grades were awarded at the Distinction or Distinction* level, while a notable 85% achieved Merit or higher grades. At GCSE level, 92% of all grades awarded to BSB students were Grade 4 or above (where Grade 4 is considered a pass).

BSB has an established French/English bilingual programme for children aged 4–14 years to complement its English-medium teaching. We introduce the teaching of Spanish, German or Dutch as optional additional languages in the Secondary School. We have developed programmes to help students with specific learning needs and to help students who join us with little or no English skills. The school also employs a counsellor.

Enrichment Activities. In addition to curricular activities, we run one of the largest extra-curricular programmes in Europe. Our dedicated teachers and coaches offer around 200 different clubs and activities, from tennis to tag rugby and choir to creative writing.

With a three-tier approach, covering all aspects of participation, we offer after-school recreational sports (dance, netball, hockey, water polo, synchronised swimming and many more), competitive sports (our ISST and SCIS seasonal formats – basketball, cross-country, golf, athletics, volleyball) and our tier 1 academy sports that run year-round (football, swimming, and gymnastics).

Elsewhere, among many other options, students can follow their artistic passions in our music, drama, art, and design clubs, and feed their curiosity through our extra-curricular science and technology programmes.

Music and Drama. The Music Department houses an extremely well-equipped music technology studio, a recording studio, and a rehearsal studio for the school's orchestras, concert bands and instrumental ensembles. Individual instrument lessons are available from visiting specialist teachers, and take place in the suite of music practice rooms. The school is the largest Associated Board centre in Europe. Each year up to fifteen drama productions – including student-directed performances – are presented across the full student age range. The 240-

seat Brel Theatre has its own workshop and Green Room, as well as a more intimate studio space that seats 80.

Careers. The school has the highest expectations of its student population and advice on careers, as well as higher and further education opportunities, is of vital importance to the further development of the students. The school takes part in many careers conventions and has its own international higher education and careers team.

Fees per annum (2023–2024). From €33,105 (Reception) to €42,360 (Years 10–13).

Past Students' Association. The school has a growing association of Alumni and has its own official BSB Alumni Facebook page. Please visit the Alumni section of the school website (Zwww.Zbritishschool.be) to see how to subscribe to the alumni newsletter and follow the school on Twitter and LinkedIn.

Patron: Her Excellency the British Ambassador to the King of the Belgians

Chairman of the Board: Mr Ian Backhouse

***Principal*: Ms Melanie Warnes**

Vice Principal and Head of Primary School: Mr Neil Ringrose

Vice Principal and Head of Secondary School (*Acting*): Mr James Johnson

The British School of Paris

38 quai de l'Ecluse, Croissy sur Seine 78290, France

Tel: 00 33 1 34 80 45 90
email: info@britishschool.fr
website: www.britishschool.fr
X/Twitter: @BritishSchParis
Facebook: @BritishSchParis
Instagram: @britishschparis
LinkedIn: /school/britishschparis

Age Range. 3–18.

Number of Pupils. 630 (Boys and Girls).

Fees per annum (2023–2024). Senior School: €29,237–€31,498; Junior School: €19,126–€26,519.

The BSP provides, in a caring environment, a high-quality British-style education for British and international students, to enable them to become caring citizens and to lead fulfilling lives.

Located just 15 kilometres from Paris, the School caters for English-speaking children of over 50 nationalities (about 30% are British) from ages 3–18. It is a not-for-profit association in France and is presided over by a governing body under the patronage of Her Excellency the British Ambassador to France.

The **Junior School** provides education for primary aged children from 3–11 years. The purpose-built Junior School is located very close to the Senior School along the banks of the river Seine. There are 35 classrooms accommodating up to 480 pupils, as well as 4 bespoke classrooms and 2 activity areas that are dedicated to our foundation stage/nursery section. Studies are based on the English National Curriculum with emphasis on English, Maths and Science, and of course, the French language. Being a holistic educator the BSP has a strong co-curricular base with a special focus on music and drama as well as a large variety of sports. (*For further information about the Junior School, see entry in IAPS section*).

The **Senior School**, which caters for pupils aged from 11–18 years, is situated beside a beautiful stretch of the Seine in Croissy sur Seine. The buildings, with the exception of two nineteenth century houses, have been built since 1990. The Science and Technology block provides excellent facilities for Science, Information Technology, Electronics and Design. There are six large, well equipped science laboratories. The other classroom blocks house Humanities, Art, Business Studies, Modern Languages, Music, English and Mathematics. Other facilities include a generously staffed and resourced student career guidance programme, a library, IT labs, a refectory, a large sports hall and fitness centre. Students enter at the age of 11 and for the first three years, a broad general education is maintained in line with the National Curriculum. Pupils are prepared for the GCSE and A Level examinations in a comprehensive range of subjects.

Music and drama are an integral part of school life; the music centre includes teaching and practice facilities as well as a well-equipped electronic studio. Specialist teachers visit the School to provide individual lessons in a wide range of instruments. Children take the Associated Board exams at regular intervals.

The School has had considerable sporting success over the years, winning the International Schools' Sports Tournament competition in girls' field hockey, and boys' rugby. Our international fixture lists provide an incentive to gain a place in school teams. As well as local matches our teams travel regularly to Belgium, Holland and the UK.

Small overall numbers, modest class sizes and a supportive pastoral system all help new pupils integrate quickly. Our examination results are outstanding. At A Level over 41% of all grades were A* and A and 96% of all grades at GCSE were between 9–4 in 2023. These results compare very favourably with high-calibre schools in the UK. Most students continue their education at prestigious universities in the UK, USA, France and worldwide. BSP students have been successfully admitted to the Universities of Cambridge and Oxford, London School of Economics, University of Pennsylvania, Stanford University, McGill University, Universidad de Madrid, Seoul National University, L'Université de la Sorbonne, to mention but a few.

Chairman of Governors: Mr E Coutts

***Headmaster*: Mr N Hammond**

Head of Senior School: Mr N Hammond

Head of the Junior School: Mr M Potter

Registrar: Mrs K Dufraisse

Other HMC International Schools

Africa

Kenya

Peponi School

PO Box 236, Ruiru 00232, Kenya
email: office@peponischool.org
website: www.peponischool.org

***Headmaster*: Mark Durston**

South Africa

Michaelhouse

Balgowan 3275, Kwazulu-Natal, South Africa
email: info@michaelhouse.org
website: www.michaelhouse.org

***Rector*: Antony Clark**

Zimbabwe

Peterhouse

Private Bag 3741, Marondera 00263, Zimbabwe
email: rector@peterhouse.co.zw
website: www.peterhouse.co.zw

***Rector*: Jon Trafford**

St George's College

3 Borrowdale Road, Harare, Zimbabwe
email: farrellyj@sgc.ac.zw
website: www.stgeorges.co.zw

***Headmaster*: Mr John Farrelly**

Asia

Brunei Darussalam

Jerudong International School

Jalan Universiti, Kampong Tungku, Bandar Seri Begawan BE2119, Brunei Darussalam
email: enrol@jis.edu.bn
website: www.jerudonginternationalschool.com

***Principal*: Nicholas E Sheehan**

China

Wellington College International Shanghai

No. 1500 Yao Long Road, Pudong New District, Shanghai 200124, China
email: info.shanghai@wellingtoncollege.cn
website: https://shanghai.wellingtoncollege.cn/

***Master*: Brendon Fulton**

Hong Kong

Harrow International School

38 Tsing Ying Road, Tuen Mun, New Territories, Hong Kong
email: info@harrowschool.hk
website: www.harrowschool.hk

***Head*: Ms Ann Haydon**

Kellett School

7 Lam Hing Street, Kowloon Bay, Kowloon, Hong Kong
email: mss@kellettschool.com
website: www.kellettschool.com

***Principal & CEO*: Diana Vernon (interim to April 2024)**, Paul Tough (from April 2024) [HMC]

Head of Kowloon Bay Prep School: Shane Nathan (*interim to Sept. 2024*) [IAPS]

India

The British School, New Delhi

Dr Jose P Rizal Marg, Chanakyapuri, New Delhi 110021, India
email: thebritishschool@british-school.org
website: www.british-school.org

***Director*: Vanita Uppal**, OBE

The Doon School

Mall Road, Dehradun 248003, Uttaranchal, India
email: info@doonschool.com
website: www.doonschool.com

***Headmaster*: Dr Jagpreet Singh**

Indonesia

The British School Jakarta

Bintaro Jaya Sector 9, Jl Raya Jombang - Ciledug, Pondok Aren, Tangerang 15427, Jakarta, Indonesia
email: principal@bsj.sch.id
website: www.bsj.sch.id

***Principal*: Mr David N Butcher**

Malaysia

Kolej Tuanku Ja'afar

Mantin, Negeri Sembilan 71700, West Malaysia
email: principal@ktj.edu.my
website: www.ktj.edu.my

***Principal*: Dr Glenn Moodie**

Marlborough College Malaysia

Jalan Marlborough, 79200 Iskander Puteri, Johor, Malaysia
email: marlborough@marlboroughcollege.my
website: www.marlboroughcollegemalaysia.org

***Master*: Alan D Stevens**

Thailand

Harrow International School Bangkok

45 Soi Kosumruamchai 14, Kosumruamchai Rd, Don Mueang Subdistrict, Bangkok 10210, Thailand
email: admissions@harrowschool.ac.th
website: www.harrowschool.ac.th

***Head Master*: James Murphy-O'Connor**

Shrewsbury International School

1922 Charoen Krung Road, Wat Prayakrai, Bang Kholame, Bangkok 10120, Thailand
email: enquiries@shrewsbury.ac.th
website: www.shrewsbury.ac.th

***Principal*: Rob Millar**

Australia and New Zealand

Australia

St Leonard's College

163 South Road, Brighton East, Victoria 3187, Australia
email: stleonards@stleonards.vic.edu.au
website: www.stleonards.vic.edu.au

***Principal*: Peter Clague**

The Scots College

Victoria Road, Bellevue Hill, NSW 2023, Australia
email: reception@tsc.nsw.edu.au
website: www.tsc.nsw.edu.au

***Principal*: Dr Ian P M Lambert**

Central, North and South America

Argentina

St George's College North

Mosconi 3500 y Don Bosco s/n, Los Polvorines, Buenos Aires B1613 FTP, Argentina
email: informes@stgeorges.edu.ar
website: www.stgeorges.edu.ar/north

***Headmaster*: Oliver Proctor**

St George's College Quilmes

Guido 800, Quilmes, CP: 1878, Buenos Aires, Argentina
email: infoquilmes@stgeorges.edu.ar
website: https://www.stgeorges.edu.ar/quilmes/

***Headmaster*: James Diver**

Brazil

St Paul's School

Rua Juquiá 166, Jardim Paulistano, São Paulo SP 01440-903, Brazil
email: spshead@stpauls.br
website: www.stpauls.br

***Head*: Titus Edge**

(*See entry in IAPSO section*)

Canada

Crofton House School

3200 West 41st Avenue, Vancouver BC V6N 3E1, Canada
email: eharrop@croftonhouse.ca
website: www.croftonhouse.ca

***Head*: Ena Harrop**

St Michaels University School

3400 Richmond Road, Victoria BC V8P 4P5, Canada
email: headofschool@smus.ca
website: www.smus.ca

***Head of School*: Mark Turner**

Chile

The Grange School

Av Principe de Gales 6154, La Reina, 687067, Santiago, Chile
email: rectoria@grange.cl
website: www.grange.cl

***Headmaster*: Mr Nicholas Eatough**

Europe

Cyprus

The English School

1 Presidential Palace Avenue and Kyriacou Matsi, 1082 Nicosia, Cyprus

email: info@englishschool.ac.cy
website: www.englishschool.ac.cy

***Headmaster*: Mr Stuart Walker**

Czech Republic

The English College in Prague

Sokolovska 320, 190-00 Praha 9, Vysočany, Czech Republic

email: office@englishcollege.cz
website: www.englishcollege.cz

***Headmaster*: Dr Nigel Brown**

Greece

Campion School

Agias Ioulianis 2, Pallini, Athens 153 51, Greece

email: mhenderson@campion.edu.gr
website: www.campion.edu.gr

***Headmaster*: Mike Henderson**

St Catherine's British School

Sofokil Venizelou 77, 141 23 Lykovrissi, Athens GR 145 10, Greece

email: headmaster@stcatherines.gr
website: www.stcatherines.gr

***Headmaster*: Mr Stuart Smith**

Italy

The British School of Milan

Via Carlo Alberto Pisani Dossi 16, 20134 Milan, Italy

email: info@bsm.school
website: www.britishschoolmilan.com

***Principal & CEO*: Dr Chris Greenhalgh**

St George's British International School

Via Cassia, La Storta, 00123 Rome, Italy

email: info@stgeorge.school.it
website: www.stgeorge.school.it

***Principal & CEO*: Dr John Knight**

Netherlands

The British School in The Netherlands

Jan van Hooflaan 3, Voorschoten 2252 BG, The Netherlands

email: admissions@britishschool.nl
website: www.britishschool.nl

***CEO*: Heath Monk**

Headteachers:

Junior School Leidschenveen: Mrs Karren van Zoest

Junior School Vlaskamp: Mrs Claire Waller

Senior School Leidschenveen: Mr James Oxlade

Senior School Voorschoten: Mr Patrick Heuff

Portugal

St Julian's School

Quinta Nova, 2775-588 Carcavelos, Portugal

email: mail@stjulians.com
website: www.stjulians.com

***Head of School*: Paul Morgan**

Spain

The British School of Barcelona
Cognita Schools Group

BSB City Main Campus, Carrer Lucà 1, 08022 Barcelona, Spain

email: school@bsb.edu.es
website: www.britishschoolbarcelona.com

***Acting Executive Principal*: Mr James Petrie**

King's College
The British School of Madrid

Paseo de los Andes 35, Soto de Viñuelas, Madrid 28761, Spain

email: info@kingscollege.es
website: https://www.madrid-soto.kingscollegeschools.org/en

***Headteacher*: Mr Matthew Taylor**, MA Oxon, MA London, PGCE, FRSA

Head of Primary Department: Paula Parkinson, BA Hons Newcastle, PGCE Manchester

Switzerland

Aiglon College

Avenue Centrale 61, Chesières 1885, Switzerland

email: info@aiglon.ch
website: www.aiglon.ch

***Head Master*: Mr Richard McDonald**, MA Oxon, PGCE

Middle East

Bahrain

St Christopher's School

PO Box 32052, Isa Town, Kingdom of Bahrain

email: office.principal@school.st-chris.net
website: www.st-chris.net

***Principal*: Dr Simon Watson [HMC]**

Head of Infant School: Ms Nat Dickinson

Head of Junior School: Mr Ian Fellows [IAPS]

Head of Senior School: Yasmine Dannawy

Oman

British School Muscat

PO Box 1907, Ruwi 112, Sultanate of Oman

email: principal@britishschoolmuscat.com
website: www.britishschoolmuscat.com

***Principal*: Mr Kai Vacher**

Qatar

Doha College

PO Box 7506, Al Niser St, Doha, State of Qatar

email: principal@dohacollege.com
website: www.dohacollege.com

***Principal*: David P. Tongue**

Senior Vice Principal, Head of Secondary: Jerome Scafe

Vice Principal, Head of Primary: Mrs Ruth Whymark

Saudi Arabia

British International School Riyadh

2786 Ibrahim Mubarak Said Ad Dusari 7693, Riyadh 13241, Saudi Arabia

website: www.bisr.com.sa

***Director*: Helen Olds**

United Arab Emirates

Brighton College Abu Dhabi

Bloom Gardens, Khalifa Park, Abu Dhabi, United Arab Emirates

email: headmaster@brightoncollege.ae
website: www.brightoncollege.ae

***Head Mistress*: Mr Scott Carnochan [HMC]**

Head of Prep: Mr Daniel Cummings [IAPS]

The British School Al Khubairat

PO Box 4001, Abu Dhabi, United Arab Emirates

email: headmaster@britishschool.sch.ae
website: www.britishschool.sch.ae

***Headmaster*: Mr Mark Leppard**, MBE

Deira International School Al Badia

Dubai Festival City, Dubai 79043, United Arab Emirates

email: Info@disdubai.ae
website: www.disdubai.ae

***Director*: Simon O'Connor**

Dubai College

PO Box 837, Dubai, United Arab Emirates

email: dcadmin@dubaicollege.org
website: www.dubaicollege.org

***Headmaster*: Mr Michael Lambert**

GEMS Wellington International School

Al Sufouh Area, Sheikh Zayed Road, Dubai, United Arab Emirates

email: reception_wis@gemsedu.com
website: www.wellingtoninternationalschool.com

***Principal & CEO*: Maryssa O'Connor**

JESS, Dubai

PO Box 24942, Dubai, United Arab Emirates

email: jess@jess.sch.ae
website: www.jess.sch.ae

***Director*: Shane O'Brien [HMC]**

Head Teacher, JESS Jumeirah Primary: Mr Luke Rees

Head Teacher, JESS Arabian Ranches Primary: Mr Jose Diez [IAPS]

Head Teacher, JESS Arabian Ranches Secondary: Mr Michael Waller

Jumeirah College, Dubai

Al Wasi Road, Dubai, United Arab Emirates

email: info_jcd@gemsedu.com
website: www.gemsjc.com

***Principal*: Mr Nicholas Brain**

The Heads' Conference

Associates

In addition to Full membership (open to Heads of independent schools in the UK and Ireland) and International membership (open to Heads of independent schools overseas), HMC also elects a small number of Associates each year.

HMC Associates are either heads of high-performing maintained sector schools proposed and supported by HMC divisions or influential individuals in the world of education, including university vice-chancellors and academics, who endorse and support the work of HMC.

The following is a list of current HMC Associates:

MARK HANLEY-BROWNE
Alpha Plus Group, London W1
website: www.alphaplusgroup.co.uk

STEPHEN GILMORE (Acting Principal)
Bangor Grammar School, Bangor, Northern Ireland
website: www.bangorgrammarschool.org.uk

DR STUART D SMALLWOOD
Bishop Wordsworth's School, Salisbury, Wiltshire
website: www.bishopwordsworths.org.uk

ANDREW MOSS
Gordon's School, West End, Surrey
website: www.gordons.school

JENNY LENDRUM
Methodist College, Belfast, Northern Ireland
website: www.methody.org

JUDITH FENN
Methodist Independent Schools Trust, London NW1
website: www.methodistschools.org.uk

RACHEL REES
Monmouth School for Girls, Monmouth, Wales
website: www.habsmonmouth.org/girls

RUSSEL ELLICOTT
Pate's Grammar School, Cheltenham, Gloucestershire
website: www.pates.gloucs.sch.uk

JON WOODS
The Judd School, Tonbridge, Kent
website: www.judd.online

JILL BERRY
Educational Consultant

DR BRENDA DESPONTIN
Former Head

PART II

Schools whose Heads are members of the Girls' Schools Association

ALPHABETICAL LIST OF SCHOOLS

GSA
GEOGRAPHICAL LIST OF SCHOOLS

The following schools, whose Heads are members of both GSA and HMC, can be found in the HMC section:

The Abbey
Berkhamsted Schools Group
Bromley High School
Bury Grammar Schools
Cheltenham Ladies' College
City of London School for Girls
Downe House
Francis Holland School, Regent's Park
Francis Holland School, Sloane Square
Godolphin and Latymer School
James Allen's Girls' School (JAGS)
Kent College Pembury
Moreton Hall
Queen Anne's School
Queenswood School
Roedean School
The Royal Masonic School for Girls
St Helen & St Katharine
St Mary's School Ascot
Sherborne Girls
Streatham & Clapham High School
Withington Girls' School
Woldingham School

The following school, whose Head is member of both GSA and The Society of Heads, can be found in The Society of Heads section:

St Gabriel's

The following schools, whose Heads are members of both GSA and IAPS, can be found in the IAPS section:

Bute House Preparatory School for Girls
Kensington Prep School
Pembridge Hall School
Sarum Hall School
Stormont School

Individual School Entries

The Abbey

Kendrick Road, Reading RG1 5DZ
Tel: 0118 987 2256
email: schooloffice@theabbey.co.uk
website: www.theabbey.co.uk
X/Twitter: @theabbeyschool
Facebook: @theabbeyschoolberkshire
Instagram: @theabbeyschoolreading
LinkedIn: /company/the-abbey-school-reading

See full entry in the **HMC** section, on **p. 7**.

Abbot's Hill School

Bunkers Lane, Hemel Hempstead, Herts HP3 8RP
Tel: 01442 240333
email: registrar@abbotshill.herts.sch.uk
website: www.abbotshill.herts.sch.uk
X/Twitter: @AbbotsHill
Facebook: @AbbotsHillSchool
LinkedIn: /abbot's-hill

Motto: *Vi et Virtute*

Founded 1912.

Abbot's Hill is a school where one size does not fit all. We know and value everyone: we know that pupils do better when they are happy and so their wellbeing is our central focus. We know that every pupil will find their own path and so we help them to navigate it alongside dedicated and expert staff, committed to ensuring that each individual thrives.

The School was founded on the present site in 1912 by sisters Alice, Katrine and Mary Baird, who founded the school to educate young women of character. Set in 76 acres of grounds within easy reach of St Albans, Berkhamsted, Kings Langley and the surrounding villages, and with excellent transport links to the M25 and the Euston train line, we pride ourselves on the broad and stimulating education we provide. One foot is firmly rooted in our heritage but the other strides forwards into the future.

The school's founding motto was *Vie et Virtute – meaning 'Strength and Power* – and this spirit lives on through our values, which underpin all that we do. Diverse pupils with wide-ranging talents and backgrounds come together in a close community that is large enough to offer choice and flexibility but compact enough to ensure that no child is overlooked.

At Abbot's Hill, academic excellence goes hand in hand with pastoral excellence. We are ambitious for all our pupils and offer exceptional learning opportunities to stretch, challenge and support the individuals in our care.

Self-belief and happiness, alongside a 'can-do' approach to every aspect of school life, enable our pupils to thrive and succeed. We are especially proud of the confidence which typifies our Year 11 leavers: they are the 'top' of the school and this means they have leadership opportunities beyond those of their contemporaries. As a result, they leave us equipped with the skills and confidence to prosper in their future lives.

We believe our pupils enjoy inspirational learning opportunities alongside challenging and enriching co-curricular activities, in a safe environment where they can be themselves and learn to be independent, resilient and confident. Beyond the classroom, our pupils' experiences are vast and varied. From our many co-curricular clubs to a comprehensive schedule of day trips and residential visits, the opportunities are endless. It is through this wealth of opportunity that each pupils finds what sparks her curiosity and love of learning.

Music and Performing Arts. The school has very strong Music and Performing Arts Departments with excellent facilities. The Performing Arts building includes studios for dance, drama and music as well as a theatre. The School Choirs and Orchestra perform regularly in concerts, recitals, plays, musicals and various functions throughout the year and there is a school production each year.

Sports. The school has a strong sporting tradition. There is a well-equipped Sports Hall, lacrosse pitches, grass and hard tennis courts, and a swimming pool. The main sports played are Lacrosse, Netball, Athletics, Tennis, Rounders and Swimming. All girls are encouraged to participate in the sporting opportunities at Abbot's Hill and currently there are a number of girls who have reached County and National standard in selected sports.

Extracurricular Activities. Many activities and clubs are held outside of school and these vary in range from Dance, Art, The Duke of Edinburgh's Award scheme, Music, Speech and Drama and all sports.

Admission. Admission to Abbot's Hill is by Entrance Examination, interview, and a report from the previous school.

Scholarships and Bursaries. Academic, Art, Drama, Music and Sport scholarships are available giving 5–10% reduction in fees. Means-tested Bursaries are also available.

Fees per term (2023–2024). Reception–Year 6: £4,421–£5,627; Year 7–11: £7,613–£7,658.

Prep School. Abbot's Hill Prep is situated in the same grounds as the Senior School. The Prep School provides Pre-Preparatory and Preparatory education for girls aged 4 and above. Abbot's Hill Nursery and Pre-School welcome boys and girls from 6 months of age. The Prep mixes the formal setting of the classroom with the wealth of opportunity provided by our physical surroundings. Children are given the freedom in which to grow, learn and play. Classrooms and corridors are bright and well decorated with children's work reflecting the diversity of the curriculum.

The Prep School plays a very important role within our school community and is an integral part of the school as a whole. It is our aim at Abbot's Hill to nurture the whole child, thus enabling our pupils to develop their talents whether they be academic, artistic or sporting. Specialist teaching is introduced from a child's earliest days; French, Music and PE are introduced in the pre-school year. This is added to as a child progresses to include Drama, Games, ICT and Geography. By the time a girl reaches Year 5 she is being completely subject taught and is able to adapt to moving around whilst being supported by a class teacher.

The small class sizes at Abbot's Hill Prep enable individual needs to be recognised and met early with the minimum disruption. For those who need extra support this is offered within the classroom setting or one-to-one as appropriate. Gifts or talents for a particular area of learning can be extended and developed to their potential.

The wider curriculum plays a key role. Educational visits are an integral part of the teaching programme and children are regularly taken on visits to galleries and museums to enhance their learning experience. Outside visitors lead workshops at school for year groups or the whole school as appropriate. The extracurricular programme is wide ranging and ever changing. It currently includes such wide-ranging pursuits as languages, trampolining, gardening and board games as well as a wealth of musical and sports clubs.

Further information. Abbot's Hill welcomes visits from prospective parents and pupils. If you would like to visit the School, please contact the Registrar for an appointment on 01442 240333 or email registrar@abbotshill.herts.sch.uk.

Charitable status. Abbot's Hill Charitable Trust is a Registered Charity, number 311053, which exists to provide high quality education for children.

Chair of the Governing Body: Mr Debashis Dasgupta

***Headmistress*: Mrs K Gorman**, BA, MEd Cantab

Head of Prep School: Miss K Bluck, MA, PGCE, QTS

Bursar: Mr Michael Waymouth, BA, MA, MCGI Cert, IoD CMgr, FCMI

Registrar: Miss A Cooper

Badminton School

Westbury-on-Trym, Bristol BS9 3BA

Tel: 0117 905 5200
email: admissions@badmintonschool.co.uk
website: www.badmintonschool.co.uk
X/Twitter: @BadmintonSchool
Facebook: @BadmintonSch
Instagram: @BadmintonSchool
LinkedIn: /school/badminton-school-limited

Motto: *Pro Omnibus Quisque Pro Deo Omnes*

Founded 1858. Non-denominational.

Badminton is an independent girls' day, boarding and weekly boarding school situated in a 15-acre site in Westbury-on-Trym on the outskirts of the university city of Bristol.

Age range of pupils. 4 to 18.

Number of pupils. 550.

Number of staff. Full-time teaching 37, Part-time teaching 16. Teacher to Pupil ratio is currently 1:7.

Educational philosophy. While the school retains an outstanding academic record, its focus continues to be on nurturing the girls' natural curiosity and fuelling their passion for learning. The enduring excellence that Badminton girls achieve, stems from the positive atmosphere in the School and the holistic approach to education, as well as the exceptional relationships between staff and pupils, which are mature, friendly and based on principles of courtesy and mutual respect. Teachers are highly qualified specialists in their field and encourage girls to develop academic confidence and to become independent learners by taking responsibility for their work and progress.

It is a characteristic of Badminton girls that they are thoughtful individuals, able to evaluate information and decide for themselves. This approach extends beyond their studies and into the day-to-day life of the School, where girls are given a wide range of opportunities to grow, develop and express themselves in an enormous range of activities. Staff also enjoy sharing their enthusiasm for their subject and often involve girls in projects and competitions in the local community and nationally.

The Badminton community gives girls a chance to develop an understanding of the viewpoints of others and to think about contributing to the world around them. Girls leave Badminton ready to face the changing and challenging wider world and, when they do, they take with them a strong network of lifelong friends developed through a wealth of shared experiences.

Boarding. The size of the campus and community at Badminton gives a homely and vibrant feel to the School. This, coupled with excellent pastoral care, leaves no scope for anonymity, but rather lends itself to strong mutually supportive relationships between girls as well as between girls and staff.

The boarding accommodation is split into three areas (junior, middle and Sixth Form) so girls get a good sense of progression and development as they move up through the school. Full-time, weekly or flexi boarding are offered and day girls are welcome to flexi board, allowing girls to easily combine their academic schedules with the many activities that are on offer after school and at weekends.

Bartlett House offers cosy bedrooms for boarders in Years 5–8 and easy access to gardens and play areas. Sanderson House, a modern boarding house opened in 2008, accommodates boarders in Years 9, 10 and 11. The Sixth Form Centre provides the Lower Sixth and Upper Sixth with a more independent environment in double or single study-bedrooms. In each House, boarders have the support of a resident Housemistress, Assistant Housemistresses and Resident Tutors and there is a broad range of clubs and activities on offer every day, as well as a full weekend programme.

The School's enrichment programme is extremely important in the overall development of the pupils and girls participate in many activities and are encouraged to do so. The activities offered vary depending on the interests of the girls; some have an academic bias, others let the girls explore their creative interests. Girls are very much encouraged to enjoy and value their own and their peers' successes and triumphs in every area of life.

Curriculum. The School's broad curriculum provides a rich and varied experience for the girls. Through Art, Drama and Music programmes, each girl has many opportunities to express her individuality and develop her own unique identity. In an increasingly global society, the importance of languages has never been greater and girls have the opportunity to study Mandarin and Greek in addition to more traditional languages such as French and Latin.

Small classes ensure that all the girls receive individual help and attention from their teachers. Badminton girls are proactive and independent learners; they are not afraid to take intellectual risks and are always happy to ask questions. The emphasis at Badminton is on a holistic education, not narrowly academic, and both the curriculum and the timetable are constructed to create a balance between academic achievement, personal development, life skills and other enterprising activity.

Academic record. Badminton has a fine academic record at GCSE and A Level. Sixth Form leavers go on to study at some of the top universities and Music Conservatories in the UK and overseas, including Oxford, Cambridge, the Royal Academy of Music and further afield.

Facilities. All facilities are situated on site and include: a new Sports Centre opened in 2018 complete with fencing piste, four-court sports hall, climbing wall and fitness suite; a 25 m indoor swimming pool; international-sized astro pitch; tennis and netball courts; as well as a fully equipped Science Centre, Creative Arts Centre and self-contained Sixth Form Centre. There are extensive fiction, careers, music and art libraries as well as a Music School.

Music, Drama and Creative Arts. All girls are involved in the Arts, both within the curriculum and as extracurricular activities, and the School attaches great importance to the development of musical and artistic talent.

Music is extremely popular at Badminton with over 85% of all pupils studying at least one musical instrument. There is a wide range of choral and instrumental groups to join including Junior and Senior Choir, Schola (choral group), orchestra, swing band, string ensembles, woodwind ensembles and other mixed musical groups. With visiting peripatetic teachers, all of whom are professional musicians, the students can study any instrument of their choice. There are a wide variety of performance opportunities including informal concerts and concerts for the local community.

There are several drama productions every year including plays directed and produced by the girls. Many girls take optional Speech and Drama lessons and LAMDA examinations.

There is an excellent Creative Arts department, with a wide choice of subjects for the girls to pursue including Fine Art, Pottery and Sculpture, Textiles, Design, Jewellery-making and Photography.

Clubs and societies. A wide range is offered including: Extended Project Qualification, The Duke of Edinburgh's Award, Italian GCSE, Sports Leaders Award, Leith's Cookery Course, Modern Languages, Debating, Drama, Musical Theatre, Mandarin, Young Enterprise, Art and Crafts, Science Outreach and The Prince's Trust.

Games and activities. Specialist PE teachers and coaches offer timetabled and optional sport including Hockey, Tennis, Netball, Swimming, Athletics, Rounders, Gymnastics, Badminton, Basketball, Self-Defence and Judo.

Optional extras. All girls participate in activities which include the full choice of Games, Creative Arts and Clubs as above and boarders have the opportunity of additional activities at weekends.

Badminton is fortunate in being sited on the outskirts of the university city of Bristol; regular visits are arranged to concerts, lectures and theatres and there is considerable contact with Bristol University. Community and voluntary work is strongly encouraged, with girls assisting with Science Outreach and reading in local primary schools, volunteering in local hospitals and charity shops.

Admission. Girls sit the Senior School entrance assessments in the November or January prior to year of entry. Entrance assessments are taken in English and Mathematics as well as an online reasoning test. Girls are also interviewed by a senior member of staff and the girls' current school is asked to provide a reference.

Girls sit Sixth Form entrance papers in the November in the year prior to joining. They choose two academic subjects they are intending to study for A Level and also sit an online reasoning test. They too will be interviewed by a senior member of staff and the girls' current school is asked to provide a reference.

Prospective Junior School pupils are assessed by spending a day in the school during which they are observed and assessed informally by staff and the Junior School Headmistress. This also helps the girls to make initial relationships with their prospective peers and gives them a real taste for life at Badminton. From Years 3–6, the tests are more formal and written papers in English, Maths, Reading and a Reasoning test are completed during the assessment day. Entry for Little Acorns (our pre-reception class) is by appointment with the Junior School Headmistress, and girls will also have a short observation session in our Little Acorns class.

Prospective parents are encouraged to visit the school individually or attend one of our Open Mornings. To obtain a prospectus and arrange a visit, please contact the Admissions Department via email at admissions@badmintonschool.co.uk or call 0117 905 5271.

Scholarships. Academic, Music, Sport and All-Rounder scholarships are available for girls entering Badminton in Years 7, 9 and 12. A STEM scholarship is also available in Years 7 and 9 and an Art scholarship is available in Years 9 and Year 12. Scholarships for entry into the upper end of the Junior School are also available. Parents of girls who are awarded scholarships are also eligible to apply for a means-tested bursary. Other awards are also available.

Scholarship application forms and more information can be obtained by emailing our Admissions Department at admissions@badmintonschool.co.uk.

Bursaries. Bursaries are means tested and awarded on the basis of parents' financial circumstances.

Application forms may be obtained by emailing admissions@badmintonschool.co.uk.

Fees per term (2023–2024). Day: Juniors £3,860–£4,420, Seniors £6,470. Boarding: Juniors £8,800–£10,100, Seniors £12,870–£15,590.

We provide a fee discount to the daughters of military families who receive Continuity of Education Allowance (CEA) funding, which caps the full boarding/tuition fees so that the parental contribution remains 10% of the total fee payable.

Charitable status. Badminton School Limited is a Registered Charity, number 311738. It exists for the purpose of educating children.

Chair of Governors: Mr Justin Lewis, MDA, BSc Hons

Bursar: Mr Jonathan Webster

***Head*: Mrs Jessica Miles**, MA Oxon, PGCE

Head of Junior School: Ms H Welch, BSc Hons, MSc Loughborough, PGCE Warwick

Bedford Girls' School

Cardington Road, Bedford, Bedfordshire MK42 0BX

Tel: 01234 361918
email: admissions@bedfordgirlsschool.co.uk
website: www.bedfordgirlsschool.co.uk
X/Twitter: @BedfordGirlsSch
Facebook: @BedfordGirlsSch
LinkedIn: /bedford-girls'-school

Foundation – The Harpur Trust.

"*Let me keep an open mind so I understand as much as I can in my lifetime and not reach the limits of my imagination.*"

Bedford Girls' School is a dynamic, forward-thinking selective independent day school for girls aged 7–18. We value creativity, technology and innovation highly, as we prepare our students to make a difference to the world around them. From Year 3 to Sixth Form, it is our belief that learning should be exciting and lifelong, so that students leave us fully equipped academically, socially and emotionally with the desire to be the creative-thinkers, the change-makers and the problem-solvers of the future.

Part of the Harpur Trust, we are under pinned by the International Baccalaureate educational philosophy; we follow the inspiring IB Primary Year Programme in our Junior School (Years 3–6) and the IB Diploma Programme is offered as well as A Levels to Sixth Formers. Our educational ethos lies in equipping them with critical thinking skills and the attributes of the IB learner profile from the moment they join us, whether in the Junior or Senior Schools. As a result, we find that the natural curiosity of the girls is heightened and sharpened and they are extremely engaged with their own independent learning and development. Our girls excel academically; we are an outstanding sports school and have an excellent reputation for Music and the Creative Arts.

Admissions. Entry to the Junior School is based on online Cognitive Ability Assessments (CAT) and a creative writing task. Entry to the Senior School is based on interview and online Cognitive Ability Assessments (CAT). Sixth Form entry is based on interviews, CAT assessments and GCSE results. A reference from the Head of the student's current school is required for all candidates.

Fees per term (2023–2024). Junior School (7–11 years) £3,907; Senior School (11–16 years) £5,491; Sixth Form (16–18 years) £5,491.

Chair of Governors: Mr N Harris

***Head*: Mrs Gemma Gibson**

Senior Deputy Head: Mr J Gardner

Deputy Head Student Engagement and Welfare: Mr M Gracie
Director of Sixth Form: Mrs H Woolley
Assistant Head: Mrs P Hooley
Director of Digital Strategy, Enterprise and Sustainability: Mrs R Finlay-Hudson
Director of Marketing, Admissions and Alumnae: Mrs J Trobe
Director of Finance and Operations: Mr M Scoble
Head of Junior School: Mrs C Howe
DSL: Mrs K Johnson

Berkhamsted Schools Group

Overton House
131 High Street, Berkhamsted, Hertfordshire HP4 2DJ

Tel: 01442 358000 (General enquiries)
01442 358001 (Admissions)
email: enquiries@berkhamsted.com
admissions@berkhamsted.com
boys@berkhamsted.com
girls@berkhamsted.com
sixth@berkhamsted.com
website: www.berkhamsted.com
X/Twitter: @berkhamstedsch
Facebook: @berkhamstedschool
Instagram: @berkhamstedschools
LinkedIn: /Berkhamsted-School

See full entry in the **HMC** section, on **p. 24**.

Blackheath High School
GDST

Senior School
Vanbrugh Park, London SE3 7AG
Tel: 020 8853 2929
email: info@bla.gdst.net
Junior School
Wemyss Road, London SE3 0TF
Tel: 020 8852 1537
email: info@blj.gdst.net
website: www.blackheathhighschool.gdst.net
X/Twitter: @BlackheathHigh
Facebook: @BlackheathHighSchool
Instagram: @blackheathhigh
LinkedIn: /blackheath-high-school-gdst

Blackheath High School GDST is an independent day school for girls aged 3–18. In 2022, we were judged by the Independent School Inspectorate to be ‘excellent in all areas’, the highest possible rating, with judges commenting not just on pupils’ outstanding academic achievement, but also on their confidence, resilience, self-esteem and positivity.

We are experts in girls’ education. As part of the GDST, global leaders in girls’ education, we share a mission to deliver an education that empowers girls to thrive. The dynamic in a girls-only setting is different: there is strong evidence that girls are more likely to boldly take intellectual risks, adopt leadership roles, and be less inclined to conform to stereotypes. Research demonstrates that GDST girls leave school prepared to face the future, with the confidence to make choices and overcome barriers in a world that is far from equal. Here, every subject is a girls’ subject.

Beyond academic excellence, our vibrant co-curricular programme offers opportunities for everyone, from charity fundraising and devising sustainability projects, to participating in the Duke of Edinburgh Award scheme and supporting the local community. Students can take part in LAMDA classes, create and perform in concerts, fashion shows and drama productions, take part in clubs from debating to politics, sports to sushi-making.

We offer a hugely varied, vibrant sports programme, designed to foster a lifelong love of sport and to nurture both physical and mental health. As well as timetabled Sports lessons, competitive fixtures and specialist coaches give students access to elite sports opportunities. Student wellbeing underpins all that we do at Blackheath High School. Staff know students as individuals; girls form strong, supportive friendships; trust is the backbone of our school. Our dedicated pastoral team is well placed to deal with any issues that may arise, supported by our School Nurse and a full-time Counsellor.

We have two school sites for Junior and Senior pupils, located just five miles from Canary Wharf and eight miles from central London, benefiting from all that our capital city has to offer while enjoying the village atmosphere and extensive heathland of Blackheath itself. We are adjacent to Greenwich Royal Park, 13 acres of open space with extraordinary views across the River Thames to St Paul’s. The Park is home to the Royal Observatory and the Greenwich Maritime Royal Heritage Site.

Chair of Local Governors: Ms Amanda Waygood

***Headteacher*: Mrs N Argile**, BSc Newcastle, MSc Hons, PGCE

Deputy Head (*Academic*): Ms K Lewis, BA Cantab, MA UCL, PGCE

Deputy Head (*Staff and Students*): Mr C Alaru, BA, BEd Hons Queensland University of Technology

Acting Assistant Head (*Learning & Staff Development*): Mrs C Beecham, BA Hons Brunel, MA Goldsmiths, PGCE

Assistant Head (*Learning & Enrichment*): Miss K Hickman, MA Hons Dundee, PGCE

Assistant Head (*Head of Sixth Form*): Ms F Cheyns, BA Universite de Lille, PGCE

Director of Finance & Operations: Mr R Ryan, AAT, DSBM

Head of Junior School: Mrs S Skevington, LLB Hons Sheffield, PGCE, EYP

Deputy Head of Junior School (*Academic*): Mrs Monica Patel, MA Open University, PGCE

Deputy Head of Junior School (*Pastoral*) : Miss A Lucas, BA Hons Sheffield Hallam

Admissions Team: admissions@bla.gdst.net

Bolton School Girls’ Division

Chorley New Road, Bolton, Lancs BL1 4PB
Tel: 01204 840201
email: seniorgirls@boltonschool.org
website: www.boltonschool.org/seniorgirls
X/Twitter: @BoltonSch
Facebook: @BoltonSch
Instagram: @bolton_sch
LinkedIn: /bolton-school

Bolton School Girls’ Division was founded in 1877 as the High School for Girls and quickly gained a reputation for excellence. In 1913 the first Viscount Leverhulme gave a generous endowment to the High School for Girls and the Bolton Grammar School for Boys on condition that the two schools should be equal partners known as Bolton School (Girls’ and Boys’ Divisions).

Bolton School – the TES’ 2019 Independent School of the Year – is a family of schools, where children can enjoy an all-through education, joining our co-educational Nursery or Infant School before moving up to our single-sex Junior and Senior Schools with Sixth Forms. We are strong believers that girls and boys from 7+ perform best in a single-sex environment, but one where there are co-educational activities – the best of both worlds.

The School occupies a stunning 32-acre site and the Girls’ Division Senior School contains over 860 day pupils. The co-educational infants’ school, Beech House, offers an education for 225 pupils aged 4–7 and up to a further 200 girls are educated in the Junior Girls' School (age 7–11). In the Senior School, 200 girls typically attend the Sixth Form.

Bolton School Girls' Division seeks to realise the potential of each pupil. We provide challenge, encourage initiative, promote teamwork and develop leadership capabilities. It is our aim that students leave the School as self-confident young people equipped with the knowledge, skills and attributes that will allow them to lead happy and fulfilled lives and to make a difference for good in the wider community.

We do this through offering a rich and stimulating educational experience which encompasses academic, extra-curricular and social activities. We provide a supportive and industrious learning environment for pupils selected on academic potential, irrespective of means and background.

Facilities. Housed in an attractive Grade II listed building the school has an impressive Great Hall which seats 900 people, spacious corridors, a theatre, two Resistant Materials workshops, two Textile studios, two Food Technology rooms, four computer rooms, seven laboratories, three Art studios and two fine libraries staffed by two qualified librarians and their staff. In September 2013, the Sixth Form moved into the purpose-built £7m Riley Sixth Form Centre, where girls and boys share a Common Room, cafe and learning areas equipped with the very latest technology. The girls' dining room was completely redeveloped in the Summer of 2015.

Besides its own fully equipped gym, the Girls' Division shares the new £1m all-weather sports surface, an award-winning Careers Department, the Arts Complex and Sports Hall, a 25-metre swimming pool, extensive playing fields, the Leverhulme Sports Pavilion and an outdoor pursuits facility at Patterdale Hall in the Lake District. Pupils also have the option of spending a week undertaking sailing lessons on Tenacity of Bolton, a ketch built by pupils in the Boys' Division.

Beech House Infants' School. The curriculum, though based on the National Curriculum, extends far beyond it. Specialist teaching is provided for older pupils in Physical Education and Music and all children are taught French. The school has recently moved to purpose-built state-of-the-art premises and in addition to its own resources, Beech House benefits from the use of Senior School facilities such as the swimming pool, playing fields and Arts Centre.

The Girls' Junior School. There are 2 classes in each of Years 3–6. In September 2010, the junior girls moved into their new £5m school which has its own hall, laboratory, art and design facility, IT suite and library, as well as large classrooms. Besides following the National Curriculum with Senior School specialists teaching PE, Music and French, pupils have additional opportunities. The many clubs and wide range of extra-curricular activities ensure a full and well-balanced programme.

The Senior School. The curriculum encompasses all the National Curriculum but also offers the study of up to three modern languages, the classics and a wide range of modules in Technology. At age 11 all girls follow a similar weekly timetable. The range of subjects offered cover: Art, English, French, Geography, History, Classical Studies, Mathematics, Music, PE, Religious Studies, Science and Technology. All pupils in Year 9 begin to study GCSE Biology, Chemistry and Physics. The above list does not fully show the great variety of opportunities available which also include: Athletics, Biology, Chemistry, Computer Graphics, Dance, Drama, Earth Science, Electronics, Food and Nutrition, Gymnastics, Information Technology, Lacrosse, Netball, Sailing, Climbing, Orienteering, PSHE, Resistant Materials Technology, Rounders, Swimming, Waterpolo, Tennis and Textiles Technology. This breadth is maintained to GCSE with a second language, German, Latin or Spanish, being offered in Year 8. In Years 10 and 11 we also offer Archery, Badminton, Basketball, Climbing, Fitness/Gym sessions, Football, Rounders, Unihoc and Volleyball.

GCSE. There is extensive choice at GCSE. All follow a common curriculum of English, English Literature, Mathematics, Biology, Chemistry and Physics (with an option to take Trilogy Award Science from Year 10) together with non-examined courses in Information Technology, PE, and Religion and Philosophy. Personal aptitude and inclination are fostered by allowing a maximum of 11 GCSEs: the core subjects plus options chosen from Art, Biology, Business and Communication Systems, Chemistry, Computing, Drama, Food and Nutrition, French, Geography, German, Greek, History, Information Technology, Latin, Music, Physics, Religious Studies, Resistant Materials Technology, Spanish and Textile Technology. Essential balance is maintained by encouraging all to include one Humanity and one Modern Language, but the choice is otherwise entirely free.

The Sixth Form. Flexibility is a key feature of the Sixth Form. Teaching in the Sixth Form is in smaller groups and single-sex teaching remains the norm, although in a very few subjects co-educational arrangements are in operation. Students choose from a list of approximately 30 AS courses. Breadth is promoted further by our complementary Curriculum Enrichment Programme. All students have the opportunity to follow a range of non-examined courses as well as Physical Education (sports include golf, football, life-saving, rugby, self-defence, tennis and yoga). Links beyond school include the Community Action Programme and Young Enterprise scheme, as well as opportunities with Business Awareness and Work Experience.

Students in the Sixth Form have greater freedom which includes wearing their own smart clothes, exeat periods and having their own Sixth Form Centre away from the Senior School. Joint social and extracurricular events are regularly organised with the Boys' Division. There are opportunities for students to assume a variety of responsibilities both within the school and in the wider community. Increasing personal freedom within a highly supportive environment helps students to make the transition to the independence of the adult world. Some students stretch themselves by taking the AQA Extended Project Qualification.

Almost all students (98%) go on to Higher Education or Degree Apprenticeships (5% typically to Oxford and Cambridge).

Music and Drama are popular and students achieve the highest standards in informal and public performances. The wide variety of concerts and productions may take place in the Arts Centre, the Great

Hall or the fully-equipped Theatre, all of which make excellent venues for joint and Girls' Division performances. The School regularly performs at Manchester's Bridgewater Hall.

Personal, Social and Health Education, and Citizenship. PSHE, RSE and Citizenship are targeted in a variety of ways and coordinated centrally. Some issues may be covered within departmental schemes of work while others will be discussed in the informal atmosphere of form groups led by the form tutor. Those areas which require specialist input are fitted into longer sessions run by experts from outside school.

Careers. The Careers Department helps prepare students for adult life. It has a resource centre giving access to all the latest information. The extensive programme starts at age 11 and includes communication skills, work sampling, and support in making choices at all stages of schooling. In addition, girls prepare their CVs and applications to Higher Education with the individual help of a trained tutor.

Extracurricular activities. Patterdale Hall, our outdoor pursuits centre in the Lake District, offers many activities including abseiling, gorge walking, orienteering and sailing on Lake Ullswater. Awards are regularly made to enable individuals to undertake a variety of challenging activities both at home and abroad while every year, the whole of Year 9 as well as many older girls embark on The Duke of Edinburgh's Award scheme. In 2017 the School won the Queen's Award for Voluntary Service, the MBE for organisations. In addition to the annual exchanges for Modern Languages students, we also offer a wide range of educational and recreational trips both at home and abroad. All have the opportunity to follow a wide range of non-examined courses of their choice, including Physical Education.

Admission. Entrance to the school is by Headteacher's report, written examination and interview in the Spring term for girls aged 7 and 11. New girls are also welcomed into the Sixth Form. Applications to other year groups are welcomed and spaces may be available depending upon migration.

One in five Senior School pupils receives assistance with their fees through the School's own bursaries. Non-means-tested Scholarships are also awarded to those pupils who achieve highly in the Entrance Examination.

Fees per term (2023–2024). Senior School and Sixth Form £4,544, Infant and Junior Schools £3,632. Fees include lunches.

Charitable status. Bolton School is a Registered Charity, number 1110703.

Chairman of Governors: Mr I Riley, MEng, MBA

***Head of Foundation*: P J Britton**, MBE, MEd

***Head of Girls' Division*: Mrs L D Kyle**, BSc

Deputy Heads:
Pastoral: Mrs A Green, BA
Academic: Mrs C Winder, MA

Assistant Heads:
Mrs S Entwistle, BA
J Hitchin, MA, MTL
Ms M Teichman, BSc

Head of Lower School: Ms S Noot, BA
Head of Sixth Form: Miss S Gunshon, BSc

Senior School:

Heads of Departments:

Art: Ms N Culican, MA
Biology: Mrs A D Furey, BSc
Business: Mrs S Foster, BA
Chemistry: Mrs S Rich, BSc
Classics: D Lamb, BA
Design Technology (*Product Design*): Miss R Langley, BA
Design Technolgy (*Textiles*): Miss R Stafford, BEd
Economics: Miss L Jones, BA
English: Mrs A Martin, MA
Food & Nutrition: Mrs N James, BA
Geography: Miss L Gillibrand, BA
History & Politics: C Owen, MA
ICT: Mrs S Brace, BSc
Mathematics: G Heppleston, BSc
Modern Languages: D O'Neill, BA
Spanish: Ms E Xerri, BA

Music: Mr P Lovatt, BMus, LRSM (*Director*)
Academic Music: Mrs S Wade, BA
Physical Education: Mrs K Heatherington, BA
Physics: B Ickringill, BSc, MInstP
Psychology: Mrs J Sanders, BSc
Religion & Philosophy: Mrs K Porter, BA
Theatre Studies, Speech & Drama: Miss S Talbot, BA, MRes (*Director*)

Careers & Higher Education: Miss L Jones, BA (*Director*)
EPQ Coordinator: Mrs S Pritchard, MA
Learning Support: Mrs M Wright, BA
Outdoor Pursuits: E Lindle, BSc

Instrumental Music Staff:
Brass, Cello, Clarinet, Flute, Guitar, Oboe, Organ, Percussion, Piano, Saxophone, Singing, Violin.

Bromley High School
GDST

Blackbrook Lane, Bickley, Bromley, Kent BR1 2TW

Tel: 020 8781 7000
email: bhs@bro.gdst.net
website: www.bromleyhigh.gdst.net
X/Twitter: @bromleyhs
Facebook: @bromleyhighschoolGDST
Instagram: @bromleyhighschoolgdst
LinkedIn: /school/bromley-high-school-gdst

See full entry in the **HMC** section, on **p. 44**.

Burgess Hill Girls

Keymer Road, Burgess Hill, West Sussex RH15 0EG
Tel: 01444 241050
email: admissions@burgesshillgirls.com
website: www.burgesshillgirls.com
X/Twitter: @BHillGirls
Facebook: @BurgessHillGirls
LinkedIn: /burgess-hill-girls

Burgess Hill Girls is a leading independent day and boarding school in Sussex for girls aged two and a half to eighteen years of age.

Whatever the stage at which your daughter joins Burgess Hill Girls you can be confident of two things: that she will be known for who she is as an individual and she will be provided with an outstanding, transformative education of the whole person.

Our school motto, 'I am, I can, I should, I will', conveys and underpins our whole approach, identifying and releasing the potential of your daughter as she proceeds, giving her the very best possible opportunities to become a successful women of the future.

As parents, success will be having a happy and healthy daughter who loves going to school, loves to learn, loves participating, and is able to make friends for life. For the girls, success may be doing well in lessons and tests, being part of a team, playing a musical instrument and having fun with friends. At Burgess Hill Girls we pride ourselves on unlocking the academic talent that is found within our girls and strongly believe each individual will thrive in our high-achieving environment.

Whilst Burgess Hill Girls aims to provide the very best opportunities for everyone to excel, we believe that success is more than obtaining the highest marks and grades. We recognise just as much all those fantastic qualities that are not materialistic or target driven. Success at our school is when we produce bright, confident and independent young women who have and will continue to achieve great things.

Burgess Hill Girls stands in 14 acres of beautiful grounds within a conservation area close to Burgess Hill's town centre in the centre of Sussex. All aspects of the school are located on this one campus; Nursery, Pre-prep, Prep, Senior, Sixth Form and Boarding Houses. The school is only a five minute walk from the railway station (on the London to Brighton line) and close to excellent road networks (10 miles from Brighton and only 20 miles from Gatwick). A flexible, daily minibus service is provided for girls across Sussex and beyond.

Chair of Governors: Dr Alison Smith, MB ChB, MRCGP

Head: **Mr Lars Fox**, MA Hons, PGCE

Director of Finance & Operations: Mr Graeme Miles

Head of Pre-Prep and Prep School and Deputy Head of School: Mrs Heather Cavanagh, BA Hons, QTS

Assistant Heads:
Academic (*Teaching & Learning*): Ms Rohaise Flint, MA Hons, PGCE
Pastoral & Boarding: Miss Nicola Donson, BMus Hons, PGCE
Head of Sixth Form: Mr Iain Regan-Smith, MA, BA Hons, GTP
Deputy Head of Prep School: Mrs Sue Collins, BA Hons, PGCE
Nursery Manager: Mrs Suzanne Roberts, BA Hons, PGCE

Bury Grammar School

Tenterden Street, Bury, Greater Manchester BL9 0HN
Tel: 0161 696 8600
email: schooloffice@burygrammar.com
website: www.burygrammar.com
X/Twitter: @BuryGrammar
Facebook: @BuryGrammarSchool
Instagram: @burygrammarschool
LinkedIn: /burygrammarschool

See full entry in the **HMC** section, on **p. 53**.

Bute House Preparatory School for Girls

Bute House, Luxemburg Gardens, Hammersmith, London W6 7EA
Tel: 020 7603 7381
email: mail@butehouse.co.uk
website: www.butehouse.co.uk
X/Twitter: @ButeHousePrep
Facebook: @butehouseprep
Instagram: @butehousepreparatoryschool

See full entry in the **IAPS** section, on **p. 630**.

Channing School

The Bank, Highgate, London N6 5HF
Tel: 020 8340 2328 (School Office)
020 8340 2719 (Bursar)
email: info@channing.co.uk
website: www.channing.co.uk
X/Twitter: @ChanningSchool
Facebook: @ChanningSchool
Instagram: @channing_school

Channing is a selective school for girls aged 4–18 in Highgate, North London.

We are unique in providing an education based on inclusive, Unitarian principles and were founded by two visionary sisters in 1885. We uphold our heritage and encourage our pupils to develop respect, tolerance and understanding of all faiths as well as individual and social responsibility.

Channing is a school of great opportunity. Our mission is to inspire pupils to develop scholarship, integrity, altruism and independence. We are a centre of academic excellence where we ensure that every girl feels empowered and valued, supported by a stimulating and vibrant educational experience that nurtures and sustains independent thinking, confidence and creativity. Our examination results bear testament to the success of our ethos, coupled with the depth and breadth of university destinations and courses onto which our students are accepted.

Most importantly, in a changing world of uncertainty and pressure, girls find at Channing an oasis of calm purpose, where pupils of all ages are encouraged to think for themselves and to keep an open mind. Every member of the School belongs to our famously warm, supportive community. Pupils, staff and visitors alike comment on the indefinable 'feel' of the School, its very special atmosphere and unique ethos, which is so different compared to other schools in the area.

Number of Pupils. 1,036.

The School is situated in Highgate Village, in attractive grounds, and offers a balanced education combining a traditional academic curriculum with modern educational developments. The complex of old and new buildings has been constantly adapted to provide up-to-date facilities, and there are strong links with the local community and local schools.

Girls usually take nine or ten subjects to GCSE and there is a wide range of A Level choices, including Physics, Further Maths, Politics and Theatre Studies. The Junior School has its own building – the elegant family home of Sir Sydney Waterlow, one-time Lord Mayor of London – set in spacious gardens, and is notable for its happy and secure atmosphere.

Most girls learn at least one musical instrument and there are frequent concerts and theatrical productions. The school is fortunate in its gardens, open space and its facilities. The school has invested £13m in new facilities including a Sixth Form Centre with bespoke study facilities, a state-of-the-art Sports Centre, a Music School and a magnificent Performing Arts Theatre.

Entry is by assessment at 4+, an examination/assessment and interview at 11+ and predicted GCSE results and interview at 16+. In addition, entry is subject to a satisfactory report from the applicant's current school. Entry assessments for occasional vacancies that arise for other years are age appropriate.

Further information can be obtained from the School prospectus and the Sixth Form prospectus available from the Registrar and the school website (www.channing.co.uk).

Scholarships and Bursaries. At Channing, we have always done our best to ensure that girls who would benefit from an education at the School are not excluded for financial reasons. We offer means-tested financial support with the payment of school fees to parents/guardians who would otherwise be unable to afford them. These bursaries may be awarded in the form of a discount of up to 100% on tuition fees, depending on the financial circumstances of applicants. All candidates who sit the 11+ entrance examination are automatically considered for a Year 7 Academic Scholarship. They do not need to make a separate application. To be considered for a Sixth Form Academic Scholarship candidates (including current pupils) must sit the Sixth Form Academic Scholarship exam which takes place in November of every year. Music Scholarships are offered at 11+ and 16+. These cover up to 50% of the tuition fees and lessons in school on one instrument for a year (renewable). Art Scholarships are offered to Sixth Form entrants based on submission of a portfolio of work. Bursaries are offered at 11+ and 16+. Please see the school website for further details.

Fees (2023–2024). Junior School: £7,500 per term, £22,500 per annum. Senior School: £8,290 per term, £24,870 per annum.

Charitable status. Channing House Incorporated is a Registered Charity, number 312766.

Governors:
Mrs L Leigh (*Chair*)
Mr J Alexander
Mrs C Chandler-Thompson
Rev D Costley
Mrs L Cristie
Mr R Hirji
Mrs C Hulme-McKibbin
Mr D Oliver
Mrs P Peck
Mr S Prior
Ms B Rentoul
Mr W Spears
Dr A Sutton
Mr K van der Sande
Mrs A Rentoul

* Head of Department
^ Part-time

Senior School
***Headmistress*: Mrs L Hughes**, BA Warwick History

Deputy Head: Mr F Meier, MA London Philosophy of Education
Deputy Head (*Academic*): Ms J Newman, MA UCL Economics
Ms S Beenstock, BA Leeds (*English^*)
Mrs G Bhamra-Burgess, MSc SOAS (*Assistant Head – Co-Curricular*)
Mrs S Blake, BSc Bristol, MA London (**Geography^*)
Mr P Boxall, GRSM, ARCO Royal Academy of Music (*Director of Music*)
Mr A Boardman, BA Hons Durham (*Geography, Assistant Head – Teaching and Learning*)
Mr G Bowman, BSc Nottingham (*Mathematics*)
Ms Z Cannell, BA Oxon (**Classics*)
Ms T Cooper, MEng Imperial (*Second in Mathematics, STEM Coordinator*)
Ms K Cronk, BA New York (*Learning Support Assistant*)
Mr P Daurat, MA Essex (*Mathematics*)
Mr R Daw, PGCE (**Physics*)
Ms S Della-Porta, BEd Wollongong, Australia (*Head of Year 10*)
Mrs W Devine, BA Reading (**Politics, MUN Coordinator*)
Miss S Donington, MA Leeds (*Second in English*)
Mrs S Elliot, MA Cantab (**Classics*)
Mr F Fallon, MA Maynooth (*Music^*)
Ms M Feeney, BA UCL, MA UCL (*History, Politics^*)
Mr S Frank, BSc Birmingham (**Biology*)
Miss S-L Fung, BSc Coventry (*Physics*)

Mrs M Gardiner, BA Hons, SENDCO A1, CCET (*SENDCO*)
Mrs C Garrill, BA Leicester (*Head of Year 7, French, Politics*)
Mr P Gittins, BA Wolverhampton (*Art, *PSHE and Wellbeing*)
Ms J Gomez, MA Sussex (*Spanish, French*)
Ms H Goodall, PGCE (*Art*)
Mr D Grossman, BSc Hons Manchester (*Assistant Head – Director of Digital Learning and Technology*)
Ms C Grierson, BA Hons Oxon English
Miss G Hadley, BSc Leeds (*Maths*)
Mr A Haworth, MA RCA (**Art*)
Dr E Hayward, BA UoL, MA UoL, PhD UoL (*English*)
Mr G Headey, MA Kent (**Religion, Philosophy and Ethics, Head of House Sharpe*)
Mrs B Hernandez, BA Hons, Alicante, Spain (*Spanish, French^*)
Ms J Hill, BA Hons Royal Conservatoire of Scotland (**Drama and Theatre*)
Miss E Hillier, BSc Durham (*Science, Partnerships Coordinator*)
Mr M Holmes, BSc Hons City (**Information and Communication Technology*)
Miss A Hosseini, BSc UCL (*Chemistry^*)
Mrs N Houston, BEd RMIT, Australia (*Physical Education, Head of Year 9*)
Ms Y Hume, BFA Hons UNSW, Australia (*Art*)
Mr R Jacobs, BA Oxon (*Teacher of Physics*)
Mrs H Kanmwaa, BA Oxon (*English*)
Ms C Kelly, MPhil Bristol (*Head of Sixth Form*) [maternity cover]
Ms A Kennedy, BA UCL (*Classics*)
Ms D Kiff, MA Kings College London (*Philosophy*)
Ms J Kung, BA USYD, Australia, DipEd MU, Australia (*History, Director of Partnerships and HE*) [sabbatical leave]
Mrs M Levontine (*Library Assistant^*)
Miss R Lindsay, BA Arts Dance/BA of Education UNSW, Australia, BA Hons Kingston (*Physical Education, Head of House Spears, Assistant Head of PSHE*)
Ms S Mackie, BA Oxon (*Art^*)
Mr P Martini-Phillips, BA Hons Leicester (*Assistant Head of Sixth Form*)
Miss C McCahill, BA Hons Birmingham (*History/ Politics^*)
Ms C McGovern, MPhil Trinity College Dublin (*English^*)
Miss R McNamara, MPhil Cambridge (*Classics*)
Mr F Meier, MA London (*Philosophy, Deputy Head*)
Ms R Mohabeer, BSc Kings College London (*Head of Year 8, Chemistry*)
Miss K Nelson, BSc Brunel (*Teacher in Charge of Netball*)
Ms E Pavlopoulos, LLB Kings/Paris I, MA Ed Open (*Extended Learning Coordinator, French, *German^*)
Mr D Pelton, BA Hons Sheffield Hallam (*Geography^*)
Ms N Quow, MA Oxon, MSc City London (*Chemistry, Years 7 & 8 Science Coordinator*)
Mr G Raine, BA St Thomas, MA Windsor (**History*)
Miss I Ramsden (*Senior School Librarian*)
Ms L Rao, PGCE (*Chemistry*)
Miss A Romero-Wiltshire, BA Nottingham (**French^*)
Ms A Rozieres, MA Grenoble, France (*French^*)
Ms V Sequeira, BSc Hons India (*Computer Science, TeenTech Coordinator*)
Mrs D Shoham, MSc LSHTM (*Biology^*)
Dr C Spinks, PhD Manchester (**Science and Chemistry*)
Mr P Starr, PGCE (**Psychology*)
Ms A Stockmann, MA Westfaelische Wilhelms, Germany (*German^*)
Mr H Thomas, BA Cambridge (*Maths*)
Miss L Vince, BA Hons Kingston (*Drama*)
Mrs S Walker, BA Durham (*Humanities Teacher, Sustainability Coordinator*)
Miss E Ward, MA UWA, Western Australia (*History of Art^*)
Mr C Waring, BS Strathclyde (**MFL and Spanish*)
Miss L Weston, MA Birmingham (*Director of Sport*)
Ms N Wilberforce, BA Oxford (*Head of Careers, HE Coordinator*)
Ms K Wilkinson, BA East Anglia (**English*)
Miss C Williams, BSc West of England (*Maths, Psychology*)
Mrs R Williams, BSc Hons UCL (*Mathematics*)
Mrs H Wootton, BSc Exeter (**Mathematics*)
Ms M Yun, BSc London (*Mathematics, Duke of Edinburgh Manager, EAL Coordinator*)
Miss L Zanardo, MEd Open BA, BMus Ed Australia, Grad Dip Australia (*Assistant Director of Music, Head of Year 11*)
Mrs D Zuluaga De La Cruz, MA Valenciennes, France (*French^*)

Junior School
***Head of Junior School*: Miss D Hamalis**, BEd Hons

Deputy Head: Mr J Entwisle, BSc Hons, PGCE
Deputy Head (*Academic*): Miss R McGinnety, BA Hons, PGCE
Head of Early Years & Key Stage 1: Mrs M Brant, BPA Hons, PGCE
Head of Key Stage 2: Miss S Kitsis, BSc, PGCE
Assistant Head Co Curricular: Miss D Wright, BA Hons, PGCE

Form Teachers & Teaching Assistants:
Reception M: Miss K Marshall (*Form Teacher*), Miss S Pala (*Teaching Assistant*)
Reception R: Miss C Robertson (*Form Teacher*), Miss F Sarkar (*Teaching Assistant*), Mrs K Lemos (*Teaching Assistant*)
Year 1A: Miss A Alfaro (*Form Teacher*), Miss H Tunkel (*Teaching Assistant*)
Year 1C: Mrs S Canning (*Form Teacher*), Miss F Shaikh (*Teaching Assistant*)
Year 1W: Miss N Walker (*Form Teacher*)
Year 2B: Mrs M Brant (*Form Teacher*), Mrs F Akram (*Teaching Assistant*)
Year 2R: Mr C Rich (*Form Teacher*), Mrs S Ibrekic (*Teaching Assistant*)
Year 3E: Miss E Evans (*Form Teacher*), Mrs K Lemos (*Teaching Assistant*)
Year 3F: Miss A Frost (*Form Teacher*), Mrs R McEwen (*Teaching Assistant*)
Year 4K: Miss D Parmar (*Form Teacher*), Mrs C Khan, Mrs A Daymer (*Teaching Assistant*)
Year 4W: Miss D Wright (*Form Teacher*)
Year 5K: Miss S Kitsis (*Form Teacher*)

Year 5S: Miss S Snowdowne (*Form Teacher*), Miss M Holmes (*Teaching Assistant*)
Year 6B: Miss K Bharucha (*Form Teacher*)
Year 6D: Ms D Davari (*Form Teacher*), Mrs N Mechik (*Teaching Assistant*)

Specialist Teachers:
Mrs M Munro (**Music*)
Mr R Fellows (**Art & DT*)
Miss A Jimenez (**MFL*)
Mrs L Lynch (**Drama*)

Cheltenham Ladies' College

Bayshill Road, Cheltenham, Gloucestershire GL50 3EP

Tel: 01242 520691
email: enquiries@cheltladiescollege.org
website: www.cheltladiescollege.org
X/Twitter: @cheltladiescoll
Facebook: @CheltLadiesColl
Instagram: @cheltladiescoll
LinkedIn: /school/the-cheltenham-ladies-college

See full entry in the **HMC** section, on **p. 63**.

City of London School for Girls

St Giles' Terrace, Barbican, London EC2Y 8BB

Tel: 020 7847 5500
email: reception@clsg.org.uk
website: www.clsg.org.uk
X/Twitter: @clsggirls
Instagram: @cityoflondonschoolforgirls

See full entry in the **HMC** section, on **p. 72**.

Cobham Hall

Brewers Road, Cobham, Kent DA12 3BL

Tel: 01474 823371
email: enquiries@cobhamhall.com
website: www.cobhamhall.com
X/Twitter: @CobhamHall
Facebook: @CobhamHall
Instagram: @CobhamHall

Cobham Hall is a Day and Boarding School for girls aged 11 to 16, and for girls and boys in the Sixth Form (ages 16 to 18). Housed in a beautiful sixteenth-century manor house in 150 acres of historic parkland near Rochester, Kent, the School enjoys exceptional transport links and is less than 30 minutes from London by train. Cobham Hall offers a range of flexi-boarding options as well as day, full and weekly boarding, providing flexibility for family life. At the heart of Cobham Hall's educational experience are the fundamental values of Trust, Respect, Honesty, Kindness and Tolerance, which underpin the journey of personal growth and development that each student undertakes at Cobham Hall.

A Cobham Hall education is an education for life. A combination of high teaching standards, small class sizes, and a wide range of co-curricular activities help students to achieve excellent results, and to develop skills and interests for life. Together with our varied and forward-thinking enrichment programme, these enable our students to look deeper, challenge themselves, and unlock talents and abilities they never realised they had. At Cobham Hall, personal and academic success, health, wellbeing, and community go hand in hand. Our innovative, skills-based curriculum is designed specifically to develop the crucial life skills young people will need in our rapidly changing world: skills in complex problem-solving, project and time management, critical thinking and creativity; resilience, communication, determination, teamwork and compassion.

Key skills lessons are timetabled throughout, culminating in our Global Perspectives GCSE course and the Extended Project Qualification. As sixth former Rhiannon explains: 'Cobham has a lovely family feel and provides so many opportunities. Through these I have been able to develop my organisational and leadership skills, giving me the confidence to take the next steps in university and beyond.' An early member of the global Round Square network, Cobham Hall has long stood for internationalism, and Round Square values of democracy, environmentalism, adventure, leadership and service remain core to our ethos. Our alumnae are at the forefront of the arts, science, medicine, politics and sport, and include Olympic Gold-winner Kate French, BBC journalist and broadcaster Mishal Husain, and Baroness Kate Fall, member of the House of Lords.

Our newly co-educational Sixth Form, with its stunning social and learning hub, offers the ideal environment for boys and girls to prepare together – academically and socially – for university and the realities of 21st century life. Alongside a broad range of A Levels, the School offers a unique enrichment programme, aimed at enhancing Sixth Formers' intellectual curiosity and creativity. All follow our unique Global Critical Thinking course and study the EPQ, prized by universities. Cobham Hall has also recently introduced the Ivy House Award, a pioneering leadership enrichment programme designed to give Sixth Form students access to life-changing personal and professional development, and build invaluable leadership and life skills.

A wide range of co-curricular activities are available, including the Duke of Edinburgh's Award and Model United Nations, which inspire students to step out of their comfort zone, try new things, and support their community; students also participate weekly in a wide range of sports. Cobham Hall achieves consistently good academic results, and almost all our students go on to university, some following highly academic routes, such as study at Oxbridge or Russell Group institutes, while others opt for more vocational courses.

Cobham Hall's small class sizes mean each student gets the academic and pastoral support needed. Looking after students' emotional and physical health forms the essence of our pastoral care practices. Wellbeing is central to school life, with timetabled lessons and a dedicated Wellbeing Centre.

Students are encouraged to explore the world around them through activities such as Model United Nations, the Duke of Edinburgh's Award, or on national and international trips. As a Round Square school, students can attend conferences both in the UK and globally. Closer to home, surrounded by an abundance of nature, there is plenty of space to reflect amongst the bluebells and daffodils, to collect data for science lessons, to be inspired for Art lessons, to boost stamina and fitness in PE or simply to run around and enjoy life.

Fees per term (2023–2024). Day students £7,600–£8,300; Boarders £12,900–£13,900. Our Boarding fees include all basic tuition, accommodation, nutritious meals, compulsory non-residential academic trips, in-school activities including our comprehensive co-curricular and Saturday programmes, and stationery. Day Students are welcome to come in early for breakfast or stay late in the evenings for supper and Prep at no extra charge.

Charitable status. Cobham Hall is a Registered Charity, number 1064758. It exists to provide high-quality education for students aged 11–18 years.

Governing Body:
Mr E Lipton (*Chairman*)
Court of Governors

Staff:
***Headmistress*: Mrs Wendy Barrett**, BSc Hons London, PGCE

Deputy Headmistress: Mrs Sue Carney, BEd Exeter
Director of Studies: Dr Patrick Drumm, BMus, MA, DPhil
Head of Boarding and Pastoral: Mrs Anna Lenton, FCCT, MBA, BA Hons
Head of Upper School: Mrs Melissa Thompson, BSc London
Head of Lower School: Mrs Emma Wilkinson, BA London
Head of Admissions and Marketing: Mrs Caroline Ward Vine, BA Hons, MA

* *Head of Faculty*

Arts Faculty (*including Music and Physical Education*):
*Mrs Charlotte Pepper, BA (*Head of Physical Education*)
Mr James Williams (*Head of Music*)
Mr Michael Turner, BA Cumbria, PGCSE (*Head of Art*)
Miss Louise Mayell, BA, PGCE Cardiff, MA Rochester (*Photography*)
Miss Danni Fautley, BSc Herefordshire (*PE*)
Dr Patrick Drumm, BMus, MA, DPhil (*Music, Director of Studies*)

English and Languages Faculty (*including Drama and Film Studies*):
*Ms Katherine Bonner, BA, MA Canterbury Christ Church (*English, Personal Discovery Framework*)
Mrs Carmel Gorman, MA Exeter (*Head of Drama*)
Mr Alex Mangan, BA Winchester (*Drama, English*)
Mr James Malcomson (*English, Film Studies*)
Mr Maciej Janowicz, BA, PGCSE, PGDip Canterbury Christ Church (*English, EFL*)
Miss Julia West, BA Oxford, MA Oxford (*English*)
Mrs Emma Wilkinson, BA London (*French, German, Head of Lower School*)
Mrs Anna Lenton, BA Hons, MBA, FCCT (*French, Director of Boarding and Pastoral*)
Mrs Maria Gutierrez, Licenciada en Lenguas Extranjeras Columbia, GTP Christ Church (*French, Spanish, Personal Discovery Framework*)
Dr Pamela Marin, MA USA, MPhil Oxon, PhD Dublin (*Latin*)
Dr Patrick Drumm, BMus, MA, DPhil (*Personal Discovery Framework, Director of Studies*)

Humanities Faculty (*including Geography, History, Economics, Psychology, Politics and Wellbeing*):
*Miss Alison Williams, BA Oxon (*History, Politics*)
Mrs Remona Puri, MBA Sheffield (*Economics*)
Mrs Rebecca Keys, BA Hons Plymouth (*Geography*)
Mrs Vicki Kipling, BSc Canterbury Christ Church (*Geography*)
Mrs Sue Carney, BEd Exeter (*Geography, Deputy Headmistress*)
Ms Jennifer Gavin, BA Hons Sussex (*History, Politics*)
Dr Pamela Marin, MA USA, MPhil Oxon, PhD Dublin (*History*)
Mrs Kelly Hickmott, BSc Middlesex (*Psychology*)
Ms Caro Russo Tomassi (*Wellbeing*)
Mrs Alexandra Chinn (*Duke of Edinburgh*)

Mathematics and Science:
*Ms Sarah Ryder, BSc, PGCE Canterbury Christ Church (*Biology*)
Mrs Anjana Ganguli (*Head of Maths*)
Mrs Melissa Thompson, BSc London (*Biology, Head of Upper School*)
Mr Andy Kirkaldy, BSc Wales, PGCE Southampton (*Chemistry*)
Mr Richard Kipling (*Computing*)
Mrs Cara Sheehan, BA Greenwich (*Maths*)
Mr Peter Hosford, BSc Thames Polytechnic (*Physics*)

Student Support Department:
*Ms K Topps
Miss M Frost, BA Hons Canterbury Christ Church (*Teaching Assistant*)

Boarding Staff:
Miss K Lucas, Hon Dip
Miss S Shipton, BA

Croydon High School GDST

Old Farleigh Road, Selsdon, South Croydon, Surrey CR2 8YB

Tel: 020 8260 7500
email: admissions@cry.gdst.net
website: www.croydonhigh.gdst.net
X/Twitter: @CroydonHigh
Facebook: @CroydonHighSchoolGDST
Instagram: @croydonhighschool
LinkedIn: /croydon-high-school

Founded in 1874, the school's original site was in Wellesley Road Croydon but is now situated in the leafy suburb of Selsdon.

Croydon High School is part of the GDST (Girls' Day School Trust). The GDST is the leading network of independent girls' schools in the UK. As a charity that owns and runs 23 schools and two academies, it reinvests all its income in its schools. For further information about the Trust, see p. xxii or visit www.gdst.net.

For over 140 years, Croydon High School has provided a superb all-round education for girls around the Croydon area and further afield. The school combines tradition with a forward-looking, aspirational and supportive atmosphere where every girl is encouraged and supported to aspire without limits to achieve her personal best. The school welcomes girls from a wide range of backgrounds; excellent pastoral care ensures that each girl is known as an individual.

Croydon High offers girls a wide range of co-curricular opportunities ensuring that each girl can find something she enjoys. The school regularly achieves local, regional and national success in Sport; its Arts are also outstanding, having recently been awarded Artsmark GOLD status, with termly west-end quality productions involving students across all year groups, a vibrant Music department offering opportunities to musicians at varying ability levels to develop their talents in all musical genres and young artists are motivated and inspired to develop their creative talents in different media.

The school aims to develop confident young women with wide-ranging interests and abilities who have also achieved excellent academic results. Emphasis is placed on ensuring that girls are happy and fulfilled in whatever career path they choose for the future and ready to excel in life beyond school.

Number of Pupils. Senior School (aged 11–18): 500 girls; Junior School (aged 3–11): 279 girls (excluding Nursery).

Facilities. The purpose-built school has outstanding facilities; including specialist music rooms with a high-spec Mac Suite and recording studio, podcast room, drama studio, language laboratory, computer suites, 10 science laboratories, 3D design technology room and a fully equipped sports block incorporating sports hall, gym, indoor swimming pool, fitness room and dance studio. The school is surrounded by spacious playing fields with netball/tennis courts, athletics track and an all-weather hockey and football pitch.

The Junior School, which has its own Nursery, is in an adjacent building on the same site, sharing many of the excellent facilities. Refurbishment, completed in December 2020, greatly enhances the Main Hall and provides additional space for the school's subject specialist teaching in Music, Drama, MFL and Computer Science, which is a specialty. It also has a new Wellbeing Hub specifically for Junior girls where the Head of Pastoral and Head of SEN can meet with girls in a calm, quiet space outside of the classroom.

The Sixth Form have their own suite of rooms, including a common room and quiet study area, adjacent to the school library and excellent Further Education, Mentoring and Careers resources are available on site. This is a real strength of the school.

Curriculum. Most girls take 9–10 GCSE subjects with the aim of providing a broad and balanced core curriculum which keeps career choices open. Over 23 subjects are offered at A Level including Politics, Psychology, Economics, Latin and Business. Almost all girls proceed to University, and, each year, the majority of girls go to Russell Group Universities and a large proportion to read medicine or STEM subjects, with increasing success in Computer Science, underpinned by a solid number studying The Arts and Languages.

Admission. A whole school Open Day is held annually in October and a Sixth Form Open Evening also in October. An additional Open Event for the Senior School is held in June. Tours and private visits are welcome and can be arranged through the Junior and Senior Admissions Registrars.

The school admits girls to the Junior School on the basis of either individual assessment (younger girls) or written tests (girls of 7+ and above). Selection procedures are held early in January for Juniors and assessments for Infants are held during the Autumn and Spring Terms for entry in the following September.

For entrance to the Senior School in Year 7, the school holds bespoke Entrance Tests in early January for entry the following September. References are taken up for all successful applicants.

Entrance Tests are held in February for Year 9 entry in September.

For the Sixth Form, the school interviews applicants and requests reports from the present school. A Sixth Form Open Evening is held in October and Scholarship and Bursary applicants sit an examination in late November.

Further details on the admissions process are available on the website or via the Registrar, admissions@cry.gdst.net.

Fees per term (2023–2024). Senior School: Years 7–9 £6,369, Years 10–13 £6,605; Junior School: Nursery (full time) £3,839, Reception £4,584, Years 1–2 £4,708, Years 3–4 £5,140, Years 5–6 £5,226.

Scholarships and Bursaries. Following the ending of the Government Assisted Places Scheme, the GDST has made available to the school a number of scholarships and bursaries.

Academic scholarships are available for entry at 11+ or to the Sixth Form. Music, art & design, drama and sports scholarships are also available at 11+ and 16+.

For entrance at Year 9, the school offers a small number of Academic Plus scholarships to applicants joining from other schools, who have chosen to be assessed academically and in one of the following subjects; art, music, drama or sport.

Bursaries are means tested and are intended to ensure that the school remains accessible to bright girls who could not otherwise benefit from the education we offer. These are available to Senior School girls only applying to Year 7 or Sixth Form.

The school has a vibrant and active Alumnae Network – The Ivy Link – which supports the school in numerous ways, including offering careers and mentoring connections.

Charitable status. Croydon High School is part of The Girls' Day School Trust, which is a Registered Charity, number 306983.

Chair of Local Governors: Ms L Lipczynski

***Head*: Ms A Davies**

Deputy Head, Pastoral: Mr D King
Deputy Head, Academic: Mr Ben Rew
Assistant Head, Sixth Form and Operations: Ms Anna Gilmour
Assistant Head, Co-Curricular: Mrs E Webb
Head of Junior School: Miss Sarah-Jane Pendleton
Deputy Head of the Junior School: Miss L Threadgold
Director of External Relations and Philanthropy: Mrs F Cook
Director of Finance and Operations: Mr J Nelson

Downe House

Hermitage Road, Cold Ash, Thatcham, Berkshire RG18 9JJ
Tel: 01635 200286
email: registrar@downehouse.net
website: www.downehouse.net
X/Twitter: @DowneHouse
Facebook: @downehouse
Instagram: @downe_house
LinkedIn: /downe-house-school

See full entry in the **HMC** section, on **p. 86**.

Edgbaston High School

Westbourne Road, Edgbaston, Birmingham, West Midlands B15 3TS
Tel: 0121 454 5831
email: admissions@edgbastonhigh.co.uk
website: www.edgbastonhigh.co.uk
X/Twitter: @Edgbaston_High
Facebook: @Edgbaston-High-School-Official-430788326941674
Instagram: @edgbastonhighschool

This independent day school, founded in 1876, attracts girls both from the immediate neighbourhood and all over the West Midlands. They come for the academic curriculum, the lively programme of sporting, creative and cultural activities, and for the individual attention and flexibility of approach. The school is renowned for its unique and distinctive programme of pastoral care and places considerable importance on wellbeing.

Personal relationships at EHS are of paramount importance. Parents, both individually and through their association, give generously of their time to support our activities; while staff, through their hard work and good relationship with the girls, create an atmosphere at once orderly and friendly.

Organisation and curriculum. There are three departments working together on one site which caters for over 850 day girls aged two and a half to eighteen. One of the features of EHS is the continuity of education it offers. However, girls can be admitted at most stages. Staff take special care to help girls settle quickly and easily. Pupils enjoy a broadly based programme which substantially fulfils the requirements of the National Curriculum and much more.

The Pre-Preparatory Department, known as Westbourne, offers facilities to girls aged two and a half to five in a spacious, purpose-built, detached house. The staff aim to create an environment in which they can promote every aspect of a girl's development. A brand new Nursery (part of the £4 million Octagon building) was opened in February 2005.

The Preparatory School accommodates over 350 girls from 5+ to 11 in up-to-date facilities, among them a new IT suite, Science Laboratory, Library and Design Technology Centre. A full curriculum, including English, Mathematics, Science and Technology, is taught throughout the department.

The Senior School and Sixth Form caters for about 500 girls aged 11+ to 18. Girls follow a well-balanced curriculum which prepares them for a wide range of subjects at GCSE and A Level.

Examination results are very good with high grades distributed across both Arts and Science subjects. The vast majority of girls in Year 13 proceed to Higher Education. Every year girls obtain places at Oxbridge and Russell Group Universities.

Co-curricular activities. Girls can take part in a broad range of activities including art, ceramics, Mandarin, drama, Duke of Edinburgh's Award, music, sport and Young Enterprise. There are clubs during the lunch hour and after school. Instrumental music lessons are available. There is a strong music tradition in the school. Girls go on visits, expeditions and work experience in this country and abroad. We encourage girls to think of the needs of others.

Accommodation. There is a regular programme of improvements to the buildings. An exciting new multi-purpose hall, The Octagon, was opened in February 2005. A floodlit all-weather surface was opened in Summer 2006. The school has its own indoor swimming pool, 12 tennis courts and 8 acres of playing fields. Work on extended Sixth Form accommodation, a new library and fitness suite, at a cost of £3.5m, was completed in January 2011. In August 2016 the school completed a building development designed to enhance the Preparatory School. At a cost of £1.6 million, the project has resulted in a newly extended library, Art room and large welcoming Reception space. A multi-purpose building, the Hexagon, was completed in early 2018. In September 2018, the Sports Pavilion underwent a refurbishment. In September 2022 the Sixth Form Centre benefitted from a full refurbishment.

Location. The school is pleasantly situated next to the Botanical Gardens in a residential area, 1½ miles south-west of the city centre. It is easily accessible by public transport and also has its own privately run coaches.

Fees per term (2023–2024). Nursery and Kindergarten: £3,369 (5 days); Prep: £3,473–£4,878; Senior: £5,176, Sixth Form: £5,250.

Scholarships and bursaries. Academic Scholarships are available at 11+, awarded on the basis of performance in the entrance examination. Sixth Form Subject Scholarships are awarded based on examination and interview.

Two Music Scholarships are also offered annually: one at 11+ and one at 16+. 11+ candidates must sit the main entrance examination in October and then have written, aural and practical tests. Candidates at 16+ attend an audition and interview in January.

At 16+ there are further subject scholarships awarded to girls of outstanding ability. Assessments take place in January.

A Bursary fund exists to help girls of good academic ability in financial need to enter at Reception, Year 3, 11+ and the Sixth Form and to assist those whose financial circumstances have changed since they entered the School. Bursaries may cover part or full fees. All scholarships can be combined with means-tested bursaries in cases of need.

Further information. Full details may be obtained from the school. Parents and girls are welcome to visit the school by appointment.

Charitable status. Edgbaston High School for Girls is a Registered Charity, number 504011. Founded in 1876, it exists to provide an education for girls.

President:
Sir Dominic Cadbury, BA, MBA
Vice-Presidents:
Mr D Cadbury, MSc
Mr I Marshall, BA
HHJ S Thomas, LLB

Members of the Governing Body appointed by the shareholders:
Chairman: Mr M Chitty, BA
Deputy Chairman: Mrs A E S Howarth, Teacher Cert, Adv Dip Ed
Mrs C Diamente, MA, GCB D
Mr T G M Downing, BA Hons
Mrs A E S Howarth, Teacher Cert, Adv Dip Ed
Mrs S Parveen, LLB Hons, PGCE, LPC, MA Ed
Ms S Priest, MA, MRICS
Mr C Pritchard, MA, BA, QTS, MInstLM
Dr S Robinson, PhD (*Psychology*), CPsychol, AFBPsS
Mr G I Scott, MA Oxon
Mrs L Smiley, BA Hons, ATT
Mrs A S Solanki, BA, FCA, PGcert
Appointed by the Old Girls' Association:
Ms E Hartley
Mrs A Lacey

***Headmistress*: Mrs C Macro,** MA Oxon

Deputy Head Academic: Miss K Purewal, BSc Coventry
Deputy Head Curriculum: Mrs J Crimp, BSc Manchester, MEd Birmingham
Deputy Head Pastoral: Mrs A Cirillo-Campbell, BA, UCE Birmingham

School Management Team:
Director Co-Curricular: Mrs L Batchelor
Director Teaching & Learning: Dr A Rajp
Director Academic Enrichment: Mr P Smith
Director Learning Support: Miss H Welsh
Head of Year 13: Mrs G Parsons
Director Systems Innovation: Mr N Southall

Farnborough Hill

Farnborough Road, Farnborough, Hampshire GU14 8AT

Tel: 01252 545197
email: admissions@farnborough-hill.org
website: farnborough-hill.org
X/Twitter: @FarnboroughHill
Facebook: @Farnborough-Hill
Instagram: @farnborough.hill
LinkedIn: /company/farnborough-hill

Motto: *Wholeheartedly*

Farnborough Hill, founded in 1889, is a leading Catholic independent day school for around 540 girls aged 11–18 years. Located on the Hampshire/Surrey border, the School has excellent transport links, both by train and road, while enjoying a beautiful setting in over 65 acres of parkland.

Farnborough Hill is a vibrant community and our vision for pupils is simple: to help them become the very best version of themselves. Teachers believe in the gifts and talents of each individual and value the uniqueness of each person. From this diversity and belief comes a unity of purpose: to develop young women, each strong, compassionate and courageous, each going into the world to play a positive role. We welcome girls of all faiths and none, who are happy to support the School's ethos.

Our girls are engaged, committed and fun-loving. They are achievers but not paralysed by perfectionism. They are risk-takers and carers. These fabulous girls are buoyed up by all the adults at Farnborough Hill, each in their specific role, sharing responsibility for the development of character and nurturing the spirit of the girls in their care.

Superb resources and facilities combined with the energy and expertise of highly-motivated staff ensure that the girls have the opportunities and self-belief to succeed in a wide variety of fields. This is a place where pupils thrive, are nourished, and are allowed to develop their individual character before launching into the world as agents of change.

Admission. Entry is by examination taken in December for the following September.

Scholarships and Bursaries. The school offers academic, drama, music, sports and art and design scholarships and also bursaries for parents who are in need of financial assistance. Academic scholarships are offered for entry at 11+. In addition music, drama, sport and art and design scholarships are awarded at 11+. Sixth Form scholarships are awarded for academic achievement, excellence in the performing arts, the creative arts and sports. An additional scholarship is awarded by Farnborough Hill Old Girls' Association.

Fees per term (2023–2024). Tuition: £5,995.

Further information. Please visit our website (farnborough-hill.org) or telephone Emma Judge, Director of Admissions, on 01252 545197.

Charitable status. The Farnborough Hill Trust is a Registered Charity, number 1039443.

Board of Governors:
Mr Gerry J McCormack (*Chair*)
Ms Helen Griffiths (*Deputy Chair*)
Mr Mark R Bernard
Mrs Ann Berry
Mr Chris J Fowler-Tutt
Miss Niamh Hills
Dr Grace Huxford
Mrs Julie L Micklethwaite
Dr Hannah Patel
Mr Gary Selby

***Acting Head*: Mrs Zoe Ireland**, BA Manchester Met, PGCE Reading

Deputy Head – Pastoral: Miss Pippa Sexton, BA Swansea, MA Hertfordshire, PGCE Oxon
Assistant Head – Assessment & Reporting: Mr Peter Forrest-Biggs, MA London, QTS
Assistant Head – Head of Sixth Form: Mr Craig McCready, BSc, PGCE Queen's Belfast, MA King's College London

Mr Joe Adams, BA, PGCE, Sussex (*Music*)
Mr Erik Anders, BA, PGCE Reading, MA Royal Holloway (*Drama*)
Mrs Christina Balsom, Lehrerin des Lehramtes an Grund-Haupt und Realschulen Lüneburg, QTS (*French*, *German*)
Mrs Katherine Bell, BA Bristol, PGCE Soton (*History*)
Mr Ciaran Bradley, QTS, PGCE Roehampton (*Design, Art and Technology*)
Mrs Denise Brennan, BA, PGCE Limerick School of Art and Design (*Art*, *Photography*)
Mrs Joanne Brereton, BA Soton, PGCE Reading (*Geography*, *History*)
Mrs Olivia Brophy, BSc LSE, PGCE Institute of Education (*English*)
Mrs Hazel Burrows, BA Loughborough, PGCE Chichester (*Physics*)
Mrs Susana Camprubí-Reches, BA Barcelona, MEd Cardiff, PGCE Barcelona (*Spanish*)
Mrs Benedikt Chamberlain, BA France and Rostock University, Germany, MA Rouen, France, QTS (*French*, *German*)
Miss Helen Clutterbuck, BSc, PGCE Warwick (*Biology*, *Chemistry*, *Physics*)
Miss Hannah Collier, BA, PGCE York (*History*, *Politics*)
Mrs Karen Davis, BSc London, PGCE Surrey (*Mathematics*)
Mrs Maria Davy, BA Surrey, PGCE St Mary's, PGCert SENCo Reading (*Religious Education*, *Philosophy & Ethics*)
Mrs Helen De Mattos, BA, PGCE Roehampton, MA Royal Central School of Speech and Drama (*Drama*)
Mr Daniel Emery, BA Chichester, QTS (*Physical Education*)
Mrs Laura Evans-Jones, BA Royal Holloway, MA, PGCE Roehampton (*English*)
Mrs Ludivine Fitzwater, Licence Valenciennes, QTS (*French*)
Mrs Mimi Fogden, BA Birmingham, PGCE Wolverhampton (*Food Technology*)
Mrs Suzanne Gibbs, BA, CNAA, PGCE Greenwich
Mrs Madeline Greene Lally, BA Queen Mary & Westfield College, MSc UCL (*English*)
Mr Simon Haddock, BSc UEA, PGCE Institute of Education (*Psychology*)
Miss Emily-Jayne Harrison, BA, QTS Brighton (*Physical Education*)
Mrs Susannah Haynes, BSc Imperial, PGCE Reading (*Chemistry*, *Physics*)
Mr James Hobbs, BA Sheffield, QTS (*Religious Education*)
Mrs Jessica Hocking, BEng Exeter, PGCE Surrey (*Mathematics*)
Mrs Helen Jones, BA, PGCE Roehampton
Ms Carmel Landowski, BA Bangor, PGCE (*Classics*, *Latin*)
Mrs Camilla Lawson, BA W Surrey College of Art and Design (*Art & Design*)
Miss Rebecca Lovelock, BSc Manchester, PGCE Reading QTS
Miss Naomi Lynch, BSc Farnborough College of Technology, PGCE Buckingham (*Physical Education*)
Mr Patrick Martin, BA, MA Cantab, PGCE, QCF
Mrs Lucy May, BSc Bristol, QTLS
Mrs Vivian McCarthy, BA Cork, PGCE Oxon (*Religious Education*, *Philosophy & Ethics*, *History*)
Mr Matthew McCarthy-Brown, BSc, PGCE Exeter (*Computing*, *Information Technology*)
Mr Aaron McGuire, BSc Brunel, QTS (*Mathematics*)
Mrs Carrie McNerney, QTS, PGCE Wales (*Mathematics*)
Mr Emanuele Maccherini, MA Siena, PGCE Cantab (*Classics*)
Mrs Susan Macey, BSc UMIST, PGCE Cantab (*Chemistry*)
Mr William Maxwell, BSc Exeter, PGCE Portsmouth (*Mathematics*)
Miss Lucy Miller, BA Reading, PGCE UWE (*Economics*, *Business*)
Mrs Jane Moseley, BSc Surrey, QTS (*Mathematics*)
Miss Jacqueline Munnings, BSc Plymouth, PGCE Sussex (*Biology*)
Miss Danni O'Laoire, MA Nottingham, PGCE King's (*Classics*)
Mrs Sarah Oscroft, BSc Sheffield, MSc Oxford Brookes, QTS (*Geography*, *History*)
Miss Katriona Pengelley, BA Nottingham, MA, PGCE Institute of Education (*Classical Civilisation*, *History*)
Mrs Sally Pollington, BEng Leeds, PGCE Greenwich (*Computer Science*)
Dr James Quinnell, BA Winchester, MA, PhD Dunelm, PGCE Lancaster (*English*)
Mr Alan Rees, BA Oxon, PGCE Oxford Brookes, QTS (*Physics*)
Dr Josephine Russell, BA Royal Holloway, MA Queen Mary College, PGCE Reading, PhD Royal Holloway (*English*)
Mr Timothy Seys, BA Southampton, PGCE (*Spanish*, *French*)
Mrs Rupinder Sidhu, BSc Coventry, QTS (*Chemistry*)
Mr Andrew Smith, BSc Open, PGCE Roehampton (*Mathematics*)
Mrs Siobhan Smith, BSc, PGCE Leeds (*Chemistry*)
Mrs Pippa Sutton, BA, PGCE Oxon (*Mathematics*)
Mrs Colleen Swire, BEd St Mary's Belfast (*Religious Education*, *Philosophy & Ethics*)
Mrs Ceri Symonds-Keates, BA Brighton, PGCE Chichester (*History*, *Politics*)
Dr Ian Taylor, BA, MSt, DPhil Oxon (*Music*)
Ms Charlotte Taylor, BA Humberside, QTS (*English*)
Mr Scott Temple, MChem, PGCE Sussex (*Chemistry*)

Dr Andrew Tytko, BSc, PhD Leeds, MA Dunelm, PGCE Kingston (*Business, Economics*)
Mrs Julia Valbonesi, BA London College of Fashion, PGCE Reading (*Design and Technology*)
Mrs Hannah Van Klaveren, BA Exeter, PGCE, MSc Oxon (*Geography*)
Miss Polly White, BA UCL, PGCE King's (*French, Spanish*)
Miss Naomi Wilcock, BA, PGCE Chichester (*Physical Education*)
Mrs Lucy Willis, BA Oxon, PGCE London, QTS (*English*)
Mrs Lori Winch-Johnson, BA Hertfordshire, MSc, PGCE Surrey, CCRS DipPerfCoach Newcastle (*English, Drama, Learning Support*)
Mrs Katherine Wood, BA Staffordshire, PGCE Canterbury Christ Church (*English*)
Mrs Taryn Zimmermann, BA Leeds, PGCE Manchester (*German, Spanish*)

Matrons: Mrs Nicola Condren, RGN
Bursar: Mr Crispin Ingham
Director of Admissions: Mrs Emma Judge, MA Hons
Chaplain: Mrs Nelle Dalton, BA, MDiv

Francis Holland School, Regent's Park

Ivor Place, London NW1 6XR
Tel: +44 (0)20 7723 0176
email: admin@fhs-nw1.org.uk
website: www.fhs-nw1.org.uk
X/Twitter: @FHSRegentsPark
Facebook: @FHSRegentsPark
Instagram: @fhsregentspark
LinkedIn: /company/francis-holland-school-regent's-park

See full entry in the **HMC** section, on **p. 120**.

Francis Holland School, Sloane Square

39 Graham Terrace, London SW1W 8JF
Tel: 020 7730 2971
email: office@fhs-sw1.org.uk
website: www.fhs-sw1.org.uk
X/Twitter: @FHSSloaneSquare
Facebook: @FHSSloaneSquare
Instagram: @fhssloanesquare
LinkedIn: /company/francis-holland-school-sloane-square

See full entry in the **HMC** section, on **p. 121**.

Godolphin and Latymer School

Iffley Road, Hammersmith, London W6 0PG
Tel: 020 8741 1936; 020 8735 9595 (Bursar)
email: office@godolphinandlatymer.com
website: www.godolphinandlatymer.com
X/Twitter: @GandLSchool
Facebook: @GandLSchool
Instagram: @GandLSchool

See full entry in the **HMC** section, on **p. 130**.

Haberdashers' Girls' School

Aldenham Road, Elstree, Herts WD6 3BT
Tel: 020 8266 2300
email: office@habsgirls.org.uk
website: www.habsgirls.org.uk
X/Twitter: @habsgirlsschool
Facebook: @habsgirlsSchool
Instagram: @habsgirlsschool
LinkedIn: /school/habsgirls

Haberdashers' Girls' School is situated on a site of over 100 acres, shared with their brother school Habs Boys, and has an excellent reputation for academic, sporting and musical achievements. Entry to the Junior School is at 4+ or at 7+; and to the Senior School, at 11+ and Sixth Form. The academic results are outstanding, a reflection of able pupils who enjoy learning and thrive on a full and challenging curriculum.

Facilities are first-class with a STEM building and Drama studio and a very wide range of co-curricular activities. Sport, music, drama, art and debating thrive and there are many other opportunities for leadership within the school community, including the Duke of Edinburgh's Award and Arts Award schemes and a very active community service programme. Life at Habs is busy and challenging, embracing new technology alongside old traditions, which include the celebration of St Catherine's Day as patron of the Haberdashers' Company and an annual Carol Service held at St Martin-in-the-Fields in London.

Over 110 coach routes, shared with Habs Boys, bring pupils to school from a thirty-mile radius covering north London, Hertfordshire and Middlesex. The provision of a late coach service ensures that pupils can take part safely in the wide range of the many clubs and societies organised after school. The St Catherine Parents' Guild, the school's parents' association, provides enormous support to the school through fundraising and social events.

Junior School. There are approximately 323 day pupils in the Junior School, with two parallel classes from Reception to Year 6.

Pastoral Care: Class teachers and Learning Support assistants maintain close contact with pupils and their parents. It is very important that our pupils feel happy and comfortable. Every adult has a responsibility for the pupils' welfare and security and there are many layers of care in place. From the outset, through the behaviour code, pupils are encouraged to be friendly, polite and caring to everyone else in the community, whether adults or children, and there is strong peer support. There are two nurses, a counsellor and two individual needs specialists, all of whom are able to provide support and to ensure each pupil understands her unique importance in the school community. Where appropriate, older pupils have responsibility for younger ones and Senior School Sixth Formers regularly help Juniors in the classroom. A programme of PSHCE (personal, social, health and citizenship education) lessons covers important issues of self-development and allows pupils to reflect on their responsibilities to each other and the wider community. Many parents are involved in the classroom, clubs and outings.

Spiritual and Moral Education: Habs is a school with a Christian tradition which welcomes the rich diversity of faiths within the community. Assemblies are held for the whole school at least twice a week and on other days are separate for Key Stage One and Key Stage Two. Values, themes, stories and reflections are drawn from a range of sources including cultures, traditions and faiths. Once a year selected classes perform an assembly to which their parents are invited. Parents are also very welcome to attend assemblies on major occasions such as St Catherine's Day and are often invited to speak to the pupils in assemblies on an area of their expertise or experience relevant to the pupils. Pupils also take part in many charitable ventures throughout the year, raising money and enhancing their awareness of lives in the wider world.

Enrichment: There is a wide range of clubs covering our pupils' interests in sport, music, arts and crafts, languages, science, maths, creative writing, reading, games and puzzles, cookery and gardening. Visits linked to the curriculum are arranged for every class and there are regular visitors to school such as theatre companies, historical re-creations, authors, illustrators, musicians and scientists. Joint events with the Boys' School occur at intervals throughout the year for the different age groups.

Sport: We have first-class sports facilities, including a sports hall, gymnasia, netball and tennis courts, a swimming pool and ample playing fields. The curriculum provides a core of gymnastics, dance, swimming, netball, tennis, athletics and rounders. Teams in netball, cricket, football, gymnastics, rounders and pop lacrosse compete against other schools.

Performance Arts: Concerts and drama productions are a major part of school life, showcasing the wide range of creative talent amongst our pupils. Our Performance Space provides many opportunities to explore and extend their interests in the performance arts. There are two major drama productions annually: an Infant production for all those in Reception and Key Stage One, and a dramatic production for Year 6. The annual Spring Concert showcases all the musical groups and ensembles as well as a massed choir of all Key Stage Two pupils. The summer Chamber Concert features performances from many of our musical ensembles. Informal lunchtime concerts occur at least once a term for Year 4 to 6 soloists or duets. Our pupils' own art and design work is displayed around the school.

Curriculum: There is a broad and challenging curriculum with the provision of opportunities for outdoor, active and independent learning, with plenty of practical tasks and problem solving, to enable pupils to develop their bright young minds. Fun is a vital ingredient. There are curriculum evenings for parents to learn about the school's approach to particular subject areas and how they can best support their daughters at home and work in true partnership with the school.

The Early Learning Goals of the Foundation Stage are met through a balance of child-initiated opportunities and teacher-led activities. There is a daily range of stimulating, play-based activities which prompts pupils to ask questions, to discover, to wonder and to learn new skills. No homework is set in Reception or Year 1 so that pupils can enjoy the precious childhood pleasures of imaginative play and being read to by a parent when they get home. Music, French and daily PE lessons are taught by specialist teachers. Phonics teaching enables pupils to make rapid progress with reading and to gain an easy independence in their writing, while the foundations of mathematical thinking are laid through carefully selected practical tasks.

Extensive use is made of IT throughout the Junior School, with a dedicated IT Suite enabling an exciting Computing curriculum, including coding and robotics. In addition, all pupils have an iPad which they can use in class under the supervision of the teacher. The use of mobile technology is not meant to replace traditional learning but to supplement and enhance it and, in some cases, to open up whole new ways of learning for the pupils.

Creativity is fostered in music and dance, in art, design technology, literacy activities, drama and role play. The school grounds provide a rich environment for building knowledge about the world of nature as well as space to develop physical skills and pupils spend one afternoon a week in our on-site Forest School.

At Key Stage One, curriculum subjects are English, Mathematics, Science, History, Geography, Religious Studies, French, Spanish, ICT, Art, Design Technology, Music, PSHCE and Physical Education, including swimming. Fostering a love of reading is paramount.

As pupils progress through Key Stage Two they encounter more subject specialists. Science lessons, which are taught in the well-equipped laboratory, strongly feature practical and investigative work. The Art Room is a magnificent space for the creation of stunning works of art, while pupils can feel transported to another culture as soon as they step into the Languages Room and they are introduced to German for the first time.

Senior School. There are approximately 847 students aged 11–18 in the Senior School.

Pastoral Care: In such a big and busy school, care for each individual is deeply important so that all can flourish and fulfil themselves in every way. Looking after them is a pastoral team consisting of the Deputy Head (Pastoral), Assistant Head (Pastoral), Heads of Year, Form Tutors, a School Nurse, a Counsellor and an Individual Needs Specialist. The provision of pastoral care is designed to help students make decisions and to care about others within the framework of a very diverse community. There is an outstanding range of opportunities for their personal development and to help them consolidate a system of spiritual beliefs and a moral code. The welfare of students is of paramount importance and it is the responsibility of all members of staff, teaching and support staff, to safeguard and promote this. From the moment a student joins the school, emphasis is placed on the partnership with parents so that, hand-in-hand, school and parents can support each child, operating on a basis of trust and with people they know from the start.

Spiritual and Moral Education: Haberdashers' is a school with a Christian tradition which welcomes the rich diversity of faiths within the community. The day begins with the whole school assembly or House meeting to reinforce the school's values and its sense of community. These meetings are often led by the students themselves. Once a week there are separate faith assemblies: Christian, Hindu, Jain and Sikh, Humanist, Jewish or Muslim. Students can choose which one they attend. Holy Communion takes place at the Boys' School. Roman Catholic Mass is celebrated each half term, either in the Girls' or the Boys' School. Students may pray at lunchtime in a room set aside for them to do so. Students organise and run many charitable events within their Houses throughout the year. This enhances their awareness of the wider world as well as raising funds for charities small and large, at home and abroad.

Enrichment: There is a wide range of clubs on offer in the Senior School, including Art, creative writing, Dance, debating, Design Technology, Drama, football, Maths, Philosophy, Science, and synchronised swimming. Trips and visits include a Year 7 adventure holiday and various trips abroad, with language exchanges, work experience, and study visits. Subject specific trips in the UK and abroad include field trips, theatre visits, trips to sites of historical importance, museums and art galleries, music and sports tours.

Sport and Performance Arts: The core curriculum includes gymnastics, dance, swimming, lacrosse, netball, tennis, athletics and rounders. For older students, there are additional options in self-defence, badminton, football, trampolining, etc. There are clubs in a range of sports for recreational enjoyment as well as for the teams. There are major drama productions in all sections of the school and symphonic concerts showcasing a variety of ensembles, including three orchestras, wind and jazz bands, percussion groups, flute choirs, and rock bands, as well as recitals and chamber concerts. There are annual Drama and Music Festivals; occasionally, there are joint productions and orchestral concerts with the Boys' School. Students' painting, sculpture and design installations are displayed around the school.

Opportunities for leadership and challenge are valued and encouraged. Activities include: The Duke of Edinburgh's Award; Community Service; European Youth Parliament; Model United Nations; etc.

Curriculum: The school follows its own wide-ranging academic curriculum tailored to the needs of its very able pupils. It preserves the best of a traditional education whilst responding positively to curricular developments. Much emphasis is placed on developing the students' ability to think and learn independently, nurturing an intellectual resilience and self confidence which will prepare them for the world beyond school. In all subjects, the curriculum aims to be something that inspires the students and stimulates discussion and ideas. A high value is placed upon creativity, imagination and the opportunity to pursue topics beyond the confines of the exam specifications. The school is not required to follow the National Curriculum but draws upon the best practice of what is happening nationally and in other schools. In the first three years of the Senior School, students follow a set curriculum, studying French, Spanish and German on a carousel and then choosing two to continue with into Year 8. As they progress through the school they are given greater choice and the opportunity to personalise their curriculum to suit their needs and interests. Thus the GCSE curriculum has space for up to four optional subjects. In the Sixth Form the students have a free choice of subjects from the subjects on offer. At each level, the curriculum is designed to prepare them for the opportunities, responsibilities and experiences of the next stage of their education and their lives.

Scholarships and Bursaries. A number of Academic Scholarships are awarded annually to pupils entering the Senior School. A smaller number of Creative Writing, Music, Art, Drama and Sports Scholarships are awarded each year to students who show additional special promise in these specific areas.

A significant number of means-tested Governors' Bursaries are awarded at age 11+, valued from a few hundred pounds to full fees, depending upon financial need. Open equally to boys progressing from the Prep School and to those applying from other Schools.

Full details of all these awards are included in the prospectus available from the School Registrar who is happy to answer enquiries.

Fees per annum (2023–2024). Senior £23,613–£23,745 exc. lunch; Junior £20,310 (R–Y2) inc. lunch, £21,642 (Y3–Y6) inc. lunch. A number of scholarships are awarded annually and means-tested financial assistance (up to full fees) is also available for students entering at 11+ or 16+.

Charitable status. The Haberdashers' Aske's Charity is a Registered Charity, number 313996. It exists to promote education.

Chair of the Board of Governors: Simon Cartmell, OBE

Executive Principal: Mr A R Lock, MA

***Headmistress*: Dr H Bagworth-Mann**, PhD Brunel

Head of the Junior School: Mrs C Brown, BSc Newcastle

Principal Deputy Head: Mrs S Wright, MEd Cantab

Deputy Head (*Academic*): Mr D Sabato, BA Nottingham

Deputy Head (*Admissions, Co-Curricular and Events*): Mr T Scott, MA Cantab

Deputy Head (*Pastoral*) *and Designated Safeguarding Lead*: Mrs L Simson, MA Cantab

Acting Assistant Heads (*Academic*): Mrs I Barrett Walsh, BSc Manchester and Mr R Yarlett, BA Leicester

Assistant Head (*Pastoral*): Mrs C Milsom, BA Brunel

Chief Operating Officer: R Dunn, MA

Head of Sixth Form: Mrs L Mee, BSc London

Joint Schools Director of Development: W Friar, MS

Director of Foundation: R de H Llewellyn, MA

Joint Schools Director of Marketing and Communications: A Tooley, BA

Director of People: Dr R McKenzie-Young, PhD

Director of Partnerships: Mr J Plotkin, MA Oxon

Director of STEM: Miss N Percy, BSc Leeds
Head of Habs Diploma: Dr K Bridge, BSc Loughborough
Director of Finance and Resources. L Karfoot, BA

Heads of Department:
Art: Miss K Shaw, BA Manchester [maternity leave], Mrs D Hobbs, BA Lancaster [maternity cover]
Classics: Mrs A Saunders, MA Oxon
Computing: Ms M Durmus-Ergul, BSc Brunel
Design Technology: Mr M Squire, BSc Southbank
Economics: Ms K Healer
English: Miss I Condon, BA Manchester
Drama: Miss A Murphy
Geography: Miss S Nanji, BA London
History: Mr R Yarlett, BA Leicester
Mathematics: Mrs I Barrett-Walsh, BSc Manchester
Modern Languages: Mrs S Bromley, BA Birmingham (*Head of French*), Mr D Foster, MEd Cantab (*Head of German*), Ms J Curtis, MA Kings College London (*Head of Spanish*)
Music: Ms M Jenkins, BMus London
Performance Music: T Taylor, MMus
Director of Sport: Miss T Dawson, BEd Greenwich
Politics: Mrs C Wilding, BA Bristol
PSHCE: Mr D Heyman, BA Oxon
Science: Dr J Havery-Barrett, BSc Newcastle (*Head of Biology*), Dr C Ruddick, BSc Exeter (*Head of Chemistry*), Dr K Bridge, BSc Loughborough (*Head of Physics*)
Religion and Philosophy: Mrs K Opie, MA London

Junior School:
Head: Mrs C Brown, BSc Newcastle
Deputy Head: Ms D Lansdown, BEd Cantab
Acting Assistant Head (*Pastoral*): Ms U Elliott

Staff lists can be found online at www.habsgirls.org.uk/about/staff-lists.

Harrogate Ladies' College

Clarence Drive, Harrogate, North Yorkshire HG1 2QG

Tel: 01423 537045
email: admissions@hlc.org.uk
website: www.hlc.org.uk
X/Twitter: @HLCNews
Facebook: @HarrogateLadiesCollege
Instagram: @harrogateladiescollege
LinkedIn: /harrogate-ladies'-college

Harrogate Ladies' College is a Boarding and Day school for 300 girls aged 11–18. Situated within the College campus, Highfield Pre-School is a pre school for over 70 boys and girls between the ages of 2–4. Highfield Prep School, which opened in 1999, is a Day Prep school for over 230 boys and girls between the ages of 4–11.

Location. The College is situated in a quiet residential area on the Duchy Estate about 5 minutes' walk from the town centre and is easily accessible by road and rail networks. Leeds/Bradford airport is 20 minutes' drive away. Harrogate itself is surrounded by areas of natural interest and beauty.

Accommodation. Approximately 40% of the pupils are full boarders. Houses are arranged in mixed age groups from Year 7 to Year 12. Year 13 pupils enjoy a greater sense of independence in their own accommodation called Tower House. This contains a large, modern kitchen, comfortable lounges and relaxation areas and girls have individual study-bedrooms. Each house has a Housemistress and Assistant Housemistress who are responsible for the well-being of the girls. There is a well-equipped Health Centre with qualified nurses.

Curriculum and examinations. The College aims to provide a broad-based curriculum for the first three years in line with National Curriculum requirements. This leads to a choice of over 28 subjects at GCSE, IGCSE and A level. Each pupil has a form tutor who continuously monitors and assesses her development.

Facilities. The central building contains the main classrooms, hall, library, and dining rooms, and a Sixth Form Centre with studies, seminar rooms, kitchens and leisure facilities. The College Chapel is nearby. An extension provides 8 laboratories for Physics, Chemistry, Biology and Computer Studies. Three dedicated computer suites, provision in the boarding houses and throughout the school, form an extensive computer network. Sixth Formers have network access using their own laptops from studies and bedrooms. Additional facilities for specialised teaching include Art, Textiles, Photography, Design and Technology, Drama and Food and Nutrition.

Our award winning Business School is where pupils are able to enjoy the academic study of Economics, Business Studies and Psychology in a state-of-the-art business-like environment which helps prepare young women of today for the global world of tomorrow.

Sport. The College has its own sports hall, a full size indoor swimming pool, gymnasium, fitness centre, playing field, netball courts, 9 tennis courts and a dance studio. Girls are taught a wide range of sports and may participate in sporting activities outside the school day. Lacrosse and netball are played in winter, and tennis, rounders, swimming and athletics are the main summer physical activities. Extracurricular sports include badminton, basketball, fencing, golf, horse riding and gymnastics.

Wellbeing. Wellness is at the heart of our school community and our wellness initiative is designed to support pupils, staff and parents. Our Wellness Centre is the hub for a wide range of activities to support and encourage all-round physical, social and mental wellbeing, including Yoga and dance classes.

Sixth form. The College has a thriving Sixth Form Community of 100 pupils. Students have a choice of 26 courses at A level. There is a broad range of general cultural study. In preparation for adult life, Sixth Formers are expected to make a mature contribution to the running of the school and many hold formal positions of responsibility. Personal guidance is given to each girl with regard to her future plans and most pupils choose to continue their education at University.

Religious affiliation. The College is Christian although pupils of other religious denominations are welcomed. We focus on inclusion, mutual respect and understanding of people of all faiths and of no faith.

Music. A special feature is the interest given to music and choral work both in concerts and in the College Chapel, and the girls attend frequent concerts and dramatic performances in Harrogate. There are Junior and Senior choirs, orchestra, string, wind and brass groups.

Scholarships. Academic, Art, Textiles, Music, Choral, Drama and Sport scholarships are available.

Fees per term (2023–2024). Boarding: £12,070, Day: £6,325. Fee remissions are available for girls with a sibling at Harrogate Ladies' College or at Highfield Prep School.

Entry. Entry is usually at age 11, 13 or at Sixth Form level. Entry is based on the College's own entrance examination and a school report. Sixth Form entry is conditional upon GCSE achievement and an interview with the Principal.

Charitable status. Harrogate Ladies' College Limited is a Registered Charity, number 529579. It exists to provide high-quality education for girls.

Chair of Governors: Dame Francine Holroyd

***Principal*: Mrs Sylvia Brett**, MA London, BA Dunelm
Financial Controller: Mrs Emma Richards
Director of Admissions and Marketing: Mrs Sarah Bowman, BA UWE, MSc Stirling
Head of Highfield: Mr James Savile, BEd Southampton
Senior Deputy: Mrs Joanna Fox, BA OU
Director of Teaching & Learning: Miss Siobhan Scully, BA Lancaster
Senior Master: Mr Peter Massey, BA, MA, MMath Cantab
Head of Boarding: Miss Laura Brookes, MA St Andrews
Assistant Head, Head of Lower School: Mrs Joanna Griffin, BA Bristol
Assistant Head, Head of Middle School: Mrs Fran Irvine, BEd Bedford
Assistant Head, Joint Head of Sixth Form: Mr Paul Dwyer, BSc Warwick
Assistant Head, Joint Head of Sixth Form: Mrs Bonnie Christie, MEd Leeds

Headington Rye Oxford

Oxford, Oxfordshire OX3 7TD

Tel: 01865 759100
01865 759 861/872/869 (Admissions)
email: admissions@headington.org
website: www.headington.org
X/Twitter: @HeadingtonSch
Facebook: @HeadingtonSch
Instagram: @headington_sch
LinkedIn: /school/Headington-School

Headington Rye Oxford is a highly successful day and boarding school in Oxford for 800 girls aged 11–18, with a Prep School for girls and boys girls aged 3–11 occupying its own site, separated from the senior school by a pedestrianised footpath. (*See Headington Rye Oxford Preparatory School entry in IAPS section.*) The school was formed from the merger of Headington School and neighbouring Rye St Antony.

The School offers pupils from Nursery to Sixth Form an unrivalled opportunity to pursue academic, sporting and artistic excellence in a caring and nurturing environment.

Set in 23 acres of playing fields and gardens, our superb facilities provide the perfect backdrop for teaching and learning that extends way beyond the classroom and curriculum. We encourage participation in all aspects of sport and culture, teamwork and leadership, challenging girls to discover and explore their own potential and achieve more than they thought possible.

Consistently in the premier league of academic schools in the UK, life at Headington Rye is about much more than exam results. Through the sheer breadth of subjects and activities at Headington, we aim to educate the complete individual, giving girls the confidence and self-awareness to compete, contribute and succeed at school, university and in their adult lives.

Facilities. Headington Rye offers a superb range of facilities to day girls and boarders to support and enhance their learning. Our Music School has fantastic acoustics, along with teaching rooms, a recording studio and electronics studio. The 240-seat Theatre, run by a professional team who provide expertise in set design, lighting and sound design, is home to the School's Drama Department. Our Dance and Fitness Centre benefits from a fully equipped gym, training rooms and a large dance studio. Other sports facilities include a floodlit all-weather pitch, sports hall and 25 m indoor swimming pool. In 2016, the School opened its award-winning Library, and an extended and refurbished Sixth Form Centre opened in early 2019. A new Creativity and Innovation Centre, the Hive, opened in 2021 and features light and airy art studios, a lens suite, 3D workshop and 3D printers, photographic studio, lecture theatre and gallery space. State-of-the-art teaching kitchens, including a demonstration kitchen, were officially opened by chef Prue Leith in 2022, while a new boathouse on the Thames for the championship-winning boat club was completed in 2023.

Curriculum. In Years 7 and 8, girls are taught in four classes of around 20 each, which increases to six slightly smaller classes in U4 after 13+ entry. They study Art, Biology, Chemistry, Computing, Creative Engineering & Design, Dance, Drama, English, Fashion and Textile Design, Food and Nutrition, French, Spanish or German (girls choose an additional language to study in Year 8), Games, Geography, History, Latin, Mathematics, Music, Physical Education, Physics, Religious Studies. By Year 9 they choose two subjects from Art, Dance, Drama, Fashion & Textile Design and Music. Most girls study nine or ten GCSE subjects, from a choice of around 30 subjects supplemented by one-year courses (the Higher Project Qualification, School Certificate in Philosophy, Certificate in Digital Communication and Award in Financial Education). The majority of students move into the Sixth Form where they can choose from 30 A Level subjects along with the EPQ and BTEC National Diplomas in Enterprise and Entrepreneurship or Sport. Many new girls, both day and boarders, also join us at this stage.

Physical Education. From Olympic rowers to recreational dancers, Headington Rye offers a genuinely inclusive approach to PE and extracurricular sport and encourages each girl to enjoy sport at the level that suits her. PE is taught throughout the school and many girls choose to study PE to GCSE. They can choose from more than 30 different sporting activities, from Dance and Fencing to Hockey and Trampolining. Sports such as Hockey, Netball and Athletics are played competitively against other schools and girls have the chance to represent the School across a range of abilities. Around 70 girls currently compete at county level and beyond and the School enjoys national success in a wide range of sports. Rowers compete at the very highest level, with the School consistently triumphing at the National Schools' Regatta. More than 150 girls row and regularly go on to represent Great Britain at international competitions.

Music. Every girl has the opportunity to enjoy music both within the curriculum and beyond. More than 430 individual music lessons take place each week and visiting teachers offer girls the opportunity to learn a wide range of instruments. The Senior School has numerous orchestras, choirs and ensembles, from junior orchestras to choose from.

Drama. There is a busy programme of productions each year and girls of all ages become involved in all aspects of theatre, from writing and producing their own plays, to lighting, costume and make-up. Drama is an option at GCSE and A Level. Many girls also elect to take Trinity Speech and Drama exams in school.

Dance. State-of-the-art Dance facilities provide a multitude of opportunities for every girl. Dance is part of the curriculum in the Lower School and girls may select it at GCSE and A Level. Outside the classroom there is a huge range of dance options, from Ballet to Street Dance and Contemporary. As well as annual Dance Shows, the Headington Dance Company competes in local and national competitions.

Extracurricular activities. More than 120 extracurricular activities take place every week during lunchtime, before and after school. A wide choice of subjects, sports, interests and hobbies ranges from The Duke of Edinburgh's Award and Drama to Astronomy and Young Enterprise. Headington Rye also has a successful Combined Cadet Force.

Higher Education and careers. Each year, girls head off to leading universities in the UK and abroad or to competitive school leaver programmes. A significant number of girls choose Oxbridge each year; some head for medical or veterinary college and others take up Art Foundation courses. Girls graduate from a wide range of arts and science degrees in subjects as diverse as civil engineering, architecture, classics and natural sciences. Detailed assistance on choice of universities is given in the Sixth Form along with special programmes for Medicine, Veterinary Science, Oxbridge, Law and Architecture. A careers programme is in place throughout the School.

Boarding. Just over a quarter of the School – around 200 girls – are boarders. The boarding houses provide girls with a 'home from home' where, supported by a team of highly experienced staff, they learn to develop into mature and independent young people. Many boarders come from the UK and the School is also very proud of its international boarding community, made up of more than 30 nationalities from all over the world. There is a choice of flexible boarding options for girls aged eleven and upwards with full, weekly and half-weekly boarding all on offer.

Entrance. The main entry points to the Senior School are at 11+, 13+ or, for the Sixth Form, 16+. Girls are occasionally able to join at other ages if places become available. Girls enter the School at 11+ via Headington's own examination day and interview in late November. Girls at UK prep schools sit the ISEB pre-tests in Year 6 or 7 for entrance at 13+. Other 13+ candidates sit the School's own examination papers in Year 8. Sixth Form entrance examinations and interviews are held in the November before the proposed year of entry and include general papers involving Maths and essay-writing, a critical thinking skills assessment and an academic interview.

Registration fees are £125 (UK) and £250 (overseas-based families). For information about admissions, please check the website, www.headington.org, or contact the School's friendly admissions team who will be happy to help.

Fees per term (2023–2024). Senior School: Full Boarders £13,1787–£15,107; Weekly Boarders £11,517–£12,770; Half-Weekly Boarders £9,238–£10,119; Day Girls £6,895–£7,505.

Scholarships and bursaries. Scholarships are awarded for academic achievement, art, dance, drama, music and sport. These awards recognise talent and achievement and most do not provide any fee reduction or financial reward, although there are a small number of special academic and music scholarships available to the highest achieving candidates at 11+ and 13+ entry. The Headington Access Programme (HAP) supports talented girls who would benefit from all that the School has to offer but who may not be able to access a Headington education without some form of financial assistance. Means-tested bursaries of up to 100 per cent of fees are available for local day girls who achieve high marks in our entrance examinations and are awarded at 11+ and 13+. Exceptional candidates at 16+ may be eligible for our Special Awards programme, worth 10 per cent of fees.

Charitable status. Headington School Oxford Limited is a Registered Charity, number 309678. It exists to provide quality education for girls.

Clerk to the Council: Miss Emma Saville

***Headmistress*: Mrs C Jordan**, MA Oxon

Head of Prep: Mrs J Crouch, BA Keele, MA London, NPQH

First Deputy Head (*Staff & Operations*): Mr S Hawkes, BA Brunel

Deputy Head (*Academic*): Dr A-M Stanton-Ife, MA Cantab, MA UCL, PhD UC

Deputy Head (*Pastoral*): Miss A Proctor, BA Oxon, MSc Dunelm

Bursar: Mr R Couzens, MBE, MA Cranfield

Heathfield School

Ascot

London Road, Ascot, Berkshire SL5 8BQ

Tel: 01344 898343

email: admissions@heathfieldschool.net

website: www.heathfieldschool.net

X/Twitter: @HeathfieldAscot

Facebook: @HeathfieldSchool

Instagram: @heathfieldascot

LinkedIn: /heathfield-school

Introduction. Pioneering high standards in girls' education since 1899, this boarding (weekly and full) and day school provides an outstanding all-round education for girls in beautiful surroundings less than an hour from London in the heart of Berkshire near the world-famous Ascot Racecourse.

The school combines exemplary standards of pastoral care with a personalised academic curriculum which adds value to every girl's achievements to provide a truly holistic education for girls aged 11–18.

Not only is Heathfield firmly on the academic map but it also produces county and national sportswomen and talented artists, photographers, actors, musicians and dancers.

Heathfield is headed by Sarah Rollings, who has an MA in Educational Leadership and Management, as well as a first-class degree from Brunel University in Secondary Education with Geography and Physical Education. Mrs Rollings was appointed Head in January 2021.

The school also boosted its growing reputation for the STEM (Science Technology Engineering and Maths) subjects with the completion of a state of the art STEM facility, officially opened by Lord Robert Winston.

Atmosphere and Ethos. The school's aim is to help every student excel, and to get the most out of life by providing the very best intellectual stimulation, physical challenges and pastoral care. The school is founded on Church of England principles but welcomes all faiths.

Pastoral Care. Heathfield's strength is in its size, meaning each student is supported throughout their school career and can never slip under the radar. Students are overseen by a dedicated team of academic staff, Heads of Year, Tutors, Housemistresses, Heads of House and Prefects. They work together to provide the highest level of pastoral care. Teachers will meet with students regularly to discuss their particular needs and to ensure they are achieving their maximum potential.

Curriculum. Heathfield offers variety in terms of the subjects on offer as well as fundamental excellence in all the traditional subjects. At A Level, students can choose from 24 subjects plus EPQ (Extended Project Qualification). Extras such as the Leiths Certificate in Food and Wine and the Duke of Edinburgh's Awards are also offered. The school is famous for its excellence in the creative arts and enjoys a close relationship with the University of the Arts, London, a unique collaboration agreement with Parsons, Paris and a new creative partnership with Falmouth University. It has also won a record five Good Schools Guide awards for Art and Design Photography at A Level.

Activities. The St Mary's Theatre, Sports Hall, playing fields and swimming pool are always hives of activity and there are many other co-curricular activities including frequent museum, art gallery and theatre trips, field trips and overseas visits.

Sport. Heathfield's outstanding facilities include a large multi-purpose sports hall, a dance studio, five lacrosse pitches, six tennis/netball courts and a 25m indoor heated swimming pool. The school competes successfully at lacrosse, netball, swimming, rounders, athletics and various equestrian disciplines including polo. Girls have represented the school regionally, nationally and internationally in a variety of sports.

Boarding Accommodation. Boarding accommodation is first-class. From Form IV onwards, all girls have single rooms. For more freedom and independence, the Upper Sixth live in Wyatt House which contains two fully-equipped kitchens and areas in which to study and socialise.

Medical Welfare. Three nursing sisters and the school doctor are in charge of the girls' medical welfare, supported by Heads of House, Housemistresses and Tutors. The Heads of House or Housemistresses are available at all times for any parental concerns.

New Facilities. A state-of-the-art STEM (Science, Technology, Engineering and Maths) block opened in January 2016 and a digital recording studio opened in 2017. A new Sixth Form Centre was completed in September 2022.

Admission. Admission points are 11+, 13+ and Sixth Form. Occasional places may be available in other year groups. Applicants are assessed using an online CEM test along with an interview with the Headmistress. Entry into the Lower Sixth Form is via predicted GCSE grades and interview. Deferred 13+ entry is also available and international students wishing to apply are guided through the procedure step by step by our Admissions team. For further information see: www.heathfieldschool.net

Scholarships and Bursaries. Scholarships and Bursaries are awarded. Bursaries are means-tested and are awarded at the Headmistress's discretion.

Fees per term (2023–2024). Senior (Forms III–UVI): Full Boarding £14,190, Weekly Boarding £13,481, Day £8,772. Lower (Forms I–II): Full Boarding £13,868, Weekly Boarding £13,174, Day £8,589.

Charitable status. Heathfield School is a Registered Charity, number 309086. It exists to provide a caring boarding education leading to higher education for girls aged between 11 and 18.

Chair of Governors: Mr Alex Popplewell, MA Cantab

Senior Leadership Team:

***Headmistress*: Sarah Rollings**, BSc Hons Brunel, MA Open

Bursar: Mrs M Frier, BSc Hons Bristol, BFP, FCA
Deputy Head (*Academics*): Mr D Mitchell, MA Hull, MSc York, BA Hons Warwick, PGCE UWE
Deputy Head (*Pastoral & Boarding*): Miss L Scott, BA Hons QTS
Director of Marketing & Admissions: Ms A Morgan, MCIM, MIDM
Assistant Head (*Co-Curricular*): Miss W Reynolds, BEd Hons Liverpool
Assistant Head (*Pastoral & Boarding*) Mr A Valner, MA, BA Nottingham PGCE London
Assistant Head (*Operations*) Miss C Wells, BSc Hons Bath, PGCE Exeter

A current full staff list can be found on our website: www.heathfieldschool.net/about-us/staff.

Howell's School Llandaff GDST

Cardiff Road, Llandaff, Cardiff CF5 2YD

Tel: 029 2056 2019
email: admissions@how.gdst.net
website: www.howells-cardiff.gdst.net
www.howellscoedcollege.gdst.net
X/Twitter: @HowellsSchool
Facebook: @Officialhowells
Instagram: @howellsschoolgdst
LinkedIn: /howell-s-school-llandaff

A magnificent Victorian gothic building right on the edge of the great, green expanse of Llandaff Fields, Howell's School Llandaff GDST has a tremendous sense of roominess for a city school, with a swimming pool, tennis courts, sports pavilion and all-weather sports pitch on the five-acre site.

Visionary Principal Sally Davis presides over excellent academic results, and in August 2023 results at Howell's were outstanding. An impressive 68% of all GCSEs were graded 9–7 (A*–A); 96% were graded 9–5(A*–B). In the co-ed Sixth Form College, 34% of all results were A* and 69% of all results were A*–A grades. These are fantastic achievements, particularly considering the significant disruption to student's education over the last three years.

Student numbers. 664: Nursery 17; Prep School 187; Senior School 306; Co-Educational Sixth Form College 154.

Founded in 1860 as a school for girls, the school was built by the Drapers' Company from the endowment left in 1537 by Thomas Howell, son of a Welshman, merchant of London, Bristol and Seville and a Draper.

Howell's School Llandaff is part of the Girls' Day School Trust GDST. The GDST is the leading network of independent girls' schools in the UK. As a charity that owns and runs 23 schools and two academies, it reinvests all its income in its schools. For further information about the Trust, visit www.gdst.net.

Howell's School puts great value on a rich and varied life outside of the classroom, with enrichment activities running from the Pride group to Poetry Club, Silent Discos to Synchronised Swimming. The extensive Enrichment Programmes, together with impressive Wellbeing and Laureate Programmes, make Howell's a special place to learn and develop in an exciting, creative and thriving environment. The school's strong Leadership Team, talented and dedicated teaching and support staff, wonderful young people and committed and interested parents are what make Howell's unique.

The Nursery at Howell's is situated in Roald Dahl's childhood home and takes inspiration from its famous former occupant. Girls who enter the nursery experience a safe, family atmosphere, making the transition from home to nursery a relaxed and happy one. The Prep School radiates an atmosphere in which every child is valued and nurtured. Great emphasis is placed on developing the self-identity, self-esteem and self-confidence of every girl.

When entering the Senior School, students are encouraged to develop skills of self-analysis and reflection, and choose the learning methods that suit them best, whilst teachers challenge and motivate them towards an appetite for lifelong learning. Howell's aims to help students acquire skills essential to tackling a competitive and rapidly changing world. The established co-educational college has a proven track record for excellence in and out of the classroom and offers students an exceptional learning experience with flexible teaching styles designed to manage the transition between school and university.

Curriculum. All National Curriculum subjects including Welsh are taught at Key Stages 1, 2 and 3. From Year 3, French, Spanish and Welsh are all taught. Latin is introduced in Year 8. First language Welsh is taught on demand. There is a broad range of subjects available in the College. Examinations in a number of AS subjects are taken at the end of Year 12. Active learning styles are an essential part of the classroom experience, and the curriculum is made more diverse by:

Educational visits, locally and abroad

Visiting authors, poets, musicians, artists and lecturers

Special activity weeks focusing on particular areas of the curriculum

Extracurricular activities. The school's aim is to fulfil the potential of all the students in all areas, which it achieves through a rich extracurricular programme. Extracurricular opportunities include:

Orchestras, choirs and jazz groups

Reading and reviewing, eco, science, mathematics, history, geography, language and cultural clubs

Concerts, plays and eisteddfodau

Tennis, hockey, cricket, swimming, athletics, cross-country, netball, rugby and football teams

The Duke of Edinburgh's Award, Rotary, public speaking and debating teams, community service and fundraising for charities

The school seeks to support the widest range of students' needs through specialist dyslexia teaching and through an extensive and comprehensive careers programme.

Admission. A selection process operates for all points of entry. Contact Admissions for further details.

Fees per term (2023–2024). Co-ed College: £5,434; Senior School: £5,388.67; Prep School: Years 3–6 £4,158.67, Reception–Year 2 £4,082.67, Nursery £3,231.67.

Fees quoted are inclusive of non-residential school trips and lunch.

Scholarships and Bursaries. Bursaries, which are means-tested, are available in the Senior School and in the co-ed College; these are intended to ensure that the school remains accessible to bright students who would benefit from a Howell's education, but who would be unable to enter the school without financial assistance.

Academic, Sports, Art and Design, Music, Drama and Product Design scholarships are available to students going into Year 7 and 12. Details of how to how apply for scholarships and bursaries are available, on request, from the school.

Charitable status. Howell's School Llandaff is part of The Girls' Day School Trust, which is a Registered Charity, number 306983.

Chair of Governors: Mrs S Thomas

***Principal*: Mrs S Davis**

Deputy Principal, Academic: Mrs C Darnton
Deputy Principal, Pastoral: Mrs Z Harvey
Deputy Principal, Prep School: Mrs A Matthews
Director of Finance and Operations: Mr G Dyer
Director of Marketing and Communications: Mrs R Eling

James Allen's Girls' School (JAGS)

144 East Dulwich Grove, London SE22 8TE

Tel: 020 8693 1181
email: enquiries@jags.org.uk
website: www.jags.org.uk
X/Twitter: @JAGSschool
Facebook: @JAGSschool
Instagram: @JAGSschool

See full entry in the **HMC** section, on **p. 156**.

Jersey College

Le Mont Millais, St Saviour, Jersey, Channel Islands JE2 7YB

Tel: 01534 516200
email: admin@jcg.sch.je
website: www.jcg.je
X/Twitter: @jcg_live
Facebook: @JerseyCollegeForGirls
Instagram: @jcgjersey/
LinkedIn: @/school/jersey-college-ci/

Motto: Aspire ·Inquire ·Excel ·Belong

Number of pupils. 761 in JCG, 392 in JCP.

Fees per term (2023–2024). £2,468 per term at JCG; £2,416 at JCP.

Jersey College for Girls is a fee paying school located on the outskirts of St. Helier in Jersey (Channel Islands). The Jersey Ladies' College, as the school was first called, opened on 20th September 1880. Its current facilities on Mont Millais were officially opened by Her Majesty The Queen Elizabeth II in 2001.

We are an academic and compassionate girls' school currently catering for 761 students aged between 11 and 18, and we offer education up to and including A-levels. Our students have many opportunities to explore and enjoy life beyond our safe walls. In addition to traditional school pastimes, such as sport and drama, we have access to all the island has to offer, both on land and sea as well as offering some truly incredible programmes, such as piloting and finance.

Our College specialist facilities include science, drama, music, textiles, design technology and art. We have a well-equipped sports complex including an astro pitch, tennis and netball courts, a swimming pool, a gymnasium, a sport hall, a cardio vascular gym, a climbing wall and a dance studio.

Our students achieve highly, and their results are the best in the island. Last year 40.1% of students achieved A*/A at A level and 64.0% achieved 9–7 at GCSE.

Admission.

Year 7 Entry – Students are not invited to take an entrance examination. The decision for admission is based on the primary school's reference, including recently sat CATs data, and the student's attitude to learning.

Years 8–11 Entry – Applicants are placed on a waiting list for testing. When a place becomes available, they will be contacted and invited to sit English and Maths entrance papers.

Sixth Form – Normally 5 grade 9–6 passes at GCSE, which must include English and Maths at Grade 5 or above, with a grade 6 in subjects (or related subjects) that students wish to study at A Level. Specific criteria is applied to certain subjects.

Jersey College Preparatory takes 44 girls and 28 boys in Reception each year. These children are organised into 3 classes of 24 in each class. JCP usually offers 5 additional places for girls from other primary schools to start at the beginning of Key Stage 2 every year. Places are gained through an assessment process, which will include information from the pupil's current school. Students are expected to be achieving age related expectation or above.

Curriculum.

Jersey College for Girls – Art & Photography, Classical Civilisation, Computer Science, Drama, Design and Technology, Economics, English & Media, Food & Nutrition, Geography, History, Mathematics, Modern Foreign Languages, Music, Physical Education, Politics, PSHE, Psychology, Religion Ethics and Philosophy, Science, Textiles

Jersey College Preparatory – Art & Design Technology, Computing, Eco School, English, Forest School, Geography, History, Maths, Modern Foreign Languages, Music, PSHE, Religious Education, Science, Sport

Extracurricular activities. Jersey College for Girls has an extensive variety of co-curricular clubs for the students to enjoy – they include sports, music, drama, creative writing, Maths, as well as an Eco Club, a Christian Union and a political discussion group.

Clubs are led by a mixture of staff, sixth form students and external agencies providing a multitude of different opportunities.

Jersey College Preparatory School offers a number of clubs including mindfulness, computing, sports, music, first aid and others.

Scholarships and Bursaries. Financial Assistance is available for students whose parents would otherwise, not be able to send their daughter to the College.

We aim to offer an education to all female students in Jersey who meet our academic entry criteria. Financial Assistance, from a number of sources, is available to help pay all or part of the school fees for families with an household income of £76,000 or below. In addition to the fees, an amount of up to £1,100 per year is also provided to support with additional costs.

Chair of Governors: Louise Read

***Head*: Carl Howarth**, Principal

Senior leadership team:
Vice Principal: Miss Toni Rollo
Assistant Headteachers: Miss Ruth Lea, Mr Peter Marett, Mr Simon Milner and Mrs Emma Silvestri-Fox
JCP Headteacher: Mrs Catherine Precious
JCP Deputy Headteacher: Miss Nadia Guglieri

Kensington Prep School
GDST

596 Fulham Road, London SW6 5PA
Tel: 020 7731 9300
email: enquiries@kenprep.gdst.net
website: www.kensingtonprep.gdst.net
X/Twitter: @KensingtonPrep

See full entry in the **IAPS** section, on **p. 702**.

Kent College Pembury

Old Church Road, Pembury, Tunbridge Wells, Kent TN2 4AX
Tel: 01892 820218
email: admissions@kentcollege.kent.sch.uk
website: www.kent-college.co.uk
X/Twitter: @KentCollegePemb
Facebook: @KentCollegePemb
LinkedIn: /kent-college-pembury

See full entry in the **HMC** section, on **p. 161**.

Kilgraston School

Bridge of Earn, Perthshire PH2 9BQ
Tel: 01738 812257
email: admissions@kilgraston.com
website: www.kilgraston.com
X/Twitter: @kilgraston
Facebook: @kilgrastonschool
Instagram: @kilgrastonschool

Kilgraston is an independent boarding and day school for children aged 5 to 18 years. It is an all-through school comprising Junior Years, Senior School and Sixth Form.

Kilgraston is set in a Georgian mansion house located in 54 acres of stunning parkland three miles from the centre of Perth, with Edinburgh and Glasgow only an hour away. The school has fantastic facilities including a state-of-the-art science centre, a sixth form study centre, a 25 m indoor swimming pool complex, and floodlit astroturf hockey pitch and tennis courts. Kilgraston is also the only school in Scotland with an on-site equestrian centre incorporating a 60 m x 40 m floodlit arena with show jumps.

Visitors to Kilgraston are struck by its warm and welcoming atmosphere, and the sense of community and friendship across the year groups. Staff know each pupil individually, and are proud of the well-rounded girls who thrive in a range of curricular and co-curricular activities. Kilgraston's Sacred Heart ethos is central to school life, providing a firm foundation for personal growth and individual contribution, while welcoming girls of all faiths and none.

The curriculum. Kilgraston follows the Scottish educational system with all the girls studying a broad curriculum before selecting subjects to continue at National 5 (GCSE equivalent). Over 18 subjects are offered at Higher/Advanced Higher (A Level equivalent). Kilgraston has a record of high academic achievement and the girls gain entrance to top UK and international universities including Oxbridge. In 2023, over 50% of pupils obtained a Grade A at Higher and Advances Higher level.

Music, Art and Drama play an important part of life at Kilgraston. The Music Department has 14 individual teaching rooms, a recording studio and two large music rooms designed to suit all needs. There are also many opportunities for pupils to perform throughout the year by participating in orchestra, string orchestra, fiddle, woodwind and brass groups or one of several choirs.

The Art Department is housed in the top of the mansion with superb views across the Ochil Hills and the school boasts an impressive number of past pupils who are practising artists.

Sports and recreation are catered for within a superb sports hall including a climbing wall and fitness gym. The extensive grounds incorporate the indoor 25 m swimming pool, nine floodlit all-weather courts, playing fields and athletics track. While the main sports are hockey, netball, tennis, rounders, swimming and athletics, other sports include football, touch rugby, skiing, cricket, badminton, yoga, karate, fencing, aerobics, ballet, modern dance and highland dancing.

Fixtures and competitions are also arranged against other schools throughout the year. Kilgraston also hosts the Scottish Schools' Equestrian Championships every Spring.

Kilgraston is divided into houses which compete against each other in games, music and debating. The girls can also take part in The Duke of Edinburgh's Award scheme and are encouraged to use all the facilities not only for curriculum lessons but also for leisure activities.

Kilgraston Junior Years, for pupils aged 5–12, is located in its own building within the same stunning parkland.

Girls are able to progress to Kilgraston Senior School, or prepare for scholarship exams for Kilgraston and Common Entrance exams for other schools. The academic standard is high with all pupils completing the Junior Years and achieving a place in their senior school of choice.

From age ten, the curriculum becomes more specialised with increasing input from specialised subject staff and use of facilities in the Senior School. Pastoral care is the responsibility of a tutor.

The Junior Years core academic curriculum is enhanced by a wide range of co-curricular subjects. Art, drama and music flourish and opportunities are provided throughout the year for pupils to perform and compete in local festivals and events. LAMDA, Associated Board and Trinity examinations are offered and there is an annual production.

Admission is normally interview and school report. Entry to the Junior Years is by interview and assessment.

Means-tested bursaries are available on application. Scholarship Examinations are held in early February. Scholarships are honorary with no remission of fees. Awards are also offered each year as a result of outstanding performance in the Academic Scholarship Examinations. Scholarships are also offered in Art, Music, Drama and Sport.

'Happy, articulate and kind children and young people who are very proud of their school. They thrive in the stimulating environment for learning, and make the most of the extensive range of enriching activities and learning experiences offered to them.' HM's Inspectorate Report, February 2019

Fees per term (2023–2024). Boarding: Senior School (Lower Fourth–Upper Sixth) £12,970, Junior School (Upper Second–Upper Third) £9,910. Day: Senior School (Lower Fourth–Upper Sixth) £7,595; Junior School: Lower Third–Upper Third £5,940, Reception–Upper Second £4,470.

Charitable status. Kilgraston School Trust is a Registered Charity, number SC029664.

Senior Leadership Team:

***Headteacher*: Mrs T Davie**, BSc Hons, MSc

Bursar: Mr N Campbell, MBA Cranfield
Deputy Head: Mrs S Fraser, MSc, MA, PGDE
Head of Boarding & Pastoral Care: Mrs S Muller, BA, PGCE

King Edward VI High School for Girls

Birmingham

Edgbaston Park Road, Birmingham B15 2UB

Tel: 0121 472 1834
email: enquiries@kehs.org.uk
website: www.kehs.org.uk
X/Twitter: @KEHSBham
Facebook: @KEHSBham
Instagram: @kehsbham
LinkedIn: /kehsbirmingham

Independent, formerly Direct Grant.

Founded in 1883, the School moved in 1940 to its present buildings and shares its 50-acre site with King Edward's School (a leading boys' independent school). There are around 660 girls from 11 to 18 years of age, all day pupils, of whom 195 are in the Sixth Form.

Ranked first academically among independent schools in the West Midlands by The Sunday Times Schools Guide 2023, Parent Power.

Curriculum. KEHS is a school synonymous with intellectual ambition, offering an unrivalled education to the brightest girls in and around Birmingham. It provides outstanding teaching through a forward-looking and challenging curriculum and culture of scholarship, going beyond the confines of exam specifications and making connections across disciplines. It seeks to impart the joy of learning and enquiry together with intellectual courage, with the resilience and adaptability requisite for this. The consistently outstanding results are a by-product of the all-round education on offer, with a highly prized co-curricular programme at the heart of the school and bespoke courses that complement the traditional curriculum.

In Year One, all students take Art, Biology, Chemistry, Computing, Design Technology, Drama, English, Food Studies, French, Geography, History, Latin, Mathematics, Music, Physical Education, Physics and Religious Education.

In Year Two, all students take Art, Biology, Chemistry, Computing, Design Technology, Drama, English, Food Technology, Geography, History, Latin, Mathematics, Music, Physical Education, Physics, PSHE and Religious Education, together with two languages from French, German, Mandarin and Spanish.

In Year Three, all students take Biology, Chemistry, Computing, English, Geography, History, Latin, Mathematics, Physical Education, Physics and Religious Education, and they continue with two languages from French, German, Mandarin and Spanish. In addition, students choose two creative options from Art, Design Technology, Drama and Music.

Core subjects in Years Four and Five are English Language, English Literature, Mathematics, at least two Sciences from Biology, Chemistry and Physics, but students can take all three, and Physical Education (non-GCSE). Students then choose their other GCSE subjects from Art and Design, Computer Science, Design and Technology, Drama, French, Geography, German, History, Latin, Music, Physical Education (as a GCSE option), Religious Studies and Spanish. Students can choose to take an additional GCSE in Classical Greek. In Year 4, students have a rotation of enrichment subjects including Enterprise Education, Food Studies, PPE (Politics, Philosophy and Economics) and Wellbeing.

In Years One to Five, all students have a weekly session of PSHE (Personal, Social, Health and Economic Education) to equip them with crucial life skills for school and beyond, enabling them to make the most of their studies, their careers and social lives, and to play a positive, influential role in the local and global community.

In the Sixth Form, students choose four A Levels from a wide range of subjects: Art and Design, Biology, Chemistry, Classical Greek, Computer Science, Economics, English Literature, French, Geography, German, History, Latin, Mathematics, Music, Physics, Politics, Psychology, Religious Studies, Spanish and Theatre Studies. Emphasis is placed on breadth at this level. The school also offers the Extended Project Qualification and Further Maths A level. All Sixth Formers take a Friday afternoon enrichment option ranging from Life Saving to Art Appreciation, and all take Physical Education. Students in the Lower Sixth have additional enrichment sessions.

Religious and moral education are considered important. Academic study of them is designed to enable students to be informed and questioning. There is no denominational teaching in the school in lessons or morning assembly. Students of all faiths or of none are equally welcome.

In Sport, world-class coaching and outstanding facilities across multiple sports, both in lessons and as part of the co-curricular programme, enable students to chase their personal bests, both individually and as part of a team. All students take part in PE, including in the Sixth Form. Sports on offer include gymnastics, hockey, netball, tennis, rounders, dance, fencing, badminton, cricket, squash, swimming, athletics, basketball, volleyball, self-defence, aerobics and health-related fitness. KEHS has its own indoor swimming pool, sports hall with indoor cricket nets, a well-equipped fitness suite with a strength and conditioning area, extensive pitches, including two astropitches, tennis courts and an international-standard athletics track.

In addition to the music in the curriculum, there are opportunities for students to perform individually, in small groups or larger ensembles with co-curricular music being offered jointly with King Edward's School. There are around 40 concerts a year, with some in venues such as Birmingham Symphony Hall and the Barber Institute. Individual (or shared) instrumental lessons, at an extra fee, are arranged in school in a great variety of instruments. Some instruments can be hired. Individual singing lessons can also be arranged.

Rich co-curricular opportunities enable students to develop leadership and other practical skills as well as character and perspective. A large number of clubs (many joint with King Edward's School) are run by students themselves with help and encouragement from staff. Help is given with activities relating to The Duke of Edinburgh's Award scheme. Some activities take place in lunch hours, others after school and at weekends.

Proactive pastoral support promotes the development of balanced, self-reflective and assertive students with a strong moral compass. Pastoral care is focused on knowing students as individuals, as well as being proactive about the issues they are likely to experience collectively.

The compassionate approach that characterises life at KEHS means that students and staff have myriad opportunities to help others, particularly through the thriving service and partnership and participation programmes. The 'Care. Do. Give.' programme raises funds for a variety of charities, and students also offer practical support to local organisations such as care homes. The school's partnership and participation programme sees free activities and use of facilities offered to local primary schools.

A spacious careers room is well stocked with up-to-date information. Individual advice and aptitude testing is given at stages where choices have to be made. The Careers Adviser has overall responsibility but many others are involved with various aspects. Students are encouraged to attend conferences, gain work experience, make personal visits and enquiries. Old Edwardians and others deliver talks about their careers either in school or online. There is good liaison with universities and colleges of all kinds. Virtually all students go on to higher education, and a wide range of subjects is studied.

Admission of pupils. Entry is normally for girls of 11 into the first year of the school in September. Applications must be made by September the year before they are due to start secondary school. The entrance examination is held in early October. Applicants are examined at the school in English and Mathematics. The syllabus is such as would be normally covered by girls of good ability and no special preparation is advised. Applicants should have reached the age of 11 years by 31 August following the examination.

Applicants aged from 12 to 15 are normally considered only if they move from another part of the country, or in some special circumstances and only on the rare occasions when a space opens up in a year group. Applications should be made to the Director of Admissions.

There is an entry into the Sixth Form for applicants wishing to study four main A Level subjects. Applications should be made to the Director of Admissions by the end of January in the preceding academic year.

Fees per term (2023–2024). £5,538.

Scholarships and bursaries. KEHS offers Academic Scholarships to the most able applicants at 11+ and 16+ at the discretion of the Principal. Academic Scholarships are available each year and there is no separate scholarship examination. Music Scholarships are available to those joining the school at 11+ and 16+, and Sports Scholarships are available to those joining at 16+.

Means-tested Assisted Places are available at 11+ and 16+.

Charitable status. The Schools of King Edward VI in Birmingham is a Registered Charity, number 529051. The purpose of the Foundation is to educate children and young persons living in or around the city of Birmingham.

Governing Body: The Independent Schools Governing Body

Leadership Team:

***Principal*: Mrs Kirsty von Malaisé**, MA Cantab, PGCE

Vice Principal (Academic): Mr Martin Lea, BSc Sheffield, PGCE
Vice Principal (Pastoral), DSL: Mrs Sarah Shore-Nye, BA Swansea, PGCE
Assistant Head (Community): Mr Andrew Duncombe, MA Cantab, PGCE
Assistant Head (Pastoral), Deputy DSL: Mrs Helen Kavanagh, BA Bristol, PGCE
Director of Enrichment: Mrs Kam Sangha, BA De Montfort, MBA UCE, PGCE
Director of Sixth Form: Mrs Joanna Whitehead, BSc Birmingham, PGCE
Bursar – Finance and Estates: Mrs Zoe Robinson, BSc Warwick, ACA
Bursar – Operations: Mrs Jenny Butterworth, BSc Sheffield Hallam, FCA
Director of External Relations: Mrs Jo Bullock, BSocSc Manchester, CIPR Diploma
Director of Admissions, Partnerships and Participation: Mrs Catherine Oakes
Development Director: Mrs Adelaide Bailey, BA Birmingham, CSBM

Lady Eleanor Holles

Hanworth Road, Hampton, Middlesex TW12 3HF
Tel: 020 8979 1601
email: office@lehs.org.uk
website: www.lehs.org.uk
X/Twitter: @LEHSchool
Facebook: @LEHSchoolOfficial
Instagram: @lehschoolofficial
LinkedIn: /school/the-lady-eleanor-holles-school

LEH is a school full of opportunity, challenge and friendship; a place to take risks and become bold; a place to discover passions, talents and yourself; a place that nurtures remarkable women.

We encourage our pupils:

- to be exactly who they are, whatever their current interests or future aspirations.
- to benefit from the warmth, respect, and support of the entire School community as they stretch themselves to become their best, most confident selves, as students, and as citizens of the world.
- to have the freedom to experiment, express opinions, explore and take on new challenges.
- to be supported by strong role models and inspired by their peers.
- to find confidence and strength, and acquire and build the skills they need to succeed throughout their lives.

This Independent Girls' School is one of the oldest in the country, founded in 1710 in Cripplegate under the Will of the Lady Eleanor Holles. In 1937, the school moved to purpose-built premises in Hampton. Numerous additions to the building have enabled the school to increase to some 999 girls, aged from 7 to 18 years, who enjoy a wealth of specialist facilities and the use of 24 acres of playing fields and gardens. Fourteen science laboratories, Learning Resources Centre, Sixth Form Library, a Product Design suite, extensive computing and multimedia language facilities and a dedicated Careers area are complemented by grass and hard tennis courts, netball courts, 5 lacrosse pitches, track and field areas and a full-sized, indoor heated swimming pool refurbished in 2017. A Boat House, shared with

Hampton School, was opened in October 2000 and a large Sports Hall, adjacent to the swimming pool, in September 2001.

September 2012 saw the opening of a new Arts Centre consisting of a 300-seat theatre, new Music and Art Departments, and Sixth Form Common Rooms, followed in September 2013 by a new dining room, a new suite of classrooms, two dedicated Drama Studios, and a Conference Room.

In 2018 the Gateway Building opened with a state-of-the-art Computing suite, and Product Design facilities. Both of these subjects are now offered at A Level.

Most recently, the Quadrant building provides dedicated teaching space for the English and Mathematics departments and a new Sixth Form expansion project will complete at the end of 2023, providing more informal study space and a refurbished and extended café area overlooking the school playing fields.

Both the Junior and Senior Schools are equipped with a lift for people with disabilities.

The School's Statement of Purpose embodies the original aim, to encourage every student to develop their personality to the full so that they may become a person of integrity and a responsible member of society. It also emphasises the value of a broad, balanced education which gives due importance to sport, music and the creative arts in general, whilst providing the opportunities for students to achieve high academic standards within a framework of disciplined, independent study.

The Curriculum. In Years 7–9 girls take two modern foreign languages (with the option of Mandarin in Y9), Latin, separate sciences, dedicated computing lessons and a PSHE programme which continues throughout the school. Selection rather than specialisation for GCSE allows girls to respond to individual abilities and attributes, and every student continues to experience a broad education in which as few doors as possible are closed. A large sixth form of over 200 students means that a wide choice of Advanced Level subjects is offered. Most students study four or five subjects in L6, proceeding to A Level with three or four. They have the option of taking the Extended Project Qualification, and emphasis is placed on leadership roles and extra-curricular activities. All sixth form students move on to further training, the majority to Russell Group universities, including Oxford and Cambridge, as well as North American universities. The supportive Careers programme, which begins in Year 9, continues throughout the school and uses external specialists, parents, past pupils, ECCTIS and other computer programmes, as well as the School's own, trained staff.

Extra-Curricular Activity. A key strength of the school is the range and diversity of its flourishing extra-curricular provision. Some 120 clubs run each week ranging from Music, Drama and Sports to Outward Bound, CCF and subject clubs, all aiming to stimulate further and inculcate a love of learning outside the classroom. Sixth Formers lead a number of groups which focus on various political, environmental and ethical issues, including 'Model United Nations', 'Amnesty' and Eco-Squad. Sixth Formers are encouraged to take the initiative and form their own clubs with a Medic Group, Law Society and Book Club formed in the recent past. The School is very much at the heart of the local community and has developed a wide range of activities to ensure that students are aware of their social responsibilities, including Service Volunteers which works with disadvantaged local school children and the elderly, and running numerous activities in local primary schools, including language and drama clubs. Pupils are strongly encouraged to participate in extra-curricular activities.

The Junior School (192 pupils aged 7–11) is accommodated in a separate building in the grounds. It is an integral part of the whole school community and uses many of the specialist facilities available for Seniors.

(*See entry in the IAPS section for more details.*)

Entrance. Pupils may enter the Junior School from the age of 7, the Senior School at 11 years, and Sixth Form at 16 years. LEH Junior School pupils are guaranteed places in the Senior School (other than in exceptional circumstances). All external applicants must sit the School's competitive entrance examinations, which are held in November for Sixth Form entry and December (7+ and 11+) each year, for admission in the following September. There are no internal hurdles for entry to Sixth Form. Registration and Entrance Examination Fee is £150, or £200 for overseas applications.

Scholarships and Bursaries.

11+ Entry Academic Scholarships: Academic scholarships are expressed as percentages of the full fee and will thus keep pace with any fee increases. Awards are non-means-tested and usually 10%. The awards are based solely on performance in the school's own Entrance Examinations and subsequent interview.

Governors' Bursaries: Candidates who sit entrance papers at any stage from 11+ onwards may be considered for a bursary award. These are available for up to 100% of fees, plus extras, and are means tested and subject to annual review.

Sixth Form Academic Scholarships: Scholarships worth 10% of fees over the two years of Sixth Form study are offered to internal and external candidates who sit the Sixth Form Entrance and Scholarship Examination in November before the year of proposed entry.

Music Scholarships: Both Scholarships and Exhibitions for Music are available at 11+ and 16+. These are for 10% and 7.5% of fees respectively, plus free tuition on one instrument. Candidates must satisfy academic requirements in entrance papers before being invited to a music audition. Full details are available from the school.

At 16+ only: Scholarships are also available in Art, Sport, Drama and STEM (one in each).

Fees per term (2023–2024). £6,867 in the Junior School; £8,291 in the Senior School. Fees are inclusive of books and stationery and exclusive of Public Examination fees.

Former Pupils' Association. Holles Connect. Address for communications: Alumnae Administrator c/o Lady Eleanor Holles; email: alumnae@lehs.org.uk.

The Cripplegate Schools Foundation

Chairman of the Board of Governors: Mr D H King, BSc, FCA

Vice-Chair: Mrs D Warman, BA (*Hons*), CFPID

Governors:
Mrs S Aziz, LLB
Ms S Bhasin
Ms A Blair, LLB
Mr P Davies
Mr M George
Mrs S Haggipavlou, BSC, FCA
Mrs A Heau, BA (*Hons*)
Mr S Hotchin, MA, BA (*Hons*)
Mr R J Milburn, MA, FCA
Mrs B Parson, CertEd, BEd Hons
Mr D Sandhu, BA (*Hons*), ACA
Mr T Woffenden, BA (*Hons*), MA, PGCE

Clerk to the Governors: Mrs A Skeffington, LLB University of Exeter, Dip LP, Assoc CIPD

***Head Mistress*: Mrs Rowena Cole**, BSc, PGCE, MBA

Deputy Head: Dr D James, PhD King's College London

Deputy Head Pastoral: Mrs A Poyner, BSc Exeter, MBA

Head of Junior School: Mrs P Mortimer, BEd Oxon
Director of Finance and Operations: Mr M Berkowitch, BSc, JD
Director of Teaching & Innovation: Mr D Piper, BA King's College London
Director of Development & Communications, Mrs L Day, MSc King's College London
Director of Outreach & Co-curricular, Dr R Taylor, PhD Brighton
Head of Sixth Form: Mr M Tompsett, MA Cantab
Head of Upper School: Ms F Ellison, MA Cantab
Head of Middle School: Mrs K Sinnett, BA Cantab

Senior School

Art and Design:
Mrs D Howorth, BA Hons Staffordshire (*Head of Art*)
Mr L Curtis, BA Slade School of Art, MA Royal College of Art
Miss E Hollaway. MA Wimbledon College of Arts
Ms A E Seaborn, BA Winchester School of Art
Miss S White, BA University of the Arts
Miss D Wellesley, BA Edinburgh

Classics:
Miss K C Eltis, BA Oxon (*Head of Classics*)
Mrs R Brown, BA Durham (*Head of Year U5*)
Ms Flora Ellison, MA Cantab (*Head of Upper School*)
Miss E Lewis, BA MA UCL
Mr D Piper, BA King's College London (*Director of Teaching & Innovation*)
Ms A Golding, BA Bristol

Computing:
Mr D Lawley, BSc Sheffield Hallam (*Head of Computing*)
Mr S Hughes, BA Lancashire, MA Bath Spa
Mr T Tovell, BA Essex
Mrs V Whiffin, MEng Southampton (*Manager of Digital Teaching & Learning*)

Drama and Theatre Studies:
Miss S Torrent, BA Greenwich (*Director of Drama*)
Miss Victoria Bedford, MA Royal Holloway (*Head of Academic Drama*)
Ms H Steele, BA Dublin
Mrs P Tate (*Music and Drama Administrator*)

Economics:
Miss C Livingstone, MA Oxford (*Head of Economics*)
Mr R Malone, BA Harvard, MA Virginia USA

English:
Mrs E Gwynne, MA Durham (*Head of English*)
Miss A-M Wright, MA Aberdeen (*Deputy Head of English*)
Miss H Barnett, BA Durham (*Head of L6*)
Mr M Grundy, BA Goldsmiths
Dr D James, PhD King's College London (*Deputy Head*)
Mrs K Mackichan, BA Leeds
Mrs U Renton, MA Aberdeen
Ms K Vines, BA Manchester
Ms E Maxey, BA Reading

Food and Nutrition:
Mrs H Boczkowski, BSc Bath Spa (*Head of Food and Nutrition*)
Mrs M Spriggs, BA Hons Leeds Metropolitan

Geography:
Mr L M O'Rourke, BA Southampton (*Head of Geography*)
Mrs K Hanna, BSc Edinburgh
Mrs R Lockett, BA Southampton
Miss A Perlowska-Goose, BSc Reading, MSc Oxford

History of Art:
Miss A Lindsay, BA Manchester (*Head of History of Art, Assistant Head of U4*)
Ms A Farnum-Ford, MA Courtauld Institute of Art

History and Politics:
Mrs N Miller, MA York (*Head of History and Politics*)
Mr N Allen, BA Nottingham
Mrs A M Bradshaw, MA St Andrews
Mr O Even, BA Oxford
Mrs B Farthing, BA Royal Holloway, University of London
Ms J FitzGerald, BA Newcastle, MA Central School of Speech & Drama (*Head of Initial Teacher Training*)
Mrs L Harding, BA Warwick

Mathematics:
Mrs J Manns, BSc Sheffield (*Head of Mathematics*)
Mr S Blatch, MSc Oxford (*Deputy Head of Mathematics*)
Mrs N Banerjee, BA Delhi
Ms N Carden, BSc Leeds
Mr M Deacon, BSc Exeter
Mrs H Doshi, BSc City University London
Mr P Manns, BSc Essex (*Head of Academic Information & Data*)
Mrs M Najjar, BSc UCL
Miss R Nicholl, BSc King's College London (*Head of Year L5*)
Miss J Orr, MMath Durham
Mr U Patel, BSc Hons Sussex, MA Ed Open University
Mrs A Poyner, BSc Exeter, MBA (*Deputy Head Pastoral*)
Mrs M Read, BSc Durham
Miss T Saunders, BSc University of Southampton
Mr C Sin, BSc, MSc Cardiff
Mrs K Sinnett, BA Cantab (*Head of Middle School*)

Modern Languages:
Mrs U Arrieta, BA Deusto, Bilbao (*Head of Spanish*)
Mr H Agulian, BA University College London (*Head of French*)
Mrs S Hewitt, MA Warwick (*Head of German & Head of MFL*)
Mrs A Buck, Universidad de Valencia, Spain (*German and Spanish*)
Ms R Hart, MA Oxon (*Spanish, Head of PSHE*)
Ms M-C McGreevy, BA Leeds, MA Bath (*German and French*)
Ms N Murray, BA, MA Leeds (*French*)
Mr H Ng (*Mandarin*)
Miss D Robbins, MA St Andrews (*French*)
Mrs A Rowe, BA Nottingham (*French and German*)
Mr M Tompsett, MA Cantab (*German, Head of Sixth Form*)
Mrs A Awbery-Maskell, BA Manchester

Music:
Mrs M Ashe, MA Oxon (*Director of Music*)
Mr B G Ashe, BA York, LRAM (*Composer-in-Residence*)
Miss C Overbury, MA Oxon
Ms A Prowse, BA Cambridge
Miss N Redman, BMus Manchester, MMus, GSMD (*Head of Thirds*)
Mrs C Zuckert, BMus Birmingham, MMus
Mrs P Tate (*Music and Drama Administrator*)

Natural Sciences:
Miss L Mercer, BSc Edinburgh (*Head of Science and Biology*)
Miss A Boland, BSc St Mary's London (*Head of Psychology*)
Mr A Hayter, BSc Durham (*Head of Chemistry*)
Mrs V Whiffin, MEng Southampton (*Head of Physics*)
Mr N Johnson, MSc Nottingham (*Physics*)
Mr A Brittain, BSc Canterbury Kent (*Physics*)
Mrs N C Camilleri, BSc Manchester (*Physics*)
Miss H Choi, PGCE UCL (*Physics*)
Mrs J Crook, BSc Nottingham (*Chemistry*)
Mrs P Earl, BSc Swansea (*Biology*)
Miss L Goodman, BSc University College London (*Psychology*)
Mr R James, BSc East Anglia (*Chemistry*)
Mrs S Jansz, BSc Bangor (*Chemistry*)
Mr S Kim, PGCE Kingston (*Science*)
Mrs H Lenox-Smith, BSc UCL (*Biology*)
Mr R Mangion, BSc King's College London (*Chemistry*)
Miss K Millar, BEng Queen's Belfast (*Physics, Head of Year U4*)
Mrs C R Nicholls, BSc Cardiff (*Biology, Head of Year L4, Deputy Head of Careers*)
Ms C Packer, BSc UCL (*Chemistry, Head of U6*)

Miss V Ranjan, BSc Durham (*Biology*) [maternity leave]
Mr P Reilly, BSc Liverpool (*Biology*) [maternity cover]
Miss C Shum, BSc UCL (*Biology*)
Mrs T Hayter, BSc King's College London (*Science*)
Miss L Mulvey, BSc Manchester (*Psychology*)

Philosophy, Religion and Ethics:
Mrs L Garcia, MA UCL (*Head of Philosophy, Religion and Ethics, Assistant Head of L6*)
Mr I Jakeway, BA Oxon, MA Reading
Mr J Winterburn, BA Cambridge

Physical Education:
Miss D Mugridge, BA Hons University College Chichester (*Director of Sport and Outward Bound Activities*)
Mrs D O'Brien, BA St Mary's Twickenham (*Head of Curriculum PE*)
Mrs E Searle, BEd Hons Exeter (*Head of Netball*)
Mr C Summers, MSc Chester (*Head of Lacrosse*)
Miss E Martin, BA University of ST Mark & St John (*Head of Swimming*)
Miss K Bruce, BSc Liverpool John Moores
Mrs K Leaney, BA Hons North Carolina, USA
Mrs C King, BEd Brighton
Miss A Fancy (*PE Graduate Assistant – Lacrosse*)
Miss A Levy (*PE Graduate Assistant – Netball*)

Mr N Cousins (*Duke of Edinburgh Manager*)
Mr D Mihailovic (*CCF Contingent Commander*)
Mr M Hanreck (*CCF School Staff Instructor*)

Product Design:
Mr S G Bicknell, BSc Brunel, PGDip (*Head of Product Design*)
Mr D Smeaton, BEng Southbank Polytechnic
Ms M Spriggs, BA Hons Leeds Metropolitan
Ms T Snook

PSHE:
Ms R Hart, BA Hons and MA Oxon (*Head of PSHE*)
Mrs A Bradshaw, MA St Andrews

Rowing:
Mr J Moon (*Acting Head of Rowing*) [maternity cover]
Mr O Night, BA Newcastle (*Assistant Head of Rowing*) [maternity cover]
Ms A Johnston, BA Newcastle (*Head of Rowing*) [Maternity leave]
Ms A Leake, BA Newcastle
Mr G Stewart, BEng Surrey
Mr T Darlow
Miss J Symons, MEng Loughborough

Careers:
Mrs N Hampstead, RCDP, CDI Qualified Careers Leader (*Head of Higher Education and Careers*)
Mrs C R Nicholls, BSc Cardiff (*Deputy Head of Careers*)
Miss E Felicien (*Careers Coordinator*)

Learning Support:
Miss M Christodoulou, BA Middlesex, MA Durham, PG Cert (*Head of Learning Support*)
Ms S Reade, BA Universidade Estadual Paulista, Brazil (*Deputy Head of Learning Support*)
Ms C Campeanu, PGCert UCL

Learning Resources Manager:
Miss G Pearce, BA Bath Spa (*Head of Library Services*)
Mrs C Didiot-Cook

Senior School Administrative Staff:
Head Mistress's Personal Assistant: Mrs F Cuddeford
Registrar: Mrs M Bradley, BA University of Cambridge
Director of HR: Mrs Natasha Geoffrey, Assoc CIPD
PA to SMT/School Office Manager: Mrs S Spight
Estates Manager: Mr P Sisodiya
Finance Manager: Mrs M Seraphimova-Spasova, BSc Oxford Brookes, ACCA Member
Director of IT Services: Mr M Taylor, BSc London, PGCE, CITP

Junior School

Head of Junior School: Mrs P Mortimer, BEd Oxon
Deputy Head of Junior School: Mrs R Yates, BA Cantab, LLM

Teaching Staff:
Mrs J E Allden, BSc London Chelsea College, MSc Kingston (*Assistant Academic Coordinator & Head of Computing*)
Mrs M Bass, BEd Natal
Miss J Chippendale, BA Brighton (*Head of Junior School PE*) [maternity leave]
Miss S Connor, BA Hons Kent at Canterbury
Mrs J Deverson, BEd Oxford Brookes
Mr J Estorninho, BEd Melbourne, Australia (*Head of Junior School Music*)
Miss L Evans, BA Kingston
Mrs M Frampton, BEd Exeter
Mrs S Harding, BEd De Montfort
Mr A Hopkins, BSc Portsmouth
Mrs K Hurley, BA Middlesex
Mrs D King, BSc Ulster [maternity cover]
Mrs K Keightley, MA Edinburgh
Mrs L Kent-Skorsepova, MA Comenius, Bratislava
Mr J Miller, BSc Durham, MSc UCL
Mrs N Rees, MA Cantab
Mrs K Sehgal, BA St Mary's London
Mrs M Walker, BA Canterbury Christ Church (*Director of Studies Junior School*)
Mrs L Cowin (*Teaching Assistant*)
Ms P Evans (*Teaching Assistant*)
Mrs E Hanreck (*Teaching Assistant*)

Junior School Administrative Staff:
Junior School Secretary & Personal Assistant to the Head of Junior School: Mrs A Rahman
Junior School Office Administrator: Mrs R Thomas Jones

School Nurses:
Senior School: Sister S Wilson, BSc Brunel NMC, DipHE South Bank
Junior School: Nurse L Parker, RCN

School Counsellors:
Senior School: Mrs G Young, BA, MBACP, Higher Diploma in Counselling
Senior School: Ms K Lacy, MA East London, Diploma in Counselling
Junior School: Mrs R Ticciati, SRCN, SRN, MBACP

Leicester High School for Girls

454 London Road, Leicester LE2 2PP
Tel: 0116 270 5338
email: enquiries@leicesterhigh.co.uk
website: www.leicesterhigh.co.uk
X/Twitter: @LeicesterHigh
Facebook: @LeicesterHigh

The school is a Trust with a Board of Governors in membership of AGBIS and the Headmaster belongs to the GSA.

Leicester High School is a well-established day school for girls situated in lovely grounds on the south side of the city. Founded in 1906 as Portland House School, it now comprises a Junior Department of approximately 100 girls (3–9 years) and a Senior School of approximately 250 girls (aged 10–18) sited on the same campus.

The Headmaster is responsible for both the Junior Department and Senior School. The staff are well-qualified specialists and the school is renowned for both its academic excellence and extra-curricular programme. At present 18 subjects are offered at GCSE Level and 21 subjects at A Level.

Facilities. The premises are a combination of modern purpose-built units and the original Victorian house, skilfully adapted to its present purpose. The facilities of the School have been systemically improved and updated over recent years. The school has a Junior Department and a Senior School in separate buildings on one site. The Junior Department has its own hall, library, IT suite, garden, playground and outdoor learning area. The Senior School has a central gym, library, drama/dance studio, ICT suites, language computer suite, 6 science laboratories, art and design studio, separate sixth form area and food studies room set around an award-winning courtyard garden. The school benefited from a £3.7m extension in 2010. The 3-acre grounds of the school have tennis and netball courts within extensive gardens. Most recently a specialist music centre has been added.

Religion. The school has a Christian foundation but welcomes girls of other faiths or of none.

Admission. All candidates over the age of 7 are required to pass an entrance examination for admission into the Junior and Senior sections. Direct entry into the Sixth Form is dependent on GCSE results. Entrance into the Early Years Unit is by assessment. A registration fee of £85 is payable for all applicants.

The Headmaster is always pleased to meet parents of prospective pupils and to show them around the school. All communications should be addressed to the Admissions Officer from whom prospectuses, application forms and details of fees may be obtained.

Fees per term (2023–2024). £3,565–£4,820.

Extras. Individual Music lessons, Speech and Drama, Ballet and Taekwondo are offered.

Scholarships and Bursaries. The Headmaster's Scholarship is a five-year scholarship for entry into Year 7 for an academic girl. All those interested must sit the January Entrance Examination. Registering for the examination costs £85.

Scholarships are awarded to any student – either existing Year 6 or external candidates – on the basis of performance in the Year 7 examination papers in English and Mathematics sat on Entrance Examination day in January.

The LHS Sixth Form Scholarship: A scholarship of up to 25% is available to one exceptional girl joining the Sixth Form. A personal statement, grades and references will be requested and shortlisted girls will be invited to attend an initial interview with the Head of Sixth Form and the subject heads of her chosen A Levels. If successful at this initial interview, girls will be invited to attend a final interview with the Headmaster.

Girls entering the Sixth Form from a state school, and resident in Leicestershire or Rutland, have been invited to apply for a Sir Thomas White Scholarship, which is 100% fees-only funded for two years. The School has had seven Sir Thomas White Scholars in recent years.

A small number of Bursaries are available from Year 6 onwards up to the value of full fees.

Charitable Status. Leicester High School Charitable Trust Limited is a Registered Charity, number 503982. The Trust exists to promote and provide for the advancement of education based on Christian principles according to the doctrines of the Church of England.

Board of Governors:

Chair: Ms J Carroll

Mrs C Flinders
Mrs H Mistry
Mrs M Neilson, BEd
Miss C Salmon
Mrs S Siesage, BA, PGCE, MBA, NPQH
Mr M Dunkley

Clerk to the Governors: Ms S Shaw

***Headmaster*: Mr A R Whelpdale**, BA, NPQH

Deputy Head: Mr J M Partridge, MA, BSc, NPQSL

Assistant Head: Mrs C Wagner-Lees, BA

Head of Years 6 and 7: Mrs K McCarthy, BSc
Head of Years 8 and 9 (*with overview of KS3*): Mrs D Morgan, BSc
Head of KS4: Mrs J Rose, BEd
Head of Sixth Form: Mr M Ryman-Tubb, BA

Teaching Staff:
* *Head of Department*

Careers:
*Mr M Ryman-Tubb, BA

Computing and Information Technology:
*Mr B Ahmed, BSc

English:
*Mrs K Penney, BA
Dr N Taylor, BA, MA, PhD

Expressive Arts:
Mr A Rose, BA (**Art and Design*)
Miss E Ikin, BA (*Art and Design/Photography*)
Miss R Proctor, BSc, MA (**Music*)
Mrs J Rose, BEd (**Drama, Head of KS4*)

Food Studies:
*Mrs J Whalley, BSc

Geography:
*Mrs K Haresign, BA

History and Politics:
*Miss A Paul, MA
Mrs F Lodder, MA

Mathematics:
*Mr M Pinnick, BSc
Dr S Hills, PhD
Miss C Taylor, BSc
Dr Z Washington, PhD

Modern Languages:
*Mrs M Watkiss, BA (*Spanish and French*)
Mrs F Lagarde (*French*)
Mrs C Wagner-Lees, BA (*French and Spanish*)
Mrs G Wheeler, BA (*French*)

Personal, Social, Health and Citizenship Education:
*Mrs D Morgan, BSc (*Head of KS3 Years 8–9*)

Philosophy and Belief (*RS*):
*Mr D Ingram, BA, MA, DipMM

Physical Education:
*Mrs K McCarthy, BSc

Science:
*Mr A McMurray, BSc, MBA (*Physics*)
Mrs K Greenwood, BSc (**Chemistry*)
Mrs H Rai, BSc, MSc (**Biology*)
Miss E Tyler, BSc (*Biology and Physics*)

Social Science:
Mrs K Haresign, BA (**Economics*)
Mr M Ryman-Tubb, BA (**Psychology and *Sociology*)

Special Educational Needs and Disabilities Coordinator:
Mrs P Oaten, MA

Highly Able Coordinator:
Mr A McMurray, BSc, MBA

Head of House:
Mrs K Greenwood, BSc

Duke of Edinburgh's Award/Adventure Service Challenge/Outdoor Education:
Mr S Tratt

School Bursar: Ms S Shaw
Accountant: Mrs K Allen, BA, FCA
Finance Officer: Mrs F Mulla
Headmaster's PA and School Administrator: Mrs I Evans
Admissions Officer: Mrs L Jaiya, BEd
Admin Officer: Mrs K Kotadia
Examinations Officer: Mrs Y Chan
Head of Marketing: Miss L Burbeck
Librarian: Mrs S Timms
ICT Network Manager: Mr K Allen
IT Technician:
Health & Wellbeing Officer: Mrs J Wright
Laboratory Technician: Mrs T Johnson
Technician: Mrs M Wormleighton
Site Manager: Mr D Parmar
Caretakers: Mr G Neary, Mr M Panter
Groundsman: Mr P Dunn

Visiting Staff:
Mrs H Barwell (*Dance*)
Mrs W Boswell (*Piano*)
Mr N Bott, BA (*Drums, Electric Guitar*)
Mrs J Bound, GBSM (*Piano*)
Mr A Hewins (*Brass*)
Mrs K Loomes, FIDTA (*Ballet*)
Mrs V A Martin, ALAM (*Speech & Drama*)
Ms A Mee (*Violin*)
Mrs C Pitchford, LRAM (*Violin*)
Miss C Smith, BMus (*Woodwind*)
Miss C Sullivan, BA (*Speech & Drama*)
Mr M Wells (*Taekwondo*)

Junior Department:

Head of Department: Mrs S J Davies, BA Ed
Assistant Head: Mrs P Gascoigne, BA
Early Years Coordinator: Mrs LHeywood, BA, PGCE

Class Teachers:
Y5: Mrs C Dryland, BA
Y4: Mrs P Gascoigne, BA, Miss S Williams, BEd
Y3: Miss F Wood, BSc
Y2: Miss E Stell, BA
Y1: Mrs S Neuberg, BA
YR: Mrs L Heywood, BA, PGCE
YF: Mrs J Jethwa, NVQ5

EYFS:
Mrs J Solanki
Mrs L Dunn

Learning Support Assistants:
Mrs R Dye
Mrs N Sturmey, NVQ5

Administrator: Mrs M Singh, NVQ

Loughborough High School

Burton Walks, Loughborough, Leicestershire LE11 2DU

Tel: 01509 212348
email: high.office@lsf.org
website: www.lsf.org/high
X/Twitter: @LboroHigh
Facebook: @LboroHigh
Instagram: @LboroHigh
LinkedIn: /loughborough-schools-foundation

Loughborough High School, one of the oldest girls' grammar schools in England, is part of the Loughborough Schools Foundation, a foundation of four schools comprising: Fairfield Prep School (boys and girls 3–11), Loughborough Grammar School (boys 10–18), Loughborough Amherst School (boys and girls 4–18) and Loughborough High School (girls 11–18). The schools operate under one governing body and are situated on two neighbouring campuses in the town. The Foundation also includes The Loughborough Nursery for children from 6 weeks to 4 years.

Loughborough High School is an 11 to 18 school of approximately 550 day girls with a large Sixth Form. Established in 1850, the School is located on a delightful 46-acre site close to the town centre with many first-rate facilities, which are being added to and improved continuously.

We have an excellent reputation for our academic, cultural and sporting achievements, and for the quality of our pastoral care. Pupils are encouraged to be kind, adaptable and resourceful individuals and are presented with opportunities that enable them to become the best version of themselves.

Since we are a comparatively small school, we are able to know our pupils as individuals and this leads to a strong community spirit. In providing a strong academic education in a disciplined atmosphere we hope to enable each girl ultimately to enter the career of her choice. We believe that our academic curriculum and extra-curricular activities nurture our pupils and encourage them to become active citizens of a modern world.

Further details about the school can be obtained by contacting the school's Registrar.

School curriculum. Applied Science, Art, Biology, Business, Chemistry, Classical Civilisation, Computer Studies, Drama, Economics, English, French, Games (hockey, netball, tennis, rounders and athletics), Geography, German, Greek, Gymnastics, History, History of Art, Latin, Mathematics, Modern Dance, Music, Physical Education, Physics, Politics, Religious Studies, Sociology, Spanish, Food, ICT, Psychology and Theatre Studies. Careful note is taken of the National Curriculum with additional subjects included within the curriculum to provide breadth and depth.

Fees per term (2023–2024). £5,300 to £5,390. Music (individual instrumental lessons): £275 (for 10 lessons).

Scholarships and bursaries.

Academic Awards: The Governors offer a number of awards at 11+ which are made on academic merit. All candidates are considered for these awards without the need for any further application.

Music Awards: Music Scholarships are available to musically promising and talented pupils who are successful in the Entrance Examinations. Auditions are held around the time of the Entrance Examinations.

Bursaries: Means-tested Foundation Bursaries of up to 100% remission of tuition fees are available. These awards are normally made only to those entering at 11+ and 16+.

Further details of all these awards are available from the School.

Charitable status. Loughborough Schools Foundation is a Registered Charity, number 1081765, and a Company Limited by Guarantee, registered in England, number 4038033. Registered Office: 3 Burton Walks, Loughborough, Leics LE11 2DU.

Chair: Mr Roger Harrison, MA Cantab, DipArch RIBA

***Head*: Dr F Miles**, BA Hons Cantab, MBBS King's College London

Senior Leadership Team:
Deputy Head (*Academic*): Dr S Reid, BA Hons Durham, MA Bristol, PhD Huddersfield
Deputy Head (*Pastoral*): Mrs R Connick, BSc Hons Leeds
Assistant Head (*Staffing and Professional Development*): Mrs L Simpkin, BA Hons Leicester
Assistant Head (*Pastoral*): Miss V Standring, BSc Hons, MSc Chester
Assistant Head (*Co-curricular & Student Experience*): Mrs D Tolley, BSc Hons Open University, MSc Loughborough
Director of Sixth Form: Mr J Travis, BSc Hons Leeds

Manor House School, Bookham

Manor House Lane
Little Bookham, Leatherhead, Surrey KT23 4EN

Tel: 01372 457077
email: admissions@manorhouseschool.org
admin@manorhouseschool.org
website: www.manorhouseschool.org
X/Twitter: @ManorHseSchool
Facebook: @manorhousesch
Instagram: @manorhouseschool_bookham
LinkedIn: /school/manor-house-school-bookham

Motto: 'To Love is to Live'

Established in 1920, Manor House School, Bookham is an Independent (private) School for girls aged 4–16 with a co-educational (boys and girls) Nursery and Lower Prep. A member of the GSA (Girls' Schools Association), Manor House School is a smaller, nurturing through-school delivering great academic results alongside a thriving extra/co-curricular programme. For more information on recent academic results, please visit www.manorhouseschool.org/academic-results

Manor House is one of three Schools in the Effingham Schools Partnership, which forms a dynamic triumvirate. Effingham Schools Trust's diamond model offers benefits of the Co-Ed classroom to very young pupils, the benefits of single-sex education in later Prep and Secondary years, before returning to a Co-Educational Sixth Form. Families joining the Trust will have provision for boys and/or girls from 2–18 years across the three Schools.

Seven school values form the foundations of school life: Academic Excellence, A Love of Learning, Happy and Healthy, Individual Challenge, Creative and Collaborative, Unforgettable Experiences and Future Leaders. The school motto 'To Love is to Live' was chosen in 1921 by the Bishop of Plymouth, Dr Masterman, who was a close friend of one of the school's original founders.

Manor House School pupils enjoy high levels of success across academic subjects as well as Sport (boasting some future world-class soccer players, cyclists, triathletes and tennis stars in its midst) and the creative and expressive arts, with additional music, singing and drama lessons a popular choice. An extensive co-curricular enrichment programme provides clubs and activities every term for every pupil to enjoy.

Facilities include an award-winning Nursery, Wellbeing Centre, Forest School, a large indoor hall which hosts sporting events and professional level theatre productions, an outdoor Swimming pool, a Tennis Academy, Netball courts and purpose-built science blocks.

Admission at Year 3 and Year 7 is by the School's own Entrance Examinations. Other main entry points are at Reception Class, although the school welcomes mid-year applications to other entry years, subject to the availability of places. Selection is determined by successful completion of an age-appropriate taster and assessment day. Offers are made following the outcome of this process at the discretion of the Headteacher.

Academic, Art, Drama, Music and Sport Scholarships are awarded at Year 7.

All Scholarships are awarded based on performance in the Entrance Examinations (preceding September entry) and attendance or submissions at our Scholarship Assessment Days. For an application pack, please contact: admissions@manorhouseschool.org.

Means-tested bursaries may also be applied for and further details are available from bursar@ manorhouse school.org

Fees per term (2023–2024). £3,660–£6,878.

Further details can be found at www.manorhouse school.org/admissions/fees

Charitable status. Manor House School is a Registered Charity, number 312063. It exists for the promotion of children's education according to their academic, social, sporting and musical abilities.

Open Mornings are typically in October, March and May. Visit our Virtual Open Day at www.manorhouse school.org/virtual-open-day.

Email: admissions@manorhouseschool.org and visit www.manorhouseschool.org for details of local minibus services.

Senior Leadership Team:

***Headteacher*: Ms T Fantham**, BA Hons, MA, NPQH

Deputy Head: Mr S Hillier, BSc Hons, PGCE, NPQH
Head of Admissions and Marketing: Mrs K McSweeney, BA Hons
Director of Finance: Mrs C Minikin
Head of Key Stage 4: Mrs T Williams, BA Hons, PGCE
Head of Key Stage 3: Mrs R Waterhouse, BSc Hons, PGCE, MA Ed
Head of Key Stage 2: Mrs H Redward, BSc Hons, QTS
Head of Early Years and Key Stage 1: Mrs Y Ferrey, BA Hons, PGCE, EYPS, NNEB

For a full staff list please visit www.manorhouse-school.org/about-us

Marymount International School London

George Road, Kingston-upon-Thames, Surrey KT2 7PE

Tel: +44 (0) 20 8949 0571
email: admissions@marymountlondon.com
website: www.marymountlondon.com
Facebook: @MMILondon
Instagram: @marymountlondon
LinkedIn: /marymount-international-school-london

Marymount International School London is an independent, day and boarding school for girls which nurtures the limitless potential of curious, motivated students (ages 11 to 18) of diverse faiths and backgrounds. Founded in 1955 through the charism of the Religious of the Sacred Heart of Mary (RSHM), the School proudly stands as the first all-girls school in the United Kingdom to adopt the International Baccalaureate curriculum (IB MYP and Diploma), where girls are inspired to learn in a creative, collaborative, interdisciplinary, and exploratory environment.

Students are empowered to build their confidence, leadership skills, and sense of self on a seven-acre garden campus conveniently located just twelve miles from Central London. The campus offers outstanding facilities, including a STEAM Hub, sports hall, dance studio, modern dining hall, and tennis courts. The School's challenging academic program is based on the International Baccalaureate curricula:

- The Middle Years Programme (MYP), offered in Grades 6 to 10 (UK Years 7 to 11), encourages students to draw meaningful connections between eight broad and varied subject groups. With a central focus on the development of conceptual understanding and effective approaches to learning (ATL) skills, the MYP is a student-centred, inquiry-based programme rooted in interdisciplinary learning.
- The International Baccalaureate Diploma Programme (DP) for Grades 11 and 12 builds on the strong foundation of the MYP, leading to independent research opportunities as well as exceptional university placement within the UK and around the world.
- Marymount's 2023 results are exceptional: an average of 37 points; the School's bespoke, student-centred college counselling programme leads to successful placements in top universities in the UK and around the world.
- The top IB Diploma mark of 45 points was also received by one of our students in 2023.

Marymount's holistic approach to learning delivers a well-rounded education that encourages critical thinking, intercultural understanding, and participation in a wide array of interesting extracurricular offerings. Robust transport service from London/surrounding areas and boarding options (full, weekly, and flexi) are available.

Marymount offers year-round rolling admission as space allows. The admissions section of the website, featuring an online application portal, provides all of the information necessary to get started. Applicant families are encouraged to learn more about the School's strong tradition of excellence by exploring the website and making contact with the Admissions team by phone/ email.

***Headmistress*: Mrs Margaret Giblin**, BA St Patrick's Pontifical University, Ireland, Higher Diploma in Teaching National University of Ireland, MA St Mary's Twickenham

Senior Leadership Team:
Bursar: Mr Alan Fernandes, MBA Oxford Brookes, BSc St Mary's Twickenham
Senior Deputy Head Academic: Mr Nicholas Marcou, BA Hons York, PGCE Roehampton, MA St Mary's Twickenham
Deputy Head Pastoral: Ms Annah Langan, MA Hons Glasgow, MA St Mary's Twickenham, PGCE Roehampton

Deputy Head Operations and Co-Curricular: Ms Victoria Mast, BA Hons Durham, PGCE Buckingham
Director of Communications and Marketing: Ms Kirsten Crossland, Dip Communications Massey
Director of Development: Miss Adriana Williams, MSc Warwick

Admissions and Communications Team:
Miss Kiera Pocock, BA Hons Cantab
Mrs Karen Semple, BA Hons Exeter
Heads of Departments:
Ms Momoko Aoe, MA Master of Education, Curriculum & Teaching, Boston, BA Health & Exercise Science/Teaching, New Jersey
Mrs Emma Burke, BA Hons, PGCE St Mary's Twickenham
Mr Stephen Clarke, MA Hons, PGCE Glasgow, TESOL
Dr Sandra Forrest, BA Denison, US, MA NYU, PGCPSE Open University
Ms Dolores García-Suárez, BA Spain, MA King's, London
Mr Jim Robertson, BA Hons Kingston, QTS
Ms Helen Szymczak, BA Dramatic Art Hons AFDA South Africa, ATCL, MA London
Residential Houseparents:
Mrs Paula Horton (*Head of Boarding*)
Mrs Annabel Plumridge, PGCE Secondary Science, BSc Biochemistry Southampton

Mayfield School

The Old Palace, Mayfield, East Sussex TN20 6PH

Tel: 01435 874623 (Headmaster and Secretary)
01435 874600 (School)
01435 874642 (Admissions)
email: enquiry@mayfieldgirls.org
website: www.mayfieldgirls.org
X/Twitter: @mayfieldgirls
Facebook: @mayfieldgirls
Instagram: @mayfieldschool
LinkedIn: /school/st-leonards-mayfield-school/

Mayfield is a leading independent boarding and day school for girls aged 11 to 18 set in the beautiful, and easily accessible, Sussex countryside less than an hour from central London. Awarded the top grade of "excellent" by the Independent Schools Inspectorate and described by Country Life as "one of the finest schools in the land", a Mayfield education combines academic rigour, breadth of opportunity and a strong sense of community. The School has an excellent academic record, exceptional pastoral care and an extensive co-curricular programme. Individuality, independence of thought and intellectual curiosity are nurtured and the School encourages equally the intellectual, creative, physical, emotional and spiritual development of each pupil.

Mayfield is successful in unlocking and developing the unique potential and talent of each girl. Every pupil is accepted for who she is and is instilled with the confidence to find her strengths, wherever they may lie, and develop them in an inspiring and nurturing environment. Mayfield's ethos reflects its Catholic foundation and encourages integrity, initiative, respect and a commitment to be the best you can be within a vibrant and inclusive community, which welcomes all. Mayfield is a lively, happy and successful School and Mayfield girls develop a lifelong love of learning, a range of transferable skills that will prepare them for their future, and friendships that will last a lifetime.

Founded in 1872 by Cornelia Connelly and her Society of the Holy Child Jesus, the School continues to fulfil its Founder's vision to educate young women to respond to the needs of the age. This is achieved through an innovative and stimulating curriculum, an extensive range of co-curricular opportunities and a strong and supportive pastoral foundation.

Curriculum. Mayfield's curriculum, both within taught lessons and beyond them, is designed to create an environment in which questioning, reflection, risk-taking and the freedom to learn from mistakes are all encouraged. Inspirational teaching, from highly-qualified and dedicated staff, enables girls to flourish and excel, reflecting the equal value placed on every subject and the breadth of curriculum offered. In Years 7, 8 and 9 pupils enjoy a broad curriculum with core subjects – English, Maths, the sciences, Religious Studies, Geography, History, Physical Education and Computer Science – complemented with a choice of languages, from Latin, French and Spanish and lessons in Art, Music, Drama, Textiles (to Year 9), Ceramics and Food and Nutrition. In Lower School (Years 7 and 8) the curriculum is structured within a Lower School Diploma programme. This provides the opportunity for girls in Year 7 and 8 to develop soft skills, such as teamwork, problem solving and resilience, alongside their academic education. Time each week is also specifically dedicated to the spiritual and pastoral education of the girls in the form of assemblies, liturgies and Mayfield's innovative Life Skills Programme.

To ensure an excellent basis for further study and a wide variety of career options, all pupils in Years 10 and 11 follow a compulsory common core, comprising English Language and English Literature, Mathematics, Religious Studies and at least two Sciences or Trilogy Science. Most pupils study 9 subjects at GCSE, selecting three choices from a wide range of optional subjects including Art & Design, Classical Civilisation, Computer Science, Drama, Food and Nutrition, French, Geography, History, Greek, Latin, Music, PE, Spanish, or a third science.

Sport is also an integral part of the timetable. Options range from traditional sports including Athletics, Cricket, Football, Hockey, Netball, Swimming and Tennis to other activities such as Badminton, Circuit Training, Volleyball and Water Polo.

The guiding principles of Sixth Form study (Years 12 and 13) at Mayfield continue to be breadth and depth and it is not unusual for girls to combine Mathematics and Science subjects (consistently the most popular choices at A Level) with Ceramics, Art or a language. Pupils choose up to four A Levels from a wide selection of over 25 options. In addition, the Sixth Form benefits from the School's Enrichment Programme, enabling girls to develop valuable life and critical thinking skills from a wide variety of options, including Sport's Leadership; Photography and Photoshop; Farming and

Land Management; Certificate in Culinary Skills and Event Management. Pupils also have the opportunity to complete an Extended Project Qualification (EPQ) on a topic of their choice, which is excellent preparation for higher education. The School's state-of-the-art Sixth Form Centre is an inspirational learning space, with a variety of study areas, dedicated group work and social spaces, providing a first-rate transition to university.

Mayfield has an excellent record of outstanding examination results and girls invariably perform well above expectation, however, the School's focus is not exclusively to this end and it encourages a balanced approach to academic studies and the development of the whole person.

Mayfield girls receive excellent careers advice and guidance throughout their school career as an integral part of the curriculum and this prepares them very well to make excellent, informed choices. Almost all pupils progress to higher education, the vast majority to Russell Group universities including Oxbridge and, increasingly, to overseas universities particularly in the USA and Europe. They study a wide variety of subjects, from Architecture to Zoology, with a regular stream of engineers, medics and vets, lawyers and economists. The School has a highly engaged alumnae community throughout the world, which is a valued support network for advice on further study and career options.

Co-curricular Activities. An extensive co-curricular provision at Mayfield accompanies learning in the classroom and girls are positively encouraged to try new activities, ranging from Riding (in the School's first class equestrian centre), Yoga and Kick Boxing to Textiles, Debating, Astronomy and Dance. The School's 'Actions Not Words' Programme, reflecting Mayfield's motto and incorporating the Duke of Edinburgh's Award scheme, provides opportunities to be involved in service in both the local community and overseas, ensuring that faith in action continues to be an important part of Mayfield life.

There are significant opportunities to become involved in the creative and performing arts. Mayfield has outstanding Arts, Ceramics and Textiles facilities and teaching and has produced award-winning artists. Pupils benefit from a variety of exhibitions and workshops throughout the year.

Mayfield has an impressive reputation for music and, with a significant number of girls learning a musical instrument, there are opportunities to perform in the School Orchestra and in the many ensembles. In addition, Mayfield's acclaimed school choir, Schola Cantorum, has performed in prestigious venues in the UK and internationally, including the Vatican, St Paul's Cathedral and Westminster Abbey.

Pupils also have the opportunity to develop their drama skills performing in the wide variety of drama productions throughout the year, together with Drama Club, LAMDA and theatre workshops.

Admissions. The main entry points are at 11+, 13+ and 16+, with applications considered for occasional places in other years. Entry at 11+, 13+ and 16+ is based on the School's own Entrance Assessments.

Registration fee: £150

Fees per term (2023–2024). Full Boarders £14,100, Day girls £8,635–£9,100.

Scholarships and Bursaries. Academic Scholarships and Creative Arts, Drama, Dance, Music, Sport and Riding Scholarships are available for entry at 11+, 13+ and 16+. Scholars are identified through a programme of examination and assessment and are expected to show a high degree of aptitude in their chosen discipline. Scholarships are offered on merit.

Means-tested bursaries up to 100% of the cost of a day or boarding place are available.

Charitable status. Mayfield School is a Registered Charity, number 1047503. It exists to provide education for girls in keeping with its Catholic foundation.

Governors:
Chair: Lady Davies of Stamford, MA Oxon, MBA[1]
Deputy Chair and Chair of Governance Committee: Dr Christopher Storr, KSG, MA, PhD[234]
Deputy Chair and Chair of Finance and General Purposes Committee: Mr Chris Buxton, BA, ACA[1]
Chair of Education Committee: Mrs Marion McGovern, BA, Cert Ed[2]
Chair of Ethos Committee: Dr Rhona Lewis, MA, PhD[24]
Mrs Angela Drew, BA, PGCE, MBA[2]
Mr Andrew Larsson, MA Cantab, MEng, MCISI[1]
Mr Tim Reid, LLB[13]
Mrs Karen Sorab, OBE[1]
Mrs Caroline Wood, BSc[1]
Rev Fr Dominic Jacob (CongOrat)[4]
Dr Veronica Cloke Browne, FEI, CEng, MIChemE[2]
Dr Luminata Henshaw

[1] *Finance and General Purposes Committee*
[2] *Education Committee*
[3] *Governance Committee*
[4] *Ethos Committee*

***Headmaster*: Mr J Forster BA**

Senior Deputy Head: Mrs D Bligh, BA Dunelm, MA, PGCE Cantab

Senior Managers:
Deputy Head, Academic: Mrs A R Bunce, MA, BSc, PGCE
Bursar: Mr R Gordon, MA, MBA
Head of Sixth Form: Mr J Doy, BA, PGCE
Head of Middle School: Mrs J M Stone, BSc, MSc, GTTP
Head of Lower School: Mrs C Baker, BSc, PGCE

The Maynard School

Denmark Road, Exeter, Devon EX1 1SJ
Tel: 01392 355998
email: admissions@maynard.co.uk
website: www.maynard.co.uk
X/Twitter: @MaynardSchool
Facebook: @MaynardSchoolExeter
Instagram: @maynardschoolexeter
LinkedIn: /company/the-maynard-school

The Maynard School in Exeter is the South-West's leading independent school for girls aged 4–18 years (Reception–Year 13). As one of the oldest girls' schools in the country, we pride ourselves on being experts in educating girls. Statistically it is a proven fact that girls in single-sex schools outperform their peers and The Maynard's long history is testament to this success. League tables consistently place us as one of the highest performing schools in the South-West and our latest ISI Inspection deemed us as 'excellent' in all five main categories.

However, a Maynard education isn't just about academic achievement. It is about so much more; we boast numerous individual and team champions in the sporting arena with access to some of the best facilities available; we are proud to offer Food & Nutrition and Textiles & Fashion classes as a life-skill; we are one of the highest achieving schools for music and drama in the county; we relish our timetable packed with trips and workshops to be enjoyed by the whole school.

We are the first school in Devon to be awarded the Wellbeing in Schools Award in recognition of the sheer breadth of provision and robustness of support that we offer to all of our students and staff. The Maynard is a warm place where everyone is nurtured individually and encouraged to carve for themselves successful futures whilst creating everlasting friendships and enduring childhood memories!

Ethos. Our vision is to be a leading school in the UK, committed to educational excellence in a caring and happy environment that fosters a lifelong love of learning. Our mission is that our team of inspiring teachers will instil in each individual the confidence to excel academically, socially and morally. Through an educational experience designed specifically for girls, we are able to give them the skills and the courage to go out into the world and make a real difference.

Numbers. There are approximately 470 day girls in the School, of whom 140 are in the Pre-Prep and Junior School and 100 in the Sixth Form.

School Buildings. The School is set in a leafy area of central Exeter in Devon, five minutes from the centre of the city. The extensive buildings include a separate Sixth Form Centre; a purpose-built block for Science, Mathematics, and Computing; well-equipped Food & Nutrition and Textiles Rooms; Music and Art Rooms and a Performing Arts Theatre which also serves as a gym, and an impressive Sports Hall which provides full-scale indoor facilities. The Junior School and Pre-Prep are situated within the grounds and are fully equipped for the education of girls aged 4–11 years.

Curriculum. The curriculum is academically rigorous and maintains a good balance between Arts and Science subjects. English, Mathematics, the Sciences and Sport are particular strengths; full scope is given to creative and practical activities, as well as ICT skills. The School prepares all girls for University, including Oxford and Cambridge. A carefully developed programme of careers advice, begun at 11+ and continuing through to the Sixth Form, ensures that all pupils are individually guided in subject options with their long-term career interests at heart.

Examinations. Candidates normally take 9 subjects at GCSE and 3 at A Level. Students are fully prepared for Oxford and Cambridge University Entrance.

Physical Education. Hockey (outdoor and indoor), Netball, Badminton, Basketball, Volleyball, Rugby, Squash, Dance and Gymnastics are offered in the winter terms; Tennis and Rounders are played in the Summer Term. Training is given in Athletics and Swimming is part of the normal timetable for all girls during the Summer Term. Kickboxing, kayaking, the CV suite and more are on offer all year round. Besides its excellent indoor facilities and the three hard courts in its own grounds, the School has access to a playing field a short walk away and is close to three swimming pools and an Astroturf playing area. The school has an extensive fixture programme in Netball, Hockey, Indoor Hockey, Badminton, Basketball, Tennis, Swimming, Athletics and Rounders. Teams have regularly reached national standard. In addition, The Maynard has a strong extra-curricular programme of outdoor pursuits including the Ten Tors, the Duke of Edinburgh's Award and Exmoor Challenge.

Admission. All admissions, except Pre-Prep, are subject to an Entrance Assessment graduated according to age and held in January each year for entry in the following September. Pre-Prep admissions attend a Taster Day where they are informally assessed. Entry into the Sixth Form is by interview.

Fees per term (2023–2024). Pre-Prep: Reception £2,642, Years 1–2 £3,043; Junior School: Years 3–5 £4,614; Senior School: Years 6–13 £5,514. Fees include wraparound care from 8.00 am to 5.30 pm. Reception fees include lunch.

There is a generous Sibling Discount Scheme.

Scholarships and the Maynard Award Programme. A range of Academic, Sport, Music and Creative Arts Scholarships are available for senior school entry at 11+, 13+ and Sixth Form. The Maynard Award Programme also offers opportunities to girls from all sectors of the community. Two 100% Scholarships are available for entry into our Sixth Form as part of the Programme.

Further Information. The Prospectus and Scholarship and Maynard Awards information are available from the Admissions Office. Visitors are very welcome by appointment, and tours and taster days can be arranged for girls considering the school. Email: admissions@maynard.co.uk; Tel: 01392 355998.

Old Maynardians. Email: office@maynard.co.uk.

Charitable status. The Maynard School is a Registered Charity, number 1099027. It exists to provide quality education for girls.

Chair of Governors: Mr H Luce

***Head*: Mrs L Gregory**

Assistant Head (*Head of Junior School*): Mrs S Lavis
Assistant Head (*Director of Studies*): Dr P Rudling
Assistant Head (*Director of Sixth Form*): Mr T Hibberd
Assistant Head (*Co-Curricular and Pastoral*): Mrs C Leigh
Assistant Head (*Designated Safeguarding Lead*): Mr M Loosemore

Marketing and Communications Manager: Mrs R Board
School Business Manager: Mrs L Beechener

Moreton Hall

Weston Rhyn, Oswestry, Shropshire SY11 3EW

Tel: 01691 773671
email: admin@moretonhall.com
website: www.moretonhall.org
X/Twitter: @moretonhall
Facebook: @moretonhall

See full entry in the **HMC** section, on **p. 234**.

North London Collegiate School

Canons, Canons Drive, Edgware, Middlesex HA8 7RJ

Tel: 020 8952 0912 (Senior School)
020 8952 1276 (Junior School)
email: office@nlcs.org.uk
website: www.nlcs.org.uk
X/Twitter: @NLCS1850
Facebook: @nlcs1850
Instagram: @nlcs1850

North London Collegiate School is a top independent day school for girls aged 4–18. Since its founding in 1850, generations of girls have received an ambitious academic education and formed a bond with NLCS, which lasts forever. We provide a carefully judged blend of support and challenge, a friendly and warm atmosphere, glorious facilities and extensive extra-curricular activities.

We are proud of our tradition of producing independent-minded young women with the drive and confidence to make the most of opportunities and make a difference in the world. That was the vision of the school's founder and it remains true of the school today.

We have a strong track record of enabling students to gain entry to their first choice of university, but examination success is only part of the picture and passionate teachers inspire pupils with a love of their subject which goes beyond the examination syllabus.

NLCS celebrates the individual and creative spirit of the pupils. We provide the springboard for our students to find their place in a world which will require not only technical skills, but also creative and communication skills to thrive. This is why we continue to invest in and enhance our music and arts provision and offer a wealth of sporting opportunities. Over 50 clubs and societies create a vibrant atmosphere that enables students to develop a relaxed self-confidence and enjoy their time at school.

NLCS has a global perspective that is unique amongst London day schools. In the Sixth Form, students can study the International Baccalaureate Diploma – a highly regarded qualification that is particularly prized by Ivy League, Russell Group and European universities. In addition to this, the opening of our sister schools in Jeju, Dubai and Singapore benefits our students through exchange and collaboration opportunities.

We believe that happy students are successful students. Our pastoral care is focused on individual support for every student, developing resilience and a sense of perspective, so that girls are able to tackle challenges head-on, learn from set-backs, and have the confidence to try again if things don't work out initially. We aim to provide an environment which promotes self-confidence, a feeling of self-worth and the knowledge that pupil's concerns will be listened to and acted upon.

The school's academic record is outstanding. It has twice been named *The Sunday Times* "Independent School of the Year" and *The Daily Telegraph* has described it as the most consistently successful academic girls' school in the country.

NLCS has offered the IB programme as an alternative to A Levels since 2004, and has a consistent record of success, ranking as one of the highest-achieving IB schools in the UK and the world.

The facilities at the school are first class, designed to offer the girls every opportunity to develop themselves both academically and socially. These facilities include lacrosse pitches, all-weather tennis courts and a Sports Centre with an indoor swimming pool, climbing wall and fitness centre.

The Performing Arts Centre, with a 350-seat auditorium, orchestra pit, galleries and rehearsal rooms, hosts over 35 productions a year. There are many Music and Drama opportunities including productions, choirs and orchestras.

There is an extensive school coach scheme.

Full details of Open Days and Taster Afternoons are on the school's website.

Bursaries. Enabling bright girls from all backgrounds is central to the ethos of the school. Many bursaries are offered to girls who do well in the 11+ test and those entering the Sixth Form, whose parents can demonstrate financial need.

Scholarships. Music Scholarships are awarded at 11+ and 16+

Fees per term (2023–2024). Senior School: £7,994; Junior School: £6,880.

Charitable status. The North London Collegiate School is a Registered Charity, number 1115843. It exists to provide an academic education for girls.

The Governing Body:
Mr R Hingley (*Chair*)
Mrs S Carter, BSc Hons, Associate CFA (*Vice Chair*)
Mr P Needleman, MA, FIA (*Vice Chair*)
Mrs E Davis, BA, Dip
Ms V Godfrey, MA Oxon, MBA, FRGS
Mrs G Gower, OBE, MSC, MA
Mrs V Harding, BMus Hons, PGDip RAM, PGCE, LRAM, ATCL
Ms R Herdman-Smith, BA
Cllr A Jogia MBE, JP, MA
Mrs N Kingsmill-Moore, MED, HDE
Ms C Marten, BA, MA, PGCE
Dr T Thomas, BSC, PhD, PGCE
Dr D Toh, PhD, CPA, PGCHE
Mr A Utermann, BSC, MA, ASIP
Mrs E Watford, MCHEM, MBA
Dr A Weller, MA, PhD
Professor B Young, BA, MA, DPhil
Mr D Baille, BSC, MSC, FRICS (*Associate Governor*)

Chief Operating Officer: Mr T Brown, BA Bournemouth, MBA Greenwich

***Headmistress*: Mrs Vicky Bingham**, MA Oxon

Deputy Heads:
Academic: (*Acting*) Mrs J Bedi, MA Cantab
Pastoral: (*Acting*) Ms G Mellor, BA Exeter, PGCE
Director of Projects: Mr A Frazer, BA Exeter

Head of Junior School: Mrs S Cartwright-Styles, BA Hons QTS Surrey, MA London

Assistant Heads:
Enrichment: Mr J Majithia, BA Oxon
Professional Development: Mr H Waddington, MA Cantab, MPhil Cantab, FRGS
Senior Tutor: Dr C Jackson, PhD Glasgow
Digital Strategy and Partnerships: Ms L Timm, MChem Oxon
University Guidance and Careers: Ms D Mardell, MA Cantab, MEd Cantab
Head of Sixth Form: Mr B Tosh, BA Greenwich
Head of Upper School: Mrs N Taberner, BA Brighton
Head of Middle School: Mrs J Demetriou, BA London

Teaching and Learning Lead: Ms V Brock, BA Oxon
SEN Advisor: Mrs K Cowan, BA Sussex, PGCE, OCR, APC SpLD, CELTA
Director of IB Diploma: Dr H Linscott, BA, MA, PhD UCL
Head of Careers: Dr R Silverman, BSc, MSc Nottingham, PhD Bristol
Head of Examinations and Data Manager: Mr V Patel, BA London

Heads of Academic Departments:
Art and Design: Miss G Holland, BA Loughborough
Classics: Mr E Pike, BA London, MA Cape Town
Computing: Mr Z Qureshi, BSc Hertfordshire
Drama: Miss H May, BA Princeton
Economics: Mrs H Waywell, BSc Loughborough, MA IoE
Engineering, Design & Technology: Mr A Duffey, BA Surrey Institute of Art & Design
English: Ms M Henson, BA, MA Cork
Geography: Miss J Payne, BA Manchester
History, Government & Politics: Dr W Van Reyk, BA, MSt, DPhil Oxon
Mathematics: Mr W Galton, BA Cantab
Modern Languages & German: Mrs A Venter, BA Hons Pretoria, MA Sorbonne
French: Miss K Bonnal, Maîtrise Avignon
Italian: Dr N Ibba, MA Bologna, PhD London
Russian: Miss E Makower, BA Oxon
Spanish: Mrs X Yerbury, MA London
Mandarin: Ms A Hickman, BA Durham
Music: Mr S McCall, BA Durham
Physical Education: Mrs G Castle, BA Liverpool John Moores
Religious Studies & Philosophy: Mr J Holt, BA Durham, MA Open
Science/ Biology: Mr M Hudson-Reeve, BSc Newcastle
Chemistry: Miss M Siddiqui, BSc London
Physics: Mrs N Timoshina, MSc Moscow

PA to the Head: Mrs D Baum

Notting Hill and Ealing High School GDST

2 Cleveland Road, Ealing, London W13 8AX
Tel: 020 8799 8400
email: enquiries@nhehs.gdst.net
website: www.nhehs.gdst.net
X/Twitter: @nhehs
Facebook: @nhehsGDST
Instagram: @nhehsgdst

Notting Hill & Ealing High School is an academically selective, independent day school for girls aged 4 to 18. It is part of the GDST (Girls' Day School Trust) which is the leading network of independent girls' schools in the UK. Founded 1873. For further information about the Trust, see p. xxii or visit www.gdst.net.

Pupils and location. Approximately 900 pupils. 590 in the Senior School (153 in the Sixth Form) and 310 in the Junior Department. Transport links are excellent (Ealing Broadway station is nearby and several buses stop outside the school) and the School runs its own bus service. Students come from Ealing and all over west London.

Ethos. This is a school with a long tradition of academic excellence and creativity within an exceptionally warm and supportive environment. Notting Hill & Ealing girls are well grounded, confident and independent. They are proud of their school and value kindness and laughter, fun and friendship. This is a place where tolerance and mutual respect are nurtured; where you can be yourself. With a wide variety of activities and opportunities, and a strong emphasis on charitable giving, everyone can enjoy being part of a vibrant community and express their passion for learning, and for life.

Pastoral care. The system of pastoral care is overseen by the Deputy Head – Pastoral, working through the Heads of Year and Form Tutors. A well-structured system that is sufficiently flexible, supports every girl and ensures she is treated as a whole person with individual strengths and needs. In the Sixth Form, the tutor team is led by the Head of Sixth Form.

Curriculum. Throughout the Junior and Senior Schools, our curriculum is broad and balanced and encourages independence of learning and thought. In Years 7–9 everyone follows courses in English, History, Geography, Mathematics, Physics, Chemistry, Biology, Design Technology, Computer Science, Religious Studies, Art, Music, and Drama. In Year 7 all girls study Mandarin plus a second modern language (French, German or Spanish). In Year 8, Latin also becomes available. Girls usually take ten subjects at GCSE, including a compulsory core of English Language and Literature, Mathematics, three Sciences and a Modern Language. 26 subjects are offered at A Level. Most girls take 3 subjects and the majority take the Extended Project Qualification (EPQ), which is highly regarded by university admissions tutors. Each department runs a special programme to support UCAS applications and there is additional support for those applying to Oxbridge or particularly competitive universities. There are also lessons in personal health, ethical and social issues, appropriate to each age and stage. Physical Education is taught throughout the school.

The Sixth Form. Our Sixth Formers play an important role in the school. They enjoy the independence of their own new Sixth Form Centre with common rooms, outdoor space for relaxing, café and fitness centre. They take responsibility for many extracurricular activities, such as organising clubs, and act as mentors for girls in the lower years. Additional leadership opportunities are offered by the House system, and voluntary and charity work. In 2023, 90% of A Level entries were graded A*–B, 66% at A*–A and 26% at A*. All go on to Higher Education and, with excellent results, successfully secure places at their choice of university (including Oxford and Cambridge).

Extracurricular activities. Students can choose from over 100 clubs and activities, covering an extensive range of sport, drama and music – as well as over 50 special-interest clubs. We take full advantage of everything London offers, with visits to theatres, museums, galleries, performances, and conferences incorporated into the curriculum. Trips abroad are arranged and there is an annual ski trip.

Careers advice. All girls are enrolled in our careers programme which entitles all students to help and advice until the age of 23. Sixth Formers receive extensive support with university applications, including mock interviews. The GDST Alumnae Network, the unique resource from the GDST, offers each student access to a database of former GDST students, who will give advice and support on careers (including helping with work experience) and universities. An annual Careers Evening, typically featuring senior representatives from almost 70 different professions and occupations, is organised by the Parents' Guild.

Creative Arts. There are three orchestras, three choirs, many chamber and ensemble groups, as well as two rock bands and a jazz band. School productions offer opportunities either to perform or to work with production, lighting, sound, costume and staging. Art thrives within the curriculum and through various art clubs. It also contributes to work in design technology and various aspects of ICT, such as web design and animation projects.

Sport. Sport is taken seriously with success in local fixtures and national championships, and we encourage participation and enjoyment at all standards. 'The Cricketer Schools Guide' have included NHEHS as one of the Top 20 UK Girls' School for Cricket for the last two years and our waterpolo teams have all competed at National level – our U15 team being the National Champions in 2023. On-site facilities include all-weather pitches, a huge sports hall with four courts and cricket nets, a dance studio and indoor 25-metre swimming pool. Lifeguard training is available for Sixth Formers. Aerobics, self-defence, kick boxing, football, fencing, dance and swimming for fun are among the extracurricular sports clubs currently available.

Fees per term (2023–2024). Junior School: £5,713; Senior School: £7,409.

Scholarships and bursaries. Academic, Music and Sports scholarships are available at 11+. At 16+ there are academic awards, as well as awards for Physical Education, Drama, Art and an All-Rounder scholarship.

Bursaries are available at 11+ and 16+ and we actively encourage applications.

Admission. Usually at 4+, 7+, 11+ and 16+, by appropriate test and/or interview.

Occasionally, vacancies may become available in other year groups.

Charitable status. Notting Hill & Ealing High School is part of The Girls' Day School Trust, which is a Registered Charity, number 306983.

Chair of Local Governing Board: Mrs Charlie Parkin Altman

***Head*: Mr Matthew Shoults**, MA, PGCE

Senior Deputy Head – Pastoral: Mrs Rebecca Irwin, BA, PGCE

Deputy Head – Academic: Ms M Copin, MA, MMath, BA

Head of Junior School: Ms Kate Bevan, BA, PGCE, MA

Nottingham Girls' High School GDST

9 Arboretum Street, Nottingham NG1 4JB

Tel: 0115 941 7663
email: enquiries@not.gdst.net
admissions@not.gdst.net
website: nottinghamgirlshigh.gdst.net
X/Twitter: @NottmGirlsHigh
Facebook: @FriendsofNGHS
Instagram: @nottmgirlshigh
LinkedIn: /school/nottingham-girls'-high-school

Founded 1875.

Nottingham Girls' High School is part of the GDST (Girls' Day School Trust), the leading network of independent girls' schools in the UK. As a charity that owns and runs 23 schools and two academies, it reinvests all its income in its schools. For further information about the Trust, see p. xxii or visit www.gdst.net.

Additional information about the school may be found on the school's website and a detailed information pack may be obtained from the school Admissions Secretary.

Number of Pupils. 670. 171 in the Junior School (including Nursery), 384 in the Senior School and 115 in the Sixth Form.

A selective day school for girls aged 3 to 18, NGHS is on a single site adjacent to a park in the middle of Nottingham. The Junior School, including a Nursery for three to four year olds, is housed in separate buildings on the same campus as the Senior School, and has been extended to include a library and ICT learning resources centre as well four additional classrooms. A major programme of refurbishment in the Senior School has included refitting the science laboratories, food technology and design technology. A state-of-the-art performing arts centre was opened in December 2016 and a brand new professional fitness centre was opened in September 2023.

There is a self-contained Sixth Form Centre providing a large coffee shop-style common room and recreational area. The tutorial rooms are light and airy, and fully equipped with the latest technology.

The school grounds include an all-weather sports pitch, climbing wall, woodland area for outdoor learning activities including a fire pit, pizza oven and low ropes course, gymnasium, sports centre and fitness suite. The modern dining hall has excellent facilities for providing a wide choice of snacks and home cooked meals throughout the day including vegetarian, vegan, and Halal options.

Examination results are among the best in the country, featuring in the top 100 schools for A Level results for all schools and the top 50 for GCSEs for girls schools. NGHS educates girls by empowering them with the skills they need for life in addition to excellent results. Leadership, confidence, passion and resilience are among the qualities increasingly demanded in today's ever-changing society. Everyone is encouraged to embrace adventure, seize opportunities to participate fully in a wide range of enrichment activities to develop skills and qualities that will lead to a happy, successful and fulfilling life with no sense of gender stereotypes or limits to what they can achieve.

Curriculum. The curriculum is designed to give a broad academic education and due regard is paid to the National Curriculum. In the Junior School, as well as following a pattern of work designed to help develop a confident grasp of core skills, the girls benefit from a stimulating and challenging integrated creative curriculum with enrichment experiences firmly embedded into teaching and learning. Girls are tested regularly and there are assessments for all girls wishing to join the school. There is liaison with the Senior School staff, helping to ensure continuity for pupils at 11+. In the Senior School girls are prepared for GCSE, A Level and EPQs as well as Advanced Mathematics and a Performing Arts Technical Award. Almost all girls go to university and individuals are encouraged to play to their strengths and do what is right for them. The personalised curriculum available for Senior School girls enables this.

Girls at all ages follow a comprehensive programme of personal and social development including aspects of careers, citizenship, health and sex education, current affairs and environmental issues.

Throughout the school girls are encouraged to develop their physical skills and the school has an excellent sports record; teams regularly win trophies at City and County level with many being selected to compete at regional or national level.

Music and Drama are also an important part of the school, with many choirs, bands, orchestras and performing arts groups taking place across all year groups. The Juniors and Year 7 Da Capo programme allows students to trial up to seven instruments to see which ones they enjoy best.

Admissions. For Nursery, girls are visited at home to assess their readiness for the NGHS environment. At 4+ entry, small groups of girls are invited to come into school and take part in a number of activities together to see if they are ready for school. Entry at 11+ is by interview and written tests which includes English, mathematics and verbal reasoning and is designed to determine potential and understanding. Most of the existing students stay on at 16+ if they meet the entrance criteria and a number of students are admitted into the Sixth Form from other schools. The entry requirement is 8 GCSE subjects at an average of grade 6, with minimum grade 7 in some subjects as specified by the department. This is supported by individual interviews and a report from the current school. The school will consider applications for admission into most year groups if there are available places and girls pass the entrance assessments.

Fees per term (2023–2024). Nursery: £58.00 per all day session (including lunch). Juniors: Reception (including lunch) £3,913; Years 1–2 (including lunch) £3,951; Years 3–6 (including lunch) £4,024; Seniors (excluding lunch): Years 7–13 £5,243. The fees cover non-residential curriculum trips, school books, stationery and other materials, games and swimming, but not optional extra subjects.

Scholarships and Bursaries. The GDST makes available a substantial number of bursaries. These are means tested and intended to ensure that the school remains accessible to bright girls who would benefit from our education but who would be unable to enter the school without financial assistance. Up to 100% of the tuition fee may be awarded. Bursary application forms are available from the Admissions team at the school.

A limited number of scholarships are available for talented Year 7 and Sixth Form based on Academic merit, Performing Arts, Sports and Music. The value of a scholarship is up to a maximum of 10% of the current tuition fee.

Charitable status. Nottingham Girls' High School is part of The Girls' Day School Trust, which is a Registered Charity, number 306983.

Chair of Local Governors: Mrs Emma Wilson

***Head*: Mrs J Keller**, BA

Deputy Head (*Academic*): Mrs R A Halse, BSc
Deputy Head (*Pastoral*): Mrs L M Wharton-Howett, BA

Deputy Head (*Teaching and Learning*): Mr James Brown

Head of Junior School: Mrs L Fowler, BA Ed

Head of Sixth Form: Mrs Maddy Sommers

Director of Finance and Operations: Mr J C Dunn, ACA

Director of Marketing: Ms C Forbes, FRSA

Admissions: Mrs C L Haddow

Oxford High School GDST

Belbroughton Road, Oxford, Oxfordshire OX2 6XA
Tel: 01865 559888
email: oxfordhigh@oxf.gdst.net
website: www.oxfordhigh.gdst.net
X/Twitter: @OxfordHighSch
Facebook: @OxfordHighGDST
Instagram: @oxfordhighschoolgdst
LinkedIn: /school/oxford-high-school

Motto: *Ad Lucem*

We are pleased to announce we have won Independent Girls' School of the Year at the Independent School Parent awards

Oxford High School is an independent day school for girls aged 4 to 18 years. Founded in 1875, it is Oxford's oldest girls' school. The school is located across three sites in Summertown in north Oxford, all within walking distance of each other. It is part of the Girls' Day School Trust (GDST) which is at the forefront of educational innovation, teaching over 20,000 girls across the UK in 25 schools, as the country's leading network of independent girls' schools.

At Oxford High School, we empower each and every student to be whoever they want to be. Those who find their way here are curious, outward-looking, and sparky; they delight in learning and questioning, they care about the world in which we live in and are fearless in the pursuit of their passions. Whether a Sixth Former organising a virtual conference and extending the invitation to other schools throughout the UK, or a Year 7 stepping up to their very first leadership role, our students embrace challenge and take every opportunity to realise their goals and aspirations, whatever they might be. With the unwavering support of their teachers and peers, OHS students forge their own paths in the world and continually push themselves to go beyond.

In the 2023 inspection report, the school was rated as 'excellent' in all areas.

Pupil numbers. 832: Prep School 230, Senior School & Sixth Form 602.

The Senior School is extremely well-resourced with a sports hall, indoor swimming pool, The Mary Warnock School of Music, separate purpose-built centres for all other subjects, and well-equipped ICT areas. Our new Sixth Form, Arts, and Well-being Centre – the Ada Benson Building – has state-of-the-art teaching and learning spaces, dedicated campus-style areas for Sixth Formers, an auditorium for talks, lectures, NT-Live events, and new teaching and gallery spaces for the Art Department. Students from the Prep sites have regular access to facilities in the Senior School.

Curriculum and Co-Curriculum. The OHS Curriculum is one that inspires as well as challenges, and girls are well-prepared for their GCSEs and A Levels. With 24 subjects to choose from, there is always something to suit a student's interests and their timetable is individually tailored around their choice of subjects. The school offers eight languages including Latin and Ancient Greek. About 90% of our Year 13s secure places at top Russell Group universities, with 10% of the year group going on to study Medicine and 1 in 4 girls regularly proceed to Oxbridge, as well as leading institutions for art, music, and the performing arts.

Many girls take examinations in Music and Speech & Drama, and multiple productions are staged each year alongside concerts at venues including the Sheldonian Theatre and Oxford Town Hall. Girls also participate in a wealth of co-curricular activities, including the Duke of Edinburgh's Award, Young Enterprise and the school's own sporting partnership, Girls on the Ball. Clubs are offered in robotics, poetry, astronomy, genome analysis and bee-keeping, to name a few. In the Sixth Form, the 360 Programme offers an innovative and academically challenging programme to prepare girls for life at university and beyond, supported by the GDST's extensive alumnae network.

Girls at the Oxford High Prep School (OHPS) also enjoy a highly varied and engaging curriculum, such as the Singapore Mathematics programme and their weekly Global Studies lessons. The PE curriculum introduces girls to a multitude of sports such as gymnastics, athletics, hockey, and cricket, to name a few. Drama and Music are a key part of life at OHPSl. Every girl is encouraged to participate in one of the many ensembles and to perform in the school plays. The girls develop great confidence and they thoroughly enjoy it.

In recent years, the Prep School has launched its Future Ready Programme, which aims to build well-rounded young people. Pupils work through progressive levels and complete a series of age-appropriate tasks, working towards the achievement of badges. The tasks are varied and wide-ranging, spanning academia, sustainability, life skills and personal development.

Admissions. The main points of entry are at Reception, Year 3, Year 7, Year 9 and Year 12. Applicants are also able to join the school at other entry points if there are places available Please contact our Admissions team for details (admissions@oxf.gdst.net or 01865 318500).

Fees per term (2023–2024). Reception: £3,505 (plus lunch £287.84); Years 1 & 2: £4,117 (plus lunch £287.84); Years 3 & 4: £4,701 (plus lunch £346.50); Years 5 & 6: £4,747 (plus lunch £346.50). Senior School (Years 7–13): £6,262 (plus lunch £346.50 for Years 7–11). Lunch is compulsory for girls from Reception to Year 11 and optional for Sixth Form girls only, who have the freedom to go to Summertown in Oxford or eat in school.

The fees cover the regular curriculum textbooks, stationery and other materials, compulsory educational visits, choral music, games and swimming, but not optional extra subjects.

Bursaries. The school offers means-tested bursaries and ensures that it remains accessible to bright girls who would profit from the education provided, but who would be unable to enter the school without financial assistance. Bursaries are available at Year 7, Year 9 and Year 12 entry to the Senior School and a confidential application can be made to the GDST. If your family's assessable income and resources are below £87,500 a year, you may be eligible for some support.

Scholarships. Scholarships are available for Year 7, Year 9, and Year 12 entry in Art, Drama, Sport, Music, Academic and the Head's Scholarship. These scholarships are held for the duration of a girl's time at

Oxford High, subject to satisfactory progress and behaviour.

Charitable status. Oxford High School is part of The Girls' Day School Trust, which is a Registered Charity, number 306983.

Chairman of the School Governing Board: Miss Katherine Haynes

***Head*: Mrs Marina Gardiner Legge**

Deputy Heads:
Dr Ed Batchelar (*Academic*)
Miss Laura Knowles (*Pastoral*)
Head of Prep School: Mrs Jessica Williams

Registrars:
Gemma Tuckey and Laura Pountney (*Senior School*)
Tash Watson (*Prep School*)

Palmers Green High School

104 Hoppers Road, London N21 3LJ

Tel: 020 8886 1135
email: office@pghs.co.uk
website: www.pghs.co.uk
X/Twitter: @PGHSGirls
Facebook: @palmersgreenhighschool
Instagram: @palmersgreenhighschool
LinkedIn: /palmers-green-high-school

Motto: *By Love Serve One Another*

Palmers Green High School, founded in 1905 by Miss Alice Hum, has provided an exceptional education for over 115 years. At PGHS we specialise in educating girls, challenging them to achieve their full potential within our warm and friendly school environment.

The School motto, "By Love Serve One Another" was carefully chosen and it still epitomises our special ethos where individuals are nurtured, successes are celebrated and their contribution to the community is greatly valued.

We provide an inspiring, challenging and supportive environment through which all pupils are given opportunities to be inquisitive, independent and develop a lifelong love of learning.

PGHS is a very special 'through-school' where pupils progress in a familiar setting and benefit from seamless transitions across the key stages in the Lower and Senior Schools. There is an authentic feeling of being one family where strong friendships are formed and extend beyond year groups.

All sections of the school, from the Nursery through to the Seniors, enjoy being part of our 'one school' community. Preps use the same facilities as the GCSE pupils in some subjects e.g. Art, Music, PE and D&T, and Years 5 & 6 enjoy Science in the laboratories. Throughout, small class sizes and excellent teaching enable rapid progress, whilst exciting extra-curricular activities encourage pupils to develop into well-rounded individuals.

Our purpose-built Nursery is designed for 3–4 year old girls, most of whom transfer to Reception at PGHS. Lower School classes from Reception through to Year 6 benefit hugely from the encouragement and expertise of their class teachers and teaching assistants. Favourable teaching group sizes, light and airy classrooms and access to Senior School facilities all lead to an inspirational learning environment. This is enriched by specialist teaching in Art, D&T, Drama, French, Spanish, Music and PE – frequently in half-class groups.

In the Senior School, small class sizes (an average of only 10 at GCSE) and a broad range of extra-curricular activities enriches the pupils' experience. In 2023, 41% of GCSE/IGCSE grades were A*/9/8 and 69% were A*/9–A/7.

Former pupils enjoy coming back to share their news with current pupils. Recent leavers have followed Sixth Form courses at The Henrietta Barnett School, St Michael's Catholic Grammar School, The Latymer School, Dame Alice Owen's School, Woodhouse College, Haberdashers' Girls' School, North London Collegiate School, Aldenham School, Channing, Haileybury and Roedean. Popular university destinations include Birmingham, Bristol, Cambridge, Durham, Exeter, Glasgow, King's College London, Liverpool, London School of Economics, Manchester, Nottingham, Oxford, University College London, University of East Anglia and Warwick.

Palmers Green High School is recognised for its all-round excellence in a small and nurturing environment and parents can be reassured that PGHS pupils not only attain excellent results in relation to their abilities and aptitudes, but also grow in confidence and poise as members of this very special school community.

Fees per term (2023–2024). Nursery £3,835 (Full time), Nursery £2,350 (Part time); Reception–Year 2 £4,455; Years 3–6 £4,770; Years 7–11 £6,375.

Scholarships and Bursaries. Academic, Art, Drama, Music and Sport Scholarships; Subject Awards, and Bursaries are available to candidates aged 11+ for entry in September.

Entrance. Admission to all year groups is by assessment and interview, the main intakes being at 3+, 4+, 7+ and 11+.

Charitable status. Palmers Green High School Limited is a Registered Charity, number 312629. It exists for the education of girls.

***Head*: Ms Sarah Proudlove**

Deputy Head: Miss Hannah Lucas
Bursar: Mrs Leonie Barnard
Chair of Governors: Mrs Melanie Curtis

Pembridge Hall School

Inspired Education Group

18 Pembridge Square, London W2 4EH

Tel: 020 7229 0121
email: contact@pembridgehall.co.uk
website: www.pembridgehall.co.uk
Instagram: @pembridgehallschool

See full entry in the **IAPS** section, on **p. 747**.

Pipers Corner School
High Wycombe

Great Kingshill, High Wycombe, Buckinghamshire HP15 6LP

Tel: 01494 718255
email: theschool@piperscorner.co.uk
website: www.piperscorner.co.uk
X/Twitter: @PipersCornerSch
Facebook: @PipersCornerSchool
Instagram: @PipersCornerSch

At Pipers Corner, from Pre-Prep through to Sixth Form, all girls are supported and challenged to achieve their full potential. In our nurturing and encouraging environment, personal development is as important as academic success and every girl is stretched as much outside as inside the classroom. We aim to know each girl as an individual and identify, develop and support her talents and strengths.

Academically successful, our students progress to further study at some of the country's top higher education institutions. In 2023, 48% of all A Level results were at grades A*/A, and 82% at grades A*–B. At GCSE there was a 100% pass rate, with 27% at grades 9–8 (A**/A*), and 50% at grades 9–7 (A**/A).

Fees per term (2023–2024). £3,590–£7,565.

Facilities. The School is set within 96 acres of picturesque Chiltern countryside, 4 miles north of High Wycombe and 2 miles from Great Missenden. The Arts Centre is the home of our 280-seat theatre, with state-of-the-art sound and lighting facilities, and a café serving nutritional and delicious food at break and lunch. Sixth Form students benefit from the modern Sixth Form Centre, with a separate quiet study room. Pipers Radio is our bespoke station, broadcasting live shows every day. Sporting facilities include the sports hall, swimming pool and triple-court astro pitch. Wraparound care is available from 7.30 am–6.00 pm.

Pastoral care. Student welfare is at the forefront of our school: we offer exceptional pastoral care with an extensive network of support. Pastoral care is enriched by a Christian ethos, encouraging the exploration of personal values and beliefs while retaining fundamental respect for the views of others. The School is made up of four Houses, consisting of students from all year groups, allowing students to integrate and make connections beyond their immediate peer group.

Enrichment. Learning is enhanced with a range of visits and excursions, both nationally and abroad, for Pre-Prep through to Sixth Form. We have a wide variety of extracurricular activities, encompassing physical, intellectual and creative pursuits. Our students are encouraged to seize every opportunity afforded to them, to take on leadership and organisational responsibilities and to be open to trying new activities.

Admissions. Girls can join Pipers at the beginning of most year groups, from Reception through to Sixth Form. The Admissions Team are the first point of contact for enquiries regarding spaces. For most year groups, an interview and day visit or assessment day will form the basis of an offer, subject to the receipt of a satisfactory reference from a current school.

Scholarships and bursaries. We are keen to encourage girls with talent and potential, and to widen access to allow as many girls as possible to take advantage of the excellent education we provide. Means-tested bursaries are available up to a maximum of 100% of fees (including any Scholarship award).

There are Academic, Art, Drama, Music and PE scholarships available for Year 7 applicants, in addition to the Jessie Cross Award which is a means-tested scholarship for students currently educated in a state primary school. Students joining Reception can apply for the Jessie Cross Foundation Award, which is means-tested and awarded for the duration of Pre-Prep education (Reception–Year 2). For Sixth Form entry, there are subject-specific scholarships in addition to the broader Academic Scholarship. Students already at Pipers and those from other secondary schools can apply.

Charitable status. Pipers Corner School is a Registered Charity, Number 310635. It exists to provide high-quality education for girls.

Visitor: The Rt Reverend The Lord Bishop of Buckingham

Chair of Governors: Mr F W Johnston, BA, FCA
Mr P S Bhullar, MCIPD
Ms E J Carrighan, MA, MBA
Mrs N Doran, BA Hons, PGCE, MEd
Mr M F T Harborne, CBII
Mr A P K McBarnett, FCMA, CGMA
Ms H F Morton, MA, MSc, CEng
Reverend H E Peters, BSc, FdA (*Vice Chair of Governors*)
Lady Redgrave, BSc, MBBS, MSc SEM
Mr H B P Roberts, BSc Eng, FCA
Miss H J R Semple, MA
Mr M Stepney, MA
Mr P B Wayne, MusB, NPQH

***Headmistress*: Mrs H J Ness-Gifford**, BA Hons, PGCE

Deputy Head Academic: Mrs C Derbyshire, BSc Hons, PGCE

Deputy Head Pastoral: Mr A McClean, BA Hons, PGCE

Assistant Head Operations: Mrs E Cresswell, BA Hons, PGCE

Assistant Head Academic: Mr A Codling, BSc Hons, GTP

Head of Pre-Prep and Prep: Mr R Urquhart, BSc Hons

Bursar and Clerk to the Governors: Mr J D Clarke, BA Hons

Director of Admissions & Marketing: Mr G Ranford, BA Hons

Director of Digital Strategy: Mr A Rees, BSc Hons, PG Dip, MSc

Portsmouth High School
GDST

25 Kent Road, Southsea, Hampshire PO5 3EQ
Tel: 023 9282 6714
email: admissions@por.gdst.net
website: www.portsmouthhigh.co.uk
X/Twitter: @portsmouthhigh
Facebook: @PortsmouthHigh
Instagram: @portsmouthhighuk
LinkedIn: /portsmouth-high-school-gdst

Portsmouth High School, founded in 1882, is part of the Girls' Day School Trust (GDST), the leading family of independent girls' schools in the UK. As a charity that owns and runs 23 schools and two academies, the GDST reinvests all its income in its schools. For further information about the Trust, see p. xxii or visit www.gdst.net.

Additional information about the school may be found on the school's website and a digital prospectus can be downloaded via the 'Request a Prospectus' button.

Number of pupils. 360 are in the senior school (11–18), 150 in the prep school (rising 3–11).

Portsmouth High School is committed to the wellbeing of each individual pupil and recently opened a dedicated wellbeing centre, Daffodil House, at the senior school. The school is ambitious for every pupil enabling each girl to become the best version of herself. Each girl is encouraged to develop her own voice and her own views and to understand and build on her strengths. There is an atmosphere of achievement across the curriculum and examination results are consistently excellent.

Just a 5-minute walk from the sea, the school attracts pupils from an extensive area of Hampshire, West Sussex and the Isle of Wight. All major transport providers serve the locality and the school runs its own extensive minibus service.

The senior school provides a broad and balanced education supported by an ongoing capital investment programme to ensure teaching spaces are bright and modern. Most recently a multi-use games area for sport and wellbeing centre at the senior school added to the portfolio of improvement.

A partnership with the University of Portsmouth gives the school joint use of the university's Langstone sports ground facilities and the school also has use of the new Ravelin Park Centre which houses a swimming pool and fitness centre.

The Sixth Form. Students have their own dedicated space in Sixth Form House which has a large common room, kitchen and separate rooms for private study. Students do not wear uniform and instead have a smart 'Dress for Work' code.

The Prep School. The prep school is located 2 minutes' walk away in a wonderful Thomas Ellis Owen period house with extensive gardens including 2 netball courts, an all-weather sports pitch, an outdoor classroom and a range of other indoor and outdoor facilities. This is a school where intellectual curiosity is developed and girls enjoy a unique explorer approach to learning through a range of opportunities, both inside and outside the classroom.

The curriculum. The aim at Portsmouth High School is to foster in each girl the confidence to take risks and tackle new challenges, within an atmosphere of ambition and enterprise, through providing appropriate teaching, advice and support. The focus on girls' learning is reflected in the design of learning spaces; the use of digital technology; a challenging and rewarding curriculum and a focus on pupils taking responsibility for their learning and having the confidence to take intellectual risks.

Co-curricular activities. There is an extensive programme of co-curricular activities in both the prep and senior schools. The lunchtime and after-school clubs range from climbing to public speaking and the programme is responsive to the interests of the pupils themselves.

There is an enthusiastic involvement in music, art, sport and drama with many performances and fixtures throughout the school calendar for prep and senior girls. Senior girls have the opportunity to become involved in The Duke of Edinburgh's Award scheme as well as a sixth form enrichment programme. There are regular overseas trips, sports and music tours.

Admission procedures/Entrance examinations. At 11+ and 13+ entry the examinations in mathematics and English are designed to test potential rather than knowledge. In addition to the 11+ examinations, all girls take part in a series of team activities in school. At 13+ girls take part in an experience day and are interviewed by the Headmistress.

Sixth-form entry is based on having at least English, mathematics and science GCSEs and applicants are invited for interview. Entry into the prep school is based on experience days, observations and reports from current schools.

Fees per term (2023–2024). Senior School: £5,386; Prep School: Years 3–6 £3,809, Pre-School to Year 2: £2,889.

The fees in the prep school include wraparound care from 7.30 am to 6.00 pm daily. The fees also cover the regular curriculum, school books, non-residential curriculum trips, stationery and other materials, public examinations, choral music, games and swimming. The fees for extra subjects, including individual lessons in instrumental music and speech training, are shown in the Admissions Handbook which can be downloaded from the school website.

Scholarships and bursaries. Bursaries are means tested and are intended to ensure that the school remains accessible to bright girls who would be unable to enter the school without financial assistance.

Academic, sport, music, art and drama scholarships are available for 11+ and 13+. At sixth form (16+) art, drama and sport scholarships are available. Please see the scholarships and bursaries page on the school website for further details.

Charitable status. Portsmouth High School is part of The Girls' Day School Trust, Registered Charity number 306983.

Chair of the School Governing Board: Mrs K Butwilowska, JP, BA, MEd

Headmistress: **Mrs J Prescott,** BSc Cardiff, PGCE, NPQH

Deputy Head: Mrs Sarah Parker, MA Hons, PGCE

Headmaster, Prep School: Mr P Marshallsay, BA Ed

Admissions Registrars: Mrs C Thomson, BSc Hons, Mrs F Cox

Queen Anne's School

6 Henley Road, Caversham, Berkshire RG4 6DX

Tel: 0118 918 7300
email: office@qas.org.uk
website: www.qas.org.uk
X/Twitter: @QASCaversham
Facebook: @QASCaversham
Instagram: @qas_caversham
LinkedIn: /school/queen-anne's

See full entry in the **HMC** section, on **p. 261**.

Queen Mary's School

A Woodard School

Baldersby Park, Topcliffe, Thirsk, North Yorkshire YO7 3BZ

Tel: 01845 575040
email: admissions@queenmarys.org
website: www.queenmarys.org
X/Twitter: @QueenMarysSch
Facebook: @Queen-Marys-School

Queen Mary's is an outstanding day and boarding school for girls aged 4 to 16 and boys aged 4 to 7. Academic excellence and exceptional extra-curricular opportunities are on offer within a nurturing environment, where education is truly tailored to the individual. The school has a unique family atmosphere with friendliness and concern for others being an important part of the school's ethos. The country setting provides a safe haven for pupils to thrive and develop self-confidence.

Location. Queen Mary's is situated at Baldersby Park in a beautiful Grade 1 Palladian mansion, with 40 acres of grounds, including formal gardens, playing fields, sports facilities and Queen Mary's Equestrian Centre. Despite its idyllic surroundings, it is only 2 miles from Junction 49 of the A1 and within ten minutes of Thirsk station. York and Harrogate are within easy reach and so are Leeds/Bradford and Teesside airports. Minibuses transport pupils to and from home on a daily basis with 32 drop-off points.

The Curriculum. Pupils at Queen Mary's are offered a great deal in terms of breadth and depth of learning. Generous time is given to core subjects, English, Mathematics, Science and Modern Languages. Strong emphasis is also placed on the supporting subjects – Geography, History, Religious Studies, Latin, Classics, Design Technology, Music, Art and a varied programme of Physical Education. Classes are kept deliberately small, which means that every girl can receive plenty of support from her teachers. The school has an excellent scholarship programme and a learning support department for those pupils who have specific learning difficulties. The two years leading up to GCSE are full and focused, with most girls taking ten subjects at GCSE. The public examination results are excellent, with 31% of entries being awarded Grades 8–9 in 2022.

Pastoral care. All girls in school have personal tutors who oversee the academic, social and emotional development of each of their tutees. Building self-confidence and developing the individual talents of each pupil is seen as a vital aspect of the education offered. Each girl is encouraged to be self-reliant from an early age and pupils are taught a real concern for the needs of others. Girls in their final year at Queen Mary's undertake a number of important responsibilities to help the school community function smoothly.

Boarding. Queen Mary's offers a number of boarding options to suit the needs of parents and their daughters. Those who choose to board may be flexi, weekly or full boarders. The boarding community is thriving. The full boarders, who stay at weekends, enjoy a broad range of activities and trips.

Extracurricular Activities. An impressive range of extracurricular activities is available to all members of the school community. Choral and orchestral music are both huge strengths of the school, as is sport, with Hockey, Lacrosse, Swimming, Netball, Gymnastics, Football, Dance, Tennis, Rounders and Athletics all on offer. Facilities include an indoor swimming pool and full sized AstroTurf pitch and sports pavilion. Performing Arts, Drama, Debating and The Duke of Edinburgh's Award are highly popular choices and the all-weather outdoor Riding facilities allow more than 90 girls to ride each week. Children enjoy the opportunity to tackle the climbing wall, canoe on the adjacent River Swale or participate in other Outdoor Adventure activities.

Religious Affiliation. The school is part of the Woodard Corporation, an Anglican foundation which promotes Christian education and high academic and pastoral standards within all its schools. The school has its own Chapel. The school Chaplain prepares girls for confirmation. Girls of other denominations are welcome.

What happens after GCSE? Specialist careers advice is offered throughout the senior school and well-informed staff support the girls as they seek to make applications and progress on to some of the most prestigious sixth forms in the country. Every senior girl was awarded a place at her first choice of sixth form destination in 2021 and a healthy proportion of the girls each year join their new schools as scholars.

Scholarships. Scholarships are offered in the Senior School to those candidates who show particular academic flair or have special talent in Art, Music, Riding or Sport. Assessments are held during the Spring Term.

Entrance. By interview with the Head. Entry can be at most stages, subject to availability. An up-to-date prospectus can be sent upon request. Visit www.queenmarys.org for more information.

Fees per term (2023–2024). Reception £3,460 (day); Pre-Prep: Years 1–3 £3,787 (day); Years 4–6 £6,266 (day), £8,652 (weekly boarding), £9,041 (boarding); Senior: Years 7–8 £6,794 (day), £9,227 (weekly boarding), £9,628 (boarding); Years 9–11 £7,708 (day), £10,214 (weekly boarding), £10,626 (full boarding).

Charitable status. Queen Mary's School (Baldersby) Ltd is a Registered Charity, number 1098410. It exists to educate children in a Christian environment.

Chair of Governors: Mr T E Fielden, BA Hons, FCA

***Head*: Mrs Carole Cameron**, MA, PGCE, NPQH, FRGS

Assistant Head: *Safeguarding and Wellbeing*: Mrs J Strawbridge, BEd Hons

Assistant Head: Mrs V Kemp, BA Hons, PCE SENCO CPT3A

Queen's College, London

43–49 Harley Street, London W1G 8BT
Tel: 020 7291 7000
email: queens@qcl.org.uk
website: www.qcl.org.uk
X/Twitter: @queenscollegew1
Facebook: @QueensCollegeW1
Instagram: @queenscollegew_1
LinkedIn: /school/queens-college-w1

Queen's College, London was the first institution to provide an academic education and qualifications for young women. It was founded in 1848 by F D Maurice, Professor of Modern History at King's College, and was housed originally at 45 Harley Street.

Today, it is a thriving girls' school of 425 pupils aged from 11–18, of whom around 100 are in the Sixth Form. Queen's College Preparatory School (020 7291 0660), which opened in 2002 at 61 Portland Place, takes girls from ages 4–11.

Queen's is situated on Harley Street, combining the beauty of four eighteenth century houses with modern facilities for science, languages, art, drama, music and computer science, as a well as a Hall and gymnasium. Two libraries, in the care of a librarian, offer the students some 10,000 books, and there is also a unique off-site archive recording the history of the College.

Curriculum. Class sizes rarely exceed twenty and the normal size of a year group is 60–65, divided into three forms. The year group is streamed for Mathematics and French during the first year and at a later stage for English, Latin and science.

Pupils usually take nine or ten subjects at GCSE, and the three sciences are taught separately. At A Level it is possible to study History of Art, Psychology, Dance, Computer Science as well as the subjects already taken at GCSE.

There is a comprehensive programme of sport offered for all year groups. There is a gym on site and outdoor games take place at Paddington Recreation Ground. Younger pupils play netball, football, cricket, rounders, hockey and tennis, while seniors can choose from a wide range of activities including Taekwondo; there are thriving clubs before and after school for swimming, running and other leisure pursuits. Regular sports fixtures are arranged against local schools. The Duke of Edinburgh's Award is organised at bronze and silver levels. Individual music lessons are offered in all instruments including voice, and the musical or dramatic productions and jazz concert are highlights of each year.

The location of the College means that theatre and other educational visits in London are an integral part of the curriculum, complemented by opportunities to travel abroad or to other parts of the country. In recent years groups of girls have visited France, Greece, Germany, Italy, South Africa, the USA and Japan. There are also regular ski trips.

Almost all pupils leaving Queen's proceed to university, including Oxford or Cambridge, and several students each year choose to take an Art Foundation course at one of the London colleges. Former students are prominent in medicine, education, writing and the media; they retain contact with each other and the college through the Old Queens' Society, which also gives bursaries to families in financial need.

Pastoral care. Queen's prides itself on its friendly and informal atmosphere, highly valued by pupils, parents and staff. Pastoral care is strong and we have a full-time nurse to support the work of form tutors and pastoral staff. A specialist in various special educational needs works individually with pupils once the need has been identified. We send reports to parents every half-term and hold regular Parents' Evenings. Parents also support the College through membership of the Parents' Association, giving practical and some financial assistance to College functions.

Admission. The College is a member of the London 11+ Consortium. Candidates for Year 7 entry sit the London 11+ Consortium entrance examination and are invited to attend an interview. As well as high academic standards we value enthusiasm and creativity, and academic, music and art awards are available to 11+ entrants.

If vacancies arise we also welcome applicants at other ages, particularly after GCSE, where there is a long-standing tradition of accepting students to undertake their A Level education at Queen's. Some scholarships are available on entry at this stage. Means-tested bursaries are available at all points of entry.

Fees per term (2023–2024). £7,995.

Charitable status. Queen's College, London is a Registered Charity, number 312726. It exists to provide education for girls. It is an Anglican foundation, open to those of all faiths or none who are prepared to subscribe to its ethos.

Patron: Her Late Majesty The Queen

Visitor: The Rt Revd and Rt Hon the Lord Bishop of London

Council:

Co-Chairman: Mrs Alexandra Gregory, BA Exeter, ACA

Co-Chairman: Mrs Rae Perry, BA Trinity Washington, MBA New York, MSc Liverpool

Vice-Chairman: Mr Matthew Hanslip Ward, MA Cantab

Mrs Marianne Austin, BSc Durham, MA Sheffield, ACA

Mrs Jenny Blaiklock, MA Oxon

Mrs Catherine Brahams-Melinek, BA UCL, MA Durham
Mr Greg Cohen, BSc Manchester
Mr Richard Ford, BSc LSE
Mrs Dina Mallett, BA Reading
Ms Holly Porter, MA Cantab, MA RCA, RIBA, FRSA
Mr Joe Silvester, BA Bristol, MA London
Mrs Linda Wei, BA Harvard, MBA INSEAD
Mrs Patricia Wilks, BA Oxon

Bursar and Clerk to the Council: R Richards, BA Leeds

***Principal*: R W Tillett**, MA Cantab

Headmistress of Queen's College Preparatory School: L Lamont, BA Hons Bristol, MA Herts

Senior Deputy Head – Pastoral: S J Abbott, BA, MA, PhD Reading

Deputy Head – Academic: S Bailey, MA Cantab, MA Open, MSc Oxon

Deputy Head – Operations & Co-curricular: E A Wilkins, MA Oxon, MA Cardiff

Registrar: B Porter, LLB Open

Queen's Gate School

131–133 Queen's Gate, London SW7 5LE
Tel: 020 7589 3587
email: info@queensgate.org.uk
website: www.queensgate.org.uk
Facebook: @QueensGateSch
Instagram: @QueensGateSchool
LinkedIn: /queen-s-gate-school

Queen's Gate School is a day school for girls aged 4–18, located in South Kensington, on the edge of the capital's educational and cultural heartland, the perfect place to inspire and indulge young hearts and minds. Our close-knit community of around 500 pupils is a special one. Our central London home affords us a diverse, multinational intake, our size allows us to know every girl as an individual, and our desire to feel 'unschooly' is brought to life in touches such as our lack of uniform.

We are unashamedly proud of our pupils' many successes. We aim to provide a learning environment in which girls feel enabled and empowered to stretch themselves both intellectually and personally. We seek for each of our girls to develop a lifelong love of learning: a readiness to question, an appetite for knowledge and the self-belief that they will find their way through any challenge. Alongside this, in line with our core values, we encourage character traits of compassion and consideration, respect and integrity. We delight in the authenticity we see emerge in our girls, their confidence to be their true selves and their enjoyment of discovering, developing and demonstrating their own personal gifts and talents.

We offer a broad and forward-thinking array of co-curricular activities, spanning the fields of Music, Drama, Sport and beyond. Pupil voice is central, with girls having the opportunity to serve on a number of committees dedicated to giving them a forum in which to put forward their ideas and share their feedback. However, all pupils are also permitted to make appointments directly with the Principal should they wish to discuss their thoughts with her directly, something she always welcomes.

High-quality pastoral care and the safeguarding of pupils is our utmost priority. Our PSHE programme is regularly reviewed to ensure we are meeting the needs of our girls, while our smaller size allows us to get to them well – vital for identifying quickly when something isn't going as well as we would hope, and for fostering the kind of staff-pupil relationships where girls feel safe to come forward and share their worries.

Junior School. We are a small, friendly school, but we enjoy all of the benefits of a broad community. Both the Junior and Senior Schools take advantage of shared resources, and many lessons, such as Science, STEAM and our six languages, are taught by specialist teachers.

Academic standards are high, and a love of learning is evident throughout the School. The Junior School Curriculum at Queen's Gate School includes a well-balanced range of diverse and exciting subjects taught by specialist teachers, with excellent enrichment opportunities.

Specialist teachers teach the sciences in our well-equipped laboratories, and we also have specialists in all six languages, art, music, design technology and PE.

Teaching groups are small, and learning is 'hands-on' investigative and collaborative; teaching methods are vibrant, dynamic and challenging. Maths challenges, entrepreneurial projects, English Speaking Board Examinations, art exhibitions and creative writing competitions run throughout the School and add extra excitement to our busy curriculum.

Junior School Pastoral Care. We are renowned at Queen's Gate Junior School for exceptional pastoral care. However, we understand that the well-being of our girls is just as important as their outstanding academic education.

Queen's Gate is a small school, with just one class for each year, enabling us to give our pupils a great deal of individual attention. Our family ethos ensures that each child is valued and nurtured; support and extension derive naturally from the built close relationships.

Senior School. Girls enter the Senior School at the age of 11–18, from our Junior School and independent and maintained feeder schools across the capital. We aim to create a secure, happy, and stimulating environment where each girl will enjoy her time and flourish academically and personally. Teaching methods combine modern technology with traditional rigour at all stages.

Senior School Pastoral Care. Pupil wellbeing is central to life at Queen's Gate and strong pupil and teacher relationships, where teachers know every pupil as an individual, are the foundations of our pastoral care structure. We believe firmly that positive self-esteem and a sense of feeling happy and well cared for are fundamental for pupil progress, both in terms of their academic attainment and their personal development.

Form Tutors see girls in the morning and at afternoon registration and will usually be the first port of call for girls and parents. Weekly Form Time sessions allow Form Tutors and pupils to explore.

All year groups benefit from a Head of Year and Deputy Head of Year who oversee both the well-being and academic progress of the girls in their care. These staff are responsible for identifying key issues for their specific age group and responding where girls might be experiencing difficulties. They also lead regular year group assemblies, again focusing on topics that are of particular relevance to the girls in their cohort.

At Queen's Gate, SEND provision comes under the auspices of our Learning Enhancement Department. Their work is crucial for the girls' academic progress, as well as playing an important part in the well-being of our girls. The Learning Enhancement Department liaises closely with our subject and pastoral staff, to ensure that any difficulties are recognised and supported in the best way possible. We also offer specialist EAL tuition which is invaluable for those girls for whom English is not their first language.

Our School Counsellors visit school each week and are available to offer extra support for pupils who need an extra listening ear. We are also able to offer 1:1 coaching for girls who may appreciate some extra help with specific issues such as exam anxiety or difficulties managing relationships with peers.

Pastoral care at Queen's Gate Senior School is overseen by the Director of Pastoral Care, who is supported by an Assistant Director of Pastoral Care. Together they plan a programme of proactive support, which seeks to meet the needs of the girls before issues can arise. Experts in working with adolescent girls, they keep up-to-date with trends and research, ensuring the provision of forward-thinking, modern and relevant pastoral care.

Sixth Form. The Sixth Form is a time for pupils to build on their experiences, to think and plan for life after school. In addition to the academic subjects offered in Sixth Form, we also offer a wide range of other opportunities. These include our:

Wider World Programme – a rolling, two-year enrichment programme of weekly lectures during the Autumn and Spring Terms, designed to widen knowledge of important issues and debates. In addition, we also offer help with topics that girls may be required to discuss at their university interviews and introduce them to university-style lectures.

Past speakers have included:

- Dr Helen Pankhurst, women's rights activist and author of *Deeds Not Words*
- Dame Helena Morrissey DBE, a British financier and campaigner
- Prof. Lyndon Da Cruz of Moorfields Eye Hospital
- Penny Marshall from ITN News

Duke of Edinburgh – The Gold Award is a fantastic opportunity to participate in physical activity, volunteer, and learn and improve skills.

The Gold programme involves:

- Volunteering for 12 months
- Doing physical activity and skill; one for 12 months, one for six months
- A residential section (four nights away from home)
- A practice expedition
- The qualifying expedition

Inspiring Women Series – was developed to provide an opportunity for staff, students, local community members and other interested parties to hear from women who have been successful in their field.

The diverse range of high-profile speakers has encouraged engagement and discussion, and the series is now a regular and essential feature in the Queen's Gate events calendar.

Speakers have included: Sally Gunnell OBE; TV presenter and vlogger, Venetia Falconer; Adventurer, Pip Stewart; and Film producer, Kate Pakenham.

Enrichment – All girls in Lower Sixth will attend a weekly enrichment tutorial from various available options.

Available Enrichment includes:

- Model United Nations (MUN)
- Extended Project Qualification (EPQ)
- Oxbridge essays and competitions
- The ARTiculation Prize
- Logical Reasoning
- SAT Preparation
- Becoming a Mental Health Ambassador
- A history of Europe through European cinema
- Current Affairs

Curriculum. Girls follow as broad a curriculum as possible and generally take GCSE in ten subjects, including English, Mathematics, Science, and a modern language.

We offer an extensive range of AS/A Level subjects; four AS Levels in the first year and three taken at A2 Level.

Games. Netball, Hockey, Tennis, Swimming, Rowing, Athletics, Basketball, Cross-Country, Biathlon and Dance.

Admission. By test and interview in the Junior School; by London 11+ Consortium entrance examination; by the School's entrance examinations for entry to other years in the Senior School.

Applicants for the Sixth Form require a minimum of six GCSEs at A Grade with A grades required in those subjects they wish to pursue to A Level.

Registration fee: £165.00.

Fees per term (2023–2024). £7,620.00–£8,442.00

Board of Governors:
Mrs Reica Gray (*Chair*)
Carol Davis KC
Mr Jonathan Dobson
Mr William Gillen
Mr Shai Hill
Mr Gary Li
Miss Camilla Trefgarne
Mr Peter Trueman
Mrs Manina Weldon

***Principal*: Miss Amy Wallace**, MA, MPhil Cantab, PGCE Oxon

Vice Principal: Mr Christian Kendall-Daw, MA Wales, BA Hons York, PhB Rome, STB Rome, QTS, FCCT, FRSA

Senior School:
Director of Pastoral Care: Ms C De La Pena, BA Hons, MA, PCGE Manchester
Assistant Director of Pastoral Care: Miss N Holgate-Smith, BA Hons, PGCE

Director of Teaching, Learning & Assessment: Mr M Crundwell, BSc Hons, MPhil London, MEd Dist, QTS
Director of Curriculum: Mr P Williams, MA
Head of Lower School: Miss C Spencer, BSc Hons, PGCE
Head of Sixth Form & Outreach: Ms C Gittens, LLB Hons, PGCE
Head of LVI: Miss C E Adler, BSc Hons, QTS
Head of UV (Academic): Mr M Crundwell, BSc Hons, MPhil London, MEd, QTS
Head of UV (Pastoral): Miss G McLister, BSc Hons, PGCE
Head of V: Mr A Cohen, MA, PGCE, QTS
Head of IV: Mrs L Sleator, BA Hons Goldsmiths, PGCE Greenwich
Head of LIV: Ms A Habib, BSc Hons Imperial, MSc UCL, PGCE
Head of Remove: Mr D Karamoutas, BA Hons, PGDE and Miss K Lamkin, BA Hons, MLitt, PGCE

Junior School:
Director of the Junior School: Mr J Denchfield, BA Hons, PGCE
Preliminary & EYFS Coordinator: Miss E Allan, BA, BEd, PGCE
Transition: Mrs Y Dhaliwal, BA, BEd, MEd
IB & KS1 Coordinator: Mrs M MacDonnell, BA, PGCE
Form Tutor IIB, Drama Coordinator, Senior Tutor: Mrs C Makhlouf, BEd Hons
Form Tutor IIA, Acting Assistant Director of the Junior School: Miss P Shingles, BA Hons, PGCE
Form Tutor III, Teaching and Learning Coordinator: Mr M Molero Segura ,BA Hons, PGCE
Head of III Form, Director of Outreach and Operations: Mrs L Kyle, BA, PGCE [maternity leave]

Queenswood School

Shepherd's Way, Brookmans Park, Hatfield, Hertfordshire AL9 6NS

Tel: 01707 602500
email: admissions@queenswood.org
website: www.queenswood.org
X/Twitter: @QueenswoodSch
Facebook: @QueenswoodSch
Instagram: @queenswoodschool
LinkedIn: /company/queenswood-school

See full entry in the **HMC** section, on **p. 265**.

Redmaids' High School

Westbury Road, Westbury-on-Trym, Bristol BS9 3AW

Tel: 0117 962 2641
email: admissions@redmaidshigh.co.uk
website: www.redmaidshigh.co.uk
X/Twitter: @RedmaidsHigh
Facebook: @redmaidshighschool
Instagram: @redmaidshigh
LinkedIn: /redmaids'-high-school

With a history dating back to 1634, we understand how valuable single-sex education can be in giving girls a great start in life. Supportive, inspirational staff, a progressive mind-set, excellent pastoral care and wide-ranging opportunities, mean we develop inspirational young women, who are fully equipped for whatever path they choose in life.

Our academic record is excellent and our students excel in a diverse range of subjects. But we are so much more than the sum of our exam results. By prioritising development of the whole girl, giving breadth and depth of knowledge and experience, as well as an international mindedness, we aim to equip girls to become the leaders of tomorrow.

Opportunities here extend far beyond the classroom. Girls are given the chance to become exceptional public speakers who excel in local and national competitions; future game-changing scientists, engineers and mathematicians; adventurers, who spend time caving, kayaking and competing in local and national sporting fixtures. We support and encourage them to be whoever they want to be.

We have the experience and expertise that enable our girls to shine whilst helping them understand the importance of curiosity, collaboration and possibility.

Our first-class facilities provide the very best learning environments, allowing girls to excel not only academically but also in sport, drama, art and music. Technology makes a central contribution to the way students work and learn – we use iPad technology in the classroom to create dynamic and independent learning environments. In addition, the international links developed over recent years and the thriving alumnae network are an integral part of the school and a hugely valuable asset for the students.

All this adds up to Redmaids' High School being one of the finest girls' schools in the UK for girls aged 7 to 18. The opportunities and facilities – combined with excellent teaching – equip young women with the skills and confidence to truly make their mark in today's world.

Character. The school provides a positive and purposeful learning environment where everything is focused on the girls; where there is no dilution of attention to their needs as young women; and where they are offered all the opportunities and hold all the responsibilities.

Facilities. The 12-acre site at Westbury-on-Trym, Bristol, just beyond the Clifton Downs, provides an inspirational backdrop for learning, with space for girls to relax and enjoy. The campus has a spacious, rural feel, despite being just a few miles from the city centre.

At the centre of the Senior School is Burfield House, built in the 19th century as a private family home. Today it houses classrooms, offices, the Pearson Library, Dining Hall and main school reception.

Redland Hall, opened in September 2017, provides a modern performance space and auditorium, complete with flexible seating, first-class lighting and acoustically engineered sound systems. It also houses new classrooms, additional music practice rooms and an area for serving refreshments at key school events.

The contemporary, self-contained Sixth Form Centre, opened in 2011, provides a university-style, independent learning space for Years 12 and 13.

Exceptional sports facilities are a hallmark of the school. There is an ethos of 'sport-for-all' balanced with elite competition. The recently redeveloped off-site sports ground, The Lawns at Cribbs Causeway, offers an International Hockey Federation certified pitch, a new multi-purpose area used for both netball and tennis and an extensive athletics, cricket and rounders space. On site at Westbury-on-Trym on our hockey pitches, netball courts and in our sports hall, girls take part in netball, basketball, fencing, judo, dance and gymnastics.

A detached former stable block is home to the music department, and includes teaching and rehearsal space. Students can also access specialist recording equipment and individual workstations with keyboards and Apple computers.

Six fully-equipped, modern laboratories provide everything the Science Department needs, while the Art Department has room to be creative with two large studio spaces, a computer suite and a library.

Extended Day. Senior girls can arrive from 7.30am and stay until 6.00pm, at no extra charge. Breakfast can be bought on an ad-hoc basis and supervised homework and extra-curricular activities take place until 5.30pm. Clubs and societies include: current affairs, choirs, orchestras, Harry Potter club, the Duke of Edinburgh's Award scheme, film production, drama and many sports clubs.

School Life. The School Council and Sixth Form leadership positions encourage students to take responsibility for others. Peer support systems, clubs run by older students and staff, and charitable fundraising demonstrate the pupils' involvement in their community. Assemblies celebrate pupils' all-round achievements, examine topical issues and offer opportunities for thought, reflection and spiritual exploration.

Curriculum. For the first three years, all Redmaids' High students follow a broad and balanced curriculum. Setting takes place in Mathematics from Year 7 and separate Sciences from Year 9. In Year 7, all girls study two languages chosen from French, German, Latin, Russian and Spanish. In Years 10 and 11, we select the best mix of qualifications from GCSE and IGCSE to prepare the girls for the next steps in their education.

Sixth Form. Redmaids' High offers Sixth Formers a wide range of A Levels. Students take three or four linear A Levels, with exams at the end of Year 13. Most girls enrich their A Level experience by taking an additional qualification such as an EPQ, Creative Writing course, an AS Level, or a Level 3 Food Science or Sports Leaders award.

Redmaids' High Sixth Formers enjoy the independence of a modern, purpose-built centre with dedicated teaching, seminar and common rooms, café, quiet study area, ICT facilities and careers library. Students achieve their full academic potential through high-quality teaching and developing habits of independent study and academic rigour. Whilst many students go on to study at university, including Oxbridge, we also assist students to access apprenticeships or plan a gap year. Sixth Formers take on many leadership roles within school and develop a broader understanding of the wider world through a varied community service programme. They also follow the Lighthouse Programme to prepare them for life beyond school and receive individual careers advice.

Fees per term (2023–2024). Years 7 to 13: £5,750. Curricular school trips are included in this fee. Lunch is compulsory for Years 7 to 11 and is invoiced termly. Other extras are individual music lessons, speech and drama lessons, optional non-academic trips, and any one-to-one tuition for those with individual needs.

Admission to Senior School. All students are admitted on the basis of an entrance examination, interview and headteacher's report. Key points of entry are at Year 7, 9 and 12. The entrance exam for Years 7 and 9 is held in January for admission the following September. Entry can take place into other years, subject to availability.

Scholarships. Scholarships are available to girls who show true potential, a dedication to learning and a lot of ambition in any subject. They are available for entry into Years 7, 9, 10 and 12 for both internal and external candidates. They may also be awarded to exceptional students entering at other stages.

Athena Development Grants. From September 2024, all students in Year 9 will be eligible to apply for a £250 Development Grant to support their personal development in a subject area of their choice. Students can reapply for a second grant in their Sixth Form.

Bursaries. The unique founding origins of Redmaids' High mean the school can offer a number of fully and partially funded places.

Junior School. *See Junior School entry in IAPS section.*

Charitable status. Redmaids' High School is a Registered Charity, number 1105017. It has existed since 1634 to provide an education for girls.

Governing Body:
Chairman: Mr Andrew Hillman
Vice-Chairman: Mrs Elizabeth Clarson and Mrs Rosemary Heald

Mrs Katie Atkins
Mr Richard Bacon
Mrs Perdita Davidson
Ms Sally Dore
Dr Bisola Ezobi
Dr Abdul Farooq
Mr James Fox
Mrs Elizabeth Fry
Mr Mike Henry
Mr Richard Page
Mrs Gillian Rowcliffe
Mrs Anne Taylor

Senior School:

***Head*: Mr Paul Dwyer**

Senior Deputy Head: Mrs Laura Beynon
Deputy Head: Ms Anya Peyton

Deputy Head, Staff and Operations: Mr Tom Johnston
Director of Sixth Form: Mrs Lisa Moyle
Assistant Head Learning and Enrichment: Dr Alice England
Assistant Head Pastoral: Ms Melissa Stimson

Director of Finance: Mr M Marshall
Director of Operations: Ms Alison Byrne

Junior School:
Headteacher: Mrs Lisa Brown

PA to Head: Mrs Hafwen Randle
PA to Directors of Finance and Operations: Mrs Susannah Wooldridge

Admissions Registrars:
Mrs Naomi Brady (*Juniors*)
Mrs Sarah Baker-Patch, Mrs Ali Wright & Mrs Antonia Firebrace (*Seniors and Sixth Form*)

RGS Dodderhill

Droitwich Spa, Worcestershire WR9 0BE

Tel: 01905 778290
email: dodderhill@rgsw.org.uk
website: www.dodderhill.co.uk
X/Twitter: @dodderhill
Facebook: @RGS-Dodderhill

Age range. 2–11 Co-educational, 11–16 Senior School for girls.

Number of pupils. 182.

Fees per term (2023–2024). £3,330–£5,598 including lunch and wraparound care.

Location. The school is set in its own grounds on the outskirts of Droitwich Spa and only minutes from the M5/M42 interchange. It serves families from Droitwich Spa, Bromsgrove and a wide area of North Worcestershire. Minibus transport is provided between school and Droitwich Spa station and many pupils take advantage of the excellent local rail network.

Curriculum and teaching. From Reception through to Year 3 emphasis is on literacy and numeracy and children are taught as a class group, with specialist input in ICT, French, Music, PE and DT. From Year 4 all subjects are specialist taught and in Year 5 and 6, increasing use is made of senior facilities to enhance learning opportunities. Throughout Years 7 and 8, in addition to the core subjects of English, Mathematics, Science, RE and PE, all girls learn French, Spanish, Geography, History, Art, Music and Textiles. Girls in Year 9 choose their GCSE options, for which all girls take English, Mathematics and Science (either triple award or dual award). There is a choice of modern languages, humanities and creative subjects. Class sizes are small, expectations are high, teachers are well qualified and experienced and the individual is paramount.

Extracurricular activities. The school offers a stimulating and diverse range of extracurricular opportunities. Creative Arts, Music, Outdoor Activities, including the Duke of Edinburgh Award and Sport are all catered for.

Scholarships. RGS Dodderhill awards three scholarships after the Entrance Examinations.

The Booker Scholarship – academic award for a current pupil moving to Year Seven, worth £1,000.

Price Scholarship – academic award for an external candidate entering Year Seven, worth the equivalent of one term's fees.

Davidson Music Scholarship – awarded to any girl entering the school in Year Seven, worth £1,000 a year. Please call the Registrar if you would like details of the audition requirements for the Music Scholarship.

Bursaries. The number of Bursaries varies each year according to need. If you do receive a means-tested award it will be reviewed annually to ensure that financial assistance is only given where there is real need.

We know it can feel uncomfortable discussing personal circumstances, which is why it is possible to go through the process without speaking to anyone. If you do have questions you'd like to discuss, please get in touch. We are well-versed in having sensitive conversations discreetly.

Charitable status. The Royal Grammar School Worcester is a Registered Charity, number 1120644.

Governors:
Mr A Robinson (*Chairman*)

Mr M Adams	Revd L Handy
Mr D Allchin	Mrs A Hines
Dr S Bowater	Mrs J E Lowe
Mrs J Cross	Mr J Ricketts
Mrs W Haines	Mrs K Wormington

***Headmaster*: Mr Thomas Banyard**

Roedean School

Roedean Way, Brighton, East Sussex BN2 5RQ

Tel: 01273 667500
email: admissions@roedean.co.uk
website: www.roedean.co.uk
X/Twitter: @RoedeanSchool
Facebook: @RoedeanSchool

See full entry in the **HMC** section, on **p. 279**.

Royal High School Bath GDST

Lansdown Road, Bath BA1 5SZ

Tel: 01225 313877
email: royalhigh@rhsb.gdst.net
website: www.royalhighbath.gdst.net
X/Twitter: @RoyalHighBath
Facebook: @TheRoyalHighSchoolBath
Instagram: @royalhighschoolbath
LinkedIn: /company/royal-high-school-bath

Royal High School Bath is a leading independent day and boarding school for **girls aged 3–18**. A pioneering girls' school founded well over a century ago with a clear remit to enable girls to learn without limits – this is as true today as it was when the School first opened.

Situated on the edge of the beautiful city of Bath and within striking distance of the M4 corridor to Bristol and London airports, Royal High School Bath is a great choice for UK based, expats and international families. Day students attend from surrounding towns and cities including Bristol, Swindon, Chippenham, Warminster, Frome, Wells, Stroud and Tetbury.

As part of the **GDST (Girls' Day School Trust)**, the leading network of independent girls' schools in the UK, Royal High School Bath has strong values – girls first, forward-thinking and fearless – providing an education which empowers girls to truly believe in themselves and value the contribution they will make on the world.

All of our lessons have been tailored to the way that girls learn. We have a long history of specialising in girls' education and are proud of our reputation as a kind, supportive and academically excellent school.

Led by an outstanding Head, our exceptional team of staff provides the support required to empower girls to truly believe in themselves and value their contribution to the wider school community, and in time, the wider world. Through innovative and creative teaching, and by focusing on the individual student, we provide the springboard girls need to develop a fearlessness for life – students leave us, ready for the world's challenges and equipped with skills for their future. We offer a broad range of subject options, ensuring our education is cutting-edge and forward-thinking. We also offer a wealth of super and extra-curricular opportunities and clubs for girls to challenge themselves beyond lessons.

Our staff are dedicated to supporting and inspiring each individual to aim high and achieve their very best. We achieve high grades, at both GCSE and A Level, with 40% of A Level students going on to study STEM subjects. The grades achieved by GDST students are 3.5% higher than the national average.

In the **Sixth Form**, students can choose either A Level or the International Baccalaureate Diploma Programme as their pathway to university. Students consistently achieve excellent grades and access to their first choice university in the UK and overseas. IB students regularly achieve well above the global average and, in 2023, achieved an average point score per student of 34.8 (5 points higher than the global average).

As the only **boarding** school in the GDST group, Royal High School Bath offers homely and stylish modern living for girls in Years 7–11 and in the separate Sixth Form boarding house. Our boarding houses are home to girls from across the world – we are very proud to be multi-cultural. Our diversity means our students learn about different cultures and live in a thriving, international community before embarking on their journey into the adult world. Our evening and weekend activities enable girls to bond, share new experiences and, of course, have a lot of fun. We encourage boarding girls to try new experiences – particularly to step outside of their comfort zone in a safe, supportive environment.

Above all, we balance academic excellence with strong pastoral care for every student, from the very youngest child in our Nursery through to the impressive young women who are our Sixth Formers. We provide a nurturing environment where students are known and can flourish, becoming confident and stronger emotionally. Girls are supported to be the best they can be today and in their lives beyond school, equipped to take on life's challenges as they leave a positive mark on the world. Here, our girls' energy and determination, yet down to earth groundedness, makes for a very special school.

Number of Pupils. 600.

Admissions. Please contact our friendly Admission Team who will offer your family a warm welcome and guide you through each step of the journey, from your initial enquiry and the assessment process, right through to admission and your daughter's first day of School. For more information, please visit: www.royalhighbath.gdst.net/admissions.

Fees per term (2023–2024). Full Boarding: £11,965–£12,577; Weekly Boarding: £10,699–£11,305; Day: £3,898–£5,526. Lunch: £244–£299 (lunch fee for day students only). Flexi boarding is available.

Scholarships & Bursaries. Scholarships are awarded to girls with exceptional academic potential as well as those with a particular gift for Music, Dance, Drama, Sport, Art and Design Technology. For more information, please visit: www.royalhighbath.gdst.net/admissions/scholarship-opportunities.

If your daughter would benefit from a Girls' Day School Trust (GDST) education, but your family is not in a position to cover the full fees, you may be eligible for a Bursary. Means-tested awards are given at Year 7, Year 9 and for entry into the Sixth Form to students who demonstrate outstanding all-round academic ability. Please refer to the website for more information: www.royalhighbath.gdst.net/admissions/financial-support.

Charitable status. The Royal High School Bath is part of The Girls' Day School Trust, which is a Registered Charity, number 306983.

Chair of Governors: Mr Richard Hall, BSc Hons

***Head*: Mrs Kate Reynolds**, LLB, PGCE

Deputy Head – Academic: Mr Hadrian Briggs, MA, PGCE

Deputy Head – Pastoral: Mrs Elizabeth Cunningham, MA Oxon, PGCE

Acting Deputy Head – Curriculum: Mr James Moyle, BSc, PGCE

Head of Sixth Form: Mr Luke Benedict, BA Hons, PGCE

Head of Prep School: Mrs Claire Lilley, BEd Hons

Head of Boarding: Mrs Emma Custodio, BA, PGCE

Director of Admissions and Marketing: Mrs Sallie Taylor

Director of Finance and Operations: Mrs Ellen Wilson, BSc Hons

The Royal Masonic School for Girls

Rickmansworth Park, Rickmansworth, Herts WD3 4HF
Tel: 01923 773168
email: admissions@rmsforgirls.com
website: www.rmsforgirls.com
X/Twitter: @RMSforGirls
Facebook: @RMSforGirls
Instagram: @RMSforGirls
LinkedIn: /school/rmsforgirls

See full entry in the **HMC** section, on **p. 289**.

St Augustine's Priory School

Hillcrest Road, Ealing, London W5 2JL
Tel: 020 8997 2022
email: admissions@sapriory.com
website: www.sapriory.com
X/Twitter: @staugustinesp
Facebook: @StAugustine's_Priory
Instagram: @st.augustines.priory
LinkedIn: /st-augustine-s-priory

Motto: *Veritas*

St Augustine's Priory is a Catholic, independent day school for girls aged 3–18 and also welcomes boys in the nursery.

Our school empowers pupils to embrace a love of learning, while exploring alternative ways of thinking and achieving outstanding results. Students thrive in an environment which has a strong focus on academic excellence and pastoral support. Girls benefit from an outstanding setting with 13 acres of unique space, which includes a working farm and impressive sports facilities. Staff are at the forefront of research-based approaches, using different platforms to inspire and engage students.

Our vision is for girls to leave St Augustine's equipped with an outstanding academic education and also with the full range of skills required to lead an effective and fulfilling life as women. As part of their journey, in a girls' school environment, they will acquire the skills of self-knowledge, of reflection, of intellectual risk-taking, of persuasiveness and team-building and of emotional strength as well as a cultural fabric for their enriched enjoyment of life. Our team of dedicated and enthusiastic teachers, teaching assistants and support staff care for the girls and encourage them in all aspects of their education and development. We believe 'Our girls will change the world'.

The school was founded in France in 1634 by Lady Mary Tredway to provide a haven where young English women could be provided with an independent education. Moving to Ealing in 1914–15, the school follows the philosophy expounded by its Patron, St Augustine of Hippo: children (and for that matter adults) achieve their best when they are happy.

Number of Pupils. There are approximately 480 girls aged from 3–18 across the school.

Location. The School is well served by public transport, with Central and Piccadilly line connections within a ten-minute stroll, Ealing Broadway Underground and main line station approximately 20 minutes' walk away and buses stopping nearby. The School sits in an idyllic setting of thirteen acres.

Admission. St Augustine's Priory is a unique and vibrant community; the best way to understand it is to come and look around the school and meet the pupils, Headteacher and staff. During the application process we invite Parents to visit us on Open Morning during the Michaelmas and Lent Terms and you are also warmly invited to visit the school for a private appointment at other times.

St Augustine's Priory operates a selective entry procedure. Selection is based upon academic merit and potential, which is assessed through an entry examination, an interview at the school and references from the candidate's previous school. Our selection process is designed to identify pupils who are able to benefit from our balanced and well-rounded education and to make a positive contribution towards the life of the school. Admission to the Prep is via interview and assessment in the Michaelmas Term. Girls in the Junior School move up seamlessly into the Senior School. External candidates for 9+, 11+, and 16+ sit entrance examinations on our various Selection Days in the Lent Term.

Those wishing to join the Sixth Form are invited to visit the school and meet with the Director of Sixth Form. Interviews are then conducted by the appropriate Heads of Department along with the Headteacher and offers are sent out with conditional GCSE pass requirements.

Faith. St Augustine's Priory is a Catholic Independent Day School for Girls. The Chapel is at the heart of school life and is used for assemblies, weekly Masses and as a place for moments of quiet reflection and prayer. We also welcome girls from other religions and faiths and learn from them.

Pastoral Care. Children from all backgrounds and all races, with a wide range of gifts, make up the community which is St Augustine's Priory. From their first day, girls become part of a community which respects the beliefs and customs of its members and learns to work together. When problems arise and questions need to be asked, we encourage a very personal approach.

Curriculum. We offer an extensive and balanced curriculum including PSHEE, and offer 20 subjects at GCSE and IGCSE and 24 subjects at AS and A2 Level. Girls will usually take ten or more subjects at GCSE.

Priory 6 (Sixth Form) and Careers. Priory 6 facilities include a common room, ICT suite, kitchen and balcony.

We expect girls to think about their next steps and to make informed decisions at every stage of their development. Priory 6 students are supported by the Careers Coordinator and Head of UCAS who provide advice and guidance. We work with the students to consider their many future options, assisting with university and course selection, preparation for Oxbridge and other university applications and subsequent interviews. This process is supplemented by a fortnightly programme of guest speakers and a biennial Careers Evening.

Working with Form Tutors and the Director of Priory 6, every girl is expected to examine her own strengths and to explore possibilities suitable for her interests and personal abilities. Talks, conferences, seminars, courses and University Open Days allow all our students to keep abreast of opportunities on offer.

All of this support builds on the guidance received throughout the school. When our girls leave here for university, they take with them not only impressive qualifications but also kindness, an understanding of, and the ability to adapt to, the world in which they live, the confidence to succeed in whatever they choose to do and above all, friendships which will last them through life.

Co-curricular Activities. A wide variety of co-curricular activities aim to ensure spiritual, moral, social and cultural development of all pupils, and to enable students to develop their talents to the full by searching for excellence. Girls will develop and practise new skills, integrate with children across year groups and be challenged and encouraged to take risks. Clubs on offer include ballet, gymnastics, fencing, yoga, life drawing, cake decorating, photography, Cipher & ink illustration and Poetry. The school excels in its extremely popular sports activities fielding winning teams in hockey, netball, swimming and cross country.

Whilst Drama forms part of the curriculum we also stage a biennial major production in the Spring at Questors Theatre, which allows involvement by the whole Senior School. We offer LAMDA, qualifications in Acting, Speaking Verse and Prose and Speaking in Public. A Musical Theatre & Drama club is run for Preps.

Music flourishes throughout the school with girls taking part in school orchestras, ensembles, choirs and concerts. A wide range of private musical instrument lessons are also on offer.

Art is outstanding and the girls' work is displayed throughout the school. An annual Art Exhibition is held each summer and is open to the public, and the department makes use of visits to the many theatres, museums and galleries in London.

A majority of girls complete The Duke of Edinburgh's Bronze, Silver and Gold Awards. Visits to Iceland, New York and Salamanca enrich Modern Foreign Languages and Geography learning, as well as History visits to Berlin, sports tours to Paris and Holland and ski trips to Italy and Canada.

Facilities. St Augustine's Priory offers superb amenities including a full-size floodlit all-weather astroturf pitch, floodlit competition-sized netball court and indoor sports hall set in stunning 13-acre grounds. A Chapel and School Hall complete with acoustics and sound-proofing.

In addition to sporting facilities, our 13 acres include a dedicated Prep meadow, orchards, Sixth Form Rose Garden, outdoor stage and Priory Farm which homes chickens, ducks and sheep. The state-of-the-art Science Wing has four laboratories and dedicated Senior and Prep music and drama rooms. To complement this there are two IT suites, music practice rooms, a Nursery block, Senior and Prep Art rooms, a Sixth Form Art studio and separate photography studio, Modern Languages Academy, dedicated Sixth Form areas, private studies and seminar rooms, and Scriptorium. Breakfast and After School Clubs are available, with Holiday Club Provision available courtesy of Camp Beaumont during Half-terms, Easter & Summer Holidays. Kitchens are on site and the Chef and catering staff serve fresh cooked lunches daily.

Fees per term (2023–2024). Nursery from £2,158 (5 mornings/afternoons + 15 free hours); Pre Preps from £4,092 (full time + 15 free hours); Preparatory Department £5,475; Senior Department £6,555.

Additional information may be found on the school's website and a more detailed prospectus may be obtained from the School.

Charitable status. St Augustine's Priory School Limited is a Registered Charity, number 1097781.

Board of Governors:
Mr P D'Arcy (*Chair*)
Mr R Beeston (*Chair of Finance & Capital Projects Committee*)
Miss M Bowler
Mr S Bristow
Mr B Cassidy (*Chair of Academic Committee*)
Mr J Davies (*Chair of Safeguarding Committee*)
Mrs J Job
Dr B Marino
Mrs A Sparks
Mr F Steadman
Mr J Philpott (*Clerk to the Governors*)

Senior Leadership Team:

***Headteacher*: Mrs C Macallister**, BA ACA ALCM, PGCE

Deputy Head (*Pastoral*) *Seniors*: Mrs A Lenton,
Deputy Head (*Academic*) *Seniors*: Mr P McCarthy
Assistant Head (*Co-Curricular*), *Head of Year Upper School & Deputy Director of Priory Sixth*: Ms L Hales
Deputy Head Preps & Pre-Preps: Olivia McLoughlin
Director of Priory 6 & UCAS: Mrs H Maclennan, MA Cantab, MEd

Bursar: Mr J Philpott, BA, MA
Registrar and Head of Communications: Mrs G Savic, BA
Director of Operations & Exams Officer: Miss L Masih, BSc, CSBMs

Welfare Staff:
School Nurse: Mrs R Finnegan, RGN
Counsellor and Play Therapist Consultant: Mrs R Good, BSc, PGCE, Dip Therapeutic Counselling

Key Administration Staff:
Mrs K Bhatti, MSc Econ, ACLIP, DipLis (*Librarian*)
Ms N Chandler (*PA to the Bursar & HR Officer*)
Miss L Naylor, MAAT (*School Office Manager, Finance and Examinations Assistant*)
Mrs T Sumpter, RGN, AMSPAR (*PA to the Headteacher*)
Mrs G Vymeris, MA (*Assistant Bursar*)

St Catherine's School
Bramley

Station Road, Bramley, Guildford, Surrey GU5 0DF
Tel: 01483 893363
email: schooloffice@stcatherines.info
admissions@stcatherines.info
website: www.stcatherines.info
X/Twitter: @stcatsbramley
Facebook: @StCatherinesBramley
Instagram: @stcatsbramley

Founded as a Church of England School for Girls in 1885, welcoming both day girls and boarders, St Catherine's is one of the UK's premier girls' schools. St Catherine's is situated in the heart of the attractive Surrey village of Bramley, three miles south of Guildford which has a mainline station (Waterloo 35 minutes). The school operates a home to school transport system which is managed by Zeelo. There is easy access to Heathrow and Gatwick and travel arrangements are made for overseas boarders. Close proximity to London allows frequent visits to theatres and galleries and the miles of countryside on our doorstep is an asset to the many girls who take part in The Duke of Edinburgh's Award scheme.

In The ISI Report, October 2016, we were pleased to receive '*Excellent*' in all three focus areas. Wherever the Inspectors visited from PP1 (Reception) to the U6, and from Day to Boarding, they encountered girls and staff who were proud to represent St Catherine's. A recurring theme of the Report was the close teamwork between the girls and their teachers. '*Pupils attitude to learning are exemplary. Teachers create an ambience of encouragement in which learning thrives*'.

Exam Results. Superb examination results are testament to the quality of teaching and learning, where students are not afraid to show enthusiasm and ambition. Lessons are taught in well-appointed classrooms by subject specialists. In 2023, 87% of girls achieved A*–B at A Level and 88% achieved Grades 9–7 at GCSE.

The outstanding results gained by our students in public examinations secure them places at the top universities, in competitive disciplines like medicine and veterinary science, law and languages. This success comes not only as a result of the fine quality of the teaching, but is also due to the individual attention received by every girl. St Catherine's places great emphasis on creating a happy environment where every girl is encouraged to work hard to maximise her talents. The atmosphere is friendly and one in which children can develop and grow in a very stimulating environment.

School Structure. A well-established House system underpins the whole School, allowing new girls to feel at home very quickly, encouraging an ethos of care and concern for others as well as a friendly competitive spirit.

Pivotal to the life of St Catherine's are the six school Houses. The girls' loyalty and affection for their Houses is impressive with memories of inter-house plays, competitions and matches enduring long after School days have ended.

A broad and varied curriculum allows all pupils to participate in many challenging and rewarding extracurricular activities. As a Church of England School girls are encouraged to think of others and impressive sums of money are raised for charity each year. The School has its own beautiful chapel which is used by the girls on a daily basis.

Activities Week is held each year in the Summer Term when every girl in the School participates in a variety of programmes organised to both support the curriculum and offer challenges not normally met in the classroom. Pupils participate in outward bound ventures, such as modern language courses in France, Germany and Spain, whilst Sixth Formers focus on university choices. Activities Week costs are included in the fees.

International links are also very important. St Catherine's has an exchange programme with St Catherine's Melbourne, Australia and there are also links with schools in Kenya, South Africa and Lebanon.

Facilities. With extensive playing fields, superb sports facilities and an auditorium which boasts better acoustics than many London venues, it is no surprise that St Catherine's is always buzzing with life after the teaching day is over.

Facilities include 3 lacrosse pitches, a multi-purpose sports hall, fitness suite and indoor pool. The auditorium provides superb acoustics for our musical and theatrical productions. The Sixth Form girls have their own Library which provides a perfect study environment right at the heart of the School. The Anniversary Halls and the Speech Hall Library were officially opened by the School's patron, Her Majesty the Queen Consort; the first Baron Ashcombe, her Majesty's Great-Great Grandfather was one of the original founders and benefactors of St Catherine's.

The successful completion of The 6, a Sixth Form centre, now offers modern boarding accommodation and a contemporary Common Room for day girls and boarders alike. Opened in 2022 is our fabulous creative art facility with Design & Technology Studios, two Textile Studios, a Photographic Studio with Dark Room and a 'MasterChef' style Culinary Art studio. A new science and digital learning space is being planned.

The School's flexible approach to boarding makes it increasingly attractive to busy, professional families; the ISI team picked out boarding as one of the outstanding features of St Catherine's. The School welcomes both weekly and full boarders who enjoy a busy and exciting programme. The Four cornerstones of boarding at St Catherine's are: Expert care from experienced and highly trained boarding staff; a huge raft of on-site activities with superb facilities; a friendly and welcoming community; and, last but not least, boarding at St Catherine's represents excellent value for money.

Enrichment Opportunities. St Catherine's has an unrivalled reputation in art, music, sport and drama; photography and Design Technology are popular options amongst the Sixth Form, and younger girls are encouraged by an enthusiastic Art and Design department to take advantage of the superb facilities, and join many after-school clubs.

Music is an important feature of school life, with numerous choirs, orchestras and concert bands rehearsing each week and performing regularly. There are in excess of 550 individual music lessons taking place each week where over half the girls learn to play a musical instrument. There are flute choirs, string quartets, recorder groups and ensembles to cater for all levels of ability. Concerts and recitals are held regularly. There is the Jennifer Bate Organ Academy and the Jennifer Bate Memorial Organ Scholarship in conjunction with Guildford Cathedral. The School boasts two organs, one in the School Chapel and a second in the Preparatory School.

Drama and Theatre Studies are extremely popular options; girls are encouraged to audition for the annual middle and senior school plays. As well as acting opportunities, pupils are also offered the opportunity to help backstage and front of house and learn many valuable skills as a result. LAMDA classes are offered to all year groups. St Catherine's also has its own very popular School of Dance.

Given the School's outstanding sports facilities it is perhaps no surprise that many girls go on to represent their county in netball, lacrosse, swimming, squash and athletics. Every girl is encouraged to take part in sport at school, whatever her level of expertise. The PE Department regularly fields four or five teams for lacrosse and netball, allowing every girl who wishes to play competitively the opportunity to do so.

The Prep School. Most girls join at 4 with a limited number of places available in other years. It aims to support families in helping younger pupils develop a strong sense of values, high standards of behaviour and consideration to others, as well as achieving excellent academic success. The girls benefit from specialist teaching, combining the best of traditional methods with modern technology to prepare them for the Entrance Examinations to all Senior Schools at 11+, including St Catherine's.

Fees per term (2023–2024). (From December 2023) Day Girls: £4,140 (Pre-Prep 1), £4,420 (Pre-Prep 2), £5,225 (Pre-Prep 3), £6,165 (Prep School), £7,465 (Senior School).

Boarders: Middle and Senior Boarding and Tuition £12,650.

Fees include the Activities Week programme for Senior School girls and lunches for all pupils aged 4–18.

Entry. This is by Entrance Examination held in November. The Prep School also holds its own entrance assessments in October.

Scholarships and Bursaries.

11+ (Year 7): There are four Academic Entrance Scholarships available for pupils at age 11. These are awarded on the results of the Entrance Examination. Two scholarships are for 20% of the fees payable and the other two are for 10% of the fees. These are for the first five years of Senior School and are extended through the Sixth Form at the discretion of the Headmistress and in consultation with the teaching staff.

Upper 5 and Sixth Form (Year 11): The following scholarships are awarded during the Summer Term to pupils already in the School in the L5 (Year 10) and in the Autumn Term U5 (Year 11). Selection for the awards is based on the results of the June examinations at the end of the L5, performance throughout the L5 year and a rigorous panel interview.

The available Sixth Form Scholarships are:

- *Margaret Kaye Scholarships:* These are scholarships of 20% of the fees payable to run for three years, through U5 (Year 11) and the Sixth Form.
- *Sixth Form Scholarships:* These are scholarships of 10% or 20% of fees. The number can be extended depending on the performance of the candidates and the recommendations of the awarding panel.
- *The Sixth Form Music Scholarship:* There are two Music Scholarships. One, to the value of 20% of the School fees is awarded during the Autumn Term of U5 to a girl who intends to study Music A Level alongside her practical music-making. The second is to the value of 10% of the School Fees and is awarded to a girl who makes a significant contribution to School music-making but will not take Music A Level.
- *The Sixth Form Art and Textiles Scholarship:* There is an Art and Textiles Scholarship to the value of 20% of the School Fees, awarded during the Autumn Term of U5 (Year 11).
- *The Sixth Form Drama Scholarship:* There is a Drama Scholarship to the value of 20% of the School Fees, awarded during the Autumn Term of U5.
- *The Clare Gregory Memorial Sports Scholarship:* This is awarded for sporting prowess and is for 20% of the day fees in the Sixth Form and is awarded internally at the end of the Spring Term in U5.
- *Scholarships for New Entrants to the Sixth Form:* There are up to three external academic, Art/Textiles and Music scholarships of up to 20% of fees and these are awarded at the discretion of the Headmistress, to new pupils joining the School in the Sixth Form. The Art/Textiles and Music scholarships are conditional upon the applicant studying Art/Textiles or Music A Level.

Music Scholarships and Awards:

An 11+ Music Scholarship of 20% of the fees and tuition on one instrument, with music and exam entry fees paid, may be awarded annually upon entry to an 11+ candidate judged by the Director of Music and an adjudication panel to have strong musical talent. A second Music Scholarship of 10% of fees and tuition on one instrument can be awarded in years where the field of applicants is particularly strong. Applications should be made by November and auditions are in January. There is an expectation that the successful candidates will take Music GCSE and A Level.

Jennifer Bate Memorial Organ Scholarship is offered in conjunction with Guildford Cathedral to a girl who is already a good organist or shows potential. This award is typically for 20% of fees payable and includes tuition on the organ and one other instrument, with music and exam entry fees. It may also involve a Bursary/Help with Fees if appropriate. Ideally, Jennifer Bate Memorial Organ Scholars are boarders who can take a full part in the Boarders' Evening Chapel Service each week.

Further Music Awards which cover music tuition, exam fees and sheet music on a range of musical instruments including chapel organ and voice are available to pupils in the Senior School. Some are specifically for those wanting to take up instruments which tend not to be the popular choice of most students, but which contribute greatly to the impact and success of the School's musical ensembles. e.g. euphonium, double bass, viola, bassoon, French horn, tuba. Auditions for Awards take place at the same time as Music Scholarship auditions.

Bursaries/Help with Fees: The School offers a number of means-tested places to girls at age 7 (Year 3), age 11 (Year 7) and at Sixth Form entry. Help can be provided for up to 100% of the fees.

For further information about any of the above Scholarships/Awards/Bursaries, please contact the Senior School Registrar or see www.stcatherines.info/admissions/bursaries-and-scholarships

Charitable status. St Catherine's School Bramley is a Registered Charity, number 1070858. It exists to provide education for girls in accordance with the principles of the Church of England.

Governing Body:
Chairman: Brigadier M P Lowe, MBE, MA, RCDS
A Alonzo Esq, BSc, PhD
J Blauth Esq, BA, FRSA, MCMI, MRAeS
Prof F Cotter, MBBS, FRCP[UK], FRCPath, FRCP[I], PhD
Mrs P Crouch, LLB
Mrs K Farrell
Mrs C Good
Mrs H Hounsell
Mrs C S Johnstone, MRCS, LRCP, MBBS, MD, FRCP
Dr J McGowan, MBBS, FRCA
Mrs Lynn Narraway
A Pianca Esq, FCA
Mrs Veronica Povey, CBE, FCMA
Mrs S E Shipway
J C M Tippett Esq, BSc, FCA, TEP
D Ulyet Esq, BSc
The Rt Revd Paul Davies
Mr Stuart Hawkes, BSc Hons, FRICS

***Headmistress*: Mrs Alice Phillips**, MA Cantab
Senior Boarding Housemistress: Mrs Helen Harkness
Director of Studies: Dr Elodie Nevin, MA Oxon, PhD, QTS
Senior Housemistress: Mrs Kirsty Meredith, BA Hons London, AKC, PGCE
Director of Staff: Mrs Claire Wyllie, MA Dunelm, PGCE
Head of Sixth Form: Mrs Kate Hawtin
School Administrator: Mrs Sheila Kelsall, MA Open, BSc Hons Open, PGCE
Head of Prep School: Miss Naomi Bartholomew, MA London, BEd Cantab, QTS, MA London
Deputy Heads – Curriculum: Mr Matthew Parry, BSc, MSc Wales, PGCE
Deputy Head – Pre-Prep: Miss Emily Jefford
Deputy Head – Staff: Mrs Wendy Gibbs, BEd Hons Winchester

Administration:
Senior School Registrar: Mrs Clare Woodgates
Prep School Registrar: Mrs Sarah Waller
Marketing Director: Ms Pippa Carte, BD, MA
PA to the Headmistress: Miss Toppy Wharton

St Catherine's School

Twickenham

Cross Deep, Twickenham, Middlesex TW1 4QJ
Tel: 020 8891 2898
email: admissions@stcatherineschool.co.uk
website: www.stcatherineschool.co.uk
X/Twitter: @stcatherinessch
Facebook: @stcatherinessch

Motto: *Not Words But Deeds*

Age range. Girls 7–18 years.

Number in school. Approx. 440 Day Girls.

St Catherine's is a Catholic School which warmly welcomes girls of all faiths.

Aims. We are proud of our Catholic ethos, which informs our commitment to a values-based education that builds character and confidence. Our broad and exciting curricular and co-curricular programmes operate within a friendly and supportive environment which encourages and challenges girls to strive to be the best they can be. Emphasis is placed on care and respect for others, self-discipline, and the nurturing of both leadership skills and the compassion to serve. Staff know the pupils as individuals and there is a strong sense of community which promotes academic success and creates a happy, purposeful school.

Situation. The school enjoys an enviable position, located next to the River Thames. It is a short distance from the centre of Twickenham and a short walk from Strawberry Hill and Twickenham Stations. Both have regular services to London (Waterloo), Surrey, Berkshire and Middlesex. There are also a number of local bus routes.

Entrance. The main point of entry is at age 11 and 16 but girls, especially those seeking a Prep place, are accepted at any stage, subject to availability. Places at the school are usually awarded on the basis of an interview, a report and reference from the candidate's previous school and an assessment or examination, depending on the pupil's age.

Scholarships and bursaries. Academic scholarships are awarded annually for Year 3, Year 7 and for Sixth form. Art, Drama, Music and Sport scholarships are also awarded annually following an audition/assessment and are conditional on the applicant achieving the school's academic requirement for entry. The Siena scholarship is an all-rounder scholarship awarded for Years 3–6 and Years 10–13.

A limited number of means-tested bursaries for Senior School pupils are offered depending on need and funds available.

Curriculum. In the Senior School, pupils follow courses in English, Mathematics, Biology, Chemistry, Physics, Religious Education, French, German, Spanish, History, Geography, Drama, Music, Art, Food and Nutrition, Computing and Physical Education. All of these subjects are offered at GCSE, when most pupils study ten subjects. All of the above subjects are available at A Level, with the addition of Politics, Graphics, Further Mathematics, Economics, Psychology, Photography, Sociology and Textiles.

There is a strong commitment to Sport, Music, Drama and co-curricular activities. The school has its own hockey pitch and indoor swimming pool as well as tennis and netball courts. Sports include swimming, netball, athletics, hockey, tennis, gymnastics, trampolining and rounders and our pupils achieve considerable success at county, regional and national level.

Music plays an important part in the life of the school; all pupils are encouraged to participate in choirs, orchestras and ensembles, and there is a varied programme of concerts and informal performances each term.

Drama is popular and, as well as opportunities to perform in school productions, regular theatre visits take place during the year.

Buildings. The Prep and Senior schools are on one site. The buildings include a large multi-purpose hall as well as a smaller assembly hall, attractive Prep and Senior Libraries, ICT Suites, spacious Art and Photography Suites and a Food and Nutrition Room. The Music Centre includes classrooms and individual practice rooms. There are fully equipped laboratories for Physics, Chemistry and Biology. A large programme of new building has recently added extra teaching blocks, a Sixth Form Centre, Drama Studio, Fitness Suite and a Chaplaincy Room, and further development is planned.

Co-curricular activities. These play a significant role in the life of the school. Activities include the Duke of Edinburgh's Award scheme, Badminton, Science Club, Football, Rugby, Rowing, Cross-Country Running, Zumba, Chess and Photography. Trips, both locally and abroad, add to the extensive range of activities on offer. Pupils also take part in community service and fundraising activities.

Fees per term (2023–2024). Inclusive of lunch: Years 1 and 2 £4,670; Years 3 to 6 £4,930; Years 7 to 13 £5,970 (excluding examination fees).

Charitable status. St Catherine's School, Twickenham is a Registered Charity, number 1014651. It aims to provide for children seeking education in a Christian environment.

Chair of Governors: Ms Sylvia Hamilton

***Headmistress*: Mrs Johneen McPherson**

Senior Deputy Head: Mrs Allison Saunders

Bursar & Clerk to the Governors: Mr Johnny Hughes

Admissions Manager: Mrs Julie Harris

St Gabriel's

Sandleford Priory, Newbury, Berkshire RG20 9BD

Tel: 01635 555680
email: admissions@stgabriels.co.uk
website: www.stgabriels.co.uk
X/Twitter: @StGabrielsNews
Facebook: @stgabrielsnewbury
Instagram: @stgabrielsnews
LinkedIn: /company/st-gabriel's-newbury

See full entry in the **Society of Heads** section, on **p. 558**.

St George's, Ascot

St George's School, Wells Lane, Ascot, Berks SL5 7DZ

Tel: 01344 629900
email: office@stgeorges-ascot.org.uk
website: www.stgeorges-ascot.org.uk
X/Twitter: @stgeorgesascot
Facebook: @StGeorgesSchoolAscot
Instagram: @stgeorgesascot
LinkedIn: /school/stgeorges-ascot

St George's, Ascot, is a thriving independent boarding and day school, offering an ambitious, connected and future-facing education for girls aged 11–18. Awarded 'excellent' in its November 2022 ISI inspection, the report speaks of:

'*Young women who demonstrate healthy self-knowledge, well-developed study skills, first-class social skills and an awareness of the world around them.*'

The St George's ethos, and education, focuses on developing Confident, Capable and Connected young women who are thoroughly prepared for the world beyond school. Learning in an all-girls environment fosters confidence as girls are emboldened to innovate, lead and express informed views free from gender stereotypes. They are, as a recent Head Girl explained, at '*the centre of their own story*' throughout their time at the school. They grow in capability as they are exposed to a wide range of opportunities both inside and outside of the classroom, developing excellence in academic, sporting, musical, dramatic and creative pursuits. Throughout their time at St George's pupils are encouraged to connect inwardly and across the diverse school community but also with the world around them and so they develop a strong sense of what they want to bring to and how they will challenge the society they will ultimately join.

Connection has been the particular focus of 2023, as the School celebrates one hundred years of excellence in girls' education since the school was purchased by Miss Anne Loveday. The school community is not only celebrating the progress made in women's education at St George's during this time, but is also looking to build towards a 'connected' future.

Pupils enjoy facilities that '*might easily belong to a school three times the size*' (2023 Good Schools Guide review), and yet the school is small enough to develop markedly strong relationships across the community. Each pupil is individually known and supported by a close network of boarding, teaching and pastoral staff who help shape and develop individual capabilities and aspirations. Examination results are excellent with regular Oxbridge success, a high percentage attending Russell Group universities and a strong number of girls choosing post-18 options in the Arts in courses ranging from visual effects, fine art, textiles and fashion to photography. The most recent value added figure for the school at GCSE placed St George's 7th out of 344 schools using a Cambridge University measure and 72% of the 2022 Upper Sixth achieved A*–B at A Level.

The school is set in 30 acres of beautiful grounds a stone's throw from the world-famous Ascot racecourse and Windsor Great Park, and less than 25 miles from London. Boarding is homely and comfortable, and an experienced team of House Staff organise an array of evening and weekend trips and excursions ranging from theatre and museum visits to 'clip and climb' and trampoline centres, as well as the frequent boarders' fire-pit nights with pizza hot from the school's Ooni ovens. All year groups also have the opportunity to regularly mix with other young people at Eton College, Winchester, and Harrow. The school is renownedly welcoming and openly celebrates the diversity and global span of its pupil body. The boarding community encapsulates the friendliness, warmth and familial nature of the school perfectly as the ISI report from November 2022 noted:

'*There is compelling evidence that pupils are inclusive of those from different backgrounds. Pupils are proud of their relationships with one another, and this extends beyond the school to their eagerness to understand the cultures and plights of others around the world. Pupils are tolerant and sensitive to the needs of others and empathise with those in varied scenarios.*'

Curriculum. Our future-facing academic curriculum is broad, balanced and contemporary and focuses on the individual talents and interests of each pupil as she progresses through the school, with the Sixth Form providing a flagship centre of excellence. Small class sizes and strong teacher-pupil relationships stretch the most able whilst allowing for individual support where required. The early adoption of innovative educational technology makes St George's a leader in this field, as evidenced by Google for Education Reference School status. St George's has a strong reputation for entry into the most academically competitive and demanding university courses and specialist creative arts, drama and music colleges alongside exciting and versatile apprenticeships and employment opportunities.

All Sixth Form pupils take the Extended Project Qualifications in addition to the recommended three A Levels, with the most recent cohort of A Level pupils achieving 47% A–A* grades.

Entrance. Entry at 11+ is by our own assessment. A reference from the current school, combined English and Mathematics examination and an online CEM (Centre for Evaluation and Monitoring) test, together with a short presentation and interview with a senior member of staff take place in the November of Year 6. For entry at 12+/13+, testing also takes place in the November preceding entry and applicants will sit papers in English, Mathematics, Science and an online CEM test. Girls will also make a short presentation and have an interview with a senior member of staff.

Girls considering an application to the Sixth Form will be invited for an interview with the Head of Sixth Form or another senior member of staff. Any offer of a place made will be contingent on meeting our minimum admissions criteria of achieving at least six, 9 to 4 grades at GCSE, with at least a 6 in any subject to be taken at A Level. A wide range of scholarships are available at 11+, 13+ and 16+.

Fees per term (2023–2024). £14,285 Boarding, £8,980 Day. Tailored flexi boarding is available.

Scholarships. Scholarships are available at 11+, 13+ and 16+ for outstanding potential, as evidenced by examination results. Academic, Art, Performing Arts, Sport, Swimming, Music and All Round scholarships and instrumental awards are available at 11+, and Academic Art, Music, Drama, Performing Arts, Swimming, All Round and Sport scholarships at 13+ and 16+.

Governors:
Mr A Mackintosh, BSc Aberdeen, MBA City (*Chair*)
[1]Dr J M Gibbons, BA, MPhil, DPhil
[2]Mr P James
[2]Mr E Luker, FRICS
[1]Mr A Miles, BSc Durham, PGCE
[2]Mrs R E S Niven Hirst, BArch Newcastle, RIBA [OG]
[2]Mr P Sedgwick, MCSI
[2]Mrs K Trueman Alexander, BA Exeter, MLitt Christie's [OG]
[2]Mrs A Felix, BA Bristol
[1]Mr J Pym, BA, MEd
[1]Member of Education sub-committee
[2]Member of Finance and Marketing sub-committee

***Head*: Mrs E M Hewer**, MA Cantab, PGCE

Bursar and Clerk to the Governors: Mr J F Anderson
Deputy Head Academic: Mr J V Hoar, BA Hull, PGCE
Deputy Head Pastoral/Designated Safeguarding Lead: Mrs H L Simpson, BA Ed Exeter
Deputy Head Co-Curricular and Connections/Deputy Designated Safeguarding Lead: Mr A J Wright, MA Oxon, MA London, PGCE

Teaching staff:
* Head of Department

Art, Textiles, Photography:
*Miss O Antolik, BA Kingston, PGCE
Ms K Gilbert, BA Chichester, PGCE
Mrs A Morgan, BA Dundee, PGCE
Ms E Townsend, BA East Anglia, PGCE

Business and Economics:
*Mr D Wilkins, BSc London, PGCE

Classics:
*Miss L Fontes, BA Leeds, PGCE
Mrs M Kalsi-Spiller, BA, MA Sussex, PGCE

Computer Science:
*Mr G Press, BSc Brunel, Certificate of Education

Drama:
*Mrs L McConville, BA Birmingham
Mrs E Gregan, BA Liverpool, PGCE

English:
*Ms L Baker, BA Sheffield, PGCE
Mrs E Gregan, BA Liverpool, PGCE
Ms M Johnston, BA East Anglia, MA London, PGCE
Mrs J Jonsson, MA Oxford Brookes, Diploma in TEFL Certificate in Education

EAL:
*Mrs N Anderson, MA East Anglia, PGCE
Mrs S Davies, CTESOL

EPQ:
*Mrs C Thomson, LLB Bristol, PGCE
Food Preparation and Nutrition
*Ms K Ashman, BSc Cardiff, PGCE

Geography:
*Mrs S Johnson, BSc Exeter, PGCE
Mr J Schofield, BA Hons Exeter, PGCE
Mrs B Dunnage, BA Birmingham, PGCE

History and Politics:
*Mrs D Kratt, BA Reading, PGCE
Mr J Hoar, BA Hull, PGCE
Mr A Wright, MA Oxford, MA London, PGCE
Mr J Schofield, BA Hons Exeter, PGCE

History of Art:
*Mrs I Fanning, BA, MA London

Learning Support:
*Ms M Johnston, BA East Anglia, MA London, PGCE

Modern Languages:
*Miss L Fontes, BA Leeds, PGCE
Miss E Pierre, Licence de Langue, Rennes, France, PGCE King's College, London [maternity leave]
Mrs R Martinez, BA Portsmouth, PGCE
Mr A Rai, BA Hons Queen Mary, London, PGCE
Mrs I Fanning, BA, MA London
Mrs C Tea, BA Birmingham, PGCE [maternity leave]

Mathematics:
*Mr P Wilson, BEng Nottingham, PGCE
Mr Naeem Mohammad, BSc, MA Punjab, HDipEd Dublin,
Mrs S Scholefield, BSc Birmingham, PGCE
Mrs B Tang, MA Harvard, PGCE

Music:
*Mr I G Hillier, GLCM, FLCM, FCSM, FGMS, PGCE
Mrs C Thomson, LLB Bristol, PGCE

Physical Education:
*Miss S Appleby
Mrs L French, BA Oxford Brookes
Mrs K Hammond, BEd Chichester [maternity leave]
Miss C Gillatt, BA Chichester, PGCE
Mrs R Tune, BSc Loughborough, PG
Mr A Hawthorn, BSc Nottingham Trent, PGCE [maternity cover]
Mrs C van Spall, England Netball Level 2 Coach
Mr D Watson
Miss L Berryman

Psychology:
*Mrs E Shingles, BSc Brunel, GTP

Philosophy, Ethics and Religion:
*Mrs M Magill, BA Bristol, MA London, PGCE
Mrs M Kalsi-Spiller, BA, MA Sussex, PGCE
Rev S Watts, BA Hons, Birmingham, BDiv Cambridge

Science:
*Mrs V Allan, BSc Bristol, PGCE
Dr C Alsop, BSc, PhD Durham, PGCE Teacher in Charge of Chemistry,
Mr Naeem Mohammad, BSc, MA Punjab, HDipEd Dublin,
Mrs E Shingles, BSc Brunel, GTP
Mrs A Sutton-Jennings, BSc Sheffield, MSc Birmingham, QTS
Mrs D Ferrer, BA Lincoln, PGCE (*Teacher in Charge of Physics*)
SGA Stretch Co-ordinator: Dr C Alsop, BSc, PhD Durham, PGCE

PSHE:
*Mrs H Simpson, BA Ed, Exeter
Miss V Alford, BSc Oxford Brookes
Ms E Townsend, BA East Anglia, PGCE

Heads of year:
Year 7: Ms E Townsend
Year 8: Mrs B Dunnage
Year 9: Mrs M Magill
Year 10: Mrs A Sutton-Jennings
Year 11: Mrs D Ferrer
Sixth Form: Mrs D Kratt
Deputy Head of Sixth Form: Mrs E Shingles

Boarding and pastoral staff:
Deputy Head (Pastoral): Mrs H Simpson, BA Ed, Exeter
School Chaplain & Charities Co-ordinator: Rev S Watts, BA Hons, Birmingham, BDiv Cantab
Health Care Professional: Mrs C Jones
Markham Housemistress: Mrs S Harmon, MA Birmingham, PGCE
Acting Markham Assistant Housemistress: Miss I Prokopenko, BA Sukhomlynski Mykolayiv National University, Ukraine
Knatchbull: Housemistress Miss V Alford, BSc Oxford Brookes
Acting Knatchbull Assistant Housemistress: Miss K Morris, BA Oxford
Loveday Housemistress: Mrs B Dunnage, BA Birmingham, PGCE
Director in Residence: Miss C Marmo Freire, BA Lancaster, PGCE
Tutor in Residence: Miss C Low, BMus Queensland Conservatorium AmusA, Master of Teaching
Artist in Residence: Miss B Smyth, BA Plymouth,
Teacher in Charge of Physics in Residence: Mrs D Ferrer, BA Lincoln, PGCE
Resident Teacher of PE and Sport: Mr A Hawthorn, BSc Nottingham Trent, PGCE
Counsellor: Mrs T Curtis

Co-curricular staff:
Head of Alexander House: Miss C Gillatt, BA Chichester, PGCE
Acting Head of Becket House: Miss C Marmo Freire, BA Lancaster, PGCE
Head of Churchill House: Mr Naeem Mohammad, BSc MA HDipEd
Head of Darwin House: Miss V Alford, BSc Oxford Brookes
Duke of Edinburgh's Award: Mr D Moran, BA, PGD
Partnerships and Outreach Co-ordinator: Mrs N Anderson, MA East Anglia, PGCE

Language and music tutors:
Arabic: Mrs M Elssadi, Degree in Arabic Literature Damascus
Chinese: Miss T Y Joyce, MA Hong Kong, PGCE
French: Ms M Boussaid, BTS
German: Mr P Scales, MA Reading, PGCE
Italian: Ms R Salera-Hounsome
Russian: Mrs M Strain, MA
Spanish: Mrs I Fanning, BA, MA
Percussion: Mr R Smith
Guitar: Mr P Williams, BA

Violin: Mr S Perkins, BMus
Double Bass: Mr Charlton, BA
Singing: Mr A Thompson, BA
Miss N Parker, BA
Piano: Miss E Krivenko, MMus
Harp: Mrs E Elliott, BA RSAMD
Flute: Mrs S Dunsdon

Visiting staff:
Learning Support: Mrs R Baxter, BA
Mrs J Hooper, BComm
Speech & Drama: Ms R Moir, BA, PGCE
Ms N Hammond-Betts, MA
Mr L Mortimore
Mrs J Brignull
Tennis: Mr N Ingham
Modern and Zumba: Ms A Lewis
Pilates: Ms K Keeling
Dance: Miss R Findlay
Miss H Fowler
Miss R Herszenhorn
Miss Z Pembroke
Miss E Horner

Support staff:
Bursar: Mr J Anderson
Operations Manager: Ms J Quinn
Finance Manager: Mrs S Clinton
Estates Compliance and Enterprise Manager: Mrs E Wiggett
Accounts Assistant: Mrs L Young
Resources Officer: Mrs T Barber
Personal Assistant to Head: Mrs J Witt
Secretary to the Senior Leadership Team: Mrs C Reader
Administrative Assistant: Miss H Austin
Director of Marketing and External Communications: Mrs N Man
Marketing Operations Officer & Alumnae Co-ordinator: Ms L Glimmerveen
Marketing Graphic Designer: Mrs G East
Marketing Videographer and Photographer: Mrs C Burnie
Director of Admissions: Mrs K Bertram
Admissions Assistant: Mrs S Holloway
Admissions Co-ordinator: Mrs S O'Brien
Director of Philanthropy: Mrs R Swan
Receptionist (*Mon to Wed*): Mrs S Davies
Receptionist (*Thurs and Fri*): Mrs E Halford
Examinations Officer: Mrs J Storm
Data Manager: Mrs C Baker
Domestic Bursar: Mrs A Craciun
Deputy Domestic Bursar: Mrs J Burns
Head Chef: Mr L McCallum
Network Manager: Mr A Attan
IT Technician: Mr M Merry
Art Technician: Mrs A Older
Theatre Technician: Mr W Turney
Science Technicians: Mrs J Bhandal, Mr P Goldsbrough, Miss J Letley
Food Technician: Ms C Dawson
Head Librarian: Mrs S van de Weg
Deputy Librarian: Mr D Moran
Clerk of Works: Mr R Cotterell
Groundsperson: Mr P Thompson
Electrician: Mr C Smith
General Maintenance Operative: Mr R MacRobbie
Estates Maintenance Assistant: Mr A Tan
Gardener: Mrs P Shepherd
Minibus Drivers: Mr C Stephens, Mr C Kerton, Mr D Fryer, Mr D Elwood, Mr D Khan, Mr A Yexley, Mr A Kennedy

St Helen and St Katharine

Faringdon Road, Abingdon, Oxfordshire OX14 1BE

Tel: +44 (0) 1235 520173
email: admissions@shsk.org.uk
website: www.shsk.org.uk
X/Twitter: @SHSKSchool
Facebook: @StHelenStKatharine
Instagram: @shskschool
LinkedIn: /shskschool

See full entry in the **HMC** section, on **p. 319**.

St Mary's School Ascot

St Mary's Road, Ascot, Berkshire SL5 9JF

Tel: 01344 296600 (Main Switchboard)
01344 296614 (Admissions)
email: admissions@st-marys-ascot.co.uk
website: www.st-marys-ascot.co.uk

See full entry in the **HMC** section, on **p. 325**.

St Mary's School
Colchester

91 Lexden Road, Colchester, Essex CO3 3RB

Tel: 01206 594256
email: registrar@stmaryscolchester.org.uk
website: www.stmaryscolchester.org.uk
X/Twitter: @stmaryscolch
Facebook: @stmaryscolchester
Instagram: @stmaryscolchester

Motto: *Scientia et Veritas*

Receiving the highest rating of 'Excellent' in ISI Inspection 2023, St Mary's is an all-girls school for pupils age 4–16. We also have a Kindergarten where children can start in the term they turn 3.

Our Kindergarten and Lower School are based on their own site on London Road while our Senior School is located on Lexden Road, Colchester. We are proud to have charitable status, meaning all fees are reinvested into the school. We are also truly independent, with no owners or shareholders, and are overseen by a committed governing body who help ensure we provide a high-quality, complete education.

At St Mary's, we believe that girls are remarkable. We recognise girls have different needs and our ambitious educational offer is tailored for girls to thrive. At St Mary's, your daughter will be inspired, build resilience, advance academically, learn what interests her and grow. We understand that the girls' wellbeing matters and is critical to achieving. Our girls are not only self-confident and capable, but also kind and considerate. We know that as parents, you want the world for your daughter – and so do we. And when she leaves us, she'll be empowered to rise to the challenges and the opportunities the world presents.

Kindergarten. St Mary's is very proud of the well-rounded education provided in our Kindergarten, where children can start in the term they turn three. They are given a solid preparation for starting school, both academically and socially, so the children can make the most of all the opportunities school life brings. The Kindergarten also provides a seamless transition to the Lower School, providing benefits from both an educational and wellbeing perspective.

St Mary's has a high ratio of staff to children and specialist teachers run sessions such as French, music and ballet. Children take part in a range of events and activities and we hold a number of events across the year for the whole family to enjoy. The indoor setting of the Kindergarten and the new outdoor learning area along with the multi-sensory play area are the perfect place for young children to flourish. The children also have access to all the Lower School facilities including the library, dance studio, school hall, playing fields and sports courts, set in nine acres of land.

We challenge girls academically. Girls learn differently and our teachers know how to challenge, engage and support our pupils so they achieve their very best. With small class sizes and high standards, our focus is on individual success.

Our Lower School pupils perform significantly higher than national average in SATs and we are consistently ranked amongst the highest performing Preparatory Schools in England by the Sunday Times. There is a high 11+ pass rate for those who choose to sit the exam, alongside a strong record of academic scholarship offers for our Senior School.

The National Association for Able Children in Education (NACE) has recently reaccredited the Lower School with the NACE Challenge Award. This award is given in recognition of commitment to high-quality provision for more able learners within the context of challenge for all.

At the Senior School we consistently see strong GCSE success in subjects from STEM to the arts and humanities, reflecting the school's commitment to delivering a strong and enriching education. St Mary's students achieved 9–7/A*–A GCSEs in nine subjects in 2023, including Biology, Chemistry, Physics, Classics and History.

We challenge girls physically. We place a great emphasis on participation in sport and physical activities and support top athletes to compete within and outside of school.

We challenge girls creatively. The creative and performing arts are highly regarded at St Mary's and, as well as providing a rich arts curriculum and extracurricular activities in school, we also support girls to perform outside of school, both locally and in the West End.

We nurture the whole person. Academic success, focus on co-curricular opportunities and high-quality pastoral care are all of equal importance at St Mary's. We nurture the whole person and provide an environment free from judgement and stereotypes, where the girls can be themselves.

We believe in instilling the values of respect and courtesy and we encourage good manners from the youngest age. Through our charity and outreach work, the pupils develop a strong sense of community and as an Eco School, girls gain a strong understanding and desire to protect the environment.

As a global member of the Round Square Organisation, a worldwide network of over 200 top schools in more than 50 countries, those who attend St Mary's also benefit from our international links, helping to broaden their horizons.

These opportunities help girls develop their personal skills and attributes, known as their 'character education'.

We provide an environment that is safe in every respect. We know that for girls to achieve their very best they must feel confident, relaxed and secure.

A strong pastoral system is essential for our girls to be happy and thrive, and we believe their wellbeing directly impacts upon their ability to grow holistically. Every girl at St Mary's has access to, and support from, a network of staff who are highly trained in pastoral matters. The size of the school means we are able to have regular, meaningful interactions with each pupil, and our staff know the girls incredibly well. The atmosphere is calm, supportive and nurturing, allowing girls to develop self-confidence.

Education goes beyond the classroom. At St Mary's there is a real focus on academic achievement, but at the same time the varied curriculum is designed to challenge girls creatively and physically, to build valuable life skills and develop the girls as active global citizens. From our enrichment programme to inspiring excursions, wide-ranging productions, focus on ecology and commitment to STEM, we encourage a wide set of interests and demonstrate the limitless opportunities available to students.

Fees per term (2023–2024). Kindergarten: from £60.50 per day; Lower School: £3,910–£4,850; Senior School: £5,700–£5,900. Fees are inclusive of lunches, drinks (including milk at the Lower School), accident insurance and certain books.

Charitable status. St Mary's School (Colchester) Limited is a Registered Charity, number 309266.

Deputy Chair of Governors: Mr Graeme Lambert

***Principal*: Mrs N Griffiths**, MA, PGCE, NPQH

Head of Lower School: Mrs E Stanhope, GMus, NPQH

Head of Senior School: Miss A Jones, BEd, NPQH

Head of Finance and Operations: Mrs E Bevan

Registrar: Mrs J Tierney

St Mary's School
Gerrards Cross

Packhorse Road, Gerrards Cross, Buckinghamshire SL9 8JQ

Tel: 01753 883370
email: registrar@st-marys.bucks.sch.uk
website: www.stmarysschool.co.uk
X/Twitter: @StMarysSchoolGX
Facebook: @St-Marys-School-Gerrards-Cross
Instagram: @stmarysgx
LinkedIn: /st-mary-s-school-gerrards-cross

Badge: *Ecce Ancilla Domini*

Founded by Dean Butler in 1872. Formerly at Lancaster Gate. Established in Gerrards Cross in 1937 as an Independent Day School catering for 400 day girls aged 3–18.

The School is situated in the attractive residential area of Gerrards Cross which is surrounded by beautiful countryside, 20 miles from London, close to the M25 and A40/M40, on the main bus routes and 10 minutes from the Railway Station.

The aim. St Mary's is committed to providing an excellent education in a caring, happy environment, where each girl develops self-confidence and achieves her very full potential. Students are actively encouraged to develop their own talents and personalities in a nurturing and purposeful environment to allow them to go on to become fulfilled, successful and empowered adults.

Curriculum. Subjects offered include English Language and Literature, History, Geography, RE, Drama, French, German, Spanish, Business Studies, Economics, Information Technology, Computer Science, Mathematics, Psychology, Sociology, Politics, Textiles, Dance, Chemistry, Biology, Physics, Music, Art & Design, History of Art, Media Studies, Food & Nutrition, Extended Project Qualification, Equestrian Team, Gymnastics, Hockey, Netball, Tennis, Rounders, Football, Badminton, Swimming, Personal, Social, Cultural and Health Education, climbing, and other sporting activities.

Regular trips are made to places of educational interest, for team building, field courses are undertaken, foreign visits including a ski trip to Canada are arranged, international sports tours, and there is highly successful participation in The Duke of Edinburgh's Award scheme, World Challenge and Young Enterprise. There is an excellent staff to pupil ratio.

Examinations. Girls are prepared for Entrance to the Universities and Colleges in all subjects; for the General Certificate of Education at A Level and GCSE/IGCSE Level; Associated Board Examinations in Music and examinations in Speech and Drama (LAMDA). The School is an 11+ centre.

The Buildings are a highly attractive mixture of old and new and include two Libraries, Dining Hall, a Science Block with Laboratories, a large open-plan Art Studio, a Home Economics Room, Textiles Room, two Computer Suites, a modern Sixth Form Centre, Cedar House which opened in 2016, two Music Rooms, Drama Studio, Chapel and two Assembly Halls/Gymnasiums equipped to the highest standards. Cherry Tree House, a new classroom block with state-of-the-art technology, opened in 2018.

The Prep Department, in the grounds of the Senior School, comprises Little St Mary's, a new build opened in 2020 for Nursery and Reception girls, Paddington House, and two modern purpose-built blocks, with a Science Laboratory, Hall, Gymnasium, Textiles/Art room and ICT suite.

The grounds include tennis and netball courts, a hockey pitch and an athletics field. There is a Sport England full-size Sports Hall and an all new Multi-use Games Area with a space for spectators.

School Hours. The hours are 8.30am–3.45pm. The School year is divided into 3 terms. Wraparound care is provided from 7.45am and after school until 6.00pm.

Reports are sent to Parents at half terms and at the end of each term and there are regular Parent/Staff meetings. The School also communicates with Parents via SchoolPost on Firefly.

Fees per term (2023–2024). £2,430–£6,870.

Scholarships and Bursaries. Academic scholarships are available at 11+ and at 16+ in the Sixth Form. There are also Art, Drama, Music and Sports Scholarships at 11+ and Sports and Expressive Arts at 16+. A means-tested Bursary scheme is in operation.

Charitable status. St Mary's School (Gerrards Cross) Limited is a Registered Charity, number 310634. It provides education for girls from Early Years to A Level in a well-structured, academic and caring environment.

Governors:
Chairman: Mr D R Wilson, BA, FCA
Mrs C Bayliss, CertEd
Mrs D Campkin, ACA, BSc Hons
Mrs S Clifford, BSc
Mrs M Hall, MA Cantab, CPA, EPA
Mr N Hallchurch, LLB Hons
Mrs R Martin, Med, NPQH, FRSA
Mr N Moss, MNAEA
Mrs H Phillips, BA Hons

Senior Leadership Team:

***Headmistress*: Mrs Patricia Adams**, MA Oxon (*French, Spanish*)

Senior Deputy Head: Mrs Jacqui Deadman, BEd Hons Exeter (*PSHCEE*)

Deputy Head: Mrs Katie Cork, BA, MEd Macquarie University (*Psychology*)

Deputy Head: Ms Joanna Croft, Maitrise de Lettres Modernes, Universite de Strasbourg (*French*)

Head of Preparatory Department: Mrs Mairead Carney, BA Hons Galway (*Year 6 Class teacher*)

Bursar, Mr Michael Boddy, LLP Warwick

Assistant Head Marketing and Communications: Ms Jess Newton, BA Hons The London Institute (*Art, Textiles*)

Assistant Head Teaching & Learning: Mrs Elain McNally, MA Open University (*English*)

Head of Sixth Form: Mrs Alex Francisco, BA Hons University of NSW (*Art*)

Heads of Department:
Mrs L Milmine, BA Hons Portsmouth (*Economics and Business Studies*)
MA Oliva, BA Hons, Warwick (*History*)
Mr J Hill, BA Hons Bangor (*Sociology*)
Mr S Cox, BA Hons East Anglia (*Politics*)
Mr T Evans, BA Hons Brunel (*Media Studies*)
Ms S Kelly, BA Hons Lancaster (*Religious Studies and PSHCE*)
Mr J Heath, BSc Hons Loughborough (*Geography/ Humanities*)
Mr J Hopkins, BSc Hons Durham (*Science*)
Mrs L Jenkinson, MA St Mary's Twickenham (*Food & Nutrition*)
Ms A Birkett, BA Glamorgan (*Drama*)
Mr A Keenan, BA Hons Queen's Belfast (*Modern Foreign Languages*)
Miss K Lasocki, BA Hons Leeds (*Dance*)
Mr J Manders-Jones, BSc University of Liverpool (*ICT*)
Ms F Brennan, BA Hons Brennan (*English*)
Mrs R Brown, BA Hons West of England (*Art & Design*)
Mrs J Phillips, MA Beds (*Director of Expressive Arts*)
Mrs M Degan, BSc Hons University of Birmingham (*Maths*)
Mrs B Taylor, PGD Leeds, BA Hons de Montfort, OCR L7 SpLD (*LEAPS*)
Mrs R Webster, BA Hons Leeds (*Physical Education*)

St Nicholas' School

Redfields House, Redfields Lane, Church Crookham, Fleet, Hampshire GU52 0RF

Tel: 01252 850121
email: headpa@stnicholas.school
website: www.stnicholas.school

Motto: *Confirma Domine Serviendo*

St Nicholas' School is a small independent day school for girls aged 3–16 and boys aged 3–7. Founded in 1935 in Branksomewood Road, Fleet, the school moved to Redfields House, Redfields Lane, Church Crookham in 1996. Redfields House, a Victorian Mansion, is set in 30 acres of glorious parkland and playing fields.

Branksomewood, the Nursery and Infant department, retains the original name of the road where the school was founded. Being built of natural wood with a wonderful airy atmosphere this building gives light and space to our younger children, creating a calming environment in which they thrive. With an adventure playground set in the woods, a large hall fitted with PE equipment overlooking the grounds, and our experienced teaching staff, it is no wonder the children are so happy.

St Nicholas' Junior department is based in Redfields House itself which keeps the charm of the old family house with its oak panelling and the senior department is located in the newer part of the school behind. All three departments have benefited from several building projects. Both Infant and Junior pupils have Forest School sessions throughout the year that take advantage of the beautiful outdoor learning space.

Facilities include a sports hall with courts, showers, changing rooms and a viewing gallery. This has enhanced the sports lessons and enabled even more sports competitions as well as extra-curricular activities. Badminton, tennis, netball, volleyball and basketball may be played throughout the year.

Our Art, Design Technology and Textiles Centre, offers three spacious rooms with large work benches, and a kiln for pottery. By having this wonderful building it has opened an opportunity for the school to adapt the old art centre into several music practice rooms. Tuition is offered in the violin, piano, guitar, harp, drums, singing, woodwind and brass.

The Pritchard Hall, named after the school's founder, was unveiled in 2009. The performing arts centre has raked seating for over 330, in the semi round and contains with an orchestra pit where concerts and plays are staged regularly. In addition, the drama department has two studios.

September 2013 welcomed the opening of state-of-the-art laboratories for juniors and seniors. The classrooms include teaching areas as well as practical learning spaces in a bright and welcoming environment.

In 2016 the addition of an all-weather pitch and two new tennis courts complemented the sports facilities. The new sand-based AstroTurf is floodlit and provides pupils with a multi-use sports facility including hockey, tennis and netball. The tennis courts are also floodlit. Hockey, athletics, football and rounders take place on the games field and the floodlit courts are used all year round. In 2018, the Junior Department benefited from a new play area. An outdoor classroom in the woodland provides Forest School lessons for all Infant and Junior pupils.

Pupils come to St Nicholas' from Hampshire, Surrey and Berkshire. School buses operate from Farnham, Odiham, Fleet, Basingstoke, Camberley, Yateley, Aldershot and Farnborough. Situated just off the A287, the Hook to Farnham road, junction 5 of the M3 is approximately 4 miles short away.

Religion. The school is a Christian foundation but children of other faiths are welcomed. Assemblies or hymn practices are held each morning. Children are encouraged to show tolerance, compassion and care for others.

Curriculum. St Nicholas' offers an extended day, from 7.30am to 6.00pm. Academic standards are high and a balanced curriculum is offered. Small classes place greater emphasis on the individual and pupils are encouraged to achieve their full potential in every area of school life. The curriculum is kept as broad as possible until the age of fourteen when choices are made for GCSE. The option choices vary year by year depending upon the girls' abilities and talents. On average each girl sits ten subjects at GCSE. More than twenty subjects are offered at this level. A carefully structured personal development course incorporates a careers programme. Our girls move confidently on to enter sixth form colleges or scholarships to senior independent schools. Choir, drama and music thrive within the school and there are frequent performances which enable the girls to develop self-confidence.

Co-Curricular Programme. Our Co-Curricular programme refers to the academic, personal, spiritual, creative and physical development of every pupil, alongside a sound understanding of community. As a through school we have the unique opportunity to monitor and support the progress of every pupil according to their strengths and abilities at each key stage. Our focus is to offer experiences that are meaningful and child-centred; whether that be mindfulness walks, relaxation classes or exploring Forest School, participating in our Duke Of Edinburgh scheme or the girls running their own lunch time club and working alongside teaching specialists during Activity Weeks.

Physical Education. Pupils take part in inter-school and local district sports matches across a large number of sports including netball, hockey, basketball, football, tennis, swimming, volleyball, badminton, tag rugby, cross-country, athletics, ultimate frisbee and Taekwondo.

Entry. Children may enter at any stage subject to interview, school report and waiting list. Scholarships and Bursaries are available. For 11+ candidates there is an entrance examination.

Fees per term (2023–2024). Infants: £3,948 (Reception), £4,220 (Year 1), £4,241 (Year 2); Junior School: £4,923 (Year 3), £4,923 (Year 4), £5,066 (Year 5), £5,116 (Year 6); Senior School: £5,843 (Years 7–11). Nursery: £10.50 per hour.

Further Information. The prospectus is available upon request from the Registrar. The Headmistress is pleased to meet parents by appointment.

Charitable status. St Nicholas' School is a Registered Charity, number 307341. It exists to provide high quality education for children.

Chair of Governors: Stephen Mellor

***Headmistress*: Dr Olwen Wright**, PhD Winchester, MA, BA Hons, PGCE

Director of Teaching and Learning and Head of Mathematics: Nicola Byrne-Chinn, BSc Hons Liverpool, GTP, NPQSL, LP, QTS

Director of Pastoral Care and Safeguarding Lead: Claire Huyton, BSc Hons Liverpool, PGCE, QTS

Head of Infants and Juniors: Lee Render, BA Hons Surrey, QTS

Bursar: D T Canning, FCCA

Teaching Staff:
Josephine Allen, BA Hons West of England, QTS (*Key Stage 2*)
Annabelle Ambrose, BA Hons Warwick, PGCE, QTS
Florence Ayache, BA Hons Glamorgan, QTS (*Spanish and French*)
Helen Barnes, BA Ed Hons Exeter (*Deputy Head of Juniors*)
Marcia Barrington, NVQ
Terri Boas, TQUK Level 3
Sophie Brown, BSc Hons Nottingham Trent, QTS
Victoria Cooper, BSc Hons Portsmouth, QTS
Gemma Cross, BSc Wales, PGCE, OTS (*Science*)
Josie Downer, BA Hons Leeds, MA King's (*Head of Drama and ELSA*)
Joanne Edwards, BA Hons Brunel, PGCE (*Head of History*)
Rachel Firth, BA Hons Bath (*Textiles*)
Amy Franke, BMus Hons, MMus Surrey (*Music*)
Dianna Gair, BEd Hons Wales, QTS (*Stage 2*)
Edwina Gross, BA Hons Trent Polytechnic
Kaeleigh Hapsa, CACHE, Level 3 Diploma
Katherine Head, PhD, BSc Hons Bristol, PGCE, QTS (*Head Of Biology*)
Rebecca Hoddinott, BA Hons South Bank (*Food Prep and Nutrition*)
Laura Homer, BA Hons Wales, PGCE (*Key Stage 2*)
Stephanie Hoskins, BA Hons Bristol, QTS
Hannah Hopkins, City & Guilds, Level 3 (*LSA and ELSA*)
Jomcy John, BSc Mahatma Gandhi University
Pilar Kimber, MA Reading (*Latin and Classical Civilisation*)
Stella Lawson, BA Nottingham Trent, QTS (*Teacher of English/Phase Leader*)
Anne-Sophie Le Mat, BA, MA France, PGCE, QTS
Deborah Martin, BA Hons Surrey (*Mathematics and ELSA*)
Lyndon Martin, BSc Surrey, QTS (*Mathematics*)
Teresa Mills, BA Manchester, PGCE, QTS
Wendy Moller, BEd South Africa (*Foundation Stage Teacher*)
Helen Molloy, BA Hons Sheffield, PGCE, QTS (*Head of Curriculum Support and Exams Officer*)
Sarah Moore, BA Hons West Of England, PGCE, QTS
Emma Munt, BCS Hons Southampton, PGCE, QTS
Paul Nicholls, BA Hons London (*Director of Co-Curricular Activities*)
Sarah Park, BA Hons Keele, QTS (*Activities*, *Head of English*)
Jo-Lesley Paxford (*LSA*)
Virginia Pearson, Perf Cert RAM, LTCL, ARCM (*Music*)
Benjamin Pont, BMus Hons (*Director of Music*)
Joanna Pont, BMus Hons (*String Tutor*)
Mary Porter, BSc Hons Southampton, MA UCL, QTS (*Geography*)
Lucy Sartori, BSc Hons Royal Holloway and Bedford New College, QTS
Louise Wallace, BA York, PGCE, QTS (*Curriculum Support*)
Steve Warriner, BA Hons Trent Polytechnic (*Forest School, DofE*)
Dan Wileman, BSc Hons OU
Hannah Willmott, BSc West of England, PGCE, QTS
Xinsheng Zhang, MEd Johannesburg SA (*Chinese Mandarin*)

Peripatetic Music:
Eleanor Bowyer, PGCE Middlesex (*LAMDA*, *Speech and Drama*)
Wendy Busby, BMus Hons (*Voice*)
Sylvia Ellison, BA Hons, PG Dip RCM (*Oboe*)
Vanessa Gynn, BA Hons, PG Dip RCM
Claire Hasted, BMus Hons (*Violin*)
Claire Hickling, BMus Hons (*Piano*, *Flute*)
Oksana Maxwell, LTCL (*Piano*)
Valerie Mitchell, LRAM (*Piano*, *Cello*)
Austin Pepper, ALCM (*Brass*)
Rachel Riordan, Adv Teaching RSM (*Saxophone*, *Clarinet*)
Rebecca Whittock, BA Hons London (*Violin*)

Administration:
Assistant Registrar: Natasha Mabilat, BA Hons
Catering: David Clayton, Chartwells, Compass Group PLC
Head of Admissions & Marketing: Paula Stelfox, AMCIS in Admissions Management
Headmistress's PA: Kathryn Killick
Laboratory Technician: Michele Axton, BA OU
Librarian: Sarah Stokes
Payroll and Pensions Administrator: Debbie Smitherman, Dip Pensions & Payroll Management
School Assistant: Amanda Bullock
School Secretary and Medical Officer: Sarah Watkins, RGN, NNEB
Teaching Assistant: Tania Negus, Level 3 Diploma EYFS

Maintenance:
Afternoon Caretaker: Peter Attwood
Assistant Maintenance Officer: Bruce Sharp, City & Guilds Levels 2 & 3
Bus Drivers: Trevor Mills; Glenn Shearer, Midas Trained
Groundsman: Maurrice Readman, Nebosh Certificate, Health & Safety, Midas Trained
Head of Maintenance: Paul Rippingale, Midas Trained
Morning Caretaker and Bus Driver: Timothy Hunt, Midas Trained

St Paul's Girls' School

Brook Green, Hammersmith, London W6 7BS

Tel: 020 7603 2288 (Front Office)
020 7605 4882 (Admissions)
email: admissions@spgs.org
frontoffice@spgs.org
website: www.spgs.org
X/Twitter: @SPGSMain
Facebook: @StPaulsGirlsSchool
Instagram: @stpaulsgirlsschool
LinkedIn: /stpaulsgirlsschool

Founded in 1904 as one of the first purpose-built schools for girls, St Paul's Girls' School embraces both tradition and innovation. The emphasis on liberal learning established by the first High Mistress, Frances Gray, finds expression today in an academically adventurous curriculum, which encourages intellectual freedom, discovery, and the joy of scholarship. School life is underpinned by the kindest and most individual of pastoral care and a strong commitment to partnerships and diversity, with a generous and growing bursary programme.

Admissions. The main ages of admission are 11 and 16. There are currently 808 students on roll. The school is committed to making an SPGS education available to the brightest students whatever their means and has an active fundraising campaign dedicated to raising funds to double the number of students on a bursary in the next 10 years. *Admissions Registrar*: Mrs Katie Smith.

Bursaries

Currently 78 students are in receipt of a financial award, which equates to 10% of student roll, with the ambition to double this over 10 years.

Junior Bursaries (11+) to a value of up to full fee remission, based on proven financial need and subject to annual review, are available. Candidates must be successful in the 11+ entrance examination. The number of junior bursaries available each year will vary.

Senior Bursaries (16+) to a value of up to full fee remission, based on proven financial need and subject to annual review, are available for candidates who have been successful in the Senior School entrance examination and are currently in their final GCSE year at another school.

Scholarships

Junior Music Scholarships (11+) to the value of lessons in two instruments/voice, currently worth £1,800 per annum, tenable for five years when scholars will be able to apply for a 16+ scholarship in Y11 for their final two years at SPGS. Music exhibitions may also be awarded following auditions at the discretion of the Director of Music. They are based on the value of lessons in one instrument/voice, currently worth £900 per annum and tenable for five years.

Senior Music Scholarships (16+) to the value of lessons in two instruments/voice, currently worth £1,800 per annum, tenable for two years (choral awards up to the value of one lesson in voice may be available). External candidates must be successful in the Senior School entrance examination.

Senior Art Scholarships (16+) of the value of £250 per annum are offered to up to two internal and two external candidates who are currently in their final GCSE year and who, if applying from another school, have previously been successful in the Senior School entrance examination. Candidates take part in a workshop and are required to submit a portfolio.

Senior Drama Scholarships (16+) of the value of £250 per annum are awarded based on an audition, workshop and interview with our Director of Drama and other drama staff to candidates who show outstanding potential as an actor or director. Please note that scholarship candidates will often study drama at A Level; however, those able to demonstrate a significant commitment to co-curricular drama will also be considered. Drama exhibitions of the value of £50 per annum are also awarded following an audition, workshop and interview with the Director of Drama.

Fees per term (2023–2024). £9,982, including lunches and personal accident insurance, and excluding textbooks. The fees per term for new entrants entering at 16+ are £10,732.

Registration & Examination Fee: £250.

Sixth Form. The Senior School is housed in our wonderful Garden Building, opened in 2018. Students have a large and comfy common room, kitchen, group working space and quiet study room at their disposal. Tutor groups are small, enabling first-class pastoral support. Students are further supported by the Senior School team, and they are guided through the university application process. One of the highlights is the weekly lecture by invited speakers.

Results and Destinations. SPGS is committed to providing an outstanding academic education within a highly encouraging environment. Students regularly achieve exceptional results (53% A* at A Level or Pre-U equivalent and 80.5% at GCSE in 2023), but the school aims to teach far beyond the prescribed curriculum, endowing students with a lifelong love of learning and the necessary tools of scholarship and enterprise. Our teaching places emphasis on creativity, innovation and entrepreneurship, while our broad and progressive curriculum is rich in opportunities to learn about new technologies, preparing students to navigate an increasingly interconnected world with ease. Students take GCSE and IGCSE examinations in Y11; alternative school directed courses in art, history of art, computer science, creative technology, drama and music are also offered for this age group. Senior students are offered 23 subjects at A Level and are prepared for university entrance by a personal higher education coordinator and an academic advisor. Students go on to study at major universities in the UK and USA, with over a third going to Oxford or Cambridge annually.

Pastoral Care. Pastoral care is also central to our ethos as evidenced by our Wellbeing Centre, five-days-a-week counselling provision and sympathetic medical staff. Students learn and thrive in a happy and supportive environment. Everyone, from Year 7 upwards, is placed in a small tutor group of approximately 14 students to ensure the delivery of targeted and empathetic pastoral care. Strong systems of support mean students always have somewhere to turn when they need a listening ear, from peer supporters to form captains and our Head of School team. The pastoral curriculum aims to introduce students to a diverse range of perspectives and demonstrates the importance of kindness, inclusion and individuality, empowering them to make a difference in the world beyond school.

Co-curriculum. There is a great depth and variety of opportunities beyond the classroom. Many of the 100+ clubs and societies on offer are run by students *for* students, and new ones are created every year to reflect passion and demand. Students are given leadership opportunities and an environment in which to experiment, innovate and push boundaries. The creative and performing arts flourish at SPGS. Composer of *The Planets*, Gustav Holst, was Director of Music at the school for over thirty years and his legacy continues. Since its foundation, music has been a particularly strong feature with well over half the student body taking instrumental lessons; there are also multiple orchestras, choirs and ensembles on offer. Art and design benefit from studio and workshop facilities and there are several major exhibitions of students' work. Drama enjoys a purpose-built theatre and a drama studio, and any student can direct her own production. The school offers the Duke of Edinburgh's Award. Volunteering is also an important feature of wider school life, with students spending time at food rescue and redistribution centres, local primary schools and residential care homes.

Community Partnerships. Partnerships play a key role at the school, and we aim to give everyone opportunities to work with students and staff from other schools. Projects include a music mentoring scheme, *The Jupiter Project*, primary reading schemes and a primary homework club, as well as a primary schools enrichment summer programme, alongside STEM courses for Years 10–13 from local secondary schools. We are founder members of the *West London Partnership*, which connects 11 schools from the state and maintained sectors in joint projects. We ensure that all our activities are open to others whenever possible, from our HE support and careers days to talks and lectures. Over 250 Paulinas and more than 500 students from other schools take part every year.

Sport. There are extensive sporting facilities on site and sport is played with verve and distinction. Facilities are some of the best offered by a central London school and include a 50 m swimming pool, four outdoor netball courts, two lacrosse pitches, an athletics track including field events, and five tennis courts. At our Sports Hall and Pavilion, we also house three dance and fitness studios and a multi-gym. SPGS prides itself on delivering a broad, balanced and exciting curriculum, offering a wide range of traditional and varied sporting opportunities, and aiming for every student to strive to discover a sport they love and in which they can achieve. The three main sports are lacrosse, netball and rowing, but students are able to take part in extracurricular clubs to broaden their participation. Fixtures are played throughout the year, ensuring every student who wants the opportunity is able.

Alumnae. SPGS is proud to have a supportive global network of over 7,000 alumnae, supported by a dedicated team in the school's Development Office. They remain connected to each other and the school in a myriad of ways, including through an exclusive alumnae networking platform, bulletins, publications and frequent events. As a vital part of the community, alumnae assist in supporting students with mentoring, careers and university guidance.

Charitable status. St Paul's Girls' School is a Registered Charity, number 1119613, and a Company Limited by Guarantee, registered in England, number 6142007 and is governed by its Memorandum and Articles of Association. It exists to promote the education of girls in Greater London. The sole member of the charitable company is the Mercers' Company.

Governors:
Chair: Mr Simon Wathen, LLB Bristol
Deputy Chair: Mrs Zeina Bain, MA Oxford
Ms Justine Archer, BSc Edinburgh
Ms Lisa Barclay, MA Cambridge, MBA London
Ms Mairi Brewis, MA Oxford
Mr Nicholas Buxton, BSc Bristol
Mr Tim Haywood, BSc Edinburgh, MBA Cranfield
Mrs Clare Hebbes, MEng MICE
Mrs Geeta Khehar, LLB Leicester
Mrs Gillian Low, MA Oxford
Mr Geoffrey Matthews, MA Cambridge
Ms Leah Morris, BA Glamorgan
Ms Joy Reymond BSc, MA, MBA USA and Australia
Professor Jane Ridley, DPhil Oxford

***High Mistress*: Mrs Sarah Fletcher**, MA Oxford

Senior Deputy Head, Director of Studies: Mr Andrew Ellams, MA Oxford

Deputy Head, Director of Pastoral Care: Mrs Lizzie Beesley, MA Oxford

Deputy Head, Director of Partnerships: Ms Simone Benn, BMus RAM

Deputy Head, Director of Innovation: Mr Giles Bennett, BA Middlesex, BSc Open, MSc Oxford, MIMA, FCCT

Deputy Head, Director of Co-Curriculum: Mr Fred Hitchcock, BA Bristol

Deputy Head, Director of Senior School: Mr Rupert Try, MA, MSt Oxford
Deputy Head, Director of Strategic Development: Mr Ellis Whitcomb, BSc Birmingham, PGCert Cambridge
Director of Safeguarding and Inclusion: Ms Coco Stevenson, MA London
Bursar: Mrs Sarah Teasdale, BSc London, FCA
Director of Operations: Mrs Barbara Sussex, BA, MPhil Birmingham
Heads of Department:
Art: Mr Matthew Bunning, BA Cambridge
Biology: Miss Harriet Newhouse, BSc Durham, PGCE Oxford
Chemistry: Dr Emma Dell, MChem Oxford, PhD Columbia
Classics: Dr Matthew McCullagh, BA, MPhil, PhD Cambridge
Computer Science and Creative Technologies: Ms Melissa Bustamante-Jenke, BSc, PGCE London
Drama: Miss Isabel Foley, BA, MA London
Economics: Mr Nicholas Hazell, BA Leeds, PGCE Brighton
English: Dr Joanna Bratten, BA Steubenville, OH, MLitt, PhD St Andrews
Geography: Ms Lucy Costello, BA Liverpool
History: Mrs Kate Snook, MA St Andrews, MPhil Cambridge
History of Art: Ms Kate Evans, BA London
Mathematics: Dr Damon Vosper Singleton, MMath Oxford, PhD London
Modern Languages (*acting*): Miss Marjorie Delage, BA Limoges
Music: Mr Joseph McHardy, BMus Edinburgh
Physical Education: Miss Jessica Basch, BA, MA St Davids, PA
Physics (*acting*): Mr Gary Davies, BSc Nottingham, MSc Cambridge, PhD London

St Swithun's School

Alresford Road, Winchester, Hampshire SO21 1HA

Tel: 01962 835700
email: office@stswithuns.com
website: www.stswithuns.com
X/Twitter: @StSwithunsGirls
Facebook: @StSwithunsSchool
Instagram: @StSwithunsGirls
LinkedIn: /school/st-swithun's-school

St Swithun's is a modern and flourishing educational organisation. The school is set on an impressive and attractive campus of 45 acres in the South Downs National Park on the outskirts of Winchester. It offers girls excellent teaching, sporting and recreational facilities. St Swithun's is a World Class High Performance Learning (HPL) School.

The school offers weekly boarding, full boarding and day options for girls aged 11–18. At present the senior school (girls aged 11–18) has 299 day girls and 223 boarders. There is an adjoining Prep School for girls aged 4–11 with a co-ed pre-school (see Prep School entry in IAPS section).

Ethos. St Swithun's is an 'appropriately academic' school which means that we celebrate intellectual curiosity and the life of the mind, but not to the exclusion of all else. We expect our pupils to develop individual passions and through them to acquire a range of skills and characteristics. These characteristics will include a willingness to take risks, to question and to debate, and to persevere in the face of difficulty. In the words of Samuel Beckett: "Ever tried. Ever failed. No matter. Try again. Fail again. Fail better." If a girl can immediately excel at everything we ask of her, we as educators must set the bar higher.

We want all girls to learn about life beyond the school gates, to appreciate the rich variety of our world, to develop an understanding of compassion and to value justice. We encourage all pupils to become involved in fundraising and community work. They should appreciate how their decisions and their actions can affect those around them.

St Swithun's was founded by Anna Bramston, daughter of the Dean of Winchester, and Christian values underpin our approach to education. We provide a civilised and caring environment in which all girls and staff are valued for their individual gifts and encouraged to develop a sense of spirituality and of kindness. We believe that kindness and tolerance are at the heart of any fully functioning community.

Location. The school is on a rural site in Winchester's 'green belt' but only a short distance from the city centre. It is easily accessible from Heathrow and Gatwick airports and is one hour from London by car (via the M3 motorway). There is a frequent train service to London Waterloo (one hour). We also offer a popular London taxi service from St Swithun's School to London on a Friday evening and a return journey on Sunday.

Curriculum. Girls at St Swithun's benefit from a broad and balanced curriculum that promotes individual choice and achievement. The timetable is designed to enable each pupil to fulfil her intellectual, physical and creative potential through a dynamic range of purposeful lessons and activities.

From their first years here girls are taught to examine social, cultural and moral issues so that they can make informed decisions about their own way of living as well as respecting the values of each individual. The PSHEE & citizenship programme is tailored for each year group and is delivered through a range of school activities and specialist speakers.

All girls follow an enrichment programme known as Stretch. This consists of taught short courses and lectures from visiting speakers. Courses are wide-ranging and topics such as magic and mathematics, biblical Hebrew, cryptic crosswords and French cinema. M5 girls will use Stretch to undertake community service.

Games and PE are taught throughout the school so that girls can participate in a wide range of team and individual sports. Both in lessons and as recreational activities, the emphasis is on personal enjoyment and the development of a healthy, active life, but all pupils receive expert coaching and the most talented individuals and teams are entered into county, regional and national competitions.

Learning support provides bespoke support for individual girls who may be experiencing difficulties in aspects of their academic studies.

Girls take 9 or 10 GCSE exams to allow time for other interests and activities. Everyone takes English language, English literature, mathematics, at least two sciences and one modern foreign language. The girls then choose a further three or four subjects from a choice of 13. Girls are encouraged to take at least one humanity or social science to ensure a breadth of knowledge and skills.

In the sixth form girls are offered 24 subjects from which they choose four at A Level (five if maths and further maths are chosen). Advice is given about the implications for their choice of university, degree course and career to ensure sensible combinations. Some girls choose to follow courses in subjects which are not offered at GCSE. Over half the sixth form study at least one science subject at A Level. Girls normally continue with three of their lower sixth subjects to complete three full A Levels.

In addition, all sixth-formers may choose to do the Extended Project Qualification (EPQ). This is worth half an A Level and is graded from A*–E. The qualification gives girls the opportunity to research an area of personal interest. Universities recognise the value of the skills required for the qualification and it attracts UCAS tariff points. Italian GCSE is also available in the sixth form.

In 2020 St Swithun's became accredited as a High Performance Learning (HPL) World Class School and was re-accredited in 2023. The philosophy and principles of HPL, that everyone can perform highly, are embedded across the curriculum and all areas of school life for all students in the school. Our unique academic enrichment programme, delivered in lunchtime and break sessions, is also open to the whole school.

Religion. The school is a Church of England foundation. There are close ties with Winchester Cathedral, where termly services and the annual confirmation and carol services are held. A full-time chaplain prepares girls for confirmation. There is a newly converted chapel at the heart of the school. Although rooted in the Anglican tradition we welcome people of all faiths and no faith, and we offer opportunities for all girls to explore the spiritual dimension of life during their time here. Students are encouraged to respect religious faith and to think for themselves: to question beliefs, to be open to possibilities and the unexpected, to respect difference and to listen to other perspectives. We are happy to enable girls of different denominations and faiths to join a local congregation if so desired.

Music. From the first hymn in the morning to the final applause on concert nights every day is enriched by music and the school enjoys a fine reputation for the excellence and variety that girls achieve. Through lessons, practice, rehearsals, exams, competitions, performances and cathedral services, the girls are drawn together to make the most of a busy and ambitious musical life: 75% have instrumental lessons and there is a choice of twenty-two instruments to study. Thirty flourishing school ensembles create a wealth of music and everyone is welcome to join in. Our most accomplished musicians are also cathedral choristers or play in county and national groups. There are endless possibilities at St Swithun's whether it is Renaissance church music, African drumming or 21st century pop music that girls wish to study, listen to, compose or perform. They are taught to appreciate many different styles of music from all over the world and from different historical eras. Learning to compose enables some to express themselves through music and we encourage performing as an integral part of what we offer. Learning a musical instrument and sharing this with an audience requires a high standard of creativity, commitment, technique and courage.

Sports. At St Swithun's we know the importance that sport and exercise plays in a pupils long term mental, physical and social health. Our goal is to ensure that every pupil leaves the school believing that sport and/or exercise is a vital part of their life and has the desire, competence and confidence to continue their journey in sport and exercise once they leave the school. We hope to achieve this by providing all pupils with a positive and purposeful journey through sport and exercise.

We understand that every pupil comes to us with different perceptions of sport and ambitions in sport. We aim to provide a tailored programme that allows each pupil to fulfil their potential. From year 7 to 9 we offer a diverse curriculum allowing the girls to experience a variety of activities. As pupils move through the school they will have the option to choose specific activities that they are more passionate about and want to develop within.

Outside of the curriculum we offer a broad range of sport and exercise classes before school, during lunch times and after school. The sports clubs available provide pupils with an additional development opportunity and our modern exercise classes aim to provide pupils with a love of movement that will serve them well beyond school.

Facilities. The original school building contains the main teaching rooms and libraries and has been extended and developed to provide specialist areas for languages, information technology, food and textiles and careers. The science wing contains eight fully equipped modern laboratories and project rooms. In addition, there is an art, design and technology centre and a performing arts building was opened in 2003. This has a 600-seat main auditorium and two smaller performance spaces. A new library, careers and ICT facility was opened in 2007. A new further education study centre for sixth form students opened in late 2021.

School Houses. There are 6 boarding houses and 4 day girl houses, each staffed by a housemistress or housemaster and assistant who take pride in the high level of pastoral care offered to each girl. The junior house is for day girls and boarders aged 11 who are then transferred to one of the senior houses after a year. They remain in the senior house until they have completed one year in the sixth form. The upper sixth house is for boarders and day girls together, with study-bedrooms for boarders, study facilities for day girls and common rooms and a kitchen for all.

Careers. Most girls continue to university, including Oxford and Cambridge, and all continue to some form of higher education and training. Each girl is counselled by one of the team of careers staff in a well-resourced department. Lectures and video presentations are organised frequently and a careers fair held annually. St Swithun's is the Oxbridge hub in Winchester.

Leisure Activities. There is an extensive range of co-curricular activities and an organised programme of visits and activities at the weekend. Girls participate in the Duke of Edinburgh's Award scheme, Young Enterprise and local community service work. The sixth form are able to assist with Stretch activities and this can count towards their UCAS tariff. Each year there are drama productions as well as regular drama activities. There are many overseas study and activity trips which include volunteer work, language trips, ski trips and watersports holidays.

Health. The school health centre forms part of the main buildings. It is staffed by qualified RGNs and visited by the school doctor twice a week.

Entrance. Entry is by means of a pre-test and the Common Entrance examination for Independent Schools. The majority of girls enter the senior school at the age of 11 or 13 years, but girls are accepted at other ages, including the sixth form, subject to satisfactory tests.

Scholarships and Bursaries. Academic scholarships, carrying a fee subsidy of up to 20%, are available for day girls and boarders entering the school at 11+, at 13+ and to the sixth form.

Music scholarships carry a subsidy of up to 10% and provide free tuition on two instruments; exhibitions provide free tuition on one instrument. Music scholars can apply for a means-tested award of up to 100% of school fees.

Sports scholarships are awarded at the end of year 9 when all girls, whether they joined the school at year 7 or year 9, will have had the opportunity to develop skills in all of the sports which the school offers. Sports scholarships are also available for internal and external candidates at 16+. These scholarships have a maximum value of 10% fee remission.

Bursaries of up to 100% of school fees are available for girls who meet the school's entrance criteria. All bursaries are subject to means-testing. In addition, the school offers a number of 20% boarding bursaries to new HM Forces families joining the school.

Fees per term (2023–2024). Senior School: Boarders £14,217; Day Girls £8,452. Prep School: £4,414–£5,938.

Charitable status. St Swithun's School Winchester is a Registered Charity, number 307335.

Chair of School Council: Mrs Alison McClure
***Headmistress*: Ms Jane Gandee**, MA Cantab

Deputy Head Pastoral: Mr Graham Yates, MA Brunel
Deputy Head Academic: Mr Charlie Hammel, AB Princeton, MLitt St Andrews
Admissions Registrar: Mrs Kate Cairns
Deputy Registrar: Miss Vikki Mitchell
Assistant Registrar: Mrs Liz Turner

Sarum Hall School

15 Eton Avenue, London NW3 3EL
Tel: 020 7794 2261
email: admissions@sarumhallschool.co.uk
website: www.sarumhallschool.co.uk
X/Twitter: @SarumHall
Instagram: @sarumhallschool

See full entry in the **IAPS** section, on **p. 799**.

Sheffield High School for Girls GDST

10 Rutland Park, Sheffield, South Yorkshire S10 2PE
Tel: 0114 266 0324
email: enquiries@she.gdst.net
website: www.sheffieldhighschool.org.uk
X/Twitter: @SheffieldHigh
Facebook: @sheffieldhighschool
Instagram: @sheffieldgirlsschool
LinkedIn: /Sheffield-High-School

Sheffield High School for Girls is the leading South Yorkshire private school, offering an engaging and enriched education for girls from age 4 right through to 18. At Sheffield Girls' we aim to bring out the best in all our pupils and encourage them within a happy, structured and nurturing environment. Our ethos is one of mutual respect and care: every girl is valued for her own talents and interests and encouraged as an individual so that she can thrive.

In 2023, Sheffield High School for Girls was named the Top Independent Secondary School of the Year in the North by the Sunday Times. In this same year, the School has also been named Independent Prep School of the Year 2023 by the Independent School Parent Magazine.

Sheffield High School for Girls is part of the Girls' Day School Trust (GDST). The GDST is the leading network of independent girls' schools in the UK. As a charity that owns and runs 23 schools and two academies, it reinvests all its income in its schools. For further information about the Trust, see p. xxii or visit www.gdst.net.

Number of pupils. 774 (166 in Sixth Form).

The School was opened in 1878 and has occupied its beautiful leafy site in the suburb of Broomhill since 1887. It draws its pupils from all parts of the Sheffield City region. Transport to and from school is available from a wide area.

The Infant School, which relocated back to No. 4 Melbourne Avenue in summer 2021, is home to Reception, Year 1 and Year 2 girls. They benefit from specialist teachers and teaching facilities, enabling them to develop an early love of music, languages, sport and drama. The facilities include the Infant School Library, music rooms, a science room and an art room where we deliver our unique fusion curriculum. Our outdoor play area was fully refurbished in 2021.

The Junior School, based at No. 5 Melbourne Avenue, is surrounded by outdoor learning spaces as well as easy access to the wider facilities in the Senior School, including indoor and outdoor sports facilities. Learning is enhanced by enrichment beyond the curriculum, which includes speakers and visitors into school, and trips to theatres and museums. In 2020 we were named as the first World Educational Robotics (WER) UK robotics HUB for Primary School children and we offer our robotics curriculum from Year 5 onwards.

In the Senior School a £3.5 million development programme over the past three years has seen the development of a new cookery room, a new drama studio and a complete refurbishment of the gym, which now incorporates a state-of-the-art fitness suite and accommodation for trampolining, gymnastics and dance. We installed brand new Biology labs in summer 2021.

A separate Sixth Form building, close to the Senior School buildings, offers well-furnished and comfortable common rooms for Years 12 and 13, a Learning Resource Centre with laptops, printers and high-speed Wi-Fi, and a fully equipped kitchen. We are very proud of our national reputation for achieving excellent results academically, but also for our outstanding success in sport, music, art and drama and for our work within the local community.

Beyond the school day. Food and refreshments are available in the dining hall from 7.30 am every morning. In the Infant and Junior School, after-school care is available daily from 3.15 pm until 5.30 pm in Tea Time Club.

Between 3.30 pm and 5.30 pm every Monday to Friday during term time, Senior pupils can stay in school to devote time to homework tasks or revision. We offer over 100 co-curricular clubs and programmes and many pupils stay in school after 3.30 pm to take part in a wide range of activities led by staff and senior students.

Curriculum. School life at Sheffield Girls' centres on an exciting and challenging curriculum. As well as the core subjects of English, Mathematics and Science, the broader Infant and Junior School curriculum includes History, Geography, Drama, Religious Studies and PSHE with specialist teaching in Music, Modern Foreign Languages (French, Spanish or German), Art and Design Technology and Physical Education.

In the Senior School, a challenging and up-to-date curriculum combines the best of traditional, modern, scientific, creative and practical subjects to provide a broad, balanced and inspiring Secondary School education. From Year 7, girls study three separate sciences, two modern foreign languages and Latin (from Year 8) in addition to the standard national curriculum. There is a full range of options in languages, humanities and technical and aesthetic subjects. Most girls study nine GCSE subjects. We are one of the only providers of the Pre-Senior Baccalaureate in the region, offered to girls in Year 7 and Year 8 in preparation for their continued studies in the upper school.

In the Sixth Form, the school offers a bespoke curriculum tailored to the needs of each individual, with a personalised timetable for each girl. The majority of Year 12 students study 3 or 4 A Levels. Students can also opt to do the Extended Project Qualification (EPQ). Our Forging Futures programme provides timetabled courses and stand-alone events for Year 12 and 13 pupils throughout the year, focusing on skills for life and skills for success.

The school has received a string of prestigious national awards for the exceptional quality of its extracurricular provision, such as PE Quality Mark with Distinction, Artsmark (Gold), GO4it, ICT Quality Mark, Eco-Schools Award and Career Mark, making it the only school in South Yorkshire to be so accredited for the quality of its careers provision. In September 2021 the School achieved the top standard in the ISI Inspection. Our pupils' academic and other achievements were rated 'Excellent' and the quality of pupils' personal development was also rated 'Excellent'.

The School academic teams and clubs often reach national competition finals in STEM subjects and debating. In September 2022 our Year 13 Economics students won the International Award at the Youth Economic Summit in Hamburg. The School's many lunchtime and after school clubs encourage excellence in sport, music, drama and art, and we offer the full Duke of Edinburgh's Award scheme. A varied programme of residential trips and expeditions at home and abroad is available, including Sport, Music, Foreign Language and Art tours. The School has strong community links and has recently received four Independent School Awards as well as being shortlisted in two further years. Awards have been for: Best Independent-Maintained School Collaboration, Outstanding Community Initiative and Best Leadership Team.

Fees per term (2023–2024). Senior School and Sixth Form: £4,995, Junior: £3,685, Reception and Infants: £3,551.

The fees cover the regular curriculum, school books, stationery and other materials, most extracurricular activities, but not school lunches. Girls are required to stay for school lunches up to Year 7 and these are charged separately per term.

Scholarships and bursaries. The GDST makes available to the School a substantial number of scholarships and bursaries. In particular, it aims as far possible to focus its support on girls for whom the chance of a GDST education would be a transformative, life-changing prospect.

Bursaries are awarded to pupils in the top 30% of performance in the entrance examinations. All bursaries are means-tested.

Scholarships are awarded on merit, irrespective of financial means. Offers are made based upon performance in the entrance examinations or audition for Year 7, or in the case of Sixth Form scholarships for outstanding ability demonstrated in individual subjects and disciplines. A Scholarship can be combined with a bursary where there is financial need.

Charitable status. Sheffield High School is part of The Girls' Day School Trust, which is a Registered Charity, number 306983.

Chair of Local Governors: Mr Jon Dunn

***Headmistress*: Mrs N Gunson**, BSc, MSc Huddersfield

Deputy Head: Mrs S White, BA Sheffield

Senior Teacher, *Assistant Head* (*Academic*): Mr Carl Adams, MChem Sheffield

Assistant Head (*Pastoral*): Mrs A Reed, BA Sheffield Hallam

Assistant Head (*Co-Curricular*): Mrs E Rodgers, BEd Liverpool John Moores

Head of Junior School: Mr C Hald, MA York

Director of Sixth Form: Mr C Spick, BSc Brunel

Director of Finance and Operations: Mr I Kane, BSc Open University

Director of Marketing and Communications: Mrs Rebecca Mills, BA Hull

Sherborne Girls

Bradford Road, Sherborne, Dorset DT9 3QN

Tel: 01935 818224 (Admissions)
01935 812245 (School)
01935 818206 (Bursar)
email: admissions@sherborne.com
website: www.sherborne.com
X/Twitter: @sherbornegirls
Facebook: @sherbornegirls
Instagram: @sherbornegirls
LinkedIn: /Sherborne-Girls

See full entry in the **HMC** section, on **p. 335.**

South Hampstead High School GDST

3 Maresfield Gardens, London NW3 5SS

Tel: 020 7435 2899
email: senioradmissions@shhs.gdst.net
website: www.shhs.gdst.net
X/Twitter: @SHHSforgirls

Founded in 1876, South Hampstead High School is a selective, independent day school for girls aged 4 to 18 in North West London – a buzzing academic powerhouse with kindness and curiosity at its core. While excellent results and university destinations place it among the country's top schools, South Hampstead is also known for its forward-looking ethos and an approach that aims to ignite a genuine joy in learning. South Hampstead was recently named the Independent Girls' School of the Year.

The school is well connected to most London postcodes, close to Finchley Road and Hampstead underground stations (Jubilee, Metropolitan and Northern lines), overground stations and numerous bus routes. It has over 950 pupils, including over 180 in the Sixth Form and 265 in the Junior School. Entry is competitive: at 4+ and 7+ to the Junior School, and 11+ and 16+ to the Senior School. Occasionally vacancies arise at other ages. Full details of the admissions procedures are available at www.shhs.gdst.net.

The Junior School occupies two large houses a few minutes' walk from the Senior School site. The Senior School is housed in a bright, modern building, designed by Hopkins Architects. Sixth Form students have their own home in Oakwood – complete with its own common room, café and garden – in a beautiful, Victorian house, connected to the Senior School. A four-acre sports ground with excellent facilities is a short walk away.

At South Hampstead, the curriculum is designed to provide a secure and imaginative basis for academic progress at each key stage of a pupil's development. The intention is that all girls develop their own enthusiasms and initiative within a broad educational framework and a balanced range of academic, cultural and aesthetic subjects. In the Junior School there is a clear focus on developing literacy and numeracy skills and an integrated approach to the curriculum whereby the focus is on learning across several subjects around a theme. In this way girls develop real depth of knowledge, as well as confidence in key skills such as research, analysing results and interpreting and presenting information. In the Senior School the curriculum has a strong academic spine and includes lessons in Critical Thinking; there is also a strong focus on empowering girls to find their voice, through the creative arts and debating.

The Sixth Form offers a range of 26 subjects at A Level and students have a strong track record in the Extended Project Qualification (EPQ). A rich and varied programme of speakers, leadership opportunities, international trips and co-curricular activities ensure that every student has the chance to grow, to give back and to shine. The school's Futures Programme provides a comprehensive framework for supporting pupils with higher education and career choices, while dynamic Free Thinking Fridays sessions encourage independent thought and debate. The vast majority are offered their first-choice university – primarily to Russell Group universities, including Oxbridge, with good numbers to medical school, prestigious art colleges and Ivy League destinations.

Pupils throughout the school participate enthusiastically in an enormous number of co-curricular activities. Creativity in art, writing, music and drama is strongly encouraged and there are many orchestras, ensembles and choirs. Tuition in almost any instrument and singing can be arranged and girls are prepared for the examinations of the Associated Board of the Royal School of Music. Large numbers participate in the Duke of Edinburgh's Award.

Fees per term (2023–2024). Senior School: £7,588, Junior School: £6,200.

The fees do not include school lunches, public exam fees or instrumental/singing lessons.

Scholarships and Bursaries. A number of scholarships and bursaries are available to internal or external candidates for entry at 11+ and to the Sixth Form. The bursaries are means-tested to ensure that the school remains accessible to bright girls who would benefit from a South Hampstead education but require financial assistance. Scholarships are currently awarded for academic, musical and sporting excellence (11+) and academic, art, drama and music in the Sixth Form.

Charitable status. South Hampstead High School is part of the Girls' Day School Trust, a leading network of independent girls' schools, Registered Charity, number 306983. As a charity that owns and runs 23 schools and two academies, it reinvests all its income into its schools. For more information, please visit www.gdst.net.

Board of Governors:
Chair: Ms A Dewinter, BA, MSc, GDL
Mr N Chandra, BA, MPhil, MBA
Mrs K Fear
Mrs V Fox, BSc
Dr J Franks, BSc, MSc
Mr R Freeman, BA, MBA
Ms A Gooch, OBE
Miss D Navanayagam, BA
Mr N Soar, BA
Mrs J Todd, BA

***Headmistress*: Mrs Anna Paul**, BA Dunelm

Senior Leadership Team:
Senior Deputy Head Pastoral: Ms Z Brass, BA Queen's University Canada
Deputy Head Co-curricular, Community, Careers: Mr C Dearmer, MA Oxon
Director of Finance and Operations: Mr R Jones, MA Oxon
Head of Junior School: Ms C Spencer, MSc Sheffield, BSc Leeds
Deputy Head Academic: Mr A Westwood, BSc Nottingham
Director of Sixth Form: Mr R White, BA Leeds
Director of Philanthropy & Alumnae: Mrs S Whitworth, MA Edinburgh

Stormont School

The Causeway, Potters Bar, Herts EN6 5HA

Tel: 01707 654037
email: admin@stormontschool.org
website: www.stormontschool.org
X/Twitter: @StormontSchool
Facebook: @StormontSchool
Instagram: @stormontschool

See full entry in the **IAPS** section, on **p. 805**.

Streatham & Clapham High School GDST

42 Abbotswood Road, London SW16 1AW

Tel: 020 8677 8400 (Senior School)
020 8674 6912 (Prep School & Nursery)
email: senior@schs.gdst.net
prep@schs.gdst.net
admissions@schs.gdst.net
website: www.schs.gdst.net
X/Twitter: @SCHSgdst
Facebook: @SCHSgdst
Instagram: @schsgdst

See full entry in the **HMC** section, on **p. 358**.

Sydenham High School GDST

19 Westwood Hill, London SE26 6BL

Tel: 020 8557 7000
email: senior@syd.gdst.net
website: www.sydenhamhighschool.gdst.net
X/Twitter: @SydenhamHigh
Facebook: @sydenham.high.gdst
LinkedIn: /sydenham-high-school-gdst

Founded in 1887, Sydenham High School is an independent day school for girls aged 4–18 and is part of the GDST (Girls' Day School Trust). The GDST is the leading network of independent girls' schools in the UK. As a charity that owns and runs 23 schools and two academies, it reinvests all its income in its schools. For further information about the Trust, see p. xxii or visit www.gdst.net.

Pupil numbers. Senior School 483, Prep School 239.

135 years ago four pioneering women championed the unfashionable cause of education for women, with the aim to provide an academic grounding, first-class teaching and an environment that developed character and personality. Radical at the time, but a shining example of the values of courage, resilience and determination that Sydenham High School is built upon. Our motto of "Fear Nothing" emboldens pupils as they forge their own path through life.

Sydenham High actively encourages its pupils to step outside their comfort zones, developing independence, curiosity of mind and the courage to take risks. This mentality is fostered throughout the school, allowing every pupil to develop academic enthusiasm and the ability and awareness to stand up for what is right. Ready to call out inequality or injustice in whatever form it may present itself, pupils have strong moral compasses, and are accepting and respectful of themselves and others.

A Sydenham High education is about so much more than an excellent set of results. The inclusive nature of the school is a point of pride, and a lifelong love of learning is fostered through tailor-made enrichment opportunities such as their Lecture Series, Socrates Programme, Plato Programme and #700STEMChallenge. Pupils are empowered with self-belief and confidence in all that they do, so that in an ever-changing world they are able to respond positively to the ever-increasing demands placed on them, both at school and in their future lives.

Alumnae are climate change consultants, doctors, authors, scientists, artists, Grammy Award-winning musicians and even a horse-racing icon. Our girls value remaining true to themselves even if that means going against the grain.

There is no mould for a Sydenham High pupil and that's what makes the school so special.

Curriculum. The school offers a broad curriculum, ensuring all our pupils are stimulated and excited by learning. English and Maths provide solid foundations while languages offered include French, German, Spanish, Italian and Latin. Pupils study Biology, Chemistry and Physics as separate sciences. Creative and practical subjects include Design Technology, Art, PE, Music and Drama, as well as Computer Science. Humanities include History, Geography, Religious Studies and Classical Civilisation.

In the Sixth Form, there are 26 subjects to choose from: Art, Biology, Chemistry, Computer Science, Design Technology, Drama & Theatre Studies, Economics, English Literature, French, Geography, German, Government & Politics, History, History of Art, Italian, Latin, Mathematics and Further Mathematics, Music, Philosophy, Physics, PE, Psychology, Religious Studies, Sociology and Spanish. Our 'Next Steps' programme ensures that sixth formers own their future and are equipped with the knowledge and skills to thrive in higher education and beyond. Following what is right for each individual is key. There is no one mould for our pupils. Our Oxbridge and Competitive Courses preparation provide targeted and focused guidance to support in making applications to Oxford or Cambridge, alongside applications for medicine, veterinary, dentistry and law. Degree apprenticeships and Art Foundation courses are increasingly popular. Another key feature is our Active Citizen Programme, incorporating a Professional Skills programme which ensures that students are well versed in the soft skills required for the workplace, Volunteering to reflect pupils' strong social conscience and Enrichment to develop skills beyond the curriculum. Alongside this, we offer a huge range of additional opportunities including the chance to take part in the Young Enterprise programme and leadership responsibilities within the school.

Personalised subject guidance at both GCSE and A Level ensures that our pupils are fully informed when choosing their options. Bespoke timetabling means we are able to offer pupils the widest range of subject combinations to suit their interests. Regular careers events and opportunities broaden pupils' knowledge of career options and sixth form students go on to read a range of subjects at competitive universities. The breadth of co-curricular opportunities ensures there is something for everyone, encouraging pupils to get involved and develop key skills. Performing Arts are an integral part of school life, whilst we offer over 20 sports, including rowing. Involvement in the wider community is encouraged through our successful involvement in The Duke of Edinburgh's Award scheme and charitable activities.

Fees per term (2023–2024). Senior School: £6,619, Prep School: £5,204.

School fees include textbooks, stationery and other materials, choral music, PE and swimming, Careers counselling. They do not include examination fees, instrumental music, speech and drama, and externally-run after-school clubs.

Scholarships and bursaries. A number of scholarships are available each year for entry to the Senior School at 11+ and the Sixth Form at 16+. Scholarships are awarded on merit for Academic, Art, Drama, Music and Sport (plus Rowing at 16+) and no financial means test is involved.

The GDST provides means-tested bursaries which are intended to ensure that the school remains accessible to bright girls who would benefit from our education, but who would be unable to enter the school without financial assistance. Bursaries are awarded on the basis of financial need and academic merit. Details can be obtained from our Registrar. It is recognised that occasions will arise when some form of short-term assistance is required – a small fund exists to help pupils in such cases.

Charitable status. Sydenham High School is part of The Girls' Day School Trust, which is a Registered Charity, number 306983.

Chair of Local Governors: Miss B Holbrooke, MSc Oxon, MSc Oxford Brookes

***Head*: Ms A Geldeard**, MA Cantab, PGCE

Deputy Head (Academic): Mr C Batty, BSc Bangor, Wales, PGCE
Deputy Head (Pastoral): Dr E Waites, PhD Birmingham, Maitrise Poitiers, BSc Liverpool, PGCE

Head of Prep School: Mrs G Panton, MA St Andrews, PGCE
Deputy Head of Prep School: Ms H Cuthbert, BA Oxford, PGCE

Assistant Head & Head of Sixth Form: Ms R Parrish, BA Southampton, PGCE
Deputy Head of Sixth Form: Mr A Hurst
Assistant Head (Enrichment): Ms L Dodds, BA Nottingham

Director of Finance & Operations: Mr A Rout, BA Nottingham Trent
Director of Marketing & Communications: Miss L Hooper, BAEcon Manchester, PGDip

Talbot Heath

Rothesay Road, Bournemouth, Dorset BH4 9NJ

Tel: 01202 761881 Senior School Admissions
01202 763360 Junior School Admissions
01202 755410 Finance
email: office@talbotheath.org
website: www.talbotheath.org
X/Twitter: @TalbotHeathSch
Facebook: @TalbotHeathSch
Instagram: @talbotheathsch
LinkedIn: /school/talbotheathschool

Motto: *Honour before Honours*

Talbot Heath is an Independent School for Girls, founded in 1886, and is among the longest-established schools in the Bournemouth area, with over a century of success. It is a Church of England Foundation and pupils of all denominations are welcome. This School is committed to safeguarding and promoting the welfare of children and young people and is also committed to a policy of equal opportunity.

There are some 347 girls in the Main School, of whom 80 are in the Sixth Forms and 40 are Boarders. There is a Junior Department for about 147 girls between the ages of 7 and 11. The Pre-Preparatory department caters for 120 girls aged 3+ to 7.

The school enjoys an attractive wooded site and outstanding facilities for Art, Drama, Music and

STEAM subjects, they are an Apple Distinguished School and Apple Regional Training Centre, with outstanding ICT provision, 1-to-1 iPad provision from Y1 and extensive modern accommodation for a wide range of sports activities. Talbot Heath have high performing Tennis and Swimming Academies.

Many believe that the future will be powered by STEAM (Science, Technology, Engineering, the Arts and Maths). The STEAM Hub, which opened in September 2019, is the heart of our vision for the future and provides an extensive flexible learning centre, dedicated to interdisciplinary learning with a creative focus. The centre includes a large auditorium, gallery space, graphic design, robotics, technology, textiles, art, drama and food studios, as well as flexible learning spaces for the use of pupils of all ages. In addition the school has a covered pool and sports facility as part of this inspirational new complex.

The school follows the best practice of the National Curriculum but does not undertake Key Stage testing at levels 1, 2 and 3.

Examinations. 21 subjects are offered to GCSE (including Core Subjects) and A Level, and girls gain places at a variety of universities, including Oxford and Cambridge, or go on to other forms of higher education or professional training.

Admission. Girls are admitted into the Junior School by examination at 7 and above and into the Main School by examination at 11+, 12+ and 13+. The Entrance Examination is held annually in January and girls must be capable of working with those of their own age. Entry to the Pre-preparatory Department requires no examination.

Boarding House. St Mary's Boarding House is located in the School grounds.

Fees per term (2023–2024). Tuition: Senior School: £5,767; Junior School: £2,719–£4,707; Kindergarten according to sessions. Boarding (in addition to Tuition Fees): £4,536 (full); £4,048 (weekly); flexi: £56 per night; 3 nights £128.

Scholarships and bursaries are available and there is also a discount for daughters of Service families and the clergy.

Charitable status. Talbot Heath is a Registered Charity, number 283708. It exists to provide high quality education for children.

Governing Body:
Chair: Dr R Day

Dr Lido Badawy	Kate Potten
Jonathan Burke	Sarah Richards
Alexandra Ewins	Dr Debbie Sadd
Gary House	Clodie Sutcliffe
Theresa Magrath	Nicholas Wells
Rebecca Newton	

***Head*: Tracy Harris**

Head of Pastoral:Anna Karanja
Head of Junior School: Mrs L Pugh
Assistant Heads:
Teaching and Learning: Mrs H Chapleo
Mr I Cradick

Assistant Heads, Junior School:
Academic: Mrs S Breeze
Pastoral: Mrs J Brown

Director of Finance: Mr G Ives
Head of Senior School Admissions: Mrs R Cambell-McLean
Head's PA/Office Manager: Mrs A Pollington
HR Manager: Mrs A Pittam
Marketing Manager: Mrs H O'Shea

Tormead School

Cranley Road, Guildford, Surrey GU1 2JD

Tel: 01483 575101
email: admissions@tormeadschool.org.uk
website: www.tormeadschool.org.uk
X/Twitter: @tormeadschool
Facebook: @TormeadSchool
Instagram: @tormeadschool

Established in 1905, Tormead is one of the leading independent day schools for girls aged 4–18 and a member of the GSA (Girls' Schools Association) and the HMC (The Heads' Conference). Located close to the town centre of Guildford, Surrey, Tormead benefits from pleasant grounds combined with the practicalities and local resources of a busy and thriving town nearby.

As an academically selective school, we achieve excellent results. Almost all Tormead students progress to higher education, reading for degrees at some of the best universities across the country. While standards and expectations are high, the teaching and learning environment at Tormead is one of fun and enthusiasm; students leave the school as confident, articulate and self-reliant young women, ready to meet the challenges of life beyond secondary school.

Our curricular enrichment programme is extensive and boasts over 108 clubs and co-curricular opportunities for girls to take part in and discover. Activities such as the Duke of Edinburgh Award, Lamda, 3D Printing Club, Rowing, Dissection Club, Forensics Society, Football and Technical Theatre Club give each girl the opportunity to experience new activities and find their niche. Tormead has a lively and active musical life, with orchestras, various chamber groups, ensembles and choirs on offer, as well as our highly popular Jazz Band that has undertaken tours to various European countries.

Tormead excels at sport, with a busy programme of fixtures in Hockey, Netball, Cricket, Athletics, Football, and Swimming taking place throughout the school year for every age group in the secondary school. Gymnastics has been a particular strength at Tormead for many years, with our teams competing successfully at national level and bringing home national championships.

We are also one of the select few schools to hold Apple Distinguished School Status meaning girls benefit from the use of iPads and Apple technology to enrich their learning and extracurricular activities. By exposing students to a vast array of apps, we feel we foster the importance of creativity within our curriculum.

The School recently opened a new Sixth Form Centre which includes a common room and café, lecture and teaching spaces and dedicated study, collaboration and social spaces, all designed to bridge the gap between secondary education and university. In 2023, the School embarked on a very exciting new development in collaboration with Guildford County School, to create a new sporting home for Tormead at the Urnfield sportsground which will provide facilities for hockey, cricket, football and athletics, as well as open the door for rugby to develop as a new sport option.

As an academically selective school, we achieve excellent results; in 2023, 90% of all A Level grades were an A* – B and 61% of all A Levels grades were an A* or A.

Fees per term (2023–2024). Reception: £3,500, Years 1 & 2: £3,700, Years 3 & 4: £5,450, Years 5 & 6: £5,520, Years 7–13: £6,325.

Scholarships. Prep – Academic scholarships are available at 7+.

11+ – Academic, Art, Drama, Music and Sports scholarships are available.

16+ – Academic, Art, Drama and Music scholarships are available.

Bursaries. Available at 11+ and 16+ and based on the level of parental income.

Alumnae. Email alumnae@tormeadschool.org.uk or visit www.alumnae.tormeadschool.org.uk.

Charitable status. Tormead Limited is a registered charity (312057). It exists to advance education for girls aged 4–18.

Board of Governors:
Mr Matthew Howse, LLB (*Chair*)
Mrs Anne Cullum, BA, PGCE, NPQH
Mr Rory Finnan, BSc Hons, MRICS
Dr Kate Jefferies, MBBS, MSc, MRCPsych
Dr Caroline Kissin, MB ChB, MRCP, FRCR
Professor Graham Miller, BSc Hons, MSc, PGCE, PhD
Mrs Suzanne Newnes-Smith, ACA
Miss Anna Spender, BSc, FIA
Mrs Fiona Thompson, LLB
Mr John Watkins, FCA
Mr Chris Zagorski, MB BChir, FRCR, MA Cantab

***Head*: Mr David Boyd**, MA Oxon, MA UCL, PGCE Cantab

Executive Group:
Mrs Karen Dabill, BSc Bangor, PGCE Surrey (*Deputy Head Academic*)
Mr Tony Breslin, BA Sussex, IPGCE Buckingham (*Deputy Head Pastoral*)
Mrs Michelle O'Brien, BA Chichester (*Deputy Head External Relations*)
Mrs Nicola Fry, BA Ed Exeter (*Head of Prep School*)
Mrs Sian Lehrter, MA Oxon, ACIB, CSBM (*Bursar and Clerk to the Governors*)

Senior Management Team:
Ms Helen Stevens, BA St Andrews, PGCE York (*Assistant Head – Teaching & Learning, English*)
Mr Christopher Ives, BA Warwick, PGCE Reading (*Assistant Head – Staff Development, Head of French*)
Mr Ed Braun, BEng Birmingham, PGCE Roehampton (*Assistant Head – Director of Studies, Head of DT*)
Mr Rob Isaacs, BSc St Andrews, PGCE Reading (*Director of Science*)
Mrs Heather Southwell, MA London, PGCE Oxon (*Assistant Head – Wellbeing & Transition, English*)
Mrs Samantha Jones, BSc Surrey, PGCE SWELTEC (*Assistant Head – Co-curricular, Geography*)
Miss Hannah Andrews (*Designated Safeguarding Lead*)
Mrs Mary Price, BA York, MA IoE, PGCE Leicester (*Deputy Head Prep School*)

Prep Senior Management Team:
Mrs Mary Price, BA York, MA IoE, PGCE Leicester (*Deputy Head*)
Miss Salaidh Insch, BEd Surrey (*Director of Studies*)
Mrs Elizabeth Alderman, BSc Leeds, PGCE Bristol (*Head of Pre-Prep*)

Tudor Hall

Wykham Park, Banbury, Oxfordshire OX16 9UR

Tel: 01295 263434
email: admissions@tudorhallschool.com
website: www.tudorhallschool.com
X/Twitter: @TudorHallSchool
Facebook: @TudorHallSchool
Instagram: @tudorhallschool
LinkedIn: /school/tudor-hall-school

Motto: *Habeo Ut Dem*

Tudor Hall is an Independent Boarding and Day School for Girls aged 11–18 years. The school was originally founded in 1850 and moved to Wykham Park in 1946. It is situated in spacious grounds 1½ miles from Banbury Station and is within easy access of London, Oxford, Bicester and Stratford-upon-Avon – M40, Junction 11. This enables the girls to enjoy a wide range of cultural and educational activities.

The school accommodates approximately 250 boarders and 75 day girls. Its buildings comprise a 17th century and an 18th century manor with a modern purpose-built house for Sixth Formers and extensive new facilities which include 5 science laboratories; designated modern languages department with a language laboratory; purpose-built drama studio, music school and sports complex; art studio and design technology workshop. The latest addition is a Teaching Centre, opened in 2019, which provides designated English and Mathematics Departments, ceramics and textiles studios and a professional kitchen. Sports facilities include floodlit tennis, netball courts, gym and AstroTurf hockey pitch, a swimming pool, grass athletics track and pitches for lacrosse, rounders and cricket.

The curriculum and co-curriculum at Tudor Hall are extensive, providing students with intellectual challenge and the opportunity to expand their horizons. Lessons are delivered in a manner which encourages confidence, gives satisfaction and enjoyment, and allows all students to learn, make progress and be successful. They develop a love of lifelong learning and acquire the necessary skills needed for university and adult life. A comprehensive careers programme ensures that students leave armed with pertinent and relevant information and experience to continue to be successful in life beyond school.

Admission is by internal examinations at 11+ and internal examinations and Common Entrance at 13+. Entry may also be made to the Sixth Form where all girls pursue courses leading to higher education or vocational training. Entry is by assessment, interview and predicted grades at GCSE. Boarders joining at 11 live in a separate and smaller house within a family environment to help them become accustomed to being away from home. Girls are divided into four competitive Houses, but residence is with their own age group.

Tudor Hall places great importance on having a friendly atmosphere, a lively and united spirit and high standards. Girls are expected to take an interest in a wide range of activities as well as following a broad educational programme. Involvement in the local community through the Duke of Edinburgh's Award and social service, and participation in events with other schools are encouraged. Debating and public speaking are strong and there is keen involvement in the Young Enterprise Scheme, Model United Nations and European Youth Parliament. Tudor Hall is an Anglican school but members of all religious groups are welcomed. There is a small chapel.

Scholarships and Bursaries. Every pupil is encouraged to aim high in all areas of Tudor life in order to fulfil their potential. The school's Aim Higher Programme offers all pupils the opportunity to broaden their horizons and excel in areas of particular interest to them. Scholarships are one element of this programme, and any pupils may apply at the appropriate entry point. Tudor Hall offers a range of Scholarships at 11+, 13+ and 16+ in recognition of an individual's potential in a particular discipline. Scholars will benefit from the expertise of Tudor staff and a mentoring programme will be tailored to their interests and goals. In return, Scholars are expected to be ambassadors for that department, demonstrate enthusiasm and leadership, and be fully involved in the co-curricular programme of their chosen discipline. Academic Scholarships are awarded for the duration of the pupil's time at Tudor Hall. Other Scholarships, awarded at 11+ and 13+ are subject to review at 16+. The following Scholarships are on offer:

- 11+: Academic, Drama, Music, Creative Arts
- 13+: Academic, Drama, Music, Creative Arts, Sport
- 16+: Academic, Dance, Drama, Music, Sport, Creative Arts, (Art, Design Technology, Photography or Textiles)

Scholarships are awards worth up to £1,000 per annum, made to pupils demonstrating a particularly high standard of achievement or potential, regardless of financial need. They will be reviewed annually and are retained subject to satisfactory performance and commitment.

A bursary may further enhance the financial award if parents can demonstrate, through a means testing process, that they would not otherwise be able to send their daughter to Tudor Hall due to limited financial means.

Fees per term (2023–2024). £15,300 for boarders; £9,250 for day pupils.

Board of Governors:
Chair: Alison Darling

Duncan Bailey
Sally Bowie
Debbie Chism
Karen Coles
Ben Evans
Jonny Hammond-Chambers
Nick Holliday
Ateh Jewel
Bob Lari
Charles Newsome
Jennifer Scarfe
Mark Sewell
Rodney Style

Senior Management Team:

***Headmistress*: Julie Lodrick**

Bursar & Clerk to the Governors: Adrian Bettridge
Deputy Head (Academic) : Simon Smith
Deputy Head (Pastoral): Kate Simlett
Director of External Relations: Lucy Keyte
Director of Co-Curriculum & Operations: Sadie Lapper
Head of Sixth Form: Justine Stephens
Director of Digital Strategy: James Wakeley

Teaching Staff:

Lucy Andrews, BA UAL, MA BCU, PGCE Exeter (*Photography*)

Jo Benlalam, BMus, AKC, PGCE London (*Head of Careers, Head of Academic Music*)

Lucinda Burton-Sims, BA Leeds, PGDipEd Birmingham (*PSHEE*)

Sophia Chichester, BA Middx (*Religious Studies*)

Alan Christopher, MA Essex, BTEC Kingshurst, HND Coventry (*Drama*)

Chloe Corani, BSc Bournemouth, PGCE Southampton (*Physical Education*)

Sheila Craske, BA Oxon, PGCE MMU (*Head of Art*)

Lindsey Cullen, MA Oxon (*Head of Classics*)

Bernard D'Souza, BA Nottingham Trent, PGCE Warwick (*Mathematics*)

Ruth Demery, BSc Portsmouth, PGCE Bristol (*Mathematics*)

Grainne Dennison, BA Durham, LPC Chester (*English, History*)

Matthew Dennison, BA Oxon, MPhil Glasgow (*Head of History, Head of Politics*)

Jane Drake, CertEd Bedford (*Food & Nutrition*)

Gerard Duncan, PGDSST, BPE University of Otago, New Zealand (*Physical Education*)

Ian Edwards, BSc Newcastle, PGCE UEA (*Mathematics, Academic Administrator*)

Samuel Edwards, BA Bath, PGCE Buckingham (*Head of Tennis*)

Scarlett Embury, BSc Newcastle, PGCE Chester (*Mathematics*)

Kate Ford, BA London, PGCE Exeter (*English*)

Sara Fordy, BA Winchester, PGCE Oxon (*Head of Textiles*)

Marie Genot, MA Provence, France, PGCE UWE (*French/Spanish*)

Shazia Gleadall, BA Birmingham, PGCE Chester (*Religious Studies*)

Victoria Gross, BA Brunel, PGCE Middx (*Head of Design & Technology*)

Elizabeth Gulliver, BA Oxon (*Psychology*)

Kerri Hadfield, BA Leeds, PGCE Canterbury (*Head of Geography*)

Clare Harding, BSc Leeds, PGCE Birmingham (*Head of Food & Nutrition*)

Louise Harper, BA Dunelm, PGCE Oxon (*Head of KS3 Geography*)

Matthew Harper, BA Oxon, PGCE Warwick (*French/Spanish*)

Kate Hart, BA MMU, PGCE Birmingham (*Head of PSHEE*)
Monica Jimenez, BA La Rioja, Spain, PGCE Canterbury (*Head of Spanish*)
Kathryn Joel, BA Warwick (*DELTA, TESOL, EAL Coordinator*)
Andrea Johnson, BSc, PGCE Durham (*Chemistry*)
Lucy Keyte, BA Nottingham, PGCE Warwick, MSc Roehampton (*French*)
Rachael Knapman, Netball Level 1 Coach UKCC (*Netball*)
Sadie Lapper, BSc Worcester, PGCert Gloucester, MSc Oxford Brookes (*Physical Education*)
Lindsey Lea-James, BMus, LTCL, ALCM, PGCE Huddersfield (*Director of Music*)
Julie Lodrick, BA Chichester, PGCE Kingston, MEd Open (*Music*)
James Long, BA, PGCE Liverpool (*Head of Hockey*)
Victoria Marsh, BSc Keele, PGCE Exeter (*Head of Mathematics*)
Harry Mitchell, BSc Bristol, PGCE Loughborough (*Mathematics*)
Rebecca Moffat, BA Durham (*Learning Support*)
Alice Montgomery, BA Newcastle, PGCE Southampton (*Head of History of Art*)
Bev Murphy, BA Wales, MA, PhD, PGCE UEA (*History, Deputy Head of Learning Support*)
Sarah Neale, BA Worcester (*Dance*)
Amanda Neil, BA Leeds, PGCIPP Chichester (*Head of Learning Support*)
Alison Osborn, BA Reading, PGCE Exeter (*History*)
Pervin Özkan, Licence Tours, France, PGCE Exeter (*Head of French*)
Charlotte Pemble, BSc, PGCE Worcester (*2 i/c Physical Education, Acting Head of Sport*)
Jonitha Peterpillai, BSc, Warwick MSc, PGCE Oxon (*2 i/c Mathematics*)
Lara Price, BLib Aberystwyth (*Librarian*)
Ryan Pickering, NPLQ, NUCO (*Sporting Facilities & Physical Education*)
James Popplestone, BSc Southampton, DPhil Oxon (*Head of Biology*)
Bob Roberts, BA, MA Warwick, PGCE Lancaster (*Head of English*)
Ian Robinson, BEng, PGCE Lancaster (*Physics*)
Emily Scates, BA London, PGCE CSSD (*Head of Drama*)
Paul Scott, BSc Newcastle, PGCE Durham (*Learning Support*)
Kate Simlett, MSc Loughborough (*Physical Education*)
Zoe Simms, BA, MA KCL, MSc Oxon, PGCE Institute of Education (*Head of Religious Studies*)
Catherine Simpson, BA, GDL, MPhil Cantab, PGCE Belfast (*English*)
Rachel Smith, BA Wales, PGCE Leicester (*Head of Psychology*)
Simon Smith, BA, PGCE York (*History, Politics*)
James Stead, BA Cumbria, PGCE Wales (*Art*)
Justine Stephens, BA London, PGCE Middx (*Drama*)
Holly Thomas, BA Bath, PGCE Coventry (*Head of Modern Languages*)
Richard Thompson, MA Oxon, PGCE London (*Head of Economics*)
Julia Thorn, BA Reading, MSt Oxon (*Classics*)
Joanne Thorne, BA Middx, MA, PGCE Warwick, MBA OU (*Head of Business Studies*)
Dane Tice, BA Lawrence University Wisconsin, DPhil Oxon (*Head of Physics*)
Henry Vigne, BA London, MA Kent, PGCE Buckingham (*Food & Nutrition*)
James Wakeley, BSc OU, PGCE Bath (*Head of Computing & IT*)
Rebecca Warrington, BA MMU, MA, PGCE Middx (*Textiles*)
Layla Williams, BA London, PGCE De Montfort (*Head of Dance*)
Stephen Williams, BEd Brighton (*Interim Director of Sport*)
James Woodward, BSc Wales, PGCE Exeter (*Biology*)

Boarding Staff:
Boarding Coordinator: Jackie Webb
Ashtons Houseparent: Lindsey Pickering
Ashtons Houseparent: Ryan Pickering
Ashtons Deputy Housemistress: Calypso Morley
Inglis Housemistress: Sophia Chichester
Inglis Deputy Housemistress: Ribh Ireland
Vs Housemistress: Ruth Demery
Vs Deputy Housemistress: Hannelie Jonas
IVs Housemistress: Sarah Lafford
IVs Deputy Housemistress: Nina Forde
IIIs Housemistress: Grainne Dennison
IIIs Deputy Housemistress: Caroline Rimmer
IIs Housemistress: Sarah Neale
IIs Deputy Housemistress: Lucy Witherspoon
Todd Housemistress: Lucinda Burton-Sims
Todd Deputy Housemistress: Chloe Corani
Boarding support: Julie Bennett, Rebecca Coleman, Penny Davies, Hannah Duckett, Jess Elliott, Sue Jenkins, Maria Rees, Georgia Thomas

Pastoral:
School Chaplain & Staff Wellbeing Lead: Alison Richardson
School Counsellor: Sarah Whitehouse

Music:
Sophie Dean (*Graduate Assistant Music*)
Serena Donnelly (*Drums*)
James Foley (*Guitar*)
Sarah Haigh (*Singing*)
Kim Keeble (*Oboe*)
Kate Pickin (*Piano*)
Miranda Ricardo (*Cello and Piano*)
Beverley Savidge (*Singing*)
Elisabeth Sharam (*Flute*)
Deborah Siepmann (*Piano*)
Kayleigh Skinner (*Singing*)
Lucy Tugwell (*Clarinet and Saxophone*)
Chris Windass (*Violin*)

Sport and PE:
Lottie Gale (*Graduate Assistant Sport*)
Godwin Abah (*Tennis Coach*)
Annabelle Bailey (*Tennis Coach*)
Lucy Brown (*Tennis Coach*)
Lee Morton (*Tennis Coach*)
Ginny Steven (*Ballet*)

Speech and Drama:
Pippa Phillips

Technicians:
Calypso Morley (*Art Technician*)
Alan Christopher (*Ceramics Technician*)

Zoe Johnson (*CDT Technician*)
Sarah Carolan (*Senior Science Technician*)
Julie Brown (*Assistant Science Technician*)
Hope Talbot Waller (*Textiles Technician*)
Samantha Sullivan (*Textiles Technician*)

Learning Support:
Stephanie Herbert (*Teaching Assistant*)
Isabel Rimmer (*Teaching Assistant*)
Sarah Skevington (*Teaching Assistant*)
Bethan Leyshon-Smith (*Learning Mentor*)
Elizabeth Smith (*Learning Mentor*)

Modern Foreign Languages:
Iris Fouquet (*French Language Assistant*)
Kubra Özkan (*French Language Assistant*)
Belen Sainz-Pardo (*Spanish Language Assistant*)
Nadine von Paledzki (*Teacher of German*)

Bursary:
Financial Controller: Kenneth Iredale
HR Manager: Nicole Hamilton
Finance Assistant: Diane Cook
Finance Assistant: Louise Sollis
Finance Assistant: Carol Edginton

Administrative and Support staff:
EA to the Headmistress: Jennifer Lewis
EA to the Bursar & Assistant Clerk to the Governors: Louise Allan
PA to the Headmistress and HR Manager: Amelia Senior
Pastoral Administrator: Zoë Ludford
Data Manager: Brian Wray
Examinations Officer: Katie Donald
School Events Coordinator: Charlotte Redman
Senior Administrative Secretary: Helen Mascall
Administrative Secretary – Music: Joanne Twelvetrees
Administrative Secretary – PE: Rachael Knapman
School Reception: Annabelle Coombs
Reception and Administrator to the Deputy Head Academic: Helen Read
Educational Visits Coordinator: Rachael Knapman
Transport Administrator: Lesley Mansfield
PA to the Headmistress and HR Manager: Susy Wood [maternity cover]

Admissions, Marketing and Development:
Registrar: Elspeth Dyer
Assistant Registrar: Fiona Gaskin
Head of Marketing & Communications: Richard Guy
Graphic Designer: Nicola Mawle
Marketing and Community Officer: Emma Walton-Pond
Alumnae Communications Manager: Lindsay Silver
Alumnae Events and Development Officer: Carrie Davidson

Grounds, Maintenance and Domestic Services:
Facilities Manager: Ben Stowe
Senior Maintenance: Sam Parkin
Senior Grounds: Charlie Cross
Facilities Administrator: Caroline Thomas
Domestic Manager: Elaine Eyre
Catering Manager: Louise Gough

ICT Systems and Network:
ICT Systems & Network Manager: Paul Smith
Systems Network Engineer: Chris Durn
ICT Technician: Melanie Bolton

Medical:
School Doctor: Dr Catriona Reid
Nurse-in-Charge: Janet Bonham, RGN
Nurse: Caroline Hutchison, RGN
Nurse: Lindsey Pickering, RGN
Nurse: Virginia Rayner, RGN

Walthamstow Hall Senior School

Holly Bush Lane, Sevenoaks, Kent TN13 3UL

Tel: 01732 451334
email: registrar@whall.school
website: www.walthamstow-hall.co.uk
Facebook: @walthamstowhall
Instagram: @walthamstowhall
LinkedIn: /school/walthamstow-hall

Walthamstow Hall is an Independent girls' day school founded in 1838 with a history of preparing academically-able individuals for stimulating, purposeful and happy lives. The belief that every pupil given the right opportunities, encouragement and inspiring teaching can develop an incredible range of skills and talents, is central to the everyday life of the School.

The School was judged as 'Excellent' in all categories by the ISI in 2019.

Facilities. Set in its own grounds within Sevenoaks, the original 1882 Arts and Crafts Senior School building is surrounded by the Swimming Pool and Sports complex, Music, Drama and 3DD rooms and The Ship Theatre. Recent developments include the expansion of Art studios, and a Sixth Form Centre with additional Science facilities opened in 2018.

Curriculum. Enriched, innovative and flexible, facilitating breadth and individual choice, without sacrificing depth of study, brought to life with inspirational teaching.

Pupils follow a curriculum of broad and balanced subjects, with a second language added in Year 8. They also receive lessons in 'Q', a mixture of practical skills and critical thinking.

Subjects include: Art, Biology, Business, Chemistry, Classical Civilisation, Computer Science, Textiles, Drama, Economics, English, Literature, EPQ, Food Preparation & Nutrition, French, History, Geography, German, Politics, Latin, Mathematics, Additional Mathematics, Further Mathematics, Music, PE, Photography, Physics, Psychology, Religious Studies, Sociology, Spanish and Three Dimensional Design.

Success in public examinations is excellent. In 2023, 84.2% of A Levels passed at grades A*–B; 72.5% of I/GCSEs passed at grades 9–7.

Religious Teaching. interdenominational.

Co-curricular. The high profile of Drama, Music, Sports, careers and study skills and personal development, together with an excellent pastoral system, provides opportunity and support for all.

A policy of 'sport for all' enables both team players and individuals to find the sporting activities that suit them best. Lacrosse, netball, swimming, athletics, cross country, badminton, hockey, cricket and tennis are on offer, with many teams and individuals achieving highly at all levels.

A high proportion participate in the DofE scheme, Enterprise, School choirs and orchestra, ABRSM and Trinity Drama.

Admission. Admission for Year 7 and deferred entry at Year 9 is through the ISEB Common Pre-Test in the Autumn Term prior to entry. Admission for Year 9 (unless deferred at Year 7) and Sixth Form is through the School's own assessment criteria. Candidates attend an interview and provide a Head's Report from their previous school. Open Mornings are usually in September and March.

Fees per term (2023–2024). £7,870.

Scholarships. Academic scholarships are available for Year 7, 9 and Sixth Form.

Music and Sport scholarships are available for Year 7 and Year 9 entry. Drama and Art can also be applied for at Year 9 and Sixth Form.

A means-tested bursary scheme includes our Founders' Bursary at nearly 100% of fees.

Charitable status. Registered Charity 1058439.

Chair of Governors: Mrs J Adams, BA Joint Hons Durham

***Headmistress*: Ms L Chamberlain**, BSc Hons Nottingham, PGCE Newcastle (*Designated Safeguarding Lead*)

Deputy Head: Mr C Hughes, BSc Hons, Cert Ed Loughborough, NPQH (*Deputy Designated Safeguarding Lead*)
Director of Studies: Ms P Evernden, MA Cantab, PGCE Oxon
Head of Sixth Form: Mrs B Brown, BA Hons, PGCE Loughborough
Head of Key Stage 4: Mrs K Franzen, BA Hons Durham, MA, PGCE King's College
Head of Key Stage 3: Mrs K Hofmann, MA St Andrews, QTS

Department Heads:

Biology: Miss T Cheney, BSc Hons Durham, MSc LSHTM, QTS
Careers: Mrs L Hayes, MA Canterbury, BCom Hons Cape Town, QCG, RCDP
Classics: Mr N Buckingham, BA Hons, MA Reading, PGCE London
Computer Science: Mr J Smith, BA Hons Canterbury Christ Church, GTP
Creative Art & Textiles: Mrs A Norman, BA Hons, MA Wales, PGCE Worcester
Drama: Mrs V Bower-Morris, BA Hons Surrey, PGCE Goldsmiths
Duke of Edinburgh Manager: Mr N Ramsden, BA Maidstone, MA Canterbury, PGCE Brighton
Economics & Business: Mr R Dewey, BA Hons Heriot-Watt, PGCE Kent & Medway
English: Miss S Mehaffey, MA, PGCE Edinburgh
EPQ Coordinator: Mrs L Thomas, BA Hons Wales, MA Open, PGCE Bristol
Geography: Mr C Sullivan, HNC, BA Hons Sussex, NPQL
History & Politics: Ms O Windle, MA, BA Hons Edgewood College, USA
Learning Support: Mr K Williams, APC PATOSS, MA CCCU, BA Hons DeMontfort, PGCE Kent
Mathematics: Mr T Dakin, BSc Hons Bristol, PGCE Sussex
Modern Foreign Languages: Mrs R Hunt, BA Hons Exeter, PGCE King's College
Music: Mr N Castell, BMus Hons, PGCE Manchester
Physics: Mr R Stewart, MEng Bath, PGCE King's College
Science & Chemistry: Dr E Doyle, BA Hons Cambridge, MSc Cambridge, MA Cambridge, PhD Cambridge, QTS
Sociology: Mr S Wilson, BA Hons Sunderland, PGCE London
Sport: Miss R Leggett, BA Hons, QTS Brighton
Theology & Philosophy: Mr D Pollen, BA Hons Bristol, MA UWE
Three Dimensional Design & Food Preparation & Nutrition: Mrs C Evans, BA Hons Greenwich, QTS

Bursar and Clerk to the Governors: Mr P A Horner, MBA, CMgr, FCMI
Admissions Registrar: Mrs A Knight

Wimbledon High School GDST

Mansel Road, London SW19 4AB

Tel: 020 8971 0900 (Senior School)
020 8971 0902 (Junior School)
email: info@wim.gdst.net
website: www.wimbledonhigh.gdst.net
X/Twitter: @WimbledonHigh
Instagram: @wimbledonhighschoolgdst
LinkedIn: /school/wimbledon-high

Founded 1880.

Wimbledon High School is part of the GDST (Girls' Day School Trust). The GDST is the leading network of independent girls' schools in the UK. As a charity that owns and runs 23 schools and two academies, it reinvests all its income in its schools. For further information about the Trust, see p. xxii or visit www.gdst.net.

Pupil numbers. Junior School: 340 aged 4–11; Senior School: 700, including 195 in the Sixth Form.

Wimbledon High School combines academic strength with a firm belief that learning should be fun. Fionnuala Kennedy became Head in September 2020, having been Deputy for 5 years prior. "This is a school with a strong sense of community – academically very successful, yet where laughter abounds. Our students live life to the full, taking themselves seriously while holding themselves lightly." Results at A Level and GCSE are consistently extremely high, music and drama are a vibrant part of school life and the school has had national representation and success in swimming, hockey, netball and rowing, amongst other sports. Activities include World Challenge, Model United Nations and The Duke of Edinburgh's Award, alongside many smaller clubs and societies, from Coding social robots to Gardening. The older students often run these themselves.

A holistic and innovative programme of pastoral care, GROW, underpins school life, with the aim for each student to be known, supported and able to shine. The student leadership team includes an equality, diversity and inclusion rep – further broadening diversity is a key focus for the school and a new Assistant Head Pastoral and Inclusion joined In September 2022. Partnership activities have expanded in recent years, with older students helping with Literacy, Maths, Latin and mentoring younger peers. The school runs SHINE, the outreach Serious Fun on Saturdays programme, as well as Teach Together and volunteering opportunities with local charities. Approximately 200 visiting pupils come weekly to the school to participate in activities during partnerships afternoons.

Junior and Senior Schools share one central Wimbledon site, with a swimming pool and sports hall, Performing Arts Centre and a new dining hall and STEAM tower (Science, Technology, Engineering, Arts and Maths). In September 2022, a new Sixth Form Centre, auditorium and Junior playground in the sky were opened. The playing fields are ten minutes' walk away at Nursery Road (the site of the original All England Club) providing a full-size, all-weather hockey pitch and five netball/tennis courts. Cricket and football are growing sports and a number of students represent their sport on a national and international stage, latterly: tennis, gymnastics, hockey, netball and swimming.

The **Junior School** provides a creative and academic education in a happy and stimulating environment, with specialist teachers for PE, languages, music and science. The curriculum, Adventum, and an enhanced co-curricular offer, Arcadia, have brought a fresh focus to learning and a growing emphasis on play and outdoor education. An after-school club offers flexibility to working parents. Sports teams do well, as do the school's chess players, actors and musicians.

The **Senior School** curriculum runs over a two week timetable. In Key Stage 3, students study English, Mathematics and Sciences; they learn two of French, German and Spanish, as well as Latin, Geography, History, Religious Studies, PE, Music, Drama, Art, Design & Technology (graphics, textiles and product design on rotation), Computer Science, study skills and PSHE (Personal, Social and Health Education). Mandarin starts as an optional club in Year 9.

At Key Stage 4, girls choose 9 GCSE subjects, of which one must be a Modern Foreign Language (Mandarin is an option), with the possibility of adding Classical Greek as a 10th GCSE. PE and PHSE continue. A bespoke Politics, Philosophy & Economics (PPE) course in Year 10 brings breadth beyond the curriculum and new this year is the school's Civil Discourse programme. The school holds regular lectures for older girls, parents and staff.

In the **Sixth Form,** students may choose from the same subjects on offer at GCSE plus Further Mathematics, Economics, Politics, Psychology, History of Art and Classical Civilisation. There is a high uptake of Maths and science subjects and in recent years students have undertaken and published novel research in scientific journals. A comprehensive programme of careers and university entrance advice is offered, including specialist support for applications to overseas universities, medical and veterinary courses, Oxbridge, and a focus on entrepreneurship.

Admissions. 4+ entry is by ballot.

For 11+ entry, candidates sit papers in Verbal and Non-Verbal Reasoning (round 1). Round 2 is a creative assessment, with group activities across a whole morning or afternoon.

The occasional entry examination for other years tests Maths and English.

16+ assessment comprises entrance exam and interviews. Offers of places are conditional upon GCSE grade 8 or above (A* or A) in candidates' chosen A Level subjects, and a minimum of eight GCSEs (grades 6–9) overall.

Fees per term (2023–2024). Senior School £7,718; Junior School £5,999.

The fees cover the regular curriculum, school books, choral music, games and swimming.

Scholarships and Bursaries. Academic scholarships are awarded to girls who do exceptionally well in the 11+ exam, typically worth 5% of the fees. There are also music and sport scholarships at 11+. At 16+ there are scholarships in Art, Drama, Music and Sport, worth up to 10%, as well as Academic scholarships. Details and application forms are available online.

Bursaries take account of academic merit, but all are means-tested. The maximum value is the full fee, and bursaries cover other costs, such as uniform, too.

Charitable status. Wimbledon High School is part of The Girls' Day School Trust, which is a Registered Charity, number 306983.

Chair of the Local Governors: Mrs R McKinlay, BA Hull

***Head*: Ms F Kennedy**, MA Oxon

Head of Junior School: Ms C Boyd, BA Royal Holloway

Director of Finance & Operations: Mrs K Jones, BA Exeter, ACMA

Senior Deputy Head: Mr B Turner, BA Hons, MA London

Director of Marketing & Communications: Mrs R Brewster, BA Oxon, MA Leeds

Withington Girls' School

Wellington Road, Fallowfield, Manchester M14 6BL

Tel: 0161 224 1077
email: office@wgs.org
website: www.wgs.org
X/Twitter: @WGSManchester
Facebook: @withingtongirlsschool
Instagram: @withingtongirlsschool
LinkedIn: /withington-girls-school

See full entry in the **HMC** section, on **p. 394**.

Woldingham School

Marden Park, Woldingham, Surrey CR3 7YA
Tel: 01883 654206
email: registrar@woldinghamschool.co.uk
website: www.woldinghamschool.co.uk
X/Twitter: @WoldinghamSch
Facebook: @woldinghamschool.co.uk
Instagram: @woldinghamsch
LinkedIn: /company/woldingham-school

See full entry in the **HMC** section, on **p 396**.

Wychwood School

72–74 Banbury Road, Oxford, Oxfordshire OX2 6JR
Tel: 01865 557 976
email: admissions@wychwoodschool.org
website: www.wychwoodschool.org
X/Twitter: @wychwoodschool
Facebook: @wychwoodschool
Instagram: @wychwoodschool
LinkedIn: /company/wychwood-school

Wychwood School is a co-educational day and boarding school for pupils aged 11–18 set in the heart of Oxford. Wychwood aims for academic excellence through creativity of thought by providing education of the highest quality in a well – rounded and unique environment, enriching pupils' education through creative approaches to learning and empowering them to face challenges head on with confidence. Wychwood focuses on innovation, teamwork, creativity, and leadership to deliver added value to all its pupils, striving to inspire the great minds of tomorrow. Its approach through creative thinking runs across the entire Wychwood School curriculum and extra-curricular and is infused in everything the pupils do, from creative subjects such as art, textiles, and photography through to STEM, the humanities and sport. The highly dedicated staff empower pupils to discover their passion and skills whilst providing first class education to enable them to find their natural space and place in the world.

Curriculum. Pupils usually take on average 9.5 subjects at GCSE; most go on to work for A Levels and University entrance. The lower school curriculum includes: English, Mathematics, Religious Studies, History, Geography, Biology, Physics, Chemistry, Psychology, French, Spanish, Computer Science, ICT, Textiles, Art, Drama, Photography, Music, PHSE and PE. In addition, pupils can also choose to study Business Studies, Economics, Film Studies, and History of Art for A Level. Staff teach other optional foreign languages and musical instruments. Wychwood has an elective extension program which allows pupils to sign up for an additional course, often not related to a specific subject, where they have the opportunity to explore new and interesting material, as well as develop high order skills such as meta cognition and critical thinking. There is a wide range of over 35 extra-curricular clubs and activities including school choir, various ensembles, dungeons and dragons, art club, fitness club, drama, LAMDA, Model United Nations, rugby, Sci-Fi appreciation, UK Space Design club, and origami to name but a few.

School Council. Day-to-day life is largely controlled by the School Council which meets weekly and consists of staff, senior pupils (elected by the school) and form representatives. This is a type of cooperative government, the mature result of a long series of experiments, which trains the pupils to deal with the problems of community life and gives everyone, in greater or lesser degree according to their age and status, an understanding of, and a voice in, the rules necessary for a sensibly disciplined life.

Sixth Form. Wychwood has a new Sixth Form hub which contains individual and communal study spaces, social areas, and a kitchenette. Members of Wychwood Sixth have considerable freedom yet play an active part in the life of the school. The choice of subjects at A Level is wide. Classes are small and stimulating. Individual help with university applications and careers is a key feature of Wychwood Sixth. Pupils are allowed to be out of school during study periods, and on a Friday, pupils do not start lessons until 9.30am. There are regular outside speakers and pupils attend a variety of lectures, conferences, exhibitions and meetings. Their participation in school plays and concerts as well as School Council is greatly valued. Sixth Form boarders have individual study bedrooms.

Entrance. A personal interview between the Head and the pupil is a key part of the admissions process. There are entrance tests in English and Maths (for years 7–10) and in chosen A Level subjects (for entry into Wychwood Sixth) to satisfy the staff that the pupil will benefit from an education of this kind. Most recent school reports and a reference from the pupil's previous school will also be taken into account.

Scholarships and Bursaries. Scholarships are awarded as academic, creative arts, drama, music sports and all-rounder.

Academic scholarships are awarded on the basis of results in the entrance examination papers at 11+ and 13+ and on the basis of the results of scholarship papers at 16+. Pupils take three scholarship papers in subjects of their choice at 16+ as well as a general paper. Wychwood awards major scholarships of £1,000 p.a. and minor scholarships of £500 p.a.

Dates and further details about all scholarship applications can be found on the website: www.wychwoodschool.org/admissions/scholarships/

Bursaries. There are bursary funds available for a limited number of pupils in particular financial need. Applicants should complete a means tested form and all applicants will be given due consideration by the Bursaries Committee; this will include a home visit.

Fees per term (2023–2024). Full Boarders UK £11,909, Full Boarders (Overseas) £12,898, Weekly Boarders £9,998, Day Pupils £6,937.

Staff:

***Head*: Mrs J Evans**

Deputy Head Academic: Mrs A Stacey (*Chemistry*)
Deputy Head Pastoral: Ms B Sherlock (*English*)
Head of Wychwood Sixth: Mr M Pennington

Miss A Wardell (*Art*)
Mrs R Humphreys (*Biology*)
Mrs G Troth (*Business Studies*, *Economics*, *PSHE*)
Mrs T Jarrett (*Careers*, *EAL*)
Mr A Chim (*Chemistry*)
Mr P Burnett (*Computer Science*)
Mrs M Constance (*Drama*)
Miss J Bettridge (*EAL*)
Mrs H Kirby (*English*)
Mrs I Mayow-Lipscombe (*English*)
Mlle S Bea Mbong (*French*)
Mr P Humphreys (*Geography*)
Mr D Haycock (*History & History of Art*)
Miss O Goodrich (*Latin & History*)
Mrs V MacKay (*Mathematics*)
Mrs R Cooper (*Mathematics*)
Mrs B Walster (*Music & History*)
Miss F Centamore (*PE*)
Miss Hope Kannor (*PE*)
Mr M Pennington (*Photography & Film Studies*)
Mr D Lorimer (*Physics*)
Mr A Mohammed (*Psychology*)
Mrs C Crossley (*RS*)
Mrs M Stephenson (*SENDCo & Head of EAL*)
Mr L Jimenez (*Spanish*)
Mrs S McCullagh (*Textiles*)
Miss Y Roberts (*TA*)
Miss A Mialkowski (*Boarding Staff*)
Mrs L Henk (*Boarding Staff*)
Mrs J Hunt (*Head of Marketing and Admissions*)
Mr Duncan Radnor (*Director of Operations*)

PART III
Schools whose Heads are members of The Society of Heads

ALPHABETICAL LIST OF SCHOOLS

THE SOCIETY OF HEADS
GEOGRAPHICAL LIST OF SCHOOLS

The following schools, whose Heads are members of both The Society of Heads and HMC, can be found in the HMC section:

Bedales School
Birkdale School
Bristol Grammar School
The Cathedral School Llandaff
City of London Freemen's School
Cokethorpe School
Gordonstoun School
Halliford School
Hill House School
Lincoln Minster School
Moreton Hall
Mount Kelly
Reading Blue Coat School
Rendcomb College
St Columba's College
Seaford College
Shiplake College
Wisbech Grammar School

The following schools, whose Head is member of both The Society of Heads and GSA, can be found in the GSA section:

St Augustine's Priory School

The following schools, whose Heads are members of both The Society of Heads and ISA, can be found in the ISA section:

Bishop Challoner School
Burlington House School
Maida Vale School
Sherfield School

Individual School Entries

Abbey Gate College

Saighton Grange, Saighton, Chester, Cheshire CH3 6EN

Tel: 01244 332077
email: admin@abbeygatecollege.co.uk
website: www.abbeygatecollege.co.uk
Facebook: @AbbeyGateCollege
Instagram: @abbeygatecollege
LinkedIn: /company/abbey-gate-college

Motto: *Audentior Ito*

Founded in 1977, Abbey Gate College is a day school for pupils from 4–18 years of age.

Location and facilities. The senior school is set in 20 acres of beautiful grounds at Saighton Grange some three miles south of the City of Chester. The history of Saighton Grange goes back long before the Norman Conquest, although most of the present building is Victorian. From 1853, the Grange was a residence of the Grosvenor family. Additional facilities include a large Sports Hall, playing fields and an Arts and Media Centre opened in March 2004 by HRH the Duchess of Gloucester. A purpose-built Art and Design & Technology Centre and new science laboratory were completed in Spring 2008 and opened by His Grace the Duke of Westminster. In 2013, developments included a new multi-purpose classroom and drama studio. In 2016, a Sports & Teaching Pavilion was opened, followed two years later by the opening of an all-weather pitch. Future developments include two fully-equipped and cutting-edge laboratories and a newly renovated Sixth Form Centre with personal study zones and a range of seminar classrooms.

The Infant and Junior School is situated in Aldford, a picturesque village only two miles from Saighton. Facilities here include a new Foundation and Infant School building opened in 2018, with three spacious classrooms with covered outdoor areas, a library area, and a space for Learning Enrichment, along with excellent playing fields, an ecology and wildlife area plus a number of other outdoor learning spaces. The Infants and Juniors benefit from shared use of the senior site facilities and specialist staff that teach throughout the age range.

Aims and mission. 'We are committed, within our safe and caring community, that each one of our pupils will become the best that they can be and have the self-belief to go forward into this changeable world with courage and with compassion.'

We pursue our whole College mission, guided by three defining and aspirational aims:

- Self: each pupil is mentally and physically well, learns and achieves to their individual potential, and is comfortable and confident to be who they are in our diverse and inclusive College.
- Service: each pupil makes a positive difference to the lives of others in our College, as well as in our local and in wider, global communities.
- Sustainability: each pupil contributes towards preserving and protecting the planet we all inherit and share, and has the opportunity to be creative and innovative; to help further humanity's progress in the future.

In achieving these aims, the College builds the self-confidence of pupils and prepares them for the opportunities, responsibilities and experiences in the next chapters of their lives.

Academic programme. The curriculum is balanced, broad, and challenging to help pupils maximise their potential, empowering them with intelligence, resilience, and the attitude to succeed. Exam results are strong across the board, with significantly positive value-added at each key stage. Pupils are constantly stretched and challenged. Small class sizes, the attention they deserve, and the school's friendly, caring approach ensure they discover and develop their personal talents.

The College is well equipped with the latest technology: interactive touch screens in every classroom, access to a range of iPads, tablets, laptops and PCs, blended learning with Bring Your Own Device in the Senior School, 3D printers, computer-aided design (CAD) equipment, Wi-Fi, and a Virtual Learning Environment (VLE), all help to develop the skills that pupils will need to succeed in the jobs of tomorrow.

The stunning woodland, gardens, and natural, green spaces on both sites contribute to pupils' curricular learning and engagement with sustainability, as well as supporting the context of wellbeing, calm, and respect.

Creativity is well-nurtured by the College's specialist Art and Design Departments, in addition to the Music Department, which enjoys an excellent reputation in the region for the quality of its choir in particular, who delight audiences in the Chester area and beyond on a regular basis.

Many pupils of all ages take music lessons and with visiting staff are prepared for the Associated Board Examinations.

Sport. All pupils participate in physical education and games. Boys play rugby, soccer, cricket and tennis; girls play hockey, netball, tennis and rounders. Athletics is popular for both boys and girls and all sports provide full fixture lists for the various College teams. The local swimming pool is reserved each week for sessions with a fully-qualified instructor for the younger pupils.

Other activities. Pupils visit all corners of the world, including History Department trips to the First World War battlefields, the USA and Poland, Geography Department trips to Iceland, Switzerland and Costa Rica and cultural trips to France. There is a well-established service project with a school in Eswatini and award-winning Young Enterprise teams. The College also have large numbers of pupils completing the Duke of Edinburgh's award at bronze, silver, and gold level.

Admission.

Senior School: Most pupils enter the senior school at age 11 following an Entrance Examination held in the Spring Term, although where occasional places occur in other year groups, assessments can be made mid-year. Each pupil is allocated to one of the Senior School Houses; the house system encourages competition, community and positive attitudes through the allocation of home points.

Junior School: Pupils are admitted to the Junior School by means of short assessment and interview at ages 7, 8, 9 and 10, dependent on spaces being available. It is expected that children already in this part of the school will move directly into the College at age 11.

Infant School: Entry at ages 4, 5 and 6 is also available. Reception places are limited and assessments run on separate occasions throughout the year.

Sixth Form: Priority is given to existing pupils but places are offered to others and are conditional on good results at GCSE.

Scholarships. Academic scholarships are available following the results of the Entrance Examination. A comprehensive Bursary Scheme also operates for pupils from Year 3 and above, widening access to deserving pupils.

For musical talent awards are offered, including the Daphne Herbert Choral Scholarship and the Music Exhibition Scholarship at Year 7.

Fees per term (2023–2024). Tuition: Infant School £3,473; Junior School £3,525; Senior School £5,054.

Abbey Gate College Alumni. All pupils are encouraged to join the Alumni Association. Further details of the Association can be obtained from the Registrar at the College.

Charitable status. Deeside House Educational Trust is a Registered Charity. number 273586. It exists to provide co-education for children in the Cheshire, Wirral and North Wales areas.

Visitor: His Grace The Duke of Westminster

Chair of Governors: A Grime

***Head*: C Jenkinson**, MA Oxon, PGCE, MInstLM

Senior Deputy Head: A Austen

Academic Staff:

J Andrews
K Anger
E Axon
T Baglole
K Bailey
S Ball
K Baty
C Bennett
S Blain
M Booth
K Burdon
A Byers
P Carter
L Chapman
C Cutler
G Darbey
M Dickins
S Dolan
S Donarski
Z Dunn
C Faithfull
E Garcia-Estrada
V Gray
S Hall
H Highton
L Hornby
C Houghton
G Hudson
D Jenkinson
L Johnson
E Jones
D Kebell
H Kitchin
F Lawrence
E Leatherbarrow
Z Leonard
D Luckwell
J Lloyd-Johnson
A Neal
G O'Leary
L Poyser
M Richardson
D Rowett
E Sanders
N Stammers
D Stockley
G Thomas
P Thomas
C Tilly
S Toosey
H Wood
E Worth
K Whitwell

Infant & Junior School:

Head of Infant & Junior School: A M Hickey

P Butcher
A Hughes
E Newman
L Parker
S Parry
W Richards
S Tomlins
C Travis
A Williams

Teaching Assistants:
G Foulkes
A Higgins
A Hughes
W Jones
A Kinsey
M Nevett
K Reid
E Turner

Finance Manager: A Williams
Admissions Manager and External Relations Manager: S MacClaren
HR & Staff Wellbeing Manager: S Moran
Finance Officer (*Operational*): S Tagg
Finance Office (*Technical*)*r*: H Keenan
Marketing and Promotions Manager: F Hodgkinson

Librarian: V Jackson

Lead First Aider & Counsellor: P Sheckley
Counsellor: V Jackson

Technicians:
R Freeman (*Art*)
S Horsefield (*DT*)
S Huxley
H Rawson

Executive PA: K Simons
PA to Head of Infant and Junior School and Receptionist/Administrator: A Ivory
Data Manager: H Goodall
Examination Officer: A Owen
Attendance Officers: K Jackson, K Lindley
Office Administrators/Reception: S Handley. K Jackson, K Lindley, N York
Digital Development and Network Manager : P Rowlands
Senior ICT Technician: A Rose
Estates Manager: Ms D Coakley
Head Gardener: Mr T Frodsham
Head Caretaker: P Hamilton
Caretakers: G Dawson, S Peers, R Tyrrell
Gardener and Maintenance: Y Laidouni, J Hughes
Mini Bus Driver: D Owen

Abbotsholme School

Rocester, Uttoxeter, Staffordshire ST14 5BS
Tel: 01889 590217
email: enquiries@abbotsholme.co.uk
website: www.abbotsholme.co.uk
X/Twitter: @AbbotsholmeSch
Facebook: @abbotsholmeschool
Instagram: @abbotsholmeschool

Abbotsholme School is an independent day and boarding school for boys and girls aged 2 to 18, situated in wonderful rolling hills and meadows on the border of Staffordshire and Derbyshire, close to the magnificent Peak District, in the UK. Our 140-acre campus offers the perfect environment to learn, achieve and enjoy a special education that focuses on academic success and character development. With superb facilities, all of our pupils from Nursery through to Sixth Form, have the opportunity to participate and excel in an extensive programme of sports, outdoor education, agriculture and equine activities as well as the creative arts, music and drama. Abbotsholme aims to prepare each pupil for the whole of life through a balanced, flexible and challenging curriculum fostering a sense of self-worth, enthusiasm for learning and ambition for the future.

ISI Inspection. Following the recent inspections by the Independent Schools Inspectorate, it was reported that at Abbotsholme the '*quality of the pupils' personal development is excellent*', *'pupils have positive attitudes towards learning'* and '*academic and other achievements are good'*.

Special Characteristics. Membership of the *Round Square* organisation (www.roundsquare.org) provides a strong international perspective. A worldwide and unique association of schools committed to personal growth and responsibility through service, challenge, adventure and international understanding, members share one aim – the full and individual development of every pupil into a whole person. Abbotsholme offers an IDEALS programme where pupils understand and learn more in-depth about these values.

Our *outdoor education* programme is both well known and well regarded. Its pioneering principles inspired such organisations as the The Duke of Edinburgh's Award scheme. With adventures both close to home and internationally, it presents pupils with personal challenges, both physical and mental, and teaches them the importance of taking responsibility for themselves and others. Many pupils are involved in The Duke of Edinburgh's Award scheme and all participate in summer camps and autumn hikes each year.

Abbotsholme is one of the very few schools in England to have a working *farm* upon which pupils are able to learn about animal husbandry and crop management and gain a healthy respect for the environment. In addition to the 70-acre farm, our British Horse Society approved *Equestrian Centre* is a popular place to be for our horse enthusiasts, who happily involve themselves in the upkeep of the stables and yard and can study for BHS exams.

We believe that the physical and mental disciplines of working together in a team are very important. *Sport* teaches the art of winning and losing with equally good grace, self-reliance and leadership, and the opportunities to compete are grasped by many of our pupils. The main sports at Abbotsholme include: hockey and cricket, with additional sports being football, netball, rugby, tennis, swimming, athletics, cross-country, badminton and basketball.

All pupils are encouraged to appreciate *Music* in some way, either by learning to play an instrument, entering the Musician of the Year competition or joining in with the inter house school singing competition.

Performing Arts flourishes, in and out of the classroom, with performances in the 120-seat theatre always oversubscribed. All pupils who are keen to be involved, whether on stage or behind the scenes, find regular opportunities to experience the fun and self-discipline characteristic of performance and improvised theatre.

The influence of the *Art* department is evident throughout school, where pupils' painting, drawing, pottery and ceramics are permanently on display. In addition many pupils enjoy the facilities of the *Design and Technology* department, which provides excellent opportunities for developing creative design into quality manufacture and 3D creations. There is an opportunity to help build electric cars in the *Automotive Engineering Club* and race them at places like Silverstone and Rockingham. Photography is a real strength of the Art department and pupils have access to a traditional darkroom as well as cutting-edge editing equipment.

Curriculum. Abbotsholme caters for a broad ability range. Academic standards are high with the majority of sixth formers going on to their first-choice university. Breadth and balance shape the curriculum, which aims to develop critical and creative thinking and self-discipline across a wide range of subjects at GCSE and A Level.

Activities. Abbotsholme firmly believes that a school should have a greater purpose beyond preparing students for College or University. As a result we seek not only to help all pupils realise their individual academic potential but also to develop in everyone a sense of responsibility for themselves and others through active participation within the community as well as a sense of adventure through challenges in and beyond the classroom. A comprehensive range of compulsory activities is integral to the curriculum as part of our carousel programme. Each half-term's activities alternately include Outdoor Education, Farm/Equestrian work and Performing Arts. Wednesday afternoons are home to sports fixtures and an array of other activities, such as equestrian, walks, rock climbing and other activities.

Home from Home. The boarding experience at Abbotsholme is a happy one, where staff and pupils know each other well and where every individual shares equal responsibility for the community's well being and progress. Small, friendly homes are run by resident houseparents as family units. Younger boarders share bright and comfortable dormitories in threes and fours whilst older pupils have single or shared study-bedrooms. A log cabin village has been added for sixth formers giving them opportunities to experience a greater degree of independence and privacy. Weekly boarding has become a popular option for families with busy lives and for our full boarders, a full programme of weekend activities provides plenty of choice and lots of fun, balancing academic work with social time. Our modern approach to boarding means that sleepover and flexi boarding are also options.

Facilities. These include: dedicated classroom areas for each subject, including specialist science laboratories, art, music, design and two IT classrooms, a purpose-built studio theatre for performing arts, sixth form centre, log cabin complex, indoor climbing wall, 70-acre working farm, equestrian centre and manège, a modern, multi-purpose sports hall, synthetic pitch, extensive playing fields and outdoor swimming pool, traditional dining hall and a chapel, which combines as the venue for morning assembly as well as concerts.

Fees per term (2023–2024). Day £3,390–£8,395; Weekly Boarding £6,995–£10,245; Full Boarding £9,295–£12,595; Occasional Boarding: £55 per night (please see full fees here: www.abbotsholme.co.uk/admissions/fees)

The Abbotsholmians' Club. The Club currently has some 2,000 members and is run by a Committee of Old Abbotsholmians, elected yearly. Members receive regular mail-outs, which give contact addresses and details of the adventures of OAs, young and old. There are also regular invitations to events, to help them keep in touch with each other and with current developments at the school. An enormous amount of networking takes place between OAs, often facilitated by the Club, ensuring that friendships are sustained and memories are relived. Website: www.abbotsholmians.co.uk.

The Club operates a small Bursary fund specifically aimed at helping to educate sons and daughters of OAs at Abbotsholme.

Abbotsholme Arts Society. The School is host to one of the most respected concert presenters in the country. Although embracing jazz, poetry and drama performances, its core programme of chamber music has brought a Who's Who of big-name musicians to the school over the years – Ashkenazy, Brendel, Galway, Hough, the Amadeus Quartet to name just a few. Pupils are able to attend any of the Arts Society concerts free of charge. Website: www.abbotsholmeartssociety.co.uk.

Abbotsholme Parents' Association. Run by parents, for the benefit of parents, children and school, the Parents' Association (APA) aims to help new families settle in and become quickly familiar with Abbotsholme and all that it has to offer. Keen to promote active parental involvement in the school, members regularly organise social activities and fundraising events.

***Head*: Mrs Helen Wilkinson**

Deputy Headteacher: Mrs Amy Thornton

Head of Prep School: Mr Richard Brindley

Director of Curriculum: Mr Gareth Pardoe

Acting PA to Headmaster: Mrs Debbie Broughton

Registrar: Mrs Charlotte Gallimore

Director of Boarding: Mrs Trish Beetar

Designated Safeguarding Lead and SENDCo: Ms Sarah Brick

Bursar: Mr Ray Morrison

Austin Friars

Etterby Scaur, Carlisle, Cumbria CA3 9PB

Tel: 01228 528042
email: office@austinfriars.co.uk
admissions@austinfriars.co.uk
website: www.austinfriars.co.uk
X/Twitter: @AustinFriarsSch
Facebook: @austinfriarsschool

Motto: *In Omnibus Caritas*

Austin Friars is a co-educational day school, founded by members of the Order of St Augustine in 1951. It is the UK's only Augustinian school and pupils of all denominations are welcome into the School which provides education for boys and girls aged 3–18.

The 3–18 profile of the School allows pupils more time to respond to the core Augustinian values of Unity, Truth and Love which are enshrined in the way the School goes about its business on a daily basis. The 3–18 model also facilitates a seamless transition from Pre-School to VI Form and presents younger pupils with access to facilities usually the preserve of secondary pupils, such as science laboratories, music suites, specialist sports facilities and design technology workshops.

The quality of pastoral care is one of the School's greatest strengths. Both the Junior and Senior Schools are divided into three Houses with the House being central to the strong sense of a community in which older and younger pupils mix freely.

Studies. The curriculum at all levels is broad and balanced which encourages academic achievement alongside sporting, musical, cultural and creative development, thus allowing each child's talents and potential to be fully pursued. Pupils are encouraged to become increasingly independent learners as they progress through the School with excellent support mechanisms available, on an individual or small group basis, for those pupils with specific learning difficulties who require specialised provision. From age 3 in the Pre-School, pupils benefit from specialist teaching. In the Senior School, class sizes are small and high standards are expected and achieved through careful monitoring of progress and a commitment by all to outstanding teaching and learning.

Activities. The School is an excellent centre for developing new and existing interests and talents. Some 50+ extra-curricular activities are available to pupils both during the School day, and in after school clubs. Music, Speech and Drama have a high profile across all phases of the School. There are regular concerts, musical performances, plays and musicals.

Sport. The school has a full-sized AstroTurf which is utilised throughout the year, and various sports pitches. The range of sporting options available is vast. The pupils regularly achieve county status in their various sports and have competed in national finals. Qualified and enthusiastic staff provide coaching in team sports from the Junior School upwards, and the School's record in inter-school competition is acknowledged far beyond Cumbria. Annual skiing trips take place.

Admissions. Children are admitted into the Pre-School in the three to four age range following a successful taster session. Entry into the Junior School at all levels, except Kindergarten, is by assessment during taster days. Entry into Kindergarten is by interview and a taster session.

The Senior School adopts a three-form entry policy. The majority of places are offered at 11+ where pupils sit the Senior School's entrance assessments; entry to the VI Form is on the basis of performance at GCSE. Admissions at other ages are considered, subject to availability of places and completion of the entrance assessment. All prospective pupils spend a taster day(s) with their prospective year group.

Fees per term (2023–2024). Pre-School: £7.60 per hour, plus £2.40 for lunch (the EYFS offers government funded hours). Junior School: £3,250 (R–Year 2), £3,650 (Years 3–4), £4,750 (Years 5–6). Senior School: £5,995 (Years 7–8), £6,200 (Years 9–11), £6,300 (Years 12–13).

Charitable status. Austin Friars is a Registered Charity, number 516289. It exists for the purpose of educating boys and girls.

Chairman of Trustees: Mr Ewen Swinton

***Headmaster*: Mr M F Harris**, BSc, PGCE

Deputy Head: Mrs J Thornborrow, BSc, PGCE
Deputy Head (*Academic*): Mr D Harte, BSc, PGCE
Head of VI Form: Mr S Parry, MEd, BSc, PGCE, Dip RSA
Head of Junior School: Mr Chris March, BSc

Bursar: Mr D Strawbridge, MSc
Admissions and Marketing Manager: Miss A Burns, BA

Bedales School

Church Road, Steep, Petersfield, Hampshire GU32 2DG

Tel: 01730 300100
01730 711733 (Admissions)
email: admissions@bedales.org.uk
website: www.bedales.org.uk
X/Twitter: @BedalesSchool
Facebook: @BedalesSchool
Instagram: @BedalesSchool
LinkedIn: /school/bedales-school

See full entry in the **HMC** section, on **p. 17**.

Bedstone College

Bucknell, Shropshire SY7 0BG

Tel: 01547 530303
email: admissions@bedstone.org
reception@bedstone.org
website: www.bedstone.org
X/Twitter: @BedstoneCollege
Facebook: @BedstoneCollege
Instagram: @BedstoneCollege

Motto: *Caritas*

Bedstone College, founded in 1948, is a fully co-educational, independent, boarding and day school catering for children between the ages of 4 and 18 years. The school enjoys a beautiful 40-acre campus within an idyllic setting amongst the south Shropshire hills, close to the ancient and beautiful market town of Ludlow, and within a 30 minute drive of both Shrewsbury and Hereford.

The school comprises the Junior School (for children aged 4 to 11 years), Senior School (for ages 11 to 16 years) and Sixth Form (for ages 16 to 18 years), all integrated within one campus. Students from the age of 9 are welcome to board at Bedstone.

Bedstone offers a broad and balanced curriculum with a wide range of subjects available at GCSE, BTEC, AS and A Levels. Bedstone is proudly non-selective and offers the opportunity for students of all ability levels to achieve beyond their expectations, including securing places at the University of their choice.

The College aims to fulfil the potential of every child wherever that potential may lie and, with an average teacher to pupil ratio of 1:8, the smaller class sizes allow individual needs to be catered for. The well-qualified and highly-motivated staff believe that each child has a unique talent which it is their job to find and to nurture.

Bedstone is very aware of the problems that learning difficulties, such as dyslexia, can cause and the nationally recognised Learning Support Department, led by its full-time director with the aid of fully-qualified staff, is central to the help provided. Bedstone is one of a small number of schools in the UK to be accredited by CReSTeD as a Specialist Dyslexia Unit.

Character of the College. Many children who join Bedstone have done so because their parents feel that the individual strengths of their child will thrive best at Bedstone, that the challenges and opportunities for fulfilling their child's unique talents do not exist at their current school, or that they wish for greater pastoral support and guidance for their child. Every parent knows that what they want is the education of the whole child – mind, body and spirit – and Bedstone provides that with its academic and extracurricular programme coupled with its outstanding pastoral care and boarding ethos. Bedstone prides itself on its supportive environment that students are proud to be a part of.

Accommodation. The main house, Bedstone Court, is a listed building of fine architectural merit and accommodates the Junior and Senior boys' houses. In addition, it houses the administration offices, library, dining hall and sixth form area. The two girls' boarding houses are on the opposite side of the campus with the senior girls accommodated within a purpose-built boarding house and the junior girls within the homely surroundings of a 19th century manor house. All boarding houses have resident staff and their families as houseparents. There is seating for 300 people in the Rees Hall Theatre with full AV facilities. There is a modern well-equipped Sports Hall, Design Technology and Art Centre, Music School, a Medical Centre staffed by RGNs, Fitness Suite, Performing Arts Studio, Learning Support and Counselling facility, and a wide range of additional facilities. The College has a campus-wide wireless LAN.

Religious Education. The formal classroom teaching of Religious Studies follows the National Curriculum which covers all the major world religions. More broadly, the college follows the teachings of the Church of England though other denominations, and children without any religious affiliation, are most warmly welcomed. Children, whose parents wish it, are also prepared for Confirmation by the Chaplain. The College enjoys a strong choral tradition and the Choir enjoys an excellent reputation.

Senior College Curriculum. From the First Form (Y7) to the Third Form (Y9) (when a number join from other Preparatory and Primary Schools) the subjects taught are: Religious Education, English Language and Literature, History, Geography, French, Spanish, Mathematics, Biology, Physics, Chemistry, Design Technology, Art, Music, Physical Education and ICT.

In the Fourth and Fifth Forms, in addition to the Core Curriculum of English, English Literature, Mathematics, one modern foreign language (French or Spanish), the three Sciences, Religious Studies, (and non-examination Physical Education), options are: History, Geography, Art, Business Studies, Music, French, Spanish, Design Technology and Sports Studies.

Throughout the College, in all classes, we help students achieve the very best that they are capable of and surpass their own expectations. With the aid of close tutorial support, industry mentor scheme, career pathways, a well-qualified staff, an excellent staff/pupil ratio, plus, of course, determined effort on the part of the students, good progress and examination success are assured. A Level courses are offered in English, History, Geography, French, Spanish, Business Studies, Art, Design Technology, Mathematics, Further Mathematics, Music, Physics, Chemistry, Biology, Psychology and Sports Studies. BTECs in Agriculture and Physical Education are also available as options.

The College has its own Learning Support Department. Excellent EAL provision is available for those who require it in addition to pre-sessional intensive English courses, a three-year A Level programme, IELTS, IGCSE and subject-specific language support.

Careers. There are specific careers staff and a well-resourced Careers Room. Bedstone makes full use of Inspiring Futures' careers services and all members of the Fifth Form take the Inspiring Futures Psychometric tests and have the opportunity to undertake work experience. Our individual guidance means that, typically, 90% or more of Sixth Former leavers gain entrance to their university of first choice.

Games and Physical Education. There are 15 acres of playing fields, with an excellent Sports Hall, fitness suite, performing arts studio and netball & tennis courts plus an astroturf. The success of the boys and girls in physical activity at school, county and district level has been nothing short of remarkable. The school has held several ISA National Championships in various disciplines including Rugby 7s, Cross Country, Tennis and Hockey.

Rugby, Football, Athletics, Cross-Country and Cricket are the main sports for the boys and Hockey, Cricket, Netball, Rounders, Cross-Country and Athletics for the girls but they can join in many more. A rotation system ensures that all students, to a greater or lesser degree, have their share of such activities as Basketball, Badminton and Tennis. Nor are the individualists forgotten. Horse riding is popular, and there are facilities for Table Tennis and Mountain Biking, whilst the South Shropshire and Powys hills provide excellent opportunities for Duke of Edinburgh's Award activities.

Clubs and Activities. The Duke of Edinburgh's Award scheme flourishes and there is a wide range of out-of-class activity, including splendid dramatic and musical productions, debating, individual music tuition. There are twice weekly 'activities' sessions which offer some 40–50 different clubs over the course of any one year. Pupils are expected to know and observe all College rules and parents to cooperate in seeing that this is done. Prefects play an important part in the pastoral system of the College. There are also a number of trips and visits that take place throughout the year, including visits to some of the most beautiful cities in Europe. Every two years there are major international sports tours for both the boys and the girls.

Bedstone Junior School is for boys and girls aged 4 to 11 years. The school is housed in its own separate accommodation and yet shares all the facilities of the senior school. Science, Modern Foreign Languages, Sport, Art and Music are all taught by senior school subject specialists within specialist areas. There is a specialist gifted and talented mathematics programme for the most able junior school students and talented sports players are developed through specialist coaching from the teachers in the senior college and entry into regional and national competitions.

The Junior School is an integral part of the College and children find the transition to the Senior College seamless. Any child accepted within the Junior School is automatically accepted into the Senior College.

Scholarships. For the academically talented, there is an opportunity to attend a Scholarship Assessment with awards available to successful students for entry into the School.

Fees per term (2023–2024). Junior School: Day: Reception to Year 2 (age 4–7) £1,872, Years 3–6 (age 7–11) £3,942; Boarding (Years 5–6, age 9–11) contact Admissions for details. Senior School: Day: Year 7 £4,680; Years 8–13 £5,440; Boarding £10,400; International Boarding (age 9–18) £13,000.

***Head*: Mr T Mullins**, BA, MBA

Deputy Headteacher: Mr C Braden, BEd, PG Dip

Houseparents:

Boys Boarding:
Pearson House: Mr and Mrs J Gray

Girls Boarding:
Bedstone House: Mr and Mrs P Singh
Wilson House: Mr and Mrs A Whitlam

Members of Common Room:
Ms C Beddow, BSc, PGCE (*Sport/PE, Science*)
Mr O Bennett, BA, PGCE (*Religious Education*)
Mr C Braden, BEd, QTS (*Head of DT*)
Mrs S Crabtree, BA, QTS (*English, Drama, Junior School teacher*)
Mrs J Crouch, BA, PGCE (*DT, Maths, i/c Art*)
Mr O Downing, BA, PGCE (*Head of English, Exams Officer*)
Ms C Evans, BMus, PGCE (*Head of Music*)
Mr H Fletcher, BA, PGCE (*Music*)
Dr D Foreman, PhD, PGCE (*Psychology*)
Mr J Gray, BA, PGCE (*Mathematics*)
Miss C Higgins, BA, PGCE (*Junior School teacher*)
Mr J Jones, BSc, PGCE (*PE*)
Mr L Kouniakis, BA, TESOL, QTS (*Head of EAL*)
Mr J Lowe MA, DipRSA Dyslexia, PGD SEN + Inclusion, PGCE, CPT3A, SpLD APC Patoss (*Head of Learning Support*)
Mr D P Marsh, BSc, PGCE (*Head of Geography*)
Mrs C Newnham, BSc, PGCE (*Biology, Computer Studies*)
Mr E Olive, BSc, PGCE (*Head of Science, Physics*)
Mrs C Pennels, BA, PGCE (*i/c French, Spanish*)
Mr J Percival, MA, PGCE (*Head of Sixth Form, Head of History*)
Mr S Pope, BSc, PGCE (*Biology*)
Mrs J Richards, MA Ed, PGCE (*Junior School teacher*)
Miss S Ross, BA, QTS (*i/c PE & Games*)
Mrs T Ruiz Blanco, MA, PGCE (*Spanish*)
Ms C Simmons, MA Oxon, PGCE (*Head of Mathematics*)
Mrs H Swift, BSc, PGCE (*i/c Chemistry*)
Mr A Whittall, BA, PGCE (*Mathematics*)
Mrs J Williams, BEd (*Junior School teacher*)
Mrs N Williams, BSc Econ, PGCE (*Head of Business Studies*)

Teaching Assistants:
Mrs L Meredith, NNEB
Mrs K Singh, BA
Ms A Bolis PhD

Learning Support:
Mr J Lowe, PGD Inclusion & SEN, PGCE

EAL:
Mr L Kouniakis, BA, TESOL, QTS

School Medical Team:
Mrs N Stead, RGN; Mrs J Jackson, RGN

Visiting Music Staff:
Mr B Welthy (*Drums*)
Mr D Luke (*Guitar*)
Mr C Lacey (*Woodwind*)
Mrs J Hargreaves (*Violin*)
Mrs J Parsons (*Piano*)
Mrs B Melling (*Vocal*)

Competitive Houses:
Hopton: Miss C Beddow
Stokesay: Miss S Ross
Wigmore: Mr J Lowe

Headmaster's PA: Mrs C Preston

Accounts Administrator: Mr P Downes
Admissions & Marketing Officer: Mrs Julia Mukho
Marketing & Communications Officer: Mr Tim Cozze-Young
Admissions, Librarian: Mrs A Whittall
Receptionists: Mrs W McKee-Wills; Miss J Goode-Naprous; Mrs H Adams-Evans
Catering/Head Chef: Mrs M Hart
Domestic Supervisor: Mrs D Gough
Transport Manager: Mr P Singh

Beechwood School

12 Pembury Road, Tunbridge Wells, Kent TN2 3QD
Tel: +44 (0)1892 532747
email: info@beechwood.org.uk
website: www.beechwood.org.uk

Beechwood is an independent co-educational day and boarding school for pupils aged 3–18. Founded in 1915, there has been a school here for well over 100 years.

The Nursery School (age 3–5), Preparatory School (age 5–11) and Senior School (age 11–18) are located in 23 acres of landscaped grounds overlooking open countryside, close to the centre of the historic town of Royal Tunbridge Wells. The Main School is based in a Victorian villa with all facilities located on a single campus. There are 325 pupils on roll.

Boarding is offered for seventy boys and girls in modern and comfortable accommodation on the school campus. After a big refurbishment programme in 2021 our junior boarders often share in two or three bedded rooms whilst older students are allocated single study-bedrooms. We receive a large number of applications for boarding places each year, so an early application is advised. The School does not operate 'Exeat' weekends.

Beechwood is noted for its genuine family atmosphere. Consideration for others underpins the code of behaviour for all pupils, making Beechwood a happy school with high academic standards being achieved through expectation and challenge, rather than prescription. We are an ambitious, caring school and that sense of confidence and generosity of spirit permeates throughout the school. At Beechwood we prepare our pupils for the future but encourage them to enjoy the present.

Curriculum. In our small classes, teachers stimulate pupils to excel in what they are good at and build confidence in areas they find difficult, from the youngest child in the Nursery through to our oldest Senior School pupils. Our Learning Development department supports the individual needs of those pupils who require extra support.

Beechwood provides a broad education. At Key Stage 3 all pupils study a range of subjects. Most subjects are taught in mixed-ability classes of boys and girls. Mathematics is setted from Year 7. French is studied in Year 7 along with either Spanish or German. Academic standards are important and we challenge our pupils to achieve their best. We also encourage our pupils to participate in a wide range of extracurricular activities, trips, and visits.

At GCSE pupils can study from a wide range of subjects. Biology, Chemistry and Physics ('triple Science') are offered as single subjects and we offer French, German, and Spanish as Modern Foreign Language options. Mathematics, English Language, RS and English Literature are compulsory at GCSE as well as at least one science subject. This enables pupils to select from a wider range of options when they construct their GCSE portfolio. Additional English language lessons are provided for international pupils. Pupils participate in a diverse PE curriculum and study PHSCE as part of their personal development.

At A Level, more than twenty subjects are offered including three Sciences, Theatre Studies, Further Mathematics, Business Studies, Photography, Product Design, Psychology, Film Studies, History, Criminology and Textiles. The Sixth Form curriculum is enhanced by an enrichment course that includes Life Skills and comprehensive Careers and University application advice. We also offer the EPQ (extended project qualification) and the Arts Award.

Sixth Formers are encouraged to show initiative and take responsibility. They have opportunities for leadership as prefects and in organising activities for younger pupils. All leavers successfully gain places at university on a wide range of courses.

Examination Results. Beechwood's record in public examinations is particularly impressive for a wide ability school, with a pass rate (9–5) of around 90% at GCSE and 100% at A Level, and is in the top 25% of schools for value-added performance at A Level.

Sports. Pupils are encouraged to experience a wide variety of sports, the emphasis being on fun and participation. Sports facilities include a MUGA (multi use games area) hockey and football pitches, netball, basketball and tennis courts, cricket nets, sports hall, badminton and volleyball courts.

Preparatory School and Nursery. Our Preparatory School and Nursery provide an excellent beginning for every child in a supportive, family atmosphere. The curriculum stimulates enquiry, academic standards being maintained through regular monitoring and assessment. French is studied from Year 1 and all pupils also enjoy cookery lessons. In addition, by sharing the facilities of the Senior School, pupils participate in a wide variety of sports and can represent the school in matches. Extra-curricular activities include chess, crafts, gardening and drama. Many pupils have instrumental music lessons.

Entry Requirements. The school is non-selective academically, selection being based on interview with the Headmaster, previous school report, performance in entrance assessments and confidential reference. All enquiries and applications should be addressed to the Registrar.

Fees per term (2023–2024). Full boarders £10,710; Weekly boarders £9,630; Day pupils £3,040–£6,237.

Scholarships. Academic, Sports, Performing Arts and Creative Arts scholarships are available on entry to Year 7, 9 and 12. Entrance Days take place in November for entry to Year 7 and 9, prior to entry the following September. Year 12 are taken prior to GCSE results.

Beechwood School is part of the Alpha schools group.

***Head*: Mr Justin Foster-Gandey**, BSc Hons, PGCE

Deputy Head: Mr Paul Kershaw, BSc Hons, PGCE, MA

Academic Deputy: Mr Jon Millward, BSc Hons, PGCE

Staff:

Heads of Division:
Mrs Rebecca Smith, BA Hons, PGCE (*Junior Division*)
Mr Joshua Rowe, BSc, PGCE (*Middle Division*)
Mr Michael Awdry, BA Hons, PGCE (*Sixth Form*)

Heads of Department:
Mrs Michelle Burton, BA, PGCE (*Drama*)
Mrs Patricia Carey, BA Hons, PGCE (*Computer Science*)
Mrs Olga Clarke, PGCE, Maîtrise MA, Licence/Deug BA (*Modern Languages*)
Mrs Kim Cook, BEd Hons, Dip Ed, AMBDA (*Learning Development*)
Mrs Maria Heslop, MBA, BA Hons, Cert Ed (*History*)
Mr Gary Hatter, MEd, PGCE (*Art*)
Ms Karen Johnson, BA Hons, PGCE (*Media and Film Studies*)
Mrs Sarah Kershaw, BA Hons, PGCE (*Music*)
Mr Toby Kyle, BSC Hons, MEd (*Mathematics*)
Mr Jonathan Millward, BSc Hons, PGCE (*Science*)
Mrs Louise Neill, BSc Hons, PGCE (*Geography*)
Ms Nicola Phipps, BA Hons, PGCE (*English*)
Mrs Candy Prodrick, BD, PGCE (*Religious Studies, PSHE*)
Mr Joshua Rowe, BSc, PGCE (*Physical Education*)
Mrs Rebecca Smith, BA Hons, PGCE (*Business Studies & Physical Education*)
Mrs Helen Startup, BSc Hons, PGCE (*Design Technology*)

Preparatory School:
Head: Ms Dani Saffer, BEcon, BPsych, MEd
Head of Pre-Prep: Mrs Melanie Ireland

Registrar: Mrs Jillian Clarke
School Secretary: Ms Inma Rivera Rios

Bethany School

Curtisden Green, Goudhurst, Cranbrook, Kent TN17 1LB

Tel:	01580 211273
email:	registrar@bethanyschool.org.uk
website:	www.bethanyschool.org.uk
X/Twitter:	@bethanyschkent
Facebook:	@bethanyschkent
Instagram:	@bethanyschkent
LinkedIn:	/Bethany School

The School was founded in 1866 by the Revd J J Kendon. It is a Charitable Trust administered by a Board of Governors, a member of the Association of Governing Bodies of Independent Schools.

Bethany has 369 pupils, aged 11 to 18. Approximately 25% board on either a weekly or termly basis, with a varied weekend programme of activities available for termly boarders. A generous staff to pupil ratio of 1:8 ensures small classes and high quality pastoral care. Individuals are encouraged to develop their potential to the full in academic and all other respects. Most teaching takes place in modern classroom blocks, the result of an ongoing building development programme. Development in ICT has been a priority at Bethany: a wireless network enables pupils from Year 7 upwards to use laptops across the curriculum.

The Orchard offers single study-bedrooms with en-suite facilities, study rooms for day pupils and communal facilities. Recent additions to the School include a brand new six-lane, 25m indoor swimming pool, a state-of-the-art fitness suite and a new Sixth Form centre as an extension of The Orchard and an extension to the outdoor events facility. Our next major project will be the Performing Arts Centre.

Situation. The School occupies a scenic, 60-acre, rural campus in the heart of the Kent countryside, easily accessible from most parts of South East England: an hour from Charing Cross (Marden Station) and easy access to Gatwick and Heathrow Airports, the Channel ports and Ashford and Ebbsfleet International railway stations.

Admission. The normal age of entry is at 11 or 13 by the School's Entrance Assessment and at Sixth Form level based on predicted GCSE grades, but the School welcomes pupils to the Bethany community at other stages if places are available.

Fees per term (2023–2024). Year 7: £6,805 (day), £10,560 (weekly boarding), £11,385 (full boarding); Year 8: £7,035 (day), £10,805 (weekly boarding), £11,635 (full boarding); Years 9–13: £7,515 (day), £11,660 (weekly boarding), £12,815 (full boarding). Dyslexia and Learning Support £795 (full time), £395 (part time); English as an Additional Language Support £795 (Years 7–11), £395 (Years 12–13).

Scholarships and Bursaries. Academic Scholarships are awarded based on performance in the Entrance Examination. Scholarships are also available in Performing Arts, Creative Arts and Sport at the main points of entry, which are Years 7 and 9 and into the Sixth Form. The Christopher Jackson Scholarship is available for pupils who attend state primary schools local to Bethany, are particularly able and have a capacity for academic excellence. Means-tested bursaries are also available. Children of members of HM Forces and the Clergy receive a 10% fee discount.

Curriculum. The broad curriculum is based on the National Curriculum. The full range of subjects is taught including Information Technology from 11+ and Spanish from 13+. We have also introduced Mandarin at Year 7 and GCSE Dance. There are 26 GCE A Level subjects, including Economics, Business Studies, Spanish, Government and Politics, Music, Photography, Politics, Textiles, Theatre Studies and Media Studies. We also offer BTECS and Applied A Levels in Business Studies, Finance, PE and Music. Almost all Sixth Form leavers proceed to degree courses at University.

Dyslexia. The Dyslexia and Learning Support department, which enjoys an international reputation, has been supporting pupils at Bethany for over 30 years.

Games and Activities. The School offers a wide range of sporting opportunities and enjoys an extensive fixture list, having established a long tradition of inter-school Sport. Facilities include a Sports Centre, climbing wall, fitness room, three squash courts, tennis courts, an indoor swimming pool and a floodlit AstroTurf. There is also a wide range of clubs and activities. The Duke of Edinburgh's Award scheme is well established at Gold, Silver and Bronze levels.

Music. There are wide-ranging opportunities for instrumental tuition. There are sectional instrumental groups including: a Symphony Orchestra, Rock School, Jazz Band, Concert Band, Brass Consort and a Choir, all making use of the fine Music School with its recording studio and music technology area.

Careers. The School is a member of Inspiring Futures and careers education is an important part of the Curriculum. Sixth Form pupils take part in the Coursefinder Analysis Scheme and receive detailed advice regarding Higher Education and Gap Year opportunities.

Chapel. The Chapel, built in 1878, is the focal point of School life. Bethany welcomes children of all faiths or none, and together they attend Chapel twice weekly.

Charitable status. Bethany School Limited is a Registered Charity, number 307937.

Governors:
Mr Jonathan Fenn, LLB (*Chair*)
Mrs Wendy Kent (*Vice Chair*)
Mr Peter Askew
Mr Keith Buckland
Mr Roger Clark
Mrs Elizabeth Connell, BA, LLB
Mr Andrew Cunningham
Mr Matthew Harman, BSc Hons, MCIOB
Mr Nigel Kimber, BSc, FCA
Mrs Gabby Power
Mrs Lindsay Roberts, BEd Hons, NPQH, FCCT
Mr Dan Shaw, BA, LLB
(To contact any member of the Governing Body please use the following address: c/o Bethany School, Curtisden Green, Goudhurst, Kent TN17 1LB Tel: 01580 211273)

Senior Staff:

***Headmaster*: Mr Francie Healy**, BSc, HDipEd, NPQ

Bursar: Mrs Clare Morey, BA Hons, ACA
Deputy Head Academic: Mrs Emily Hill, BA Hons, PGCE (*English*)
Deputy Head Pastoral: Mr Alan Sturrock, BEd Hons (*DSL, Games, Geography*)
Director of HR: Miss Toni Carter, Chartered MCIPD
Director of Marketing and Admissions: Mrs Wendy Owens

Teaching and House Staff:
Mr Jack Allsopp (*Religious Studies*)
Mr Ritchie Beckham, BA Hons (*English and Media*)
Mr Dariius Bell, BA Hons, MRes, PGCE (*English, Media and History, Second Assistant Housemaster The Orchard*)
Mr Alex Bolton, BA Hons, NPQSL (*Director of Performing Arts, Head of Key Stage 4*)
Mrs Nicola Clough, BDes, PGDE (*Art and Textiles, Assistant Head of Key Stage 4, Head of Kiplings*)
Mr Richard Clough, BA Hons, PGCE (*History, Assistant Head of Year 7 and 8*)
Mr Cliff Cooper, MSc (*Director of Extra Curricular Activities, Teacher of Maths*)
Mr Simon Davies, BA Hons (*Head of History & Politics, Housemaster The Orchard*)

Mr Simon Duff, BEd, TEFL, NPQML (*Head of Business Economics, Second Assistant Housemaster The Orchard, Head of 6th Form, UCAS Co-ordinator*)
Mr Anton Evans (*Head of Geography*)
Miss Mathilda Fuller, BA Hons (*Mathematics, Second Assistant Housemistress The Orchard*)
Mrs Sarah Fuller, BSc Hons (*Speech Pathology and Therapy, Learning Support Assistant and Exam Access Arrangements*)
Mr Alejandro Garcia (*Spanish*)
Mr Steve Hampton, BSc, PGCE (*Food and Nutrition*)
Mrs Kate Harper, BSc Hons, QTS PGCert SpLD (*School SENCo, Head of Dyslexia and Learning Success, Learning Support, Specialist Teacher*)
Mrs Samantha Harris-Green, BA Hons, PGCE (*Assistant Director of Performing Arts*)
Mrs Frances Healy, BA SpLD (*English*)
Mr Tomorrow Henson, BA Hons (*Games, First Assistant Mount House*)
Mr Anthony Khan, BA Hons, PGCE (*Business Studies, Head of Student Enterprise*)
Miss Sam King, BA (*Head of Girls' Sport*)
Mr Adam Manktelow, BSc Hons, PGCE (*Head of Maths*)
Miss Claire Mills, BEd Hons, PGCert SpLD (*Learning Support Specialist Teacher, Head of Year 7 and 8*)
Mr Marcus Norman, BEd Hons (*Head of Design & Technology*)
Dr Clare Notley, BSc Hons, PhD, PGCE (*Lead Teacher of Biology*)
Mr Matt Payne, BSc Hons, PGCE (*Director of Sport*)
Mrs Rachael Payne, BA Hons, PGCE (*Lead Teacher of Dance*)
Mr Devin Reilly, BSc Hons (*Science, Competitive House Coordinator*)
Ms Nicola Rendall-Jones, BA Hons, DTEFLA, PGCE (*Head of EAL*)
Mr Ceri Roberts, MSc, BSc Hons, PGCE (*Geography*)
Mrs Caroline Rowell, BA Hons (*Teaching Assistant Apprentice*)
Ms Debby Sanjaya, MSc, PGCE (*Lead Teacher for A Level Maths*)
Mrs Carly Shapland, BA Hons (*Head of English and Media*)
Mrs Sarah Smart, BA Hons, PGCE, NPQML (*Head of Art*)
Mrs Anne-Marie Sturrock, BEd Hons (*DLS, EAL, PSHCE Coordinator*)
Mr Mike Thomas, MSc, PhD (*Head of Science, Lead Teacher of Physics, Second Assistant Housemaster Mount*)
Mr James Vickerman, BSc Hons, PGCE (*Lead Teacher of Chemistry, Housemaster Mount*)
Mrs Jules Wareham, BEd Hons (*Maths and Games, Head of Year 9, Careers, Second Assistant Housemistress The Orchard*)
Mr Michael Watts (*Head of Computer Science*)
Ms Laura Williams (*Music*)
Mr Michael Willis, BA Hons, PGCE (*Head of Modern Foreign Languages*)
Ms Leaf Ye Zhao, BA PGCE (*Mandarin*)

Key Support Staff:
Registrar: Mrs Sally Martorell, BA Hons
PA to Headmaster: Mrs Andrea Discombe
Finance Manager: Miss Hayley Rigg
Marketing Assistant: Mrs Sara Cooper
Communications Officer: Sam Harris
School Receptionists: Mrs Amy Mewse and Mrs Ruth DeSouza
Exams and Data Manager: Ms Katja Thornton
Librarian and Archivist: Mrs Claire Rendell
Senior Sister, Wellness Centre: Ms Rhiannon Eyre, RN, BSc Hons

Birkdale School

Oakholme Road, Sheffield S10 3DH

Tel: 0114 266 8408
0114 266 8409 (Admissions)
email: headmaster@birkdaleschool.org.uk
admissions@birkdaleschool.org.uk
enquiries@birkdaleschool.org.uk
website: www.birkdaleschool.org.uk
X/Twitter: @BirkdaleSchool
Facebook: @BirkdaleSchool

See full entry in the **HMC** section, on **p. 26**.

Bishop Challoner School

228 Bromley Road, Shortlands, Bromley, Kent BR2 0BS

Tel: 020 8460 3546
email: office@bishopchallonerschool.com
website: www.bishopchallonerschool.com
X/Twitter: @challoner_head
Instagram: @bishop.challoner.school

See full entry in the **ISA** section, on **p. 862**.

Bournemouth Collegiate School

Senior School:
College Road, Southbourne, Bournemouth, Dorset BH5 2DY

Tel: 01202 436550
email: registrar@bcschool.co.uk
Facebook: @Bournemouthcollegiateschool
Instagram: @bcs_school

Prep School:
40 St Osmund's Road, Poole, Dorset BH14 9JY

Tel: 01202 714110
email: prep-admin@bcschool.co.uk

website: www.bournemouthcollegiateschool.co.uk

Together we #achievetheextraordinary

Bournemouth Collegiate School offers the very best in independent co-education for ages 3–18 with boarding from age 11. Our Senior School is situated in a beautiful coastal location just a few minutes from Bournemouth beach and our Preparatory School is located in a spacious woodland setting in Lower Parkstone, Poole.

BCS provide a holistic teaching experience to all students, understanding that academic success is not the only principal factor in a child's education. Our mission is to equip our students with the tools and experiences for a successful and enriching future; helping them to realise their full potential for personal and academic excellence.

BCS provides a nurturing environment where the happiness of our pupils comes first. Our 'added value' extends to our variety of co-curricular opportunities and sporting and music programmes, that allow our pupils to cultivate new skills and develop into well-balanced, confident and versatile young people. BCS runs a successful Sports Academy for talented athletes that utilises our outstanding facilities across both sites, including indoor swimming pools at both schools, this was recognised at the Independent School's Association Awards 2021, when BCS were announced as winners of the award for Outstanding Sport (Large School).

We encourage independent learning and intellectual curiosity by providing pupils with a wide range of experiences including trips, seminars, talks by guest speakers and the opportunity for fun, expression and friendship in the many school events on offer. Our aim is to inspire each pupil to make the most of their talents. This way the pupils at BCS, of any age, grow in self-esteem, develop resilience, have a sense of adventure and are equipped to flourish as young adults.

Fees (2023–2024)

Prep School (termly): £2,570–£4,230.

Senior School (annual): Day Pupil £15,990, Weekly Boarder £29,875, EU/Full time Boarder £33,140, International Boarder £38,650.

For more information regarding fees please visit bournemouthcollegiateschool.co.uk.

Scholarships and Bursaries. Each year, we are proud to award a limited number of scholarships to pupils who are capable of extremely high levels of achievement and who we believe will make a significant contribution to the life of the school.

Bursary support is also available through a means-tested application process. For more information please visit our website or contact us at registrar@bcschool.co.uk.

***Headteacher*: Mrs Maria Coulter**, BSc Hons, PGCE, NPQH, Dip Ed

Senior Deputy Head: Mrs Helen Pike, BSc Hons, PGCE, PGCE in Dyslexia and Literacy

Head of Prep School: Mrs Karen Wyborn, BA Hons, PGCE

Box Hill School

Mickleham, Dorking, Surrey RH5 6EA

Tel: 01372 373382
01372 385002 (Registrar for Overseas Admissions)
01372 384240 (Registrar for UK Admissions)
email: registrar@boxhillschool.com
website: www.boxhillschool.com
Facebook: @BoxHillSchool
Instagram: @boxhillschool
LinkedIn: /box-hill-school

Affiliations: The Society of Heads, Round Square, BSA, AGBIS, ISBA, BAISC, IBO, DofE, NAGC.

Box Hill School, nestled in twenty-six acres of Surrey countryside, offers a nurturing and diverse co-educational environment for students aged 11–18. Embracing day, flexi, weekly, and full boarding options, we stand out by recognising and fostering the unique talents of each individual. Our focus lies in unlocking their potential, fostering confidence and building resilience.

Renowned for our robust educational, artistic and sporting traditions, our commitment to discovering and nurturing every student's abilities is what sets us apart. Our academic standards are notably high despite our non-selective approach, with students consistently surpassing national averages in public exams – a testament to our dedication to academic excellence.

Key School features:

- International opportunities via Round Square membership.
- IB World School status.
- Small classes and robust academic support.
- Exceptional pastoral care.
- Diverse weekly and termly co-curricular activities, ranging from Chamber Orchestra to High Ropes.
- International Study Centre.

In our Sixth Form, students have the choice between the IB Diploma Programme or A Levels, benefitting from flexible subject combinations within our timetable system. We aim to accommodate a wide array of choices to suit individual aspirations.

As a proud founding member of Round Square, a global network of 200+ schools, we are guided by its core 'IDEALS': Internationalism, Democracy, Environment, Adventure, Leadership and Service, ingrained in our school's ethos.

Our small, friendly Houses create a supportive 'home away from home' atmosphere. Full-time boarders relish weekend outings, and a staffed on-site medical centre ensures their wellbeing during term time. Notably, there are no 'exeat' weekends.

We strongly believe in the value of extracurricular activities, woven into our extensive timetabled program. Students engage in UK expeditions twice a year, with a strong emphasis on programmes like the Duke of Edinburgh's Award and Round Square expeditions focusing on community-based projects globally.

Our vibrant Parents Association, comprising supportive parents and friends, fosters community links through social functions and fundraising events, encouraging all parents to actively participate.

Courses offered. GCSE: Mathematics, English Language, English Literature, Biology, Chemistry, Physics, Geography, History, Business Studies, Computer Science, French, Spanish, Music, Art, Textiles Design and Fashion, Drama, Physical Education, Design Technology.

IB: Biology, Environmental Systems, Business and Management, Mathematics – Analysis & Approaches, Mathematics – Applications & Interpretation, Chemistry, Psychology, Economics, English Language and Literature, Visual Arts, Geography, History, Russian, Italian, French, Spanish, German, Physics. We aim to offer all other IB approved languages in any year, subject to demand.

A Level: Art, Biology, Business Studies, Chemistry, Economics, English, French, Further Mathematics, Geography, History, Mathematics, Media Studies, Physics, Psychology. BTEC Sport can be taken with an additional A Level subject.

Sports. Athletics, basketball, cricket, football, hockey, netball, rounders, rugby and tennis as competitive sports but many others as part of the activities programme such as dance, kickboxing, pilates, golf, swimming, volleyball, mountain biking and multi-gym.

Drama, Music and Art. Art students gain excellent examination grades each year, with many going on to be accepted at major art schools. Our purpose-built Music School enables a wide range of musical opportunities within school, including a choir, rock band and performance opportunities for individual vocalists and instrumentalists. The school stages senior and junior productions each year and has performed *The Great Gatsby, The Addams Family, Wendy & Peter Pan* and an innovative and original festival. There are lunchtime recitals where staff and students perform while others enjoy their lunch on the picnic benches. LAMDA coaching is available and the school has an excellent record in these examinations.

Fees per annum (2023–2024). Day from £21,120; Flexi Boarding (2 nights) from £26,040; Weekly Boarding from £30,960; Full Boarding from £35,145.

Scholarships. A variety of awards are offered for entry to Box Hill School; the latest information can be found on the school's website. Scholarships are available for those entering Years 7, 9 and the Sixth Form, under the following categories: Academic, Art, Drama, Music and Sport.

Bursaries are available on application following registration and are subject to means-testing and are offered on the basis of a formula laid out in the school's Scholarships and Bursaries Policy which is available on request from the school. All bursaries are reviewed annually.

Method of entry. Entry is based on an interview, the two most recent reports from the pupil's present school, and written tests in Maths and English. Sixth Form entry is based on report, interview and GCSE predictions. For overseas pupils a personal interview on site is desirable but we are happy to conduct a virtual interview if necessary. Main school entrance ages are 11, 13 and 16 years. Under normal circumstances, we like to meet prospective pupils and their parents or guardians – this also gives you an opportunity to have a look around our campus facilities and meet key staff and students.

Charitable status. Box Hill School Trust Limited is a Registered Charity, number 312082. It exists to promote the advancement of education.

Chairman of Governors: Mr Trevor Johnson

***Acting Headmistress*: Mrs Hayley Robinson**

Chief Operating Officer: Mr Stuart Ansell

Registrar for Overseas Students: Mrs Kirstie Hammond

Registrar for UK Students: Mrs Claire Jordan

Headmaster's PA: Mrs Kate Kench

Bredon School

Pull Court, Bushley, Tewkesbury, Gloucestershire GL20 6AH

Tel: 01684 293156
email: admissions@bredonschool.co.uk
website: www.bredonschool.org
X/Twitter: @BredonSchool
Facebook: @Bredon-School
LinkedIn: /bredon-school-2002-limited

Teaching dyslexic pupils since 1962.

Age Range. 8–18.

Number of Pupils. 240: Boarders 100, Day 140.

Bredon School is a co-educational independent boarding and day school located in the beautiful Gloucestershire countryside. As a dyslexia specialist since 1962, the School supports children with dyslexia to achieve their potential in a caring, nurturing environment. The inspiring location, wide-ranging curriculum and vast outdoor environment enables all pupils to find an area in which to shine; whether that is on the school farm, within the forest school, out on the sports fields, taking part in outdoor education and adventure activities, or joining our thriving Combined Cadet Force. The opportunities are endless.

Ethos. Bredon educates the whole child through sound, realistic academic provision, sympathetic pastoral care delivered through a House system, regular leadership challenges and a varied sports programme. The small and friendly environment allows children of all ages to thrive and achieve academic success.

Learning Support. The school is internationally-renowned for its expertise in supporting children with dyslexia and is CReSTeD-accredited, holding Dyslexia Specialist Provision (DSP) status. Within its dedicated Learning Support Centre, an extensive range of specialist software and specialist tuition allows pupils to organise their thoughts, practice their skills and use voice-activation to enhance their individual progress.

Curriculum. Bredon provides a broad academic curriculum that progresses from its Junior School to Sixth Form. From Years 10 to Year 13 Bredon's curriculum is organised into 'Academic', 'Vocational' and 'Professional' pathways. The Academic Pathway includes a range of GCSEs and A Levels. Subjects within this pathway include Art and Design, Mathematics, History, Geography, Environmental

Studies (to name but a few). Bredon's vocational pathway features BTECs that make use of Bredon's inspiring facilities. For example, our Engineering workshops and Farm offer vocational pathways for those interested in pursuing a career in engineering, agriculture or animal care. Bredon's professional pathway includes a desirable IT industry CISCO qualification. Across the school class sizes average 12 pupils.

Sports. Bredon offers pupils a wide variety of sporting opportunities including rugby, hockey, netball, football, cricket, kayaking, mountain biking, running, horse riding, golf, football, tennis, athletics, chess, swimming, shooting and fishing. Pupils frequently take part in fixtures with local schools. Pupils also have access to a fully equipped gymnasium, a 30 metre sports hall, a climbing wall, shooting range and bouldering course.

Outdoor Activities. Bredon school offers a number of outdoor activities for pupils at all ages. The Bredon Farm allows pupils to learn outside the classroom. The farm is home to rare breed pigs, cattle, sheep, Shetland ponies and fowl. The Forest School is a firm favourite with Junior Pupils. Extensive opportunities such as Duke of Edinburgh scheme at Bronze, Silver and Gold levels, Combined Cadet Force and extra curricular trips are organised by the school.

Clubs and Activities. There are many thriving lunchtime clubs including coding, cooking and sports. In addition, once a week, the afternoon lessons are given over to activities and the children can choose from options as varied as cycling, dancing, music, art, cookery, engineering, farming and clay pigeon/air rifle shooting.

Boarders. There is provision for boarders from age 9 and they are cared for by house parents, creating a real home-from-home environment. Accommodation is in dormitory-style rooms until Year 12 when children move into individual study-bedrooms. Boarders have an extensive range of after school activities to participate in and there is a lively schedule of weekend events too.

Pupils join us from the local area, the UK and the wider world, and come together to form a vibrant community of learners who are socially and morally responsible and who support one another on their journey towards becoming happy, healthy, confident and capable young people.

Admissions. Admission is by potential not just attainment, and all lessons are taught with dyslexia-friendly teaching in mind. There is no entrance examination, instead school reports and any specialist reports will be requested and assessed, followed by a 3 or 5-day 'taster' visit to the school to assess suitability. A place is usually offered upon completion of a satisfactory taster stay.

Fees per term (2023–2024). Day: £4,410–£8,770. Termly Boarding Supplement: £5,270. International Boarding Supplement: £5,950.

Chairman of Governors: Mr Aatif Hassan

***Headteacher*: Mr Nick Oldham**, BA Hons, QTS Dip NLP

Bursar: Mr S Giles, BSc, FCCA

Registrar: Esther O'Reilly-Cain

Deputy Head (*Co-Curricular*): Mr J Richardson, BA, PGCE

Deputy Head (*Safeguarding*): Miss C Eaton, PGCE, QTLS, NPQSL, MInstRE

Academic Development Lead: Mrs L Saunders

Director of Learning and Development: Mrs Jodie Grant, BEd, BQTS, SpLD Level 5, CPT3A

Bristol Grammar School

University Road, Bristol BS8 1SR

Tel: 0117 973 6006
email: headmaster@bgs.bristol.sch.uk
website: www.bristolgrammarschool.co.uk
X/Twitter: @bgsbristol
Facebook: @bgsbristol

See full entry in the **HMC** section, on **p. 42**.

Burlington House School

Bishop's Avenue, Fulham, London SW6 6EG

Tel: 020 7610 9018
email: office@burlingtonhouseschool.com
website: www.burlingtonhouseschool.com
X/Twitter: @Burlington_HS
Facebook: @BurlingtonHouseSchool
LinkedIn: /@company/burlington-house-school

See full entry in the **ISA** section, on **p. 864**.

The Cathedral School Llandaff
A Woodard School

Llandaff, Cardiff CF5 2YH

Tel: 029 2056 3179
email: registrar@cathedral-school.co.uk
website: www.cathedral-school.co.uk
X/Twitter: @cslcardiff
Facebook: @cslcardiff
Instagram: @cslcardiff

See full entry in the **HMC** section, on **p. 58**.

City of London Freemen's School

Ashtead Park, Ashtead, Surrey KT21 1ET

Tel: 01372 822400
email: admissions@freemens.org
website: www.freemens.org
X/Twitter: @HelloFreemens
Facebook: @HelloFreemens
Instagram: @hellofreemens

See full entry in the **HMC** section, on **p. 67**.

Clifton High School

College Road, Clifton, Bristol BS8 3JD
Tel: 0117 973 0201 (School Office)
0117 933 9087 (Admissions)
email: admissions@cliftonhigh.co.uk
website: www.cliftonhigh.co.uk
X/Twitter: @cliftonhigh1877
Facebook: @CliftonHighSchoolBristol
Instagram: @cliftonhighschoolbristol

Clifton High School is centrally located in Clifton Village, a picturesque area set in the heart of Bristol. In a city renowned for its culture, architecture and beautiful green spaces, the School immerses itself in the local community and while we embrace tradition, we are unafraid of change.

Clifton High School is a thriving, co-educational independent day school for over 775 pupils ranging from 3 to 18 years old. Previously a traditional girls' School, founded in 1877 and steeped in history, we continue to offer a solid education focused on holistic values with an emphasis on an exceptionally nurturing approach to learning.

As an all-through School, Clifton High School children are driven by our core values of Curiosity, Empathy, Love and Direction with each step of their educational journey, from The Hive Pre-School through to the Sixth Form, perceived as an integral transition in their growth of freedom. As children learn within small class sizes and are nurtured by a well-administered community safety net that sits alongside the triangular collaborative investment and communication links between teachers, parents and pupils, their individual brilliance is more clearly transparent. We provide them with the privilege of personal success, create a culture strengthened by a united community that openly recognises and applauds our differences whether it be in gender, age, race, colour, nationality, ethnicity, disability, religion or culture.

While our academic results speak for themselves and we are proud of the achievements of all our pupils, it is our School ***aims, ethos and values*** that reinforce the supremacy of wellbeing. Realising the individual brilliance of each and every pupil is the most authentic way to achieve our **aims** by offering a well-rounded, bespoke education, delivered by staff who grow to recognise each child's gifts so to offer them unique opportunities to shine. The **ethos** of the School is one of belief in the worth of a holistic education, encouraging all pupils to become passionate in their interests while learning to deal with both success and defeat. They are encouraged to reach milestones as well as set personal standards with confidence, as they work towards and embark upon successful and self-fulfilled futures.

Curiosity – The bedrock of any school is when curiosity is embedded into the learning structure. At Clifton High School, our pupils are educated to be informed individuals. They develop the ability and knowledge to apply the art of questioning and debating that builds confidence in themselves to explore the development of new and independent ideas.

Empathy – Consideration of alternative perspectives directly relates to the formation of relationships with one another. As a School, we aim to foster empathy in our pupils, allowing them to appreciate a world based upon human interaction and nature. Our embedded pastoral system equips them with the ability and desire to change the world in positive ways, maintaining a foundation of kindness throughout their life.

Love – Relationships are enhanced when the value of love, for oneself and others, is achieved. We encourage pupils to believe that love for others directly equates to an inclination of prioritising personal wellbeing. Effectiveness is heightened when individuals develop the confidence and resilience of self-love. Loving the natural world, feeling passionate about the outdoors and nurturing a desire to preserve our planet for future generations are lessons constantly celebrated within the School.

Direction – Collectively, Clifton High School's values direct pupils to aspire and achieve in the education that they receive, beyond the parameters of a standard curriculum. We actively encourage pupils to strive for ambition through a commitment and dedication to accomplishing their personal goals, all of which provide direction, purpose and drive motivation.

Facilities. Clifton High School pupils have access to a wealth of on-site and external facilities and resources that benefit their education. These include a newly designed Sixth Form Centre, built to meet the evolving needs of young people, a Science Department hosting seven laboratories, a STEM Room and Design Workshop, Food and Nutrition room, heated 25-metre indoor swimming pool with spectator's gallery, a gymnasium featuring a climbing wall, cardio, strength and conditioning suites and floodlit multi-games courts. Our valued and esteemed sporting partnerships with the University of Bristol, Henleaze Performance Swimming Club and Bristol Sport afford our pupils access to world-class professional coaching at off-site and state-of-the-art facilities including indoor and outdoor floodlit tennis courts, 3G artificial pitches (sand dressed and floodlit), grass pitches for football and rugby, cricket squares and nets, and netball courts.

Class sizes. Throughout Clifton High School, class sizes remain small. We base our intake on accommodating no more than eighteen pupils in the Infant School, twenty in the Junior and Senior School and twelve in each Sixth Form class.

Classrooms. Clifton High School's large, bright and airy teaching spaces are intentionally designed and organised to be creative in their approach to learning, engaging all pupils in practical and interactive opportunities, constantly encouraging a growth mindset and a love of learning.

Curriculum. *The Hive Pre-School and Infant School* follows the latest Early Years Foundation Stage Curriculum which places a strong emphasis on exploration, investigation, discovery and problem-solving. Our young learner's education is complemented by proactive Adventure, Sport and Co-Curricular Programmes. Teachers in the Hive primarily observe how children play, considering their interaction with hands-on activities to adopt pedagogy while developing and challenging an enquiring mind. As children seamlessly transition from the Pre-School environment into the Infant School, they instinctively thrive from an increase in independence. Our bespoke curriculum encourages a responsive approach to learning with the offering of a range of subjects and opportunities that are designed with individualism in mind.

The Junior School's approach is offering excellent pastoral care and academic teaching with a qualified teaching body that encapsulates development on all levels. A broad, pupil-centric, bespoke curriculum allows an optimal learning environment to be created which together with annual curriculum audits, ensure lessons cater for each child's evolving needs. Junior School children benefit from lessons taught by specialist subject teachers including Mathematics, Science, Modern Foreign Languages, Drama and Physical Education.

The Senior School is built upon a community that truly understands their role in the wider world, with a confidence instilled through our esteemed secondary education and service to pupils' wellbeing. Our excellent academic results are clear evidence of the incorporation of the successful Diamond Edge Model into our teaching methods. This allows pupils to be supported in their individual dynamic needs, teaching boys and girls separately in the core subjects of Mathematics, English and the Sciences during Years 7, 8 and 9. Evidence of success is clearly demonstrated in our excellent academic results. As an academically selective School, pupils are recommended to choose nine GCSE subjects with each individual understanding how to work collaboratively and independently to achieve excellent results, which as a School, consistently meets and exceeds baseline grade predictions in every subject.

The Sixth Form is distinctive in its approach to a selective, co-education for 16–18-year-olds in purpose-built facilities that support outstanding teaching. Our broad A level curriculum is exemplary in its offering of twenty-seven subjects alongside a range of additional ancillary courses and the bespoke 'Above and Beyond' Programme. Students are expected to choose three A levels and up to two additional ancillaries, ensuring their academic experience is tailored to their future pathway. They are guided through our inspiring Careers Guidance Programme, with every student receiving 1:1 support on their UCAS application or alternative vocation. While we very much value our students for who they are, we firmly believe that from happiness and self-confidence, success will follow. Their excellent academic results and the value we add to their academic outcomes consistently set us above other parallel schools.

International. Clifton High School has a proven track record in successfully educating international students and is a sponsor for UK Visas and Immigration. Despite not being an International Boarding School, we embrace the cultural and social diversity that international students contribute to our community. We welcome those families seeking a first-class English education for their child, which offers them a true integration into British culture. We also deliver the Centre National d'Education àDistance (CNED) Programme to native level French speakers enrolled at the School, who are enabled to study the relevant French curriculum for their age alongside the British curriculum. Clifton High School was the first to do so in the Bristol area. This is a popular offering, particularly with French expatriates who may be living in Bristol for a number of years before returning to France. It allows their children to seamlessly transition and enrol back into the French education system.

Sport. Sport is not only a social and positive aspect of life at Clifton High School, but also serves as a dynamic force that brings joy and a sense of belonging to every member of our community. We pride ourselves on promoting inclusivity, welcoming every pupil, regardless of their experience or skill level, to participate in our Sports Programme. While our School site hosts multiple physical education environments including a gymnasium, outdoor multi-use games area, 25m indoor swimming pool, lawn and studio space, we also enjoy partnerships with the University of Bristol, Bristol Sport (Bristol Bears Rugby and Bristol Flyers Basketball) and Henleaze Performance Swimming Club, benefitting from their elite coaching programmes and facilities. These sport offerings enable pathways to international standard, forging links with other local schools and often resulting in county and national honours in relevant leagues and tournaments.

Music and drama. With over 150 music lessons being offered in any one School week, all pupils have the opportunity to perform in orchestras, wind bands, drama groups and choirs as well as participate in a variety of concerts and productions throughout the year. Many pupils work towards Associated Board and LAMDA examinations, consistently achieving outstanding results and being awarded places in top music and drama establishments with careers extending into the Performing and Creative Arts.

Charitable programmes. Clifton High School actively supports local and national charities through numerous fundraising events held within and beyond the parameters of the School campus. These endeavours contribute on many levels to charitable initiatives while also contributing to our community ethos, drawing upon a supportive network of generous members.

Co-curricular programmes. We pride ourselves on our enviable reputation for the breadth of enrichment learning we offer through our co-curricular clubs, Adventure Programme and external national and international educational trips. An extensive array of over one hundred and fifty options, thoughtfully curated into the three spheres of Skills Development, Academic Progress and Individual Brilliance aims to embrace a holistic approach to individual growth and professional development, equipping pupils with the tools to embrace new challenges and navigate relationships. As a School, we believe it is both vitally important to complement classroom skills with the development of these diverse skills and interests to ignite our pupils' passions as they develop into engaged and empathetic responders to the world around them. A partnership with The Mendip Activity Centre, together with our offering of a wealth of activities that include Construction, Coding, Choir, Chess, Tennis, Swimming, Gymnastics and Taekwondo, ensure that all innovative opportunities are carefully interwoven into the School co-curricular programme, truly realising 'Individual Brilliance'. As pupils progress into the Sixth Form, the wealth of co-curricular opportunities afforded to them provide a genuinely holistic learning environment, learning skills in leadership and instilling our core values of Curiosity, Empathy, Love and Direction. They are assigned roles as Head Prefects, House Captains, Sports Captains, ambassadors for charitable initiatives and lead on Diversity and Inclusion, Environmental Change and Sustainability all with the motivation to act as mentors for the younger years and represent Clifton High School as socially aware individuals.

Clifton High School participates in many initiatives that act as platforms for like-minded individuals to unite and engage. These include the Excelsior Forum, Duke Of Edinburgh Award, The Young Enterprise Club and as a Green Flag awarded Eco School, pupils work on environment focused projects with a real-world context.

Admissions. Clifton High School's dedicated Admissions Team are experienced in guiding families in the process of starting your child's educational journey with us. Entry into The Hive Pre-School is after a child's third birthday with Reception class being the first point of entry into the Infant School. Infant School places (up to Year 3) are offered after an in-class assessment during a Taster Day. For Junior School places (Year 4-Year 6), children are invited to sit entrance examinations in English and Mathematics before attending a Taster Day in their current year group. For entry into Senior School, prospective Year 7 pupils are invited to attend a Taster Day before sitting entrance examinations in English, Mathematics, Verbal and Non-Verbal Reasoning and on occasions places that arise entry into Year 8 to 10 will require entrance examinations to be sat in English and Mathematics and, if successful, pupils will attend a Taster Day. Prospective Sixth Form pupils are invited to attend a Sixth Form Experience Day, before submitting an application to express an interest in joining the School, consisting of a registration form, predicted and/or mock grades and a written statement by the pupil. On consideration of the application, pupils will be invited to interview with the Head of Sixth Form, before an offer of a place being made.

Scholarships. *Scholarships* are typically awarded upon entry into Year 7, however, scholarships can be awarded in other Senior School year groups at the discretion of the Head of School. All pupils applying for Year 7 entry are automatically considered for an academic scholarship from the result of the entrance examinations. The School also extends scholarships in Sport, Music as well as an Individual Brilliance Award. Sixth Form scholarships can be applied for in any one of a pupil's chosen A level subjects, Music or Sport. Once shortlisted, pupils will be invited to attend a Scholarship Interview Evening. Further information on all Scholarships may be obtained from our Admissions Team.

Fees per term (2023–2024). Sixth Form: £5,840; Senior School: £5,840; Junior School: £4,035; Infant School: £3,295–£3,560 (Free Early Education Entitlement (FEEE) – 15 hours per week for children under 5 years old accepted); Hive Pre-School: £68.00 per day (FEEE – 15 hours per week for children under 5 years old accepted).

Charitable status. Clifton High School is a Registered Charity, Number 311736. It exists to provide a first-class education for pupils aged 3 to 18 years.

Patron: Dr Richard Gliddon, PhD, BSc, FI Biol

Chair: Mr J Caddy, BSc

***Head of School*: Mr Luke Goodman**, BA Hons Birmingham, PGCE

Head of Infant and Junior School: Mrs Alice Taylor, BSc, PGCE Cardiff [maternity leave]
Head of Sixth Form: Miss Katherine Rich, BA Birmingham, PGCE
Estates and Operations Director: Mrs Louise Brennan
Director of Finance: Mr Mike Stewart, BEng Southampton
Deputy Head – Staff: Mr Manolis Psarros, BA Hons UCW Lampeter, MA Bristol, MEd Bristol
Senior Deputy Head: Dr Mark Caddy, BSc Hons, PhD Warwick
Deputy Head Academic: Ms Louise Brackenbury, BSc Hons UWIC, PGCE
Deputy Head Pastoral: Mr Christopher Collins, MA Oxon, PGCE
Assistant Head – Pupil Voice and Staff Development: Mrs Louise Brackenbury, BSc Hons UWIC, PGCE
Miss Rebecca Brown: Director of Admissions, Communications, Events and Marketing, BA Birmingham [maternity leave]
Child Protection and Safeguarding:
Mr Christopher Collins, MA Oxon, PGCE (*Designated Safeguarding Lead*)
Ms Alison Taylor, BSc Hons Reading, MEd Bristol, PGCE (*Deputy Designated Safeguarding Lead*)
Mrs Alice Taylor, BSc, PGCE Cardiff (*Deputy Designated Safeguarding Lead*)
Miss Claudia Mulholland, BSc Hons Swindon, PGCE (*Deputy Designated Safeguarding Lead*)

Admissions, Development, Communications and Marketing:
*Miss Rebecca Brown (*Admissions, Communications and Marketing Manager*) [maternity cover]
Miss Esme Gottesman (*Digital Marketing Executive / Marketing and Communications Manager*)
Ms Eileen Unwin (*Communications Officer and Copywriter*)
Miss Rebekah Malvern (*Admissions Manager*)
Mrs Sarah Maidment (*Admissions Officer*)
Mrs Lye (*Admissions Officer*)

Cokethorpe School

Witney, Oxfordshire OX29 7PU

Tel: 01993 703921
email: hma@cokethorpe.org
admissions@cokethorpe.org
website: www.cokethorpe.org
X/Twitter: @CokethorpeSch
Facebook: @CokethorpeSch
Instagram: @CokethorpeSch
LinkedIn: /company/cokethorpe-school

See full entry in the **HMC** section, on **p. 75**.

Concord College

Acton Burnell Hall, Shrewsbury, Shropshire SY5 7PF

Tel: 01694 731631
email: enquiries@concordcollege.org.uk
website: www.concordcollegeuk.com
X/Twitter: @ConcordCollege
Facebook: @ConcordCollegeUK
Instagram: @concordcollege
LinkedIn: /concord-college-uk

Concord College is a highly successful, academic, co-educational international school for day and boarding students aged 13–18, providing GCSE/IGCSE and A Level courses. Set in 80 acres of Shropshire parkland, the College combines outstanding facilities with first-rate academic performance. The College is regularly rated in the top 10 schools in the UK. Students are cared for by a dedicated staff in a safe and beautiful environment. Concord is an international community dedicated to rigour, kindness and creativity and provides a vibrant and friendly environment in which students can flourish and fulfil their potential. Students are expected to display mutual respect and to promote harmony, decency and trust. The result is a happy and kind community in which students are polite, articulate and conscientious without ever losing their sense of fun.

Number of students. 577 (approximately equal numbers of boys and girls) of whom over 460 are boarders.

Facilities. The campus is centred around an historic hall which, with other college buildings, is set in beautifully maintained grounds. There has been considerable investment in high-quality modern facilities. Lessons are taught in well-equipped classrooms with excellent IT provision. The state-of-the-art Science block comprises 22 laboratories including a special projects lab. The academic departments are well supported by a modern library complex in the Jubilee Building which students can access for their studies and reading for pleasure. There is a well-resourced theatre and music school, an excellent sports centre and indoor swimming pool, as well as extensive grounds including sports pitches, tennis courts and a high ropes course. All students have individual study-bedrooms, many with en-suite bathrooms. Meals are eaten in the College Dining Room where students can select from a variety of international cuisine. The wide range of facilities also includes common rooms and a student kitchen.

Wellbeing. All students have Tutors who have oversight of their pastoral wellbeing (as well as monitoring their academic progress). Boarding students also have boarding parents who focus on providing boarders with the emotional and practical support they need when they are away from home. Concord also offers support to students via Heads of Year in the Lower School and via our House system in the Upper School. Medical provision is available 24 hours-a-day, there is a modern and well-equipped medical centre and a dedicated nursing team. Mental health is taken very seriously, and support and counselling are available. The campus is secure and security staff are on duty at all times.

Education. Teaching groups average 16 students at GCSE and 14 students at A Level. Teachers are experts in their subjects. At GCSE, English, Mathematics and Sciences are compulsory. Optional subjects include Art, Astronomy, Computer Science, Economics, French, German, Geography, History, Music, Statistics, Religious Studies and Spanish. For GCSE sciences, Biology, Chemistry and Physics are taught as separate subjects and emphasis is placed upon laboratory experience.

Sixth Form students normally study at least three A Levels. There is also an opportunity to study for a further AS level or an EPQ which is an independent research project. Subjects include Art, Biology, Chemistry, Economics, English Language and Literature, French, Geography, History, Mathematics, Further Mathematics, Music, Physics and Spanish. All students who do not have a GCSE in English are expected to study English. There is a comprehensive careers programme to support all students with their university applications in the UK or overseas.

Reports to parents are sent at half term in the first term and subsequently at the end of each term. Parents also receive the results of weekly Saturday Tests.

Examination Results and University Entry. The College's students achieve excellent examination results; In 2023, 90% of GCSE/IGCSE results were 7/8/9 and over 50% were grade 9. Over half of our A Level students achieved AAA or better in their exams and 33 achieved A*A*A* or more. This year, students went on to study at top-flight UK Universities including 12 students to Oxford and Cambridge. Others went to Imperial College London, UCL and LSE. Internationally, students went to Cornell, UC San Diego, Chicago, Melbourne and many others. Altogether over 100 leavers went to World Top 100 universities.

Clubs, Sports and Extracurricular Activities. Students at Concord can choose from a multitude of activities. Many clubs and societies have an academic focus and are part of Concord's well-developed super-curriculum, for example the Medics Society, the Philosophy Club and numerous academic discussion groups.

Sports, music, dance and drama are also all available in our own facilities. There is a sports hall, squash courts and gymnasium as well as outdoor facilities including for football, athletics and tennis. A wealth of sporting activities are on offer ranging from archery to fencing and badminton to volleyball. There is a purpose-built dance studio and a range of gym equipment available for students to use after lessons and in the evenings.

Musicians can have individual instrumental tuition and join one of the chamber groups. Choir and singing lessons can develop all levels of vocal talent. Many other activities are also offered ranging from public speaking and chess to horse riding and charity fundraising. Students take part in Concord's outdoor education programme and the Duke of Edinburgh's Award scheme is also available. Whatever their talents, students are able develop them at Concord.

The School Week. Lessons run from 9.00am to 4.00pm Monday to Friday with Wednesday afternoon allocated to sport and an optional trip to Shrewsbury for senior students. There is compulsory supervised study (prep) each evening Monday to Friday.

Saturday mornings are used for subject testing. Subjects are tested in rotation allowing teachers and students alike to monitor academic progress. These tests are taken under examination conditions to help students to prepare for their GCSEs and AS and A Levels.

Selection for Entry. Applicants are selected on the basis of school reports, academic achievement, entry tests and interviews. Applicants are required to sit Concord's entry tests to assess their potential for future study. Entry normally takes place into Year 9 (Form 3), Year 10 (Form 4) or Year 12 (Sixth Form).

Fees per annum (2023–2024). Full boarding fees are £53,400 per annum. Boarding fees are due for payment on a half yearly basis and invoices are issued accordingly. Day student fees are £18,300 per annum (£6,100 per term).

Scholarships and Bursaries. A number of scholarships exist for the most able students and means-tested bursaries are available separately for those who require financial assistance with fees. In all cases the candidate must complete the Application Process first before applying for a scholarship.

Charitable status. Concord College is a Registered Charity, number 326279. It exists to provide high quality education for secondary age students.

Chair of the Governors: Dr Iain M Bride

Clerk to the Governors and Bursar: Matthew Hodge

***Principal*: Michael R Truss**, PhD, MPhys Oxon

Vice-Principal (Academic): Robert Pugh, PhD, BA
Vice-Principal (Pastoral): Jeremy Kerslake, MA
Head of Lower School: Ms Sue Correll, BA, MA
Assistant Principal: Phil Outram, PhD, BSc
Assistant Principal: Daniel Wilson, MA
Assistant Principal: Diane van Dongen, BSc, PGCE

Principal's Personal Assistant & Admissions Registrar: Mrs Wendy Hartshorne

Dover College

Effingham Crescent, Dover, Kent CT17 9RH

Tel: 01304 205969
email: admissions@dovercollege.org.uk
website: www.dovercollege.org.uk
X/Twitter: @DoverCollege
Facebook: @DoverCollege
LinkedIn: /dover-college

Dover College was founded in 1871 in the historic grounds of the old St Martin's Priory.

We are the closest school to continental Europe, one hour to Central London by train and within easy reach of London's airports.

We are a small, family-style school with a vibrant mix of local and international pupils. We expect academic excellence from our pupils, but also encourage them to find their talents in other areas such as art, drama, music and sport.

Co-education. Dover College (age 3–18) has been fully co-educational since 1975 and the 300+ boys and girls are integrated at all levels. There are 100 boarders.

Organisation. Our Nursery & Prep School are located in their own comfortable building on the main College campus and accept day pupils aged 3–11. Our Senior School is for pupils aged 11–18 and we can accept day, weekly boarding and full boarding pupils. We have two boarding houses for girls and two for boys. Pupils in Shell (year 7) have their own dedicated house, Priory, to help them with the transition from Prep to Senior School.

Catering. The catering team provides delicious, healthy, well-balanced homemade food and meals are taken in our historic Refectory.

Curriculum. We are academically ambitious. We take the time to really get to know each child so that the right balance of challenge and support is in place based on their needs. We recognise that success is as unique as the individual and we celebrate achievement where it represents the personal best for each child.

Our distinctive curriculum, connecting Early Years right through to Sixth Form, focuses on not only achieving results but also developing inquisitive and creative minds ready for the challenges ahead. We are a member of the Round Square organisation, a group of 150 worldwide schools, and share their commitment to an all-round education. We prize their values of Internationalism, Democracy, Environmentalism, Adventure, Leadership and Service.

Sixth Form. The Sixth Form is overseen by a Head of Sixth Form and pupils are able to choose A Levels and BTECs. Traditional academic subjects are provided, as are the practical subjects of art, design and technology, textiles, photography, drama and music.

Sixth Formers wear business attire and are given more choice and freedom than younger pupils, being expected to respond positively to their treatment as young adults. A well-equipped Sixth Form Centre is used as a meeting place and social club.

The School's Careers Adviser works in liaison with external agencies to plan, deliver and evaluate an integrated careers education and guidance programme. This enables pupils to gain the necessary knowledge, skills and understanding in order to make informed career plans before attending the universities of their choice.

International Study Centre (ISC). The International Department was started in 1957 and backed at the time by members of NATO, although international boarding has a far longer history than this starting point. The International Study Centre provides intensive English courses for pupils whose first language is not English. These courses vary in length and the aim is to enable all pupils to integrate fully into the life of Dover College as soon as possible after their arrival.

Individual Support. There is an Individual Needs Department in which pupils with learning difficulties (e.g. Dyslexia) receive 1:1 tuition. Each pupil has a member of staff as a personal tutor. The tutor supervises his/her pupils' general academic progress.

Learning Resources Centre. It provides cutting-edge facilities and resources to all pupils, including Careers information.

Sport. The School's main playing fields are a short distance away; on site are tennis courts, an astroturf, basketball court, Eton Fives court, cricket nets and an excellent Sports Hall with a fitness suite. Sports include Athletics, Badminton, Basketball, Cricket, Cross Country, Running, Football, Hockey, Netball, Rugby, Sailing, Tennis, Volleyball and various PE activities. Swimming takes place at the indoor swimming pool in the local leisure centre. Golf may be played on local courses and horse riding is also offered locally through the School.

Extracurricular Activities. In addition to sport, pupils have the opportunity of taking part in a wide range of over 50 activities including Adventure Training, Art, Chess, Computing, Debating, Duke of Edinburgh's Award, Dancing, Horse Riding, Language Clubs, Music, Photography, Stage Management and Technology. The London West End theatres are within easy reach and regular trips to a variety of productions are made.

Pastoral Care. All pupils benefit from a carefully designed system of outstanding pastoral care. Every Dover College student belongs to a House and Boarders are provided with comfortable accommodation in one of four boarding houses. All pupils have single study-bedrooms. A Housemaster or Housemistress, supported by a team of tutors, runs each House; it is their role to give pastoral support as well as supervising the pupils' academic progress.

Pupils have access to a fully equipped and professionally staffed Medical Centre, which can accommodate pupils overnight.

Religious Life. College has its own Chapel and is a Church of England school. All pupils are encouraged to respect each other's beliefs and faiths from a position of tolerance and understanding.

Entry. Pupils are typically admitted into the Senior School at 11, 13 or 16 years old, but may come at any age. Most pupils join the College in September, but entry in January and April is possible.

Entry into Nursery and Prep is by interview and an informal assessment carried out during a 'Taster Day' at the school. Entrance into the Senior School at 11+ and 13+ is dependent on previous school reports as well as an interview with the Headmaster. Provision is made for direct entry into the Sixth Form for boys and girls. This is normally conditional upon GCSE results. Further information can be obtained from Admissions.

Fees per term (2023–2024). Nursery & Prep Day: £3,438–£4,585; Senior Day: £5,459–£6,559; Senior Weekly Boarding (up to 6 nights per week): £9,371–£12,067; Full Boarding: £12,000–£13,505.

Scholarships. Academic Scholarships are awarded by competitive examinations.

Scholarships for Music, Drama, Art, Sport and All-Rounder are available by competitive interview.

Scholarships are available to pupils at 11+, 13+ and 16+ entry. Scholarships are not awarded to pupils in the Prep School.

Sibling Bursaries (5%) and Service Bursaries are automatically awarded. Members of HM Armed Forces and the Diplomatic Service who are eligible for the boarding allowance only pay a parental contribution of 10% of the full boarding fee.

Further details may be obtained on application to Admissions.

Old Dovorian Club. President: Ms Margo Mayhew, c/o Dover College.

Charitable status. Dover College is a Registered Charity, number 307856. The School exists to develop confidence and individual talents.

Chairman of Governors: Dr Claire Scholfield-Myers

***Headmaster*: Mr Simon Fisher**

Director of Finance: Mrs Susan Davis

Deputy Head: Mme Therese Taylor

Deputy Head of Prep School: Mrs Tracey Mills

Head of International Study Centre: Mrs Clara Hebblethwaite

Director of Admissions & Marketing: Ms Alison Wilson

PA to the Headmaster: Mrs Jo Proctor

d'Overbroeck's

333 Banbury Road, Oxford OX2 7PL

Tel: 01865 688600
email: mail@doverbroecks.com
website: www.doverbroecks.com
X/Twitter: @doverbroecks
Facebook: @doverbroecksoxford
Instagram: @doverbroecks_oxford
LinkedIn: /company/doverbroecks-oxford

Age Range. 11–18. (11–14: day only; 14–18: day and boarding.)

Number in School. 744.

Fees per term (2023–2024). Years 7–11: £7,250; Sixth Form: £9,515; The International School: £10,700–£11,615.

Boarding fees per term (2023–2024). Sixth Form boarding houses: £7,740; The International School boarding: £6,975.

d'Overbroeck's is a leading co-educational independent school in Oxford, UK, offering an exceptional academic and extra-curricular programme. We teach the GCSE, IGCSE and A Level curriculum to students aged 11–18 on three school sites: Years 7–11, the Sixth Form and The International School. We have day students only at the Years 7–11 site, a mixture of boarding and day students in the Sixth Form, and mainly boarding at our International School. A 2021 Independent Schools Inspectorate report rated us 'Excellent' across the board for academic achievement and personal development.

We have small classes so that every student gets the attention they need from our highly qualified teachers in a supportive and encouraging environment. Teaching is interactive to generate enthusiasm for the subject, sound academic skills, and effective working habits – while at the same time providing a thorough preparation for public examinations. We offer a caring, creative, nurturing and relatively informal environment where, no matter what a student's interests are, they will find plenty of opportunities to explore. The range of opportunities on offer at d'Overbroeck's is outstanding, so we encourage you to read on to find out more and visit our website.

Our school is high-achieving and academically rigorous, and students will receive expert guidance on how to make the most of their experience with us considering their long-term goals. We expect high standards of commitment and effort from our students and have a track record of strong GCSE and A Level results. Once enrolled at the school, our staff work closely with each student to make sure they are getting the advice and support they need. Pastoral care and support for each student is an essential feature at d'Overbroeck's, where wellbeing and happiness are prioritised alongside responsibility and achievement.

Our Principal, Patrick Horne says:

'As well as providing the expert teaching and support for academic success, we provide an array of excellent opportunities for students to develop their passions and explore new possibilities. There is no typical d'Overbroeck's student or single experience here, and we value the distinctiveness of every person. Our exciting learning environment is characterised by a shared love of learning, with our brilliant teachers encouraging curiosity, innovation and compassion. The broad and fulfilling opportunities here ensure that students can build the skills, discipline and character needed for their futures, while also inspiring a lifelong love of learning.'

A brief description of Years 7–11. Years 7–11 at d'Overbroeck's is the secondary school branch of the d'Overbroeck's family of sites. It is co-educational, and also boasts a range of opportunities for students. Here you will find a broad range of GCSE subjects on offer, along with non-academic co-curricular activities, and pastoral care. We are Oxford's only fully co-educational independent school from age 11 through to Sixth Form. Our aim is for every one of our students to meet his or her personal potential. That journey begins aged 11 in Year 7 (or aged 13 in Year 9 for those joining us from Prep schools), where this potential is identified, challenged and given every opportunity to grow. At the heart of our ethos is the knowledge and celebration of each of our students as an individual. Our consistently proven academic excellence comes as a result of this ethos, as does our community of students who are engaged, happy and at ease with themselves and their peers. d'Overbroeck's has always been a place of positive relationships and shared purpose; a place where academic and extra-curricular achievement, personal development and hearty laughter all come on the same wavelength.

A brief description of the Sixth Form. Students in the Sixth Form are aged 16–18 years of age. 35 A Level subjects are currently on offer, plus a comprehensive academic enrichment programme to stretch our students beyond the standard curriculum. Further to this, we offer a range of non-academic co-curricular activities for students to get involved in across drama, music, sport, and more, as well as a packed programme of trips, excursions, and regular social events. Many students at the Sixth Form choose to do an Extended Project Qualification (EPQ) as part of their academic enrichment activities. The broad range of academic subjects that students can learn means that d'Overbroeck's an ideal place for bright, ambitious students to achieve their full potential academically, but also a place they can thrive outside of the standard curriculum. The majority of students go on to university, and we have an excellent record of success with entry to Oxford and Cambridge, as well as prestigious medical, law, veterinary and art schools. We offer significant Higher Education and Careers support including application writing advice and interview practice.

A brief description of The International School. The International School is made up of students generally aged 14–16 years from all over the world who choose to study with us in our vibrant and friendly school. At d'Overbroeck's we help students to prepare for academic success in the English education system. On one of our IGCSE programmes, and in a small, caring atmosphere, our specialist teachers will help students improve their spoken and written English and teach them a full range of academic subjects. English as an Additional Language, non-academic co-curricular activities, TRACK (Theory of Research, Active Citizenship and Knowledge), and Sixth Form and University Progression are just some of the options available to international students who join us. Students will receive pastoral care throughout their time with us, to make sure they receive the support they need academically and in their co-curricular pursuits. Students coming from abroad will be warmly welcomed and there are opportunities for them to mix with English students through activities that interest them. Trips and excursions relating to British heritage are also on offer, allowing students to learn more about British culture and history.

Main entry points to the school are: at ages 11, 13 and directly into the Sixth Form aged 16 following GCSE exams.

For all other information and to apply please visit our website: www.doverbroecks.com.

***Principal*: Patrick Horne**

Vice Principal (*Staff and Curriculum*): Stephen Creamer (*Chemistry*, *Physics*)
Vice Principal (*Head of Years 7–11*): Nick Haines (*Maths*)
Vice Principal (*Head of The International School*): Ted McGrath
Vice Principal (*Head of Sixth Form*): Alasdair MacPherson (*English*)

Academic Director: Andrew Gillespie
Pastoral Director: Sarah Squire

Head of Admissions: Joanne Baird
Head of Boarding: Hannah Mungall

Director of Operations: Tammy Heavens

Chair of Governors: Brian Cooklin

Dunottar School

United Learning

High Trees Road, Reigate, Surrey RH2 7EL

Tel: 01737 761945
email: info@dunottarschool.com
website: www.dunottarschool.com
X/Twitter: @dunottarschool
Facebook: @Dunottar
Instagram: @dunottarschool

The aim of Dunottar is to offer an outstanding education to boys and girls and, through excellent teaching and high levels of individual support, to enable pupils to achieve added value which is comparable with what is achieved in the top schools in the UK. Dunottar is a vibrant, co-educational secondary school which, as part of United Learning's family of schools, shares the group's core values of ambition, confidence, determination, creativity, respect and enthusiasm along with the objective of bringing out the "Best in Everyone". Dunottar celebrates achievement in its broadest sense resulting in a community of happy, confident pupils who achieve their first choice ambition for their future education and employment.

The School was founded in 1926 and joined United Learning in 2014. It is situated in 15 acres of beautiful grounds and woodland on the outskirts of Reigate, convenient to mainline stations and bus routes. The main building is a handsome Palladian mansion and purpose-built wings include additional classrooms, art and design suites, the main hall, Sixth Form Centre, a 25-metre heated indoor swimming pool and large sports hall. Outdoor space includes a sports field, several courts and an outdoor classroom and arrangements with Old Reigatian RFC, South Park FC and local cricket clubs extend the off-site sporting facilities. In 2021, a £4.5 state-of-the-art performing arts centre was opened, including a 500-seat theatre, drama studio, music classrooms and music practice rooms.

Religion. The School holds the Christian ethos paramount and welcomes children from any denomination or none.

Curriculum. The school offers a broad education and preserves a balance between arts and science subjects. Early specialisation is avoided, though some subject options become necessary from the beginning of the GCSE year. Subjects include English Language and Literature, Mathematics, French, Spanish, History, Geography, Religious Studies, Biology, Physics and Chemistry, Business and Economics, Three-Dimensional Design, Computer Science, Physical Education, Drama, Food and Nutrition, Music, Art and Design & Technology.

Dunottar has strong sporting and music traditions. Teaching is given in a wide range of musical instruments and pupils are encouraged to join the orchestras, music groups and choirs. A busy fixtures list offers many opportunities for competitive sport and 'sport for all' is encouraged within school and through the co-curricular programme. Rugby, football, athletics, netball, swimming and cricket are amongst the sports on offer. Co-curricular clubs are designed to broaden horizons and encourage new skills, hobbies and interests and range from beekeeping to science based groups such as 'dissection club' and sports including badminton and swimming. Students also participate in The Duke of Edinburgh's Award scheme at Bronze, Silver and Gold levels.

Careers. Dunottar offers an interesting and varied careers programme for pupils, from online careers research tools through to careers networking lunches and suppers. The school welcomes a range of speakers from a diverse range of fields to offer our pupils an insight into application processes, daily life of employees and the skills employers are looking for.

Examinations taken. GCSE and A Levels, Associated Board of the Royal School of Music, London Academy of Music and Dramatic Art, Imperial School of Dancing, Royal Society of Arts.

Admissions. The admissions process at Dunottar is designed to identify those pupils who will thrive at the school. The admissions process is as friendly and relaxed as possible. The main intake is in Year 7 and Year 12. We are happy to consider pupils joining into other year groups where spaces are available. Prospective pupils can be registered at any time prior to the registration deadline. Please check the Admissions Process page on our website for all the current registration process details and deadlines. The Admissions Department are happy to answer any questions.

Fees per term (2023–2024). Years 7 to 13: £6,970, payment by BACS/Credit Card; £6,880, payment by monthly or termly Direct Debit.

Scholarships. Academic Scholarships are awarded annually in Year 7 to those who reach the highest standard in the entrance tests and show the greatest potential for growth. Year 12 Academic Scholarships are awarded at the discretion of the Headmaster based on the outcome of the students' GCSE examinations. Scholarships are also available in Year 7 and Year 12 for those who show exceptional promise and talent in Music, Art, Performing Arts and Sport. Further details can be found on the website.

Scholarships and bursaries

Scholarships Offered: Academic, Art, Music, Sport

Other Scholarships: Performing Arts

Bursaries / Discounts: New entrant bursary

Charitable status. Dunottar School is part of United Learning which comprises: UCST (a Company Limited by Guarantee, Registered in England, number 2780748, and a Registered Charity, number 1016538) and ULT (a Company Limited by Guarantee, Registered in England, number 4439859, and an Exempt Charity).

Senior Leadership Team:

***Headmaster*: Mr M Tottman**, MA Oxon, MBA, QTS

Deputy Head (*Pastoral*) *and Designated Safeguarding Lead*: Mr J Weiner, BA Hons Worcester, MEd

Deputy Head (*Academic*): Mrs J Hislop, BA Hons Southampton, PGCE

Deputy Head (*Operations*): Mrs R Stringer, BA Hons Warwick, PGCE

Embley

United Learning

Embley Park, Romsey, Hampshire SO51 6ZE

Tel: 01794 512206 (Senior School)
01794 515737 (Prep School)
email: info@embley.org.uk
website: www.embley.org.uk
X/Twitter: @EmbleySenior
Facebook: @EmbleyHampshire
LinkedIn: /school/embleyhampshire

Embley is an independent day and boarding school for girls and boys aged 2–18. The school is nestled in 130 acres of private parkland, which includes woodlands, playing fields, tennis courts, AstroTurf pitches, a swimming pool and a golf course. It also runs a comprehensive sailing programme with its own boats moored at Lymington.

The school is academically ambitious for its children and motivates them to achieve their personal best. It encourages an appropriate belief in oneself while being mindful that the world does not end at the tip of one's nose and that happiness in life is through success in enriching the lives of others.

Constitution. Over 640 pupils, with 485 in the Senior School and Sixth Form and 155 in the Prep School.

Boarding. Flexi and full time boarding are available from 11+. The Heads of Boarding reside in the Boarding House. The house family includes dedicated nurses and matrons who specialise in the welfare and medical needs of all boarders.

Curriculum.

Prep School: A broad curriculum is offered, including French, Music, Computer Science, Design Technology and Physical Education taught by specialists.

Senior School: The GCSE curriculum offers a choice of many subjects (including separate subject sciences).

Sixth Form: 24 A Level subjects are available and a Pre-A Level for international students whose first language is not English. All students are expected to take an Extended Project Qualification (EPQ).

Further details can be found at www.embley.org.uk

Co-curricular and enrichment. The school has an extensive co-curricular programme which includes sailing, skiing, horse riding, golf, rugby, football, cricket, hockey, netball, cross country, basketball, swimming, tennis, athletics and golf. The school has a thriving drama, art and musical life. All Senior School pupils are encouraged to undertake The Duke of Edinburgh's Award scheme and join the Combined Cadet Force.

Higher Education & Careers. The school runs a regular series of industry career events and all Sixth Form students attend termly Nightingale Lectures (black-tie events with eminent guest speakers).

Admission procedures.

Nursery: No formal assessment

Prep School: Entry at any age from 4 to 11. Informal assessment Reception and Year 1. Assessment Year 2 to Year 6.

Senior School: Entrance assessments, interview and a suitable reference from the head teacher of the pupil's current school.

Sixth Form: Offers made usually on the following conditions: A minimum of 5 GCSE grades 9 to 5 and at least grade 7 or 8 in the A Level subjects to be studied or equivalent. A suitable reference from the head teacher of the pupil's current school.

Scholarships. Scholarships are available at 11+, 13+ and 16+ and are awarded for: Academic, Art & Design, Music, Drama and Sport.

Fees per term (2023–2024). Nursery: £3,429 (full time). Prep School £4,070–£6,250; Senior School: £6,350 (day), £11,100 (UK boarding), £11,210 (EU Boarding), £12,540 (International Boarding), £12,770 (Pre-A Level). Please refer to www.embley.org.uk/admissions/fees for further information.

Local Governing Body:
Professor Tom Thomas (*Chairman*)
Mr C M Canning (*Headmaster*)
Mrs K Smith
Dr L Black
Mrs R Brooks
Mr R Butler

***Headmaster*: Mr Cliff Canning**, BA Hons, BD Hons, HDipEd, NUI

Deputy Head: Mr Jose Picardo, MA, PGCE
Deputy Head (*Pastoral*): Mrs Leah Goodey, BA, PGCE
Bursar: Mrs Claire Brighton, MBA
Head of Prep School: Ms Sheina Wright, BA, QTS
Assistant Head Co-Curriculum, Head of Year 7, Deputy Designated Safeguarding Lead: Mrs Rebecca Clayton, BSc, PGCE
Director of Marketing, Admissions & Communications: Mrs Charlotte Welland, BA

Ewell Castle School

Church Street, Ewell, Surrey KT17 2AW

Tel: 020 8394 3576 (Admissions)
020 8393 1413 (Main Office)
email: admissions@ewellcastle.co.uk
website: www.ewellcastle.co.uk
X/Twitter: @EwellCastleUK
Facebook: @EwellCastleSchool
Instagram: @ewellcastleschool
LinkedIn: /school/ewell-castle-school

Ewell Castle is an independent, co-educational day school in North Surrey, twenty minutes from London. It was built as a castellated mansion in 1814. It offers Early Years (Nursery and Reception) Preparatory School, Senior School and a Sixth Form.

The gardens and playing fields of the Senior School cover some fifteen acres and were once part of Nonsuch Park. The Senior School is accommodated at The Castle. The Preparatory School occupies two other premises in Ewell village: the Nursery and Reception in a Georgian house minutes from the Senior School; and the Preparatory School, the former Rectory to the parish church, opposite the Senior School. Further Sixth Form teaching and study facilities are housed in nearby Fitzalan House in Ewell Village High Street.

The School, which was founded in 1926, is registered as an educational charity and is administered by a Board of Governors, which is in membership of AGBIS (Association of Governing Bodies of Independent Schools). The Principal is a member of The Society of Heads and the Head of the Preparatory School is a member of IAPS (Independent Association of Prep Schools).

The School comprises approximately 665 pupils in total, with 508 pupils in the Senior School and 157 pupils in the Preparatory School.

Buildings. The School is located on four sites within the village of Ewell: Chessington Lodge accommodating the Nursery and Reception (3–5 years); Glyn House accommodating the Preparatory School (6–11 years); The Castle accommodating the Senior School (11–16 years) and Sixth Form (16–18 years); plus additional teaching facilities in Fitzalan House in the village for Sixth Formers. Academic departments are well resourced and accommodated. Recent developments on the Senior School site include the refurbishment of the Pledger building incorporating the Science labs and Maths classrooms.

School Mission. We will inspire our children and young people to thrive, engaging them to excel in a creative and academic environment. We will instil a growth mindset to develop: confidence, contentment and emotional intelligence.

We are a genuinely mixed ability co-educational selective day school.

Aims and Ethos. We are a vibrant learning community, inspiring every child to thrive: discovering strengths, deepening intellectual curiosity and cultivating wellbeing.

Values. Personal integrity, mutual respect, social responsibility and lifelong resilience.

Organisation. The Preparatory School is co-educational and accepts pupils from three years of age. Most pupils transfer to the Senior School, whilst others go to a range of Independent and selective/non-selective schools at 11+. The Sixth Form has been co-educational since September 2013 and the Senior School became fully co-educational in September 2015.

Curriculum. National Curriculum requirements are incorporated into Senior and Preparatory School schemes, although the broad and flexible curriculum extends beyond such criteria. Breadth at KS3 (11–13 years) is replaced at KS4 (14–16 years) by a core of Mathematics, English, Science and PSHE, supplemented by a wide-ranging option scheme covering the languages, arts, humanities and technologies. There is an increased range of subjects available at A level and BTEC in the Sixth Form

Work experience is undertaken by pupils in Year 11. Specialist HE/Careers guidance is available from Year 7 within the Senior School.

After the Sixth Form the majority of pupils proceed to universities and colleges, with most pupils achieving their first choice of institution.

Extracurricular Activities. The principle sports are rugby, football, hockey, netball and cricket. In addition there are numerous pursuits which include: athletics, badminton, basketball, table tennis, skiing, and tennis. There is an extensive music and drama programme and other activities such as The Duke of Edinburgh's Award scheme. Regular language, sports and field trips embarked for America, Austria, Belgium, France, Germany, Iceland, Ireland, Italy, Romania and Spain in recent years.

The School benefits from an active PTA.

Admissions. Girls and boys are admitted to the Preparatory School at the age of three. There are no entry requirements at this stage. Older children are invited to attend the School for a day's assessment in November for entry into the Senior School and Sixth Form.

At the Senior School the standard points of entry are at 11+ and 16+. Subject to availability, there may be places at other levels. Entry requirements include a report from the current/previous school and written assessments.

Visitors are welcome to the School on scheduled Open Days or by appointment.

Scholarships. Scholarships are available for pupils entering the school at 11+, 13+ and 16+. At 11+ awards are made on the basis of competitive examination/assessment in the designated category. Awards are made for Academic excellence and also in the categories of Art, Design and Technology, Drama, Music, Dance, Performing Arts and Photography (both Sixth Form only) and Sport.

Fees per term (2023–2024). Senior School: £6,731, Preparatory School (Years 1–6): £4,160–£4,702, and Nursery & Reception: £3,695.

Preparatory School. *For further information, see Ewell Castle Preparatory School entry in IAPS section.*

Charitable status. Ewell Castle School is a Registered Charity, number 312079. The aim of the charity is to achieve potential and excellence over a broad field: in academic, in sport, in the arts, and in numerous other extracurricular activities and aspects of school life.

Chairman of the Governing Body: Mr C Griffith

***Principal*: Mr Silas Edmonds**, MA, NPQH

Head of Preparatory School & Vice Principal: Mrs L Macallister BA, PGCE, NPQSL
Senior School Deputy Head (*Academic*): Mrs B Hart, BSc
Senior School Deputy Head (*Pupil Wellbeing*) *& Vice Principal*: Mr S Leigh, BA, PGCE
Deputy Head of Preparatory School & Assistant Principal: Mrs S Fowler, BSc, PGCE
Deputy Head of Preparatory School & Assistant Principal: Mrs G Bean, MA, PGCE
Bursar: Ms J Abraham, BSc, FCCA
Marketing, Development & Alumni Director: Ms C Hernandez, BA, CIM Grad Dip
Registrar: Mrs E Porter, BA, CIM Grad Dip

Heads of Department:
Art & Design & Photography: Ms D Carrick, BA, QTS
Business: Mrs R Rudd, BA,QTS
Computing and Information Technology: Mr R Brooks, LLB, PGCE
Design Technology: Mrs D Sarmiento, MA, BA, GTP
Drama: Mr L Bader-Clynes, BA, RADA Dip
Economics: Mrs R Rudd, BA, QTS

English: Ms K Wallace, BA, PGCE
Geography: Miss S Earthrowl, BSc, PGCE
History & Classics: Mr J C W Blencowe, BA, PGCE
Learning Support: Miss S Kuti, BA, QTS, PGCert NASENCO
Mathematics: Mr J Baldwin, BSc, QTS
Modern Foreign Languages: Miss P Hernandez, Licence LLC, PGCE (*Deputy DSL*)
Music: Mr J Hargreaves, BA, PGCE, MMus
Performing Arts: TBC
Philosophy and Religious Studies: TBC
Physical Education: Mr N Turk, BSc, GTP
Politics: Mrs E Harrison, BA, PGCE
Psychology: Mr J D'Souza, BSc, PGCE
Sociology: Mrs G Evans, BSc, QTS
Science: Mr B Visser BSc, PGCE

Executive Assistant to the Principal : Mrs K El-Dahshan, BA Cantab

Fulneck School

Pudsey, Leeds, West Yorkshire LS28 8DS

Tel: 0113 257 0235
email: enquiries@fulneckschool.co.uk
website: www.fulneckschool.co.uk
X/Twitter: @FulneckSchool
Facebook: @FulneckSchool
Instagram: @FulneckSchool
LinkedIn: /fulneck-independent-school

Fulneck fulfils…

Fulneck has a warm, family atmosphere and is a vibrant, inclusive community in which to live, learn and achieve. The wonderful rural location in the historic and unique settlement of Fulneck provides an inspirational and stimulating environment for children and young people to fulfil their potential.

For over two hundred and seventy years, Fulneck has delivered a distinctive education which values individuals, and it is the quality of the relationships and the personalised approach that makes our school so successful. Our students are at the heart of everything we do; they are happy, creative, aspirational and form life-long friendships. Small acts of kindness are valued in equal measure alongside achievements in national competitions.

We pride ourselves on setting high expectations for every individual which allow them to achieve at levels well above the national average, instilling good manners and fostering an ethic of hard work. Pupils experience outstanding opportunities inside and outside the classroom, learning how to work in a team and how to provide the leadership that our society needs.

Fulneck School's academic results speak for themselves and the School is proud of its position in the top 5% of all schools and colleges in England in 2021. With our diverse curriculum, we are constantly able to help our pupils to fulfil, if not exceed, their academic potential. Whether it be pupils with Oxbridge aspirations or those needing expert care from our award-winning Learning Support Unit, Fulneck School is equipped to help each individual succeed.

Just as important, however, are the ambitions, skills and personal attributes that are developed through a Fulneck education. Whether it be music, sport, drama or the Duke of Edinburgh Award scheme, pupils learn how to succeed as individuals and as teams. As adults, we know that these characteristics are, in the end, as important as exam qualifications in determining our success in the real world.

A Fulneck education opens doors for its pupils, giving them the tools and skills they need to approach the next stage of their careers with confidence and enthusiasm. Our committed and expert staff inspire our pupils to gain a love of learning, an inquisitive mind, the confidence to try new things and old-fashioned Yorkshire grit to pick themselves up if at first they don't succeed.

Where we differ from other schools, however, is in our emphasis on making a positive contribution to the society around us, whether that be in West Yorkshire, the UK or further afield like 18th-century architect and alumnus, Benjamin Latrobe. Our pupils are outward looking, empathetic and humble.

We are a diverse yet close-knit community with a family feel to it. Our community is enriched by its diversity, with pupils coming to us from across Yorkshire, the UK and all over the world. Our small boarding house provides a real family atmosphere and is a 'home away from home' whether that is for the occasional night, weekly or full, termly boarding.

We are a small school and therefore offer a more personalised education than many other schools. This only gives a flavour of what Fulneck School has to offer and we warmly invite you to visit us in person to understand why **Fulneck fulfils…**

Sport. Netball, Football, Cricket and Rounders are the main games of the School.

Activities. Music education is strong with Performing Arts in the Junior and Senior school.

There are a number of clubs and societies such as Art, Computer Coding, Languages, Golf, Netball, Table Tennis, Forensic Club, Science, Eco, Strength & Conditioning, Dance and Rock Band.

The Duke of Edinburgh's Award scheme is available to pupils over the age of 14, together with a wide range of trips and residential visits, walking and skiing. The school has regularly participated in World Challenge expeditions.

Pre-School and Early Years. Fulneck School has been an excellent centre for education for over 260 years. Our Pre-School benefits from our many years of educational experience, meaning we know how to balance learning and development with exploration, play and imagination to give your child a well-rounded start and prepare them for school life.

Primary School (Key Stage 2). We are values driven and in particular, our two values of 'work hard' and 'be kind' are very visible from the moment you arrive. We focus on our remaining values of 'be useful' and 'go well' by placing emphasis on serving our community and being mentally and physically fit.

Our children study a knowledge-rich curriculum and our talented teachers bring it to life by creating memories that will last a lifetime.

We have small class sizes, enabling teachers to give precise feedback and next steps to children throughout the day, thus accelerating their academic performance. With our skilled staff, friendly children and small numbers, all the children are highly visible, and the school has a real family feel.

Senior School and Sixth Form. Our Senior Students are nurtured to develop into successful and compassionate young adults who can take the 21st century by storm. With our diverse cultural mix within the boarding community, the Senior School offers a truly international experience which prepares our young people for life beyond school.

In our classrooms, our highly qualified, dedicated teachers deliver teaching and learning which is at the cutting edge of education. We are never complacent; Challenge, enquiry and engagement are key to every Fulneck lesson and inspirational teaching is an expectation. To sum up our Senior School, our aim is to ensure that, collectively and individually, we are the best we can be.

The Sixth Form years are best seen as a co-operative partnership between the teachers and students, with both working together to secure the very best academic results and outcomes. We are ambitious for our pupils, supporting many to achieve places at top UK universities. Fulneck students are encouraged to develop themselves and follow their dreams. Dedicated staff encourage each individual student to reach their goals and be the best they can be. We take pride in preparing and equipping our Sixth Formers for the challenges of university, employment and life beyond Fulneck. Excellent teaching in a brand new Sixth Form study centre, a wide programme of enrichment activities and outstanding pastoral care make Fulneck a fantastic place to study.

International students: Fulneck is a diverse and inclusive school and we welcome students of all nationalities to join us. We offer both day and boarding places to international students.

Learning Support Unit. The aim of the LSU is to support pupils with special learning needs, providing teaching programmes and strategies to allow access to the curriculum at a level commensurate with intellectual ability. The Unit is CReSTeD approved and has repeatedly confirmed its 'DU' status, the highest grade awarded to mainstream schools.

Parents and Friends Association. There is a flourishing organisation which acts as a fundraising body, and also supports the School in a variety of other ways. This is a living example of the belief that education is a partnership between home and school.

Admission. Admission to the school is welcomed at any age depending on the availability of places. Direct entry to the Sixth Form is also possible.

Fees per term (2023–2024). Primary School Day: Nursery (mornings only) £1,790, Foundation Stage (full day) £2,900, Years 1 & 2 £3,149, Years 3–6 £3,944. Senior School and Sixth Form: Day £5,216, Weekly Boarding £9,397, Full Boarding £11,152, Flexi Boarding £60 per night. These fees are the same for international students.

Fulneck Former Pupils' Association. Mr R Tordoff, Fulneck School, Pudsey, West Yorkshire LS28 8DS.

Charitable status. Fulneck School is a Registered Charity, number 251211. It exists to provide a traditional, Christian education for boys and girls between the ages of 3 and 18.

The Governing Body:
Mrs E Dawson (*Chair*)
Ms L Christopher (*Vice Chair*)
Mr C Smith (*Chair of Finance and Resource Committee*)
Ms C Shotton (*Chair of Safeguarding, Risk and Compliance Committee*)
Mr E Whitehead (*Chair of Education Committee*)
Ms Rehana Cusworth
Mr S Kader
Mr N Tucker
Mr L Wall

***Principal*: Mr D Cassidy**

Vice Principals, Senior School: Mrs H Stewart and Mr A Smyth

Vice Principal, Head of Junior School: Mr L Downes

Gordonstoun

Elgin, Moray IV30 5RF
Tel: +44 (0)1343 837837
email: admissions@gordonstoun.org.uk
principalpa@gordonstoun.org.uk
website: www.gordonstoun.org.uk
X/Twitter: @gordonstoun
Facebook: @GordonstounSchool
Instagram: @gordonstounschool
LinkedIn: /company/gordonstoun-school

See full entry in the **HMC** section, on **p. 132**.

Halliford School

Russell Road, Shepperton, Middlesex TW17 9HX
Tel: 01932 223593
email: registrar@hallifordschool.co.uk
website: www.hallifordschool.co.uk
X/Twitter: @hallifordhead
Facebook: @hallifordschool
Instagram: @hallifordschoolshepperton
LinkedIn: /halliford-school-limited

See full entry in the **HMC** section, on **p. 140**.

Highclare School

10 Sutton Road, Erdington, Birmingham B23 6QL
Tel: 0121 373 7400
email: enquiries@highclareschool.co.uk
website: www.highclareschool.co.uk
X/Twitter: @HighclareSchool
Facebook: @highclareschool
Instagram: @highclareschool
LinkedIn: /company/highclare-school

Founded 1932.

Age range. 2+ to 18 years. Co-educational.

Number of pupils. 518.

Fees per term (2023–2024). £3,525–£5,325.

Location. The School is situated on three sites on the main road (A5127) between Four Oaks, Sutton Coldfield and Birmingham. The Senior Department and Sixth Form are on direct train and bus routes from Birmingham city centre, Tamworth, Lichfield and Walsall as well as being serviced by our own buses. There are two preparatory schools, known as Highclare Preparatory School: Woodfield and Highclare Preparatory School: St Paul's. Wraparound care operates from 7.30 am until 6.00 pm for the parents who require it. Holiday cover is available for Pre-School only. The ethos of the school lies in the fulfilment of potential for each pupil, outstanding pastoral care and a belief in the education of the 'whole person'. Our latest ISI inspection report (April 2023) stated 'The quality of the pupils' academic and other achievements is excellent' and 'The quality of the pupils' personal developments is excellent.'

Organisation. Four departments:

Pre-Preparatory Department (age 2+ to 4 years, co-educational). An educational setting, with qualified teachers, integrated into the School, it has the support of facilities and resources of the Preparatory School. MFL, dance and music are taught from Pre-Prep 2.

Preparatory Departments (age 4+ to 11 years, two co-educational departments). The Preparatory School, with classes of up to a maximum of 22 pupils, follows National Curriculum guidelines. Pupils also have the benefit of specialist tuition in MFL, PE/games, music and science. Other foundation subjects are taught by subject and by class teachers. Entry by School's own assessment procedure.

Senior Department (age 11 to 16, co-educational). The full curriculum is covered at KS3. At GCSE all students study English Language and English Literature, Mathematics, Combined Science or separate sciences, and most study a modern foreign language, (French, German or Spanish) with a wide choice of options. In addition PSHCE, Physical Education, Music and Performing Arts form an important part of the curriculum. Through a wide programme of enrichment activities every child has the opportunity to enjoy activities beyond the academic. Entry by School's own assessment procedure.

Sixth Form (age 16+). The Sixth Form is co-educational and accepts external candidates as well as pupils transferring from Highclare Senior School. A wide range of A Level subjects is available for study alongside the extended project qualification. Excellent pastoral, higher education and careers guidance is also offered and timetables are structured to meet the individual requirements of each student.

All parts of the School participate in extensive lunchtime and after-school activities.

The School is multi-denominational. Further information may be obtained from the School or the website and prospective parents are always welcome to visit. Open mornings are held throughout the year including school-in-action weeks on all three sites.

Charitable status. Highclare School is a Registered Charity, number 528940.

Chair of Governors: Mrs L Flowith

School Leadership Team:
***Head*: Miss Francine Smith**, BSc Hons, PGCE, FRSA

Head of Preparatory School: Mrs P Bennett, BA Hons, PGCE Liverpool
Business Manager: Mrs M P A McGoldrick, BA Hons, MSc Manchester, MAAT, AInstAM Dip
Deputy Head of Senior School Pastoral: Mrs S Cassell, BA Hons Oxon, PGCE Keele
Deputy Head of Senior School Academic: Mr Matthew Coles, BSc Hons Warwick, PGCE Bristol
Deputy Head of Preparatory School: Mrs J Griffiths, BA Hons, QTS York, MA Wolverhampton
Designated Safeguarding Lead: Mrs H Good, BEd Hons Worcester

Senior School Staff:
Assistant Head of Senior School: Mrs H Bate, BSc Hons Bimingham
KS5 Coordinator: Mrs M Sharman-Everton, BA Hons Birmingham QTS
KS4 Coordinator: Mrs A Green, BSc Econ Aberystwyth, PGCE Warwick
KS3 Coordinator: Mr R Linfield, BA Hons, PGCE Birmingham

Heads of Departments:
Art: Mrs K Stott, BA Hons, PGCE Birmingham, QTS
Business Studies: Mrs A Green, BSc Econ Aberystwyth, PGCE Warwick
Design & Technology: Mrs H Good, BEd Hons Worcester
Drama: Mrs M Sharman-Everton, BA Hons Birmingham QTS
English: Mrs K J Dawson, BA Hons Exeter, PGCE Oxon
Geography & Religious Studies: Mrs J Palmer, BSc Hons Open University, PGCE Birmingham
History: Miss M Watson, BA Hons Durham, MA Warwick, PGCE Glos
Food & Nutrition: Mrs S Williamson, BA Hons Liverpool, PGCE Birmingham
Information Technology/Computing: Mr L Sneary, BSc Hons Brunel, PGCE Brunel
Law: Ms J Campbell, LLB Law Sheffield, CertEd Greenwich
Mathematics: Mr S Parkinson, BSc Hons Southampton, PGCE Birmingham
Modern Languages: Mrs J Lightfoot, BA Hons Newcastle, PGCE Warwick
Music: Mr B Barlow, BMus Hons Bangor, PGCE Leeds

Psychology: Miss K Stanley, BSc Hons, PGCE Worcester
Physical Education: Mr R Linfield, BA Hons, PGCE Birmingham
Science: Mr W Murray-Smith, BSc, MA Warwick, QTS Nottingham Trent
Sociology: Dr D Edwards, BA Hons Liverpool, PGCE Leics, MA, PhD Manchester

Posts of Additional Responsibility (Senior):
Learning Support Coordinator: Mrs C Roberts, BA Hons, PGCE Hull

Preparatory School Staff:

Head of Preparatory School: Mrs P Bennett, BA Hons, PGCE Liverpool
Deputy Head of Preparatory School: Mrs J Griffiths, BA Hons, QTS York, MA Wolverhampton

Highclare Preparatory School, St Paul's:
Assistant Head and KS2 Coordinator: Mrs J O Quigley, BA Hons Birmingham, PGCE UCB
KS1 Coordinator (Acting): Mr J Goddard, BA Hons History Nottingham Trent, PGCE Newman College
EYFS Coordinators:
Mrs T Tweedie, MA Hons Edinburgh, PGCE Leeds
Mrs P Mitchell, BEd Hons Wolverhampton

Highclare Preparatory School, Woodfield:
Assistant Head and KS2 Coordinator: Mr P Greenfield, BSc Hons Manchester, PGCE Cumbria
KS1 Coordinator: Mrs K S Tidman, BA Hons UCE, PGCE
EYFS Coordinators:
Mrs T Tweedie, MA Hons Edinburgh, PGCE Leeds
Mrs P Mitchell, BEd Hons Wolverhampton

Hill House School

Sixth Avenue, Auckley, Doncaster, South Yorkshire DN9 3GG

Tel: 01302 776300
email: info@hillhouse.doncaster.sch.uk
website: www.hillhouse.doncaster.sch.uk
X/Twitter: @HillHouseSchool
Facebook: @hillhouseschool
Instagram: @hillhouseschool
LinkedIn: /school/hill-house-school-doncaster

See full entry in the **HMC** section, on **p. 149**.

Kingsley School

Northdown Road, Bideford, Devon EX39 3JR

Tel: 01237 426200
email: admissions@kingsleyschoolbideford.co.uk
website: www.kingsleydevon.com
X/Twitter: @KingsleyDevon
Facebook: @KingsleySchoolBideford
Instagram: @kingsleyschool
LinkedIn: /company/kingsley-school-bideford

Kingsley Devon, which is a co-educational boarding and day school accommodating pupils between the ages of 2 and 18, is wholeheartedly dedicated to promoting positive mental health and wellbeing for each of its students, with an aim to achieving both academic success and happiness. Such level of commitment makes it an excellent choice for families within and outside the United Kingdom, who share the belief that every child is unique and deserving of personalised attention and support.

As a relatively small school of around 420 boys and girls from Nursery to Sixth Form, Kingsley's atmosphere is like a large family where everybody knows each other well. The school's philosophy encourages personal qualities such as courage, generosity, honesty, imagination, tolerance and kindness. In addition, we develop the students' broader interests and skills in sport, music, outdoor education, surfing, art, and drama. Overall, a Kingsley education develops each student's individual character and talents both inside and outside the classroom.

Location. Kingsley School is situated in the beautiful North Devon market town of Bideford, a historic port beside the estuary of the River Torridge. The spectacular scenery of the North Devon coast and beautiful beaches are on our doorstep, and there is easy access to the National Parks of Exmoor and Dartmoor. The North Devon link road, which passes close to Bideford, provides a direct route to the M5 motorway.

Earth Centre. The development of the Earth Centre offering, based in the heart of Devon's UNESCO biosphere, is a destination for excellence in educating and developing students to be future leaders and experts in environmental protection and sustainability. Environmental sustainability is of significant importance and is seen as an integral part of the curriculum and the way Kingsley School is run and operated. In particular, climate action, biodiversity restoration and nutrition from healthy food are at the forefront of the schools' policy on environmental sustainability. Through its investment in the Earth Centre concept, Kingsley is driving its school operations towards carbon neutrality, investing in ecology zones to restore and enhance biodiversity on its school sites; and developing commercial-scale market gardens to provide nutrient-dense healthy food for its pupils and the wider community. These activities also aim to cultivate a range of academic and vocational skills relevant to the environmental challenges we face and the new career opportunities that become available.

Organisation. Kingsley School is entirely co-educational and comprises a Senior School with approximately 240 pupils aged 11 to 18 years and a Prep School with approximately 130 pupils aged 2½ to 11 years, as well as 50 in our Pre-Prep, which offers wraparound care for children from 2 to 3 years old. In addition, Kingsley has a nationwide reputation for outstanding dyslexia provision, serving around 25% of the school's pupils.

Site and buildings. Situated on a beautiful 25-acre site, the school has two Boarding Houses for boys and one for girls, all of which have immediate access to extensive playing fields, theatre, studio, an all-weather pitch, playing fields, netball and tennis courts.

In recent years, an investment programme has led to the provision of excellent facilities for surfing, drama, gymnastics, art and science. The Library provides an excellent environment for study, research and career guidance.

Curriculum. In Senior School, for GCSE study, the core subjects include English, Mathematics, Biology, Chemistry, Physics, Modern Languages and Religious Studies. In addition, subjects such as Art and Design, CoPE, Computer Science, Drama, Engineering, Geography, History, Hospitality, Music and Sports Science and PSE complete the programme of study. In the Sixth Form, there is a wide choice of A Level and vocational subjects, including Applied Science, Art, CoPE, Biology, Business Studies, Chemistry, Drama, Economics, EAL, English Literature, EOQ, Geography, History, Horticulture, Hospitality, Maths, Further Maths, Modern Foreign Languages, Music, Photography, Physics, Psychology and Sport. Tuition in English for speakers of other languages is also available.

Sport and Physical Education. All pupils, girls and boys, are encouraged to participate in various sports, including rugby, hockey, netball, cross-country, handball, cricket, gymnastics, badminton, basketball, football, rounders, tennis, judo, swimming and health-related fitness. The Judo Academy has a unique link with the elite Team Bath. The school's gymnasts compete at a local, regional and national level. Our cross-country athletes compete at regional and national ISA levels. Our new Surfing Academy, supports all students to become confident, competent and healthy surfers.

Clubs and activities. There is an extensive range of extracurricular activities organised and supervised by staff. The Duke of Edinburgh's Award scheme, Ten Tors, Eco club, gardening, filming, choir, orchestra, judo, computing, art, music, climbing and surfing are among the most popular clubs available for our pupils to enjoy. Numerous expeditions and field trips are organised each year, both in the UK and abroad. Musicals, plays and concerts are regularly presented in the school's purpose-designed theatre.

Careers. From Year 9 onwards, pupils are offered a planned programme of careers education and guidance as part of the tutorial programme. This is complemented by presentations from visiting professionals, visits to careers events and close contact with Careers Advisers from Connexions Cornwall and Devon. All pupils have access to the latest careers information in the School Library.

Pastoral care. In addition to their Year Heads, all pupils have a Personal Tutor responsible for monitoring their academic progress and personal wellbeing. For boarders, care is also the responsibility of the Houseparents.

Admission. Boys and girls join the Nursery from 2 years. Entry to the Prep and Senior Schools is by interview and taster day. For pupils with recognised learning difficulties, entry is by interview and an up-to-date educational psychologist's report. 13+ admission is through our own Entrance Examination or Scholarship Examination. An interview and a report from their present school are required for older pupils.

Scholarships. Many of our scholarship programmes are combined with a fee reduction and this can be as much as 100% with some of our Sixth Form scholarships. Entrance scholarships are offered annually for pupils joining Year 7, Year 9 and Year 12 based on the results of entrance tests held in the preceding January. Candidates may be considered for an academic scholarship along with individual scholarships in Music, Performing Arts, Sports, Judo, Gymnastics, Netball, Surfing, Art, Top Universities Programme and Earth Centre. Scholarships will be awarded on the basis of an interview, audition or assessment at the School, together with a supporting portfolio of achievements in the relevant subject. Assessment for Year 7, 9, 12 academic scholarships is made through written tests in Mathematics, English and Science, and a verbal reasoning test.

Fees per term (2023–2024). Prep School: Day £2,496/term (Reception), £2,616 (Years 1 and 2), £3,228 (Years 3 and 4), £4,132 (Years 5 and 6); Boarding (from Year 7) £7,765 (flexi), £11,545 (full). Senior School: Day £5,220.

More details. Please contact the Admissions team, email: admissions@kingsleyschoolbideford.co.uk, tel: 01237 426200 or online via the school's website: www.kingsleydevon.com. Visitors are most welcome to tour the school by appointment.

***Headteacher*: Mr Robert Pavis**, MA Ed

Assistant Headteacher (*Pastoral*): Ms. Katrina Venner
Assistant Headteacher (*Academic*): Mr Adam Kilner
Head of Prep/Pre School/Nursery: Mr Andrew Trythall, BA
Head of Marketing: Mrs Lucy Goaman, BA, MA, MCIM
Director of Admissions: Mrs Melanie Gray
Head of Boarding: Mrs Jess Willoughby
Bursary: Mr Stephen O'Brien

Leweston School

Sherborne, Dorset DT9 6EN

Tel: 01963 210691
email: admin@leweston.dorset.sch.uk
website: www.leweston.co.uk
X/Twitter: @LewestonSchool
Facebook: @Leweston
Instagram: @leweston1891

Leweston School is a co-educational boarding (full, weekly and flexi) and day school situated in 46 acres of beautiful Dorset parkland, 3 miles south of Sherborne.

The school offers all the advantages of both the traditional and modern in education with excellent facilities, particularly in the Sciences, Art, Design & Technology and Sport. The school is also a Pentathlon GB Modern Pentathlon Training Hub, one of only 9 in the country, thanks to its impressive record in the field of multisport disciplines. The school runs dedicated training programmes for these disciplines and hosts a number of popular training camps and competitions throughout the year. There is also a popular and successful Equestrian team who are NSEA Regional Points League winners for the sixth year running. Leweston pupils achieve outstanding results in many sports as representatives of the school, the county and Team GB.

Founded by the Religious of Christian Instruction in 1891, the school is a Catholic foundation but has a large percentage of pupils from other denominations. There are approximately 600 pupils in the whole school, (250 Prep and 350 Senior) of whom around 100 are boarders. The ethos of the school is based on a wide social mix with a spread of talents, firm but friendly discipline and a keen sense of Christian and moral values. The Headmaster is forward looking with a strong sense of leadership and vision.

The academic standard of the school is high. At both GCSE and A Level pass rates are consistently over 95% and the school's reputation for excellence in Music and Drama runs parallel with academic achievement in Sciences and the Arts. Each year pupils gain places at leading universities and go on to read a wide range of degrees. The real success of the school, however, is achieved by realising the full potential of each individual pupil; much emphasis is placed upon the rich extracurricular offering, which helps to discover and nurture a wide range of talents.

Teachers are dedicated and imaginative, including specialist teachers for Dyslexia and EAL. The school's special quality is its ability to encourage in each pupil a sense of their own worth and ability. Pupils are outgoing and well-mannered. While Leweston has a high proportion of day pupils, the school is fully committed to boarding, offering a wide programme of activities in the evenings and at the weekends which are open to day and boarding pupils.

Sherborne is an attractive historic abbey town with few of the distractions of a large city but at the same time, it is served by regular Network Express trains to and from London and good road links to Salisbury, Exeter and Bath.

Leweston Prep (IAPS) for girls and boys aged 3 months to 11 years, with boarding provision from age 8, is situated on the same campus, thus offering continuity of education to age 18. The early years provision includes French, Spanish and weekly swimming lessons from Nursery and was recently award outstanding in all areas by Ofsted for the second time. The school hosts a weekly Forest School Playgroup and Toddler Swimming Group. (*For further details, see entry in IAPS section.*)

Scholarships are awarded at 11+, 13+ and Sixth Form entry. Academic scholarships are available as well as Music, Art/Design, Drama, Sport, Equestrian and Pentathlon. Dates of examinations: Late November for Sixth Form scholarships, late January for others. Further details and entry forms can be obtained from the Registrar or found on the school website.

Fees per term (2023–2024). Senior School: Full Boarding £9,846–£10,930; Weekly Boarding (5 nights) £8,494–£9,405; Day £6,062; Flexi Boarding (including supper) £58 per night.

Charitable status. Leweston School Trust is a Registered Charity, number 295175. It is a charitable foundation set up for educational purposes.

Governing Body:
Mr I Lucas
Deacon Mark Brown
Mrs V de Fontanals Simmonds
Mr D McKechnie
Mrs R Peacock
Prof T Meehan
Mr G Best
Mr M Brunel-Cohen
Mr S Greenwood
Mrs J Schofield
Mr P Felbeck
Lt-Gen Sir James Dutton

***Head*: Mr John Paget-Tomlinson**, BA Hons Reading, MA King's College London, MRes London, PGCE

Deputy Head (*Academic*): Mr S Whittle, BSc Hons Birmingham

Deputy Head (*Pastoral*): Mr O McManus, BA Hons Nottingham Trent, PGCE Bath

Bursar: Lt Col Gus Scott-Masson

A full teaching staff list can be found on the School website.

Lichfield Cathedral School

The Palace, The Close, Lichfield, Staffordshire WS13 7LH

Tel: 01543 306170
email: admissions@lichfieldcathedralschool.com
website: www.lichfieldcathedralschool.com
X/Twitter: @lichfieldcschl
Facebook: @lichfieldcschl
Instagram: @lichfieldcschl

Age range. 2½–18.

Number of pupils. 570 including 28 Cathedral choristers.

Fees per term (2023–2024). Tuition: £3,539–£5,547.

Lichfield Cathedral School is an outstanding co-educational day school for children aged 2½ to 18. Our mission is to be an internationally recognised school that serves its local area by creating an inclusive school community devoted to Christian ideals of learning, faith, leadership and service, raising the aspirations of each of its members and fulfilling their potential in body, mind and spirit.

The ethos of the school is that of a community where Christian values are upheld and, whilst most pupils are members of the Church of England, children of other denominations and religions are welcomed.

The school occupies two main sites: the Junior Years are located 3½ miles north of Lichfield city centre in six acres of countryside at Longdon Green, while the Middle and Senior Years occupy several buildings in the Cathedral Close, one being the magnificent 17th century Palace, the home of the Bishops of Lichfield until 1952.

The link with the Cathedral remains strong with a twice-weekly school service, as well as concerts and services throughout the year. The boy and girl choristers (aged 7–13) are supported by scholarships provided by the Cathedral Chapter and the School. Former choristers continue their choral training in Cantorum, the scholarship-based chamber choir and Sixth Form Choral Scholars rejoin the Cathedral Choir to sing with the Lay Vicars Choral. Academic, art, drama, sport and music scholarships are available to internal and external students entering Year 7 and Sixth Form.

Learning in the Early Years Foundation Stage is planned around half-termly topics and the children take part in a range of activities which are balanced between adult-led and child-initiated opportunities. Activities are carefully structured to challenge children, encouraging them to develop confidence and the skills needed to solve problems. The outdoor facilities offer children an exciting environment in which to explore and investigate, and we ensure children have the time for free play.

Forest School is a popular element of the curriculum up to Year 9 that provides a holistic, individualised approach to outdoor learning, with a strong focus on developing self-esteem, confidence, resilience, communication skills and social and emotional awareness.

The spirit of intellectual enquiry is at the heart of teaching and learning at the school. Academic results are strong, particularly at GCSE and A Level. Throughout Key Stages 1 to 3, pupils follow a broad and balanced curriculum of English, Mathematics, Science, Computing, French, Spanish, German, Latin, History, Geography, Religious Studies, Art, Design, Music, Drama, Physical Education & Games and Personal, Social & Health Education. ICT skills are developed across every subject.

We offer a wide range of GCSE subjects, including Art and Design, Biology, Business Studies, Chemistry, Computer Science, Design Technology, Drama, English Literature, English Language, French, Geography, German, History, Mathematics, Music, Music Technology, Physical Education, Physics, Product Design, Religious Studies, Spanish and Travel & Tourism. The same subjects are offered for Sixth Form in a mixture of A Levels and BTECs, with the addition of Criminology, Economics, Further Mathematics, Government & Politics, Law, Philosophy, Ethics & Theology, Psychology and Drama & Theatre.

A co-curriculum of activities ensures students are well-rounded and gain valuable skills for higher education, employment and life beyond school. Extracurricular activities every day after school cover a wide range of subjects from chess to cooking and from Taekwondo to tennis. Several orchestras and ensembles are extremely active, as are the five main school choirs.

The unique, whole-school Ethical Leadership Programme helps pupils and students to develop both the life skills and the strength of character to make a positive contribution to the world and do what is right, because they know it to be so.

All pupils have access to a rich variety of residential and day trips as well as pupil exchanges, overseas expeditions and cultural immersion opportunities. Many are directly linked to the curriculum, but the benefits to pupils go far beyond the purely educational. The Duke of Edinburgh's Award scheme is thriving. Sixth Form students take part in overseas volunteer work through World Challenge.

Parents are welcome to contact the school for a tour and a meeting with the Head or to attend any of the school Open Events held throughout the year.

Charitable status. Lichfield Cathedral School is a Registered Charity, number 1137481.

Governors:
Chair: Mrs N Dawes, OBE
Mrs C Evans
Mr E Lunt
Mrs J Mason
Rt Revd J McFarlane, Interim Dean
Mr J Morris
Mr J Neville
Mr R Oakley
Mr C Rickart
Mrs N Roy
Revd Canon A Stead
Director of Finance and Clerk to the Governors: Mr E Fenn

***Head Teacher*: Mrs Susan Hannam**, BA Hons, MA, PGCE

Deputy Head: Mr A Harrison, BEd Hons
Head of Junior Years: Mrs J Churton, BSc Hons, PGCE

Assistant Head (Pastoral): Mrs J Owens, BA Hons, PGCE
Assistant Head & Head of DT: Mr R Hoddle, BA Hons, PGCE
Assistant Head & Head of Science: Mrs M Gardner, BSc Hons, PGCE
Assistant Head & Head of Geography: Mr M Amison, BSc Hons, PGCE, MSc, FRGS
Assistant Head & Head of Sport: Mr M Turner, BSc, MEd, PGCE

Heads of Year:
EYFS: Mrs W Williamson, MBA, PGCE
Years 5 & 6: Mr S Coleman, BA Hons, PGCE
Year 7: Mrs A Bent, BSc Hons, PGCE
Years 8 & 9: Mr M Mayne, BSc Hons, QTS
Years 10–11: Mrs M Goodwin, BA Hons, PGCE
Head of Sixth Form: Mrs F Goodlet, BA, MA

Other Heads of Department:
Mrs S Croft, BA, PGCE (*Drama*)
Mrs S Essex, BA Hons, NASENCO (*SENDCO & Learning Support*)
Mr J Gardiner, BA Hons, PGCE (*Computing*)
Mrs I Johnson, BA Hons, PGCE (*Religious Studies*)
Dr P Jones, BA, MRes, PGCE, PGCES, PhD (*History*)
Mrs S Kundra, BComm Hons, PGCE (*Business Studies*)
Dr S Lane, BEd Hons, PhD (*Chaplaincy Lead*)
Mrs C Lamb, MA, ARCO (*Performance Music & Director of Music Outreach*)

Mr A Nicholson-Ward, BA Hons, PGCE (*English*)
Mrs J Reynolds, BSc Hons, PGCE (*Mathematics*)
Mrs D Rice, BA Hons, ALCM, PGCE (*Music*)
Mrs N Smith, BA Hons, PGCE (*Languages*)
Mrs S Whatley, BA Hons, PGCE (*Art*)

Lincoln Minster School

Part of United Learning

The Prior Building, Upper Lindum Street, Lincoln, Lincolnshire LN2 5RW

Tel: 01522 551300
email: admissions@lincolnminsterschool.co.uk
website: www.lincolnminsterschool.co.uk
X/Twitter: @MinsterSchool
Facebook: @LincolnMinsterSchool
Instagram: @LincolnMinsterSchool
LinkedIn: /Lincoln-Minster-School

See full entry in the **HMC** section, on **p. 208**.

Longridge Towers School

Longridge, Berwick-upon-Tweed, Northumberland TD15 2XQ

Tel: 01289 307584
email: enquiries@lts.org.uk
website: www.lts.org.uk
X/Twitter: @LongridgeTowers
Facebook: @LongridgeTowersSchool
Instagram: @LongridgeTowers

Motto: *Carpe Diem*

The school occupies a Victorian Mansion set in 80 acres of woodland in the beautiful Tweed Valley and enjoys excellent road and rail links with England and Scotland. Daily school bus services operate within a radius of 35 miles from the school.

Longridge Towers, refounded in 1983 under its founder and President, the late Lord Home of the Hirsel, has grown from 113 pupils to 337 pupils. It is probably unique in offering the close personal relationships between pupils, staff and parents which creates a genuine 'family atmosphere'. The school has a reputation for turning out well-rounded and confident young people, the vast majority of whom continue their education at university.

Alongside the excellent academic results, the school offers many opportunities through its sporting and extra-curricular enrichment activities. All of these combine to give all pupils the chance to participate and acquire a variety of skills.

Sport figures strongly in the life of the pupils and many gain representative honours at county and national level in a variety of sports, such as rugby, hockey, cross-country running, athletics, tennis and cricket. Art, Music and Drama are also very popular and successful activities.

Entry. The school caters for a wide spectrum of abilities among its pupils who are taught in small classes. Special provision is made for the needs of pupils with mild dyslexia and for the small proportion of pupils for whom English is their second language.

Assessments upon entry to the Senior School in Mathematics and English are diagnostic and have no fixed pass mark.

The school is divided into 2 departments, Junior and Senior, and caters for pupils throughout their school career, from three to eighteen years. Pupils may enter at any age provided that a vacancy exists. Classes are small with less than 20 pupils per teaching set, reducing to about half this in the Sixth Form.

Activities. Longridge Towers is a school where the development of the pupils outside the academic sphere is considered to be vital. Every afternoon there is an extensive Enrichment programme offering a wide range of activities including: archery, rocket making, football, computer construction, dance, drama, creative writing, wildlife and gardening, young engineers, science club, debating, along with many others. The major team games are rugby, hockey, tennis, cross-country running, athletics and cricket. Many senior pupils participate in the Duke of Edinburgh's Award scheme. The musical activities within the school are varied and numerous. There are five Choirs, two Orchestras and various instrumental groups. Almost a third of the pupils take private instrumental lessons and the taking of grade examinations is encouraged. Over half of the pupils also take LAMDA examinations. No visitor to the school could fail to be aware of the variety and excellence of the artwork on display which includes clay modelling and photography.

Public Examinations. Sixteen subjects are offered at GCSE level, including Physics, Chemistry and Biology and 19, including Economics, Psychology, Sports Studies and Drama, are offered in the Sixth Form at A Level.

Boarding. The Boarding House and pastoral care are in the hands of resident non-teaching house parents. There is medical and dental care. Pupils have access to telephones and email and may send or receive fax messages using the facilities in the school office. Boarders may attend on a weekly or termly basis from age 8 years onwards. At weekends the boarders participate in a wide range of activities.

Scholarships and Bursaries. Academic awards at various levels are available annually to pupils aged 9–14 and 16 (into Sixth Form). Music, Sports, Art and All-Rounder Scholarships are also available to pupils aged 11–14 and 16.

Bursaries are available to children of serving members of the Armed Forces.

Bursaries are also available to pupils; the value of these is determined after consideration of a statement of parental income.

Fees per term (2023–2024). Full Boarders: £9,400 (Junior), £9,650 (Senior). Weekly Boarders: £7,310 (Junior), £7,890 (Senior). Day pupils: Government-funded Nursery with charges for extra hours, £3,630 (Junior age 5–7), £4,620 (Junior age 7–11), £5,200 (Senior age 11–18).

Charitable status. Longridge Towers School is a Registered Charity, number 513534. It exists to provide an academic education for boys and girls.

Board of Governors:
Chairman: Mr T M Bramald
Mrs P Derries
Mrs S Dunford
Mrs A Marshall
Dr E C Miller
Mr M Mole
Mr E Roney
Dr J Watson

***Headmaster*: Mr J C E Lee**, MA Hons, ACA, PGCE

Deputy Head: Mrs J Arnott, BSc, PGCE
Head of Junior Department: Mrs S Maddock, BEd
Deputy Head of Junior Department: Mrs S Bullen, BA, QTS, NASENCo
Senior Teachers:
Mrs C Barber, MEd, PGCE, NASENCo, PGCSpLD (*SENDCo/Senior DSL/PSHE*)
Dr N Dalrymple, PhD, MLitt, BA, PGCE (*Director of Learning*)
Mr A Skeen, BA, QTS (*Pastoral, Economics, Games*)
Teaching Staff:
Ms D Bryden, BEd (*Junior Department*)
Mr M Caddick, BA, PGCE (*German*)
Mrs C Cairns, BA Hons (*Junior Department*)
Miss A Coulson, PGCE (*Junior Department*)
Mr D Crowe, BA, PGCE (*History*)
Mr R Davie, BSc, PGCE (*Mathematics, Computing, Head of Sixth Form*)
Mr P Dodd, BEng, DIS, PGCE (*Head of Maths*)
Mrs S Douglas, BA (*Junior Department*)
Mrs A Gettins, BA (*Librarian, English*)
Mrs N Green, BA, PGCE (*EFL*)
Mr D Gunn, MA, PGCE, QTS (*Humanities*)
Dr D Hardy, MA, PhD, LRSM, QTS (*Music*)
Mrs H Humphreys, BA, PGCE, (*Music*)
Mrs K Hutton, BA (*Drama*)
Mr R Johnson, BA, MA, PGCE (*English*)
Mrs L Johnson, BA, MA, PGCE (*English*)
Mr C Johnston, BA (*Geography*)
Mr B Jones, BA, BEd (*Art*)
Miss D Kirk, BA, PGCE, (*Drama*)
Mr D Massie, BEd (*Head of Sport*)
Mrs B Mayhew, BA, PGCE (*French/Spanish*)
Miss J McCalvey, BSc, PGCE (*Science*)
Mrs J McDougall Welch, BSc, PGCE (*Science*)
Mrs R Mole, BSc, PGCE (*Junior Department*)
Mr R Moscrop, BA, QTS (*Junior Department*)
Mrs S Murray, BA, PGCE (*Junior Department*)
Ms H Norbury, BA, PGCE (*Junior Department*)
Mrs L Peters, BEd (*Girls Games, Sports Studies*)
Mrs E Shaw, BA, PGCE (*Girls Games, Sports Studies*)
Mrs G Skeen, BSc, QTS (*Junior Department*)
Mrs M Smith, BSc, PGCE (*PE, CDT*)
Mr A Westthorp, BEng, PGCE (*CDT, Computing*)
Mrs K Westthorp, MA, PGCE (*French*)
Mrs M Wood, BSc Hons, PGCE (*Maths*)
Mr R Woodrow, MEng, PGCE (*Science*)

Teaching Assistants:
Mrs K Czerwinska
Miss E Dixon
Mrs C Handley, BA, HLTA
Mrs D Johnston, FD Level 5
Mrs Z Jones
Miss K Redpath, HLTA
Mrs A Young, FDTA

Boarding Staff:
Mr G Hattle, Cert. of Prof. Practice (*Senior House Parent*)
Mrs E Crossan
Mrs A Ireland, BA, PGCE, Cert. of Prof Practice (*Residential Senior House Parent*)
Mr M Short, Cert. of Prof. Practice (*House Parent*)

Matron: Mrs M Hattle, RGN
Administration:
Director of Finance/Bursar: Mrs V Bryson, BA, Chartered Accountant
Bursar's PA/HR Manager: Mrs J Sherratt
Finance Manager/Assistant Bursar: Mrs J Aitchison, BSc
Head's PA: Mrs C Craze, BSc
PA to Head of Junior Dept: Mrs A Allis, BA
H&S Co-ordinator: Mrs S Fleming
IT Manager: Mr M McCarter
IT Apprentice: Mr J Dickson
IT Assistant: Mr T Burns
Registrar/Marketing Manager: Mrs M Burns
Reception: Mrs R Flatman & Mrs L Eden
Science Technician: Mr K Toomey
Site Manager: Mr C Smith

Luckley House School

Luckley Road, Wokingham, Berkshire RG40 3EU
Tel: +44 (0)118 978 4175
email: registrar@luckleyhouseschool.org
website: www.luckleyhouseschool.org
X/Twitter: @LuckleyHouse
Facebook: @LuckleyHouseSchool
Instagram: @luckleyhouseschool
LinkedIn: /Luckley-House-School

Luckley House School is a thriving co-educational independent school, located in Wokingham, Berkshire.

Offering day and flexible boarding provision for pupils aged 11 to 18 years. The School is set in attractive grounds with excellent facilities, and at just 40 miles from London, is the perfect location for boarders.

Our uniqueness lies in the combination of our size, Christian ethos and flexibility to meet the needs of individual pupils and their families. We provide a distinctly academic education that is tailored to the individual needs of each pupil. This is offered in the context of a broad curriculum which celebrates the arts and sports, as much as academic achievement.

When a young person leaves Luckley, for whatever pathway they choose, we recognise their success. If they are properly equipped and full of excitement and enthusiasm for the next stage of their life, then they are already successful. For some, this may mean a clutch of the highest grades, but for others it will be a spread of grades in the exams. And these grades will not be the whole story; every young person will have learnt and developed along the way. For every list of grades there is a young person full of potential.

Luckley was founded on its present site in 1918. In 1959, it amalgamated with Oakfield School, established in 1895 in the Lake District. Initially the school was administered by the Church Society but in 1969 it became an independent educational trust.

Luckley boasts fantastic facilities: the school is set in beautiful, safe and secure grounds, with modern classrooms, new science laboratories, contemporary boarding accommodation, a state-of-the-art music centre and stunning performing arts centre and conference theatre, well-equipped art studios and a large sports centre with extensive playing fields, an all-weather pitch, tennis courts, fitness suite, climbing wall and fully sprung dance floor.

The curriculum is broad and challenging with pupils taking 9.5 subjects for GCSE. A wide variety of A Level courses is offered and almost every student goes on to higher education as a preparation for careers in, for example, languages, medicine, engineering, law, business and design.

The School has a well-deserved reputation for Art, Drama, Music and Sport and offers a range of other activities including The Duke of Edinburgh's Award scheme and Combined Cadet Force. Boarders and Day students are encouraged to join in this extensive programme of extracurricular activities.

Boarding. Weekly and flexi boarding offer the opportunity to experience the fun of boarding while keeping close links with home and avoiding long daily journeys. Full boarding, with an extensive weekend activity programme, can provide a stable and secure education for pupils whose schooling would otherwise be interrupted.

Ethos. Luckley House School is built on the Christian foundations of love and service. We enable our students to thrive in a secure and encouraging environment, thereby equipping each pupil to be resourceful and resilient, and ready to take on the challenges and opportunities that lie ahead.

Fees per term (2023–2024). Full Boarders: £11,983, Weekly Boarders: £9,446, Day Pupils: £6,798.

Scholarships and bursaries. Scholarships are awarded at 11+ and 13+ on the results of the Entrance Examination and on entry to the Sixth Form. Music, Drama, Art and Sports scholarships are also on offer.

Means-tested Bursaries and Forces Bursaries are also available.

Charitable status. Luckley House School Limited is a Registered Charity, number 309099.

Mrs Claire Tao (*Chair*)
Headmistress**: Mrs Areti Bizior**, MBA UCL, BSc, BEd Hons, PGCE, UNISA

LVS Ascot

London Road, Ascot, Berkshire SL5 8DR
Tel: 01344 882770
email: registrar@lvs.ascot.sch.uk
website: www.lvs.ascot.sch.uk
X/Twitter: @lvsascot
Facebook: @LVSAscot
Instagram: @lvs_ascot

LVS Ascot is a non-selective, co-educational day and boarding school of over 800 pupils aged 4–18. It is an all-through school so pupils can begin their school career at LVS Ascot at age 4 and remain there until they complete Sixth Form.

GCSE exam results in 2023 saw an overall pass rate of 90.8% (grades 9–4). At A Level the overall pass rate was 96%, with 67.3% achieving grades A*–C.

Numbers. 840 pupils.

Organisation. Pupils aged 4 to 11 (Years R to 6) are taught in the Infant & Junior School, in separate classes each with a class teacher. Houses are used for sports and other competitions. Junior School pupils may board from Year 3 (age 7) and join a mixed House (Kew House), which is an integral part of the Junior School buildings.

Senior School pupils, aged 11 to 18 (Years 7 to 13), are placed in tutor groups and a school House, with a tutor who monitors their pastoral care and oversees their academic performance. Students are taught in ability groups with a maximum class size of 20. Boarders are accommodated in four separate boarding Houses, each supervised by Housemasters/mistresses: Kew (junior house) is mixed for pupils from Year 3 to Year 7; Osborne (girls' house) for pupils from Year 8 to Year 11; Hampton (boys' house) for pupils from Year 8 to Year 11; Blenheim (mixed sixth form house) for pupils in Years 12 and 13.

Location. LVS Ascot is north of the A329, close to Ascot Racecourse and Royal Windsor. The school is easily accessible from the M3, M4 and M25 motorways as well as Heathrow and Gatwick airports. The school bus service connects with trains at Ascot Station, as well many surrounding towns within a 20 miles radius including locations in West London.

Facilities. LVS Ascot is a modern day and boarding school in the UK. The purpose-built facilities, set in 25 acres of landscaped grounds, include: boarding accommodation and classroom blocks, a sports centre, all-weather pitch, indoor swimming pool, fully-equipped 250-seat theatre and a music technology suite. LVS Ascot hosts over five-hundred networked computer workstations, with every classroom equipped with ICT resources for digital and interactive learning. Wireless networking provides additional facilities for centrally-managed student laptops, eBooks and other devices in a secure environment. There is a dedicated Sixth Form Centre, and a Learning Resource Centre, that has an extensive range of books and journals.

Curriculum. The curriculum is broad and based on the national curriculum 'plus'. Pupils follow a common core curriculum of English, Mathematics, Science, one/two foreign languages, plus PE and PSHE. Science is taught as separate subjects. At GCSE, students select their choices from: Business Studies, Technology, Art & Design, Geography, History, Food Technology, Music, Drama, Media Studies, Economics, Physical Education, Computer Science, Spanish, German or French.

A wide range of A Level and vocational options are provided, including Mathematics, Physics, Chemistry, Biology, Music, Geography, History, Economics, Business Studies, English, Art & Design, Theatre Studies, Design & Technology, Media Studies, Photography, Psychology, French, Spanish, German, ICT, Computer Studies, Engineering and Physical Education.

Sport. The school has superb indoor and outdoor facilities with a large sports hall, dance studio with ballet bars, a 25-metre swimming pool and a well-equipped gym as well as rugby, football and hockey pitches, tennis courts and an all-weather pitch. The school has achieved considerable success in providing County, Regional and National standard players in a wide range of sports. Whilst all pupils play team games such as Rugby, Football, Cricket, Hockey, Tennis, Netball, Basketball or Athletics in their early years, the range of options widens as pupils become older to encourage fitness for life, with opportunities such as skiing, skating, polo, fencing and playing squash.

Clubs and Activities. LVS Ascot is an accredited Duke of Edinburgh's Award training centre and runs a vibrant and popular award scheme. Alongside this there is a range of co-curricular activities such as music ensembles, newspaper club, riding, canoeing, rowing, climbing, cookery, animation and film club. In September 2015 LVS Ascot Junior School introduced a range of 25 co-curricular after-school clubs.

Admissions. There is no entrance examination; reports are requested from a student's current school. All students are interviewed prior to acceptance. Prospective students and their families are welcome to visit the school. Personal tours can also be arranged by appointment.

Fees per term (2023–2024). Infants £4,105; Junior: £4,915 (day), £10,305 (boarding); Senior: £6,985 (day), £12,215 (boarding); Sixth Form: £7,365 (day), £12,695 (boarding).

A loyalty discount of 5% is given to pupils in Year 7 who have been at the school from the beginning of Year 4.

Scholarships and Bursaries. Academic, Music, Art, Drama, Sport Scholarships are available at Year 7 entry and various Scholarships are available for entry to the Sixth Form (Year 12).

Fee discounts and Bursaries are available to assist parents working in the Licensed Drinks Trade, MoD and British Diplomats. Third child discount is also available.

Charitable status. The Society of Licensed Victuallers is a Registered Charity, number 230011. It exists to provide education for boys and girls.

Patron: Her Majesty The Queen

Executive Director of Education & Operations: Mr I Mullins, BEd Hons, MSc, MBIM

***Principal*: Mrs C Cunniffe**, BA Hons, MMus, MBA

Senior Deputy Head and Wellbeing (*Infant & Junior School*): Mrs K MacKrell, BA Hons, NPQSL, MCCT
Deputy Head Academic/Director of Studies (*Senior School*): Mrs S Petrault, BA Hons, CELTA
Deputy Head Academic/Director of Studies (*Infant & Junior School*): Mrs F Izod, BA Hons, MCCT
Deputy Head Wellbeing, Personal Conduct Designated Safeguarding Lead & Compliance (*Whole School*): Mrs L Collins, BA Hons
Deputy Head Pupil Outcomes/Pupil Development & Co-Curricular and Head of Years 10 & 11: Mrs F Wall, MA, Med, BSc Hons
Senior Assistant Head Co-curricular & Personal Development, Head of Years 7–9: Mr R Fraser, MA Hons
Senior Assistant Head, Head of Sixth Form: Mr S Moore, BEd
Assistant Heads (*Senior School*): Mrs C Robinson, MA RCA, Mrs R Sandford, BA Hons

Head of Infant & Junior School: Mr T Wintle, BEd Hons
Deputy Head of Infant & Junior School: Mrs K Mackrell, BA Hons, NPQSL

Head of Boarding: Mr J M Wilder, FASC, BMus Hons, BSA Certified

Housemasters/mistresses:

Boarding Houses:
Blenheim: Mr C Drummond
Hampton: Mr J M Wilder, FASC, BMus Hons, PGCE, BSA Certified
Kew: Mrs G Windsor, BA Hons
Osborne: Miss P Swiech, BA Hons

Day Houses:
Heads of Melbourne-Brake: Mr S McDonnell-Roberts, BSc (*Snr*); Mrs R Roberts, (*Jnr*)
Heads of Buchanan-Coburg: Mrs C Robinson, MA RCA (*Snr*); Mr J Matthews, (*Jnr*)
Heads of Kennington-Hart: Mrs R Sandford, BA Hons (*Snr*); Mrs K Stearns, (*Jnr*)

Designated Safeguarding Lead: Mrs L Collins, BA Hons
Deputy Designated Safeguarding Leads:
Mrs N Cowell, BSc Hons (*Snr*)
Mr C Drummond (*Snr*)
Mrs F Izod, BA Hons, MCCT (*Jnr*)
Mrs K MacKrell, BA Hons, NPQSL, MCCT (*Jnr*)
Mr S Moore, BEd (*Snr*)
Mrs R Roberts, BA Hons (*Jnr*)
Mr J M Wilder, FASC, BMus Hons, BSA Certified (*Snr*)

Heads of Departments:
Art and Design: Mrs R Sandford, BA Hons
Biology: Mrs L Chappell, BSc Hons
Business Studies/Economics: Mr R Furse, BA Hons
Chemistry: Mr P Unitt, BSc
Computer Science: Mr M Dripps, BSc
Design & Technology: Mrs C Robinson, MA RCA
English: Mr J Gardner, BA
Food & Nutrition: Mrs C Steer, BSc Hons
Geography: Mrs M McAuley, BA, H Dip Educ, FDE
History: Mrs T Bason, BA Hons
LAMDA: Mrs T Grimsditch, MA
Mathematics: Ms G Els, BA
Media Studies: Mrs J Westwood, BA Hons
Modern Languages: Dr J Roucka-Brown, Med, PhD
Music: Mr J Wilder, FASC, BMus Hons, BSA Certified
Neurodiversity: Ms M Ash, BA Hons, MA, PGCert NASENCO
Performing Arts: Miss J Clark, BA Hons
Philosophy: Mr S Martin, BA Hons
Physical Education: Mrs E Pearce, BA Hons (*Maternity leave*); Mr J Hill, BSc Hons [maternity cover]
Physics: Ms S Sookhun, BSc Hons, MinstP, PhD
Psychology: Mrs K Jones, BA Hons
Science: Mr P Unitt, BSc

Head of Digital Transformation: Mr J McNaughton, BSc

Head of Learning Resources: Mrs E Bartle-Jones

Administrative Staff:
Head of Admissions: Ms L Smit
Executive PA: Mrs C Clark, BA Hons
Principal's PA: Mrs C Gedge
Examinations Officer: Mrs R Jacobs
Senior School Administrator: Mrs N Smith
Senior School Receptionist: Mrs J Gammons
Junior School Secretary: Mrs D Pearce
Junior School Receptionists: Mrs V De Barros; Mrs R Johal

Maida Vale School

Gardener Schools Group

18 Saltram Crescent, London W9 3HR

Tel: 020 4511 6000
email: schooloffice@maidavaleschool.com
website: www.maidavaleschool.com
X/Twitter: @MaidaValeSchool
Facebook: @MaidaValeSchool
Instagram: @MaidaValeSchool
LinkedIn: /company/maidavaleschool

See full entry in the **ISA** section, on **p. 895**.

Milton Abbey School

Milton Abbas, Blandford Forum, Dorset DT11 0BZ

Tel: 01258 880484
email: admissions@miltonabbey.co.uk
website: www.miltonabbey.co.uk
X/Twitter: @MiltonAbbey
Facebook: @MiltonAbbeySchool
Instagram: @MiltonAbbey

At Milton Abbey, we recognise that every child learns differently. Our purposefully small school size, coupled with an extensive range of subjects, puts us in a unique position to recognise and respond to these differences, giving every child the chance to thrive.

We tailor each pupil's education to make the most of their individual skills and talents in a way which nurtures and cultivates their natural abilities so that they can achieve their best possible results, both inside and outside the classroom.

Our school promotes individuality and the pursuit of personal strengths and preferences. Care, guidance and carefully targeted support is available wherever required, resulting in greater confidence and enhanced self-esteem.

We inspire pride in pupils' individual work, whether in sport, academia, the creative arts or in our range of outdoor and practical subjects. Milton Abbey offers parallel learning pathways to a common destination, giving pupils the opportunity to study GCSEs and A Levels, alongside the widest range of vocational subjects in the independent school sector.

Our small size allows for a great involvement in school life, huge opportunity for pupils to represent the school and to master a chosen subject or activity. Lasting and fulfilling friendships are forged, and everyone has the chance to get to know one another. Class sizes are very small – even by independent schools' standards – so no one is overlooked or left behind.

Organisation. Milton Abbey is proud of its full-boarding status and the comprehensive co-curricular and recreational programmes this allows.

Curriculum. An innovative 'carousel curriculum' allows joining Third Form pupils to study core subjects throughout the year, while sampling a huge range of courses usually only available as GCSEs or BTECs. This helps them make informed course choices for study in later years. The Sixth Form provides a wide range of academic, technical and vocational courses including traditional A Levels, BTECs and top-up GCSEs.

Situation. Stunning countryside surroundings offer space, yet safety and security, providing an inspirational setting for learning.

Facilities. The Abbey is the School Chapel, and the dining room, the Abbot's Hall, dates back to the medieval era. Alongside a mansion house, modern facilities include boarding houses, a music school, art studio, fashion studio and creative media suite, a 370-seat theatre, plus a farm and stables. Sporting facilities include all-weather pitches, an indoor pool, cricket nets and golf course.

Admissions. Most pupils join the School at age 13 in the Third Form (Year 9). The School gives quick and unconditional offers to prospective pupils, after they undertake an individual Admissions Visit. This provides clarity and certainty for families. Students seeking to join the Sixth Form are judged on individual merit and suitability for their chosen courses.

Offers are dependent on a satisfactory current school reference, including CAT4 or equivalent cognitive test scores, and an interview with the Head or Deputy Head. Offers are not dependent on Common Entrance results, however all applicants receiving an offer must maintain high levels of effort and application at their current school.

Prospective pupils with Special Educational Needs will be assessed by the Head of Learning Development, to make sure that the School can offer them the correct level of support.

Fees per term (2023–2024). Lower School: Boarding £16,545, Day £8,690.

Supplement for Sixth Form entrants. £500 per term

Charitable status. The Council of Milton Abbey School Limited is a Registered Charity, number 306318.

Chair of Governors: Ian G Bromilow, MSc, PhD
Visitor: Revd Canon C W Mitchell-Innes, MA

***Head*: James Watson**, MA Hons, FCA, PGCE

Senior Deputy Head: Chris Barnes, BA Hons

Deputy Head (*Academic & Head of Sixth Form*): Josh Bradbury, BA Hons, MA, PhD, PGCE
Deputy Head (*Co-Curricular*): Will Fraser, MA, MEd
Deputy Head (*Development & Admissions*): Claudia Hindle, MA, PGCE, MEd

Director of Finance: Stephen Lane, BSc, ACA

SENDCo & Lead Practitioner: Laura Kleiser
Head of Operations: Tracey Edwards

Head of Marketing & Events: Nick Cloke
ICT Manager: Brendan Picknell
Milton Abbey Association (Alumni) Manager: Hugo Mieville, BA, MA, PG Dip

Moreton Hall

Weston Rhyn, Oswestry, Shropshire SY11 3EW

Tel: 01691 773671
email: admin@moretonhall.com
website: www.moretonhall.org
X/Twitter: @moretonhall
Facebook: @moretonhall

See full entry in the **HMC** section, on **p. 234**.

Mount House School

Camlet Way, Hadley Wood, Barnet, Hertfordshire EN4 0NJ

Tel: 020 8449 6889
email: schooladminofficer@mounthouse.org.uk
website: www.mounthouse.org.uk
X/Twitter: @MountHouseSch
Facebook: @MountHouseSchoolBarnet
Instagram: @mounthouse_school/?hl=en
LinkedIn: /school/mount-house-school

Age Range. 11–18 co-educational.
Number in School. 243 Day Girls & Boys.
Fees per term (2023–2024). £6,710.

Our mission at Mount House School is to inspire lifelong learning within a nurturing, culturally creative and intellectually dynamic community.

At Mount House, every individual is valued and each child's unique talents will be identified and nurtured. Students leave as able, articulate, balanced, caring, and well-rounded individuals with a genuine love of learning, ready to take on life's challenges and opportunities, aware of the needs of others and confident in their ability to make a difference.

Mount House expects students to be the very best they can be and inspires them to make their best even better. Our overarching aim is that Mount House is a happy and successful School, with an excellent record of GCSE and A level results and an outstanding record of students achieving places at top universities. The School is equally concerned to foster the wide range of skills that help young students grow into capable adults with a sense of self-worth. Mount House supports students as they strive for academic excellence within a clear framework of personalised pastoral care and wellbeing that brings success without stress.

Board of Directors:
Mr Ian Davies (*Chairman*)
Mr Emil Gigov, FCA
Mr Adam Chirkowski, BA Hons, MA FCA

School Staff:

***Head*: Mrs Sarah Richardson**, BA Hons, PGCE

Senior Leadership Team:

Senior Deputy Head: Mr J Cooper, MA Hons, PGCE
Deputy Head Pastoral & DSL: Mr T Phillips, BA Hons, PGCE
Assistant Headteacher, Head of Lower Schoo, Director of Sport & Co-Curricular: Mrs N Hillcoat-Hyde, BA, MA, PGCE
Assistant Head (Pastoral), Whole School Mental and Wellbeing Lead, DDSL: Ms P Smyth, BA Hons, PGCE
Assistant Head (Academic): Mr C McCormick, BA Hons, MA, PGCE
Assistant Head (Pastoral), Head of Faculty Technology & Computing: Mrs Sara Trickey, NPQLTD, NPQSL, MA Education, PGCE, BA Hons
Deputy Head Pastoral and Designated Safeguarding Lead (DSL): Mr Gerrard Crosby, BA
Bursar and Clerk to the Board of Directors: Mrs N Nathwani

Mr Phillip Allman, BA Hons, PGCE (*Sociology & Politics*)
Mrs Satbir Allman, MA, PGCE (*Sociology*)
Miss Kulsum Ansari, BSc, MA, PGCE (*Business, Economics & Mathematics, Head of Careers*)
Mr Douglas Badger (*Teaching Assistant*)
Miss Victoria Bailey, BA (*Classics & Latin*)
Ms Amy Baird, BA Hons (*Art*)
Ms Carole Berry (*French*)
Mr Peter Brozny, BSc (*Science*)
Miss Amy Buckland, BSc (*Physical Education & Food Technology, Head of House*)
Miss Antonia Christofi, MA, PGCE (*English*)
Mrs Sue Colebrook (*Learning Support*)
Miss Libby ColetBSc, PGCE (*Geography*)
Mrs Dolores Conchillo Hernandez (*Language Assistant*)
Mr Jon Cooper, MA Hons, PGCE (*History, Senior Deputy Head*)
Miss Lynsey Cosham, BA Hons (*Textiles & Food Technology*)
Mr Gerrard Crosby, BA (*Deputy Head (Pastoral), History & Classics*)
Miss Natalie DalcherGraduate Teaching Assistant
Mrs Abisoye Da Rocha, BA Hons, PGCE (*French and Spanish*)
Ms Fiona Dawson, PGCE (*Drama*)
Miss Flaminia Di Dio, BSc, MSc, QTS (*Science*)
Mrs Kathryn Fallon, BA Hons, MLDP, PGCE (*Classics*)
Mr Patrick Gallagher, BSc Hons, MSc (*Mathematics*)
Miss Maria Gregoriou (*Mathematics*)
Miss Samira Hassan, BA (*Humanities*)
Mrs Natasha Hillcoat-Hyde, BA, MA, PGCE (*PE*)
Miss Molly Hopping (*Graduate Teaching Assistant*)
Ms Semra Kazim, PGCE, MSc (*Science*)
Ms Clare Kelly (*Drama*)
Mrs Melani Lazouras, BA Hons, PGCE (*MFL*)
Mrs Rebecca MacDonald, MA Hons, PGCE (*English*)
Ms Eleonora Mariottini, Class 3 University, Italy QTS (*Spanish*)
Ms Glynis Marshall (*Teaching Assistant*)
Mr Dan Mather, BA (*PE*)
Mr Craig McCormick, BA Hons, MA, PGCE (*History*)
Mr Paul Nancarrow, PG Cert TEAL, PG Dip, MA (*English*)
Mr Siraj Peara, BSc (*Science*)

Ms Melissa Petinou (*Learning Support*)
Mrs Sophie Rosenfeld, BSc, PGCE (*Science*)
Mrs Solene Roy, BSc, PGCE (*Psychology, Science*)
Mr Sayful Sayeed, BSc, MSc, PGCE (*Computer Science*)
Ms Meliz Shukru (*Learning Support*)
Miss Sophie Simon, BSc, PGCE (*Physics & Chemistry, Head of Digital Teaching & Learning*)
Ms Patrice Smyth, BSc, PGCE (*Physical Education, Assistant Head*)
Ms Elizabeth Somerville, BA Hons, PGCE (*Co-Head of Faculty, Art & Design*)
Mrs Sara Trickey (*Head of Faculty, Technology, Assistant Head*)
Mr Ronald Van Leeven (*Science*)
Ms Malgorzata Wachowska, MA, PGCE (*English*)
Mr Sam Whitehouse, BA Hons, PGCE (*Music*)
Mrs Melanie Wiltshire, BSc, PGCE (*PE, Dyslexic Specialist*)
Ms Gabrielle Wong (*Business, Economics, Maths*)

Mount Kelly

Parkwood Road, Tavistock, Devon PL19 0HZ

Tel: 01822 813193
email: admissions@mountkelly.com
website: www.mountkelly.com
X/Twitter: @Mount_Kelly
Facebook: @MountKellyFoundation
Instagram: @mount.kelly
LinkedIn: /mount-kelly

See full entry in the **HMC** section, on **p. 236**.

The National Mathematics & Science College

2 The Oaks, Westwood Way, Westwood Business Park, Coventry, Warwickshire CV4 8JB

Tel: 02475 092950
email: admissions@natmatsci.ac.uk
website: www.natmatsci.ac.uk
X/Twitter: @natmatsci
Facebook: @natmatsci
Instagram: @natmatsci_
LinkedIn: /natmatsci

Number of pupils. 133.

Fees per term (2023–2024). Boarding £15,299 per term. Day £4,999 per term.

The National Mathematics and Science College is the top specialist STEM college in the UK. Science, Technology, Engineering and Mathematics (STEM) subjects are more important today than they have ever been. For those students looking to excel in these areas, the specialist education we can provide is designed to enable them to thrive both at A-level and beyond.

We recognise that a high-quality specialist education must go beyond the narrow confines of the curriculum and must expose our students to the breadth and joy contained within these subject areas in an integrated way. We are geared to help students learn how to think, not what to think, which will allow them to thrive at College, at University and beyond.

Students of The National Mathematics and Science College should go on to achieve at the highest levels, pushing the boundaries of our mathematical and scientific understanding. Our collective role at the College is to work in partnership with our students to establish an effective foundation and help light the spark! We do all of this as part of a caring and supportive community, which encourages students to think creatively about the links both within and outside of their subject domains.

The National Mathematics and Science College is an inspiring place, where we support the development of some exceptionally gifted young people. It has recently been named Independent School of the Year in the Outstanding New Initiative category for its STEM Communication programme.

Admission. The National Mathematics and Science College operates on a selective entry basis, with entry upon the successful completion of the College entrance exams along with an interview with a senior member of staff.

Scholarships are offered and details regarding these can be found on our website: www.natmatsci.ac.uk.

Curriculum. Pre-A-Level: Mathematics, Chemistry, Biology, Physics, Economics and Computer Science, and English as an Additional Language.

A-Levels: Mathematics (including Further Mathematics), Chemistry, Biology, Physics, Economics, Computer Science and the EPQ (Extended Project Qualification).

We believe in the value of specialism, and our two-year A-level programme presents the pinnacle of specialist pre-university study anywhere in the world. Most of our students will study four A-levels choosing from Mathematics (including Further Mathematics), Chemistry, Biology, Physics, Economics, Computer Science and the EPQ (Extended Project Qualification).

Alongside our A-level programme we have a specialist 'preparation for medicine programme' which builds on the A-level programme to provide a rich programme of activities and opportunities which help ensure that our budding medics are fully prepared. This programme includes a range of visiting speakers, lectures and visits as well as specialist mentoring and preparation for the relevant entrance papers. All our medics last year received interviews and offers to read medicine.

For those not yet ready to start the two-year A-level programme, either because of age, experience or language skills, we offer a one-year Pre A-Level programme designed to get students ready to thrive at A-Level. Students will learn Mathematics, Chemistry, Biology, Physics, Economics and Computer Science as well as developing their English language skills.

A Level Results. In the summer of 2023, we achieved outstanding results with 69% of results being awarded A* or A grades and almost 40% of grades being awarded the top A* grade.

University Destinations. Students from The National Mathematics & Science College regularly go on to gain places at some of the very best universities around the world, those universities which can change the trajectory of their life. Over the last three years almost 1 in 5 of our students gained places in Oxbridge with over 1 in 3 students having gained places at GS universities, with many others going on to excellent universities in the UK and internationally.

Location. The National Mathematics and Science College is situated on the edge of Warwick University in the leafy and picturesque area of Westwood Heath in Warwickshire. With excellent transport links, it is easily accessible by rail, bus and car.

Boarding. Boarding students live together in specialist accommodation next door to the teaching centre in the heart of leafy Warwickshire. Each student has their own luxury en-suite study bedroom with a three-quarter sized double bed, desk, wardrobe, under-bed storage and highspeed wifi. The rooms provide a calm and comfortable space for students to study and live independently, within a university-style environment.

The boarding residence has a large number of open-plan kitchen and living rooms, with ample space for relaxing, socialising and eating together. Kitchens are fully equipped and have dining space as well as comfortable seating and televisions. Meals are fully catered for in the College's onsite Alchemist's Restaurant which serves three hot meals a day plus snacks and our barista coffee service. However, students are also welcome to use the kitchens to prepare additional food and snacks outside of mealtimes. There are also a number of indoor and outdoor communal spaces for the students to enjoy including a gaming area, coffee hub, collaborative working spaces and gym.

Chair of Governors: Michael O'Sullivan

***Principal*: Dr Andy Kemp**

Newcastle School for Boys

Senior School:
34 The Grove, Gosforth, Newcastle upon Tyne NE3 1NH

Tel: 0191 255 9300

Junior School:
30 West Avenue, Gosforth, Newcastle upon Tyne NE3 4ES

Tel: 0191 255 9300

email: enquiries@newcastleschool.co.uk
website: newcastleschool.co.uk
X/Twitter: @NSB_Boys @nsb_sport
Facebook: @NewcastleSchoolforBoys

Age Range. 3–18.

Number of Boys. 370.

Fees per term (2023–2024). £3,924 (Reception), £4,577 (Years 1–2), £4,721 (Years 3–6), £5,782 (Year 7 and above).

Newcastle School for Boys is the only independent school in the north east providing continuous education for boys from ages 3 to 18. Situated in Gosforth, Newcastle upon Tyne, the Senior School site on The Grove covers 5 acres of playing fields and buildings that currently house Years 7 to 11. Opposite the Senior School, Years 12 and 13 are housed in their own dedicated Sixth Form Centre, opened in September 2017. Our Junior School is housed on nearby sites on West Avenue and North Avenue. The School currently has 390 pupils on role from Nursery to Year 13.

The academic curriculum starts in the Infants and provides boys with opportunities for stretch and challenge from the outset. This leads through the Juniors to GCSE, A Level and vocational qualifications in a wide range of disciplines at the Senior School and Sixth Form.

Pastoral care is outstanding throughout the school and boys receive plenty of individual attention so that they grow in confidence and independence.

Newcastle School for Boys believes strongly in enhancing learning beyond the classroom and runs an extensive trips and visits programme. Residential and day visits are offered to all pupils from age 5 onwards and culminate in major overseas trips and Duke of Edinburgh's Gold Award expeditions in the Sixth Form.

Senior School. The Senior School starts at Year 7 (11+) and runs through to Year 13 (18+).

We offer an enhanced curriculum leading up to GCSE, where most boys study 10 subjects. The Senior School provides an extensive co-curricular programme of music and a wide range of sports, including a number of major overseas trips. The School enhances its sporting provision using a number of excellent local facilities including at South Northumberland Cricket Club and Northern Rugby Club.

Sixth Form. The School has established a successful and growing Sixth Form offering students a wide choice of A Level and vocational qualifications. The Sixth Form provides the learning and support the boys need to achieve their best possible academic and personal outcomes.

Entrance and scholarship Examinations are offered in January for boys entering Year 7 (11+), Year 9 (13+) and Year 12 (16+). Entry at other points is possible following a full academic assessment and interview.

Junior School. The learning environment across our Junior School is tailored to the needs of the younger boys, taking into account their energy and enthusiasm for challenge and discovery. The curriculum offered is a blend of the traditional and the innovative and is designed to balance the need for adventure and fun, while maintaining progress in numeracy and literacy. The boys are provided with opportunities to develop their individual academic talents and to pursue their creative goals. Excellence is also pursued in the sporting arena where boys have opportunities including football, rugby, cricket, golf and table tennis.

Regular drama performances and musical productions encourage teamwork and build confidence from an early age.

Breakfast club and after-school clubs and activities provide full wraparound care.

Charitable status. Newcastle School for Boys is a Registered Charity, number 503975.

Chairman of Governors: T J Care

***Headmaster*: D J Tickner**, BA, MEd

Deputy Heads:
G Hallam, BSc
A Newman, BA

Head of Junior School: T White

Bursar: C Dobson, FCCA

Director of Marketing and Admissions: A Kingsland, BA, MSc

Our Lady's Abingdon

Radley Road, Abingdon-on-Thames, Oxfordshire OX14 3PS

Tel: 01235 524658
email: office@ola.org.uk
website: www.ola.org.uk
X/Twitter: @OLAabingdon
Facebook: @OLAabingdon
Instagram: @OLAabingdon
LinkedIn: /our-ladys-abingdon

Motto: *Age Quod Agis – Whatever you do, do it well*

Founded in 1860 by Mother Clare Moore of the Sisters of Mercy, Our Lady's Abingdon (OLA) is an independent, co-educational, Catholic day school, for ages 7–18. The school welcomes pupils of all faiths and none who wish to benefit from its nurturing and outward-looking ethos. OLA offers outstanding pastoral care and a wide range of academic and co-curricular activities, ensuring that pupils are confident and engaged and leave school excited about their next steps in life.

Small class sizes allow staff to get to know every single pupil, giving them the support and encouragement they need to fulfil their academic and personal potential.

Numbers. There are 388 pupils aged 11–18 in the Senior school and 37 pupils aged 7–11 in the Lower school.

Facilities and buildings. Bright, spacious classrooms and an excellent library provide a pleasant ambience conducive to study and learning. Grounds surround the building, providing an attractive setting in which pupils can play and relax during breaks. Sports facilities include football and rugby pitches, a multi-use games area, tennis courts, a sports hall, hockey and athletics provision and a 25-metre indoor swimming pool. The school has dining rooms and a 50-seat café, with other building projects including a 6th form garden, a Design & Technology centre, an auditorium and library, the latest in ICT equipment and additional Science laboratories. The Music department benefits from facilities to aid composition and support the wide variety of instruments taught in the school.

Curriculum. The school teaches a balanced range of subjects both academic and practical during the first three years. All lessons are one hour long to maximise learning on a 2-week timetable to increase flexibility and maintain a broad and deep curriculum. The School day starts at 8.30am and ends at 4.00pm. We strive for all pupils to fulfil their potential, whatever their level of ability, and they are supported in making the most of the opportunities available. We are constantly developing our Academic Enrichment which enables all pupils to discover and explore their intellectual curiosities. In addition, the extensive enrichment opportunities available allows us to stretch and challenge the most able, and empower their university and career decision-making. We have introduced alternative pathways into our curriculum so that we can cater for all pupils. There is BTEC Film and Media in OLA 6th, which is a more accessible and vocational course than many A-Levels, and is accepted as equivalent to one A Level by all UK universities. Pupils are able to study either Separate Sciences or Combined Science at GCSE. French and Spanish are no longer compulsory subjects at GCSE. We value the study of languages, and we recommend that pupils choose a broad and balanced set of subjects for GCSE, including a language, a creative subject and one of the humanities. However, the study of French or Spanish is not always appropriate for some pupils and, in these cases, they can opt for another subject. The great majority of OLA 6th students go on to Higher Education, but some have also succeeded in gaining places on highly competitive professional placement programmes. There is also support throughout the school for pupils with special educational needs and for pupils for whom English is not their first language.

Co-curricular activities. The school provides an extensive programme of co-curricular activities including drama, music, art, public speaking and many forms of sport. There is also a strong commitment to local community schemes and an impressive record in the Duke of Edinburgh's Award scheme. OLA has regularly been accredited with the British Council's International School Award for the links it has fostered with schools in Uganda.

Fees per term (2023–2024). Senior School: £6,175; Lower School: £4,145–£4,975.

Admission. We have developed an assessment process that is kinder to your child while yielding in-depth information for our admissions decisions. Our new process uses a test designed to identify each child's potential and aptitude for learning, not simply their current performance. This gives us a deeper understanding of each individual child; whilst also minimising the impact of lost learning due to Covid-19. Our move away from formal written assessments in large examination halls provides a kinder and less daunting experience for your child.

Pupils may apply for Scholarships for entry to Year 7, Year 9 and OLA 6th. Candidates may also apply for bursaries, which are awarded at the discretion of the Governors.

Charitable status. Our Lady's Abingdon Trustees Limited is a Registered Charity, number 1120372, and a Company Limited by Guarantee, registered in England and Wales, number 6269288.

Board of Governors:
Chairman: Mr F Elturk, BSc
Mr G Ayling, MA
Dr L Bergmeier, PhD, CBiol, MRSB, FHEA
Mrs A Freeman, BEd
Revd J McGrath, STB, MA
Mr F Peck
Mrs H Ronaldson
Dr Jacqueline Woodman, MB ChB, MRCOG, MA, MEd Ed, DPhil

Leadership Team:
Chief Operating Officer & Executive Leader: Mr P Karian, CIPD

Head of OLA: **Mr D Gibbons**, BA Hons Leeds, PGCE, MMU
Senior Deputy Head: Mrs S Machen
Deputy Head Academic: Mrs F Bayly
Deputy Head Pastoral & DSL: Mr A Jackson

Heads of Sections:
OLA 6: Dr E Lawson, BA, MA, PhD
Upper School: Miss J Simpson
Middle School: Mr J Cooper, BA, PGCE
Head of Transition & Year 7: Mr A Raszpla

Heads of Departments:
Art: Mrs L Bainbrigge
Careers: Mr C Sissons, BEd
Classics: Miss P Smith, BA
Design & Technology: Mr N Humphreys, BEd
Drama: Dr E Lawson, MA, PhD
Economics & Business Studies: Mrs L Webster, BA, Grad Dip, MEd
English: Mrs C Phippen
Geography: Mrs S Dutton, BSc, PGCE
History: Mrs N Nicholls
Learning Support: Mrs C Roberts, SENCo
Mathematics: Mr A Bartoli-Edwards
Modern Languages:
Mrs S Machen, BA Lille, PGCE Sc, PGCE Liv
Music: Mr G Damiani
Physical Education (Girls): Mrs M Barnett, BA
Physical Education (Boys): Mr L Allen, BSc, PGCE
Psychology: Mrs J James, BSc, PGCE, GTP
Religious Studies: Mr J Cregan
Science: Mrs L Read
Textiles: Mrs C Sharkey, BA, PGCE

Director of Admissions & Marketing: Ms K Sutton, CIM Dip
Head's PA: Mrs J Braley, BSc, Assoc CIPD
School Business Manager: Ms T Wheatley, AAT
School Development Manager: Mrs Z Doy, FIOS

The Peterborough School
A Woodard School

Thorpe Road, Peterborough PE3 6AP

Tel:	01733 343357
email:	office@tpsch.co.uk
website:	www.thepeterboroughschool.co.uk
X/Twitter:	@PeterboroughSch
Facebook:	@ThePeterboroughSchool
Instagram:	@thepeterboroughschool
LinkedIn:	/company/thepeterboroughschool

The Peterborough School is the City's only independent day school for boys and girls from Nursery to Sixth Form. Situated in beautiful surroundings in the heart of Peterborough, the School enjoys excellent road and rail links. The School is a member of the Woodard Corporation, the largest group of Church of England Schools in England and Wales.

Situation and buildings. The School is located in beautiful secluded grounds, near the centre of Peterborough, 50 minutes by fast train from King's Cross and easily accessible by road from the A1, A14 and A47. The elegant Victorian house is the centre of a modern, purpose-built complex of classrooms, laboratories, Music School, Art Block, Sixth Form Centre, Library and a modern Computing Suite. The Sports Facility was completed in September 2012.

The Preparatory School. Boys and girls are admitted into the Reception Class from the age of 4+. The whole range of Key Stage subjects is covered in addition to a variety of other subjects and activities, e.g. Reasoning, French and other languages. Some subjects are taught by specialist staff from the Senior School. There is emphasis on academic standards, good manners, Physical Education, Music and Drama.

The Senior School. The curriculum of the Senior School is characterised by small classes and an emphasis on individual guidance and target-setting. A balanced programme leads to high achievement at GCSE. English, Mathematics, Sciences, Religious Education, Games and PE remain compulsory throughout; Languages, Computer Science, Food Tech, History and Geography, Art, Art Textiles and Design Technology, Music, Drama and Physical Education form the matrix of options. Spanish has recently been added to the curriculum.

External candidates are selected from the entrance examinations and opportunities for Scholarships exist at Year 7 and Sixth Form entry.

The School has a modern Computing Suite with state-of-the-art equipment, including iPads and laptops. All classrooms are networked.

There are specialist laboratories for all sciences and a new Sixth Form science lab.

In the Sixth Form students usually take three A Level subjects but may in some circumstances undertake four. These are linear qualifications, with examination at the end of the two-year course of study: there are no AS examinations available at the end of the Lower Sixth. In addition to their academic studies, Sixth Formers undertake a significant enrichment programme that includes volunteering, the Extended Project Qualification (EPQ) and an electives programme.

As a School with pupils from Reception and children in the Nursery from 6 weeks and above, older pupils have many opportunities to develop a sense of involvement and responsibility, and carry out valuable service in the wider School community. Business sense is developed through the Young Enterprise scheme, in which the School is very successful. The Duke of Edinburgh's Award Scheme is also prioritised.

The Nursery. The Peterborough School Nursery offers daycare for babies to preschoolers. Optional lessons include French, Ballet and Key Sports.

Religion. Weekly Chapel Services are held and attendance is compulsory, although participation is optional.

Music and Drama. The music of the School, in particular its choral tradition, is renowned and the School competes in festivals as well as singing at events across the city. Tuition in singing, piano and all orchestral instruments is available. Major theatrical and musical productions take place several times a year, and the School presents an Art & Design Exhibition each summer. Speech & Drama is a popular extracurricular activity, with many students gaining LAMDA or New Era qualifications.

Games and Physical Education. The pupils achieve outstanding success in team and individual sports and athletics. Many pupils have represented the county, the region, and Team GB. The School estate is spacious with several pitches and all-weather courts. The many and varied sporting facilities of the city are within easy reach for swimming, rowing and athletics. The School is benefiting from the major development of its Sports Facility, including a Fitness Suite and Climbing Wall.

Extracurricular activities. Many clubs and societies operate in extracurricular time, and field visits and excursions illuminate classroom work. Many pupils undertake the Duke of Edinburgh's Award Scheme at both Bronze and Gold levels, with outstanding success and the School has its own St John Ambulance division. Cubs, Scouts and Beavers are also run from the School.

Fees per term (2023–2024). Reception: £3,997; Years 1–2: £4,367; Years 3–6: £5,295; Years 7–9: £6,330; Years 10–Upper Sixth: £6,448.

Tuition fees include a mid-morning snack and lunch.

Scholarships. Academic, Art, Music and Sport are the main scholarships available to those entering Year 7. Woodard All-rounder Scholarships are also available for Senior students at the Headmaster's discretion. Sixth Form Academic Scholarships are also available. Please apply to the Admissions Team for more information.

The Peterborough School Alumni (Westwoodians' Association). Secretary: Mrs Ivana Zizza who is based at the School.

Charitable status. The Peterborough School Limited is a Registered Charity, number 269667. It is an independent school which exists to promote the education of children.

School Council:
Chair: Mr K Craig, BA Hons, FCCA, CTA
Deputy Chair: Mr P Simmons
The Revd Canon T Jones, Vice Dean of Peterborough
Ms L Ayres, LLB
Mr K Chakraborty
Mrs S Dixon, BA Hons, PGCE
Mrs K Hart, BA Hons
Mr P Hayes
Prof C J Howe, SCD, MA, FLS
The Rt Revd R Ladds, SSC, LRSC, BEd Hons
Dr N Menon, MRCS, BMBS Hons, BMedSci Hons
Mrs H Milligan-Smith, LLB Hons
Dr E Nisbet
Mrs E Payne
Dr J S Thompson, LMSSA, MBBS, DRCOG

***Head*: Mr A Meadows**, BSc Hons Manchester, NPQH

Bursar: Mr S Dharamraj, MBA, MA, BSc Hons, FCMI
Deputy Headmaster: Mr R Cameron, BA Hons Southampton
Head of the Preparatory School: Mrs A-M Elding, MA OU, BEd Hons Derby
Head of Pastoral Care: Mr M Pryor
Director of Sixth Form: Mr A Stroud, BA Hons Oxon

Staff:
Miss H Adams, BSc Hons (*Mathematics*)
Mrs L Andrew, BEd Hons (*Preparatory*)
Mr P Baldwin, BA Hons (*Preparatory*)
Mr K Bingham, BA Hons (*Preparatory*)
Mr D Bocking (*Maths*)
M A Boxall (*Head of Boys' Sport*)
Mr C Brocklesby, BA Hons (*Geography*)
Mrs H Brookes, BA Hons (*English, Head of Key Stage 3*)
Mrs Burgess (*Speech and Drama*)
Miss A Buxcey, BA Hons (*Religious Education*)
Miss Z Chappell, BA Hons Cantab (*Preparatory*)
Miss S M Clarkson, BA Hons Cantab (*History*)
Miss H Clisset, BA Hons (*Dance*)
Mr G Cloke, BSc Hons (*Preparatory*)
Miss S Cummings, BA Hons (*Chemistry, Head of Key Stage 4*)
Mrs K Davis, BSc Hons (*Chemistry*)
Mrs R Ditcher, BSc Hons (*Preparatory*)
Dr L Fox-Clipsham, PhD, BSc (*Science*)
Mrs H Graves, BA Hons (*Drama, PSHE*)
Miss M Gray (*Head of Individual Learning*)
Mrs L Grinyer, BA Hons (*English*)
Ms A Garala, BSc Hons (*Preparatory*)
Mrs R Hampson, BA Hons (*Art, Textiles*)
Mr A Harwin, BA Hons (*Art*)
Miss M Johal (*Sociology/Psychology*)
Miss C Johnson, BSc Hons (*Biology, PSHE*)
Mrs E Kay, BSc Hons (*Physical Education*)
Ms A Kupara, BA (*Computing & Digital Strategy*)
Mrs L Lane (*PE, Head of Girls' Sport*)
Mr S Law, BSc Hons (*Physics*)
Miss L McChlery, BEd (*Preparatory*)
Mrs L McClarnon, BEd Hons (*Preparatory*)
Mr J Marsden, BSc Hons (*Physical Education*)
Mrs G Mason, OND Hotel & Catering (*Food Technology & Preparatory Teaching Assistant*)
Mrs S Noone, BEd (*Preparatory*)
Mrs E Porsz, BA Hons (*Physical Education*)
Ms E Potbury, BA Hons (*French*)
Mrs C Raitt (*PE*)
Mrs J Roberts, BA Hons (*English*)
Mr P Schavier, Masters Degree (*German*)
Mrs M Silvester, BSc Hons (*Mathematics*)
Mrs A Skelton, BA Hons (*Preparatory*)
Mr S Stevenson (*PE*)
Miss C Steward, BA Hons (*Preparatory*)
Mr M Twigg, BA Hons (*Product Design*)
Mrs C Wagner-Lees, BA Hons (*German*)
Mrs L Wisdom, BSc (*Geography*)
Mrs J Young, BSc Hons (*Physical Education*)

Instrumental Music/Speech & Drama:
Miss K Birtles, BMus Hons (*Flute & Oboe*)
Mr R Brain, BA Hons, MA (*Director of Music*)
Mr J Cranfield, BA Hons (*Guitar*)
Mr R Haylett, BA Hons Cantab (*Singing*)
Mr M Jewkes (*Jazz Piano & Saxophone*)
Mrs M McAuliffe, Dip ABRSM (*Violin*)
Mr J Nessfield, BA Hons (*Brass*)
Mrs P Samuels, LGSM Cert Acting GSMD (*Speech & Drama*)
Miss E Smith, BMus Hons (*School Accompanist*)

Administrative Officers:
Head's PA: Mrs L Hale
Marketing Executive: Miss A Salmon
Admissions and Alumni Manager: Mrs I Zizza
Admissions Officer: Mrs W Short
Administrative Assistant: Mrs K Woods
Accounts: Mrs J House, BA Hons; Mrs R Forman
Operations Manager: Mr K Green

Estate Manager: Mr C Lang
Laboratory Technician: Mrs A Albon, BSc
Art and Food Tech Technician: Miss A Prebble
Network Manager: Mr A Nicholls
IT Technician: Mr K Rossall
LRC Manager: Mrs C Thomson
Receptionist: Mrs R Adcock
Office: Mrs K Kett
Teaching Assistants & Supervisors:
Mrs A Brennan
Miss C Callow
Mrs W Cohen
Miss F Cupoli
Ms E Drew, BA Hons
Mrs Z Green
Mrs E Penniston, BA Hons
Miss D Pepper
Mrs J Reade
Mr C Howitt
Mr R Westbrook

Medical Staff:
Mrs F Aylmore, BSc Hons (*Senior Nurse*)
Mrs M Lay, BSc Hons (*School Counsellor*)

Pitsford School

Pitsford Hall, Pitsford, Northamptonshire NN6 9AX

Tel: 01604 880306
email: office@pitsfordschool.com
website: www.pitsfordschool.com
X/Twitter: @Pitsford_School
Facebook: @PitsfordSchool
Instagram: @pitsfordschool

Age range. 3–18 Co-educational.

Number of pupils. 290 boys and girls.

Fees per term (2023–2024). Junior School: £3,200–£5,190; Senior School: £5,552. Lunches: £304.

The School was founded in 1989 to offer a traditional Grammar School standard of education to boys in Northamptonshire. Today, the School still offers the same high standards of education but to boys and girls from 3–18 years of age.

Thirty acres of beautiful parklands and outdoor sporting areas mean there is a real emphasis on being outside and enjoying nature. This emphasis is shown in our activities and extracurricular clubs and includes camp-outs in the grounds, marshmallow toasting, planting of new woodland areas and gardening.

Pastoral care. The School's academic success is complemented by exemplary pastoral support. By keeping class sizes small, a friendly, family atmosphere is evident, allowing pupils to grow and develop in confidence as they progress through the School.

Admissions. Nursery, Reception, Year 7 and Sixth Form are the most common years of entry to the School, although pupils may be admitted in other years when required, if space is available.

Pupils are invited into school to spend a day with their current year group and carry out the school's entrance assessment.

Learning support programmes are available where a need is identified and likewise stronger pupils can be challenged where needed. Pupils generally take 10 GCSEs before transferring to the Sixth Form at the end of Year 11.

The Sixth Form is structured to provide a stepping stone from the discipline of Senior School to the demands of Higher Education. Sixth Formers take a full part in the life of the School and are encouraged into positions of responsibility including mentoring younger years and leading House and Sporting events. A new Sixth Form Centre building will open in 2024.

Sport and extracurricular activities. Rugby, netball, cricket, rounders, swimming and tennis are just some of the sports played throughout the School. In addition, the School's Cross Country Team enjoys ongoing success when competing against other Schools. The Pitsford Run is a well-known local event.

Junior School students have access to a huge variety of extracurricular activities – from the School Council, Eco Club, Choir, Cooking, Rugby, Netball, Arts and Craft, plus many others.

Senior School pupils have over 60 extracurricular activities to choose from – including Duke of Edinburgh award, Service and Adventure Programme, Astronomy and Engineering Club, Politics Club, Yoga, Musical Theatre, Robotics Club and many more.

Music. Music is an integral element of school life at Pitsford School.

Musical Recitals are held regularly in Pitsford Hall and in addition, the School holds termly evening concerts. Individual music lessons are available and encouraged in a wide range of instruments and group participation and performance opportunities include: woodwind, guitar, percussion, strings, sax and flute ensembles and two choirs.

A number of Junior and Senior performances take place throughout the year, ranging from plays to musicals. The most recent production is The Wizard of Oz.

Charitable status. Northamptonshire Independent Grammar School Charity Trust Limited is a Registered Charity, number 298910.

Governing Body:
Chairman: Mr S Phipps

Mr J Brown	Mr A Moodie
Mrs J Harrop	Mr A Ross
Mrs B Hill	Reverend S Trott
Miss L Mohess	Mr J Weitzel

***Headmaster*: Dr Craig Walker**, MA Glasgow, DPhil Balliol Oxon, Winston Churchill Memorial Trust and Farmington Institute Fellow, FRSA

Deputy Head: Mrs F M Kirk, BA, Med
Head of Junior School: Mr P Edwins, BA Hons

Bursar: Mrs S Sherlock

Assistant Head: Dr J Ewington, BSc, MSc, PhD
Assistant Head: Mr B Harrison
PA to the Headmaster: Mrs J Ross

Portland Place School

Alpha Plus Group

56–58 Portland Place, London W1B 1NJ
Tel: 020 7307 8700
email: admin@portland-place.co.uk
website: www.portland-place.co.uk
X/Twitter: @PortlandPlaceHd
Facebook: @PortlandPlaceSchool
Instagram: @PortlandPlaceSchool

Age Range. 10–16 year olds. Co-educational.

Number of Pupils. 225.

Fees per term (2023–2024). Day School: £8,395. Portland Place Hybrid: from £4,280.

Aims and Philosophy. Portland Place School is a leading independent co-educational day school for children aged 10–16, located in the heart of central London. It was founded in 1996 with a particular purpose in mind: to be an alternative to the intense, large, examination-focused independent day schools in London.

Ethos. The school is small, nurturing and inspirational – enabling students to achieve their very best, with space to develop and express their creativity.

Portland Place School encourages aspiration, resilience and a love of learning within a supportive and inclusive environment. Aiming to ensure each pupil achieves their best personally, socially and academically.

Happiness Gets Results. Portland Place School believe the importance of happiness in education should never be underestimated. It is only when children feel comfortable that they are truly in the right frame of mind to welcome new ideas and actively engage in their learning. Portland Place School adds significant value with usually 1 or 2 grades added to those predicted by externally administered baseline testing.

Curriculum. Portland Place School believe that exceptional teaching, combined with a modern curriculum inside and outside the classroom, provides the best stimulus for children to become inquisitive, open-minded and creative learners and achieve beyond exams.

The school's creative approach to academic study helps the child find their own path to learning. The curriculum at Portland Place is developed from the English National Curriculum and taught in small classes of up to 16 students. Full advantage is taken of its central London location with its excellent local facilities. The school caters for a range of abilities and learning styles, achieving strong results at GCSE.

Class music is a compulsory part of the curriculum in Years 6–9 and free individual tuition is offered to all Year 7 students.

Sport. Portland Place School offers a wide range of sport including athletics, basketball, cricket, cross country, dance, fencing, football, hockey, netball, rounders, swimming, tennis and rugby. Outdoor sports take place in Regent's Park a short walk from the school. Indoor activities include basketball, swimming and fencing. Specialist facilities are used where required. The school offers after-school sports activities and clubs and participates in inter school competitions across London and the UK.

Extracurricular Activities & Enrichment. There is a wide and ever evolving range of extracurricular activities that are offered during lunchtimes and after school. These range from yoga, extreme dance, Arabic, Shakespeare and table tennis. Whole school productions, concerts, choirs and performances take place throughout the year. The Duke of Edinburgh award is facilitated and encouraged for the older years. The students enjoy regular outdoor activities, day trips, charity projects and overseas trips including Lisbon, Paris, Iceland, Barbados, Washington, New York and even Tanzania.

The weekly Enrichment Programme allows the students to participate in activities not tied to examinations and explore and develop new interests. Activities range from horse riding to carpentry; boxing to forest school; LEGO design to musical theatre.

Pastoral. Portland Place has an emphasis on supporting students' mental health and improving their personal resilience. There are school counsellors, plus a coaching programme that is integrated into the curriculum.

Location and Buildings. Portland Place is ideally located in the centre of London, less than five minutes' walk from Regent's Park (where much of the outdoor sporting activities take place) and ten minutes' walk from Oxford Circus. The school is housed in two magnificent Grade II listed James Adam houses in Portland Place with a separate Art, Drama and Science building in Great Portland Street. The buildings are refurbished to an exceptionally high standard with specialist faculty facilities.

Portland Place Hybrid School. Portland Place have extended their ethos into an innovative hybrid learning offer, that runs in parallel to the main school: Portland Place Hybrid School. A cost-effective blended learning approach, combining live online teaching with an optional one-day-a-week on site to access facilities for practical subjects such as science, creative arts and sport; creating a unique educational offering for ages 10–16.

Admission. Entry to the day school is usually in Year 6, 7 or 9 by baseline assessments in English and Mathematics (along with Science for Year 8 onwards) and an interview. Interviews for September entry are held in the autumn term prior to entry and the school's assessments are held in January.

Governance. Portland Place School is part of the Alpha Plus Group of schools.

Senior Leadership Team:

***Headmaster*: Mr David Bradbury**, MSc Keele, MA Open, MInstP, CPhys, FRSA

Deputy Head: Mr Jamie Whiteside, BSc, PGCE, Edinburgh
Assistant Head (*Welfare*): Mr Paul Jones
Assistant Head (*Co-Curriculum*) *and Director of Music*: Mr Steve Hill, MA Ed, BMus Hons, PGCE, Cert GSMD (P), ALCM
Assistant Head (*Student Support*): Ms Patricia Pieri, BSc London, MA
Finance & Operations Manager: Ms Vicki Bromley

The Purcell School

Aldenham Road, Bushey, Hertfordshire WD23 2TS
Tel: 01923 331100
email: info@purcell-school.org
website: www.purcell-school.org
X/Twitter: @PurcellSchool
Facebook: @PurcellSchool
Instagram: @the_purcell_school

The Purcell School is Britain's oldest school for young musicians. Situated on the outskirts of London in Bushey, Hertfordshire, the co-educational boarding and day school is home to around 196 musically talented young people aged 11–18.

The School aims to provide young musicians, of remarkable ability and promise from all backgrounds, with the best possible teaching and environment in which to fulfil their potential. We deliver the very highest world-class musical instruction and hold the UNESCO Mozart Gold Medal in recognition of the School's unique contribution to music, education and international culture.

The school affords ideal opportunities for practising, performing and developing musicianship, while also providing a balanced academic education which helps to prepare our students for life-long careers as musicians. The high quality of teaching and outstanding pastoral support is further complemented by a nurturing environment in which students can form stimulating and mutually supportive friendships with similarly gifted children.

Music Department. The Music Department at The Purcell School aims to provide a stimulating and challenging musical environment, at the heart of which is an individually tailored programme for every student. A flexible timetable, designed to enable students to practise, sustains this. Students in Years 7 to 8 are able to practise up to 3 hours each day, with those in Years 9 and 10 between 3–4 hours, and Sixth Formers in the region of 4–5 hours, depending on academic commitments. Practice supervisors are provided, themselves graduate musicians, and work with students up to Year 11 to ensure practice time is used effectively. The School's expert instrumental teachers also set practice goals and teach practice strategies.

Students have twice-weekly contact with their first study instrumental teacher for up to 2 hours' tuition. All of Purcell's instrumental teachers have considerable experience of working with motivated young musicians and have proven ability in enabling their students to succeed. They are all active performers and practitioners, and many teach at the London conservatoires as well as those further afield. As such, they are distinguished industry professionals, who understand exactly what is necessary to succeed in the music business today.

In addition, the Music Department offers an enriched musical programme that includes chamber music, orchestras, piano classes, choirs and aural and theory training. Frequent performing opportunities range from daily lunchtime concerts at School and in the surrounding area to formal recitals around the UK and in the capital's leading venues. The School's proximity to London provides regular performance opportunities at some of the world's finest venues, an experience unmatched by any other musical school. Students, for example, can audition for the chance to play concertos with the School's orchestras, to give solo and chamber music recitals at Cadogan Hall, Wigmore Hall, Milton Court Concert Hall, Queen Elizabeth Hall and other prestigious venues.

The School also facilitates frequent visits from the world's leading musicians for masterclasses, recitals, courses and collaborative projects to enhance the work of our regular teachers.

The importance of providing an outstanding all-round educational experience is paramount at The Purcell School, so that students can leave with the skills they need to meet the challenges of an ever-changing and complex world. Purcell therefore endeavours to deliver an integrated curriculum in which music, academic, pastoral and social provision are treated equally. The School recognises that intellectual curiosity and social empathy are vital components of being a great musician, and that it is imperative to develop the whole person for a student to be truly happy and healthy.

Academic Studies. The School's curriculum allows students to fulfil their musical potential without limiting their choices. A range of subjects are offered including Mathematics, English, Sciences, Modern Languages and Humanities, which provide an essential complement to performing skills.

The size of the School ensures that classes are generally small, which allows for a great deal of individual attention from experienced and dedicated teachers.

All students are set homework each day and time is allocated in the boarding houses each evening for this to be completed. Students' academic progress is closely monitored and parents receive frequent progress reports.

Boarding. With approximately 76% of students boarding, the School feels like a home from home and boarders lead very full lives. As travel time is reduced there is more time to practise, to ensure academic work is completed to a high standard, to be involved in a breadth of musical and co-curricular activities, and to build life-long friendships. Boarding also prepares students for the independence they will have in further education.

The Purcell School has three boarding houses – Avison, New Boarding House and Sunley – which are run by a dedicated team of warm and caring boarding and pastoral staff, who are responsible for each student's welfare and wellbeing. Great care is taken to ensure a student's stay is safe, productive and most of all as enjoyable as possible.

All boarders eat together in the main dining hall, however there are also common rooms and small kitchens in each corridor of the boarding houses. Weekend activities, evening events and social gatherings are regularly organised, and students are able to travel into London to attend the junior departments of the capital's music colleges and conservatoires or enjoy concerts and events.

Boarders have access to school facilities, such as practice rooms and computers, at evenings and weekends.

In each half of the term there is normally an exeat weekend when all students go home or to their guardian or to friends. There is also a half-term period in each of the three terms.

Admission. Entrance is by musical audition and interview – please see the School website for further details. The Registrar, Natasha Vallance, can answer queries.

Fees per term (2023–2024). Day £10,366; Boarding £13,236.

Bursary funding is available, for those students who meet the eligibility criteria, under the Department for Education Music and Dance Scheme, and there is the possibility of means-tested financial support from the School for those who do not. Parents are welcome to consult the Bursar for guidance.

Charitable status. The Purcell School is a Registered Charity, number 312855. It aims to offer specialist musical training, combined with an excellent general academic education, to children of exceptional musical ability.

Patrons:
Sir Simon Rattle, CBE, OM (*President*)
Vladimir Ashkenazy, CBE
Sir Andrew Davis, CBE
Donatella Flick
Dame Kiri Te Kanawa, DBE
Evgeny Kissin
Julian Lloyd Webber, OBE

Artists in Association:
Robert Saxton

Governing Body:
Dr Bernard Trafford, MA Oxon, MEd, PhD Birmingham (*Chairman*)
William McDonnell, BA Oxon (*Chairman of Finance and General Purposes Committee*)
Kirsty Von Malaisé, MA Cantab (*Chair of Music of Education Committee*)
Sophia Coles, BA, LLM
Gautam Dalal, FCA, FRSA
Jeffrey Hewitt, MA Oxon, MBA Stanford
Richard Hill, MA Cantab
Timothy Jones, MA, DPHIL, Hon RAM
Dr Diana Salazar, FHEA, PGCE Kul, PHD Manc, BA, PGDipMus, MMus RSA

Senior Leadership Team:

***Principal*: Paul Bambrough**

Vice-Principal: Thomas Burns
Director of Music: Paul Hoskins
Bursar: Adam Wroblewski
Director of Boarding: Kate Caley
Director of Boarding: Jane Mitchell
Director of Operations: Emma Bantock
Director of Teaching and Learning: Michael Long
Head of Sixth Form & DSL: Ziggy Szafranski

Music Department:

Strings:
Charles Sewart (*Head of Strings*, *Violin/Viola*)
Richard Jenkinson (*Assistant Head of Strings*)
Pál Banda (*Cello*)
Aiste Dvarionaite Berzanskiene (*Violin*)
Anna-Liisa Bezrodny (*Violin*)
Sascha Boyarsky (*Cello*)
Sarah-Jane Bradley (*Viola*)
Ben J Davies (*Cello*)
Alda Dizdari (*Violin*)
Cathy Elliott (*Double Bass*)
Tanja Goldberg (*Violin*)
Sadagat Mamedova-Rashidova (*Violin*)
Francesco Mariani (*Guitar*)
Julian-David Metzger (*Cello*)
Joo Yeon Sir (*Violin*)
Nathaniel Vallois (*Violin*)
Jacky Woods (*Viola*)

Keyboard:
William Fong (*Head of Keyboard*, *Piano*)
Lidia Amorelli (*Piano*)
Ben de Souza (*Accordion*)
David Gordon (*Harpsichord & Improvisation*)
Caterina Grewe (*Piano*)
Morte Grigaliunaite (*Piano*)
Gareth Hunt (*Piano*)
Ilya Kondratiev (*Piano*)
Jianing Kong (*Piano*)
Alla Kravchenko (*Piano*)
Ching-Ching Lim (*Piano*)
Florian Mitrea (*Piano*)
Tessa Nicholson (*Piano*)
Vitaly Pisarenko (*Piano*)
Danielle Salamon (*Piano*)
Tatiana Sarkissova (*Piano*)
Deborah Shah (*Piano/Accompanist*)
Daniel Swain (*Accompanist*)
Patsy Toh (*Piano*)
Nafis Umerkulova (*Piano*)

Percussion, *Brass*, *Harp & Voice*:
Ryan Hepburn (*Head of Percussion*, *Brass*, *Harp & Voice*, *Percussion*)
Daphne Boden (*Harp*)
Tony Cross (*Trumpet*)
Timothy Ellis (*French Horn*)
Daniella Ganeva (*Percussion*)
Tom Marandola (*Voice*)
Ruth Molins (*Trombone*)
Mike Poyser (*Tuba*)
Charlotte Seale (*Harp*)
Karen Vaughan (*Harp*)
Jill Washington (*Voice*)

Woodwind:
Joy Farrall (*Head of Woodwind*, *Clarinet*)
Joanna Bailie Stark (*Bassoon*)
Izzie Couch (*Clarinet*)
Amy Green (*Saxophone*)
Graham Hobbs (*Bassoon*)
Sarah Humphrys (*Recorder*)
Clare Jefferis (*Flute*)
Andrew Marriner (*Clarinet*, *Associate Artist*)
Melanie Ragge (*Oboe*)
Mark Taylor (*Flute*)
James Turnbull (*Oboe*)
Stephen Williams (*Clarinet*)

Jazz:
Simon Allen (*Head of Jazz*, *Jazz Saxophone*)
Sebastiaan de Krom (*Jazz Drums*)
Sam Dunn (*Jazz Guitar*)
David Gordon (*Jazz Piano*)

Oli Hayhurst (*Jazz Bass*)
Jacqueline Hicks (*Jazz Voice*)
John Turvills (*Jazz Piano*)

Commercial and Popular Music:
Simon Allen (*Head of Commercial and Popular Music*)
Pete Billington (*Songwriting*)
James Clark (*Guitar*)
Chris Draper (*Drums*)
Daniel Drury (*Electric Bass Guitar*)
Jacqui Hicks (*Vocals*)

Composition:
Alison Cox (*Head of Composition*)
Jacques Cohen (*Composition*)
Daniel Fardon (*Composition*)
Silvia Lim (*Composition*)
Gareth Moorcraft (*Composition*)
Michael Small (*Junior Composer in Association*)
Simon Speare (*Composition*)

Audio Production Department:
Aidan Goetzee (*Head of Audio Production*)

Academic Music Staff:
Andrew Williams (*Interim Head of Academic Music*)
Alison Cox (*Composition*)
Daniel Fardon
Ryan Hepburn
Edward Longstaff
Alberto Martin Entrialgo
Irina Walters

Academic Staff:
Michael Long (*Director of Teaching and Learning, Head of English*)
Adriana Blond (*English*)
John Brookes (*Head of PE*)
Margaret Brookes (*Chemistry, Head of Science*)
Aidan Goetzee (*Head of Music Technology*)
Victoria Hill (*Head of History*)
Anisha Kochhar (*Maths*)
Kinga Kozak (*EAL*)
Heloise Gille (*French*)
Robert Matthews (*Head of EAL, German*)
Nicky Morris (*Counsellor, Arts Therapist*)
Craig Nunes (*Drama, English*)
Ashvin Patel (*Science, Chemistry*)
Zara Pradhan (*English*)
Victoria Samuel (*Head of Art*)
Jyoti Shah (*Mathematics*)
Alexandra Stone (*Head of Mathematics*)
Martina Swift (*EAL*)
Jim Titmuss (*Science, Physics*)
Ziggi Szafranski (*Drama*)
Sally-Ann Whitty (*Head of Learning Support*)

Boarding Houses:
Bethan Baker (*Resident Graduate Assistant, Sunley*)
Olena Bilash (*Resident Boarding Assistant, Avison*)
Emily Black (*Resident Graduate Assistant, NBH*)
Adriana Blond (*Assistant Houseparent, Sunley*)
John Brookes (*Avison Assistant Houseparent*)
Margaret Brookes (*Avison Houseparent*)
Tiffany Buxton (*Resident Graduate Assistant, Sunley*)
Kate Caley (*Director of Boarding*)
Ross Conquer (*Resident Graduate Assistant, NBH*)
Annette Cook (*Avison Assistant Houseparent*)
Samuel Cubarsi-Fernandez (*Assistant Houseparent, NBH*)
Susie Hunter (*Sunley House Day Matron*)
Katharine Mendes da Costa (*NBH Day Matron*)
Jane Mitchell (*Director of Boarding*)
Carol Morgan (*Residential Medical Practioner*)
Dominika Mrozek (*Assistant Houseparent, NBH*)
Isabelle Norwood (*Resident Graduate Assistant, NBH*)
Sofia Pan (*Resident Graduate Assistant, NBH*)
Deborah Prescott (*Houseparent, NBH*)
Rachel Price (*Sunley Houseparent*)

Admin & Non-Teaching Staff:
Hilary Austin (*School Nurse*)
Emma Bantock (*Director of Operations*)
Fletcher Barrett (*Music Technology Assistant*)
Tony Bond (*Estates Officer*)
Charlotte Buck (*Development Officer*)
Ryan Bunce (*Librarian*)
Robin Collingwood (*Specialist Art and Teaching Assistant*)
Susannah Curran (*PR & Communications Manager*)
Fiona Duce (*Music Timetabler*)
Caroline Fletcher (*Overseas Student Co-ordinator*)
Sarah Graham (*Executive Assistant to Principal*)
Linda Griffiths (*School Office Administrator*)
Chris Harbour (*Head of Development and Philanthropy*)
Simon Kingsbury (*IT Network Manager*)
Charlotte Lee (*Concerts Assistant*)
Fei Liu (*International Partnerships & Recruitment Representative (China)*)
Marie Lynch (*School Office Administrator*)
Jane McGuinness (*Data and Payroll Specialist*)
Andy Milner (*Estates Supervisor*)
Carol Morgan (*Residential Medial Practioner*)
Caroline Murphy (*Exams Officer*)
Hawreen Osman (*Science Technician*)
Susan Pickard (*Assistant Bursar*)
Sharanha Senguttuvan (*School Office Administrator*)
Elisabeth Stemson (*School Office Administrator*)
Helena Thomas (*Art Technician*)
Sarah Upjohn (*Physiotherapist*)
Nicole Holmes (*Senior Housekeeper*)
Natasha Vallance (*Executive Administrator*)
Tony Whitman (*Estates Assistant*)

The Read School

Drax

Drax, Selby, North Yorkshire YO8 8NL

Tel: 01757 618248
email: enquiries@readschool.co.uk
website: www.readschool.co.uk
X/Twitter: @Read_School
Facebook: @readschool
Instagram: @read_school1667

Age range. Co-educational 4–18, Boarding 8–18.

Number in School. Total 248: Day 228, Boarding 20; Boys 138, Girls 110.

The school is pleasantly situated in the rural village of Drax and is very convenient for main rail (Doncaster, York, Leeds) and road access (M62, M18, A1).

Manchester is the nearest international airport (1½ hours distant). It is a relatively small school where children are well known to each other and to the staff.

The school has been a focal point for education in the Selby-Goole area since the 17th century and is proud to be one of the oldest educational establishments in the UK. The school has been co-educational since 1992 and offers a wide range of academic studies at GCSE and A Level. Within school, our small class sizes, inspirational teaching and wide array of extracurricular activities, including an excellent sports programme, Combined Cadet Force, Duke of Edinburgh programme and Leith's Food Academy sections, provide an outstanding education. There is one class in each Junior School year from Reception to Year 6. There are three classes in each of the Senior years (8–11); 2 classes in Year 7. There is a small Sixth Form (24 pupils) following BTEC and A Level courses. High standards are expected in all aspects of endeavour, and in behaviour and manners.

Although we are a small school our pupils enjoy a full and vibrant sports curriculum. Alongside hockey, netball, rounders (girls); rugby, football and cricket (boys) we also offer additional sports and activities such as tennis, badminton, table tennis, cross country, athletics and trampolining.

Fees per term (2023–2024). Boarders: £7,732–£11,788; Day: £3,230–£5,096.

Admission. An offer of a place in the school is made after interview (and verbal reasoning and mathematics tests for admission to the Senior School) and satisfactory report from the pupil's current school.

Charitable status. The Read School is a Registered Charity, number 529675. It exists to provide a proper education for boys and girls aged 4–18.

Chairman of Governors: Brian Watt

***Head*: Mrs R A Ainley**, MA Oxon (*Modern Languages*)

Bursar: vacant

Deputy Head: M A Voisey, BA (*English*)

Teaching Staff:
Mrs P Anderson, BEd (*English*)
Dr P Armstrong, BSc (*Economics*)
Mrs S Ashworth-Lilley, BSc (*Psychology*)
Mrs S Black, BA (*Drama*, *English*)
Miss J Bullock, BSc, MSc (*Head of Science*, *English Additional Language*)
Mrs V Burnell, BA (*Lower Junior School*)
Mr J Calderwood, BSc, (*Mathematics*)
Ms S L Campbell, BSc (*Junior School*)
Mrs S Chambonnet, BA (*French*)
Mrs E Cressey, BA (*DT*)
Mrs H Crompton, BMus (*Head of Music*)
Dr P Duggan, BSc, PhD (*Biology*, *Chemistry*)
Mrs L Fairhurst, BA (*EYFS Teacher*)
Mrs J Fildes, BA (*Mathematics*)
Miss L Fletcher, BSc (*Mathematics*)
Mr S Franks, PGCE (*Computer Science*, *Geography*)
Ms H Hewson, BA (*English*)
Miss J Hutchinson, PGE (*History*)
Mr G Hill, BA (*Head of Junior School*)
Mrs K Ives, BA (*Spanish*)
Mr L Johnson, BSc (*PE & Games*)
Mrs P Kavanagh, BA (*Business Studies*)
Miss M Keenoy, BA (*Head of Inclusive Learning*)
Mrs L Li, MEd (*Mandarin*)
Mr J Matthews, BSc (*Head of PE*)
Miss F M Newman, BA (*Junior School*, *KS3 Art*, *Dance*)
Mrs A Oliver (*Latin*, *Classic Civilisation*)
Mr M Perkins, BA (*History*, *Religious Studies*)
Mrs S Prosser, BA (*PE and Games*)
Miss S Rothwell, BEd (*Head of Creative Arts*, *Design Technology*, *Food*)
Mrs S Scholefield, BSc (*Head of Humanities*)
Mr C Sharples, BSc (*ICT*, *Computer Science*)
Mrs E Stark, BSc (*Chemistry*)
Mr R Stark, BSc (*Physics*)
Mrs N Suttill, BA (*Art*)
Mrs R M Wake, BA (*Junior School*)
Mrs S A Warren, BA (*Head of Girls' Sport*)
Mr A Woods, PGCE (*Chemistry*, *Science*)

Reading Blue Coat School

Holme Park
Sonning Lane, Sonning-on-Thames, Berkshire RG4 6SU

Tel: 0118 944 1005
email: reception@rbcs.org.uk
website: www.rbcs.org.uk
X/Twitter: @ReadingBlues
Facebook: @ReadingBlueCoat
Instagram: @readingbluecoatschool

See full entry in the **HMC** section, on **p. 271**.

Rendcomb College

Rendcomb, Cirencester, Gloucestershire GL7 7HA

Tel: 01285 831213
email: admissions@rendcombcollege.org.uk
website: www.rendcombcollege.org.uk
X/Twitter: @RendcombCollege
Facebook: @Rendcombcollege
Instagram: @rendcombcollege
LinkedIn: /rendcomb-college

See full entry in the **HMC** section, on **p. 273**.

Rishworth School

Oldham Road, Rishworth, Sowerby Bridge, Halifax, West Yorkshire HX6 4QA

Tel: 01422 822217 (Main School)
email: admissions@rishworth-school.co.uk
website: www.rishworth-school.co.uk
X/Twitter: @Rishworth1724
Facebook: @RishworthSchool
Instagram: @rishworthschool
LinkedIn: /rishworth-school-trading-limited

Rishworth is an exceptionally friendly, caring community, in which pupils are as strongly encouraged to rejoice in each other's achievements as to take pride in their own. The School succeeds in combining a disciplined environment with a relaxed and welcoming atmosphere.

Rishworth's magnificent buildings, extensive grounds and superb Pennine location, which chart a 300-year heritage, provide all members of this friendly community with a physical environment which is conducive both to the clarity of mind required for academic study and to pursuits which provide for a full and balanced development of personal character.

At Rishworth, students develop:

- a lifelong love of learning, curiosity and discovery;
- a sense of responsibility, purpose and ambition;
- a capacity for both self-reliance and cooperation; and
- an appreciation of personal virtues and spiritual values, such as honesty, dependability, perseverance, commitment, humility and respect for others.

General organisation. Founded in 1724, Rishworth is a co-educational day and boarding school comprising a nursery for children from age 3, a Preparatory School, Heathfield, which has its own separate site where children are taught up to the age of 11, and the Senior School up to age 18. Rishworth is a Church of England foundation, but welcomes children of all faiths, or of none. Numbers stand at over 400 pupils.

Facilities and location. Superbly located in 140 acres of a beautiful Pennine valley, the School has a mix of elegant older buildings and excellent modern facilities including: a capacious sports hall with fitness suite, a separate sports club with 25-metre indoor swimming pool and squash courts, a large expanse of games pitches, a music block, 3 modern ICT suites, wireless (and cabled) internet and intranet connection across the whole site, a Performing Arts Theatre, a centre dedicated to sixth-form study, cosy and friendly boarding houses and science laboratories.

Access to the School by road is easy, with the M62 within five minutes' drive. School buses run to the Halifax, Todmorden, Rochdale, Oldham and Huddersfield areas.

Welfare and pastoral. The unusually high degree of attention afforded to pupils by small teaching groups, the careful monitoring of progress, coordinated pastoral support and a close working partnership with parents enables pupils to build on their strengths and allows specific needs to be addressed. Each boarding pupil is under the direct care of a Houseparent, who is ably supported by assistant staff in each boarding house.

Teaching. Taught by a dedicated staff of qualified specialists, the curriculum, both academic and non-academic, is broad and stimulating, and offers every pupil the chance to be challenged and to excel. A general curriculum, broadly in line with the National Curriculum, is followed until Year 9, after which pupils select GCSE options in consultation with their parents, tutors and subject teachers. A Level, Diploma and BTEC options are also selected via consultation.

Support is given by qualified specialists for certain special needs including dyslexia and English where this is not the pupil's first language.

Academic. In 2023, Nearly 85% of GCSEs were achieved at grades 4–9, well in excess of both national and regional levels. Noteworthy results were recorded in Mathematics and English, in which Rishworth students achieved over 20% above national average. Similarly, the traditional strength in STEM subjects was exemplified in grades which were also more than 20% above the national average.

Results in Humanities subjects have been exceptional this year, seeing Rishworth students continue to perform well in Art, Design Technology, French, Food and Nutrition and the Performing Arts, with students attaining 100% achievement in the highest possible grading bands in these subjects. In the Higher Project Qualification (HPQ), 100% of grades awarded were A*–B.

A Level grades of A*–C were well above national average, securing students places at university to study subjects ranging from Economics and Psychology to Medicine and Accounting and Business Management at Russell Group Universities including York, Manchester, and Leeds.

The proportion of top grades awarded between A* and B was almost 15% above national average, which demonstrates a consistent trend over the past four years.

Our students' success this year ensured the school maintained its traditional strengths in STEM subjects. Students obtained 100% A*–B success in: Maths, Further Maths, Physics and Computer Science, while performing equally well at A*–B in Art and Design, and International Languages including: Spanish, Italian, and Chinese.

Those studying BTEC and Vocational qualifications including Sport and Food Science and Nutrition, celebrated 100% achievement, with 96% of grades being within the higher grading boundaries of Distinction* to Merit.

Further success was celebrated by students who achieved their Extended Project Qualification (EPQ), with 100% of grades awarded at A*–B.

Enrichment and extension. In order to help our pupils to become the confident, balanced and considerate young men and women we wish them to be, we encourage participation in a wide range of activities because at Rishworth we understand that learning doesn't just take place in the classroom.

Sports are well appointed and well taught, and each term boys and girls enjoy excellent results. The School also has a justly high reputation in music and drama.

Additionally we have nearly 90 enrichment and extension activities! From Duke of Edinburgh through to our Medical Society, from skiing through to podcasting. There really is something for everyone.

Boarding. We have no dormitories. Boarders (from age 9) are accommodated in individual study-bedrooms, almost all single occupancy which allow pupils their personal space. These are located in spacious houses, overseen by house staff. The boarding houses are cosy and family-centric, the secure havens needed by young people away from home. The character of the historic buildings has been retained, alongside the provision of top-rate modern amenities. A full programme of activities is arranged for the evenings and weekends, and there are good recreational facilities reserved for the boarders, including dedicated social areas.

Admission. Places in the Junior School, Heathfield, are given, subject to availability, on individual assessments appropriate to each applicant's age and previous education. Entrants for Rishworth at Year 7 are asked to sit the School's entrance assessment, which also forms the basis for the award of scholarships.

Those who wish to join the School at other stages are assessed individually.

Fees per term (2023–2024). Reception to Year 2: £2,700; Years 3 to 6: £3,800; Years 7 & 8: £4,600 day, £10,600 full boarding, £9,600 weekly boarding; Years 9 to 13: £5,000 day, £11,400 full boarding, £10,350 weekly boarding. The School operates a number of schemes, including monthly payments, to ease the financial burden on parents. Fees are subject to change; please refer to the website.

Scholarships and bursaries. Scholarships & bursaries are available, the former on merit, the latter for demonstrable financial need. The extent to which these awards can be offered will also be determined by other factors, such as the School's own circumstances and the nature of a given cohort of applicants.

Scholarships may be awarded, up to a value of 30% of Tuition fees, for excellence in academic work, sport, music or drama.

For Year 7 entry scholarships, applicants are formally assessed. For Year 12 entry, awards are made on the basis of an individual's past record (including examination results).

Most awards are made to applicants on entry to Year 7, 9, or 12.

Substantial discounts are available for siblings of pupils in the School, for children of serving members of the Armed Forces and of ordained members of the Church of England. Bursaries may also be available in cases of financial need.

The Old Rishworthian Club maintains a fund for the grant of scholarships to children of ORs.

For more information contact the Bursar.

Charitable status. Rishworth School is a Registered Charity, number 1115562. It exists to provide education for boys and girls.

The Governing Body:
Revd Canon H Barber (*Chairman*)
Mrs F Ellam (*Vice Chair*)
Mrs M Garbett (*Vice Chair*)
Mr C Bell
Mrs E Davies
Mr B Moore, Esq
Dr R Viney
T M Wheelwright, Esq

Senior Leadership Team:

***Head*: Dr A M Wilkins**, BA, MA Lit, MA Hist, PhD

Acting Head: Ms J Sheldrick, BSc (*DSL*)

Bursar and Clerk to the Board of Governors: Mrs C Walsh

Director of Marketing and Admissions: Mr Richard Danks, BA

Head of Heathfield Prep: Mr D Baker, BEd

Key Business Support Staff:
Head of Admissions: Mrs R Miller, BA, MA
Matron: Mrs D K Robinson
Librarian: Mrs B Day

Ruthin School

Mold Road, Ruthin, Denbighshire LL15 1EE

Tel: 01824 702543
email: registrar@ruthinschool.co.uk
website: www.ruthinschool.co.uk
X/Twitter: @ruthinschool
Facebook: @RuthinSchool

Motto: *Dei gratia sum quod sum*

Ruthin School was originally founded in 1284. Refounded in 1574 by Gabriel Goodman, Dean of Westminster, and granted a Royal Charter, the School is a centre of academic excellence in North Wales.

The School is co-educational with around 250 students, comprising approximately half boarders and half day students. Ruthin School is an international community committed to high academic standards, dedication and mutual respect. Safeguarding and wellbeing are at the core of the School's ethos and informs all decision-making. The School is run on the principle of collegiality and provides a safe, modern and friendly environment in which students can fulfil their potential. Students are expected to behave in a way that promotes decency, harmony and trust. They should strive to achieve their best at all times and our staff support them in this goal.

Organisation. Places (both day and full boarding) are offered to students from the age of 11.

The four boarding houses – Goodman, Trevor, Wynne and Gladstone – have their own House system under the guidance of resident Houseparent, Boarding Assistant, Housekeeper and Graduate Assistant.

Admission. The normal method of entry to the School is by interview, examination and reports.

Activities. Our Electives programme is wide ranging. Our Electives include many sports such as football, netball, badminton, basketball and volleyball. However we also have a large timetable of popular electives centred around wellbeing including cooking classes, chess, lego robotics, choir, debating, and arts and crafts. Students are encouraged to participate in the Duke of Edinburgh's Award scheme at the age of 14 until they have completed the Bronze Award; several go on to complete the Silver and Gold Awards. Many students receive individual instrumental tuition from professional music staff. A programme of weekly trips is organised for boarders in the evenings and at weekends. The trips allow students to experience the best the area has to offer with arts and culture experiences in our closest cities of Liverpool and Manchester and outdoor pursuits activities on the north Wales coast and in Snowdonia National Park.

Bursaries and awards. In addition to academic awards, remissions are available for siblings, children of members of the armed forces and of Old Ruthinians. All awards are means tested and reviewed annually.

Curriculum. A wide curriculum is offered and includes English, Mathematics, History, Geography, Latin, separate Biology, Physics and Chemistry, Psychology, Business Studies, Art, Music, Computer Science, French, and Spanish. Astronomy and Economics are added at GCSE level. Further Mathematics and Politics are taught in the Sixth Form.

Pastoral. All Students have a pastoral tutor who in the Upper Sixth support university applications. Careers guidance is also offered to all Sixth Form Students from a dedicated UCAS coordinator.

Fees per annum (2023–2024). Day: £13,650–£16,540; Boarding: £42,700. Fees are payable twice yearly, at beginning of August and February. British parents have the option to pay monthly by Direct Debit.

Transport. The School provides daily transport to and from the North Wales coast, the Chester area and the Wrexham area. Transport is provided for boarders from Manchester airport to the School, at the beginning and end of each term.

The Old Ruthinian Association fosters close links between past and present students of the School.

Board of Management
N Grenfell-Marten, FCMI

***Head*: V Gamble**, BSc, PGCE
Bursar: S Harris

Deputy Head, Miss S Frencham, BSc, PGCE

Director of Safeguarding: R Searle, BA Hons, PGCE AdvDip Oxon
Director of Studies: D Kynes, BSc Chemistry, MSc, PGCE
Director of Electives: M Orchard, BSc, PGCE

Teaching Staff:
J S Bartlett, BSc, PGCE
Mrs S M Bellis-Whitworth, BA, MA, PGCE
N J R Blandford, BA, MA, PGCE
Mrs J Brass
Mrs E T Brodzinska, LLB, MA, DELTA
Mrs E M Brown, BA, MA Ed, PGCE, TEFL, AMBDA
Mrs Y Brown, BSc, PGCE, MSc
B Cribb, BA, PGCE, MEd
Mrs R Crowther, BA, PGCE
F Dewar, BSc Sports Coaching, PGCE
Dr D G Edwards, BA Hons, DPhil
I G Evans, BA, PGCE
Mrs S J Eve, BSc, PGCE
Dr N Fairbank, BSc, MA, PhD
Dr M Galvin, BSc Hons, PhD, PGCE
Dr G H Green, BSc, MA, PhD
J P Hamer, BA, PGCE
Dr M D Hannant, PhD, PGCE
Mrs I Haywood, BSc, MBA, PGCE
J R Henry, BA, PGCE
M H L Hewer, MA Oxon, DipEd
Dr A W Hughes, BEng, PhD, PGCE
Mrs K Hughes, BA, PGCE
Mrs M Kenworthy, BSc, PGCE
M Lamprecht
Mrs J Morton, MA Hons, PGCE
D A Owen Booth, MGCI, BEd, DipHE
S Parry, BA Hons, PGCE
C Perry, BSc, PGCE
Mrs C Peters, BSc, PGCE
Dr J Roberts, BSc, MSc, PhD
S D Stark, BSc, MEng, PGCE
R A Wadon, BSc, PGCE
Miss H Webb, BSc, PGCE
B Welsby
Miss D A Williams, BSc, PGCE
Dr M Wilton, BSc, PhD, PGCE

Registrar and PA to the Head and Bursar: Mrs S E Williams
Deputy Bursar: Mrs J Rainford
School Nurse: Mrs T Beaver, RGN, RSCN
School Nurse: Miss Ffion Jackson, RGN
School Nurse: Mrs J Wordsworth, RGN
School Counsellor: Ms K Comrie

St Augustine's Priory School

Hillcrest Road, Ealing, London W5 2JL

Tel: 020 8997 2022
email: admissions@sapriory.com
website: www.sapriory.com
X/Twitter: @staugustinesp
Facebook: @StAugustine's_Priory
Instagram: @st.augustines.priory
LinkedIn: /st-augustine-s-priory

See full entry in the **GSA** section, on **p. 473**.

St Columba's College

King Harry Lane, St Albans, Hertfordshire AL3 4AW

Tel: 01727 855185
email: admissions@stcolumbascollege.org
website: www.stcolumbascollege.org
X/Twitter: @StColumbasHerts
Facebook: @StColumbasCollege
Instagram: @stcolumbascollege
LinkedIn: /school/stcolumbascollege

See full entry in the **HMC** section, on **p. 304**.

St Edward's Senior & Sixth Form

Cirencester Road, Charlton Kings, Cheltenham, Gloucestershire GL53 8EY

Tel: 01242 388555
email: reception@stedwards.co.uk
website: www.stedwards.co.uk
X/Twitter: @StEdwardsChelt
Facebook: @StEdwardsSchoolCheltenham
Instagram: @stedwardscheltenham

Motto: *Quantum Potes Aude*

A wealth of opportunity exists for students at St Edward's Senior & Sixth Form. We teach that there is no ceiling to potential, focussing on the individual needs of each and every pupil, and valuing their unique gifts and talents.

Located in the heart of Cheltenham, with a range of creative and sporting facilities to enrich our academic provision, the School offers a strong and vibrant school community, based on Christian values, in which all children can thrive.

We have high expectations of all members of our school community. Excellent teaching and pastoral care in our nurturing and encouraging environment allows our pupils to flourish. Our small class sizes mean that our teachers really know pupils as individuals and can provide tailored support to maximise achievement. A broad range of subjects is offered at GCSE, together with 24 subjects at A Level. Our School motto means to strive for the best and that is exactly what we want for all our students.

We encourage our pupils to become fully involved in all aspects of school life, offering an extensive range of extra-curricular clubs, sporting and cultural activities. It is important to us that our pupils are challenged to step outside of their 'comfort zone' and realise that they can achieve beyond their perceived potential.

Most importantly, our aim is to provide an education that will last a lifetime and enable our pupils to develop into happy, confident, resilient, compassionate and aspirational individuals who are ready to become positive and life-long contributors to society.

Admission. The main entry to the Senior School is at Year 7 and at Sixth Form. However, pupils are welcome to join at any point, providing there are spaces in the year group. Entry into all year groups is subject to successful completion of an Entrance Examination.

Fees per term (2023–2024): £5,595–£6,620.

Scholarships are available for entry to Year 7 and Sixth Form in the following areas: academic, art, music, drama and sport.

Further information is available on the School's website, www.stedwards.co.uk. To request a prospectus or arrange an appointment to visit the School, please contact our Admissions Manager at senioradmissions @stedwards.co.uk or on 01242 388555.

Charitable status. St Edward's is a Registered Charity, number 293360.

Chair of Trustees: Dr Susan Honeywill

***Principal*: Mr M Burke**, BA Hons, PGCE, Ad Dip Ed, NPQH

St Gabriel's

Sandleford Priory, Newbury, Berkshire RG20 9BD

Tel: 01635 555680
email: admissions@stgabriels.co.uk
website: www.stgabriels.co.uk
X/Twitter: @StGabrielsNews
Facebook: @stgabrielsnewbury
Instagram: @stgabrielsnews
LinkedIn: /company/st-gabriel's-newbury

Independent Day School, in membership of Society of Heads, GSA and IAPS.

Number of Pupils. 495 through Nursery, Junior, Senior and Sixth Form.

St Gabriel's is a co-educational day school, where pupils excel and reach their true potential through a balanced and inspiring education, which combines academic rigour, breadth of opportunity and a strong sense of community. As a school, our responsibility is to provide each pupil with the right combination of opportunities and challenges to create a pathway for academic success while at the same time unlocking and developing the talents of each individual pupil to give them the confidence and self-belief to pursue their ambitions.

In September 2022, we welcomed boys into Year 7 of the Senior School. The Sixth Form, alongside Year 9, will accept boys from September 2024. This incremental approach will ensure a measured and smooth transition to a fully co-educational school from Nursery to Sixth Form in 2026.

Curriculum. The curriculum is regularly reviewed to ensure that it is broad and well-balanced, providing an education that is relevant for the 21st Century. Inspirational teaching delivered by highly qualified and dedicated staff encourages pupils to question, to think critically, to work collaboratively, to persevere and to celebrate each other's achievements, while equipping them with the skills and experiences required to succeed in their careers beyond St Gabriel's.

A choice of 26 subjects is offered at GCSE of which English Language, English Literature, Mathematics, all three Sciences, and a Modern Foreign Language are compulsory.

At Sixth Form, students choose three subjects to study to A Level from the 26 offered. All students also undertake the Extended Project Qualification (EPQ), which is equivalent to half an A Level, and is designed to develop key skills such as researching, project management, academic writing, and referencing in preparation for university study.

Results. Examinations are seen as a pathway to achieving personal goals and our academic team encourage, motivate, and support all our pupils to pursue their aspirations. St Gabriel's is justifiably proud of its students' achievements and it is not surprising that they go on to study a wide and diverse range of courses at their chosen universities.

Inspection. The latest Independent Schools Inspection took place in November 2019. St Gabriel's was rated Excellent & Outstanding. They reported: "At all stages in the school, pupils make excellent progress in terms of their attainment".

Extra and Co-Curricular Activities. The school provides a wide range of opportunities outside of the classroom and by encouraging pupils to express themselves in different ways creates a happy and rewarding educational environment. Numerous activities and visits extend and enrich pupils' learning experience and pupils are positively encouraged to try new things. The performing and creative arts, sport and a wide range of clubs and societies ensure that pupils progress to the next stage of their education with confidence. Whether it is through The Duke of Edinburgh's Award, Debating Society, on the pitch or performing in front of an audience, our pupils constantly rise to meet new challenges.

Music. A variety of choirs, orchestras and instrumental groups ensure able musicians have the opportunity to perform at the highest levels. Most orchestral instruments can be learned with bespoke guidance from our peripatetic music staff, and music theory tuition is given to pupils who show a considerable aptitude for composition.

Sport. Football, Netball, Basketball, Hockey, Swimming, Rounders, Athletics, Cricket, Cross-Country, Dance, Gymnastics, Rugby, Badminton and Tennis. The school also has an equestrian team.

Facilities. Specialist IT suites, state-of-the-art science laboratories and MFL rooms, multi-disciplinary sports hall, theatre and dance studio.

Our Ethos. Children join St Gabriel's with many different interests, strengths and aspirations. Our responsibility is to create a pathway to academic success and to acquiring the personal skills to pursue their ambitions.

Push too hard and we fall over; the same is true in education. Our pupils succeed academically because we give them the space and time to mature, to be confident, fulfilled and happy in their studies and co-curricular life. The pastoral care offered individually, in tutor groups and across the school community is exemplary and essential to the wellbeing of our pupils, enabling them to manage the pressures of the world in which we live.

We are proud to be a school that allows the strength of personal relationships to form and develop. It is our size that makes us what we are; a school for the individual, a school where your child will be noticed for all the right reasons, a school where we can enjoy community. It is from this position that we work in partnership to ensure that your child becomes the success they deserve to be.

St Gabriel's: a school founded on community, inspiration, understanding and balance.

Supervised Prep. This is provided on a daily basis between 4.00pm and 6.30pm.

Scholarships & Bursaries. Academic, Sport, Art, Dance, Drama and Music scholarships are awarded at 11+ and 13+. Sixth Form scholarships are also awarded at 16+. Bursaries covering up to 100% of fees are available through the Montagu Award scheme, which aims to ensure that St Gabriel's is accessible to pupils who would otherwise not be able to enjoy the unique education the school offers.

Admission. Entry to the Junior School for children aged 6–10 years is by assessment. Entrance examinations is held in November for entry at 11+ and 13+. Students are accepted in to the Sixth Form on the basis of their GCSE results and an interview.

Fees per term (2023–2024). £6,778–£7,026.

Junior School. (*See entry in IAPS section*).

Charitable status. The St Gabriel Schools Foundation is a Registered Charity, number 1062748. It seeks to promote and provide for the advancement of education of the pupils at the school.

Governing Body:
Chairman: Mr N Garland, BSc Hons
Mr S Barrett
Mrs S Bowen
Mrs J Heywood
Mrs S Hutton
Mr D Peaple
Mr N Rankin
Mr S Ryan
Mr M Scholl
Mrs J Whitehead

***Principal*: Mr R Smith**, MEd, MA, PGCE

Vice-Principal: Mrs A Chapman, BA Hons, PGCE, QTS
Bursar & Clerk to Governors: Mrs P Setter, BA Hons
Deputy Head (*Academic*): Mrs Anna Chicken, MA, BA Hons, PGCE
Deputy Head (*Pastoral*): Mrs Emma Hammons, LLB, PGCE
Head of Sixth Form: Mrs H Trevis, BSocSc Hons, PGCE
Head of Upper School (*Years 9, 10 & 11*): Mrs J Shillaw, BA Hons, PGCE
Head of Lower School (*Years 7 & 8*): Mrs R Wright, BSc Hons, PGCE
Head of Junior School: Mr P Dove, BA Hons, PGCE
Deputy Head of Junior School: Miss A Smith, BEd Hons, QTS
Nursery Curriculum Manager: Mrs C Lawrence, BA Ed, QTS
Nursery Manager: Mrs K Noonan, BA Hons, EYTS
Nursery Deputy Manager: Mrs Naomi Kelly, NVQ3
Compliance Coordinator: Mrs V Vaughan, BSc Hons, QTS
Challenge & Extension (*Senior School*): Mrs A Chicken, MA, BA Hons, PGCE
Challenge & Extension (*Junior School*): Miss A Smith, BEd Hons, QTS

St Joseph's College

Belstead Road, Ipswich, Suffolk IP2 9DR
Tel: 01473 690281
email: admissions@stjos.co.uk
website: www.stjos.co.uk
X/Twitter: @MyStJos
Facebook: @StJosephsCollegeIpswich
LinkedIn: /St-Joseph's-College-Ipswich

St Joseph's College is a lively and purposeful day and boarding school offering girls and boys aged 2 to 19 space to thrive. The Nursery, Prep, Senior and Sixth Form provision offers a broad, well-rounded and all-through education.

Located on a 60-acre parkland site near to the centre of Ipswich, the College lies just 10 minutes' walk from Ipswich train station and a five-minute drive from the A12/A14 interchange.

Traditional values are at the heart of the school community, which, at the same time, is forward-thinking, meeting the challenges of an ever-changing world. Pupils are provided with every opportunity to develop their talents to the full.

Ethos. The uniqueness of St Jo's is shaped by its ethos, combining Christian values with a distinctive approach to supporting and nurturing children individually within a friendly, family environment. Along with the pursuit of excellence, this approach is reflected in all aspects of life at the College – academic, sporting, spiritual and cultural.

Developments. December 2019 saw the reopening of the College Chapel following a £750K upgrade. During the refurbishment, a new meeting space was created – The ARC, named after the school's three core values, Aspiration, Respect and Confidence. The Pavilion, with dual-aspect views over the sports fields, also opened that year. It supports the school's move to four performance sports: rugby, cricket, football and netball. New cricket nets were installed and an indoor cricket training facility updated.

There is a striking, post-industrial Sixth Form Centre and a colourful, curving Prep School building with maltings-style windcatcher towers. The College's Technology Centre caters for Engineering, while award-winning sports pitches, floodlit AstroTurf, sports hall and fitness suite serve PE, Games and recreational sport.

ISI Inspection. St Joseph's College was top rated by the Independent Schools Inspectorate for EYFS, Prep School, Senior School, Sixth Form and Boarding. ISI rated the school 'Excellent' across both mandatory inspection judgement areas: the quality of pupils' achievement and the quality of pupils' personal development. St Joseph's was commended for academic achievement, teacher subject knowledge, and student study skills, self-discipline and social awareness. The school also met all requirements on its Compliance Inspection in 2023.

Boarding. Flexible, weekly, short-term and full boarding is offered in two family-run, spacious and warm boarding houses, recently redecorated and upgraded. Accommodation includes both single and shared rooms, with kitchens, studies and recreational facilities.

Curriculum. The curriculum is designed to provide a broad and balanced education for all pupils. Strong foundations in the core skills of reading, writing and numeracy are laid down in the Infant Department and consolidated in the Juniors. Science, Spanish, Music, PE and Engineering are taught by specialists. Work is cross-curricular and there is an emphasis on STEM subjects.

The Senior School students are set according to ability in certain subjects. In Years 7 to 9, the emphasis remains on the core subjects while developing the knowledge and skills required for more advanced studies. At GCSE, Mathematics, English Language & Literature and Double Science Award are compulsory, with PE and Faith, Life & Wellbeing also studied by all. There is a wide range of optional subjects.

The majority of students proceed to the Sixth Form to complete their A level and vocational courses. Subjects available include: Art, Biology, Business (A Level and BTEC), Chemistry, Computer Science, Digital Media (CTEC), Drama and Theatre Studies, Economics, Engineering (BTEC), English, French, Geography, History, Law, Mathematics, Further Mathematics, Mathematical Studies, Music, Photography, Physics, Politics, Psychology, Sociology, Spanish, Sport Coaching and Development (BTEC) and Textiles. St Joseph's also offers EPQ, IELTS and EAL, and is a national test centre for SATs.

The well-regarded Learning Support department operates throughout the College to provide individual and small group assistance to students of all abilities with specific learning needs and differences. Comprehensive careers guidance is available from Year 9, and the College has a highly experienced Futures Advisor.

Extracurricular activities. Sport, Art, Music and Drama are strongly encouraged, as is participation in the Duke of Edinburgh's Award. The College stages a musical production annually, together with plays and concerts. A large number of extracurricular clubs meet weekly. Regular ski trips, activity holidays and language exchanges are organised throughout the College, including a Year 9 exchange with two leading schools in Sydney, Australia.

Admission. Entry to the College is normally at 2+, 7+, 11+, 13+ and the Sixth Form, with applications for vacancies at other ages subject to spaces being available. The entry process includes an interview, a Taster Day, a formal assessment and a report from the applicant's previous school. For the Sixth Form, the academic assessment is replaced by GCSE results.

Fees per term (2023–2024). Nursery: £66–£68 (per full session); Infants (Reception to Year 2): £3,689; Juniors (Years 3–6): £5,167 (day); Senior School: Years 7–8 £6,112 (day), £10,825 (weekly boarder), £10,926 (full boarder); Year 9–11 £6,503 (day), £11,825 (weekly boarder), £14,526 (full boarder); Sixth Form: £6,503 (day), £11,825 (weekly boarder), £14,526 (full boarder).

Scholarships and bursaries. The College offers a number of scholarships each year at select points of entry into Prep, Senior and Sixth Form, including academic, all-round and subject specific, including Sport. Means-tested bursaries may also be available in cases of need. Please contact the Admissions team for further information.

Charitable status. St Joseph's College is a Registered Charity, number 1051688. It exists to provide high-quality education for children.

Governing Body:
Chair: Mr Perry Glading
Vice Chair: Mr Richard Stace, LLB

Mr John Button
Mr Kevyn Connelly
Mr Phil Dennis
Mrs Emma Hardwick
Mr Patrick Lewis
Mrs Jo Ludlam
Mr Anthony Newman
Mr Matthew Potter
Mr Christopher Richardson-Smith
Mr Christian Ross

Senior Leadership Team:

***Principal*: Mrs Danielle Clarke**, BA Hons, NPQH

Deputy Principal: Mr Sacha Cinnamond, BA Hons, MA, NPQH
Vice Principal, Head of Prep School: Mrs Amanda Childs, MA, BA Hons, QTS, PGCPS, Dip Ed
Vice Principal, Pastoral: Mrs Gina Rowlands, BA Hons, PGCE, NPQH
Vice Principal, Co-curricular: Mrs Vicki Harvey, BA, PGCE, DipEd, NPQH, MCCT
Director of Business Development and Sport: Mr Anthony O'Riordan, NPQSL, NPQH
Director of Finance: Mrs Julie Keech, FCCA
Director of Admissions, Marketing and Communications: Mrs Sarah Edwards, BA Hons

Senior School Heads of Faculty and Pastoral Leads:
Dr Jen Stimson (*Director of Academic and International Projects*)
Mrs Katherine Simpson-Jacobs (*Head of Sixth Form*)
Mrs Mychaela Frost (*Head of Technology*)
Mrs Jane Wicks (*Head of Learning Support/SENDCo*)
Mr James Ingle (*Deputy Director of Sport*)
Mrs Sally Hosking-Burtle (*Head of English*)
Mr Chris Fletcher (*Senior Pastoral Manager*)
Mr Dominic Briffa (*Head of Science*)
Mr Colin McNicholas (*Head of Humanities*)
Ms Morag Strong (*Head of MFL & EAL*)
Miss Helen Rolls (*Head of Mathematics*)
Mrs Vicki Harvey (*Head of Creative and Performing Arts*)

Prep School:
Mrs Lucy Dhanak (*Head of EYFS & Infant*)
Mrs Dianne Searle (*Deputy Head*)

Scarborough College

Filey Road, Scarborough, North Yorkshire YO11 3BA

Tel: 01723 360620
email: admin@scarboroughcollege.co.uk
website: www.scarboroughcollege.co.uk
X/Twitter: @ScarColl
Facebook: @ScarboroughColl
Instagram: @scarboroughcollege

Motto: *Pensez Fort*

Scarborough College, founded in 1896, is a thriving co-educational day and boarding school for children aged 3–18 with an exceptional academic pedigree and an unrivalled reputation for making the most of every child's potential. The College, its Prep School and Pre-School all share the same site. Our beautiful campus overlooks the spectacular North Yorkshire coast and is ten minutes' walk from the centre of the stunning seaside town of Scarborough. The boarding houses are merely a 15-minute walk from the beach. The College has fine views overlooking the South Bay of the town and Scarborough Castle.

Although the ethos of the College is firmly based upon wholesome traditional principles, we have a progressive approach to education, which has led to us offering the International Baccalaureate in our Sixth Form since 2007, a qualification that is highly prized throughout the world. Our average staff to student ratio of 1:8 ensures we develop the full potential of every child.

Superb facilities – including 20 acres of sports pitches, a fully floodlit AstroTurf, a performing arts centre with 400-seater theatre, sports hall and neighbouring 18-hole golf course – all ensure a truly first-class education can be delivered to nurture the talents of all.

Scholarships for academic performance, sport, music and as an 'all-rounder' are awarded at all entry points. Means-tested bursaries are also available.

Admission. *Prep School:* Admission is by visit to the school and an interview with the Head of Prep School. Taster days can be arranged.

Senior School: Admission at age 11 is following an Entrance Assessment and interview. Admission at all other ages is subject to recommendation from the previous school, an interview and satisfactory performance in a general assessment.

Sixth Form: Admissions are subject to the achievement of a minimum of five GCSEs at Grades 9 to 6 and an interview with the headmaster. *Overseas Students* are required to submit: school reports for the previous two years; academic certificates, if appropriate (GCSE or equivalent and any other exams taken); written reference from the Head of current/previous school. They are also required to sit our English and maths assessments and undergo an interview either during a visit to the school or via Skype. Scholarships and bursaries are available.

Senior School. Students join us in all year groups with especially high numbers of new arrivals in Years 7, 9 and 10 for GCSE, Year 11 for our bespoke Pre-IB course and the Lower Sixth for the IB Diploma.

Students in Years 7, 8 and 9 study three modern languages and three sciences, providing them with a firm foundation for further study. Along with English and maths, they also study traditional subjects including history, geography, music, art, religious education, classics, ICT, drama, and design and technology. Further options appear as GCSE subject choices in Year 10.

A dedicated Learning Support and English as an Additional Language team of staff ensures all individual needs are fully met.

Sport, music, and drama are very important parts of the daily College life with over 50 clubs and societies on offer every year. Horse riding is particularly popular and the College has both a Cricket Academy and Golf Academy.

Prep School. Our educational vision is simple: the pursuit of excellence in every aspect of school life in an environment which will develop active, questioning, confident, thinking children.

At the core of our school is a traditional academic approach and a challenging curriculum. We provide the best pastoral care and support for every child. We also pride ourselves on the breadth of our education inside and outside the classroom. Dedicated subject specialists deliver a stimulating programme including art, drama, design technology, French and music, as well as daily games and outdoor pursuits. The enrichment programme is rich and varied and includes our own Forest and Beach school too.

In addition we offer free wraparound care before and after school for our busy working parents.

Sixth Form and the IB Diploma. The International Baccalaureate Diploma programme provides our Sixth Form students with a stimulating and challenging post-16 curriculum. Our experience has shown that the IB encourages the development of inquisitive, critical and reflective thinkers who engage fully in the learning process to acquire knowledge. 29 separate subject course options are available.

In our Sixth Form, students develop a new relationship with their teachers within a university-style tuition setting. They have many opportunities to show and develop their leadership skills and become very involved in the School Council, hosting and organising school, house and social events as well as prefect duties and helping younger students in roles such as mentors and sports coaches. There is a rich programme of visiting speakers and exchange visits, and they have their own dedicated Study Centre, Café and Common Room. This is a caring, friendly and warm environment which is a great place to develop and grow into inquisitive and confident young adults.

Boarding. There are three traditional and charming boarding houses at Scarborough College, offering boarding accommodation for pupils aged 11–18 years from all around the world. These really do provide a warm family environment with a home-from-home feeling for all our students, both British and foreign.

A busy programme of weekend entertainment is planned each term to keep the students active. More spontaneous events also include house barbecues, impromptu sports, trips to the beach, go karting, mountain biking, surfing and cinema trips, just to name a few.

Our boarding staff are all experienced members of staff with families of their own, so know how challenging and demanding teenagers can be from time to time, but also are very caring, understanding and sympathetic to the needs of each and every individual child.

Day pupils benefit from all of the extras that being part of a boarding school brings, including the opportunity for occasional boarding. The school bus service operates daily to Bridlington, Whitby, Driffield, Malton and Pickering.

For further up-to-date information on the school, please visit the College's website.

Fees per term (2023–2024). Senior School Day: £5,389–£6,005; UK Weekly Boarding: £7,519–£8,488; Full UK boarding: £9,623–£10,828; Overseas boarding: £11,439–£12,663.

Charitable status. Scarborough College is a Registered Charity, number 529686.

Governors:
Mr G Robinson (*Chairman*)
Mr A Green (*Deputy Chairman*)
Mr J Cliffe
Mr S Fairbank
Mrs V Gillingham
Mr R Guthrie
Mr A Ingham
Mr R Marshall
Mrs W Martin
Dr J Renshaw
Mr J Rowlands
Mr J Swiers
Mr G Young

Senior Management Team:

***Headmaster*: Mr Guy Emmett**

Head of Prep School: Mr Chris Barker

Deputy Head: Mr Timothy Cashell

Assistant Head (*Academic*): Mrs Kate Hill

Assistant Head (*IB*): Ms Katherine Cook

Assistant Head (*Boarding*): Mr Timothy Cashell

Assistant Head (*Teaching & Learning*): Mr Daniel Vickery

Business Manager & Clerk to the Governors: Miss Alison Higgins

Director of Marketing and Admissions: Mr Remco Weeda

Seaford College

Lavington Park, Petworth, West Sussex GU28 0NB

Tel: 01798 867392
email: info@seaford.org
website: www.seaford.org
X/Twitter: @seafordcollege
Facebook: @seafordcollege
Instagram: @seafordcollege
LinkedIn: /company/seaford-college

See full entry in the **HMC** section, on **p. 332**.

Shebbear College

Shebbear, Beaworthy, Devon EX21 5HJ
Tel: 01409 282000
email: admissions@shebbearcollege.co.uk
website: www.shebbearcollege.co.uk
X/Twitter: @ShebbearCollege
Facebook: @ShebbearCollege
Instagram: @ShebbearCollege
LinkedIn: /company/shebbearcollege

Founded in 1841 and steeped in history, Shebbear College is a thriving day and boarding school for girls and boys aged 4 to 18. Our 85-acre campus is situated in the beautiful Devon countryside, close to Exmoor and Dartmoor National Parks and the fantastic surfing beaches of the North Cornwall coast. Life at Shebbear is busy, filled with academic purpose, co-curricular activity, creative discovery and outdoor adventure. We are a community where everyone is known and cherished and life-long friends are made within our supportive and caring environment.

Pupil numbers. In the Senior School there are around 200 pupils, of whom around 50 are boarders, and around 60 pupils in our Prep School.

Situation and location. Shebbear College borders on Dartmoor National Park and stands in 85 acres of unspoilt countryside. It can be easily reached by main road and rail links; only 40 miles west of Exeter and 40 miles north of Plymouth. Both cities have their own regional and international airport.

Buildings. Shebbear College boasts impressive facilities in all areas of the curriculum. The extensive buildings include a separate Sixth Form Centre; a purpose-built block for Science; a modern Computing suite; a superbly equipped modern Music Centre; Art Rooms and two Performing Arts halls. Our Sports Hall, gym and dance studio provide full-scale indoor facilities. The Pre-Prep and Prep School are situated within the grounds and are fully equipped for children aged 4–11 years. There are two boarding houses, Ruddle girls and Pollard boys.

Admission. Admissions into all year groups are accepted all year round, with an Entrance Day for those looking to join Year 7 and Year 9 taking place each January. We are a non-selective school and this day is simply designed to help us establish the academic ability and level of each child. Entry into the Sixth Form is by interview.

Houses. Every pupil belongs to a House – Pollard, Ruddle, Thorne or Way. These Houses organise activities and games competitions throughout the year. The House Tutors watch each child's progress academically as well as their general development.

Curriculum. All pupils at Shebbear College follow the National Curriculum until the age of 14. A wide choice of subjects is available in the following two years, leading to GCSE, but everyone is obliged to take English, Mathematics, Science and, usually, a foreign language. In the Sixth Form there is not only a wide choice of A Levels, but there is particularly flexible timetabling which enables students to mix Arts and Science subjects. We also offer a variety of BTEC courses which pupils can study alongside A Levels and/or the Extended Project Qualification (EPQ).

Sport. With more than 25 acres of playing fields, modern sports hall with multi-gym, dance studio, cricket nets, all-weather pitch, tennis and netball courts, pupils have the security to exercise within the school grounds confidently. The main games covered for the boys are rugby and football, and for girls, netball and hockey. We also offer mixed cricket, athletics and tennis. A variety of other sports are also on offer including rounders, volleyball, badminton, basketball, gymnastics and dance.

Outdoor education. Shebbear College is well known for its strong Outdoor Education programme, and its vision is to become the best school for Outdoor Education in the South West. Pupils take part in weekly lessons which include Forest School, learning bushcraft skills, building, trekking and tree planting. Pupils take part in the Ten Tors Challenge and Duke of Edinburgh Award each year.

Music and drama. Music and drama play a central role in life at Shebbear. Our choir has over 40 members and our orchestra, also with over 40 members, represents most instruments. Players perform regularly in concerts and instrumental ensembles. Every year, a theatrical or musical production is performed to a very high standard. Following successful completion of A Levels, we regularly have pupils going on to the Cardiff University School of Music and other prestigious Conservatoires.

Societies and activities. All pupils participate in at least 4 afternoons a week of extracurricular activities. This widens their interests and develops their self-confidence. The list of activities is endless and includes the usual and unusual. Many pupils enjoy getting involved with Ten Tors training, hillwalking, camping, sailing, canoeing, and surfing. Many pupils are involved in the Duke of Edinburgh's Award scheme.

Careers. Our innovative careers department, Horizons, prepares all of our pupils for their lives beyond school. In the Sixth Form, pupils have access to our excellent programme dedicated to university applications, apprenticeships and gap years.

Scholarships and Bursaries. We offer Scholarships at 11+, 13+ and 16+ for talented pupils in the areas of academia, sport, music, drama and art. Bursaries are available to all pupils but are based on parental income. We also offer transitional bursaries to talented students looking to join our Sixth Form which can account for up to 100% of fees.

Fees per term (2023–2024). Prep School: £2,185–£3,980. Senior School: Day £5,400–5,540, Weekly Boarding £7,035–£7,500, Full Boarding £7,870–£13,225.

Charitable status. Shebbear College is a Registered Charity, number 1142794.

Chairman of the Governors: Mr N Buckland

***Head*: Mr Charlie Jenkins**

Senior Deputy Head (*Pastoral*): Mrs F Lovett
Deputy Head Academic: Miss E Southern
Head of Prep School: Mr M Foale
Director of Finance and Operations: Mr K Maukonen
Head of Marketing & Admissions: Mrs J Conway

Heads of Departments/Senior Staff:
Head of Additional Learning Needs: Mr S Sansom, BA, PGCE
Art: Miss H Kaur, BA Hons, PGCE
Creative, Digital and Performing Arts: Mrs R Sadler-Smith, BMus Hons, PGCE
Digital Learning: Mr R Giles, MEng, MSc, QTS
English: Mrs F Shamsolahi, BA Hons
English & Languages/Horizons: Mrs J Aliberti, BA Hons, PGCE
Drama: Mr J Pomroy, BA Hons, PGCE, MEd
Humanities: Mr E Grey, BA Hons, PGCE
Mathematics: Mr R Giles, MEng, MSc, QTS
Sport & Personal Development: Mr P Nicholls, BA, GTP, QTS
Science (Physics): Mrs A Kingsland, BSc, PGSE
Head's PA: Mrs A Stairs

Sherfield School

Education in Motion Group

Sherfield-on-Loddon, Hook, Hampshire RG27 0HT

Tel:	01256 884800
email:	info@sherfieldschool.co.uk
website:	www.sherfieldschool.co.uk
X/Twitter:	@SchoolSherfield
Facebook:	@SherfieldSchoolHampshire
Instagram:	@sherfieldschool
LinkedIn:	/school/sherfield-school

See full entry in the **ISA** section, on **p. 923**.

Shiplake College

Henley-on-Thames, Oxon RG9 4BW

Tel:	0118 940 2455
email:	registrar@shiplake.org.uk
website:	www.shiplake.org.uk
X/Twitter:	@ShiplakeCollege
Facebook:	@ShiplakeCollege
Instagram:	@ShiplakeCollege
LinkedIn:	/shiplakecollege

See full entry in the **HMC** section, on **p. 337**.

Sibford School

Sibford Ferris, Banbury, Oxon OX15 5QL

Tel:	01295 781200
email:	admissions@sibfordschool.co.uk
website:	www.sibfordschool.co.uk
X/Twitter:	@SibfordOxon
Facebook:	@SibfordOxon
Instagram:	@Sibfordoxon
LinkedIn:	/sibfordoxon

Founded 1842. A Co-educational Independent Boarding (full, weekly, and flexi) and Day School. Membership of The Society of Heads, BSA, AGBIS.

There are over 400 pupils in the school aged between 3 and 18: 345 pupils in the Senior School and 96 pupils in the Junior School. There are 85 teachers plus visiting staff.

Curriculum. Sibford School offers an extensive, innovative and diverse education where pupils are encouraged to 'live adventurously'. Broad and balanced curriculum which reflects our view that while some may have talent for maths or history, others may be gifted in the arts or horticulture. Renowned dyslexia tuition and support for a small number of pupils with other learning difficulties.

Junior School (age 3–11): wide-ranging curriculum with an emphasis on outdoor education. Literacy, numeracy, science and technology skills are emphasised alongside art, music, drama and PE. Enriched Curriculum in Year 6 with Senior School Staff. Specialist teachers help individual children with specific learning difficulties. No SATS.

Senior School (age 11–16): all pupils follow courses leading to GCSE, in a curriculum expanding on the National Curriculum. Information Technology is introduced at an early age and the use of laptop computers is widespread.

Dyslexic pupils have special tuition in small groups on a daily basis. Highly regarded Support for Learning Department provides specialised support within the timetable. Personal and Social Development runs through the school.

Sixth Form (age 16–18) students take A Levels and/or BTEC Diplomas. The Sixth Form curriculum leads to higher education and offers a particularly wide range of opportunities for further study.

Overseas pupils are welcomed into the school community. The school has a specialist ESOL department and English as an additional language is taught by ESOL qualified teachers.

Entry requirements. Admission is by interview and internal tests. Where applicable a report from the candidate's current school is required. No religious requirements.

Examinations offered. A Level, GCSE, BTEC Diploma, Associated Board Music Examinations, LAMDA, Oxford and Cambridge IELTS Examinations.

Academic and leisure facilities. Exceptional Performing & Creative Arts in purpose-built facilities. Multi-purpose Sports Centre, including a state-of-the-art Climbing Wall. 25 m indoor swimming pool. Well-equipped Library and Information Technology Centres. Design Technology Centre. Separate Sixth Form Centre. Wide range of indoor and outdoor activities. 50 plus-acre campus set in beautiful North Oxfordshire countryside. Three boarding houses (for girls, boys and sixth form). Easy access to Stratford, Oxford, Cheltenham, Birmingham, London.

Religion. Established as a Quaker school, Sibford welcomes pupils of all faiths, backgrounds and nationalities, encouraging in each of them genuine self-esteem in a purposeful, caring and challenging environment.

Fees per term (2023–2024). Full Boarders: £11,750–£11,985, Weekly Boarders: £10,165–£10,280.

Occasional Boarding: £75 per night, Day Pupils: £6,045–£6,165. Junior School: Day Pupils £3,840–£4,650.

Scholarships and bursaries. The School offers general academic scholarships and specific scholarships in Art, Drama, Music and Sport. A limited number of bursaries is offered to both Quaker and non-Quaker children.

Charitable status. Sibford School is a Registered Charity, number 1068256. It is a company limited by guarantee under number 3487651. It aims to give all pupils a vehicle to educational and personal success.

***Head*: Rebecca Evans**

Deputy Head and Designated Safeguarding Lead: Phil Tattersall-King
Director of Studies: Jessica Boyle
Co-Heads of Sixth Form: Helen Gormley and Darren De Bruyn
Head of Junior School: Edward Rossiter

Business Manager: Ally Lynch
Admissions Registrar: Elle Kitching
Marketing Manager: Harriet Canavan

Stover School

Newton Abbot, South Devon TQ12 6QG
Tel: 01626 354505 (Main switchboard)
01626 359911 (Registrar)
01626 335240 (Finance Office)
email: schooloffice@stover.co.uk
website: www.stover.co.uk

Stover School is a leading independent, co-educational, non-selective, day and boarding school for pupils aged 3 to 18. It is set in 64 acres of beautiful and historical grounds in the heart of Devon's glorious countryside between the foothills of Dartmoor and the South West Coastline. In the last ISI Inspection the School was judged as fully compliant and in the previous quality inspection as excellent in teaching, pastoral care, welfare, health and safety, quality of leadership and management and governance.

Stover School delivers a cutting edge Research Based Learning Curriculum across the entire age range while retaining a healthy focus on traditional Christian morals, values and manners. Happy children are at the very centre of the school's ethos, reflecting the robust system of pastoral care. Children who feel safe, valued, respected and who trust those around them are free to focus on learning to their maximum potential.

Pupils are encouraged, motivated and supported in achieving their aspirations in all areas of the academic and broader curriculum. Successes are celebrated wherever they occur, be that be in Bushcraft, French, Hockey, Science, Fencing, Art or Computer Programming.

The extensive activities and enrichment programmes ensure that everyone can enjoy, develop and challenge themselves. In this relatively small school every pupil is well known. The strong House system provides a framework for pupils to develop a sense of collectiveness within the supportive environment. Pupils learn respect for themselves and others through the teaching of moral values and good standards of behaviour.

The aim is to ensure that every child enjoys their experience at Stover School, having achieved the best they are capable of in the broadest education sense and having equipped themselves with the qualifications and skills required for future success and fulfilment.

Recent developments include a refurbished Art Studio, Sixth Form Centre and boarding accommodation, a newly established tennis academy, the creation of a music ensemble practice suite and recording studio, the establishment of a clay shooting and rifle range and the arrival of the first vegetable beds, chickens and beehives, coupled with an outdoor classroom.

Examinations. Public examinations set by all examination boards include GCSE, BTEC and A Level. Music examinations are set by the Associated Board of the Royal Schools of Music. Speech and Drama examinations are set by LAMDA. Sixth Form pupils can also take CoPE and CSL/HSL qualifications, set by ASDAN and Sports Leaders UK respectively.

Physical Education. Hockey, rugby, netball, table tennis, football, rounders and cricket are the core team games. Individual sports include athletics, gymnastics, golf, tennis, badminton and cross country. Other sports throughout the year include adventure development, orienteering, shooting and skiing.

The school has extensive grass pitches, six tennis courts (3 floodlit and one cover all-weather), a 9-hole golf course, cross-country tracks, clay pigeon and rifle range and cricket nets. We run a full range of school sports activities, clubs and fixture lists for both Senior and Prep.

Optional subjects. In addition to a wide variety of activities organised by Stover's own staff there are specialist peripatetic staff for instrumental and voice tuition, speech and drama, riding, fencing, judo, golf, clay pigeon and rifle shooting and tennis coaching.

Fees per term (2023–2024). Preparatory School: Day: Reception £3,240, Years 1–3 £3,505, Years 4–6 £4,355. Weekly Boarding: Years 4–6 £7,565. Full Boarding: Years 4–6 £8,740, International £9,190 (inclusive). Senior School: Years 7–13: £5,330 (day), £9,165 (weekly boarding), £11,065 (full boarding), £11,500 (International, inclusive).

Entrance and Scholarships. Compatibility of new pupils is assessed through a Head's interview, school tours, a series of taster days and submission of previous school's full written report. Academic, Music, Sport and Arts Scholarships are available and can be sat at point of entry or on our Scholarship Assessment Day in January. In addition, means-tested bursaries are available. Stover School, in association with Plymouth University, also offers the Excellence in Mathematics Scholarships to International students. This attracts a 10% remission of fees at Plymouth University for the duration of the Undergraduate Degree course (3 years).

Health. Nursing care is provided by our on-site Matron who is a Registered General Nurse. All boarders are registered with the school's GP.

Old Stoverites. c/o Stover School.

Charitable status. Stover School Association is a Registered Charity, number 306712. Stover School is a charitable foundation for education.

***Headmaster*: Mr R W D Notman**, BCom Birmingham

Deputy Head Teacher: Dr J Stone, BSc Wales, MEd Open, PhD S'ton, HDipEd Dublin
Head of Preparatory School: Mr B Noble, BSc Hertfordshire

Senior Leadership Team:
Mr P Jenkins (*Bursar*)
Mrs H Notman, BSc, UMIST, MSc Ed Res Manchester (*Assistant Head Pastoral*)
Mr M Mooney, BEd Cheltenham & Glos (*Assistant Head Operations*)

Middle Leadership Team Senior School:
Mrs S-J Avery, BA Plymouth (*Senior Teacher Pastoral*)
Mr S Griffin, BEd Cheltenham & Farnborough (*Head of KS3, Geography*)
Mrs D Robinson, BA Twickenham (*Head of Sixth Form*)
Mrs A Stone, BA Angers, HDipEd Dublin, CELTA (*Deputy Head of Sixth Form, Head of EAL*)

Senior School Teaching Staff:
* *Head of Department*

*Dr D Allway, BSc, MSc, PhD Manchester (*Science*)
Mrs H Bailey, MSc Swansea (*Mathematics*)
*Mr J Balfour, MA Exeter (*Drama*)
Mr P Barter, BA Exeter (*Humanities, Duke of Edinburgh Award Coordinator*)
Mr J Brown, MA (*Science*)
Mrs Debbie Burman (*MFL*)
*Mr S Cocker, BSc, QTS Marjon (*Mathematics*)
*Miss R Cocks, BSc Southampton (*Humanities*)
*Mrs T Craven, BA, QTS Brighton (*Sport*)
Miss Emma Davies (*Dance*)
Mrs Sarah Farleigh (*Music*)
*Mrs R Fenton, BA Manchester (*English & Media*)
Mr G Forsyth, BA Sheffield, TEFL (*English*)
*Mr G Foxley, BA Plymouth (*MFL*)
Mrs K Gardner, BA Nottingham (*History*)
Mrs Davina Gunn-Hawking (*PSHE*)
Mr J Hartley, BA Exeter (*Business*)
Miss J Henwood, BSc Bath (*Mathematics*)
*Mrs C Howard, BA Wales (*Art & Photography*)
Mrs Melanie Hulbert (*Mathematics*)
*Mr Alex Lloyd (*Sport*)
Mr David May (*Computer Science*)
Mrs E McEwen, BA Oxford Brookes (*English*)
Mrs J Mooney, PGCE Exeter (*Science, Mathematics*)
Miss A Morgan, BSc Wales (*Biology*)
Mrs H Rice, BA Wales (*MFL*)
*Mrs B Seward, BA Middlesex (*Philosophy & Ethics*)
*Mrs C Sewell, BA, MA Edinburgh (*Psychology, German*)
Mr Matt Warton (*Mathematics*)
*Mrs C Wightman, BA Wolverhampton (*Art and Photography*)
Revd F Wimsett, BA Wales, Cert Theology Exeter (*School Chaplain & Teacher of Religious Studies*)

Tettenhall College

Wood Road, Tettenhall, Wolverhampton, West Midlands WV6 8QX
Tel: 01902 751119
email: head@tettcoll.co.uk
website: www.tettenhallcollege.co.uk
Facebook: @TettColl
Instagram: @tettcoll
LinkedIn: /company/tettenhall-college

Motto: *Timor Domini Initium Sapientiae*

Founded in 1863, Tettenhall College provides a stimulating learning environment for girls and boys, boarders and day pupils aged 2–18. The emphasis at Tettenhall College is on a personalised education that develops the whole person, both in and beyond the classroom with exceptional extra-curricular opportunities that complement the rigorous academic environment. The School ensures that everyone will find their niche and grow in confidence.

Life skills and real-world preparation are integral from Nursery to Sixth Form. The Preparatory School's diverse enrichment programme ranging from chess to Mandarin and philosophy to debating, enhances pupils' experiences alongside daily emphasis on English, reading, and mathematics remaining at the heart of the curriculum.

Academic success is a major focus across the whole School, with consistently high GCSE and A Level grades above national averages. In 2021, at A Level an impressive 57% of grades were awarded at A*/A, 85% achieving A*–B grades and 96% gaining A*–C grades.

For a non-selective school, equally important to measure is 'value-added,' comparing pupils predicted grades at entry to the school with actual grades achieved at 16. On this measure, Tettenhall College surpasses many highly selective state and independent schools. Small class size enables pupils to flourish whilst those requiring support are given this at no extra cost.

Situation and Buildings. Nestled in 33 acres of beautiful woodland grounds, Tettenhall College comprises of historic buildings and modern amenities allowing pupils to thrive within a caring family atmosphere. Located in the picturesque village of Tettenhall, only 40 minutes from Birmingham International Airport, the School is one of the leading independent day and boarding schools in the region.

Amenities include renovated boarding facilities and outstanding sporting facilities including an indoor heated Swimming Pool, Sports Hall, Squash Courts, Sports Pavilion, floodlit artificial courts for football, netball, tennis and hockey, two cricket squares and playing fields for rugby, football and athletics.

Religion. Services in the College Chapel are interdenominational.

Entry. Preparatory School: assessed during a taster day/session with completion of informal assessments.

Senior School entry (Years 7–9) pupils will be invited to attend the College Entrance Assessment in the January prior to entry the following September. Year 12 is determined by Entrance Assessment, GCSE results (or equivalent), school reports, and a successful interview with the Headmaster.

Organisation. Preparatory School (Reception to Year 6) and Senior School (Years 7–13) are divided into four Houses which compete in activities, work and games. Nursery comprises Day Nursery and Pre-School from the age of 2 to 4.

Senior School & Sixth Form Curriculum. Years 7–9 in Senior School are designed to give our pupils a sound basis for studies at GCSE and beyond.

As well as a strong emphasis on the core subjects of English, Mathematics and Science we consider languages to be important therefore offer French and Spanish. Creativity abounds in our Art, Music and Drama programmes, and History and Geography lessons teach pupils about our world, both past and present.

Computing offers exciting possibilities to explore new technologies. Physical Education and Games encourage health and fitness and provides opportunities to acquire and develop skills and attitudes to individual endeavour and teamwork. Add to the mix the moral and ethical dimensions discussed in PSHE and Religious Education and you have an academic programme that is broad and balanced, enjoyable and intellectually demanding.

In Year 9, Business and Electronics are introduced, ensuring pupils experience all of our GCSE subjects before choosing which subjects they wish to study further. EAL is offered as a specialist subject throughout Senior School.

A Levels are academically challenging and entry into the Sixth Form (Years 12–13) has a minimum of 5 GCSEs at grade 5 or above for entry. Our A Level curriculum offers a wide range of subjects, with small class sizes ensuring the best possible results. Visit our website to see the curriculum subjects offering.

Careers. Extensive careers guidance is provided by the Head of Careers, with each Sixth Former assigned a Personal Tutor for support. Regular visits from universities, local companies, and alumni who host career talks and seminars enrich the guidance process.

Societies and Activities. All pupils are encouraged to engage in community life and to play a part in the social and cultural organisations.

Pupils take part in The Duke of Edinburgh's Award scheme, working for Bronze, Silver and Gold Awards. Beyond sporting opportunities, school plays and musicals are produced annually; there is a house festival of Performing Arts and the Music Department has a deservedly strong reputation for its quality of performance and opportunities. All pupils from Year 6 take part in the extended day programme where activities range from climbing and mountain biking to the Extended Project Qualification for older pupils.

Preparatory School. The Preparatory School is housed separately in a purpose-designed building, sharing some facilities with Senior School. Senior School Staff help with games and specialist teaching.

The curriculum extends beyond the national standards. Younger pupils are taught by a form teacher with a focus on key skills in Literacy and Numeracy. As children move through the years they are introduced to teaching from subject specialists.

Athletics, Cricket, Netball, Hockey, Rounders, Rugby, Football, Swimming and Tennis are the main sports, and all pupils have PE and two afternoons of games each week. Extracurricular activities change regularly but include clubs in all the previously mentioned sports.

Fees per term (2023–2024). Boarding: Years 5–9 £8,838 (full), £6,982 (weekly); Years 10–13 £12,486 (full), £9,881 (weekly). Day: Nursery £3,550 (full-time), Reception £2,880, Year 1 £3,220, Year 2 £3,490, Years 3–6 £4,120, Years 7–13 £5,491.

Scholarships and Bursaries. Senior School Academic Scholarships may be offered to outstanding pupils. Scholarships are also awarded for Academic, Music, Art, Performing Arts and Sport.

Means-tested Bursaries are available. There is a reduction in fees for the children of the Clergy, members of HM Forces and children of former pupils.

The Old Tettenhallians' Club. Membership is automatic on reaching 18 years of age.

Charitable status. Tettenhall College Incorporated is a Registered Charity, number 528617.

Chairman of Governors: Mr Jeremy F Woolridge, CBE, DL, BSc Hons

Senior Leadership Team:

***Headmaster*: Mr Christopher McAllister**, NPQH, BA Hons

Bursar: Mr C Way, BSc Hons
Senior Deputy Head: Miss C Troughton, BSc Hons, MSc Hons, QTS
Head of Preparatory School Division: Mr J Gomersall, BSc Hons, PGCE, MCCT
Director of Admissions & External Relations: Mrs V McAllister, BA, MA

Assistant Heads:
Pastoral: Mrs J Hollinshead, BSc Hons, PGCE
Academic: Mr D Matthews, BScEcon, LLM, PGCE
Preparatory School: Mrs A Marshall-Walker, BA Hons, QTS

Thetford Grammar School

Bridge Street, Thetford, Norfolk IP24 3AF

Tel: 01842 752840
email: office@thetgram.norfolk.sch.uk
website: www.thetfordgrammar.co.uk
X/Twitter: @ThetGram
Facebook: @thetfordgrammarschool

Thetford Grammar School is a co-educational independent boarding school that teaches pupils aged 3–19. We are one of the oldest schools in the country and have been educating young people since the 7th century. Our pupils benefit from an academically robust, yet rounded education that includes a range of extracurricular activities and a strong pastoral system. We understand that children learn best when they are relaxed and at ease and our school is very much focused on providing an environment that encourages this. Children flourish at Thetford Grammar School because they feel safe and supported.

Buildings and situation. Situated close to the centre of Thetford, the school occupies a well-established site graced by several buildings of architectural interest and the ruins of a medieval priory. There are extensive playing fields with a refurbished pavilion within walking distance of the main buildings, as well as an award-winning Sixth Form Centre built around the original Cloisters.

Organisation. Prep Department pupils (age 3–11) are taught in their own premises with independent facilities. Older Prep pupils have contact with specialist teachers in several subject areas and benefit from similar integration into many other aspects of school life. Main School education from 11 follows a two-form entry pattern in core subjects to GCSE. Sixth Form students play a full part in the life of the school.

Curriculum. Prep Department teaching follows National Curriculum lines with strong emphasis on the English/Mathematics core with the other curriculum subjects taught as part of the Exploration Curriculum, a project based learning style of teaching. Music, Art and Modern Foreign Languages are taught by subject specialists, while a full programme of PE and Games allows for the development of team sports and individual fitness.

Main School education through to GCSE is based on a common core of English, English Literature, Mathematics, a Modern Language (French, Spanish or German) and the Sciences. Options allow students to develop skills and interests in History, Geography, RS, Business Studies, Languages, the Expressive Arts, Physical Education and Technology. IT is strongly represented across the curriculum. AS and A2 courses are offered in all these subjects. Mathematics and Science lead a strong pattern of results at this level and Sixth Form students proceed to university degree courses.

Sport and extracurricular activities. The life of the school extends widely from the classroom into sport, community service, dramatic and musical presentation.

Winter sports are Rugby, Football, Hockey, Netball and Cross-Country with Cricket, Tennis, Rounders and Athletics in the Summer. Popular indoor sports such as Basketball, Aerobics, Badminton, Volleyball and Gymnastics are also followed. Sixth Form students are able to enrol in the local gym which is situated opposite the school.

A majority of pupils take part in training for The Duke of Edinburgh's Award scheme. A lively concert programme supports individual instrumental tuition and choral rehearsal while opportunities for theatre are provided termly by House and School productions.

There is a varied programme of curricular and extracurricular clubs and trips including expeditions and foreign visits.

Admission. Admission into the Prep Department follows a day in school with the appropriate year group during which an assessment is made. Admission into Main School is by formal examination with interview and school report. Sixth Form entrance is on the basis of interview and school report, with subsequent performance at GCSE taken into consideration. The main Entrance Examination is held in January but supplementary testing continues throughout the year. Full details from the Admissions Officer, admissions@thetgram.norfolk.sch.uk.

Fees per term (2023–2024). Prep Department: Reception–Year 2 £3,120, Years 3–6 £4,435; Main School £5,165, including books and tuition but excluding uniform, lunches, transport, examination entry fees and some specialised teaching such as instrumental music lessons. Nursery funding of 15 hrs per week is available and there are fee awards for Service families across the school. Sibling discount is applicable when a family has 2 or more children in the school at any one time from Reception year upwards and where the family is not in receipt of a bursary or other remission assistance. Fees are subject to an annual fee increase.

Scholarships and bursaries. Bursaries can be available from Year 3 upwards. Scholarships of an honorary nature may be awarded to the top performers in the entrance examinations. Academic Scholarships are available in Year 3, Year 7, Year 9 and Sixth Form. Art, Music, Drama and Sport are also available in Year 7, Year 9 and Sixth Form for both internal and external candidates. Pathways Scholarships are available on entry into Year 12. Details of all awards may be obtained from the Head.

***Head*: Mrs A Faye**, BSc, PGCE

Deputy Head: Mr M Glassbrook, BSc Northumbria, PGCE

Head of Preparatory Department: Mrs H Butler-Hand, BA, MEd Cantab

Head of Sixth Form: Mr A Ward, BSc London, PGCE

Deputy Head of Sixth Form: Mrs K Clark, BSc Kent, PGCE

Academic Staff:

Mrs A Alecock, BA Manchester
Mrs L Arbuthnot, BA University of the Arts Norwich
Miss E Bell, PGCE
Mrs T Beukes, BSc Stellenbosch SA
Mrs M Blanco, BA Exeter
Miss R Callaghan, BA Hons Newcastle
Mr T Casemore, BA Hons Middlesex
Mrs S Collins
Ms S Cornell, BA Hons University of East Anglia
Mrs R Dimminger, Dip Ed Bulawayo
Mrs J Foreman, BA Warwick
Mr M Foreman, BEd Nottingham
Mrs A Glassbrook, BA Hons Sheffield
Mrs T E Granger, BSc Wolverhampton, PGCE
Miss C Griffiths, BA LCC, PGCE
Mr M Hill, BA Bedfordshire
Mrs V Horner, BA Ed Fontys
Dr C Kingsnorth, BSc University of London
Mr D Mitchell, BA Hons Liverpool
Ms W Naylor, BA Hons Salford
Miss N Nunn, BA Lincoln
Mrs N Peace, BA Hons Hull
Mrs H Pringle, BA Teesside Polytechnic
Mr E Rose, BSc Maths, PGCE University of East Anglia
Mrs C Salt, BEd Exeter
Mrs D Skeels, BEd Nottingham Trent
Mr J Snipe, BSc Bristol, PGCE
Miss F Travers, BA Nottingham Trent

Miss Z Venables, BA Anglia Ruskin, PGCE
Mrs P Weyers, MMus Wales, PGCE

LAMDA:
Mrs S Cornell, BA Hons UEA

Teaching Assistants:
Mr A Doyle
Mr B Doyle
Mr J Dunn
Mrs K Hill
Ms M Kheder
Ms S Northmore
Mrs L Steeds
Mr P Taylor
Miss M Trussell
Miss S Wookey

Learning Support:
Mrs K Jones, BSc QTS, Dip SpLD, AMBDA, SpLD APC Patoss

Visiting Music Staff:
Mrs S Brotherhood (*Woodwind*)
Ms F Levy, LLCM TD, ALCM (*Violin*)
Mrs N Pakenham (*Violin*)
Mr J Rowland (*Drum Kit and Jazz Piano*)

Administrative Staff:
Miss C Addinall (*Admissions Officer*)
Mrs L Collings (*Marketing Officer*)
Mr M Glassbrook (*Examinations Officer*)
Miss P Hall (*Receptionist*)
Mrs C Huggins (*Accounts Secretary*)
Mr A Koch (*Accounts Assistant*)
Mrs C Reynolds (*Senior School Secretary/HR Admin*)
Mrs J Settle (*Librarian*)
Mrs H Stocks (*Receptionist*)

Technicians:
Mr B Cockett
Mrs T Evans
Mr A Gatward

Maintenance and Compliance:
Mr D Ford
Mr R Gray
Mr M Mosby
Mr M Reynolds

School Nurse:
Mrs J Theobald

Tring Park School for the Performing Arts

Mansion Drive, Tring, Hertfordshire HP23 5LX

Tel: 01442 824 255
email: info@tringpark.com
website: www.tringpark.com
X/Twitter: @TringParkSchool
Facebook: @TringParkSchool
Instagram: @tringpark_school

Tring Park School for the Performing Arts is the UK's leading vocational and academic boarding and day school. We offer an exceptional opportunity to young people aged 7–19, enabling them to study a dual curriculum with specialist training in the performing arts alongside an exceptional academic education.

Number in School. Boarders: 204 Day: 151

Pupils are provided with the necessary training required to forge influential careers in the performing arts; with notable alumni including Daisy Ridley, Lily James, Drew McOnie, Ella Henderson and Joe Griffiths-Brown. Alternatively, if pupils wish to do so, they can secure places at top Russell Group universities, with many of our alumni becoming lawyers, doctors and scientists.

Entrance is via audition. Scholarships are available for the dance course via the Government's Music and Dance Scheme and Dance and Drama Awards (DaDAs) for Sixth Form. School scholarships and bursaries are available for the Acting, Musical Theatre and Commercial Music courses.

Performance Foundation – Lower and Middle School Course

In Lower School, the course aims to build confidence and performance skills whilst consolidating basic technique. Pupils on the Performance Foundation Course take part in core technique classes in classical ballet, modern and tap dance, solo and group singing classes and acting classes which cover script work, voice work and improvisation.

In Middle School, pupils have the opportunity to develop their skills and talents in technique classes and live performances, so that they can make the right choices about the future direction of their career and education. Pupils will continue to study core classes in ballet, modern and tap dance, solo and group singing and acting.

Dance – Lower, Middle and Sixth Form Course

At Sixth Form level, students study classical ballet, contemporary and jazz dance. The curriculum is enhanced by additional classes in pointe work, repertoire, virtuosity, pas de deux, body conditioning, weights classes, Pilates and commercial dance. Second year students continue to develop their skills and contemporary improvisation is introduced. During the third year of training, dancers join Encore Dance Company and have the opportunity to work with internationally known guest professional choreographers.

Commercial Music – Sixth Form Course

The two-year Commercial Music Course focuses on Pop, Rock and Jazz music. The creative aspects of the Commercial Music Course allow students to write original material, create their own arrangements and write for commissions.

Acting – Sixth Form Course

The two-year Acting Course includes classes covering: voice, classical and modern text, physical theatre, movement for actors, acting study, improvisation, dance and singing. All students on the Acting Course also benefit from screen acting lessons and workshops. A strong theatre company ethos is fostered as part of the Acting Course activities, and students participate in a variety of performances throughout the year.

Musical Theatre – Sixth Form Course

The two-year Musical Theatre Course provides students looking to forge a career in the performing arts with a strong understanding and knowledge of technique in the three essential specialist skills. Students study an intensive two-year course focussed on singing, dance and acting.

Fees per term (2023–2024).

Prep Department (Years 3–6): Boarders £8,730 (Year 5), £8,990 (Year 6). Day £5,135 (Year 3–5), £5,290 (Year 6).

Lower School (Years 7–9): Boarders £12,780, Day £8,170.

Middle School (Years 10 & 11): Boarders £12,970, Day £8,300.

Sixth Form: Boarders £13,880, Day £9,190.

*Sibling discount available: 10% of termly fees. Forces discount available – please enquire.

Charitable status. The AES Tring Park School Trust is a Registered Charity, number 1040330. It exists to provide vocational and academic education.

Board of Governors:
Chair: Mrs Angela Odell
Vice-Chair: Mr Mark Hewitt
Robert Breakwell
Vanessa Champion
John Clark
Michael Harper
Rachel Joseph
Jan Kitteridge
Simon Knee
Eric Pillinger
Mark Taylor
Edward Williams
Daniel Zammit

Senior Management Team:

***Principal*: Simon Larter-Evans**

Deputy Principal: Anselm Barker, MSt Oxon, BA Harvard, ARCM
Director of Studies: Elizabeth Odell, BA, AVCM, AISTD, FDI, QTS
Business Director: Stephen Robinson, MBA, MA, DMS

Vocational Directors:
Director of the Dance Course, Head of Dance: Lorraine Jones, LISD (MTH, Tap), AISTD CB NT
Artistic Director of Encore and Graduate Programmes: Antony Dowson, ARAD, PDTC Dip
Head of Drama and Director of the Acting Course: Edward Applewhite, BA Hons, Dip Acting GSA, QTS
Head of Music and Director of the Commercial Music Course: Harmesh Gharu, MA, BMus Hons, PGCE
Director of Musical Theatre Course: Donna Hayward, FISTD
Directors of Performance Foundation Course: Donna Hayward and Jane Verrall

Academic Management Team:
Deputy Director of Studies (Academic): Dr Anu Mahesh, PhD, MSc Hons, PGCE
Head of the Preparatory Department: Amanda Deer, BEd
Head of Lower School: Sarah Bell, MA, BA Hons, PGCE
Head of Middle School, Head of Careers and UCAS: Imogen Myers, BA Hons, CAP, MA
Head of Sixth Form: Dr Sarah Coren, PhD, BSc Hons, QTS
Head of Humanities: Robert Brown, MA, BA, IPGCE
Head of Arts: Jo Myers, BA Hons, PGCE

Trinity School

Buckeridge Road, Teignmouth, Devon TQ14 8LY

Tel: 01626 774138
email: admissions@trinityschool.co.uk
website: www.trinityschool.co.uk

Foundation and Ethos. With a joint Anglican/Catholic foundation, Trinity School's Christian ethos and family atmosphere are complemented by a commitment to excellence in both academic and personal development. With recent inspections by both ISI and Ofsted rating the School as 'Outstanding' in many areas, the School has successfully demonstrated a determination to deliver the best education possible for the pupils in its care.

Pupil Body. 250 pupils from age 3 to 19 years, with around 50 boarders.

Location and Facilities. The School offers excellent facilities in a very attractive environment with panoramic views of Lyme Bay. Facilities include a purpose-built Design Technology building, IT laboratories, a Music Centre, a Science block, a Food Technology Centre, en-suite boarding accommodation for Sixth Formers, indoor and outdoor tennis facilities, a 25m heated swimming pool, and an Art Centre. The School is very well connected by road and rail, with the nearest railway station being under a mile away and on the London main line.

Academic Record. At the upper end of our ability profile, we have a proven track record of sending pupils to Russell Group universities. We have gained 6 Good School Guide Awards for performance in English, Business Studies and Science. Prep pupils' performance considerably exceeds expectations at KS1 and KS2. 95% of Sixth Form students in recent years have progressed to university or apprenticeships. A mix of BTEC and A Level subjects are taught (inc. all facilitating subjects) in the Sixth Form.

Pastoral Care and Welfare. The quality of the School's pastoral care is an established and considerable strength as proven by the recent inspections. Our Anglican/Catholic ethos permeates all that we do. We believe that for care to be effective, it is essential that school and family work closely together – the relationship needs to be dynamic, honest and built on mutual trust and understanding. This approach, and the fact that Trinity provides education for girls and boys of all ages, helps to generate the School's warm, 'family' atmosphere.

Personal Development. Extensive sporting, cultural, charitable and leadership opportunities are available at all ages: rich musical life with yearly musical productions involving Prep and Senior department pupils; choir; one of the most active CCF sections in the country; Ten Tors and DofE regulars; Lawn Tennis

Association centre of excellence with one national LTA champion and regular Independent Schools Association (ISA) champions; in swimming, athletics, cross country, tennis – Prep and Senior.

Admissions. Trinity is a non-selective school, so there are no entrance examinations required for entry. Assessments are carried out for new students in order to gauge ability and tailor education. Scholarships are by open competition at 11+, 13+ and 16+, for academic, creative arts, sport and all-rounder Notre Dame Awards (selection in January). Bursaries and HM Forces Bursaries.

Fees per term (2023–2024). Tuition (day pupils) £3,125–£4,930; Boarding: £7,710–£9,975 (weekly), £8,300–£10,400 (full), £8,460–£11,150 (international students).

Charitable status. Trinity School is a Registered Charity, number 276960.

Patrons:
Rt Revd Robert Atwell, Bishop of Exeter
Rt Revd Mark O'Toole, Bishop of Plymouth

Proprietor and Director: Mr Ali Khan

Senior Leadership Team:

***Headmaster*: Mr Robert Robinson**

Head of Preparatory Department: Mr Sean Lovett

Deputy Heads:
Mrs Frances Baxter
Mrs Anna Brown
Mrs Julia Bryant
Mrs Jade Connelly

Assistant Heads:
Mrs Lucy Atkins
Mr Robert Larkman

Bursar: Mr Shaun Dyer

Westholme School

Meins Road, Pleasington, Lancashire BB2 6QU

Tel: 01254 506070
email: secretary@westholmeschool.com
website: www.westholmeschool.com
X/Twitter: @westholmeschool
Facebook: @WestholmeSchool
Instagram: @westholme_school
LinkedIn: /company/westholme-school

Westholme School comprises: Prep (Boys and Girls aged 4–11), Senior (Boys and Girls aged 11–16) and INSPIRED Sixth Form (Boys and Girls aged 16–18). There are currently 750 day pupils at Westholme: 577 in the Senior School and INSPIRED Sixth Form, 173 in Prep.

Westholme School is administered by Governors and includes three nominated Governors representing current parents. Although the school is non-denominational, its Christian foundation is regarded as important – the emphasis being placed on the moral aspect of Christian teaching.

Westholme provides a distinctive educational approach rooted in unrivalled holistic excellence that educates the whole child. Equal importance is placed on academia, sport and the creative and performing arts, and a plethora of experiences are offered inside and outside the classroom which fosters confident, well-rounded young people.

Set in the rural Lancashire countryside of Pleasington, Westholme School is situated on one site with the newly constructed state-of-the-art Prep. The first-class facilities on site provide a stimulating environment to inspire students and includes a full-sized professional theatre that seats 500; a fully equipped professional Music Department; seven modern laboratories that support the three separate sciences; a 20 m swimming pool; 7 hard courts for tennis and netball, a floodlit astroturf, sports pitches, fully equipped sports hall and a new strength and conditioning gym to come soon. The Learning Resource Centre has open-access multimedia giving students full research facilities. The INSPIRED Sixth Form wing offers excellent facilities complete with common room, computer workstations and café.

The Performing Arts are a special feature of the school. There are several school choirs and students have the opportunity to learn a string, brass or wind instrument and to play in the school orchestras or wind ensembles. Co-curricular Drama includes the full-scale spectacular musical, in-the-round productions, club and house competitions, while make-up and costume design are popular options at GCSE.

The extensive co-curricular provision is the cornerstone of the education ethos with many clubs and societies.

Prep. The newly purpose-built Prep building is a fabulous addition to Westholme now providing a truly unique through-school experience. Children aged 4–18 are wholeheartedly empowered with access to a plethora of superb facilities and academic opportunities provided by whole-school faculty leads. A rich co-curricular provision enables children to develop 21st century skills as well-rounded young adults and progress into Seniors as articulate, confident and delightful individuals. There's no Prep like Westholme!

Senior. Westholme offers a warm family feel, academic rigour and an extensive holistic curriculum which is extensive in both breadth and depth. Our pupils are happy, foster intellectual curiosity, are independent learners and develop 21st century skills in a wide range of disciplines. Small class teaching is combined with an unsurpassed pastoral care where every pupil is known and valued. The progress of each pupil is carefully monitored by teaching staff, form tutors and Heads of Year and the school believes in a close partnership with parents. Most of the students continue their studies at INSPIRED Sixth Form as the culmination of our unrivalled holistic excellence.

INSPIRED Sixth Form. Students experience incomparable 1:1 support and guidance during every step of their INSPIRED Sixth Form journey to ensure each individual is motivated to reach their own exciting aspirations. Every member of the INSPIRED Sixth Form takes full advantage of the Westholme innovative leadership programme and develops invaluable skills for the 21st century workplace. We are absolutely elated to win the Independent School of the Year 2023 for our Careers programme and proud to receive national recognition for our excellent students' careers provision. Over 90% receive their first choice university and a significant number of students continue their further education at Oxbridge universities, studying Medicine and Law. As the highest-achieving Sixth Form in Lancashire, we are proud of our exceptional outcomes and our wonderfully well-rounded young adults make friends for life. Once a Westholmian – always a Westholmian!

Admission. While most children make transitions at typical points of Prep R, Year 7 or Year 12, this is by no means the binding rule as midstream entries are welcome at any point throughout the year providing the year group is not full. Due to demand for places, parents are advised to make an early application by completing a registration form online. Prospective parents are welcome to book appointments to meet the Principal and have a tour of the school. The Annual Open Evening is held on the first Thursday of October each year.

Transport. Private coaches run from Accrington, Blackburn, Bolton, Burnley, Colne, Chorley, Clitheroe, Darwen, Leyland, Preston, Standish, Ribble Valley, South Ribble, the Rossendale Valley and Wigan.

Fees per term (2023–2024). Senior: £4,550; Upper Prep: £3,535; Lower Prep: £3,405.

Academic scholarships are available for entry into Year 7 and Year 12 for students who demonstrate exceptional academic ability (4x8s and above at GCSE for Year 12) and a small number of means-tested bursaries are available.

Charitable status. Westholme School is a Registered Charity, number 526615. It exists for the education of children between the ages of 4 years and 18 years.

Governing Body:
Chairman: Mr B C Marsden, FCA
Vice Chairman: Mr P Forrest, MRICS, FCIOB
Mr D J Berry, BA, FCMA, MIBM
Mrs J Conlon, BSc Hons, MRICS
Ms H Crosby
Dr R Dobrashian, MBChB, FRCR
Mr O McCann, BA Hons
Mrs D Northin
Mrs L Robinson, BA Hons, MA (*Co-Opted*)
Mrs V Robinson-Hoy, BA Hons
Miss P Williamson

Clerk to the Governors: Mr J Backhouse, LLB Hons

***Principal*: Dr Richard Robson**, BA Hons, PGCE, MA, EdD

Commercial Director: Mrs Vivienne Davenport, MA Oxon

Deputy Head: Mrs Jude Gough, BA Hons, PGCE, MISTC

Deputy Head: Mrs Carla Hornby, BSc Hons

Windermere School

Patterdale Road, Windermere, The Lake District, Cumbria LA23 1NW
Tel: +44 (0)15394 46164
email: admissions@windermereschool.co.uk
website: www.windermereschool.co.uk
X/Twitter: @windermeresc
Facebook: @Windermereschool
Instagram: @windermereschool/
LinkedIn: /company/windermere-school-uk

A visit to Windermere School or a look at our website tells you this is a very special place indeed. Our stunning location has been the inspiration for world-famous artists, poets, and authors, a sanctuary and the antidote to congested city life, a fascination to scientists, a home for adventurers as well as part of the masterpiece of human creative genius that affords us UNESCO World Heritage status. It is a daily inspiration to every one of us fortunate enough to call it our school.

Schools are what we build together and the Windermere community is as special as the place itself. Every child is different, talented, and special and every child matters. Here their differences are respected, their talents developed and their individuality encouraged. Our staff are dedicated to bringing out the very best in everyone and our examination results, university destinations, and the confidence of our pupils bear testimony to this commitment.

The beauty of our location, expertise of our staff, and wealth of facilities are enhanced by our size. Windermere is a deliberately small school. Pupils are known and cherished for who they are, every family is a vital part of our community and the voices of everyone are heard. Our classes are small, our pupils are happy, our education is bespoke and the results are stunning.

It is a rare privilege to be part of a school with Windermere's history and potential and we would be delighted to welcome you and your family to our school.

Numbers. There are approximately 320 pupils in total. The Senior School has approximately 243 pupils, of whom around 40% are boarders. The size of the community has the advantage of providing a friendly atmosphere of understanding and fosters good staff-pupil relationships. Many members of the teaching staff hold additional qualifications in outdoor adventure.

Curriculum. The curriculum offered at Windermere School reflects the belief that students should be exposed to as many opportunities as possible and leave the school as well-rounded individuals. It is tailored to the needs of each child, with small class sizes. Each pupil is provided with a personal tutor that stays with them throughout their years at the school, to oversee work on a daily basis and act as an advocate. One-year and two-year GCSEs and IGCSEs are taken in Years 10 and 11. Sixth Form students undertake the internationally recognised International Baccalaureate Diploma or International Baccalaureate Careers Programme. Sixth Form students also have the opportunity to study BTEC Business.

There are qualified staff and programmes in place for Special Educational Needs, English as an Additional Language, and Gifted and Talented pupils.

Music, Art, and Drama play an important part in the life of the school. There are two choirs, and individual instruction leading to chamber groups and orchestra. Students are prepared for the written and practical music exams of the Associated Board of the Royal Schools of Music. The school participates in regional Music Festivals. The Central School of Speech and Drama and LAMDA's examinations are also taken in Speech and Drama. Art and Design Technology provide considerable scope and opportunity. The Art Studios contain facilities for History of Art and an Art History Library. Drama classes are included in the curriculum, and there are several productions staged each year.

Extracurricular activities. Windermere School's watersports centre, Hodge Howe, with over 160 metres of lakefront on the shores of Windermere, hosts a wide range of activities during the school's timetabled curriculum, and as part of the extra-curricular activity programme. The centre has accreditation from the Adventure Activities Licensing Authority, as well as being a Royal Yachting Association Training Centre. In 2018, the School was announced as a British Youth Sailing Recognised Club by the Royal Yachting Association for its race training. Windermere was the first school in the UK to be awarded this status.

There are traditional competitive sports teams in hockey, netball, tennis, athletics and more. Many students play for regional and national teams, as well as for the school.

Religion. The school is Christian in outlook and welcomes other denominations.

Boarding. There is a strong boarding tradition at Windermere School that benefits the whole school community. Each Boarding House has live-in staff supervised by a House Mistress or House Master. Each evening, academic staff oversee prep and are available for extra tuition and advice. There are weekend activities, we offer on-site activities along with staff-led excursions throughout the Lake District and beyond. It is a safe and caring extended family environment where pupils can excel both academically and personally.

Round Square. The School is a member of the international Round Square group of schools. Exchanges and Overseas Service Projects are regularly arranged between the schools involved in Australia, Canada, Germany, India, Switzerland, South Africa and USA and Brunei.

Infant and Junior School. The nearby Infant and Junior School is in the care of a Head, and takes boarders from age 8, along with day children up to Year 6. The Infant and Junior School is fully integrated with the Senior School giving continuity of teaching programmes and use of joint facilities.

Fees per term (2023–2024).

Average Day Fees per term (including lunch): Reception £3,251, Years 1–2 £3,731, Years 3–6 £5,519, Years 7–8 £6,318, Years 9–11 £7,012 Year 12 £7,134, Year 13 £10,701 for 2 terms only.

Average Weekly Boarding Fees: Years 3–6 £7,990, Years 7–8 £9,720, Years 9–11 £11,321, Year 12 £11,448, Year 13 £17,172 for 2 terms only.

Average Full Boarding Fees: Years 3–6 £8,720, Years 7–8 £10,700, Years 9–11 £12,825, Year 12 £12,955, Year 13 £19,433 for 2 terms only.

Discounts are available for Forces families eligible for the MOD Continuity of Education Allowance (CEA).

Charitable status. Windermere Educational Trust Limited is a Registered Charity, number 526973, with a mission to provide education of the highest quality.

Chair of Governors: Mr P Hogan

***Headmaster*: Mr F Thompson**, MA, MPhil Cantab, PGCE London, NPQH

Senior Deputy Head: Mrs J Overton
Deputy Head Academic: Mrs L Moses

Headteacher, Junior School: Mrs J Davies

Administrative Staff:
School Business Manager: Mrs S Ross
Head's PA: Mrs P Thistlewood
School Secretary: Mrs S Dougherty
Head of Admissions and International Recruitment: Mrs A Hennah

Wisbech Grammar School

Chapel Road, Wisbech, Cambridgeshire PE13 1RH

Tel: 01945 583631
01945 586750 Admissions
email: office@wisbechgrammar.com
website: www.wisbechgrammar.com
X/Twitter: @wisbechgrammar
Facebook: @wisbechgrammar
Instagram: @wisbech_grammar

See full entry in the **HMC** section, on **p. 393**.

The Yehudi Menuhin School

Stoke d'Abernon, Cobham, Surrey KT11 3QQ

Tel: 01932 864739
email: admin@menuhinschool.co.uk
website: www.menuhinschool.co.uk
X/Twitter: @menuhinschool
Facebook: @yehudimenuhinschool

The Yehudi Menuhin School was founded in 1963 by Lord Menuhin and is situated in beautiful grounds in the Surrey countryside, close to London and within easy reach of both Gatwick and Heathrow.

The School provides specialist music tuition in stringed instruments, piano and classical guitar for approximately 90 musically gifted boys and girls aged up to 19 and aims to enable them to pursue their love of music, develop their musical potential and achieve standards of performance at the highest level. The School also provides a broad education within a relaxed open community in which each individual can fully develop intellectual, artistic and social skills. We are proud that our pupils develop into dedicated and excellent musicians who will use their music to inspire and enrich the lives of others and into friendly, thinking individuals well equipped to contribute fully to the international community.

Music. At least half of each day is devoted to musical studies. Pupils receive a minimum of two one-hour lessons each week on their first study instrument and at least half an hour on their second study instrument. Supervised practice is incorporated into the daily programme ensuring that successful habits of work are formed. All pupils receive guidance in composition and take part in regular composers' workshops and concerts. Aural training and general musicianship studies are included in the music curriculum. To awaken feeling for good posture, training in Alexander Technique is provided. GCSE and A Level Music are compulsory core subjects for all pupils.

Regular opportunity for solo performance is of central importance to the musical activity of the School, and pupils also perform chamber music and with the String Orchestra. Concerts are given several times each week within the School and at a wide variety of venues throughout the United Kingdom and overseas. The most distinguished musicians have taught at the school, including Boulanger, Perlemuter, Rostropovich and Perlman. Lord Menuhin visited the school regularly. Selection of pupils is by stringent audition which seeks to assess musical ability and identify potential. Special arrangements are made for applicants from overseas, who account for around half of the School's pupils.

Since 2006, the School has a state-of-the-art Concert Hall seating 315 with outstanding acoustics, where concerts and outreach programmes are presented. Purpose-built Music Studios opened in September 2016.

Academic Studies and Sport. The curriculum is designed to be balanced and to do full justice to both the musical and the general education of each pupil. Academic studies including the understanding of art, literature and science are considered vital to the development of creative, intelligent and sensitive musicians. All classes are small with excellent opportunities for individual attention, and as a result GCSE and A Level examination grades are high. To broaden their artistic and creative talents, all pupils work in a wide variety of artistic media including painting, ceramics and textiles. Pupils from overseas with limited English receive an intensive course in the English Language from specialist teachers.

The extensive grounds with an indoor swimming pool allow plenty of scope for relaxation and sport, including tennis, dance, badminton, football, swimming and yoga.

An International Community. The international reputation of the School brings pupils from all over the world who find a happy atmosphere in a large musical community. Pupils are cared for by the resident House Staff and Nurse. Both boarding houses include a mixture of shared and single rooms, with single en-suites for the most senior pupils. Special attention is paid to diet with the emphasis on whole and fresh food.

Fees and Bursaries. All pupils fully resident in the UK are currently eligible for an Aided Place through the Music and Dance Scheme which is subsidised by the Department for Education (DfE). Parents pay a means-tested contribution to the school fees based on their gross income assessed on a scale issued by the DfE. After two calendar years pupils from overseas may be able to obtain support through the Music and Dance Scheme. Until that time they pay full fees, although the school has some bursary funds available to assist with fees for pupils until they become eligible for the Music and Dance Scheme.

Admission. Entry to the School is by rigorous music audition, and prospective pupils are auditioned at any time during the year. Candidates may audition at any age between 10 and 16.

Charitable status. The Yehudi Menuhin School is a Registered Charity, number 312010. It exists to provide musical and academic education for boys and girls.

President Emeritus: Daniel Barenboim, KBE
Co-President: Tasmin Little, OBE

Vice-Presidents:
Barbara R-D Fisher, OBE
The Hon Zamira Menuhin Benthall

Governors Emeritus:
Daniel Hodson
Anne Simor

Music Patrons:
Steven Isserlis, CBE
Robert Levin
Sir András Schiff

Governors:
Chairman: David Buckley
Vice-Chairman: Geoffrey Richards

Dominic Benthall	Andrew Hunter Johnston
Lord Norman Blackwell	John Pagella
George Bruell	Alice Phillips
Andrew Burton	Vanessa Richards
Kate Costeloe, CBE	Benedict Vanderspar
Hilary Cowan	Jonathan Willcocks
John Everett	

Staff:

***Headmaster*: Ben Gudgeon**, MA, BA, FRSA, AMusTCL

Director of Music: Ashley Wass
Director of Studies: David Bruce

Interim Bursar: Philippa Stanfield

Director of Development & External Relations: Gerald Carew

Director of Pastoral Care: Melanie Bloor-Black

Director of Staff & Boarding: Robin Harskin

Academic Staff:
Art and Craft: Pryanka Rana
Biology and Science:
Jenny Dexter
Karen Lyle
English & Drama: Alan Humm
French & German: Robin Harskin
German: Christiane Wagner-Tree
History:
Sarah Howell
Jeanne Rourke
Mathematics:
David Bruce
Sarah Lee

English as an Additional Language: Naomi Roberts
Japanese: Akiko Kubo
Chinese: Xiang Yun Bishop
Russian: Anna Wall
Philippa Brown (*Teaching Assistant*)
Swimming: Lucy Ashdown-Parkes
Yoga: Jennifer Garcia
Hannah Juliano
Dance: Katie Brewer

Music Staff:
Deputy Director of Music: Marco Galvani

Violin:
Boris Brovtsyn
Ning Kam
Boris Kucharsky
Sebastian Mueller
Akiko Ono
Alex Redington
Robin Wilson

Viola:
Louise Lansdown
Elliott Perks

Violin Assistants:
Gergana Raykova
Anna Ziman

Cello:
Matthijs Broersma
Alex Chaushian

Cello Assistant:
Eun Cho

Double Bass:
Caroline Emery

Guitar:
Richard Wright

Piano:
Ruth Nye, MBE
Anahit Chaushyan
Dinara Klinton

Piano Assistant:
Ayaka Shigeno

Piano Supporting Study:
Mariko Brown
John Turville
Alexis White

Harpsichord:
Carole Cerasi

Harp:
Keziah Thomas

Staff Pianists:
Nigel Hutchison
Miho Kawashima
Edward Leung

Choir:
David Condry

Composition:
John Cooney

General Music:
Freddie Meyers
Matthew Taylor

Alexander Technique:
Fuensanta Zambrana-Ruiz

Junior Menuhins Staff:
Junior Menuhins Lead: Suzanne Evans
Little Menuhins tutor: Aaliyah Booker
Little Menuhins Project Assistant: Catherine Lett

VMS (*Virtual Menuhin School*) *Staff*:
VMS Piano Tutor: Ron Abramski
VMS Violin Tutor: Alison Stringer
VMS Musicianship Tutor: Frank Zielhorst

Pastoral Staff:
Housemaster, Harris House: Robin Harskin
Housemistress, Music House: Melanie Bloor-Black
Assistant Housemaster: Bertie Duncan
Assistant Housemistress: Victoria Hiscock
School Nurse: Pollyanna Richardson,
Day Matron: Nikki Davies
Resident Music Assistant: Stuart Bramwell
Resident Boarding Assistant: Niamh Poole
Boarding Assistant: Steve Black
Boarding Assistant: Tony Chipps

Support Staff:
Registrar and Head's PA: Cheryl Poole
Head of Concerts and Artistic Engagement: Tamas Reti
Music Studies Co-ordinator: Catharine Whitnall
School Office Manager: Lesley Moon
Receptionist: Adele Hunt
Examinations Officer: Jeanne Rourke
Partnership & Outreach Officer: Keelan Carew

Bursary:
Assistant Bursar (*Estates*): Gerry Vermeulen
Business Development Co-ordinator: Niamh Poole
Accounts Assistant: Helen Rendell
IT Support Assistant: Vacancy
HR Administrator: Gemma Lawrence
Commercial Manager: Thomas Gerstenmeyer

External Relations:
Head of Individual Giving: Marion Chow
Trusts and Foundations Manager: Vacancy
Fundraising and Events Administrator: Maria Porter
Head of Marketing and Communications: Christine Brown
Marketing and Communications Assistant: Rosie McCance

Estates:
Estates Supervisor: Brian Harris
Estates Caretaker: Brendan Marshall
Estates Groundsman: Jack Heaslewood
Science Lab Technician: Kerry-Louise Fenn

Catering:
Head Chef: Samuel Bartlett
Weekend Chef: Jo Busby
Sous Chef: Vacancy
Lunchtime Assistant: Julie-Ann Sage

Housekeeping:
Cleaning supervisor: Nikki Davies
Cleaner: Irma Barbosa
Cleaner: Pedro Barbosa
Cleaner: Julian Bell
Cleaner: Tracy Bell
Cleaner: Susan Eyre

Menuhin Hall:
Visitor Experience Supervisor: Nic Belfrage
Production Manager: Jon Griffin
Menuhin Hall Technician: Will Hallworth-Cook
Box Office Assistant: Lindsay Bould
Front of House: Anna Larson
Front of House: Adrian Whyte

The Society of Heads

Alliance Members UK

Berkhamsted Boys School, Berkhamsted, Herts
email: enquiries@berkhamsted.com
website: www.berkhamsted.com/boys

King's Ely, Cambs
email: reception@kingsely.org
website: www.kingsely.org

Kingswood House School, Epsom, Surrey
email: office@kingswoodhouse.org
website: www.kingswoodhouse.org

The Royal School, Wolverhampton, West Midlands
email: info@theroyal.school
website: https://theroyalschool.co.uk

Alliance Members Overseas

Brummana High School, Brummana, Lebanon
email: info@bhs.edu.lb
website: www.bhs.edu.lb

International Christian School, Hong Kong
website: www.ics.edu.hk

Jeddah Prep and Grammar School, Jeddah, Saudi Arabia
email: hmsec@jpgs.org
website: https://jpgs.org

King's College International School, Bangkok, Thailand
email: info@kingsbangkok.ac.th
website: www.kingsbangkok.ac.th/en

Leerwijzer School, Oostduinkerke, Belgium
email: info@leerwijzer.be
website: www.leerwijzer.be

Nymphenburger Schulen, München, Germany
email: sekretariat@nymphenburger-schulen.de
website: www.nymphenburger-schulen.de

Peponi School, Ruiru, Kenya
email: office@peponischool.org
website: www.peponischool.org

St Andrew's Senior School, Turi, Molo, Kenya
email: officesenior@turimail.co.ke
website: www.standrewsturi.com

St George's International School, Luxembourg
email: info@st-georges.lu
website: www.st-georges.lu

The English International School, Baghdad
website: https://eis.edu.iq

The English School of Kyrenia
email: info@englishschoolkyrenia.org
website: www.englishschoolkyrenia.com

The Junior and Senior School, Nicosia
website: www.tjss.ac.cy

The Roman Ridge School, Accra, Ghana
email: enquiries@theromanridgeschool.com
website: www.theromanridgeschool.com

PART IV
Schools whose Heads are members of the Independent Association of Prep Schools

ALPHABETICAL LIST OF SCHOOLS

IAPS
GEOGRAPHICAL LIST OF SCHOOLS

The following schools, whose Heads are members of both IAPS and HMC, can be found in the HMC section:

The Abbey
Bedales School
Bromley High School
Bryanston School
Campbell College
The Cathedral School Llandaff
Dulwich College
Elizabeth College
Eltham College
Farringtons School
Frensham Heights
Gordonstoun
Hill House School
Immanuel College
King Henry VIII School
King's Ely
The King's School, Macclesfield
The King's School Worcester Foundation
Latymer Upper School & Latymer Prep School
The Grammar School at Leeds
Lincoln Minster School
Magdalen College School
Moreton Hall
Mount Kelly
Nottingham High School
Plymouth College
Pocklington School
The Portsmouth Grammar School
Queen Elizabeth Grammar School
Ratcliffe College
Rendcomb College
Repton School
Royal Grammar School, Newcastle upon Tyne
St Edmund's School Canterbury
Solihull School
The Stephen Perse Foundation
Strathallan School
Wellingborough School
West Buckland School
Wisbech Grammar School
Wolverhampton Grammar School

The following schools, whose Heads are members of both IAPS and GSA, can be found in the GSA section:

Abbot's Hill School
Blackheath High School
Channing School
Harrogate Ladies' College
North London Collegiate School
Notting Hill and Ealing High School
Pipers Corner School
Queen's College, London
The Royal High School Bath
St Catherine's School, Bramley
St Mary's School, Colchester
Sheffield High School for Girls
Sydenham High School
Tormead School
Wimbledon High School

The following schools, whose Heads are members of both IAPS and The Society of Heads, can be found in the Society of Heads section:

Bournemouth Collegiate School
Clifton High School
Kingsley School
Newcastle School for Boys
St Gabriel's
St Joseph's College
Scarborough College

The following schools, whose Heads are members of both IAPS and ISA, can be found in the ISA section:

Ballard School
Belmont School
Cranford House
Duke of Kent School
Queen Ethelburga's Collegiate

IAPS Member Heads and Deputy Heads

Individual School Entries

The Abbey

Kendrick Road, Reading RG1 5DZ

Tel: 0118 987 2256
email: schooloffice@theabbey.co.uk
website: www.theabbey.co.uk
X/Twitter: @theabbeyschool
Facebook: @theabbeyschoolberkshire
Instagram: @theabbeyschoolreading
LinkedIn: /company/the-abbey-school-reading

See full entry in the **HMC** section, on **p. 7**.

Abbot's Hill School

Bunkers Lane, Hemel Hempstead, Herts HP3 8RP

Tel: 01442 240333
email: registrar@abbotshill.herts.sch.uk
website: www.abbotshill.herts.sch.uk
X/Twitter: @AbbotsHill
Facebook: @AbbotsHillSchool
LinkedIn: /abbot's-hill

See full entry in the **GSA** section, on **p. 418**.

Abercorn School

Lower School
28 Abercorn Place, London NW8 9XP

Tel: 020 7286 4785
email: lower@abercornschool.com

Senior School
60 Paddington Street, London W1U 4JA

Tel: 020 7723 8700
email: senior@abercornschool.com
website: www.abercornschool.com
X/Twitter: @abercornschool
Facebook: @abercornschool
Instagram: @abercornschool

Founder & High Mistress: Mrs Andrea Greystoke, BA Hons

***Headmaster*: Mr Christopher Hammond**

Age Range. 2 to 14+ Co-educational.

Number of Pupils. 300.

Fees per term (2023–2024). £3,670–£8,190. Fees include all extras, apart from lunch and school transport.

Since 1987, Abercorn School has proudly offered children from the age of 2 to 14 years the perfect balance of a rigorous academic curriculum, delivered in a warm and nurturing environment in central London.

The school has gained an enviable record of achievement for both boys and girls graduating at 11+ and 13+. We guide both pupils and parents through the education process to ensure our pupils attain the highest standard and meet their potential. From September 2022, Abercorn will be accepting Year 9 pupils, with the capacity to expand to Year 11 and beyond.

The children are continuously evaluated, supported and challenged in order to foster their individual talents and skills. We are firm believers in traditional values and standards, including excellent pastoral care. However, we are committed to embracing the best of what the 21st century offers, and preparing each child to face the challenges of the modern world with confidence and competence.

Happiness is an essential prerequisite to the acquisition of knowledge. At Abercorn learning is serious but fun!

'Pupils are extremely well prepared for the responsibilities, opportunities and experiences of the next chapter of their lives.' *Independent Schools Inspectorate 2018.*

Discover Abercorn, discover their future.

Aberdour School

Brighton Road, Burgh Heath, Tadworth, Surrey KT20 6AJ

Tel: 01737 354119
email: enquiries@aberdourschool.co.uk
website: www.aberdourschool.co.uk
X/Twitter: @aberdourschool
Instagram: @aberdour_preparatory_school
LinkedIn: /company/aberdour-school

The School is an Educational Trust run by a Board of Governors. Founded in 1928, Aberdour is a thriving and extremely successful preparatory school for 360 girls and boys aged 2 to 11 years old. At all levels, we aim to provide every child with an individually tailored education that identifies their potential and maximises their opportunities to learn, grown and succeed. Finding the brilliance in every child.

Chairman of the Governors: Mr D Davie, MSc Dist, MBCS

***Headmaster*: Mr S D Collins**, CertEd

Deputy Head: Mrs E Hoskins, BSc Hons
Head of Middle School: Mrs S Couper, BA Hons, QTS
Head of Pre-Prep: Mrs A Terry, BA Hons

Age Range. 2–11.

Number of Pupils. 338 Day Boys and Girls.

Fees per term (2023–2024). £1,810–£6,030 inclusive.

Children can start from 2 years old in Nursery, which is part of our brand new Pre-Prep Department (opened

September 2023) and transfer to Middle School, which comprises Years 2 and 3 (ages 6 to 7). Senior School follows, which includes Years 4, 5 and 6 (ages 8 to 11). Children are prepared for all the major 11+ senior schools and many scholarships have been won. This last academic year, pupils in Year 6 gained 61 scholarships to independent senior schools. Set within 12 acres, there are ample playing fields, climbing wall, two all-weather areas, a large sports hall and indoor heated swimming pool. There are two science laboratories, a design technology room and an Arts & Innovation Centre with a STEAM room, languages studio, classrooms, music rooms, VR and Creativity studio and dance studios. All the usual games are coached and the general character of the children is developed by many interests and activities.

Charitable status. Aberdour School Educational Trust Limited is a Registered Charity, number 312033. Its aim is to promote education.

Aldro

Lombard Street, Shackleford, Godalming, Surrey GU8 6AS

Tel: 01483 813530 (Headmaster)
01483 813535 (Admissions)
01483 810266 (School Office)
email: hmsec@aldro.org
website: www.aldro.org
X/Twitter: @AldroSchool
Facebook: @AldroSchool
Instagram: @aldroschool

Chairman of the Governors: Mr J B H Geffen

***Headmaster*: Mr Chris Carlier**, MA Oxon, MEd, PGCE

Age range. 7–13.

Number of pupils. 237: 66 boarders, 171 day pupils.

Fees per term (2023–2024). Boarding: Form 3 £9,260, Form 4 £10,210, Forms 5–8 £10,365. Day: Form 3 £6,880, Form 4 £7,830, Forms 5–8 £7,985.

Aldro is a co-ed independent day and boarding prep school set in a beautiful rural location yet within a mile of the A3 and 45 minutes of central London, Gatwick and Heathrow airports.

Aldro aims to offer an exceptional all-round education in a happy, purposeful community. It has a Christian foundation and this underpins the values and ethos of the school. Each school day starts with a short service in the lovely Chapel, beautifully converted from an eighteenth-century barn.

The school is fortunate in having a spacious site including a lake and about 20 acres of playing fields. We have our own rowing lake, the new sports centre, four all-weather tennis courts, brand new netball court, two shooting ranges, swimming pool and a croquet lawn. The Centenary Building opened in 2000 and houses most of the classrooms, the CIL centre, an outstanding library and, in the basement, changing rooms and a large common room. The Crispin Hill Centre incorporates a Music School and Theatre. Two science laboratories and the Art and Design & Technology Centre have been developed in eighteenth century buildings either side of the Chapel. The Argyle Building including a new dining hall and kitchen was opened in late 2003. The dormitories in the main building have recently been refurbished. The boarders enjoy high-quality pastoral care and a varied programme of activities in the evenings and at weekends.

In the classroom, there is a balance between the best traditional and modern approaches, while firm and friendly encouragement of each individual has led to an outstanding academic record of success at Common Entrance and Scholarship level. Many academic awards have been won in the last four years (2019 being a record breaking year) to leading schools such as Charterhouse, Eton, Sherborne, Winchester, Radley, Tonbridge and Wellington College.

Aldro is committed to giving pupils real breadth to their education and much emphasis is placed on extracurricular activities. There are many opportunities for the arts, with a good record of success in Art and Music scholarships – 20 awards have been won in the past four years. An astounding 85% of our children learn musical instruments and there are three choirs, brass group, and numerous more ensembles. Drama also features prominently with several productions each year.

The major sports are football, netball, rugby and hockey in the winter, with cricket, tennis and swimming in the summer. Athletics, cross-country running, sailing and shooting are secondary sports and high standards are achieved. A huge range of activities are available including badminton, ballet, croquet, dodge ball, pioneers and pétanque. The school has an enviable record for Chess with 9 teams winning National championships in the past six years.

Pupils at Aldro are treated as individuals with talents to develop. They lead cheerful and purposeful lives, and are well-prepared for a wide range of leading senior schools.

There is a focus on excellence and achievement, whether that is in the classroom, music room or on the sports field. Aldro prepares children for the rest of their lives.

Charitable status. Aldro School Educational Trust Limited is a Registered Charity, number 312072. It exists to provide education for boys and girls.

Aldwickbury School

Wheathampstead Road, Harpenden, Herts AL5 1AD

Tel: 01582 713022
email: office@aldwickbury.org.uk
website: www.aldwickbury.org.uk
X/Twitter: @aldwickbury
Facebook: @aldwickburyschool
Instagram: @aldwickburyschool
LinkedIn: /school/aldwickbury-school

Chair of Governors: J Bromfield, MBE, BA, PGCE

***Headmaster*: P Symes**, BSc Hons Brunel

Deputy Head: C Schanschieff, BSc Hons Exeter

Age Range. 4–13.

Number of Boys. 385.

Fees per term (2023–2024). Day Boys: Pre-Prep £4,925–£5,285, Years 3–8 £5,815–£6,565. Flexi-Boarding Fee: £48.50 per night.

Aldwickbury is a day and flexi-boarding school for boys set in 20 acres on the outskirts of Harpenden in Hertfordshire.

At the heart of the Aldwickbury community lies our belief that pastoral care should form the bedrock for academic success. Every boy is nurtured and encouraged to try their best, embrace challenge and most importantly; be kind.

We allow them to flourish as individuals in an environment that challenges and stimulates them whatever their interests, passions or talents. Our teaching mixes traditional approaches together with modern ideas and methods. We aim to equip all the boys with the skills to be happy and confident, build relationships with their peers and staff and develop strategies for coping with the challenges life presents.

The breadth of opportunities on offer at Aldwickbury is something we are incredibly proud of. The boys are challenged and engaged academically but also benefit from a wide-ranging co-curricular programme making full use of our extensive grounds and facilities. The school offers boys of all abilities a myriad of exciting opportunities to develop their confidence and unearth their talents in the arts, STEM, on stage, in music and on the sports field.

The journey through the school prepares the boys to leave at 13 when we believe they are truly ready for senior school education. The boys move onto a wide range of senior schools, both day and boarding. The recent results at Common Entrance, entry tests and scholarships have been a reflection on the excellent teaching that the boys receive. In 2023 all 33 of our Year 8 leavers were offered a place at their first choice of senior school and 12 boys were awarded scholarships.

The maximum class size for Pre-Prep is 16 and 18 for Years 3–8. Wraparound care is available in the form of breakfast and after-school clubs and flexi-boarding is also available from Year 5 upwards.

The school has excellent facilities based around a large Victorian House. Purpose-built teaching blocks, including a modern self-contained Pre-Prep department, ensure that the education is of a high standard. Other facilities include an indoor swimming pool, tennis courts and playing fields.

Over the last ten years, there has been extensive redevelopment of the school's facilities, including a new hall complex, a new music department, refurbishment of the science labs, total renovation of the Coach House providing a new Art and DT department, and a makeover of the boarding house. A new £4 million sports centre was completed in Autumn 2022 and a new building with additional science labs, an ICT suite and multi-use classroom was completed in September 2023 to further enhance the facilities and demonstrate our curriculum commitment to STEAM subjects (science, technology, engineering, arts and maths).

The school continues to invest in its facilities to create the best possible learning environment for the boys and plans for the next development project are underway.

Charitable status. Aldwickbury School Trust Ltd is a Registered Charity, number 311059. It exists to provide education for children.

All Hallows School

Cranmore Hall, East Cranmore, Somerset BA4 4SF

Tel: 01749 881600 (School Office)
01749 881609 (Admissions)

email: admissions@allhallowsschool.co.uk

website: www.allhallowsschool.co.uk

X/Twitter: @AllHallowsSch

Facebook: @allhallowssch

Instagram: @allhallowssch

LinkedIn: /all-hallows-cranmore-hall-school-trust-limited

***Head*: Dr Trevor Richards**, CPsychol

Age range. 3–13 Co-educational.

Number of pupils. 240: 134 Boys, 106 Girls.

Fees per term (2023–2024): Full Boarding (all years): £9,900 per term. Weekly Boarding: £8,640 per term.
Nursery: £60 per day, Reception: £3,275 per term, Years 1 and 2: £3,365 per term, Year 3: £5,455 per term, Year 4: £5,845 per term, Years 5 and 6: £6,255 per term, Years 7 and 8: £6,545 per term.

Ethos and values

All Hallows Prep is a well-established school which forms part of the Monkton Family of Schools. This allows All Hallows the independence to lead an education framework which is believed to give children the best start of their education, as well as the security that comes from being part of a larger collective of schools. All Hallows is dedicated to nurturing the all-round development of every child within the school.

The school's vision and ethos have always revolved around the inspiration of young minds, empowering them to unlock their full potential. Our approach places a strong emphasis on happiness and wellbeing, serving as the cornerstone of our educational philosophy.

Carving their own curriculum

The school maintains high academic standards across a diverse spectrum of subjects, with a strong emphasis on experiential learning, whether in the classroom or outdoors. A passionate staff team collaborates closely with parents to prepare children for the ever-evolving world they are destined to grow up in. Starting from Nursery age and beyond, pupils have access to a vast and diverse curriculum. Pupils can explore creative design through robotics, acquire survival skills in Forest School, engage in swimming lessons, explore music, learn modern foreign languages, and build strong foundations in traditional core subjects such as English, Maths and Science. All Hallows values the input of its pupils, who have a voice in shaping the curriculum and campus.

Extensive focus on co-curricular

All Hallows offers a wide array of co-curricular opportunities through an extensive after-school and Saturday enrichment programme. This programme includes activities like clay-pigeon shooting, swimming lessons, tennis coaching, drama productions, Forest School sessions, art workshops and creative design lessons, golf and music, among others. It's a school supporting children in discovering their unique interests and passions, encouraging them to embrace their individuality, creativity, and what makes them unique.

Boarding at its best

Our family-orientated boarding house is dedicated to creating a positive and welcoming home-away-from-home. The school offers a blended approach to boarding, accommodating both full-time boarders and day pupils, enriching the All Hallows experience for all. Supported by parents and an experienced residential team, children can settle into boarding life, have fun, build lasting friendships, and enjoy their childhood, all while experiencing the independence of living away from home. With an average of 40 boarders at any given time, boarders quickly get to know one another as well as their boarding parent, supporting them so they quickly feel at home.

All Hallows' extensive and diverse programme of weekend trips, including activities like hosting their own 'mini Glastonbury Festival', sailing at the UKSA, visits to the historic city of Bath, attending local sports matches, ice-skating day trips and so much more, ensures there's something for everyone to look forward to, fostering the growth of their boarding family and ensuring lifelong memories.

Nursery and Reception – building foundations

Our All Hallows Early Years Foundation Stage (EYFS) Nursery and Reception classes are ideally situated side by side at the heart of the school. These dedicated indoor and outdoor spaces provide children with a joyful, calm, safe, stimulating and fun environment. By being part of a prep school, our children benefit from access to specialist teaching staff in subjects such as Music, Art, Forest School, Sports and Activities. They also have access to all prep school resources and facilities, including All Hallows' nine-acre woodland for Forest School, on-site Tennis Academy, Creative Design Centre, swimming pool, and various music and sports facilities. The School's teaching approach is rooted in a play-based curriculum, guided by children's interests, supplemented by adult-led activities drawing upon specialist expertise, ensuring the best possible outcomes through a holistic approach.

Sports – excelling both on and off the pitch

All Hallows has a rich tradition of regional and national sporting success, both as a team and at an individual level. The school's commitment lies in achieving excellence within a 'sport for all' framework. Tennis, in particular, holds a special place at All Hallows, with strong connections to the Tennis Performance Centre at Bath University. Most children engage in traditional team sports at least three to four times a week, with many participating in the Somerset Development Pathway. All Hallows offers a Saturday fixtures and training programme for those in Year 3 and above, allowing pupils to compete against various independent schools across the South-West.

Impressive facilities

The school boasts generous facilities, including a brand-new, all-weather Astro pitch, extensive sports grounds, a 6-acre Forest School, Creative Design Centre, Art Workshop, Swimming Pool, Tennis Academy and a Sports Hall, to name just a few. This, combined with small class sizes and a network of experienced teachers, provides the best possible foundations for your child's education.

Supporting every step of the way

All Hallows recognises that choosing the right school for your child can be a challenging decision. The School offers support every step of the way, ensuring that each parent's choice aligns with both their child's needs and the school's values.

The decision of moving on to a senior school can have a profound impact on children's lives. As part of the Monkton Family of Schools, while preserving independence, All Hallows offers valuable guidance and support to help you select the most suitable senior school for your child, whether this be Monkton Senior, or further afield. Children who move on to their chosen senior schools leave All Hallows confident and well prepared to embrace the opportunities that lie ahead.

Alleyn's Junior School

Townley Road, Dulwich, London SE22 8SU

Tel: 020 8557 1519
email: juniorregistration@alleyns.org.uk
website: www.alleyns.org.uk
X/Twitter: @Alleyns_Junior
Instagram: @alleyns_junior

Chair of Governors: Mrs L Malkin

***Head*: Mr Simon Severino**, MA Hons, PGCE

Registrar: Mrs Felicity Thomas

Age Range. 4–11.

Number of Pupils. 296 boys and girls.

Fees per term (2023–2024). £7,650 including lunches, most clubs, out of school visits and one residential trip per year for Years 3–6.

Alleyn's is a selective, co-educational school and we attract families and children from diverse backgrounds with a range of personalities, talents and interests which need to be met. So, we aim to create an environment for each child to achieve their best academic progress by developing the children's sense of confidence. To this end we offer small class sizes in a well-structured school where teachers work towards creating a calm, purposeful and vibrant atmosphere, so that high levels of participation are possible for all children.

Diverse interests and talents should be nurtured outside the classroom too. So, there is a wealth of co-curricular opportunities for pupils to develop their individual strengths and passions. With over one hundred clubs each term to choose from, the children can explore new interests, learn new skills, mix with different children and develop new passions.

Bright children with bright futures need to have opportunities to develop a sense of team spirit and to take individual responsibility for themselves and for others. The school's pastoral care is supported by a strong house system that extends from Reception all the way through the school to Year 6. Our children love their school very much and this is because the relationships they have with each other, as well as with their teachers, are mutually supportive.

Alleyn's has a wonderful history that we cherish along with a desire to remain at the forefront of education. We aim to prepare our children for the demands of an ever-changing society and world. The school's origins can be traced back to Edward Alleyn in 1619 who was arguably the most famous Shakespearean actor of the Elizabethan age. From its origins, Alleyn's has continued to create a school where children and teachers respect each other in a friendly, safe and happy environment. In doing this we lay the foundations for future personal and academic fulfilment.

Charitable status. Alleyn's School is a Registered Charity, number 1161864, and a Charitable Company Limited by Guarantee, registered in England and Wales, number 09401357. Registered office: Townley Road, London SE22 8SU.

Alpha Preparatory School

21 Hindes Road, Harrow, Middlesex HA1 1SH
Tel: 020 8427 1471
email: sec@alpha.harrow.sch.uk
website: www.alpha.harrow.sch.uk

Chair of the Board of Governors: Ms K Brookes

***Headmaster*: Mr Pádraic Fahy**

Age range. 3–11.

Number of pupils. 140 boys and girls (day only).

Fees per term (2023–2024). Inclusive of lunch, with no compulsory extras: Nursery: £1,857–£3,000; Reception to Year 2: £4,209; Years 3 to 6: £4,638.

The School, situated in a residential area of Harrow, was founded in 1895, and in 1950 was reorganised as a non-profit-making Educational Charity, with a Board of Governors elected by members of the Company; parents of pupils in the School are eligible for membership.

The children enter Reception at the age of 4 by an informal, 'light-touch' assessment in November the year before entry. Should a space be available in Year 1 to Year 6, your child will be invited to spend time with their potential class group and will also meet a range of staff and sit an English and maths assessment.

The Alpha Community consists of a team of experienced and qualified staff members, happy children and supportive parents. We offer specialist teaching in music, languages, computing, PE and games (from Nursery), and English and maths in preparation for 11+. Alpha also offer peripatetic music lessons in guitar, violin, clarinet, flute, piano and drums, not to mention our choirs and a select Ensemble Band. Our Games Department have been successful in football, cricket, netball, swimming galas and rounders. Other sporting events consist of a wonderful cross-country meet, athletics, tennis and basketball House Competitions.

Our enhanced curriculum, alongside our before- and after-school clubs, prepares our children to be active, engaged and enthusiastic towards their learning, their progression and their development, placing each and every one of them in good stead to be independent and forward-thinking individuals of the future. In fact, the children have described our approach to the curriculum in the following way: '*Whether it is the explosions of volcanoes in science or the calming music in art, the staff provide a variety of opportunities to discover, making it a fun, positive and enjoyable learning environment. Ideas are shared in lessons and everyone is included...*' Innovative ideas are created by the staff to suit each particular age group. Our curriculum ignites a hunger for learning and the potential to achieve. Kindness pervades the school, giving the pupils both the reason and power to show compassion.

Over the past two years or so, Alpha's extracurricular offerings have increased and the children now have quite an eclectic mix of activities from which to choose. For example, judo, cookery club, street dance, musical theatre, scrabble, ballet, yoga, board games club, Lego club, science documentary club and sign language club, to name but a few. All of our before- and after-school activities enhance our broad, independent and forward-thinking curriculum.

Religious Education is non-sectarian in nature, and follows upon the School's Christian foundation and tradition by using the nationally recognised 'Jigsaw' PSHE resources. Children of all faiths are accepted at Alpha and our one school rule is to 'Be kind!'

Outside visits to theatres and museums form an integral part of the curriculum and, during the Lent Term, pupils in Year 6 visit the Isle of Wight for a week's residential. In March 2022, Alpha completed a highly successful music tour to France where 41 children performed for dignitaries and for French school children, and they were the first primary school children ever to perform in Notre Dame, Laon, a tremendous achievement. Years 5 and 6 are hoping to go on a Residential Music Trip to Spain in the Lent Term 2024.

Excellent successes are obtained in entrance and scholarship examinations, with 12 scholarships being awarded to the Class of 2023. Alpha is a small school, but it is mighty in achievement and success!

Alpha Preparatory School is proud to have its own Nursery, called Alphabets, on site for children aged 3+.

Further details can be obtained from our friendly Office Team by contacting us on 0208 427 1471 or emailing us on sec@alpha.harrow.sch.uk

Charitable status. Alpha Preparatory School is a Registered Charity, number 312640, existing to carry on the undertaking of a co-educational preparatory school in Harrow in the County of Middlesex.

Altrincham Preparatory School

Marlborough Road, Bowdon, Altrincham, Cheshire WA14 2RR
Tel: 0161 928 3366
email: admin@altprep.co.uk
website: www.altprep.co.uk
Facebook: @altprep
Instagram: @altrinchampreparatoryschool

***Headmaster*: Mr N Vernon**
Deputy Head (*Academic*): Mrs H Finnie
Deputy Head (*Pastoral*) : Mrs C Finch
Head of Educational Operations : Mrs A Stewart

Age Range. 2+ to 11.

Number of pupils. 278 Day Boys.

Fees per term (2023–2024). £2,867–£3,743.

With an engaging curriculum designed to capture the imaginations of its boys and a reputation for outstanding academic, musical and sporting achievements, Altrincham Preparatory School is widely regarded as one of the very best schools for 2–11 year olds in the North-West.

Altrincham Preparatory School believes in delivering academic excellence; its boys go on to some of the best selective grammar schools in the region, including Altrincham Grammar School and The Manchester Grammar School. Yet while recent examination results are hugely impressive, Altrincham Preparatory School is also a music school, an arts and technology school and a sports school. The culture of participation means the boys want to be part of everything and two full-time specialist PE teachers have guided the boys to national finals in a range of sports.

Altrincham Preparatory School was successfully inspected by the Independent Schools Inspectorate in May 2023, receiving the highest grading of 'Excellent' for both the pupils' academic achievement and the pupils' personal development. The school was also found to be compliant in all areas of the inspection. The pupils demonstrate an excellent attitude to learning and show strong self-confidence, perseverance and motivation. The inspection team recognised that the 'pupils are achieving highly compared to national standards' and are 'academically well prepared for entry to their future school'. Pastoral care is at the heart of everything the school does and it is 'successful in building a community which encourages all its members to develop a healthy respect for each other'.

Altrincham Preparatory School is committed to providing such high-quality education in a happy, safe and state-of-the-art environment. The Early Years Foundation Stage Centre at Bank Place opened in 2015 with a beautiful 16-place Nursery for boys aged 2 and above feeding into the Pre-School. Boys there are able to access the adjacent Bell Field for outdoor exploration, while the use of Bowdon Cricket, Hockey and Squash club's facilities means games can take place on high-quality artificial and grass surfaces. With bright, well-equipped and attractive classrooms, Altrincham Preparatory School is welcoming, nurturing, and most important of all, happy.

Amesbury

Hazel Grove, Hindhead, Surrey GU26 6BL

Tel: 01428 604322
email: L.Turner@amesburyschool.co.uk
website: www.amesburyschool.co.uk
Facebook: @amesburyschoolhindhead
Instagram: @amesburyschool

Chair of Governors: Karen Davies

***Head*: Gavin Franklin**

Age Range. 9 months–13 years.

Number of Pupils. 349.

Fees per term (2023–2024). Prep School: £5,725–£6,610; Pre-Prep & Reception: £4,275–£4,320; Early Years (Babies, Pre-Nursery & Nursery): please visit website for details: www.amesburyschool.co.uk/admissions/fees/.

Amesbury is a co-educational day school founded in 1870 and is the only co-educational Prep school in the Hindhead/Haslemere area. The main building is unique, as the only school to be designed by Sir Edwin Lutyens, and stands in its own 34-acre estate in the heart of the Surrey countryside.

We are a family school, keen for siblings to study together and to feel equally valued irrespective of their aptitudes and abilities. There is no competitive entry. Entry is based on registration plus a visit – not a formal assessment but the opportunity for child and school to get acquainted.

Classes are small guaranteeing individual attention. Study programmes currently lead to senior school entrance and scholarship examinations at 11+ and at 13+. We have a proud tradition of academic, sporting and artistic achievement. The school has excellent purpose-built facilities with an award winning Visual Arts Facility which opened in September 2015 and a Library which opened in 2019.

We pride ourselves on sending children to the best senior schools in the country at both 11+ and 13+. Amesbury's academic record is excellent with an average of 20% of pupils receiving senior school scholarships. "Many a school may claim to be 'academically rigorous'. Not all would also make such a virtue out of also being 'relaxed' …this one does." (Good Schools Guide).

In addition to a compelling academic record, Amesbury has a thriving Performing Arts Department: "Music embraces everything from formal chapel choir to semi-secret bands formed each year, strutting stuff at annual concert. There's plentiful dance and drama including ambitious takes on Shakespeare" (Good Schools Guide). As for sport, the site is 34 acres, with an all-weather astro, indoor sports hall and an all-school tennis programme. Our Extra Curricular programme runs a whole host of activities including Judo, Golf, Chess, Music Technology, Drama and many more.

Amesbury understands its role as part of your family life. We believe weekends should be your time; there is no Saturday school and prep can be done at school. We offer Breakfast Club and After School Care. Our Pre-Nursery and Nursery offer early drop-offs, late pick-ups and holiday care.

ISI Inspection.

The last full ISI Inspection was in November 2018 some highlights are below. The last ISA Compliance Inspection was in July 2022 which was passed fully.

- The quality of the pupils' academic and other achievements is excellent.
- Pupils of all abilities make excellent progress during their time at school.
- Pupils are highly independent and confident communicators, who keenly articulate their views and opinions to enhance their learning.
- Pupils have extremely well-developed study skills and relish opportunities for analytical and hypothetical thinking in their learning.

- Pupils have outstanding attitudes to learning and enjoy the breadth of the curriculum.

The quality of the pupils' personal development is excellent:

- Pupils develop high levels of confidence and warmly embrace new challenge.
- Pupils speak passionately about all that the school provides and the strong support that staff provide.
- Pupils have excellent moral awareness and a mature understanding towards the importance of positive behaviour.
- Pupils' empathy towards the needs of their peers is exemplary.

Focused Compliance:

Eight standards are reviewed and the highest accolade one can hope for is that the school will be found to be compliant in all eight areas. Amesbury was found to be fully compliant.

Open Mornings take place in October, February and May.

Charitable status. Amesbury School is a Registered Charity, number 312058. It exists to provide education for boys and girls. It is administered by a Board of Governors.

Ardvreck School

Crieff, Perthshire PH7 4EX

Tel: 01764 653112
email: office@ardvreckschool.co.uk
admissions@ardvreckschool.co.uk
website: www.ardvreckschool.co.uk
X/Twitter: @ArdvreckSchool
Facebook: @ArdvreckSchool
LinkedIn: /ardvreck-school

***Headmistress*: Mrs Ali Kinge**, BA, PGCE, BCAv

Chair of the Governors: Jeremy Garrett-Cox

Age Range. Co-educational 3–13.

Number of Pupils. 130. Main School: 30 Full Boarding, 20 Step-up Boarding, 60 day. Little Ardvreck 20

Fees per term (2023–2024). Main School: £10,520 (boarders), £7,020 (day); Little Ardvreck £3,350.

Ardvreck, an extraordinary boarding and day preparatory school, located in the heart of rural Perthshire and within an hour's reach of Glasgow and Edinburgh, offers a unique, educational experience to children from the age of 3 to 13.

Known for our sense of adventure and creativity, we are most definitely the school every grown-up wishes they had attended as a child. It's where kindness, courtesy and good manners are at the forefront of every human interaction. It's an environment where working hard and playing hard are of equal importance and where good humour and fun permeate every undertaking.

Our dedicated boarding house, Dalvreck, accommodates up to 70 boarders on any given night. Refurbished in 2020, Dalvreck House is filled with the latest technologies as well as many home comforts taking into account your children's suggestions and needs.

We see time as the most important currency for our boarders who are given the time to enjoy being children within our beautiful 40-acre estate and beyond into our extended "garden", the foothills of the highlands. The boarders at Dalvreck benefit from our sector-leading outdoor provision, together with the weekend and evening activities which brim with fun and inspiration.

We offer bespoke travel options which include chaperoned, direct trains from London to Gleneagles. Boarders can be escorted to and from Scottish airports; all necessary documentation can be handled by the School if required.

You will soon realise that we firmly believe classrooms do not need walls. As well as outdoor lessons, the entire school regularly adventures into the exciting, natural playground on our doorstep to undertake Barvicks (expeditions) and a regular Ard Challenge.

A modern and well-equipped Music School provides the best possible opportunities for music-making. There is an orchestra, choir and pipe band, all of which regularly participate in both school and local music events. Music and drama play an important part in the life of the school and a major production is staged annually with several smaller productions and numerous concerts taking place throughout the year.

There is a heated, indoor swimming pool (all children are taught to swim), an Astroturf surface for hockey, tennis and netball, and a superb sports hall.

This is not just a school; this is Ardvreck School. Here the children are prepared to be resilient and well equipped, with a daring spirit to succeed and to overcome anything that is thrown at them on their life journeys; they are courageous pioneers.

We burst with pride at each speech day when we celebrate the achievements of the children whose lives we have helped shape. They are happy, well-rounded and fulfilled children who are full of hope and ambition for their futures. It will come as no surprise then, that Head Teachers from public schools all over the UK are very keen to enlist Ardvreck pupils. Since 2019, 82% of our pupils have been awarded scholarships to a total of 27 of senior schools across the UK, including Eton and St Mary's, Ascot. Our pupils have secured scholarships for Music, Sport, Academic, Drama and Art to name a few.

Ardvreck has an unbelievable team of staff; they are the movers and shakers, optimists, can-doers, smilers and, above all, all care about the education and wellbeing of every single child in our school.

Financial assistance is available through means-tested bursaries.

Charitable status. Registered Charity, number SC009886.

Arnold House School

1 Loudoun Road, St John's Wood, London NW8 0LH
Tel: 020 7266 4840
email: office@arnoldhouse.co.uk
website: www.arnoldhouse.co.uk

Chair of the Board of Governors: Sumita Honey

***Headmaster*: G F Tollit**

Age Range. 3–13.

Number of Boys. 370 (Day Boys only).

Fees per term (2023–2024) Reception to Year 8 £8,311, Pre-Reception £7,480.

Arnold House School was founded in 1905 in St John's Wood, London. It is an independent preparatory school for boys aged 3–13, and a member of IAPS. A thriving school, with 350 boys, Arnold House aims to provide an education of breadth and excellence and to serve the boys' best interests across the ability range. The School aims to do so in a supportive, purposeful and stimulating environment, to provide a foundation for the boys' development within a generous Christian ethos, to help them mature into well-rounded individuals by developing their enjoyment of music, the arts and sport, and to promote good citizenship through the virtues of courtesy and industry.

The school works across three sites including 7 acres of playing fields at Canons Park, which also houses a 150-seat auditorium. More recently, the School acquired 38 Marlborough Place (The Huxley Building) in St John's Wood allowing for the expansion of an Early Years offering. The main point of entry is in Pre-Reception (aged 3). Occasional places may become available further up the school and bursary places are offered from Year 5.

Boys transfer to their chosen independent senior schools and Arnold House has an enviable record of success in placing each boy in the school that is right for him. More than half of the boys move on to the most sought-after London day schools: City of London, St Paul's, Mill Hill, UCS and Westminster. Others transfer to renowned boarding schools: Eton, Harrow, Marlborough, Bradfield, Radley, Rugby, Tonbridge and Winchester have been popular destinations in recent years.

Charitable status. Arnold House School is a Registered Charity, number 312725. It exists to provide education for boys in preparation for transfer to senior independent schools.

Ashford Prep School

United Learning

Great Chart, Ashford, Kent TN23 3DJ
Tel: 01233 620493
email: ashfordprep@ashfordschool.co.uk
website: www.ashfordschool.co.uk
X/Twitter: @AshfordPrep
Facebook: @AshfordSchool
Instagram: @ashfordschool
LinkedIn: /school/ashford-school

Ashford Prep School (part of Ashford School) is home to over 350 children from 3 to 11 years of age. Based in the leafy village of Great Chart on a site of 44 acres, the Prep School provides an inspiring environment that encourages both personal growth and a sense of community.

***Head*: Mr Nick Tiley-Nunn**

Deputy Head, Teaching and Learning: Mrs R Clifford, BSc

Deputy Head, Pastoral: Mr C Neesham, BA

Fees per term (2023–2024). Prep Nursery: £3,318 (full time). Reception, Years 1 & 2: £4,050, Years 3 to 6: £5,787.

We believe that the formative years at Ashford Prep are crucial to building the firm foundations required for a lifelong love of learning. Our aim is to provide an environment that inspires the minds and souls of those who are part of our warm school community. We are committed to providing an education experience that recognises the right that every child has to be provided with diverse opportunities and skilful guidance to optimise their potential.

Within our school, we recognise the importance of the individuality in each child. Everyone plays a vital role in ensuring that Ashford Prep is a happy environment in which to learn, play and grow. We cherish every child and encourage them to take care of those that are around them. In turn, each child contributes to an overwhelmingly warm and positive atmosphere. We have a simple motto that sums up what we expect from everyone who forms part of our Prep School: Always Be Caring (ABC). Our 'ABCs' are a set of nine values that sit the heart of our commitment to ensuring that our students not only become great pupils, but more importantly, great people.

Children normally progress to Ashford Senior School (see HMC entry) without the need to take an entrance test, unless they wish to sit scholarship exams. The Prep School has had considerable success in preparing children for scholarships at leading independent schools as well as other entrance tests including the Kent Test.

Ashford Prep School is a member of the **Pre-Senior Baccalaureate (PSB)**, a prestigious charity that represents several world-class, forward-thinking Schools. The school has a strong commitment to adventurous learning and as such, is embracing the PSB framework with very positive results. The ability to award the Pre-Senior Baccalaureate at the end of pupil's time at Ashford Prep School helps children to celebrate and recognise the pursuit of becoming a true all-rounder.

The Head of the Prep School, Mr Nick Tiley-Nunn, believes that learning should be the ultimate adventure. In order for a Prep School to truly prepare its pupils for their onward journey, they need to experience an education that is broad and allows them the space to explore what it is that they are passionate about. His team's aim is for every child to leave Ashford Prep as a vastly skilled all-rounder with a kind heart and positivity running through their veins, with their eyes open wide to the inspiration that surrounds them.

Campus and facilities. The Prep School is a very modern, well-resourced environment which presents a stimulating, purpose-built learning space for the pupils. The campus comprises: two Halls, specialist music, science, art, DT, and food rooms in addition to a wonderful library and extensive outdoor play areas. The vast outdoor sports facilities extend over the beautiful 40-acre site, including a state-of-the-art pavilion and changing facility. There is also a floodlight all-weather Astroturf, swimming pool and Sports Hall.

The school enjoys both classroom-based and excellent specialist teaching with well-designed facilities for science, art, music, PE, ICT and Design Technology. The school is fully networked and has exceptional provision for ICT with ACTIVboards in all classrooms, iPads for each pupil, a computer room capable of accommodating entire classes and broadband access to the Internet throughout.

Team sports include rugby, hockey, netball, football, rounders, athletics, and cricket. Regular fixtures are held with local and regional schools. Children also participate in PE and swimming as part of their curricular programme. An extensive range of co-curricular activities is provided during lunchtime and after school. Individual music tuition with a wide range of instruments is available. Music, drama, dance, and public speaking are all important opportunities; productions and presentations are performed by all age groups to a high standard and take place throughout the year. The choir and orchestra meet regularly.

A programme of educational trips and visits provides a stimulating and important addition to the all-round education and development of the 'whole' child and the costs of these are included in the fees.

The Ashford Prep School Nursery (3 to 4 years) offers an exciting and vibrant environment for engaging children in a broad range of learning activities. All children have the best possible individual care and education, supported by exceptional and experienced staff. They are encouraged to explore, play, and learn whilst developing independence and resilience, amongst other skills.

The Nursery follows the Early Years Foundation Stage Curriculum, which covers the areas of Personal, Emotional and Social Development, Communication and Language, Physical Development, Literacy, Mathematics, Understanding the World and Expressive Arts and Design.

The thriving Nursery operates on a flexible basis and the Prep School offers full, wraparound care from 7.30 am to 6.30 pm for all our children. The school operates Mondays to Fridays. Holiday Clubs operate during school breaks.

Charitable status. Ashford Prep School is part of United Learning which comprises: UCST (a Company Limited by Guarantee, Registered in England, number 2780748, and a Registered Charity, number 1016538) and ULT (a Company Limited by Guarantee, Registered in England, number 4439859, and an Exempt Charity).

Avenue Pre-Prep & Nursery School

2 Highgate Avenue, Highgate, London N6 5RX
Tel: 020 8348 6815
email: office@avenueprep.co.uk
website: www.avenueprep.co.uk

Principal: Mrs Mary Fysh

***Head*: Mrs Sarah Tapp**

Age range. 3–7 Co-educational.

Number of pupils. 90.

Fees per term (2023–2024). £4,000–£6,350.

The ethos of the School is the happiness and success of every child through a secure, friendly and exciting environment. The provision of a wide and varied programme of activities, all of which are timetabled and included in the fee, contributes considerably towards achieving this aim. The high staff/child ratios enable children to learn and achieve in small groups thus progressing successfully throughout the curriculum. External assessments are introduced in the Nursery and continued through Reception, Years 1 and 2. The results are collated and provide a useful means of tracking the progress of each child: it also aids the planning and learning needs of different children. The School is non-denominational and children of all denominations or none are welcome. Children are made aware of major religious festivals including Christmas.

Pre-Nursery children enter the School when rising 3. The children enjoy participating in many different activities designed to promote speech and language skills, hand/eye coordination and the development of social skills. The large garden provides many opportunities for physical activities, role play and social interaction.

The Nursery takes children from the age of 3+ for four and a half days a week. A new purpose-built nursery wing was completed in 2021 in the grounds which enables the nursery children to enjoy full days at school until 3.00 pm. The Nursery children build on the skills they have learned in Pre-Nursery and are also introduced to letters and numbers. Singing, using the Kodály teaching approach, is introduced in the Pre-Nursery and continues throughout all the classes, as does Drama. Visits to places of interest off site are also introduced in the Nursery year.

The Reception Class is taught Literacy and Numeracy each morning. French and swimming are added to the curriculum along with Dance, Woodwork and Swimming. Children remain at school until 3.00 pm and either bring a packed lunch or sign up for a school lunch.

The class teacher remains with them throughout Key Stage 1 to ensure a seamless transition from Years 1 to 2, greatly benefitting the children's preparations for their future 7+ assessments. The classes follow a curriculum based on the National Curriculum but designed to enable each child to progress towards a successful outcome at 7+. Learning the violin or cello is introduced and mandatory for all Year 1 children. This is continued through Year 2. After-school clubs are available free of charge for all Years 1 and 2 children. These clubs are held on four afternoons a week and finish at 4.00 pm.

Children are prepared for the 7+ entry to their next school, and advice and support is provided for parents throughout their child's time at The Avenue.

We have built up good relationships with other schools in the area and, as members of the IAPS (since November 2009), enjoy meeting and visiting member schools.

Aysgarth School

Newton-le-Willows, Bedale, North Yorkshire DL8 1TF

Tel: 01677 450240
email: admissions@aysgarthschool.co.uk
website: www.aysgarthschool.com
X/Twitter: @AysgarthSchool
Facebook: @aysgarthschool
Instagram: @aysgarthschool
LinkedIn: /company/aysgarth-school

Chairman of Governors: P J S Thompson, Esq
***Headmaster*: Mr Jonthon Anderson**, BA Hons Exeter, QTS
Senior Deputy Headmaster and Deputy Head Pastoral: Mr Paul Barlow, BEd Hons De Montfort
Deputy Head Academic: Dr Ed Canning, BSc Leeds, PGCE Canterbury, PhD

Age Range. 3–13.

Number of Pupils. 196. Pre-Prep Department: 73 boys and girls aged 3–8. Prep School: 124 boys aged 8–13.

Fees per term (2023–2024). Boarders (full and weekly) £10,890, Day £8,370, Pre-Prep £3,405–£4,525, Nursery £875–£3,405.

The Prep School is a day and boarding school for boys set in 50 acres of grounds in North Yorkshire about 6 miles from the A1. It attracts boys from all over the UK, and boys go on to the country's leading independent senior schools, many of them in southern England. Some boys start as day boys or weekly boarders to enable them to adjust to boarding gently, some boys will remain as day boys throughout their time at the School. For exeats, boys can be escorted on trains from Darlington to the north and south. International children are offered escorted service to all northern airports.

Boys of all abilities are welcomed and academic standards are high. All boys are prepared for Common Entrance and several gain scholarships. Before entry, each boy is assessed to ensure that any special needs are identified early and given fully integrated specialist help where necessary. Class sizes are typically around 12. Recent developments include newly refurbished science labs and rifle ranges, and all pupils have access to Chromebooks, particularly at the top end.

The activities in which boys can participate are enormously varied. The facilities include a new heated indoor swimming pool, a state-of-the-art sports hall, a climbing wall, 17 acres of excellent playing fields and a floodlit all-weather pitch. Cricket, Football and Rugby are the main school sports, however there are opportunities to participate in a wide range of other sports including Tennis and Water polo. Music is one of the strengths of the school with more than 75% of boys playing a musical instrument and boys are regularly awarded music scholarships at their senior schools. There are three choirs and the school musicians have regular opportunities to perform both in the school and locally. Each term different year groups produce a play or musical. Art & Craft and Design & Technology are taught by specialist teachers from Form 1 (age 8).

The school has a fine Victorian chapel, and boys are encouraged to develop Christian faith and values in a positive, caring environment. Pastoral care is the first priority for all staff. The headmaster and his wife, a housemaster and his wife and three matrons, are all resident in the main building. A wide range of exciting activities in the evenings and at weekends ensure that boys are keen to board, and they are encouraged to do so particularly in their last two years as preparation for their next schools.

The school aims to encourage boys to be well mannered and courteous with a cheerful enthusiasm for learning and for life and a determination to make the most of their abilities.

There is also a flourishing Pre-Prep Department including a Nursery for day boys and girls aged 3 to 8.

Charitable status. Aysgarth School Trust Limited is a Registered Charity, number 529538. Its purpose is to provide a high standard of boarding and day education.

Badminton Junior School

Westbury-on-Trym, Bristol BS9 3BA

Tel: 0117 905 5271
email: admissions@badmintonschool.co.uk
website: www.badmintonschool.co.uk
X/Twitter: @BadmintonSchool
Facebook: @BadmintonSch
Instagram: @BadmintonSchool
LinkedIn: /school/badminton-school-limited

Chair of Governors: Mr Justin Lewis MDA, BSc Hons

***Head of Junior School*: Ms Heidi Welch**, BSc Hons, MSc, PGCE

Age Range. 4–11.

Number of Girls. 130.

Fees per term (2023–2024). Day: £3,860–£4,420 inclusive of lunch and extended day. Boarding (from Year 5): £8,800–£10,100.

Educational Philosophy. Children learn best when they are interested, happy and supported in their work. Our girls thrive in a stimulating environment where high standards of work and behaviour are expected. All subjects in the Junior School are taught by enthusiastic subject specialists in classes of no more than 16 girls. We provide a welcoming and friendly atmosphere so that all of our girls feel secure whilst we encourage them to develop their own particular talents and interests. Our philosophy is centred on the development of self-confidence, a healthy respect for one another and the nurturing of curious, critical minds.

We believe children enjoy being kept busy and acquiring new skills, so we try to create a balance between academic work in the classroom, plenty of physical exercise, a range of extra-curricular activities and opportunities for recreational and creative play. The girls are given the opportunity to explore and develop their language skills and study French, Latin, German and Spanish whilst additional languages, such as Mandarin and Italian, are offered in after-school clubs.

Facilities. The Junior School is well appointed with light airy classrooms, dedicated rooms for Art and Music, a Science laboratory, and an ICT suite. We have a well-stocked library and a Hall in which various activities including ballet, drama and musical concerts take place. There is a wonderful, secure adventure playground that the girls make the most of during break and lunch times.

Being on the same campus as the Senior School, the girls make use of all the facilities on site which include the 25m indoor swimming pool, the new Sports Centre complete with climbing wall, fencing piste, fitness centre and four-court sports hall, and the all-purpose sports pitch. There are excellent facilities for music, which plays an important part both inside and outside the curriculum.

With our extended day facilities we aim to provide a warm and caring environment to suit the needs of all our pupils and their parents. Every day clubs such as gardening, chess, drama, art or playground games take place after school and girls are welcome to stay on for prep or late stay until 5.45pm, at no additional cost

For further information on Badminton School, see entry in GSA section. A prospectus is available on request from our Admissions Department (admissions@badmintonschool.co.uk).

Charitable status. Badminton School Limited is a Registered Charity, number 311738. It exists to provide education for children.

Ballard School

Fernhill Lane, New Milton, Hampshire BH25 5SU

Tel: 01425 626900
email: registrar@ballardschool.co.uk
website: www.ballardschool.co.uk
X/Twitter: @BallardSchool
Facebook: @BallardSchoolNewMilton
LinkedIn: /BallardSchool

See full entry in the **ISA** section, on **p. 859**.

Bancroft's Preparatory School

High Road, Woodford Green, Essex IG8 0RF

Tel: 020 8506 6751
020 8506 6774 (Admissions)
email: prepoffice@bancrofts.org
website: www.bancrofts.org
X/Twitter: @BancroftsSchool
Facebook: @bancroftsschool
Instagram: @bancrofts_social_media

Chairman of the Governors: Sir Andrew Ford

***Head*: J P Layburn**, MA

Deputy Head, Pastoral: Mrs L Life, BA
Director of Studies: Mr T Paramour, BA
Assistant Head, Lower Phase: Mrs L Dalton, BA
Assistant Head Upper Phase: Miss A Adams, BA

Age Range. 7–11.
Number of Pupils. 123 girls, 138 boys.
Fees per term (2023–2024). £6,365.

Bancroft's Preparatory School was established in September 1990 in the attractive grounds of Bancroft's School in Woodford Green (*see entry in HMC section*) and in 2000 the Head at that time became a member of IAPS. Academic results are excellent and places are much sought after – the school is heavily oversubscribed with numbers of registrations rising year by year.

The Prep School has its own distinct character within the Bancroft's community and has the advantage of being able to use the excellent Senior School facilities. The Prep School is housed in an attractive modern building with its own performing arts studio for drama, music and dance, a science lab and a children's adventure play area. There are three classes of 22 (maximum) children in each of its four year groups.

The Prep School is a truly academic school but its vision of education is about much more than academic results. It's about character development, about the life of the school outside the classroom as well as in it. The Prep School believes the bright children it recruits can 'have it all': outstanding academic qualifications which will enable them to pursue their enthusiasms; rich and formative experiences from a wide ranging co-curricular programme which will help to develop them as people; and an active, reflective approach to learning which will set them up for life.

Children are assessed for entry at the age of six/seven, visiting the school in small groups and tested by the Head and the Deputy Head, Pastoral. The experience is friendly and low-key. Once accepted, pupils have guaranteed transfer to Bancroft's Senior School (on the same site) at the age of eleven. Bancroft's Prep School offers up to two assisted places for pupils entering the School at the age of 7 each year. These awards are based on family finances and performance in the entrance tests. The administration of the Prep School and Senior School are closely linked and the Head is a member of the Senior Leadership Team of Bancroft's School.

Charitable status. Bancroft's School is a Registered Charity, number 1068532. It exists to provide a rounded academic education for able children.

Barfield Prep School

Guildford Road, Farnham, Surrey GU10 1PB
Tel: 01252 782271
email: admin@barfieldpst.org
website: www.barfieldpst.org
X/Twitter: @Barfield_School
Facebook: @BarfieldSchool
Instagram: @barfieldschool
LinkedIn: /barfieldschoolsurrey

Barfield School is part of the Prep Schools Trust.

Chair of the Board of Trustees: Emma McKendrick

***Headmaster*: Mr Andy Boyle**

Age range. 2–11 Co-educational.
Number of children. 286.
Fees per term (2023–2024). Reception–Year 1: £4,000; Year 2: £4,320; Years 3–4: £5,700; Years 5–6: £5,890; Nursery: £1,356–£4,855.

Barfield Prep School, set in 12 acres of beautiful grounds, was awarded 'Excellent' in all eight areas of inspection by the ISI in June 2023. The school is co-educational and takes children between the ages of 2 and 11 years.

In 2021, we underwent a complete brand identity change. Headmaster Andy Boyle, who has now been at the school for four years, felt that it seemed like the right time, alongside the school transitioning from a 13+ school to an 11+ school, to consolidate his vision for the school and to fully engage the staff, parents and pupils in the process.

Our brand defines our culture, so it's essential that it represents who we are, what we believe, and what we value. We have kept our owl that has been the school's emblem since it was founded in 1933, but modernised it and tried to capture the school's key values of Integrity, Compassion, Resilience, Tolerance and Enthusiasm in its creation.

The brand relaunch coincided with the official opening of a £1million+ investment building project which has provided the school with fantastic new classrooms, a science lab and a food tech room. We are also in the process of building a new dining hall which we hope to open in the Spring Term.

Barfield School is a family-orientated school with an excellent reputation for high academic standards and caring staff. Facilities include an Outdoor Treehouse Classroom, Auditorium, ICT Suite, Library, Music and Music practice rooms, art and DT rooms. The school has a flourishing PE and Outdoor Pursuits Department, with a full-size climbing wall, high ropes course and zip line. There is a magnificent indoor heated swimming pool and children are encouraged to participate in a wide range of extracurricular activities. Activity courses are run throughout the school holidays and are enjoyed by children from Reception to Year 6.

Children are taught in small classes and are prepared for Common Entrance and Scholarship examinations, as well as Grammar School entry.

The Nursery is an integral part of the school and is bright and airy, with plenty of green free-flow space. Open 50 weeks of the year from 8.00 am to 6.15 pm, experienced and qualified staff nurture, encourage and support all the children, ensuring they feel both happy and secure. The children have use of all the school facilities and access to specialist teachers for swimming and music.

Visitors are always welcome. Please contact the school.

Charitable status. Barfield School is part of the Prep Schools Trust, which is a Registered Charity, number 309639.

Barlborough Hall School
Preparatory School to Mount St Mary's College

Park Street, Barlborough, Chesterfield, Derbyshire S43 4ES
Tel: 01246 810511
email: headteacher@barlboroughhallschool.com
website: www.barlboroughhallschool.com
X/Twitter: @BarlboroughHall
Facebook: @MSMBHS
LinkedIn: /company/mount-st-mary-s-college-barlborough-hall-school

***Head Teacher*: Mrs Karen Keeton**

Deputy Headteacher: Mrs Cath Chadbourne
Key Stage 2 Coordinator: Mrs Fran Wilson
Key Stage 1 Coordinator: Mrs Cath Chadbourne
Early Years Coordinator: Mrs Andrea Booth
Admissions Officer: Claire Adams

Age Range. 3–11 Co-educational.
Number of Pupils. 210.
Fees per term (2023–2024). £3,150–£4,250.

We are a Jesuit, Catholic co-educational independent day school and nursery for children aged three to 11. We work to inspire a love of learning from the moment your child joins us, to the day they leave. From the classroom, to the sports track, from the extra-curricular, to the great outdoors, there's more to discover at Barlborough Hall School.

Learning together, playing together and sharing the joy together is fundamental to the way we care for and develop children to the best of their academic abilities, but also in cultivating good interpersonal relationships, as well as encouraging their extra-curricular interests.

Whilst we are always striving for excellence, our school is a place full of laughter. Every corridor, every classroom and every playground is filled with the sounds of happiness. The children's smiles are infectious. We are one big happy community. It is truly a wonderful place to be.

The school is a few minutes' drive from Junction 30 of the M1. Worksop and Rotherham are 20 minutes by car. It is the preparatory school to Mount St Mary's College and is true to the Jesuit principles of a Catholic education.

You want the best for your child, and so do we. From specialist teaching and facilities, to the nurturing and friendly atmosphere – children thrive at Barlborough Hall School.

Each class has its own teacher who delivers the majority of the curriculum, including Mathematics, English, Humanities and Science. Our teachers get to know your child as an individual, and will work closely with both you and them, to encourage progress, build on their strengths and development in other areas. This goes much further than the classroom for us.

We have an exceptional sporting reputation, and regularly emerge victorious at sporting fixtures.

Our musical repertoire is no different, with most of our children playing at least one instrument, whilst also participating in our choir or instrumental ensembles.

We recommend coming to visit us for a private tour of Barlborough Hall School, so you can meet our teachers and pupils, and see for yourself why we're in the top 50 prep schools in the country.

For further details of the admissions process and a prospectus, please contact the Admissions Team at admissions@barlboroughhallschool.com.

Barlborough Hall pupils can automatically transfer at age 11 to Mount St Mary's College (*see entry in HMC section*).

Charitable status. Mount St Mary's is a Registered Charity, number 1117998.

Barnard Castle Preparatory School

Westwick Road, Barnard Castle, County Durham DL12 8UW

Tel:	01833 696032
email:	prep@barneyschool.org.uk
website:	www.barnardcastleschool.org.uk
X/Twitter:	@barney_school
Facebook:	@BarnardCastleSchool
Instagram:	@barnardcastleschool
LinkedIn:	/company/barnard-castle-school

Chair of Governors: Mrs C J Sunley

***Headmistress*: Mrs Laura Turner**, MA
Deputy Head: Mrs Sarah Leonard, BA
Deputy Head (*Pastoral*): Mrs Lianne Taylor, BA

Age range. 4–11 years.

Number of pupils. 173 girls and boys, including 10 boarders.

Fees per term (2023–2024). Prep: £10,000 (International Boarders), £8,580 (Boarders), £4,410 (Day), Pre-Prep: £2,988.

Barnard Castle Preparatory School is the junior school of Barnard Castle School and offers an all-round, high-quality education for boys and girls aged between 4 and 11 years. The School offers both day and boarding places and is situated in a beautiful setting on the edge of a traditional English market town.

The campuses of the two schools are adjoining, allowing shared use of many excellent facilities. At the same time the Preparatory School is able to provide a separate, stimulating environment, with small classes, a wide range of co-curricular activities and an exciting school excursion programme.

The School is well served by a bus network system, a breakfast club and after-school supervision is readily available. The boarders reside in a fully-functional boarding house, Old Courts, which creates a warm and friendly environment supported by a full range of facilities including the School's medical centre. Flexi boarding (minimum of 4 nights) is also available.

Sport, Drama and Music occupy important places in the life of the School. All children have numerous opportunities to participate in each of these, as well as an extensive co-curricular programme. The School also offers a qualified learning support service to those children who require further assistance.

Charitable status. Barnard Castle School is a Registered Charity, number 1125375. Its aim is the education of boys and girls.

Barnardiston Hall Preparatory School

Barnardiston, Nr Haverhill, Suffolk CB9 7TG

Tel:	01440 786316
email:	registrar@barnardiston-hall.co.uk
website:	www.barnardiston-hall.co.uk
X/Twitter:	@barnardiston
Facebook:	@barnardiston
Instagram:	@barnardistonhall

***Headmaster*: Mr Gavin Sinnott**, BSc Econ Hons, PGCE, NPQH

Registrar: Mrs L P Gundersen

Bursar: Mrs A Gregory

Age Range. Co-educational 6 months–13 years.

Number of Pupils. Day: 180, Boarding (full and weekly): 27.

Fees per term (2023–2024). Day Pupils: £3,460–£5,425; Weekly Boarders: £7,500; Full Boarders: £8,140; International Boarders: £6,825 (Day), £9,370 (Boarding).

Barnardiston Hall, set in 36 acres of grounds on the borders of Suffolk, Essex and Cambridge, offers an individual all-round education for boys and girls, both day and boarding. High standards are achieved by small classes taught by graduate and teacher-trained staff, a caring approach and close liaison with parents.

The School has good facilities, including a Nursery, a Pre-Preparatory Block and Art Room / CDT complex, a computer room, assembly hall, Music Block, science laboratory, library, tennis/netball courts, AstroTurf and extensive sports fields. For the boarders, the dormitories are bright, uncluttered and home-like.

The curriculum is designed to allow pupils to reach Common Entrance standards in the appropriate subjects. The best of traditional methods are mixed with modern ideas to provide an enjoyable and productive learning environment. Spanish is taught from the age of 3; French from age 8 and Forest School starts at age 3. The School is CReSTeD registered. Pupils go on to a wide range of secondary schools, both in the local area and further afield.

Sports in the Michaelmas and Lent Terms are hockey, swimming (Pre-Prep only) and cross-country/orienteering for all pupils, rugby for the boys and netball for the girls. During the Summer, all do athletics, cricket and tennis/short tennis. The School has won the National Orienteering Championships many times over the past few years including 2021.

There is a wide range of clubs and activities including 3 choirs, an orchestra, recorders, chess, painting, drama, carpentry, cookery and pottery. Ballet, speech and drama, piano, guitar, woodwind, violin, brass, string and singing lessons are also offered.

Throughout the term, there are weekend activities for boarders (optional for day pupils) which include mountain walking. Derbyshire Dales at 7, Ben Nevis at 8, camping, visits to museums/historic buildings and other places of interest and theatre trips.

Barrow Hills School

Roke Lane, Witley, Godalming, Surrey GU8 5NY

Tel: 01428 683639
email: info@barrowhills.org
website: www.barrowhills.org
X/Twitter: @BarrowHills
Facebook: @Barrow-Hills-School

Chair of the Governors: Mrs Justine Voisin

***Headmaster*: Mr John Towers**

Age Range. 2–13.
Number of Pupils. 221.
Fees per term (2023–2024). Tuition: £3,995–£6,500 (including meals). Nursery and Kindergarten according to sessions.

Barrow Hills School is an independent, co-educational day school and nursery.

We strongly believe that a happy child is a successful one. Children are challenged within a positive, diverse community of learners and are stretched at a time appropriate to them, helping them to aspire to achieve their individual best. Balanced with an ethos of strong pastoral care, children become well-rounded high achievers.

Teaching is based on the understanding that children vary in academic ability, learn and mature at different rates and discover areas of the curriculum which they enjoy and excel at. The family feel of the School is evident and the children clearly benefit from being members of a small community. Class sizes allow for more individual attention from staff, who value and understand every child and spend quality time with them to enhance their learning and confidence. The intimate atmosphere is a particular strength of the School and enables us to build warm relationships with our families.

Education at Barrow Hills is for life, not just the classroom and we are committed to being leaders in Prep School education; promoting mutual respect, curiosity of mind and independence of spirit; prepared for greater things. Our extensive grounds provide excellent facilities that encourage play and exploration. Children experience a wide variety of activities in order to develop their abilities without fear of failure.

We provide devices for every child in the Prep department. Access is also provided for younger children along with Wi-Fi, large screen digital displays and air printers across the school.

Music and theatre is in our DNA and our children are part of a culture that sees everyone, every year, be part of a production. Sport matters; by Year 3 all children have five hours of sport a week, including competitive matches against rival schools. Major team sports are: hockey, netball, rounders, tennis, cricket, swimming and some lacrosse for girls; football, rugby, hockey, swimming and cricket for boys. We have strong links with excellent senior schools, in particular with King Edward's Witley, our partner school. We are proud of our 100% success at Common Entrance with all children gaining entry to their chosen senior school at 13+. Many of our children are awarded scholarships. We offer a broad range of extracurricular activities and a comprehensive programme of educational and residential visits.

Our main building is an attractive Arts and Crafts house, with 33 acres of beautiful gardens, playing fields and woods. We are close to Guildford, Godalming and Haslemere.

Key entry points: Nursery, Kindy, Reception, Year 3, Year 7.

Charitable status. Barrow Hills School Witley is a Registered Charity, number 311997.

Bassett House School

60 Bassett Road, London W10 6JP

Tel: 020 8969 0313
email: info@bassetths.org.uk
website: www.bassetths.org.uk
X/Twitter: @bassetths
Facebook: @Bassett-House-School
Instagram: @bassetthouseschool
LinkedIn: /showcase/bassett-house-school

Motto: *Quisque pro sua parte ~*
From each to the best of his or her ability

Chair of Governors: Libby Nicholas

***Headmistress*: Kelly Gray**

Age Range: 3–11 Co-educational.
Number of Pupils: 151.
Fees per term (2023–2024): Nursery (5 mornings) £3,606; Pre-Prep £7,212; Prep £7,511.

Bassett House School also teaches the value of endeavour and of staying power, of developing social skills and forming respectful relationships. It has an extensive programme of extra-curricular activities and clubs, day outings and residential trips, as well as a lively schedule of music, drama and sports.

Bassett House provides a thorough and broad educational grounding following the national curriculum and embracing different teaching techniques (including

Montessori). The school has invested heavily in the latest classroom technology to give teachers additional tools to make learning lively, fun and effective. It has specialist teachers in maths, English, science, computing, French, music, physical education, art/design technology, eurhythmics, Latin and dance.

The school was built towards the end of the 19th century and what was originally designed as a large family house now provides modern spacious and airy classrooms. The school premises include use of a separate annex comprising an assembly hall with a stage and gymnasium, three classrooms, a kitchen and a garden. There is also a brand new building, with three Early Years classrooms, an interactive learning zone for child-initiated learning and a performing arts studio for music, dance and drama. The main school building has a playground and the school also uses excellent local play and sports facilities. Included in the school's facilities is an edible garden and new playground.

Beachborough

Westbury, Nr Brackley, Northants NN13 5LB

Tel: 01280 700071
email: admissions@beachborough.com
website: www.beachborough.com
X/Twitter: @Beachborough
Facebook: @Beachborough
Instagram: @beachboroughprep
LinkedIn: /beachborough-school-trust-limited

Chair of Governors: Mrs S Barrett

***Head*: Mrs S L Mitchell**, BA, PGCE, MEd

Age Range. 2½–13.

Number of Children. Main School 225 (40% flexi boarding), Pre-Prep 180.

Fees per term (2023–2024). Prep School: Years 5–8 £6,745, Years 3–4 £6,186, Reception, Years 1 & 2 £4,295. Nursery from £360 for one session per week. Flexi boarding from £45 per night.

Beachborough is a friendly and energetic Independent Prep School ideally situated on the borders of Buckinghamshire, Oxfordshire and Northamptonshire. We provide an outstanding all-round education for around 300 boys and girls, a quarter of whom take advantage of our flexible boarding provision. We are large enough to have a diverse and lively community, yet small enough for each individual to be known and nurtured.

We believe that a good prep school education will give children opportunities that will equip them intellectually, physically, culturally and emotionally for the challenges of the twenty-first century. At whatever stage your child joins us, be it Early Years (pupils aged 2½ to 5), Pre-Prep (pupils aged 6 to 7) or Prep School (pupils aged 8 to 13) they will be warmly welcomed into the school. We are not obsessed with reflecting on past glories or the latest headline-grabbing news, but have an active desire to find each child's individual talent and help them surpass their personal best. Our parents use words such as inclusive, nurturing and rounded to define our school, so if you share in our belief that happy children thrive, please come and visit.

Charitable status. Beachborough is a Registered Charity, number 309910.

The Beacon

Chesham Bois, Amersham, Bucks HP6 5PF

Tel: 01494 432764
email: admissions@beaconschool.co.uk
website: www.beaconschool.co.uk
X/Twitter: @Beacon_School
Facebook: @beaconschoolamersham
Instagram: @beaconschooluk
LinkedIn: /the-beacon-school

Chair of the Governors: Charles Miller

***Headmaster*: Nick Baker**, BA Hons, PGCE

Age Range. 3–13.
Number of Boys. 510.

Fees per term (2023–2024). Nursery: £1,980 (5 mornings/week), £385 (one afternoon/week), £3,700 (reduced full-time fee). Reception: £4,525; Y1 & Y2 £5,250; Y3 & 4 £6,650; Y5 £6,950; Y6–Y8 £7,275.

The Beacon is one of the UK's leading independent prep day schools for boys aged 3 to 13 years, set in the heart of the idyllic Chiltern countryside in Amersham. The ISI inspection report rated The Beacon 'Excellent' in all areas and the school has as a well-founded reputation in Buckinghamshire and the surrounding counties for being exceptional. The Beacon is a happy school where no boy is ever overlooked and each individual is inspired to fulfil his own academic, creative and physical potential, both in and beyond the classroom.

The Beacon and Beyond. From the earliest steps in initial learning, The Beacon prepares boys for secondary education through a curriculum that offers both richness and diversity of opportunity. The Beacon is proud to prepare its boys for entry to over 25 senior independent day and boarding schools, with a variety of scholarships being awarded each year. The school also enjoys impressive success at 11+ for entry into Grammar Schools.

Life at The Beacon. The Beacon is located in the idyllic Chiltern countryside and the boys are educated in extremely well-resourced buildings with first class facilities; a beautiful blend of old: 17th-century farmstead and barns; and new: including a 220-seat Theatre, a Design and Technology Suite, Cooking and Nutrition Room, Science Labs, a 25m Swimming Pool, Drama Studio, Music Technology Suite, two Libraries, a large Sports Hall, two AstroTurfs, and 16 acres of playing fields.

All class sizes are small and whilst academic core skills are at the heart of the school, The Beacon is also dedicated to teaching boys 'how to learn', instilling key core learning skills such as independent thinking, teamwork and resilience, preparing them for this ever-changing world.

Music and Drama are also real strengths at The Beacon, with over five choirs, eight ensembles and numerous opportunities for all boys to perform.

Sport is all-inclusive and exemplifies teamwork, emphasising the school ethos that everybody matters. Boys regularly compete at County level in cricket, hockey, tennis, athletics, cross country, swimming and rugby. The Beacon has an excellent record of success in many national and regional competitions.

The Performing Arts Department has numerous instrumental ensembles and choirs, and a range of weekly Music and Drama clubs for all ages.

There are 21 visiting Music and Drama specialists with over 400 weekly lessons taking place. Every boy at The Beacon is given a chance to perform throughout the year in a range of musical productions, playlets, showcases and concerts, with international choir tours and performances at the Edinburgh Festival Fringe being particular highlights.

Pastoral Care. The Beacon's ethos of kindness underpins every aspect of school life as the dedicated Wellbeing Team actively promotes and creates a happy and healthy environment for all to thrive. The Beacon runs a mindfulness programme and a hugely successful peer-mentoring scheme for the boys. There is also a dedicated on-site Counsellor who provides incredible support for both the boys and their families when needed.

The Little Beacons. Little Beacons is an inspiring and nurturing educational Nursery welcoming boys from the age of 3, offering early school experiences to encourage development of a love and curiosity for learning. Located within a wonderfully spacious Early Years setting, Little Beacons take their first steps on their educational journey, supported, and encouraged throughout by a dedicated Nursery team. Boys also have weekly lessons with specialised staff to enjoy Music, French, Swimming and Games.

Wraparound Care & Transport. Wraparound care is available for all boys from 7.30am (Breakfast Club) until 6pm (Prep and After-School Care and Clubs).

The Beacon also offers a wide range of minibus routes as well as an under 6 car service (fully fitted with ISOFIX car seats) for families living in Beaconsfield, Gerrards Cross, Chorleywood, High Wycombe and the surrounding villages.

Charitable status. The Beacon Educational Trust Limited is a Registered Charity, number 309911. It exists to provide education for boys.

Beaudesert Park School

Minchinhampton, Stroud, Gloucestershire GL6 9AF

Tel: 01453 832072

email: office@bps.school

website: www.beaudesert.gloucs.sch.uk

X/Twitter: @beaudesertpark
@beaudesertsport

Facebook: @Beaudesert-Park-School

Instagram: @beaudesertparksch

LinkedIn: /company/beaudesert-park-school

Chairman of Governors: S C I Jones MSc MLitt

***Headmaster*: C D Searson**, BA

Age Range. 3–13, boys and girls.

Number of Pupils. 395 (209 boys and 186 girls). 121 children in Pre-Prep, and 274 in Prep. 160 children (from Year 4 upwards) board at least once a week, the vast majority of whom flexi-board for between 1 and 3 nights per week. Most families live within 20 miles of the School.

Fees per term (2023–2024). Nursery from £2,350, Reception–Year 2 £3,900, Year 3 £5,200, Year 4 £6,150. Day Years 5–8 £7,200, Boarding Years 5–8 £8,900. All fees include lunch. Boarding and flexi-boarding fees also include breakfast and supper.

Thriving country prep. A thriving prep school with a family feel, Beaudesert sits in glorious grounds on the edge of 500 acres of National Trust common land, surrounded by Cotswolds countryside.

Parents speak of a happy, confidence-building school with excellent teachers and knockout facilities – a place where children are able to enjoy the important business of childhood for as long as possible. Children are encouraged to lay deep roots, grow with confidence, branch out in many directions, and live to reach for ever increasing heights.

At the heart of Beaudesert is the warmth and strength of its relationships, creating an unrivalled atmosphere where all members of the school community feel valued, supported and inspired.

Be curious, be yourself, belong. The School is non-selective but is ambitious for every child to reach their full potential. An embedded culture of growth mindset and an encouragement to be curious, questioning and critical thinkers, underpins the philosophy within Beaudesert classrooms. As a truly independent prep school, Beaudesertians move on to over 20 different senior schools, many with scholarships and awards to their chosen schools.

From Nursery to Year 8, children are inspired to participate in sport, step out of their comfort zone in the arts, and pursue their personal passions through the many clubs and activities on offer.

Boarding evenings are full of spirit and excitement, with different activities on offer each evening, all supported by teachers and our close-knit team of boarding houseparents, tutors and matrons.

Stand-out facilities. The School is very well equipped and includes a high-spec, multi-functional Performing Arts Centre, three science labs, indoor and outdoor swimming pools, sports hall, Art Studio and Design Technology department – not to mention a thriving Forest School. The Nursery and Reception class areas were refurbished in 2019 to include free flow inside-outside spaces, and part of the dormitories were refurbished in 2021. There are also AstroTurf tennis courts and hard courts within the 30-acre site, and 15 acres of sports fields. Despite its rural location, the School is within half an hour of the M4 and M5 motorways and within easy reach of the surrounding towns of Gloucester, Cheltenham, Cirencester, Swindon, Bath and Bristol.

Rich heritage brought up to date. Founded in 1908 in Warwickshire, the School moved lock, stock and barrel to its hill-top spot in Gloucestershire in 1918. In 2018, Beaudesert celebrated 100 years of being in glorious Gloucestershire. The School celebrated receiving international accreditation with its 'Green Flag' award in 2022, which recognised its commitment to supporting the local and global environment.

Charitable status. Beaudesert Park is a Registered Charity, number 311711. It exists to provide education for boys and girls in a caring atmosphere.

Bedales Prep, Dunhurst

Alton Road, Steep, Petersfield, Hampshire GU32 2DR

Tel: 01730 711558
email: admissions@bedales.org.uk
website: www.bedales.org.uk
X/Twitter: @BedalesPrep
Facebook: @BedalesSchool
Instagram: @bedalesprep
LinkedIn: /school/bedales-school

Chairman of Governors: Stephen Nokes

***Head*: Colin Baty**, BA Ed

Deputy Head (*Pastoral*): Graeme Thompson, BA Southampton

Deputy Head (*Academic*): Andy Wiggins, BA Kent, PGCE Portsmouth

Age range. 8–13.

Number in school. 219 pupils: 104 boys; 115 girls; 24 boarders.

Fees per term (2023–2024). Day: £6,745–£7,335. Boarding: £9,750; Half-boarding (3 nights): £8,680; Flexi-boarding available (£54 per night).

Established in 1902 to join with Bedales Senior School, Bedales Prep takes root in the shared conviction that education is about 'head, hand and heart'. The school's progressive ethos sets to empower its pupils through opportunity and experience, and the unique approach to learning helps students to excel academically. The pupils at Bedales Prep are encouraged to explore their ambitions, aiming as high as they can while simultaneously enjoying their childhood and the accompanying natural learning processes that accompany. The curriculum is unique and rigorous, offering a breadth of teaching beyond what is standard for a prep school. Unbound by the Common Entrance syllabus, teachers can pursue topics in depth to allow a rounded education and apply relevant teaching to the real world. Pupils engage with a large scope of subjects at Bedales Prep, with many opportunities for STEM, Arts, Humanities and Sports. The school follows the principle of 'learning by doing'; this approach to education nurtures pupils in a creative learning and teaching environment, which promotes personal growth and confidence through challenge and problem-solving. While underpinning the curriculum with quality and rigour, the school maintains as much freedom from the pressures of testing and exam results as possible.

Matches against other schools take place regularly in athletics, cricket, football, hockey, netball, rounders, rugby, swimming and tennis. A wide range of other sports and outdoor activities is also offered, including squash, karate and fencing. Bedales Prep makes full use of the first-rate facilities at Bedales, which include a theatre, sports hall, floodlit netball and tennis courts, an all-weather pitch and indoor swimming pool. This, and the common ethos, makes for an easy transition for pupils moving from Bedales Prep to Bedales Senior at the age of 13.

A unique and indispensable element of life at Bedales is the contribution to Outdoor Work for the Prep students, harmonious with Bedales Pre-prep and Senior schools. Pupils are actively involved in the growing and harvesting of vegetables, livestock management and the process of constructing shelters with natural materials. In Blocks 1 and 2 (Years 7 and 8) children employ these skills to give back to the community through the community service programme. This may include building outdoor learning areas for a local school or redesigning the garden at a GP surgery. The programme encourages pupils to help others and evaluate their position in the wider world. Cultivating an environment where learners are inquisitive and independent, pupils have timetabled 'Greens'. Flexible periods in which pupils manage their time and work, these sessions can be dedicated to a series of co-curricular endeavours. Time may be spent completing prep, undertaking further academic studies, engaging in instrumental lessons or participating in sports. The number of Greens timetabled increases as pupils progress through the school, building upon the individual management skills that will prepare them for Bedales Senior and life beyond.

Bedales Prep takes pride in its strong pastoral system, which nurtures pupils to recognise their own worth, collaborate with others and feel supported within the Bedales community. Timetabled wellbeing lessons provide the foundation for children to lead confident, happy lives, recognising the importance of supportive relationships and making informed decisions. In alignment with Bedales' founding beliefs, mutual respect is the cornerstone of teaching and learning at Bedales Prep. Pupils are encouraged to use their voices to positively shape their own experiences, with a dedicated School Council comprising representatives from all age groups.

Boarding is an inclusive and cherished aspect of life at Bedales Prep. For pupils aged 8 to 13, the provision of full, half and flexi boarding options offers academic, social and pastoral benefits and recognises the need for flexibility in families' lives. The newly refurbished co-educational boarding house was designed in collaboration with staff and boarders and is a warm and secure environment for pupils to live. The boys occupy the top floor, and the girls the lower, with communal spaces available for all to ensure peers can socialise in a welcoming and homely setting, irrespective of gender.

Applicants for both boarding and day places sit residential entrance tests. The main points of entry are at 8+ and 11+. Entry at other ages is dependent on the availability of places.

For information about Bedales Pre-Prep (3–8 years), see the Bedales entry in HMC section.

Charitable status. Bedales School is a Registered Charity, number 307332. It exists to provide a sound education and training for children and young persons of both sexes.

Bedales School

Church Road, Steep, Petersfield, Hampshire GU32 2DG

Tel: 01730 300100
01730 711733 (Admissions)
email: admissions@bedales.org.uk
website: www.bedales.org.uk
X/Twitter: @BedalesSchool
Facebook: @BedalesSchool
Instagram: @BedalesSchool
LinkedIn: /school/bedales-school

See full entry in the **HMC** section, on **p. 17**.

Bede's Preparatory School

Duke's Drive, Eastbourne, East Sussex BN20 7XL

Tel: 01323 734222
email: prep.school@bedes.org
website: www.bedes.org
X/Twitter: @bedesprep
Facebook: @bedesprepschool
Instagram: @bedesprep

Co-educational day and boarding school with Nursery and Pre-Prep departments.

Chair of Governors: Mrs Geraldine Watkins, JP

***Headteacher*: Mrs Leigh-Anne Morris**, BCom Accountancy, GTP

Deputy Head (*Pastoral*): Ms Katie Jackson, PCert, PDip, MA, QTLS, OTHM

Deputy Head (*Academic and Operations*): Mr Matt Bennett-Tomlin, BSc Hons, QTS, MA

Age Range. 3 months–13 years Co-educational.

Number of Pupils. 305: Prep 189, Pre-Prep 33, Nursery 83.

Fees per term (2023–2024). Tuition: Prep £5,550–£6,790, Pre-Prep £3,835 (Reception, Years 1 & 2). Nursery prices per session.

Bede's Prep was founded in 1895 with a roll of just four boys. In 1902, it moved to its current grander premises, where it is nestled on a clifftop above Beachy Head, affording stunning views of the sea.

Bede's Prep is a vibrant, energetic and forward-thinking school, which focuses on promoting learning, personal growth and development. Pupils are valued as individuals and enjoy a broad range of opportunities inside and outside the classroom to suit their interests and passions.

Our core values of compassion, courage, conscientiousness and curiosity shape a pupil's educational experience. A Bede's education is based upon academic rigour through excellent teaching, encouraging our pupils to explore, question, take risks, and develop their creativity, communication and teamwork – all central to successful life-long learning.

Bede's offers academic, sport, music, dance, art and drama scholarships and bursaries for children from the ages of 7 to 12 years.

Pastoral. Our exceptional pastoral care is evidenced as happy pupils who are engaged in their learning and are actively involved in the wider life of the school, embracing every opportunity provided to them. Pupils who are kind to themselves and each other and are gracious about success and failure.

At the Prep School, in the junior years, most teaching is done by the pupils' Form Teacher and they therefore develop a rich learning understanding of each child's needs and their learning journey. As they progress into the senior years at the Prep School and begin to be taught by specialist teachers, the Form Teacher's role evolves to be more akin to the Personal Tutor they will have as they move into the Senior School. They see pupils daily and take an overview of their progress, helping them to plan their goals and reflect on the young person that they are becoming.

All of our pupils benefit from small class sizes and belong to one of four Sections. They compete throughout the year for Section points and in competitions such as Section Music.

Academic. The curriculum for each year group at Bede's Prep School focuses on promoting learning, personal growth and development. We provide pupils with a curriculum that is broad, stimulating and designed to facilitate the highest possible levels of attainment by those who follow it – programmes of study that imbue children with a wealth of skills, a depth of knowledge and an irrepressible curiosity.

By the time the children have reached Year 5, lessons have become more formally structured and delineated by subject, but this does not mean they are less wide-ranging in approach. Rather, the opposite is true, with the children being increasingly capable and hungry for new challenges.

As the children move through the year groups, each curriculum also includes an ever-evolving and increasingly rigorous 'hidden curriculum' – a set of skills the children develop from the ways they are treated and the expectations set by their teachers, informed by communication between teachers, tutors and Heads of Year. This hidden curriculum is, like everything else at Bede's, tweaked and personalised to suit the needs, talents and propensities of each individual. What is right for one child may not be for another and as such, every pupil will finish their time at Bede's Prep with a uniquely distinguished academic record, a set of high personal ideals and a clear set of aspirations particular to them.

Co-Curricular. Bede's provides an all-round education where academic pursuits are supported by wonderful co-curricular opportunities and where pupils learn lessons that books cannot give; courage and joy, resilience and self belief, developing into confident globally minded young people.

The activities programme is varied each term and is carefully crafted to develop pupils' soft skills such as cooperation, negotiation and empathy – valuable in every aspect of life. Pupils can try anything from debating, to creative writing, to chess.

Performing Arts forms an integral part of the school. There is a thriving orchestra and the majority of pupils learn one or more instruments, with children as young as six playing in recorder groups. Informal concerts take place during the school year and there are several choirs.

There are annual Christmas nativities, the Pre-Prep pupils produce a Christmas play, and there are frequent productions throughout the year.

For Pre-Prep pupils onwards, there are specialist dance classes held during the school day as part of the Dance Programme or there are dance clubs and activities, whether they want to learn for fun or are looking to train for a career in the performing arts.

Sport. Few Prep Schools can offer the calibre of coaching found at Bede's Prep and these opportunities deepen year on year, exposing our pupils to an expansive training and fixtures programme.

Bede's provides the very best coaching for pupils of all abilities to give pupils the chance to grow in confidence, capacity and accomplishment. Pupils have training sessions with the professional coaches at the Senior School in Cricket, Football, Hockey, Tennis and Netball. They also utilise the market-leading facilities offered at the Senior School.

All the pupils use the indoor 20-metre swimming pool. The fixture list is very comprehensive and, while the top teams enjoy a high standard of coaching and performance, special emphasis is placed on ensuring that the other teams also have the opportunity to play matches against other schools. The Sports Hall covers two indoor tennis courts and is used to house a huge variety of sports. There is also an astro court for hockey, cricket and other sports.

Learning Enhancement. There is a Learning Enhancement department staffed by qualified learning support staff which can cater for pupils who require additional or particular support. The school also has an EAL centre which is run by highly trained and experienced staff. Gifted children are placed on a Curriculum Enhancement Programme to maximise their potential.

Nursery and Pre-Prep. Bede's Nursery offers care from the age of just three months. The nursery is open 51 weeks of the year and offers extended day care for busy families. Bede's provides a home away from home for the children, preparing everything on site, from their home cooked, locally grown, nutritious meals to a fantastic range of activities and learning resources.

The children move through the Baby and Toddler Unit, to the Starfish Room, to the Rainbow Fish room, until they finally move to the Preschool area where they spend a year before moving to Reception class.

The children enjoy a lot of outdoor activities including beach school and forest school, and they also have weekly swimming and dance lessons.

Entry to Bede's Prep School is by taster day, assessment and a recent school report.

Charitable status. St Bede's School Trust Sussex is a Registered Charity, number 278950. It exists to provide education for boys and girls.

Bedford Girls' School Junior School

Cardington Road, Bedford, Bedfordshire MK42 0BX

Tel: 01234 361918
email: admissions@bedfordgirlsschool.co.uk
website: www.bedfordgirlsschool.co.uk
X/Twitter: @BedfordGirlsSch
Facebook: @BedfordGirlsSch
Instagram: @bedfordgirlssch

Foundation – The Harpur Trust.

"*Let me keep an open mind so I understand as much as I can in my lifetime and not reach the limits of my imagination.*"

Chair of Governors: Mr N Harris

Head of Bedford Girls' School: Mrs G Gibson

***Head of Bedford Girls' School Junior School*: Mrs C Howe**

Deputy Head: Mr S Powell

Age Range. 7–11.

Number of Pupils. 230 in the Junior School (980 across the whole school).

Fees per term (2023–2024). £3,907.

Bedford Girls' School is a dynamic, forward-thinking selective independent day school for girls aged 7–18. We value creativity, technology and innovation highly; we are preparing our students to make a difference to the world around them. From Years 3 to Sixth Form, it is our belief that learning should be exciting and lifelong, so that students leave us fully equipped academically, personally and emotionally, with a desire to be the creative thinkers, the change-makers and the problem-solvers of the future. We embrace the International Baccalaureate philosophy of education and are an accredited IB World School offering the IB Primary Years Programme in the Junior School and a choice of IB Diploma Programme or A Levels in the Sixth Form.

This journey begins in the Junior School where our expert teachers recognise and ignite the curiosity of every individual, harnessing her natural curiosity and fuelling her confidence to develop her own thoughts, opinions and talents. Students not only excel intellectually, but also as well-rounded, insightful, caring girls with a joy and passion for life and learning.

The atmosphere of our school is unique and exciting. Classrooms fizz with energy and enthusiasm and each day brings forth new discoveries and achievements. We would be delighted to welcome you to visit, either for one of our Open House events or a private tour, to experience at first hand a true flavour of life at Bedford Girls' School. Please visit www.bedfordgirlsschool.co.uk for further information or contact our Admissions Team: Tel: 01234 361918, email: admissions@bedfordgirls school.co.uk.

Admissions. Entry to the Junior School is based upon Cognitive Ability Testing (CAT) and a creative writing task. Entry to the Senior School is based on an interview with the Headmistress and Cognitive Ability Testing (CAT). Sixth Form entry is based on interviews, Cognitive Ability Testing, and GCSE results. A reference from the Head of the student's current school is required for all candidates.

Charitable status. Bedford Girls' School is part of the Harpur Trust which is a Registered Charity, number 1066861.

Bedford Modern Junior School

Manton Lane, Bedford, Bedfordshire MK41 7NT

Tel: 01234 332513
email: reception@bedmod.co.uk
website: www.bedmod.co.uk
X/Twitter: @BedfordModern
Facebook: @BedfordModernSchool
Instagram: @bedfordmodern
LinkedIn: /bedford-modern-school

Chair of Governors: Mrs S Jackson

***Head of Junior School*: Mrs P Pacyna**, BA Hons, QTS

Deputy Head of Junior School (*Academic*): Mrs K Harpin, BA Hons

Deputy Head of Junior School (*Pastoral*): Mr M Redmond, BA Hons, PGCE, PGDip, MA, NPQSL

Junior School Head's Assistant and Office Manager: Miss K Harding

Head of Junior School Sports Development: Mr T Bucktin, BSc, PGCE

Age Range. 7–11 Co-educational.

Number of Pupils. 268 (M: 45%; F: 55%).

Fees per annum (2023–2024). £12,324.

The Junior School is housed in its own separate building adjacent to the Senior School. Facilities include specialist rooms for Art and Science, ICT, Design Technology and a refurbished Library, with designated Year 3 classrooms and playground as well as a superb state-of-the-art School Hall.

The whole site overlooks the school playing fields and the Junior School has extensive views over the Ouse Valley. Many of the Senior School facilities are available to the Junior School, including full use of the playing fields, Sports Hall, Gymnasium, covered and heated Swimming Pool and all-weather pitches. The Howard Hall, the 300-seat theatre in the Senior School, provides facilities for full-scale drama productions and concerts.

The school enjoys a strong musical, dramatic and sporting tradition.

Students are admitted to the Junior School at ages 7, 8, 9 and 10 following assessments in January. Most of these are computerised and include English, Maths and non-verbal reasoning. Students proceed to the Senior School at 11, unless special circumstances prevent this.

(*See* Bedford Modern School entry in HMC section.)

Charitable status. Bedford Modern School is part of the Harpur Trust which is a Registered Charity, number 1066861. It includes in its aims the provision of high quality education for all students.

Bedford Prep School

De Parys Avenue, Bedford MK40 2TU

Tel: 01234 362216
email: admissions@bedfordschool.org.uk
website: www.bedfordschool.org.uk
X/Twitter: @bedfordschool
Facebook: @p/Bedford-School-100057414311854
Instagram: @bedfordschool_uk
LinkedIn: /school/bedfordschool

Chairman of Governors: Mr John Holland-Kaye

***Headmaster*: Mr Ian Silk**

Age range. 7–13.

Number of boys. Day Boys: 358, Boarders: 14, Weekly Boarders: 3, Flexi Boarders: 9.

Fees per term (2023–2024). Day: £5,286–£6,927, Full Boarding: £9,410–£11,172, Weekly Boarding: £8,559–£10,731.

Bedford Prep School is a thriving and vibrant independent day and boarding school for boys aged 7–13.

We believe that boys learn best when they're happy and confident, and their curiosity is stimulated, so we feel it's paramount that learning is fun, creative, inspirational and active. We also recognise boys learn differently from girls, and this informs our teaching.

Whether it's music and the arts, science and technology, language and literature, or sports and games, boys are encouraged to learn new skills and embrace new experiences.

Visit our classes and you'll find boys thoroughly engaged in their learning, inspired by challenge, competition, high expectations and risk within a safe environment. Our expectations are high but achievable, and our curriculum encompasses and transcends the National Curriculum. Our bespoke Future Skills Curriculum teaches content and subject-specific skills for each subject while also explicitly developing **skills, attributes and characteristics** to ensure that every boy continually practises these skills and competencies and reflects on our school values. We believe that this enables boys to achieve success not only in the Prep School, but also as they move up to the Upper School, as well as throughout life in general.

Our extensive campus offers boys outstanding academic, sporting, music, drama and art facilities. We share the swimming pool, recreation centre, playing fields, Astro and tennis courts with the Upper School and make use of the school's fantastic theatre and other specialist facilities.

Working with each and every boy, we help them to develop their sporting talents. We provide expert coaching in a wide variety of sports, including rugby, hockey, cricket, golf, skiing, horse riding, cross country, swimming, badminton and rowing.

Creative arts are a big part of school life, with boys taking part in concerts, exhibitions and performances throughout the year. In our dedicated music building, with a state-of-the-art music technology suite and well-equipped practice rooms, many of our boys learn to play one or more instruments, with boys in Years 5 and 6 offered free starter lessons.

Boys can also get involved in a broad range of extracurricular activities: from cookery to steel band, chess to climbing – there is something for every boy.

A full range of wraparound care options is available to working parents. Boys can stay at school, free of charge, until 5.45 pm in our Late Room or join one of our before- and after-school 'Day Plus' sessions.

Eagle House, our purpose-built junior boarding house, is a real home from home for our boarders, who flourish in its warm, family atmosphere. Full, weekly, flexi and occasional boarding is available, enabling boys and their parents to find an option that is just right.

Admissions. Entrance assessments for the Prep School are held during the spring term, and all boys are assessed in English, maths and underlying ability. We will also request a report from your son's current school.

We recommend that families come and visit us to see the school in action and meet the boys and staff. Please call admissions on 01234 362216 or email admissions@bedfordschool.org.uk to arrange a visit or request a prospectus.

Charitable status. Bedford Preparatory School is part of the Harpur Trust, which is a Registered Charity, number 1066861.

Beechwood Park

Pickford Road
Markyate, St Albans, Hertfordshire AL3 8AW

Tel: 01582 840333
email: admissions@beechwoodpark.com
website: www.beechwoodpark.com
X/Twitter: @BWPSchool
Facebook: @BWPSchool
Instagram: @bwpschool
LinkedIn: /company/beechwood-park-school

Chairman of Governors: Mr M Hammond
***Headmaster*: Mr Christian Pritchard**

Age range. 3–13.

Number of pupils. 504: 52 boarders (aged 9–13), 270 day boys and 182 day girls (aged 3–13), including pre-school children at the Woodlands Nursery, which is housed in new purpose-built premises on the main school site.

Fees per term (2023–2024). Day pupils: Years 5–8 £6,925, Years 3 and 4 £5,590, Years 1 and 2 £5,475, Reception £4,785. Boarders (up to 4 nights per week in addition to day fees): £1,645. No compulsory extras. Fees are inclusive of lunches, most trips and visits.

Beechwood Park occupies a large mansion, with a fine Regency Library and Great Hall, in 60 acres of surrounding grounds, which provide ample space for the Forest School (complete with outdoor classroom). Modernisation has added Science laboratories, computer suites, Design Technology workshop, gymnasium and sports facilities, including a large sports hall and two squash courts, two netball courts, an all-weather pitch and an indoor swimming pool complex. Boarding House with modern facilities and spacious common rooms. Two purpose-built classroom blocks house the Middle and Junior Departments. The Music Department has a song room, 14 practice rooms and a newly-opened Music Technology Suite and Recording Studio. A large Performance Hall provides space for assemblies and the many music and drama productions.

Many day pupils use private buses serving Harpenden, St Albans, Berkhamsted and the surrounding villages. Many subsequently convert to boarding under the care of the Acting Head of Boarding, Mr I Griffiths.

Class size is around 20 (15 in Reception); Maths is streamed from Year 3 onwards, English from Year 5 and other major subjects from Year 6. There is a resident Chaplain. The Director of Music has a staff of visiting instrumentalists in a flourishing Music Department.

The number of scholarships gained each year and Common Entrance results affirm a high standard of work, against a background of wide-ranging co-curricular activities.

Football, Rugby, Cricket (boys and girls), Netball, Hockey, Swimming, Athletics and a Sport for All programme, which includes an unusually wide range of minor sports, are all coached by well-qualified PE Staff.

Charitable status. Beechwood Park School is a Registered Charity, number 311068. It exists to provide education for boys and girls from 3–13.

Beeston Hall School

West Runton, Cromer, Norfolk NR27 9NQ

Tel: 01263 837324
email: office@beestonhall.co.uk
website: www.beestonhall.co.uk
X/Twitter: @beestonhall
Facebook: @beestonhall
Instagram: @beestonhall

Chairman of Governors: Mrs H Lindsell / Mr H Hammond

***Headmaster*: W F de Falbe**, BA Hons, PGCE
Bursar: Mrs S Lubbock

Age range. Co-educational 4–13 years.

Number of pupils. 176: 32 Full Boarding, 30 Flexi, 144 Day Pupils; 83 Boys, 93 Girls.

Fees per term (2023–2024). Boarding: £7,750 (Year 3), £10,750 (Years 4–8); Day Pupils: £3,845 (Pre-Prep), £5,270 (Year 3), £7,680 (Years 4–8).

Beeston Hall was established in 1948 in a Regency house set in 30 acres in North Norfolk, close to the sea and surrounded by 700 acres of National Trust land. The Beeston Brief outlines the core values of purpose, resilience and empathy which underpin a small school with a family atmosphere, which is true to its motto of *floreat fiducia* – let confidence flourish.

The scale, and strength, of the pastoral care system ensures that every child is closely watched over and cared for. Beeston has a boarding ethos, the majority full, with weekly or flexi for younger ones, or those progressing towards boarding; most children experience boarding before they leave. Relatively non-selective, Beeston is very proud of the value-added in children's development. Recent destinations have been: Ampleforth, Eton, Downe House, Framlingham, Gresham's, Harrow, The Leys Cambridge, Oakham, Oundle, Queen Margaret's York, Norwich School, Norwich High School for Girls, Radley, Repton, Rugby, Shrewsbury, Stowe, Tudor Hall, Uppingham and Wycombe Abbey. The school enjoys great success at scholarship level, with an average of over 60% of leavers winning awards in the last 6 years.

In addition to the usual examinable subjects, art, music, DT, computing, PHSEE, reasoning and theatre studies are all timetabled, providing children with a wealth of opportunities to find activities in which they can excel. Qualified EAL staff support overseas pupils with a minimum of 90 minutes per week and the Learning Support department is holistic in approach, responding to academic, social and emotional needs which are swiftly identified and acted upon.

Every child takes part in at least one production each year, with an emphasis on developing confidence through participation and presentation. Four choirs and twelve music groups meet each week and 88% of the school learn a musical instrument. The school is equally proud of its record on the sports field where all children are coached, regardless of ability, by a dedicated team of staff, and are given the opportunity to represent the school. In 2016, cricket was introduced for girls, several of whom are county players. The 2023 cohort of boys were county champions for 3 years running and national finalists in the 2021 ESCA competition. Hockey is strong, with both boys' and girls' teams regularly reaching IAPS regional and national stages. In addition to the usual major sports, children compete in cross country, athletics, swimming, tennis, surfing and sailing (IAPS champions in 2019), while a comprehensive activities programme provides opportunities to suit all tastes: shooting, roller-skating, skiing, metal-detecting, chess, cooking or scuba, to name a few. Forest School is a timetabled part of the week for Year 5 and below.

The 2017 ISI Inspection Report comments thus: 'Pupils' attitudes to work are outstanding, nurtured by the high expectations of staff …many awards also reflect pupils' exceptional achievements in areas such as sport, music, art, drama …Pupils can apply their outstanding numeracy skills effectively across a range of subjects …Pupils show outstanding social skills and are highly respectful of people …'.

Religious denomination. Mainly Church of England; 15% Roman Catholic.

Charitable status. Beeston Hall School is part of the Prep Schools Trust, which is a Registered Charity, number 309639. It exists to provide preparatory education for boarding and day boys and girls.

Belhaven Hill School

Belhaven Road, Dunbar, East Lothian EH42 1NN

Tel: 01368 862785

email: secretary@belhavenhill.com

website: www.belhavenhill.com

Facebook: @BelhavenHill

Instagram: @bebelhaven

Chair of Governors: Camilla Gray Muir

***Headmaster*: Olly Langton**, MA Hons History Edinburgh

Deputy Head: John Marriott, BA Hons, MA, PGCE, MBA

Deputy Head Pastoral: Katie Gale, BSc Hons, PGCE, CCRS

Age Range. 5–13 Co-educational.

Number of Pupils. 61 girls, 82 boys; 58 Boarders, 53 Day (in Prep School 8–13yrs).

Fees per term (2023–2024). Day: £4,500–£8,500 per term; Boarding: £10,900 per term.

Religion. Non-denominational.

Overlooking the sea in an idyllic East Lothian location, Belhaven Hill School is a co-educational, independent boarding and day school for 5 to 13-year-olds. Since its establishment in 1923, the school has focused on developing well-rounded, happy, confident children through a strong academic curriculum, lots of sport and a broad extracurricular programme. Ideally placed just off the A1, it is close to a mainline London–Edinburgh railway station, only 30 miles from central Edinburgh and less than an hour to Edinburgh airport.

A boarding and day school, Belhaven has a long tradition of providing a first class all-round education before sending its pupils far and wide to all the leading public schools in both Scotland and England. These include Ampleforth, Eton, Downe House, Fettes, Glenalmond, Gordonstoun, Harrow, Loretto, Marlborough, Merchiston, Oundle, Radley, Rugby, Sherborne, Stowe, Strathallan, Tudor Hall, Uppingham and Winchester. Committed and enthusiastic members of staff work with small classes of between 10–16 pupils. There is ample opportunity for scholarship and extended work, resulting in an impressive number of awards being gained every year. A strong learning support department with four dedicated, trained staff provides one-to-one and small group tuition.

Belhaven pupils are renowned for being happy children and this is in no small part due to the outstanding pastoral care provided for day pupils and boarders alike. The majority of staff live on site and the policy of the governors has been to keep the school comparatively small in order to retain a family atmosphere. A full-time School Nurse and a team of matrons (day and night) take care of the children around the clock. A Deputy Head Pastoral is in overall charge of pastoral care.

The school has an excellent reputation for sport with rugby, netball, hockey, cricket, tennis and athletics, making up the main part of the sporting programme. Swimming takes place from April to October in the school's heated outdoor pool. In addition, many opportunities abound for a wide variety of other recreational activities: skiing, surfing, horse riding, golf on the adjacent links course and gardening for those who want to grow their own produce in the school's walled garden. An extensive Activity Programme offers something for everyone to discover and enjoy such as charity work, debating, 'mastermind', knitting, model-making, computer programming and coding, cookery, crafts, chess, fencing, girls' rugby, mixed football, water polo, Highland dancing and reeling to name but a few.

Music and Drama flourish at Belhaven and every child has ample opportunity to perform in regular concerts and productions throughout the year. LAMDA tuition is available and Academic Music and Drama lessons are now included in the timetable. A stand-alone music building houses a vibrant department which caters for a wide range of instrumental ensembles including its own Pipe Band and two choirs. Over 90% of the children play one or more instruments, with specialist tuition provided by a team of peripatetic music staff. Outdoor Education has always been on the agenda at Belhaven, but is now taking on a more prominent profile, with timetabled lessons for the junior years and expeditions for all.

Belhaven is now preparing for its next major phase of development which forms the focus of its Centenary Campaign. Together with ambitious plans for bursaries, the developments include a new facility to further strengthen digital education and to build on the provision for swimming, indoor sport, drama and musical performance.

Belhaven places the child at the core of everything it does. The school's values of Courage, Creativity and Courtesy, encourage every child to 'have a go' and to do so with ingenuity, good grace and kindness, instilling a belief that they can have a positive influence on the world around them. The 'Belhaven Award', structured in line with these three core values, invites the children to challenge themselves by learning a variety of life skills from bronze to gold level. Ultimately, Belhaven aims to provide the children with the practical skills and the mindset to be able to shape the world around them and meet with confidence the challenges of the 21st century.

Means-tested bursary support is available. Fee concessions are available for children of members of the armed forces. For a prospectus and more information please see our website www.belhavenhill.com or contact Olivia Reynolds our Admissions and Development Officer at admissions@belhavenhill.com.

Charitable status. Belhaven Hill School Trust Ltd is a Registered Charity, number SC007118. Its aim is to educate children in the fullest sense of the word.

Belmont
Mill Hill Prep

The Ridgeway, Mill Hill Village, London NW7 4ED
Tel: 020 8906 7270
email: office@belmontschool.com
website: www.millhill.org.uk/belmont
X/Twitter: @MillHillBelmont
Facebook: @MillHillBelmont
Instagram: @millhillbelmont

Motto: *Instilling values, inspiring minds*

Co-educational Preparatory Day School for 7 to 13 year olds. Awarded 'Excellent' in quality of education in academic achievement and personal development – ISI Inspection January 2020.

Chair of Governors: Mr Elliot Lipton, BSc Hons, MBA, FRSA, FRICS

***Head*: Mr Leon Roberts**, MA

Age Range. 7–13 Co-educational.

Number of Pupils. 292 Boys, 275 Girls. Total 567.

Fees per term (2023–2024). £7,550 Years 3–6, £7,800 Years 7–8).

Overview. Belmont, Mill Hill Prep is a co-educational prep day school, in Mill Hill which educates boys and girls from age 7 to 13. Situated on 35 acres, Belmont is just a short walk from Mill Hill School, which sits on 115 acres of magnificent parkland on the edge of the North London Green Belt and just ten miles from Central London. Awarded 'Excellent' in quality of education in academic achievement and personal development in their last ISI Inspection (January 2020). A part of the Mill Hill Education Group, a charitable collection of independent schools.

Belmont is a warm and caring prep school which believes that the children's happiness and wellbeing is integral to a fulfilling education. Entry at 7+ is automatic from Grimsdell, Mill Hill Pre Prep and selective for external candidates. Entry at 11+ is selective and gives automatic transfer to Mill Hill School at 13+. The school achieves high academic standards, with a significant number of pupils regularly achieving academic, music, art, design, drama and sports awards. The School has a strong reputation for outstanding pastoral care and the personal development of every child as well as a friendly environment in which pupils enjoy learning; the extra-curricular programme is extensive and of high quality.

Academic. Belmont, Mill Hill Prep is proud to offer a curriculum that is academically rigorous and engaging and goes far beyond the national curriculum, in order to instil a love of learning in the pupils. The curriculum runs seamlessly through every school across the Mill Hill Education Group and is designed to prepare pupils for life in the 21st century. It teaches children to think creatively and critically, and builds flexible skills for a fast-changing world of new technologies. Teachers are highly skilled, motivated and love their work. Traditional teaching are both used and learning methods, and innovative approaches using IT, inquiry based projects and peer-to-peer learning.

Pastoral Care. The school believes that a child who is happy and safe in their environment will flourish. The excellent pastoral care underpins all aspects of school life. Therefore, Belmont, Mill Hill Prep actively delivers the values of 'Be Kind, Be Brave and Be You' in every subject, activity, sporting or musical performance the pupils take part in. The backbone of the pastoral system is based on a team of outstanding tutors, who get to know every child and support them on each step of their journey through the School. The pastoral care is individually tailored through the mentoring programme, well-being clubs and additional support for pupils and families is available, if necessary, through the team of School Counsellors.

Activities and Sports. Over 100 clubs are run each term, and always make sure a breadth and variety of activities are offered in each year group that guarantee that every child can find their niche. Pupils perform with skill, energy and commitment. The School has its own sports hall with a climbing wall and cricket nets, secure play areas and an adventure playground. The sports grounds are second to none, and they are set in a stunning landscape. With 30 acres, the school have maintained rugby and football pitches, AstroTurf for hockey, netball courts and cricket squares (including artificial surfaces), cricket nets, tennis courts, and a woodland cross-country course. In addition, the School makes use of further facilities on offer at Mill Hill School, including sports fields, Fives Courts, swimming pool and theatre.

Entry Points. The usual and main point of entry is at 11+ but 7+, 8+, 9+ and 10+ entry is considered as vacancies occur.

Charitable status. Mill Hill Education Group is the brand name for The Mill Hill School Foundation, a Registered Charity, number 1064758. It exists to provide excellence in education.

Belmont Grosvenor School

Swarcliffe Hall, Birstwith, Harrogate, North Yorkshire HG3 2JG

Tel: 01423 771029
email: admin@belmontgrosvenor.co.uk
website: www.belmontgrosvenor.co.uk
X/Twitter: @BelmontGrosvenor
Facebook: @BelmontGrosvenor
Instagram: @belmontgrosvenorschool
LinkedIn: /belmont-grosvenor-school-and-nursery

Chair of Governors: Mrs Charlie Brooksbank

***Headmaster*: Mr Nathan Sadler**, BEd Hons, NPQH

Age range. 3 months–11 years Co-educational.
Number of pupils. 143.

Fees per term (2023–2024). Prep: £4,539, Pre-Prep: £3,832, Pre-Reception: £3,832 full time. Nursery: Under 2s £40.00–£78.00 per session; Over 2s £37.00–£69.00 per session.

Belmont Grosvenor School is a magical place where children make outstanding progress in all that they try, giving them the foundations to thrive in an ever-changing world.

Set in 20 acres of stunning grounds, just a short drive from the centre of Harrogate, North Yorkshire, independent co-educational Belmont Grosvenor School, along with its nursery, welcomes children from three months to 11 years.

The happiness and well-being of our pupils is at the heart of all we do. By using our unrivalled Yorkshire Dales setting, BGS aims to provide a breadth of learning experiences both inside and outside the classroom.

Whether it's building fires in our Forest School area, practising front crawl in our indoor swimming pool or enjoying guided reading in our very own Magic Tree on the front lawn, staff at BGS ensure learning is not confined to four walls.

Smaller class sizes allow high-qualilty personalised learning to take place; teachers at BGS know exactly how to motivate their pupils and help them progress in all they try.

After a decade of education at Belmont Grosvenor School, children continue their successes at a wide range of senior and secondary schools from across the area, but always remain part of BGS!

Belmont Grosvenor is a warm and friendly family school and community that always welcomes new children and families with open arms. It's vision is to nurture and challenge children to make outstanding progress in all they do.

Belmont School

Feldemore, Holmbury St Mary, Dorking, Surrey RH5 6LQ

Tel: 01306 730852
email: admissions@belmont-school.org
website: www.belmont-school.org
X/Twitter: @BelmontDorking
Facebook: @BelmontDorking
Instagram: @BelmontDorking
LinkedIn: /BelmontSchool (Surrey)

See full entry in the **ISA** section, on **p. 862**.

Berkhamsted Pre-Prep

Chesham Road, Berkhamsted, Hertfordshire HP4 2SZ

Tel: 01442 358188 (Pre-Prep)
01442 358276 (Berkhamsted Day Nursery)
email: preprep@berkhamsted.com
website: www.berkhamsted.com/pre-prep
www.berkhamsted.com/day-nursery
X/Twitter: @BerkoPrePrep
Facebook: @berkhamstedschool
Instagram: @berkopreprep
LinkedIn: /berkhamsted-school

Chair of the Governors: Mrs C Copland

Principal: Mr Richard Backhouse, MA Cantab

***Headteacher, Pre-Prep*: Ms Karen O'Connor**, BA, PGCE, NPQH

Age Range. Pre-Prep: 3–7 years. Day Nursery: 5 months–3 years. Co-educational.

Number in School. 112 Boys, 112 Girls.

Fees per term (2023–2024). £3,675–£4,175.

Berkhamsted Pre-Prep is a co-educational independent day school for ages 3–7. Berkhamsted Pre-Prep offers a balanced approach to learning where children are equally nurtured and challenged to extend themselves. Taking risks and being adventurous in all aspects of school life underpin an ambition to aim high with integrity, for every individual child. The extensive grounds and innovative approach to learning which develop not only knowledge but also the skills of being a learner, ensure that the children bound into school excited and hungry to learn more. The family atmosphere, where experienced staff place pastoral care and wellbeing at the heart of school life, provides children with a safe and secure environment to grow emotionally and socially. In addition, children have opportunities to learn French, music, drama, dance, sport and art, all taught by specialist teachers, as well as an outdoor education that takes full advantage of our exceptional grounds.

Knowing that future success is dependent on the firm foundations of academic and personal growth, the excellent educational start at Pre-Prep enable children to progress through the family of schools at Berkhamsted and beyond, with key skills of leadership, independence and high levels of communication. Pupil voice and placing the child at the centre is seen in all aspects of school life with the evidence being considerate, empathetic and confident children who embrace every day with curiosity and a smile.

After-school clubs, outings and trips further enhance an exciting curriculum and extend children's experiences. Wraparound care, from 07.30 to 18.00, supports parents and provides a healthy breakfast and home-from-home experience after a long day. Camp Beaumont, our holiday activities camp at the school designed for 3–11 year olds, is usually available every holiday from 08.00 to 18.00.

Berkhamsted Day Nursery (0–3+ years) is open 50 weeks per year from 07.30 to 18.00, and is situated on the school site. Children can join Berkhamsted Day Nursery from 5 months of age and can move on to Berkhamsted Pre-Prep, which is just next door. Berkhamsted Day Nursery caters for children up to the September that they begin in the Nursery class at Berkhamsted Pre-Prep (when they can use the school's out-of-hours clubs).

In June 2016, the Independent Schools Inspectorate found the quality and standards of the early years provision at Berkhamsted Day Nursery and Berkhamsted Pre-Prep to be '*outstanding*' across all five key areas. The ISI also concluded that 'All children make excellent, continuous progress in relation to their individual starting points and capabilities due to the nurturing and supportive environment that recognises each child as an individual'.

Berkhamsted Prep

Doctors Commons Road, Berkhamsted, Hertfordshire HP4 3DW

Tel: 01442 358201/2
email: prep@berkhamsted.com
website: www.berkhamsted.com/prep
X/Twitter: @berkhamstedprep
Facebook: @berkhamstedschool
Instagram: @berkopreprep
LinkedIn: /berkhamstedschool

Chair of the Governors: Mrs C Copland

Principal: Mr R P Backhouse, MA Cantab

***Head of Pre-Prep and Interim Head of Prep*: Mrs Karen O'Connor**, BA, PGCE, NPQH

Deputy Head: Mr P D Whitby, BA, MA

Age Range. 7–11.

Number of Pupils. 155 boys, 165 girls.

Fees per term (2023–2024). £5,390–£5,960.

Berkhamsted Prep School is part of Berkhamsted School, a school with a 'Diamond' structure that combines single-sex and co-educational teaching. Boys and girls are taught together at the Pre-Prep (Haresfoot site) from age 3 to 7, and at the Prep (Doctors Commons Road site) from age 7 to 11. They are then taught separately from age 11 to 16 (Berkhamsted Boys and Berkhamsted Girls), enabling them to flourish academically, with numerous co-educational activities, trips and events, before coming back together again in a joint Sixth Form. Berkhamsted Prep pupils entering Berkhamsted Senior Schools will not be required to take any entrance exams from the 2025 Year 7 entry onwards: this affects pupils in Year 3 in September 2021, and following years.

Berkhamsted Prep School offers first-class facilities for the 7 to 11 age group, in conjunction with the highest standards of teaching and educational development. All classes offer a happy, caring environment where children are encouraged to investigate and explore the world around them. Classes at all levels have access to computers. Key features include a multi-purpose hall, modern dining facilities and a full range of specialist classrooms (e.g. Science laboratory, a DT and an ICT suite with mobile device accessibility for all year groups, Drama Studio, new Food Technology and Art classrooms). The school has also added a netball court, Eton Fives courts and an outdoor learning area. The Prep School also has use of Senior School facilities including extensive playing fields, tennis and netball courts, a Sports Centre, a swimming pool and a 500-seat theatre.

All children are encouraged to develop to their full potential and grow in confidence and independence. The School's general approach is progressive, while retaining traditional values and standards; courtesy and politeness towards others are expected at all times. Academic achievement is of great importance, but the emphasis on other activities such as sports and music ensures that pupils receive a well-rounded education.

The most recent ISI Inspection Report (September 2017) found that the school was excellent in all areas, in particular in terms of the quality of pupils' academic and other achievements and also their personal development.

A wide range of voluntary extracurricular activities is offered at lunch-time and the end of the school day, including art, drama, music and sport. Choirs and orchestras perform in concerts and services throughout the year and school teams compete successfully in a variety of sports.

In addition, the school operates a holiday care facility with Camp Beaumont, with activity programmes available for 3–11 year olds, tailored by age group. There is something for everyone: craft a new creation in clay, take part in sports and games, relax and unwind with mindfulness and yoga, or have lots of fun with water-based games including aqua Olympics and Wet, Wild and Wacky. There is also extended care from 08.00 to 18.00 each day.

Charitable status. Berkhamsted Schools Group is a Registered Charity, number 310630.

Bickley Park School

24 Page Heath Lane, Bickley, Bromley, Kent BR1 2DS

Tel: 020 8467 2195
email: info@bickleyparkschool.co.uk
website: www.bickleyparkschool.co.uk
X/Twitter: @bickleyparksch
Facebook: @bickleyparksch
Instagram: @bickleyparksch

Chairman of Governors: Mr M Hansra

***Head*: Mr Tom Quilter**

Age Range. Boys 2½–13, Sibling Girls 2½–4.

Number of Pupils. 364 Boys, 6 Girls.

Fees per term (2023–2024). From £2,607 (Nursery) to £6,105 (Boys in Years 4–8). There are no compulsory extras.

Bickley Park School, founded in 1918, is a boys-only day school which occupies two spacious and attractive sites in Bickley, Bromley: the Prep Department at 24 Page Heath Lane and the Pre-Prep Department at 14 Page Heath Lane. The school has excellent facilities to complement the original Victorian buildings, including a five-acre sports field, state-of-the-art science labs, a large sports hall, swimming pool, Theatre and Art Studios.

The Independent Schools Inspectorate (ISI) awarded Bickley Park a 'double excellent' standard, the highest possible grading for an Independent School, following an inspection in March 2023. The school also won Prep School of the Year at the end of 2021 for its 'well-articulated, coherent and holistic Four Quadrants of Learning programme'.

The Nursery Pre-Prep Department provide a first-class foundation before the children progress into Prep. The educational approach combines an inspiring academic and creative curriculum with passionate teaching, outstanding pastoral care and exciting outdoor learning programme.

In the Prep Department, the children are introduced to more specialist teaching and setting for Mathematics, English, Science, Spanish and French. The curriculum is built around Four Quadrants of Learning that espouse academic rigour alongside exceptional opportunities in the wider curriculum.

Most children leave at 13+ to attend some of the UK's leading independent schools, whilst some leave at 11+, usually to join local Grammar Schools.

The school is very outward-looking and enjoys a vibrant community feel.

Charitable status. Bickley Park School Limited is a Registered Charity, number 307915. It exists to provide a broad curriculum for boys aged 2½–13 and girls aged 2½–4.

Bilton Grange

Dunchurch, Rugby, Warwickshire CV22 6QU

Tel: 01788 810217
email: admissions@biltongrange.co.uk
website: www.biltongrange.co.uk
X/Twitter: @biltongrange
Facebook: @biltongrangeschool
Instagram: @biltongrangeprepschool

***Headmaster*: Gareth Jones**, BA Hons, PGCE, MEd

Deputy Headmaster: Colin Langley, BSc Hons, PGCE

Assistant Head – Pastoral: Mireille Everton, BA Hons
Assistant Head – Academic: Greg Das Gupta, BSc, BCom, PGCE
Assistant Head – Boarding: Mark Tovey, BEd Hons
Assistant Head – Teaching and Learning: Nicola Sodhi, MA, BA Hons, QTS
Assistant Head – Pre Prep: Katie Gedye, BA, QTS

UK Registrar: Liz Graham, BSc Hons
International Admissions Registrar: Caroline Morgan, MA Oxon

Age Range. 3–13.

Number of Pupils. 384 boys and girls of whom 90 are full, weekly, or flexi-boarders. Preparatory (8–13 year olds): 251 pupils; Pre-Preparatory and Early Years (3–8 year olds): 133 pupils.

Nestled in 90-acres of parkland and woods, Bilton Grange is a safe and wonderful place where a child's imagination can run free. Whenever and wherever a child's mind is thrilled, they will learn, and here, in this environment, each child can grow up better because they can stay younger longer. They can be the hero of his or her story because Bilton Grange makes learning the adventure it should be.

The hugely popular Headmaster, Gareth Jones, ensures pupils benefit from an impressive range of opportunities designed to support individual interests. Children share common values of respect, awareness of others and courtesy. They are usually 'all-rounders', willing to take advantage of all that is on offer – be it on the sports field, in the classroom or on an adventure weekend. The school demonstrates all the advantages of a traditional prep school curriculum with the benefits of an innovative approach to teaching and learning. Expect small class sizes, a broad range of subjects and specialist teaching staff, plus the '90-acre classroom' to enhance the learning landscape even further.

Bilton Grange is non-selective and yet maintains the highest standards across the board, delivered in a relaxed setting suited to the young learner. Children are entered for the Common Entrance Examination and take their next step to some of the top senior schools across the UK including Rugby, Oundle, Eton, Repton, Oakham, Bloxham and Uppingham. Every year many of our children achieve awards and scholarships to senior schools and, in recent years, all Year 8 leavers have moved up to the senior school of their choice.

Full, weekly and (the very popular) flexible boarding is offered with more than 80 boys and girls enjoying these options. A close knit team of house parents and matrons create a nurturing environment where children feel comfortable, safe and secure, whether they are staying for an occasional night a week or boarding full time.

Impressive facilities feature a purpose-built theatre and separate Music School, an atmospheric panelled library, chapel, sports hall, 25m indoor swimming pool, nine-hole golf course, shooting range and a floodlit artificial grass hockey pitch located within Pugin's walled garden. Sporting success is achieved at regional and national level, while creative arts are a big part of school life with scholarship successes and achievements across Music, Art, Drama and Design Technology.

Fees per term (2023–2024) Preparatory: Full Boarding £11,000, Weekly Boarding £10,210, Day £7,120–£8,080. Pre-Preparatory: £4,530–£5,020. (Fee discounts for Services' children.)

Bursaries and academic scholarships are awarded annually and open to both internal and external candidates in Year 6, to start in Year 7. Bursaries are awarded on a financial need basis – please see the school website for more information.

We encourage all prospective parents and children to visit and see why Bilton Grange is the first step in the adventure of life.

Charitable status. Bilton Grange is part of the Rugby School Group. Charity number 528752.

Birkdale Prep School

Clarke House, Clarke Drive, Sheffield S10 2NS

Tel: 0114 267 0407
email: prepschool@birkdaleschool.org.uk
website: www.birkdaleschool.org.uk
X/Twitter: @BirkdalePrep
Facebook: @BirkdaleSchool
LinkedIn: /company/birkdaleschool

Chairman of Governors: P Houghton, FCA

***Head of Prep School*: C J Burch**, BA, PGCE

Age range. 4–11.

Number of pupils. 250 day.

Fees per term (2023–2024). Pre-Prep Department: £3,586; Prep Department: £4,397. Lunch included.

Birkdale Prep School is a co-educational school specialising in quality education and care for children 4–11. Continuous education is offered from 11–18 at Birkdale Senior School.

Birkdale Prep School is based at Clarke House, situated in a pleasant area near the University, close to the Senior School. The school has a firm Christian tradition and this, coupled with the size of the school, ensures that pupils develop their own abilities, whether academic or otherwise, to the full.

The Pre-Prep Department is based in a separate building, Belmayne House. The facilities are outstanding and designed specifically to meet the needs of 4–7 year olds. Specialist subject teaching across the curriculum starts at age 7 and setting in core subjects in the final two years enhances, still further, the pupil to teacher ratio.

The school has its own Matron and pastoral care is given high priority. Pupils are encouraged to join a wide variety of clubs and societies. Music plays a significant part in school life, both in and out of the timetable. There is a large choir, brass band and orchestra.

Cricket, Rugby and Football are played on the School's own substantial playing fields, which are within easy reach of the school. Netball and Hockey are also played. A broad range of activities is available as part of the extensive extracurricular programme.

The majority of pupils pass into the Senior School.

Charitable status. Birkdale School is a Registered Charity, number 1018973, and a Company Limited by Guarantee, registered in England, number 2792166.

Bishop's Stortford College Prep School

Maze Green Road, Bishop's Stortford, Hertfordshire CM23 2PH

Tel: 01279 838607
email: psadmissions@bishopsstortfordcollege.org
website: www.bishopsstortfordcollege.org
X/Twitter: @BSCollege
Facebook: @bishopsstortfordcollege
Instagram: @thebishopsstortfordcollege
LinkedIn: /school/bishops-stortford-college

Chairman of Governors: Mr G E Baker, BSc, MRICS

***Head*: Mr W J Toleman**, BA

Age Range. 4–13.

Typical Number of Pupils. 36 boarders and 597 day pupils.

Fees per term (2023–2024). Full Boarders £10,215; Overseas Boarders £10,430; Weekly Boarders £9,738; Day £6,141–£6,473; Pre-Prep £3,983. There are no compulsory extras.

Academic qualifications are a prime focus for us, yet we know that qualifications alone will not suffice for a life fully lived. Together, qualifications and qualities are what an education for today and tomorrow must deliver.

There are opportunities. So many opportunities. In the classroom, on the sports fields, in the clubs and societies. We offer every pupil the chance to unearth new talents and to develop valuable life skills.

Underpinning everything is a strong, community spirit that empowers each pupil to thrive and succeed. We have created a community of togetherness where none of us is as important as all of us.

These days standing still is moving backwards. Bishop's Stortford College is not standing still. We are the modern face of independent education.

Charitable status. The Incorporated Bishop's Stortford College Association is a Registered Charity, number 311057. Its aims and objectives are to provide high quality co-educational independent day and boarding education for pupils from age 4 to 18.

Bishopsgate School

Bishopsgate Road, Englefield Green, Surrey TW20 0YJ

Tel: 01784 480222 (Admissions)
01784 432109 (School Office)

email: headmaster@bishopsgatesch.uk
office@bishopsgatesch.uk
admissions@bishopsgatesch.uk

website: www.bishopsgateschool.com

X/Twitter: @BishopsgateSch

Facebook: @bishopsgateschool

Instagram: @bishopsgateschool

LinkedIn: /school/bishopsgateschool

Chair of Governors: Mr Christiian Marriott, BA Hons

***Headmaster*: Mr Peter Thacker**, MEd, BA Hons, PGCE, FRGS

Age Range. 3–13.

Number of Pupils. 400.

Fees per term (2023–2024). £6,173 (Years 5–8), £5,030 (Years 3–4), £5,382 (Years 1–2), £4,506 (Reception), Nursery: £3,895 (5 days), £2,180 (5 mornings).

Set in 20 acres of beautiful woodland, close to Windsor Great Park, Bishopsgate is blessed with a glorious learning environment. The heart of the school remains as a large, Victorian house, but many additional modern buildings have been added offering parents outstanding on site facilities for their children.

The most exciting projects that have been completed are the new Science lab, the new Food Tech room, the sound clouds in the Dining Room and the new astro turf pitch that is situated next to the fabulous brand new state-of-the-art Sports Hall which opened in September 2020. These developments and other future projects are part of the Governors long term plan to ensure Bishopsgate continues to offer excellence in teaching along with progressive facilities.

The School also has a four-lane 25-metre swimming pool and swimming is included in the curriculum from Nursery. In addition, the school has a well equipped Design & Technology Suite and an upgraded IT Suite which includes touch-screen computers and the procurement of laptops and Chromebook for the pupils. The completion of a major upgrade of the School All Weather Facility, the Performing Arts Studio, the building of a new cricket square, and the redevelopment of the current all-weather surface has vastly enhanced the facilities.

Children may enter Bishopsgate from the age of 3 into our Nursery. Our trained staff and well-equipped Nursery ensure that each child is given the best possible start to life. There is a warm family atmosphere as we recognise how important it is for children to feel happy and secure. We place great emphasis on building a solid foundation of social skills and a love of learning, which will enable each child to settle confidently into school life. A wide variety of activities is on offer with plenty of opportunities for healthy outdoor learning for all year groups.

Beyond Nursery, a class teacher remains at the core of each child's learning. Emphasis is placed on establishing a firm foundation in literacy and numeracy, but the curriculum is broad with a range of educational visits planned to enrich and extend the children's learning. The teaching of French, Music, PE, Singing and Dance is provided by specialist teachers. Good use is made of our glorious grounds as an Outdoor Learning resource.

Form-based teaching continues in Years 3 and 4, but by Year 5 all teaching is by subject specialists. Programmes of study in Upper School are full and varied, covering the traditional academic subjects as well as Art, Design, Music, Computer Studies, PSHE and PE. The children are prepared carefully for entrance to a range of senior schools and we are proud of our record of success. We prepare children for 11+ entry to senior schools, but we also encourage our children to remain with us to age 13.

In Upper School, opportunities to represent the school in sports teams, plays, choirs and instrumental groups are all part of the 'Bishopsgate Experience'. In addition, a busy programme of extracurricular activities ensures that all children have the opportunity to shine at something.

Music plays an essential part in the life of the school with many of our pupils enjoying individual music lessons. There are choirs and ensembles. Participation by children of all abilities, with ample opportunities to perform, is our aim. Drama productions, dance and public speaking events all provide additional occasions when the children can develop their presentation skills.

Our vibrant Art and Design Department occupies a spacious studio equipped with a kiln for ceramics and a printing press for design projects. There is an annual ArtsFest for the whole School and the children's work is displayed proudly around the school and in our annual School magazine.

Team Games, Swimming, Rowing, Athletics, Dance, Golf, Tennis, Gymnastics and much more are all included in a varied and exciting sporting programme within the school day. An extensive programme of inter-school fixtures is arranged each term and we like to see as many parents in support as possible! We like to win, but our priorities are participation, enjoyment and teamwork.

A prospectus and further details can be obtained from the Admissions Office.

Charitable status. Bishopsgate School is a Registered Charity, number 1060511. It aims to provide a broad and sound education for its pupils with thorough and personal pastoral care.

Blackheath High School GDST

Senior School
Vanbrugh Park, London SE3 7AG
Tel: 020 8853 2929
email: info@bla.gdst.net
Junior School
Wemyss Road, London SE3 0TF
Tel: 020 8852 1537
email: info@blj.gdst.net

website: www.blackheathhighschool.gdst.net
X/Twitter: @BlackheathHigh
Facebook: @BlackheathHighSchool
Instagram: @blackheathhigh
LinkedIn: /blackheath-high-school-gdst

See full entry in the **GSA** section, on **p. 422**.

Blackheath Prep

4 St Germans Place, Blackheath, London SE3 0NJ
Tel: 020 8858 0692
email: info@blackheathprep.co.uk
website: www.blackheathprep.co.uk
X/Twitter: @BlackheathPrep
Facebook: @blackheathprepschool
Instagram: @blackheathprep

An outstanding co-educational day school in Blackheath, South East London.

Chairman of Governors: Mr Peter Doyle

***Head*: Mr Alex Matthews**, MA, PGCE, MA Ed

Age Range. 3–11.

Number of Pupils. 163 Boys, 191 Girls.

Fees per term (2023–2024). Nursery: £4,915; Reception–Year 2 £5,520; Years 3–6 £5,975.

The school is located close to Blackheath village, overlooking the heath itself and borders of Greenwich Park. The five-acre site includes attractive playing fields, cricket nets, tennis courts and two playgrounds, providing enviable sporting opportunities and room for children to play.

A well-equipped learning environment includes specialist rooms for Science, ICT, Art, DT, Maths and Music. A spacious multi-purpose hall and music suite enhance the opportunities for Music, Drama, Sport and extracurricular activities. Over 70 activities are offered in a wide-ranging extracurricular programme.

Most children join the school in the Nursery at the age of three and progress through the Pre-Prep (4–7) and Prep (7–11) before leaving to transfer to selective senior schools. Academic standards are high and pupils are well prepared for selection at 11 and achieve consistent success in obtaining places at their first choice of grammar or independent senior school. On average over the last five years more than 50% of Year 6 pupils have been awarded academic scholarships each year and scholarships in Art, Music, Drama and Sport.

The form teacher of every class is responsible for the pastoral welfare of each child, supported by a robust pastoral framework across the school. In the Nursery and the Pre-Prep the key worker and the form teacher are primarily responsible for teaching the children. However, there is a strong emphasis on specialist teaching from the very beginning. Music, French, PE, Drama and Dance are introduced in the Nursery. As the children progress through the school, specialist teachers are responsible for Art, ICT, Design Technology, Maths, English and Science. The quality of teaching is recognised as one of the many strengths of the school and pupils are encouraged to develop a sense of curiosity about the world around them and nurture a lifelong love of learning.

The school positively encourages parental involvement in the daily life of the school. The strong ethos and vision of the school of kindness, curiosity, ambition and courage is underpinned by the vibrant enthusiasm of all involved and by a strong sense of community.

The Blue Coat School Birmingham

Somerset Road, Edgbaston, Birmingham B17 0HR
Tel: 0121 410 6800
email: admissions@thebluecoatschool.com
website: www.thebluecoatschool.com
X/Twitter: @bcsbirmingham
Facebook: @bluecoatbirmingham
Instagram: @bcsbirmingham
LinkedIn: /Blue-Coat-School-Birmingham

Founded 1722. Co-educational Day Preparatory School.

Chair of Governors: Mrs K Gilmore

***Headmaster*: Mr N G Neeson**, BEd Hons, NPQH

Age Range. 3–11.

Number of Pupils. The total enrolment is 624 children. Nursery and Pre-Prep have 262 girls and boys from 3–7 years, while Prep has 362 from 7–11 years.

Fees per term (2023–2024). Pre-Prep: £2,899–£4,401; Prep: £5,217–£5,307. The fees quoted include lunches and morning and afternoon breaks. Over 80 co-curricular activities take place each week, some of which are charged as extras.

Assisted Places are available to children with a demonstrable need, entering Years 3 and 4.

7+ Scholarships are offered for academic and musical excellence (entry to Year 3).

The Blue Coat School celebrated its 300th anniversary in 2022, however, its current 15-acre leafy green site in Harborne dates back to 1930 when the school relocated three miles from the city centre.

Behind the impressive facade and clock tower, its state-of-the-art facilities include two brand new science laboratories; an impressive auditorium hall which regularly showcases music and drama performances; a range of grass and AstroTurf pitches for rugby, hockey, cricket, football and netball; a multi-purpose sports centre with a 25-metre indoor swimming pool, sports hall and studios; a computing suite equipped with Apple Macs, a green screen recording studio and an audio recording room; a fully equipped music centre for creating and producing music; an art studio and a dedicated hub for year 6 pupils to simulate a more independent and mature environment for moving up to senior school.

Additional features include a Forest School, an outdoor classroom, a school garden, two libraries and a recently refurbished dining hall.

Spiritual and wellbeing support is integral to upholding the fundamental Christian principles of the School. The on-site Chapel was renovated in 2022 and parents are welcomed into the weekly Chapel services. The 'Lighthouse' also provides a tranquil space for pupils to visit the in-house pastoral team.

All classrooms are equipped with an interactive whiteboard, Apple and Windows technology and an array of resources to achieve the School's vision for limitless learning. Lessons in the classroom are complemented by outings including field courses and residential trips.

Children are prepared for scholarships and examinations to prestigious local schools. The school enjoys particular success in the 11+ examinations to Birmingham's grammar schools and the schools of the King Edward VI Foundation.

The Statutory Framework for the Early Years Foundation Stage is followed for children aged 3 to 5, and the National Curriculum is incorporated at Key Stages 1 and 2 as part of a wider academic structure.

The school is well known for musical excellence. The robed Chapel Choir is affiliated to the RSCM, and there are five further choirs and a significant number of instrumental groups and ensembles. Musicals, concerts and recitals feature in abundance, involving the great majority of the children. Over 300 instrumental lessons are given weekly.

The main sports at Blue Coat are hockey, netball, rounders, rugby, football, cricket, athletics and swimming. The School encourages all children to develop their skills in sport to support both their physical and mental health. The School's teams enjoy considerable success in inter-school and national competitions.

The School also offers exceptional facilities for before and after school and an extensive co-curricular programme to maximise the development of the whole child. The playgrounds feature an array of equipment including a bouldering wall; there are four Houses equipped with music and television facilities, table tennis and social spaces for before and after school socialisation. And a Breakfast Club is offered to Years 2 to 6 from 7.30am. After school care, as well as after school activities are available until 5.45pm for all year groups. The rich co-curricular programme includes gymnastics, judo, creative arts, LAMDA, modern languages and chess.

The House system is also used to facilitate a sense of belonging for Prep children, as they take part in House competitions, charity events and social impact initiatives.

The Blue Coat School has been shortlisted for The Times Prep School of the Year for three consecutive years between 2020 and 2022.

Charitable status. The Blue Coat School Birmingham Limited is a Registered Charity, number 1152244, and a Company Limited by Guarantee, registered in England, number 8502615.

Blundell's Preparatory School

Milestones House, Blundell's Road, Tiverton, Devon EX16 4NA

Tel: 01884 252393
email: prep@blundells.org
website: www.blundells.org

Chairman of Governors: Mr N P Hall, MA, FCA

***Head Master*: Mr A Southgate**, BA Ed Hons

Age Range. 3–11 years.

Numbers of Pupils. 248 (153 boys, 95 girls).

Fees per term (2023–2024). Nursery £201.20–£2,088.05, Prep £2,740–£4,905.

Blundell's Preparatory School is a family school and all the staff adopt a personal interest in every child and work in partnership with the parents. The school places great emphasis on children being happy, secure and confident, thus offering individuals every opportunity to achieve their full potential within a caring family atmosphere. The rural setting is within easy reach of the market town of Tiverton and is conveniently placed less than ten minutes from the M5 motorway and Tiverton Parkway Station.

The School has an excellent reputation for providing sound academic standards which are based on providing the core subjects of Maths, English and Science taught to an extremely high standard. Added to this is the bonus of a wide range of supplementary subjects, well taught by specialist teachers in specialist teaching areas, including a fully-equipped Science Lab, Dance Studio, Art & Design Centre and a Food Technology Suite.

Drama, music and art flourish at Blundell's Preparatory School with all the children participating fully both in lessons and as part of co-curricular activities. Specialist music teachers offer an extensive variety of different instruments. The drama and music departments have their own dedicated facility.

The sports department has an enviable reputation of producing good all-round sporting pupils, as well as nurturing and extending those with talent. Amongst the sports offered are rugby, football, netball, hockey and cross-country in the winter and cricket, tennis, athletics and swimming in the summer. The Preparatory School has access to the extensive sporting facilities within Blundell's senior campus.

There is a comprehensive choice of co-curricular activities offered to the pupils which includes ballet, chess, fencing, golf, art, judo, Bushcraft Club, Wild Wonders and woodwork.

(*See also Blundell's School entry in HMC section.*)

Charitable status. Blundell's School is a Registered Charity, number 1081249. It exists to provide education for children.

Bootham Junior School

Rawcliffe Lane, York YO30 6NP

Tel: 01904 655021
email: junior@boothamschool.com
website: www.boothamschool.com
X/Twitter: @BoothamSchool
Facebook: @BoothamSchool
LinkedIn: /bootham-school

Clerk to the School Committee: Cathy Woodbine

***Head*: Helen Todd**, BA Hons, MA Ed, QTS

Age Range. 3–11 Co-educational.

Number of Pupils. 151.

Fees per term (2023–2024). £2,625–£4,200 inc. lunch for full-time pupils.

Bootham Junior School stands apart by treating each member of its community, in a practical application of Quaker principles, as equally important. We welcome all faiths or none, encouraging our children to develop their own convictions while learning to respect those of others. The Independent Schools Inspectorate reports '*A sense of calm and a quiet pace to the working of the school that enables individuals to flourish*'. Although our children are as boisterous as any others, and, indeed, enjoy a tolerance to behave as children, quietness is important. The values of cooperation, community, and quietness grow from the Quaker tradition, but they resonate with the modern world of work, where teams find solutions individuals can't, where knowledge is seen as interrelated and not separate, and where values-driven responses earn our respect.

At Bootham Junior School, we aim to encourage a lifelong love of learning and inspirational teaching is a good place to start. Equally important is the mutual high regard and understanding that children and teachers enjoy. This relationship provides the very best environment for learning to take place. High standards are achieved because children feel happy, confident, motivated and respected. Education is more than examination preparation; it is about unlocking potential skills and aptitudes. We want our children to find their particular strengths: through sport, through music, through the Arts, through outdoor education, through social debate and action.

Bootham Junior School has a beautiful sports field, a swimming pool at the senior school dating from 1912 and hard courts for tennis and netball. The range of sports taught include: gymnastics, dance, athletics, netball, tennis, swimming, football, basketball, cricket and rounders. Our Director of Music has a range of musical groups including: two choirs, orchestra, flute group, string group, clarinet group and recorder group. Individual music lessons are also available in all instruments should parents wish it. Engagement with the community is in line with a Quaker sense of responsibility and extends to children's activities too. Drama flourishes both within and beyond the formal curriculum. Regular productions of plays and musicals cater for different age groups and allow talents to be explored, nurtured and showcased. Children also take part in LAMDA schemes for recital and public speaking. Our Outdoor Classroom is an extremely well-used resource and all children have the opportunity to take part in residential experiences, from nursery age onwards. We believe in building adaptable, resilient young people who can respond to the world around them. Whatever their interests, this is the place where all our children can find inspiration and where they will be inspired. The small size of our school means that everyone has the chance to try something new. The result is a sense of personal achievement both in and outside the classroom.

Charitable status. Bootham School is a Registered Charity, number 513645.

Boundary Oak School

Roche Court, Wickham Road, Fareham, Hampshire PO17 5BL

Tel: 01329 280955
email: admissions@boundaryoak.co.uk
office@boundaryoak.co.uk
website: www.boundaryoakschool.co.uk
X/Twitter: @boundaryoak
Facebook: @boundaryoakschool

***Director*: Mr James Polansky**, MA Cantab, PGCE
***Headmistress*: Mrs Sophie Savage**, BA Hons, PGCE

Age Range. 2–16.

Number of Pupils. 22 Boarders, 450 Day Pupils.

Fees per term (2023–2024). Boarding Supplement (Years 6–11): £2,415 (Weekly boarding 5 nights); £3,185 (Full boarding 7 nights). Day Pupils: £3,580–£5,860 (Reception–Year 11), Pre-School £68 for all-day session.

The school was founded in 1918 and moved to Roche Court in 1960. A new 99 year lease was secured in 1994. The school is set in 30 acres of pleasant, self-contained grounds between Fareham and Wickham in Hampshire and enjoys extensive views of the countryside around.

The Pre-School takes children from the age of 2 to rising 5 and this group is housed in a purpose-built centre offering the most up-to-date facilities. This department is structured to the needs of this age group and the day can extend from 8.00am to 5.30pm.

The Pre-Prep Department has its own purpose-built buildings and other facilities within the school, and caters for children from rising 5 to 8 years of age (Reception to Year 3).

At 8 years the children move to the Preparatory Department where they remain until they are 11 years old (Year 6). From here they move to Seniors in Year 7 and choose their GCSE options in Year 9 from a large array of subjects. Full and weekly boarding is offered to pupils from the age of 11 years and the school has a policy of admitting boarders in a flexible system that is of great benefit to all. Pupils are prepared for a wide number of independent schools throughout the United Kingdom in a friendly and caring environment.

Apart from the historic main house of Roche Court where the boarders live, there are the Jubilee and Kellett Blocks of classrooms, three science laboratories, the Widley Block, Library and the Music Centre. The School has three ICT Suites and two purpose-built Art and Design Technology Centres that incorporate work areas for Fine Art, Cooking, Photography, Pottery and Carpentry. The school has an Assembly Hall that is also used for Drama and Physical Education.

As well as extensive playing fields with woods beyond for cross country and a woodland classroom for Outdoor Learning, the all-weather AstroTurf pitch is utilised for football, hockey, netball, basketball and tennis. In addition, there is a large sports hall on site and an outdoor, heated swimming pool.

Many sports are taught as part of the curriculum and there is a wide selection of optional extra-curricular clubs and activities available for both day and boarding pupils, these include judo, swimming, horse riding, art, camp craft, chess, and many more.

For a copy of the prospectus and details of scholarships and bursaries, please apply to the Registrar, email: admissions@boundaryoak.co.uk or look at our website www.boundaryoakschool.co.uk.

Bournemouth Collegiate School

Senior School:
College Road, Southbourne, Bournemouth, Dorset BH5 2DY

Tel: 01202 436550
email: registrar@bcschool.co.uk
Facebook: @Bournemouthcollegiateschool
Instagram: @bcs_school

Prep School:
40 St Osmund's Road, Poole, Dorset BH14 9JY

Tel: 01202 714110
email: prep-admin@bcschool.co.uk
website: www.bournemouthcollegiateschool.co.uk

See full entry in the **Society of Heads** section, on **p. 517**.

Bradford Grammar Junior School

Keighley Road, Bradford, West Yorkshire BD9 4JP

Tel: 01274 553742
email: chsec@bradfordgrammar.com
website: www.bradfordgrammar.com
X/Twitter: @JuniorGrammar_BGS
@bradfordgrammar
Facebook: @BGSclockhouse
Instagram: @bradfordgrammarschool
LinkedIn: /bradfordgrammar

Chairman of Governors: Lady Morrison, LLB

***Headmaster*: Mr R Ribeiro**

Age range. 6 to 11 (4 to 11 from September 2024).

Number of pupils. 151 pupils: 79 boys, 72 girls.

Fees per term (2023–2024). £3,665 (Year 2) and £3,863 (Years 3–6).

Bradford Grammar Junior School is a selective school for boys and girls aged 6 to 11 (from age 4 in September 2024), holding no catchment boundaries and a strong reputation for specialist teaching.

The school seeks to inspire happy, respectful and grounded children, who are ready for the transition to Senior School. The school's aim is to provide exceptional care in a nurturing atmosphere so that each child can thrive.

Location. Bradford Grammar Junior School is located at the same site as the Senior School at Keighley Road, Bradford. It is housed in an original seventeenth century manor house called Clock House.

Specialist facilities. The school offers pupils a wide range of specialist facilities, including a swimming pool, theatre, an outdoor classroom, instrumental music tuition and dedicated Computer Science and Design Technology rooms. Full use is made of the Senior School facilities including Science laboratories, Sports facilities and Art rooms.

Specialist teaching. In Years 2, 3 and 4 (ages 6 to 9), pupils are taught the majority of subjects by form teachers and are based in their classrooms, with specialist teaching for Art, Modern Foreign Languages, Music, Computing, and Games. In Years 5 and 6, pupils have increasing input from specialist teachers utilising the extensive facilities throughout the whole school.

Co-curricular activities. The Junior School offers a wide and varied range of co-curricular activities which mainly take place during the lunch break. All pupils are encouraged to participate in at least two different activities each week. These may include: netball, hockey, rugby, swimming, cross country, cricket, football, rounders, athletics, table tennis, dance, design technology, computing, Lego, craft, art, board games, gardening, choir, orchestra, wind band, string group, guitar group and samba band.

Pastoral care. Form Teachers are closely involved with the wellbeing of the children in their form and all of our teachers have a good knowledge of, and relationship with, the pupils. We encourage open communication between school and home and hope parents will keep in close contact with us. A child's progress and happiness are our priorities. We promote good manners and respect for others throughout the School and believe that this is an important aspect of all pupils' education.

After-care. Bradford Grammar Junior School provides before and after-school care from 7.45 am to 6.00 pm.

Transport links. The school organises private coach transport for pupils travelling to and from Huddersfield, Halifax, Bramhope, Horsforth, Rawdon, Wharfedale and Oxenhope. It is situated a short walk from Frizinghall Railway Station, which is on the Airedale and Wharfedale lines. There are half-hourly rail services, taking approximately 30 minutes, to Leeds, Skipton, Ilkley and Apperley Bridge.

Entry. The school is selective and takes a number of pupils each year for entry from Year 2 (age 6 to 7) through to Year 6 (age 10 to 11). Entry to Years 2, 3 and 4 (age 6, 7 and 8) is by assessment. Entry to Years 5 and

6 (age 9 and 10) is by entrance examination and involves tests in Maths and English.

Pupils who progress from Bradford Grammar School Junior School to the Senior School are not required to sit the 11+ entrance exam. The close relationship between the two schools enables a smooth transition from Junior to Senior School.

Charitable status. Bradford Grammar School (The Free Grammar School of King Charles II at Bradford) is a Registered Charity, number 529113. It exists to provide education for children.

Brambletye

Lewes Road, East Grinstead, West Sussex RH19 3PD

Tel: 01342 321004
email: registrar@brambletye.com
website: www.brambletye.co.uk
X/Twitter: @brambletweet
Facebook: @brambletyeschool
Instagram: @brambletyeschool

Chairman of Governors: Mr N J Perry, MA
***Headmaster*: Mr W Brooks,** BA, PGCE, MBA Ed

Age range. 2–13 Co-educational.

Number of pupils. 321 day/boarding pupils.

Fees per term (2023–2024). Boarders: £10,095–£10,330; Day Pupils: £7,430–£8,275; Pre-Prep: £4,125 (Years 1 & 2), £3,840 (Reception), Nursery £3,800 (5 full days) – varied pricing if doing fewer sessions.

Brambletye is an independent day and boarding Preparatory School for boys and girls aged 2–13 years, situated in beautiful grounds in rural Sussex. Brambletye is a large country house in its own wooded estate of 140 acres, overlooking Ashdown Forest and Weir Wood Reservoir. The school stands one mile south of East Grinstead. Gatwick Airport is only 20 minutes by car and Heathrow is an hour away. London is 30 miles by road and 50 minutes by rail. There is escorted travel to and from London at the beginning and end of all exeat weekends and half-term holidays.

The school has outstanding academic, sporting, music, drama and arts facilities. These include a new modern classroom block, two redeveloped science laboratories, an up-to-date Arts Room and Design Technology workshop, a brand new Library, an ICT room, a large theatre and music rooms. There is also a Sports Hall, large astro pitch, tennis and netball courts, two squash courts, a swimming pool, a golf course and several playing fields. We aim to produce happy, confident, well-rounded children who work hard, enjoy drama, games and music, play a part in some of the numerous societies and hobbies, and take a full share in the daily life of the school. These facilities, in conjunction with high-quality teaching staff, generate regular awards for the children from the schools that inherit them.

Brambletye has always been run along family lines, with a distinctive warm and friendly atmosphere. Traditional values such as high standards of manners and good behaviour provide a platform for academic and personal development. As a co-educational day and boarding school, pupils enjoy and benefit from living and working in a community. At weekends, there is a full programme of activities for the boarders and children are encouraged to make constructive use of their spare time. The environment is inspirational and pupils develop a love of learning which creates a positive interaction with the staff and a curiosity about the world around us.

The Nursery and Pre-Prep Department is situated in a self-contained purpose-built state-of-the-art building. The main aim of the Department is to provide a secure, friendly and structured environment in which all children are encouraged to achieve their full potential and to develop at their own rate.

Children may join the Nursery class at the age of two before progressing to Reception at four. Boys and girls transfer to the Prep School at the age of seven. All children acquire the basic skills, while following the breadth of the National Curriculum. Religious Studies, Physical Education, Art, Music, Science and Technology are all integrated into the weekly timetable. Children have swimming lessons throughout the year in the indoor pool, and teachers from the Prep School visit regularly to teach Music and to coach games. The Pre-Prep has an exciting School in the Woods project.

Enquiries about admissions and our scholarships and bursary programme are welcomed throughout the year. Brambletye offers generous discounts for Armed Forces and Foreign Office Families.

Charitable status. Brambletye School Trust Limited is a Registered Charity, number 307003. It aims to provide an all-round education for the children in its care.

Brentwood Preparatory School

Shenfield Road, Brentwood, Essex CM15 8BD

Tel: 01277 243300
email: prep@brentwood.essex.sch.uk
website: www.brentwoodschool.co.uk
X/Twitter: @Brentwood_Prep
Facebook: @BrentwoodSchoolUK
Instagram: @brentwood_prep
LinkedIn: /brentwood-school-uk

Chairman of Governors: Sir Michael Snyder, DSc, FCA, FRSA [OB]

***Headmaster*: Mr K J Whiskerd,** BA, PGCE

Age range. 3–11.

Number of children. Prep: 575.

Fees per term (2023–2024). £5,977.

Brentwood Preparatory School's award-winning, multi-million pound development provides the Prep with the kind of learning spaces that most schools can only dream of. In addition, the growth of the School enables Brentwood to offer a breadth and depth of academic courses and co-curricular programmes that few schools in the country can match: maintaining a small school feel, but with big school opportunities.

A major programme of improvement works; new buildings, refurbishment and upgrading of existing buildings and improvements to external areas and landscaping, now sees the co-educational Preparatory School, which opened in 1892, at the forefront of cutting-edge educational facilities. The Prep also shares the use of Brentwood School's chapel, indoor swimming pool, Sports Centre and world-class athletics track.

Children in EYFS and KS1 are primarily taught in the spacious Higgs Building and South Prep within very well-equipped classrooms. Entrance is by an informal assessment at age 3. With Bayman Forest as the home to our extensive Forest School programme, and the chance to participate in drama and musical performances, our EYFS and KS1 pupils are enriched with opportunities, alongside their structured curriculum.

Older children in KS2, are mainly based in Middleton Hall, an elegant building which has its own extensive grounds, sports pitches and all-weather Astroturf. Entrance is at age 7 by an academically-selective test and candidates come from a wide range of schools. Small class sizes and a team of well-qualified and specialist teachers, provide a caring and challenging environment. Designated rooms for art, design and food technologies, drama, MFL (French, Spanish, German and Chinese), ICT, music, science and our forward-thinking Futures Room provide outstanding facilities and a stimulating environment in which children can thrive.

There is an extensive programme of house and inter-school sports matches. All pupils have the opportunity to represent the school at an appropriate level. Choirs, orchestras and a variety of ensembles perform regularly both in and out of school. Every child has the opportunity to take part in a major drama production. There are a huge range of co-curricular lunchtime and after-school clubs that are offered through our ACES (Arts, Community, Enrichment, Sport) programme. All Prep pupils participate annually in Enrichment Week and weekly in our Activities Programme to complement school-based work. They also enjoy annual residential trips both at home and overseas.

The Preparatory School has a strong academic tradition and a reputation for providing an excellent all-around education. The vast majority of pupils transfer to the Senior School (founded in 1557) at age 11.

With the increase in the Preparatory School roll; expanded and re-organised Early Years facilities; new Assembly and Dining amenities; and a suite of state-of-the-art specialist teaching areas, the School is proud of its offering.

The Preparatory School offers various Foundation options and all Prep pupils, from 3 years of age, can extend their school day from 7.30 am–6.00 pm by using our Wraparound.

Charitable status. Brentwood School (part of Sir Antony Browne's School Trust, Brentwood) is a Registered Charity, number 1153605. It exists for the purpose of educating children.

Brighton College Prep School

Years 4 to 8:
Walpole Lodge, Walpole Road, Brighton, East Sussex BN2 0EU
Tel: 01273 704210
email: prepoffice@brightoncollege.net

Nursery to Year 3:
Eastern Road, Brighton, East Sussex BN2 5JJ
Tel: 01273 704259
email: preprepoffice@brightoncollege.net
website: www.brightoncollege.net
X/Twitter: @bcpsuk
Facebook: @bcpsuk
Instagram: @bcpsuk

Chair of Governors: The Lord Mogg, KCMG

***Headmaster*: Ant Falkus**, BSc Hons

Senior Deputy Head:
Ms T Hoyles, BA Hons, QTS

Deputy Heads:
Mrs J Tooke, BA Hons, PGCE
Mr P Smith, BA Hons, PGCE
Mr D Lawson, BA Hons
Mr G Jackson, BSc Hons, PGCE
Ms L Amos, BA Hons, PGCE

Registrar: Alison Westbrook, BA Hons, PGCE

Age Range. 3–13.

Number of Pupils. 512.

Fees per term (2022–2024). From £4,340 (Reception) to £7,960 (Year 8).

Brighton College Prep School is a co-educational school, which offers a broad curriculum taught to high standards by dedicated and energetic staff. The Pre-Prep cares for children from Nursery to Year 3 in a purpose-built building with playing fields, overlooking the sea. Years 4 to 8 are housed on their own site situated adjacent to the College. Both sites are urban but enjoy close proximity to the sea, the South Downs and the vibrant sports and culture of Brighton, where an annual arts festival is held in May. Some of the excellent facilities provided by Brighton College are shared, including the College Chapel, the School of Science and Sport, playing fields, a purpose-built Recital Hall and the Great Hall.

From Reception, our children benefit from specialist lessons in art, music, French, Mandarin, library, PE, games and swimming on its own well-equipped site. From Year 4 upwards, specialist teaching is broadened to include design technology, LAMDA, our innovative HEALTH curriculum and Spanish and German.

Pastoral care is strong and a culture of kindness is commonplace and reinforced in assemblies, within the curriculum and during form time. The motto from Nursery to Year 8 is 'Be Kind, Be Curious, Be Confident. Be the Best You'.

Academic standards are high and are one of the foundations upon which school life is built, along with the broad range of subjects taught. A variety of teaching methods is used – the key principle being that children enjoy their lessons and thus develop a love for learning.

Learning Support teachers can provide specialist teaching on a 1:1 basis or in small groups for pupils with an identified need.

Sport is a very important part of life at the school. The teaching of girls' and boys' games begins in Year 1 and includes netball, hockey, football, rugby, cricket, athletics and swimming.

The school is well known for its strength across the performing arts. Thirty-five visiting music teachers provide tuition for a large number of pupils who learn a wide variety of instruments. There are two orchestras, a concert band and three choirs organised by the music department.

Drama clubs and lessons are available from Year 3 and there are opportunities for children to perform during the academic year through assemblies, recitals, Chapel services and annual drama productions and musicals. The Brighton College School of Dance is thriving, and many pupils attend classes after school during the week and on Saturdays.

The school runs over 100 clubs and activities after school and at lunchtimes for pupils from Reception and there is a range of school bus routes for pupils from Year 4. Children attending Nursery can stay for optional, themed afternoons, including yoga, French and art.

The Admissions team hold regular events for prospective pupils and their families or can arrange individual visits. Open Mornings, taster days and themed mornings take place throughout the year, alongside taster and assessment days for pupils wishing to join the school. For more information, contact prepadmissions@brightoncollege.net or 01273 704343.

Charitable status. Brighton College is a Registered Charity, number 307061. It exists to provide high-quality education for boys and girls aged 3–18.

BGS Infants and Juniors

Elton Road, Bristol BS8 1SR

Tel: 0117 973 6109
email: admissions@bgs.bristol.sch.uk
website: www.bristolgrammarschool.co.uk
X/Twitter: @bgsbristol
Facebook: @bgsbristol

Chairman of Governors: Romesh Vaitlingam, BA Hons Oxon, MBE

***Head*: Miss Heidi Hughes**, BA Hons, MEd, PGCE

Deputy Head: Mrs Veryan Rookes, BSc Hons, PGCE
Deputy Head: Mrs Vicky Drew, BA Hons, QTS

Assistant Head: Mrs Lucy Bendall, BA Hons, PGCE
Assistant Head: Mrs Kate Conway, BA Hons, PGCE

Age Range. 4–11.

Number of Pupils. 336. Infants 108; Juniors 228

Fees per term (2023–2024). Juniors: Years 3–6 £3,951. Infants: Years 1 & 2 £3,671, Reception £3,362. Fees include lunch.

BGS Infants and Juniors is an independent co-educational day school. It was founded in 1900 and since 2010 has offered Infant as well as Junior provision. The School occupies self-contained buildings on the same site as the Senior School, Bristol Grammar School (*see entry in HMC section*). The School's facilities include a Hall, Library, Music, Art, Science and Technology rooms. Some facilities are shared with the Senior School, particularly the Sports Hall, Performing Arts Centre and Dining Hall. The School now thrives on the happy and purposeful demands of approximately 340 girls and boys aged 4–11 years.

Entry into BGS Infants is by an informal assessment session. Entry for the Junior School is by test and is normally at seven or nine years old (entry to other age groups is subject to the availability of places). Peloquin bursaries are awarded annually and are means-tested. Children who have been members of the School since the start of Year 5 or earlier are offered places in the Senior School following continuous assessment of their progress; other children take the normal Senior School entrance test.

BGS Infants and Juniors aims to provide a rich, broad and balanced curriculum while also maintaining a nurturing environment for children to flourish. The School encourages all pupils to develop their own ideas, giving support so they gain skills and confidence and offering challenges to stretch their thinking. Many subjects are taught by subject specialists, including specialists from the Senior School. Music, art, dance and drama are particularly encouraged with the annual MADD Evening being a particular highlight. There are many clubs and activities including Lego, Gardening, Mindful Colouring, Russian, Board Games, Ukulele, and Coding, as well as extra sports and musical opportunities. One afternoon per week is dedicated to the Activity programme, where children can choose a new challenge or a favourite hobby. In addition, all children in the Infant School, and many Juniors, take part in Forest School and swimming lessons. The children have many opportunities to develop leadership and responsibility; the Infant and Junior School Councils meet regularly with the Head and there is a Charity Committee as well as an Eco-Committee.

A wide range of sports is offered to the pupils at the School's superb playing fields at Failand with its state-of-the-art pavilion. The impressive purpose-built Sports Hall on the main campus provides facilities for indoor PE and has a climbing wall. Pastoral care is provided by the Form Tutors and the Assistant Heads, supported by all teaching staff and the Head. Form Tutors take a lead in ensuring that children are learning and progressing well. A prosperous House system produces many friendships between age-groups, with mentors and buddies showing new pupils the ropes, making sure that things are running smoothly for them. This leads to a strong sense of family and community within the School owing much to the warm and trusting relationships between children, with each other and with their teachers.

Charitable status. Bristol Grammar School is a Registered Charity, number 1104425. The object of the Charity is the provision and conduct in or near the City of Bristol of a day school for boys and girls.

Brockhurst & Marlston House Schools

Hermitage, Newbury, Berkshire RG18 9UL
Tel: 01635 200293
email: r.harper@brockmarl.org
website: www.brockmarl.org.uk

***Headmaster*: Mr D J W Fleming**, MA Oxon, MSc

Age Range. 2–13.

Number of Girls. 346, Girls 114, Boys 129, Pre-Prep 103.

Fees per term (2023–2024). Full Boarding £9,700 (UK), Full boarding International Pupils £10,200 (includes transfers, uniform provision and EAL). Armed Forces & Diplomatic Service Families £7,700. Reception to Year 2 £4,450. Day (full, Year 3 to Year 8) £7,400, includes tuition, lunches, sport and many of our extracurricular activities. Flexi-day fee £4,750, covers the full academic programme which is timetabled until 3.00 pm. Flexi-day fee pupils are welcome to take part in as many of the activities as suits you. Each activity session costs £28.50 and there are over 80 activities to choose from each week. You can opt in to as many activity sessions as you would like to. This enables you to design a timetable from the very wide range of activities to suit the interests of your child.

Established in 1995, Marlston House is situated in 500 acres of its own grounds in countryside of outstanding beauty, only four miles from access to the M4. The school is situated beside Brockhurst Boys' Preparatory school and occupies separate listed buildings. Boys and girls are taught separately, but the two schools join together for drama music and activities. In this way Brockhurst and Marlston House combine the best features of the single-sex and co-educational systems: academic excellence and social interaction. The schools are proud of the high standard of pastoral care established within a family atmosphere. (*See also entry for Brockhurst School.*)

The Pre-Prep School, Ridge House, is a co-educational department of Brockhurst and Marlston House Schools for children aged 3–6 years, and is situated on the same site in new self-contained, purpose-designed accommodation. Our Pre-Prep also includes a 51 week a year Nursery.

Girls are prepared for entry to a variety of leading Independent Senior Schools through the ISEB Common Entrance and Scholarship Papers at 11+ and 13+.

All girls play Netball (outdoor and indoor courts), Hockey, Rounders and Tennis (outdoor and indoor courts) and take part in Athletics, Cross Country and Swimming (25m indoor heated pool). Additional activities include riding (own equestrian centre), fencing, judo, shooting (indoor rifle range), dance and ballet. Facilities for gymnastics and other sporting activities are provided in a purpose-built Sports Hall. Year 7 pupils make a week-long visit to a Château in France as part of their French studies.

Music and Art are important features of the curriculum and a number of girls have won scholarships and awards to senior schools in these subjects recently. The school has a dedicated Music School and professionally designed Theatre.

Transport is provided by the school to and from airports and between Newbury and Paddington stations. Pupils are accompanied by school staff to their destinations.

Bromley High School GDST

Blackbrook Lane, Bickley, Bromley, Kent BR1 2TW
Tel: 020 8781 7000
email: bhs@bro.gdst.net website:
www.bromleyhigh.gdst.net X/Twitter:
@bromleyhs
Facebook: @bromleyhighschoolGDST
Instagram: @bromleyhighschoolgdst
LinkedIn: /school/bromley-high-school-gdst

See full entry in the **HMC** section, on **p. 44**.

Bromsgrove Preparatory & Pre-Preparatory School

Old Station Road, Bromsgrove, Worcs B60 2BU
Tel: 01527 579679
Pre-Preparatory:
Avoncroft House, Hanbury Road, Bromsgrove, Worcs B60 4JS
Tel: 01527 579679
email: admissions@bromsgrove-school.co.uk
website: www.bromsgrove-school.co.uk
X/Twitter: @BromsSchool
Facebook: @BromsgroveSchool
Instagram: @bromsgroveschool

Chair of Governors: Mr Michael Luckman

***Headmaster*: Mr M Marie**, BSc, PGCE

Age Range. 2–13.

Number of Pupils. Prep School (7–13): 218 day boys, 211 day girls, 57 boy boarders, 37 girl boarders. Pre-Preparatory (4–7): 69 boys, 60 girls. Nursery: 56 pupils.

Fees per term (2023–2024). Nursery: £68.20 per day; Pre-Prep: £3,250–£3,580; Prep: £4,690–£6,080 (day), £9,770–£12,055 (full boarding), £7,125–£8,630 (weekly boarding).

Forces Bursaries and, from 11+, scholarships (academic, art and music) are available.

Bromsgrove Preparatory School feeds the adjacent 1000-strong Senior School. (*See Bromsgrove School entry in HMC section.*) The sites covering 100 acres offer exclusive and shared facilities, with a combined Prep and Senior Performing Arts Complex opened in November 2017, which gives outstanding performance and rehearsal facilities to the School. Boarding at prep is thriving with a dedicated boarding house (Page House) for 100 boys and girls, this has recently been extended by the addition of Conway Page for pupils in Year 8. This allows the School's youngest boarders to live together in modern and comfortable surroundings. Other recent improvements include a new suite of classrooms, an upgrading of the dining hall, a new science laboratory, refurbishment of the library, main hall and sports hall. Pupils have access to a flourishing Forest School. Teachers working in both Senior and Preparatory Schools ensure continuity of ethos and expectation.

Academic, sporting and cultural facilities are extensive and outstanding.

Pupils are admitted at the age of 7+ with another substantial intake at 11+ but pupils, including boarders, are admitted throughout the age range up to 13. Admission to the School is by Entrance Test supported by a report from the current school. Year 5 and 6 pupils are assessed during the course of the year; the outcome of these assessments allow them to be guaranteed a place in Bromsgrove Senior School two years later. Pupils admitted at age 11 are also guaranteed entry to the Senior School.

Prep School boarding is flourishing and the junior boarding houses are lively, homely environments where pupils are cared for by resident houseparents and a team of tutors. The School aims to make a boarder's first experience of life away from home enjoyable and absorbing.

All academic lessons are timetabled from Monday to Friday, with Saturdays offering an optional and flexible programme of activities and sports fixtures, the majority of pupils attend for activities on a Saturday. The School has a national reputation in a number of sports.

The aim of the School is to provide a first-class education, which identifies and develops the potential of individual pupils, academically, culturally and socially. It prepares them to enter the Senior School with confidence. In the Preparatory School, there is a purposeful and lively atmosphere. Mutual trust, respect and friendship exist between staff and pupils. The high quality and dedication of the teaching staff, favourable teacher to pupil ratio and regular monitoring of performance ensure that the natural spontaneity and inquisitiveness of this age group are directed purposefully. The latest ISI Inspection (June 2023) found the School to be excellent in both categories covered by the inspection.

The pastoral care system is rooted in the School's Christian heritage and firmly founded on the form tutor. It is designed to ensure that every pupil is recognised as an important individual and that their development is nurtured.

The School has its own feeder Pre-Preparatory School which takes children from the age of 2. The clear majority of children transfer to the Prep School at the end of Year 2. Situated just a mile away from the Prep and Senior Schools, in the spacious tree-lined grounds of an old manor house, the Pre-Preparatory School has spacious and light classrooms and delightful outdoor areas including the popular Forest School. The Headmaster is Head of both the Preparatory and Pre-Preparatory sections, giving good continuity and communication between the School. High teacher to pupil ratios and small class sizes ensure each pupil's individual needs are met.

Charitable status. Bromsgrove School is a Registered Charity, number 1098740. It exists to provide education for boys and girls.

Brontë House

The Junior School of Woodhouse Grove

Apperley Lane, Apperley Bridge, Bradford, West Yorkshire BD10 0PQ

Tel: 0113 250 2811
email: enquiries@brontehouse.co.uk
website: www.woodhousegrove.co.uk
X/Twitter: @BronteHouse_
Facebook: @brontehouseschool
Instagram: @brontehouseschool

Chair of Governors: Mr A Wintersgill, FCA

***Head*: Mrs S Chatterton**

Deputy Head (*Pastoral*): Mrs F Pearson
Deputy Head (*Academic*): Mrs H J Simpson
Head of Early Years: Mrs H Foster
Assistant Head (*Operations*): Mr J Gallucci

Office Manager: Mrs K Bedford
Admissions: Mrs J Amos

Age Range. 2–11 Co-educational.

Number of Pupils. 308 Boys and Girls.

Fees per term (2023–2024). £3,640–£4,650. Fees are graduated according to age. Ashdown Lodge Nursery and Reception: £3,640 (term-time only)–£4,675 (51-week place). The day fee covers an extended day from 7.30am to 6.00pm; there are no extra charges for breakfast, tea or the majority of supervised activities after lessons.

At Brontë House we welcome children into Ashdown Lodge, our Early Years setting, from the age of two years old. In Pre-Nursery and Nursery, there are two types of child care options to meet the different requirements of our families: term-time only and 51-week contracts.

The School is situated in its own grounds, a short distance from the Senior School, close to both Leeds and Bradford and with easy access to Leeds/Bradford Airport and the Yorkshire Dales National Park.

Our hard work has been recognised by the latest Independent Schools Inspectorate inspection which rated both Brontë House and Woodhouse Grove as Excellent. The inspectors came away with very clear evidence of the values that we seek to promote. They recognised our outstanding academic and co-curricular programme and our aim to ensure that all our pupils reach their full potential.

During their time in Foundation Stage, we aim to develop a child's ability and self-confidence, encouraging good behaviour and consideration for others. Children are provided with a stimulating programme of learning and play within a calm and relaxed atmosphere, providing a framework for every individual to fulfil their potential ready for the next stage of their education.

The EYFS curriculum is followed, beginning in Nursery and lasting for two years. Language and literacy, mathematics, knowledge and understanding of the world, physical and creative development are promoted in preparation for the transfer to Key Stage One.

By encouraging a child's intellectual, creative, sporting and personal development, we aim to get the best from our children in the classroom, on the games field, in music, drama and all other activities. We maximise the use of our outdoor surroundings to promote learning. The broad academic curriculum covers a wide range of subjects, including foreign languages, but with particular emphasis on ensuring a strong foundation in reading, writing, mathematics and science.

As children progress through the school they are encouraged to take increasing responsibility and to show consideration for others. Friendship, trust and courtesy are promoted so our children have a sound foundation as they move up to Woodhouse Grove at the end of Year Six.

We aim to encourage every pupil to develop his or her potential across both curricular and co-curricular areas by participating in a variety of activities. As they progress through the school, sport plays an increasingly significant role in the life of the children and there are plenty of opportunities for pupils to be involved in team games and individual sports, which encourage not only physical achievement, but also a healthy outlook for enjoying school life to the full.

As with sports, music and drama also play an important part of life at Brontë House. All children are encouraged to learn an instrument. The music curriculum is a mixture of traditional and modern with opportunities for composing and performing. There are many choirs and ensembles and the children are regularly offered the chance to take part in concerts and festivals. Housed in spacious rooms on the top floor of Brontë House, our children are given excellent opportunities to develop musically and creatively.

Charitable status. Woodhouse Grove School is part of the Methodist Independent Schools Trust, which is a Registered Charity, number 1142794.

Brooke Priory School

Station Approach, Oakham, Rutland LE15 6QW
Tel: 01572 724778
email: communications@brooke.rutland.sch.uk
website: www.brooke.rutland.sch.uk
X/Twitter: @Brooke_Priory
Facebook: @brookepriory
Instagram: @brookeprioryschool

***Headmaster*: Mr Duncan Flint**, BSc Hons, PGCE

Age Range. 2 to 11 years (co-educational).

Number of Pupils. 134: 114 (age 4+ to 11); 20 (Nursery, age 2 to 4).

Fees per term (2023–2024). £2,395–£4,065.

Staff. There are 17 qualified members of the teaching staff.

Brooke Priory is a day Preparatory School for boys and girls. The school was founded in 1989 and moved into its own purpose-built building in February 1995. Since then it has doubled its classroom provision, established a Nursery, fully-networked Computer Suite, state-of-the-art Resources Centre, Theatre, Art & DT Studios, individual Music Practice Rooms, Sports Hall and Astroturf.

Brooke Priory provides a stimulating, caring environment in which children are encouraged to attain their highest potential. Class sizes average 14, and children are grouped according to ability in Mathematics and English (reading and spelling).

The school delivers a broad and varied curriculum, where every child will participate in Art, Drama, French and Music. Many children in the Prep Department enjoy individual music lessons and are encouraged to join one of the Choirs and Ensembles.

The curriculum is enriched with a variety of trips, visits (and residential trips for Forms III–VI) which support learning in the classroom.

In recent years, the school has enjoyed 100% pass rate at 11+ to independent schools and local select entry grammar schools. Some children are offered scholarships to independent schools each year including academic, music and sport. In 2021, a record number of scholarships were awarded to children progressing to a variety of senior independent schools. Children progress to senior schools as confident and independent learners.

Sport is an important part of the curriculum. Children swim weekly throughout the year and are taught in a wide variety of games by specialist staff. The main sports are Football, Rugby, Hockey, Netball, Cricket, Rounders, Tennis and Athletics.

The original Brooke Priory, which is situated just 1 mile outside Oakham, is set in 30 undulating acres and everyone, from the Nursery to Year VI, visits regularly for Welly Days.

The school's aims include 'positive relationships'; the teachers know the children as individuals and develop a level of trust which allows children to flourish in a safe, inspiring environment. Outstanding teaching, with bespoke levels of challenge for all children ensure every child reaches their potential.

The school offers a wide choice of extracurricular activities. Before and after school care is available and holiday clubs are enjoyed by many children. Many holiday courses specialise in sport, dance/drama and music.

Broughton Manor Preparatory School

Newport Road, Broughton, Milton Keynes, Buckinghamshire MK10 9AA

Tel: 01908 665234
email: info@bmprep.co.uk
website: www.bmprep.co.uk

Chair of the Governors: Mrs Vivianne Thompson, BA Hons, QTS (Early Years Specialism), MHFA (Mental Health First Aider)

***Headmaster*: Mr Jeremy Smith**, BA, QTS
***Headmistress*: Mrs Rachel Smith**, BA, PGCE

Age range. Nursery: 2 months–2 years. Pre-Prep: 2–7 years. Preparatory Department: 7+–11 years.

Number of pupils. 350 Day Pupils.

Full time fees per term (2023–2024). Nursery (per week): £332 (2 months–2 years). Pre-Preparatory: £4,660 (2–5 years), £4,900 (6–7 years). Preparatory: £5,330 (8–11 years).

Broughton Manor Preparatory School is part of the Chatsworth Schools family, who have a proven track record of outstanding educational leadership with real integrity, a passion for schools as learning communities and a commitment to excellence.

The opening hours are 7.30 am to 6.30 pm, providing care before and after the core hours of the school day. The school is open for 46 weeks per year, which includes a 35-week academic year and 11 weeks of in-house play schemes during the school holidays.

Staff are highly qualified experts, who are committed to delivering the very best teaching and levels of care.

The Nursery can be found in the Manor House, within the grounds of the Preparatory School. Its safe and nurturing environment, for children from 2 months to 2 years, provides a rounded learning environment for children to grow and thrive.

The Early Years professionally led staff team consists of qualified and experienced practitioners.

The Nursery is surrounded by beautiful outdoor spaces where the children have access to a large lawned area, sandpits, astro and the Spinney.

The Pre-Preparatory and Preparatory Departments are housed in a modern, purpose-built building. The school offers the absolute best in teaching and learning at every age. The academic core is intertwined with a wide raft of subjects and opportunities.

Academic standards are excellent, with pupils being prepared for entry to senior independent schools, both locally and nationally, and to grammar schools. Teaching is structured to take into account the requirements of the National Curriculum, with constant evaluation and assessment for pupils.

With an average class size of 14, every child receives individual, tailored learning.

All departments have access to outdoor learning and extensive playground areas; there is a multi-purpose Sports Hall, a separate Assembly Hall and Astroturf court.

State-of-the-art facilities include an Art Studio, high-tech Computing Suite and STEM laboratories.

Music, Drama and Sport play an important part in the life of the school. Concerts are held, and a wide variety of sport is played, with teams competing regularly against other schools, and additional clubs are held for those wanting to learn specialist activities such as karate, yoga, tennis and ballet.

The school aims to incorporate the best of modern teaching methods and traditional values in a friendly, caring and busy environment, where good work habits and a concern for the needs of others are paramount.

Broughton Manor aims to develop skills for life; self-confidence, resilience, independence, respect for others and the environment, creativity and imagination.

Broughton Manor welcomes children of all ages, all year round.

Bruern Abbey School

Chesterton House, Chesterton, Oxfordshire OX26 1UY

Tel: 01869 242448
email: secretary@bruernabbey.org
website: www.bruernabbey.org

***Executive Head*: Mr J Floyd**, MA, PGCE

Age Range. Boys 8–16.

Number of Pupils. 152.

Fees per term (2023–2024). Day £9,630–£10,220, Boarding £11,235–£12,295, Flexi Boarding £68 per night.

Bruern Abbey School is unique in the marketplace because it is the only school in the country that caters exclusively for children diagnosed with learning difficulties and prepares them for Common Entrance to mainstream public schools; learning difficulties should not preclude academic success. ISI has stated that 'pupils are successfully educated in a secure and nurturing environment where they are given every possible help and encouragement to overcome the challenges presented by their specific learning difficulties'. Bruern provides a tailored education in beautiful surroundings and maintains high expectations for the academic future. We aim to enhance boys' self-esteem, in the firm belief that confidence is the key to academic success. A recent Crested report stated that 'Bruern Abbey is a unique school with its own special way of delivering an all-round education for its pupils. It successfully prepares boys for the Common Entrance Examination whilst at the same time developing each boy into a happy and confident individual'.

Bruern Senior School opened in September 2022, extending provision to provide boys with invaluable support throughout their GCSEs and beyond.

In most other respects, Bruern models itself on traditional preparatory schools, with breadth to the curriculum, including French to Common Entrance, full and varied sports, activities and cultural programmes, and the adherence to good manners, self-discipline and common courtesy. We encourage boys to share their aspirations and their anxieties. Ofsted has stated that 'the school has an incredibly warm and compassionate approach to all the boys' and also that 'pastoral care is exceptional – very understanding and caring staff'.

At Bruern we place great emphasis on experiencing all that prep school life has to offer; specialist teaching should not mean missing out on all the fun. We also make every effort, despite our somewhat diminutive size, to give the boys an action-packed time – be it musical, theatrical, cultural or sporting.

Bruern differs from traditional preparatory schools in many ways which allow our boys to succeed at Common Entrance and be ready for life beyond. These are regarded as the 'pillars' upon which the School's ethos and reputation, founded by the Principal in 1989, still stand, not to be compromised under any circumstances, and ingrained within the mission statement. They are not necessarily in any order of priority, but are:

- a clear focus on literacy and numeracy, with nine periods each of English and Mathematics a week. We have approximately twice as many English and Maths lessons as standard prep schools for all our Junior School boys, and there are two teachers in each class for these key subjects;
- small classes (eleven pupils or fewer) which allows boys more individual attention in class;
- limited withdrawal for remedial support, as boys needs are met in class;
- the extensive use of IT as a tool with which to deliver the curriculum;
- the use of laptops in lessons. For those who have difficulty in expressing themselves as swiftly or as coherently on paper as they do in speech, this is an absolute godsend;
- the teaching of reading as a distinct curriculum subject;
- the importance attached to good food and to finding the time for children within their busy schedule to eat, talk, play and relax together without the distraction of television or electronic games.

Bryanston School

Blandford, Dorset DT11 0PX
Tel: 01258 484632
email: head@bryanston.co.uk
website: www.bryanston.co.uk
X/Twitter: @BryanstonSchool
Facebook: @bryanstonschool

See full entry in the **HMC** section, on **p. 50**.

The Buchan School

Westhill, Castletown, Isle of Man IM9 1RD
Tel: 01624 820110
email: admissions@kwc.im
website: www.kwc.im
X/Twitter: @kwciom
Facebook: @kwciom
Instagram: @kwcandthebuchanschool
LinkedIn: /school/king-william's-college

Chairman of the Governors: Mr P B Clucas, BA, BSc Hons

***Headteacher*: Mrs Janet Billingsley-Evans**, BSc

Age Range. 4–11.

Number of Pupils. 160.

Fees per annum (2023–2024). Day only: £11,595 (P1), £11,995 (P2–P3), £15,145 (Forms 1–2), £15,555 (Forms 3–4).

After more than a century of independence, mainly as a Girls' School, The Buchan School amalgamated, in 1991, with King William's College to form a single continuous provision of Independent Education on the Isle of Man.

As the Preparatory School to King William's College (*see entry in HMC section*), The Buchan School provides an education of all-round quality for boys and girls until the age of 11 when most pupils proceed naturally to the Senior School although the curriculum meets the needs of Common Entrance, Scholarship and Entrance Examinations to other Independent Senior School.

The school buildings are clustered round Westhill House, the centre of the original estate, in fourteen acres of partly wooded grounds. The whole environment, close to the attractive harbour of Castletown, is ideally suited to the needs of younger children. They are able to work, play and develop their potential in every direction.

A well-equipped Nursery provides Pre-School education for up to 65 children. At the age of 4, boys and girls are accepted into the Pre-Preparatory Department. They work largely in their own building in bright, modern classrooms and also make use of the specialist Preparatory School facilities where they proceed three years later.

The School is particularly well-equipped with ICT facilities extending down to the Pre-Prep Department. It is also home to a STEAM Studio, providing a great opportunity to extend learning in this area. There is a Pavilion with fields marked out for a variety of team games and a multi-purpose area which is used for Rugby, Football, Hockey and Netball.

There is emphasis on traditional standards in and out of the classroom, with an enterprising range of activities outside normal lessons. Music is strong – both choral and instrumental – and there is energetic involvement in Art, Drama and Sport.

The school strives for high academic standards, aiming to ensure that all pupils enjoy the benefits of a rounded education, giving children every opportunity to develop their individual talents from an early age.

Entry is usually by interview and school report (if applicable) and the children may join The Buchan School at any time, providing there is space. The School is a happy, friendly community where new pupils integrate quickly socially and academically.

Charitable status. King William's College is a Registered Charity, number 615. It exists for the provision of high quality education for boys and girls.

Buckingham Preparatory School

458 Rayners Lane, Pinner, Middlesex HA5 5DT
Tel: 020 8866 2737
email: office@buckprep.org
website: www.buckprep.org
X/Twitter: @BuckinghamPrep
Facebook: @buckinghamprep
Instagram: @buckinghampreparatory

Chair of Governors: Mrs Lynn Grimes

***Headteacher*: Mr Michael Doyle**

Age Range. Boys 3–11.

Number of Pupils. 95.

Fees per term (2023–2024). £3,700–£4,750 (includes lunches).

Buckingham Preparatory School (BPS) is a small school which offers its pupils an extremely high level of academic education and pastoral care. An ISI inspection in May 2017 rated BPS as "Excellent" and "Outstanding" in each and every aspect of our offering in every part of the school.

Our teaching staff have been universally praised for their "constantly warm and encouraging guidance" and pupil progress is put down to our teachers' "highly effective use of clear explanations" and "because all teachers focus strongly on improving individual pupils' learning and achievement".

With a maximum class size of 18 throughout the school, individual attention is guaranteed.

BPS pupils consistently achieve excellent academic results due to the inspirational teaching, commitment and professionalism of its highly qualified teaching staff. Each year, Year 6 pupils gain offers to the major Independent and Grammar schools in the area and beyond. In the majority of cases, this is to the boys' first-choice schools, often with scholarships.

BPS also prides itself in its results in other areas of the curriculum; areas which are vital in building confidence and self-esteem. Achievement in sport, music and drama is excellent. The pupils regularly take part in local fixtures, often winning inter-school tournaments in cricket, unihoc, football, rugby swimming and cross-country, and other sports. A thriving choir and school plays allow the pupils plentiful opportunities for performance. Speech & Drama classes (LAMDA) and individual instrumental tuition are also on offer.

The Expressive Arts Week, when pupils have the opportunity of participating in approximately 14 categories of events, is also a focal point of the academic year allowing all boys from the very youngest to demonstrate their individual talents.

The School also believes in forging a strong Parent/Teacher partnership so that parents feel they have a vital role to play in the education of their child. A thriving Parent/Teacher Association also organises as many as three major fundraising events during the academic year which are always well supported and are highlights of the year.

At BPS we do not select pupils based simply on their current academic abilities, but on their desire to learn and achieve. We believe in potential. We believe that if your child wants to succeed, then we will enable him to do so.

Charitable status. The E Ivor Hughes Educational Foundation is a Registered Charity, number 293623.

Bute House Preparatory School for Girls

Bute House, Luxemburg Gardens, Hammersmith, London W6 7EA
Tel: 020 7603 7381
email: mail@butehouse.co.uk
website: www.butehouse.co.uk
X/Twitter: @ButeHousePrep
Facebook: @butehouseprep
Instagram: @butehousepreparatoryschool

Chair of Governors: Mr Jonathan Beckitt

***Head*: Ms Sian Bradshaw**, BEd Hons

Age Range. 4–11.

Number of Pupils. 324 Day Girls.

Fees per term (2023–2024). £7,545 inclusive of lunches.

Bute House has a unique non-competitive academic ethos where every girl runs her own best race. The school offers a broad curriculum that develops skills alongside knowledge, and provides exceptional pastoral care in a happy, safe and inspiring environment. Through the implementation of our Learning Powers, our goal is to cultivate opportunities for students to foster connections across diversity, valuing differences as assets. We champion their voices, recognising their unique identities. These bonds create inclusive learning spaces, encouraging students to embrace risk-taking and collaboration.

Bute House overlooks extensive playing fields and is housed in a large, bright, modern building. Facilities include a science laboratory, an art room, a food technology room, a music studio, a drama studio, a multi-purpose hall and a spacious, well-stocked library which extends to separate reading pods. A well-qualified, enthusiastic and experienced staff teach a broad curriculum, which emphasises both the academic and the pastoral side of school life. Information Technology is an integral part of the curriculum and the Computing classrooms are all equipped with multimedia machines. Laptops, iPads and Chromebooks are also widely used for individual or class work. French and Spanish are taught from Year 1.

Sports include swimming, gymnastics, dance, tennis, football, netball, kwik cricket and athletics which are taught on our excellent on-site facilities. Full use is made of our local area and all that London has to offer. Residential trips further afield are also offered to the girls from Years 3–6.

Girls are encouraged to take an active part in school life from the start. There is a democratically elected School Council and regular school meetings, run by the girls, when all pupils are able to put their views forward, as well as to volunteer for key roles around the school. A wide variety of extracurricular activities are also available, such as cookery, debating, curve stitching, drama, knitting, karate, musical theatre and goblin car building, to name but a few.

There is a flourishing Parents Association who are closely involved with events throughout the school year, as well as a very active Governing body who participate in the running of the school.

Entry is by ballot at age 4 and by assessment at age 7.

Caldicott

Crown Lane, Farnham Royal, Buckinghamshire SL2 3SL

Tel: 01753 649300
email: admissions@caldicott.com
website: www.caldicott.com
X/Twitter: @CaldicottSchool
Facebook: @Caldicott.School
Instagram: @caldicottschool
LinkedIn: /company/caldicott-school

Chairman of the Board of Governors: M S Swift

***Headmaster*: Jeremy Banks**, BA Hons, MEd

Age Range. 7–13.

Number of Boys. 100 Boarders and 150 Day Boys.

Fees per term (2023–2024). Year 7 and 8 Boarding: £11,811; Year 5 and 6 Boarding: £10,630; Year 5 and 6 Day: £7,936; Year 3 and 4 Day: £7,114.

Caldicott is a thriving day and boarding prep school for boys aged 7–13. Situated in 40 acres of Buckinghamshire countryside, we are located just 15 miles from Heathrow Airport and 30 minutes from West London where we operate a daily return bus service from Chiswick, Brook Green, Notting Hill, Barnes Bridge, and the local area. We are always looking to expand and adapt our bus network each year, depending on demand from parents.

Our founder, Mr J Heald Jenkins, believed decency, tolerance and humanity would enable each boy to 'shine their light on the world'. Today, his vision remains relevant and a source of inspiration.

At Caldicott we place each individual boy at the centre of our day and boarding experience and believe happiness is key to fulfilling potential. Offering flexi and occasional boarding to Years 3–6 allows our busy parents some manoeuvrability in their schedules; it also eases the boys' transition into boarding in Years 7 and 8. For those boys that aren't ready for boarding at Year 7, we are delighted to offer Day Plus from 2024, which is effectively a day place that includes two nights of non-compulsory boarding a week. Despite being a school with a strong boarding culture, we felt that it was time to adapt our model to reflect the individualised needs of our boys. We were also delighted to receive the BSA's Award for 'Supporting Junior Boarders' in 2022, as well as being highly commended for our Pastoral Care in the 2022 Muddy Stilettos Awards.

We have the reputation as one of the best prep schools in the UK with an excellent record in preparing boys for scholarships and Common Entrance to top UK boarding schools including Eton, and Harrow, as well day schools including St Paul's and Merchant Taylors'. We have a strong and dynamic staffroom of dedicated and inspirational teachers and professionals. As a result, we have high academic standards and expectations, an outstanding record in art, sport, music and drama scholarships, an innovative pastoral provision and a wide range of extra-curricular activities in which all boys can take part.

The wellbeing of each boy is our priority; our goal is to develop individuals who thrive and flourish in the fullest sense. We aim to equip our children to be happy and confident, form lasting relationships with others and develop strategies for coping with the challenges life throws at them – essential skills for succeeding in today's complex, fast-moving world. Our community is not only warm and welcoming from the staff and pupil body, but also our parents form the Friends of Caldicott who add another layer of friendship and happiness.

We are a school where boys fulfil their academic potential and are guided to become all-rounders, with the character and grit to succeed.

Charitable status. Caldicott is a Registered Charity, number 310631. Its purpose is to provide education for the young.

Campbell College

Belmont Road, Belfast, Co Antrim BT4 2ND, Northern Ireland

Tel: +44 (0)28 9076 3076
email: hmoffice@campbellcollege.co.uk
website: www.campbellcollege.co.uk
X/Twitter: @CampbellCollege
Facebook: @CampbellCollege1894
Instagram: @campbellcollege
LinkedIn: /school/campbell-college-belfast

See full entry in the **HMC** section, on **p. 55**.

Cargilfield School

45 Gamekeeper's Road, Edinburgh EH4 6HU
Tel: 0131 336 2207
email: admin@cargilfield.com
website: www.cargilfield.com
X/Twitter: @cargilfield
Facebook: @cargilfield
Instagram: @cargilfieldschool

Chairman of the Board of Governors:
Lord Sinclair, MRICS

***Headmaster*: Mr Rob Taylor**, BA, PGCE

Deputy Heads:
Mrs Emma Buchanan, MEd, BEd
Ms Anjali Dholakia, MA Hons, LLB, Dip LP, PGDE
Mr Ross Murdoch, BEd Hons

Age range. 3–13.

Number of children. 308.

Fees per term (2023–2024). Boarding: £8,410 (weekly). Day Pupils: £6,865, Pre-Prep £4,255, Nursery £2,475–£4,145.

About Cargilfield. Cargilfield is a unique Scottish independent boarding and prep school in Edinburgh for 308 girls and boys aged 3 to 13 and has been educating and inspiring children since 1873. With its 13 acres of picturesque grounds, our campus is conveniently located just 10 minutes away from the centre of Edinburgh.

We believe in developing vital life skills such as independence, curiosity, kindness and positive self-esteem, alongside academic advancement, to prepare children for their later education journey and provide them with lifelong memories. We offer a flexible approach to learning, where the individual needs of each student are attended to, ensuring that every girl and boy can realise their potential to the fullest.

In September 2023, Education Scotland published Cargilfield School's Inspection Report and the School received an outstanding report in all four inspection categories, with an excellent for raising attainment and achievement; and very good for leadership of change learning; for learning, teaching and assessment and for ensuring well-being, equality and inclusion.

Education Scotland reports that "the School's motto 'Where Learning is an Everyday Adventure' is evident in the exciting and motivating experiences for children". The inspection states the School successfully strikes "a balance between achieving outstanding academic standards and expectations while ensuring children's emotional and mental well-being is nurtured".

Academic excellence. We nurture all children to leave Cargilfield with active, enquiring minds and with confidence in who they are, in their values, and in the contribution they make to their community. We achieve this by teaching each individual within small classes, setting high expectations for the children, and making sure that learning happens in all aspects of daily school life.

Co-curricular range. At Cargilfield, your child will experience a broad and comprehensive academic experience well beyond the conventional curriculum expectations for 13+ through a coherent programme of learning from Nursery and Pre-Prep, towards success in Common Entrance and Scholarship examinations in Form 8. Beyond the more conventional academic disciplines, such as Latin, French and Greek, there is an abundance of specialist offerings such as Music and Drama, Art and Design, and Outdoor Education. Students can take part in daily sports, and both computers and ICT are seen as integral parts of the curriculum, never as an end in themselves. This year, a total of 31 scholarships were offered to our Leavers from prestigious senior schools throughout Scotland and Britain, causing us to take immense pride in our students' accomplishments.

Boarding. Cargilfield is a family school, with boarding at the heart of what we offer. This is an extension of our family. A place where children are valued members of the community and secure in their place within the school environment.

We understand the demands of modern family life and the importance of excellent pastoral care for your child's success and happiness. That's why Cargilfield can also offer tailored and flexible boarding in addition to our day school, creating a unique home-away-from-home experience for your child. Our boarding house system provides every pupil with opportunities to thrive in a supportive and inclusive community.

Our committed pastoral team understands and meets the needs of each pupil, guiding them through all aspects of their individual school lives. The strong relationships forged in our boarding house underpin our pupils' confidence, independence, and character, and the friendships they make last a lifetime.

We are able to accommodate up to 60 children during weekdays; the evenings are filled with great banter and relaxation after an active and busy day of learning, sports, and club activities.

Charitable status. Cargilfield School is a Registered Charity, number SC005757.

Carrdus School

Overthorpe Hall, Nr Banbury, Oxfordshire OX17 2BS
Tel: 01295 263733
email: office@carrdusschool.com
website: www.carrdusschool.co.uk
X/Twitter: @carrdusschool
Facebook: @carrdusschool
Instagram: @carrdusschool

Chair of Governors: Mr Simon Beale
***Head*: Mrs Samantha Bagshaw**, BA, PGCE, MA, NPQH
Deputy Head: Mrs Laura Mills, BA Hons, PGCE

Age range. Boys & Girls 3–11 (Nursery Class for children 3–4½).

Number of day pupils. 120.

Fees per term (2023–2024). From £4,450–£4,995 (Sibling discounts available).

Carrdus School is a co-educational day prep school for girls and boys aged 3–11 years, nestled within 11 acres of beautiful grounds, located on the outskirts of Banbury, Oxfordshire and bordering nearby Northamptonshire, Buckinghamshire and Warwickshire. The Carrdus Pathway is a holistic approach to learning, forming strong relationships, instilling confidence and nurturing each child as they make their way through the school; ensuring they achieve their full potential and setting the foundations for academic success.

The teaching staff consists of highly qualified individuals, including the advantage of a plethora of specialist subject teachers in Music, Art, Drama, Science, Sport, French, Latin and Computing. The school has an excellent record of success in examinations, regularly sending pupils to well-known independent senior schools, with many achieving Academic Scholarships.

The on-site facilities are vast for this modest school and include a heated outdoor swimming pool which the children use on a weekly basis, two full-sized tennis courts, a purpose-built Art Studio, Science Lab, a multi-use Sports Hall and new Sports pitches. Music, Sport, Drama and Art are highly valued in the curriculum. There are regular sessions of Outdoor Learning and STEM where children can get really hands on and are encouraged to learn through doing. The girls and boys at Carrdus also have the advantage of daily use of Tudor Hall's extensive Sports, Arts and Science facilities.

The aim of the school is to produce confident, independent and resilient children, who are happy and engaged in all that they do, and who have the satisfaction of reaching their own highest academic and personal standards.

Charitable status. Carrdus School is part of Tudor Hall School, which is a Registered Charity, number 1042783.

Casterton, Sedbergh Preparatory School

Casterton, Kirkby Lonsdale, Cumbria LA6 2SG

Tel: 015242 79200
email: prepoffice@sedberghprep.org
website: www.sedberghprep.org
X/Twitter: @Sedbergh_Prep
Facebook: @SedberghPrep
Instagram: @Sedbergh_Prep_School
LinkedIn: /casterton-sedbergh-preparatory-school

Chairman of Governors: Mr Richard Gledhill

***Headmaster*: Mr Will Newman**, MA

Age Range. 6 months–13 years, Co-educational.

Number of Pupils. 200.

Fees per term (2023–2024). Day: £3,335–£6,640, Full Boarding: £8,160–£9,845, Weekly Boarding: £7,610–£9,295.

At Casterton, Sedbergh Preparatory School we develop happy, confident children with a 'can-do' attitude; independent yet always with a sense of team before self. Through careful and sensitive teaching, we aim to foster a spirit of adventure, both inside and outside the classroom.

Our curriculum is ambitious and equips pupils with the necessary skills for future success, yet is delivered in a setting of timeless beauty where pupils have the space and time to enjoy their childhood. Breadth of opportunity and depth of involvement is what sets us apart. Maths competitions, explosions and dissections in Science lessons, pony care at our stables and collecting eggs from the School chickens – all these create outstanding memories for the children at Sedbergh Prep.

Our facilities are first class and include a high-spec Design, Technology and Engineering Department, seven Science laboratories, floodlit astro and tennis courts, a theatre, heated pool, equestrian centre and several computer suites. We are excited by the curiosity and thirst for learning that each child, regardless of their academic ability, naturally displays. We work hard to allow each child the time to question and develop their thoughts independently, leading to fresh discoveries in an innovative learning environment.

One of our strengths is a focus on the individual. We are not a School of rote and regurgitation. Rather, we understand that a child's future success is dependent upon their ability to use what they know in a variety of creative ways. Every area of School life, therefore, provides fantastic opportunities for creativity of all kinds. Day in, day out, we encourage pupils to live our ethos of 'give it a go and try your best', supporting them to face and overcome challenges in all areas of their schooling and beyond.

Our three boarding houses – Beale, Thornfield and Cressbrook – are very much 'home from home' environments and our House Parents support and nurture our boarders, who provide the School with a unique family atmosphere. The Prep School's holistic approach to pastoral care aims to bring out the best in every child. We look to develop young people who are kind, responsible, creative, ambitious, collaborative and courageous – the values that make up our 'Ways of the Wolf' and guide the ethos of the entire Prep School.

The Cathedral School Llandaff
A Woodard School

Llandaff, Cardiff CF5 2YH

Tel: 029 2056 3179
email: registrar@cathedral-school.co.uk
website: www.cathedral-school.co.uk
X/Twitter: @cslcardiff
Facebook: @cslcardiff
Instagram: @cslcardiff

See full entry in the **HMC** section, on **p. 58**.

Channing School

The Bank, Highgate, London N6 5HF
Tel: 020 8340 2328 (School Office)
020 8340 2719 (Bursar)
email: info@channing.co.uk
website: www.channing.co.uk
X/Twitter: @ChanningSchool
Facebook: @ChanningSchool
Instagram: @channing_school

See full entry in the **GSA** section, on **p. 425**.

Charlotte House Preparatory School

Nursery, Pre-Prep & Preparatory School for Girls

88 The Drive, Rickmansworth, Herts WD3 4DU
Tel: 01923 772101
email: office@chpschool.co.uk
website: www.charlottehouseprepschool.co.uk
Facebook: @CharlotteHousePrepSchool
Instagram: @charlottehouseschool

Chairman of Governors: Mr Simon Reader

***Headmistress*: Miss P Woodcock**, BA Hons QTS

Age range. 3–11.
Number of pupils. 120 Girls.
Fees per term (2023–2024). £2,035–£5,249.

Charlotte House is a forward-thinking dynamic school built on traditional values. This winning combination means we instil in our girls all the social and academic tools they need to become independent, successful, confident and caring women.

Our pupils aspire to be the best. We help them discover their talents and encourage them to persevere when they meet challenges. To aid this, we teach them a varied curriculum and they are fortunate to have specialist teachers right the way through the school commencing in Nursery.

We are passionate about the learning that goes on outside the classroom walls, whether it is their manners as they move around the school, discovering mini beasts in our beautiful garden or meeting up with their French pen-pals in France; we provide the girls with a wealth of experiences to learn more about themselves and the world around them.

Charlotte House encourages the girls to be confident so that they meet challenges head on. We enter many academic and sporting inter-school competitions. We encourage the girls to be confident on stage with termly class assemblies and each girl is involved in an annual play.

At Charlotte House, we recognise the importance of strong links between home and school and provide many opportunities for parents to visit us and find out more about their daughter's progress.

Charlotte House has an excellent record at Secondary Transfer and we have a thorough programme in place to ensure both the girls and their parents feel supported and ready for the challenges secondary transfer poses. Our girls go on to a wide range of schools including state and private schools and the secondary schools often comment on how pleased they are to welcome our girls as they know they will be of a high calibre.

We are a dynamic school whose girls achieve great things!

Charitable status. Charlotte House School Limited is a Registered Charity, number 311075.

Cheam School

Headley, Newbury, Berkshire RG19 8LD
Tel: 01635 268242
01635 267822 (Registrar)
email: registrar@cheamschool.co.uk
website: www.cheamschool.co.uk
X/Twitter: @CheamSchool
Facebook: @CheamSchool
Instagram: @cheamschool
LinkedIn: /company/cheam-school-educational-trust

Cheam is a leading independent, day and boarding prep school, nestled in 100 acres on the Hampshire/Berkshire border, for pupils aged 3 to 13 years.

Chair of Governors: Sir Mark Harford

***Headmaster*: W Phelps**, MA New York, BA AKC King's College London

Deputy Headmaster: T C Haigh, BA Birmingham, PGCE Westminster College, Oxford

Age range. 3–13.
Number of pupils. 90 boarders, 380 day children.
Fees per term (2023–2024). £9,995–£10,345 Boarders (5 nights per week); £3,995–£7,995 Day children.

Cheam is a leading day and boarding school for children aged 3 to 13 years, set in 100 acres on the Berkshire/Hampshire border. We provide broad and extensive opportunities across academics, sport, drama, art, DT, music and outdoor learning. Our vibrant boarding provision is increasingly popular and provides families with flexible and weekly boarding, in a homely and caring environment.

Our committed and passionate team of professionals deliver their subjects with energy, wisdom and creativity. Learning at Cheam is engaging, collaborative, child-focused and inspired, using the best technology, resources and experiences available.

At Cheam we nurture every child in our care, with a focus on individual happiness, development, and confidence. An outstanding team of teachers and highly effective pastoral systems ensure that all pupils are included, supported and nurtured. Cheam Pre-Prep Department offers a supportive and caring environment for our youngest pupils. We develop children socially and emotionally and instil a love of learning through a wide range of topics and a vibrant, hands-on and child-centred curriculum.

Classes are small and academic ambitions are both high and appropriate for all. Cheam has a long history of preparing children for many of the top senior schools in the UK, with children gaining an impressive range of scholarships year on year. Pupils are prepared for the major senior independent schools with Marlborough, Bradfield, St Edward's Oxford, Radley, Eton, Wellington, Sherborne Girls', Pangbourne, St Mary's Calne, Harrow, St Mary's Ascot and Downe House featuring frequently.

The School is situated halfway between Newbury and Basingstoke on the A339 and is within easy reach of the M3 and M4 motorways and the A34 trunk route from Portsmouth, Southampton and Winchester to Oxford and the Midlands. London Heathrow Airport is within an hour's drive.

Charitable status. Cheam School Educational Trust is a Registered Charity, number 290143. It provides high-class education for boarding and day pupils; traditional values; modern thinking; education for the 21st century.

Chinthurst School

52 Tadworth St, Tadworth, Surrey KT20 5QZ

Tel: 01737 812011
email: office@chinthurstschool.co.uk
website: www.chinthurstschool.co.uk
X/Twitter: @ChintSchool
Facebook: @ChinthurstSchool
Instagram: @chinthurst.school

Chair of Governors: Mr Mark Elsey

***Headteacher*: Miss Cathy Trundle**, BA Hons, QTS

Age Range. 2–11.

Number of Pupils. 290.

Fees per term (2023–2024). Little Chicks: £1,290 (min. 3 mornings). Kindergarten: £2,150 (min. 5 mornings). Lower School: £4,430; Upper School £6,040.

Chinthurst is located between the Surrey villages of Walton on the Hill and Tadworth, close to Epsom, Banstead, Kingswood and Reigate, and is rated 'Excellent in all areas' by the independent Schools Inspectorate (March 2023). Founded in 1908, it is a co-educational day school and nursery for children aged 2 to 11, and a junior school of the multi award-winning senior school, Reigate Grammar. Central to the school's ethos is a bespoke and comprehensive wellbeing programme called Wellbeing at Heart, which has been designed to help children understand how their bodies and minds work, and give them the skills to navigate life's inevitable challenges.

Building strong relationships is a key part of this approach and ensures children know they are truly valued as individuals. This gives them the confidence to try new things and the resilience to learn from their mistakes. Most importantly, the children are really happy, and visitors often comment on the buzz of energy, warmth of atmosphere and sense of fun around the school buildings and grounds. Chinthurst was shortlisted for an ISP 2022 Independent School of the Year award in the wellbeing category in recognition of this.

Sport is an important part of life at Chinthurst, and school teams are extremely successful in a variety of sports. Boys and girls at Chinthurst choose the sport they want to play and are not constrained by gender norms, and the school's competitive teams reflect this gender mix. The children love it, seeing themselves as equals on the pitch with no preconceived limitations. Chinthurst was named 2022 Independent School of the Year for Sporting Achievement in recognition of this ground-breaking approach to gender and sport. A strong extracurricular programme provides additional sporting opportunities, as well as a broad range of other popular clubs, including dance, drama, martial arts and craft.

An emphasis on outdoor learning means the children spend as much of the timetable as possible learning outside and younger children enjoy regular forest skills sessions in addition to this. Every child is a member of one of four Houses and this gives them a sense of belonging and peer support, as well as providing plenty of opportunities for friendly inter-house competitions.

The school is renowned for their music, drama and art provision. The children gain outstanding marks in LAMDA drama exams and there is a strong peripatetic music programme. There are many opportunities to perform throughout the year at assemblies, musical showcases and drama productions as well as in choirs and ensembles. Standards are always extremely high and the children also enjoy performing in the community and at local festivals. A well-equipped art studio allows the children to explore their creative potential.

Academic outcomes are excellent and children leave as well-rounded individuals with an enthusiasm for life which is very much a reflection of the Chinthurst spirit. Most move on to Reigate Grammar School and the remaining children move to other top senior schools, both locally and further afield.

Charitable status. Chinthurst School is a Registered Charity, number 1081898.

Christ Church Cathedral School, Oxford

Independent Day School for Boys 3–13 & Girls 3–5, Flexi-Boarding for Boys 8–13

3 Brewer Street, Oxford OX1 1QW

Tel: 01865 242561
email: schooloffice@cccs.org.uk
website: www.cccs.org.uk
Facebook: @Christ-Church-Cathedral-School-Oxford
Instagram: @cccsoxford

Chairman of Governors: The Reverend Canon Professor Sarah Foot, Dean of Christ Church

***Headmaster*: Mr Richard Murray**, BA, MA

Age Range. 3–13 (co-ed Nursery).

Number of Boys. 20 boarders, all are Cathedral Choristers and required to board, and 140 day pupils.

Fees per term (2023–2024). Day boys (including lunch) from £6,896; Pre-Prep from £4,856 (including lunch); Cathedral Choristers £4,350; Probationer Choristers: £4,815 (Chorister fees are subsidised by the Cathedral); Nursery £1,790 and Reception £3,847 (inc. EY Funding).

Christ Church Cathedral School, Oxford, is an independent Pre-Prep and Prep School for Boys with a co-ed Nursery.

The School provides Choristers for the choirs of Christ Church Cathedral, Pembroke College and Worcester College, and is governed by the Dean and Canons of Christ Church, with the assistance of lay members drawn from the city's professional community, some of whom are past or current parents.

The School was founded in 1546 when provision was made for the education of eight Choristers in King Henry VIII's foundation of Christ Church on the site of Cardinal Wolsey's earlier foundation of Cardinal College. In the latter half of the nineteenth century, at the initiative of Dean Liddell, father of Alice Liddell, the inspiration for 'Alice in Wonderland', the boarding house was established at No 1 Brewer Street, and in 1892, during the Headship of the Reverend Henry Sayers, father of Dorothy L Sayers, the Italian Mediaeval scholar and creator of Lord Peter Wimsey, the present building was erected.

The School is centrally situated off St Aldates, two hundred yards from Christ Church. It therefore enjoys the unique cultural background provided by Oxford itself, as well as beautiful playing fields on Christ Church Meadow. Buildings include a former residence of Cardinal Wolsey and the Sir William Walton Centre, which contains a recital hall and spacious classrooms.

Charitable status. Christ Church Cathedral School Education Trust is a Registered Charity, number 1114828.

Churcher's College Junior School and Nursery

Midhurst Road, Liphook, Hampshire GU30 7HT

Tel: 01730 236870
email: hello@churcherscollege.com
website: www.churcherscollege.com
X/Twitter: @ChurchersJunior
Facebook: @ChurchersJunior
Instagram: @ChurchersJunior

Chairman of Governors: Charles Strick, BSC MechEng, MBA, CEng

***Head*: Ffion Robinson**, BA, MA
Deputy Head: Philipa Yugin-Power, BSc Leeds, MA Ed Open
Head of Infant Department: Kerry M Humphreys, BEd Plymouth
Head of Middle School: Sarah-Jane Moore, ARCM, GRSM
Head of Upper School: Nathan Rushin, BSc, MSc Southampton
Senior Teacher (*Academic*): Geraldine Norton, BA Nottingham
Senior Teacher (*Operations*): Matt Forbes, BSc Gloucester

Age Range. 3–11 Co-educational.

Number of Pupils. 250 (excluding Nursery).

Fees per term (2023–2024). Reception-Year 6: From £3,176 to £4,455. Early Years Funding is available for children from the term after the pupil turns 3 years old and for Reception children up to and including the term in which they turn 5 years old.

Joining Us. The main entry point is at Nursery. We welcome children the term after their third birthday. Please get in touch if you are interested in joining Churcher's College from Reception or Year 3 (7+) as places are limited and in high demand.

Churcher's College Junior School and Nursery is the perfect place to start your child's learning journey.

We are a haven for learning and adventure with a 'have a go' philosophy and an overarching aim for each child to reach their personal best inside and outside the classroom. With a broad and rich curriculum, the children enjoy a range of subjects and fully seize the array of opportunities on offer. From the academic to the activities that feed the soul, the children love it here.

Set just off the South Downs in Liphook, Hampshire, your child can experience a real countryside childhood and then make a very smooth transition at eleven years old as she/he moves to the Senior School in Petersfield. We fully support each child at every step of the entrance process. Every child's happiness is paramount to their achievement and we pride ourselves on our high-quality pastoral care, excellent teaching and learning, all within a warm, family atmosphere.

The Nursery. Nestled in the grounds of our Junior School, Churcher's College Nursery is a warm and creative environment where children are encouraged to explore, question and discover. Every child is unique and we want to give each boy and girl every opportunity to grow and flourish in a safe and nurturing environment so that they become happy, self-confident and thoughtful children who respect each other and the wonderful natural space they are sharing.

Pastoral. Happy children make happy learners. We strive to create a secure and friendly place of learning in which our children feel valued and where they can grow personally, socially, spiritually and intellectually. Class teachers take responsibility for day-to-day pastoral care. Heads of School support pupils, parents and staff. Our close-knit community enables us to talk freely with parents and vice versa. We work hard to make sure pupils thrive here. The House system fosters great community spirit, allowing friendships to form between year groups.

Academic. Academic rigour is at the heart of our teaching.

Junior Curriculum: A broad and balanced curriculum, combining academic, creative and cultural elements, gives children a varied day and also develops a lifelong love of learning in preparation for Senior School and beyond.

Nursery and Reception: Pupils in the Nursery and Reception Class follow the Early Years Foundation Stage curriculum.

Sport. We offer a broad range of sports to help develop fitness and skills, teamwork and a healthy attitude towards competition through PE and Games. There are many opportunities to represent the school in a variety of matches from Year 2 onwards. The pupils learn a great deal from these: etiquette, collaboration, organisation, sportsmanship. They enjoy the experiences immensely.

Music and Drama. The Arts play a significant role throughout school life at the Junior School.

Music is made accessible to all pupils, from the Nursery to Year 6 and whatever their abilities, whether being inspired for the first time or developing existing skills. With plenty of opportunities, including timetabled music lessons, teatime concerts, an orchestra, choirs, and a jazz band, the pupils' confidence is positively built. From the harp to the trombone, individual music lessons are also available.

Drama plays a key part in helping our pupils to gain confidence and to develop their imagination and communication skills. There are many opportunities for children of all ages (including Nursery) to perform, with a host of drama showcases, year group productions, dance festivals and many extra-curricular clubs. Assemblies and workshops also provide more opportunities for pupils to unleash their dramatic flair and build every child's confidence. In addition, children can attend small group LAMDA (London Academy of Music and Dramatic Arts) sessions and work towards an examination which gives them techniques to increase their memory and recall skills, speaking and listening as well as improving self-expression.

Adventure. Building confidence and self-esteem is important for all of our children. We do this by providing challenging and adventurous activities that include the opportunity to take risk in a controlled environment. This is achieved through our Outdoor Adventurous Activities Programme and embedding Learning Outside the Classroom throughout the curriculum. From onsite campfire events to residential trips off site, the children relish the opportunity to learn outside their comfort zone. Children remember these adventures and experiences fondly.

Clubs and After-school Activities. Pupils at Churcher's are encouraged to be involved in a wide range of activities, to broaden their interests and try new things. There is a great deal of choice, with activities ranging from sports and drama to music and dance. We love giving our children every opportunity to discover something a bit different or try out a new activity, and we find they thoroughly enjoy doing so.

The Guild Award. Unique to Churcher's College Junior School and Nursery, the Guild Award is a DofE-style programme of challenges, which is very popular and available from Year 3. The award helps pupils to develop themselves through attaining new skills and abilities, think beyond themselves, develop a resilience to difficulty through new challenges and develop leadership skills.

Charitable status. Churcher's College is Registered Charity, number 1173833, and a Charitable Company Limited by Guarantee, registered in England and Wales, company number 10813349.

City of London Freemen's School

Ashtead Park, Ashtead, Surrey KT21 1ET

Tel:	01372 822400 (School Reception)
	01372 822423 (Admissions)
email:	admissions@freemens.org
website:	www.freemens.org
X/Twitter:	@HelloFreemens
Facebook:	@HelloFreemens
Instagram:	@hellofreemens

A co-educational day and boarding school, located on a magnificent 57-acre site in Ashtead Park, Surrey.

Assistant Head **(*Head of Junior School*): Mr Matthew Robinson**

Assistant Head of Junior School: Mrs Louise Jowitt
Head of Year 3 (*Form 1*): Mrs Emma Smith
Head of Year 4 (*L2*): Mrs Vanessa Symonds
Head of Year 5 (*U2*): Mrs Janet Wilby-King
Head of Year 6 (*L3*): Mrs Sarah Gillespie

Board of Governors:
Deputy Philip Woodhouse (Chairman)
Jamel Banda (Deputy Chairman)
Deputy Graham Packham
Alderman Robert Howard
Alderman Christopher Makin
Alderman Tim Levene (ex-officio)
Councillor Chris Townsend
Roy Anklesaria
John Foley
Nicholas Goddard
Michael Hudson
Andrew McMillan
Clare Verga
Lady Gillian Yarrow

Support Officer: Melanie Peel

Age range. 7–10.

Number of pupils. 230.

Fees per term (2023–2024). £5,856.

Freemen's Junior School is located on a magnificent 57-acre site in Ashtead Park, Surrey, where the many outstanding facilities are available to all pupils (see separate entry in HMC section).

Happy children learn. It's no surprise to us that the most popular word that comes to pupils' minds when describing the Junior School is 'fun'.

Fun is one of the three main disciplines we discuss, repeat and reinforce. Kindness is the priority – if everybody (adults and children alike) is kind to everybody else then the School functions well.

Honesty is expected from everybody at all times – on occasion home truths have to be shared between parents, children and staff but, because they are shared in an environment of kindness, all is well. Finally, fun is to be had at all times (provided it's enjoyed in a kind and honest way). And there's a lot of fun to be had in the Junior School.

We won't rush your child through the curriculum. We want them to have a steady education with depth and breadth, so that they have solid foundations on which to build upon when they progress up into the Senior School. There are no exams to progress up into the Senior School, meaning your child can focus on thriving in a welcoming, flexible and secure learning environment.

One of the first questions your child will be challenged with when joining the Junior School is 'What do you think?' This question is displayed in every single classroom because it is a great way to develop your child's resilience, to get them to think for themselves and to draw out their ideas and thoughts. There are so many people around to talk to in the Junior School in an environment of kindness, honesty and fun.

In Key Stage 2, Heads of Year work in liaison with the subject coordinators and the Heads of Departments to ensure that the programmes of work are compatible and stimulating. The aim is to establish a secure foundation in traditional core subjects within a curriculum which will broaden experience and excite the imagination of each child. While academic excellence throughout the Junior School is still a major aim, there is also an enrichment programme and a very full programme of co-curricular activities including drama, music and sports.

There are three Houses in the school providing pastoral care while also promoting healthy competition in many activities. In both the Junior and the Senior School, outstanding work and good progress, inside and outside the classroom, are recognised by the award of appropriate merits and distinctions.

The purpose-built Junior School is warm and comfortable and provides a safe base for your child, as they explore the wider campus and its impressive swimming pool, sports facility and music department, as well as the all-important play areas. Importantly, as they discover Freemen's, your child will come into contact with older, inspiring pupils, who will become important role models to them. We are passionate about co-education and have been since our foundation. Our classes have approximately 20 pupils and come from a broad range of feeder schools and backgrounds. We mix up classes every year so that new pupils are made to feel part of the group straight away. When new children arrive, they are each given a buddy, a child in their class who knows the school well.

Clifton College Pre-Preparatory School

Guthrie Road, Clifton, Bristol BS8 3EZ

Tel: 0117 315 7160
email: prepadmissions@cliftoncollege.com
website: www.cliftoncollege.com
X/Twitter: @Clifton_College
Facebook: @CliftonCollegeUK
LinkedIn: /clifton-college

Chairman of College Council: Mr Nick Tolchard

***Headmaster*: Mr Sam Morgan**, BA

Age Range. 4–8.

Number of Pupils. 143.

Fees per term (2023–2024). Reception (full time) £4,100; Year 1 £4,330; Years 2–3 £4,760.

Clifton College Pre-Preparatory School is a vibrant co-educational school for children aged 4–8, there is a Preschool next door for children aged 3+. The College prides itself on creating an environment where children are fully engaged, and who are creatively immersed in their learning, making firm friendships along the way. The highest possible standard of education is provided for all, and places strong emphasis on building the core skills of literacy and numeracy, the essential foundations for future learning.

Life at the Pre-Preparatory is busy and exciting. Year 2 and 3 pupils may take part in a range of co-curricular activities at lunchtimes or after school, with around 16 clubs and societies taking place. These change termly and include a variety of sports, sewing club, craft club, science club, ukulele club, book club and Lego club. Services and concerts are held every term in the Chapel, and an annual musical is performed at the wonderful Redgrave Theatre. There is a full programme of educational visits and outings for all ages, including a youth hostelling trip for Year 3.

Each class benefits from a dedicated class teacher, along with support from a teaching assistant. Qualified specialist class teachers deliver a topic-based curriculum, with specialist teachers for Music, Dance, Sport, French and Mandarin.

Piano and instrumental lessons are available from Year 2, and all children in Years 2 and 3 learn the recorder, strings and sing in the choir.

The Pre-Preparatory benefits from aspects of the Preparatory school, it is governed by the same Council and enjoys the considerable advantages of sharing many of Clifton College's impressive facilities. These include the swimming pool, sports hall, library, multi-activity hall, Chapel and Theatre. The Pre-Preparatory school is situated in two buildings either side of a superb playground, with a variety of exciting play equipment available.

Recent investment has seen the creation of an outdoor area leading from the reception classrooms. This is designed to give reception classes easy access to an outdoor space which they can use to extend and enhance their learning.

Another exciting provision is the Forest School at our Beggar's Bush Sports Ground. All year groups, from Reception to Year 3, visit the Forest School, it provides a range of stimulating outdoor experiences for the children, enabling them to learn, achieve and develop confidence through curriculum-linked activities and free exploration of the natural woodland.

Charitable status. Clifton College is a Registered Charity, number 311735. It provides boarding and day education for boys and girls aged 3–18.

Clifton College Preparatory School

The Avenue, Clifton, Bristol BS8 3HE
Tel: 0117 315 7160
email: prepadmissions@cliftoncollege.com
website: www.cliftoncollege.com
X/Twitter: @Clifton_College
Facebook: @CliftonCollegeUK
Instagram: @CliftonCollegeUK
LinkedIn: /clifton-college

Chairman of College Council: Mr Nick Tolchard

***Headmaster*: Mr Jim Walton**, BA

Age Range. 8–13.

Number of Pupils. 313.

Fees per term (2023–2024). Years 4–6: Boarders £9,980; Flexi Boarders (3 nights) £6,730; Day Pupils £5,435. Years 7–8: Boarders £11,825; Flexi Boarders (3 nights) £8,490; Day Pupils £7,105.

There is no 'one size fits all' approach at Clifton College Preparatory School, a friendly and inspiring co-educational boarding and day school for pupils aged 8–13. Each child is considered and treated as an individual with a unique profile of skills, passions, talents and undiscovered potential. Clifton College offers a stimulating and challenging curriculum, which combines traditional methods with programmes of study relevant to the needs of the next century.

Clifton College Preparatory School aims to provide the highest possible standard of education, and to help pupils develop the key skills of literacy and numeracy, as well as observation, information-seeking, posing questions and problem-solving. In addition, we aim to develop their ability to co-operate and work productively with others, as well as to work and learn independently.

A wide range of subjects are studied, and pupils are supported and encouraged to become high achievers across the varied curriculum. Small class sizes, first-class facilities and teaching excellence enables pupils to aim high, reaching their academic potential, and beyond.

The vast majority of pupils move through to the Upper School, but those who choose to move elsewhere are prepared for, and often win, scholarships to other schools.

As part of Clifton College, the Preparatory School benefits from being governed by the same Council and enjoys the considerable advantages of sharing many of Clifton College's impressive facilities. These include the Redgrave Theatre, Sports Complex, Indoor Swimming Pool, Gymnasium, Squash and Rackets Courts, and over 90 acres of playing fields off-site at Beggar's Bush. This includes an Olympic-standard water-based Hockey pitch, a 3G pitch, an indoor Tennis and Netball Centre and Activity Centre. The School has its own impressive Science laboratories, Arts Centre, ICT suites, Music facilities and Chapel.

There are six Houses in the Prep School, three day Houses for Years 4–6, two day Houses for Years 7–8, and a boarding House for Year 4 upwards. Pupils benefit from a supervised environment where they can meet, work or relax, and provides a true home away from home. Each House is led by a Housemaster/Housemistress and their spouse, along with Tutors, Matrons and the occasional House dog.

The excellent and well-rounded co-curricular programme encourages children to try something new, find new interests, and to engage with the world around them – boosting their confidence and self-esteem.

The youngest pupils (aged 3–8) learn next door at the Pre-Preparatory School, under the care of their own teachers. (See separate IAPS entry for Clifton College Pre-Preparatory School.)

Charitable status. Clifton College is a Registered Charity, number 311735. It provides boarding and day education for boys and girls aged 3–18 years.

Clifton High School

College Road, Clifton, Bristol BS8 3JD
Tel: 0117 973 0201 (School Office)
0117 933 9087 (Admissions)
email: admissions@cliftonhigh.co.uk
website: www.cliftonhigh.co.uk
X/Twitter: @cliftonhigh1877
Facebook: @CliftonHighSchoolBristol
Instagram: @cliftonhighschoolbristol/

See full entry in the **Society of Heads** section, on **p. 521**.

Colfe's Junior School

Horn Park Lane, London SE12 8AW
Tel: 020 8463 8240 Junior Head
020 8463 8266 Junior Office
email: junioroffice@colfes.com
website: www.colfes.com
X/Twitter: @ColfesSchool
Facebook: @ColfesSchool

Chair of the Governors: Mr Matthew Pellereau, BSc, FRICS

***Head of the Junior School*: Mrs M-C Gilfedder-Bonnar**, LLB, BSc, PGCE

Deputy Head and Head of EYFS: Mrs S Gurr, BEd Hons
Director of Studies: Miss L Kirkland, BA Hons, PGCE
Head of Learning Support: Mrs G Fisher, HND, OCR Level 7 Cert SpLD

Age Range. 3–11.

Number of Pupils. 460 boys and girls.

Fees per term (2023–2024). Junior School, KS2: £5,640 (excluding lunch); KS1: £5,335 (including lunch); EYFS: £5,110 (including lunch).

Colfe's Junior School is an independent day school for boys and girls 3–11. Entrance is academically selective. The Junior School offers a broad curriculum and aims to provide an excellent all-round education. Small class sizes and a team of well-qualified teachers provide a caring and vibrant environment. Children normally enter at the ages of 3 or 4, although the occasional vacancy arises at other times.

For the children starting school it is the beginning of an exciting and inspiring journey; this begins in our Nursery and Reception classes which together form the Early Years Foundation Stage (EYFS). Children gain confidence and thrive in a warm, friendly and nurturing atmosphere where they feel secure and valued. Through a specialised play-based curriculum teachers plan for a rich learning environment which provides opportunities for the children to flourish in all aspects of their development. In Years 1 and 2 children begin to study all National Curriculum subjects, building on the skills, knowledge, understanding and experience gained during their time in Nursery and Reception. Moving into KS2 the focus shifts to three aspects of every child – talent, potential and character. Strong curriculum and expert teaching is underpinned by a rich programme of music, art, sport, drama, outdoor pursuits. Each pupil belongs to a House and they compete to earn the most points, helping them to develop a real sense of community.

The majority of Junior School pupils transfer to the Senior School at the end of Year 6, providing they achieve the qualifying standard.

The Junior School is housed in modern purpose-built accommodation with spacious and well-equipped classrooms. Excellent library facilities and specialist accommodation for art and design, ICT and science provide pupils with a stimulating environment in which to learn. Full use is made of the school's swimming pool, sports centre, visual and performing arts centre and extensive on-site playing fields.

PE specialists teach a wide range of sports and there is an extensive programme of House and inter-school sports matches. A school choir, orchestra, strings group and numerous ensembles perform frequently both in and out of school. Drama productions normally take place each term. There is a wide range of after-school clubs on offer (over 50 each week for the 7–11 year olds) and a Breakfast Club from 7.30am and Late School scheme until 6.00pm each day.

Charitable status. Colfe's School is a Registered Charity, number 1109650. It exists to provide education for children.

Collegiate Prep School

Park Road, Stapleton, Bristol BS16 1BA

Tel: 0117 965 5297
email: admissions@collegiate.org.uk
website: www.collegiate.org.uk
X/Twitter: @CSBprep
Facebook: @CollegiateSchoolBristol
Instagram: @collegiateschoolbristol

Chair of Governors: Mr N Baker

***Head of Prep School*: Mr D A H Edwards**, BEd, MA
Assistant Head of Prep: Mr O Barwell, BA Hons
Assistant Head of Pre-Prep: Miss S Evans, BEd Hons
Assistant Head Academic: Miss K Fitchett

Age Range. 3–11.

Number of Pupils. 230 Day Pupils.

Fees per term (2023–2024). Reception, Years 1 & 2 £3,250, Years 3–6 £3,925.

Collegiate Prep School is located in Stapleton village, north Bristol. It is less than one mile from Junction 2 of the M32 and therefore easily accessible from north Bristol and South Gloucestershire. In addition to its own specialist facilities for Science, ICT, Music, Design & Technology, Art and Games, the Prep School has full use of facilities at the neighbouring Collegiate Senior School including 30 acres of playing fields, plus the theatre, concert hall and sports centre.

At the end of Year 6, pupils move from the Prep to the Senior School *(see entry in HMC section)*. They work in small classes on a broad and engaging curriculum that extends and enthuses a community of highly active learners. It incorporates the full range of academic subjects together with French, Design and Technology, ICT, Art, Music, Forest School and competitive sports. The School benefits from a highly efficient Learning Support Unit for those needing additional support and a Gifted and Talented programme for those who show particular strengths.

To find balance in their learning all children are encouraged to explore their strengths in music, drama, languages, sport and art. School sport fixtures, trips, residential visits and clubs all enhance school life and each child's enjoyment of their community. In the onsite woodland, the Forest School sees children learn new skills, both within and beyond the national curriculum. They enjoy the time and space to develop their natural curiosity through hands-on practical experiences.

Pastoral care is at the core of life at Collegiate Prep.Pupils have a form tutor and are part of a deeply supportive traditional house system that celebrates all elements of school life, from sports day to inter-house competitions and regular house gatherings. Older pupils form bonds with Pre-School and Reception classes in the weekly reading buddies sessions, which mutually support the reading skills of younger pupils and give Year 6 children a taste of responsibility and relationship building.

Collegiate Prep School offers a wide range of extra-curricular clubs and activities, and pupils are able to start the day with Breakfast Club at 7.30am and stay on at school under supervision for an extended day until 6pm.

Charitable status. Collegiate School is a Registered Charity, number 1079552. Its aims and objectives are the provision of education.

Copthorne Preparatory School

Effingham Lane, Copthorne, West Sussex RH10 3HR
Tel: 01342 712311
email: office@copthorneprep.co.uk
website: www.copthorneprep.co.uk
X/Twitter: @copthorneprep
Facebook: @copthorneprep
Instagram: @copthorneprep
LinkedIn: /copthorne-prep-school

Chair of Governors: S Coutinho BA Hons, FCCA, IRM Cert

***Headmaster*: N Close BA Hons**, PGCE

Deputy Head: S Janman BEd (Music)

Age Range. 2–13.

Number of Boys and Girls. 260.

Fees per term (2023–2024). Day: Reception £3,734, Year 1 £3,825, Year 2 £3,911, Year 3 £5,157, Year 4 £5,666, Years 5–8 £6,500. Occasional boarding £38 per night.

Copthorne is a flourishing IAPS Prep School with approximately 260 boys and girls aged from 2 to 13. Children are prepared for independent school scholarships or common entrance. In the last 5 years Copthorne children have been awarded 48 scholarships or awards to a variety of Senior Schools.

We believe that, in order to learn, children must be happy and feel secure in their environment. Copthorne Prep School is full of happy children and the environment is caring but still allows children the freedom to develop as individuals.

The school helps to develop each child's confidence, to raise self-esteem and to make children feel good about themselves. Nothing does this more than children enjoying success in all areas of school life. This is why art, music, ICT, DT, drama and sport are all just as important as the pursuit of academic excellence.

Copthorne Prep School has developed an outstanding reputation for helping children to realise their full potential. By providing opportunities for all to succeed, children leave us as confident individuals, well prepared for their progression to senior schools of their choice. We inspire all our pupils to become lifelong learners, responsible global citizens and be the very best that they can be.

Our mission is to develop confidence, provide opportunities and realise potential as well as promoting imagination and happiness in our pupils.

The school is very proud of its 120-year history and retains all the important traditions of the past whilst developing a very forward thinking approach. The children receive a child-centred education, where their individual needs come first, in an environment that is parent-friendly, with very high levels of communication and pastoral care.

Charitable status. Copthorne School Trust Limited is a Registered Charity, number 270757. It exists to provide education to boys and girls.

Cottesmore School

Buchan Hill, Pease Pottage, West Sussex RH11 9AU
Tel: 01293 520648
email: admissions@cottesmoreschool.com
website: www.cottesmoreschool.com
X/Twitter: @cottesmoreprep
Facebook: @cottesmoreprepschool
Instagram: @cottesmore_school_open

Tatler School Awards 'Prep School of The Year 2020/21' and TES 'Boarding School of The Year 2019'.

***Headmaster*: T F Rogerson**, BA Hons, PGCE

Age Range. 4–13.

Number of Pupils. 200.

Fees per term (2023–2024). Prep: £7,032 (Day), £10,528 (Boarding); Pre-Prep: £3,756–£5,009.

Cottesmore is an award-winning co-educational Preparatory school for girls and boys in West Sussex, less than an hour from London.

Curriculum. Boys and girls are taught together in classes averaging 12 in number. Children are fully prepared for Common Entrance and Scholarship examinations. Cottesmore achieves excellent academic results. The strength of Cottesmore's academic programme lies within its breadth. There are 21 different curriculum subjects taught. Through this rich variety of intellectual experience, each girl and boy finds her or his particular strength and this in turn lifts their all-round potential.

Music. The musical tradition is strong – more than 90% of children learn a variety of instruments; there are three Choirs, a School Orchestra and several musical ensembles.

Sport. The major games are Football, Rugby, Cricket, Hockey, Swimming, Tennis, Netball, Athletics and Rounders. Numerous other sports are taught and encouraged. These include Archery, Riding, Basketball, Shooting, Short Tennis, Canoeing, Snooker, Cross-Country Running, Squash, Table Tennis, Gymnastics, Trampoline, Golf, Chess and Judo. The School competes at a national level in several of these sports.

Recent Developments. Our Technology Centre houses a constantly developing Information Technology Suite, a Design Technology room for metal, woodwork, plastic and pneumatics, a Craft room, Kiln, two Science laboratories and Art Studio.

Hobbies and Activities. These include Pottery, Drone Club, Photography, Bridge, Model-Making, Model Railway, Tenpin Bowling, Gardening, Rollerblading, Ballet, Modern Dancing, Drama, Craft, Carpentry, Printing, Cooking and Debating.

The boys and girls lead a full and varied life and are all encouraged to take part in as wide a variety of activities as possible. Weekends are a vital part of the school life and are made busy and fun for all.

Headmaster's Philosophy: Everyone has a talent. Whatever creative or academic outlet makes a child tick, Cottesmore finds and nurtures it. Endeavour and fun are the most important elements of intellectual life at

Cottesmore. Success follows this explosion of discovery and purposefulness.

Entry requirements. Entry is by Headmaster's interview and a child's last three terms' school reports, if necessary. For a prospectus or more information, please contact the Registrar, Lottie Rogerson, at admissions@cottesmoreschool.com or telephone 01293 520648.

Coworth Flexlands School

United Learning

Valley End, Chobham, Surrey GU24 8TE

Tel: 01276 855707
email: secretary@coworthflexlands.co.uk
registrar@coworthflexlands.co.uk
website: www.coworthflexlands.co.uk
X/Twitter: @CoworthFlexSch
Facebook: @CoworthFlexSch
Instagram: @coworthflexlands
LinkedIn: /coworth-flexlands-prep-school-and-nursery-675ab7210

Chairman of Governors: Mr Matthew Close

***Headmistress*: Miss Nicola Cowell**

Age range. 2½–11 years.

Number of pupils. 130.

Fees per term (2023–2024). From £4,080 to £5,498.

Coworth Flexlands Prep School and Nursery is an Independent Prep School and Nursery for children aged 2½ to 11 years. Nursery is fully immersed in school life. The school is nestled in between the villages of Sunningdale, Windlesham and Chobham. Rated excellent in all areas by the Independent Schools Inspectorate March 2023.

Inspiring Minds and Nurturing Spirit is at the heart of the School's approach. The result of this approach sees every pupil reaching and growing their potential at a pace which is right for them. Through highly specialist teaching led by staff who are passionate and knowledgeable about their curriculum area, pupils show high levels of understanding and attainment. Pupils are well known to staff and, as such, their individual trajectory of progress is carefully planned and monitored. Talents are nurtured and pupils are encouraged to follow their passions.

Coworth Flexlands is a school where happiness gets results! Pupils leave Coworth Flexlands as happy, confident and curious learners, ready to embrace new opportunities and make the most of the world ahead of them.

The school offers the convenience of optional wraparound care and clubs for busy parents from 7.30 am to 6.00 pm and a wide range of on-site holiday activities.

Charitable status. Coworth Flexlands School School is part of United Learning which comprises: UCST (a Company Limited by Guarantee, Registered in England, number 2780748, and a Registered Charity, number 1016538) and ULT (a Company Limited by Guarantee, Registered in England, number 4439859, and an Exempt Charity).

Crackley Hall School

Kenilworth, Warwickshire CV8 2FT

Tel: 01926 514444
email: post@crackleyhall.co.uk
website: www.crackleyhall.co.uk
X/Twitter: @CrackleyHallSch
Facebook: @crackleyhallandlittlecrackersofficial
Instagram: @crackleyhall_littlecrackers

Co-educational Nursery and Prep School.

Leadership Team:

***Headmaster*: Mr Robert Duigan**, BComEd, MEd

Deputy Head: Mr Duncan Cottrill, BSc, PGCE, PSHCE
Assistant Head – Early Years Foundation Stage and KS1: Mrs Susan Glen-Roots, BEd (English and Drama)
Assistant Head – Key Stage 2 and Academic: Ms Sharon McAloon, BA, ATS
Foundation Principal: Ed Hester, MA Oxon, PGCE

Age range. 2–11 years.

Number of pupils. 236.

Fees per term (2023–2024). Prep School: £4,064–£4,290. Reception: £3,855. Nursery: £309 per week (full time, term-time only), £300 per week (full time, all year).

Crackley Hall is a co-educational independent Catholic day school which welcomes pupils of all denominations. The school is part of The Princethorpe Foundation comprising Little Crackers Nursery, Crackley Hall School, Crescent School and Princethorpe College.

Crackley Hall continues to go from strength to strength following the merger with Abbotsford School in September 2010. Under the leadership of Headmaster, Robert Duigan, pupil numbers have risen considerably and we are now well known for our high academic standards, sporting provision and excellence in the performing arts.

In 2017, the ISI Inspectors judged the school to be 'excellent' in every area.

In 2019, in its Canonical Inspection Report, the Archdiocese of Birmingham rated the 'Catholic Life' and 'Collective Worship' at Crackley Hall School as 'outstanding'.

Building work that provided more classrooms, specialist teaching rooms for Art and Music, greatly enhanced IT, Science and Technology suites, and improved sports changing rooms was completed in 2013, and the second phase of major development, a new multi-purpose hall with additional teaching space, was completed in Spring 2016.

Situated on the outskirts of Kenilworth, Crackley Hall occupies a pleasant and safe setting with playing fields a short distance across the road. An extended day facility is offered; pupils may be dropped off from 7.45am and can stay at school until 6.00pm. Nursery attendance times are flexible, with term-time and year-round (51 weeks) places available.

Crackley Hall bases its care for individuals on the sound Christian principles of love and forgiveness; children become strong in the understanding of themselves and others. There is a keen sense of community between pupils, staff and parents. We encourage fairness, freedom, friendship and fun.

Small class sizes promote individual attention. The curriculum is based on national guidelines, but pupils are encouraged to achieve well beyond these targets. During the early years, great emphasis is placed on developing key skills in reading, writing, speaking, listening, mathematics and science. The learning of tables and spellings is actively developed through simple homework tasks. Specialists teach Art, Design Technology, French, Music, Games, ICT and RE. Recent investment has resulted in specialist teaching rooms for Art and Music, greatly enhanced IT, Science and Technology suites and improved sports changing facilities.

Sports are very strong with football, rugby, cricket, hockey, netball, tennis, athletics, swimming, rounders, trampolining, gym and karate all available. There is a strong and thriving music department and all pupils together with members of the choir, choral group and orchestra participate in concerts and stage productions to enrich their learning and to build confidence and self-esteem. Pupils have the opportunity to study a wide range of individual instruments under the guidance of a team of peripatetic staff and specialist teachers offer classes in music, theatre, speech and drama and dance. Other activities are offered before and after school as well as during lunch breaks including art, chess, craft, ICT, Mandarin, cookery, rock school, Lego, Latin, brass, climbing, sewing and mindfulness.

Admission is through interview with the Head, assessments in English and Mathematics, and a taster day at the school. We also ask for a reference from the child's current school. The admission information is considered as a whole so that as accurate a picture as possible of the child can be obtained. The pastoral elements are as important to us as academic ability.

Parents are welcomed into school for Friday morning assembly when the children's good work is celebrated. An active Parent Teacher Association organises social and fundraising events. Pupils are encouraged to maintain their links with the school by joining the Past Pupils' Association.

Charitable status. The Princethorpe Foundation is a Registered Charity, number 1087124. It exists solely for the purpose of educating children.

Craigclowan School & Nursery

Edinburgh Road, Perth PH2 8PS

Tel: 01738 626310
email: head@craigclowan-school.co.uk
website: www.craigclowan-school.co.uk
X/Twitter: @craigclowan
Facebook: @craigclowan
Instagram: @craigclowan

Chairman of Governors: Bill Farrar

***Head*: Liz Henderson**

Bursar: Tom Kerrigan
Registrar: Jennifer Trueland

Age range. 3–13.

Number of pupils. 209: 123 boys, 86 girls.

Fees per term (2023–2024). £5,730.

Craigclowan provides a warm and nurturing environment for boys and girls aged 3–13 to learn and grow. Set in stunning grounds with magnificent views over Perthshire, the school has a distinguished history, a reputation for the highest standards and expectations and a passion for childhood.

Craigclowan delivers a modern education within a framework of traditional values. With a dedicated, caring and supportive ethos, the staff are very close to the children, and the families, in their care, and treat them as individuals in all they do. Every child is encouraged to achieve their all-round potential, in the classroom, on the sports fields, on the stage and in the music and art departments.

The school aims to make the most of the world outside the classroom through a wide range of outdoor activities that build confidence and resilience, encourage creativity and problem-solving and ensure rosy cheeks and muddy boots. Wellies and waterproofs are a must! When it comes to moving on to senior school, pupils go on to attend a wide variety of top UK schools, both north and south of the border, many with scholarships under their belts. The values that are instilled in children during their journey through Craigclowan are the qualities that allow them to thrive after they leave.

School is a hive of activity from 7.30 am until 6.00 pm, with a family-friendly wraparound care programme before and after lessons. The school minibus fleet collects children from across the region and Craigclowan's ever-popular holiday activity camps operate throughout the year. Grant funding is available for nursery pupils setting out on their Craigclowan adventure.

Why not come along and find out what a Craigclowan education has to offer to your family? You will be assured of a very warm welcome and will find a school in a stunning location with tremendous spirit.

Charitable status. Craigclowan School Limited is a Registered Charity, number SC010817. It exists to promote education generally and for that purpose to establish, carry on and maintain a school within Scotland.

Cranford School

Moulsford, Wallingford, Oxfordshire OX10 9HT

Tel: 01491 651218
email: admissions@cranfordschool.co.uk
website: www.cranfordschool.co.uk
X/Twitter: @CHSMoulsford
Facebook: @CranfordHouse
Instagram: @chsmoulsford

See full entry in the **ISA** section, on **p. 871**.

Cranleigh Preparatory School

Horseshoe Lane, Cranleigh, Surrey GU6 8QH
Tel: 01483 542058
email: cjs@cranprep.org
website: www.cranprep.org
X/Twitter: @CranleighPrep
Facebook: @CranPrep

Chairman of Governors: Mr Adrian Lajtha
Leadership Team:

***Head*: Mr Neil R Brooks**

Mrs Sarah Awwad
Mr Toby Batchelor
Ms Alison Bridges
Mrs Tracy Brooks
Mr Paul Dunn
Mr Mark Halstead
Mrs Emma Lewis
Mrs Hannah Pakenham-Walsh
Mr Jeremy Reid
Mr Chris Stone
Miss Jane Underdown
Mrs Emma Unwin

Age range. 7–13.

Number of pupils. 315 (70 Boarders, 245 Day).

Fees per annum (2023–2024). Boarders: £28,515; Day Pupils: £18,195 (Forms 1 & 2), £23,610 (Forms 3–6). A discount of fees is available for the third (20%) and subsequent (30%) siblings attending either the Prep, Senior School or Sixth Form at any one time.

The School stands in its own beautiful and spacious grounds, set in 40 acres of stunning Surrey countryside, just 50 minutes from London. Cranleigh Preparatory School is a co-educational boarding and day school. A teaching staff of 50 enables classes to be small. The Head and his wife live just at the bottom of the school drive. The boarding Houseparents and their families both live on the school site. They are fully involved with the health and happiness of the boys and girls, together with pastoral staff, including matrons. A great source of strength is the close partnership with Cranleigh School 'across the road', with both schools sharing an innovative 7–18 programme across sport, music and computing. The Preparatory School has use of Senior School sports facilities, including an indoor pool, artificial pitches, the stables and golf course.

The boys and girls are prepared for Common Entrance and scholarships. Pupils have achieved over 200 scholarships in the last five years to some of the country's leading schools, including Cranleigh School, Brighton College, Charterhouse, Eton, KCS Wimbledon, Marlborough, RGS Guildford, Tonbridge, Wellington and Winchester.

Boarding life is busy and fun, with a wide array of exciting activities on offer. There is the opportunity to board all week or flexi board for one or more nights during the week; all pupils return home every weekend and there is a weekly bus service to and from London.

The curriculum is broad, balanced and covers all and more than that laid down by the National Curriculum. The School teaches Computing, and technological problem solving is encouraged. Art, Food Technology, Design and Music are included in the curriculum at all levels. Individual instrumental lessons are available and peripatetic music staff teach at both schools. There are choirs, orchestras, bands and several ensembles. Boys and girls are given every incentive to develop spare time interests and a choice of activities is built into the timetable.

The School is fortunate to have excellent facilities including a full-sized artificial pitch, a large Sports and Drama Hall, a Dance Studio, a Music School and very light, airy classrooms. The School has recently opened a brand new teaching block, housing three new Science laboratories, two Art Studios and state-of-the-art Design and Food Technology areas. Boarding numbers are steadily increasing, and the boarding facilities are being updated again later this year.

Rugby, football, hockey, netball, cricket, athletics, tennis, swimming, squash, cross country, basketball, fencing, riding, golf, Eton Fives, archery and badminton, are among the sports.

Main entry age is at 7 or 8, with limited availability at 11. Places are sometimes available in the intervening year groups.

Charitable status. Cranleigh School is a Registered Charity, number 1070856, whose Preparatory School exists to provide education for boys and girls aged 7–13.

Cranmore

Epsom Road, West Horsley, Surrey KT24 6AT
Tel: 01483 280340
email: office@cranmore.org
website: www.cranmore.org

Joint Chair of Governors: Mr Michael Henderson & Mrs Annette Turner

***Headmaster*: Mr B Everitt**, BSc, MEd, PGCE

Deputy Head (*Academic*): Mr J Pulford, BSc, PGCE
Assistant Head (*Pastoral*): Ms J Schembri, BA, PGCE
Assistant Head (*Academic*): Mr T Heaver, BSc, MSc Oxon, PGCE
Head of Lower Prep School: Miss S Gallop, BA, PGCE
Director of Finance: Mrs C Minikin, BA, ACA
Director of Operations: Mr A Ellison

Age Range. 2+ co-educational diamond model.

Number of Pupils. 525 Day Pupils.

Fees per term (2023–2024). Nursery (5 full days/week) £3,875; Reception £4,350; Years 1 & 2 £4,695; Year 3 £5,050; Year 4 £5,300; Years 5 & 6 £5,795; Years 7 & 8 £6,995; Years 9 upwards £7,195.

On 1 September 2019, the school formed a partnership with St Teresa's Effingham, The Effingham Schools Trust, offering education to girls and boys aged 2 to 18. Cranmore is equidistant between Leatherhead and Guildford and is easily accessible from Cobham, Esher, Weybridge, Dorking and Woking with school transport available. Normal entry points are Nursery, Reception, Year 3 (7+), Year 7 (11+) and Year 9 (13+). Entry is non-selective in the early years and assessments are held for other year groups. There is a Scholarship programme for 11+ and 13+ entry offering Academic, Sport, Music, Art and Drama Scholarships. In the most recent Inspection in February 2022, the school was rated 'Excellent' for the quality of pupils' academic and other achievements, as well as the quality of their personal development. In addition to the overall judgment of 'Excellent', each of the eight sub-categories for these areas were graded as 'Excellent'.

An ongoing programme of investment over several years has given the school many outstanding facilities based on the extensive 25-acre site. These include a £250,000 redevelopment of the Cranmore Nursery outdoor learning area, car park redevelopment, a forest school, refurbishment of the 25m swimming pool and an Athletic Development Centre. In 2023, a brand new purpose-built science and technology building was added, providing four more science labs, an ICT suite, a modernised DT room and two classrooms. The dining room has also been completely refitted for the academic year 2023–24. The sports facilities include: a sports hall, gymnasium, 25m swimming pool, 4 AstroTurf tennis courts and hockey pitch, 5-a-side astro, 9-hole golf course, large playground with rubberised surface, 3 squash courts and athletic development centre, plus extensive playing fields.

Cranmore Nursery (from age 2) has its own dedicated accommodation which includes several rooms and outdoor learning area. The Lower Prep School (Nursery to Year 3) offers all children access to tremendous resources including the sports hall, gymnasium, swimming pool, forest school and music facilities. Pupils are taught by specialist subject teachers from Year 4. Cranmore's academic standards are high and pupil development enables all pupils to fulfil their individual potential.

Sports teams compete in galas, tournaments at local and national level; Inter-School and Inter-House competitions allow all pupils to take part. All children have the opportunity to represent the school at one of the main sports: rugby, football, cricket, netball and hockey. Our swimming squads compete successfully at national level. There is also a long tradition of other sports including golf, tennis and rowing – with boats housed at a local rowing club on the Thames. Skiing is supported by weekly training at Sandown with plans to install a ski simulator within school. There is a thriving extracurricular programme as well as trips to support curriculum learning and to develop team building and leadership skills.

The Drama, Speech and Music school offers every pupil the opportunity to learn an instrument, sing in one of our choirs and play in a wide variety of ensembles and orchestras.

Cranmore is a Catholic school, welcoming families from all religious backgrounds and none. Our Christian ethos is central to supporting every child's development underpinned by our core values: Community, Faith, Character, Compassion and Intellect.

Charitable status. Effingham Schools Trust is a Registered Charity, number 1095103. It exists to provide education for children.

Crescent School

Bawnmore Road, Bilton, Rugby, Warwickshire CV22 7QH

Tel: 01788 521595
email: admin@crescentschool.co.uk
website: www.crescentschool.co.uk
X/Twitter: @CrescentSchRug
Facebook: @cres.school
Instagram: @crescentschoolrugby

Leadership Team:

***Headmaster*: Joe Thackway**, BA, PGCE

Deputy Head, Head of Curriculum & Assessment: Ms Bryony Forth, BSc, PGCE, NPQH (Year 5 Teacher – Mathematics, Geography)
Finance Manager and Registrar: Mrs Helen Morley
Head of Wellbeing, Deputy DSL: Mrs Sam Stapleton, BSc, QTS (Year 1 Teacher – RE and PSHE)
Assistant Head, Head of Pre-Prep, Designated Safeguarding Lead, Head of Pastoral Care: Alan Webb, BEd (Year 2 Teacher)
Assistant Head, Educational Visits Co-ordinator, Events Manager: Mrs Sarah Webb, BEd (Year 6 Teacher – English)

Foundation Principal: Ed Hester, MA Oxon, PGCE

Age range. 4–11.

Number of pupils. 157 Day Boys and Girls (73 boys, 84 girls).

Fees per term (2023–2024). £3,785–£4,121.

The Crescent School is an independent co-educational preparatory school for day pupils aged 4–11 years. It merged with the Princethorpe Foundation in September 2016 joining the other schools in the Foundation – Little Crackers Nursery, Crackley Hall School and Princethorpe College.

The school was founded in 1948, originally to provide a place of education for the young children of the masters of Rugby School. Over the years the school has steadily expanded, admitting children from Rugby and the surrounding area. In 1988, having outgrown its original premises, the school moved into modern, purpose-built accommodation in Bilton, about a mile to the south of Rugby town centre. The buildings provide large and bright teaching areas, with a separate annexe housing the Nursery and Reception classes. There are specialist rooms for Science, Art, Design Technology, ICT and the Performing Arts. In addition, there is also a spacious Library and Resource Area. The multi-purpose hall provides a venue for daily assemblies, large-scale music-making, is fully equipped for physical education and has all the necessary equipment to turn it into a theatre for school productions. The school is surrounded by its own gardens, play areas and sports field.

The requirements of the National Curriculum are fully encompassed by the academic programme and particular emphasis is placed on English and mathematics in the early years. All pupils receive specialist tuition in Information and Communication Technology, Music and Physical Education. Specialist teaching in other subjects is introduced as children move upwards through the school. Spanish is introduced in Reception, followed by French in Year 3. The pupils are prepared for the local 11+ examination for entry to maintained secondary schools, including local grammar schools, and specific entrance examinations also at 11+ for independent senior schools.

The performing arts are a particular strength of the school and lessons are given in speech and drama, singing, percussion, musical theory and appreciation and recorder playing. Instrumental lessons (piano, brass, woodwind and strings) are offered as an optional extra. There is a school choir, orchestra, brass, string and wind ensembles and recorder groups.

Charitable status. The Princethorpe Foundation is a Registered Charity, number 1087124. It exists solely for the purpose of educating children.

The Croft Preparatory School

Loxley Road, Stratford-upon-Avon, Warwickshire CV37 7RL

Tel: 01789 293795
email: office@croftschool.co.uk
website: www.croftschool.co.uk

Chair of The Board of Directors: Mrs L Thornton, Cert Ed Lond, FRSA

Chair of the School's Governing Committee: Mrs V Aris, MBE, MSc

***Headmaster*: Mr M Cook**, BSc Hons, PGCE

Deputy Headmaster: Mr E Bolderston, BSc Hons, PGCE

Age range. 3–11.
Number of pupils. 403: 215 boys, 188 girls.
Fees per term (2023–2024). £552–£4,806.

The Croft Preparatory School is a co-educational day school, for children from 3 to 11 years of age, situated on the outskirts of Stratford upon Avon. Founded in 1933, the school occupies a large rural site with superb facilities and extensive playing fields, offering children some of the most exciting educational opportunities in the area. There is also a nature conservation area with a lake.

A family-based school, The Croft provides specialist teaching in small groups, where good discipline and a wider knowledge of the world around us, both spiritual and geographical, is encouraged. Music, Sport and Drama each play an important part in the curriculum. The resulting high educational standards provide the all-round excellence which is at the heart of the school.

The scope of the grounds and facilities enable a wide range of activities and opportunities – sporting, creative and recreational. From the Sports Hall, swimming pool and games pitches, to the Music practice rooms, Performance Space, small arenas in the playgrounds and the 600-seat Theatre; the Croft Cabin and conservation area, to the imitation Motte and Bailey castle, Geology Museum and Train Shed. The opportunities are endless at The Croft.

The children are prepared for 11+ entry to the local Grammar Schools or Senior Independent Schools.

Entrance requirements. Children can be accepted in Little Crofters from the age of 3 years. Prospective pupils registered for Years 1–6, where a place is available, are invited into School for a taster day. They will spend a day in the classroom with their age group and be assessed by the Class Teacher. Parents provide a copy of their child's latest school report and if deemed necessary, an assessment of literacy, numeracy, and sometimes other appropriate tests will be given by the SENDCo.

Crosfields School

Shinfield Road, Reading, Berks RG2 9BL

Tel: 0118 9871810
email: admissions@crosfields.com
website: www.crosfields.com
X/Twitter: @WeAreCrosfields
Facebook: @CrosfieldsSchool
Instagram: @CrosfieldsSchool

Chair of Governors: Mr C Bradfield

***Head*: Mrs Caroline Townshend**, BSc Southampton, PGCE Gold Smiths

Deputy Head Academic (*Seniors*): Mr Richard Ebbage, BSc Roehampton, MSc Southampton, QTS, NPQSL UCL

Deputy Head Pastoral (*Seniors*): Mr Adam Mallins, BSc Birmingham, PGCE Buckingham

Head of Pre-Prep: Mrs Janey McDowell, BSc Hons Reading, PGCE Cantab

Deputy Head Academic (*Juniors*): Mr John Ireland, BA Kent, PGCE, PGCert, Med Reading

Deputy Head Pastoral (*Juniors*): Mr Tom Goodhew, BSc Winchester, PGCE Reading

Age range. 3–16.
Number of pupils. 750.

Fees per term (2023–2024). £3,992–£6,552 inclusive of food, educational day visits, curriculum residentials, textbooks and many co-curricular sessions. After-school care options are available.

Crosfields is an independent, co-educational day school in Shinfield, Reading, situated in over 40 acres of wood and parkland. Offering education to Nursery children through to Year 11, Crosfields is a modern, well-resourced school boasting an outstanding reputation for academic excellence, and holds a strong track record in preparing pupils for the most academically demanding schools.

A recent Independent Schools Inspection awarded Crosfields 'Excellent', with inspectors commenting that, 'Academic attainment is in advance of that expected at the relevant levels of age and stage of development.' Pupils benefit from small class sizes where they receive individual attention from experienced and dedicated teaching staff, all housed in purpose-built, spacious classrooms. With contemporary science labs and well-stocked libraries, the school offers a broad curriculum that develops confident and independent learning, enhanced by exciting day and residential trips.

Facilities at Crosfields are considered unrivalled in the Reading area, where children enjoy an abundance of green space. Six Forest School outdoor learning sites, age-appropriate play equipment and sports areas are just some of the many jewels in the Crosfields crown. A floodlit artificial turf pitch provides four netball courts or hockey pitches, and is complemented by many natural turf sports pitches, cricket wickets, nets and pavilion. Pupils enjoy an on-site sports centre that houses a sports hall and dance studio, as well as a swimming pool with moveable floor so that children of all ages can learn to swim confidently.

From 2021, Crosfields welcomed pupils into Year 9, with the School's first full set of GCSE results expected in 2024. This past summer, a handful of pupils voluntarily sat Spanish, German and RS (Short Course). 100% of pupils achieved a strong pass with 62% achieving grade 7–9.

In addition to its outstanding academic reputation and facilities, Crosfields offers working parents wraparound care that includes an early morning Breakfast Club that opens at 7:30 am (7:45 am for EYFS), and after-school collection times up to 17:50. A comprehensive, co-curricular programme caters for all children and interests, pupils can choose from a range of options which provides challenges and opportunities to investigate areas of interest, enhancing learning and expanding the school experience at Crosfields. Activities include cookery, golf, drama classes, judo, dance, fencing, choir singing and music, science and, most recently, rowing, to name but a few!

The school is easily accessible from junction 11 of the M4 and the A33 Basingstoke Road. Several transport routes for pupils travelling into the school are available for families who may require additional support with the school run. Routes run between neighbouring towns, including Emmer Green, Caversham, Bucklebury, Mortimer Common, Winnersh, Woodley and Sonning.

Charitable status. Crosfields School Trust Limited is a Registered Charity, number 584278. The aim of the school is solely to provide education for children between the ages of 3 and 16.

Culford Prep School

Bury St Edmunds, Suffolk IP28 6TX

Tel: 01284 385308

email: admissions@culford.co.uk

website: www.culford.co.uk

X/Twitter: @CulfordSchool

Facebook: @OfficialCulfordSchool

Instagram: @culfordschool

Chair of Governors: Mr Mark Donougher, BSc ACA

***Head*: C Bentley**, MEd

Age Range. Co-educational 7–13.

Number of Pupils. 260 (Day), 40 (Boarders).

Fees per term (2023–2024). Day: £4,720–£6,180; Boarding: £9,195–£9,880 (full), £8,730 (3-night), £8,150 (2-night).

Admission is by entrance examination at all ages, though the majority of pupils enter at age 7 or 11 and scholarships are available at 11+.

Culford Prep School has its own staff and Head, but remains closely linked to the Senior School. This allows the School to enjoy a significant degree of independence and the ability to focus on the particular needs of Prep School age children while benefiting from the outstanding facilities and community spirit of Culford.

Facilities. Culford Prep School is situated in its own grounds, within Culford Park. The heart of the School is the impressive quadrangle at the centre of which lies the Jubilee Library. Other facilities include two science laboratories and two state-of-the-art ICT suites which, in common with the rest of the Prep School's classrooms, have networked interactive whiteboards.

Outside Prep have a mix of playing fields for all the major sports and the perennially-popular adventure playground.

Teaching & Learning. Prep School pupils are given a thorough grounding in the essential learning skills of mathematics and English and the enhanced curriculum broadens beyond the confines of the National Curriculum. Work in the classrooms is augmented by an extensive Activities Programme which offers pupils a wide range of opportunities and experiences, including trips out and visits from guest authors and experts in their field.

Music & Drama play a significant part in Culford Prep School life, and a variety of theatrical performances, choirs and ensembles are performed each year, either in the Prep School hall or in Culford's purpose-built Studio Theatre. Specialist speech and drama lessons are also offered.

Sports Facilities. Culford Prep School have access to the fantastic Sports and Tennis Centre, a state-of-the-art facility, which comprises a four-court, championship-standard Indoor Tennis Centre, a 25m heated indoor pool, gym, strength and conditioning suite, golf swing studio, golf short game area, driving range and a large sports hall with a climbing wall and indoor cricket nets. Outside there are further tennis courts, two of which are seasonally covered, two artificial turf pitches (one in partnership with Bury Hockey Club) and numerous rugby and hockey pitches. Pupils can also pursue athletics, horse riding, archery and other outdoor activities. Culford launched a new Football Academy programme to sit alongside its already well-established tennis, golf and swimming programmes.

Boarding. Prep School boarders live in Cadogan House, a mixed boarding house located next to the School overlooking the playing fields. Boarders are able to take advantage of a comprehensive programme of weekend activities and are looked after by a team of dedicated staff under the direction of the Housemaster. Recent trips have included visiting Harry Potter World, the Oasis Camel Park and the North Norfolk Coast.

Religious affiliation. Methodist: pupils from all faiths, and those of none, are welcome.

Charitable status. Culford School is part of the Methodist Independent Schools Trust, which is a Registered Charity, number 1142794.

Cumnor House School

Cognita Schools Group

Boys School:
168 Pampisford Road, South Croydon, Surrey CR2 6DA
Tel: 020 8660 3445

Girls School:
1 Woodcote Lane, Purley, Surrey CR8 3HB
Tel: 020 8668 0050
email: admissions@cumnorhouse.com
website: www.cumnorhouse.com
X/Twitter: @wearecumnor
Facebook: @WeAreCumnor
Instagram: @cumnorhouseschool
LinkedIn: /company/cumnorhouseschool

***Head of School, Cumnor Boys*: Miss Emma Edwards**
***Headmistress, Cumnor Girls*: Mrs Amanda McShane**

Age Range. Boys 4–13, Girls 4–11. Co-educational Nursery 2–4 years.

Number of Pupils. Prep & Pre-Prep: 360 Boys, 185 Girls. Nursery: 149.

Fees per term (2023–2024). £4,725–£5,746 (including lunch and school trips).

Cumnor House School for Boys – shortlisted for Sporting Achievement, Independent School of the Year 2021 – is one of Surrey's leading Preparatory Schools and prepares boys for scholarships and common entrance examinations to leading senior independent schools and local grammar schools.

Scholarships have been won recently to Charterhouse, Epsom, Dulwich, Harrow, Tonbridge, Westminster and the local senior independent schools, Caterham, Trinity and Whitgift.

Music, Sports, Art and Drama play a large part in the life of the School and all contribute to the busy, happy atmosphere.

Choir, sports tours and matches, ski trips, regular stage productions and a broad spectrum of clubs and options, give the boys the opportunity to pursue a wide range of interests.

This school is located in a residential area in South Croydon with access to good transport links.

Entry requirements: Taster Day with Assessment.

At **Cumnor House School for Girls – shortlisted for Small Independent School of the Year 2021** – our main aim is to give parents and their daughters as much choice as possible when selecting their senior schools in Year 6. This journey starts in the Early Years; by developing confidence and a positive attitude to learning, we lay vital foundations for the future.

Practical experiences complement the curriculum and encourage the love of learning needed to embrace the academic, cultural, sporting and musical opportunities that Cumnor House School for Girls provides. The girls are encouraged to develop all their interests and talents, both within the extensive curriculum and through involvement in a wide range of clubs and activities.

Scholarships have been won recently to Caterham, Croydon High, Ewell Castle, Old Palace, Reigate Grammar, Royal Russell, Streatham and Clapham High, Sutton High and Woldingham.

The school is located in a quiet, leafy, private road in Purley – a hidden gem of a school!

Entry requirements: Taster Day with Assessment.

Cumnor House Sussex

Danehill, Haywards Heath, West Sussex RH17 7HT
Tel: 01825 790347
email: registrar@cumnor.co.uk
website: www.cumnor.co.uk
Facebook: @cumnorhouse
Instagram: @cumnorhousesussex

***Headmaster*: Fergus Llewellyn**

Deputy Head Pastoral: Michael Matthews
Deputy Head Academic: Bruno Shovelton
Head of Pre-Prep: Jacqui Freeman
Bursar: Leigh Stark

Age range. 2–13.

Number of pupils. 347: 191 boys, 156 girls. (Nursery 31 boys, 37 girls.)

Fees per term (2023–2024). Boarding: Weekly £8,990, Flexi £7,860–£8,780; Day: Years 5–8 £7,790, Year 4 £6,850, Year 3 £5,950, Year 2 £4,700, Year 1 £4,170, Reception £3,560 (£2,710 after free entitlement).

Cumnor House Sussex is one of the country's leading independent day and flexible boarding schools for children from the ages of 2 to 13. Situated at the heart of the Ashdown Forest in Sussex, we provide an empowering education for active and ambitious boys and girls.

Cumnor is a School that lives by its motto of 'Aim High, Be Kind and Dare to be Different'. It places the child at the centre of all it does, looking each day to help them become the very best version of themselves, in whatever area that might be. It aims to strike the balance between the modern and the traditional. It looks to include every member of its community, from the Nursery child through to its parents. It wants its children to be happy and to thrive.

Set in 60 acres of beautiful Sussex countryside, our award-winning Cumnor Nursery is a truly wonderful, bespoke space for young children to explore, investigate, create and discover through play. The Nursery is a caring, friendly and nurturing environment where children are encouraged to make the most of the joys of living and learning. We are the only independent school in Sussex offering truly flexible childcare from 7.00 am to 7.00 pm, 50 weeks of the year, for children aged 2 to 4, and offering up to 30 hours EYEE.

Cumnor House Pre-Prep provides a happy, safe and nurturing environment in which children can begin to develop a lifelong love of learning and interest in the world around them. Our self-contained Pre-Prep is the hub of Cumnor, with easy access to the Prep school's wider facilities including Woodpeckers, the theatre, swimming pool, home economics, music barn, sports pitches and 60 acres of Sussex countryside to explore. Our dedicated, passionate and devoted teachers support and encourage pupils to become well-rounded, inspired and confident individuals who are kind, tenacious and eager to do their best.

We are focused on individuals and every child is known to us. The happiness and wellbeing of each child is of paramount importance and in all decision making the impact on the child is considered first. We are ambitious for every child in our care and offer a fully rounded education within a community that nurtures childhood. We value kindness – to others and ourselves – above all else and believe this is central to enabling children to achieve their full potential while at school and to succeed in later life.

The breadth and depth of our curriculum is evident through our long-standing track record of academic achievement, scholarship success and an unrivalled range of destination senior schools. Our children consistently achieve impressive academic results, moving on to over 20 different senior schools, with over 50% in any one year doing so with an Award or Scholarship.

Cumnor is a warm, friendly community with family at its heart. We offer preparation for boarding life at senior school with flexible boarding options for children in Years 7 and 8 in a home-from-home environment where they can develop personally, socially and creatively alongside their friends.

At Cumnor, we believe passionately that what makes us stand out as a school community is the collective will to bring out the very best in each and every child in our care. Pastoral care is right at the heart of a Cumnor education, seeking out a child's individual spark and being attentive in helping it burn brightly as they grow.

As part of this journey, we also acknowledge that there will be bumps along the way and sometimes pupils, teachers and parents need signposting as to how best to navigate these. The initiatives detailed in 'The Next Chapter' (The Cumnor Holistic Approach to Pastoral Thinking and Emotional Resilience) set out a number of additional tools designed to complement the work already undertaken by tutors, form takers, in assemblies and by all teachers across the curriculum.

Charitable status. Cumnor House School Trust is a Registered Charity, number 801924. It exists for the advancement of education.

Dair House School

Bishop's Blake, Beaconsfield Road, Farnham Royal, Buckinghamshire SL2 3BY

Tel: 01753 643964
email: schooloffice@dairhouse.co.uk; admissions@dairhouse.school
website: www.dairhouse.co.uk
X/Twitter: @DairHouseSchool
Facebook: @dairhouse

Chairman of Governors: Mrs Jane Masih

***Head*: Mrs Janine Bull**

Age Range. 3–11 Co-educational.

Number in School. 125 Day pupils.

Fees per term (2023–2024). £1,270–£5,335.

Located on the A355 in Farnham Royal, we are conveniently placed for Farnham Common, Farnham Royal, Gerrards Cross, Beaconsfield, Stoke Poges, Burnham and Slough.

Dair House School offers an exciting and personalised education to boys and girls from 3–11 years old.

We take pride in our warm, friendly, individual care, catering for each child's abilities. We provide our children with a firm sense of belonging and a sure foundation from the start in classes which are no larger than 19.

The school has excellent facilities and each class is fully resourced with smartboards. Our Nursery is very much part of the school with the children attending assemblies once a week and and enjoying a fantastic outdoor play environment.

Dair House School is situated in 4 acres of wonderful tree-lined grounds with a forest school area, large sports field and an all-weather sports surface.

We offer a breakfast club from 7.30 am and an after-school tea club until 6.00 pm, as well as a plethora of lunchtime and after-school activities.

Charitable status. Dair House School Trust Limited is a Registered Charity, number 270719. Its aim is to provide 'a sure foundation from the start'.

Danes Hill School

Leatherhead Road, Oxshott, Surrey KT22 0JG

Tel: 01372 842509 (General), 01372 849203 (Adnmissions)
email: registrar@daneshill.surrey.sch.uk
website: www.daneshillschool.co.uk
X/Twitter: @Danes_Hill_Sch
Facebook: @Danes Hill School
Instagram: @danes_hill_school
LinkedIn: /company/danes-hill-school

***Head*: Mrs Maxine Shaw**, BSc, PGCE, PG Dip, NPQH
***Head of the Pre-Prep*: Mrs Ruth Samson**

Fees per term (2023–2024). Nursery: £510–£540 per morning/afternoon. Pre-Prep (Reception and Year 1): £5,300. Prep (Years 2–8): £7,500.

Scholarships offered. Scholarships are available for pupils in Year 3, 5 and 7 and include Academic, Art, Design and Technology, Drama, Music and Sport.

Danes Hill is a co-educational day school providing children aged 3 to 13 with an exciting and dynamic curriculum. This unique educational environment gives the children a chance to develop academically and socially before embarking on their Senior School journey.

The Pre-Prep

The Pre-Prep takes children from 3 to 6 years and is situated separately, but within easy walking distance of the Prep site. Located on Steels Lane in Oxshott Surrey, the Pre-Prep is home to our Nursery, Reception and Year 1 children with the Head, Mrs Ruth Samson at the helm of the school. Alongside their dedicated Class Teacher, the children are taught by talented specialist teachers. This includes lessons such as Forest School, sport, swimming, performing arts, French and Spanish. The school recognises that young children thrive, and their minds and bodies develop best when they have access to stimulating outdoor environments. At the Pre-Prep, pupils have regular timetabled days when learning takes place outdoors. The children regularly visit our outdoor learning environment, The Paddock, with their trained Forest School teachers. Facilities include a heated swimming pool which the children swim in weekly, an expansive playground with a sandpit, mindfulness garden and pirate ship, an ICT suite and a Library.

The Prep

High academic success combines happily with a strong tradition of sporting prowess, to ensure that all children are exposed to a kaleidoscope of opportunity on a peaceful 55-acre site in the heart of Oxshott Village in Surrey. The facilities are designed to enhance the excellent standard of teaching that is offered at Danes Hill: state-of-the-art classrooms and five Science Labs are just the beginning of this. A refurbished Library offers a wonderful learning atmosphere, opening out onto the Head's Terrace when the weather permits. There is an outstanding Dining Room and catering facilities, offering a range of lunch options for all pupils. The children also enjoy the new state-of-the-art Sports Hall with climbing wall. Both Pre-Prep and Prep sites have swimming pools.

The curriculum is dynamic and exciting, and a wide range of extra-curricular activity is encouraged. The Danes Hill Extra Curricular Activities (ECA) programme aims to deliver fun and stimulating pursuits to children who wish to take part. It has been created in order to offer an opportunity to enjoy and participate in interests beyond the normal school day. The programme is an integral part of school life, providing pupils with an opportunity to expand their horizons or harness an existing skill or talent.

Pastoral care and pupil welfare are closely monitored. The Pastoral system is one of the school's greatest strengths, and parents and visitors comment on the excellent knowledge that our staff have of our pupils as individuals. The school is divided into sections, the Pre-Prep, Junior School and Upper School, allowing focus on individual pupils and their needs. The school has an onsite School Counsellor who supports the pupils, parents and staff. The school's Learning Support Centre provides a high level of support both for those children with specific learning needs, as well as running a programme for our more able pupils.

Residential and day trips are seen as an essential part of the school experience and a range are offered on an annual basis. These may include language, ski, choir and drama trips, as well as sports tours. The annual Trips Week is a very special feature of the School Calendar, with the pupils leaving site for various residential destinations in the UK and abroad.

Sport is a major strength and specialist Games staff ensure that all the major sports are expertly coached. A floodlit astroturf pitch allows all-weather training and team spirit is valued alongside ability. There are extensive programmes of inter-school fixtures for all age groups. Every child is encouraged to participate. We also hold annual Games Dinners for the senior teams and their parents to celebrate the end of each season. In-house Christmas, Easter and Summer holiday activity courses are also very popular options with the pupils.

Head Maxine Shaw says: '*Childhood is precious and as adults we have a true responsibility to our children to make it as special as possible. We want our children to have breadth to their lives, to recognise the importance of sport, the arts, philosophical debate, friendships, teamwork ...I could go on. At Danes Hill your child's emotional wellbeing will be strengthened by this breadth and they will become rounded and emotionally intelligent human beings. We want them to have great EQ, to learn to be kind and to understand that a Danes Hill education is a privilege that brings with it the responsibility to give back to others. We want to work with you, as parents, to help your children to become thoroughly decent human beings.*'

Charitable status. Danes Hill School (administered by The Vernon Educational Trust Ltd) is a Registered Charity, number 269433. It exists to provide high-quality education for boys and girls.

Please contact our Admissions Team at registrar@daneshill.surrey.sch.uk to find out more. Book a place on Danes Hill School's Open House here.

Davenies School

Beaconsfield, Buckinghamshire HP9 1AA

Tel: 01494 685400
email: office@davenies.co.uk
website: www.davenies.co.uk
X/Twitter: @DaveniesSchool
Facebook: @DaveniesSchool
Instagram: @daveniesschool
LinkedIn: /company/davenies-school

Chairman: Mr N Edwards

***Headmaster*: Mr C Rycroft**, BEd Hons

Age range. 4–13.

Number of boys. 348 (day boys only).

Fees per term (2023–2024). Pre-prep: £4,485 (Reception), £5,220 (Years 1 and 2); Junior School: £6,440 (Years 3 and 4), £6,520 (Middle School, Years 5 and 6); Senior School: £6,870 (Years 7 and 8).

Davenies is a thriving IAPS day school for boys aged 4–13. Our ethos and philosophy enable the boys to make the most of their preparatory years, supported by high-quality pastoral care, a broad and stimulating curriculum and numerous extracurricular opportunities.

Davenies has its own distinct character and from their earliest years children are encouraged to relish the learning experience.

We are committed to an education both in and out of the classroom, thereby enabling the academic, artistic, musical, creative and physical potential of each child to flourish. The school environment is a warm, caring and happy one, where self-esteem is nurtured and grown; we believe that by fostering a wide range of interests and passions we provide the boys with every opportunity to develop in confidence. Our high-quality teachers have an excellent track record of preparing children for life at the country's leading senior schools and beyond.

Enterprises such as unique Davenies Award Scheme and the permeation of technology in our teaching and learning ensure we offer a truly independent educational experience.

At Davenies, our outstanding facilities support us in providing a positive learning experience with our own language of learning that nurtures each boy's understanding of how he learns. Davenies' boys are polite and friendly with their own individual characters, personalities, passions and interests.

Davenies offers a wide range of scholarships to those boys who display an outstanding talent. Exhibitions are also available for individuals who show tremendous potential in their chosen area. Areas where awards are offered include Academic, Music, Sport, Art, Drama and Design and Technology. As well as the accolade of receiving a scholarship, there is a fee remission of 10% from the published school fees, and an Exhibition receives a remission of £300 per term. Successful candidates are automatically enrolled onto our Gifted and Talented programme, which aims to help boys flourish within their specific talent.

The Governors of Davenies are committed to broadening access to the School in Years 7 and 8 by offering to eligible parents/guardians means-tested financial support with the payment of school fees. Bursaries may be awarded in the form of a discount of up to 85% on tuition fees payable, depending on the financial, compassionate or other pertinent circumstances of applicants. The child's suitability for the school is the first consideration in granting support.

Charitable status. Beaconsfield Educational Trust Ltd is a Registered Charity, number 313120. It exists to provide high standards and the fulfilment of each child's potential.

Dean Close Pre-Preparatory School

Lansdown Road, Cheltenham, Gloucestershire GL51 6QS

Tel: 01242 258079
email: squirrels@deanclose.org.uk
website: www.deanclose.org.uk
X/Twitter: @DeanCloseSchool
Facebook: @DeanCloseSchool

Chairman of Governors: Mrs K Carden, MPhil, BA

***Head*: Mr James Cowling**

Age Range. 2–7 Co-educational.

Number of Pupils. 142.

Fees per term (2023–2024). £3,125–£3,400.

Dean Close Pre-Preparatory School is a co-educational, Christian, family school which occupies the same campus as Dean Close Preparatory and Dean Close School and is, therefore, able to share their outstanding facilities including the swimming pool, sports hall, tennis courts, theatre and art block.

The Pre-Preparatory School is based in a purpose-built school building opened by Lord Robert Winston in June 2004. The School has a large hall surrounded by classrooms on two floors. There are two playgrounds – one for the Nursery and Kindergarten and one for Reception and Years 1 and 2.

The curriculum within the Pre-Preparatory School offers a wide range of learning opportunities aimed at stimulating and nurturing children's development and interests in an intellectual, physical, spiritual, social and emotional sense. Speech and Drama, Dance, Tennis, Music, Orchestra and Choir are some of the extracurricular activities available. All children participate in Forest School, which inspires creativity, thinking skills and cooperation, together with a love of the natural world.

Charitable status. Dean Close School is a Registered Charity, number 1086829.

Dean Close Preparatory School

Lansdown Road, Cheltenham, Gloucestershire GL51 6QS

Tel: 01242 258000
email: dcpsoffice@deanclose.org.uk
website: www.deanclose.org.uk
X/Twitter: @DeanCloseSchool
Facebook: @DeanCloseSchool
Instagram: @deanclose_prepschool

Chairman of Governors: Mrs K Carden, BA, MPhil

***Headmaster*: Mr P Moss**, BA

Age Range. 7–13.

Number of Pupils. 298: Boarding Boys 35, Boarding Girls 40, Day Boys 111, Day Girls 112.

Fees per term (2023–2024). Boarders £7,945–£10,195, Day Boarders £5,240–£8,490, International Boarders £8,945–£11,195; Day Pupils £4,445–£7,695.

Dean Close Preparatory School is a co-educational, Christian, family school which occupies the same campus as Dean Close School and is, therefore, able to share the outstanding facilities. These facilities include: 25m swimming pool, amphitheatre, shooting range, performance hall, 550-seat theatre and chapel. There are also extensive playing fields and sports facilities including hard tennis courts, floodlit astroturf hockey pitches and the new sports hall, which houses indoor tennis and cricket nets, as well as a large gymnasium and dance studio.

The Prep School also has its own teaching blocks and Music School, and a £4.5m building which opened in autumn 2013. This contains an additional 360-seat theatre and 8 teaching areas located over two floors, with a dedicated IT suite and drama rooms.

The new building also contains a music suite, which links to the existing Music School, and comprises 6 music practice rooms including a dedicated guitar room. The building has a formal reception area where parents and visitors are welcomed into the School.

There are two additional classroom blocks. One consists of 10 specialist teaching rooms including 2 laboratories and a computer centre. The other has 7 purpose-built classrooms, together with day house facilities, a staff Common Room, a new Library and an Art and Technology block. There is also a separate dining hall and kitchens.

Although the Preparatory School is administered by the same Board of Governors as the Pre-Prep and the Senior School, it has its own Headmaster and staff. There are 48 teaching staff who either hold degrees or diplomas in education. As well as a dedicated Director of Music, Director of Sport and Director of Drama. The music department is also supported by a team of excellent peripatetic music teachers specialising in a variety of instruments.

Pupils in Years 7 and 8 are taught in ability based form classes. All pupils follow an Independent Curriculum, aligned to the Common Entrance for: English, Mathematics, Biology, Chemistry, Physics, French, History, Geography, Religious Studies and Spanish. Pupils in the top two forms study Latin from Year 7.

The School has three boarding houses one for girls, one for boys and a mixed boarding house for the younger children. Each boarding house has a team of resident Houseparents, 2 House Tutors and a resident matron.

The day pupils are accommodated in three purpose-built houses. Each is run by a Housemaster/ Housemistress, assisted by House Tutors.

The main games for boys are rugby, hockey and cricket, and for girls, hockey, netball, cricket and tennis. Swimming, athletics and cross-country running are also taught and use is made of the School's covered playing area. Golf and horse riding are available nearby.

A wide range of additional activities is also available: camping, canoeing, hillwalking, orienteering, judo, climbing, cooking, watercolour painting and all forms of dance, to name but a few.

With a Prep School population of 298, the sense of family-like community is developed in such a way that it is possible for every child to know each other and to be individually known, valued and cared about. The Prep School offers Foundation, Art, Drama, Music, Academic and Sports scholarships at 11+ and educates the Choristers who sing Evensong at Tewkesbury Abbey.

Charitable status. Dean Close School is a Registered Charity, number 1086829. It exists to provide education for children.

Dolphin School

Waltham Road, Hurst, Berkshire RG10 0FR

Tel: 0118 934 1277
email: enquiries@dolphinschool.com
website: www.dolphinschool.com
X/Twitter: @DolphinSch
Facebook: @dolphinschoolhurst
Instagram: @dolphinschoolberkshire

Founded in 1970.

***Head*: Adam Hurst**

Age Range. 3–13.

Number of Pupils. 223: 132 Day Boys, 91 Day Girls.

Fees per term (2023–2024). Nursery £3,965 (8.45 am to 3.00 pm, 5 days); Reception £4,185; Years 1–2 £4,610; Years 3–4 £5,520; Years 5–6 £5,675; Years 7–8 £5,730.

We believe that all children have their own interests, skills and talents, but all too often these remain hidden. Dolphin School offers an environment which encourages individuality to flourish. Children leave Dolphin with self-belief, a strong sense of identity, intellectual curiosity, and the ability to adjust sensitively to different schools and social situations. Throughout life, in a rapidly changing world, our students will have the adaptability to successfully pursue their goals and interests, in order to lead happy and fulfilled lives.

Dolphin children are encouraged to develop as individuals and are guided to fulfil their potential, in small classes, under the careful guidance of specialist teachers. Abundant academic, artistic, social and sporting stimulation is provided through a varied, broad, well-rounded curriculum. We encourage lateral thinking and the ability to link concepts and ideas across subject and topic areas. Expectations for all children are high and academic rigour is a key component in all lessons.

The average class size in Years 3–8 is 16, although this can vary year-to-year. Children learn to take part in constructive and dynamic dialogue, to consider and respect the opinions of others, to take pride in their own achievements, but also the accomplishments of others. They are encouraged to accept responsibility and to develop leadership skills.

Dolphin School provides the friendly, family atmosphere of a small school. There is no school uniform, and most staff are addressed by their first name; this informality creates a strong bond between all members of our community fostering a culture of warmth and familiarity. All members of staff are actively engaged in the pastoral care of our children, and form teachers assume special responsibility for the daily wellbeing and overall progress of their small group of children.

In a world where children are encouraged to demonstrate independence, resilience, confidence and individuality, Dolphin School strives to realise this aim through its forward-thinking and progressive approach to teaching and learning.

Courses offered. At Dolphin, children are taught by subject specialists from Year 3, and in some cases, from

Nursery! In Early Years we provide a firm grounding in literacy and articulacy. French begins in Nursery, Latin in Year Six, and Spanish in Year Seven. Laboratory based Science is taught from Year 3. English, Mathematics, Geography, History, ICT, Global Citizenship, Classics, Art, Drama, Music and PE are all taught by subject specialists from Year 3 upwards. Teachers seek ways and create opportunities to link their own subject to others, with a strong cross-curricular approach integral to teaching and learning at Dolphin. Throughout the year, children in Years 3–8 now have the opportunity to complete their DPQ (Dolphin Project Qualification), which is tailored to suit lesson content and teaching in school, and to stretch and inspire our students. Our DPQs give students the chance to develop life skills – collaboration, independent research, analysis, IT use and oral presentations – that will serve them well in the years ahead.

Activities. A unique feature of a Dolphin School education is our extensive residential field trip programme. These start from Year 3. Annual field trips include visits to East Sussex, Dorset, Ironbridge, North Wales, Northumbria and Italy, while the French and Drama departments organise residential trips to Boulogne and Stratford respectively. We also offer an extensive mountain-walking programme, with staff and children participating in graded fell-walking from Year 5 onwards. Locations include the Brecon Beacons, the Lake District, Snowdonia and the Alps.

We believe in 'hands-on' learning, whether in or outside the classroom, and all Dolphin students also benefit from an extensive range of inspiring and stimulating day trips throughout the year.

Almost all costs associated with field, walking and day trips are included in the fees, as are lunchtime and after-school clubs which usually include: athletics, tennis, cricket, computer programming, swimming, football, netball, arts and crafts, hockey, chess, cross-country, rugby, art, music, orienteering, gardening, team building, engineering, debating, exam skills and drama.

We field teams from Year 2 in football, hockey, cricket, netball, swimming, cross-country and athletics. We are well represented at county level and a large number of our students play with distinction for local clubs.

Facilities. Our hall offers a splendid venue for assemblies, school concerts and plays. We stage several major productions each year. Grounds include a swimming pool, two tennis courts, netball courts, a brand new AstroTurf, and large playing fields. We also have our very own 'copse', where our highly acclaimed forest school takes place. Cricket matches are hosted at the nearby Hurst Cricket Club, with hockey matches played on our own Astro or the excellent facilities at Cantley Park.

Entry. We welcome new students into any year group and children can join us at any point in the school year. Our staff and pupils are open and friendly, providing a warm welcome. Nursery at age 3+, Reception at age 4+, and at any time throughout Years 1–8.

Examination results. Our examination results are very strong and we frequently win scholarships (academic, drama and sport) to leading senior independent schools, including Abingdon, The Abbey, Queen Anne's and Leighton Park. We have a thriving Old Delphinian organisation. Most past pupils gain good degrees with a disproportionately high number going on to study at Oxbridge.

The Downs Malvern

Brockhill Road, Colwall, Malvern, Worcestershire WR13 6EY

Tel: 01684 544 100

email: registrar@thedownsmalvern.org.uk
website: www.thedownsmalvern.org.uk
Facebook: @TheDownsMalvern
Instagram: @thedownsmalvern
LinkedIn: /company/thedownsmalvern

Chair of Governors: Mr Carey Leonard

***Headmaster*: Mr Andrew Nuttall**, BSc Hons, PGCE, MEd

Age Range. 3–13 years Co-educational.

Number of Pupils. 196 children.

Fees per term (2023–2024). Full Boarding: £5,760–£8,900; Weekly boarding: £5,070–£7,830; Flexi boarding: £42.00 per night; Day: £4,770–£6,720; Pre-Preparatory: £2,795–£3,780; Early Years: £28.35 per am/pm session, £56.70 per day (8.30 am–3.30 pm), £61.20 per day (8.30 am–5.00 pm).

"It is impossible for all but the hard of heart not to get swept along in the magic of The Downs. It has the very best ingredients of a rural prep, somehow keeping children young while also prepping them for next steps." The Good Schools Guide, 2023

The junior arm of the prestigious Malvern College, The Downs Malvern offers a robust and inspiring education for children aged 3–13 years in one of the most beautiful areas in the UK.

Situated on a rural 55-acre campus in the village of Colwall, the school is located 3 miles west of Malvern, just 15 miles from the M5 motorway, and also served on the main line from London Paddington.

We continually strive to exceed the confines of the National Curriculum in academic, as well as cultural, sporting, and environmental accomplishments, and in 2023 were awarded Best Eco Initiative in the Muddy Stilettos Best School Awards, in addition to being shortlisted for Small Independent School of the Year in the Independent Schools of the Year Awards. Further to this, the school was also rated as 'Excellent' in its most recent ISI inspection.

Following a seamless transition from Pre-Prep to Prep School at age 7, pupils progress to a variety of independent senior schools including Malvern College. With this in mind, the emphasis in Years 7 and 8 is not only on specific preparation for 13+ scholarships and Common Entrance exams, but also on our new, bespoke two-year course of study called the TDM Baccalaureate. This is unique to The Downs Malvern and is underpinned by a rigorous and stimulating academic curriculum. It also focuses on the development of a forward-thinking skill set that prepares children for their future studies and lifelong learning.

Sports, especially team games, are a significant part of the curriculum, as are Art and Music; with more than half the number of pupils learning to play a musical instrument. There is also an ever-expanding Saturday Hobbies programme that includes activities as far-reaching as Farming, Horse Riding, Yoga, Sports, Art, and even Engineering on our very own miniature railway. Introduced almost 100 years ago as an educational tool, The Downs Light Railway is believed to be one of the world's oldest miniature railways and features its own station and track that runs around the school.

Boarding. Our refurbished Boarding House provides a home for up to 60 boarders and is offered on a full, weekly, or flexible basis. Bright, comfortable and inviting dorms are offered throughout, in addition to two large common/games rooms and a wide range of activities are available in the evenings and at weekends, including sports, outdoor pursuits, creative activities and trips.

Pastoral care is of the utmost importance and a team of dedicated, resident staff, led by our Houseparents, is always available, spending mealtimes, evenings and weekends with the children and providing a kind, caring and dependable source of support. The team also includes two resident matrons, providing the reassurance of 24-hour medical care should it be needed.

Facilities. The Downs Malvern boasts excellent facilities across all areas of the school including a 300-seat capacity Concert Hall; self-contained Music and Art buildings; well-equipped Science laboratories and a new Design and Technology suite. Additional facilities include a large indoor sports complex, supplemented by an all-weather pitch, 3 Netball/Tennis courts and 55 acres of grounds set aside for games pitches, Forest School lessons and relaxation.

Scholarships and Bursaries. 11+ Scholarships and Exhibitions are awarded annually to pupils who evidence exceptional talent in Academics, Art, Music, Drama, or Sport. Bursaries are also available subject to the completion of a means-tested bursary application, as are discounts for current serving members of the Armed Forces.

Charitable status. The Downs, Malvern College Prep School, trading as The Downs Malvern, is a Registered Charity, number 1120616. It exists to provide education for girls and boys from 3–13 years.

Downsend School

Cognita Schools Group

1 Leatherhead Road, Leatherhead, Surrey KT22 8TJ

Tel: General 01372 372197
Admissions 01372 372311
email: admissions@downsend.co.uk
website: www.downsend.co.uk
X/Twitter: @DownsendSchool
Facebook: @DownsendSchool
Instagram: @downsendschoolsurrey
LinkedIn: /company/downsend-school

***Executive Head*: Ian Thorpe**, BA Ed Hons Exeter, MA Ed Open University

Head of Little Downsend: Lisa Burns, BA Hons Winchester, PGCE

Head of Junior School: Clare Kirkham, BA Hons London, PGCE

Interim Head of Senior School: Marc Broughton, BA Hons, MA Ed Bucks

Age range. 6 months–16 years co-educational.

Fees per term (2023–2024). Little Downsend Nursery (Bright Beginners, Early Learners, First Steps, Rising Reception): £1,324–£4,943. Please note, that we provide monthly payment options for our nursery year groups. Little Downsend School: Reception & Year 1 £4,880, Year 2 £5,156. Downsend School: Years 3–4 £6,570, Years 5–6 £6,591, Years 7–8 £6,725, Years 9–11 £7,445. Sibling discounts apply for more than one child in reception or above.

Downsend is a co-educational day school for children aged between 2 and 16 years.

Downsend (Junior & Senior) is located at the Leatherhead Road site and stands on a pleasant, open site just outside the town, surrounded by its own playing fields, tennis courts, Astro pitch, cricket nets and sports pavilion. The Sports Complex includes a large indoor swimming pool and sports hall. The comfortable and vibrant library, expanded networked ICT provision, bespoke facilities for Design Technology, Textiles and Food Technology, a Music Suite (complete with soundproof practice rooms) and Drama Room extend the curriculum to support pupil's learning and development.

Little Downsend (age 0.6 months to 7). There are three co-educational nursery and pre-preparatory school sites in Ashtead, Epsom and Leatherhead. Pupils work in a welcoming and stimulating environment, in small classes, where a strong focus on education builds solid foundations in Numeracy and Literacy. Dance and Drama, French, Music and Swimming are all taught by specialists and enhance the curriculum across all year groups. An enhanced afternoon programme, further supported by a wide range of after-school clubs including Spanish, is also on offer. An extended day facility is available. At the age of 7, the children move on to Downsend Junior where they are joined by children from other local independent and state schools.

Downsend Junior & Senior (ages 7 to 16). Founded in 1891, Downsend was an established academic prep school which extended its provision to age 16 from September 2020. The school is a thriving community where children are encouraged to develop their talents both in and outside the classroom. A huge variety of extracurricular opportunities are offered to allow children to try new activities during and after school.

The standard of work is high and there is a broad and engaging curriculum. Our approach to learning sees English, Science, Maths, Languages, Humanities, Art and Technology being lifted off the pages of textbooks and worksheets through creativity and enthusiasm. In addition to the usual subjects, children study Art, Drama, Food Technology, ICT, Music, Design Technology, Textiles and PSHE. There is a termly curriculum collapse day for STEAM projects. Parents are kept informed of their children's progress through regular parents' evenings and termly reports, and are welcome at all times to communicate with teaching staff and the management team.

The school has a strong reputation for music, with regular and varied concerts throughout the year, as well as orchestras and choirs for the Junior and Senior Schools. A large number of children learn musical instruments and all pupils in Year 3 enjoy the instrumental scheme where they try different instruments before choosing which one to learn for the rest of the school year. Drama is equally important and there is a production at the end of each term. Pupils can take part in a full range of sports not only in school but also at local, regional and national levels. Regular visits occur outside school and trips abroad are also offered.

The holiday club scheme, Downsend+, gives pupils access to exciting and absorbing workshops, courses, themed days and thrilling days out. Run by qualified Downsend staff, this provision is available to children from age 5 (Reception) from 8.00 am to 5.30 pm, including breakfast, lunch and tea as appropriate. Little Downsend+ is also available as a dedicated facility for our younger children aged 2–5 and is held at Little Downsend Leatherhead. Additionally, we offer holiday provision at Little Downsend Nursery in Ashtead for ages 6 months to 2 years old.

Please contact our Admissions Team at admissions@downsend.co.uk for more details.

Dragon School

Bardwell Road, Oxford OX2 6SS
Tel: 01865 315 405
email: admissions@dragonschool.org
website: www.dragonschool.org
X/Twitter: @thedragonschool
Facebook: @DragonSchoolOxford
Instagram: @dragonschooloxford

Motto: *Arduus ad solem* – 'reach for the sun'

Chair of Governors: Andrew Webb, MA, MBA

***Head*: Emma Goldsmith**, BA

Age Range. 4–8 (Pre-Prep), 8–13 (Prep).
Number of Pupils. 806.

Fees per term (2023–2024). Prep Day: £8,550; Prep Boarding: £12,630; Pre-Prep: £4,850–£6,380.

Since 1877, Dragon School has cultivated kindness, courage, and respect in its young learners. Today, it is an extraordinary co-ed day and boarding school in Oxford for children aged 4–13.

In terms of location, the Dragon enjoys the best of both worlds. The nurturing Pre-Prep is in vibrant Summertown, and the North Oxford Prep boasts expansive playing fields rolling down to the banks of the River Cherwell. In classrooms, you'll feel the energy, excitement and aspiration which define a Dragon education. And elsewhere around school – on the playing fields, in the boathouse, art studio, science labs or the homely boarding houses – you'll get a sense of the strong relationships and the powerful ethos that binds the school community.

The Dragon's progressive outlook is built on a legacy of intellectual curiosity. The school was founded as the Oxford Preparatory School in the 19th century to educate the sons of Oxford University dons. The name was soon changed to Dragon School and it was run for many years by the Lynams, a family with progressive educational views. Today, the Dragon's aims and ethos remains true to its founding tenets: that school should be a place of inspiration, wonder and, above all, fun.

The Curriculum. Dragons are academically rigorous, creative, independent and ambitious free thinkers. The pupils are inspired and encouraged to *reach for the sun* in their learning, and to strive for excellent academic outcomes and experiences through a rich and progressive curriculum.

Co-Curricular. The Dragon has an enviable programme of over 100 co-curricular activities, guaranteeing something for everyone. From animation club to yoga, rock group to roller skating, skiing to surfing and gardening to coding, there are countless opportunities for children to develop their creative talents and build their confidence, physical health, and general wellbeing.

We make the most of our location on the River Cherwell with our extensive sports and leisure facilities, meaning that activities such as paddle-boarding, sculling and lifeguarding are always on offer.

Pastoral. At the Dragon, pupils live by their values: they are kind, courageous and respectful. The Dragon spirit is like no other – ambitious, caring, spirited, curious and always reaching for the sun.

This spirit is instilled through the unique pastoral approach. Dragons love the family feel of the school, and the focus on fun and playful exploration balanced with intellectual ambition. The pastoral mission is for pupils to end their time there with an understanding of what it means to be a human, to know their place in the world, and to have a grasp of their potential.

Dragons' differences are celebrated, whether they're playful or thoughtful, sensitive or loud, expressive or analytical. That's why the three key values are instilled – kindness, courage and respect – from Day 1, so that every member of the Dragon community feels valued and nurtured.

Boarding. Boarding is the beating heart of the Dragon. In the nine vibrant boarding homes, the focus is very simple: family, friends and having fun. If you arrange to visit the Dragon, make sure you speak to a young boarder for their view – we're sure you'll hear about all of the above – and more!

Boarding is an experience that endures in the most positive of ways. Former boarders regularly talk about the long-lasting friendships, strong relationships with staff and the powerful sense of independence they developed at the Dragon.

Head's Philosophy. It is important to harness the vitality, imagination and natural curiosity of young people to develop the mindset of 'why not?'. If this culture of questioning is embedded at an early age, it will encourage an enthusiasm to lead a lifetime of learning. *Arduus ad solem* – 'reach for the sun' – is the School's motto and is as relevant today as it was when the school was founded. We want all of our children to become resilient and ambitious, ready to take on the challenges of being a global citizen of the 21st century. The Dragon has a well-earned reputation of providing a community which will nurture these characteristics with the values of kindness, courage and respect underpinning all that we do.

Outstanding Characteristics. The 2022 ISI inspection rated Dragon School as 'outstanding', and teaching and learning as 'exceptional'. The School ethos promotes a warmly enthusiastic, genuinely respectful and a naturally unpretentious approach to learning. It manages to be nurturing yet ambitious while fostering an intellectual curiosity, a strong sense of community and a keen pursuit of excellence in all its forms.

For further information or to arrange a visit please contact Dr Kate Heath, Registrar, on 01865 315 405 or admissions@dragonschool.org. Please visit www.dragonschool.org for more information. Personal tours available by appointment.

Charitable status. The Dragon School Trust Ltd is a Registered Charity, number 309676. Aim: to provide education for boys and girls between the ages of 4 and 13.

Duke of Kent School

Peaslake Road, Ewhurst, Surrey GU6 7NS

Tel: 01483 277313
email: office@dokschool.org
website: www.dukeofkentschool.org.uk
X/Twitter: @DoKSchool
Facebook: @Duke-of-Kent-School/100063860978283
Instagram: @dukeofkentschool

See full entry in the **ISA** section, on **p. 875**.

Dulwich College

Dulwich Common, London SE21 7LD

Tel: 020 8693 3601
email: info@dulwich.org.uk
website: www.dulwich.org.uk
X/Twitter: @DulwichCollege
Facebook: @DulwichCollege
Instagram: @dulwichcollege
LinkedIn: /school/dulwich-college

See full entry in the **HMC** section, on **p. 88**.

Dulwich Cranbrook

Coursehorn, Cranbrook, Kent TN17 3NP

Tel: 01580 712179
email: admissions@dulwichcranbrook.org
website: www.dulwichcranbrook.org
X/Twitter: @DPCranbrook
Facebook: @dulwichcranbrook
Instagram: @dulwichcranbrook
LinkedIn: /dulwichcranbrook

Chair of Governors: Mrs Susanna Rynehart
***Head*: Mrs Sophie Bradshaw**

Age range. 2–16.

Number of boys and girls. Day and Flexi Boarding: 105 (Senior), 227 (Prep), 60 (Nash House).

Fees per term (2023–2024). Day: £7,410 (Years 7–11), £6,995 (Years 5–6), £6,240 (Years 3–4), £5,840 (Year 2), £4,710 (Year 1), £4,350 (Reception). Nursery: £3,815 (full day), £2,400 (mornings). Pre-Nursery (Fledglings): £3,350 (full day), £2,060 (mornings). Boarders: from £45 per night.

The School, which is one mile from the country town of Cranbrook, has extensive grounds (50 acres) and offers a broad and varied education to boys and girls from 2 to 16 years. To ensure that children receive the personal attention that is vital for this age rang, the School is divided up into three separate, self-contained, departments. These are Nash House (2–5 year olds), Prep (5–11 year olds) and Senior (11–16 year olds). Each department has its own staff, teaching equipment, sports facilities, playgrounds, swimming pools, etc. With Dulwich Cranbrook's recent expansion to Year 11, pupils are offered a rich GCSE curriculum. While the majority of pupils choose to progress from the Prep School to the Senior School, some pupils are prepared for Common Entrance and Scholarship examinations for Year 9 entry to other senior schools of their parents' choosing. The wide scope for sporting activities – Football, Rugby, Cricket, Hockey, Netball, Athletics, Cross Country, Swimming, Tennis – is balanced by the importance attached to Art, DT, Drama, Computer Science and Music. Over 165 pupils have weekly individual music lessons. There are multiple choirs, an orchestra, a jazz band, flute ensemble, rock school, guitar ensemble, brass band, ukulele ensembles, and recorder ensembles. The flexi-boarders are housed in the Manor House, boys and girls each under the care of House staff. The happiness of the boarders is a particular concern and every effort is made to establish close and friendly contact between the School and the parents. There is a flourishing Parents Association, and the school prides itself on its open door policy and friendly atmosphere.

The School is a Charitable Trust, under the same Governing Body as Dulwich Prep London, although in other respects the two schools are quite separate. The link with Dulwich College is historical only.

Charitable status. Dulwich Cranbrook is a Registered Charity, number 1174358.

Dulwich Prep London

38–42 Alleyn Park, London SE21 7AA
Tel: 020 8766 5500
email: admissions@dulwichpreplondon.org
website: www.dulwichpreplondon.org
X/Twitter: @dulwichprep
Facebook: @DulwichPrepLondon
Instagram: @dulwichpreplondon
LinkedIn: /dulwich-prep-london

Since 1885 Dulwich Prep London has been at the forefront of preparatory schooling in England.

Chair of Governors: Mrs Kate Kelleher

***Head Master*: Miss Louise Davidson**

Bursar and Clerk to the Governors: Mrs Caroline Skillings
Director of HR: Mr Paul James
Deputy Head Academic: Mr Ed Matten
Assistant Head: Mr Piers Young
Head of Early Years: Dr Christopher Halls
Head of Pre-Prep: Mrs Shelley Whitehead
Head of Lower & Middle School & Designated Safeguarding Lead: Mrs Karen McDonald-Tuckwell
Head of Upper School: Mr Sasanka Velagapudi
Professional Tutor: Miss Jeannie McElroy

Age Range. Boys 3–13, Girls 3–4.

Number of Children. 794 boys, 15 girls.

Fees per term (2023–2024). Tuition: Day fees £5,375–£7,795, inclusive of lunch (there are no compulsory extras).

Dulwich Prep London is an independent preparatory school with a national reputation for excellence, the 'Launchpad for life'. Our eight School Values of Love, Courage, Gratitude, Humility, Justice, Self-Discipline, Service and Honesty are at the forefront of everything we do.

While we are a boys' school, with around 800 pupils aged between 3 and 13, we start with Early Years, which also caters for nursery-aged girls. There are four other sections to the school: the Pre-Prep (Years 1 & 2), the Lower School (Years 3 & 4), and the Middle & Upper Schools (Years 5 & 6 and 7 & 8).

At 13+, our boys go on to more than fifty excellent day and boarding schools throughout the country. Alleyn's, Harrow, Dulwich College, Eton College, Marlborough College, Tonbridge, St Paul's, Wellington College, Westminster, and Winchester College are just a selection of our leavers' destination schools. For the academic year, 2022–2023, 95% of our Year 8 pupils achieved their first-choice senior school. A total of 41 scholarships (20 Academic, 2 Art, 4 Music and 15 Sport) were won by Year 8 pupils.

Situated in SE21, we have incredible facilities akin to a senior school. These include very spacious classrooms, a science block containing three labs, a design technology suite, a cookery suite, an observatory, a dedicated music school, a large sports hall, a studio theatre, an ICT suite, a superb art studio, a six-lane 25 m swimming pool, woodland and more than 25 acres of playing fields – unique given our privileged location.

Some of the opportunities available to our pupils are:

- We promote an inclusive approach to sport, enabling every pupil to be involved. We run more than ten sports teams each term, with the top teams regularly doing well in national competitions. Competitive fixtures happen in Football, Rugby, Athletics, Swimming, Water Polo, Cross Country and Biathlon.
- More than 700 individual music lessons take place every week, and boys have the opportunity to perform regularly in a range of groups and ensembles. 90% of pupils play one instrument, with many playing two.
- Over 30 groups regularly perform in our 300-seat concert hall. Many also appear on the programme for our gala concerts at prestigious venues such as Southwark Cathedral.
- We provide more than 150 clubs and extracurricular activities, stimulating boys' intellectual and sporting interests. From Lego club to Table Tennis club, we like to think that there is something that interests everyone.
- We run residential trips for pupils in Years 3 to 8 within the curriculum built into the fee structure; these include outdoor pursuits trips to Wales and cultural visits to York. We also offer a range of trips during the holidays ranging from skiing or sailing trips, to sports tours to South Africa, to Geography trips to Iceland.
- Forms and year groups stage drama productions from Reception to Year 8. Pupils start with the foundational skills of Drama through structured play. Exploring spatial awareness, role play and creating character through story-telling, language and listening skills forms the basis for students to flourish in various performance opportunities. In Year 8, every class has a two-week-long intensive drama workshop in which pupils create a live performance with a theatre professional.
- As the school approaches its 140th Anniversary in 2025, its commitment to boys' education will deepen by opening a senior section to welcome their first Year 9 cohort. The school wants to offer something different; therefore, we will not become 'just' an all-through school but strongly continue to be a school that supports families in finding the right school at the right time for their son, supporting the transition to senior school or sixth form in Year 7, Year 9, and Year 12.

The senior section will be deliberately smaller in comparison to most senior schools (a maximum of 60 in each year group), enabling the offer to be more personalised with a familiar education environment where the boys are well-known by staff.

Finally, in September 2024, the school will change its name to better represent its future offering and become Dulwich Prep & Senior.

Dumpton School

Deans Grove House, Deans Grove, Wimborne, Dorset BH21 7AF

Tel: 01202 883818
email: secretary@dumpton.com
website: www.dumpton.com
X/Twitter: @dumpton
Facebook: @dumpton
Instagram: @dumpton_school

Chairman of Governors: Mr H Cocke

***Headmaster*: Mr C Saenger**, BA Hons, QTS

Age Range. 2–13.

Number of Pupils. Girls and Boys: 218 aged 7–13 and 92 aged 2–7.

Fees per term (2023–2024). Prep School (Years 3–8) £6,354; Pre-Prep (Reception, Years 1 & 2) £3,554; Nursery charged at £8.95 per hour. The school week is from Monday to Friday. All fees include meals and there are no compulsory extras.

Dumpton School is a co-educational day school for pupils aged 2 to 13 years. The school is set in a beautiful rural setting with 26 acres of grounds but is nevertheless only one mile from Wimborne and school buses run daily to and from the nearby towns of Blandford, Bournemouth, Dorchester, Ferndown, Poole, Ringwood, Verwood and Wareham.

Despite record numbers in the school, class sizes are small. Children enjoy excellent teaching as well as incomparable opportunities for Music, Art, Drama and Sport in which the school excels. Dumpton is renowned for its caring approach in which every child is encouraged to identify and develop his or her abilities and personal qualities as fully as possible. This safe and supportive environment sees the children thrive and reach their full potential. The framework of family and Christian values emphasises the importance of teamwork and mutual respect that pervades the school. It is a very happy and successful school and children regularly win scholarships to their Senior Schools or places at the local Grammar Schools. Over the past twelve years, Dumpton pupils have been awarded over 278 scholarships to schools such as Bryanston, Canford, Clayesmore, Millfield, Milton Abbey, Talbot Heath and Sherborne.

Recent developments have included a new multi-purpose Performing Arts venue complete with music recital room, a new outdoor adventure playground for the Prep School, a new Science and Maths Block, a full-size floodlit Astroturf, a covered swimming pool, a new Art, Design and Food Technology Centre, an outdoor classroom, climbing wall and environmental area, complete with ponds, pontoons, beehives and pupil allotments. In addition, the school has been awarded Green Flag status by Eco-Schools for 4 years running as well as the South West Environmental Award for 2018. The building of a new state-of-the-art sports hall was completed in the summer of 2019.

The school motto 'You can because you think you can', lies at the cornerstone of teaching at Dumpton and our aim is for pupils to leave us having reached their full potential, as confident communicators and appreciating good manners and tolerance.

For a copy of the prospectus, please apply to the Headmaster's Secretary.

Charitable status. Dumpton School is a Registered Charity, number 306222. It exists to provide education for boys and girls.

Durlston Prep and Senior School

Becton Lane, Barton-on-Sea, New Milton, Hampshire BH25 7AQ

Tel: 01425 610010
email: admissions@durlstonschool.co.uk
website: www.durlstonschool.co.uk
X/Twitter: @DurlstonSchool
Facebook: @DurlstonSchool
Instagram: @durlstonschool

Chairman of Governors: Mr Chandra Ashfield

***Headmaster*: Mr Richard May**, BA, PGCE

Age Range. 2–16 Co-educational.

Number of Pupils. 250 Day Pupils.

Fees per term (2023–2024). Reception: £3,250, Years 1–2: £3,595, Year 3: £5,350, Years 4–11: £6,695.

Our purpose is to provide an exceptional education in an environment where each child is properly known by all members of staff. It is the quality of the relationship between our staff and children that makes Durlston such a very special place to learn and grow. Our small class sizes and 'family feel' ensure that we truly know your children.

Durlston has a long-standing reputation for all-round educational excellence – combining academic, creative and sporting opportunities with the pastoral support to help our children grow in ability and confidence and, ultimately, to achieve their very best. We focus on good manners and behaviour while promoting ever-evolving, tailor-made challenges for each child. Our highly committed staff genuinely enjoy encouraging the mindset and skills that will enable all to flourish now and post-Durlston.

We welcome children at any point. Our Pre-Prep children enjoy a vibrant and nurturing environment where they can experience their journey of discovery at their own pace. Children in Middle Prep explore new and exciting opportunities as they grow in independence and are encouraged to find what they love. Children in Upper Prep continue to grow with Durlston confidence as they are supported and challenged by our highly dedicated, specialist staff team.

We are thrilled that we can now offer children the opportunity to continue their education at Durlston through to Year 11 and to GCSE examinations. Our senior pupils are well supported both academically and socially as they develop into determined young adults.

Charitable status. Durlston Prep and Senior School is a Registered Charity, number 307325, which exists to provide quality education for children from 2–16 years.

Durston House

12–14 Castlebar Road, Ealing, London W5 2DR

Tel: 020 8991 6530
email: info@durstonhouse.org
website: www.durstonhouse.org
X/Twitter: @DurstonHouse
Facebook: @DurstonHouse
Instagram: @durstonhouse
LinkedIn: /durston-house-school

Chairmen of Governors: Mr K Mahoney, BSc, MRICS & Mr D G Henshall

***Headmaster*: Mr G Entwisle**, BA Hons

Deputy Head: Miss L Vallely, BEd Hons, QTS
Head of Pre-Prep: Ms D Finlayson, BSc Hons, PGCE
Assistant Head, Pastoral: Miss P Orr, BEd
Assistant Head, Academic: Mrs C Saigau, BA, PGDip, MTeach, QTS
Assistant Head, Co-Curricular: Mr D Stock, BSc Hons, PGCE
Assistant Head, Studies Administration: Miss J Chisholm, BEd, QTS
Head of Early Years (*Reception*): Mrs A Stiglingh, MA, QTS
Head of Early Years (*Pre-School*): Mrs A Cannon, BA Hons, PGCE
Bursar: Mrs J Twyford

Age Range. 3–13.

Number of Pupils. 389 day (55 Girls, 334 Boys).

Fees per term (2023–2024). £4,750–£6,180.

Durston House is a leading prep school located in Ealing, West London, providing an outstanding education in an inclusive, warm and dynamic environment for girls and boys aged 3–13.

In September 2023, Durston House became co-educational, welcoming boys and girls from Nursery through to Year 8. An education at Durston House is based upon academic rigour through excellent teaching, encouraging our pupils to explore, question, take risks, and develop their creativity, communication and teamwork – all central to successful life-long learning.

Pupils are recognised and appreciated for who they are as individuals. There is a whole-hearted commitment to a holistic education, in which each individual and their talents come first. Our pupils shape the community and are supported and nurtured by teachers who really care. The excellent pastoral care at Durston allows for the school to flourish as the happy and relaxed place that it is.

Durston House has a long, proud and impressive history of preparing pupils for the most prestigious senior schools in London and beyond. Our pupils leave heading to top Independent Schools, such as Hampton School, John Lyon School, Merchant Taylors' School and St Paul's School.

We are non-selective at Pre School and Reception, which is our main point of entry. Durston believes that academic success is achieved through excellent teaching and creating an environment where respect and values matter. In 2023, Durston House was awarded 17th on the '*Top 20 Schools for Academic Results*' according to The Sunday Times Parent Power List, and while this is a superb accolade to have, we know the key to success is through hard work and a desire to improve continually. We place our pupils at the centre of everything we do and make sure every opportunity is taken so that each pupil is able to flourish.

Charitable status. Registered Charity, number 294670.

Eagle House

Crowthorne Road, Sandhurst, Berkshire GU47 8PH

Tel: 01344 772134
email: info@eaglehouseschool.com
website: www.eaglehouseschool.com
X/Twitter: @EagleHouseSch
Facebook: @EagleHouseSch
Instagram: @eaglehousesch

Chairman of Governors: William Jackson, MA Oxon

***Head*: Mr Edward Venables**

Age Range. 3–13.

Number of Children. 386: 50 Boarders, 336 Day Children.

Fees per term (2023–2024). Prep School: £9,910 (boarders), £7,120–£7,375 (day pupils). Pre-Prep: £4,715. Nursery: £2,585 (5 mornings including lunch).

Eagle House is a co-educational, boarding and day Prep, Pre-Prep and Nursery located in Berkshire. The school's superb grounds and excellent facilities are the background to an experience where success, confidence and happiness are paramount. The school is proud of its academic record, preparing children for a host of top independent schools and boasting a diverse and robust curriculum. A new Pre-Prep and Music School opened in 2021.

Younger pupils follow the International Primary Curriculum and our older children embark on Curriculum 200, that links subjects through topics and themes. Great teaching, new technology and a focus on the basics mean that children make good progress and love to be in the classroom. Independent learning is a focus for all children and our Extended Project programme helps drive inquisitive minds.

Eagle House offers a diverse and varied extra-curricular programme and we unashamedly offer lots as part of our Golden Eagle activities experience. Children benefit from a huge range of opportunities in sport, music, drama, art, outward bound and community programmes. Busy children are happy and fulfilled children and we like to think that all pupils are Learning for Life.

Learning for Life means that children benefit from the best all-round education. They can feel confident in the classroom, on the games field, on stage, in the concert hall and in the community. Everyone is given the chance to stretch themselves in every area. Challenge is an important part of growing up and at Eagle House we learn that success and failure are both positive experiences.

Bright learning environments, outdoor learning areas and wonderful sporting facilities are important, but it is the community that shapes a young person. Through the excellent pastoral care and tutor system, coupled with a buddy structure, ensuring children have an older pupil to support them, Eagle House seeks to develop wellbeing from the youngest to the oldest.

Recognising how to be a positive influence within a community is also part of the Eagle House journey. Through our wonderful Learning for Life programme that teaches children about themselves and the wider community, we aim to make all our pupils responsible and independent as well as able to show empathy and understanding towards others. Time for reflection in chapel and assemblies also improves the way we look at the world and mindfulness sessions help us all take stock.

Boarding is a popular option and allows children to experience a varied evening programme of activities as well as being part of a vibrant and caring community. Boarding encourages independence, but it is also great fun and whether full, weekly or flexi, boarders have the most wonderful time.

We often say that Eagle House children have the time of their lives and we firmly believe this. Learning for Life at Eagle House opens the doors to all sorts of opportunities and this results in children who are highly motivated and enthusiastic in all they do. Eagle House buzzes with achievement and laughter – not a bad way to grow up!

Charitable status. Wellington College is a Registered Charity, number 309093. Eagle House School is owned by Wellington College and is part of the same charity registration.

Eaton House Belgravia Pre-Prep, Prep and Nursery

3–5 Eaton Gate, Belgravia, London SW1W 9BA

Tel: 020 7730 9343
email: sfeilding@eatonhouseschools.com
website: www.eatonhouseschools.com
X/Twitter: @eatonhousesch
Facebook: @eatonhouseschools
Instagram: @eatonhouseschools.belgravia

***Head*: Mr Ross Montague**

Age Range. Co-educational Nursery: 2–4, Boys' School: 4–11.

Number of Pupils. 180.

Fees per term (2023–2024). £7,740–£8,575. Nursery prices according to sessions attended.

Eaton House Belgravia is an outstanding independent boys' school and co-educational nursery, educating children between the ages of 2 and 11. Founded in 1897, the school has become part of the very fabric of Chelsea and Belgravia, offering a diverse and intellectually stimulating education in the heart of London.

Boys are thoroughly prepared for 7+, 8+ and 11+ examinations, according to choice. The school is ambitious for its pupils, committed to igniting each boy's potential beyond academic excellence, into the realms of first-rate music, drama, creative arts and sport. As a result, boys achieve extraordinary results each year. In 2023, among a cohort of 33 boys sitting 7+ and 8+ exams, we received an outstanding 18 offers for Westminster Under, King's College Wimbledon and St Paul's Juniors.

Mr Ross Montague joined Eaton House Belgravia from Hampstead Hill School as Head Teacher in January 2024. He aims to maintain the traditional academic values of Eaton House Belgravia, while bringing a fresh eye to the school, building on the school's philosophy of 'stretch and support'.

Boys will experience a happy, confident and ambitious start to their education, in a traditional, yet modern and welcoming academic environment. Wellbeing is central to the school's philosophy and the 'teachers have a lovely supportive dynamic' – The Good Schools Guide (2023). Staff prioritise the mental health of their pupils and, in turn, happy children achieve great results. The Good Schools Guide (2023) says, 'Pastoral care is excellent, accommodating and proactive, picking up on any potential anxieties very quickly.' Therefore, each pupil is well supported to start their academic career and journey into adulthood.

Entrance Procedure. Entrance to the nursery and reception is non-selective. Registration is accepted from birth and early application is advised. Boys and girls are welcomed to the nursery in the September following their second birthday. The majority of the nursery pupils go on to attend reception, where they are joined by those who register for 4+ entry.

For Years 1 to 6, children registered to join Eaton House Belgravia after the initial reception entry point will be invited to visit the school for an admissions assessment before a place can be offered (subject to availability). Prospective pupils are asked to complete a formal 8+ assessment for external entry into Year 4.

Eaton House The Manor Boys' School

58 Clapham Common Northside, London SW4 9RU

Tel: 020 3917 5050
email: sfeilding@eatonhouseschools.com
website: www.eatonhouseschools.com
X/Twitter: @eatonhousesch
Facebook: @eatonhouseschools
Instagram: @eatonhouseschools.themanor

***Principal of EHS and Headmistress of Prep*: Mrs Sarah Segrave**

***Headmaster of Pre-Prep*: Mr David Wingfield**

Age Range. Co-educational Nursery: 2–4, Boys' School: 4–13.

Number of Pupils. 430.

Fees per term (2023–2024). £6,740–£8,090. Nursery prices according to sessions attended.

Eaton House The Manor Boys' School, rated excellent' by ISI, is an academically outstanding independent school and co-educational nursery, set opposite the leafy green stretches of Clapham Common.

Eaton House The Manor has sent many generations of boys to Eton, Westminster, St. Paul's and other top secondary schools. Pupils achieve scholarships every year, including, in 2023, two to St Paul's, four to Alleyn's School, two to Dulwich College, one to Lancing College, and one to Royal Russell.

The school offers an inspiring and dynamic education to boys between the ages of 2 and 13 and is non-selective at its reception entry point. Mrs Segrave, Principal of Eaton House Schools and Headmistress of Eaton House The Manor Prep School says, 'We aim to identify and nurture each boy's budding strengths and interests, encouraging his curiosity so that he will have the confidence to pursue them.'

A wide range of extra-curricular opportunities are available to the boys, with up to 50 clubs each term from School of Rock to Rugby and Gardening. The school is committed to the individual learning and pastoral care of their boys, instilling in them an academic and social confidence that they carry through life. Staff prioritise the mental health of their pupils and, in turn, happy children achieve great results. The House system, dedicated form tutors, and an extensive wellbeing hub, contribute to a strong framework of pastoral care, ensuring that every child is championed and supported throughout their education at the school.

Eaton House The Manor Boys' School is located on the same extensive premises as Eaton House The Manor Girls' School, making it the ideal place for siblings to enjoy the benefits of a single-sex education on one site. In 2022, the ISI reported at both Eaton House the Manor schools, 'respecting others is an innate quality exhibited by all pupils, with diversity and inclusion being openly celebrated'.

Entrance procedure. Entrance to the nursery and reception is non-selective. Registration is accepted from birth and early application is advised. Boys and girls are welcomed to the nursery in the September following their second birthday. The majority of the nursery pupils go on to attend reception, where they are joined by those who register for 4+ entry.

From Years 1 to 8, children registered to join Eaton House The Manor Boys' School after the initial reception entry point will be invited to visit the school for an admissions assessment before a place can be offered (subject to availability). Prospective pupils are asked to complete a formal 8+ assessment for external entry into Year 4

Eaton House The Manor Girls' School

58 Clapham Common North Side, London SW4 9RU
Tel: 020 3917 5050
email: sfeilding@eatonhouseschools.com
website: www.eatonhouseschools.com
X/Twitter: @eatonhousesch
Facebook: @eatonhouseschools
Instagram: @eatonhouseschools.themanor

***Headmistress*: Mrs Claire Fildes**

Age Range. Co-educational Nursery: 2–4, Girls' School: 4–11.

Number of Pupils. 220 Girls.

Fees per term (2023–2024). £6,740–£7,875. Nursery prices according to sessions attended.

Eaton House The Manor Girls' School is an outstanding independent school and nursery, set opposite the leafy green stretches of Clapham Common. The school offers a balanced, highly academic education to girls between the ages of 2 and 11, and is non-selective at its reception entry point. A philosophy of 'the sky-is-the-limit learning' allows each girl to reach her fullest potential, supported by specialist subject teaching and an exceptional pastoral network. A stimulating classroom environment promotes intellectual curiosity and the girls prize both academic exploration and risk-taking highly. Consequently, pupils leave for a range of top secondary schools, including St Paul's Girls' School, JAGS, Alleyn's and Wycombe Abbey. In 2022 and 2023, the girls received an outstanding 41 Scholarships and Awards across Academics, Sport, Drama, Music and Art. This year, these included Woldingham, Brighton College, Streatham & Clapham High School, Emanuel and Royal Russell.

Beyond an excellent core curriculum of literacy and numeracy, an equal emphasis is given to the arts and STEM subjects. Each girl is encouraged to pursue her interests through an increasingly co-curricular attitude to learning and a sophisticated range of extracurricular activities. The wellbeing of the girls is of paramount importance to all staff. The House system, 'Big Sister' scheme, excellent form teachers and visible senior management team combine to ensure that each girl feels supported in her learning. A Head of Wellbeing and school nurse are on hand to support all parents and pupils whenever a concern is raised. Mrs Claire Fildes, the Head Teacher says, 'When the girls really feel that they're cared for and happy in their learning environment, I really believe that the learning falls into place.' (*The Good Schools Guide*, 2023).

Eaton House The Manor Girls' School is located on the same extensive premises as Eaton House The Manor Boys' School, making it the ideal place for siblings to enjoy the benefits of a single-sex education on one site. In 2022, the ISI reported both Eaton House the Manor schools as 'Excellent', with 'diversity and inclusion being openly celebrated'.

Entrance Procedure. Entrance to our nursery and reception is non-selective. Registration is accepted from birth and early application is advised. We welcome girls to our nursery in the September following their second birthday. The majority of our nursery pupils go on to attend reception, where they are joined by those who register for 4+ entry.

From Years 1 to 6, children registered to join Eaton House The Manor Girls' School after the initial reception entry point will be invited to visit the school for an admissions assessment before a place can be offered (subject to availability). Prospective pupils are asked to complete a formal 8+ assessment for external entry into Year 4.

Eaton Square Prep School

55–57 Eccleston Square, Pimlico, London SW1V 1PH

Tel: 0207 225 3131
email: registrar@eatonsquareschools.com
website: www.eatonsquareschools.com
X/Twitter: @EatonSquareSch
Instagram: @eatonsquareprepschool
LinkedIn: /company/eaton-square-school

Principal: Mrs Suzie Longstaff

***Headmistress*: Mrs Trish Watt**

Age Range. 2–11 Co-educational Nursery and Prep School.

Number of Pupils. 316.

Fees per term (2023–2024). Reception & Year 1: £8,200, Years 2–4: £8,745, Years 5 & 6: £8,825.

Ethos. The School ignites a passion for learning in all pupils, exposing them to a broad curriculum, dynamic classrooms and opportunities to discover who they are and what place they wish to take in the world. A nurturing 'home from home' environment is underpinned by the School's 'POISE' values: perseverance, ownership, integrity, service and empathy.

Pupil wellbeing at Eaton Square is truly outstanding. Pastoral support rated 'Excellent' by all recent ISI inspections. The school offers the unique 'Listening Space' programme for all pupils, plus 'worry post boxes' for children to post any concerns in confidence. In 2021 the School was one of the Top three ISA Schools for its commitment to Equality, Diversity and Inclusion.

Academic Life. Eaton Square is renowned for its stimulating, rigorous and tailored academic programme, enabling pupils to fulfil their potential in all areas of the curriculum. Based on the National Curriculum, consistently exceptional 11+ and 13+ Common Entrance results are achieved.

A wide range of subjects are encompassed in the curriculum, including Latin, French and Spanish. Digital skills are an integral part of the syllabus: the School has a device-per-child programme and interactive whiteboards.

Pupils are prepared for entry into both selective London Day schools and leading Boarding schools through London Day School examinations and Common Entrance examinations at 11+.

Sport & the Arts. Sport and Physical Education include Swimming, Rugby, Cricket, Hockey, Fencing, Gymnastics, Football, Sailing, Skiing, Karate, Ballet and Tennis. National success is a routine part of school life: recent accolades included IAPS Football winners, ISA Nationals Swim champions and RYA Sailing Gold Medallist.

Creative self-expression is a valued, integral part of the curriculum, be it through Art, Music, Drama, Debating or Public Speaking. Appreciation of music, singing, composition and theory are taught by specialists at all ages. There are active School Choirs, an orchestra and a variety of ensembles that rehearse throughout the week. The Debating team is renowned; the School is even an accredited Tedx Talks centre. Drama is integrated within the curriculum and each child takes part in at least two performances every year.

Eaton Square Schools are part of the Dukes Education Group.

Edge Grove

Aldenham Village, Watford, Herts WD25 8NL

Tel: 01923 855724
email: admissions@edgegrove.com
website: www.edgegrove.com
X/Twitter: @EdgeGrove
Facebook: @Edge-Grove
Instagram: @edgegrove

Chair of Governors: Howard Clayden

***Head*: Edward Balfour**, BA Hons, PGCE

Age Range. 3–13.

Number of Pupils. 450.

Fees per term (2023–2024). Day: Nursery (5 mornings only; optional afternoons are available every day) £2,820; Junior Department: Reception £5,150, Year 1/2 £5,170; Middle Department: Year 3 £5,830, Year 4 £5,940, Year 5 £6,850; Senior Department Years 6–8: £6,890.

Edge Grove is a vibrant and successful independent school for boys and girls aged 3–13 years. It is set in 48 acres of parkland, only 15 miles from central London and conveniently located close to the M1 and M25 motorways. Our wonderful setting and facilities ensure our children enjoy a wide range of experiences and develop confidence in a challenging, fun and inspirational environment.

The School was inspected by the Independent Schools Inspectorate (ISI) in February 2023, and was rated as 'EXCELLENT' in ALL areas. The ISI stated that at all stages of the school "the quality of pupils' academic and other achievements is excellent. The report noted that "Pupils enjoy excellent levels of achievement, particularly in entrance examinations and scholarships to selective senior schools." They also observed that pupils "Pupils show excellent levels of initiative and independence as well as a self-evident willingness to work collaboratively.". Pupils' personal development was also commented on, with inspectors praising how "Pupils show a very high level of self-understanding. They gain high levels of self-confidence and self-esteem through the support and nurturing of staff who know them well.". The importance the School places on belonging and inclusivity was also commented upon: "The school successfully fulfils its aim of providing a warm, welcoming educational community in which pupils with a broad diversity of backgrounds develop a genuine sense of belonging and pride."

The Junior Department at Edge Grove (previously called the Pre Prep) caters for children between the ages of 3 and 7. The Edge Grove Nursery is located in a purpose-built building close to the main school site and can accommodate up to 40 children aged 3–4 years. The Junior Department (Reception to Year 2) is situated within the main school grounds, close to the main school. There are around 20 pupils in each class size, and each is supervised by a teacher and teaching assistant. A broad curriculum is offered with French, Music, Sport and Forest School taught by specialist teachers.

Pupils move on to a wide variety of senior independent schools across the country and the school has an excellent record of Scholarship and Common Entrance success. Music and Art are also particularly strong and Edge Grove is a leading player in the world of prep school sport. There is a great range of after-school activities on offer every day until 6.00pm.

Facilities include an outdoor covered learning hub; two Forest School sites; an adventure playground; a language classroom with a dedicated 'virtual language lab'; Chromebooks throughout the school and 1:1 from Year 5; a fully-equipped textiles room and two science laboratories; and purpose-built and state of the art facilities for home economics. Sports facilities include a 20-metre heated swimming pool; vast playing fields with ten junior football fields; a 3-court badminton Sports Hall; an AstroTurf hockey pitch; two tennis/netball courts and six outdoor/four indoor cricket nets.

Charitable status. Edge Grove School Trust Ltd is a Registered Charity, number 311054.

Edgeborough

84 Frensham Road, Frensham, Farnham, Surrey GU10 3AH

Tel: 01252 792495
email: office@edgeborough.co.uk
website: www.edgeborough.co.uk
X/Twitter: @edgeborough
Facebook: @edgeborough
Instagram: @edgeboroughschool
LinkedIn: /company/edgeborough-educational-trust-limited

Chair of Governors: Mr John Olsen, BA (Interim)

***Head*: Mr Daniel Cox**

Age Range. 2–13.

Number of Children. Total: 379 Flexi-boarders 60, Day 273, Pre-Prep 67, Nursery 39.

Fees per term (2023–2024). Years 5–8 £7,130, Years 3–4 £6,430, Pre-Prep Years R–2 £4,390. Weekly Boarding (4 nights): £45 per night.

Edgeborough is a co-educational Independent School for children aged 2–13, with day and flexi boarding. The school is situated within 50 acres of rolling countryside in Frensham, Surrey.

Edgeborough offers a carefully balanced, all-round education with a focus on outdoor learning, which aims to develop skills, interests and an aspiration within pupils to do anything and everything to the best of their ability. A strong and enthusiastic team of experienced specialist teachers enrich the curriculum, while small class sizes ensure that each child's progress is recognised and encouraged.

Boarding at Edgeborough enhances the overall experience of pupils in the school and is a vital factor in creating a vibrant family atmosphere. Boarding at Edgeborough offers a modern take, providing a safe, home-from-home environment. It is an exciting opportunity to stay overnight with friends, while the schedule is as flexible as possible to tailor the experience to each family's needs.

Excellent educational opportunities at Edgeborough enable pupils to regularly gain scholarships to prestigious senior schools. During the past academic year, Edgeborough Year 8 pupils were awarded 13 scholarships to the senior school of their choice for excelling in sports, art, drama, music and all-round skills.

A range of extra-curricular activities and clubs provide the opportunity for teachers to nurture and develop pupils' self-esteem. Our vast outdoor space is ripe for discovering and is a constant source of enjoyment for pupils. The specialist facilities help make learning fun, enriching the academic, social and cultural aspects of school life. Facilities include state-of-the-art ICT and science labs, music suites, an art and pottery studio, a fully-equipped indoor theatre, dance and drama studios, a large sports hall, floodlit astro pitches and a heated swimming pool.

Charitable status. Edgeborough is part of the Charterhouse family of schools (Registered Charity: 312054)

Elizabeth College

The Grange, St Peter Port, Guernsey, Channel Islands GY1 2PY

Tel: 01481 726544
email: office@elizabethcollege.gg
website: https://elizabethcollege.gg
X/Twitter: @Eliz_Coll
Facebook: @ElizabethCollegeGuernsey

See full entry in the **HMC** section, on **p. 96**.

Elm Green Preparatory School

Parsonage Lane, Little Baddow, Chelmsford, Essex CM3 4SU
Tel: 01245 225230
email: admin@elmgreen.essex.sch.uk
website: www.elmgreen.essex.sch.uk

Principal: **Mrs A E Milner**, BTech Hons, MSc, PGCE

Age Range. Co-educational 4–11 years.

Number of Day Pupils. 220.

Fees per term (2023–2024). £3,270

Religious affiliation. Non-denominational.

Elm Green was founded in 1944 and enjoys a lovely rural setting, surrounded by National Trust woodland.

Children enter in the September after their fourth birthday and in their final year are prepared for scholarships, entry to other independent schools and for entry to maintained schools. Many of the pupils take the Essex 11+ and the school has an excellent record of success in this examination.

The school maintains a high standard of academic education giving great emphasis to a secure foundation in the basic subjects whilst offering a wide curriculum with specialist teaching in many areas.

Information technology and design technology form an integral part of the curriculum and there are flourishing art, music and PE departments. The school competes successfully in a wide range of sports – football, rugby, netball, swimming, cricket, gymnastics, athletics, rounders and tennis.

There are many extra-curricular activities and all the children are encouraged to work and to play hard in order to fulfil their potential.

The school aims to foster intellectual curiosity and to encourage individual and corporate work. Kindness and thought for others are given a high priority.

The Elms School

Colwall, Malvern, Worcestershire WR13 6EF
Tel: 01684 540344
email: office@elmsschool.co.uk
website: www.elmsschool.co.uk
X/Twitter: @theelmsschool
Facebook: @ElmsSchoolColwall
Instagram: @theelmsschool_colwall

Founded 1614.

Chairman of the Governors: Mr J Rose
Head: **Mr Ed Lyddon**

Age range. 3–13.

Number of pupils. 160. Boys 90, girls 70.

Fees per term (2023–2024). Full boarding: £8,660–£10,430; Flexi-boarding: £50 per night; Day fee: Year 3 £4,920, Year 4 £5,800, Years 5 and 5 £6,990, Years 7 and 8 £7,580. Pre-Prep (ages 3–7): £2,940–£4,920. Fees are payable termly in advance.

The Elms is run as a charitable, non-profit making company with a Board of Governors. Children are taken in the Main School from the age of rising 8 and there is a Montessori and Pre-Preparatory Department for 3–7 year olds.

The Elms is a leading, independent, co-educational preparatory school for children aged between 3 and 13. Welcoming day pupils, flexi-boarders and full-boarders, we provide a special place of children to enjoy their education while receiving exceptional pastoral care and every opportunity to flourish. The strong values and ethos are evident throughout all areas of school life. The Elms seeks to find each child's talents by giving all children the freedom, space and endless opportunities to discover and develop themselves while growing in confidence. We recognise that all children are unique and hugely special and we provide a safe and secure environment for all children to be stretched to their potential.

'I can honestly say that what you have done for my daughter has been outstanding. Absolutely outstanding. What has been returned to me at the end of the process is a daughter who is confident, articulate, sports mad, and has an appetite for learning and is above all happy with herself and others. I couldn't have made a better choice…' *A Testimonial from the Parent of a Year 8 Leaver*

The Elms is situated in stunning countryside, surrounded by the Malvern Hills. There is a quiet ambition that emanates throughout the school and we enjoy celebrating the success of our children while embracing positive failure in a secure and nurturing environment. The curriculum is rich and diverse and delivered by our outstanding and dedicated staff. The house system and extensive extracurricular programme provides vast opportunities in all of areas of school life. All children have the opportunity to care for our animals on the farm and they also have the chance to take riding lessons.

We are very lucky to have such fantastic facilities in all forums. Our children enjoy intensive sport sessions every day from our highly qualified staff. The sessions take place on the floodlit astroturf, in our recently refurbished indoor swimming pool and on the professionally prepared cricket, rugby and football pitches.

Bursaries are available on entry. Our Year 8 leavers go on to a variety of leading senior schools that we ensure are carefully chosen for their individual needs and many achieve scholarships in a wide variety of areas.

At The Elms we pride ourselves on the strong community and family feel of the school. The relationship between staff and children is truly distinctive and allows children to flourish and have belief in themselves. While recognising the absolute importance of academic achievement, we educate and nurture the whole child to ensure they are fully ready for their next school and life beyond.

Charitable status. The Elms (Colwall) Limited is a Registered Charity, number 527252. It exists to provide education for boys and girls.

Eltham College

Grove Park Road, Mottingham, London, LONDON SE9 4QF

Tel: 020 8857 1455
email: mail@eltham-college.org.uk
website: www.eltham-college.org.uk
X/Twitter: @ElthamCollegeUK
Facebook: @ElthamCollegeOfficial
Instagram: @ElthamCollegeLondon
LinkedIn: /Old-Elthamians

See full entry in the **HMC** section, on **p. 100**.

Embley Prep School
United Learning

Embley Park, Romsey, Hampshire SO51 6ZA

Tel: 01794 515737
email: prep@embley.org.uk
website: www.embley.org.uk
X/Twitter: @embleyprep
Facebook: @EmbleyHampshire
LinkedIn: /school/embleyhampshire

Chairman of the Local Governing Body: Professor Tom Thomas

Headmaster: Mr Cliff Canning, BA Hons, BD Hons, HDipEd, NUI

***Head of Prep School*: Ms Sheina Wright**, BA, QTS

Age Range. 2–11 Co-educational.

Number of Pupils. 170 day pupils.

Fees per term (2023–2024). Nursery: £3,429 (full-time excluding EYE funding). Prep School: £4,070 (Reception, Years 1 and 2); £4,670 (Year 3); £6,250 (Years 4–6).
Please refer to www.embley.org.uk/admissions/fees for further details.

Embley's Prep School provides an education with character that uncovers and nurtures each child's niche and inspires ambition and academic achievement. Children are encouraged to be independent and push themselves to find out more, giving a real sense of purpose to their learning adventures.

Specialist subject staff work across every year group to give children the very best learning experiences. Academic opportunities are combined with a diverse co-curricular programme including performing arts, drama and music alongside sports such as sailing, skiing, golf and tennis. Many varied initiatives and activities, such as the Prep School Stock Market Investment Club and Natural Sciences, provide a variety of complex, multi-layered, problem-solving experiences and develop articulate, reasoned and informed children with analytical minds.

The school is nestled in 130 acres of private parkland, which includes woodlands, playing fields, tennis courts, AstroTurf pitches, a swimming pool and a golf course. It also runs a comprehensive sailing programme with its own boats moored at Lymington.

Embley's Nursery operates for 48 weeks of the year, offering an exciting introduction to learning to ensure that each child will love going to school. From the early years, children are encouraged to be resilient in their approach and take responsibility for their learning adventures. They leave the Nursery with a calm confidence and independence: the perfect learning foundation.

At the end of Year 6, children progress to Embley's Senior School which is within the same campus.

Eton End School

35 Eton Road, Datchet, Slough, Berkshire SL3 9AX

Tel: 01753 541075
email: admin@etonend.org
website: www.etonend.org
X/Twitter: @EtonEndSchool
Facebook: @EtonEndSchool
Instagram: @etonendschool
LinkedIn: /company/eton-end-school

Board of Governors:
Chair: Mr J Clark
Deputy Chairs: Mrs N Brewster and Mr A Boothroyd

***Headmistress*: Mrs Rachael Cox**, BA Hons, PGCE, NPQSL, MA, FCCT

Age range. 3–11 Co-educational.

Number of pupils. 182: 83 girls, 99 boys.

Fees per term (2023–2024). Nursery: £1,999–£3,999; Pre Prep: £4,054–£4,655; Prep: £5,095–£5,465. Fees include lunch and after-school care.

Eton End is a co-educational day school and Nursery for children aged 3 to 11 years, situated on the fringes of Datchet and Eton and positioned in six acres of semi-wooded land. Having been established in 1936 to educate the children of Eton Masters, it is a school which successfully merges tradition with a forward-thinking approach to teaching and learning. The links with Eton College continue to this day, enabling our pupils to experience numerous opportunities which extend and enrich their learning.

The children at Eton End achieve excellent academic standards, developing a lifelong love of learning, in small classes. The highly qualified specialist staff bring the broad curriculum alive with their enthusiasm and expertise, and use of the outdoor space is maximised to enhance this.

Eton End children are confident and articulate with strong communication skills, displaying excellent attitudes to learning from an early age. Encouraging the children to be resilient and to persevere, showing self-awareness and an ability to reflect on their progress is key. The children at Eton End display a strong sense of self-confidence, resilience and commitment to improve their learning and performance in readiness for the next stage of their lives. Empathising with peers, encouraging others and, most importantly, learning to respect one another, are essential skills for life which are developed and nurtured at Eton End.

The opportunities available to the pupils at Eton End enable every child to find their strengths, both inside and outside of the classroom. With the wonderful space available and our bespoke 'Outdoor Learning Centre', the opportunities for outdoor learning are endless. An Eton End Education is not only about teaching the children a body of knowledge but also about preparing them for life in the 21st century.

A full after-school programme of clubs and activities is available for pupils to enjoy, enabling them to develop alternative skills in the comfort of the school environment. Happiness and wellbeing are pivotal to an Eton End education and we work hard to ensure that our happy children thrive.

Eton End offers pupils an excellent all-rounded education, while ensuring they experience a childhood they will cherish.

Please contact us to chat to our Registrar or make an appointment to meet the Headmistress and tour the school on 01753 54107

Charitable status. Eton End School Trust (Datchet) Limited is a Registered Charity, number 310644. The aim of the charity is to provide a well-balanced education for children whose parents wish them to attend Eton End School.

Eversfield Preparatory School

Warwick Road, Solihull, West Midlands B91 1AT

Tel: 0121 705 0354
email: enquiries@eversfield.co.uk
website: www.eversfield.co.uk
X/Twitter: @eversfield647
Facebook: @EversfieldPrep
LinkedIn: /eversfield-preparatory-school-trust-limited

Chairman of Governors: Dr T Brain

***Headmaster*: Mr R Yates**, MA, BA, PGCE, FCTT

Age range. 2¾–11 years.

Number of pupils. 336 boys and girls.

Fees per term (2023–2024). Nursery and Kindergarten: £1,424–£3,950 according to age and sessions. Lower, Middle and Upper School from £4,066–£4,647 according to age and inclusive of lunch, books and swimming lessons.

Eversfield is a Nursery and Day Preparatory School in Solihull preparing boys and girls for entry to the leading independent and grammar senior schools in the Midlands. The school was founded in 1931 and its mission is to provide an outstanding, broad education within a safe, caring, happy, family atmosphere where the talents of every child are valued and nurtured.

The curriculum focuses on academic excellence while retaining the breadth which nurtures the creative, sporting, technical and social skills of each child. The School's aim is for all their pupils to achieve beyond any boundaries set by expectations, whatever their talents and ability, and to instil a lifelong love of learning.

Eversfield was named Independent Prep School of the Year 2023.

Future schools. The wide range of scholarships regularly awarded demonstrates the breadth of high-quality teaching across the school. Children benefit by being individually guided through the process of carefully selecting the senior school that is right for them and pupils advance to the leading independent and grammar schools in the UK. The children are extremely happy and leave as confident, enthusiastic and inquisitive learners.

Co-curricular activities. There is a rich variety of lunchtime and afterschool clubs on offer which provide opportunities to develop intellectual, creative and physical skills both inside and outside the classroom. The choice is impressive and includes choirs, chess, speech and drama, creative arts, dance, musical ensembles, STEM clubs and multiple sports disciplines.

Achievement in sport is strong and teams perform to a high standard against local opposition. Talented sports players are encouraged to attend trials for county teams and individual pupils compete at a very high level.

Pastoral care. At the heart of everything lies a deep care for each child and family values permeates through the whole school. The school code of conduct, CARE, is central to the pastoral programme and helps children develop essential life skills: Compassion, Aspiration, Respect and Endeavour. The School promotes high moral standards and responsible attitudes based upon clear and relevant Christian teaching. A strong sense of community exists where small classes, a well-ordered routine and excellent pastoral support helps pupils to feel secure and develop their self-confidence.

Facilities. Set on an attractive five-acre site impressive facilities are akin to those found at a senior school and include specialist rooms for teaching art, design and technology, science, food technology, music and computing. Sporting facilities comprise a gymnasium, extensive playing fields and all-weather courts.

The sports and performing arts centre is an impressive state-of-the-art building featuring an indoor heated swimming pool, three badminton courts, indoor cricket nets and is also marked for netball. The customised lighting and sound system, theatre curtains, modular staging and retractable seating for over 200 make it the perfect venue for performances. Children in Kindergarten and Nursery have access to all the facilities on the site and are cared for in a warm and welcoming dedicated purpose-built building with its own secure outdoor all-weather play area.

Bursaries. Thanks to the School's charitable status a number of fee assisted places are made available each year. This financial support, ranging from 10% up to 100% reduction in school fees, is available for pupils entering Form 3, and above.

Charitable status. Eversfield Preparatory School Trust Limited is a Registered Charity, number 528966. It is under the direction of a Board of Governors and exists to carry out the work of an Independent Preparatory School.

Ewell Castle Preparatory School

Glyn House, Church Street, Ewell, Surrey KT17 2AP
Tel: 020 8394 3579
email: admissions@ewellcastle.co.uk
website: www.ewellcastle.co.uk
X/Twitter: @ECSPrep
Facebook: @EwellCastleSchool
Instagram: @EwellCastleSchool
LinkedIn: /school/ewell-castle-school

Chairman of Governors: Mr C Griffith

Principal: Mr Silas Edmonds, MA, NPQH

***Head of Preparatory School*: Mrs L Macallister BA,** PGCE, NPQSL

Deputy Head of Preparatory School & Assistant Principal: Mrs S Fowler, BSc, PGCE
Deputy Head of Preparatory School & Assistant Principal: Mrs G Bean, BA, PGCE
Registrar: Mrs E Porter, BA, DipM

Age Range. 3–11.

Number of Pupils. 157 Girls and Boys.

Fees per term (2023–2024). £4,160–£4,702.

School Mission. We will inspire our children and young people to thrive, engaging them to excel in a creative and academic environment. We will instil a growth mindset to develop: confidence, contentment and emotional intelligence.

Aims and Ethos. We are a vibrant learning community, inspiring every child to thrive: discovering strengths, deepening intellectual curiosity and cultivating wellbeing.

Values. Personal integrity, mutual respect, social responsibility and lifelong resilience.

Ewell Castle Preparatory School is an independent co-educational day school, located on two sites in the heart of Ewell Village. Nursery and Reception (EYFS) pupils (ages 3–5 years) are based at Chessington Lodge in Spring Street, while Years 1 to 6 (ages 6–11) are based at Glyn House in Church Street, opposite the Senior School (co-educational 11–18 years), with which a close liaison is maintained.

There are no entry requirements for Nursery/Reception children, but older pupils attend the school for a day's assessment, which will include assessment through lesson observation. The majority of pupils at the Preparatory School proceed to the Senior School and a number of bursaries and scholarships are available at 11+, 13+ and 16+ entry. The National Curriculum is incorporated within a broad curriculum.

The creative arts play an important part in school life. Apart from the timetabled music lessons, there is the opportunity for pupils to learn a variety of instruments under professional teachers. Drama productions take place regularly. Pupils' art work can be seen on display in the local community and is always to be found decorating the School walls. All pupils join in various sporting activities as part of the weekly curriculum. In addition, a wide variety of activities are available after school and during the holidays.

All pupils use the five acres of attractive gardens and playing fields at Glyn House for outdoor play (including Forest School) and games lessons. In addition, Preparatory School pupils benefit from full access to the excellent sporting facilities, including a sports hall and playing fields, on the 15-acre site at The Castle. The main games are football, netball, hockey, cricket and tennis. There are also athletics and cross country events, including a School sports day. All pupils receive swimming instruction.

Outside speakers include police liaison officers and actors and authors who conduct workshops with pupils. A number of visits occur to places of interest which are relevant to a particular area of study. There are regular School visits abroad.

The School also enjoys close links with St Mary's Church, where regular assemblies are held throughout the year.

The Preparatory School aims to provide a caring, responsive and stimulating environment in which pupils are able to fulfil their potential. Hard work and high standards together with courtesy and consideration to others are of prime importance.

Who we are It is not just the family feel which characterises interactions at the school gates, within the classroom and in extracurricular pursuits, at both the Prep sites at Chessington Lodge and Glyn House. It is also the wonderful blend of academic aspiration and challenge, pastoral care and inclusivity, and a real sense of warmth and community. This comes from our parents, colleagues and pupils as they interact with each other across all sites.

Developing independent learners and critical thinkers Potential is key in every school. Key to unlocking it in each child comes from providing that environment of psychological safety for children to try new things, to chance success or redirection; and with staff being happy for children to both learn from their mistakes as well as rejoice in their triumphs. Sampling life experiences, learning new things and not being afraid to try is what teaches pupils to know themselves and become architects of their own learning, in order to benefit from that self-awareness with life's big decisions later on. Developing critical thinkers who are compassionate and curious is what we are all about.

What is at the heart of Ewell Castle Prep? Simple: there is something for everyone. Our values are embedded within our rich and varied curriculum, designed to both stretch and support, so that we provide genuine conditions for personal integrity, life-long resilience, mutual respect and social responsibility to be lived and breathed. Our values are not just on our website: they are inherently a part of who we are and we attract those for whom this is magical and important.

Parents trust us to support their children in one of the biggest decisions they can make and we don't take that trust lightly. We are a school of choice, in both meanings of the word, and understand that who children become is as important as what they know. It must be so if they are to relish their childhood without wishing it away, if they are to be prepared for the future and, most importantly, if they are to enjoy the journey to become the best versions of themselves.

Charitable status. Ewell Castle School is a Registered Charity, number 312079. It exists to provide education for boys and girls.

Exeter Cathedral School

The Chantry, Palace Gate, Exeter, Devon EX1 1HX

Tel: 01392 255 298
email: reception@exetercs.org
website: www.exetercathedralschool.co.uk
X/Twitter: @ECSPrepSchool
Facebook: @ExeterCathedralSchool
Instagram: @ecsprep

Chairman of Governors: Mr Charles Beer

***Headmaster*: Mr James Featherstone**, BA Hons, PGCE

Age range: 3–13.

Number of pupils: 221 pupils.

Fees per term (2023–2024): Reception: £3,216; Years 1–2: £3,291; Years 3–4: £4,822; Year 5: £4,993; Years 6–8: £5,390.

Exeter Cathedral School is Exeter's oldest school offering boys and girls aged 3–13 a remarkably tailored education.

Proudly educating the 40 boy and girl choristers of Exeter Cathedral, today we are a thriving independent school, fostering a happy and purposeful learning environment where every child can reach their full potential.

Our size means we are large enough to have the vibrancy, energy and expertise to deliver truly first-rate educational opportunities, yet small enough to know each and every one of our pupils as individuals. This, coupled with our passionate focus on character development, is why we believe our pupils flourish academically, creatively and socially… for a lifetime.

Pastoral care and pupil wellbeing are at the forefront of all that we do, and we believe very firmly that happy children are best placed to be successful learners and engaged members of the community.

Curriculum: We offer a broad and balanced curriculum that focuses on developing the whole child, aiming to ensure that each pupil leaves Exeter Cathedral School ready for the challenges ahead and understanding their responsibility to others.

Music: Founded as a choir school in the 12th century, and as one of today's 44 Cathedral Schools in the UK, Exeter Cathedral School has music at its heart. We are known for providing a breadth of musical opportunity, and for being a school which promotes 'music for all' while offering high-calibre training to our most gifted elite musicians.

Our choristers receive a scholarship to attend the school, which is awarded by the Dean and Chapter of Exeter Cathedral. As well as being fully involved in the life of the school, our choristers are trained to a professional standard to sing alongside the adult members of the choir, benefitting from world-class musical coaching and unparalleled opportunities.

Sport: Exeter Cathedral School is serious about sport, with a philosophy of 'sport for all'. We focus on participation, development and enjoyment, while still catering to our elite athletes. We are proud of our long-standing association with some of the region's top sporting clubs and venues. We train and play at the world-class Exeter University Sports Hub, including the astroturf pitches and indoor sports hall, as well as Exeter Cricket Club and County Ground, Exeter Athletics Arena and Victoria Park Tennis Club. These first-rate venues are just minutes away in one of our minibuses, allowing our pupils and staff to make the most of the best sporting facilities in the city.

Charitable status: Exeter Cathedral School is a Registered Charity, no. 1151444.

Exeter Junior School

Victoria Park Road, Exeter, Devon EX2 4NS

Tel: 01392 307080 Headmistress
01392 307080 Director of Admissions & Marketing
email: admissions@exeterschool.org.uk
website: www.exeterschool.org.uk
X/Twitter: @ExeterSchoolUK
Facebook: @ExeterSchoolUK
Instagram: @exeterschooluk
LinkedIn: /school/exeter-school

Exeter School is a co-educational day school. Exeter Junior School is situated in the grounds of Exeter School and provides for girls and boys aged 7–11.

Exeter Pre-Prep (formerly known as The New School) joined the Exeter School family in March 2021 and is a co-educational pre-prep from nursery to Year 2. It is situated in Exminster, about 10 mins drive from the Exeter School campus.

Chairman of Board of Governors: Mr James Gaisford, BSc, ACA

***Headmistress*: Mrs Saskia van Schalkwyk**, BA Hons, QTS

Deputy Head: Mr J Wood
Head of Upper School: Mr R W I Evans, MA Exeter (Form Tutor, Lower Two/Year 5)
Head of Lower School: Mrs L L Hardy, MA Lancaster (Form Tutor, Form One/Year 3)

Age range. 7–11.

Number of pupils. 198: 127 Boys, 71 Girls.

Fees per term (2023–2024). Form One/Upper One (Years 3 and 4): £4,400, Lower Two/Upper Two (Years 5 and 6): £4,600.

Exeter Junior School is housed in a spacious, Victorian building in the grounds of Exeter School. The close proximity of the junior school to the senior school enables the pupils to take full advantage of the facilities on site, which include a chapel, music centre, science laboratories, sports hall with dance studio, fitness suite and squash courts, indoor swimming pool, playing fields, all-weather astroturf arena and tennis courts. The junior school was extended in 2017 to provide additional changing room facilities and a STEAM room for DT, science and cookery.

The junior school retains its own playground and green space, therefore giving the school a separate and clearly recognisable identity. The playground benefitted from a substantial refurbishment over the summer of 2021 including bespoke wooden playground equipment and an outdoor classroom.

Liaison between junior and senior staff is a positive feature of this thriving junior school.

The school aims to offer, in academic, cultural and sporting terms, the widest possible range of opportunities thus helping each pupil to identify the activities which will give the greatest scope for development and fulfilment in years to come. Music, drama, art, sport and expeditions all have an important part to play in the life of the school.

The majority of pupils enter the school at age 7 or 9, and entrance is by informal assessment in January. This includes a report from the child's previous school, classroom sessions in the company of other prospective pupils, literacy and numeracy tasks. Pupils may enter the school at other ages where space is available.

Pupils are offered an academic programme which incorporates the National Curriculum model with the addition of French which is introduced from Year 3.

Exeter Junior School offers free lessons on string instruments to all pupils entering Year 3.

Specialist teaching is offered from the outset, with the additional support of senior school staff in science, French, German, Spanish, music, sport and Latin.

A wide variety of clubs are available during the week including art & craft, dance, modern languages, calligraphy, sewing, football, hockey, netball, rugby, coding, Minecraft, chess and drama. After-school care is available until 5.30 pm.

(*For further information about the Senior School, see Exeter School entry in HMC section.*)

Charitable status. Exeter School is a Registered Charity, number 1093080. It exists to provide education for children.

Exeter Pre-Prep School

The Avenue, Exminster, Exeter, Devon EX6 8AT

Tel: 01392 496122
email: preprep@exeterschool.org.uk
website: www.exeterschool.org.uk
X/Twitter: @exeterpreprep
Facebook: @exeterpreprep
Instagram: @exeterpreprep
LinkedIn: /company/thenewschoolexeter

Chair of Governors: Mrs Helen Clarke
***Head*: Mr Daniel Ayling**, MA Cantab, PGCE, NPQH, MCCT
Senior leadership team:
Head of Exeter School: Ms Louise Simpson, BSc
Headmistress of Exeter Junior School: Mrs Saskia A Van Schalkwyk, BA
Bursar: Mr Miles C M MacEacharn, BSc FCA
Deputy Head (*Co-curricular*, *Compliance*, *ICT*): Mr Graham S Bone, BSc Ed
Deputy Head (*Pastoral*): Miss Ali Dunning, BA
Deputy Head (*Academic*): Dr James L Wilson, DPhil
Deputy Head (*Junior School*): Mr John S Wood, BA
Director of Admissions & Marketing: Mrs Elizabeth S Williams
Assistant Head (*Character*): Miss Bethan V Rose, MA
Assistant Head, Head of Sixth Form: Mr Luigi Chu, BA

Number of Pupils. 72.

Fees per term (2023–2024). From £2,900 per term.

Founded in 1992, we have maintained a consistently strong reputation for academic excellence and a caring, familial ethos over the last 30 years, previously as The New School. We pride ourselves on offering the very best introduction to school life, especially during those early years when key skills, attitudes and learning foundations are laid for life. As a small school with significant expertise in early years education, we are able to take a highly personalised approach, finding the brilliance in every child and supporting them to achieve their full potential. We take the time to develop strong relationships with all our children and parents to provide the best possible experience for each individual pupil in the time that they are with us. Having joined the Exeter School family in March 2021, we are very proud that our well-established relationship has been strengthened, and excited that our children can continue to experience and enjoy a full Exeter School education, from the early years through to the sixth form. There has been significant investment in sympathetically refurbishing our beautiful building and grounds to provide further outstanding facilities while retaining their unique charm and period features.

Admission. Please contact our friendly admissions team at 01392 307080 or admissions@exeterschool.org.uk.

We run open events throughout the year and personalised visits are welcomed. Please check www.exeterschool.org.uk for details.

Curriculum. EYDS and NC.

Extracurricular activities. Wide range including drama, tennis, football and individual music lessons.

Charitable status. Registered Charity, number 1093080.

Fairfield Prep School

Leicester Road, Loughborough, Leicestershire LE11 2AE

Tel: 01509 215172
email: Fairfield.office@lsf.org
website: www.lsf.org/fairfield
X/Twitter: @LboroFairfield
Facebook: @LboroFairfield
Instagram: @LboroFairfield
LinkedIn: /loughborough-schools-foundation

Chair of the Governors: Mr Roger Harrison, MA Cantab, DipArch RIBA

***Head*: Mr A Earnshaw**, BA Lancaster, NPQH

Age range. 3–11.

Number of pupils. 235 Boys, 218 Girls (numbers exclude Kindergarten).

Fees per term (2023–2024). Kindergarten (5 days): £4,330, Pre-Prep: £4,450, Upper Prep: £4,560. Lunches and individual music lessons extra.

Fairfield is the prep school for the Loughborough Schools Foundation, a foundation of four schools comprising: Fairfield Prep School (boys and girls 3–11), Loughborough Grammar School (boys 10–18), Loughborough Amherst School (boys and girls 4–18) and Loughborough High School (girls 11–18). The schools operate under one governing body and are situated on two neighbouring campuses in the town. The Foundation also includes The Loughborough Nursery for children from 6 weeks to 4 years.

Recently the School embarked on an ambitious building project to provide pupils with additional space and improved accommodation, including new classrooms for pupils in Reception and Years 1–3, an extended gymnasium with spacious changing rooms for pupils and staff, a specialist arts and craft room and an additional performance hall. Accommodation also includes a purpose-built Kindergarten unit for children aged 3+ during term time, which can cater for up to 44 children.

Fairfield's partnership with pupils, parents and the wider community ensures every child is given the ability to reach their full potential through a combination of academic, cultural, sporting and artistic opportunities.

Learning is extended through a wide range of activities, utilising iPads and other technologies, along with specialist teaching in science, ICT, modern foreign languages, PE, and music. Music is a vital part of the school's culture and the facilities available to pupils are second to none. All Year 2 pupils follow a course in instrumental playing, and children in the Upper Prep have the opportunity to have individual instrumental lessons with one of the Foundation Music department's peripatetic staff. In September 2015, the Music department became the only All-Steinway School in the Midlands, demonstrating the Foundation's commitment to providing pupils with the very best instruments on which to learn, practise and perform.

Fairfield provides access to an extensive range of extracurricular activities. There are a greater number of sports, and more teams, clubs and opportunities for extracurricular music on offer than ever before. Practically every single member of staff at the school runs at least one extracurricular session, ensuring that our programme of activities meets the diverse and ever-changing interests of our pupils.

In a nurturing, happy atmosphere, children are guided along their educational journey through purposeful, academic work and are constantly encouraged to succeed. Staff help develop each child's confidence, courtesy and self-worth so they grow stronger, not only as individuals, but also as members of their local community. By taking individual differences into account, the successful Fairfield Prep School pupil of today acquires the skills and values which allow them to make a valuable contribution to the success of the senior schools, and through their lives, to the society of tomorrow.

The Headmaster is happy to show prospective parents around the school by appointment. Further information can be found on the school website at www.lsf.org/fairfield.

Charitable status. Loughborough Schools Foundation is a Registered Charity, number 1081765, and a Company Limited by Guarantee, registered in England, number 4038033. Registered Office: 3 Burton Walks, Loughborough, Leics LE11 2DU.

Fairstead House School & Nursery

Fordham Road, Newmarket, Suffolk CB8 7AA

Tel: 01638 662318

email: registrar@fairsteadhouse.co.uk

website: www.fairsteadhouse.co.uk

Chair of Governors: Mr David Day

***Head*: Mr Michael Radford**, BEd Hons, MEd

Age Range. 3 months–11 years Co-educational.

Number of Children. 207.

Fees per term (2023–2024). Tuition (including lunches): Reception, Year 1 & 2 £3,970, Years 3–6 £4,425. Please visit our website for information on current Nursery fees.

Fairstead House is situated in the heart of Newmarket and offers a combination of an excellent academic education with an emphasis on creativity and imagination in a caring, happy community with a unique family ethos, closely linked to the local community.

From Nursery onwards, we offer a broad and stimulating curriculum which provides the children with a solid foundation for their onward journeys to senior schools in both Independent and State sectors. The curriculum is complemented by Art, DT, Music, Drama and Sports.

Pupils take part in a variety of sports such as rugby, football, cricket, hockey and netball. All children play rounders and take part in cross-country running and athletics.

Extracurricular Speech & Drama lessons are available, as is private tuition in a wide selection of musical instruments. All children take part in the many theatrical productions that are held at School.

A programme of development has ensured the provision of first-class facilities throughout the School including a state-of-the-art Music & Drama Centre with specialist facilities, an ICT suite, iPads, interactive whiteboards in every classroom and a dedicated Science & DT area.

As well as a breakfast club and after-school care club providing wrap-around care, there is a diverse range of after-school activity clubs available. A Holiday Club is also available for all children out of term time.

Throughout the year, pupils go on a variety of trips and excursions, both day and residential. The residential trips to Norfolk and Snowdonia for the older pupils are designed to encourage independence and cultivate a spirit of adventure as well as personal responsibility and development.

Charitable Status: Fairstead House School Trust Limited is a Registered Charity, number 276787. It exists to provide education for boys and girls.

The Falcons School
Alpha Plus Group

11 Woodborough Road, Putney, London SW15 6PY
Tel: 020 8992 5189
email: admissions@falconsgirls.co.uk
website: www.falconsgirls.co.uk

***Head Teacher*: Mrs Sara Williams-Ryan**, L-ès-Lettres Geneva, MA, PCGE

Age Range. Co-educational, 2–11.

Number of Pupils. 286 Boys; 96 Girls.

Fees per term (2023–2024). Nursery & Pre-Prep: £3,075–£5,005, Reception £5,190; Years 1–6 £6,025.

The Falcons School enjoys a well-deserved reputation for excellence. Exit results to leading London Day Schools are impressive, as too is the specialist teaching on offer throughout the schools. The schools provide a safe outdoor space for play and sport and a school hall for gym, assemblies and lunch. Nearby sports facilities are used to enhance an exciting sports programme. There are well-equipped libraries, music rooms, ICT suites, with much-admired art and science facilities. Our overriding emphasis is on achieving excellence in numeracy and literacy whilst offering a broad and creative curriculum. The Falcons school offers uniquely caring and stimulating environments, where learning is seen as fun and the pursuit of excellence is embraced by all.

Farleigh School

Red Rice, Andover, Hampshire SP11 7PW
Tel: 01264 710766
email: office@farleighschool.com
website: www.farleighschool.com
X/Twitter: @FarleighSchool
Instagram: @farleighschool
LinkedIn: /farleigh

Chair of Governors: Mrs Jane Vyvyan

***Headmaster*: Fr Simon Everson**

Age range. 3–13. Boarding from age 7.

Number of pupils. 460 (120 full and weekly boarders; 340 day pupils – 110 in Kindergarten and Pre-Prep).

Fees per term (2023–2024). Boarders: £10,875 (Years 7 and 8), £9,810 (Years 4–6), £9,385 (Year 3); HM Forces boarders: £8,950 (Years 7–8), £8,525 (Years 3–6); Day pupils: £8,210 (Years 4–8), £7,750 (Year 3); Pre-Prep: £4,510 (Reception–Year 2), £2,245 (Kindergarten).

Farleigh is a contemporary, Catholic, co-educational boarding and day school, which welcomes children of all faiths, or none. Situated in a stunning Georgian country house standing in 70 acres of magnificent parkland and landscaped woodland in the Test Valley of Hampshire, near Andover, Farleigh is just over an hour from London and within easy reach of Southampton and London airports.

High standards are achieved both in and out of the classroom and excellent academic results are the norm, with leavers going on to a large number of leading senior schools and more than a third each year gaining awards/scholarships to their chosen destination.

Farleigh has outstanding facilities, which include an all-weather pitch, a purpose-built music school with 12 practice rooms, Recital Hall, rehearsal room, soundproof 'rock' room and recording studio. The Junior and Senior Boarding Houses have also undergone significant refurbishment. There is a spacious and light Art and Design Technology building, computer rooms with state-of-the-art technology, newly refurbished Theatre with tiered seating, fully adaptable staging and built-in LED lighting, a drama/dance studio, spacious recreation rooms, a fine Chapel, gymnasium, 22-metre heated indoor swimming pool, tennis courts and separate purpose-built Pre-Prep and Kindergarten with its own landscaped and secure playground. In addition, the school has three science laboratories and a food technology room, as well as additional circulation space with a well-lit ball play area and a small amphitheatre to the rear of the existing Farleigh Theatre.

The teaching staff is complemented by a committed pastoral team including Year Heads, House Parents, a Senior Nurse and a further Boarding Nurse and Day Matron. Many staff are resident, giving the school a welcoming family atmosphere, often commented upon by visitors. The latest ISI inspection of the school's boarding provision was 'Outstanding' in all areas inspected, 'with no recommendations'. The inspectors added, 'Pupils demonstrate an extensive range of skills, knowledge and understanding well beyond the expectations for their age and ability across all areas of learning.'

The school provides a vibrant and active evening and weekend activity programme for boarders. Regular dinner nights, barbecue parties, annual X-Factor competition, theatre trips, quiz nights and bowling are just some of the weekend events organised for pupils. Weekday activities include bushcraft, forest school, cooking, cycling, community service, debating, golf, archery, yoga, winter cricket nets, swimming, water polo, tennis and additional sport sessions.

Drama, music and art play an important part in school life with two-thirds of the school learning at least one musical instrument and a quarter of the school taking up LAMDA drama lessons. A programme of major musical productions and informal concerts take place throughout the year and the children's artwork is displayed around the school.

The major sports for boys are rugby, football, cricket, athletics and cross country; for girls they are netball, hockey, cricket, athletics and cross country. Swimming lessons and extra tennis coaching are offered throughout the year.

Charitable status. Farleigh School is a Registered Charity, number 1157842. It exists for the purpose of educating children.

Farringtons School

Perry Street, Chislehurst, Kent BR7 6LR
Tel: 020 8467 0256
email: fvail@farringtons.kent.sch.uk
website: www.farringtons.org.uk
X/Twitter: @OneFarringtons
Facebook: @OneFarringtons

See full entry in the **HMC** section, on **p. 113**.

Felsted Prep School

Braintree Road, Felsted, Essex CM6 3JL
Tel: 01371 822610
email: prepadmissions@felsted.org
website: www.felsted.org
X/Twitter: @felstedprep
Facebook: @felstedschool
LinkedIn: /school/felsted-school

***Head*: Mrs Miranda Norris**, BEd, ILMP, MEd

Deputy Head: Mr Jeremy P Fincher, BSc, PGCE
Director of Learning: Mrs Christina F Bury, BA Ed
Head of Stewart House (*Reception–Year 2*): Mrs Jacqueline A Atkins, BEd
Head of Frome Court (*Year 3 & 4*): Mrs Julie E Green, BA
Head of Cloisters (*Years 5 & 6*): Mrs Gemma Paine, BA
Head of Courtauld House (*Years 7 & 8*): Mr Mark C Stringer, BA
Boarding House Parents: Mr Nick F Thomas & Mrs Victoria J Ellis-Thomas
Director of Co-Curricular: Mr Hector Bevitt-Smith, BSc
Head of Support for Learning: Mrs Georgina L Clifford-Smith, PGCE

Governing Body:
Chair of Governors: Robert Brown
Julia Abel Smith, DL, MA
Geoffrey Bault, BA
Mike Beale
Ann Carrington, LLB, LLM, JP
Jane Crouch, BA, MA
John Davies, OBE, MA
Bobbi Davy
James Nicholson, DM, MA, MB BChir, FRCPCH
Lucilla Poston, CBE, PhD, FMedSci
Alison Sefton, BSc
Oliver Stacken, CBE
Nic Stuchfield, MA
Patricia Wardell, BA
Jason Windsor, BA
Stephen Wolfe, BSc, MRICS, IRRV

Age Range. 4–13. Co-educational.

Number of Pupils. 475 pupils (of which 3 are full-time boarders, 3 weekly and 103 flexi boarders).

Fees per term (2023–2024). Day: Prep £5,370–£7,275, Pre-Prep £3,705. Weekly Boarding: £9,415, Full Boarding: £9,995, Flexi Boarding (1–4 nights): £60.75–£143.50 per week.

The staff, excluding the Head, consists of over 50 full-time qualified teachers and there are additional part-time teachers for instrumental music and games. There are six matrons and two sisters in charge of the Medical Centre.

The School was rated 'excellent' in every category by the Independent School Inspectorate in 2019, in addition to a legacy rating of 'Outstanding' by Ofsted for EYFS and Boarding. Winner of TES for Boarding School of the Year 2023.

The Prep School, set in its own area on the main Felsted School campus, has many of its own facilities, including a modern well-equipped library, an excellent theatre/assembly hall, music practice rooms, a multi-purpose sports hall and floodlit, multi-purpose, hard play/games area. Use is made of Felsted School's extra amenities at regular times, including the indoor swimming pool, two Astroturf hockey pitches, small-bore rifle shooting, squash and tennis courts, a state-of-the-art Music School and another indoor sports hall. Pupils in Years 6–8 also lunch at the senior school every day as part of a smooth transition process.

Rugby, netball, hockey, cricket, tennis are core sports, with squash, swimming, athletics, cross country and football also played. Music plays an important part in the School's life, with an excellent Chapel Choir. Regular instrumental, orchestral and rock concerts are given and those children showing particular talent can study at the Junior Guildhall on Saturdays, subject to passing their auditions. The School has a deserved reputation for its drama productions, while Art, Design and Technology, Spanish. PSHE, and Computing are part of the weekly timetable. Out-of-class activities include public speaking and debating opportunities, horse riding, chess, football, golf, karate, cookery and dance/ballet, among others.

Pupils joining at 11+ can be guaranteed assured transfer to Felsted Senior School at 13, as can pupils of a similar age already at the Prep School, following successful completion of assessment tests. The majority of pupils proceed to Felsted Senior School itself, some move on to other major independent senior schools. There is an excellent record of academic, art, music, sport, drama and Design & Technology scholarships. (*For further information about Felsted, see entry in HMC section.*)

Scholarships and Awards are open to pupils joining Felsted Prep School at ages of 11+ in the September of the year of entry. Top-up bursaries may also be available on a means-tested basis. One 100% bursary is available each year to a child who meets the right criteria and is given at the discretion of the Head.

Charitable status. Felsted School is a Registered Charity, number 310870. It exists to provide education for boys and girls.

Feltonfleet School

Byfleet Road, Cobham, Surrey KT11 1DR
Tel: 01932 862264
email: office@feltonfleet.co.uk
admissions@feltonfleet.co.uk
website: www.feltonfleet.co.uk
X/Twitter: @Feltonfleet
Facebook: @feltonfleet
Instagram: @feltonfleetschool

Chair of Governors: Mr Giles Ashbee

***Headmistress*: Mrs Shelley Lance**, BD, PGCE

Director of Admissions: Mrs Catherine Pinder

Age Range. 3–13.

Number of Pupils. 496; of whom 54 are Boarders.

Fees per term (2023–2024). Weekly Boarders £8,458, Day Pupils £4,761–£6,997; Nursery £2,554 (5 mornings).

Feltonfleet School was founded in 1903 and became an Educational Trust in 1967. The School is situated in 25 acres of scenic grounds within easy reach of London and the southern Home Counties. There are 56 full-time and 4 Gap Year members of the teaching staff. The School became fully co-educational in September 1994 and offers both weekly boarding (Monday to Thursday) and day education, as well as a flexible boarding option. There is a flourishing, purpose-built Pre-Preparatory Department with two form entry.

Academics. Academic results are high and pupils routinely gain entry to their first choice senior school. The staff team are 100% committed to drawing out the best in each and every child and this really shines through in Feltonfleet's results. In the Upper School pupils follow the Pre-Senior Baccalaureate – a broad and rich curriculum which thoroughly prepares them for success in their senior schools and beyond. Academic rigour lies at its heart, with a focus on developing core skills of 'thinking and learning', 'reviewing and improving' and 'communicating'.

Ethos. Our ethos is values driven and our day-to-day living begins with identifying and understanding our four core values of honesty, responsibility, respect and kindness. These are our community's fundamental beliefs and the principles we consider to be worthwhile and desirable. It is about teaching children to flourish emotionally, socially, spiritually and physically. This is essential in developing a child's sense of well-being, nurturing their resilience, self-esteem, sense of respect for others and a sense of social responsibility. At Feltonfleet we encourage pupils to enjoy both their learning and their childhood by celebrating who they are as individuals and not just what they achieve.

Pastoral. Feltonfleet is a happy, safe and caring environment where a very high priority is given to pastoral care. So much so that there is a dedicated Deputy Head (Pastoral Care). The division into Pre-Prep, Lower, Middle and Upper Schools means that, at each stage of a child's learning journey, their needs are met so that they can continue to grow in self-confidence and independence. Class teachers and Form Tutors take a close interest in their pupils' pastoral welfare. They are supported in their roles by the Year Leaders who are responsible for the welfare of children in each year group, and by the Deputy Head (Pastoral). Feltonfleet is an environment conducive to mindfulness and positive mental health. 'Time To Think' sessions are an explicit part of the curriculum and Form Tutor system throughout the school.

Entry. Children are admitted from the age of three into the two-form Nursery in the Pre-Prep Department. Places are allocated on a first come first served basis with priority given to siblings. Moving into the Main School at the age of seven, pupils are joined by more children to create three forms. For entry into the Main School pupils are required to sit an entrance assessment and informal interview. Academic, Art, Music, Drama, DT, All-Rounder and Sports Scholarships are offered at 11+.

Facilities. A brand new, state-of-the-art, 400-seat Performing Arts Centre opened in May 2015, where dramatic productions, dance shows and music are performed by all year groups. Well-equipped Science, Art, DT and Digital Learning Departments and Library. 'Calvi House', for Pre-Prep pupils Nursery to Year 1, has its own hall, gardens and outdoor classrooms. 'Year 2 House' provides a dedicated space giving increased access to the extensive facilities and further specialist teaching available on the main campus. There are landscaped play areas throughout the school and a stunning tree house, pond and wildlife area with bird hide.

Sport. The Feltonfleet Sport aim is to 'create better athletes… for life'. The Department prides itself on its ability to encompass both excellence and sport-for-all within a very busy prep school environment. All pupils receive high quality teaching and coaching in a variety of sports and activities in a positive and safe learning environment. Facilities include a magnificent sports hall, sports fields, a 15m indoor swimming pool, a shooting range for air and .22 rifles, a large floodlit Astro pitch and a climbing wall.

Games played are rugby, football, hockey, netball, athletics and cricket.

Extra-Curricular Activities. The School has an active policy of preparing children for the challenges of today's world and an exceptional activities programme is offered to all pupils both during and after the school day. Pupils in the prep school are offered the opportunity to attend residential activity courses as well as subject-related overseas trips. In the final two years pupils attend residential leadership courses. After Common Entrance examinations, Year 8 pupils take part in a varied programme of activities, lectures and trips in preparation for leaving Feltonfleet and moving on to their senior schools.

Charitable status. Feltonfleet School Trust Limited is a Registered Charity, number 312070.

Fettes College Preparatory School

East Fettes Avenue, Edinburgh EH4 1DL
Tel: +44 (0)131 332 2976
email: prepschool@fettes.com
website: www.fettes.com
X/Twitter: @Fettes_College
Facebook: @FettesCollegeFettesPrep

Chair of Governors: Lady M Wise

Chair of Preparatory School Committee: H Bruce-Watt

***Headmaster*: C Minogue**, BSc Hons, PGCE, MEd

Age Range. 7–13.

Number of Pupils. 182: 49 boarders, 133 day pupils; 96 boys, 86 girls.

Fees per term (2023–2024). Boarders: £10,230; Day Pupils: £6,970, including all meals and textbooks.

Fettes Prep School lies within the Fettes College grounds, on 100 acres of parkland in the heart of Edinburgh. The Prep School has its own separate campus adjacent to Fettes College and takes full advantage of all the excellent facilities on the site.

Learning. The curriculum is structured to reflect the strengths of the Curriculum for Excellence, the National Curriculum of England and Wales and IAPS guidance. A strong emphasis is placed on a thorough grounding in the traditionally important subjects of Maths and English. Class sizes are no larger than 18 and pupils from the age of 7 are taught by specialist Science, Language, Art, Music and Drama teachers.

Life. The two Boarding Houses are Iona for the girls and Arran for the boys. The pastoral teams of each house provide around the clock care to create a fun, happy and secure home away from home. We make the most of our fabulous location with plenty of action and adventure trips at weekends when we can be found visiting attractions far and wide.

Sport. We aim to balance 'sport for all' with our ethos of sporting excellence and each Prep pupil, irrespective of their sporting talents, has access to our state-of-the-art, on-site facilities. In addition to expanding their skills, we want our pupils to enjoy the camaraderie of playing in a team and to inspire them to develop a lifelong love of sport and physical activity.

The Arts. We firmly believe that art, drama and music are vital to every child's development, which is why specialists teach all three subjects from age 7. Our tailored curriculum gives the children the chance to explore their creativity, gain the confidence to perform, learn new techniques and experience the thrills and spills of shared endeavour.

Co-curricular. There are annual trips abroad to bring learning to life and other tours are regularly organised. Every child is involved in an array of trips, talks, social events and activities, utilizing the beautiful city of Edinburgh, the surrounding countryside and beyond. The top two year groups are involved in a programme designed at the school to increase and improve resourcefulness, initiative and provide personal challenge.

Entry. Entry at the age of seven, eight or nine is by assessment tests and at 10+, 11+ and 12+ by the Entrance Examinations, taken in late Jan/early Feb. All applicants can apply for a means-tested bursary which can cover up to 100% of the fees. There is a finite amount of funding available each year and therefore not all applicants will be successful. Bursaries are awarded independently of any Scholarship or Award.

Further information and a prospectus can be obtained from the Admissions Team (Tel: +44 (0)131 311 6744, email: admissions@fettes.com) who will be very happy to arrange a visit.

Charitable status. Fettes College is a registered Scottish Charity, No SC051259

Finton House

171 Trinity Road, London SW17 7HL
Tel: 020 8682 0921
email: office@fintonhouse.org.uk
website: www.fintonhouse.org.uk
X/Twitter: @FintonHouseSch
Facebook: @Finton.House.School
Instagram: @fintonhouseschool

Terry O'Neill and Finola Stack founded Finton House in 1987 as a charitable trust with two principles in mind: firstly, that children joining in Reception should not have to face the pressures of a competitive entry system, and secondly that of providing an inclusive educational environment where every child is able to shine.

Chair of Governors: Ms Liz Buckley

***Headmaster*: Mr Ben Freeman**

Age Range. 4–11.

Number of Pupils. 170 Girls, 170 Boys.

Fees per term (2023–2024). Reception to Year 2 £6,287; Years 3–6 £6,405.

Entrance. Non-selective – first come/first served.

Exit. Boys and Girls at 11 for London Day, Prep or Boarding.

Aims to provide a broad education, embracing technology and outdoor learning, encouraging children to live a healthy life in order to flourish in a rapidly changing world. Pastoral care is central to the ethos of the school, with the Finton Goals of self-belief, kindness, resilience, curiosity, respect, communication and morality at the heart of the child's development. Academic subjects, music, art, computing, design and technology, languages and sports are all taught to a very high standard. High success rate in entrance exams to excellent 11+ senior schools, mainly London Day plus some boarding schools, with over a third of leavers winning scholarships and awards. Strong policy of inclusion with a percentage of children with special needs.

Charitable status. Finton House is a Registered Charity, number 296588. It exists to provide a broad, inclusive education for children.

Forest Preparatory School

College Place, Snaresbrook, London E17 3PY
Tel: 020 8520 1744
email: PSOffice@forest.org.uk
website: www.forest.org.uk
X/Twitter: @ForestSchoolE17
Facebook: @ForestSchoolE17
Instagram: @forestschoole17

Co-educational Day School.

Chairman of Governors: David Wilson, LLB

***Head*: James Sanderson**, FRSA, FCCT, BMusPerf Hons Elder Conservatorium, BMus Adelaide

Age range. 4–11.
Number of pupils. 336.
Fees per term (2023–2024). £5,749–£6,625.

Forest Preparatory School is part of Forest School (HMC), with which it shares a 50-acre site at the foot of Epping Forest on the East London/Essex border. Its aims are to offer an education of high quality, and to encourage and develop each child academically, physically and creatively. Pupils are taught in small co-educational classes and at age 11, they proceed to the Senior Section of Forest School (*see separate entry in HMC section*).

Entry to the school is by selection, at 4+ by means of an informal assessment.

The Pre-Prep has 3 forms of 16 pupils in each year group who are taught predominantly by form teachers and supported by qualified teaching assistants and a team of specialist staff.

From the age of 7, there are 24 pupils in two forms in each year group. Starting in Reception, specialist teaching staff provide lessons in computing, music, drama, swimming, Forest Schools and PE/Games with the addition of dance, art, engineering, science, French, Italian, Spanish and Mandarin as pupils progress through the school.

Academic standards, sport and music are all strengths of the school in equal measure. The main sports played are football, cricket, netball and rounders, and teams compete locally and regionally. Athletics, swimming and cross-country are all coached to a high standard. The musical life of the school is enriched by its choirs, orchestra and several chamber groups, and all pupils in Years 3 to 6 are provided with 4 years' free tuition on a musical instrument as part of the School Gloucester programme. There are endless opportunities for pupils to perform in concerts or recitals throughout the year, in and out of School, at venues ranging from St Paul's Cathedral, Great St Bartholomew's Church and Cadogan Hall, as well as Chapel services. Form assemblies and school competitions also provide occasions for public-speaking and performance.

Clubs take place at lunchtime, before school and after school, with a wide variety of extracurricular clubs on offer. Breakfast club commences at 7.30 am and after-school care is available until 6.00 pm each day. Forest School also has an extensive school bus service in operation.

Charitable status. Forest School, London is a Registered Charity, number 312677. The objective of the school is education.

Frensham Heights

Rowledge, Farnham, Surrey GU10 4EA
Tel: 01252 792561
email: admissions@frensham.org
website: www.frensham.org
X/Twitter: @FrenshamHeights
Facebook: @frensham
Instagram: @frensham_heights
LinkedIn: /frensham-heights-school

See full entry in the **HMC** section, on **p. 122**.

The Froebelian School

Clarence Road, Horsforth, Leeds LS18 4LB
Tel: 0113 258 3047
email: office@froebelian.co.uk
website: www.froebelian.com
X/Twitter: @FroebelianS
Facebook: @FroebelianSchool
Instagram: @froebelian_school
LinkedIn: /FroebelianSchool

"We knew from our first visit to the school that it was perfect. Every day our instincts are justified, as we watch our little girl blossom into a confident, delightful and happy little person." A Parent

Chair of Governors: Mr Simon Bickerton
***Head*: Mrs Anna Coulson**

Deputy Head (*Pastoral*): Mrs Judith Giles
Deputy Head (*Academic*): Mrs Lisa Soutar
Admissions: Mrs Hannah Borkala
For full staff details, visit www.froebelian.com

Age Range. 3+ to 11+ years (3–4 years, four compulsory mornings and optional afternoons).
Number of Pupils. 150.
Fees per term (2023–2024). £2,085–£3,100. Compulsory extras for full-time pupils.

A limited number of bursary-assisted places are available for eligible families. 30 hours funding available to those eligible.*

Religious Affiliation: Christian, non-denominational.

Entry Requirements: Interview and assessment; written tests for older children.

Entry is usually at 3+ and limited places are sometimes available throughout the school.

"We chose Froebelian because it feels like a family." – Mrs Canavan, Parent

The Froebelian School, Horsforth is one of the leading independent preparatory schools in the North for children aged **3 to 11 years**. School life is varied, exciting, and fast-paced and there is never a dull moment as we embody our ethos of **'Giving a Flying Start to the Citizens of Tomorrow'**.

Since The Froebelian School's foundation in 1913, influenced by German educationalist, Friedrich Froebel, it has become one of the North's leading educational success stories. Academic results are outstanding, but the school offers much more than an excellent academic education: firmly believing in laying solid foundations for a lifelong love of learning, to gain knowledge and skills and develop personal attributes, relevant to each and every child's future.

Children are at the heart of everything we do, and we are passionate that they enjoy a positive experience, in a warm, safe, friendly, caring, structured and secure environment.

The sense of community at Froebelian is second to none and we value our place in our local community, too. The breadth of opportunity on offer means that there is something for everyone to discover and in which to thrive. Our pupils are confident and our talented and passionate staff guide and support each individual on their personal journeys of discovery.

Our pupils are encouraged to step outside their comfort zone and take risks in a safe and supportive environment, discovering new talents and interests which provide much happiness at school and, critically, develop their self-confidence, problem solving abilities and interpersonal skills.

Sport, Drama and Music all play important roles in school life. Games receives a more generous time allocation than in many schools and our pupils represent the school in fixtures in a wide range of sports. There are a multitude of opportunities to be involved in musical ensembles, groups and performances. House Drama competitions give large numbers of pupils the opportunity to tread the boards, and our end of year productions are of exceptional quality, playing to large audiences at Yeadon Town Hall.

We have a very active Outdoor Education Curriculum which provides residential experiences across the UK and all pupils in Year 6 undertake our very own version of the Duke of Edinburgh's Award Scheme – The FIVe (sic) Steps Challenge – through which they acquire self-reliance, resilience and teamwork whilst learning the importance of service to the community.

With 51 weeks a year provision for all children, we have made significant investment in our early years provision, creating bespoke-designed classrooms and continuous access to an exceptional outdoor space including our hidden, secret forest and treehouse.

Our children adore their school and are justly proud of all they do. They love learning and there is a true sense of fun. We would love you to experience the warmth of our Froebelian Family for yourselves – please do come and see us!

The school is an educational charity where ultimate responsibility rests with a School Council (Governors). The day-to-day running of the school is delegated to the Headteacher, supported by a senior leadership team.

Charitable status. The Froebelian School is a Registered Charity, number 529111. It exists to provide education of the highest quality at affordable fee levels.

Garden House School

Turk's Row, London SW3 4TW

Tel: 020 7730 1652 (Girls)
020 7730 6652 (Boys)

email: info@gardenhouseschool.co.uk

website: www.gardenhouseschool.co.uk

Joint Principals: Mr Christian Warland and Mrs Sophie Strafford

***Head, Girls' School*: Mrs Emma Studd**
***Head, Boys' School*: Mr Dan Jameson**
***Head, Early Years*: Mrs Julia Adlard**

Age Range. 3–11 Girls, 3–11 Boys.

Number of Pupils. 263 girls, 202 boys, taught in single-sex classes.

Fees per term (2023–2024). Kindergarten (all day) £6,600; Reception–Year 6 £8,650–£9,200. There is a 5% reduction for siblings.

Buildings and facilities. The School is housed in a light, airy building in Chelsea. Original artwork hangs in every classroom and facilities include libraries for different age groups, a ballet/performance/drama hall and dedicated science and art rooms.

Sport is played in various locations close to the School. The school has its own garden within the grounds of the Royal Hospital where children enjoy science lessons and attend a Gardening Club.

School drama productions are staged at the Royal Court Theatre in Sloane Square.

Aims, ethos and values. Garden House provides a stimulating and supportive environment in which our children gain an enthusiasm for learning. Our children achieve strong academic results in a calm, constructive manner, being encouraged to have inquiring and independent minds. We teach our boys and girls separately, delivered in teaching styles relevant to the difference audiences. Emphasis is placed not only on academic, sporting and artistic excellence but on manners and consideration to others. Our Kindness Code is adhered to and constantly re-emphasised.

Curriculum. English, Mathematics, Science, History, Geography, Religious Education, French (from Kindergarten), Latin, Computing, Life & Culture, Current Affairs, Art, Drama, Singing and Music, Dancing, Fencing and Physical Education (netball, tennis, rounders, gymnastics, swimming, athletics, cricket, hockey, rugby and football). We have many sports squads, sports clubs and matches. The Learning Support Department helps both children with special needs and those who are gifted, catered for in small groups, taught by two full-time and visiting specialist teachers. 80% of children learn at least one musical instrument. The School runs four choirs and a chamber orchestra.

A diverse range of early morning and after-school clubs include Chess, Coding, Debating, Harry Potter, Lego, Maths Monsters, Music Technology, French, Spanish and German to name a few of the fifty on offer every week.

Benefiting from our central London location, visits to museums, galleries and churches form an essential part of the Curriculum, as do annual field study and outward bound trips. Girls and boys spend a week in France after CE and boys enjoy a camping expedition among others including Outpost trip, a geography and science trip and a Bushcraft trip. The choir sings around the country; this year at Stratford-upon-Avon in a combined music/drama trip.

School Successes. Girls are prepared for the Common Entrance, with the majority leaving for the premier girls' Schools, 75% to leading London senior Schools, 25% to major boarding schools. Some boys leave us at eight, having been well prepared for entrance to leading London Prep Schools and 10% to top boarding Preps. Other boys remain at Garden House, being educated to the age of 11. Our children achieve several scholarships each year.

Entrance. We encourage you to visit the School. Girls and boys join Garden House in September after they reach 3 or 4 years of age. A Registration Form can be obtained from the School website and once completed and returned with the relevant fee, your child's name is placed on the Main List. Entry interviews are held one year before entry. We look forward to welcoming you and your children to Garden House School.

Gatehouse School

Sewardstone Road, Victoria Park, London E2 9JG

Tel: 020 8980 2978
email: admin@gatehouseschool.co.uk
website: www.gatehouseschool.co.uk
X/Twitter: @GatehouseSch
Facebook: @GatehouseSch

***Headteacher*: Mrs S Korbay**

Age Range. 3–11 Co-educational.

Number in School. 528 Day Pupils.

Fees per term (2023–2024). £4,696–£4,951.

Gatehouse School is an Independent Co-educational School for girls and boys aged 3 to 11.

Founded by Phyllis Wallbank, in May 1948, in the gatehouse of St Bartholomew, the Great Priory Church near Smithfield, London, the School was a pioneer of much that is now generally accepted in education. Gatehouse is based on the Wallbank plan whose guiding principle is that children of any race, colour, creed, background and intellect shall be accepted as pupils and work side by side without streaming or any kind of segregation with the aim that each child shall get to know and love God, and develop their own uniqueness of personality, to enable them to appreciate the world and the world to appreciate them.

Gatehouse is now located in Sewardstone Road, close to Victoria Park, and continues to follow this philosophy.

The Nursery is accommodated in a self-contained building with an outdoor play area. Pupils follow a balanced curriculum of child-initiated and teacher-led activities.

Lower Juniors are taught most subjects by their own qualified teacher and assistant, but have French, PE, Drama and Music with a specialist teacher.

In Upper Juniors from the age of 7, teaching is by subject and is conducted by highly qualified specialist staff. This is a special feature of Gatehouse and gives children from an early age, contact with subject specialists, not available to many children until secondary school.

Gatehouse has a specialist Nurture teacher who delivers extended learning for those children exceeding their targets.

We send children to schools such as City of London Boys and Girls, Forest, Bancroft's and Highgate, often with scholarships.

Charitable status. Gatehouse Educational Trust Limited is a Registered Charity, number 282558.

Gayhurst School

Bull Lane, Gerrards Cross, Bucks SL9 8RJ

Tel: 01753 882690
email: enquiries@gayhurstschool.co.uk
website: www.gayhurstschool.co.uk
X/Twitter: @GayhurstSchool
Facebook: @gayhurstschool
Instagram: @gayhurstschool

Chair of Governors: Mr Rob Skinner
***Headmaster*: Mr G R A Davies**, BA Hons, PGCE, MEd

Age range. 3–11 Co-educational.

Number of children. 360.

Fees per term (2023–2024). £4,300–£6,175 (inclusive of lunch). Nursery: from £2,350 per term.

Gayhurst is a happy, thriving and vibrant independent preparatory school for girls and boys aged 3–11. For over 100 years, the school has endeavoured to bring out the best in every child in its care by focusing on individual talents and supporting children to achieve their full potential. Since becoming co-educational in 2008, Gayhurst has built a reputation as a family school, providing first-class co-education in Gerrards Cross.

Life at Gayhurst is engaging and exciting with regular activities organised to enrich the education of its pupils. Children are encouraged to participate in sport, with a busy programme of fixtures against other schools. Creativity is evident throughout the school with opportunities to learn an instrument, become a member of one of the many musical ensembles or take part in the annual year group drama productions. There are also numerous visits to places of interest on both day and residential trips.

Gayhurst strives to ensure that pupils are given every opportunity to achieve the best start in life. The school's commitment to continual improvement and development means that the children benefit greatly from the facilities offered on the school's five acre site, including IT rooms, Science laboratories, woodland adventure playground and an all-weather AstroTurf.

Pupils consistently achieve strong academic results, progressing to both local Grammar Schools and to Senior Schools, day and boarding, in the Independent sector.

Headmaster, Gareth Davies says, 'Pupils' social and personal development is enhanced by the co-educational experience that they get at Gayhurst. In my experience, boys and girls enjoy learning and socialising together and at such a young age, the elimination of gender stereotypes and access to different perspectives and ideas proves only to be beneficial. The family ethos, excellent pastoral care, support and guidance from our caring staff and parent partnership also reinforce the children's positive experiences at school.'

For more information about the school, or to arrange a visit, please contact the Admissions Coordinator on 01753 882690 or email admissions@gayhurstschool.co.uk.

Charitable status. Gayhurst School Trust is a Registered Charity, number 298869.

The Gleddings Preparatory School

Birdcage Lane, Savile Park, Halifax, West Yorkshire HX3 0JB

Tel: 01422 354605
email: admin@thegleddings.co.uk
website: www.thegleddings.co.uk

***Headmistress*: Mrs Jill Wilson CBE**

Age Range. 3–11 Co-educational.

Number of Pupils. 200.

Fees per term (2023–2024). £3,920 including meals.

"The Gleddings is very special. It is precious to several generations of families in the locality and beyond. We are now educating the children of our past pupils. We consider it a great privilege to do so.

The staff and I remember, all of the time, the trust that parents bestow in us. We promise our best efforts for every child.

Our academic results speak for themselves but The Gleddings is about much more. We develop self-discipline, self-respect and confidence within The Gleddings' unique "YOU CHOOSE" ethos. We encourage children to THINK! and to learn how to learn."

Jill Wilson CBE, Headteacher.

Godstowe Preparatory School

Shrubbery Road, High Wycombe, Bucks HP13 6PR

Tel: 01494 529273
01494 429006 Registrar
email: schooloffice@godstowe.org
website: www.godstowe.org
X/Twitter: @GodstoweSchool
Facebook: @GodstoweSchool
Instagram: @godstoweprepschool
LinkedIn: /godstowe-preparatory-school

Motto: *Finem Respice*

Chair of Governors: T Leaver

***Headmistress*: Ms K Bailey**, MA, PGCE

Age Range. Girls 3–13, Boys 3–7.

Number of Pupils. Preparatory: 334 (boarding and day). Pre-Preparatory: 115.

Fees per term (2023–2024). Day Children: £4,500–£6,995, Boarding Supplement: £3,500. Nursery: £2,175 (£435 per additional session, 5 minimum).

Since its foundation in 1900, Godstowe Preparatory School has been at the forefront of education. It has a distinguished tradition as the first British boarding preparatory school for girls, in a foundation that includes Wycombe Abbey, Benenden and St Leonards.

Today, Godstowe is a flourishing boarding and day school with around 450 pupils, enjoying an unparalleled academic reputation. It has a Pre-Prep department for boys and girls aged between three and seven, and a Preparatory School for girls from seven to thirteen years old. Class sizes are small allowing children to benefit from individual attention.

A new indoor swimming pool opened in May 2019. The school underwent an ISI inspection in June 2018 and was regarded as 'excellent' in every respect.

Academic Record. Godstowe enjoys an excellent and unparalleled academic reputation amongst British independent schools. Despite its non-selective entry policy, Godstowe consistently achieves unrivalled academic results. In 2019, 33 scholarships and distinctions were awarded. By the age of nine, pupils are taught by specialists in 16 subjects across the curriculum. Language teaching includes French, Spanish and Latin. Sport, ICT, Art and Music are all outstandingly taught within first-rate facilities.

Boarding. Girls' boarding life is focused within three houses in the grounds, one of which is a dedicated junior house. Each has three resident staff and a warm and supportive atmosphere. A combination of professional and caring staff and beautifully refurbished accommodation ensures a safe and relaxing environment. Each house has its own garden, reinforcing the feeling of 'going home' at the end of the school day. Weekends are packed full of activity and fun, with many weekly boarders often choosing to stay at School for the weekend.

The **Enrichment Curriculum** offers 50 after-school activities each week, most of which run after school between 4.30pm and 6.30pm. The 'E-Curriculum' gives children the chance to try many exciting and challenging new pursuits including poetry writing, judo, cooking, Chinese Mandarin, football and debating. In addition, supervised homework sessions are offered every evening. Day children may join the boarders for breakfast and supper. Other than those sessions supervised by outside instructors all activities are offered free of charge. An Enrichment programme is also in place for Pre-Prep children.

Charitable status. The Godstowe Preparatory School Company Limited is a Registered Charity, number 310637. It exists to provide education and training for young girls and boys.

Gordonstoun

Elgin, Moray IV30 5RF
Tel: +44 (0)1343 837837
email: admissions@gordonstoun.org.uk
principalpa@gordonstoun.org.uk
website: www.gordonstoun.org.uk
X/Twitter: @gordonstoun
Facebook: @GordonstounSchool
Instagram: @gordonstounschool
LinkedIn: /company/gordonstoun-school

See full entry in the **HMC** section, on **p. 132**.

Grange Park Preparatory School

13 The Chine, Grange Park, London N21 2EA
Tel: 020 8360 1469
email: office@gpps.org.uk
website: www.gpps.org.uk
X/Twitter: @gpprepschool
Facebook: @grangeparkprep
Instagram: @grangeparkprepschool

Day School for Boys and Girls from 3–11.

Chair of Governors: Mr Amit Metha

***Head*: Mrs Flavia Rizzo**, BSc, PGCE, MA

Age Range. 3–11.

Number of Children. 144.

Fees per term (2023–2024). Reception to Year 6: £3,951.15.

Grange Park Preparatory School is a long established, happy and successful school that provides a broad and stimulating education. It is situated in the pleasant residential area of Grange Park.

We remain committed to educating boys and girls in a small school with small class sizes, thus allowing every child to be known as an individual. The children enjoy a broad curriculum taught by experienced staff who encourage excellence in all areas of school life.

We have a Nursery class for boys and girls aged 3 and 4. Nursery staff and children have access to the excellent resources available at GPPS, including outside space, the gym and a cooked lunch for those children staying the whole day. The children follow the Early Years Curriculum with additional specialist teaching in French, Dance, Drama and Music.

In KS1 the children are taught mostly by form teachers with specialist teaching being introduced gradually in KS2. From Reception specialist teachers teach PE and Games, French, Music, Dance and Drama. Individual music tuition is also available from Reception.

In Key Stage 2 preparation for 11+ state selective and independent secondary schools starts from as early as Year 3, where children undertake verbal and non-verbal reasoning as part of the curriculum. In addition, from the spring term in Year 4, children wishing to sit for selective schools attend extra prep classes, thus equipping them with the tools to achieve their maximum potential in terms of academic attainment. Every year we are proud to announce that our Year 6 children do extremely well in the secondary school entrance exams, with some being awarded scholarships.

Children enjoy a very busy school life and benefit from an excellent variety of extra-curricular activities, including LAMDA, Judo, football, tennis, gymnastics, cookery and chess to name a few, further enriching their experience and creating lifetime memories.

The school has a healthy eating policy. Lunches are cooked in school using only fresh ingredients; no processed food is used. There is always a vegetarian and vegan option and salads and fresh fruit are available daily.

Places for Reception are offered after the Headteacher has met with parents and their child. Children taking up chance vacancies in other classes will be invited to spend a day in school to ensure they will fit into the class successfully.

Before leaving GPPS every child will have been given a responsible role at some level, instilling in them a sense of duty and ingrained confidence, preparing them for today's challenges.

Grange Park Preparatory School is a part of The Inspired Learning Group, company number 11458444,

The Granville School

2 Bradbourne Park Road, Sevenoaks, Kent TN13 3LJ
Tel: 01732 453039
email: secretary@granvilleschool.org
website: www.granvilleschool.org
X/Twitter: @granville_prep
Facebook: @TheGranvilleSchool

Chairman of Governors: Mrs N Coll

***Headmistress*: Mrs Louise Lawrance**, BPrimEd Hons

Age Range. Girls 3–11, Boys 3–5.

Number of Pupils. 200.

Fees per term (2023–2024). Pre-School: £3,013 (mornings only) or £4,125 (all day). Reception, Years 1 & 2: £4,850; Years 3, 4, 5 & 6: £6,185. Lunch included.

Breakfast Club (7.30am until the start of school day): £7.50 per session, After School Care: £8.50 per session until 5.00pm, £16.50 per session until 6.00pm.

Extras: Private Lessons: Singing, Pianoforte, Violin, Cello, Oboe, Clarinet, Flute, Recorder, Brass: £242 per term. LAMDA Individual Lessons: £175 per term; Shared Lessons: £130/£95. Ballet: £88 per term.

The Granville School was founded on VE Day, 8th May 1945, with the Dove of Peace and Churchill's victory sign chosen to form the school crest.

The Granville is an exceptional school which combines the very best of a Prep school tradition with a vibrant, forward-looking outlook where change is embraced and innovation celebrated. Girls aged three to eleven, and boys aged three to four, thrive on individual attention and achieve their best in a happy, secure and stimulating environment. Our highly-qualified, specialist teachers make learning enjoyable, develop inquiring minds and raise levels of expectation.

The school maintains Christian principles and traditional values within a broad and stimulating curriculum. The Granville has a strong record of academic achievement and children are prepared for 11+ entry into independent schools and state grammar schools. Granville pupils excel in music, art, drama and sport. There is a wide range of extra-curricular activities available for all age groups.

The school is set in five acres of garden and woodland close to Sevenoaks Station. The original house and new buildings enable pupils to enjoy a high-quality learning environment with light and airy classrooms. The Granville has its own indoor heated Swimming Pool, a Sports Hall, Science Lab, Studio for Music and Drama, French room, ICT Suite, individual teaching rooms and Junior and Senior Libraries. A new building, opened in January 2014, provides high-quality Early Years facilities together with a large Art and DT room. Outside facilities include three netball/tennis courts, sports/playing field, junior activity playgrounds and a woodland classroom. Plans are under way to further develop the Hall, Computing Suite and Performing Arts Studio.

Means-tested bursaries are available on request.

Charitable status. The Ena Makin Educational Trust Limited is a Registered Charity, number 307931. Its aim is to run any school as an educational charity for the promotion of education generally.

Great Walstead School

East Mascalls Lane, Lindfield, Haywards Heath, West Sussex RH16 2QL

Tel: 01444 483528
email: GWmail@greatwalstead.co.uk
website: www.greatwalstead.co.uk
X/Twitter: @greatwalstead
Facebook: @GreatWalstead

Chairman of the Board of Governors: P Thurston

***Headmaster*: C B Calvey**, BEd Hons

Deputy Head: W Fuller, BSc Hons, PGCE

Deputy Head Academic: E Scotland, BMus Hons, PGCE, NPQSL

Age Range. 2½–13.

Number of Pupils. 309: Main School 209; Pre-Prep 50; Pre-School & Reception (EYFS) 50.

Fees per term (2023–2024). Tuition: Pre-School £695 (per day); Reception £3,315; Pre-Prep £3,860–£4,475; Main School £5,705–£6,325.

Founded in 1925 by Mr R J Mowll in Enfield, the school moved to its present location in the heart of Sussex two years later. Staff and pupils came to a large country house set in over 260 acres of fields and woodland, where children could learn and play in unspoiled surroundings.

From these beginnings, Great Walstead has developed into a thriving co-educational prep school, catering for children from 2½ to 13 years of age. It is a school which values children as individuals and regards it as vital that each child develops his or her potential – academically, creatively, socially and spiritually. Above all, the school is built on the strong values of Christian Faith, Success, Communication, Environment and Dedication, creating an essential foundation for the whole of a pupil's education and life.

The Early Years Foundation Stage incorporates Pre-School and Reception classes, welcoming children from the age of 2½ until it is time to enter the Pre-Prep at 5. It provides a full, rich and varied Early Years education, laying firm foundations in basic skills and understanding for future learning. They share a dedicated outdoor learning and play space with a giant covered sandpit, mud kitchen and music area.

The Pre-Prep covers the ages from 5 to 7 within its own section of the school. It has its own library, ICT suite and play area. The aim here is to ensure that the foundation skills of reading, writing and maths are taught while, at the same time, teachers add a breadth of interest through specialist lead classes in French, computer skills, PE and Music.

Children enter the Junior School at 7. For the next two years they will have a class teacher who supervises them closely for a good proportion of the day, but have specialist teachers for French, Music, ICT, Art, Craft, Design & Technology, Sport and PE. They have games or outdoor activities each day and gradually learn to become more independent.

Children in the senior age group, from 9 to 13 years of age, are taught by graduate specialist teachers in preparation for the Common Entrance examination and senior school scholarships at 13. In the past ten years, Great Walstead pupils have won over 200 scholarships or awards to senior schools and in the last four years over 50% of pupils gained such success. Facilities in the Senior School include two computer rooms with 21 linked PCs, a well-equipped science laboratory, and a fine Library.

The 269 acres of farmland, playing fields, and woodland make many outdoor activities possible. The woods host learning activities in Eco-School and Forest School and fun exercises in camp-building, as well as teddy bear picnics for the younger children. In the summer, the older children camp out overnight. In addition, the purpose-built challenge course gives enormous pleasure all year round for all ages.

The Art department is housed in the Cedar building. The Great Walstead Secret Garden is a wonderful addition to the curriculum, providing a fantastic walled garden space for academic and creative exploration using all of the senses.

The school's extensive grounds allow a wide range of major sports. Swimming is possible all year round in our own heated pool. We have a superbly equipped sports hall and facilities including a wonderful new AstroTurf. Match Day on Wednesdays for Years 5–8 and Thursdays for Juniors are weekly events with emphasis on sportsmanship, healthy competition and sport for all. All children (Years 3–8) have the opportunity to be involved in competitive sport at least once per season.

The school has a Learning Enhancement department where specialist staff are able to give the extra support required. The department helps children with all their learning needs whether helping with a specific difficulty or extending those children who are gifted and talented.

Music has long been a strength at Great Walstead, with a high proportion of the children learning instruments and playing in groups, bands and orchestras. Singing is encouraged from Pre-School upwards. Drama is also an important part of the Arts here. All children are given the opportunity to act, with both major productions and form performances.

Matron, the school nurse, tends to the health of the children in the whole school. The school, through the Keep and Wrap Around Care, provides flexible holiday, pre- and after-school care, as well as other holiday activities to meet the needs of today's parents.

Parents are always made most welcome at the school. There is a thriving parents' organisation called FOGWA (Friends of Great Walstead Association) which provides a number of successful social events and raises substantial sums for the benefit of the school.

Academic, Music and Sports Awards are offered at 9+, and Academic, All-Rounder, Art, Drama, Music, Performing Arts and Sport Scholarships at 11+.

Charitable status. Great Walstead School is a Registered Charity, number 307002. It exists to provide a good education on Christian foundations.

Greenfield School

Old Woking Road, Woking, Surrey GU22 8HY

Tel: 01483 772525
email: admissions@greenfield.surrey.sch.uk
website: www.greenfield.surrey.sch.uk
Facebook: @greenfieldwoking
Instagram: @greenfieldwoking
LinkedIn: /greenfieldwoking

TES Prep School of the Year 2022

Chair of Governors: Mrs Janet Day

***Headmistress*: Mrs Tania Botting**, BEd, MEd

Deputy Head: Mr David Brown, BSc Hons, GTP, MEd

Age range. 6 months to 11 years.

Number of pupils. Nursery (0–3): 40, Main School (4–11): 314.

Fees per term (2023–2024). Reception–Year 6: £4,598–£5,400.

Greenfield School is an academically non-selective, co-educational school and nursery for children aged from 6 months to 11 years. We aim to offer every possible opportunity for children to reach their full potential and recognise that all children have talents and strengths in many different areas. We are proud of our academic and non-academic successes and have a strong track record of achieving scholarships to a wide range of senior schools for music, art, sport, drama and academic excellence.

In 2022, Greenfield School was awarded the *TES Prep School of the Year* title. This national recognition places Greenfield amongst the top schools in the country and shines a light on the school's contemporary approach to education.

With just two forms per year group, Greenfield is able to offer 'big school' facilities and functionality alongside 'small school' ethos and pastoral care. This magic combination helps us to attract superb staff and create enviably small teaching groups, whilst also allowing the children the freedom to learn and experience new things with greater independence.

Occupying an impressive purpose-built building on a green and leafy site close to Woking town centre, Greenfield strikes the perfect balance between modern-day facilities and the great British countryside. The school has its own sports hall, drama & dance studio, music recital space, soundproof practice rooms, multimedia suite, breakout spaces, art studio, design & technology room, science lab, stage, gymnasium, and numerous bright, airy classrooms. Outside, two netball courts and two Forest Schools complement the large playing fields and playground areas.

Charitable status. Greenfield School is a Registered Charity, number 295145. It aims to offer an excellent all-round education to children of all abilities.

Grimsdell
Mill Hill Pre-Preparatory School

Winterstoke House, Wills Grove, Mill Hill, London NW7 1QR

Tel: 020 8959 6884
email: office@grimsdell.org.uk
website: www.millhill.org.uk/grimsdell
X/Twitter: @millhillpreprep
Facebook: @millhillpreprep
Instagram: @millhillpreprep

Awarded 'Excellent' in quality of education in academic achievement and personal development – ISI Inspection January 2020.

Chairman of Court of Governors: Mr Elliot Lipton, BSc Hons, MBA, FRSA, FRICS

***Head*: Mrs Kate Simon**, BA Hons, PGCE

Deputy Head: Mrs Jenny Ticehurst, BEd Hons

Assistant Head Teaching & Learning: Miss Yuka Matsushita, BA Hons, QTS
Assistant Head Early Years: Mrs Hannah Holwerda, BA Hons
Assistant Head Pastoral/SENCO: Ms K Vanstone, BEd, MEdPsyc, PG Cert SpLD, ATS SENCO

Age range. 3–7 Co-educational.

Number of pupils. 105 Boys, 109 Girls.

Fees per term (2023–2024). Reception–Year 2: £6,300, Nursery: £5,400.

Grimsdell, Mill Hill Pre-Prep, is situated in the Green Belt on the boarders of Hertfordshire and Middlesex and just ten miles from Central London. A part of The Mill Hill School Foundation which is set in 160 acres of beautiful grounds, we make extensive use of the outdoors in all subject areas and Forest School has a firm place within our curriculum. We provide a happy, secure and rich learning environment for boys and girls aged 3 to 7. Belmont, Mill Hill Preparatory School, is less than a quarter of a mile away and educates pupils from age 7 to 13, the majority of whom move on to the senior school – Mill Hill, which educates boys and girls from age 13 to 18.

We pride ourselves on the delivery of our creative curriculum which seeks to embed dynamic experiences into the children's learning. Grimsdell children are inspired to learn while being encouraged to explore and enjoy their childhood. Our pupils learn through hands-on experience with the support and guidance of professional and caring staff aided by excellent resources and equipment. Our approach combines traditional skills of reading, writing and mathematics with the breadth and balance offered by an enhanced Early Years Foundation Stage and KS1 Curriculum. Every pupil will benefit from the many opportunities offered at Grimsdell including lessons from specialist teachers in Science, Technology, French, Drama, Music, PE and Forest School. Our Nursery children enjoy a hybrid learning environment, spending half their day in the traditional classroom environment – with access to the outdoor early years play area – and half their day in our dedicated Forest School, complete with outdoor classroom.

The school is housed in a large Victorian building with its own secure play areas and adventure playgrounds, taking advantage of further facilities on the Mill Hill site including a Forest School area, sports fields, swimming pool and theatre.

We have two main entry points at 3 years old (Nursery) and 4 years old (Reception), with occasional vacancies occurring in Years 1 and 2. It is expected that most children will pass to Belmont at the end of Year 2.

Charitable status. The Mill Hill School Foundation is a Registered Charity, number 1064758. It exists to provide education for boys and girls.

Guildford High School – Junior School

United Learning

London Road, Guildford, Surrey GU1 1SJ

Tel: 01483 561440
email: admissions@guildfordhigh.co.uk
website: www.guildfordhigh.co.uk
X/Twitter: @guildfordhigh
Facebook: @GuildfordHigh
Instagram: @GuildfordHigh

Chair of Local Governing Body: Ms Kate Richards

***Head of Junior School*: Mr Allistair Williamson,** BPhEd Auckland

Deputy Head of Junior School: Mrs Kathryn L Hughes, BSc Hons London

Age Range. Girls 4–11.

Number of Pupils. 300.

Fees per term (2023–2024). Reception–Year 1: £4,622. Year 2: £5,268. Years 3–6: £5,913.

Awarded *'Independent Preparatory School of the Decade 2022'* by *The Sunday Times, 'The Best Prep School for Academic Results'* in The Week magazine 2023 and '*Best School for Pastoral Care*' in The Week magazine 2018, the Junior School at Guildford High School is situated on the same site as the Senior School. It is a modern, bright, self-contained school with the third floor especially dedicated to Art, Music, Science, IT and the Library.

The girls normally start in the Reception classes (4 years) or at Year 3 (7 years), however, they are welcome in any year group depending on spaces available, and work their way through the Junior School with natural progression on to the Senior School at Year 7 (11 years).

The breadth and depth of the curriculum encompasses 15 fast paced subjects, with an embedded thinking skills programme. Three modern foreign languages are included, with Spanish starting in Year 1 for five year olds. Music, Drama and Sport play an important part in the curricular and co-curricular programmes. Specialist teachers and resources are employed throughout the Junior School. Parents and teachers work closely together to ensure excellent differentiation and a nurturing environment with strong pastoral care.

Guildford High School Junior School girls are confident, happy and well-prepared for entry to the Senior School. (*See Guildford High School Senior School entry in HMC section.*)

Charitable status. Guildford High School Junior School is part of United Learning which comprises: UCST (a Company Limited by Guarantee, Registered in England, number 2780748, and a Registered Charity, number 1016538) and ULT (a Company Limited by Guarantee, Registered in England, number 4439859, and an Exempt Charity).

Haberdashers' Boys' Prep & Pre-Prep School

Butterfly Lane, Elstree, Hertfordshire WD6 3AF
Tel: 020 8266 1779
email: prepoffice@habsboys.org.uk
website: www.habsboys.org.uk
X/Twitter: @habsboys
Facebook: @habsboys

Chair of the Board of Governors: Mr S Cartmell, OBE

Headmaster: Mr R D Sykes

***Head of Prep School*: Ms K Umpleby**

Deputy Head (Pastoral): Mr P Swindell
Deputy Head (Academic): Mrs M Best

Head of Pre-Prep School: Ms V Huggett

Age range. Prep 4–11.

Number of boys. Prep 223, Pre-Prep 120.

Fees per term (2023–2024). Pre-Prep: £6,348 (including lunch); Prep: £7,747.

The Preparatory School at Habs has been the top-performing independent boys' school in the country. It is vibrant with the energy and curiosity of over 300 boys aged 4–11 from a wide range of local schools and communities. It is a very special place to work and play.

It is housed in a purpose-designed building, opened by HRH The Princess Margaret, Citizen and Haberdasher, in 1983, on the same campus as the Senior School. The bright, cheerful classrooms provide a welcoming and stimulating environment. The Prep enjoys a unique mix of family atmosphere and close links with the Senior School. The boys are able to share the wonderful facilities and grounds of the Senior School, including the Sports Centre, the heated indoor Swimming Pool, the Music School and the Dining Room. The brand new Pre-Prep building opened in January 2023, housing students from Reception–Year 2.

The relationship between the Preparatory staff and their forms is close and friendly, within a context of firm discipline. In this environment, brimming with opportunities, the school ensures an education of breadth and depth extending well beyond national guidelines.

Sport and games play a major role in the boys' week, offering fitness and fun to all. Indeed, the sporting ethos of team spirit and fair play underpins the whole structure of Prep School life.

The arts spring to life in a wealth of musical, dramatic and artistic activity, guided by specialists whose passion for their subject is matched by the enthusiasm of their pupils.

Every boy is a musician for at least one year when he studies an orchestral instrument of his choice, free of charge, through the Music Scheme; many of these fledgling musicians eventually make their way into the Senior School's First Orchestra.

There are many clubs and societies; however, boys with some special interest often start their own, supported by staff, and eagerly attended by those of like mind. Some boys also stay on to enjoy extra play time with their friends or to do their homework and to have tea. The After-school Care Facility is equipped with bean bags, games and sports equipment.

Boys are admitted each September after assessments to the Pre-Prep at the age of 5+ and to the Prep at 7+. Boys are expected to move into the Senior School at 11. Most boys will flourish in the Senior School as they have in the Prep, and the transition is made as natural as possible. A qualifying examination assures candidates that the Senior School is right for them and they are given help preparing for the different pace and rhythms they will find there. (*For further details, please see entry in HMC section.*)

Charitable status. The Haberdashers' Aske's Charity is a Registered Charity, number 313996. It exists to promote education.

Hall Grove

London Road, Bagshot, Surrey GU19 5HZ
Tel: 01276 473059
email: office@hallgrove.co.uk
website: www.hallgrove.co.uk
X/Twitter: @hallgroveschool
Facebook: @hallgroveschool
Instagram: @hallgroveschool

Principal: Alastair R Graham, BSc, PGCE

***Headmaster*: Neil Tomlin**, OBE, BA, MA

Age Range. 3–13.

Number of Children. Pre-Preparatory (age 4–7) 110; Preparatory (age 7–13) 300.

Fees per term (2023–2024). Day fees: Pre-School £2,350 (mornings)–£4,200 (full days); Reception £4,200; Years 1 & 2 £4,350; Lower Juniors (Years 3 & 4) £5,200; Years 5 to 8 £5,650. Weekly boarding: £1,485 supplement per term. Pre-paid flexi-boarding: £45 per night. Sibling discount.

Hall Grove is a happy, vibrant school of over 400 boys and girls aged 3–13 with a separate pre-school in its grounds for those aged 3 and 4. Weekly/Flexi boarding is offered for up to 12 pupils. The main entry ages are 3, 4, 7 and 11.

The school was founded in 1957 by the Graham Family, Alastair Graham is Principal of the school. At its centre is a most attractive Georgian house set in beautiful gardens and parkland. Recent additions have provided some modern rooms and specialist teaching areas, an impressive computer facility and new classroom blocks. Despite this building programme, the character and atmosphere of a family home has been retained.

The academic standards are high and there is a very strong emphasis on Sport and Music. A wide range of activities flourish; woodwork, ceramics, food technology, drama and a host of major and minor sports including soccer, rugby, hockey, netball, rounders, cricket, tennis, athletics, swimming, golf, judo, basketball, badminton and dance. Riding and stable management is an added attraction.

Under the leadership of new boarding parents, Hall Grove completely refurbished their boarding facilities in time for the start of the new school year in September 2022. The "Hall Grove Boarding World" consists of 20 beds, 10 for boys and 10 for girls, in six themed rooms. Each room is decorated to reflect a continent and boarders enjoy the modern, airy environment at the top of the main school house. They also enjoy the freedom to explore the extensive grounds and use the facilities including the swimming pool, riding stables, forest school, performing and visual art blocks, and the sports fields.

Boarding nights take place for year groups from Year 4 upwards. Regular boarders enjoy in-house events as well as local visits and excursions. The boarding house has been designed to cater for weekly boarders and flexi boarders, booked in for one to four nights a week. Some parents and children like to use the boarding facilities to prepare them for their year group visits to the School's off-site house in Devon, Battisborough House. Boarding is also useful preparation for children heading away to their Senior Schools where boarding may be an option,

Hall Grove has its own residential field study centre situated on the South Devon coast called Battisborough House and there are many field trips and expeditions both in Devon and overseas. Battisborough is available for hire by other schools and can accommodate up to 60 in comfort.

Halstead St Andrew's School

Nursery to Year 2:
Woodham Rise, Horsell, Woking, Surrey GU21 4EE
Tel: 01483 760943
Year 3 and above:
Church Hill House, Wilson Way, Horsell, Woking, Surrey GU21 4QW
Tel: 01483 760943
email: admissions@hsaschool.co.uk
website: www.hsaschool.co.uk
X/Twitter: @hsa_school
Facebook: @halsteadstandrews
Instagram: @halsteadstandrews

Chair: Mr Simon Brookhouse

***Head*: Mr Fitzgerald**, BEd Hons NPQH

Deputy Heads: Mr Jonathan Spooner, MA Hons and Miss Melanie Eaton, BA Hons

Age Range. 2–13, Co-educational.

Fees per term (2023–2024). Prep £5,420–£6,135. Pre-Prep £1,425–£4,580.

Halstead St Andrew's School is a partnership between Halstead Preparatory School for Girls and St. Andrew's School, Woking. Opened in September 2023, we are a co-ed school, with the aim to educate around 500 pupils aged 2–16 across our two sites in Woking.

Halstead and St. Andrew's School are both long-established schools; proud of the fact that between us we can claim nearly 200 years of experience in educating prep school children.

Our vision is to build on the success of both schools, to develop the best we both offer and to create a dynamic and exciting new school that prepares pupils for an ever-changing world.

The partnership provides more opportunities and greater career enhancement for our staff. This in turn enables us to develop the already outstanding educational provision we offer and preserve the well-known, well-loved family atmosphere that both schools provide.

Our Nursery and Pre-Prep are based at our Woodham Rise site: a stimulating and age-appropriate environment for our youngest pupils, which creates a happy and secure learning environment. There are expert, class-based and specialist teachers to inspire and nurture our pupils.

From Year 3, pupils move to Church Hill House. Here they enjoy continuing outstanding teaching and facilities including a swimming pool, astroturf pitch, state-of-the-art theatre and extensive playing fields. From 2026 pupils will have the opportunity to stay with us through to GCSE.

Having two dedicated sites allows us to maintain a small and nurturing school atmosphere in each, while the resources and security that are part of a larger school ensures that the teaching and learning environment is entirely appropriate for the different age groups.

One of the defining features of Halstead St Andrew's is freedom of choice. Whilst we hope that pupils will progress from our Prep School to our Senior School, we will continue to prepare pupils opting for other senior schools at both 11+ and 13+. We will also continue to support parents in finding the next stage school that is best suited to their child's individual needs. This flow of incoming pupils at key transition points creates a stimulating and energised educational environment.

We support all our pupils in taking their place in the community and wider world, demonstrating civic duty and interpersonal skills alongside the ability to think creatively. In an ever-changing world, we believe the environment we create fosters adaptability and reflects society today.

At Halstead St Andrew's, a successful education goes beyond academic studies. We are confident that pupils will leave us as well-rounded, determined young adults who are prepared for the future.

Charitable status. Halstead St Andrew's School Trust is a Registered Charity, number 297580, established to promote and provide for the advancement of education of children.

Hampton Pre-Prep & Prep School

Gloucester Road, Hampton, Middlesex TW12 2UQ
Tel: 020 8979 1844
email: admissions@hamptonprep.org.uk
website: hamptonprep.org.uk
X/Twitter: @Hampton_Prep

Chairman of Governors: A H Munday, LLB QC

***Headmaster*: Mr Tim Smith**, BA, NZ Dip Tchg, MBA

Age Range. Boys 3–11, Girls 3–7.

Number of Pupils. 229.

Fees per term (2023–2024). Kindergarten (3–4 years): £2,493 (mornings), £4,616 (all day). Pre-Prep (4–7 years): £5,265. Prep (7–11 years): £5,775. All fees include lunch for full day pupils.

The School is situated in a quiet, leafy part of Hampton and is easily accessible by road and rail. After a merger with Hampton School in 1999, Hampton Pre-Prep & Prep is part of the Hampton School Trust. Both schools are served by the same Board of Governors and the Headmaster of Hampton Pre-Prep & Prep reports to the Headmaster of Hampton School. The amalgamation produces economies of scale from which Hampton Pre-Prep & Prep benefits. Boys transfer to senior schools at 11+.

Approximately 75% of Prep pupils transfer to Hampton School each year. Since September 2004, Hampton has been offering Assured Places for 11+ entry. These can be gained from Year 2 through to the end of Year 5 via an ongoing programme of assessment of the boys. In addition, those boys who perform very well in the 11+ Hampton entrance examinations, but who do not gain an award from Hampton, will be considered for the W D James Award made by Hampton Prep, which will be in the form of a reduction in the child's first term's fees at Hampton.

The Pre-Prep accepts boys and girls from 3 years to 7 years and is situated a five-minute walk from the Prep building in an attractive period property which is homely and inviting. The children enjoy playing in a well-equipped playground and in the spacious, lawned garden. There is one class per year group of 22 pupils.

The Prep School is two-form entry with approximately 18 pupils per class and backs onto an attractive local park. The Prep has undergone significant redevelopment including the construction of a state-of-the-art building in March 2016. The new facilities have played a large part in the transformation of the School, its academic life included. The School's curriculum has a number of distinct elements including its own bespoke philosophy schemes of work, engineering instead of DT, computing instead of ICT, all of which sit alongside timetabled mindfulness and dance lessons for the boys in the Prep. Major school sports are Football, Rugby and Cricket. An extensive programme of co-curricular activities includes: art club, chess, drama, music technology, computing, Lego and a variety of minor sports. There is a School choir, an orchestra, and a flourishing tradition of drama. Individual music tuition and LAMDA lessons are also available.

There is a thriving Parents' Association and families share in the life of the School as fully as possible.

Charitable status. Hampton Pre-Prep & Prep School is part of the Hampton School Trust, which is a Registered Charity, number 1120005. It exists to provide a school in Hampton.

Hanford School

Child Okeford, Blandford Forum, Dorset DT11 8HN

Tel: 01258 860219
email: office@hanfordschool.co.uk
website: www.hanfordschool.co.uk
Facebook: @HanfordSchool
Instagram: @hanfordschool

Chairman of Governors: Mrs Louise Hall

***Head*: Hilary Phillips**

Age Range. 7–13.
Number of Girls. 100.

Fees per term (2023–2024). Boarders £8,480, Day Girls £6,500.

Hanford School, located between Blandford and Shaftesbury in Dorset, was founded in 1947 by the Revd and Mrs C B Canning. It is housed in a beautiful 17th Century Jacobean manor house set in 45 acres of land in the Stour valley. The amenities include a Chapel, Laboratories, a Computer Room, a Music School, an Art School, a Gymnasium, a Swimming Pool, a Handwork Room, two Netball/Tennis Courts (hard) and an indoor covered Riding School.

Girls arrive from the age of seven onwards and leave at 13 after taking Common Entrance. Hanford is non-selective and prides itself on bringing out the best in each and every girl. Pupils are prepared for entry to Independent Senior Schools including: Marlborough, Bryanston, St Mary's Shaftesbury and Sherborne Girls.

Hanford believes children should be children for as long as possible, climbing trees, building dens, riding ponies and playing in the garden. Giving girls free time is something Hanford has always believed in as it encourages girls to become lost in their own imagination and develop creatively. Hanford took the decision to switch off all 'Smart devices', iPhones, tablets etc. during term time. Unplugging the girls from social media, games and communications was not done to protect them but to encourage them to make their own fun; they will have plenty of time to use social media but a relatively short time in which to be silly, fun-loving children. The girls use their free time to play games such as British Bulldog, riding the Hanford ponies, tending the chickens, gardening or climbing trees.

Hanford teaches girls to combine having fun with working hard. A strong and committed teaching staff seeks to bring out the best in each and every girl. This combination of fun and hard work pays dividends when it comes to Common Entrance and Scholarships. Evidenced in year on year Scholarships for the past 27 years: academic, art, drama, sport and all-round. Class sizes are small, normally 10–12, and there is learning support available if required. Alongside the core curriculum girls are taught handwork, where they make their own school uniform skirt, and Art Appreciation (Art Apre) where they can begin to understand and appreciate the cultural world around them. Music has always been central to life at Hanford with almost all girls learning at least one instrument or joining one of the choirs or folk group; music composition is also offered as an activity.

Sport is also strong at Hanford. The rounders, tennis and athletics teams have all been county champions. Hanford is perhaps most famous for its ponies and stables with most girls choosing to have riding lessons and some testing their equestrian skills at local and national events including tetrathlons.

Harrogate Ladies' College

Clarence Drive, Harrogate, North Yorkshire HG1 2QG

Tel: 01423 537045
email: admissions@hlc.org.uk
website: www.hlc.org.uk
X/Twitter: @HLCNews
Facebook: @HarrogateLadiesCollege
Instagram: @harrogateladiescollege
LinkedIn: /harrogate-ladies'-college

See full entry in the **GSA** section, on **p. 437**.

Hazelwood School

Wolfs Hill, Limpsfield, Oxted, Surrey RH8 0QU

Tel: 01883 712194
email: schoolsec@hazelwoodschool.com
website: www.hazelwoodschool.co.uk
X/Twitter: @hazelwoodoxted
Facebook: @HazelwoodSchoolOxted
Instagram: @hazelwoodschooloxte

Chair of Governors: Mr Roger Heaton
***Head*: Mrs Lindie Louw**

Head of Senior School Transition: Mr Will Fagg
Assistant Head: Mr Howard Garlick
Director of Finance: Mr Mark Hugall
Director of Teaching and Learning: Mrs Charlotte MacDougall
Head of Innovation: Ms Nichola Trojanowski
Head of Operations: Mrs Melanie Mercer
Head of Organisation: Mrs Clare Hargrave
Director of Marketing and Admissions: Mrs Kate Whitehead

Age range. 9 months–13 years Co-educational.
Number of pupils. 583.
Fees per term (2023–2024). Day Pupils from £3,800 (Reception) to £6,055 (Year 8).

Founded in 1890, Hazelwood stands in 20+ acres of superb grounds, commanding a magnificent view over the Kent and Sussex Weald.

Pupils enter at age 4 into the Pre-Prep or at 7+ to the Prep School, joining those pupils transferring from the Pre-Prep to the Prep School. Entry at other ages is possible if space permits. Hazelwood School's Nursery and Early Years, open all year round for children from 9 months to 4 years, opened in September 2009 on the Laverock site which offers unrivalled accommodation and facilities.

A gradual transition is made towards subject specialist tuition in the middle and upper forms. Pupils are prepared for the Common Entrance examinations at 11+ and 13+, and also for Scholarships to Senior Schools. Over 200 academic, all-rounder, sporting, music and art awards have been gained since 1995. The school has a balanced curriculum with Forest Schools and Philosophy for Children sitting alongside the more traditional subjects of Maths, English, Science and Modern Languages. In the Upper Years, children also learn Graphics and Design and Technology.

Extracurricular activity is an important part of every pupil's education. Excellent sports facilities, which include games fields, heated indoor swimming pool, gymnasium, many games pitches, tennis courts and a brand new all-weather astro pitch (completed in the Summer of 2022) – all of which allow preparation of school teams at various age and ability levels in a wide range of sports. Our aim is that every pupil has an opportunity to represent the School. In September 2016 the Baily Building was opened containing 14 classrooms, a Recital Room, a Food Tech Kitchen, a Lower School Art Room and a 450-seat auditorium, The Bawtree Hall.

Art, Technology, Music and Drama are also strengths of the school. Our Centenary Theatre incorporates a 200-seat theatre, music school and Chapel. All our pupils are encouraged to play an instrument and join one of the music groups catering for all interests and abilities. Further extracurricular activities include tap, ballet and jazz dance, judo, art, gymnastics, scuba, debating, fantasy football, Forest Skills, computing, Lego modelling and chess.

For children in Years 7 and 8, our outstanding 2-year foundation programme helping prepare children for transition into Senior School education, also includes an Electives programme which enables children to choose between a range of subjects from stockbroking, forensic science, home economics, Mandarin, fashion and more.

Our pupils develop a curiosity about the world in which they live and a real passion for learning. Most importantly of all they become confident learners, mature and articulate individuals who love coming to school each day. The school's Community Fund was set up to benefit from pupil and parent fundraising. Each year, grants totalling £8,000 are awarded to community organisations with an educational bias.

Charitable status. Hazelwood School Limited is a Registered Charity, number 312081. It exists to provide excellent preparatory school education for girls and boys in Oxted, Surrey.

Hazlegrove Prep School

Sparkford, Yeovil, Somerset BA22 7JA

Tel: 01963 442606
email: admissions@hazlegrove.co.uk
website: www.hazlegrove.co.uk
X/Twitter: @HazlegrovePrep
Facebook: @HazlegrovePrep

Senior Warden: Stephen Edlmann, MA

***Headmaster*: Edward Benbow**, BA, MEd, PGCE

Deputy Headmaster: Matthew Bartlett, BSc Hons, PGCE

Head of Pre-Preparatory Department: Hannah Strugnell, BSc Hons, PGCE

Age Range. 2–13.

Number of Pupils. 385 boys and girls of whom 100 are boarders. Preparatory (7–13 year olds) 290 pupils; Pre-Preparatory 95 (2–7 year olds) pupils.

Fees per term (2023–2024). Preparatory: Boarders £8,051–£10,272 (fees are inclusive, with few compulsory extras); Day pupils £5,442–£6,940. Pre-Preparatory: £3,423. Nursery: Morning session £34, Afternoon session £22.50, Lunch £9.95.

Scholarships and Bursaries. Armed Forces Bursaries are available to serving members.

Hazlegrove is an exceptional coeducational full boarding and day school for children between 2–13, the school enables children to be children and is committed to celebrating childhood. A vibrant and creative curriculum, exceptional pastoral care and stunning rural Somerset location combine to make children feel nurtured, motivated, inspired and encouraged to love learning for life. The school was judged "Excellent" in all areas of assessment in its last ISI Inspection.

Every child is unique, the breadth and depth of the learning experience at Hazlegrove ensures that all of the pupils have the opportunity to discover their strengths and interests, The children are grounded in their approach to the world, inclusive in the warmth that they show to others and happy in the knowledge that they are growing up in an environment which supports a broad range of interests. When a pupil moves on from the school, as a Hazlegrovian in the 21st century, they are a child who is empathetic, kind and connected to the world; one who is independent but knows that developing relationships and a sense of duty to the community are integral to a successful life.

Sitting in 200 acres of glorious Somerset parkland, with exceptional facilities and opportunities for the children, Hazlegrove ticks all of the boxes. Hazlegrove Pre-Prep provides children with a wonderful start to school life ensuring that children have a positive first experience of education, building a foundation for a life-long love of learning. The Pre-Prep is run by caring, creative and experienced staff who know exactly how to bring out the best in each pupil, and, most importantly, make learning fun! As part of the Hazlegrove school, the Pre-Prep children have access to an amazing array of resources including a 25m indoor swimming pool, theatre, dance studio and sports pitches.

Alongside the superb facilities there is a dedicated and passionate team of teachers who help the children achieve across the board. Both past and present pupils have gained Great Britain selection in a wide range of sports – hockey, riding, rowing, laser run, triathle, biathle, cricket and pentathlon. The Music Department is thriving offering a wealth of opportunity both in and out of the classroom. Children are introduced to a wide variety of musical styles and cultures through creative classroom and instrumental teaching, from traditional classical and jazz to rock, pop, rap and dance music.

What makes the school unique is the fact that the facilities and settings are enjoyed by a minimum of 60 boarders every weekend, with 100+ boarders, including 20–30 flexi boarders. The popularity of the boarding and the enthusiasm that all of the pupils' display comes down to the calibre and dedication of the people who deliver the education and care to the children.

The school has excellent links with a broad range of senior schools, about 60% of Year 8 go to major senior schools such as Bryanston, Eton, Sherborne, Sherborne Girls, Millfield, King's College Taunton, Radley, Marlborough and Winchester, while around 40% move through to the senior school, King's School Bruton. Between 25 and 30 scholarships and awards are gained by pupils each year.

Charitable status. King's School, Bruton is a Registered Charity, number 1071997. It exists to provide education for children.

Headington Rye Oxford Prep School

26 London Road, Headington, Oxford, Oxfordshire OX3 7PB

Tel:	01865 759400 Admissions 01865 759116
email:	prepadmissions@headington.org
website:	www.headington.org
X/Twitter:	@HeadingtonPrep
Facebook:	@HeadingtonSchool

Chair of Board of Governors: Mrs Carol Oster Warriner, MA Oxon

***Head of Prep*: Mrs Jane Crouch**, BA Keele, MA London, NPQH

Deputy Head (*Teaching and Learning*): Miss Caroline Crookes, BA Ed Exeter, MA Edgehill, NPQSL

Deputy Head (*Pastoral Care*): Mrs Tessa Davey, BA Cape Town

Deputy Head – Operations: Mrs Edwina West, BEd West of England

Head of Early Years: Miss Ruth Sibly, BSc Bristol

Head of Key Stage 1: Mrs Joanna Haynes, BEd Cantab

Age Range. Girls and Boys 3–11.

Number of Pupils. 262.

Fees per term (2023–2024). Day: £3,615–£5,530.

Following the merger between Headington School and Rye St Antony, Headington Rye Oxford Prep School will open in September 2024 on the former Rye St Antony site in Headington. The School for girls and boys aged 3–11 occupies a beautiful, secluded 12-acre oasis of green space separated from the Senior School by just a pedestrianised lane, one mile from the centre of Oxford. Children benefit from a wealth of teaching expertise, unrivalled facilities and exceptional pastoral care.

The Prep School's friendly, family atmosphere means pupils develop as happy individuals with a sense of responsibility and self-awareness, enjoying a wealth of experiences inside and out of the classroom as part of an outstanding education.

The Early Years Foundation Stage includes Nursery for children aged 3–4 and Reception for children aged 4–5 and offers

- Family dining in Nursery
- Specialist teaching in French, Ballet, Music, Sport and Forest School
- Learn to read music and play the piano in Reception

Children are expertly guided by qualified teachers from Nursery upwards with Specialist EYFS learning assistants.

As children progress through the School beyond EYFS, they also receive specialist teaching in Art, Computing, Dance, Drama and Science in addition to the subjects taught by specialists from age three.

Across the Prep School there are 24 nationalities represented, reflecting Oxford's multicultural and diverse setting, and 16 languages spoken. There are currently 12 sports on offer along with more than 80 clubs and activities to choose from, while theatre productions are held for pupils all the way from nursery up to Year 6. Each week, over 120 individual music lessons take place and pupils sit ABRSM and Trinity Music exams, along with Trinity Guildhall Speech and Drama exams. Many pupils excel in the arts and the sporting arena and are awarded scholarships to senior school. There are a large number of after-school clubs and activities from Fencing to Coding and Trampolining and aftercare runs every day incorporating a range of activities, tea and prep.

Unrivalled facilities include dedicated Science Labs, a Theatre, Music School, ICT suites, Art Room, Spots Hall, all-weather pitch, Tennis Courts, Teaching Kitchens, Swimming Pool, outdoor play areas and substantial woodlands for Forest School.

For pupils entering Nursery and Reception (EYFS), entry is by informal assessment at a taster session. Children are assessed in small groups, with experienced staff supporting them as they play. For Reception age pupils, emergent literacy and numeracy tasks are included in their activities. For those entering Year 1 and Year 2 (Key Stage 1), entry is by informal assessment within the class setting. Literacy, numeracy and problem-solving tasks are included within their activities.

For those entering into Years 3 to 6, entry is by assessment in Mathematics, English and Non-Verbal Reasoning (NVR). Pupils will also have a short interview and then spend the afternoon with their peer group at the Prep School.

The majority of girls continue to the Senior School, with a number being awarded scholarships every year. (*See Headington Rye Oxford entry in GSA section.*)

Charitable status. Headington School Oxford Limited is a Registered Charity, number 309678. It exists to provide quality education for girls.

Heath Mount School

Woodhall Park, Watton-at-Stone, Hertford, Hertfordshire SG14 3NG

Tel: 01920 830230
email: registrar@heathmount.org
website: www.heathmount.org
X/Twitter: @heathmountsch
Facebook: @heathmountsch
Instagram: @heathmountschool

The school became a Trust in September 1970, with a Board of Governors.

Chair of Governors: Mrs J Hodson

***Headmaster*: Mr C Gillam**, BEd Hons

Deputy Head Academic: Mrs R Archer, BEd

Age Range. 3–13.

Number of Pupils. 262 Boys, 233 Girls. Flexi/Sleepover boarding offered.

Fees per term (2023–2024). Boarding (1–4 nights): £565–£1,935 (Lent/Summer). Tuition: Nursery £2,850–£4,770, Pre-Prep £5,505, Years 3–6 £7,125, Years 7–8 £7,355.

There is a reduction in fees for the second and subsequent children attending the School at the same time.

Heath Mount School is situated five miles from Hertford, Ware and Knebworth, at Woodhall Park – a beautiful Georgian mansion with 40 acres of grounds set in a large private park. A dedicated Nursery, Pre-Prep and Lower School are situated a short walk from the main house. The fabulous facilities are inspiring – a Performing Arts Centre and excellent sports facilities which include a sports hall, covered swimming pool, an all-weather pitch for hockey and tennis, netball courts and cricket nets. The main house contains an imaginatively developed lower ground floor housing modern science laboratories and rooms for art, pottery, textiles, film making, food technology and design technology. There is a further information technology room and well-stocked research and fiction libraries. The boys board in a wing of the main house and the girls in a dedicated house in the adjoining park. Resident boarding house parents provide a welcoming environment for both the boys and girls.

The School has an excellent academic record, as well as outstanding art and sport and some of the finest school music in the country. Illustrating this, in 2023 an outstanding 50% of our leavers achieved scholarships to their senior schools across a range of areas.

Charitable status. Heath Mount School is a Registered Charity, number 311069.

Heatherton

Copperkins Lane, Amersham, Buckinghamshire HP6 5QB

Tel: 01494 726433
email: office@heatherton.com
website: www.heatherton.com
X/Twitter: @HeathertonSch
Facebook: @HeathertonSchool
Instagram: @heathertonschool
LinkedIn: /berkhamsted-school

Chair of the Governors: Mrs C Copland (Chair of Berkhamsted Schools Group)

Principal: Mr R P Backhouse, MA Cantab

***Head*: Mrs N Nicoll**, MEd, BSc

Age Range. Girls rising 3–11, Co-Ed Nursery rising 3–4.

Number of Pupils. 157 Girls, 3 Boys.

Fees per term (2023–2024) £392–£680 for Nursery; £3,525–£5,300 for Reception to Year 6.

Founded in 1912, Heatherton is set in an attractive green and leafy location on the outskirts of Amersham.

Heatherton provides an excellent all-round education. An experienced staff of specialist teachers encourage each child's individual academic and emotional development. High standards are achieved across a broad curriculum with small classes, a caring ethos and a close relationship with parents.

At 11 pupils progress to both local independent girls' senior schools and Buckinghamshire grammar schools. Excellent results are produced at all stages of school performance tests and the girls are tracked from an early age, both pastorally and academically.

Musical, artistic and sporting talents flourish at Heatherton. A thriving orchestra, individual instrument lessons and many drama, ballet and music productions are an important part of life in a school year. Art and design skills are celebrated in displays and exhibitions, both internally and externally. Each pupil is offered a wide range of sporting activities – swimming, netball, gymnastics, dance, athletics, tennis, lacrosse and cross country.

An extensive range of educational visits and activities in the UK and Europe are organised each year. The school has recently introduced an additional Enrichment Curriculum to its pupils' timetables, offering the girls exciting opportunities to expand their knowledge, with topics as diverse as mindfulness, team-building and Tudor cooking.

Heatherton offers wrap-around care from 07.30 until 18.00 for all pupils from Nursery to Year 6.

In September 2015, the Heatherton Nursery became Co-Educational, providing for both boys and girls. Heatherton has been recognised for its 'outstanding quality of provision' in the Early Years Foundation Stage. Its 'calm, purposeful environment' and 'a host of stimulating learning opportunities', were just some of the features highlighted by the Independent Schools Inspectorate who are now citing Heatherton's EYFS as an example of very best practice. Heatherton remains a girls' school from Reception class to Year 6.

Following a merger with Berkhamsted School in 2011, Heatherton pupils are increasingly enjoying the benefits of initiatives such as joint curriculum days, music and drama workshops, sports coaching and residential trips in partnership with Berkhamsted Prep, as well as access to the significant resources and infrastructure of the Berkhamsted Schools Group. Heatherton pupils entering Berkhamsted Girls will not be required to take entrance exams for the Senior School, this affects pupils in Year 3 and Year 4 in September 2022, and following years, making their journey through to Berkhamsted Girls as smooth and seamless as possible.

Charitable status. Heatherton School is a member of the Berkhamsted Schools Group, which is a Registered Charity, number 310630.

Heathfield Prep

The Preparatory School to Rishworth School

Oldham Road, Rishworth, Halifax, West Yorkshire HX6 4QF

Tel: 01422 823564
email: admin@heathfieldjunior.co.uk
website: www.rishworth-school.co.uk
X/Twitter: @HeathfieldPrep
Facebook: @RishworthSchool
Instagram: @rishworthschool
LinkedIn: /rishworth-school-trading-limited

Motto: *Deeds Not Words*

Chairman of the Board of Governors: Canon Hilary Barber

Head of Rishworth: Dr A M Wilkins, BA, MA, MA, PhD

***Head of Heathfield*: Mr D Baker**, BEd

Age Range. 3–11 co-educational.

Number of Pupils. 100 day boys/girls and 30-place Foundation Stage Unit. Boarding is available from Year 5: details on request.

Fees per term (2023–2024). Day: Reception–Year 2 £2,700; Years 3–6 £3,800.

Staffing. 9 full-time teaching and 6 part-time teaching and a number of teaching assistants. Specialist teachers deliver: music, art, PE, French, dance and drama, with additional peripatetic staff providing further individual tuition in Music and the Arts.

Location. Heathfield stands in its own substantial grounds and enjoys an outstanding rural position in a beautiful Pennine location with easy access via the motorways to Manchester and Leeds.

Facilities. Well-equipped classrooms; Foundation Stage Unit and purpose-built Infant classes; designated teaching rooms for Music, Science, Art and Design Technology; modern ICT Suite; library; a multi-purpose Hall for assemblies and productions; heated indoor swimming pool; netball court and football/rugby pitch; eco-classroom; outdoor music area; and the Forget-Me-Not sensory garden.

Wraparound Care. Pre/After School Care and Holiday School available.

Forest School. Children learn through playing and the hands-on forest school approach gives them plenty of opportunity to do just that, we have our own river, waterfall and even a brand new eco-classroom!

Aims. To provide a stimulating and challenging environment in which individual attainment is nurtured, recognised and celebrated.

To ensure each child receives their full entitlement to a broad, balanced curriculum which builds on a solid foundation in literacy and numeracy.

Curriculum. An extensive programme of study which incorporates the Foundation Stage, Key Stage 1 and Key Stage 2. An emphasis on developing an independence in learning and analytical thinking through Literacy, Numeracy, Science, French, History, Geography, Religious Studies, Design Technology, Information and Communications Technology, Music, Art and Physical Education.

Enrichment and Extension. There are over 90 different enrichment and extension activities on offer every term including activities such as: Drama, Choir, Orchestra, Baking, Brass, Recorder, String Groups, Art, Board Games, Lego, Astronomy and Mystery Solving Club.

Sports. Include Swimming, Rounders, Netball, Football, Rugby, Cross-Country, Cricket, Athletics, Gymnastics, Hockey and Biathlon.

Trips and Performances. Each term there are plays and musical concerts incorporating most children in the School. Residentials include Outdoor Pursuits, Camping and Environmental Studies.

Charitable status. Rishworth School is a Registered Charity, number 1115562. It exists to provide education for boys and girls.

Hereward House School

14 Strathray Gardens, London NW3 4NY
Tel: 020 7794 4820
email: office@herewardhouse.co.uk
website: www.herewardhouse.co.uk

***Headmaster*: Mr P J E Evans**, MA

Deputy Headmaster: Mr P Cheetham, BA, PGCE
Head of Middle School and Lead Teacher: Mr M Blakey, MA, PGCE
Head of Junior School and EYFS: Ms L Kay, DipEd
Bursar: Mr A Jenne, BA
Headmaster's PA/Admissions: Mr J Jones, MSc

Age Range. 4–13.

Number of Pupils. 165 Day Boys.

Fees per term (2023–2024). £6,870–£7,095.

Hereward House provides a warm and welcoming atmosphere in which every child feels valued, secure and thrives. The school works hard to create a stimulating, purposeful and happy community, within which boys are encouraged and assisted to develop academically, morally, emotionally, culturally and physically. The school's aim is for boys to enjoy their school days yet at the same time be well prepared for the demands of Common Entrance and Scholarship examinations.

The school's academic success is built upon excellent teaching and the highly individual educational teaching programmes created to meet individual boy's needs. Great care is taken to ensure that a boy gains a place at the school which is right for him.

Boys are prepared for the Common Entrance and Scholarship examinations to highly sought after independent schools, both day and boarding. Two-thirds of boys proceed to top London Day Schools, such as City of London, Highgate, St Paul's, UCS and Westminster, others to leading boarding schools such as Eton, Harrow and Winchester. Scholarships and Awards have been won by our boys to several of the above schools.

The school takes pride in the breadth of education it offers. Music plays a major role in the boys' education. Almost all boys learn at least one instrument, most of them two or even three. There is a full school orchestra which gives a performance each term. Weekly concerts are held throughout the year.

Team Games play an integral part in the sports syllabus. We regularly field teams against other schools and have an enviable record of success in Cricket, Football and Cross-Country Running. Swimming, Tennis, Hockey and Athletics are included in our sports programme.

Art has a valued place in the syllabus. Chess, Judo, Fencing, Coding, Yoga, ICT and Music Theory are among the clubs available to the boys.

High March School

23 Ledborough Lane, Beaconsfield, Bucks HP9 2PZ
Tel: 01494 675186
email: office@highmarch.co.uk
admissions@highmarch.co.uk
website: www.highmarch.co.uk
X/Twitter: @HighMarchSchool
Instagram: @highmarch1

Established 1926.

Chairman of the Governing Board: Mr C Hayfield, BSc, FCA

***Headmistress*: Mrs Kate Gater**, MA, PGCE Warwick

Age Range. Girls 3–11, Boys 3–4.

Number of Pupils. 292 day pupils.

Fees per term (2023–2024). £2,275–£6,235 inclusive of books, stationery and lunches, but excluding optional subjects.

High March consists of 3 school houses set in pleasant grounds. Junior House comprises Nursery and Key Stage 1 classes, ages 3–7 years, while Upper School covers Key Stage 2, ages 7–11 years. Class sizes are limited. Facilities include a state-of-the-art 20-metre indoor heated swimming pool, a Gymnasium, as well as Science, Music, Art, Design Technology, Drama, Information Technology rooms and a Library. Recent refurbishments include re-landscaping of the gardens at Junior House as well as an extensive re-design of the outdoor classrooms for both Nursery and Reception.

High March is within easy reach of London, High Wycombe, Windsor and within a few minutes' walk of Beaconsfield Station.

Under a large and highly qualified staff and within a happy atmosphere, the girls are prepared for Common Entrance and Scholarships to Independent Senior Schools and for the 11+ County Selection process. All subjects including French, Spanish, Latin, Music, Art, Technology, Speech and Drama, Dancing, Gymnastics, Games and Swimming are in the hands of specialists. The academic record is high but each child is nevertheless encouraged to develop individual talents.

Highfield & Brookham School

Highfield Lane, Liphook, Hampshire GU30 7LQ

Tel: 01428 728000
email: headspa@highfieldandbrookham.co.uk
admissions@highfieldandbrookham.co.uk
website: www.highfieldandbrookham.co.uk
X/Twitter: @HighfieldSch
Facebook: @HighfieldandBrookham
Instagram: @highfieldandbrookham
LinkedIn: /highfield-and-brookham-schools

Chair of Directors: Mr W S Mills

***Head*: Mrs Suzannah Cryer**

Age Range. 2–13.
Number of Children. 470.
Fees per term (2023–2024). Day Pupils: £4,550 (Reception with 15 hours free entitlement) to £8,775 (Year 8); Full Boarding: £10,075 (Year 4) to £11,050 (Year 8). Weekly boarding and Steps to Boarding is available. Discounts are available for siblings and Forces families.

Highfield and Brookham School is a Nursery, Pre-prep and Prep School in Liphook for boys and girls aged 2–13, offering both day and boarding options. We are situated in the South Downs National Park on the borders of Surrey, Hampshire and West Sussex.

At Highfield and Brookham, we provide a coherent academic journey right the way from Nursery through to Year 8. Children experience a dynamic, seamless and rich education based on experience and robust research delivered by passionate teachers in an inspirational setting. Our transformative approach empowers children to become critical thinkers, curious questioners and compassionate, creative contributors. Our education embraces change, diversity, and the progressing demands of the modern world.

Children are at heart of everything we do and every decision is made in their best interests. Our timetable is designed to ensure children are fully prepared for exams by providing plenty of time for the core subjects, as well as providing breadth and added value. Children at Highfield and Brookham develop a positive attitude, love learning and understand that mistakes are an important part of the process and encourage resilience and ambition.

We believe in the importance of developing essential skills that will support your child socially, increase their learning outcomes and enhance career opportunities. Highfield and Brookham look beyond the curriculum to skills that children can learn through sport, music, drama and art. There are over 50 extracurricular activities and sports on offer throughout the year which enable children to broaden their horizons and foster lifelong passions.

We take every aspect of pupil care very seriously, which is why keeping your child safe and ensuring they are happy at school are our biggest priorities. As the world is ever changing, children need to learn to adapt and change with it. We pride ourselves on our exceptional pastoral care, our integral learning support department and our first-class medical centre. These three elements are fundamental for ensuring every child is truly happy at Highfield and Brookham and we have no doubt that happy, healthy children are the best learners.

The school enjoys 175 acres of fields, sports pitches and woodlands. Children learn beyond the walls of the classroom every day as teachers take learning outside at every opportunity. Complementing the numerous natural playing fields, and providing all-year-round play, the school also benefits from a floodlit all-weather pitch.

We provide a supportive and collaborative process for parents to help them identify the right educational path for their child. We feed the very top senior schools, including Marlborough, Winchester, Radley, Sherborne School for Girls and Eton, and have an excellent scholarship success rate at 11+ and 13+ to schools such as Canford, Charterhouse, Cranleigh, Harrow and Wellington.

Choosing Highfield and Brookham, whether day or boarding, is your opportunity to make a positive impact on your child's educational journey, ensuring they leave as a happy and well-rounded individual and ready to tackle the next stage of their learning journey.

Highgate Pre-Prep & Junior School

Bishopswood Road, London N6 4PL

Tel: 020 8347 4490 (Admissions)
email: admissions@highgateschool.org.uk
website: www.highgateschool.org.uk
X/Twitter: @highgate1565
Facebook: @HighgateSchoolLondon
LinkedIn: /school/highgate-school

Founded over 450 years ago, Highgate is one of the UK's leading co-educational independent schools with pupils from a diverse range of backgrounds across North London and beyond.

***Principal of Junior School*: Philippa Studd**

***Principal of Pre-Preparatory School*: Sally Hancock**

Age Range. Pre-Prep, age 4–7; Junior age 7–11.

Number of Pupils. Pre-Prep: 180; Junior: 448.

Fees per term (2023–2024). Pre-Prep: £7,365 (Reception–Year 2); Junior (Years 3–6): £7,800.

Highgate Pre-Preparatory School is situated in a light, airy and colourful building on Bishopswood Road, overlooking the open spaces of our grounds, with its own playground, separate music room and learning support room. The building has recently undergone improvements with a two-storey extension offering three new classrooms, a covered play space, a library with enclosed terrace and secure viewing area for children to observe the green planted roof. Pupils also benefit from their own dining hall and a secure outdoor woodland space for Forest School lessons. Our small class sizes are led by qualified early-years teachers and support staff, together with specialists in music, drama, sport and exercise. We take a creative and reflective approach to education, with a focus on how children learn, not just what they learn. Through immersion in project-based learning, the children develop resilience, creativity and a sense of responsibility not only as a learner, but also as a member of the school community and wider society.

Highgate Junior School is located on Bishopswood Road in a bright and spacious building which opened in September 2016. Built to the highest specification, there are specialist facilities for computing, science, art, design and technology, drama and music, as well as its own library, a large hall, outdoor play area and gardens.

We pride ourselves on providing an innovative curriculum which challenges our pupils to be curious, creative and brave in their learning. Our timetable is designed to incorporate both an intellectually rigorous approach to studies alongside skills-based learning. We aim for our pupils to develop a genuine love of learning whilst acquiring a knowledge of how they learn, how to take responsibility for their learning and how to apply their skills and knowledge in a variety of different contexts. We nurture in our pupils how to be a reflective and proactive member of the community, with a sense of social responsibility and a deep understanding and appreciation of the wide range of heritages, cultures and backgrounds in our diverse society.

Wellbeing is at the heart of our school. We understand that developing a child who feels happy, healthy and confident in themselves, with skills to manage ups and downs, is of utmost importance, not only during their time here but when they leave and move into the adult world. We nurture confidence and strength of character, supporting pupils to grow and thrive in their emotional, mental and physical health. We retain close links across the three Highgate schools to provide a continuity of education for the majority of pupils that transition from Pre-Prep to Junior School at age 7 and on into Senior School at age 11.

Sport and Exercise is taught by specialist teachers to ensure a high-quality experience. Our extensive outdoor playing fields and all-weather pitches are complemented by excellent indoor facilities in the Mallinson Sports Centre which includes a swimming pool, gym and sports courts for a variety of activities.

Co-curricular activities provide countless opportunities for pupils to have fun, make new friends and learn something new. Time is set aside each week for every pupil to take part in at least one co-curricular venture. Our wide offering continues to evolve and develop in response to the changing needs of our pupils and the world around us and aims to:

- Develop qualities of self-reliance, endurance and leadership;
- Serve the community; and
- Develop interests and enthusiasms.

Admission. Prospective families should fill out an online application form if they would like their child to be considered for a place.

Invited Pre-Prep candidates are asked to attend a group assessment together with other children.

Invited Junior School candidates will sit an English and Maths test, with a further proportion invited back for a taster lesson and group interview. We aim to make these assessments as fun and stress-free as possible.

Bursaries are available for 7+ and 11+ entry, please visit our website for more information: www.highgateschool.org.uk/bursaries

Charitable status. Highgate School is a Registered Charity, number 312765.

Hilden Grange School

Alpha Plus Group Ltd

Dry Hill Park Road, Tonbridge, Kent TN10 3BX

Tel: 01732 351169 / 01732 352706
email: office@hildengrange.co.uk
website: www.hildengrange.co.uk
X/Twitter: @HildenGrange
Facebook: @HildenGrange
Instagram: @hildengrangeschool

***Headmaster*: Mr M Gough**, BA, LLB Rhodes, LLM Cape Town, PGCE OU

Deputy Head: Mrs R Jubber, BSc, HDE

Age Range. 2½–13 Co-educational.

Number of Pupils. 294: 187 Boys and 107 Girls.

Fees per term (2023–2024). Prep School (Years 5–8): £5,925, Prep School (Years 3–4): £5,325, Pre-Prep (Years 1 and 2): £4,320, Reception: £3,745, Nursery: £1,295 per term (minimum five sessions per week). Lunches are provided at £275–£320 per term.

At Hilden Grange, we provide a stimulating, friendly and secure environment in which an individual child's potential is developed in the academic, creative, physical and spiritual areas. Through encouragement, outstanding teaching and a positive, inclusive atmosphere, we aim to help pupils strive for high standards, both inside and outside the classroom, take a pride in their endeavours and enjoy participating in the life of the school with all its wide-ranging opportunities. The wellbeing of each child underpins their success and is of paramount importance to us. Courtesy, good manners and mutual respect are expected at all times within our community. We aim for each individual to feel valued and very much a part of our school family.

Though links are especially strong with Tonbridge and Sevenoaks, boys and girls are prepared for all

Independent Senior Schools and Grammar Schools at 11+ and 13+. We have an unequalled record of success in this area. Examination results rank among the highest in Kent, and in the past ten years, all pupils gained entry to their chosen school at 13. Boys and girls who show special promise sit for scholarships to the school of their choice, and our track record in this area is excellent. 71 scholarships have been gained since 2019 in areas as diverse as music, drama and sport, as well as traditional academic scholarships. Pupils benefit from specialist teaching in all subjects from Year 3, dedicated staff, and class sizes that average 16.

The School stands in about twenty acres of attractive grounds in the residential area of North Tonbridge. Boys and girls are accepted into the Nursery at 2½+ or at 4+ into the Pre-Preparatory Department within the school grounds, and at 7 into the main school.

There is an outdoor heated swimming pool, a dedicated Sports Hall, all-weather tennis courts, Science Laboratories, Music Rooms, an Art and Design area, a Library, a Learning Support Area, a dining hall and two Information Technology Rooms, with networks of personal computers.

The Headmaster, staff and children welcome visitors and are pleased to show them around the School.

Hill House School

Sixth Avenue, Auckley, Doncaster, South Yorkshire DN9 3GG

Tel: 01302 776300
email: info@hillhouse.doncaster.sch.uk
website: www.hillhouse.doncaster.sch.uk
X/Twitter: @HillHouseSchool
Facebook: @hillhouseschool
Instagram: @hillhouseschool
LinkedIn: /school/hill-house-school-doncaster

See full entry in the **HMC** section, on **p. 149**.

Hoe Bridge School

Hoe Place, Old Woking, Surrey GU22 8JE

Tel: 01483 760018
email: info@hoebridgeschool.co.uk
website: www.hoebridgeschool.co.uk
X/Twitter: @HoeBridgeSchool
Facebook: @hoebridgewoking
Instagram: @hoebridgeschool
LinkedIn: /company/hoe-bridge-school

Independent school in Old Woking for boys and girls aged 2 to 16 years old.

Chairman of Governors: Ian Katté

***Headmaster*: Christopher Webster**, MA, BSc Hons, PGCE

Deputy Headmaster: Adam Warner, BA Hons

Head of Pre-Prep: Amanda Willis, BA Hons, QTS

Age Range. 2–16 years.

Number of Children. 532.

Fees per term (2023–2024). £4,160–£6,130 (including lunch).

We are very fortunate to enjoy the historic and inspirational site which is home to Hoe Bridge School. The 22-acre estate is a hidden gem in the heart of Surrey and a stone's throw from Woking town centre.

The school has invested strategically to ensure the best facilities in the area, with a high standard of classrooms to provide the perfect learning environment. These are complemented by specialist suites for subjects such as Art, Design & Technology, ICT, Science, Music and indoor exercise. Staff and children alike are justifiably proud of the recently built 110-seat Performing Arts Centre.

Sport and exercise are all-important in the school week, and are amply catered for with two sports halls, three large playing fields, all-weather pitch, heated outdoor swimming pool, outdoor and indoor cricket nets, cross country course and grass and artificial cricket squares.

Beyond, the Hideout outdoor classroom, pond with its own pontoon, meadow and woods provide a natural wonderland for outdoor learning, inspiration and exploration for inquiring young minds.

Within our estate, Pre-Prep enjoys its own purpose-built building with assembly hall, fully equipped gym, well-stocked library, ICT suite, art and music rooms, as well as modern classrooms with indoor and outdoor learning areas. All classrooms have interactive whiteboards and we make extensive use of iPads.

Transition to the Prep Department is seamless and as children mature they become increasingly independent learners in preparation for the move to senior school. The results achieved by the children across the ability range are outstanding leading to success at some of the country's leading schools. The pupils are inspired by dedicated staff, lessons are rigorous and interactive and achievement is excellent. 2022 Common Entrance Exam Results were outstanding.

Alongside the academics sport, music, art and drama play a major part throughout the school and children excel in many areas: end-of-year productions; sporting excellence achieving national success in netball and hockey, county success in cricket and football; individual musical success in national youth orchestras and choirs and a spectacular annual art exhibition. Scholarships in all these areas are won every year to a variety of schools across the country. "The pupils' successes in academic work, sport and music, both individually and in groups, are due to their excellent attitudes to learning." Latest ISI Inspection Report.

Older pupils take part in regular activities such as Bush Craft weekends, French trips, cricket and netball tours and are challenged by preparing and presenting a gourmet meal to their parents. It is at this stage of their time at Hoe Bridge that they take on extra responsibility becoming prefects and role models to the younger children.

Recognising the pressing need for an independent senior school in Woking, we have established Hoe Bridge Senior School. This ensures that your child can benefit from our outstanding education in preparation for GCSE and their choice of further education or career within easy reach of the local area. From September 2022, pupils in or joining Year 6 and below will be able to stay at the school until Year 11, when GCSEs are taken.

We are passionate in the belief that the role of educators is to provide a wide-ranging framework in which children can grow and develop creatively in a continually changing and often unpredictable world. We have an unwavering commitment to empowering those within our community: inspiring, challenging and motivating both children and adults in all that we do. We have an environment which grows and adapts, allowing all children to learn and understand from their many different strengths. Empathy and caring for others are our principal values, which are intrinsic within our ideology and shown in the special qualities within our community. Each child is known and valued for who they are.

In providing a safe and secure environment where children can explore their potential, confidence and self-esteem we nurture each individual enabling them to achieve the highest of standards. Learning is best achieved in a collaborative community which inspires and encourages ambitious minds with high quality and dynamic teachers being the driving force behind such a setting.

Charitable status. Hoe Bridge School is a Registered Charity, number 295808. It exists to provide a rounded education for children aged 2 to 16.

Holme Grange School

Heathlands Road, Wokingham, Berkshire RG40 3AL

Tel: 0118 9781566
email: school@holmegrange.org
website: www.holmegrange.org
X/Twitter: @holmegrange
Facebook: @holmegrange
Instagram: @holmegrange
LinkedIn: /company/holme-grange-school

Chair of Governors: Mrs Sue Northend, Director of HR for REAch2 Academy Trust

***Head*: Mrs Claire Robinson**, BA, PGCE, NPQH

Deputy Head Operations: Mr Matthew Jelley, BA Hons, PGCE, MEd

Deputy Head Safeguarding, Welfare & Wellbeing: Ms Tanya Bobela, BA Hons, PGCE

Age Range. 2–16 Co-educational.

Number of Pupils. 664 (excluding Nursery): 344 boys, 320 girls.

Fees per term (2023–2024). Little Grange Nursery from £65.50 (per day); Pre-Preparatory £4,180 (Reception), £4,180 (Years 1–2); Prep £5,300 (Years 3–4), £5,500 (Years 5–6), £5,755 (Years 7–8), £5,935 (Years 9–11) with an option to pay over 10 months. Reductions for second and subsequent children.

Holme Grange is a co-educational day school for girls and boys aged 2–16 years. The school provides pupils with a toolkit to live their lives and when they eventually enter the adult world, they will do so well prepared with a real-life foundation for every challenge they will face. Set in 21 acres of Wokingham countryside, Holme Grange offers a unique educational journey in an idyllic setting, delivering a creative experience, sporting prowess and academic excellence.

The School occupies a large country mansion, to which many additional facilities have been added over recent years, including outdoor classrooms, three additional science laboratories, food technology room, common room and additional classrooms. 2016 saw the opening of a 300-seat Performing Arts Theatre, Music School and Drama Suite and a new block housing a dining room, kitchens and eight additional classrooms. The Sports Hall was also extended, offering a fitness gym and changing facilities. Further expansion saw the opening of a new senior building in 2019 and this year a fourth science laboratory was added to the senior facilities. Pre-Prep and Prep also have a dedicated Science Laboratory. Reception pupils moved into new classroom facilities in September 2019, with direct access to an adventure playground. A Recording Studio was introduced for the start of the 2020–21 academic year.

The School is set in an idyllic environment of grounds comprising grass pitches, all-weather surfaces, swimming pool, Cricket, Football, Hockey and Rugby pitches, Netball and Tennis courts, 3 Forest schools and woodland walks for the children to explore. Specialist teaching and facilities for Music, Art and Technology, Dance, Performing Arts, Science, ICT and Sport enhance our fully comprehensive provision and support the individual development of all our pupils. Holme Grange is one of the first schools in the area to have gained Forest School status and has a number of qualified Forest Leaders on the Staff, thus allowing opportunities for children to achieve and develop confidence and knowledge through hands-on learning in a woodland environment. The erection of a second Polytunnel, together with a market garden shop, provides opportunities for pupils to learn about sustainable education whilst the development and expansion of the School farm with its goats, pigs, chickens and ducks enable the pupils to learn about life cycles and animal husbandry in a very hands-on manner.

We have recently acquired an established Day Nursery down the road from our School premises and have relocated our existing Nursery to those premises. Little Grange Nursery is equipped to the highest standard and is located in a safe and secure environment and will offer flexible day care from 8.00 am to 6.00 pm Monday to Friday for children from the age of two years through to when they start in Reception. Little Grange, though not now within our School grounds, will, very much, continue to be part of Holme Grange, with our teaching staff regularly going up to Nursery to teach Sport and Music. The Nursery children will also participate in activities at the main school site from time to time.

We welcome and cater for pupils with a wide range of ability. Entry is based upon an assessment day where baseline assessment tests are taken in verbal and non-verbal reasoning. This entry process is designed to identify pupils who are able to benefit from our balanced and well-rounded education. We aim to foster confidence and a love of learning across the age range. Pupils are accepted from the age of two years, providing outstanding continuous education up to and including GCSE, and also preparing students for the Common Entrance examinations. We celebrated another fantastic set of GCSE results in 2023, with 9.5% of all grades being 9, 26% of all grades being 9–8 and 44.3% of all grades being 9–7. The pass rate across the board was 96%.

The Headteacher is assisted by a highly qualified and experienced teaching staff with classroom assistants in the Pre-Prep and NNEB assistants in Little Grange. There is an Accelerated Learning Centre giving help to those children with special needs.

The School's policy is to set high standards, to establish good all-round personalities and to give inspiration for each pupil's life. Our aim is to create an environment where every child can thrive. Our Mission is to inspire achievement beyond the bounds of expectation within an environment where every child can succeed. A bold statement but one that we believe every child deserves. We appreciate children's differences and respond to their individual needs. In 2013, we were awarded the prestigious NACE Challenge Award for More Able, Gifted and Talented Pupils in recognition of the high quality work by the whole school in challenging all pupils to achieve their best, gaining re-accreditation in 2017 and 2021. Holme Grange is one of only 100 schools in the country to be re-accredited twice and is recognised as a Regional Hub for NACE in the local area. In 2020, we were awarded a Gold SMSC National Quality Mark, in recognition of the spiritual, moral, social and cultural development Holme Grange provides, and also an Artsmark Gold Award from Arts Council England.

At Holme Grange we offer excellence in personalised learning – a rare school that caters equally well for pupils at both ends of the academic continuum. We believe in our pupils and instil a belief in themselves.

We develop intellectual character through our learning habits and the ethos throughout the school is one of warmth and friendliness – questioning, divergent thinking and the freedom to learn from mistakes are all encouraged. Pupils are inspired to take responsibility for their own learning, develop good work habits and gain a sense that learning can thrill and invigorate.

We deliver a rounded education by providing opportunities in sport, the arts, languages, technology and a wide range of activities, maximising opportunities for success for all. We hope to inspire your child both in and outside of the classroom. At Holme Grange School, we foster self-reliance, self-discipline and self-confidence in a caring community where children gain interests and characteristics that give them a head start for life.

We will not only unlock your child's potential but will also foster within them, a passion for learning. Our pupils are prepared to succeed in an ever changing, competitive world. We offer challenge, we strive to inspire, develop confidence, provide opportunity and realise potential in every child up to the age of 16.

We are committed to providing the very best education. Academic standards are excellent. Life in our school is a journey of exploration and discovery. We are a holistic school offering an all-round education, bursting with life and vitality.

The School is a Trust, administered by a board of Governors who have considerable experience in education and business.

Charitable status. Holme Grange Limited is a Registered Charity, number 309105. It exists to serve the local community in providing an all-round education for boys and girls.

Holy Cross Preparatory School

George Road, Kingston upon Thames, Surrey KT2 7NU

Tel: 020 8942 0729
email: admissions@holycrossprep.com
website: www.holycrossprepschool.co.uk
Facebook: @holycrossprepschool
Instagram: @holycrossprepschool

***Headteacher*: Mrs Sarah Hair**

Age range. 3–11.

Number of girls. 290.

Fees per term (2023–2024). £5,380.

Location. Holy Cross Prep is located on the private Coombe estate on Kingston Hill, just a short drive from the centre of Kingston upon Thames. The pre-school opened in September 2021 admitting girls from 3 years old into a newly refurbished and extended building within the grounds.

Educational philosophy. Holy Cross Prep provides a warm, nurturing and stimulating environment for girls aged 3–11, welcoming all faiths and cultures. We offer two-form entry, with small class sizes to provide our pupils with the skills and knowledge they need to thrive and succeed in today's modern world. We are a compassionate, vibrant community, working together to inspire a true love of learning in our pupils.

Curriculum. Our broad and dynamic curriculum is delivered by exceptional, dedicated teachers, ensuring that our high academic standards are upheld across every subject. Specialist subjects include sport, music, drama, computing, art and French. Our staff take great pleasure in nurturing and guiding the girls on their individual learning journeys, and are justifiably proud of the great success they have with senior school entrance exams. Our girls engage and participate fully in school life, regularly performing academically above the national average. Academic success not only enables access to highly selective senior schools, it also offers opportunities for academic scholarships, as reflected in the large number awarded to Holy Cross girls each year. Pupils are awarded scholarships based on their academic achievement, as well as their talents in sport, music, drama and art. Our pupils are happy, curious individuals, encouraged to nurture their natural inquisitiveness and a healthy attitude towards learning.

Our dynamic curriculum is supported by a diverse extra-curricular programme, with a wealth of activity clubs running before, during and after school. To support working parents, our wraparound care provision is available from 7.30 am until 6.00 pm on each full school day.

Facilities. Our state-of-the-art facilities are set in eight acres of beautiful, historic grounds, with plenty of outdoor space for the girls to explore. From our much-loved woodland walk and adventure playground, to our floodlit sports pitch and pavilion, pupils are actively encouraged to spend time enjoying the outside world. Completed in 2019, our tailor-made, all-weather facilities are perfect for a wide variety of sports, including hockey and football. We also have dedicated specialist classrooms and a spectacular multi-purpose hall, which hosts countless activities and events, including PE lessons, assemblies and drama productions, as well as our daily lunch provision. Large-scale productions benefit from a curtain theatre and retractable tiered seating for approximately 300 guests, which transforms the space into an auditorium.

Charitable status. Holy Cross Preparatory School is a Registered Charity, number 1200167. It is a Roman Catholic School providing excellence in Christian education to local children.

Homefield Preparatory School

Western Road, Sutton, Surrey SM1 2TE
Tel: 020 8642 0965
email: enquiries@homefieldprep.school
website: www.homefieldprep.school
X/Twitter: @HomefieldSchool
Facebook: @homefield.school
Instagram: @homefieldprep
LinkedIn: /company/homefield-preparatory-school-trust-limited

'*I don't believe we could have found a better school in the country to bring out the best in both our sons.*'

Chair of Governors: Ms Meg Gardiner Boiling, MA Cantab, Graduate LLB Hons, DipABRSM

***Head*: Mr Sam Naismith BEd**, BPE

Age range: 4–13.

Number of boys: 280.

Fees per term (2023–2024): Reception: £3,730, Years 1 & 2: £4,620, Years 3–8: £5,410. (Siblings are eligible for a 5% discount on the youngest sibling's fees.)

Homefield Prep is an academically selective independent day school for boys aged 4–13. Founded in 1870, it is one of the oldest prep schools in England and has been renowned for its academic success and family atmosphere for over 150 years. To mark the 150th anniversary, the school reflected on its mission and its vision for the coming decades and created a statement that captures what the school holds dear for its students and the community. 'At Homefield, we aim to provide a safe and happy environment, with a real depth of specialist teaching, to enable academic success. We invest in an ambitious curriculum for all our boys. This goes beyond English, Mathematics and the Sciences. Quality and vitality also underpin the humanities, the arts and sport. This breadth and depth ensure a wider fulfilment of our boys' individual potential, in "head, hand and heart". We seek to develop deeper study skills and aptitudes toward learning, such as research and collaboration, in order to inspire independent thinkers, who work well with others and are eager for challenge. We aspire to be a truly cosmopolitan school with a rich diversity both reflecting and supporting our place as a charity within the wider community of London. We aim for a generous education of knowledge and skill, but also ethical character, so that our boys not only "do well", but "do good". With roots in the 19th century, our mission embraces the 21st century, where wellbeing and civic virtue are key to our school's character and success.'

The school offers a safe and happy environment, with a real depth of specialist teaching, which ensures the fulfilment of the students' individual potential. The school is truly cosmopolitan, with students coming from diverse backgrounds and nationalities, which is a real strength. A generous education is provided, aimed at building knowledge and increasing skills, as well as building resilience, perseverance and good character. At Homefield, we produce well-rounded students, who go on to some of the very best senior schools in the country, including KCS Wimbledon, Eton, Harrow & Epsom College.

'Pupils have extremely well-developed and positive attitudes towards their learning. They are highly productive when collaborating on work, and focused and determined when working independently. Pupils listen and engage with high levels of respect to each other and to adults and are eager to learn.' (ISI Inspection, December 2021)

From December 2019–June 2022, the school invested in a complete redevelopment of the school site to provide the highest-quality facilities for our students now and for future generations.

The redevelopment included a purpose-built block of new classrooms, constructed to a very high specification, overlooking the playing fields and a brand new Performance Hall, Dining Room and Kitchen. At the same time, the school created new music facilities, a STEAM/Computing suite, a Library Hub over two floors, a multi-use games area and adventure playgrounds.

Due to the redevelopments, the school has gained around 10% more green space. The school has also added to its eco-credentials through solar power, low energy underfloor heating and a 'green roof'.

Awareness of others is encouraged and the boys are involved in many fundraising charity events. A wide range of opportunities are available to extend gifted boys, and learning support is available for children with special needs. Mental Health and Emotional Wellbeing are embedded into the school curriculum.

Academic, sporting, art and music scholarships are offered as well as occasional bursaries.

Daily minibuses serve Carshalton, Epsom, Wimbledon and Worcester Park areas to transport boys before and after school.

Breakfast, after-school and complimentary clubs are available, as well as wraparound care.

Charitable status. As a charitable trust since the 1960s, a keen sense of civic and community responsibility is important at Homefield. We believe that positive values influence character and attitude. In the 21st century it's more important than ever for our boys to feel rooted within a strong moral community.

Homefield Preparatory School Trust Limited is a Registered Charity, number 312753.

Hornsby House School

Hearnville Road, London SW12 8RS

Tel: 020 8673 7573
email: school@hornsbyhouse.org.uk
website: www.hornsbyhouse.org.uk
X/Twitter: @hornsbyhousesch
Facebook: @Elementary-School/Hornsby-House-School
Instagram: @hornsbyhousesch

Chair of Governors: Ms Corinne Aldridge

***Headmaster*: Mr Edward Rees**, BA Ed Hons

Age range. 4–11.
Number of pupils. 215 Girls, 228 Boys.
Fees per term (2023–2024). £6,010 (Reception to Year 2), £6,450 (Years 3 to 6). Lunch: £375 per term.

Hornsby House is a thriving IAPS co-educational prep school in Wandsworth, southwest London. At their most recent inspection in October 2016, the Independent Schools Inspectorate judged Hornsby House pupils' overall achievement as 'excellent' and found that 'pupils achieve highly from the wide-ranging curriculum that provides for all abilities'. Pupils' personal development was described as 'excellent' and stated that 'pupils have high levels of self-esteem, positive relationships, healthy lifestyles and social awareness'. Hornsby House provides a nurturing environment where attainment and happiness are key aims and the children achieve outstanding educational outcomes as a result. In 2023, our Year 6 children won over scholarships and awards between them. There are three classes in each year group, a generous staff to pupil ratio and around 440 pupils in the school. Entry into Reception classes is unassessed and is on a first-come, first-served basis with priority being given to siblings. Children wishing to enter the school in year groups above Reception are required to attend an assessment.

There is an extensive co-curricular programme with over 50 clubs, as well as before- and after-school care from 7.30 am to 6.00 pm. Over half the children in the school play a musical instrument and a third sing in one of the three choirs. Sport is a central part of the curriculum, the staffing level is excellent and the benefits of teamwork are seen clearly in school life as a whole. The school has an outstanding IT infrastructure to support the children's learning. The majority of leavers go to one of seven London day schools: Dulwich College, JAGS, Alleyn's, Emanuel, King's College School Wimbledon, Streatham & Clapham High School and Whitgift. The remainder move on to other day or boarding schools.

To arrange a visit to see the children at work, please contact the Registrar.

Charitable status. Hornsby House Educational Trust is a Registered Charity, number 800284.

Horris Hill

Newtown, Newbury, Berkshire RG20 9DJ

Tel: 01635 40594
email: office@horrishill.com
website: www.horrishill.com
X/Twitter: @HorrisHill
Facebook: @HorrisHillSchool
Instagram: @horrishillschool
LinkedIn: /company/horris-hill-school

***Headmaster*: Mr Rob Stewart**

Deputy Headmaster: Miss Melanie Lewis

Chairman of the School: Mr J Forsyth

Age range. 2–13.
Number of children. 119.
Fees per term (2023–2024). Full Boarders from £11,900; Transition Boarders (3/4 nights per week) from £7,600; Day Pupils from £4,560.

Horris Hill is one of the leading prep schools in the UK. The school's emphasis is on the development of the whole child, without compromising the 130 year record of academic excellence. Horris Hill School has a unique ethos which develops every child as an individual and provides a rigorous and extensive academic, sporting, musical and artistic foundation. From September 2023, Horris Hill is co-educational across the whole school.

We deliver success by achieving places and awards at the very best senior schools and developing children with impeccable manners, good humour, kindness and self-confidence. Recent awards to senior schools have included academic scholarship to Harrow and Winchester, Music Exhibition to Eton and Harrow, and sport scholarships at Cheltenham, Radley and Sherborne.

We nurture and challenge every child to see school as an exciting adventure and lessons are carefully planned to excite and interest with stimulating activities to foster each child's development.

Life outside the classroom is just as important to us at Horris Hill, enhancing your child's experience and enjoyment of their school days. Almost all of the children in the upper school take individual music lessons in our purpose-built music school, and, in the new dedicated theatre, pupils take part in weekly drama lessons, LAMDA classes and workshops with local theatre companies. The theatre also hosts quizzes, talks, lectures and movie nights.

Playing sport is a very important part of school life and we aim to give every child the confidence to participate on the games field, to provide high quality coaching for every age group and to see pupils develop a number of sports which they enjoy playing. Horris Hill pupils are very competitive on the pitch, but also understand the vital importance of playing fairly and of being great hosts.

With 65 acres of parkland and a wide variety of sports, activities, clubs and hobbies on offer, there is no chance of your child being bored.

A significant proportion of our pupils, and nearly all of those in the lower school, are day pupils. Our local families form a considerable and vital part of our close-knit school community. In the upper school, day pupils all eat supper and complete their prep at school, just like their boarding counterparts. Boarding is a wonderful opportunity for your child to grow as an independent individual. Our younger boarders sleep in the heart of the school, where they learn how to thrive in a 'home away from home', in a nurturing and supportive environment. Life in our senior boarding house on the estate encourages its residents to develop the independence and confidence to prepare them for life at senior school. A variety of flexible boarding options are available, including as few as three nights at school for the youngest boarders, to weekly or full boarding.

To see for yourself what a difference a Horris Hill education could make for your child, please come and visit us. Simply email admissions@horrishill.com to arrange an appointment. We look forward to welcoming you to Horris Hill.

The school is owned and governed by Forfar Education who help to maintain the family-centred ethos whilst generating a safe, well-rounded education for its pupils. The proprietor of Horris Hill Preparatory School is Forfar Hampshire Ltd.

Hunter Hall School

Frenchfield, Penrith, Cumbria CA11 8UA
Tel: 01768 891291
email: office@hunterhall.cumbria.sch.uk
website: www.hunterhall.co.uk
X/Twitter: @hunterhall_sch
Facebook: @hunterhallschool
Instagram: @hunterhallschool

Chairman of Governors: Mrs Natalie Harling

***Head*: Mr Paul Borrows**, BA Hons, PGCE, MEd

Deputy Head: Mrs Kirsten Fletcher, BA Hons, PGCE, QTS

Foundation Stage Manager and KS1 Coordinator: Mrs Ella Tarrant, BA Hons, PGCE

Bursar: Mr David White, BA Hons, FCCA

Age Range. 3–11 co-educational.

Number of Pupils. 100.

Fees per term (2023–2024). £3.199–£3,260 Lower School (Reception to Year 2), £3,778–£3,849 Upper School (Year 3 to Year 6) including after-school activities. Pre-School paid per hour.

Who we are

Hunter Hall is a school like no other.

Housed in 19th century farm buildings in the Eden Valley on the edge of the Lake District, we combine specialist teaching, small class sizes and a tranquil rural setting to create a unique learning environment where children can learn, grow and become the best that they can be.

Our Approach

Hunter Hall is first and foremost a family school. Our families are at the heart of our community, and as a school we greatly value their contribution in making Hunter Hall a unique place to learn and grow up. Fundamental to the success of every child at Hunter Hall is the strength of relationships between the children and their teachers.

We know that happy children who feel a genuine sense of belonging will flourish in everything they do. What is more, we know, and value, every child as an individual, and work with them as individuals to ensure they fulfil their potential.

As well as ensuring all children feel a profound sense of place, providing them with a safe and happy environment in which to learn, we also want all children to enjoy a real sense of purpose in everything they do. Whether it be in the science laboratory or on the stage, when problem-solving in Maths or on the sports field, we want the children to engage purposefully in all that they do, understanding that the more that they actively engage in learning and school life the more rewarding it will be for them.

Our Values

As a prep school, we are true to our name and always have one eye on a more distant horizon. We are looking ahead to what comes next, to the challenges that the children will face when they move on from Hunter Hall. Our values are intended to ensure that the children are able to thrive at secondary school and beyond.

Kindness and respect

In everything that we do, we recognise that empathy and consideration of others come first. We also recognise the importance of respecting school property and equipment as well as the wider environment.

Resilience and receptiveness

We understand that making mistakes and overcoming challenges are a fundamental part of both learning and growing up, and we recognise the value of persevering and being open to a different way of seeing things.

Curiosity and creativity

We recognise that the joy of learning is rooted in both curiosity and creativity. The exhilaration of exploring and discovering new ideas never leaves us, nor does our appreciation of the freedom to approach learning in our own way and to express ourselves as individuals.

Self-awareness and self-belief

We understand that through self-awareness, we are able to determine our own path and strive for our own goals. Self-belief gives us the confidence to achieve our goals, supported by those around us

Charitable status. Hunter Hall School Ltd is a Registered Charity, number 1059098.

Hurlingham School

Main School:
122 Putney Bridge Road, Putney, London SW15 2NQ
Tel: 020 8103 1083
email: admin@hurlinghamschool.co.uk
website: www.hurlinghamschool.co.uk

Nursery:
The Old Methodist Hall, Gwendolen Avenue, Putney, London SW15 6EH

Head: **Mr Simon Gould**, BA Hons, QTS

Age range. 2–11 Co-educational.

Number of pupils. 411.

Fees per term (2023–2024). Main School: £6,575–£6,800; Nursery from £2,875.

Location and facilities. Hurlingham is a non-selective independent preparatory school in Putney. The modern and spacious buildings provide excellent facilities which include bright classrooms, a large gym and dance and drama studios, as well as a science laboratory, art studio and several music rooms. Recreational space includes two large playgrounds, an adventure playground and the adjacent Wandsworth Park. The Nursery School is located at our new refurbished site in Gwendolen Avenue and provides families with the option of nursery provision for children aged 2 to 4.

Ethos. The School's ethos is to provide a happy, secure atmosphere in which children flourish both academically and personally. Experienced and enthusiastic teachers provide opportunities for the children that strongly promote creativity and independence of thought, essential attributes for a child growing up in the 21st century. Self-confidence, self-discipline, self-motivation, self-esteem and, above all, a thirst and enjoyment for learning are nurtured.

Academic. The curriculum is broad, with the aim of providing a balanced and rounded education in which every child is treated as an individual and is encouraged to make the most of their particular talents. The important skills of reading, writing and numeracy are given a high priority in everyday teaching; these are delivered through many exciting cross-curricular topics which bring the children's learning alive and allow them to make sense of the world around them. All children on the main site learn French and Spanish in Reception, then choose one for the remainder of their time in school. Latin is taught from Form IV. Pupils are developed, nurtured and challenged to become critical thinkers who are thirsty for knowledge and can apply the skills that they have learnt.

Sport. All Hurlingham children participate enthusiastically in games and PE. Seasonal team games skills are taught in football, rugby, hockey, netball, cricket, gym and athletics. Numerous matches are organised with other local schools throughout the sporting year. Every summer term the whole school joins in with traditional Sports Day activities.

Music. Hurlingham has an excellent music department. The youngest children are encouraged to sing, play simple instruments and enjoy performing. The after-school Arts programme is open to all children from January of the Reception year through to the end of Year 6, enabling additional activities in music, art, drama and dance to be undertaken. For older pupils there are many extra opportunities to learn individual instruments, play in ensembles and participate in music concerts. There are several very popular choirs and ensemble groups.

Pastoral care. The focus is ensuring a culture that cultivates a psychologically safe space for all to flourish and cares deeply about emotional wellbeing. Children are encouraged to consider their place in the world and seek opportunities to have impact in their community and care for each other. All staff foster an intimate and welcoming environment centred on family values, with a clear focus on good manners, kindness and respect for one another. The House System, School Council and various pupil committees provide the children with wonderful opportunities to support each other and express their views about their school.

Clubs. Children are encouraged to participate in a wide range of clubs which include: art, ballet, chess, drama, karate, music, modern dance, table tennis and science. Older children are able to do their homework in school if parents wish and after-school care is available.

Starting out. A newly refurbished nursery close to the main site provides cutting-edge pre-school experiences, including a unique 1:4 forest school option. Children begin their life on the main campus in Reception which, although contained within the school building, is a separate area allowing children to feel part of the whole school but not overwhelmed by it. The three parallel classrooms all have direct access on to the playground, thus enabling the teaching of the curriculum to extend outside. There is also a cosy dedicated activity hall for Reception pupils which provides space for all three forms to join together for group activities, regular access to computers and a quiet place for reading.

Entry. For entry to Nursery and Reception there is no entrance test or interview. Places are offered in order of registration, although all pupils attending the Nursery are guaranteed the offer of a place at the prep-school. Siblings, and those living within 1.2 km of the school, are also given priority. Older children are invited to spend a day at Hurlingham and take part in lessons in order to assess their academic ability.

School visits. Appointments should be arranged with the School offices at either the main school or Nursery or sign up via the school website for half-termly Open Mornings.

Hurstpierpoint College Prep School

A Woodard School

Chalker's Lane, Hurstpierpoint, West Sussex BN6 9JS

Tel: 01273 834975 (Prep and Pre-Prep)
email: prepadmissions@hppc.co.uk
website: www.hppc.co.uk
X/Twitter: @Hurst_Prep
Facebook: @HurstCollege
Instagram: @hurst_prep

Chair of Governors: Mr A Jarvis, BEd, MA, FRSA

***Head of Senior Prep*: Mr Simon Lilley**, BSc Loughborough, MA Buckingham, PE & Sports Science

***Head of Junior Prep*: Mr Nick J Oakden**, BA Wales, MEd Buckingham, NPQH

Head of College: Mr Dominic W Mott, MA Queens' College, Cantab, Spanish

Deputy Head of College: Mr Lloyd P Dannatt, MEng Imperial College, London, Physics

Admissions Officer: Mrs Christina Treadaway

Age Range. 4–13 Co-educational.

Number of Pupils. Prep 304; Pre-Prep 52.

Fees per term (2023–2024). £3,670–£7,045. There are no compulsory extras.

The Prep and Pre-Prep Schools of Hurstpierpoint College (*see entry in HMC section*) share a beautiful 140-acre campus with the College. Although both Schools operate independently of the Senior School, having their own timetable, staff, buildings and Heads, the schools work closely together to offer a first-class programme of education for pupils from the age of 4 to 18.

The Prep School has joint use of many of the College's superb facilities, including a 25m heated indoor swimming pool, new theatre, drama and dance studios, music school, large sports hall, tennis courts and three full-size AstroTurf hockey pitches.

The aim of the Prep and Pre-Prep is to provide an outstanding education in a secure and happy environment.

The academic programme is exciting and innovative, with independent learning at the heart of teaching. The children are provided with an excellent grounding in the more traditional subjects and, as they progress through the school, they are encouraged to take more responsibility for their learning in order to develop the qualities and skills required for academic success in the Senior School.

The sports programme is extensive with netball, hockey, rugby, football, cricket, swimming, tennis, and athletics on offer. In addition, there is a wide-ranging activity programme which caters for the interests of all pupils.

The Music, Drama and Dance Departments are also very strong; about half the pupils learn musical instruments. The Preparatory School choir performs at the weekly Chapel service. There are at least three musicals or plays each year involving many children throughout the School.

The College has a dedicated Medical Centre with fully-qualified staff.

Each year a number of scholarship awards are available for entry into Year 7 (11+).

Charitable status. Hurstpierpoint College is a Registered Charity, number 1076498. The College provides a Christian education to pupils between the ages of 4 and 18.

Immanuel College

Elstree Road, Bushey, Hertfordshire WD23 4EB

Tel: 020 8950 0604
email: enquiries@immanuelcollege.co.uk
website: www.immanuelcollege.co.uk
X/Twitter: @ICBushey
Facebook: @ImmanuelCollegeUK

See full entry in the **HMC** section, on **p. 154**.

James Allen's Junior School

144 East Dulwich Grove, London SE22 8TE

Tel: 020 8693 0374
email: prep@jags.org.uk
website: www.jags.org.uk
X/Twitter: @JAGS_Prep
Facebook: @JAGSschool

Chair of Governors: Dr Jane Marshall, FRCPsych

***Headteacher*: Ms Victoria Goodson**, BA, MA

Age range: 4–11.

Number of pupils: 303.

Fees per term (2023–2024): £6,705.

James Allen's Junior School is an independent day school for girls aged between 4 and 11, offering a high quality of education provided by a team of skilled, motivated and dedicated teachers and support staff. The curriculum is broad and well-balanced and enriched by a varied and stimulating programme of extra-curricular clubs and activities.

Warmth, happiness and vitality are at the heart of everything we do at the Junior School. Children are encouraged to work to the best of their abilities, but we also want them to have fun and be curious in their learning. We see the primary years as vital to the success of all children's education.

The Junior School has an excellent staff-to-pupil ratio and provides specialist teachers in Art, DT, ICT, Music, PE and Science from Year 3. In French the children are taught from 4 years of age using the immersion method. Prep School girls enjoy specialist teaching for most of their subjects whilst regularly being taught by their Form Teacher. Our specially designed Computing suite, along with the Science, Design Technology and Art rooms, enable girls to enjoy their learning in a practical as well as a theoretical way. Enriching our exciting and diverse curriculum is an extensive range of extra-curricular activities to develop and extend the girls' own interests, teamwork and leadership skills.

The Pre-Prep School (for pupils aged 4–7) is housed in a separate Edwardian building with a large outside green space, including a sensory garden, new library and Forest Schools activities. The Prep School (for pupils aged 7–11) is a large, modern building on the same site as the Senior School sharing their theatre, swimming pool and games fields. The contemporary Vaughan Williams Auditorium offers an exceptional musical performance and event space for the school and local community.

Pupils normally enter the school in the year in which they are 4 or 7 at the beginning of the Autumn Term. Assessments take place the preceding December and January. At 11, girls normally progress to JAGS where Prep girls regularly win scholarships.

Charitable status. James Allen's Girls' School is a Registered Charity, number 1124853. The purpose of the charity is the conduct at Dulwich of a day school in which there shall be provided a practical, liberal and religious education for girls.

John Lyon School (Prep)

Hindes Road, Harrow HA1 1RX

Tel: 020 8515 9500
email: admissions@johnlyon.org
website: www.johnlyon.org
X/Twitter: @Johnlyonharrow
Facebook: @JohnLyonSchool
Instagram: @Johnlyonharrow
LinkedIn: /school/johnlyonharrow

Chairman of the Board of Governors (*a committee of the John Lyon Governing Body*): Mr N Enright, MA Oxon, MBA, NPQH, FRSA

***Head*: Mrs Sonal Chatrath**

Age Range. Boys and Girls 3–11.

Number of Pupils. 235.

Fees per term (2023–2024). Reception–Y2 £4,792 per term, Y3–Y6 £5,427 per term (fees include lunch). Nursery: £4,000 per term. Breakfast and late sessions available. (www.johnlyon.org/admissions/fees).

For more than 125 years, Quainton Hall, now John Lyon School (Prep) has served families in and around Harrow. The School became a part of John Lyon School in 2020. Together as one school, John Lyon provides the very best education for pupils aged 3–18, from the very youngest in the Nursery right the way through to A-Level students in the Sixth Form.

The life and work of the school is planned to enable children to shine in those areas and activities that they are good at and to reach their full potential. All members of staff have this objective as their aim. We also encourage the notion that learning is fun and that the acquisition of knowledge brings its own rewards. All that we do is conducted in an atmosphere and ethos that is personal, caring and family-orientated. We promote good order and self-discipline, consideration, and tolerance towards others as well as personal motivation and group endeavour.

Curriculum. Children enjoy a broad and inclusive education, firmly centred on the core values of respect, integrity, determination, and humility. With an emphasis on achievement, we believe in setting high expectations, leading by example, and creating a secure, positive and inspiring learning environment where our pupils can feel challenged and supported to aim high and develop their individual talents.

Our results are consistently impressive and many of our leavers gain scholarships to the senior schools of their choice. In a recent ISI School Inspection, we were rated the highest possible 'Excellent', for both our pupils' academic achievement and personal development.

Nursery. As soon as children walk through the doors of our Nursery they become part of the caring John Lyon family. Set within a large, recently refurbished and well-equipped building, with lots of access to outside space, our Nursery children are given the space to be inquisitive about the world around them while being supported to discover a love of learning that will benefit them for the rest of their lives.

Pre-Prep. From Reception to Year 2 our emphasis is on making our pupils feel excited about their learning and showing children how they can develop to the best of their ability in a caring yet challenging environment. We focus on building firm foundations in Literacy and Mathematics whilst ensuring children learn through cross-curricular themes and topics. The small classes have one class teacher and one teaching assistant, which means that each individual child is able to receive all the attention and support needed.

Prep. From Year 3 to Year 6, pupils begin to attend lessons with subject specialists in English and Mathematics, as well as other subjects including Science, Computing, Art, and French, together with a full Games programme, which includes some competition against other schools. Great care is taken by form teachers and subject staff to develop in each child a good sense of purpose and drive, supported by sound and effective organisational skills. Each child's effort and attainment is regularly assessed and homework becomes a feature of school life. Children are also expected to have a reading book with them at all times. By the age of 11, John Lyon pupils are ready to make the leap into secondary education with great confidence.

Admissions. Choosing the right nursery and first school for your child can be a daunting prospect, so we are here to guide parents every step of the way.

Children typically join the Prep School in either Nursery or Reception years and continue to the end of Year 6, aged 11. However, some children do join us at other stages, and we are always pleased to welcome them. We are proud to serve the families of Harrow and surrounding areas. Our families typically come to us from a Northwest London catchment area including the Boroughs of Barnet, Brent, Ealing and Hillingdon, as well as parts of Middlesex, Berkshire, Buckinghamshire and Hertfordshire.

The most common senior school destination for pupils is John Lyon School (Senior). Other school destinations include Merchant Taylor's, the two Haberdasher's schools, and City of London.

Pastoral care. The School is very much a family school where children are always our highest priority and where teachers and other staff operate an open-door policy. Our pastoral care is of paramount importance to us and our approach is rooted in a strong sense of community based on the belief that happy children can achieve great things.

Facilities. Through an ongoing desire to improve and enhance our provision, we are proud to boast first rate facilities including a recently refurbished swimming pool and Art and Design Centre, an AstroTurf pitch, a new ICT suite and modern classrooms with interactive whiteboards. We also have extensive use of sporting facilities at our Senior School.

Charitable status. The Keepers and Governors of the Free Grammar School of John Lyon is a Registered Charity, number 310033.

Keble Prep

A member of the Mill Hill Education Group

Wades Hill, Winchmore Hill, London N21 1BG
Tel: 020 8360 3359
email: office@kebleprep.co.uk
website: kebleprep.co.uk
X/Twitter: @kebleprep
Instagram: @kebleprepschool

***Head*: Mr P Gill**, BA Hons

Age Range. 3–13 Co-educational.
Number of Pupils. 165.
Fees per term (2023–2024). £4,400–£5,915.

As confirmed by the ISI Inspectors in the Spring of 2022, the warm and friendly atmosphere that exists at Keble ensures that the pupils are well-motivated, keen to learn and able to mature at their own pace. Strong pastoral care is regarded as a key element in the children's overall development and well-being, along with the encouragement of courteous and considerate behaviour.

The academic staff comprises 20 qualified graduate teachers, 7 classroom assistants and 3 Learning Support teachers. The buildings are well maintained and facilities are regularly updated. The school has an ambitious ICT development programme.

The average class size in the school is 16–18, although many classes are taught in half-groups and sets as the pupils progress through the school. Pupils follow the EYFS Curriculum in Pre-Prep. General subject teachers cover the academic curriculum in Years 1 to 4, with subject specialists following on from Year 5 onwards. The National Curriculum is used as a guide to curriculum development. Art, Music, PE, ICT, PSHE and Games are introduced at appropriate stages and are included within the timetable. Pupils are encouraged to learn a musical instrument, sing in the choir, perform in plays and concerts and play an active part in the wide range of sports on offer.

Football, rugby, netball, hockey and cricket are the major team games. Further opportunities exist to participate in swimming, basketball, athletics, cross country and tennis. There is a wide range of lunchtime and after-school activities and clubs, including drama, gardening, chess, eco and karate. There are also numerous educational outings and four residential trips.

Pupils are not required to pass an assessment to gain entry into the school at Nursery or Reception. Pupils wishing to join the school at a later stage in Year 1 or above are assessed in order to ensure that they will fit comfortably into their new surroundings.

Pupils are prepared for entry to senior independent schools through Common Entrance and Scholarship examinations at 11+ and 13+. The school has a strong record of success in placing pupils in the senior school which is right for them. In recent years, these schools include Mill Hill, Highgate, City of London, UCS, Haberdashers' Aske's, Haileybury, St Albans, St Columba's, Mount House and Westminster.

Charitable status. Keble Prep School became part of the Mill Hill Education Group (Registered Charity, number 1064758) on 1 April 2022.

Kensington Prep School

GDST

596 Fulham Road, London SW6 5PA
Tel: 020 7731 9300
email: enquiries@kenprep.gdst.net
website: www.kensingtonprep.gdst.net
X/Twitter: @KensingtonPrep

Founded in 1873.

Kensington Prep School is part of the GDST (Girls' Day School Trust). The GDST is the leading network of independent girls' schools in the UK. As a charity that owns and runs 23 schools and two academies, it reinvests all its income in its schools. For further information about the Trust, see p. xxii or visit www.gdst.net.

***Head*: Mrs Caroline Hulme-McKibbin**, BEd Hons Cantab

Age Range. 4–11 years.
Number of Girls. 300 (approx.).
Fees per term (2023–2024). £6,954.

Since 1997 Kensington Prep has been based in Fulham.

At Kensington Prep the focus is on growing great minds that are curious and creative, healthy and happy with an excellent, broadly-based but strongly academic curriculum. Independence, individuality and questioning thinkers are encouraged. Girls enjoy challenging and interesting work in a stimulating and nurturing environment, whilst being prepared for entry to leading day and boarding schools at 11+.

The school is set in an acre of grounds and has bright classrooms and specialist spaces for ICT, Art, Drama, Music and Science. The large playground provides fantastic play facilities, netball and tennis courts and great resources for outdoor learning including a Pocket Park.

Kensington Prep's innovative building project 'Creating Spaces for Growing Minds' has transformed the school and provides ground-breaking facilities for independent exploration, self-directed learning and collaborative work. These include spacious and flexible classrooms with breakout areas and retractable doors, a high-tech 'Explore Floor', a multimedia recording studio, and an Eco-Greenhouse. The beautiful school library puts reading at the heart of the school, with a child-friendly design and an extensive range of fact and fiction books. Three lifts make the school fully accessible.

The School achieved the highest possible grades across the board in its last Inspection by the Independent Schools Inspectorate and the quality of pupils' achievements and learning was rated 'exceptional'.

Entry to the School is selective and the main entry point is at 4+/Reception. Occasional places do occur throughout the School from time to time.

Charitable status. Kensington Prep School is part of The Girls' Day School Trust, which is a Registered Charity, number 306983.

Kensington Wade

Fulham Palace Road, London W6 9ER
Tel: 020 3096 2888
email: admissions@kensingtonwade.com
website: www.kensingtonwade.com

Chair of Governors: Mr Rodney Harris

***Head*: Mr Huw May**

Senior Leadership Team:
Ms Mary-Anne Malloy (Deputy Head)
Ms Jing Wang (Deputy Head and Head of Chinese Programme)
Mrs Lindsey Kavanagh (Head of Marketing)

Age Range. 3–11 years.

Student numbers. 105.

Fees per term (2023–2024). £6,830.

Admission. Children are able to join Kensington Wade at the start of the term in which they turn three.

Curriculum. We follow the British curriculum except in mathematics where we follow the Shanghai Approach (also called the Mastery Approach). The unique advantage at Kensington Wade is that we teach the curriculum in a fully immersive bilingual English-Chinese setting.

Extracurricular activities. We offer a wide range of curricular activities. Clubs offered include: African drumming, ballet, Bilingual Beats, board games, chamber choir, chess, Chinese art, Chinese calligraphy, Chinese dance, Chinese music, Chinese storytime, choral group, coding, cookery, drama, football, games, homework, Karate, multi-sports, musical ensemble, musical theatre, orchestra, passport, programmable robotics, Spanish, tennis and yoga.

Kent College Junior School

Harbledown, Canterbury, Kent CT2 9AQ
Tel: 01227 762436
email: prepenquiries@kentcollege.co.uk
website: www.kentcollege.com
X/Twitter: @kcsimonjames
Facebook: @kentcollege
Instagram: @kcjuniorschool
LinkedIn: /kent-college-canterbury

Chair of Governors: Mrs L Cocking

Head of Kent College: Mr M Turnbull

***Head of Junior School*: Mr S James**, BA Hons, MBA

(The full staff list can be found on the Kent College website.)

Age range. 0–11 Co-educational.

Number of pupils. Juniors (Day and Boarding): 200.

Fees per term (2023–2024). Juniors: Boarders £10,072; Day Pupils (including lunch): Year 6 £6,237, Year 5 £6,168, Year 4 £5,886, Year 3 £5,410, Year 2 £4,317, Year 1 £4,291, Reception £3,964, Pre-Reception £4,163 (full days, full week). Nursery: (0–3 years) £66.00 a day.

Kent College is a very happy and successful school for boys and girls aged 0–18, which is situated in the south-east of England on the outskirts of the beautiful and historic city of Canterbury. Canterbury is less than one hour from the centre of London by train and very close to all of the London airports.

The Garden Cottage Nursery (0–3 years) and Prep School (3–11 years) are based in an idyllic 14-acre site, just one mile from the centre of Canterbury. This day and boarding school offers a British education with an innovative approach to learning, full of opportunities for children to grow and develop their skills and talents.

The school has a thriving Music Department. The Choristers regularly perform at national level and have frequent success in competitions such as the BBC's Songs of Praise 'Junior Choir of the Year', and the prestigious Barnardo's National Choral Competition, in which they were 2022 winners. There is a wide range of sports on offer, from hockey to football, and the school hosts regular athletic and cross-country events, as well as taking students on sports tours during the year. Art and drama are also well catered for with the installation of a new Art department in the main school house (which was previously owned by Sidney Cooper, the Victorian landscape artist) and with the development of an outdoor theatre, The Dell, in the grounds. Children thrive in this progressive environment where the emphasis is on finding the right pace of education for each individual child.

There is a strong belief in making the timetable appropriate for each individual child. All children in the junior school take part in the Gifted, Really Enthusiastic, Able and Talented Programme, which enables the children to increase their performance even further in their chosen area. These lessons are given curriculum time and are delivered by specialist teachers who develop individual programmes for each pupil based on their needs and interests.

The areas of choice are geared towards maximising each child's chances of winning a scholarship to senior school and gaining entry to the school of their choice.

Boarding. Kent College has a long history of welcoming boarding pupils from abroad, as well as from British families resident in the UK or working overseas. The Junior boarding house, Sidney Cooper House, takes children from the age of 7 upwards and has a cosy family environment. Boarders can participate in evening and weekend activities as well as joining up to 30 Sunday excursions over the school year, from ice skating at the Natural History Museum in London, to going to the theatre or paintballing. We have a popular range of innovative one-term or one-year residential courses available to boarders to develop talent and excellence in English language, music or sport.

Beyond the classroom. Our full range of 50 after-school clubs offer a variety of interesting, challenging and fun activities for the children to enjoy while expanding their skills and knowledge.

There are clubs each evening from 4.10 pm–5.00 pm and 5.10 pm–6.00 pm which enable the children to be purposefully occupied until their parents can collect them. Many children choose to stay until six every evening, such is the range and variety.

For busy parents early care is also available in the mornings before school starts.

School farm and horse riding. The school is lucky to have a working farm where students can join the Farm Club and learn to care for and show animals at the Kent Show. Horse riding lessons are also available in the school's riding arena and the NESA team successfully competes in events all over the country.

Charitable status. Kent College, Canterbury is part of the Methodist Independent Schools Trust, which is a Registered Charity, number 1142794. The School was founded to provide education within a supportive Christian environment.

Kew College Prep

24–26 Cumberland Road, Richmond TW9 3HQ
Tel: 020 8940 2039
email: enquiries@kewcollegeprep.com
website: www.kewcollegeprep.com
Instagram: @kewcollegeprep

Chairman of Governors: Mrs Andrea Samuelson

***Head*: Mrs Jane Bond**, BSc, MAEd, PGCE

Age Range. 3–11 Co-educational.
Number of Pupils. 296.
Fees per term (2023–2024). £2,730–£5,105.

Kew College Prep was established in 1927 and was made into a charitable trust in 1985 by its founder, Elizabeth Hamilton-Spry, to ensure the long-term continuity of the school. The school's ethos is to ensure all pupils have an excellent grounding in the basics, but with a strong emphasis on areas such as art, music, drama and sport to develop the whole child.

Kew College Prep's style is described as traditional, yet imaginative and the atmosphere is happy and lively with a team of enthusiastic, caring and dedicated staff to help fulfil each child's potential. Pupils enjoy excellent facilities including specialist ICT and science labs. The ISI inspection in October 2010 concluded that '*Pupils achieve well across the curriculum and extra-curricular activities, and standards are exceptionally high in all aspects of English and Mathematics. The quality of their reading, writing and mathematical skills is in advance of their years.*'

In the ISI Regulatory Compliance Inspection of November 2016 the school was deemed to have met all of the ISI standards, with no action points.

The welfare and happiness of the children is of primary importance. This was highlighted in the ISI Inspection report of October 2019 which concluded that, '*the quality of the pupils' personal development is excellent*'.

Beyond the core curriculum pupils enjoy a wide range of weekly after-school clubs including chess, computer, debating, Building Imagination, STEMKids, M:Tech – music technology, fencing, skateboarding and yoga, with arts and crafts, Lego and Robotics for the younger pupils. There are also school choirs, a wind band and string orchestra. The school takes full advantage of its London location for educational visits. There are residential field trips in Years 3, 4, 5 and 6. In their final term, Year 6 pupils enjoy a week-long stay at a château in France improving their language skills, cultural knowledge and doing outward bound team activities.

At 11+ pupils not only achieve places through competitive entrance examinations to selective London day schools but also win a good number of awards. Year 6 pupils this year gained 27 scholarships.

Charitable status. Kew College Prep is a Registered Charity, number 286059.

Kew Green Preparatory School

Gardener Schools Group

Layton House, Ferry Lane, Kew Green, Richmond, London TW9 3AF
Tel: 020 8948 5999
email: secretary@kgps.co.uk
website: www.kgps.co.uk
X/Twitter: @KewGreenPrep
Facebook: @KewGreenPrep
Instagram: @kewgreenprep
LinkedIn: /company/kewgreenprep

***Headteacher*: Mrs Sasha Davies**

Age Range. 2–11 Co-educational.
Number of Pupils. 280.
Fees per term (2023–2024). £6,695.

Kew Green Preparatory School is housed in an attractive building and grounds directly next door to the Royal Botanical Gardens. The front of the school overlooks Kew Green, which is used for games and the back of the school has a good-sized playground which looks onto the River Thames.

In a non-pressurised, caring environment, KGPS produces excellent academic results, sending its pupils to London's best independent senior schools.

The children are encouraged to use philosophy and ethical thinking throughout the curriculum, which includes English, maths, science, French, RE, music, design & technology, art, games/PE and computer studies. All Upper School children attend a summer term Residential Week where cross-curricular studies are applied in a non-urban environment.

There are many after-school clubs and sports activities including three choirs, an orchestra and rock band. Individual tuition is offered in piano, violin, brass, woodwind, cello, saxophone, guitar, drums and singing.

An 8.00am to 6.00pm All-Day Care service is offered to parents at an extra charge.

The school is noted for its warm, happy atmosphere where parents play a full part in enriching the curriculum and social life. Off-site visits and guest workshops presented by noted visitors are a regular feature of education at Kew Green.

The school is always heavily over-subscribed and registration is recommended from birth. A prospectus can be downloaded on the school website and the registration form is now online.

The school opened a nursery in September 2022 for children aged 2 to 4 years old. Kew Green Nursery is a beautifully spacious environment situated opposite Kew Green and moments away from Kew Green Preparatory School. The children that attend Kew Green Nursery have the opportunity to transition to the Reception class at Kew Green Preparatory School, should this be the desired choice for parents.

Kimbolton Preparatory School

Kimbolton, Huntingdon, Cambs PE28 0EA
Tel: 01480 860281
email: prep@kimbolton.cambs.sch.uk
website: www.kimbolton.cambs.sch.uk
X/Twitter: @KimboltonSchool
Facebook: @KimboltonSchool
Instagram: @kimbolton_school

Motto: *Spes Durat Avorum*

Chair of Governors: Cllr J A Gray
***Headmaster*: J P Foley**, BA, NPQH

Age Range. 4–11 Co-educational.

Number of Children. Over 300.

Fees per term (2023–2024). £4,150–£5,385 (including lunch). These figures include a 2% discount which is applied if fees are paid by termly direct debit.

Mission Statement. Kimbolton School creates a caring, challenging environment in which pupils are encouraged to fulfil their potential and are given opportunities to flourish in a wide variety of curricular and extra-curricular interests.

We provide a close family environment where young people are educated to be tolerant, socially responsible and independent of mind, equipping them for our changing world. We are a community that challenges pupils to discover their talents, develop socially and excel.

Our Preparatory School is located at the western end of Kimbolton village in a mix of modern and Victorian buildings, while our Senior School is based at the opposite end of the village in Kimbolton Castle, among 120 acres of parkland and playing fields. We are very much one school: the curricula of the Prep and Senior Schools are aligned; our warm, caring ethos starts at the Reception Year and continues through to the Upper Sixth; and some of our staff teach at both the Prep and Senior Schools.

Our normal entry points for the Prep School are 4+, and 7+, with the assessment process taking place in February. We are able to accept applications into other year groups and/or at times other than September when space permits; this is subject to passing an appropriate assessment.

Pupils join our Reception year and are then split into two classes in Year 1 and Year 2. Years 3–6 have three classes each. Each has its own class teacher and pupils throughout the Upper Prep also benefit from a good deal of specialist teaching. We have provision for academically gifted children and provide one-to-one and small group tuition as needed.

We offer an extensive range of trips, visits and competitions to complement the curriculum, as well as regularly welcoming visiting speakers. From Year 3 onwards, children have the option of participating in residential trips.

There is a vibrant musical scene throughout Kimbolton School. The majority of children in Years 3–6 take individual music lessons in addition to class music; those in Years 1 and 2 may opt for small group string sessions. Performance opportunities abound, with formal and informal concerts plus an annual orchestral afternoon.

Lower Prep is located in Aragon House, a purpose-built facility for 4–7 year olds, recently furbished and extended, which provides a safe, welcoming and happy environment. Children in Lower Prep also use the facilities on offer throughout the Prep School. Children automatically progress to the Upper Prep, with the expectation that at age 11 pupils will continue to the Senior School. (*See entry in HMC section*).

The Prep School has, on its own site, a dining hall, library, digital suite, assembly hall, music teaching and practice rooms, science laboratory, art and design technology room and sports hall, as well as large, light and airy classrooms. There is a full-time nurse on site.

Our outdoor facilities include tennis and netball courts, 400m grass athletics track, rounders fields, floodlit all-weather pitches, plus football, hockey and cricket pitches. Pupils also enjoy regular access to the first-class facilities at the Senior School, including a 25-metre swimming pool. We have a full programme of sports fixtures and tournaments and have achieved notable successes across a range of sports.

Out of hours options provide high-quality support to working parents. Children may arrive for breakfast at 7.30 am and our 'Kim Club' facility is available after school until 6.00 pm. There is also an extensive range of extracurricular activities, clubs, and supervised homework to extend the school day. Many of our children use our daily bus service to travel to and from school.

Kimbolton Preparatory School was inspected by ISI in 2017.

Charitable status. Kimbolton School Foundation is a Registered Charity, number 1098586.

King Edward's Junior School
Bath

North Road, Bath BA2 6JA
Tel: 01225 463218
email: junior@kesbath.com
website: www.kesbath.com
X/Twitter: @KESBathJunior
Facebook: @kesbath
Instagram: @kesbath

Chair of Governors: Mrs W Thomson, MEd, BEd Hons, LLCM TD

***Head Teacher*: Mr S Price**, BA, PGCE

Age range. 7–11 Co-educational.

Number of pupils. 195.

Fees per term (2023–2024). £4,470.

Our award-winning, purpose-built Junior School on the same North Road site as the Senior School is extremely well equipped for learning, with dedicated specialist teaching rooms for Science, Art, Design Technology and Music and a state-of-the-art ICT Suite and Technology Centre, all housed around a lovely central library. The School also includes a large multi-purpose hall and dining room.

Externally, the Junior School has its own adventure playground, dipping ponds, wildflower garden, multi-sport play area, an astro, Activity Trail, as well as access to the Meadow, a delightful and spacious area with beautiful views over Bath.

The Junior School is an integral part of the King Edward's foundation and is governed by the same Board. It joins with the Senior School in major events, such as the Founder's Day Service in Bath Abbey, and shares various games facilities and specialist teaching staff.

All children learn the strings (violin, viola, cello and double bass) in Year 3, recorder in Year 4, whole class orchestra/band and Gamelan in Year 5 and Steel Pans in Year 6. Well over half of the children learn additional instruments under the tutelage of a strong peripatetic music team. A mixture of French, German and Spanish is taught throughout the School while purpose-built facilities in Art, Science, Technology and IT, coupled with specialist teaching, ensure high standards of achievement in those areas. The School is a very busy one renowned for its co-curricular programme. The wide variety of activities on offer include table tennis, gymnastics, fencing, judo, chess, dance, Eco Club and Crafty Club. This is not to mention the various musical and instrumental groups and the many opportunities to play rugby, football, hockey, netball, cricket, tennis, cross country and athletics. Frequent educational trips are arranged in and around the local area and during the summer Activities Week; residential trips for Years 3–6, include destinations such as France and Devon. Sporting tours also take place each year.

The House system plays a central role in the life of the School. All children belong to one of four Houses and take part in many events and competitions during the year.

Pre-Prep & Nursery and Senior School. For details of the Pre-Prep and Nursery please see separate IAPS entry and for Senior School details please see King Edward's School's entry under HMC.

Charitable status. King Edward's Junior School is part of King Edward's School Bath which is a Registered Charity, number 1115875.

King Edward's School Pre-Prep and Nursery
Bath

Weston Lane, Bath BA1 4AQ
Tel: 01225 421681
email: pre-prep@kesbath.com
website: www.kesbath.com
X/Twitter: @KESBathPrePrep
Facebook: @kesbath
Instagram: @kesbath

Chair of Governors: Mrs W Thomson, MEd, BEd Hons, LLCM TD

***Head Teacher*: Ms J Gilbert**, BEd Hons, NPQH

Age range. 3–7 Co-educational.

Number of pupils. 85.

Fees per term (2023–2024). £3,330–£4,035.

King Edward's Pre-Prep and Nursery offers an exciting and stimulating world in which to start school life. A desire to make learning 'irresistible' in a nurturing environment is at the heart of everything we do. Personalised learning, combined with academic rigour, ensures that every child thrives and is provided with the extension and support that they need. New initiatives, fresh challenges, concerts, trips, visiting experts and inspiring projects all help to enrich our broad and creative curriculum.

Ethos. Child focused – First and foremost we want every child to feel safe, encouraged and happy in school. We place children at the centre of learning, creating a close match between your child and the curriculum. This helps to increase a child's eagerness to learn, builds self-esteem and encourages positive attitudes.

Family focused – Visitors to the Pre-Prep often remark on the wonderful 'family feel' that they sense in the school. We work very hard to be as family-focused as possible and are very fortunate to have such supportive parents; we are never short of volunteers for the many school trips that the children enjoy and for all the varied events that take place. It is lovely to see not only parents but grandparents taking an active role in the school.

Outdoor focused – At King Edward's the outdoor environment is a natural extension of the classroom and we are proud of our status as a Forest School. As well as allowing children to engage directly with the environment, outdoor learning also brings together many different elements of the curriculum and enriches school life.

Facilities. Our Pre-Prep and Nursery is situated in a beautiful Victorian house close to Royal Victoria Park, Bath. In addition to the light and airy classrooms, we have a well-equipped school hall. There is also Teddy's Lodge for pre- and after-school care, an art room and library. Children make full use of the spacious and safe grounds to the rear of the main house, with a dedicated outdoor cedar lodge classroom, storytelling corner, surfaced playground, wooden fort, wooded area and an amazing adventure climbing frame. The grounds also boast an extensively landscaped gardening area with greenhouse, where the children cultivate their own vegetables, as well as a dipping pond for Science investigation. There is also a magical sensory garden and an all-weather Astro pitch for team games.

Junior School and Senior School. For details of the Junior School please see separate IAPS entry and for the Senior School please see King Edward's School's entry under HMC.

Charitable status. King Edward's Pre-Prep and Nursery is part of King Edward's School Bath which is a Registered Charity, number 1115875.

King Henry VIII School

Part of the Coventry School Foundation

Warwick Road, Coventry CV3 6AQ

Tel: 024 7627 1111
email: info.khviii@bkhs.org.uk
website: www.kinghenrys.co.uk
X/Twitter: @KHVIIISchool
Facebook: @KingHenryVIIISchool
Instagram: @kinghenryviiischool

See full entry in the **HMC** section, on **p. 172**.

King's College Prep School

A Woodard School

Kingston Road, Taunton, Somerset TA2 8AA

Tel: 01823 285920
email: admissions@kings-taunton.co.uk
schooloffice@kingshalltaunton.co.uk
website: www.kings-taunton.co.uk
X/Twitter: @KingsCollPrep
Facebook: @KingsCollegePrepSchool
LinkedIn: /kings-college-prep-school

***Headmaster*: Mr Justin Chippendale**

Deputy Head (*Academic*): Mr Alistair Wilkinson
Deputy Head (*Pastoral*): Mr Steve Watson
Head of Pre-Prep: Mrs Claire Luckhurst
Head of Boarding: Mrs Anna Hardy
Director of Finance and Operations: Mr Simon Worthy
Director of Admissions & Marketing: Mrs Kate Rippin
Chaplain: The Revd Mark Smith
PA to the Headmaster: Mrs Emma Guppy

King's College Prep is a leading pre-prep and prep school with around 300 girls and boys. Set in a beautiful countryside location surrounded by farmland, the school is only a couple of minutes' drive from the centre of Taunton.

The school respects traditional values and boarding is a strong feature which contributes to the tangible family atmosphere that exists in the school. Children enjoy a challenging all-round education in a progressive and stimulating environment.

The 2022 ISI report recognised that pupils at King's Prep have 'been brought up in a school where they feel happy and confident …they appreciate their natural environment and understand the positive impact on their wellbeing'. It also commented on 'the effective teaching and balanced educational experience that leads to pupils leaving equipped with a diverse set of skills'.

Pre-Prep. We have a very popular Pre-Prep, located in its own dedicated area of the school with full access to our extensive facilities and grounds. Our Nursery is a friendly, happy and welcoming setting for children aged two to four years, and every child has their own key worker who focuses on individual needs and supports each child through their time with us. When the time comes to move up to Reception, we take the children and their parents on a tour of the facilities so they can see more of what we have to offer for the next stage of their child's development. This gentle and smooth transition helps children become familiar with their new surroundings and feel like part of one big school family.

Prep School. When children first join the Prep School, the door to an exciting new world of opportunities and challenges is opened, both inside and outside the classroom. Our teachers are experts in their fields, and welcoming, engaging and passionate. All children study core subjects: English, maths, science, geography, history, modern foreign languages (MFL) and religious studies, and our broad curriculum also embraces Latin, the visual and creative arts (including music, art and drama), design technology, and an imaginative programme of PE and games.

Activities. Sporting facilities and opportunities are extensive, as is the school's co-curricular, offering includes Forest School, riding lessons at the school's off-site Equestrian Centre, archery, ballet, fencing, cookery, multi-sports and outdoor adventure.

Facilities. Across the school site, pupils benefit from traditional and modern facilities such as a bright modern science facility, cookery school, adventure playground, outdoor swimming pool, Astros and extensive grass pitches, a huge indoor sports centre and gym equipment, as well as an arts centre that acts as the hub for music and performing arts events. The school's 2.5 km 'King's Loop' is popular for cross-country running at lunch times.

King's Prep has a partner senior school, King's College, Taunton, and the two schools benefit from their own independent sites, furnished with excellent age-appropriate facilities to maximise the opportunities for the children in their care. There is a close working relationship between King's Prep and the senior school, and the majority of pupils progress to King's College at age 13.

Fees per term (2023–2024). Pre-Prep: £3,200–£3,330, Prep: £4,015–£6,800, UK boarding: £7,750–£9,995.

Charitable status. Woodard Schools Taunton Ltd is a Registered Charity, number 1103346. King's College Prep exists to provide high quality education for boys and girls aged 2–13.

King's College School, Cambridge

West Road, Cambridge, Cambridgeshire CB3 9DN

Tel: 01223 365814
email: office@kcs.cambs.sch.uk
website: www.kcs.cambs.sch.uk

Chairman of Governors: The Revd Dr S Cherry

***Head*: Mrs Y F S Day**, BMus Cape Town, MMus London, GDL College of Law

Deputy Heads:
Mr T Coe-Hales, BA Hons Cantab, MA Cantab, PGCE Cambridge
Mr J Rist, MA Cantab, PGCE University of East Anglia

Age Range. 4–13 Co-educational.

Number of Pupils. 391 day pupils, 35 boy boarders including 24 choristers, 12 flexi/weekly girl boarders.

Fees per term (2023–2024). Weekly Boarders: £9,750; Choristers: £3,215; Day Pupils: £6,295; Pre-Prep: £4,960.

King's College School is a leading independent prep school with 410 boys and girls aged 4–13. We are large enough to provide a full range of options and facilities, but small enough to give a 'family feel' where the teachers can get to know all the children.

The school enjoys an excellent academic reputation, with a huge number of leavers winning scholarships to senior schools in various disciplines.

Situated in the centre of Cambridge, the school is ideally placed on a leafy campus to combine the strengths of traditional academic and cultural excellence with modern and innovative educational ideas.

Admission. Prospective parents are invited to come to King's for an individual tour of the School with the Registrar. Entry to all year groups is by assessment and by taking into account current school reports (Years 1–8).

Curriculum. Our curriculum embraces the Common Entrance and Independent Schools Scholarship syllabuses, as well as meeting the requirements laid down in the National Curriculum. We also teach French from the age of 4, Latin from age 8, and Ancient Greek to older children. Standards of literacy and numeracy are high at King's. While external examination success is the final goal, children are encouraged to develop a sense of achievement, enjoyment and attainment of potential in all subjects. The School has a history of winning numerous academic, art, music, drama and sports awards annually.

Choristers. In 1441 Henry VI founded King's College and decreed that there should be 16 choristers to sing at services in his chapel. Now over 550 years later, our choristers are famed throughout the world and each year millions of listeners and viewers tune in on Christmas Eve to enjoy the 'Festival of Nine Lessons and Carols' from King's College Chapel. For more information about the choir and choristerships at King's please visit our website: www.kcs.cambs.sch.uk/kings-choristers.

Schola Cantorum. A choral training programme for girls in Years 4 to 8 was launched in 2020, giving them opportunities for rehearsal and performance both here in Cambridge and further afield.

Facilities. A newly built Sport and Culture Centre is situated at the heart of the school. The Wiles Centre for Technology has first-class facilities for ICT and DT. The Performing Arts Centre includes 16 music rooms and a multi-purpose hall used for plays and concerts; it also doubles as a fully-equipped gym.

A modern classroom block contains 2 well-equipped science labs as well as classrooms for modern languages, English and maths; our purpose-built library houses over 15,000 books.

Music. King's has a strong tradition of musical excellence and encourages pupils to participate on all levels. We have many choral and instrumental groups including jazz groups, 2 orchestras of some 80 players each and about 40 chamber groups.

Sports. Our new sports and cultural centre is now complete and includes facilities for badminton, netball, basketball, cricket, dance, concerts, lectures and assemblies. We also have two large playing fields, tennis courts, a heated outdoor swimming pool, floodlit astroturf, and two recently-built squash courts. Games include Rugby, Football, Hockey, Cricket, Girls' Cricket, Netball, Rounders, Athletics, Tennis, Squash, and Swimming. We run Sports Performance and Sports Development programmes, to enable all children to enjoy sports regardless of their underlying ability.

Activities. Drama, Art, Computing, Craft, Touch-typing, Spelling, Gardening, DT, Music and Mindfulness, Gardening, PE, Chess, Science, Wildlife Explorers, Library, Orienteering, Yoga, Ballet, Spanish, Electronics, Karate, Jazz Dance, Street Dance, Airfix, Ballet, Cookery, Cross Stitch, Spelling, Board Games, French Films, and Mandarin Chinese.

Staff. The Head is assisted by 51 full-time and 22 part-time teachers. There are 40 full or part-time music staff.

Bursaries. Means tested bursaries are available for children applying for places in Year 3 from a state school.

Leaving King's. Pupils are prepared for local senior school entrance assessments as well as for Common Entrance and academic scholarship examinations. Nearly all children are offered places at their first-choice senior school and many achieve scholarship awards. Some pupils also transfer to local state schools.

Charitable status. King's College School is an integral part of King's College, Cambridge, which is a Registered Charity, number 1139422. Its aim is to provide an excellent education for girls and boys of mixed ability aged 4 to 13.

King's College Junior School

Wimbledon Common, London SW19 4TT

Tel: 020 8255 5335
email: jsadmissions@kcs.org.uk
HMJSsec@kcs.org.uk
website: www.kcs.org.uk
X/Twitter: @KCJSWimbledon

Chairman of the Governing Body: Lord Deighton, KBE

***Headmaster*: Mr E Lougher**, BA, MSc

Age range. 7–11.

Number of boys. 286 (day boys only).

Fees per term (2023–2024). £7,250 (Years 3–4), £7,805 (Years 5–6).

The Junior School was established in 1912 as an integral part of KCS, to prepare boys for the Senior School. It shares with it a common site and many facilities, in particular, the Music School, the Art and Design Engineering School, the Dining Hall, the Sports Halls, the swimming pool and extensive playing fields. For the rest, Junior School boys are housed in their own buildings. The Priory, rebuilt in 1980, contains twelve classrooms, including specialist rooms for languages, mathematics, history, geography, information technology and multimedia work. The youngest age groups have their own special accommodation in Rushmere, a spacious Georgian house whose grounds adjoin the Junior School. The School also has its own purpose-built library, science laboratories and well-equipped theatre and assembly hall.

The School is separately administered in matters relating to admission, curriculum, discipline and day-to-day activities. There are thirty-nine members of staff in addition to those teaching in specialist departments common to both Schools.

The work and overall programme are organised in close consultation with the Senior School to ensure that boys are educated in a structured and progressive way from 7 to 18, having the benefit of continuity, while enjoying the range and style of learning that are best suited to their age.

Boys come from both maintained and pre-preparatory schools and are admitted at the age of 7, 8 or 9. Entry is by interview, activity session and examination.

Charitable status. King's College School is a Registered Charity, number 310024. It exists to provide education for children.

King's Ely

The Old Palace, Palace Green, Ely, Cambridgeshire CB7 4EW

Tel: 01353 660701 (Principal's PA)
01353 660707 (Admissions)
email: admissions@kingsely.org
website: www.kingsely.org
X/Twitter: @Kings_Ely
Facebook: @KingsElyOfficial
Instagram: @kingselyofficial
LinkedIn: /kingselyofficial

See full entry in the **HMC** section, on **p. 179**.

King's House School

68 King's Road, Richmond, Surrey TW10 6ES

Tel: 020 8940 1878
email: admissions@kingshouseschool.org
website: www.kingshouseschool.org
X/Twitter: @kingshousesch
Facebook: @kingshousesch
Instagram: @kingshousesch
LinkedIn: /company/kings-house-school

King's House School is an independent day preparatory school and nursery in Richmond for children aged 3 to 13.

Chair of Governors: Mrs Christine Laverty

***Head*: Mr Mark Turner**, BA, PGCE, NPQH

Age Range. Co-ed 3–13, including Nursery.

Number of Pupils. 430.

Fees per term (2023–2024). Nursery Department: £2,870–£5,580; Junior Department: £5,280–£6,190; Senior Department: £6,890 (all fees inclusive of lunch excluding Nursery).

King's House School is a mixed-ability inclusive independent day preparatory school in Richmond for children aged 3 to 13. Founded in 1946, we provide a happy and relaxed environment for our pupils, where they can thrive and flourish. We offer a broad and balanced education to all our pupils, enabling them to discover their unique talents and passions. The first girls will join Reception and Year 1 from September 2024 as the school moves to full co-education.

King's House Nursery opened in 2009, providing a wealth of resources to inspire little minds and create a love of learning. The team of highly experienced staff help children to become independent, settle into nursery life and develop key social skills. Children move up to Reception ready for their next steps at school.

A broad curriculum ensures that pupils explore their different interests, and specialist teaching starts in the nursery with Computing, PE, Music, Drama, yoga and French lessons. By the time they reach the Senior Department (Years 4–8), pupils enjoy a wide range of specialist subjects across the arts, science, humanities, sport and much more. Pupils move onto a huge range of senior schools at 11 or 13, including day, boarding, single sex or co-ed. Staff work closely with families to find the right school for each child.

Pastoral care is at the heart of the King's House community, where children who are happy can thrive and succeed. The positive relationships that we enjoy with our parents, the local community and charities are all key to the pupils' sense of responsibility. We aim to ensure that the school keeps pace with global developments so that pupils are ready to take their place in an ever-changing world. When pupils leave us, they are not only armed with outstanding academic results, but also with a sense of self-awareness, respectfulness and independence. Academic success is a result of the happy atmosphere of King's House, which allows pupils to simply be themselves.

The school is based on three sites on Richmond Hill and also benefits from its own 35-acre Sports Ground in Chiswick. The three main school sites have spacious state-of-the-art facilities, and pupils have close access to all that London has to offer.

King's House is a mixed-ability inclusive school at our two main entry points, Nursery and Reception. All children in the Nursery are guaranteed a place in Reception. There are also small intakes at 7+, 8+, and 11+.

For more information visit the school's website or contact our Registrar, Sally Bass, on 020 8940 1878 or admissions@kingshouseschool.org.

Charitable status. Kings House School Trust (Richmond) Limited is a Registered Charity, number 312669. It exists for the education of children.

Junior King's School

Milner Court, Sturry, Canterbury, Kent CT2 0AY

Tel: 01227 714000
email: office@junior-kings.co.uk
website: www.junior-kings.co.uk
X/Twitter: @JuniorKingsSch
Facebook: @JuniorKingsSch
Instagram: @JuniorKingsSch
LinkedIn: /company/junior-king-s-school-canterbury

Chairman of Governors: Count Benoit De Vitry D'Avaucourt

***Headmistress*: Mrs Emma Károlyi**

Age range. 3–13.

Number of pupils. 359 (67 Boarders; 292 Day Pupils, including 77 Pre-Prep).

Fees per term (2023–2024). Boarders: £9,545; Day Pupils: £5,610–£6,785; Pre-Prep: £4,055 (including meals).

Junior King's was founded in 1879 as the preparatory school to The King's School Canterbury, which can trace its roots back to the sixth century when St Augustine established a monastery in Kent.

Set in eighty acres of attractive countryside, just two miles from Canterbury city centre, Junior King's pupils enjoy a calm, happy and purposeful atmosphere drawing upon a rich Christian heritage. Girls and boys from the ages of three to thirteen years achieve their potential, both inside and beyond the classroom, whatever their ability.

The school has an outstanding reputation for academic excellence and scholarship due to a varied and stimulating curriculum. This is supported by first-class teaching and opportunities to enjoy a wide range of sports, music, drama and extracurricular activities.

The school is in the grounds of Milner Court, a 16th century Manor House. This historic building, along with a Kentish Oast House used by the Pre-Prep, a newly refurbished Tithe Barn used for theatre and musical productions, and a flint stoned church for services and assemblies, has been sensitively augmented over the years. Other impressive facilities include specialist art, science, ICT and design suites.

Spacious and comfortable boarding accommodation for around 80 boarders with social rooms, kitchens and games rooms are at the heart of the school in the main building.

The school has a fine reputation for music, both instrumental and choral, as well as for art, design and drama. The school year includes a programme of concerts, recitals and exhibitions involving children of all ages.

In 2013, Mr Hugh Robertson, MP and Minister of State for Sport, Olympic Legacy and Tourism opened a stunning new all-weather sports pitch and tennis courts. In 2016, a magnificent new music school was officially opened by Dr Harry Christophers, CBE, OKS.

A large and modern sports hall is used for PE lessons, basketball, volleyball, badminton, and netball, as well as indoor hockey, soccer and tennis. Rowing and sailing take place on nearby lakes. Pupils make use of the large indoor swimming pool at the senior school.

For boys, cricket, soccer hockey and rugby are the main team games, while girls play netball, hockey and rounders. Athletics, tennis and fencing are joint pursuits.

Children can join the Nursery from the age of three in our impressive purpose-built 'Little Barn'. In its delightful Kentish Oast House setting, the Pre-Prep has its own spacious hall, library and seven bright classrooms complete with the latest ICT facilities. Outside, pupils have their own extensive adventure playground as well as sharing the main school facilities such as the sports hall, tithe barn, sports fields and dining hall.

Junior King's pupils progress at 13+ to The King's School Canterbury and other leading public schools, with a sense of achievement, maturity and self-confidence. Academic standards are high and the record of success in Scholarships and Common Entrance is outstanding.

(*See entry for The King's School Canterbury in the HMC section.*)

Charitable status. The King's School of the Cathedral Church of Canterbury is a Registered Charity, number 307942. It exists to provide education for boys and girls.

The King's School
Macclesfield

Alderley Road, Prestbury, Macclesfield, Cheshire SK10 4SP
Tel: 01625 260000
email: mail@kingsmac.co.uk
website: www.kingsmac.co.uk
X/Twitter: @kingsmac
Facebook: @kingsinmacc
Instagram: @explore/tags/kingsmac

See full entry in the **HMC** section, on **p. 188**.

The King's School Worcester Foundation

Senior School
5 College Green, Worcester WR1 2LL
Tel: 01905 721700
email: info@ksw.org.uk
website: www.ksw.org.uk
X/Twitter: @KingsWorcester
Facebook: @KingsWorcester

King's St Alban's Prep
Mill Street, Worcester WR1 2NJ
Tel: 01905 354906
email: ksa@ksw.org.uk

King's Hawford Prep
Hawford Lock Lane, Claines, Worcester WR3 7SD
Tel: 01905 451292
email: hawford@ksw.org.uk

See full entry in the **HMC** section, on **p. 190**.

Kingshott School

Stevenage Road, St Ippolyts, Hitchin, Hertfordshire SG4 7JX
Tel: 01462 432009
email: pa2head@kingshottschool.com
website: www.kingshottschool.com
Facebook: @kingshottschool
Instagram: @kingshottschool
LinkedIn: /school/kingshott-school

Chairman of Governors: Mr James Bentall

***Headmaster*: Mr David Weston**, BA Hons, QTS

Age Range. From September 2024 onwards, the school will grow, incrementally, to educate pupils age 3–16, with our first Year 9 year group in September 24.

Number of Pupils. There are currently around 400 day pupils in the school, from Nursery through to Year 8.

Fees per term (2023–2024). (including lunch) Nursery £2,430 (5 mornings), Pre-Prep £4,285, Prep £5,225.

Kingshott School is delighted to be expanding its 'excellent' ISI-rated education up to GCSE. For many years, Kingshott families have been asking us to continue our education through to GCSE, and we are now pleased to be expanding, with three additional year groups (Years 9, 10 and 11) being incrementally added to the School from September 2024 onwards. Current Kingshott pupils will be able to automatically move through to join our Senior School. New pupils, from Hitchin and across Hertfordshire, Bedfordshire and Cambridgeshire, will be able to join Kingshott in Year 7, 8 or 9, after successfully completing our admissions process.

The Kingshott community – which is focused on being **caring** and **inclusive** – encourages children to be **confident** and **ambitious** for themselves and each other. Going forward, we will be supporting and stretching children, from age 3 up to 16, to achieve their full potential at every stage of their educational journey, culminating in their GCSEs. At Kingshott we welcome every child's unique character and approach to learning. There is no 'one-size-fits-all' education. At the core of every decision we make lies pupil development and happiness.

Our modern facilities, set within 23 acres on the edge of Hitchin, inspire the staff and children alike to strive for their best. Over the last 20 years, Kingshott has invested in state-of-the-art facilities including a standalone Nursery building, and purpose-built Pre-Prep and Prep School buildings. The fabulous sports hall converts into a drama theatre, and the recently refurbished heated swimming pool enables pupils to benefit from year-round swimming. As well as extensive sports and astroturf pitches, there are plenty of areas for our children to enjoy playing. Our developments continue with our move to offer GCSEs, with new science facilities being created, along with improved Design Technology and dining facilities.

Our emphasis on a rounded education ensures our children experience the very best teaching available, whether it be through the academic subjects or our broad and comprehensive wider curriculum. This is complemented by a full and varied after-school programme (until 6.00 pm) which includes a wide variety of creative and sporting activities and hobbies. Breakfast Club and After-School Care is also available for all pupils.

Kingshott is open to pupils between the ages of 3 and 13 (rising to 16), irrespective of gender, race, religion, culture, sexual orientation or disability. Entry into Nursery and Reception is non-selective. Early registration is encouraged, as waiting lists are in place for most year groups. Entry into older year groups (including Year 7+ to join Kingshott for Senior School) is by an assessment which is appropriate to the child's age. Year 7 Scholarships (Academic, Art, Drama, Music and Sport) are available, and Year 9 Scholarships will be added as the school grows.

Kingshott is conveniently situated on the outskirts of Hitchin, with plenty of convenient parking for busy parents. Families join Kingshott from across Hertfordshire and beyond – including Luton,

Letchworth, Baldock, Stevenage and Welwyn. The A1(M) Motorway is within just two miles of the school.

The School, founded in 1931, is currently a Charitable Educational Trust, with a Board of Governors. Kingshott School Trust Limited is Registered Charity number 280626. It exists to provide education for boys and girls. In January 2024, Kingshott was delighted to announce that it is joining forces with a charitable foundation, the Mill Hill Education Group. This proactive initiative enables Kingshott to action its ambitious goals over the years ahead.

Kingsley School

Northdown Road, Bideford, Devon EX39 3JR

Tel: 01237 426200
email: admissions@kingsleyschoolbideford.co.uk
website: www.kingsleydevon.com
X/Twitter: @KingsleyDevon
Facebook: @KingsleySchoolBideford
Instagram: @kingsleyschool
LinkedIn: /company/kingsley-school-bideford

See full entry in the **Society of Heads** section, on **p. 534**.

Kingswood House School

56 West Hill, Epsom, Surrey KT19 8LG

Tel: 01372 723590
email: office@kingswoodhouse.org
website: www.kingswoodhouse.org
X/Twitter: @kingswoodhouse
Facebook: @p/Kingswood-House-School-100057209630206/
Instagram: @kingswood_house

The school is an educational trust, overseen by a board of governors.

Chairman of Governors: Richard J Evans, BEd Hons, MEd

***Interim Headmaster*: Liam Clarke**, BSc Open, PGCE

Age Range. 4–16; co-educational.

Number of Pupils. 227 day pupils.

Fees per term (2023–2024). Reception–Year 2 £3,940; Years 3–4 £5,610; Years 5–6 £5,855; Years 7–8 £5,925; Years 9–11 £6,280. Free after-school care provided until 5.00 pm in Prep Club.

At Kingswood House, we have long enjoyed an outstanding reputation as a leading school for boys but we are embracing the future and moved to co-education in September 2021. Our Senior division opened in September 2016, thereby extending our exceptional academic and pastoral provision through to GCSE; this year our cohort achieved 78% success at Level 9–4 with many of those grades showing much individual value-added. We offer a genuine all-round education, underpinned by exciting curricular and co-curricular opportunities, with a strong emphasis on character development and preparation for life beyond the school gate.

Kingswood House is situated in a leafy suburb of Epsom with excellent transport links. We are ambitious for our pupils and challenge each individual to achieve their potential in a conducive environment of small classes and high expectations.

Accredited as "excellent in all areas" in our last ISI inspection in April 2023, Kingswood House is also endorsed by the Independent Association of Preparatory Schools (IAPS) and inclusion in The Good Schools Guide.

We are proud to be finalists for an ISY award in 2021 and shortlisted in 2022 and again in 2023 – most recently for Student Wellbeing. Furthermore, we won the National 'Best School Trip' Award in 2019 for our bespoke "Making of Modern Britain" residential trip for our Year 9 pupils.

Our values promote tolerance, respect and friendship and we welcome families from all faiths, or none. We offer a well-rounded education and a purposeful, supportive ethos in which each child will grow in independence, resilience and self-esteem. All boys and girls are encouraged to participate in every aspect of school life and this provides a wonderful platform for them to take themselves out of their comfort zone within a supportive environment. A rich variety of opportunities, both inside and outside the classroom, engenders an avid natural curiosity and propagates a willingness to try new things.

With the advent of our flourishing Senior Years, parents are able to consider their options carefully, secure in the knowledge that Kingswood House offers an excellent pathway for the pupils through to GCSE. We are also developing KHS for the future and have recently built an impressive Lower Prep and Upper Prep Department. The new Peter Brooks Building, boasting customised teaching accommodation for our Senior Years, opened in September 2018, and recent enhancements include a new Design Technology suite, Drama studio and Music Recording booth as well as the acquisition of superb playing fields off-site.

You are warmly invited to explore the benefits of a KHS education online, or better still, in person.

Charitable status. Kingswood House School is a Registered Charity, number 312044. It exists to provide educational support in the form of bursaries for the parents of children in need.

Kingswood Prep School

College Road, Lansdown, Bath BA1 5SD

Tel: 01225 734460
email: kpsreception@kingswood.bath.sch.uk
website: www.kingswood.bath.sch.uk
Facebook: @KingswoodSchool
Instagram: @kingswoodschool
LinkedIn: /school/kingswoodschool

Chairman of Governors: Mr T Lindsay

***Headmaster*: Mr Mark Brearey**

Deputy Head / Deputy DSL: Ms Helen Worrall

Assistant Head (*Academic*): Mrs Helen D'Souza
Assistant Head (*Pastoral*): Mrs Naomi Harding

Head of The Garden Nursery and Head of EYFS: Mrs A Ballanger
Head of Key Stage 1: Miss Rebecca Howe
Senior Teacher, Head of Year 3 and 4, Head of Performing Arts: Mrs Marie McGlynn
Senior Teacher, Head of Innovation, Health and Safety: Mr David Murphy
Senior Teacher, Head of Year 5 and 6, Academic Number 2: Mrs Alexandra St Quintin

Age range. 9 months to 11 years.

Fees per term (2023–2024). £3,991–£4,846.

Kingswood Prep School is like no other, with an abundance of outdoor learning space and boundless opportunities. Here, we celebrate individuality and uniqueness in an unrivalled woodland setting in one of the most beautiful cities in England.

We are a co-educational boarding and day school welcoming children between the ages of nine months to 11 years (up to age 18 in the Senior School and offering boarding from Year 7 onwards), located in Lansdown, Bath. Providing a happy, secure and family friendly environment, our children are encouraged to fulfil their academic, artistic, sporting and musical potential. Each one of our exceptional teachers helps each child to develop their personality and finding the essence of what it means to be themselves; all with the Kingswood spirit and ethos.

The garden at Kingswood. Our purpose-build nursery, nestled into our stunning grounds, welcomes children from nine months old for 50 weeks of the year. Learning comes through play, experimentation, investigation and discussion; starting from the children's own experiences and interests.

All children make full use of the outdoor spaces, and the curriculum is enriched by specialist teaching of Swimming, Games, Languages, Outdoor Learning, Music and Art in our Preschool and Reception rooms.

Opportunities. We provide opportunities to challenge and excite every one of our children both in and out of the classroom, including Bath's first education-based STEAM and Innovation Centre. This equips our pupils with the practical skills needed in an ever-changing workplace. Pupils have opportunities to explore a range of creative and innovative processes from Robotics and Programming in the STEAM rooms, to ceramics and printing in the Art room.

Co-curricular activities. At Kingswood Prep, we aim to provide the best all round experience for your children, both in and out of the classroom. We offer an extensive and varied activity programme with more than 80 co-curricular activities each week, giving children experiences that go well beyond a normal school day.

We believe that every child has strengths and many have hidden talents; our challenge is to unlock and then nurture them. The activity programme is a key vehicle in enabling this process, as well as in helping our children to become more confident and self-motivated.

Charitable status. Kingswood Preparatory School is a Registered Charity, number 309148.

Knightsbridge School

67 Pont Street, London SW1X 0BD

Tel: 020 7590 9000
email: registrar@knightsbridgeschool.com
website: www.knightsbridgeschool.com
X/Twitter: @Knightsbridge06
Facebook: @KnightsbridgeSchoolLondon
Instagram: @knightsbridge_school
LinkedIn: /company/knightsbridge-school-2006

***Principal and Founder*: Mr Magoo Giles**

***Head*: Ms Shona Colaço**

Age range. 4–16.

Number in school. 424.

Fees per term (2023–2024). £7,975–£8,940.

Knightsbridge School is a co-educational, all-through school for pupils aged 4–16, based in the heart of central London.

Knightsbridge School (KS) believes in the power of community: of being connected as a family within the school and being part of the community outside. The school aims to be an unashamedly happy and vibrant school. Our ethos is based on a set of values known as the KS Code: shared beliefs centred on caring for each other and fulfilling our individual potential every day.

The school has an amazing atmosphere where children can be themselves, where they can discover their many strengths, and challenge their weaknesses, supported by an unbelievably dedicated team of teachers and staff. We are a 'joined-up' community at KS – each and every member of staff is connected with every child.

KS has real academic rigour, our children excel across the curriculum, but we are not, and never will be, an academic hothouse. Instead, we provide an enriching and truly rounded education; we have more than 70 extracurricular clubs at the school. A strong spirit of can-do attitude runs throughout the school from children, to staff, to the wonderful parents who support us every step of the way.

KS is deeply involved with the local community; it has meaningful partnerships with two local primary schools, Ashburnham Community Primary School and Marlborough Primary School, and during lockdown we set up and ran a food bank at a third primary school in Lambeth. Before Christmas, KS delivered 'a Christmas Fair in a box' to Ashburnham pupils and has provided much-needed mental health support for them by establishing Place2Be at the school.

In a new venture, KS, Marlborough and Ashburnham pupils will together nurture oak saplings to create a new oak forest. Each class will germinate acorns in special vases, and watch their sapling grow before they are replanted in the KS forest Scotland.

KS pupils are encouraged to think of their own ways to support the local community; the eco-committee created wrapping paper out of waste paper which was sold at Christmas to raise money for charity. KS staff and parents took part in a sleep-out for the homeless last term, raising more than £50K for Restart Lives, a charity based in the church opposite the school.

Children learn best when they are happy. And we believe much of human happiness comes from being part of a community, so we do everything we can to create a warm, vibrant community both inside and outside our school.

Lady Eleanor Holles Junior School

Burlington House, 177 Uxbridge Road, Hampton TW12 1BD

Tel: 020 8979 2173
020 8979 1601 (Registrar & Senior School)
email: junior-office@lehs.org.uk
website: www.lehs.org.uk
X/Twitter: @LEHSchool
Facebook: @LEHSchoolOfficial
Instagram: @lehjuniors

Chairman of Governors: Mr D H King, BSc, FCA

Head Mistress: Mrs Rowena Cole, BSc, PGCE, MBA

***Head of Junior School*: Mrs Paula Mortimer**, BEd

Age range. 7–11.

Number of pupils. 192 day girls.

Fees per term (2023–2024). £6,867.

Lady Eleanor Holles Junior School is housed in its own separate building in one corner of the school's spacious twenty-four-acre grounds. Junior School pupils make full use of the school's extensive facilities, such as the heated indoor 25 m pool, Sports Hall, Activity studio, 240-seat theatre and floodlit netball courts. (*See The Lady Eleanor Holles School's entry in the GSA section for more details.*) They also take advantage of a fleet of school coaches serving most of West London and Surrey.

The school is academically selective, with most girls joining in Year 3. Entrance exams in English and Maths are held the December before entry. The vast majority of Junior School pupils are given guaranteed places in the Senior School.

The school's teaching is firmly based on the National Curriculum and there are specialist teachers for Science, Art, French, IT, Music and PE from the beginning. The school is very well resourced and staff use a wide variety of teaching styles and activities to ensure pace, stimulation and progression.

There is a wide range of extracurricular activities so girls can develop their own interests and abilities, and all achievements and progress are valued and praised.

Extracurricular clubs include Drama, Chess, Gardening and various Art, Music and Sports activities.

While LEH is a broadly Christian foundation, it welcomes girls of all faiths, and none. School Assemblies, some of which are performed by the girls for their parents, may feature Hindu, Islamic, Sikh or Jewish festivals and stories, as well as Christian.

Burlington House, the home of the Junior School, boasts superb facilities for a 21st-century education including a spacious Art and Design Technology studio, Science lab, computing suite; a much-loved library as well as a separate reading room and large, bright classrooms. As well as the great sports facilities, there are additional spaces including a giant Teepee and Nature Garden for outdoor learning.

The staff work hard to establish and maintain a caring, supportive atmosphere in which girls feel confident to be themselves, to respect and care for everyone in the community, to be proud of their achievements and to persevere with things they find challenging. Pastoral care is a priority and we are proud of the happy, lively, hard-working pupils of the Junior School.

Charitable status. The Lady Eleanor Holles School is a Registered Charity, number 1130254.

Lancing College Preparatory School at Hove
A Woodard School

The Droveway, Hove, East Sussex BN3 6LU

Tel: 01273 503452
email: hove@lancing.org.uk
website: www.lancingcollege.co.uk/prep-hove
X/Twitter: @LancingPrepHove
Facebook: @LancingPrepHove
Instagram: @lancingprep.hove

Co-educational day school for children aged 3–13 years.

Chairman of Governors: Mr M Slumbers, BSc, ACA

***Head*: Mrs K Keep**, BEd Hons

Age Range. 3–13 Co-educational.

Number of Pupils. 280.

Fees per term (2023–2024). £3,027–£6,595 (including lunch).

Lancing College Preparatory School at Hove is situated on a superb 7-acre campus in the heart of Hove.

We aim to inspire a desire for excellence, to develop independent, searching minds and to foster creativity. We encourage the children entrusted to us to explore and achieve their potential, academically and creatively. Academia is rightly important to us but of equal importance is our pupils' personal development.

Whilst proud of our traditions, we are also a forward-thinking school, looking to build upon our past successes to achieve even greater heights in the future. By the time our pupils leave, they will have acquired a confidence and a self-belief, together with a set of values that will remain with them throughout their lives.

Our pupils are taught by our fully-qualified staff of 30 in our wonderful facilities, inside and out. A new school hall and library space opened in 2017, with the relocation of our much improved Pre-School within the heart of the Pre-Prep and new Music School with practice rooms and classroom/performance space in 2019. We have a fully-equipped science laboratory and art, design and technology room. Outside, our leafy grounds include an adventure playground, school garden, science garden, forest school area, two grass fields and a brand new, extended floodlit all-weather Games Area was completed in 2023. Sports include: cricket, football, hockey, netball, rounders, rugby and tennis. Co-ed sporting opportunities were introduced in 2022, with a termly co-ed tournament for visiting prep schools. Our pupils also access the extensive cultural and sporting facilities at Lancing College, where Years 7 and 8 also take part in the weekly language programme, learning Spanish or German, along with a carousel of co-curricular activities. Scholarships with means-tested bursaries are available for entry into Year 7.

Charitable status. Lancing College is a Registered Charity, number 1076483. It exists to provide education for boys and girls.

Lancing College Preparatory School at Worthing

A Woodard School

Broadwater Road, Worthing, West Sussex BN14 8HU

Tel: 01903 201123
email: worthing@lancing.org.uk
website: www.lancingprepworthing.co.uk
X/Twitter: @LancingPrepWthg
Facebook: @lancingprepworthing
Instagram: @lancingprep.worthing

Co-educational day school for children aged 2–13 years.

Chairman of Governors: Mr M Slumbers, BSc, ACA

***Head*: Mrs F Milling**, BSc Hons, PGCE, MA Ed

Age range. 2–13 Co-educational.

Number of pupils. 213.

Fees per term (2023–2024). Preparatory termly fee (Years 3–8): £4,865. Pre-Preparatory termly fee (Reception–Year 2): £3,540).

Lancing Prep Worthing is based in a lovely Georgian manor house on a site of two acres, with space to run and play, in the Broadwater area of Worthing. It is located some six miles from Lancing College.

Our ethos is made up of three elements: Love Learning, Be Kind and Go out in the World and Do Good. Parents choose Lancing Prep at Worthing for these aims, which are fundamental to everything that happens here, but also because they recognise that its family feel, outstanding pastoral care and small classes are good for children starting on their learning journey and whose childhood is protected and cherished. When children leave us at 13+, they are role models and mentors to their younger peers, and they have achieved their potential.

In the most recent ISI inspection of June 2022, the school was judged 'excellent' for educational quality in all areas, the highest possible grading, in all 16 categories. Academic achievement is outstanding due to our passion for learning and high expectations, but Lancing Prep at Worthing is not a crammer, more of a place where children are engaged, supported and encouraged. Pupils consistently earn top scholarships in a broad range of subjects, academic of course, but also sport, music, drama, art and as all-rounders.

Our broad and balanced curriculum is enriched with high-quality creative and physical activities to provide a vibrant learning environment. We nurture in all our pupils a love of learning to enable them to maximise their academic potential. We encourage our pupils to think for themselves and to find ways in which they may enrich the lives of others, whether inside or outside the school community. This ensures that, as our children leave us for their next school, they do so as thoughtful members of society, well prepared to face the challenges that life sends their way.

Outdoor space comprises hard courts and a large grass field for the coaching of our main sports: cricket, football, hockey, netball, rounders, athletics and tennis. Our children also benefit from sharing the extensive cultural and sporting facilities at Lancing College. Children in Years 7 & 8 take part in a language programme learning Spanish or German, led by Lancing College. Scholarships with means-tested bursaries are available for entry into Year 7.

Charitable status. Lancing Prep at Worthing is a Registered Charity, number 1155150. It exists to provide education for boys and girls.

Latymer Upper & Prep School

Upper School
King Street, Hammersmith, London W6 9LR

Tel: 020 8629 2024
email: head@latymer-upper.org
website: www.latymer-upper.org
X/Twitter: @LatymerUpper
Facebook: @latymerupper
Instagram: @latymerupperschool
LinkedIn: /latymer-upper-school

Prep School
36 Upper Mall, Hammersmith, London W6 9TA

Tel: 020 7993 0061
email: principal@latymerprep.org
website: www.latymerprep.org
X/Twitter: @latymerprep

See full entry in the **HMC** section, on **p. 198**.

Laxton Junior School

East Road, Oundle, Peterborough PE8 4BX

Tel: 01832 277275
email: info@laxtonjunior.org.uk
website: www.laxtonjunior.org.uk
X/Twitter: @LaxtonJunior
Instagram: @laxtonjuniorschool

Governors: The Worshipful Company of Grocers
Chairman, Oundle Corporation of Schools: Mr Robert Ringrose
Chair, Laxton Junior School: Mrs Debbie McGregor

Senior Leadership Team:

***Head*: Mrs Lydia Waller**, MA Birmingham

Deputy Head: Ms Stacey Crump, BSc Hons Herts, PGCE Herts

Assistant Head Academic: Mrs Sumitha Hill, BA Hons Liverpool, PGCE Glos, MEd Glos

Assistant Head Admissions: Mrs Rachel Waterhouse, BEd Hons Derby

Assistant Head Co-Curricular: Mrs Claire Henderson, BSc Hons Trent, PGCE Plymouth

Assistant Head Pastoral: Mrs Jackie Ormston, BA Hons, QTS Northampton, MA Warwick

Age Range. 4–11.

Number of Children. 250.

Fees per term (2023–2024). £3,880–£5,640.

Part of Oundle School, Laxton Junior School (LJS) is an independent day school with 250 children aged 4 to 11. The school prides itself in providing an innovative and progressive education of the very highest standard, offering each unique child the best possible start to a life of learning.

Fantastic teaching staff take the time to really understand every single child, what motivates and excites them, and how we can harness this to challenge them at just the right level in every lesson and in every activity. The school's approach to staffing ensures children get the individual attention they need, building their confidence and resilience and allowing them to take risks and not to fear failure. The result is children who are inspired by the opportunities they have, who have the confidence to learn from mistakes and who ultimately develop real mastery of their subjects. Recent investment in re-imagined EYFS and STEAM learning environments have further empowered teaching staff to deliver the curriculum in a bespoke, exciting and adaptable way.

Outdoor learning is part of daily life at LJS and its beautiful, bespoke-designed Woodland Garden is an intrinsic element of learning, whatever the weather. A tailor-made outdoor learning curriculum allows children to find out more about nature and living outdoors – including making fires, using tools and building dens – but teachers also use the many spaces to inspire children and energise lessons across the curriculum.

Five core values sit at the heart of an LJS education: care, a love of learning, opportunity, community and quality. These values are evident across everything the school does, ensuring pupils are equipped with the skills to thrive in all aspects of their future lives. LJS is proud of the high academic standards its children achieve, the vast majority moving up to Oundle School at the end of Year Six, but prouder still of the intellectually curious, open-minded, kind-hearted and well-rounded young people they become.

Charitable status. Laxton Junior School, part of the Corporation of Oundle School, is a Registered Charity, number 309921. It exists to provide education for boys and girls.

The Grammar School at Leeds

Alwoodley Gates, Harrogate Road, Leeds LS17 8GS

Tel: 0113 229 1552
email: enquiries@gsal.org.uk
website: www.gsal.org.uk
X/Twitter: @theGSAL
Facebook: @TheGSAL
Instagram: @thegsal
LinkedIn: /the-grammar-school-at-leeds

See full entry in the **HMC** section, on **p. 200**.

Leicester Grammar Junior School

London Road, Great Glen, Leicester, Leicestershire LE8 9FL

Tel: 0116 259 1950
email: junioroffice@leicestergrammar.org.uk
website: www.lgs-junior.org.uk
X/Twitter: @LGS_Junior
Facebook: @LeicesterGrammarJuniorSchool
Instagram: @lgs_junior

Chair of Governors: Mr S Gasztowicz, QC

***Headteacher*: Mrs S Ashworth Jones**, BEd

Deputy Head (*Academic*): Mr D Fulton, BEd

Deputy Head (*Pastoral*): Mrs R Strong, BSc

Age Range. 3–11 Co-educational.

Number of Pupils. 420.

Fees per term (2023–2024). Years 3–6: £4,586; Kinders to Year 2: £4,316.

Founded in 1992, Leicester Grammar Junior School (LGJS) moved on to the purpose-built site in Great Glen in 2008. Our formula for success is steeped in academic tradition and is wrapped up in outstanding pastoral care. To love learning for a whole lifetime is our mission for each of our pupils and their all-round wellness and self-belief is at our heart.

Nestled within the Leicester Grammar School campus and surrounded by fields and farmland, it is hard to believe that we are so close to the city. With direct access from parking to playground, our parents find it easy dropping off and collecting their child every day.

Leicester Grammar School facilities are second to none. Academic subjects are enhanced by science laboratories, an art studio and a truly magical library, just for Juniors. Extra-curricular activities and interests catered for on-site too. A 25-metre indoor swimming pool, dance studio, drama theatre, Astroturf and acres of sports fields mean that taking up everything from Indian dancing, cricket or cheerleading is child's play!

Teachers, parents, children and visitors abide by LGJS values which are at the heart of the school: respect, community, curiosity, courage and trust. These values can be seen and felt in all corners of the school.

We look forward to welcoming you to our school.

Admissions. Pupils are admitted at all ages between 3+ and 10+ although the vast majority enter in the September following their third or fourth birthday (Kinders or Reception). Applications are online via the website, where assessment dates are also displayed.

Parents wishing for their child to be admitted to LGJS at times other than in September should call reception to speak with Mrs Dubois. She will do her best to organise an ad-hoc assessment visit, if there are places available.

Charitable status. Leicester Grammar School Trust is a Registered Charity, number 510809.

Leweston Prep School

Sherborne, Dorset DT9 6EN

Tel: 01963 210790
email: admissions@leweston.dorset.sch.uk
website: www.leweston.co.uk
X/Twitter: @LewestonSchool
Facebook: @lewestonprep
Instagram: @lewestonprep

Clerk to the Board of Governors: Lt Col G Scott-Masson, Manchester School of Business

***Head of Leweston Prep*: Mr Richard Thompson**, BA Hons, PGCE Oxford Brookes

Deputy Head of Leweston Prep: Mrs E Winter, BA Hons Warwick, PGCE Bath Spa

A full staff list can be found on the School website.

Age Range. 3 months–11 years Co-educational.

Number of Pupils. 137 Girls, 121 Boys.

Fees per term (2023–2024). Day: Reception–Year 1 £2,499, Years 2–3 £3,060, Years 4–5 £3,796, Year 6 £4,528. Boarding: £6,728 (weekly), £8,132 (full). Nursery (per day): £45.00–£50.00 (full day), £28.00–£32.00 (half day).

Setting. Leweston Prep School is an independent Catholic school for boys and girls with boarding provision from Year 4 and above. The school is situated in forty-six acres of Dorset parkland three miles south of Sherborne and occupies an enviable setting in a skilfully converted former Coach House providing a unique range of bright spacious classrooms. The beautiful rural site is shared with Leweston School, offering continuity of education right through to A Level. The Prep enjoys the benefit of many excellent facilities including a modern, well-equipped Art and Design Centre, an all-weather sports pitch, a swimming pool, a large sports hall, tennis courts and extensive playing fields. A new Prep Hall opened in September 2019 to support the school's expansion. Prep pupils take advantage of the specialist teaching in Languages, Art, Maths, Home Economics, Music and Sport. The parkland setting offers many opportunities for study and recreation. An accredited Forest School opened in September 2017 and every year group has a Forest School session once a week.

Ethos. Traditional excellence in teaching is combined with modern facilities and resources in a stimulating, happy and purposeful environment. The school motto 'Gaudere et Bene Facere' (Rejoice and Do Well) exactly reflects the importance of high academic standards together with artistic, musical and sporting excellence achieved in an atmosphere of joy and vibrancy. Each child is encouraged to develop individual talents within the caring and supportive school community. A friendly family ethos, and traditional values of work and behaviour are appreciated by parents. Full and flexi boarding options provide flexibility for pupils to enjoy a wide variety of extracurricular activities, whilst no Saturday morning school allows for rest and relaxation. Wrap-around care is available from 8.00am to 5.45pm.

Curriculum. Programmes of study encompass the National Curriculum without being constrained by it. Basic subjects are taught to a high standard concentrating on literacy and numeracy acquisition in the early years before expanding into a broader curriculum in Years 3–6. Well-qualified class teachers and specialist subject teachers foster independent learning and encourage the development of problem solving and investigative skills in all areas of the curriculum. Academic standards are high and many pupils gain awards to senior school.

There is a strong tradition in the creative arts and sport. Music and Drama are taught within the curriculum. A high percentage of pupils learn to play musical instruments and take additional Drama. There is a school orchestra and choir and many opportunities throughout the year for performance and grade examinations in both Music and Drama. All pupils in Years 4–6 undertake English Speaking Board assessments. Individual and team sports are considered important as part of the healthy, active lifestyle and the school enjoys a particular reputation for hockey and cross-country. The school is one of only nine Pentathlon Academies in the UK and is regarded as a centre of excellence by Pentathlon GB. Art, Ceramics and Design Technology are taught by specialist teachers using the exceptional facilities in the Art and Design Centre.

Charitable status. Leweston School Trust is a Registered Charity, number 295175. It exists to provide for children a contemporary education in the Catholic tradition.

Lincoln Minster School
Part of United Learning

The Prior Building, Upper Lindum Street, Lincoln, Lincolnshire LN2 5RW

Tel: 01522 551300
email: admissions@lincolnminsterschool.co.uk
website: www.lincolnminsterschool.co.uk
X/Twitter: @MinsterSchool
Facebook: @LincolnMinsterSchool
Instagram: @LincolnMinsterSchool
LinkedIn: /Lincoln-Minster-School

See full entry in the **HMC** section, on **p. 208**.

Littlegarth School

Horkesley Park, Nayland, Colchester, Essex CO6 4JR

Tel: 01206 262332
email: office@littlegarth.org
website: www.littlegarth.org
Facebook: @LittlegarthPrep
Instagram: @littlegarthschool

Chairman of Governors: Mr Jim Keohane

***Head*: Ms Kathy R Uttley**, BA Hons, PGCE, MEd

Deputy Head Curriculum: Miss Helen Smith, BA Hons, QTS
Deputy Head Pastoral: Mr Keith Dawes, BA Hons, QTS

Age range. 2½–11.

Number of pupils. Day: approximately 162 Boys, 153 Girls.

Fees per term (2023–2024). £552–£4,795.

Littlegarth has grown steadily following the School's move to our current premises of Horkesley Park in 1994. The Grade II listed Georgian house is situated in delightful Stour Valley countryside, designated as an Area of Outstanding Natural Beauty. The 30 acres of School land boast a number of purpose-built teaching rooms, including a multi-purpose Sports Hall, Science Laboratory, and numerous classrooms. A brand new purpose-built facility opened in January 2018, which provides outstanding specialist teaching rooms for music, drama and art, a large library incorporating a computer room, a learning support room and six substantial new teaching rooms. In 2019, existing rooms were refurbished to create outstanding facilities for Food Technology and Engineering. These facilities provide the children with increased opportunities to develop a wide range of skills, supported by our exciting and broad curriculum.

Outdoors, we make good use of our sports field with up to eight pitches and four outdoor cricket nets. Our outdoor play area has climbing and activity structures, and a vegetable garden with a recent extension to the green area enhancing the natural space around our covered outdoor reading areas. Our innovative adventure woodland provides an excellent environment for nature walks and Forest School activities, which run from Nursery through to Year 4. This area has been enriched by the planting of wildflower meadows and the erection of an outdoor stage which has hosted productions and concerts by the children.

Children from the age of 2½ are provided with excellent specialist teaching in Drama, French, Music and Sport. Small class sizes ensure that children receive a high level of individual attention and the Early Years Foundation Stage (EYFS) framework provides a springboard for individualised learning which continues throughout the school. Pre-Prep teachers provide a firm foundation in the core subjects, supported by caring teaching assistants and learning support staff. In Year 3, the number of lessons taught by subject specialist teachers increases and from Year 4 all timetabled lessons are taught by subject specialists.

Pastoral care is one of the key strengths of Littlegarth, as highlighted in our inspection report. Year 6 children are given considerable opportunities to take on responsibilities and further develop their self-confidence as Prefects, supporting children and staff in a variety of ways.

The School produces many plays each year and strong drama links with the local community are being forged. As well as supporting the school library, parents are also actively involved in helping on school trips, running a wardrobe department and there is a flourishing 'Friends of Littlegarth' parent body.

A wide variety of clubs and extracurricular activities are available each day and the School also provides pre- and after-school care which includes the provision of an Early Birds Club each morning.

Charitable status. Littlegarth School Limited is a Registered Charity, number 325064. It exists to provide education for children.

Lochinver House School

Heath Road, Little Heath, Potters Bar, Herts EN6 1LW

Tel: 01707 653064
email: ameir@lochinverhouse.com
website: www.lochinverhouse.com
X/Twitter: @LHSPrep

Chairman of the Governors: Nick Gilbert

***Headmaster*: Jonathan Wadge**, BA Hons

Age Range. 4–13.

Number of Boys. 331 day boys.

Fees per term (2023–2024). £4,750–£6,075 with no compulsory extras.

The academic staff consists of 35 qualified and graduate teachers supported by Laboratory, ICT, Art and DT technicians, Teaching Assistants, a School Nurse and a Child and Family Support Worker.

The school, founded in 1947, is situated in a pleasant residential area on the edge of green belt land in South Hertfordshire, and yet is conveniently placed for access to London. At the heart of the school is a late Victorian house. Facilities on our 8½ acre site are extensive and include a separate Sports Hall, Gymnasium & Theatre, Music Centre, two Science Laboratories and specialist IT, DT, and Art rooms. Lochinver is fully advanced with the teaching of and integration of Computing and Digital Learning, including the provision of iPads to older boys.

Boys are prepared for 11+ and 13+ entrance and scholarship examinations to a wide range of world-class day and boarding Independent Schools.

The school has its own extensive playing fields on site, including an all-weather Astro pitch. The major sports of football, rugby, cricket, athletics and basketball are complemented by opportunities to take part in a very wide range of further sports and physical activity. Optional residential trips take place both within the UK and overseas, such as a European Football and Classics trip, and a Rugby Tour to South Africa. During their time at the school, each boy will spend some time in

France as this is an important and much valued part of the French curriculum. All senior boys learn Latin from Year 5.

Music, Art, Drama, Design Technology, Food Technology and PE are part of the timetabled curriculum for all boys. The school encourages boys to learn at least one musical instrument and currently 75% of the children are doing so. There is a school orchestra, junior and senior choirs, together with a variety of instrumental groups. Parents appreciate our provision of co-curricular activities and extended care at both ends of the day.

The school is a non-profit making Educational Trust administered by a Board of Governors.

Charitable status. Lochinver House School is a Registered Charity, number 1091045. It aims to provide a quality education.

Lockers Park

Lockers Park Lane, Hemel Hempstead, Hertfordshire HP1 1TL

Tel: 01442 251712
email: secretary@lockerspark.co.uk
website: www.lockerspark.co.uk
X/Twitter: @lockerspark
Facebook: @LockersParkSchool
Instagram: @lockersparksch

Chair of Governors: C Lister, BSc Hons, MBA

***Headmaster*: G Taylor**, BEd Hons

Admissions: C Hampton

Age Range. 4–13. Prep and Pre-Prep for Boys.

Number of Pupils. 202, of whom almost half are boarders or flexi boarders.

Fees per term (2023–2024). Boarders £10,270, Day Boys £4,380–£6,950. Day fees include the flexible day, which runs from 7.30 am to 6.00 pm/7.30 pm (Pre-Prep/Prep) with the option to have breakfast, stay for supper and participate in evening activities at no extra cost.

Further details are outlined in the prospectus, available on application.

Lockers Park is a day and boarding school nestled in 23 acres of Hertfordshire woodland with boys from St Albans, Harpenden, Berkhamsted, Tring and the surrounding villages. The school is located near to excellent road and rail links serving London and the Home Counties as well as being in close proximity to London airports including Heathrow and Luton.

Lockers Park has its own particular magic. Being purposefully small it allows the boys to achieve excellent results and develop an enthusiasm for life. Lockers Park boys move on to the country's leading senior schools, with many achieving scholarships and exhibitions. Whilst the school pursues a programme of Academic excellence, the Arts, Music, Sport and Co-Curricular success are also celebrated.

The happiness and wellbeing of the boys is at the heart of Lockers Park. Teachers know each pupil not only by name but by personality and learning style. Simply put, Lockers Park know what makes each boy tick. The family-like community, which actively encourages and involves parents, gives the school a special, caring feel built on a well-established framework of respect.

The school's heritage and experience is rooted in providing an education for boys. The structure and educational content of the school day is tailored to help develop boys academically, socially and behaviourally. Lessons are deliberately designed so that they are interactive, practical and varied. The timetable is created with frequent breaks and plenty of outdoor activities built into the day which enables the boys to return to classrooms having expended healthy energy and allowing heightened concentration when they attend academic lessons.

Small class sizes (an average of 14 with a pupil to staff ratio of 8:1) and a staff of experienced teachers expect and encourage the best from every pupil, providing all the support and encouragement that growing boys need. The school's recent ISI evaluation concluded that "Pupils aspire to high achievement as a result of a culture where success is respected and celebrated."

A rich palette of opportunities is accessible to all at Lockers Park. Whether it's Sport, Science & Technology, Music, Art, Drama, Beavers, Cubs and Scouts or Chess and Debating, there really is something for everyone. Pupils are encouraged to try new things, to take on personal challenges and learn from their experiences. The school believes that trying out something new can help pupils to apply themselves, as well as developing teamwork skills and an appreciation of working towards goals. This inclusive attitude also means every boy is given the opportunity to represent the school termly in sports fixtures throughout their Lockers Park career.

At Lockers Park there are day boys, weekly boarders, flexi-boarders and full boarders, as well as many families who make the most of the school's popular inclusive wraparound care programme. The flexibility the school offers is indispensable for many parents; approximately half of pupils board and many day boys also stay for activities and prep in the late afternoons and evenings. Wraparound care for Prep School pupils runs from 7.30am–7.30pm, including a cooked breakfast and supper. This exclusive feature is included within the termly fees and can be accessed on an ad-hoc basis with no need to pre-book.

Ask any boarder and they will confirm boarding at Lockers Park is a hugely enjoyable experience. With cheerful, homely dormitories, a well-equipped Common Room and a dedicated boarding team on hand to provide care, comfort and support, every boarder enjoys a secure family structure. Boys who board at weekends have an enviable array of activities including visits to sporting events, museums and theatre trips. The school's wonderful grounds are also well-used, especially in the summer when popular pursuits involve swimming in the outdoor heated pool and playing mini golf.

Bursaries & Scholarships. Lockers Park is committed to offering financial help to deserving candidates, subject to financial resources. Scholarships are available, which may be increased with a means-tested bursary.

Bursaries/Discounts: New entrant bursary, Existing pupil bursary/hardship award, Local resident bursary,

HM forces discount, Sibling discount, Draper Bursary to celebrate 150th.

Charitable status. Lockers Park School Trust Ltd is a Registered Charity, number 311061. It aims to provide an all round, high quality education on a non-profit making basis.

Longacre School

Hullbrook Lane, Shamley Green, Guildford, Surrey GU5 0NQ

Tel: 01483 893225
email: office@longacreschool.co.uk
website: www.longacreschool.co.uk
X/Twitter: @longacreschool
Facebook: @longacreschool
Instagram: @longacreschool

***Headmaster*: Mr Matthew Bryan**, MA PGCE Cambridge, MA MSc Oxford

Age Range. 2–11.

Number of Pupils. 264 boys and girls.

Fees per term (2023–2024). £4,375–£6,790.

Longacre School is a thriving, co-educational preparatory school for boys and girls aged 2 to 11 years. Set in a beautiful rural location on the outskirts of the picturesque village of Shamley Green, between Guildford and Cranleigh, the school offers a wonderful environment for young children.

The school buildings comprise the original large 1902 house plus modern, purpose-built classrooms standing in nine acres of grounds. Facilities include a new dining room, sports hall and Astroturf, sports fields, woodland and an adventure playground. Longacre has a proud history and the motto of the school's founder, Ursula Fairfax-Cholmeley, "A happy heart goes all the way" is still very much part of the school's ethos.

The cheerful and purposeful atmosphere at Longacre is apparent as soon as you enter the school. Here, children are valued as individuals and are encouraged to fulfil their potential in every facet of school life. Personal and social development is highly valued, enabling pupils to grow in confidence as they mature.

At Longacre, we believe that children learn more effectively when they are happy, and that excellent academic results can be achieved without subjecting pupils to hothouse pressure. The fact that our pupils gain a range of scholarships, and that they transfer successfully to their senior school of choice, is evidence that this approach works.

Academic progress is closely monitored and regularly tested. Small class sizes enable pupils to be taught at an individual level, with increasing subject specialist tuition as children progress through the school. Alongside the core curriculum, Longacre offers a wide range of activities, sporting opportunities, stimulating off-site visits and exciting workshops. There are after school clubs every day, ranging from cooking to judo, and regular masterclasses for able pupils.

Longacre is a community where parents are welcome. The school has a thriving and supportive PTA and parents are kept well informed about school events and their children's progress through a weekly newsletter, formal and informal meetings and written reports. The Head and staff work closely with parents to ensure that their children are happy, successful and fulfilled.

Loyola Preparatory School

103 Palmerston Road, Buckhurst Hill, Essex IG9 5NH

Tel: 020 8504 7372
email: office@loyolaprepschool.co.uk
website: www.loyola.essex.sch.uk

Chair of Governors: Mrs A M Fox

***Headmistress*: Mrs Kirsty Anthony**, BA Hons, PGCE

Age range. 3–11.

Number of boys. 150.

Fees per term (2023–2024). £4,237 (incl. lunch, books & some after-school extracurricular sessions).

Loyola Preparatory School is a long established school educating boys for over a century, originally as part of St Ignatius College. As a caring Catholic School, it welcomes boys of all denominations offering a weekly mass to celebrate faith, ethos and values.

As a boys-only school, Loyola focuses its teaching techniques to harness the attention of boys by applying the extensive studies made into 'the ways boys learn best'. These practices encourage greater stimulation and enjoyment which is demonstrated by their overall behaviour and results.

Loyola has a high teacher-to-pupil ratio, facilitated by enthusiastic and committed teachers, supported by a generous quota of quality teaching assistants.

Loyola boys are encouraged to be kind and respect each other, with the older boys acting as role models for the younger boys. Year 6 boys are given Prefect responsibilities as well as the opportunity to be elected to the position of Head Boy and Deputy Head Boy. All boys regularly take part in community events including fundraising for national and local charities.

Loyola supports their boy's progression for the next step in their learning journey by preparing them for entrance and scholarship exams with English and Maths being taught in small ability sets from Year 3 upwards.

The curriculum covers all the normal primary subjects and includes Spanish, science and computer studies. There are Schola, choir and orchestra opportunities available in school, with additional tuition for piano, strings, woodwind, brass and guitar.

Loyola is proud of its range of sporting activities for the boys, aided by a large all-weather pitch on site. Sporting activities include soccer, cricket, rugby, swimming, athletics and sailing (Year 6) of which many are available during the school day and others offered as an after-school club.

During their time at the school, Loyola boys experience a wide range of trips and activities including a 5-day residential trip (Year 6), a 3-day residential trip (Year 5), together with many day trips across the school years selected to stimulate and enrich their learning experience.

The school prospectus is available on the school website and prospective parents are welcome to telephone to register and for an appointment to be given a personal tour of the school.

Charitable status. Loyola Preparatory School is a Registered Charity, number 1085079. The school is established in support of Roman Catholic principles of education.

Ludgrove

Wokingham, Berks RG40 3AB

Tel: 0118 978 9881
email: office@ludgroveschool.co.uk
registrar@ludgroveschool.co.uk
website: www.ludgrove.net
X/Twitter: @_Ludgrove
Instagram: @Ludgrove_School

Chairman of Governors: C Butterworth

***Head*: S W T Barber**, BA Durham, PGCE

Registrar: Mrs Rebecca Philpott

Age Range. 8–13.

Number of Boys. 185 Boarders.

Fees per term (2023–2024). £11,100.

Ludgrove is a thriving bi-weekly boarding boys prep school situated in 130 acres of beautiful grounds in Berkshire. It is a magical place to spend five years of childhood, where outstanding pastoral care lies at the heart of everything.

The principal aims of the school are for boys to grow and develop in a happy caring environment, to explore and expand their potential and to learn to develop an awareness and concern for others around them. We aim to prepare our boys to meet the demanding challenges they will experience at the next stage of their education with confidence and good humour.

We are unashamedly ambitious for every boy and are proud of our strong academic record. In recent years we have sent over 70% of boys on to Eton, Harrow and Radley, in addition to other distinguished public schools. The boys have a wealth of opportunities: a stimulating curriculum, exceptional facilities and a vibrant extracurricular programme with exposure to music, drama, sport and art.

Our extensive facilities include a stunning 350-seat theatre, a refurbished sports hall and well-stocked library. Opened in 2021, the state-of-the-art Exploration Centre provides one of the finest prep school scientific and creative learning environments in the country. In addition to the impressive 130 acres of grounds incorporating numerous games pitches, a 9-hole golf course, squash courts, fives courts, an astroturf, tennis courts, a 20m indoor pool and adventure playground.

Charitable status. Ludgrove School Trust Limited is a Registered Charity, number 309100.

Lyonsdown School

3 Richmond Road, New Barnet, Hertfordshire EN5 1SA

Tel: 020 8449 0225
email: admissions@lyonsdownschool.co.uk
website: www.lyonsdownschool.co.uk
X/Twitter: @LyonsdownSchool
Facebook: @LyonsdownSchool
Instagram: @lyonsdownschool

***Head*: Mrs Rittu Hall**, BSc Hons, PGCE

Age Range. Girls 3–11.

Number of Pupils. 180.

Fees per term (2023–2024). Nursery: £1,345–£2,830; Reception–Year 2 £3,995; Years 3–6 £4,325.

Lyonsdown School is a small, friendly school for girls aged three to eleven which, since September 2020, has fully embraced an all-girls education. Situated in the leafy suburb of New Barnet, within easy access to the North Circular and both Northern Line and mainline rail services.

Lyonsdown nurtures both potential and ability, allowing all pupils to thrive and achieve personal excellence. The school is non-selective at entry into Nursery and Reception. Year 6 girls gain entry and scholarships to top London senior schools, both independent (day and boarding) and selective maintained schools.

Class sizes are small with high teacher to pupil ratios, ensuring that both teaching and pastoral care are of the highest standards. A broad and balanced curriculum provides personalised learning with a high degree of specialist teaching. This allows pupils to flourish and discover their passions and abilities, whatever they might be.

Lyonsdown has significant strengths in Music, Drama and Art with recent successes coming in the North London Music Festival and the ISA Art competition and being shortlisted for the National ISA awards. The school runs two lively and popular choirs and individual instrumental lessons are taught by visiting specialists.

"Lyonsdown learning" is at the heart of the school and the pupils develop those skills that will prepare them for their senior school and a life of learning beyond the classroom. They are critical thinkers, exploring their lessons and activities with independence, responsibility and imagination.

The school is housed in a beautiful Edwardian building with modern facilities including a Science Laboratory, Library and Dining Room, an Outdoor Learning Area, Art Studio, Computing Suite and Music Room. Sport is both popular and important at Lyonsdown and the school makes good use of its own purpose-built hall and local facilities for PE and Games.

An extensive co-curricular programme, including breakfast and after-school clubs, traditional dancing, prep club and karate, runs throughout the year. Visiting speakers, theatre groups and workshops are very popular with pupils and parents alike. The school makes excellent use of its location with visits into London are a regular feature of the calendar and Year 5 and 6 pupils enjoy an annual residential trip.

Specialist learning support is also provided to those pupils who need additional focus, be it a specific need such as dyslexia, or for those who need a temporary boost. More able girls have their learning extended in lessons and in a variety of additional activities, and pupils of all abilities are challenged.

Lyonsdown is an inclusive community with a Christian ethos, welcoming a diverse mix of pupils of all faiths. The school is a community of learning and the partnership between home and school is of central importance. Regular communication ensures parents are well-informed and celebrates the pupils' many successes.

The school is a member of the Independent School's Association

Charitable status. Lyonsdown School became a member of the Mill Hill School Foundation (Registered Charity, number 1064758) on 1 April 2022.

Magdalen College School
Oxford

Cowley Place, Oxford OX4 1DZ

Tel: 01865 242191
email: enquiries@mcsoxford.org
website: www.mcsoxford.org
X/Twitter: @MCSOxford
Facebook: @MCSOxfordUK
Instagram: @mcsoxford
LinkedIn: /school/magdalen-college-school-oxford-limited

See full entry in the **HMC** section, on **p. 216**.

Maidwell Hall

Maidwell, Northampton, Northamptonshire NN6 9JG

Tel: 01604 686234
email: thesecretary@maidwellhall.co.uk
website: www.maidwellhall.co.uk
X/Twitter: @MaidwellHall
Facebook: @Maidwell-Hall

Chair of Trustees: Barbara Matthews, MBE

***Headmaster*: A Rendall**, BA, PGCE

Age range. 4–13.

Number of pupils. 147: 97 Day, 50 Boarders (23 Flexi, 27 Full).

Fees per term (2023–2024). £4,030–£10,584, dependent on age and whether a child is boarding or day. Please see our website for further details.

Maidwell Hall is a co-educational fortnightly boarding and day school. Occupying a substantial 17th century hall, the school is situated in beautiful countryside and is characterised by its rural location and by 44 acres of grounds. The school aims to encourage all the children to discover and develop all their talents through the academic curriculum, the games programme, Music, Art, Drama and an impressive range of hobbies and activities.

The school is organised as a seven-day-a-week boarding school with a comprehensive programme of club activities in the evenings, supplemented by a choice of outings or school-based, free-time activities on Sundays. Day children are fully involved in all aspects of school life, including all the after-school clubs, for which there is no extra charge. Children from Year 3 to Year 8 can board for two or three nights a week or fortnightly board, with a leave-out every other weekend. The children benefit greatly from the freedom and security of the school's spectacular grounds including its famous arboretum (wilderness) and its large lake for fishing and boating. The pastoral care for the boarders is overseen by the House Parents, the Headmaster and his wife and a team of matrons. In addition, each pupil has an individual tutor.

The Pre-Prep is nestled in a woodland setting within the School's extensive grounds. It is a place where the youngest pupils, from ages 4–7, come together to play, learn and explore. The Pre-Prep focuses on the core skills of reading, writing and numeracy, as well as plenty of opportunities to enjoy the Forest School and extra teaching from French, Music and Art teaching specialists.

Pupils are prepared for Common Entrance to the major independent senior schools (typically Uppingham, Oundle, Stowe, Rugby, Shrewsbury, Eton and Harrow) and every year, several sit scholarships. In addition to core subjects, all pupils study Art, Design, ICT, Latin, Music and Religious Studies and there are also timetabled lessons in PE, Swimming, PSHE and Drama. There is a specialist carpentry shop which operates as a club activity.

The school has a strong reputation for sport. The major games for the boys are rugby, football, hockey and cricket and there are also matches against other schools in athletics, cross-country running, golf, squash, swimming and tennis. The major games for girls are hockey, netball, tennis and rounders, as well as a strong equestrian team. In addition to impressive games pitches, sporting facilities include a multi-purpose sports hall with climbing wall, a squash court, a 6-hole golf course, astroturf, hockey pitch, tennis courts and a heated indoor swimming pool. There is particular emphasis on outward bound activities and leadership. There is a strong musical tradition and 90% of the pupils play one or two musical instruments; there is a thriving church choir and strings, wind and guitar groups. There are regular concerts throughout the year and each year there is a major school play.

Charitable status. Maidwell Hall is a Registered Charity, number 1147280. It exists for the purpose of educating children.

The Mall School

185 Hampton Road, Twickenham, Middlesex TW2 5NQ

Tel: 020 8977 2523
email: admissions@themallschool.org.uk
website: www.themallschool.org.uk
X/Twitter: @Themallschool
Facebook: @themallschool
Instagram: @themallschool
LinkedIn: /the-mall-prep-schoolandnursery

Chair of Governors: Mrs Natasha Page

***Headmaster*: D Price**, BSc, MA, PGCE

Deputy Head: J Fair, BA

Age range. 6 months–11.

Fees per term (2023–2024). Reception–Year 2: £4,980, Years 3–6: £5,600.

The Mall School recently celebrated its 150th year, coinciding with the school's decision to move to a co-educational model, with the first girls joining Reception in September 2023. With the school's nursery located three minutes away, the school now educates boys and girls from 6 months and will be fully co-educational in all year groups by 2029.

Our 2022 and 2023 11+ leavers were offered places at over 25 senior schools. Between them, they were offered 26 scholarships including academic awards to Hampton, King's College Wimbledon, Epsom College, Radnor House and St George's College and non-academic awards including Claremont Fan Court (music), Epsom College (music), Kingston Grammar (music), Hampton (sport and drama), Reed's (music) and St James (sport). Increasing numbers of pupils are gaining entry to selective state grammar schools including Tiffin and Wilson's.

Children are welcomed into Reception at 4+ where entry is non-selective. Places are allocated on a first-come-first-served basis. Pupils also join at 7+ and 8+, and other year groups (subject to availability) where entry follows a successful assessment. Pupils are taught by a well-qualified staff consisting of 15 full-time and 3 part-time members with an additional 10 full-time and 9 part-time staff in The Mall Nursery. The average class size is 15. We teach a broad curriculum with subject specialists, including art, DT, music, drama, history and French, in addition to sport and PE.

Cricket, rugby, football, swimming and athletics are the main sports played at the school. We have our own 20 m indoor swimming pool and a large sports hall. All pupils have weekly swimming and PE lessons at school with specialist staff. From Year 3, pupils have two afternoons of games each week at Sunbury Cricket Club including competitive fixtures against local schools.

We encourage all pupils to participate in our lively music and drama departments. All children in Years 2 and 3 join the choir, performing in local events and there are many performance opportunities in school. A number of different ensembles rehearse every week including: the string orchestra, the wind band, the brass ensemble, the samba band, choirs, recorder groups, and a rock band. Eleven visiting music teachers also give weekly lessons in all orchestral instruments plus piano, guitar, singing and music theory.

Operating across 50 weeks each year, our nursery is open every day from 7.30 am to 6.30 pm with extended hours on request. At the school we provide wraparound care from 7.30 am to 6.00 pm with an extensive range of after-school clubs, such as chess, judo, cookery, computing and music technology. Holiday camps run during most of the school holidays.

In addition to bright modern classrooms, facilities include science laboratories, music practice rooms, IT suite, library and a creative and performing arts centre, which provides a 160-seat theatre and large-sized art and design technology studios. Morning and afternoon minibus services are in operation and children are collected from and returned to various locations in the Teddington, Kingston, Richmond, Isleworth and Chiswick areas.

More information is available via the website or the Headmaster's PA who manages admissions to the school.

Charitable status. The Mall School Trust is a Registered Charity, number 295003. It exists to promote and provide for the advancement of the education of children.

Maltman's Green School

Maltmans Lane, Gerrards Cross, Bucks SL9 8RR

Tel: 01753 883022
email: office@maltmansgreen.com
website: www.maltmansgreen.com
X/Twitter: @MaltmansGreen
Facebook: @MaltmansGreenSchool

***Headmistress*: Mrs Jill Walker**, BSc Hons, PGCE, QTS, MA Ed

Age Range. 2–11.

Number of Girls. Approx. 320.

Fees per term (2023–2024). Nursery (5 mornings and 1 afternoon) £2,850 rising to £6,500 in Year 6.

Our Approach. At Maltman's Green we believe in the pursuit of excellence whilst maintaining a sense of enjoyment. Girls are inspired to do their best inside and outside of the classroom through an exceptional academic curriculum and extensive extra-curricular opportunities. We prepare girls for the modern world through a relevant, adaptable and innovative approach that is supported by a foundation of traditional values. Our girls are given every opportunity to succeed across multiple disciplines, fostering confidence and self-belief, and empowering them for whatever future awaits.

We believe that the emotional, social and physical wellbeing of our girls is paramount. By providing a personalised learning experience in an encouraging and nurturing environment, we ensure our girls feel happy, confident and valued – a perfect foundation from which children can flourish. This ethos has been recognised by the ISI who applauded our "outstanding" pastoral care.

Games and The Arts. Our sports provision is an outstanding feature of the School, with dedicated facilities and daily lessons. All girls enjoy friendly tournaments between houses and within year groups where those with the talent and inclination can progress to squad level to compete locally, regionally or nationally with exceptional results.

Music is a very important part of life at Maltman's Green. Specialist teaching, exceptional facilities and lots of choice give our girls plenty of opportunity to explore and showcase their musical talents. Many girls participate in our various choirs and we have a variety of different musical instrument lessons available as well as instrumental ensemble groups to join. Drama too has a big part to play in school life where regular performances and workshops give girls a strong sense of confidence and creative expression. Our dedicated performance space with high-quality staging, lighting, costumes and props give our shows a professional feel.

Achievements. Our girls are encouraged to be independent thinkers, to challenge themselves and to always try their best. Maltman's Green provides a firm foundation, preparing girls to face senior school and beyond with confidence, determination and a lifelong love of learning. This is reflected in our impressive 11+ results (84% qualification rate in 2021) and a record number of scholarships awarded to Independent Senior Schools. This, combined with our girls' impressive achievements across sport, music and drama affirm our position as one of the foremost prep schools in the country.

Outstanding Characteristics. 2018 marked our 100th Anniversary and, since the School was founded in 1918, we have seen numerous developments and upgrades to our facilities, including dedicated subject classrooms, a 6-lane, 25-metre indoor swimming pool, a Science Lab, STEAM lab, IT hub, Art hub, Music hub a multi-use gymnasium, a state-of-the-art theatre space and a dedicated 2–3yr olds day-care centre. We place great importance on outdoor learning and have an extensive Woodland School as well as a discovery garden and landscaped grounds that offer a secluded, peaceful and nurturing environment. This excellent suite of facilities is complemented by our highly committed, well-qualified and experienced body of staff who enable us to provide an outstanding and unique breadth of challenging opportunities for our girls.

Charitable status. Maltman's Green School Trust Limited is a Registered Charity, number 310633.

Manor Lodge School

Rectory Lane, Ridge Hill, Shenley, Hertfordshire WD7 9BG

Tel: 01707 642424

email: enquiries@manorlodgeschool.com
website: www.manorlodgeschool.com
X/Twitter: @manor_lodge
Facebook: @ManorLodgeSchool
Instagram: @manorlodgeschool

Chair of Governors: Mr D Arnold, MBE

***Head*: Mrs Alyson Lobo**, BEd Hons

Age range. 3–11.

Number of pupils. Nursery (age 3) 15; Infants (age 4–7) 198; Juniors (age 7–11) 237.

Fees per term (2023–2024). Nursery: £4,100; Infants: £4,370; Juniors: £4,800.

There are three forms of 18–20 children in Reception to Year 6 inclusive. We have specialist teachers for French, PE, IT, DT, Art, Drama, Science (Years 5 & 6), and Music, as well as numerous instrumental teachers for piano, brass, woodwind, percussion and strings. All staff are fully qualified.

The main school building consists of an 18th century manor house with classrooms, a new Modern Foreign Languages section, as well as a stunning new building dedicated specifically to STEAM subjects. There is also a building housing further classrooms for Year 6 and a sports hall/theatre provides additional space for sports, music and the performing arts.

The cottage at the end of the drive houses our Nursery. The children must be siblings of pupils in the main school and are eligible to attend from the term in which they turn three.

Our classrooms are bright and well equipped and the standard of work displayed is very high. We aim to provide excellent teaching and learning opportunities within a caring environment in which high standards of behaviour and good manners are encouraged and expected. We thus ensure that all pupils achieve their full potential and are prepared for entry to senior schools, both independent and state.

Music plays an important part in the life of the school. There are several choirs, an orchestra, jazz band and various ensembles and almost half the children in school learn an instrument. Music is of course linked to our Drama activities. Reception to Year 5 children take part in at least two performances a year and, in Year 6, the children all take part in the much anticipated Year 6 production. Art is of a particularly high standard and the children use a variety of media, producing excellent original work. We strongly believe in children being allowed a childhood and with this in mind, have created an all-weather Outdoor Learning area and will endeavour to create an environment that makes it simple to integrate traditional learning with an outdoor space. Our aim is to create physical spaces where students are able to develop key concepts that help meet their wellbeing needs as well as promote our ethos of a classroom without walls, leading children to understand that learning can come from any environment. The twelve acres of grounds also include pitches, an all-weather court and play areas with climbing activity equipment and other outdoor toys. The children are offered a wide range of sporting activities including football, rugby, hockey, cricket, netball, rounders, swimming and athletics.

Our caterers provide a delicious selection of fresh, healthy lunches and cater for a number of dietary requirements.

Extra activities available at the school include chess, drama and ju-jitsu. There are numerous clubs run by the staff after school until 4.30 pm, for example, cooking, football, rugby, cricket, netball, dance, athletics and choir.

Charitable status. Manor Lodge School is a Registered Charity, number 1048874. The school exists to provide an education which will maximise the potential of the girls and boys in our care.

The Manor Preparatory School

Faringdon Road, Abingdon, Oxon OX13 6LN
Tel: 01235 858458
email: admissions@manorprep.org
website: www.manorprep.org
X/Twitter: @ManorPrep
Facebook: @ManorPrepSchool
Instagram: @manor_prep_school

Chair of Board of Governors: Mr Shaun Forrestal
***Headmaster*: Mr Alastair Thomas**, BA Hons, PGCE

Age Range. Girls and Boys 2–11.
Number of Pupils. 379 pupils.
Fees per term (2023–2024). £5,445 (Reception)–£6,630 (Year 6).

Founded in 1907 and situated in Abingdon, The Manor Preparatory School is an independent, co-educational day school that welcomes children aged 2–11.

The school offers a wonderfully happy, creative and varied learning experience where every child is challenged, cherished and inspired to reach their potential. The Manor's most recent ISI Inspection saw the school receive the highest possible rating of '*Excellent*' in all areas. Inspectors commented that *"Pupils approach every day with an overwhelming passion to learn and develop."*

Parents often comment on how happy the children are and on the feeling of warmth which fills every corner of the school; laughter is an essential part of the school day. The children's personal development is further strengthened by staff who act as excellent role models.

Every child is encouraged to push themselves to new challenges; the school aims to foster a 'have a go' attitude ensuring the children always give their best resulting in outstanding results academically, on the sports field, and in the creative and performing arts. Headmaster, Alastair Thomas, says "Our job is to prepare children for life, not just senior school and to ensure they collect happy memories along the way."

The Manor has an excellent record of ensuring that its Year 6 leavers move on to the senior school that is perfectly suited to them. Scholarships, awards and exhibitions feature highly in all areas with an impressive 31 offered to Year 6 pupils in 2023.

At the heart of the school sits a lovely, historic Manor House building, and surrounding this are the light, spacious, purpose-built classrooms and facilities which ensure the school strikes the perfect balance between old and new. Always aiming to improve its facilities, there is an exciting development plan in place to extend the breadth of opportunities on offer even further.

The Manor aims to simplify the logistics of family life with access to an extensive daily bus service covering Oxfordshire, Berkshire, Buckinghamshire and Wiltshire. The school also provides fully flexible wraparound care from 7:30am to 6:00pm, most of which is free of charge.

To find out more about how The Manor challenges, cherishes and inspires every child or to arrange a tour, please visit www.manorprep.org or contact Mrs Nicole Burroughs, Director of Admissions and Marketing on 01235 858462 or admissions@ manorprep.org.

Merchant Taylors' Prep

Moor Farm, Sandy Lodge Road, Rickmansworth, Herts WD3 1LW
Tel: 01923 825648
email: office@mtpn.org.uk
website: www.mtpn.org.uk
X/Twitter: @MTSPrep
Facebook: @MerchantTaylorsPrep

Chair of Governors: Mr D Eggar

***Head*: Dr Karen McNerney**, BSc Hons, PGCE, MSc, EdD

Deputy Head: Mr Tony McConnell, MA Hons, PGCE, FHA
Deputy Head: Mr Andrew Crook, BA Hons, PGCE

Age Range. 3–13.
Number of Pupils. 371 Day Boys.
Fees per annum (2023–2024). £13,395 (Nursery), £18,606 (Reception, Years 1 and 2), £19,530 (Years 3–8).

The School is located amidst 14 acres on a former farm in an idyllic park and woodland setting. The Grade II listed buildings have been stylishly converted to provide a complete and unique range of classrooms and ancillary facilities. The medieval Manor of the More, once owned by King Henry VIII and used as a palace by Cardinal Wolsey, was originally located within the grounds and provides some interesting and historical associations.

The School is divided as follows: an off-site Nursery & Reception School for children aged 3+ and 4 + based at Merchant Taylors' School; then on the Merchant Taylors' Prep School site, there is the Pre-Prep (Year 1 to Year 2) and the Prep Department (Year 3 to Year 8).

Pupils are admitted to the school after an assessment by Heads of Section. The main entry is into Nursery at 3+ when boys are admitted in the September after their third birthday. We also have a small 4+ and 7+ entry. Pupils are expected to remain until the age of thirteen. Parents of pupils at the Prep School will be given an assurance at the end of Year 5 as to whether their son will be able to progress to Merchant Taylors' School at the end of Year 8. Continuity scholarships are awarded to some pupils in the Prep School in Year 6.

Work of a high standard is expected of everyone. The curriculum is interpreted as richly as possible and includes Technology, Music, Art, Drama, Physical Education and Games. We focus on a genuinely holistic education that emphasizes values and dispositions as much as academic skills. The School has a fully-qualified and experienced staff team that complements modern teaching facilities including The Sir Christopher Harding Building for Science and Technology with two state-of-the-art laboratories, a new Art Design Technology workshop that opened in 2018, an ICT suite and a Library. A 200-seat theatre with tiered seating and a separate music school provide a Centre for the Performing Arts. A Centenary Trail and outdoor classroom accommodate a range of outdoor learning activities. A bespoke nursery school was opened in the grounds of Merchant Taylors' School in April 2008 known as The Manor. Additional classrooms were added as part of our centenary celebrations in 2010. In 2014 a new dining hall, kitchen and common room were added. In September 2016, the Reception Year joined the Nursery in The Manor to create a specialist Early Years Foundation Stage.

Swift access to London by train from nearby Moor Park Station (Metropolitan line) allows easy access to places of historical and cultural interest as well as concerts and lectures.

The school was originally founded as Christian, but children of all faiths have always been welcomed.

There is an extensive programme of extra-curricular activities in which all pupils are encouraged to take part. A key feature of the School's ethos is a strong tradition of caring, both for those within our community and for the wider community through regular charitable activities.

Rugby Football, Hockey, Association Football and Cricket are the principal team games. Athletics, Golf, Swimming, Table Tennis and other sports are also coached. The School has the benefit of a fully-equipped Sports Hall with indoor cricket nets and a floodlit AstroTurf facility.

The School has a flourishing Parents' Association which arranges social and fundraising activities, and an association for former pupils, The Old Terryers.

Charitable status. Merchant Taylors' School is a Registered Charity, number 1063740.

Micklefield School

10 Somers Road, Reigate, Surrey RH2 9DU
Tel: 01737 224212
email: office@micklefieldschool.co.uk
website: www.micklefieldschool.co.uk
X/Twitter: @MicklefieldPrep
Facebook: @MicklefieldSchoolReigate
Instagram: @micklefield_prep
LinkedIn: /company/micklefield-school

Chair of the Council: Mrs Joosje Hamilton

***Headmaster*: Mr Ryan Ardé**

Bursar: Mrs Laura Butterfield

Age Range. Rising 3–11.

Number of Pupils. 224.

Fees per term (2023–2024). £1,460–£4,930.

At Micklefield we pride ourselves on providing a nurturing, family environment that delivers a first class tailored education and dedicated pastoral care. As the only truly independent school in Reigate, we have a reputation for achieving excellent academic results, preparing children for the next stage of their educational journey and supporting their successful entry to a senior school of their choice.

What makes our children stand out is what they have to offer over and above their excellent academic results. Our small class sizes and specialist teachers enable us to develop children's unique gifts and provide a vibrant array of extracurricular activities in sports, science, arts, music, performing arts, academic and creative subjects. Micklefield pupils become well-rounded individuals with good character, self-belief and the willingness to seize new opportunities.

'Igniting a passion for learning' is the foundation of our educational philosophy which we share with all our pupils. We aim to deliver a creative, innovative curriculum that is exciting and fun. Our vision is to deliver an outstanding educational experience for our children whilst balancing our traditional values with the very best elements of a 21st century education.

Visit the website or telephone for a prospectus on 01737 224212. Mr Ardé, the Headmaster, is always pleased to show prospective parents around by appointment.

Charitable status. Micklefield School (Reigate) Limited is a Registered Charity, number 312069. It exists to provide a first-class education for its pupils.

Millfield Prep School

Edgarley Hall, Glastonbury, Somerset BA6 8LD
Tel: 01458 832446
email: office@millfieldprep.com
website: www.millfieldschool.com
X/Twitter: @millfieldprep
Facebook: @millfieldprep
Instagram: @millfieldschool

Chair of Governors: Mr Roland Rudd

***Head*: Mr Dan Thornburn**, BA Hons, FCMI, MEd

Head of Prep Admissions: Mrs Kirsty Drawer

Age Range. 2–13.

Number of Pupils. 468; 251 Boys and 217 Girls.

Fees per term (2023–2024). Prep: Full and Weekly Boarding: £11,650; Day: £4,375–£7,570; Flexi Boarding: £1,350 (2 nights); £2,020 (3 nights); £2,700 (4 nights). Occasional boarding: £73 per night. Pre-prep: Day: £3,445.

The school is administered by the same Board of Governors and on the same principles of small-group teaching as Millfield (made possible by a staff to pupil ratio of approximately 1:8) which ensures breadth and flexibility of timetable. It has its own attractive grounds of 185 acres some four miles from the Senior School, and its extensive facilities include games fields, art, design and technology centre, drama hall, music school, science laboratories, sports hall, astroturf, gymnasium, golf course, tennis courts, squash courts, sport pavilion, equestrian centre, 25-metre indoor swimming pool, three IT laboratories and chapel. The pupils also have access to some of the specialist facilities at Millfield including a water-based astro, Olympic-sized swimming pool, tartan athletics track and indoor tennis centre.

Small class sizes allow the individual pupil to be taught at his or her most appropriate pace. The range of ability within the school is comprehensive and setting caters for both the academically gifted and those requiring additional learning support. The curriculum is broadly based and provides a balance between the usual academic subjects and the arts. Junior pupils study French and in Year 6 there is a choice of Spanish or French, plus a taster in Latin for more able pupils. In Years 7 and 8 there is a choice of French, Spanish and Latin. Children may choose either one or two foreign languages, dependent on ability. Pupils are also given a choice of extra-curricular languages which vary depending on demand. Science is taught throughout the school and as three separate subjects from the age of 10.

There is a full games programme organised by qualified teachers of physical education, with the help of other staff. The programme includes athletics, basketball, climbing, cross country, cricket, fencing, football, golf, hockey, netball, riding, rugby, sailing, squash, swimming, tennis, outdoor pursuits and multi-sports, to name but a few. Over 70 different clubs are available.

Within music the offering includes multiple choirs and orchestras, wind band and an exciting and ever-expanding range of ensembles, ranging from rock bands and brass bands to percussion ensembles and a guitar group. Over 250 pupils learn at least one musical instrument. There are regular opportunities for performance and all pupils are coached in performance and presentation skills. Highlight events include themed large ensemble evenings such as the annual Rock and Pop Concert, Summer Concert, Saturday morning breakfast masterclasses with visiting international artists and the whole school House Singing competition.

Admission usually depends on interview, assessment and reports from the previous school. A number of academic, art, drama, music and sports scholarships are awarded each year for entry into Years 6, 7 and 8. Drama scholarships will be awarded for the first time in September 2024, recognising candidates who want to actively engage in all areas of the subject and who have an obvious flair and enthusiasm for drama. The Millfield Prep Award was launched last year, recognising Prep pupils who are talented all-rounders.

There are five boarding houses for pupils aged 7 years and above (three for boys and two for girls). Each house is under the care of resident house parents and assistant house parents. The Medical Centre is staffed by three qualified nurses, a physiotherapist, and the School Doctor attends daily.

Charitable status. Millfield is a Registered Charity, number 310283. The Millfield Schools provide a broad and balanced education to boys and girls from widely differing backgrounds, including a significant number with learning difficulties, and many for whom boarding is necessary.

Milton Keynes Preparatory School

Tattenhoe Lane, Milton Keynes, Buckinghamshire MK3 7EG

Tel: 01908 642111
email: info@mkps.co.uk
website: www.mkps.co.uk
X/Twitter: @prep_mk
Facebook: @mkprepschool

Chairman of the Governors: Mr David Pye, BA Hons, Cert Ed (Distinction), MA Ed (Distinction), SEDA III, HETC, FFSC, FGMS, FCSCM, FGGRS, AFNCollM, FRSA

Proprietor/Principal: Mrs Hilary Pauley, BEd

***Headmaster*: Mr Simon Driver**, BA, PGCE, QTS

Deputy Head: Mrs Katherine Foulger, BA Hons, PGCE, QTS

Age range. Nursery: 2 months–3 years. Pre-Prep Department: 3–7 years. Preparatory Department: 8–11 years.

Number of pupils. 369 Day Pupils.

Fees (2023–2024). Nursery (per week): £115 (2 mornings)–£365 (5 days). Pre-Preparatory Department (per term): £1,608–£4,712 (2–5 years), £4,868 (6–7 years). Preparatory Department (per term): £5,528 current pupils (8–11 years), £5,944 new pupils (10–11 years).

Milton Keynes Preparatory School is a well-established school, with an additional Nursery in the group, also in Milton Keynes, for children of 2 months to 4+ years.

Opening hours are 7.30 am to 6.30 pm for a 35-week academic year and an extra 11 weeks in school holidays, enabling pupils to join play schemes and to be cared for outside normal core school hours.

Staff are highly qualified and committed to delivering the very best teaching and levels of care. Academic standards are 'Excellent', as identified in recent inspections, with pupils being prepared for entry to senior independent schools locally and nationally and to local grammar schools. Teaching is structured to take into account, and extend, the requirements of the National Curriculum, with constant evaluation and assessment for each pupil. Scholarships are offered from Year 3 for those with excellent academic and sporting abilities.

Housed in purpose-built accommodation, specialist facilities include a CTS suite, a Music Technology studio, Sports Hall and AstroTurf courts, Science Laboratory, Engineering & Design workshop and a large Art studio.

The Nursery and Pre-Preparatory Department have extended artificial grass gardens to enable year-round outdoor learning and activities.

The Environmental Studies Centre provides a state-of-the-art outdoor learning resource room and extensive outside areas for gardening and wildlife. There is a large Music and Drama Studio and a Fitness Room.

Music and Sport play an important part in the life of the school. Concerts are held, and a wide variety of sport is played, with teams competing regularly against other schools. A broad range of extracurricular activities is offered in the Preparatory and Pre-Preparatory Departments.

The school aims to incorporate the best of modern teaching methods and traditional values in a nurturing and busy environment, where good work habits and a concern for the needs of others are paramount.

Monmouth Prep School

Haberdashers' Monmouth Schools

The Grange, Hadnock Road, Monmouth NP25 3NG

Tel: 01600 732426
01600 732382
email: prep.enquiries@habsmonmouth.org
prep.admissions@habsmonmouth.org
website: www.habsmonmouth.org/prep
X/Twitter: @Habsmonmouth
Facebook: @Habsmonmouth
LinkedIn: /haberdashers'-monmouth-schools

Foundation Bursar: Mrs T Norgrove, MBA
Director of Boarding: Mr A Peace, BSc

***Head*: Mr N Shaw**, MA

Deputy Heads:
Mrs K Kirman, BSc
Mr T Evans, BA, PGCE

Nursery to Year 2
Mrs J Cameron
Mrs S Chowns, BA
Mrs K Davies, BA
Mrs A Lewis, BEd
Mrs S Reynolds, BEd
Mrs L Shepherd, BA
Mrs V Taylor, BA

Years 3–6
Mrs S Beaumont, BA, PGCE
Mrs A Copley, BHEd
M K Fradd, BSc
Mrs A Griffiths, BA
M S Holmes, BEd
Mrs S George, BA, PGCE
Dr T Murcott, BSc, PhD
Mr D Murray, MA
Mrs L Partridge, BA
Miss N Price, BEd
Miss R Forester-Bennett, BA
Mrs H Rees BA, PGCE
Mrs S Ridyard, BEd, MA Ed
Mrs A Roskilly-Green, BA PGCE
Miss R Sanderson, PGCE
Mr K Shepherd, BA
Mr F Somerset-Norris, BA, PGCE, MSc
Mr C Stonier, BSc
Mrs A Taylor, LRSC, PGCE
Dr S Wall, BSc, PhD
Mr J Walton, BMus

Age Range. 3–11.

Number of Pupils. 231 (boys and girls).

Fees per term (2023–2024). Day £3,187–£4,670, Boarding (Years 3–6) £8,572.

Monmouth Prep School is fully co-educational and welcomes day and boarding pupils aged 3–11, where we focus on developing enthusiastic, inquisitive, resilient girls and boys with high aspirations.

A child's educational journey at Haberdashers' Monmouth Schools begins at Monmouth Prep School, where boys and girls thrive and flourish with inspired and engaging subject-specialist teaching delivered across two sites.

Based at Agincourt, a delightful old rectory set in picturesque grounds, children in Nursery to Year 2 enjoy the beautiful, open spaces for learning and enrichment activities.

The Grange is modern and home to pupils from Years 3 to 6 where enhanced outside areas combine to create a dynamic and engaging space for children aged 7 to 11.

Pupils at Monmouth Prep School make the most of the outstanding facilities for science, languages, music, culture, sports and dance on offer across our family of schools.

Girls and boys immerse themselves in a breadth and range of educational opportunities, trips and expeditions, social and co-curricular events and shared community projects.

Children are motivated to learn with a sense of fun, enjoyment and excitement, both in and out of the classroom.

Carefully planned and coordinated, the curriculum focuses on developing enthusiastic, inquisitive and resilient boys and girls and provide a strong bedrock for learning across the whole of our integrated prep school.

Boarding, from the age of 7, creates a real sense of community throughout the school, where children thrive in a safe and friendly environment.

We will provide additional support for pupils who need it, confident that your child will flourish to their full potential.

There is a sense that anything is possible for children at Monmouth Prep School, ensuring a confident step up to the senior school.

Aims. We aim to provide an excellent education as the foundation for future achievement and to develop personal qualities of confidence, independence and social conscience.

Location. Nursery to Year 2 are based at Agincourt, a delightful old rectory set in picturesque grounds with beautiful, open spaces for learning and enrichment activities. Years 3 to 6 are based at modern premises at The Grange, next to Monmouth Schools Sports Club with its own 25-metre swimming pool, indoor sports hall and an all-weather pitch, with enhanced outside areas.

Facilities. We have well-equipped classrooms, hall, library, art studio, science laboratory, computer suite, music room and music studios. We have kitchens and the grounds provide a safe, spacious area for recreation, games and outdoor projects. In addition, we share the facilities of Monmouth School for Boys and Monmouth School for Girls, including the School Chapel, large playing fields, sports complex, gymnasium, artificial pitches, sports pavilion, drama studio, Performing Arts Centre and our professional theatre, The Blake Theatre.

Curriculum. Our curriculum is broad and varied and takes account of, though is not constrained by, the National Curriculum. We teach English, mathematics, science, Latin, humanities, information and communication technology and computing, history, geography, religious education, art, design technology, music, physical education, games, drama, French and study skills.

Extra-curricular Activities. We have a full programme of activities that take place both in the lunch break and after school. This includes hockey, rugby, netball, gymnastics, football, cricket, tennis, swimming, golf, karate, cross-country running, string orchestra, wind band, choir, fencing, art, gardening, computing and chess.

Entry is usually at 7+ following assessment, though recruitment is currently across all year groups.

We award a number of scholarships each year to pupils moving on to our senior schools. Various scholarships are available for girls and boys joining in Year 7 (11+) and Year 9 (13+) and applications are open for all candidates, whether boarders or day pupils. Scholarship allocation is based on entrance results, an interview, an audition or trial, and a clear display of outstanding potential. (For further details, *see* Monmouth School for Boys and Monmouth School for Girls entries).

Charitable status. William Jones's Schools Foundation is a Registered Charity, number 525616. Its aims and objectives are to provide an all-round education for girls and boys at reasonable fees.

Moor Park School

Richard's Castle, Ludlow, Shropshire SY8 4DZ

Tel: 01584 876061
email: registrar@moorpark.org.uk
website: www.moorpark.org.uk
Facebook: @MoorParkSchool
Instagram: @moorparkludlow

Chairman of Governors: Julian Rogers-Coltman

***Headmaster*: Mr Brendan Brady**

Deputy Head: M. J-M Collin

Age Range. 3 months to 13 years.
Number of Pupils. 235.
Fees per term (2023–2024). Boarding: £8,805–£10,540, Day: £2,565–£7,105.

Founded in 1964, Moor Park is an IAPS, Catholic, co-educational boarding and day school accepting children from 3 months to 13 years of age. A family atmosphere pervades, resulting in happy, rounded and grounded children.

Children often start at Moor Park in the Tick Tock Nursery (from 3 months) located at the heart of the school, which provides a secure environment for our very youngest children. The learning environment (inside and outside) is maximised to allow real potential for exploration and creativity. The children transfer to the Pre-Prep Kindergarten in the term that they turn 3, where they are carefully prepared to start more formal schooling by a team of well-qualified and caring staff.

All our children make full use of the 85 acres of stunning grounds, but Moor Park is not just about getting muddy and exploring. Our schemes of work and teaching methods from Nursery to Year 8 have been designed to deliberately encourage the thinking skills, as well as the knowledge, that young people will need in a fast-changing world. Creativity, curiosity, critical thought, confidence, independence and resilience are all deliberately fostered, and the results are plain to see. In the last five years, our leavers have won over 100 scholarships to senior schools, and this from a non-selective intake. Being a truly independent school has helped our children gain entry to the full range of schools nationally, and these scholarships include academic and extra-curricular awards to some of the top senior schools in the country.

It is also worth saying that Moor Park is emphatically not simply an academic hothouse and is a school where children of all abilities thrive. All of this is underpinned by a carefully maintained culture of kindness which ensures that all children are valued for who they are. Passionate teachers and an average class size of around 14 also make a difference, with specialist staff offering extra-curricular activities throughout the school.

The Head, Brendan Brady, started in September 2022 bringing with him a wealth of experience, high aspirations and a passion for ensuring that every child has a chance to reach their potential whilst enjoying the wholesome, well-rounded education that Moor Park offers.

Not every child can be good at everything but every child can be good at something, and finding that something for every child we take seriously. Moor Park's facilities and, more importantly, enthusiastic and dedicated staff, ensure that the school is well placed to get the best out of every child.

Moor Park – More than just a school!

Charitable status. Moor Park School is a Registered Charity, number 511800, which exists to provide education for young people.

Moorfield School

Wharfedale Lodge, 11 Ben Rhydding Road, Ilkley, West Yorkshire LS29 8RL

Tel: 01943 607285
email: enquiries@moorfieldschool.co.uk
website: www.moorfieldschool.co.uk
X/Twitter: @MoorfieldIlkley
Facebook: @MoorfieldSchoolIlkley

Moorfield is an Education Charitable Trust and the Headmistress is a member of IAPS.

Chairman of Governors: Mr Richard Wallace

***Head*: Mrs Tina Herbert**

Bursar: Mrs Michelle Holland
Admissions Secretary: Mrs Debbie Firth

Age Range. 2–11 Co-educational.
Number of Pupils 116 Girls and Boys.
Fees per term (2023–2024). Nursery £30.95 per session; Main School £3,887 including lunch.

Staff: 10 full-time, 16 part-time, 11 peripatetic teachers.

Religious affiliation: Interdenominational.

Excellence in Education inspiring Kindness, Confidence & Creativity

Moorfield School is situated in a beautiful setting on the edge of Ilkley Moor. It prides itself in providing inspirational teaching within a giving and caring school.

Independence and individuality are encouraged and confidence nurtured. The whole child is important and we work together to grow hearts, minds and strength of character.

Our child-led approach to teaching and learning from ages 2 to 6 is unique and results show that children at the end of Reception (90%) are way above the national average (67%) across the curriculum.

Further up the school, high standards in English and Maths are the bedrock of academic success enabling all our pupils to get into their secondary school of choice. Outstanding teaching from a vibrant staff gives pupils confidence to succeed in all subjects. With specialist teaching in many subjects, pupils are given the opportunity to develop skills and interests in Computer Science, Drama, Music and Sport, Art, Cookery and Bushcraft.

Support for working parents is provided by offering wrap-around care in term time from 7.45am to 6.15pm and throughout school holidays from 8.00 am to 4.00 pm.

Pupils leave Moorfield with a secure foundation of learning, a strong work ethic and the confidence to be successful.

Moorfield is recommended by *The Good Schools Guide*.

Charitable status. Moorfield School Ltd is a Registered Charity, number 529112.

Moorlands School

Foxhill Drive, Weetwood Lane, Leeds LS16 5PF

Tel: 0113 278 5286
email: info@moorlands-school.co.uk
website: www.moorlands-school.co.uk
X/Twitter: @MoorlandsLeeds
Facebook: @MoorlandsLeeds
Instagram: @moorlands_school

***Headteacher*: Jacqueline Atkinson**, GMus Hons, PGCE, MEd

Age Range. 2–11 Co-educational.

Number of Pupils. 150 Day Boys and Girls.

Founded in 1898, Moorlands is the oldest prep school in Leeds and is dedicated to providing a first-class education for girls and boys aged 2 to 11 years in a warm, friendly environment.

The school is conveniently located off the Ring Road at Weetwood Lane, yet sat in beautiful grounds providing all the outdoor space required for children to play in a safe and secure environment. The school boasts fantastic wrap-around care facilities, excellent teaching standards, an on-site swimming pool and small class sizes.

Being part of the Methodist Independent Schools' Trust enables us to deliver outstanding value for money. Unlike many other schools, our inclusive fees, for children in Reception (starting the term after they turn 5) to Year 6, includes:

- Supervised breakfast club from 7.30 am, after-school care and a cooked tea from 5.00 pm–6.00 pm.
- Educational day visits which form part of the learning experience on the curriculum.
- A choice of around 20 free-to-attend clubs which take place between 4.00 pm and 5.00 pm.
- Regular learning support sessions for those children who would benefit from it.
- For KS1 and KS2, weekly bushcraft and outdoor learning sessions held in our extensive grounds, taught by Yorkshire Dales Bushcraft.
- For Reception, Forest School sessions held within the Early Years woodland area in the school grounds.
- Weekly swimming lessons held in the on-site heated indoor pool, with qualified instructors.
- Specialist teaching in Music, Drama, Modern Foreign Languages and Art.

The aim of the school is to develop the full potential of every child within a happy and caring environment fostered by small classes and the professional skills of a highly qualified staff. Strong links between the parents and the school are encouraged to facilitate the provision of an effective education.

Admission is by assessment and observation. Pupils are accepted at 2 years old for entry into the Nursery and are expected to progress through the school in preparation for entry to senior independent day and boarding schools. The school has a well-developed specialist facility to provide assistance to pupils with any learning issue such as dyslexia or to gifted children.

Blended with this traditional core of academic work is offered a comprehensive range of sporting activities, outdoor education and a wide range of musical and extra-curricular pursuits.

At Moorlands, we have a simple yet beautiful motto, 'Intrepide', or 'be brave'! In school, we talk about how being brave or intrepid takes many forms. Being brave isn't always a grand gesture; sometimes it simply means 'having a go', such as attempting that difficult question, offering an answer in class when you're not quite sure or trying something new. This culture of intrepidness allows children to try new things in a safe, nurturing and stimulating environment.

Religious affiliation: Methodist.

Fees per term (2023–2024). EY: £3,633, Reception: £3,783, Years 1–2: £3,836 (lunch £250), Years 3–4: £4,250, Years 5–6: £4,280 (lunch £280).

Charitable status. Moorlands School is a Registered Charity, number 529216. It exists to provide children with the finest education possible, using the best resources in an environment of care.

Moreton Hall

Weston Rhyn, Oswestry, Shropshire SY11 3EW

Tel: 01691 773671
email: admin@moretonhall.com
website: www.moretonhall.org
X/Twitter: @moretonhall
Facebook: @moretonhall

See full entry in the **HMC** section, on **p. 234**.

Moulsford Preparatory School

Moulsford-on-Thames, Wallingford, Oxfordshire OX10 9HR
Tel: 01491 651438
email: heads.pa@moulsford.com
website: www.moulsford.com
X/Twitter: @Moulsford
Facebook: @Moulsford
Instagram: @moulsford

The School is a Charitable Trust controlled by a Board of Governors.

Chairman of the Board of Governors: Mr E L A Boddington

Headmaster: **B Beardmore-Gray**, BA Hons, QTS

Age range: 3–13.
Number of children: 380.
Fees per term (2023–2024): Prep School Day fee (Years 3–8): £7,035, Pre-Prep fee (Reception–Year 2): £4,710, Pre-School up to £4,010 for 5 full days. Weekly boarding (Years 5–8): £1,765 (in addition to day fees).

Moulsford is a thriving independent day and boarding Prep School for children aged 3–13 years set on the banks of the River Thames in South Oxfordshire. The Pre-Prep is co-educational for boys and girls aged 3–7 years, and the Prep school is for boys aged 7–13 years. We aim for our pupils to receive the broadest possible education, while remembering that they will learn best when happy and settled. Our down-to-earth, family-focused approach embraces the fact that children of this age should be having fun at the same time as learning.

Moulsford offers pupils superb opportunities for learning while having fun, with a curriculum designed not only to prepare them for senior schools, but also to ensure they have the skills for life beyond. The curriculum promotes intellectual agility, encourages them to think and analyse critically, makes connections across the subjects and gives plenty of opportunity for creativity and collaboration. Children are encouraged to build resilience by having a go, taking a well thought-out risk, and, on occasion, failing.

Through Moulsford's Activities programme, the school aims to offer opportunities to develop new skills and talents, while becoming a conscientious citizen. Working towards the Moulsford Award, children can try bike maintenance, cookery, bushcraft, photography, climbing, drama, chess, pantomime, parkour, geocaching and many more activities covering the five key elements of performance and arts, community, self-development, adventure and healthy living.

Moulsford's reputation for sport remains extremely strong with all boys in the Prep school in teams A to F regularly playing competitive matches. Major sports are football, rugby, hockey, cricket and athletics. Minor sports have also seen significant successes in golf, skiing, fencing and judo. Music and drama remain very popular with roughly three-quarters of the boys from Years 3–8 playing an instrument.

Boys leaving in Year 8 progress to the UK's leading independent day and boarding schools at 13+ including Abingdon, Eton, Harrow, Radley, Magdalen College School, St Edward's Oxford, Wellington, Marlborough, Pangbourne, Bradfield and The Oratory.

The riverside setting provides a different dimension to prep school life with kayaks, canoes and stand-up paddleboards all put to good use. At Forest School there are opportunities for fire-building, whittling and making bows and arrows.

A new state-of-the-art Pre-Prep building opened in September 2022. The Pre-Prep building is home to a Pre-School, Reception, Year 1 and Year 2, and welcomes boys and girls throughout.

Moulsford sits on the border of South Oxfordshire and West Berkshire and is easily accessible within the Newbury, Oxford and Reading 'triangle' with the M40 and M4 motorways and the A34 close by. School transport services are provided throughout the local area.

Charitable status. Moulsford Preparatory School is a Registered Charity, number 309643.

Mount Kelly

Parkwood Road, Tavistock, Devon PL19 0HZ
Tel: 01822 813193
email: admissions@mountkelly.com
website: www.mountkelly.com
X/Twitter: @Mount_Kelly
Facebook: @MountKellyFoundation
Instagram: @mount.kelly
LinkedIn: /mount-kelly

See full entry in the **HMC** section, on **p. 236**.

Naima Jewish Prep School

21 Andover Place, London NW6 5ED
Tel: 020 7328 2802
email: secretary@naimajps.co.uk; headmaster@naimajps.co.uk
website: www.naimajps.org.uk

Chair of Governors: Mr Julian Levy

Headmaster: **Mr J W Pratt**, GRSM Hons, CertEd

Age Range. 2–11 Co-educational.
Number of Pupils. 152 girls and boys.
Fees per term (2023–2024). £4,375–£5,155.

Naima JPS is centred on the belief that an excellent secular education and strong Jewish grounding are mutually attainable. As such, our twin goals merge as we aspire to prepare our children for a successful life in society imbued with Torah values. We aim to provide a secular education on a par with the top national private schools with a curriculum that extends beyond the minimum guidelines provided by the National Curriculum. As a private school, we provide both the environment and teaching resources to monitor each individual, and to help children of all abilities to reach their full potential.

Naima JPS challenges all children, together with their parents, no matter what their level of religious observance, to pursue ongoing spiritual growth as individuals. We encourage children on their journey to spiritual maturity in a harmonious and nurturing community environment of tolerance, respect and care for one another.

The school has a one-form entry. Given that class sizes seldom exceed 22 and the favourable ratio of teachers and assistants to children – as little as 1:5 depending on the age and need – programmes of learning have the flexibility for differentiation. The school has a high number of particularly able children with specific intellectual gifts.

During the crucial early years at school it is important that children define themselves by things they can do well. Self-esteem, that essential by-product of success, empowers strength and gifts. Once children understand how their minds work, as they learn in many different ways, they can feel comfortable about entering any environment and mastering it. Children who truly understand, value and like themselves are better equipped to flourish and embrace fresh challenges. Confidence through success contributes to strong identities that welcome new horizons. Resiliency, discovery, independence and spiritual maturity are nurtured at all levels. At Naima JPS education is not about coveting garlands for the few, but ensuring that all children reach their full potential.

Charitable status. Naima JPS is a Registered Charity, number 289066.

The New Beacon

Brittains Lane, Sevenoaks, Kent TN13 2PB

Tel: 01732 452131
email: admin@newbeacon.org.uk
website: www.newbeacon.org.uk

Chairman of the Governors: Mr James Thorne

***Head*: Mrs S Brownsdon**, BA Hons

Age Range. Rising 3–13.

Number of Boys. 340 Boys (Girls in nursery only). Predominantly Day Pupils, but flexi boarding is available from Monday to Thursday.

Fees per term (2023–2024). £4,446–£6,385. Fees include lunches.

Boys are prepared for both grammar and senior independent schools and enjoy considerable success at 11+ and 13+, with many achieving scholarships (including music, sport, art, design technology and drama) to a wide range of first-class senior schools.

The School divides into Senior, Middle, Junior and Nursery sections in which boys are placed according to age and ability. Initiative is encouraged by organising the School into 4 houses or 'companies'. The well-equipped main School building is complemented by several modern, purpose-built facilities: separate Pre-Prep and Junior School buildings for nursery girls and boys from rising 3, and for boys aged 4–9; a Sports Hall with modern changing facilities; a multi-purpose, AstroTurf sports pitch; a Theatre; a heated indoor Swimming Pool; a centre for Art and Music; and modern facilities for Science and Technology. Football, Rugby Union and Cricket are the major games. During the summer months Tennis and Athletics are available. Swimming and Shooting are available all year round. A very extensive range of extra-curricular activities is offered (including many interesting and exciting trips) together with a programme of pre- and after-school care. Music, sport, art and drama at the School are highly regarded.

The New Beacon merged with Tonbridge School in August 2021. While the two Governing Bodies work together to align in terms of overall strategy, each school retains its own site, leadership and management teams.

Following the merge in 2021, The New Beacon is overseen by the Skinners' Company – a major not-for-profit organisation which supports seven other schools (including Tonbridge School).

New College School

Savile Road, Oxford OX1 3UA

Tel: 01865 285560
email: office@newcollegeschool.org
website: www.newcollegeschool.org

Governors: The Warden & Fellows of New College Oxford

***Headmaster*: Dr Matthew Jenkinson**, BA Dunelm, MEd Buckingham, MSt, DPhil Oxon, FRHistS

Age range. 4–13 years.

Number of boys. 169 Day Boys, including 20 Choristers.

Fees per term (2023–2024). Reception: £4,490; Year 1: £5,260; Year 2: £6,350; Years 3–4: £6,410; Years 5–8: £7,010; Choristers: £2,795.

New College School was founded in 1379 when William of Wykeham made provision for the education of 16 Choristers to sing daily services in New College Chapel. Situated in the heart of the city, a few minutes' walk from the College, the school is fortunate in having the use of New College playing fields for sport and New College Chapel for school services.

The staff consists of some 22 full-time teachers and a full complement of visiting music teachers. In their final year, all boys complete the Pre-Senior Baccalaureate, while there is also a separate academic scholarship form and pupils are prepared for their destination schools' entrance exams when applicable. The school broadly follows the national curriculum subjects, but also teaches French, Latin, Design Technology and Greek.

Sports, played on New College Sports Ground, include soccer, hockey, cricket, rounders, athletics and rugby. Activities include archery, art, craft, pottery, design, chess, sport, computing, drama, and science clubs. There is a Choral Society for parents.

Music plays a major part in school life with orchestra, ensembles, concert and junior choirs and form concerts, in addition to individual tuition in a wide range of instruments. An optional Saturday morning music education programme is followed by boys from Year 5 upwards.

Boys are admitted by gentle assessment to the Pre-Prep Department at 4 years and to the Prep School at 7 years. Potential Choristers are tested between the ages of 6 and 7 at annual voice trials.

Newbridge Preparatory School

51 Newbridge Crescent
Tettenhall, Wolverhampton, West Midlands
WV6 0LH

Tel: 01902 751088
email: office@newbridgeprepschool.org.uk
website: www.newbridgeprepschool.org.uk

Chairman of Board: Mr G Birkett

***Headmistress*: Mrs S Fisher**, BEd Hons

Age Range. Girls 2–11. Boys 2–7.

Number of Pupils. 138.

Fees per term (2023–2024). £2,160–£3,370 including dance, recorder, drama, gym, netball, singing for various year groups.

Newbridge Preparatory School, founded in 1937, occupies a super site on the outskirts of Wolverhampton, convenient for parents travelling from Telford, Bridgnorth, Shropshire, and Stafford.

The school is divided into Lower School (Pre-Nursery–Year 2) and Upper School (Years 3–6). Upper School is housed in the main building which is a substantial house set in huge, beautiful mature gardens. There are specialist facilities in Art and Design, ICT, Science, Music and PE. The school also has netball and tennis courts.

The staff to pupil ratio is high. Specialist teaching takes place in Key Stage Two in English, Mathematics, Music, Science, French, PE, Dance and Drama. In Key Stage One: Dance, PE, Music and French.

Lower School enjoys a separate Nursery and purpose built accommodation for Pre-Nursery to Year 2. There is a multi-use sports hall.

Children with Special Needs are well supported and nurtured with 1:1 support and a SENCo.

Upper School girls take drama and dance and enter examinations. They also enter the annual local festival for Music and Drama.

The school offers a Breakfast Club (7.30 am to 8.00 am), an Early Club (8.00 am to 8.30 am), an After-School Club (3.15 pm to 6.00 pm) and a Holiday Club (8.00 am to 5.30 pm).

Standards are high in all areas of the curriculum. Senior School results are excellent. Places are gained at local selective Independent and Maintained Schools but also Boarding Schools. Sporting, Academic and Speech and Drama Scholarships are attained for entrance into Senior School. Girls leave Newbridge well equipped to face the challenges of a Senior School.

Educational visits and visitors take place each term for Year 1 to Year 6. Nursery children enjoy a Forest School experience. Residential visits occur in Years 3–6. The visits vary from outdoor activities and challenges and cultural visits to London.

Emphasis is placed on traditional values, personal development and responsibility. The curriculum is very broad, including many opportunities in Sport, Dance, Drama and Music.

Our school mission statement is: *Aiming High, Building Bridges and Preparing for Life*. Our motto is: *Dare to dream it, Work to achieve it.*

Children are taught to do their best in all areas, strive for a challenge and succeed at their own level.

Emphasis is placed on self-discipline, inclusion, equal opportunity and respect.

Charitable status. Newbridge Preparatory School is a Registered Charity, number 1019682. It exists to advance the education of children by conducting the school known as Newbridge Preparatory School.

Newcastle Preparatory School

6 Eslington Road, Jesmond, Newcastle-upon-Tyne, Tyne and Wear NE2 4RH

Tel: 0191 281 1769
email: office@newcastleprep.co.uk
website: www.newcastleprepschool.org.uk
X/Twitter: @NclPrep
Facebook: @newcastleprep
Instagram: @newcastleprep1885

The School was founded in 1885 and is now a Charitable Trust with a Board of Governors.

Chair of Governors: Mrs Susan Blair

***Head Teacher*: Miss Gemma Strong**

Assistant Head Teacher: Mr Peter Fargher
Assistant Head Teacher: Mrs Natalie Johnson
Assistant Head Teacher: Mrs Amy Porter

Bursar: Mrs Susan Easton

Age Range. 3–11.

Number of Pupils. 279 Day Pupils (163 boys, 116 girls).

Fees per term (2023–2024). £4,251.

The School is situated in a residential part of Newcastle with easy access from all round the area.

Newcastle Preparatory School is a fully co-educational day school for children aged 3 to 11 years. It is a warm, caring environment in which all pupils are encouraged to reach their full potential.

Children may join 'First Steps' at NPS from the age of 3 years. 'First Steps' is an exciting and colourful nursery with excellent resources and well qualified staff who look after the needs of each individual.

At age 4, children make the easy step into School where they experience many 'steps to success'.

The curriculum offered throughout school is broad and balanced so that children enjoy learning in a variety of ways. French is taught from age 4 with music and PE being taught by specialist teachers. As children progress through School they become independent learners, following a varied timetable and class sizes are small to provide individual attention.

Music is an important part of life at NPS. There is a choir and an orchestra.

Sporting achievements too are very good. There is a purpose-built Sports Hall and a wide range of sport is offered with extracurricular activities including rugby, football, cricket, hockey, netball, athletics, tennis and swimming.

Also there are many clubs and activities to enrich the curriculum, e.g. Drama, Dance, Chess, Philosophy, Art, ICT, Design, Food Technology and there is an effective School Council as well as a Buddy System.

Outdoor learning is offered throughout the school. In 2017 a dedicated Forest School area was opened and pupils also run a a local allotment.

The variety of opportunities ensures that the children leave NPS well equipped for an easy transition to senior school. The academic results are very good and the children receive an all-round education, so that they are confident, eager learners.

Charitable status. Newcastle Preparatory School is a Registered Charity, number 528152. It exists to provide education for boys and girls.

Newcastle School for Boys

Senior School:
34 The Grove, Gosforth, Newcastle upon Tyne NE3 1NH
Tel: 0191 255 9300

Junior School:
30 West Avenue, Gosforth, Newcastle upon Tyne NE3 4ES
Tel: 0191 255 9300
email: enquiries@newcastleschool.co.uk
website: newcastleschool.co.uk
X/Twitter: @NSB_Boys @nsb_sport
Facebook: @NewcastleSchoolforBoys

See full entry in the **Society of Heads** section, on **p. 545**.

Newland House School

Waldegrave Park, Twickenham TW1 4TQ
Tel: 020 8865 1234
email: admissions@newlandhouse.net
website: www.newlandhouse.net
X/Twitter: @newlandhouse
Facebook: @Newland-House-School-Twickenham
Instagram: @newlandhouseschool.uk

Founded in 1897, Newland House is an Independent Prep School and Nursery for children from the ages of 3–13.

Located on a quiet residential street on the borders of Twickenham and Teddington, it is ideally situated for parents living in Richmond, Kingston, Whitton and Hampton. As one of the oldest and largest Prep schools in the area, Newland House offers history and tradition alongside modern facilities, progressive teaching methods and a vibrant community.

Chairman of Governors: Mr Andrew Gumpert
***Head*: Mr Chris Skelton**, BSc, NPQH

Age Range. 3–13.

Number of Pupils. 267 Boys, 181 Girls.

Fees per term (2023–2024). Nursery from £2,690, Pre-Prep: £4,771, Prep: £5,323. Lunch is included in the fees.

Newland House School is divided into Nursery, Pre-Prep (Reception to Year 2), and Prep (Years 3 to 8). The Pre-Prep and Prep School sit on a 5-acre site, with Nursery just over the road. Classrooms are well equipped with interactive whiteboards and touch screens, and there is plenty of access to outdoor space. Facilities include two science labs, an excellent Design and Technology workshop, a purpose-built music block, as well as a state-of-the-art ICT suite and a well-stocked library. There are two large multi-functioning halls, one of which has been recently updated to include retractable seating and a new lighting and sound system to support the school's ambitious drama productions.

Onsite sports facilities include two artificial grass pitches, a hard court and cricket nets. Just a short distance away, we use the extensive grounds of Bushy Park Sports Club for field sports.

The main entry points for joining Newland House School are at age 3 (into Nursery) and age 4 (into Reception). Entry to Nursery and Reception is non-selective, and places are offered on a first-come, first-served basis. Some pupils join in Year 7 for the Senior Prep years, but otherwise, there are no additional defined entry points. Admissions in Year 1 upwards are dependent on a place becoming available, and you can join the waiting list at any time. An offer will be subject to an informal assessment (Pre-Prep) or a more formal assessment (Prep).

The school is committed to providing a broad and balanced curriculum and bringing out the full potential in every child. The school's ISI Inspection in the summer of 2022 found that the quality of pupils' academic and other achievements is 'excellent' and that the quality of pupils' personal development is 'excellent'.

The staff currently consists of 47 teachers. There are two Nursery assistants, each class up to Year 2 has a dedicated Teaching Assistant, and in the Prep, there are Teaching Assistants in Years 3 and 4. There is a well-resourced Learning Enrichment department that offers group interventions and one-to-one sessions as required. Pupils who are more able are challenged through interventions led by the More Able Pupils co-ordinator.

In the Early Years, the class teacher's role is complemented by specialist teaching in Music, PE and French. Children in Years 3 and 4 are taught by specialists in Design and Technology, Music, Art, Drama, Games and PE, Swimming, French and Computing (ICT). From Year 5, Mathematics and English are taught in sets by specialist teachers. Science, History, Geography and Reasoning are also specialist subjects. In Year 6 upwards, Latin is introduced, and Spanish is taught from Year 7.

Children are well prepared for their senior school exams at 11+ or 13+ and leave as confident, empathic, and well-rounded individuals with a strong moral compass and an understanding of the role they play in society. They go on to a range of excellent schools, including Hampton, LEH, Kingston Grammar School, Surbiton, Epsom College, Reed's, Halliford and St George's. In 2023, 20 students achieved scholarships across academics, sports, and the Arts.

The core sports of football, netball, hockey, rugby and cricket are introduced through the Games curriculum. The ethos is 'sport for all', where each child gets the opportunity to develop to the best of their ability. Girls and boys have equal opportunities to participate in all sports offered. A commitment to inclusivity goes hand in hand with fostering a spirit of healthy competition. There are teams from A–F in many sports, so children get a chance to represent the school in regular competitive fixtures. Swimming is offered from Year 3 upwards. Every two years, there is a Senior cricket tour, with previous years' destinations including Barbados and St. Lucia.

Pupils have timetabled Music lessons from Nursery to Year 8. Fifteen peripatetic music teachers offer lessons from Year 1 in a huge range of instruments, singing, music theory and music technology. Around 70% of children learn a musical instrument at school. There are 5 choirs, several wind and brass ensembles, 2 orchestras, and a jazz band. Each year there are around 25 concerts, as well as an annual European choir tour and the opportunity to perform in external competitions and local events.

In Design and Technology, pupils have access to a range of modern CAD/CAM equipment. Robotics, programming and problem-solving are taught as part of the curriculum and in STEM Club through VEQ Robotics and Sphero Education.

Pastoral support is excellent and ensures that every single child in the school feels safe, valued and cared for, allowing them to thrive and be happy. The Wellbeing Coordinator, along with Tilly, the therapy dog, offers extra support if needed.

The educational visits program is extensive, and children benefit from local trips as well as international ones to enrich the curriculum and broaden their horizons.

Over 70 extracurricular clubs are on offer, allowing children to explore their passions or discover new ones, hone their skills and build confidence. The options available include fencing, golf, karate, chess, entrepreneur club, Money Matters, African drumming, dance, mindfulness and coding, and many more.

The school provides wraparound care from 7.30 am to 8.20 am and from 3.50 pm until 6 pm, and there are three daily bus services before and after school to support busy parents.

Charitable status: The Newland House School Trust Limited is a Registered Charity, number 312670. It exists to promote and provide for the advancement of education for children.

Newton Prep

149 Battersea Park Road, London SW8 4BX
Tel: 020 7720 4091
email: admissions@newtonprep.co.uk
website: www.newtonprepschool.co.uk
X/Twitter: @NewtonPrepSch
Facebook: @NewtonPrepSch
Instagram: @newtonprepschool
LinkedIn: /company/newtonprepsch

Chairman of Council: Dr Farouk Walji
***Head*: Mrs A E Fleming**, BA, MA

Age range. 3–13.
Number of pupils. 646: 54% Boys, 46% Girls.
Fees per term (2023–2024). £3,780–£7,980.
Average size of class. <20.
The current teacher to pupil ratio is 1:11.
Religious denomination. Non-denominational.

Newton Prep is a vibrant school which offers a challenging education for inquisitive children who are eager to engage fully with the world in which they are growing up. The school aims to:

- inspire children to be adventurous and committed in their learning;
- provide balance and breadth in all aspects of a child's education: intellectual, aesthetic, physical, moral and spiritual;
- encourage initiative, individuality, independence, creativity and enquiry;
- promote responsible behaviour and respect for others in a happy, safe and caring environment.

Entry requirements. Children joining Reception are assessed individually: a gentle process, with offers made in November the year before entry. Older children come to an assessment morning in the Spring Term (on a case-by-case basis at other times) during which they will be assessed in English, Maths and some diagnostic, age-appropriate reasoning tests. Means-tested top-up bursaries are available in and after Year 3.

Examinations offered. The school prepares children for the wide range of entrance exams required for senior school entry. About half of the Year 6 cohort move on at 11+ with the remainder staying until Year 8. Newton Prep believes that there is no one 'best' school but instead it is a matter of finding the right school for each child. Each year, children head off to between 40 and 50 different day and boarding schools including Westminster, St Paul's, Wycombe Abbey, Latymer, Alleyn's, City of London, Eton, Wellington and Brighton College. Over the past three years, they have been offered 66 scholarships.

'Bright children, exceptional opportunities.'

First-time visitors to the school are invariably impressed by the scale and range of the secondary-school-level facilities and by the wide open outdoor spaces enjoyed by the children on a large site so close to the centre of London. As well as the three school gyms there are two huge outdoor spaces for PE/Games and free play: behind the school, an all-weather pitch and, in front, a large, tree-fringed playground for the littler children. The school also has a large garden with a wildlife area and an activity area with a pirate boat.

Newton Prep occupies an early 20th-century elementary school building, which has been extensively remodelled internally, and behind which stands large modern extensions containing classrooms, the dining hall and kitchen, two gymnasiums, a 300-seat auditorium and a state-of-the-art recital hall (along with a recording studio and a music technology suite). The top floor of the Edwardian building provides one large general-purpose space as well as two art studios. Below are two floors of classrooms, including three collegiate-style science labs, three ICT suites and a library that is the envy of the many visiting authors, who all say it is one of the most vibrant and popular reading spaces they have come across in a school.

Despite the excellence of their education, Newton Prep children are notable for their lack of arrogance and entitlement. The kindness and generosity shown by the pupils towards their peers is remarkable and the engagement between the older children and the little ones is heartwarming, especially when it comes to inter-house events, when children up and down the school are united by their love for their house!

Newton is not a blazers and boaters kind of school. As one current parent put it, '*Newton combines a quirky nature and knowledge of families with great space and facilities ...All the teachers understand my (very different) children, the management is open to fresh ideas and the school is large enough to accommodate variety.*'

Scholarships and bursaries:

Bursaries are available for children entering the School from Year 3.

Norfolk House School

4 Norfolk Road, Edgbaston, Birmingham B15 3PS

Tel: 0121 454 7021
email: info@norfolkhouseschool.co.uk
website: www.norfolkhouseschool.co.uk

***Headmistress*: Mrs Susannah Palmer**

Age Range. 3–11.
Number in School. 147.
Fees per term (2023–2024). £2,865–£4,144.

Norfolk House School is an Independent, co-educational school, situated in the pleasant suburb of Edgbaston. It is ideally located for pupils and parents all over Birmingham and the surrounding areas.

The school aims to provide individual attention to each pupil, thus enabling each child to fulfil his or her potential. Small class sizes and favourable pupil to teacher ratios culminate in the best possible academic results. Many pupils move on to the various King Edward Schools, or to other grammar schools or senior independent schools as the direct result of the high standards achieved at Norfolk House.

The curriculum is designed to give each child a thorough academic education over a wide range of subjects, taking fully into account the requirements of the Eleven Plus and the various entrance examinations to senior independent schools.

A wide range of extra curricular activities and enrichment sessions ensure that all children receive a rounded education. They are encouraged to pursue their interests, whether sporting, musical or artistic, alongside the rigorous academic work they encounter. The School has access to first class sports pitches and other facilities nearby.

In addition, the School aims to instil in each child good manners, consideration and respect for others, and recognition of personal responsibility. Norfolk House is a small school with an emphasis on caring and traditional values, yet forward thinking in outlook. It is a happy school with high attainment, competitive fees and a family atmosphere.

Norland Place School

162–166 Holland Park Avenue, London W11 4UH

Tel: 020 7603 9103
email: registrar@norlandplace.com
website: www.norlandplace.com
Instagram: @norlandplace

***Headmaster*: Mr P Mattar**

Age Range. Girls & Boys 4–11.
Number of Children. 228.
Fees per term (2023–2024). £6,316–£7,020.

A thriving Preparatory School founded in 1876 and still standing on the original site in Holland Park Avenue. Children are well-prepared for competitive London day schools and top rate boarding schools. The curriculum is balanced with an emphasis on English, Mathematics and Science. Music, Art and Games are strong. The school contains a Library in addition to specialist Music, Science and Art Rooms.

Early registration is essential but it is worth checking with the Registrar regarding late applications and occasional place enquiries.

North London Collegiate School

Canons, Canons Drive, Edgware, Middlesex HA8 7RJ

Tel: 020 8952 0912 (Senior School)
020 8952 1276 (Junior School)
email: office@nlcs.org.uk
website: www.nlcs.org.uk
X/Twitter: @NLCS1850
Facebook: @nlcs1850
Instagram: @nlcs1850

See full entry in the **GSA** section, on **p. 457**.

Northbourne Park

Betteshanger, Deal, Kent CT14 0NW
Tel: 01304 611215
email: office@northbournepark.com
website: www.northbournepark.com
X/Twitter: @northbournepark
Facebook: @Northbourne-Park-School

Chair of Governors: Susie Barter

***Headmaster*: Mark Hammond**, BA Hons, PGCE, MA

Age Range. Nursery–13, Co-educational.

Number of Pupils. 189 boys and girls, including 46 boarders.

Northbourne Park is a co-educational day and boarding school set in 100 acres of beautiful park and woodland in rural Kent, close to Canterbury and within easy reach of central London, Eurostar and Gatwick Airport.

We provide children with a first-class education focusing on the individual needs of every child, inspiring them to succeed across a wide range of learning experiences. We offer each child the freedom and space, together with countless opportunities, to grow in confidence and succeed.

Academic. From the Nursery and Pre-Prep through to the Prep School all our pupils gain confidence in their learning, and through inspirational teaching from dedicated staff, the pupils adapt well to an engaging and stimulating curriculum with a real sense of achievement. Although non-selective, we consistently achieve 100% pass rate in examinations – entry to top Independent Senior and local Grammar schools, LAMDA and the Associated Board of the Royal Schools of Music. Many of our pupils gain scholarships to prestigious Senior Schools.

Northbourne Park's unique Language Programme helps every child develop foreign languages in an integrated learning environment. French is introduced at 3 years and we have a unique Bilingual programme for French pupils joining Years 7 and 8 who study the French academic curriculum. The result is a clear advantage when they move on to Senior Schools.

Sport. We are passionate about sport and through an excellent sports programme the pupils develop key skills and learn the importance of teamwork and leadership. There are many opportunities to try a variety of sports from the traditional to the more diverse such as archery and trampolining. The school has recently installed a new all-weather sports pitch with floodlighting.

Creative Arts. We nurture a love for all the Arts. Many pupils learn one or more instrument in our purpose-built Music suite. They have the opportunity to take part in the choir, band, orchestra, string and brass groups performing regularly within the school and the local area. Other opportunities include LAMDA lessons, regular drama productions and Public Speaking that ensure pupils are articulate and confident in their performances. Artistic talents are encouraged through a range of media including sculpture, costume design, film-making on iMacs and pottery.

Community. Pupils are provided with a first-rate level of pastoral care in safe and nurturing surroundings with a real family atmosphere. Our welcoming boarding community provides a home-from-home environment and a continuous boarding service at weekends throughout the term. Boarders enjoy regular excursions and activities, and the accompanied services to London and Paris provide opportunities for weekends at home.

Extracurricular. We provide the pupils with a fun and extensive programme of clubs that help develop their interests and skills in hobbies that can endure long into adult life. Love of the outdoors and respect for the environment begins in the Pre-Prep and develops through into the Prep School with fun physical adventures. Whether they are playing in the woods, camping out overnight or following our pioneering Outdoor Education Programme, children love Northbourne Park life.

Fees per term (2023–2024). Boarders: £7,830 (weekly), £9,066 (full); French Programme £9,509. Day Pupils: £3,266–£3,976 (Pre-Prep), £4,633–£6,221 (Years 3–8), Flexi 3-night package £7,473. Fees include customary extras and many extracurricular activities. We offer bursaries and a wide range of scholarships. Sibling, HM Forces and Clergy discounts are generous and popular.

Charitable status. Northbourne Park is a Registered Charity, number 280048.

Norwich School, The Lower School

30 Bishopgate, Norwich, Norfolk NR1 4AA
Tel: 01603 728485
email: admissions2@norwich-school.org.uk
website: www.norwich-school.org.uk

Chairman of Governors: P J E Smith, MA, FIA

***Head of the Lower School*: J K Ingham**, BA

Age range. 4–11.

Number of pupils. 252.

Fees per term (2023–2024). £4,516–£6,069.

The Lower School is the Infant and Junior Day School for Norwich School (*see entry in HMC section*). It is delightfully located in the Cathedral Close, between the East End of the Cathedral and the River Wensum. The Cathedral Choristers are educated at Norwich School, which is a member of the Choir Schools' Association.

The Lower School provides depth and breadth of education through a challenging curriculum. It seeks to recognise, nurture and develop each pupil's potential within an environment which encourages all-round emotional, physical, social and spiritual growth and to foster positive relations between pupils, teachers and parents. The dedicated teaching staff is committed to providing a stimulating programme of active learning which has rigour and discipline but avoids unnecessary pressure.

With one form in Reception, Year 1 and Year 2, three forms in Year 3, two forms in Year 4 and three forms in Years 5 and 6, the Lower School is the ideal size for ensuring a lively environment within a warm family atmosphere. The main building has bright, spacious areas for activities and lessons. As well as the library, there are specialised facilities for science, art, technology and ICT. There is an excellent play area in addition to the adjacent, extensive playing fields. A new Infant department opened in September 2018, offering bespoke facilities for the EYFS and Key Stage 1 curriculum.

A wide range of extracurricular activities and school trips is offered. Music is a strong feature of school life. Many pupils choose to learn a musical instrument and participate in the various instrumental music groups. Rugby, netball, hockey, cricket and tennis are taught and the games programme is designed to encourage pupils of all abilities to enjoy games and physical activity.

The School aims to attract pupils who will thrive in a challenging academic environment and is therefore selective. All pupils are assessed by age-appropriate means. The principal entry points are at 4+, 7+ and 9+ with a smaller number of places available in other year groups.

Application forms and further details can be found on the website: www.norwich-school.org.uk

The vast majority of pupils from the Lower School progress to the Senior School at age eleven, and the curriculum is designed to prepare the pupils effectively for the next stage of their Norwich School education.

Charitable status. Norwich School is a Registered Charity, number 311280.

Notting Hill and Ealing High School
GDST

2 Cleveland Road, Ealing, London W13 8AX
Tel: 020 8799 8400
email: enquiries@nhehs.gdst.net
website: www.nhehs.gdst.net
X/Twitter: @nhehs
Facebook: @nhehsGDST
Instagram: @nhehsgdst

See full entry in the **GSA** section, on **p. 458**.

Nottingham High Infant and Junior School

Waverley Mount, Nottingham NG7 4ED
Tel: 0115 845 2214
email: juniorinfo@nottinghamhigh.co.uk

Lovell House Infant School:
13 Waverley Street, Nottingham NG7 4DX
Tel: 0115 845 2222
email: lovellinfo@nottinghamhigh.co.uk
website: www.nottinghamhigh.co.uk
X/Twitter: @NottsHighIJS
Facebook: @NottsHigh
Instagram: @nottshighijs
LinkedIn: /school/nottshigh

Chairman of Governors: Mr Steven Banks

***Head*: Mrs C Bruce**

Deputy Head (*Academic*): Miss L Thorpe
Deputy Head (*Pastoral*): Mr C Cordy

Age Range. 4–11 Co-educational.
Number of Pupils. 329 Day pupils.

Fees per term (2023–2024). Infant School £4,094; Junior School £4,763.

Parents often tell us they seek an environment that is stimulating, challenging and which helps their child recognise and share their individuality, interests and talents. It should be safe, warm and kind, balancing aspirations and expectations with a holistic approach. Like all excellent schools, we prize academic effort and resultant achievement, but we also value community, laughter, fun and the development of personal qualities just as much. We want your child to be happy at Nottingham High Infant & Junior School, your child will feel recognised, appreciated, respected and valued. We will foster your child's confidence to learn, be curious, make friends and relish new opportunities, and we will support them as they grow and develop, academically and as people personally.

The verdict of our recent 'Good Schools Guide' independent reviewer was that ours is 'a happy school that stands out for championing individual talents and gets these boys and girls good and ready for the more academic senior school'.

The Junior School is housed in purpose-built premises on the main school site, having its own Classrooms, ICT Suite, Library, Art Room, Science Laboratory, Outdoor play area and more.

Entrance Assessments are held in January, based around the core subjects of Mathematics and English, including reading, along with some measures of general ability. The tests are all set at National Curriculum ability levels appropriate for each age group.

The Junior School has an experienced and well-qualified staff. The curriculum is designed for those who expect to complete their education at Nottingham High School. The subjects taught are English, Mathematics, History, Geography, Science, Languages and PSHE. Full provision is made for Music, Art, Design

Technology, Information Communication Technology, Swimming, Physical Education and Games.

The Junior School has its own Orchestra and about 100 pupils receive instrumental tuition. All Year 3 pupils play an instrument of their choice. A Concert and School Plays are performed annually. A wide range of supervised activities and hobbies takes place during every lunch time.

School games are Football, Netball and Rugby with some Hockey and Cross Country in the winter, Cricket and Tennis in the summer.

Lovell House Infant School opened in September 2008 for children in Reception, Year 1 and Year 2. Lovell House is situated across the road from the main High School in its own secure and self-contained grounds. The school features state-of-the-art classrooms and facilities, and extensive play areas, all in a friendly, home-from-home surrounding. In fact, the main school building is very much like a large house, making the transition between nursery and the early stages of a formal school education so much easier.

Classes are deliberately kept small (a maximum class size of 18), so that our teachers are able to devote time to the children as individuals. The majority of subjects are taught by class teachers, although specialist teachers are used for ICT, Swimming, Music and languages. All subjects are taught in an integrated curriculum to allow time for play and problem-solving activities to take place.

Beyond the classroom we offer an excellent range of extracurricular activities, giving real breadth to our curriculum. We make full use of some of the Nottingham High School facilities, such as the swimming pool, the extensive games fields and both the music and drama facilities. Thus whilst Lovell House is largely self-contained we are also able to use the High School's wider facilities to expand the horizons of the children in our care.

Entry to Lovell House is by assessment; the admissions process is designed to assess the numeracy and literacy skills of the children applying for a place in Years 1 and 2, and a range of activities are used to assess school readiness and the potential for learning for those applying for a place in Reception. In addition, all children are invited to school for a final classroom-based assessment where they are observed completing practical activities.

As part of Nottingham High School, Lovell House not only benefits from the continuity of education and community from entry at age 4 right through to A Level at age 18, but also from the extensive recreational and cultural facilities provided by the High School.

Charitable status. Nottingham High School is a Registered Charity, number 1104251. It exists to provide education for boys and girls between the ages of 4 and 18 years.

Nottingham High School

Waverley Mount, Nottingham NG7 4ED
Tel: 0115 978 6056
email: info@nottinghamhigh.co.uk
enquiries@nottinghamhigh.co.uk
website: www.nottinghamhigh.co.uk
X/Twitter: @NottsHigh
Facebook: @nottshigh
Instagram: @nottshigh
LinkedIn: /nottshigh

See full entry in the **HMC** section, on **p. 242**.

Old Buckenham Hall School

Brettenham Park, Ipswich, Suffolk IP7 7PH
Tel: 01449 740252
email: admissions@obh.co.uk
website: www.obh.co.uk
X/Twitter: @OBHSchool
Facebook: @OBHSchool
Instagram: @obhschool
LinkedIn: /Old Buckenham Hall School

Chair of Governors: A McGregor, MA Cantab

***Headmaster*: J Large**, BSc Hons, PGCE

Age Range. 3–13 years.

Number of Pupils. 198 (Boarders: 21 Girls, 40 Boys).

Fees per term (2023–2024). Full Boarding: £9,335–£10,956, Day pupils: £6,185–£7,805, Pre-Prep: £3,848, Nursery: £32 per session.

Give your child a third of an acre…

Old Buckenham Hall is recognised as one the leading preparatory schools in the UK. We have tremendous academic results with entry to many of the top public schools in the country. Our pastoral provision is outstanding, our boarding houses are beautiful and our facilities incredible. What really makes us special, though, is the happiness of our children, who bound around our magical setting. With each child having a third of an acre to play in, they can climb the trees, fly down the zip wire, they can take on the challenge of the rope swings, have a round of golf or explore the big woods.

The staff to pupil ratio is approximately 1:8, giving an average class size of 14. All members of staff, including part-time staff, contribute to a wide range of afternoon, evening and weekend extracurricular activities – where every child has the opportunity to participate. Activities on offer include arts and crafts, tennis, dance, drama, golf, music, climbing, cookery, cross country, gymnastics, debating, pistol shooting and clay pigeon shooting.

Winter sports include hockey, netball and tag rugby for the girls, and hockey, football and rugby for the boys. In the summer, girls and boys play cricket and take part in athletics. The school offers excellent tennis facilities, with pupils receiving specialist tennis coaching on six tennis courts and a purpose-built, state-of-the-art AstroTurf. The school also has a 9-hole golf course.

The boarding model is flexible, offering children the opportunity to board anything from 2 nights a week to full boarding on an eleven-day cycle. Children boarding at the weekend enjoy a varied programme of exciting activities, such as campfires, the 'Great OBH Bake Off', 'Bush Tucker Trials', a Masquerade Ball and trips out to the coast and other local attractions. The boarding houses at OBH give boarders a warm, nurturing boarding environment, while being in the care of very experienced and caring staff.

Children develop a wide range of life skills through the outdoor education programme – the OBEs (Old Buckenham Explorers) for pupils in Years 3–8 and the MBEs (Mini Buckenham Explorers) for pupils in the Pre-Prep. The construction of two outdoor classrooms has proved to be very innovative and exciting – where children learn to camp, shelter, cook and learn vital survival skills in preparation for Bronze, Silver and Gold expeditions.

Old Buckenham Hall was founded in Lowestoft in 1862 and moved in 1937 to Old Buckenham in Norfolk. In 1956, the school moved to its present site in Brettenham Park, Suffolk, which is 4 miles from Lavenham, 11 miles from Bury St Edmunds, 18 miles from Ipswich, 23 miles from Colchester and an hour and a half by direct train from London. The school became an Educational Trust in 1967.

The school prospectus can be obtained on application to the Registrar, Kate Walmsley.

Charitable status. Old Buckenham Hall (Brettenham) Educational Trust Limited is a Registered Charity, number 310490. It exists to provide education for boarding and day pupils.

The Old Hall School

Stanley Road, Wellington, Shropshire TF1 3LB

Tel: 01952 223117
email: admissions@oldhall.co.uk
office@oldhall.co.uk
website: www.wrekinoldhall.com
X/Twitter: @oldhallschool
Facebook: @The-Old-Hall-School
Instagram: @theoldhallschool
LinkedIn: /company/old-hall-school

Chair of the Governors: Mr R J Pearson, BSc

***Head*: Mrs Anna Karacan**, BA Hons, CELTA, PGCE, EYPS, NPQH

Age Range. 4–11.
Number of Pupils. 230: 132 boys, 98 girls.
Fees per term (2023–2024). Lower School: £3,300 (Reception), £3,680 (Years 1–2); Upper School: £5,180 (Years 3–6).

Founded in 1845, Old Hall School is a co-educational day school (4–11 years), which is housed in spectacular premises, located alongside Wrekin College. The school offers first-class facilities; a double sports hall, 25-metre indoor swimming pool, an artificial playing surface and grass pitches offer an excellent sports and games environment, while specialist music and drama facilities help to promote high standards in the performing arts. A dedicated Art Room, innovation lab, Science lab, library and IT Suite, as well as a suite of specialist learning support rooms, reflects the School's commitment to the needs of the individual.

The broad curriculum is enriched by a dedicated team of professionals who encourage pupils to fulfil their potential in a happy and secure environment.

Through the academic curriculum and caring pastoral system, the school aims to lay solid foundations in the development of well-motivated, confident and happy individuals who are always willing to give of their best on the road to high achievement.

Charitable status. Wrekin Old Hall Trust Limited is a Registered Charity, number 528417.

Old Vicarage School

48 Richmond Hill, Richmond, Surrey TW10 6QX

Tel: 020 8940 0922
email: office@oldvicarageschool.com
website: www.oldvicarageschool.com
X/Twitter: @ovsrichmond
Facebook: @ovsrichmond
Instagram: @ovsrichmond
LinkedIn: /old-vicarage-school

Chairman of Governors: Mr C Heidl

***Head*: Mrs C Strickland**, MA, BA, PGCE Cantab

Age Range. 3–11.
Number of Pupils. 220 girls.
Fees per term (2023–2024). £5,900 Reception–Year 6; £4,930 5 full days at Little Vic.

The Old Vicarage school is a non-selective girls' prep school based in a beautiful Grade 2* listed "castle" on Richmond Hill. The School was established in 1881 and became a Charitable Educational Trust in 1973. Whilst retaining traditional values, there is a clear vision for the future and teaching and facilities combine the very best of the old and the new. Girls are admitted into Little Vic pre-school in September following their third birthday. Older girls may be admitted further up the school if a vacancy arises, following a day spent at the school to ensure it is a good fit for them. Girls are expected to remain until the age of 11, being prepared for Common Entrance Examinations at 11+ and for entry to the London Day Schools. A good range of academic, sporting, drama and arts scholarships to senior schools has been awarded to girls over the years.

Work of a traditionally high standard is expected of the girls and they are challenged and supported in classes of up to 15 girls, encouraging self esteem and enabling them to fulfil their potential. Girls in the Lower School are taught by a Form Teacher, with some specialist input. Girls in the Upper School are taught by subject specialists who impart a real enthusiasm and love for their subject areas. They will also have a form tutor to provide the pastoral support the school is known for. A system of older buddies, prefects and the Student Council ensures that all girls feel an integral part of the school from the beginning.

Music and drama are active throughout the school. Individual music tuition is provided in a wide range of instruments in purpose-built facilities and active choirs sing at numerous competitions and collaborations. All girls take part in at least one dramatic production a year, as well as in assemblies to which parents are invited.

The major sports are netball, hockey, football, cricket, athletics and swimming and the school has sports facilities near Ham House as well as our own gym and playground. Girls compete in fixtures against other schools from Year 3 and have had notable successes in recent years in borough-wide championships. They are the current Richmond Borough Netball and Swimming Champions.

Extra-curricular activities cater to a range of interests and include art, fencing, sports, computing, chess, school newspaper, eco-warriors and drama clubs. All girls in the Upper School attend a residential trip to Sussex, Dorset, Oxfordshire or France and up to fifty join the biennial ski trip to Italy.

Charitable status. The Old Vicarage School is a Registered Charity, number 312671.

The Oratory Prep School

Goring Heath, Reading, South Oxfordshire RG8 7SF
Tel: 0118 9844511
email: office@oratoryprep.co.uk
website: www.oratoryprep.co.uk
X/Twitter: @OPS_OratoryPrep
Facebook: @oratoryprepschool
Instagram: @oratoryprepschool

***Headmaster*: Mr Andrew De Silva**, BA QTS, MSc, NPQH, FGMS, AFNCollM

Number of Pupils. 338 (189 boys, 149 girls), including 40 full, weekly or flexi-boarders.

Fees per term (2023–2024). Boarders: £8,535 (weekly); £9,910 (full). Day: Senior Prep (Years 5–8) £6,635; Junior Prep (Reception–Year 2) £3,855; (Years 3 & 4) £6,410. Visit our website to view a full breakdown of the fees for Nursery, Kindergarten and Pre-Reception.

We provide an enriched education to boys and girls aged 2–13. Set within 65 acres of Oxfordshire countryside with outstanding facilities, we nurture happy, balanced, confident and inquisitive children. Our commitment to the pastoral care, wellbeing and all-round development of each child, with an ethos of broad-minded and inclusive learning, is at the core of our education. We strive to strike a balance between encouraging children to step out of their comfort zone, seek adventure and develop resilience, while ensuring they feel stretched, fulfilled, secure and supported in being the very best that they can be.

Academic challenges and pursuits combined with self-expression through sport, music, art and drama are central to the confidence and self-discovery of our children and equip them with essential skills for life beyond school. In all that we do and teach, our children grow and learn under our founder St John Henry Newman's, motto 'Cor Ad Cor Loquitur' [Heart speaks to Heart]; encouraging our children to model the key values of compassion, humility and forgiveness. Such values, including our school virtues: Curiosity, Kindness and Wisdom, are at the heart of our education, shaping the moral awareness and convictions of our pupils.

Pupils become ambitious and independent learners, immersed in a skills-based, thematic curriculum, meaningful and highly relevant to their everyday experiences and life beyond school. We enable our children to make connections across subjects and think more deeply about their significance, applying their learning across different contexts and developing core, transferable skills, such as critical thinking and strong reasoning skills, to judge the value of ideas and knowledge presented to them. This includes Forest School from the age of two, science experiments in our woodlands and art classes in our gardens.

The school boasts an Astroturf for an array of sporting fixtures. The 25-metre indoor swimming pool for Year 3 upwards is the venue for galas and a starting point for Mini-Triathlons. The smaller pool for children from Kindergarten upwards allows for weekly lessons.

The children have so many opportunities to discover themselves and their talents through our after-school activities programme. Running on Saturdays during term time, The Newman Programme is open to pupils in Year 5 upwards and is designed to further develop skills in leadership, collaboration and critical thinking. Modules range from entrepreneurship and presentation skills to Artistic Hour, Yoga and Podcast Club.

The school's Boarding House has a mix of nationalities with pupils in Year 3 upwards from China, Spain, France and Nigeria.

The Oratory Prep School is part of Bellevue Education (www.blvue.com).

Orchard House School

16 Newton Grove, London W4 1LB
Tel: 020 8742 8544
email: info@orchardhs.org.uk
website: www.orchardhs.org.uk
X/Twitter: @orchardhs

Chairman of Governors: Mr Aatif Hassan

***Headmaster*: Mr Kit Thompson**

Age Range. Girls and Boys 3–11.

Number of Pupils. 305: 160 Girls, 145 Boys.

Fees per Term (2023–2024). Nursery (min 5 sessions) £3,550, Pre-Prep £7,100, Prep £7,398.

Orchard House School is part of Dukes Education. It provides an excellent all-round education for boys and girls from 3 to 11, preparing them for the competitive entry examinations for the London day and country boarding schools whilst maintaining a happy, purposeful atmosphere.

There is an emphasis on teaching traditional values tailored for children growing up in the 21st century. Uniform is worn and good manners are expected at all times. Children shake hands with the staff at the end of each day and are encouraged to take part, with the deputy head or head, in describing the school to prospective parents and other visitors. Appetising lunches are provided and all food is cooked freshly on site each day.

The main premises were designed by the well-known architect Norman Shaw and built around 1880; the building is Grade 2 listed. The school enjoys a corner site in Bedford Park and the classrooms have good natural lighting as well as overlooking a large playground.

Children aged 3 or 4 are admitted on a first come, first served basis. Occasional places higher up are filled following assessment. Selected aspects of the Montessori philosophy are used to deliver the Early Years Foundation Stage curriculum; at KS1 and KS2 the curriculum is based on the National Curriculum and the demands of the future schools. Specialist teachers are employed for many subjects and support teachers provide one-on-one or small group tuition where necessary. Staff turnover is low.

Orchard House is proud of the excellent results the children achieve at their future schools which include many of the most academic schools in this country. The school is within easy reach of St Paul's schools, Latymer Upper, Hampton School, Notting Hill & Ealing High School and Godolphin & Latymer and many pupils have taken up places at one of these schools.

The school boasts state-of-the-art ICT resources and attractive playgrounds/garden with all-weather surfaces. The children make good use of additional local facilities to enhance their sport and drama lessons.

Orchard House participates in the Nursery Education Grant. There are occasional means-tested scholarships available through the Orchard House School Educational Trust for children entering Year 3. Contact: info@orchardhs.org.uk for further information.

Orchard School

Higham Road, Barton-le-Clay, Bedfordshire MK45 4RB

Tel: 01582 882054
email: admin@orchardschool.org.uk
website: www.orchardschool.org.uk

Chair of Friends: Mrs Anna Gingell

***Headmistress*: Mrs Anne Burton**, MEd Cantab, Cert Ed, HV SRN

Deputy Head, Designated Safeguarding Lead, Prep: Miss Louise Burton, BEd Hons Cantab, QTS

Co-educational Day School.

Age Range. 4–9 years; Nursery for children aged 0–4.

Number of Pupils. Preparatory School 65; Nursery 30.

Fees per term (2023–2024). Tuition (including lunch) £3,402.50; (including breakfast, lunch & tea) £4,263.00.

8:00am – 5:45pm – per term

Location. Orchard School is a Preparatory School for boys and girls, ideally situated on the outskirts of a large village in south Bedfordshire.

The School has been established for 20 years, and the Nursery for 30 years. Located in a beautiful setting and backed by the Barton Hills (thought to be The Delectable Mountains in Pilgrim's Progress) both School and Nursery are surrounded by rolling countryside that hosts an abundance of wildlife.

Ethos. The school's motto – "to be the best that you can be" is reflected in all areas of school life. Orchard's aim is to enable each child to value and strive for the highest levels of achievement, and to nurture a pride in success. Praise and encouragement are the primary motivational tools employed, tempered by the recognition that every child develops at their own pace. Skilful and careful observations are undertaken by the teaching team to help the children meet and surpass key learning targets. The school also encourages an 'esprit de corps' and a sense of true belonging. Emphasis is placed on the moral, social and personal development of all pupils in order to expand their confidence and self-esteem.

100% academic success. The school boasts an exemplary academic record with (for example) a 100% pass rate into the nearby Harpur Trust schools in Bedford.

The combination of a progressive, structured, yet genuinely friendly family atmosphere creates an ideal environment for the children to thrive both academically and in other activities that they pursue.

Activities. We encourage each child to experience as wide a range of activities as possible; for example, music lessons, choir, ballet, dance and philosophy.

A comprehensive sporting programme including swimming and rugby is also included within the well-rounded curriculum. Further opportunities include craftwork, running, lacrosse, badminton and recorder are offered via lunchtime and after-school clubs. There are several visits a term across all year groups to complement topic learning and to provide a real-life context to the subjects being studied. Years 3 and 4 also enjoy residential trips to specialist adventure-based facilities where activities such as abseiling, kayaking and raft building help increase fun, team spirit and pupil confidence.

Friends of Orchard. Orchard is proud of its strong and supportive parent base and there is a well-established 'Friends of Orchard School' group which organises social gatherings and fundraising events, further enhancing the friendly and family inclusive atmosphere at the school.

Bursaries. Bursaries are available for year 1 and above.

Summary. Our aim is to develop well-motivated and confident children who are considerate to others, well-mannered, who know the value of hard work.

We are happy to say that virtually all Orchard School pupils have been proven to excel at their subsequent schools and seats of learning.

Orley Farm School

South Hill Avenue, Harrow on the Hill, Middlesex HA1 3NU

Tel: 020 8869 7600
email: office@orleyfarm.harrow.sch.uk
website: www.orleyfarm.harrow.sch.uk
X/Twitter: @orleyfarmschool
Facebook: @orleyfarmschool
Instagram: @orleyfarmschool
LinkedIn: /company/orley-farm-school

The school is a Charitable Trust administered by a Board of Governors.

Chairman of Governors: Dr M Short

***Headmaster*: Mr T Calvey**, BA Ed Hons

Age Range. 4–13 Co-educational.

Number of Pupils. 505 Day pupils, including 188 in Pre-Prep (age 4 to 7).

Fees per term (2023–2024). Pre-Prep: £5,572; Years 3–4: £5,926; Years 5–8: £6,429 (inclusive of lunch).

At Orley Farm School we are in the fortunate position of being a London day school blessed with boarding school acreage and facilities. Founded in 1850, the school has grown and developed to become one of the leading and largest co-educational prep schools in Greater London. Entry is by assessment at 4+ and when occasional places appear in the rest of the school. The academic journey of the children begins in Reception and ends when pupils transfer successfully to their senior schools – at the end of Year 6 for our girls and at the end of Year 8 for our boys attending more traditional senior schools. Pupils enter a range of very impressive senior schools, including Aldenham, Haberdashers' Aske's Boys and Girls, Haileybury, Harrow, John Lyon, Merchant Taylors', Mill Hill, Northwood College, North London Collegiate, Royal Masonic, Rugby, St Helen's, St Paul's and Westminster, to name but a few. However, most impressively, Orley Farm has served over 61 senior schools over the past 7 years. We pride ourselves in finding the right future step for every child. Scholarships are regularly awarded to our senior pupils – 37 awards were offered in 2021–2022 including a Queen's Scholar for Westminster.

Success, happiness and future fulfilment start with a deep love of learning. So firmly do we believe in this philosophy, that we have invested £9 million in our facilities (a Music and Drama School, three state of the art Science Laboratories, a new Humanities department, a new Dining Hall and at the very heart, a cutting-edge Library).

'Breadth, Balance & Excellence …The Orley Farm Way!'

Alongside academic excellence, we pride ourselves on giving pupils experiences and opportunities that foster a lifetime and love of learning. All pupils are expected to contribute to the broader curriculum and a packed programme of Drama, Art and Music and Design & Technology. Over 200 individual music lessons take place each week and are supported by many musical groups and choirs. Productions, concerts and competitions offer all pupils the chance to showcase their talents and dedication in a variety of different settings.

Sport plays a very large part in our school life. We have over thirty six acres of land and full use is made of this in providing a venue for training and matches. Pupils will compete internally and externally in athletics, cricket, football, hockey, netball and rugby. In addition basketball, cross-country, fencing, fives, gymnastics and tennis also thrive through activities, clubs and matches. A Gym, Sports Hall and full-sized AstroTurf pitch enable our strong PE and Games Department to help our pupils develop their sporting talents.

This rich blend of curricular and co-curricular education is exemplified by our Expeditions Week. All pupils and staff from Year 4 and above travel to a variety of venues to spend a week extending their curriculum in a host of new challenges and adventures.

We are privileged to be working with young learners at a point where we can 'hardwire' key traits and values that we believe are essential to happiness and success in an ever-changing world. Our 10 Thinking Skills are the bedrock of 'The Orley Farm Way' and we have no doubt that we are giving voice to the *ambitious*, the *creative*, the *curious*, the *focused*, the *resilient* and the *risk-takers* as they'll possess *empathy*, *flexibility of mind*, *initiative* and *good judgement* in all that they do!

We pride ourselves on preparing our young learners for life and, therefore, we go well beyond assessment preparation and this is reflected in an Alumni who know the power and value of an outstanding start in life but more importantly, how to find fulfilment, purpose, joy and wonder in making a difference to others. We are blessed and privileged to work with pupils, colleagues and parents who know the power of these years and who recognise this wonderful African proverb:

'*It takes a village to bring up a child*'

The Orley Farm Family is a special place and we would encourage anyone and everyone who might be searching for something a little more than the superficial to come and visit but be warned, there's no room for passengers, we are all committed to doing something with this privileged start…!

Orley Farm School is located in North West London close to Harrow on the Hill and is only twenty minutes on the Metropolitan Line from Baker Street Station.

Entry to this exciting place of learning is by assessment. For further details contact the Registrar, Mrs Anita Patel, on 0208 869 7634.

Charitable status. Orley Farm School is a Registered Charity, number 312637.

Orwell Park

Nacton, Ipswich, Suffolk IP10 0ER
Tel: 01473 659225
email: admissions@orwellpark.org
website: www.orwellpark.co.uk
X/Twitter: @OrwellParkSch
Facebook: @orwellpark

Chairman of Governors: James Davison, BA

***Headmaster*: Guy Musson**

Age Range. 2½–13.

Number of Pupils. 250 pupils including 33 full, 22 weekly, and 60 flexi boarders.

Fees per term (2023–2024). Nursery: £63 per day/ £30 per session. Pre-Prep: from £3,213 (Day).
Prep: Day from £6,891, Weekly Boarding from £9,228, Full Boarding from £9,406.

The school has one of the most beautiful and expansive settings in the UK, housed in an 18th century mansion, within 110 acres of stunning grounds on the banks of the River Orwell. The adjacent pre-prep building is a new, purpose built facility that combines innovative indoor spaces with an interactive forest school setting.

This is a busy and exciting education that makes the most of superb facilities to provide an unparalleled co-curricular experience with outstanding preparation for senior schools.

The timetable is especially designed to be very flexible, with setting in most subjects, a potential scholars' set in Year 7 and a scholarship set in Year 8. The curriculum, both in and out of the classroom, is unusually broad. Children are encouraged to enjoy their learning and good learning support is offered. Thinking Skills and other opportunities for academic enrichment are also offered, including a weekly evening lecture programme to challenge the older children. There is a host of extracurricular activities (just under 100) run by permanent or visiting staff.

Over 90% of the school learn a musical instrument and the school has a number of orchestral and ensemble groups. Drama is strong – all children have opportunities to perform regularly in school productions, and LAMDA lessons are offered as an extracurricular activity. All children take part in annual Reading and Public Speaking Competitions.

The very large Georgian style building and 110 acres of grounds (sandy soil) on the banks of the River Orwell have the following special features: 21 recently refurbished themed dormitories, 22 bright classrooms with modern audio-visual equipment, beautiful Orangery used as an Assembly and Lecture Hall, 2 ICT suites, large Design Centre including metal, wood and plastic workshop plus electronics, mechanics, home economics, radio and model-making areas, Music Technology Room, Music Room and 40 Practice rooms, Music Recording Studio, 2 Laboratories plus associated areas, brand new Library, Art Room including large pottery area and kiln, Observatory with 10' Refractor Telescope, Photographic Room, 17 Games pitches and one Astroturf pitch, one Multi-Use Games Area, large Sports Hall with permanent stage, Climbing Wall, Games Room, large heated Swimming Pool, 3 Squash Courts, 5 Hard Tennis Courts, Nine-hole Golf Course (approximately 1,800 yards) and a purpose-built Assault Course.

Good sports coaching is given and fixtures are arranged in the following sports: Rugby, Hockey, Cricket, Netball, Tennis, Athletics, Squash, Sailing, Swimming and Cross-Country Running. Emphasis is also placed on individual physical activities and we offer a wide range including Gymnastics, Fencing, Ballet, Canoeing, Sailing, Modern Dance, Karate, Riding and Clay Pigeon Shooting.

The School aims to introduce the pupils to a broad and varied set of experiences and opportunities. It tries to see that every activity, whether academic, sporting, social or character building, is properly taught using the best possible facilities and that each is conducted in an atmosphere which is friendly but disciplined. Under the overarching value of integrity, the school's core values are: kindness, collaboration, courage, spirit and respect.

Charitable status. Orwell Park School is a Registered Charity, number 310481. It exists to provide education for boys and girls.

Packwood Haugh

Ruyton XI Towns, Shrewsbury, Shropshire SY4 1HX
Tel: 01939 260217
email: admissions@packwood-haugh.co.uk
website: www.packwood-haugh.co.uk
X/Twitter: @packwoodhaugh
Facebook: @packwoodhaugh
Instagram: @packwoodschool

Chairman of Governors: Mr J Pitt, BSc Hons, MBA

***Headmaster*: Robert Fox**, BSc Hons, PGCE

Deputy Heads
Tim Leverton-Griffiths, BEd
Sue Rigby, BA Hons, PGCE, Dip SpLD

Age range. Co-educational 4–13.

Number of children. 230. Boarding: 40 boys, 18 girls. Day: 86 boys, 50 girls. Pre-Prep 36.

Fees per term (2023–2024). Boarding: UK £9,310, International £10,500; Day: £5,175–£7,285, Pre-Prep (Acorns) £3,500. No compulsory extras. Extras available on request.

Set in the heart of the Shropshire countryside, between Shrewsbury and Oswestry, Packwood Haugh is a co-educational day (4–13) and boarding (7–13) school which provides an excellent all-round education in a happy and caring environment. Children benefit from a wide range of academic, sporting, musical, artistic and cultural activities which encourage them to develop enquiring minds and an enthusiasm for learning. The school espouses an atmosphere of cooperation and understanding between pupils, staff and parents and encourages good manners and consideration towards others at all times.

Packwood has always striven for academic excellence; class sizes are small (average 13) and children are prepared for all the major independent schools across the country winning a number of academic, music, sports, art and all-rounder scholarships and awards each year. Packwood is part of the Shrewsbury School family of schools and at least a third of pupils head to Shrewsbury. The school has a thriving pre-prep department (Packwood Acorns), which takes children from Reception.

The school's facilities are superb; a state of the art sports hall allows for fencing, indoor tennis, badminton, indoor cricket nets, judo, gymnastics and five-a-side football. Incorporated in the building are fully equipped DT and Art departments and a linked computer suite. A 280-seat theatre is used for assemblies, concerts and drama productions throughout the year.

As well as the classrooms in the main school buildings and a purpose-built new block, there are three science laboratories, two libraries, a Year 8 study area and two further computer suites. Park House, which accommodates Packwood Acorns and girls' boarding, is a short distance from the main school building.

Packwood has a very strong sporting tradition. Set alongside 66 acres of grass playing fields, there is a newly resurfaced full-size, floodlit AstroTurf pitch, an additional hard court area, tennis courts, squash courts, an indoor, heated swimming pool and a golf course. In the winter terms the boys play rugby, football and hockey while the girls play netball, hockey and lacrosse. There is also cross country running on a course within the grounds. In the summer both boys and girls play cricket as well as tennis, athletics and swimming.

Additional facilities include Forest School, a shooting range, cooking room and an adventure playground. Children can take part in over 70 activities throughout the year, including horse riding, sailing and gardening to name but a few.

Charitable status. Packwood Haugh is a Registered Charity, number 528413. It exists to provide day and boarding education for boys and girls from the age of 4 to 13.

Papplewick

Windsor Road, Ascot, Berks SL5 7LH

Tel: 01344 621488
email: schoolsec@papplewick.org.uk
registrar@papplewick.org.uk
website: www.papplewick.org.uk
X/Twitter: @PapplewickAscot

Chairman of Board of Governors: A A M Try, DL

***Headmaster*: T W Bunbury**, BA University College Durham, PGCE

Age range. 6–13.
Number of boys. 224: 89 Boarders, 135 day boys.
Fees per term (2023–2024). Boarding Fees: £12,095 (International £13,520). Day Boys: £6,690 (Year 2), £8,765 (Years 3–4), £9,290 (Years 5–6).

Papplewick is a boys only, day, weekly and full boarding school with an exceptional scholarship record to top Independent Schools. Day boys do prep at school and come in to board from the summer term of Year 6. Three very popular daily transport services run to and from London, one from Chiswick, one from Brook Green and one from near the Millennium Gloucester Hotel. Also, a daily service runs to and from Maidenhead/South Bucks. Situated between the M3 and M4, the school boasts easy access to London airports. A new Year 8 standalone boarding house has now opened with two Year 5 classrooms underneath and staff accommodation.

Papplewick exists to provide a high-quality education where – for all our academic, cultural and sporting success – the happiness of the boys come first, and kindness is a top priority.

Papplewick was awarded Tatler's Prep School of the Year 2018–2019.

Charitable status. The Papplewick Educational Trust is a Registered Charity, number 309087.

The Paragon
Prep School of Prior Park College

Lyncombe House, Lyncombe Vale, Bath BA2 4LT

Tel: 01225 310837
email: office.tps@priorparkschools.com
ehughes@priorparkschools.com
website: www.paragonschool.co.uk
Facebook: @TheParagonJunior
Instagram: @paragonjunior

Chair of Trustees: Mrs Anne Shepherd

***Head of School*: Mrs Rosie Allen**, BA Hons, PGCE

Admissions and Marketing: Ms Emily Hughes

Age Range. 3–11 years.
Number of Pupils. 135 Boys, 121 Girls.
Fees per term (2023–2024). Juniors: Years 5–6 £4,311, Years 3–4 £4,206. Infants: Reception, 1 & 2 £3,780. Pre-School: Full-time £3,497, Part-time £710 (per day 9.00 am–3.00 pm), £520 (per morning 9.00 am until 1.00 pm). Fees include lunch. Sibling discounts available. Registration Fee (non-refundable): £125. Deposit: £300.

60+ qualified teachers including peripatetic teachers.

The Paragon is an independent, co-educational day school based in a beautiful Georgian house situated a mile from the centre of Bath. The school is set in eight acres of grounds with woodland, conservation areas, lawns and streams. It's the perfect 'outdoor classroom' and we use it right across the curriculum. We also enjoy regular access to the superb sport, science, D & T and drama facilities at our Senior School, Prior Park College.

An undoubtedly homely feel comes from being based in a beautiful, former family home. Then there's our Christian ethos and strong pastoral care, as well as our belief that school at this age is about being stimulated and inspired, about laughter and spontaneity and about having fun.

We offer a broad curriculum taught in small classes by teachers with real passion. Academic life at The

Paragon cultivates a love of learning and encourages independent and creative thinking. Our results are impressive. Our children consistently achieve well above the national average and a high proportion of Year 6 children win senior school scholarships and Head's Awards. Our facilities include a library, large gymnasium/dining hall, Pre-School with secure indoor and outdoor play areas, art studio, modern languages and dedicated Music Lodge.

Sport is particularly strong at The Paragon. Our sports teams take part, with considerable success, in a wide range of tournaments and festivals. We also offer a vast range of sports clubs that all children can join regardless of ability. Prior Park College offers us an indoor swimming pool, AstroTurf and grass pitches, tennis courts, athletics track and sports centre.

The Paragon's extracurricular programme is extensive. Staff run more than 60 lunchtime and after-school clubs that range from pottery and chess, to drama and cross-country running. The school also enjoys an enviable reputation for Music. All children receive weekly music lessons from a specialist teacher. Our Year 2 students will learn the recorder, Year 3s a string instrument and Year 5s will spend a term learning Samba. In addition, visiting instrumental teachers offer tuition in a wide range of instruments. We offer an excellent choice of extracurricular music activities including the orchestra, two choirs, a wind band, brass group, flute choir, string ensemble, African drumming group and an ever-growing Samba band.

The Paragon is proud of its consistently impressive academic results but we strive for much more than success in exams. We believe in developing the whole person – physically, spiritually, and emotionally as well as intellectually. As W B Yeats said: 'Education is not filling a bucket but lighting a fire.'

Charitable status. Prior Park Educational Trust is a Registered Charity, number 281242.

Parkside School

The Manor, Stoke d'Abernon, Cobham, Surrey KT11 3PX

Tel: 01932 862749
email: reception@parkside-school.co.uk; head.pa@parkside-school.co.uk; admissions@parkside-school.co.uk
website: www.parkside-school.co.uk
X/Twitter: @parksideprep
Facebook: @parksideprep
Instagram: @parkside_prep

Chairman of Governors: Robin Southwell

***Head*: Ms Nicole Janssen**, BA Hons, PGCE, NPQH

Interim Bursar: Mr J Taylor
Deputy Head, Head of Pre Prep, DDSL: Mrs M McMurdo, BEd Hons

Age Range. Boys 2–13 years old. Co-educational Nursery 2–4 years old.

Numbers. Total 260: Prep 162, Pre Prep 53, Nursery 45.

Fees per term (2023–2024). Prep Boys £6,467, Pre Prep £4,652, Nursery £825–£4,125.

Parkside School is a wonderful environment where children's curiosity is awakened. Their journey is one of discovery; where talents and passions are nurtured and developed, and pupils are encouraged to take responsibility for their learning. It is an independent boys' school with a co-educational nursery set in 45 acres of beautiful Surrey countryside with school bus routes including to and from South West London. **A recent ISI Inspection (Oct 2022) has highlighted the outstanding teaching and learning provision offered by the School – and it's results speak for themselves.**

Parkside was founded in 1879 and became a Charitable Trust in 1960. The School moved from East Horsley to its present site, The Manor, in 1979, its centenary year. Since the move, a continual development programme has seen the development of a purpose-built, well-equipped Science block, an extension of the main building to provide more Pre Prep classrooms, a Performance Hall, a Music School and six practice rooms. A new Food Technology Room and Forest School were opened in 2019, and an additional science lab was added in 2021 along with the new Outdoor Learning Area. The Pre Prep department had a complete refurbishment in the Summer of 2022 along with the Play Areas and resurfacing of the Tennis Courts.

There is also a 20m indoor swimming pool and Sports Hall complex with a stage for drama, and a £2 million classroom block was added to further enhance the facilities in the school. The Design Technology Department, Nursery and new STEM ICT suite are housed in a delightful Grade II-listed barn which has been skilfully refurbished to provide spacious, well-lit classrooms and workshops. The newly refurbished second Computer Room 'CHQ' opened in Autumn 2021 with the Art and Music facilities housed in dedicated buildings.

The school is large enough to be flexible and offer setting in major subjects, yet small enough for each pupil to be known and treated as an individual. On average there are between 8–15 pupils in a 'set'. All teaching staff are highly qualified and are passionate about boys' learning; specialist teaching begins in Year 1 in Sport, ICT, Music and Forest School and for all subjects from Year 3 to Year 8. The children in Parkside's Nursery also enjoy specialist teaching, including individual swimming lessons, French and Forest School, alongside the Early Years Curriculum. Each boy is a member of a House and this helps to stimulate friendly competition for work points and many other inter-house contests.

At Parkside, pupils develop the courage to rise to each challenge, persevere when the going gets tough and face their fears with confidence. The positive message of 'make it happen' underpins the whole approach to the learning journey and is at the forefront of all the pupils' minds. They are supported to take risks and persist with any obstacles they may encounter on their journey. Areas of improvement, as well as strengths, are celebrated and used to develop skills in order to achieve goals. The belief is that taking risks ensures complete development, resulting in a sense of pride and determination coupled with an unrivalled work ethic; invaluable in gaining success for their future.

All boys pass Common Entrance exams to their first choice Senior Schools and results in these examinations are impressive. **Parkside School achieved a 100% CE pass rate in 2021 & 2022, with 100% scholarships gained** to Tonbridge, RGS, Charterhouse, Reed's and commendation to Harrow. The curriculum is broad based, and boys are taught Art, Music, PE, Food Tech, Forest School and Technology in addition to the usual Common Entrance subjects. There is a School Choir, Chamber Choir, Big Band, a School Orchestra and several smaller musical groups. During the year, there are many opportunities for boys to perform in musical and dramatic productions.

A Parkside education is forward thinking and based on a creative curriculum; however, traditional values are woven through all learning in day-to-day life. Success is supported by an emphasis on manners and etiquette; thus, ensuring the boys leave Parkside as outstanding and well-rounded gentlemen.

The School has a very well-known sporting record and many tournaments in different sports and at different age groups have been won, with Parkside coming in the top 10 in the country at IAPS Finals. A new Director of Sport (ex Wasps) started in Autumn term 2022, bringing a more competitive edge to the sports offering. In addition, a number of boys have gone on to represent their County and Country in various sports. The main sports are football (taught by Chelsea FC professionals), rugby, hockey and cricket, but boys are also able to take part in swimming, athletics, water polo, tennis, cross-country running, basketball and judo, as well as yoga. An extensive After School Activity Programme (including supervised homework sessions) is available, with over 40 different activities on offer, from gardening to kayaking, touch typing and coding to mindfulness with the newly added shooting club and bike trail club. Many boys have also represented the school at a high level (County and England) in chess. The 45 acre beautiful estate and the River Mole, which runs through the grounds, are also used to contribute to the all-round education each pupil receives both in and out of the classroom.

All children from Nursery to Year 8 can be supervised from 7.30am–6.00pm daily. Breakfast Club runs from 7.30–8.15am in the Nursery and Main School where a choice of hot and continental breakfast is offered. After school care is available for Nursery children from 3.00–6.00pm, Pre Prep boys from 4.00–6.00pm and Prep boys from 5.00–6.00pm. A hot meal is served between 5.00 and 6.00pm and sandwiches between 4.00 and 5.00pm. Snacks are provided in Nursery between 3.00 and 4.00pm. Boys staying from 5.00–6.00pm will have the opportunity to complete their prep. After school care may be booked in advance or on an ad hoc basis by 9.00am in the morning. The new All Year Round Nursery provision started in September 2022 and has proved very popular, with wait lists now being held.

Parkside was selected as one of five finalists in the UK as Best Independent Boys' School 2020 (ISOTY) as well as being finalists in the 2021 and 2022 awards. This has been largely accredited, not only to the values, aims and ethos mentioned, but also to its colossal efforts in providing a continued outstanding education during the Covid-19 crisis and the teaching and learning ethos implemented by Nicole Janssen, Head, following her appointment in 2019.

Virtual and individual tours are available by appointment only. For further details, contact Parkside's Registrar, Mrs Lindre Scott via email: admissions@parkside-school.co.uk or call 01932 62749

Charitable status. Parkside School is a Registered Charity, number 312041

Parsons Green Prep

1 Fulham Park Road, London SW6 4LJ

Tel: 020 7371 9009
email: office@parsonsgreenprep.co.uk
website: www.parsonsgreenprep.co.uk
X/Twitter: @pgpschoollondon
Facebook: @parsonsgreenprep
Instagram: @ParsonsGreenPrep

Head of Governance: Mr Tim Cannell (proprietorial so Head of Governance)

***Head*: Dr Pamela Edmonds**

Senior leadership team:
Deputy Head: Miss Beth Dinsmore
Head of Pre-Prep: Mr Lee Bradshaw
Head of Teaching and Learning: Miss Samantha Porter

Student numbers. 150.

Fees per term (2023–2024). Reception to and including Year 2: £6,983–£7,350. Years 3–6: £7,529–£7,925. Registration fee £200, Deposit £3,500.

Admission. Selective.

Curriculum. EYFS, Enhanced National Curriculum, ISEB, 11+.

Extracurricular activities. Netball, Football, Chess, Irish Dancing, Ballet, Table-tennis, Yong Journalist, Debating, Quiz Club, Baking, Coding, Performing Arts, Young Engineers, Choir to name a few.

Charitable status. Registered Charity, number 4216973.

Pembridge Hall School

Inspired Education Group

18 Pembridge Square, London W2 4EH

Tel: 020 7229 0121
email: contact@pembridgehall.co.uk
website: www.pembridgehall.co.uk
Instagram: @pembridgehallschool

***Head*: Mrs Sophie Banks**, BA, QTS, MEd

Age Range. 4–11.
Number of Girls. 459.
Fees per term (2023–2024). £8,735.

Pembridge girls take advantage of a vast array of learning experiences, both inside and out of the classroom. Pembridge Hall offers a 'three-dimensional education', believing that it is only by creating an environment in which teaching is inspiring and imaginative that girls will thrive. Sport and the Arts feature strongly on the curriculum.

Teachers, girls and parents work in a close partnership, ensuring that each girl is happy and achieving her maximum potential in every area of school life. Girls transfer at the end of Year Six to some of the finest senior day and boarding schools in the country.

Pennthorpe

Church Street, Rudgwick, Nr Horsham, West Sussex RH12 3HJ

Tel: 01403 822391
email: enquiries@pennthorpe.com
website: www.pennthorpe.com
X/Twitter: @PennthorpeSch
Facebook: @PennthorpeSchool
Instagram: @PennthorpeSchool
LinkedIn: /Pennthorpe

***Headmaster*: Mr Chris Murray**, BA Hons, PGCE

Clerk to the Governors: Mr Vincent Rapley
Deputy Head: Mr Jon Marler, BA Hons
Head of Pre-Prep: Mr James Davis, BSc, MA, QTS
Registrar: Mrs Sam Curling, BA Hons
Head of Marketing: Mrs Lucy Brearley, BA Hons

Age range: Co-educational 2–13.

Number of pupils: 250 Day Pupils.

Fees per term (from January 2024): £2,780–£6,625.

Whether it's academic achievement, consideration and kindness towards others, or an energetic and positive attitude – excellence underpins all that we do at Pennthorpe, and all that we strive to be.

Pennthorpe is a place of discovery, where the happiness of children takes precedence and the focus on learning, and dedication to every child's confidence and success, is relentless.

At Pennthorpe, children are uniquely valued for who they are, and for their individual strengths and passions. Whether in maths or textiles, cello or rugby, all skills are celebrated – everybody is somebody at Pennthorpe.

Children are deeply involved in their learning, demonstrated by their enthusiasm, their desire to learn new things and take risks, and their willingness to be in the driving seat of their own destiny. Children take responsibility for who, and what, they are becoming, in addition to who they aspire to be. Hopes and dreams become a reality at Pennthorpe.

Our broad and skills based curriculum requires our children to be authentic, independent learners; to trust their instincts and to be bold.

We teach our children *how* to learn, and then give them the tools and inspiration to challenge themselves. We embrace our failings; enabling our children to experience and overcome disappointment and fear, as well as gain perspective. Our innovative curriculum enables our children to dabble in everything, whilst giving them time to become thinkers, time to reflect, time to work slowly as well as quickly. We work hard to develop young people who can confidently take their place in the world, and prepare them to set about making it a better place for others.

Our exceptional staff team is integral to Pennthorpe's happy environment. The knowledge, passion, care and diversity of our team, complemented by our bespoke Wellbeing Curriculum, with its innovative elements such as our termly Happiness Tracker, creates Pennthorpe's very exciting atmosphere. We are committed to helping our children be happy, healthy and flourish. This is the foundation upon which academic success is built.

Topping it all off with our 26 acre, tardis-like campus, which is crammed with first rate, extensive facilities, means Pennthorpe offers a desirable education few could contend! The Independent School Inspectorate (ISI) agree; Pennthorpe achieved 'Excellent' in all categories in its latest inspection in October 2018. The inspectorate's report states 'Pupils' attitudes to learning are excellent. As a result, they persevere, are resilient, confident and active learners who involve themselves fully in all they do.'

Charitable status: Pennthorpe School is a Registered Charity, number 307043. It exists to provide an excellent education for boys and girls and to benefit the community.

Perrott Hill

North Perrott, Crewkerne, Somerset TA18 7SL

Tel: 01460 72051
email: admissions@perrotthill.com
website: www.perrotthill.com
X/Twitter: @perrotthill
Facebook: @PerrottHillSchool
Instagram: @perrotthill
LinkedIn: /perrott-hill-prep-school

Chair of the Board of Directors: Timothy Fisher
Chair of the Board of Governors: Paul Brewster

***Headmaster*: Mr Alexander McCullough**, BA Hons Dunelm, PGCE, NPQH

Age range. 3–13.

Number of pupils. 96 boys and 90 girls, with a range of day, flexi, weekly and full boarders.

Fees per term (2023–2024). Day pupils: £2,697–£6,599. Boarders: £8,044 (weekly), £9,526 (full), £10,000 (international).

Perrott Hill is an award-winning day and boarding school set in 28 acres of beautiful grounds in the heart of the countryside, near Crewkerne on the Somerset/Dorset border. It is served by excellent road and rail networks, being around two and a half hours from London.

The school has repeatedly been recognised across the sector for numerous awards and was a finalist for Small Independent School of the Year 2023, Highly Commended for Outstanding Pastoral Care 2023 and Creative Learning through Play 2023 with Muddy Stilettos, as well as Finalist for Best Prep School 2022 at the Tatler Awards, shortlisted for Prep School of the

Year 2022 at TES awards and Finalist Supporting Junior Boards 2022 at BSA Awards.

Perrott Hill is a thriving country preparatory school where children are nurtured and encouraged in all areas, whether in the classroom, on the sports field, on the stage and beyond. Staff are dedicated and highly qualified. Sports facilities include an all-weather pitch, purpose-built sports hall, games fields, outdoor swimming pool and a four-hole pitch and putt course. There is a theatre, an eco-build music school, Tinker Lab and extensive Forest School.

The award-winning Nursery and Pre-Prep are housed within the converted stable courtyard next to the main school buildings, which gives the younger children their own safe, secure environment whilst allowing them to take advantage of the grounds and facilities of the Prep School. There is an emphasis on outdoor learning including weekly on-site Forest School sessions, and all children in Reception to Year 8 swim every week.

Music, drama and art are taught within the timetable alongside core curriculum subjects. The choir and orchestra perform regularly at concerts such as 'The Beaminster Festival' and school events such as 'The Perrott Promenade', and there are drama productions throughout the school year. Teaching is largely class-based until Year 5 and subject-based in the middle and upper school, where all lessons are taught by specialist teachers. French, Music, IT and PE, however, are taught by specialists from Nursery upwards.

Sport is played every day, and matches take place on Tuesdays and Wednesdays as well as on Saturdays for Years 5–8. Emphasis is placed upon skills and teamwork and games played include rugby, football, hockey, netball, cricket, tennis, athletics, rounders and swimming. The school takes part in national events, such as the National Small Schools Rugby Sevens. Optional extras include fencing, pinhole photography, carpentry, archery, karate, riding, ballet, speech and drama, cookery and golf. The school was highlighted as 'great for extracurricular' in The Week's Independent Schools Guide 2019.

Perrott Hill combines extremely high standards of academic and pastoral care and provides a 'home from home' for its pupils. The boarding Team is a dedicated and talented group of residential boarding staff. The school has an enviable scholarship record, with 82 scholarships across the past five years, including an art scholarship to Harrow and a rugby scholarship to Millfield. Leavers' destinations include Blundell's, Bryanston, Canford, Downside, Eton, Harrow, King's Bruton, King's College Taunton, Marlborough, Millfield, Milton Abbey, Queen's College Taunton, Sherborne, Sherborne Girls, Taunton School, Radley and Winchester. The school offers 9+ and 11+ scholarships to internal and external candidates who can demonstrate significant potential in one or more of the following areas: academic, music, sport, art and drama.

The combination of countryside, space, a family atmosphere and a forward-looking academic programme creates an ideal environment for children to thrive both academically and in their leisure pursuits. Parents are encouraged to attend one of the school's Open Mornings which take place termly, and individual tours are available throughout the year.

The Perse Pelican Nursery and Pre-Preparatory School

92 Glebe Road, Cambridge CB1 7TD

Tel: 01223 403940
email: pelican@perse.co.uk

website: www.perse.co.uk

Chairman of Governors: J W Scott, MA

***Head*: Mrs Francesca Heftman**, BA

Age range. 3–7.

Number of pupils. 150.

Ethos. We aim to awaken a thirst for learning, helping children to develop an understanding and enjoyment of the world around them. The children are enthusiastic and inspired by the opportunities on offer and delight in meeting challenges and taking risks whilst benefiting from a safe and secure environment. They learn through a range of play-based activities as well as more formal methods of learning and have many opportunities to develop their independence.

Our aim is to ensure that the children in our care are sociable, rounded, confident and inquisitive. We are proud of our broad, challenging, enticing curriculum and the spirit with which our pupils approach their learning.

Admissions. The main entry point for the Pelican is Nursery, which is for children who are three years old by 1 September in the year of entry. There are also a few spaces available for new children in Reception.

History. The buildings of the Nursery and Pre-Prep began life in 1911 as a boarding house for the Upper School. The School has been sympathetically extended inside and out, so that it provides exceptional space and excellent facilities, yet still feels like a home from home.

School life. Our pastoral care is second to none. Every single child in the School is known to all and is valued for their individual characteristics. All achievements are celebrated.

Classroom routines are quickly established from the start of a child's time at the Pelican, and from day one they feel they belong. Every class benefits from a full-time teaching assistant who works alongside the teacher.

Dance, Games, Languages and Music are all taught by specialist teachers. An inclusive choir is open to everyone in Years 1 and 2 and a range of music ensembles are formed each year appropriate to the needs of the children in those year groups at the time. Our musicians regularly perform in regional and national festivals.

The children relish challenge and aim high, knowing that there is always someone to support them. We work in partnership with parents to nurture children's interests and provide opportunities to develop their potential. Pupils begin to acquire essential skills through play, topic work and a wide range of experiences and activities.

A rounded education. Regular school trips bring learning to life and being close to the centre of Cambridge, the School is able to take advantage of trips to local museums and wildlife parks.

Out-of-school care. Children may be dropped at school from 8.00 am and may stay until 5.30 pm each day. We run an extended range of after-school clubs catering to all tastes, from ballet to science, chess to football, and drama to gymnastics. In addition, children may attend our own holiday club, known as Club Pelican, which runs for 7 weeks of the year: five weeks in the summer holidays and one week in each of the Christmas and Easter holidays.

Moving on. By the end of Year 2, children are ready to move onto the Prep with confidence and enthusiasm. Their move is gradual and carefully managed.

Fees per term (2023–2024). Full time (Reception, Years 1 and 2): £5,518 per term; Part time (Nursery – six sessions per week): £3,718 per term; Additional Nursery sessions: £50,15 per session.

Charitable status. The Perse School is a charitable company limited by guarantee (company number 5977683, registered charity number 1120654) registered in England and Wales whose registered office is situated at The Perse School, Hills Road, Cambridge CB2 8QF.

The Perse Preparatory School

Trumpington Road, Cambridge CB2 8EX

Tel: 01223 403920
email: prep@perse.co.uk
website: www.perse.co.uk
X/Twitter: @PersePrep
Facebook: @theperseschool
Instagram: @theperseschoolcambridge

Chairman of Governors: Mr Jonathan W Scott, MA

***Head*: James Piper**, BA Hons, PGCE, MEd

Age Range. 7–11.

Number of Pupils. 283.

Ethos. At the Prep we are committed to helping your child develop as a confident, smiling, interesting and interested individual. Our School has a strong academic edge, attracting an outstanding group of specialist staff who encourage in the children academic curiosity and a love of learning. Prep children thrive on challenges outside the classroom with great emphasis placed on developing breadth and balance through first-rate sport, clubs, music, art, drama and outdoor pursuits. Excellent pastoral care is at the heart of our work and ensures that our children feel completely at ease and secure in their surroundings.

Admissions. The main entry point to the Prep is Year 3 (7+) with about 25 places available. Admissions to Years 4, 5 and 6 is dependent on availability of places with about 3 places available in each year. Entrance tests assess the applicant's abilities in English, Maths and reasoning, and a reference from the child's current school is also sought. Selection for all year groups takes place in mid-January of the year of intended entry.

Facilities. The Prep is set in spacious mature parkland on Trumpington Road. Traditional and modern buildings are successfully combined on site, from the Victorian Leighton House to the 'New School' classroom block, and the state-of-the-art Science block which opened in 2019, reconfigured Music Department and refurbished Year 3 classrooms in 2022. The Prep has nine acres of playing fields on its doorstep, including a full-size AstroTurf.

Educational success. The Prep is an academically selective school with pupils of above average ability who relish challenge. Most pupils progress to the Upper School in Year 7. Pupils follow a broad curriculum which promotes intellectual curiosity and a love of learning, and we nurture creativity through a vibrant programme of drama, music and art.

The depth of academic ability throughout the School allows intellectual curiosity to flourish and pupils thrive on challenges both inside and outside the classroom. Enjoyment of learning, mutual respect and the celebration of achievement characterise life at the Prep and as a result children become independent, confident and responsible.

A supportive environment. Pastoral care is first class: Form Teachers, Heads of Year and the Assistant Head (Pastoral) all support pupils, who have access to a medical room, with a qualified nurse, and to our counselling service. Self-confidence and happiness are prerequisites to academic and extra-curricular success which is why we focus so much on a supportive community for children, parents and staff; this is characterised by mutual respect, reassurance and encouragement.

A rounded education. We make good use of technology, based on our philosophy that it should be effective, meaningful and engaging. Resources include two dedicated computer rooms and bookable laptops and iPads. All classrooms are equipped with Interactive Whiteboards. We use Teams and SharePoint as our Virtual Learning Environments.

We encourage every pupil to make the most of our extra-curricular provision. There is a wide range of lunchtime and after school clubs – more than 90 currently. The majority of pupils learn a musical instrument and there are over 30 different ensembles (including numerous choirs and an orchestra comprising a quarter of the School). Further opportunities to perform publicly come with Drama productions which involve every child in the year, from Year 3 to Year 6. Sport is a major part of a Prep education, and all children compete against other schools. The games programme (football, rugby, netball, hockey, cricket, athletics and tennis) is designed to encourage all pupils to enjoy games and physical exercise.

Moving on. The School plans carefully for a smooth transition to the Upper School. Year 5 and 6 pupils spend days on the Upper site as part of their subject learning, helping to prepare them for the move up.

Fees per term (2023–2024). £6,405.

Charitable status. The Perse School is a charitable company limited by guarantee (company number 5977683, registered charity number 1120654) registered in England and Wales whose registered office is situated at The Perse School, Hills Road, Cambridge CB2 8QF.

The Pilgrims' School

The Close, Winchester, Hampshire SO23 9LT
Tel: 01962 854189
email: admissions@pilgrims-school.co.uk
pilgrims@pilgrims-school.co.uk
website: www.thepilgrims-school.co.uk
X/Twitter: @PilgrimsSchool
Facebook: @PilgrimsSchool
Instagram: @thepilgrimswinchester
LinkedIn: /the-pilgrims-school

Chairman of Governors: Jeremy Griffith

***Headmaster*: Tim Butcher**

Age range. Boys 4–13.

Number of pupils. 234 Boys (74 boarders/weekly boarders, 160 day boys, with 74 Juniors, 129 Seniors and 31 boys in Pre-Prep).

Fees per term (2023–2024). Boarders: £9,669, Day boys: £6,544–£7,624, Pre-Prep: £4,233.

About us. The Pilgrims' School is a day and boarding school for boys age 4–13. With its outstanding academic results it feeds the top independent schools in the country. A double choir school in a unique position, between Winchester Cathedral and Winchester College.

Curriculum. Pilgrims' is a place of outstanding personalised learning and teaching. We take great care to ensure that the interests and specific talents of each boy are valued and developed across our broad curriculum, co-curriculum, and extra-curriculum.

Sports and the Arts. A progressive approach to games; traditional sports are played daily. Winter games are football, rugby and hockey. In the summer, cricket and athletics. Art, drama and design & technology are much loved. Music is an exceptional strength.

Pastoral care. Our pastoral care is exemplary and we were delighted to be recognised as a school that is 'Great for Pastoral Care' in The Week's Independent Schools Guide 2022. Not only do we have a Deputy Head Pastoral, a Director of Wellbeing and a lay chaplain, we also have heads of year, form teachers and vertical tutor groups looking after not just the academic but also the pastoral life of the boys. In addition, we have a team of boarding house parents, nurses and matrons working together to provide excellent care.

Scholarships. We have had recent scholarships to Winchester College, Eton College, Tonbridge, Radley College, Canford, Sherborne, Marlborough College, Magdalen College School in academic, music, art and sport.

The Pilgrims' School is the perfect place for boys from reception to year 8 to learn and grow up – to find their passions and nurture them. It is a place of outstanding personalised learning and teaching. All boys move onto their senior schools with confidence having made excellent progress academically and pastorally.

Our Pre-Prep. The Pilgrims' Pre-Prep is a joyful place in the heart of Winchester full of happy boys and staff. The boys experience an active day which is timetabled to provide opportunities for learning and development in all areas of the curriculum. We have close links with Winchester Cathedral and use The Bishop's Palace Garden, as well as the Winchester College grounds for our Forest School and 2-hour weekly outdoor learning sessions.

We have excellent pupil/teacher ratios and teach a creative curriculum. The boys learn cursive handwriting and letter formation from the very beginning.

Wraparound care is provided for families who need it with a breakfast club and after school care or activities.

Our Positive Behavioural Policy reflects our ethos of praising positive behaviour. We celebrate the boys' achievements in all sorts of ways in class and assemblies.

Charitable status. The Pilgrims' School is a Registered Charity, number 1091579.

Pinewood

Bourton, Shrivenham, Wiltshire SN6 8HZ
Tel: 01793 782205
email: office@pinewoodschool.co.uk
website: www.pinewoodschool.co.uk
Facebook: @Pinewoodprepschool
Instagram: @pinewoodprepschool

***Headmaster*: Neal Bailey**

Deputy Head: Timothy Knapp

Age Range. 3–13.

Number of Pupils. 405 boys and girls of which Nursery and Pre-Prep: 100 and Prep: 305.

Fees per term (2023–2024). Day £3,685–£7,490 inclusive, with no compulsory extras. Weekly boarding supplement of £1,980 per term and regular boarding available at £58 per night. Boarding is available from Year 5 upwards and exeats are fortnightly.

Established in 1875, Pinewood is a thriving traditional country prep school with modern values in which staff, parents and children work together to find and realise the potential in every child. Set in 84 acres of rolling countryside on the Wiltshire/Oxfordshire border, it offers a warm family-based environment where children are encouraged to think for themselves and given the space to let their personalities and talents shine. The children are encouraged to learn through their adventures and a strong emphasis is placed on self-discipline, manners, kindness, trust and selflessness.

Resources include a purpose-built Music School and Science Labs, a flourishing Pre-Prep and Nursery, Art and Design Workshops, Research and Reference Library, ICT Rooms and a state-of-the-art Sports Hall. Recent investment has included the newly-created Hoyland building (a £2.5million six-classroom teaching block) and £750,000 of funding for AstroTurfs for children to enjoy hockey, netball, tennis and 5-a-side-football.

Excellent academic results are achieved through a mixture of traditional and forward-thinking teaching within a happy, friendly and stimulating learning atmosphere. Learning outside the classroom is key and trips are frequent and varied, as are residential trips. Great successes have been achieved in Music, Art and

Drama. The Pinewood SKILLS programme is an exciting new addition to the school week and provides the opportunity for children to experience a wide range of sessions allowing them to gain new attributes and experiences with academic, pastoral and social benefits. Over 40 dynamic sessions are on offer from clay pigeon shooting, to mountain biking, mosaics and Young Engineers.

Sport is keenly coached and matches are played at all levels on the picturesque playing fields, which incorporate a nine-hole golf course. Families are encouraged to join the school community to support the matches on a Wednesday afternoon and Saturday morning, following which they can enjoy Pinewood's famous match tea in the drawing room.

Boarding is popular and fun, with a multitude of activities on offer every night from the infamous 'Spotlight' tag game in the grounds, to cooking, craft, neon discos, and 'the floor is lava' in the sports hall. Children feel very at home in the warm and cosy atmosphere created by the houseparents, relishing the opportunity to spend more time with their friends.

Exit Schools: Bradfield College, Cheltenham College, Clifton College, Cokethorpe School, Dean Close School, Downe House School, Eton College, Marlborough College, Monkton Combe School, Pangbourne College, Radley College, Rendcomb College, Sherborne School, Sherborne Girls School, St Edward's School Oxford, St Mary's School Calne, Stowe School, Tudor Hall School and Wellington College.

Charitable status. Pinewood is a Registered Charity, number 309642.

Pipers Corner School
High Wycombe

Great Kingshill, High Wycombe, Buckinghamshire HP15 6LP

Tel: 01494 718255
email: theschool@piperscorner.co.uk
website: www.piperscorner.co.uk
X/Twitter: @PipersCornerSch
Facebook: @PipersCornerSchool
Instagram: @PipersCornerSch

See full entry in the **GSA** section, on **p. 463**.

Plymouth College

Ford Park, Plymouth, Devon PL4 6RN

Tel: +44 (0)1752 505100
email: admissions@plymouthcollege.com
mail@plymouthcollege.com
website: www.plymouthcollege.com
X/Twitter: @PlymouthCollege
Facebook: @PlymouthCollege
Instagram: @plymcollege

See full entry in the **HMC** section, on **p. 250**.

Pocklington School

West Green, Pocklington, York, East Yorkshire YO42 2NJ

Tel: 01759 321200
email: admissions@pocklingtonschool.com
website: www.pocklingtonschool.com
X/Twitter: @pockschool
Facebook: @PocklingtonSchool
Instagram: @pockschool
LinkedIn: /school/pocklington-school

See full entry in the **HMC** section, on **p. 252**.

Port Regis

Motcombe Park, Shaftesbury, Dorset SP7 9QA

Tel: 01747 857800
email: admissions@portregis.com
website: www.portregis.com
X/Twitter: @PortRegisSchool
Facebook: @PortRegis
Instagram: @portregisschool

Chairman of the Governors: Mr James Hussey
***Headmaster*: Mr Titus Mills**, BA, PGCE

Age range. 2–13.

Number of pupils. 292.

Fees per term (2023–2024). Boarders: £11,125 (full); Day: £6,610–£8,270. Pre-Prep: £3,530.

Port Regis is a co-educational day and boarding school for children aged 2–13. Located in the beautiful Dorset countryside, the school provides the perfect environment in which boys and girls can flourish and enjoy school.

Message from the Headmaster: Founded in 1881, Port Regis is steeped in history and yet it remains a community that is, at its core, forward-thinking and innovative in its approach to educating young children.

Few other prep schools can provide the breadth of experience on offer at Port Regis. It is renowned for its exceptional staff and academic credentials, as well as its first-class facilities, set within 150 acres of stunning grounds in rural Dorset. These facilities (which eclipse many at senior schools) enable Port Regis to deliver an outstanding holistic education that inspires the head, the hand and the heart.

However, I believe it is the engagement of the heart, in education, that is foundational. I have come to understand that the best schools do not just focus on the expansion of pupils' intellects, artistic creativity or physical health. The best schools go deeper still. They nurture the character and moral values of their pupils. As a preparatory school, not only are we preparing girls and boys for life at senior school, but we're preparing them for the great adventure of life itself. So, it is entirely fitting that Port Regis has a compelling motto: 'We seek higher things.' It seems to me that this gets to the heart of the matter. Our passion is to help pupils hone an array of qualities – generosity and endeavour, courage and creativity, good manners and friendship. These things underpin a Port Regis education. These things propel Portregians far in life.

And an education such as this should not only be purposeful and stretching, but also great fun! The best schools should be joyful schools. Joy and wonder are integral parts of childhood and should be visible and audible in every corridor, classroom and playground.

We would love you to come and visit Port Regis. It is a very special place. You will find a school in a stunning location, with a distinctive ethos and a tremendous spirit!

Titus Mills, Headmaster

Port Regis is located in 150 acres of parkland in the stunning Dorset countryside and enjoys a beautiful campus with facilities that are second to none in the Prep school world. Extensive woodland with nature trails sits alongside lawns, several ponds and a lake, so that the children can enjoy the space and freedom of the grounds. There are also 35 acres of games pitches, a nine-hole (18 tees) golf course, hockey pitch, hard tennis and netball courts, a 25m indoor swimming pool, a rifle range and an indoor sports complex, which includes two sports halls. An equestrian centre is conveniently situated close to the School.

The school's enviable reputation attracts the best teaching staff from all over the country. We are extremely fortunate to have an immensely accomplished team of staff dedicated to achieving this and who provide the happy, family atmosphere in which a child can realise their full potential. Port Regis is extremely proud of its 100% Common Entrance success record and the high number of scholarships and awards won to senior schools every year. Learning Support is available for children with mild-to-moderate specific learning difficulties.

2022 ISI Inspection: The school was inspected by the Independent Schools Inspectorate (ISI) in September 2022 and was rated 'Excellent' in every single judgement.

Extensive opportunities are provided for Music (about three-quarters of the School learn an instrument), Drama (there are up to six productions a year) and Art (in a wide choice of media), with Woodwork, Electronics, Riding, .22 Rifle Shooting, Karate, Gymnastics and Canoeing included in a list of over 70 hobby options. Major team games are Rugby, Hockey, Soccer, Netball and Cricket. Inter-school, county and national standard competitions are entered. Home and abroad trips take place.

The high standard of boarding provision is an impressively strong feature of the school, which explains why so many boys and girls choose to board (awarded 'Excellent' by ISI inspection).

Open Mornings take place each term and include tours of the school with pupils. Personal visits are also available.

Academic, Music, Gymnastic, Sport and All-Rounder entrance scholarships may be awarded annually.

Charitable status. Port Regis School Limited is a Registered Charity, number 306218.

The Portsmouth Grammar School

High Street, Portsmouth, Hants PO1 2LN
Tel: 023 9236 0036
email: admissions@pgs.org.uk
website: www.pgs.org.uk
X/Twitter: @PGS1732
Facebook: @ThePortsmouthGrammarSchool
Instagram: @theportsmouthgrammarschool
LinkedIn: /school/pgs1732

See full entry in the **HMC** section, on **p. 253**.

Pownall Hall

Carrwood Road, Wilmslow, Cheshire SK9 5DW
Tel: 01625 523141
email: genoffice@pownallhallschool.co.uk
website: www.pownallhallschool.co.uk
X/Twitter: @PownallHallSchool
Facebook: @Pownall-Hall-School
Instagram: @pownallschool

Chair of Governors: Mrs Eileen MacAulay

***Head*: Mr D Goulbourn**, BA Hons, PGCE Distinction

Age Range. 6 months–11 years. Co-educational.
Number of Boys and Girls. 308 (Day Children)
Fees per term (2023–2024). £3,860–£4,295.

Pownall Hall, a preparatory day school for children aged 6 months to 11 years old and set in its own beautiful and extensive grounds, has been established for over 100 years. It is situated on the north-western side of Wilmslow, 12 miles from Manchester and within easy reach of motorway, rail and air travel.

The school has highly-trained teaching staff, who prepare children for the Entrance Examinations to the Independent Day schools and Grammar schools in the area. A thorough grounding is given in all academic subjects extending well beyond the confines of the National Curriculum. An excellent mixture of traditional and modern techniques is used through the implementation of cutting-edge technology in and around every classroom. In Key Stage 2 each major subject has specialist teaching staff and subject rooms including a fully-equipped Science Laboratory, Art Studio, D&T Studio, Maths, English, Information Technology, and MFL rooms and, in addition, a computer-aided Library. Spanish, French and German are taught from the age of two.

Pownall Hall School has three pre-school rooms, with children entering the Robin Room Nursery from 6 months old, transferring to the Owls Room at age 2 years, and then to Kindergarten at the age of 3 or 4. From Kindergarten the pupils then enter Reception and go through the school to Year 6, by which point the school will have guided parents as to where best for their child to continue their education at the age of 11.

At Pownall Hall there is an excellent staff to pupil ratio throughout the school, ensuring that pastoral care is of a very high level and also supporting the learning of children of all abilities, in conjunction with a specialist SEND provision. Children are taught in small class sizes, which are capped at a maximum of 18 children per class from Reception to Form 6, gaining from the individual attention they receive.

Great importance is attached to Sport, Music and Drama in order to develop the rounded education that allows all children to achieve, wherever their ability lies. The school has its own well-equipped theatre where all children perform on stage during the year. Music is offered as part of the curriculum and also additionally through a full range of peripatetic teaching staff, providing chances for the children to perform in and outside school. As well as subject specialist rooms with an outstanding range of specialist equipment, the implementation of mobile technology for both staff and children provides opportunity for outstanding teaching and learning across the school.

The facilities for sport are very impressive with the school having its own extensive grounds, alongside a fully-equipped Sports Hall, Astro Pitch and both outdoor and indoor facilities for Netball, Hockey, Football, Rugby, Tennis and so much more.

All children experience outdoor learning, with Forest School, Extra-Curricular clubs, day and residential trips arranged as well as utilising our on-site woods for free-flow teaching and learning at all ages. Children in Years 3 to 6 also experience outdoor pursuits at a range of well-equipped sites which enhance their learning experiences. There is an extensive provision of co-curricular clubs, complementing our out-of-hours Breakfast Club and After School Care. Holiday Quest runs on site throughout all school holidays.

The school received an outstanding Full Inspection Report in 2017 and an outstanding EYFS Inspection in 2014.

Charitable status. Pownall Hall School is a Registered Charity, number 525929. It exists to provide education for boys and girls, aged 6 months – 11 years old.

The Prebendal School

52–55 West Street, Chichester, West Sussex PO19 1RT

Tel: 01243 772220
email: office@prebendalschool.org.uk
website: www.prebendalschool.org.uk
X/Twitter: @theprebendal
Facebook: @ThePrebendalSchool
Instagram: @the_prebendal_school
LinkedIn: /company/the-prebendal-school

Proprietor: Mr Ali Khan, BSc Hons, MBA

***Head*: Mrs A Napier**, BEd

Deputy Head: Miss L Johnstone, BSc Hons, PGCE, QTS
Chaplain: Reverend Canon Dr D Inman

Age range. 3–13.

Number of pupils. 104 pupils in total (including 23 boarders): 64 in the Prep School (Years 3–8) and 40 in the Pre-Prep (Nursery–Year 2).

Fees per term (2023–2024). Full Boarders: £8,355. Day Pupils: Years 5–8 £5,780; Years 3–4 £5,356. Weekly Boarding: £1,750 in addition to Day Fee. Reception–Year 2: £3,100–£2,595. Nursery: £45.00 per morning £30.00 per afternoon and £65.00 for the whole day. Compulsory extras: laundry and linen for Full Boarders.

The Prebendal is the oldest school in Sussex and has occupied its present building at the west end of the Cathedral (though with later additions) for hundreds of years. The Cathedral Choristers are among the pupils educated at the school and they receive Choral Scholarships in reduction of fees. A range of scholarships and means-tested bursaries are available. Music and Academic scholarships are open to pupils entering the prep school and there are Academic, Art, Music & Sport scholarships available for Year 7 entry. Sibling discount, former Prebendalian discount and Armed Forces discount are also available. Year 8 Leavers achieve an impressive range of scholarship awards to a range of prestigious senior schools every September. In 2020, 82% of Year 8 leavers achieved awards.

There are excellent playing fields in the heart of the city. The sports are football, hockey, netball, cricket, athletics, tennis, rugby and rounders. Younger children enjoy Beach School and the school unveiled a new outdoor classroom and amphitheatre in September 2018. A new Pavilion is being built in 2022. The Pre-Senior Baccalaureate (PSB) and Quadrivium, a programme of academic excellence for children in Years 6–8, were also introduced in 2018. Pupils in Years 6–8 use iPads as an additional tool to enrich their learning.

Approximately 95% of the children learn to play musical instruments and the school has a large range of ensembles and choirs along with Concert Band and 1st Orchestra. There are many optional extras and after-school clubs, such as Forest School and Sailing. Flexi boarding is a popular choice and there is a growing demand for the extended day programme, from Breakfast Club to supper, for busy families. Pelicans Nursery opened in September 2019, with 7.00 am to 7.00 pm provision for three- and four-year-olds so they can be Reception-ready.

Former pupils, parents and staff are known as The Prebendal Associates and events are held regularly throughout each academic year. The School also has its own thriving Toddler Group on Wednesday mornings during term time.

Charitable status. The Prebendal School is a Registered Charity, number 1157782. Registered Company No. 09038149.

Prestfelde

London Road, Shrewsbury, Shropshire SY2 6NZ

Tel: 01743 245400
email: office@prestfelde.co.uk
website: www.prestfelde.co.uk
X/Twitter: @prestfelde
Facebook: @prestfelde
LinkedIn: /Prestfelde

Shrewsbury's Co-educational Prep School for all aged 3–13.

Chair of Governors: Mr Rex Sartain

***Head*: Mr N Robinson**, MSc, PGCE, DMS Portsmouth

Age Range. 3–13.

Number of Pupils. 335 (190 boys, 145 girls).

Fees per term (2023–2024). Flexi Boarding: £40 per night. Day: Year 8 £6,400, Years 6–7 £6,370, Year 5 £6,300, Year 4 £6,050, Year 3 £5,180, Year 2 £3,960, Year 1 £3,870, Reception £3,800, Nursery 2,040 (5 mornings).

Prestfelde is one of the UK's leading Prep schools. Children benefit from the nurturing environment, first class facilities, and progressive, high quality education. We pride ourselves on providing the best school experience a child can have, one that enriches their happiness in school, enables them to pursue their individual interests and develop confidence to grow into the person they want to be. Our excellent teachers build trusting relationships and impart their knowledge through inspirational teaching and learning experiences. Guiding and transforming pupils through a broad range of experiential learning; children at Prestfelde gain the skills, qualities and knowledge to set them up to succeed.

Situated in the heart of Shrewsbury, the beautiful tree lined site extends over 30 acres and is an inspirational environment for children to learn.

Academic highlights are underlined by the level of success and quality of scholarships gained by pupils to a range of leading senior schools. In 2022, Year 8 pupils achieved consistently high pass rates at Common Entrance with 100% of Year 8 children, successfully gaining places to their first-choice senior schools. Each year pupils gain scholarships to a number of aspirational independent schools, covering every section of the curriculum from academics, art, design, technology and drama to music and sport

Whilst many pupils maintain high levels of competitive sport in their disciplines, we recognise the importance of children enjoying the challenges of team sport at school. Outstanding coaching and mentoring in football, netball, rugby, lacrosse and cricket have encouraged pupils to become outstanding team players. Additional hours of coaching in these and other sports, together with physical education lessons, swimming (on site) and outdoor fitness by specialist coaches, enhance the physical well-being of Prestfelde pupils, resulting in the enjoyment of competition in a variety of sporting environments.

The extra-curricular offering at Prestfelde is designed to build on children's experiences with the aim of improving outcomes in all areas of their learning. Purposefully building on pupils' interests, we aim to light that spark for learning and to develop talents. Activities range from bushcraft and outdoor gardening to construction and minecraft. Pupils enjoy the many and varied inter-house competitions and the friendly rivalry enhances the will and enjoyment of achievement.

Charitable status. Prestfelde School is a Registered Charity, number 1102931. It aims to provide education for boys and girls.

Prospect House School

75 Putney Hill, London SW15 3NT

Tel: 020 8780 0456
email: info@prospecths.org.uk
website: www.prospecths.org.uk
X/Twitter: @prospecths
Facebook: @Prospect-House-School-163116433760812
Instagram: @prospect_house_school

Managing Governor: Mrs L Nicholas

***Head*: Mr Michael Hodge**, BPrimEd Rhodes QTS

Age Range. 3–11 co-educational.

Number of Pupils. 310 day pupils.

Fees per term (2023–2024). Nursery (5 mornings) £3,490, Reception–Year 2 £6,975, Years 3–6 £7,510.

Prospect House is a leading co-educational prep school with a village feel, overlooking Putney Heath in south-west London. We provide a bespoke curriculum which is designed and delivered to be intellectually exciting, academically engaging and imaginatively stimulating.

The school enjoys two large sites on Putney Hill situated just a short walk apart. Children aged 3 to 7 years occupy the Lower School and children aged 7 to 11 years are based in the Upper School. Both sites have large grounds including all-weather sports pitches. There are multi-purpose halls where assemblies, music concerts, gymnastics and drama productions take place together with dedicated rooms for music, computing, art and DT.

Children join the school at 3 or 4 years old and admittance is by date of registration with priority given to siblings of pupils already in the school. Occasional places for older children higher up the school are sometimes available. An equal balance of boys and girls is kept throughout the school. Children are prepared for a wide range of leading day and boarding schools for entry at 11 years old with a high number of students taking academic, all-rounder, music and sports scholarships.

Core subjects are complemented by a wide range of arts, languages and humanities as well as a keen focus on sport and PE. To ensure personal attention, the ratio of staff to pupils is high. Without exception our teachers are highly qualified and ably supported by our carefully chosen team of teaching assistants. We have an extensive range of specialist teachers covering maths, English, computing, French, music, physical education, art & design technology and Latin. Other highly trained staff are available to identity and support children who may display specific learning needs. Specialist staff such as speech therapists are also available to work with pupils.

Our dynamic staff and external specialists offer over 40 different clubs each term catering to a wide range of interests. The variety and quality of the club provision encourages the learning and development of new skills and helps to develop friendships with children in other year groups. Residential trips, day outings, workshops and visiting performers enhance and embed curriculum learning.

Queen Elizabeth Grammar School Wakefield

Senior Section (Boys 11–18)
154 Northgate, WF1 3QX
Tel: 01924 373943
email: qsoffice@wgsf.net

Junior Section (Boys 7–11)
158 Northgate, WF1 3QY
Tel: 01924 373821
email: qjoffice@wgsf.net

website: www.wgsf.org.uk
X/Twitter: @QEGSYorkshire
Facebook: @QEGSYorkshire
Instagram: @QEGSYorksire
LinkedIn: /school/queen-elizabeth-grammar-school-wakefield

See full entry in the **HMC** section, on **p. 262**.

Queen Elizabeth's Hospital (QEH) – Junior School

9 Upper Berkeley Place, Clifton, Bristol BS8 1JS
Tel: 0117 930 3087
email: juniors@qehbristol.co.uk
website: www.qehbristol.co.uk
X/Twitter: @qehjuniors
Facebook: @qehjuniorschool
Instagram: @qehjuniorschool

Chairman of Governors: Mr K Riley,

***Junior School Headteacher*: Mr D M Kendall**, MA, MEd

Age Range. Boys 7–11.

Number of Pupils. 113 day boys.

Fees per term (2023–2024). £3,895 Fees include pre- and after-school supervision until 5.00 pm.

The QEH Junior School was opened in September 2007 and is located in gracious Georgian town houses in Upper Berkeley Place backing onto the Senior School, which means it can share its first-class facilities including science, drama, music and sport. The cultural facilities of the city, such as the city museum and art gallery, are also on its doorstep.

Pupils travel to the school from across the region and there is a hub for public transport on the nearby Clifton Triangle. The school also offers timed parking facilities for parents in the adjacent NCP West End multi-storey car park, to pick up and drop off pupils, at no extra cost.

As the only boys' junior school in the city, QEH Juniors is unique in Bristol. Being small, it focuses on the individual, fostering a love of learning whilst nurturing the interests and talents of each boy. In addition there is a wealth of extracurricular activities available.

QEH Juniors offers a values based education with outstanding pastoral care, a nurturing academic environment and an ethos building kindness, confidence and resilience.

Boys can enter in Year 3 or Year 5, though places occasionally become available in other Years. Boys are expected to move into the Main School at 11. (*See QEH entry in HMC section.*)

Charitable status. Queen Elizabeth's Hospital is a Registered Charity, number 1104871, and a Company Limited by Guarantee, number 5164477.

Queen Ethelburga's Collegiate

Thorpe Underwood, York YO26 9SS
Tel: 01423 333330
email: admissions@qe.org
website: www.qe.org
X/Twitter: @qethelburgas
Facebook: @queenethelburgas
Instagram: @queenethelburgas/
LinkedIn: /queen-ethelburga's-college

See full entry in the **ISA** section, on **p. 905**.

Queen's College, London

43–49 Harley Street, London W1G 8BT
Tel: 020 7291 7000
email: queens@qcl.org.uk
website: www.qcl.org.uk
X/Twitter: @queenscollegew1
Facebook: @QueensCollegeW1
Instagram: @queenscollegew_1
LinkedIn: /school/queens-college-w1

See full entry in the **GSA** section, on **p. 466**.

Radnor House Sevenoaks – Prep School

Combe Bank Drive, Sundridge, Kent TN14 6AE

Tel: 01959 564320
email: enquiries@radnor-sevenoaks.org
website: www.radnor-sevenoaks.org
X/Twitter: @radnorsevenoaks
Facebook: @radnorsevenoaks
Instagram: @radnorsevenoaks

Chairman of Board of Directors: Mr Colin Diggory, BSc Hons, PGCE, MA, EdD, CMath, FIMA, FRSA

Head: Mr Fraser Halliwell, BSc Hons, PGCE, MEd, FRSA

***Head of Prep School*: Ms Philippa Lang**

Radnor House Sevenoaks Prep School is a flourishing independent school with entry from the day a child turns 2 up to the age of 11 (Nursery to Year 6).

Aims and Ethos. As the world becomes more complex, diverse and fast paced, the school's mission is to future-proof its pupils to give them the very best start in life. Academic qualifications are an important aspect of this but so too are interpersonal skills such as emotional intelligence and leadership. Underpinning their approach to education is a set of core values – excellence, respect, courage and perseverance – which form the bedrock of the school and provide a moral compass for children from school through to adulthood. Pupil happiness is their first priority as a happy child is one who will thrive, grasp opportunities to learn and develop and will become a confident and well-balanced young person. One key focus is to be a pioneer in preparing the children for the digital age by working with Microsoft as one of their flagship schools as they aim to build adults who can thrive in the world of tomorrow by using technology to propel their learning forward.

Location. Situated in a Palladian Mansion and set in superb grounds with 27 acres of parkland just outside Sevenoaks, the school has excellent facilities. The Nursery and Prep School are on the same site as the Senior School and Sixth Form and there are many positive links between them, so that all pupils have guaranteed access through the school until they leave at 18. The Prep School is housed in an original stable block and affords a unique environment in which the students feel secure and comfortable.

Curriculum. A modern and broad range of subjects is taught at all age levels. The school boasts a strong Art Department with an innovative graphic design suite, alongside a popular Music Department with regular exhibitions and musical performances in which wide participation is achieved. Radnor House Sevenoaks has a well-earned reputation for competitive success in a wide range of sports. Swimming in the 25-metre covered pool is a particularly popular activity throughout the whole school. Outdoor Adventurous Education has taken a firm place on the curriculum in the form of Forest School and Bush Craft.

Transport. Coach transport is organized for pupils from Year 4 onwards for five significant routes, to be paid for on a termly basis.

Fees per term (2023–2024). Preparatory School £4,315–£5,570 (Lunch £325).

Ratcliffe College

Fosse Way, Ratcliffe on the Wreake, Leicester, Leicestershire LE7 4SG

Tel: 01509 817000 School Office
01509 817072/817031 Admissions Office
email: admissions@ratcliffecollege.com
website: www.ratcliffecollege.com
X/Twitter: @RatcliffeColl
@RatcliffePrep
@RatcliffeSport
Facebook: @RatcliffeCollege
Instagram: @RatcliffeCollege
LinkedIn: /school/ratcliffe-college

See full entry in the **HMC** section, on **p. 268**.

Ravenscourt Park Preparatory School

Gardener Schools Group

16 Ravenscourt Avenue, London W6 0SL

Tel: 020 8846 9153
email: office@rpps.co.uk
website: www.rpps.co.uk
X/Twitter: @RPPSLondon
Facebook: @RPPSLondon
Instagram: @rppslondon
LinkedIn: /company/rppslondon

***Headmaster*: Mr Carl Howes**

Age Range. 4–11 co-educational.

Number of Pupils. 416 boys and girls.

Fees per term (2023–2024). £6,995.

Ravenscourt Park Preparatory school provides education of the highest quality for boys and girls, preparing them for transfer to the best independent schools at 11 years of age. The Lower School caters for pupils aged 4–7 and the Upper School for 7–11 years. All pupils are housed in one of the three main buildings that make up the RPPS site. The Gardener Building is home to a theatre, a state-of-the-art science laboratory and an art studio. The secure site includes a large play area, a newly refurbished outdoor learning area for Early Years and the school makes use of the extensive facilities of Ravenscourt Park which it adjoins.

The curriculum includes French, humanities, music, art and craft, RE and PE for all pupils in addition to the usual core subjects. In the Upper School the majority of subjects are taught by specialists. All Upper School pupils attend a Residential Week where studies across the curriculum are applied to a non-urban environment.

There are many after-school clubs and sports activities, as well as three choirs and two orchestras. Individual tuition is offered in piano, harp, violin, brass, woodwind, cello, saxophone, clarinet, flute, percussion and singing. The drama productions and concerts are a highlight of each school year.

A wraparound care service, before and after school, is offered to parents at an extra charge.

The school is noted for its warm, happy atmosphere where parents play a full part in enriching the curriculum and social life. Off-site visits and guest workshops presented by noted visitors are a regular feature of education at RPPS.

The school is very popular in the local area and registration is strongly recommended on the child's first birthday. A prospectus and registration form may be obtained from the school secretary and online. Open Mornings take place each month (dates are available on the school website).

The school was inspected by ISI in November 2021 and received 'excellent' in both key outcomes. The full inspection report is available on the school website.

Reddiford School

38 Cecil Park, Pinner, Middlesex HA5 5HH

Tel: 020 8866 0660
email: office@reddiford.org.uk
website: www.reddiford.co.uk
Facebook: @reddifordschool
LinkedIn: /company/reddiford-school

Chairman of Governors: Mr A Cairns

***Head*: Mrs J Batt**, CertEd, NPQH

Age Range. 2 years 9 months to 11.

Number of Pupils. Prep: 80 Boys, 68 Girls; Pre-Prep: 38 Boys, 23 Girls; Early Years: 29 Boys, 26 Girls.

Fees per term (2023–2024): Early Years (before Reception Year): £3,980, Pre-Prep/Reception: £4,330, Prep: £4,460.

Reddiford School has been established in Cecil Park, Pinner since 1913. Whilst the school maintains its Church of England status, children from all faiths and cultures are welcomed. Throughout the school the ethos is on respect for one another. Reddiford prides itself on being a town school based in the heart of Pinner; a few minutes' walk from local transport facilities.

Reddiford possesses a fine academic record, preparing its pupils for entrance at 11+ into major independent schools, many at scholarship level, and local Grammar schools. There is a high teacher to pupil ratio ensuring small classes leading to a friendly caring environment where all children are valued.

The Early Years Department is situated in its own building and caters for children from 2 years nine months to rising 5 years. It offers a stimulating and attractive environment where children are encouraged to be independent and active learners. The Early Years Department follows the Early Years Foundation Stage Curriculum.

The Pre-Prep Department builds on the knowledge and skills acquired in the Early Years placing the emphasis on developing confidence and the ability to learn and work independently and with others. The Pre-Prep Department has its own computer suite and interactive whiteboards in classrooms. There is specialist teaching in French, Music and PE from reception upwards and all children are taught to swim.

In the Prep Department children are taught by specialist teachers in properly resourced subject rooms. There is a fully-equipped science laboratory, dedicated art and music rooms and an ICT suite. Pupils are prepared for entry to the many prestigious senior schools in the area, a process which involves consultation with parents from an early stage.

There is an extensive programme of extra-curricular activities throughout the school including: sports (football, cricket, netball, gymnastics), languages (French, Latin, Mandarin), art and science. We also offer before and after school care (7.55am–6.00pm).

Assessments for Reception upwards require the child to be in school for the day. They complete English and Mathematics assessments and their ability to cope with the educational and social demands for the year group are evaluated.

Charitable status. Reddiford School is a Registered Charity, number 312641. It exists to provide education for boys and girls.

Redmaids' High Junior School

Grange Court Road, Westbury-on-Trym, Bristol BS9 4DP

Tel: 0117 962 9451
email: junioradmissions@redmaidshigh.co.uk
website: https://www.redmaidshigh.co.uk/junior/
X/Twitter: @RedmaidsJuniors
Facebook: @redmaidshighschool
Instagram: @redmaidshigh

Chairman of Governors: Mr Andrew Hillman

***Headteacher*: Mrs Lisa Brown**, BSc Hons Leicester, PGCE Oxford Brookes

Headteacher's PA/Admissions: Mrs Naomi Brady

Age Range. 7–11.

Number of Girls. 132 Day Girls.

Fees per term (2023–2024). £3,675 plus lunch.

At Redmaids' High Junior School, girls receive an outstanding educational experience. Our mission is for your daughter to wake up every morning eager to be at school. Small class sizes, dedicated teachers and a friendly, nurturing atmosphere, make that a reality.

We set the bar high academically, stretching our pupils to ensure they become the best they can be. Each week, time is given to all subjects in our broad curriculum. Alongside the core areas, the foundation subjects and creative arts are just as valued. Sport is integral to our timetable, instilling positive attitudes towards physical activity. A focus on teamwork and specific skills lead to success in competitive fixtures.

Our single-sex setting means no dilution of attention to the needs of the girls as young women. They are offered all the opportunities, hold all the responsibilities, and enjoy everything in their path without any self-consciousness or stereotypical judgement.

Extra-curricular activities are an essential part of the Redmaids' High experience. Girls learn resilience and determination through trying new things. Whether it is playing chess, football or hockey, taking part in a concert or book group, joining art or fencing clubs, caving on the Mendips or sailing in Bristol docks, they enjoy busy, active and purposeful days.

We value diversity and embrace internationalism; we are forward thinking in our teaching, preparing our pupils for an ever-changing technological future filled with careers that have not even been dreamed of yet.

The House system enables girls to work and make friends with children in all year groups. There is a happy and relaxed atmosphere within the school, with easy access for parents to speak to teachers, a regular discussion group with the headteacher and many social events bringing families, staff and pupils together.

Assessment of pupil progress is built into every subject area. We moved away from SAT testing some years ago, preferring Durham University's INCAS test for monitoring performance and progression, and individual target setting.

Pastoral care is one of our major strengths. New pupils are supported by a buddy system and through school meetings and class activities, pupils learn about good citizenship, taking responsibility for themselves, for each other and for the care of their community and environment.

Close links are fostered between the Junior and Senior schools. Pupils benefit from use of the science laboratory, extensive PE facilities including an all-weather pitch, shared dining facilities and award-winning catering. At age 11, transition occurs to the Senior School (conditions apply) having sat the entrance examination and applied for academic, sport and music scholarships alongside those joining from other schools. (*See Redmaids' High School entry in GSA section*.)

The School occupies a spacious site nestled in a quiet residential neighbourhood. We have a mix of well-maintained traditional and purpose-built buildings including a library, music room, art studio and lofty assembly hall, plus a large garden for outdoor play complete with sports and climbing equipment.

Admission: All girls are assessed prior to entry. Potential Year 3 pupils are assessed in pairs, with girls spending half the day in class and half working alongside the headteacher. Year 4, 5 and 6 taster days are conducted in groups. Interested families are encouraged to visit the school individually or at one of our visiting events.

Charitable status. Redmaids' High School is a Registered Charity, number 1105017.

Reigate St Mary's Preparatory and Choir School

Chart Lane, Reigate, Surrey RH2 7RN

Tel: 01737 244880
email: office@reigatestmarys.org
website: www.reigatestmarys.org
X/Twitter: @rsmprepschool
Facebook: @ReigateStMarys
Instagram: @rsmprepschool

Chairman of Governors: Mr Mark Elsey

***Headmaster*: Marcus Culverwell**, MA Ed

Age Range. 2–11.

Number of Pupils. 390.

Fees per term (2023–2024). Green Shoots: £1,335 (min. 3 mornings); Kindergarten: £2,225 (min. 5 mornings); Lower School (Reception, Years 1 & 2): £4,820; Upper School (Years 3–6): £6,040.

Reigate St Mary's (RSM) is a co-educational day school for children aged 2 to 11 years old. It is a junior school of Reigate Grammar School (RGS), the top co-educational day school in Surrey and typically, 80 percent of pupils transfer to RGS each year. RSM believes that a good education should be a challenging, inspirational and exciting journey, preparing children for happy and fulfilled future lives. The aim is to produce confident, resilient and creative young people who will one day become leaders who care deeply about a sustainable and equitable future for everyone.

This is achieved by a relentless focus on wellbeing, and by prioritising the building of strong relationships with the children and their families over everything else. From their earliest days, right through to their transition to senior school, each child is supported according to their individual needs and strengths. By doing this, the children know they are truly valued at school and this gives them the confidence to take challenges, learn from mistakes and ultimately reach their full potential. The school has been shortlisted for Independent School of the Year in the Wellbeing category in recognition of this.

The children enjoy busy days filled with imaginative teaching and exciting adventures focusing on teamwork, creativity, digital learning, and communication. Lessons are taken outside whenever possible and with 15 wonderful acres of grounds, there is plenty of space to roll down hills, explore dens and enjoy the school's many nature areas and playgrounds.

The youngest children joining Early Years are in the safe hands of warm and caring teachers and teaching assistants. The team focus on making sure each child feels happy and secure as they know that ultimately, happy children learn. Days in Early Years are designed to harness natural curiosity and ensure the children become enthusiastic and happy learners, eager to come to school every day.

As they move up through the school, the children learn to be good citizens, with the confidence to make the right decisions and the skills to thrive in the workplace of tomorrow. The school is passionate about teaching the children to be independent and resilient thinkers, fully equipped to reach their individual potential, whatever form that takes. An Education for Social Responsibility (ESR) curriculum is central to this and helps children to think about the core values that will lead to worthwhile and content lives, within stable and caring communities while protecting the planet for the future.

There is significant and ongoing investment in technology throughout the school and IT is embedded in all teaching. Classrooms are exciting and inspiring places where children use technology to explore. There is an impressive IT Lab and Mac Suite and the school's Lego robotics team have been UK finalists in the worldwide Lego robotics competitions many times.

Rendcomb College

Rendcomb, Cirencester, Gloucestershire GL7 7HA
Tel: 01285 831213
email: admissions@rendcombcollege.org.uk
website: www.rendcombcollege.org.uk
X/Twitter: @RendcombCollege
Facebook: @Rendcombcollege
Instagram: @rendcombcollege
LinkedIn: /rendcomb-college

See full entry in the **HMC** section, on **p. 273**.

Repton Prep

Milton, Derbyshire DE65 6EJ
Tel: 01283 707100
email: admissions@repton.org.uk
website: www.reptonprep.org.uk
X/Twitter: @reptonprep
Facebook: @repton prep
Instagram: @ReptonPrep

Chairman of Governors: Mr E M Shires, BA, FCA
***Repton Prep Head*: Mrs Victoria Harding,** BMus Hons, PGDip RAM, PGCE, LRAM, ATCL
Senior Deputy Head: Mr James Aldred, BSc Hons, QTS
Deputy Head Academic: Mrs Samantha Krbacevic, BSc Hons, PGCE, MPhil
Deputy Head Pre-Prep: Ms Kellee-Anne Cavill, BA Hons, PGCE
Deputy Head Pastoral & Boarding: Mr Stuart Elks, BA Hons, PGCE (QTS)

Gender. Co-ed.

Age range. 3 to 13.

Day/Boarding. Day, Full Boarding, Weekly Boarding, Home & Away Boarding, Flexi Boarding.

Location. Derbyshire.

Repton Prep is the 3–13 campus of Repton School, a co-educational boarding and day school providing an exceptional education for children aged 3 to 18 years. With over 400 pupils, around 40 of which board, the school offers a caring and inspirational environment with enviable facilities paired with excellent pastoral care. Repton Prep firmly believes that learning is a collaborative endeavour. There is a strong community of pupils, teachers and staff, and a united belief that the most valuable education is one that is broad, balanced and allows children to enjoy their childhood, while benefitting from a range of opportunities both in and out of the classroom. With a rich heritage and as part of Repton School, pupils enjoy a wealth of facilities and a plethora of resources, enabling a curriculum where academic excellence and an enriching co-curricular programme provides a rounded education. Set in the 55-acre grounds of a Palladian mansion, nestled in the glorious Derbyshire countryside with its own lake and woodland, what makes Repton Prep truly special is the team of dedicated teachers and staff; a highly experienced, gifted and committed community who strive for each child to develop a lifelong curiosity in the world. During their time at Repton Prep, children benefit from deep and nurturing relationships that motivate and inspire them to succeed.

Repton Prep is located two miles away from Repton School and the close relationship between the two schools ensures a fluid transition from Repton Prep to Repton, although pupils who opt for other senior schools are fully supported to achieve Common Entrance. Both campuses offer fantastic travel links and can be easily reached by road from the M1, M6 and M5 via the A50, by rail from East Midlands Parkway and Lichfield, or from nearby Birmingham and East Midlands airports.

Admission. Repton Prep welcomes applications for both boarding and day places throughout the academic year, starting at age 3 and up to age 13. Boarding is available from Year 3, and from that point of entry upwards, all candidates – day and boarding – will undergo an age-appropriate admissions process involving assessments, taster days and interviews. School reports and references will be obtained from their current school before formal offers are made.

Fees per term (2023–2024). Pre-Prep: £3,769–£4,395; Prep: Boarders £8,870–£10,485; Day £6,480–£8,100.

Curriculum. A varied curriculum with a breadth of subjects is offered to pupils. The Pre-Prep syllabus provides pupils with the skills and experiences that will form the foundation for their future learning, including the benefits of lessons taught by specialist teachers from an early age. The Prep curriculum builds on prior experience so that pupils become more independent and active learners. Teaching groups are streamed by ability with setting in place for Mathematics, English and French. This is designed to maximise the efficiency of teaching programmes and ensures that the work presented to pupils is 'just right'.

In Year 8, pupils are prepared for entrance examinations or, if applicable, scholarship examinations. However, it is the aim of Repton to produce young pupils at 13 who are well prepared for the senior phase of their education, as well as being well on the way to being a major contributor to society in their lives beyond school.

Outdoor learning. Repton Prep's setting plays no small part in the broader education of its pupils. Lessons often spill out into the woods, spinneys, formal ponds (all the pupils are expert pond dippers!) or around the lake, as teachers take full advantage of the glorious Derbyshire countryside. During playtime at Repton Prep, the youngest pupils have their own Teletubbies-style playground, with tunnels, surfboards, blackboards and play equipment to spark their imaginations. Older pupils build dens, climb trees and explore the natural surroundings with unbounded curiosity. Every experience at Repton Prep is seen as a learning opportunity.

Beyond Repton Prep. With Repton offering pupils an education from 3–18, 90% of leavers move on to Repton, with a number of pupils also receiving places at other highly acclaimed schools.

Facilities. Repton Prep is surrounded by 55 acres of woodland, playing fields and a lake. The School has a plethora of facilities including a striking purpose-built dining hall, three science laboratories, and a sophisticated computer technology suite. The Quad development houses a contemporary Music facility, language laboratory, an Art department complete with kiln, a fully equipped DT classroom and a Greenpower garage for Repton Prep's award-winning electric cars. An extensive library is situated in the main Hall, and there is an indoor competition-sized swimming pool, a sports hall and floodlit Astroturf. Pupils are fortunate to also have access to the world-class facilities at Repton School and shared resources across campuses.

Creative Arts. From Nursery onwards, all pupils are given the opportunity to participate in a wide variety of classroom and extracurricular music activities. The Music Department's three full-time members of staff are supported by 20 specialist visiting music teachers offering over 200 lessons a week, and they work closely with the Director of Music at Repton School to deliver outstanding opportunities to pupils, from masterclasses to one-to-one tutorials with visiting musicians. Pupils are encouraged to take part in the School's wide variety of ensembles and choirs and they have an enviable number of pupils who are part of regional and national orchestras and ensembles. The Drama department affords many opportunities for all pupils to design, direct and perform in the multiple productions that take place during the school year. Extracurricular activities include all aspects of theatre production including technical and backstage. Pupils are able to improve their confidence and love of performing without fear through LAMDA examinations. The personalised programme is tailored to individual needs and abilities from Year 3 upwards. Lessons are available within and outside of school hours. Repton Prep has enjoyed considerable success, with high uptake and consistently outstanding LAMDA examination results.

The Design and Technology Centre is home to a fully equipped workshop which enables pupils to develop a greater understanding of the real-world applications of Design Technology. It is the home of Greenpower, where pupils design, build and eventually race their own electric car.

Sport. Repton Prep recognises the importance of young people being involved in sport, whatever their ability and whatever their eventual chosen discipline. Pupils are actively encouraged to participate at the best level they can, and the aim is to equip every pupil with confidence and enthusiasm to enjoy sport and an active lifestyle both in school and beyond. Squads are fielded in the major sports of football, hockey and cricket for boys and girls, with second, third, fourth and even fifth teams formed. There is a wide range of different sporting opportunities from tennis, athletics, golf and kayaking to fencing and orienteering. The School also has its own equestrian team.

Houses. Day pupils join a House and, throughout the year, they can earn points by participating in various competitions, for positive behaviour and for special accomplishments. This not only fosters a sense of community but also forms an integral part of life at the School. Boarders are assigned a Boarding House and are welcomed into a warm, caring and fun environment, where they are looked after by Houseparents and the boarding staff team in a relaxed setting, where the emphasis is on enjoying a happy childhood.

Boarding. Boarding at Repton Prep is a highly rewarding experience; as well as developing lifelong friendships with people from all over the world, our boarders build a strong sense of self by immersing themselves in every opportunity that Repton Prep provides. There are four boarding houses at Repton Prep, with two of these being dedicated to flexi-boarding. Each House has its own relaxed atmosphere where children can be children, enjoying running around in the fresh air, playing games with their friends, reading, catching up with their favourite TV programme or simply chatting with friends and boarding tutors.

Scholarships. Academic, Music, Sport, Drama, Art and DT scholarships are available for new pupils joining Repton Prep in Year 7. Bursaries may be available to families looking to access an independent education for their child, subject to means testing. These may, in appropriate circumstances, be used to supplement scholarship awards. Additional bursaries are also available for Forces families.

Charitable Status. Repton Prep (1093165) is a Registered Charity. Repton Prep exists to provide high-quality education for boys and girls.

Repton School

Repton, Derbyshire DE65 6FH

Tel: 01283 559222 (Admissions)
01283 559200 (Reception)
email: admissions@repton.org.uk
website: www.repton.org.uk
X/Twitter: @ReptonSchool
Facebook: @ReptonSchool
Instagram: @ReptonSchool
LinkedIn: /school/repton-school

See full entry in the **HMC** section, on **p. 274**.

RGS Prep

Maori Road, Guildford, Surrey GU1 2EL
Tel: 01483 880650
email: rgsp-office@rgsg.co.uk
website: www.rgsg.co.uk
X/Twitter: @RGSprep
Facebook: @RGSprep
Instagram: @rgsprep

Chairman of Governors: Mrs S K Creedy, MA Cantab

***Head*: Mr T Freeman-Day**, BA Hons

Age range. 3–11.

Number of boys. 350 day boys.

Fees per term (2023–2024). £4,389–£6,300.

RGS Prep is the Preparatory School of the Royal Grammar School and the choir school for Guildford Cathedral. Cathedral choristers qualify for choral scholarships.

The main entry points are Nursery, Reception and Year 3. Many of the pupils gain entry to the Royal Grammar School at age 11.

The School is divided into four Houses for House competitions. Pastoral care and supervision of academic progress are shared by the Head, Housemasters, Form and subject teachers. Extracurricular activities include music, art, chess, drama, computer club, judo, fencing, tennis, basketball, science and general knowledge.

Music is a strong feature of the life of the school, which is a member of the Choir Schools Association. In addition to the Cathedral Choir, there are senior and junior choirs, an orchestra, wind and string groups. Private tuition by qualified peripatetic teachers is available in most instruments. There are music concerts and the school Carol Service at the Cathedral has achieved wide acclaim. Music scholarships to Independent senior schools are gained each year.

Art plays an important part in the curriculum also, with boys receiving tuition throughout the school.

The well-equipped performance space further enhances drama productions.

Games are association football, rugby, cricket, athletics, swimming, basketball, hockey and badminton. There is a school field, gym and astroturf. A brand new, purpose-built Sports Hall opened in September 2016, and a bespoke performance space for drama and music.

Regular school visits are undertaken to local places of interest. School parties also go abroad, e.g. for skiing, watersports, football and on cultural visits.

The Pre-Preparatory department (for boys aged 3–7 and including a Nursery unit) is housed in a separate building, but shares many of the facilities of the main Prep School.

There is an active and very supportive Parents' Association.

Charitable status. Royal Grammar School Guildford is Registered Charity, number 1177353, and a Company Limited by Guarantee, incorporated in England and Wales, Company number 10874615. Registered Office High Street, Guildford, Surrey, GU1 3BB.

RGS Springfield

Britannia Square, Worcester WR1 3DL
Tel: 01905 24999
email: springfield@rgsw.org.uk
website: www.rgsw.org.uk
X/Twitter: @RGSSpringfield
Facebook: @RGS-Springfield

Chair of Governors: Mr Quentin Poole

***Headmistress*: Mrs L Brown**, BA Hons, PGCE

Age Range. 2–11 Co-educational.

Number of Pupils. 111.

Fees per term (2023–2024). £3,330–£5,370 including lunch and wraparound care.

Introduction from the Headmistress. 'I am delighted to have this opportunity to welcome you to RGS Springfield, with its wonderful family atmosphere and nurturing co-educational environment, which together creates a uniquely friendly school.

Our aim is to ensure that children develop their full potential academically, socially and emotionally in a safe, caring environment.

All our pupils benefit from individual care, small class sizes, professional and dedicated teaching; all of which help children become confident, secure and considerate of the needs of others.

The school has scored highly in recent inspections, rated as consistently excellent in all areas by ISI inspectors in 2022. There are a wealth of academic and extra-curricular opportunities to provide children with an enriching and stimulating environment, preparing them for the challenges of the 21st century, underpinned by traditional family values. The digital learning programme adds a new dimension to classroom learning with all teachers trained as Apple teachers and Showbie educators. The family of RGS schools is recognised internationally as an "Apple Distinguished School" for the third time running.

The school has wonderful grounds, which allow pupils to play outside in all weathers, learn from the natural environment and take part in all the fun that Forest School offers; wellies are very much encouraged!

The school, tucked away within the beautiful Georgian Britannia Square in the heart of Worcester, will provide a safe and happy place for your child to grow and develop. This website conveys only some of the ethos and spirit of RGS Springfield. Please visit us and see for yourself the happy, smiling faces of children having fun and learning in a stimulating environment. We are very much a happy family with Bumble our school dog as a much loved part of school life.

I look forward to welcoming you in person to our school.'

Overview. RGS Springfield is the co-educational junior school for RGS Worcester (*see HMC entry*). The school educates children between the ages of 2 and 11 and is situated within a large, beautiful Georgian Town House and gardens in the centre of Worcester.

High academic standards are expected as the children are prepared to enter RGS Worcester at 11. There is a wide range of extra-curricular activities on offer and, while the school is noted for academic, creative and sporting excellence, it is of the greatest importance that the children are encouraged to be kind, considerate and well-mannered.

In 2009 an extensive refurbishment was undertaken to restore and develop the original historic site, Springfield, providing excellent modern facilities including art, design technology, science and ICT rooms alongside large, airy and warm well-equipped classrooms.

The school is set in two acres of maintained grounds, unique for a city centre location, and offers fantastic games facilities and outdoor space, including an extended Forest School, Walled Garden and Paddock Play Area. We can use senior school facilities very easily such as a full-sized astroturf, science labs, textile rooms and gym/dance studios as we are located over the road from RGS Worcester.

Charitable status. The Royal Grammar School Worcester is a Registered Charity, number 1120644.

RGS The Grange

Grange Lane, Claines, Worcester WR3 7RR
Tel: 01905 451205
email: grange@rgsw.org.uk
website: www.rgsw.org.uk/the-grange
X/Twitter: @rgsthegrange
Facebook: @RGS-The-Grange
Instagram: @rgsthegrange

Chairman of Governors: Mr Quentin Poole

***Headmaster*: G W Hughes**, BEd Hons

Age range. 2–11 Co-educational.

Number of pupils. 376.

Fees per term (2023–2024). £3,330–£5,370 including lunch and wraparound care from 7.45 am–6.00 pm.

Introduction from the Headmaster. 'Welcome to a nurturing school with a big personality.

Giving a child the best possible foundations for a bright future is a true privilege. Our fantastic facilities give pupils tremendous scope for achieving the academic, sporting and creative excellence that we encourage. Just as important is the safe, secure and caring framework that we provide, giving children the support and self-belief they need to make their own individual strides forward.

I get huge satisfaction from seeing each one cross barriers and shine in a way that is uniquely theirs and with two children myself, I know the pride parents feel when they see their child thriving.

I look forward to helping your child thrive too.'

Overview. RGS The Grange is one of two co-educational junior schools for RGS Worcester (*see HMC entry*). The school educates children between the ages of 2 and 11 and is situated in open countryside three miles north of Worcester in Claines.

High academic standards are expected as the children are prepared to enter RGS Worcester at 11. There is a wide range of extracurricular activities on offer and, while the school is noted for academic, creative and sporting excellence, it is of the greatest importance that the children are encouraged to be kind, considerate and well mannered.

The school has scored highly in recent inspections, being acknowledged as 'Outstanding' and 'Excellent' in all areas by ISI inspectors. The Digital Learning Programme adds a new dimension to classroom learning across all four RGS schools and RGS The Grange is a leading school of excellence for digital innovation.

RGS The Grange provides excellent modern facilities including specialist art, design technology, science, food technology, French and Computing & IT rooms alongside large, airy, well-equipped classrooms.

The school is set in 50 acres of grounds and offers exceptional games facilities and outdoor space, including a full-sized floodlit Astroturf, cricket pavilion, Forest School, traverse wall and adventure play area.

Charitable status. The Royal Grammar School Worcester is a Registered Charity, number 1120644.

The Richard Pate School

Southern Road, Leckhampton, Cheltenham, Glos GL53 9RP
Tel: 01242 522086
email: hm@richardpate.co.uk
website: www.richardpate.co.uk
Facebook: @RichardPateSchool
Instagram: @richardpate_school

Chairman of Trustees: Mrs Jane Williams

***Headmaster*: Mr R A MacDonald**, MEd, BA

Deputy Heads:
Mr P Lowe
Mrs J Miller-Howell

Age Range. 3–11 Co-educational.

Number of Pupils. 290 (approximately an equal number of boys and girls).

Fees per term (2023–2024). Nursery: £1,487 (5 mornings), £1,884 (any 3 full days), £3,140 (5 full days). Preparatory: £3,189 (Reception), £3,388 (Year 1), £3,607 (Year 2). Junior: £3,956 (Year 3), £4,131 (Year 4), £4,393 (Year 5), £4,587 (Year 6).

Hot lunches are provided and included in the fees, except for 'mornings only' nursery.

The School, occupying an 11½ acre semi-rural site at the foot of the Cotswold escarpment, is part of the Pate's Grammar School Foundation which is a charity founded by Richard Pate, a Recorder of Gloucester, in 1574.

It is a non-denominational Christian school which in its present form began in 1946. The aim of the school is to provide a high academic standard and continuity of education up to the age of 11 years. The curriculum is broadly based with strong emphasis being attached to music, art, drama and sport, for these activities are seen as vital if a child's full potential is to be realised.

Facilities include a music centre with individual practice rooms; a fully equipped computer suite; an all-weather astroturf with floodlights and a woodland area with enclosed pond for environmental studies. There is also a specialist wing with science labs, language suite and art studio. After-school care is available through until 5.30 pm.

At present the School is divided into three sections: Nursery 3–4 years; Preparatory Department 4–7 and Junior 7–11. Entrance is dependent upon the availability of places but most pupils join the school at the commencement of the Nursery, Preparatory or Junior Departments.

No entry tests are taken by younger pupils but assessments are conducted for pupils who enter at Year 3 and beyond.

The teaching takes full account of national curriculum guidelines with children in the upper part of the school following the normal preparatory school curriculum leading to Common Entrance and Scholarship at 11+. Pupils leave at age 11 for local Grammar Schools and a variety of independent secondary schools, particularly, but not limited to, those in Cheltenham.

The Headmaster is assisted by two deputies and 22 fully qualified teachers including specialists in Latin, French, Art/Design, Science, Music and Learning Support. The School employs music and dance teachers, who prepare children for participation in various competitions, in particular the Cheltenham Festival and LAMDA exams.

Charitable status. The Richard Pate School is owned and operated by Pate's Grammar School Foundation which is a company limited by guarantee in England and Wales under Registration No. 14111232, and Registered Charity No. 1202002.

Richmond House School

170 Otley Road, Leeds, West Yorkshire LS16 5LG

Tel: 0113 2752670
email: enquiries@rhschool.org
website: www.rhschool.org
X/Twitter: @RHSchoolLeeds
Facebook: @RHSchoolLeeds
Instagram: @RHSchoolLeeds
LinkedIn: /richmond-house-school

Chair of the Board of Governors: Ms Catherine Shuttleworth

***Headteacher*: Mrs Sharon Young**

Age Range. 2–11.

Number of Day Pupils. 225 boys and girls.

Fees per term (2023–2024). Nursery: £2,330 (5 half days only), £3,643 (full time, including lunch), Reception to Year 6 £3,643, Lunches £260.

Rated 'Excellent in all areas' by ISI in its most recent full inspection, Richmond House School is an independent co-educational preparatory school providing an outstanding standard of education for children aged 2 to 11 years, within a happy, stimulating, family environment.

At Richmond House School, a team of dedicated staff are committed to giving each child the opportunity to develop into confident, hard-working and successful individuals, realising the school's mission of developing the unique potential of every child.

All pupils are given the chance to learn and achieve across a broad range of activities and subject areas, nurturing the talents of each individual child. The breadth of activities offered aims to challenge pupils, build self-confidence, and lead pupils to discover new interests and skills.

The school boasts outstanding 11+ exam success, with pupils having their choice of senior school, and a substantial number being awarded scholarships.

In addition to strong academic credentials, Richmond House School is committed to providing all pupils with the opportunity to excel in all areas. The school is situated in 10 acres of land, providing excellent sports facilities and a dedicated Outdoor Learning area. The school offers pupils a wide range of sports to participate in, as well as specialist teaching in Art, Design Technology, ICT, Languages, Outdoor Learning, Music and Science.

Pastoral Care and pupil well-being is an important aspect of life at Richmond House School. Our Headteacher designed and oversees the Pastoral and Wellbeing Programme, working closely with staff, including the SENDCo, to ensure the physical and emotional wellbeing of all pupils.

Excellent Pre and After School Care, a Holiday Club, and an easily accessible car park and drop-off zone are available for busy families.

Charitable status. Richmond House School is a Registered Charity, number 505630. It exists to provide high quality education for boys and girls aged 2–11 years.

Ripley Court School

Rose Lane, Ripley, Surrey GU23 6NE

Tel: 01483 225217
email: headmistress@ripleycourt.co.uk
website: www.ripleycourt.co.uk
X/Twitter: @RipleyCourtPrep
Facebook: @ripleycourtschool
Instagram: @ripleycourt
LinkedIn: @ripleycourtschool

Chair of Governors: R Mohindra

***Headteacher*: Ms A Clarke**

Age Range. 3–11 Co-educational.

Number of Pupils. Day: 105 Upper Court (Y3–Y6), 80 Little Court (R–Y2); Nursery and Transition (age 3+): 20.

Fees per term (2023–2024). Years 5–6: £5,680; Year 4: £5,380; Year 3: £5,250; Years 1–2: £4,190; Reception: £3,890; Nursery/Transition: £3,690 full-time (10 sessions) or £1,110 part-time (min. 3 sessions).

The main intakes are Nursery, Reception and Year 3. Scholarships are available from Year 3. Children may enter at other times if there is space. Children are thoroughly prepared for 11+ pre-testing and Common Entrance and Scholarship Examinations for a wide range of independent senior schools. There is a very high academic standard, and many Scholarships are won for academic performance as well as for sport, music and art.

Ripley Court School is renowned for its outstanding pastoral care and providing a warm and nurturing environment; children are encouraged to be themselves and grow into individuals able to explore their potential. The broad and balanced curriculum with subject specialist teaching, weekly enrichment programme and a wealth of extra-curricular activities, inspires children to reach their full potential and creates opportunities for independent learning, creativity, critical thinking and problem-solving skills.

In addition to the academic subjects, PE, Music, Art and Food Technology are a part of every child's timetable. Forest School sessions are also taught on-site from Nursery to Year 6. There are opportunities for all in orchestral, choral and dramatic productions – the school prides itself on ensuring every child can participate in all areas, including in competitive sports fixtures. The varied and enhanced curriculum, underpinned by our values of perseverance, aspiration, curiosity and kindness, further equips each individual to reach their full potential.

Facilities include a library, science laboratories, a gymnasium, computer suite, art, music and food tech rooms. There are banks of iPads to support learning. There are 19 acres of playing fields, on which Football (Association and Rugby), Hockey, Netball, Cricket, Tennis (2 hard, 2 grass courts), Athletics and Rounders are played in season. Swimming and Life Saving are taught in a large, covered, heated swimming pool.

Little Court uses all the facilities and much teaching expertise. The nursery, delivers specialist tuition in French, music, swimming and dance.

School transport serves Woking, Pyrford and West Byfleet.

Charitable status. Ripley Court School is part of The London Orphan Asylum (Reed's School), a Registered Charity, number 312008.

Rokeby School

George Road, Kingston upon Thames, Surrey KT2 7PB

Tel: 020 8942 2247
email: reception@rokeby.org.uk
website: www.rokebyschool.co.uk
X/Twitter: @RokebyPrep
Facebook: @rokebyprepschool

Maxim: *Smart, Skilful and Kind*

Chair of the Governors: Mrs Deirdre Davidson

***Headmaster*: Mr J R Peck**

Age Range. 4–13.

Number of Boys. 404.

Fees per term (2023–2024). £5,686–£7,081 (including lunch and morning snack, books, day trips and some residential trips, personal accident and dental insurance and all compulsory extras).

Rokeby has an outstanding record of success in Common Entrance and Scholarships to leading Independent Senior Schools. Boys are accepted at 4+ to the Pre-Prep and at 7+ to the Prep School.

In recent years a fabulous two-storey, energy-efficient new building was opened by HRH Princess Alexandra. It has six spacious classrooms, a multi-purpose Performing Arts Hall, as well as other lovely spaces built to house Reception, Year 1 and Year 2 boys. The spacious and exciting playground area is enjoyed by all year groups and includes an outside classroom, an adventure playground with balance wall and an area for gardening club to grow seeds and encourage wildlife.

Science is taught in three well-equipped Laboratories. There is a large Computer Room and a spacious Art and Design Technology Centre. Football, Rugby, and Cricket are played while other sports include Swimming, Athletics, Hockey and Basketball. There are two large Halls and an Astroturf. A full activities programme is available for boys from Chess Club to Golf. The Music Department provides Orchestra, Ensembles and four Choirs and there are fourteen visiting peripatetic teachers, who work within a sound-proofed music block.

Many educational school trips are arranged as well as trips overseas, including France, Italy, Iceland and a number of overseas sports tours, including India.

Charitable status. Rokeby Educational Trust Limited is a Registered Charity, number 312653. It exists to provide an excellent education for boys aged 4–13.

Rose Hill School

Coniston Avenue, Tunbridge Wells, Kent TN4 9SY

Tel: 01892 525591
email: admissions@rosehillschool.co.uk
website: www.rosehillschool.co.uk
X/Twitter: @rosehillschool
Facebook: @RoseHillSchool
Instagram: @rosehillschool
LinkedIn: /rose-hill-school

Chairman of Governing Body: Mr Nevil Phillips

***Head*: Ms E Neville**, BA Hons, MEd

Age range. 3–13.

Number of pupils. 250.

Fees per term (2023–2024). Kindergarten: £2,675–£3,195, Reception–Year 2: £4,585, Years 3–6: £6,165, Years 7–8: £3,035.

Rose Hill School is an inspiring place to learn: a warm, caring school with inspirational teachers, an enriching curriculum, first-class facilities and creative indoor and outdoor learning spaces.

A modern school rich with tradition, we offer a rare mix: academic excellence; sporting achievement; exceptional pastoral care; and the freedom to explore the creative arts. Set in 18 acres of grass and woodland, the school has countryside on its doorstep and yet the town centre is just five minutes away.

With 250 pupils, everyone knows each other well. All the faces in the corridor are familiar and every teacher knows every pupil. This friendly and supportive family atmosphere means that children feel happy and secure and provides them with the confidence to embrace new challenges and opportunities with gusto.

A wide spectrum of co-curricular activities, including music, art, sport, drama and design, makes it possible for every child to fulfil his or her potential, whilst the school supports and nurtures their emotional and academic growth – helping them develop the leadership skills that will play a vital part in their future lives.

Expectations are high and pupils are encouraged to make the most of every day. Together, pupils, teachers and staff apply themselves with enormous energy to create a truly stimulating environment for learning.

Charitable status. Rose Hill School is a Registered Charity, number 270158. It aims to provide a high-quality education to boys and girls aged 3–13.

Rosemead Preparatory School and Nursery

70 Thurlow Park Road, West Dulwich, London SE21 8HZ

Tel: 020 8670 5865
email: admissions@rosemeadprepschool.org.uk
website: www.rosemeadprepschool.org.uk
X/Twitter: @RosemeadPrep
Facebook: @rosemeadprep
LinkedIn: /rosemeadprep

***Headmaster*: Mr Graeme McCafferty**, BEd Hons, MCCT, NPQH

Age Range. 2½–11.

Number of Pupils. Day: 144 Boys, 140 Girls.

Fees per term (2023–2024). £2,985–£5,606.

Our school aims are at the very core of everything we do. They are:

- To encourage confidence from a young age, preparing children for the next stages of their own brilliant futures
- To meet the intellectual, physical and emotional needs of each child and embrace excellence across the curriculum
- To create an inclusive, nurturing community that enables children to be creative, reflective and compassionate
- To inspire a thirst for learning, providing opportunities that extend far beyond our curriculum
- To work in close partnership with our parents and the wider community

Our motto, Inspiring Brilliant Futures, reflects our desire to develop a passion for learning that will enable children to aim high and achieve their goals. The school's success is evident in our pupils' enviable record of entry to leading senior schools locally in both the independent and maintained sectors.

Although we set the highest academic standards, we are committed to providing a well-rounded and inclusive education. With bursaries and Academic scholarships available from Year 3, we work hard to identify and nurture talents in, for example, sport, the arts or leadership and allow all children to thrive. Outstanding pastoral support and the school's unique status under the auspices of the Thurlow Educational Trust, of which every parent is a member, results in an exceptionally strong school community.

All religious denominations welcome.

Charitable status. Rosemead Preparatory School (The Thurlow Educational Trust) is a Registered Charity, number 1186165. It exists to provide a high standard of education in a happy, caring environment.

Rowan Preparatory School
United Learning

6 Fitzalan Road, Claygate, Esher, Surrey KT10 0LX

Tel: 01372 462627
email: school.office@rowanprepschool.co.uk
website: www.rowanprepschool.co.uk
X/Twitter: @Rowan_Prep
Facebook: @RowanPreparatorySchool
Instagram: @rowanpreparatoryschool
LinkedIn: /rowan-preparatory-school

With a solid foundation of family and community and a progressive curriculum, Rowan Preparatory School provides a nurturing and inspiring learning environment that encourages girls (aged 2–11) to have a strong sense of self, a life-long love of learning and confidence in themselves to reach for the stars.

We see the best in every girl, embracing their individuality and the unique contribution they each make to school life. All we ask is that they trust in us to take them on the exciting educational journey that our school has to offer. And that they are willing to listen, learn and embrace our school motto of 'I can, I can, I know I can'.

Chair of the Local Governing Body: Mrs Jo Marr

***Headmistress*: Mrs Sarah Raja**, BA Hons, MSc

Age Range. 2–11 (Pre-Preparatory age 2–7, Preparatory age 7–11).

Number of Pupils. 300 Day Girls.

Fees per term (2023–2024). Preschool (based on number of sessions attended), Reception: £4,505, Years 1 & 2: £5,168, Years 3 to 6: £5,978.

In 1936, Miss Katherine Millar was determined to breathe new life into the English educational system. She wished to create an environment that inspired a passion for learning. The doors of Rowan were opened wide to enable girls to develop a strong sense of self and establish lasting friendships. Three quarters of a century on, Katherine Millar's core values are firmly established in the school. Girls achieve personal excellence in a warm, family environment.

As our motto says '*Hic Feliciter Laboramus*'; here we work happily.

The school is located on two sites very close to each other in a leafy part of Claygate. Rowan Brae accommodates the Preschool and Pre-Prep and Rowan Hill, the Prep.

Upon entering the Brae you cannot fail to notice the warm, friendly and happy atmosphere. The stimulating learning environment, both indoors and outdoors, creates an inspiring and engaging place to learn. Outstanding lessons and excellent resources allow all pupils to thrive and reach their potential. Girls in Year 2 are fully prepared for the seamless transition and exciting challenges which lay ahead at the Hill.

Girls at the Hill develop a thirst for knowledge, an appreciation of all subject areas and a deeper understanding of how to analyse and apply information across different areas of learning and in everyday life. The varied creative and outdoor curriculum continues to stimulate and inspire in all subject areas of day-to-day learning. Dynamic and challenging lessons, adapted to suit the girls' needs ensure that they can truly achieve personal excellence. There is a superb ICT Suite, which was funded by the very supportive parents association, The Friends of Rowan, and well-equipped playgrounds and adventure walkways with a wooded area called The Spinney, which is held in great affection by the girls.

Girls are prepared for entry to a wide variety of senior independent day and boarding schools. There is an excellent record of 100% of girls moving on to a first-choice senior school with over 40 scholarships and awards being offered this year for academic, music, drama, sports or art.

Rowan offers a broad-based curriculum of work so that each pupil is able to develop her own talents and maximize her potential through an adventurous learning approach. The school welcomes visiting speakers and performers to enhance the curriculum. Day trips are also included in each term and the annual residential trips to Sayers Croft, The Isle of Wight, European ski resorts and France are both popular and highly educational in content. In addition, a wide variety of clubs are offered before and after school and at lunchtimes; they include drama, chess, art, science, foreign languages and a host of sports and musical activities. In addition, breakfast club and after-school prep clubs are available to support families.

Rowan has an outstanding Music Department, with all girls singing in a choir and playing the recorder. In addition, three-quarters of girls at the Hill play a further instrument. There are various ensembles, which the girls can also join in preparation for the orchestra. Girls at Rowan Brae are invited to play the violin or cello as part of the school's String Initiative during Year 1, a fantastic opportunity to learn about music and performance.

The school has excellent sporting opportunities and achievements. Girls have the chance to represent the school both locally and nationally for sports such as swimming, gymnastics, tennis and biathlon. Games are developed throughout the school with girls taking part in their first matches from Year 2.

Rowan is very proud of its art, providing stunning displays around both the Brae and the Hill expressing the girls' individuality and excellent capabilities.

With small classes on both sites and strong pastoral care it is Rowan's aim to provide the essential early grounding in a happy, stimulating and secure environment where every child's needs are catered for.

Prospective parents are encouraged to attend one of the Open Mornings held each term or to make an appointment to view the school during a normal working day. Admission in the Early Years is non-selective and early registration is advisable if a place in the Preschool is to be assured. Girls entering the school at 7+ will be invited to take part in a Discovery Day which takes place in November.

Assisted places are available and details may be obtained upon request from our Head of Admissions.

Charitable status. Rowan has a Local Governing Body that plays an active and supportive role in the school. Rowan is part of United Learning which is an educational trust controlled by a Board of Governors and chaired by Mr Richard Greenhalgh which comprises: UCST (a Company Limited by Guarantee, Registered in England, number 2780748, and a Registered Charity, number 1016538) and ULT (a Company Limited by Guarantee, Registered in England, number 4439859, and an Exempt Charity).

Royal Grammar School
Newcastle upon Tyne

Eskdale Terrace, Newcastle upon Tyne NE2 4DX

Tel: 0191 281 5711
email: communications@rgs.newcastle.sch.uk
website: www.rgs.newcastle.sch.uk
X/Twitter: @RGSNewcastle
Facebook: @newcastleroyalgrammarschool
Instagram: @rgs_newcastle
LinkedIn: /school/royal-grammar-school-newcastle

See full entry in the **HMC** section, on **p. 285**.

Royal High School Bath
GDST

Lansdown Road, Bath BA1 5SZ

Tel: 01225 313877
email: royalhigh@rhsb.gdst.net
website: www.royalhighbath.gdst.net
X/Twitter: @RoyalHighBath
Facebook: @TheRoyalHighSchoolBath
Instagram: @royalhighschoolbath
LinkedIn: /company/royal-high-school-bath

See full entry in the **GSA** section, on **p. 471**.

The Royal Masonic School for Girls – Nursery School and Prep School

Rickmansworth Park, Rickmansworth, Herts WD3 4HF

Tel: 01923 725337 (Cadogan House Prep School)
01923 725316 (Ruspini House Nursery School)
email: admissions@rmsforgirls.com
website: www.rmsforgirls.com
X/Twitter: @RMSforGirls
Facebook: @RMSforGirls
Instagram: @RMSforGirls
LinkedIn: /school/rmsforgirls

Chair of Governors: Mr Simon Staite

***Headteacher*: Mr Kevin Carson**, BA, MPhil Cantab, PGCE

***Head of Cadogan House Prep School*: Mrs Melanie Horn**, BA

***Head of Ruspini House Nursery School*: Mrs Vicky Greig**, BA

Age Range. Nursery School, Ruspini House: 2–4 (boys at 2+, girls only from 3+). Prep School, Cadogan House: Girls 4–11.

Number of Pupils. Nursery 54, Cadogan House 214.

Fees per term (2023–2024). Cadogan House: Boarders (Years 3–6) £9,095 (Full), £8,625 (Weekly); Day Pupils £4,530 (Reception), £4,760 (Years 1 and 2), £5,670 (Years 3–6). Ruspini House: £1,660–£4,764. Please visit our website for the range of flexible nursery fees.

Ruspini House is a small, friendly, caring community within the larger RMS family, guided by the same ethos. We understand that every child is unique and offer an individualised education to reflect this. Our curriculum draws inspiration from Montessori, Reggio Emilia and Forest School, and incorporates the latest research in child psychology and neuro-development. We are committed to learning through play, helping children to develop critical thinking, collaboration and communication skills.

Learning doesn't just take place in the classroom. We offer a wide range of co-curricular activities to ensure our children have broad horizons and happy minds.

Outdoor learning is a crucial part of an RMS pupil's wellbeing and development. In our spacious and inviting outdoor spaces, children explore, discover new passions and learn to take risks. Pupils participate in RMS Go, led by our experienced Forest School leader, they explore the wider campus and all it has to offer.

Cadogan House is the home of the RMS Prep for girls aged 4 to 11 years. Recognised as excellent in all areas, Cadogan House is a warm and vibrant community alive with the buzz of happy, enthusiastic, and motivated young learners, each of whom is valued as an individual.

The learning opportunities are exceptionally broad with outstanding teaching from both subject specialists and class teachers. Small class sizes ensure that teachers quickly get to know the pupils and focus on nurturing their individual talents and strengths to enable them to become well-rounded independent young people. In Pre-Prep, Reception to Year 2, English and Maths are taught each day as individual subject areas, whilst Science and Humanities are covered through cross-curricular work. In Years 3 to 6, girls study English, Mathematics, Science, Art, DT, French, Geography, History, Computing, Music, PE, PSHCE and Religious Studies, with several subjects taught by subject specialists.

Our wide and varied curriculum encourages excellence and empowers girls to reach their full potential. An array of themed days, visiting speakers and trips all help to bring classroom learning to life.

An abundance of opportunities exist for pupils beyond the classroom. From music, sports, drama, and the creative arts, there is space for every girl to hone their talents, develop new skills and to have plenty of fun with friends along the way. Being part of a through school gives us access to facilities that most prep schools could only dream of. We seek to foster a natural curiosity, enthusiasm and love of learning in every girl.

Year 6 pupils transfer seamlessly onto RMS Senior School, where they are guaranteed a place in Year 7.

Charitable status. The Royal Masonic School Limited is a Registered Charity, number 276784.

Royal Russell Junior School

Coombe Lane, Croydon, Surrey CR9 5BX

Tel: 020 8651 5884
email: juniorschool@royalrussell.co.uk
website: www.royalrussell.co.uk
X/Twitter: @Royal_Russell
@RRS_Sport
Facebook: @RoyalRussellSchool
Instagram: @royal_russell_school
LinkedIn: /royal-russell-school

Chair of Governors: Mr A Merriman

***Headmaster*: Mr John Evans**

Deputy Head (*Learning & Teaching*): Mrs Ruth Bannon
Deputy Head (*Pastoral*): Mrs Sarah Pain
Head of EYFS: Ms Tanya Mawanda
Assistant Head (*Operations*): Mrs Alys Netherway

Age range. 3–11.

Number of pupils. 195 Boys, 130 Girls.

Fees per term (2023–2024). Upper Juniors: £5,444 (Years 3–4), £5,665 (Years 5–6); Lower Juniors: £4,444 (Reception–Year 2), Nursery £2,668–£4,444.

The Junior School stands on a magnificent campus extending to over 110 acres, which it shares with Royal Russell Senior School (11–18 years). (See Royal Russell School entry in HMC section.) The school is well served by road, tram and rail links and is one of the few co-educational schools in the South London area.

Alongside the outstanding class teaching that takes place, the children in the Junior School benefit from the knowledge, guidance and expertise of specialist teachers in a large number of vital curriculum areas. These specialists are dedicated to progression and build authenticity into everyday learning. The school has a broad and deep curriculum which seeks to blend the highest standards of academic achievement with a wide range of co-curricular activities developing the whole child.

There are opportunities for all pupils to participate in football, netball, hockey, swimming, trampolining, gymnastics, cross-country and cricket as team sports alongside a PE and Health Related Fitness curriculum. There is an extensive fixture list of matches against other schools and Royal Russell regularly competes regionally and nationally, with significant success.

Artistic development extends to include full dramatic and musical productions, and many pupils learn musical instruments and achieve scholarships to Senior Schools. All forms of art, design and technology are entwined within our curriculum and benefit from our bespoke Art and Design workspace.

There are excellent teaching facilities with the latest interactive technology, which are complemented by Science Laboratories, Music and Art Rooms, Computer Suite, School Chapel and a Performing Arts Centre with a 200-seat Auditorium. For sport, the impressive facilities include a large Sports Hall, Gymnasium, floodlit all-weather pitch for hockey and tennis, multi-use games area, netball courts, 4 grass pitches for athletics, football and cricket and an indoor swimming pool. The Forest School is central to our Early Years and Lower Junior curriculum, and, at play time, children enjoy our adventure playground and huge estate.

The majority of the pupils join the school at 3 years into the Nursery, and transfer to the Senior School at 11+. Candidates for entry to the Lower Juniors and Early Years are assessed informally, while all other entrants sit assessments in English, Mathematics and Cognitive Ability appropriate to their ages. Prospective parents are very welcome to come and meet the Headmaster and to tour the school, by appointment.

Charitable status. Royal Russell School is a Registered Charity, number 271907. It exists solely to provide education to girls and boys

Ruckleigh School

17 Lode Lane, Solihull, West Midlands B91 2AB
Tel: 0121 705 2773
email: office@ruckleigh.co.uk
website: www.ruckleigh.co.uk

Headmaster: **Mr Dominic Rhys Smith**, MA Oxon

Age range. 3–11.
Number in School. Day: 120 Boys, 120 Girls.
Fees per term (2023–2024). £1,359–£3,897.

Ruckleigh is an independent day school offering education to boys and girls between the ages of 4 and 11, with a Nursery catering for children from the age of 3.

Although a high standard of work is expected this is related to the individual child, and the school is able to provide opportunities within a wide range of academic ability. Each child has every chance to develop his or her talents to the full, often resulting in achievements beyond initial expectations.

The comparatively small classes mean that every child is well known individually throughout the school, creating a friendly environment.

Pupils are guided into habits of clear thinking, self-reliance and courtesy. Sound practical judgement, sensitivity towards the needs of others, and a willingness to 'have a go' are the qualities that the school seeks to promote.

Rupert House School

90 Bell Street, Henley-on-Thames, Oxon RG9 2BN
Tel: 01491 574263
email: office@ruperthouse.oxon.sch.uk
website: www.ruperthouse.org
X/Twitter: @ruperthouse
Facebook: @RupertHouseSchooll
Instagram: @rupert_house_school
LinkedIn: /company/rupert-house-school

Chair of Governors: Mr C Lowe

***Head*: Mr N Armitage**, BA Hons University of East Anglia, PGCE Cambridge University

Age Range. Girls and Boys 3–11.
Number of Pupils. 206.
Fees per term (2023–2024). £4,033–£5,571.

At Rupert House, we welcome boys and girls aged 3 to 11 into our happy and high-achieving school. In September 2020 the school became fully co-ed – enabling both boys and girls to stay for the duration of their primary education from Nursery through to Year 6. Since making this move, Rupert House has seen pupil numbers rise 29 per cent.

From the moment a child enters our care, they are encouraged to adopt a Growth Mindset, enabling them to believe that their skills and abilities are not set in stone. Setbacks are re-framed as hurdles to overcome, and the children are encouraged and rewarded for stepping out of their comfort zone in their learning and for their willingness to embrace challenge. Our small class sizes enable us to focus on each child as an individual, helping them to climb their own ladder to success – whatever their goal may be!

Academic and co-curricular success at Rupert House goes from strength to strength, as we prepare pupils for entry to senior school at both 11+ and 13+. Once again, our Year 6 pupils this year all obtained places at their first-choice senior schools, with a total of 7 scholarships and awards won by the cohort of 22 children in Academic, Performing Arts, Sport and Art categories, and considerable success in the 11+ Grammar School assessments and the ISEB Pretest exams.

Our location, in the heart of Henley-on-Thames, enables Rupert House to provide a whole host of opportunities for our pupils. We have our own newly revamped onsite forest school and playing fields, as well as an all-weather pitch, tennis and netball courts. Our close links with Henley Cricket, Rugby, Tennis and Rowing Clubs and Henley Leisure Centre, mean that our pupils have access to expert coaching and fantastic facilities on a regular basis, both during sports lessons and after-school clubs. Children in Year 3 to 6 play regular sports fixtures against nearby prep schools, and have the opportunity to experience a variety of river sports including rowing, paddleboarding, kayaking and bell-boating. In addition to this, the Town Hall and The Kenton Theatre are just a short walk away and are professional settings in which pupils are regularly given the opportunity to display their skills in music and the performing arts.

There are over 50 extra-curricular activities to choose from at Rupert House, including cricket, golf, rugby, tennis, ballet, breakdancing, cross-country, orchestra, design technology, animation, paddle-boarding, robotics, rowing and drama. We offer wraparound care from 7.30am to 5pm and have a number of minibus routes in order to make sure Rupert House is accessible to everyone.

Charitable status. Rupert House School is a Registered Charity, number 309648. It exists to provide quality education for boys and girls.

Russell House

Station Road, Otford, Sevenoaks, Kent TN14 5QU

Tel: 01959 522352
email: head@russellhouse.kent.sch.uk
website: www.russellhouseschool.co.uk
X/Twitter: @RussellHouseSch
Facebook: @RussellHouseSchool
Instagram: @russell_house_school

***Head*: Mr Craig McCarthy**

Age Range. Co-educational 2–11.
Number of Pupils. Approx. 200.

Fees per term (2023–2024). Russell Robins (Under 3s): £930 (for 2 mornings); Nursery: £1,485 (for 3 mornings); Transition: £2,550 (for 5 mornings). Extra sessions are available and charged separately. Reception: £4,400; Years 1–2: £4,865; Year 3: £5,100; Year 4: £5,425; Years 5–6: £5,590. Fees are inclusive of lunch.

Russell House is a family-friendly school for girls and boys aged from 2 to 11, with a warm, caring and inclusive atmosphere where every child has access to a myriad of opportunities for extra-curricular activities. Our size enables us to promise and deliver exceptional levels of personal care, ensuring each child is authentically treated as an individual throughout their time with us.

We have a reputation for achieving remarkable results across the board; from academic subjects to music, art, drama and sport. All our children leave at 11 and we have a well-established reputation for success in the Kent Test and other super-selective Grammar tests at 11+, and competitive entry to independent schools such as Sevenoaks, Caterham and King's Rochester. We have a consistently good record in gaining scholarships in academics, sport and music, which goes hand in hand with an ethos which encourages individuality, self-expression, curiosity to learn and the ability to challenge accepted wisdom.

The school is careful to cultivate a calm, happy atmosphere and there is also a strong emphasis on building skills for the future and developing a sensitive awareness of the world beyond the school. Russell House is idyllically set in the beautiful village of Otford, with sweeping views of the North Downs.

Ryde School with Upper Chine (Nursery, Pre-Prep and Prep)

Queen's Road, Ryde, Isle of Wight PO33 3BE

Tel: 01983 612901
email: prep.office@rydeschool.net
website: www.rydeschool.org.uk
X/Twitter: @RydeSchool
Facebook: @RydeSchool
Instagram: @rydeschoolprep

Chairman of the Board of Governors: Christoph Lees, MB BS, BSc, MD

***Head of Prep*: Mr E Marsden**, BSc
***Head of Pre-Prep*: Mrs E Willetts**, BA

Age Range. 2–11.

Fees per term (from September 2023). Tuition: Foundation Stage – please see School website; Pre-Prep £3,128–£4,415. Prep School £5,358, Boarding (excluding tuition) £6,741, (full) £5,408 (weekly). Rates for payment by Direct Debit. Lunch included.

Scholarships may be awarded on merit to external or internal candidates for entry at 11+. Scholarships open up bursaries which are means tested.

The Prep School at Ryde, is an independent Coeducational Nursery, Pre-Prep & Prep, providing an ambitious, happy and supportive environment, one in which children thrive and develop a lifelong love of learning. Children aged 2–11 years benefit from a varied and relevant programme of study, supplemented by enriching extracurricular activities, as we seek to prepare our pupils for an exciting future in an ever-changing world.

Westhill Nursery, is a beautifully restored Victorian villa in the grounds of Ryde School, run by a fully qualified team in a nurturing social environment that operates a year round provision, 8.00 am – 6.00 pm, 47 weeks a year. Fiveways, in its own separate building, is home to the Pre-Prep, whilst Prep sits on the main school site. Through creative and imaginative teaching in purpose-built classrooms, a sound foundation of key skills is established from Nursery to Year 6. Pupils receive the support of a well-qualified and dedicated staff, enjoying a full range of specialist facilities including a continually upgraded IT facility, with Internet access across the school, the new HIVE creative centre, including the Lego studio, Science Laboratory, Music room and Theatre.

A broad, balanced and rich curriculum is followed. Pupils have the unique opportunity to study and develop a love of languages from an early age. As the original host school for the Isle of Wight Literary Festival

Schools' programme, our children benefit from the thrill of visiting authors, poets and script writers. Pupils are encouraged to develop their full range of talents. In Music they are able to compose and perform, with all Pupils in Year 4 learning an instrument for free. Many pupils undertake individual instrumental lessons. There are choirs, music groups and an orchestra. As well as weekly classroom drama lessons, we enter children into LAMDA examinations and they take part in shows and festivals across the Island. Art and Design Technology are taught as discrete subjects and clubs, competitions and exhibitions also allow the children to develop their talents. Sports teams start at U8 level and we compete successfully against Island and mainland prep schools in netball, hockey, rugby, football, athletics (indoor and outdoor), cricket, rounders and cross country. Every child has the opportunity to sail by the end of Year 6 and swimming and tennis also make up part of our extensive sports programme. Our new outdoor education programme and outdoor classroom provides an inspirational environment for the children to learn, grow and develop. There is a full and wide-ranging programme of clubs and activities (which changes each term) during lunchtime and after school, offering something for everyone.

The Senior School is on the same campus, enabling Prep School pupils to benefit from the use of the Sports Hall and pitches. Careful liaison between the staff and induction days in the Summer Term ensure a smooth transition for pupils to the Senior School (see entry in the HMC section for Ryde School with Upper Chine).

The Prep School takes flexi, weekly and full boarders from Year 6. The boarding community is run with an emphasis on family values and boarders enjoy a large range of extra curricular activities. Prep pupils board in a newly renovated Victorian Villa called Millfield; opened in 2020 within the school grounds, pupils enjoy twin and triple rooms, most with en-suite facilities.

Charitable status. Ryde School with Upper Chine is a Registered Charity, number 307409. The aims and objectives of the Charity are the education of boys and girls.

Rydes Hill Preparatory School

Rydes Hill House, Aldershot Road, Guildford, Surrey GU2 8BP

Tel: 01483 563160
email: admissions@rydeshill.com
website: www.rydeshill.com
X/Twitter: @rydeshillprep
Facebook: @RydesHill

Chairman of the Governors: Mrs Katie Cardona

***Headmistress*: Mrs Sarah Norville**

Age Range. Girls 3–11, Boys 3–7. Pre-school Nursery for children 3–4.

Number of Day Pupils. 145.

Fees per term (2023–2024). £3,165 (Reception)–£5,034 (Year 6) including lunch.

Nursery. Term-time and all-year-round places are offered with flexible hours from 7.30 am to 6 pm

Rydes Hill is a Catholic Prep School educating girls from 3 to 11 and boys from 3 to 7. As a non-selective, one-form entry school, they are blessed with small class sizes in bright airy rooms, set in beautiful grounds in the Guildford suburbs. Rydes Hill is open to families of all faiths and beliefs and they are immensely proud of the deep bonds that unite their close-knit community.

The parents at Rydes Hill often coin a phrase that the School is 'small but mighty' as their achievements reach far beyond their small stature. Indeed, it is their small size that enables the teachers to have a genuine understanding of what makes every child tick, which, in turn, informs the individualised learning paths. Far from expecting the children to march to the beat of the same drum, Rydes Hill empowers the children to embrace their unique passions and talents and stay true to themselves. This is reflected in the breadth of scholarships awarded, with the 2022 leavers receiving 10 scholarships from academic to drama, music, art and sport.

Rydes Hill emboldens their children to find their voice and public speaking is gently encouraged at every opportunity. All 210 children who sat Speech and Drama exams during the course of the last three years were awarded a distinction. Witnessing shy or timid children transform into confident orators through their Rydes Hill journey is one of the School's greatest sources of pride.

The School's 'small but mighty' spirit is evident on the sporting field where Rydes Hill frequently out-competes prestigious independent schools triple or quadruple their size. Rydes Hill recently reached the IAPS National Championships in both Netball and Swimming spurred on by the collective roar from their supporters!

The undoubted heartbeat and driving force of Rydes Hill is the Headmistress, Mrs Norville who can be summed up in the words of one of the parents:

"By far and away the real understated (but somewhat self-effacing) gem at Rydes Hill is Mrs Norville. She is wonderfully passionate about what she does, she seems to emanate contagious energy, she is kind, she has good humour, and she has a profoundly holistic approach to the development of every single child at Rydes Hill. The School, under the leadership of Mrs Norville, is nothing short of magnificent."

Rydes Hill were selected as a finalist in the Small Independent School of the Year in 2022 and ranked 22nd in the Top Independent Preparatory Schools in the Sunday Times Parent Power 2021, placing the School amongst the academically elite. Whilst they wear these accolades as a badge of pride, they know the real secret to their success is far from being elite. Their doors are open to all, they celebrate difference and they have both feet firmly planted on the ground.

Charitable status. Rydes Hill Preparatory School and Nursery is a Registered Charity, number 299411.

St Andrew's Prep

Meads, Eastbourne, East Sussex BN20 7RP
Tel: 01323 733203
email: admissions@standrewsprep.co.uk
website: www.standrewsprep.co.uk
Facebook: @StAndrewsprepEB
Instagram: @standrewsprep_eastbourne
LinkedIn: /st-andrew-s-prep

Chairman of the Governing Body: Mr P A J Broadley

***Head*: Mr Tom Gregory**

Age range. 9 months–13 years.

Number of pupils. 239 (Prep School), 104 (Pre-Prep and Nursery).

Fees per term (2023–2024). Full boarding: £10,305; Weekly Boarding: £9,070; Flexible boarding: supplements from £29 per night. Day children: £7,250 (Years 7–8), £7,100 (Years 5–6), £6,600 (Year 4), £6,000 (Year 3); Pre-Prep: £4,100.

Nursery sessions: We offer the EYEE grant and sessions start from £33.10 for 3- to 4-year-olds claiming the EYEE grant. For 2- to 3-year-olds, sessions start from £48.50. For babies aged 9 to 24 months, sessions start from £51.00. Sessions run from 8.00 am to 1.00 pm, 1.00 pm to 6.00 pm, 8.00 am to 4.00 pm and 8.00 am to 6.00 pm. Please contact the Registrar for more details.

St Andrew's is positioned within 12 acres of beautifully tended grounds at the foot of the South Downs and is just a five-minute walk to the beach. The school, founded in 1877, has a highly qualified teaching staff and children are taught in classes with a maximum size of 20 and an average number of approximately 16. A number of children in the Prep department are boarders and the school operates a popular scheme of flexi boarding allowing day children to stay any number of nights during the week on a flexible basis.

The Head is supported by the Deputy Head and a strong management team. All children in the school have a Form Teacher or Form Tutor who is responsible for their pastoral welfare and academic progress. Each section of the school has its own Head (Nursery and Pre-Prep, Junior, Middle and Senior) who coordinates, together with the Deputy Head and Pastoral Heads, the overall pastoral and academic work of the staff.

In addition to the expanse of playing fields, St Andrew's benefits from its newly refurbished netball and tennis courts and a new state-of-the-art sports hall and dance studio, which was opened by Baroness Tanni Grey-Thompson in September 2016, to provide excellent sporting provision for its pupils. During summer 2018, the boarding house was also refurbished together with the Pavilion which now forms a superb space for hosting events and presentations as well as a Senior Common room for pupils in Years 7 and 8.

There are three computer/iPad suites equipped with up-to-date software and hardware including a wireless network connection. There is an interactive whiteboard in every classroom. The equipment in the Pre-Prep suite is designed specifically for children from 3 to 7 years of age.

Other facilities include a modern purpose-built music block, an extensively equipped research and resource centre, a chapel, a Woodland Classroom and a creative arts centre with an art studio and design and technology facilities. The school strongly encourages music and drama and more than three quarters of the children play instruments and participate in orchestras, bands and choirs.

As well as music, drama is a timetabled subject and plays take place every term.

From the age of nine, children are taught by subject specialists. French is taught from the age of 5 and Latin is introduced from the age of 9. Children are introduced to working on computers from the age of two. The breadth of the curriculum means that, while the requirements of the National Curriculum are fulfilled, the children are able to experience a variety of other stimulating activities.

Accelerated sets exist from Year 5 to provide more challenging opportunities for those who are academically gifted. Academic, art, drama, music, and sports awards have been achieved to many major senior schools and, over the past five years, almost 140 scholarships have been won by St Andrew's pupils. The charity running St Andrew's Prep amalgamated with Eastbourne College in 2010 and the two schools are part of the Eastbourne College Incorporated Charity. The school benefits from the use of College facilities including an indoor touch pad swimming pool, astroturf pitches, a contemporary performing arts centre and specialist staff. Approximately 65–70% of St Andrew's Prep leavers each year progress to Eastbourne College. However, it should be noted that although the schools are inter-dependent, they are also independent of each other and the Headmaster of St Andrew's advises on any number of other schools too, as appropriate to each individual.

There is a wide range of activities on offer. The extracurricular programme, which runs for children in Years 5 to 8, offers opportunities for all children to develop areas of interest and strength or to discover new ones. Each activity offered has its own educational objectives and challenges designed to improve children's skills and broaden their horizons. Optional Saturday morning activities for Years 4 to 8 pupils are also very popular. An extensive programme of after-school activities has always been a strong feature of St Andrew's. This starts at the Pre-Prep and runs through to Year 8.

The school's strong sporting reputation manifests itself in national honours regularly achieved in many different sports. Specialist coaches are employed to teach the skills required for all to enjoy participating in team games and opportunities are available to anyone wishing to represent the school.

Charitable status. Eastbourne College Incorporated is a Registered Charity, number 307071. The aim of the Charity is the promotion of Education.

St Andrew's School

Buckhold, Pangbourne, Reading, Berks RG8 8QA

Tel: 0118 974 4276
email: secretary@standrewsberkshire.co.uk
website: www.standrewsberkshire.co.uk

The School is an Educational Trust controlled by a Board of Governors.

Chair of the St Andrew's Committee: Mr A Nott

***Headmaster*: Mr Ed Graham**, MA Hons, QTS

Age range. 3–13. Flexi Boarding Years 3–8.

Number of pupils. 320.

Fees per term (2023–2024) Flexi Boarders: £45 per night, £140 per week (four nights). Day Pupils: £4,260–£7,310. Nursery from £2,130 (5 mornings).

The School is fully co-educational and set in over 54 acres of private wooded estate and parkland. Our vision is to nurture happy, grounded and kind children, who are stretched but not stressed, and who leave the School with a zest for learning and for life.

We avoid a one-size-fits-all approach to education by offering strong, personalised academic learning in small classes, alongside outstanding pastoral care, which is provided by our experienced and dedicated group of staff.

Children in Years 7 and 8 complete the PSB assessment, and the school's curriculum includes all the traditional subjects, with an emphasis on Music, Sport, Speech and Drama and Modern Languages. Senior School preparation and Study Skills are an important part of the senior pupils' timetable and Information Technology is well resourced.

Academic and Sporting standards are high and there is a state-of-the-art Sports Centre with a 25 m indoor swimming pool and a full-size Astro pitch.

Charitable status. St Andrew's School, part of The Bradfield Group, is a Registered Charity, number 309089. It exists to provide education for boys and girls.

S. Anselm's

Stanedge Road, Bakewell, Derbyshire DE45 1DP

Tel: 01629 812734
email: admissions@anselms.co.uk
website: www.sanselms.co.uk
Facebook: @s.anselms
Instagram: @sanselmsschool

Tatler Prep School of the Year 2021

Chairman of Governors: Mr Paul Houghton, BSc FCA

***Headteacher*: Mrs L Donnelly**, BEd Hons

Age Range. 3–13.

Numbers. 145 (83 boys, 62 girls).

Fees per term (2023–2024). Boarders: £9,840 (weekly), International £12,500 Day: Prep £6,450–£7,815; Pre-Prep £4,135–£4,700.

Welcome to S. Anselm's School, the only independent co-educational prep school in Derbyshire. Situated in the heart of the glorious Peak District it offers outstanding academic, sporting and extra-curricular opportunities to all pupils. We actively welcome children of all abilities to the school and pride ourselves on cherishing each individual child and allowing their full potential to shine through.

S. Anselm's sits on the crest of a hill in the heart of the Peak National Park – a beacon of excellence in all it does. All parents seek an environment where their children can remain children for as long as possible. Here at S. Anselm's it is just so. Through everything we do this ethos remains steadfast. We are proud of our tradition and are not ashamed to say that the values we hold dear are the very reason this school is quite unique.

With an 18-acre campus in the Peak District the children are surrounded by beauty and opportunities to explore. We have 5 netball courts, an indoor swimming pool, a recently renovated sports hall, a theatre with a permanent stage, a dedicated music block, 3 fully equipped science laboratories, 2 art rooms, Innovation Centre, engineering lab and library. The school is forward looking in its approach to IT having invested heavily in it over the last 2 years with iPads for learning, fully interactive whiteboards and Wi-Fi throughout the school.

The boarders enjoy a varied programme of activities including the debating club and fiercely fought tournaments of dodgeball. Those who learn music practise for 20 minutes every evening and cocoa and toast every night give a homely feel to bedtime.

Here our pupils are encouraged to be themselves; they are genuinely excited about learning and have a real thirst for knowledge. They thrive in the music and art rooms, and on the games field and stage. Pupils adore this school and are justly proud of all they do. They love learning and there is a true sense of fun.

Our small class sizes mean our staff can plan their teaching to ensure every pupil is treated as an individual. Each child is cared for and nurtured in every way they need. Our teaching staff simply want the very best for all our pupils and will do all they can to help them achieve their own personal best.

At the very centre of our values is creativity – whether through the individual or the community. It is creativity in thought and every aspect of life that sets a S. Anselm's pupil apart from others. We encourage our children to be creative in their thinking and their play and strongly believe in the importance of nurturing an environment where they can fully and confidently explore their individuality. This is a kind, caring and tolerant school and we are quite sure this wonderful environment will make a lasting impression on all who visit.

Charitable status. S. Anselm's School is part of the Birkdale family of schools, registered charity number 1018973. It exists to provide an excellent all-round education for boys and girls.

St Anthony's School for Boys
Alpha Plus Group

90 Fitzjohn's Avenue, Hampstead, London NW3 6NP

Tel: 020 7435 3597 (Junior House)
020 7431 1066 (Admissions)
email: PAHead@stanthonysprep.co.uk
website: www.stanthonysprep.org.uk
Facebook: @stanthonysprep
Instagram: @stanthonysprep

***Headmaster*: Richard Berlie**, MA Cantab

Age Range. 2.5–4 years (Nursery); 4–7 years (Junior House); 7–13 years (Senior House).

Number of Boys. 272 Day Boys.

Fees per term (2023–2024). Nursery: £3,220 for 5 half days or £5,520 for 3, 4 or 5 full days; Junior House: £7,555 including lunches; Senior House: £7,795 including lunches.

Founded in the 19th century and now set in the heart of Hampstead village, St Anthony's is an academically selective IAPS co-educational nursery and preparatory school for boys between the ages of 2.5 – 4 years and 4 – 13 years respectively. It is Roman Catholic, but welcomes boys of all faiths and cultures. Boys transfer at both 11+ and at 13+, via scholarship or CE, to leading independent senior schools (both day and boarding) with transfers to Westminster, University College School, Habs, St Paul's, Highgate, Eton, Harrow, Bedford, Dulwich and Oundle topping the list, amidst many other top UK schools. A number of boys also transfer to leading state Catholic schools. It is part of the prestigious Inspired Education Group which is a leading group of premium schools across the world. The co-educational nursery opened in September 2023 and offers places to children from the age of 2½ to 4 years. Children feed directly into the prep school via an assessment at 4+ and the school provides an excellent education.

The boys' school is housed in two large Victorian buildings situated in close proximity to each other. Both have their own grounds and separate playgrounds. There are six forms in the Junior House, where boys range in age from four to eight, and eight forms in the Senior House, where boys range in age from eight to thirteen. The specialist Design and Technology room, Music Rooms, Dance & Drama Studios, Computer Suites, Science Laboratories and the swimming pool are all contained within the Senior House but are accessible by both the Juniors and the Seniors.

Religious Education follows the Catholic curriculum set by the Diocese of Westminster which includes learning about world religions. The subject also introduces boys to philosophical discussions on religion, beliefs and faiths of all cultures and communities. Mass is attended by the boys once per term.

St Anthony's aims to educate the whole person so that each individual child can fulfil their potential. We value growth in knowledge and virtue within a pastoral context. The school is focused on excellence in all its endeavours and tapping into the potential of every child.

The school curriculum is stimulating and challenging: for example, it is possible for boys to study five foreign languages. All pupils study French from Year 1; Latin and Greek are available from Year 6 and pupils can study Philosophy from Year 4 upwards. The arts have an important place in the school with a majority of boys learning to play a musical instrument and all boys involved in drama. Sport is a further strength of the school with many pupils achieving success on a national stage. The school has use of a superb local sports club at Brondesbury, with extensive facilities. It has recently introduced Computer Programming and Robotics courses which have been very successful. There has, in fact, been a significant increase in co-curricular provision recently which includes coding, public speaking and debating, karate, chess, table tennis, boxing, fencing and a host of others. Full details of co-curricular provision is available on the school's website. Children also take part in academic competitions such as the Primary and Junior Maths Challenges.

Furthermore, enhancing communication, we feel, has been key to academic success and the school now reports on progress in Maths, English and Science every six weeks by issuing Learning Snapshots. Full reports and parents' meetings have also been made more effective but the most important change has been to emphasise the role of the Form (or Class) Teacher as the main link between home and school. All teachers' email addresses are shared with parents who are encouraged to get in touch with any queries or concerns. The sooner a problem is raised and discussed the sooner a solution can be reached.

St Anthony's still retains its famous commitment to fostering individuality, with alumni such as David Suchet, Anthony Gormley and Bombay Bicycle Club underlining its notable commitment to the liberal arts. Recently, pupils have been awarded Music, Arts and Academic scholarships to many of the leading academically selective top-tier UK secondaries. Boys have also achieved Sports awards at several leading secondaries – all information can be found on our website.

The school works hard to instil in its pupils a sense of social responsibility and charity fundraising is a key feature of school life. It has a long tradition at the school and the boys raise thousands of pounds each year for the Catholic Children's Society, Mary's Meals, The Passage and the Cardinal Hume Centre (to name a few). A former pupil was awarded the Gusi Peace Prize (Asian equivalent of the Nobel).

St Anthony's Boys is maintaining a steady climb up the league tables and values being more of a greenhouse than a hot house. We believe that there is nothing mutually exclusive between being a kind school and delivering fantastic outcomes for the boys, whether that is academically or in sport or co-curricular activities, and the fantastic leavers' results bear witness to this. The school sets a high standard for its pupils within a context of a kind and caring community and boys flourish here on so many levels because they are happy.

St Aubyn's School

Bunces Lane, Woodford Green, Essex IG8 9DU
Tel: 020 8504 1577
email: school@staubyns.com
website: www.staubyns.com
X/Twitter: @st_aubyns
Facebook: @St-Aubyns-School
Instagram: @st_aubyns_school

The School was founded in 1884 and is governed by a Charitable Trust.

The school motto of 1884 still reflects the School's ethos and approach to teaching and learning today: *fortiter, fideliter, feliciter – bravely, faithfully, happily.*

Chairman of the Governors: Mr Michael Foster

***Headmaster*: Mr Louis Taylor**, BA Hons, PGCE

Deputy Heads:
Mrs Carol Porter, BA (acting)
Mr Marcus Shute, BEd Hons

Age range. 3–11.

Number of children. 500 Day.

Fees per term (2023–2024). £3,953 (Nursery) to £4,898 (Year 6) fully inclusive.

St Aubyn's provides an all-round preparatory education for pupils aged 3–11. The School is non-selective at its main point of entry for children aged 3. There are entry assessment tests for older children, principally at ages 4+ and 7+.

There are two departments within the School: Pre Prep (including EYFS) and Upper Prep and each has its own base and resources.

Classes are small, taught by well-qualified, dedicated staff. Nursery and Reception pupils are also supported by teaching assistants. Qualified nurses deal with all medical issues and emergencies.

The School offers a wide-ranging curriculum within a traditional framework, encompassing all National Curriculum requirements. French is introduced from Nursery onwards and Latin in Year 6. French, Music and PE are specialist-taught from an early age. All subjects are specialist-taught in Year 6. The Head of Music leads a thriving department with a School orchestra and various instrumental groups and choirs. Pupils are regularly involved in performances both within and outside the School. Sport is very important and games include football, cricket, hockey, rugby, netball, athletics and swimming, all coached to a high standard.

The School is pleasantly situated on the borders of Epping Forest, yet is close both to the North Circular and the M11. Facilities are extensive with 8 acres of grounds, a large sports centre, all-weather pitches, fully-equipped performing arts centre and music department, science laboratory, art, design and technology studio, library, dance and drama studio and two IT suites. The School expanded and upgraded its changing room facilities in the sports hall in 2018. Most recently, an extension to the performing arts centre and refurbishment of the Upper Prep facilities, the Reception classes and science laboratory were completed.

Pupils progress to a range of selective, independent and state schools at 11 and gain a range of scholarships. In 2023, a total of 32 awards were made and pupils were awarded academic scholarships as well as awards in music and sport.

St Aubyn's School is a registered charity and all income from fees is for the direct benefit of its pupils. There is a means-tested assisted places scheme at 7+.

Charitable status. St Aubyn's (Woodford Green) School Trust is a Registered Charity, number 270143. It exists to provide education for children.

St Benedict's Junior School

5 Montpelier Avenue, Ealing, London W5 2XP
Tel: 020 8862 2250
email: juniorschool@stbenedicts.org.uk
website: www.stbenedicts.org.uk
X/Twitter: @stbenedicts
Facebook: @StBenedictsSchool
Instagram: @stbenedictsschool
LinkedIn: /st-benedicts-school

Governing Body:
The Governing Board of St Benedict's School

***Headmaster*: Mr R G Simmons**, BA Hons, PGCE

Deputy Head: Mrs T Scott, BEd

Age range. 3–11 Co-educational.

Number of pupils. 308.

Fees per term (2023–2024). Nursery: £3,850–£5,789; Pre-Prep: £5,321; Junior School: £5,914.

St Benedict's is London's leading independent Catholic co-educational school, located in leafy Ealing. Within a caring, happy community, St Benedict's has strong academic standards. The Junior School and Nursery offers a holistic education for children aged 3 to 11, which continues through the Senior School and Sixth Form. St Benedict's, which welcomes children of other Christian denominations and faiths, is committed to supporting all children to develop their full potential.

Inspirational teaching and exceptional pastoral care are at the heart of the education we offer.

The Junior School and Nursery provide a supportive, friendly and vibrant co-educational environment in which to learn. In the Nursery a carefully-planned and child-centred programme enables and extends learning and development. The Junior School provides a broad and balanced curriculum based on a rigorous academic core. Sharing excellent facilities with the Senior School, and participating in a programme of cross-curricular activities, helps ease the transition at 11+ to the Senior School, which is on the same site.

There are extensive opportunities in music, art, sport and drama. St Benedict's has a proud sporting tradition, which promotes the highest sporting aspirations while encouraging everyone to enjoy sport, fitness and teamwork. Music is excellent, with several choirs (including the renowned Ealing Abbey Choir) and many instrumental ensembles. A wide range of co-curricular activities is offered, and an after-school club is available at the Junior School.

There has been huge investment in building and facilities at St Benedict's, providing our youngest pupils with a first-rate learning environment.

St Benedict's School is unique. Come and visit and see what we have to offer. You can be sure of a warm welcome.

Charitable status. St Benedict's School Ealing is a Registered Charity, number 1148512, and a Charitable Company Limited by Guarantee, registration number 8093330.

St Bernard's Preparatory School

Hawtrey Close, Slough, Berkshire SL1 1TB
Tel: 01753 521821
email: info@stbernardsprep.org
website: www.stbernardsprep.org
X/Twitter: @stbernardsprep
Facebook: @stbernardspreparatory
Instagram: @stbernardsprep

***Headteacher*: Mrs A Verma**, LLB Hons, NPQH, GTP

Acting Deputy Headteacher & Head of Early Years: Mrs M Biscardi, BA Hons
Assistant Headteacher: Mrs A Underwood, BEd Hons, MEd

Age Range. 2½–11 co-educational.
Number of Pupils. 218.
Fees per term (2023–2024). £3,690–£4,395.

St Bernard's Preparatory has a unique ethos. We are a Catholic school, teaching the Catholic faith and living out the Gospel values which are shared by all faiths and are the foundation of all our relationships and the daily life of our school. We welcome and embrace children of all faiths and we recognise and celebrate our similarities and differences, developing mutual respect, understanding and tolerance.

We recognise the value and uniqueness of each individual, both child and adult. We celebrate the talents and gifts of each child and enable them to develop to their full potential spiritually, morally, academically, socially and physically. Our children are happy, courteous, confident, articulate young citizens, committed to the ideal of service to others.

We work in partnership with parents, recognising that they are the first and best educators of their child. We consider ourselves to be very privileged that parents have entrusted us with the care and education of their child. We ensure that parents are kept fully informed of their child's progress.

We are committed to offering a broad, balanced, creative and challenging curriculum, enriched by experiences and opportunities which enhance and consolidate the learning process. Small class sizes enable our team of highly qualified, caring, committed and enthusiastic teachers to be responsive to the needs of the individual child ensuring continuity and progression for all our children. We have developed a wide and varied range of after-school activities which broaden the curriculum and enrich the children's lives. Children are encouraged to develop new skills.

We are proud of our reputation as a school with a strong ethos and nurturing pastoral care coupled with academic excellence reflected in consistently outstanding results in local and national tests.

Our school motto 'Dieu Mon Abri' meaning 'God is my Shelter', is an inspiring reminder of God's love for each one of us. The three swords represent 'Love, Work and Prayer' which underpin and permeate the life of our school.

St Catherine's School
Bramley

Station Road, Bramley, Guildford, Surrey GU5 0DF
Tel: 01483 893363
email: schooloffice@stcatherines.info
admissions@stcatherines.info
website: www.stcatherines.info
X/Twitter: @stcatsbramley
Facebook: @StCatherinesBramley
Instagram: @stcatsbramley

See full entry in the **GSA** section, on **p. 475**.

St Cedd's School

178a New London Road, Chelmsford, Essex CM2 0AR
Tel: 01245 392810
email: info@stcedds.org.uk
website: www.stcedds.org.uk

Chair of Governors: Mr G C Allen
***Head*: Mr M Clarke**, BEd Hons Cantab

Age Range. 3–11 Co-educational.
Number of Pupils. 400.
Fees per term (2023–2024). £3,490–£4,470 including educational visits, curriculum-linked extra-curricular activities, lunch and the majority of after-school clubs.

St Cedd's School, founded in 1931, is a leading co-educational day school and Pre-School for children aged 3 to 11. The grounds and facilities create a vibrant and purposeful learning environment where children are encouraged to become independent, confident and caring individuals. A St Cedd's School education focuses on high standards of literacy and numeracy within an expansive academically broad and balanced curriculum, supplemented by a superb programme of sport and an extraordinarily creative output of music and the performing arts. PE, Music, Art and MFL are taught by specialist teachers from Pre-School; Swimming and Recorders are introduced in Year 2 and International Studies in Years 5 and 6. Following the 11+ entry and Independent School Examinations, a baccalaureate-style curriculum in Year 6 leads to the HOLDFAST Award which celebrates the breadth of children's achievements and talents. Music is a particular strength of the school with outstanding individual instrumental examination results. St Cedd's School is a Choir Schools' Association School and a member of the Chelmsford Choral Foundation. This link to Chelmsford Cathedral provides the opportunity for our choirs to perform at Choral Evensong.

The grounded confidence the pupils have, as a result of excellent teaching and differentiated learning in a happy and supported environment, where children have fun and are encouraged to take risks, results in great personal achievements. Our children aspire to the highest levels of attainment and we boast a successful track record of outstanding results at entry to Grammar Schools and scholarships to Independent Senior Schools.

Breakfast is available from 7.30 am and there is an extensive array of after-school activities with wraparound care in our TLC provision until 6.00 pm.

Charitable status. St Cedd's School Educational Trust Limited is a Registered Charity, number 310865. It exists to provide education for girls and boys.

Saint Christina's RC Preparatory School

25 St Edmund's Terrace
St John's Wood, London NW8 7PY

Tel: 020 7722 8784
email: headteacherspa@saintchristinas.org.uk
website: www.saintchristinas.org.uk
X/Twitter: @saintchristinas
Facebook: @saintchristinas
Instagram: @saint.christinas.school

***Headteacher*: Mr Alastair Gloag**, BA

Age range. Girls and boys 3–11.

Number of pupils. 95 girls, 68 boys.

Fees per term (2023–2024). £5,750 (inclusive).

Saint Christina's was founded in 1949 by the Handmaids of the Sacred Heart of Jesus. Educating children in the Catholic tradition means being part of a warm, caring and compassionate community in which everyone is encouraged to think about others and care for our environment. A key feature of our Catholicism is the way in which we tend to each child's individual needs. At Saint Christina's we talk about 'stewardship'. For us this means that we hold your child in trust. It means taking each child by the hand and walking their path so that, in their time with us, they have the opportunity to become the very best that they can be.

Saint Christina's offers a contemporary curriculum, characterised by variety and innovation. We enjoy an enviable reputation for our STEM provision and Intellectual Curiosity Programme which has already provided opportunities for the children to launch their own space probe, build their own robots, code their own creations, and engineer, design and race their own mini-Formula 1 racing cars as part of the F1 in Schools programme.

Children at Saint Christina's approach all that they do with great enthusiasm. In sport, they are successful in their leagues; in music and drama they perform as soloists, and within ensembles, orchestras, musicals and choirs. They successfully combine impressive intellectual endeavour with passion and engagement well beyond the curriculum.

Boys and girls are prepared for entrance exams to day and boarding schools.

The School nestles in a quiet terrace at the foot of Primrose Hill and within a few minutes of Regent's Park. Prospective parents are warmly invited to visit the School.

Charitable status. Saint Christina's is a Registered Charity, number 221319.

St Christopher's Prep School, Hove

A Brighton College School

33 New Church Road, Hove, East Sussex BN3 4AD

Tel: 01273 735404
email: office@stchristophershove.org.uk
website: www.stchristophershove.org.uk
X/Twitter: @stchrishove
Facebook: @StChristophersPrep
Instagram: @stchrishove

Chairman of Governors: Mr A Underwood

***Head*: Ms E Lyle**, BSc, QTS

Age Range. 4–13 co-educational.

Number of Pupils. 284.

Fees per term (2023–2024). £3,456–£5,167.

Since its foundation in 1927, St Christopher's School has expanded to become a highly successful academic preparatory school, located in the middle of Brighton & Hove, England's youngest and most vibrant city.

St Christopher's School aims to provide a traditional academic education within a supportive family environment where individual talents are developed to produce confident, articulate and well-balanced children. Pupils regularly obtain top academic scholarships and awards for art, music, drama and sport. St Christopher's is a Brighton College school and many of its pupils go on to Brighton College.

Entry to the School is at 4+, however, places are occasionally available in other age groups. In the Pre-Prep, pupils are taught mainly by their form teachers. Particular emphasis is placed upon reading, writing and mathematics, but the curriculum is broad and a wide range of subjects is taught by specialist teachers, including French, Latin, Science, Music, Art, ICT, PE and Games.

Pupils move into the Middle School in Year 4, where the curriculum reflects the syllabuses of the Common Entrance and Brighton College Academic Scholarship Examinations. Formal homework is introduced at this stage. In the Upper School (Years 7 and 8), all subjects are taught by specialists, who make full use of the interactive ICT suite, music technology suite, science laboratory, art studio and library. A variety of educational day trips, an annual residential visit to France and sports trips ensure that children receive a broad and stimulating educational experience.

The boys achieve an enviable record of success in football, rugby and cricket and the girls match that success in hockey, netball and rounders. The musical life of St Christopher's is enriched by three choirs and the choice of a wide variety of instrumental and vocal tuition. All pupils are encouraged to perform on stage as part of a wide programme of drama and the development of confidence is a central aim of the school. A wide range of extra-curricular activities is on offer. After-school care is available until 5.30pm each evening.

The Head is always delighted to welcome prospective parents. Please contact the Registrar to arrange a visit.

Charitable status. St Christopher's Prep, Hove is a member of the Brighton College Family of Schools and is a Registered Charity, number 307061

St Columba's College Preparatory School

King Harry Lane, St Albans, Hertfordshire AL3 4AW

Tel: 01727 862616
email: prepadmin@stcolumbascollege.org
website: www.stcolumbascollege.org
Facebook: @StColumbasCollege
Instagram: @stcolumbascollege
LinkedIn: /school/stcolumbascollege

Acting Chair of Governors: Mrs Barbara Elliot, MA Cantab

***Head of Preparatory School*: Mr R McCann**, BA

Deputy Head of Prep: Mr K Boland, BA
Deputy Head of Prep & SENCo: Miss C Maton, BA

St Columba's College Prep School is a unique and happy place, with a strong reputation for academic achievement in a nurturing and supportive environment. The school strives to create a welcoming community in which each pupil is valued as an individual, and endeavours to promote positive relationships based on mutual respect and understanding. There is a rigorous academic curriculum with an extensive range of extra-curricular opportunities. A full curriculum and sports programme is offered at Key Stage 1 and 2.

Age range. 4–11.

Number of pupils. 200 Students.

Fees per term (2023–2024). Reception–Prep 2: £4,238: Prep 3: £4,998; Prep 4–6: £5,502. Fees include personal accident insurance. Additional charges are made for coaches and consumables.

Entry. Admission to the Lower Prep is by an informal assessment, where children spend an hour with our teaching staff. Admission to the Upper Prep is by age-appropriate Maths, English and Reasoning assessments, and a reference and the latest report will be sought from the child's school.

Examinations. Most pupils progress at 11+ to St Columba's College, on the same site. In their final year, most Preparatory School pupils are offered unconditional places at St Columba's College Senior School, following recommendations by Prep School staff.

Facilities. Academic facilities include: modern form rooms with specialist facilities for Science, IT, ADT, Music, PE, Games, RE and French, and a professionally staffed extensive library. Sports facilities include: MUGA pitches, cricket nets and square. A swimming pool and athletics track are adjacent to the site.

There are a number of scholarships available to Prep School pupils on entry to St Columba's College Senior School. These include academic and music scholarships. Candidates for the music scholarships should be established performers on one or more instruments, are likely to have reached Grade 4 or above (or the equivalent), and will have good musical skills.

(*See also St Columba's College entry in HMC section.*)

Charitable status. St Columba's College is a Registered Charity, number 1088480. It exists to provide a well-rounded Christian education for pupils from 4–18 years of age.

St Dunstan's College Junior School

Stanstead Road, London SE6 4TY

Tel: 020 8516 7225
email: jsoffice@stdunstans.org.uk
website: www.stdunstans.org.uk
X/Twitter: @StDunsJunior
Facebook: @StDunstansColl
Instagram: @stdunstansjunior
LinkedIn: /school/st-dunstans-college

Chairman of Governors: Mr Paul Durgan, BA, FCA

***Head of Junior School*: Miss Laura Whitwood**

Age Range. Co-educational 3–11.

Number of Pupils. Pre-Preparatory (Age 3–7) 140, Preparatory (Age 7–11) 240.

Fees per term (2023–2024). Nursery £5,337, Pre-Preparatory £5,387, Preparatory £5,487–£6,724. Fees include lunch.

We see that our ambitious, co-educational Junior School is the perfect starting point for pupils to make their first marks on their St Dunstan's shield as they begin their College adventure, learning who they are and discovering a true love of lifelong learning from the very earliest stages. Our academic ambition is cultivated by a balance of rigour, challenge, immersive real-life learning experiences and independent exploration.

Our pupils thrive from our forward-thinking and innovative approach to education, where they are well-prepared for the unexpected of tomorrow's world and ready to embrace any challenges that may come their way in the future. Pupils from Nursery to Year 6 are able to make excellent progress and achieve their academic potential in every area of our curriculum, whilst also reaping the benefits of the broad co-curricular programme available to them. The St Dunstan's curriculum is engaging, broad, balanced and unashamedly aspirational for each and every pupil, regardless of their starting point. We see that it equips them with the necessary skills they will need to thrive as proactive citizens within a rapidly changing world.

There is no better time to join St Dunstan's College Junior School. True to our forward-thinking and ambitious approach to education, we were absolutely delighted to move into our new building development in April 2021. Our new Junior School includes state-of-the-art, bright, modern and stimulating working environments, as well as dedicated specialist spaces for art, ICT, music and performance, along with a new library and Woodland Classroom. In addition, whether your child is in Nursery or Year 6, they will have their own dedicated outdoor learning space on each floor. Redesigned Junior School playing fields and two multi-use Games Areas will also ensure pupils have unrestricted access to age-appropriate, exceptional sporting facilities. With the new Junior School building as the first phase of a five-phase project, your child will reap the benefits of our first-class facilities from their very first day in school, through to their final day of Sixth Form.

Our pupils see that through learning, they gain a better sense of who they are, what they can achieve, and what they will be able to accomplish in the future. Learning at St Dunstan's does not just take place within our state-of-the-art classrooms; learning opportunities are embraced and appreciated in any setting, whether it is through our co-curricular 'Forder' Programme (with over 80 activities taking place each week), performing a production in our Great Hall or on the professional stage, by facing a fear on a residential visit, or playing a match to understand the benefits of teamwork and sportsmanship. Our pupils relish the learning for their own personal development and fulfilment.

We take pride in our broad and balanced curriculum which is taught by our highly-skilled teachers and provides children with the skills, knowledge and understanding they need to develop into curious, creative and courageous individuals. No day is ever the same at St Dunstan's and it is through our rich, exciting and vast selection of activities that we can focus on a holistic approach to education, in order that our pupils can thrive as well-rounded individuals, who feel happy and safe in school. They enjoy forming positive and trusting relationships with both their Form Teacher and specialist teachers in art, design technology, drama, music, ICT, swimming, PE, Modern Foreign Languages (Spanish in Pre-Prep and Spanish and French in Prep) and Stuart lessons (PSHE). As such, our pupils make rapid progress in every subject, and it is through exposure to a number of subject areas and enrichment opportunities that our pupils thrive. Our offering enables pupils to discover what sparks their interest, relishing new skills, but within a supportive environment, created by strong teacher/pupil relationships.

Boys and Girls are admitted at all ages from 3+ to 10+ but principally at 3+ and 4+ (Nursery and Reception) and at 7+ (Year 3). We also welcome applications for occasional place entry within the other Junior School year groups.

Charitable status. St Dunstan's Educational Foundation is a Registered Charity, number 312747. It exists to provide education for boys and girls.

St Edmund's Prep School

Old Hall Green, Ware, Hertfordshire SG11 1DS
Tel: 01920 824239
email: prep@stedmundscollege.org
website: www.stedmundscollege.org
X/Twitter: @stedmundsware
Facebook: @stedmundscollegeandprep
Instagram: @stedmundscollegeandprep

Chairman of Governors: Mr Paul Raynes, MA Cantab

***Head*: Mr S Cartwright**, BSc Hons Surrey

Deputy Head: Dr F J McLauchlan, MA, PhD Cantab
Assistant Head: Mr G Duddy, BEd Wales
Head of EYFS: Mrs V Penfold, BA London Metropolitan

Age Range. 3–11 Co-educational.

Number of Pupils. 195.

Fees per term (2023–2024). Day (inc. Lunch): £1,923–£5,629.

St Edmund's Prep, founded in 1874, is a co-educational, independent Catholic Nursery, Pre-Prep and Prep school, situated in beautiful surroundings of wood and parkland in Old Hall Green, easily accessible from the main thoroughfares of Hertfordshire. The school embraces family values to lay the foundation for a happy and successful life. Education is seen as a joint venture involving staff, parents and children.

When you arrive at the Prep you will experience a welcome from us all that invites you and your child to be part of a very special community.

Guided by the principles of our Catholic faith and acknowledging Christ as our leader and teacher, we strive for excellence and creativity in forward-thinking education. We commit ourselves to the preparation of our children by instilling in them a sense of responsibility and strive to ensure that they leave St Edmund's Prep with a solid foundation on which to build their future in the College and beyond.

Small class sizes allow focused attention to ensure that your child becomes a confident learner both inside and outside the classroom. Our facilities shared with the College and our committed teachers ensure our pupils have the experiences they need to develop fully in all aspects of their lives. With a heritage and ethos deeply rooted in the Catholic tradition, we welcome families from all faiths who will appreciate the all-round education that we offer.

The school has a broad, balanced curriculum and it seeks to cater for the individual child at the different stages of their development. The curriculum offered is intended to improve the learners' knowledge, introduce them to a wide range of educational experiences and develop skills needed to deal critically and creatively with the world.

For students who join in or before Year 4, there is the possibility to not sit the entrance examination for the College at 11+, thus offering straight-through entry.

The Prep is a proud holder of the Gold sports mark for Sport and the England Arts Council Silver award.

The Prep is committed to healthy living and we deliver this through daily home-cooked, well-balanced meals; fresh fruit is provided at break times and sport and activity for all is a priority.

Co-curricular is the norm in the Prep with a stimulating, fun range of activities run every day from chess club to junior cadets; from cookery in dedicated facilities to sport.

A breakfast and tea-time club is offered and a school bus service runs for children over 7 in Year 3.

We are fortunate to share facilities with St Edmund's College and as a result, the Prep children have an opportunity to use the floodlit AstroTurf, all year round use of the indoor swimming pool, a large gymnasium as well as acres of grounds which the children, with supervision, can explore.

We are committed to being leaders in education in these changing times. We invite you to join us as a member of St Edmund's Prep.

Charitable status. St Edmund's College is a Registered Charity, number 311073.

St Edmund's School Canterbury

St Thomas Hill, Canterbury, Kent CT2 8HU

Tel: 01227 475601 (Admissions)
01227 475600 (General Enquiries)

email: admissions@stedmunds.org.uk

website: www.stedmunds.org.uk

X/Twitter: @StEdsCanterbury

Facebook: @StEdsCanterbury

Instagram: @stedscanterbury

See full entry in the **HMC** section, on **p. 311**.

St Edmund's School

Portsmouth Road, Hindhead, Surrey GU26 6BH

Tel: 01428 609875

email: admissions@saintedmunds.co.uk

website: www.saintedmunds.co.uk

Facebook: @StEdmundsSurrey

Instagram: @stedmundshindhead

Chairman of Governors: Mrs J Alliss

***Headmaster*: Dr A J Walliker**, MA Cantab, MBA, EdD, PGCE

Age Range. 2–16 Co-educational.

Number of Pupils. Senior, Prep and Lower Prep: 566 day pupils.

Fees per term (2023–2024). Lower School £3,810–£5,490, Prep and Senior £6,830. Lunch and snack fee (compulsory) £440.

The fees are inclusive of all ordinary extras including supervised prep, orchestra/choirs, games, swimming, lectures, optional Saturday activities etc, as well as a free hour of after-school care activities for children in the Lower Prep.

Scholarships and means-tested bursaries are available.

We are a fully co-educational school from age 2 through to 16. Through a rich curriculum, small teaching groups and exemplary pastoral care, St Edmund's seeks to provide an excellent all round education by encouraging its pupils to achieve their very best in all that they do. "I like St Ed's, I can be myself." These words, spoken by one of our pupils, capture much of what we strive to do at St Edmund's: to instil in every child a sense of self-esteem and belonging by building on their own talents, opening their eyes to new ones and giving them focused and personal support whenever it is needed. Academically, it is an approach that continues to pay dividends, with our pupils going on to a wide range of senior schools at both 11+ and 13+ and 16+ including St Edmund's Senior.

Yet of equal importance are the discoveries, excitements and good old-fashioned fun that St Edmund's Lower Prep, Prep and Senior create inside our 40 beautiful acres with facilities including professional MTB trails, an immaculate 9-hole golf course, indoor swimming pool, cross-country running course, games fields, rifle range, a floodlit all-weather sports pitch and Dance and Drama Studio. A brand new multi-use sports hall opened in January 2021. The list of co-curricular activities is endless at St Ed's, from mountain biking to cookery, scuba-diving to den building and from street dance to giant chess, including our unique optional Saturday Activity programme that allows us greater depth in the number of activities on offer to our pupils.

St Edmund's Senior School offers a rare and unique educational experience for those who join us. In contrast to the many larger institutions available, our dedication to small teaching groups and our strong sense of community creates an environment where pupils' confidence can be invigorated. Through high-quality teaching and resources, our aim is to provide our pupils with an inspiring and notable experience that naturally encourages an appreciation for lifelong independent learning. Our broad curriculum across Forms 7 to 11 presents a firm foundation upon which to make future educational choices, and our distinctive tutorial system enables our pupils a platform to discuss progress and achievements as well as any pastoral issues that require guidance and consideration. In 2023 St. Edmund's again achieved an outstanding set of GCSE results and posted a fantastic 96% pass rate (grades 9–4) against a national average of 68.2%. Notably, 50% of the grades attained were at grades 9–7 (equivalent to the old A*/A grades), more than double the national average of 22%. At the top end, 40% of St Edmund's students achieved the most demanding and coveted grade 9.

During our latest Independent Schools Inspection in June 2021, the report noted, "The quality of St Edmund's pupils' achievements and learning is 'Excellent'. Pupils' have positive attitudes to learning and they are well motivated. They show exemplary behaviour and their care for each other is special".

Charitable status. St Edmund's School Trust Limited is a Registered Charity, number 278301. Its aim is the education of children.

St Faith's School

Trumpington Road, Cambridge, Cambridgeshire CB2 8AG

Tel: 01223 352073
email: info@stfaiths.co.uk
website: www.stfaiths.co.uk
X/Twitter: @St_Faiths
Facebook: @StFaithsSchool
Instagram: @stfaithscambridge
LinkedIn: /st-faith's-school-cambridge

Chair of Governors: Mrs A Brunner

***Headmaster*: Dr C Hyde-Dunn**, MA Oxon, PGCE, MA Ed, NPQH, PhD

Deputy Head: Mr J P Davenport, PGCE Camb, BEd Camb, MBA

Age Range. 4–13.

Number of Pupils. 577.

Fees per term (2023–2024). £5,245 (Pre-Prep), £6,440 (Years 3 and 4), £6,605 (Years 5 to 8).

Judged "excellent" for pupils' academic and other achievements and "excellent" for pupils' personal development (Independent Schools' Inspectorate October 2021), as well as being named *Prep School of the Year* in 2019 by The Times Educational Supplement, St Faith's is a co-educational day school for children aged 4–13. Located on the south side of central Cambridge, approximately one mile from the city centre, the school benefits from a beautiful and spacious setting of 9 acres of grounds, with access to a further 20 acres of sports fields just 2 minutes' walk away. St Faith's is part of The Leys and St Faith's Foundation and each year approximately half of the children move on to The Leys at the end of Year 8, while others prepare for entry to a variety of senior schools.

At St Faith's, each child is developed, nurtured and challenged, to equip them with skills for life, whatever path they choose to take. Passionate teachers share their knowledge, explore new ideas and instill a lifelong passion for learning. We strive to provide a genuinely tailored approach for each individual child, helping every pupil to thrive and fulfil their potential. In 2023, a total number of 37 awards and scholarships to Senior Schools were achieved by our pupils, across the whole curriculum.

With a focus on the St Faith's 'Learning Habits' of curiosity, collaboration, independence, listening, reflection, creativity, ambition and resilience, children are encouraged to understand how they learn best and to make confident choices. Our approach of top-down excellence in all lessons ensures that pupils are engaged and inspired. Our academic curriculum is ground-breaking in its innovative content and has been commended by the University of Cambridge and the Times Educational Supplement, with an award for 'Strategic Education Initiative of the Year' (2018) for the introduction of Engineering to the curriculum.

Ambitious, forward-looking and appropriately rigorous academic subjects are interspersed each day with sporting endeavours, social impact work, musical experiences, artistic creations, and dramatic performances. Assemblies, tutor time and plenty of playtime ensure children have a chance to express themselves away from the classroom. Owing to small class sizes, exceptional teachers and the above average ability of our children, all subjects follow an accelerated curriculum. The vast majority of pupils work at a higher level than that commensurate with their age, with their high levels of focus in lessons recognised by the Inspectors in our recent ISI Inspection (2021).

Our green and spacious site provides some of the best facilities of any prep school. Every classroom is equipped with modern teaching technology. The shelves in our library brim with over 12,000 volumes with relevance to our youngest and most mature readers. Engineering suites provide access to tools and equipment beyond many inventors' wildest dreams. Fully-equipped science laboratories and computer suites are used by all year groups. Our new £2m STEM Hub includes state of the art science laboratories, flexible large indoor spaces for interdisciplinary projects, a rooftop greenhouse and a night sky viewing platform. Our magnificent sports hall and pitches have been instrumental in training St Faith's National Champions in a variety of sports, including Hockey, Athletics, Gymnastics and Trampolining. We promote sport for all, as a conduit for developing mental as well as physical fitness and all pupils have the opportunity to enjoy a variety of fixtures against other schools. Our large 'Ashburton Hall' provides an outstanding venue for concerts and performances, with children also having opportunities to perform at other venues locally and nationally.

We recognise the crucial importance of children feeling happy in our school community and we work hard to promote staff and pupil wellbeing. Parents are closely involved with the school through a range of social events as well as having regular contact with teaching staff. Our excellent pastoral care provision is supported by a range of initiatives, including a buddy system and kindness certificates. Pupils develop leadership skills in our School Council and Eco-Committee, and we were delighted that the ISI commented in 2021 on the outstanding behaviour and moral understanding of St Faith's pupils.

Charitable status. The Leys and St Faith's Schools Foundation is a Registered Charity, number 1144035. The aim of the charity is the provision of first-class education.

St Francis School

Marlborough Road, Pewsey, Wiltshire SN9 5NT

Tel: 01672 563228
email: stanleyc@stfpewsey.co.uk
schooloffice@stfpewsey.co.uk
website: www.stfpewsey.co.uk
X/Twitter: @stfrancispewsey
Facebook: @StFrancisPewsey
Instagram: @stfrancispewsey

Chair of Governors: P Humphries-Cuff

***Headmaster*: Mr David Lee**, BA, MA. PGCSE, QTS

Age range. 0–13.

Number of boys and girls. 208: 104 Boys, 104 Girls.

Fees per term (2023–2024). Reception–Year 8: £2,817–£5,450 including lunch. Nursery Fees available on application.

St Francis is a co-educational day school for children age 0 to 13. Established in 1941, the School is situated alongside the Kennet and Avon Canal in the beautiful Vale of Pewsey, five miles south of Marlborough. Pupils travel from a wide area of Wiltshire; daily minibus services operate from Marlborough and Devizes and surrounding villages. Wraparound care is available for all pupils, from 7.45 am until 6.00 pm.

Providing every child with the opportunity to fulfil their full potential is a feature of the School, and staff are positive and encouraging in their teaching. If a child needs additional support with their learning this is provided by the highly regarded Learning Support Department. The modern Burden Block and George Cannon centre provides a Design Technology room, Art room, Science Lab, Drama loft and specialist subject teaching rooms, as well as form rooms.

The curriculum is diverse, which enables the older pupils to have, for example, STEAM, Art, Drama and Music in their timetable, alongside their lessons of English, Maths and Science. French is also a key part of the curriculum and is taught from the age of three. Pupils can take individual music lessons with specialist peripatetic music teachers, who offer a wide range of instruments. Many pupils enter local music, public-speaking and choral competitions.

The pupils are offered plenty of opportunity to develop and excel in their sport. All the major sports are taught both outdoors on the playing fields and also inside the Hemery Sports Hall which is also used for drama performances. Swimming lessons are held weekly for pupils in Reception – Year 2 and there is a Swimming Squad for Year 3 and above. Regular matches take place against other schools and a policy of 'sport for all' allows all pupils to be involved.

Little Saints Nursery caters for children from 0 to 4 years of age for 51 weeks a year (both term time and full-time contracts are available). Little Saints Nursery makes use of all the facilities including the school's gardens, playground and woods.

The beautiful 17-acre school grounds include a Forest School and a wooden adventure playground, the St Francis Fortress, which was built in 2019, providing an exciting area for pupils to let off steam after their lessons.

Results are excellent. The pupils are mainly entered for the local senior schools, St Mary's Calne, Godolphin, Dauntsey's, Marlborough College, Stonar and Warminster, but scholarships and common entrance are also taken for boarding schools further afield. Awards are regularly achieved to all of the aforementioned.

Please telephone 01672 563228 or email admissions@stfpewsey.co.uk if you would like more information or to arrange a tour of the school with the Headmaster. Virtual Tours of the school and nursery are available on our website. Open Mornings are usually held during the Autumn and Spring terms.

Charitable status. St Francis is a Registered Charity, number 298522. It exists solely to provide education for boys and girls.

St Gabriel's

Junior School

Sandleford Priory, Newbury, Berkshire RG20 9BD

Tel: 01635 555680
email: admissions@stgabriels.co.uk
website: www.stgabriels.co.uk
X/Twitter: @StGabrielsNews
Facebook: @stgabrielsnewbury
Instagram: @stgabrielsnews
LinkedIn: /company/st-gabriel's-newbury

Chairman of Governors: Mr N Garland, BSc Hons

Principal: Mr R Smith, MEd, MA, PGCE

***Head of Junior School*: Mr P Dove**, BA Hons, PGCE

Age Range. 6 months to 11 years Co-educational.

Number of Pupils. 245.

Fees per term (2023–2024). £4,303–£5,783.

The Nursery and Junior School are situated adjacent to the Senior School in 33 acres of parkland on the southern outskirts of Newbury.

Our Nursery lies at the heart of St Gabriel's and provides high-quality nursery care and Early Years education for children aged 6 months to 4 years. Open across 50 weeks a year and with an extended day, the Nursery has a warm and homely atmosphere where children become happy, confident and independent learners. As a natural progression, most of our Nursery children continue into the Reception class of the Junior School.

The Junior School is situated adjacent to the Senior School in 33 acres of parkland on the southern outskirts of Newbury.

Junior School subjects taught include English, Mathematics, Science, Art, Computing, Dance, Drama, Humanities (History, Geography), French, Music, Outdoor Education, PE, Religious Studies, Technology (Food Technology, Design Technology), Thinking Skills and PSHE.

The excellent range of facilities includes a multi-discipline sports hall, theatre, dance studio, junior science laboratory, library, computing suites, orienteering courses and woodland trails.

Sport plays an important and integral role in the life of the school and there is a comprehensive fixtures list from Year 3 to Year 6. The wide range of sports offered includes, Athletics, Basketball, Cricket, Cross-Country, Dance, Football, Gymnastics, Hockey, Netball, Rugby, Rounders and Tennis, which are included in the curriculum for all pupils. Swimming takes place during the Summer Term in the outdoor heated swimming pool.

Music holds an equally high profile. In addition to curriculum Music lessons, there are numerous co-curricular music-making opportunities for all children with an interest in the subject. A large number of pupils learn instruments in school and there are many opportunities to perform in front of an audience, ranging from informal lunchtime events to major end of term extravaganzas.

In addition, pupils are offered a wide range of co-curricular activities, including Art Club, Ballet, Book Club, Chess Club, Choir, Climbing Club, Cricket Club, Dance Club, Drama, Fencing, Football, Gymnastics, Judo, Junior Duke, Languages Clubs, Music Theory, Netball Club, Pathfinders, Recorder, Science Club, Tennis Club, Trampolining Club and Training Orchestra. Pupils in Years 3–6 are elected on to a School Council which plays an important role in school, particularly with charity work. Pupils also participate in the Junior Duke Awards starting in Year 3 with the Bronze Award, leading to the Platinum Award in Year 6.

Pupils in Year 3 and above are provided with a managed school iPad as a tool to support teaching and learning in school and at home.

In 2021, the Junior School was awarded the gold level from The Woodland Trust *Green Tree Schools Award*, demonstrating a commitment to using and improving the school grounds to develop pupils' environmental awareness.

There is no assessment for children joining the Nursery setting. Prospective pupils entering the Junior School in Year 1 and 2 are assessed by the class teacher and subject staff; prospective pupils entering Year 3 to 6 are assessed by the Individual Needs Department. Pupils who apply for entry to Year 6 will also be assessed on their ability to pass the 11+ entrance examinations to the co-educational Senior School.

(For further information about the Senior School, see St Gabriel's entry in Society of Heads.)

Charitable status. The St Gabriel Schools Foundation is a Registered Charity, number 1062748. It seeks to promote and provide for the advancement of education of the pupils at the school.

St Gabriel's

Sandleford Priory, Newbury, Berkshire RG20 9BD

Tel: 01635 555680
email: admissions@stgabriels.co.uk
website: www.stgabriels.co.uk
X/Twitter: @StGabrielsNews
Facebook: @stgabrielsnewbury
Instagram: @stgabrielsnews
LinkedIn: /company/st-gabriel's-newbury

See full entry in the **Society of Heads** section, on **p. 558**.

St George's Junior School, Weybridge

Thames Street, Weybridge, Surrey KT13 8NL

Tel: 01932 839400
email: contact@stgeorgesweybridge.com
website: www.stgeorgesweybridge.com
X/Twitter: @sgweybridge
Facebook: @stgeorgescollegeuk

Chair of Board of Governors: Mr D Nowlan

***Headmaster*: Mr A J W Hudson**, MA Cantab, PGCE, NPQH

Age Range. 3–11.

Number of Pupils. 590.

Fees per term (2023–2024). Nursery £2,270 (mornings only), £3,715 (full days); Reception–Year 2 £4,280; Years 3–6 £5,870. Lunches (compulsory): £330.

St George's Junior School is a fully co-ed Roman Catholic Day School, with a Senior School on a separate site nearby. The Junior School was established in 1950 by a Religious Order of Priests and Brothers known as "The Josephites" as a development of the educational provision of St George's College which celebrated its 150th Anniversary in 2019.

In September 2000, the Junior School moved from its previous co-located site a mile down the road, to its present 50-acre site on the outskirts of Weybridge close to the River Thames. Huge development has taken place since then, most notably, a new Kitchen and Dining Room, and a state-of-the-art Lower Years building for children aged 3–7 – The Ark – which was opened and blessed by Cardinal Cormac Murphy-O'Connor in 2016, at the same time as a new Performing Arts Centre. Along with the recent development of a Forest School and the Eco Garden, as well as extra playing fields for cricket, rugby and rounders, the Master Plan has given the Junior School first-rate facilities which provide the children with a wonderful start to their education. The School operates a very extensive bus service and an option for parents using cars to drop off their children at either the Junior School using the 'Kiss and Drop' system, or the College, using the minibus shuttle service.

The Junior School has a genuinely happy atmosphere in which every pupil is respected and treated as an individual. The Headmaster considers the staff, pupils and parents to be constituent parts of an extended family – 'The Georgian Family'. The School has always placed great emphasis on the importance of maintaining excellent channels of communication between members of staff, parents and pupils.

Pupils who are 'rising three' are admitted into the Nursery, after which children can be admitted to any year group, subject to available spaces. The size of classes ensures that the School is a learning community by creating the correct balance between pupil interaction and pupil-teacher contact. The pupils in the top two years of the School are taught by subject specialists. French is offered to all pupils from Year 1. In November 2019, the ISI Educational Quality Inspection found the School to be 'Excellent' in all areas, following on from the Diocesan Inspection Report in May 2018 which noted that 'the school's pastoral care is a particular strength' and the 'teachers manifest an enthusiasm for sharing their love and knowledge of subject, and communicate high expectations'.

All pupils are assessed on entry and when they leave at the end of Year 6, the vast majority transfer to St George's College. In 2021, 7 Academic, 5 Sports, 4 Music and 1 Art Scholarship along with 1 Art Exhibition were awarded. While the pursuit of academic excellence is highly valued, the Mission Statement of the School stresses the importance of pupils being the very best versions of themselves. The School requires its pupils to have high moral values especially those of its school motto: "Honesty and Compassion".

The Junior School has four Houses which compete against each other across a wide range of activities inside and outside the classroom including Music, Public Speaking and Sport.

Extracurricular and other enrichment activities are, likewise, considered to play an important role in the educational development of children. The extensive range of activities include dance (ballet, modern and tap), gymnastics, and clubs based on the academic subjects taught in the School. Mandarin is offered to Upper Years pupils if they so wish, and pupils are taken to places of educational interest regularly, including theatre, music and art trips, and there is an annual Book Week during which pupils meet and listen to visiting authors and storytellers. The School recently hosted its own Literature Festival, inviting over 500 children from local schools to attend.

Considerable emphasis is placed on the Creative and Performing Arts. The school stages six major Drama Productions a year. All children in Year 2 learn the ukulele and recorder as part of the Music Curriculum. There is an orchestra, choirs and various ensembles. Individual music lessons are very popular, with over 50% of the children in Years 3 to 6 learning at least one additional instrument. Since September 2016 an Instrumental Tuition Scheme has been implemented which subsidises free peripatetic lessons for all children in Years 3 or 4, in order to encourage them to take up strings, woodwind or brass instruments, which has been a great success. Concerts take place at least once a term, and music lessons are supported by the use of the latest computer-based technology. Pupils have achieved considerable success at Public Speaking Competitions and achieve a very high level of attainment in their external Spoken English, LAMDA and instrumental music exams.

Apart from its own on-site sports facilities, comprising an artificial sports pitch, netball and tennis courts, a sprung floor gymnasium and a swimming pool, the School has use of outstanding sports facilities at the College including its brand new Activity Centre, a four-court indoor tennis centre, and a tartan athletics track. The Junior School has a track record of great sporting success with Hockey & Rugby teams regularly reaching the final stages of IAPS National Finals and more recently excelling at Boys' and Girls' Gymnastics. In the midst of this tangible success, the Junior School prides itself on ensuring that all pupils from Year 3 upwards have the opportunity to represent the school at least once each term in one of the mainstream sports, i.e. Rugby, Hockey and Cricket for boys and Netball, Hockey, Rounders & Cricket for girls.

School lunches, which are compulsory for children in Upper Nursery staying on for afternoon activities and for all from Reception Year onwards, are prepared on site and eaten in the dining room which can seat 320 people. Since November 2020, the School has engaged the services of an external provider – 'The Gap Club' – for pre- & after-school care for all children who so wish from 7.30am – 6.30pm. Children in Years 1 & 2 can sign up for 2 after school clubs per week until 4.30pm, while those in Years 3–6 can sign up for clubs which continue until 5.00pm each day.

For the last few years, the School has usually had more applications for places than it can accommodate in all year groups. When vacancies do occur, pupils are admitted as long as they meet the School's entry criteria and successfully complete an assessment day at the School, as well as receiving a satisfactory report from their current school where this is appropriate. Priority is afforded to siblings and children from Roman Catholic families.

Charitable status. St George's Weybridge is a registered Charity, number 1017853. The aims and objectives of the charity are the Christian education of young people.

St George's School Windsor Castle

Windsor, Berkshire SL4 1QF

Tel: 01753 865553

email: enquiries@stgwindsor.org

website: www.stgwindsor.org

X/Twitter: @stgwindsor

Facebook: @stgwindsor

Instagram: @stgwindsor

Chair of the Governors: Mr Ian Canning

***Head*: Mr William Goldsmith**, BA Hons Durham, MSC Oxford, FRSA, FCCT, FTIOB

Deputy Head, Head of Prep School: Mr Kevin Wills, BSc Hons, PGCE

Deputy Head, Head of Pre-Prep: Mrs Emma Adriano, BA Hons, PGCE, PG Dip

Head of Senior Prep, Mr Henry Knight, BA Hons, PGCE, MEd

Age Range. 3–13, co-educational.

Number of Pupils. 335 (including 23 weekly boarders, with capacity for additional flexi-boarding up to a maximum of 46).

Fees per term (2023–2024). Pre-Prep (Kindergarten to Year 3): £2,631–£6,210; Prep (Years 4–6): £6,210–£6,957; Senior Prep (Years 7 & 8): £6,957. Weekly boarding: £8,637.

St George's School Windsor Castle is an award-winning day and boarding school for girls and boys aged 3–13, offering extensive facilities in a truly iconic setting at the foot of Windsor Castle in Berkshire.

The first standalone prep school in the UK to be designated an IB World School, St George's prides itself on combining a pioneering, 'world-class', International

Baccalaureate curriculum, with exciting opportunities to collaborate across the globe through Round Square, and a school-wide approach which prioritises mental wellbeing and nurturing children to be kind, resilient, inquisitive, internationally minded and *Real World Ready*.

Alongside an exceptional reputation for musical excellence, including a 675-year history of educating the choristers of the world-famous St George's Chapel in Windsor Castle, the school offers diverse opportunities across sport, performing arts, design and technology, both via the taught curriculum as well as through an exciting co-curricular programme offering more than 80 activities across the year, ranging from scuba diving to street dance, cookery and Eco Club.

The only school in Windsor to feature in the Tatler Schools Guide 2024, St George's is described by Muddy Stilettos as ideal 'for progressive families who want a modern education fit for the future' and by The Good Schools Guide as somewhere 'families who want a liberal, outward-looking education delivered by bright-eyed teachers in a small and nurturing urban haven (plus castle) may find their child's happy ever after'.

The school was rated 'excellent' in all areas by the Independent Schools Inspectorate in November 2022 and in 2023 won the hieda Creating a Mentally Healthier Workplace Award in recognition of its proactive approach to mental wellbeing for both students and the wider school community. In addition, St George's were shortlisted in the Independent Pre-Prep School of the Year category at the Independent Schools of the Year Awards 2023, as well as being named a double finalist in the 2023 Muddy Stilettos Best Schools Awards, the only co-ed school in the Royal Borough of Windsor and Maidenhead to feature.

With a school bus service operating from both Maidenhead and Gerrards Cross, as well as Windsor & Eton Riverside Station directly opposite, the school is easily accessible from across the borough and beyond.

Families are warmly invited to attend one of the school's open events throughout the year, or contact the school's registrar to arrange a personal tour.

Charitable status: St George's School Windsor Castle is a Registered Charity, number 1100392. It exists to provide an excellent all-round education for children aged 3–13.

St Helen's College

Parkway, Hillingdon, Middlesex UB10 9JX

Tel: 01895 234371
email: admin@sthelenscollege.com
website: www.sthelenscollege.com

Principals:
Mr D A Crehan, ARCS, BA, BSc, MSc, CPhys, MEd
Mrs G R Crehan, BA, MA, PGCE

***Head Teacher*: Ms S Drummond**, BEd Hons, MLDP, FCCT

Age Range. 2–11 co-educational.
Number of Pupils. 380 Day Pupils.
Fees per term (2023–2024). £3,660–£4,560.

St Helen's College has been described by inspectors as a 'Haven of Harmony' and was deemed 'outstanding/excellent' in its most recent educational quality inspection. It is a happy, family-run school, based on three enduring values: Love, Harmony and Growth.

The aims of St Helen's College are to develop as fully as possible each child's academic potential, to provide a wide, balanced, stimulating and challenging curriculum, and to foster true values and good character based on moral and spiritual principles. The children enjoy a purposeful and happy 'family' atmosphere and are taught by committed, professional, specialist teachers.

Children are prepared for independent senior schools and local grammar schools, and records of success are very good indeed. In addition to the academic subjects, sport, music and drama play an important part in the lives of the children.

An extraordinarily wide range of extra-curricular activities is offered and pupils enjoy outings, day and residential, to many places of interest. There is a breakfast club, after-school club and summer school, and a holiday club which runs throughout the year.

Individual tours for prospective parents are run during term time and on regular Open Mornings. Please telephone 01895 234371 or contact susmith@sthelenscollege.com to make an appointment.

St Hilary's Preparatory School

Holloway Hill, Godalming, Surrey GU7 1RZ

Tel: 01483 416551
email: admissions@sthilarysschool.com
website: www.sthilarysschool.com
X/Twitter: @StHilarysSchool
Facebook: @profile.php?id=100026420866007
Instagram: @sthilarysschool

Chair of Governors: Mr Richard Thompson, BSc Hons, MBA

***Headmistress*: Mrs J Whittingham**, BEd Cert, Prof Prac SpLD

Age range. Boys and Girls 2–11.
Number of pupils. 260 Day Pupils.
Fees per term (2023–2024). Including lunch: Reception £4,093; Year 1 £4,398; Year 2 £5,161; Year 3 £5,421; Years 4 to 6 £6,022. Kindergarten £35.50 and Nursery £37.00 per am/pm session with lunch extra.

St Hilary's is an independent preparatory day school which provides a stimulating, safe environment in which boys and girls can develop, be happy and flourish.

Situated in the heart of Godalming, St Hilary's prides itself in providing an outstanding all-round education, equipping pupils not only with strong academic standards but also the essential qualities and skills required beyond their time at our school. Ultimately we strive to ensure that all our pupils develop a real thirst for learning.

The Independent Schools Inspectorate judged our main school to be 'Excellent' in all areas in December 2016 and our Early Years Foundation Stage achieved 'Outstanding' at its last inspection. St Hilary's was also judged as 'Independent Prep School of the Year 2020', by the *Independent School Parent* magazine.

Every child enjoys the benefits of well-qualified, enthusiastic staff and a broad curriculum combined with splendid facilities. Amenities include well-equipped classrooms, music wing, spacious hall for the performing arts, science room, library, modern ICT suite, design & technology, art studios, all-weather pitch, the Hiorns Centre for drama, a Lego Innovation Studio and a wellbeing centre 'The Nest'. Small class sizes allow children to achieve their best in a dynamic and vibrant environment.

Outside the classroom, pupils can enjoy the woodland in our Forest School and play opportunities with the very popular Trim Trail and exciting adventure play area. Pupils share a love of growing things in our gardens and appreciate the safe, beautiful surroundings.

Physical Education and sport features highly at St Hilary's. The Sports Department gives all pupils equality of opportunity to participate in a broad range of activities. All pupils experience a variety of competitive and challenging situations. Our House system encourages healthy competition with matches, a swimming gala and sports days.

Children are given the opportunity to participate in a wide, varied number of extra-curricular activities, such as, gardening, football skills, skateboarding, tennis, netball, drama, LEGO, science, art, pottery, textiles, debating, First Aid, French, chess, gym, cross country, judo, cricket, dance, tap, choirs, woodwind, string ensemble, percussion, orchestra, recorder groups and violin.

Speech & Drama is a highly popular option for many with pupils preparing for LAMDA (London Academy of Music and Dramatic Art) examinations. The school takes advantage of its ideal location and access to London for visits to galleries, museums and theatres.

Parents are expertly guided in next school options and have the opportunity to make informed choices at a time when a child's true academic potential can be accurately predicted and talents in other areas identified. We have an excellent reputation in securing first-choice schools for our pupils when they leave. Our leavers successfully move on to prestigious schools; every year many obtain academic, art, music, sport and drama scholarships.

Please do come and visit us; we will be delighted to welcome you and discuss your child's education. We hold two Open Days in April and in October, or we are happy to arrange 1:1 tours and taster days; please contact our Admissions Manager for more details.

Charitable status. St Hilary's School Trust Limited is a Registered Charity, number 312056. It exists to provide education for children.

St Hugh's

Carswell Manor
Carswell, Faringdon, Oxfordshire SN7 8PT

Tel: 01367 870700
email: office@st-hughs.co.uk
registrar@st-hughs.co.uk
website: www.st-hughs.co.uk
Facebook: @people/St-Hughs-Oxfordshire
Instagram: @sthughsschooloxfordshire

Chairman of Governors: Mr Neill Lawson-Smith

***Headmaster*: David Griffiths**, BA Cardiff, PGCE, MEd

Age Range. 3–13.

Number of Pupils. 342: 191 Boys (62 Boarders), 151 Girls (51 Boarders).

Fees per term (2023–2024). Upper School: £8,350; Middle School: £7,500; Pre-Prep £4,830–£5,280. (All fees inclusive, with very few compulsory extras.) Weekly boarding (Mon-Fri inclusive): Termly Fee £1,780.

The School's main building is a fine Jacobean house with extensive grounds. Boys and girls are prepared for Pre-Test, Common Entrance and Scholarship examinations to senior independent schools. The school is organised into four departments: Nursery (3–4), Pre-Prep (4–6), Middle School (7–8) and Upper School (9–13). Careful liaison ensures a strong thread of continuity throughout the school. The main entry points are at 3, 4, 7 and 9.

The School is not academically selective and both welcomes and accepts children from all backgrounds and a wide range of academic abilities. We aim to foster confidence and a love of learning across this range: an impressive pre-test, scholarship and CE record and the provision of integral specialist support both bear testimony to our inclusive approach. The arts and sport feature strongly and pupils are encouraged to develop their talents and interests as broadly as possible.

St Hugh's is described by the Good Schools Guide as a school which "personifies what is best in prep school education".

Charitable status. St Hugh's is a Registered Charity, number 309640. It exists to provide a centre of excellence for the education of children.

St Hugh's

Cromwell Avenue, Woodhall Spa LN10 6TQ

Tel: 01526 352169
email: office@st-hughs.lincs.sch.uk
website: www.st-hughs.lincs.sch.uk
X/Twitter: @sthughslincs
Facebook: @sthughslincs
Instagram: @sthughswoodhall

Chairman of Governors: R Bussell

***Headmaster*: Mr Jeremy Wyld**, BA Hons, PGCE

Age range. 2–13.

Number of pupils. 174. Prep 50 boys, 53 girls. Pre Prep: 18 boys, 26 girls. Nursery: 27 children.

Fees per term (2023–2024). Boarding: £7,595 (4 nights); Day: £5,425–£5,975; Pre Prep: £3,695. The fees are fully inclusive.

St Hugh's School was founded by the Forbes family in 1925 and today is fully co-educational, offering both day and boarding places. The Headmaster is assisted by 21 qualified and experienced teachers and is a member of IAPS (The Independent Association of Prep Schools) as well as the Boarding Schools' Association.

Pupils are prepared for the Common Entrance and Scholarship examinations. The school's academic record is excellent, with regular awards being gained to major Independent Schools, as well as 11+ and 13+ places at Lincolnshire Grammar Schools. Children with special learning needs are treated sympathetically within the mainstream, with support from specialist staff. The aim of the school is to give every child a good all-round education and to discover and develop his or her own particular talents.

The major school games for boys are rugby, hockey and cricket, and for girls netball, hockey and cricket. Pupils can also enjoy cross-country, tennis, athletics and swimming. All children have PE each week and swimming lessons.

The school lays heavy emphasis on extracurricular activities including music, art, drama, forest school and sport. There is also a strong and continuing Christian tradition at St Hugh's.

The school has excellent facilities including a modern sports hall, an assembly hall with stage and lighting, a heated indoor swimming pool, extensive playing fields including an all-weather pitch, a library, and dedicated classrooms for Music, Science, Art & Design, and Technology.

Weekly and flexi boarders are accommodated in a well-appointed House under the close supervision of a Houseparent, and dormitories and common rooms are bright and cheerful. Contact with parents and guardians is well maintained. Minibus transport for day pupils is provided across the county.

The Pre Preparatory department caters for approximately 40 children aged from 4 to 7 and is located in its own building with separate play area and staff.

The Nursery for children aged between 2 and 4 is attached to the Pre Prep and accommodates approximately 30 children.

Charitable status. St Hugh's School (Woodhall Spa) Limited is a Registered Charity, number 527611. It exists to provide a high standard of education and care to pupils from the age of 2 to 13.

St John's
A Merchant Taylors' School

Potter Street Hill, Northwood, Middlesex HA6 3QY

Tel: 020 8866 0067
email: office@st-johns.org.uk
website: www.st-johns.org.uk
X/Twitter: @stjsnorthwood
Facebook: @profile.php?id=100089827154136
Instagram: @stjohnsnorthwood
LinkedIn: /company/st-john's-school-northwood

Chair of Governors: Mr J Fowler

***Headmaster*: Mr T W Jenkin**, MA

Age Range. 3–13.

Number of Boys. 350 Day Boys.

Fees per annum (2023–2024): Nursery £12,655; Pre-Preparatory £16,995; Preparatory £18,360.

Facing south, on a 35-acre site, we have outstanding views over London. Since the Merchant Taylors' Educational Trust took the School under its wing, impressive development has taken place. St John's now has two completely refurbished science laboratories, a state of the art Design & Technology Workshop including 3D printer, a set of sewing machines and sublimation printing equipment, an ICT Centre and a large Music Department. Outside the classroom, we have an all-weather multi-purpose sports pitch, four rugby pitches and an athletics track, which have been levelled and provided with excellent drainage and irrigation. We also have an expansive nature trail and woodland area which is used by the Pre-Prep for Forest School on a daily basis and by older boys for ecological and environmental study. These areas are in addition to our extensive playing fields and formal gardens.

Our Pre-Preparatory Department provides dedicated Nursery facilities, an Information Technology Suite and Library. There are six purpose-built Pre-Prep classrooms in a self-contained area of the School leading to a covered outdoor play area and wooden climbing frame.

Recently completed is a brand new two-floor sports hall with changing area and a dedicated site for our wraparound care providers. We have also recently introduced a purpose-built tree house which will benefit all pupils at St John's.

Most of the boys enter the School at either the age of three into the Nursery or at four into the Pre-Prep; there is a separate entry into the Prep School at seven. St John's has an excellent record of success in scholarship and senior school entrance examinations. Boys are prepared for all independent schools, but our links with Merchant Taylors' School, Northwood, are particularly strong.

Although the School was originally a Church of England foundation, boys of all religions and denominations are welcome.

Charitable status. St John's School, part of the Merchant Taylors' Educational Trust, is a Registered Charity, number 1063738. It exists for the purpose of educating boys.

St John's Beaumont Preparatory School

Priest Hill, Old Windsor, Berkshire SL4 2JN
Tel: 01784 494053
email: sjb.admissions@sjb.email
website: www.SJBWindsor.uk
X/Twitter: @SJBWindsor
Facebook: @SJBWindsor
Instagram: @sjbwindsor.uk

Chairman of Governors: Mr Andrew Johnson

***Headteacher*: Mr Philip Barr**, MA, FCCT

Age range. 3–13.

Number of children. 220 (40 Full, Weekly, Tailored Boarders; 180 Day Pupils).

Fees per term (2023–2024). Pre-Prep: £4,200–£4,800, Prep: £5,600–£7,877, Boarding: £1,590–£4,000.

St John's Beaumont is a day and boarding preparatory school for children aged 3 to 13, located on a stunning 75-acre campus near Windsor, on the Berkshire–Surrey border. St John's was founded as a Jesuit school for boys in 1888, and has had an outstanding track record of secure places and scholarships to all the top senior schools for its pupils.

This year, the school is entering an exciting new phase of its development with a move to co-education. From September 2023, girls will be welcomed into the Pre-Prep section of the school (Nursery–Year 2) with the intent that co-education will move up through the year groups with the passing of each academic year. The intent is to provide the same quality and breadth of learning and co-curricular activities for girls and boys.

We welcome children of all backgrounds, faiths and abilities, whose parents value high academic attainment and the development of the values, skills and attributes to enable successful navigation through life. Pupils from St John's have always secured places at top senior schools, but our emphasis is on making sure that wherever the destination, each child is a 'round peg in a round hole' and that they continue to thrive.

To this day, St John's still values the Jesuit approach to education, which is based upon a clear set of values to guide the development of the whole person and their interactions with those around them. Accordingly, St John's offers a high-quality academic, co-curricular and external engagement programme that propagates a myriad of talents in all our pupils. But more than anything, we aim to nurture the development of the confidence and leadership skills that enables each pupil to lead others and themselves at every stage of life.

ISI rated excellent in all areas

Shortlisted Small Independent School of the Year (ISOTY 2023)

To arrange a visit and find out what makes St John's so special, email sjb.admissions@sjb.email.

Charitable status. St John's is a Registered Charity, number 230165.

St John's College School

73 Grange Road, Cambridge, Cambs CB3 9AB
Tel: 01223 353532 Reception
01223 353652 Admissions Secretary
email: shoffice@sjcs.co.uk
bhoffice@sjcs.co.uk
website: www.sjcs.co.uk

Chair of Governors: Lindsay Dodsworth

***Headmaster*: Mr Neil R Chippington**, MA, MEd, FRCO

Age range. 4–13.

Number of children. 438 girls and boys (including 22 Choristers/ Non-Chorister boy and girl boarders).

Fees per year (2023–2024). Day: £16,020–£19,800; Boarding: £31,200; Choristers: £10,401 pa. Bursaries available for Choristers.

Profile. St John's prides itself on the quality of the academic and pastoral care it provides for each child. Through relaxed and friendly relations with children in a well-structured environment rich with opportunity; through close monitoring of progress; through communication and cooperation with parents; through expert staffing and, above all, through a sense of community that cares for the strengths and weaknesses of each of its members, St John's has consistently achieved outstanding results exemplified by over 70 scholarships during the last three years. While its Choristers maintain the tradition of choral services and tour the world, St John's status as an Expert Centre for ICT, and other innovations, ensure the school's commitment to the future. Mr Neil Chippington joined St John's as the Headmaster in September 2016, having been Head at St Paul's Cathedral School in London.

Entry. At 4–7 by parental interview; at 7–12 by parental interview, report from previous school and, as appropriate, assessment.

Curriculum. The curriculum surrounds the core of formal skills teaching with a breadth of enrichment and extension for each child's talents. In addition to the usual subjects including specialist taught DT, ICT, Art, Music, Dance and Drama, and PE for all pupils, the following are also available: French (from 4+), Latin (from 9+), Greek (optional from 11+), Spanish (11+). Pupils prepared for CE and Scholarship examinations. Philosophy and Study Skills are now regularly taught to pupils in certain year groups and all pupils are being introduced to Mindfulness.

Leavers. Virtually all go to senior independent day or boarding schools. The School works closely with parents to assist them in finding the best school for their child.

Consultation. Tutorial system (1 teacher to 10 pupils) with daily tutorial session timetabled. Half yearly academic assessments, end of year examinations, termly Parents' Evenings and weekly staff 'surgery' times.

Sports. Athletics, Badminton, Basketball, Cricket, Cross Country, Football, Golf, Gymnastics, Hockey, Netball, Rounders, Rowing, Rugby, Short Tennis, Squash, Swimming, Table Tennis, Tennis. All games are timetabled and therefore given significant status. All major sports strong.

Activities. Numerous clubs including Art, Chess, Dance, Drama, Pottery, Sketching, Design Technology, Craft, Information Technology, Maths games and puzzles, Magic, Touch-typing, Cycling Proficiency, General Knowledge, Debating, Poetry, Sewing and Wardrobe. College Choir of international status, Chamber Groups, Orchestras, School Chapel Choir, Junior Chamber Choir, Parents' Choir, Major theatrical productions, e.g. *Oliver!*, *Hamlet*, and theatrical opportunities for all children. A range of visits relating to curriculum plus French, Classics, skiing and outward bound trips.

Facilities. School on two sites with facilities used by all pupils.

Byron House (4–8). Outstanding facilities including Science, DT Centre, two large suites of networked PCs, newly-designed Library, Drama Studio, Gym, Hall, and specialist Music wing. The Byron House site has also been redeveloped and the children can now use the newly landscaped and planted 'Forest Garden'. The site has completely redesigned classrooms and a large learning space for child-initiated learning and digital learning. The rooms are fitted with bespoke, streamlined storage. Investigative and collaborative skills have been fostered by the use of the new 'working walls' and 'writeable tables'.

Senior House (9–13). The Senior House site has been completely redeveloped. In addition to existing facilities such as the Chapel, Theatre, Gymnasium Science Laboratory, Art Room, ICT Room, Swimming Pool and Music School, the site boasts 14 new classrooms, an outstanding Library, a new DT and Computer Control and Graphics facility, a second Science Laboratory, a new Drama Studio, new Music facilities, a Quiet Garden, a new Multi-Sports Court and changing block, extensive storage and excellent staff facilities.

Boarding. From age 8. Girl and boy boarders form an integral part of life at St John's and benefit from all the School's facilities while living in the homely, caring atmosphere of a Boarding House. The Boarding House accommodates up to 40 boys and girls and facilities include recreation areas, a library, TV, table tennis and use of all Senior House facilities. Day boarding and 'Waiters' facilities allow the School to be flexible to the needs of parents and children alike.

Charitable status. St John's College School is part of St John's College Cambridge, which is a Registered Charity, number 1137428.

St Joseph's College

Belstead Road, Ipswich, Suffolk IP2 9DR

Tel: 01473 690281
email: admissions@stjos.co.uk
website: www.stjos.co.uk
X/Twitter: @MyStJos
Facebook: @StJosephsCollegeIpswich
LinkedIn: /St-Joseph's-College-Ipswich

See full entry in the **Society of Heads** section, on **p. 560**.

St Leonards Junior Years

St Andrews, Fife KY16 9QJ

Tel: 01334 460470
email: contact@stleonards-fife.org
website: www.stleonards-fife.org
X/Twitter: @StLeonards_Head
Facebook: @stleonardsschool
Instagram: @stleonardsschool
LinkedIn: /school/st-leonards-school

Chair of the Board of Governors: Danny Campbell

***Head*: Simon Brian**, MA Hons Edinburgh

Age range. 5–11.

Number of pupils. 140 (75 girls, 65 boys).

Fees per term (2023–2024). Day: £3,862 (Years 1–3), £4,787 (Years 4–6). Boarding (Year 6 upwards): £9,464.

St Leonards School in St Andrews spans Years 1 to 13, with Years 1–6 classed as the 'Junior Years'. The school is administered by the Board of Governors and offers day and boarding education – boarding is available from age 10.

Pupils typically continue to Year 7, the first of the Senior Years, and beyond to Year 13. With specialist teachers and small classes, children benefit from individual attention. In addition to a strong academic tradition, drama, music, languages, art, ICT and sport are included in the timetable. Swimming is taught every week, and sports are on rotation each term – hockey and rugby in the autumn, hockey and lacrosse in the spring, and tennis, cricket and athletics in the summer.

St Leonards was the first school in Scotland to be accredited to teach the inspiring International Baccalaureate Primary Years Programme, which encourages boys and girls to develop a love of learning. Since its accreditation for the PYP, St Leonards has become one of just two IB continuum schools in the UK, actively offering the PYP, MYP, CP and DP.

Pupils enjoy a dynamic and refreshing approach to teaching and learning both in and outside the classroom. The diverse programme of co-curricular activities offers up to 50 options each year, varying from term to term to encourage young people to develop new passions. Favourites include ballet, bushcraft, beekeeping, Green Team, judo and yoga.

The St Leonards Croft offers pupils opportunities to engage in 'farm to fork' activities, growing their own vegetables and pollinating plants (to encourage the resident bees). Vegetables are harvested and prepared for lunch, which brings a real sense of satisfaction.

St Andrews is known as the 'Home of Golf' and St Leonards offers an outstanding Golf Programme. With six tiers catering to all abilities, the youngest pupils start in the St Leonards Minis before progressing up through the levels and benefitting from famous golf courses and state-of-the-art tracking technology.

Outdoor learning is part of the ethos in the Junior Years, including camping, whittling and Beach School, which is delivered close to home at the East Sands, just a four-minute walk from the campus. A classroom at St

Leonards is not bound by four walls, and the children spend lessons at the beach whenever possible, the teachers making the most of the school's stunning surroundings and natural resources to bring learning to life.

Boarding in the Junior Years is available from Year 6 upwards, with the younger and middle years boarders living in St Rule, a mixed house which was refurbished to the highest standard in 2019. Everyone's favourite pastime is walking 'up town' to Jannettas Gelateria for a scoop of ice cream as a treat!

Charitable status. St Leonards School is a Registered Charity, number SC010904. It exists to provide education to children between the ages of 5 and 18.

St Martin's School

40 Moor Park Road, Northwood, Middlesex HA6 2DJ

Tel: 01923 825740
email: office@stmartins.org.uk
website: www.stmartins.org.uk
X/Twitter: @stmartinsprep
Facebook: @stmartinsschoolnorthwood
Instagram: @stmartinsschoolnorthwood

Chairman of Governors: Andy Harris

***Headmaster*: Mr Simon Dunn**, BEd Hons

Age Range. 3–13.

Number of Boys. 400 Day Boys.

Fees per term (2023–2024). Main School £5,885; Pre-Prep £5,445; Nursery £4,520. Bursaries are available, details on request.

St Martin's aims to provide boys aged 3–13 with the breadth of education and experience necessary for them to realise their full potential in a safe and friendly environment. An enthusiastic staff of 40 experienced and well-qualified teachers maintains high academic standards and provides broad sporting, musical and cultural opportunities. The atmosphere is friendly and lively with great emphasis on pastoral care.

The School, which is an Educational Trust, administered by a Board of Governors, prepares boys for entry to all the Independent Senior Schools. One hundred and two Scholarship awards have been won to senior schools during the last five years. The School, which is in a pleasant residential area, stands in 12 acres of grounds. Facilities include a Nursery and separate Pre-Preparatory building; two Science Laboratories; a Performing Arts Centre; a Sports Centre including an indoor swimming pool; a playground; two ICT suites; an Art Studio with facilities for Design Technology; 3 Tennis Courts and a Nature Reserve.

Computing, Art, DT, and Music are included in the curriculum for all boys, and a large proportion of the boys in the School learn a musical instrument. There is a varied after-school activity programme for boys to pursue their interests.

There is a pre-school and after-school club from Nursery age upwards enabling parents to work a full day.

The School is divided into Patrols for competitions in work and games, and senior boys make a responsible contribution towards the running of the School. Boys are taught football, rugby, cross-country running, hockey, cricket, swimming, athletics and tennis. The school has a fine reputation in inter-school matches.

Charitable status. St Martin's (Northwood) Preparatory School Trust Limited is a Registered Charity, number 312648. It exists to provide education for boys.

St Mary's School
Colchester

91 Lexden Road, Colchester, Essex CO3 3RB

Tel: 01206 594256
email: registrar@stmaryscolchester.org.uk
website: www.stmaryscolchester.org.uk
X/Twitter: @stmaryscolch
Facebook: @stmaryscolchester
Instagram: @stmaryscolchester

See full entry in the **GSA** section, on **p. 481**.

St Mary's School, Hampstead

47 Fitzjohn's Avenue, Hampstead, London NW3 6PG

Tel: 020 7435 1868
email: office@stmh.co.uk
website: www.stmh.co.uk

Chairman of Governors: Mr Sean Murphy, MA Cantab
***Headmistress*: Miss Charlotte Owen**, BA, QTS

Deputy Head: Ms Philippa d'Aquino, BA, QTS

Age Range. Girls 2¾–11.

Number in School. 300 pupils.

Fees per term (2023–2024). Nursery £3,345 (5 mornings a week), £53.00 each additional afternoon per week; Reception to Year 6 £6,180.

St Mary's School Hampstead provides an outstanding and inspirational Catholic education to girls from 2 years 9 months–11 years.

St Mary's School celebrates the uniqueness of every pupil and their achievements. The rigorous, challenging curriculum places a strong emphasis on high academic achievement within a culture of care and support.

The School aims to instil four key habits of learning in their pupils. The children are encouraged to be risk-takers, not only in their play, but also in their learning. They are also taught to be resilient and not to fall at the first hurdle. Staff ask the children to make mistakes, as through the process of challenging themselves, they make more academic progress and in turn excel not only in the classroom, but in their own self-confidence. The girls at St Mary's School are respectful, not just of each other, but of themselves. Finally, pupils are encouraged to be reflective on their faith, behaviour and academic work.

The School has invested in an extensive refurbishment programme to deliver the most up-to-date and stimulating learning spaces. The Global Learning Centre is a cutting-edge space that includes an Engineering and Robotics Lab, Virtual Reality Launch Pad, Art and Design Studio as well as a Green Room.

Another key priority has been incorporating the latest technology to bring learning to life with iPads and Google Chromebooks accessible to every pupil. The spacious classrooms are flooded with natural light and offer innovative flexible seating, making for a very appealing learning space for both individual and collaborative study.

The focus on technology is equally balanced with an emphasis on creative and physical development. Music, drama, art and sports are an essential part of school life and involve everyone. The unique and extensive outdoor area allows girls the space to breathe and consists of climbing equipment and a full-size netball court which affords each child the opportunity to take part in football, tag rugby, netball, cricket and tennis.

The unique combination of integrated technology, flexible seating and a broad curriculum allows St Mary's girls to flourish. They are adopting habits of learning and being encouraged to make independent choices which they can take forward into their secondary education.

Leavers achieve impressive results, gaining offers and Academic Scholarships from the best schools in the country, including Channing School, City of London School for Girls, Francis Holland School, Highgate School, North London Collegiate, South Hampstead High School, St Mary's Ascot and St Paul's Girls' School.

St Mary's Preparatory School

Melrose

Abbey Park, Melrose, Roxburghshire TD6 9LN

Tel: 01896 822517
email: office@stmarysmelrose.org.uk
website: www.stmarysmelrose.org.uk
X/Twitter: @SchoolMarys
Instagram: @melrosestmarys

Founded 1895.

Chairman of Governors: Mr G T G Baird

***Headmaster*: William J Harvey**, BEd Hons

Age range. 2–13 co-educational.

Number of pupils. 171.

Fees per term (2023–2024). Day: Pre-Prep £5,568, Prep £6,518; Weekly Boarding: £7,418.

Curriculum. A healthy variety of subjects including traditional core studies reflecting both the Scottish and English Curriculums (English, Maths, Science, Computer Studies, French, Geography, History, Classics, Latin, Spanish, RE, Art, Music, Drama and PE). The School's intention is to provide a genuinely nourishing environment allowing for the development of the whole child.

Entry requirements. Application by letter or telephone, followed by a visit to the school, if possible, and a tour guided by senior pupils. All pupils can be offered an 'In-day' to help with placement.

Examinations offered. Common Entrance to Scholarship for independent senior schools in Scotland and England.

Academic, sports, games and leisure facilities. Classroom computers, Science Laboratory and a big open Art Room. Theatre-Arts and Assembly Hall for concerts and drama. Spacious games pitches supporting a strong tradition in rugby, cricket, hockey, netball and rounders. There is a cross-curricular Study Support Programme for talented and gifted children as well as for children with Specific Learning Difficulties.

Religious activities. Morning Assembly with hymn-singing and readings, stressing pupil participation and contribution through drama and music.

Charitable status. St Mary's School, Melrose is a Registered Charity, number SC009352. Its aim is to provide education for primary school children.

St Michael's Preparatory School

La Rue de la Houguette, Five Oaks, St Saviour, Jersey, Channel Islands JE2 7UG

Tel: +44(0)1534 856904
email: clt@stmichaels.je
admissions@stmichaels.je
website: www.stmichaels.je
X/Twitter: @stmichaelsprep
Facebook: @St-Michaels-Preparatory-School-Jersey
Instagram: @stmichaelsschooljersey
LinkedIn: /st-michael-s-school-a54955264

***Head*: H J N Marshall**, BSc Hons, PGCE

Academic Assistant Head: G S Green, BEd Hons

Pastoral Assistant Head: Mrs F F Clayton, BA Hons, PGDE

Age Range. 3–14.

Number of Pupils. 155 Boys, 143 Girls.

Fees per term (2023–2024). Pre-Prep (Reception, Years 1 and 2) £4,305–£4,845; Juniors (Years 3 & 4) £5,985; Middle School (Years 5 & 6) £6,615; Senior School (Years 7, 8 & Shell) £6,768. Lunch £435.

Boys and girls are prepared for scholarship and entrance to all Independent Senior Schools. Hockey, rugby, football, gymnastics, netball, rounders, cricket, athletics and tennis are taught on spacious playing fields with pavilion and hard tennis courts and hockey astro, which adjoin the school. The school also has a purpose-built Sports Hall (4 badminton court size), indoor swimming pool and dance studio. Regular tours are made to Guernsey and England for sporting fixtures.

The school has flourishing and well equipped computer, art and engineering departments, in addition to networked computers across the school, including individual devices available for every pupil in Years 1 to Shell. A wide variety of clubs and hobbies function within the school, including activities such as Martial Arts, coding, engineering, yoga, cross-country and many other outdoor activities. Our Shell Year (Y9) take part in the Duke of Edinburgh's (Bronze) Award and play an integral role in the School's Social Impact programme.

Music, drama and art (including pottery), are all encouraged and a wide range of musical instruments are taught. There are three school choirs, two orchestras and a number of ensemble groups. The choirs participate locally and nationally in events and competitions.

For Middle and Senior School pupils there is an annual Activities Week, which takes Years 6, 7 and 8 to different locations in the UK and France; Year 5 take part in island-based activities. Every year a party of children from Years 3 to Shell ski in Europe.

Care, consideration and courtesy form the School's Ethos and are important aspects of behaviour that the School holds dear.

The academic and physical development, in addition to the spiritual, moral and cultural growth of the whole child, is the main aim of the school and every child is encouraged to do 'a little better' than anyone thought possible.

St Michael's Prep School

Otford

Otford Court, Row Dow, Otford, Sevenoaks, Kent TN14 5RY

Tel: 01959 526042
email: jthornton@stmichaels.kent.sch.uk
website: www.stmichaels.kent.sch.uk
X/Twitter: @StMichaels_Prep
Facebook: @StMichaelsPrepSchool
Instagram: @stmichaelsprep
LinkedIn: /st-michael's-prep-school

Chair of Governors: Mr Rashid Chinchanwala

***Head*: Mr Nik Pears**, BEd Hons Cantab

Head of Pre-Prep: Mrs Zerrin Leech, BA Hons, PGCE

Age Range. 2–13 Co-educational.

Number of Pupils. 479.

Fees per term (2023–2024). £910–£5,885.

Joy is at the heart of life at St Michael's: the joy of our children, the joy of our community and the Joy and Wonder of Learning. St Michael's is driven by a passionate belief in the value and power of learning: for children, for teachers, for parents and everyone who comes into contact with us.

St Michael's is an inclusive school where each individual is known, valued and celebrated. We want our children to embrace each day and be inspired by their lessons and co-curricular activities.

We believe in providing a rounded education where children can pursue their passions, challenge themselves and enjoy a creative and innovative curriculum. We are continually looking for ways to improve our curriculum and facilities, making them more vibrant, inspiring and in step with our ever-changing world. Access to our 100 acre site plays an important role in the pupils' learning and growth, developing them into mindful and knowledgeable citizens who will care for their environments throughout their lives.

Our growth mindset approach to teaching and learning ensures that every child understands the value of failure in their path to success. St Michael's children are not afraid to get things wrong, or judgemental of others' mistakes, and this is something they carry with them.

Our school motto: perseverantia, sapientia, gratia (perseverance, wisdom and gratitude) encapsulates our ethos of striving for success and using our skills to make a difference. These values are instilled daily throughout the St Michael's journey.

We strongly believe that in order to teach our children about the importance of life-long learning, we must first model this ourselves. Our staff undergo regular professional development and parents are also invited to a range of workshops on relevant topics.

We are confident that when our pupils move on from St Michael's, they will use the wisdom, skills and values that we taught them to make a positive change in the world.

A message from Nik Pears our Head:

"I would be delighted to welcome you to St Michael's and give you the opportunity to meet some of the extraordinary children and staff who make our school such a special place to grow up. In the first instance, please do visit our website where you will be able to take a virtual tour of our grounds and facilities and gain an insight into life at St Michael's."

Charitable status. St Michael's is a Registered Charity, number 1076999. It exists to provide education for boys and girls.

St Neot's Preparatory School

St Neot's Road, Eversley, Hook, Hampshire RG27 0PN

Tel: 0118 973 2118 (Office)
0118 973 9650 (Admissions)
email: office@stneotsprep.co.uk
admissions@stneotsprep.co.uk
website: www.stneotsprep.co.uk
X/Twitter: @stneotsprep
Facebook: @stneotsprep
Instagram: @stneotsprepschool

Chair of Governors: Mr David Hertzell

***Head*: Mr Jonathan Slot**

Age Range. 2–13 years co-educational.

Number of Pupils. 313.

Fees per term (2023–2024). Years 5–8 £6,414, Years 3–4 £5,983, Reception–Year 2 £4,483, Nursery £81 per day (core hours), £47 per morning session.

St Neot's, founded in 1888, is a happy, vibrant community for boys and girls from 2 to 13 years. The school is situated on the border of Hampshire and

Berkshire and is set in 70 acres of beautiful grounds and woodland.

The school's educational philosophy is to inspire children to develop a love of learning in a supportive and happy environment, where each individual is encouraged to achieve their full academic potential and beyond. Children are motivated to discover their full range of talents and to develop the passion to pursue them. They are given the opportunity to embrace challenge, think creatively, develop self-confidence and foster empathy towards others, preparing them both intellectually and emotionally for success in the 21st Century.

We aim to provide the highest standards in teaching and learning, within a well rounded educational experience and St Neot's has a very strong record of success in achieving Scholarships and Awards to numerous Senior Schools.

St Neot's is committed to providing a world of opportunity in every aspect of school life. Stimulating learning environments ensure that engaged pupils work towards the highest academic standards, whilst also enjoying a breadth of experience in sport, music, art, drama and dance.

Emphasis is placed on developing independence, self-confidence, curiosity and collaboration. Forest School and Outdoor Education programmes encourage children of all ages to develop these attributes, which are so vital in the modern world. The St Neot's journey culminates in the Years 7 and 8 leadership programme, which draws together a mix of skills through the Pre Senior Schools Baccalaureate (PSB).

Sport is a strength of the school and our state-of-the-art sports complex, comprising sports hall, 25m indoor swimming pool, all-weather astro, cricket nets, hard tennis and netball courts, significantly supplement the extensive playing fields. There is also an on-site mountain bike track and a traversing wall. Judo, dance and tennis are taught by specialist coaches and there are many after-school clubs and activities covering a wide range of interests. Holiday Clubs run in all school breaks and offer a wealth of opportunities, both sporting and creative.

St Neot's holds a Gold Artsmark award, giving recognition to our achievements in art, music, drama and dance. A number of plays, concerts and recitals take place throughout the school year for all age groups, either in the school grounds or in the Performing Arts Centre.

Open Mornings take place termly and details of these can be found on the school website: www.stneotsprep.co.uk. We would also be delighted to arrange an individual tour and a meeting with the Head. Please contact Admissions on 0118 9739650; email: admissions@stneotsprep.co.uk.

Charitable status. St Neot's (Eversley) Limited is a Registered Charity, number 307324. The aim of the Charity is to try to provide the best all-round education possible to as many pupils as possible, with bursarial help according to need.

St Olave's Prep School

106–110 Southwood Road, New Eltham, London SE9 3QS

Tel:	020 8294 8930
email:	office@stolaves.org.uk
website:	www.stolaves.org.uk

Chair of Trustees: Peter Houillon

***Headteacher*: Miss Claire Holloway**, BEd QTS

Age Range. 3–11.

Number of Pupils. 215 Day Boys and Girls.

Fees per term (2023–2024). Nursery £2,320–£4,552; Reception & Year 1 £4,772; Years 2–6 £5,120.

In a single sentence, the school aims to bring out the best in everyone. It seeks to achieve this aim by providing an all-round education for both boys and girls aged 3 to 11 in a warm and caring environment in which each child can thrive and be happy knowing that each is accepted for who they are.

A Christian ethos permeates the pastoral life of the school, where care for others through thoughtful and responsible behaviour is expected. Praise and encouragement are emphasised and relationships between staff and pupils are relaxed and friendly. A close partnership with parents is sought.

The children in the EYFS (Nursery and Reception) and Pre-Prep (Year 1 and Year 2) are taught in mixed-ability classes where each child's progress is carefully monitored by the Class Teacher. In the Upper School (Years 3–6) the children are set across the year group for Mathematics. Throughout the school individual differences are appropriately met, with the very able and those with mild learning difficulties receiving additional support where this is thought beneficial. The school is noted for the broad curriculum it offers and for its excellent achievements in Music and Drama. A range of sporting activities is taught as part of the curriculum and there is a wide range of after school clubs and activities. Music and PE are taught by specialist teachers from the age of three, French is introduced at four years old and Latin at ten years old. The classrooms are equipped with computers and there is a networked suite which supports all areas of the curriculum. A specialist ICT teacher teaches all year groups from Reception to Year 6. Digital panels and portable devices are used to enhance learning.

St Olave's feeds a wide range of secondary schools and parents are given help in choosing the school most appropriate to meet the needs of their child.

Charitable status. St Olave's School is a Registered Charity, number 312734. It exists to provide high quality education for boys and girls.

St Paul's Cathedral School

2 New Change, London EC4M 9AD
Tel: 020 7248 5156
email: office@spcs.london.sch.uk
website: www.spcslondon.com
X/Twitter: @StPaulsCathSch
Facebook: @StPaulsCathedralSchool
Instagram: @stpaulscathedralschool
LinkedIn: /spcslondon

Chairman of Governors: Robert-Jan Tremmink, KC

***Head*: Judith Fremont-Barnes**, MA Hons, MEd

Bursar: Steve Vickery
Registrar: Clare Morgan

Age Range. 4–13 Co-educational.

Number of Pupils. Boarding Choristers circa 30, Day Boys circa 160, Day Girls circa 110, Pre-Prep circa 100.

Fees per term (2023–2024). Choristers: £3,421; Day pupils: £5,656–£6,090.

St Paul's Cathedral School has existed since the 12th century, originally established to educate the now world-class choristers of St Paul's Cathedral. Since moving to its present site, set to the east end of the Cathedral, it is also a vibrant day school, educating the children of professionals living and working in the City and local boroughs.

It is a school in high demand, and is noted for its friendly atmosphere, sense of purpose, care and kindness. Teaching staff are recruited carefully, and the school invests in their continual professional development, meaning that children benefit from staff that are fully focused on the pupil's wellbeing and learning outcomes.

Providing boys and girls with the firm foundations for the future and preparing them for the next stage in their education in a safe and comfortable environment is central to our aims and principles. There is real breadth to the educational experience here. Recent enlargement of the school has provided additional classrooms, extended dining facilities and created fantastic play areas. The school is self-contained, and given it is surrounded on three sides by trees and gardens, the air quality is excellent.

Our location means that we can make the most of what London has to offer: trips to museums and galleries and other places of interest are a regular occurrence, not to forget our privileged access to the Cathedral, our school chapel. We use a wide range of London's sporting facilities, and enjoy success in fixtures against other schools.

Ultimately, the most important thing we aspire to do as a school is instil a lifelong love of learning.

The boys and girls go on to a wide variety of senior schools at 11+ and 13+: co-educational; single sex; boarding and day. We have a good record of scholarships, particularly music scholarships, to many of the top schools in London and beyond.

We pride ourselves on the high calibre of pastoral care given to all our pupils and resident staff take on the particular role of looking after the choristers who board in a separate building on the school's site.

All pupils are encouraged to play a musical instrument (most pupils play two) and there are music and theory lessons with school orchestras and chamber groups.

A wide variety of games is offered including field sports at local playing fields. The children have their own playground and the use of the hall for indoor games and gymnastics.

Admissions procedure. Prospective pupils of 7+ years in September are given academic tests in verbal and non-verbal reasoning, in January of the year of entry.

Pre-Prep children (4+) are assessed in an informal play situation in the November prior to entry.

11+ entry is becoming popular, and scholarships at 11+ offering 10% fee remission are available to exceptional candidates in music, art, sport and academic ability. For more information see: www.spcs.london/admissions/scholarships

Occasional places sometimes come up.

For prospective boy and girl choristers, voice trials and tests are held throughout the year for pupils in years 3, 4 and occasionally 5.

The Head is always happy to invite prospective parents to see the school.

St Paul's Juniors

Lonsdale Road, London SW13 9JT
Tel: 020 8748 3461
email: spjheadpa@stpaulsschool.org.uk
website: www.stpaulsschool.org.uk
X/Twitter: @StPaulsSchool
Facebook: @StPaulsSchool1509
Instagram: @stpaulsschoollondon
LinkedIn: /school/st-paul's-school

Chairman of Governors: Richard Cassell, BA, LLB

***Head*: Oliver Snowball**, BA, MA, PGCE

Age Range. 7–13.

Number of Boys. 511.

Fees per term (2023–2024). £7,910.

St Paul's Juniors is the junior division for St Paul's School (*see entry in HMC section*) and attracts bright, enthusiastic boys who are inquisitive and eager to learn.

Working closely alongside St Paul's senior school to inform the curriculum ensures continuity and a more holistic learning experience, with some teaching staff working across both schools. Pupils at St Paul's Juniors hold a place at St Paul's School and transfer automatically at the end of Year 8, subject to ongoing good work and conduct, rather than a formal examination. Our aim is to offer a broad education to every pupil, along with the opportunity to enjoy a wide range of activities. Music, Art, Drama and Sport are all strong, but additional activities range from history and debating to chess, coding and cookery.

Boys join the School at 7+, 8+ and 11+. Fifty-four boys join Year 3 into three classes of 18 and a further eighteen join them at 8+. Thirty-six boys join in Year 7 creating a total of six classes in Years 7 and 8. Entrance at all levels is by competitive examination and interview. Means-tested bursaries are available at all points of entry.

St Paul's School sits on the south bank of the Thames. St Paul's Juniors is on the same campus as St Paul's School. The Juniors are currently housed in recently refurbished accommodation, which is separate but adjacent to the senior school's main teaching block. Two major new buildings, now under construction on the campus, will ultimately become the long-term home for St Paul's Juniors and are due for completion in 2025. Whilst SPJ shares some amenities with the senior school, including the dining hall, the sports complex, engineering workshops, the music centre and playing fields, it also has its own science laboratories, art studios, computer suites, drama studio and library.

Charitable status. St Paul's School is a Registered Charity, number 1119619. The object of the charity is to promote the education of boys in Greater London.

St Peter's 2–8
The Pre-prep School of St Peter's School, York

Clifton, York YO30 6AB

Tel: 01904 527361
email: enquiries2–8@stpetersyork.org.uk
website: www.stpetersyork.org.uk
X/Twitter: @stpetersyork
Facebook: @stpetersyork
Instagram: @stpeters.york
LinkedIn: /school/stpetersyork

Chairman of the Governors: Mr W Woolley

***Head*: Mrs Antonia Clarke**, BA Nottingham

Age Range. 2–8 co-educational.

Number of Pupils. 155 boys, 121 girls.

Fees per term (2023–2024). Nursery (term-time): £3,190 (full-time nursery is available through the holidays but booked separately); Reception, Years 1 & 2: £3,570; Year 3: £3,840. Nursery Education Grant accepted for 3 and 4 year olds.

A sense of belonging, infinite opportunities and unlimited possibilities is what it feels like to be a child at St Peter's 2–8. As part of the St Peter's School family, the school represents the start of an exciting and rewarding learning adventure. In April 2021, St Peter's 2–8 was declared *Pre-prep School of the Year* in the national Tes Independent School Awards for its 'outstanding innovative and broad curriculum, which encourages curiosity in an ever-changing world'.

Curriculum. A vibrant and dynamic thematic skills-based curriculum is covered, which offers variety, challenge and opportunities for everyone to discover what they love. Small classes, individual attention, Forest School and a huge range of after-school activities enable high standards to be achieved. French is offered to all children from Nursery upwards.

Music and Drama. All children throughout the school have ample opportunity to be creative and express themselves. Nursery children have a session of music and movement, and all other classes have weekly lessons with a dedicated music teacher. From Year 2, children have the opportunity to learn to play a variety of instruments in personal lessons. Each year there are opportunities for children to participate in performances to a wider audience. All classes have weekly drama lessons, and there is the opportunity for Y2 and Y3 to do speech and drama as an after school activity.

Sport and Co-Curricular Activities. Physical Education starts in the Nursery. As children grow older, games and swimming are added. The pupils have access to the impressive sports facilities and 47-acre green campus at St Peter's School. Co-curricular activities include: Art, Drama, Animation, Ballet, Karate, Explorers, Lego and The Green Team.

Assessments. Throughout Nursery and Reception, children work towards achieving the Early Learning Goals, culminating in the completion of the Foundation Stage Profile. Work is assessed continuously and children's progress is discussed at staff meetings. Incas is used in Years 1 to 3 for assessment purposes which informs future planning. There is ongoing communication between parents and staff through a reports system, invitations to visit the school and parent evenings.

An ISI Inspection in April 2017 found St Peter's School 2–18 to be 'excellent' in all areas for the quality of its education – the highest grading that any school can achieve.

Charitable status. St Peter's School, York, is a Registered Charity, number 1141329. It exists to provide education for boys and girls.

St Peter's 8–13
The Prep School of St Peter's School, York

Queen Anne's Road, York YO30 7WA

Tel: 01904 527416
email: enquiries8–13@stpetersyork.org.uk
website: www.stpetersyork.org.uk
X/Twitter: @stpetersyork
Facebook: @stpetersschoolyork
Instagram: @stpeters.york
LinkedIn: /school/stpetersyork

Chairman of the Governors: Mr W Woolley

***Head*: Mr P C Hardy**, BA, PGCE

Deputy Head: Mr M C Ferguson, HDE Cape Town

Age Range. 8–13 co-educational.

Number of Pupils. 223 Boys, 186 Girls.

Fees per term (2023–2024). Day: £5,110–£6,180; Boarding: £9,600–£10,595. Non-EEA Boarder: £10,380–£11,430.

Tuition fees include the costs of stationery and textbooks. There are no compulsory extras except for examination fees. Lunches are included in day fees.

St Peter's 8–13 (formerly St Olave's) was founded in 1876. With its own halls, music school, practical subjects workshops, sports hall and magnificently appointed specialist teaching rooms, St Peter's enjoys some of the best facilities for a prep school of its type and is proud to be the Choir School for York Minster.

The school puts praise, encouragement and pastoral care of the individual as its highest priority. There is a demanding wide curriculum from the earliest age with specialist subject areas – modern foreign languages, information technology, science and music, amongst others – being taught by specialist teachers from Year 4. Progress is monitored through a regular system of effort grades, and attainment is measured through internal and externally moderated tests.

Boarding, available for children in Year 7 and above, is a flourishing aspect of the school, with a co-educational House under the constant care of resident Houseparents and their own family. Weekly and flexi boarding are also available. There are also five Day Houses.

Music plays an important part in the life of the school with 22 music teachers, two orchestras, a wind band and 14 ensembles playing and practising weekly. Over 200 pupils learn individual instruments, and all are encouraged to join larger groups. York Minster's girl and boy choristers are educated at St Peter's 8–13.

Sport has an equally high profile where football, hockey, cricket, netball, rugby, tennis and swimming are major sports. Athletics, cross-country running, squash, badminton, basketball and volleyball are also available for all. The school has 23 tennis courts, a synthetic pitch and a 25 m 6-lane swimming pool.

Drama has an increasing profile, and out-of-school activities flourish through clubs such as eco club, science society, chess, photography, art and trampoline.

The vast majority of boys and girls move on to St Peter's 13–18.

Entrance assessments are held in January/February each year, and assessments can also be arranged at other times. Entry is possible in most year groups, although the school is heavily oversubscribed at most stages. Means-tested fee assistance is available from age 11.

Charitable status. St Peter's School, York, is a Registered Charity, number 1141329. It exists to provide education for boys and girls.

St Piran's

Gringer Hill, Maidenhead, Berkshire SL6 7LZ

Tel: 01628 594300
email: registrar@stpirans.co.uk
website: www.stpirans.co.uk
X/Twitter: @stpirans_school
Facebook: @StPiransSchool
Instagram: @stpirans
LinkedIn: /company/stpiransschool

Chair of Governors: Mrs Kate Taylor

***Headmaster*: Mr Sebastian Sales**

Age range. 2 to 11 Co-educational.

Number of pupils. 431 day pupils.

Fees per term (2023–2024). £4,211 to £6,624. Nursery (5 full days, including food): £3,620.29 (funded).

St Piran's is a thriving co-educational IAPS day school set amid 10 delightful acres just to the north of Maidenhead town centre. Founded as a small school in Blackheath, London in 1805.

Class sizes are small with a maximum of 20 children. Boys and girls benefit from individual attention in all subjects. They are provided with a wide range of exciting opportunities both inside and outside the classroom. Numerous trips to castles and museums, theatres and shows, history re-enactments, geographical fieldwork and religious sites extend the children's understanding of the world around them. In addition to the academic subjects, pupils take part in a wide range of other activities each week.

Academically, the school offers a broad curriculum at all levels in the school. French starts with our youngest classes where confidence in the spoken language is encouraged. By Year 6 we are introducing Latin and Spanish. The children enjoy specialist teaching in art, games and PE, IT, swimming and music from an early age. We support children with their entrance exams at 11+ to Grammar Schools or other Senior independent schools. Our results over the years have been excellent, supporting our desire to encourage independent thinkers, confident individuals and strong leaders of the future.

The main sports that pupils take part in are rugby, football, netball, hockey, cricket (both girls and boys) and swimming. The school has its own indoor swimming pool and large sports hall. St Piran's also has a dance studio and pupils are encouraged to take an active part in the performing arts. We are blessed with wonderful facilities which serve to enhance the varied sports programmes that we offer the children at all levels.

The school has its own Leadership programme and regular visits off-site are arranged for all the children, including residential trips.

Pupils may enter the school at any age, although the main intakes occur at Nursery and Reception.

The school is proud of its outstanding record of achievement and the fully rounded education that it provides within a friendly caring atmosphere. We are proud of our Christian tradition and family ethos which foster high expectations and successful, happy children.

Children and parents are warmly invited to visit St Piran's to see for themselves the excellent facilities that we offer and to meet some of the staff and pupils.

Charitable status. St Piran's School Limited is a Registered Charity, number 309094.

St Pius X Prep School

200 Garstang Road, Fulwood, Preston, Lancashire PR2 8RD

Tel: 01772 719937
email: enquiries@st-piusx.lancs.sch.uk
website: www.stpiusx.co.uk
Facebook: @StPiusXCatholicPreparatorySchool
Instagram: @stpiusxprepschool

Chairman of Governors: Mr Raj Luthra

***Headmaster*: Mr Charlie Long**

Age range. 2–11.

Number of children. 120 Day Girls and Boys.

Fees per term (2023–2024). Main School: £2,756–£2,966 per term, Nursery: £25 per session.

The School is a non-profit-making charitable trust administered by a Board of Governors, providing education from 2–11, set in six acres of its own grounds in a pleasant suburb of Preston.

The children are prepared for the entrance examinations to independent schools and Grammar Schools and it has an excellent record of scholarships to senior schools and SATS results at KS1 and KS2.

The school has an outstanding EYFS setting which covers the Reception classes and the Nursery, in open-plan Nursery rooms.

All preparatory curriculum subjects are covered, as well as sign language, Health & Wellbeing, and STEM.

Sports taught are Association Football, Cricket, Tennis, Hockey, Netball, Rugby, Rounders, Athletics and Cross Country.

Creative and Performing Arts, including Music and Drama, thrive alongside Outdoor Education and Forest School. Ballet, piano, wind, bass-guitar, percussion, string and singing lessons are some of the optional extras offered.

Charitable status. St Pius X School is a Registered Charity, number 526609. Its purpose is to equip the children with an outstanding academic and social education in a Catholic Christian environment, which will enable them to achieve their full potential – the school welcomes pupils of all faiths.

St Swithun's Prep School

Alresford Road, Winchester, Hampshire SO21 1HA

Tel: 01962 835750
email: prepoffice@stswithuns.com
website: www.stswithuns.com
X/Twitter: @stswithunsprep
Facebook: @StSwithunsPrepSchool
Instagram: @stswithunsprep

Established 1884. Girls day preparatory school with a co-ed pre-school. Church of England.

School Council:
Chair: Mrs Alison McClure

***Head*: Mrs Liz Norris**, BSc King's College, London, PGCE Anglia Ruskin

Deputy Head: Mrs Katherine Grosscurth, BSc Hons Plymouth, PGCE Exeter

Age Range. Girls 4–11, with a co-ed pre-school.

Number of Pupils. 220 pupils. Average class size 18. Pupil to teacher ratio 12:1.

Fees per term (2023–2024). Pre-school: £4,414 (all day including lunch); Reception, Years 1 & 2 £4,414; Year 3 £5,854; Years 4–6 £5,938.

Profile. Welcome to St Swithun's Prep School, a school in which every child is known, cherished and at the same time encouraged to be fearless.

Our modern, purpose-built prep school provides a simply spectacular and inspiring teaching and learning environment. It is an environment in which pupils and staff have warm, respectful relationships. The building includes specialist teaching rooms, a science laboratory, an art studio, a media/computing room, a performing arts space and a gym. Prep school children also have access to the school's athletics track and indoor swimming facilities, including a teaching pool. Swimming is part of the curriculum for all students. There is also a Forest School on campus. The children enjoy going to school and the staff relish having the opportunity to share adventures, interests and laughter.

While united in their enthusiasm and energy, the children are all individuals and we encourage them to sample a wide range of experiences so that they each develop individual passions. We look always to celebrate characteristics such as the ability to bounce back from disappointment, to show compassion for others, to rise to challenges and to keep a sense of perspective. We want your children to go home every evening with slightly grubby knees and tales of what they have done at school that day.

Entry. At 3.

Curriculum. Usual subjects taught plus French, art, technology, drama, ICT, music and PE, with due regard for National Curriculum requirements.

Leavers. Girls go on to a range of senior independent schools, with the majority going to St Swithun's Senior School.

Consultation. Biannual reports, regular parents' evenings and PTA.

Sports. Gymnastics, netball, pop lacrosse, rounders, tag rugby, tennis, short tennis, swimming, football, and athletics.

Activities. These include tennis, art, drama, gymnastics, judo, science, cookery, swimming, football and dance.

Musical concerts and productions are regularly held. Three annual residential trips in Years 4–6, and regular visits from Nursery to Year 6 take place.

Special needs. Qualified Learning Support teacher.

Charitable status. St Swithun's School Winchester is a Registered Charity, number 307335.

Salisbury Cathedral School

1 The Close, Salisbury, Wilts SP1 2EQ

Tel: 01722 555300
email: admissions@salisburycathedralschool.com
website: www.salisburycathedralschool.com
X/Twitter: @salisburycathsc
Facebook: @Salisbury-Cathedral-School
Instagram: @salisburycathedralschool
LinkedIn: /company/salisbury-cathedral-school

Founded in 1091. Co-educational Day and Boarding Preparatory, Pre-Preparatory and Choir School.

Chairman of Governors: Mr James Fletcher

Head: Sophie Baber (until Sept. 2024); Sally Moulton (from Sept. 2024)

Age Range. 3–13.

Number of Pupils. Day pupils: 180; Boarders: 40.

Fees per term (2023–2024). Pre-Prep: £3,563 (Reception, Years 1 & 2), £5,341 (Year 3). Preparatory School: £6,418 (day), £3,013 (boarding supplement).

'Warm', 'caring', 'happy' – these are the three most popular words used by parents to describe Salisbury Cathedral School. Our unique setting, adjacent to one of England's finest cathedrals, helps to cultivate a strong spiritual awareness and Christian values underpin everything that we do.

Our wonderful 21st century school is based in the 800 year old Bishops Palace within Salisbury Cathedral's grounds.

We believe a child's self-esteem is vital to their success. At SCS, we foster an unpressured environment where pupils are encouraged and congratulated every step of the way, celebrating their achievements and promoting a strong sense of self-worth. Our focus on the individual child means that all staff play a role in discovering strengths and areas that need guidance and support.

This approach works. Our academic results are impressive and consistently out-perform competing schools but, more than this, the children who leave us are confident, self-assured, well-rounded and comfortable in their own skins.

Facilities include: over 20 acres of beautiful grounds, an all-weather sports pitch, swimming pool, outstanding music facilities, a variety of performance spaces, specialist science laboratory, art, design technology and computer suites and extensive playground facilities.

Talented sports staff coach all the major team sports and every child plays in regular fixtures.

There are many after-school clubs open to all children in the Preparatory School. (Quality wrap-around school care is available for children in the Pre-Prep). The boarding house staff operate an "open door" policy to parents, organise many outings and activities and have achieved an enviable reputation for running a truly happy and caring boarding house.

For more information and/or to arrange a visit to the school, please telephone Jojo Orange, Registrar on 01722 555300 or visit our website.

Charitable status. Salisbury Cathedral School is a Registered Charity, number 309485. It exists to provide high quality education for children.

Sandroyd School

Rushmore Park, Tollard Royal, Salisbury, Wiltshire SP5 5QD

Tel: 01725 530124
email: admissions@sandroyd.com
website: www.sandroyd.org
X/Twitter: @SandroydSchool
Facebook: @sandroydschool
Instagram: @sandroydschool
LinkedIn: /company/sandroyd-school

Chairman of Governors: R G L Thomas, MRICS, FAAV

***Headmaster*: A B Speers**, BSc, MEd

Age Range. 2–13 co-educational.

Number of Pupils. 140 boarders, 50 day, plus 40 in pre-prep.

Fees per term (2023–2024). Boarding: £10,620 (Years 4–8), £8,410 (Year 3); Day: £10,620 (Years 7–8), £8,780 (Years 4–6), £6,530 (Year 3). Pre-Prep: £3,660 (Reception–Year 2). Nursery: £28 (per morning), £41 (all day including lunch).

Sandroyd is a co-educational day and boarding school for children aged 2–13 years. It is a wonderfully unique family school that 'prepares' children in the very broadest sense. It nurtures a child's confidence and self-esteem whilst encouraging each individual pupil to fulfill all aspects of their potential: academic, artistic, cultural, sporting, and social.

Sandroyd pupils stand out from the crowd – or at least that's what Senior Schools report back. We're repeatedly told that our pupils are better prepared to face the demands of senior school successfully. Not just in their academic abilities, but, just as importantly, in the vital 'soft skills' of confidence, resilience, and self-motivation.

We believe that childhood should be relished, enjoyed, and remembered fondly. That's why pastoral care is absolutely central to everything that we do at Sandroyd – in both our Pre-Prep, (for children aged 2–7), and in our Prep School (for children aged 7–13).

Academic Excellence within a Balanced Curriculum

We have a deserved reputation as one of the top academic prep schools in the country. This academic success is not assessed solely by our consistently excellent scholarship and Common Entrance results but by the value added across all ability ranges and throughout the school. Our day is broadly split into academic work in the mornings and after lunch, children spend the majority of time outside. Our timetable ensures equal time and importance is given to extra-curricular activities and the academic curriculum; neither is at the expense of the other.

Pastoral Care. Outstanding pastoral care is the lynchpin of a Sandroyd education. It ensures that each child feels safe to develop, explore and make mistakes in a nurturing environment. At the core of our pastoral care is our commitment to boarding (offering full, weekly, or flexi options).

Our Size. We are unequivocally proud of the size of our school, creating a wonderful family atmosphere that allows us to properly focus on the individual needs of each child. A size that allows us to invest in the best staff, appropriate facilities, and equipment. We are large enough to provide stimulating opportunities yet small enough to maintain the family feel that is so pertinent.

Location. Our location, in the centre of over 500 acres of parkland, is idyllic. Our stunning environment allows pupils to take part in a wide variety of sports, to learn outside, and, most importantly, to be able to just romp about outdoors. There is untold value in giving children the freedom and space to grow and develop in a safe setting.

Ethos. At Sandroyd we aim to inspire each child to strive for excellence in all aspects of school life; academic, cultural, and sporting. We seek to combine the best in modern educational methods with an emphasis on the time-honoured virtues of good manners, self-discipline, and respect for others. We strive to ensure that the children in our care are happy, self-confident, and well-prepared to meet the challenges of the future.

Sarum Hall School

15 Eton Avenue, London NW3 3EL

Tel: 020 7794 2261
email: admissions@sarumhallschool.co.uk
website: www.sarumhallschool.co.uk
X/Twitter: @SarumHall
Instagram: @sarumhallschool

The School, which has a Christian (Church of England) foundation, is an educational trust with a Board of Governors.

Chair of Governors: Dr C Sayer
***Headmistress*: Miss Karen Coles**, BEd Hons

Age Range. 3–11.
Number of Pupils. 185 Day Girls.
Fees per term (2023–2024). £5,865–£6,350.

Founded in 1929, the school has, since 1995, been housed in new purpose-built premises which provide excellent, spacious facilities, including a large playground, gym, dining room and specialist art, IT, music and science rooms, in addition to a French room, wellbeing room, multi-purpose room and individual music teaching rooms. The school has a purpose built Food Studio to support Food Technology teaching, as well as cross-curricular links and the opportunity to foster relevant and practical skills across the wider curriculum.

Girls are prepared for senior London day schools and for 11+ Common Entrance. The main point of entry is into the Nursery at 3+ where there is no assessment; occasional places further up the school are subject to an age appropriate performance in a short English and Maths test. The school is ambitious for its girls and believes that in a caring, supportive and imaginative environment, every girl can achieve her full potential. The pupils are encouraged to develop a set of transferable life skills that they can apply to a variety of scenarios, and develop as individuals with a sense of purpose in the school community and beyond. The school has a well-established record of scholarship and examination success; destination schools include Channing, City of London School for Girls, Downe House, Francis Holland, Godolphin & Latymer, Highgate, Mill Hill Foundation, North London Collegiate, Queen's College, Queen's Gate, Queenswood, South Hampstead High School, St Helen's, St Marylebone School for Girls, St Paul's Girls and Wycombe Abbey.

A broad curriculum is followed and a major investment in IT ensures that each girl has access to the latest technology, which expands and enriches their educational provision. Languages are taught from Reception, Chess and a comprehensive games programme, which primarily takes place on site, ensures that girls have the opportunity to experience a variety of sports. We believe in offering a broad and balanced curriculum, therefore there is a strong emphasis on music, art, design and drama. Woodwind, violin, piano, cello and singing are offered. There are also two choirs, an orchestra and ensemble groups. Other extra-curricular activities include theory of music, fencing, junior and senior football, gardening, modern art, nature, netball, tennis, ICT, yoga, philosophy, photography, drama, craft, chess, cooking, classical civilisations, board games, dance and performance.

Scarborough College

Filey Road, Scarborough, North Yorkshire YO11 3BA

Tel: 01723 360620
email: admin@scarboroughcollege.co.uk
website: www.scarboroughcollege.co.uk
X/Twitter: @ScarColl
Facebook: @ScarboroughColl
Instagram: @scarboroughcollege

See full entry in the **Society of Heads** section, on **p. 561**.

Seaford College Prep School
Wilberforce House

Lavington Park, Petworth, West Sussex GU28 0NB

Tel: 01798 867893
email: wilberforce@seaford.org
hrichardson@seaford.org
website: www.seaford.org
X/Twitter: @seafordcollege
Facebook: @seafordcollege
Instagram: @seafordcollege
LinkedIn: /company/seafordcollege

Chairman of Governors: R Venables Kyrke

***Head of Prep School*: Mr Alastair Brown**, BEd

Age Range. 5–13 Co-educational.

Number of Pupils. 241.

Fees per term (2023–2024). Day £4,240–£8,785; Weekly boarding: £8,825 (Year 6), £9,345 (Year 7), £11,895 (Year 8); Full Boarding £13,580.

Seaford College Prep School (Wilberforce House) is an integral part of Seaford College, having the same board of governors, but with its own buildings, playground and corporate organisation. There is very close cooperation between the two schools and there are many shared facilities such as the games fields, a new Sports Centre, the Music School, Science Department, and Art and Design Department. Wilberforce House is named after Samuel Wilberforce, the son of the anti-slavery campaigner William Wilberforce. Samuel is buried in the grounds of the School's chapel. The School is set in a magnificent 400-acre site adjacent to the South Downs National Park.

The Prep School educates boys and girls from the age of 5 and the vast majority of children continue their education at Seaford College until 16 or 18. The main entry points for the Prep School are at 7+ and 11+ although children are welcome to join the school at any age.

The school aims to nurture a love of learning through a broadly based curriculum and classroom activities are often complemented by day and residential visits. In Years 1–5, the majority of lessons are taught by form teachers with subjects such as Music, French, PE/Games and Design and Technology taught by specialist staff. Year 6 are form based for English, Maths, History and Geography with all other subjects taught by subject specialists. From Year 7 all subjects are taught by specialist staff, many of whom also teach in the Senior School. All classrooms are equipped with interactive whiteboards while a Special Educational Needs Coordinator oversees the school's learning support provision which further enhances learning and achievement. The majority of children complete most of their homework in school and the school day finishes at 5.20pm.

Boarding provision, from Year 6 upwards, is an important aspect of life in the school with the aim being to be as flexible as possible in order to meet parents' and pupils' needs as well as providing a warm and caring home-from-home atmosphere.

Pupils are able to benefit from the impressive range of games facilities on site, including the new Sports Centre, an AstroTurf hockey pitch, indoor swimming pool and a 9-hole golf course, with practice greens and driving range as well as the services of a golf professional. Expert coaching is provided in the main sports of football, rugby, hockey, cricket, netball, rounders, tennis, athletics and swimming. The school also has excellent facilities for music, art and design and technology.

The standard of pastoral care is high and the school has its own Chaplain who takes a weekly assembly. The Prep School aims to treat each pupil as an individual and to establish the firm foundations necessary for success in the Senior School and beyond. (*See Seaford College entry in HMC section.*)

Charitable status. Seaford College is a Registered Charity, number 277439.

Sevenoaks Prep School

Godden Green, Sevenoaks, Kent TN15 0JU

Tel: 01732 762336
email: admin@theprep.org.uk
website: www.theprep.org.uk
X/Twitter: @Sevenoaksprep
Facebook: @sevenoaksprep
Instagram: @sevenoaksprep

Chairman of Governors: Jan Berry

***Headmaster*: Luke Harrison**, BA Hons, PGCE

Head of Pre-Prep: Helen Cook, BSc, PGCE Primary and Early Years, NPQH

Age Range. 2 to 13.

Number of Children. 370 pupils.

Fees per annum (2023–2024). Reception: £12,996; Years 1–2: £14,823; Years 3–8: £17,793. Nursery & kindergarten: £445 one session/week per term or £880 for a full day/week per term.

Founded in 1919, Sevenoaks Prep School stands on a spacious 25-acre site of playing fields and woodland bordering the 1,000-acre Knole Estate. We welcome girls and boys from 2 to 13 years of age. Our small class sizes and family atmosphere enables us to build special relationships with the children and their parents.

The curriculum is tailored to the needs of the pupils and their future aspirations. Whilst due regard is paid to the National Curriculum, our children are taught to the highest standard achievable by the individual. To this end, our teachers enhance their Programmes of Study to ensure that every pupil is motivated, challenged and prepared for 11+ or 13+ entry tests to local grammar schools or via ISEB Common Entrance examinations and scholarships to independent schools. Our academic achievements are consistently high and our pupils compete successfully for academic, sport, music and other scholarships.

Throughout the school all classes regularly participate in a programme of visits, workshops and field trips to support their learning. Education at Sevenoaks Prep is for life not just the classroom – it is the balance of academic study and co-curricular activities that prepare the children for their future.

The school had their latest ISI Inspection in March 2022 which is available to view on their website. They were delighted to have received a glowing report and were graded as 'Excellent' for both pupils' personal and academic achievements, the highest outcome that a school can receive.

The school comprises the Pre-Prep (Nursery–Year 2), and the Prep School (Years 3–8).

Nursery and Kindergarten are staffed by teachers who are specially qualified in Early Years education, with a high teacher to pupil ratio. The education provided is specifically designed to match each child's needs, so that child-initiated play and teacher-directed activities are thoughtfully planned and carefully balanced.

Full-time education starts in the Reception class in Pre-Prep and from this point, through Years 1 and 2, class teachers and their assistants provide a rich and stimulating environment where curiosity and enthusiasm to learn are fostered. Pupils benefit from using the Prep facilities for their computer and art lessons and these subjects, along with PE and games, are taught by Prep teachers.

On entering the Prep school in Year 3, class teaching is continued for core subjects (with specialist teaching for drama, languages, music, ICT, PE and games). By the age of ten, our pupils are taught by specialist teachers in all subjects whilst each class continues to have a form teacher who monitors their progress. Years 7 and 8 are the secondary school years and this is reflected in the teaching and levels of responsibility offered to the children. At Sevenoaks Prep they are at the top of the school and are provided with leadership opportunities and responsibilities. Heads of our destination schools say that children from Sevenoaks Prep enter Year 9 as rounded individuals, confident both academically and socially.

Facilities include a large multi-purpose sports hall, a state-of-the-art drama and music suite, 'Forest School' outdoor education area, and modern Early Years classrooms and hall. A new Centenary Centre housing science, art, humanities, ICT and a library opened in 2020. The location provides a useful and natural extension to the teaching facilities and a vast playground, where children are trusted and encouraged to explore safely.

The school provides after-school care until 6.00pm each evening and the extra-curricular activities are extensive. The school is supported by an active Social Events Committee who regularly arrange social events for parents to meet each other and to raise money for the school.

Sheffield High School for Girls GDST

10 Rutland Park, Sheffield, South Yorkshire S10 2PE

Tel: 0114 266 0324
email: enquiries@she.gdst.net
website: www.sheffieldhighschool.org.uk
X/Twitter: @SheffieldHigh
Facebook: @sheffieldhighschool
Instagram: @sheffieldgirlsschool
LinkedIn: /Sheffield-High-School

See full entry in the **GSA** section, on **p. 490**.

Sherborne Preparatory School

Acreman Street, Sherborne, Dorset DT9 3NY

Tel: 01935 812097
email: admissions@sherborneprep.org
website: www.sherborneprep.org
X/Twitter: @Sherborneprep
Facebook: @sherborneprepschool
Instagram: @sherborneprep
LinkedIn: /sherborne-preparatory-school

Chair of Governors: Lieutenant General David Leakey, CMG, CVO, CBE

CEO Sherborne Group: Dr Dominic Luckett, DPHIL, FRSA, FHA, FCCT

***Head*: Annie Gent**, BA Hons, MEd

Age range. 3–13.
Number of boys and girls. 201.
Fees per term (2023–2024). Boarders: £7,680–£8,995. Day: Nursery £3,200, Pre-Prep £3,200, Prep Year 3 £4,895, Years 4–6 £5,995, Years 7–8 £6,250.

The school accepts CEA, but for those military families not eligible for CEA they offer a military discount of 10% (with further means-tested bursaries also available). Scholarships are available from Year 6 upwards (scholarship assessments are held at the beginning of the Spring term each year). Bursaries available on a means-tested basis.

Sherborne Prep's curriculum follows the Pre-Senior Baccalaureate (PSB), which is a framework that aims to develop the children's knowledge, skills, attitudes, and values, enabling them to succeed and flourish in an ever-changing world. Children are encouraged, recognised, and celebrated in their achievements, and are directly prepared for the next step of their educational journey. Ultimately, Sherborne Prep pupils will leave school with a toolbox full of skills rather than just a briefcase of grades.

The school, part of the Sherborne School Group, is a co-educational day and boarding school for children aged 3–13 years. Founded in 1858, it is set in twelve acres of attractive grounds and gardens in the centre of Sherborne and is well served by road and rail links. On 1 April 2021, Sherborne Prep merged with Sherborne

School and now sits with Sherborne School and Sherborne International under the same governance. It also enjoys a long and close association with its neighbour, Sherborne Girls.

The Prep School (Years 3–8) offers a broad education, leading to Common Entrance and Scholarship examinations in the penultimate and final year groups. Despite being non-selective ourselves, a large proportion of pupils gain scholarships or awards to leading independent schools, including Sherborne School, Sherborne Girls, Blundell's, Bryanston, Canford, Charterhouse, Cheltenham Ladies' College, Clayesmore, Downside, Eton, Godolphin, King's Bruton, King's College Taunton, King's School Canterbury, Leweston, Marlborough, Milton Abbey, Monkton Combe, Queen's College Taunton, Radley, Rugby, Taunton and Winchester.

We encourage every child to embrace all the wonderful opportunities on offer, and to discover and develop his or her talents and interests to the full. Our children grow to question and reason, so that they are fully prepared to embrace opportunity and fulfil their potential as resilient and responsible members of the community. Outdoor Learning is integral within the curriculum, offering a great opportunity for pupils to develop curiosity, confidence and independence, as well as enriching their knowledge of the natural environment.

Sherborne Prep offers a full Saturday morning programme of various sporting, artistic, musical, and cultural activities, including introductory language classes and informative lectures. At the end of each school day, the pupils can choose to attend an imaginative after-school enrichment and academic support programme until 6.00 pm.

The Pre-Prep Department is housed in a fully equipped and purpose-built classroom building, with experienced and well-qualified staff, providing an excellent ratio of teachers to children. The children enjoy weekly swimming lessons and a varied programme of after-school activities, including, sports, music, and crafts.

The School's ISI report in January 2023 stated The Prep as being 'Excellent in all areas' and described the quality of the pupils' academic and other achievements as 'excellent'. Sherborne Prep was awarded Independent School of the Year for Sporting Achievement in 2021.

Charitable status. Sherborne Preparatory School is a Registered Charity, number 4002575. It exists to provide an all-round education for children.

Solihull School

Warwick Road, Solihull, West Midlands B91 3DJ

Tel: 0121 705 0958
email: admin@solsch.org.uk
website: www.solsch.org.uk
X/Twitter: @solsch1560
Facebook: @SolihullSchool
Instagram: @solsch1560
LinkedIn: /SolihullSchool

See full entry in the **HMC** section, on **p. 342**.

Sompting Abbotts

Church Lane, Sompting, West Sussex BN15 0AZ

Tel: 01903 235960
email: office@somptingabbotts.com
website: www.somptingabbotts.com
Facebook: @somptingabbotts

Principal: Mrs P M Sinclair

***Headmaster*: Mr C Gunn**, BA Hons

Bursar: Mr D A Sinclair

Age Range. 2–13 Co-educational.

Number of Pupils. 120.

Fees per term (2023–2024). Day £3,645–£4,620 (including lunches).

The only independent, family-run school in the area!

Set in a magnificent site on the edge of the South Downs, Sompting Abbotts overlooks the English Channel with views towards Beachy Head and the Isle of Wight. The imposing Victorian house has some 30 acres of sports fields, woodlands, gardens and activity areas.

The aim of the school is to provide a well-balanced education in a caring environment, recognising and developing the individual needs of each child, so that maximum potential academic achievement may be gained. Within the community of the school an emphasis is laid on the cultivation of courtesy, self-discipline and respect for one another in order to engender a happy atmosphere.

The school has a vibrant Pre-Preparatory Department, which includes lively Early Years classes. In the Preparatory Department, well-equipped Science Laboratory and Computer Room are enjoyed by all ages. The Art and Drama departments offer wide scope for creativity, and peripatetic teachers provide tuition for a range of musical instruments. Free wraparound care is provided from 8.00am to 6.00pm.

Book your child in for a Taster Day to see what life is like at our wonderful school!

Spratton Hall

Smith Street, Spratton, Northampton NN6 8HP

Tel: 01604 847292
email: office@sprattonhall.com
website: www.sprattonhall.com
X/Twitter: @SprattonHall
Facebook: @sprattonhallschool
Instagram: @sprattonhall
LinkedIn: /company/spratton-hall-school

Chairman: Mr James Coley

***Head Master*: Mr Simon Clarke**, BA

Deputy Head Master: Mr Robert Dow, BA Hons, PGCE

Age range. 4–13 Co-educational.

Number of pupils. 400.

Fees per term (2023–2024). Prep: £5,450–£6,200, Pre-Prep: £3,995.

Spratton Hall embodies the values of a traditional prep school, as academic achievement is always encouraged and rewarded. However, we are not an academic hot house and as such, we help children develop their strengths wherever they lie, be they in Sport, Drama, Art, STEM, or Music.

We have 50 acres of first-rate facilities, including: a purpose-built theatre, art studios, Forest School science labs, an indoor sports dome, floodlit AstroTurf and multiple sports courts, tracks, pitches and nets. Combined with our 65 extracurricular activities, we definitely have something to delight and inspire every child.

In our Pre-prep, determination and kindness are woven into all areas of the curriculum, and children receive daily individual support from highly-experienced Early Years teachers. To complement their classroom-based learning, they also enjoy regular PE, Dance, Music, Art, Drama and Forest School sessions.

With a 100% pass rate at Common Entrance and multiple annual scholarships to top public schools, the rigorous academic curriculum is balanced with fun inter-house competitions, school trips and exceptional pastoral care.

Our dedicated Head of Pastoral Care oversees the wellbeing and welfare of all pupils, and a well-resourced learning support team are always on hand to help children overcome any academic obstacles they may meet. Meanwhile parents are supported with extended school days, free wraparound care, and local minibus routes.

To experience a typical school day, the School holds Open Mornings in May and October. There are also termly Discovery Days for pre-school children aged 2 to 4. Open Mornings and private tours can be booked at www.sprattonhall.com.

Charitable status. Spratton Hall is a Registered Charity, number 309925. It exists to provide education for boys and girls.

Spring Grove School

Harville Road, Wye, nr Ashford, Kent TN25 5EZ

Tel: 01233 812337
email: office@springgroveschool.co.uk
website: www.springgroveschool.co.uk
X/Twitter: @SG_School
Facebook: @Spring-Grove-School-Wye
Instagram: @springgroveschool

Chair of Governors: Mrs Dawne Sweetland

***Head*: Mrs Therésa Jaggard**, BA Hons, Cert Ed, NPQH
tjaggard@springgroveschool.co.uk

Bursar: Mrs Vicky Jones, BA Hons, CA
bursar@springgroveschool.co.uk

Head of Marketing and Admissions: Mrs Nicky Lee-Browne, MA
admissions@springgroveschool.co.uk

Age Range. 2–11 Co-educational.

Number of Pupils. 230.

Fees per term (2023–2024). £2,475–£4,905.

Spring Grove is a co-educational Day Preparatory School for children aged 2 to 11, widely known for its family ethos and feel. It is located in a stunning rural location just outside the village of Wye, between Ashford and Canterbury. The school offers a first-class education, preparing children for both grammar and senior independent school entry.

The facilities include an award-winning Nursery, School Hall, Art Room, Science Room, Music Room, well-equipped Classrooms, and Multi-Use Games Area. The grounds contain the main school buildings and 14 acres of playing fields.

Spring Grove has a strong tradition of academic excellence, exceptionally lively music, drama and art departments, Forest School, and children who are inspired with a sense of wonder about the world. Emphasis is placed on innovative and creative teaching in a caring yet well-structured atmosphere with close contact maintained between parents and teachers. Typically around 55% of leavers go to grammar schools, and around 35% to senior independent schools, many with scholarships.

The curriculum includes Music, Drama, Art, Dance, Forest School, PE and extracurricular activities. Athletics, Cricket/Kwik Cricket, Cross-Country, Football, Hockey, Netball, Tennis, Swimming and Rugby are the principal games.

Enquiries concerning places and admissions should be made to the Registrar (email: admissions@springgroveschool.co.uk, tel: 01233 812337).

Charitable status. Spring Grove School 2003 is a Registered Charity, number 1099823.

Staines Preparatory School

3 Gresham Road, Staines upon Thames, Surrey TW18 2BT

Tel: 01784 450909
email: admissions@stainesprep.co.uk
website: www.stainesprep.co.uk
X/Twitter: @StainesPrep
Facebook: @StainesPrepSchool
Instagram: @stainesprep

Staines Preparatory School has been 'Educating today's children for the Challenges of Tomorrow' for over 85 years and is a happy and welcoming non-selective school that prides itself on creating a genuine family atmosphere alongside a first rate education.

Chair of Governors: Mr M Hall

***Headmistress*: Ms Samantha Sawyer**, BEd Hons, MEd, NPQH

Bursar: Mr J Philpott, BA Hons, ACMA

Age Range. 3–11 Co-educational.
Number of Pupils. 291: 155 Boys, 136 Girls.
Fees per annum (2023–2024). £11,925–£14,610.

At Staines Prep, our ethos of 'Educating today's children for the Challenges of Tomorrow' is more than our excellent academics. We will be with you and your child every step of the way throughout their first stage of education.

Our Staines Prep Way values, Growth Mindset approach and wellbeing initiatives define a culture of community and respect and your child will learn the importance of commitment to successful learning, develop discipline, self-esteem and a sense of responsibility. We are proud of how successful our pupils subsequently are in senior school entrance and scholarship exams.

We were delighted to be shortlisted for the Independent School Awards three years in a row, and we are proud to have received an EYFS and Primary Quality Mark for our curriculum and Practice. This followed our ISI inspection in December 2019 where we were found to be excellent in all areas.

We offer state-of-the-art teaching, sporting, music and performance facilities to all of our pupils with our Upper School pupils also benefitting from dedicated senior school standard Science lab and Art Design Technology suites. Our Digital learning suite not only caters for a full class to access their own desktop, it includes a dedicated space with green screen technology and lighting effects for multimedia learning and a flexible and larger space to enable coding with robotics and roamers and group work with iPads and laptops. This year, we have added a Home Economics room.

Our environmental area, The Sanctuary, allows the children to bring science to life and learn to safely explore the great outdoors. We use Forest School principles to teach skills that can be used in the classroom and beyond, encouraging team work, responsibility and communication as well as building self-esteem and independence. The children are not limited in what they can do but instead are taught how to access and manage the risks in nature. Our Outdoor Classroom provides additional space for pupils to learn.

We understand how hard our parents work and we aim to support them by providing wraparound care from 7.30am until 6.30pm. We are less than 5 minutes' walk from Staines railway station and operate a school minibus service from the surrounding areas, making pick-up and drop-off that little bit easier.

To come and experience the school first hand, you can arrange a private tour to fit in around your commitments or visit us at one of our popular Open Events which run throughout the year. Details of these can be found on our website www.stainesprep.co.uk.

Stamford Junior School

Kettering Rd, Stamford, Lincolnshire PE9 2LR
Tel: 01780 484400
email: headjs@ses.lincs.sch.uk
website: www.stamfordschools.org.uk
X/Twitter: @SJS_Head
Facebook: @stamfordendowedschools
Instagram: @StamfordSchools

Stamford Junior School, along with Stamford High School (girls) and Stamford School (boys), is one of three schools in the historic market town of Stamford comprising the Stamford Endowed Schools. The schools are under a single Governing Body and overall management and leadership of the Principal and allow continuity of education for boys and girls from 2 to 18, including boarding from age 8. Each school has its own Head and staff.

Principal: William Phelan, MBA

***Headteacher*: Matthew O'Reilly**

Chairman of Governors: Mr Tom Cartledge

Bursar and Clerk to the Governing Body: Dean White

Age Range. 2–11.
Number of Children. 350.
Fees per annum (2023–2024). Day: Reception £12,425, Years 1–2 £13,200, Years 3–6 £15,850; Boarding: 7 Day £27,460, 5 Day £24,760, 4 Day £23,585, 3 Day £21,725.

The Junior School educates boys and girls up to the age of 11 (including boarders from age 8), when boys move on to Stamford School and girls to Stamford High School. Admission from the Junior School to the two senior schools is based on progress and without further entrance testing.

The Junior School occupies its own spacious grounds, bordering the River Welland, overlooking the sports fields and open countryside, the boarding houses, the sports hall, floodlit artificial hockey pitch and the swimming pool on the same site. It is on the south-west outskirts of Stamford within easy reach of the A1.

Entry to the School is according to registration at 4+ and assessment.

The lively and broad curriculum offers an ILIC-based (Independent Learning and Intellectual Curiosity) foundation to all academic, creative, and sporting subjects. Lessons are stimulating, energetic, and fully engaging so that the natural curiosity of our pupils can flourish. Extensive facilities, sporting opportunities, and the wide-ranging co-curricular programme promote the rounded development that we believe is essential for our children.

In addition to teaching staff, the Junior School has a number of specialist teachers in physical education, swimming, art, music, and speech and drama, with a number of visiting teachers offering a variety of sports, dance and modern foreign languages.

There is a purpose-built nursery in the grounds of the school – Stamford Nursery School – offering first-class care and early learning for children aged 2–4. Pupils then head to the adjacent Early Years Reception Classes.

Boarding. The co-educational Boarding House (St Michael's) is run in a homely, family style. Boys and girls are accepted as full or weekly boarders from the age of 8. Occasional or flexi-boarding is accommodated where possible and according to family need. A full programme of activities takes place at weekends so that boarders enjoy a rich and varied week.

Stephen Perse Foundation

Union Road, Cambridge, Cambridgeshire CB2 1HF

Tel: 01223 454762
email: admissions@stephenperse.com
website: www.stephenperse.com
X/Twitter: @SPFSchools
Facebook: @stephenpersefoundation
Instagram: @stephenpersefoundation
LinkedIn: /stephen-perse-foundation

See full entry in the **HMC** section, on **p. 349**.

Stormont School

The Causeway, Potters Bar, Herts EN6 5HA

Tel: 01707 654037
email: admin@stormontschool.org
website: www.stormontschool.org
X/Twitter: @StormontSchool
Facebook: @StormontSchool
Instagram: @stormontschool

The school is administered by a Board of Governors.

Chairman of Board of Governors: Mr Andrew Newland

***Headteacher*: Miss Louise Martin**

Age range. 4–11.

Number of pupils. 160 Day Girls.

Fees per term (2023–2024). £4,655–£5,148 (including lunch). There are no compulsory extras.

The School was founded in 1944 and has occupied its attractive Victorian house since then. There is a spacious, bright, purpose-built Pre-Prep building where the classrooms flow from a central play and study area, which adjoins an outdoor play area for EYFS, Year 1 and 2. Prep girls move to the main house in Year 3 and move around each area on their timetable.

The well-equipped Art, Pottery, Design Technology, Science and French rooms are housed in The Courtyard and provide inspirational learning areas for all the girls. The Millennium Building houses our Drama and Music Classroom with separate studios on the ground floor and our ICT Suite on the first floor. Within this building, music is taught on the curriculum and individual music lessons are taught in the designated music studios by our peripatetic music teachers.

The Johnston Sports Hall, with its own changing rooms, provides a fabulous space for gymnastics and a wide variety of team sports, including netball, which take place whatever the weather. The school has outdoor tennis courts that double up as netball courts, a two-acre playing field and use of a swimming pool at Queenswood School.

The large and spacious Pearson Hall enables us to have whole-school assemblies, class assemblies for parents to watch, concerts and various whole-school activities or larger events. The stage is one that can be adapted depending on the occasion and some after-school clubs also take place here.

Our Library has been relocated to the Dyson Room, within its high-vaulted ceiling and decorative woodwork panelling. Spaces for study, discussion or reading a good book have been created and new furniture installed.

Our well-qualified, specialist teachers and experienced staff prepare the girls for entry to a wide range of both independent and maintained senior schools at the age of eleven, many of whom gain Scholarships at their chosen school.

Charitable status. Stormont School is a Registered Charity, number 311079. It exists to establish and carry on as a school where children receive a sound education.

Stover Preparatory School

Newton Abbot, Devon TQ12 6QG

Tel: 01626 354505
email: schooloffice@stover.co.uk
website: www.stover.co.uk
X/Twitter: @StoverSchool
Facebook: @StoverSchool
Instagram: @StoverSchool

Chairman of Governors: Mr S Killick, ND, ARB

***Head*: Mr Ben Noble**, BSc

Age Range. 3–11 Co-educational.

Number of Pupils. 142.

Fees per term (2023–2024). Preparatory School: Day: Reception £3,240 Years 1–3 £3,505, Years 4–6 £4,355. Weekly Boarding: Years 4–6 £7,565. Full Boarding: Years 4–6 £8,740.

Stover Preparatory School enjoys a beautiful rural setting on the edge of Dartmoor National Park, close to the South Devon coast. Set in 64 acres there is ample space for pupils of all ages to experience the great outdoors, be that through play, nature walks, sport, orienteering, bushcraft, learning in our outdoor classroom or researching the history of our fine old buildings. Stover Preparatory School shares its fine site with Stover Senior School, making transfer at aged 11 years a smooth process for our pupils.

We pride ourselves on our warm, welcoming atmosphere where each individual is nurtured and encouraged to reach their full potential. Visitors frequently comment on the positive, happy feeling they experience upon entering the school. Teachers are aware of pupils' individual needs and provide support in an approachable and friendly manner.

We offer a broad, balanced curriculum with high academic standards, complemented by a wide range of extra-curricular activities. Spanish begins in Reception and French is also introduced at Year 3. Languages, PE and music are taught by specialist teachers across the school. All other subjects are taught by the class teacher to enable cross-curricular links to thrive. Underpinning everything we do is our firm belief in Research Based Learning, where pupils develop their inquiry skills, taking ownership of their learning from a young age. Sport and the Performing Arts play a vital role in each child's development. We have a full fixture list for our U9 and U11 teams as well as involvement with the local Schools' Sports Partnership. Our regular school performances and concerts are a highlight of the calendar. More than 80% of our Prep School pupils choose to participate in the Prep School Choir. In addition, we offer a Pre-Prep Choir and a Chamber Choir for talented pupils in Years 5 and 6. Residential and day trips into our beautiful local environment further complement the curriculum.

Facilities include an extensive Outdoor Classroom, Sports Fields, Tennis Courts, Art room, Music room, Multi-Purpose Hall, Library and ICT suite.

Flexi, weekly and full boarding are available from the age of 8 years. Scholarships are offered at 11+. The majority of our pupils move on to Stover Senior School.

See also Stover School senior entry in The Society of Heads section.

Charitable status. Stover School Association is a Registered Charity, number 306712.

Strathallan School

Forgandenny, Perth, Perthshire PH2 9EG

Tel: 01738 812546
email: admissions@strathallan.co.uk
website: www.strathallan.co.uk
X/Twitter: @StrathallanSchl
Facebook: @strathallanschool
Instagram: @Strathallanschoolofficial
LinkedIn: /company/strathallanschool

See full entry in the **HMC** section, on **p. 354**.

Streatham & Clapham Prep School GDST

Wavertree Road, London SW2 3SR

Tel: 020 8674 6912
email: prep@schs.gdst.net
website: www.schs.gdst.net
X/Twitter: @SCPSgdst
Facebook: @SCPSgdst

Motto: *ad sapientiam sine metu*

Chair of Local Governors: Mr Angus Wrixon, BSc Hons

***Head*: Mrs H Loach**, BEd Cantab

Age range. Girls 3–11.

Number of pupils. 227.

Fees per term (2023–2024). Prep School: £5,441, Nursery: £4,145 (cost less EYS funding).

Streatham & Clapham Prep School is a division of Streatham & Clapham High School GDST (*see entry in the HMC section*), situated on its own extensive campus in Streatham Hill, within a mile of the Senior School. The School provides a specialist academic curriculum as part of a liberal and challenging educational experience for its girls within a caring culture of warm relationships and diversity, all the while nurturing their personal development and confidence. Its facilities include a full-size gymnasium, all-weather pitch, state-of-the-art outdoor learning and play areas and specialist drama, music, IT and art and design rooms. Admission to the school is by selective assessment, with informal assessment of pupils for Nursery, Reception, Year 1 and Year 2, and an entrance examination for Year 3 candidates. Places in other year groups are occasionally available.

The school's distinctive features.

1. Its suffragist heritage: as a school where Millicent Fawcett sent her daughter and as a member of the GDST family of schools, the school is a pioneer in, and the shaper of, girls' education;
2. Its curricular specialisation from an early age;
3. Its trailblazing and innovative approach, supercharging its girls with life skills enabling them to embrace and instigate change;
4. Its family, not factory, environment, supporting individual families' needs; and
5. Its buzzy, diverse community, celebrating difference and drawing strength from all that is great about London.

Curriculum. The school's broad and varied curriculum benefits from leading specialist teachers in all areas. Girls enjoy distinctive and invigorating learning through programmes such as Philosophy for Children, the Learning Tree Programme, PE, Music, Art, Drama, Computer Science, Design & Technology, Mandarin, French and Latin.

Personal & pastoral development. Great emphasis is placed on nurturing well-balanced and considerate individuals, who are ready for the challenges of adolescent and adult life. Strong pastoral and House systems reinforce this ethos, as do lessons in philosophy, myriad opportunities to build resilience, and overseas residential trips.

Co-curricular programme & family support. The school offers an extensive co-curricular programme with over 30 free clubs as well as other after-school activities, societies and events. Wraparound childcare is offered from 7.30 am to 5.55 pm, five days a week, during term-time. The school is conveniently located near major transport links and also offers nine minibus routes serving most of south London.

Stroud School
King Edward VI Preparatory School

Highwood House, Highwood Lane, Romsey, Hampshire SO51 9ZH

Tel: 01794 513231
email: registrar@stroud-kes.org.uk
website: https://stroud.kes.school/
X/Twitter: @Stroud_School
Facebook: @stroudschool

Chair of Governors: Mr A J Morgan, MA Oxon, FCA, ATII
Chair of Stroud Committee: Mrs C Musker

***Headmistress*: Mrs Rebecca Smith**, MBA

Deputy Head (*Pastoral*): Mr Jonty Stewart

Deputy Head (*Academic*): Mrs Sarah Mason-Campbell

Age Range. 3–11.

Number of Pupils. 260.

Fees per term (2023–2024). Upper Prep £6,525; Lower Prep £4,980–6.525; Pre-Prep £4,060–£4,285; Nursery – price available on enquiry depending on term-time only, 51 weeks, full or part-time.

Stroud is a co-educational day school for children aged 3 to 11 years. Pupils are prepared for entrance to Senior Independent or Grammar Schools.

The School stands on the outskirts of Romsey in its own grounds of 22 acres, which include playing fields, a full-sized sports hall, a heated outdoor swimming pool, tennis courts, riding arena, a wellbeing centre, lawns and gardens and a purpose-built Pre-prep building and Art and Design Pod. The main team games for boys are cricket, hockey, rugby and football, and for girls hockey, cricket and netball. Both boys and girls play tennis.

Music and drama play an important part in the life of the School. A wide variety of instruments is taught and children are encouraged to join the school orchestra. Each year there is a musical production and the Christmas Carol Service is held at Romsey Abbey.

The Stroud School Association, run by the parents, holds many social activities and helps to raise money for amenities, but its main function is to generate goodwill.

Summer Fields

Mayfield Road, Oxford OX2 7EN

Tel: 01865 459204
email: admissions@summerfields.com
website: www.summerfields.com
X/Twitter: @SFSOxford
Facebook: @Summer-Fields-Oxford
Instagram: @summerfieldsoxford
LinkedIn: /Summer-Fields-Oxford

Chairman of Governors: J Rooth, BSc, MBA

***Headmaster*: David Faber**, MA Oxon

Age Range. 4–13.

Number of Boys. Prep: 169 boarders, 93 day; Pre-Prep: 69.

Fees per term (2023–2024). Prep: £12,530 Boarding, £8,735 Day. Pre-Prep: £4,950 Reception, £5,570 Years 1 & 2, £6,440 Year 3.

Set in 72 acres of delightful grounds which lead down to the River Cherwell and yet only a few miles from the city centre, Summer Fields is often known as Oxford's *Secret Garden*.

The School, comprising of a Pre-prep and Prep, offers an exceptional education for boys aged 4–13.

The Pre-prep for day boys, opened in 2018, is state of the art and benefits from the use of all of the Prep facilities. It is the perfect start to learning and an excellent introduction to Summer Fields Prep, which has always had a strong academic reputation, with Summerfieldians regularly securing scholarships, awards and exhibitions to top independent schools, including Eton, Harrow, Radley and Winchester. Each year, boys pass Common Entrance to a wide variety of top public schools.

The facilities are outstanding. They include the refurbished chapel and the Mark Shvidler Library – a wonderful addition to the school's infrastructure – custom-built pottery studio, Design and Technology and ICT centre, a magnificent Sports Hall, with squash and Eton fives courts, a shooting gallery and swimming pool, and the Salata Pavilion which includes purpose-built changing rooms for the boys and a large multi-functional space on the first floor.

Sport has a high profile and proud history at Summer Fields, with many children representing the school at local, county and national levels. Football, Rugby and Cricket are the major sports, but by no means the only ones. The school's ethos supports sport for everyone, encouraging and enabling pupils to participate and develop skills in their sports of choice.

Huge emphasis is placed on providing the highest standards of pastoral care. Each boy has a personal tutor, who is responsible for his academic progress and social welfare, and will be in regular contact with the boy's parents. Wraparound care is provided at the Pre-prep.

Prep boarders live in Lodges within the school grounds and are looked after by an experienced and dedicated husband and wife team of Lodgeparents. The modern award-winning boarding facilities offer a home from home for the boys. Around two-thirds of the staff live on site, making a significant contribution to school life both in and out of the classroom, ensuring evenings and weekends are packed full of activities for the boys to enjoy.

Pupils participate in a wide variety of music groups, choirs, orchestras and ensembles, with 80% taking music lessons. The Choir regularly sing Evensong in Oxford Colleges and tour abroad. LAMDA is offered, with many pupils achieving distinctions, and at least one Drama production takes place every term in Macmillan Theatre onsite.

Outside in the grounds, a beautiful tree house, Forest school and camping site enhance the outdoor learning provision throughout the school, but especially in the Pre-prep. There are also impressive outdoor sports facilities including AstroTurf, tennis courts and all-weather cricket nets, a nine-hole golf course, birdwatching hut, outdoor pool, and adventure playground. A huge range of sports, activities and hobbies is on offer to the boys.

Bursaries are available up to a value of 100%.

For further information or to arrange a visit, please contact Mrs Christine Berry, Registrar Tel: 01865 459204 or email: admissions@summerfields.com

Sunninghill Prep School

South Court, South Walks Road, Dorchester, Dorset DT1 1EB
Tel: 01305 262306
email: registrar@sunninghill.dorset.sch.uk
website: www.sunninghillprep.co.uk
Facebook: @SunninghillPrepSchool
Instagram: @sunninghillprep

***Head*: Mr David Newberry**, BSc Hons, GTP

Age range. 2 years–13 years.
Number of pupils. 130 (approximately).
Fees per term (2023–2024). £3,390–£5,997.

Sunninghill is a co-educational day school of approximately 130 children with single-form entry throughout the school from Nursery to Year 8. Classes are deliberately small so we can focus on the academic and personal development of the individual. This helps us fulfil our mission which is to find the unique brilliance of every child.

The School was founded in 1939 and became a Charitable Trust in 1969. It moved to its present site in January 1997 where it enjoys its own swimming pool, all-weather sports pitch, superb teaching facilities and extensive grounds. The surrounding local area and stunning Jurassic Coast is our extended playground.

Academically and pastorally, every child's attainment, potential and wellbeing are tracked, and we have a highly able and talented programme for children in all classes across the school. Children in Years 4, 6 and 8 are CAT4 tested in the autumn term, which provides a valuable indicator for potential. Standardised assessments in maths, English and science, along with diagnostic, formative and summative assessments, provide important attainment benchmarks, giving us the tools to ensure all our children thrive.

Over the years the school has attained many academic successes, but the broad curriculum also includes drama, art, craft, music and physical education. Our comprehensive Friday Enrichment programme encourages greater cross-curricular links for Years 1 to 8, enhancing their learning further.

Team and individual sports are played, with PE and Games taking place at least three times a week from Years 3–8. These include hockey, netball, cricket, rounders, rugby, football, athletics, swimming and tennis.

Out-of-school activities include academic clubs, preparing for scholarships, humanities and art, plus debating, chess, creative arts, ballet, dance, kickboxing, LAMDA and various music clubs including choir and string quartet. We offer multi sports across a wide age group. Residential expeditions are a feature of the curriculum from Year 3 upwards and we are a member of the National Sailing Academy, with our own race team.

Our expanding nursery will be welcoming 2-year-olds from April 2024, and will be moving to an all-year-round provision. Nursery children enjoy the beautiful grounds of Sunninghill, as well as specialist lessons in PE, music & drama, French and gardening. Children in our nursery are given first consideration for places in our Reception class.

Sunninghill Prep prides itself on its nurturing, family ethos. The school values of compassion, creativity, commitment and courage are deeply embedded into the school, and rewarded on a weekly basis in our celebration assemblies. The school's flourishing Parents' Association ensures that parents and staff all know each other and work together for the good of the children and the school.

Sunninghill welcomes children of all ages at any point during the school year. Prospective families are warmly invited to visit the school either at one of our termly Open Mornings, or for individual appointments. Our prospectus is available on request or downloadable from our website.

In December 2023, Sunninghill Prep was acquired by the Inspired Learning Group.

Sussex House

68 Cadogan Square, London SW1X 0EA
Tel: 020 7584 1741
email: schoolsecretary@sussexhouseschool.co.uk
website: www.sussexhouseschool.co.uk

Chairman of the Governors: John Crewe, Esq

***Headmaster*: Nicholas Kaye**, MA Magdalene College Cambridge, ACP, Hon FCOT, FRSA, FRGS
***Executive Headmaster*: Tony Chan**, BA, LLB Sydney, GradDipEd Wesley Institute Sydney

Deputy Headmaster: Martin Back, BA, PGCE Sussex

Age Range. 8–13.
Number of Boys. 186.
Fees per term (2023–2024). £8,660.

Founded in 1952, Sussex House is situated in the heart of Chelsea in a fine Norman Shaw house in Cadogan Square. Its Gymnasium and Music School are housed in a converted chapel in Cadogan Street. The school is an independent charitable trust. At Common Entrance and Scholarship level it has achieved a record of consistently strong results to academically demanding schools. The school enjoys its own entirely independent character and the style is traditional yet imaginative.

There is a full-time teaching staff of 25. Creative subjects are given strong emphasis and throughout the school boys take Music and Art. Team sports take place at a nearby site and the school's football teams have an impressive record. Cricket is the main summer sport and there are opportunities for a variety of other sports, including tennis, swimming, athletics and golf. Sussex House is a centre of excellence for fencing and its international records are well known.

Cultural and creative activities play a major role, including theatrical productions at the Britten theatre, a major annual exhibition of creative work featuring large-scale architectural models and an annual competition of poetry written by boys. There is a strong bias towards music and an ambitious programme of choral and orchestral concerts. A large number of pupils play musical instruments and there is an impressive record of music awards to senior schools. The school provides a range of sporting and cultural trips.

The school has a Church of England affiliation. There is a school chaplain and weekly services are held in St Simon Zelotes Church, Chelsea. Boys of all religions and denominations are welcomed.

Charitable status. Sussex House is a Registered Charity, number 1035806. It exists to provide education for boys.

Sutton Valence Preparatory School

Church Road, Chart Sutton, Maidstone, Kent ME17 3RF

Tel: 01622 842117
email: admissions@svs.org.uk
website: www.svs.org.uk
X/Twitter: @SVPS_News
Facebook: @SuttonValencePrepSchoolNews

Chair of Governors: Mrs G Swaine, BSc Hons, MEd

***Head*: Mr M Scholey**, BA Hons, PGCE, QTS, MEd Cantab, MCCT

Deputy Head: Mr J Watkins, BSc Hons, PGCE Primary

Academic Deputy Head: Ms R Harrison, BEd Hons

Age Range. 2–11.
Number of Pupils. 300.
Fees per term (2023–2024). Reception £4,153, Years 1 to 2 £4,898, Years 3 to 4 £5,422, Years 5 to 6 £5,864.

The values of our School community and the happiness of our children are central to everything we do. These provide pupils with a strong feeling of structure and security which enables them to work effectively.

At whichever point children join us they embark on their own journeys, each one different and each one with differing emphasis on the four areas we hold dear: Academic, Enrichment, Community and Leadership and Service.

By the time they leave us at the age of 11, it is our responsibility to have equipped the children during their formative years with the essentials of character to thrive in an increasingly competitive world. To put firmly in place the qualities which will make them clear thinking, lateral thinking, robust, hardworking, determined and yet kindly citizens, who will go on to influence many people in the coming years.

We have high expectations of ourselves and of our children, both inside and out of the classroom, and we have a long history of successful preparation of children for the next stage of their education, be that for our Senior School, the Kent grammars, or other schools.

None of this should come at the expense of childhood and what the School does so successfully is find that balance between delivering in terms of education, and yet doing so kindly and with many broad, interesting and high-quality opportunities. The School is very proud of its articulate and confident pupils who move on well-equipped to work things out for themselves, so crucial in an increasingly challenging world.

To achieve this we have dedicated Art, Science and ICT facilities and a new Library. Classes are small throughout the school. The 40 teaching staff are all well qualified and there is an extensive peripatetic staff for music. Special needs are addressed by the SENCO and three part-time teachers. The Kindergarten to Year 2 classes all have qualified classroom assistants.

The School is situated in 18 acres of countryside overlooking the Weald and includes a hard and grass play areas, heated outdoor swimming pool, four hard tennis courts, a Sports Hall, a 13-acre games field, a full-size Astroturf and a newly established 'forest school' area, all of which support our co-curricular programme.

A solid foundation in the core subjects of English, Mathematics, Science and ICT is supplemented by Languages, Music, Drama, Art, Design Technology and Sport which are all taught by specialist teaching staff. The co-curricular programme is wide and varied providing many opportunities for children to perform in drama productions and in concerts, occasionally in conjunction with the senior school. Children are prepared for our senior school, Sutton Valence, the local Grammar schools and other independent schools with an 11+ entry.

Cricket, football, hockey, netball, rugby and rounders are the major sports, with athletics, swimming and cross-country also being available. The proximity of the senior school, Sutton Valence, allows the children to benefit from their staffing and facilities, including the use of the Sports Hall, athletics track and the indoor swimming pool. After-school activities include chess club, art, 5-a-side football, gymnastics, drama, craft, croquet, science club, ballet and judo.

The school is a Christian foundation. Assemblies, for celebration, and the use of the local church are an important facet of our lives, with the school's Chaplain visiting regularly. The school provides a fulfilling education for all its children, a thriving network for its parents and a happy workplace for all who dedicate their lives to it.

Charitable status. The United Westminster and Grey Coat Foundation is a Registered Charity, number 1181012. It exists to provide education for boys and girls and provides valuable resources and support.

Swanbourne House

Part of The Stowe Group

Swanbourne, Milton Keynes, Buckinghamshire MK17 0HZ

Tel: 01296 720264
email: office@swanbourne.org
website: www.swanbourne.org
Facebook: @SwanbourneHouse
LinkedIn: /school/swanbournehouse

Chairman of Governors: Mr C Creedy-Smith

***Head*: Mr N Holloway**

Age Range: 3–13.

Number of Pupils: 300 (mix of day pupils and full, weekly and flexi borders).

Fees per term (2023–2024): Boarding: Full £9,936; Weekly £9,288; Day: Year 5–8 £7,290; Year 4 £6,156; Year 3 £5,724; Reception–Year 2 ££4,266; Pre-Reception: Various.

At Swanbourne House, greatness is not solely about what you can do but about who you are, where qualities such as resilience, self-belief and risk-taking are developed as companions on the road to success. We provide a dynamic & challenging curriculum, small class sizes, inspirational extra-curricular activities and extensive facilities, all set in 55 acres of Buckinghamshire countryside, near Milton Keynes and Aylesbury.

The quality of teaching and innovative approach to learning at Swanbourne House inspires and engages young minds in new ways, broadening horizons and creating opportunities, while giving a platform to develop new skills and develop minds. Our exceptional facilities help provide the environment for the teaching of an inspiring, challenging and flexible curriculum that stimulates and engages.

Understanding and promoting the whole child is our priority as we prepare to send each one off to their carefully chosen senior school with the energy, enthusiasm and resilience to thrive.

Our extensive sporting facilities include rugby, football and cricket pitches, two astro-turf pitches, golf course, indoor sports hall, dance and gymnastics studio and indoor 20m swimming pool.

Our sports include rugby, hockey, netball, football, lacrosse, cricket, athletics, swimming and tennis, with more opportunities available across dance, gymnastics, clay pigeon shooting, triathlon, fencing, skiing, badminton, golf and yoga.

Performing Arts at Swanbourne House plays an integral part of School life for every child. The broad curriculum encompasses all areas of music, learning not just about the technical side of a piece of music, but really diving into the emotional too. We ask how do we feel when we listen to a piece of music, and we introduce our pupils to music from across the spectrum from Bach to Bernstein, Chopin to Coldplay. The School productions represent an extraordinary opportunity for pupils to be involved in large-scale shows with professional set design, lighting and sound. Giving opportunities to perform and helping develop a life-long love of drama is something the School is passionate about providing to every child. Our recent productions show the breadth of the programme, with performances of Chitty Chatty Bang Bang, Matilda the Musical, Fame and Shrek The Musical.

As a result of the breadth and depth of experience and learning at Swanbourne House, the number of scholarships our Year 8 children have secured in recent years in Academics, Art, Drama, D&T, Music and Sport is very impressive indeed. Recent leavers' destinations include Stowe, Eton, Harrow, Cheltenham Ladies' College, Radley, Bradfield, Wellington College, Oundle, and Rugby.

We're a proud member of The Stowe Group of schools.

Charitable status. Swanbourne House is part of Stowe School which is a registered charity.

Sydenham High School

GDST

19 Westwood Hill, London SE26 6BL

Tel: 020 8557 7000
email: senior@syd.gdst.net
website: www.sydenhamhighschool.gdst.net
X/Twitter: @SydenhamHigh
Facebook: @sydenham.high.gdst
LinkedIn: /sydenham-high-school-gdst

See full entry in the **GSA** section, on **p. 493**.

Talbot Heath Junior School

Rothesay Road, Bournemouth BH4 9NJ

Tel: 01202 763360
email: jsoffice@talbotheath.org
website: www.talbotheath.org

Chair of Governors: Dr Richard Day

***Head Teacher*: Mrs Elizabeth Pugh**

Number of Pupils. 217.

Age Range. Girls, 3–11.

Our Ethos. Talbot Heath is a flourishing, vibrant and dynamic school, with a focus on both high academic standards as well as outstanding pastoral care. It is a forward thinking school with a 137-year history, catering for girls aged 3 to 18.

Our pupils are confident, happy, articulate, and they have a genuine love of learning. We strive to make sure that each pupil reaches their full potential and every individual feels valued. The School's motto, 'Honour Before Honours', underpins everything we do. We care for each other and support one another with integrity and compassion.

Being selective, we value our academic tradition and encourage our pupils to be self-motivated, hard-working, diligent and resilient within a nurturing and supportive environment. We have strong links and communication with all our parents, which fosters a thriving community.

Our results, right from the first steps in EYFS, are outstanding, but our school places value on so much more than just results. Emphasis is placed on becoming rounded individuals, experiencing the full breadth of an extensive and rich curriculum.

Facilities. The Junior School, housed in its own buildings on our woodland campus, is split into two departments; Pre-Prep (age 3–7) and Junior (age 7–11). Alongside large, spacious classrooms, our pupils enjoy extensive grounds including two playgrounds and a designated area for our Forest School which forms part of the curriculum. In addition to pupils having their own school iPad, we deliver a computing curriculum within our own IT suites.

Pupils also have access to our Senior School facilities which encourages a smooth and familiar transition from our Junior to Senior School at the end of Year 6. These include our state-of-the-art STEAM Hub with interactive floors and walls, plus studios for Design, Art, Graphics, Textiles and Drama. These combined with our Music School, Sports Hall, large dedicated grounds for various sporting activities, indoor swimming pool and Science Block, mean that our pupils have the opportunity of fully exploring and developing their skills in different areas. Pupils are taught by subject specialists for subjects such as Music, PE, Art and French.

Fees per term (2023–2024). £2,719–£4,707.

Charitable status. Talbot Heath School Trust Limited is a Registered Charity, number 283708.

Terrington Hall School

Terrington, North Yorkshire YO60 6PR

Tel: 01653 648227
email: office@terringtonhall.com
website: www.terringtonhall.com
X/Twitter: @TerringtonHall
Facebook: @TerringtonHall
Instagram: @terringtonhall.school
LinkedIn: /company/terrington-hall-school

Chair of Governors: Mrs Katharine Lamont

***Headmaster*: Mr Simon Kibler**, BA Hons

Age range. 3–13 years.

Number of children. 198.

Fees per term (2023–2024). Day: £3,480 (Nursery and Reception); £3,695 (Years 1 & 2); £5,595 (Years 3 & 4); £5,990 (Years 5–8). Weekly boarding: £7,573 (Years 3 & 4); £7,970 (Years 5–8). Flexible boarding is available at £30 per night.

Terrington Hall is a vibrant and purposeful co-educational day, weekly and flexi-boarding school situated in the Howardian Hills, an Area of Outstanding Natural Beauty 15 miles north of York.

We blend forward thinking learning with a traditional prep school ethos to develop kind, confident and well-mannered children who have the courage to take calculated risks without fear of failure and the resilience to pursue their talents and interests.

Every day is aimed at expanding our children's horizons through a journey of discovery which makes learning fun and lights a spark in their hearts and minds. Our ethos is underpinned by the key values represented in the school crest: Confidence; Kindness; Growth and Courage. The high level of individual care and attention extended to every child is supported by small class sizes, an excellent staff/pupil ratio, specialist teaching staff and strong emphasis on wellbeing. Our nurturing yet focused environment develops children who are critical thinkers, self-directed and willing to seize opportunities.

Terrington's broad curriculum and excellent facilities are supplemented by an exceptional range of co-curricular activities and events. Our unique TALL Programme helps children acquire a depth of skills and experience outside their academic work, from critical thinking to teamwork and other life-skills. The ad astra Programme stretches and challenges pupils with a wide range of intellectual challenges. Collaborative leadership skills are prized across the school, along with a clear sense of service and empathy. We aim to develop children who have an awareness of their social and environmental responsibility to the world around them.

As truly independent school with no ties to any other, we place special emphasis on preparing each child for entry into the senior school best suited to them, whether locally or further afield. Pupils regularly win scholarships for academia, art, sport, drama and all-round excellence.

The school has a strong boarding community, with over 90% of Year 3–8 pupils opting to stay for weekly or flexi boarding during the school year to make the most of the exciting evening activity programme.

Our excellent sporting facilities include eight acres of playing fields, AstroTurf pitches, tennis courts, an indoor heated swimming pool and sports hall. All major sports are played and an extensive fixture list ensures that every child has ample opportunity to represent the school. Specialist peripatetic tuition is available in Tennis, Cricket and Swimming (either 1:1 or small group sessions) throughout the year. All children have the opportunity to join residential adventure trips in the UK and beyond.

Teaching facilities are modern and well-equipped and include both computer and science suites. Music, art and drama are an integral part of the curriculum. Individual tuition is available for most instruments, voice and drama. Children prepare for concerts, external festivals and exams. The Junior and Senior choirs perform within school and at local venues, and our instrumental ensembles run during enrichment throughout the year. All children have the opportunity to perform in termly recitals held in our Music Centre, as well as our more large-scale concerts and services.

The Headmaster, his wife and children live in the school grounds and parents are fully involved in the life of the school. There is a flourishing 'Friends of Terrington Hall' parents' social committee.

Bursaries are available on a means-tested basis. Discounts are available to siblings and Old Terringtonians.

Charitable Status. Terrington Hall is a registered charity, number 532362. It exists to provide a quality education for boys and girls.

Thorngrove School

The Mount, Pantings Lane, Highclere, Newbury, Hampshire RG20 9PS

Tel: 01635 253172
email: admin@thorngroveschool.co.uk
website: www.thorngroveschool.co.uk
X/Twitter: @thorngroveprep
Facebook: @ThorngrovePrep
Instagram: @thorngroveprep

Proprietors: Mr Nicholas and Mrs Connie Broughton

***Headmaster*: Mr N Graham**, BA Hons Oxford Brookes, PGCE, MEd

Senior Deputy Head: P Swinden, BA Hons, MA
Deputy Head Academic: Mrs L Street, SCITT, QTS
Deputy Head, Head of Lower School & EYFS: Mrs V McSorland, BA QTS

Age Range. 2½–13 Co-educational.
Number of Pupils. 220 Day Pupils.
Fees per term (2023–2024). Reception–Year 2: £4,910; Years 3 & 4: £6,495; Years 5–8: £7,255.

Thorngrove School was founded in 1988 and is an IAPS co-educational day preparatory school for children aged 2½ to 13 years. The purpose-built facilities are set in former farmland in the village of Highclere, 5 miles south of Newbury and 12 miles north of Andover. Children are currently prepared for Common Entrance at 13+, from where their paths lead to a wide range of senior day and boarding schools.

Thorngrove is set in 25 acres of beautiful Hampshire countryside. There is an extensive range of sports pitches within the grounds. In addition to this, there is an astro, two further hard courts and an all-weather cricket net facility. The purpose-built teaching spaces provide an excellent learning environment with specialist areas for Music, DT, Science, Art and PE.

Thorngrove's IT provision is excellent and all pupils from Years 3–8 benefit from their own Chromebook to support their learning and enhance their skills for the 21st Century. We are committed to ongoing development and during the past school year, Thorngrove has benefitted from a canopied area for Forest School and a new play area for the Lower School pupils. Our new 'break-out' classroom is being successfully used for drama, ballet classes and parents' match teas, among other things. To further develop our provision for the Performing Arts, the School is looking into the development of a Performing Arts Centre for Music, Drama and Dance.

Thorngrove offers a unique environment where children can grow and learn independently. We value our intimate and friendly community and the benefit that brings; we are proud of our small class sizes and the individual attention we can offer to each of our pupils.

Thorngrove has a relaxed yet purposeful atmosphere, where working relationships between staff and pupils flourish. We are forward-thinking in our approach – providing children with the skills they need to succeed, supported through technology, while at the same time remaining true to traditional values.

Pupil progress is tracked continuously, and communication with parents plays an important part in this process. Above all, our aim is that all pupils reach their potential in terms of confidence, creativity and achievement; allowing them to thrive in the 21st Century.

The most recent ISI inspection report (March 2020) judged the school to be 'Excellent' in all areas.

Thorpe House School

Oval Way, Gerrards Cross, Bucks SL9 8QA

Tel: 01753 882474
email: office@thorpehouse.co.uk
website: www.thorpehouse.co.uk
X/Twitter: @thorpehousesch
Facebook: @thorpehousesch
Instagram: @thorpehousesch
LinkedIn: /company/thorpehousesch

Independent Boys' School of the Year 2021 Finalist
Independent Boys' School of the Year 2022 Shortlisted

Chairman of the Governors: Mr Richard Tufft

***Headteacher*: Mr Jake Burnett**

Age Range. Boys 4–16.
Numbers of Pupils. 299 Day Pupils.
Fees per term (2023–2024). Y9–Y11 £6,900, Y7–Y8 £6,750, Y6 £5,875, Y5 £5,700, Y4 £5,650, Y3 £5,375, Y1–Y2 £4,295, Reception £3,800.

Thorpe House is an Independent boys' school based in the beautiful town of Gerrards Cross in Buckinghamshire. We offer education for boys from Reception to Year 11.

At Thorpe House our aspirations push us to achieve higher: there is no such thing as failure, only a desire to learn and become the best version of ourselves.

As soon as our boys start in Reception, we look to prepare them for the world to which we believe we should all aspire, one in which there is an emphasis on encouragement and recognition of our diversity and where we want the boys to consider not what they can do for themselves but what they can do for others.

Through an enrichment programme that runs throughout our three-year GCSE course, we build on the confidence that has already been nurtured in the earlier years to develop skills and empathy that will make them the leaders that we want and need; to direct the course of our society in the future.

Charitable status. Thorpe House School Trust is a Registered Charity, number 292683. It exists to provide education to boys.

Tockington Manor School and Nursery

Washingpool Hill Road, Tockington, Bristol BS32 4NY

Tel: 01454 613229
email: admin@tockingtonmanorschool.com
website: www.tockingtonmanorschool.com
X/Twitter: @TockingtonManor
Facebook: @tockingtonmanorschool
Instagram: @tockingtonmanorschool
LinkedIn: /tockington-manor-school-limited

Chairman of Governors: Mr A Ramsay

***Headmaster*: Stephen Symonds**, BA Ed Hons

Age Range. Boys and Girls aged 2–13+.

Number of Pupils. 144 Upper School, 74 Lower School, 50 Nursery.

Fees per term (2023–2024). Upper School Day £5,375–£6,165 (including meals and wraparound care); Lower School £3,960.

Tockington Manor School and Nursery is an independent co-educational Preparatory school set in 28 acres of lovely countryside in the picturesque village of Tockington, South Gloucestershire. Pupils are welcomed from age 2 to 13+.

Our small friendly classes and family approach to education provides bespoke learning for every child. We pride ourselves in delivering a varied timetable geared to the needs of each pupil but with emphasis on the core subjects of English, Mathematics and Science. We aim to provide an environment that is positive, supportive and disciplined within a warm, caring family atmosphere. Pupils are encouraged to be confident, considerate and accomplished free thinkers. All pupils take part in all aspects of school life, academic or otherwise, making the most of every moment.

The school works closely with parents to prepare every pupil for Common Entrance and Scholarships to appropriate Independent Senior Schools. We have an enviable success rate in delivering entry into their first-choice Senior Schools, with many being awarded scholarships in Academia, Sport, Music, Drama and Design Technology. Our new Pathway Programme for Year 7 and 8 pupils offers an exciting programme of events and support for those with exceptional talent in sport, music, academia, art and drama.

Nursery. Tockington Manor Nursery is set in a refurbished converted barn within the school grounds. Each child is encouraged to learn through 'hands on' experience overseen by their dedicated Nursery Practitioner who is specially trained to nurture and extend the development of every child. Children benefit from the wider school facilities, tending to their own "cottage style" vegetable garden, discovering nature and forest skills on "welly walks" or enjoying weekly swimming lessons in the school's indoor heated pool.

The School website has further details or a copy of the School's prospectus is available on request by emailing the Registrar, email: registrar@tockington manorschool.com. The Headmaster will be delighted to give a tour of the School to prospective parents upon request.

Charitable status. Tockington Manor School is a Registered Charity, number 311716.

Tormead School

Cranley Road, Guildford, Surrey GU1 2JD

Tel: 01483 575101
email: admissions@tormeadschool.org.uk
website: www.tormeadschool.org.uk
X/Twitter: @tormeadschool
Facebook: @TormeadSchool
Instagram: @tormeadschool

See full entry in the **GSA** section, on **p. 495**.

Tower House School

188 Sheen Lane, East Sheen, London SW14 8LF

Tel: 020 8876 3323
email: admissions@thsboys.org.uk
website: www.thsboys.org.uk
X/Twitter: @towerhousesch
Facebook: @p/Tower-House-School-100072290408154
Instagram: @towerhouseschool
LinkedIn: /tower-house-school

Chair: Mr Antony Phillips

***Head*: Mr N Lunnon**, BSc, PGCE

Age range. 4–13.

Number of boys. 180.

Fees per term (2023–2024). Reception and Year 1: £5,250, Years 2 and 3: £5,800, Senior School: £5,950 (including residential trips and all school lunches).

Our boys want to be part of everything. Whether it be sports teams, musical ensembles or our famous drama productions, pupils are enthusiastic because they know they are valued and have an important contribution to make.

Small class sizes in each year leads to a unique, nurturing and incredibly friendly environment where no boy is left behind. Great emphasis is placed on the development of each boy's individual character and confidence from an early age – encouraging resilience, humility and kindness to others. This happens alongside a fun and forward-looking learning environment with highly skilled staff that inspire pupils to be intellectually curious and ambitious.

Our strong links with Old Vicarage School enable our boys to work and socialise with girls as they grow up, leading to a healthy understanding of how positive and happy relationships are formed.

We are proud of our outstanding academic record, preparing boys for a wide range of senior schools across the country, carefully chosen to suit their academic and extracurricular strengths.

We are delighted to welcome prospective parents to our termly Open Mornings, where they can meet staff, current parents and, most importantly, have a tour of our magical school with our pupils. Alternatively, we are very happy to arrange personal tours of the school with our Headmaster or Deputy Headmaster, if this is more convenient.

For more information visit the school's website or contact our Head of Admissions, Caroline Booth at admissions@thsboys.org.uk.

Charitable status. Tower House School is a Registered Charity, number 1068844.

Town Close School

14 Ipswich Road, Norwich, Norfolk NR2 2LR

Tel: 01603 620180
email: admissions@townclose.com
website: www.townclose.com
X/Twitter: @townclose; @townclosehead
Facebook: @towncloseschool

Chairman of Governors: Sarah Anthony

***Headmaster*: Christopher Wilson**, BA Cantab, PGCE

Age Range. 3–13 Co-educational.

Number of Pupils. Prep: 290, Pre-Prep: 175.

Fees per term (2023–2024). £3,413–£5,176 including lunch and all single-day educational excursions. No compulsory extras.

Town Close School was founded in 1932 and became a Charitable Trust in 1968. The School is fully co-educational and is situated on a beautiful wooded site near the centre of Norwich. This location provides pupils with space and freedom and contributes substantially to Town Close's reputation as an outstandingly happy school.

There is a team of talented teachers who aim to produce well-motivated, balanced, confident children, who are caring and sociable and who know the value of hard work. The children receive excellent teaching and are prepared for all major senior schools. In recent years, pupils have achieved highly in entrance and scholarship assessments to a range of the country's leading senior schools.

A modern teaching building stands at the heart of the School, containing a large, well-equipped library, an art room, an IT centre and 16 purpose-built classrooms. There are many other outstanding facilities including an indoor heated swimming pool, a high-specification sports hall, a performance hall and a full-size, floodlit Astroturf. Science and DT are taught in specialist buildings and the school places a high value on innovation, engineering and scientific discovery. The Pre-Prep occupies a magnificent converted house on the campus and also contains a multi-purpose hall, kitchens, and a new and purpose-built Nursery wing that opens onto fantastic outdoor facilities.

Nursery and Reception classes follow the Foundation Stage curriculum, an important element of which is outdoor learning. Children progress through a broad and varied programme of activities with a strong emphasis on the development of personal and social skills and on establishing positive attitudes to learning and to school life. Swimming, music and dance are taught by specialist teachers, while the rest of the curriculum is delivered by class teachers, ably supported by well-qualified teaching assistants.

Throughout the children's time at Town Close particular attention is paid to the teaching of good handwriting and spelling. Traditional core skills are valued very highly in addition to promoting children's use of digital technology. IT provision is extensive allowing children to become confident and proficient users. The Pre-Prep pupils use a range of children's software to develop key skills and Prep Department children build on this foundation using more sophisticated software, either in the computer room or on laptops and tablets. All sections of the School have filtered access to the internet across the network. The School Intranet contains interactive activities, images, lesson material and links to carefully selected websites. Interactive whiteboards are used throughout the School to support the curriculum.

Town Close has an excellent academic reputation and is also known for the quality of its sport, music, art, drama and its extensive co-curricular programme. Trips and expeditions form a valuable part of what is offered, and provide the balance essential for a full and rounded education. Activities take place during the lunch hour, after school, and occasionally at weekends. In terms of music, the School has a full orchestra, a variety of choirs and a wide range of ensembles. All children are encouraged to perform with regular high-quality concerts and plays.

Physical Education plays an important part in the development of each child, be they in the Nursery or in Year 8. Emphasis is placed on fostering healthy exercise, as well as encouraging a positive, competitive attitude, individual skills and teamwork. As well as providing all the usual opportunities for the major sports (rugby, netball, hockey, cricket and athletics), coaching is offered in many other sports.

A visit to www.townclose.com will provide a fuller picture of the School, including a sight of the most recent inspection report, in which Town Close was given the highest rating in every area.

Charitable status. Town Close Educational Trust Limited is a Registered Charity, number 311293. It exists to provide education for children.

Truro School Preparatory

Highertown, Truro, Cornwall TR1 3QN

Tel: 01872 272616
email: prepenquiries@truroschool.com
prepadmissions@truroschool.com
website: www.truroschool.com/prep-school/contact-prep

Chairman of the Governors: Mr R Thomas

Head of Truro School: Mr A Johnson, MA

***Head of Preparatory School*: Mr R Morse**, BEd Hons

Key Stage I Coordinator: Mr L Keveren, BA Hons
EYFS Coordinator: Ms Kate Williams, BEd Hons

Age Range. 3–11.
Number of Pupils. 283: 172 Boys, 111 Girls.
Fees per term (2023–2024). Prep (including lunch): £4,940 (Years 3–4), £5,130 (Years 5–6). Pre-Prep (including lunch): £3,480 (Nursery and Reception), £3,655 (Years 1 and 2).

Optional extras: Individual music lessons, fencing, ballet, judo, photography, Bushcraft, badminton, LAMDA (Speech & Drama), Pre-Prep tennis.

Truro School Prep opened as Treliske School in 1936 in the former residence and estate of Sir George Smith. The school lies in extensive and secluded grounds to the west of the cathedral city of Truro, three miles from Truro School. The grounds command fine views of the neighbouring countryside. The drive to the school off the main A390 is almost 800 metres and Truro Golf Course also surrounds the school, producing a campus of beauty and seclusion.

The keynote of the school is a busy and positive atmosphere in which children learn the value of contributing positively to the school community and the wider world through a structured framework of academic study and extracurricular interests. The approach is based firmly in Christian beliefs and the school is proud of its Methodist foundation.

Building development has kept pace with modern expectations and Truro School Prep has its own large sports hall, an indoor heated swimming pool, a design and technology workshop with a computer room adjoined and purpose-built Pre-Prep.

The games programme is designed to encourage all children and the excellent facilities coupled with the talented and professional staff enable us to offer a rich variety of sporting and recreational pursuits. There are over 70 clubs that run before school, during lunch break or after school (from 4.00pm to 5.00pm).

There is a strong school tradition in music and drama and the arts. Children may choose to learn a musical instrument from the full orchestral range. Each year the Spring concert, with Truro School, allows the school to show the community the excellent talents, which flourish in both schools.

Close links are maintained with the Senior School and nearly all pupils progress through at age 11 on the Head's recommendation to Truro School; the only Independent Headmasters' and Headmistresses' Conference School in Cornwall (*see entry in HMC section*).

The prospectus and further details can be obtained from the Head's PA, and the Head will be pleased to show prospective parents around the school.

Charitable status. Truro School is part of the Methodist Independent Schools Trust, which is a registered Charity, number 1142794.

Twickenham Preparatory School

Beveree, 43 High Street, Hampton, Middlesex TW12 2SA

Tel: 020 8979 6216
email: admissions@twickenhamprep.co.uk
website: www.twickenhamprep.co.uk
X/Twitter: @twickenhamprep
Facebook: @twickenhamprepschool
Instagram: @twickenham_prep

Chairman of Governors: Mr H Bates

***Headmaster*: Mr O Barrett**, BA Hons, QTS

Age Range. 4–13.
Number of Pupils. Boys 150, Girls 120.
Fees per term (2023–2024). £4,320–£4,815. Lunch £250–£285.

Founded in 1969, Twickenham Prep is an independent, co-educational school situated in Hampton. We are a happy, vibrant, and thriving school where every child is valued as an individual and inspired to achieve their full potential, personally, socially and academically. The pupils benefit from small classes, first-class facilities, specialist subject teaching and excellent pastoral care.

Our pupils achieve great success, both academic and extracurricular, moving on to excellent independent secondary schools with regular academic, sporting, musical, art and all-rounder scholarships. We are committed to working in partnership with our parents so that our pupils leave TPS as well-rounded individuals. All pupils sit their secondary entrance exams in Year 6, with offers made to girls for Year 7 entry and for boys, the possibilities of a Year 7 or Year 9 entry. The majority of boys stay on at TPS Senior Prep which allows them to access our robust KS3 provision alongside the Pre-Senior Baccalaureate (PSB) framework, which has a core skills focus and is designed to be in tune with the requirements of the 21st century workplace. PSB allows us to maintain high academic standards through a knowledge-rich curriculum, alongside the explicit teachings of key skills that pupils need to be lifelong learners.

Our Pre-Prep and Prep curriculum is based on the National Curriculum with specialist teaching of PE, Games, ICT, French, Music and Think Tank (formerly Mind Lab, an innovative thinking skills programme) from Reception, ensuring a balanced educational experience. Art/Design and Technology is introduced in Year 3 and, from Year 4, pupils have specialist teaching in all subjects, with Latin being introduced in Year 5. Class sizes are no more than 20, developing each pupil to their full academic potential and promoting high academic standards. The school is well equipped to cover the full range of subjects, with purpose-built Art/DT, Science and Music facilities and a modern sports hall used for PE and termly productions.

Strong emphasis is placed on participation by all in sporting, musical and extracurricular activities. The school plays a wide range of sports and has recently formed an affiliation with Kempton Cricket Club to provide 10 acres of dedicated sporting facilities for rugby, football, cricket and athletics. The girls also play netball, hockey and cricket, with athletics and swimming also part of the sporting curriculum. Music and drama play a large part in the school with full-scale productions and concerts annually involving all pupils. There is a school choir and individual instrumental lessons are taught by visiting specialists.

TPS is a leading Chess school and we are also the current National Mind Lab Champions; we have represented the UK for the last 7 years at the International Mind Lab Olympics.

There are also many extracurricular clubs during and after school to choose from, including coding, LAMDA, chess, DT, Music technology and many sports options, and we also provide on-site wraparound care from 7.30 am to 6.30 pm.

Located in Hampton, we offer morning minibus services to children living in Richmond, Twickenham, Teddington, St Margaret's, Hampton Wick, Feltham, Sunbury, Thames Ditton and East Molesey.

Following the recent renovation of our new premises, 'The Hub', located at 51 High Street in Hampton, we are excited to have launched the TPS radio station. This new facility complements our Digital Media Suite which includes broadcast cameras and an editing suite. These state-of-the-art facilities provide excellent opportunities for children to develop their AV skills through recording and podcasts and short films, alongside broadcasting live radio shows.

Last year we were delighted with the results of our school inspection, carried out by the Independent Schools Inspectorate. We achieved the highest rating of 'Excellent' in both categories of the educational quality aspect: 'Pupils' Academics and Other Achievements' and 'Pupils' Personal Development'. This impressive result is testament to the hard work and dedication of the whole TPS community, including staff, governors, pupils and our families.

Entry to the school is non-selective at Reception with limited places available in other year groups subject to an assessment.

Regular Open Days are held and personal tours are available – the pupils and Headmaster would be delighted to show you around. Please contact the school office.

Charitable Status. Twickenham Preparatory School is a Registered Charity, number 1067572. It exists to provide education for boys and girls.

Twyford School

Twyford, Winchester, Hampshire SO21 1NW

Tel: 01962 712269
email: twyford@twyfordschool.com
website: www.twyfordschool.com
X/Twitter: @TwyfordSchool
Instagram: @twyfordschool

Chairman of Governors: Mr Colin Howman

***Headmaster*: Mr Andrew Harvey**

Age range. 2–13.

Number of children. 433. Main School: 277, of whom 13 are weekly boarders, 105 are flexi boarders; Pre-Prep: 156.

Fees per term (2023–2024). Weekly boarding: £9,906. Day: Prep Years 4–8 £7,331, Year 3 £6,543; Pre-Prep: £1,198–£4,404. Fees are inclusive of all outings/trips run during the term.

Twyford School is situated at the edge of the beautiful South Downs, just two miles from the historic city of Winchester and the M3. Twyford is a family school that aims to offer an all-round, top-rate education with a Christian ethos. Most pupils are day pupils, but from Year 4, many board one or two nights a week through the school's flexi boarding system. By the final year, many weekly board, which makes an excellent preparation for their move to senior school. The contrast between the modern facilities (classrooms, laboratories, music school, creative arts and ICT block, swimming pool and sports centre) and the Victorian chapel and hall creates a rich and stimulating environment.

The school regularly achieves scholarships – 62 awards (academic, art, design, sport and music) in the last 5 years – to major senior schools such as Winchester College, St Swithun's, Canford, Marlborough, Wycombe Abbey, Godolphin, Wellington College, Bradfield, Radley, Bryanston, Eton, Sherborne Boys and Sherborne Girls.

Charitable status. Twyford School is a Registered Charity, number 307425. It exists to provide education for children.

Unicorn School

238 Kew Road, Richmond, Surrey TW9 3JX

Tel: 020 8948 3926
email: registrar@unicornschool.org.uk
website: www.unicornschool.org.uk
Instagram: @unicornschoolkewroad

Chair of Governors: Mr Paul Rathbone

***Headteacher*: Mrs Polly Fraley**

Age Range. 3–11.

Number of Children. 171 Day Pupils: 84 boys, 87 girls.

Fees per term (2023–2024). £2,995 (Nursery half days), £4,950 (Nursery full days)–£5,870.

Unicorn is a parent-founded IAPS co-ed primary school founded in 1970. Situated opposite Kew Gardens, the school occupies a large Victorian house and converted coach house with a spacious, superbly-equipped playground and garden.

The school has access to Kew Gardens and the sports facilities at the nearby Barnes Hockey Pitch fields are used for games and Pools on the Park for swimming. The school offers breakfast club from 7.30am and wraparound care until 6.00pm daily.

Our aim is for Unicorn to be a successful, forward-thinking school that embraces children, staff and parents in an evolving, exciting, dynamic and nurturing community, enriched with creativity and supported by excellent leadership and management. Pupils are encouraged to become independent, responsible, self-aware and confident young people, who reap the benefits of a very broad curriculum to achieve considerable success.

There are normally 22 children per class, where a variety of teaching methods are used with the children regularly assessed. Importance is placed upon the development of the individual and high academic standards are achieved. The main point of entry is to the nursery at 3+. Children are prepared for entry at 11+ to the leading London day schools, as well as a variety of boarding schools.

Teaching methods are thoughtfully planned to encourage, accelerate and support each child's abilities. The school's individual approach helps the less able, as well as the more talented, through small separate groups in reading and maths. We cover all areas of the National Curriculum and more besides, so that every child can find areas of personal strength.

Our broad curriculum includes computing, science, music, creative arts, drama, French and PE, all taught by specialist teachers and often in small groups. All classes have a specific time each day for reflection and to develop their thinking skills. In the Junior Classes, Years 3 and 4 have 'Brain Time' and Years 5 and 6 enjoy philosophy lessons and current affairs. Individual music lessons offered in piano, violin, cello, drums, clarinet, saxophone, flute, guitar and trumpet, as well as singing. Recorder groups, choirs, an orchestra, rock band, violin group, music theory and tutti fluti also flourish.

Every child from Year 2 up is assigned their own iPad; there is a Science suite, music rooms, library and a state-of-the-art fully-equipped Art and DT room and interactive whiteboard technology in all classrooms.

In addition to the major games of football, hockey, netball, cricket and rounders, there are optional clubs for chess, French, karate, Little Voices, MTech, Virtual Reality, Lego, Swim, Touch Typing and Musical Theatre. Other club activities include computer, cookery, dance, debate, design and technology, golf, poetry, pottery, riding, sailing and padel tennis. There are regular trips, including visits to the theatre and museums as well as the galleries of Central London. All children, from the age of seven upwards, participate in residential field study trips to Surrey, Devon and Cumbria and Years 5 and 6 have an optional biennial ski trip.

An elected School Council, with representatives from each age group, meets weekly with the Headteacher and a weekly newsletter for parents is also produced.

A happy, caring environment prevails and importance is placed on producing kind, responsible children who show awareness and consideration for the needs of others.

Unicorn seeks to be diverse, open minded and foster a culture of compassionate and conscious inclusion. We stand against everything to do with discrimination, exclusion, harassment, bullying and hatred in whatever form it takes.

Charitable status. Unicorn School is a Registered Charity, number 312578. It exists to provide education for boys and girls.

University College School – Junior Branch

11 Holly Hill, Hampstead, London NW3 6QN

Tel: 020 7435 3068
email: juniorbranch@ucs.org.uk
website: www.ucs.org.uk

Chair of Council of Governors: Mr Stephen Warshaw

***Headmaster*: Mr L R J Hayward**, MA

Age Range. 7–11.
Number of Boys. 250.
Fees per term (2023–2024). £7,757.

The School was founded in 1891 by the Governors of University College, London. The present building was opened in 1928, but retains details from the Georgian house first used. It stands near the highest point of Hampstead Heath and the hall and classrooms face south. Facilities include a Science Laboratory, Library, Drama Studio, Music and Computer Rooms, and a Centre for Art and Technology. Boys receive their Swimming and PE lessons in the pool and Sports Hall at the Senior School, 5 minutes' walk away. The Junior School has full use of the 27 acres of playing fields on games days.

Boys enter at 7+ each year and they are prepared for transfer to the Senior School at 11+. (*See entry in HMC section.*)

Charitable status. University College School, Hampstead is a Registered Charity, number 312748. The Junior Branch exists to provide education for boys aged 7+ to 11 years.

University College School Pre-Prep

36 College Crescent, Hampstead, London NW3 5LF

Tel: 020 7722 4433
email: pre-prep@ucs.org.uk
website: www.ucs.org.uk/UCS-Pre-Prep

Chairman of Council: Mr Stephen Warshaw, BA

***Headmistress*: Dr Z Dunn**, BEd, PhD, NPQH

Age range. Boys 4–7.
Number of pupils. 100 Boys.
Fees per term (2023–2024). £7,077.

At UCS Pre-Prep, we firmly believe that happiness and self-esteem are the keys to success in every pupil's learning journey. The well-qualified and highly supportive staff accompany each child on a voyage of educational and social discovery during the first years of school life.

The Pre-Prep fully supports the aims and ethos of UCS: intellectual curiosity and independence of mind are developed, self-discovery and self-expression are fostered and a cooperative and collaborative approach to learning is of great importance.

For every child in our care, we provide a continuously positive and creative learning environment that allows the individual the opportunity to develop personal qualities and talents. Children enjoy specialist teaching in music, art and Physical Education and the full primary curriculum in well-resourced classrooms. All pupils enjoy the use of the swimming pool and experience a wide range of different sports. The outdoor learning programme takes advantage of the school's allotment and extensive space at the fields. At the end of Year 2, the boys transfer to the Junior Branch of UCS.

Charitable status. UCS Pre-Prep Limited is a Registered Charity, number 1098657.

Upton House School

115 St Leonard's Road, Windsor, Berkshire SL4 3DF

Tel: 01753 862610
email: info@uptonhouse.org.uk
registrar@uptonhouse.org.uk
website: www.uptonhouse.org.uk
X/Twitter: @UptonHouseSch
Facebook: @UptonHouseSch
Instagram: @UptonHouseSch

Chair of the Council: Mrs V Barker

***Headmistress*: Mrs Rhian Thornton**, BA Hons, NPQL, LLE, PGCE

Deputy Head: Mrs Kate Newcombe, BEd Hons
Head of Pre-Prep: Mrs Emma Pritchard, BSc Hons, QTS, NVQ3
Head of Early Years/Transition: Mrs Susi Broad, BSc Hons, QTS, DipTH

Age Range. Girls and Boys 2–11 years.

Number of Pupils. 295 Day: 185 Girls, 110 Boys.

Fees per term (2023–2024). Nursery: please contact the school for details. Transition and Pre-Prep: From £3,531 per term. Forms 3–6: From £5,950–£5,980 per term. Bursaries available.

Our aim at Upton House is to foster a happy and stimulating environment in which each child can prosper academically, socially and emotionally. The school prepares all children for their continuing education and equips them with life skills for the future.

Upton House School was founded in 1936 by benefactors and has evolved over the years to provide a well-equipped modern environment where children thrive.

At Upton House we aim to provide the best possible education for each child. We give encouragement and stimulation to develop their academic abilities and we develop pupils individual strengths, whether it is from our broad curriculum or from our wide range of extracurricular activities. This combined with a loving nurturing environment, develops a set of pastoral values which makes Upton very special.

Our arts block houses a music room, recording studio and art studio. Our newly opened Broadcasting Studio offers the facility to livestream many of our events to parents and their families, and the opportunity for older pupils to try their hand at broadcasting. Our kitchen serves freshly prepared, nutritious meals on site. Facilities also include a drama/dance studio and gymnasium.

Specialist subjects include PE and French from 3 years old. Educational robots, iPads, laptops, and interactive whiteboards are used across the school to enhance learning. Diverse sporting activities include judo, fencing and ballet.

Our enhanced curriculum is rich with cross-curricular digital innovations and our pioneering live-streamed events run by our Broadcasting Club share our activities with our global family online.

Boys and girls leaving us gain places at a wide range of excellent senior schools and regularly win scholarships.

Entry is non-selective and means-tested bursaries are available for those entering the school.

We provide care from 7.45am in our Early Birds breakfast club as well as an extended day until 6pm for children from age 3. A wide variety of clubs are offered in the extended day programme as well as teacher-supervised prep for older children.

We have an active PTA which organises many fundraising events through the year and helps to forge close links between the school and parents. Please visit our website for details of forthcoming virtual open mornings. Personal tours are also welcome.

Charitable status. Upton House School is a Registered Charity, number 309095. It exists to provide an excellent all-round educational foundation for boys and girls.

The Ursuline Preparatory School Ilford

2–4 Coventry Road, Ilford, Essex IG1 4QR

Tel: 020 8518 4050
email: urspsi@urspsi.org.uk
website: www.urspsi.org.uk
X/Twitter: @URSPSI
Facebook: @URSPSI

Chair of Governors: Mr Simon Bird

***Headteacher*: Mrs Natasha Boyce**

Age range. 3–11 Co-educational.

Number of pupils. 100.

Fees per term (2023–2024). Nursery: £2,902 (full-time including lunch, pre- and after-school care, net of government funding), Reception–Year 6: £3,833 (including lunch, pre- and after-school care).

The Ursuline Preparatory School Ilford is a Roman Catholic day school in the trusteeship of the Ursuline Sisters. The Ursuline Sisters first came to England in 1862, settling at Forest Gate from where they established the school in Ilford in 1903 at 73 Cranbrook Road. The school has since flourished. Formerly part of The Ursuline Academy, The Ursuline Preparatory School Ilford is now a fully independent school in its own right, but continues to share close and valued links with the Academy.

As a Catholic school, we firmly believe that Religious Education is the foundation of the entire educational process. Prayers and liturgical celebrations are an important aspect of school life, unifying the hearts and minds of all associated with the school and ensuring we are all working to achieve the best possible education for the children in our care.

We provide a safe, secure and stimulating environment for our pupils to thrive. We recognise each child's unique value and are committed to encouraging self-esteem and developing each child's potential. We encourage the children to become independent learners by building on their curiosity and desire to learn and developing their skills, concepts and understanding.

While the school continues to set its own high standards, we complement these with the integration of the best of the National Curriculum. English and mathematics form the core subjects together with Religious Education, science, history, geography, ICT, PE, drama, design technology, art, music, MFL and stimulating project work. The Performing Arts have a high profile in school and the children are regularly given the opportunity to develop their talents. Well-stocked libraries, audio-visual aids and a specialist Information Communication Technology department are all available throughout the nursery and school.

We offer a wide range of extracurricular activities including ballet, speech and drama and Irish Dancing. Other clubs and sports clubs including football, cricket, basketball, netball, gymnastics and trampolining are held weekly. Individual instrumental tuition can be arranged for piano, violin, guitar and ukulele. There is also an award-winning school choir.

All teaching staff are fully qualified, experienced and dedicated to the ideals of the school. They work in close partnership with parents to ensure that each child's special individual needs are recognised. In addition, we have the help of experienced general assistants. Our pupil to teacher ratio is excellent and we are able to engage in small group teaching.

Pre- and after-school care is available. Holiday club is run by an outside company at an additional cost.

Charitable status. The Ursuline Preparatory School Ilford is a Registered Charity, number 245661.

Ursuline Preparatory School

Wimbledon

18 The Downs, Wimbledon, London SW20 8HR
Tel: 020 8947 0859
email: headteachersoffice@ursulineprep.org
website: www.ursulineprep.org
X/Twitter: @ursulineprep
Facebook: @Ursulineprep

Chair of Governors: Ms Merinda D'Aprano

***Head Teacher*: Mrs Caroline Molina**

Age range. Ursuline Prep School Girls 4–11, Ursuline Pre-School Boys and Girls 3–4.

Number of pupils. 128+.

Fees per term (2023–2024). £4,660 full time, Pre-School £4,600 full time and from £2,796 part time.

Ursuline Preparatory School is a Roman Catholic school that welcomes children of all faiths and none. Non-selective by choice, the school offers a values-driven, academic education to girls from 4–11 years of age. Our Ursuline Pre-School offers provision for boys and girls age 3–4.

Established in 1892 to promote the values of St Angela Merici OSU, Ursuline Preparatory School places equal value on the education of heart, mind and soul in the certain knowledge that only through the equal development of all three can a child truly excel. The school's mission is to develop a community that lives each day working together *(Insieme)* and united in harmony, valuing the contributions of all and championing the virtues of love, compassion, kindness and generosity. The children are encouraged to be grateful for the gifts they have been given and to develop these gifts to the full, in generous service to others. The school seeks to pass on the living and faith-filled tradition of Jesus Christ by having unswerving faith in every single one of our pupils and by encouraging them, in turn, to have faith and hope in others. A keen focus is to educate and create future leaders in the spirit of *Serviam* (I will serve), keeping justice at the centre of their lives.

The core provision of this school is threefold:

- A strong Ursuline ethos;
- An academic provision, that prepares children fully for secondary school;
- A strong partnership between pupils, parents and staff.

Our children enjoy a rich diversity of experiences, both inside and outside of the classroom. Our 11+ preparation curriculum, full sporting programme and developed range of extracurricular activities provide an enriching and engaging provision.

The girls at Ursuline Preparatory School follow an academic curriculum and are fully supported, securing places in their senior school of choice. As a result of the Ursuline ethos, and the academic preparation put in place, the girls here can face the 11+ process with confidence. Last year, girls received offers from the following schools: City of London, Epsom College, Guildford High School, Ibstock Place, Kingston Grammar, Lady Eleanor Holles, Notre Dame, Putney High, Surbiton High, Sutton High, St John's Leatherhead, St Paul's Girls School, Ursuline High School and Wimbledon High.

While we are a non-selective school, our girls exceed expectations at 11+ with many scholarships offered.

An Ursuline education seeks to help the young people here grow and flourish in an environment in which every child is loved and valued. On such sure foundations, we help them become the very best that they can be. Please do come and visit; you will be made most welcome.

Charitable status. Ursuline Preparatory School, Wimbledon is a Registered Charity, number 1079754.

Victoria College Preparatory School

Pleasant Street, St Helier, Jersey, Channel Islands JE2 4RR

Tel: 01534 723468
email: admssions@vcp.sch.je
website: www.vcp.sch.je
X/Twitter: @JerseyVcp
Facebook: @VCPJERSEY
Instagram: @victoriacollegeprep
LinkedIn: /company/vcpjersey

***Headteacher*: Mr Dan Pateman**, BA Hons

Chair of Governors: Mr Richard Stevens

Age range. 7–11.

Number of boys. 275 Day Boys.

Fees per term (2023–2024). £2,469 (£7,407 per annum).

Victoria College Preparatory School was founded in 1922 as an integral part of Victoria College and is now a separate School under its own Headteacher, who is responsible for such matters as staffing, curriculum and administration. The Preparatory School shares Governors with Victoria College, whose members are drawn from the leaders of the Island of Jersey with a minority representation from the States of Jersey Education Committee. Members of staff are all experienced and well-qualified teachers, including specialists in Art, Dance, Music, PE, French and Science. Entry to the Prep School is at 7 and boys normally leave to enter Victoria College at the age of 11. The school games are cricket, football, athletics, swimming, hockey, cross-country and rugby. Sporting facilities are shared with Victoria College. Special features of the school are exceptionally high standards of sport, drama, music, and French. Many visits, both sporting and educational, are arranged out of the Island.

A separate Pre-Preparatory School (5 to 7 years) is incorporated in a co-educational school situated at Jersey College Preparatory School and offers places for boys whose parents wish them to be educated at both Victoria College and the Preparatory School. Candidates for Pre-Prep entry should be registered at Jersey College Prep, St Helier, Jersey.

Vinehall School

Robertsbridge, East Sussex TN32 5JL

Tel: 01580 880413
email: admissions@vinehallschool.com
website: www.vinehallschool.com
Facebook: @VinehallSch
Instagram: @vinehallschool

Chairman of Governors: Mr Daniel Lewis

***Headmaster*: Mr Joff Powis**, BSc, QTS, NPQH

Age range. 2–13 co-educational.

Number of children. 220.

Fees per term (2023–2024). Prep: Years 6–8: £7,225 (day), £9,975 (full boarding), £8,975 (weekly boarding); Years 3–5: £7,000 (day), £9,975 (full boarding), £8,975 (weekly boarding); Pre-Prep: Reception, Years 1 & 2 £3,750; Nursery (without Early Years funding): £42.50 per morning session, £25 per afternoon session, £67.50 per full day session. Please contact the Bursary for further details about Early Years Funding. 50-week Nursery provision was introduced in September 2023 and full wraparound care for 50-weeks of the year for children from Nursery to Year 2 is also available.

Vinehall is a leading co-educational day, boarding school and nursery for children between the ages of 2 and 13 and is a proud member of the Repton Family of Schools. Our family of schools share an outward-looking, forward-thinking philosophy of how to give children the very best chances in the world that awaits them.

Founded in 1938, Vinehall School is located in 50 acres of picturesque East Sussex countryside, and provides a unique learning experience that allows our children to thrive in an expansive and nurturing family environment. Our goal is to give every child the opportunity to succeed both academically and personally while allowing them to remain children for as long as possible.

Our wonderful site means our pupils have a freedom rarely found these days, providing opportunities to explore and play outside, including climbing trees and building dens. This environment fosters a love for nature and encourages our children to become responsible stewards of the environment. We are fortunate to boost exceptional facilities including a magnificent Millennium Building, comprising classrooms, IT suite and library, a science block, music building, art, design and technology centre, a purpose-built theatre with seating for 250, a sports hall and adjoining indoor swimming pool, an AstroTurf pitch, an adventure playground and a nine-hole golf course.

At Vinehall, we have high academic expectations for our children, supported by dedicated teachers who inspire them to work with enthusiasm and enjoyment in preparation for their senior schools and beyond. We take great pride in preparing our pupils for their next educational journey. In Years 7 and 8, our dedicated teachers focus on preparing pupils for Common Entrance and scholarships to various independent senior schools at 13+.

Our school has a history of sending pupils to some of the most prestigious senior schools in the country, including Battle Abbey, Bede's, Benenden, Brighton College, Charterhouse, Cranbrook, Eastbourne College, Eton, Harrow, Hurst, King's Canterbury, Mayfield, Repton, Sevenoaks, Sutton Valence, Tonbridge and Winchester. Our aim is to help parents make informed decisions and ensure that every child is matched with the most suitable school for them.

Located within the heart of the main school, our boarding house is very much an extended family. It is valued as a home away from home for our boarders; creating a relaxed and comfortable environment separate from academic life at the school.

Boarding has always been an integral part of Vinehall life, and we recognise that many working parents need additional support from the school, whilst at the same time letting children develop independence and spend time with their friends in a safe and caring environment.

Whether you are looking for full boarding or flexible boarding options, Vinehall can cater to the needs of all in a safe and family centred boarding house.

We know that choosing the right school for your child is one of the most important decisions you can make. Our Admissions team will support and guide you through the process from your first enquiry right the way through to your child's first day and will ensure you have a full understanding of our school, its ethos and the opportunities on offer.

Vinehall School offers a happy and inspiring environment for boys and girls from Nursery through to Year 8. The best way to find out more about what makes our School so inspiring is to come and see for yourself at one of our Open Days or you can arrange a private tour with our Head.

To find our more, contact our Admissions Department on admissions@vinehallschool.com or call 01580 883090. Visit www.vinehallschool.com/admissions.

Charitable status. Vinehall School is a Registered Charity, number 307014. It exists to provide a secure, quality education, in particular for those in need of residential schooling.

Walhampton School

Lymington, Hampshire SO41 5ZG

Tel: 01590 613300
email: registrar@walhampton.com
website: www.walhampton.com
X/Twitter: @Walhamptonprep
Facebook: @walhamptonprep
Instagram: @walhamptonprep
LinkedIn: /walhampton-independent-preparatory-school

Chairman of Governors: Victoria Speers

***Head*: Mr Jonny Timms**, BA, MA

Age Range. Boys and girls, 2–13.

Number of Pupils. 370 pupils: 50 boarders, 235 Prep School.

Fees per term (2023–2024). From (day) £2,815–£7,180 and up to £10,280 for full boarding. Pre-prep reception to year 2, £3,785 per term, prep (day) junior to year 3, £5,640–£7,180 per term, (day) years 4–8, £7,180 per term, boarding (in addition to the fees above) full boarding £3,100 per term, weekly boarding £3,025 per term, flexi boarding £55 per night.

Set within one hundred acres of lawns, lakes and woodlands in the idyllic New Forest close to the sea, Walhampton is a remarkable independent day, flexi and full-time boarding school for boys and girls aged 2–13.

With small class sizes and innovative teaching, Walhampton pupils achieve consistently impressive academic results. Walhampton's Year 8 leavers recently gained entrance to Brighton College, Bryanston, Canford, Durlston Court, King's Bruton, King Edward VI, Embley, Sherborne, Radley College, Royal High School Bath and Winchester College. Walhampton pupils have a 100% success rate in senior school admissions, with 45% awarded scholarships across a variety of disciplines.

A Walhampton education allows children to be children for longer whilst also preparing them for their life after Walhampton and in the world of tomorrow. Pupils are encouraged to find their voice and develop the strength of character through the Pre-Senior Baccalaureate (PSB) framework and CE curriculum, and the School's focus on nurturing curiosity and global thinking instils passion and purpose.

Digital learning and STEAM (Science, Technology, Engineering, Arts and Maths) features highly with STEAM and Boat Modelling challenges and competitions. The School's location and facilities enables Walhampton to offer a broad, holistic and dynamic curriculum, which stretches beyond the classroom. Lessons are also taught in the permanent outdoor classroom, in Forest School, by the lakes and in the kitchen garden, bringing subjects like Maths, English, History and Science to life while making sure sports, music and the arts flourish alongside academic disciplines.

Walhampton has one of the ultimate prep school settings and offers a varied programme of enrichment activities during the timetabled "SPARK" curriculum (Society & Service, Play & Train, Adventure & Exploration, Radical, Kindle & Create) as well as after school activities. The SPARK sessions reinforce the School's focus on the outdoors and eco-school Green Flag status with activities including gardening club, beekeeping, conservation groups and cookery. A central part of our programme includes a range of sports undertaken in our grounds such as our Rugby and Netball Academies, horse riding in our dedicated equestrian centre, watersports and fishing on our lakes, and sailing at our partner club in Lymington. Performing arts activities such as orchestra and LAMDA also help to further our children's passions.

The network of daily bus routes for local day pupils; wraparound care (breakfast and supper clubs); and popular flexi boarding are all designed to support families with busy lives. For those considering a Walhampton education but living further afield, the Walhampton Express brings this remarkable country school closer. The escorted train service stops at mainline stations from Brockenhurst to London Waterloo. Boarding staff collect children on Sunday evening and escort them on Friday after chapel. Full, weekly and flexi boarders enjoy the relaxed and homely, family orientated atmosphere of Bradfield House, surrounded by stunning grounds with views over the Solent to the Isle of Wight.

Scholarships and Bursaries. Walhampton offers a number of bursary awards and scholarships, together with means-tested financial support to help with fees. In addition, the School offers a 10% military discount for forces families. Our Governors are keen to encourage academic excellence and are committed to broadening access to the school. The School has set up the Walhampton Foundation Trust to give every child the opportunity of a Walhampton education. For our School community, bursaries will not only provide life-changing opportunities, but also help to raise standards across the School through an infusion of bright young talent.

Find out more: www.walhampton.com/joining-walhampton/financial-assistance/

Walthamstow Hall Junior School

Bradbourne Park Road, Sevenoaks, Kent TN13 3LD

Tel: 01732 453815
email: registrar@whall.school
website: www.walthamstow-hall.co.uk
X/Twitter: @WalthamstowHall
Facebook: @Walthamstow-Hall
Instagram: @walthamstowhall
LinkedIn: /company/walthamstow-hall

Chair of Governors: Mrs J Adams, BA Joint Hons

***Headmistress of Walthamstow Hall School*: Ms Louise Chamberlain,** BSc Nottingham, PGCE Newcastle

Deputy Head of the Junior School: Mrs C Conway, BA Hons, MA Witwatersrand South Africa, PGCE Canterbury Christ Church

Day School for Girls; co-ed Nursery only.

Age Range. 2–11.

Number of Pupils. 125.

Fees per term (2023–2024). Nursery: £38.40 per session (2–10 sessions per week); Reception–Year 2: £4,505; Years 3–6: £5,770.

Walthamstow Hall Junior School is a happy and vibrant school with a proud tradition of providing the highest quality education for boys and girls aged 2 up to Reception (4/5 years), and girls-only from Reception–11 years.

From Reception upwards pupils benefit from being in small classes with two parallel classes in most year groups. Optimum-sized classes throughout the Junior School guarantee individual attention, with obvious benefits including a seamless and highly effective preparation for senior school entrance exams without last-minute cramming and changes to routine.

A well-planned programme of education brings out the potential of each child as she progresses through the Junior School. A broad curriculum is enriched with many co-curricular activities and clubs. Wraparound care provision is available from 7.15 am until 6.15 pm Monday–Friday.

Girls are well prepared for a range of senior schools and have won awards to prestigious independent schools, including Walthamstow Hall Senior School (*see entry in GSA section*). Entry to our Senior School is from 11+, 13+ and 16+ with Awards, Scholarships and Bursaries offered. Equally, our track record in the Kent 11+ test is excellent.

Walthamstow Hall was founded in 1838 and is one of the oldest girls' schools in the country. It has built a reputation for all-round excellence and achievements by girls are outstanding. Over recent years, many facilities have been enhanced or added, and our specialist facilities include our ICT Suite and Science Laboratory, Design and Technology, Art and Cookery Rooms, well-stocked computerised Library, Tennis and Netball Courts and dedicated Music Centre. Girls also have access to facilities at the nearby Senior School including the Ship Theatre, Swimming Pool, and Sports Centre. The school is situated in the centre of Sevenoaks within easy reach of road and rail networks.

Warwick Preparatory School

Banbury Road, Warwick CV34 6PL

Tel: 01926 491545
email: admissions@warwickprep.com
website: www.warwickprep.com
X/Twitter: @WarwickPrep
Facebook: @warwickprep
Instagram: @warwickprep

Chairman of the Governors: Mrs Sally Austin

***Headmistress*: Mrs Hellen Dodsworth**

Age range. Boys 3–7, Girls 3–11.

Number of children. c. 500.

Fees per term (2023–2024). Nursery: £3,326 (full time, after Nursery Education Funding, lunch included). Lower School (4–6 years): £4,022; Middle School (7–9 years): £4,643. Upper School (9–11 years): £4,930. Lunch: £255 (mid-morning fruit included).

Instrumental music tuition optional extra.

Warwick Preparatory School is an Independent School, purpose built on a 4½ acre site on the outskirts of Warwick. It is part of the Warwick Schools Foundation, which includes King's High School, Warwick School and The Kingsley School.

The Prep School has an exceptionally large staff, with specialist tuition in Art, French, Science, Music, Drama, DT, Physical Education and Computing.

Boys and girls are admitted from the age of 3+, subject to the availability of places. At the age of 7, the majority of boys continue to Warwick School, while the girls normally remain with us until they are 11.

Entry to King's High School is based on girls' progress at Warwick Prep and their aptitude, and girls may be offered a guaranteed place. If there are any concerns, the Entrance Examination will be used to determine a place, as with candidates outside the Foundation.

Early registration is advised if a place in the Pre-Prep Department is to be ensured. Entry to the School at the age of 7 and later requires a satisfactory level of attainment in the basic skills and may be competitive.

Charitable status. Warwick Schools Foundation is a Registered Charity, number 1088057.

Wellesley Prep School

Stratfield Turgis, Hook, Hampshire RG27 0AR
Tel: 01256 882707
email: office@wellesleyprep.co.uk
website: www.wellesleyprepschool.co.uk
X/Twitter: @WellesleyPrep
Facebook: @wellesleyprep
Instagram: @wellesleyprepschool

Headmaster: **Mr A McDonald**, BSc, PGCE

Age Range. 3–13.
Number of Pupils. Day Boys 147, Day Girls 147.
Fees per term (2023–2024). Nursery on application; Reception £4,365; Year 1 £4,490; Year 2 £4,860; Year 3 £5,235; Years 4–8 £5,905. Lunch included. There are no compulsory extras.

Founded in 1950, Wellesley Prep School (formerly Daneshill) has always prided itself on the collective qualities of its teaching staff and their ability to interact with pupils and deliver a stimulating learning experience.

Set in over 100 acres of beautiful Hampshire countryside, the School provides the perfect environment and atmosphere for each pupil to grow and prosper as an individual with a strong set of core values.

In September 2023, Daneshill changed its name to Wellesley Prep School. The school was acquired by The Wellington Estate in 2018. The school continued to thrive under the careful guidance of its new proprietors and Governors, and established its place as a key part of the Wellington Estate. As such, the school's name should reflect this and was changed to Wellesley Prep School – Wellesley being the family name of the Duke and Duchess of Wellington.

Academically, the Wellesley curriculum has always maintained the expectations of the national curriculum, while also offering so much more in respect of what we would regard as real education. Traditional values form the basis of a learning experience that engenders an enthusiasm for knowledge and encourages hard work as a means to academic success. This broadly based curriculum also allows the development of high academic achievement, to sit comfortably alongside our enthusiasm for pupils to become actively involved in all areas of the performing arts as well as the pursuit of sporting excellence.

Our aim has always been to develop enthusiastic learners who will make a strong contribution to their senior schools as good citizens, and as pupils who are prepared to work hard in order to achieve success. This is certainly made easier by the children at Wellesley who possess a self-confidence and natural carefree joy which makes them a pleasure to teach. Each of them is a living testament to our belief that self-esteem is crucial to their development and success. We are also justifiably proud of the way our pupils exude courtesy, honesty, warmth and respect for others. They develop responsible attitudes to learning and life, and are a credit to themselves and their families.

Visitors to the School will be made very welcome and straight away they will experience the atmosphere that makes Wellesley unique.

Wellingborough School

London Road, Wellingborough, Northamptonshire NN8 2BX
Tel: 01933 222427
email: admissions@wellingboroughschool.org
website: www.wellingboroughschool.org
X/Twitter: @wboroschool
Facebook: @WboroSchool
Instagram: @wboroschool
LinkedIn: /wellingborough-school

See full entry in the **HMC** section, on **p. 379**.

Wellington Prep School

South Street, Wellington, Somerset TA21 8NT
Tel: 01823 668700
email: prep@wellington-school.org.uk
website: www.wellington-school.org.uk
X/Twitter: @wellingtonsch1
Facebook: @WellingtonSchool
Instagram: @wellingtonschool1

Chair of Governors: Mrs Anna Govey, MSc

***Head*: Mrs Victoria Richardson**, BSc, PGCE

Head of Pre-Prep: Mrs Jan Wheller, BEd Hons, PGCE
Head of Year 3 & 4: Mrs Angela Needs, BEd Hons
Head of Year 5 & 6 : Mr Roger Hitchen, BEd Hons, PGCE

Age range. 3–11 Co-educational.
Number of pupils. 200.
Fees per term (2023–2024). Day: £2,695–£4,995.

Wellington Prep School opened in September 1999 in purpose-built accommodation to provide one of the most stimulating educational environments for children anywhere in the country.

Wellington Prep School provides an education of unrivalled quality which both complements and enhances the national reputation of Wellington School and enables us to deliver educational excellence from nursery level through to university entrance. Our school is a place of endeavour, teamwork, integrity and laughter; a place where each child is nurtured.

We believe whole-heartedly in our three core principles and these influence all we do in the classroom and out:

- love of learning
- outstanding relationships
- the pursuit of excellence.

We value education in its widest sense; making the most of today in order that we can make even more of tomorrow and the days, weeks, months and years that lie ahead. This is 'Learning for Life'. Our education is unbounded, as we encourage our children to be curious, to be creative and to be compassionate. At WPS Learning is not a spectator sport.

We believe that every child deserves to be inspired every day. The qualities our children will need in life are as important as their skills. This is why we have high expectations for each child, nurture and support each child and develop each child's leadership skills. We encourage our children to think independently and to 'have a go', secure in the knowledge that they can learn from mistakes.

While the headline ratio of one fully-qualified and experienced teacher for every ten children in the Prep School is striking, it is the quality of these relationships that really matters and this cannot be gauged by a simple statistic. The range of experiences our teaching team provide for our children is superb. Every person cares deeply about the children in their care and each child's happiness and fulfilment.

Our children benefit from sharing some facilities with our Senior School, giving them access to:

- eighteen purpose-designed, modern classrooms;
- a large, attractive, central school hall, the hub of our school;
- the most modern and up-to-date education resources;
- purpose-built ICT suite and library;
- spacious grounds including a large playground with wooden amphitheatre;
- our forest school in the Blackdown Hills;
- the Princess Royal Sports Complex;
- numerous sports pitches, hard courts and the astro;
- music and drama resources across the whole school 3–18;
- dedicated performance space;
- an indoor swimming pool.

School is open from 8.00 am and there is an extensive clubs programme followed by STAR club, which is available to all children from 5.00 pm to 6.00 pm during term time. For children in Reception and older, holiday clubs operate at Christmas, Easter and during the summer holidays to accommodate busy working families. Our Nursery setting has a holiday club that runs during some weeks of the Prep School holidays.

Our prospectus is available from the School Registrar and can be requested via our website.

Charitable status. Wellington School is a Registered Charity, number 1161447.

Wells Cathedral Prep School

Jocelyn House, 11 The Liberty, Wells, Somerset BA5 2ST

Tel: 01749 834400
email: prep@wells.cathedral.school
website: wells.cathedral.school
X/Twitter: @wellscathschool
Facebook: @From Pre-Prep to Prep School at Wells
Instagram: @from_pre_prep_to_prep_at_wcs

Acting Chair of Governors: Mr David Brown, OBE
Head Master: Alastair Tighe

Head of the Prep School: **Mr Jody Wells**
Registrar: Joanna Prestidge

Age range. 2–11 years.

Number of pupils. 146 plus 42 in the Nursery.

Fees per term (2023–2024). Day: £3,112–£6,261. Boarding: £9,553–£10,604. Weekly Boarding: £8,276–£9,326.

The Prep School is made up of the Pre-Prep department (age 2–7) and the Prep School (age 7–11). Pupils accepted into the Prep School normally make a smooth transfer to the Senior School at age 11 when scholarships may be awarded.

Academic work. The School prepares children for the academic demands in the Senior School. Pupils complete internal standardised baseline tests throughout each academic year. The School is not restricted by the National Curriculum; the aim is to ensure high academic standards within a friendly, creative and stimulating environment.

Children are assessed regularly for both academic achievement and effort, and feedback is given to both children and parents. There are several opportunities throughout the year for parents to meet with teachers to discuss their child's progress.

As well as driving high academic standards, there is an important focus on developing 'Learning Powers' such as resilience, curiosity and motivation.

Boarding. We offer boarding for pupils from Year 4. Our youngest boarders live in the beautiful house and grounds of Claver Morris with a priority to create a warm, caring family environment for them. The children are very well looked after by a resident family – community living lies at the heart of their daily lives. They all eat breakfast and most evening meals together; the House is extremely spacious and includes excellent facilities, including separate rooms for games, music and relaxing. The House has a lovely family feel and yet is large enough for the children to form lots of strong friendships.

Creativity. We have close ties to Wells Cathedral and all their boy and girl Choristers attend our School, which is set in beautiful grounds just to the north of the Cathedral. A number of pupils are Specialist Musicians who enjoy the expert tuition of the music department, which is one of the four in the UK designated and grant-aided by the Government's Music and Dance Scheme. Scholarships are available.

Drama, music and dance are considered vital activities to bring out the best in children. In our state-of-the-art Cedars Hall, we offer a full programme of concerts during the year for all age groups as well as big productions and small year-group dramas. The School has established drama exchange links with schools in other European countries.

A whole-school arts week each summer allows all aspects of creativity to come to the forefront for every pupil. Themes have included the Caribbean, Somerset and China; pupils experience workshops in the areas of art, dance, drama and music. Regular exhibitions and performances are a feature of the School.

Sport. The School has many excellent facilities, such as the sports hall, dance studio, astroturf pitch and swimming pool. Pupils experience a wide range of activities on the games field. Sport is played to a high standard with rugby, cross country, netball, hockey, cricket, swimming, athletics and gymnastics being the main sports; basketball and badminton are also available. A full programme of inter-school matches and house matches is available for all pupils in Year 3 to 6. Many clubs and activities run at lunchtimes or after school.

West Buckland School

Barnstaple, Devon EX32 0SX
Tel: 01598 760000
email: admissions@westbuckland.com
website: www.westbuckland.com
X/Twitter: @westbuckland
Facebook: @wbsdevon
LinkedIn: /westbuckland

See full entry in the **HMC** section, on **p. 387**.

West House School

24 St James Road, Edgbaston, Birmingham B15 2NX
Tel: 0121 440 4097
email: secretary@westhouseprep.com
website: www.westhouseprep.com
X/Twitter: @westhouseschool
Facebook: @westhouseschool

Chair of Governors: J Gittins

***Headmaster*: A M J Lyttle**, BA Hons, PGCE Birmingham, NPQH

Age Range. Boys: 4–11 years; Co-educational Nursery: 6 months to 4 years.

Number of Pupils. A maximum 230 boys aged 4–11 (Reception to Year 6) plus 100 boys and girls aged 12 months–4 years.

Fees per term (2023–2024). 4–11 year olds: £3,485–£4,725 according to age. The fees include lunches and breaktime drinks. Under 4: fees according to number of sessions attended per week. Fee list on application.

West House was founded in 1895 and since 1959 has been an Educational Trust controlled by a Board of Governors. The school has a strong academic reputation and pupils are regularly awarded scholarships to senior schools at 11+. The well-qualified and experienced staff provides a sound education for boys of all abilities. The National Curriculum has been adapted to suit the aptitudes and interests of pupils and to ensure that it provides an outstanding preparation for entry into selective senior schools. Pupils are taught in small classes which ensures that they receive much individual attention. Specialist help is available for children with Dyslexia or who require learning support. Music teachers visit the school to give individual music tuition.

The school occupies a leafy five-acre site a mile from Birmingham city centre. As well as the main teaching blocks there are two well-equipped science laboratories and a sports hall.

The Centenary Building, opened in 1998, accommodates the art and design technology department, ICT room and senior Library. Extensive playing fields, two all-weather tennis courts and all-weather cricket nets enable pupils to participate in many games and sports. Pupils also enjoy a wide range of hobby activities, and drama and music play important roles in school life.

The school is open during term time between 7.00am and 6.00pm. On-site Holiday Clubs are run by members of staff during the holidays.

Charitable status. West House School is a Registered Charity, number 528959. It exists to provide education for boys.

Westbourne House School

Coach Road, Shopwyke, Chichester, West Sussex PO20 2BH
Tel: 01243 782739
email: admissions@westbournehouse.org
website: www.westbournehouse.org
X/Twitter: @WestbourneHse
Facebook: @westbournehouseschool
Instagram: @westbournehouseschool
LinkedIn: /school/westbourne-house-school

Chairman of the Governors: James Patrick

***Headmaster*: Martin Barker**

Head of Pre-Prep and Nursery: Caroline Oglethorpe

Age Range. 2–13.

Number of Pupils. 360 pupils: 70 boarders, 267 Prep School; 86 Pre-Prep.

Fees per term (2023–2024). Day £6,300–£7,365 (Years 3–8); Full Boarding £2,596 (7 nights/in addition to day fees); Pre-Prep £1,590–£4,405 (Nursery to Year 2).

"Fizzing energy, small family feel and top-drawer academics." Talk Education

Westbourne House School, for children aged 2½–13, is set in 100 acres of parkland between the South Downs and south coast, just outside Chichester.

In 2022, Westbourne House was the inaugural winner of a special award: The Alice Rose Award in the Talk Education Awards for Innovation in Education. The judges were looking for *"a school where children are allowed to be children, one that supports growth and learning but allows them to climb trees and get muddy knees, where confident, nurtured, happy children enjoy their childhood. A true home-from-home."*

The Westbourne Way

At Westbourne House, we uncover the character, dreams, potential – the magic – of each child. We ensure pupils make the most of the world of experiences offered to them – from canoeing adventures on our lake to awe-inspiring science experiments – building their confidence and sparking a love of learning. In our kind, happy and supportive environment, we cultivate curiosity, encourage wellbeing and prepare them with skills for the future. Our children leave with the tools they need to make brave and ambitious decisions on the way to their chosen future.

Celebrating Individuality

Focusing on every child as an individual is at the heart of everything we do, ensuring each pupil feels valued, supported and appreciated for who they are and their contributions to our community.

A World of Opportunities

Designed to be holistic and stimulating, the curriculum at Westbourne House is exceptionally broad and inclusive. Encouraging our children to have a go and persevere is a key part of our ethos. It gives children the opportunity to develop self-knowledge and an enviable adventurous attitude that is remarked upon time and time again by the heads of senior schools. Teachers make the most of the school's extensive facilities, woods, grounds and lake as well as its location near Chichester, seaside and countryside.

Ready to Shape the Future

Throughout the school's long history, our focus has gone beyond that of academic achievement to the growth of the whole child. Pupils develop key life skills, values and attributes and are rewarded for applying them. These skills empower our pupils to be open-minded, work well in teams, think flexibly and develop resilience.

The Wonderful Pre-Prep and Nursery

We place much emphasis on outdoor learning. Our teachers and pupils make the most of the gardens, play equipment, woods and lake for play and learning. Pupils enjoy an 'all round' experience sparking a love of art, drama, music and sport. *"A huge shout-out to the splendid Pre-Prep. It offers a gentle transition from Nursery to Reception and is one of the loveliest, most uplifting Pre-Preps we've seen." Talk Education*

Boarding

Westbourne House is known for is its gentle introduction to the boarding experience. Supportive houseparents, family-style houses and a vibrant boarding community provide the perfect environment for children starting their boarding journey.

Exceptional results

We believe every child can succeed if given the right opportunities, encouragement and practice. Our pupils go on to some of the best senior schools including Bede's, Brighton, Canford, Churcher's, Cranleigh, Eton, Harrow, Hurstpierpoint, Lancing, Marlborough, Millfield, Portsmouth Grammar, Radley, Seaford, Sherborne, Wellington and Winchester. In 2023, Year 8 pupils were awarded 26 scholarships: academic (7), art (2), music (1), drama (1), dance (1), sport (11) and all-around ability (3).

"Westbourne House School is excellent preparation for a move to Brighton College in Year 9. Their pupils are adventurous, keen to get involved, responsible and academically they are extremely well prepared." Leah Hamblett, Deputy Head Brighton College

"A deeply fun experience." Tatler Schools Guide

"Best for Music." The Week

"Westbourne House is brimming with original ideas." The Week

"Boarding at Westbourne House School has been the best decision of my life so far." Isobel (Year 8 Spanish student)

Westbourne School

60 Westbourne Road, Sheffield, South Yorkshire S10 2QT

Tel: 0114 266 0374

email: enquiries@westbourneschool.co.uk

website: www.westbourneschool.co.uk

Facebook: @WestbourneSheffield

Instagram: @westbournesheffield

Chair of the Governors: Mr D Peters

***Headmaster*: Mr Chris Hattam**, BA Edinburgh, BA Manchester, MEd Buckingham

Bursar and Registrar: Mr Adam Anderson

Age Range. 3–16.

Number of Pupils. 370 day pupils, boys and girls.

Fees per term (2023–2024). £3,688–£5,300.

The co-educational School, founded in 1885, is an Educational Trust with a Board of Governors, some of whom are Parents. The number of entries is limited to maintain small class sizes – with an average class size of 14 throughout the school and a staff to pupil ratio of less than 1:10.

A new £3 million development opened in 2022 for the expanding Pre-School and Junior School including three new classrooms, a gymnasium and a state-of-the-art hall for music and drama. French, Music, Drama and Games are taught by specialists, some in subject specialist rooms. Specialist Science and Technology are introduced from Year 4 (8+), as well as specialist teaching in Computing, Art and Design. French, Science, Computers, Drama and Sports are introduced from the age of 4.

In the Junior School, Forest School, in the school's historic Dell, provides an innovative programme of curricular outdoor learning. There are also ICT, Drama, Art and Music Rooms, Fiction and Reference Libraries, and a Hall with a Stage.

The Senior School provides teaching to GCSE from Year 7 to 11, up to age 16. It has its own campus immediately adjacent to the Junior School. Years 7 and 8 have the benefit of their own designated building with access to all the facilities available in Senior School. The school has a 3-form entry in Year 7 with a scholarship class. External and internal scholarships are taken in January of Year 6. All Senior School children are placed in sets in Maths (from Year 5), Science and English.

The school focuses on individualised learning, where close support and monitoring enable teachers to bring out the best in every pupil according to their ability. There is a tailored programme of additional curricular and extra-curricular activities for More-Able Pupils (MAPS) and a Special Educational Needs (SEN) team. Great emphasis is laid on courtesy and the school's values of respect, resilience, excellence and inclusion

An enrichment programme open to all pupils enables a wide range of cultural activities. Art, Music and Drama are strongly encouraged throughout the school, with regular concerts, plays and art exhibitions. Tuition in several instruments is available. A new Drama Studio opened in June 2015 and new Chemistry and Biology laboratories in September 2017.

The main sports are Rugby, Football, Hockey, Cricket, Athletics, Netball, Rounders and Cross-Country Running with regular matches against other schools. There are also opportunities for Short Tennis, Swimming, Basketball, Volleyball, Fencing, Skiing, Badminton, Climbing, Golf and Scuba Diving. Numerous educational visits are on offer with annual trips abroad.

A supervised breakfast club runs from 7.30am to 8.15am. While the length of day depends on the age of the child, there are after-school facilities for all pupils until 5.15pm, with some going on until 5.45pm. There is no school on Saturdays.

Charitable status. Westbourne School is a Registered Charity, number 529381. It exists to provide education of the highest quality for boys and girls.

Westbrook Hay School

London Road, Hemel Hempstead, Herts HP1 2RF

Tel: +44 (0)1442 256143/230099
email: admin@westbrookhay.co.uk
website: www.westbrookhay.co.uk
X/Twitter: @WestbrookHaySch
Facebook: @Westbrook-Hay-Prep-School
Instagram: @westbrook_hay
LinkedIn: /westbrook-hay-prep-school

Chair of Governors: Diana Robinson

***Headmaster*: Mark Brain**, BA Ed Hons

Director of Marketing and Admissions: Kate Woodmansee

Age Range. 3–16.
Number of Pupils. Day: 220 Boys, 155 Girls.
Fees per term (2023–2024). £4,400–£6,260.

Westbrook Hay is an outstanding independent school educating boys and girls from 3–16 years. The school's beautiful location boasts 26 acres of parkland overlooking the Bourne valley in Hertfordshire, and is just off the A41, between Berkhamsted and Hemel Hempstead. This unique setting offers a secure environment, within which children explore and enjoy all that childhood has to offer.

We know that our childhood is a most precious time. Here, at Westbrook Hay, we want it to be the best time of your children's lives. We believe that it is one filled with happiness, rich and varied experiences, in an ambitious, yet nurturing environment. This is what we strive to provide at Westbrook Hay and what makes our boys and girls the confident, well-mannered young people of whom we are so proud.

Currently offering an education up to Year 8, from 2025 Westbrook Hay is expanding to offer a senior provision up to Year 11 and GCSEs. This is a wonderful opportunity for pupils to be educated in a nurturing, family, coeducational environment focussing on an exciting academic curriculum without the distraction of 11+ and 13+ entrance exams.

Our most recent Independent Schools Inspectorate (ISI) regarded the school as 'Excellent' in all areas of the inspection:

"Pupils make excellent progress during their time at the school, as seen in their high attainment in senior school examinations."

"Pupils have excellent relationships with peers and adults and exhibit a strong sense of community through the school's ethos of 'happiness, confidence, success'."

Classes are small and each individual is encouraged and helped to achieve their potential. Individuality, honesty, a sense of humour, and self-reliance are attributes that are stimulated and valued in this most friendly school, which maintains a caring, family atmosphere.

The wonderful Pre-Prep for children in Nursery to Year 2, benefits from a modern purpose-built facility, a woodland school and an exciting outdoor classroom. Children in Years 3 and 4 are class taught primarily by their form teacher, before a move to a subject-based curriculum in Year 5. Already well established, our Lower Seniors in Year 7 & 8 benefit from learning the skills of the Pre Senior Baccalaureate. The PSB has skills, attitudes and behaviours at the heart of its assessment and these skills fit beautifully into our already rigorous academic curriculum. In Year 8 pupils take part in the kids MBA, a recognised qualification introducing the children to entrepreneurship and the world of business. The Upper Senior Years of 9–11 will be working towards an exciting GCSE programme. There is a diverse array of options that allow the children to leverage their strengths while enjoying a broad range of experiences.

The facilities of the school have benefited from significant improvements including a £2 million lower school building, an art studio with pottery kiln, and a £3 million Performing Arts Centre, with 300-seat theatre and full music practice and performance facilities. The state-of-the-art Outdoor Classroom for our youngest children and the modernisation of the classrooms for our senior pupils are amongst the most recent additions to the outstanding facilities. We have further enhanced our outdoor play areas for the older children with a generously sized adventure playground. Our Upper Seniors will enjoy a purpose built facility that will meet their academic and pastoral needs. Although located separately to our younger pupils, it will be within the far reaching grounds of Westbrook Hay and accessible to all.

Extensive playing fields give ample room for rugby, football, cricket, golf, and athletics. All-weather netball courts and a heated swimming pool are complemented by a Sports Hall which provides for basketball, POP lacrosse, hockey, badminton, table tennis, cricket nets, five-a-side football, gymnastics and many other indoor sports. Westbrook Hay continues to boast a reputation of not just excellent sports results, but an all inclusive programme for every child.

An exciting range of after school activities is provided by our Westbrook+ programme including Taekwondo, skiing, fencing, ballet, drama, shooting, golf, choir, sewing and model making, to name just a few. We offer breakfast club from 7:30am, supper club until 6:00pm and a school bus service is also available to accommodate the needs of working parents. School bus routes are extended to enable children from Buckinghamshire and Hertfordshire to attend the school with shuttle buses allowing children to catch the train to local train stations.

Our Westbrook Adventure is a range of exciting residential trips for children encouraging independence, courage, resourcefulness and teamwork. The trips become progressively more adventurous as the children get older. In Year 3 our children experience a first night away from home by camping in our teepee-style bell tents in the grounds of the school. By the time the children are in Year 6, they enjoy a 5-night language immersion, history and cultural trip to France, and in Years 7 & 8 the children can participate in the trip to Iceland, a curriculum residential trip and a national sports tour. Our Upper Seniors will enjoy a wide range of domestic and international trips that will complement their GCSE studies and will be encouraged to take part in DofE to expose the children to new challenges and situations.

Charitable status. Westbrook Hay School is a Registered Charity, number 292537. It exists to provide education for boys and girls.

Westminster Abbey Choir School

Dean's Yard, London SW1P 3NY

Tel: 020 7654 4918
email: headteacher@westminster-abbey.org
website: www.abbeychoirschool.org

Chairman of Governors: The Dean of Westminster

***Headteacher*: Dr Emma Margrett**

Age range. 8–13.

Number of boys. Up to 35 all chorister boarders.

Fees per term (2023–2024). £3,540 inclusive of tuition on two instruments. Additional bursaries may be available in cases of real financial need.

Westminster Abbey Choir School is the only school in Britain exclusively devoted to the education of boy choristers. Boys have been singing services in the Abbey since at least 1384 and the 30 boys in the school maintain this tradition.

Westminster Abbey Choir School is a special place, offering boys from eight to thirteen a unique and exciting opportunity to be a central part of one of our great national institutions. Boys sing daily in the Abbey and also take part in many special services and celebrations both in the UK and abroad.

The small size of the school, the fact that all boys are boarders and the high proportion of staff who live on the premises, allow the School to have an extended family atmosphere.

A full academic curriculum is taught by specialist staff, and boys are prepared for the Common Entrance and academic scholarship examinations; most boys win valuable scholarships to secondary independent schools when they leave at 13.

Music obviously plays a central part in the school. Every boy learns the piano and at least one orchestral instrument and there are 15 visiting music teachers. Concerts, both inside and outside school, are a regular feature of the year.

Besides music and academic lessons there is a thriving programme of other activities and there are many opportunities for boys to develop interests outside music.

Sports played include football, cricket, athletics, hockey, sailing, canoeing and tennis.

Entry is by voice trial and academic tests. Further details are available from Jennifer Benjamin (Headteacher's PA and Admissions Officer). The Headteacher is always pleased to hear from parents who feel that their son might have the potential to become a chorister.

Charitable status. Westminster Abbey is a Registered Charity, number X8259. It is a religious establishment incorporated by Royal Charter in 1560.

Westminster Cathedral Choir School

Ambrosden Avenue, London SW1P 1QH

Tel: 020 7798 9081
email: office@choirschool.com
website: www.choirschool.com

President: HE Cardinal Vincent Nichols, Archbishop of Westminster

Chair of Governors: David Heminway

***Headmaster*: Neil McLaughlan**, BA Hons

Age Range. 4–13.

Number of Boys. 269 (22 Choristers, 247 Day Boys).

Fees per term (2023–2024). Chorister Boarders £3,667; Day Boys (Reception to Year 2) £6,974; Day Boys (Year 3) £7,204; Day Boys (Years 4 to 8) £7,942.

Founded in 1901, Westminster Cathedral Choir School is a day prep and pre-prep school and boarding choir school. Choristers must be Roman Catholic, but day boys of all denominations are welcome.

The school forms part of the precincts of Westminster Cathedral and enjoys such facilities as a large playground and a Grade 1 listed Library.

Choristers and day boys alike achieve a high level of music making. The Choristers sing the daily capitular liturgy in the Cathedral and are regularly involved in broadcasts, recordings and tours abroad. There is also a day boy choir, two orchestras and a substantial programme of chamber music. Boys can learn the piano and any orchestral instrument in school.

The major sports include football, rugby and cricket and the boys travel to Vincent Square, Battersea Park and the Queen Mother Sports Centre for games.

There is a wide range of extracurricular activities available including: chess, computing, debating, fencing, football, judo, drama and a Saturday rugby club.

The school is justly famed for its fantastic food!

Assessment for Choristers is by academic assessment and voice trial, generally in November and February.

Day Boy assessments are held in November (pre-prep) and January (7+ and 8+).

Charitable status. Westminster Cathedral Choir School is a Registered Charity, number 1063761.

Westminster Under School

Adrian House, 27 Vincent Square, London SW1P 2NN

Tel: +44 (0)20 7821 5788
email: wusreception@westminster.org.uk
website: www.westminsterunder.org.uk
X/Twitter: @WestminsterUS
Facebook: @westminsterUS
Instagram: @westminsterus

Westminster Under School is a happy, high-achieving prep school for boys aged seven to 13. Pupils who love to learn are offered a supportive, dynamic and inspirational environment to fuel their curiosity.

Chairman of Governors: Mr Mark Batten

***Master*: Mrs Kate Jefferson**, MA Cantab, LLM, PGCE, NPQH

Deputy Master: Michael Woodside, BSc

Age Range. 7–13.
Number of Boys. 286.
Fees per term (2023–2024). £8,136–£8,340.
For more information see www.westminsterunder.org.uk/admissions/school-fees.

About the School. Westminster Under School has a rich history, originating in 1943 when it was opened as an independent preparatory school for boys aged 7 to 13. It shares a close connection with Westminster School, sharing the same Governing Body and the same ethos of a liberal education.

Located in the heart of London, Westminster Under School overlooks the beautiful school playing fields in Vincent Square and is just a few moments' walk from Westminster Abbey and the Houses of Parliament. The Under School's premises were extended in 2011 with a new dining hall and a specialist suite of Art rooms located in an adjacent site, George House.

Academic. The school's curriculum is broad and diverse, aiming to foster a sense of wonder and curiosity in children and encourage independent thought. The teaching programme goes above and beyond the National Curriculum and teachers are not tightly bound by syllabus. Pupils are taught a wide range of subjects by expert teachers who embrace opportunities for growth and promote diverse thinking. English, Mathematics, Science, History and Geography are all taught by the pupil's form teacher for Year 3 and 4, allowing pupils to become familiar with their surroundings and facilitating the discussion and dissection of cross-curricular topics and ideas. Pupils then receive specialist teaching outside of their form classrooms in Art, Drama, Music, French, ICT, Religious Studies, and Sport. As they progress more of their lessons are taught by specialists, such as Latin and Greek. In addition to this, the same broad range of subjects are available.

Admissions. The main entry points for Westminster Under School are at 7+, 8+ and 11+. Each year approximately 22 new boys are admitted to the Under School into both 7+ and 8+, with 28 joining at 11+. At all ages the School looks for potential, and for boys who have natural curiosity and aptitude and thrive in an academic environment. The School seeks boys with great potential, valuing those who are eager to learn, develop their skills, and achieve their fullest potential. At 7+ and 8+ the entrance assessment includes papers in Mathematics, English, verbal reasoning and non-verbal reasoning. Based on the results of these, selected boys are called back to the second round, which includes classroom activities and an interview session, at which we find out more about each boy as an individual. Entry at 11+ begins with ISEB Common Pre-tests in Mathematics, English, verbal reasoning and non-verbal reasoning, before selected boys sit further papers in Mathematics and English. Interviews with each boy then follow. Entry into the Under School at age 11+ guarantees a place at Westminster School at 13+.

Bursaries and Scholarships. The purpose of a bursary is to give financial support to a child who has the academic ability to benefit from a Westminster education but whose parents would not be able to afford the fees either wholly or in part without unacceptable hardship. Means-tested bursaries up to 100% are available at 11+, as are Music scholarships, and many boys apply at this entry point from London primary schools. Bursaries that are awarded at 11+ entry will continue, subject to satisfactory academic performance, until a pupil leaves Westminster School, should they opt to stay at Westminster.

Co-curricular and Sport. Westminster Under School encourages boys to experience and develop a wide range of interests outside of the classroom. Music is a particular strength of the School and most boys play at least one instrument. Boys join a plethora of musical groups, including the renowned Senior Choir, Junior Choir, orchestra, and string, brass, and jazz bands. Chess plays a key part in School life and the School fosters much talent in this area. In recognition of this, this School received the British Chess Education Award this year. Recently, WUS was the first prep school to reach the U19 Chess Finals, competing against sixth forms and performing admirably.

Art is housed in a wonderful facility for all kinds of creative activity. The Art Department also organises competitions in photography and model-making. There are other school competitions in areas such as public speaking, creative writing, chess, and Scrabble. Dramatic productions are always a highlight of the calendar, and each section of the school participates in their own performance across the year, with previous highlights including Oliver!, Private Peaceful and Guys and Dolls.

Games are played on the 13-acre field at Vincent Square, or nearby in the impressive art deco Sports Hall, complete with a range of excellent facilities, from a rowing suite and weights gym to the dojo and climbing wall. Seasonal sports such as football, cricket, hockey, and rugby are played, and there are also opportunities to participate in athletics, basketball, cross country, swimming, skiing, rowing, and tennis. There is vast array of after-school clubs in such activities as fencing, judo, karate, climbing and table tennis.

Pastoral care. Pastoral care is a core focus at Westminster Under School and each child is supported to flourish through its values-driven care. The School gives boys the tools to develop into happy, fulfilled, and resilient young individuals who enjoy their time at the school. There is a strong culture in which boys look out for others and always act thoughtfully and compassionately, encouraged through systems such as vertical House Families, our 'Caught Being Great' initiative and Enterprise programme, which focusses on fundraising, sustainability, and community involvement. To support pupils' well-being, everyone has a dedicated form teacher and a form support teacher. The school also provides access to a BACP-accredited Child and Adolescent Counsellor, and we have an in-house therapy dog. All pupils have a weekly timetabled PSHE lesson, delivered by trained and resourced staff, which guides boys and helps them to make constructive choices in life. Each week, there is dedicated time for personal, spiritual, and philosophical reflection during our weekly Church service – it is a real highlight of the week where boys take time for quiet contemplation.

Charitable status. St Peter's College (otherwise known as Westminster School) is a Registered Charity, number 312728.

Wetherby School
Alpha Plus Group

11 Pembridge Square, London W2 4ED

Tel: 020 7727 9581
email: learn@wetherbyschool.co.uk
website: www.wetherbyschool.co.uk

Headmaster: **Mr Paul David**

Age Range. Boys 4–8.
Number of Pupils. 360.
Fees per term (2023–2024). £8,945.

Wetherby School is situated at 11 Pembridge Square and 19 Pembridge Villas. The four Reception classes are based at 19 Pembridge Villas. Each class occupies a whole floor level and there is a playground at the back for the boys to run around in. The rest of the school (Years 1, 2 and 3) are based at 11 Pembridge Square.

Whilst proud of its academic attainments for London Day School entry at 7+ and 8+ and top Boarding Schools, the priority is in producing happy, respectful, thoughtful, sociable and motivated boys. The curriculum is well balanced, with excellent sport, music and art opportunities. There is also a wide range of extra-curricular activities available. There is a library and specialist teaching rooms for art, ICT and music.

Wetherby operates a non-selective admissions procedure; registration is at birth.

Willington Independent Preparatory School

Worcester Road, Wimbledon, London SW19 7QQ

Tel: 020 8944 7020
email: admissions@willingtonschool.co.uk
website: www.willingtonschool.co.uk
X/Twitter: @WillingtonHead
Facebook: @willingtonprep
Instagram: @willingtonprep
LinkedIn: /company/willingtonprep

Chair of Governors: Mrs Deborah Streatfield

Headmaster: **Mr Keith Brown**, MA, BSc Hons, PGCE

Age Range. 3–11.
Number of Pupils. 197.
Fees per term (2023–2024). £5,390–£6,055 according to age.

Based in the heart of Wimbledon, Willington Prep offers an education for life for girls and boys aged 3 to 11.

Offering a high quality education to all, where pupils are self-confident and happy, we instil the values of kindness, humility, respect and honesty in all that we do. Our quietly confident Year 6 pupils go on to a vast range of destination schools, many with scholarships from academic through to music, art and sport.

A broad curriculum and rich co-curricular programme is offered from Nursery onwards, led by passionate, supportive teachers, who hold true to the school's motto, *non scholae sed vitae discimus* – we do not learn for school, but for life.

Charitable status. Willington School Foundation Limited is a Registered Charity, number 312733. Its aim is to devote itself to the continuation and development of the School.

Wilmslow Preparatory School

Grove Avenue, Wilmslow, Cheshire SK9 5EG

Tel: 01625 524246
email: secretary@wilmslowprep.co.uk
website: www.wilmslowprep.co.uk
X/Twitter: @wilmslowprep
Facebook: @wilmslowprep

Co-ed Day School founded 1909.

Chair of Board of Trustees: Mrs D Stephenson, BSc Hons

Headteacher: **Mr B Lavagna-Slater**, HDipEd, BA Hons, NPQH

Bursar: Miss S J H Davies, BSc Hons, IPFA Hons
Secretary: Miss L Kendal, BA Hons, PGCE

Age Range. 3–11.
Number of Pupils. 133 day pupils.

Fees per term (2023–2024). £1,200–£4,545 (lunches extra).

The School is registered as an Educational Trust. It is purpose built and is situated in the centre of Wilmslow in its own spacious grounds. The facilities include an Assembly Hall, modern Sports Hall, a Science Room, refurbished dedicated Music Suite, Computer Room with networked Chromebooks, suites of iPads, classroom-based interactive TVs, a specialist Art Room with a kiln, two well-stocked libraries and a Classroom Block with its own outdoor area for 3–5 year olds. There is a Tennis/Netball Court, a Sports field with its own stand-alone Sports Hall, outdoor long jump pit and new all-weather pitch, and ample play areas including an outdoor woodland/forest classroom.

The School aims to provide extensive educational opportunities for all its pupils. Class sizes are intentionally small, enabling all staff to know pupils individually and to provide tailored, focussed teaching. It has a long-established excellent academic record and caters for a wide variety of entrance examinations to Independent Senior Day and Boarding Schools.

Wilmslow Preparatory School offers an engaging curriculum, designed to inspire young minds. Additionally over 40 extracurricular activities are offered, which include fencing, lacrosse, craft, coding, STEM as well as music, art and drama clubs. Principal sports include gymnastics, netball, football, cricket, hockey, tennis and athletics.

There are sixteen qualified and experienced teachers on the staff, as well as a highly knowledgeable and expert team of teaching support staff and management.

Charitable status. Wilmslow Preparatory School is a Registered Charity, number 525924. It exists to provide full-time education for pupils aged between 5 and 11, and part-time or full-time education to kindergarten children from the age of 3.

Wimbledon Common Preparatory School

113 Ridgway, Wimbledon, London SW19 4TA

Tel: 020 8946 1001
email: info@wcps.org.uk
website: www.wcps.org.uk
Instagram: @wimbledoncommonprepschool

Chairman of Governors: Lord Deighton, KBE

***Head*: Mr Andrew Forbes**, BA

Age Range. Boys 4–7.
Number of Pupils. 175.
Fees (2023–2024). Effective from September 2023: Per Term £5,690; Per Annum £17,069.

Wimbledon Common Preparatory School is a pre-prep for boys situated in Wimbledon village, south-west London. It was founded in 1919 as a preparatory school for King's College School and other local prep schools. It moved to its present site in 1957. In 2006 it was bought by the King's College School and is now part of their Co-operation. WCPS is governed by the King's College Co-operation and benefits greatly from their shared facilities.

The school aims to provide challenging, exciting and modern learning and teaching; to develop an intrinsic love of learning: to offer exciting extracurricular activities; to engender a culture that promotes self-confidence, generosity, respect for others and a strong sense of community; to instil skills that will enable pupils to make a positive contribution to their wider global society; to develop strong parent and family partnerships.

The school teaches boys aged from four to seven years, broadly following an accelerated Early Years and Foundation Stage curriculum in its Reception classes.

Charitable status. Wimbledon Common Prep School is owned by King's College School, which is a Registered Charity, number 310024.

Wimbledon High School GDST

Mansel Road, London SW19 4AB

Tel: 020 8971 0900 (Senior School)
020 8971 0902 (Junior School)
email: info@wim.gdst.net
website: www.wimbledonhigh.gdst.net
X/Twitter: @WimbledonHigh
Instagram: @wimbledonhighschoolgdst
LinkedIn: /school/wimbledon-high

See full entry in the **GSA** section, on **p. 500**.

Winchester House School

44 High Street, Brackley, Northamptonshire NN13 7AZ

Tel: 01280 702483
email: office@winchester-house.org
website: www.winchester-house.org

Chairman of Governors: Mr Simon C Creedy Smith, BA, FCA

***Head*: Antonia Lee**

Age Range: 3–13.
Number of Children: 316.
Fees per term (2023–2024). Nursery: £3,327 (5 days), Reception £4,212, Year 1 £4,320, Year 2 £4,428, Year 3 & 4 £5,940, Years 5–8 £7,236. Weekly Boarding (Years 3–8) £9,072.

Our vision

We teach the future, nurture ambition, grow potential, and change the world, one pupil at a time.

We are Winchester House.

About

Winchester House is a haven of exploration, a home of questioning minds and risk takers, where passions meet success and the future opens up with fun, opportunity and excitement. It's a place where ambition, courage and laughter go hand in hand and are nurtured in a family, friendly and fun atmosphere.

Our Nursery to Year 4 Creative Curriculum where the children access their learning through a term long topic creates excited and thoughtful young learners ready to take on the responsibility of independent and collaborative study and challenging specialist subject teaching from Years 5 to 8 as pupils prepare for Common Entrance.

Small classes, an experienced and passionate teaching team, and subject specialist teachers from an early age, provide powerful academic foundations for our pupils to succeed. Strong academic results and a number of pupils achieving scholarships to their chosen Senior Schools every year is just the beginning. Winchester House pupils are learning how to thrive as Change Makers in our ever changing world, becoming critical thinkers and trouble shooters, leaders and pioneers.

Our comprehensive and inspiring co-curricular programme offers a programme of discovery, growth and challenge, where new passions can be uncovered and talents developed. Horizons are broadened, with pupils learning how to navigate challenges as they build self-confidence, learn to look at things in different ways and master new skills. Our commitment to the whole child means that Academic success is important but no more important than succeeding in Sport, Drama or Music or indeed sustainability, kindness, questioning and responsibility.

Winchester House pupils have a global outlook and a community perspective, with our motto 'not for ourselves alone' coursing through the heart of the School.

The school is set in the heart of the market town of Brackley, on the borders of Northamptonshire, Oxfordshire and Buckinghamshire. We're a town school with an outdoor feel, with extensive playing fields, an outdoor pool, integrated inside/outside learning areas and a Secret Garden for outdoor education.

We're a proud member of The Stowe Group of schools.

Pupils return from Winchester House each day or after boarding excited by their learning, well fed, nurtured and often victorious from sporting success and usually fairly muddy!

Charitable status. Winchester House is part of Stowe School which is a registered charity.

Winterfold House School

Part of the Bromsgrove School Family

Chaddesley Corbett, Worcestershire DY10 4PW

Tel: 01562 777234
email: info@winterfoldhouse.co.uk
website: www.winterfoldhouse.co.uk
X/Twitter: @winterfoldhs
Facebook: @Winterfoldhs

Chairman of Governors: Mr Michael Luckman

***Headmistress*: Mrs Denise Toms**, BA Hons, QTS, NPQH

Age Range. 0–13 Co-educational.

Number of Pupils. 327 Day Boys and Girls.

Fees per term (2023–2024). Preparatory: £4,415–£5,155; Pre-Prep: £3,250–£3,580.

Set in over forty acres of grounds with views to the Malvern Hills, Winterfold offers excellent facilities which meet the needs of a broad and balanced curriculum. The School is just half an hour from the centre of Birmingham, 10 miles away from Worcester, and a mere 10 minutes from the M5 and M42.

Winterfold is a non-selective school and there are no formal entry requirements or tests. It is a Roman Catholic co-educational day preparatory school but children of all faiths are warmly welcomed and made to feel valued members of the community. The nursery offers day care for babies and toddlers.

The School has an excellent academic record at all levels. There is a highly regarded Learning Support Unit which provides one-to-one help for children with specific learning difficulties such as dyslexia. Pupils continue to Bromsgrove School, assessments take place in Years 5 and 6 which, if successful, will guarantee entry to Year 9 at Bromsgrove Senior School.

Winterfold places a great emphasis upon educating the whole child and aims to produce well-rounded and confident boys and girls with high moral standards and good manners. In order to develop self-belief, every child is encouraged to achieve success in some area and thus the school fields a number of teams and not just in the main sports of rugby, soccer, cricket, netball, hockey and rounders; but also in sports such as golf, tennis, swimming, athletics, basketball and fencing. There are also a large number of clubs and societies, and regular visits to theatres, concerts and other places of educational interest, providing fullness and breadth to the educational experience. Music and Drama are real strengths of the School and a new Performing Arts Centre is at the heart of Music in the School.

In recent years, there has been considerable investment into the School which has seen the development of a new classroom block with eight new classrooms, state-of-the-art Science labs and Art and CDT rooms. The School also boasts a splendid sports hall, new AstroTurf, hockey pitches and tennis courts, ICT suite, chapel and a library. Adventure playgrounds cater for the demands of the full age range of pupils.

Charitable status. Winterfold House School is part of the Bromsgrove School family which is a Registered Charity, number 1098740. It exists solely to provide education for boys and girls.

Wisbech Grammar School

Chapel Road, Wisbech, Cambridgeshire PE13 1RH

Tel: 01945 583631
01945 586750 Admissions
email: office@wisbechgrammar.com
website: www.wisbechgrammar.com
X/Twitter: @wisbechgrammar
Facebook: @wisbechgrammar
Instagram: @wisbech_grammar

See full entry in the **HMC** section, on **p. 393**.

Witham Hall

Witham-on-the-Hill, Bourne, Lincolnshire PE10 0JJ
Tel: 01778 590222
email: office@withamhall.com
website: www.withamhall.com
X/Twitter: @withamprep
Facebook: @withamhallschool
Instagram: @withamhallschool
LinkedIn: /company/witham-hall-school-trust

Witham Hall is a happy and thriving boarding and day school for boys and girls aged 4 to 13 years. We are committed to an education both in and beyond the classroom, thereby enabling the academic, artistic and physical potential of each child to flourish. Coupled with their purpose and determination to succeed, this broad programme enables our children to acquire a strong sense of achievement, a quiet confidence and an awareness of both themselves and each other.

Chairman of Governors: Mr A R Riddington

***Headmaster*: Mr W S D Austen**, BSc Hons, PGCE

Age Range. 4–13.

Number of Pupils. 233. Prep (age 8–13): 157 pupils – 82 Boys (48 boarders, 34 day pupils); 75 Girls (42 boarders, 33 day pupils); Pre-Prep (age 4–8): 76 pupils.

Fees per term (2023–2024). Boarders: £7,575–£9,225, Day pupils: £6,850, Pre-Prep: £4,050–£4,525.

The School is situated in a superb country house setting in the village of Witham-on-the-Hill, close to the Lincolnshire–Rutland border just eight miles from Stamford. Boarding is very popular (weekly and flexi are available from Year 4) and benefits from first-class provision within the original Queen Anne house at the heart of the School.

There is a teaching staff of 36, and additional visiting teachers for instrumental music. The maximum class size is 19 and pupils benefit from outstanding pastoral care across the school. The majority of pupils join at the Pre-Prep stage, and then continue through to Common Entrance. Pupils progress to their first-choice senior school both locally (Oundle, Oakham, Uppingham and Stamford) and further afield (Eton, Wycombe Abbey, Downe House, Rugby, Repton, Shrewsbury and Stowe). The School has a proud and enviable scholarship record across a range of disciplines, including academic, art, drama, music and sport.

Facilities are outstanding with modern, purpose-built Prep and Pre-Prep teaching areas. Significant developments have taken place in the last four years, the most recent being a superb Sports Centre (that includes a Dance/Drama Studio and Fitness Suite), new ICT suites, a Treehouse and a new Games Room. The Stimson Hall, serving as a Concert Hall and Theatre, underpins a strong commitment to both Creative and Performing Arts. Most of the children learn one instrument or more and there are three bands and four choirs. Inclusivity is strong; within sport all Prep pupils represent the school on a regular basis each term. The standard is high, with teams regularly reaching National Finals in Rugby, Hockey, Netball, Cricket and Rounders. An Olympic-size all-weather AstroTurf complements magnificently maintained grass surfaces, including county-standard cricket facilities and a nine-hole golf course. The school has seen considerable growth in numbers in recent years and in almost every year group early registration is recommended.

Charitable status. Witham Hall School Trust is a Registered Charity, number 507070. It exists for the purpose of educating children.

Wolverhampton Grammar School

Compton Road, Wolverhampton, West Midlands WV3 9RB
Tel: 01902 421326
email: admissions@wgs.org.uk
website: www.wgs.org.uk
X/Twitter: @WGS1512
Facebook: @WolverhamptonGrammarSchool
Instagram: @wolverhamptongrammarschool
LinkedIn: /company/wolverhampton-grammar-school

See full entry in the **HMC** section, on **p. 398**.

Woodcote House

Snows Ride, Windlesham, Surrey GU20 6PF
Tel: 01276 472115
email: info@woodcotehouseschool.co.uk
website: www.woodcotehouseschool.co.uk
X/Twitter: @woodcotehouse
Facebook: @woodcotehouseschool
Instagram: @woodcotehouse.school

***Headmaster*: Oliver Paterson**

Deputy Headmaster, Academic: Andrew Monk
Deputy Headmaster, Pastoral: Tim Ramage

Age Range. 7–13.

Number of Boys. 94 (21 full boarders, 36 part boarders, 37 day).

Fees per term (2023–2024). £9,250 (Boarding), £6,875 (Day), £11,000 (Overseas boarders). No compulsory extras. Scholarship offered at the Headmaster's discretion.

Location. Originally a Coaching Inn on the old London to Portsmouth Road, Woodcote enjoys a beautiful, rural setting in 30 acres of grounds. The school is easily accessible from London and runs 2 daily bus services from SW & W London, 25 miles from Fulham via the M3 (Junction 3), 25 minutes from Heathrow and 40 minutes from Gatwick.

Pastoral care. Woodcote House has been owned and run by the Paterson family for over 90 years. With a settled and committed staff, many of whom live on site with their own families, Woodcote provides an exceptionally caring and supportive environment for both Boarders and Day Boys. Our unique, graduated approach to boarding has helped solve the modern boarding conundrum faced by parents torn between Full and Weekly options. A strong emphasis is placed on manners, consideration and respect for others. The school has its own Chapel in the woods and parents are welcome to Saturday services, as well as to school matches on Wednesdays and Saturdays (after which legendary Match Teas are served), so there is plenty of opportunity to see their boys and talk to staff and fellow parents.

Academic. There are two forms in each year group, with an average of 10 boys in each class, enabling the staff to offer all boys an enormous degree of individual attention. With SEN and EFL teaching also available, academic standards are high and the school is proud of its 100% Common Entrance and excellent Scholarship record. Woodcote boys go on to a wide variety of independent senior schools and the Headmaster takes particular care in assisting parents to choose the right school for their son.

Music and Drama. 80% of boys learn at least one musical instrument, and the young and innovative Director of Music has ensured that it is considered 'cool' to be in the excellent choir. There is an orchestra and a jazz band and the school holds regular concerts so that the boys are comfortable with public performance, both individually and as part of a group. The school produces a Junior and a Senior Play each year, in which all boys are involved one way or another.

Sports. Rugby, football, cricket and hockey are coached to a high standard and there are teams at all levels of age and ability, with a high success rate for a small school. Individual sports include tennis (the school has five courts), swimming, athletics, golf, judo, fencing, and rifle-shooting.

Hobbies and free time. With 'prep' done at school, there are numerous opportunities for the boys to pursue hobbies after lessons and games. These activities are also available at weekends, along with the traditional activities of 'hutting' (camp building in the woods), 'cooking' (frying potatoes on camp fires), and overnight camping in the grounds. Boys are encouraged to read and have a quiet time after lunch each day for this, as well as before lights out in the evening.

Ethos. The school motto, "Vive ut Discas et Disce ut Vivas" (Live to Learn and Learn to Live), embodies the school's aim to give all boys a love of learning and to discover and nurture their individual talents in a happy and positive atmosphere.

Woodford Green Preparatory School

Glengall Road, Woodford Green, Essex IG8 0BZ

Tel: 020 8504 5045
email: bursar@wgprep.co.uk
website: www.wgprep.co.uk
X/Twitter: @wgprep
Facebook: @wgprep1
Instagram: explore/locations/387087353/woodford-green-preparatory-school

The School is an Educational Charity and registered company, controlled by a Board of Governors who are also its Directors and Trustees.

Chair of Governors: Mrs Gillian Haddon

***Head*: Miss Lisa McDonald**, LLB Hons, PGCE

Age Range. 3–11.

Number of Pupils. 388 (Boys and Girls).

Fees per term (2023–2024). Please see our website www.wgprep.co.uk/388/school-fees.

Established in 1932 as a Christian, co-educational school, we are proud to have been entrusted with delivering a first-class education for generations of pupils. We are a forward-thinking, diverse and inclusive community, welcoming children of all faiths and none; our approach is to enable children to learn with enthusiasm and flair. We aim to equip children with the skills and knowledge that will prepare them for the next phase of their education and beyond.

We are quietly ambitious for every pupil in our school. Our curriculum is broad, creative, and designed to adapt to the ever-changing world. We encourage all our pupils to have a 'can-do' attitude and place great emphasis on developing intellectual curiosity, depth of thought and scholarship. At the heart of the school is a strong commitment to personal development and pastoral care, for we recognise that happiness, confidence and high levels of involvement and wellbeing are the linchpins of academic success.

In May 2023, the school underwent a full inspection by the Independent Schools Inspectorate. The results of the evaluation were excellent, with the school receiving the highest commendation across all assessed areas.

There are modern facilities throughout the school, including a fabulous library which is regularly used by the whole school to foster a love of reading for pleasure. Children are taught by specialist teachers for art, music, modern foreign languages and sport and they benefit from a dedicated music room, science lab and art studio. In the Early Years, highly qualified staff ensure that children have an outstanding foundation for the rest of their education, both here at WGPS and beyond.

To complement the broad curriculum, there are a wide selection of co-curricular clubs on offer. Similarly, there are a wealth of sports fixtures, musical events, house and curriculum competitions, both inside and outside of school.

The school provides an exceptional learning environment in which children achieve their best, feeling valued and secure. We have an outstanding record of success in 11+ examinations to Senior Independent and Grammar Schools, and demand for places at Nursery (3+) and Reception far outstrips availability. We value, with pride, the offers that our pupils gain through their 11+ assessments. Recent offers include City of London School, City of London School for Girls and Westminster School, as well as numerous offers for local independent and grammar schools such as Bancroft's, Forest, Chigwell and Brentwood. 2023 saw a record number of scholarships being awarded at 11+, which is testament to both the academic rigour of our curriculum and the breadth of opportunity available.

Parents are advised to make a very early application to the school via the website, and are encouraged to attend Open Events which are also advertised on the website. Means-tested assisted places, of up to 100% of the full fees, are available for 7+ entry or above.

We want to ensure that each child's curiosity and love of learning is harnessed, nurtured and developed, so that they are inspired and prepared for their life-long journey of discovery. We promote kindness, resilience, curiosity, creativity and independence. We want every child to do their very best and we are dedicated to ensuring all are given the necessary support and challenge. Our school crest reminds us that we are here to ignite a passion for learning and to '*let each flame burn brighter*'.

Charitable status. Woodford Green Preparatory School is a Registered Charity, number 310930.

Yarlet School

Yarlet, Nr Stafford, Staffordshire ST18 9SU

Tel: 01785 286568
email: julia.bryan@yarletschool.org
website: www.yarletschool.uk
Facebook: @yarletschool

Chair of Governors: Jo Betteley (Acting)

***Headmaster*: Mr Ian Raybould**, BEd Hons, ALCM, NPQH

Age range. Co-educational 2–13.

Number of pupils. 155 pupils: 96 Girls and Boys in the Preparatory and Senior School (aged 7 to 13) and 59 Girls and Boys in the Early Years, Pre-Prep School (aged 2 to 7).

Fees per term (2023–2024). £3,595–£5,240. Flexi boarding available (Wednesday and Thursday nights) at £36 per night.

Established in 1873, Yarlet stands in 33 acres of grounds in unspoiled open countryside 3 miles north of Stafford. The school offers small classes, enthusiastic, qualified teachers, excellent facilities and a warm, friendly environment conducive to active learning. All teachers keep fully abreast of senior school entry requirements and ensure that pupils are prepared for the next stage of their education.

Pupils have access to a wide range of facilities which include a new, state-of-the-art Science Laboratory, an Information Technology Centre, a CDT Centre, a purpose-built Art Studio, an indoor Sports Hall; and extensive outdoor facilities which include a large Forest School area, a heated swimming pool, four playing fields (for football, tag-rugby, hockey, cricket and athletics), three tennis courts, a netball court, an all-weather Astroturf pitch (for football, hockey and netball) and a cross-country running course. These facilities support an extensive sports curriculum, which features a one-hour daily games lesson run by a team of qualified sports coaches.

Music and Drama complete the picture of a Yarlet education, with termly performances from the Music Department. The arts are brought to life at Yarlet, instilling self-belief and creative confidence in all our pupils. Whatever their talent, Yarlet pupils have the chance to shine. Clubs and extracurricular activities are a further feature of Yarlet and include Music, Drama, Computing, Poetry, Golf, Tennis, Cricket, Football, STEM, Dance, Gymnastics, Fitness and Animal Kingdom.

Yarlet has high expectations of all its children. Children are prepared for entry to a wide variety of senior schools and their achievements in Common Entrance and Scholarship examinations are a source of great pride. In 2022, 82% of children left with one or more award/s to their Senior School.

Charitable status. Yarlet is a Registered Charity, number 528618. It exists to provide education for boys and girls from 2 to 13.

Yateley Manor Preparatory School

51 Reading Road, Yateley, Hampshire GU46 7UQ

Tel: 01252 405500
email: office@yateleymanor.com
registrar@yateleymanor.com
website: www.yateleymanor.com
X/Twitter: @YateleyManorSch
Facebook: @YateleyManorSchool
Instagram: @yateleymanorschool

Chairman of the Inspired Learning Group: Mr David Tidmarsh

***Headmaster*: Robert Upton**, BSc Hons, PGCE, MA Ed, NPQH

Age range. 2–13.

Number of pupils. Pre-Prep and Nursery: 50 Girls, 50 Boys; Prep: 90 Girls, 110 Boys.

Fees per term (2023–2024). £4,361–£5,978. Fees are fully inclusive of all normal activities, extended supervision from 8.00 am until 6.30 pm, meals, educational visits and residential field trips for Years 5, 6, 7 and 8.

Yateley Manor has a long and successful history of educating children from the age of 2 to 13.

Its focus on rigorous academic standards, coupled with a broad and balanced curriculum, delivers an education for the twenty-first century. Yateley Manor's six core values: Happiness, Reflectiveness, Community, Resilience, Teamwork and Relationships run like a vein through the community. They help guide behaviour and actions so that they are in alignment with the school's beliefs. They also bring the community together and provide children with opportunities, which will lead to successful adult lives.

The School's emphasis on educating the whole child is supported by a broad enrichment programme. Activities include chess, dance, horse riding, drama and modern pentathlon and the school is always keen to find new opportunities for children to find their talents and strengths.

Nurtured in a warm, friendly and safe environment with excellent facilities and limited class sizes, children are given new experiences to explore, building confidence and stimulating a desire to learn.

Innovative, enthusiastic and committed teachers embrace the different learning styles of children and incorporate varied approaches into lessons. The result is that children may spend a day being Vikings, visiting the Houses of Parliament, creating maths games to bolster understanding of probability or fractions or cooking during science to reinforce the difference between physical and chemical changes.

There is a strong culture of continuing professional development with staff attending external courses, as well as weekly after-school workshops and sharing best practice. This ensures the School's innovative and committed staff are constantly challenging their own practice.

A building housing a state-of-the-art Music School, spacious and light rooms for Art and DT, a Modern Foreign Languages Department and a drama venue provides children with opportunities in performing and creative arts. The School's superb teaching facilities are complemented by excellent sports amenities including a heated indoor swimming pool, a large sports hall with indoor cricket nets and provision for football, netball and basketball, a gymnasium, a climbing wall, Aeroball and several pitches.

The Woodland Learning Area is an inspirational educational environment which gives children the freedom to explore nature in a hands-on and child-led approach. This helps build confidence, independence and self-esteem as well as giving children new life skills.

The school welcomes children of all ages at any point during the school year. The speed at which children new to the school settle demonstrates the strength of pastoral care. Means-tested bursaries are available.

A network of school coaches serves the surrounding areas including Camberley, Church Crookham, Farnborough, Fleet, Frimley, Hartley Wintney, Hook and Odiham.

Yateley Manor is part of the Inspired Learning Group.

IAPS Overseas

ALPHABETICAL LIST OF SCHOOLS

GEOGRAPHICAL LIST OF SCHOOLS

Individual School Entries

Brighton College Abu Dhabi

Bloom Gardens, Khalifa Park, Abu Dhabi, United Arab Emirates

email: headmaster@brightoncollege.ae
website: www.brightoncollege.ae

See full entry in the **HMCI** section, on **p. 413**.

The British School Al Khubairat, Abu Dhabi

PO Box 4001, Abu Dhabi, United Arab Emirates

Tel: 00 971 2 446 2280
email: registrar@britishschool.sch.ae
website: www.britishschool.sch.ae
X/Twitter: @BSAKAbuDhabi
Facebook: @BSAKAbuDhabi
Instagram: @BSAK_AbuDhabi
LinkedIn: /bsakabudhabi

Abu Dhabi's leading British, not-for-profit, co-educational day school. A member of HMC, IAPS and BSME and BSO Inspected.

Chair of Governors: Faisal Raja

***Headmaster*: Mark Leppard**, MBE

Head of Secondary School: Nigel Davis

Head of Primary School: Elaine Rawlings

Age Range. 3–18.

Number of Pupils. 1000 Boys, 975 Girls (all day).

Fees per term (2023–2024). Nursery: AED14,816; Reception: AED16,720; Years 1–6: AED18,056; Years 7–9: AED23,353; Years 10–13: AED24,246.

The British School Al Khubairat (BSAK) is Abu Dhabi's leading British, not-for-profit, co-educational day school.

From Nursery to Sixth Form, their award-winning dynamic school culture offers students an enriching experience and outstanding results. Founded in 1968 on donated land, they are the British Embassy School of the UAE, and under the ongoing patronage of the British Ambassador and the current President of the United Arab Emirates.

The School's mission is to deliver excellence in teaching and learning, bringing everything that is outstanding about the British curriculum to the UAE. They are a member of IAPS, HMC and BSME.

They are rated outstanding across all performance standards, by both the local Government Agency inspection (ADEK) and the British Schools Overseas (BSO). In 2019 and 2021 BSAK was awarded Best British School in the UAE and Best Post-16 Education in the Schools Compared, Top Schools Award.

BSAK provides a full and broad education. In addition to offering a wide range of GCSEs and A Levels, it also offers the BTEC Level 3 Diploma in Engineering, Business and Sport, and subsidiary BTECs in Sport.

The School fosters a welcoming environment for its BSAK families, that is genuinely friendly and happy. It engenders an inclusive community spirit, in which everyone is valued; reinforcing cultural diversity and empathy. It is a caring school, with the safety and well-being of its students always at the forefront.

It is through their academic excellence, outstanding sport and music programmes, and wide co-curricular activities, that BSAK supports its students to exceed expectations, ensuring their education becomes the foundation for happiness and success.

All of these exciting elements are set in a stunning campus and superbly housed in its purpose-built facility, which includes:

- Large, creative classrooms
- A 25m swimming pool
- Learner pool
- Grass pitch
- Two synthetic turf pitches
- Auditorium
- Theatre
- Gym
- Multimedia suites equipped with Apple Macs

The British School in The Netherlands

Jan van Hooflaan 3, Voorschoten 2252 BG, The Netherlands

email: admissions@britishschool.nl
website: www.britishschool.nl

See full entry in the **HMCI** section, on **p. 412**.

The British School of Paris – Junior School

12 rue Hans List, Croissy sur Seine 78290, France

Tel: 00 33 1 30 15 88 30
email: junior@britishschool.fr
website: www.britishschool.fr
X/Twitter: @BritishSchParis
Facebook: @BritishSchParis
Instagram: @britishschparis
LinkedIn: /school/britishschparis

Chairman of Governors: Mr E Coutts

Headmaster: Mr N Hammond

***Head of the Junior School*: Mr M Potter**

Age Range. 3–11 Co-educational.
Number of Pupils. 250.
Fees per annum (2023–2024). €19,126–€26,519.

The Junior School educates pupils aged 3–11 and is located very close to the Senior School along the leafy banks of the river Seine. This campus opened in September 2010; there are 35 classrooms accommodating up to 480 pupils, as well as 4 bespoke classrooms and 2 activity areas that are dedicated to our foundation stage/nursery section. The school was specifically designed to meet the educational and social welfare needs of junior school pupils. It is bristling with new technology and up-to-the-minute IT facilities to assist the pupils' learning and development.

The British School of Paris' philosophy of education permeates throughout the Junior School and has at its core the goal of unlocking the potential of all students, by identifying strengths and supporting areas of development, while having fun and enjoying happy and strong social relationships. Studies are based on the British National Curriculum with emphasis on English, Maths and Science, and of course, the French language. Various sports, music, drama and many other extracurricular activities are also provided.

For further details and applications, please contact the Registrar, email: registrar@britishschool.fr.

Doha College

PO Box 7506, Al Niser St, Doha, State of Qatar
email: principal@dohacollege.com
website: www.dohacollege.com

See full entry in the **HMCI** section, on **p. 413**.

The English School
Kuwait

PO Box 379, 13004 Salmiya, Kuwait
Tel: 00 965 22271385
email: admissions@tes.edu.kw
website: www.tes.edu.kw
X/Twitter: @tes_kuwait
Facebook: @theenglishschoolkuwait
Instagram: @tes_kuwait
LinkedIn: /company/teskuwait

Owner: Mr Emad Mohamed Al-Bahar

Chair of the Governing Committee: Brigadier Gavin Thompson

***Head*: Alison Peterson**

Age range. 3–13.
Number of pupils. 660.
Fees per annum (2023–2024). Kindergarten: KD1,741; Pre-Preparatory (Rec, Year 1 and Year 2): KD2,735; Lower Preparatory (Years 3–6): KD3,135; Upper Preparatory (Years 7 and 8): KD3,435.

The English School, founded in 1953 under the auspices of the British Embassy, is the longest established school in Kuwait catering for the expatriate community. The school operates as a not-for-profit, private co-educational establishment providing the highest standards in education for children of Pre-Kindergarten to Preparatory school age. The school is registered with the UK Department for Education (DfE No 703 6052) and the Head is a Member of the Independent Association of Prep Schools.

TES is an Accredited Member of BSME, of COBIS, and is also accredited as a British School Overseas with the DfE and listed as a 'world class British school'. Uniquely in Kuwait, the language of the playground is English. The roll is predominantly British, as are the resources and texts. With the exception of foreign language teachers, the teaching staff are also predominantly British and qualified in the UK. The number of pupils in the school continues to increase although the average class size remains around 22. The school is housed in well-resourced and spacious, fully air-conditioned premises in a pleasant residential suburb of Kuwait City.

The curriculum is British, contemporary and delivers the best of traditional standards within a broad-based structure. Class teachers are supported by specialist coordinators in Art, Science, Design and Technology, Information Technology, Music, Library and PE and Games. Music is taught to all ages and French is introduced from Year 4. The National Curriculum for England is used as the core for the curriculum, although the most able are challenged and those in need of support benefit from individual tuition.

Formal end of key stage assessment takes place in Years 2 and 6. In addition the pupils are prepared for entrance tests to other schools including, where appropriate, Common Entrance Examinations at 11+, 12+ and 13+, and scholarship examinations. Pupils in Years 3–8 use iPads as an integral tool and part of their teaching and learning. Pupils in Year 2 and below have access to banks of school iPads. The school's VLE (Virtual Learning Environment) is also at the heart of the pupils' studies and the development of skills for learning drive the school's innovative approach to teaching and learning.

Responsibility for the school is vested in the Governing Committee whose members serve in a voluntary capacity. The school provides a learning environment within which children develop their individual capacity for achievement to its fullest potential. The school's core values of Confidence, Empathy, Integrity, Positivity and Respect are at the heart of all that it does. Strong emphasis is placed on academic study, together with a wide range of non-academic activities to provide breadth and balance. The school aims to ensure that, by achieving standards at least equivalent and often better than those of competitive private and state schools in Britain, pupils are well prepared for the subsequent stages of their academic development whether in Britain, Kuwait or elsewhere in the world.

In the first instance application for enrolment should be made online via the website: www.tes.edu.kw/594/admissions/admissions-form.

The Admissions Team will confirm receipt of the Online Application Form. If there are places in the year requested, the School will ask for copies of current academic reports and arrange a date for the child(ren) to be assessed. Where possible for children entering Year 3 and above, part of this assessment will be an online test. Pupils and parents will then be invited to attend one of the school's 'Welcome and Assessment Days' prior to the start of the academic year.

The Grange Preparatory School

Chile

Av Principe de Gales 6154, La Reina, 687067, Santiago, Chile

Tel: 00 562 598 1500
email: rectoria@grange.cl
website: www.grange.cl

Co-educational Day School.

***Headmaster of The Grange School*: Mr Nicholas Eatough**

Vice-Rector of The Grange School and Head of Senior: Mr Carlos Packer-Comyn

Head of the Upper Preparatory School: Ms Kate Ingamells

Head of the Lower Preparatory School: Mrs Renuka Chinnadurai

Age Range. 4–12.

Number of Pupils. 1,300.

Fees per annum (2023–2024). Approximately £7,000 payable in one annual sum or 11 monthly instalments. There is a one-off incorporation fee payable on entry.

The Grange Preparatory School is the junior section of The Grange, founded in 1928 by John Jackson and based upon the British independent school which he had attended.

The Prep School is divided into the Lower Prep, which takes children from the age of 4 to the age of 8, and the Upper Prep, taking children from 8 to 12. Almost all pupils will transfer into The Grange senior school.

The ethos of the school is strongly based on giving a broad, all-round educational experience to find strengths for each child. The school may be very large but each child is valued as an individual within the team.

Entry to the school is usually at the age of 4, though entry at ages over 4 may be possible as vacancies occur in the course of the year. All teaching is in English except in those areas where the Chilean National Curriculum requires that they be taught in Spanish. The majority of the pupils are Chilean and begin an immersion course in English upon entry.

International assessment criteria are used at various stages of each pupil's career. The core curriculum is based largely upon the National Curriculum of England and Wales, fully encompassing and surpassing the local National Curriculum. Teaching is mainly by class teachers, though older children will find themselves being taught by specialists in many subjects. All heads of department are specialists. Approximately 20 of the teachers are expatriates.

Over the last few years strong progress has been made in the areas of Science, Music, Drama and Art and Design Technology, with new rooms having been dedicated to these subjects. There is a comprehensive after-school extracurricular programme in which children from the age of 7 upwards are strongly encouraged to take part.

JESS, Dubai

PO Box 24942, Dubai, United Arab Emirates

email: jess@jess.sch.ae
website: www.jess.sch.ae

See full entry in the **HMCI** section, on **p. 413**.

King's College

The British School of Madrid

Paseo de los Andes 35, Soto de Viñuelas, Madrid 28761, Spain

email: info@kingscollege.es
website: https://www.madrid-soto.kingscollegeschools.org/en

See full entry in the **HMCI** section, on **p. 412**.

Pembroke House School

P.O. Box 31, Gilgil 20116, Kenya

Tel: +254 711875972
email: registrar@pembrokehouse.sc.ke
website: www.pembrokehouse.sc.ke

Chairman of Council: Mr Richard Vigne

***Headmistress*: Mrs Deborah Boyd-Moss**

Age Range. 6 months–13 years.

Number of Pupils. 100 boy boarders, 93 girl boarders plus 34 Pre-Prep who are day pupils.

Fees per term (2023–2024). Nursery Kshs 102,100, Pre-School Kshs 228,800, Year 1 Kshs 604,200, Year 2 Kshs 906,300, Year 3 to 8 Kshs 1,007,000 (approx. £556–£5,485 however exchange rates vary).

Founded in 1927, Pembroke House has been educating children for almost a century. Owned by the Kenya Educational Trust Limited, it is located in amongst 140 acres in the heart of the Rift Valley, 120 km north of Nairobi. Sitting at an elevation of 2000m, the climate offers year-round sunshine, affording every day opportunities for an outdoor education.

Excellent facilities include a Science Lab, Chapel, Theatre, Swimming Pool, Music School, Library, Art and Design Technology Centre, STEAM Centre, IT Room, Squash Courts and Tennis Courts, access to a neighbouring Golf Course, and a multi-purpose Sports Hall with Astro Turf, Horse Riding Stables, MotoX course and Café. The school has a well-equipped onsite Nurses' clinic.

The main sports are Cricket, Hockey, Rugby and Netball plus Tennis, Swimming, Athletics, Cross Country, Squash, Golf, Horse Riding and Football on offer as well.

A full range of clubs and various extras are offered, including individual music instruction, LAMDA, Street Dance, Taekwondo and Chess. Drama is strong with several productions put on each year. Pembroke has a vibrant and varied weekend programme to support the full boarding ethos of the school. This involves camping and other adventurous outdoor pursuits that strengthen team-building and develop leadership skills.

Pembroke House follows a British Curriculum and term dates. The school is non-selective and currently has 28 different nationalities on roll. Children are well prepared for the Common Entrance exams taken at the end of Year 8. From Y5 all children have access to their own Chrome Books. The Coach House offers additional SEN support from a team of 6 specialist teachers; talented & gifted pupils are stretched in enrichment classes and scholar sets. CE qualifies them for entry into top flight Independent senior schools both within Kenya but predominantly the UK and South Africa. Every year, Pembrokians achieve great scholarship success, both in academics and music or sporting awards.

Small class sizes with a maximum of 14 students and a pupil/teacher ratio of 1:6 enable tailored learning experiences and strong outcomes. Pembroke House has a reputation for producing outstanding pupils who are full of character, integrity and grit. The Headmistress and her motivated teaching staff, help instil manners, kindness and courage into the well balanced Pembroke children.

Peponi House

PO Box 23203, Lower Kabete, Nairobi 00604, Kenya

Tel: +254 20 2585710–712, 734881255, 722202947

email: registrar@peponihouse.sc.ke

website: www.peponischool.org/house

Facebook: @peponihouseschool

***Head*: Tracy Handford**

Age Range. 5–13.

Number of Pupils. 373 boys and girls, all day.

Fees per term (2023–2024). Year 1: Kshs 382,360; Year 2: Kshs 672,210; Years 3 to 8: Kshs 730,275.

Founded in 1986, Peponi House has grown to become one of the leading preparatory schools in East Africa. The attractive and spacious site in Lower Kabete houses all that a thriving prep school requires to get the very best out of the children, both in and out of the classroom. The school was rated as 'Outstanding' in all respects in an inspection carried out in February 2018.

An ambitious building programme has started that will provide the finest school accommodation and that will reflect the school's forward-thinking curriculum. Phase One is nearing completion, comprising a new school hall, library, drama studio, spacious and bright classrooms and office accommodation, as well as spaces for computing, design, learning support and extended learning. A variety of landscaped outdoor learning areas are also integral to the project.

The Peponi curriculum is also undergoing change, with self-directed learning being allocated its own time in the week, alongside the traditional subjects. Children are encouraged to enquire and all children have access to either iPads or LearnPads. A virtual learning environment allows for clarity of communication between home and school.

Whilst always striving for academic excellence, it is central to Peponi's philosophy that education is not limited to the classroom. In addition to the numerous scholarships to senior schools that our pupils have won in the last three years, we have had notable successes in sport, music, art and drama. Peponi teams have won competitions at a national level, with many individuals going on to represent their country.

We follow the British National Curriculum but this is seen very much as a framework on which we build, adapt and extend. In addition to the core subjects of Literacy, Numeracy, Science and Computing, pupils in the Junior School (Years 2 to 4) also have lessons in Music, PE and Games, Swimming, Kiswahili, Art and DT, Tennis and, from Year 3, Spanish. Junior children are taught these subjects by specialist teachers while the class teachers deliver the core subjects and humanities. All children are taught in a way that best suits their individual needs and some children do require additional support. This is carried out by our learning support teachers who will help children either individually or in small groups, but mainly through integrated support in the classroom. Our learning support teachers also play a vital role in advising colleagues as to the strengths and weaknesses of particular children so that teaching can be differentiated to suit everyone.

In Year 5, children are taught Humanities and English by their form teachers, who also play a vital pastoral role in preparing the children for life in the senior school. In Year 6, all subjects are delivered by subject specialists. The sciences are taught separately and there is an option for children to study Kiswahili or Latin, or they can return to Spanish. French is taught from Year 5, with a busy French club that is open to all.

We also have a wide and varied range of extra-curricular activities. The whole school joins in the Activity Programme on Friday afternoons, with children from all year groups taking part in activities together. On Mondays, children in Years 5 to 8 take part in HOTS: higher order thinking skills activities.

Our music department flourishes in its own purpose-built accommodation. In addition to weekly class music lessons, the children have the opportunity to play in the orchestra or in one of the ensembles, or sing in either the Junior or Senior Choir. As well as the two major school concerts during the year, all children have the opportunity to perform in front of their peers and parents at our termly "Tea-Time Concerts". The Carol Service and Peponi Schools Concert offer other chances for our choirs to perform and all the children are encouraged to take part in the plays that are staged in December, March and June.

We have children from many different cultures and ethnic backgrounds and we encourage understanding and above all respect for each other. We are a Christian school and the ethos of "Love one another" is a recurring theme in our Monday Assemblies, but we are proud of our multi-faith society where children learn to appreciate and value their differences as well as their similarities.

The school's motto, "A School of Many Nations, a Family of One" encapsulates all that we hold most dear. First and foremost, we are a school and the academic side of things lies at the heart of all that we do. However, we are also a family and that makes itself very clear in the day to day life of the school. We have an open door policy with our parents and encourage them to be very active in their support of what we do, either through our energetic PTA or through close consultation with the staff.

At Peponi House, we believe that our role as educators is to give our children the best possible foundation for what lies ahead. We are, after all, a preparatory school and excellent preparation is what we set out to achieve. By the time they leave us, our pupils will be confident young adults who are ready to face the future with poise and self-belief.

The Roman Ridge School

No. 14 Onyasia Crescent, Roman Ridge, Accra, Ghana

Tel: 00 233 302 780456 / 780457
email: enquiries@theromanridgeschool.com
website: www.theromanridgeschool.com

Postal Address:
PO Box GP 21057, Accra, Ghana

Co-educational Day School.

Governors:
Chairman: Dr Frank B Adu Jnr, BA Hons, MBA
Chair, Academic Board: Revd Dr Joyce Aryee, BA Hons, PG Cert Public Administration

***Principal*: Mrs Valerie Mainoo**, BSc Psych, MA Ed

Head of Middle School: Mr Bruno Ted Waze
Head of Junior School: Ms Gloria Dakwa

Age Range. 4–18.

Numbers of Pupils. 373 Boys, 386 Girls.

Fees per term (2023–2024). Junior School (Reception–Class 6): US$1,840; Senior School (Forms 1–5) US$2,185; Sixth Form US$2,300.

Established in September 2002, The Roman Ridge School aims to provide the very best of British Education whilst being firmly rooted in Ghanaian life and culture. The school is a unique facility in Ghana as it offers small class sizes (20), individual pupil attention, a family atmosphere, firm discipline, emphasis on good manners, a sound Christian foundation, a caring environment and a full programme of Sports and extra-curricular activities.

The school is noted for its Individual Learning Programmes and its dedication to all pupils including the high and low ability learners and scholars. Pupils are carefully monitored and assessed regularly in order to achieve academic success and parents are encouraged to help in this process.

All teaching is initially based on the English National Curriculum for the Foundation Course and Key Stage One, after which the pupils progress to the 11+ examination, then take the full range of academic subjects at the 13+ Common Entrance and the IGCSE Courses (Cambridge Assessment International Education). The school runs a thriving AS & A Level programme and offers a comprehensive range of courses.

There are forty-two classrooms at present, three ICT suites, two Multimedia Centres, two up-to-date Libraries with full audio-visual facilities, E-Learning facilities, Primary & Secondary Science Labs, a Dance Studio, a Drama Studio, two Art Rooms and sporting facilities. Two clinics are on site staffed by two qualified SRNs.

Pupils play Football, Basketball, Volleyball, Netball, Hockey and Rounders and also enjoy a very successful Swimming programme. Pupils also benefit from an extensive extra-curricular programme which includes Karate, Ballet, Tennis, Drama Club and a highly successful Choir programme, which includes a Parent Choir. School productions and concerts take place at the end of each term.

The school also runs an excellent internal and external Community Literacy Programme, with Senior Pupils spearheading reading programmes for all age groups.

The school is open on Saturdays for extra work and pupil support programmes, swimming, games, music lessons, art and computer clubs, and special events.

Pupils thrive in The Roman Ridge School and are reluctant to go home at the end of the day.

St. Paul's School

Rua Juquiá 166, Jardim Paulistano, São Paulo, Brazil/ São Paulo SP 01440–903, Brazil

Tel: 00 55 11 3087 3399
email: contact@stpauls.br
website: www.stpauls.br
X/Twitter: @stpaulsschoolsp
Facebook: @StPaulsschoolSP
Instagram: @stpaulsschoolsp
LinkedIn: /school/stpaulsschool

Chairman of the Board of Governors: Mr Philip Reade

***Headmaster*: Mr Titus Edge**

Deputy Head: Mrs Zeba Clarke
Senior Master: Dr Barry Hallinan
Head of Junior School (*Pre-Preparatory & Preparatory Schools*): Miss Amy Clifford
Head of Senior School: Mrs Martina Oparaocha

Age Range. 3–18.

Number of Pupils. 1,183: Pre-Preparatory 235, Preparatory 393, Senior 539.

Fees per annum (2023–2024). R$98,508–R$126,060.

St. Paul's School was the first British School to be established in São Paulo (Brazil) and continues to offer an Anglo-Brazilian curriculum, embracing the best of both cultures. As an all-through (ages 3–18) co-educational school, offering the IGCSE and IB Diploma Programme courses to pupils, we are affiliated to a global network of top UK Schools through our membership of HMC (Headmaster's Conference) and COBIS (Council of British International Schools). Almost 100 years old, we draw on our proud heritage as the first British school in Latin America to be recognised as a British School Overseas (BSO) by the UK government. Yet, we look forward with creativity and confidence.

At St. Paul's we always strive to be our better selves. We have the courage of our convictions, essential values, freedom to imagine and create. This is achieved through our high quality British and Brazilian holistic education which drives the personal and academic development of pupils, within a framework of a caring, inclusive and united community.

It is our aim to discover the passion and talents of every pupil, and create the right environment to develop these. The school prides itself on an excellent enrichment programme ranging from MUN to Duke of Edinburgh, from knitting classes to a robotics programme, from mathematical Olympiads to outstanding drama and music. The school is a positive agent of change, helping its pupils to be caring individuals ready to inspire and mobilise those around them to impact the world for the best. Our commitment to broad educational experiences opens many opportunities for pupils who go on to leading universities in the United Kingdom, America and Brazil.

St Saviour's School, Ikoyi
Lagos, Nigeria

54 Alexander Avenue, Ikoyi, Lagos, Nigeria
Tel: 00 234 1 8990153
email: info@stsavioursschikoyi.org
website: www.stsavioursschikoyi.org

St Saviour's is an Associate Member of COBIS.

Chairman of Board of Trustees: Mr L N Mbanefo, MA, LLM Cantab, SAN

***Head Teacher*: Mr Craig Heaton**, BA Hons

Age Range. 4–11 Co-educational.

Number of Pupils. 320.

Fees per term (2023–2024). Naira 1,875,442.

A truly rounded education is a preparation for life. Grounded on our core values, St Saviour's seeks to provide an education that is challenging, relevant, exciting and delivered in a caring and thoroughly professional manner. We look, unashamedly, for academic achievement in each pupil alongside equal progress in spiritual growth, friendship, independence, confidence and some appreciation of their place in the world and their responsibilities towards others.

Christian principles are integrated into the daily life of the school which is an Anglican foundation. Children of a number of denominations and faiths attend the school and are warmly welcomed. Parents are welcomed as part of the learning cycle; communication with them is regular and their support of the school is exceptional.

The development of the whole child is at the heart of education at St Saviour's. Learning is about developing personal, emotional and social skills as well as being an intellectual and academic process. We aim to help children find their voice – their own unique, personal significance. We encourage them to think about what their contribution will be in the world – how they will try to make a difference as responsible and engaged members of the School community as well as citizens of the world.

St Saviour's has high expectations for all its learners. We pride ourselves on knowing each child as an individual in order to help them make progress. Teachers plan to scaffold success for all learners from their point of entry. This means that learning opportunities are planned so that all students are challenged appropriately, sometimes by providing work that is a little too hard and then providing support systems to enable students to work through their difficulties to achieve success.

Above all, we are interested in the learning process – learning how to learn and how to apply skills and knowledge across an ever-increasing spectrum of experience. From the earliest age we ensure that children have an enjoyable experience of school and are motivated to learn and improve. This positive attitude is supported by a team of highly professional teachers who are themselves engaged in lifelong learning and model effective habits of mind. The curriculum is based on that of the National Curriculum for England and Wales and the International Primary Curriculum adapted to reflect the needs of an increasingly international and multicultural student body We aim to build on the children's background knowledge and experience to equip them with the skills, strategies and a love of learning that will inspire them to succeed whatever the next step on their educational journey.

The school has developed and renewed its own sports facilities over the past few years and now has its own 25m swimming pool and extensive sports field, including football pitch and running track as well as informal play areas. Routinely, about 30 extracurricular Clubs operate after school each week and they are very well supported. Events such as Assemblies, Independence Day, Foundation, KS1 and KS2 Productions, Sports Day, International Week, Flower Show, Fun Day and Harvest Festival add greatly to the school's character. Our support of local orphanages flows from monies raised at some of these events.

Pupils leave the school from Y6 to attend leading Secondary schools in Nigeria and approximately 40% move on to outstanding independent schools in the UK, where they prove to be excellent ambassadors of the holistic education they have received at St Saviour's.

Tanglin Trust School

95 Portsdown Road, Singapore, Singapore 139299
Tel: +65 6778 0771
email: admissions@tts.edu.sg
website: www.tts.edu.sg
Facebook: @TanglinTrustSchool
Instagram: @tanglintrust
LinkedIn: /tanglin-trust-school

Chair of Governors: Mr Dominic Nixon (Acting Chair)

***Chief Executive Officer*: Mr Craig Considine [HMC]**

Head of Infant School: Mrs Paula Craigie [IAPS]
Head of Junior School: Mrs Clair Harrington-Wilcox [IAPS]
Head of Senior School: Mr Chris Seal

Age range. Nursery through Senior School (3–18 years).

Number of pupils. 2,829 across Infant, Junior, Senior School and Sixth Form.

Fees per annum (2023–2024). Nursery to Reception: S$31,695–S$38,910; Years 1 to 6: S$39,690–S$41,550; Years 7 to 13: S$46,875–S$50,865.

Established in 1925, Tanglin Trust School is the oldest British international school in Southeast Asia. It provides the English National Curriculum with an international perspective to students from 3–18 years.

Tanglin is a vibrant co-educational school of 2,800 students representing over 50 nationalities and provides a unique learning environment for children from Nursery right through to Senior School. As a not-for-profit school, tuition fees are devoted to the provision of an outstanding education.

As the only school in Singapore to offer A Level or the IB Diploma in Sixth Form, all Sixth Formers study a programme that is tailored both to the subjects they are passionate about and to the style of learning that most suits them, ensuring they thrive and flourish.

The school has an excellent academic reputation. Students' examination results consistently surpass Singapore and global averages, with around 96% of graduates typically receiving their first or second choice university, which are among the best in the world.

Tanglin is inspected every year within the British Schools Overseas (BSO) framework, recognised by Ofsted. In the most recent inspection, Tanglin Infant, Junior and Senior school went through a single inspection process for the first time ever, and was awarded the highest possible grade of 'Outstanding'. The outcome bears witness to the dedication, skill, care and quality of the staff and speaks volumes about the abilities and learning of the students across the three schools.

Drawing on professional and dynamic staff, the school aims to nurture students to achieve their intellectual, cultural, social and physical goals. Tanglin strives to make every individual feel valued, happy and successful. Responsibility, enthusiasm and participation are actively encouraged, and integrity is prized. Working together in a safe, caring yet stimulating environment, the School sets high expectations whilst offering strong support, resulting in a community of lifelong learners who can contribute with confidence to the world.

Tanglin encourages both broad participation and the achievement of excellence in Arts, Sport, Outdoor Education and Co-curricular activities.

Tanglin aims to nurture and inspire a lifelong participation in sport. Tanglin teams play over 500 fixtures across Singapore and compete in more than 40 different tournaments across the region. With the launch of the new Centenary Building, Tanglin's sports facilities have reached new heights, featuring a roof-top Aquatics Centre with Olympic-size pool, 15-metre-high climbing wall, fully equipped Gymnastics Centre, Athletic Development Gym, and Physiotherapy Clinic. All students at Tanglin have access to these world-class facilities, with those aspiring for excellence supported through the Lions IMPACT programme.

Tanglin has a thriving and energetic Arts programme which plays an important part in school life. Students develop their skills in Art, Design, Drama, Music, and Film-making; facilitating creative, social and intellectual development. Tanglin has recently invested in a range of new drama teaching spaces, including a White Studio, a new Black Box drama studio and the Chandran Theatre, which can seat an audience of 140. The drama programme provides specialist teaching, along with visits from international theatre companies, theatre practitioners and regular opportunities to perform in both intimate and large-scale performances. Last year, Tanglin performed 24 drama productions as part of the 2023 creative arts CCA programme.

At the start of 2023 Tanglin unveiled its new Centenary Building. This impressive 11 storey inspirational learning space is home to a diverse range of exceptional educational facilities including Tanglin's new music school. Located over two floors of the Centenary Building it is a central music hub, where Seniors and Juniors can participate in individual and group lessons, and ensembles and performances can happen.

A highlight of the new department are two beautifully designed performance rooms. The larger one can seat up to 100 persons and is designed for a symphony orchestra, symphonic chorus or wind band. The smaller recital space which seat 70 is designed for solo or recital performances. Both are truly aspirational performances spaces, crafted from beautiful materials, and are acoustically perfect.

Impressive facilities attract impressive talent and in September 2023 Tanglin launched a new music scholarship, providing students entering the Senior School the chance to achieve their potential with an enhanced musical studies programme and financial support.

Outdoor education at Tanglin is designed to provide transformational experiences and opportunities to develop greater independence and resilience. 2023 saw 1226 students involved in residential trips both in and outside of Singapore including destinations like Malacca, Japan and India. The Duke of Edinburgh programme also saw strong cohorts across Bronze, Silver and Gold levels.

'At Tanglin there is an unwavering commitment to provide not just education, but also genuine care and guidance. Through my time at Tanglin, I have grown in confidence to voice my opinions and ask questions.' *Harriet, Lead Student 2023/24*

'The school's commitment to sporting excellence is evident in every aspect, from the dedicated coaches to the state-of-the-art facilities. Alongside this, the Lions ethos and camaraderie makes playing sports at Tanglin an unparalleled experience. As a Touch and Netball player, progressing through the school allowed me to gain invaluable skills such as commitment, leadership and collaboration, and has given me the rare opportunity to compete at a high international level.' *Skylar, Head Team Member 2023/24*

What the inspectors say:

'The quality of teaching, learning and assessment is outstanding across the whole school and contributes to pupils of all ages and abilities making rapid progress and achieving consistently high standards in all subjects. Ongoing assessment and tracking of pupils' progress are used very effectively to inform teachers' planning and to ensure that all pupils are appropriately supported and challenged to achieve their aspirational targets. This leads to the majority exceeding age-related expectations at the end of every phase and achieving grades in IGCSE, A level and IB examinations which are significantly above UK and international averages. As a result, the school is consistently placed among the strongest performers worldwide, with pupils achieving Top in the World awards for their examination performance in a number of subjects.' *2022 UK Ofsted British Schools Overseas (BSO)*

PART V
Schools whose Heads are members of the Independent Schools Association

ALPHABETICAL LIST OF SCHOOLS

ISA
GEOGRAPHICAL LIST OF SCHOOLS

PAGE

ENGLAND

The following schools, whose Heads are members of both ISA and HMC, can be found in the HMC section:

ACS International Cobham
The Grange School
Leighton Park School
Lingfield College
New Hall School
Princethorpe College

The following schools, whose Heads are members of both ISA and GSA, can be found in the GSA section:

Abbot's Hill School
Farnborough Hill
St Catherine's School, Twickenham
St James Senior Girls' School
St Mary's School, Colchester
St Mary's School, Gerrards Cross

The following schools, whose Heads are members of both ISA and The Society of Heads, can be found in The Society of Heads section:

Abbey Gate College
Bedstone College
Bournemouth Collegiate School
Bredon School
Highclare School
Kingsley School, Bideford
Luckley House School
LVS Ascot
Mount House School, Barnet
Pitsford School
Portland Place School
St Edward's School, Cheltenham
Shebbear College
Tettenhall College
Tring Park School for the Performing Arts
Trinity School, Teignmouth

The following schools, whose Heads are members of both ISA and IAPS, can be found in the IAPS section:

Abercorn School
Boundary Oak School
Crackley Hall School
Cranmore
Crescent School
Crosfields School
Downsend School
Eaton Square Prep School
Gatehouse School
Holme Grange School
Kensington Wade
Knightsbridge School
Littlegarth School
Lyonsdown School
Newbridge Preparatory School
Norfolk House School
Orchard School
Parsons Green Prep
Reddiford School
Rosemead Preparatory School and Nursery
Ruckleigh School
Russell House
S. Anselm's
St Mary's School, Hampstead
St Olave's Prep School
Wilmslow Preparatory School

Individual School Entries

Abbey College Cambridge

Homerton Gardens, Cambridge CB2 8EB
Tel: 01223 578280
email: admincam@abbeycambridge.co.uk
website: www.abbeycambridge.co.uk
X/Twitter: @abbeycambridge
Facebook: @abbeycollegecambridge
Instagram: @abbeycollegecambridge
LinkedIn: /abbey-college-cambridge

Chair of Governors: Mr Tim Haynes

***Principal*: Dr Ellen Hesse**, PaedDr, MSc, Associate CIPD, CELTA

Senior leadership team:
Dr Carolyn Dunn (Vice Principal Pastoral)
Andrew Humpries (Vice Principal Academic)
Helen Walker (Director of Boarding)
Stephanie Stafford (Director of Operations)

Student numbers. 435, age 13–20.

Fees per term (2023–2024). UK Day fees £9,300; Boarding from £17,835.

Abbey College Cambridge is a community energised by a love of learning and the pursuit of outstanding academic achievement for all.

Founded in 1994, Abbey College Cambridge has grown from strength to strength to now be a thriving successful school with over 450 students from over 40 nationalities.

We are renowned around the world for academic excellence that stems from our students' ambition, their academic discipline and high-quality teaching. Further aided by an engaging enrichment programme, empowering pastoral support, leadership programmes and a series of lectures. Abbey College Cambridge students make friends from all over the world, share unforgettable experiences, and go on to achieve amazing things together.

Our purpose-built campus provides the perfect study environment, light airy classrooms, with modern technology. We find that we don't need the acres of sports fields or grand music halls. Cambridge itself can offer us everything we need. Our students can benefit from the most amazing sports facilities within Cambridge. This allows us to offer a wide range of sports and allow students the choice as to which sports they wish to participate in.

Our robust curriculum delivered by our high calibre teachers allows our students to engage with their studies effectively. Students appreciate the small classes and supportive environment and feel comfortable to be able to ask questions and participate in class discussions. The diverse and international community allows class discussions to take a wider focus, providing students with a different view to many aspects of the world. This allows our students to be truly global citizens and prepared for a globalised work environment.

However, we recognise that students need more than just lessons and Abbey Cambridge has an extra curricular programme with over 50 clubs and activities weekly. Wednesday afternoons are dedicated to enrichment. Enrichment is divided into five categories Active, Community, Thinking, Science and Technology, Music and Creative Arts. Each Enrichment activity has outcomes which are specifically tailored to give students experiences they will treasure for the rest of their lives, but also, very importantly, experiences they can talk about at university or job interviews in the future.

There are also dedicated programmes for students wishing to progress to Oxbridge or competitive university courses such as medicine. Our medicine preparation programme with the provision of seven additional lessons a week is globally respected. The outcome – 100% medical offers year on year and 30% of our A Level students progress to G5 universities.

Our clubs and activities don't stop for the holidays. The college is open to all during the half term and Easter holidays. Our dedicated staff arrange activities, trips, courses to upskill our students and study support during these times with many boarders choosing to stay in Cambridge.

We focus on supporting young people to take responsibility for their own learning and provide them with opportunities to develop life skills such as critical thinking, leadership, teamwork and time management to name a few.

Admission. Enquiries to the college at admincam@abbeycambridge.co.uk.

Curriculum. UK Curriculum Year 9–Year 13, GCSEs and A Levels. We offer an International Foundation Programme for International Students aged over 17.

Extracurricular activities. We have over 40 clubs and activities every week for students to participate in. Clubs and activities are grouped into: Active, Creative Arts, Community, Music, Science & Technology and Thinking

Scholarships and Bursaries. Scholarships are available.

The college is part of the Abbey DLD Group of Colleges.

Abbey College Manchester
Abbey DLD Group of Colleges

5–7 Cheapside, King Street, Manchester M2 4WG
Tel: 0161 817 2700
email: admin@abbeymanchester.co.uk
website: www.abbeymanchester.co.uk
X/Twitter: @AbbeyManchester
Facebook: @AbbeyCollegeManchester

***Principal*: Mr Chris Randell**

Age Range. 15–19.

Number of Pupils. 212.

One Year GCSE, Two Year A Level, One Year A Level Retake, Combined Studies Programme, International Foundation Programme; Academic Studies with Football, Basketball or Tennis Training.

An independent day school with a college environment

- Year 11, Lower Sixth and Upper Sixth entry
- Very small classes (a maximum of 12 students in each) ensure excellent progress
- Unique one year GCSEs and A Levels for those sitting for the first time or retaking
- A Combined Studies Programme, which is an alternative to A Level and is now accepted by several universities
- High levels of personal support and individual responsibility gives good preparation for university life
- Expert advice is delivered for entry onto all university courses leading to strong relationships with the top universities in Britain
- City centre location means students will benefit from the unlimited arts, business, science, sports and music resources on offer

Flexible learning programmes mean that students can join at any time during the academic year, not just September.

Fees per annum (2023–2024): Year 12 (A Level or Combined Studies) £15,000; Year 13 (A Level or Combined Studies) £15,000; One Year A Level (1 subject) £7,800; One Year A Level (2 or 3 subjects) £15,000; Year 11 (GCSE – up to 6 subjects) £13,400.

Fees per annum (2024–2025): To be confirmed.

Fees are inclusive of exam charges.

Abbey Gate College

Saighton Grange, Saighton, Chester, Cheshire CH3 6EN

Tel: 01244 332077
email: admin@abbeygatecollege.co.uk
website: www.abbeygatecollege.co.uk
Facebook: @AbbeyGateCollege
Instagram: @abbeygatecollege
LinkedIn: /company/abbey-gate-college

See full entry in the **Society of Heads** section, on **p. 508**.

Abbot's Hill School

Bunkers Lane, Hemel Hempstead, Herts HP3 8RP

Tel: 01442 240333
email: registrar@abbotshill.herts.sch.uk
website: www.abbotshill.herts.sch.uk
X/Twitter: @AbbotsHill
Facebook: @AbbotsHillSchool
LinkedIn: /abbot's-hill

See full entry in the **GSA** section, on **p. 418**.

Abercorn School

Lower School
28 Abercorn Place, London NW8 9XP

Tel: 020 7286 4785
email: lower@abercornschool.com

Senior School
60 Paddington Street, London W1U 4JA

Tel: 020 7723 8700
email: senior@abercornschool.com
website: www.abercornschool.com
X/Twitter: @abercornschool
Facebook: @abercornschool
Instagram: @abercornschool

See full entry in the **IAPS** section, on **p. 590**.

Abingdon House School
Cavendish Education Group

Broadley Terrace, London NW1 6LG

Tel: 020 3750 5526
email: office@abingdonhouseschool.co.uk
website: www.abingdonhouseschool.co.uk
X/Twitter: @AbingdonHouseSC
Instagram: @AbingdonHouseSC

***Principal*: Ms Tanya Moran**
***Headteacher*: Mr Rory Vokes-Dudgeon**

Head of Senior: Mr James Gilbert-Farrell
Assistant Head of Senior: Ms Nadia Carella
Head of Prep: Mr Christopher Lloyd
Assistant Head of Prep: Ms Cullen
Head of SEN: Ms Susannah Harris
Bursar: Ms Jenny Fromer
Senior Administrator, Marketing and Admissions: Ms Claire Essien
Senior Administrator, Office Manager and H&S: Ms Karen Franklin

Age range. 7–19 Co-educational.
Number of pupils. 131.
Fees per term (2023–2024). £15,317.

Abingdon House Senior is located in a refurbished Victorian building in London NW1 on four levels with facilities to educate up to 90 pupils aged between 11–19 years of age (Years 7–13). The school has specific expertise in the education of children who have Specific Learning Difficulties, such as dyslexia, dyspraxia and ADD/ADHD, autistic spectrum condition, social communication difficulties and other associated needs.

Abingdon House Prep was established in September 2022. It is located in South Kensington with facilities to educate up to 90 pupils aged between 7–13 years of age (Years 3–8).

The school provides a warm, nurturing and aspirational learning environment where the specific individual learning needs of our students are fully supported in a mainstream styled environment. At

Abingdon House School we provide an integrated, whole-school multidisciplinary approach to meeting the needs of students with unique learning profiles based on understanding your child's individual needs, nurturing their academic and social development and caring for their well being.

We foster a sense of pride and belonging that encourages your child to progress and achieve at school, and prepares them for independence beyond our doors.

Effective learning and teaching is based on understanding a child's individual needs, nurturing a child's academic and social development and caring for a child's wellbeing. The environment is therefore warm and friendly and we are committed to each child's holistic development.

We deliver this through:

- The provision of a holistic and individually tailored education programme.
- A whole-school teaching regime of small classes with teaching assistants, therapists and trained staff using a range of teaching strategies and therapeutic interventions. There is an appropriately low pupil to teacher ratio. Many pupils have integrated successfully into various London day schools.
- Developing, monitoring and implementing an IEP (Individual Education Plan) for each pupil, which details SMART (Specific, Measurable, Achievable, Realistic and Timely) targets and describes the strategies and supports required to achieve those targets.
- Monitoring pupil progress through a rigorous system of assessment and tracking.
- Implementing a consistent system of positive behaviour support.
- Facilitating pupil-centred active learning.
- Placing special emphasis on the development of literacy and numeracy, social skills, language and communication and coordination, sequencing and movement.

Effort and achievement are praised and rewarded to build self-esteem. Pupils are given the opportunity for their efforts and achievements to be recognised and celebrated on a regular basis culminating in an end-of-term Musical Performance and Prize Giving.

We offer a full curriculum. PE/Games take place on a weekly basis at school and in local community facilities. Reading, Literacy and Maths lessons are ability grouped to enable pupils to progress as soon as they are ready. After-school clubs are offered several times a week.

We value teamwork and the partnership between parents and staff.

ACS International School Cobham

Heywood House, Portsmouth Road, Cobham, Surrey KT11 1BL

Tel: 01932 867251
email: cobadmissions@acs-schools.com
website: www.acs-schools.com/cobham
X/Twitter: @ACSintschools
Facebook: @ACSCobham
Instagram: @acscobhamschool
LinkedIn: /school/acs-international-schools

See full entry in the **HMC** section, on **p. 7**.

ACS International School Egham

Woodlee, London Road (A30), Egham, Surrey TW20 0HS

Tel: 01784 430800
email: eghamadmissions@acs-schools.com
website: www.acs-schools.com/egham
X/Twitter: @ACSEgham
Facebook: @ACSEgham
Instagram: @acseghamschool
LinkedIn: /school/acs-international-schools

***Head of School*: Mr Mark Wilson**

Age range. 4–18.

Number in school. Day only: 485 students.

Fees per annum (2023–2024). Tuition: £12,780–£29,990.

At ACS Egham. We offer the International Baccalaureate (IB) – an aspirational, global, and modern curriculum that inspires children to become the drivers of their own success. Rather than forcing students to jump through hoops, the IB awakens their inner curiosity, challenging students to think for themselves, exceed expectations, and make the most of their talents, so that they take command of their learning journey.

Just 25 miles from London, we are home to just under 500 students, co-educational aged 4 to 18, and 120 expert faculty staff from around the world. The school's global outlook informs our curriculum, building on the very best of international educational standards. And providing our students with a world-class education that is fit for the 21st century

Academic programmes. ACS Egham was the first school in the UK to have full authorisation to offer all four International Baccalaureate (IB) programmes, providing our students with a globally recognised, reassuringly independent and seamless route to success – both in and out of the classroom. These programmes are the IB Primary Years (IB PYP), the Middle Years (IB MYP) and IB Diploma (IB DP) Programmes, as well as the IB Career-related Programme (IB CP).

These programmes share a common philosophy and characteristics: they develop the whole student, helping them to grow socially, physically, aesthetically, and culturally; and provide a broad and balanced education that includes science, humanities, languages, mathematics, technology, physical education, and the arts.

This academic programme challenges students to fulfil their potential, and offers a broad-based selection of courses and levels to meet individual needs and interests. An important characteristic of ACS Egham is individual attention to students' needs facilitated by an exceptionally well-qualified, experienced, and empathetic faculty; many of whom are IB examiners, moderators, and teacher trainers. The success of our programme is reflected in our IB Diploma pass rate over the last ten years, which has enabled our graduates to continue their studies at top universities around the world, including the UK and Europe as well as the US.

ACS Egham runs small class sizes which afford a greater opportunity for individual attention and support for various learning styles. Specialist staff meet with individual students' teachers, administrators and parents, to ensure that every child is appropriately challenged and encouraged. A Language Coordinator assists families in organising native language lessons.

Facilities. Providing a great all-round education requires an amazing range of facilities. Our beautifully landscaped campus features: 20-acre site with Mansion House and multi-use sports fields; a 700 square-foot design technology and art annexe with 3D printers, laser cutter and interactive modular classrooms; a science wing with five labs and a prep room; two IT labs; a student centre with performing arts centre; a dedicated IB centre for Grades 11 and 12; and two libraries. We also offer three music practice rooms as well as dedicated music classrooms and a forest school with a pond and chicken coop.

Sport and extracurricular activities. Our Woodlee Sports Centre comprises a dance studio, fitness suite, indoor climbing wall, two FIBA-sized basketball courts that can also convert to eight badminton courts and an outdoor traversing wall. ACS Egham offers an extensive range of extracurricular clubs and community service activities both locally and internationally. Students also participate in international theatre arts programmes, as well as maths, literature and music competitions in the UK and across Europe. The campus sports programme runs three seasons, fielding teams in football, volleyball, cross-country, basketball, dance, tennis and athletics. We also offer tournament sports competitions across the UK and Europe.

Accreditation. ACS Egham is accredited by the New England Association of Schools and Colleges (NEASC) and is authorised by the International Baccalaureate (IB) to offer the IB PYP, IB MYP, IB DP and IB CP. The School holds memberships in the European Council of International Schools (ECIS), the Council of International Schools (COIS) and the Independent Schools Association (ISA).

Four schools, one world-class education. ACS Egham is part of ACS International Schools. Founded in 1967 to serve the needs of international and local families, ACS International Schools now educates 3,500 students up to age 18, from more than 70 countries, at three London area campuses in England and one in Doha, Qatar.

Contact the admissions team. The admissions team is available throughout the year to answer questions, book campus visits, and assist families through the enrolment process. Students are accepted in all grades throughout the year, on a non-selective criteria. Partial and full bursaries in Grade 6/Year 7, Grade 8/Year 9 and Grade 11/Year 12 are now available.

ACS International School Hillingdon

Hillingdon Court, 108 Vine Lane, Hillingdon, Middlesex UB10 0BE

Tel: 01895 259771
email: hillingdonadmissions@acs-schools.com
website: www.acs-schools.com/acs-hillingdon
X/Twitter: @ACSintschools
Facebook: @ACSHillingdon
Instagram: @acshillingdonschool
LinkedIn: /school/acs-international-schools

***Head of School*: Martin Hall**

Age Range. 4–18.

Number in School. Day only: 600 Students – boys and girls

Fees per annum (2023–2024). Tuition: £12,510–£28,870.

ACS Hillingdon is a beautifully green and welcoming campus close to central London, bursting with innovation and enterprise.

We're home to around 600 students, aged 4 to 18, from over 50 countries, taught and supported by 150 teachers and staff members. Our global perspective reflects our world-renowned curriculum that builds on the very best of leading education standards, giving our students the flexibility to tailor their studies from a wide range of options.

Academic programme. The broad and flexible curriculum at ACS Hillingdon is designed to help students excel, ensuring they're ready for the next stage of their academic career. Underpinned by the International Baccalaureate, Advanced Placement courses and the US High School Diploma, our curriculum emphasises life skills as much as academic excellence, with a focus on experiential learning and leadership that ensures we nurture confident, caring, well-rounded individuals. ACS Hillingdon also has a new Film Programme working with Pinewood studios and working with film industry mentors. The School has also introduced the IBCP (Career Pathway) in Expressive Arts and Digital Arts where lessons take place in a state-of-the-art computer suite.

Facilities. ACS Hillingdon campus boasts a stunning mansion house and modern wing extension with libraries, science and IT labs, art studios, cafeteria, gym, auditorium, and a dedicated music centre. Our grounds are home to an all-weather playing field, tennis and basketball courts, and adventure play areas, with off-site facilities for soccer, rugby, swimming, track and field. We have 13 acres of grounds including a G4 all-weather pitch and tennis courts, 14 acres of offsite playing fields, including a clubhouse, changing rooms and four sports fields for football, rugby, hockey and baseball.

Our science wing has seven labs and a prep room. We also have a range of facilities including an auditorium with tiered theatre-style seating, an art gallery space, Think Tank/Maker space classrooms for Coding, Media and Design, dedicated indoor gym for basketball/volleyball and other sports and Harmony House, with music practice rooms and recording studio. Our three divisional libraries are equipped with computers and our IT labs have film/media capability.

Enrichment. ACS Hillingdon also offers extensive and varied extracurricular clubs and community service activities both locally and internationally, which encourage students to participate in the richness of school life. Students also participate in international theatre arts programmes, maths, literature and music competitions in the UK and across Europe.

Four schools, one world-class education. Founded in 1967 to serve the needs of global and local families, ACS International Schools educate over 3,700 students, aged 2 to 18, day and boarding, from more than 100 countries. Our schools – 3 in Greater London and 1 in Doha, Qatar – are all non-sectarian and co-educational.

Contact the Admissions Team. The admissions team is available throughout the year to answer questions, book campus visits, and assist families through the enrolment process. Students are accepted in all grades throughout the year. Bursary applications are now closed, and will re-open in September 2023 for academic year 2024. Partial and full bursaries in Grades 6/year 7, Grade 8/year 9 and Grade 11/year 12 are available.

Alton School

Anstey Lane, Alton, Hampshire GU34 2NG

Tel: 01420 82070
email: enquiries@altonschool.co.uk
website: www.altonschool.co.uk
X/Twitter: @AltonSchool1938
Facebook: @altonschool1938
LinkedIn: /company/altonindependentcatholicschool

Motto: Be the best that you can be

Chairman of Governors: Mr Clive Hexton
***Headmaster*: Mr Andrew Reeve**
Deputy Head: Mrs Susie Brooks, BA Hons, PGCE

Age Range. 6 months to 18 years.
Number in School. 450.
Fees per term (2023–2024). Lower School £4,192–£5,073, Senior £5,949–£6,052, Sixth Form £5,432.

Entrance. Nursery and Lower School – non-selective; Senior School – entrance assessment (Cat 4) and interview; Sixth Form – GCSE results and interview.

Details of Awards programme (scholarships) on website.

Alton School is an independent co-educational Catholic school located on the north Hampshire/Surrey border, on the outskirts of the market town of Alton. It is an all through School with a clear educational and pastoral pathway for boys and girls, from Nursery through to Sixth Form. Formerly known as Alton Convent, Alton School prides itself on its pastoral care and outstanding progress that it achieves for every child.

The minute you step foot in Alton School you feel the sense of family, care and community. We are a happy and friendly school, but we are also bold and ambitious in our approach and in our aspirations for our pupils. We guide our pupils in finding their moral compass, in understanding themselves and what they can contribute to the world.

Achieving and Caring. We know each of our pupils individually and understand how best to balance the challenge, support and encouragement that every student needs to succeed. Our A Level and GCSE results are consistently strong and our pupils regularly outperform expectations at every stage of their education.

At Alton School results matter but it is the progress that each individual makes that is of the greatest value. Progress is developed and monitored as pupils move through the School all the way from Nursery, through Prep and Senior school and often into Sixth Form. The effect of this is seen in the excellent Value-Added scores students obtain – this is the measure of progress that students achieve based on where a student started from and the progress they make relative to other similar students.

Extra-Curricular. Alton School students are invited to develop their talents and interests through a fantastic range of stimulating and inspiring learning experiences. There really is something for everyone including award-winning Science, thought-provoking field trips, and reflection time on spiritual retreats. There are a wide range of sports for boys and girls, music for all age groups, drama and art as well as CCF and Duke of Edinburgh.

International Opportunity. We are fortunate to be part of a vibrant international community. Our students have the opportunity to go to India to support the work of our sister school in Varanasi, join the annual pilgrimage to Lourdes and experience a fully immersive language programme in Columbia. Students regularly tell us that these trips are life changing.

Remote Learning. We are committed to preparing our students for the future and this need has never been more real than it is today. Our interactive Alton@Home Remote Learning Programme offers a full and structured timetable of remote, interactive lessons using Microsoft Teams.

Charitable status. The Alton Convent School Charity is a Registered Charity, number 1071684.

Argyle House School

19/20 Thornhill Park, Tunstall Road, Sunderland, Tyne & Wear SR2 7LA

Tel: 0191 510 0726
email: office@argylehouseschool.co.uk
website: www.argylehouseschool.co.uk

***Head*: Mr C Johnson**

Age Range. 3–16.
Number in School. 250 Boys and Girls.

Fees per term (2023–2024). £2,600–£3,170.

Argyle House School was established in 1884 as a small independent day school for boys and girls, situated in the centre of Sunderland. Students travel from all parts of the region, by our buses, or local forms of transport. The school has maintained its high standards of academic achievement, whilst catering for a wide variety of abilities.

At Argyle House School, we believe in the individual, and work with him or her to enable the achievement of each student's potential. This is due to attention to detail by fully qualified and dedicated staff, who help to mould the individual into a well-mannered and accomplished young individual, who will be able to meet future challenges.

Small class sizes and a friendly environment facilitate learning, but not all work is academic, as the school takes an active part in many sporting leagues, both within the school, and locally with other schools. We aim to offer all the facilities of a much larger school, whilst remaining at present student levels to keep the intimacy and friendliness of a smaller school, for both parents and students.

ArtsEd Day School & Sixth Form

Cone Ripman House, 14 Bath Road, Chiswick, London W4 1LY

Tel: 020 8987 6600
email: pupils@artsed.co.uk
website: www.artsed.co.uk
X/Twitter: @ArtsEdLondon
Facebook: @ArtsEdLondon
Instagram: /artsedschool

***Interim Headteacher*: Mr Peter Middleton**

Deputy Headteacher: Mrs Claire Parker-Wood
Director of Performing Arts: Ms Natalie Bareham
Director of Curriculum: Mr Thamir Elzubaidi
Director of Sixth Form: Mr Mark Ferrington
Director of Operations: Mr Christopher Reynolds
Director of Teaching and Learning: Charly Swingler
Head of BTEC: Ms Elizabeth Bellamy

Age Range. 11–18.

Number in School. Day School: 137 Sixth Form: 150.

Fees per term (2023–2024). £5,918–£6,788.

ArtsEd Day School and Sixth Form offers pupils an outstanding education and training in a truly unique environment. Highly skilled staff create exciting opportunities for pupils to explore and develop their creativity, at the same time as enabling excellent academic achievement. Every member of the school community is committed to our supportive and welcoming ethos, demonstrated in the warm and friendly atmosphere that is evident from the moment you walk into our lively foyer.

ArtsEd is consistently the most academically successful performing arts school in the country. Pupils achieve excellent exam results at all levels and value-added scores place ArtsEd in the top 1% of all schools in the UK. With 100% of Year 13 BTEC students achieving Triple Distinction or better in Acting, Musical Theatre, and Dance in the last three years, ArtsEd is the UK's leading centre for Level 3 BTEC Performing Arts.

Autumn 2020 saw the completion of a £10 million capital project and the opening of a new wing on the Chiswick site. This new space adds dance studios and cutting edge classrooms to ArtsEd's training facilities, which include the industry standard Andrew Lloyd Webber Foundation Theatre.

Judged as Excellent in all areas in the ISI Educational Quality Inspection in 2019, ArtsEd continues to go from strength to strength and in 2020 was awarded the Best Contemporary Performing Arts Provider in the National Education and Training Awards. These accolades join many others over recent years including the ISA Excellence Award, The Stage's School of the Year and BE OPEN Foundation's recognition of the ArtsEd as one of the top five schools and colleges in the UK.

For over 100 years, ArtsEd alumni have significantly influenced the creative industries and beyond. They include doctors, lawyers and high-flying executives, as well as leading choreographers, directors and producers. The enthusiasm and expertise of our teachers fuels pupils' passion for performance and cultivates a zest for learning right across the curriculum. Outstanding pastoral care and the support and encouragement that pupils give one another makes enjoyment, as much as excellence, part of everyone's day.

"I wanted my daughter to be somewhere where she could continue her academic successes, but in a warm and happy environment that's fun and supportive, and ArtsEd was the answer." ArtsEd parent

"My daughter's maths grade has really shot up because of the brilliant teaching and small class sizes here." ArtsEd parent

"I am delighted with my son's progress since he's been at ArtsEd. The small class sizes and the creative environment have really helped him thrive." ArtsEd parent

Ashley Manor Preparatory School

252 London Road, Charlton Kings, Cheltenham, Gloucestershire GL52 6NR

Tel: 01242 388550
email: prepschool@ashleymanorprep.co.uk
website: www.ashleymanorprep.co.uk
Facebook: @AshleyManorPrep
Instagram: @AshleyManorPrep

Co-educational day school for pupils aged 1–11.

***Headmaster*: Mr Paul Fathers**, BA, PGCE

A wealth of opportunity exists for students at Ashley Manor Preparatory School. We teach that there is no ceiling to potential, focussing on the individual needs of each and every pupil, and valuing their unique gifts and talents.

Located in the heart of Cheltenham, the School is set in over 40 acres of grounds, with a range of creative and sporting facilities to enrich our academic provision. The

School offers a strong and vibrant school community, based on Christian values, in which all children can thrive.

We provide a supportive family atmosphere in which pupils from Kindergarten right through to Year 6 are encouraged to develop their individual potential – academic, social, physical, creative and spiritual – in preparation for their secondary education.

Excellent teaching and pastoral care in our nurturing and encouraging environment allows our pupils to flourish. Our small class sizes mean that our teachers really know pupils as individuals and can provide tailored support to maximise achievement. Our School motto means to strive for the best and that is exactly what we want for all our students.

We encourage our pupils to become fully involved in all aspects of school life, offering an extensive range of extra-curricular clubs, sporting and cultural activities. It is important to us that our pupils are challenged to step outside of their 'comfort zone' and realise that they can achieve beyond their perceived potential.

Most importantly, our aim is to provide an education that will last a lifetime and enable our pupils to develop into happy, confident, resilient, compassionate, and aspirational individuals who are ready to become positive and life-long contributors to society.

Admission: The main entry points are at Kindergarten, Pre-School, Reception and Year 3. However, pupils are welcome to join at any point, providing there are spaces in the year group.

Fees per term (2023–2024): £2,660–£4,825.

Further information is available on the School's website, www.ashleymanorprep.co.uk.

Ashton House School

50–52 Eversley Crescent, Isleworth, Middlesex TW7 4LW

Tel: 020 8560 3902
email: school@ashtonhouse.com
website: www.ashtonhouse.com

Proprietor: Mr S J Turner, BSc

***Head Teacher*: Mrs Angela Stewart**

Age Range. 3–11.

Number in School. 100 Day Pupils

Fees per term (2023–2024). £3,428–£4,716.

Founded 1930. Proprietor: S J Turner. Entry by interview and assessment. Prospectus on request.

Choosing a school for your child is one of the most important decisions you will be making on their behalf and we fully understand that you want to get it right. At Ashton House we do our very best to deliver a first-class education in a calm and happy atmosphere, where children learn and develop while still enjoying their childhood. Our results at 11 indicate that we are succeeding while our pupils have grown into confident, caring young people ready for the next phase in their education. Our most recent inspection judged us to be "excellent in all areas".

Ayscoughfee Hall School

Welland Hall, London Road, Spalding, Lincolnshire PE11 2TE

Tel: 01775 724733
email: admin@ahs.me.uk
website: www.ahs.me.uk
Facebook: @Ayscoughfee-Hall-School-Life
Instagram: @ayscoughfeehallschoollife

***Head*: Mrs Theresa Wright**

Bursar/Company Secretary: Mrs Emma Gibson

Age range. 3–11 Co-educational.

Number of pupils. Maximum capacity 160 Day Pupils.

Fees per term (2023–2024). £1,940–£2,865.

Founded in 1920, Ayscoughfee Hall School is centred around a beautiful Georgian family home. A purpose-built extension complements the already spacious accommodation. The School houses Kindergarten, Infant and Junior Departments and has further developed its facilities to include enlarged classrooms, a dedicated Science/Art Room, Music Department, Cookery Room, Library, a large Sports Hall and a Foreign Languages Room.

Following a full inspection in September 2021, Ayscoughfee Hall School was judged to be 'Excellent' in all areas. A very thorough inspection was carried out by the Independent Schools Inspectorate in which the school was awarded the highest possible grade.

The guidelines and principles of the National Curriculum are followed in all subjects but go far beyond the basic requirements in order to give each child a broader, more varied understanding. Academic standards are high, and progress is well monitored throughout the school. The vast majority of pupils are successful in the Lincolnshire County Council 11+ selection examination (average pass rate of 96% over the last 3 years) and progress to secondary selective school education very well equipped to tackle all subjects. The curriculum is continually reviewed and class teachers are supported by specialist teachers for PE, ICT, languages, music and Forest School. French and Spanish are taught from Reception class.

iPads support learning in the classrooms and pupils receive weekly, dedicated ICT tuition in our up-to-date ICT suite.

The School excels with its music and drama productions over the academic year, in which all children perform in front of their parents and guests.

The school competes successfully in local and regional sports activities, including football, rugby, hockey, netball, cross-country and athletics.

There is a thriving programme of extracurricular activities, including sport, drama, cookery, chess, poetry, textiles, choir, stop motion, mindfulness/wellbeing, gardening, eco club and Forest School. A wide variety of educational visits is offered, with the older children having the opportunity to participate in alternate cultural and activity residential trips, accompanied by the staff. Furthermore, regular visits by professional groups and individuals take place in school.

As a small school with small class sizes, we aim to provide a happy and caring environment where the individual child may flourish. We are proud of our academic standards but we also strive to give a broad and balanced education placing the child's wellbeing at the heart of everything we do. Above all, we want our boys and girls to use and develop their different abilities and to enjoy the success this brings.

Charitable status. Ayscoughfee Hall School Limited is a Registered Charity, number 527294. It exists to provide education for boys and girls.

Babington House School

Grange Drive, Chislehurst, Kent BR7 5ES

Tel: 020 8467 5537
email: enquiries@babingtonhouse.com
website: www.babingtonhouse.com
Facebook: @BabingtonBR7
Instagram: @babingtonhouseschool
LinkedIn: /Babington-House-School

Chair of Governors: Mr C Turner

***Headmaster*: Mr T W A Lello**, MA, FRSA, NPQH, PGCE

Head of Seniors: Mr P Showell, BMus Hons, QTS, FRSA

Head of Preparatory: Mr J Mole, BA Hons, PGCE

Age range. Co-educational 3–18.

Number in School. 489 Day Pupils: 243 boys, 246 girls.

Fees per term (2023–2024). £5,255–£6,550.

Babington House School is an independent day school for pupils aged 3 to 18 years, situated in a beautiful group of buildings on Grange Drive in Chislehurst, near Bromley and close to Elmstead Woods station.

Our commitment is to provide an academic and well-rounded education with small class sizes which is tailored to the needs of our pupils, believing that bright children benefit from carefully monitored and well-directed learning, where self-discipline is highly prized and where each pupil is known as an individual. This helps Babington House pupils grow into confident, accomplished, creative young people with emotional intelligence and high standards.

Babington is an academic school. Our academic, social and sporting endeavours are underpinned by core Christian values which include a respect for others and an awareness of a purpose greater than ourselves. There is a strong sense of community at Babington House.

Over the past four years, Babington has achieved 82% A* to B grades at A Level.

In its last inspection, Babington House was praised by the ISI for achieving outstanding academic success at all key stages and providing exemplary pastoral care. The boys and girls receive a first-class education in a nurturing and supportive environment, set in pleasant suburban surroundings. Full range of courses for examinations at all levels. 'Excellent' in all areas of the school and across every age group from 3–18 (ISI report November 2016).

Specialist facilities for Science, Music, Drama, Art, Sport, ICT, Languages, Maths & English.

Small classes: Maximum size 20 pupils. Careers guidance by a specialist.

Wide range of sports (Athletics, Swimming, Tennis, Netball, Gymnastics, Football, Cross Country) and extracurricular activities (Drama, Gym Club, Horse Riding, Cookery, Rock Climbing, Taekwondo, Choir, and Instrumental Tuition).

Charitable status. Babington House School is a Registered Charity, number 307914. It exists to provide exemplary education.

Ballard School

Fernhill Lane, New Milton, Hampshire BH25 5SU

Tel: 01425 626900
email: registrar@ballardschool.co.uk
website: www.ballardschool.co.uk
X/Twitter: @BallardSchool
Facebook: @BallardSchoolNewMilton
LinkedIn: /BallardSchool

Chairman of the Board of Governors: Mr P Goodfellow

***Headmaster*: Mr Andrew McCleave**

Age Range. 2 to 16 Co-educational.

Number of Children. 470 day children.

Fees per term (2023–2024). Years 9–11 £6,055; Years 6–8 £5,755; Year 5 £5,600; Year 4 £5,425; Year 3 £4,950; Reception–Year 2 £3,290. Fees include the cost of school lunches and most extra-curricular clubs. Sibling discounts available.

'Pupils are reflective and have high levels of self-esteem and empathy. They are highly successful in displaying these characteristics through academic study as well as the wealth of sporting performing arts and extra-curricular opportunities in which they participate.' ISI Inspection November 2017.

Ballard is an award-winning, independent, co-educational day school for children from Nursery to GCSE. Rated 'excellent & outstanding' by ISI, we believe in a bespoke education for your child within a nurturing and engaging environment. Set in 34 acres of beautiful grounds located between the New Forest National Park and the Solent, we serve Hampshire and Dorset.

Ballard pupils achieve excellent examination results: this year over 40% of pupils achieved grades 9–7 which is double the national average.

Subject specialist teaching staff, alongside small class sizes and a diverse and inspiring range of activities and trips, nurture self-confidence, aspiration and help develop each child's personality.

A family school with Christian values, Ballard offers inspiring teaching and excellent pastoral care; children are encouraged to take on responsibilities from an early age including a mentoring programme whereby older children help younger children.

Extra-curricular: 120+ activities and GCSE 'Raising Attainment' sessions a week, Ballard's co-curricular programme is designed to give pupils of all ages a breadth of opportunities, from Archaeology to Zumba! Whatever their individual strengths or curiosities, there is something for everyone.

Notable Achievements and Alumni: 'Excellent and Outstanding' (ISI); shortlisted for Independent School of the Year – Co-Educational (2020 and 2022) and Student Wellbeing (2021); shortlisted for a Wilder School award (2021); finalist for Independent School of the Year – Performing Arts (2022) and ISA Award for Excellence and Innovation in Art and Design (2022); Highly commended in the ISA Award for Outstanding Sport – Large School (2022). Current awards include: Artsmark Gold Award, Schools Sport Gold and Eco Schools Green Flag (the highest accolade), alongside National championships in several sports and an ISA Musician of the Year Award. Our alumni include World Champions and Olympic medallists as well as an international opera star, pop bands and harpists.

There is a wealth of information on our website – www.ballardschool.co.uk – including our Open Morning dates. So come along and see for yourself why more parents are choosing a Ballard education for their children.

"*Quite simply a remarkable school.*"

"*A warm, friendly school in a glorious setting, where pupils enjoy their learning, throw themselves into a plethora of activities and have fun. The performing arts are outstanding and children seem genuinely sad to leave for pastures new at 16.*" Good Schools Guide

"*My son's predicted grade for Maths GCSE has gone from a D/C to an A* because of the way he has been taught.*"

"*The attitude at Ballard is very much 'You can do it' not 'Can you do it?'* "

"*It's been the making of both of our boys.*"

"*You are not just a number.*"

"*Ballard has given me everything I need so that I can go forward and achieve anything I want.*"

Charitable status. Ballard School Ltd is a Registered Charity, number 307328. It exists for the education of children.

Bedford Greenacre Independent School & Nursery

58–60 Shakespeare Road, Bedford MK40 2DL

Tel: 01234 352031
email: admissions@bedfordgreenacre.co.uk
website: www.bedfordgreenacre.co.uk

Chair of Governors: E Coley, MEd Cantab, BMus Hons Lond

***Principal*: I M Daniel**, BA, NPQH

Age Range. 6 weeks to 18 co-educational
Number in School. 665 Day Pupils.
Fees per term (2023–2024). £2,566–£4,295.

Bedford Greenacre Independent School was formed on 1st May 2021 by the merger of Rushmoor School and St Andrew's School and Nursery.

Rushmoor School moved to Bedford in 1918 and had grown and improved over 104 years by investing greatly to provide excellent facilities. Rushmoor formed an alliance in 2013 with St Andrew's School and the formal merger and rebranding was the next step in this process. St Andrew's School had an equally strong reputation in Bedford, initially opening in 1896.

We appreciate the importance of selecting the right school for your child; childhood is something which can be experienced only once. With this in mind, and the belief that children learn best when they feel happy and secure, we aim to develop in our pupils a lifelong interest in learning – one which encompasses the full range of intellectual, cultural, artistic and sporting achievements of our society.

We believe in individual care and attention. Visitors to the school are impressed by the friendly, positive attitude of the pupils and their energetic sense of purpose. The staff are caring and understanding, yet know the importance of effort and personal discipline in enabling pupils to achieve the highest academic standards.

At the school we ensure that all children have opportunities to develop their intellectual, physical and creative gifts, across a broad and balanced curriculum. Children in Reception and Junior classes benefit greatly from a wide range of specialist teachers.

We emphasise the individual, recognising that all children are different and value each child in their own right. Encouraging children to develop their strengths improves their self-esteem, enabling them to find their role in the community. We promote children's personal development, encouraging lively and enquiring minds, respect for others and a high regard for truth. The stability of continuous education, spanning the school age ranges, is a major factor in helping us achieve this.

We pride ourselves on our ability to integrate children with Specific Learning Differences within mainstream school life, whilst still providing extended challenges for our gifted and talented pupils. We believe that every child should be allowed to embrace any aspect of the curriculum. Enabling children to receive support without undermining their confidence amongst their peers is of primary importance.

In 2019, under our former names, we won the *ISA Award for Outstanding Provision for Learning Support*. We have also won the *ISA Award for Excellence and Innovation in Early Years*. We boast successful sporting records, with many pupils gaining county and national honours. Under our former name, we won the *ISA Award for Outstanding Provision in Sport* in 2016. Children have also gained much success in national and local drama competitions and festivals, together with art and photography competitions. In 2014, under our former name, we were a finalist in the *ISA Award for Excellence* and winner of the 'Financial Innovation' category.

We are excited about the future where we will be on one site with new, purpose-built facilities. To find out more, please visit our website www.bedfordgreenacre.co.uk.

Prospective parents and children can tour the school at any time with the Principal and 'taster days' can be arranged. Come and experience our caring ethos which enables our children to develop the confidence and flexibility which allows them to face the demands of modern life. To view our excellent inspection reports please visit our website. Contact us on hello@bedfordgreenacre.co.uk.

Charitable status. Bedford Greenacre Independent School Limited is a Registered Charity, number 1194080. It exists to provide education.

Bedstone College

Bucknell, Shropshire SY7 0BG
Tel: 01547 530303
email: admissions@bedstone.org
reception@bedstone.org
website: www.bedstone.org
X/Twitter: @BedstoneCollege
Facebook: @BedstoneCollege
Instagram: @BedstoneCollege

See full entry in the **Society of Heads** section, on **p. 512**.

Beech Hall School

Beech Hall Drive, Tytherington, Macclesfield, Cheshire SK10 2EG
Tel: 01625 422192
email: secretary@beechhallschool.org
website: www.beechhallschool.org
X/Twitter: @beechhall_macc
Facebook: @beechhallschool

***Headmaster*: Mr J D Allen**, BA Ed Hons, MA, NPQH, FCoT

Deputy Headmistress: Mrs G Yandell, BA Hons, PGCE, L2 Elklan
Director of Teaching & Learning: Mr Colin Richards, BA Hons
Director of Finance & Operations: Mrs V Parkes, BA Hons, MSc, PGCE
Registrar: Miss J Lord

Age Range. 6 months–18 years.

Number of Pupils. 225.

Fees per term (2023–2024). Infants £3,930 Junior School £4,820, Lower Senior School £5,350, Upper Senior School £5,400. The fees are inclusive of lunches, snacks and wrap-around care.

Nursery, Infant, Junior and Senior departments offer education between 8.30am and 4.00pm with further supervised sporting and leisure activities available until 5.00pm. If required, there is supervised care up until 6.00pm for all children.

Beech Hall is a co-educational Day school situated in spacious and attractive grounds with extensive playing fields, a heated outdoor swimming pool, new food technology lab and many other facilities.

Pupils are prepared for entry to a wide variety of Independent Schools and Sixth Form Colleges. Classes are kept small, making individual attention possible in every lesson.

There is a very popular Nursery, Pre-School and Reception department, consisting of children between the ages of 6 months and 5 years under the care of their own specialist teachers. These classes were started with the objective of giving children a good grounding in reading, writing and arithmetic.

Beech Hall aims to provide a sound all-round education. Rugby, football, hockey and netball are played in the winter terms and in summer, cricket, athletics, and rounders are taught. There is an extensive sporting fixture list covering all sports with children playing representative sport from Year 3 upwards. Swimming is taught throughout the year and other activities include badminton and fives.

The school is situated off the main Stockport–Macclesfield road, within easy reach of Manchester International Airport and the M6 and M62 motorways.

Further details and illustrated prospectus are obtainable from the school or via the school's website.

Beech House School

184 Manchester Road, Rochdale, Greater Manchester OL11 4JQ
Tel: 01706 646309
email: info@beechhouseschool.co.uk
website: www.beechhouseschool.co.uk

***Principal*: Mr Kevin Sartain**, BSc Hons, PGCE, Dip Spo Psy, CBiol, FIBiol

Age range. 2–16 Co-educational.

Number of pupils. 180.

Fees per term (2023–2024). £2,203–£2,627.

Founded pre 1850, Beech House School is an independent co-educational school for students aged two to sixteen years. An Upper Preparatory department for children aged eight to eleven years and a Senior department for those aged eleven to sixteen years have been based on the Manchester Road site in Rochdale for its entire history. The Lower Preparatory department for children aged two to seven has been based at Broadfield Style.

Offering tailored education that is as unique as each individual child, Beech House is an award-winning school that makes a difference to the lives of every student it admits. Its average class consists of 12 students, ensuring ample room for young people to learn, grow and succeed as they embark on their academic journey. With small class sizes, the school is able to ensure each child receives the support they need to achieve excellence.

Taking on children as young as two years old, Beech House nurtures students to their full potential through quality primary and secondary education. The incredible academic achievement it fosters in its students is what sets it apart from other independent schools. Its student body is small yet bursting with success in a multitude of areas.

Beech House welcomes pupils from a variety of social and economic backgrounds, including those with special educational needs. All children, regardless of their abilities, are encouraged to participate in a variety of activities. Through this, the school enables students to build confidence and discover new talents.

Part of Beech House's success comes from the fact that it operates differently to other independent schools. Dedicated to inclusiveness, the school does not just pick the best children, but instead ensures that everyone is performing together. It supports those who are falling behind, enabling them to catch up. Thanks to its small population, the school is able to treat each child as the individual they are.

Teachers at Beech House are talented professionals who enjoy drawing the best out of their students. Thanks to their hard work, these students go on to achieve some incredible things. For example, some have gone on to attend Oxford University, while others have become international athletes.

Former students of Beech House reflect on their time at the school with great fondness and affection. For this very reason, Beech House often has the pleasure of teaching multiple generations of the same family. The school is proud to change its students' futures for the better, giving them opportunities that they may never have otherwise had.

Parents interested in viewing Beech House are invited to contact the school to make an appointment and discuss any queries they may have. The school recommends that they visit during operational hours so that they can witness the joyful, caring atmosphere that fills the grounds when the students are there.

Belmont School

Feldemore, Holmbury St Mary, Dorking, Surrey RH5 6LQ

Tel: 01306 730852
email: admissions@belmont-school.org
website: www.belmont-school.org
X/Twitter: @BelmontDorking
Facebook: @BelmontDorking
Instagram: @BelmontDorking
LinkedIn: /BelmontSchool (Surrey)

Chairman of the Governors: Mr A Baker

***Head*: Mr M Broughton**, BA, MEd

Age Range. 3–16.

Number of Pupils. 200 Boys and Girls: Day, Weekly and Flexible Boarding.

Fees per term (2023–2024). Day Pupils: Pre-Reception £4,050, Reception £4,050, Years 1–2 £4,760, Year 3 £5,880, Year 4 £6,290, Years 5–6 £6,660, Years 7–8 £6,820 and Years 9–11 £7,280. Boarding Pupils: day boarding £12/£24 per day (until 6.30pm/8.30pm), flexi-boarding is £46 per night and weekly boarding is £1,885 (for 4/5 nights per week, Sunday/Monday to Friday and seat on London minibus).

Founded in London in 1880, the School is now established in 65 acres of woodland overlooking the picturesque village of Holmbury St Mary, between Guildford and Dorking in the Surrey Hills. Outstanding facilities include an impressive sports hall, well-equipped theatre, extensive sports pitches, mountain bike tracks, music school, swimming pool, woodland adventure courses, food technology room and our latest development, the Aquileon, which boasts art & photography studios, black box performance area, additional senior classrooms and a well-being centre. Our friendly, well-qualified and talented staff focus upon developing confident, happy and capable pupils. In addition, we seek to smooth the logistics of family life by delivering flexible arrangements for parents and by providing a minibus service.

We offer co-educational day education for pupils aged 3 to 16, and optional weekly, flexible and day boarding arrangements for pupils from 7 years old. Breakfast club is available from 3 years old and extended day arrangements in the evening for pupils from Reception upwards.

At Belmont, we seek to discover and to develop what is best in each pupil, seeking to inspire and to unfurl the hidden strengths of every child. There is a happy, industrious atmosphere and high expectations pervade throughout all aspects of school life. We have a challenging curriculum and an extensive array of extra-curricular opportunities that together are designed to captivate the imagination, to nurture independence and to harness academic ambition for every pupil.

The curriculum covers all the requirements leading from Early Years education to GCSE including Drama, Art, Design Technology, Music, PSHE, Computing, PE and Games. Sports include Netball, Rugby, Football, Cross-Country, Hockey, Tennis, Swimming, Cricket, Athletics and Sailing (Seniors only). Pupils have a busy life at Belmont; they are passionate and proud of their school and talk enthusiastically about how the educational experience shapes itself according to the age of the pupils, and the needs of the individual.

Children in Year 1 and above attend for a half day or full day visit prior to entry. Further details can be obtained from the Registrar, Charlotte Smith on 01306 730852 or admissions@belmont-school.org.

Charitable status. Belmont School (Feldemore) Educational Trust Limited is a Registered Charity, number 312077.

Bishop Challoner School

228 Bromley Road, Shortlands, Bromley, Kent BR2 0BS

Tel: 020 8460 3546
email: office@bishopchallonerschool.com
website: www.bishopchallonerschool.com
X/Twitter: @challoner_head
Instagram: @bishop.challoner.school

***Headteacher*: Mr Mark Wallace**, BA Hons, MBA

Deputy Headteacher: Mrs Kate Brooker, LLCM, FLCM, GLCM Hons, PGCE, AdvDip Ed Mgmt, NPQH, FCCT

Age range. 3–18.

Number in school. 310 Day Pupils.

Fees per term (2023–2024). Seniors: £5,208, Juniors: £4,048, Infants: £3,644, Nursery: £1,047 (min. 3 sessions), £3,334 (full time).

This is a Roman Catholic Independent Co-educational School for pupils aged 3–18 years.

Happiness, self-fulfilment and personal success are all embraced at Bishop Challoner.

The school's motto is '*Quantum potes, tantum aude*' – Dare to do your best.

The School welcomes all faiths and none.

Admissions to the School follows the successful completion of an entrance examination/assessment and an interview with the Headteacher.

Scholarships and Bursaries are available.

Charitable status. Bishop Challoner School is a Registered Charity, number 1153948. It exists to provide an excellent education for boys and girls.

Boundary Oak School

Roche Court, Wickham Road, Fareham, Hampshire PO17 5BL

Tel: 01329 280955
email: admissions@boundaryoak.co.uk
office@boundaryoak.co.uk
website: www.boundaryoakschool.co.uk
X/Twitter: @boundaryoak
Facebook: @boundaryoakschool

See full entry in the **IAPS** section, on **p. 620**.

Bournemouth Collegiate School

Senior School:
College Road, Southbourne, Bournemouth, Dorset BH5 2DY

Tel: 01202 436550
email: registrar@bcschool.co.uk
Facebook: @Bournemouthcollegiateschool
Instagram: @bcs_school

Prep School:
40 St Osmund's Road, Poole, Dorset BH14 9JY

Tel: 01202 714110
email: prep-admin@bcschool.co.uk
website: www.bournemouthcollegiateschool.co.uk

See full entry in the **Society of Heads** section, on **p. 517**.

Bowbrook House School

Peopleton, Nr Pershore, Worcs WR10 2EE

Tel: 01905 841242/841843
email: enquiries@bowbrookhouseschool.co.uk
website: www.bowbrookhouseschool.co.uk
X/Twitter: @bowbrookhouse
Facebook: @Bowbrook-House-School
Instagram: @bowbrookhouse

***Headmaster*: Mr C D Allen**, BSc Hons, CertEd, DipSoc

Age Range. 3½–16.

Number in School. Day 212: 111 Boys, 101 Girls.

Fees per term (2023–2024). £2,250–£4,750.

Bowbrook House is set in 14 acres of picturesque Worcestershire countryside yet within easy reach of Worcester, Pershore and Evesham. The school caters for the academic child and also those of average ability, who can benefit from the small classes. All pupils are able to take full advantage of the opportunities offered and are encouraged to participate in all activities. As well as the academic subjects, the school has a flourishing art department, a computer room, hard tennis courts and an open air swimming pool in addition to extensive games fields.

The Pre-Prep department of 3½–8 year olds is a self-contained unit but enjoys the use of the main school facilities.

Whilst stressing academic achievement, the school aims to provide a structured and disciplined environment in which children of all abilities can flourish, gain confidence and achieve their true potential. The small school size enables the head and staff to know all pupils well, to be able to accurately assess their strengths and weaknesses it enables each pupil to be an important part of the school and to feel that their individual attitudes, behaviour, efforts and achievements are important.

There is an extended school day from 8.15am to 5.30pm, with supervised prep sessions. There is also an extensive and varied extracurricular programme run by specialist coaches from basketball, gym and dance to kickboxing and fencing.

Bredon School

Pull Court, Bushley, Tewkesbury, Gloucestershire GL20 6AH

Tel: 01684 293156
email: admissions@bredonschool.co.uk
website: www.bredonschool.org
X/Twitter: @BredonSchool
Facebook: @Bredon-School
LinkedIn: /bredon-school-2002-limited

See full entry in the **Society of Heads** section, on **p. 519**.

Bridgewater School

Drywood Hall, Worsley Road, Worsley, Salford, Greater Manchester M28 2WQ

Tel: 0161 794 1463
email: admin@bwslive.co.uk
website: www.bridgewater-school.co.uk
X/Twitter: @BridgewaterScho
Facebook: @BridgewaterConnected
Instagram: @bridgewater_school
LinkedIn: /bridgewater-school-worsley

Chair of Governors: Mrs K Mort, BA Hons

***Headmistress*: Mrs J A T Nairn**, Cert Ed Distinction

Age Range. 3–18 Co-educational.

Number of Pupils. 461: 248 Boys, 213 Girls.

Fees per term (2023–2024). £3,373–£4,542.

In 1950, a group of parents wanted to find an alternative to schools in the area, believing that every child deserved access to the best education possible. Out of this shared vision, Bridgewater School was born.

Today, seventy years later, this aspiration remains at the heart of everything we do. Bridgewater School provides independent education for boys and girls aged 3–18 years in an inspirational setting that is inclusive, stimulating, supportive and totally focused on achieving every pupil's individual goals.

Ever since the school's inception, our family ethos has ensured that each young person is treated very much as an individual and, although the scale and academic stature of the school have grown alongside our new buildings and facilities, we are still small enough to know each young person by name and develop a true understanding of their specific needs and abilities.

Whether your child joins us at the very start of their learning journey, as a Prep pupil, Senior School student or at Sixth Form level, they will enjoy consistently high teaching standards and a wonderfully varied extra-curricular programme. A programme designed to enrich their experiences, enhance their personal development and give them the opportunity to develop their individuality their way. The result is a vibrant community where children can flourish and thrive, learning together and achieving together.

The exceptional focus we can bring to all students through the intimacy and support of small classes can make all the difference. A difference which manifests itself in exceptional A Level and GCSE exam results, year after year. However, we believe that exam results are an end product of an outstanding, fully rounded education rather than an end in themselves. Our students are successful and achieve their personal best because they study a broad and challenging curriculum in a stable, happy and reassuring environment. They are given the opportunity to discover previously undiscovered talents both within and beyond the classroom, which explains why so many of our young people go on to make so much of their lives.

Our unique, outwardly focused approach to education engenders high standards of behaviour and self-discipline amongst pupils, as well as building a mature awareness of their personal and social responsibilities. This approach, together with the importance we place on the relationship between family and school, produces articulate, well-rounded individuals who take pride in their achievements and who are fully prepared to meet the exciting challenges yet to come.

We are committed to a programme of continuous development and improvement and the school governors, staff and pupils all share a real sense of excitement about both our recent accomplishments and Bridgewater's future.

If you have not yet visited us then may we recommend that you do so soon. We would be delighted to meet you and show you the uniquely individual features which set our school apart.

Charitable status. Bridgewater School is a Registered Charity, number 1105547.

Bronte School

Mayfield, 7 Pelham Road, Gravesend, Kent DA11 0HN

Tel: 01474 533805
email: enquiry@bronteschool.co.uk
website: www.bronteschool.co.uk

***Headmistress*: Mrs Emma Wood**, BA Hons

Age Range. 3–11.

Number in School. 143 Day Pupils: 72 Boys, 71 Girls.

Fees per term (2023–2024). £4,081.

Bronte is a small, friendly, family-orientated, co-educational day school serving Gravesend and surrounding villages. The children are taught in small classes and are prepared for all types of secondary education. In 1999 the school moved to its present building which has since been expanded to accommodate specialist teaching rooms. A broadly-based curriculum and an extensive number of activity clubs provide the children with every opportunity to develop their individual interests and abilities. We achieve excellent 11+ results every year.

Entry is preferred at Kindergarten (age 3) following a parental visit to the school and an interview with the Head. Children joining at a later stage are assessed informally prior to entry.

Burlington House School

Bishop's Avenue, Fulham, London SW6 6EG

Tel: 020 7610 9018
email: office@burlingtonhouseschool.com
website: www.burlingtonhouseschool.com
X/Twitter: @Burlington_HS
Facebook: @BurlingtonHouseSchool
LinkedIn: /company/burlington-house-school

***Principal*: Koen Claeys**, BA GLSE Belgium

Headmaster: Matthew Potger, BA Hons, Post Cert Dysl & Lit, PGCE, Level 3 Success with People with Autistic Spectrum Disorder ASD York

Head of Sixth Form: Steve Proctor, BA Hons, PGCE, QTLS, BOA, SENCo

Head of Prep School: Nicola Lovell, BEd Hons, Level 5 SpLD, Cert Reading Recovery, Cert Competency Educational Testing CCET, ADG

Co-educational Day School.

Age Range. 7–19.

Number of Pupils. 114 Boys, 62 Girls.

Fees per term (2023–2024). £10,247–£13,897.

Set within the historic conservation area of Fulham Palace, Burlington House School is a specialist school for secondary-age SpLD pupils. Mainstream in structure and specialist in nature, Burlington House caters successfully for the needs of pupils with specific learning difficulties. Alongside the curriculum, the school also offers expertise in speech and language therapy, occupational therapy and a school counsellor.

Burlington House Sixth Form was established in September 2020, providing pupils post-16 from Burlington House (previously The Moat School) and other schools a chance to take A Level and BTEC options. It also offers a full range of GCSE re-sit options as well as therapeutic benefits for KS5 pupils with SpLDs and others with additional needs.

Burlington House Prep was established in September 2022, providing a space for prep-aged pupils to work with expert staff from an early age. The Prep facilities at Burlington House were shortlisted for 'Prep School of the Year' at the 2023 TES awards.

All teachers complete a postgraduate BDA-approved course in teaching students with SpLD within their first 2 years of appointment. Qualified Learning Support Assistants accompany pupils throughout their lessons at Key Stage 3, where class sizes are a maximum of 10. Class sizes are even smaller at Key Stage 4.

Multi-sensory teaching is combined with advanced IT provision, each pupil being provided with a laptop computer for use in school and at home. Touch-typing is taught in Year 7 and there is a state-of-the-art wireless network which enables staff and pupils to access the school intranet with its wide range of learning resources and data, as well as the internet.

At Key Stage 3, pupils follow a mainstream curriculum (with the exception of foreign languages) before selecting their GCSE options alongside the core subjects of English, Mathematics and Single or Dual Award Science. Burlington House offers excellent facilities for learning, with a suite of Design Technology workshops offering state-of-the-art facilities for Food Technology, Resistant Materials and Graphics. Art, Music, Drama, ICT and Business Studies each have dedicated studios or specialist classrooms.

Burlington House has an extensive enrichment programme of extracurricular activities designed to widen experience and develop self-confidence. In Drama, all Year 9 pupils take part in an annual Shakespeare play and there are several productions and workshop performances each year. Burlington House's proximity to the River Thames enables pupils to experience rowing as a sport, swimming is popular and 2012 saw the introduction of Martial Arts and boxing. The Duke of Edinburgh's Award encourages pupils to test their own limits and since 2020 we have also offered the Duke of Edinburgh Gold award with a full set of dedicated DofE accredited staff across both the school and Sixth Form.

Burlington House School is part of the Cavendish Education Group.

Buxlow Preparatory School

5/6 Castleton Gardens, East Lane, Wembley, Middlesex HA9 7QJ

Tel: 020 8904 3615
email: admin@buxlowschool.org.uk
website: www.buxlowschool.org.uk

***Head*: Mrs Christine McLelland**

Deputy Head: Mrs N Zaman
Deputy Head (*Assessment*): Mr Hamilton-Turner
Head of EYFS: Mrs M Jobe
Sendco: Mrs P Kelly
School Secretary and Headteacher's PA: Ms Da Cunha

Age Range. 2–11 Co-educational, Nursery to Year 6.

Number of Pupils. 75.

Fees per term (2023–2024). Reception £3,492.70, Years 1–6 £3,685.80.

Founded in 1927, as an independent preparatory school for boys, Buxlow Preparatory School is now fully co-educational and offers quality education to children between 2 and 11 years of age. Buxlow is a calm, nurturing, stimulating, education based setting. We ensure the children are engaged in their learning and are provided with appropriate resources and opportunities to become active, independent learners

Our nursery provision is available for 51 weeks of the year, with a variety of different sessions. The children enjoy a range of activities to support them in reaching their potential through curriculum based learning that promotes independence from a young age. Children can join our Nursery when they are 2 years old and age appropriate children are given first consideration for our sought after Reception places.

The curriculum has a thematic approach and where possible, cross curricular links are made to motivate the children and promote creativity. We also ensure that children gain experiences of the curriculum outside the classroom through off site visits or workshops. We promote high levels of achievement and effort and encourage pupils to take pride and a greater responsibility in their work. As the year progresses the children's sense of pleasure in their self-motivated achievements grows, laying a solid foundation for future study habits.

We also focus on independent thinking skills through verbal and non-verbal reasoning. We take the learning beyond school through educational visits. Through motivational teaching and attention to every child's needs our pupils experience an inspiring learning journey.

During the Spring Term in Year 5, the children are introduced to 11+ preparation in the form of weekly preparation sessions, involving practice papers and guidance to improve examination technique. The children become familiar with the style and expectations of the papers and these are embedded into their weekly learning, with any marks and general feedback going home to parents. Interview preparations also begin, with the children seen by the Headteacher and Year 6 teacher. LAMDA lessons also support this practice. As a result of this gradual yet thorough preparation, our pupils go into their exams confident and self-assured and our senior school successes speak for themselves.

Our aim is to establish a nurturing environment and an atmosphere where children feel valued and can thrive both emotionally and academically.

Cambridge Tutors College

Water Tower Hill, Croydon, Surrey CR0 5SX

Tel: 020 8688 5284
email: info@ctc.ac.uk
website: www.ctc.ac.uk

***Principal*: Dr Chris Drew**, BSc Sussex, MA Bath, EdD Bath, PGCE, Dip RSA, FCCT

Age Range. 14–23.

Number of Pupils. 60.

Fees per annum (2023–2024). International fees from £17,330 excluding accommodation; up to £33,920 including homestay accommodation. UK fees from £17,900 excluding accommodation; up to £26,825 including homestay accommodation.

2021 A Level results: 65% A*/A and 75% of students entering their first choice universities, mostly Russell Group.

Since 1958 Cambridge Tutors College (CTC) has been offering a very high quality academically focused education to young people from the United Kingdom and from across the world. Fundamental to the College's ethos is small group teaching – our average class size is just over 5 students – and regular testing: students sit weekly tests in every subject, under examination conditions. This combination of small classes, regular testing and expert teaching has proved to be highly successful in giving students the motivation and confidence to succeed.

CTC offers: A Level courses (two-year and 18-month), NCUK International Foundation Year and an accelerated 6 month course, one-year GCSE course and a one-year pre-GCSE course. CTC also offers one and two-term pre-sessional courses linked to the two-year A Level programme.

The College's most recent ISI Inspection reports in 2017 and 2020 were outstanding.

The college enjoys a particularly strong reputation for helping students to gain entry to the UK's most prestigious universities.

Situated in a pleasant parkside location in South Croydon, CTC is just a few minutes' walk from the town centre, East Croydon station and bus and tram routes. It is close to Central London, just 15 minutes away by train, but surrounded by parkland and quiet residential streets.

Facilities and resources are modern and well-appointed. The College has excellent technological infrastructure with fast Wi-Fi, and there is an ambitious development programme in place.

The College's welfare provision includes a team of trained professionals and all students have a personal tutor. A varied weekly programme of sporting and other activities is offered, as well as weekend excursions.

Charitable status. Cambridge Tutors Educational Trust Limited is a Registered Charity, number 312878.

Canbury School

Kingston Hill, Kingston-upon-Thames, Surrey KT2 7LN

Tel: 020 8549 8622
email: reception@canburyschool.co.uk
website: www.canburyschool.co.uk
X/Twitter: @canbury_school

***Acting Head*: Mrs P Rich**, BA Hons, PGCE
Assistant Head Academic: Ms S Ridley, BA Hons, PGCE, PGCert NASENCo
Bursar & Clerk to the Governors: Mrs Lusia Anindita-Beckman, BA Hons, MSc, LLB, CMgr MCMI
Consultant Bursar: Mrs C O'Neill, MBA
Head's PA and Registrar: Ms Louise Boggi

Age range. 11–18.

Number in school. 75 students.

Founded in 1982, Canbury School is a unique and happy co-educational independent day school for students from the ages of 11 to 18 on the outskirts of London beside Richmond Park. We actively embrace difference and harness talent at Canbury. With excellent transport links to the school, students come from various nearby areas such as Barnes, Putney, Wandsworth, New Malden, Richmond, Teddington, Twickenham, Hampton, Epsom and other areas in Surrey such as Esher and Effingham. We also welcome overseas students. Located on the top of Kingston Hill, the school affords our students the opportunity to experience the vast resources London has to offer such as museums, parks, galleries and theatres. At Canbury, we recognise that we all learn in different ways, and at different paces, and this is reflected in our teaching style. With class sizes of 15 students or less, enthusiastic teaching, excellent pastoral care and a determination to target the needs of individuals, Canbury School is an inclusive environment in which to thrive.

Entry requirements. We don't look for students to fit a Canbury mould; we look for students whom we can help to grow. All applicants undertake a baseline assessment. For 11+ entry, we consider reports from Junior/Primary schools and other documentation and then invite those selected to spend a day with us. If all goes well, we may make an offer. For occasional places in other year groups, the candidate would be invited to spend three days with us in order to secure a place. Any educational reports need to be submitted prior to an interview with the Head.

Curriculum. Broad range of GCSE subjects. Functional Skills. BTEC subjects up to Level 3 at KS5.

Students may take up to seven GCSEs and/or BTEC level 2 equivalent.

In Years 7–9, the students' timetable includes the following subjects Art, Drama, English, Geography, Graphics, History, ICT, Mathematics, Music, Science, Spanish, Physical Education and Well Being.

Games are taught throughout all Key Stages. In Games, students are set into groups of equal ability for each sport. Winter sports may include cross country, kayaking, dodgeball, football, climbing and netball. Summer sports may include athletics, cricket, tennis and rounders. Teams participate in inter-school matches. In PE lessons, classes are mixed ability and activities such as basketball, badminton, gymnastics and health-related fitness are taught, thereby providing a wide diversity of opportunities for all.

In addition to their studies, students have a structured PHSE programme throughout the year. This includes a careers programme with work experience – a week in Year 10 and one day a week in Sixth Form.

At KS4, students study a number of GCSEs suitable to their academic ability and personal inclination. They are encouraged to keep their choices as balanced and broad as possible. The school offers the facility to study seven subjects, with the compulsory ones being Mathematics, English and Science. Students may then choose from a range of other options, including Art & Design, Business Studies, Drama, Geography, History, ICT, History, Photography and Spanish, as well as BTECs in Travel & Tourism and Sport. All students continue to have lessons in Physical Education and Games.

Where appropriate, Functional Skills Maths and/or English can be taught as an alternative to a GCSE programme. Functional Skills are taught across all levels (Entry 1–Level 2). Level 2 Functional Skills is universally recognised as an alternative qualification to GCSE, enabling students to progress to college or on to an apprenticeship.

The final programme for each GCSE cohort is determined by the curriculum structure (distributed on Options Evening) and will be confirmed in consultation with students, parents, subject teachers, the student's tutor and the Senior Leadership Team.

We run a wide range of extracurricular activities and clubs including (but not limited to) drama, art, self-defence, sports, board games, chess and lego. Students may ask for a club to be run, or lead one, if there is enough interest.

Students participate in the school council which is led by our two Head Students. The Prefect Team is responsible for Charity, Sport, and House activities. Students are all members of our very active House system led by Heads of Houses from the Prefect team.

Facilities. We are a small, friendly school with well-equipped classrooms. We have a dedicated science laboratory, classrooms, Art/DT Studio with pottery area and kiln, playground and a separate Sixth Form building. We access local facilities for a wide range of seasonal sporting activities including athletics, cricket, netball, softball, swimming, watersports, badminton, soccer, hockey, basketball, netball, dance, tennis and rock climbing.

Fees per term (2023–2024). £6,386 Years 7–11, £6,948 Sixth Form. Bursaries are means tested and are available at the discretion of the School subject to satisfactory completion of the School's Bursary Form.

Charitable status. Canbury School is a Registered Charity, number 803766. It exists to provide education to a broad range of students who find working in a smaller environment much better.

Cardiff Sixth Form College

1–3 Trinity Court, 21–27 Newport Road, Cardiff CF24 0AA

Tel: 02920 493121
email: admissions@ccoex.com
website: www.ccoex.com
X/Twitter: @csfcofficial
Facebook: @csfcofficial
Instagram: @csfofficial
LinkedIn: /school/cardiff-sixth-form-college

Motto: *Ignite Your Future, Ignite Your Passion, Ignite Your Interest*

***Director*: Gareth Collier**
Principal: Tom Arrand

Deputy Head (*Pastoral*) *& Designated Safeguarding Person*: Lisa Morton
Deputy Head (*Academic*): Paula Downey
Director of Marketing and Admissions: Henrietta Lightwood
Financial Director: Sharon Wright

Age Range. 14–19 Co-educational.
Number of Students. 405.

Cardiff Sixth Form College's results are outstanding. In 2023, 95% of students received A*–A grades, with 100% of students achieving A*–B grades. These results saw the college top the league table as the best independent school in the UK as reported by The Daily Telegraph. Excellent teaching, one-to-one support, superb academic materials, nearly double the amount of teaching hours of any other school and developing academic students with programmes designed to enhance their careers is what really makes the difference. The staff offer outstanding one-to-one support, tutorials and academic enrichment on top of their extensive teaching programme.

Cardiff also runs one-year and two-year GCSE courses. GCSE results in 2023 were outstanding with 84% of students achieving 9–7 grades and 91% 9–6. This course provides a unique opportunity for younger students, many of whom aspire to progress on to the award-winning Sixth Form, to be able to take advantage of the inspirational teaching, excellent career development and modern boarding environment at the top school in the UK. Designed as a four-way career path into top universities, this new course gives students the opportunity to study up to 11 key academic subjects as well as improve their English proficiency in small class sizes with intensive teaching.

Cardiff Sixth Form College has an enviable careers department with five full-time careers advisors, personal tutors and a full-time work experience coordinator. In addition, the College is part of Dukes Education with expertise in medical applications, Oxbridge and Russell Group university placements, giving its students access to top industry specialists from across the professions. A two-year super programme of UCAS support, assistance with university entrance exams, lectures and work experience programmes, interview technique and one-to-one tutoring for personal statements ensures that Cardiff students are expertly prepared for the competitive courses they are applying to.

The College also offers a wide range of super-curricular activities. Internationally, students undertake voluntary and work placement programmes in Malaysia, Tanzania, India and Europe, join medical, architectural or finance societies and enter national academic competitions such as science Olympiads, Model United Nations and Maths challenges. The Debating Team's performance this year has been outstanding, coming first in the South Wales round of the Oxford Union Schools Debating Competition and for five years in a row Cardiff students have won NASA's International Space Settlement Design Competition in Florida.

From an extra-curricular perspective, students have plenty of opportunities to get involved with sports, performing and creative arts with highlights including an annual Sports Day, the Cultural Event, Talent Show and annual Glee production. Many are talented musicians and gold awards have been won this year in the Duke of Edinburgh's Award scheme.

Pastoral care is award winning with boarding staff and progress tutors constantly monitoring each student. Boarding accommodation is outstanding with every student having a university-style, single bedroom or studio apartment.

For more information or to find out about upcoming Open Days and the application process, please go to www.ccoex.com.

Fees per annum (2023–2024). Day £22,300; Boarding £52,800–£58,000.

Carfax College Oxford

39–42 Hythe Bridge Street, Oxford, Oxfordshire OX1 2EP

Tel: 01865 200676
email: enquiries@carfax-oxford.com
website: www.carfax-oxford.com
X/Twitter: @CarfaxEducation
Facebook: @carfaxoxford
Instagram: @carfax_college
LinkedIn: /company/carfax-college

***Principal*: Iwan Lloyd**

Fees per term (2023–2024). Fees are individual, depending on the student's needs.

Age Range. The majority of GCSE pupils are between 14 and 16 years old, and most A level pupils are between 16 and 19 years old. However, the College can offer courses which are suitable for both younger and older pupils.

Admission. Carfax College does not operate a selective admissions policy. The college is suited to a range of abilities, and the levels of individual attention can also be of particular help to pupils with special educational needs.

Curriculum. COURSES | carfax-college The exam-focused curriculum is taught in individual sessions by experienced tutors. The exam boards are chosen on an individual basis during the course to reflect previous qualifications and different learning styles. There is regular exam practice, and arrangements are made for at least five hours of additional supervised study per week. Monthly reports are sent to parents or guardians. In addition to individual one-to-one A level tuition, pupils at Carfax College receive full UCAS support and careers guidance. With regards to GCSE, there are a mix of core and supplementary subjects. Students are also encouraged to study for an extra two GCSEs in additional subjects, which will help them with admission to sixth form at British independent schools.

Extracurricular activities. Football, Tennis, Golf, Polo, Swimming, Horse Riding, Gym Membership and fitness instructions, Art and Design, Photography and Architecture.

Carleton House Preparatory School

145 Menlove Avenue, Liverpool L18 3EE

Tel: 0151 722 0756
email: schooloffice@carletonhouse.co.uk
website: www.carletonhouse.co.uk
X/Twitter: @carletonhouse

Chair of Governors: Mrs Lynsey Morrison

***Head Teacher*: Mrs S Coleman**, BEd Hons SLE

Age Range. 3+–11 Co-educational.
Number in School. 182.
Fees per academic year (2023–2024). £9,660 inclusive of lunch, day trips, Spanish lessons and personal insurance cover.

Located in the leafy suburbs of south Liverpool, Carleton House is Merseyside's leading co-ed Preparatory School (13th in the Sunday Times Parent Power 2019). We are a Catholic school that welcomes children of all denominations.

Our most recent external ISI Educational Quality inspection judged both the achievement of our pupils, including their academic development and personal development, to be 'Excellent' – the highest possible judgement. All regulatory requirements were fully met.

"The quality of the pupils' academic and other achievements is excellent. The school's aim to develop a love of learning, foster intellectual curiosity and expand cultural horizons are successfully met."
Carleton House Preparatory School ISI Report June 2022.

Our school motto, *"They can because they think they can"* truly embodies the spirit of Carleton House. Our school is a lively, vibrant community that gives its pupils a first-class education for the 21st century.

Small class sizes (maximum of 23) and a high ratio of teaching staff to pupils enable the well-qualified and experienced staff to provide individual attention in a friendly, caring atmosphere. We nurture the development of the whole child – academically, spiritually and in the sporting and cultural aspects of their lives. Through excellent teaching and the close relationship that exists between school and home, our pupils are challenged, encouraged and supported to achieve their very best.

The implementation of all National Curriculum subjects ensures a broad, well-balanced curriculum is followed, but great importance is given to Maths and English as success in these subjects is central to development in other areas. Additional specialist teaching is provided for children requiring support in the basic subjects.

The children are taught Spanish throughout the school from Nursery to Year 6.

All children receive curriculum music lessons from our specialist teacher. Children in Year 3 to 6 benefit from instrumental music lessons through our external music tuition partner Pulse. Individual piano and guitar lessons are also available.

Children in Years 3 to 6 take part in weekly swimming and gym lessons at a local pool.

Emphasis is placed on high academic standards with our children being prepared for a variety of Entrance examinations at 11. A high percentage of our pupils successfully gain places at selective schools of their choice.

Our children are prepared for and take part in the English Speaking Board (ESB) examinations in year 5 and 6, supporting their public speaking skills.

We place a high importance on the development of computing skills for all pupils, with children from Year 1 to Year 6 benefiting from specialist computing teaching in our newly refurbished computing suite. This is complemented through the use of iPads in class based lessons.

A wide range of sports and extracurricular activities are offered to both boys and girls, including football, netball, cricket, rounders, chess, debate club, orchestra, cookery, singing and speech choir. The children compete in local sporting events as well as choral festivals and national quiz competitions.

Theatre and educational visits to enhance our curriculum are provided in all year groups. Our residential trips start in Year 3 with an overnight stay in Barnstondale, followed by a two-night stay in Shropshire in Year 4, a weekend in Lockerbie in Year 5 and culminating in a week long residential for our Year 6 pupils. These residentials provide field and adventure activities that help build confidence and self-esteem outside of the usual classroom environment.

Our open door policy encourages positive engagement with our parents, with regular parent/teacher meetings and biannual written reports on pupils progress.

A thriving Parent Teacher Association provides social functions for parents while raising funds for extra equipment for school and our chosen school charity.

After-school provision is provided by the 'Kids Club'. This operates daily from 3.30pm until 6.00pm and school is open from 8.00am for early drop-offs.

Parents are welcome to visit the school by appointment.

Charitable status. Carleton House Preparatory School is a Registered Charity, number 505310. It exists to provide education for boys and girls.

Claires Court

1 College Avenue, Maidenhead, Berkshire SL6 6AW

Tel: 01628 327710
email: registrar@clairescourt.com
website: www.clairescourt.com
X/Twitter: @clairescourt
Facebook: @clairescourt
Instagram: @clairescourtschool

Principals:
Mr H Wilding, BA, MCIM, FRSA
Mr J Wilding, BSc, FRSA

Head of Senior Boys: Mr J Wilding, BSc, FRSA
Head of Senior Girls: Mr S Richards, BA, PGCE, QTS
Head of Juniors & Nursery: Mrs L Kirby, BA, QTS, MA
Head of Sixth Form: Mr G Hope, MA, BSc, QTS

Age Range. 2–18.
Number of Pupils. 958.
Fees per term (2023–2024). £3,495–£6,330.

Claires Court is a school for families, run by a family, providing education for young people aged 2 to 18 years. Based on three sites across Maidenhead, we are a broad ability 'diamond model' day school where boys and girls are educated separately during their main school years, but come together for trips and visits, whilst the Nursery School and Sixth Form pupils benefit from a co-educational learning environment.

It is the feeling of belonging and the school's ethos that helps young people thrive and flourish in our school community. At Claires Court, we treat everyone as an individual, evaluating each child's ability to ensure we can enable them to reach their full potential, helping them achieve great results, whether that is in the classroom, on the sports field or in the creative arena. By offering the best education, strong pastoral care and a wealth of opportunities, our pupils achieve academically, feel valued and have a strong sense of self-belief and self-worth.

Pupils have access to excellent facilities across the sites, with indoor swimming pools, drama studios, extensive playing fields and music suites. Senior pupils have access to top-class facilities for training and playing rugby, football, cricket and hockey through our partnership agreements with local sports clubs. Sailing and rowing are also part of our sport offering with much success in regional and national competitions.

At the core of our learning philosophy are the Claires Court Essentials. Right from Nursery we make learning fun but challenging and from that springboard we focus on developing a variety of skills and behaviours that young people need to be a successful learner and individual in our fast-paced world. As they mature, pupils are expected to stretch themselves, push their own boundaries and limitations; we believe it is good to be wrong as long as we learn from that experience and bounce back. We develop boys and girls who are confident and resilient, learners who are critical thinkers and risk-takers, who can solve problems and communicate, as well as be creative and work collaboratively with others.

In the junior years, the creative, topic-based curriculum inspires a passion for learning and children quickly develop a taste for success. There is a focus on mastering the fundamental skills as well as academic attainment. Further up the school, the breadth and balance of the curriculum allows senior pupils to develop new interests and talents before focusing on their GCSEs.

The Sixth Form offers just as much variety with more than 27 subjects including A Levels and Level 3 BTECs. Claires Court is committed to excellence in sport and is pleased to offer four specific Sports Development Programmes in rugby, football, netball and rowing. Our value added surpasses that of most other Sixth Forms, meaning our students achieve over and above their predicted grades. Alongside this, the team also offers development and training for the personal, social and work skills that are desired by universities and employers.

For a prospectus or to arrange a visit, call Ms Tidey, Head of Admissions, on 020 8647 4607.

Collingwood School

3 Springfield Road, Wallington, Surrey SM6 0BD

Tel: 020 8647 4607
email: schooloffice@collingwoodschool.org.uk
website: www.collingwoodschool.org.uk
X/Twitter: @Collingwood_Sch
Facebook: @Collingwood-School

***Headmaster*: Mr Leigh Hardie**

Age Range. 2–11 Co-educational.

Number in School. Day: 100.

Fees per term (2023–2024). £3,331 (Reception)–£3,526 (year 1 to 6). There is a reduction for siblings.

Collingwood was founded in 1928

It is a school that has deliberately remained small in order to foster a very friendly and caring environment.

Our aim is to give children a first-class academic and sporting education while at the same time instilling the virtues of courtesy, respect and consideration for others. These traditional values, coupled with a modern, relevant education, make Collingwood the happy, purposeful and unique place that it is.

We offer an exciting range of subjects including ICT, DT, Music, French and Spanish. Currently we have over twelve extracurricular activities taking place each week including, drama, football, judo, gymnastics, robotics, construction, debating and Mandarin. Children are also able to learn to play a musical instrument such as piano, keyboard, drums, violin, cello, guitar or recorder. We also offer a breakfast and after-school club.

Although we are a non-selective school, many of our children over the years have gained entry into the local Grammar or Independent Selective Schools.

Copthill School

Barnack Road, Uffington, Stamford, Lincolnshire PE9 3AD

Tel: 01780 757506
email: mail@copthill.com
website: www.copthill.com
X/Twitter: @copthill
Facebook: @copthill
Instagram: @copthillschool

***Principal*: Mr J A Teesdale**, BA Hons, PGCE
Headteacher: Mrs H Schofield, BA Hons, PGCE

Departmental Leads:
Upper School Lead: Mrs I Hesford
Middle School Lead: Mr T Fournier
Lower School Lead: Mrs J Dimbleby
SLT Pastoral – Mr S Willson and Mrs A Teesdale
Early Years Lead: Miss B Hanham
SENCO Wellbeing Lead: Mrs R York-Forward
Head of Sport: Mrs G Alcoran
Head of Music: Mrs S Over

Age range. Co-educational 2–11 years.

Number of pupils. 300 total: Main School (age 4+ to 11) 240 and Nursery/Pre-School (age 2 to 4) 60.

Fees per term (2023–2024). £3,590–£4,210.

Educational aims.

- Put the child at the heart of their education, making the education fit the child rather than trying to make the child fit into a one-size-fits-all system.
- Care for our children as individuals within a supportive family community, learning and growing together; happy pupils learn.
- Have the highest expectations of our children across all areas of their education and development, with flexibility in our approach.
- Challenge and support our children to be confident in recognising their own and each other's strengths and talents across the broad Copthill curriculum.
- Acknowledge that learning can be difficult and aim to reassure our children that making mistakes is part of the process of learning.
- Work to instil in our children the curiosity, excitement, desire and drive to be lifelong learners, seizing every opportunity to pursue their dreams and to write their own success stories at each stage of their journey.
- Grow pupils as Copthill Learners (responsible citizens, independent explorers, team players, problem solvers, creative thinkers and reflective learners), respecting each other, our environment and ourselves and preparing for the next stage in life, whatever that might be.

Location. Purpose-built, modern facilities set within 350 acres of farmland, including river and woodland. 2 miles from Stamford and the A1 and 15 miles from Peterborough.

School day. Monday to Friday from 8.35 am to 4.40 pm. After- and before-school care from 7.45 am to 6.00 pm. Breakfast and tea available.

Facilities. Creative Suite, Music Suite, Library, Languages Suite, Sports Hall and playing fields including AstroTurf and a well-established on-site Forest School, High-quality catering, River, Farmland, School Animals.

Pastoral care. In addition to their forms, pupils from Year 5 upwards are also placed in small tutor groups in which their progress is closely monitored in preparation for senior school entrance. There is a genuine 'open door policy' throughout the School. Parents' Evenings are hosted twice a year and written reports are distributed at least 3 times a year.

Curriculum. A modern curriculum based on the National Curriculum. Combines traditional and innovative teaching methods. Learning support offered throughout the school where a specific need has been assessed.

Music, Speech & Drama. Music and Drama are taught as part of the curriculum. Regular drama productions encourage all pupils to participate. Pupils can also receive expert individual tuition and perform at school concerts, assemblies and in local music and drama festivals.

Sport. Rugby, Hockey (boy and girls), Netball, Cross-Country, Athletics, Cricket (mixed), Swimming, Tennis plus many extracurricular sports including Climbing and Archery.

Future schools. Pupils leave Copthill at 11 years old with great confidence and the ability to think for themselves. Copthill is a truly independent school, offering thorough preparation to a wide variety of independent and state senior schools, both local and national, achieving a large number of scholarships and awards.

Crackley Hall School

Kenilworth, Warwickshire CV8 2FT

Tel: 01926 514444
email: post@crackleyhall.co.uk
website: www.crackleyhall.co.uk
X/Twitter: @CrackleyHallSch
Facebook: @crackleyhallandlittlecrackersofficial
Instagram: @crackleyhall_littlecrackers

See full entry in the **IAPS** section, on **p. 642**.

Cranford School

Moulsford, Wallingford, Oxfordshire OX10 9HT

Tel: 01491 651218
email: admissions@cranfordschool.co.uk
website: www.cranfordschool.co.uk
X/Twitter: @CHSMoulsford
Facebook: @CranfordHouse
Instagram: @chsmoulsford

Chair of Governors: Mr Stuart Wallis

***Head*: Dr James Raymond**, PhD, BA Hons, PGCE, NPQH

Senior Assistant Head & DSL: Mrs K Heard, BA Hons, PGCE
Deputy Head (*Calendar/Compliance*): Mrs M Carter, BA, PGCE
Deputy Head (*Junior Academic and Whole School SenCo*): Miss R Hudson, BA Hons, PGCE, QTS
Director of Finance: Mrs S Whipp, BSC, CPFA
Director of Operations: James Stockford
Deputy Head (*Academic*): Mr A Atkinson, BA Hons, MA, PGCE, QTS
Assistant Head Pastoral Care (*Senior*): Mrs C Viggers, MA, BSc, PGCE, QTS
Assistant Head/Director of Music: Mrs J Powell, BA Hons, Dip Adv Studies RAM
Director of Communications: Mr B Monet, BFA
Director of Admissions: Mrs K French, BA Hons

Fees per term (2023–2024). £4,000–£7,125.

Cranford is a leading co-educational independent day school for boys and girls aged 3–18 years. It has an excellent reputation for providing its pupils with a balanced, all-round education within a warmly nurturing environment. Set in over 14 acres of rural South Oxfordshire, the small class sizes, close community and committed staff ensure each pupil is ably supported and challenged to achieve their full potential. The school was rated as 'Excellent' in all categories in its ISI Inspection of November 2022. "Pupils are highly motivated, have extremely positive attitudes to learning and are determined to make the most of the opportunities available to them at the school." ISI Inspection. The school recently opened a new co-ed Sixth Form Centre, with more than 20 A Level option choices and an extensive co-curricular programme.

At Cranford, the aim is to encourage pupils to achieve their full potential, becoming motivated, confident and happy individuals, recognising the importance of respect and support for others, but ready to seize life's opportunities.

The Early Years Foundation Stage (EYFS) encompasses Pre-School and Reception, catering for boys and girls aged 3–5 years. Pupils benefit from a large, Pre-School in a beautiful setting with plenty of green space for free-flow activities and Forest School outdoor learning. There are many links with Reception, which include swimming lessons and whole-school productions and activities.

The Junior School comprises Years 1 to 6. Juniors benefit from Senior School facilities and specialist subject teachers are used in a variety of disciplines. The school's all-inclusive approach sees all pupils taking part in competitive sports matches from Year 3 upwards. Lesson content is based on the National Curriculum, but supplemented to ensure pupils develop their own collaborative, reflective and reasoning skills and abilities. Results are excellent. Responsibility is offered at a young age through posts such as Junior Head Girl/Boy and team captains.

In the Senior School, pupils follow a common core curriculum, as well as an extensive range of extra-curricular opportunities. Academic ambition for each pupil is high and every child is supported in achieving to the very best of their ability. Pupils consistently achieve on average 60% 9–7 (A*–A) at GCSE demonstrating the consistent academic excellence for which the school is renowned. The exceptional value-added score of +1.3 indicates that pupils continue to achieve well over a grade above their nationally standardised baseline targets.

Pupils benefit from an excellent pastoral offering, key to which is a vibrant House System which encourages both a sense of community and leadership. On reaching Year 11, pupils enjoy further positions of responsibility. The school has extensive recreational and games fields. In winter, hockey, football and netball are played, and in summer, tennis, cricket and athletics. Swimming takes place on site. Dramatic, musical and dance productions are an important aspect of school life and all are encouraged to take part.

The new purpose-built Sixth Form Centre celebrated its first set of A Level results in summer 2022 with 70% of all grades awarded at A*–B and 42% A*/A. These inaugural set of marks from the newly opened Sixth Form demonstrate excellent academic and personal achievements and allowed for 95% of students to head off to their chosen university.

In addition to the extensive range of enrichment activities offered throughout the school, all pupils have the opportunity to join educational trips and excursions. For Senior pupils, Bronze and Silver levels of The Duke of Edinburgh's Award scheme are offered, in addition to far-flung expeditions with World Challenge. Opportunities for overseas travel are also offered through exchanges, ski and sports trips and choir tours. School transport operates over a wide area throughout both Berkshire and Oxfordshire.

Scholarships, bursaries and awards are offered for Year 7 and Year 12 entry points.

Charitable status. Cranford School is a Registered Charity, number 280883.

Cranmore

Epsom Road, West Horsley, Surrey KT24 6AT

Tel: 01483 280340
email: office@cranmore.org
website: www.cranmore.org

See full entry in the **IAPS** section, on **p. 644**.

Crescent School

Bawnmore Road, Bilton, Rugby, Warwickshire CV22 7QH

Tel: 01788 521595
email: admin@crescentschool.co.uk
website: www.crescentschool.co.uk
X/Twitter: @CrescentSchRug
Facebook: @cres.school
Instagram: @crescentschoolrugby

See full entry in the **IAPS** section, on **p. 645**.

Crosfields School

Shinfield Road, Reading, Berks RG2 9BL

Tel: 0118 9871810
email: admissions@crosfields.com
website: www.crosfields.com
X/Twitter: @WeAreCrosfields
Facebook: @CrosfieldsSchool
Instagram: @CrosfieldsSchool

See full entry in the **IAPS** section, on **p. 646**.

Cundall Manor School

Cundall, North Yorkshire YO61 2RW

Tel: 01423 360200
email: admissions@cundallmanor.org.uk
website: www.cundallmanorschool.com
X/Twitter: @CundallManor
Facebook: @CundallManor
Instagram: @CundallManor
LinkedIn: /cundall-manor-school

***Headmaster*: Mr Christopher James-Roll**, BSc Hons, MEd

Age Range. 2–16. Co-educational.
Number of Pupils. 350.

Cundall Manor School is a thriving independent co-educational boarding school, catering for 350 boys and girls from two to sixteen years of age. Set in 28 acres of beautiful grounds between Harrogate, Ripon and York, it is easily accessed from the A1(M) and A19.

Cundall Manor School blends the best traditions of honour, integrity and courtesy with up-to-the-minute teaching facilities and approaches. The school has developed a reputation for ensuring that each and every child feels happy, safe, supported and celebrated. Within this environment, children engage fully with the educational challenges and risks that maximise learning and achievement. The rural setting allows pupils to embrace their childhoods while the innovative and unique curriculum provides opportunity for all to develop the confidence, judgement and personal skills that will benefit their futures.

Children are encouraged to participate in a number of sports and events outside of the curriculum, including outward bound courses, travel, charity/community work, daily enrichment activities and extracurricular sports. While many children do achieve top standards and awards across academia, sports and music, competing and succeeding at area, county and national level, our aim is to ensure every child has the opportunity to participate in the full range of activities, whatever their level of ability and experience. We do this by cultivating a 'yes' mentality amongst our pupils, encouraging them to engage with the wider world and to think and act independently and without inhibition.

Fees per term (2023–2024).

Nursery: Full day 8.30 am–15.30 pm (excluding lunch) £40.

Reception–Year 2: Day £3,847, After-school care/prep 5–6 No charge.

Years 3 & 4: Day £6,138, Weekly Boarding £7,466 International Boarding £8,378.

Years 5–8: Day £6,369, Weekly Boarding £7,697; International Boarding £8,610.

Years 9–11: Day £6,466, Weekly Boarding £7,794, £8,687.

Charitable status. Cundall Manor Limited is a Registered Charity, number 529540.

The Daiglen School

68 Palmerston Road, Buckhurst Hill, Essex IG9 5LG

Tel: 020 8504 7108
email: admin@daiglenschool.co.uk
website: www.daiglenschool.co.uk
X/Twitter: @DaiglenSchool

Perstare et Praestare – Persevere and Excel

***Head Teacher*: Mrs P Dear**, BEd

Age Range. 3–11.

Number in School. 130.

Fees per term (2023–2024). £3,790–£4,295 sibling discount available. Extras: music tuition, trips.

The Daiglen School is a small preparatory school which provides a happy and secure environment for all pupils. Kindness to others is valued above all, and pupils are polite and considerate with each other as well as with adults. We have a strong sense of family and community, underpinned by warm supportive relationships and mutual respect, which ensures that all pupils are valued and given the chance to shine.

Confident children relish challenge and the school promotes a culture of excellence. We celebrate individual and group successes as children learn the importance of pursuing their ambitions with determination and perseverance. They are inspired to do well both by the infectious enthusiasm of their excellent teachers and by the example of older children who become their role models. Our pupils flourish in this environment and leave as caring, confident, articulate and well-mannered young people, fully prepared for the next stage in their journey through life. We are justifiably proud of our pupils' academic achievements, as well as those on the sports field and other areas, and a good proportion leave with scholarships to selective independent and state secondary schools.

Founded in 1916, The Daiglen School is rich in history and tradition. The school is built around an elegant Victorian house with much of its stained glass and cornices intact. Modern features include a purpose-built gymnasium/hall and art room. It is pleasantly situated on the borders of Epping Forest and is well served by public transport.

Inspection: The Daiglen School was inspected in June 2022. The full report is available to read on our website.

Choosing a school is arguably the most difficult decision you will make for your child, and one which will have the greatest consequences in his or her life. Most of our pupils come to Daiglen on personal recommendation from parents of past or present pupils. We encourage a close and mutually supportive partnership with parents. To find out more about us, you can visit our website or make arrangements to visit the school; you will receive a warm welcome.

Charitable status. The Daiglen School Trust Limited is a Registered Charity, number 273015.

Dallington School

8 Dallington Street, London EC1V 0BW

Tel: 020 7251 2284
email: admissions@dallingtonschool.co.uk
website: www.dallingtonschool.co.uk
Facebook: @Dallingtonschoollondon
Instagram: @dallington_school
LinkedIn: /company/dallington-school-london

Motto: *Value your own worth and understand the differences in others*

Chair of Governors: Cortina Butler & Fiona Naylor

***Head*: James Griffiths**

Senior leadership team:
James Griffiths, Victoria Highfield, Tina Saedi, Eileen Fletcher

Student numbers. 69.

Fees per term (2023–2024). £4,420–£5,560.

Admission. Non-selective.

Curriculum. Enhanced British Curriculum.

Extracurricular activities. Lego robotics, science, animation, drama, cookery, football, art, instrumental lessons.

The Dixie Grammar School

Market Bosworth, Leicestershire CV13 0LE

Tel: 01455 292244
email: info@dixie.org.uk
website: www.dixie.org.uk
X/Twitter: @DixieGrammar
Facebook: @the.dixie.grammar
Instagram: @dixie_grammar

***Headmaster*: Mr Richard J Lynn,** BA Cardiff

Age Range. 3–18.

Number in School. 475.

Fees per term (2023–2024). Reception, Years 1 and 2 £3,680, Years 3 to 5 £4,175, Year 6 to Sixth Form £4,995. Scholarships, Bursaries, Vouchers/Government Funding, Monthly Payment Scheme available.

The earliest records we have of the School's existence date from 1320, but the School gained its present name when it was re-founded in 1601 under the will of an Elizabethan merchant and Lord Mayor of London, Sir Wolstan Dixie.

The most distinguished of the School's former pupils is Thomas Hooker, founder of Hartford, Connecticut, and Father of American Democracy. The best known of its teachers is undoubtedly Dr Johnson, moralist, poet and author of the famous dictionary, who taught at the School in the mid-eighteenth century.

The main building of today's School was built in 1828 and faces the historic market square of Market Bosworth, making a distinctive landmark. However, in 1969 the School was closed, as new, much larger comprehensive schools found favour.

It was to revive the best aspects of the grammar school tradition that the Leicestershire Independent Educational Trust was formed in 1983, and four years later the School was reopened as a selective, independent, day school for boys and girls of all backgrounds between the ages of 10 and 18. Three years later our Junior School opened, moving to its present premises, Temple Hall in Wellsborough, in 2001, where we have The Pippins Nursery.

The emphasis remains the same as it ever was: to provide an excellent academic education that will be of lasting value to our children as they face the challenges of the future.

Both schools are selective and have academic achievement as their central aim. Music, drama, sport and service are also an integral part of the education offered. Both schools have an interdenominational Christian basis. The relative smallness of the schools ensures that they combine great friendliness with excellent discipline, providing a secure and well-ordered framework in which children can confidently achieve their full potential. We are ambitious for each of them.

The Grammar School offers academic, music, art, sports and sixth form scholarships.

Charitable status. The Leicestershire Independent Educational Trust is a Registered Charity, number 514407.

DLD College London
Abbey DLD Group

199 Westminster Bridge Road, London SE1 7FX

Tel: 020 7935 8411
email: dld@dld.org
website: www.dldcollege.co.uk
X/Twitter: @DLDcollege
Facebook: @DLDcollege
Instagram: @dldcollege
LinkedIn: /company/dldcollegelondon

***Principal*: Mr Irfan Latif,** BSc Hons, PGCE, FRSA, FRSC

Age Range. 13+ Co-educational.

Number of Pupils. 402 Day and Boarding.

Fees per annum (2023–2024). £27,300.

DLD College London is a co-educational, independent day and boarding school of diverse thinking and influences. Housed in a purpose-built, futuristic building with cutting-edge facilities and with 5* urban boarding on-site, it sits opposite the Houses of Parliament on the vibrant South Bank. London is very much our classroom!

With a caring, supportive and student-focused environment, our students benefit from amazing learning and teaching opportunities with many progressing to join some of the finest universities. Our multi-award-winning provision is available to students aged 13–19.

In addition to a number of significant national award wins, DLD College London is also proud to be named by The Good Schools Guide, Tatler and Talk Education as one of the top schools in the UK. DLD is a distinctive, multi-award-winning school on the South Bank with many advantage points which include:

- developing confident and independent young people
- first-class teaching and award-winning wellbeing support
- expert university guidance with destinations including Oxbridge and Russell Group universities
- unique learning opportunities including the Urban Schools Project for Year 9
- having London as our classroom
- innovative 5* boarding uniquely located directly above the school.

Much like the city that we call home, DLD College London is a fusion of the historic and the modern. Our history dates back to 1931, and we still hold close traditional values such as academic rigour, discipline, and exam success. We have combined these values with a focus on student wellbeing and personal development which means that DLD graduates are well prepared for life after college.

As central London's only purpose-built on-campus boarding school, studying at DLD puts you in the heart of the city. Students wake up to the iconic London skyline, and our home on the South Bank puts some of London's best leisure, cultural and entertainment experiences on your doorstep. Our onsite facilities include:

- over 200 secure, ensuite student bedrooms above the school
- a dedicated wellbeing centre
- a Global Kitchen, including a Grumpy Mule Coffee franchise
- six high-specification laboratories
- custom-built E-sports lab
- art, photography and media studios, plus a state-of-the-art drama studio
- over 40, fully air-conditioned classrooms
- learning hub, digital eHub, study and ICT facilities
- wellbeing garden and outdoor basketball court
- access to swimming pool, sauna and gymnasium facilities.

Our extensive co-curricular programme includes over 50 activities for students to join. At DLD we encourage students to get involved in co-curricular activities to further enrich their wider learning and personal development, as well as helping to improve the quality of their UCAS personal statement and CV in the future. After school and weekend clubs make the most of our amazing location in central London while ensuring that students remain safe and focused on their studies.

Downsend School

Cognita Schools Group

1 Leatherhead Road, Leatherhead, Surrey KT22 8TJ

Tel: General 01372 372197
Admissions 01372 372311
email: admissions@downsend.co.uk
website: www.downsend.co.uk
X/Twitter: @DownsendSchool
Facebook: @DownsendSchool
Instagram: @downsendschoolsurrey
LinkedIn: /company/downsend-school

See full entry in the **IAPS** section, on **p. 654**.

Duke of Kent School

Peaslake Road, Ewhurst, Surrey GU6 7NS

Tel: 01483 277313
email: office@dokschool.org
website: www.dukeofkentschool.org.uk
X/Twitter: @DoKSchool
Facebook: @Duke-of-Kent-School/100063860978283
Instagram: @dukeofkentschool

Chairman of the Governing Body: Mr Richard Brocksom

***Head*: Mrs Sue Knox**, BA Hons UCNW, MBA Cranfield, Grad DipEd & MEdLead Macquarie University Sydney

Age range. 3–16.

Number of pupils. 330.

Set in inspirational grounds high in the Surrey Hills, surrounded by forest land, Duke of Kent School provides an excellent co-educational option for pupils from 3 to 16 years. Coming from Guildford, Horsham, Dorking and surrounding local villages, many pupils use the School minibus service.

Extended day arrangements for those pupils who wish to arrive before or stay beyond the end of lessons (7.30 am to 7.30 pm) provide families with exceptional flexibility. At the end of the School day, pupils can choose to complete their homework at School under supervision or at home, and can also choose from a varied programme of sport, academic and social activities.

The small size of the School enables us to know our pupils very well and to ensure that all pupils can reach their potential. All pupils receive the appropriate combination of academic challenge and support to enable them to achieve. A Duke of Kent School pupil is expected to contribute and participate to the very best of their ability, take an active role in community life and take responsibility for their learning. Our able and committed teaching and support staff work in partnership with pupils and their families. The expectation is that each pupil will strive to achieve a string of 'personal bests': in the classroom, on the sports field, in personal development, in exploring the arts and in a wide range of activities. We focus on each child's attitude to learning in order to ensure that they are fully equipped to make maximum progress. Teaching and learning is supported by a well-established 1–1 iPad and Chromebook programme, with all pupils encouraged to learn to touch type.

Pupils are prepared for GCSE/IGCSE examinations in the context of a curriculum which aims to take pupils above and beyond exam preparation. There is a focus throughout the School of encouraging pupils to adopt a growth mindset in order to become successful learners. Building on the work of our Prep School in which Creative Curriculum provides excellent stretch and challenge for pupils, our rigorous GCSE programme prepares pupils for A Level and university study and sparks what may be lifelong intellectual passions. Learning beyond the classroom, whether on educational visits or through outdoor learning on site, is a crucial aspect of our pupils' experience. Personal development receives close attention. Our pupils develop confidence and self-esteem from opportunities to lead and to serve. Kindness is expected and encouraged from pupils of all ages.

The School maintains a busy fixtures calendar at all ages. We have extensive playing fields, an all-weather astroturf, all-weather tennis courts, a swimming pool and a full-sized sports hall. More than half of our pupils are learning a musical instrument. Music and Drama activities take place in a purpose-built Performing Arts Hall with facilities for Music Technology. The quality of Art on display and in production is a particular strength of the School.

In 2023, our Year 11 cohort achieved an overall pass rate of 98% with a commendable 92% of our pupils gaining at least one grade 7. In recent years our pupils have gone on to successful courses of further study at day schools, boarding schools and colleges, both locally and further afield.

Prospective pupils are invited to attend a visit day during which they will be interviewed by the Head or another senior member of staff, and will take a range of cognitive tests (CAT4). No preparation is required for our admissions testing. We are looking for evidence of enthusiasm and willingness to get fully involved in our lively community.

Fees per term (2023–2024). £2,820–£7,420.

Charitable status. The Duke of Kent School is a Registered Charity, number 1064183.

Dwight School London

6 Friern Barnet Lane, London N11 3LX

Tel: 020 8920 0600
email: admissions@dwightlondon.org
website: www.dwightlondon.org
X/Twitter: @DwightSchoolUK
Facebook: @Dwight-School-London
Instagram: @Dwight-School-London
LinkedIn: /dwight-school-london

***Head of School*: Chris Beddows**

Junior School Principal: Matt Parkin
Senior School Principal: William Bowry

Age Range. 2–18.

Number in School. 284 Boys and Girls.

Fees per term (2023–2024). Nursery fees can be viewed on our website. Reception–Year 2 £6,550, Years 3–6 £7,000, Years 7–11 £8,075, Years 12 & 13 £9,650.

Dwight School London is part of a network of international schools in New York, Seoul, Shanghai, and Dubai, as well as Dwight Global Online School. Each Dwight School shares the same commitment to igniting the spark of genius in every child. No matter where in the world students attend Dwight, they are inspired to find their passions and receive the same high-quality IB education.

Being part of a global network affords students numerous benefits and countless opportunities. Travel and exchange programs, cross-campus curricular and creative collaborations, online learning programs, international athletic competitions, and global leadership conferences all foster the development of global citizens.

We are truly international with more than 50 nationalities represented at Dwight!

Our learners are proud to come from diverse backgrounds; they celebrate and learn from each others' perspectives, and they take pride in taking action to make a better world.

Our open-minded approach that values diversity and innovation is underpinned by the academically rigorous International Baccalaureate programmes that open pathways to the top universities across the globe. Our students are critical and creative thinkers, empowered by inquiry-led learning and an expectation that they will be independent learners who create meaning from their experiences.

IB Programmes

We offer the following programmes:

The Primary Years Programme (IBPYP) – ages 2 to 11
The Middle Years Programme (IBMYP) – ages 11 to 16
The Diploma Programme (IBDP) – ages 16 to 18

To learn about the benefits of the IB Curriculum visit www.dwightlondon.org/theib

Mission and Pillars

Through the academic breadth and depth of the International Baccalaureate programmes, Dwight London nurtures confident, compassionate young people who influence the future.

Our students thrive in a curriculum rooted in our three educational pillars:

Personalised learning: an education just for the student

Dwight School London prides itself on really getting to know each of our students and their families. We shape students' education around them: how they best learn, where their skills lie, what sparks their interest, and where we can best help them.

Community: earn your place in the wider world

Our students are best placed to make a positive difference: to their school, to their neighbours and the world beyond. For this, they need more than academic learning. We develop the aptitudes our students will need, through local and global projects, as well as joint ventures with the world-wide family of Dwight schools.

Global vision: for the future global citizen

With students representing the UK and more than 50 other nations, Dwight London is a culturally and socially rich and diverse school. We are committed to developing confident, compassionate, intellectually mature young people who will be a force for good across the world.

Our vision is to produce students who are inquiring, knowledgeable and caring, while fostering their academic growth. Dwight School London prepares students to move on to further education, to be active, and be desirable citizens and learners gaining places at top universities around the world.

Eaton Square Prep School

55–57 Eccleston Square, Pimlico, London SW1V 1PH

Tel: 0207 225 3131
email: registrar@eatonsquareschools.com
website: www.eatonsquareschools.com
X/Twitter: @EatonSquareSch
Instagram: @eatonsquareprepschool
LinkedIn: /company/eaton-square-school

See full entry in the **IAPS** section, on **p. 662**.

Egerton Rothesay School

Durrants Lane, Berkhamsted, Herts HP4 3UJ
Tel: 01442 865275
email: admin.dl@eger-roth.co.uk
website: www.eger-roth.co.uk

A School with a Difference

***Headteacher*: Mr Colin Parker**, BSc Hons, Dip Ed, PGCE, CMath

Age Range. 6–19 years: Poplar 6–11 years; Senior School 11–16 years; Sixth Form 16–19 years.

Number in School. 128 boys, 40 girls.

Fees per term (2023–2024). £6,547–£9,316 (lunches included).

ERS aims to provide an exciting and relevant educational experience for pupils who need that little bit more support from their school, whilst studying a mainstream curriculum.

It focuses especially on students who have found, or would find, it difficult to make progress and succeed within another school – perhaps because of an earlier, negative, educational experience or perhaps because of a specific learning difficulty, such as dyslexia or dyspraxia, a speech and language difficulty or an autistic spectrum condition. If your child has other educational difficulties the school may also be able to help with these.

Children come with a variety of learning styles and use is made of a wide range of teaching strategies in order to match these. The school provides additional levels of support both in the classroom and on an individual basis, varying to suit the need of the child. Throughout the school children are taught in small classes to match their need for support, to the level of teaching and support staff provided. The team of therapists includes Speech and Language, Occupational Therapy, Social Emotional Development and visiting physiotherapists. Our specialist teaching team provide individual lessons in literacy and numeracy.

The Sixth Form provides for students who continue to mature beyond the age of 16 and require an additional amount of support and time in order to enable them to transfer successfully into a further education establishment or employment. The school has developed both one and two year educational programmes within a high-quality, secure and supportive environment, in which students are able to continue to mature, develop and learn whilst studying for additional examinations including GCSE, BTEC, Foundation and ASDAN awards. Examination results enable pupils to enter colleges and sixth forms in both state and independent schools to continue their education before university entrance, if appropriate.

Every child at Egerton Rothesay is seen as a unique person and an individual student. The school aims to make an excellent contribution into the life of each one ensuring that they can be supported in the way that they personally need to maximise their individual learning potential.

The school wants more than just to deliver a curriculum and has a learning skills approach throughout the school – aiming to prepare students not just for school and exams but for life in today's complex society and an ever changing world of work.

A child can often be able and talented in one aspect of the curriculum, yet find it difficult to make good progress in another. Some students will need support for the duration of their time in school, whilst others may only need a short amount of support to address a specific problem or to build confidence.

All activities takes place within an environment offering exceptional pastoral care and spiritual development that is driven and informed by the school's Christian foundation and its Chaplaincy team.

Transport: Egerton Rothesay is also more than just a local school – students travel to the school from all directions, many using the comprehensive bus service that the school runs over a 35-mile radius.

If you think this may be the right type of school for your child you can obtain more information from the Registrar on 01442 877060 or visit the website at www.eger-roth.co.uk.

Fairfield School

Fairfield Way, Backwell, Bristol BS48 3PD
Tel: 01275 462743
email: bursar@fairfieldschool.org.uk
website: fairfield.school
X/Twitter: @fairfieldpneu
Facebook: @fairfieldschoolbackwell
Instagram: @fairfieldpneu

***Headteacher*: Mrs Lesley Barton**, BA Hons, PGCE

Age Range. 2–11.

Number in School. 64 Boys, 55 Girls.

Fees per term (2023–2024). Lambs Nursery from £64.20 per day, Upper Nursery from £56.45 per day; Reception, Years 1–2 £3,200; Years 3–6 £3,525.

Fairfield is an independent day school for boys and girls aged 2–11. The school was founded in 1935 and aims to provide a broad, traditional education. We encourage each child to maximise his or her potential through creating a family ethos in which children feel happy, secure and valued. A fundamental aspect of our ethos is our commitment to small classes, usually of 18–20. Fairfield offers a broad and balanced curriculum, informed by the National Curriculum. Teachers and visiting coaches provide a wide range of extracurricular lessons including music, dance, sport, drama and creative activities. Pupils are prepared for entry into all local independent senior schools as well as for the local maintained sector schools.

For further details please apply to the Facilities Bursar.

Charitable status. Fairfield PNEU School (Backwell) Limited is a Registered Charity, number 310215.

Fairley House School

Junior Department:
218–220 Lambeth Road, London SE1 7JY
Tel: 020 7976 5456
email: junior@fairleyhouse.org.uk

Senior Department:
30 Causton Street, London SW1P 4AU
Tel: 020 7976 5456
email: senior@fairleyhouse.org.uk

website: www.fairleyhouse.org.uk

Head of School: **Michael Taylor**, BA Hons, PGCE, FRGS

Age Range. 6–16.

Number of Pupils. Day: 134 Boys, 78 Girls.

Fees per term (2023–2024). £12,413.

We are London's leading day school for children with specific learning differences specialising in the support of children with dyslexia, dyspraxia and dyscalculia. We have transformed the lives of hundreds of families since opening in 1982 and remain at the forefront of the latest in SpLD knowledge and provision.

Our deep expertise is core to Fairley House and led to the creation of our magic formula we know works from Day 1. Our flexible approach and small class sizes allow us to see each child as an individual, so we can tailor their learning experience. When one approach isn't working, we change and adapt until we are able to achieve progress and remove their barriers to learning.

The provision of on-site Speech and Language Therapy (SLT) and Occupational Therapy (OT) and an in-house Educational Psychologist (EP) is key as it is our transdisciplinary approach which truly differentiates us from mainstream schools.

Our specialist teachers work together with subject teachers to implement multisensory teaching across subjects, applying our own formulated frameworks for everything from emotional regulation to memory.

We identify learning gaps to be plugged and regularly provide opportunities for re-learning. We understand not all brains are wired the same, so we adapt our teaching for the different neural pathways of each child.

This focus on the needs of each individual child is integral to helping them regain their confidence in a learning environment. Undoubtedly this is enhanced by the kinship they feel by being with like-minded children which is cultivated through collaborative work, co-curricular opportunities and after school clubs.

Importantly, we continually monitor and track progress to steer development and boost learning outcomes. As a result we often find children may only need a year or two at Fairley House to rebuild their skills and confidence to subsequently re-enter mainstream education.

And when we don't find the right tools and methods, we develop our own! That pioneering spirit is what has kept Fairley House at the forefront of SpLD education for over forty years.

From humble beginnings in the living room of our founder Daphne Hamilton-Fairley, Fairley House has expanded over the years to now offer a first-class education across Key Stages 2, 3 and 4 with our tailored GCSE programme. We are thrilled with the consistently fantastic results our pupils achieve with many going onto success in fields as diverse as jewellery design and film production. It is our guiding mission that children with speech and language differences are not defined or limited by their learning challenges, but are inspired and empowered to realise their ambitions and reach their full potential.

Falkner House

Girls' School:
19 Brechin Place, London SW7 4QB
Tel: 020 7373 4501
email: office@falknerhouse.co.uk

Boys' School:
20 Penywern Road, London SW5 9SU
Tel: 020 7373 2340
email: office20pr@falknerhouse.co.uk
website: www.falknerhouse.co.uk

Principal: **Mrs Anita Griggs**, BA Hons, PGCE

Headmistress, Girls' School: Mrs Flavia Rogers, BA Hons, PGCE

Headmistress, Boys' School: Mrs Eleanor Dixon, MA Cantab

Age Range. Girls 4–11, Boys 4–11, Co-educational Nursery (ages 3–4).

Number of Pupils. Girls: 188. Boys: 160 (including nursery children).

Fees per term (2023–2024) Girls' School: £7,760; Boys' School: £7,910; Nursery: £3,880.

Girls' School. The development of self-confidence and happiness are seen as key goals at Falkner House. A family feeling underpins the busy yet friendly environment and as a result, pupils have an engaging openness, intellectual curiosity and courtesy beyond their years. "We like the girls to be engaged and driven," says Mrs Rogers, "but not to be sassy or precocious." Academic success comes with this positive atmosphere and pupils achieve notable success at 11+ to the very top day and boarding schools.

Excellent facilities include a science laboratory, art room, library and playground. State-of-the-art IT facilities including individual iPads from Year 4 are integrated into the curriculum. A strong musical tradition lies alongside an excellent sporting record. Pre/post school care is offered, as well as a wide range of after-school activities.

Entrance at 4+ by assessment.

Boys' School. The Boys' School started on a separate site nearby in September 2017, with the same ethos and values as the Girls' School.

Falkner House offers a unique environment in which the boys can flourish and are given the opportunity and confidence to excel. The Falkner House teachers are undoubtedly unique in how they know, nurture and genuinely value the boys as individuals. Small but mighty, Falkner House boys are confident without being macho. They show grit and determination, and are good sports at all times. The years children spend at school are few and precious. The process of teaching and learning is at the heart of the school, and the very reason for its existence.

Excellent facilities include an art room, library and playground – a hardworking space that the school is particularly proud of given its central London location. It helps the boys learn, both directly and indirectly. State-of-the-art IT facilities including individual iPads from Year 4 are integrated into the curriculum. A strong musical tradition lies alongside an excellent sporting record. Pre/post school care is offered, as well as a wide range of after-school activities.

Entrance is at 4+ by assessment.

Falkner House Nursery caters for boys and girls aged 3–4 years. Children thrive in a stimulating atmosphere under the care of professional and thoughtful teachers. Children are encouraged to be curious, to experiment and to learn through play. Specialist staff teach subjects such as music and PE to enrich the nursery curriculum.

Entrance at rising 3 is by date of registration. Registrations accepted within nine months of birth.

Faraday Prep School

Old Gate House, 7 Trinity Buoy Wharf, London E14 0FH

Tel: 020 7719 9342
020 8965 7374 (Admissions)
email: admissions@faradayschool.co.uk
head@faradayschool.co.uk
website: www.faradayschool.co.uk

Head Teacher: **Lucas Motion**

Age Range. 4–11 Co-educational.
Number of Pupils. 102.
Fees per term (2023–2024). £4,653.

Founded in 2009, Faraday Prep School offers inspirational learning in an inspirational setting. A happy, vibrant and diverse independent primary school in East London, the school's historic and artistic riverside location, provides a magical environment and access to a stimulating, creative community that offers exciting learning opportunities.

We give every child a first-class education rooted in a creative curriculum, with small classes, quality teaching and a personal approach in a caring and kind environment.

In these formative years our aim is to inspire a love of learning and that the desire to explore, grow and create will stay with our pupils for life. We place a strong focus on literacy and numeracy, with a targeted approach that enables each child to progress at their own level.

Our lessons stretch, challenge and engage pupils of all abilities and interests. We present children with the great literature, music and works of art to help them acquire an increased understanding of the world in which they live and build a thorough understanding of knowledge in each subject. As such, our curriculum is broad and stimulating, and includes specialist teaching in French, Music, Drama and Physical Education.

Children join our Reception class in their fifth year and leave for senior school at the age of eleven. The school day runs from 8.45am until 3.30pm, with our private buses running before and after school from a range of East London locations. We support busy parents by welcoming children from 8.15am and by offering after-school care until 5.30pm each day, with a wide range of extra-curricular activities on offer from gardening to robotics.

Entry into Reception is non-selective and based on the date the completed registration form is returned to our Registrar, with siblings given priority. Entry higher up the school is by interview and informal assessment in the classroom. We offer regular open days and welcome private tours.

Faraday was awarded 'Excellent' in all areas by the ISI in November 2020.

Farnborough Hill

Farnborough Road, Farnborough, Hampshire GU14 8AT

Tel: 01252 545197
email: admissions@farnborough-hill.org
website: farnborough-hill.org
X/Twitter: @FarnboroughHill
Facebook: @Farnborough-Hill
Instagram: @farnborough.hill
LinkedIn: /company/farnborough-hill

See full entry in the **GSA** section, on **p. 432**.

Forest Park Preparatory School
Bellevue Education

Lauriston House, 27 Oakfield, Sale, Cheshire M33 6NB

Tel: 0161 973 4835
email: post@forestparkprep.co.uk
website: www.forestparkprep.co.uk
X/Twitter: @ForestParkPrep
Facebook: @forestpark
Instagram: @forestparkprepschool

Headteacher: **Mr Nick Tucker**, BEd Hons Prim Ed, MA Ed Leadership & Mgt

Age Range. 3–11.
Number in School. 84 Day Boys, 72 Day Girls.
Fees per term (2023–2024). £2,760–£2,950.

Forest Park occupies a pleasant site in a quiet road surprisingly close to the centre of Sale, easily accessible from motorways and surrounding areas.

The school aims to discover and develop each child's particular abilities by offering a varied curriculum in a stimulating and happy atmosphere. Forest Park has a good pupil to teacher ratio and offers a wide range of subjects with priority given to the traditional disciplines of English, mathematics and science. Pupils from three years of age are taught information technology by specialist staff. Swimming is taught from the age of five and games offered are football, cricket, netball, tennis and hockey. Pupils are taught Spanish from Pre-Prep. Older children have the opportunity to enjoy residential and activity trips to broaden their knowledge and develop self-confidence.

The confidence and social ease one expects of a private education is a product of the school. Our aim is to develop skills and knowledge through a habit of hard work in a secure and happy environment within a disciplined framework. The school prepares pupils for all independent grammar school examinations and has an excellent record in this respect.

The school prides itself on strong links and communication with a most supportive Parents' Association.

Gad's Hill School

Higham, Rochester, Kent ME3 7PA
Tel: 01474 822366
email: admissions@gadshillschool.org
website: www.gadshill.org
X/Twitter: @GadsHillSchool
Facebook: @GadsHillSchoolOfficial
Instagram: @gadshillschoolofficial

***Headmaster*: Mr Paul Savage**, BA Hons, PGCE

Age Range. Co-educational 3–16.

Number in School. 380.

Fees per term (2023–2024). Spring Term £3,944–£5,720.

Gad's Hill School is set in the expansive and beautiful grounds of the former, family home of Charles Dickens in the historic village of Higham, just on the outskirts of Rochester, Kent.

Our wonderfully happy and vibrant independent day school educates girls and boys aged 3–16 years in the Lower and Upper School. The site boasts modern facilities, courtesy of its main building, which include a theatre, refectory and sports hall, while also retaining the famous literary heritage of the 18th Century Grade I Listed Gad's Hill Place, where Dickens lived for the final 14 years of his life, and many of the traditions established since its foundation as a school in 1924.

Pupils are taught in classes of no more than 20 and benefit from a friendly and purposeful learning environment where teachers know and cater for each child as an individual across an exciting and engaging curriculum. This allows teachers greater knowledge of pupils' individual strengths, from Nursery to GCSE. The curriculum values the creative and practical alongside the more traditionally academic: an innovative Combined Cadet Force programme, for example, results in qualifications including Institute of Leadership and Management, BTEC, Duke of Edinburgh and First Aid awards delivering vital life skills. Indeed, the School's ethos is that the development of self-confidence, resilience, leadership and teamwork is essential for successful adulthood.

We are different from other schools and are rightly proud of this. We stand for traditional values, self-respect, self-discipline and have a strong sense of friendship, family and community spirit. Through the school's curriculum, children learn how to look after their own wellbeing and develop compassion for the wider world. Our School is a caring and compassionate environment offering outstanding pastoral care which encourages the children to give their best.

Enrichment activities throughout Gad's Hill include London Academy of Music and Dramatic Art (LAMDA) courses, fencing, rock climbing, karate, air rifle, dance, singing and instrumental music lessons. Our younger pupils make wonderful use of the on-site Forest School, a child-centred, hands-on learning experience in a beautiful natural setting.

Gad's Hill provides bus services throughout the surrounding area and to South East London and offers wraparound care from 7.30am–6pm to support working parents of Lower School-aged children.

Gatehouse School

Sewardstone Road, Victoria Park, London E2 9JG
Tel: 020 8980 2978
email: admin@gatehouseschool.co.uk
website: www.gatehouseschool.co.uk
X/Twitter: @GatehouseSch
Facebook: @GatehouseSch

See full entry in the **IAPS** section, on **p. 677**.

Gidea Park Preparatory School and Nursery

2 Balgores Lane, Gidea Park, Romford, Essex RM2 5JR
Tel: 01708 740381
email: office@gideaparkprep.co.uk
website: www.gideaparkprep.co.uk
Facebook: @gideaparkcollege

***Headmaster*: Mr Callum Douglas**, BA Hons, PGCE

Age range. 2–11 Co-educational.

Number in School. 110 Day Pupils.

Fees per term (2023–2024). £4,000.

Gidea Park Preparatory School and Nursery is a very special school. Founded in 1917 we have been educating, nurturing and challenging children for over 100 years. Children are at the heart of everything we do; our small classes and school environment truly allow us to know our pupils as individuals and tailor our teaching and curriculum accordingly. We have high expectations of our pupils' academic progress and personal development and work closely with our parents to ensure that all our pupils get the very most from their time with us.

The school has an enviable academic record and a long tradition of sending pupils to grammar and selective independent schools. But there is a great deal more to Gidea Park Prep than that. We believe that happy children make better progress and to achieve this children need to be understood, listened to and valued.

The School has been part of the Inspired Learning Group since 2020 and has seen significant investment since then. All pupils from Reception to Year 6 have the use of 1:1 iPad devices and a new nursery was opened in January 2022, which now accepts pupils from age 2, and is a 51-week-a-year setting.

The Grange School

Bradburns Lane, Hartford, Northwich, Cheshire CW8 1LU

Tel: 01606 539039
email: office@grange.org.uk
website: www.grange.org.uk
X/Twitter: @Grange_Cheshire
Facebook: @GrangeCheshire
Instagram: @Grange_Cheshire
LinkedIn: /the-grange-school

See full entry in the **HMC** section, on **p. 134**.

Grantham Preparatory International School
An IES School

Gorse Lane, Grantham, Lincolnshire NG31 7UF

Tel: 01476 593293
email: contact.grantham@iesmail.com
website: www.tgps.co.uk
X/Twitter: @tgps_school
Facebook: @GranthamPrep

***Head*: Mrs Kathryn Korcz**, BSc Hons, CertEd

Age range. 3–11 Co-educational.
Number of pupils. 115.
Fees per term (2023–2024). £3,110–£3,762.

The Grantham Preparatory International School is a non-denominational independent day school for boys and girls between the ages of three and eleven. The school was established in 1981 and moved to a modern purpose-built building in 1987. It is set in nearly four acres of grounds and playing fields and, being close to the A1, it is easily accessible.

The school is owned by International Education Systems. IES is a network of ten schools (three in South Africa, two in the UK, one in Hungary, one in the United States, one in Panama and one in Italy). IES's mission is to provide excellence in education provision within an international perspective. Here at The Grantham Preparatory International School we are committed to excellence in all areas of the curriculum, and we aim to provide the best for all our children in a happy family environment. We are now delighted to be a member of the ISA family after being accredited in November 2011.

We received an ISI inspection in January 2023 and were found to be 'Excellent in all areas'.

Our children are prepared for entrance examinations to Independent senior schools and for Grammar school selection examinations. Children benefit from many specialist teachers who bring their own enthusiasm and knowledge to a particular subject. This ensures high academic standards and our broad and balanced curriculum enables our children to experience sport, art, music and drama and have the opportunity to pursue and develop their strengths, achieving their full potential. Specialist music teachers provide individual tuition in a wide variety of instruments.

The school wind band, choir and recital groups continue to delight audiences with their stunning performances. The school has been awarded the Platinum Award for Sport for five years in succession as well as other awards for Sport.

Learning is fun in our Early Years Foundation Unit. In our care, children thrive and make excellent progress in all areas of learning and development.

We believe that every child is an important unique individual that should be valued and nurtured during their time with us. We expect our children to leave us at age 11 as independent, confident individuals, tolerant of others and well prepared for the next stage of their education.

Greenbank Preparatory School and Day Nursery

Heathbank Road, Cheadle Hulme, Cheshire SK8 6HU

Tel: 0161 485 3724
email: office@greenbankschool.co.uk
website: www.greenbankschool.co.uk
Facebook: @Greenbank-Preparatory-School

***Headteacher*: Mr Malcolm Johnson**

Age Range. 6 months–11 years.
Number in School. Day: 64 Boys, 60 Girls. Daycare: 109.

Fees per term (2023–2024). £3,550 including lunches from Reception to Year Six.

Greenbank is an independent co-educational school for pupils aged three to eleven years. A separate Nursery, open fifty weeks of the year, cares for babies and children from six months to four years old.

Greenbank School was founded in 1951 by Karl and Linda Orsborn. Since 1971 the School has been administered by an Educational Trust and is registered with the Department for Education.

Greenbank is situated within extensive grounds, comprises a mixture of traditional and modern buildings including an IT Suite and Library, separate play areas for Foundation, Infant and Junior children, playing fields with a cricket pavilion, an Astroturf area and netball court. 2009 saw the opening of state-of-the-art Science, Art and Music classrooms within a new administration building. Further developments in 2012 included a new Pre-school offering greater flexibility to parents.

The school day begins at 8.40am and ends at 3.30pm, however we provide wrap-around care from 7.30am until 6.00pm. The school also runs activity and sports clubs in the holidays.

Through its varied curricular and extracurricular activities the School provides pupils with the opportunity of expanding their natural abilities to the full. Music, drama, sport, computing and educational visits are some of the activities which play their part in providing a well-rounded programme of education. We strive to meet the social, emotional and intellectual needs of all pupils and the success of this philosophy is proven by the consistently outstanding examination results throughout the school, particularly at age eleven.

Charitable status. Greenbank School Limited is a Registered Charity, number 525930.

Greenfields Independent Day & Boarding School

Priory Road, Forest Row, East Sussex RH18 5JD

Tel: 01342 822189
email: admissions@greenfieldsschool.com
website: www.greenfieldsschool.com
Facebook: @greenfieldsIndependentschool
Instagram: @greenfieldsindependentschool

Executive Head: **Jeff Smith**, BSc Eng, AMIMechEng

Age Range. 3–18.

Number in School. Day: 100 Boys, 77 Girls. Boarding: 25 Boys, 13 Girls.

Tuition Fees per term (2023–2024). Day: £1,400–£4,800, Boarding: (Full) £4,500, (5 Nights) £3,784 (added to tuition fee) ESL/EFL: £2,000–£5,167. Fees are reviewed annually.

Greenfields Independent Day and Boarding School is an Independent Schools Association school with a Preschool and a Reception class (forming the Early Years Foundation Stage), an Infant and Junior School, and a Senior School including Sixth Form and long and short-term (6 Month) English as a Second/Foreign Language courses.

Students aged 3 to 18 receive an all-round education for life, using the Cambridge and National Curriculum from Infants upwards. Greenfields utilises a unique study method that ensures children can apply what they learn for use in life – not just to pass examinations (please see our website for a full explanation). It has a strong moral code and zero tolerance for bullying, drugs, smoking and alcohol. Maximum to a class in Infants and Juniors, 16 and in Seniors, 20.

Situated on beautiful grounds, with its adventure playground backing onto the Ashdown Forest itself, the school is a safe and inspirational place to learn. We have also just acquired 19 more acres of ground in which to extend our sports facilities.

The main difference between Greenfields and other schools is the unique teaching method it uses. This method isolates the barriers preventing or hindering a child from learning and then provides precise tools to deal with them. Its use allows any child of any ability to learn anything. We are the only school in the UK licensed by Applied Scholastics International to use this amazing Study Technology.

There is a high level of open communication between students and staff which the school takes pride in and parents have full access to keep up with their child's progress via the Parent Portal.

Every student is individually programmed and targeted to ensure each one achieves the success they are capable of. No student is left behind or held back from studying more advanced work if needed.

The classes are small and an excellent curriculum using the Cambridge and National framework, providing core subjects and peripheral studies, is available up to GCSE and Advanced Levels.

A "Qualifications" department exists to check that students have fully understood each step of their studies, and also provides extra help for any student having any trouble in class. There is also a Student Consultant who helps to resolve any personal problems the student may have.

Entry is by assessments (not entry tests – Greenfields is non-selective) for literacy, science and numeracy. There is a pre-entry section for those who need a short programme to catch up and be ready to join their correct class.

Trains take under an hour from London to East Grinstead, which is a ten-minute car ride from the school. Gatwick Airport is a twenty-minute car ride away.

Charitable status. Greenfields Educational Trust is a Registered Charity, number 287037. The object for which the trust is established is the advancement of education.

The Gregg Preparatory School

17–19 Winn Road, Portswood, Southampton SO17 1EJ

Tel: 023 8055 7352
email: office@thegreggprep.org
website: www.thegreggprep.org
Facebook: @thegreggprep
Instagram: @thegreggprep

Chair of Board of Trustees: Mrs J Preston

***Head Teacher*: Mr Matt Pascoe**, BA Hons, PGCE

Age Range. 4–11 Co-educational.

Number of Pupils. 100.

Fees per term (2023–2024). £3,342 (Lunch £210).

The Gregg Preparatory School is a small school, on a pleasant, urban road in central Southampton, close to the university. It exists to make *the most of Individual Talent – nurturing every child*. The school caters for children aged 4–11; The school provides before and after care from 8.00am until 6.00pm.

The School aims to provide for the whole child through a varied curriculum, with a wide programme of study and opportunities to develop all aspects of every pupil's talents. The core subjects, English, Maths and Science, as well as the development of ICT skills, are at the centre of learning throughout the school. Pupils are encouraged and helped to develop a disciplined approach to personal study skills at all ages. Group and class activities help everyone to experience cooperative work and gain useful understanding of others skills and feelings.

Details of the curriculum can be found on our website. A structured academic program is covered by all age groups. This is delivered by specialist staff that enable every pupil to achieve their potential. Continuous assessment and tests prepare the upper school pupils for their entrance exams and for further achievement at secondary school.

The School provides regular feedback about pupils' progress at Parents' Evenings and through reports. Weekly newsletters are emailed to parents informing them of events pupils are involved in as well as activities happening within the school. Parents are encouraged to be involved in their children's education where ever possible.

The School is proud of its achievements in music, drama, games, swimming and dance. As well as our own two indoor hall spaces and playground, the school takes advantage of The Gregg School's sporting facilities. Weekly games, swimming and gym/dance sessions with qualified staff are provided, as well as a variety of after-school activities.

Upper school pupils gain valuable experience whilst preparing for Communication examinations. Each year many pupils achieve distinctions and merits but, most importantly, all gain much personal satisfaction and confidence that will help them in later life.

Further opportunities are provided, through extracurricular activities, to develop pupils' individual talents and personal strengths and interests. Monthly Achievement Assemblies celebrate individual and group interests in and out of school as well as focusing on pupils Endeavour and Courtesy within school. These are an opportunity for every individual to learn their own self-worth.

For taster days and further information, please contact the school secretary or visit our website.

Charitable status. The Gregg Schools Trust is a Registered Charity, number 1089055.

The Gregg School

Townhill Park House, Cutbush Lane, Southampton SO18 3RR

Tel: 023 8047 2133
email: office@thegreggschool.org
website: www.thegreggschool.org
X/Twitter: @TheGreggSchool
Facebook: @TheGreggSchool
Instagram: @thegreggschool

Chair of Board of Trustees: Mrs J Preston

***Headteacher*: Mrs S Sellers,** MSc, BSc Hons, NPQH, PGCE

Age Range. 11–16 years.

Number in School. 330.

Fees per term (2023–2024). £5,169.

The Gregg School is situated to the east of Southampton and set in 23 acres of beautifully landscaped grounds. The School has a unique family atmosphere and an excellent reputation for its outstanding pastoral care. A high value is placed on identifying and developing each child's individual talents and abilities, and small classes, taught by experienced and dedicated staff, ensure that every student has the opportunity to achieve their very best.

A broad and balanced curriculum is supplemented by a wide range of extracurricular clubs and activities, ranging from orienteering to yoga, bouldering, first aid and the Duke of Edinburgh award.

The School's music and drama departments provide a host of opportunities for students to perform to a range of audiences, and the School regularly achieves success in sporting disciplines at both city and county level.

A comprehensive transport service is provided for students living within a 15 mile radius of the School.

Our Trust Partner, The Gregg Preparatory School, offers a high-quality educational experience for children aged 4–11.

Scholarships. A small number of academic, art, music and sports scholarships are awarded each year, which attract a reduction in fees of between 10%-33%. Entry into the Academic Scholarship is automatic for those entering the main Entrance Assessment day.

Bursaries. In addition to the Scholarship awards, parents can apply for a Bursary. This is a means-tested application where household income and expenditure will need to be declared. To request a Bursary Application Pack email Mrs Gibson, Deputy Bursar: amg@thegreggschools.org

Hale Preparatory School

Broomfield Lane, Hale, Cheshire WA15 9AS

Tel: 0161 928 2386
email: mail@haleprepschool.com
website: www.haleprepschool.com
Instagram: @haleprepschool

Principal: J Connor, JP, BSc, FCP
***Headteacher*: Mrs Ruth Vayro MA NPQH**

Age Range. 4–11.

Number in School. Day: 116 Boys, 93 Girls.

Fees per term (2023–2024). £3,000.

Hale Preparatory School is a completely independent, co-educational school for children from the age of 4 to 11.

The school's most recent ISI inspection was in February 2023. The overall summary of the report reads, "*Hale Prep is a very successful school. Throughout, the teaching is excellent and the pupils' industrious approach to their studies is reflected in their rapid progress and substantial academic achievement at all levels. Indeed, in some cases, levels of progress and achievement are exceptional. The pupils reach high standards of personal fulfilment and participate enthusiastically in a wide range of extra-curricular activities. The quality of the pupils' personal development is excellent, reflecting the school's highly effective emphasis on their welfare, safeguarding and well-being."*

In recent years, the school was considered the Prep School of the Year by the Sunday Times and was referred to in two studies presented to the Department of Education: firstly, on "Best Practice in the Independent Sector" and secondly, as one of five examples of successful private schools.

One of the aims of the school is to develop each child to his or her fullest potential. This can only be achieved in a situation that emphasises a disciplined approach to school work. Teaching is carried out in a formal, traditional manner but one which also incorporates modern teaching aids. Homework is set every night.

The curriculum of the school is designed to create well-rounded children. Thus, whilst 50% of the curriculum is devoted to the core subjects of maths, English and science, all children have weekly lessons in drama, music, dance, art and design, information technology, history, geography, French, Spanish, ethics, physical education/games and Latin in year 6. Additionally, the school offers a range of extra-curricular activities including a dance club, theatre club, fencing, chess, sewing, gardening, choir, orchestra, a range of sports and outdoor pursuit holidays.

Heathcote School

Eves Corner, Danbury, Essex CM3 4QB

Tel: 01245 223131

email: enquiries@heathcoteschool.co.uk

website: www.heathcoteschool.co.uk

Headteacher: **Mrs Samantha Scott**

Age Range. 2–11+.

Number in School. 112

Fees per term (2023–2024). £3,500.

Founded in 1935, Heathcote School has achieved a high reputation and won many accolades including ISA Junior School of the Year 2021–2022. One of our newly qualified teachers was also a silver award winner in the *2021 TES National Awards*.

Heathcote is a small, village school that encourages excellence in all areas to ensure pupils leave as confident, capable well-rounded citizens.

Children may start in our Nursery from 2 years old. We offer wrap-around care from 7.30am to 6.00pm with holiday club provision ensuring 48 week cover and have many extra-curricular activities throughout the day to give a plethora of opportunities.

Specialist subject teachers ensure the success of the high teaching standards expected at this school. Children are prepared for scholarships, entrance examinations and the Essex Selective Schools Examination at 11+. A very high pass rate is attained across these examinations.

The School participates in many sporting fixtures including netball, football, cricket and swimming and is particularly successful in horse jumping, cross country and triathlon.

Pupils are expected to show courtesy and consideration at all times and encouraged to develop self-discipline and pride in themselves and their environment. Regular consultations with parents are held and the Head Teacher is always available for any discussions that parents consider necessary. We have an active and dedicated "Friends of Heathcote School" who regularly hold social events, e.g. Heathcote Ball, and raise funds for charity and for the school.

For more information please contact us or visit our website.

Heathfield Knoll School

Wolverley, Kidderminster, Worcestershire DY10 3QE

Tel: 01562 850204

email: admissions@hkschool.org.uk

website: www.hkschool.org.uk

Facebook: @HeathfieldKnollSchool

Instagram: @heathfieldknoll

LinkedIn: /company/heathfield-knoll-school-and-nursery

Headmaster: **Mr Lawrence Collins**, MA, PGCE

Age Range. 3 months to 18 years.

Number in School. 238.

Fees per term (2023–2024). Main school £3,371–£5,325 per term. Nursery from £34 (half day) to £71 (full day). Preschool £40–£58 per day. Sixth Form on application.

Heathfield Knoll School is a mixed-ability independent day school that believes pupils learn, play and interact when their happiness is placed at the forefront of all we do. Fostering happiness involves embracing all aspects of a child's development, listening to their concerns and responding to needs as appropriate.

Nestled within the Wolverley countryside just outside Kidderminster, Heathfield Knoll School encompasses a large section of school life onto one site (from 3 months to 19 years). Heathfield Knoll has an enviable reputation as the leading school in the Wyre Forest District and Worcestershire, as well as the wider region.

Heathfield Knoll **Nursery and Preschool** accepts children as early as 3 months old right through to age 4 when they continue their journey to **Lower School (Reception–Year 4)**. As pupils grow they move into **Middle School (Years 5–8)** and then subsequently into **Upper School (Years 9–11)** and their GCSE years. Once pupils reach their post-16 choices they are able to attend Heathfield Knoll **Sixth Form (Years 12–13)** where they benefit from a flexible and tailored curriculum.

The school is centred around a large country house in beautiful surroundings which includes extensive playing fields, woodland and grassland. Heathfield Knoll's generous grounds are frequently used to support a creative curriculum, including Outdoor Learning and Land-Based Studies. Heathfield Knoll aims to provide a traditional, well-structured education in small, nurturing teaching groups. This means that children's needs are catered for and they thrive in a well-ordered atmosphere of mutual respect. Heathfield Knoll is concerned with more than just academic achievements; we encourage children to approach adulthood as confident, articulate and courteous individuals.

Heathfield Knoll School's mission is to

- **enrich** our pupils through a broad and inclusive education, in a nurturing and supportive environment where wellbeing is paramount.
- **challenge** our pupils to find their own pathway by encouraging curiosity, critical thinking and inquisitive minds.
- **prepare** pupils for their future by encouraging resilient learners, leaders and compassionate global citizens.

To learn more about Heathfield Knoll School please contact admissions@hkschool.org.uk or call 01562 850204.

Herne Hill School

The Old Vicarage, 127 Herne Hill, London SE24 9LY

Tel: 020 7274 6336
email: enquiries@hernehillschool.co.uk
website: www.hernehillschool.co.uk

Headteacher: **Mrs Ngaire Telford**

Age Range. 2–7.

Number in School. 300 boys and girls.

Fees per term (2023–2024). £2,760–£6,090.

Herne Hill School is the largest independent Pre-School and Pre-Prep in the UK focusing exclusively on 2–7 year olds, i.e. the period research has shown to be the most important educational years in a person's life. Children join Kindergarten in the academic year they become 3 years old, with an option to join early for half-day play sessions the term after the child has become 2 years old. Kindergarten is by far the greatest entry point, followed by Pre-Reception and Reception. There are usually only chance vacancies for Years 1 and 2.

The school is well known as an oasis of happy learning and as the ideal setting for young children to acquire the key values and cognitive, physical, social, emotional and self-regulatory skills they will require to lead happy, successful and balanced lives. At 7+, the children graduate to move on to a number of local independent and state schools, 'ready to shine with that special Herne Hill sparkle', as one of the heads of the receiving schools has described his Herne Hill School intake.

By focusing on Early Years education, Herne Hill School has developed strong expertise in making the critical transition from Nursery to School seamless. Children joining the Kindergarten can avoid the disruption of a 4+ change and enjoy continuity of care for up to five years in what are arguably their most important educationally-formative years. Children joining in Reception benefit from the smooth progression from a play-based learning approach to more structured lessons.

"*Love • Care • Excellence*" encapsulates the school philosophy that love, nurture and a caring environment foster the children's self-confidence, sense of achievement and happiness, thereby stimulating their curiosity and desire to learn. The school's atmosphere lives this philosophy. It is a caring, friendly and stimulating place, and at the same time there is an air of achievement, respect and discipline.

The curriculum is finely balanced to develop all skills and interests of 'the whole child' and take account of each child's individual needs as well as the requirements of the 7+ entry tests – and to make learning fun! It is also designed to develop the skills of independent learning and to sustain the children's innate joy of learning. Music, drama, gym, dancing and French are emphasised and taught by specialists.

The last ISI inspection delivered a strong endorsement of the school's ethos, staff, curriculum, *modus operandi* and infrastructure by giving the highest possible rating of 'excellent' on the two overarching domains of quality of education, the pupils' academic and other achievements and the pupils' personal development. The full report can be found on the school's website.

The school holds two open mornings a year, typically on a Saturday in March and September. Prospective parents may also see the school 'in action' by joining one of the regular tours held during school hours. The school's website contains relevant information about life at the school, its curriculum, the destination of its leavers and some useful links.

Herries Preparatory School

Dean Lane, Cookham Dean, Berks SL6 9BD

Tel: 01628 483350
email: office@herries.org.uk
website: www.herries.org.uk
X/Twitter: @Herries_School
Facebook: @HerriesPrepSchool
Instagram: @HerriesWindintheWillows

Chair of Governors: Christine Weaving

Headmaster: **Mr Robert Grosse**, MEd, BA Ed Hons

Age Range. 2–11 Co-educational.

Number of Pupils. 120 Day Boys and Girls.

Fees per term (2023–2024). £3,687–£4,323. Fees are inclusive of swimming tuition, if applicable, sports transport, morning snacks, homework clubs and personal accident insurance. A discount is given for second, third and subsequent children attending school at the same time.

Herries has a delightful location alongside National Trust land and is close to Maidenhead and Marlow; all children can make use of the neighbouring Quarry woods. Small class sizes enable each child to receive individual attention and to flourish in a secure environment. The curriculum is broad and balanced and there is a wide range of extra curricular clubs after school and holiday clubs. After school clubs include football, dance, coding, create/art, cookery, fencing, home work club (Free of charge to Y3 and above), chess, cross country, tennis and multi sports. Wrap-around care is available to all pupils from 8am until 5.30pm Monday to Friday. Herries has a distinctive family atmosphere and happy pupils who progress to the grammar, state and independent secondary schools of their choice.

Curriculum. The National Curriculum is covered and we teach beyond the levels expected of children in each age group. Class teachers deliver the core and foundation subjects in Key Stage 1 while there is subject specialist teaching in all subjects in KS2. Herries offer enrichment and study skills as part of the fees from Y3 upwards.

Examinations. Children are assessed through the NFER testing scheme and a variety of standardised tests. Emphasis is placed on preparing pupils for their next school of choice and the timetable includes 'Thinking Skills' which helps pupils learn to cope with a variety of different tests and exams.

Facilities. Set in a beautiful building which was the house in which Kenneth Grahame wrote 'The Wind in the Willows', the nursery occupies a purpose-built and spacious suite of rooms. ICT, coding and many lessons are taught on the school chrome books, all homework is set through Google classrooms. Class rooms are equipped with interactive Smart Boards and there is an excellent library. Games are played at the National Sports Centre at Bisham Abbey, only a few minutes away by coach; swimming at Wycombe Leisure Centre; cricket at Cookham Dean Cricket Club; athletics events at a local Sports Centre. There are weekly fixtures against other schools from Y3 upwards. Herries is a warm, friendly school where happy children achieve great things.

ISI Inspection Result 2022: Excellent in All Areas.

Highclare School

10 Sutton Road, Erdington, Birmingham B23 6QL
Tel: 0121 373 7400
email: enquiries@highclareschool.co.uk
website: www.highclareschool.co.uk
X/Twitter: @HighclareSchool
Facebook: @highclareschool
Instagram: @highclareschool
LinkedIn: /company/highclare-school

See full entry in the **Society of Heads** section, on **p. 533**.

Highfield Priory School

Fulwood Row, Fulwood, Preston, Lancashire PR2 5RW
Tel: 01772 709624
email: schooloffice@highfieldpriory.co.uk
website: www.highfieldpriory.co.uk

***Headmaster*: Mr J Duke**

Age Range. 2–11 years.

Number in School. Day: 106 Boys, 93 Girls.

Fees per term (2023–2024). £3,140.

Highfield is set in 8 acres of landscaped gardens, woodlands and playing fields and is a co-educational preparatory school for children aged 18 months to 11+ years. It is fully equipped with its own established Nursery and prepares children for all Independent, Grammar and Senior Schools in Lancashire, for which it has an excellent academic record.

Class numbers average 20 and children are taught by fully-qualified and experienced staff. Specialist facilities and teachers ensure that children are challenged and fulfilled across the curriculum, most notably in Art and CDT with a new studio in 2005, an ICT suite (since 1994), a Science Laboratory (2006) and, most recently, a Performing Arts Studio in 2013. Children from Nursery through to Year Six are also able to enjoy the school Library, Sports Hall and the school's own nature reserve, Highfield Haven.

The school has strong musical, dramatic and sporting traditions. Every child in the Junior School is given the opportunity to take part in competitive sporting fixtures and to perform in a full-scale dramatic production each year. In addition, Highfield examines the Junior children in the disciplines of Public Speaking, Elocution and Drama twice a year thereby greatly improving the children's eloquence and confidence.

Highfield holds a Step into Quality Award for its Early Years and Foundation Stage and Potential Plus UK's Three Star Gold Membership for its work with Gifted and Talented children. Highfield encourages its pupils to 'Aim High' and gives them every opportunity to achieve this.

Highfield offers an extended day from 7.15am until 6.00pm. Extra-curricular activities include Ballet, Gardening, Choir, Design, Dance, Judo, Public Speaking, Chess, Spanish, Homework Club and Instrument Tuition. The school is well supported by an enthusiastic Parents' Association. Prospective parents, and children, are encouraged to visit the school, have a tour with the Headmaster and to experience a school day.

Charitable status. Highfield Priory School is a Registered Charity, number 532262. It exists to provide independent education to all children between the ages of 2 and 11 years within Preston and surrounding areas for all who wish to participate and to provide access to the community at large to all sporting, musical and artistic provision within the school.

Highfields School

London Road, Newark, Nottinghamshire NG24 3AL
Tel: 01636 704103
email: admissions@highfieldsschool.co.uk
website: www.highfieldsschool.co.uk
X/Twitter: @HighfieldsNG24
Facebook: @highfields.newark
Instagram: @highfields_school

***Head*: Mrs Sarah H Lyons**, BEd Hons Primary Early Years

Age Range. 2–11 Co-educational.

Number in School. 125.

Fees per term (2023–2024). Reception £3,820, Pre-Prep £3,920, Prep £3,985 including lunch. Day Nursery from £19.50 per three-hour session to £45.10 per school day (8.30am–3.30pm), £60.25 per full day (7.30am–6.00pm).

Highfields Independent School & Day Nursery is a thriving and supportive environment with a strong sense of family and well embedded values and traditions of which the school is very proud.

Set in fourteen acres of mature parkland, including wonderful sports fields, the grounds provide a beautiful setting for children to explore, whilst enjoying their education. The Highfields school building is steeped in history, with an exquisite entrance hall, and stain glass windows, with a warm and welcoming feel.

Personal growth and wellbeing are valued as highly as academic success with an emphasis on the holistic development of the individual. Highfields provide children with a wealth of contextualised learning experiences to create meaningful connections, skills and memories which last a lifetime.

Sport, Music, Forest School, Speech and Drama as well as the Arts are all equally important components of the full and exciting curriculum that has been developed in order to build well rounded young individuals.

At Highfields, curiosity is championed and pupils are encouraged to realise their potential and discover new talents across all areas of the curriculum through very high levels of engagement and participation.

We develop 'Highfeldians' who are prepared not only for senior school, but life beyond. Flexible, independent thinkers and learners with a love of adventure and a strong sense of identity, Highfields pupils are spirited, resourceful and self-motivated with respect for both themselves and others. Able to identify and appreciate opposing opinions and beliefs, Highfields build proactive, tolerant and considered global citizens of the future with a well-developed sense of responsibility, and a desire to make a difference to our world.

In 2023 100% of our Form 6 leavers were accepted into their first choice Grammar or Independent School – many with scholarships.

The School is administered by a Board of Governors, including parent governors.

Charitable status. Newark Preparatory School Company Limited is a Registered Charity, number 528261. It exists to provide and further the education of children.

Holme Grange School

Heathlands Road, Wokingham, Berkshire RG40 3AL
Tel: 0118 9781566
email: school@holmegrange.org
website: www.holmegrange.org
X/Twitter: @holmegrange
Facebook: @holmegrange
Instagram: @holmegrange
LinkedIn: /company/holme-grange-school

See full entry in the **IAPS** section, on **p. 694**.

Hulme Hall Grammar School

Beech Avenue, Stockport, Cheshire SK3 8HA
Tel: 0161 485 3524
email: secretary@hulmehallschool.org
website: www.hulmehallschool.org
X/Twitter: @HulmeHallGS
Facebook: @Hulme-Hall-Grammar-School
Instagram: @hulmehall

***Headmaster*: Mr D Grierson**, BA Econ Hons, MEcon, PGCE

Business Manager: Mr M Lynch, BA Hons, ACMA, CGMA
Assistant Headteacher (*Curriculum*): Mr P Bradford, BSc, PGCE
Assistant Headteacher (*Pupil Progress*): Mrs J Smith, BEd Hons
Head of Pre-School: Mrs H Khinda, BEd Hons, QTS

Age range. 2–4 and 11–16 Co-educational.
Number in school. 200.
Fees per term (2023–2024). £4,320.

Hulme Hall Grammar School is a non-selective school with an excellent reputation for providing a friendly, warm and positive atmosphere in which all pupils thrive and succeed. Its small class sizes, high quality teaching and superb enrichment programmes ensure that it provides the best possible educational journey for every pupil.

Situated in a beautiful conservation area in Stockport, Hulme Hall is split into two schools – the Pre-School and Senior School.

The **Pre-School** (2–4 years) builds relationships with families and has one shared goal: to create a place of awe and wonder where children can explore, create and grow. The setting has both indoor and outdoor learning environments where children are encouraged to become curious, confident and happy learners.

The **Senior School** (11–16 years) aims to provide every pupil with a challenging, dynamic and relevant education that enables them to attain their academic and personal potential and to prepare them fully and effectively for the next stage of their educational journey.

It delivers a curriculum covering a wide range of academic, creative and practical subjects. An extensive choice of GCSE and other external examinations enables pupils at KS4 to choose learning programmes tailored to the individual. This allows them to fulfil, if not exceed, expectations and achieve academic success.

Achievement out of the classroom is important too. Hulme Hall offers a wide and varied co-curricular programme including opportunities for trips abroad and the Duke of Edinburgh's Award Scheme.

There are numerous clubs available at lunchtime and after school and termly enrichment days that take the children outside the classroom.

Caring for the individual has always been at the heart of Hulme Hall's philosophy and an outstanding pastoral provision ensures that each child can thrive within the school and wider community. Pupils are nurtured through a vital phase in their growth and development focusing on all aspects of education – academic, personal, social and moral – to create confident and respectful individuals. All of Hulme Hall's pupils will continue their education at local colleges studying A Levels and other equivalent courses or an apprenticeship.

Charitable status. Hulme Hall Educational Trust is a Registered Charity, number 525931. The school aims to promote the personal, moral, social and academic development of all pupils.

Hurtwood House School

1 Radnor Ln
Holmbury St Mary, Dorking, Surrey RH5 6NU

Tel: 01483 279000
email: info@hurtwood.net
website: www.hurtwoodhouse.com
X/Twitter: @hurtwoodhouse
Facebook: @hurtwoodhouse
Instagram: hurtwoodhouse/?hl=en
LinkedIn: /hurtwood-house

***Headmaster*: C M Jackson**, BEd

Age range. 16–18.

Number in School. 365 (235 girls, 130 boys).

Fees per term (2023–2024). Boarding: £17,409, Day: £11,606.

Hurtwood House is the only independent boarding school specialising exclusively in the Sixth Form. It concentrates on the 16–18 age range and offers students a caring, residential structure and a commitment to a complete education where culture, sport, friendship and a full range of extracurricular activities all play an important part. Hugely successful across the whole range of academic subjects, Hurtwood House is also widely recognised as having the best Creative and Performing Arts and Media departments in the country and is therefore especially attractive to aspiring actors, directors, film directors, dancers, singers, artists and fashion designers.

Many students now want to leave the traditional school system at 16. They are seeking an environment which is structured and safe, but which is less institutional and better equipped to provide the challenge and stimulation which they are now ready for, and which is therefore better placed to develop their potential. They also require teaching methods which will prepare them for an increasingly competitive world by developing their initiative and encouraging them to think for themselves.

It is a small and personal school, but it is a large and powerful sixth form which benefits from having specialised A Level teachers. The examination results put Hurtwood House in the top independent school league tables, but it is equally important to the school that the students develop energy, motivation and self-confidence.

In short, Hurtwood House is a stepping stone between school and university for students who are all in the same age group and who share the same maturity and the same ambitions.

The school is situated in its own grounds high up in the Surrey Hills and offers excellent facilities in outstandingly beautiful surroundings.

Ipswich High School

Woolverstone, Ipswich, Suffolk IP9 1AZ

Tel: 01473 780201
email: admissions@ipswichhighschool.co.uk
website: www.ipswichhighschool.co.uk
X/Twitter: @IpswichHigh
Facebook: @ipswichhighschool
Instagram: @ipswichhighschool
LinkedIn: /school/ipswich-high-school

***Head*: Mr Dan Browning**

Head of Senior School: Kaye Extance
Director of Teaching & Learning and CPD: Laura Massey
Director of Boarding & Pastoral: Tom Collishaw
Director of Curriculum & Achievement: Mark Speakman
Head of Prep School: Mrs Lisa Finch
Head of Sixth Form: Mrs Imogen Vickers
Registrar: Mrs Sue Burden

Ipswich High School is a vibrant day and boarding school for boys and girls aged 3–18, set in an idyllic 87-acre campus in Woolverstone on the banks of the River Orwell. With approximately 500 pupils, we are a small school with big school facilities. We have small classes of hard-working pupils and inspirational teachers who help to instil a love of learning, the results of which are exceptional academic outcomes year-on-year.

We are just as ambitious outside the classroom and pride ourselves on the huge breadth of our co-curricular programme (we call this 'Enrichment'). The 300 clubs and activities we offer as part of our Enrichment Programme are embedded as part of the school day and underline our commitment to the holistic education of the whole child.

We offer a high class 'boutique' boarding experience in our two small, award-winning boarding houses; the Barns and The Dairy House. This offer includes full, weekly, flexi and occasional boarding for pupils from Year 7 to Year 13.

We believe in getting to know every pupil and use these positive relationships to ensure that everyone in our community is inspired, happy and successful; above all building the foundations to flourish.

The school was founded in 1878 and since 1992 has been situated in the Grade I listed Palladian mansion, Woolverstone Hall. The school occupies 87 acres of beautiful parkland in a rural location just four miles outside the county town of Ipswich. The spacious site has been adapted well to the needs of a forward-looking school with superb facilities, including a theatre, ICT suites, 25m indoor heated swimming pool, Sixth Form Centre, cookery rooms and AstroTurf pitch. The school capitalises on its outstanding natural surroundings: the woodland provides an outdoor learning area for the Prep School and the pond and parkland are often used for scientific research.

Pupils follow a broad and balanced curriculum from which they enjoy great academic success. In 2023, for GCSE 10% more pupils achieved a 9–8 grade than the previous year. Likewise, our Sixth Form saw remarkable A Level results this year as 24% of students achieved A* grades and over 48% of students achieved A*-A grades.

Admissions. Admission to Nursery is after the child's 3rd birthday. Admission into Reception is based on an informal assessment in a play situation. Entry to the rest of the Prep School is based on an assessment including written and numerical testing. Entry to the Senior School involves an interview, written test, and a school report. Sixth Form entry is based on an interview, GCSE results and a school report. International boarding entry is based on written assessments and a school report.

Fees per term (2023–2024). Day: Reception £3,785, Years 1–2 £3,985, Years 3–6 £4,400, Year 7–8 £5,630, Year 9–13 £5,985.

Boarding per annum including school fees (from Year 7): Full £40,110, Weekly £29,925. Flexi Boarding options are available.

Woolverstone Scholarship Programme. Our Woolverstone Scholarship Programme is for our scholars from Years 7–13, with scholarships being awarded in Year 7, Year 9, and Year 12. This programme ensures that our scholars continue to develop their considerable talents by providing them with additional support and unique opportunities. Academic Scholars are supported to complete independent scholar projects, whilst Sport Scholars, Music Scholars, Art Scholars, Dance Scholars and Drama Scholars will enjoy scholarship programmes designed by the relevant Head of Department. These scholars are also able to access the academic scholar projects should they wish to do so.

Year 7 & Year 9 Academic Scholarships. Upon receipt of a completed application form, all students will be invited into school to sit our Entrance Examination. The results of this assessment are combined with the information provided from recent school reports to decide who is eligible to receive an Academic Scholarship offer. These are then awarded by the Head, and you do not apply.

Year 7 Arthur Ransome Scholarships. All students entering Year 7, including those from our Prep School, may apply for one or more of the following Arthur Ransome Scholarships: Art, Dance, Drama, Music and Sport. These Scholarships, which may attract a tuition fee award, are awarded from Years 7 through to 11, provided the Scholar continues to demonstrate commitment to their chosen area.

Year 9 George Orwell Scholarships. George Orwell Scholarships are for pupils joining Ipswich High School for our GCSE programme in Year 9. Students can apply for one or more of the following: Art, Dance, Drama, Music and Sport. These Scholarships, which may attract a tuition fee award, are awarded for Years 9 through to 11, provided the Scholar continues to demonstrate commitment to their chosen area.

Year 12 Woolverstone Scholarships. All students entering our Sixth Form, including those progressing from our GCSE programme, may apply for a Woolverstone Scholarship.These are our most prestigious Academic Scholarships and are awarded for Years 12 and 13 to pupils who demonstrate strength in any academic discipline, as well as being predicted a strong set of GCSE grades.

Those applying to Ipswich High School from state-funded schools are also eligible to apply for our Elliston Award.

Year 12 Sophie Youngman Scholarships. Named after the founder of Ipswich High School, this Scholarship exists to recognise any Sixth Form student who is currently excelling in Art, Dance, Drama, Music and Sport. Like the Woolverstone Scholarships, these are awarded for both Years 12 and 13.

Kensington Wade

Fulham Palace Road, London W6 9ER

Tel: 020 3096 2888
email: admissions@kensingtonwade.com
website: www.kensingtonwade.com

See full entry in the **IAPS** section, on **p. 703**.

Kew House School
Gardener Schools Group

Kew House, Capital Interchange Way, London TW8 0EX

Tel: 020 8742 2038
email: secretary@kewhouseschool.com
website: www.kewhouseschool.com
X/Twitter: @KewHouseSchool
Facebook: @KewHouseSchool
Instagram: @KewHouseSchool
LinkedIn: /company/kewhouseschool

***Headmaster*: Will Williams**

Age Range. 11–18 Co-educational.
Number of Pupils. 592.
Fees per term (2023–2024). £8,517.

Kew House School is a co-educational, independent school for 11–18 year olds. Situated in two modern buildings close to the River Thames, it is the third school to open of the Gardener Schools Group.

Kew House School takes a modern and pioneering approach to every aspect of school life. The school recognises and enhances the individual abilities of each child, welcoming pupils with varying academic profiles and placing emphasis on confidence, self-esteem and creativity. We benefit from having a smaller student roll than many independent senior schools, which allows us to provide the flexibility and individualised attention needed to enable students to fulfil their potential.

The school boasts modern, cutting edge facilities that capture every part of school life, whether the focus is on academia, sports, or the arts. We have multiple science laboratories, music suites, a theatre, multi-use games area, a basketball court and a purpose-built Independent Learning Centre for Sixth Formers.

Our aim is to provide a rich and broad education to all pupils whatever their specialism, pursuing excellence in all areas, examinable or not. The daily timetable is six taught hours, plus the extracurricular programme involving academic, non-academic and sports-based clubs. Core GCSEs as well as a variety of options are available to pupils. For the Sixth Formers, we offer a large selection of A levels, and work with pupils to guide them through the selection process to ensure their futures are well prepared for.

We try to enrich our pupils lives as much as possible, one way we achieve this is by offering pupils the chance to learn and grow in a new environment by visiting various different places worldwide. Trips can range from a theatrical troupe seeing France, geographers travelling to Laos, outdoor enthusiasts getting sporty in Cornwall, to art appreciation in Rome. These trips are designed specifically to bolster confidence and independence, as well as to provide inspiration.

We aim for a family and social hub giving emotional support and security to all pupils and employees. Each pupil receives individual attention both educationally and pastorally. Our approach is holistic, as we believe that there can be no artificial barriers between a pupil's intellectual, emotional, social and spiritual growth. A number of staff are involved in the life of each pupil, but in particular, the personal tutor who meets their tutee on a daily basis. Pupils have the same tutor throughout their seven years with us.

To find out more about joining Kew House School, view our admissions procedure via our website: www.kewhouseschool.com/admissions

The King Alfred School

Manor Wood, 149 North End Road, London NW11 7HY

Tel: 020 8457 5200
email: kas@kingalfred.org.uk
website: www.kingalfred.org.uk
X/Twitter: @kingalfredsch
Facebook: @TheKingAlfredSchool
Instagram: @the_king_alfred_school
LinkedIn: /school/king-alfred-school

***Head*: Robert Lobatto**, MA Oxon, NPQH London

Deputy Head Upper School: Alistair McConville, MA Cantab, PGCE Gloucestershire

Head of Lower School: Karen Thomas, BEd Goldsmiths

Age range. 4–18.

Number in school. Primary: approximately 315; Secondary: approximately 400.

Fees per term (2023–2024). Reception, Years 1–2: £6,353, Years 3–6: £7,321, Upper School (Years 7–13): £7,660.

The King Alfred School is unique among independent schools in North London. Apart from being all-age (4–18), co-ed and secular, it takes in a range of ability as opposed to its academically selective neighbours in the private sector.

The school's beginnings are unusual: it was founded in 1898 by a group of Hampstead parents and its governing body comprises mainly current and ex-parents. Visitors tend to comment on the pretty site (on the edge of Hampstead Garden Suburb), the 'village' layout (carefully preserved by a succession of architects), and the friendly atmosphere – this is a no-uniform establishment and all are on first-name terms.

Academic results are consistently impressive and constantly improving, and almost 100% of the KAS Sixth Form go on to universities and some go to Art Foundation courses, music colleges and conservatoires. The school prides itself on its reputation as a relaxed, informal and vibrant community that focuses on the development of the whole child and achieves academic success within a non-pressured environment.

Bursaries for Year 7 and the Sixth Form are available.

Charitable status. King Alfred School is a Registered Charity, number 312590. It exists to provide quality education for boys and girls.

Kings Monkton School

6 West Grove, Cardiff CF24 3XL

Tel: 029 2048 2854
email: mail@kingsmonkton.org.uk
website: www.kingsmonkton.org.uk
X/Twitter: @kings_monkton
Facebook: @kings-monkton-school

***Principal*: Mr Paul Norton**

Vice Principal and Head of Primary: Mrs Karen Norton

Age range. 3–18.

Number in school. 290.

Fees per term (2023–2024). £3,740–£5,464.

Kings Monkton School is a co-educational day school in the heart of Cardiff for pupils aged 3 to 18. Family owned, by Paul and Karen Norton, the school takes a different approach to learning and teaching. They believe that with the right support and in the right environment, all children can succeed and achieve their life dreams. Their recipe is simple: inclusivity, achievement for all, and choice.

Kings Monkton School is inclusive and warmly welcomes pupils of all abilities; they do not have entrance exams, they embrace diversity and celebrate differences, and they work with their families to create bespoke learning pathways for every pupil. They also listen, and their exceptional wellbeing and pastoral teams provide support to enhance the learning experience – Kings Monkton School is a place for all.

The school motto is 'Be the best you can be', and they believe that achievement means achievement for all. It is not the starting point for pupils that is important, but their academic journey. Many achieve several grades higher than predicted and leave the school as well-rounded, resilient life-long learners, which is accomplished by small classes, great teaching and inspirational staff. Kings Monkton School wants your child to aspire, believe and achieve and they will guide their path.

But choosing the right path can be difficult, so the school offers choice. Their personalised curriculum offers over 33 different options at GCSE and post-16, and an array of assessments from A levels, GCSEs, BTEC and diplomas, while their bespoke Baccalaureate encourages pupils to go beyond the classroom and develop their own interests and passions, to be explored through their extensive range of extracurricular activities. The school also believes that with the New Curriculum for Wales, the need remains for some pupils to master specific subject knowledge, so they continue to offer options in science, maths and English.

The school has excellent public transport links and offers a school transport service. To support families, placement fees for this academic year have been frozen, primary pupils have free lunches, there are no exam fees or charges for curricular trips. The school also offers bursaries and scholarships.

The Kingsley School

Beauchamp Hall, Beauchamp Avenue, Royal Leamington Spa, Warwickshire CV32 5RD

Tel: 01926 425127
email: schooloffice@kingsleyschool.co.uk
website: www.thekingsleyschool.co.uk
X/Twitter: @Kingsley_School
Facebook: @thekingsleyschool
Instagram: @thekingsleyschool
LinkedIn: /company/thekingsleyschool

Part of the Warwick Independent Schools Foundation
Principal of Warwick Independent Schools Foundation: Mr R Nicholson, MA Oxon

***Headteacher*: Dr Sarah Howling**

Deputy Head (*Pastoral*): Mrs C McCullough, BA QTS SENCO
Assistant Headteacher (*Academic*): Mrs R Rogers, BSc, PGCE, MA
Head of Sixth Form: Mrs D Morgan, BA, PGCE
Interim Head of Preparatory School: Mrs Jennie Phillips

Independent Day School for Girls aged 3 to 18, and boys up to 11 years, founded in 1884.

For over 135 years The Kingsley School has had an excellent reputation for high academic standards and first class pastoral care. What sets The Kingsley School apart from other schools is its distinctive family ethos and friendly atmosphere. We are immensely proud of the fact that everyone who visits us remarks on the happy staff–student relationships and the sense of community it fosters. At Kingsley, pupils have a positive and purposeful approach to learning. The atmosphere is unique; enthusiastic and approachable teachers inspire pupils to learn; behaviour is excellent and pupils are challenged and supported according to individual need. Where practical, we aim to personalise the curriculum so that pupils can reach their potential whatever their gifts and talents.

The Kingsley **Preparatory School** is friendly and purposeful and offers a rich, vibrant and creative curriculum for girls and boys aged 3–11. Outstanding teaching encourages a love of learning by providing a balance between the sound foundations for academic progress with character-building creativity. Kingsley has a well-established core curriculum in which the focus is on excellence within English, mathematics and science, supported by bespoke teaching in music, drama, modern foreign languages and physical education. In support of the core curriculum we have developed an exciting Creative Curriculum which sets our pupils a challenge; to explore and discover the real world. Most girls progress to The Kingsley Senior School, and boys move on to the next stage with self-assurance, some having been awarded scholarships for entry into local schools.

The **Senior School** provides continuity of academic and pastoral care. We offer a broad, balanced and stimulating academic experience. The curriculum at Kingsley is structured to maximise progress, building on girls' prior learning to encourage creativity, intellectual curiosity and independence. Our GCSE results are excellent, with high attainment year on year. At GCSE our curriculum provides opportunities for girls to study examinations in the core subjects of English, mathematics and the three separate sciences, as well as in the humanities subjects, the performing arts, physical education and modern foreign languages. The school delivers an academically rigorous timetable, yet has the flexibility and scope to offer additional subjects such as Latin and classical civilisation. Girls also experience a range of design subjects, for example food technology and textiles. Academic standards are high, as demonstrated by the 2021 GCSE results, with top marks awarded across the board in all subjects. Of all grades, 35% were awarded at level 9–8, 52% at level 9–7 and 99% at level 9–4.

The Kingsley School's **Sixth Form** provides a wide range of opportunities for all students. We offer a high-quality A Level curriculum and cater for a wide range of interests and post-16 aspirations. Students' academic achievements are outstanding and the diversity of their goals is embraced, with most progressing to their first-choice university, choosing to take apprenticeships within prestigious commercial organisations or studying further Higher Education courses. In the 2021 A Levels, 37% of all grades were awarded at A*, 68% at A*–A and 97% at A*–C, with a 100% pass rate. Destinations of recent leavers include Medicine at UEA, Law at Birmingham, Leeds and Liverpool, Medieval and Modern Languages at Cambridge, Neuroscience at Manchester, Dentistry at Bristol, English at Cardiff, Geography at Leeds, Maths at Swansea, Music at Edinburgh and Leeds, Marine Zoology at Newcastle, Zoology at Exeter, Business Management at Exeter, Veterinary Science at Liverpool, Pharmacology at Leeds, Agriculture with Animal Science at Harper Adams, Nursing at Leeds, Conservation and Forestry at Bangor, Fashion with Marketing at Southampton and a Pharmaceutical Apprenticeship at Boots PLC.

The school operates a tiered system of Learning Support where pupils benefit from a broad and balanced curriculum, with small classes and excellent relationships with teachers. Lessons provide opportunities for challenge and extension, as well as scaffolded learning, with teachers making dynamic assessments of need on an individual basis. In every area of school life, pupils are supported to be the very best version of themselves and fulfil every aspect of their potential.

Kingsley runs a formal Enrichment Programme which aims to extend and enhance the core curriculum. The inclusive programme takes place within the school day, enabling all pupils to enjoy new experiences and develop essential life skills. Many of the clubs and activities are tailored towards particular year groups or Key Stages and themed by skill base. Academic clubs are generally subject specific, while STEM clubs – aimed at developing enquiry skills – focus on exciting scientific and technological advances. Pupils also have access to a wide range of performing arts clubs – including choirs, instrumental groups and drama workshops – and wellbeing activities. Our affiliation with Round Square enables us to offer clubs with more of an international focus, giving pupils greater exposure to different cultures and languages and the opportunity to develop their communication skills, leadership abilities and more. Aligned to our formal Enrichment Programme are wider opportunities for character development such as the Duke of Edinburgh's Award and Young Enterprise and World Challenge schemes. There are also a variety of both local and international trips.

Sport and physical education are a vital part of life at Kingsley; each child is encouraged to achieve their personal best. We recognise that mental and physical fitness go hand in hand with developing wellbeing and academic potential. Sport helps to develop resilience, teamwork and leadership skills and lifelong health and fitness. Each week there is an inclusive programme of extracurricular sports offered, and we compete regularly against local and regional opposition, with thriving sports teams. Kingsley also runs its own competitive riding squad and an award-winning ski team.

We offer tuition in the performing arts leading to national music and drama qualifications. There are Kingsley choirs, musical ensembles and bands with regular opportunities to perform and showcase talent; both Prep and Senior School have annual musical theatre and drama productions.

Fees per term (2023–2024). Preparatory School: £4,256 (Reception to Year 2), £4,955 (Years 3–6). Senior School & Sixth Form: £5,317.

Scholarships and Bursaries. Academic, all-rounder, art, music, drama, sport and performing arts scholarships are available at 11+. Academic, all-rounder, drama, music, art, photography, textiles and PE scholarships are available in Sixth Form.

Bursaries are available.

Our fleet of school minibuses serves a wide area and before and after-school care is available.

Charitable status. The Kingsley School is part of the Warwick Independent Schools Foundation, a Registered Charity (number 1088057).

Kingsley School

Northdown Road, Bideford, Devon EX39 3JR

Tel: 01237 426200
email: admissions@kingsleyschoolbideford.co.uk
website: www.kingsleydevon.com
X/Twitter: @KingsleyDevon
Facebook: @KingsleySchoolBideford
Instagram: @kingsleyschool
LinkedIn: /company/kingsley-school-bideford

See full entry in the **Society of Heads** section, on **p. 534**.

Knightsbridge School

67 Pont Street, London SW1X 0BD

Tel: 020 7590 9000
email: registrar@knightsbridgeschool.com
website: www.knightsbridgeschool.com
X/Twitter: @Knightsbridge06
Facebook: @KnightsbridgeSchoolLondon
Instagram: @knightsbridge_school
LinkedIn: /company/knightsbridge-school-2006

See full entry in the **IAPS** section, on **p. 713**.

Leehurst Swan School

19 Campbell Road, Salisbury SP1 3BQ

Tel: 01722 333094
email: registrar@leehurstswan.org.uk
reception@leehurstswan.org.uk
website: www.leehurstswan.org.uk
X/Twitter: @LeehurstSwanSch
Facebook: @officialleehurstswanschool
Instagram: @leehurstswanschool
LinkedIn: /leehurst-swan

Chair of Governors: Mr Ian Macdonald

***Headteacher*: Mrs Mandy Bateman**, BA Hons, MA, PGCE

Age Range. 4–16 Co-educational.

Number of Children. 200.

Fees per term (2023–2024). Senior School: £5,750–£5,883; Prep School: £2,650–£4,450.

Leehurst Swan is an independent day school, just a 10 minute walk from Salisbury city centre, which has been inspiring and educating pupils for over 100 years. We are the only independent day school in Salisbury offering education for girls and boys from Reception to GCSE. The benefits of an all-through education are widely recognised, eliminating the problems of transfer between the stages of education.

Our mission is to encourage every pupil to find their voice. Everything we do is carefully sculpted to create a community of learners with character, passion, resourcefulness, independence skills, knowledge and qualifications. So everyone can become the best possible version of themselves and make a great contribution to a challenging world.

We love that every child is different. It's our privilege to help each child to find their voice and shine.

Children surprise themselves when they try something new. Seeing a bashful child confidently take to the stage, or an academic child take joy in sport, is rewarding for us all.

In the Senior school we offer a fresh approach to GCSE options with our 'Find Your Voice' curriculum, by offering, alongside the core subjects of English language, English literature and mathematics, the choice of seven subjects from a list of seventeen. In Year 9, our pupils have an exciting choice of subjects to choose from which are not limited by option blocks and allow our pupils to choose any combination from four sciences (computer science, physics, biology and chemistry); four creatives (music, drama, photography and art); three modern foreign languages (German, French and Spanish); three humanities (history, geography and religious studies); alongside additional choices of business studies, design technology and physical education.

At Leehurst we believe that education is not about forcing pupils to fit a pre-determined mould. Uniqueness matters and as a school we encourage all pupils to 'find their voice' and explore their passions and potential; preparing them to be adaptable in an ever-changing world. Our bespoke approach empowers pupils to be fully involved in their education, increasing their chances of success and enabling them to realise their potential and fulfil their dreams.

The size of our school means that all of our staff get to know each of our pupils. We all work together to share information and insight and as a result, we're able to provide levels of individual support and guidance to pupils and their families.

School is an emotional as well as an academic journey and we are with you every step of the way.

In our last inspection Leehurst Swan achieved the grade of 'Excellent' in every aspect of educational quality; the highest possible outcome from the Independent Schools Inspectorate (ISI).

The inspectors reported, 'The quality of the pupils' personal development is excellent. Pupils of all ages are happy and confident individuals who feel supported by the school community.'

Further comments included: 'The quality of the pupils' academic and other achievements is excellent. Pupils of all ages make excellent progress.'

In 2020 the Regulatory Compliance Inspection found that Leehurst Swan was compliant in all components of the Compliance Inspection and that GCSE performances (for years 2017–2019) were reported to be 'above the national average for maintained schools'. Inspectors stated that our 'teaching enables pupils to make good progress, encompasses effective behaviour management and is supported by suitable resources'.

Leehurst Swan welcomes visitors to the school to come and see them at work and play.

Charitable status. Leehurst Swan Limited is a Registered Charity, number 800158. It exists to provide education for children.

Leighton Park School

Shinfield Road, Reading, Berkshire RG2 7ED
Tel: 0118 987 9600
email: admissions@leightonpark.com
website: www.leightonpark.com
X/Twitter: @LPSchool
Facebook: @leightonparkschool
Instagram: @leightonparkschool
LinkedIn: /leighton-park-school

See full entry in the **HMC** section, on **p. 205**.

Lime House School

Holm Hill, Dalston, Carlisle, Cumbria CA5 7BX
Tel: 01228 710225
email: office@limehouseschool.co.uk
admissions@limehouseschool.co.uk
website: www.limehouseschool.co.uk
X/Twitter: @limehouseschool
Facebook: @p/Lime-House-School-100087187012676
Instagram: @limehouseschool

***Headteacher*: Mr Andrew Guest**, BSc Dunelm

Age Range. 7–18. Boarders from age 9.

Number in School. Day: 24 Boys, 29 Girls; Boarding: 57 Boys, 50 Girls.

Fees per term (2023–2024). Boarding £11,500–£12,500; Day £4,000–£5,000.

Compulsory extras: Activities, Laundry.

Lime House School is a fully independent co-educational boarding and day school for pupils aged 7 to 18. Our aim is to ensure that each pupil achieves his or her potential both academically and socially, with each child treated individually. Our pupils are cared for in a safe rural environment and we work hard to ensure that they develop confidence and self-esteem. Boarding is available to all pupils, with the majority being full boarders.

Foreign students whose first language is not English add to the cosmopolitan atmosphere of the school. They are prepared for Cambridge English examinations (iGCSE & IELTS) and follow the same curriculum as all other students.

Games and sport form an important part of school life. All students participate and a wide range of team and individual sports is offered. Academically, Lime House offers a wide range of subjects at both GCSE and A Level. In 2023, the GCSE pass rate was 88% and at A Level 45% of grades were A* to B.

We would welcome a visit to our school to see it in action. Simply contact the school and we will arrange a time convenient for you.

Lingfield College

St Piers Lane, Lingfield, Surrey RH7 6PH

Tel: 01342 832407
email: office@lingfieldcollege.co.uk
website: www.lingfieldcollege.co.uk
X/Twitter: @LingfieldColl
Facebook: @LingfieldCollege
Instagram: @lingfieldcollege
LinkedIn: /company/lingfield-college

See full entry in the **HMC** section, on **p. 209**.

Littlegarth School

Horkesley Park, Nayland, Colchester, Essex CO6 4JR

Tel: 01206 262332
email: office@littlegarth.org
website: www.littlegarth.org
Facebook: @LittlegarthPrep
Instagram: @littlegarthschool

See full entry in the **IAPS** section, on **p. 718**.

London Christian School

40 Tabard Street, London, Greater London SE1 4JU

Tel: 020 3130 6430
email: admissions@londonchristianschool.com
website: www.londonchristianschool.com

Motto: An Excellent Christian Education for Children in London

Chair of Governors: Rev'd Chris Fishlock
***Head*: Miss Nicola Collett-White**, LLB Hons, PGCE

Fees per term (2023–2024). £3,810.

We are a small independent primary school set in a historic and central part of London, with St Paul's, Southwark Cathedral, The Shard, The Globe, Tower Bridge, HMS Belfast and The Tower of London on our doorstep. We are a Christian School but there is no requirement that a child come from a Christian background or from any faith at all. The school started in 2007 with 4 pupils and now sits at 120. We have recently purchased the adjoining premises and aim to expand over the next few years, though class sizes will remain small.

We are non selective at entry but have an excellent record at 11+ with the vast majority of our pupils going on to top independent London day schools, a number with academic, music and/or dramatic arts scholarships. Our children are cheerful and confident communicators. London Christian School is accredited for using technology well and we have rich cross curricular provision with many opportunities for service and leadership. We are a vibrant and friendly school community with many of our families living locally.

Charitable status. London Christian School Ltd is a Registered Charity, number 1133692.

Loughborough Amherst School

Gray Street, Loughborough, Leicestershire LE11 2DZ

Tel: 01509 263901
email: Amherst.office@lsf.org
website: www.lsf.org/amherst
X/Twitter: @LboroAmherst
Facebook: @LboroAmherst
Instagram: @LboroAmherst
LinkedIn: /loughborough-schools-foundation

Chair of Governors: Mr Roger Harrison, MA Cantab, DipArch RIBA
***Headmaster*: Mr James Neville**, MA Oxon, MPhil Cantab

Age Range. Co-educational 4–18.

Number of Pupils. Approximately 300+.

Fees per term (2023–2024). Pre-Prep: £4,040, Prep: £4,160, Senior: Years 7–9 £5,160, Years 10–11 £5,230, Sixth Form £5,270. (Please email amherst.admissions@lsf.org for boarding fees.)

Loughborough Amherst School is a Catholic co-educational day and boarding school. Welcoming children of all faiths and non, the School is part of the Loughborough Schools Foundation, a foundation of four schools comprising: Fairfield Prep School (boys and girls 3–11), Loughborough Grammar School (boys 10–18), Loughborough Amherst School (boys and girls 4–18) and Loughborough High School (girls 11–18). The schools operate under one governing body and are situated on two neighbouring campuses in the town. The Foundation also includes The Loughborough Nursery for children from 6 weeks to 4 years.

We hold an open day each term, but encourage all prospective parents to see our Senior and Preparatory School departments in action on a normal working day, view our facilities and meet our Headmaster. Visitors continually note the happy classroom environment and the mutual respect between pupils, staff and visitors. Some of our children are with us from 4 to 18, but we welcome new pupils at all stages of their education.

Our focus is very much on the individual child and his/her personal progress and character growth. At all stages of their education, our pupils receive individual attention in small classes. The emphasis is on giving 'added value' through the patient nurturing of confidence and 'growth mindset' in our pupils. Our progressive approach to learning and character growth is embodied in the School philosophy we call 'Minerva'.

From our Sixth Form, students have recently taken up places at The Courtauld Institute of Art, Oxford, Durham, Lancaster and Warwick universities amongst others. Our results demonstrate excellent value-added, which is a result of diligent and expert teachers, high behavioural standards and a strong teaching and learning culture.

Our membership of the Loughborough Schools Foundation places us in a wonderful position, where we can combine all that is best in a small school community with the benefits of the human and physical resources of a campus of over two thousand students. This provides numerous enrichment possibilities for our pupils, whatever their personal interests. To give just four examples:

- Our budding musicians have access to one of the finest music provisions in the country
- Our Sixth Formers can choose from a very large range of A Level courses
- Our youngest pupils can enjoy outdoor learning in a Forest School and a year of free string instrument lessons
- Applicants for Oxford, Cambridge or the leading US universities will be able to access subject specialist mentoring from a large body of teaching staff stretching across three schools

In addition to the traditional sporting teams we offer morning fitness sessions for all, swimming, basketball, trampoline and football practices with the aim to enter local and ISA competitions. We also run a popular triathlon club. We have a new AstroTurf and sports hall, fitness suite and dance studio.

The School successfully participates in the Combined Cadet Force (CCF), The Duke of Edinburgh's Award and the Young Enterprise scheme.

The Nursery at the Loughborough Schools Foundation is based on our campus and offers childcare 51 weeks a year from age 6 weeks to 4 years.

For further information visit our website: www.lsf.org/amherst.

Charitable status. Loughborough Amherst School is part of the Loughborough Schools Foundation, which is a Registered Charity, number 1081765, and a Company Limited by Guarantee, registered in England, number 4038033. Registered Office: 3 Burton Walks, Loughborough, Leics LE11 2DU.

Luckley House School

Luckley Road, Wokingham, Berkshire RG40 3EU

Tel: +44 (0)118 978 4175
email: registrar@luckleyhouseschool.org
website: www.luckleyhouseschool.org
X/Twitter: @LuckleyHouse
Facebook: @LuckleyHouseSchool
Instagram: @luckleyhouseschool
LinkedIn: /Luckley-House-School

See full entry in the **Society of Heads** section, on **p. 539**.

LVS Ascot

London Road, Ascot, Berkshire SL5 8DR

Tel: 01344 882770
email: registrar@lvs.ascot.sch.uk
website: www.lvs.ascot.sch.uk
X/Twitter: @lvsascot
Facebook: @LVSAscot
Instagram: @lvs_ascot

See full entry in the **Society of Heads** section, on **p. 540**.

Lyonsdown School

3 Richmond Road, New Barnet, Hertfordshire EN5 1SA

Tel: 020 8449 0225
email: admissions@lyonsdownschool.co.uk
website: www.lyonsdownschool.co.uk
X/Twitter: @LyonsdownSchool
Facebook: @LyonsdownSchool
Instagram: @lyonsdownschool

See full entry in the **IAPS** section, on **p. 721**.

Maida Vale School

Gardener Schools Group

18 Saltram Crescent, London W9 3HR

Tel: 020 4511 6000
email: schooloffice@maidavaleschool.com
website: www.maidavaleschool.com
X/Twitter: @MaidaValeSchool
Facebook: @MaidaValeSchool
Instagram: @MaidaValeSchool
LinkedIn: /company/maidavaleschool

***Head*: Magnus Bashaarat**

Age Range. 11–18 Co-educational.

Number of Pupils. 160.

Fees per term (2023–2024). £8,517.

Maida Vale School, part of the Gardener Schools Group, is a co-educational, independent school for 11–18 year olds. We take a fresh approach to all areas of school life, while retaining core traditional values, we also have a broad curriculum, a vast enrichment programme, and an extended school day. This provides variety and flexibility, which allows our Pupils to develop their individual talents and fulfil their fullest potential.

For those interested in STEM, Maida Vale offers multiple science laboratories, computing suites, as well as D&T and CAD design spaces. Although academic rigour is at the centre of our school, sports and the arts form an important part of the day to day at Maida Vale. The school houses spacious studio facilities for dance, yoga and HIIT (high intensity interval training) classes.

We have access to a number of nearby sports grounds and facilities allowing our dynamic PE department to thrive, whilst our theatre and art studios provide a wide variety of drama, musical and artistic opportunities.

Each pupil receives individual attention both educationally and pastorally. We believe that children and young adults flourish when their self-esteem and confidence is bolstered. Our Personal Tutor Group system contributes greatly to this with each tutor meeting their tutee daily and remaining the same member of staff throughout the Pupil's seven years with us. We cultivate values of respect, tolerance, and community responsibility in everyone that attends Maida Vale.

Taking advantage of the school's location close to the heart of London, we use the city as a valuable resource, both within our learning and within extra-curricular activities. We frequently have guest speakers that give talks entrenched in their own life experiences. We also offer pupils the chance to experience residential activity-based courses in the UK, and cultural excursions abroad.

To find out more about joining Maida Vale School, view our admissions procedure via our website: www.maidavaleschool.com/admissions.

Maldon Court Preparatory School

Silver Street, Maldon, Essex CM9 4QE
Tel: 01621 853529
email: enquiries@maldoncourtschool.org
website: www.maldoncourtschool.org

***Principal*: Mrs L F Guest**, BEd Hons
Headteacher: Mrs E Mason

Age Range. 1–11 co-educational.
Number of Pupils. 144 Day pupils.
Fees per term (2023–2024). Reception £3,710; Years 1–6 £3,760.

Welcome to Maldon Court Preparatory School, a small, happy and caring school community where young children can flourish in a positive and supportive environment. Originally established in 1956, the school has maintained its vision of being run as a family-owned, friendly school with high expectations and standards.

Children here are encouraged to develop in all aspects of the broad and balanced curriculum. Each pupil is valued as an individual and allowed to develop at their own pace. Strengths and weaknesses are identified at an early age and our dedicated staff ensure that every child is challenged and supported to achieve their full potential through exploring the huge range of possibilities open to them.

Within this framework of close care and encouragement, Maldon Court delivers a first-class education, laying down strong foundations for the future. At the same time, great emphasis is placed on pastoral care, which is strengthened by a close partnership with parents and a strong family atmosphere that is evident throughout the school. The success of this ethos is reflected in the school's achievement of 'excellent' (the highest inspection rating) in every area in 2013. We are also delighted to have been graded 'Outstanding' in our Ofsted Nursery inspection in May 2017 and 'Outstanding' in our Nursery ISI Inspection in May 2017.

There is a love of sport at Maldon Court which has been nurtured and developed by the dedicated members of our PE Department. We aim for high levels of physical fitness and coordination, in turn fostering confidence and encouraging participation from children at all levels. The school enters teams both locally and nationally in a wealth of sporting events and competitions.

At the end of their time at Maldon Court, we are proud to see our boys and girls emerge as articulate, well-informed and interesting young people, comfortable in their abilities, buoyed by their achievements, ambitious and well equipped for the challenges that lie ahead.

Mander Portman Woodward (MPW)
London

90–92 Queen's Gate, London SW7 5AB
Tel: 020 7835 1355
email: london@mpw.ac.uk
website: https://www.mpw.ac.uk/locations/london/
X/Twitter: @mpwlondon
Facebook: @MPWLondon
Instagram: @mpw_london
LinkedIn: /school/mander-portman-woodward-limited

***Principal*: Sally Powell**, BA, PGCE, MPhil, PhD
Vice Principals:
Dee Robins
Rachel Sherman
Simon Horner

Age Range. 14–19+.
Number in School. 600.
Fees per term (2023–2024). From £11,411.

Tailored, not uniform. Founded in 1973, MPW London is one of the UK's leading Sixth Form colleges. Situated in the heart of one of the capital's most exclusive and vibrant locations, the college offers small classes in a socially relaxed yet highly academically disciplined environment.

A unique teaching method. We have a distinct approach to education with small classes of no more than nine students and a strong emphasis on exam techniques which have been proven over decades. Our Director of Studies system offers a high level of personal care, supporting welfare and academic progress.

Unrivalled range of courses. We offer a highly flexible curriculum of unrivalled depth and breadth, comprising A level, GCSE, retakes and university foundation programmes. We also run an acclaimed programme of Easter Revision courses each year.

Strong results and progression. Despite having a non-selective admissions policy and a wide variety of courses targeted at students of different academic abilities, our students achieve outstanding overall results year after year. In 2023, A*/A was the commonest grade at A level. These results unlock the doors to some of the UK's best universities – each year, approximately two-thirds of our students progress to top tier universities (Russell Group, University of London and specialist institutions).

Stunning location. MPW London is located in South Kensington (Zone 1), one of the most exclusive and affluent parts of the capital. MPW London is just a few minutes' walk from Hyde Park, Imperial College and many world-famous museums, including the Science Museum, the Natural History Museum and the Victoria & Albert Museum.

Rating 'Excellent' by ISI. In our latest Independent School Inspectorate (ISI) report published in February 2022, we received the highest rating of 'Excellent', prompting the inspectors to report: 'Students make rapid progress from their various starting points, in small-sized classes, due to highly effective specialist teaching and closely focused pastoral support.'

Maple Hayes Hall
Specialist School for Dyslexics

Abnalls Lane, Lichfield, Staffordshire WS13 8BL

Tel: 01543 264387
email: office@dyslexia.school
website: www.dyslexia.school
Facebook: @Maple-Hayes-Hall-School

***Co-Principals*: Dr E N Brown**, PhD, MSc, BA, MSCME, MINS, AFBPsS, CPsychol and Dr D J Brown, DPhil, MEd Psychology of SpLD, MA Oxon, PGCE

***Headteacher*: Mr David Lowe**

Age Range. 7–17.
Number in School. 120 Day Boys and Girls.
Fees per term (2023–2024). £5,690–£7,600.

Maple Hayes is a specialist independent day school approved under the 1996 Education Act as a co-educational school for children of average to very high intelligence who are not achieving their intellectual potential by normal teaching methods.

This school is under the direction of Dr E Neville Brown whose work in the field of learning strategies has achieved international recognition and includes a major breakthrough in the teaching of dyslexic children. Attention is paid to the individual child by teaching the basic literacy and numeracy skills required for the child to benefit from a full curriculum (with the exception of a foreign language). The school had an outstanding Ofsted report in November 2017.

The very favourable teacher to pupil ratio of 1:10 or better ensures a high standard of educational and pastoral care. The children's learning is under the supervision and guidance of a qualified educational psychologist.

Maple Walk Prep School

62A Crownhill Road, London NW10 4EB

Tel: 020 8963 3890
020 8965 7374 (Admissions)
email: admissions@maplewalkschool.co.uk
website: www.maplewalkschool.co.uk

***Head Teacher*: Claire Murdoch**

Age Range. 4–11 Co-educational.
Number of Pupils. 169.
Fees per term (2023–2024). £4,518.

Maple Walk, judged excellent in all areas (ISI Inspection, March 2020), is a happy, vibrant, exceptional value prep school for boys and girls aged 4–11 in north west London, nurturing children's wellbeing and academic best through fun, kindness and respect for one another.

We provide a safe, supportive and stimulating environment with small class sizes for outstanding learning and personal development where children flourish, developing self-confidence, self-esteem and social awareness.

Cultivating a growth mindset, Maple Walk's innovative, creative curriculum underpinned by academic rigour instils a love of learning and resilience ensuring each child is well prepared for whatever the future holds.

The numerous opportunities outside the classroom are fundamental to the school day. Through sporting activities, first class music, art and drama, we encourage every child to find their own particular strength with many gaining scholarships at top independent secondary schools.

Our enriching selection of after school clubs allows pupils to explore a diverse range of activities beyond the school day including skateboarding, gymnastics, animation, robotics and plenty more.

This educational journey is housed in purpose-built accommodation and comes with a host of eco credentials, including a ground source heat pump for our heating and hot water, solar PV panels for electricity and a growing sedum roof to attract local wildlife.

Entry into Reception is non-selective and based on the date the completed registration form is returned to our Registrar, with siblings given priority. Entry higher up the school is by interview and informal assessment in the classroom. We offer regular open days and welcome private tours.

The Mead School

16 Frant Road, Tunbridge Wells, Kent TN2 5SN
Tel: 01892 525837
email: office@themeadschool.co.uk
website: www.themeadschool.co.uk
X/Twitter: @TheMeadSchoolTW
Facebook: @themeadschoolTW
Instagram: @meadschooltunbridgewells

Headmistress: **Mrs C E Openshaw**

Age range. 3–11.
Number in School. 237.
Fees per term (2023–2024). Infants: £4,115; Juniors: £4,615 (nursery fees depending on sessions).

The Mead School is a thriving, co-educational prep school situated in the heart of Tunbridge Wells. The school, which was rated 'Excellent' in all areas in its most recent ISI Inspection Report (March 2023), is a true community and runs as a large family living under one roof.

The Mead's ethos is that a child who is happy and secure in school is one who is going to learn, thrive and aspire. School must be an exciting, fulfilling and safe place where every day is a new adventure and is positively anticipated, whether you are aged three or eleven.

The Mead enjoys a reputation of high academic standards within a caring, happy environment. Children are prepared for the highly selective Tunbridge Wells and Tonbridge Grammar Schools as well as a wide range of Independent and maintained secondary schools.

The Mead has exceptional music, drama and sport provision and over 30 extracurricular clubs to choose from. Fully catered provision is offered from 7.45 am to 5.30 pm.

Mill Hill International School

Milespit Hill, Mill Hill Village, London NW7 2RX
Tel: +44 (0)20 3826 3333
+44 (0)20 3826 3366 (Admissions)
email: office@millhillinternational.org.uk
international@millhillinternational.org.uk
website: www.millhill.org.uk/international
X/Twitter: @millhillintl
Facebook: @MillHillIntl
Instagram: @millhillintl

Motto: *Instilling values, inspiring minds*

Head: **Ms Sarah Bellotti**, BEd

Age Range. 13–17 Co-educational
Number of Pupils. 140.
Fees per term (2023–2024). Day £10,320 (including lunch), Weekly Boarding £14,165 (including meals), Full Boarding £16,417 (Year 9 and Year 10 & 11): Two Year GCSE course), Full Boarding £16,917 (Year 11: One Year GCSE course).

Overview. Mill Hill International is a co-educational boarding and day school for international pupils aged 13–17. The ground is a short walk from Mill Hill School, which sits in 115 acres of magnificent parkland on the edge of the North London Green Belt and just ten miles from Central London. Providing a wonderful environment in which to learn. Mill Hill International forms a part of the Mill Hill Education Group, a charitable collection of independent schools. Day, weekly and full boarding places are available for entry at Year 9, Year 10 and Year 11. Pupils from all over the world come together in an inspiring school to gain internationally recognised qualifications a transformational educational and cultural experience.

At Mill Hill International your child will develop habits of mind that will equip them for their educational journey in the UK and prepare them to face the challenges of life in the 21st century with confidence, resilience and creativity. Pupils are guided to seek courage and curiosity within themselves and apply them in all their endeavours. A traditional British educational experience is offered as well as an academic curriculum up to GCSE/IGCSE and specialist EAL teaching. Pupils for whom English is not their first language receive English language tuition while at the same time studying an appropriate range of other subjects in order to equip them for further study whether at Mill Hill School or elsewhere. Suitable also for British pupils returning to the UK after a period abroad, Mill Hill International offers a year 9 course to help pupils prepare for GCSE, an intensive one-year GCSE course for pupils entering Year 11 and a two-year GCSE programme in Year 10 where students will study between 8 and 12 subjects. In addition, there is a Spring and Summer School which offer courses to ages 12–17, combining English learning with academic subjects, including mathematics and science or sport. These core elements are complemented by a varied programme of creative activity classes including music, dance, drama and art.

The teaching is rigorous, challenging and exciting and have high expectations of every pupil. Class sizes are small and all teachers are qualified or trained in teaching English as an additional language so every pupil can progress quickly. In addition to the impressive resources of the Mill Hill International campus, pupils also have access to Mill Hill School's sports facilities, including the indoor heated swimming pool, sports hall, theatre and music school situated within over 115 acres of grounds Pupils are fully integrated with those from Mill Hill School throughout their time and share boarding houses

Charitable status. Mill Hill Education Group is the brand name for The Mill Hill School Foundation, a Registered Charity, number 1064758.

Moon Hall School

Specialist School for Dyslexic Children

Flanchford Road, Leigh, Reigate, Surrey RH2 8RE

Tel: 01306 611372
email: schooloffice@moonhall.co.uk
website: www.moonhallschoolreigate.co.uk
X/Twitter: @MoonHallReigate
Facebook: @moonhallschoolreigate
LinkedIn: /company/moon-hall-school-reigate

Chair of Governors: Mr Adrian Turner

***Headmistress*: Mrs Michelle Catterson**, BSc, PGCE

Age range. 7–16.
Number of children. 185.
Fees per term (2023–2024). £7,380–£8,793.

Moon Hall School is a thriving mainstream specialist school for Dyslexic children. We are *hugely* ambitious for our pupils in all aspects of their school life, we all champion them to be the very best version of themselves.

We tailor our curriculum to meet the needs of our pupils; our pupils will be challenged to push on and aim higher whatever their ability may be. Challenge and being able to push themselves is of great importance, in order to achieve the very best in their studies, whether this be on the sports field, the stage or in their academic lessons. Our curriculum includes a wide range of creative subjects in which our pupils can excel. We want our pupils to enjoy learning and the excitement to be gained from having an enquiring mind, to appreciate the wonder and complexity of the world and to have opportunities to be innovative.

GCSE results 2023: 52% overall GCSE pass rate across all subjects. 22% English Language Pass, 86% English Literature Pass, 36% Maths Pass. Given our pupils have dyslexia, this is a phenomenal achievement for all staff and pupils and demonstrates the value added that being a pupil at Moon Hall can bring.

Admission is based on a review of specialist reports relating to the child's educational needs or developmental progress and attendance at taster days. As a small school with a limited number of places, currently at full capacity, we have to carefully assess the suitability of each pupil before making a decision as to whether we can offer a place.

With high adult:pupil ratios our staff know our pupils individually and help them to develop independent learning strategies. Our pastoral support is exemplary, we know each pupil as an individual and we work with our families to create a supportive and enriching learning opportunity for them all. We work closely in partnership with our parents in all aspects of their child's development and wellbeing.

We provide our pupils with opportunities for teamwork and leadership, in which their personalities can develop and flourish. We encourage them to be positive, compassionate and know the value of making a contribution to their community. Our aim is for all our pupils to leave us with the qualifications they need for the next stage of their education and their adult life. Above all, we expect them to leave as confident, independent individuals, with integrity and enthusiasm for the future.

Charitable status. Moon Hall School is a Registered Charity, number 803481.

Moorland School

Ribblesdale Avenue, Clitheroe, Lancashire BB7 2JA

Tel: 01200 423833
email: enquiries@moorlandschool.co.uk
website: www.moorlandschool.co.uk
X/Twitter: @MoorlandSchool1
Facebook: @MoorlandPrivateSchool

***Headteacher*: Mrs Deborah Frost**

Head of Juniors: Ms Rachel Peachey

Age Range. 3 months–18 years.
Number of Pupils. 190 including 74 boarders.
Fees per term (2023–2024). Day (Reception–Year 13): £3,167–£5,333; Full Boarding: £8,667–£11,000; Weekly Boarding: £7,333–£10,000.

Moorland School is a thriving co-educational day and boarding school located in the historic town of Clitheroe within the picturesque Ribble Valley, in the North-West of England. The school enjoys excellent transport links to Manchester. We have an outstandingly beautiful site with more than 15 acres of grounds. Nearly half of the children at Moorland are boarders and we find it makes for a good social mix with our day pupils from the surrounding area. The opening of our purpose-built new building means our boarders can enjoy modern and spacious facilities, fully equipped with satellite television and Wi-Fi. Moorland can now offer the seamless transition from GCSE to A Level or BTEC study, through our thriving new Sixth Form Centre, which provides our students with the opportunity to settle in one place rather than having to move from school to school. Furthermore, the School boasts an outstanding elite football and elite ballet, unique to any British boarding school. These courses are led by field professionals in their respective areas.

Admission to Moorland. Parents and children are encouraged to visit the school to meet the Headteacher and see the school in action. Boarding or Day children are also welcome to attend Moorland for a one or two day 'taster visit'.

Kindergarten & Nursery. As well as having its own indoor soft-play area, the nursery also has a large outdoor play area within its extensive grounds, with unbroken views over Waddington Fell. The Nursery's superb layout of colourful rooms and equipment make it an ideal and exceptional learning environment.

Junior School. The Preparatory Department takes children between the ages of 4 and 11. The children have their own play area and IT suite and benefit from using the facilities of the Senior School such as science laboratories and sports hall.

The children follow Key Stages 1 and 2 of the National Curriculum with particular emphasis on numeracy and literacy. Our small class sizes allow every child to read to the Teacher on a daily basis. French is also included in the Junior curriculum.

The Senior School follows the criteria set down in the National Curriculum. We enter our pupils for the Standard Attainment Tests and for GCSE at the end of Key stage 4.

Football at Moorland. Our FA approved coach, Charles Jackson, is one of the UK's most innovative and well-respected football coaches. He teaches to a Premier League standard. He has worked at Moorland since November 2002. He also worked at the Manchester United Advanced Coaching Centre up to July 2005 and is now the Under 14 academy technical skills Development Coach at Manchester City FC. Mr Jackson is a full-time teacher at Moorland School, teaching children from age 4–18.

Pastoral Care. At Moorland children benefit from continuous pastoral support within a friendly family environment. By day, teaching staff provide continual support within small classes. Evening and weekend care is undertaken by the House Parent team.

More House School

Moons Hill,
Frensham, Farnham, Surrey GU10 3AP

Tel: 01252 792303
email: schooloffice@morehouseschool.co.uk
website: www.morehouseschool.co.uk
X/Twitter: @MHSFrensham
Facebook: @morehouseschoolfrensham
Instagram: @morehouseschoolfrensham
LinkedIn: /more-house-school-frensham

***Headmaster*: Mr Jonathan Hetherington**, BA Hons, MSc Ed, QTS

Age range. 8 to 18.

Number in school. 494: 74 Boarders, 420 Day Boys.

Fees per term (2023–2024). Full Boarding: £10,275–£11,400; Weekly Boarding: £9,416–£10,541; Day: £6,275–£7,400.

The largest school in the country for intelligent pupils with Dyslexia, Developmental Language Disorders and associated special educational needs.

More House School in Frensham, a registered charity, is rated 'Outstanding' by the government's schools inspectorate, Ofsted, in all aspects of its provision, including School, Sixth Form and Boarding, following an integrated inspection in March 2023 and a further Boarding and Welfare inspection in November 2023.

The school, for up to 515 boys, aged eight to 18, is nationally recognised as a centre for excellence in supporting pupils with specific learning and language difficulties; it also offers training in special educational needs for teachers and other educational professionals across the region and nationally.

Founded over eighty years ago, the school prides itself on using the best modern practices to increase confidence, make children feel valued and happy, and equip them with the tools they need to fulfil their potential at GCSE, A Level and other public examinations.

Boarding is run by caring staff. Situated in beautiful grounds, there are always ample opportunities to enjoy outdoor pursuits. The school's extensive extracurricular timetable encourages both day boys and boarders to make good use of their leisure time. There is a strong sense of community.

Facilities are good across all departments and there is an ongoing programme of building development.

Please visit our website for more information, including the dates of our biannual Open Days and to make an admissions or training enquiry.

Charitable status. More House School is a Registered Charity, number 311872. A Catholic foundation, we are open to all faiths and none, committed to helping boys succeed.

Mount House School

Camlet Way, Hadley Wood, Barnet, Hertfordshire EN4 0NJ

Tel: 020 8449 6889
email: schooladminofficer@mounthouse.org.uk
website: www.mounthouse.org.uk
X/Twitter: @MountHouseSch
Facebook: @MountHouseSchoolBarnet
Instagram: @mounthouse_school/?hl=en
LinkedIn: /school/mount-house-school

See full entry in the **Society of Heads** section, on **p. 543**.

Moyles Court School

Moyles Court, Ringwood, Hampshire BH24 3NF

Tel: 01425 472856
email: sally.spark@moylescourt.co.uk
website: www.moylescourt.co.uk
Facebook: @moylescourt

***Headmaster*: Mr Richard Milner-Smith**

Please see school website for full Staff list.

Age Range. 2½–16.

Number in School. Boarders: 22 boys, 16 girls. Day: 74 boys, 82 girls.

Fees per term (2023–2024). Senior Day £5,370–£5,660; Senior Boarding £9,840; Junior Day £2,695–£4,820; Junior Boarding £7,975; Nursery: please contact the school for session rates.

Moyles Court School is a non-selective day and boarding co-ed school taking pupils from 3 to 16 years and is housed in a 16th Century Manor house close to Ringwood, set within the beautiful New Forest National Park. It offers individualised learning, affordable fees and traditional core values. The boarding environment at Moyles Court School aims to provide a welcoming and supportive setting where boarders can flourish and develop within a safe and beautiful campus environment. It is an environment in which children grow, where confidence and self-belief are heightened and where values and skills are learnt that will stay with them for the rest of their lives.

In 2021 100% of pupils gained 5 or more GCSEs at Grade 4 and above (including Maths, English and Science), with 99% of all grades being above Grade 4. Over half the grades awarded (51%) were at Grade 7 or above (A and A*), with 32% of all grades reaching either 9 or 8.

We are proud of our academic results, with all our pupils showing that with great effort and determination, from both teacher and pupil alike, they can secure GCSE results way above their national predictions. However, we are also committed to educating the whole child, on the understanding that academic results will only take you so far in life. Sport, music and drama all flourish here and a vast range of extra-curricular activities ensure children are exposed to an exciting range of opportunities that will help shape and develop them as individuals.

In 2016, Moyles Court partnered with Broadway Education, owned by Lymington family Mark and Jo Broadway, in order to further capitalise on Moyles Court's success. The new strategic relationship complements Broadway Education's portfolio of schools.

Small class sizes, individualised learning, great teaching, extensive after-school provision, tailored transport and excellent pastoral care provide your children with the best possible start in life. Parents are welcome to book an appointment at any time to see the school and find out why everyone is talking about Moyles Court School. For further details visit the website at www.moylescourt.co.uk or contact Mrs Sally Spark, Admissions Registrar.

Mylnhurst Preparatory School & Nursery

Button Hill, Woodholm Road, Ecclesall, Sheffield S11 9HJ

Tel: 0114 236 1411
email: enquiries@mylnhurst.co.uk
website: www.mylnhurst.co.uk

A Catholic Foundation Welcoming Families of All Faiths – maximising the potential of your children through partnership within a challenging and supportive Catholic Christian Community.

***Headmaster*: Mr Michael Hibbert**

Age Range. 3–11 Co-educational.
Number of Pupils. 163.
Fees per term (2023–2024). £4,125.

Situated in extensive private grounds, Mylnhurst provides a state-of-the-art teaching environment supported by our outstanding school facilities, which include a 25m pool, dance studio, sports hall, Apple Mac suite and outdoor classroom.

With a strong emphasis on school-parent partnership, Mylnhurst embraces your high expectations and ensures each child benefits from an exciting and stimulating curriculum.

Top performing Sheffield School in the Times Top 100.

Be assured of a very warm welcome and the opportunity to work closely with our committed and talented staff. So, whether it be an informal chat or a school open day, we look forward to sharing our vision with you and discussing the exciting future of your children.

Charitable status. Mylnhurst Limited is a Registered Charity, number 1056683.

New Hall School

The Avenue, Boreham, Chelmsford, Essex CM3 3HS

Tel: 01245 467588
email: admissions@newhallschool.co.uk
website: www.newhallschool.co.uk
X/Twitter: @NewHallSchool
Facebook: @newhallschool
Instagram: @newhallschool_1642
LinkedIn: /school/new-hall-school

See full entry in the **HMC** section, on **p. 238**.

Newbridge Preparatory School

51 Newbridge Crescent
Tettenhall, Wolverhampton, West Midlands
WV6 0LH

Tel: 01902 751088
email: office@newbridgeprepschool.org.uk
website: www.newbridgeprepschool.org.uk

See full entry in the **IAPS** section, on **p. 733**.

Norfolk House School

4 Norfolk Road, Edgbaston, Birmingham B15 3PS

Tel: 0121 454 7021
email: info@norfolkhouseschool.co.uk
website: www.norfolkhouseschool.co.uk

See full entry in the **IAPS** section, on **p. 736**.

Notre Dame Preparatory School

147 Dereham Road, Norwich, Norfolk NR2 3TA

Tel: 01603 625593
email: headspa@notredameprepschool.co.uk
website: www.notredameprepschool.co.uk
Facebook: @notredameprepnorwich

Chair of Governors: Mr Kevin Long

***Headmaster*: Mr Rob Thornton**, MA Ed

Age Range. 2–11 Co-educational.

Number of Pupils. 180 Day.

Fees per term (2023–2024). £2,390–£2,590.

Notre Dame Prep School was originally founded by the Sisters of Notre Dame de Namur in 1864. The school transferred to its present site in 1971 and is now a Limited Company with charitable status. The school maintains the traditions and the spirit of the Sisters of Notre Dame and the former name and ethos.

As a Catholic school we endeavour to nurture a love of God through Jesus Christ in all the children. The school has an ethos of love and care and embraces children of all faiths or none.

Children are treated as individuals, respected, nurtured and encouraged to embrace and fulfil their potential in all areas of school life. We have excellent links with High Schools in both the maintained and independent sectors.

The school achieves well above-average results in external tests and has a strong academic reputation. Children are prepared carefully for entry to selective independent schools. Subjects include English, Maths, Science, Computing, Design and Technology, Art, Geography, PE, History, Music, RE, French and Personal, Social and Health Education.

The school has a very strong musical tradition and has a wide range of extra-curricular musical activities on offer including Choir, Chamber Choir, Recorder, Piano, Guitar, Flute, Violin, Saxophone, Clarinet lessons, Drums and Singing. Particularly strong singers are able to audition for chorister positions for St John's Cathedral which is a 1,000 yd walk from school.

Sports include Football, Cricket, Rugby, Netball, Rounders, Hockey, Tennis and Swimming.

The school offers a wide range of extra-curricular activities including Speech and Drama, Chess, Cookery, Debating, Photography, Arts and Crafts, Science, Sewing, Young Explorers, Creative Writing, Badminton and other sports and activities.

Catering is provided in house and lunches and dinners are excellent. We have an After-School Activities Club which runs until 5.45 pm incorporating homework club (Prep) and games activities for younger children. Holiday clubs are available in school holidays at agreed times.

Charitable status. Notre Dame Preparatory School (Norwich) Limited is a Registered Charity, number 269003.

Oakfield Preparatory School

125–128 Thurlow Park Road, West Dulwich, London SE21 8HP

Tel: 020 8670 4206
email: admissions@oakfield.dulwich.sch.uk
website: www.oakfield.dulwich.sch.uk
X/Twitter: @oakfieldprep
Facebook: @OakfieldPrep
Instagram: @oakfieldprep

***Head*: Mrs Moyra Thompson**, MA Cantab, PGCE, NPQH

Age Range. 2–11

Number in School. 163 Boys, 149 Girls.

Fees per term (2023–2024). Years 1–6: £4,831. Fees for Early Years Foundation Stage fees based on chosen sessions and Early Years funding where applicable.

Oakfield is a nurturing, diverse co-educational prep school, founded in 1887 in the heart of Dulwich, which blends a modern curriculum with strong pastoral values. It is committed to supporting every child to be the absolute best that they can be and helping them find the right senior school for them at 11+.

The school site of nearly three acres allows plenty of space for play and games and we enjoy strong regional and national success in both sport and drama. We offer specialist teaching in Spanish, music and art and have taught philosophy for children for many years.

We offer full wraparound care and there are more than 40 after-school clubs available to children in Upper Foundation and above. These include Mandarin, Karate, Music Tech and Fencing among many others.

We are a non-selective school but we conduct observations to ensure Oakfield will be the best environment for your child. Entry to the 2+ Nursery is by observation. Once accepted, the child will progress automatically into the Foundation Years (subject to the admissions policy) and Main School. Entry at 3+ and 4+ is also by observation. Entry at 7+ follows an assessment and observation in a class setting.

Prospective parents – and children – would be very welcome to join one of our Open Mornings or arrange a private tour with our registrar.

Oakhyrst Grange School

160 Stanstead Road, Caterham, Surrey CR3 6AF

Tel: 01883 343344
email: office@oakhyrstgrangeschool.co.uk
website: www.oakhyrstgrangeschool.co.uk

Chair of Board of Governors: Mrs Pauline Clark

***Headmaster*: Mr Alex Gear**, BEd

Age Range. 4–11.

Number in School. 147 Day Boys and Girls.

Fees per term (2023–2024). £1,654–£3,836.

Oakhyrst Grange School is an independent, co-educational preparatory day school for boys and girls between 4 and 11 years.

The School was established in 1950 and moved to its present premises in Stanstead Road in 1957. Since September 1973 the School has been administered by a non-profit making trust.

Standing in five acres of open country and woodland and surrounded by the Green Belt, the School enjoys a fine position amongst the Surrey Hills.

The school has a wide and imaginative curriculum, which includes traditional teaching combined with innovative ideas. Small class sizes, with a maximum of 20 pupils, and an excellent teacher to pupil ratio enable pupils to work at their own rate and capabilities whilst being encouraged to meet new challenges.

Our pupils secure the offer of places at prominent senior schools, including scholarships and awards across the range of academic, all-rounder, drama, music, art and sport.

There are many sporting opportunities offered and particularly high standards have been reached in cross-country, swimming, football, judo and athletics where ISA National level has been achieved. The pupils compete in many inter house, inter school and area competitions. The school also has its own heated indoor swimming pool, all-weather floodlit multi-use games area, tennis, netball, hockey and 5-a-side court, sports pitch, cross-country course and gymnasium.

Extra-curricular music lessons are offered and much music making also takes place as part of the normal school timetable. The school has an orchestra, in addition to flute, guitar, string and cello ensembles along with a chamber choir, all of whom perform regularly.

In addition to the curriculum the pupils can enjoy an extensive range of clubs and activities throughout the week. At Oakhyrst Grange School we are very proud of our Forest School status. A senior leader is fully trained in Forest School Activities and it is an integral part of our Year 3 curriculum and whole school extra-curricular activities.

Academic excellence is encouraged, every child is expected to attain his or her individual potential. The School helps children to develop self confidence, independence and a readiness for their next school.

Charitable status. Oakhyrst Grange School Educational Trust is a Registered Charity, number 325043. It exists to provide an all-round education, to give the children success and the best possible start.

Orchard School

Higham Road, Barton-le-Clay, Bedfordshire MK45 4RB

Tel: 01582 882054
email: admin@orchardschool.org.uk
website: www.orchardschool.org.uk

See full entry in the **IAPS** section, on **p. 742**.

Park School

45 Queens Park South Drive, Bournemouth BH8 9BJ

Tel: 01202 396640
email: office@parkschool.co.uk
website: www.parkschool.co.uk
Facebook: @ParkSchoolPrep

***Headteacher*: Mrs Melanie Dowler**, BSc Hons, PGCE

Age range. 3 months to 11 years.

Number in school. 278 in total – 157 Boys, 121 Girls.

Fees per term (2023–2024). £2,910–£3,990.

Park School is a thriving co-educational junior day school in a pleasant residential area near Bournemouth town centre. Our last full ISI Educational Quality and Compliance Inspection in February 2023 awarded the school 'Excellent' across all academic and pastoral areas of the School and EYFS.

Pupils are taught in small classes in a caring, happy environment. The school is geared principally towards academic achievement, with an emphasis on nurturing individual progress. At the heart of all we do is the belief that children will achieve their best when they are happy. We foster a positive ethos and the development of the all-round child. This covers not only work in the classroom, but all other aspects of school life: games, music, the arts and other activities. Sport is an important part of Park School life and we use our stunning facility at Dean Park for games lessons and sports fixtures.

Pupils are prepared for entry to Senior Independent Schools and Bournemouth and Poole Grammar Schools through tests at 11+ years. Many children gain scholarships to Senior Independent Schools.

Most pupils join us in the Nursery and Reception years but there are occasionally vacancies further up the School. An offer of a place is made only after prospective pupils have been assessed.

Park School Nursery is open between 8.00 am and 6.00 pm Monday to Friday all year round with the exception of Christmas week and Bank Holidays.

Parsons Green Prep

1 Fulham Park Road, London SW6 4LJ

Tel: 020 7371 9009
email: office@parsonsgreenprep.co.uk
website: www.parsonsgreenprep.co.uk
X/Twitter: @pgpschoollondon
Facebook: @parsonsgreenprep
Instagram: @ParsonsGreenPrep

See full entry in the **IAPS** section, on **p. 747**.

Pitsford School

Pitsford Hall, Pitsford, Northamptonshire NN6 9AX

Tel: 01604 880306
email: office@pitsfordschool.com
website: www.pitsfordschool.com
X/Twitter: @Pitsford_School
Facebook: @PitsfordSchool
Instagram: @pitsfordschool

See full entry in the **Society of Heads** section, on **p. 549**.

Portland Place School

Alpha Plus Group

56–58 Portland Place, London W1B 1NJ

Tel: 020 7307 8700
email: admin@portland-place.co.uk
website: www.portland-place.co.uk
X/Twitter: @PortlandPlaceHd
Facebook: @PortlandPlaceSchool
Instagram: @PortlandPlaceSchool

See full entry in the **Society of Heads** section, on **p. 550.**

Prenton Preparatory School

Mount Pleasant, Oxton, Wirral CH43 5SY

Tel: 0151 652 3182
email: enquiry@prentonprep.co.uk
website: www.prentonprep.co.uk
Facebook: @PrentonPreparatorySchool

Directors: Prenton Preparatory School Ltd is part of the Forfar Education Group

Chairman: Mr John Forsyth

***Headteacher*: Mr M T R Jones**

EYFS Lead: Miss J Orme
KS1 Lead: Mrs A Beecroft
KS2 Lead: Mrs C Taylor
SENCo: Dr A Pemberton

Age Range. 2½–11.

Number in School. Day: 74 Boys, 38 Girls.

Fees per term (2023–2024). From £2,615 part-time in Foundation Stage (with free places available for up to 30 hours) to £3,630 (Juniors).

Founded in 1935.

Prenton Preparatory School is an ISI excellent rated, co-educational day school for children aged 2½–11 years, situated on the Wirral about a mile from Junction 3 of the M53.

The building is a large Victorian house which has been carefully converted into the uses of a school. There is a large playground and gardens. Facilities include an ICT/Science block and an Art block. The Foundation Stage outdoor play area is also a valuable addition to the school.

The children benefit from small classes and individual attention in a holistic approach to their education within a disciplined environment which enables them to realise their full potential.

The school offers a broad curriculum covering the whole National Curriculum and more with a particular emphasis on the three main National Curriculum core subjects: English, Mathematics and Science. French is taught from an early age and swimming forms a regular part of the curriculum from Year 1 upwards.

Children are prepared for entrance examinations to county, independent and grant-maintained grammar schools, gaining well above-average pass rates.

Childcare facilities are available from 8.00am to 6.00pm. Clubs are provided at lunchtime and after school. They include football, cricket, computers and technology, karate, swimming, dance, netball, music group, speech & drama and musical instruments.

The school has a wide range of sporting teams that compete in local and regional fixtures and competitions. These include: swimming, water polo, cross-country, football, netball, cricket, rounders and athletics. Several of these teams have been successful enough to qualify for National tournaments in recent years.

Art, drama, dance and music also play an important part in school life and parents and members of the wider school community enjoy the regular performances that are part of the annual calendar.

Princethorpe College

Princethorpe, Rugby, Warwickshire CV23 9PX

Tel: 01926 634200
email: post@princethorpe.co.uk
website: www.princethorpe.co.uk
X/Twitter: @PrincethorpeCol
Facebook: @princethorpecollege
Instagram: @ThePrincethorpeFoundation

See full entry in the **HMC** section, on **p. 255**.

Priory School

Sir Harry's Road, Edgbaston, Birmingham B15 2UR

Tel: 0121 440 4103
email: enquiries@prioryschool.net
website: www.prioryschool.net
X/Twitter: @PrioryEdgbaston
Facebook: @prioryschooledgbaston

Chair of Governors: Ms Heather Somerfield

***Headmaster*: Mr Jonathan Cramb**, BA Hons, PGCE, MEd

Age Range. 6 months to 18 years.

Number in School. 400.

Fees per term (2023–2024). £3,870–£5,860.

The school, founded on its present site in 1936 by the Sisters of the Society of the Holy Child Jesus, stands in 17 acres of parkland in the pleasant suburb of Edgbaston, only 2 miles from the centre of Birmingham. The school has extensive playing fields, excellent AstroTurf tennis courts, a multi-gym, athletics facilities and football and cricket pitches. There are minibuses running to and from school and frequent bus services to all parts of the city.

The school has an excellent Early Years Department on site which offers care for 51 weeks per annum and accepts children from the age of 6 months. All pupils are able to remain in After Care until 6.00pm if preferred.

The school has a diverse, inclusive pupil community built on strong Catholic heritage values and attitudes, welcoming children of all faiths and none. Pupils are taught by specialist teachers from the age of 9 and in the Senior School the curriculum is broad and balanced with pupils benefiting from small class sizes and individual attention, enabling them to make excellent progress in their academic development.

The school, whilst remaining proudly multi-ability, is justly proud of the academic achievements of the pupils. A wide range of subjects is available for GCSE and A Level, with good facilities, including well-equipped science laboratories, language resources rooms, Information Technology facilities, sports centre, multi-gym and performing arts Suite. The new Mayfield building opened in 2019, housing six new Preparatory classrooms, it marks the initial stage of a five-year development programme.

Priory School aims to develop the whole child, so that as well as achieving academic excellence, its pupil grow into confident, articulate, well-rounded individuals.

Entry to the school is by interview, assessment and day visit. Scholarships are awarded at 11+. Means tested bursaries may be awarded in cases of financial need.

Parents are warmly welcomed into the school to discuss individual needs. Full details prior to the visit may be obtained from the Admissions Registrar.

Charitable status. Priory School is a Registered Charity, number 518009.

Priory School of Our Lady of Walsingham

Beatrice Avenue, Whippingham, Isle of Wight PO32 6LP

Tel: 01983 861222
email: mail@prioryschool.org.uk
website: www.prioryschool.org.uk
X/Twitter: @PriorySchoolIW
Facebook: @prioryschoolwhippingham

***Principal*: Mr David EJJ Lloyd**

Age Range of pupils. 4–18 years.
Number of pupils. 182, Boys 93, Girls 89.
Fees per annum. £7,350–£11,850.
Maximum teaching class size. 16.

Priory School is an independent co educational day school for boys and girls aged 4–18 years. We are a non-denominational school, run with a Christian ethos under the patronage of Our Lady of Walsingham, the national shrine to Mary the Mother of Christ. Originally founded in Shanklin in 1993 out of Upper Chine School, the Matyjaszek family (Edmund & Fiona) took over ownership in 2009, and in 2012 the school moved to the historic site of Queen Victoria's school at Whippingham.

We are all immensely proud that Priory School maintains a family atmosphere where pupils feel safe, secure and can thrive in all areas of school life, curricular and co-curricular. The values of kindness and respect, and the development of the individual underpin all that we do, and our small class sizes facilitate expert knowledge of the child and very strong relationships between staff and pupils. Staff are skilled in helping pupils to fulfil their potential and deliver personalised and flexible pastoral care and excellent academic results. Our results are some of the best, if not the best, on the Isle of Wight each year. Moral and ethical decision making are central to our provision, and we encourage all members of our school community to be upstanders and not bystanders. Pupil voice is very important to us and pupils take responsibility for the continuous improvement of the school.

The aim of Priory School is to offer a first class education at an affordable cost in a well structured and compassionately run environment in order to become and remain the school of choice for parents and pupils on the Isle of Wight. We operate an 'open house' policy and parents considering Priory School are encouraged to book a tour of the school to see us in situ. All applicants come for three taster days to fully experience all that Priory School has to offer, and we are very proud of how much pupils enjoy their time with us. Happy pupils make for successful pupils and not the other way round.

For more information, please visit our website, www.prioryschool.org.uk.

Queen Ethelburga's Collegiate

Thorpe Underwood, York YO26 9SS

Tel: 01423 333330
email: admissions@qe.org
website: www.qe.org
X/Twitter: @qethelburgas
Facebook: @queenethelburgas
Instagram: @queenethelburgas/
LinkedIn: /queen-ethelburga's-college

Motto: *To be the best that I can with the gifts that I have.*

Co-educational Day and Boarding School.

***Principal*: Daniel Machin**

Head of Chapter House: Karen Kilkenny
Head of King's Magna: Joseph Birchall
Head of the College: Steven Turner
Head of the Faculty: Lauren Blakeley

Age Range. 3 months–19 years.
Number of Pupils. 1,400.
Fees per term (2023–2024). Day: £4,100–£6,950; Boarding: £11,150–£12,600 (UK students), £18,450–£19,950 (International students).

Set in more than 220 acres of beautiful North Yorkshire countryside, Queen Ethelburga's has provided students with a vibrant and supportive school community since 1912.

Queen Ethelburga's is an Excellent rated Collegiate (ISI 2019). We are known locally, nationally, and internationally as a group of four schools that promotes the highest standards in all that it does. The Collegiate welcomes girls and boys from 3 months and supports them through four schools – Chapter House (3 months to Year 5), King's Magna (Year 6 to 9), The College and The Faculty (both Year 10 to 13).

This unique make up of four smaller schools is designed to maintain a nurturing family atmosphere and some individuality, each having their own Heads and

Staff teams. This allows the staff to know students thoroughly and form outstanding student teacher relationships based on mutual respect and unwavering support. QE's Hill Standard is 'To be the best that I can with the gifts that I have' providing every child with a springboard to their individual successes, whichever pathway they choose. We place great emphasis on our children growing into resilient, caring, compassionate and confident adults, who develop independence and initiative, and who can take responsibility for their own learning and futures.

Our exam results speak for themselves, consistently ranking us amongst the top day and boarding schools in the UK, with students benefiting from incredible study, boarding and leisure facilities as part of campus life.

In 2023, students in The Collegiate (QE College and QE Faculty) achieved 80% A*/A at A Level with students in The Faculty also achieving 76% Distinction in BTECs. In addition, our Year 11s scored 63% 7–9 (A*-A equivalent) at GCSE Level.

Alongside academic success, at Queen Ethelburga's Collegiate (QE) we aim to provide a holistic education which supports students to develop their knowledge, skills, and experience beyond the classroom. We provide a broad enrichment curriculum to ensure students become well-rounded individuals, gaining skills in leadership and teamwork, as well as developing self-confidence and self-awareness, respect for others, and their environment.

Care is the most important element within the QE community; every member of the Collegiate, staff and student, is responsible for the pastoral care and happiness of the site. QE offers support and guidance to all students and parents to ensure that we are all working to support individual student needs and equipping them with the right skills, not only to be successful in education, but to excel in their chosen career and life in general. Our dedicated THRIVE@QE programme offers all students a huge range of activities to support their positive mental health and wellbeing.

Our reputation has grown considerably over recent years, and we believe this is due to our drive to ensure that our outcomes for QE students, across all areas of their endeavour and aspiration, match those of the world's best schools.

Radnor House Sevenoaks School

Combe Bank Drive, Sundridge, Kent TN14 6AE

Tel: Senior School 01959 563720
Preparatory School 01959 564320
email: admissions@radnor-sevenoaks.org
website: www.radnor-sevenoaks.org
X/Twitter: @radnorsevenoaks
Facebook: @radnorsevenoaks
Instagram: @radnorsevenoaks

Chairman of Board of Directors: Mr Colin Diggory, BSc Hons, PGCE, MA, EdD, CMath, FIMA, FRSA

***Head*: Mr David Paton**

Head of Prep School: Ms Philippa Lang

Radnor House Sevenoaks is an independent school with entry from the term that pupils are aged 2 up to the age of 18. (*See also Preparatory School entry in IAPS section.*) In September 2014, the school became co-educational and in 2016, the school name was changed from Combe Bank to Radnor House Sevenoaks. Radnor House is proud to be a member of the Round Square global community of schools.

Aims and ethos. The school's mission is to future-proof pupils to give them the very best start in life. Academic qualifications are an important aspect of this but so too are interpersonal skills such as emotional intelligence and leadership and global citizenship. Underpinning their approach to education is a set of core values – excellence, respect, courage and perseverance – which form the bedrock of the school and provide a moral compass for children from school through to adulthood. Pupil happiness is a priority, as a happy child is one who will thrive, grasp opportunities to learn and develop into a confident and well-balanced young person. A focus of Radnor House Sevenoaks is to be a pioneer in preparing the children for the digital age by working with Microsoft to become one of their flagship schools as they aim to build adults who can thrive in the world of tomorrow by using technology to propel their learning forward.

Location. Situated in a Palladian Mansion and set in superb grounds with 28 acres of parkland just outside Sevenoaks, the school has excellent facilities. The Nursery, Prep School, Senior School and Sixth Form are on the same site and there are many positive links between them, so that all pupils have access through the school until they leave at 18.

Curriculum. A modern and broad range of subjects is taught at all age levels. English, Mathematics, Sciences and an MFL are compulsory at GCSE. Pupils can then choose from Art, Computer Science, Drama, Economics, English Literature, RE, Geography, History, Mathematics, iMedia, Business, Modern Languages, Music, PE, Psychology, Science, Sociology and Photography subjects at A Level. The school boasts a strong Art department with an innovative graphic design suite, alongside a popular Performing Arts faculty with regular drama and musical performances in which wide participation is achieved. Radnor House Sevenoaks has a well-earned reputation for competitive success in a wide range of sports with its focus sports being football, hockey, cricket and swimming for both boys and girls. Swimming in the 25-metre indoor pool is a particularly popular activity from Nursery through to Sixth Form. Outdoor Adventurous Education has taken a firm place on the curriculum in the form of Forest School and Bush Craft for the Prep school, and Outdoor Education forming part of the Senior School curriculum alongside the option to participate in DofE awards.

Admission. Children enter the Prep school in Nursery from their 2nd birthday. Other entry points are Reception and Year 4. For the Senior School, pupils take the School's entrance examination at 11+ and 13+. Deferred entry is offered for Year 9. Good passes at GCSE are also expected for the A Level subjects of choice in order to join the Sixth Form. There are a number of places available for Sixth Form entry, with offers conditional on GCSE results.

Transport. Private bus transport is organised for 6 significant routes, to be paid for on a termly basis.

Fees per term (2023–2024). Senior School: £7,200–£7,760 (Lunch £350); Preparatory School: £4,315–£5,570 (Lunch £325); Nursery: £1,140 for 3 sessions per week and Transition £1,900 with an additional session being £380 (includes lunch).

Scholarships. Radnor House Sevenoaks offers a range of Academic, Art, Drama, Music, Sport and All-Rounder scholarships for entry into Year 7, Year 9 and the Sixth Form. There are also Academic scholarships awarded into Year 4.

Scholarships are typically worth 10% of the annual tuition fee but may, in exceptional circumstances, be increased through the award of an Outstanding Scholarship which is entirely at the Head's discretion. In addition, means-tested bursaries worth up to 50% of the tuition fee, are also available but only after a scholarship has been awarded.

Reddiford School

38 Cecil Park, Pinner, Middlesex HA5 5HH

Tel: 020 8866 0660
email: office@reddiford.org.uk
website: www.reddiford.co.uk
Facebook: @reddifordschool
LinkedIn: /company/reddiford-school

See full entry in the **IAPS** section, on **p. 758**.

RGS Dodderhill

Droitwich Spa, Worcestershire WR9 0BE

Tel: 01905 778290
email: dodderhill@rgsw.org.uk
website: www.dodderhill.co.uk
X/Twitter: @dodderhill
Facebook: @RGS-Dodderhill

See full entry in the **GSA** section, on **p. 471**.

Rochester Independent College

254 St Margaret's Banks, Rochester, Kent ME1 1HY

Tel: 01634 828115
email: admissions@rochester-college.org.uk
website: www.rochester-college.org.uk
X/Twitter: @rochesterindcol
Facebook: @RochesterIndependentCollege
Instagram: @rochesterindcollege
LinkedIn: /school/rochester-college

***Principal*: Alistair Brownlow**, MA Hons St Andrews, MPhil Glasgow, MEd Buckingham

Senior Vice Principal: Kelly Flatman, BA Hons Leeds (Graphic Design)

Vice Principal (*Sixth Form*): Ian Pay, BA Hons, MA Lancaster, MEd Buckingham (History, Politics)

Vice Principal (*Lower School*): Leighton Bright, BA Hons Reading, PGCE, MA (SEN) CCCU, SENCO

Age range. 11–19 Co-educational.

Number of pupils. 370 (including 120 single-room boarding places).

Fees per annum (2023–2024). Tuition: £15,600–£22,800. Weekly Boarding: £15,600; Full Boarding: £12,660–£18,000.

Rochester Independent College is an alternative to conventional secondary education with a happily distinctive ethos. Accepting day students from the age of 11 and boarders from 14, the focus is on examination success in a lively, supportive and informal atmosphere. Students are encouraged to be themselves and achieve exam results that often exceed their expectations. There is no uniform, no bells ring and everybody is on first-name terms. The average class size is 8.

Students enjoy being here and are treated as young adults. We encourage them to search for their own answers, to voice their opinions, to think critically, creatively and independently. They leave not only with excellent examination results but with enthusiasm for the future and new confidence about themselves and their education.

Personal tutors work closely with sixth-form students to give advice about course combinations and help ensure that their courses are designed to meet the requirements of university entrance. With such small class sizes individual attention is not only available, it's practically inescapable.

The College has particular academic strengths in the Sciences, Mathematics, English Literature, Social Sciences and the Creative and Visual Arts including Film, Photography and Digital Media.

The College's reputation for academic excellence is founded on almost 40 years' experience of rigorous teaching. Students come to us for a variety of reasons and from many different backgrounds. We are not academically selective; our only entrance qualification is an honest determination to work hard. Our results however are always ranked among the best of the academically selective schools and students secure places at top universities. Direct entry into any year group is possible and the College also offers intensive one year GCSE and A Level courses as well as retake programmes. International students benefit from specialised English Language teaching support.

In 2021, Rochester Independent College won the Independent Schools Association 2021 award for Excellence and Innovation in Fine Arts. The judges were impressed with the huge range of ways in which the College values, promotes and gives profile to the arts and considered the College an inspiration to the whole sector. The link between an aesthetic appreciation of the visual arts and personal development runs through all aspects of school life and is highly valued by the whole school community.

The College Halls combine the informality of a university residence with the supervision and pastoral support appropriate for young adults. The College offers students the opportunity to thrive in an atmosphere of managed independence and acts as a stepping stone between school and university. All accommodation is on campus and in single rooms.

Rochester Independent College is part of the Dukes Education Group.

Rookwood School

Weyhill Road, Andover, Hampshire SP10 3AL
Tel: 01264 325900
email: office@rookwoodschool.org
website: www.rookwoodschool.org
X/Twitter: @rookwood_school
Facebook: @rookwoodschool

***Headmaster*: Mr A Kirk-Burgess**, BSc, PGCE, MSc Oxon [on sabbatical]

Acting Head: Mrs J Jellard
Deputy Head: Mrs E Hacker
Head of Senior School: Mr A Kirk-Burgess
Head of Lower School: Mrs E Ozanne

Age Range. Co-educational 2–18 with boarders from age 7.

Number in School. 215: 116 girls, 99 boys (EYFS 43).

Fees per term (2023–2024). Boarding: £8,849–£10,565. Day: £3,684–£6,265. Nursery: £6.00 per hour (Early Years Education Funding accepted). Flexi and occasional boarding also available.

Hailed by the ISI as an "outstandingly happy and successful school", Rookwood is an independent non-selective day and boarding school for girls and boys aged 2–18 years in Andover, Hampshire.

Described as "warm, welcoming and nurturing", Rookwood is known for its family atmosphere and strong pastoral care which encourages each and every child to achieve their very best with excellent results. In 2022 40% of all GCSEs were awarded at Grade 7 or above and 94% of our students achieved GCSEs at Grade 4 or above.

Set in almost ten acres of private grounds Rookwood has an impressive range of amenities including a state-of-the-art sports hall, outdoor swimming pool, excellent art and science facilities. Rookwood's Private Sixth Form opened in September 2021.

Both Music and Drama thrive at Rookwood, with every child encouraged to take part, whilst the Physical Education department is equally busy with several pupils advancing to represent their favourite sports at national level in recent years.

In addition to its many tangible achievements Rookwood is committed to delivering excellent pastoral care and takes great pride in seeing its pupils develop into confident, resilient and principled young adults. The School also offers a rich and varied programme of extra-curricular activities for all ages and interests giving pupils the opportunity to develop new skills, discover new passions, grow socially and emotionally and to simply enjoy themselves.

Rookwood's boarding provision was recently rated as 'excellent' in all areas by the ISI with boarders receiving a unique 'home-from-home' experience. Family-style meal times, experienced and supportive boarding staff and busy weekends all combine to ensure that Rookwood's boarders receive the best possible care.

Prospective pupils and their parents are warmly invited to visit the school (please see website for latest information). Alternatively, if you require any further information or would like to make an individual appointment, please do not hesitate to contact the Registrar directly on 01264 325910.

Admission is by school reports and individual visits. Scholarships are available at 11+, 13+ and 16+. Means-tested bursaries are available throughout the school.

Rookwood is conveniently situated close to Andover town centre and less than 10 minutes' walk to Andover railway station, with good services to Salisbury, Basingstoke and London Waterloo. By road, there is easy access from the A303 and A343, with the journey from Andover to London taking about one and a half hours. School bus services are also available from Newbury and North West Hampshire.

Charitable status. Rookwood School is a Registered Charity, number 307322. It exists to provide education for children.

Rosemead Preparatory School and Nursery

70 Thurlow Park Road, West Dulwich, London SE21 8HZ
Tel: 020 8670 5865
email: admissions@rosemeadprepschool.org.uk
website: www.rosemeadprepschool.org.uk
X/Twitter: @RosemeadPrep
Facebook: @rosemeadprep
LinkedIn: /rosemeadprep

See full entry in the **IAPS** section, on **p. 766**.

Ruckleigh School

17 Lode Lane, Solihull, West Midlands B91 2AB
Tel: 0121 705 2773
email: office@ruckleigh.co.uk
website: www.ruckleigh.co.uk

See full entry in the **IAPS** section, on **p. 769**.

Russell House

Station Road, Otford, Sevenoaks, Kent TN14 5QU
Tel: 01959 522352
email: head@russellhouse.kent.sch.uk
website: www.russellhouseschool.co.uk
X/Twitter: @RussellHouseSch
Facebook: @RussellHouseSchool
Instagram: @russell_house_school

See full entry in the **IAPS** section, on **p. 770**.

Sacred Heart School

Mayfield Lane, Durgates, Wadhurst, East Sussex TN5 6DQ
Tel: 01892 783414
email: admin@sacredheartwadhurst.org.uk
website: www.sacredheartwadhurst.org.uk
Facebook: @sacredheartwadhurst
Instagram: @sacredheartwadhurst

Chair of Governors: Mrs Hilary Blake

***Head Teacher*: Mrs Johanna Collyer**, MA, NPQSL, PGCE

Age range. 2–11 Co-educational.
Number of pupils. 145.
Fees per term (2023–2024). £3,310.

Sacred Heart School is a small independent Catholic primary school and Nursery, nestling in the heart of the Sussex countryside.

We welcome boys and girls from 2–11, and with pupil numbers around 145, we have the opportunity to know each child individually, to recognise and encourage their strengths and support them in overcoming areas of difficulty.

Our pupils enjoy a high degree of academic success, regularly obtaining places at their first choice of school, including passes at 11+ and Scholarships.

Courtesy and care for each other are important values nurtured at Sacred Heart School where children play and work well together.

Charitable status. Sacred Heart School, as part of the Arundel and Brighton Diocesan Trust, is a Registered Charity, number 252878.

St Anne's Preparatory School

154 New London Road, Chelmsford, Essex CM2 0AW
Tel: 01245 353488
email: admin@stannesprep.essex.sch.uk
website: stannesprep.co.uk
X/Twitter: @StAnnesPrep1925
Facebook: @stannespreparatory1925

***Head Teacher*: Mrs V Eveleigh**

Proprietor: Mr P Robson
DSL: Mrs V Eveleigh
Pastoral Lead: Mrs A McClymont

Age Range. 3–11.
Number of Children. 137.
Fees per term (2023–2024). £3,175–£3,400.

Recently ranked 10th nationally in *The Sunday Times* Parent Power Survey, St Anne's is a co-educational day school, with its own excellent nursery facility. Established in 1925, the school is conveniently situated in the centre of Chelmsford. The building is a large Victorian house, which has been carefully converted into the uses of a school. Extensive lawned areas, AstroTurf, playground and Nursery play area provide ample space for both recreation and games lessons. In addition, older pupils benefit from the use of the excellent sports facilities at the nearby Essex County Cricket Club.

The children benefit from small classes and individual attention in a disciplined but happy environment, which enables them to realise their full potential. Provision is made in the school for the gifted as well as those pupils less educationally able. Classrooms are bright and well equipped and the teachers are chosen for their qualifications, experience and understanding of the needs of their pupils.

St Anne's combines modern teaching with the best of traditional values. The school maintains a high standard of academic education giving great emphasis to a secure foundation in the basic subjects whilst offering a wide curriculum with specialist teaching in many areas.

Examination results at both KS1 and KS2 levels are excellent and many pupils gain places at the prestigious Grammar and Independent schools in the county.

The school offers a wide range of extra-curricular activities and an excellent after-care facility is available for all age groups. St Anne's is rightly recognised for its friendly and supportive ethos. Parents are particularly supportive of all aspects of school life. Visitors are always welcome.

S. Anselm's

Stanedge Road, Bakewell, Derbyshire DE45 1DP
Tel: 01629 812734
email: admissions@anselms.co.uk
website: www.sanselms.co.uk
Facebook: @s.anselms
Instagram: @sanselmsschool

See full entry in the **IAPS** section, on **p. 773**.

St Catherine's School
Twickenham

Cross Deep, Twickenham, Middlesex TW1 4QJ
Tel: 020 8891 2898
email: admissions@stcatherineschool.co.uk
website: www.stcatherineschool.co.uk
X/Twitter: @stcatherinessch
Facebook: @stcatherinessch

See full entry in the **GSA** section, on **p. 477**.

St Christopher's School

6 Downs Road, Epsom, Surrey KT18 5HE
Tel: 01372 721807
email: office@st-christophers.surrey.sch.uk
website: www.st-christophers.surrey.sch.uk
Facebook: @StChrisEpsom
Instagram: @stchrisepsom

***Headteacher*: Mrs B Grehan**

Age Range. 3–7.

Number in School. 190.

Fees per term (2023–2024). £4,150 (Full time including lunch), £2,100 (5 mornings).

St Christopher's School (founded in 1938) is a co-educational, non-denominational, Nursery and Pre-Prep for children from 2¾ to 7 years of age. Set halfway between Epsom Town and Downs in a quiet residential area it has attractive, secure grounds and a generous Nursery setting. As confirmed in the last ISI inspection, St Christopher's is successful in their aim to offer the best possible start to their pupils who are subsequently well-prepared for a variety of Surrey and London schools, enjoying a significant first choice pass rate for 7+ assessments.

St Christopher's won the ISA Junior School of the Year in 2020 and was a Finalist in the Independent School of the Year Awards 2022 for Pre-Prep School of the Year. We are also proud to be named by DayNurseries as one of the Top 20 Nurseries in South East England 2023. The school enjoys the support of an active parents association that organises a wide variety of social and fundraising events.

Breakfast Club opens at 7.45am and After School Care is available until 6pm. There is also a rich range of after-school clubs available.

For further information please visit the website: www.st-christophers.surrey.sch.uk and follow us on social media @StChrisEpsom. Parents are welcome to visit the school by appointment with the Headteacher or attend our termly Open Mornings, further information is on our website.

Charitable Status. St Christopher's School Trust (Epsom) Limited is a Registered Charity, number 312045. It aims to provide a Nursery and Pre-Preparatory education in Epsom and district.

St Christopher's School

71 Wembley Park Drive, Wembley Park, Middlesex HA9 8HE
Tel: 020 8902 5069
email: admin@stchristophersschool.org.uk
website: www.stchristophersschool.org.uk
X/Twitter: @StChrisPrep
Facebook: @St-Christopher-School-104683814794567
Instagram: @stchristophersprepschool
LinkedIn: /company/stchristophersschool

***Head*: Mr Jonathan Coke**

Age Range. 2–11.

Number in School. 47 Boys, 46 Girls.

Fees per term (2023–2024). £3,430–£3,753 (includes lunch). Advance payment and Sibling discounts available.

Entry requirements: Interview and Assessment.

St Christopher's Prep School and Nursery, a large Victorian building on Wembley Park Drive, offers a caring family atmosphere coupled with an equal emphasis on good manners, enthusiastic endeavour and academic excellence. The School, originally a Christian foundation dating from 1928, welcomes children of all faiths and cultures.

Caring and supportive staff provide a well-structured, disciplined and stimulating environment in which pupils are nurtured and encouraged to develop the necessary skills – academic, social and cultural – so that when they leave us at the age of 11 they can be certain of future success. All pupils at St Christopher's are equal and we emphasise the qualities of equality, justice and compassion. Pupils benefit from a fast paced holistic curriculum that offers both breadth and depth, an activity programme that teaches skills and develops talents, and a pastoral programme that develops social responsibility.

The full range of academic subjects are taught based on an enriched National Curriculum. Sport and Music are seen as central elements in school life with sports fixtures, regular concerts and an annual carol service. In addition there are a variety of clubs and activities both at lunchtime and after school; these include Arts & Crafts Club, Book Club, Booster Club, Choir, STEM, Football, Multi Sports, French Club, Supervised Study, Latin Club and Recorders.

Pupils are prepared for the full range of examinations at 11 years. Historically leavers have gained entry to a wide range of excellent schools including Haberdashers' Aske's Boys' and Girls' Schools, Merchant Taylors', Northwood College, St Helen's, North London Collegiate, Henrietta Barnett, Queen Elizabeth's Boys' School, City of London Boys and Girls, UCS, Aldenham, John Lyon, St Paul's Boys' and Girls' Schools and South Hampstead High.

St Christopher's offers both Morning and After School Care, from 8.00am until 6.00pm.

Please phone for an appointment to view the school. We look forward to welcoming you.

St Clare's, Oxford

139 Banbury Road, Oxford OX2 7AL
Tel: 01865 552031
email: admissions@stclares.ac.uk
reception139@stclares.ac.uk
website: stclares.ac.uk
Facebook: @stclaresoxford
Instagram: @stclaresoxford
LinkedIn: @stclaresoxford

***Principal*: Mr Duncan Reith**, MA Oxon, MA Open University, PGCE Roehampton, MBA Durham

Vice Principal Pastoral: Rebecca Allen, BA, MA Warwick
Vice Principal Academic: David White, BA Southampton, PGCE Bath, PG Dip Glasgow, MA Staffordshire

Age range. 15–19 Co-educational.

Number of students. 280.

Fees per annum (2023–2024). Boarding: £45,636, Day: £22,256.

Established in 1953, St Clare's is an Oxford-based international school with the mission 'to advance international education and understanding'. We embrace internationalism and academic excellence as core values. St Clare's is a co-educational day and boarding school which has been offering the International Baccalaureate Diploma for over 40 years, longer than any other school or college in England.

Students regularly achieve the maximum of 45 points, achieved by only 0.2% of candidates worldwide and a quarter achieve scores high than 40 points, placing them in the elite top 5% globally.

Students from over 40 countries study at St Clare's with a core group of British students. The caring atmosphere is informal, positive and friendly with an equal emphasis on hard work, tolerance and developing personal responsibility. Each student is paired with a personal tutor who oversees their welfare and progress and is the first point of contact for parents.

St Clare's has an especially wide range of IB Diploma subjects on offer at Higher and Standard level and, in addition, currently teaches a wide variety of foreign languages.

For students not yet ready to begin the IB Diploma, the college also offers a Pre-IB course of either one, two or three terms duration.

As part of the Creativity, Activity, Service requirements of the Diploma, there is an extensive programme of social, cultural and sporting activities and students are encouraged to take full advantage of the opportunities that Oxford provides.

During the summer months, we run a 3-week introduction to the IB Diploma.

St Clare's is also authorised by the IBO to run IB workshops for teachers.

St Clare's is located in an elegant residential area that is part of the North Oxford Conservation Area. It occupies 25 large Victorian and Edwardian houses to which purpose-built facilities have been added. The campus is made up of classrooms, a dining room, a popular café, music department and activities department plus library (over 35,000 resources), an IT suite and a Careers and Higher Education Information Centre. Stunning buildings in college grounds and gardens provide science laboratories, prep rooms and a mathematics department, plus two modern boarding houses arranged around a quad with a beautiful art studio. There is Wi-Fi throughout both the academic facilities and student houses which are no more than five minutes' walk from the central campus.

We welcome applications from UK and international students. Entry is based on academic results, an interview and a placement test. There is a competitive scholarship and bursary programme awarded by interview and group exercises.

Charitable status. St Clare's, Oxford is a Registered Charity, number 294085.

St David's School

23–25 Woodcote Valley Road, Purley, Surrey CR8 3AL

Tel: 020 8660 0723
email: office@stdavidsschool.co.uk
website: www.stdavidsschool.co.uk

***Head Teacher*: Miss Cressida Mardell**

Age Range. 3–11.

Number in School. 145 Day: 76 boys, 69 girls.

Fees per term (2023–2024). £2,865–£4,652 (including lunch).

We look forward to welcoming you to our happy and creative school, where we aim to achieve the highest academic standards. At St David's we offer a rich and stimulating curriculum, delivered by a talented and caring staff, giving your child the best possible start. The School has undergone many changes and developments since its foundation in 1912 and in 2022 entered into partnership with the Royal Russell School Trust. Please visit our website to find out more about all the exciting things that have been going on.

The small school atmosphere is, we believe, a strength and reassuring to parents and children alike. We aim to balance nurture with independence to equip your child to succeed academically and we are extremely proud of our results. Please do contact us to experience the warm inspiring environment that is the "St David's Family". Please telephone the School Office to arrange an appointment and we look forward to showing you round our school.

St David's is registered for appropriate early years funding and accepts Childcare Vouchers.

Charitable status. Royal Russell School Trust is a Registered Charity, number 271907. St David's aims to provide a quality education for boys and girls from 3+ to 11 years old.

St Dominic's Grammar School

Bargate Street, Brewood, Staffordshire ST19 9BA

Tel: 01902 850248
email: secretary@stdominicsgrammarschool.co.uk
website: www.stdominicsgrammarschool.co.uk
X/Twitter: @StDomsBrewood
Facebook: @StDominicsGrammar

***Headmaster*: Mr Peter McNabb**, BSc Hons, PGCE

Bursar: Mr Paul Tudor
Head of Preparatory School: Mrs Kay Parker-McMahon, MEd, MA, PGCE
Head of Senior School & Sixth Form (*Safeguarding*): Mrs Nicola Hastings Smith, BA Hons, PGCE, NPQH
Admissions & Marketing: Mrs Samantha Emery

Heads of Faculty:
Mathematics: Mr Warren Baker, BEd Hons
Science & Technology: Mr Ian Henderson, BSc Hons, MRSC, PGCE, QTS
Expressive Arts: Miss Chloe Fisher, BA Hons
Communications: Mrs Nicola Hastings Smith, BA Hons, PGCE, NPQH
Humanities: Mr Graham Saul, BA Hons, PGCE

St Dominic's Grammar School Brewood provides education for over 210 girls and boys from the ages of 4 to 18.

Development of the 'whole person' is at the heart of our school. We believe each child has special talents and we work to enable them to achieve their full potential within a caring environment. We nurture the pupils academically, socially, creatively and spiritually.

Teaching & Learning. Small class sizes facilitates individual attention so strengths and weaknesses are diagnosed and all work is tailored to match individual's needs. We believe in a close partnership with parents, keeping you informed about your child's progress.

Curriculum. We offer a broad and balanced curriculum with enhancement and enrichment. The National Curriculum is taught throughout the school. This is enhanced with additional subjects including performing arts, dance, drama and singing which are integrated into the weekly timetable. We offer a comprehensive range of subjects at AS and A Level.

Sports. We offer a broad curriculum including netball, hockey, dance, gymnastics, aerobics, football, volleyball, basketball, badminton, rounders, tennis, athletics and cross-country. Our all-inclusive extra-curricular programmes provide further sporting variety including Zumba, gymnastics, trampolining, modern dance and ballet, with all abilities encouraged to attend.

There is a comprehensive fixtures programme incorporating inter-house events and annual Preparatory and Senior Sports Days. We take part in ISA sporting events at local, regional and national level.

The facilities include brand new outdoor cricket nets, newly-resurfaced netball and tennis courts, hockey, football and rounders pitches and an athletics track. We also have an excellent fully-equipped sports hall with cricket nets and electronic basketball hoops.

Expressive Arts. We are renowned for our musical and dramatic excellence. Our contemporary Performing Arts Centre houses a Drama and Dance Studio, a Music Suite and a Recording Studio. Pupils are encouraged to join the choirs, play an instrument, take up dance, singing or tread the boards. Throughout the year there are a variety of performances ranging from the Pre-Preparatory Christmas play, to productions such as *Thoroughly Modern Millie* and *High School Musical*. The pupils participate in many local and regional competitions, take part in local festivals and public speaking events. Many do LAMDA examinations and all Year 7s take English Speaking Board examinations.

Extra-Curricular Activities. Four days a week there is an all-inclusive after-school programme where pupils can undertake a variety of activities ranging from The Duke of Edinburgh's Award scheme to debating, cooking, bushcraft, Young Enterprise and STEM Club.

Throughout the year, pupils are encouraged to become involved in fundraising for local and national charities. These activities help each child develop a good community spirit with respect and consideration for others.

Pastoral Care. Our outstanding pastoral care system and Christian ethos create an atmosphere which fosters trust and mutual respect between pupils and teachers. Pupils feel relaxed and secure and develop their self-respect, self-confidence, personal discipline and consideration for others.

Examination Results. Our pupils achieve outstanding exam results year on year outperforming the national averages of both comprehensive and independent schools at Key Stage 2, GCSE and A Level. In 2021 we achieved a 100% pass rate in all subjects at both GCSE and A Level; English Baccalaureate was 94%.

Facilities. We have a purpose-built Preparatory building, which encompasses a brand new state of the art Science Laboratory, a Preparatory Hall, IT room, Home Economics room and library. The Senior building has fully-equipped science laboratories, IT room and library. All classrooms have networked computers and interactive whiteboards. The Sixth Form and Performing Arts Centre is a modern, state-of-the-art facility housing the latest technology in music, IT and the Performing Arts. It has a common room with terraces and a well-equipped Library with Wi-Fi technology.

Admissions. Although selective, we draw our pupils from a wide ability range, which makes our record of results outstanding. Assessment is made during trial days at school. Entry into Year 7 is dependent on the entrance examination held in October. Applications for all other year groups are considered, depending on availability. A place in the Sixth Form is conditional upon GCSE results.

Fees per term (2023–2024). Reception including lunch £2,166, Year 1 including lunch £2,184, Year 2 including lunch £2,316, Years 3–6 please enquire, Year 7 £2,883.33, Year 8 £3,094, Year 9 £3,245, Year 10 £3,367, Year 11 £3,700, Year 12 £3,000, Year 13 £2,975.

Scholarships and Bursaries. Scholarships may be available for Senior School applicants. Academic, Sport, Art and Performing Arts non-financial scholarships may be awarded for entry into Years 7 and 12.

St Dominic's Priory School, Stone

37 Station Road, Stone, Staffordshire ST15 8ER

Tel: 01785 814181
email: info@stdominicspriory.co.uk
website: www.stdominicspriory.co.uk
Facebook: @stdominicsprioryst one
Instagram: @stdominicsprioryst one
LinkedIn: /st-dominic's-priory-school-stone

Chair of Governors: Mrs Karen Champ

***Headteacher*: Mrs Rebecca Harrison**

St Dominic's Priory School, Stone is an independent Catholic school, educating boys and girls from pre-school to 16 years.

We are proud of our strong academic tradition alongside our reputation for nurturing individuals. Our high-quality teaching and small classes creates an environment in which true potential can be maximised at all times.

Not only are we ranked as one of the top performing schools in Staffordshire, we are non-selective, accepting children of all abilities. Our teachers are engaging and our low teacher-to-child ratio ensures that each child receives a high quality education with the individual support that they need.

The redevelopment of our school site has seen us benefit from brand new, state-of-the-art teaching facilities and landscaped recreational areas. The teaching block accommodates 10 new classrooms, all with interactive walls, state-of-the-art science laboratories and specialist art, music, performing arts and drama studios. We even have a roof-top classroom for vegetable growing, a bee hive, weather projects, outdoor performances and much more.

Location. Centrally located within North Staffordshire, the school is situated in the picturesque canal town of Stone, Staffordshire, within easy reach of Newcastle-under-Lyme, Stoke-on-Trent, Stafford, Uttoxeter, Cheadle and the surrounding villages. We provide school transport from a number of locations and Stone Railway Station is only a 5 minute walk from school.

Aims and Ethos. Our school mission statement is: Living and Learning with Christ as our Guide. We aim to create a love of learning in a friendly and happy environment, nurture individuality and instil in our students a sense of community spirit rooted in Dominican values. We wish to provide each child with tools that will equip them to not only succeed academically, but contribute positively to a society in which values of justice and compassion are paramount.

St Dominic's welcomes children of all faiths and within our school community diversity is embraced and respected.

Once again, our students achieved fantastic examination results in their end-of-year GCSEs in 2023, which only highlights the school's strong academic tradition and reputation for giving an excellent all-round education. Students leave St Dominic's with superb academic grades, self-confidence and friends for life.

Religion. St Dominic's Priory is a Catholic school where children of all faiths are welcomed.

The Arts. The school excels in the creative and performing arts, and our busy programme of cultural events, visits and activities ensures that there is something for everyone at St Dominic's. With a dedicated dance and drama studio, together with our art studio and music suite, our students regularly take part in productions, festivals, concerts, recitals and exhibitions, both within and outside the school.

Sport. The school has a strong sporting tradition and we excel in competition across local, regional and national level. Our facilities include a sports hall, multi-use-games area (MUGA), climbing wall and outdoor playing fields. Sports include: athletics, badminton, basketball, boccia, cricket, cross country, football, hockey, netball, table tennis, tennis, trampolining, tri-golf and volleyball.

Extra-Curricular Activities. Numerous clubs and activities are held after school and during lunchtimes for both the prep and senior schools. These include the Duke of Edinburgh's Award, choir, design and technology, LAMDA, sports, STEM and percussion ensemble.

Admission. Please contact Charlotte Brindley, our admissions secretary on 01785 814181 ext 1 or email admissions@stdominicspriory.co.uk or visit the website.

Scholarships and Bursaries. Scholarships are awarded irrespective of financial means in the senior school.

All students entering Year 7 the following academic year, are automatically entered for the academic scholarships. They also have the opportunity to apply for our performing arts, music, art and sport scholarships.

Bursaries will be considered if bursary funds are available and depending on the financial, compassionate or other circumstances of applicants.

Fees per term (2023–2024). Pre-School: £30 per session, £45 per day, 5 full days £210 per week. Reception: £3,346; Primary: 1–2 £3,721; Primary: 3–6 £3,831; Year 7: £4,081; Years 8–11: £4,204.

Charitable status. St Dominic's Priory is a Registered Charity, number 1141147, providing quality education for boys and girls aged 3 to 16 years.

St Edward's Senior & Sixth Form

Cirencester Road, Charlton Kings, Cheltenham, Gloucestershire GL53 8EY

Tel: 01242 388555
email: reception@stedwards.co.uk
website: www.stedwards.co.uk
X/Twitter: @StEdwardsChelt
Facebook: @StEdwardsSchoolCheltenham
Instagram: @stedwardscheltenham

See full entry in the **Society of Heads** section, on **p. 558**.

St Faith's Prep School

5 The Street, Ash, Kent CT3 2HH

Tel: 01304 813409
email: info@stfaithsprep.com
website: www.stfaithsprep.com
Facebook: @stfaithsprep
Instagram: @stfaithsprep
LinkedIn: /company/st-faiths-prep-school

Motto: *I Can & I Will*

***Head*: Mrs Helen Coombs**
Senior leadership team:
Deputy Head (*Pastoral*): Mr Duncan Andrews
Deputy Head (*Academic*): Mr David Mackenzie
Director of Studies: Mrs Joanna Woodhead
Learning Enhancement Coordinator: Mrs Yvette Allen
Sustainability Lead: Mrs Katie Ross

Student numbers. 240.

Fees per term (2023–2024). £2,440 to £4,248.

Admission. Non-selective.

Curriculum. Broad, balanced and imaginative.

Set in the heart of the Kent countryside, St Faith's Prep is a happy, high-achieving prep school & nursery for children aged 2–11.

Academic. Our children are taught in small classes (our average class size is 16) by our cohort of inspirational teachers. We are known for our outstanding academic results (typically 80–90% of Year 6 leavers attain grammar school places and many are offered scholarships to local independent schools), a determination to provide a bespoke education for every child, and our welcoming and nurturing family atmosphere.

We offer a broad and balanced curriculum which offers every child the opportunity to shine. Our teaching staff ensure that every child is nurtured and achieving at the best of their ability. For some, this is excelling academically, winning spelling bees or tackling the toughest of maths challenges. For others it is programming LEGO robots, driving a football or hockey ball towards the goal, creating unique works of art or playing the trumpet in a concert.

Specialist Teachers. Children have access to our subject specialist teachers from the very youngest classes. Every child at St Faith's plays a musical instrument and by the end of Year 6 most children have a solid understanding of sheet music. Expert sporting tuition means our teams play to a very high standard and our children proudly don the purple and gold kit to represent the school in matches. All children learn German, French and Spanish during their time with us, with Latin also on offer for those particularly keen on languages. From Year 2 onwards our children learn coding, and our digital strategy means that from Year 4 each child has their own Surface Go device, used across the curriculum as part of their learning.

Facilities. Our brand new, state of the art Sport Hall offers the perfect place to hone skills and learn new ones, and the Summer Term sees our heated saltwater pool full to the brim with happy, splashing children. From Upper Nursery onwards, our children all receive swimming lessons as part of their PE lessons, learning important skills to keep them safe (and having fun!) Our extensive outdoor space offers views across the countryside and provides the backdrop to sports lessons, and our Nature Garden is the perfect place to really bring learning to life through hands on opportunities to explore the world around them, from pond-dipping to growing vegetables and tending to the school rabbit.

Extracurricular. We offer a wide range of clubs and activities, including 3 choirs, 2 orchestras, cooking, dance, cheer, netball, art, LAMDA, basketball, fencing, yoga and quidditch (yes you read that right!).

Ethos and Community. Our school motto 'I Can & I Will' embodies the atmosphere of St Faiths; we are approachable and friendly, committed to giving all our pupils a strong education together with a raft of experiences and opportunities. St Faith's is a place where children will make friendships, build confidence and develop a love of learning.

St Gerard's School
Bangor

Ffriddoedd Road, Bangor, Gwynedd LL57 2EL

Tel: 01248 351656
email: sgadmin@st-gerards.org
website: www.st-gerards.org
X/Twitter: @stgerardsbangor
Facebook: St-Gerards-School-Trust
Instagram: @stgerardsbangor
LinkedIn: /company/ysgol-st-gerard-s

Chairman of the Governing Body: Mrs M Benson

***Headteacher*: Mr C Harrison**

Age Range. 4–18.

Number in School. Day: 54 Boys, 57 Girls.

Fees per term (2023–2024). £3,025–£4,580.

St Gerard's is a small independent day school that has a happy, secure, family atmosphere in which the pupils thrive. Since its foundation over a hundred years ago the school has maintained a kind and caring ethos which also sets high standards of behaviour for the students.

Children from the earliest years learn to share with and care for others and the older children work and interact in an atmosphere free from bullying that encourages them to be resilient, compassionate and trustworthy. There are lots of different activities that the children can take part in to enrich their learning experience.

Through the hard work of staff and pupils and the support of parents we hope to develop analytical, critical and compassionate thinkers who are capable of achieving happiness and success in their life. We achieve fantastic results year on year and last year were ranked second in the UK for small independent schools. We are very proud of our school and all that is achieved here. The best advertisement for our school is our students and we invite you to come and meet them and see the school in action.

During the summer term 2022 we welcomed Estyn to the school. Inspectors spent a week in the school. They certainly managed to get a detailed view of the school and we are delighted with the excellent findings in the report. You can read the full report here: www.estyn.llyw.cymru/inspection-reports.

Our senior school offers a small educational community that is focused on the potential of each pupil. Our pupils, staff and parents work in partnership towards our aim of achieving optimum progress together. The senior school at St Gerard's is located in the original convent building with two more recent extensions to house purpose-built classrooms. The senior school is in close proximity to the junior school. This allows the interchange of staff expertise and the opportunity for interaction between junior and senior pupils' with the aim of benefiting the pupils' education. At the senior school our teachers are subject specialists and individual year groups move from classroom to classroom to curricular need. Each member of staff in the senior school is linked to a form group to help monitor pupils' personal welfare as well as their academic progress. Our small class sizes in the senior school allow for individual attention for each pupil. Teachers are aware of individual pupils' strengths and target individual areas for improvement. Our junior school offers every child the opportunity to achieve his or her potential. Our children, staff and parents work in partnership towards our aim of achieving together.

Arrangements can be made to visit throughout the whole of the year.

Charitable status. St Gerard's School Trust is a Registered Charity, number 1001211.

St Hilda's School

28 Douglas Road, Harpenden, Hertfordshire AL5 2ES

Tel: 01582 712307
email: office@sthildasharpenden.co.uk
website: www.sthildasharpenden.co.uk
Facebook: @sthildasharpenden

***Headteacher*: Mr D Sayers**, BA Hons, QTS

Deputy Head: Mrs N Comer, BA Hons, QTS
Business Manager: Mrs D Taylor, ACMA

Age Range. 3–11.

Number in School. 180 approximately.

Co-educational Nursery, all other year groups for female pupils.

Fees per term (2023–2024). £4,830 (Forms IV to VI*); £4,735 (Forms II & III*), £4,560 (Reception & Form I*), Nursery: flexible options with variable pricing. (* including lunch and free wraparound care from reception classes).

St Hilda's School was founded in 1891, it is privately owned and situated in a residential site of 1¼ acres in the beautiful village of Harpenden. The premises include an outdoor swimming pool, a hard tennis/netball court, an adjacent playing field used for outdoor learning, sport and break times, together with attractive play areas for all age ranges. The original building has been substantially improved with two extensions and includes a fully-equipped stage in the modern hall, a sound-proofed Performing Arts Studio, a suite of music rooms, a dedicated computer suite, a science lab, a purpose-built EYFS unit, an art room, and a lovely library in the old building.

Caring, Curious & Confident At St Hilda's School, we welcome all children irrespective of race, religion, culture, disability or ability. Christian values and an appreciation of British values are essential to the life of the school and our core values are those of tolerance, respect for others, integrity, industry, and achievement.

Our aim is to achieve the highest standard of education in a happy, safe and purposeful working environment, instilling in all pupils a love of learning, independent thinking and good manners.

We strive to nurture each child's individuality, developing talent and ability to the full.

St Hilda's has a mixed ability intake but enjoys a reputation for high academic standards. For example, pupils in our Nursery access a full phonics programme and access reading as soon as they are ready, prior to joining the Reception class. Throughout, the foundations for success are carefully laid. Careful consideration is given to ensure each child enters the secondary school best suited to their needs. Preparation for the exams starts in Form IV and progresses further from Form V, where additional setting and specialist teaching in Maths, English and Reasoning enables our pupils to achieve highly; including an impressive range of scholarships each year.

The school is well known for its high musical standards with almost all pupils learning an instrument, many two or three. The standards in drama, art and sport are also consistently high.

St Hilda's is a member of the Independent Schools Association and the Independent Schools Council. The School received an '*excellent in all areas*' rating in October 2019, and previously in November 2016 a Focused Compliance Inspection was successfully passed in all areas.

The School website has a wealth of information and links to our virtual tour, a prospectus is also available on application to the School Secretary.

Please call us if you would like to arrange a visit to our beautiful School.

St James' School

22 Bargate, Grimsby, North East Lincolnshire DN34 4SY

Tel: 01472 503260
email: enquiries@saintjamesschool.co.uk
website: www.saintjamesschool.co.uk
X/Twitter: @StJamesSchoolGY
Facebook: @stjamesschoolgrimsby

***Head*: Ms T Harris**
Assistant Head (*Academic*): Mr D Rose
Finance and Accounts: Mrs J Dunn

Age Range. 11–18.

Fees per term (2023–2024). Day fees: Senior School £4,237, Sixth Form £3,302. Weekly boarding: £6,825. Full Boarding: £8,665.

St. James' School is built upon the tenet of family; caring, encouraging, supporting, and inspiring. Deliberately small, we passionately believe an extraordinary education is built upon strong, trusting relationships. At St. James', these are immediately obvious.

St. James' pupils are allowed time to follow their own passions within an environment that creates opportunities both in the 'here and now', but also for the future.

Outwardly facing and globally aware, we welcome pupils from across the globe into our school. Boarding remains central to the St. James' ethos, where the benefits of 'living your education' are available to all pupils.

Blending together a love of learning with the development of 'character', at St. James' our goal is not only to educate, but to 'Future Proof'; securing the qualifications to stand out, building the character to endear, and instilling the core values to succeed.

The School offers academic, musical, sporting and all-round scholarships as well as means-tested bursaries.

The School operates a morning and evening bus services calling in at villages from the Louth, Brigg areas as well as local collections.

St John's School

47–49 Stock Road, Billericay, Essex CM12 0AR

Tel: 01277 623070
email: registrar@stjohnsschool.net
website: www.stjohnsschool.net
Facebook: @StJBillericay
Instagram: @stjohns_billericay

***Headteacher*: Mr A Angeli**, BA Hons

Age range. 2–16.
Number in school. Day: 155 Boys, 141 Girls.
Fees per term (2023–2024). £782–£5,241.

From the moment a child enters St John's, whatever their age, they are treated as an individual. Our aim is to ensure that learning, creativity and success is enjoyed by everyone and that when a child leaves our school they have fully achieved their potential. Set on eight acres of land overlooking Lake Meadows Park in Billericay, St John's is ideally located for public transport links and is only a five minute walk from Billericay train station.

Pupils benefit greatly from lessons with specialist teachers. In the Kindergarten, children have lessons in Music, Singing, Computing, PE and visit our own Forest School. In the Junior School, pupils have additional specialist teachers for PE, Art, Music, Computing, and French and Spanish in Year 6. Senior School pupils follow a broad curriculum, which leads to GCSE courses commencing in Year 10. Subjects include English Language, English Literature, Maths, Statistics, Double Science, Triple Science, Art, Drama, French, Spanish, Geography, History, Sociology, Religious Studies, Music, PE, Food Technology, Business and Computer Science. Pupils make excellent progress throughout the school and GCSE pass rates are consistently high.

Sport is not only an integral part of our curriculum but also part of our extracurricular programme. Our Sport England standard Sports Hall hosts a wide range of activities including trampolining, table tennis, badminton, and basketball to name but a few. The school participates in ISA Regional and National sporting events.

A wide range of extracurricular clubs and activities are offered, including karate, cookery, ballet, dance, tennis and homework club. Pupils have the opportunity to participate in instrumental lessons, perform in the school orchestra and join one of the vocal groups. In addition, the performing arts are a pivotal part of our school, with fantastic success rates for our LAMDA examination entrants. A number of day and residential trips are offered each year.

A child's education is one of the most important factors in their well-being and success. We instil all the virtues of politeness, integrity and consideration of others into our pupils.

Although our academic success over the years has been exceptional, we are equally proud that we have educated thousands of children who are confident, successful and who genuinely make a positive contribution to society when they leave.

Means-tested scholarships are available for Year 7 places in the Senior School. For more information and to arrange a tour of the school, please contact our Registrar on 01277 623070 or by email to registrar@stjohnsschool.net.

St Joseph's School

St Stephen's Hill, Launceston, Cornwall PL15 8HN

Tel: 01566 772580
email: registrar@stjosephscornwall.co.uk
website: www.stjosephscornwall.co.uk
X/Twitter: @StJosephsSch
Facebook: @StJosephsSchoolLaunceston
Instagram: @stjosephscornwall

***Head Teacher*: Mr Oliver Scott**

Deputy Headteacher: Mr Sam Matthews
Junior School Headteacher: Mrs Caroline Skerry
Bursar: Mr Ian Barton
Registrar: Miss Rebecca Walker

Age Range. 4–16 Co-educational.
Number in School. 240.
Fees per term (2023–2024). £2,160–£5,475.

St Joseph's School, Launceston, is an award-winning independent day school for boys and girls between the ages of 4 and 16. Having been inspected by the Independent Schools Inspectorate in December of 2022, we would be delighted for your to read our report at www.isi.net/reports to get a clear view of the school as it is today.

St Joseph's has a truly unique family atmosphere that is apparent from the moment you enter the school. The school's small size means that it is possible both to keep sight of strong family values, giving children the confidence necessary to succeed, and to allow staff and pupils to work happily together. Due to the high teacher to pupil ratio, St Joseph's is able to encourage each pupil to reach their full potential through positive encouragement and commendation. The ethos of care, compassion and community is integral to the daily life of the school and student voice is a genuine driver for change.

In both the Junior and the Senior sides of the school, St Joseph's provides an excellent academic and pastoral education for all, regardless of ability and background. Our individualised academic curriculum runs alongside a wide variety of extra-curricular activities that challenge, stimulate and inspire all pupils to unlock their potential in a safe and supportive environment. St Joseph's offers equal prospects to every child and it is the positive response to the school's ethos that sees pupils rising to challenges both within the classroom and as highly valued members of the wider school community. High expectations and excellent relationships are key to success.

St Joseph's GCSE pupils achieve superb results across the curriculum, and results both prior to and post the pandemic bear this out. The school regularly achieves results higher than those of academically selective schools at local and national level. This is a remarkable achievement as St Joseph's is a non-selective school, meaning there is no entrance exam and admission is possible at any point during a child's education. Fees are set at levels which offer great value for money, particularly in light of what is available to all pupils at the school, coupled with excellent academic results.

During the Covid-19 pandemic full online timetables were followed by all in the Senior School, with an engaging mix of live lessons and teacher interaction, while live teacher time and individualised work across the Junior School ensured high-quality learning continued throughout lockdown.

Academic and Sports Scholarships are offered from age 7+ and Music and Art Scholarships from 11+. Bursaries are available and considered on an individual basis.

An extensive daily bus service (currently 9 bus routes) allows pupils from a wide area across Devon and Cornwall to attend St Joseph's.

St Joseph's School offers a number of open events throughout the year for prospective parents. To arrange an individual visit please contact the Registrar. Further information can be found at www.stjosephscornwall.co.uk or by contacting the Registrar on 01566 772580, registrar@stjosephscornwall.co.uk.

Charitable status. St Joseph's School is a Registered Charity, number 289048.

St Mary's School
Colchester

91 Lexden Road, Colchester, Essex CO3 3RB

Tel: 01206 594256
email: registrar@stmaryscolchester.org.uk
website: www.stmaryscolchester.org.uk
X/Twitter: @stmaryscolch
Facebook: @stmaryscolchester
Instagram: @stmaryscolchester

See full entry in the **GSA** section, on **p. 481**.

St Mary's School
Gerrards Cross

Packhorse Road, Gerrards Cross, Buckinghamshire SL9 8JQ

Tel: 01753 883370
email: registrar@st-marys.bucks.sch.uk
website: www.stmarysschool.co.uk
X/Twitter: @StMarysSchoolGX
Facebook: @St-Marys-School-Gerrards-Cross
Instagram: @stmarysgx
LinkedIn: /st-mary-s-school-gerrards-cross

See full entry in the **GSA** section, on **p. 483**.

St Mary's School, Hampstead

47 Fitzjohn's Avenue, Hampstead, London NW3 6PG

Tel: 020 7435 1868
email: office@stmh.co.uk
website: www.stmh.co.uk

See full entry in the **IAPS** section, on **p. 790**.

St Michael's School

Bryn, Llanelli, Carmarthenshire SA14 9TU

Tel: 01554 820325
email: admissions@stmikes.co.uk
office@stmikes.co.uk
website: www.stmikes.co.uk
X/Twitter: @StMikes
Facebook: @St-Michaels-School
Instagram: @stmikeswales

***Headmaster*: Benson Ferrari**, MA, PG Cert, BA Hons, FRSA, FCIEA

Deputy Head: Kay Francis, BSc Hons, PGCE

Head of Prep School: Melony Rees-Davies, BA Hons, PGCE, PGradDip

Age Range. 3–18.

Number in School. 418.

Fees per term (UK resident students 2023–2024). Tuition: Preparatory School £1,965–£3,180; Senior School £4,665–£4,830. Full Boarding: Years 7–10 £10,590 (twin), £9,690 (single); Years 11–13 £10,590 (twin), £11,685 (single). Weekly Boarding: Years 7–10 £8,595 (twin), £9,690 (single); Years 11–13 £8,595 (twin), £9,690 (single). Sibling allowances available.

International Students per annum (2023–2024): Years 7–8 £39,480 (twin & single rooms), Year 9 £39,480 (twin and single rooms), Year 10 (GCSE) £39,480 (twin and single rooms), Year 11 (GCSE) £40,980 (single en-suite room), Sixth Form (A Level) £40,980 (single en-suite room).

St Michael's combines great learning and excellent pastoral care as part of a well-rounded education. The school has a traditional approach to learning, which does not mean it lives in the past, but places emphasis on the importance of hard work and homework in the school curriculum. The high academic standards of the school are reflected in the National League Tables. In 2021, St Michael's was the recipient of the *Sunday Times* Wales Independent Secondary School of the Decade award. Previous accolades have included the 2019 *Sunday Times* Welsh Independent Secondary School award and in 2017, the school was ranked a Top 20 school in *The Times* Top 100 Co-Educational Schools in the UK. In the same year, St Michael's was also named top school in Wales for GCSE results.

In 2023, the school reached 13th place in *The Telegraph*'s 'Best UK Private Schools by A Level Results'; this is the highest position the school has ever achieved nationally. In 2023, 79.1% of pupils A Level grades were A* or A and 94.3% received A*–B grades. No school can build up such a strong reputation without a competitive, but well-disciplined atmosphere and a highly qualified and dedicated staff. This is where we feel St Michael's is particularly fortunate.

Our boarding houses are excellent: Parc House for Years 7 to 10 is a handsome and historic mansion set in an acre of grounds in the village of Llangennech nearby and Tenby House is a purpose-built, on-site, state-of-the-art, 31-bedroom boarding house for those in Years 11 to 13. Both houses offer a high standard of comfort where every pupil feels safe, happy and protected. Pupils are accommodated in well-furnished and equipped, single en-suite or shared study-bedrooms. The houses provide spacious recreation rooms and pleasant grounds in which pupils may relax, play or watch TV.

We have well-equipped computer laboratories where pupils have access to a computer each from 3 years of age. Languages taught in the school are French, Spanish, Welsh and Chinese (Mandarin).

The school has an envied reputation for its academic achievement but is also proud of the wide range of traditional games and activities it offers. Pupils from Year 10 onwards pupils can also take part in The Duke of Edinburgh's Award scheme to Gold Award standard. We have a large choir and school orchestra and pupils may take music examinations at GCSE and A Level.

One of the main reasons behind the school's success is the thorough grounding that pupils receive in the 'basics' – English, Mathematics, IT/Computing and Science in the Prep and Pre-Prep Schools, continuing into the Senior School.

We have enjoyed outstanding sporting success over the last few years in netball, rugby, football, tennis, cricket and athletics.

Every pupil is encouraged to develop their full potential whether in academic work or in all the extracurricular activities on offer.

Saint Nicholas School

Hillingdon House, Hobbs Cross Road, Old Harlow, Essex CM17 0NJ

Tel: 01279 429910
email: office@saintnicholasschool.net
admissions@saintnicholasschool.net
website: www.saintnicholasschool.net
X/Twitter: @SaintNicksSch
Facebook: @SaintNicksSch
Instagram: @saintnickssch
LinkedIn: /saintnickssch

***Headmaster*: Mr Terence Ayres**, BA Hons, PGCE

Age Range. 3 Months–16 Years.

Number in School. 472 Day Pupils: 248 Boys, 224 Girls.

Fees per term (2023–2024). Reception, Years 1 & 2: £3,838. Years 3, 4 & 5: £4,219. Years 6, 7 & 8: £4,721 and Years 9, 10 & 11: £5,148. Pre-school fees: £26 per session.

Saint Nicholas is situated in a delightful rural location and combines a fresh and enthusiastic approach to learning with a firm belief in traditional values.

It is in the perfect location for professional families who want their children to benefit from an education in beautiful, countryside surroundings and require close links to Central London and the rest of the world.

The academic record of the school is excellent, reflected in high pupil success rates in all competitive examinations. The dedicated team of staff involves itself closely with all aspects of pupils' educational progress and general development. While the academic core skills are at the heart of the school, Saint Nicholas School is dedicated to teaching pupils how to learn, instilling key learning skills, such as initiative, resilience, collaboration, teamwork and independent thinking. High standards of formal teaching are coupled with positive encouragement for pupils to reason for themselves and develop a high degree of responsibility.

The pupils follow the national curriculum which is adapted to provide more challenge and engagement. Pupils choose their GCSE options at the end of Year 8 and the school has recently introduced new GCSE subjects which include Astronomy, Business Studies and Photography.

As part of the school's commitment to providing affordable, quality care to children in the community, Little Saints Pre-School opened its doors in September 2014 to children from 2½ years old and an onsite nursery, the Rocking Horse Nursery, has also recently opened, taking babies from as young as three months old.

The school has recently achieved a grading of 'Excellent', in all areas, from the Independent School Inspectorate, and boasts superb facilities including extensive outdoor learning spaces. Facilities include magnificent junior and infant department buildings, a theatre, a science and technology centre, swimming pool and sports hall, and on-site catering facilities.

The school also has a Forest School and a large muddy discovery area set within our stunning grounds –

they are a real strength of our provision and we recognise the importance of these areas and the learning opportunities they afford to enrich our children's experiences.

Main sports include netball, rugby, tennis, football, cricket, swimming, athletics and gymnastics. There are many optional extracurricular activities available including ballet, individual instrumental lessons, karate, performing arts, sewing and a Law Society, to name but a few.

Charitable status. Saint Nicholas School (Harlow) Limited is a Registered Charity, number 310876. It exists to provide and promote educational enterprise by charitable means.

St Olave's Prep School

106–110 Southwood Road, New Eltham, London SE9 3QS

Tel:	020 8294 8930
email:	office@stolaves.org.uk
website:	www.stolaves.org.uk

See full entry in the **IAPS** section, on **p. 793**.

St Peter's School

52 Headlands, Kettering, Northamptonshire NN15 6DJ

Tel:	01536 512066
email:	stpsoffice@st-peters.org.uk
website:	www.st-peters.org.uk
Facebook:	@stpetersschoolkettering

Headteacher: **Mark Thomas**, BEng Hons, PGDE

Age range. 3–11.

Number in School. Day: 44 Boys, 61 Girls.

Fees per term (2023–2024). £3,475–£4,246 (incl. lunch).

Established in 1946, St Peter's is a small day school set in secure and beautifully green grounds in a quiet residential area of Kettering. It offers an enriched education based upon Christian values for boys and girls from the term of their third birthday to age 11. Pupils are thoroughly prepared for entry to a secondary school of their choice and have a high rate of success in entrance and scholarship examinations.

The School is situated in a leafy part of Kettering, which has excellent transport links via road and rail. Housed in the former family home of William Timpson, the school occupies a beautiful and secure campus. The School has grown from its 1946 beginnings, and now houses St Peter's Pre School, Reception and KS1 within the gardens of the Victorian house. The latest addition in the development plan is a new eco teaching space housing Art and the wraparound care facility in the Cedar Hub building.

With academic excellence at our core, in addition to fulfilling the requirements of the National Curriculum, the School emphasises the importance of Music, Art, Sport and Information Technology in its curriculum, providing children with a wide and rich spectrum of opportunities in which to thrive. Many of our children take part in additional instrumental lessons ranging from violin to saxophone, and all children from Year 2 upwards swim every Friday.

St Peter's School is a lively, friendly school with a strong family atmosphere and our highest pastoral care is noted at inspection. The School encourages all children to develop their individual strengths and talents. It aims to promote a respect for traditional values, a sense of responsibility and a concern for the needs of others. Each child is encouraged and nurtured to fulfil their own potential. Inspection reports detail the excellent progress made together with a strong extracurricular activity timetable.

Charitable status. St Peter's School is a Registered Charity, number 309914. It was originally incorporated in 1946 with an intention to maintain and manage a school for boys and girls in the town of Kettering. In addition to this it provides local employment and seeks to source from the local community wherever economically viable.

St Piran's School, Hayle

14 Trelissick Road, Hayle, Cornwall TR27 4HY

Tel:	01736 752612
email:	admin@stpirans.net
website:	www.stpiranshayle.net

Headteacher: **Miss Louise Adams**

Age range. 4–16.

Number of pupils. 81.

Fees per term (2023–2024). £1,980–£2,550.

Established in 1988, St Piran's School is set in attractive and well-maintained premises which, at present, accommodates around seventy-five children, aged from four to sixteen. It is a friendly, well-ordered community with a positive ethos where pupils make good friendships with each other and relate well to staff. Pupils are treated with respect and valued equally. They have a clear sense of right and wrong. There is a good sense of community within the school and new pupils are quickly made to feel welcome. The school places a strong emphasis on good manners and politeness. Visitors often comment about the warm friendly atmosphere and how happy the pupils are.

The curriculum is broad and balanced and helps to prepare the children for the next stage in their education. A wide variety of after school and lunchtime clubs provide additional activities and experiences for pupils of all ages. Educational visits to local places of interest and annual residential visits (for Year 5 and up) further enrich the curriculum.

From Years 5 and 6 there is a greater emphasis on subjects being taught by specialists. Class size remains low, with thc maximum class size being twelve. Well-qualified, conscientious and hard-working staff teach children in a supportive learning environment. Children are given the opportunity to explain their ideas and be involved in activities. There is a very well-equipped and effectively-organised computer suite, which ensures that the children are at the cutting edge of technology.

We offer our senior pupils all of the opportunities offered by larger secondary schools. Every pupil is encouraged to find their own strengths and build on that feeling of confidence in every subject and area of their lives.

St Winefride's RC Independent School

Shrewsbury

Belmont, Shrewsbury, Shropshire SY1 1TE

Tel: 01743 369883
email: reception@stwinefridesircs.co.uk
website: www.stwinefrides.com
Facebook: @st.winefrides
Instagram: @st.winefrides

Motto: *Soli Deo*

***Headteacher*: Mr. R. Goody**, BA Hons (History), QTS, MCCT, NPQSL.

Age range. 4+–11. Nursery: 3+–4.
Number in School. Day: 51 Boys, 55 Girls.
Fees per term (2023–2024). £1,885–£1,953.

Founded in 1868 by the Sisters of Mercy, it has been furnishing children with precious opportunities, experiences and memories for over 155 years. What lies at the heart of pupils' achievements is their happiness and enthusiasm for learning. This is nurtured by dedicated staff who provide a secure environment and curriculum designed to stimulate on all levels of development: spiritual, emotional, physical and academic.

The National Curriculum provides the basis for our programmes of study. This is enhanced and enriched to reflect the interests of our pupils. We have specialist teachers to deliver PE, French, Art, Music, Gymnastics and Dance. We have a school librarian who oversees the well-stocked library and all pupils have the opportunity to attend a library session once a week.

Children of other religions and Christian denominations are very welcome at St. Winefride's and share in the Religious Ethos of the School, which is summed up in our motto, 'Soli Deo'. Arising from the Christian values of the school is an awareness of the plight of others around the world, for whom the school raises money through a number of fundraising events.

Our aim is to ensure that the needs of our children are met in all areas of school life and that each child is given a wealth of experience and opportunities. By working collaboratively in a caring and compassionate environment, the children will be supported to reach their full academic, social and personal potential. This, in turn, will guarantee they leave St. Winefride's as confident, responsible and resilient members of society, ready to tackle whatever comes their way.

Our pupils have always achieved well academically and St. Winefride's was number 28 in the Sunday Times Top Independent Prep Schools 2021. We are proud to be the only Shropshire school to have been included in the top 50 national list.

Parents and carers can book a personal tour of the School by contacting the School office.

For admission enquires during term time contact: reception@stwinefridesircs.co.uk; during school holidays contact: head@stwinefridesircs.co.uk.

St Wystan's School

High Street, Repton, Derbyshire DE65 6GE

Tel: 01283 703258
email: head@stwystans.org.uk
website: www.stwystans.org.uk
X/Twitter: @StWystans
Facebook: @stwystansschool
Instagram: @stwystansschool

Chairman of Governors: Mr D Lewis
***Headteacher*: Ms K Lebihan**, BA Hons, PGCE

Number of Pupils. Day: Boys 35, Girls 37.

Fees per term (2023–2024). £3,560 per term (plus compulsory extras), lunches: £358.

Founded in 1926, St Wystan's is an independent preparatory day school for pupils aged 4 to 11 years of age. The School is situated in the heart of Repton and is only a short distance from Burton-on-Trent and the city of Derby.

St Wystan's is a thriving non-selective school that prides itself on its reputation for producing happy, confident and successful children. Every child is recognised and cherished for their individual strengths and characteristics in an inspiring and warm learning environment. Dedicated staff encourage a love for learning and warm, respectful relationships are nurtured between the pupils, their peers and the staff. The children enjoy going to school and the staff relish having the opportunity to share learning experiences, adventures and interests.

St Wystan's has a varied and stimulating curriculum so that pupils can develop, be happy and flourish. Specialist teaching in Music, Physical Education, French and Woodland School is introduced from Reception through to Year 6, with Drama introduced for Years 3 to 6 and Science from Form 1.

St Wystan's provides a comprehensive level of pastoral care through popular wraparound care and smaller class sizes, which ensures each child receives a tailored learning experience to prepare for the wider world with confidence. There are a range of extracurricular clubs and many pupils undertake individual instrumental, music and LAMDA tuition.

The School enjoys an excellent reputation in music, sport and drama, with pupils progressing to regional and national championships in swimming, tennis, athletics and music competitions. There is a thriving choir and pupils are actively encouraged to participate in clubs and groups in the wider community.

The benefits of a holistic education are valued and implemented to equip pupils with strong academic standards and behaviour, but also the essential qualities and skills required beyond their time at our school. The School has strong links with local secondary independent and state schools and leavers have an excellent reputation for securing scholarship offers and first-choice destinations.

St Wystan's benefits from being part of the Repton Family of Schools and pupils are fortunate to be able to share world-class facilities, including a Sports Centre with 25 m swimming pool.

Beyond St Wystan's. The School has a real gift for unlocking potential. Pupils achieve outstanding results with all 2023 leavers achieving their first choice of independent senior school and a number of scholarships being awarded across academia, creative arts, drama and sport. Pupils move on to a range of senior schools in the surrounding area, both in the state and independent sectors.

Charitable status. St Wystan's School Limited is a Registered Charity, number 527181. It exists to provide a quality education for both boys and girls.

Salesian College

119 Reading Road, Farnborough, Hampshire GU14 6PA

Tel: 01252 893000
email: office@salesiancollege.com
website: www.salesiancollege.com
X/Twitter: @SalesianFboro
Facebook: @Salesiancollegefarnborough

***Headmaster*: Mr Gerard T Owens**, MA Hons, PGCE

Age range. Boys 11–18 years, Girls 16–18. Co-educational Sixth Form.

Number in School. 587.

Fees per term (2023–2024). £4,901.

As a Catholic school in the Salesian tradition, the College provides a Home that welcomes; a Church where Gospel values are shared and lived out on a daily basis; a School which educates for Life and prepares for future success and realisation of individual potential; and a Playground where personal, social, moral, sporting and cultural enrichment, beyond the academic curriculum, takes place and where lasting friendships are formed. Therefore, the formation of character and the development of social conscience are at the heart of our mission. Students of other Christian denominations and religious faiths are warmly welcomed.

Salesian College forms well-educated, happy and well-rounded, confident young men and women; good Christians; honest citizens who are comfortable with themselves and those around them. Students are decent, courteous, selfless people; well equipped to take their place in and make a significant contribution to society.

Staff are caring and provide an excellent all round education. Salesian has outstanding levels of academic, cultural, spiritual and physical achievement, exemplary student behaviour and a caring ethos. We are a happy and highly successful school.

Although selective, we admit students of a wide range and believe in the pursuit of excellence for all. As such it caters excellently for all levels of ability, providing stretch for the most able and support for those with additional learning needs.

Excellent relationships between staff and students, and the students themselves, are a key feature of the College which seeks at all times to provide a holistic approach to the education and formation of those entrusted to our care.

The recent ISI Inspection report rated Salesian College as excellent in all areas, stating that, 'The excellence of academic achievement owes much to the excellence of the curriculum and the teaching. Pupils find the collaborative approach of the teaching staff very helpful and supportive. Teachers know their pupils extremely well; they plan their lessons carefully to include a variety of approaches which succeed in engaging pupils' interest and, in almost all cases, in enabling them to maintain strong progress.'

The school has its own chapel, chaplaincy and resident chaplain.

Prospective parents are always welcome to make an appointment to visit the College while in session. Please see our website for up-to-date details.

Charitable status. Salesian College Farnborough Limited is a Registered Charity, number 1130166. It exists to provide education in North East Hampshire and neighbouring counties.

Sancton Wood School

Sancton Wood Nursery:
17 Station Road, Cambridge CB1 2JB

Tel: 01223 471703 (whole school)
email: office.Nurseries@sanctonwood.co.uk

Sancton Wood Pre-Prep and Prep:
2 St Paul's Road, Cambridge CB1 2EZ

email: office.Prep@sanctonwood.co.uk

Senior School:
57 Bateman Street, Cambridge CB2 1LR

email: office.Seniors@sanctonwood.co.uk

website: www.sanctonwood.co.uk
X/Twitter: @SanctonWood
Facebook: @SanctonWood
Instagram: @sancton_wood_school
LinkedIn: /company/sancton-wood-school-cambridge

***Principal*: Mr Richard Settle**, BA Hons, PGCE

Age Range. 9 months–16.

Number of Pupils. 365.

Fees per term (2023–2024). Nursery £2,730 (3 days/week, minimum)–£4,550 (5 days/week); Reception–Year 2: £4,200; Years 3–6: £4,550; Years 7–11: £5,500.

Sancton Wood is a small independent, family-orientated co-educational day school in the heart of Cambridge, for pupils aged 9 months to 16 years. They believe that a happy child is a learning child. An innovative and creatively enriched curriculum and exceptional pastoral care allows each child to thrive. Their nurturing approach to academic excellence delivers impressive GCSE results, proven by a final outcome of a 1.5–2 grade increase on predicted grades given on entry to the school, and regularly feature in top GCSE results tables. Sancton Woods' recent inspection awarded the highest ratings in every category and they have been named as a finalist in the Independent School Awards for three years running.

Their class sizes offer an excellent teacher: pupil ratio. Staff can really get to know and spend time with each individual child. They understand what motivates them, what pace they work at, and which approach suits their talents and personality. This is key to a philosophy focused on providing a tailored educational journey for each child. It facilitates the early identification of strengths to be nurtured and challenges to be overcome with individual support.

With the world we are living in changing at an ever-increasing rate, Sancton Wood pride themselves on instilling a passion for life-long learning in their pupils. A love of learning and intellectual curiosity will be key to the continuous educational development needed as their students forge long-lasting, successful careers. They don't just teach towards tests: they are creative about their pupil's learning and nurture the characteristics of creativity, leadership, problem-solving and kindness (to name but a few) which will help them navigate a different career structure.

Clever timetabling allows for an enrichment programme to be offered as part of the school day. The breadth and diversity of the programme gives students access to a whole host of new experiences, helping them to develop a range of interests and skills and to build a sense of confidence to support them in the classroom and beyond.

Students are offered opportunities to explore and discover in a wide range of activities across STEM, Sport, The Arts, Humanities, Culture, and Debate and Discussion, as well as wider advanced qualification opportunities, a careers programme and pupil leadership positions.

Learning is regularly brought to life with school trips. There are plenty of rich learning resources right on their doorstep in Cambridge as well as offering international trips to places such as New York, Iceland, Japan, Spain and skiing destinations.

Sancton Wood offers specialist facilities and truly inspirational teaching. In sport they take advantage of the best professional standard facilities the city has to offer. Talented students are given the chance to thrive through their affiliation to a selection of outstanding local and national sports organisations, but every student has the opportunity to participate in team or individual events.

Scholarships. Scholarships at Sancton Wood are prestigious awards available to students demonstrating outstanding talent and ability in the spheres of Academic Study, STEM, the Creative Arts or Sport.

Pupils are offered exciting programmes and opportunities to develop their skills to the maximum and are also expected to act as role models, promoting their area of excellence and encouraging others to follow their example. All scholarships are won in open competition and are awarded solely on merit. Candidates must be registered with the school prior to entering the scholarship process or must going through the application process with our admissions team.

Scholarships are available to pupils entering Sancton Wood at Y3, Y7 and Y9. The application process is open in September for the following academic year. The school reserves the right to vary the number of awards according to the strength of applications and all scholarships awarded are reviewed at the start of a new key stage.

Scholarships are usually awarded at a fee reduction of 5%. In the interests of inclusivity, no student will be awarded more than two scholarships although applicants may apply for more than two.

In addition to a fee reduction, scholars receive support in their area of talent from an assigned academic mentor. Scholars also act as role models to their peers and contribute to wider school life, and in doing so will benefit from additional enrichment opportunities in their chosen area. Pupils with scholarship awards meet regularly with their scholarship mentor, and all those on the Gifted and Talented Register, to offer support with time-management, study-skills and other pressures and challenges beyond the academic sphere.

With their mentor, pupils explore and identify their academic and vocational aspirations. Mentors will then alert them to the opportunities available to them, helping them to expand their horizons and fulfil their potential, ensuring that their CVs are strong for their chosen sixth form, and exposing them to their academic competition.

When to apply. Year 3, Year 7 and Year 9 scholarship applications are open from 11th September and close on 19th January. Interview day is on 15th March and offers are made on 27th March.

The benefits of being a scholar:

- 5% reduction in school fees
- Free consultation session with Oxbridge Applications in Y9
- 25% reduction in all consultancy fees with Oxbridge and US Applications
- Free Summer School place for one of the school's Summer Courses
- Priority access to appropriate elements of the school's Accelerated Learning Provision
- All scholars are part of the Dukes' Scholars programme
- Scholarship opportunities at Cardiff 6th Form College (Cambridge)

Scholarships are offered to both internal and external candidates in Y3, Y7 and Y9. Interviews and Scholarships Days are competitive. Candidates may apply for more than one scholarship. All external candidates wishing to apply must complete a Scholarship Application Form together with a completed Registration Form and pay the Registration Fee (unless already on roll).

The application form can be found at: www.sanctonwood.co.uk/admissions/scholarships/.

Seaton House School

67 Banstead Road South, Sutton, Surrey SM2 5LH
Tel: 020 8642 2332
email: office@seatonhouse.sutton.sch.uk
website: www.seatonhouse.sutton.sch.uk
Facebook: @SeatonHouseSchool

Chair of Governors: Mrs J Evans

***Headteacher*: Mr Carl Bates**

Age range. Girls 3–11 years.

Number of pupils. Main School: 140; Nursery: 36.

Fees per term (2023–2024). £2,427–£4,097.

Seaton House School was founded in 1930 by Miss Violet Henry and continues to have a strong family feel to this day. The school provides all children with an excellent start to their learning journey and girls consistently gain both academic and scholarship success at both grammar and local independent schools. In 2023, 93% of our Year 6 girls who sat the 11+ were offered a grammar school place.

Seaton House has consistently been ranked in the top 5 Prep Schools in the *Sunday Times* list and was 'Prep School of the Year' in 2018–19 and currently number 2. ISI in its Educational Quality report judged the school to be 'Excellent in All Areas'.

Small class sizes ensure that every pupil is known as an individual and supported to ensure that they make the most of their gifts and talents. Alongside excellent academic teaching, the girls have opportunities to develop artistic, musical, dramatic and sporting talents. There are specialist teachers for almost all subjects to ensure that the girls receive the very best education in every area of the curriculum. The girls also compete in a range of events ranging from ISA young musician of the Year, musical concerts, full-scale productions to regular sports fixtures. We have a school choir, orchestra, drama groups and sports teams as well as a range of lunchtime and after school clubs which include: fencing, rock choir, ballet, musical theatre and various sports clubs.

Outside speakers and educational visits are an integral part of the School's curriculum as first hand experiences are so important to both inspire and give context to the girls' learning. Alongside regular workshops and termly external day visits, the girls in Key Stage Two also have the opportunity to engage in an annual residential course. These are carefully planned and provide a wealth of outdoor learning and adventurous activities to aid the development of leadership skills, teamwork and resilience.

Pastoral care is of the highest calibre with all staff taking a keen interest in the personal development of all the pupils. Courtesy, good manners and kindness are expected as the norm and pupils are encouraged to develop initiative, independence and confidence. The School has a strong house system and the pupils are encouraged to engage in community and fund raising events.

By the end of Year Six every girl will leave us as a confident, curious, creative individual who is fully prepared for the next step in her education and has made lasting memories and friendships. Please do come and see what makes Seaton House such a special place where you will always be assured of a warm welcome.

Charitable Status. Seaton House School is a Registered Charity, number 800673.

Shebbear College

Shebbear, Beaworthy, Devon EX21 5HJ
Tel: 01409 282000
email: admissions@shebbearcollege.co.uk
website: www.shebbearcollege.co.uk
X/Twitter: @ShebbearCollege
Facebook: @ShebbearCollege
Instagram: @ShebbearCollege
LinkedIn: /company/shebbearcollege

See full entry in the **Society of Heads** section, on **p. 563**.

Sherfield School
Education in Motion Group

Sherfield-on-Loddon, Hook, Hampshire RG27 0HT
Tel: 01256 884800
email: info@sherfieldschool.co.uk
website: www.sherfieldschool.co.uk
X/Twitter: @SchoolSherfield
Facebook: @SherfieldSchoolHampshire
Instagram: @sherfieldschool
LinkedIn: /school/sherfield-school

***Head of School* (*Interim*): Mr Neil Richards**

Age Range. 3 months–18 years, Co-educational.

Number in School. 620.

Fees per term (2023–2024). Day: £4,035–£6,725; Boarding: £8,705–£11,990.

Are you ready for an adventure?

You can start your Sherfield journey at any age, from 3 months to 18 years! We combine excitement and curiosity with new ventures and learning. Based in Hook, Hampshire, we offer plenty of boarding options as well as a day school.

Our school is bursting with excitement, energy and enthusiasm – perfect for students who are ready to have some serious fun while learning! You'll be swept away by the exciting opportunities that await you.

At Sherfield School, we believe that learning should be engaging, exciting and interactive. That's why we offer a curriculum that's full of surprises and fun activities designed to keep you on your toes. From science experiments to artistic creations, our teachers will inspire you to think outside the box and unleash your creative potential.

But that's not all – our school is also home to some of the coolest extracurricular activities around! Whether you want to join our championship-winning sports teams, showcase your talents in our music and drama departments, or explore your adventurous side through our outdoor education offerings, we've got something for everyone.

From the moment your child enters our outstanding nursery, they will start to develop their social and learning skills within our warm and nurturing school environment.

As they progress through the Prep and Senior schools, the children start to develop rigorous academic skills and enjoy world-class sports, arts and music programmes. With our small class sizes and bespoke learning, we regularly achieve outstanding results in academic league tables. Sixth Formers are exceptionally well prepared by our dedicated staff for further education, and gain entry into some of the best colleges and universities in the world. Regular fieldwork, sports exchanges and cultural trips round out their development and this integrated education instils a lifelong love of learning and culture.

We immerse our pupils in school life from day one of their journey here. Sherfield School is always a hive of activity. Our gifted and talented student body includes many musicians, artists, world-class players in tennis and golf, plus national and international equestrian, figure skating, cross-country and swimming stars. The school also plays host to many music and arts events throughout the school year.

Alongside academic learning and sports, we tailor pastoral care to meet your child's individual needs and aim to foster their unique talents and character, building confidence and respect.

And with our Grade II listed manor house set in many acres of beautiful grounds, woods and gardens, plus a new, purpose-built playground, there are plenty of opportunities for all ages to get outside in the fresh country air.

So what are you waiting for? Come and visit us to get a feel for our dynamic community and see how your child could benefit from The Sherfield Experience.

Sherrardswood School

Lockleys, Welwyn, Hertfordshire AL6 0BJ

Tel: 01438 714282
email: headmistress@sherrardswood.co.uk
website: www.sherrardswood.co.uk
Facebook: @sherrardswoodschool.co.uk

***Headmistress*: Mrs Anna Wright**

Head of Prep: Mr Matt Capuano
Assistant Head – Academic: Mrs Koulla Theodoulou
Assistant Head – Pastoral: Mrs Nicci Venn

Age range. 2–18.

Number in School. Day: 506.

Fees per term (2023–2024). £4,079–£6,339.

Sherrardswood, founded in 1928, is a co-educational day school for pupils aged 2–18. The School is set in 40 acres of attractive parkland two miles north of Welwyn Garden City. The Prep Department is housed in a beautiful 18th century building whilst the Senior Department occupies a purpose-built facility. Games fields, tennis courts and woodlands trail are available on the Lockleys site for both departments.

Entry to the school is by interview and individual assessment. A broad curriculum is offered to GCSE level and a wide range of A Level subjects is available. We pride ourselves on being a successful and ambitious non-selective school where students make excellent academic progress. Our approach is to nurture and ensure that the students are happy and enjoying their time at school. With this ethos, our academic results rival those of other highly competitive local schools. A range of sport and extracurricular opportunities is available, both within the school day and out of school hours. There is a strong focus on music and drama, with performance playing a valuable part in developing the confidence of our students. We are a happy and focused community.

Shoreham College

St Julian's Lane, Shoreham-by-Sea, West Sussex BN43 6YW

Tel: 01273 592681
email: info@shorehamcollege.co.uk
website: www.shorehamcollege.co.uk
X/Twitter: @ShorehamCollege
Facebook: @shorehamcollege

***Principal*: Mrs Sarah Bakhtiari**, BA, MA Brighton, QTS

Age Range. 3–16.

Number in School. Total 391: 227 Day Boys, 164 Day Girls.

Fees per term (2023–2024). £3,800–£6,100.

Shoreham College offers all the advantages of an all-through integrated education. Children learn together and thrive in our welcoming community. We choose to be co-educational, teaching girls and boys together from the ages of 3 to 16, knowing that this better prepares our pupils for a world in which the sexes live and work alongside each other.

We recognise that every child has their own strengths and challenges, and we believe that by learning together in an inclusive and kind environment, our pupils learn to respect and value one another, irrespective of gender and other differences.

Shoreham College pupils benefit from excellent facilities, caring support staff and specialist teachers. From a young age, our junior pupils gain from specialist senior resources as well as from regular interaction and friendship with older pupils. In turn, our senior pupils become leaders and role models to our youngest children. Our learning community enables each member to grow and flourish.

We offer a broad and balanced curriculum, designed to develop a range of transferable skills and talents and to appeal to every interest. As they progress through the school, our children benefit from the continuity our integration provides and from being a valued individual within our community. Our knowledge of our pupils' needs and passions means these remain a focus, and as our attainment data shows, our children are protected from the attainment dip that too often characterises the move from KS2 to KS3. Smooth transition between year groups and key stages ensures pupils maintain and build on their progress without interruption.

Charitable status. Shoreham College (The Kennedy Independent School Trust Limited) is a Registered Charity, number 307045. It exists to provide high-quality education for boys and girls.

Snaresbrook Preparatory School

75 Woodford Road, South Woodford, London E18 2EA

Tel: 020 8989 2394
email: office@snaresbrookprep.org
website: www.snaresbrookprep.org
X/Twitter: @SnaresbrookPrep
Facebook: @SnaresbrookPrep
LinkedIn: /snaresbrook-prep-school-ltd.

***Head*: Mr Ralph Dalton**

Age range. 3½–11.
Number in School. 165.
Fees per term (2023–2024). £4,606–£5,416.

Snaresbrook Preparatory School is a vibrant independent day school for boys and girls aged from 3½ to 11 years. Founded in the 1930s, the school occupies a substantial Victorian building, once a large private family home – something that contributes to the strong community spirit within the school. We aim to cultivate an intimate, caring family atmosphere in which children feel secure and valued. Snaresbrook Values have been introduced and embedded by the current Head – they include Respect, Enjoyment and Excellence. The values are posted all around the School and even on the hopscotch in the playground!

The Lower Foundation Stage is extremely popular and is our main point of entry. Most children join the school at age 3½ and stay with us until they reach 11 when they leave for their senior schools.

We provide a rounded education covering every aspect of your child's early development. The curriculum has broadened in the last few years and is designed to prepare pupils for life as well as entrance and scholarship examinations to senior independent and grammar schools. The curriculum includes Mathematics, English, Science, Current Affairs, ICT, Art, DT, Music, Drama, French, PE/Games, RE, Wellbeing and PSHEE. Latin and Swimming are introduced in the Juniors.

Areas such as Music, Drama, Sport, Computing and Languages are very strong and are led by passionate specialists. Ambitious School Development Plans have moved the School forward. At age 11, we find that Snaresbrook children are confident, cheerful and courteous, with a good sense of community and a readiness to care for each other and the world around them. They have learned how to work in the ways that suit them best, are receptive to teaching and are well prepared for the next stage of their education and development. We see ourselves as joint trustees, with parents, of the young lives in our care, bearing equal responsibility for their happiness, wellbeing and development.

In 2017, Snaresbrook came through its Regulatory Compliance Inspection fully compliant and without any action needed. The school feeds many of the top independent schools in the area including the City of London Schools, Forest, Chigwell and Bancroft's.

Anyone interested in the School is encouraged to contact the office to book a personal tour.

Steephill School

Off Castle Hill, Fawkham, Longfield, Kent DA3 7BG

Tel: 01474 702107
email: secretary@steephill.co.uk
website: www.steephill.co.uk
X/Twitter: @steephillonline
Facebook: @Steephill-School

***Head*: Mr John Abbott**, BA Hons, PGCE

Age range. 3–11 co-educational.
Number of pupils. 120.
Fees per term (2023–2024). £3,800. Pre School Fees are pro rata.

Steephill School provides an excellent all-round education, as evidenced in its academic, sporting, arts and musical achievements. The vast majority of Year 6 pupils gain entry to selective schools. Success at local music and drama festivals is very high, with individuals and group performances often winning top awards. The latest ISI inspection rated all areas of the school as 'Excellent'.

Steephill School believes in high-quality teaching within a disciplined but relaxed atmosphere. The School holds traditional values and beliefs; working with and supporting one another is an important part of the ethos. There are close links with the church opposite the School. Four services per year are held there and the Rector takes regular assemblies. The setting is very rural despite being only a few minutes' drive from the M2 and five miles from the M20 and M25. The School enjoys beautiful views of the countryside with very little traffic nearby.

The classes are small with only 120 pupils in the School. There is a close liaison between all members of the school community: children, staff, family members and governors. Parents are welcomed into the School and work closely with the teachers. There is regular feedback to parents on children's progress. Parents are also active in Friends of Steephill School, the Parents Association, to provide social and fundraising activities.

The children join the School aged 3 in the Pre School and they leave at age 11. The curriculum is designed to support all abilities to achieve academically, and in all the broader aspects of education such as drama, the arts and sports. Information Technology has been developed well over the last few years and is being continually updated.

There is a large selection of extracurricular activities at lunchtime and after school. We are very fortunate to have large grounds with a superb sports field, orchard and forest school, despite being a small school.

There is a care facility both before and after school so we are open from 7.00 am to 5.30 pm. The School is also very proud of the lunches. All the food is sourced from local shops: butcher, baker and greengrocer. The meals are carefully balanced and freshly made.

Charitable status. Steephill School is a Registered Charity, number 803152.

Stratford Preparatory School

Church House, Old Town, Stratford-upon-Avon, Warwickshire CV37 6BG

Tel: 01789 297993
email: secretary@stratfordprep.co.uk
website: www.stratfordprep.co.uk
Facebook: @stratfordprep

Motto: *Lux et Scientia*

***Executive Headteacher*: Mr David Preston**
Deputy Head: Ms Samantha Scorah

Age range. Preparatory School 4–11 years. Montessori Nursery School 2–4 years.

Number in School. 70: 39 Boys, 31 Girls.

Fees per term (2023–2024). Juniors: £4,250; Infants: £3,750; Reception: £3,750 (funded); Lunch: £200. Nursery School: according to sessions attended.

Stratford Preparatory School is situated in the heart of the historic town of Stratford-upon-Avon. The Preparatory school opened in September 1989 and has developed around a large town house. An additional detached house within the school's grounds provides accommodation for the Reception and Nursery children, a gymnasium, a science room and design and technology room.

The Nursery implements the Montessori philosophy of learning which encourages a structured learning environment. French and ballet are taught from the age of 2 years.

The main school offers a broad, balanced learning plan adapted to the individual needs of the children using traditional teaching methods and with specific reference to the National Curriculum. All children are entered for the 11+ and independent school entrance examinations.

The school offers a high level of pastoral care and attention to personal development.

Physical education activities include: sailing, swimming, football, cricket, tennis, netball, rounders, ballet and athletics.

There are opportunities for the children to learn a variety of musical instruments. The school has two choirs and an orchestra.

Reduction in fees is offered for families with two or more children in the School.

The Headmistress is pleased to provide further details and meet prospective parents.

The Study Preparatory School

Wilberforce House, Camp Road, Wimbledon Common, London SW19 4UN

Tel: 020 8947 6969
email: admissions@thestudyprep.co.uk
website: www.thestudyprep.co.uk
X/Twitter: @thestudyprep
Facebook: @thestudyprep
Instagram: @thestudyprep

Chairman of Governors: Mr John Tucker

***Head*: Sharon Maher**

Admissions: Connie Cherrett

Age range. 4–11.

Number of girls. 320 (approximately).

Fees per term (2023–2024). £5,565.

The Study Preparatory School provides a happy and stimulating learning environment for girls from 4 to 11 on two very attractive and well-equipped sites adjacent to Wimbledon Common.

The girls enjoy a rich diversity of experiences, both in and out of the classroom. The school is renowned for its creative ethos, and has had Artsmark Gold status by Arts Council England since 2009. Each girl is encouraged to do her best academically, and excellent teaching standards encourage academic rigour and challenge. Music and sport are exceptionally strong, while drama, public-speaking and a varied clubs programme play an important part. Guest speakers, fundraising events, workshops and school trips all help the children to understand important issues beyond the school gates. Good manners and consideration for others are encouraged at all times. Girls leave at 11+, very well prepared for the next stage of their education, with a zest for learning and many happy memories. Girls receive offers from leading day and boarding senior schools, many with academic or performance scholarships, with a total of 57 scholarships and awards offered in 2022 for 2023 Secondary school entry.

Entry is non-selective at Reception and by assessment thereafter.

Charitable status. The Study (Wimbledon) Ltd is a Registered Charity, number 271012. It exists to provide education for girls from 4 to 11.

Sylvia Young Theatre School

1 Nutford Place, London W1H 5YZ

Tel: 020 7258 2330
email: info@syts.co.uk
website: www.syts.co.uk

Principal: Mrs Sylvia Young, OBE

***Headteacher*: Mrs Anne-Marie Kennedy**, BSc Hons, PGCE, NPQH

Age range. 10–16.

Number in School. Day: 50 Boys, 161 Girls.

Fees per term (2023–2024). Key Stage 2, 3 & 4: £5,070.

The School has a junior department (Year 6 only) and a secondary department (Years 7–11). We aim to provide an appropriately balanced academic and vocational experience for our students. We are proud of the caring and well disciplined environment that prevails and promotes a very positive climate of individual success.

Academic subjects are delivered by highly qualified staff to the end of Key Stage 4.

GCSE Examination subjects include English, English Literature, Mathematics, Combined or Triple Science, Art, Drama, Music, Media Studies, Spanish and History.

Theatrical training is given by experienced professional teachers. Pupils are prepared for examinations in Speech and Drama – LAMDA (London Academy of Music and Dramatic Art). Entry is by audition with academic ability assessed.

TASIS The American School in England

Coldharbour Lane, Thorpe, Surrey TW20 8TE

Tel: +44 (0)1932 565 252
email: ukadmissions@tasisengland.org
website: www.tasisengland.org
X/Twitter: @tasisengland
Facebook: @TASIS The American International School in England
Instagram: @tasis_england_official
LinkedIn: /school/tasis-the-american-school-in-england

***Head of School*: Bryan Nixon**
Head of Upper School: Stephanie FeoHughes
Head of Middle School: Dr Megel Barker
Head of Lower School: Melodi Jordan

Number of Pupils. 639. Girls: 363, Boys: 276, Total boarders: 238.

Fees per year (2023–2024). Early Years Program (Ages 3–5) full year tuition fees £13,280; K–3 £22,800; 4–8 £26,630; 9–13 £29,080. Boarding Fees Full Year (Grades 8–13) £54,510.

TASIS The American School in England provides a truly international learning experience for day and boarding students aged 3 to 18. Our caring teachers are committed to providing the balance of academic challenge and support that will enable our students to realize their full potential and contribute to their community as they discover their passion and follow their own pathway.

- Average class size of 10–12 students
- American curriculum leading to an American High School Diploma
- Advanced Placement (AP) courses
- International Baccalaureate (IB) Diploma Programme
- Individualized four-year university counseling
- Excellent university placement in the UK, US & worldwide
- 60 nationalities & 30 languages spoken on campus
- 45 minutes from central London
- 20 minutes from Heathrow Airport

Set in the beautiful Surrey countryside, our spacious 46-acre campus is close enough to London to take advantage of all the culture and excitement it offers for field trips and weekend activities. The TASIS boarding program provides a safe and welcoming home-away-from-home for students aged 13 to 18 (Grades 8–12).

In Upper School, our impressive academic offerings include Advanced Placement courses developed by the American College Board and the IB Diploma Programme. Both provide well-defined pathways to universities in the US, the UK, or anywhere in the world. A broad range of co-curricular, leadership, and service opportunities round out our students' educational experience.

TASIS England also offers an award-winning residential Summer Program for ages 11–17. Our program attracts bright and adventurous students from around the world who take one major academic course and one elective, complemented by sports, activities, and weekend excursions. We offer two three-week sessions starting in late June and ending in early August.

Tettenhall College

Wood Road, Tettenhall, Wolverhampton, West Midlands WV6 8QX

Tel: 01902 751119
email: head@tettcoll.co.uk
website: www.tettenhallcollege.co.uk
Facebook: @TettColl
Instagram: @tettcoll
LinkedIn: /company/tettenhall-college

See full entry in the **Society of Heads** section, on **p. 566**.

Thames Christian School

12 Grant Road, London SW11 2FR

Tel: 020 7228 3933
email: admissions@thameschristianschool.org.uk
website: www.thameschristianschool.org.uk
X/Twitter: @ThamesCSchool
Facebook: @Thameschristianschool
Instagram: @thameschristianschool

***Head*: Dr Stephen Holsgrove**, PhD

Age range. 11–18 Co-educational.
Number of pupils. 167.

These are exciting times for Thames. As we begin our third decade, there is increased awareness that young people require an education that prepares them to navigate life successfully. Faced with a fluid, and at times uncertain, world, they increasingly need to develop exceptional soft skills, resilience and deep-rooted values.

Academic rigour is foundational for us at Thames. However, we are passionate about far more than this. We enjoy seeing young people understand their value, learn to honour and encourage others and contribute to the wider school community.

Small classes and excellent pastoral care enable us to challenge and support each individual in their learning and in building good interpersonal skills. Our ethos of compassion, respect and humility enables young people to grow in confidence and their appreciation of each other.

With our new building adjacent to Clapham Junction station complete, our pupils now have the state-of-the-art facilities that they deserve. At five times the floor area of our old facility, the new space includes multiple science laboratories, DT workshops, a food technology room, library, PE hall/theatre and a dance/drama studio.

As well as A levels from September 2023, our new sixth form will offer a co-curricular and pastoral programme that will see our pupils further develop their leadership skills and understanding of the world so that they are prepared for a successful future.

GCSE Results 2022. Our Year 11s have moved to their next phase of education well prepared despite the disruption of Covid, with almost all entering their first choice sixth forms. In 2022 the percentage of grades at 9–7 was 35% and 9–4 was 82%. 31% of pupils achieved at least five 9–7 grades and 69% at least one 9–7 grade.

ISI Inspection April 2022. We are delighted with the judgements of the Independent Schools Inspectorate in its Educational Quality Inspection in April 2022. Key findings were:

- The quality of the pupils' academic and other achievements is excellent
- Pupils are highly effective communicators
- Pupils show highly positive attitudes to their learning
- Pupils value the opportunities they are given to pursue interests beyond the classroom and many achieve success in them
- The quality of the pupils' personal development is excellent
- Pupils show real compassion for each other and have a genuine appreciation of the strength of the school community
- Pupils develop strong self-confidence and self-worth because they feel accepted for who they are
- Pupils have high standards for their own behaviour and encourage the same of their peers
- In this diverse community pupils demonstrate high levels of cultural awareness and celebrate each other's differences as well as everyone's common humanity.

We are able to offer individual tours of the school, by appointment, to Year 6 parents. To make an appointment, please phone 020 7228 3933.

For further information please visit: www.thameschristianschool.org.uk.

Fees per term (2023–2024). £7,440.

Charitable status. Thames Christian School is a Registered Charity, number 1081666.

Thorpe Hall School

Wakering Road, Thorpe Bay, Essex SS1 3RD
Tel: 01702 582340
email: sec@thorpehallschool.co.uk
website: www.thorpehallschool.co.uk
X/Twitter: @ThorpeHall
Facebook: @ThorpeHallSchool
Instagram: @thorpehallschool

***Headteacher*: Mr Stephen Duckitt**

Age range. 2–16 years.

Number in School. Approximately 400 girls and boys.

Fees per term (2023–2024). £3,240–£5,028. Nursery: £29.70 per session (excluding Early Years Funding).

Thorpe Hall School is a co-educational independent day school, pleasantly situated on green belt land on the outskirts of Southend-on-Sea, Essex. The buildings are modern and purpose built.

Communications to London are good via the A13 and A127 and the Liverpool/Fenchurch Street railway lines. The nearest station is approximately 10 minutes' walk.

Founded in 1925, the school has been educating children for nearly 100 years years and consistently achieves excellent academic results with special emphasis being placed on the traditional values of good manners, behaviour, dress and speech.

The school has won many awards for its excellence and innovation across a number of different aspects. Best Senior School – ISA 2017; Best Early Years – ISA 2017, Best Pupil Wellbeing – ISA 2019. Top 100 Prep School in the Sunday Times every year since 2015. Nominated by the TES for Wellbeing initiative of the Year 2019 and 2020.

The school runs Forest School sessions and Beach School sessions in the Early Years along with French, yoga and dance. In the Prep school, pupils learn to read and write super-fast and are supported by the Read Write Inc and Accelerated Reader programmes. In the Senior School, pupils can choose what they do on a Wednesday afternoon from a list that includes drone flyer, radio-controlled car racing, archery, diving, Stage Make-up, Film Making, Kung Fu and many other activities. GCSE results are consistently good and outstrip national norms every year. Around 80% of leavers go to university 2 years after leaving.

The Charitable Trust status enables fees, which are very competitive, to be kept to a minimum. Nursery vouchers are accepted and some bursaries are available. The School is regularly inspected by the Independent Schools Inspectorate.

Charitable status. Thorpe Hall School Trust is a Registered Charity, number 298155. It exists to provide good-quality education for boys and girls in South East Essex.

Tower College

Mill Lane, Rainhill, Merseyside L35 6NE

Tel: 0151 426 4333
email: msbingley@towercollege.com
office@towercollege.com
website: towercollege.com
Facebook: @towercollege

***Principal*: Ms A Bingley**

Vice-Principal: Mrs R Wright
Registrar: Ms C McNamara

Age range. 3 months–16 years.

Number in School. Day: 231 Boys, 230 Girls.

Fees per term (2023–2024). £2,716–£3,322.

Tower College is a non-denominational Christian Day School housed in a beautiful Victorian mansion set in 11 acres.

We believe children thrive in our safe and secure environment where they do not have to conform to a peer group. They are free to become their best selves, to achieve the best possible academic results and are given every opportunity to excel in Sport, Art and Music.

Charitable status. Tower College is a Registered Charity, number 526611.

Trevor-Roberts School

55–57 Eton Avenue, London NW3 3ET

Tel: 020 7586 1444
email: trsenior@trevor-robertsschool.co.uk
website: www.trevor-robertsschool.co.uk

***Headteacher*: Mr Simon Trevor-Roberts**, BA

Age Range. 5–13 Co-educational.

Number in School. 170 Day Pupils: 100 boys, 70 girls.

Fees per term (2023–2024). £6,300–£6,950.

Trevor-Roberts School was founded in Hampstead in 1955 by the headmaster's late father and moved to its present site in 1981. The school is made up of two departments but operates as one school and occupies two adjacent much-adapted late Victorian houses in Belsize Park. In addition to on-site facilities, the school makes use of nearby playing fields and a local leisure centre swimming pool and astroturf pitch.

Central to the education provided is the school's aim for all pupils to become happy and confident individuals who fulfil their potential. Strong emphasis is placed on personal organisation and pupils are encouraged to develop a love of learning for its own sake. In a happy, non-competitive atmosphere, pupils are well cared for and teachers' responses are tailored to the individual needs of pupils. It is the School's strong belief that much can be expected of a child if he or she is given self-confidence and a sense of personal worth and does not feel judged too early in life against the attainment of others.

High success rates throughout the school are achieved through small classes, individual attention and specialist teachers. The standards achieved enable almost all pupils to gain places in their first choice of school at either 11+ or 13+ into the main London day schools and academically selective independent boarding schools. In recent years a number of pupils have been awarded academic, art and music scholarships to these schools. The school aims to make pupils prepared for this process and give them the confidence to enjoy the academic challenges they will be offered.

The school provides a broad range of curricular and extra-curricular activities, contributing to pupils' linguistic, mathematical, scientific, technological, social and physical development in a balanced way. Aesthetic and creative development is strongly encouraged through art, drama and music. In the Senior Department the syllabus is extended to include Classical History, Latin and Greek. The curriculum is enriched at all stages by a variety of one-day educational visits as well as by residential trips for Years 5–8 on activity trips, a sailing weekend and a geography field trip.

A range of extra-curricular activities and sporting opportunities appropriate for boys and girls of all ages is offered two afternoons a week and after school. The school's founder believed passionately in music and drama as a means of developing pupils' confidence and self-esteem and both subjects are a strong feature of the school today. All classes prepare and perform two drama performances each year in which every pupil has a speaking and/or singing part.

Pupils thrive in a caring family atmosphere where the emphasis is on individual progress and expectation, and where improvement is rewarded as highly as success. It has a broadly Christian tradition, but welcomes pupils of all faiths and of none.

Tring Park School for the Performing Arts

Mansion Drive, Tring, Hertfordshire HP23 5LX

Tel: 01442 824 255
email: info@tringpark.com
website: www.tringpark.com
X/Twitter: @TringParkSchool
Facebook: @TringParkSchool
Instagram: @tringpark_school

See full entry in the **Society of Heads** section, on **p. 569**.

Trinity School

Buckeridge Road, Teignmouth, Devon TQ14 8LY

Tel: 01626 774138
email: admissions@trinityschool.co.uk
website: www.trinityschool.co.uk

See full entry in the **Society of Heads** section, on **p. 570**.

Ursuline Preparatory School

Great Ropers Lane, Warley, Brentwood, Essex CM13 3HR

Tel: 01277 227152
email: headmistress@ursulineprepwarley.co.uk
website: www.ursulineprepwarley.co.uk

Independent Preparatory School of the Year 2021.

Headmistress: **Mrs Pauline Wilson**, MBE, MSc

Age Range. 3–11.
Number in School. Day 180.
Fees per term (2023–2024). £2,525–£4,705.

Founded in the early 1930s, the Ursuline Preparatory School enjoys a reputation as a happy family school, where pupils strive to give of their best in all areas of school life. Consequently, much emphasis is placed on encouraging the children to develop to the full their individual talents and interests, as well as fostering in each pupil a strong sense of well-being, self-reliance and team spirit.

This is achieved by the frequent use of praise, by adherence to an agreed policy of consistent and fair discipline and by the high standards, moral code and caring attitudes deriving from the strongly Catholic ethos which underpins the life of the whole school.

The Ursuline Preparatory School has well qualified and very experienced teachers and support staff.

It is committed to offering to all its pupils the distinct advantages of a broad and balanced curriculum. This includes a rigorous academic curriculum supplemented by the provision of an excellent PE, Drama, Music, ICT and Language programme.

A comprehensive range of extracurricular activities are offered to the pupils. These are often taught by specialist staff and include subjects such as Theatre Club, Art Appreciation, ICT, Maths, Chess, Ballet and Speech and Drama. As well as many Instrumental Classes and Sporting Activities, with which the School has considerable success in gaining individual and team awards at competition level.

The School successfully prepares children for entry to local and national independent schools, both day pupils and boarding, Grammar Schools or local Secondary Schools.

The relatively small size of the School allows for very close contact between staff, pupils and parents and provides each child with the opportunity to fulfil his or her academic potential. The pupils are encouraged to follow their own interests and to develop a sense of self-confidence and self-worth which will hopefully remain with them throughout their lives, allowing them to reflect the school motto: *A Caring School that strives for excellence.*

Charitable status. The Ursuline Preparatory School is a Registered Charity, number 1058282, which is a non-profit making and managed by an independent board of voluntary trustees. It exists to provide Roman Catholic children and those of other denominations with the opportunity to reach the highest individual standards possible in every area of School life.

Waverley Preparatory School and Nursery

Waverley Way, Finchampstead, Wokingham, Berkshire RG40 4YD

Tel: 0118 973 1121
07768 708743 (Admissions)
email: admissions@waverleyschool.co.uk
website: www.waverleyschool.co.uk
www.waverleynursery.co.uk
X/Twitter: @waverleyschool
Facebook: @waverleyschool
Instagram: @waverleyprepschool
LinkedIn: /waverley-preparatory-school-&-nursery

Chair of Governors: Mr Blair Jenkins

***Head Teacher*: Mr Guy Shore**, BA Hons, QTS

Assistant Head: Mr Henry Mitchell
Bursar: Mrs Carole Barke
Head of Admissions: Mrs Helen Jenkins
Deputy Head of Teaching and Learning: Mrs Pippa Eden

Age range. 3 months–11 years.
Number of pupils. 240.

Class sizes. Average of 21 pupils with 2 teachers per class. Single-form entry (one class per year group).

Fees per term (2023–2024). Reception–Year 6 Core School Day: £3,622–£4,331. Extended day package (Breakfast Club and After-school Clubs) also available. Wraparound care available for children from 7.30 am to 6.00 pm, 51 weeks a year. Early Years Funding available and can also be used in our Reception class until the term of a child's 5th birthday. Core school fees and wraparound care (Breakfast Club and After-school Club) are charged separately so that parents only pay for the wraparound care required. Nursery fees are according to the broad range of flexible sessions attended, including term-time only or 51-weeks-a-year contracts. Sibling discounts are available. A discount is also available for fees paid annually in advance.

Ethos. Waverley is ranked 'Best in Berkshire', 33rd in the UK out of over 20,000 Prep and Primary schools and also no. 1 primary and Prep School in the Wokingham and Reading area based on our academic results. Waverley is rated 'Double Excellent' in our ISI (Independent Schools Inspectorate) inspection. At the same time, Waverley provides a warm, family environment with small class sizes (an average of 21 pupils per class) and an excellent pupil/teacher ratio. Despite being non-academically selective, last year all our Year 6 pupils were offered a place at their chosen secondary school, including to some of the most reputable independent senior schools in the country. We are a purpose-built Preparatory school which combines a traditional ethos towards a rewarding and thorough education, with a modern feel and the latest teaching technology. Located on the edge of the Berkshire countryside, we enjoy a rural setting and spacious playing fields as well as a large woodland area for our Forest School.

Our priority at Waverley is to challenge every pupil to achieve academic excellence. We recognise, however, that only happy children, who feel supported and confident, learn to the best of their ability. Waverley's unique cheerful, nurturing environment enables every child to succeed and reach his or her full potential.

Academic excellence. Waverley is ranked 33rd in the UK out of over 20,000 Primary and Prep School. The school is also ranked 'Best in Berkshire' by the *Top 100 Prep Schools in the UK* (The Sunday Times) having been the only school to be consistently in these rankings for the past 12 years. Our rankings are based purely on our academic success. Our educational prowess is also reflected in the exceptional exam results of our Year 6 students and the secondary schools they move on to – most of our students attain scholarships, or places at selective secondary schools. On average 85–95% of our pupils pass the 11+ each year.

We operate small class sizes, giving each child individual attention and enabling us to closely monitor every child's progress. Our purpose-built school enables daily school life to flow and function easily in a modern, welcoming and spacious learning environment. Our family atmosphere means that our teachers not only know every child by name – they also know what makes a child tick. This warm ethos is also visible amongst our children who play with each other freely across the year groups in the playground.

In addition to academic success, we aim to encourage self-discipline, respect, tolerance and kindness and to provide a broad, rich curriculum going far beyond national expectations. Our school motto is 'We Are Kind, We Are Honest, We Do Our Best' which we believe should apply to everything a child undertakes whether academic work, sporting performance or relationships with friends, teachers and family.

Curriculum. Waverley's curriculum provides children with a solid foundation, particularly in the areas of literacy and numeracy. Pre-prep and Preparatory children engage in a full curriculum of subjects including English, Mathematics, ICT, French, History, Geography, Latin, Science and Art. We enjoy a high number of specialist teachers across many of our core curriculum and supporting subjects.

Gifted and talented. We have development programmes for gifted and talented children.

Sports. Waverley School's physical education curriculum includes football, rugby, hockey, tennis, netball, cricket, athletics and rounders. Swimming also takes place weekly throughout the year as part of our ethos that every child needs to learn this life skill. The children regularly take part in sports matches and swimming galas against other local independent schools and also participate in ISA (Independent Schools Association) competitions. Waverley is proud that our recent results included being finalists in the ISA football tournament.

The Arts. We have extremely strong Speech and Drama, and Music (both choral and instrumental) departments. As well as termly productions, the School regularly takes part in local concerts both in the local community and with other schools to build children's self-confidence.

Wraparound care. Our After-School Clubs include Cookery, Fencing, Tennis, Gardening, Rugby, Cheerleading, Prep Club, Lego, ICT, Yoga and Cross Country. We offer over 75 different after-school activities each academic year which change every term.

Moving on. As Waverley is not an affiliated feeder for any one Senior School, we have excellent relationships with many local and national Senior Schools, including grammar, independent and state. We pride ourselves in ensuring that our pupils move on to the right secondary school for them by providing them with excellent preparation to attain their place at their preferred secondary school. The majority of our students attain scholarships, or places at selective secondary schools. All our Year 6 students last year were offered places at their first choice. Senior Schools that our pupils move on to include Wellington College, Reading Blue Coat, Lord Wandsworth and local and national grammar schools.

West Lodge School

36 Station Road, Sidcup, Kent DA15 7DU
Tel: 020 8300 2489
email: info@westlodge.org.uk
website: www.westlodge.org.uk

Chair of Governors: Mrs Chris Head-Rapson

***Head Teacher*: Mr Robert Francis**, BEd Hons

Age Range. 3–11.
Number of Pupils. 176 Day Boys and Girls.
Fees per term (2023–2024). £2,218–£3,711.

West Lodge was founded in 1940 and is now an educational trust. The main building is an extended Victorian house, well adapted to use as a school, whilst still retaining its homely atmosphere. Facilities include a science/cookery room and art room/crèche, which can also be used together as an additional hall facility, a fully-equipped gymnasium, Astroturf surfaced playground, art studio, music rooms and a computer suite. There are eight classes of up to 22 pupils, one class in each year group from Nursery through to Year 6. The staff to pupil ratio is extremely high and the children are taught in smaller groups by specialist teachers for many subjects. The school is open from 7.30 am and an after-school crèche and homework club operate until 6.00 pm.

The school has a strong academic tradition and a purposeful atmosphere permeates each class. The National Curriculum is at the core of our teaching but it is enhanced and enriched by the inclusion of a wider range of subjects. These include: English, mathematics, science, French, information technology, design technology, history, geography, religious education, music, art and craft, physical education and games, swimming and drama.

Great emphasis is placed on a thorough grounding in basic learning skills, with literacy and numeracy seen as key elements in the foundation, upon which future learning will be built. Particular care is taken to extend the most gifted children and support the less able. West Lodge has a consistent record of a high level of entry to local authority selective schools and independent schools.

Music has a particularly high profile within the school and all of the children are encouraged to develop their talents. Well-qualified peripatetic staff teach both group and individual lessons and children of all ages are encouraged to join the school orchestras and choir. Concerts and dramatic performances are staged regularly and parents are warmly invited to attend.

Sports of all sorts are taught and we are keen to get involved in both competitive and friendly sporting fixtures with other schools.

The school promotes a caring attitude between all its members and aims to help each child towards the achievement of self-control and self-discipline. The Head Teacher and the class teachers know each of the children well and the excellent pastoral care and family atmosphere are major features of the school.

Home-school links are strong and the open door policy gives parents immediate access to members of staff should worries occur. The school also has strong contacts with the local community.

Extracurricular activities are given the highest priority and clubs run each afternoon after school. Regular school outings form part of the curriculum for all children, the older pupils enjoying residential visits.

Charitable status. West Lodge School Educational Trust is a Registered Charity, number 283627. It exists for the provision of high quality education for boys and girls between 3 and 11 years.

Westbourne School

Hickman Road, Penarth, Vale of Glamorgan CF64 2AJ

Tel: 029 2070 5705
email: admissions@westbourneschool.com
website: www.westbourneschool.com
Facebook: @WestbourneSchool
Instagram: @westbourne.school
LinkedIn: /company/westbourne-international

***Head of School*: Miss Joanne Chinnock**

Global Academic Director & IB Coordinator: Ms Lisa Phillips
Digital Director: Mr Stuart Ayres
Pastoral Coordinator & IB Deputy: Mrs Nia John
GCSE Coordinator (*Yr 9-PreIB*): Mrs Jodi Barber
Middle Years Coordinator (*Yr 6–8*): Mr Jason Murray
Upper Prep Coordinator (*Yr 3–5*): Mrs Laura Doidge
Early Years Coordinator (*Reception–Yr 2*): Mrs Victoria Edwards
Little Westbourne Nursery Manager (*Age 2–4*): Ms Louise Dwyer

Age Range. 2–18.
Number in School. 194 Boys, 169 Girls.
Boarding. From Senior School upwards.
Day fees per term (2023–2024). £3,309–£5,815.

Boarding fees per annum (2023–2024). £43,820 (Boarding House accommodation), £41,820 (local home stay accommodation); both fully inclusive of tuition, accommodation during term time and half term breaks, all meals (including weekends), guardianship costs and annual airport transfers, with no exeat weekends.

Westbourne Nursery accepts children from 2 years and is open for 51 weeks a year at a cost of £68 per day from 7.30am until 6.00pm, or £41 per half day session.

Big Ideas, Infinite Possibilities

Westbourne develops globally-minded, well-rounded young scholars who progress to the best universities in the world (90% graduate entry rate to elite Russell Group universities and international equivalents). Graduates possess the skills, knowledge, confidence and character to become the STEM and business leaders of the future, securing careers in competitive fields including medicine, law, engineering and business.

One of the UK's most outstanding schools

Westbourne is one of the UK's leading academic schools for children aged 2–18, ranked 1st in the UK for 5 consecutive years (Daily Telegraph), voted No.1 IB Sixth Form and called "one of the most consistently high-achieving independent schools in Britain" (Sunday Times Best School Guide 2021): 2023 saw outstanding results in both the IB Diploma at Sixth Form (92.75% A*-B (7–5 IB Points), 100% A*-C), and at GCSE (2023 A*-B results: 61% A*, 85% A*/A and 92% A*-B, with 100% Distinctions in Additional Maths).

With an illustrious 126-year history of academic excellence, Westbourne is recognised as an innovator in education, leading the way with a cutting-edge approach that not only nurtures students academically, but also offers them the best global learning opportunities thanks to privileged links with leading global academic organisations including INSEAD Business School and a number of universities. In 2023, the school was honoured with the Global EdTech Award for Best School Digital Transformation for a world-leading use of technology, and was one of the first schools in Wales to use artificial intelligence to enhance classroom learning. In addition to virtual collaboration with their peers across the global schools, students develop advanced computing skills, with an impressive grasp of high-level programming and robotics.

Leading the global education frontier – now on 3 continents

The UK school is the hub of a groundbreaking international network of academically elite schools – the world's first truly global network of leading IB schools – which has grown to Westbourne College Sydney, ranked 1st in Australia with its first graduating class, and Westbourne College Singapore in August 2023.

A visionary approach sees students collaborate across continents, working together to solve problems and discuss global issues, supported by cutting-edge technology that allows real-time interaction. Students benefit from unmatched learning and personal development opportunities, participating in global webinars, lessons and international exchange trips.

A home-away-from-home

Westbourne offers boarding from Senior School upwards, either in the school's Boarding House or via homestay with friendly local families. Westbourne's Boarding House accommodation is safe, secure and comfortable, with options for single or shared rooms, as well as dining, quiet study and socialising spaces. The boarding community is small, supportive, family-like and multicultural, providing the opportunity to meet and make friends with students from all over the world. Westbourne prides itself on being a distinctly British school complemented by a student body representing over 25 different nationalities.

Smaller class sizes, with a focus on wellbeing

Students benefit from smaller class sizes than at other schools, allowing personalised attention and one-to-one support. Offering a small, friendly community where every student is known by name by every teacher, Westbourne is described as having a family feel, blending traditional values with outstanding teaching and the latest technology.

Westbourne offers the International Baccalaureate (IB) Diploma Programme in Sixth Form, and GCSEs from Year 9, which allows students opportunity to study a wider range of subjects as excellent preparation for the IB. A broad co-curricular programme enhances the competencies learned in class, with opportunities to engage in a wide range of leadership roles, student council, music and drama, and an exhilarating programme of after school clubs making use of the best facilities in the local area including climbing, sailing, horseriding, kayaking, skiing, yoga, ice skating and more.

Prep School pupils also benefit from a diverse curriculum, including early exposure to foreign languages, the arts, mathematics and science, as well as a range of excellent sporting opportunities, including a thriving Saturday Sports fitness club and team sports. All children participate in a regular STEM afternoon and attend Westbourne's FaB (Forest and Beach) School half termly – an immersive outdoors learning and wellbeing initiative set in local coastal and countryside settings, including the school's private forest site on a 20-acre farm – in addition to an equally wide range of after school clubs and personal development opportunities.

One of the best places to live in the UK

Westbourne is located in Penarth, an affluent seaside suburb voted one of the best places to live in 2021 for health and wellbeing (*The Times*) and one of the Top 10 best places to live in the UK (*Sunday Times*). Ten minutes from vibrant, historic Cardiff (ranked by the EU Quality of Life Survey as the 3rd best European capital city) Westbourne offers the perfect blend of modern metropolis, suburban safety, seaside and countryside.

The school enjoys excellent transport links, with easy access to the M4. There is a convenient train service from Penarth to Cardiff Central, which offers direct trains to London and across the UK. The school has minibuses running each day across the Vale of Glamorgan and Cardiff.

Weston Green School

Weston Green Road, Thames Ditton, Surrey KT7 OJN

Tel: 020 8398 2778
email: info@westongreenschool.org.uk
website: www.westongreenschool.org.uk
X/Twitter: @westongreensch
Facebook: @westongreenschool
Instagram: @westongreensch
LinkedIn: /company/weston-green-school

Motto: Inspiring Individuals, Nurturing Potential, Successful Futures

***Head*: Mrs Sarah Evans**

Senior leadership team:
Mrs Azmina Hansraj (*Deputy Headteacher, Designated Safeguarding Lead, Head of Pastoral Care and PSHE*)
Mrs Azmina Hansraj (*Deputy Headteacher, Designated Safeguarding Lead, Head of Pastoral Care and PSHE*)
Mrs Sara Wilson (*Assistant Head and Director of Studies*)
Mrs Harriet Doughty (*Head of Lower Prep*)
Mrs Catherine White (*Head of Upper Prep*)
Mrs Emma Nicholas (*School Business and Operations Manager*)

Student numbers. 190.

Fees per term (2023–2024). See website www.westongreenschool.org.uk/admissions/fees/

As an excellent rated school, Weston Green fosters learning and opportunities for each child to reach their full academic potential where they feel valued, confident and emotionally secure. Small class sizes and specialist teaching programme ensure 11+ success to highly regarded senior schools, many with scholarships.

Extracurricular activities. Examples include: art, craft, origami, STEM and Lego Clubs, Yoga and a variety of team sports.

Clubs change per term you can find a full list of clubs here: www.westongreenschool.org.uk/school-life/extra-curricular-clubs/

Scholarships and Bursaries. Yes – at the discretion of the school and awarded on an individual basis.

Whitehall School

117 High Street, Somersham, Cambs PE28 3EH

Tel: 01487 840966
email: office@whitehallschool.com
website: www.whitehallschool.com
Facebook: @Whitehall-School

***Head of School*: Mr Chris Holmes**, BSc Hons, MA, PGCE

Age Range. 6 months to 11 years.

Number in School. 107 Day children: 48 boys, 59 girls.

Fees per term (2023–2024). £3,165–£3,550.

'*A Unique School in Rural Cambridgeshire: A Dynamic, Forward-Thinking environment.*'

Set in extensive grounds with excellent facilities, Whitehall School provides a small, family environment where children are supported to achieve their best academically whilst also developing personality, creativity and social consciousness.

The school consists of an Edwardian house and 18th Century coach house and is set within approximately 1.5 acres of stunning grounds. Facilities include a covered heated swimming pool, playground, sensory garden, games field, library and iPad suite.

Small class sizes allow us to support children to access the curriculum at their own pace, catering for the specific needs of each child so that they excel. Our Individual Performance Programme allows us to work in partnership with parents to encourage children to become active, independent learners.

Wilmslow Preparatory School

Grove Avenue, Wilmslow, Cheshire SK9 5EG

Tel: 01625 524246
email: secretary@wilmslowprep.co.uk
website: www.wilmslowprep.co.uk
X/Twitter: @wilmslowprep
Facebook: @wilmslowprep

See full entry in the **IAPS** section, on **p. 830**.

Windrush Valley School

The Green, Ascott-under-Wychwood, Chipping Norton, Oxfordshire OX7 6AN

Tel: 01993 831793
email: info@windrushvalleyschool.co.uk
website: www.windrushvalleyschool.co.uk
Facebook: @Windrush-Valley-School

Headteacher: **Mrs A Douglas**, BA Hons, QTS

Age range. 3–11 Co-educational.

Number of pupils. 119.

Fees per term (2023–2024). £2,755–£2,845.

We believe that every child deserves the best possible start. With class sizes currently averaging 15, our pupils receive one-to-one attention, and the highest standards of education. We build self-esteem, self-confidence and independence; preparing boys and girls aged 3–11 for a successful future in either the independent or state senior school sectors. Over the last 25 years all pupils have passed their senior school entrance examination and attended their first-choice secondary school.

The school is ranked in the top 30 independent preparatory schools in England by the Sunday Times – earning it the prestigious accolade of Best Prep School Oxfordshire. The School has also received an Award for Excellence by the Independent Schools Association.

Our inspiring and stimulating curriculum is delivered within a nurturing, supportive and positive environment, and includes; literacy, language, mathematics, science, technology, human & social, sports, art and music. In addition, adventure trips and foreign residential weeks away, further enrich the curriculum and the children's life-experience.

All children regularly play in the school band, perform in musicals on stage, compete in public speaking competitions and sing in the choir. Our sporting pedigree has resulted in children competing at the highest level in swimming, athletics and cross country. For the last 10 years, our pupils have competed at a national level at the Independent Schools Association championship.

We also provide a comprehensive after-school programme in which children enjoy a wide range of additional activities, including cooking, first aid, forest school, horse whispering and cycling proficiency.

To support the needs of working parents we provide supervised wraparound care daily, from 8.00 am to 6.00 pm.

Our affordable fees underpin our commitment to make educational excellence accessible to as many children as possible.

If you want to give your child the best possible start – *excellence starts here.*

Woodlands School – Great Warley

Warley Street, Great Warley, Brentwood, Essex CM13 3LA

Tel: 01277 233288
email: info@woodlandswarley.co.uk
website: www.woodlandsschools.co.uk

Head Teacher: **Mrs Kirsty Kernaghan**

Age Range. 2–11 years.

Number in School. 100.

Fees per term (2023–2024). £2,929–£5,783.

Woodlands School at Great Warley is set in attractive, spacious grounds, with excellent facilities for outdoor activities. The school also uses the extensive facilities of our sister school at Hutton Manor.

The principal aim of the School is to ensure that all the children are happy and secure and are as successful as possible. They are encouraged to work hard and to show kindness and consideration to their peers. The resulting ethos of the School is one of warmth, support and mutual respect.

The School provides an exciting learning experience that enables the pupils to achieve full academic potential and to develop qualities of curiosity, independence and fortitude. Classes are small. The school aims to develop high levels of self-esteem and a good attitude to learning. The School has an excellent record in public examinations. Pupils are highly successful in gaining places at the schools of their choice. Examination results in Music and LAMDA are also excellent.

A varied programme of team and individual sports aims to offer something for everyone.

There is a strong music tradition and a variety of dramatic and musical concerts and productions are staged throughout the year for children of each age group.

Modern languages are taught to a very high standard, with French introduced at the age of 3 and Spanish in the Upper School.

Pastoral care is a major feature. An 'Open House' policy is in place for parents, which results in any concern being dealt with promptly and effectively.

It is the School's view that the education of the whole child is the most important priority and is confident that the learning experience it provides is fun, truly stimulating and memorable.

The school offers places for children from 2 years in Lower Kindergarten who will then progress automatically into Upper Kindergarten at age 3.

Woodlands School – Hutton Manor

428 Rayleigh Road, Hutton, Brentwood, Essex CM13 1SD

Tel: 01277 245585
email: info@woodlandsschools.co.uk
website: www.woodlandsschools.co.uk

Head Teacher: **Mrs Donna Burkert**, BA Hons

Age Range. 3–11 Co-educational.

Number of Pupils. 125–130.

Fees per term (2023–2024). £4,617–£6,057.

Woodlands School at Hutton Manor is set on attractive, spacious grounds, with excellent facilities for outdoor activities. The school also uses the extensive facilities of our sister school at Great Warley.

It is the School's principal aim to ensure that all the children are happy and secure and are as successful as possible. They are encouraged to work hard and to show kindness and consideration to their peers. The resulting ethos of the School is one of warmth, support and mutual respect.

The School provides an exciting learning experience that enables the pupils to achieve full academic potential and to develop qualities of curiosity, independence and fortitude. Classes are small. The school aims to develop high levels of self-esteem and a good attitude to learning. The School has an excellent record in public examinations. Pupils are highly successful in gaining places at the schools of their choice. Examination results in Music and LAMDA are also excellent.

A varied programme of team and individual sports aims to offer something for everyone.

There is a strong music tradition and a variety of dramatic and musical concerts and productions are staged throughout the year for children of each age group.

Modern languages are taught to a very high standard, with French introduced at the age of 3 and Spanish in the Upper School.

Pastoral care is a major feature. An 'Open House' policy is in place for parents, which results in any concern being dealt with promptly and effectively.

It is the School's view that the education of the whole child is the most important priority and is confident that the learning experience it provides is fun, truly stimulating and memorable.

The school has an onsite day-care nursery, Little Acorns, which operates for 51 weeks of the year from 7:30–18:00 offering places for children from the age of 3 months.

INDEX OF ENTRANCE SCHOLARSHIPS

Academic Scholarships

Academic Scholarships .../cont'd

Academic Scholarships .../cont'd

Academic Scholarships .../cont'd

All-Rounder Scholarships

PAGE

Art Scholarships .../cont'd

PAGE

PAGE

Art Scholarships .../cont'd

Art Scholarships .../cont'd

Dance Scholarships

PAGE

Design Technology Scholarships

Drama Scholarships

PAGE

Drama Scholarships .../cont'd

PAGE

Drama Scholarships .../cont'd

Music Scholarships

Music Scholarships .../cont'd

PAGE PAGE

Music Scholarships .../cont'd

PAGE

Sport Scholarships .../cont'd

PAGE

Sport Scholarships .../cont'd

Sport Scholarships .../cont'd

Other Scholarships

Arkwright Engineering

Boarding

Chess

Choral

Computing

Creative Arts

Cricket

Design

Drumming

Economics

Equestrian

Expressive Arts

Fencing

Golf

Hockey

Humanities

IT

Mathematics

PAGE

Modern Languages

Musical Theatre

Ogden Trust Science

Organ

Performing Arts

Photography

Piping

Rugby

Sailing

Science

INDEX OF BURSARIES AND DOUBTS

PAGE

New entrant bursary

New entrant bursary .../cont'd

PAGE

New entrant bursary .../cont'd

New entrant bursary .../cont'd

Existing pupil bursary/hardship award

PAGE PAGE

Existing pupil bursary/hardship award ..../cont'd

Existing pupil bursary/hardship award .../cont'd

Local resident bursary

Clergy discount

HM forces discount

PAGE

HM forces discount .../cont'd

Sibling discount

Sibling discount .../cont'd

PAGE

Sibling discount .../cont'd

Former pupil discount

INDEX OF EXAMINATIONS OFFERED

A Level

A Level ... /cont'd

PAGE

A Level .../cont'd

A Level ... /cont'd

AS Level

PAGE

AS Level .../cont'd

Extended Project Qualification (EPQ)

PAGE

Extended Project Qualification (EPQ) .../cont'd

PAGE

PAGE PAGE

Extended Project Qualification (EPQ) .../cont'd

International Baccalaureate (IB) Diploma

International Baccalaureate Middle Years Programme

BTEC

GCSE

GCSE .../cont'd

GCSE .../cont'd

GCSE .../cont'd

IGCSE

IGCSE .../cont'd

Applied A Level

Pre-U

Common Entrance to Senior

PAGE

Common Entrance to Senior .../cont'd

PAGE

PAGE PAGE

Common Entrance to Senior .../cont'd

Current School to Senior

PAGE

Current School to Senior .../cont'd

Scottish National 4

Scottish National 5

Scottish Highers

Scottish Advanced Highers

INDEX OF SCHOOLS BY AGE RANGE

Pre-Nursery

Nursery

PAGE

Nursery .../cont'd

PAGE

Nursery .../cont'd

PAGE

Nursery .../cont'd

PAGE

Nursery .../cont'd

PAGE

Nursery .../cont'd

Pre-Prep/Infants

PAGE

Pre-Prep/Infants .../cont'd

PAGE PAGE

Pre-Prep/Infants .../cont'd

PAGE

Pre-Prep/Infants .../cont'd

PAGE PAGE

Pre-Prep/Infants .../cont'd

PAGE

Pre-Prep/Infants .../cont'd

PAGE PAGE

Pre-Prep/Infants .../cont'd

Prep/Junior to 11

Prep/Junior to 11 .../cont'd

PAGE

Prep/Junior to 11 .../cont'd

PAGE

Prep/Junior to 11 .../cont'd

PAGE

Prep/Junior to 11 .../cont'd

PAGE

PAGE

Prep/Junior to 11 .../cont'd

Prep/Junior to 13

PAGE PAGE

Prep/Junior to 13 .../cont'd

Prep/Junior to 13 .../cont'd

Senior to 16

Senior to 18

PAGE

Senior to 18 .../cont'd

PAGE

Senior to 18 .../cont'd

PAGE

PAGE PAGE

Senior to 18 .../cont'd

PAGE

Senior to 18 .../cont'd

PAGE

Sixth Form only

GEOGRAPHICAL INDEX OF SCHOOLS

OVERSEAS SCHOOLS

ALPHABETICAL LIST OF SCHOOLS